D0849307

# THE EXPOSITOR'S BIBLE COMMENTARY

*with the New International Version*

# VOLUMES AND CONTRIBUTORS

**Volume 1**
Introductory Articles: General, Old Testament, New Testament

**Volume 2**
Genesis: *John H. Sailhamer*
Exodus: *Walter C. Kaiser Jr.*
Leviticus: *R. Laird Harris*
Numbers: *Ronald B. Allen*

**Volume 3**
Deuteronomy: *Earl S. Kalland*
Joshua: *Donald H. Madvig*
Judges: *Herbert Wolf*
Ruth: *F. B. Huey Jr.*
1, 2 Samuel: *Ronald F. Youngblood*

**Volume 4**
1, 2 Kings: *Richard D. Patterson and Hermann J. Austel*
1, 2 Chronicles: *J. Barton Payne*
Ezra, Nehemiah: *Edwin Yamauchi*
Esther: *F. B. Huey Jr.*
Job: *Elmer B. Smick*

**Volume 5**
Psalms: *Willem A. VanGemeren*
Proverbs: *Allen P. Ross*
Ecclesiastes: *J. Stafford Wright*
Song of Songs: *Dennis F. Kinlaw*

**Volume 6**
Isaiah: *Geoffrey W. Grogan*
Jeremiah: *Charles L. Feinberg*
Lamentations: *H. L. Ellison*
Ezekiel: *Ralph H. Alexander*

**Volume 7**
Daniel: *Gleason L. Archer Jr.*
Hosea: *Leon J. Wood*
Joel: *Richard D. Patterson*
Amos: *Thomas E. McComiskey*
Obadiah: *Carl E. Armerding*
Jonah: *H. L. Ellison*
Micah: *Thomas E. McComiskey*
Nahum, Habakkuk: *Carl E. Armerding*
Zephaniah: *Larry Walker*
Haggai: *Robert L. Alden*
Zechariah: *Kenneth L. Barker*
Malachi: *Robert L. Alden*

**Volume 8**
Matthew: *D. A. Carson*
Mark: *Walter W. Wessel*
Luke: *Walter L. Liefeld*

**Volume 9**
John: *Merrill C. Tenney*
Acts: *Richard N. Longenecker*

**Volume 10**
Romans: *Everett F. Harrison*
1 Corinthians: *W. Harold Mare*
2 Corinthians: *Murray J. Harris*
Galatians: *James Montgomery Boice*

**Volume 11**
Ephesians: *A. Skevington Wood*
Philippians: *Homer A. Kent Jr.*
Colossians: *Curtis Vaughan*
1, 2 Thessalonians: *Robert L. Thomas*
1, 2 Timothy: *Ralph Earle*
Titus: *D. Edmond Hiebert*
Philemon: *Arthur A. Rupprecht*

**Volume 12**
Hebrews: *Leon Morris*
James: *Donald W. Burdick*
1, 2 Peter: *Edwin A Blum*
1, 2, 3 John: *Glenn W. Barker*
Jude: *Edwin A. Blum*
Revelation: *Alan F. Johnson*

# THE EXPOSITOR'S BIBLE COMMENTARY

*with the New International Version*

## *Deuteronomy, Joshua, Judges, Ruth, 1 & 2 Samuel*

**VOLUME 3**

*Deuteronomy* - Earl S. Kalland

*Joshua* - Donald H. Madvig

*Judges* - Herbert Wolf

*Ruth* - F. B. Huey Jr.

*1 & 2 Samuel* - Ronald F. Youngblood

Frank E. Gæbelein general editor

GRAND RAPIDS, MICHIGAN 49530

ZONDERVAN.COM/
AUTHORTRACKER

We want to hear from you. Please send your comments about this book to us in care of zreview@zondervan.com. Thank you.

ZONDERVAN®

*The Expositor's Bible Commentary, Volume 3*
Copyright © 1992 by Zondervan

Requests for information should be addressed to:

Zondervan, *Grand Rapids, Michigan 49530*

ISBN-10: 0-310-60893-7
ISBN-13: 978-0-310-60893-6

This edition is printed on acid-free paper.

All Scripture quotations, unless otherwise indicated, are taken from the *Holy Bible: New International Version*®. NIV®. Copyright © 1973, 1978, 1984 by International Bible Society. Used by permission of Zondervan. All rights reserved.

All rights reserved. No part of this publication may be reproduced, stored in a retrieval system, or transmitted in any form or by any means—electronic, mechanical, photocopy, recording, or any other—except for brief quotations in printed reviews, without the prior permission of the publisher.

*Printed in the United States of America*

08 09 10 11 12 • 10 09 08 07 06 05 04 03 02

# CONTENTS

# CONTRIBUTORS TO VOLUME 3

**Deuteronomy: Earl S. Kalland**

Th.B, Bible Institute of Los Angeles; Th.B., Gordon College; B.D., Th.D, Gordon Divinity School.

*Former Professor of Old Testament, President, Western Baptist Seminary; Former Professor of Old Testament, Dean of Faculty, Denver Theological Seminary*

**Joshua: Donald H. Madvig**

B.A., Bethel College; B.D., Bethel Theological Seminary; Th.M., Fuller Theological Seminary; M.A., Ph.D., Brandeis University

*Senior Pastor, Beverly Evangelical Covenant Church, Chicago, Illinois*

**Judges: Herbert Wolf**

B.A., Wheaton College; Th.M., Dallas Theological Seminary; M.A., Ph.D, Brandeis University

*Professor of Theological Studies, Wheaton College*

**Ruth: F.B. Huey**

B.B.A, University of Texas at Austin; M.Div., Ph.D., Southwestern Baptist Theological Seminary

*Professor Emeritus of Old Testament, Southwestern Baptist Theological Seminary*

**1, 2 Samuel: Ronald F. Youngblood**

B.A., Valparaiso University; B.D., Fuller Theological Seminary; Ph.D., Dropsie College for Hebrew and Cognate Learning

*Professor of Old Testament, Bethel Seminary West*

# PREFACE

The title of this work defines its purpose. Written primarily by expositors for expositors, it aims to provide preachers, teachers, and students of the Bible with a new and comprehensive commentary on the books of the Old and New Testaments. Its stance is that of a scholarly evangelicalism committed to the divine inspiration, complete trustworthiness, and full authority of the Bible. Its seventy-eight contributors come from the United States, Canada, England, Scotland, Australia, New Zealand, and Switzerland, and from various religious groups, including Anglican, Baptist, Brethren, Free, Independent, Methodist, Nazarene, Presbyterian, and Reformed churches. Most of them teach at colleges, universities, or theological seminaries.

No book has been more closely studied over a longer period of time than the Bible. From the Midrashic commentaries going back to the period of Ezra, through parts of the Dead Sea Scrolls and the Patristic literature, and on to the present, the Scriptures have been expounded. Indeed, there have been times when, as in the Reformation and on occasions since then, exposition has been at the cutting edge of Christian advance. Luther was a powerful exegete, and Calvin is still called "the prince of expositors."

Their successors have been many. And now, when the outburst of new translations and their unparalleled circulation have expanded the readership of the Bible, the need for exposition takes on fresh urgency.

Not that God's Word can ever become captive to its expositors. Among all other books, it stands first in its combination of perspicuity and profundity. Though a child can be made "wise for salvation" by believing its witness to Christ, the greatest mind cannot plumb the depths of its truth (2 Tim. 3:15; Rom. 11:33). As Gregory the Great said, "Holy Scripture is a stream of running water, where alike the elephant may swim, and the lamb walk." So, because of the inexhaustible nature of Scripture, the task of opening up its meaning is still a perennial obligation of biblical scholarship.

How that task is done inevitably reflects the outlook of those engaged in it. Every Bible scholar has presuppositions. To this neither the editors of these volumes nor the contributors to them are exceptions. They share a common commitment to the supernatural Christianity set forth in the inspired Word. Their purpose is not to supplant the many valuable commentaries that have preceded this work and from which both the editors and contributors have learned. It is rather to draw on the resources of contemporary evangelical scholarship in producing a new reference work for understanding the Scriptures.

A commentary that will continue to be useful through the years should handle contemporary trends in biblical studies in such a way as to avoid becoming outdated when critical fashions change. Biblical criticism is not in itself inadmissable, as some have mistakenly thought. When scholars investigate the authorship, date, literary characteristics, and purpose of a biblical document, they are practicing biblical criticism. So also when, in order to ascertain as nearly as possible the original form of the text, they deal with variant readings, scribal errors, emendations, and other phenomena in the manuscripts. To do these things is essential to responsible exegesis and exposition. And always there is the need to distinguish hypothesis from fact, conjecture from truth.

The chief principle of interpretation followed in this commentary is the grammatico-historical one—namely, that the primary aim of the exegete is to make clear the meaning of the text at the time and in the circumstances of its writing. This endeavor to understand what in the first instance the inspired writers actually said must not be confused with an inflexible literalism. Scripture makes lavish use of symbols and figures of speech; great portions of it are poetical. Yet when it speaks in this way, it speaks no less truly than it does in its historical and doctrinal portions. To understand its message requires attention to matters of grammar and syntax, word meanings, idioms, and literary forms—all in relation to the historical and cultural setting of the text.

The contributors to this work necessarily reflect varying convictions. In certain controversial matters the policy is that of clear statement of the contributors' own views followed by fair presentation of other ones. The treatment of eschatology, though it reflects differences of interpretation, is consistent with a general premillennial position. (Not all contributors, however, are premillennial.) But prophecy is more than prediction, and so this commentary gives due recognition to the major lode of godly social concern in the prophetic writings.

THE EXPOSITOR'S BIBLE COMMENTARY is presented as a scholarly work, though not primarily one of technical criticism. In its main portion, the Exposition, and in Volume 1 (General and Special Articles), all Semitic and Greek words are transliterated and the English equivalents given. As for the Notes, here Semitic and Greek characters are used but always with transliterations and English meanings, so that this portion of the commentary will be as accessible as possible to readers unacquainted with the original languages.

It is the conviction of the general editor, shared by his colleagues in the Zondervan editorial department, that in writing about the Bible, lucidity is not incompatible with scholarship. They are therefore endeavoring to make this a clear and understandable work.

The translation used in it is the New International Version (North American Edition). To the International Bible Society thanks are due for permission to use this most recent of the major Bible translations. It was chosen because of the clarity and beauty of its style and its faithfulness to the original texts.

To the associate editor, Richard P. Polcyn, and to the contributing editors—Dr. Walter C. Kaiser, Jr., Dr. Bruce K. Waltke, and Dr. Ralph H. Alexander for the Old Testament, and Dr. James Montgomery Boice and Dr. Merrill C. Tenney for the New Testament—the general editor expresses his gratitude for their unfailing cooperation and their generosity in advising him out of their expert scholarship. And to the many other contributors he is indebted for their invaluable part in this work. Finally, he owes a special debt of gratitude to Dr. Robert K. DeVries, publisher, The Zondervan Corporation, and Miss Elizabeth Brown, secretary, for their assistance and encouragement.

Whatever else it is—the greatest and most beautiful of books, the primary source of law and morality, the fountain of wisdom, and the infallible guide to life—the Bible is above all the inspired witness to Jesus Christ. May this work fulfill its function of expounding the Scriptures with grace and clarity, so that its users may find that both Old and New Testaments do indeed lead to our Lord Jesus Christ, who alone could say, "I have come that they may have life, and have it to the full" (John 10:10).

FRANK E. GAEBELEIN

# ABBREVIATIONS

## A. General Abbreviations

A — Codex Alexandrinus
Akkad. — Akkadian
א — Codex Sinaiticus
Ap. Lit. — Apocalyptic Literature
Apoc. — Apocrypha
Aq. — Aquila's Greek Translation of the Old Testament
Arab. — Arabic
Aram. — Aramaic
b — Babylonian Gemara
B — Codex Vaticanus
C — Codex Ephraemi Syri
c. — *circa*, about
cf. — *confer*, compare
ch., chs. — chapter, chapters
cod., codd. — codex, codices
D — Codex Bezae
DSS — Dead Sea Scrolls (see E.)
ed., edd. — edited, edition, editor; editions
e.g. — *exempli gratia*, for example
Egyp. — Egyptian
et al. — *et alii*, and others
EV — English Versions of the Bible
fem. — feminine
ff. — following (verses, pages, etc.)
fl. — flourished
ft. — foot, feet
gen. — genitive
Gr. — Greek
Heb. — Hebrew
Hitt. — Hittite
ibid. — *ibidem*, in the same place
id. — *idem*, the same
i.e. — *id est*, that is
impf. — imperfect
infra. — below
in loc. — *in loco*, in the place cited
j — Jerusalem or Palestinian Gemara
Lat. — Latin
LL. — Late Latin
LXX — Septuagint
M — Mishnah
masc. — masculine
mg. — margin
Mid — Midrash
MS(S) — manuscript(s)
MT — Masoretic text
n. — note
n.d. — no date
Nestle — Nestle (ed.) *Novum Testamentum Graece*
no. — number
NT — New Testament
obs. — obsolete
OL — Old Latin
OS — Old Syriac
OT — Old Testament
p., pp. — page, pages
par. — paragraph
Pers. — Persian
Pesh. — Peshitta
Phoen. — Phoenician
pl. — plural
Pseudep. — Pseudepigrapha
Q — Quelle ("Sayings" source in the Gospels)
qt. — quoted by
q.v. — *quod vide*, which see
R — Rabbah
rev. — revised, reviser, revision
Rom. — Roman
RVm — Revised Version margin
Samar. — Samaritan recension
SCM — Student Christian Movement Press
Sem. — Semitic
sing. — singular
SPCK — Society for the Promotion of Christian Knowledge
Sumer. — Sumerian
s.v. — *sub verbo*, under the word
Syr. — Syriac
Symm. — Symmachus
T — Talmud
Targ. — Targum
Theod. — Theodotion
TR — Textus Receptus
tr. — translation, translator, translated
UBS — Tha United Bible Societies' Greek Text
Ugar. — Ugaritic
u.s. — *ut supra*, as above
v., vv. — verse, verses
viz. — *videlicet*, namely
vol. — volume
vs. — versus
Vul. — Vulgate
WH — Westcott and Hort, *The New Testament in Greek*

**B. Abbreviations for Modern Translations and Paraphrases**

| | |
|---|---|
| AmT | Smith and Goodspeed, *The Complete Bible, An American Translation* |
| ASV | American Standard Version, American Revised Version (1901) |
| Beck | Beck, *The New Testament in the Language of Today* |
| BV | Berkeley Version (The Modern Language Bible) |
| JB | The Jerusalem Bible |
| JPS | *Jewish Publication Society Version of the Old Testament* |
| KJV | King James Version |
| Knox | R.G. Knox, *The Holy Bible: A Translation from the Latin Vulgate in the Light of the Hebrew and Greek Original* |
| LB | The Living Bible |
| Mof | J. Moffatt, *A New Translation of the Bible* |
| NAB | The New American Bible |
| NASB | New American Standard Bible |
| NEB | The New English Bible |
| NIV | The New International Version |
| Ph | J. B. Phillips *The New Testament in Modern English* |
| RSV | Revised Standard Version |
| RV | Revised Version — 1881–1885 |
| TCNT | Twentieth Century New Testament |
| TEV | Today's English Version |
| Wey | *Weymouth's New Testament in Modern Speech* |
| Wms | C. B. Williams, *The New Testament: A Translation in the Language of the People* |

**C. Abbreviations for Periodicals and Reference Works**

| | |
|---|---|
| AASOR | *Annual of the American Schools of Oriental Research* |
| AB | *Anchor Bible* |
| AIs | de Vaux: *Ancient Israel* |
| AJA | *American Journal of Archaeology* |
| AJSL | *American Journal of Semitic Languages and Literatures* |
| AJT | *American Journal of Theology* |
| Alf | Alford: *Greek Testament Commentary* |
| ANEA | *Ancient Near Eastern Archaeology* |
| ANEP | Pritchard: *Ancient Near Eastern Pictures* |
| ANET | Pritchard· *Ancient Near Eastern Texts* |
| ANF | Roberts and Donaldson: *The Ante-Nicene Fathers* |
| A-S | Abbot-Smith: *Manual Greek Lexicon of the New Testament* |
| AThR | *Anglican Theological Review* |
| BA | *Biblical Archaeologist* |
| BAG | Bauer, Arndt, and Gingrich: *Greek-English Lexicon of the New Testament* |
| BAGD | Bauer, Arndt, Gingrich, and Danker: *Greek-English Lexicon of the New Testament* 2nd edition |
| BASOR | *Bulletin of the American Schools of Oriental Research* |
| BC | Foakes-Jackson and Lake: *The Beginnings of Christianity* |
| BDB | Brown, Driver, and Briggs: *Hebrew-English Lexicon of the Old Testament* |
| BDF | Blass, Debrunner, and Funk: *A Greek Grammar of the New Testament and Other Early Christian Literature* |
| BDT | Harrison: *Baker's Dictionary of Theology* |
| Beng. | Bengel's *Gnomon* |
| BETS | *Bulletin of the Evangelical Theological Society* |
| BH | *Biblia Hebraica* |
| BHS | *Biblia Hebraica Stuttgartensia* |
| BJRL | *Bulletin of the John Rylands Library* |
| BS | *Bibliotheca Sacra* |
| BT | *Babylonian Talmud* |
| BTh | *Biblical Theology* |
| BW | *Biblical World* |
| CAH | *Cambridge Ancient History* |
| CanJTh | *Canadian Journal of Theology* |
| CBQ | *Catholic Biblical Quarterly* |
| CBSC | *Cambridge Bible for Schools and Colleges* |
| CE | *Catholic Encyclopedia* |
| CGT | *Cambridge Greek Testament* |

CHS Lange: *Commentary on the Holy Scriptures*
ChT *Christianity Today*
DDB *Davis' Dictionary of the Bible*
Deiss BS Deissmann: *Bible Studies*
Deiss LAE Deissmann: *Light From the Ancient East*
DNTT *Dictionary of New Testament Theology*
EBC *The Expositor's Bible Commentary*
EBi *Encyclopaedia Biblica*
EBr *Encyclopaedia Britannica*
EDB *Encyclopedic Dictionary of the Bible*
EGT Nicoll: *Expositor's Greek Testament*
EQ *Evangelical Quarterly*
ET *Evangelische Theologie*
ExB *The Expositor's Bible*
Exp *The Expositor*
ExpT *The Expository Times*
FLAP Finegan: *Light From the Ancient Past*
GKC Gesenius, Kautzsch, Cowley, *Hebrew Grammar*, 2nd Eng. ed.
GR *Gordon Review*
HBD *Harper's Bible Dictionary*
HDAC Hastings: *Dictionary of the Apostolic Church*
HDB Hastings: *Dictionary of the Bible*
HDBrev. Hastings: *Dictionary of the Bible*, one-vol. rev. by Grant and Rowley
HDCG Hastings: *Dictionary of Christ and the Gospels*
HERE Hastings: *Encyclopedia of Religion and Ethics*
HGEOTP Heidel: *The Gilgamesh Epic and Old Testament Parallels*
HJP Schurer: *A History of the Jewish People in the Time of Christ*
HR Hatch and Redpath: *Concordance to the Septuagint*
HTR *Harvard Theological Review*
HUCA *Hebrew Union College Annual*
IB *The Interpreter's Bible*
ICC *International Critical Commentary*
IDB *The Interpreter's Dictionary of the Bible*
IEJ *Israel Exploration Journal*
Int *Interpretation*
INT E. Harrison: *Introduction to the New Testament*
IOT R. K. Harrison: *Introduction to the Old Testament*
ISBE *The International Standard Bible Encyclopedia*
ITQ *Irish Theological Quarterly*
JAAR *Journal of American Academy of Religion*
JAOS *Journal of American Oriental Society*
JBL *Journal of Biblical Literature*
JE *Jewish Encyclopedia*
JETS *Journal of Evangelical Theological Society*
JFB Jamieson, Fausset, and Brown: *Commentary on the Old and New Testament*
JNES *Journal of Near Eastern Studies*
Jos. Antiq. Josephus: *The Antiquities of the Jews*
Jos. War Josephus: *The Jewish War*
JQR *Jewish Quarterly Review*
JR *Journal of Religion*
JSJ *Journal for the Study of Judaism in the Persian, Hellenistic and Roman Periods*
JSOR *Journal of the Society of Oriental Research*
JSS *Journal of Semitic Studies*
JT *Jerusalem Talmud*
JTS *Journal of Theological Studies*
KAHL Kenyon: *Archaeology in the Holy Land*
KB Koehler-Baumgartner: *Lexicon in Veteris Testament Libros*
KD Keil and Delitzsch: *Commentary on the Old Testament*
LSJ Liddell, Scott, Jones: *Greek-English Lexicon*
LTJM Edersheim: *The Life and Times of Jesus the Messiah*
MM Moulton and Milligan: *The Vocabulary of the Greek Testament*
MNT Moffatt: *New Testament Commentary*

| | |
|---|---|
| MST | McClintock and Strong: *Cyclopedia of Biblical, Theological, and Ecclesiastical Literature* |
| NBC | Davidson, Kevan, and Stibbs: *The New Bible Commentary*, 1st ed. |
| NBCrev. | Guthrie and Motyer: *The New Bible Commentary*, rev. ed. |
| NBD | J. D. Douglas: *The New Bible Dictionary* |
| NCB | *New Century Bible* |
| NCE | *New Catholic Encyclopedia* |
| NIC | *New International Commentary* |
| NIDCC | Douglas: *The New International Dictionary of the Christian Church* |
| NovTest | *Novum Testamentum* |
| NSI | Cooke: *Handbook of North Semitic Inscriptions* |
| NTS | *New Testament Studies* |
| ODCC | *The Oxford Dictionary of the Christian Church*, rev. ed. |
| Peake | Black and Rowley: *Peake's Commentary on the Bible* |
| PEQ | *Palestine Exploration Quarterly* |
| PNF1 | P. Schaff: *The Nicene and Post-Nicene Fathers* (1st series) |
| PNF2 | P. Schaff and H. Wace: *The Nicene and Post-Nicene Fathers* (2nd series) |
| PTR | *Princeton Theological Review* |
| RB | *Revue Biblique* |
| RHG | Robertson's *Grammar of the Greek New Testament in the Light of Historical Research* |
| RTWB | Richardson: *A Theological Wordbook of the Bible* |
| SBK | Strack and Billerbeck: *Kommentar zum Neuen Testament aus Talmud und Midrash* |
| SHERK | *The New Schaff-Herzog Encyclopedia of Religious Knowledge* |
| SJT | *Scottish Journal of Theology* |
| SOT | Girdlestone: *Synonyms of Old Testament* |
| SOTI | Archer: *A Survey of Old Testament Introduction* |
| ST | *Studia Theologica* |
| TCERK | Loetscher: *The Twentieth Century Encyclopedia of Religious Knowledge* |
| TDNT | Kittel: *Theological Dictionary of the New Testament* |
| TDOT | *Theological Dictionary of the Old Testament* |
| THAT | *Theologisches Handbuch zum Alten Testament* |
| ThT | *Theology Today* |
| TNTC | *Tyndale New Testament Commentaries* |
| Trench | Trench: *Synonyms of the New Testament* |
| TWOT | *Theological Wordbook of the Old Testament* |
| UBD | *Unger's Bible Dictionary* |
| UT | Gordon: *Ugaritic Textbook* |
| VB | Allmen: *Vocabulary of the Bible* |
| VetTest | *Vetus Testamentum* |
| Vincent | Vincent: *Word-Pictures in the New Testament* |
| WBC | *Wycliffe Bible Commentary* |
| WBE | *Wycliffe Bible Encyclopedia* |
| WC | *Westminster Commentaries* |
| WesBC | *Wesleyan Bible Commentaries* |
| WTJ | *Westminster Theological Journal* |
| ZAW | *Zeitschrift für die alttestamentliche Wissenschaft* |
| ZNW | *Zeitschrift für die neutestamentliche Wissenschaft* |
| ZPBD | *The Zondervan Pictorial Bible Dictionary* |
| ZPEB | *The Zondervan Pictorial Encyclopedia of the Bible* |
| ZWT | *Zeitschrift für wissenschaftliche Theologie* |

## D. Abbreviations for Books of the Bible, the Apocrypha, and the Pseudepigrapha

### OLD TESTAMENT

| | | |
|---|---|---|
| Gen | 2 Chron | Dan |
| Exod | Ezra | Hos |
| Lev | Neh | Joel |
| Num | Esth | Amos |
| Deut | Job | Obad |
| Josh | Ps(Pss) | Jonah |
| Judg | Prov | Mic |
| Ruth | Eccl | Nah |
| 1 Sam | S of Songs | Hab |
| 2 Sam | Isa | Zeph |
| 1 Kings | Jer | Hag |
| 2 Kings | Lam | Zech |
| 1 Chron | Ezek | Mal |

### NEW TESTAMENT

| | |
|---|---|
| Matt | 1 Tim |
| Mark | 2 Tim |
| Luke | Titus |
| John | Philem |
| Acts | Heb |
| Rom | James |
| 1 Cor | 1 Peter |
| 2 Cor | 2 Peter |
| Gal | 1 John |
| Eph | 2 John |
| Phil | 3 John |
| Col | Jude |
| 1 Thess | Rev |
| 2 Thess | |

### APOCRYPHA

| | |
|---|---|
| 1 Esd | 1 Esdras |
| 2 Esd | 2 Esdras |
| Tobit | Tobit |
| Jud | Judith |
| Add Esth | Additions to Esther |
| Wisd Sol | Wisdom of Solomon |
| Ecclus | Ecclesiasticus (Wisdom of Jesus the Son of Sirach) |
| Baruch | Baruch |
| Ep Jer | Epistle of Jeremy |
| S Th Ch | Song of the Three Child (or Young Men) |
| Sus | Susanna |
| Bel | Bel and the Dragon |
| Pr Man | Prayer of Manasseh |
| 1 Macc | 1 Maccabees |
| 2 Macc | 2 Maccabees |

### PSEUDEPIGRAPHA

| | |
|---|---|
| As Moses | Assumption of Moses |
| 2 Baruch | Syriac Apocalypse of Baruch |
| 3 Baruch | Greek Apocalypse of Baruch |
| 1 Enoch | Ethiopic Book of Enoch |
| 2 Enoch | Slavonic Book of Enoch |
| 3 Enoch | Hebrew Book of Enoch |
| 4 Ezra | 4 Ezra |
| JA | Joseph and Asenath |
| Jub | Book of Jubilees |
| L Aristeas | Letter of Aristeas |
| Life AE | Life of Adam and Eve |
| Liv Proph | Lives of the Prophets |
| MA Isa | Martyrdom and Ascension of Isaiah |
| 3 Macc | 3 Maccabees |
| 4 Macc | 4 Maccabees |
| Odes Sol | Odes of Solomon |
| P Jer | Paralipomena of Jeremiah |
| Pirke Aboth | Pirke Aboth |
| Ps 151 | Psalm 151 |
| Pss Sol | Psalms of Solomon |
| Sib Oracles | Sibylline Oracles |
| Story Ah | Story of Ahikar |
| T Abram | Testament of Abraham |
| T Adam | Testament of Adam |
| T Benjamin | Testament of Benjamin |
| T Dan | Testament of Dan |
| T Gad | Testament of Gad |
| T Job | Testament of Job |
| T Jos | Testament of Joseph |
| T Levi | Testament of Levi |
| T Naph | Testament of Naphtali |
| T 12 Pat | Testaments of the Twe Patriarchs |
| Zad Frag | Zadokite Fragments |

### E. Abbreviations of Names of Dead Sea Scrolls and Related Texts

| | |
|---|---|
| CD | Cairo (Genizah text of the) Damascus (Document) |
| DSS | Dead Sea Scrolls |
| Hev | Nahal Hever texts |
| Mas | Masada Texts |
| Mird | Khirbet mird texts |
| Mur | Wadi Murabba'at texts |
| P | Pesher (commentary) |
| Q | Qumran |
| 1Q, 2Q, etc. | Numbered caves of Qumran, yielding written material; followed by abbreviation of biblical or apocryphal book. |
| QL | Qumran Literature |
| 1QapGen | Genesis Apocryphon of Qumran Cave 1 |
| 1QH | *Hodayot* (Thanksgiving Hymns) from Qumran Cave 1 |
| 1QIsa a,b | First or second copy of Isaiah from Qumran Cave 1 |
| 1QpHab | Pesher on Habakkuk from Qumran Cave 1 |
| 1QM | *Milhamah* (War Scroll) |
| 1QpMic | Pesher on portions of Micah from Qumran Cave 1 |
| 1QS | *Serek Hayyahad* (Rule of the Community, Manual of Discipline) |
| 1QSa | Appendix A (Rule of the Congregation) to 1Qs |
| 1QSb | Appendix B (Blessings) to 1QS |
| 3Q15 | Copper Scroll from Qumran Cave 3 |
| 4QExod a | Exodus Scroll, exemplar "a" from Qumran Cave 4 |
| 4QFlor | Florilegium (or Eschatological Midrashim) from Qumran Cave 4 |
| 4Qmess ar | Aramaic "Messianic" text from Qumran Cave 4 |
| 4QpNah | Pesher on portions of Nahum from Qumran Cave 4 |
| 4QPrNab | Prayer of Nabonidus from Qumran Cave 4 |
| 4QpPs37 | Pesher on portions of Psalm 37 from Qumran Cave 4 |
| 4QTest | Testimonia text from Qumran Cave 4 |
| 4QTLevi | Testament of Levi from Qumran Cave 4 |
| 4QPhyl | Phylacteries from Qumran Cave 4 |
| 11QMelch | Melchizedek text from Qumran Cave 11 |
| 11QtgJob | Targum of Job from Qumran Cave 11 |

# TRANSLITERATIONS

## Hebrew

| | | | | |
|---|---|---|---|---|
| א = ʾ | ד = ḏ | י = y | ס = s | ר = r |
| בּ = b | ה = h | כּ = k | ע = ʿ | שׂ = ś |
| ב = ḇ | ו = w | ך כ = ḵ | פּ = p | שׁ = š |
| גּ = g | ז = z | ל = l | ף פ = p̄ | תּ = t |
| ג = ḡ | ח = ḥ | ם מ = m | ץ צ = ṣ | ת = ṯ |
| דּ = d | ט = ṭ | ן נ = n | ק = q | |

| | | | |
|---|---|---|---|
| (ה)◌ָ = â (h) | ◌ָ = ā | ◌ַ = a | ◌ֲ = $^{a}$ |
| ◌ֵי = ê | ◌ֵ = ē | ◌ֶ = e | ◌ֱ = $^{e}$ |
| ◌ִי = î | ◌ֹ = ō | ◌ִ = i | ◌ְ = $^{e}$ (*if vocal*) |
| וֹ = ô | | ◌ָ = o | ◌ֳ = $^{o}$ |
| וּ = û | | ◌ֻ = u | |

## Aramaic

ʾ *b g d h w z ḥ ṭ y k l m n s* ʿ *p ṣ q r ś š t*

## Arabic

ʾ *b t ṯ ǧ ḥ ḫ d ḏ r z s š ṣ ḍ ṭ ẓ* ʿ *ġ f q k l m n h w y*

## Ugaritic

ʾ *b g d ḏ h w z ḥ ḫ ṭ ẓ y k l m n s s̀* ʿ *ġ p ṣ q r š t ṯ*

## Greek

| | | | | | | | |
|---|---|---|---|---|---|---|---|
| α | — | *a* | π | — | *p* | αι | — *ai* |
| β | — | *b* | ρ | — | *r* | αὐ | — *au* |
| γ | — | *g* | σ,ς | — | *s* | ει | — *ei* |
| δ | — | *d* | τ | — | *t* | εὐ | — *eu* |
| ε | — | *e* | υ | — | *y* | ηὐ | — *ēu* |
| ζ | — | *z* | φ | — | *ph* | οι | — *oi* |
| η | — | *ē* | χ | — | *ch* | οὐ | — *ou* |
| θ | — | *th* | ψ | — | *ps* | υι | — *hui* |
| ι | — | *i* | ω | — | *ō* | | |
| κ | — | *k* | | | | ῥ | — *rh* |
| λ | — | *l* | γγ | — | *ng* | ʽ | — *h* |
| μ | — | *m* | γκ | — | *nk* | | |
| ν | — | *n* | γξ | — | *nx* | ᾳ | — *ā* |
| ξ | — | *x* | γχ | — | *nch* | ῃ | — *ē* |
| ο | — | *o* | | | | ῳ | — *ō* |

# DEUTERONOMY

Earl S. Kalland

# DEUTERONOMY

## Introduction

1. Name
2. Character and Author
3. Purpose
4. Summary
5. Canonical Status
6. Critical Theories
7. Text
8. Theological Values
9. Bibliography
10. Outline

### 1. Name

The name Deuteronomy results from a mistranslation of Deuteronomy 17:18 in the LXX and the Vulgate. For the Hebrew "a copy of this law," the LXX and the Vulgate have terms meaning "the second law" or "a repetition of this law."

The Jews identify the book by its first words—*'ēlleh hadd[e]ḇārîm* ("These are the words")—or by the phrase in 17:18 cited above, or by "The Book of Admonitions" or reproofs or corrections. It is also known as "The Fifth" or "Fifths of the Law."

Internal data locate Deuteronomy as beginning in the desert east of the Jordan in Moab on the first day of the eleventh month of the fortieth year—forty years after the Exodus from Egypt (1:3). This was after Moses and the Israelites had defeated Sihon and Og, kings of the Amorites in Transjordan (1:4).

### 2. Character and Author

In addition to the many statements about Moses' speaking these words, there are statements made within the book itself that indicate that he was the author (at the direction of the Lord: 1:5; 31:9, 22, 24, 30). Other OT books similarly assert Mosaic authorship of Deuteronomy (1 Kings 2:3; 8:53; 2 Kings 14:6; 18:6, 12), as do Jesus and others in the NT (Matt 19:7–8; Mark 10:3–5; 12:19; John 5:46–47; Acts 3:22; 7:37–38; Rom 10:19).

Deuteronomy may be approached from several angles: (1) as a "Book of the Law"; (2) as a series of addresses with materials both repetitive of formerly given content (from Exodus, Leviticus, and Numbers) and additions that occasionally are more or less extemporaneous; (3) as a covenant-treaty in both form and content (29:1; 31:9–13, 24–26), including the narratives of the adoption of that agreement and the exhortations to not only adopt the covenant-treaty but also to adhere to the stipulations of it. It also may be approached (4) as a compendium of the directives of the Lord given through Moses to prepare the people for the conquest, settlement, and occupation of Canaan. In addition to its original purpose for Israel, Deuteronomy should be read also for the spiritual truths that pertain to the redemption offered to all people and for those truths concerning God and man that never change.

Traditional Mosaic authorship has been attacked mainly on literary-critical grounds. The alternate theories, however, are quite diverse and have been subject to much emendation. (For a limited review of various theories of the authorship of Deuteronomy, see R.K. Harrison, EBC, 1:239–43.)

Deuteronomy is law, but it is also exposition and application of the law; and the whole of it is in the covenant-treaty form and contains repetitive exhortation to give heed to the sovereign Lord and to the other stipulations of the covenant.

The historical and literary similarity of the second millennium B.C. to the early first millennium B.C. clearly identifies the Mosaic covenant-treaty elements and their order with those of the fourteenth and thirteenth centuries B.C.

The procedure for the establishment and continuity of these treaties, as well as their schematic literary structure, lends itself strikingly to the relationship between the Lord (Yahweh) and his people Israel as made known through Moses.

One most important variation, however, concerns the position of the Lord God in the Deuteronomic covenant-treaty. The Near Eastern treaties have recourse to their god or gods as witnesses to the treaty. To be sure, the Lord God also is witness to the proclamation of the Deuteronomic covenant-treaty (31:19, 26; 32:1–47), but that is not his most important role. He is the Sovereign who dictates the terms of the covenant-treaty and declares what the acceptance and the rejection of its terms involve. This relationship of the Lord God as sovereign goes beyond the rule over Israel. In Deuteronomy he is sovereign over all people and things, but his relationship with Israel under the covenant-treaty makes him especially their sovereign. They are his vassal people whose attitude and disposition toward him entail faith, love, and obedience.

Moses' position was that of a representative of the Lord to his people. The term applied to him is "prophet"—the spokesman of God to the people. The Lord revealed his will to Moses, and Moses made this known to Israel. Moses was also the leader and judge of and for the people.

The main features of the Near Eastern treaties of the thirteenth and fourteenth centuries B.C. are (1) preamble; (2) historical prologue; (3) stipulations, laws, and regulations; (4) arrangements for depositing treaty copies; (5) arrangements for regular reading of the treaty; (6) witnesses; and (7) curses and blessings.[1] The Deuteronomic addresses of Moses follow this order, though, in addition to the historical prologue, historical allusions are often intermixed with exhortations to the Israelites to give heed to the Lord their God and to obey the covenant-treaty stipulations.

Because of the nature of the participants, the sovereignty of God becomes a vastly more potent factor in the Deuteronomic covenant-treaty than that of any other state. Nevertheless, this historical framework makes the relationship of Israel to the Lord God and his government and its stipulations, laws, and regulations very vivid and life

[1] Kitchen, *Ancient Orient*, pp. 90–102; Kline, *Biblical Authority;* Mendenhall, "Covenant Forms," pp. 52–67.

giving, while the rejection of the Lord's sovereignty results not only in the destruction of the nation as a nation but of the people as individuals as well.

Another similarity between the suzerain-vassal treaties and Deuteronomy is the succession when a sovereign dies. No notion of the death of God exists in the book; rather, the succession from Moses to Joshua as the human leader of the nation covers this likeness. This similarity is mentioned in the commentary.

Vocabulary similarities are also occasionally indicated. The similarity of the structure of Deuteronomy especially to the treaties of the last half of the second millennium B.C. strongly buttresses the basic unity of the book and therefore the Mosaic authorship of it, as Kitchen, Kline, and others have clearly shown. See above and in the following notes.

## 3. Purpose

The Mosaic purpose for the proclamation and writing of Deuteronomy is distinctly stated, beginning with 4:1–2, 5–6, 9–14, and continuing under such injunctions as "Hear, O Israel . . . ," "These are the commands . . . ," and "Be careful to do." Such exhortations are often followed by reasons for obedience to the Lord. The basic existential occasion grew from the rescue of the people from Egypt and their position on the southeastern border of Canaan—poised there to enter and to occupy that land as their own in fulfillment of the promises first made to Abraham, Isaac, and Jacob, and now reiterated to the descendants of the patriarchs. It was the purpose of God to form their nation and give Canaan to them as their national homeland as recorded in 6:18: "Do what is right and good in the LORD's sight, so that it may go well with you and you may go in and take over the good land that the LORD promised on oath to your forefathers."

The Book of Deuteronomy calls for the enactment (renewal) of the covenant as a preparation for the entrance into Canaan—its conquest and occupation—and presents the way of life that the Israelites were to follow in the Promised Land. Incidental to this covenant enactment are such corollaries as the curses that will fall on Israel if they fail to observe the stipulations and the blessings they will receive when they obey the Lord their God. In the purpose of God, these curses and blessings are to fix firmly in the mind of the people their resolve to adhere to the Lord and to serve as a continual warning against traitorous infidelity. In view of later history, they also predict times of disaster as well as ultimate blessing.

## 4. Summary

The report of the addresses of Moses "in the desert east of the Jordan" begins with a preamble in 1:1–5 giving the locale and the time of the addresses relative to the Exodus and the conquest of Transjordan.

The introductory clause of 1:1 covers all the messages of Moses. Similar clauses appear throughout the book introducing particular addresses or parts of addresses.

The historical prologue, which follows the preamble and is the substance of the first address (1:6–4:43), covers the experiences from Mount Horeb (Sinai) to the Jordan River in the plains of Moab and the appointment of the Transjordan cities of refuge.

The first address stresses the graciousness of God, in spite of the recalcitrance of Israel, and provides the spiritual foundation for the commands of the next address.

The grace of God in the first address is indicated by references to his gift of the land (1:8, 21, 25, 35–36, 39; 3:18), his support of the people in its acquisition (1:31, 39; 2:31, 36; 3:3), and his continued presence (4:7, 31, 37–38).

The second address, presenting the stipulations of the covenant-treaty, is covered in 5:1–26:19 and begins similarly to the first, with an introductory statement including geographical and temporal elements (4:44–49). It sets forth the Ten Commandments and, to some degree, their exposition (ch. 5), together with related rules including the basic commandment of love toward God (chs. 6–11) and certain stipulations demanding obedience to the Lord and governing the people's way of life in the Promised Land (chs. 12–26). This conforms to the Hittite suzerain-vassal treaty order of (1) preamble; (2) historical prologue; (3) stipulations, laws, and regulations; and then the other elements covered in the treaty form.

Whether or not the second address includes 27:1 to 28:68, the next section of Deuteronomy speaks of the ratification of the covenant-treaty (27:1–30:20). The inclusion of the first part (27:1–28:68) of this section in the second address stems from the use of the introductory formula: "These are the terms of the covenant the LORD commanded Moses to make with the Israelites in Moab, in addition to the covenant he had made with them at Horeb" (29:1). This supposedly signals the beginning of the third address.

The end of the third address is even more problematic, as a review of various outlines of Deuteronomy shows, and is thought to be at any of several places from 30:20 to 33:29. It is unlikely that the addresses can all be discretely divided. In any case, the message is clear. From 27:1 to 30:20 Moses delineates the ratification procedure of the covenant-treaty with its future ancillary elements of locale and blessings and curses together with anticipations for Israel for either acceptance or rejection of the covenant.

The concluding narratives (31:1–34:12) include still more similarities to the Near Eastern treaties, such as the succession of the leader and the deposition of copies of the law. The Song of Moses, the blessing of Moses on the tribes (a patriarchal tradition), and the death and burial of Moses complete the book.

As noted above, Deuteronomy can be outlined as a series of addresses by Moses to the Israelites preparing them for entrance into Canaan, the conquest of the land, and their settlement there as God's people. The addresses are indicated by (1) "These are the words Moses spoke to all Israel in the desert east of the Jordan" (1:1); (2) "This is the law Moses set before the Israelites. These are the stipulations, decrees and laws Moses gave them when they came out of Egypt and were in the valley near Beth Peor east of the Jordan" (4:44–46); and (3) "These are the terms of the covenant the LORD commanded Moses to make with the Israelites in Moab, in addition to the covenant he had made with them at Horeb" (29:1).

Moses' last major address once more emphasizes the character of the covenant: "You are standing here in order to enter into a covenant with the LORD your God, a covenant the LORD is making with you this day and sealing with an oath, to confirm you this day as his people, that he may be your God as he promised" (29:12–13).

## 5. Canonical Status

From intertestamental times on into the NT period and beyond, God's people have recognized the Book of Deuteronomy as canonical Scripture. In the prologue to

Ecclesiasticus, written in 180 B.C., reference is made to "the Law and the prophets and the others who followed after them." The Law undoubtedly includes Deuteronomy.[2] Josephus (*Contra Apion* 1:8) mentions among the twenty-two "divine" books five that "belong to Moses." Moreover, the inclusion of Deuteronomy in the LXX and other early translations and the quotations from Deuteronomy found in the NT reckon Deuteronomy as canonical.

Deuteronomy was a favorite book of the Qumran community. Among the fragments of the DSS, all but eight chapters of Deuteronomy are represented (Craigie, pp. 84–86).

How the original and earliest MSS were kept and copied is unknown. Within the corpus of the OT, however, whenever reference is made to the covenant law of God, the authentic and basic Word of God stems from that which came through Moses. Illustrative of this are the phrases and clauses from the Song of Moses that erupt here and there. Verbatim quotes from the song appear again and again in the Psalms and Prophets (even in 2 Macc 2:3) and on into the NT. What changes in the text might have occurred prior to the oldest extant textual materials are, of course, unknown. Many variants have appeared during the history of the known text. Doubtless other variants occurred during earlier periods. Nevertheless textual history shows that significant variations that would change the basic message of the Scriptures have not appeared. The text now known can be trusted as essentially the text of the autographs: "Jewish fidelity and scrupulousness in handing down the sacred page is a strong guarantee for the essential soundness of the text, outweighing the want of age."[3] Walter C. Kaiser, Jr., points out that when our Lord declared that the Scriptures spoke of him (Luke 24:27), he was referring to the canonical OT Scriptures ("The Theology of the Old Testament," EBC, 1:290).

Deuteronomy 1:36 is cited in Joshua 14:9, while 2 Kings 14:6 quotes Deuteronomy 24:16. The NIV lists in its footnotes thirty-four passages in Deuteronomy that are quoted one or more times in the NT, making forty-three NT quotations. Many more allusions and partial quotes occur, but these forty-three are indicated as quotations in the text of the NT. Moreover, these forty-three are made as the authoritative revelation of God to support theological positions.

In the gospel narratives the Lord Jesus specifically quotes ten passages from Deuteronomy, including the celebrated answers to the Devil during the temptation in the desert, saying, "It is written" (Matt 4:4, 7, 10; Luke 4:4, 8, 12). The rest of the NT quotes are found in Acts, the writings of Paul, and the Epistle to the Hebrews.

Though not a few ancient and especially modern scholars have doubted that Deuteronomy was what the Scriptures claim it to be, the uniform historical testimony declares its canonicity as Scripture. For a good review of the canonicity of the OT with several specific references to Deuteronomy, see Milton Fisher's "The Canon of the Old Testament" (EBC, 1:385–92).

## 6. Critical Theories

From early Christian times until the rise of the documentary hypothesis of Pentateuchal formation in the nineteenth century, biblical scholars generally held to

[2] Edgar J. Goodspeed, "Ecclesiasticus," *The Story of the Apocrypha* (Chicago: University of Chicago Press, 1939), p. 20.

[3] Aage Bentzen, *Introduction to the Old Testament* (Copenhagen: G.E.C. Gad, 1952), 1:65. See also Alan R. Millard, "In Praise of Ancient Scribes" BA 45, 2 (Summer 1982): 143–53.

the Mosaic authorship of the Pentateuch. The influence of such men as Julius Wellhausen on the continent, S.R. Driver in Britain, and Robert Pfeiffer in the United States at the close of the nineteenth and during the first half of the twentieth centuries swept biblical scholarship into the documentary fold.

Wellhausen, following earlier suggestions, declared that the basic elements of Deuteronomy (D) were written in the fifty years prior to 622 B.C. and were the basis for Josiah's 621 B.C. reformation. This reconstruction of Pentateuchal formation included two "historical documents" whose authors used the terms "Yahweh" and "Elohim" (J and E) for God and P to signify later priestly writers. The temporal order of production was JEDP.

This theory of biblical provenance did not lack critics, who, though they accepted the documentary theory, developed many variations of the basic scheme. Those who defended the Mosaic authorship rejected this whole rationalistic, evolutionary approach.

As discussion continued no consensus relative to the formation or the date of the writing of Deuteronomy appeared. In 1946 H.H. Rowley wrote, "One of the most debated questions in the field of O.T. scholarship during the last twenty-five years has been that of the date of Deuteronomy."[4] Rowley mentioned dates from "the formation of the monarchy" to "a time after the fall of Jerusalem in 586 B.C."[5]

Forty years after Rowley's work, the setting of dates has not ceased. A sampling of dates includes von Rad, 701 B.C.; Rowley, 680; Bright, 600; Noth, 550; Holscher, 520; and Pedersen, 400. The differences of opinion arise from attempts to fit Deuteronomy into the historical slot (or slots) that the evidence is thought to suggest. Evidence of a new understanding of the history, the cultural life, and the religions of the ancient Near East have forced reconstruction—if not the abandonment—of the documentary theory.

Nevertheless, attempts to harmonize various points of view continually appear. Richard Clifford says that the formation of Deuteronomy began in the mid-eighth century and was completed in the mid-sixth century. The process was in three principal stages. Stage one produced Deuteronomy 1:1 to 3:29 and 31:1–8. Stage two brought forth 4:1 to 33:29 (except for 31:1–8, which was part of stage one), and stage three added chapter 34. The second stage, especially, covered most of the two hundred years involved and included various writers and editors.[6]

Current theories stress such subjects as the centrality of worship. Is this of prime importance or is it not? Is the locale of "the place the LORD your God will choose as a dwelling for his Name" of leading significance (Deut 12:11)? Is this the one place or several or a series? Is Deuteronomy itself covenant renewal? Was Deuteronomy written to protect Israel from Canaanite influence? Is it law or is it preaching? Or both—and more? What was the effect of Deuteronomy on subsequent eras? Some observations on these and similar questions will be found in various locations in the commentary where these subjects appear.

A cardinal question concerns the method of the formation of Deuteronomy (see above). Was Deuteronomy the result of God's revelation through Moses, or was it a gradual accretion of Israelite ideas based on a limited initial experience? Is Deuteronomy truly Mosaic as the Scriptures aver, or is it the result of a "Deutero-

[4] *Studies in Old Testament Prophecy* (Edinburgh: T. & T. Clark, 1950), p. 157.

[5] Ibid.

[6] *Deuteronomy* (Wilmington: Michael Glazier, 1982), pp. 1–3.

nomic history" (Deuteronomy through Kings) during which "Deuteronomists" produced it? The existence of the "Deuteronomic school" owes more to the ingenuity and fertile imaginations of the critics than to the demands of the Scriptures themselves.

The most enlightening element in the elucidation of Deuteronomy in recent times is that of the knowledge of the ancient Near Eastern suzerain-vassal treaties, especially the Hittite treaties of the second millennium B.C. Mendenhall pointed out the remarkable similarities between the Hittite suzerainty treaties and the biblical covenant. Kitchen, Kline, and others showed how these similarities give evidence for the unity of Deuteronomy and for the Mosaic date for its authorship.[7]

## 7. Text

The Hebrew Bible (BHS) lists more than 750 variants in the text of Deuteronomy; but many more exist, and some appear significant. For instance, instead of reading Deuteronomy 22:6 as "do not take the mother with the young," the Severus Codex has "do not take the mother on the laying nest," because the Severus MS has an additional letter giving the spelling of the word meaning "delivery stool," as in Exodus 1:16.[8]

In addition to spelling variations, there are differing divisions of letters into words and varying vocalizations (i.e., insertions of vowels). In some instances words may be missing while in other places words may have been introduced for various reasons—like being taken from another verse where a fuller phrase was original.

In 4:48 an ancient confusion of the consonants "resh" and "yod" in addition to a change in vocalization have resulted in the Masoretic "Siyon" rather than the Sidonian name "Sirion" for Mount Hermon (as in 3:9).

In 5:10 the MT has a "waw" for a "yod" in the word for "my commandments." The correct form is in Exodus 20:6.

In 11:24 apparently the word *'aḏ* was dropped from before "Lebanon." The same thing occurs in Joshua 1:4. The meaning may be different.

Variations in vocalization occur also in 20:8, 19; 28:22; 31:7; and 32:26. For details see the Notes on these verses.

The texts of Deuteronomy are in substantial agreement. Some of the variants above have been followed in the NIV.

The oldest extant witnesses to the text of Deuteronomy include the Nash papyrus, with an excerpt from Deuteronomy 5:6–6:5, and twenty-five MS fragments from the DSS. These are dated variously from 200 B.C. to A.D. 100. The earliest complete text of Deuteronomy is from the early eleventh century.

The observation of C.F. Keil in the midst of the nineteenth-century controversies on the text of the OT as a whole can certainly be said of the text of Deuteronomy: "The text of the Bible was faithfully and carefully handed down by the Masoretes. For the results which have been brought to light have shown that, without an exception, the various readings obtained from the manuscripts exert no influence of importance on

[7] George E. Mendenhall, "Ancient Oriental and Biblical Law," BA 17 (May 1954): 26–46; id., "Covenant Forms," pp. 50–76; Kitchen, *The Bible*, pp. 79–85; id., *Ancient Orient*, pp. 90–102; Kline, *Treaty*, pp. 28–30; id., *Structure*, pp. 131–53.

[8] The Severus Codex, supposedly part of the plunder brought to Rome in A.D. 70, contains thirty-two variant readings of a Pentateuch MS from the synagogue of Severus in Rome (E. Würthwein, *The Text of the Old Testament* [Oxford: Basil Blackwell, 1957], p. 27).

the meaning and the contents of Scripture, so far as concerns the subject matter of the faith."[9]

## 8. Theological Values

The Book of Deuteronomy is definitely spiritual and intensely theological. In character it is an interpretation and an application of the relationship of the Lord to Israel and his revelation in covenant-treaty form to his people.

The theological values of Deuteronomy can hardly be exaggerated. It stands as the wellspring of biblical historical revelation. It is a prime source for both OT and NT theology. Whether the covenant, the holiness of God, or the concept of the people of God is the unifying factor of OT theology, each finds emphasis and remarkable definition in Deuteronomy.

When the prophets speak of God, they speak of the God and the message of Deuteronomy and of the relationship embodied in its covenant-treaty. The warnings of doom in the prophets (esp. Jeremiah) are the warnings or curses of Deuteronomy. The promises of blessing for Israel when she lives in faith, love, and obedience to the Lord (or returns to the Lord after a period of doom) are the blessings of Deuteronomy. The loving, righteous, all-powerful, wonder-working Lord of Deuteronomy is the God of the prophets—and of the NT as well!

The way of life of the people of God forms the basis for all subsequent revelation of the way of life acceptable to him. These people belong wholly to the Lord; they are his treasured inheritance. He redeemed them from the bondage of Egypt. He is about to fulfill his promise to Abraham, Isaac, and Jacob by giving them the Promised Land, their inheritance. The later NT teachings on the love of God, the redemption offered through Christ, the saved as the inheritance of God, and the fulfillment of the promises of God to the saved as their inheritance from him rest on Deuteronomy.

God in Deuteronomy is personal, eternal, omnipotent, sovereign, purposeful, loving, holy, and righteous. The knowledge of his person and will is communicated by propositional, directive, exhortative, informative, and predictive revelation. No other God exists, though cognizance is taken of the gods believed in by other nations.

The most important element of subjective theology in Deuteronomy is that of the absolutely unqualified, total commitment of the people to the Lord. Nothing less is acceptable. No dissimulation, no assimilation, no syncretism with other gods or religions or religious practices are to be tolerated. The people belong to the Lord alone. He is the absolute—though benevolent—sovereign, whose people uniquely and completely belong to him.

Deuteronomy clearly indicates the Judeo-Christian idea of law and the basis for it. Here is no man-made agreement based on interpersonal, intertribal, or even international experience; rather, the decrees of God produce the notion of law. These decrees stem from the nature of God himself and from his disposition toward mankind.

This understanding of the source of the concept of law underlining the development of civilization in the Western world is of the utmost importance in retaining the rights of man in a society free from coercion.

---

[9] *Introduction to the Old Testament* (Grand Rapids: Eerdmans, 1959), p. 331.

## 9. Bibliography

### Commentaries


Blair, E.P. *The Book of Deuteronomy; The Book of Joshua*. The Layman's Bible Commentary. Richmond: John Knox, 1964.

Craigie, P.C. *Deuteronomy*. The New International Commentary on the Old Testament. Grand Rapids: Eerdmans, 1976.

Cunliffe-Jones, H. *Deuteronomy*. Torch Bible Commentaries. London: SCM, 1964.

Driver, S.R. *Deuteronomy*. International Critical Commentary. Edinburgh: T. & T. Clark, 1902.

Gottwald, N.K. "Deuteronomy." *The Interpreter's One-Volume Commentary on the Bible*. Edited by C.M. Laymon. Nashville: Abingdon, 1971.

Harrison, R.K., and Manley, G.T. "Deuteronomy." *The New Bible Commentary: Revised*. Edited by D. Guthrie et al. Grand Rapids: Eerdmans, 1970.

Keil, C.F. *Deuteronomy*. Biblical Commentary on the Old Testament. Grand Rapids: Eerdmans, 1949.

Kline, M.G. *Treaty of the Great King*. Grand Rapids: Eerdmans, 1963.

Phillips, A. *Deuteronomy*. Cambridge Bible Commentary on the New English Bible. Cambridge: University Press, 1973.

Reider, Joseph. *Deuteronomy With Commentary*. Philadelphia: Jewish Publication Society of America, 1937.

Robinson, D.W.B. *Josiah's Reforms and the Book of the Law*. London: Tyndale, 1951.

Robinson, H. Wheeler. *Deuteronomy and Joshua*. New York: Oxford University Press, 1907.

Schultz, Samuel J. *Deuteronomy: The Gospel of Love*. Chicago: Moody, 1971.

Smith, G.A. *The Book of Deuteronomy*. The Cambridge Bible. Cambridge: University Press, 1918.

Thompson, J.A. *Deuteronomy*. Tyndale Old Testament Commentary. London: Inter-Varsity, 1974.

von Rad, G. *Studies in Deuteronomy*. London: SCM, 1953.

______. *Deuteronomy*. Philadelphia: Westminster, 1966.

Watts, J.D.W. *Deuteronomy*. The Broadman Bible Commentary. Nashville: Broadman, 1971.

Wright, A.E. *Deuteronomy*. The Interpreter's Bible. Edited by G. Buttrick. Nashville: Abingdon, 1953.


### Selected Studies


Ackyrod, P.R., and Linders, B. *Words and Meanings*. Cambridge: Cambridge University Press, 1968.

Allis, O.T. *The Five Books of Moses*. Philadelphia: Presbyterian and Reformed, 1943.

______. *God Spoke by Moses*. Philadelphia: Presbyterian and Reformed, 1943.

Baltzer, K. *The Covenant Formulary in Old Testament, Jewish, and Early Christian Writings*. Oxford: Blackwell, 1971.

Baly, Dennis. *The Geography of the Bible*. New York: Harper, 1957.

Beegle, D.M. *Moses, the Servant of Yahweh*. Grand Rapids: Eerdmans, 1972.

Boecker, H.J. *Law and the Administration of Justice in the Old Testament and Ancient Near East*. Minneapolis: Augsburg, 1980.

Boman, Thorleif. *Hebrew Thought Compared With Greek*. New York: Norton, 1970.

Brichto, H.C. *The Problem of "Curse" in the Hebrew Bible*. Philadelphia: Society of Biblical Literature, 1968.

Bridges, Ronald, and Weigle, Luther A. *The Bible Word Book*. New York: Thomas Nelson and Sons, 1960.

Brinker, R. *The Influence of Sanctuaries in Early Israel*. Manchester: University Press, 1946.

Carmichael, C.M. *The Laws of Deuteronomy*. Ithaca: Cornell University Press, 1974.

Charles, R.H. *The Decalogue*. Edinburgh: T. & T. Clark, 1923.

DEUTERONOMY


Clements, R.E. *God's Chosen People.* Valley Forge, Penn.: Judson, 1969.
Coogan, M.D. *Stories From Ancient Canaan.* Philadelphia: Westminster, 1978.
Cross, F.M. *The Ancient Library of Qumran.* Garden City: Doubleday, 1961.
Cross, F.M., and Freedman, D.N. *Studies in Ancient Yahwistic Poetry.* Missoula: Scholars, 1975.
de Vaux, R. *The Bible and the Ancient Near East.* Garden City: Doubleday, 1971.
Dupont-Sommer, A. *The Essene Writings From Qumran.* Cleveland: World, 1967.
Eissfeldt, O. *The Old Testament, an Introduction.* New York: Harper and Row, 1965.
Ellenbogen, M. *Foreign Words in the Old Testament.* London: Luzac, 1962.
Frank, H.T., and Reed, W.L., edd. *Translating and Understanding the Old Testament.* Nashville: Abingdon, 1970.
Garstang, John. *Foundations of Bible History, Joshua, Judges.* London: Constable, 1931.
Gibson, J.C.L., and Driver, G.R. *Canaanite Myths and Legends.* Edinburgh: T. & T. Clark, 1978.
Green, A. *The Role of Human Sacrifice in the Ancient Near East.* Missoula: Scholars, 1975.
Hillers, D.R. *Covenant: The History of a Biblical Idea.* Baltimore: Johns Hopkins University Press, 1969.
———. *Treaty-Curses and the Old Testament Prophets.* Rome: Pontifical Biblical Institute, 1964.
Hodges, Henry. *Technology in the Ancient World.* New York: Knopf, 1970.
Hulst, A.R. *Old Testament Translation Problems.* Leiden: Brill, 1960.
Jocz, J. *The Covenant—A Theology of Human Destiny.* Grand Rapids: Eerdmans, 1968.
Kitchen, K.A. *Ancient Orient and Old Testament.* Chicago: InterVarsity, 1966.
———. *The Bible in Its World.* Exeter: Paternoster, 1977.
Kline, M.G. *Treaty of the Great King.* Grand Rapids: Eerdmans, 1963.
———. *The Structure of Biblical Authority.* Grand Rapids: Eerdmans, 1972.
McCarthy, D.J. *Old Testament Covenant: A Survey of Current Opinions.* Richmond: John Knox, 1972.
Manley, G.T. *The Book of the Law.* Grand Rapids: Eerdmans, 1957.
Mendenhall, G.E. *Law and Covenant in Israel and the Ancient Near East.* Pittsburgh: Biblical Colloquium, 1955.
———. *The Tenth Generation.* Baltimore: Johns Hopkins University Press, 1973.
Moscati, S. *The World of the Phoenicians.* New York: Praeger, 1968.
Muilenburg, J. *The Way of Israel.* New York: Harper and Row, 1965.
Neufeld, E. *The Hittite Laws.* London: Luzac, 1951.
Nicholson, E.W. *Deuteronomy and Tradition.* Philadelphia: Fortress, 1967.
Nielsen, E. *The Ten Commandments in New Perspective.* Naperville: Allenson, 1968.
Noth, M. *The Old Testament World.* Philadelphia: Fortress, 1964.
Pfeiffer, Charles. *Ras Shamra and the Bible.* Grand Rapids: Baker, 1962.
Phillips, A. *Ancient Israel's Criminal Law: A New Approach to the Decalogue.* Oxford: Blackwell, 1970.
Polzin, R. *Moses and the Deuteronomist.* New York: Seabury, 1980.
Ridderbos, H.N. *The Epistle of Paul to the Churches of Galatia.* The New International Commentary on the New Testament. Grand Rapids: Eerdmans, 1965.
Stamm, J.J., and Andrew, M.E. *The Ten Commandments in Recent Research.* Naperville, Ill.: Allenson, 1967.
Thomas, D. Winton, ed. *Documents From Old Testament Times.* New York: Harper and Row, 1961.
Thompson, J.A. *The Ancient Near Eastern Treaties and the Old Testament.* London: Tyndale, 1964.
———. *The Bible and Archaeology.* Grand Rapids: Eerdmans, 1972.
Weinfeld, M. *Deuteronomy and the Deuteronomic School.* Oxford: Clarendon, 1972.
Welch, A.C. *The Code of Deuteronomy.* London: J. Clarke, 1924.
———. *Deuteronomy, the Framework of the Code.* London: Oxford University Press, 1932.
Wijngaards, J. *The Formulas of the Deuteronomic Creed.* Tilburg: Reijen, 1963.

Wiseman, D.J. *The Alalakh Tablets*. London: British Institute of Archaeology at Ankara, 1953.
______. *The Vassal-Treaties of Esarhaddon*. London: British Institute of Archaeology in Iraq, 1958.
Wright, G.E. "The Lawsuit of God: A Form Critical Study of Deuteronomy 32." *Israel's Prophetic Heritage*. Edited by B.W. Anderson and W. Harrelson. New York: Harper, 1962, pages 26–27.
______. *Discoveries in the Judean Desert of Jordan*. 4 vols. Oxford: Clarendon, 1965.

## Periodicals

Albright, W.F. "Some Remarks on the Song of Moses in Deuteronomy." *Vetus Testamentum* 9 (October 1959): 339–41.
Brueggemann, Walter. "Trajectories in Old Testament Literature and the Sociology of Ancient Israel." *Journal of Biblical Literature* 98 (June 1979): 161–85.
Clements, R.E. "Deuteronomy and the Jerusalem Cult Tradition." *Vetus Testamentum* 15 (July 1965): 300–315.
Cross, F.M., and Freedman, D.N. "The Blessing of Moses." *Journal of Biblical Literature* 67 (September 1948): 191–201.
Cross, L.B. "Commentaries on Deuteronomy." *Theology* 64 (May 1961): 184–88.
Emerton, J.A. "Priests and Levites in Deuteronomy." *Vetus Testamentum* 12 (April 1962): 129–38.
______. "Considerations of Some Alleged Meanings of ידע in Hebrew." *Journal of Semitic Studies* 15 (Autumn 1970): 145–46.
Fretheim, T.E. "The Ark in Deuteronomy." *Catholic Biblical Quarterly* 30 (January 1968): 1–14.
Hertz, J.H. "Deuteronomy: Antiquity and Mosaic Authorship." *Journal of the Transactions of the Victoria Institute* 72 (1940): 86–103.
Hillers, D.R. "A Note on Some Treaty Terminology in the Old Testament." *Bulletin of the American Schools of Oriental Research* 176 (December 1964): 46–47.
Hoffner, H. "Some Contributions of Hittitology to Old Testament Study." *Tyndale Bulletin* 20 (1969): 41–42.
Kaufman, Stephen A. "The Structure of Deuteronomic Law." *Maarav* 1 (Spring 1979): 105–58.
Kitchen, K.A. "The Old Testament in Its Context, 2." *Theological Students Fellowship Bulletin* 60 (1972): 3–11.
______. "The Old Testament in Its Context, 6." *Theological Students Fellowship Bulletin* 64 (1976): 2–10.
McBride, S. "The Yoke of the Kingdom—An Exposition of Deuteronomy 6:4–5." *Interpretation* 27 (July 1973): 273–306.
Manley, G.T. "Problems in Deuteronomy." *Evangelical Quarterly* 28 (October-December 1955): 201ff.
Mendenhall, G.E. "Covenant Forms in Israelite Tradition." *Biblical Archaeologist* 17 (September 1954): 50–76.
Moran, W.L. "The Ancient Near Eastern Background of Love of God in Deuteronomy." *Catholic Biblical Quarterly* 2 (1963): 77ff.
______. "A Note on the Treaty Terminology of the Sefire Stelas." *Journal of Near Eastern Studies* 22 (July 1963): 173–76.
Muilenburg, J. "The Form and Structure of the Covenantal Formulations." *Vetus Testamentum* 11 (October 1959): 347–65.
Nielsen, E. "Moses and the Law." *Vetus Testamentum* 32 (January 1982): 87–88.
Reif, S.C. "Dedicated to חנך." *Vetus Testamentum* 22 (October 1972): 495–501.
Rofé, A. "The Monotheistic Argumentation in Deuteronomy IV 32–40: Contents, Composition, and Text." *Vetus Testamentum* 35 (October 1985): 434–45.
Segal, M.H. "The Book of Deuteronomy." *Jewish Quarterly Review* 48 (1957/58): 315–51.

Skehan, P. "The Structure of the Song of Moses in Deuteronomy (Deut. 32:1–43)." *Catholic Biblical Quarterly* 13 (April 1951): 153–63.

———. "A Qumran Fragment." *Bulletin of the American Schools of Oriental Research* 136 (December 1954): 12–15.

Weinfeld, M. "Traces of Assyrian Treaty Formulae in Deuteronomy." *Biblica* 46, 4 (1965): 417–27.

———. "Deuteronomy—the Present State of the Inquiry." *Journal of Biblical Literature* 86 (September 1967): 249–62.

———. "Review of Frank Cruseman's *Der Widerstand Gegen das Königturn . . . israelitischen Staat.*" *Vetus Testamentum* 31 (January 1981): 99–108.

Wenham, G.J. "Deuteronomy and the Central Sanctuary." *Tyndale Bulletin* 22 (1971): 103–18.

Williams, D. "Deuteronomy in Modern Study." *The Review and Expositor* (Fall 1964): 265–73.

Wiseman, D.J. "Is It Peace? Covenant and Diplomacy." *Vetus Testamentum* 32, 3 (July 1982): 311–26.

Wright, G.E. "The Levites in Deuteronomy." *Vetus Testamentum* 4 (October 1954): 325–30.

## 10. Outline

I. Preamble (1:1–5)

II. First Address: The Historical Prologue (1:6–4:43)
- A. Experiences From Horeb to the Jordan (1:6–3:29)
  - 1. The command to leave Horeb (1:6–8)
  - 2. The appointment of leaders (1:9–18)
  - 3. The spies sent out (1:19–25)
  - 4. The rebellion against the Lord (1:26–46)
  - 5. The journey from Kadesh to Kedemoth (2:1–25)
  - 6. The conquest of Transjordan (2:26–3:20)
    - a. The defeat of Sihon (2:26–37)
    - b. The defeat of Og (3:1–11)
    - c. The division of the land (3:12–20)
  - 7. Moses forbidden to cross the Jordan (3:21–29)
- B. Israel Before the Lord (4:1–40)
  - 1. Exhortation to obey the Lord's commands (4:1–14)
  - 2. Idolatry forbidden (4:15–31)
  - 3. Acknowledgment of the Lord as God (4:32–40)
- C. The Transjordanian Cities of Refuge (4:41–43)

III. The Second Address: Stipulations of the Covenant-Treaty and Its Ratification (4:44–28:68)
- A. Introduction (4:44–49)
- B. Basic Elements of Life in the Land (5:1–11:32)
  - 1. The Ten Commandments (5:1–33)
    - a. Exhortation and historical background (5:1–5)
    - b. The commandments (5:6–21)
      - 1) The Lord as God and the prohibition of other gods (5:6–7)
      - 2) Prohibition of images (5:8–10)
      - 3) Prohibition against misusing God's name (5:11)
      - 4) Observance of the Sabbath (5:12–15)
      - 5) Honoring one's parents (5:16)
      - 6) Prohibition of murder (5:17)
      - 7) Prohibition of adultery (5:18)
      - 8) Prohibition of stealing (5:19)
      - 9) Prohibition of false testimony (5:20)
      - 10) Prohibition of coveting (5:21)
    - c. Ratification of the covenant-treaty (5:22–33)
  - 2. The greatest commandment: Love the Lord (6:1–25)
    - a. The intent of the covenant (6:1–3)
    - b. The greatest command: total commitment (6:4–5)
    - c. Propagation of the command (6:6–9)
    - d. Ways to preserve the command (6:10–25)
  - 3. Problems of achieving the covenant of love in the land (7:1–26)
    - a. Relations with the people of the land and with the Lord (7:1–10)
    - b. Blessing of the conquest (7:11–26)

4. Exhortation not to forget the Lord (8:1–20)
   a. The discipline of the desert and the coming Promised Land (8:1–9)
   b. Remembrance of the Lord who led them from Egypt to Canaan (8:10–20)
5. Warning based on former infidelity (9:1–10:11)
   a. The coming defeat of the Anakites (9:1–6)
   b. The golden calf provocation (9:7–21)
   c. Israel's rebellion and Moses' prayer (9:22–29)
   d. New tablets (10:1–11)
6. Exhortation to revere and love the Lord (10:12–11:32)
   a. The requirement of allegiance (10:12–22)
   b. Love and obedience toward the Lord (11:1–25)
      1) The requirements of the disciplined (11:1–7)
      2) Allegiance necessary to possess the land (11:8–25)
   c. Directives for the blessing and curse recital (11:26–32)

C. Specific Stipulations of the Covenant-Treaty (12:1–26:19)
1. For worship and ceremony (12:1–16:17)
   a. At the place of the Lord's choosing (12:1–32)
      1) The sanctuary and its sacrifices (12:1–14)
      2) Prohibitions and regulations regarding eating blood and meat (12:15–32)
   b. Worship of other gods forbidden (13:1–18)
   c. Clean and unclean foods (14:1–21)
   d. Time-related activities (14:22–16:17)
      1) Tithes (14:22–29)
      2) The year of canceling debts (15:1–11)
      3) Freeing servants (15:12–18)
      4) Firstborn animals (15:19–23)
      5) Passover (16:1–8)
      6) Feast of Weeks (16:9–12)
      7) Feast of Tabernacles (16:13–17)
2. National concerns (16:18–19:21)
   a. Judges (16:18–20)
   b. Asherah poles, sacred stones, and flawed animals (16:21–17:1)
   c. Procedures for punishment of covenant violators (17:2–13)
   d. Appointment of and rules for a king (17:14–20)
   e. Shares for priests and Levites (18:1–8)
   f. Detestable practices of Canaan (18:9–13)
   g. The prophet like Moses (18:14–22)
   h. Cities of refuge (19:1–14)
   i. Witnesses to a crime (19:15–21)
3. Rules for warfare (20:1–20)
4. Interpersonal relationships (21:1–25:19)
   a. Atonement for unsolved murder (21:1–9)
   b. Family relationships (21:10–21)
   c. Relations to land, animals, and things (21:22–22:12)
   d. Marriage violations (22:13–30)

- e. Family, neighborhood, and national relationships (23:1–25:19)
  - 1) Situations requiring exclusion from the assembly (23:1–14)
  - 2) A miscellany of personal relationships (23:15–25:19)
    - a) Sundry laws (23:15–25)
    - b) Marriage, divorce, and remarriage (24:1–5)
    - c) Concern for others (24:6–22)
    - d) Civil situations (25:1–4)
    - e) Levirate marriage (25:5–10)
    - f) Belligerent behavior and honest measures (25:11–16)
    - g) Destruction of Amalek (25:17–19)
- 5. Firstfruits and tithes (26:1–15)
- 6. Concluding exhortation and the declaration of the covenant-treaty compact (26:16–19)

D. Ratification of the Covenant-Treaty (27:1–26)
- 1. The law and the altar on Mount Ebal (27:1–8)
- 2. The curses from Mount Ebal (27:9–26)
  - a. The standing and the stance of the tribes (27:9–13)
  - b. Curses and response (27:14–26)

E. The Blessings and the Curses (28:1–68)
- 1. The blessings (28:1–14)
- 2. The curses (28:15–68)

IV. Third Address: The Terms of the Covenant (29:1–30:20)

A. Recapitulation of Historical Background: Warnings and Results of Abandonment of the Covenant-Treaty (29:1–29)
- 1. Introduction (29:1)
- 2. Recapitulation of desert situation (29:2–8)
- 3. Clarification of covenant-treaty situation (29:9–21)
- 4. Results of the Lord's anger on those who abandon the covenant (29:22–29)

B. Prosperity After the Return to the Lord (30:1–10)

C. The Covenant Offer of Life or Death (30:11–20)

V. Concluding Narratives (31:1–34:12)

A. Charge to Joshua and Deposition of the Law (31:1–29)
- 1. Joshua to be leader (31:1–8)
- 2. Recitation of the law at every seventh Feast of Tabernacles (31:9–13)
- 3. Some last words on leadership transfer (31:14–23)
- 4. The deposition of the law book and its witness (31:24–29)

B. The Song of Moses (31:30–32:47)
- 1. Moses' recitation before the assembly (31:30)
- 2. Literary introduction (32:1–2)
- 3. The theme: the proclamation of the Lord (32:3–4)
- 4. The indictment of Israel (32:5–6)
- 5. Israel as God's inheritance (32:7–9)
- 6. The Lord's early care of Israel (32:10–12)
- 7. The Lord's care of Israel in Canaan foreseen (32:13–14)

8. Affluent Israel's rejection of God (32:15–18)
9. God's rejection of Israel (32:19–30)
10. The punishment of Israel's enemies (32:31–35)
11. The Lord's compassion toward Israel and vengeance on the enemies (32:36–43)
12. Moses' presentation of the song and his exhortation to obey the law (32:44–47)

C. Directives for Moses' Death (32:48–52)
D. The Blessing of Moses on the Tribes (33:1–29)
1. Introduction (33:1–5)
2. Reuben (33:6)
3. Judah (33:7)
4. Levi (33:8–11)
5. Benjamin (33:12)
6. Joseph (Ephraim and Manasseh)(33:13–17)
7. Zebulun and Issachar (33:18–19)
8. Gad (33:20–21)
9. Dan (33:22)
10. Naphtali (33:23)
11. Asher (33:24–25)
12. Peroration of God and Israel, his people (33:26–29)

E. The Death of Moses and the Succession of Joshua (34:1–12)

# Text and Exposition

## I. Preamble

### 1:1–5

> 1 These are the words Moses spoke to all Israel in the desert east of the
> Jordan—that is, in the Arabah—opposite Suph, between Paran and
> Tophel, Laban, Hazeroth and Dizahab. 2 (It takes eleven days to go from
> Horeb to Kadesh Barnea by the Mount Seir road.)
> 3 In the fortieth year, on the first day of the eleventh month, Moses
> proclaimed to the Israelites all that the LORD had commanded him
> concerning them. 4 This was after he had defeated Sihon king of the
> Amorites, who reigned in Heshbon, and at Edrei had defeated Og king
> of Bashan, who reigned in Ashtaroth.
> 5 East of the Jordan in the territory of Moab, Moses began to expound
> this law, saying:

The Book of Deuteronomy is described as the words Moses gave to the people of Israel when they were east of the Jordan near the Dead Sea. The places mentioned are locations on Israel's journey from Mount Horeb to their current encampment. The forty years include the time the people spent on the journey from Egypt to Sinai (Horeb), the time spent at Sinai, and the time that elapsed on the journey to Kadesh Barnea.

The journey from Horeb to the southern entrance into Canaan at Kadesh Barnea ordinarily took eleven days; but because Israel did not obey the Lord's command to go north from Kadesh, the Lord turned them back into the desert. Now, in the fortieth year since they had left Egypt, they were at the southeastern entrance into Canaan proper. The time is more specifically indicated as after the conquest of Gilead and Bashan and the killing of the Amorite kings Sihon, king of Heshbon, and Og, king of Bashan.

Heshbon was the capital city of Moab, but Sihon had captured it and made it his capital. Bashan was the territory east of the Lake of Galilee. Ashtaroth, the capital of Og, was a little more than twenty miles east of the Lake of Galilee while Edrei, where Israel defeated Og, was a little less than twenty miles southeast of Ashtaroth.

A most crucial, stirring moment in the experience of the new nation was at hand. It was time for the realization of the Lord's promises from the past—a time for the fulfillment of the hope that began at the Exodus. The Lord's concern—and Moses'—was to prepare the people for the conquest and occupation of Canaan. Now, on the brink of crossing the Jordan, Moses reviewed the salient historical events and Israel's covenant-treaty with the Lord.

The terms used in these initial verses indicate the nature of the book. "These are the words" (v.1) suggest a suzerain-vassal treaty preamble. "All that the LORD had commanded him" (v.3) indicates the source of the material in the book, the nature of Moses' ministry as communicator of the Lord's commands rather than that of an author, and the authoritative character of the addresses as commands of the Lord. The character of the book as regulatory instruction is seen in the designation "this law" in v.5. Moses "spoke" (v.1), "proclaimed" (v.3), and "began to expound . . . saying" (v.5) what the Lord had commanded him. One could expect, therefore, that "these words" would be highly interpretive and hortatory, and that is what they are.

In 1:3, 6, 10, 11, et al., "The LORD," "The LORD our God," "The LORD your God,"

"The LORD, the God of your fathers" all signify strong emphasis on Yahweh as the originator of all that follows in Deuteronomy.

The position of the Lord in Deuteronomy immeasurably transcends that of any king (or any god) in the suzerain-vassal treaties (where gods are mentioned as empowering the kings and where their temples may be repositories for the treaties) because, not only is the Lord superior to all other gods, but he is the suzerain also, and so is the supreme author, enactor, and benefactor of the covenant-treaty. In 1:3 Moses declared that the addresses to come would be "all that the LORD had commanded him." In v.6 "the LORD our God" stands first in the sentence in an emphatic position. Though some deny this syntactical rule, normally the verb stands first. The same position (of the subject standing first) is true of "the LORD your God" in v.10 and of "the LORD, the God of your fathers" in v.11.

"The LORD, the God of your fathers" appropriately fits into the context of v.11 because of its hope and wish that the blessing of the promise to Abraham and the other patriarchs for a largely increasing progeny would be realized. The phrase "the LORD, the God of your fathers" prominently advertised "the LORD" (YHWH) as the God of history to Moses in the burning bush experience, when the Lord commissioned him to lead Israel out of Egypt and into the Promised Land (Exod 3:6, 13, 15–16). Elsewhere in Deuteronomy wherever the phrase "the LORD, the God of your fathers" occurs, the promise of the land is in view. In 29:25 the variant "the LORD, the God of their fathers" appears in retrospect of the Exodus as well as in the promise of the land as in 26:7.

**1** The geographical references, though not now clear, were evidently known in Moses' time. The NIV punctuation suggests that "the desert east of the Jordan," the Arabah, and the series of places that follow are, in general, explications of "desert east of the Jordan." This, however, may not be the case. In Deuteronomy Moses often presents subjects disjunctively; some item under explanation or some description is introduced for further exposition before the main subject is developed. The commissioning of Joshua, for instance, is first mentioned in 3:28 (cf. 1:39; 3:21); but most of the book intervenes before this subject is taken up again, and then other subjects appear between descriptions of the commissioning process (31:3, 7, 14, 23; 34:9). So it may be that these locations identify a few of the places where Moses had earlier imparted some of "these . . . words" to the people. Certainly the addresses in Deuteronomy are not all new material. Moreover Laban and Hazeroth appear to be two of the stations on the journey from Egypt to Canaan (Num 33:18, 20–21 [Hazeroth and Libnah]).

The reference to the journey from Horeb to Kadesh Barnea also suggests this reminiscence. The locations of the other places are not certain, though there was a Paran northwest of Mount Sinai and a Tophel about twenty miles southwest of the Dead Sea.

**2** Mount Horeb is interchangeable with Mount Sinai. Horeb is used more often in Deuteronomy (1:2, 6, 19; 4:10, 15; 5:2; 9:8; 18:16; 29:1 [28:69 MT]) but also occurs in Exodus 3:1; 17:6; 33:6; 1 Kings 8:9; 19:8; 2 Chronicles 5:10; Psalm 106:19; and Malachi 4:4 (3:22 MT). In Sirach 48:7 Sinai and Horeb are used synonymously. Sinai occurs in Deuteronomy 33:2.

**3** "In the fortieth year" terminates the period that the Lord had determined for Israel to live in the deserts of Sinai, the punishment for their refusal to enter Canaan at his command at Kadesh. These forty years represented a generation—specifically the one that disobeyed the command at Kadesh.

The forty years included all the time from Israel's exodus from Egypt till they were to cross the Jordan and enter Canaan from the southeast (Num 14:29–35; 32:13; Deut 8:2–5; 29:5–6; Heb 3:7–19).

**4–5** The defeats of Sihon and Og (v.4) are described in 2:24–3:11. The Amorites had spread widely throughout Mesopotamia and into Syria and Canaan since the third millennium B.C. The term "Amorite" (and also Canaanite) sometimes is used widely of the people in Canaan and Transjordan and sometimes more specifically of people in certain sections of the country. Sihon and Og were Amorite kings of Amorite peoples (ZPEB, 1:140–43). Canaan proper, west of Jordan, is labeled "the hill country of the Amorites," as is seen from the command of the Lord (v.19) and that of Moses (v.20) when Israel advanced to Kadesh Barnea with the expectation of entering Canaan from the south. Sihon controlled southern Transjordan and Og the northern sector, mainly the area east of the Lake of Galilee. So here, "east of the Jordan," Moses began his sermon (v.5).

## Notes

**5** בֵּאֵר (*bē'ēr*, "expound") is a rare word that means "to make clear, distinct, or plain." At the end of Deuteronomy, "all the words of this law" (27:8; cf. 32:46) were to be written "very clearly" (בַּאֵר הֵיטֵב, *ba'ēr hêṭēḇ*) on large stones on Mount Ebal. Habakkuk 2:2 speaks of writing "plain" (*bā'ēr*) on clay tablets so that one could easily read the message.

"East of Jordan" as a translation of בְּעֵבֶר הַיַּרְדֵּן (*bᵉ'ēḇer hayyardēn*, "the region of, by, or near the Jordan") is rendered according to its context. The phrase is used of the area on either side of the Jordan and often appears with an accompanying phrase to clarify it (Manley, *Book of the Law*, pp. 48–49).

## II. First Address: The Historical Prologue (1:6–4:43)

### A. *Experiences From Horeb to the Jordan (1:6–3:29)*

#### 1. *The command to leave Horeb*

1:6–8

6 The LORD our God said to us at Horeb, "You have stayed long enough at this mountain. 7 Break camp and advance into the hill country of the Amorites; go to all the neighboring peoples in the Arabah, in the mountains, in the western foothills, in the Negev and along the coast, to the land of the Canaanites and to Lebanon, as far as the great river, the Euphrates. 8 See, I have given you this land. Go in and take possession of the land that the LORD swore he would give to your fathers—to Abraham, Isaac and Jacob—and to their descendants after them."

**6–8** In this historical prologue to his addresses to Israel, Moses followed the pattern of the suzerain-vassal treaties, which begin by delineating their historical context. For Israel the covenant finds its beginning in the promise the Lord gave to Abraham (Gen 15:18), the promise that made Canaan and environs "the Promised Land."

Moses began by reciting God's order to leave Horeb (v.6) and to go to Canaan (v.7). What the Lord commanded the people at Horeb was a new bit of information. That he gave such a command is mentioned in Numbers 10:11–13, but its content is given only here.

The Lord's gift of Canaan to Israel (v.8) and his command to them to enter and to possess the land began here and was reiterated and emphasized repeatedly in the speeches of Moses recorded in Deuteronomy. They are cardinal elements of the teaching of the book and show that, as Baly has said, "Palestine was, in fact, the Chosen Land for the Chosen People; not, it should be noticed, chosen *by* them, but chosen *for* them" (p. 303). This land was given to them in perpetuity, but their possession of it had definite contingencies, as are often repeated in Moses' addresses.

The description of the extent of the land Israel was to occupy coincides with that of the land promised on oath to the fathers of the nation and to their descendants (Gen 15:18). The geographical terms delimit the land by sections: "The Arabah" (v.7, as in v.1) is the Jordan Valley from Lake Galilee to the area south of the Dead Sea (part of the deepest rift on earth); "the mountains," the central hill country; "the western foothills," the slopes toward the Mediterranean; "the Negev," the area north of the Sinaitic peninsula but south of the central hill country; "the coast," the land along the Mediterranean, while "the land of the Canaanites" and "Lebanon, as far as . . . the Euphrates" is the northern section.

## Notes

---

**8** The promise—"I have given you this land. Go in and take possession"—was irrevocable, but the fulfillment in time and personnel was contingent on the people's obedience to the Lord's directives to enter, conquer, and take possession of the land. יָרַשׁ (*yāraš*, "to take possession," usually by force) appears about fifty times in Deuteronomy relative to Israel's occupation of the land. Of course, when one nation possesses another nation's land, it also dispossesses that nation. *Yāraš* may also mean "to inherit," though this nuance more definitely resides in נָחַל (*nāḥal*), which frequently appears in Deuteronomy. See Notes on v.38.

"I have given you this land" as a translation of נָתַתִּי לִפְנֵיכֶם אֶת־הָאָרֶץ (*nāṯattî lip̱nêḵem 'eṯ-hā'āreṣ*) is based on the usual meaning "give" for נָתַן (*nāṯan*). *Nāṯan*, however, must be contextually understood; its semantic range is large.

The use of the prepositional phrase לִפְנֵי (*lip̱nê*) usually means "in the presence of" or "before," though it may mean no more than the preposition לְ (*l*ᵉ). In Deuteronomy נָתַן (*nāṯan*) with the simple preposition לְ (*l*ᵉ) commonly is used of God giving the land to the patriarchs or to their descendants. Moreover, *nāṯan* with *lip̱nê* represents placing something before one, as the Lord places before Israel the blessings and the curses in 30:1, 15, 19. Verse 8, therefore, means that the Lord has set the land before them as a gift, but they must go in and take possession of it.

The translation "their descendants after them" for זַרְעָם אַחֲרֵיהֶם (*zar'ām 'aḥ*ᵃ*rêhem*) is pleonastic. "Descendants" means those of the same blood who come after. It has a wider semantic range than the Hebrew זֶרַע (*zera'*, "seed," "issue"), which often by itself relates to the source rather than the succession. The English word "descendants" covers the whole Hebrew phrase *zar'ām 'aḥ^a^rêhem.* "Their seed after them" means "descendants." "After them" is redundant.

The promise was given "to Abraham, Isaac and Jacob—and to their descendants." The land, then, was first promised to Isaac as the only son of Abraham and Sarah and then limited to Jacob and his sons, the heirs of the promise (Gen 12:7; 15:18; 26:3–4; 28:4, 13–15). This promise was reaffirmed at the burning bush (Exod 3:8, 17). This gradual delimitation of the sphere of application of the promise gave the land to Israel, that is, the sons of Jacob, alone. When Abraham interceded with the Lord for Ishmael, the Lord promised to bless Ishmael in other ways, but not under the covenant that bequeathed the land to Abraham's descendants (Gen 17:18–21). Esau got a secondary blessing from Isaac, but Esau was not included in the covenant blessing of the land (Gen 27:26–29; 28:13–15).

---

## 2. *The appointment of leaders*

### 1:9–18

9 At that time I said to you, "You are too heavy a burden for me to carry
alone. 10 The LORD your God has increased your numbers so that today
you are as many as the stars in the sky. 11 May the LORD, the God of your
fathers, increase you a thousand times and bless you as he has
promised! 12 But how can I bear your problems and your burdens and
your disputes all by myself? 13 Choose some wise, understanding and
respected men from each of your tribes, and I will set them over you."

14 You answered me, "What you propose to do is good."

15 So I took the leading men of your tribes, wise and respected men,
and appointed them to have authority over you—as commanders of
thousands, of hundreds, of fifties and of tens and as tribal officials.
16 And I charged your judges at that time: Hear the disputes between
your brothers and judge fairly, whether the case is between brother
Israelites or between one of them and an alien. 17 Do not show partiality
in judging; hear both small and great alike. Do not be afraid of any man,
for judgment belongs to God. Bring me any case too hard for you, and I
will hear it. 18 And at that time I told you everything you were to do.

**9–14** The increased number of Israelites presented too many problems for Moses to care for alone (vv.9–10). Consequently, political and juridical appointments were initiated. In his address as recorded in Deuteronomy, no mention is made of the instigation of this procedure by Moses' father-in-law (cf. Exod 18:13–26; see also Num 11:14 for wording similar to v.9). Here Moses simply stated that he saw the need for leaders for political and judicial activity as his assistants. In Exodus it would seem that Moses himself appointed these leaders; but it is apparent from v.13 that the people chose the leaders as representative of the various tribes, and then Moses appointed them to their several tasks (vv.15–18). The leaders were to be characterized by wisdom, understanding, and experience (v.13).

**15–18** The use of the word "commanders" (v.15) and the size of the groups—thousands, hundreds, fifties, and tens—suggest a military arrangement; but neither the Exodus narrative nor this one speaks of military matters. Moreover, the current need was for assistant judges, not for military men as commanders and tribal officials. It is not clear in this context, however, whether commanders and tribal officials are the same men. When in v.16 Moses recalled what he had done "at that time," he spoke only of his charge to judges. Were these also the same men? The designations of the men as commanders, tribal officials, and judges seems to indicate three distinct classes; but these are not clearly delineated otherwise. The context begins and ends with reference to a judicatory. The command over a group of a thousand, a hundred, or fifty is ordinarily a military division, though a group of ten in such lists is not known elsewhere than in Exodus 18:21, 25. Most likely Moses' use of these terms indicates no clearly defined classes of appointments, such as military, political, and juridical. This arrangement proved to be satisfactory to the people (v.14).

Four matters regarding justice are mentioned.

1. Disputes between fellow Israelites or with foreign inhabitants in the land were to be arbitrated (v.16).

2. The directives for making decisions include no partiality; small and great were to be heard on an equal basis (v.17a).

3. Judges were not to fear man because juridical process rested on the realization that "judgment belongs to God" (v.17b).

4. Cases too difficult for the judges were to be referred to Moses (v.17c).

## Notes

---

**9** בָּעֵת הַהִוא (*bā'ēt hahiw'*, "at that time") occurs eleven times in the first address, the historical prologue (1:9, 16, 18; 2:34; 3:4, 8, 12, 18, 21, 23; 4:14), and five times in the other addresses (5:5; 9:20; 10:1, 8; 32:35). The time of 1:9, 16, 18, and 4:14 preceded the departure from Horeb. The other occurrences in the first address relate to the time of the conquest of Transjordan. The later occurrences concern experiences at Horeb relative to the giving of the law, except 32:35, where reference is made to the time when the foot of the disobedient will slip. This latter passage was the basis for Jonathan Edward's famous sermon, "Sinners in the Hands of an Angry God." *Bā'ēt hahiw'* appears occasionally in other OT historical books, and in some of the prophets it refers either to the past or to the future.

**10** The promise "as many as the stars in the sky" was first made to Abraham and then repeated in reference to that promise (Gen 15:5; 22:17; 26:4; Exod 32:13).

**13** The "wise, understanding and respected" men are also called "leading" men in v.15. חֲכָמִים (*ḥᵃkāmim*, "wise") means men who know how to apply their knowledge. נְבֹנִים (*nᵉbōnîm*, "understanding") means those who have discernment and so are able to judge matters. יְדֻעִים (*yᵉdu'îm*, "respected") means those who are well known or, possibly, experienced. This passive form of יָדַע (*yāda'*, "know") occurs also in Isa 53:3, where the NIV translates it as "familiar with suffering." It may well be "experienced in suffering" (Emerton, "Considerations," pp. 175–76).

**15** רָאשִׁים (*rā'šîm*, "leading men") are literally "heads." Moses said he took the heads of their tribes and made them heads over them, which the NIV correctly renders "have authority over." Verse 13, with v.15, tells how they were leaders (heads), and vv.15b–16 show the nature of their leadership.

---

### 3. *The spies sent out*

#### 1:19–25

[19]Then, as the LORD our God commanded us, we set out from Horeb
and went toward the hill country of the Amorites through all that vast
and dreadful desert that you have seen, and so we reached Kadesh
Barnea. [20]Then I said to you, "You have reached the hill country of the

Amorites, which the LORD our God is giving us. 21 See, the LORD your God
has given you the land. Go up and take possession of it as the LORD, the
God of your fathers, told you. Do not be afraid; do not be discouraged."
22 Then all of you came to me and said, "Let us send men ahead to spy
out the land for us and bring back a report about the route we are to
take and the towns we will come to."
23 The idea seemed good to me; so I selected twelve of you, one man
from each tribe. 24 They left and went up into the hill country, and came
to the Valley of Eshcol and explored it. 25 Taking with them some of the
fruit of the land, they brought it down to us and reported, "It is a good
land that the LORD our God is giving us."

**19–23** In response to the Lord's command (v.7), the Israelites went "as the LORD . . . God commanded" (v.19) toward the hill country of the Amorites (see comment on v.4). This difficult journey of more than 150 miles through the Desert of Paran—called "vast and dreadful" (v.19)—brought them to Kadesh Barnea on the southern perimeter of the Land of Promise. There Moses reiterated the Lord's command (v.8) to take possession of the land the Lord had set before them and exhorted them not to be afraid (vv.20–21), an exhortation often renewed in these last addresses of Moses, obviously indicating that the Israelites were afraid.

Being fearful of what lay before them, the people suggested that some men be sent into the land to explore it (scout or spy out) and bring back information about routes of travel and cities they would encounter (v.22). Noting the narrative in Numbers 13:1–3, in addition to what is written here, it appears that the people first suggested that this reconnoiter be made, then Moses approved the idea, referred the request to the Lord who agreed to it, and ordered that each tribe send out one representative (v.23).

**24–25** Moses, recalling that event, left out the details of the command, the description of the exploration, and the report of the spies (but cf. Num 13:3–33). In these reminiscences Moses said only that the spies returned with a report that the land was good and that they brought back some fruit from the Valley of Eschol as evidence (v.25).

"Eschol" specifically refers to the stalk or stem of some fruit or flower. From this it comes to represent a whole bunch or cluster. The Valley of Eschol lies about two miles north of Hebron (ZPEB, 2:364). Grapes are still grown there.

Beginning in v.21 and continuing through this section, the plural verbs and pronouns change to singular and then vary. Several theories have been offered to explain these variations, but none is altogether satisfactory. The variation is most likely due to the speaker's thought encompassing the people as a group (collective use) and then as so many individuals. This variation appears again toward the end of the book and is not unknown elsewhere.

S.R. Driver (*Deuteronomy,* p. 21) notices that this variation in number is very frequent in Deuteronomy, sometimes taking place even within the limits of a single sentence. Kenneth A. Kitchen ("Ancient Orient, 'Deuteronomism,' and the Old Testament," in J. Barton Payne, ed., *New Perspectives on the Old Testament* [Waco: Word, 1970], pp. 4–5) declares that variation in number and person is not restricted to Deuteronomy but appears in the treaties of the first and second millennia B.C. These variations as a "criterion for literary analysis" must be "abandoned as worthless. . . . Its significance for literary prehistory is nil." For further illustration of shifts of personal pronouns elsewhere, see Walter C. Kaiser, Jr., *Toward Old Testament Ethics* (Grand Rapids: Zondervan, 1983), p. 108.

## Notes

**19** "All that vast and dreadful desert" was a forbidding limestone plateau: hot, dry, rugged, and usually bare of any sustainable vegetation. "Dreadful" translates the Niphal passive participle of יָרֵא (*yārē'*, "fear"; see also 8:15). In the OT it often is used of the Lord and is rendered "awesome" (see 7:21).

**20** The tense translated "is giving us" may be rendered "about to give" as an immediate future participle (W.F. Stinespring, "The Participle of the Future and Other Matters," in H.T. Frank and W.L. Reed, edd., *Translating and Understanding the Old Testament* [Nashville: Abingdon, 1970]). The NIV translates the Piel participle this way in 4:1 ("I am about to teach"), but the use of נֹתֵן (*nōṯēn*) in 11:32 ("laws I am setting before you today") militates against the immediate future because some of the laws were already given. The laws in the addresses were then in the process of being given.

**21** On the phrase "the LORD your God has given you the land," see the Notes on v.8.

The exhortation "Do not be afraid; do not be discouraged" appears a half-dozen times in Deuteronomy; and, as here, it is usually יָרֵא (*yārē'*, "fear") in combination with a synonym: in 1:21 and 31:8 with חָתַת (*tēḥāṯ*, "discouraged, dismayed, or frightened"); in 1:29; 20:3; and 31:6 with עָרַץ (*'āraṣ*, "tremble, panic, be terrified or alarmed"). Synonyms are used in this way for emphasis.

**24** The verb רָגַל (*rāgal*, "explored") stems from the noun *regel* ("foot") and means "to walk about" and so "to explore."

### 4. *The rebellion against the Lord*

1:26–46

26But you were unwilling to go up; you rebelled against the command
of the LORD your God. 27You grumbled in your tents and said, "The LORD
hates us; so he brought us out of Egypt to deliver us into the hands of
the Amorites to destroy us. 28Where can we go? Our brothers have
made us lose heart. They say, 'The people are stronger and taller than
we are; the cities are large, with walls up to the sky. We even saw the
Anakites there.'"
29Then I said to you, "Do not be terrified; do not be afraid of them.
30The LORD your God, who is going before you, will fight for you, as he
did for you in Egypt, before your very eyes, 31and in the desert. There
you saw how the LORD your God carried you, as a father carries his son,
all the way you went until you reached this place."
32In spite of this, you did not trust in the LORD your God, 33who went
ahead of you on your journey, in fire by night and in a cloud by day, to
search out places for you to camp and to show you the way you should
go.
34When the LORD heard what you said, he was angry and solemnly
swore: 35"Not a man of this evil generation shall see the good land I
swore to give your forefathers, 36except Caleb son of Jephunneh. He
will see it, and I will give him and his descendants the land he set his
feet on, because he followed the LORD wholeheartedly."
37Because of you the LORD became angry with me also and said, "You
shall not enter it, either. 38But your assistant, Joshua son of Nun, will

enter it. Encourage him, because he will lead Israel to inherit it. 39 And
the little ones that you said would be taken captive, your children who
do not yet know good from bad—they will enter the land. I will give it to
them and they will take possession of it. 40 But as for you, turn around
and set out toward the desert along the route to the Red Sea."
41 Then you replied, "We have sinned against the LORD. We will go up
and fight, as the LORD our God commanded us." So every one of you put
on his weapons, thinking it easy to go up into the hill country.
42 But the LORD said to me, "Tell them, 'Do not go up and fight,
because I will not be with you. You will be defeated by your enemies.'"
43 So I told you, but you would not listen. You rebelled against the
LORD's command and in your arrogance you marched up into the hill
country. 44 The Amorites who lived in those hills came out against you;
they chased you like a swarm of bees and beat you down from Seir all
the way to Hormah. 45 You came back and wept before the LORD, but he
paid no attention to your weeping and turned a deaf ear to you. 46 And so
you stayed in Kadesh many days—all the time you spent there.

**26–28** In spite of the good report and evidence of the productivity of the land, the people refused to enter because the rest of the report discouraged them. The size and strength of the inhabitants, the high fortifications of their large towns, and the presence of the Anakites made the Israelites so fearful (v.28) that they added to their rebellion against the Lord their misconstruing his attitude toward them and their unbelief in his promises (v.26). Grumbling in their tents, they said, "The LORD hates us" (v.27), when in truth he loved them. (The Lord's love for his people and their obligation to love him are main themes in Deuteronomy.) They said that the Lord brought them from Egypt to have them destroyed by Amorite hands; but the contrary was true—when they would advance in obedience into the land, the Lord would crush the Amorites.

**29–31** Again Moses urged the people not to be afraid (v.29). The Lord their God would go ahead of them and fight for them as he had in Egypt and Sinai (vv.30–31a). Before their very eyes God had carried them along "as a father carries his son" (v.31b). A similar illustration is given in Numbers 11:12, when Moses was troubled by the wailing of the people for food other than manna. He complained to the Lord saying, "Why do you tell me to carry them in my arms, as a nurse carries an infant?"

**32–36** In spite of the promise of the Lord's leadership—the same leadership that had brought them thus far—the people refused to enter the land; so the Lord declared that they would not see that good land. Out of the vast throng of Israelites, only those under twenty years of age and Caleb and Joshua would enter it (vv.36, 38–39; Num 14:30–31). Caleb would receive the area he had explored.

**37** Moses told the people that the Lord was angry with him also "because of you"; so Moses himself would not be allowed to enter the land. "Because of you" can only refer back to the experience of the Israelite quarrel with the Lord at the waters of Meribah (Kadesh), which took place years later than the time of the spies' reconnaissance. There the Lord said that Moses and Aaron would not enter the land because they did not trust him enough to honor him as holy in the sight of the people (Num 20:12); for Moses had struck the rock twice to produce water, though the Lord had said that Moses was to speak to the rock. Moses in these last addresses to the people looked behind his own failure and referred to the cause of his action, which was the people's criticism of the Lord's provision of food.

**38** Joshua is called Moses' assistant. In Hebrew *hā'ōmēḏ lᵉp̄āneḵā* (lit., "he who stands before you"; cf. 17:12; 18:7; Judg 3:19; 20:28; 1 Kings 12:6, 8; 2 Chron 9:7; Neh 12:44) is an assistant serving in some official capacity. Joshua, as well as Caleb (v.36), would enter the country. Joshua, however, would lead the Israelites in the acquisition of the land. The causative verb *yanḥilennāh* ("will lead") gives this sense.

**39–40** The "little ones" (v.39, persons with some sort of incapacity, and so dependent) and "children" (usual word for son, child) are used here, not to distinguish younger and older children, but synonymously. These children who were then helpless and uninformed (not knowing good or bad is a Hebrew way of describing not knowing anything) would acquire the country that the generation at Kadesh had faithlessly failed to invade and possess. Rather than achieving the promised homeland, that generation was condemned to return to the desert by the Red Sea road. The two verbs "turn" and "set out" (v.40) are commonly used together with the sense of going on a journey. The way of the Red Sea was doubtless a well-known route through Sinai and does not imply destination necessarily. One might traverse part of the road.

**41** Being sent back into the vast, dreadful desert (v.19) was more than the people could take; so they confessed their sin, put on their weapons, and presumptuously went up into the hill country. This admission of guilt for failing to follow the Lord's former command was frivolous as is evident from their immediate failure to follow the command to return to the desert. Without due consideration of the Lord's later command, their action of going up into the hill country, now without the Lord's approval, was foolhardy.

**42–43** Not only did the Lord declare that he would not go with the people, he also prophesied their defeat (v.42). But the Israelites' obstinacy was such that they would not listen; so they marched up to battle against the Amorites (v.43). The three verbs—in Numbers 14:44 ("they went up"), here in v.41 ("we will go up"), and in v.43 ("marched up")—all suggest audacity, foolhardiness, presumption, rashness, and arrogance.

**44** The Amorites met the Israelite army somewhere north of Kadesh Barnea and then routed the Israelites toward the south or southeast. The Amorites' pursuit "like a swarm of bees" describes numerical greatness, persistence, and ferocity. Hormah lies about fifty-five miles northeast of Kadesh Barnea.

**45** "You came back" might refer to the changing of the mind of the people and be translated "You changed your minds" (about entering Canaan from the south), but the action involved favors the NIV. On any account, both happened—the army did return to Kadesh, and the people did not attempt again to invade the land from the south contrary to the Lord's command in v.42. "You came back and wept before the LORD" means that the Israelites returned to the tabernacle (tent) and wept there.

**46** The Hebrew phrase noting the time Israel spent in the Kadesh Barnea area figuratively expresses a long, indefinite time and suggests that a large part of the next thirty-eight years was spent there.

## Notes

**28** בְּנֵי עֲנָקִים (*bᵉnê ʿᵃnāqîm,* lit., "sons of the Anakim") is a pleonastic gentilic. The plural form *ʿᵃnāqîm* ("Anakites") is the simpler gentilic form. The Anakites were early inhabitants of Canaan described as "giants" (2:10, 21; 9:2; Num 13:32–33).

**36** Of Caleb it is said, מִלֵּא אַחֲרֵי יהוה (*millēʾ ʾaḥᵃrê YHWH,* "he followed the LORD wholeheartedly"). This uncommon phrase in Num 14:24 describes Caleb; in Num 32:11 it is said that the Israelites did not wholeheartedly follow the Lord, but Caleb and Joshua did (v.12); in Josh 14:8, Caleb said that he had done so and referred to Moses' testimony to this fact (v.9). This testimony is repeated in v.14. This phrase also appears in 1 Kings 11:6, where it is said that Solomon did not follow the Lord wholeheartedly (NIV, "completely") as his father, David, had. The idea of full commitment resides in the meaning of the stative verb *mālēʾ* ("to be filled"), which lends itself to such ideas as completeness and totality. Caleb was totally committed to the Lord and consequently followed the Lord's directive with all-out obedience.

**37** Three times in the Deuteronomic addresses (here; 3:26; 4:21), Moses spoke of God being angry with him "because of you," i.e., the Israelites; and on that account he prohibited Moses' entrance into the Promised Land. Though the phrases vary in Hebrew, the meaning is much the same. The verb used here and in 4:21, אָנַף (*ʾānap̱*), is a common word for anger, while עָבַר (*ʿāḇar*) in 3:26 has a stronger meaning. It occurs rarely of God's anger as furious (Deut 3:26; Pss 78:21, 59, 62; 89:38 [39 MT], all of which the NIV translates as "very angry"). The cognate adjective occurs, especially in the prophets, expressing the wrath of God. The prepositional phrases also differ in form but not basically in meaning. See comment on 4:21 for a possible difference of meaning there.

Though the occasions for these statements vary, they all speak of the Lord's unrelenting attitude regarding his decree that Moses was not to enter the Promised Land. The reason for this arose over the altercation about the water at Meribah-Kadesh. Again and again Moses pled with the Lord to relent, but to no avail. The Lord, however, did not forget his promise to Israel. Though Moses was not to lead Israel into the land, Joshua as Moses' successor would lead them in the Conquest.

**38** הָעֹמֵד לְפָנֶיךָ (*hāʿōmēḏ lᵉp̱āneyḵā,* "your assistant") has much the same sense as מְשָׁרְתוֹ (*mᵉšārᵉṯô,* "his aide") in Exod 24:13; 33:11; Num 11:28; and Josh 1:1. These words describing Joshua's relationship to Moses are often used of priests and Levites who assist, serve, or stand ministering.

יַנְחִלֶנָּה (*yanḥilennāh,* "will lead . . . to inherit it"), from נָחַל (*nāḥal*), embodies significant theological as well as historical connotations in both testaments. Here it relates to the land Israel was to receive as a permanent possession in fulfillment of God's promise. See TWOT, 2:569–70.

**41, 43** The use in v.41 of הוּן (*hûn,* "be easy") implies a cavalier attitude on the part of those who before were afraid to challenge the Canaanites in battle. Now without the Lord's assistance, they unconcernedly went to war when before with his assistance they were afraid to do so. In v.43, זוּד (*zûḏ,* "to boil up," consequently, to act insolently, presumptuously, rebelliously, arrogantly, etc.) indicates more intensely the reactionary character of their act. They needed to learn the lesson that with God they could win the land; without him they were impotent.

## 5. *The journey from Kadesh to Kedemoth*

### 2:1–25

1Then we turned back and set out toward the desert along the route to
the Red Sea, as the LORD had directed me. For a long time we made our
way around the hill country of Seir.
2Then the LORD said to me, 3"You have made your way around this hill
country long enough; now turn north. 4Give the people these orders:
'You are about to pass through the territory of your brothers the
descendants of Esau, who live in Seir. They will be afraid of you, but be
very careful. 5Do not provoke them to war, for I will not give you any of
their land, not even enough to put your foot on. I have given Esau the
hill country of Seir as his own. 6You are to pay them in silver for the food
you eat and the water you drink.'"
7The LORD your God has blessed you in all the work of your hands. He
has watched over your journey through this vast desert. These forty
years the LORD your God has been with you, and you have not lacked
anything.
8So we went on past our brothers the descendants of Esau, who live
in Seir. We turned from the Arabah road, which comes up from Elath
and Ezion Geber, and traveled along the desert road of Moab.
9Then the LORD said to me, "Do not harass the Moabites or provoke
them to war, for I will not give you any part of their land. I have given Ar
to the descendants of Lot as a possession."
10(The Emites used to live there—a people strong and numerous, and
as tall as the Anakites. 11Like the Anakites, they too were considered
Rephaites, but the Moabites called them Emites. 12Horites used to live in
Seir, but the descendants of Esau drove them out. They destroyed the
Horites from before them and settled in their place, just as Israel did in
the land the LORD gave them as their possession.)
13And the LORD said, "Now get up and cross the Zered Valley." So we
crossed the valley.
14Thirty-eight years passed from the time we left Kadesh Barnea until
we crossed the Zered Valley. By then, that entire generation of fighting
men had perished from the camp, as the LORD had sworn to them. 15The
LORD's hand was against them until he had completely eliminated them
from the camp.
16Now when the last of these fighting men among the people had
died, 17 the LORD said to me, 18"Today you are to pass by the region of
Moab at Ar. 19When you come to the Ammonites, do not harass them or
provoke them to war, for I will not give you possession of any land
belonging to the Ammonites. I have given it as a possession to the
descendants of Lot."
20(That too was considered a land of the Rephaites, who used to live
there; but the Ammonites called them Zamzummites. 21They were a
people strong and numerous, and as tall as the Anakites. The LORD
destroyed them from before the Ammonites, who drove them out and
settled in their place. 22The LORD had done the same for the descendants of Esau, who lived in Seir, when he destroyed the Horites from
before them. They drove them out and have lived in their place to this
day. 23And as for the Avvites who lived in villages as far as Gaza, the
Caphtorites coming out from Caphtor destroyed them and settled in
their place.)
24"Set out now and cross the Arnon Gorge. See, I have given into your
hand Sihon the Amorite, king of Heshbon, and his country. Begin to
take possession of it and engage him in battle. 25This very day I will
begin to put the terror and fear of you on all the nations under heaven.

**They will hear reports of you and will tremble and be in anguish because of you."**

**1** In obedience to the Lord's command in 1:40, the chastised Israelites returned to the desert, the area between Kadesh and the Seir range. This range east of the Arabah in Edom ran roughly from the area south of the Dead Sea to the Gulf of Aqabah (see comment on 1:6–8). The period probably encompassed both departures from Kadesh recorded in Numbers 14:25 and 20:22. The phrase "for a long time" in 1:46 (NIV, "many days") and 2:1 suggests that the time spent at Kadesh and around Seir took up the period between the abortive attempt to enter Canaan from Kadesh in the south and the end of the wanderings that brought them to the vicinity of Edom and Moab to enter Canaan from the east.

**2–7** If the command to go northward (v.3) was given in Kadesh, then the order gives the general direction only. It was necessary for them to proceed both south and east from Kadesh before the northward march began. The objective and the journey as a whole were to the north.

The people had spent the time the Lord had decreed on the nation as punishment for disobedience at Kadesh. With the exception of Caleb, Joshua, and Moses, the generation of men twenty years old or more who had refused to enter Canaan from Kadesh at the Lord's command were now dead (vv.14–15); and Moses also would die before the crossing of the Jordan. Therefore the Lord said that they had gone around the hill country of Seir long enough (v.3).

The wanderings of the previous generation had been to the west of the territory of the Edomites. Though the area was called the hill country of Seir, it is not the same as that called the territory of the Edomites who live in Seir (v.4). Approaching Edomite lands brought Israel in or near the area the Lord had promised to Esau and his descendants. So the Lord commanded the Israelites not to make war on their Edomite relatives (v.5); neither were they to take their land or anything in it. From the Edomites they were to buy with "silver" food to eat and water to drink (v.6). Before this, as v.7 shows, the Israelites had lived off the land. The Lord had supplied manna and other food and water as needed. Now they were to buy food and water as they moved through (and around) Edomite territory. Manna, however, did not completely cease until the day after the first celebration of the Passover at Gilgal in Canaan under Joshua (Josh 5:10–12). Perhaps the manna was gradually phased out. Exodus 16:35 says that the people ate manna "until they came to a land that was settled; . . . until they reached the border of Canaan."

**8** The order of the journey, picked up again here, reviews the travel from Ezion Geber or Elath at the head of the Gulf of Aqabah northward to the plains of Moab.

**9** As the Lord had forbidden Israel to attack the Edomites because they were blood brothers, so now he warned them not to fight with the Moabites. They were descendants of Lot, and he had given them the land they controlled. Nor were the Israelites to fight with the Ammonites east of the Jabbok River; they too were descendants of Lot (v.19).

**10–12** The mention of these territories elicited historical references to former inhabitants, which the Moabites (vv.9–11), Ammonites (vv.19–21), Edomites (vv.12,

22), and Caphtorites (v.23) had displaced. These ancient nations are described as numerous, tall, and strong. Yet they were destroyed by invading brothers of the Israelites—surely a suggestion that Israel too would succeed in conquering the land they were about to invade.

The reference to Israel's destruction of former inhabitants "in the land the LORD gave them as their possession" (v.12) may indicate the point of view of Moses referring to the conquest of Transjordan or of some later copyist after the conquest of the land no earlier than the latter days of Joshua.

The parenthetical, explanatory nature of vv.10–12 and vv.20–23 has been cited as evidence that these are later additions rather than part of Moses' original speech. However, these speeches in Deuteronomy were made subsequent to the conquest of Transjordan (1:3–4), which (in 3:20) is called the "possession" of the two and a half tribes. Perhaps v.12 should be translated "just as Israel has done in the land the LORD has given to them as their possession"—meaning, just as Israel has done in destroying the Amorites under Sihon and Og in the land the Lord has given to the two and a half tribes in Transjordan as their possession.

**13–15** Since the fighting men of the generation that had failed to enter the land from the south at Kadesh Barnea had died off and were eliminated from the camp, the Lord's hand was no longer against Israel (v.15). The Lord directed the new generation to cross the Zered, which flows into the southern end of the Dead Sea from the east (v.13), and then to cross the Arnon (v.24), which flows into the sea halfway up its eastern side. This brought them into the area controlled by the Amorites.

**16–19** When the Israelites came near the northeastern border of Moab at Ar, they were next to the territory occupied by the Ammonites, who at that time lived east of the Amorites under Sihon. Sihon controlled the area between the Arnon River on the south, the Jordan on the west, the Jabbok on the north, and the border of the Ammonites on the east. The Israelites were not to disturb the Ammonites but rather were to turn northwestward into the country of Sihon. The Ammonites were the descendants of Lot, and the Lord had given that country to Lot and his descendants.

**20–23** This parenthetical portion mentions how the Lord had destroyed the Zamzummites and had given their land to the Amorites. He had also destroyed the Horites, the Avvites, and the Caphtorites and had given their land to the descendants of Esau.

It is evident from v.21 that the Rephaim (Zamzummites) and Anakites were large people who could be called giants. The size of the bed of Og king of Bashan (3:11), who was a Rephaite, supports this.

**24–25** While Israel was not to disturb the Edomites, Moabites, or Ammonites, such prohibition did not extend to the Amorites. The Lord declared that he had put Sihon and his kingdom into Israel's hands (v.24). The conquest was certain; it was only for Israel to accomplish it. They were to cross the Arnon into Amorite territory and confidently engage Sihon's army in battle. God would put the fear of Israel into all the nations in the area. "All the nations under heaven" (v.25) is an idiomatic hyperbole signifying all the nations in the vicinity; that is, at least from horizon to horizon (under heaven). In 11:25 fear is said to fall on all the land Israel would tread on, and in Exodus 15:15–16 fear falls on the inhabitants of Palestine—Edom, Moab, and

Canaan—while in Exodus 23:27 all the people they meet are included. It is evident that the Lord through Moses was establishing belief in his control over the fluctuation of Canaanite national groups of the past in order to inspire Israel for the conquest ahead of them and to faith in his promises.

Moses' objective was focused on Canaan proper, west of the Jordan River. However, the land of the Amorites too had been promised to Abraham and his descendants (Gen 15:18–21), though, because of tribal or national movement, the labeling of areas by its inhabitants at a given time may not be accurate for a later time. Nevertheless, it appears that Transjordan comes within the area of the promise to Abraham (v.24).

## Notes

---

1 The "long time" of 2:1 and "many days" of 1:46 are from the same Hebrew words, יָמִים רַבִּים (*yāmîm rabbîm*), and signify a long period of time. The additional phrase in 1:46, כַּיָּמִים אֲשֶׁר יְשַׁבְתֶּם (*kayyāmîm 'ašer yešabtem*, lit., "according to the days you lived"; NIV, "all the time you spent there") indicates an indefinite period.

4 The Hebrew for "be very careful," שָׁמַר (*šāmar*) with מְאֹד (*me'ōd*), suggests that Israel was to exercise strong restraint.

6 The word כֶּסֶף (*kesep*, "silver") means a medium of exchange or "money" rather than silver as such, though the money may well have been the metal silver.

While כָּרָה (*kārāh*, "buy [water]") also means "dig," the parallel with שָׁבַר (*šābar*, "buy food") and the reference to buying with "silver" show that *kārāh* is used here as in Hos 3:2.

7 In the Hebrew idiom "the LORD your God has blessed you in all the work of your hands," the people are addressed in the singular and יָדְךָ (*yādekā*, "your hand") is also singular, though to conform to English idiom the plural "hands" is required. The phrase also occurs in 14:29; 16:15; 24:19; 28:12; and 30:9. Some evidence exists in these places (and others) for a plural Hebrew reading.

8 Elath and Ezion Geber apparently were situated near the head (north) of the Gulf of Aqabah. These names may refer to two places or are two names for the same place (see ZPEB, 2:468–70).

10 "Emites" (Emim) may be Moabite nomenclature meaning "terrors" or "terrible ones" and may be descriptive rather than strictly ethnic (ZPEB, 2:99). Rephaim may also be descriptive, meaning "the dead." See the parallelism in Ps 88:10 (11 MT); Prov 2:18; and Isa 26:14 (where the NIV translates rephaim as "departed spirits" parallel to "dead"). Rephaim generally refers to certain ancient peoples no longer in existence except, in some places, as disembodied spirits (ZPEB, 5:64–65). See also Coogan, pp. 48–49. For "Anakites" see the Notes on 1:28 and NBD, pp. 34–35.

12 These Horites were Hurrians, possibly non-Semitic people who established themselves especially in Mesopotamian and Aramean territories beginning as early as the eighteenth century B.C. See Noth, p. 240, and H. Hoffner's article on "Horites" in ZPEB, 2:202.

20 Three words גִּבּוֹר (*gibbôr*, "mighty one"), רָפָא (*rāpā'*, or the plural *repā'îm*, "fearful one[s]"), and נְפִילִים (*nepîlîm*, "fallen ones") have been sometimes translated "giants"—in the KJV and elsewhere—though none of these words specifically means "giant," and they are not so translated in the NIV. Only *repā'îm* appears in Deuteronomy. Anakites were descendants of the Nephilim (Num 13:33). However, the contexts in some cases certainly indicate that large men were in view (cf. vv.10, 21; 3:11; Num 13:32–33; 2 Sam 21:16, 20; 1 Chron 20:6).

"Zamzummites" probably means "murmurers" and is descriptive rather than ethnic. They may be identified with the Zuzites of Gen 14:5.

**23** The Avvites are mentioned elsewhere in the OT in Josh 13:3 in connection with the Philistine area not yet taken over by the Israelites and in 2 Kings 17:29 in connection with idolatrous worship. The more ancient Avvites were dispossessed of southwest Canaan by Caphtorites (Gen 10:14; 1 Chron 1:12), most probably early Philistine invaders from Crete (Kitchen, *Ancient Orient*, pp. 80–81; G.A. Wainwright, "Caphtor-Cappadocia," VetTest 6 [April 1956]: 199–210).

---

## 6. *The conquest of Transjordan (2:26–3:20)*

### a. *The defeat of Sihon*

#### 2:26–37

26From the desert of Kedemoth I sent messengers to Sihon king of
Heshbon offering peace and saying, 27"Let us pass through your
country. We will stay on the main road; we will not turn aside to the right
or to the left. 28Sell us food to eat and water to drink for their price in
silver. Only let us pass through on foot—29as the descendants of Esau,
who live in Seir, and the Moabites, who live in Ar, did for us—until we
cross the Jordan into the land the LORD our God is giving us." 30But
Sihon king of Heshbon refused to let us pass through. For the LORD your
God had made his spirit stubborn and his heart obstinate in order to
give him into your hands, as he has now done.
31The LORD said to me, "See, I have begun to deliver Sihon and his
country over to you. Now begin to conquer and possess his land."
32When Sihon and all his army came out to meet us in battle at Jahaz,
33the LORD our God delivered him over to us and we struck him down,
together with his sons and his whole army. 34At that time we took all his
towns and completely destroyed them—men, women and children. We
left no survivors. 35But the livestock and the plunder from the towns we
had captured we carried off for ourselves. 36From Aroer on the rim of
the Arnon Gorge, and from the town in the gorge, even as far as Gilead,
not one town was too strong for us. The LORD our God gave us all of
them. 37But in accordance with the command of the LORD our God, you
did not encroach on any of the land of the Ammonites, neither the land
along the course of the Jabbok nor that around the towns in the hills.

**26–35** Though the Lord had said that he had given Sihon into Israel's hands (v.24), Moses approached Sihon with messengers bearing a request to pass peaceably through his country (vv.26–27). But Sihon, from a heart made stubborn by the Lord, refused the request and came south to Jahaz to battle against the Israelites (vv.30, 32). Sihon, his sons, his army, his people, and his towns were destroyed (vv.33–34). So southern Transjordan was subjected to total destruction except that the Israelites kept for themselves the livestock and objects of value (quite properly called "plunder" in the NIV) rather than give them over to the Lord by destruction (vv.34–35). Such exceptions were not allowed when the Lord required a strict following of the *ḥerem* principle (total destruction; cf. the story of Achan in Josh 7 and Saul in 1 Sam 15).

It is said of Sihon that the Lord God "had made his spirit stubborn and his heart obstinate" (v.30) for the definite purpose of placing him into the hands of the Israelites, or "to deliver Sihon and his country over to you" (v.31). This may account for Moses' initial offer of peace to Sihon. He was sure that the Lord would, in his own way, give him victory over the Amorite king. The attribution to the Lord of making Sihon stubborn and obstinate without mentioning mediate or contributing circumstances or persons is not an uncommon procedure in the OT. Sihon by his own conscious will refused Israel passage; yet it was certain that God would give Sihon's land to Israel.

**36–37** So all the territory from the Arnon Gorge (from an unknown town in the gorge) on the south to Sihon and Og's boundary in Gilead on the north, and from the Jabbok River on the east (i.e., the upper reaches of the Jabbok flow north before flowing west and hence is reckoned as an eastern boundary) to the Jordan on the west fell to the Israelites. Israel, however, did not encroach on any of the Ammonite land—land that the Lord expressly commanded them to avoid (see v.19).

## Notes

**33** The Masoretic consonantal text would be translated "we struck him down and his son and all his army [עַמּוֹ (*'ammô*, lit., 'his people') often used as army]." The *Qere*, with different vowel pointing, together with the versions generally read "his sons," which the NIV follows.

**34** The *ḥerem* principle—חֵרֶם ("a devoted thing," and, consequently, a thing to be destroyed)—was an ancient Near Eastern practice that in its complete application required the extermination of everyone and everything that could be destroyed. Things metallic that could not be destroyed, Israel put in a place under the Lord's protection. This destruction kept captured people and things from the people but put them into the hands of God. The practice, however, was sometimes limited by the Lord's decree, as here, where the livestock and other valuable plunder were kept by the Israelites. A variation in application of *ḥerem* can be seen in the rules for war in 20:10–18. This was one of the means used to bring destruction on the sinful inhabitants of Canaan and to isolate the Israelites from them and their wicked practices. The verb חָרַם (*ḥāram*) sometimes carries the sense of "devote." Someone or something is devoted to the Lord; i.e., it is given altogether to the Lord. From this stems the practice of destroying whoever or whatever is devoted, for then it goes to God and cannot be used by the giver.

**36** On the location of Aroer and the town in the gorge, see *World of the Bible*, 1:254.

"Not one town was too strong for us" is an adequate translation into English idiom, but it obscures a possible relationship to the adverse majority report of the spies sent out from Kadesh (1:28), who said, "The cities are large, with walls up to the sky." The word translated "strong" in 2:36 is שָׂגַב (*śāgab*), which means "to be high." Moses used the victory over all the walled cities of Sihon as an indication that the spies—and the people who listened to them—were wrong to suppose that the cities of Canaan were too "high" (strong) to be conquered. The victory was an assurance that they would also conquer the high-walled cities of Canaan.

### b. *The defeat of Og*

#### 3:1–11

[1]Next we turned and went up along the road toward Bashan, and Og
king of Bashan with his whole army marched out to meet us in battle at
Edrei. [2]The LORD said to me, "Do not be afraid of him, for I have handed
him over to you with his whole army and his land. Do to him what you
did to Sihon king of the Amorites, who reigned in Heshbon."
[3]So the LORD our God also gave into our hands Og king of Bashan and
all his army. We struck them down, leaving no survivors. [4]At that time

we took all his cities. There was not one of the sixty cities that we did
not take from them—the whole region of Argob, Og's kingdom in
Bashan. 5All these cities were fortified with high walls and with gates
and bars, and there were also a great many unwalled villages. 6We
completely destroyed them, as we had done with Sihon king of
Heshbon, destroying every city—men, women and children. 7But all the
livestock and the plunder from their cities we carried off for ourselves.
8So at that time we took from these two kings of the Amorites the
territory east of the Jordan, from the Arnon Gorge as far as Mount
Hermon. 9(Hermon is called Sirion by the Sidonians; the Amorites call it
Senir.) 10We took all the towns on the plateau, and all Gilead, and all
Bashan as far as Salecah and Edrei, towns of Og's kingdom in Bashan.
11(Only Og king of Bashan was left of the remnant of the Rephaites. His
bed was made of iron and was more than thirteen feet long and six feet
wide. It is still in Rabbah of the Ammonites.)

**1–3** The conquest continued by pressing north to engage Og king of Bashan in battle because the Lord had signified that Og's army and territory would also become Israel's (v.2). King Og and his army were met at Edrei (v.1), a city on the Yarmuk River at the southeast frontier of his land. Og was vanquished; and here too both population and cities were destroyed (v.3), but the livestock and valued goods were kept by the Israelites (v.7).

**4–7** The geographical limits of the country conquered are in general clear, though certain specific designations are not. The exact location and extent of Argob (v.4) are unknown, though they appear in the text to coincide with Bashan in a general way.

The fertile region between the eastern shore of Lake Galilee and Mount Hauran contained many cities, sixty of which were walled, in addition to unwalled towns of lesser size. The description of the sixty cities as "fortified with high walls and with gates and bars" (v.5) indicates that they were formidable obstacles and that their capture was a remarkable success. This success was fixed in Israel's memory (Num 32:33; Josh 9:10; Pss 135:10–11; 136:18–22). The term "city," however, need not imply that these were places with large populations. While some cities had thousands of inhabitants, others had only a few hundred.

**8–11** Preparatory to allocating the captured lands to the Reubenites, Gadites, and the half-tribe of Manasseh (the Marirites), Moses described the whole area taken from the Amorite kings. The names Sirion and Senir (v.9) for Mount Hermon occur elsewhere. In the Scriptures Sirion is found in Psalm 29:6 and Senir in 1 Chronicles 5:23; Song of Songs 4:8; and Ezekiel 27:5. Reference to Salecah and Edrei (v.10) apparently fix the southern border of Bashan controlled by Og. His iron bed might have been a black basal sarcophagus (v.11 NIV mg.), many of which have been found in that country, although *barzel* apparently means "iron."

## Notes

11 The Hebrew עֶרֶשׂ (*'ereś*) means "couch" or "bed." Sarcophagus has been suggested as an extension from "last couch." See S.R. Driver, *Deuteronomy*, pp. 53–54, and BDB (s.v.).

### c. *The division of the land*

### 3:12–20

[12]Of the land that we took over at that time, I gave the Reubenites and
the Gadites the territory north of Aroer by the Arnon Gorge, including
half the hill country of Gilead, together with its towns. [13]The rest of
Gilead and also all of Bashan, the kingdom of Og, I gave to the half-tribe
of Manasseh. (The whole region of Argob in Bashan used to be known
as a land of the Rephaites. [14]Jair, a descendant of Manasseh, took the
whole region of Argob as far as the border of the Geshurites and the
Maacathites; it was named after him, so that to this day Bashan is called
Havvoth Jair.) [15]And I gave Gilead to Makir. [16]But to the Reubenites and
the Gadites I gave the territory extending from Gilead down to the Arnon
Gorge (the middle of the gorge being the border) and out to the Jabbok
River, which is the border of the Ammonites. [17]Its western border was
the Jordan in the Arabah, from Kinnereth to the Sea of the Arabah (the
Salt Sea), below the slopes of Pisgah.

[18]I commanded you at that time: "The LORD your God has given you
this land to take possession of it. But all your able-bodied men, armed
for battle, must cross over ahead of your brother Israelites. [19]However,
your wives, your children and your livestock (I know you have much
livestock) may stay in the towns I have given you, [20]until the LORD gives
rest to your brothers as he has to you, and they too have taken over the
land that the LORD your God is giving them, across the Jordan. After that,
each of you may go back to the possession I have given you."

**12** The geographical description of the territories given to the two and a half tribes is difficult to follow in its entirety. The southern boundary at the Arnon Gorge and the western border at the Jordan are clear, but the boundary between the half tribe of Manasseh and the other two tribes cannot be clearly plotted.

**13–15** Throughout the NIV this half of the tribe of Manasseh is called "the half-tribe of Manasseh" (v.13; 29:8; most often in Joshua). The other half of Manasseh, which received its allotment in Canaan proper, is not as often mentioned; when it is, however, the specific designation "the half-tribe of Manasseh" is not used.

The Geshurites and Maacathites (v.14) were two smaller kingdoms, Geshur being east of Lake Galilee and Maacah east of the Waters of Merom and north of Geshur. Israel did not drive out the Geshurites and Maacathites. Those people continued to live on their land within Israel and under the governance of Israel (Josh 13:11, 13).

Makir (v.15) was the progenitor of the half-tribe of Manasseh; the half-tribe is called the Makirites in Numbers 26:29 and 32:40.

In v.13 "the rest of Gilead" (a northern part other than that given to Reuben and Gad) is given to the half-tribe of Manasseh, while in vv.15–16, not "the rest of Gilead," but simply "Gilead" designates this northern portion of the area. In other occurrences also, Gilead sometimes refers to the area between the Jabbok and the Yarmuk (the northern sector), sometimes to the central area south of the Jabbok but north of Heshbon and the Dead Sea, and sometimes to the area including both sections. The area secured by the clan of Jair was in the northern sector of Gilead, reaching beyond the Yarmuk Valley up to the territory of the Geshurites and Maacathites who occupied the land east of Lake Galilee and the Waters of Merom. The boundary between Gilead and Bashan is not clearly defined. The territory of Jair seems to be in both Gilead and Bashan. Judges 10:3–5 records that a later Jair of this clan judged Israel for twenty-two years.

# EXODUS AND CONQUEST OF CANAAN

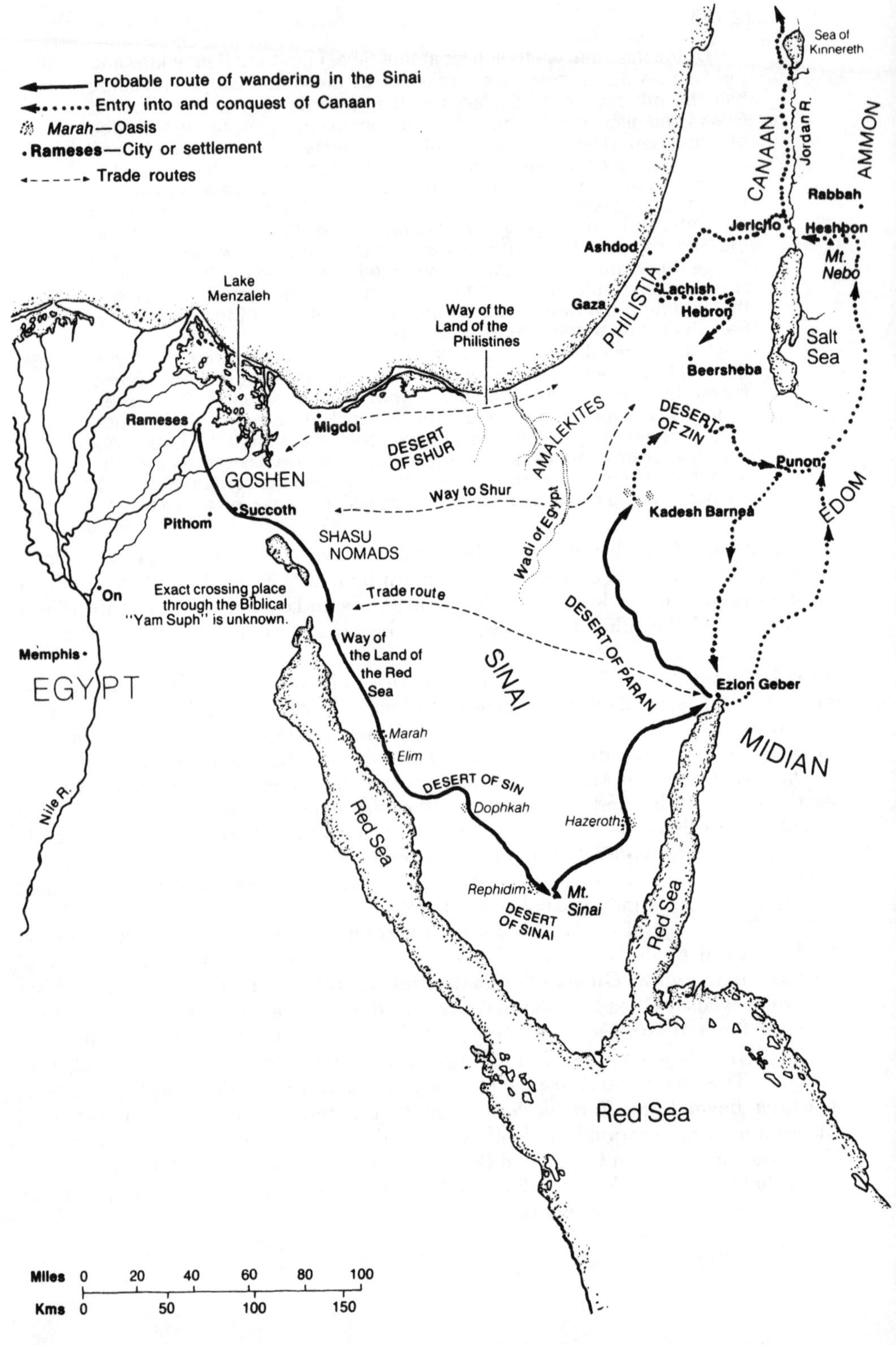

**16–17** This appears to be a clarification of what is written in v.12 about the area given to Reuben and Gad. In v.12 it is said that the Reubenites and Gadites' area included half the hill country of Gilead. This makes the southern part of Gilead the northern part of Reuben and Gad, the southern border of Reuben and Gad being the Arnon Valley, and the eastern border being the Jabbok River from its headwaters in the south. The eastern border continues northward until the river bends and flows westward to the Jordan. Its western border was that part of the Jordan River and the Dead Sea that closed the gap between the northern and southern borders.

"Kinnereth" (v.17) is an older name for Lake Galilee, a town on its northwest perimeter, or the area. Gennesaret in the NT is a corruption of Kinnereth (Luke 5:1). The western border of the Gadites and Reubenites' allotment extended from Lake Galilee (Kinnereth) along the Jordan and the eastern side of the Dead Sea (the Salt Sea) as far as the Arnon Gorge, approximately half the length of the sea.

**18–20** Moses reminded the men of the two and a half tribes of their responsibility to cross the Jordan with the rest of the Israelites in order to win the land there before they settled down in their Transjordanian possessions. All the "able-bodied men, armed for battle" (v.18) must represent a special body of soldiers. Surely some men, also armed, must of necessity have remained in Transjordan to protect the women and children (v.19).

## Notes

---

**12** The NIV, following the text of BHS, translates עַל־נַחַל אַרְנֹן (*'al-naḥal 'arnōn*) as "by the Arnon Gorge." An alternate reading supported by some Hebrew MSS and major versions, which introduces שְׂפַת (*śᵉpaṯ*) between עַל and נַחַל, meaning "on the rim of the Arnon Gorge," may be the correct reading. This reading occurs in 2:36 and 4:48. A possible alternate translation of the whole phrase would be "on the bank of the Arnon River." The topographical detail is not certain.

**16** The prepositional phrase מִן־הַגִּלְעָד (*min-haggil'āḏ*, "[the territory extending] from Gilead") agrees well with the boundaries of the rest of the description. It of necessity calculates—as is noted in the commentary—that Gilead is used to represent varying parts of Transjordan. For an alternate view, see Hulst, *Translation Problems*, p. 13.

**17** The additional phrase תַּחַת אַשְׁדֹּת הַפִּסְגָּה מִזְרָחָה (*taḥaṯ 'ašdōṯ happisgāh mizrāḥāh*) describes that part of the Dead Sea coast as lying "below the slopes of Pisgah"; e.g., Pisgah is the range of mountains to the east (*mizrāḥāh*) of the northern sector of the Dead Sea. *Mizrāḥāh* occurs in the Hebrew text, but this Hebrew method of repetitive description sometimes confuses rather than clarifies descriptions for the English reader. If Pisgah is taken as a ridge of the mountain range (rather than a proper name), the meaning is the same. Nebo seems to be a high mountain in the Pisgah Range (32:49; 34:1).

---

### 7. *Moses forbidden to cross the Jordan*

#### 3:21–29

**21** At that time I commanded Joshua: "You have seen with your own eyes all that the LORD your God has done to these two kings. The LORD

will do the same to all the kingdoms over there where you are going.
22 Do not be afraid of them; the LORD your God himself will fight for you."
23 At that time I pleaded with the LORD: 24 "O Sovereign LORD, you have
begun to show to your servant your greatness and your strong hand. For
what god is there in heaven or on earth who can do the deeds and
mighty works you do? 25 Let me go over and see the good land beyond
the Jordan—that fine hill country and Lebanon."
26 But because of you the LORD was angry with me and would not listen
to me. "That is enough," the LORD said. "Do not speak to me anymore
about this matter. 27 Go up to the top of Pisgah and look west and north
and south and east. Look at the land with your own eyes, since you are
not going to cross this Jordan. 28 But commission Joshua, and encourage and strengthen him, for he will lead this people across and will
cause them to inherit the land that you will see." 29 So we stayed in the
valley near Beth Peor.

**21–29** Two subjects are intertwined in these verses: the commissioning and encouragement of Joshua (vv.21–22, 28) and the Lord's unequivocal denial of Moses' plea that he be allowed to enter the land (vv.23–27). The additional statement of v.29 indicates more precisely their locale as given in 1:5 (see Notes). The location had ready access to the top of Pisgah and to the place where Israel would cross the Jordan. Here the messages of Deuteronomy were delivered (4:45–46), and in this valley Moses was buried (34:6).

After encouraging Joshua with the assurance that God would fight for him (v.22) in Canaan as he did in Transjordan, Moses referred to his appeal to God that he might go into "the good land beyond the Jordan" (v.25). The Lord refused this request and directed him to ascend to the top of Pisgah so that he might look over the Promised Land, even though he would not enter it (vv.26–27). Joshua, not Moses, was to lead the people in conquering the land (v.28). The succession of Joshua appears also in 1:38; 31:3–8, 14, 23; and 34:9. The reason Moses gave for the Lord's order that he not enter the land is mentioned in 1:37 (see comment there), here in v.26, and in 4:21. See also 31:2; 32:48–52; and 34:1–4.

The intertwining of the two subjects mentioned above in this fashion stems from the extemporaneous character of this part of Deuteronomy. Such parts tend to be repetitive and seem to rise from the immediate occasion without express preparation. As Manley (*The Book of the Law,* p. 175) suggests, the sequence of thoughts expressed is "true to life." The directive to go to the top of Pisgah to view the Promised Land (v.27) was fulfilled after Moses had delivered the messages of Deuteronomy (those involving the renewal or reaffirmation of the covenant-treaty) to prepare the people for life in the Promised Land (see 31:7–8, 14, 23).

## Notes

**21, 23** On "at that time," see Notes on 1:9.

**24** The translation of אֲדֹנָי יהוה (*'ᵃḏōnāy YHWH*) as "Sovereign LORD" (cf. 9:26) is superior to "Lord God" (KJV et al.) since LORD translates YHWH and *'āḏôn* means "Lord" in the sense of sovereign when applied to God. In Deuteronomy "Sovereign LORD" occurs in two prayers of Moses in a most fitting way, for Moses was emphasizing God's sovereign control over history and the physical universe as seen in his "mighty works" of redemption. He realized that the decision to prohibit his entrance into the land, or to allow it, was totally within the sovereign power of the Lord. The ascription "Sovereign LORD" appears also in Genesis, Exodus, Joshua, Judges, 2 Samuel, and 1 Kings, as well as in some psalms and prophets, especially Isaiah, Jeremiah, Amos, and, most often, Ezekiel. It often is used in prayer and, among the prophets, in the phrase "this is what the Sovereign LORD says" (Amos 1:8; 3:11; et al.).

**28** On "inherit the land," see the comment on 32:8 and see 1:38; 12:10; 19:3, 14; 20:16; 31:7.

**29** "Beth Peor" (cf. 4:46; 34:6; Josh 13:20) probably was about twenty-five miles west of where the Jordan enters the Dead Sea and about six miles west of Heshbon.

---

## B. *Israel Before the Lord (4:1–40)*

### 1. *Exhortation to obey the Lord's commands*

4:1–14

[1]Hear now, O Israel, the decrees and laws I am about to teach you. Follow them so that you may live and may go in and take possession of the land that the LORD, the God of your fathers, is giving you. [2]Do not add to what I command you and do not subtract from it, but keep the commands of the LORD your God that I give you.

[3]You saw with your own eyes what the LORD did at Baal Peor. The LORD your God destroyed from among you everyone who followed the Baal of Peor, [4]but all of you who held fast to the LORD your God are still alive today.

[5]See, I have taught you decrees and laws as the LORD my God commanded me, so that you may follow them in the land you are entering to take possession of it. [6]Observe them carefully, for this will show your wisdom and understanding to the nations, who will hear about all these decrees and say, "Surely this great nation is a wise and understanding people." [7]What other nation is so great as to have their gods near them the way the LORD our God is near us whenever we pray to him? [8]And what other nation is so great as to have such righteous decrees and laws as this body of laws I am setting before you today?

[9]Only be careful, and watch yourselves closely so that you do not forget the things your eyes have seen or let them slip from your heart as long as you live. Teach them to your children and to their children after them. [10]Remember the day you stood before the LORD your God at Horeb, when he said to me, "Assemble the people before me to hear my words so that they may learn to revere me as long as they live in the land and may teach them to their children." [11]You came near and stood at the foot of the mountain while it blazed with fire to the very heavens, with black clouds and deep darkness. [12]Then the LORD spoke to you out of the fire. You heard the sound of words but saw no form; there was only a voice. [13]He declared to you his covenant, the Ten Commandments, which he commanded you to follow and then wrote them on two stone tablets. [14]And the LORD directed me at that time to teach you the decrees and laws you are to follow in the land that you are crossing the Jordan to possess.

**1–2** The basic historical milieu, the usual account of which is common to suzerain-vassal covenants, having been given (1:1–3:29), Moses next turned to the stipulations of the covenant-treaty. Historical references continued as Moses proceeded, but these were now ancillary to the presentation of the stipulations of the covenant.

This beginning section on stipulations (4:1–14) is largely hortatory, though what the Israelites were exhorted to do necessitates introductory reference to the stipulations. Kitchen (*Ancient Orient*, p. 97, 3.B) points out that vv.5–11 present the "basic" form of the stipulations of an ancient Near Eastern covenant. In vv.1 and 5 these stipulations, decrees, and laws are mentioned; and in v.2 the word "commands" is added, while in v.45 stipulations are mentioned together with decrees and laws.

By these terms Moses emphasized the importance and necessity of adhering to the codes the Lord had given the people. What God declared was sufficient to guard their lives and to guarantee their possession of the land (v.1). They needed no additional rules or directives, and none of those given were superfluous; so the people were not to add to them or subtract from them (v.2).

The covenant-treaty stipulations are all sufficient. Whatever adulterates, contradicts, or makes these stipulations ineffective cannot be allowed. God's word remains settled, if a satisfactory relationship with him is to be maintained. For further development of this aspect of revelation, see 12:32; Proverbs 30:6; Galatians 3:15; and Revelation 22:18. Not the exact wording, but the meaning or sense is covered by this dictum, as a comparison of Deuteronomy 5 and Exodus 20 shows.

The phrase "I am about to teach you" (v.1) indicates the nature of the Deuteronomic messages. They are not only the citation (or repetition) of laws but also an educative instrument explaining, interpreting, and sometimes adjusting the laws as they would relate to the circumstances that Israel would face in Canaan. Coupled with these expositions of the law are the exhortations to "follow" the laws and "keep the commands of the LORD" (vv.1–2).

**3–5** Failure to follow the Lord results in death—as following Baal of Peor proved (v.3; Num 25). The historical recital in the Thanksgiving Psalm (Ps 106:28) about the experience at Baal Peor served as a constant reminder to the people of later years that the Lord had loved his people though they had grievously sinned against him and the covenant. In Psalm 106:28 it is said, "They yoked themselves to the Baal of Peor/ and ate sacrifices offered to lifeless gods." Hosea made the indictment even sharper by focusing on the immorality involved: "They consecrated themselves to that shameful idol and became as vile as the thing they loved" (Hos 9:10). Numbers 25 tells the story of the seduction of Israel by the Moabite women at Baal Peor. This name designates both the place (and in this usage may be equated with Beth Peor) and the god (or idol) of the place. The worship of the Canaanite Baal as the god of fertility involved human sexual acts to stimulate agricultural fertility. Baalism continued to be a serious breach of the first commandment among the Israelites and, consequently, of the covenant.

Loyalty to the Lord is an absolute requirement for those who would follow him. Here at the entrance to Canaan, Israel failed to heed the warnings about the "other gods" of Canaan. The punishment, therefore, was immediate destruction. Moses recalled the incident to indicate that only those who held fast to the Lord could expect to remain alive in the land they were about to enter.

**6** Obeying the Lord's codes would make them known to the nations, who would esteem the Israelites as wise and understanding people.

**7–8** With two potent rhetorical questions, Moses pointed up the distinctive character of these codes: (1) the Lord was near them when they prayed; (2) no other nation had such righteous laws. These righteous laws were communicated and operated through prayer. Not that Israel asked for the laws, but the giving of them brought Israel close to God; and this induced the necessity for communication by prayer (vv.10–14). The nature of the Lord's prologue to the laws and their character produced the same necessity for prayer. The experience of receiving the law was to teach Israel to revere the Lord always (v.10)—to revere him through praise in prayer.

The Lord's presence in the center of the camp ("the way the LORD our God is near us," v.7) was symbolized in the glory over the ark of the covenant and the tabernacle (tent) in which the ark was placed and in the pillar of cloud by day and of fire by night (Exod 40:34–38; Num 23:21).

**9–14** This whole section (vv.1–40) carries the characteristic style of the Deuteronomic messages as a series of personalized and internalized interpretations of the laws and regulations of the covenant constitution given at Sinai and along the way as occasion arose. Interspersed with these are Moses' exhortations urging the countrymen to remember their experiences with the Lord, to adhere to the Lord, and to follow his orders and teach them to their children and to the generations to come. This should be done to insure their occupation of the land—both to acquire it and to retain control of it—and to prosper there.

Moses was concerned not only that the generation before him would be taught the stipulations of the covenant-treaty (vv.1–2, 14) but that the generations to follow would be taught what he was teaching to the people (vv.9–10). This communication involved memory and observance. "Do not forget" and do not "let them slip from your heart" (and "remember" in v.10) go along with the exhortation of v.2: "Do not add to" and "do not subtract from" the Lord's commands, and "do not forget the things your eyes have seen" (v.9). But knowledge of the codes and the Lord's communication of them (vv.9–14) was not enough; the people were to "follow them" (vv.1, 5, 13–14) and "observe them carefully" (v.6). Active obedience was essential.

Israel was called on to remember the day at Horeb (Sinai) when the Lord spoke to them "out of the fire," because, though they met God, they could not see him (v.12). They were to remember his presence through "the sound of words . . . only a voice." This is elaborated further by such terms as "his covenant, the Ten Commandments," and by what was written "on two stone tablets" (v.13). The "Ten Commandments" (lit., "ten words") epitomize all the commands the Lord gave to Israel through Moses, though the phrase occurs only here, in 10:4, and in Exodus 34:28. In 5:22 the words "these are the commandments" refer directly to the Ten Commandments. In the NIV, in deference to tradition, the word "commandments" is used for the Ten Commandments. Elsewhere "command" or some such synonym is used.

The "two stone tablets" (v.13) are two tablets rather than one tablet having two lists of commands inscribed on them. This coincides with the two copies of a suzerain-vassal treaty. Each participant was to have a copy (see Kline, *Biblical Authority*, pp. 189–24).

## Notes

---

**1–2, 5, 45** Several words used in these verses are descriptive of the stipulations of the covenant-treaty developed in 4:45–26:9. The חֻקִּים (*ḥuqqîm*, "decrees") are words cut into rock or wood and so fixed (either used physically or metaphorically) and therefore fittingly describe a monarch's decree. Used of God's laws given through Moses, *ḥuqqîm* emphasizes the divinely authoritative character of the Lord's decrees.

A judicial notion specifying the idea of a decision made on the merits of a matter resides in מִשְׁפָּטִים (*mišpāṭîm,* "laws," v.1). It suggests that these laws are God's judgments on what is right.

A basic word for laws, מִצְוֹת (*miṣwōṯ,* v.2) stems from the verb "to command," "to give a charge," "to commission"; consequently the verb is here translated "command" and the noun, "commands."

In a similar way עֵדֹת (*'ēḏōṯ*) identifies regulations ratified by some authority—an ordinance or stipulation. It is used of the Ten Commandments ("Testimony") in Exod 25:21 and in the phrases "the ark of the Testimony" (Exod 25:22) and "the Tent of the Testimony" (Num 9:15). *The Torah* (New York: Jewish Publication Society of America, 1962) has "the ark of the Pact" and "the Tent of the Pact," respectively, in these places. The Ten Commandments are the epitome of the stipulations of the covenant-treaty, the "ark" being the depository of the covenant and the "Tent" being the place where the ark was placed.

**1** For "the LORD, the God of your fathers," see the comment in the introduction to 1:1–5.

**2** The vassal treaties of Esarhaddon contain a like warning not to alter the stipulations of the treaties. See Wiseman (*Vassal-Treaties*), Kline (*Treaty,* p. 43), and Kitchen (*Ancient Orient,* p. 97) on adhering to the treaty stipulations in Deut 4:5–11.

**6** חָכְמָה וּבִינָה (*ḥoḵmāh ûḇînāh,* "wisdom and understanding") were prized elements in the socio-political life of the ancient Near East. Wise men as a class were teachers and advisers (consultants) especially to governments. The vocabulary of wisdom literature appears in significant frequency in Deuteronomy. See J. Malfroy, "Lagresse et Loi Dans Le Deuteronome," VetTest 15, 1 (January 1965): 49–65. Wisdom and understanding would be shown among the Israelites when they observed carefully the decrees and laws given by the Lord. Wise and understanding men (as well as experienced) were to be chosen as leaders in Israel (see Notes on 1:13), and Joshua as successor to Moses "was filled with the spirit of wisdom because Moses had laid his hands on him" (34:9).

**7** אֱלֹהִים (*'ᵉlōhîm*) here has been interpreted as "a god," "god," "gods," or "God." Though the contrast is between Israel and other nations, it involves a contrast between other nations' gods and the Lord as Israel's God (the true God). The contrast does not appear to be the lack of nearness of the nations to God as over against Israel's nearness to him but rather the nations' distance from their gods and Israel's nearness to the Lord, who was personally with them and could be personally entreated in prayer. Balaam seems to have understood this situation (Num 23:21–23).

**9** The restrictive רַק (*raq,* "only") lends special emphasis to Moses' twofold exhortation: "Be careful, and watch yourselves closely."

הִשָּׁמֶר לְךָ (*hiššāmer lᵉḵā,* "Be careful"), a Niphal imperative (also in v.23; 6:12; 8:11; 11:16; 12:13, 19, 30; 15:9) with *lᵉḵā,* focuses the command definitely on Israel's responsibility to guard themselves from participation in any idolatry.

שְׁמֹר נַפְשְׁךָ מְאֹד (*šᵉmōr napšᵉḵā mᵉ'ōḏ,* "watch yourselves closely") achieves a like emphasis by the use of the same verb in the Qal imperative with *napšᵉḵā* (lit., "your soul") used in the sense of "self," together with the emphatic particle *mᵉ'ōḏ*. All this constitutes a very strong and urgent appeal.

---

## 2. *Idolatry forbidden*

### 4:15–31

[15]You saw no form of any kind the day the LORD spoke to you at Horeb out of the fire. Therefore watch yourselves very carefully, [16]so that you do not become corrupt and make for yourselves an idol, an image of any shape, whether formed like a man or a woman, [17]or like any animal on

earth or any bird that flies in the air, [18]or like any creature that moves
along the ground or any fish in the waters below. [19]And when you look
up to the sky and see the sun, the moon and the stars—all the heavenly
array—do not be enticed into bowing down to them and worshiping
things the LORD your God has apportioned to all the nations under
heaven. [20]But as for you, the LORD took you and brought you out of the
iron-smelting furnace, out of Egypt, to be the people of his inheritance,
as you now are.

[21]The LORD was angry with me because of you, and he solemnly swore
that I would not cross the Jordan and enter the good land the LORD your
God is giving you as your inheritance. [22]I will die in this land; I will not
cross the Jordan; but you are about to cross over and take possession
of that good land. [23]Be careful not to forget the covenant of the LORD
your God that he made with you; do not make for yourselves an idol in
the form of anything the LORD your God has forbidden. [24]For the LORD
your God is a consuming fire, a jealous God.

[25]After you have had children and grandchildren and have lived in the
land a long time—if you then become corrupt and make any kind of
idol, doing evil in the eyes of the LORD your God and provoking him to
anger, [26]I call heaven and earth as witnesses against you this day that
you will quickly perish from the land that you are crossing the Jordan to
possess. You will not live there long but will certainly be destroyed.
[27]The LORD will scatter you among the peoples, and only a few of you
will survive among the nations to which the LORD will drive you. [28]There
you will worship man-made gods of wood and stone, which cannot see
or hear or eat or smell. [29]But if from there you seek the LORD your God,
you will find him if you look for him with all your heart and with all your
soul. [30]When you are in distress and all these things have happened to
you, then in later days you will return to the LORD your God and obey
him. [31]For the LORD your God is a merciful God; he will not abandon or
destroy you or forget the covenant with your forefathers, which he
confirmed to them by oath.

This section (vv.15–31) begins with an exhortation to eschew idolatry and ends with a warning to that generation and to the generation to come—a warning of what will happen to them if they turn to the worship of idols, which would abrogate the covenant. In between the exhortation and the warning, Moses once more said that he would not be able to enter the land because the Lord had forbidden it (vv.21–22).

**15–18** To begin the exhortation to eschew idolatry, Moses repeated his observation (v.12) that the people saw no form when the Lord spoke to them from Horeb (v.15). Because the Lord has no physical form, no physical representation could be tolerated. The description of the forms of creatures (vv.16–18) is slightly more explicit than that in the second commandment (Exod 20:4; Deut 5:8) and reminiscent of the Creation narrative (Gen 1:20–26). The Lord is not like the idols of the peoples of Canaan.

**19** Neither were the Israelites to worship the sun, the moon, and the stars. "Things the LORD your God has apportioned to all the nations under heaven" cannot mean that God gave the sun, moon, and stars as objects of worship to the nations—prohibiting such worship on the part of Israel only. This clause simply states that these celestial objects were given to all mankind for the physical benefit of the earth and were not proper objects of worship at all (Gen 1:14–18).

**20** The Lord, said Moses, had dealt with Israel as a special people. He brought them "out of the iron-smelting furnace, out of Egypt," for a purpose. The use of metal by heating certain ores and then hammering the metallic residue or welding it to other parts while still hot may have appeared in the Near East in the first half of the third millennium B.C., but the manufacture of iron objects (usually weapons) was very limited till 1500 B.C. and later. Though the "furnaces" of the OT world could not be heated sufficiently to make molten iron, artisans had learned to use bellows to make the hottest fire then known; and they knew that the hottest fire they could produce was necessary for their iron productions. "Out of the iron-smelting furnace, out of Egypt" does not mean to imply that iron-smelting furnaces were in Egypt at that time. Rather, bringing Israel out of Egypt was like bringing her out of an iron-smelting furnace—the heavy bondage of Egypt with its accompanying difficulties and tensions being likened to the hottest fire then known.

In vv.15 and 23 Moses strongly exhorted the people to watch themselves very carefully (see Notes on v.9). Idolatry corrupts and the nature of that corruption is infidelity to the Lord. This infidelity is not consonant with their standing as the people of his inheritance, the citation of which is followed by the simple, common (but here delightful) phrase "as you now are." In the same way in the NT, the apostle John writes: "How great is the love the Father has lavished on us, that we should be called children of God! And that is what we are!" (1 John 3:1; the latter clause is missing in the KJV). Here in Deuteronomy it has just been said that Israel had been brought out of Egypt "to be the people of his inheritance." "As you now are" says that the expectation had been realized. At that moment Israel was "the people of his inheritance" in actuality.

Israel as God's inheritance is seen in Psalm 78:62, 71 and Isaiah 19:25. God had promised Abraham that the land of Canaan would become the land of his offspring, so it fell to the Israelites as their inheritance; the land became their property. Using this figure Moses stated that God had brought Israel out of Egypt so that they should be his very own people—his inheritance.

**21** Moses, however, was to die in Moab, and for the third time he referred to the Lord's refusal to let him cross the Jordan and enter Canaan proper (1:37; 3:26–27). Each time he spoke of the Lord's anger toward him "because of you." (Though the Hebrew expressions are not identical, they are synonymous.) Moses appeared to feel that the Israelites were to bear the blame for his predicament (see comment on 1:37). Certainly the repetitious reference to the Lord's prohibition reflects his keen disappointment.

**22–24** The people, nevertheless, were to enter the land (v.22). So Moses reiterated his exhortation that they be very careful not to forget the covenant the Lord made with them (v.23), the central character of which is the nature of Yahweh himself, who is "a consuming fire" (v.24), a jealous God, intolerant of idols in any form. The Lord as "a jealous God" (5:9; 6:15; Exod 20:5; 34:14; cf. Josh 24:19; Nah 1:2) is not to be taken in any pejorative or petulant sense. God cannot tolerate the worship of anyone or anything else on the part of his very own people because such worship is the essence of sinfulness and self-corruption.

**25–28** The spirit of the prophets moved in Moses as he looked into the future of Israel relative to idol worship. Seeing that the generations to come might become corrupt through idolatry (v.25), he called heaven and earth as witnesses of his warning of destruction against the Israelites (v.26), the scattering of them among the nations (v.27), and their extremely limited numerical survival. He seemed sure that such a situation would prevail because he proceeded to tell how, in those foreign lands, the Israelites would "worship man-made gods" (v.28) but eventually would seek and find the Lord their God. He would not abandon, destroy, or forget them—or forget his covenant with them (cf. vv.29–31).

The temporal element mentioned in v.25—"After you have had children and grandchildren and have lived in the land a long time"—is not to be limited to two generations. It is only an alternate way of saying "later generations" (29:22) or "generations that follow" (Josh 22:27).

The indictment of idolatry in v.28 portrays the spiritual nature of Deuteronomy. No ground is given for the notion that the idol is a representation of a spiritual presence. The idol has no senses like hearing; nor does it have the ability to eat or to smell the offerings given to it. The idols are only fabrications of man using common, insensate materials.

**29** The only way out of any future predicament resulting from infidelity rested on unequivocal recommittal to the Lord—a returning to him "with all your heart and with all your soul." This same spiritual commitment is mentioned in 6:5; 10:12; 11:13; 26:16; and 30:2, 6, 10.

**30–31** The nation may fail to uphold the covenant; the people may forget their Lord; but when they turn back to him in faith and obedience (v.30), he will mercifully accept them. He will not forget the covenant based on his promises (v.31).

## Notes

---

**16** Becoming corrupt and making idols are equated. שָׁחַת (*šāḥat̲*, "to corrupt") is "to ruin or destroy."

פֶּסֶל (*pesel*), a general word for "idol," when used specifically describes an idol chiseled from stone or carved from wood (vv.23, 25; 5:8; 27:15).

The people were not to make תְּמוּנַת כָּל־סָמֶל (*t*[e]*mûnat̲ kol-sāmel*, "an image of any shape"), any formed statue (or some such representation of any formed idol). The gods of Egypt may have been in mind. They were often pictured as animals, though some were portrayed as human beings with animal heads (see F.G. Bratton, *Myths and Legends of the Ancient Near East* [New York: Crowell, 1970], pp. 57ff., and C.F. Pfeiffer, *Egypt and the Exodus* [New York: Baker, 1967], pp. 21–25). Israel was not to depict the Lord in any such corrupting fashion.

**20** On iron-working in the ancient world, see ZPEB, 3:307–8, and Hodges, pp. 144–46.

כּוּר הַבַּרְזֶל (*kûr habbarzel*) was an "iron-smelting furnace" rather than a furnace made of iron (cf. KJV), which was then nonexistent. The earliest "furnaces" were holes in the ground into which the ore and charcoal were placed. This mixture was set afire and superheated through blow pipes. Such pipes were later replaced by bellows. The iron-smelting furnace of affliction is mentioned also in 1 Kings 8:51 and Jer 11:4.

The word כּוּר (*kûr*, "furnace") appears to be originally Sumerian and reached Hebrew by way of the Akkadian *kēru* (Ellenbogen, p. 83).

לִהְיוֹת לוֹ לְעַם נַחֲלָה (*lihyôt̲ lô l*[e]*'am naḥ*[a]*lāh*, "to be the people of his inheritance") is literally "to be to him an inherited people" and can be compared with לִהְיוֹת לוֹ לְעַם סְגֻלָּה (*lihyōt̲ lô le'am seg̱ullāh,* "to be to him a people of treasure"), which can be translated as "to be his people, his treasured possession" (7:6; 14:2; et al.).

**21–22** On the pathos of Moses' repeated reference to the Lord's decree that he was not to enter the Promised Land, see the comment on 34:4.

**25** לְהַכְעִיסוֹ (*lehak̲'îsô,* "provoking him to anger") relates particularly to the ideas of provocation and vexation, perhaps even exasperation. The anger involved is that incident to being aggravated and grieved by the infidelity of his people (9:18; 31:29; 32:16, 21).

**26** Calling heaven and earth as witnesses follows the Near Eastern treaty pattern of calling the gods to witness the treaty stipulations and the parties to it (Kline, *Biblical Authority,* pp. 137, 141). Heaven and earth are not thought of as gods but rather as either personifications, which is not likely, or those who live in heaven and on earth; the thought being that witnesses both celestial and earthly would make God's creation the broadest possible assembly of witnesses to the Lord's proclamation.

---

## 3. *Acknowledgment of the Lord as God*

### 4:32–40

32 Ask now about the former days, long before your time, from the day
God created man on the earth; ask from one end of the heavens to the
other. Has anything so great as this ever happened, or has anything like
it ever been heard of? 33 Has any other people heard the voice of God
speaking out of fire, as you have, and lived? 34 Has any god ever tried to
take for himself one nation out of another nation, by testings, by
miraculous signs and wonders, by war, by a mighty hand and an
outstretched arm, or by great and awesome deeds, like all the things the
LORD your God did for you in Egypt before your very eyes?
35 You were shown these things so that you might know that the LORD
is God; besides him there is no other. 36 From heaven he made you hear
his voice to discipline you. On earth he showed you his great fire, and
you heard his words from out of the fire. 37 Because he loved your
forefathers and chose their descendants after them, he brought you out
of Egypt by his Presence and his great strength, 38 to drive out before
you nations greater and stronger than you and to bring you into their
land to give it to you for your inheritance, as it is today.
39 Acknowledge and take to heart this day that the LORD is God in
heaven above and on the earth below. There is no other. 40 Keep his
decrees and commands, which I am giving you today, so that it may go
well with you and your children after you and that you may live long in
the land the LORD your God gives you for all time.

**32** Waxing eloquently as he tried to press home the greatness of the Sinaitic experience—the making of the covenant-treaty with the Lord—Moses grandly asserted by a series of questions that the revelation of the Lord at Horeb was the greatest event of history. From the creation of man until that time, nowhere else on earth had such an observable event happened.

The Hebrew idiom for the whole phenomenal earth, "from one end of the heavens to the other" (i.e., from horizon to horizon), equals the whole known world.

**33–38** God spoke to the people out of the fire, and they still lived (v.33)! Stacking word upon word for clarity and emphasis, Moses described what the Lord had done for them in Egypt and through the deserts. The "testings" (*massōt̲,* v.34) probably relate primarily to the plagues or "great trials" (as NIV translates this word in 7:19). This "testing" is immortalized in the experience at Rephidim where the Israelites tested the Lord's patience by asking, "Is the LORD among us or not?" (Exod 17:7). So the place was called Massah and Meribah, Massah meaning "to test or plague" and Meribah, synonymously, meaning "to contend or strive."

The rest of these seven more or less synonymous expressions in v.34 indicate the extraordinary display of the Lord's power. They all indicate that Yahweh (the LORD) is God and that he is stronger than the gods of Egypt. Moreover, all these "awesome deeds" had been done for them "before [their] very eyes" with a specific intent. The people were to (1) learn that he was the only true God, (2) be corrected of any false notions or wrong behavior, and (3) be prepared for entrance into the land of their inheritance (vv.35–38).

The Lord's love for his people finds its first mention here (v.37). The reference to the Lord's choice of Israel, based on his love for their forefathers (v.37), and the reference to his gift of Canaan to them as an inheritance (v.38) go back to the covenant with Abraham and to the promises of that covenant (Gen 12:3; 17:4–8; 18:18–19). Further development of this love follows in 7:8–9, 13; 10:15; and 23:5. Reciprocating love from the people for the Lord is urged in 5:10; 6:5; 7:9; 10:12; 11:1, 13, 22; 13:3; 19:9; 30:6, 16, 20. One is reminded of 1 John 4:19: "We love because he first loved us"; John 14:15: "If you love me, you will obey what I command"; and many similar passages.

**39–40** Moses again emphasized personal commitment to the Lord. In v.39 this commitment is based on the fact that the Lord is the only God and that he exists both in heaven and on earth. The people therefore are to acknowledge him as such and fix in their minds that he alone is God. This commitment would result in prosperity and continued possession of the land that the Lord was giving them. The Hebrew structure of the last clause of v.40 suggests purpose rather than result—in order that you may continue to live in the land.

## Notes

**32** The rare לְמִן (*lᵉmin*), the pleonastic form of מִן (*min*), used here as "from" in "from the day God created," occurs when the terminus from which an event occurs (temporal) or a place from which someone or something comes (spatial) is meant (cf. BDB, p. 583).

כַּדָּבָר הַגָּדוֹל הַזֶּה (*kaddāḇār haggāḏôl hazzeh,* "has anything so great as this") is in the singular and conveys the idea that Moses was looking at the whole experience—the Exodus, the Sinaitic revelation of the Lord himself and the giving of the covenant, and the desert wanderings—as one great testimony to the Lord's person and power. And all this was to their great benefit.

**33** On living after a revelation from God, see the Notes on 5:26.

**34** On מַסֹּת (*massōṯ,* "testings"), see 7:19 and 29:3, where the NIV has "trials." On "miraculous signs and wonders," see Exod 7:3; "wars," Exod 14:14; 15:3; "mighty hand," Exod 3:19–20; 6:1; "outstretched arm," Exod 6:6; and for "great and awesome deeds," see the experiences recorded in Exod 12:31–36. Here in 4:34 the phrase בְּמוֹרָאִים גְּדֹלִים (*bᵉmôrā'îm gᵉḏōlîm,* "by great and awesome deeds") is plural. In another list, however, of much the same words in 26:8 ("testings" and "war" are missing), the singular בְּמֹרָא גָּדֹל (*bᵉmōrā' gāḏōl*) occurs; and NIV translates it as "great terror." Doubtless the works of God mentioned inspired both awe and terror.

**37** Wiseman (*Vassal-Treaties*, 1:268) says that "political loyalty was generally expressed by the term 'love'." And Moran ("Love of God," pp. 77ff.) observes that this expression (love) served a political need in the ancient Near East. Moran shows that as early as the eighteenth century B.C., the term "love" was used to describe the loyalty due a vassal king to his suzerain. This loyalty required unqualified obedience to the suzerain and to all the stipulations expressed in the suzerain-vassal treaty. So too the love required by the Lord involved the unqualified obedience of his people. On the love of God as total commitment in Deuteronomy, see comment on v.29 and the passages cited.

**39** יָדַעְתָּ (*yāḏa'tā*, "acknowledge") and הֲשֵׁבֹתָ אֶל־לְבָבֶךָ (*h^a šēḇōṯā 'el-l^e ḇāḇeḵā*, "take to heart") surely are synonymous expressions, the second reinforcing the first. "Take to heart" does not carry all the force of the Hebrew. The verb *ḥāšaḇ* means "to think, desire, esteem, or value ideas that evoke active thought"; so *lāḇaḇ* is mind rather than heart, and the expression describes a definite mental decision. The use of *yāḏa'* as "acknowledge" supports this. *Yāḏa'* surely has the sense here of its synonym *nāḵar*, with the meaning of "acknowledge" in the parallelistic structure in Isa 63:16. TWOT (1:467) says that in some instances as here, *lāḇaḇ* "virtually becomes a synonym for such ideas as 'mind'."

---

## C. *The Transjordanian Cities of Refuge* 4:41–43

**41**Then Moses set aside three cities east of the Jordan, **42**to which anyone who had killed a person could flee if he had unintentionally killed his neighbor without malice aforethought. He could flee into one of these cities and save his life. **43**The cities were these: Bezer in the desert plateau, for the Reubenites; Ramoth in Gilead, for the Gadites; and Golan in Bashan, for the Manassites.

**41–42** Verses 41–43 constitute a historical observation situated between two addresses, probably because the cities were chosen at this particular time.

Bezer, Ramoth Gilead, and Golan are designated as sanctuaries (refuges)—elsewhere called cities of refuge—for whoever unintentionally and without malice aforethought killed someone. The regulations appropriate to the use of these cities are elaborated in 19:1–13 and in Numbers 35:9–28, but only here are the names of the Transjordanian cities of refuge expressly mentioned in the Pentateuch (but see Josh 20:8).

**43** The desert plateau extends eastward from the upper part of the Dead Sea. Bezer lies about twenty miles east of the northeast corner of the Dead Sea. Ramoth Gilead was about thirty miles southeast of Lake Galilee, and Golan, twenty miles east of a centerpoint on the east bank of Lake Galilee. Bezer, then, was accessible to the people in southern Transjordan, Ramoth Gilead to those in the central part, and Golan to the ones in the north. The identification and location of these places are not certain but are probably correct.

## Notes

---

**42** The Hebrew word for "these" (הָאֵל, *hā'ēl*) here ("these [cities]") and in 7:22 ("those [nations]") illustrates an orthographic peculiarity of the letter ה (*h*) occasionally found in the MT. The word is obviously the demonstrative pronoun ordinarily spelled הָאֵלֶּה (*hā'ēlleh*).

---

## III. The Second Address: Stipulations of the Covenant-Treaty and Its Ratification (4:44–28:68)

### A. *Introduction*

#### 4:44–49

> [44]This is the law Moses set before the Israelites. [45]These are the
> stipulations, decrees and laws Moses gave them when they came out of
> Egypt [46]and were in the valley near Beth Peor east of the Jordan, in the
> land of Sihon king of the Amorites, who reigned in Heshbon and was
> defeated by Moses and the Israelites as they came out of Egypt. [47]They
> took possession of his land and the land of Og king of Bashan, the two
> Amorite kings east of the Jordan. [48]This land extended from Aroer on
> the rim of the Arnon Gorge to Mount Siyon (that is, Hermon), [49]and
> included all the Arabah east of the Jordan, as far as the Sea of the
> Arabah, below the slopes of Pisgah.

**44–49** The NIV heading for this passage agrees with the judgment of many scholars that the section is an introduction to the law—specifically the law as delineated in chapters 5–26. The first words—"This is the law" (v.44)—and also the beginning of the next verse (v.45)—"These are the stipulations"—are said to be forms that designate what follows rather than that indicate a summary of what precedes. That this is usually the case can be seen often in Leviticus in the introduction to the regulations for certain offerings (Lev 6:9, 14, 20, 25; 7:1, 11, et al.). However, these clauses sometimes designate what has preceded, as in Leviticus 26:46 and 27:34. So it may be that vv.44–49 summarize what precedes or, as Kline (*Biblical Authority*, p. 136 n. 17) suggests, they may be transitional relating to both what proceeds and what follows. Certainly the material relates to both.

As an introduction to the stipulations, the paragraph presents something of the character of what follows—viz., "stipulations, decrees and laws" (v.45). It mentions also the people on whom the stipulations were imposed—"the Israelites" (v.44); the time—"when they came out of Egypt" (v.45); and the place—"in the valley near Beth Peor" (v.46); and a brief description of the extent of the lands that they had captured from the Amorites Sihon and Og (vv.47–49).

Why another introduction? (Notice 1:1–5.) It may be that this is a second beginning after the preamble followed by the historical prologue as suggested by Kline (*Treaty*, p. 30). Perhaps this follows the procedure of updating the treaty at treaty renewal time. It may be an instance of the repetitive character of Deuteronomy as a device for emphasis and instruction. Certainly notations beginning with "These are the laws" or "stipulations" or some such term occur frequently elsewhere in the Pentateuch.

## Notes

---

**45** For stipulations, decrees, and laws, see the comments and Notes on 4:1.

**46** On Beth Peor, see the Notes on 3:29.

The campaign against Sihon is found in 2:26–37.

**47** For the campaign against Og, see 3:1–11.

**48** Aroer on the rim of the Arnon Gorge at that time was the northern border of Moab and the southern border of the Transjordanian area held by the Amorites. Mount Hermon, here called "Siyon"—שִׂיאֹן (*śî'ōn;* in Syriac, "Sirion")—is the northern border of the area conquered. See the comment on 3:9 and on the Text in the Introduction.

---

## B. *Basic Elements of Life in the Land (5:1–11:32)*

### 1. *The Ten Commandments (5:1–33)*

#### a. *Exhortation and historical background*

5:1–5

1 Moses summoned all Israel and said:
Hear, O Israel, the decrees and laws I declare in your hearing today.
Learn them and be sure to follow them. 2 The LORD our God made a
covenant with us at Horeb. 3 It was not with our fathers that the LORD
made this covenant, but with us, with all of us who are alive here today.
4 The LORD spoke to you face to face out of the fire on the mountain. 5 (At
that time I stood between the LORD and you to declare to you the word of
the LORD, because you were afraid of the fire and did not go up the
mountain.) And he said:

**1–2** Moses' main address begins much as his introduction to the historical prologue, his first address (4:1). He urged that the people personally learn these decrees and laws and that they personally adhere to them (v.1). He reminded the people that they themselves had received the covenant from the Lord who had spoken to them out of the fire on Mount Horeb (v.2). Though the people he was then talking to were less than twenty years of age at the time of the Horeb experience, they were nevertheless there and were representative of Israel. Caleb and Joshua were exempted from the decree of death in the desert and were older. Whether the people then standing before him were individually at Horeb was not important. The covenant-treaty was made by the nation represented at Horeb, and the covenant remained in force to all succeeding generations until abrogated or qualified by the Lord.

**3** The "fathers" were not the people's immediate fathers who had died in the desert and who were recipients of the covenant but their more distant ancestors, the patriarchs (see 4:31, 37; 7:8, 12; 8:18).

**4–5** The immediacy of the Lord's relationship with the people is pointed up in the phrase "face to face" (v.4). Almost the same phrase describes the Lord's unusual relationship with Moses (34:10; cf. Exod 33:11), Jacob's vision of God at Peniel (Gen 32:30), and Gideon's experience with the angel of the Lord (Judg 6:22). However, as soon as Moses mentioned their face-to-face encounter with the Lord at Horeb, he explained that this was through his mediatorship, because of their fear of the fire on the mountain. That fear, in any event, was not only due to the fear of God whose theophanic presence induced the fire (Exod 20:18–20; Deut 5:24–26). The character of Moses' mediation can be seen in the contrast between the Israelites' hearing the sounds of the voice of God (4:12, 15; 5:4, 22, 24; 10:4) but not with sufficient clarity to distinguish the words (Exod 19:7, 9; 20:19, 21–22). A similar situation occurred at Paul's conversion (Acts 9:7).

## Notes

---

1 עַתָּה יִשְׂרָאֵל שְׁמַע (*'attāh yiśrā'ēl š$^e$ma'*, "Hear now, O Israel") in 4:1 and the more common שְׁמַע יִשְׂרָאֵל (*š$^e$ma' yiśrā'ēl,* "Hear, O Israel," 5:1; 6:4; 9:1; 20:3; 27:9, where "listen" has the same Hebrew form) contain the sense of more than "pay attention." Obedience is expected. Thompson (*Ancient Treaties*, p. 36) illustrates this use of the form in Near Eastern treaties.

2 This covenant bound Israel to the Lord as her absolute suzerain-monarch. Jeremiah later spoke of a new covenant that would put the Lord's "law in their minds and write it on their hearts" (Jer 31:33). And the author of the Epistle to the Hebrews says that the new covenant made the old one obsolete. Jesus Christ, the Mediator of the new covenant, by his person and work saves from their sins those under the new covenant; and they "receive the promised eternal inheritance" (Heb 9:15; cf. Heb 7:22; 8:7–13; 10:15–17).

---

### b. *The commandments (5:6–21)*

#### 1) *The Lord as God and the prohibition of other gods*

#### 5:6–7

**6 "I am the LORD your God, who brought you out of Egypt, out of the land of slavery.**
**7 "You shall have no other gods before me.**

**6–7** The Ten Commandments sit appropriately at the beginning of Moses' elucidation of the basic legislation for the Israelites. These commands are not only to be learned but are also to be obeyed. They are apodictic. They come directly from the Lord their God—the God who brought them up from Egypt, the land of slavery. Their relationship with God is rooted in history, and that history is one of God's intervention for their benefit. Apodictic law has been variously defined. Here what is meant may be tersely summarized as fiat, divine commands—commands that come directly from the Lord.

The suzerain-vassal treaty form began with a historical prologue that portrayed the benefactions of the suzerain as the basis for obeying him as the stipulations required. Verse 6 is an epitome of God's benefaction toward Israel. Moses elaborated and repeated this throughout the Lord's messages as recorded in Deuteronomy and elsewhere (Exod 20:2; Lev 26:13; Num 15:41; Deut 13:4–5; et al.; see Nielsen, *Ten Commandments*, pp. 60ff.).

The phrases "other gods" and "before me" (v.7) also speak of the relationship of the people to God. The God who brought the people out of Egypt does not allow the people to have "other gods"—whatever they might be. The Hebrew phrase translated "before me," "besides me," or any similar English phrase calls for the exclusive commitment of the people to the Lord. The subsequent prohibition of idolatry and the use of idolatrous forms surely indicate that the prohibition against other "gods" rules out Israelite recognition of any other "god" as the true "God."

#### 2) *Prohibition of images*

#### 5:8–10

**8 "You shall not make for yourself an idol in the form of anything in heaven above or on the earth beneath or in the waters below.**

[9]You shall not bow down to them or worship them; for I, the LORD your God, am a jealous God, punishing the children for the sin of the fathers to the third and fourth generation of those who hate me, [10]but showing love to a thousand ⌊generations⌋ of those who love me and keep my commandments.

**8–10** The proscription of making or using idols is total (vv.8–9a). Nothing in Israel's environmental experience may be the basis for an idolatrous form to be honored and worshiped as God.

The reason given for the prohibition is definitely personal, both on the part of the Lord and on the part of the people (vv.9b–10). The people either hate the Lord or love and obey him, and they receive from him punishment or love commensurate with their hate or love and obedience. Those who adhere to the covenant-treaty stipulations get its promised benefits; those who do not adhere to them get its punishments. The effect of one generation on succeeding generations is noted often in the OT. Here, however, the children are not punished for the sins that their father committed; the children who sin as their fathers sinned are punished for their own sins (cf. 24:16). The punishment goes on "to the third and fourth generation of those who hate me," just as his love continues toward "a thousand [generations] of those who love me and keep my commandments." The distinction between punishment unto the third and fourth generation of those who hate the Lord and love extended to thousands who love him and keep his commandments suggests that God's love far surpasses his retribution.

### 3) *Prohibition against misusing God's name*

5:11

[11]"You shall not misuse the name of the LORD your God, for the LORD will not hold anyone guiltless who misuses his name.

**11** "You shall not misuse the name of the LORD your God" concerns, among other practices, the use of his name in oaths or vows.

In OT times oaths were part of the common process of making authoritative and firm statements or promises. The Israelites were not to use the Lord's name to seal such declarations in a light or frivolous manner or without the intention of fulfilling the oath, vow, or promise.

Jesus taught that his disciples should always simply tell the truth and "not swear at all" (Matt 5:33–37; cf. James 5:12). In the NT, however, the Lord confirms his promise to Abraham by swearing an oath in his own name. This was historically enacted (Gen 22:15–18; Heb 6:13–20).

The "misuse" or "lifting up" (lit. Heb.) of the name of the Lord for an unworthy cause or in an unworthy manner destroys the proper use of the name in prayer, praise, and thanksgiving and substitutes a blasphemous manipulation of witchcraft and other supposed sources of power for a holy invoking of God's name. Such unworthy methods are denounced in 18:9–14. They will not go unpunished.

Other sworn promises of God are mentioned in the NT. In Acts 2:30–32, Peter said that God promised David on oath that one of his descendants would be placed on his throne and that this prophesied Christ's resurrection. In Hebrews 7:20–22, it is argued that the eternal priesthood of Jesus was assured by the Lord's sworn declaration in Psalm 110:4, that Christ would be a priest forever in the order of

Melchizedek, that is, like Melchizedek. On the use of the name of the Lord in Deuteronomy, see the comment on 32:3.

### 4) *Observance of the Sabbath*

#### 5:12–15

> [12]"Observe the Sabbath day by keeping it holy, as the LORD your God has commanded you. [13]Six days you shall labor and do all your work, [14]but the seventh day is a Sabbath to the LORD your God. On it you shall not do any work, neither you, nor your son or daughter, nor your manservant or maidservant, nor your ox, your donkey or any of your animals, nor the alien within your gates, so that your manservant and maidservant may rest, as you do.
> [15]Remember that you were slaves in Egypt and that the LORD your God brought you out of there with a mighty hand and an outstretched arm. Therefore the LORD your God has commanded you to observe the Sabbath day.

**12–15** Deuteronomy is more explicit than Exodus regarding the Sabbath commandment. The emphatic statement "as the LORD your God has commanded you" (v.12) looks back to the earlier initial declaration.

The prohibition against making animals work on the Sabbath is also more emphatic here than in the Exodus statement: "nor your animals" (Exod 20:10). Not only are certain common draft animals mentioned, but the totality of the Israelite animal holdings are included in "any of your animals" (v.14). Moses next gave a reason why their servants were to be granted cessation of work on the Sabbath: "so that your manservant and maidservant may rest, as you do." This concern for the lower strata of society is further developed in v.15 in the exhortation to remember that they themselves were slaves in Egypt and that it was through the Lord's intervention that they were "brought . . . out of there." The Lord's bringing the Israelites out of Egypt, here given as the reason for the Sabbath command to rest, does not preclude other reasons for the law of the Sabbath—as in Exodus, where God's rest on the seventh day (after Creation) is the reason given (Exod 20:11).

The anthropomorphisms "mighty hand" and "outstretched arm" are used a half-dozen times in Deuteronomy and about twenty times in the rest of the OT, where they refer mostly to the hand being extended to signify the powerful intervention of God in history.

The fourth commandment begins on a positive note. The people were to observe the seventh day by keeping it holy; that is, they were to recognize that the Lord had set the day apart as being holy, as a special day of rest, just as he had rested after his creative work (Exod 20:11). In addition to the remembrance of the initial creative work of God, the people were to remember the Sabbath because the Lord had brought them out of Egyptian slavery and had created them as a nation (v.15; Exod 15:16).

Ideas involved in the observation of the Sabbath are perpetuated in the NT revelation by the analogy of the creating of a new people of God through the ministry of the Lord Jesus. The time reference, however, is now changed from the last day to the first day of the week, commemorating the resurrection of our Lord and the new creation that followed on faith in Christ and his saving grace (Matt 28:1–7; Mark 16:1–6; Luke 24:1–6; 1 Cor 16:2; Rev 1:10; cf. Eph 2:4–10; 4:24).

The Sabbath rest goes far beyond the cessation of work on the seventh day after six days of labor, not only in the Sabbatical years in the Mosaic economy, but also in the much wider connotations of fulfillment of the rest of the soul of those who trust in Jesus as Savior (Heb 4:1–11).

The obviously ceremonial aspects of the observance of the Sabbath are based on moral and spiritual considerations as evidenced by the command to make the day holy by activity separate from the labors of the six days and by concern for not only one's self but also for others in the family, the servants in the household, the aliens, and the animals he owns. "As the LORD your God has commanded you" (v.12) points up the necessity of obedience, and the words "may rest, as you do" (v.14) indicate concern for others' well-being. Moreover, the reference to the Lord as the one who brought them out of Egypt (v.15) surely suggests that they should remind themselves of his kind providence of liberation from Egypt and of support through the desert wanderings. This would strengthen their faith.

In the NT the ritual elements of the Jewish Sabbath are superseded by the work of Christ and by faith in him. The Sabbath observance changed to the first day of the week, now called the Lord's Day, to focus on the new life effected and epitomized by the resurrection of Christ Jesus. However, even now the observance of the Lord's Day must subscribe to Colossians 2:16–17: "Therefore do not let anyone judge you . . . with regard to . . . a Sabbath day. . . . the reality . . . is found in Christ" (cf. John 20:1, 19, 26; Acts 2:1; 20:7; 1 Cor 16:2; Rev 1:10).

### 5) *Honoring one's parents*

#### 5:16

16 "Honor your father and your mother, as the LORD your God has commanded you, so that you may live long and that it may go well with you in the land the LORD your God is giving you.

**16** The tendency to elaborate the statement of the commands appears again in the fifth command. After the specific command, "Honor your father and your mother," Exodus 20:12 says, "so that you may live long in the land the LORD your God is giving you." Moses, preparing the people for the conquest and settlement of the land, added: "that it may go well with you."

To honor is to respect, glorify, and venerate. By contrast the offering of improper sacrifices is described as despising and dishonoring God—on the part of both Eli's sons and the priests of Malachi's day. To Eli's house a man of God said, "Those who honor me I will honor, but those who despise me will be disdained" (1 Sam 2:30). God through Malachi equates the failure of the priests to honor God with despising him; i.e., they "show contempt for [his] name" (Mal 1:6).

Children are to hold parents in high regard because of the parental position in the family, a position not only in God's scheme of authority in human relationships but also in the covenant relationship that called for continuation of the people's status with the Lord. The children's regard for their parents led to regard for their parent's relationship to God.

It should be noted that both father and mother are to be honored. The results of failure to honor parents can be seen in the law concerning an incorrigibly rebellious son (21:18–21).

Jesus criticized the Pharisees and teachers of the law for setting aside the commandments by observing their own traditions. He illustrated this by their breaking of this commandment to honor father and mother (Matt 15:4; Mark 7:10).

Paul cited this commandment as essential to Christian behavior and productive of well being and longevity (Eph 6:1–3).

The apostle Paul referred to the fifth commandment as "the first commandment with a promise," the promise being "that it may go well with you and that you may enjoy long life on the earth" (Eph 6:2–3). Paul did not limit the promise either temporally (to OT times) or geographically (to Canaan or Palestine). Doubtless the reference to "land" here in Deuteronomy was to Canaan as the Land of Promise. That promise was specifically offered to Israel. Nevertheless, the honoring of father and mother as ethical revelation, together with its promise, carries over into all time and everywhere. Furthermore, the promise of an ultimate resting place (homeland) reaches its greatest fulfillment in "a new heaven and a new earth" (2 Peter 3:13; Rev 21:1).

When a certain rich man asked Jesus what good thing he had to do to obtain eternal life, Jesus answered, "Obey the commandments" (Matt 19:17). To clarify this Jesus specifically mentioned certain of the Ten Commandments that related to behavior toward others (Deut 5:16–20; Matt 19:18–19) and added, "Love your neighbor as yourself" (Matt 19:19; Lev 19:18). Jesus did not abrogate the moral law established in the Ten Commandments; rather he declared them essential to it (see also Mark 10:19; Luke 18:20). Paul declared that the commandments are summed up and fulfilled in love toward one's neighbor (Rom 13:9–10).

### 6) *Prohibition of murder*

#### 5:17

17"You shall not murder.

**17** The NIV correctly translates the sixth command as a prohibition of murder rather than of killing. Murder is a personal, capital crime. Killing may be done as representative of the nation in judgment on a criminal or in war. In OT times persons were put to death in obedience to the command of God, but private or personal killing is murder and is proscribed.

God in his covenant with Noah placed responsibility on man for his fellowman who bears the image of God: "Whoever sheds the blood of man, by man shall his blood be shed" (Gen 9:6). Capital punishment is the penalty for willful homicide (Exod 21:12; Num 35:16; Deut 19:12), the worshiping of other gods (Deut 17:2–7), and other acts of disobedience to the Lord (Deut 22:22; Josh 8:24–26; et al.).

The Ten Commandments do not allow the pandering of the criminal who takes the life of a fellow human being. Yet the person who without malice aforethought accidentally kills another is protected (4:41–42). So the covenant-treaty restricts the passions that lead to murder but requires proper punishment of criminal homicides.

Jesus got behind the prohibition to murder by teaching that the anger driving one to such violence was sinful (Matt 5:21–22). James cited this command and the one on adultery in his argument that breaking one command makes one guilty of breaking them all (James 2:10).

### 7) *Prohibition of Adultery*

#### 5:18

18"You shall not commit adultery.

**18** The starkly simple sentence "You shall not commit adultery" carries an immense load of social and spiritual implications and provides the basis for the later development of these implications. Specific laws regarding male and female relationships are found in Moses' address in chapters 21–25. The marriage relationship and its dissolution continues throughout the OT as a figure of the covenant relationship between the Lord and his people. The Lord remains true to his love for his people, even though they are often guilty of infidelity, which is "spiritual adultery" (Jer 3:8–9; Ezek 16:15–63; Hos).

Does the proscription against adultery in the Ten Commandments extend beyond the social structure between men and women? Is this commandment humanistic only? It should be noted that the Hebrew word *nā'ap̱* ("adultery") occurs only here in Deuteronomy, though the subject of adultery appears in 22:22–27. However, *nā'ap̱* occurs elsewhere, especially in Hosea, Jeremiah, and Ezekiel, in the sense of apostasy as marital infidelity.

Apostasy is marital infidelity (figuratively), and total commitment must be Israel's relationship to the Lord; marriage under the covenant must be marked by the same faithful commitment. In Leviticus 20 further explication of the prohibition of adultery shows the analogy of the marriage relationship to the people's relationship to the Lord.

Nielsen (*Ten Commandments*, p. 107) averred that "the sixth commandment came . . . to be directed not only against every form of sexual offense (including sodomy and homosexuality) but also against apostasy," and he cited the use of *nā'ap̱* in Jeremiah, Ezekiel, and Hosea as proof.

Jesus went beyond the commandment against adultery by declaring that a man who entertains lustful thoughts has sinned before the act or without the act (Matt 5:27–28).

### 8) *Prohibition of Stealing*

5:19

19 "You shall not steal.

**19** Both here and elsewhere all thievery is condemned in the OT as well as in the NT. The right to personal property is basic to the whole Mosaic economy. The word *gānaḇ* ("to steal") reoccurs in Deuteronomy only in 24:7 in relation to kidnapping—a particularly serious violation of the eighth commandment, because it resulted in slavery.

Among the Jewish laws (in Sanhedrin [courts] 86a, the fourth tractate of the fourth order, *Nezikim* ["damages"] of the Mishnah), the eighth commandment is limited to kidnapping because its penalty was capital punishment—a punishment not exacted for stealing property. But this interpretation of the rabbis did not coincide with Exodus 22:2, where burglary comes under the prohibition of theft, and in Exodus 21:16 so does kidnapping. The indictment of the eighth commandment, then, extends to both manstealing, or kidnapping, and the theft of goods.

The experience of Joseph being sold by his brothers (Gen 37) and Nehemiah's charge (which was very much later) that brothers were selling brothers (Neh 5:5–9) illustrate the selling of fellow Israelites for personal gain.

The protection granted by the eighth commandment under the covenant provided freedoms that are still essential to a free society; the freedom from involuntary servitude and the right to hold property are protected by this law against theft.

The eighth commandment, however, involves spiritual values also. These values rest on the covenant relationship that the Lord proffers to his people. By keeping his commands the people will experience the Lord's blessing "so that it may go well with" them and so that they "may live long in the land" (4:40).

### 9) *Prohibition of false testimony*

5:20

[20]"You shall not give false testimony against your neighbor.

**20** The truth, the whole truth, and nothing but the truth was a most important matter in Israel. Though these terms in this combination of words were not used, the sense of them was required and sought. Judges were required by the Lord to make their decisions on the basis of truth without prejudice or partisanship (1:16–17). False testimony, when discovered, brought severe penalty. In the later section on witnesses (19:15–21), the lex talionis appears: "Show no pity: life for life, eye for eye, tooth for tooth, hand for hand, foot for foot" (v.21). Both here and in Exodus 20:16, this commandment is directed to false witness against one's neighbor, that is, another Israelite under the covenant.

God is "the God of truth" (Isa 65:16). His words are true (Ps 119:142, 151), and he hates "a lying tongue" and "a false witness who pours out lies" (Prov 6:17, 19). If a witness cannot establish a charge made before the authorities but is shown to be a liar, that witness must pay the penalty that he had sought against the person who was charged with the crime (Deut 19:15–21). If one has evidence of a public charge against anyone and withholds that evidence, "he will be held responsible" (Lev 5:1). Upholding the truth was important in Israel.

## Notes

---

**20** The "false" witness here is שָׁוְא (*šāw'*); שֶׁקֶר (*šeqer*) is used in Exod 20:16. The NIV quite properly translates both words as "false" since they are synonymous in these places. The meaning of *šeqer* is commonly "false" while *šāw'* is translated by "false" in such places as Exod 23:1 ("false reports"); Ezek 12:24; 13:6–7, 9, 23; 21:29 (34 MT); 22:28 ("false visions").

---

### 10) *Prohibition of coveting*

5:21

[21]"You shall not covet your neighbor's wife. You shall not set your desire on your neighbor's house or land, his manservant or maidservant, his ox or donkey, or anything that belongs to your neighbor."

**21** There is a slight variation from Exodus in the order of the tenth command. Exodus 20:17 first prohibits coveting "your neighbor's house" and then prohibits coveting "your neighbor's wife," while Deuteronomy mentions the prohibition against coveting "your neighbor's wife" first. Deuteronomy uses a different verb relative to coveting the neighbor's house or land ("land" is added in Deuteronomy), but the words for coveting are synonyms.

The last of the Ten Commandments goes beyond what people do; it probes into their minds and desires. The prohibition to covet catches wrongdoing at its source.

Coveting stems from the set of one's soul, from one's intentions, from one's motivations, from one's "heart." As purity of one's desires is required by the Lord in 6:5: "Love the LORD your God with all your heart and with all your soul and with all your strength," the possibility of its antithesis lies behind the warning of 1 Chronicles 28:9: "Acknowledge the God of your father, and serve him with wholehearted devotion and with a willing mind, for the LORD searches every heart and understands every motive behind the thoughts." The motives that might be found surely include the covetousness proscribed by the tenth commandment.

The prohibition against coveting a neighbor's land would have no meaning if family rights in marriage ties, domestic tranquility, and property ownership did not exist. To insure family rights after the land in Canaan was allotted, the Lord forbade coveting not only a neighbor's wife, servants, animals, and whatever other goods he owned, but also his house and land, neither of which any of them had at that time. It was anticipated, however, that each Israelite family would have a house and land in Canaan. These are protected by the prohibitions against theft and covetousness.

In the NT the apostle Paul said that the knowledge of the law, through the command "Do not covet" (Rom 7:7), elicited every kind of "covetous desire" (v.8) in him because of his "sinful nature" (v.18).

For a more thorough review of the tenth commandment, See Kaiser, *Old Testament Ethics*, pp. 235–44.

## Notes

**21** While Exod 20:17 uses חָמַד (*ḥāmaḏ*) for coveting a neighbor's house and coveting a neighbor's wife, Deut 5:21 uses *ḥāmaḏ* for coveting a neighbor's wife but the reflexive Hithpael תִּתְאַוֶּה (*tiṯ'awweh*, "desire," from אָוָה [*'āwāh*]) for coveting another's house or land. It is evident that not literal likeness but the sense of the words used is important.

### c. *Ratification of the covenant-treaty*

#### 5:22–33

22These are the commandments the LORD proclaimed in a loud voice
to your whole assembly there on the mountain from out of the fire, the
cloud and the deep darkness; and he added nothing more. Then he
wrote them on two stone tablets and gave them to me.
23When you heard the voice out of the darkness, while the mountain
was ablaze with fire, all the leading men of your tribes and your elders
came to me. 24And you said, "The LORD our God has shown us his glory
and his majesty, and we have heard his voice from the fire. Today we
have seen that a man can live even if God speaks with him. 25But now,
why should we die? This great fire will consume us, and we will die if we
hear the voice of the LORD our God any longer. 26For what mortal man

has ever heard the voice of the living God speaking out of fire, as we
have, and survived? 27 Go near and listen to all that the LORD our God
says. Then tell us whatever the LORD our God tells you. We will listen and
obey."
28 The LORD heard you when you spoke to me and the LORD said to me,
"I have heard what this people said to you. Everything they said was
good. 29 Oh, that their hearts would be inclined to fear me and keep all
my commands always, so that it might go well with them and their
children forever!
30 "Go, tell them to return to their tents. 31 But you stay here with me so
that I may give you all the commands, decrees and laws you are to teach
them to follow in the land I am giving them to possess."
32 So be careful to do what the LORD your God has commanded you;
do not turn aside to the right or to the left. 33 Walk in all the way that the
LORD your God has commanded you, so that you may live and prosper
and prolong your days in the land that you will possess.

**22** These "ten words" (commands) are made still more emphatic by Moses' declaration that at the particular time the Ten Commandments were given, these commands and these alone were spoken to the Israelites directly by God. He uttered them in a loud voice from the mountain, out of the fire, the cloud, and the deep darkness. The rest of the stipulations of the covenant were given to Moses who in turn gave them to the Israelites.

He "added nothing more" (v.22) refers to these Ten Commandments that were spoken and then written by God on the two stone tablets. They constitute the basic behavioral code that was to determine not only their allegiance and life-style but also that of all succeeding generations as well. No other such short list of commands begins to compare with the effect that these have had in world history. In spite of being constantly broken, they stand as the moral code par excellence.

**23–28** Moses referred to recent history to recount a strange inconsistency of the leaders and elders of Israel (v.23), an inconsistency that necessitated the mediatorial character of Moses' ministry (for references to a covenant-mediator as in the suzerain-vassal treaties, see Kline, *Biblical Authority*, pp. 61ff., and Phillips, *Deuteronomy*, pp. 44, 51–53, 196, 204–5). The leading men and elders acknowledged that they had seen the Lord's glory and majesty and had heard his voice and yet remained alive (v.24). Nevertheless, they were afraid that continuous exposure would cause their death (vv.25–26). No reason for this contradiction was offered, but they wanted Moses to be their intermediary (v.27). They asserted that they would do whatever God told Moses they should do. Moses reminded them that the Lord had accepted this arrangement (v.28). Moses had been their intermediary ever since he had returned to Egypt to lead the people out of bondage. At Horeb, however, Moses became the intermediary between the Lord and the people for the establishment of the covenantal stipulations. The people accepted the covenant with all these stipulations (v.27; Exod 20:19; 24:3).

**29** With an outburst of emotion, the Lord added, "Oh, that their hearts would be inclined to fear me and keep all my commands always, so that it might go well with them and their children forever!" The best interests of his people are deep in the heart of God. This view of divine compassion shows how the Lord's love focuses on what is best for his people. Here is no vindictive god in contrast to a loving NT Lord.

No, this glimpse into the heart of God is in harmony with the most compassionate depictions of Christ in the NT.

**30–31** The Israelites were directed to return to their tents (v.30). However, at the direction of God, Moses stayed to receive additional commands, decrees, and laws that the people were to follow in the land they were about to acquire (v.31).

**32–33** Moses drew the attention of the people back to the giving of the law at Horeb—to the people and to their children forever. As long as the nation remained true to the Lord and the covenant-treaty, the people as a nation would live and prosper and could prolong their days in the land. Before once again stating and explaining the specific laws, Moses urged the people to do what the Lord had commanded—and exactly what he had commanded (v.32). No deviation was to be practiced. The result of obedience would be long residence in the land they would win for themselves in Canaan (v.33). Individual longevity may not be precluded from this promise for following the Lord, but the main reference was to the national welfare—as is the case elsewhere in Deuteronomy (cf. 6:2 for individual reference).

## Notes

---

**22** On the two stone tablets, see the comment and Notes on 9:15 and the NIV mg. See also Kline, *Biblical Authority*, pp. 35–36, 121, and id., *Treaty*, pp. 14ff.

**26** The idea that no one can see God and live appears in the narrative of Moses' seeing the Lord's glory (Exod 33:18–23), in the experience of Gideon (Judg 6:22–23), and in that of Manoah and his wife (Judg 13:22).

"Mortal man" translates בָּשָׂר (*bāśār*), which elsewhere in Deuteronomy is "meat" (12:15, 20, 23, 27; 14:8; 16:4) or the flesh of human beings (28:53, 55; 32:42). In other places it sometimes depicts living beings subject to death (Gen 6:17, 19) or just human beings subject to death (Gen 6:12–13; Num 16:22 ["mankind"]). See also Isa 40:6–8, where the moral frailty of mankind is described: "All men [*bāśār*] are like grass."

**29** כָּל־הַיָּמִים (*kol-hayyāmîm*, "always"; lit., "all the days") is coextensive with עֹלָם (*'ōlām*, "forever") at the end of the verse.

---

### 2. *The greatest commandment: Love the Lord (6:1–25)*

#### a. *The intent of the covenant*

6:1–3

[1]These are the commands, decrees and laws the LORD your God directed me to teach you to observe in the land that you are crossing the Jordan to possess, [2]so that you, your children and their children after them may fear the LORD your God as long as you live by keeping all his decrees and commands that I give you, and so that you may enjoy long life. [3]Hear, O Israel, and be careful to obey so that it may go well with you and that you may increase greatly in a land flowing with milk and honey, just as the LORD, the God of your fathers, promised you.

**1–3** Since "these are the commands" (v.1) in Hebrew is singular here and "decrees and laws" are plural (as in 5:1, without "these are the commands"), the meaning, as Keil suggests, is probably "This is the legislation, the decrees and laws," the latter being in apposition to "the commands" (the legislation) and explaining what the legislation involves, and so refers to both what precedes and what follows.

As the intermediary between the Lord and the people (5:27–30), Moses began to teach them what the Lord wanted them to do in the land across the Jordan. The reference to the Jordan is implicit rather than explicit in the Hebrew text.

The reason for this instruction is that the people and their descendants should "fear" (v.2) the Lord their God throughout their lifetime. The nuances of the Hebrew word for "fear" are obscured in many people's minds. That being afraid is part of the meaning can be seen in many places—the experience of the Israelites at Horeb (Sinai) with its loud thunder, lightning flashes, earthquake, and darkness being one illustration. The derived sensation of standing in awe of God and then of holding him in utmost reverence and respect is, however, essential to the understanding of "fearing God" especially in Deuteronomy. In the wisdom literature the "fear of the LORD" becomes a distinctive expression for the totality of right and devout relationship to God. The same notion is here—though it may not be as developed as in the Psalms, Proverbs, et al.

The reason for Moses' teaching is elaborated by explaining why the people should hear and obey: to insure the nation's well-being and to increase in number and wealth. These would follow their adherence to the Lord, as he, the Lord, the God of their fathers, had promised (see Exod 13:5).

The description of the country as "a land flowing with milk and honey" (v.3) occurs eighteen times in the OT from Exodus 3:8 to Ezekiel 20:15—fourteen of these occurrences are in the last four books of the Pentateuch when the people were looking toward the Promised Land. Once it refers to Egypt (Num 16:13), but all the other references are to Canaan. The figure describes a land of plenty, a land of fertility. In Sinuhe's report of his travels (1920 B.C.), he depicted the fertility of Canaan, mentioning both milk and honey (ANET, pp. 19–20).

The intent of the covenant builds step on step (v.2): *so that* the people and their descendants would reverence the Lord by keeping the stipulations, *so that* they may enjoy long life, *so that* it may go well with them, and *so that* they may increase in number (v.3).

## Notes

---

1 The Hebrew does not have a word for "me" in this verse, but the sense requires it. See 5:31. אֲשֶׁר אַתֶּם עֹבְרִים (*'ᵃšer 'attem 'ōḇᵉrîm*) says only "that you are about to cross," but the meaning is "that you are about to cross the Jordan." However, the Hebrew—as שָׁמָּה (*šāmmāh*, "to there"; untr. in NIV) shows—focuses on the other side rather than the crossing.

2 תִּירָא (*tîrā'*, "fear") has wide connotations. In Deuteronomy יָרֵא (*yārē'*) refers to piety, obedience, and service inspired by awe and reverence toward God (TDNT, 9:201).

3 The Hebrew syntactical order of the latter part of this verse is unusual, being "just as the LORD, the God of your fathers promised you, a land flowing with milk and honey."

Sometimes, however, words fall at the end of Hebrew sentences as clarifications or afterthoughts.

---

### b. *The greatest command: total commitment*

#### 6:4–5

> 4Hear, O Israel: The LORD our God, the LORD is one. 5Love the LORD your God with all your heart and with all your soul and with all your strength.

**4–5** Moses as God's spokesman (his revelatory intermediary) belied thoroughly his former excuse before God when he said, "O Lord, I have never been eloquent, neither in the past nor since you have spoken to your servant. I am slow of speech and tongue" (Exod 4:10), unless this refers exclusively to how Moses spoke, not to what he said. God's response at that time—"Who gave man his mouth?" (Exod 4:11)—was altogether appropriate. The uneloquent Moses was used of the Lord to give the world some of the most eloquent declarations in all the history of speech when he extolled the being and nature of the Lord and described the relationship that his people should have with him.

Various interpretations have been given to the "*shema*" (lit., "Hear," v.4, but the term applies to the whole verse) as indicated in the NIV margin. Does the text teach monotheism? or monolatry for Israel? or does it teach only a uniqueness in the Lord as over against various Baals and gods of other peoples? That the Israelites (at least some of them) often believed in the reality of other deities is obvious, but it does not follow that *this* declaration of the nature of the Lord admits of the real existence of other gods. The consistent teaching of Moses and the prophets, as well as the psalmists and the wise men, admits of the Lord only as true deity.

While the primary assertion of v.4 is that there is only one true God, it is also asserted that this true God is Israel's God. The Israelites should acknowledge no other god. The Lord, Israel's God, cannot be known or acknowledged in many forms like the Canaanite Baals could. There is no Lord of Sinai differentiated from a Lord of Mount Nebo or a Lord of Beersheba differentiated from a Lord of Reuben. Neither can the Lord be identified with any heathen god syncretistically. There is only one Lord, and he alone is God. Furthermore, he is Israel's God, and they have entered into a covenant-treaty with him.

Jesus taught that Deuteronomy 6:4–5 constituted the first, the greatest, and the most important commandment, and that by obeying it one would live (Matt 22:37–38; Mark 12:29–30; Luke 10:27).

So what was to be Israel's relationship to the Lord? They were to love him totally (v.5). The exhortation to love "with all your heart and with all your soul and with all your strength" is not a study in faculty psychology. It is rather a gathering of terms to indicate the totality of a person's commitment of self in the purest and noblest intentions of trust and obedience toward God. The verse does not invite analysis into ideas of intellectual, emotional, and physical parts. The words behind heart, soul, and strength basically relate to what a person is or how a person directs himself toward another person. It is, therefore, not inaccurate for the NT writers to quote (or translate) the Hebrew words, which are often synonymous, by differing Greek words, which are also often synonymous, since the words taken together mean to say that the people are to love God with their whole selves.

The covenant-treaty itself, based on the love of God for his people, required their love for the Lord in return. The teaching on God's love and the love of the people toward God and toward one another permeates the OT in such a manner that it cannot be limited by the use of words for love in the Near Eastern treaties. It is nevertheless true that this was treaty language and so to some degree adds to the meaning of love in Deuteronomy. It ties love tightly together with the sense of obedience and loyalty.

## Notes

**4** For שְׁמַע (*šᵉmaʿ*, "hear"), see Notes on 5:1.

The majuscula on the beginning word and on the last word of this verse have been the subject of many notions. These letters at least indicate an attempt to draw special attention to the verse.

To the Jews v.4 is not only an assertion of monotheism, it is also an assertion of the numerical oneness of God contradictory to the Christian view of the Trinity of the Godhead. This kind of oneness, however, runs contrary to the use of אֶחָד (*'eḥāḏ*) in the sense of a unity made up of several parts. In Exod 26:6, 11, the fifty gold clasps are used to hold the curtains together so that the tent would be a unit (*'eḥāḏ*). Ezekiel said that the Lord directed him to join two sticks to represent Judah and Ephraim, for he was going to make the two kingdoms one, i.e., a single nation made of two parts (Ezek 37:17, 19, 22). This Jewish view of oneness also contradicts those statements in Scripture that show that God is Father, Son, and Holy Spirit. The verse declares the unity of the Godhead, viz., one God in three persons—though the Trinity of the Godhead is not taught in this passage.

**5** On "love" in Near Eastern treaties, see J. McKay, "Man's Love for God in Deuteronomy," VetTest 22 (1972): 426–35; Moran, "Love of God," pp. 77–87; and Weinfeld, *Deuteronomic School*, pp. 333–34.

The quotations of v.5 in the NT vary: Matt 22:37 has καρδίᾳ (*kardia*, "heart"), ψυχῇ (*psychē*, "soul"), and διανοίᾳ (*dianoiā*, "mind"). Mark 12:30 has the same series but adds ἰσχύος (*ischyos*, "strength"). Luke 10:27, on the other hand, follows the order: *kardiā*, *psychē*, *ischyi*, *dianoiā*—the last two words being a conflate rendering of the Hebrew מְאֹד (*mᵉ'ōḏ*, "strength"). The Talmud (*Sanhedrin* 74a et al.) translates the last phrase: "and with all your money."

These words are paralleled in the vassal treaties of Esarhaddon. See H.J. Franken, "The Vassal-Treaties of Esarhaddon and the Dating of Deuteronomy," *Old Testament Studies* 14 (1965): 122–54, and Wiseman, *Vassal-Treaties*.

### c. *Propagation of the command*

#### 6:6–9

**6**These commandments that I give you today are to be upon your hearts.
**7**Impress them on your children. Talk about them when you sit at home and when you walk along the road, when you lie down and when you get up. **8**Tie them as symbols on your hands and bind them on your foreheads. **9**Write them on the doorframes of your houses and on your gates.

**6–9** The people were not to concern themselves only with their own attitudes toward the Lord. They were to concern themselves with impressing these attitudes on their children as well. The Israelites were to talk about God's commands always, whether at home or on the road.

Since in Exodus 13:9–16 the consecration of the firstborn is said to be "like a sign on your hand and a reminder on your forehead that the law of the LORD is to be on your lips" (Exod 13:9), it would seem that here also (vv.8–9) the tying of these words as symbols on their hands and binding them on their foreheads and writing them on their doorframes and gateposts should be taken metaphorically or spiritually rather than physically. The symbols tied on the hands and forehead (phylacteries) and others placed on doorposts and gates drew attention to the injunctions in vv.5–7 immediately preceding. For the forms of these objects, see Notes on vv.8–9.

## Notes

**7** The NIV's "impress" translates שִׁנַּנְתָּם (*šinnantām*), from שָׁנַן (*šānan*, "sharpen"). Ugaritic suggests that *šānan* may mean "repeat," "second time," or "say again." See G.R. Driver, *Canaanite Myths and Legends* (Edinburgh: T. & T. Clark, 1956), p. 151, and KB, pp. 998–99.

**8–9** "And bind them" translates וְהָיוּ לְטֹטָפֹת (*wehāyû leṭōṭāpōṯ*; lit., "and they shall be encircling bands") and looks back to the antecedent idea of symbols. Both the Hebrew word *ṭōṭāpōṯ* and the NT word "phylactery" are of uncertain origin. See Reider, p. 74.

The Hebrew expression for forehead is "between the eyes."

שְׁעָרִים (*še'ārîm*, "gates") frequently refers to city gates and, figuratively, sometimes means the cities themselves (5:14 and in 12:12, 15, 17, 21, where NIV has "towns"). However, *še'ārîm* is also used of the gates of the temple, of palaces, and of other official residences, and in Prov 14:19 of a private residence. If "house" is meant here, שַׁעַר (*ša'ar*, "gate") and בַּיִת (*bayiṯ*, "house") are synonymous.

The history of the use of מְזוּזוֹת (*mezûzōṯ*, "phylacteries") is not clear. Available evidence suggests that they were first used in Hasmonean times (early second century B.C.). See IBD, pp. 1227–28; ZPEB, 4:213. Phylacteries were little boxes or small metal cylinders with accompanying straps to bind them on the arm or forehead. At least later ones had four parchment rolls inscribed with Exod 13:1–10, 11–16, and Deut 6:4–9; 11:13–21.

### d. *Ways to preserve the command*

6:10–25

[10]When the LORD your God brings you into the land he swore to your
fathers, to Abraham, Isaac and Jacob, to give you—a land with large,
flourishing cities you did not build, [11]houses filled with all kinds of good
things you did not provide, wells you did not dig, and vineyards and
olive groves you did not plant—then when you eat and are satisfied,
[12]be careful that you do not forget the LORD, who brought you out of
Egypt, out of the land of slavery.

[13]Fear the LORD your God, serve him only and take your oaths in his
name. [14]Do not follow other gods, the gods of the peoples around you;
[15]for the LORD your God, who is among you, is a jealous God and his
anger will burn against you, and he will destroy you from the face of the
land. [16]Do not test the LORD your God as you did at Massah. [17]Be sure to

keep the commands of the LORD your God and the stipulations and
decrees he has given you. [18]Do what is right and good in the LORD's
sight, so that it may go well with you and you may go in and take over
the good land that the LORD promised on oath to your forefathers,
[19]thrusting out all your enemies before you, as the LORD said.

[20]In the future, when your son asks you, "What is the meaning of the
stipulations, decrees and laws the LORD our God has commanded you?"
[21]tell him: "We were slaves of Pharaoh in Egypt, but the LORD brought us
out of Egypt with a mighty hand. [22]Before our eyes the LORD sent
miraculous signs and wonders—great and terrible—upon Egypt and
Pharaoh and his whole household. [23]But he brought us out from there
to bring us in and give us the land that he promised on oath to our
forefathers. [24]The LORD commanded us to obey all these decrees and to
fear the LORD our God, so that we might always prosper and be kept
alive, as is the case today. [25]And if we are careful to obey all this law
before the LORD our God, as he has commanded us, that will be our
righteousness."

**10–12** Again Moses gave a warning in the context of history. The land that was to be Israel's had been promised years before to Abraham, Isaac, and Jacob (v.10). This promise was to be fulfilled in Israel's experience. It involved much wealth: barns, houses, wells (cisterns), vineyards, and olive groves that they had not built, provided, dug, or planted (v.11). When they would eat and be satisfied, they might forget the Lord who brought them out of a less felicitous situation in Egypt, the land of slavery (v.12). The warning was wise, for the people later did what Moses warned against. This sets the exclamation of God in 5:29 in bold and poignant relief.

**13–19** The warnings continue, focused on the necessity of recognizing and obeying "the LORD your God" (v.13) because of who he is and what he would do if they did not acknowledge and obey him. Many find the jealousy ascribed to God (v.15) very difficult to understand because jealousy can be such a vicious sin, producing much grief and animosity. But one must recognize that the provocations that give rise to the Lord's anger are most severe. Biblical history shows that such provocations frustrate the love of God until his patience with their idolatry ceases to be a virtue. Only then does his jealousy call for redress. Notice the illustration in the Song of Moses, especially in Deuteronomy 32:16–26.

The people must adhere to the Lord God so that it may "go well" with them and so that they may thrust out all their enemies from the "good land" and take it over (vv.18–19). If they do not devote themselves to him (fear him), worship and work for him only (serve him), and speak of him in their daily relationships to one another (take oaths in his name; v.13) but instead follow other gods (v.14), his jealous anger will destroy them as a nation (v.15).

So the Israelites were not to test the Lord by the denial of his efficacious presence as they did at Massah (v.16), where they criticized him because of the lack of drinking water and said, "Is the LORD among us or not?" (Exod 17:1–7).

**20–25** An expansion of the teaching procedure follows—a procedure to inculcate the lessons of the covenant in the children. The answer to a son's query, "What is the meaning of the stipulations?" is a historical resume of the Exodus (vv.21–22), the making of the covenant-treaty, and the giving of the legislation for the nation, together with the Lord's commands to obey and reverence him (vv.23–24). The Lord who gave them the covenant-treaty with its stipulations was active on their behalf in freeing them from Egypt and from the control of Pharaoh by his mighty hand, by miracles that taught lessons, and by wonderful acts that were great and terrible—a fit description of the plagues. God had brought them out of Egypt in order to bring them into Canaan, the country that he had promised to their forefathers. Obedience was necessary for their prosperity and continuance as a people. Obedience to all the Lord's legislation would constitute their righteousness (v.25; see 24:13).

These items must be impressed on each succeeding generation. This recital contains the main elements of the covenant-treaty relationship—its history and requirements. These elements are often reiterated in the Deuteronomic addresses.

## Notes

**11** בֹּרֹת (*bōrōṯ*, "wells"), especially coupled with חָצַב (*ḥāṣaḇ*, "hew," "cut"), would include cisterns, which were very common in Canaan. See *World of the Bible*, 1:257.

On "eat and are satisfied," see Notes on 8:10, 12.

**13** The Hebrew word order of this sentence puts emphasis on the objects, which precede the verbs: The LORD your God you are to fear (reverence), and him you are to serve (worship), and in his name you are to swear (to him give allegiance). שָׁבַע (*šāḇa'*, "swear") probably primarily speaks of their giving allegiance to the Lord as basic to the covenant-treaty.

Jesus quoted from this verse, adapting it verbally to Satan's temptation. Satan said, "All this I will give you, . . . if you will bow down and worship me" (Matt 4:9). In response Jesus said, "'Worship [*προσκυνήσεις*, *proskynēseis*] the LORD your God, and serve him only [*μόνῳ*, *monō*]'" (Matt 4:10; Luke 4:8). The LXX has *φοβηθήσῃ* (*phobēthēsē*), to which the Hebrew תִּירָא (*tîrā'*, "fear") agrees. The sense of "worship," however, is certainly within the semantic reach of both the Hebrew and the Greek. Jesus added *monō* as the sense of the whole passage in Deuteronomy in its application to Satan's temptation.

On the use of the name of the Lord in Deuteronomy, see comment on 32:3.

**15** On "a jealous God," see the comment on 4:22–24.

**16** See text and margin note at Exod 17:7. Jesus cited the first half of this verse to answer Satan's quotation of Ps 91:11–12 during the temptation in the desert (Matt 4:7; Luke 4:12). "Test" or "put to a test" rather than "tempt" is the meaning of נִסָּה (*nissāh*, Piel form). The Greek *εκπειράζω* (*ekpeirazō*, Matt 4:7; Luke 4:12) also means "to prove or test thoroughly." "Massah" (from *nissāh*) means "testing" (Exod 17:7 mg.).

**20** "In the future" is an extended meaning of מָחָר (*māḥār*, "tomorrow"). It is obvious that a son's question would arise in many generations, and the hypothetical case here proposed is meant to emphasize the necessity of keeping the knowledge of these elements fresh in the minds of succeeding generations. The phrasing, however, speaks as though those involved in the experiences are asked about the "laws the LORD our God has commanded you [אֶתְכֶם, *'eṯkem*]." In the response also the speakers identify themselves as those who had these experiences. By such dramatic presentations each succeeding generation identifies itself with the nation that had experienced these events.

### 3. *Problems of achieving the covenant of love in the land (7:1–26)*

#### a. *Relations with the people of the land and with the Lord*

7:1–10

1 When the LORD your God brings you into the land you are entering to
possess and drives out before you many nations—the Hittites, Girgash-

ites, Amorites, Canaanites, Perizzites, Hivites and Jebusites, seven
nations larger and stronger than you—2and when the LORD your God
has delivered them over to you and you have defeated them, then you
must destroy them totally. Make no treaty with them, and show them no
mercy. 3Do not intermarry with them. Do not give your daughters to their
sons or take their daughters for your sons, 4for they will turn your sons
away from following me to serve other gods, and the LORD's anger will
burn against you and will quickly destroy you. 5This is what you are to
do to them: Break down their altars, smash their sacred stones, cut
down their Asherah poles and burn their idols in the fire. 6For you are a
people holy to the LORD your God. The LORD your God has chosen you
out of all the peoples on the face of the earth to be his people, his
treasured possession.

7The LORD did not set his affection on you and choose you because
you were more numerous than other peoples, for you were the fewest of
all peoples. 8But it was because the LORD loved you and kept the oath he
swore to your forefathers that he brought you out with a mighty hand
and redeemed you from the land of slavery, from the power of Pharaoh
king of Egypt. 9Know therefore that the LORD your God is God; he is the
faithful God, keeping his covenant of love to a thousand generations of
those who love him and keep his commands. 10But

those who hate him he will repay to their face by destruction;
he will not be slow to repay to their face those
who hate him.

**1–2** These Hittites were remnants of the great Hittite Empire that began about 1800 B.C. and continued to 1200 B.C. Smaller Hittite states existed prior to this empire period and after the empire's collapse. The Hittites that the people had to contend with in Canaan in Moses' time were fringe states. (On the Hittites, see Noth, pp. 254, 274; and ZPEB, 3:165–72.)

The Girgashites were an otherwise unknown group. They are mentioned in Ugaritic literature (see G. Douglas Young, *Concordance of Ugaritic* [Rome: Pontificium Institutum Biblicum, 1956], p. 14, and C.H. Gordon, UT, p. 381).

The Amorites were situated west of the Jordan near the Canaanites who were on the southwest coast on the Mediterranean (Josh 5:1). Canaanites lived farther north also (Josh 11:3; 13:4).

From Judges 1:4–5 it would seem that the Perizzites lived in the southern area allotted to Judah and Simeon. However, the Perizzites also appear to be in the area of Ephraim in the center of the country (Josh 17:15).

At this time the Hivites were found in Gibeon (Josh 9:7; 11:19). In David's time there were Hivite towns south of Tyre (2 Sam 24:7).

The Jebusites lived in Jerusalem and its surroundings (Josh 18:28; Judg 1:21).

Israel would win the land from its inhabitants by driving them out and destroying the ones remaining. In 7:1 and 22 it is said that the Lord would drive out their enemies. But v.2 speaks of when "you have defeated them," and in v.17 they ask the question, "How can we drive them out?" Moreover, v.22 says, "You will not be allowed to eliminate them all at once." And v.24 says, "No one will be able to stand up against you; you will destroy them." The Lord will drive out the Canaanites and "deliver them over to" Israel (vv.2, 16, 23); but the Israelites will be the instrument used to accomplish this destruction—though the Lord may use other persuaders also, such as the hornet (v.20). This ambivalence is common throughout the settlement narratives. The Lord will accomplish what he says he will, but he uses the means he chooses. In the conquest of Canaan, the Israelite army is the usual instrument.

Seven of the many nations to be driven out (v.1) are mentioned (cf. Josh 3:10; 24:11). In 20:17; Exodus 3:8, 17; 23:23; and 33:2, the Girgashites are not included. In the promise to Abraham, Kenites, Kenizzites, Kadmonites, and Rephaites also are included, though Hivites are not (Gen 15:19–21). Elsewhere, all these groups are included under Canaanites or sometimes Canaanites and Amorites. These references mean to be general and are representative of the pre-Israelite population. They are not always an exhaustive portrayal. The inhabitants who were not driven out of the country were to be destroyed. No treaty was to be made with them; no mercy shown to them (v.2). The covenant-treaty of the Lord with Israel excludes other treaties.

**3–5** The young Canaanite men were not to be given Israelite daughters as wives and young Canaanite women were not to be taken by Israelite men as wives. Such relationships would lead to forsaking the Lord and to worshiping other gods, which would anger the Lord and would lead to Israelite destruction. Intermarriage would tend to compromise faithfulness to the covenantal relationship of Israel with the Lord by the amalgamation of Canaanite life with that of Israel. Only by total commitment to the Lord and to the covenant-treaty could the unique status of Israel with the Lord be preserved.

Albright mentions that the Canaanite Baalism was much cruder and more debased than the religions of Egypt and Mesopotamia. His depiction of some of the acts of Canaanite gods and goddesses in *From the Stone Age to Christianity* (Baltimore: Johns Hopkins University Press, 1946, pp. 175–79) clearly bears this out.

The prohibition of intermarriage was not absolute. The regulation for the marriage of an Israelite man to a foreign woman taken as a prize of war is given in 21:10–14. Ezra and Nehemiah strongly disparaged intermarriage between Israelites and non-Israelites (Ezra 9–10; Neh 13:23–27). The experience of Solomon and Ahab (among others) indicates how intermarriage adversely affected Israel.

The antecedent of "them" (v.5) is the "many nations" of v.1. "Destroy them totally" and "show them no mercy" (v.2) are explicated more fully by "break down their altars, smash their sacred stones, cut down their Asherah poles and burn their idols in the fire" (v.5). These objects of Canaanite religious worship were to be destroyed by means proper to their structure. The altars of earth and stone were to be broken down; the sacred stones smashed (broken to pieces); the Asherah poles, whether live trees or wooden poles, cut down; and the idols burned up.

**6–10** The destruction of people and things that would be inimical to their concentrated absorption in the Lord as God follows from their position as holy to the Lord; that is, set apart to the Lord. This holiness is partially explained by the Lord's choice of the Israelites as his people out of all the nations on earth (v.6). They were his "treasured possession" (*s^e^g̱ullāh*), i.e., something of great value owned completely by him.

These two ideas—personal ownership and treasured value—are evident in *s^e^g̱ullāh*'s use in David's statement that he was giving his own personal treasures for the building of the temple in addition to what he had officially gathered from many sources (1 Chron 29:3). The writer of Ecclesiastes also had amassed for himself the treasures of kings (Eccl 2:8). Via the LXX this notion of God's people as his treasured possession appears in the NT where the church is "God's possession" (Eph 1:14), "a people that are his very own" (Titus 2:14), and "a people belonging to God" (1 Peter 2:9).

Moses' concern that Israel would keep the right perspective in her relationship with the Lord surfaces again in v.7. He mentioned that the large number of people in the Israelite community was not the reason for the Lord's choice of them as his people. In 9:4–6 he says that it is not because of Israel's righteousness or integrity that the Lord was giving Canaan to them. They were few in number (in contrast to the large Near Eastern empires, or even in comparison with the seven nations they were to displace; cf. 4:38; 9:1; 11:23)—or perhaps the reference is to their small beginnings. Elsewhere, Israel is said to be "as many as the stars in the sky" (1:10; 10:22) and "a great nation" (4:6; 26:5)—doubtless in fulfillment of the promise to Abraham. On any account Israel was not to rest on or glory in the numbers of her people but in her Lord.

Because he loved them and kept the promise of his covenant with their forefathers, the Lord brought the Israelites out of Egypt and redeemed them from the land of slavery and the power of Pharaoh (v.8). Why God loved them is not stated in the Pentateuch, but the focus of thought is obvious—it is the character of God rather than any excellence in the people that accounts for the choice. This is more evident by the reiterated assertion that the Lord their God was God, was faithful and true in himself and true to his covenant-treaty, and would be true in his covenant love toward his people into the distant future—"to a thousand generations of those who love him and keep his commands" (v.9). But those who hate him, who do not love and obey him, he will repay with destruction "to their face"—viz., individually (v.10). Both the singular suffix on "face" and the figurative use of "face" suggest the meaning "to each personally."

## Notes

---

**1, 22** The word נָשַׁל (*nāšal*) can mean "to drop off, draw off" (the sandal, Exod 3:5; Josh 5:15) or "to throw off, clear out, drive out" (2 Kings 16:6) and is surely used in the later sense here. It indicates that the Canaanites were to be driven out of the land. Those remaining were to be made subject to חֵרֶם (*ḥerem*, "total destruction," v.2).

A more common word for driving out is יָרַשׁ (*yāraš*, "to dispossess"), and הָדַף (*hādap̱*) occurs a few times with a similar meaning (6:19; 9:4; and elsewhere outside of Deuteronomy).

**2** For "destroy them totally," see the comment and Notes on 2:34.

בְּרִית (*berîṯ*, "treaty") is usually translated "covenant" and indicates that a covenant or treaty made with anyone other than the Lord would be contrary to his covenant-treaty with Israel. Other Near Eastern treaties also bear this stipulation (ANET, p. 204).

**4** עָבַד (*'āḇaḏ*, "to serve") may include the idea of worship and often is its specific meaning (e.g., Exod 3:12; 4:23; 23:33; Deut 4:19, 28; 2 Kings 21:3; 2 Chron 33:3).

**5** מִזְבְּחֹת (*mizbeḥōṯ*, "altars") were made of earth or stones (Exod 20:24–25), and מַצֵּבֹת (*maṣṣēḇōṯ*, "sacred stones") were probably stone pillars (*World of the Bible*, 2:258). אֲשֵׁירִים (*'ašērîm*, "Asherah poles") were made of wood (Judg 6:26). They were "set up" (Deut 16:21) and were representations of the goddess Asherah who was worshiped by the Canaanites and others.

פְּסִילִים (*pesîlîm*, "idols") is used often for idols generally and so here.

**6** סְגֻלָּה (*s^egullāh*) in the OT describes something or someone as a "treasured possession," "personal property," or movable "personal treasure." Israel was the prized, personal property of the Lord (Exod 19:5; 1 Chron 29:3; Eccl 2:8).

**8–9** God's "love" (אָהַב, *'āhab̲*) for his people appears in 4:37; 7:8, 13; 10:15; and 23:5 (6 MT). The people's required love for God is always represented in Deuteronomy by *'āhab̲* (5:10; 6:5; 7:9; 10:12; 11:1, 13, 22; 13:3 [4 MT]; 19:9; 30:6, 16, and 20). The term חֶסֶד (*ḥesed̲*) occurs in 5:10; 7:9, 12, referring to the Lord's love for his people and his covenant of love. The conjunction ו (*w*) joins the words חֶסֶד (*ḥesed̲*, "love") and בְּרִית (*b^erît̲*, "covenant") and closely identifies them—thus NIV's "covenant of love"—and so indicates the dominant force of the Lord's love in the formation and perpetuation of the covenant. Although "love" meant political loyalty in Near Eastern treaties, it meant vastly more in Deuteronomy. See observations on Deuteronomic terminology and Near Eastern treaties in Moran, "Love of God," pp. 77–78; Weinfeld, *Deuteronomic School*, pp. 83–84; and Wiseman, *Vassal Treaties*, 1:268.

---

## b. *Blessing of the conquest*

### 7:11–26

11 Therefore, take care to follow the commands, decrees and laws I give you today.

12 If you pay attention to these laws and are careful to follow them, then the LORD your God will keep his covenant of love with you, as he swore to your forefathers. 13 He will love you and bless you and increase your numbers. He will bless the fruit of your womb, the crops of your land—your grain, new wine and oil—the calves of your herds and the lambs of your flocks in the land that he swore to your forefathers to give you. 14 You will be blessed more than any other people; none of your men or women will be childless, nor any of your livestock without young. 15 The LORD will keep you free from every disease. He will not inflict on you the horrible diseases you knew in Egypt, but he will inflict them on all who hate you. 16 You must destroy all the peoples the LORD your God gives over to you. Do not look on them with pity and do not serve their gods, for that will be a snare to you.

17 You may say to yourselves, "These nations are stronger than we are. How can we drive them out?" 18 But do not be afraid of them; remember well what the LORD your God did to Pharaoh and to all Egypt. 19 You saw with your own eyes the great trials, the miraculous signs and wonders, the mighty hand and outstretched arm, with which the LORD your God brought you out. The LORD your God will do the same to all the peoples you now fear. 20 Moreover, the LORD your God will send the hornet among them until even the survivors who hide from you have perished. 21 Do not be terrified by them, for the LORD your God, who is among you, is a great and awesome God. 22 The LORD your God will drive out those nations before you, little by little. You will not be allowed to eliminate them all at once, or the wild animals will multiply around you. 23 But the LORD your God will deliver them over to you, throwing them into great confusion until they are destroyed. 24 He will give their kings into your hand, and you will wipe out their names from under heaven. No one will be able to stand up against you; you will destroy them. 25 The images of their gods you are to burn in the fire. Do not covet the silver and gold on them, and do not take it for yourselves, or you will be ensnared by it, for it is detestable to the LORD your God. 26 Do not bring a detestable thing into your house or you, like it, will be set apart for destruction. Utterly abhor and detest it, for it is set apart for destruction.

**11–16** If the Israelites followed the Lord's stipulations (v.11), he would keep his "covenant of love" with them (v.12). The keeping of his covenant of love is explicated in vv.13–15. He would love and bless them and increase their number. In particular he would bless them with many children and with productivity in crops and animal husbandry. These blessings were of things close to the soil and natural productivity (v.13): grain from the field, not bread prepared from it; fresh grape juice, not fermented wine; and fresh olive oil, not products prepared from it. This series occurs fairly often elsewhere (11:14; 12:17; 14:23; 18:4; 28:51; 33:28 [minus oil]). "Grain, new wine and oil" or "grain and new wine" designates a fruitful land in the OT (2 Kings 18:32; 2 Chron 31:5; Neh 13:5, 12; Isa 36:17; Jer 31:12; Hos 2:8 [10 MT], 22 [24 MT]; 7:14; Joel 1:10; 2:19; Hag 1:11).

The obedient Israelites would also have many calves and lambs from herds and flocks. Neither they nor their livestock would fail to have offspring, and their blessings would exceed that of all other people. Good health too would be theirs. Those terrible diseases they knew in Egypt would not come on them (Exod 15:26; 23:25) but would be inflicted on their enemies (v.16).

To secure these advantages, the Israelites were to destroy without pity the Canaanites the Lord would give over to them. The Canaanite gods were not to be worshiped, for that would be a snare to the Israelites. In Exodus 23:33, Judges 2:3, and Psalm 106:36, the gods (idols) of Canaan are said to be snares, while in Exodus 34:12 and Joshua 23:13 the Canaanites themselves are snares.

**17–26** The Israelites were not to be intimidated by thinking that the nations of Canaan were stronger than they, making it impossible for them to drive out the Canaanites (v.17). As an antidote to such fear, the Israelites were to remember what the Lord had done to Pharaoh and all Egypt (v.18). That was not something the Israelites had heard from others; with their own eyes (v.19) they had seen how the Lord had brought them out with great trials ("testings" in 4:34), by miraculous signs and wonders, by the mighty hand and the outstretched arm (cf. 4:34, where "war" and "great and awesome deeds" are added). The Lord would do to the Canaanites what he had done to other enemies. He would also send the "hornet" (v.20) among them so that even those who survived the onslaught and hid themselves would die.

Moses reminded the people that the great and awesome Lord was among them (v.21); so they should not be terrified by the Canaanites. However, as mentioned in Exodus 23:30–31, their driving out the Canaanites would be little by little so that the wild animals would not multiply to Israel's detriment (v.22).

Though the conquest was not to be immediate over the whole land, the Lord, nevertheless, would deliver the Canaanites into Israel's hand (v.23). None would be able to withstand them; Israel would wipe out their kings' names from under heaven (v.24), i.e., remove them from the earth. The destruction of the Canaanite idols was to be complete. Every part of the images (including the tempting silver and gold on them) was detestable to the Lord and therefore was to be detested by the Israelites (v.25). No detestable thing was ever to be taken into an Israelite house (v.26). Two strong words for disapprobation—"Utterly abhor and detest it"—indicate the abhorrence the people were to hold toward the idols. The idols were to be set apart for destruction.

## Notes

**13** A result of the Lord's love toward Israel was that "He will . . . increase your numbers." The Hiphil הִרְבְּךָ (*hirbeḵā*, "increase") is forceful: "He will . . . make you to increase in number."

**15** מַדְוֵי מִצְרַיִם הָרָעִים (*madwê miṣrayim hārā'îm*, "horrible diseases . . . in Egypt") is literally the "evil, bad, distressing, malignant, or horrible diseases of Egypt." Ancient and modern sources confirm that some virulent and malignant diseases, such as elephantiasis, ophthalmia, and dysentery, were common in Egypt (Pliny the Elder, *Historia Naturalis* 26:1).

**16** מוֹקֵשׁ (*môqēš*, "snare"), a bait or a lure placed with a net to catch birds, is used figuratively for anyone or anything that ensnares prey.

**20** The הַצִּרְעָה (*haṣṣir'āh*, "hornet" or "wasp") was a large, virulent insect that was common in Canaan. The reference, however, more likely is metaphorical of the sense of fear, panic, or discouragement that the Lord would inflict on the Canaanites (11:25). Garstang (p. 259) suggests that the hornet was a symbol of the Pharaohs.

**22** On הָאֵלֶּה (*hā'ēlleh*, "those") rather than הָאֵל (*hā'ēl*), which is in the Hebrew text, see the Notes on 4:42.

**26** The noun תּוֹעֵבָה (*tô'ēḇāh*, "abomination") and the verb תָּעַב (*tā'aḇ*, "abhor" or "abominate") are strong words of disapproval or rejection. The noun occurs seventeen times in Deuteronomy, indicating the Lord's firm disapproval of unclean food, objectionable and wicked acts, and idolatrous objects and practices.

The parallel verb שִׁקֵּץ (*šiqqēṣ*, "abhor") elsewhere also describes the detestation the Israelites should show toward anything unclean (Lev 11:11, 13, 43) and the defilement they were to avoid by following the rules for refraining from contact with the unclean (Lev 20:25). Psalm 22:24 (25 MT) says that the Lord has not "disdained" (*šiqqaṣ*) the suffering of the afflicted.

The infinitive absolutes with the imperfect verbs in the Piel constitute a very forceful way of declaring that Israel must "utterly abhor and detest" both the idols and the valuable silver and gold ornamenting them.

---

### 4. *Exhortation not to forget the Lord (8:1–20)*

#### a. *The discipline of the desert and the coming Promised Land*

#### 8:1–9

1 Be careful to follow every command I am giving you today, so that
you may live and increase and may enter and possess the land that the
LORD promised on oath to your forefathers. 2 Remember how the LORD
your God led you all the way in the desert these forty years, to humble
you and to test you in order to know what was in your heart, whether or
not you would keep his commands. 3 He humbled you, causing you to
hunger and then feeding you with manna, which neither you nor your
fathers had known, to teach you that man does not live on bread alone
but on every word that comes from the mouth of the LORD. 4 Your clothes
did not wear out and your feet did not swell during these forty years.
5 Know then in your heart that as a man disciplines his son, so the LORD
your God disciplines you.

6 Observe the commands of the LORD your God, walking in his ways
and revering him. 7 For the LORD your God is bringing you into a good
land—a land with streams and pools of water, with springs flowing in
the valleys and hills; 8 a land with wheat and barley, vines and fig trees,
pomegranates, olive oil and honey; 9 a land where bread will not be
scarce and you will lack nothing; a land where the rocks are iron and
you can dig copper out of the hills.

**1–5** Chapter 8 reaffirms certain admonitions and warnings already made to impress these particular points on the Israelites. The chapter covers the discipline of the prior forty years from which they were to remember and learn that they were to be humble and rely on the Lord. Moses also spoke again of the natural benefits of Canaan, for which they were to praise the Lord rather than follow their proclivity to forget him in their coming prosperity. Furthermore, they were warned that forgetting the Lord and turning to other gods would result in Israel's destruction.

Moses first focused on the necessity of following every command of the Lord, as with the remembrance motif beginning at 4:10, so that Israel would be able to enter and possess the Land of Promise (v.1). They were to remember the discipline of the forty years of the Lord's leading in the desert (v.2). This remembrance was to teach them that "man does not live on bread alone but on every word that comes from the mouth of the LORD" (v.3) and that "as a man disciplines his son, so the LORD . . . disciplines" them (v.5). (The discipline of sons by fathers is mentioned in Prov 3:12 and developed in Heb 12:5–11.) He had made them hungry, then fed them with manna (see Exod 16). Under his providence during those forty years their clothes did not wear out and their feet did not swell (v.4), in spite of the heat and rough terrain of the desert.

In response to Satan's suggestion that he make bread from stones to satisfy his hunger, the Lord Jesus quoted v.3: "Man does not live on bread alone but on every word that comes from the mouth of the LORD" ("the mouth of God" in Matt 4:4; cf. Luke 4:4). During the temptation experiences Jesus used other quotations from Deuteronomy also (Deut 6:13 in Matt 4:10; Deut 6:16 in Matt 4:7).

**6–9** The Israelites were urged to walk in the ways of the Lord and to revere him (v.6), not only as in the past days of hunger and thirst, but when the affluence of Canaanite productivity became theirs (vv.7–9). The country he was leading them into had great natural benefits: streams, pools, and springs flowing in the valleys and from the hills (v.7). This contrasted both with Egypt proper and with Sinai. Egypt relied on one river while Sinai had none; Canaan had more rivers and, in addition, had springs in valleys and hills (fed from the water in the limestone base of much of the country; see Baly, p. 20). This good land—productive of wheat, barley, grapes, figs, pomegranates, olives, and honey—would sustain them; they would lack nothing. The iron (v.9) was probably that in southern Lebanon, in the mountains of Transjordan, and, perhaps, in the Arabah south of the Dead Sea. The basalt of the volcanic region east of the Lake of Galilee was 20 percent iron.

The copper mines of Solomon at Ezion Geber are well known. Werner Keller (*The Bible as History* [New York: Morrow, 1956], pp. 123–25) gives a dramatic description of the discovery in Sinai of ancient Egyptian copper and turquoise mines. See also Baly, pp. 98, 212, 215.

## Notes

---

**4** The NIV translates בָּצֵקָה (*bāṣēqāh*), which occurs elsewhere only in Neh 9:21, a quotation of this passage, as "swell," probably referring to blisters or sores. The LXX, however, translates it by ἐτυλώθησαν (*etylōthēsan*), which in the passive (as here) means "to grow hard or calloused." The Hebrew cognate noun means "dough." (That swells!)

**7** The נַחֲלֵי מָיִם (*naḥ$^a$lê māyim*, "streams of water") may be perpetual streams or intermittent ones dependent on periodic rainfall. The עֲיָנֹת (*$^a$yānōṯ*, "pools") are springs as distinct from cisterns, and the תְּהֹמֹת (*t$^e$hōmōṯ*, "springs") are streams gushing in hills and valleys.

**7–9** In the Near Eastern treaties, grants of land often included a description similar to that in this section and elsewhere (Weinfeld, *Deuteronomic School*, pp. 71–72).

**8** זֵית שֶׁמֶן (*zêṯ šemen*, "olive oil") was from cultivated olive trees whereas זֵית יִצְהָר (*zêṯ yiṣhār*) refers to the wild olive (2 Kings 18:32).

---

## b. *Remembrance of the Lord who led them from Egypt to Canaan*

### 8:10–20

10 When you have eaten and are satisfied, praise the LORD your God for
the good land he has given you. 11 Be careful that you do not forget the
LORD your God, failing to observe his commands, his laws and his
decrees that I am giving you this day. 12 Otherwise, when you eat and are
satisfied, when you build fine houses and settle down, 13 and when your
herds and flocks grow large and your silver and gold increase and all
you have is multiplied, 14 then your heart will become proud and you will
forget the LORD your God, who brought you out of Egypt, out of the land
of slavery. 15 He led you through the vast and dreadful desert, that thirsty
and waterless land, with its venomous snakes and scorpions. He
brought you water out of hard rock. 16 He gave you manna to eat in the
desert, something your fathers had never known, to humble and to test
you so that in the end it might go well with you. 17 You may say to
yourself, "My power and the strength of my hands have produced this
wealth for me." 18 But remember the LORD your God, for it is he who
gives you the ability to produce wealth, and so confirms his covenant,
which he swore to your forefathers, as it is today.

19 If you ever forget the LORD your God and follow other gods and
worship and bow down to them, I testify against you today that you will
surely be destroyed. 20 Like the nations the LORD destroyed before you,
so you will be destroyed for not obeying the LORD your God.

**10–18** When the Israelites had eaten and were satisfied, after they were settled in the land, they were to praise the Lord for the good land (v.10). In their prosperity they were not to forget him or fail to observe his laws (v.11). After they had built fine homes and settled down and acquired large herds (cattle) and flocks (sheep and goats), with much silver and gold, they might forget the Lord their God who had brought them out of Egypt and had led them through the desert, that desert vast and dreadful, thirsty and waterless, inhabited by venomous snakes and scorpions (vv.12–15). They had lived through the hard life of that desert by God's providence, but the future prosperity in a better land might lead them astray. In that desert experience the Lord had brought water out of the hard rock (v.15; cf. Exod 17:1–7 and Num 20:2–13); in Canaan they would find streams and pools in both valleys and hills. In that desert the Lord gave them manna (v.16), a new substance unknown to their fathers. In Canaan bread would not be scarce (v.9). In their pride in their prosperity, they might claim that the power and strength of their hands produced their wealth, not remembering that the Lord their God gave them the ability to produce wealth in confirmation of his covenant with them (vv.17–18).

**19–20** Once more Moses warned that forgetting and disobeying the Lord and turning to follow other Gods to worship and bow down before them would mean the destruction of Israel as a nation as surely as those who followed other gods were destroyed by the Israelites as they displaced the inhabitants of Canaan.

## Notes

---

**10, 12** The combination of אָכַל (*'āḵal*, "eat") and שָׂבַע (*śāḇa'*, "satisfy," "satiate") suggests not only the satisfaction of eating good and sufficient food but also general well-being (cf. 6:11; 14:29).

**15** The נָחָשׁ שָׂרָף (*nāḥāš śārāp̱*, "venomous snakes"), a collective, were those that bit the Israelites as recorded in Num 21:6. Isaiah also uses *śārāp̱* for venomous snakes (Isa 14:29; 30:6). See D.S. Wiseman, "Flying Serpents?" in *Tyndale Bulletin* 23 (1972): 108–10.

The עַקְרָב (*'aqrāḇ*, "scorpion"), an eight-legged arachnid, was common in Canaan. Its sting was in the tip of its long, jointed, whiplike tail. The pass through the hills southwest of the Dead Sea was called "Scorpion Pass" (Num 34:4; Akrabbim in Heb.), perhaps because of the abundance of scorpions there.

**19** עָבַד (*'āḇaḏ*, "worship") and חָוָה (*ḥāwah*, "bow down") occur often together synonymously, being descriptive of both legitimate and illegitimate worship practices.

**20** The point of view here is that of Israel after Canaan is conquered, the Hiphil participle מַאֲבִיד (*ma'aḇîḏ*, "destroyed") encompassing all the defeated Canaanites. It is possible, however, that Moses was referring to their status and by the participle meant the conquest of Sihon and Og or simply the Canaanites they were about to destroy. The introductory phrases "when you have eaten and are satisfied" (v.10), however, mitigate against this.

---

### 5. *Warning based on former infidelity (9:1–10:11)*

### a. *The coming defeat of the Anakites*

#### 9:1–6

1 Hear, O Israel. You are now about to cross the Jordan to go in and dispossess nations greater and stronger than you, with large cities that have walls up to the sky. 2 The people are strong and tall—Anakites! You know about them and have heard it said: "Who can stand up against the Anakites?" 3 But be assured today that the LORD your God is the one who goes across ahead of you like a devouring fire. He will destroy them; he will subdue them before you. And you will drive them out and annihilate them quickly, as the LORD has promised you.

4 After the LORD your God has driven them out before you, do not say to yourself, "The LORD has brought me here to take possession of this land because of my righteousness." No, it is on account of the wickedness of these nations that the LORD is going to drive them out before you. 5 It is not because of your righteousness or your integrity that you are going in to take possession of their land; but on account of the wickedness of these nations, the LORD your God will drive them out before you, to accomplish what he swore to your fathers, to Abraham, Isaac and Jacob. 6 Understand, then, that it is not because of your righteousness that the LORD your God is giving you this good land to possess, for you are a stiff-necked people.

**1–6** Chapter 9 begins a section that points out once more that the greatness of the Lord, not any excellence of the Israelites, was to be the basis for Israel's acquisition of Canaan. Prior to this Moses had made it clear that God's choice of them was not because of their numerical superiority (7:7). Here he added that their entrance into the land would not be because of their righteousness either (v.5). To support this Moses launched into a long narration of the people's former recalcitrance and of the Lord's goodness and greatness.

First Moses recognized the difficulties these people would face in the country they were about to cross over Jordan to possess. The current inhabitants, as earlier described by the Israelite scouting party, were greater and stronger than the Israelites (4:38), with large cities with walls up to the sky (v.1; cf. 1:28).

"Who can stand up against the Anakites?" (v.2) was a popular saying indicating Anakite strength. But Moses had an adequate answer to this proverbial question: The Lord can, or you can, under the Lord's guidance and power (v.3). The Lord was the one who "goes across" (an apocopated way of saying "crosses the Jordan") ahead of them. The assertion that the Lord would lead Israel into the Promised Land appears throughout the narratives of the Exodus, the desert wanderings, and the conquest of Canaan, and becomes a major theme throughout the OT (Exod 13:21; Deut 1:30, 33, et al.). The Lord would lead his people, and he would destroy and subdue the Canaanites by empowering the Israelites.

Almost in the same breath, Moses said that Israel would drive out the inhabitants (v.3) and that the Lord would have driven them out, indicative again that Israel's abilities were from the Lord. At best they were the Lord's instruments.

Not Israelite righteousness but Canaanite wickedness caused Canaanite dispossession (Lev 18:1–30 gives more detail on "the wickedness of these nations," v.4). Three times in this context Moses said that the Lord would drive out the Canaanites (vv.4, 5, 6). As a matter of fact, Israel's own behavior shows that she was an intractable people and, consequently, not deserving of the good land.

## Notes

1 The הַיּוֹם (*hayyôm*, "this day") of this verse does not mean "this twenty-four-hour day." More than a month was to pass before the Israelites crossed the Jordan (34:8). As the NIV translates—"now about to"—the reference is to the crossing as relatively near, a use of *hayyôm* that is not uncommon.

2 בְּנֵי עֲנָקִים (*benê ʿanāqîm*, "sons of Anak"; lit., "sons of Anaks") is a gentilic expression. As "sons of Israel" means "Israelites," so "sons of Anak" means "Anakites." See Notes on 1:28.

3 The Lord would "destroy"—שָׁמַד (*šāmad*, "exterminate")—and "subdue"—כָּנַע (*kānaʿ*, "to humble," "to bring under one's control")—the Canaanites; and the Israelites would "drive them out"—יָרַשׁ (*yāraš*, "to dispossess")—and they would "annihilate"—אָבַד (*'ābad*)—them, meaning, like שָׁמַד (*šāmad*), "to exterminate" them.

4 In the Hebrew figure בִּלְבָבְךָ (*bilbābekā*, "in your heart"), לֵבָב (*lēbāb*) equals "self," the whole clause meaning "Do not say to yourself" (NIV).

5 יֹשֶׁר לְבָב (*yōšer lebāb*, "integrity") also occurs in 1 Chron 29:17; Job 33:3; Ps 119:7. A synonymous expression, בְּתָם־לֵבָב וּבְיֹשֶׁר (*betām-lēbāb ûbeyōšer*), appears in 1 Kings 9:4 as "in integrity of heart and uprightness," while תֹּם־וָיֹשֶׁר (*tōm-wāyōšer*, "integrity and uprightness") is in Ps 25:21. Not Israel's righteousness or integrity, but Canaanite רִשְׁעָה (*rišʿāh*, "wickedness") would bring about Canaanite downfall.

**6** קְשֵׁה־עֹרֶף (*qešēh-ʿōrep̱*, "stiff-necked"; lit., "hard of neck") is a figurative expression for stubborn, intractable, obdurate, and hardheaded (cf. 10:16; 31:27; Exod 32:9; 33:3, 5; 34:9; 2 Kings 17:14; 2 Chron 30:8; 36:13; Neh 9:16–17, 29; Prov 29:1; Jer 7:26; 17:23; 19:15. See also Acts 7:51).

---

### b. *The golden calf provocation*

#### 9:7–21

[7]Remember this and never forget how you provoked the LORD your
God to anger in the desert. From the day you left Egypt until you arrived
here, you have been rebellious against the LORD. [8]At Horeb you aroused
the LORD's wrath so that he was angry enough to destroy you. [9]When I
went up on the mountain to receive the tablets of stone, the tablets of
the covenant that the LORD had made with you, I stayed on the mountain
forty days and forty nights; I ate no bread and drank no water. [10]The
LORD gave me two stone tablets inscribed by the finger of God. On them
were all the commandments the LORD proclaimed to you on the
mountain out of the fire, on the day of the assembly.
[11]At the end of the forty days and forty nights, the LORD gave me the
two stone tablets, the tablets of the covenant. [12]Then the LORD told me,
"Go down from here at once, because your people whom you brought
out of Egypt have become corrupt. They have turned away quickly from
what I commanded them and have made a cast idol for themselves."
[13]And the LORD said to me, "I have seen this people, and they are a
stiff-necked people indeed! [14]Let me alone, so that I may destroy them
and blot out their name from under heaven. And I will make you into a
nation stronger and more numerous than they."
[15]So I turned and went down from the mountain while it was ablaze
with fire. And the two tablets of the covenant were in my hands. [16]When
I looked, I saw that you had sinned against the LORD your God; you had
made for yourselves an idol cast in the shape of a calf. You had turned
aside quickly from the way that the LORD had commanded you. [17]So I
took the two tablets and threw them out of my hands, breaking them to
pieces before your eyes.
[18]Then once again I fell prostrate before the LORD for forty days and
forty nights; I ate no bread and drank no water, because of all the sin
you had committed, doing what was evil in the LORD's sight and so
provoking him to anger. [19]I feared the anger and wrath of the LORD, for
he was angry enough with you to destroy you. But again the LORD
listened to me. [20]And the LORD was angry enough with Aaron to destroy
him, but at that time I prayed for Aaron too. [21]Also I took that sinful thing
of yours, the calf you had made, and burned it in the fire. Then I crushed
it and ground it to powder as fine as dust and threw the dust into a
stream that flowed down the mountain.

**7–14** With "Remember this and never forget (v.7)," Moses sought to impress strongly on the people that they must not provoke the Lord by disobedience as they began the conquest of Canaan.

Continuing his warnings against failure in their allegiance to the Lord, Moses reminded Israel of their behavior from the time they left Egypt till they arrived at Jordan. He exhorted them to remember how they had rebelled against the Lord, provoking his anger and arousing his wrath (v.8). He had been angry enough to slay them at Horeb (Sinai; see the comment on 1:2). Moses had gone up on the mountain to receive the tablets with the Ten Commandments that the Lord had proclaimed to them on the day of the assembly (v.10; Exod 19–20; 31:18). After forty days and nights, the Lord told Moses to go back down to the people who had become corrupt with idolatry (vv.11–12). God told Moses that the people were stiff-necked (v.13, as Moses had just reminded them, v.6). The Lord asked Moses not to interfere with his intention to destroy the rebellious people and offered to make Moses into an even stronger and more numerous nation (v.14).

**15–17** Moses proceeded to tell how he went down from the fiery mountain, carrying the two stone tablets in his hands (v.15), or perhaps (cf. NIV mg.) one in each hand (the same expression occurs in v.17 but not in 10:3).

When he saw that the people had sinned against the Lord by making an idol, Moses threw down the two tablets, breaking them before the people's eyes (vv.16–17). The nature of their sin is indicated not only by the indictment of making the calf-idol but also by their turning away quickly from the Lord's commands. The first two commands on the tablets that were physically broken by Moses had already been broken by the people's disobedience and idolatry.

**18–21** Moses did not mention here how he went back up the mountain for the second period of forty days and nights. Neither did he mention the remonstrance made at the time on Sinai when the Lord told him that the people had sinned and that he would destroy them. Moses spoke of the second period of forty days and nights and also referred to two prayers on their behalf (v.18, "once again"; v.19, "again the LORD listened to me"). The two prayers are telescoped, a reference to the destruction of the calf-idol being at the end of the narrative. So the narrative is not in strict chronological order but rather in an order that emphasizes the peoples' wrongdoing.

Moses said he feared the anger and wrath of the Lord because he was angry enough to destroy the Israelites (v.19; cf. v.8). But Moses' intercession was successful both for the people as a whole and for Aaron individually (v.20; Exodus fails to mention this). Moses destroyed the calf (the sinful thing they had made) by heating it, grinding it to fine dust, and throwing the dust into a mountain stream (v.21).

This prayer of Moses (vv.19–20) is one of the most critical interventions in Israel's history (Exod 32:9–14). Another prayer of the same dimension was Samuel's at Mizpah (1 Sam 7:5, 8–9). The Lord reminded Jeremiah of these extraordinarily efficacious prayers when he told him that his heart would not go out to Judah in the last days of the empire (Jer 15:1).

The designation "that sinful thing of yours, the calf you had made" (v.21) contrasts the golden calf as a man-made piece of metal with the Lord himself as the Almighty Creator. While the calf incident may have been an attempt to combine worship of the Lord with Egyptian and Canaanite calf worship (Exod 32:4, 8), such syncretism was no better than outright exchange. No other gods were to be tolerated (5:6–8; 6:4–5; et al.).

The phrase "that flowed down the mountain" (v.21) is not in Exodus 32:20. On the other hand, the clause "and made the Israelites drink it" occurs only in Exodus. Moses threw the dust into the stream "that flowed down the mountain" and then "made the Israelites drink" from the stream—surely an ignominious exercise!

## Notes

---

**7** Moses often called on Israel to "remember" (זָכַר, *zākar*) the Lord or some episode or situation in the past, or he urged them to remember in the future something he was currently telling them. Here, for emphasis, he added the negative statement אַל־תִּשְׁכַּח (*'al-tiškah,* "never forget"). The whole expression could well be rendered "Remember! Don't forget!"

**10** The phrase "day of the assembly," which looks back to Exod 19:17–25, appears again in Deut 10:4 and 18:16, which refers back to Exod 20:19.

**13, 16** The interjection הִנֵּה (*hinnēh,* untr. in NIV), translated in the KJV and elsewhere as "behold," "see," "lo," makes the sentence an exclamatory one: "They are a stiff-necked people indeed!" (so NIV). In v.16 in combination with the parallel verb רָאָה (*rā'āh,* "look," "see"), *hinnēh* becomes "I saw."

**15** The reports on the way Moses held the tablets are diverse. Here the NIV text has "in my hands," but the meaning of עַל שְׁתֵּי יָדָי (*'al šᵉtê yāḏāy,* "in my hands") could be "one in each hand" (NIV mg.). This supposes that there were two separate tablets (or copies) rather than one stone with two columns. Notice, however, that in Exod 32:15 the Hebrew has יָד (*yāḏ*) with the singular suffix, viz., "his hand"—though this may be a collective. The LXX has ἐν ταῖς χερσὶν ἀυτοῦ (*en tais chersin autou,* "in his hands").

**16** The עֵגֶל מַסֵּכָה (*'ēgel massēḵāh,* "calf-idol"; NIV, "an idol cast in the shape of a calf") was probably made in the likeness of a contemporary bull-calf idol of the Goshen area of Egypt or of Canaanite Baal worship or a blending of the two fertility cults (Kitchen, NBD, p. 180).

**18** Moses fasted for his people's sinful behavior: כָּל־הַטַּאתְכֶם אֲשֶׁר חֲטָאתֶם (*kol-haṭṭa'ṯᵉkem 'ᵃšer ḥᵃṭā'ṯem,* "all your sin that you sinned [NIV, 'had committed']"), which is a cognate expression found most often in Lev 4 and 5. His fasting during this period of intercession indicated the depth of his anxiety for the people who had defamed the Lord by their wicked idolatry. Once more Moses' prayer prevailed (v.19).

**19** יָגֹרְתִּי (*yāgōrᵉtî,* "I feared"), a rare word, is translated in the LXX by the strong word ἔκφοβος (*ekphobos*), which means "exceedingly frightened" or "stricken with terror." The author of Hebrews (12:21) quotes the LXX ἔκφοβός εἰμι (*ekphobos eimi*) and couples it with καὶ ἔντρομος (*kai entromos,* "trembling"), which the NIV translates "I am trembling with fear."

אַף (*'aḏ,* "anger") and חֵמָה (*ḥēmāh,* "wrath") are joined together in 29:23 (22 MT), where the NIV has "in fierce anger," and in 29:28 (27 MT), "in furious anger." Here also synonyms coupled together by a conjunction intensify the meaning.

---

### c. *Israel's rebellion and Moses' prayer*

### 9:22–29

22You also made the LORD angry at Taberah, at Massah and at Kibroth
Hattaavah.
23And when the LORD sent you out from Kadesh Barnea, he said, "Go
up and take possession of the land I have given you." But you rebelled
against the command of the LORD your God. You did not trust him or
obey him. 24You have been rebellious against the LORD ever since I have
known you.
25I lay prostrate before the LORD those forty days and forty nights
because the LORD had said he would destroy you. 26I prayed to the LORD
and said, "O Sovereign LORD, do not destroy your people, your own
inheritance that you redeemed by your great power and brought out of
Egypt with a mighty hand. 27Remember your servants Abraham, Isaac
and Jacob. Overlook the stubbornness of this people, their wickedness
and their sin. 28Otherwise, the country from which you brought us will
say, 'Because the LORD was not able to take them into the land he had

> promised them, and because he hated them, he brought them out to put them to death in the desert.' [29]But they are your people, your inheritance that you brought out by your great power and your outstretched arm."

**22–24** It was not only at Horeb (Sinai) that the people showed themselves rebellious (vv.7–8) and stiff-necked (v.13) and thus angered the Lord. At Taberah (Num 11:1–3), Massah (Exod 17:1–7; Deut 6:16), Kibroth Hattaavah (Num 11:4–34), and Kadesh Barnea (Deut 1:19, 21, 26), also, they rebelled (vv.22–23). So Moses made the overall indictment: "You have been rebellious against the LORD ever since I have known you" (v.24). The source of this rebellion was their lack of trust in the Lord and, consequently, their disobedience to him (v.23).

The actual time sequence is Massah (Exod 17:1–7; Num 33:15 [Rephidim is Massah]), Taberah (Num 11:1–3), Kibroth Hattaavah (Num 11:34), and then Kadesh Barnea (Num 13:26; 33:36; Deut 1:19) (see KD in loc.). Here, perhaps for rhetorical effect, Moses rose from the less serious breach of loyalty to the most serious one. The people were facing the same situation as at Kadesh, being poised at an entrance to the land for conquest.

**25–29** Again Moses mentioned how he had interceded successfully for Israel. From a most humble position—lying prostrate before the Lord (v.25)—Moses addressed God as "Sovereign LORD" and prayed eloquently, reminding God that these were his people, his own inheritance, and that he had redeemed them from Egypt by his great power and mighty hand (v.26). He called on the Lord to remember Abraham, Isaac, and Jacob (v.27)—doubtless a reference to the covenantal promises. If God's people were destroyed, the Egyptians would indict him on the dual charge of his inability to bring Israel into the land, on one hand, and of his trickery of leading them into the desert to slaughter them (because he hated them), on the other hand (v.28). Moses did not at all deny the people's guilt but pled with the Lord to overlook their stubbornness, wickedness, and sin (v.27).

When God spoke to Moses about the peoples' sin while he was on Horeb the first time, God called the Israelites "your people whom you brought out of Egypt" (v.12); but when Moses prayed, he said that they were "your people, your (own) inheritance" (vv.26, 29). Why this change of identification? God was constantly portrayed by Moses as gracious and loving toward his people. His anger was only aroused by considerable provocation. Was God trying to evoke Moses' concern for his people by identifying them as Moses' people whom Moses had brought from Egypt? Probably so. Moses did show his concern by his great intercessory prayer in which he insisted that the people belonged to the Lord, and this brought the desired result.

## Notes

**26** The clause "you redeemed by your great power and brought out" is reemphasized in v.29: "you brought out by your great power." פָּדָה (*pāḏāh*, "redeemed") gives the meaning of the Lord's act of bringing the people out of Egypt. It means to free or rescue. In bringing the people out of Egypt, he freed them from Egyptian slavery. Moses used *pāḏāh* six times in Deuteronomy—always of the Lord bringing the Israelites out of Egypt and relative to freeing them from the slavery of Egypt (7:8; 9:26; 13:5 [6 MT]; 15:15; 21:8; 24:18). In the OT sacrificial system, גָּאַל (*gā'al,* "redeem") is more technically used of redemption by ransom or vengeance. Redemption by ransom focuses on deliverance by the payment of a price. On the other hand, redemption through vengeance relates to an act that settles a just recompense as in Isa 63:4: "For the day of vengeance was in my heart, and the year of my redemption has come."

**27** "Overlook" translates the Hebrew figurative expression אַל־תֵּפֶן אֶל (*'al-tēpen 'el*), which is literally "do not turn the face to" or "do not look back to."

**28** The Samaritan Pentateuch and the LXX have "The people of the land," a translation of the metaphor "land" (NIV, "country"). Exodus 32:12 has "the Egyptians."

**29** See the comments and Notes on 4:20; 7:6; and the comment on 14:1–2 for "your people, your inheritance." נַחֲלָה (*nahªlāh,* "inheritance") means "one's own particular possession."

---

## d. *New tablets*

### 10:1–11

[1]At that time the LORD said to me, "Chisel out two stone tablets like the
first ones and come up to me on the mountain. Also make a wooden
chest. [2]I will write on the tablets the words that were on the first tablets,
which you broke. Then you are to put them in the chest."
[3]So I made the ark out of acacia wood and chiseled out two stone
tablets like the first ones, and I went up on the mountain with the two
tablets in my hands. [4]The LORD wrote on these tablets what he had
written before, the Ten Commandments he had proclaimed to you on
the mountain, out of the fire, on the day of the assembly. And the LORD
gave them to me. [5]Then I came back down the mountain and put the
tablets in the ark I had made, as the LORD commanded me, and they are
there now.
[6](The Israelites traveled from the wells of the Jaakanites to Moserah.
There Aaron died and was buried, and Eleazar his son succeeded him as
priest. [7]From there they traveled to Gudgodah and on to Jotbathah, a
land with streams of water. [8]At that time the LORD set apart the tribe of
Levi to carry the ark of the covenant of the LORD, to stand before the
LORD to minister and to pronounce blessings in his name, as they still do
today. [9]That is why the Levites have no share or inheritance among their
brothers; the LORD is their inheritance, as the LORD your God told them.)
[10]Now I had stayed on the mountain forty days and nights, as I did the
first time, and the LORD listened to me at this time also. It was not his will
to destroy you. [11]"Go," the LORD said to me, "and lead the people on
their way, so that they may enter and possess the land that I swore to
their fathers to give them."

**1–5** Moses next rehearsed the second experience regarding the two stone tablets of the covenant (Exod 34:1–4). "At that time" refers to the period during which Moses offered the prayer of 9:26–29. At the Lord's command he had chiseled out two stone tablets similar to the first ones (v.1). God said that he would write on them the words that had been on the first tablets. Moses was also to construct a wooden chest for the tablets (v.2). In deference to traditional and now technical terminology, the NIV from v.3 and on uses the term "ark" for this particular chest. "Ark" was a common household word for box, chest, or basket in seventeenth-century England.

The narrative here is severely truncated, and the order of events is not immediately discernible. One might suppose from vv.3 and 5 that Moses himself made the chest before he went up Horeb the second time and that immediately after he came down he put the tablets in that chest. The history that is given in Exodus, however, indicates that the ark was built by Bezalel after Moses' return (Exod 37:1–9). It is too much to say, as S.R. Driver (*Deuteronomy,* in loc.) does, that these "differences do not admit reconciliation." The collocation of clauses in v.3 does not necessarily mean that the actions mentioned are in chronological order. Dischronologized narrative is not uncommon in the OT. The same is true of v.5. The text does not say that no time elapsed between Moses' descent of the mountain and his placement of the tablets in the chest.

Neither is it uncommon that a leader of a venture is said to do something when the actual physical accomplishment of it is done by someone else, as is the case here.

**6–9** The sequence of the places mentioned is not that of Numbers 33:31–33, which is Moseroth, Bene Jaakan (Num 33:31), Hor Haggidgad, Jotbathah, but rather that of the later journey back to Kadesh before the return mentioned in Numbers 33:37. The "wells of the Jaakanites" (v.6) is to be identified with Bene Jaakan, Moserah with Moseroth (Num 33:31), and Gudgodah (v.7) with Hor Haggidgad (Num 33:32). Jotbathah is common to both itineraries. It appears that after leaving Kadesh, Israel went toward Edom and then later returned to Kadesh before starting on the last trip around Edom and up onto the plains of Moab. Consequently the order here is the reverse of that in Numbers 33:31–33.

Moserah was evidently a larger area that included Mount Hor. So it was quite correct to identify Aaron's place of death as either Mount Hor (Num 20:22–29; 33:38–39; Deut 32:50) or Moserah (Deut 10:6). Moserah, like Taberah, Massah, and Meribah, appears to be first a common noun, as the plural form in Numbers 33:30–31 suggests. Moserah (Moseroth) means "chastisement(s)" and might be Moses' designation of the area and not a generally used name (see Manley, "Problems in Deuteronomy," pp. 203ff.).

None of the places mentioned have been located with certainty. Possible locations are in the Arabah opposite Edom (see S.R. Driver, *Deuteronomy,* pp. 120–21).

Verses 6–9 are a historical aside, parenthetical in style but not really parenthetical in the flow of Moses' thought. His mind moved along the course of events relating to the ark and then proceeded to the Israelites' journey beginning just before the death of Aaron and includes Aaron's death, the succession of Eleazer, the ministry of the Levites relative to the ark (v.8), as well as their broader ministries and their special situation regarding landed inheritance (v.9). The Lord himself in a special way—not land—was to be their inheritance. "At that time" (v.8) is the same time as v.1 (q.v.).

**10–11** The climax of this recital is Moses' declaration that the Lord listened to his plea on the Israelites' behalf (v.10). It was not the Lord's will to destroy them. The grace of God—not because they were numerous or righteous—kept them from destruction, and by his grace Moses' orders were renewed to "lead the people on their way" to occupy the Promised Land (v.11).

## Notes

---

**1–2** For אֲרוֹן (*'arôn,* "chest") as coffin, see Gen 50:26; as chest other than the ark, see 2 Kings 12:10; 2 Chron 24:8, 10–11; and Ellenbogen, p. 40. On the meaning of ark in seventeenth-century English, see Bridges and Weigle, p. 27, and *The Oxford English Dictionary,* (Oxford: Oxford University Press, 1955), p. 1330.

**2, 5** Mendenhall ("Covenant Forms," p. 60) writes of the provision for deposit of the vassal treaties that a copy of the treaty was deposited in the sanctuary of the vassal state. The Lord required the same of Moses. See also Kitchen, *Ancient Orient,* p. 93; Kline, *Treaty,* pp. 14ff.; id., *Biblical Authority,* pp. 35–36, 121; and ANET, p. 205.

**3** "Acacia wood," the Hebrew שִׁטִּים (*šiṭṭîm*) or שִׁטָּה (*šiṭṭāh*), was useful in carpentry. It was common in Sinai and Canaan. The encampment in the plains of Moab near the Jordan had as one of its boundaries "Abel Shittim" (Num 33:49), אָבֵל הַשִּׁטִּים (*'ābēl haššiṭṭîm,* lit., "the meadow of the Acacias"), elsewhere simply "the Acacias" (see *Fauna and Flora of the Bible,* [London: United Bible Societies, 1972], pp. 87–88).

**5, 10** Because of the change from first person in vv.5, 10 to the third person in vv.6–9, some have suggested that vv.6–9 are a later insertion. It may be that Moses quoted here from a travel document (cf. Craigie, p. 200 n. 6). Such changes are not unknown elsewhere.

**8** The series of Levite responsibilities—to carry the ark, to stand before the Lord, to minister to him, and to pronounce blessings in his name—constitute a succinct delineation of the duties of Levites and the priests as elaborated elsewhere, especially in Num 3 and 8.

On the use of the "name" of the Lord in Deuteronomy, see the comment on 32:3; and on blessing in his name, see 21:5.

---

## 6. *Exhortation to revere and love the Lord (10:12–11:32)*

### a. *The requirement of allegiance*

### 10:12–22

[12]And now, O Israel, what does the LORD your God ask of you but to
fear the LORD your God, to walk in all his ways, to love him, to serve the
LORD your God with all your heart and with all your soul, [13]and to
observe the LORD's commands and decrees that I am giving you today
for your own good?

[14]To the LORD your God belong the heavens, even the highest
heavens, the earth and everything in it. [15]Yet the LORD set his affection
on your forefathers and loved them, and he chose you, their descendants, above all the nations, as it is today. [16]Circumcise your hearts,
therefore, and do not be stiff-necked any longer. [17]For the LORD your
God is God of gods and Lord of lords, the great God, mighty and
awesome, who shows no partiality and accepts no bribes. [18]He defends
the cause of the fatherless and the widow, and loves the alien, giving
him food and clothing. [19]And you are to love those who are aliens, for
you yourselves were aliens in Egypt. [20]Fear the LORD your God and serve
him. Hold fast to him and take your oaths in his name. [21]He is your
praise; he is your God, who performed for you those great and awesome
wonders you saw with your own eyes. [22]Your forefathers who went
down into Egypt were seventy in all, and now the LORD your God has
made you as numerous as the stars in the sky.

This exhortation, most eloquent in order and content, reminiscent and somewhat repetitive of chapter 6, fittingly climaxes this section, which precedes the giving of specific covenant-treaty stipulations that Moses held to be especially important as the people faced entrance into the land.

**12–13** In answer to the question "What does the LORD your God ask of you?" five phrases are piled one on the other, phrases that occur again and again through these speeches. The people are urged to (1) "fear the LORD [their] God" (expressive of highest reverence vv.12, 20); (2) "walk in all his ways" (with utmost devotion, v.12; 11:1, 13, 22); (3) "love him" (totally, v.12; 6:5; 13:3; 30:6); (4) "serve" him (in worship and daily living, vv.12, 20; 11:13); and (5) "observe [his] commands and decrees" (in obedience, v.13). More ore less synonymous with "observe" are the words and phrases "keep," "obey," "fix in your hearts and minds," and "teach his commands, requirements, laws, and decrees." All this was for their own good (v.13).

**14–16** This call to allegiance to the Lord reiterates the call of 6:4–9. The Lord who loved the Israelites issued his requirement of their love. This is far beyond legalism. It touches the deepest wells of spiritual relationship between the Lord and his people. Though God, to whom they were to give their fealty, owns the farthest reaches of the "heavens, the earth and everything in it" (v.14), yet he set his affection and love on their forefathers and chose these, their descendants, above all other nations (v.15). Because of this gratuitous position they had in relation to the true God, the Israelites were urged to circumcise their hearts and cease being stiff-necked (v.16). The circumcision of the heart contrasts with being stiff-necked, which means being stubborn and rebellious. Circumcision of the heart connotes being open, responsive, and obedient to the Lord.

In the promises of restoration—restoration in the distant future, when the people return in obedience to the Lord—it is said that the Lord would circumcise the people's hearts, and this act would cause them to love him (30:6). Jeremiah took up this refrain, calling on the people of his day to circumcise their hearts (Jer 4:4). The people are said to have uncircumcised hearts in Leviticus 26:41; Jeremiah 9:26; and Ezekiel 44:7, 9.

**17–22** The relationship of the Lord with his people is based on his being. The majestic sovereignty of the Lord is reemphasized and reiterated in vv.17–22. His greatness is portrayed by the names ascribed to him as well as by the characteristics and acts attributed to him (vv.17–18, 21). "God of gods" and "Lord of lords" (v.17) are Hebrew superlatives. The designations do not suggest that there are in reality other divine gods or lords over whom God rules. Rather, as God and Lord he is supreme over all. The superlative is based on the idea that other gods are said to exist but does not admit of their reality.

As the great, mighty, and awesome One, the Lord performed the "great and awesome wonders" that the people had seen with their own eyes (v.21). The majesty of the Lord extends to righteous behavior (vv.17–18), showing no partiality, accepting no bribes. He defends the fatherless and the widows and loves the alien, giving him food and clothing. The people were to be like the Lord; they too were to love aliens, for they had been aliens in Egypt (v.19).

Not only were the people to reverence and worship the Lord, they were also to hold fast to him and make oaths only in his name (v.20). Moreover, the Lord their God was to be the object of their praise (v.21)—the Lord who brought up out of Egypt the descendants of the seventy (Gen 46:27; Exod 1:5), who had gone down into Egypt and had become "as numerous as the stars in the sky" (v.22). In contrast to the few who went down into Egypt with Jacob, this generation had become numerous indeed. In contrast with the Eastern empires and even with other nations around them, the Israelites were the "fewest of all peoples" (7:7).

## Notes

**12–13** Weinfeld (*Deuteronomic School*, pp. 83ff.) points out that the expressions to love, fear, hold fast, obey, etc., are similar to the diplomatic terminology of the Near East. Moran ("Love of God," pp. 77ff.) notes that "love" served a political need in the ancient Near East. See also Wiseman, *Vassal-Treaties*, 1.268.

**17** "Shows no partiality" in the Hebrew idiom is לֹא־יִשָּׂא פָנִים (*lō'-yiśśā' pānîm*), which is literally "does not lift up faces [persons]." All persons are considered on the same level and are equal in the Lord's eyes.

**18** Similar expressions to "he defends the cause of the fatherless and the widow" are used of Danel in Aqhat. See Coogan, pp. 35, 41, and Thomas, p. 134.

**18–19** A גֵּר (*gēr*) is a resident "alien," and in Israel he was granted many rights that an Israelite as an alien in Egypt did not have. See "foreigner" in ZPEB, 2:590.

**20** "Hold fast to him" comes from the verb דָּבַק (*dāḇaq*), which means "stick to," "cling to," or "hold onto," as a man is to be united to his wife (Gen 2:24) and as Ruth clung to Naomi (Ruth 1:14) (cf. also Deut 11:22; 13:4; 30:20).

**22** For "seventy" the LXX has seventy-five in Gen 46:27 and Exod 1:5 but seventy here in v.22. Stephen (Acts 7:14) took seventy-five from the LXX. Both numbers have been justified by inclusion or exclusion of certain persons. (For a discussion of those who went to Egypt with Jacob, see KD, *The Pentateuch*, 1:369–74.)

### b. *Love and obedience toward the Lord (11:1–25)*

#### 1) *The requirements of the disciplined*

11:1–7

**¹Love the LORD your God and keep his requirements, his decrees, his laws and his commands always. ²Remember today that your children were not the ones who saw and experienced the discipline of the LORD your God: his majesty, his mighty hand, his outstretched arm; ³the signs he performed and the things he did in the heart of Egypt, both to Pharaoh king of Egypt and to his whole country; ⁴what he did to the Egyptian army, to its horses and chariots, how he overwhelmed them with the waters of the Red Sea as they were pursuing you, and how the LORD brought lasting ruin on them. ⁵It was not your children who saw what he did for you in the desert until you arrived at this place, ⁶and what he did to Dathan and Abiram, sons of Eliab the Reubenite, when the earth opened its mouth right in the middle of all Israel and swallowed them up with their households, their tents and every living thing that belonged to them. ⁷But it was your own eyes that saw all these great things the LORD has done.**

**1–7** In this section the Exodus and desert experiences of Moses' audience are called to remembrance (notice the recurrence of the remembrance motif). The constant repetition of ideas, words, and phrases characterizes the messages of Deuteronomy. The repetition shows the intensity of the Lord's desire to remold his people to prepare them for the conquest and settlement of Canaan. By this repetition Moses attempted to plant firmly in the minds of the people the necessity of total allegiance to the Lord. Chapter 11 is markedly illustrative of this hammerlike repetitive style. The exhortations to love, remember, observe, worship (serve), obey, teach, and walk in the Lord's ways are all here. So also are the words used to describe the basic content of the messages as requirements, decrees, laws, commands, words, and symbols. Reference is made to what God did for them and how he did it by his majesty, his mighty hand, and his outstretched arm. If they would live and obey the Lord, he would drive out the nations then in Canaan, settle the Israelites in the land, and provide for them to their satisfaction; but if not, they would be destroyed. Other elements of this chapter have been mentioned before, but not so emphatically.

The dominant personnel in the nation were those who had seen what the Lord had done for them in Egypt (v.3) and in the desert (v.5). They had seen this with their own eyes (v.7). They were not of the generation doomed to die in the desert for their disobedience at Kadesh Barnea (1:35–36) but those who ranged from infancy to the age of twenty (Num 14:29–30). These were the children who remained alive (14:31), whom their fathers had said would be taken as plunder in the desert (14:3, 31). Though they were then young, they too had seen the great redemptive acts of God and were thus about to enter the Promised Land.

Moses focused his attention on those who were the leaders. In v.1 he repeated the exhortation formula: "Love the LORD . . . and keep his requirements." Then, in a seminegative way, he built up the responsibility of the dominant body in the nation—the ones who were under twenty years of age at Kadesh Barnea (1:35–36). Not their children but they themselves had had the experiences in the Exodus and the desert that should have taught them to love the Lord and to keep his requirements: "as they were pursuing you" (v.4), "what he did for you in the desert" (v.5). The exhortation is picked up again in v.8.

Those who knew (experienced) and saw what the Lord did in the Exodus (vv.2–4) and the desert (vv.5–6) were to remember (understand) that discipline of the Lord. In 5:3 Moses said that it was not with their fathers but with them that the covenant was made.

Though Korah was a leader of the rebellion described in Numbers 16:1–35, he is not mentioned with Dathan and Abiram here (v.6) as an illustration of what the Lord had done in the desert. Perhaps as Keil (in loc.) surmises, Korah is not named with those who were swallowed up with all their goods (tents) and adherents (servants) (every living thing that belonged to them) because Korah's sons were not destroyed (Num 26:9–11). From these experiences the Israelites were to learn that they should obey the Lord's commands (vv.8ff.).

## Notes

---

**1** The verb שָׁמַר (*šāmar,* "keep," "guard") is common in Deuteronomy.

The noun form מִשְׁמַרְתּוֹ (*mišmartô,* "his requirements") is not used elsewhere in Deuteronomy, though it occurs frequently in Numbers.

**2** The מוּסָר (*mûsār,* "discipline") is an admonition of a moral nature (BDB, p. 416) or moral education (S.R. Driver, *Deuteronomy,* p. 125).

**3** The NIV's "in the heart of Egypt" for בְּתוֹךְ מִצְרָיִם (*b*ᵉ*ṯôḵ miṣrāyim* ) is an attempt to give the sense of *b*ᵉ*ṯôḵ* ("in the middle"), which here may be no more than a simple locative "in," as NEB et al.; JB has "in Egypt itself."

**4** "He overwhelmed them with the waters of the Red Sea" expresses the Hebrew for "he made the waters of the Red Sea to overflow their faces." Here פְּנֵיהֶם (*p*ᵉ*nêhem*) means "their persons," i.e., "them."

"Lasting ruin," which translates עַד הַיּוֹם הַזֶּה (*'ad hayyôm hazzeh,* lit., "to this day"), is the NIV's way of saying "major destruction."

**5** To put the text into clear English, the NIV has escaped awkward syntax by repeating the negation relative to the children. "Your children were not the ones who saw" in v.2 is repeated in v.5: "It was not your children who saw." This was done to carry this sense throughout the passage without making too long a sentence and so losing the thought. The MT does not have this clause at the beginning of v.5.

On "what he did for you in the desert," see Num 10:1–31:54.

---

## 2) *Allegiance necessary to possess the land*

### 11:8–25

[8]Observe therefore all the commands I am giving you today, so that
you may have the strength to go in and take over the land that you are
crossing the Jordan to possess, [9]and so that you may live long in the
land that the LORD swore to your forefathers to give to them and their
descendants, a land flowing with milk and honey. [10]The land you are
entering to take over is not like the land of Egypt, from which you have
come, where you planted your seed and irrigated it by foot as in a
vegetable garden. [11]But the land you are crossing the Jordan to take
possession of is a land of mountains and valleys that drinks rain from
heaven. [12]It is a land the LORD your God cares for; the eyes of the LORD
your God are continually on it from the beginning of the year to its end.
[13]So if you faithfully obey the commands I am giving you today—to
love the LORD your God and to serve him with all your heart and with all
your soul—[14]then I will send rain on your land in its season, both
autumn and spring rains, so that you may gather in your grain, new wine
and oil. [15]I will provide grass in the fields for your cattle, and you will eat
and be satisfied.
[16]Be careful, or you will be enticed to turn away and worship other
gods and bow down to them. [17]Then the LORD's anger will burn against
you, and he will shut the heavens so that it will not rain and the ground
will yield no produce, and you will soon perish from the good land the
LORD is giving you. [18]Fix these words of mine in your hearts and minds;
tie them as symbols on your hands and bind them on your foreheads.
[19]Teach them to your children, talking about them when you sit at home
and when you walk along the road, when you lie down and when you get
up. [20]Write them on the doorframes of your houses and on your gates,
[21]so that your days and the days of your children may be many in the
land that the LORD swore to give your forefathers, as many as the days
that the heavens are above the earth.
[22]If you carefully observe all these commands I am giving you to
follow—to love the LORD your God, to walk in all his ways and to hold
fast to him—[23]then the LORD will drive out all these nations before you,
and you will dispossess nations larger and stronger than you. [24]Every
place where you set your foot will be yours: Your territory will extend
from the desert to Lebanon, and from the Euphrates River to the
western sea. [25]No man will be able to stand against you. The LORD your
God, as he promised you, will put the terror and fear of you on the whole
land, wherever you go.

**8–15** To be able to conquer the land and to live long in it as a nation, the people were to observe the Lord's commands (vv.8–9). The description of the land has a new element. Not only was it "flowing with milk and honey" (v.9; see comment on 6:3), but it was a land that drank "rain from heaven" (v.11). It was not like Egypt, where the planted seed was irrigated by foot because water had to be brought from the Nile (v.10).

There is no archaeological evidence from this period of an apparatus for irrigation that was foot-operated. However, one would expect that an Egyptian would use his feet to clear a channel for the flow of water to where he wanted it in his garden. Irrigation by foot may also simply mean carrying buckets of water from the source of the water to the field: that is moving it on foot. The Torah translates this clause in v.10 as "watered by your own labors," which at least focuses the meaning in the right direction. In Egypt water for growing grains, vegetables, and fruits depended on the people's labors. In Canaan the water came in its season from the heavens by the providence of God; and if the people faithfully obeyed him, he would send the rain (vv.12–15; see the comment on 4:29).

**16–21** However, if the Israelites were enticed to turn away from the Lord and to worship other gods, he would shut the heavens so that it would not rain (vv.16–17). This enticement would be everywhere present in Canaan because of the prevailing Baalism. Baal (Hadad) was said to control the rains that brought fertility to Canaan. But Moses contended that it was the Lord who governed the incidence of rainfall; and if the people did not worship and obey him, he would shut the heavens so that no rain would fall and the ground would not produce (28:23–24; Lev 26:19–20). Conversely, Malachi 3:10 promises that the heavens would be opened when the people obeyed God.

In vv.16–21 Moses reiterated what he had said in 6:6–9, with some variation, as would be expected in a more or less hortatory, extemporaneous discourse. Clearly, these important practices would guard the people against being deceived by the Canaanites.

**22–25** The land that the people would acquire by obedience to the Lord (vv.22–23) under the covenant was limited in two ways: (1) by "every place where you set your foot" (v.24a) and (2) by geographic boundaries (v.24b). The Lord confirmed this promise to Joshua (Josh 1:3). He also had made a particular promise of this sort to Caleb (1:36), a promise that was fulfilled (Josh 14:9–13).

The geographical boundaries of the desert to Lebanon are on the south and the north, while the Euphrates and the Mediterranean ("the western sea") are east and west. These are generalized boundaries in harmony with other such promises and prophecies (1:7; Gen 15:18).

On "the terror and fear of you" (v.25), see the comment on 2:24–25.

## Notes

---

**13–15** The change of persons in vv.13–15 is very abrupt. The "I" in "I am giving you today" is Moses, while the "I" in "I will send" and "I will provide" is the Lord. This kind of transition occurs in the prophetic writings, too. However, the Samaritan Pentateuch, some LXX MSS, the Vulgate, and a Mezuzah quotation from Qumran (Wright, *Discoveries*, p. 161) suggest "he" rather than "I" in vv.14–15.

**14** The "autumn rains"—יוֹרֶה (*yôreh*, "former")—fell from October-November to January, while "spring rains"—מַלְקוֹשׁ (*malqôš*, "latter")—came in March and April.

**16–17** On Baal's controlling rain, see Pfeiffer, *Ras Shamra*, p. 30.
**17** עָצַר (*'āṣar*, "he will shut") means literally "to hinder, shut up, or imprison."
**18** On "symbols" see comments and Notes on 6:8–9.
**21** A description indicating perpetuity—"enduring like the days of heaven"—occurs on an ancient pottery jar from Saqqarah in Egypt. It is similar to the statement here: "as many as the days that the heavens are above the earth" (Thomas, p. 251).

---

### c. *Directives for the blessing and curse recital*

11:26–32

[26]See, I am setting before you today a blessing and a curse—[27]the
blessing if you obey the commands of the LORD your God that I am
giving you today; [28]the curse if you disobey the commands of the LORD
your God and turn from the way that I command you today by following
other gods, which you have not known. [29]When the LORD your God has
brought you into the land you are entering to possess, you are to
proclaim on Mount Gerizim the blessings, and on Mount Ebal the
curses. [30]As you know, these mountains are across the Jordan, west of
the road, toward the setting sun, near the great trees of Moreh, in the
territory of those Canaanites living in the Arabah in the vicinity of Gilgal.
[31]You are about to cross the Jordan to enter and take possession of the
land the LORD your God is giving you. When you have taken it over and
are living there, [32]be sure that you obey all the decrees and laws I am
setting before you today.

**26–32** The most important addition to the highly repetitive directives of chapter 11 is that of the blessing and curse recital to be proclaimed from Mounts Gerizim and Ebal. The blessings and the curses form an important part of the covenant-treaty articles that make up the Book of Deuteronomy. Here they constitute both a conclusion to this first section and an introduction to what follows, in the more detailed delineation of the Lord's decrees under which the people were to live. The blessing was to be theirs for obedience and the curse for disobedience (vv.27–28; cf. 27:9–28:68). The basic element is adherence to the Lord as God, and the basic error is following other gods. The recognition of the Lord as God, and therefore as suzerain who must be obeyed, is the basic commitment. It is the Lord who says, "Obey!"

No certain clue exists to explain why Gerizim and Ebal (v.29) were chosen as the places for the proclamation of the blessings and curses. No doubt they were chosen because of their centrality and natural adaptability for such an event. They are close to each other and are both about 3,000 feet above sea level, Ebal being about 230 feet higher than Gerizim. The location as "west of the road" (v.30) refers to the main north-south road, and "near the great trees of Moreh" indicates a location a little south of the center of the valley between the two mountains. The Arabah is surely the Jordan Valley, but which Gilgal is meant is not certain since there may be as many as six in the OT (see ZPEB, 2:725–27). Perhaps the NIV is correct in relating the reference to the headquarters of these Canaanites who controlled that territory.

## Notes

---

**26–30** This is the initial record of the blessings and the curses in Deuteronomy. For the fuller recital see chs. 27 and 28.

**30** Both אַחֲרֵי (*'aḥ$^a$rê,* lit., "behind," the general stance from which the Israelites indicated directions when facing east) and מְבוֹא הַשֶּׁמֶשׁ (*m$^e$ḇô' haššemeš,* "the setting of the sun") mean "west."

Instead of "the great trees of Moreh," the LXX and other ancient versions have the singular "tree" as in Gen 12:6. Here the Lord appeared to Abraham, and here he built an altar to the Lord.

---

## C. *Specific Stipulations of the Covenant-Treaty (12:1–26:19)*

### 1. *For worship and ceremony (12:1–16:17)*

#### a. *At the place of the Lord's choosing (12:1–32)*

##### 1) *The sanctuary and its sacrifices*

12:1–14

1 These are the decrees and laws you must be careful to follow in the
land that the LORD, the God of your fathers, has given you to possess—
as long as you live in the land. 2 Destroy completely all the places on the
high mountains and on the hills and under every spreading tree where
the nations you are dispossessing worship their gods. 3 Break down
their altars, smash their sacred stones and burn their Asherah poles in
the fire; cut down the idols of their gods and wipe out their names from
those places.
4 You must not worship the LORD your God in their way. 5 But you are to
seek the place the LORD your God will choose from among all your tribes
to put his Name there for his dwelling. To that place you must go; 6 there
bring your burnt offerings and sacrifices, your tithes and special gifts,
what you have vowed to give and your freewill offerings, and the
firstborn of your herds and flocks. 7 There, in the presence of the LORD
your God, you and your families shall eat and shall rejoice in everything
you have put your hand to, because the LORD your God has blessed you.
8 You are not to do as we do here today, everyone as he sees fit, 9 since
you have not yet reached the resting place and the inheritance the LORD
your God is giving you. 10 But you will cross the Jordan and settle in the
land the LORD your God is giving you as an inheritance, and he will give
you rest from all your enemies around you so that you will live in safety.
11 Then to the place the LORD your God will choose as a dwelling for his
Name—there you are to bring everything I command you: your burnt
offerings and sacrifices, your tithes and special gifts, and all the choice
possessions you have vowed to the LORD. 12 And there rejoice before the
LORD your God, you, your sons and daughters, your menservants and
maidservants, and the Levites from your towns, who have no allotment
or inheritance of their own. 13 Be careful not to sacrifice your burnt
offerings anywhere you please. 14 Offer them only at the place the LORD
will choose in one of your tribes, and there observe everything I
command you.

**1–14** Chapter 12 begins a new section of this major address of Moses. This chapter by itself presents some crucial elements for the Israelites' national and individual spiritual lives.

1. The people were to worship the Lord their God in the place he chose to put his Name (v.5), the place he identified himself with and where his presence would be manifested (v.7). This relates the regulations regarding the worship of the Lord in the Tent of Meeting (from Exod 27:21, throughout Exodus, Leviticus, and Numbers) to

the settled life in Canaan, which is anticipated. That one specified place surely contrasts to the many places Canaanite gods were worshiped (cf. vv.2, 5, 11, 13–14, 26, et al.).

The centrality of worship also had political and social benefits in unifying the people. While the one place the Lord would choose might vary from time to time (as it did), the tendency of the directive was toward stability and unification.

2. The people were not to worship the gods of the Canaanites but were rather to destroy them, their articles, and their places of worship. By this destruction the Israelites would wipe out the Canaanite names and memory from these places (vv.2–3).

It is not clear whether the names of the Canaanite gods or the names of the Canaanite peoples were to be wiped out. Doubtless in actuality both were involved. In 7:24 mention is made of wiping out the Canaanite kings, including, of course, their subjects.

The "high mountains," the "hills," and "under every spreading tree" (v.2) were the common places for Canaanite worship that were frequently castigated by the prophets throughout Israel's history. Every spreading tree, used only here in the Mosaic books, occurs often with hills as places of pagan worship (see 1 Kings 14:23; 2 Kings 16:4; 17:10; et al.). All the paraphernalia of pagan worship was to be completely destroyed. In 7:5 the Asherah poles were to be cut down and the idols burned, while here (v.3) the Asherah poles were to be burned and the idols cut down. The variation could be due to the extemporaneous nature of the messages.

The people were to bring all their offerings to the place the Lord chose (vv.4–6). The "burnt offerings" were whole offerings consumed on the altar (Lev 1:1–17; 6:8–13). The "sacrifices" when in combination with "burnt offerings" were fellowship offerings (Lev 3; 7:11–21). "Tithes" cover that tenth of the returns from the soil that was to be brought to the sanctuary (Lev 27:30–32). The "special gifts" were contributions made to the Lord at any time (Lev 22:21; 27:2). The "lifting up of the hand," as the Hebrew has it, seems to be a more general expression for contributions ("special gifts") than the traditional translation "heave offering" suggests. The "vows" cover an almost limitless array of things that a worshiper might vow to the Lord—anything evoked by whatever emotion or experience that leads one to promise something to the Lord, either conditionally or unconditionally. "Freewill offerings" were voluntary communal offerings that were less restricted than some of the others. The categories of offerings are not altogether exclusive but may overlap. Moses meant to emphasize that all the offerings were to be made in the place the Lord chose to put his Name.

3. Israel was not to worship the Lord in the way or with the means that the inhabitants of Canaan worshiped their gods (vv.4, 30–31). Neither were they to be as free as they had been in the desert wanderings (vv.8–9). Everyone doing "as he sees fit" (v.8) indicates that the camp life of the desert years was less controlled than the settled life in Canaan under the regimen of the covenant-treaty stipulations was to be. The messages of Deuteronomy were needed as preparation for that new life to come. They emphasize particularly those aspects of the commands of God that were most important in Moses' sight as he was led by divine revelation. The basic elements of love and obedience toward God and concern for others are still the requirements for a new life in Christ (Matt 22:37–39; 1 Cor 13; Heb 5:9).

4. Israel's burnt offerings, sacrifices, tithes, special gifts, vows, freewill offerings, and the firstborn of their flocks and herds were all to be brought to the place in the

Promised Land where the Lord chose to put his Name (vv.5–6, 11–14, 17–18, 26–28).

"The resting place" (vv.9–10) as a description of the land begins with Jacob's blessing when he called the allotment of Issachar "his resting place" (Gen 49:15). Numbers 10:33 states that the ark was to find a place of rest for the people as they journeyed from one place to another, but those resting places gave merely temporary relief. Canaan was to be a settled place of rest. Solomon, after the prayer of dedication for the temple, said, "Praise be to the LORD, who has given rest to his people Israel just as he promised" (1 Kings 8:56). Isaiah used this term with reference to the messianic age (Isa 11:10; 28:12; 32:18; 66:1); and Micah enjoined the false prophets about the Jerusalem of his time, saying, "Get up, go away! For this is not your resting place" (Mic 2:10).

David said of the Lord, his shepherd, "He leads me beside quiet waters [*mê menuḥôṯ*, the waters of rest or restful waters]" (Ps 23:2); and in Psalm 132:8, 14, Zion is extolled as the resting place for the ark and for the Lord.

Psalm 95:11 becomes the source for vital NT teaching. The psalmist says that the Lord had declared of the people who disobeyed him in the desert, "They shall never enter my rest." The author of Hebrews, quoting from Psalm 95:11, says that those who disbelieved, disobeyed, and rebelled did not enter into his rest (ch. 3). Neither did later Israelites, for Joshua did not give them rest since the Lord was still offering this rest in the days of David. To fulfill the promise of God, a rest was still to be provided. That rest was for the soul in Jesus as Savior from sin: "We who have believed enter that rest" (Heb 4:3). Jesus is the *menûḥah* ("the resting place") for the believer. On "rest" see Leon Morris, EBC, 12:33–43, and also John Owen, *An Exposition of Hebrews* (Marshallton, Del.: National Foundation for Christian Education, 1969), 1:263–460.

## Notes

1 Manley (*Book of the Law*, p. 71) shows how 11:21–32 proves a fitting introduction and setting for chs. 12–26.

2 הֶהָרִים הָרָמִים (*hehārîm hārāmîm*, "high mountains"), הַגְּבָעוֹת (*haggeḇa'ôṯ*, "the hills"), and תַּחַת כָּל־עֵץ רַעֲנָן (*taḥaṯ kol-'ēṣ ra'anān*, "under every spreading tree") are places used in Canaanite worship. Throughout the kingdom period, בָּמָה (*bāmāh;* KJV, "high place") is commonly used for heights. However, see Lev 26:30; Num 33:52; and Deut 33:29, where *bāmāh* occurs. *Giḇ'āh* ("hill") is often associated with *bāmāh* in the prophets as descriptive of places of Canaanite idolatry.

The adjective רַעֲנָן (*ra'anān*) means "luxuriant," "fresh," "flourishing," "green," or "leafy," and consequently is descriptive of a luxuriant, "spreading" tree.

5 שֵׁם (*šēm*, "name") is one of the Hebrew words signifying "self." Boman (p. 106) says that it speaks of "his essence . . . his spiritual personality." On the use of the "Name of the LORD" in Deuteronomy, see the comment on 32:3.

6 In v.11 the נְדָרִים (*neḏārîm*, "freewill offerings") are called מִבְחַר נִדְרֵיכֶם (*miḇḥar niḏrêḵem*, "the choice possessions"), and in v.26 all these are subsumed under the general term קָדָשֶׁיךָ (*qoḏāšeyḵā*, "your consecrated things") and the phrase "whatever you have vowed."

When in combination with burnt offerings, the זְבָחִים (*zeḇāḥîm*, "sacrifices") are fellowship offerings, in this term's broadest sense (27:7; Exod 20:24; 24:5; 29:28). The שְׁלָמִים (*šelāmîm*, "fellowship offerings"), traditionally translated "peace offerings," have a wider connotation than cessation of conflict or a pleasant condition or relationship. Fellowship with God and fellow worshipers better conveys the overall thrust of these offerings.

"Special gifts" translates תְּרוּמַת יֶדְכֶם (*t^erûmaṯ yeḏkem*, lit., "the lifting up of the hand"). This expression is peculiar to Deuteronomy though תְּרוּמָה (*t^erûmāh*) occurs in Exodus, Leviticus, and especially Numbers to designate this offering, which in the KJV is "heave offering." The NIV in other places—places where *yeḏkem* is not in combination with *t^erûmāh*—translates *t^erûmāh* in verbal form as "present" or "present an offering." Perhaps the word or phrase indicates that the offering was indeed strictly a voluntary contribution, though some other offerings were also voluntary. The name of this offering may reflect the way it was offered, that is, presented to the Lord.

On sacrifices and offerings, see ZPEB, 5:194–210.

**8** Everyone doing "as he sees fit" is English idiom for אִישׁ כָּל־הַיָּשָׁר בְּעֵינָיו (*'îš kol-hayyāšār b^e'ênāyw*, "each according to whatever is right in his eyes").

**9** For the land as inheritance, see the comment on 4:20.

**11, 21** On the use of the "Name of the LORD" in Deuteronomy, see the comment on 32:3.

---

## 2) *Prohibitions and regulations regarding eating blood and meat 12:15–32*

[15]Nevertheless, you may slaughter your animals in any of your towns
and eat as much of the meat as you want, as if it were gazelle or deer,
according to the blessing the LORD your God gives you. Both the
ceremonially unclean and the clean may eat it. [16]But you must not eat
the blood; pour it out on the ground like water. [17]You must not eat in
your own towns the tithe of your grain and new wine and oil, or the
firstborn of your herds and flocks, or whatever you have vowed to give,
or your freewill offerings or special gifts. [18]Instead, you are to eat them
in the presence of the LORD your God at the place the LORD your God will
choose—you, your sons and daughters, your menservants and maidservants, and the Levites from your towns—and you are to rejoice before
the LORD your God in everything you put your hand to. [19]Be careful not
to neglect the Levites as long as you live in your land.

[20]When the LORD your God has enlarged your territory as he promised
you, and you crave meat and say, "I would like some meat," then you
may eat as much of it as you want. [21]If the place where the LORD your
God chooses to put his Name is too far away from you, you may
slaughter animals from the herds and flocks the LORD has given you, as I
have commanded you, and in your own towns you may eat as much of
them as you want. [22]Eat them as you would gazelle or deer. Both the
ceremonially unclean and the clean may eat. [23]But be sure you do not
eat the blood, because the blood is the life, and you must not eat the life
with the meat. [24]You must not eat the blood; pour it out on the ground
like water. [25]Do not eat it, so that it may go well with you and your
children after you, because you will be doing what is right in the eyes of
the LORD.

[26]But take your consecrated things and whatever you have vowed to
give, and go to the place the LORD will choose. [27]Present your burnt
offerings on the altar of the LORD your God, both the meat and the blood.
The blood of your sacrifices must be poured beside the altar of the LORD
your God, but you may eat the meat. [28]Be careful to obey all these
regulations I am giving you, so that it may always go well with you and
your children after you, because you will be doing what is good and
right in the eyes of the LORD your God.

[29]The LORD your God will cut off before you the nations you are about
to invade and dispossess. But when you have driven them out and

**settled in their land, [30]and after they have been destroyed before you, be careful not to be ensnared by inquiring about their gods, saying, "How do these nations serve their gods? We will do the same." [31]You must not worship the LORD your God in their way, because in worshiping their gods, they do all kinds of detestable things the LORD hates. They even burn their sons and daughters in the fire as sacrifices to their gods.**

**[32]See that you do all I command you; do not add to it or take away from it.**

**15–28** While sacrificial offerings were to be brought to the central sanctuary, the butchering and eating of meat for regular sustenance could be engaged in anywhere (vv.15, 20–25). The only restriction on eating nonsacrificial meat (except for the rules relative to unclean foods) prohibited eating the blood, which is the life and so must not be eaten. The blood was to be poured out on the ground like water (vv.16, 23–24). The nonsacrificial meat may be eaten by anyone—the ceremonially unclean person as well as the clean (v.22).

The proscription of eating blood and the reason for such proscription are developed in Leviticus 3:17; 7:26–27; 19:26; and especially 17:10–14. The life of the creature is its blood; so the spilling of the lifeblood is the giving of its life as the atoning sacrifice. This central characteristic of the sacrificial system in the OT becomes all important in the NT, when the typical aspects of the OT sacrifices are fulfilled in Christ by the shedding of his blood on the cross as the atonement for sin (Acts 20:28; Rom 3:25; 5:9; Eph 1:7; Col 1:14 [NIV mg.], 20; Heb 9:11–28; 10:19–20; Rev 1:5).

The emphasis and repetitions of this section of the Mosaic regulation are doubtless due to the changes that would follow the new conditions of settlement in the land as mentioned in v.10—"But you will cross the Jordan and settle in the land"—and in v.20—"When the LORD your God has enlarged your territory." The freedom enunciated in v.15 and repeated in vv.20–22 is conditioned by the prohibitions of vv.17–19. Tithes, vows, and certain offerings were to be eaten only in the place the Lord chose. Notice that "you, your sons and daughters, your menservants and maidservants, and the Levites" (v.18) fall under the prohibition.

**29–32** The Israelites were to resist the influences of the Canaanite culture and were not to conform to Canaanite religious practices. Concerning Canaanite worship v.31 says: "They do all kinds of detestable things," including burning "their sons and daughters in the fire as sacrifices."

Death was the penalty for anyone who sacrificed a child by passing him through the fire (Lev 18:21; 20:2–5). *The Wisdom of Solomon* 12:5–6 says that the Canaanites were merciless murderers of their defenseless children.

This section on the place of worship ends with Moses' warning neither to add to nor to subtract from all that he had said (12:32)—a warning given before (4:2) and reiterated elsewhere (Prov 30:6; Rev 22:18–19).

## Notes

---

31 For a description of child sacrifice by fire, see W.F. Albright, *Archaeology and the Religion of Israel* (Baltimore: Johns Hopkins University Press, 1942), pp. 162ff.; Green, pp. 179–87; and Moscati, pp. 141ff.

**32** This verse is 13:1 in BH. Since chapter 13 speaks of apostasy, the verse could be declaring that altering God's law is equal to apostasy. See Kaufman, pp. 126–27.

On the similarity to Near Eastern treaties, see the Notes on 4:2.

---

## b. *Worship of other gods forbidden*

### 13:1–18

1 If a prophet, or one who foretells by dreams, appears among you and
announces to you a miraculous sign or wonder, 2 and if the sign or
wonder of which he has spoken takes place, and he says, "Let us follow
other gods" (gods you have not known) "and let us worship them," 3 you
must not listen to the words of that prophet or dreamer. The LORD your
God is testing you to find out whether you love him with all your heart
and with all your soul. 4 It is the LORD your God you must follow, and him
you must revere. Keep his commands and obey him; serve him and hold
fast to him. 5 That prophet or dreamer must be put to death, because he
preached rebellion against the LORD your God, who brought you out of
Egypt and redeemed you from the land of slavery; he has tried to turn
you from the way the LORD your God commanded you to follow. You
must purge the evil from among you.

6 If your very own brother, or your son or daughter, or the wife you
love, or your closest friend secretly entices you, saying, "Let us go and
worship other gods" (gods that neither you nor your fathers have
known, 7 gods of the peoples around you, whether near or far, from one
end of the land to the other), 8 do not yield to him or listen to him. Show
him no pity. Do not spare him or shield him. 9 You must certainly put him
to death. Your hand must be the first in putting him to death, and then
the hands of all the people. 10 Stone him to death, because he tried to
turn you away from the LORD your God, who brought you out of Egypt,
out of the land of slavery. 11 Then all Israel will hear and be afraid, and
no one among you will do such an evil thing again.

12 If you hear it said about one of the towns the LORD your God is giving
you to live in 13 that wicked men have arisen among you and have led the
people of their town astray, saying, "Let us go and worship other gods"
(gods you have not known), 14 then you must inquire, probe and
investigate it thoroughly. And if it is true and it has been proved that this
detestable thing has been done among you, 15 you must certainly put to
the sword all who live in that town. Destroy it completely, both its people
and its livestock. 16 Gather all the plunder of the town into the middle of
the public square and completely burn the town and all its plunder as a
whole burnt offering to the LORD your God. It is to remain a ruin forever,
never to be rebuilt. 17 None of those condemned things shall be found in
your hands, so that the LORD will turn from his fierce anger; he will show
you mercy, have compassion on you, and increase your numbers, as he
promised on oath to your forefathers, 18 because you obey the LORD your
God, keeping all his commands that I am giving you today and doing
what is right in his eyes.

**1–5** To hinder and thwart rebellion against the Lord and adherence to the deities of the country that they were soon to enter, Moses gave the Israelites directions on how to deal with insurrectionists from the Lord's authority.

If a prophet, or one who foretells by dreams, should predict a miraculous sign or a supernatural event that comes to pass (vv.1–2) but should say, "Let us follow other gods . . . and worship them" (v.3), this prophet must not be listened to but rather must be put to death (v.5).

Dreams were used in prophecy both legitimately (Num 12:6) and illegitimately (Jer 23:25). Moses said that such illegitimate prophets were being used by the Lord to test the people's love for him (v.3). They were not to be followed (cf. v.4) but were to be put to death so that the evil would be purged from among the people (v.5).

This test of the prophet or of prophecy overrides all other tests. In Deuteronomy Moses got down to basics. The *sine qua non* of life is total love, total commitment, and total allegiance to the Lord. Elsewhere the fulfillment of prophecy establishes a prophet as a prophet. In such a case, however, the one who claims to be a prophet does so in the name of the Lord (18:19–22; Jer 28:9).

**6–11** Not only rebellious prophets, but one's closest relatives (one's very own brother, a son or daughter, or dear wife) or closest friend who said, "Let us go and worship other gods" (v.6), was to be put to death (vv.9–10). This was to be done when such enticement was made secretly as well as openly.

When speaking of the gods of the people who would be around them in Canaan (v.7), Moses referred to them three times in this chapter either as "gods you have not known" (vv.2, 13) or as "gods that neither you nor your fathers have known" (v.6). It is not that the Israelites had never heard of these gods but rather that neither they nor their fathers had ever acknowledged them as gods. They had never known them as their gods in day-to-day experience. Craigie (p. 223) says, "The Israelites *knew* God from their experience of his presence with them and word to them, but they had no such knowledge of any other supposed gods."

A panoply of words cautions the people not to be seduced by intimates to the worship of other gods. They were not to yield to, listen to, show pity to, spare, or shield an enticer (v.8). Not only was the defector to be stoned to death (v.10), but the first stone was to be thrown by the near relative or friend that the defector had attempted to drive from the Lord (v.9). The NIV's "turn" (v.10; cf. v.5) seems not strong enough. The word is used for driving a nation from its lands, either driving the Canaanites out before Israel or driving Israel out of the land into exile (30:1, "disperses"; Jer 8:3, "banish"; 23:2–3, "driven"). This extreme punishment is expected to produce good results. Though many modern sociologists declare that punishment—especially capital punishment—is no deterrent to crime, the message Moses proclaimed as the Word of God says that it would be a deterrent. The observation of v.11 is repeated in 17:13; 19:20; and 21:21. (On the theological and social implications of the death penalty, see Kline, *Biblical Authority*, pp. 154–67. See also the comments and Notes on 17:7, 12.)

**12–18** Towns that defected from the Lord were to be punished also. Israel, however, was to investigate thoroughly and prove that an allegation of this sort was true. Then the town was to be completely destroyed. Inhabitants, livestock, and all plunder were to be a whole burnt offering to the Lord. Such a town was to be an eternal ruin, never to be rebuilt. This doom, which goes contrary to the common practice of rebuilding towns on the ruins of the site, as the stratigraphic remains of tells in the Middle East plainly show, indicates how serious the Lord considered any defection from him.

In other circumstances some alleviation of these rigorous rules for destruction was allowed, but under these circumstances no "condemned things" (v.17) could be salvaged. When Israel would keep the Lord's commands and do what was right in his eyes, he would have compassion on them, and they would grow numerically as a nation—according to his promise to their forefathers. The contrast between doing what was right in the eyes of the Lord and what was right in one's own eyes can be seen in 12:8, 25, 28.

## Notes

The versification of BHS begins chapter 13 with what is 12:32 in the EV. Consequently, 13:1 in the NIV is 13:2 in the Hebrew text and so on throughout the chapter.

**1–2** (3–4 MT) אוֹת (*'ôṯ,* "miraculous sign") and מוֹפֵת (*môp̱ēṯ,* "wonder") are sometimes combined with other such terms (see 4:34; 7:19; 26:8) and most often describe the great acts of the Lord, especially those relative to the Exodus (6:22; 28:46; 29:2–3 [1–2 MT]; 34:11).

**6** (7 MT) The Hebrew figure for "the wife you love" is "the wife of your bosom," אֵשֶׁת חֵיקֶךָ (*'ēšeṯ ḥêqeḵā*) and "closest friend" is "a friend who is as oneself [soul]," רֵעֲךָ אֲשֶׁר כְּנַפְשְׁךָ (*rē'ᵃḵā 'ᵃšer kᵉnap̱šᵉḵā*).

בַּסֵּתֶר (*bassēṯer,* "secretly") is literally "in the hiding place," "in secret," where (or when) a person could easily overlook or deliberately keep secret this enticement. Not only is the perpetrator guilty, but so is the one who fails to report the crime. Secret sin is indicted also in the curses in 27:15, 24, and in 2 Sam 12:12 and Job 31:27.

**7** (8 MT) It has been supposed that מִקְצֵה הָאָרֶץ וְעַד־קְצֵה הָאָרֶץ (*miqṣēh hā'āreṣ wᵉ'aḏ-qᵉṣēh hā'āreṣ,* "from one end of the land to the other") speaks of "whatever gods there might be upon the whole circuit of the earth" (KD, *Pentateuch,* 3:364) or, as S.R. Driver (*Deuteronomy,* p. 153) has it, "nations at a distance (e.g., from Syria or Assyria)." But Moses' main perspective here was surely the land that Israel was soon to invade; and, as often elsewhere, *hā'āreṣ* means "the Land" of Promise. The designation of the people as those around them points in the same direction. Supporters of the idea that *hā'āreṣ* means "the whole earth" can point to the same phrase in Deut 28:64, where it does mean the whole earth, but this is obviated by the same phenomenon appearing in Jeremiah. In Jer 12:11–12, *hā'āreṣ* refers to the land of Israel, and in 25:33 it encompasses the whole world. The context determines the meaning.

**8** (9 MT) The psalmist in Ps 81:11 (12 MT) presents God as saying that his people would not "listen" to him—שָׁמַע (*šāma'*)—or "submit [yield]"—אָבָה (*'āḇāh*)—to him. The command of the Lord was the direct opposite to Israel's behavior. The rejection they were to exercise toward other gods they turned toward the Lord himself.

**13** (14 MT) אֲנָשִׁים בְּנֵי־בְלִיַּעַל (*'ᵃnāšîm bᵉnê-ḇᵉlîya'al,* "wicked men") is literally "men, sons of belial (worthlessness)," a Hebrew way of saying base, worthless, or wicked men (Judg 19:22; 1 Sam 2:12; 1 Kings 21:10, 13).

**14–15** (15–16 MT) Every care was to be taken to insure that the facts of the case were known. The authorities were to "inquire" (דָּרַשׁ [*dāraš,* "seek," "consult," "study"]), "probe" (חָקַר [*ḥāqār,* "search," "examine"]), and "investigate" (שָׁאַל [*šā'al,* "ask," "inquire"]); and this was to be done "thoroughly" (הֵיטֵב [*hêṭēḇ,* "diligently," "well"]). When the report "has been proved" (נָכוֹן הַדָּבָר [*nāḵôn haddāḇār*]), they were to punish the offender.

**15, 17** (16, 18 MT) On complete destruction, חָרַם (*ḥāram*), see the Notes on 2:34.

**16** (17 MT) תֵּל (*tēl,* "ruin") corresponds to the Arabic tell, "a mound or heap," the remains of an ancient town.

### c. *Clean and unclean foods*

### 14:1–21

**[1]You are the children of the LORD your God. Do not cut yourselves or shave the front of your heads for the dead, [2]for you are a people holy to**

the LORD your God. Out of all the peoples on the face of the earth, the
LORD has chosen you to be his treasured possession.
3 Do not eat any detestable thing. 4 These are the animals you may eat:
the ox, the sheep, the goat, 5 the deer, the gazelle, the roe deer, the wild
goat, the ibex, the antelope and the mountain sheep. 6 You may eat any
animal that has a split hoof divided in two and that chews the cud.
7 However, of those that chew the cud or that have a split hoof
completely divided you may not eat the camel, the rabbit or the coney.
Although they chew the cud, they do not have a split hoof; they are
ceremonially unclean for you. 8 The pig is also unclean; although it has a
split hoof, it does not chew the cud. You are not to eat their meat or
touch their carcasses.
9 Of all the creatures living in the water, you may eat any that has fins
and scales. 10 But anything that does not have fins and scales you may
not eat; for you it is unclean.
11 You may eat any clean bird. 12 But these you may not eat: the eagle,
the vulture, the black vulture, 13 the red kite, the black kite, any kind of
falcon, 14 any kind of raven, 15 the horned owl, the screech owl, the gull,
any kind of hawk, 16 the little owl, the great owl, the white owl, 17 the
desert owl, the osprey, the cormorant, 18 the stork, any kind of heron, the
hoopoe and the bat.
19 All flying insects that swarm are unclean to you; do not eat them.
20 But any winged creature that is clean you may eat.
21 Do not eat anything you find already dead. You may give it to an
alien living in any of your towns, and he may eat it, or you may sell it to a
foreigner. But you are a people holy to the LORD your God.
Do not cook a young goat in its mother's milk.

**1–2** Israel's relationship to the Lord as his son, which relationship had been declared to Pharaoh even before the Exodus (Exod 4:22), is highlighted here: "You are the children" (v.1). It was incumbent on all the Israelites to behave themselves according to the injunctions of the Lord. They were his holy, treasured possession (v.2). Moses before had referred to the Lord as Israel's father and to Israel as his son. This relationship was indicated by the way he had led them through the desert—caring for them (1:31) and disciplining them (8:5). He had also said that they were holy to the Lord and were his treasured possession (4:20; 7:6) when he told them that they were to destroy the religious paraphernalia of the Canaanites. Now, on the basis of this relationship, they were commanded not to follow the ways of mourning for the dead that the nations of Canaan practiced (Lev 19:27–28; 1 Kings 18:28).

In later years, at least, they did not all obey this injunction; for further prohibition is given in Jeremiah 16:6, and certain Israelites are said to have cut themselves while in mourning (Jer 41:5). The prohibition of shaving the forehead was a particular practice for mourning (see Craigie, pp. 229–30; S.R. Driver, *Deuteronomy*, pp. 155ff.; on the Ugaritic custom of gashing the skin in mourning, see Coogan, pp. 45–46).

**3–21** Because the Israelites were the Lord's children, they were not to eat any "detestable thing" (v.3), neither unclean animals, aquatic creatures, birds, flying insects, nor dead creatures. These prohibitions were more fully and legalistically given in Leviticus 11, except that Leviticus does not give these specifications of the clean animals. As the chosen people of God—chosen "out of all the peoples on the face of the earth" (v.2)—and as his holy, treasured possession, Israel was to follow God's injunctions to distinguish themselves from the surrounding peoples, because the pagan Canaanite culture was inimical to the holiness of the Lord and to the holiness required of his people. As Kaiser (*Old Testament Ethics,* pp. 140–41) has said, "In the last analysis that was what distinguished Israel from the nations: Their call to holiness had separated them from the nations and from all that was 'common' or 'profane.' "

The reason, then, for these injunctions is basically spiritual, though there may be other reasons growing out of psychological and sanitary considerations as well. Some of the unclean animals, etc., had associations with Canaanite religions. Some of the unclean creatures appear as reprehensible and others dangerous to the health of any who ate them. Eating anything dead (v.21) probably relates to the prohibition of eating blood. This also would constitute a religious reason for the prohibition. The meat would not be worth selling to a foreigner or giving to an alien if it were not edible.

Any animal that has a completely divided hoof and chews the cud could be eaten, but an animal that has only one of these characteristics is unclean and was not to be eaten (vv.6–8).

In Leviticus 17:13–16 both Israelite and alien were not to eat meat with blood in it; if either Israelite or alien ate anything found dead, he was to cleanse himself. Yet here an Israelite was allowed to give such meat to an alien, and he could eat it. The variation in the prohibition could be due to the changed situation. In Deuteronomy Moses prepared the people for the situation in Canaan, where they would be in a head-on clash with pagan culture in which the alien would not yet be integrated into Israelite culture. In Leviticus the alien comes within the culture of Israel and has the benefits of adhering to that culture. However, even during the period of conquest, the Israelites were always to be kind to the alien, remembering that they were aliens in Egypt (10:18–19; 14:29; et al.). Yet in the Deuteronomic messages Moses emphasized over and over again (as in v.21) the unique relationship of Israel as holy to the Lord. This is the basis for even ritualistic stipulations.

The prohibition against cooking a young goat in its mother's milk (v.21b) is apparently in reaction to an ancient Canaanite and Syrian custom dated as early as the fifteenth century B.C. (for sources on Israelite-Canaanite cultural variations, see Reider, pp. 138ff. See also the comments by Walter C. Kaiser, Jr., "Exodus," EBC, 2:445, and R. Laird Harris, "Leviticus," EBC, 2:519, 621).

## Notes

---

3–21 For identification of these animals, aquatic creatures, birds, and flying insects, see S.R. Driver, *Deuteronomy,* pp. 159–63; Reider, pp. 138–44; and *Fauna and Flora of the Bible.* On unclean creatures, see NBCrev, pp. 219–20, and ZPEB, 1:884–85.

21 On גֵּר (*gēr,* "alien"), see the Notes on 10:18–19 and TWOT, 1:155–56.

---

### d. *Time-related activities (14:22–16:17)*

#### 1) *Tithes*

14:22–29

[22]Be sure to set aside a tenth of all that your fields produce each year.
[23]Eat the tithe of your grain, new wine and oil, and the firstborn of your

herds and flocks in the presence of the LORD your God at the place he
will choose as a dwelling for his Name, so that you may learn to revere
the LORD your God always. 24 But if that place is too distant and you have
been blessed by the LORD your God and cannot carry your tithe (because
the place where the LORD will choose to put his Name is so far away),
25 then exchange your tithe for silver, and take the silver with you and go
to the place the LORD your God will choose. 26 Use the silver to buy
whatever you like: cattle, sheep, wine or other fermented drink, or
anything you wish. Then you and your household shall eat there in the
presence of the LORD your God and rejoice. 27 And do not neglect the
Levites living in your towns, for they have no allotment or inheritance of
their own.

28 At the end of every three years, bring all the tithes of that year's
produce and store it in your towns, 29 so that the Levites (who have no
allotment or inheritance of their own) and the aliens, the fatherless and
the widows who live in your towns may come and eat and be satisfied,
and so that the LORD your God may bless you in all the work of your
hands.

**22–29** The tithes required in the Pentateuch have been the subject of much debate. In Numbers 18:21–28 the tithe is given to the Levites who in turn tithe their receipts for the use of the Aaronic priests. In Deuteronomy the tithe is taken to the place the Lord shall choose as a dwelling for his Name, and there it is eaten joyfully in the presence of the Lord (v.23). Moses had already mentioned in 12:6 the tithes along with the other things the people were to bring to the chosen sanctuary, where they should eat and rejoice. Surely the people in a few days would not consume a tenth of their total annual production! Having already given directions for the support of the Levites by the tithes (Num 18:21–28), Moses here spoke of the festal communal meals that the people were to enjoy when the tithes were brought to the tabernacle (v.26)—situated somewhere in one of the tribal allotments after settlement in Canaan.

Every three years these tithes were to be brought to local city centers where they were stored for the use of the Levites, the aliens, and the poor (vv.28–29). This care for nonlanded people would lead to God's blessing on the work of their hands. The garnering of tithes was to come the third year and the sixth year. After the sixth year, the sabbatical year was observed as a year when the fields lay fallow, after which the cycle commenced again. "At the end of every three years" (v.28) is Hebrew idiom for the third year, as is seen from the reference to the sabbatical year, especially in 15:12, where the sabbatical year obviously starts immediately after the passage of six years.

The Jewish rabbis have usually held that there were three tithes: (1) for the priests and Levites, (2) for the communal meals, (3) every third year for the nonlanded (i.e., the Levites, aliens, fatherless, and widows).

It is obvious that the observations on tithes in Leviticus, Numbers, and Deuteronomy overlap one another. The Levites had interest in all three tithes, as did the general populace. The tithes were often the source of sacrifices and so within the control of the priests and Levites, at least to the extent that the tithes were used in sacrifices. The sacrificial system included communal meals, participation in which varied. In one place one aspect of these variants is emphasized and in another a different aspect is mentioned. The garnering of the tithes of the third year in the towns surely indicates that every third year the tithes of v.22 were not to be taken to the central sanctuary.

So all the designations of tithes speak of one basic tithe to be put to various uses.

The contributions of the Israelites to the economy, however, extended beyond the tithes; they included other sacrifices, vows, gifts, etc.

The logistics of transporting the tithes of all production would be difficult—perhaps impossible for families living at a distance from the tabernacle, wherever it might be. An interesting and modern adjustment is offered. The people could turn the tithe into cash and then, at the place the Lord would choose, convert it into food and drink desired for the celebration of God's blessing on the work of their hands (vv.24–26).

## Notes

---

**22–29** Josephus (Antiq. IV, 205, 240–43 [viii.8, 22]) distinguishes three tithes: one for the Levites (Num 18:20–32); the second for the Israelites to eat and enjoy in the chosen place (Deut 14:22–27); and the third granted every third year to the poor, the widows, and the orphans (Deut 14:28–29). Tobit 1:7–8 reads: "A tenth part of all my produce I would give to the sons of Levi, who officiated at Jerusalem, and another tenth I would sell, and go and spend the proceeds in Jerusalem each year, and a third I would give to those to whom it was fitting to give it, as Deborah my grandmother had instructed me." While this indicates that three tithes were known in the second century B.C., the second and third tithes are more freely interpreted than one might adduce from Deuteronomy; and this is not necessarily the correct interpretation of the data in Numbers and Deuteronomy.

**22–23** On "tenth" and the "tithe," see 12:6, 11, 17; 14:23, 28; 26:12; and the Notes on 12:6 and ZPEB, 5:756–57.

**23** On "the place he will choose," see the comment on 12:4–7.

**23–24** On "his Name," see the Notes on 12:5 and the comment on 32:3.

**25** Pieces of silver of varying weights were the medium of exchange and served much as modern money does. Coinage had not yet come into use.

The procedure of exchanging produce for silver and vice versa at the temple led to the abuse that the Lord Jesus dealt with when he forced the money changers from the temple (Matt 21:12–13; Mark 11:15–17).

---

### 2) *The year of canceling debts*

15:1–11

[1]At the end of every seven years you must cancel debts. [2]This is how it
is to be done: Every creditor shall cancel the loan he has made to his
fellow Israelite. He shall not require payment from his fellow Israelite or
brother, because the LORD's time for canceling debts has been proclaimed. [3]You may require payment from a foreigner, but you must
cancel any debt your brother owes you. [4]However, there should be no
poor among you, for in the land the LORD your God is giving you to
possess as your inheritance, he will richly bless you, [5]if only you fully
obey the LORD your God and are careful to follow all these commands I
am giving you today. [6]For the LORD your God will bless you as he has
promised, and you will lend to many nations but will borrow from none.
You will rule over many nations but none will rule over you.

[7]If there is a poor man among your brothers in any of the towns of the
land that the LORD your God is giving you, do not be hardhearted or
tightfisted toward your poor brother. [8]Rather be openhanded and freely
lend him whatever he needs. [9]Be careful not to harbor this wicked
thought: "The seventh year, the year for canceling debts, is near," so

that you do not show ill will toward your needy brother and give him
nothing. He may then appeal to the LORD against you, and you will be
found guilty of sin. 10Give generously to him and do so without a
grudging heart; then because of this the LORD your God will bless you in
all your work and in everything you put your hand to. 11There will always
be poor people in the land. Therefore I command you to be openhanded
toward your brothers and toward the poor and needy in your land.

**1–4** Whether the year for canceling debts involved a release of repayment for one year or a cancellation in perpetuity has long been debated, and the debate continues. The NIV has interpreted the regulation as a cancellation of debt (v.1). This seems most appropriate to the spirit of Deuteronomy as a whole and to this context. Israel was to have a very special internal relationship of brotherhood in its citizenry. If followed, there would be no poor, no needy among them, because of the Lord's blessing (vv.4–6, 10). The cancellation of debt would itself go a long way toward producing that blessing. It would result in the limitation of the centralization of monetary assets in the hands of the more well-to-do. No evidence exists that the Mosaic economy in its details was ever fully implemented with its sabbatical years and years of Jubilee. Fulfillment would have brought a considerable redistribution of assets and nullification of indebtedness. As an economic system, it is an interesting approach to economic and social well-being.

Though the notion that the year of release as a relaxation of payment for one year only fits well with the sabbatical year prohibitions (Lev 25:1–7, 20–22) on gathering the produce of the land (Exod 23:10–11)—when the produce was not harvested, the debtor would lack the means to pay debts—that is no proof that the release was only a year's relaxation of payment. Surely there would be more cause for one to hesitate to grant a loan that would soon be canceled than one whose repayment would be withheld for a year. Consequently, if the debt were canceled, there would be more occasion for the warning of v.9.

The assertion of v.4 that "there should be no poor" among them at first glance may seem to conflict with v.7 ("If there is a poor man among your brothers") and especially v.11 ("There will always be poor people in the land"). But the same kind of situation appears in the NT in 1 John 2:1: "I write this to you so that you will not sin. But if anybody does sin." Both Moses and John kept on proclaiming and urging the ideal situation while being doubtful that the ideal would be fully realized. Perhaps Jesus was thinking of v.11 when he said, "The poor you will always have with you" (Matt 26:11; Mark 14:7; John 12:8).

**5–6** Israel would realize the ideal situation only if the people would fully obey (infinitive absolute construction indicating intensity) the Lord. Obedience would not only bring rich blessings so that no poor would be among them, but they would also have monetary superiority over the nations around them. They would lend to many nations but borrow from none and would rule over nations but not be ruled by them. This rule over nations is either by economic control or is a military and political extension of their economic advantage.

**7–11** Moses moved into the subjective bases for the Israelites' behavior—their thoughts and emotions—when he said that they should not be hardhearted (not harden their hearts) but, conversely, openhanded (open wide their hands), freely lending a brother whatever he needs (vv.7–8). They must exercise care not to harbor a base thought that would limit generosity, such as "the year for canceling debts, is near" (v.9). This being the case, giving generously to a brother would limit the possibility of getting a beneficial return on a loan. They must give generously without a grudging heart (v.10; the Hebrew figure, an evil [?] heart, may be rendered variously to give the English equivalent of a sad or unfriendly or grudging heart).

A warning is appended: the brother can appeal to the Lord, and the grudging-hearted will be found guilty of sin. How the appeal is made is not indicated—whether it be an informal prayer or a formal petition through a priest. Likewise, the indictment "You will be found guilty of sin" (v.9) may be either one made directly by the Lord to the conscience or a formal one made by a priest (23:21–22; 24:15; cf. Lev 20:20; Num 9:13; 18:22).

## Notes

---

**1–3, 9** שְׁנַת הַשְּׁמִטָּה (*šenaṯ haššemiṭṭāh,* "year for canceling debts," v.9) is "the year of dropping, letting fall, or releasing." "Debts" comes from the context as indicated in v.2: "cancel [שָׁמוֹט, *šāmôṭ*] the loan [מַשֵּׁה, *maššēh*]."

**1** For arguments for a temporary, one-year release of debt payment, see Keil, pp. 369–70.

**4, 7** אֶבְיוֹן (*'eḇyôn,* "poor") is probably an Egyptian loan word meaning poor in the sense of needy and wretched (Ellenbogen, p. 1).

**4** The action of the infinitive absolute coupled with the imperfect verb—בָּרֵךְ יְבָרֶכְךָ (*bārēḵ yeḇāreḵā,* "he will richly bless you")— is consequent on the same construction in v.5. The Lord will honor their full obedience ("fully obey") with his rich blessings; or, Moses seems to be saying, the blessings will be absolutely certain, and they will be true benefits.

**5** שָׁמוֹעַ תִּשְׁמַע (*šāmôa' tišma',* "fully obey"), an infinitive absolute with the imperfect verb, intensifies the meaning of "obey" to "really, truly obey," as compared with simulated or half-hearted obedience, or complete obedience in contrast to partial obedience, or immediate obedience as over against hesitant obedience. The Lord demands of his people wholehearted, total, immediate obedience.

**6** In the complement and converse of this in 28:12, 44, the verb לָוָה (*lāwāh,* "lend") is not the same, but the meaning is. Among the curses that would fall on disobedient Israel is economic debasement. Aliens among them would lend to them, but Israel would not have the resources to lend to aliens (v.44).

---

### 3) Freeing servants

#### 15:12–18

[12]If a fellow Hebrew, a man or a woman, sells himself to you and
serves you six years, in the seventh year you must let him go free. [13]And
when you release him, do not send him away empty-handed. [14]Supply
him liberally from your flock, your threshing floor and your winepress.
Give to him as the LORD your God has blessed you. [15]Remember that you
were slaves in Egypt and the LORD your God redeemed you. That is why I
give you this command today.

[16]But if your servant says to you, "I do not want to leave you,"
because he loves you and your family and is well off with you, [17]then
take an awl and push it through his ear lobe into the door, and he will
become your servant for life. Do the same for your maidservant.

> 18 Do not consider it a hardship to set your servant free, because his service to you these six years has been worth twice as much as that of a hired hand. And the LORD your God will bless you in everything you do.

**12–18** Concern for the poor relates also to one's attitude toward those who are in servitude, for servitude among Israelites was usually due to poverty. That such persons should go free after no more than six years of bondage had already been given in Exodus 21:2–6. One's liberality should go beyond manumission. The manumitted should be given liberal supplies from their former owner's flock, threshingfloor, and winepress. Remembering that they were redeemed by the Lord from slavery in Egypt, they were to give liberally of their possessions to manumitted servants, as God had blessed them.

If a servant did not want to be set free, the master was to push an awl through the lobe of his ear and into the door or doorpost (v.17), thereby marking him for a life of servitude. Exodus 21:6 mentions that the servant is first brought publicly to the judges and then has his ear attached with an awl to the door or doorpost. Neither Exodus nor Deuteronomy reveals where this is done.

Two reasons for this choice of life servitude are given (v.16): love for the master and the well-being of the servant under the master. In Exodus 21:5 love for one's wife and children acquired during servitude constitutes an additional reason. The servant who does not want to leave his wife and children, as the law required, chooses life servitude instead.

After speaking about servants who do not want to be set free (vv.16–17), the subject of attitude to freed servants appears again (v.18). Anticipating possible reaction to this largess required of the master, the Israelites were advised not to consider this action a hardship but rather to realize that the indentured servant during his six years of servitude has been worth twice as much as a hired hand. How he was worth twice as much is not said. Some suggest that such indentured servants worked twice as long each day as hands hired for the day. Others suppose that they worked twice as hard, and still others that six years of service is double what was required elsewhere; that is, two times three years. The text seems to say only that such a servant was worth twice as much as a hired hand (double the hire). Perhaps what is meant is that through the years the servant's labor was equivalent to that of a hired hand (see Notes) yet he had not received the daily wage of a hired hand. He had, however, worked off his debt. Thus the servant was worth double because the owner not only had the service of the servant, but he did not have to pay out anything for that service as he would have for a hired hand.

## Notes

---

**12–18** This slave law or emancipation law in Deuteronomy differs in some respects from that of Exod 21:2–11. In Deuteronomy women have certain legal rights including possession of property given them when they are emancipated. Also in Deuteronomy the maidservant has the same right as men, while in Exodus a daughter sold into servitude "is not to go free as menservants do"(v.7). Under certain situations, however, they are to go free (v.11), and they may be redeemed (v.8). The variations appear to be due to the situation the people faced as they looked toward the new life in Canaan (see Boecker, pp. 181–83).

**12** אָחִיךָ הָעִבְרִי (*'āhîkā hā'ibrî*, "fellow Hebrew") is literally "your brother, a Hebrew"—the article merely denotes a gentilic—and surely means an Israelite. Deuteronomy concerns itself with Israelites as brothers, and the notion of showing such liberality to foreigners when released from servitude to Israelites goes beyond the general attitude toward non-Israelites in this historical context. See TWOT, 2:641–42. For contrary opinion see David O'Brien, "David the Hebrew," JETS 23, 3 (September 1980): 197, and Thompson, pp. 189–90.

**14** הַעֲנֵיק תַּעֲנִיק (*ha'anêq ta'anîq*, "supply liberally") is a Hebrew figure for liberality that literally means "you should make a rich necklace," i.e., "be liberal with gifts."

**15** On "redeemed" see the Notes on 9:26.

**17** The law in Exod 21:6 says that first the servant is brought "before the judges, אֶל־הָאֱלֹהִים (*'el-hā'elōhîm*), which may mean "to God," i.e., to the sanctuary. See also Exod 22:8–9.

עֶבֶד עוֹלָם (*'ebed 'ôlām*, "servant for life"), according to Josephus (Antiq. IV, 273 [viii.28]) and others, was limited to the period before the Jubilee so that after every fifty years even those who chose to remain with masters were manumitted (Lev 25:39–46). This is purely theoretical; the laws relating to Jubilee appear never to have been implemented.

**18** Instead of "six years" the Code of Hammurabi has "three" (see ANET, p. 171).

If the מִשְׁנֶה (*mišneh*, "twice as much") reflects *mištannu* in the texts from Alalakh, then "equivalent to" would be the sense (D.J. Wiseman, NBD, p. 67). However, the Babylonian Code of Lipit-Ishtar allows the manumission of a slave after giving service amounting to twice his debt, or when he pays twice his purchase price (ANET, pp. 159–61).

---

### 4) Firstborn animals

#### 15:19–23

[19]Set apart for the LORD your God every firstborn male of your herds and flocks. Do not put the firstborn of your oxen to work, and do not shear the firstborn of your sheep. [20]Each year you and your family are to eat them in the presence of the LORD your God at the place he will choose. [21]If an animal has a defect, is lame or blind, or has any serious flaw, you must not sacrifice it to the LORD your God. [22]You are to eat it in your own towns. Both the ceremonially unclean and the clean may eat it, as if it were gazelle or deer. [23]But you must not eat the blood; pour it out on the ground like water.

**19–23** Reference had already been made to offering firstborn males (12:6, 17; 14:23). The firstborn of herds and flocks were to be brought to the place the Lord would choose to put his Name, and there in the Lord's presence the people were to eat and rejoice. It is specified in 12:7 and 12 that they, their sons and daughters, menservants, maidservants, and Levites were to eat and rejoice in that place. In 14:23–26 directions are given for conversion of the tithes into money for reconversion into food and drink in the place the Lord chooses, if that is necessary. Now it is said that the firstborn of herds should not be worked and the firstborn of sheep not sheared (v.19). They belong to the Lord and are not to be used secularly or for private gain. In Numbers 18:8–19 certain parts of the firstborn animals are given to the priests and their families, and nothing is said of the general populace eating with the priests. That Numbers would specify what is now referred to in this more general way in the speeches of Deuteronomy is not surprising. Numbers mentions the priests, for instance, while Deuteronomy speaks of the Levites, the priestly tribe.

All the people were to eat and rejoice together at the annual festivals (v.20). The regulations of Deuteronomy are, generally, given to all the people, including the priests. The logistics of consuming all the specified parts of all the firstborn of herds and flocks annually might well demand the participation of the whole populace at these specified periods.

The animals with serious defects were not to be sacrificed (v.21); they were to be eaten as common food by the people, whether the people were ceremonially clean or unclean (v.22). The constant prohibition against eating blood with the meat remained in effect always (v.23). The blood must be poured out on the ground like water. These regulations emphasize anew that God's people were to follow a holy way of living.

## Notes

---

**19–23** The consecration of all the firstborn of men and animals rests on the historic occurrence of the plague of death of the firstborn in Egypt (Exod 12:12, 29; 13:1–2).

**23** On "you must not eat the blood," see the comment on 12:16.

---

### 5) *Passover*

16:1–8

1 Observe the month of Abib and celebrate the Passover of the LORD
your God, because in the month of Abib he brought you out of Egypt by
night. 2 Sacrifice as the Passover to the LORD your God an animal from
your flock or herd at the place the LORD will choose as a dwelling for his
Name. 3 Do not eat it with bread made with yeast, but for seven days eat
unleavened bread, the bread of affliction, because you left Egypt in
haste—so that all the days of your life you may remember the time of
your departure from Egypt. 4 Let no yeast be found in your possession in
all your land for seven days. Do not let any of the meat you sacrifice on
the evening of the first day remain until morning.

5 You must not sacrifice the Passover in any town the LORD your God
gives you 6 except in the place he will choose as a dwelling for his Name.
There you must sacrifice the Passover in the evening, when the sun
goes down, on the anniversary of your departure from Egypt. 7 Roast it
and eat it at the place the LORD your God will choose. Then in the
morning return to your tents. 8 For six days eat unleavened bread and on
the seventh day hold an assembly to the LORD your God and do no work.

**1–4** The directions for the three pilgrimage festivals—Passover-Unleavened Bread, Weeks, and Tabernacles (Booths, Lev 23:42–43)—vary somewhat from those in Exodus 23:14–19, Leviticus 23, and Numbers 28:16–29:38. But the variations are consonant with the character of the books. In Deuteronomy the whole Passover Festival is in mind, including the Feast of Unleavened Bread, and so the sacrificing of the Passover animal (or animals) includes the sacrifices of animals from the herd as well as the sacrifice of a lamb from the flock for the main Passover meal.

Moreover, the Passover, which began as the culmination of the Egyptian residence and was at that time observed in the homes (tents) of the people (Exod 12:1–28), soon, when they were settled in the land, was to be held in the place the Lord would "choose as a dwelling for his Name" (v.2). The historical occasion for the Passover now would have an added significance—that of the agricultural year, in conjunction with the other major festivals.

The yeast (or leaven of any kind) is said to be suggestive of decay and, consequently, not fitted for the symbolism of the Passover; but in this text bread without yeast, the bread of affliction, a reference to the affliction the people experienced in Egypt (Exod 3:7), was to be eaten because they had left Egypt in apprehensive haste. Unleavened bread can be made in less time than leavened bread (and it keeps better); so it is reminiscent of the precipitate nature of their departure from Egypt after the death of the firstborn of the Egyptians (v.3). Bread needed at once occurs in the narrative of Lot feeding the angelic visitors in Sodom (Gen 19:3), Gideon preparing a meal for the Angel of the Lord while he waited under the oak in Ophrah (Judg 6:19–21), and the spiritist-medium of Endor fixing a meal for Saul and his men after the confrontation with Samuel (1 Sam 28:24).

The statement "so that all the days of your life you may remember the time of your departure from Egypt" (v.3) makes it clear that the date of the Passover Feast rests on a historical basis rather than on the agricultural year. "All the days of your life" (and similar phrases) is a Hebrew idiom for the lifetime of an individual or a series of individuals or the nation's whole existence (4:9–10; 6:2; 12:1; 17:19; 31:13). "Day" or "time" is used in v.3 for the time of their departure from Egypt, while in v.6 a "set" or "appointed time"(*mô'ēḏ*) is used, supported by "in the evening, when the sun goes down." A set time could conceivably refer to the hour of the day (S.R. Driver, *Deuteronomy*) or, as the NIV translates, to "the anniversary" (so also NAB), with which the analogy of the set annual feasts in Leviticus 23 would agree.

"On the evening of the first day" (v.4) by Hebrew calculation, which counts the evening as the beginning of the day, would be the beginning of the fifteenth of Nisan (March/April) (Lev 23:6).

**5–8** After eating the main Passover meal, the people were to return to the places where they were staying; that is, where they were staying during their visit to the place the Lord would choose (v.6). The Passover meal was complete in itself; none of the meat sacrificed in the evening was to remain until the morning.

"To your tents" (v.7) as a Hebrew idiom for going to one's dwelling (whether temporary or permanent) continued in use for many years after Israel had settled in towns and no longer used tents (2 Kings 8:21; 13:5; 14:12; the NIV renders each occurrence as "home[s]"). The Passover-Unleavened Bread Festival ended with a special closing assembly (v.8).

In the NT the last Passover that Jesus ate with his disciples became the Lord's Supper (Matt 26:17–29; Mark 14:12–25; Luke 22:7–22), and Christ's death on the cross became the Passover sacrifice to take away sin (1 Cor 5:7–8; cf. John 1:29).

## Notes

---

**1–17** The three festivals—Passover-Unleavened Bread, Weeks, and Tabernacles (Booths)—are חַגִּים (*ḥaggîm*, "pilgrim festivals"), from חָגַג (*ḥāg̲ag̲*, "to leap, dance," "to walk in procession," or "to keep a pilgrimage feast"). The Ārabic *ḥajj* is commonly used of a pilgrimage to Mecca (KB, pp. 275–76).

**2** In v.16 Passover is not mentioned in the list of festivals; the first festival listed is the Feast of Unleavened Bread, חַג הַמַּצּוֹת (*ḥag hammaṣṣôṯ*), which is part of the Passover Festival.

**2, 6, 11** On the use of the Name of the Lord, see the comment on 32:3.

**3** The emphasis on the place where the festivals were to take place, as seen in the sixfold occurrence in this chapter of "the place the LORD will choose" (vv.2, 6–7, 11, 15–16) and the threefold mention of "before the LORD your God" (vv.11, 16 bis), may lend credence to the suggestion of Dahood (followed by Craigie, p. 242) that עָלָיו (*'ālāyw*) should be translated "in his presence," though this is doubtful. If *'ālāyw* is to be so rendered, the verse would begin: "Do not eat bread made with yeast [חָמֵץ, *ḥāmēṣ*] in his presence; for seven days eat bread without yeast [מַצּוֹת, *maṣṣôṯ*], the bread of affliction, in his presence."

On the meaning of בְּחִפָּזוֹן (*beḥippāzôn*, "in haste"), notice the use of the verb in 20:3, where it means "being apprehensive, frightened, or alarmed," and where the NIV has "do not be terrified." Here it is "apprehensive haste."

**7** The word בָּשַׁל (*bāšal*, "roast") means "to cook." How the cooking is to be done can only be discerned from the context or from other accounts of the same experience. Exodus 12:9 indicates that in this instance "roast" is meant (so also in 2 Chron 35:13, where *bāšal* refers to roasting with fire).

**8** An עֲצֶרֶת (*'aṣereṯ*, "assembly") to the Lord is called in Exod 13:6 a חַג (*ḥag*, "festival"); in Exod 12:16; Lev 23:7–8; and Num 28:18, 25, it is called a מִקְרָא־קֹדֶשׁ (*miqrā'-qōḏeš*, "sacred assembly," "holy gathering"). The word *'aṣereṯ* comes from a root signifying "to restrain, hold in, confine, or enclose," and from the sense of enclosing the festival means "closing assembly." It is used to identify the last day of the Feast of Unleavened Bread here and the last day of the Feast of Tabernacles (Booths) in Lev 23:36, where the NIV translates it "closing assembly."

---

### 6) *Feast of Weeks*

#### 16:9–12

[9]Count off seven weeks from the time you begin to put the sickle to the standing grain. [10]Then celebrate the Feast of Weeks to the LORD your God by giving a freewill offering in proportion to the blessings the LORD your God has given you. [11]And rejoice before the LORD your God at the place he will choose as a dwelling for his Name—you, your sons and daughters, your menservants and maidservants, the Levites in your towns, and the aliens, the fatherless and the widows living among you. [12]Remember that you were slaves in Egypt, and follow carefully these decrees.

**9–12** The accounts of the Feast of Weeks are elsewhere given in Exodus 23:16 (where it is called the Feast of Harvest); 34:22; Leviticus 23:15–20; and Numbers 28:26–31, where it is "the day of firstfruits" as well as the Feast of Weeks.

This feast was to begin seven weeks from the time the sickle was put to the standing grain (v.9). More specifically, Leviticus 23:15 says that the count was to be made from "the day after the Sabbath, the day you brought the sheaf of the wave offering," which was on the second day of the Passover Festival (Abib 16). The phrase "fifty days" in Leviticus 23:16 in the LXX led to the designation of the Feast of Weeks as Pentecost. It falls on Sivan 6 (May/June).

The Feast of Weeks was a harvest celebration, and the freewill offering made at that time was to be commensurate with the blessing the Lord had given the people (v.10; cf. vv.16–17).

In the NT the Feast of Weeks becomes significant as the time of the outpouring of the Holy Spirit in fulfillment of the prophecy of Joel 2:28–32 and the beginning of the church in the NT. (For a discussion on the relationship of the Feast of Weeks with Pentecost in Acts 2, see R. Longenecker, EBC, 9:268–71.)

## Notes

---

**9** The LXX's πεντήκοντα ἡμέρας (*pentēkonta hēmeras,* "fifty days") in Lev 23:16 was the basis for the later designation ἡ ἡμέρα τῆς πεντηκοστῆς (*hē hēmera tēs pentēkostēs,* "the day of Pentecost").

**10** מִסַּת (*missat,* "proportion") occurs only here in the Hebrew, but in the Aramaic it occurs extrabiblically as "sufficiency." The sense is clear from the context.

---

### 7) *Feast of Tabernacles*

16:13–17

[13]Celebrate the Feast of Tabernacles for seven days after you have gathered the produce of your threshing floor and your winepress. [14]Be joyful at your Feast—you, your sons and daughters, your menservants and maidservants, and the Levites, the aliens, the fatherless and the widows who live in your towns. [15]For seven days celebrate the Feast to the LORD your God at the place the LORD will choose. For the LORD your God will bless you in all your harvest and in all the work of your hands, and your joy will be complete.

[16]Three times a year all your men must appear before the LORD your God at the place he will choose: at the Feast of Unleavened Bread, the Feast of Weeks and the Feast of Tabernacles. No man should appear before the LORD empty-handed: [17]Each of you must bring a gift in proportion to the way the LORD your God has blessed you.

**13–17** The Feast of Tabernacles or Booths is celebrated for seven days after the processing of the grain at the threshing floor and the grapes in the winepress (v.13). In Exodus 23:16 and 34:22, it is called the Feast of Ingathering; and the time of the feast is more explicitly given in Leviticus 23:34, 36, 39, and Numbers 29:12 as extending from the fifteenth to the twenty-first of the seventh month, which is Tishri (Sept./Oct.). It was followed by an additional day with an assembly (or closing assembly; see Notes on v.8). This seven-day feast was for everybody (v.14). The populace was urged to be joyful at the feast; and because of God's blessing on the work of their hands, their joy would be complete (v.15).

A summary and reiteration of the command that all Israelite men were to appear before the Lord for these three festivals annually concludes this review (v.16). One was not to attend the festivals empty-handed; he was to bring a contribution proportionate to the Lord's blessing on his labor (v.17).

## Notes

---

**15** "Your joy will be complete" is a positive way of translating אַךְ שָׂמֵחַ (*'ak śāmēaḥ,* "only joy," "nothing but joy," or "unmixed joy").

---

## 2. *National concerns (16:18–19:21)*

### a. *Judges*

#### 16:18–20

> 18 Appoint judges and officials for each of your tribes in every town the
> LORD your God is giving you, and they shall judge the people fairly. 19 Do
> not pervert justice or show partiality. Do not accept a bribe, for a bribe
> blinds the eyes of the wise and twists the words of the righteous.
> 20 Follow justice and justice alone, so that you may live and possess the
> land the LORD your God is giving you.

**18–20** Verses 18–20 begin a section that concerns itself with Israel's judicial system and is more fittingly attached to chapter 17.

In modern societies with tripartite governments of executive, legislative, and judicial branches, ancient Israel's government system appears less than clearly defined. One must remember, however, that a strong, patriarchal substratum with its tribal traditions and practices existed in Israel.

At first Moses was the sole judge for the people. At Sinai other judges as assistants were provided (1:9–18; Exod 18:13–26). Here, however, when the nation was contemplating the new settlement in Canaan, further arrangements were necessary; so Moses instructed the people to appoint "judges" and other "officials" in every town the Lord was about to give them (v.18).

These "judges" were civil magistrates, not like those in the Book of Judges, where judges were not limited to their towns nor were restricted to magisterial activities but were often military leaders and sometimes, at least, area or national chieftains, though not kings.

The "officials" were subordinate leaders who implemented the decisions of the judges. The word used can depict subordinates in the military and in other spheres of communal life (20:5, 8–9; 29:10; 2 Chron 19:11; 34:13 [NIV, "secretaries"]).

The specifics following v.18 were both for the judges particularly and the populace generally, as can be seen from the observation that the judges were to "judge the people fairly"; and the people were admonished to follow justice alone, so that they would be able to continue living as a nation in possession of the land (v.20).

The judges were not to pervert (twist) justice or show partiality (v.19). A bribe was not to be accepted, because a bribe blinds the eyes of the wise and twists the words of the righteous. Pure justice is required. The Lord demands ethical dealings of the highest order.

## Notes

---

**18** The שֹׁפְטִים (*šōp̱eṭîm,* "judges") served strictly within the judicial system. Later the *šōp̱eṭîm* of the Book of Judges were often political and military leaders as well—and sometimes primarily so (TWOT, pp. 947–48).

שֹׁטְרִים (*šōṭerîm,* "officials") were subordinate leaders of various kinds. "Secretaries" may be a more original sense, being an Akkadian loan word meaning a writer of documents—a sense basic to the work given to Israelite foremen by the Egyptians. See Exod 5 ("foremen," passim); TWOT, pp. 918–19; and Ellenbogen, p. 161.

בְּכָל־שְׁעָרֶיךָ (*bekol-še'āreykā*, "in all your gates") is Hebrew idiom for "in all your towns" (cities)—equal to city halls(?).

**19** "Show partiality" renders the Hebrew figure "recognize faces" (Exod 23:3; Lev 19:15; 2 Chron 19:7; Ps 82:2; Prov 18:5; Mal 2:9).

The latter half of v.19 is verbatim for Exod 23:8, except that Exodus has פִּקְחִים (*piqḥîm*, "open-eyed"; NIV, "those who see") instead of עֵינֵי חֲכָמִים (*'ênê ḥakāmîm*, "the eyes of the wise").

The bribe "twists," סָלַף (*sālap*), a word that NIV variously translates: "overthrows" (Prov 13:6); "ruin" (Prov 19:13; 21:12); "frustrates" (Prov 22:12)—all of which express the idea of "to render a thing ineffective."

דִּבְרֵי (*dibrê*, "words of [the righteous]") in judicial references like this means "the case of [the righteous in court]."

**20** The Hebrew repetition צֶדֶק צֶדֶק (*ṣedeq ṣedeq*, "justice, justice") is a way of emphasis. It could be rendered "real justice" or, as in the NIV, "justice and justice alone." Muilenburg (*Way of Israel*, p. 71) says: "Nowhere is the demand for justice more impassioned and stirring than in Deuteronomy." He then translates the beginning of v.20 as "justice, only justice you must pursue" (ibid.).

---

### b. *Asherah poles, sacred stones, and flawed animals*

#### 16:21–17:1

**[21]Do not set up any wooden Asherah pole beside the altar you build to the LORD your God, [22]and do not erect a sacred stone, for these the LORD your God hates.**

**[17:1]Do not sacrifice to the LORD your God an ox or a sheep that has any defect or flaw in it, for that would be detestable to him.**

**16:21–17:1** The mind of the speaker returned momentarily to the idolatry Israel would find in Canaan, and once more he warned against using an Asherah pole or a sacred stone in their worship (vv.21–22). The worship of the Lord must not be with the paraphernalia of the gods of Canaan in an eclecticism that would allow Asherah poles and sacred stones alongside the altar of the Lord who hates those items of worship.

Central to the covenant-treaty of Deuteronomy is the relation of the people to the Lord. An important element in proper worship was the quality of the offerings brought to him—offerings that would indicate the esteem the worshipers showed toward him. In 15:21 the firstborn offered had to be without "serious flaw," and in Leviticus "without defect" (Lev 1:3 et al.) or "perfect." This rule is here applied to the sacrifice of any ox or sheep (17:1).

## Notes

---

**21–22** On Asherah poles and sacred stones, see 7:5; 12:3; and S.R. Driver, *Deuteronomy*, pp. 201–4; Albright, *Archaeology*, pp. 73–78; and Bratton, *Myths and Legends in the Ancient Near East*, pp. 109–29.

---

### c. *Procedures for punishment of covenant violators*

#### 17:2–13

[2]If a man or woman living among you in one of the towns the LORD
gives you is found doing evil in the eyes of the LORD your God in
violation of his covenant, [3]and contrary to my command has worshiped
other gods, bowing down to them or to the sun or the moon or the stars
of the sky, [4]and this has been brought to your attention, then you must
investigate it thoroughly. If it is true and it has been proved that this
detestable thing has been done in Israel, [5]take the man or woman who
has done this evil deed to your city gate and stone that person to death.
[6]On the testimony of two or three witnesses a man shall be put to death,
but no one shall be put to death on the testimony of only one witness.
[7]The hands of the witnesses must be the first in putting him to death,
and then the hands of all the people. You must purge the evil from
among you.

[8]If cases come before your courts that are too difficult for you to
judge—whether bloodshed, lawsuits or assaults—take them to the
place the LORD your God will choose. [9]Go to the priests, who are Levites,
and to the judge who is in office at that time. Inquire of them and they
will give you the verdict. [10]You must act according to the decisions they
give you at the place the LORD will choose. Be careful to do everything
they direct you to do. [11]Act according to the law they teach you and the
decisions they give you. Do not turn aside from what they tell you, to the
right or to the left. [12]The man who shows contempt for the judge or for
the priest who stands ministering there to the LORD your God must be
put to death. You must purge the evil from Israel. [13]All the people will
hear and be afraid, and will not be contemptuous again.

**2–3** How are deviations from the worship of the Lord to be handled? Such deviant worship is called "doing evil in the eyes of the LORD," a "violation of his covenant" (v.2), and "contrary to my command" (v.3). Specifically, the worship of other gods consists of "bowing down to them" or "to the sun or the moon or the stars of the sky" (v.3). The reference to the sun or the moon certainly suggests that the rendering "stars of the sky" accurately indicates physical phenomena as the sun and moon do. This is not to say that the sun, moon, and stars were not symbols of gods or even thought to be gods by the nations round about. Israel was not to worship the sun, moon, and stars of the sky either as physical entities or as representations of pagan deities. In OT theology the sun, moon, and stars along with other physical elements—as mountains and seas—show the glory of the Lord; but they are by no means idolatrous, pantheistic, or animistic representations of the Lord (Pss 8:3; 19:1; 148:3–6; Jer 10:10–13; see also Rom 1:20).

**4–13** Any alleged case of deviation from the worship of the Lord should be thoroughly investigated (v.4). If the allegation proves true (as in 13:14) on testimony of two or three witnesses—one witness being insufficient (v.6)—the guilty party is to be stoned to death (v.5), the witnesses being the first to throw stones (v.7). The seriousness of this defection and the purpose of the punishment are seen in the declaration, "You must purge the evil from among you (Israel)" (vv.7, 12).

The place the Lord will choose is to be the juridical as well as the spiritual, social, and political center of the nation (cf. 16:18–20; Matt 18:16). The categories of cases cover generally the whole corpus of criminal and civil law. The Hebrew forms "between blood and blood," "between lawsuit and lawsuit," and "between assault and assault" mean any kind of bloodshed, lawsuit, or assault (v.8). All cases too difficult for lower local court decision were to be taken to the priests and the current judge at the chosen center for decisions (vv.8–9). Their decision was final and was to be followed in detail. No ameliorating or avoiding of strict adherence to their decision was to be tolerated (vv.10–11). Contempt of court was a capital offense (v.12). It is said that when these procedures are followed, "all the people will hear and be afraid, and will not be contemptuous again" (v.13)—obviously referring to the general public, which had heard of the death penalty being exacted. As in 13:11, the Lawgiver plainly asserted that capital punishment would be a deterrent to crime.

The local judges were to appeal (perhaps together with the litigants) to the higher court. They were not to decide in the cases that were appealed to the higher court; they simply decided to refer the case to the higher court for decision, and that decision was then implemented by the local judges. The tenor of the law as given, however, places the responsibility for the application of the law on the whole populace. "The man who shows contempt" (v.12) may not only be the local judge who does not want to exact punishment decided by the priests and the judge in the place the Lord would choose; such a man may be anyone in Israel—as is obvious from the idea that none of the people will be "contemptuous" (v.13) when they learn of the one in contempt being put to death.

## Notes

---

**6** "Two or three witnesses" was a standard requirement (19:15; cf. Exod 20:16; 23:1; see also Matt 18:16; 2 Cor 13:1). Notice especially Boecker's work.

**7** The hands of the witnesses were to be the first to administer punishment (cf. John 8:7). See the comment on 13:6–11.

**7, 12** When Paul told the Corinthian church members that they should expel the wicked man from among them, he quoted this injunction, which appears, with slight variation, nine times in Deuteronomy. The NIV margin on 1 Cor 5:13 cites only the passages that have ἐξαίρω (*exairō*, "to expel") as the verb, though the Pauline citation has the second person plural form while the LXX for Deuteronomy has the verb in the singular. For some unknown reason the LXX has a synonym, ἀφανιεῖς (*aphanieis*, "to put out of view"), in Deut 13:5; so it is not cited in the 1 Cor 5:13 margin. The Hebrew text has the same verbal form in all nine instances. The translation from the MT, "You must purge the evil from among you," could also be the translation of the LXX and the NT in 1 Cor 5:13. See the comment on 13:1–5.

**8** יִפָּלֵא מִמְּךָ (*yippālē' mimmeḵā*, "too difficult [wonderful] for you") signifies something beyond their knowledge or ability to handle. For "too difficult," "too wonderful," or "too hard," see Gen 18:14; Deut 30:11; Job 42:3; Ps 131:1; Jer 32:17.

**9** This first occurrence of הַכֹּהֲנִים הַלְוִיִּם (*hakkōhanîm halewîyim*, "the priests, the Levites") is translated by the NIV as "the priests, who are Levites" to suggest positively that the priests were of the tribe of Levi and negatively that there were no other priests, as the phrase "the Levitical priests" might suggest.

In Deuteronomy priests are sometimes called simply כֹּהֲנִים (*kōhanîm*, "priests"); sometimes הַכֹּהֲנִים הַלְוִיִּם (*hakkōhanîm halewîyim*, "the priests who are Levites"); and at other times הַכֹּהֲנִים בְּנֵי לֵוִי (*hakkōhanîm benê lēwî*, "the priests, the sons of Levi"), *benê lēwî* being another way of indicating a gentilic, and therefore equal to "the priests who are Levites" (ZPEB, 4:853ff.; WBE, pp. 1394ff.; NBD, pp. 1029, 1033).

## d. *Appointment of and rules for a king*

### 17:14–20

**14When you enter the land the LORD your God is giving you and have
taken possession of it and settled in it, and you say, "Let us set a king
over us like all the nations around us," 15be sure to appoint over you the
king the LORD your God chooses. He must be from among your own
brothers. Do not place a foreigner over you, one who is not a brother
Israelite. 16The king, moreover, must not acquire great numbers of
horses for himself or make the people return to Egypt to get more of
them, for the LORD has told you, "You are not to go back that way
again." 17He must not take many wives, or his heart will be led astray. He
must not accumulate large amounts of silver and gold.**

**18When he takes the throne of his kingdom, he is to write for himself
on a scroll a copy of this law, taken from that of the priests, who are
Levites. 19It is to be with him, and he is to read it all the days of his life so
that he may learn to revere the LORD his God and follow carefully all the
words of this law and these decrees 20and not consider himself better
than his brothers and turn from the law to the right or to the left. Then
he and his descendants will reign a long time over his kingdom in Israel.**

**14–15** Attention turns to the concept of a kingship for Israel, a subject not elsewhere mentioned in the Pentateuch. Supreme leadership in Israel, and, for that matter, the whole structure of government for Israel, rests on the idea of theocracy; the Lord, not man, was their leader.

It was not until the latter days of Samuel that the kingdom of Israel was first instituted under Saul. Prior to that human representatives of the Lord in the sphere of government in all Hebrew life avoided the term "king" as well as the idea of kingship (with the exception of the usurper Abimelech, Judg 9). Moses, in spite of his authoritative position, was not a king. Joshua, his successor, received an appointment charismatically, as did Moses. The judges that followed were not kings, though the Hebrew for "judge" may lean to some degree in that direction.

Here in Deuteronomy the possible future institution of kingship comes not as a command. It does not rise out of the Lord's immediate plan for government but out of a supposition that the people will want a king because the surrounding peoples had kings. It would appear from this text that the Lord's purposes would be thwarted should Israel ask for a king, even as later experience in the time of Samuel shows (1 Sam 8:4–9).

Nevertheless, the Lord, in developing revelation, revealed his eternal plan of using kingship as the vehicle of central importance in messianic prophecy and fulfillment. It is evident that the supreme, eternal rulership of the Lord, as enunciated, for instance, in the Song of Moses and Israel at the crossing of the Red Sea (Exod 15:18), can be proclaimed either with or without a human representative. This legislation exercises controls for the foreseen desires of the people. Given that desire, they were to find the king the Lord would choose (v.15). How the choice was to be made is not said, but the field was narrowed by the specification that he must be a brother Israelite.

**16–17** Restrictions too were placed on the king: (1) he must not acquire many horses (v.16); (2) he must not take many wives (v.17a); (3) he must not accumulate much silver and gold (v.17b); (4) he must adhere to the law (vv.18–19); and (5), as a corollary, he must not consider himself better than the people (v.20).

The accumulation of horses is linked to the prohibition that the people were not to return to Egypt (v.16). Egyptians dealt in horse trading. Having many horses signified either riches or military resources or both. Doubtless both indicated a reliance on one's own resources rather than more direct reliance on the Lord.

A large harem of many wives also represented a likeness to the Oriental courts of other kingdoms, and having many wives envisaged the usual procedure of acquiring those wives from families of other kings and so sealing treaties by marriage. Such wives would bring the impact of foreign cultures into the palace, particularly the worship of other gods, and so lead the heart of the king astray (v.17).

The accumulation of ever larger amounts of silver and gold would also tend toward reliance on riches rather than on the Lord. Later history—especially the experience of Solomon (1 Kings 10:1–11:13)—illustrates the wisdom of these prohibitions.

**18–20** Following the procedures for vassal treaties, a copy of the covenant-treaty including all its stipulations, warnings, etc., was deposited in the dwelling of the Lord (see comments and Notes on 10:1–5; cf. 31:9, 24–26). From this the king was to make a copy for himself and keep the copy with him, reading it regularly (vv.18–19). This preoccupation with the "words of this law" had a threefold purpose—that the king may (1) learn to serve the Lord, (2) follow carefully all the words of the law and its decrees, and (3) keep on the same level as his brothers before the law of the Lord. The result of this behavior would be a long reign (v.20).

It has been charged that these observations are idealistic and impractical, but no such notion is implied in the text of Deuteronomy. Even though the subsequent history of Israel, especially in the kingdom period, lacks evidence that the kings followed these injunctions, that failure is no basis for supposing such impracticality. The history of Israel is replete with illustrations showing that when Israel's kings went astray of the laws of the Lord, they were punished; but when they followed the dictates of the Lord (including those written beforehand), they were successful—illustrated by such common phrases as "he did evil in the eyes of the LORD" (1 Kings 15:26), "he . . . walked in the ways of his father David" (2 Chron 34:2), and "just as his father David had done" (2 Chron 29:2). This is the interpretation that the historical writers as well as the prophets and psalmists placed on the events.

## Notes

**14** מֶלֶךְ (*melek*, "king") comes into approved usage for Israel in the OT during Samuel's time, and even then—in agreement with this prediction here—both Samuel and the Lord indicate that kingship was not really approved (1 Sam 8:6–9; 10:17–19). Only under David was kingship seized on as ideal, and then it became a vehicle of messianic expectation. The Lord as king, however, remains a key ideal in both current and messianic rule.

**17** Ancient Near Eastern history is loaded with illustrations of kings giving daughters in marriage to other kings for security reasons or for control of other lands. The effects of Solomon's many marriage alliances are summarized in Leon Wood, *A Survey of Israel's History* (Grand Rapids: Zondervan, 1970), p. 293. First Kings 11:1–11 speaks of the adverse results of Solomon's wives' presence. The marriage of Ahab and Jezebel illustrates the evil inherent in such alliances.

On יָסוּר לְבָבוֹ (*yāsûr lᵉbābô*, "his heart will be led astray"), see 4:9; 28:14.

**18** This verse does not mean that the king wrote the copy himself. See comment on 10:1–5.

Kline (*Biblical Authority*, pp. 27–28) says that the treaty tablet played a central role in the preservation of the covenant. Duplicates were made for the parties to the covenant-treaty, and the several copies were each deposited in the presence of the gods of the states involved. Periodically they were taken out and publicly read in the vassal kingdom. See also 10:2; 31:9, 24–26.

The phrase מִשְׁנֵה הַתּוֹרָה (*mišnēh hattôrāh,* "a copy of this law"), which was mistranslated in the LXX as *τὸ δευτερονόμιον τοῦτο* (*to deuteronomion touto,* "the second law") and followed by the Vulgate, was the basis for the English name for the book as "Deuteronomy." See the Introduction: Name.

As a result of failing to follow carefully the law, notice the mistake David made when he first attempted to bring the ark of the covenant to Jerusalem and the correction of that mistake at the second and successful attempt (1 Chron 13:1–10; 15:2, 13).

---

## e. *Shares for priests and Levites*

### 18:1–8

**[1]The priests, who are Levites—indeed the whole tribe of Levi—are to have no allotment or inheritance with Israel. They shall live on the offerings made to the LORD by fire, for that is their inheritance. [2]They shall have no inheritance among their brothers; the LORD is their inheritance, as he promised them.**

**[3]This is the share due the priests from the people who sacrifice a bull or a sheep: the shoulder, the jowls and the inner parts. [4]You are to give them the firstfruits of your grain, new wine and oil, and the first wool from the shearing of your sheep, [5]for the LORD your God has chosen them and their descendants out of all your tribes to stand and minister in the LORD's name always.**

**[6]If a Levite moves from one of your towns anywhere in Israel where he is living, and comes in all earnestness to the place the LORD will choose, [7]he may minister in the name of the LORD his God like all his fellow Levites who serve there in the presence of the LORD. [8]He is to share equally in their benefits, even though he has received money from the sale of family possessions.**

**1** A wide, sweeping presentation (common throughout the Deuteronomic review)—a presentation telling of the support of the Levites—is added to the stipulations relative to judges and possible kings. The designations the "priests," the "Levites," and the "whole tribe of Levi" indicate that the priests and Levites were not always coextensive terms; the "priests" were those Levites who were the descendants of Aaron, and the "Levites" included all those who belonged to the tribe of Levi, whether or not they were descendants of Aaron (Num 18:20, 23–24).

**2** The Levites as a tribe were not to have a tribal allotment in Canaan, as the other tribes would have. The Lord was their inheritance, that is, as far as material possessions were concerned. Their special relationship to the Lord brought with it a share of that which belonged to the Lord in Israelite economy. They would have certain cities within the boundaries of some other tribes and, under certain situations, could also have private holdings (see v.8; Num 35; Josh 20–21).

The daily sustenance of the Levites came from the offerings made to the Lord and from the firstfruits. Particular portions of the offerings were to be given to the priests, those who were the sons of Aaron (Lev 7:31–35).

**3–5** The word for sacrifice in v.3 normally refers to sacrificing animals for religious feasts. Here, however, as in 12:15, 21, the word has a broader coverage and includes the meals of the festivals that are in addition to the fellowship offerings.

"The share due the priests" (v.3) was the part they were to receive, based on the procedure established by the Lord because he chose them and their descendants to minister in his name always (v.5). Designations of the Levites as the priestly tribe sometimes refer to their tribal position as a whole and at other times to the sons of Aaron, a more limited group. It is often difficult for interpreters to recognize this distinction, even though most languages exhibit this characteristic.

**6–8** All Levites were to share in tribal benefits when they so desired. Whatever be the reason, when a Levite from anywhere in Israel desired to move to the place the Lord would choose, to engage in service in the presence of the Lord (in tabernacle or temple), he could do so; and he was to have an equal share in the benefits of his position. No mention is made here of the various levels of Levitical service—levels available because of one's identification with a certain family line within the tribe of Levi (Lev 21:17; Num 3–4). The benefits here mentioned accrue to any Levite even though he may have other assets from the sale of family possessions—whatever they may be (v.8). The Hebrew phrase does not clearly establish what these possessions might include.

## Notes

---

1 אִשֵּׁי יהוה (*'iššê YHWH*, "offerings made to the LORD by fire") is used only here in Deuteronomy though it appears more than forty times in Leviticus and fifteen times in Numbers. Many of the offerings that are wholly or partly burned on the altar are called fire offerings. These include burnt, grain, fellowship, and guilt offerings and also the offering at the consecration of Aaron and his sons (Lev 8:28) (G.F. Oehler, *Theology of the Old Testament* [Grand Rapids: Zondervan, n.d.], p. 282; J. Gray, *The Legacy of Canaan* [Leiden: Brill, 1957], p. 198).

3 The מִשְׁפָּט (*mišpāṭ*, "share") is an extension of the idea of one's right, in the sense of rightful share, viz., that which is due the priests. The same sense can be discerned in 21:17, where the "right" of the firstborn is the "double share."

5 שָׁרַת (*šārat*, "minister") is used of domestic and royal service but most often of religious service.

5, 7 On the use of the Name of the Lord in Deuteronomy, see the comment on 32:3.

---

### f. *Detestable practices of Canaan*

#### 18:9–13

[9]When you enter the land the LORD your God is giving you, do not
learn to imitate the detestable ways of the nations there. [10]Let no one be
found among you who sacrifices his son or daughter in the fire, who
practices divination or sorcery, interprets omens, engages in witchcraft,
[11]or casts spells, or who is a medium or spiritist or who consults the
dead. [12]Anyone who does these things is detestable to the LORD, and
because of these detestable practices the LORD your God will drive out

**those nations before you. [13]You must be blameless before the LORD your God.**

**9–13** Because of the difficulty of bridging the gap between the Lord God and the people (Exod 20:18–21)—their beliefs and behavior—leadership in Israel included several roles. Judges, possible kings, and priests were to have their areas of responsibility and authority in interpreting and applying the basic elements of the written codes. In Deuteronomy's addresses both the office and the procedures were being presented by Moses in preparation for the new national life the people were to face in Canaan. However, the Canaanites employed other means of communication with their pagan gods, and those means might lure the Israelites to emulate them. Such emulation would mean rebellion and defection from the Lord and the covenant-treaty with him.

References to these "detestable ways" (v.9) are not uncommon in the OT, but the list in vv.10–11 is more full than elsewhere. The precise identification of the prohibited behavior cannot now always be clearly discerned by means of the terms used. Comparison with other such prohibitions shows that several of the words are sometimes generalizations and at other times more specific or discreet. The various procedures proscribed seek magical and spiritistic assistance for solutions to problem situations.

These evil practices were the reason the Lord was going to drive the Canaanites out of the land. Not only adherence to the false gods of Canaan was proscribed, but also the means by which the Canaanites attempted to communicate with them. Both the objects and the methods of Canaanite religious life were to be abhorred totally and rejected completely.

The Israelites were not to "imitate" (v.9) the nations of Canaan but rather were to be "blameless" (v.13). They were to be without any taint of these detestable practices, which were to be absolutely shunned.

## Notes

**9** לֹא־תִלְמַד לַעֲשׂוֹת (*lō'-tilmaḏ la'ᵃśôṯ*, "Do not learn to imitate") is a strict injunction not to copy, imitate, or do what the Canaanites did. The means the Lord gave the Israelites to know his will were adequate for all circumstances. On the ancient Near Eastern background of these "detestable ways," see Kitchen, *The Bible*, pp. 116–17; T. Witton Davies, *Magic, Divination and Demonology Among the Hebrews and Their Neighbors* (New York: KTAV, 1969); and Harry Hoffner, "Second Millennium Antecedents to the Hebrew *'ÔB*," JBL 86 (December 1967): 385–401.

**9, 12** There are nine words or phrases that explicate what תּוֹעֵבֹת (*tô'ᵃḇōṯ*, "detestable ways") are. They designate various forms of occult communication. The first of these—"one . . . who sacrifices his son or daughter in the fire"—is considered in the commentary and Notes on 12:31.

**10** קָסַם (*qāsam*, "divining" or "divination") covers many kinds of occult practices, and the list that follows may be meant to specify kinds of divination or mantic or magic ways to get information from the supernatural False prophets are accused of divination in Jer 29:8 and Ezek 13:9; 22:28.

מְעוֹנֵן (*me'ônēn*, "sorcery"), a Polel participle of עָנַן (*'ānan*), is unclear in both root and usage. Generally it is thought to be some kind of soothsaying—predicting the future by means of physical signs (astrology). The NIV translates a locale in Judg 9:37 as "the soothsayers' tree."

The etymology of מְנַחֵשׁ (*menaḥēš*, "interprets omens") is uncertain. In some way it may be related to נָחָשׁ (*nāḥāš*, "snake"), either likening the practice to the sound of a snake's hiss or to the use of snakes in understanding the omen.

The etymology and procedures of מְכַשֵּׁף (*mekaššēp*, "[one who] engages in witchcraft") are doubtful. The LXX translates the word by φαρμακός (*pharmakos*), possibly one who induces magical effects by drugs or some sort of potion.

**11** חֹבֵר חָבֶר (*hōber ḥāber*, "casts spells"; lit., "speller of spells," "a charmer of charms") seems to speak of the sound made by these practitioners in Ps 58:5 (6 MT) and that of a quarrelsome woman in Prov 21:9 and 25:24. Though both verb and noun occur in other senses in the OT, the nature of this occult practice is not clear.

שֹׁאֵל אוֹב (*šō'ēl 'ôḇ*, "inquiring medium"), in "who is a medium or spiritist or who consults the dead," is illustrated by the בַּעֲלַת אוֹב (*ba'alat 'ôḇ*, "medium" or "possessor of a spirit") of Endor (1 Sam 28:7–25).

יִדְּעֹנִי (*yidde'ōnî*, "spiritist") is "a known one," "an intimate acquaintance," "a familiar spirit," or "a medium."

דֹּרֵשׁ אֶל־הַמֵּתִים (*dōrēš 'el-hammēṯîm*, "[one] who consults the dead") is one who investigates, looks into, and seeks information from the dead.

These last three designations are different ways of expressing the same practice. As illustrations see "Akkadian Oracles and Prophecies" and "Divine Revelations" in ANET, pp. 449–52, 623–26, 629–32.

---

## g. *The prophet like Moses*

### 18:14–22

[14]The nations you will dispossess listen to those who practice sorcery or divination. But as for you, the LORD your God has not permitted you to do so. [15]The LORD your God will raise up for you a prophet like me from among your own brothers. You must listen to him. [16]For this is what you asked of the LORD your God at Horeb on the day of the assembly when you said, "Let us not hear the voice of the LORD our God nor see this great fire anymore, or we will die."

[17]The LORD said to me: "What they say is good. [18]I will raise up for them a prophet like you from among their brothers; I will put my words in his mouth, and he will tell them everything I command him. [19]If anyone does not listen to my words that the prophet speaks in my name, I myself will call him to account. [20]But a prophet who presumes to speak in my name anything I have not commanded him to say, or a prophet who speaks in the name of other gods, must be put to death."

[21]You may say to yourselves, "How can we know when a message has not been spoken by the LORD?" [22]If what a prophet proclaims in the name of the LORD does not take place or come true, that is a message the LORD has not spoken. That prophet has spoken presumptuously. Do not be afraid of him.

**14–19** Israelite reliance was to be wholly on the Lord, who would send them prophets like Moses, whose prophetic ministry would be in marked contrast to the occult practices of the Canaanites (vv.14–15). Moses became the spokesman for God at Horeb (Sinai) at the people's request (v.16; Exod 20:18–19), but it is obvious that the Lord had already chosen him and used him as his spokesman. Being the spokesman for God is the central characteristic of a prophet.

These prophets would be selected by the Lord from their own brothers (v.18). The Lord would put his words in their mouths, and they were to tell the Israelites what the Lord commanded them to speak. The Lord would call to account anyone who did not listen to the words spoken in the Lord's name (v.19).

**20–22** The prophet who presumed to speak in the Lord's name (without authorization), or, on the other hand, one who spoke in the name of other gods, would be put to death (v.20). The latter could be readily discerned—he broke the first commandment and merited capital punishment. But the former could be difficult to determine. So Moses concerned himself with the question, "How can we know when a message has not been spoken by the LORD?" (v.21).

The answer relates only to predictive messages. If the prediction *is not* (as the Hebrew succinctly says) or does not happen (synonymous expressions), the message is not spoken by the Lord. This answer is not comprehensive: it speaks of only one of the ways to determine the validity of a prophet and a prophecy. It does not cover all circumstances. In fact, the predictive proof alone cannot be used to nullify the second referent of v.20 (a prophet who speaks in the name of other gods) as seen in chapter 13, where prediction that comes true when spoken in the name of another god is a capital offense (13:1–5). Verse 14 clearly states that sorcery and divination were not permitted, which is one of the main ways pagans get messages from their gods. Adherence to the Lord and his written word is the highest law; one is not to be afraid of any false prophet or of his predictions.

This section on prophets and prophecy was very important to Israel and has had an immensely important position in interpretation. Israel has been given a written covenant with all its historical, religious, legislative, and promissory elements as a revelation from the Lord. Priests have been provided to implement its religious aspects. Judges and a possible kingship are to care for legislative and executive matters, but how will the people know the will of God in day-to-day circumstances? The prophets as spokesmen for the Lord, as Moses was, supply this lack. So now there were priests, judges, possible kings, and *prophets*. (Lesser offices such as elders also existed.)

The promise of the prophetic movement, however, did not exhaust the promise of vv.18–19. The "prophet like you from among their brothers" (v.18) was seen as a messianic prediction, a prophet par excellence. This interpretation was widespread in NT times, being mentioned in the NT and among the Essenes as well as among the Jews, Gnostics, and others (cf. John 1:21; 6:14; 7:40; Acts 3:22–23; Cross, *Ancient Library*, p. 219; J.T. Milik, *Ten Years of Discovery in the Wilderness of Judaea* [Naperville: Allenson, 1959], p. 124).

The question was raised whether any of the prophets was equal to Moses. As the Lord's spokesman, the one through whom the whole initial covenant-treaty that established the nation was brought, Moses was superior to all the prophets who followed him—except the Prophet, Jesus. Moses' superiority is distinctly appended in the epilogue of Deuteronomy (34:10–12), though, of course, this is limited somewhat by the time of the writing of this portion of the book.

John the Baptist, in answer to the priests and Levites, said that he was not "the Christ, nor Elijah, nor the Prophet" (John 1:21, 25); and later the people are reported to have said on two occasions: "Surely this is the Prophet" (John 6:14), and "Surely this man is the Prophet" (John 7:40). Philip also, referring to the one Moses wrote about in the law, applied this to Jesus, saying, "We have found the one Moses wrote about" (John 1:45).

Was not Jesus himself calling this Deuteronomic passage to mind when he said of Moses, "He wrote about me" (John 5:46)? Moreover, Jesus claimed to fulfill the requirements of the prophet like Moses when he said, "For I did not speak of my own accord, but the Father who sent me commanded me what to say and how to say it. . . . So whatever I say is just what the Father has told me to say" (John 12:49–50).

Peter, when speaking to the people at the Beautiful Gate of the temple, explicitly applied this passage to Jesus (Acts 3:22–23). To this can be added the testimony of Stephen (Acts 7:37).

Though the statement in Deuteronomy promised a series of prophets, and so included the prophetic movement in the providence of God for the direction of his people, it looks beyond the prophetic movement to the One who is the supreme revealer of God; it looks to Jesus.

## Notes

---

**15** Etymologically, as Albright (*Stone Age*, pp. 231–33) and others suggest, נָבִיא (*nāḇîʾ*, "prophet") may come from the Akaddian meaning, "one who is called," e.g., one called by a god. However, following common linquistic experience—in the Scriptures here and elsewhere—usage, not etymology, determines the meaning of the word. See TWOT, 2:544.

The singular *nāḇîʾ* and the singular forms that follow imply a series or a succession of prophets as the context clearly shows. Notice the generalization of vv.20–22.

**18** For the DSS reference to the messianic prophet, see Cross, *Ancient Library*, p. 219, and Dupont-Sommer, pp. 316–18.

**19** שָׁמַע (*šāmaʿ*) means "listen" in the sense of accept or obey, depending on whether the message is informational as a prediction or calls for action.

**19–20, 22** On the use of the "name" of the Lord in Deuteronomy, see the comment on 32:3.

**21** "You may say to yourselves" is a good rendering of the Hebrew idiom "You may say in your heart."

---

### h. *Cities of refuge*

#### 19:1–14

[1]When the LORD your God has destroyed the nations whose land he is
giving you, and when you have driven them out and settled in their
towns and houses, [2]then set aside for yourselves three cities centrally
located in the land the LORD your God is giving you to possess. [3]Build
roads to them and divide into three parts the land the LORD your God is
giving you as an inheritance, so that anyone who kills a man may flee
there.

[4]This is the rule concerning the man who kills another and flees there
to save his life—one who kills his neighbor unintentionally, without
malice aforethought. [5]For instance, a man may go into the forest with
his neighbor to cut wood, and as he swings his ax to fell a tree, the head
may fly off and hit his neighbor and kill him. That man may flee to one of
these cities and save his life. [6]Otherwise, the avenger of blood might
pursue him in a rage, overtake him if the distance is too great, and kill
him even though he is not deserving of death, since he did it to his

neighbor without malice aforethought. [7]This is why I command you to
set aside for yourselves three cities.
[8]If the LORD your God enlarges your territory, as he promised on oath
to your forefathers, and gives you the whole land he promised them,
[9]because you carefully follow all these laws I command you today—to
love the LORD your God and to walk always in his ways—then you are to
set aside three more cities. [10]Do this so that innocent blood will not be
shed in your land, which the LORD your God is giving you as your
inheritance, and so that you will not be guilty of bloodshed.
[11]But if a man hates his neighbor and lies in wait for him, assaults and
kills him, and then flees to one of these cities, [12]the elders of his town
shall send for him, bring him back from the city, and hand him over to
the avenger of blood to die. [13]Show him no pity. You must purge from
Israel the guilt of shedding innocent blood, so that it may go well with
you.
[14]Do not move your neighbor's boundary stone set up by your
predecessors in the inheritance you receive in the land the LORD your
God is giving you to possess.

**1–4** Moses had already established Bezer, Ramoth, and Golan as cities of refuge for the tribes of Reuben, Gad, and the half-tribe of Manasseh east of the Jordan. Anyone who killed a neighbor unintentionally could flee to one of these cities to save his life (4:41–43). Now he directs Israel to likewise set up three cities of refuge in Canaan proper when they occupy it.

When Israel's control would extend over the whole Land of Promise (v.1), three more cities were to be selected for this purpose (v.2). The whole Land of Promise, according to the oath to their forefathers (v.8), apparently extended from Egypt (WBE, 14:74; ZPEB, 5:121) to the Euphrates (Gen 15:18). In those parts of this larger area outside Canaan, three more cities were to be chosen (vv.8–9), making nine in all—if the larger area became identified as Israelite lands. Even under David and Solomon, this did not occur; so the third set of cities of refuge was never appointed.

The designation of cities of refuge develops what is stated in Exodus 21:13. Exodus 21:12 and 14 cover deliberate homicide. The altar as sanctuary is an alternate, temporary refuge for guilty parties. In Numbers 35:6–34 the most detailed presentation of the cities of refuge appears. The actual choice of these cities in Canaan proper was made by Joshua (Josh 20–21).

The cities were to be centrally located in three divisions of the country so that anyone who killed another would have reasonably close sanctuary (vv.2–3). Cities of refuge constituted a means to thwart a hasty application of blood revenge (v.6), which might result in the death of an innocent man—one who killed another unintentionally and without malice aforethought (vv.4–5).

**5–13** The shedding of innocent blood in Israel's land would be a social evil that would bring guilt on the nation (v.10). It would be wrong both to allow the innocent to be killed and to allow the guilty to go unpunished (v.13).

The process of determining the innocence or guilt of the one who kills another is not given here—other than that the elders of the town of the accused should send for the killer to be returned from the city of refuge to which he had fled (v.12). If guilty, they are to hand him over to the avenger of blood for execution. Acquittal or guilt would be determined on bases indicated elsewhere, as in v.15: "A matter must be established by the testimony of two or three witnesses." See also Numbers 35:9–34, where more of the procedure appears, including the instruction that the judicatory is the town assembly. The elders are to act as administrators of the decisions of the assembly.

That capital offenses were to be punished by capital punishment rigorously applied is seen in the declaration of v.13—"Show him no pity"—and in the repetition of this clause in v.21 together with the famous lex talionis.

**14** The territorial imperative was of basic importance in the economy that the Lord revealed through Moses. The land—and private ownership of the land—made possible the most equitable distribution of wealth. Moses looked ahead to the time when Israel would be settled in the land within the tribal and family boundaries and when these boundaries could be subject to dispute. The boundaries once allotted in the original division of the land were to be inviolate; so moving a boundary stone was to be strictly forbidden.

The Lord had given the land to the people. Their descendants were never to disturb the boundary stones. The right to hold property was a cornerstone of Israel's inheritance from the Lord. It is still a primary right of free people on the earth, and without it freedom is greatly limited.

## Notes

---

**4–7** E.C. Brewer (*Dictionary of Phrase and Fable* [New York: Harper and Row, 1970], p. 678) says: "In addition to its common meaning, *malice* is a term in English law to designate a wrongful act carried out against another intentionally, without just cause or excuse. This is commonly known as malice prepense or malice aforethought."

**6** גֹּאֵל הַדָּם (*gō'ēl haddām*, "the avenger of blood") vindicates or redeems the rights of the dead person. In various applications of the participle, a *gō'ēl* is a person who redeems someone or something; i.e., he does something to return someone or something to a former estate. In the case of the avenger, vindicator, or redeemer of blood (Num 35:19–27; Josh 20:3, 5, 9; 2 Sam 14:11), the *gō'ēl* is to implement the law of blood for blood, life for life (v.21), which doesn't bring the dead back to life but does rectify the injustice caused by the shedding of innocent blood (cf. Num 35:33; TWOT, pp. 144–45).

**8** כָּל־הָאָרֶץ אֲשֶׁר דִּבֶּר (*kol-hā'āreṣ 'ᵃšer dibber*, "the whole land he promised") is the territory God promised on oath to the patriarchs. Promised is a meaning mainly attached to the Piel perfect of the common verb דָּבַר (*dāḇar*, "say," "speak") when used of the promise of the land or the promise of Israel's increase in number in the land. See also 1:11; 6:18; 9:28; 12:20; 15:6; 27:3.

**9** "Three more cities" is a plain English way of translating עוֹד שָׁלֹשׁ עָרִים עַל הַשָּׁלֹשׁ הָאֵלֶּה (*'ōḏ šālōš 'ārîm 'al haššālōš hā'ēlleh*), which is literally "three cities more in addition to these three." *Haššālōš hā'ēlleh* ("these three") must refer to the three cities of v.2, so that *'ōḏ šālōš 'ārîm* are a third three cities.

The first three cities were situated in Transjordan (4:41–43); the second three were to be located in Canaan proper (19:2–3, 7); the third three were projected for the enlarged territory in the other parts of the whole land promised to the forefathers (vv.8–9).

---

### i. *Witnesses to a crime*

#### 19:15–21

**15**One witness is not enough to convict a man accused of any crime or offense he may have committed. A matter must be established by the testimony of two or three witnesses.

[16]If a malicious witness takes the stand to accuse a man of a crime,
[17]the two men involved in the dispute must stand in the presence of the
LORD before the priests and the judges who are in office at the time.
[18]The judges must make a thorough investigation, and if the witness
proves to be a liar, giving false testimony against his brother, [19]then do
to him as he intended to do to his brother. You must purge the evil from
among you. [20]The rest of the people will hear of this and be afraid, and
never again will such an evil thing be done among you. [21]Show no pity:
life for life, eye for eye, tooth for tooth, hand for hand, foot for foot.

**15** Jurisprudence must have rules of evidence, and in Israel witnesses were required to supply evidence or be punished (Lev 5:1). The rule for witnesses in capital offenses (17:7) is here applied to any crime or offense. Two or three witnesses are required (17:6; Num 35:30; Matt 18:16; 2 Cor 13:1).

**16–20** The designation of a false witness as "malicious" (v.16) probably indicts one using harsh and injurious language. When one accuses another after this fashion, the two of them, the accused and the accuser, are to stand in the presence of the Lord before the incumbent priests and judges (v.17). "In the presence of the LORD" refers to the tribunal meeting in the place in the central sanctuary designated for this purpose (17:9). The investigation must be "thorough" (v.18; 13:14; 17:4); and if the accuser is proved to be a liar, the punishment sought for the accused will be meted out to the accuser (v.19a).

Two formulas recurring in Deuteronomy follow: (1) the necessity of purging out evil (v.19b; see comment on 13:5) and (2) the declaration that punishment will be a deterrent to evil on the part of the populace (v.20; see comment on 13:11).

**21** The lex talionis (as cited also in Exod 21:23–25; Lev 24:18–20) is given as the guide to punish offenders.

The Lord Jesus negated the Deuteronomic rule in Matthew 5:38–42 and substituted for "eye for eye, and tooth for tooth" the turning of the other cheek. It must be remembered, however, that Deuteronomy is the law that the officials of the nation were to follow to protect the public, punish offenders, and deter crime. Jesus spoke to individuals about violence against themselves personally. One must not take the law into his own hands, returning evil for evil. Such action should be referred to the officials responsible before God to adjudicate and to punish offenders.

## Notes

**16** עֵד־חָמָס (*'ēḏ-ḥāmās*, "malicious witness") might be either one whose words indicate a malicious spirit or one who witnesses with the intent to harm—to bring violence on the accused. The former is most likely, but both might be true in a given circumstance.

**19** The Code of Hammurabi begins: "If a citizen has accused a citizen and has indicted him for murder and has not substantiated the charge, his accuser shall be put to death" (ANET, p. 166). Other laws in the same vein of compensatory punishment follow (see Thomas, p. 29).

"You must purge the evil from among you" is quoted in 1 Cor 5:13. See comment on 13:1–5.

### 3. *Rules for warfare*

#### 20:1–20

1When you go to war against your enemies and see horses and
chariots and an army greater than yours, do not be afraid of them,
because the LORD your God, who brought you up out of Egypt, will be
with you. 2When you are about to go into battle, the priest shall come
forward and address the army. 3He shall say: "Hear, O Israel, today you
are going into battle against your enemies. Do not be fainthearted or
afraid; do not be terrified or give way to panic before them. 4For the
LORD your God is the one who goes with you to fight for you against your
enemies to give you victory."

5The officers shall say to the army: "Has anyone built a new house
and not dedicated it? Let him go home, or he may die in battle and
someone else may dedicate it. 6Has anyone planted a vineyard and not
begun to enjoy it? Let him go home, or he may die in battle and
someone else enjoy it. 7Has anyone become pledged to a woman and
not married her? Let him go home, or he may die in battle and someone
else marry her." 8Then the officers shall add, "Is any man afraid or
fainthearted? Let him go home so that his brothers will not become
disheartened too." 9When the officers have finished speaking to the
army, they shall appoint commanders over it.

10When you march up to attack a city, make its people an offer of
peace. 11If they accept and open their gates, all the people in it shall be
subject to forced labor and shall work for you. 12If they refuse to make
peace and they engage you in battle, lay siege to that city. 13When the
LORD your God delivers it into your hand, put to the sword all the men in
it. 14As for the women, the children, the livestock and everything else in
the city, you may take these as plunder for yourselves. And you may use
the plunder the LORD your God gives you from your enemies. 15This is
how you are to treat all the cities that are at a distance from you and do
not belong to the nations nearby.

16However, in the cities of the nations the LORD your God is giving you
as an inheritance, do not leave alive anything that breathes. 17Com-
pletely destroy them—the Hittites, Amorites, Canaanites, Perizzites,
Hivites and Jebusites—as the LORD your God has commanded you.
18Otherwise, they will teach you to follow all the detestable things they
do in worshiping their gods, and you will sin against the LORD your God.

19When you lay siege to a city for a long time, fighting against it to
capture it, do not destroy its trees by putting an ax to them, because you
can eat their fruit. Do not cut them down. Are the trees of the field
people, that you should besiege them? 20However, you may cut down
trees that you know are not fruit trees and use them to build siege works
until the city at war with you falls.

**1–2** Chapter 20, as some other parts of Deuteronomy, seems to have a somewhat haphazard relationship with what precedes and what follows. This may be due to the extemporaneous character that appears here and there in this book.

These rules for warfare are quite extraordinary. They run counter to much of ancient as well as modern procedures for war, though certainly the psychological preparation of troops for battle in vv.1–4 breathes a modern spirit.

There is no new message from the mouth of Moses, nor does it cease with the settlement of the tribes in Canaan. Reliance on the Lord against all odds is a main theme of Joshua and the Book of Judges as well as of the prophets and the more godly kings during the monarchy (monarchies during the divided kingdom).

The Israelites were not to be frightened by the panoply of their enemies: horses, chariots, and a greater army than theirs should cause them no fear, because the Lord who had brought them up from Egypt (a phrase suggestive of his miraculous assistance and of the historical prologue of the covenant-treaty) would be present with them (v.1).

**3–4** The priest was to prepare the army for battle by assuring the troops of the Lord's presence to fight their enemies and to give them victory. The fourfold expostulation is dramatic: (1) Do not be fainthearted; (2) Do not be afraid; (3) Do not be terrified; (4) Do not give way to panic.

**5–9** The officers too were to speak to the inductees, and this in a most extraordinary way—they were to articulate the ways to be excused from service. Only men ready and willing for battle were wanted. This was no conscripted army. If one could not fit any of the specific categories of exemption, the last general category, "Is anyone afraid," would certainly relieve him of duty, if he so desired.

The responsibilities that would exclude one from military service generally relate to settled society and indicate—as commonly in Deuteronomy—the preparation of the people for settled life in Canaan. They also relate to the importance of the family in Israelite life.

The first exemption (v.5) was for one who had just acquired a home. He should have opportunity to live in it before serving in the military.

The second exemption is for one who plants a vineyard but has not brought it to the time when he can enjoy its fruit.

A third exemption, due to recent marriage, is mentioned again in 24:5, where the exemption lasts one year.

So that discouragement will not infect the ranks, the fearful and fainthearted are also exempt (a fourth cause for exemption), or else his brothers' hearts will melt (v.8).

When the troops were psychologically ready for battle, commanders were appointed. Who was to do the appointing is not clear; the subject of the clause is indefinite (v.9).

**10–15** When in the more distant future Israel would attack a city beyond the boundaries of Canaan proper, different rules would apply. These cities at a distance from them do not belong to the nations nearby; that is, within Transjordan and Canaan proper. The cities of Canaan were to be totally destroyed, but the distant cities were first to be offered peace (v.10). If they accepted that offer and opened their gates, they were to become a work force for the Israelites (v.11).

When one of these cities fell, after refusing a peace offer, the men were to be executed; but the women, the children, the livestock, and everything else in the city were to become booty for Israel (vv.12–14).

**16–18** In contrast to this treatment, the cities within Canaan proper were subject to *ḥērem* ("total destruction"; see Notes on 2:34). "Anything that breathes" (v.16), as elsewhere (except in Gen 7:22), refers to human beings. All the inhabitants that remained in the conquered cities of Canaan were to be completely destroyed so that Israel would not be enticed into the supreme sin of defecting from the Lord and turning to the worship of other gods.

**19–20** When Israel needed logs for building siege works during the investiture of a city, the immediate need was not to outweigh the long term value of fruit trees. They were not to be used for siege implements. They had value in the production of food. Evidently orchards were not common and were considered valuable. These "trees of eating" covered all trees that bear something edible.

Warfare ancient and modern is filled with violence, anguish, and inhumanity. These directions given to Israel must be measured relative to the war tactics of the world they lived in and to the heinousness of the sins of the cultures of Canaan.

## Notes

---

1 On war and warfare in the Bible, see ZPEB, 5:894–900.

The Deuteronomic laws concerning war (listed by von Rad, *Studies in Deuteronomy*, p. 50) include laws concerning war, 20:1–9; captured cities, 20:10–18, 19–20; female prisoners of war, 21:10–14; hygiene in the camp, 23:10–14; exemption for the newly married, 24:5; and Amalek, 25:17–19. After his observations on "the Deuteronomic laws concerning wars," von Rad discusses "the Deuteronomic speeches concerning war" and "Deuteronomy's atmosphere of war." In these three von Rad asserts that the references to waging war in Deuteronomy indicate an ancient background that was reinterpreted by a later writer about 701 B.C. It should be noted that these laws are for aggressive warfare and look forward to conquest. No need for positing an additional later writer exists (see Manley, *Book of the Law*, pp. 112–13).

3 יֵרַךְ לְבַבְכֶם (*yēra<u>k</u> l<sup>e</sup><u>b</u>a<u>bk</u>em*, "Do not be fainthearted") connotes being soft or tenderhearted. "Do not be terrified," from חָפַז (*ḥā<u>p</u>az*), suggests "frightened into precipitous flight."

עָרַץ (*'āraṣ*, "panic") together with מִפְּנֵיהֶם (*mipp<sup>e</sup>nêhem*) means "fleeing in panic from them."

5 According to the usual translation of חָנַךְ (*ḥāna<u>k</u>*, "to dedicate"), the first exemption speaks of the dedication of a house, a practice unknown in Israel. It seems more likely that Rashi, Qunhi, O.S. Rankin, S.C. Reif, Craigie, and others are right in asserting that the basic meaning of "begin" for *ḥāna<u>k</u>* is the meaning here. The NIV and many others translate *ḥāna<u>k</u>* in Prov 22:6 as "train," but NEB uses "dedicate." Craigie's translation is apropos: "and another man started to live in it." Rashi had "take up residence." See Reif, pp. 495–501, and Craigie, pp. 272–73.

The שֹׁטְרִים (*šōṭ<sup>e</sup>rîm*) are subordinate military officers here (cf. 1:15; 16:18).

6 The one who plants a vineyard must not use the fruit for three years. On the fourth year the fruit is holy and is to be an offering of praise to the Lord. Finally, in the fifth year its fruit may be eaten. It is this process that appears to be described by חִלְּלוֹ (*ḥill<sup>e</sup>lû*), which the NIV renders "begun to enjoy it," i.e., brought it into common use. See also 28:30; Jer 31:5.

8 מָסַס (*māsas*, "to melt"; NIV, "become disheartened") probably should be the Hiphil form, as in 1:28, thus giving a stronger, causative effect to the spread of discouragement. Only vocalization of the verb is involved.

14 The human population—other than combatants—is meant by הַנָּשִׁים וְהַטַּף (*hannāšîm w<sup>e</sup>haṭṭa<u>p</u>*, "the women, the children"). *Ṭa<u>p</u>* sometimes means little children (1:39), sometimes children in general, including youth (2:34), and sometimes dependents (2 Sam 15:22); and so here, as Reider (p. 192) and others allege, it means noncombatants.

17 The list of nations is the same as that in 7:1 except that "Girgashites" is missing here.

19 Instead of "Are the trees of the field people," the MT has "man is the tree of the field." The slight change of הָאָדָם (*hā'ā<u>d</u>ām*, "the man") to the interrogative הַאָדָם (*he'ā<u>d</u>ām*, "Is man?") is in conformity with the LXX and other early versions.

For illustrations of the proscription of felling fruit-producing trees, the building of siege works, and the taking of booty, see *World of the Bible*, pp. 275–77.

---

### 4. *Interpersonal relationships (21:1–25:19)*

#### a. *Atonement for unsolved murder*

21:1–9

**[1]If a man is found slain, lying in a field in the land the LORD your God is**
**giving you to possess, and it is not known who killed him, [2]your elders**
**and judges shall go out and measure the distance from the body to the**
**neighboring towns. [3]Then the elders of the town nearest the body shall**
**take a heifer that has never been worked and has never worn a yoke**
**[4]and lead her down to a valley that has not been plowed or planted and**
**where there is a flowing stream. There in the valley they are to break the**
**heifer's neck. [5]The priests, the sons of Levi, shall step forward, for the**
**LORD your God has chosen them to minister and to pronounce blessings**
**in the name of the LORD and to decide all cases of dispute and assault.**
**[6]Then all the elders of the town nearest the body shall wash their hands**
**over the heifer whose neck was broken in the valley, [7]and they shall**
**declare: "Our hands did not shed this blood, nor did our eyes see it**
**done. [8]Accept this atonement for your people Israel, whom you have**
**redeemed, O LORD, and do not hold your people guilty of the blood of an**
**innocent man." And the bloodshed will be atoned for. [9]So you will**
**purge from yourselves the guilt of shedding innocent blood, since you**
**have done what is right in the eyes of the LORD.**

**1–4** After the digression on warfare (20:1–20), the speaker returns to the subject of homicide and adds some detail to chapter 19.

What is the responsibility of an area where an unsolved homicide occurs? How is the area guilty? Israel was to take crime seriously, because crime was against the Lord and his law (see comments on 19:5–15).

When murder or manslaughter has been committed (Num 35:32–33), the justice of God is affronted. There is an identification of the criminal with both the land and the people; and unless the criminal is punished, justice is not met. When the perpetrator of the crime cannot be detected, some method of removal of the guilt that then falls on the land and people must be secured.

A like instance of communal or corporate guilt occurred in the experience at Ai (Josh 9) and that of Saul's slaughter of certain Gibeonites (2 Sam 21). The procedure given in this section of Deuteronomy provides the means for satisfying the Lord's justice by the removal of corporate guilt. The regulation has two important focuses: (1) the realization of the seriousness of the pollution of sin, (2) the grace of God that offers this means for the removal of that pollution.

The personal guilt of a murderer cannot be readily removed. As Numbers 35:33 says, "Atonement cannot be made for the land on which blood has been shed, except by the blood of the one who shed it."

W.R. Smith (*The Religion of the Semites* [New York: Meridian Books, 1959], p. 420) places corporate guilt as a belief "in the oldest state society" (meaning early Near Eastern society) and says that sacrifice is necessary to "restore the harmony between the community and its god." In the Code of Hammurabi (ANET, p. 167), it is obvious that a territory and district are responsible for payment to a victim of an unsolved robbery; and in the case of undetected murder, the city and government must pay one mina to the victim's family. In the Hittite laws the responsibility for an unsolved killing falls on the owner of the property; but if there is no owner, "the responsibility falls on the neighboring village" (Neufeld, *Hittite Laws*, p. 135). (For corporate guilt in the Nuzi tablets, see C.H. Gordon, "Biblical Customs and the Nuzu Tablets," *The Biblical Archaeologist Reader*, 2, edd. D.N. Freedman and E.F. Campbell, Jr. [Garden City: Anchor Books, 1975], p. 31.)

How can a place be purged of its guilt "if a man is found slain" (v.1) there? First, the guilty area is determined by the elders and judges who measure the distance from the body to the nearby towns (v.2). The elders of the town closest to the body are required to make atonement for the bloodshed. An unworked heifer was led into an uncultivated valley that had a flowing stream in it. Presumably the place where the heifer was led was as near as possible to where the body lay.

**5** The priests needed to be present, for they had been given authority and responsibility to decide difficult cases of dispute and assault. Moreover, they represented the Lord (10:8; 18:5).

**6–9** Atonement was made for the bloodshed when the elders broke the heifer's neck and washed their hands over the heifer's body while they declared that they, representing the people, were innocent of the homicide. Then they prayed that the Lord's redeemed people would be held guiltless. This action, described as "right in the eyes of the LORD" (v.9), purged the people from the guilt of spilling innocent blood.

Though the word *kāpar* ("atone") appears twice in v.8, the atonement mentioned is not an atonement within the sacrificial system; for the blood of the heifer was not offered. It is rather an atonement for justice; the heifer suffered death in place of the unknown criminal, in order to clear the land of guilt.

## Notes

**1** Calum Carmichael ("A Common Element in Five Supposedly Disparate Laws," VetTest 29, 2 [April 1979]: 129–42) contends that "Subjects related to life and death" is the unifying factor in chapter 21.

**2** The ascription of guilt to the area where one is killed is illustrated by Danel in "Aqhat" when he cursed three towns near the spot where his son Aqhat was killed. In each case he pronounced a woe on the city, "for near you Aqhat the hero was killed" (Coogan, p. 45).

**3** The age of a heifer is not given. Webster's *Third New International Dictionary* says that a heifer is a young cow less than three years old. A three-year-old heifer was sacrificed by Abraham in Gen 15:9. Heifers were used for both plowing (Judg 14:18) and threshing (Jer 50:11; Hos 10:11).

**4** אֵיתָן (*'êṯān*, "flowing stream") was a constant flow, not one flowing only after a rain.

**5** On the use of "the name of the LORD" in Deuteronomy, see the comment on 32:3.

On כָּל־רִיב וְכָל־נָגַע (*kol-rîḇ wᵉḵol-nāga'*, "all cases of dispute and assault"), see 17:8–10.

**8** On "redeemed" see the Notes on 9:26.

**8–9** On "the bloodshed will be atoned for" (v.8) and the removal of "the guilt of shedding innocent blood" (v.9), see S.R. Driver, *Deuteronomy*, pp. 425–26; TDNT, 3:302–10; TWOT, 1:452–53; and Oehler, *Theology of the Old Testament*, pp. 276–80.

## b. *Family relationships*

### 21:10–21

[10]When you go to war against your enemies and the LORD your God
delivers them into your hands and you take captives, [11]if you notice
among the captives a beautiful woman and are attracted to her, you may
take her as your wife. [12]Bring her into your home and have her shave
her head, trim her nails [13]and put aside the clothes she was wearing
when captured. After she has lived in your house and mourned her
father and mother for a full month, then you may go to her and be her
husband and she shall be your wife. [14]If you are not pleased with her, let
her go wherever she wishes. You must not sell her or treat her as a
slave, since you have dishonored her.

[15]If a man has two wives, and he loves one but not the other, and both
bear him sons but the firstborn is the son of the wife he does not love,
[16]when he wills his property to his sons, he must not give the rights of
the firstborn to the son of the wife he loves in preference to his actual
firstborn, the son of the wife he does not love. [17]He must acknowledge
the son of his unloved wife as the firstborn by giving him a double share
of all he has. That son is the first sign of his father's strength. The right
of the firstborn belongs to him.

[18]If a man has a stubborn and rebellious son who does not obey his
father and mother and will not listen to them when they discipline him,
[19]his father and mother shall take hold of him and bring him to the
elders at the gate of his town. [20]They shall say to the elders, "This son of
ours is stubborn and rebellious. He will not obey us. He is a profligate
and a drunkard." [21]Then all the men of his town shall stone him to
death. You must purge the evil from among you. All Israel will hear of it
and be afraid.

**10–14** Various family matters are regulated in vv.10–21. The first relates to the marriage of an Israelite man to a foreign, unmarried woman captured in warfare (vv.10–11). This was not warfare within Canaan or with contiguous Canaanite neighbors but with those who were "at a distance" (20:15). The woman would not be under the ban of *ḥerem* (20:16–18). She and the man would be subject also to the other rules regarding the marriage of Israelites. This legislation could have two basic results: the men would be restrained from rape, and the women would have time to become adjusted to their new condition.

Symbolic of casting off her former life, the woman was to remove the clothing she wore when captured (v.13a), shave her head and trim her nails (v.12), and put on new clothes. These cleansing rites (cf. Lev 14:8; Num 8:7; 2 Sam 19:24) initiated the woman into the Israelite family, but she would have a full month to mourn her separation from her father and mother before she became the wife of the Israelite (v.13b). She was also protected from being sold for money or treated as a commodity.

After marriage, if her husband was not pleased with her, he must let her go free because he had intercourse with her (v.14).

**15–17** Polygamy, while not officially approved, was condoned in ancient biblical times; so problems relating to the responsibilities and privileges of succession would arise, as seen in the patriarchal narratives of Genesis and elsewhere in the OT. The narratives about Jacob, Leah, and Rachel show how custom and favoritism could affect life in the polygamous family (Gen 29:15–30:24).

The succession of Jacob and that of Solomon illustrate the problem of primogeniture in a polygamous situation. Not the favoritism of the father, but the temporal order of birth in the family governed succession normally. This rule was not followed in the case of Solomon. The rule here established for Israel existed elsewhere in the ancient Orient (cf. Middle Assyrian law, ANET, p. 185 [B1]).

In Israel the responsibilities and privileges of the firstborn stayed with the firstborn regardless of the father's desires. A father was not to make a will to frustrate this law or otherwise dispose of his property. The Hebrew idiom for "double share" (v.17) became indicative of the position of successor. When Elisha requested a double portion of Elijah's spirit, he sought the role of successor to Elijah (2 Kings 2:9).

The first son, the first sign of his father's strength, describes the son as the first result of the father's procreative power.

**18–21** The rules for behavior in domestic and civil life generally provided protection for the less fortunate, which Neufeld (p. 98) observes is in contrast to Hittite law. In the case of a recalcitrant son, however, no mercy was allowed. The description of such a son alleviates what seems to be a less humanitarian approach. This son was stubborn, rebellious, and disobedient in the face of remonstrance (v.18). These words describe incorrigible wickedness. Moreover, when the parents leveled charges against the son before the elders, they made the specific accusations of his being both a drunkard and a profligate (v.20).

Rebelliousness was a serious sin. Moses designated his people as rebellious at Kadesh. Before he brought water from the rock, he said, "Listen, you rebels, must we bring you water out of this rock?" (Num 20:10).

This son was not only stubborn and rebellious, he was incorrigibly disobedient. No hope remains for such a person. His parents made their accusation before the elders sitting in the place of judgment in the gate of the city, and the punishment of being stoned to death was meted out by the townspeople so that evil would be purged from among them (v.21; see comments and Notes on 17:7, 12). The fear of punishment was expected to restrain each filial rebelliousness (13:11; 17:13; 19:20). This kind of rebelliousness was strictly forbidden by the fifth commandment (5:16; Exod 20:12; notice also Exod 21:15). The OT does not contain an instance of this punishment being applied.

## Notes

---

**11** חָשַׁק (*ḥāšaq*, "attracted") in 7:7 and 10:15 describes the Lord as setting his affection on his people. In this place the attraction is physical, based on the beautiful appearance of the woman: אֵשֶׁת יְפַת־תֹּאַר (*'ēšeṯ yᵉp̄aṯ-tō'ar*, "a woman of beautiful form and appearance").

**13** On rules of Israelite marriages, see ZPEB, 4:92–102.

**14** The Piel of שָׁלַח (*šālaḥ*, "let her go") may mean divorce, as in 22:19, 29, where the NIV so translates. Jewish interpretation of *šālaḥ* as "divorce" has a long history. Reider (p. 199) notes that the comment in *Sifre*, the Halakic midrash to Numbers and Deuteronomy, implies that a formal divorce as in Jer 34:16 ("had set free") is meant. See also Isa 50:1 and Jer 3:8.

The meaning of תִּתְעַמֵּר (*tiṯ'ammēr*), occurring only here and in 24:7, is not certain. Its parallelism with being sold for money suggests the translation "treated as a commodity," which in this context would be "treated as a slave" (Hulst, *Translation Problems*, p. 16, and id., VetTest 1 [1951]: 219–21; 2 [1952]: 153ff.).

The verb עָנָה (*'ānah*) means "to subdue," "to treat as a dependent," and from this meaning various nuances emerge: afflict, humiliate, or dishonor. It is used thirteen times of men having sexual intercourse with women (Gen 34:2; Deut 21:14; 22:24, 29; Judg 19:24; 20:5; 2 Sam 13:12, 14, 22, 32; Lam 5:11; Ezek 22:10–11).

**15–17** On rules of primogeniture in the ancient Orient, see ANET, p. 185 (B.1), and Kitchen, *The Bible*, p. 69.

**17** פִּי שְׁנַיִם (*pî šenayim*, "mouth of two"), a Hebrew idiom for "double share" (NIV), appears in 2 Kings 2:9 as "double portion," meaning successor, or in Zech 13:8 as "two-thirds," being twice "one-third."

On "first sign of strength," see Ackroyd and Lindars (p. 99).

**18** סוֹרֵר וּמוֹרֶה (*sôrēr ûmôreh*, "stubborn and rebellious") occur paired together in Jer 5:23 where Israelite wickedness, which was bringing on the destruction of the nation, is described. In Ps 78:8 the forefathers who were not loyal to God are called "a stubborn and rebellious generation." Jeremiah uses *sôrēr* with a cognate form (6:28) to depict the people the Lord was rejecting as "hardened rebels." *Môreh* also means "rebellious," and English translations—"out of control" (NEB), "unruly" (NAB), "refractory" (Craigie)—imply the rebelliousness of a malcontent.

**19** The gate of the city was a walled enclosure where it was customary for the elders to meet as judges (22:15; 25:7; Ruth 4:1; cf. ZPEB, 2:656).

---

## c. *Relations to land, animals, and things*

### 21:22–22:12

22If a man guilty of a capital offense is put to death and his body is
hung on a tree, 23you must not leave his body on the tree overnight. Be
sure to bury him that same day, because anyone who is hung on a tree is
under God's curse. You must not desecrate the land the LORD your God
is giving you as an inheritance.
22:1If you see your brother's ox or sheep straying, do not ignore it but
be sure to take it back to him. 2If the brother does not live near you or if
you do not know who he is, take it home with you and keep it until he
comes looking for it. Then give it back to him. 3Do the same if you find
your brother's donkey or his cloak or anything he loses. Do not ignore it.
4If you see your brother's donkey or his ox fallen on the road, do not
ignore it. Help him get it to its feet.
5A woman must not wear men's clothing, nor a man wear women's
clothing, for the LORD your God detests anyone who does this.
6If you come across a bird's nest beside the road, either in a tree or on
the ground, and the mother is sitting on the young or on the eggs, do
not take the mother with the young. 7You may take the young, but be
sure to let the mother go, so that it may go well with you and you may
have a long life.
8When you build a new house, make a parapet around your roof so
that you may not bring the guilt of bloodshed on your house if someone
falls from the roof.
9Do not plant two kinds of seed in your vineyard; if you do, not only
the crops you plant but also the fruit of the vineyard will be defiled.
10Do not plow with an ox and a donkey yoked together.
11Do not wear clothes of wool and linen woven together.
12Make tassels on the four corners of the cloak you wear.

**22–23** When a person is put to death for wrongdoing and his body is hanged on a tree, the body must not remain exposed overnight: the dead body is under God's curse, and more exposure would desecrate the land. Hanging the body (cf. Josh 8:29; 10:26–27) exhibited the person to public humiliation. The criminal was under the curse of God, that is, under the indictment of death by God's judgment. The exposure of his body was the utmost desecration. Such humiliation, however, has limits. Continued exposure would desecrate the land, not particularly due to putrefaction of the body, but to the effect that the continual remembrance of the crime and its punishment would have symbolically on the land.

The meaning of "under God's curse" (v.23) has long been debated. Since judgment basically is God's (1:17), the judgment that takes a person's life out of the covenant community as a perpetrator of the worst kind of sin (*ḥēṭ'*, "capital offense") and displays that judgment by the humiliation of hanging his body in public shows that that person is under God's curse. Paul's citation of this verse to illustrate the extent of Jesus' humiliation on the cross as a curse of one exposed as a criminal—though he was bearing the sins of others—is very apt (Gal 3:13).

**22:1–4** In Exodus 23:4 concern for the animals of an enemy is required. Here concern for a brother's animals is stipulated—whoever that brother may be. At the very least he is a fellow Israelite.

Straying domestic animals are not to be ignored (v.1); they must be returned to their owner, if he is known. When an owner does not live nearby, or for any other reason is unknown, the one who saw the stray must take it to his own place for safekeeping until the owner comes searching for it; then the animal is to be restored to the owner (v.2). This same rule applies to anything one loses and another finds (v.3). Concern for an animal fallen on the road requires that anyone passing by should help it to its feet (v.4). This does not necessarily refer to an animal that had strayed. More likely it envisages an animal fallen under a load with the owner beside him (Exod 23:5). Because of the weight of the load, the owner alone is unable to assist the animal to its feet. In any case, the fallen animal was to be helped to its feet.

Legislation for the life-style in the Land of Promise went far beyond rules to control wrongdoing. Involvement in a fellow citizen's plight (or that of his animal) demanded that assistance be given, and that without reward—except for the satisfaction of having helped one in difficulty.

**5** The prohibition against a woman wearing the habiliments of a man and of a man wearing the clothing of a woman can scarcely refer to transvestism. Though evidence for religious transvestism in ancient Canaanite religion is not conclusive, the inclusion of this rule under the proscription of the things the Lord detests suggests a serious problem, one that involves alienation from the Lord because of the adoption of proscribed religious practices. Most probably illicit sexual practices—including homosexuality (Lev 18:22; 20:13)—are included in this prohibition. Nevertheless, as elsewhere, Scripture considers the natural differences between male and female to be the Lord's creation and so should not be disregarded or camouflaged, though in many relationships between people and God, people are considered as human beings without regard to sexuality.

**6–7** The injunction here relates to any discovery of a mother bird on her nest with eggs or newly hatched young. The most common nesting places were in trees or on the ground; so mention is made of these.

Concern of the "be kind to animals" type or for animal parenthood or for saving the mother in the interest of continuing productivity (as modern hunting laws) may have occasioned this legislation. It should be recalled that God had said to Adam and Eve, "Rule over the fish of the sea and the birds of the air and over every living creature that moves on the ground" (Gen 1:28). After the Flood the covenant God made was with Noah, his descendants, and every living creature that was with him in the ark (Gen 9:9–10). Long life and well-being follow obedience to this command, the same promise as that which follows the honoring of father and mother (5:16).

**8** Protection of self and property from the guilt of bloodshed underlies the concern for persons who may be on the flat roof of one's house (Josh 2:6; 2 Sam 11:2). A balustrade, parapet, or railing was to be built as a safety precaution. The roofs of houses were often used for various purposes. Consequently, without some kind of restraining wall, one could easily fall off and be hurt. In 1 Samuel 9:25–26, Samuel conversed with Saul on the roof and spent the night there. David was walking on the roof of the palace when he saw Bathsheba (2 Sam 11:2). A tent was pitched on the roof so that Absalom "lay with his father's concubines in the sight of all Israel" (2 Sam 16:22).

**9–10** The prohibitions of mixing seeds for planting, plowing with diverse animals, and wearing clothes woven of differing kinds of thread expand slightly on Leviticus 19:19. The ancient rationale for these regulations is not known. However, the practices prohibited seem to have occurred throughout history in the Bible lands. Perhaps the idea is that the distinctions that God ordained in Creation are to be preserved. Israelite behavior was to be differentiated from that of its neighbors. Possibly the mixing of animals pulling plows was thought to be unkind because of the differing strengths of the animals or ways of pulling under harness (see esp. the comment on Lev 19:19 by R. Laird Harris in EBC, 2:606–7).

Verse 9 declares that when vines and other plants are mixed, both the grapes and the other crop are "defiled" (*tiqdaš*, "become holy," and so "untouchable") and no longer permissible for personal use. The aim of the legislation again seems to be to maintain the natural distinctiveness of certain objects of Creation by keeping them separate from one another. The NIV margin suggests an alternate meaning of "set apart" in the sense of being forfeited to the sanctuary (cf. Lev 27:10, 21). Because of the negative nature of the immediate context, the translation of the NIV text is the most likely emphasis here.

**11** The mixing of kinds of thread in garments is prohibited in Leviticus 19:19, but in this place the specific kinds of thread—"wool and linen"—are mentioned. Perhaps these are illustrative.

**12** In Numbers 15:38–40 the regulation for the wearing of tassels includes the reason for the custom: "You will have these tassels to look at and so you will remember all the commands of the LORD, that you may obey them and not prostitute yourselves by going after the lusts of your own hearts and eyes. Then you will remember to obey all my commands and will be consecrated to your God" (vv.39–40).

## Notes

---

**22** חֵטְא (*ḥēṭ'*, "offense," "sin"; NIV, "guilty of") is clarified by מִשְׁפַּט־מָוֶת (*mišpaṭ-māwet*, "the sentence of death") (in apposition) and so "a capital offense." *Mišpāṭ-māwet* is "deserving of death" in 19:6 and "sentenced to death" in Jer 26:11, 16.

עֵץ (*'ēṣ*) may be a "tree," wood from a tree, or an object made from the wood, e.g., a "gallows" (Esth 5:14). In the NT ξύλον (*xylon*) has about the same semantic reach and is sometimes used for "cross" (Acts 5:30; 10:39; 13:29; Gal 3:13; 1 Peter 2:24), though usually translated "tree"; however, NEB has "gibbet" and JB has "cross" in 1 Peter 2:24.

**22:1–3** In comparison to Hittite law on lost animals, the law of the Lord for Israel shows more concern for both people and animals. Hittite law says: "If anyone finds an ox or a horse or mule, he shall bring it to the royal gate. But if he finds it in the country, it shall be brought to the elders and he may continue to harness it. But if its owner finds it and receives it as it was, he shall not hold him as a thief. If he does not bring it before the elders he is a thief" (Neufeld, *Hittite Laws*, p. 23).

**1** הִתְעַלַּמְתָּ מֵהֶם (*hiṯ'allamtā mēhem*, "do not ignore it") is literally "hide yourself from them," or, as in Isa 58:7, "turn away from" them; that is, ignore them. The NIV translates the Hebrew plural as "it" to conform to English syntax.

**5** כְּלִי־גֶבֶר (*kᵉlî-geḇer*, "men's clothing") and שִׂמְלַת אִשָּׁה (*śimlaṯ 'iššāh*, "women's clothing") probably refer to clothes in general, though *kᵉlî* would seem to describe all the trappings of a man, while *śimlāṯ* suggests a covering or clothes as a covering.

**9–11** Prohibitions against mixture based on Lev 19:19 and Deut 22:9–11 are given in detail in the First Order of Mishnah, Tractate 4, *Kilaim*. This prohibition seems to refer to deviant sexual practice (transvestism?). It falls under the indictment of what is detestable to the Lord as do idols and the paraphernalia of their worship (7:25), occult practices (18:12), and homosexualism (Lev 18:22; 20:13).

**12** While Num 15:38–39 has the technical term צִיצִת (*ṣîṣiṯ*) for "tassel" (lock of hair, Ezek 8:3), Deuteronomy has גְּדִלִים (*gᵉḏilîm*, "twisted cords"). Pictures of ancient painting and sculpture showing tassels on garments are known from the fifteenth and twentieth centuries B.C. (*World of the Bible*, 1:280).

---

### d. *Marriage violations*

### 22:13–30

[13]If a man takes a wife and, after lying with her, dislikes her [14]and
slanders her and gives her a bad name, saying, "I married this woman,
but when I approached her, I did not find proof of her virginity," [15]then
the girl's father and mother shall bring proof that she was a virgin to the
town elders at the gate. [16]The girl's father will say to the elders, "I gave
my daughter in marriage to this man, but he dislikes her. [17]Now he has
slandered her and said, 'I did not find your daughter to be a virgin.' But
here is the proof of my daughter's virginity." Then her parents shall
display the cloth before the elders of the town, [18]and the elders shall
take the man and punish him. [19]They shall fine him a hundred shekels of
silver and give them to the girl's father, because this man has given an
Israelite virgin a bad name. She shall continue to be his wife; he must
not divorce her as long as he lives.
[20]If, however, the charge is true and no proof of the girl's virginity can
be found, [21]she shall be brought to the door of her father's house and
there the men of her town shall stone her to death. She has done a
disgraceful thing in Israel by being promiscuous while still in her
father's house. You must purge the evil from among you.

22If a man is found sleeping with another man's wife, both the man
who slept with her and the woman must die. You must purge the evil
from Israel.
23If a man happens to meet in a town a virgin pledged to be married
and he sleeps with her, 24you shall take both of them to the gate of that
town and stone them to death—the girl because she was in a town and
did not scream for help, and the man because he violated another man's
wife. You must purge the evil from among you.
25But if out in the country a man happens to meet a girl pledged to be
married and rapes her, only the man who has done this shall die. 26Do
nothing to the girl; she has committed no sin deserving death. This case
is like that of someone who attacks and murders his neighbor, 27for the
man found the girl out in the country, and though the betrothed girl
screamed, there was no one to rescue her.
28If a man happens to meet a virgin who is not pledged to be married
and rapes her and they are discovered, 29he shall pay the girl's father
fifty shekels of silver. He must marry the girl, for he has violated her. He
can never divorce her as long as he lives.
30A man is not to marry his father's wife; he must not dishonor his
father's bed.

**13–21** Marital fidelity looms large in the Mosaic legislation. Even though Jesus later said that Moses allowed divorce "because your hearts were hard" (Mark 10:5), divorce was subject to a number of restrictions. A husband's charge of premarital infidelity on the part of his newly acquired wife followed certain procedures. If the husband, after lying with his bride, disliked her and declared that she was not a virgin when she came to him, her parents could come to her aid by displaying the proof of her virginity to the town elders at the gate (the court of justice in the city gate) (vv.13–17). If the elders decided that the man was guilty of defaming his bride, he must give a hundred shekels of silver to the girl's father, and she remained as his wife; he was never to divorce her (vv.18–19). If no acceptable proof of the girl's virginity was presented, she was to be stoned to death at the door of her father's house (vv.20–21).

The law protected the innocent bride from the caprice of her husband and discouraged premarital infidelity among young women. It did not, however, protect young women from getting a husband who had previously had sexual relations. But other laws do concern themselves with men's extramarital relations (e.g., vv.22–29).

The proofs of virginity (vv.14, 17), the blood-spotted bedclothes or garments, which, though not infallible, were widely accepted in the ancient Near East as indications of prior virginity, are still accepted among some peoples today (Reider, pp. 207ff.).

**22** It is noteworthy that the Deuteronomic formula "You must purge the evil from among you" or "from Israel" is given three times (vv.21, 22, 24) in this series of capital offenses—an indication of the seriousness of crimes against marital fidelity.

Under the conditions expressed, adultery is not only forbidden but, as a capital offense, demands the death penalty (v.22). Neither here nor in Leviticus 18:20, 29, and 20:10 is the manner of death indicated, but analogy with v.24 suggests stoning.

**23–27** If the adulterous persons are a man and a woman "pledged to be married" to someone else and the act occurs in a town, without any voiced protest by the woman, stoning is required (vv.23–24). If rape occurs in the country, where a girl's screams could not be heard, only the man's life is required; the girl goes free (vv.25–27).

**28–29** The law is more lenient with a man who forces a virgin who is not pledged in marriage to another. The penalty, however, is not light. The offender must pay a fine of fifty shekels of silver, marry the girl, and keep her as his wife as long as he lives; she cannot be divorced. It was customary to pay a purchase price for a wife, but a set price is not indicated (Gen 34:12; Exod 22:16; 1 Sam 18:25) except in the case of Hosea's buying Gomer (Hos 3:2). The Deuteronomic legislation lessens the responsibility of the court, limits its freedom, and also inhibits those inclined toward such a crime. By contrast the price of a slave was thirty shekels (Exod 21:32).

**30** The prohibition of intercourse with one's father's wife undoubtedly refers to a wife other than one's own mother since a father's wife in this sense is in view elsewhere (27:20; Lev 18:8, 11; 20:11). Moreover, Jacob condemned his son Reuben for his incest with Bilhah, which Jacob denounced as defiling his couch (Gen 35:22; 49:3–4). In Leviticus death is decreed on both persons involved in such incest (Lev 18:8, 29; 20:11). Hebrew has several euphemisms for sexual intercourse; the phrase here is "uncover his father's skirt," translated as "dishonor his father's bed" (cf. 27:20).

## Notes

**13–14** The man's attitude, שָׂנֵא (*śānē'*, "dislikes," v.13), and his charges stemming from this attitude, עֲלִילֹת דְּבָרִים (*'ălîlōṯ debārîm*, "slander"; lit., "acts of words," v.14), giving her "a bad name," שֵׁם רָע (*šēm rā'*), lead to the accusation of the girl's "being promiscuous while still in her father's house" (v.21). The intensity of *śānē'* can be determined only from the context. In 21:15–17 a cognate form represents the unloved wife in contrast to the loved wife. The derivation of *'ălîlōṯ* is subject to dispute, but here it certainly relates to derogatory speech.

**19** Hebrew does not carefully indicate antecedents as English requires. The subject of הוֹצִיא (*hôṣî'*, "has given") is not the father, who is mentioned in the immediately preceding clause, but the slanderer. The NIV translates "this man" to clarify the antecedent.

**23–27** The Near Eastern law codes contain similar laws on sexual aberrations. See Neufeld, *Hittite Laws*, p. 56.

**25** The girl is presumed to have resisted because in this case she was raped; i.e., the man forced her, seized her violently—הֶחֱזִיק (*heḥezîq*, "rapes")—and lay with her.

### e. *Family, neighborhood, and national relationships (23:1–25:19)*

#### 1) *Situations requiring exclusion from the assembly*

23:1–14

1 No one who has been emasculated by crushing or cutting may enter the assembly of the LORD.

2 No one born of a forbidden marriage nor any of his descendants may enter the assembly of the LORD, even down to the tenth generation.

3 No Ammonite or Moabite or any of his descendants may enter the
assembly of the LORD, even down to the tenth generation. 4 For they did
not come to meet you with bread and water on your way when you came
out of Egypt, and they hired Balaam son of Beor from Pethor in Aram
Naharaim to pronounce a curse on you. 5 However, the LORD your God
would not listen to Balaam but turned the curse into a blessing for you,

because the LORD your God loves you. [6]Do not seek a treaty of friendship
with them as long as you live.
[7]Do not abhor an Edomite, for he is your brother. Do not abhor an
Egyptian, because you lived as an alien in his country. [8]The third
generation of children born to them may enter the assembly of the LORD.
[9]When you are encamped against your enemies, keep away from
everything impure. [10]If one of your men is unclean because of a
nocturnal emission, he is to go outside the camp and stay there. [11]But
as evening approaches he is to wash himself, and at sunset he may
return to the camp.
[12]Designate a place outside the camp where you can go to relieve
yourself. [13]As part of your equipment have something to dig with, and
when you relieve yourself, dig a hole and cover up your excrement.
[14]For the LORD your God moves about in your camp to protect you and
to deliver your enemies to you. Your camp must be holy, so that he will
not see among you anything indecent and turn away from you.

**1–2** Chapter 23 begins its miscellany of laws with those regarding three categories of persons who are excluded from the assembly of the Lord: eunuchs, illegitimate children, and both Ammonites and Moabites. In Deuteronomy the assembly is usually the Israelite community gathered at Sinai (5:22; 9:10; 10:4; 18:16); but in 31:30 those assembled were all the elders and officials (v.28)—and possibly others; but the specific mention of elders and officials would seem not to include the whole populace.

In vv.1, 2, 3, and 8 (vv.2, 3, 4, and 9 MT), the assembly is expressly called "the assembly of the LORD" and is probably restricted to the religious community. Most likely this law did not exclude one from residence in areas where Israel was to live but rather from the benefits of full-fledged citizenship and most particularly (and maybe only) from participation in religious rites in the homes and at the tabernacle and later at the temple.

At this period in Israel's national existence as the people of God, external, physical, and material means had spiritual significance and were used to teach lessons on the nature of their relationship to the Lord and the nature of the holiness that was required of them. Any defect in the body was considered less than acceptable to God—as were the results of sinful acts, whether personal (as illegitimacy) or national (as the behavior of the Ammonites and the Moabites during the Israelite trek around the east of the Dead Sea when they approached the Promised Land).

The eunuchs excluded from the assembly were those who were deliberately made eunuchs either by crushing or surgically removing their private parts (v.1). Probably this rule was directed particularly to men who had been emasculated in dedication to foreign gods—and also to those who had official positions under foreign governments—as well as against deliberate mutilations abhorrent to the position of God's people as holy.

Isaiah, however, predicted that in the future, in glorious Zion, eunuchs who did what pleased the Lord would have a better name than the sons and daughters of Israel (56:4–5). In the NT the evangelist Philip, under guidance of an angel of the Lord and the Holy Spirit, led an Ethiopian eunuch to trust in Christ and then receive Christian baptism (Acts 8:26–39).

What persons come under the ban of those born out of wedlock is not clear (v.2, NIV mg.). That all persons born out of wedlock would be meant seems unlikely because prohibited marriages are so clearly delineated, and unmarried persons known to have had intercourse were either put to death, required to be married, or in some cases to remain in protective custody of a family.

The Deuteronomic prohibitions, often if not always, relate in some way to the religious differences between Israelites under the covenant stipulations of the Lord and the pagan nations of Canaan. Consequently, this regulation might well be aimed at the offspring of cult prostitutes or of other promiscuous sexual practices related to the fertility religions of Canaan. It seems possible, however, that the law covers, as the NIV translates, the offspring of all "forbidden marriages."

The temporal reference in vv.2–3 "to the tenth generation," as v.6 indicates, means as long as the nation exists. The generations are not to be counted but should be understood rather as in the Lord Jesus' statement that one's brother should be forgiven seventy-seven times (i.e., always; cf. Matt 18:22).

**3–6** Ammonites and Moabites were excluded from the assembly of the Lord (v.3) because they failed to show concern for the Israelites when they moved toward Canaan. Israel had sought nothing from either Ammon or Moab except the right to purchase food and water (2:28–29). Israel skirted their lands and, at the express direction of the Lord, showed no hostility toward them (2:9, 16–19). But Moab hired Balaam to curse Israel; and even though the Lord turned the curse to blessing, Moab came under the indictment of not supporting the Israelites. This appears to be the failure of showing brotherly love based on the blessing to Abraham beginning in Genesis 12:3.

The clauses of v.4 are generally ascribed to the subjects of v.3. It was Balak king of Moab who hired Balaam to curse Israel (v.4). The act of the king is naturally the responsibility of the whole kingdom because he represents and acts for the people.

Balaam son of Beor was a northwest Mesopotamian sorcerer who was compelled by the Lord to bless rather than to curse Israel (v.5; Num 22–24).

Israel as a nation was never to seek peace or good relations with these two nations (v.6)—a statement prohibiting any treaty of friendship or mutual assistance. The prophets also denounced the Ammonites and Moabites (Isa 15:1–16:13; Jer 48:1–49:6; Ezek 21:28–32; 25:3–4; Zeph 2:8–9). This rule has a notable exception in Ruth, a Moabitess who was accepted in Israel and whose descendants included the Davidic line eventuating in the Messiah.

**7–8** Though Edomites and Egyptians also failed in kindness toward Israel—and even oppressed her—these two nations were not to be abhorred; Edom because of near kinship, and Egypt because Israel lived as an alien in that country. Great grandchildren of the then current population could be integrated into the assembly of the Lord.

**9–14** Rules for the holiness and cleanliness of the camp during military engagements, such as those the Israelites were soon to experience in Canaan, are in mind. A man who has an emission at night must go outside the camp and remain there until the next evening when, after washing himself, he may reenter at the going down of the sun (vv.10–11). For the disposal of excrement, a place outside the camp was to be chosen (v.12). In addition to weapons, some sort of instrument like a spade was to be used for digging a hole (v.13). The excrement was to be covered over so that the Lord would not be offended and turn away from the people because indecencies were evident as he went through the camp to protect them and deliver their enemies to them. Holiness is identified with cleanliness. Only the clean person can approach the

Lord in worship (Exod 19:10–11; 30:18–21; Josh 3:5; Ps 51:7, 10; see Kaiser, *Old Testament Ethics*).

## Notes

**1–7** (2–8 MT) The כָּל־קְהַל (*kol-qᵉhal*, "the whole assembly") of 5:22 is clarified by כָּל־יִשְׂרָאֵל (*kol-yiśrā'ēl*, "all Israel") in 5:1; and the occurrences of קָהָל (*gāhāl*, "assembly") in 9:10; 10:4; and 18:16 all refer to the same gathering of the people at Horeb (Sinai). The assembly in 31:30 appears to be limited to leaders, according to 31:28. קְהַל יהוה (*qᵉhal YHWH*, "the assembly of the LORD") specifies a more limited group—one that has all the advantages of the theocratic commonwealth, including all the religious advantages. In Deuteronomy *qᵉhal YHWH* appears only in 23:2, 3, 4, and 9 (1, 2, 3, and 8 EV), and it occurs a few times elsewhere in the OT. On the basis of this passage, Nehemiah "excluded from Israel all who were of foreign descent" (Neh 13:3).

**1** (2 MT) On eunuchs see ZPEB, 2:415–17.

**2** (3 MT) A מַמְזֵר (*mamzēr*) has been variously identified as one born out of wedlock (LXX, Vul., et al.), one born of a forbidden marriage (particularly the unlawful unions of Lev 18:16–20; 20:10–12, 14, 17–21) (so NIV), or one born of a cult or religious prostitute (vv.17–18). The word *mamzēr*, which occurs only here and in Zech 9:6, is of uncertain origin (see Keil, p. 414, and Craigie, p. 297).

**2–3** (3–4 MT) דּוֹר עֲשִׂירִי (*dôr 'ᵃśîrî*, "to the tenth generation") is repeated as עַד־עוֹלָם (*'aḏ-'ôlām*), which in v.3 is "even down to the tenth generation" or "never."

**6** (7 MT) Hillers ("Treaty Terminology," pp. 46–47) translates v.6 as "you shall never, as long as you live, seek (a treaty of) friendship and peace with them," the Hebrew terms שָׁלוֹם (*šālôm*, "peace") and טוֹבָה (*ṭôḇāh*, "good relation") being equated with the terms of Near Eastern treaties.

**12** (13 MT) יָד (*yāḏ*), which the NIV has translated "place," might carry the meaning of "sign," a meaning BDB suggests for Ezek 21:24 (19 EV), where the NIV has "signpost." BDB (p. 390), however, gives "place at one side" here. If "sign" is meant, the directive would be: "Have a sign outside the camp, and go to the place outside."

**14** (15 MT) The going about in the camp seems not to describe the Lord moving about within the confines of the camp but rather to speak of him being situated in the camp and moving with the Israelites on their military expeditions. The presence of the Lord could refer to his presence in the tabernacle, but that would necessitate the transportation of the tabernacle with the army in the field, or at least the presence of the ark with the army, an action that proved disastrous when fighting the Philistines (1 Sam 4), and one that is unknown elsewhere in the OT. The reference is most likely to the Lord's personal, spiritual presence.

עֶרְוַת דָּבָר (*'erwaṯ dāḇār*, "anything indecent") means the nakedness or indecency of a thing or any indecent thing (a construct serving in place of an adjective). This phrase has been the subject of much discussion, most especially as it appears in 24:1 relating to divorce. See comment and Notes on 24:1. Here, however, it refers to excrement.

## 2) *A miscellany of personal relationships (23:15–25:19)*

### a) Sundry laws

#### 23:15–25

15 If a slave has taken refuge with you, do not hand him over to his
master. 16 Let him live among you wherever he likes and in whatever
town he chooses. Do not oppress him.

17No Israelite man or woman is to become a shrine prostitute. 18You
must not bring the earnings of a female prostitute or of a male prostitute
into the house of the LORD your God to pay any vow, because the LORD
your God detests them both.
19Do not charge your brother interest, whether on money or food or
anything else that may earn interest. 20You may charge a foreigner
interest, but not a brother Israelite, so that the LORD your God may bless
you in everything you put your hand to in the land you are entering to
possess.
21If you make a vow to the LORD your God, do not be slow to pay it, for
the LORD your God will certainly demand it of you and you will be guilty
of sin. 22But if you refrain from making a vow, you will not be guilty.
23Whatever your lips utter you must be sure to do, because you made
your vow freely to the LORD your God with your own mouth.
24If you enter your neighbor's vineyard, you may eat all the grapes you
want, but do not put any in your basket. 25If you enter your neighbor's
grainfield, you may pick kernels with your hands, but you must not put a
sickle to his standing grain.

**15–16** A fugitive slave was not to be handed over to his master but was to be given asylum and the freedom to go anywhere he desired within the domain of Israel. These were slaves who had fled from foreign parts, since they were not to be oppressed as the Israelites themselves had been oppressed in Egypt (Exod 22:21; Lev 19:33–34).

**17–18** Temple prostitution was practiced among Baal worshipers of Canaan in their fertility rites. Israel was strictly forbidden to indulge in this demoralizing practice (v.17). The earnings of prostitutes are tainted and are not to be offered to pay any vow to the Lord. "Vow" (v.18) covers any contributions promised to the Lord. Whatever is acquired by evil means as well as what is evil in itself is not to be offered to the Lord. Such things do not belong in the house of the Lord; nor are they acceptable to him.

**19–20** When the nation was first established, the Israelite economy was by no means mercantile; and loans were made to help persons who had become too poor to support themselves. Assistance to such persons was to be given without interest—not interest of silver (equals "money"), food, or anything that might earn interest (v.19). But since merchants from other nations might come for business reasons to Israel, or make loans on interest to Israelites, foreigners could be charged interest (v.20). This rule alleviates the plight of the poor and made it more possible for them to work themselves out of their low estate. Interest is also regulated in Exodus 22:25 and Leviticus 25:36–37. The Lord's blessing on their labors in the land they were about to enter was contingent on their following this directive. Reider (p. 218) reminds us that a foreigner was permitted to require interest from an Israelite.

**21–23** Vows were common in the OT world. They became a part of the OT system of offerings and are mentioned frequently with the sacrificial offerings. Vows were never required, however, but properly handled would have the Lord's approval (v.22). Sometimes the payment of a vow was contingent on the occurrence of some specific event, as Jephthah's rash vow (Judg 11:30–31). The regulations for vows of various kinds and by differing persons had already been given in Leviticus 27 and Numbers 30. Here Moses urged the people to fulfill vows with dispatch (v.21).

Payment of vows is often mentioned by psalmist and prophet (Pss 22:25; 50:14; et al.; Isa 19:21; Jonah 2:9; Nah 1:15). Jeremiah and Malachi speak of improper vows (Jer 44:25; Mal 1:14).

As in Numbers 30:2, Moses here stressed that the payment of vows cannot be escaped. The Lord requires it. Failure to pay is sinful (v.21). Since it is certain that the vow must be paid, delay in payment should be avoided. In Numbers 30 certain persons within the family structure are not under responsibility to pay their vows unless certain conditions prevail. The avoidance of reckless making of vows seems to underlie vv.22–23. The same notion is explicit in Proverbs 20:25 and Ecclesiastes 5:4–7, which appear to be an exposition of these verses in Deuteronomy.

**24–25** The right to pick a few grapes from a neighbor's vineyard or to pluck a few kernels of grain in his field as one goes along the way appears to stand on somewhat the same level as gleaning during harvest. It is based on a concern for the immediate need for food. On the other hand, this advantage was not to be abused by putting grapes in a basket or putting a sickle to the neighbor's grain for one's future use.

According to one Jewish tradition, these verses refer only to persons who were hired to work in the vineyard or field. In NT times the Pharisees declared that Jesus' disciples who picked heads of grain in the field and rubbed them in their hands were doing what was unlawful on the Sabbath (Matt 12:1–2). On other days this action would not have been forbidden. Edersheim (LTJM, 2:56) points out that the disciples were guilty of a breach of rabbinic law, not biblical law.

## Notes

**16** (17 MT) בְּאַחַד שְׁעָרֶיךָ (*be'aḥaḏ še'āreyḵā*, "in whatever town") is literally "in any of your gates," gates representing cities.

**18** (19 MT) אֶתְנַן (*'eṯnan*, "the earnings" or hire of a prostitute) and מְחִיר (*meḥîr*, the "price" of a dog) are synonymous and refer to the earnings of female and male prostitutes.

זוֹנָה (*zônāh*) is the common word for "a female prostitute," and כֶּלֶב (*keleḇ*, "dog") is probably a common name for "a male prostitute." Notice the derogatory use of "dog" in Phil 3:2.

**19** (20 MT) There is a distinction between נֶשֶׁךְ (*nešeḵ*) here and תַּרְבִּית (*tarbîṯ*) in Lev 25:36–37. Speiser holds that these references were not to interest per se but to kinds of interest. Interest subtracted from the amount of the loan before the loan was made was *nešeḵ*. Any interest that was excessive (usury) was prohibited (E.A. Speiser, *Oriental and Biblical Studies* [Philadelphia: University of Pennsylvania Press, 1967], pp. 131–35).

**21** (22 MT) It is doubtful that the sin was incurred by delaying payment. The guilt came from the nonpayment of the vow. The limits of time for payment of vows is nowhere indicated. Of course, some vows have the time limit involved in the vow itself.

**24–25** (25–26 MT) "All [the grapes] you want" translates כְּנַפְשְׁךָ שָׂבְעֶךָ (*kenapšeḵā śāḇe'eḵā*), which is literally "according to your appetites," or "your fill" (*nep̱eš* as "appetite").

מְלִילֹת (*melîlōṯ*, "kernels") occurs only here in biblical Hebrew but often in postbiblical Hebrew. These two laws on picking grapes and heads of grain appear only in this place. Josephus (Antiq. IV, 231–39 [viii.21]) has an eloquent passage extolling a very liberal and kindly attitude on the part of farmers toward passersby and those in need.

### b. *Marriage, divorce, and remarriage*

#### 24:1–5

**1 If a man marries a woman who becomes displeasing to him because
he finds something indecent about her, and he writes her a certificate of
divorce, gives it to her and sends her from his house, 2 and if after she
leaves his house she becomes the wife of another man, 3 and her second
husband dislikes her and writes her a certificate of divorce, gives it to
her and sends her from his house, or if he dies, 4 then her first husband,
who divorced her, is not allowed to marry her again after she has been
defiled. That would be detestable in the eyes of the LORD. Do not bring
sin upon the land the LORD your God is giving you as an inheritance.**
**5 If a man has recently married, he must not be sent to war or have any
other duty laid on him. For one year he is to be free to stay at home and
bring happiness to the wife he has married.**

**1–4** Divorce in the books of Moses (Lev 21:7, 14; 22:13; Num 30:9) appears as a fact of social life; while under certain circumstances it was permitted, it was to be regulated. Divorce was initiated only by men, not by women. Verses 1–3 are the protasis of a conditional sentence, and the first part of v.4 is the apodosis containing the prohibition. The first three verses set the stage: a man marries a woman who subsequently displeases him because of some indecency. The man divorces the woman, and she remarries another man who also dislikes her and divorces her—or dies, leaving her without a husband. This law says that the first husband cannot marry the woman because she has been defiled by the second marriage. This act (of remarriage), should it occur, would be detestable in the Lord's eyes and would bring sin on the land (v.4). This required procedure for divorce is not given elsewhere but is referred to by Jeremiah (Jer 3:1) and Jesus (Matt 5:31–32).

The basis for divorce is not to be whimsical or frivolous. The man who desires to divorce his wife must show that there is "something indecent" (v.1) about her. Jewish commentators have had differing opinions about what things are covered by "something indecent." In NT times the schools of Shammai and Hillel made lists of what could constitute the basis for divorce, with the school of Shammai being more restrictive than that of Hillel. Something less than adultery must be meant here, since the punishment for adultery is death (22:22–27; Lev 20:10). Being guilty of "something indecent," however, is more than trivial. It must have sufficient grounds to be alleged as "something indecent."

When grounds for divorce existed, the man must have "a certificate of divorce" (v.3) served on his wife. Only then may he send her from his home.

**5** In 20:7 a man engaged to a woman is exempt from military duty. Here exemption is extended to the newly married and lasts for one year, doubtless because in war he might be killed (20:7). However, other conscriptions of like kind are not to be laid on him either. Happy family life and family continuity were held in great respect in the Mosaic economy.

## Notes

---

**1–4** Jesus said that Moses permitted divorce "because your hearts were hard" (Matt 19:8); and Jesus pointed out that what obtained at the beginning, at the creation of mankind, was monogamy (Matt 19:3–9; see also Matt 5:31–32).

1 עֶרְוַת דָּבָר (*'erwat dābār*, "something indecent"; lit., "the indecency of a thing") could be any kind of impurity or indecency. In 23:9 (10 MT), a synonymous phrase, כֹּל דְּבַר רָע (*kōl dābār rā'*, "everything evil") is translated as "everything impure" and includes what is mentioned in 23:14.

The "certificate of divorce"—סֵפֶר כְּרִיתֻת (*sēper kerītut*, "a writing of cutting off")—was a formal document or writ of separation. The man was to put this certificate "into her hand," בְּיָדָהּ (*beyādāh*); i.e., it was his responsibility to see that she had the document in her possession. He could not send her from his house until he had given her such a certificate.

4 הֻטַּמָּאָה (*huttammā'āh*, "defiled") is an unusual form of the verb occurring only here; but the stative verb occurs frequently with the meaning "to be unclean, impure, or defiled," and specifically depicts the result of adultery in Lev 18:20 and Num 5:13–14, 20. So here it refers to whatever defilement is associated with adultery.

5 In the Code of Hammurabi, laws on a man captured in war are elaborated relative to the wife's behavior, which is often determined by her economic situation. For instance, if she can support herself, she is to remain at home and not remarry (Code 133–35, ANET, p. 171).

---

## c. *Concern for others*

### 24:6–22

[6]Do not take a pair of millstones—not even the upper one—as
security for a debt, because that would be taking a man's livelihood as
security.
[7]If a man is caught kidnapping one of his brother Israelites and treats
him as a slave or sells him, the kidnapper must die. You must purge the
evil from among you.
[8]In cases of leprous diseases be very careful to do exactly as the
priests, who are Levites, instruct you. You must follow carefully what I
have commanded them. [9]Remember what the LORD your God did to
Miriam along the way after you came out of Egypt.
[10]When you make a loan of any kind to your neighbor, do not go into
his house to get what he is offering as a pledge. [11]Stay outside and let
the man to whom you are making the loan bring the pledge out to you.
[12]If the man is poor, do not go to sleep with his pledge in your
possession. [13]Return his cloak to him by sunset so that he may sleep in
it. Then he will thank you, and it will be regarded as a righteous act in
the sight of the LORD your God.
[14]Do not take advantage of a hired man who is poor and needy,
whether he is a brother Israelite or an alien living in one of your towns.
[15]Pay him his wages each day before sunset, because he is poor and is
counting on it. Otherwise he may cry to the LORD against you, and you
will be guilty of sin.
[16]Fathers shall not be put to death for their children, nor children put
to death for their fathers; each is to die for his own sin.
[17]Do not deprive the alien or the fatherless of justice, or take the cloak
of the widow as a pledge. [18]Remember that you were slaves in Egypt
and the LORD your God redeemed you from there. That is why I
command you to do this.
[19]When you are harvesting in your field and you overlook a sheaf, do
not go back to get it. Leave it for the alien, the fatherless and the widow,
so that the LORD your God may bless you in all the work of your hands.
[20]When you beat the olives from your trees, do not go over the branches
a second time. Leave what remains for the alien, the fatherless and the
widow. [21]When you harvest the grapes in your vineyard, do not go over
the vines again. Leave what remains for the alien, the fatherless and the

widow. [22]Remember that you were slaves in Egypt. That is why I command you to do this.

**6** The millstones that ground the grain (a basic life sustenance) for a family were not to be taken as security for a loan. The family's life was involved. Not even the upper millstone—the most easily carried part—was to be taken. The lower millstone by itself could not grind grain.

**7** The death penalty would be exacted of one who kidnapped a brother Israelite for involuntary servitude under the captor or as merchandise to sell. The victim's free life was involved; so the death penalty was decreed for the culprit—life for life.

Once more the relationship of crime to the responsibility of the commonwealth and to its moral condition is emphasized by the demand: "You must purge the evil from among you" (see comment on 13:1–5).

**8–9** Twice the people were exhorted to exercise special care to follow the commands of the Lord regarding infectious skin diseases or other malignant infections in the houses, etc. The experience of Miriam illustrates the dire results of disobedience—the consequences for those who contracted leprous diseases (Num 12:1–15). The reference to leprous diseases presupposes acquaintance with the legislation of Leviticus 13–14.

**10–13** The grant of a loan to a neighbor should be made discreetly with consideration for the neighbor's privacy (v.10). What is given as security is chosen by the neighbor privately within the walls of his home and brought out to the one granting the loan (v.11). If the neighbor is so impoverished that his cloak, which serves as his bedclothes at night as well as his outer garment during the day, has to be given as security, the cloak must be returned to him by sunset (vv.12–13). God will approve this act as a righteous one, and the debtor will thank his creditor.

**14–15** One was not to take advantage of the poor workingman living in any Israelite town, whether he be Israelite or alien (v.14). Wages were to be paid each day because the worker expected it to cover his daily expenses (v.15). In contrast to the thankfulness of the man whose garment was returned at sunset, the man who was denied his daily wage at sunset may cry to the Lord against his employer, and sin would be registered against him—rather than the righteousness with which the creditor would be reckoned (v.13).

**16** The law of individual responsibility under which the courts decreed punishment inflicts that punishment only on the criminal. Though shame and other consequences of crime fall naturally on one's family and descendants according to the governance of God, the punishment to be exacted for a crime falls on the perpetrator alone. As in 7:10, "those who hate him he will repay to their face." Therefore, the Israelites as a community are not to put fathers to death for their children's crime, but "each is to die for his own sin."

One has to reckon, however, that the OT brings us face to face with experiences that involve what Kaiser (*Old Testament Ethics*, pp. 67–72) calls corporate solidarity. In such situations the group as a whole is implicated, and the individuals in the group are either punished with the group or are benefitted by union with it. David, for instance, after his sin with Bathsheba, said, "I have sinned against the LORD" (2 Sam 12:13). David admitted that he had sinned, but God said that the sword would never depart from his house, not just from David (2 Sam 12:10).

**17–18** Concern for the underprivileged, a concern that appears again and again in Deuteronomy (10:18–19; 14:29; 16:11; 24:6, 10–15 as well as the rest of this chapter), is based on Exodus 22:21–24; 23:6, 9; and Leviticus 19:9–10; 23:22. Israel's slavery in Egypt should have made the people sensitive to the needs of the less fortunate. Moreover, that experience is said to be the reason for God's commands that they act kindly toward the alien, the widow, and the orphan (vv.18, 22). This compassionate consideration arising from one's own former, less-fortunate condition contrasts with the common psychology that excuses criminal action on the basis of some former mistreatment of the criminal.

The alien and fatherless are not to be deprived of justice, and the widow's cloak must not be taken in pledge (though taking a cloak in pledge, temporarily, was allowed for others, vv.12–13).

**19–22** The overlooked sheaf of grain was to be left for the underprivileged so that the Lord's blessing may rest on the owner's endeavors (v.19). Only once are the olive trees to be beaten with poles to harvest olives (v.20). The remaining olives were for the alien, the widow, and the orphan. In grape harvest also the vines were gone over only once so that the needy could have the remainder (v.21).

Underlying these rules for noble behavior is concern for the disadvantaged and the underprivileged. Again the remembrance motif is cited as reason for Israel's consideration of the needy. The Israelites were to remember that they had been redeemed from Egypt (v.22).

## Notes

---

**7** In the Code of Hammurabi, kidnapping is punishable by death, but so is robbery (Codes 14 and 22, ANET, pp. 166–67).

**8** In נֶגַע־הַצָּרַעַת (*nega'-haṣṣāra'at*, "in case of leprous diseases"), *nega'*—which is used of the plagues of Egypt as well as the "plague" of leprosy—at least sometimes refers to the marks of a "leprous disease" (cf. Lev 13:3). The sense here in v.8 may be "carefully watch for the marks of leprous diseases." The rest of the verse indicates that Moses had given the priests detailed instructions on leprous diseases prior to this time (see Lev 13–14).

On "priests, who are Levites," see the Notes on 17:9.

**14** For לֹא־תַעֲשֹׁק שָׂכִיר (*lō'-ta'ašōq śākîr*, "do not take advantage of a hired man"), Craigie (p. 309) suggests vocalizing שׂכר (*śkr*) as a construct, שְׂכַר (*śekar*); so the sentence would read: "Do not withhold the wages of the poor and needy." The NEB has "the wages of a man who is poor and needy." "Poor and needy" occur together in 15:11 and as a set phrase in Job, Psalms, Proverbs, Isaiah, Jeremiah, Ezekiel, and Amos, but not as modifiers of another term.

**15** Solicitude for the laboring poor and needy is in contrast to Hittite law where the rights of the laborer are not a matter of concern (see Neufeld, *Hittite Laws*, p. 157).

קָרָא (*qārā'*, "cry") means "make an appeal," as that of the needy brother who is denied help because a sabbatical year is near (15:9). This is in contrast to the more emotive cry—צָעַק (*ṣā'aq*, "scream," "cry out")—of the girl attacked by a rapist (22:24, 27) or the anguished cry of the Israelites in Egypt (26:7).

**17** In numbers of Near Eastern texts as early as the third century B.C., concern for the poor, the widow, and the orphan is enunciated (*World of the Bible*, 1:282).

---

## d. *Civil situations*

### 25:1–4

[1]When men have a dispute, they are to take it to court and the judges will decide the case, acquitting the innocent and condemning the guilty. [2]If the guilty man deserves to be beaten, the judge shall make him lie down and have him flogged in his presence with the number of lashes his crime deserves, [3]but he must not give him more than forty lashes. If he is flogged more than that, your brother will be degraded in your eyes.
[4]Do not muzzle an ox while it is treading out the grain.

**1–3** When a dispute arises between persons, they are to take the matter to court (v.1). The alternative would be to take matters into their own hands, and that is not acceptable in a nation governed by law. Moreover, the judge has been given the responsibility and the authority to make decisions and to make sure that the punishment, if any, is inflicted on the guilty party.

A guilty man, who deserves to be beaten, must be beaten with the number of blows commensurate with the nature of his crime (v.2). Moreover, the number of blows must not exceed forty lashes because more blows would be inhumane; the brother would be degraded (humiliated) in the public's eyes (v.3). The guilty man is to lie down in front of the judge who has sentenced him and is to be flogged there so that the punishment will conform to the judge's decision.

**4** Animals too must be treated with kindness. They are to be worked with their need of food in mind. In the threshing process oxen or other heavy animals (especially donkeys) were led around a threshing floor, sometimes harnessed to a central pivot. The stalks of grain were laid on the floor, and the hooves of the animals and sometimes a sledge drawn by animals would separate the kernels from the stalks and hulls (Isa 28:28; 41:15; Hos 10:11).

This law concerning threshing animals occurs only here in the OT, but the apostle Paul twice quoted it to illustrate that "the thresher threshes . . . in the hope of sharing in the harvest" (1 Cor 9:9–10; 1 Tim 5:18). Paul was not saying that God is unconcerned about oxen but rather that the Deuteronomic law can be applied to human beings as well (see EBC, 10:242–43, and W.C. Kaiser, Jr., "The Current Crisis in Exegesis and the Apostolic Use of Deuteronomy 25:4 in 1 Corinthians 9:8–10," JETS 21, 1 [March 1978]: 3–13).

## Notes

---

**1** אֶל־הַמִּשְׁפָּט (*'el-hammišpāṭ*, "to the judgment") here is "to the place of judgment," that is, "to court."

The verbal and substantival forms of צָדַק (*ṣāḏaq*) and רָשַׁע (*rāša'*) in this place mean, respectively, "to declare the innocent innocent and the guilty guilty."

**2** בִּן הַכּוֹת (*bin hakkôṯ*, "a son of beating") is, according to Hebrew idiom, equal to "one who deserves to be beaten"; as in 1 Sam 2:12, "sons of Belial" means "wicked men," and in 1 Sam 20:31, "a son of death" means "he must die." On flogging see *World of the Bible*, 1:283.

**4** On threshing see W.M. Thomson, *The Land and the Book* (Grand Rapids: Baker, 1954), 2:314–15; *World and the Bible*, 1:282; and ZPEB, 5:739.

---

## e. *Levirate marriage*

### 25:5–10

**5 If brothers are living together and one of them dies without a son, his**
**widow must not marry outside the family. Her husband's brother shall**
**take her and marry her and fulfill the duty of a brother-in-law to her.**
**6 The first son she bears shall carry on the name of the dead brother so**
**that his name will not be blotted out from Israel.**
**7 However, if a man does not want to marry his brother's wife, she shall**
**go to the elders at the town gate and say, "My husband's brother**
**refuses to carry on his brother's name in Israel. He will not fulfill the duty**
**of a brother-in-law to me." 8 Then the elders of his town shall summon**
**him and talk to him. If he persists in saying, "I do not want to marry her,"**
**9 his brother's widow shall go up to him in the presence of the elders,**
**take off one of his sandals, spit in his face and say, "This is what is done**
**to the man who will not build up his brother's family line." 10 That man's**
**line shall be known in Israel as The Family of the Unsandaled.**

The "discrepancies" or "contradictions" between Genesis 38 (the affair of Judah, Onan, and Tamar), the Book of Ruth, and Deuteronomy 5–10 have been given several solutions. M. Burrows ("The Ancient Oriental Background of Hebrew Levirate Marriage," BASOR 77 [1940]: 2–15) suggests that the variations are due to historical development, while Thomas and Dorothy Thompson ("Some Legal Problems in the Book of Ruth," VetTest 18 [January 1968]: 79–99) suppose that the differences come from a too rigid interpretation of the three sources. Kaiser (*Ethics*, pp. 190–92) recognizes that the discrepancies are real but that by sanctioning levirate marriage God has simply made an exception to prohibitions regarding incest in marriage. Was the law of levirate marriage an approval of polygamy? Hardly! It was rather an alternate arrangement under specific bounds to make possible the retention of landed property throughout the families of Israel. It had a subsidiary result of protecting widows without children. E. Neufeld (*Ancient Hebrew Marriage Laws* [London: Longmans, 1944], pp. 23–55) says that among the Jews of postbiblical times there was a tendency to discourage levirate marriage.

In the Mishnah the first tractate (*Yabamot*, "sisters-in-law") of the third order (*Nashim*, "women") covers the subject of levirate marriage with considerable detail. In addition, see especially Donald A. Leggett, *The Levirate and Goel Institutions in the Old Testament With Special Attention to the Book of Ruth* (Cherry Hill, N.J.: Mack, 1974), pp. 29–62; 83–142.

**5–6** The social structure based on family and tribal divisions and relationships and the ownership of property by tribes and families were of prime importance in the Mosaic economy. Consequently, levirate marriage, an ancient custom in the Near East, under which a brother (or nearest relative by marriage) takes a childless brother's widow into his home to raise up a descendant, was of considerable importance relative to the continuity of the family and the distribution of landed property.

In the history of the interpretation of this Deuteronomic law, difference of opinion existed among Jewish expositors whether *bēn* in v.5 meant "son" or "child." The LXX and Josephus render it "child." Moses had already established that when no male heir existed, daughters would be heirs of their father's property (Num 27:1–8). So a basic reason for levirate marriage did not exist if a man died without a male heir but did have a daughter. Many interpreters, however, consider that a male heir is meant here. The rule that the widow must not marry outside the family is similar to that which grew from the experience of Zelophehad's daughters, who were limited to the clan of their father (Num 36:10–12).

If the husband's brother fulfilled the law of the *levir,* the first son (child?) the widow bore was to carry on the name of the dead brother (v.6). The estate would belong to him.

**7–10** If the man did not want to marry his brother's wife, the widow could hold him up to public shame and disapproval by bringing the matter to court (the city gate) before the elders (v.7). There she would indict her husband's brother for his refusal to carry on her late husband's name. If the elders failed to break the man's persistence in not marrying the woman (v.8), she was to take off one of his sandals, spit in his face, and denounce him as one who would not build up his brother's family line (v.9). His family line would then be known as "The Family of the Unsandaled" (v.10). This procedure is given as law only here, but the narratives in Genesis 38 and Ruth 4 indicate similar if not the same practice. The legislation makes possible the release of the brother-in-law from his duty, while definitely discouraging such failure by the shame involved in being brought to court, spit upon, and labeled as "The Family of the Unsandaled."

## Notes

**5** יָבָם (*yāḇām,* "husband's brother") and the Piel verb יִבֵּם (*yibbam,* "to act as a *yāḇām*") are technical words used only here in biblical Hebrew. The giving of a special designation to this relationship might show the importance that the Israelites attached to this situation, as S.R. Driver (*Deuteronomy,* pp. 282–83) suggests.

*Levir* is the Latin equivalent of the Hebrew *yāḇām* ("husband's brother").

The Levitical law prohibited marriage between a man and his brother's wife and says that such a union will be childless (Lev 20:21). This appears to be directly opposed to levirate marriage. The application of this Levitical law, however, probably refers to sexual intercourse and possibly to marriage while the brother is still alive.

Verse 5 limits the law's application to brothers who are living together, but it can only be surmised how close "together" means. It may well mean within the family landed inheritance. As the people on the plains of Moab contemplated the allocation of the land of Canaan among their tribes, their clans, and their families, brothers living together would most likely be within their family allotment.

**5–6** בֵּן (*bēn*) may be either "son" or "child." Josephus (Antiq. IV, 254 [viii.23]) speaks of the husband having no children but then goes on to speak of the son that would be born of the levirate marriage. See also WBE, 2:1083, and Reider, pp. 230–31.

**7–10** Boaz was not Ruth's brother-in-law, but near kinship and taking the widow with the property, as well as using the sandal as a symbol, indicate levirate marriage (Ruth 4:1–10).

**8** The Hebrew idiom וְעָמַד וְאָמַר (*wᵉʿāmaḏ wᵉʾāmar*, "be steadfast and say") means "persists in saying," as in Ruth 2:7: "worked steadily" or "persistently."

---

## f. Belligerent behavior and honest measures

25:11–16

[11]If two men are fighting and the wife of one of them comes to rescue
her husband from his assailant, and she reaches out and seizes him by
his private parts, [12]you shall cut off her hand. Show her no pity.
[13]Do not have two differing weights in your bag—one heavy, one
light. [14]Do not have two differing measures in your house—one large,
one small. [15]You must have accurate and honest weights and measures,
so that you may live long in the land the LORD your God is giving you.
[16]For the LORD your God detests anyone who does these things, anyone
who deals dishonestly.

**11–12** Indecency in sexual situations is said to be illustrated by the law against a woman laying hold of the private parts of an assailant of her husband (v.11). The circumstance here cited would not be common but is rather a case law, which would cover all such actions. The punishment of having the offending hand cut off was a severe one, necessitating the additional statement: "Show her no pity" (v.12). Once again the Deuteronomic law appears to be based on the use of law and punishment as a deterrent to crime.

**13–14** An Israelite was to be honest in any commercial dealing (Lev 19:35–36). That requirement is even more particularized here. The phrase "differing weights" (v.13) is stone and stone, a Hebrew way of indicating variety. This is made more specific by adding "heavy" and "light." A large stone for buying (to acquire more for one's money) and a small stone for selling (to give less) were unlawful. Weights were carried in a bag for transactions anywhere.

Neither were the people to have differing quantitative measures in their homes (v.14). These are also specified—"one large, one small."

**15–16** The Lord detests those who deal dishonestly (v.16); but, on the other hand, when people follow his ethical standards, he will reward them with long life in the land he is about to give them (v.15).

Jesus taught that one should give a good measure: "For with the measure you use, it will be measured to you" (Luke 6:38).

## Notes

---

**13** Palestinian weights in OT times were not accurate and often not honest (Prov 11:1; 20:23; Amos 8:5). The weights that have been found vary greatly. This variation was due to the difficulty in finding accurate weights when stones were used as measuring instruments. No Bureau of Standards existed; however, there was some uniformity for the current weight of the shekel among the merchants (Gen 23:16), the "sanctuary shekel" (Exod 30:13 et al.), or the shekel by the "royal standard" (2 Sam 14:26); but these also varied.

Quantitative measurements were even more difficult to determine. The law in Leviticus and Deuteronomy was possible to follow, however, in each individual's dealings. He, at least, could use the same measure for buying and selling (see Thomas, pp. 227–30).

**13–14** אֶבֶן וָאָבֶן (*'eben wā'āben*, lit., "stone and stone") means "differing weights," and אֵיפָה וְאֵיפָה (*'êpāh we'êpāh*, "ephah and ephah") means "differing measures." The ephah was the most commonly used quantitative measure.

**15** Weights and measures were required to be שְׁלֵמָה (*šelēmāh*, "accurate") and צֶדֶק (*ṣedeq*, "honest"). They were to be accurate in the sense of whole, full, complete, and honest as right, fair, and just.

---

## g. Destruction of Amalek

### 25:17–19

**[17]Remember what the Amalekites did to you along the way when you came out of Egypt. [18]When you were weary and worn out, they met you on your journey and cut off all who were lagging behind; they had no fear of God. [19]When the LORD your God gives you rest from all the enemies around you in the land he is giving you to possess as an inheritance, you shall blot out the memory of Amalek from under heaven. Do not forget!**

**17–19** The Amalekites sprang from Esau's son Eliphaz and his concubine Timna (Gen 36:15–16; 1 Chron 1:36). They were a nomadic, marauding, desert tribe living in the Negev south of Beersheba and in upper Sinai including the deserts of Zin and Shur. When the Israelites were at Rephidim early in the Exodus, they were attacked by the Amalekites (Exod 17:8–16). The Israelites eventually won those battles because Aaron and Hur upheld Moses' hands—"lifted up to the throne of the LORD" (Exod 17:16)—while Joshua and the army fought. At that time the Lord told Moses, "Write this on a scroll as something to be remembered and make sure that Joshua hears it, because I will completely blot out the memory of Amalek from under heaven" (Exod 17:14). Later, after Israel rejected the directive of the Lord to enter Canaan from the south, in an abortive war Israel suffered defeat at the hands of the Amalekites and the Canaanites (Num 14:39–45). Once more Moses called the Israelites to remember the Amalekite harassment on their journeys in Sinai and the Negev. He reminded them that the Amalekites attacked the "weary and worn" stragglers (v.18). Nowhere else is this experience mentioned; so it most probably refers to a more common harassment than that of the definite battles at Rephidim and Hormah.

In these attacks against God's people, the Amalekites showed "no fear of God" (v.18) and so came under his indictment. The call to remember what the Amalekites had done and the Lord's directive concerning them are emphasized by the totality of the destruction decreed: "You shall blot the memory of Amalek from under heaven," and by the additional admonition: "Do not forget!" (v.19).

The reminder (v.19) comes quite properly in this series of directives that were to prepare the Israelites for entrance into Canaan. As people under covenant-treaty with the Lord, it was necessary that they obey the stipulations of that covenant. One of the stipulations written into the record, according to Exodus 17:14, included the statement "I will completely blot out the memory of Amalek from under heaven." The Amalekites disappeared from history after the time of Hezekiah (1 Chron 4:43).

God's declaration concerning the Amalekites must be interpreted with the circumstances that developed. Moses in Deuteronomy spoke of the Lord as a God of love, with concern not only for his people but for others—even for animals. Yet the Amalekites and the nations of Canaan were to be rigorously destroyed. This destruction rests on the same basis as the destruction of the pre-Noahic people (Gen 6:5–7) and the people of Sodom and Gomorrah (Gen 18:20–21; 19:24–25). Their incorrigible wickedness was such that annihilation was necessary. Besides this the Amalekites, by their attacks on God's people—and that against the weak and worn-out ones—indicated that "they had no fear of God" (v.18).

## Notes

---

**18** The Niphal participle in כָּל־הַנֶּחֱשָׁלִים אַחֲרֶיךָ (*kol-hanneḥ[e]šālîm 'aḥareyḵā*, "all who were lagging behind") indicates that the ones lagging behind (*'aḥareyḵā*) were broken down, incapacitated, by the desert travel. Therefore, they were unable to keep up with the main body of people, who themselves were "weary," עָיֵף (*'āyēp̱*, being faint from exertion, thirst, and hunger), and "worn out," יָגֵעַ (*yāḡē[a]'*, worn out from labor, etc.). Because of the depleted strength of the stragglers, the attacks of the Amalekites on them were the more wicked and despicable.

---

### 5. *Firstfruits and tithes*

#### 26:1–15

[1]When you have entered the land the LORD your God is giving you as
an inheritance and have taken possession of it and settled in it, [2]take
some of the firstfruits of all that you produce from the soil of the land
the LORD your God is giving you and put them in a basket. Then go to the
place the LORD your God will choose as a dwelling for his Name [3]and say
to the priest in office at the time, "I declare today to the LORD your God
that I have come to the land the LORD swore to our forefathers to give
us." [4]The priest shall take the basket from your hands and set it down in
front of the altar of the LORD your God. [5]Then you shall declare before
the LORD your God: "My father was a wandering Aramean, and he went
down into Egypt with a few people and lived there and became a great
nation, powerful and numerous. [6]But the Egyptians mistreated us and
made us suffer, putting us to hard labor. [7]Then we cried out to the LORD,
the God of our fathers, and the LORD heard our voice and saw our
misery, toil and oppression. [8]So the LORD brought us out of Egypt with a
mighty hand and an outstretched arm, with great terror and with
miraculous signs and wonders. [9]He brought us to this place and gave us
this land, a land flowing with milk and honey; [10]and now I bring the
firstfruits of the soil that you, O LORD, have given me." Place the basket
before the LORD your God and bow down before him. [11]And you and the
Levites and the aliens among you shall rejoice in all the good things the
LORD your God has given to you and your household.

[12]When you have finished setting aside a tenth of all your produce in
the third year, the year of the tithe, you shall give it to the Levite, the
alien, the fatherless and the widow, so that they may eat in your towns

and be satisfied. [13]Then say to the LORD your God: "I have removed from my house the sacred portion and have given it to the Levite, the alien, the fatherless and the widow, according to all you commanded. I have not turned aside from your commands nor have I forgotten any of them. [14]I have not eaten any of the sacred portion while I was in mourning, nor have I removed any of it while I was unclean, nor have I offered any of it to the dead. I have obeyed the LORD my God; I have done everything you commanded me. [15]Look down from heaven, your holy dwelling place, and bless your people Israel and the land you have given us as you promised on oath to our forefathers, a land flowing with milk and honey."

**1** Deuteronomy 26 consists of a remarkably compact presentation of salient features of Israel's early history, religion, and economy. It begins with Moses again mentioning that these particular directives he was about to give them were to be followed when they entered, possessed, and settled in the land.

Once more the land is referred to as the people's inheritance, a reference to the Abrahamic covenant (Gen 12:7). The key word "inheritance" is first used as a part of the Promised Land in Genesis 48:6. There Jacob explained some matters regarding the succession of Joseph's sons in the tribal structure of Israel based on the reiteration to Jacob of the promise of the land to Abraham.

**2–4** When the people were settled in the land, each leader of a family was to take in a basket some of the first produce of the soil to the place the Lord would choose as a "dwelling for his name"; that is, the locale of the tabernacle (v.2). There each man was to say to the priest officiating at that time, "I declare today to the LORD your God that I have come to the land the LORD swore to our forefathers to give us" (v.3). This is tantamount to saying, "I have received my part of the land as an inheritance according to the promise of God." The landowner then was to present to the priest the basket of produce as a token of the land's fruitfulness, and the priest was to set the basket down in front of the altar (v.4). Though v.10 says that the man was to place the basket before the Lord and bow down before him (in worship), this is not contradictory (or in addition) to v.4, which says that the priest was to set it down in front of the altar. Not infrequently one statement speaks as though a certain person does a thing while another statement clarifies the action by stating more precisely that another person actually performs the deed for him.

Since only priests were allowed in the tabernacle, the altar spoken of must be the altar of sacrifice outside the tent.

These tokens of the first produce of the land together with the declarations made by the offerer, while similar to the law of the regular offering of firstfruits (Exod 23:19; 34:26), surely refers to an initial offering to be made after the first harvest in the land—subsequent, of course, (for orchards) to the years required by the legislation of Leviticus 19:23–25. The first statement of the declaration (v.3), particularly, is not fitting for annual repetition.

**5–6** The terse historical review (vv.5–9), replete with phrases and descriptive clauses used elsewhere, witnesses to the Israelites' faith in the Lord their God. Jacob, the wandering Aramean, went down into Egypt with a few individuals but became a numerous and powerful people, who, after mistreatment and suffering under hard labor, were brought out of Egypt by the Lord.

**7–11** The Lord was the God of their fathers (v.7), an expression reminiscent of the discussion between God and Moses at the burning bush. At that time when he was to appear before the enslaved Israelites in Egypt, Moses was to identify the God who spoke to him and who directed him to lead his people out of Egypt as "the LORD, the God of your fathers" (Exod 3:16). And so it was that the Israelites were to now assert that they cried out in distress to the God of their history, not to any newly found or newly revealed God, and that the God of their fathers had brought them out of Egypt and into the Promised Land.

The highly descriptive terms "misery" and "oppression" (v.7), the "mighty hand," the "outstretched arm," the "great terror," the "miraculous signs and wonders" (v.8) are used elsewhere of the Exodus experience.

Israel's escape from the oppression in Egypt and from the trials of the Exodus and the blessings of residence in the land "flowing with milk and honey" (v.9; cf. 6:3) are all credited to the Lord with thankfulness, worship, and rejoicing. Levites and aliens were to be included as participants in this festivity (v.11).

**12–15** Appended to this initial giving of the firstfruits is the rule for the setting aside of the tithe of every third year for the support of the Levites and the underprivileged (v.12). This triennial tithe was probably presented in the donor's town. It would be logistically wasteful to carry these tithes to a central sanctuary and then return them to the towns from which they came and there distribute them to the Levites, the aliens, the fatherless, and the widows.

In substance the declaration to be made (vv.13–15) says that the tenth of the produce had been removed from the donor's premises and was given to the Levites and the underprivileged alien, fatherless, and widow. None of it had been diverted or mishandled. So because the donor had obeyed the Lord's command, he could pray for the Lord's blessing on the people and on the land the Lord had given to the people—a good illustration of being on praying ground.

The part of the produce of the land given to the Levites and the underprivileged is called the "tenth" or "tithe" (v.12; see 12:6) and the "sacred portion" (v.13). Being sacred, the tenth is definitely not for the donor's use. This sacred tithe was not conceived of as merely a secular tax for the welfare of the poor but as an act inspired by the Lord. Both the giving of it by the donor and the reception of it by the Levite or underprivileged were spiritual acts, and the tithe itself was to be recognized as holy. The eating of it was expected to satisfy the receptor because of its abundance. None should be hungry.

Several specific situations illustrate the speaker's assertion that he himself had not eaten any of the tenth (v.14). He had not eaten any of it while in mourning. The participant in mourning would be unclean as the next situations also attest. The tenth was not removed when the donor was unclean for any reason. Neither was any of the food ever offered to the dead. Whether this refers to putting food in the grave with the dead body or to being given to relatives for their sustenance during the mourning period or even to being sold to defray the expenses of a funeral, the donor was not guilty of any improper use of the sacred portion that took place when he could be considered ritually unclean. Putting food in a grave with a dead body was a common Egyptian and Canaanite practice, which is most likely what the Israelites were not to emulate.

The worshiper's reiteration of having obeyed the commands of the Lord is surely meant to instill in him that this procedure was indeed a stipulation in the Lord's covenant and that he was obeying it to the letter, an assertion equal to that of a modern notarized affidavit. Observe the repetitions (vv.13–14): "according to all you commanded. . . . [I have not] forgotten any of them. . . . I have obeyed the LORD my God; I have done everything you commanded me."

The affirmation ends with prayer recognizing that God's dwelling place is in heaven and that he had given the Israelites the land flowing with milk and honey as he had promised to their forefathers (v.15). Thus continued blessing on both people and land was requested.

## Notes

**1** נַחֲלָה (*naḥ*[a]*lāh,* "inheritance") stems from the Lord's promise to Abraham: "To your offspring I will give this land" (Gen 12:7). On his deathbed Jacob repeated these words to Joseph and then—using the verb form נָחַל (*nāḥal,* "inherit")—said that Ephraim and Manasseh would inherit an allotment in Canaan (Gen 48:6). This was the basis for the idea that Canaan was Israel's by inheritance. Though they had not possessed it, the land belonged to those who were descendants of Abraham through Jacob. See the comment on 4:20; TWOT, 2:569–70; and TDNT, 3:769–76.

**2** On the use of "the name of the LORD" in Deuteronomy, see the comment on 32:3.

**4, 10** Notice, for instance, that 2 Kings 24:13 says that Solomon made all the gold articles for the temple when actually artisans did the work.

For a different interpretation of who set the basket in front of the altar, see Craigie (p. 320), who suggests that two actions are involved, with the priest returning the basket to the offerer who then puts it down before the altar. This appears to be a bit artificial.

**5** אֲרַמִּי אֹבֵד ('[a]*rammî 'ōḇēḏ,* "a wandering Aramean") describes Jacob who had left home in Canaan, lived with his mother's people in Haran, and from them took his two wives, Leah and Rachel. When he returned to Canaan, he continually moved about as a herdsman—a wandering Aramean.

Some commentators take אֹבֵד (*'ōḇēḏ,* "wandering") as meaning impoverished, lost, or ailing—all taken from the meaning of "perishing" (cf. KJV). Most modern translators have "wandering" taken from the idea of strayed or lost property (22:3; 1 Sam 9:3, 20). In Jer 50:6 *'ōḇēḏ* describes the people of Judah as sheep lost and gone astray; in Ezek 34:4 the shepherds of Israel are castigated for failure in bringing back his lost, straying people; and in Ezek 34:16 God says he will search for the lost and bring back the strays. In Ps 119:176 the psalmist says that he has strayed as a lost sheep. The NIV often translates *'ōḇēḏ* (or cognate form) as "lost," but the sense in this context, as the parallels in these verses show, relate to straying and wandering people.

**7** נִצְעַק (*niṣ'aq,* "we cried out") describes an outcry for help in anguish, distress, or grief.

**7–8** For עָנָה (*'ānāh,* "misery"), see Gen 15:13; Exod 1:11–12; לַחַץ (*lāḥaṣ,* "oppression"), see Exod 3:9; יָד חֲזָקָה (*yāḏ ḥ*[a]*zāqāh,* "mighty hand") and זְרֹעַ נְטוּיָה (*z*[e]*rō*[a]*' n*[e]*ṭûyāh,* "outstretched arm"), see Deut 4:34; 5:15; מֹרָא גָּדֹל (*mōrā' gāḏōl,* "awesome deeds"; NIV, "great terror"), see Deut 4:34; 34:12; and וּבְאֹתוֹת וּבְמֹפְתִים (*ûḇ*[e]*'ōṯôṯ ûḇ*[e]*mōp̄*[e]*ṯîm,* "and with miraculous signs and wonders"), see Deut 4:34; 6:22; 7:19; 13:1.

**12–13** On מַעְשַׂר (*ma'śar,* "tenth [tithe]") and הַקֹּדֶשׁ (*haqqōḏeš,* "sacred portion," "the holy thing," used of anything set apart for God—and for God himself), see the comment on 12:1–14.

**13** S.R. Driver (*Deuteronomy,* in loc.) et al. say that the declaration to be made לִפְנֵי יהוה (*lip̄nê YHWH;* lit., "before the LORD") meant before the Lord in the tabernacle (later in the temple). However, in some places this prepositional phrase means no more than the shorter inseparable preposition לְ (*l*[e], "to"), as in 1 Sam 1:12, where the NIV translates "praying to the LORD." So here in Deut 26:13, the NIV text says, "Then say to the LORD your God," which prayer could be made anywhere.

**14** בְּאֹנִי (*be'ōnî*, "in mourning") is most probably from אָוֶן (*'āwen*, "sorrow"), as in Ps 90:10 or Hos 9:4. Craigie (in loc.) suggests the basic meaning "strength," implying one's own strength as over against God's strength, giving the sense: I have not eaten of it "trusting in my own strength." The context supports the notion of something relating to ritual uncleanness.

**15** This is the first reference to God's dwelling place as a מְעוֹן קָדְשְׁךָ (*mā'ôn qodšekā*, "holy dwelling place"). The same phrase occurs later in 2 Chron 30:27; Ps 68:5 (6 MT); Jer 25:30; and Zech 2:13 (17 MT). This does not suggest that the Lord does not dwell in the tabernacle—or, for that matter, anywhere else—no more than the Lord's prayer (Matt 6:9–13) directed to "Our Father in heaven" excludes him from earth.

---

## 6. *Concluding exhortation and the declaration of the covenant-treaty compact*

### 26:16–19

16The LORD your God commands you this day to follow these decrees
and laws; carefully observe them with all your heart and with all your
soul. 17You have declared this day that the LORD is your God and that
you will walk in his ways, that you will keep his decrees, commands and
laws, and that you will obey him. 18And the LORD has declared this day
that you are his people, his treasured possession as he promised, and
that you are to keep all his commands. 19He has declared that he will set
you in praise, fame and honor high above all the nations he has made
and that you will be a people holy to the LORD your God, as he promised.

**16–19** Chapter 26—and this whole section of Deuteronomy (12:1–26:19)—concludes with an exhortation to adhere carefully to the stipulations of the covenant-treaty the Lord has given to the Israelites. "This day" (v.16) points to a particular day when the command to follow God's decrees and laws was reiterated on the plains of Moab and when the people declared that the Lord was their God and the Lord declared that they were his people (vv.17–18). The Hiphil of *'āmar* ("declared"), used for the declaration of the people and that of the Lord, is unique to this passage and appears to be Moses' special word for the covenant-treaty formula. Moses also exhorted the people—as he often did in the speech preceding this declaration—to be careful to observe (i.e., to rigorously keep) the stipulations, not only formally, and certainly not grudgingly, but with a total commitment of themselves—with all their "heart" and "soul" (v.16; cf. 6:5).

The Lord declared on his part that the Israelites in a special sense were his people (though all people are his creation), and they were further defined again as his "treasured possession" (v.18; see 7:6; 14:2). He had promised their forefathers that they would be his people, his treasured possession, and a people holy to the Lord (7:7–8; 14:2; see also Gen 15:7–21; Exod 19:5–6).

As the Lord was to be the object of their praise (10:21), so his people would be the object of the praise of the nations (v.19). They would have a name with a fame high above other nations, far more than any of those peoples. The words translated "praise" and "honor" (v.19) are used together to describe the Lord in Psalm 71:8: "My mouth is filled with your praise,/ declaring your splendor all day long."

This exhortation and declaration concludes the section on the stipulations of the covenant-treaty covering individual, family, tribal, national, and international relationships. These stipulations were especially important for the Israelites at this juncture in their budding national existence. One relationship towers above all others in importance: Israel must be loyal and obedient to the Lord their God, the Suzerain who presented this covenant to them.

The character of the address is historical, legal, reminiscent, sometimes extemporaneous, and often repetitive, exhortative, or parenthetic.

In this last section (vv.16–19) the treaty form involves the people's acceptance of the Lord as suzerain and Moses' acceptance of Israel as the Lord's vassal people. Moses served as the covenant's mediator.

## Notes

**16–19** As Nicholson (p. 45) says, "An actual covenant ceremony is presupposed by XXVI. 16–19." See also Kline, *Biblical Authority,* pp. 132–39.

**16** הַיּוֹם הַזֶּה (*hayyôm hazzeh,* "this day") and הַיּוֹם (*hayyôm,* "today," vv.17–18 [NIV, "this day"]) are more explicit than יוֹם (*yôm,* "day") by itself, but the length of time meant must be determined by the context.

"Decrees and laws" refer to the stipulations of both the first and the second addresses. The words occur together in many places, and sometimes more or less synonymous words occur with them. See especially 4:1, 14, 45; 5:1; 6:1; 7:11; 11:32; and the introduction to the second address in 12:1.

The use of three words in 6:5—לֵבָב (*lēḇāḇ,* "heart"), נֶפֶשׁ (*nep̱eš,* "soul"), and מְאֹד (*m^e'ōḏ,* "strength") rather than two words here—*lēḇāḇ* and *nep̱eš*—does not imply greater adherence in 6:5. It is simply a slightly more descriptive way of saying the same thing.

## D. *Ratification of the Covenant-Treaty (27:1–26)*

### 1. *The law and the altar on Mount Ebal*

### 27:1–8

[1]Moses and the elders of Israel commanded the people: "Keep all these commands that I give you today. [2]When you have crossed the Jordan into the land the LORD your God is giving you, set up some large stones and coat them with plaster. [3]Write on them all the words of this law when you have crossed over to enter the land the LORD your God is giving you, a land flowing with milk and honey, just as the LORD, the God of your fathers, promised you. [4]And when you have crossed the Jordan, set up these stones on Mount Ebal, as I command you today, and coat them with plaster. [5]Build there an altar to the LORD your God, an altar of stones. Do not use any iron tool upon them. [6]Build the altar of the LORD your God with fieldstones and offer burnt offerings on it to the LORD your God. [7]Sacrifice fellowship offerings there, eating them and rejoicing in the presence of the LORD your God. [8]And you shall write very clearly all the words of this law on these stones you have set up."

Chapters 27–28 constitute the instruction for impressing the covenant-treaty on the people by two specific programs: (1) the setting up on Mount Ebal of stones on which the law was written and building a fieldstone altar on which burnt offerings and fellowship offerings were to be sacrificed for this event, (2) the presentation by the people of the cursings and blessings. Some of the tribes were to be on Mount Gerizim to bless the people for obedience, and the others were to be on Mount Ebal to pronounce curses for disobedience.

In the specific procedures that immediately follow (vv.14–26), the Levites, presumably standing in the middle of the valley between the mountains, actually recited the curses; and the people affirmed their agreement by saying, "Amen."

Because the tribes to represent the blessings are mentioned first, one would expect the blessings to precede the curses; but the blessings are not given. Why they are not given cannot now be ascertained. Perhaps the recitation of the curses are merely illustrative of the procedure to be followed. Blessings together with more development of the curses are given in the further revelation in chapter 28. When Joshua followed these injunctions, both blessings and curses were read, "just as it is written in the Book of the Law" (Josh 8:34).

**1** Chapter 27 has an unusual introduction. Not Moses alone, but Moses and the elders of Israel commanded the people. Nowhere else in Deuteronomy are the elders associated with Moses as spokesmen to the people. Perhaps this is due to the prospect of the imminent death of Moses and, consequently, to his absence when the ceremony at Gerizim and Ebal was to be enacted. Perhaps it was to enhance their authority at the coming covenant renewal in the land.

**2–4** The temporal focus of being on the verge of entering Canaan, as in all Deuteronomy, is mentioned again (vv.2–3), and once more with the participial form of the verb *nāṯan* ("to give"), which the NIV generally translates—in more than thirty-five places in Deuteronomy when referring to the land—as "is giving." This translation does not convey quite the sense of imminency that the Hebrew may intend. "Is about to give" is better. Yet the Lord had already given them the land. Nevertheless, it had not yet been appropriated. In Deuteronomy the sense of anticipation of the imminent appropriation of the land as a gift from the Lord is meant.

Large stones set up on Mount Ebal (vv.2, 4) were to be coated with plaster and then inscribed with "all the words of this law" (v.3). Writing laws on stones (or even sides of mountains as the later inscriptions of Darius I on the Behistun Rock attest) was common in the ancient Near East. Whitewashing stones before writing on them was a practice in Egypt. Large writing stones, some eight feet high, from before Moses' time have been found at Byblos.

What is meant by "all the words of this law" cannot be definitely determined. It is surely not the Pentateuch, which contains more than law—or even all of Deuteronomy with its geographical and historical sections. Its length too might be prohibitive for such inscription. Most likely the salient parts of the laws reiterated in Deuteronomy would be all that was necessary. In Hebrew (and in Greek) the semantic range of the word for "all" must be determined by its context. Doubtless "all these commands that I give you today" in v.1 are said of the arrangements for the covenant-treaty renewal at Mount Gerizim and Mount Ebal. "Today" limits the commands to what Moses had said to them in that twenty-four-hour period and so differs from the days in the discourses on the plains of Moab prior to this day.

**5–8** In addition to the stones to be set up on Mount Ebal for displaying the law, an altar made of fieldstones was to be erected (vv.5–6). "Burnt offerings" (v.6) and "fellowship offerings" (v.7) were to be sacrificed there, and the people were to eat the fellowship offerings while rejoicing in the presence of the Lord. Just as the people were instructed at the incidence of the giving of the law at Sinai, so now, at the renewal of the covenant-treaty, burnt offerings and fellowship offerings were to be made.

In agreement with the rule for altars of stones in Exodus 20:25, no iron tool was to be used in building this altar (v.5). Iron tools normally would be used to shape the stones, which was prohibited here. So the limitation of the material to fieldstones is similar to the prohibition in the use of dressed (cut) stones in Exodus 20:25.

This altar did not take the place of the altar in front of the Tent of Meeting. This kind of altar was for temporary use on a special occasion, like the altars erected by the patriarchs.

## Notes

---

**2** שַׂדְתָּ אֹתָם בַּשִּׂיד (*śaḏtā 'ōṯām baśśîḏ*), a cognate accusative, is literally "lime them with lime" or "plaster them with plaster," a Hebrew idiom for "coat them with plaster."

**4** The Samaritan Pentateuch and the Old Latin have Gerizim substituted for Ebal here, apparently due to Samaritan desire to buttress their claim that Gerizim was the mountain on which to worship.

**5** The use of iron was related to the life-style of Canaan and so was inimical to the life-style that the Lord sought to instill in the Israelites. In Exod 20:25 the use of an iron tool for building an altar of stones is said to profane the altar. This suggests that such use would in some way be contrary to the means allowed for Israelite worship of the Lord and was associated with Canaanite worship (see Craigie, p. 329). Maybe because Israel did not work in iron, using an iron implement would be deemed as subservience to the Canaanites as it was later to the Philistines (1 Sam 13:19–22).

**8** That these laws are written for instruction rather than for ritual display is indicated by the directive for the people to write them on the large stones "very clearly," בָּאֵר הֵיטֵב (*ba'ēr hêṭēḇ*, "plainly," "well"). At the inception of the Deuteronomic record, it is said that Moses "began to expound this law" (1:5); that is, he began "to make clear" (*bē'ēr*) this law.

---

### 2. *The curses from Mount Ebal (27:9–26)*

#### a. *The standing and the stance of the tribes*

27:9–13

9Then Moses and the priests, who are Levites, said to all Israel, "Be silent, O Israel, and listen! You have now become the people of the LORD your God. 10Obey the LORD your God and follow his commands and decrees that I give you today."

11On the same day Moses commanded the people:

12When you have crossed the Jordan, these tribes shall stand on Mount Gerizim to bless the people: Simeon, Levi, Judah, Issachar, Joseph and Benjamin. 13And these tribes shall stand on Mount Ebal to pronounce curses: Reuben, Gad, Asher, Zebulun, Dan and Naphtali.

**9–11** The authority of the elders coupled with that of Moses began this series of directives (v.1); now that of the priests is added (v.9). Again, however, Moses speaks in the first person ("decrees that I give you today," v.10).

The repetition of the declaration of the people becoming the people of the Lord their God is noteworthy. Basically three occasions of this declaration occur or were about to occur: the first at Horeb (Sinai) (Exod 19:3–8), the second on the plains of Moab (Deut 26:16–19; 27:9–10), and the third on Mount Ebal (Josh 8:30–35). In every instance aspects of the treaty formula are present. Most notable is the relationship established between the Lord and Israel. But this relationship goes beyond the usual treaty form. The Lord is their God, and they are his people. Not only is he the Creator of the people humanly, but he is the Creator of Israel politically—as a special nation whose laws relate to their personal commitment to the Lord as their God as well as to their behavior and to their motivation for their behavior. Rewards and punishments too stem from this relationship.

**12–13** The tribes to stand on Mount Gerizim to bless the people are all descendants of Jacob's two wives, Leah and Rachel, while the tribes that uttered curses were Reuben and Zebulun, both sons of Leah, plus the tribes of the sons of the handmaids Zilpah and Bilhah. Preference is given to the sons of the wives of Jacob who had higher standing than the sons of the handmaids, though the division into two groups of six necessitated putting two sons of Leah with those of the handmaids. The basis for the choice of Reuben and Zebulun is not evident. Reuben did forfeit his birthright (Gen 49:4), but no particular defection of Zebulun is known.

## Notes

**9** On "the priests, who are Levites," see Notes on 17:9.

**12–13** In regard to the blessings and curses, etc., see the summary in Kitchen, *The Bible*, pp. 79–85.

### b. *Curses and response*

27:14–26

14 The Levites shall recite to all the people of Israel in a loud voice:

15 "Cursed is the man who carves an image or casts an idol—a thing detestable to the LORD, the work of the craftsman's hands—and sets it up in secret."

Then all the people shall say, "Amen!"

16 "Cursed is the man who dishonors his father or his mother."

Then all the people shall say, "Amen!"

17 "Cursed is the man who moves his neighbor's boundary stone."

Then all the people shall say, "Amen!"

18 "Cursed is the man who leads the blind astray on the road."

Then all the people shall say, "Amen!"

19 "Cursed is the man who withholds justice from the alien, the fatherless or the widow."

Then all the people shall say, "Amen!"

20 "Cursed is the man who sleeps with his father's wife, for he dishonors his father's bed."

Then all the people shall say, "Amen!"

[21]"Cursed is the man who has sexual relations with any animal."
Then all the people shall say, "Amen!"
[22]"Cursed is the man who sleeps with his sister, the daughter of
his father or the daughter of his mother."
Then all the people shall say, "Amen!"
[23]"Cursed is the man who sleeps with his mother-in-law."
Then all the people shall say, "Amen!"
[24]"Cursed is the man who kills his neighbor secretly."
Then all the people shall say, "Amen!"
[25]"Cursed is the man who accepts a bribe to kill an innocent
person."
Then all the people shall say, "Amen!"
[26]"Cursed is the man who does not uphold the words of this law
by carrying them out."
Then all the people shall say, "Amen!"

**14** While in vv.12–13 we read that six tribes were to stand on Mount Gerizim to bless the people and the other six on Mount Ebal to pronounce curses, v.14 further explains that the Levites were to recite the words and the people were to say, "Amen" (v.15b et al.). This indicates that the actual voicing of blessings and curses was made by priests and that "to bless" and "to pronounce curses" of vv.12–13 refers, not to the voicing of blessings and curses, but to the representation of blessings and curses in the ceremony. The Levites mentioned as actually voicing the blessings and curses (v.14) are apparently priests who have the care of the ark of the covenant (Josh 8:33). The rest of the tribe of Levi was among the tribes on Gerizim (v.12).

The list of curses in vv.15–26 tells on whom and why the curses would fall. Who would be cursed? Everyone who makes an idol and sets it up in secret, who dishonors father or mother, who moves his neighbor's boundary stone, who leads the blind astray on the road, etc.

The sinful actions that evoke the curses are illustrative rather than comprehensive. Why these and not others should be mentioned is not clear. The addition to the law on making idols (i.e., making them "in secret") and the reference to killing one's neighbor "secretly" (v.24, same Heb. word) suggest that Moses was emphasizing that the curse of the Lord would be on those Israelites who did such wicked acts even though the authorities were unaware of their guilt and therefore did not publicly punish them. All these actions are condemned elsewhere, though not necessarily in identical phraseology.

**15** The first curse covers an Israelite's relationship to his Lord. No one was to make an idol, either carved of wood or cast in metal. This was detestable to the Lord. This summarizes the first two commandments of the Decalogue (Exod 20:3–4) but adds the Deuteronomic phrase "detestable to the LORD" and comments that the idol set up in secret is of human manufacture (in contrast to the Lord himself, who created everything). This indictment is repeated by Isaiah (Isa 40:19–20; 41:7; 44:9–20; 45:16), Jeremiah (Jer 10:3, 9), and Hosea (Hos 8:6; 13:2).

**16** The second curse falls on the one who dishonors his father or mother. This command is stated positively in the Decalogue (Exod 20:12; Deut 5:16) and, as Paul said, "is the first commandment with a promise" (Eph 6:2).

**17** The third curse relates to the division of the land. Each family's allotment was to be respected; consequently, moving boundary stones came under God's curse (see 19:14).

**18–19** The next two curses concern the disabled and the underprivileged. Leviticus 19:14 prohibits putting "a stumbling block in front of the blind." Here the curse falls on the one "who leads the blind astray on the road" (v.18).

The next curse is on the man who withholds justice from the disadvantaged (v.19): the alien, the fatherless, or the widow. The requirement of equal justice for everyone is frequently stated in Mosaic legislation (Exod 22:21–24; 23:9; Lev 19:33–34; Deut 10:17–19; 24:17).

**20** Here the first of four curses involving incest is indicative of the importance of sexual morality in the Mosaic order and of the common practice of such immorality even in the religious ceremonies among the Canaanites, making sexual deviation an ever-present evil. Some Israelites had already succumbed to such behavior in the affair at Peor when many died under divine punishment (Num 25:18; 31:16).

The "father's wife" refers to a wife of one's father other than one's mother. The euphemism "dishonors his father's bed" (Heb. "uncovers his father's skirt") may mean that he violates his father's marriage. To cover one's skirt is a way of saying to take one in marriage (cf. Ruth 3:9). Sexual relations are only for those lawfully married.

**21** Having sexual relations with animals, though plumbing the depths of depravity, was not unknown in the ancient Near East (see Hoffner, pp. 41–42). Among the Hittites bestiality was practiced with "sacred" animals to bring people into union with their gods. Exodus 22:19 and Leviticus 18:23; 20:15–16, as well as the reiteration by Moses here in Deuteronomy 27:21, indicate that bestiality on the part of both men and women was practiced in Canaan. When this sin was discovered, death was the penalty. If not discovered, the participants were nevertheless under the curse of God.

**22–23** Curses eight and nine fall on those who commit incest with a half-sister or one's mother-in-law (see also Lev 18:9, 17; 20:14, 17).

**24–25** The tenth and eleventh curses fall on those who kill secretly and those who accept fees for killing innocent persons. These actions, along with those that precede, appear to place a curse on criminal actions that are not publicly known, which allow the criminal to escape punishment by his peers. The Lord, however, denounces that person, and the Lord's curse ever hangs over him, eventuating in unknown punishment.

The explication of these curses for disobedience indicate that punishment would be most severe (28:15–68). The laws against murder are enunciated in both Exodus (20:13; 21:12) and Leviticus (24:21). The acceptance of any bribe is prohibited in Exodus 23:8 and Deuteronomy 16:19. Only here is a curse placed on anyone who accepts a bribe (or payment) for the specific crime of murder of the innocent, but Ezekiel 22:3–12 indicts Jerusalem's rulers and citizens for crimes such as these in the Deuteronomic curses.

**26** The last of the twelve curses sums up them all but includes more than the curses specified. The Israelites must "uphold," or make effective, this law by following it. It is not enough to assent to it; one must confirm, uphold, and establish it by one's life in action. This covers all the law as enunciated by Moses on the plains of Moab. It is essentially the revelation of God governing the Israelites' individual and national lives in Canaan under the covenant—under the form of treaty stipulations.

To the recitation of each of these curses, the people were to respond with a definite "Amen." This did not mean simple acquiescence or approval but a solemn assertion confirming the validity of the curses. The people declared that they were placing themselves under the consequences of breaking the covenant stipulations, which was tantamount to saying, "We formally accept the terms and agree to all the provisions."

Paul used v.26 in Galatians 3:10 as an indication of the ineffectiveness of the law as a saving instrument. But this is quite contrary to its original intention. Certainly Deuteronomy 27:26 is a curse, but that curse is meant to forestall the failure to follow the law. One must remember, as Ridderbos (p. 123) says, "As for the difference of intention between the use of this passage here in Galatians and in Deut 27, we ought not to forget that the whole development of Jewish legalism lies between Deut 27 and Gal 3."

The Deuteronomic curses were warnings not to break the law, given with the intent that paying heed to the warning would keep Israel in good relationship with the Lord. Those living in OT times who were faithful to the Lord were not under the curse but rather had the witness from the Spirit of God that they were acceptable to him.

## Notes

---

**15–26** A vassal response similar to "Amen" appears in Esarhaddon's Nimrud treaty (Wiseman, *Vassal-Treaties*, p. 26) and in the response of Hittite soldiers in ANET, pp. 353–54. This use of amen as "agreement" is the basis for the NIV marginal note on Judg 11:20.

**18** מַשְׁגֶּה (*mašgeh,* "leads . . . astray") in Prov 28:10 speaks of one who leads astray an upright person along an evil path.

**25** The use of שֹׁחַד (*šōḥaḏ*), which means "gift," "reward," or "payment" as well as "bribe," suggests that this curse covers more than judicial corruption. It covers also murder for hire.

**26** The Hiphil imperfect of קוּם (*qûm,* "establish," "raise up") coupled with the infinitive of עָשָׂה (*'āśāh,* "do," "make") may mean to persist in upholding the law or to continually uphold the law by following it.

The MT has דִּבְרֵי הַתּוֹרָה־הַזֹּאת (*diḇrê hattôrāh-hazzō'ṯ,* "the words of this law"), and the LXX has *πᾶσιν τοῖς λόγοις τοῦ νόμου τούτου* (*pasin tois logois tou nomou toutou,* "all the words of this law"), while Gal 3:10 reads, *πᾶσιν τοῖς γεγραμμένοις ἐν τῷ βιβλίῳ τοῦ νόμου* (*pasin tois gegrammenois en tō bibliō tou nomou,* "everything written in the Book of the Law").

---

### E. *The Blessings and the Curses (28:1–68)*

#### 1. *The blessings*

28:1–14

[1]If you fully obey the LORD your God and carefully follow all his commands I give you today, the LORD your God will set you high above

all the nations on earth. 2All these blessings will come upon you and accompany you if you obey the LORD your God:

3You will be blessed in the city and blessed in the country.
4The fruit of your womb will be blessed, and the crops of your land and the young of your livestock—the calves of your herds and the lambs of your flocks.
5Your basket and your kneading trough will be blessed.
6You will be blessed when you come in and blessed when you go out.

7The LORD will grant that the enemies who rise up against you will be defeated before you. They will come at you from one direction but flee from you in seven.

8The LORD will send a blessing on your barns and on everything you put your hand to. The LORD your God will bless you in the land he is giving you.

9The LORD will establish you as his holy people, as he promised you on
oath, if you keep the commands of the LORD your God and walk in his
ways. 10Then all the peoples on earth will see that you are called by the
name of the LORD, and they will fear you. 11The LORD will grant you
abundant prosperity—in the fruit of your womb, the young of your
livestock and the crops of your ground—in the land he swore to your
forefathers to give you.

12The LORD will open the heavens, the storehouse of his bounty, to
send rain on your land in season and to bless all the work of your hands.
You will lend to many nations but will borrow from none. 13The LORD will
make you the head, not the tail. If you pay attention to the commands of
the LORD your God that I give you this day and carefully follow them, you
will always be at the top, never at the bottom. 14Do not turn aside from
any of the commands I give you today, to the right or to the left,
following other gods and serving them.

**1–2** The often-repeated reference to the "commands I give you today" (v.1; cf. vv.9, 13, 14, 15, 45, 58, 62) introduces the blessings for obedience. The first part of v.1 is virtually identical with 15:5, where the blessings of the Lord in the land are anticipated. The day seems to be the day stressed in 26:16–18. Whether translated "today" or "this day," *hayyôm* should be translated variously according to its context. Full obedience to the Lord results in blessing for his people. Among these blessings is eminence. If Israel obeyed the Lord, she would be set high above all the nations of the world (26:19).

Moreover, the blessings seem to be personified. They will come to the people and go with them (v.2), much like goodness and love in Psalm 23:6, which, as servants to the psalmist in the Lord's encampment, always closely follow the psalmist to respond to his every need.

**3–4** Two sections of blessings and curses (generalizations or specific areas of blessing or curse as representative of life elements) balance each other in vv.3–6 over against vv.16–19. After the section on blessing in vv.3–6, the nature of the blessed state that will result from obedience is portrayed; and after the curses of vv.16–19, the condition of disobedient Israel is depicted in a much longer section. These are not the blessings and curses to be repeated on Gerizim and Ebal. Rather, Moses gave a fuller explanation, largely in a prophetic vein, of the options that stood before Israel as she was about to enter and settle in the land under the covenant-treaty with the Lord.

The blessing or the curse would be nationwide, covering "city and country" (vv.3,

16). Every productivity would be under either the blessing or the curse: children, crops, and livestock, including both herds and flocks (v.4). The blessing of reproduction had been in the promise to Abraham and was repeated throughout the revelation through Moses (Gen 15:5; Exod 32:13; Deut 1:10).

**5** Blessing or curse would extend to the Israelites' daily sustenance (vv.5, 17), the basket and kneading trough being used to gather food products and to prepare them for meals.

Among a desert-dwelling people, food products were scarce (notwithstanding the manna) and hunger and thirst common. An abundance of foodstuffs was a notable blessing indeed!

**6** The Lord's goodness would cover the Israelites' daily labor. Going out and coming in (the order, coming in and going out, in vv.6 and 19 is unusual) is a common descriptive phrase of going out to one's daily tasks and returning home after the day's work is done, whatever that activity entails. Coming in from labor and going out to work have the same meaning.

Though the references to the basket and kneading trough and to their offspring are in opposite order, in the same areas of life in which obedience would bring blessing, disobedience would bring the curse (vv.17–18).

**7–8** Further specification of the Lord's blessing under the covenant tells of victory over enemies and utopian prosperity in the land. When enemies come from one direction, they will flee in defeat in seven directions (v.7). External foes will be decisively disoriented and scattered, unable to carry on warfare.

By using a jussive verbal form and a particle probably signifying accomplishment, Moses personified God's blessing. The Lord would eagerly command blessing to be with them on their barns (granaries) and on everything they put their hands to (v.8).

**9–11** Once again Moses conditioned Israel's blessed relationship to the Lord on keeping his commands and walking in his ways (v.9). If Israel would do this, the Lord would fulfill his sworn promise to establish them; he would confirm his oath by establishing whatever he promised.

This establishment of the people as the Lord's holy people would make all the other people of the world recognize that the Israelites were "called by the name of the LORD" (v.10), and this would make the nations afraid of them. The name of the Lord being called on them (cf. 2 Chron 7:14; Jer 14:9; 15:16; Amos 9:12) is like a badge of his ownership identifying them as his. (In contrast notice Isa 63:19.)

The blessing of v.4 to be experienced in the land is expanded into "abundant prosperity" (v.11).

**12** The particular blessing of rain would provide fertility to the soil and, consequently, an abundance of crops to the farmer. "All the work of your hands" in this place refers especially to the workers of the soil. Rain was essential in Canaan and constituted part of the description and promise of the fertile land in contrast to that of Egypt, which relied totally on the Nile (11:10–11, 14).

The Lord promised to bless the people by opening the treasure house of his bounty in the skies so that the seasonal rains would fall. The prosperity of v.8 is now his "bounty," describing the goodness and sufficiency of his treasures of rain. The figure of rain, snow, etc., being stored in the heavens occurs in Job 38:22; Psalms 33:7; 135:7; and Jeremiah 10:13; 51:16.

The Israelites were facing a land where belief in the fertility gods of Baalism was common. The various Baals were thought to be in control of rain. The Canaanites believed that Baal had a house in the heavens with an opening in the roof from which the rains were sent. Whether this constitutes the background for the figure underlying the storehouse in the heavens here, Moses did insist that it was the Lord who would either bless Israel with abundant rain or withhold rain because of her disobedience. As in 15:6, so it is said here that because of the blessing of the Lord, Israel was destined to be rich and so would "lend to many nations but borrow from none."

**13–14** Israel would move upward from her current status to that of the head among the nations, rather than become (or continue to be) the tail (v.13). She would "always be at the top, never at the bottom." But all this would be determined by the adherence of the people to the stipulations of the covenant-treaty that they had accepted from the Lord. They must "carefully follow them" and "not turn aside . . . to the right or to the left" (v.14) from any of the commands Moses was rehearsing to them that day.

The essence of following the Lord's commands lies in fidelity and loyalty to him. The essence of disobedience was following and serving (worshiping) other gods. At the end of this section on blessings, Moses again exhorted the people not to turn aside from the Lord their God.

## Notes

---

Chapter 28 is one of the most eloquent and moving passages in the Bible. "In sustained declamatory power, it stands unrivalled in the O.T." (S.R. Driver, *Deuteronomy*, p. 303).

**1** The emphatic infinitive absolute with the imperfect verb—שָׁמוֹעַ תִּשְׁמַע (*šāmôaʿ tišmaʿ*, "if you fully obey")—stresses complete obedience; and the Hebrew figure of listening to the voice—meaning obeying—underlies the strong demand to fully obey.

הַיּוֹם (*hayyôm*) may be translated "the day," "today," or even "this day," with the article having some demonstrative force. See Notes on 26:16.

עֶלְיוֹן עַל (*ʿelyôn ʿal*, "high above") repeats what is promised in 26:19. *ʿElyôn* when ascriptive of God is translated "Most High." See 32:8.

**5** The טֶנֶא (*ṭene'*, "basket"), used only here and in 26:2, 4, where the representative firstfruits are carried in a basket and placed before the altar, is most probably an Egyptian loan word. Baskets were used in Egypt before 5000 B.C. In postbiblical Hebrew a *tenî* was a metal container (Ellenbogen, p. 77; Hodges, p. 48 fig. 40; NBD, p. 135).

The מִשְׁאֶרֶת (*miš'ereṯ*, "kneading trough"), here and in Exod 8:3 (7:28 MT) and 12:34, must have been either a large, shallow bowl or a stone like the lower section of an ancient, hollowed-out handmill (Hodges, p. 34 fig. 22).

**6** "When you come in . . . when you go out" appears again in the more usual order—go out and come in—in the Hebrew of 31:2, where Moses speaks of his inability to lead the people any longer.

**8** The אָסָם (*'āsām*, "barns"), here and in Prov 3:10 only, appear to be granaries. A letter from about the sixth century B.C. carries a statement from a worker to the military commander that he had harvested, measured, and stored grain (a verbal cognate of *'āsām*) (Ackroyd and Lindars, p. 41).

**10** שֵׁם יהוה נִקְרָא עָלֶיךָ (*šēm YHWH niqrā' 'āleykā*, "called by the name of the LORD") differs in meaning from הַנִּקְרָא בִּשְׁמִי (*hanniqrā' bišmî*, "the ones called by my name"). The identification is stronger in the longer form and denotes that the Lord is sovereign. They are the property of God, and so all peoples will fear them who are under his protection. On the use of the "name of the LORD" in Deuteronomy, see the comment on 32:3.

**11** "Abundant prosperity" renders לְטוֹבָה . . . הוֹתִרְךָ (*hôtirkā . . . leṭôbāh*), which means he will make abundant (or expansive) prosperity for you (by productivity).

**12** אוֹצָר (*'ôṣār*, "storehouse") can be the treasure itself or the place where anything valuable was kept, whether a building or a room. Here it appears to refer to the heavens as the storehouse, and the bounty is the treasure of rain.

On "you will lend," see Notes on 15:6.

---

## 2. *The curses*

### 28:15–68

15 However, if you do not obey the LORD your God and do not carefully
follow all his commands and decrees I am giving you today, all these
curses will come upon you and overtake you:

16 You will be cursed in the city and cursed in the country.
17 Your basket and your kneading trough will be cursed.
18 The fruit of your womb will be cursed, and the crops of your
land, and the calves of your herds and the lambs of your flocks.
19 You will be cursed when you come in and cursed when you go
out.

20 The LORD will send on you curses, confusion and rebuke in
everything you put your hand to, until you are destroyed and come to
sudden ruin because of the evil you have done in forsaking him. 21 The
LORD will plague you with diseases until he has destroyed you from the
land you are entering to possess. 22 The LORD will strike you with wasting
disease, with fever and inflammation, with scorching heat and drought,
with blight and mildew, which will plague you until you perish. 23 The sky
over your head will be bronze, the ground beneath you iron. 24 The LORD
will turn the rain of your country into dust and powder; it will come
down from the skies until you are destroyed.
25 The LORD will cause you to be defeated before your enemies. You
will come at them from one direction but flee from them in seven, and
you will become a thing of horror to all the kingdoms on earth. 26 Your
carcasses will be food for all the birds of the air and the beasts of the
earth, and there will be no one to frighten them away. 27 The LORD will
afflict you with the boils of Egypt and with tumors, festering sores and
the itch, from which you cannot be cured. 28 The LORD will afflict you with
madness, blindness and confusion of mind. 29 At midday you will grope
about like a blind man in the dark. You will be unsuccessful in
everything you do; day after day you will be oppressed and robbed, with
no one to rescue you.
30 You will be pledged to be married to a woman, but another will take
her and ravish her. You will build a house, but you will not live in it. You
will plant a vineyard, but you will not even begin to enjoy its fruit. 31 Your
ox will be slaughtered before your eyes, but you will eat none of it. Your
donkey will be forcibly taken from you and will not be returned. Your
sheep will be given to your enemies, and no one will rescue them.
32 Your sons and daughters will be given to another nation, and you will
wear out your eyes watching for them day after day, powerless to lift a
hand. 33 A people that you do not know will eat what your land and labor
produce, and you will have nothing but cruel oppression all your days.

34The sights you see will drive you mad. 35The LORD will afflict your
knees and legs with painful boils that cannot be cured, spreading from
the soles of your feet to the top of your head.
36The LORD will drive you and the king you set over you to a nation
unknown to you or your fathers. There you will worship other gods,
gods of wood and stone. 37You will become a thing of horror and an
object of scorn and ridicule to all the nations where the LORD will drive
you.
38You will sow much seed in the field but you will harvest little,
because locusts will devour it. 39You will plant vineyards and cultivate
them but you will not drink the wine or gather the grapes, because
worms will eat them. 40You will have olive trees throughout your country
but you will not use the oil, because the olives will drop off. 41You will
have sons and daughters but you will not keep them, because they will
go into captivity. 42Swarms of locusts will take over all your trees and
the crops of your land.
43The alien who lives among you will rise above you higher and
higher, but you will sink lower and lower. 44He will lend to you, but you
will not lend to him. He will be the head, but you will be the tail.
45All these curses will come upon you. They will pursue you and
overtake you until you are destroyed, because you did not obey the LORD
your God and observe the commands and decrees he gave you. 46They
will be a sign and a wonder to you and your descendants forever.
47Because you did not serve the LORD your God joyfully and gladly in the
time of prosperity, 48therefore in hunger and thirst, in nakedness and
dire poverty, you will serve the enemies the LORD sends against you. He
will put an iron yoke on your neck until he has destroyed you.
49The LORD will bring a nation against you from far away, from the
ends of the earth, like an eagle swooping down, a nation whose
language you will not understand, 50a fierce-looking nation without
respect for the old or pity for the young. 51They will devour the young of
your livestock and the crops of your land until you are destroyed. They
will leave you no grain, new wine or oil, nor any calves of your herds or
lambs of your flocks until you are ruined. 52They will lay siege to all the
cities throughout your land until the high fortified walls in which you
trust fall down. They will besiege all the cities throughout the land the
LORD your God is giving you.
53Because of the suffering that your enemy will inflict on you during
the siege, you will eat the fruit of the womb, the flesh of the sons and
daughters the LORD your God has given you. 54Even the most gentle and
sensitive man among you will have no compassion on his own brother
or the wife he loves or his surviving children, 55and he will not give to
one of them any of the flesh of his children that he is eating. It will be all
he has left because of the suffering your enemy will inflict on you during
the siege of all your cities. 56The most gentle and sensitive woman
among you—so sensitive and gentle that she would not venture to
touch the ground with the sole of her foot—will begrudge the husband
she loves and her own son or daughter 57the afterbirth from her womb
and the children she bears. For she intends to eat them secretly during
the siege and in the distress that your enemy will inflict on you in your
cities.
58If you do not carefully follow all the words of this law, which are
written in this book, and do not revere this glorious and awesome
name—the LORD your God—59the LORD will send fearful plagues on you
and your descendants, harsh and prolonged disasters, and severe and
lingering illnesses. 60He will bring upon you all the diseases of Egypt
that you dreaded, and they will cling to you. 61The LORD will also bring
on you every kind of sickness and disaster not recorded in this Book of
the Law, until you are destroyed. 62You who were as numerous as the

stars in the sky will be left but few in number, because you did not obey
the LORD your God. 63Just as it pleased the LORD to make you prosper
and increase in number, so it will please him to ruin and destroy you.
You will be uprooted from the land you are entering to possess.
64Then the LORD will scatter you among all nations, from one end of
the earth to the other. There you will worship other gods—gods of
wood and stone, which neither you nor your fathers have known.
65Among those nations you will find no repose, no resting place for the
sole of your foot. There the LORD will give you an anxious mind, eyes
weary with longing, and a despairing heart. 66You will live in constant
suspense, filled with dread both night and day, never sure of your life.
67In the morning you will say, "If only it were evening!" and in the
evening, "If only it were morning!"—because of the terror that will fill
your hearts and the sights that your eyes will see. 68The LORD will send
you back in ships to Egypt on a journey I said you should never make
again. There you will offer yourselves for sale to your enemies as male
and female slaves, but no one will buy you.

**15** As the blessings of the Lord seem to be personalized (v.2), so also the curses take on personal action; they would come and overtake a disobedient Israel. Verse 45 says that the curses would come, pursue, and overtake the disobedient people.

**16–19** After the basic coverage of the curse (vv.16–19), following the same plan as that of the blessings (vv.3–6), Moses developed—but with about six times the length—the description of the disaster that would follow when Israel was disobedient to the Lord. Curses, confusion, and rebuke would fall on everything disobedient Israel did—until destruction and sudden ruin enveloped her. Disobeying the Lord is equated with forsaking him, because national and personal commitment to the Lord is the central command, and forsaking him is the central evil.

**20–21** The Lord would send plagues of many kinds. Some would attack the Israelites physically, and others would affect their lands and goods.

**22–24** The bodily aspects of the curse that would come on the people include illnesses of various sorts and the shameful desecration of their dead bodies (v.26). Disturbance of their emotional and mental balance would follow. The word translated "diseases" (v.21) is not uncommon, but "wasting disease" and the word for "fever" (v.22) occur only here and in Leviticus 26:16. While inflammation is limited to this reference, the cognate verb occurs elsewhere, sometimes in the sense of burning. A precise identification of these diseases is not possible.

Not only were diseases to be the people's punishment, the physical land too would suffer. In the alternate blessings and curses (vv.3–6, 16–19), the crops of the land and the domestic animals that live off those crops were either blessed or cursed. The nature of that curse is developed as drought and its accompanying evils. The specific diseases mentioned in v.22 relate in some way to the excessive heat of fever or inflammation; then mention is made of the heat of drought and its consequences: scorching heat from a bronze sky, drought producing dust rather than rain from the Lord, and a soil made as hard as iron by the hot east wind off the desert (vv.23–24; Gen 41:6, 23, 27).

"Blight and mildew" (v.22) is an idiom for disaster to crops (1 Kings 8:37; 2 Chron 6:28; Amos 4:9; Hag 2:17). It signifies contrasting degenerative actions. Blight is the result of the hot, dry sirocco winds coming from the eastern deserts scorching all crops, while the mildew appears because of the excessive humidity of a moist, hot climate. Together the words depict the dearth of productivity and the destruction of the crops.

**25** Israel under the curse of disobedience would also suffer defeat in warfare. Under the blessing their enemies would come from one sector, united to attack, but flee, disorganized and routed, in seven directions (v.7). Under the curse the opposite would be true. Israel would attack her enemies from one direction and flee in seven. Seven in both cases depicts complete, disorganized rout.

**26** The Israelite's dead bodies would not be given burial but would be eaten by the birds and wild animals, a most shameful desecration. Jeremiah similarly portrayed the frightful future in the Valley of Hinnom, after which it would be called the Valley of Slaughter (Jer 7:32–33; cf. 1 Sam 17:44, 46; 1 Kings 14:11; Ps 79:2; Jer 16:4; 19:7; 34:20).

**27** The "boils of Egypt" are doubtless the boils of the sixth plague, which so discomfited the Egyptian magicians, as well as all other Egyptians, that they could no longer stand before Moses (Exod 9:9–11). This may have been a form of leprosy known in Egypt (see Keil, p. 439).

The "tumors" that were to come on disobedient Israel were like those the Philistines later contracted when the ark of the covenant was held by them (1 Sam 5–6). The Hebrew word *'ōp̱el* means "a swelling" and is usually thought to be hemorrhoids, tumors, bubonic plague, or leprosy.

The "festering sores" appear to be some kind of eruptive sore. A descendant of Aaron so afflicted could not serve as a priest offering sacrifices (Lev 21:20), and an animal so afflicted could not be offered as a sacrifice (Lev 22:22).

The "itch" is some sort of skin disorder that induces scratching. These skin eruptions will be incurable.

**28–29** Following on these diseases afflicting the skin come debilitating dysfunctions: madness, blindness, and mental confusion (v.28). This blindness will be so complete that in the brightness of noon the people will grope about as blind men—as though in total darkness. Instead of success in all that they do (v.12), they will be unsuccessful in everything (v.29). Day after day, with a maddening, inexorable regularity, they would be oppressed and robbed of whatever they labored for; and there would be no one to rescue them from their plight.

Many attempts have been made to identify the incapacities of vv.27–28—e.g., various stages of advancing syphilis, kinds of leprosy (mostly so-called)—but none are certain. In any case, the afflictions that the Lord said would fall on disobedient Israel were dire indeed.

**30** From v.30 and on, by citing specific troubles, Moses portrayed the miserable existence and, finally, utter destruction of Israel as a nation. The greater detailed length of the description of Israel under the curse makes Moses' expectation of Israel's future very bleak. The possibility of a blessed future remained, but the possibility of the horrors of Israel under the curse of the Lord because of infidelity seemed more sure. With calamity heaped on calamity, this section of Moses' speeches to the Israelites ready to enter the Promised Land more eloquently and luridly pictures the results of infidelity to the Lord than anywhere else in the Bible.

To be pledged to be married was a more certain relationship than modern engagement; so having that status broken, probably by one's betrothed being taken captive and forced into sexual compliance by violent means, would be a very trying experience.

Building a house will be useless labor: "you will not live in it." The same frustration will follow attempts at viticulture; not even the beginning of the enjoyment of the fruit will be experienced—an enjoyment that was not to be taken from one who might be conscripted for military service (20:6). Yet under the curse no enjoyment of the fruit of the vine could be expected.

**31–32** One's ox would be slaughtered in plain view, but the Israelite owner, obviously helpless, would have none of it to eat (v.31). So also his donkey, his conveyance and work animal, would be forcibly taken from him and never returned, and his sheep given to his enemies. Sons and daughters (v.32) would be taken captive to other nations; and day after day parents helplessly would wear out their eyes watching for the return of those who would never come back.

**33** Instead of the abundance that an obedient Israel would receive from the soil (vv.4–6, 8, 11–12), disobedient Israel would have the people of an unknown land eat what their "land and labor" produced while they themselves would experience cruel oppression throughout their lives. Another nation in v.32 and the unknown nation in v.36 both signify foreign people.

**34–35** Blow upon blow continues. What the people would see—the devastated land, ruined by drought and marauding armies; their possessions gone; their bodies sickened; the many dead; their children taken captive into a wretched condition—would drive them insane (v.34). The specifics of this dirge are picked up again (v.35). Painful, incurable boils that particularly afflicted the knees and the legs would spread from the soles of their feet to the top of the head (cf. Job 2:7–8; 7:3–5; 17:7; 19:17, 20; 30:17). This may have been a kind of elephantiasis.

**36–37** So far Moses has said that disobedient Israel would be plagued until they were "destroyed . . . from the land" (v.21) and that their children would be given to another nation. Here he introduced national captivity, a subject he developed with increasingly vivid detail to the end of the chapter. In this reference to captivity, Moses announced the fact and then described their situation in the foreign land in bold outline, before he reverted again to the agonizing situation they would face in Canaan as a people under the curse (vv.38–63).

The Lord would drive the Israelites and their king to a distant, foreign nation unknown to them or their fathers (v.36; see also v.33), and there they would worship idols. Among the nations they would be driven to by the Lord, they would become an object of horror, scorn, and ridicule (v.37; 1 Kings 9:7; 2 Chron 7:20; Jer 24:9), the butt "of sharp and cutting remarks" (S.R. Driver, *Deuteronomy*, p. 312).

**38–42** Again the curse on the land, resulting in unproductive farming, is elaborated (in contrast to the blessings of vv.8, 11–12). This time the produce itself is attacked, and the harvest is lost (v.38). Abundant planting of grains will not be harvested because the grasshoppers will eat it. The grapes of cultivated vineyards will not be gathered; and, consequently, the people will not drink the wine that might have been made—worms will eat the grapes (v.39). The olive oil, which would have been the Israelites, will not be available for their use (v.40). The locust swarms will take over all the trees and crops of the land (v.42).

In this scene of unproductivity everywhere, the Israelites will not be able to keep their children either, because their children will go into captivity (v.41).

**43–44** In contrast to vv.12b–13a, aliens rather than the nations will lend to the Israelites; and the alien will be the head and Israel the tail. Moreover, the Israelite condition under the curse would be more of a curse than their blessing would be a blessing, because of their continual deterioration.

**45–48** Verse 45 picks up the curse formula of v.15 and adds to it. All these curses will not only come on the people and overtake them, but these curses will pursue them until they are destroyed for their disobedience (see comment on v.15).

The Lord who had brought the Israelites out of Egypt by signs and wonders (4:34) would make the curses to be "a sign and a wonder" to them and their descendants forever (v.46). In view of 4:29–31 and 30:1–10, Moses was not saying that the curses would be on the people and their descendants forever but that the curses on the disobedient generations would be a sign and a wonder to the people and their descendants forever.

Because the people did not serve the Lord, they would serve the enemies he would send against them. The text, taking a stance in the future, as though the people had already come under the curse, uses the perfect tense in the casual clauses of vv.45 and 47.

In the time of their prosperity, the people had an abundance of everything. In spite of this abundance, they did not serve the Lord joyfully and gladly (v.47). Serving the Lord involved committal to him in worship and obedience to all the stipulations of the covenant-treaty. This life of obedience was to bring the joy and happiness of an abundant and affluent prosperity inwardly and outwardly. But if they did not under these conditions continue to serve the Lord, they would experience the dire consequences of the curse: hunger, thirst, nakedness, poverty, and servitude would come on them from the Lord, like an iron yoke on their necks, until they were destroyed (v.48).

**49** The destruction of disobedient Israel was to come from a distant, foreign nation; and the experience of siege, defeat, and dispersal of the population was to bring the destruction of national Israel to a frightful conclusion. This distant enemy would strike swiftly and unerringly like an eagle swooping on its prey. The Assyrians are likened to an eagle in Hosea 8:1 and the Babylonians similarly in Jeremiah 48:40 in their attack on Moab and on Edom in 49:22.

This foreign nation would have a language not understandable to the Israelite population. Though the languages of Assyria and Babylon were cognate Semitic languages, they differed from Hebrew sufficiently so as not to be understood by the populace in Israel (Isa 28:11; 33:19).

The apostle Paul in 1 Corinthians 14:21 quotes Isaiah 28:11–12 and Deuteronomy 28:49 in reference to the tongues problem in the Corinthian church. The tongues mentioned in Isaiah and Deuteronomy were the regular languages of foreign peoples that were unknown by the Israelites.

**50–52** This "fierce-looking nation" (v.50; cf. Dan 8:23, "a stern-faced king"), without regard for either the aged or the young, will mercilessly eat up both the choice livestock and the crops (v.51). No grain, wine, oil, calves, or lambs will be left. That they would "besiege all the cities throughout the land" (v.52) seems to include cities of any size or importance in the land the Lord had given to Israel. However, only walled cities were subject to siege. The word for cities here is "gates" (frequently meaning cities), and gates are only in walled cities. Israel's trust in the strength of their fortified walls rather than in their Lord would be shown to be misplaced trust when those walls fell down.

**53–57** The illustrations of the frightful horrors the victims of the siege will perpetrate on one another as food gives out and of how they will resort to cannibalism show the same descriptive power that runs through this whole portrayal of Israel under the curse for disobedience to her Lord.

Those children given to the people under the blessing of God will now be eaten by their parents (v.53); and when the flesh of children is insufficient to go around, there will be no sharing of flesh with a starving brother or sister (vv.54–55). Women, raised in delicate fashion, at the time of giving birth will begrudge their husbands and older children the afterbirths of their wombs and the children themselves who are born during the siege, eating them as food—so extreme will be the hunger, debasement, and hopelessness (vv.56–57). Not only rough, coarse characters will do such things, but the most gentle and sensitive man and woman will descend to this debased state.

The actual occurrence of such cannibalism is reported in 2 Kings 6:24–31 and Lamentations 2:20 and 4:10. All these frightful experiences result "because of the suffering that your enemy will inflict on you during the siege." Three times this phrase occurs (vv.53, 55, 57), bearing down on the terrible experience the Israelites could expect if they disobeyed their Lord.

**58–61** These verses are a reiterative summary or conclusion to this curse section of the covenant-treaty. They are also a powerful contrast to the blessings promised to Israel under the covenant and portray the dreadful condition Israel would face under the curse. The Israelites will experience not only the diseases of Egypt (v.60) but every other sickness or disaster as well (v.59)—even all those "not recorded in this Book of the Law" (v.61). They will no longer experience the freedom from these diseases that were inflicted on their enemies when Israel was under the protective blessing of the Lord (7:15; Exod 15:26).

In v.58 the people are told that they will fall under the curse if they do not carefully follow "all the words of this law, which are written in this book"; and in v.61 this book is "this Book of the Law," the capitalization signifying that a definite, particular written document is meant. This is evident from 17:18–19, where an anticipated king is instructed to "write for himself on a scroll a copy of this law, taken from that of the priests." He is to "read it all the days of his life." Moreover, in vv.60–61 the curse will bring on them "all the diseases of Egypt" as well as "every kind of sickness and disaster not recorded in this Book of the Law." In Exodus 24:4, 7, reference is made to Moses' writing "the Book of the Covenant" and reading it to the people.

While the precise contents of the Book of the Law are uncertain, it covered the basic laws and the historical episodes relating to the establishment of the covenant-treaty—its laws, stipulations, and regulations (Keil [p. 443] says it covered "the Pentateuch," so far as it was already written).

Failure to follow all the stipulations of the book results in failure to revere the glorious and awesome name: "the LORD your God" (v.58). The name of God carries great importance in the Mosaic revelation. It identifies him as the Creator and as the God of historical revelation; the God of Abraham, Isaac, and Jacob; the God who revealed himself as the one who made covenant promises to Abraham, promises that were being fulfilled in the Exodus and in the settlement in Canaan as their inheritance as heirs of the promises to Abraham. This glorious and awesome name speaks of his essence, character, and reputation as the God of the promises, the true and living God revealed to the people, particularly at Horeb (Sinai).

In v.59 the Hebrew idiom for "the LORD will make your plagues astounding or extraordinary, or exceptional or virulent, powerful or fearful" (NIV, "will send fearful plagues on you") emphasizes the intensity of the plagues he will place on his disobedient people and on their descendants.

**62–64a** Israel's growth as a nation will also be reversed. Under the covenant flowing from the promise to Abraham, Isaac, and Jacob, Israel had increased and would continue to increase in number as the stars in the sky (1:10; 10:22; 26:5); but under the curse a reversal would return them to being few in number.

The promise of the land as their very own was central in the promise to Israel—a promise repeated again and again in these messages in Deuteronomy. But under the curse the few people left would be torn from the land and scattered worldwide (v.64a).

**64b–68** Instead of following the Lord exclusively, the Israelites would turn from him and engage in idolatrous worship of other gods, gods not previously acknowledged by them. Instead of the repose and rest of the Promised Land, anxiety, wearisome longing, despair, constant suspense, and fear would be their lot among the nations (v.65). In the Promised Land under the blessing of the Lord, the nations would fear them (v.10); but under the curse in foreign lands, the Israelites would be in constant fear of the nations (v.66). So low would they sink that the offering of themselves as slaves in Egypt, from which bondage they had been redeemed by the Lord, would be rejected (v.68).

The psychological state of the people (vv.65–67) dispersed among the nations is depicted with no less descriptive power than the foregoing calamities, especially when seen from the viewpoint of the utopian rest and peace in Canaan that obedient Israel was given by the Lord. Certainly this graphic portrayal of disobedient Israel under the curse should have been a most effective warning—as it was intended to be.

## Notes

**20** עַד הִשָּׁמֶדְךָ (*'ad hiššāmedkā*, "until you are destroyed") is sounded with insistent repetition as a tolling death knell that haunts one in vv.20, 21, 24, 45, 48, 51, 61, 63. This is the converse of the promise given in 7:24, where it is said that no king would be able to stand up against

Israel. Israel would destroy everyone of them—עַד הִשְׁמִדְךָ אֹתָם (*'ad hišmidka 'ōtām,* "you will destroy them").

**22** Though the MT has the vowels as חֶרֶב (*hereb,* "sword"), this has been almost universally reckoned as חֹרֶב (*hōreb,* "drought").

"Blight and mildew"—שִׁדָּפוֹן (*šiddāpôn*) and יֵרָקוֹן (*yērāqôn*)—occur together here and in 1 Kings 8:37 (2 Chron 6:28), Amos 4:9, and Hag 2:17.

**27** The Masoretes suggested that עֳפָלִים (*'ᵒpālîm,* "tumors," most probably hemorrhoids) should be טְחֹרִים (*ṭᵉhōrîm*), a *Qere* reading, which in Syriac meant "dysentery" (see BH note and BDB, p. 377). Twice (1 Sam 6:11, 17) *ṭᵉhōrîm* is in the text for *'ᵒpālîm.*

The noun form חֶרֶס (*heres,* "itch") occurs only here and is said to come from a verb meaning to scratch, as in Arabic et al.

**30** שָׁגַל (*šāgal,* "ravish"), a strong term implying violence, was apparently thought by the Masoretes to be obscene (see Jer 3:2); so they substituted שָׁכַב (*šākab,* "to lie with"). See the footnote in BHS.

**33** For "cruel oppression," the NIV has taken the two passive participles עָשׁוּק וְרָצוּץ (*'āšûq wᵉrāṣûṣ*), both of which mean "to be oppressed," as a Hebrew intensive, a common use of repetition of meaning. In 1 Sam 12:3–4 where these two words as finite verbs appear in separate clauses, the NIV translates עָשַׁק (*'āšaq*) as "cheat" and רָצַץ (*rāṣaṣ*) as "oppress." In Amos 4:1 the same pair of words in tandem clauses is translated as "oppress" and "crush."

**36, 41, 64** Taking a people captive was not uncommon in the ancient Near East. Kitchen (*The Bible,* pp. 120–22) lists numbers of captivities of smaller nations by more powerful ones.

**38** אַרְבֶּה (*'arbeh,* "grasshoppers" or "locusts") occur also in the locust plague in Egypt (Exod 10) and as one of the forms of locusts mentioned by Joel (1:4; 2:25). The Midianites and Amalekites that were driven out of Canaan by Gideon were likened in numbers to swarms of *'arbeh* (Judg 6:5; 7:12). The designation may come from the Hebrew word meaning "many."

יַחְסְלֶנּוּ (*yahsᵉlennû*) means "will bring it to an end" and, consequently, "devour it" or "consume it." The verb occurs only here, but a noun form is one of the Hebrew words for grasshopper or locust and occurs a half-dozen times in the OT, evidently meaning one who devours or destroys.

A third word for grasshopper or locust, צְלָצַל (*ṣᵉlāṣal*), is mentioned in v.42 and occurs only there; the particular kind of locust meant is unknown.

**40** The Hebrew for "oil," שֶׁמֶן (*šemen*), refers particularly to oil used as a cosmetic for protecting, conditioning, or soothing, as in Mic 6:15. The verb translated "to use"—סוּךְ (*sûk*)—means "to anoint," and so the clause refers to using oil cosmetically.

**43** The repetition of מַעְלָה (*ma'ᵃlāh,* "high") and מַטָּה (*maṭṭāh,* "low") indicates the comparatives higher and lower. With the verbal forms they mean that the alien would continue to rise higher and higher while Israel would constantly sink lower and lower.

**45** This verse adds רָדַף (*rādap,* "pursue") to the words for "come upon" and "overtake" in v.15 (see TWOT, p. 834).

**47** בְּטוּב לֵבָב (*bᵉṭûb lēbāb,* "gladly") is "with gladness of heart." At Isa 65:14 the NIV translates טוּב לֵב (*tôb lēb*) "the joy of their hearts."

מֵרֹב כֹּל (*mērōb kōl,* "prosperity") is literally "an abundance of everything."

**49** The נֶשֶׁר (*nešer*) in most places in the OT is the eagle rather than the vulture (*Fauna and Flora,* pp. 82–84).

**51** The destruction theme is sounded twice here (as in vv.20–21); once with שָׁמַד (*šāmad,* "destroy") and once with אָבַד (*'ābad,* "ruin").

**53, 55, 57** בְּמָצוֹר וּבְמָצוֹק אֲשֶׁר־יָצִיק לְךָ אֹיְבֶךָ (*bᵉmāṣôr ûbᵉmāṣôq 'ᵃšer-yāṣîq lᵉkā 'ōyᵉbekā,* lit., "in the siege and in the distress that your enemy will distress you with"; NIV, "because of the suffering that your enemy will inflict on you during the siege") has a cacophony of sounds, making its repetition more of a dirge than English can readily translate.

**58** The reference to "the name" is meant to communicate vastly more than the way the name was spoken, but evidence for how the name was pronounced is less than certain. It comes to us in abbreviated and fuller forms, some of which are certainly inaccurate, as the form Jehovah, which is the consonants יהוה (*YHWH*) and the vowels of אֲדֹנָי (*'ᵃḏōnāy*, "lord[s]"). The literature on "the name" is immense. See NBD, p. 478; WBE, p. 694; and ZPEB, p. 761. See also the Notes on 32:3.

**65** לֹא תַרְגִּיעַ (*lō' targîᵃ'*, "no repose") means "no cessation of wandering, moving to and fro, or activity," perhaps both in spirit and in body. There will be "no resting place" for disobedient Israel (Lam 1:3). In contrast the Lord leads his sheep "beside quiet waters"—the waters of rest (Ps 23:2).

**67** In the Talmud (*Sotah* 49a) it is said that cries of "If only it were evening!" and "If only it were morning!" refer to the past, since the future becomes increasingly unbearable. In this view the future is hopeless. If these cries refer to the next evening and then the next morning, the focus is on the unbearable nature of the present. Doubtless, in actuality, both points of view were experienced.

---

## IV. Third Address: The Terms of the Covenant (29:1–30:20)

### A. *Recapitulation of Historical Background: Warnings and Results of Abandonment of the Covenant-Treaty (29:1–29)*

#### 1. *Introduction*

29:1

**[1]These are the terms of the covenant the LORD commanded Moses to make with the Israelites in Moab, in addition to the covenant he had made with them at Horeb.**

**1** BHS prints 29:1 of the most common EVV as 28:69, making "These are the terms of the covenant . . . " refer to the foregoing rather than to what follows. No agreement on the matter exists among older or current expositors. It is said that the reference to "the terms of the covenant" necessitates mentioning the terms and that these terms precede but do not follow the statement. On the other hand, the central theme basic to everything in the covenant-treaty is in v.13: "to confirm you this day as his people, that he may be your God as he promised you." Moreover, "the terms of the covenant" are again referred to in v.9, and the covenant itself, or the "words," "law," or "Book," are more often mentioned in chapters 29–32 than in any other section of Deuteronomy (see vv.9, 12, 14, 19, 21, 25, 29; 30:10; 31:9, 11, 12, 13; 32:46; et al.). Reference is also made to the blessings and curses, which are part of the "terms." It is, of course, true that whether "these" in v.1 refers specifically to what follows or not, it was spoken from the background of the addresses of Moses that had preceded it.

In the introduction to Deuteronomy's addresses, the locale had been given as in Moab (1:5); and reference was made to Horeb (1:6; 4:10, 15), where the law and the covenant were first given. Here Moses differentiated between the two declarations of the covenant, though this by no means indicates any conflict between the two. Only comparison can establish the variations. The covenant is one; the affirmations or renewals of allegiance to the Lord and the terms of the covenant could be several. Through further revelation additional stipulations or applications and interpretations of stipulations could be made, and to this Deuteronomy attests. Deuteronomy is an exposition of the covenant of Horeb (Sinai), a revelation of additional stipulations, an application of many of the terms to the new situation they will face in Canaan, and an extensive and repetitive exhortation to adhere wholly to the Lord and the covenant, together with warnings for nonadherence.

## 2. *Recapitulation of desert situation*

### 29:2–8

2Moses summoned all the Israelites and said to them:

Your eyes have seen all that the LORD did in Egypt to Pharaoh, to all his officials and to all his land. 3With your own eyes you saw those great trials, those miraculous signs and great wonders. 4But to this day the LORD has not given you a mind that understands or eyes that see or ears that hear. 5During the forty years that I led you through the desert, your clothes did not wear out, nor did the sandals on your feet. 6You ate no bread and drank no wine or other fermented drink. I did this so that you might know that I am the LORD your God.

7When you reached this place, Sihon king of Heshbon and Og king of Bashan came out to fight against us, but we defeated them. 8We took their land and gave it as an inheritance to the Reubenites, the Gadites and the half-tribe of Manasseh.

**2–3** The rest of the Book of Deuteronomy concerns the ratification (renewal) of the covenant-treaty (vv.1–15), the results of acceptance or rejection of it (v.16–30:20), Moses' Song (31:19–32:43) and his final blessing on the tribes (33:1–29), Joshua's induction as Moses' successor (31:1–8, 14–15, 23; 32:44; 34:9), and Moses' death (34:1–12). In these culminating addresses of his life, Moses at first identified the people with the whole immediate past history. This historical perspective is all-important. They—the ones now before him—had seen all that the Lord had done in Egypt (v.2). They saw his wonderful miracles and experienced his sustenance through the desert (v.3). But Moses lamented that they really did not yet understand all the implications of the Lord's actions (vv.4–6).

Many of those in front of Moses had not been in Egypt; they were born in the desert. However, many of them were under the age of twenty at Kadesh, two years after leaving Egypt, and were eighteen years of age or younger at the time of the Exodus (they were now thirty-nine to fifty-six years old). These had seen the "miraculous signs and great wonders" (v.3; 4:34; 7:19) that the Lord had loosed on the Egyptians during the plagues, though the youngest of them would have no memory of what happened when they were infants. Moses' message, however, was directed to the nation. The community had been in Egypt and had seen the wonderful things that the Lord had done for them. Even the specific mention of "your own eyes" (v.3) is doubtless directed to the whole community comprising the nation, as vv.10–11 indicate.

**4** When Moses said that the Lord had not given the Israelites the realization of his intervention in the experiences of their history, he did not deny that they had knowledge of his part in the action; rather, he was asserting that the ultimate directive and operative power in all their national life—including immediate needs—was the Lord himself. This, he said, they had not yet fully realized. Only by a total commitment to the Lord in the covenant-treaty and by a grasp of all that meant in every aspect of their life and in their relationships with the rest of the nations of the world would that understanding be produced. Consequently, Moses gave a review of some of God's providences as a basis for his final exhortation to induce their total commitment.

**5** The Lord's providence (as in 8:4 and Neh 9:21) included provisions of clothing and food. "Your clothes did not wear out" does not demand that as the children grew up their clothes enlarged as their bodies did or that additional supplies of clothing (as additional supplies of manna and water) were not found. Specific miracles of supplying clothes and of keeping clothing from falling from their bodies in tatters are not mentioned, but uniting the durability of their clothing and sandals with the giving of manna puts this supply from the Lord on the same plane for the same purpose—"that you might know that I am the LORD" (v.6).

Care should be taken to keep one from supposing that such a declaration of purpose for God's providence indicates that he is only interested in bringing the people under his sovereignty without regard for their welfare inspired by their need—soliciting his compassion for them. The best situation possible for the people was their commitment to the Lord as God. No higher and more satisfactory state was conceivable than that of obedient Israel under the covenant-treaty with the Lord.

**6** The Israelites neither ate bread nor drank wine, the staple elements of sustenance, while homeless and wandering in the desert; but the Lord supplied their needs, nevertheless. He provided them with manna and water—often in miraculous ways.

"That you might know that I am the LORD" had already been declared, particularly in the narrative of the Exodus. Pharaoh and the Egyptians, as well as the Israelites, were to know "I am the LORD" by the signs and wonders during the plagues on Egypt resulting in the escape of the Israelites (Exod 6:7; 7:5, 17; 10:2; 14:4, 18). Also, by his providence of quail and manna in the desert (Exod 16:12) and by his presence among them in the tabernacle (Exod 29:46), Israel was to learn the reality of "I am the LORD."

Later a prophet would tell Ahab that he would learn this truth when the Lord gave him victory over the vast Aramean army of Ben-Hadad (1 Kings 20:13, 28). But it remained for Ezekiel to make the most use of the phrase (over fifty times) as he revealed the punishment and the mercies of the Lord to the Israelites in exile.

**7** "When you reached this place" refers to the area immediately north of the Arnon, an area controlled by Sihon the Amorite king (2:24–37) who had won it in warfare with Moab (Num 21:26); so the plains of Moab were in Amorite hands until Moses conquered that area.

Og had been king of the northern sector of Transjordan. He also was defeated by Moses (3:1–11). The allotment of these areas to Reuben, Gad, and the half-tribe of Manasseh followed the defeat of the Amorites (3:12–17).

## Notes

---

**4** (3 MT) The apostle Paul in Rom 11:8 related this verse and Isa 29:10 to Israel's inability to become believers. In Deuteronomy it is said that God did not give Israel the mind to understand, the eyes to see, and the ears to hear. Paul said (as Isaiah also does) that God gave them a spirit of stupor so that they could not understand, see, or hear.

**5–6** (4–5 MT) An abrupt change in person indicates that these verses are spoken by the Lord, possibly to emphasize the phrase "I am the LORD your God."

**8** (7 MT) On "inheritance" see comments and Notes on 4:20; 7:6; and 14:1–2.

---

## 3. *Clarification of covenant-treaty situation*

29:9–21

[9]Carefully follow the terms of this covenant, so that you may prosper in everything you do. [10]All of you are standing today in the presence of the LORD your God—your leaders and chief men, your elders and officials, and all the other men of Israel, [11]together with your children and your wives, and the aliens living in your camps who chop your wood and carry your water. [12]You are standing here in order to enter into a covenant with the LORD your God, a covenant the LORD is making with you this day and sealing with an oath, [13]to confirm you this day as his people, that he may be your God as he promised you and as he swore to your fathers, Abraham, Isaac and Jacob. [14]I am making this covenant, with its oath, not only with you [15]who are standing here with us today in the presence of the LORD our God but also with those who are not here today.

[16]You yourselves know how we lived in Egypt and how we passed through the countries on the way here. [17]You saw among them their detestable images and idols of wood and stone, of silver and gold. [18]Make sure there is no man or woman, clan or tribe among you today whose heart turns away from the LORD our God to go and worship the gods of those nations; make sure there is no root among you that produces such bitter poison.

[19]When such a person hears the words of this oath, he invokes a blessing on himself and therefore thinks, "I will be safe, even though I persist in going my own way." This will bring disaster on the watered land as well as the dry. [20]The LORD will never be willing to forgive him; his wrath and zeal will burn against that man. All the curses written in this book will fall upon him, and the LORD will blot out his name from under heaven. [21]The LORD will single him out from all the tribes of Israel for disaster, according to all the curses of the covenant written in this Book of the Law.

**9** Moses' reasoned exhortation, based on the history of Israel's Exodus experience till that current time, emphasized the participation of the people in the covenant-treaty. Only by their adoption of the covenant and the following of its stipulations would prosperity come.

**10–13** All the Israelites—from their leaders to their alien servants—standing there in the presence of the Lord were called on to enter into the covenant-treaty. The Lord, said Moses, was making the covenant-treaty with them and sealing it with an oath (vv.10–12). In this renewal the central characteristic and purpose of the covenant was again affirmed as the establishment of the people as the people of the Lord and their acceptance of him as their God in accordance with what he had promised to Abraham, Isaac, and Jacob by an oath. The oath in v.12 is like the oath to Abraham, and the formation of Israel as the people of God (v.13) is in fulfillment of the promise to Abraham.

**14–15** To focus on the national character of this covenant renewal—and the future benefits to the nation and the responsibilities of the national entity—Moses declared that not only those who were standing there at that time (notice the frequent "today") but those who were not there at that time but would appear in later generations were involved in making this covenant-treaty (as in 5:3 and Acts 2:39).

**16–18** The statements "How we lived in Egypt" and "how we passed through the countries on the way here" (v.16) provide the locale and historic background for the people's knowledge of the gods in those places and the nature of their worship. This is evident from the definite reference to the detestable images and idols that they saw among the people there (v.17). The Israelites were exhorted to "make sure" that no one's heart turned away from the Lord and that there was no source in them to produce such "bitter poison" (v.18).

"How we passed through the countries on the way here" (v.16) may not communicate quite the indefiniteness of the Semitic style, though the meaning is in general conveyed by "on the way here." The Hebrew is something like "we passed through the countries we passed through" and means that they passed through certain countries without saying explicitly what countries they were.

The people were to "make sure" (v.18) that not only individual apostasy (man or woman) but also group apostasy (clan or tribe) should not occur. Later they were to be concerned with the defection on the part of the army of Reuben, Gad, and the half-tribe of Manasseh—a supposed defection (Josh 22:10–34)—and with the defection of the tribe of Benjamin involving their failure to follow the moral codes. This brought on the Benjamite war (Judg 20–21). Both northern and southern kingdoms were often guilty of national defection. Moses' exhortation was well taken; he had no optimism about his people's inclinations (31:27, 29).

The source of "bitter poison" (v.18) was the person who turned away from the Lord to worship the gods of Egypt and those of the other nations that the Israelites passed through on their journey from Egypt to the plains of Moab.

**19–21** Moses, by the Spirit of God, expressed the thoughts of such a "bitter-poison" person when he heard "the words of this oath" (v.19); that is, the terms of the covenant-treaty, perhaps with special reference to the curses of it as a specific warning. Such a person invokes a blessing on himself saying, "I will be safe, even though I persist in going my own way."

The aphorism that follows (v.19b) has been variously interpreted, and the NIV puts one interpretation in the text and another in the margin. The text suggests that the attitude and action of rebellion will bring disaster both on the one who perpetrates this folly and on others as well. Perhaps the perpetrator of apostasy supposes that he can exercise his own desires and still enjoy the blessings of the majority. This is not likely. The expression appears to be the conclusion of Moses, not that of the apostate, and consequently refers to the dire result, which would not be the expectation of the apostate who says, "I will be safe."

The footnote translation of the aphorism—"I will be safe, even though I persist in going my own way, in order to add drunkenness to thirst"—means that the punishment of the apostate involves a disaster that results from the exercise of his desires. The apostate's stubborn recalcitrance toward the Lord is his thirst, and that results in drunkenness, a deplorable condition.

The text's translation is preferable. The punishment the Lord will send is noteworthy in two respects. In line with the tone of the passage from v.18 where the community is no longer in view, individuals are in view. From the "no man or woman" of v.18 through v.21, an individual apostate condition is considered. Individual apostasy cannot hide in the blessed state of the believing community. One's apostasy will bring disaster on the innocent (if that is the meaning of the proverbial expression in v.19). Whether this be so or not, at least the individual apostate will feel the result of the Lord's burning wrath and zeal (strong words for anger). No more dreadful state can be imagined than "the LORD will never be willing to forgive him" (v.20). The appalling results of apostasy are heaped one on the other: all the curses in the book, the blotting out of one's name on earth (a figure used of the Amalekites, 25:19; Exod 17:14), and being singled out for disaster (v.21). All these results will fall on the apostate.

That "the LORD will never be willing to forgive" (v.20) the apostate does not properly contrast with the NT statement of 2 Peter 3:9, that God does not want "anyone to perish"; so some suppose a difference between the God of the OT and the God of the NT. Moses' declaration is reaffirmed in Hebrews 6:4–8 and in 2 Peter 2 and 3:16–17 as well as elsewhere. The Petrine Epistles indicate that there are grounds on which God's forgiveness rests. He is not willing to forgive anyone in rebellion against him, whether under the OT or the NT. His love reaches out to all, but those who reject that love have recourse to no other means to save themselves from the dire consequences of apostasy. Such apostasy includes the severance of the apostate from the source of forgiveness.

## Notes

---

**10** (9 MT) נִצָּבִים (*niṣṣāḇîm*, "standing") means "to station themselves" and suggests that the people were not simply standing there physically but were taking a stand on an issue—the elements of the covenant-treaty.

For "your leaders and chief men," the MT reads רָאשֵׁיכֶם שִׁבְטֵיכֶם (*ro'šêḵem šiḇṭêḵem*, "your leaders, your tribes"). The NIV follows the suggestion that *šiḇṭêḵem* should be שֹׁפְטֵיכֶם (*šōpṭêḵem*, "chief men"), as in Josh 8:33; 23:2; 24:1, where NIV has "judges." Others suggest רָאשֵׁי (*ro'šê*) for *ro'šêḵem* and read "the leaders of your tribes," citing LXX support.

**11** (10 MT) On טַפְּכֶם (*ṭappᵉḵem*, "your children"), see Notes on 20:14.

**13** (12 MT) הָקִים (*hāqîm*, "to confirm"), the Hiphil infinitive of קוּם (*qûm*, "to rise up, stand"), is used in Deuteronomy to describe establishing, confirming, or performing something actively and effectively. In 8:18 the Lord "confirms" his covenant; in 9:5 he drives out the Canaanites "to accomplish" what he had promised; in 22:4 one is to "help" a donkey get on its feet; and in 25:7 one is to "fulfill" his duty. Here it speaks of an effective confirmation or establishment of the covenant.

**14** (13 MT) The word אָלָה (*'ālāh*, "oath") also may mean curse and may refer to the making of the covenant with its curses as warnings to those who might turn from its stipulations.

**16** (15 MT) The same kind of idiom as "on the way here," indicating a generalization, is found in 1:46 ("many days" = all the time you spent there); 1 Sam 23:13 ("kept moving from place to place" = they went according to where they went); 2 Sam 15:20 ("when I do not know where I am going" = when I am going where I am going); and 2 Kings 8:1 ("stay for a while wherever you can" = stay wherever you will stay).

**18** (17 MT) פֶּן (*pen*, "make sure") in the NIV, as in the NAB et al., is taken as introducing an exhortation to make certain that idolatry does not occur.

Defection is likened to a root that bears ראשׁ ולענה (*rō'š wᵉla'ᵃnāh,* "bitter poison"), the familiar gall and wormwood. But *rôš* (or *rō'š*) is used of the poison or the venom of snakes as well as of a plant (possibly hemlock), while *la'ᵃnāh* may be *artemisia judaica,* the juice of whose leaves has a bitter taste. The repetition—using two somewhat synonymous words—often heightens the meaning rather than distinguishing two discrete things; thus the NIV's "bitter poison" (cf. *Fauna and Flora,* pp. 167–68, 198).

**19** (18 MT) שׁרר (*šārar,* "hard," "firm") together with לב (*lēb,* "heart") occurs eight times in Jeremiah (3:17; 7:24; 9:14; 11:8; 13:10; 16:12; 18:12; 23:17) and once in Ps 81:12 (13 MT) always in the bad sense of stubborn or persistent evil resistance to the Lord; thus NIV's "persist" here. Jeremiah 18:12 depicts the same situation that Moses predicted here.

**20** (19 MT) The blotting out of one's name on earth was a very serious matter in Israel. Notice the importance of levirate marriage to avoid the blotting out of a dead brother's name (25:6). See also Exod 32:32–33; Rev 3:5; and the imprecations of Pss 69:28 and 109:13.

---

## 4. *Results of the Lord's anger on those who abandon the covenant*

### 29:22–29

22Your children who follow you in later generations and foreigners who come from distant lands will see the calamities that have fallen on the land and the diseases with which the LORD has afflicted it. 23The whole land will be a burning waste of salt and sulfur—nothing planted, nothing sprouting, no vegetation growing on it. It will be like the destruction of Sodom and Gomorrah, Admah and Zeboiim, which the LORD overthrew in fierce anger. 24All the nations will ask: "Why has the LORD done this to this land? Why this fierce, burning anger?"

25And the answer will be: "It is because this people abandoned the covenant of the LORD, the God of their fathers, the covenant he made with them when he brought them out of Egypt. 26They went off and worshiped other gods and bowed down to them, gods they did not know, gods he had not given them. 27Therefore the LORD's anger burned against this land, so that he brought on it all the curses written in this book. 28In furious anger and in great wrath the LORD uprooted them from their land and thrust them into another land, as it is now."

29The secret things belong to the LORD our God, but the things revealed belong to us and to our children forever, that we may follow all the words of this law.

**22–24** From v.22 to the end of the chapter, the nation as a whole is again in view, and the conditional nature of the address (v.19, "when") changes to prediction. Both the inhabitants and foreigners from distant lands will see the devastation and diseases resulting from the Lord's punishment (v.22)—a punishment likened to that of Sodom, Gomorrah, Admah, and Zeboiim, the cities in the southern Dead Sea area destroyed in the time of Abraham and Lot (v.23; Gen 14:2; 19:24–29).

Utter desolation will prevail. No more will the land flowing with milk and honey be so productive that "abundant prosperity" will be present (28:11). The Promised Land will become a burning waste of salt and sulfur. The dramatic translation of the NIV portrays well the utter desolation—"nothing planted, nothing sprouted, no vegetation growing" (v.23). The pictorial representation is dramatized further by the reaction of later generations of Israelites and of the nations, who ask the universal question when confronted by events that adversely affect lives or properties: "Why? Why did the Lord do this? Why was he so angry?" (cf. v.24).

**25–28** The answer contains (again) the warning that Israel "abandoned the covenant of the LORD" (v.25), though the answer, as well as the preceding paragraph, is cast in the form of accomplished prediction. The people did abandon the covenant; they did go off and worship other gods. Therefore, the Lord's "furious anger" and "great wrath" (v.28) uprooted them from their land and thrust them into another land. Those strong and highly descriptive words appear also in Jeremiah 21:5 and 32:37.

"As it is now" (v.28) appears to be spoken from the point of view of "all the nations" (v.24) who would see the devastation in the future.

**29** The gnomic character of this verse has led some expositors to suppose that this observation was inserted in the text at a later time, when questions were being asked about the providence of God relative to his kindness toward his people or to their punishment. But this is by no means the only aphoristic wisdom statement in Deuteronomy, as our former observations have shown. The statement fits well between chapters 29 and 30, both of which relate very particularly to Israel's allegiance to the Lord and to his revealed word as well as relating to the results stemming from either the people's allegiance or their disobedience.

The "secret" or hidden things are at least the future experiences of Israel whether they are obedient or disobedient—experiences then hidden but eventually realized by future fulfillment. The nation has been given the covenant-treaty with its stipulations including its blessings and curses. This constitutes a way of life that they must follow. Its central characteristic necessitates their adherence to the Lord their God as their suzerain. They have specific promises of his help in conquering and settling in Canaan—if they abide by his revealed word. The hidden things of the future are known only to the Lord, but his people, nevertheless, have reason for great expectations allied with great responsibilities; they have the things revealed. These are within the area of their knowledge and that of their children forever, and that for a definite, specific reason—that they should "follow all the words of this law."

Other, wider theological meanings spring from this declaration, especially regarding the secret things known only to the Lord, in harmony with such verses as Isaiah 55:8–9:

> "For my thoughts are not your thoughts,
> neither are your ways my ways, . . ..
> "As the heavens are higher than the earth,
> so are my ways higher than your ways
> and my thoughts than your thoughts."

So God knows all things, and human knowledge in comparison is severely limited. But people do have the revelation of God in his Word, and to that they should give obedient attention. Moses in this place aptly relates the hidden things to the future of his people as they stand on the brink of Jordan facing the Promised Land. So once more he exhorted them to follow "all the words of this law."

## Notes

**23** (22 MT) The exact locations of Sodom, Gomorrah, Admah, and Zeboiim are not known. Sodom is mentioned often in both the OT and the NT (about fifty times) and Gomorrah about half as often, while Admah and Zeboiim are mentioned only in Gen 10:19; 14:2, 8; Deut 29:23; and Hos 11:8. See the *Illustrated Bible Dictionary*, 3:1237; ZPEB, 5:466–68.

**24–25** (23–24 MT) The prediction of these verses is repeated by the Lord to Solomon after the building of the temple and applied to its destruction—if the people turn to other gods (1 Kings 9:8–9). Jeremiah predicted the same future for Jerusalem in Jer 22:8–9.

**26** (25 MT) Though in 4:19 Israel was told not to worship the "sun, the moon and the stars," which had been given "to all the nations," nowhere is it said that God gave the "idols" to other nations. It should not be supposed that the negative statement that the idols of the nations were not given to Israel means that they were given to the nations by the Lord, as some have averred, supposing this to be a recognition of natural theology under the control of God.

**28** (27 MT) בְּאַף וּבְחֵמָה וּבְקֶצֶף גָּדוֹל (*be'ap̱ ûḇeḥēmāh ûḇeqeṣep̱ gāḏôl*, "in furious anger and in great wrath") is literally "in anger and rage and great wrath." The first two words for anger taken together mean "furious anger," and the additional phrase, "in great wrath," indicates a very great anger indeed (cf. Zech 8:2).

It is possible that the phrase "as it is now" was inserted after the devastation actually occurred in 586 B.C., but it is not necessary to suppose this. It may simply be a prediction of what a person at that time in the future would say to one who questioned, "Why has the LORD done this?" (v.24).

הַנִּסְתָּרֹת (*hannistārōṯ*, "the secret things") is the feminine plural Niphal participle of סָתַר (*sāṯar*, "to hide") and therefore means the things in general that are hidden from mankind, the secret things.

The Hebrew texts have a series of dots called *puncta extraordinaria* over לָנוּ וּלְבָנֵינוּ (*lānû ûleḇānênû*, "to us and to our children"). This Masoretic device brought special attention to the words; but the reason for its use is not now known, though many notions have been suggested. It surely highlighted the fact that "the things revealed" belonged to all generations of Israelites and that they should adhere to the revealed word. This is applicable to all people as the NT especially clearly shows.

---

## B. *Prosperity After the Return to the Lord*

### 30:1–10

**1 When all these blessings and curses I have set before you come upon
you and you take them to heart wherever the LORD your God disperses
you among the nations, 2 and when you and your children return to the
LORD your God and obey him with all your heart and with all your soul
according to everything I command you today, 3 then the LORD your God
will restore your fortunes and have compassion on you and gather you
again from all the nations where he scattered you. 4 Even if you have
been banished to the most distant land under the heavens, from there
the LORD your God will gather you and bring you back. 5 He will bring you
to the land that belonged to your fathers, and you will take possession
of it. He will make you more prosperous and numerous than your
fathers. 6 The LORD your God will circumcise your hearts and the hearts
of your descendants, so that you may love him with all your heart and
with all your soul, and live. 7 The LORD your God will put all these curses
on your enemies who hate and persecute you. 8 You will again obey the
LORD and follow all his commands I am giving you today. 9 Then the LORD
your God will make you most prosperous in all the work of your hands
and in the fruit of your womb, the young of your livestock and the crops
of your land. The LORD will again delight in you and make you
prosperous, just as he delighted in your fathers, 10 if you obey the LORD
your God and keep his commands and decrees that are written in this**

**Book of the Law and turn to the LORD your God with all your heart and with all your soul.**

**1–3** In 29:22 the tenor of Moses' address turns predictive and leads to the notion that Moses was not optimistic about all of Israel's future. Now in 30:1 there appears a mixture of hesitant and contingent prediction relative to Israel's return to the land in blessing after a period of dispersion and captivity throughout the world. In v.1 Moses looked beyond the period when Israel has had a time of blessing and after a subsequent time when Israel would be under the curse of the Lord while dispersed among the nations.

It is not clear whether the destruction by a nation whose language they would not understand (28:36, 49) is the same experience as the scattering among the nations in 28:64; 29:22; and 30:1. Neither is it clear that there would be two basic dispersions, as later Scriptures and history have shown—one after the destruction of the kingdom(s) culminating in 586 B.C. and another after A.D. 70, a dispersion that is still in effect even though an Israeli national state is in control of part of the Promised Land.

When the people who are dispersed among the nations return to the Lord in obedience to all the commands of the covenant with all their heart and soul (v.2), then the Lord, having compassion on them, will restore their fortunes after regathering them from the nations (v.3).

The Hebrew phrase translated "restore your fortunes" signifies a total change, a return to a former state, and indicates that Israel would return to the position of being under the blessing of the Lord in their own land. This is what the following verses describe.

**4–8** The hypothetical particle translated "even if" (v.4) is often used to make a very strong assertion, as in Numbers 22:18: "Even if Balak gave me his palace filled with silver and gold, I could not do anything great or small to go beyond the command of the LORD my God." So here from the most extreme distance, as the ancient Israelites conceived distances, out on the perimeter of the known nations, even from there the Lord would regather his people.

This future return of God's people to their land will be occasioned by the resolve of their heart and soul to return to him, and it will also be characterized by their new, wholehearted love for him and by their obedience to all his commands (vv.6, 8). This new state of blessing, however, will be due not only to the renewal of Israel's allegiance to the Lord but also to his compassion. The Lord's compassion makes possible the return from banishment even in the most distant lands (vv.3–4). That compassion will not only return the people to their land; it also (as "restore your fortunes" [v.3] suggests) rehabilitates them. His compassion not only makes them prosperous; it makes them more prosperous and more numerous than their fathers (v.5). Three times in vv.5, 9, Israel is promised a new and greater prosperity than she ever has experienced before.

The curses of disobedience will then fall on Israel's enemies, not on Israel herself. The Lord will circumcise the people's hearts so that they will love him with heart and soul. This work of God in the innermost being of the individual (you and your descendants), as well as what appears to be a central disposition of the individual himself (6:5–6; 10:16), is characteristic of the spiritual nature of Deuteronomic revelation. See the comment on 10:14–16.

**9–10** The initial promises the Lord had been giving the Israelites as they were being prepared for entrance into Canaan would be renewed. They would be prosperous in everything they did (v.9). Fecundity would again mark their families, livestock, and crops (28:11). The Lord would again delight in his people (as in the first part of 28:63, where the same verb *śûś* is translated "pleased"); he would return to being pleased to make them prosper.

This look into the distant future ends with a warning that prosperity will come only if the people return to the original demands of the covenant-treaty—obedience to the Book of the Law, the central character of which is total allegiance to the Lord their God (v.10).

## Notes

This section is largely a reiteration or summary of statements made in 4:29–31 and chapter 28. For an interesting chart of parallels, see Craigie, p. 363.

**1–5** That a dispersion of Israel is still in effect can be seen by the population distribution of Jewish people. In 1990 according to various almanacs and encyclopedias, there were about 13 million Jews scattered throughout the world and only about 4.4 million in Israel—for a total of 17.5 million.

**3** The Hebrew clause וְשָׁב . . . אֶת־שְׁבוּתְךָ (*wešāḇ . . . 'eṯ-šeḇûṯeḵā,* "will restore your fortunes") in the KJV is "turn thy captivity." But the more probable idea of "to turn a turning" (i.e., "to restore their fortunes") has a long history, being anticipated as far back as Aquila's translation (A.D. 130), and is adopted generally by most modern exegetes because it is contextually more appropriate. This supposes that *šeḇûṯ* comes from שׁוּב (*šûḇ,* "return") rather than from שָׁבָה (*šāḇāh,* "to take captive"). It should be noticed that the verse ends with the promise that the Lord would gather them again from all the nations. See also Jer 29:14; 30:3; 32:44 (NIV mg.); 33:7, 11, 26; 49:6; Ezek 29:14; 39:25. See Reider, p. 382.

**4** The Hebrew figure בִּקְצֵה הַשָּׁמָיִם (*biqṣēh haššāmayim,* "under the heavens"; lit., "at the end of the heavens") focuses on the horizon and refers to the most distant land.

### C. *The Covenant Offer of Life or Death*

#### 30:11–20

11 Now what I am commanding you today is not too difficult for you or
beyond your reach. 12 It is not up in heaven, so that you have to ask,
"Who will ascend into heaven to get it and proclaim it to us so we may
obey it?" 13 Nor is it beyond the sea, so that you have to ask, "Who will
cross the sea to get it and proclaim it to us so we may obey it?" 14 No,
the word is very near you; it is in your mouth and in your heart so you
may obey it.

15 See, I set before you today life and prosperity, death and destruction. 16 For I command you today to love the LORD your God, to walk in
his ways, and to keep his commands, decrees and laws; then you will
live and increase, and the LORD your God will bless you in the land you
are entering to possess.

17 But if your heart turns away and you are not obedient, and if you are
drawn away to bow down to other gods and worship them, 18 I declare to
you this day that you will certainly be destroyed. You will not live long in
the land you are crossing the Jordan to enter and possess.

**[19]This day I call heaven and earth as witnesses against you that I have set before you life and death, blessings and curses. Now choose life, so that you and your children may live [20]and that you may love the LORD your God, listen to his voice, and hold fast to him. For the LORD is your life, and he will give you many years in the land he swore to give to your fathers, Abraham, Isaac and Jacob.**

**11–14** From v.11 to v.20, Moses turned back to the options that were placed before Israel as they stood by the Jordan facing the future in Canaan. He first set before them the availability of the resources for responding affirmatively to the commands he was giving them. The commands (all the revelation of God given through Moses in the covenant-treaty) were neither too difficult nor beyond their reach (v.11). Their proximity and intimacy are illustrated by assertions and rhetorical questions. It is neither in heaven nor beyond the sea; so questions like "Who will ascend into heaven?" (v.12) or "Who will cross the sea to get it?" (v.13) are superfluous and nonsensical. Even in these rhetorical questions, Moses emphasized the necessity of the proclamation and fulfillment of the commands by obedience to them. The positive assertion of the nearness of the revelation (v.14) is even more specific; the word is in their mouth (they can repeat it) and in their heart (they can think it and understand and react to it). Obedience is possible!

**15–20** In this peroration the issue is set out plainly: life and prosperity or death and destruction (v.15). Starkly clear, the Lord through Moses set the choice before his people. Will it be obedience or disobedience—life and prosperity or death and destruction? Which will it be? The route of obedience itself is twofold: It requires one "to love the LORD" and "to walk in his ways" (v.16). As in a covenant-treaty, the "love" required is that set of the soul that involves the committal of one's self in loyal devotion to the Lord. It relies on faith in his saving grace and goes hand in hand with obedience as walking "in his ways," that is, obeying his precepts. That route will lead to life; it will increase the size of the nation and bring the Lord's blessing on them in the land.

The obverse, however, will be Israel's lot if the people turn their hearts away from the Lord in disobedience, if they are drawn away from him to bow down to other gods and to worship them (v.17). Disobedient Israel, Moses declared, will be destroyed; the nation separate from the Lord will not live long in that land across the Jordan, which they were contemplating to enter and take for themselves (v.18).

After invoking both heaven and earth to witness that he has placed the options of life and death, blessings and curses, before Israel (4:26), Moses made his final appeal to his people.

"Choose life!" he exhorted (v.19).

Why? Because they and their children will then live; and they will love the Lord, listen to him, and hold fast to him (v.20).

As elsewhere, now at the end of his addresses, Moses stressed the personal involvement of the people with the Lord. When they are committed wholly to him, he will give the nation many years in the land he promised to Abraham, Isaac, and Jacob.

## Notes

---

**11** The subject of "What I am commanding" is a singular noun, a collective, as in 8:1 and 27:1. It refers to the whole legislation or all the elements of the covenant-treaty as a corpus.

"Not too difficult" renders לֹא־נִפְלֵאת (*lō'-niplē't*), which also means "not too mysterious, hard to understand or incomprehensible" (see 17:8). "Beyond your reach" renders לֹא רְחֹקָה (*lō' reḥōqāh*), which means "not far distant."

**11–14** There may be a reflection here on Near Eastern religious literature, especially the Gilgamesh Epic in which Gilgamesh has to search heroically for life. Moses said that God's life-giving revealed word was very near them. It does not need to be searched out (cf. ANET, "Gilgamesh Epic," 1:63–75).

**12** "It is not up in heaven" is not a denial of passages similar to Ps 119:89, which speaks of the eternal and fixed state of the revelation of God. The Deuteronomic statement relates to the revelation being given to the Israelites in their locale on earth.

**12–14** In Rom 10:6–10 the apostle Paul cited Deut 30:12–14 to prove that salvation is by faith. He used Moses' rhetorical questions regarding the revealed commands of God as illustrative of attempting salvation by bringing Christ down from heaven or up from the grave—neither of which is necessary or effective. It is rather that the word of faith is "in your mouth and in your heart" as Moses declared. This then became the basis for Paul's great affirmation, "That if you confess with your mouth, 'Jesus is Lord,' and believe in your heart that God raised him from the dead, you will be saved." As in Moses' time, so in NT times, the Word of God was in their mouths and in their hearts. See EBC, 10:111–12.

**16** The syntax of the beginning of this verse is awkward. It appears to lack a conditional clause. The LXX solved the problem by inserting into the text (unless this comes from another Hebrew textual tradition that had it) at the beginning of the verse: "If you listen to the commands of the Lord your God." This is much as the MT in 11:27, as well as the LXX text. The NIV has translated אֲשֶׁר (*'ašer*) as "For," and this may be correct, though this usage is disputed (see BDB, pp. 83–84).

**17** חָוָה (*ḥāwāh*, "to bow down in worship") and עָבַד (*'ābad*, "to perform acts of worship") are commonly used together to give the sense "to bow down to other gods and worship them" (cf. 11:16; 17:3; 29:26 [25 MT]).

**19** On "I call heaven and earth as witnesses," see Notes on 4:26.

**20** For "love," "listen," and "hold fast," see Notes on 10:12–13 and 10:20.

In 32:46–47, "all the words of this law" are said to be their "life." See Joshua's decision and commitment in Josh 24:15. "All the words of this law" constitute their life because the central requirement of "this law" is total commitment to the Lord who gives them life, with all its ramifications of blessing. See Ps 36:9; Prov 8:35; John 14:6.

---

## V. Concluding Narratives (31:1–34:12)

The basic historical element of 31:1–34:12 is the succession of Joshua, but the narrative of this succession is broken by several long sections relating to the last acts and the death of Moses. A symphonic structure lies almost hidden throughout the narrative. The main theme of Joshua's succession appears in 31:1–8, 14, 23; 32:44; and 34:9.

Another theme appearing in these last narratives is the death of Moses (31:1–2, 14, 16, 26–29; 32:48–52; 33:1; 34:1–8, 10–12). The last acts of Moses include the writing of the law and the giving of instructions for its communication, the Song of Moses, and his blessing on the tribes.

The literary order of this last section moves the action toward the death of Moses. First Moses speaks of what will transpire as the people make conquest of Canaan. He exhorts both the people and Joshua to be "strong and courageous" (vv.6–7). Then mention is made of writing down the law, giving it to the priests, and adding instructions for its septennial reading during the Feast of Tabernacles. In vv.14–23 messages from the Lord to Moses about the commissioning of Joshua, the death of Moses, the prediction of future disaster for Israel, and a directive for Moses to write down and teach to the Israelites what follows in chapter 32 as Moses' Song are interwoven with the commissioning of Joshua. Reference is made again in 31:24–29 to Moses' writing the words of the law in a book, and further directions are given for depositing it in the tabernacle and for its use. Moses' Song, the Lord's final directive for Moses' death, Moses' blessing on the tribes, and the report of his death complete the book.

## A. *Charge to Joshua and Deposition of the Law (31:1–29)*

### 1. *Joshua to be leader*

#### 31:1–8

[1]Then Moses went out and spoke these words to all Israel: [2]"I am now
a hundred and twenty years old and I am no longer able to lead you. The
LORD has said to me, 'You shall not cross the Jordan.' [3]The LORD your
God himself will cross over ahead of you. He will destroy these nations
before you, and you will take possession of their land. Joshua also will
cross over ahead of you, as the LORD said. [4]And the LORD will do to them
what he did to Sihon and Og, the kings of the Amorites, whom he
destroyed along with their land. [5]The LORD will deliver them to you, and
you must do to them all that I have commanded you. [6]Be strong and
courageous. Do not be afraid or terrified because of them, for the LORD
your God goes with you; he will never leave you nor forsake you."
[7]Then Moses summoned Joshua and said to him in the presence of all
Israel, "Be strong and courageous, for you must go with this people into
the land that the LORD swore to their forefathers to give them, and you
must divide it among them as their inheritance. [8]The LORD himself goes
before you and will be with you; he will never leave you nor forsake you.
Do not be afraid; do not be discouraged."

**1–2** Most of the material in chapter 31 is given elsewhere in Deuteronomy. This material appears to be in the nature of a summary with, here and there, some specific additions—just as one who knows that his ministry is coming toward its end repeats, for emphasis' sake, things said before.

The chronological incidence and sequence of chapter 31 cannot be determined, other than that in broad outline the various items relate to the last days of Moses' life. He was 120 years old and unable to lead the people (Heb., unable "to go out and come in," a common idiom for engaging in a day's work). Moses' statement, however, should be considered as his own humble assessment. Moses did not die because his natural strength was gone (34:7) but because the time for Israel's entrance into Canaan had come, and Moses was not to enter the land. That was precluded by his arrogance before the people at the waters of Meribah when he struck the rock twice to bring out water though the Lord had told him only to speak to the rock. It may be, however, that Moses did not feel competent to lead the Israelites in the wars of conquest, which they would soon face.

**3–6** Though Moses himself was not to cross the Jordan, he encouraged the Israelites by the assurance that the Lord himself would cross over ahead of them and that he would destroy the nations of the land as he had destroyed Sihon and Og (vv.3–4). He exhorted them not to be afraid of the Canaanites (v.6). The Lord would not only go with them, he would never leave them or forsake them. Moses would soon remind them that this presence of the Lord was contingent on their allegiance to him. Moses also assured the people that Joshua would cross over the Jordan with them.

**7–8** In the presence of "all Israel" (v.7), Moses repeated to Joshua personally what he had just said to the people, adding that Joshua was to divide the land among the people. What land each would receive would be his inheritance. The reference to Joshua is picked up again in v.14, where the Lord directed Moses to present Joshua and himself at the Tent of Meeting for Joshua's commissioning.

The substance of Moses' exhortation to Joshua in vv.7–8 is repeated in v.23 as the Lord's command to him. In 32:44 it is said that Moses came with Joshua the son of Nun when he spoke the words of his song to the people, and in 34:9 Joshua becomes Moses' successor in fact.

The exhortation "Be strong and courageous" (v.7) given to Joshua and to the people by Moses at the end of his career is repeated by the Lord to Joshua after the death of Moses (Josh 1:6, 9) and also urged on Joshua by the people (Josh 1:18). When the army had triumphed over the five-king southern coalition, Joshua exhorted the people to be strong and courageous. David also picked up these words to urge Solomon to follow the decrees the Lord gave Moses, as David encouraged Solomon to build the temple (1 Chron 22:13; 28:20).

## Notes

---

**1** S.R. Driver (*Deuteronomy*, pp. 333–34) and others assert that "then Moses went out and spoke these words to all Israel" must refer to words previously uttered because, if the following words were meant, the infinitive לֵאמֹר (*lē'mōr*, "saying") would have been used rather than "these words." That this is common cannot be denied, but such introductory formulas vary a great deal and cannot be pressed into exact molds.

**2** The Hebrew idiom for "to lead you" is "to go out and come in." See the comment and Notes on 28:6.

**3** Regal succession was a concern of Near Eastern treaties; and though neither Moses nor Joshua were kings, they represented the Lord as King, and so a successor for Moses was a concern of this covenant-treaty (Kline, *Biblical Authority*, p. 143).

**4** On Sihon and Og, see 2:26–3:11.

**6, 8** As elsewhere indicated, the Lord never leaves his people. When it appears that he has left them (or it is so stated), he is with them to punish them for their evil. "The Lord has left me" is always an anthropomorphic or anthropopathic statement.

Apparently the LXX considered that the Hebrew לֹא יַרְפְּךָ וְלֹא יַעַזְבֶךָּ (*lō' yarpeḵā welō' ya'azḇeḵā*, "he will never leave you nor forsake you") was emphatic, for they made the negative strong with οὐ μή . . . οὔτε μή (*ou mē . . . oute mē*). The writer of Hebrews quotes the LXX, and so the NIV renders the verse in Heb 13:5 in emphatic English order.

**7** A few Hebrew MSS, the Samaritan Pentateuch, and the Vulgate support reading "you will bring this people" as it is in v.23: "you will bring." This involves reading the Qal תָּבוֹא (*tāḇô'*, "go") with the preposition אֶת (*'eṯ*) as the Hiphil תָּבִיא (*tāḇî'*, "bring") and *'eṯ* as the sign of the direct object. The NIV follows most MSS of the MT.

## 2. *Recitation of the law at every seventh Feast of Tabernacles* 31:9–13

9So Moses wrote down this law and gave it to the priests, the sons of Levi, who carried the ark of the covenant of the LORD, and to all the elders of Israel.
10Then Moses commanded them: "At the end of every seven years, in the year for canceling debts, during the Feast of Tabernacles,
11when all Israel comes to appear before the LORD your God at the place he will choose, you shall read this law before them in their hearing.
12Assemble the people—men, women and children, and the aliens living in your towns—so they can listen and learn to fear the LORD your God and follow carefully all the words of this law.
13Their children, who do not know this law, must hear it and learn to fear the LORD your God as long as you live in the land you are crossing the Jordan to possess."

**9** Like the rest of these observations, commands, and historical notations at the end of Deuteronomy, the paragraph on the writing and reading of "this law" (vv.9–13) comes rather abruptly on the scene. However, all the materials of these chapters relate to things of great importance to Israel and to Moses as his career ends. The time when Moses wrote down the law and what "law" is meant in each of the cases mentioned here cannot easily be determined. This "law" has been interpreted as extending to the whole Pentateuch on the one hand and as limited to the central legal core of Deuteronomy on the other. It surely included all that was essential to the covenant-treaty documents that are constantly referred to in Deuteronomy—and that includes historical, hortative, and legal elements, substantially all of Deuteronomy.

The statement about writing down the law serves as an introduction to the depositing of the revelation with the priests and elders and to the command to have it read at the septennial sabbatical Feast of Tabernacles (v.10).

The priests designated as the sons of Levi (v.9) are also so designated in 21:5. The more common Deuteronomic designation is "the priests, the Levites." Both designations indicate that the priests are of the tribe of Levi. The additional description of the priests as those "who carried the ark of the covenant of the LORD" was apropos especially to the wandering and residence in the deserts of Sinai where Israel was always thought to be en route to Canaan.

As was customary in covenant-treaty procedures, a copy of the treaty was deposited in the sanctuary of the suzerain; and the covenant-treaty stipulations were to be read before the vassal people at stated times.

**10–13** The stated time for reading "this law" (v.11) was at seven-year intervals (v.10), at the time of canceling debts (15:1), that is, the sabbatical year. More specifically, it was to be during the Feast of Tabernacles of the sabbatical year, when all Israel was "to appear before the Lord at the place he [was to] choose" (v.11; i.e., where the tabernacle was placed).

Attendance at the feast was to be a joyous occasion for all the people: men, women, sons, daughters, menservants, maidservants, Levites, aliens, fatherless, and widows (16:14). The law was to be read before all these people (v.12). The children were singled out for special mention because they did not know the law (v.13). This reading of the law once every seven years would not be sufficient to inculcate its teachings in the minds of either the children or the adults. This septennial reading does not obviate the teaching ministry of the home (6:1–9) or that of the priests (17:11; 24:8;

Lev 10:11). It is meant, rather, to strengthen these other teaching procedures, to focus the attention of the people as a nation on the revelation of God on a dramatic and joyful occasion. It would also dramatize the learning of the law for those children and others who had not been reached by the other teaching procedures in home and tabernacle.

The arrangement for a covenant renewal is missing from this septennial reading of the law. It should not be considered as a basis for a regular covenant-renewal experience. The reading was to inspire the people to reverence (fear) the Lord and to follow carefully all the covenant stipulations. The children especially must hear it to learn to reverence the Lord. That this process should go on "as long as you live in the land" (v.13) is not to suggest that elsewhere knowledge of the Lord and his word was not necessary. Rather, the process of making known the revelation of God should never cease so that reverence for the Lord and obedience to his word would never cease.

## Notes

---

**9–11** There were set times for reading the treaties in the Near East, to remind the parties of the stipulations involved. The reading of "this law" every seven years conforms to this practice. See Kline, *Biblical Authority*, pp. 121–23, and Kitchen, *Ancient Orient*, p. 97; by way of illustration, see ANET, p. 205.

---

### 3. *Some last words on leadership transfer*

#### 31:14–23

[14]The LORD said to Moses, "Now the day of your death is near. Call
Joshua and present yourselves at the Tent of Meeting, where I will
commission him." So Moses and Joshua came and presented themselves at the Tent of Meeting.
[15]Then the LORD appeared at the Tent in a pillar of cloud, and the
cloud stood over the entrance to the Tent. [16]And the LORD said to Moses:
"You are going to rest with your fathers, and these people will soon
prostitute themselves to the foreign gods of the land they are entering.
They will forsake me and break the covenant I made with them. [17]On
that day I will become angry with them and forsake them; I will hide my
face from them, and they will be destroyed. Many disasters and
difficulties will come upon them, and on that day they will ask, 'Have not
these disasters come upon us because our God is not with us?' [18]And I
will certainly hide my face on that day because of all their wickedness in
turning to other gods.
[19]"Now write down for yourselves this song and teach it to the
Israelites and have them sing it, so that it may be a witness for me
against them. [20]When I have brought them into the land flowing with
milk and honey, the land I promised on oath to their forefathers, and
when they eat their fill and thrive, they will turn to other gods and
worship them, rejecting me and breaking my covenant. [21]And when
many disasters and difficulties come upon them, this song will testify
against them, because it will not be forgotten by their descendants. I
know what they are disposed to do, even before I bring them into the

**land I promised them on oath." [22]So Moses wrote down this song that day and taught it to the Israelites.**

**[23]The LORD gave this command to Joshua son of Nun: "Be strong and courageous, for you will bring the Israelites into the land I promised them on oath, and I myself will be with you."**

**14–15** At the commissioning of Joshua, Moses and Joshua presented themselves before the Lord at the "Tent of Meeting" (v.14); and the Lord spoke of future apostasy of Israel, not only to Moses, but in the hearing of Joshua as well. In this way Joshua too was warned to resist the tendency of the people to turn to foreign gods. The solemnity of the event is apparent in the description of the Lord appearing in the "pillar of cloud" (v.15), with the cloud standing over the entrance to the tent.

**16–18** After mentioning that Moses was soon to rest with his fathers, the Lord told him and Joshua that the people would soon prostitute themselves to the foreign gods of the land they were about to enter (v.16). Turning to Canaanite gods had its counterpart in forsaking the Lord and breaking the covenant-treaty. When the people forsake the Lord, he will forsake them in anger against their wickedness (vv.17–18) and will hide his face from them. Hiding his face (vv.17–18; 32:20) is the converse of making his face to shine on his people and turning his face toward them as in the Aaronic blessing (Num 6:25–26). It is equal to saying that the Lord would hide himself from his people so that he and the help he could give them would not be available to them. On the contrary, many disasters and difficulties would come on them (v.17); and they will raise a rhetorical question about the reason for the disasters, which would indicate that they knew that the disasters came because God was not with them.

**19** In view of the apostasy to come, the Lord told Moses and Joshua to write down (plural verb) this song. Though the verbs after the initial plural form become singular, this agrees with the fact that Moses and Joshua were there before the Lord (v.14) and with 32:44, where it is said, "Moses came with Joshua son of Nun and spoke." Again, however, the writer changes immediately to say, "When Moses finished reciting" (v.45).

"Teach it to the Israelites and have them sing it" (v.19) implies sufficient repetition to fix it in the minds of the people. Only then would they be able to sing it, and only then would it be a witness to the Lord's admonition, not only to those of that generation, but to their descendants who will not have forgotten it (v.21). The song was to be taught nationally from generation to generation.

**20–22** The apostasy was to come after the fulfillment of the promise made to their fathers that they would realize a satisfying and thriving economy in the land flowing with milk and honey (v.20; Exod 3:8, 17; 13:5; et al.). Under affluence they would become apostate, turning to other gods, rejecting the Lord, and breaking the covenant-treaty. So when the many disasters and difficulties (as in v.17) come on them, the Song of Moses would testify against them.

Moses had shown his pessimistic view of Israelite allegiance to the Lord before. Here he reported that the Lord himself had the same expectation. The Lord said that he knew their disposition toward disobedience—disobedience that appeared even before he brought them into the Land of Promise (v.21). Therefore, this song was given, and Moses wrote it down and taught it to the Israelites (v.22).

**23** The succession of Joshua, the writing down of the law, the prediction of the people's rebellion with its attendant results, and the Song of Moses are intertwined in chapter 31. For the Lord's commission to Joshua, see the comments on vv.1–8 and vv.14–15.

## Notes

**14, 23** The succession to the throne is an important concern in the suzerain-vassal treaties. See Notes on v.3.

**14–15** אֹהֶל מוֹעֵד (*'ōhel mô'ēḏ*, "Tent of Meeting") occurs twice in v.14 and *'ōhel* alone twice in v.15, referring to the same tent (tabernacle). These are the only occurrences in Deuteronomy, though the Tent of Meeting is mentioned often in Exodus, Leviticus, and Numbers.

**16** "You are going to rest with your fathers" is a euphemism for death. In Gen 47:30, Jacob said to Joseph, "When I rest with my fathers, carry me out of Egypt." Another euphemism for death in the earlier books is "gathered to his people" (Gen 25:8; 35:29; et al.).

The verb זָנָה (*zānāh*, "prostitute") may refer to either literal, physical prostitution (Gen 38:24; Deut 22:21) or metaphorical, spiritual turning from allegiance to the Lord and worshiping other gods (Hos 1:2). Since religious prostitution was a feature of Canaanite religion, both ideas may be meant.

**17** For God forsaking his people, see Notes on vv.6, 8.

**19, 21, 26** Both the Song of Moses (vv.19, 21) and the Book of the Law (v.26) are to be witnesses against Israel in any defection from the Lord. In Near Eastern treaties the pagan gods as well as the copies of the treaties themselves were to be witnesses (Kitchen, *Ancient Orient*, p. 97; Kline, *Biblical Authority*, p. 92).

**19** The most common word for "to sing" is שִׁיר (*šîr*), with its noun forms שִׁיר (*šîr*, "song") and שִׁירָה (*šîrāh*), the feminine form, which is used of Moses' song in vv.19, 21–22, 30; 32:44. While songs of various sorts appear in the OT, here the song is an instructional and a mnemonic device.

### 4. *The deposition of the law book and its witness*

#### 31:24–29

24After Moses finished writing in a book the words of this law from
beginning to end, 25he gave this command to the Levites who carried
the ark of the covenant of the LORD : 26"Take this Book of the Law and
place it beside the ark of the covenant of the LORD your God. There it will
remain as a witness against you. 27For I know how rebellious and stiff-
necked you are. If you have been rebellious against the LORD while I am
still alive and with you, how much more will you rebel after I die!
28Assemble before me all the elders of your tribes and all your officials,
so that I can speak these words in their hearing and call heaven and
earth to testify against them. 29For I know that after my death you are
sure to become utterly corrupt and to turn from the way I have
commanded you. In days to come, disaster will fall upon you because
you will do evil in the sight of the LORD and provoke him to anger by
what your hands have made."

**24–29** As in v.9, so in vv.24 and 26 it is said that Moses wrote the "Book of the Law" and gave it to the Levities who carried the ark of the covenant of the Lord. Only in v.11 did the command of Moses concern the regulation for reading the book every seven years. In v.24 it is said that Moses finished writing the book from the beginning to the end, a statement not made before. The command of the Lord to write down the song was given so that it would be a witness against sinning Israel (v.19). In the same way the Book of the Law as a witness (v.26) suggests that the Song of Moses is included in this completed book. It may be supposed that Moses also wrote down his blessing on the tribes (ch. 33) and that someone else may have added it to the book. Nothing is said in Deuteronomy about writing down the blessings on the tribes.

The procedure for making the song known to the people seems to have three steps: Moses wrote it down (vv.19, 22), then he spoke these words in the hearing of the elders and officials (v.28), and finally he recited them in the hearing of the whole assembly (v.30). This reconstruction rests on the idea that "these words" (v.28) refer to the song, not to the Book of the Law (the whole corpus) just mentioned in v.26, and on the idea that "the whole assembly of Israel" (v.30) refers to all the people rather than to the assembly of elders and officials of v.28.

The instruction that the Lord gave Moses indicates that initially Moses directly taught the song to the Israelites (vv.9, 22; 32:44–45). Whether the song was recited originally as a poem or sung as a song is not certain. The usual verb "to sing" is not used here; but the Hebraic figurative expression "put it in their mouths" (v.19), where the antecedent of "it" is this song, may well be correctly translated "and have them sing it." The full expression would be "put this song in their mouths," which in English idiom equals "have them sing it."

Moses last words are replete with his warning (and the Lord's) against apostasy. This warning is directed to all the Israelites (29:2, 16–28; 30:17–19; 31:30–32:47), to Joshua (vv.14–22), to the Levites (the priests) (vv.24–27), and to the elders and officials (vv.28–29).

The Book of the Law was to be placed beside the ark of the covenant as a witness against the people, according to the command to the Levites, because the Lord knew how rebellious and stiff-necked the people were—a statement abundantly supported by a recount of their experiences between the Exodus and their arrival at the Jordan. The Lord had said to Moses (vv.14–18) that after his death the people would soon become apostate. Here Moses conveyed this pessimism in a more direct and personal way to the people by telling them that after he was gone they would be even more rebellious than when he was alive (v.27). His pessimism was well founded both in experience and in the predictive warnings from the Lord. The conduct of Israel fluctuated between obedience and disobedience with gray areas of partial obedience all through their history as a nation.

The references to the renewal of the covenant-treaty on the plains of Moab at the Jordan were over. In response to Moses' command, the last act was to be the placement of the Book of the Law beside the ark of the covenant, which was in the tabernacle for safekeeping. This was to be a witness against any breaking of the covenant-treaty by Israel's failure to maintain allegiance to the Lord their God. This placement of the records of the covenant-treaty in a sanctuary is one of the "standard elements of the classic treaty structure" (Kline, *Biblical Authority*, p. 141).

## Notes

**24–26** Kline argues for the inclusion of chapters 31–34 in the completed covenant records (*Biblical Authority*, pp. 141–42; cf. Wiseman, *Vassal Treaties*, p. 28).

**27–29** Moses' pessimistic view of at least part of Israel's future is most evident in these verses. His assessment of the people's rebellious nature is viewed as history by Stephen in Acts 7—summarized in Stephen's charge to that generation in Acts 7:51–53.

Among the Qumran cave 1 fragments are *The Sayings of Moses*, which rest heavily on Deuteronomy 31 and relate particularly to the proclamation of the law as a witness against apostate Israel (Dupont-Sommer, p. 307).

## B. *The Song of Moses (31:30–32:47)*

The Song of Moses, like all other poetic sections in the historical books of the OT (especially those attributed to the more ancient periods), has been subjected to a great amount of discussion. Also, as with other poetic sections, the song and the blessing on the tribes are replete with textual and translation questions. The main themes are, nevertheless, quite clear.

After the call to listen (vv.1–2), the Lord is proclaimed and praised (vv.3–4). Then in vv.5–6 the people are chided for their reaction toward the Lord. This leads the speaker into a recital of the Lord's goodness toward Israel (vv.8–14), Israel's response to that goodness (vv.15–18), his rejection of them (vv.19–20), and their estrangement and future punishment (vv.21–30) and that of their enemies (vv.31–35). The poem ends with the Lord's salvation for his people and his judgment on his (and their) enemies (vv.36–43).

### 1. *Moses' recitation before the assembly*

31:30

30 And Moses recited the words of this song from beginning to end in the hearing of the whole assembly of Israel:

**30** The command to write down the song and to teach it to Israel and have them sing it (v.19) is said to have been obeyed (v.22). This is now made more explicit as an introduction to the song itself. The Hebrew word behind "recite" (*dāḇar*) has a very wide semantic spread. But because the writing of the song has already been mentioned, because it was recounted from the beginning to end, and because it was to be taught to the Israelites, the use of the word "recite" describes well what Moses did before the whole assembly.

### 2. *Literary introduction*

32:1–2

1 Listen, O heavens, and I will speak;
hear, O earth, the words of my mouth.
2 Let my teaching fall like rain
and my words descend like dew,
like showers on new grass,
like abundant rain on tender plants.

**1–2** In his introduction Moses called heaven and earth to listen to what he was about to say. Isaiah and Micah did the same in several places (Isa 1:2; 34:1; Mic 1:2; 6:1–2). Yet the message of the song is not directed to heaven and earth but to the nation of Israel. The "they" of v.5 is Israel; so also are the "you" and the "people" of v.6. The Lord is the Father and Creator of national Israel. The rest of the song directs its message to Israel in either the second or the third person. However, when the song comes to its conclusion, the nations again are addressed—this time to rejoice with Israel for the Lord's punishment of his enemies and his atonement for his people (v.43).

The call to the heavens and the earth to listen is a figure for all sentient creation as an audience to hear the message to Israel—a poetic way of emphasizing the importance of the song's themes. As in the treaty form, all creation is a witness to the covenant-treaty between the Lord and Israel.

It should also be remembered that this song was to be repeated by the Israelites themselves both as a warning against disobedience and as a basis for hope when "their strength is gone" (v.36).

The remainder of the introduction (v.2) expresses Moses' wish that his song would have a beneficent and pleasing reception and result. To this end he revealed his desire in four references to the beneficial results of water coming onto the land—an effective simile in a country of limited rainfall.

Like rain, dew, showers, and abundant rain bringing fertility to the new grass and tender plants, Moses hoped that his teaching—his words—would prove pleasant and beneficial.

## Notes

---

**2** The masculine noun לֶקַח (*leqah*), from the verb לָקַח (*lāqah*, "to take"), probably means "teaching," "instruction," "learning," as what was received. It occurs only here and in Isa 29:24 aside from the wisdom literature (Job 11:4 ["beliefs"]; Prov 1:5; 4:2; 7:21 ["persuasive words"]; 9:9; 16:21, 23).

שְׂעִירִם (*śeʿîrim*, "showers") is a *hapax legomenon* that possibly means "raindrops."

רְבִיבִים (*rebîbîm*, "abundant") is from רֹב (*rōb*), which means "multitude," "abundance," i.e., copious rain.

---

### 3. *The theme: the proclamation of the Lord*

32:3–4

> 3 I will proclaim the name of the LORD.
> Oh, praise the greatness of our God!
> 4 He is the Rock, his works are perfect,
> and all his ways are just.
> A faithful God who does no wrong,
> upright and just is he.

**3** The song proper begins with the declaration that Moses proclaimed the name of the Lord and called on others to ascribe greatness to him. Moses has proclaimed the name of the Lord throughout Deuteronomy. He has transmitted the third commandment—

"You shall not misuse the name of the LORD your God"—and warned that such misuse would bring punishment (5:11). The people were to make oaths only in the Lord's name (6:13; 10:20). To the priests, the Levites, was given the responsibility to bless the people in the Lord's name (10:8; 21:5; Num 6:22–27). The priests were also to minister in the Lord's name always (18:5, 7). The prophet that the Lord was to raise up in Moses' stead would speak in the Lord's name, but one who presumed to speak in the Lord's name something the Lord had not said was to be put to death (18:19–20). One who predicts in the Lord's name what does not come to pass is declared to be false (18:22). The blessings that will come on obedient Israel will cause the nations to realize that Israel is "called by the name of the LORD" (28:10).

It is this name, the glorious and awesome name, that Moses called the people to revere (28:58). Basically, the name of the Lord signifies his person (see Notes on 12:5; 28:10; and 28:58).

The most common reference to the Name in Deuteronomy speaks of the place the Lord would choose as a dwelling for his name (12:5, 11, 21; 14:23–24; 16:2, 6, 11; 26:2). In these places the Name most significantly relates to his person, his being. Consequently, the NIV in these places capitalizes Name. This not only signifies that the Lord (*YHWH,* "Yahweh") is God but that the Lord is the God of history, the God of the promises, the God who was fulfilling the covenant promises, the God whose people they now were, under the covenant-treaty. His Name is significant of himself. His Name dwelling over the ark in the tabernacle in the place he would choose signifies that he placed himself in the midst of his people and that that place would be the center of worship. The place could be anywhere that the Lord might designate.

"Our God" signifies Israel's God. The verbal structure of v.3b is also found in Psalm 29:1–2, where the NIV has translated, "Ascribe to the LORD." After the same fashion the translation here could be, "Ascribe greatness to our God."

The Hebrew word for "greatness" (*gōḏel*) occurs five times in Deuteronomy: 3:24; 5:24 ("majesty" [21 MT]); 9:26; 11:2 ("majesty"); 32:3; see also Numbers 14:19; Psalms 79:11 ("strength"); 150:2; Isaiah 9:9 ("arrogance" [8 MT]); 10:12 ("pride"); and Ezekiel 31:2 ("majesty"), 7 ("majestic"), 18 ("majesty"). All these passages—except those in Isaiah and Ezekiel—refer to the greatness of God, the greatness described in the following verses of the song.

**4** The grammatical structure of v.4 makes its assertion of the nature of God stand out forcefully and dramatically. The first word, "the Rock," is a *casus pendens,* a nominative absolute. The metaphor declares that the Lord is strong and stable, one who can be relied on. The following four parallel lines indicate how the Lord as "the Rock" stands in contrast to Israel who acted corruptly toward him (vv.5–6). The Lord as "the Rock" is a major theme of the song, being mentioned in vv.15, 18, and 30–31, and is used of other gods in v.31 and v.37. Elsewhere the Rock is used metaphorically of the Lord in the same way (see 1 Sam 2:2; 2 Sam 22:2–3, 32, 47 [bis]; 23:3; Pss 18:31, 46; 28:1; 31:2; 61:2; 62:2, 7; 78:35; 89:26; 92:15; 94:22; 95:1). (Other Hebrew words for rock are also used to portray God as "the Rock.")

The rest of the song suggests that the main "works" of the Lord are activities of creating, aiding, and guiding Israel. These "works are perfect, and all his ways are just" (cf. Ps 18:30). His character is marked by faithfulness; no wrongdoing exists in him. He is upright and straightforward.

## Notes

3 גֹּדֶל (*gōḏel*, "greatness") is properly ascribed of God; but when used of others it may be assumed greatness, e.g., pride or arrogance. See Isa 9:9 (8 MT); 10:12.

4 The NEB, following the suggestion of a few ancient Hebrew, Samaritan, and Syriac sources and some questionable parallels, accepts a different reading from יָצַר (*yāṣar*) meaning "maker," hence "Creator" rather than "Rock."

The NIV levels the parallel of the Hebrew singular "work" and the plural "ways," making both plural, "works" and "ways."

In this verse two words are translated "just"; the first synonym מִשְׁפָּט (*mišpāṭ*) basically means "that which is right," and the second, יָשָׁר (*yāšār*), "that which is straight or straightforward," used metaphorically as in Isa 40:3.

## 4. *The indictment of Israel*

### 32:5–6

5They have acted corruptly toward him;
to their shame they are no longer his children,
but a warped and crooked generation.
6Is this the way you repay the LORD,
O foolish and unwise people?
Is he not your Father, your Creator,
who made you and formed you?

**5–6** The Lord's governing of his people is on the highest moral and ethical level, but in contrast the Israelites "have acted corruptly" (v.5). Acting corruptly (as in 9:12) expresses that, while the Lord is always right in his handling of Israel, Israel has been wrong and devious in rejecting him. The idolatry of the golden calf illustrates this corruption that broke their relationship to the Lord so that they were "no longer his children"; they were "no sons." This condition of being "no sons" was to their shame and disgrace.

The first two lines of v.5 come from five words in Hebrew that appear to form two clauses, which have been variously translated and by some exegetes reconstructed. The Hebrew is more abrupt than the NIV and other translations. This, however, is not unusual in Hebrew poetry, which frequently makes an assertion in only one or two words. The English therefore must be construed more fully to bring out the force of the Hebrew text. The NIV follows quite closely to the words of the Hebrew text even though this requires fifteen English words to represent five Hebrew words. In their state of idolatrous corruption and their "no sons" status, the people are described further by two synonyms that speak of twisting and turning from the right path.

To drive home even more forcefully the deplorable, shameless state of the nation, two questions are asked. In these questions the Israelites are labeled as foolish and unwise—though the Lord is their Father, their Creator (v.6). The questions not only look back on the outrageous behavior of the Israelites in turning from God to idols and their consequent loss of sonship but also are preparatory to the following history of the Lord's kind providence toward Israel and their unfortunate reaction to his blessings.

The Lord as Father appears infrequently in the OT (Isa 63:16; 64:8; Mal 2:10), but the corollary of Israel's sonship is more common. Here the word "Father" assists in building up the idea that the formation of the nation of Israel is a creative act of God.

As Father he is the progenitor and originator of the nation and is also the one who has matured and sustained them.

In v.6b three Hebrew verbs translated "Creator," "made," and "formed" describe aspects of the same Father-Creator relationship. The first of the three, though not commonly indicating obtaining something by purchase, sometimes carries the nuance of producing, as here and in Genesis 14:19, 22. However, buying the nation from Egyptian slavery may be an overtone of the word in this place because the act is part of bringing Israel into existence.

The second and third verbs, the making and forming (fashioning and preparing), describe the Lord's directive process establishing the nation through the ministry of Moses in giving them the covenant-treaty with all its ramifications and in leading them by revelation through the Exodus and desert experiences.

The effect of these questions is to magnify the position of the Lord as the one who brought Israel into existence and to stigmatize Israel for her failure to recognize him in this position.

## Notes

---

**5** On the first two lines, see Hulst, p. 17.

The reduplicated form פְּתַלְתֹּל (*p*$^{e}$*ṯaltōl*, "crooked"), from פָּתַל (*pāṯal*, "to twist, wrestle, or torture"), occurs only here.

---

### 5. *Israel as God's inheritance*

32:7–9

7 Remember the days of old;
  consider the generations long past.
Ask your father and he will tell you,
  your elders, and they will explain to you.
8 When the Most High gave the nations their inheritance,
  when he divided all mankind,
he set up boundaries for the peoples
  according to the number of the sons of Israel.
9 For the LORD's portion is his people,
  Jacob his allotted inheritance.

**7** To develop his accolade for the Lord and his indictment of Israel, Moses in the song begins a recital of historical episodes. First, however, there is an introduction to this recital. The song calls on Israel—at whatever time it would be recited—to remember the past, some episodes of which would soon be mentioned.

Moses had called Israel before to remember how they had provoked the Lord (9:7); here he called on the people to remember the divine acts of kindness. The time element referred to has been debated. The words are strong and seem to thrust one into the distant past. The "days of old" does not seem quite applicable to the last forty years. The NIV has translated the Hebrew figure of "generation and generation" by "generations long past"—a rather strong translation. The Hebrew figure may have a distributive function meaning many generations or even every generation. Some (e.g.,

S.R. Driver) have said that this indicates that the song was written late in Israel's history when the events described were in the distant past. Others (e.g., Keil) hold that Moses deliberately took a future stance from which he looked back on the events of the Exodus and desert wanderings. As the text stands (and there is no variant text), the context depicts two elements. Moses was giving this song to the Israel that was then existent, and he was speaking about events that occurred in the past half-century. It would seem, therefore, that the Hebrew phrase must be taken as poetic hyperbole with some expectation of the use of the song in days to come (cf. 31:21). The stress is not on the distant past with the precision a scientific age would require but on the solemnity of the utterance from the viewpoint that older people among them had from the wisdom of years of experience.

In the manner of 4:32 and Job 8:8, the people were urged to ask for information from their fathers and their elders (v.7). These fathers and elders would "tell them" (i.e., explain to them) what had occurred. Then, supposing the people had asked for this explanation, the song proceeds to give it.

**8–9** Here Israel is geographically and religiously set in the context of the Lord's sovereignty over all nations, apparently based on Genesis 10, where the record of the division of mankind is given. When speaking of God's allocating geographical areas for the nations, he is the "Most High" (v.8; used only here in Deuteronomy). Most High is in contrast to his name "Lord" (Yahweh) as the God of Israel (v.9). Most High is an elative form; Melchizedek is priest of the God Most High (Gen 14:18–20, 22). In Psalms 83:18 and 97:9, the Lord is "the Most High over all the earth." Most High as a name for God appears more than twenty times in the Psalms.

That Canaan was Israel's inheritance (v.8) by the Lord's decree, based on the promise to Abraham, is of major importance in the developing doctrine of the Lord's relationship to his people and his redemption for them and providence toward them. This inheritance was soon to be divided among the tribes, providing each tribe with boundaries for its patrimony; and this division proceeds down to each family and to each man's (and in some cases woman's) inheritance. In this way the ownership of private, landed property becomes a basic right of Israelite social structure and economy. And much more than this, the idea of inheritance, that is, ownership on the basis of inherent right, describes the relationship of Israel to the Lord—and sometimes of the Lord to Israel (especially the Levites). Israel is the Lord's inheritance.

However, this cardinal figure, basic to the Lord's promise of Canaan to Israel, is applied to all nations, though in a more general way. Not only did the Lord give Canaan to Israel, he also gave certain lands to other nations. While this reference probably falls back on Genesis 10, that does not suggest that this division was made all at once in the distant past. It suggests, rather, that the Lord rules over the disposition of land to all nations in the sovereign exercise of his will in every generation. This is illustrated by several national geographical changes in chapter 2.

While the latter part of v.8 is unclear, the most probable meaning is that the boundaries of the nations were determined with the intent that Israel would have Canaan because her numbers could be supported in that area. This was done because Israel was central in the Lord's affection and sovereign planning. The use of Jacob for Israel contributes to the poetic style of the song.

As the people looked across the Jordan at the country that was to be their share of the world's lands, the Song of Moses told them that they were the Lord's portion, allotment, and inheritance.

## Notes

8 The term פָּרַד (*pāraḏ*, "divided") is used both here and in Gen 10:32 ("spread out").

9 "Portion" translates חֵלֶק (*ḥēleq*), which means "a part" or "a share." It is used to represent that part of the land or territory given to a certain tribe, family, or person. It is also used of relationship as "What share do we have in David?" (2 Chron 10:16) and "The LORD is my portion" (Lam 3:24). The word *ḥēleq* is combined with נַחֲלָה (*naḥ*ᵃ*lāh*, "inheritance") in 10:9; 12:12; 14:27, 29; 18:1.

חֶבֶל (*heḇel*) is a "cord" or a "measuring line" that was used to determine what one's allotment would be; so what is here translated "allotted" is also used to represent one's part or portion of land. It is nowhere else used of Israel as the Lord's portion or allotment.

### 6. *The Lord's early care of Israel*

32:10–12

10 In a desert land he found him,
in a barren and howling waste.
He shielded him and cared for him;
he guarded him as the apple of his eye,
11 like an eagle that stirs up its nest
and hovers over its young,
that spreads its wings to catch them
and carries them on its pinions.
12 The LORD alone led him;
no foreign god was with him.

**10–11** In a bold, dramatic way it is said that Israel was found "in a desert land" and "a barren, howling waste" (v.10). This cannot be Egypt as some suppose. It is part of the moving description of how the Lord found Israel in a desolate and desperate—if not hopeless—plight in the Sinai Desert (like he found Hagar? [Gen 21:14–20]). This figure is also used by Jeremiah (2:2) and Hosea (9:10). By depicting this impressive scene, Moses did not denigrate the wonders of the Exodus; he simply focused on the people as largely an unorganized body in an inhospitable environment at the time God entered into the covenant-treaty with them and from this rude beginning brought them into national affluence.

There in the inhospitable desert the Lord "shielded" and "cared" for Israel (v.10). He shielded them by surrounding them with his protection, and he attentively thought of them and concerned himself with them (as the distinctive Poel form of the verb *bîn* ["care for"] intimates). The frequentative imperfect verbs beginning with "shielded" in v.10 and continuing into v.13 suggest the Lord's constant care.

The "apple of his eye" (v.10) is an English idiom for "anything held extremely dear" or "much cherished" and is a fitting translation for the Hebrew "the little man of his eye," that is, the pupil.

The Lord exercised his loving care for Israel like an eagle caring for its young, especially as they are taught to fly (v.11). The eagle by stirring up the nest thrusts the eaglets out into the air to try their wings but does not leave them altogether on their own resources. The parent eagle catches the fluttering little ones on its outspread wings and again deposits them in the nest. Similarly the Lord took Israel out from Egypt into the deserts of Sinai but did not leave them without his help. His widespread wings supported them throughout the learning years in Sinai.

**12** The gods of the Egyptians, the desert tribes, and the Canaanites were multiple. Not so the Lord! He was alone as the leader and supporter of Israel. The parallel line, "no foreign god was with him," augments and explains the word "alone."

## Notes

**10** אֶרֶץ מִדְבָּר (*'ereṣ miḏbār,* "a desert land") is a common designation for Sinai as well as for other desert areas. The next phrases in the Hebrew order are "in a waste, a howling, barren place." יְשִׁמֹן (*yᵉšîmōn,* "waste") is synonymous with *miḏbār*. The masculine noun form יְלֵל (*yᵉlēl,* "howling") appears only here; but the feminine noun, and especially the verb, occurs more than thirty times in the OT, mostly in the sense of howling in distress or anguish. תֹהוּ (*tōhû,* "barren") is a vacant, desolate place or "trackless waste" (Job 12:24; Ps 107:40).

On "the apple of his eye," see E.C. Brewer, *Brewer's Dictionary of Phrase and Fable,* revised by I.H. Evans (New York: Harper and Row, 1970), p. 43.

**11** The word נֶשֶׁר (*nešer,* "eagle") occurs more than twenty-five times throughout all parts of the OT, mainly ascriptive of a regal bird of prey, possibly the imperial eagle, *Aquila heliaca.* The names of birds are not always used with precision in the OT. See the preface to the NIV and the margin note on Lev 11:19. See also *Fauna and Flora of the Bible,* pp. 82–84.

A גּוֹזָל (*gôzāl*) is a "young" bird, here a young נֶשֶׁר (*nešer,* "eagle"). In Gen 15:9, the only other occurrence, it appears to be a "young pigeon."

כְּנָפָיו (*kᵉnāp̄āyw,* "its wings") and אֶבְרָתוֹ (*'eḇrāṯô,* "its pinions," or "flight feathers," "wings") are synonyms, the former being very common and the latter infrequent and more poetic.

**12** אֵל נֵכָר (*'ēl nēḵār,* "foreign god") describes what is separate and different from one's own family, country, or culture. In the OT *nēḵār* identifies gods, people, altars, lands, or anything foreign, as that from which Nehemiah purified the priests and Levites (Neh 13:30).

### 7. *The Lord's care of Israel in Canaan foreseen*

32:13–14

13 He made him ride on the heights of the land
  and fed him with the fruit of the fields.
He nourished him with honey from the rock,
  and with oil from the flinty crag,
14 with curds and milk from herd and flock
  and with fattened lambs and goats,
with choice rams of Bashan
  and the finest kernels of wheat.
You drank the foaming blood of the grape.

**13** How then does Moses' song eulogize the Lord's acts for Israel? It says that he fed them with the finest foods—not the prepared foods of the sophisticated, but the best that comes directly from God's natural provisions. The introductory phrase to this list of foods gives the contextual time and place. It is the life of Israel in Canaan in anticipation. Causing Israel to ride on the high places of the land pictures their advance and conquest of Canaan, which was known as a high, mountainous country. The song views Israel as fed and nourished with the fruit of the fields (food, produce), honey from the rock, and olive oil from the trees in the flinty crags. Bees in Canaan often built their combs between the rocks. Olive trees flourished and produced bountiful crops of olives in the unlikely limestone soil in rocky places.

**14** The animals too contributed to this good life, with curds and milk and the meat of the best of lambs and goats. Curds might refer not only to the curds of cattle's milk but also to cream (Job 29:6) and butter (Prov 30:33). The fat of lambs describes not the fat itself as such but the best of lambs, which is the meaning of "fattened lambs and goats."

Bashan produced fine livestock, being noted for bulls and cows (Ps 22:12; Amos 4:1) as well as rams, which are here literally called "rams of the sons of Bashan," meaning rams of Bashan's breed or quality, to convey the notion of choice rams of Bashan.

In addition the people were to have the "fat of the kidneys of the wheat" (see Notes)—i.e., the choicest, richest, or finest wheat—and fine wine of the blood of grapes (blood indicating the red grapes of Canaan).

Grammatical shifts in person are common in Semitic poetry and account for the shift to second person at the end of v.14. There highly figurative descriptions of the best of the types of food productivity in Canaan that were to be available to Israel stand in stark contrast to Israel's response to the Lord who provided these abundant, choice foods.

## Notes

**13** Though "the heights of the land" is a highly figurative, poetic phrase, the word אֶרֶץ (*'ereṣ*, "land") here, as often elsewhere, refers to Canaan and not to land as the world (Reider, p. 304).

On "oil from the flinty crag," see Baly, p. 175; Thomson, *The Land and the Book*, pp. 51–57; and ZPEB, 4:528.

**14** כָּרִים (*kārîm*, "lambs"), a synonym for the more common כְּבָשִׂים (*keḇāśîm*, "young rams or lambs") may refer here to "a tender lamb," i.e., a special delicacy (S.R. Driver, *Deuteronomy*, p. 360). On "fattened lambs," see *World of the Bible*, p. 294.

חֵלֶב כִּלְיוֹת חִטָּה (*ḥēleḇ kilyôṯ ḥiṭṭāh*) is literally "the fat of the kidneys of wheat," meaning "the choicest, richest wheat" (BDB, p. 480) or "the finest kernels of wheat" (NIV).

### 8. *Affluent Israel's rejection of God*

32:15–18

15 Jeshurun grew fat and kicked;
filled with food, he became heavy and sleek.
He abandoned the God who made him
and rejected the Rock his Savior.
16 They made him jealous with their foreign gods
and angered him with their detestable idols.

17 They sacrificed to demons, which are not God—
gods they had not known,
gods that recently appeared,
gods your fathers did not fear.
18 You deserted the Rock, who fathered you;
you forgot the God who gave you birth.

**15** The song portrays the people's expected apostasy in vv.15–16. But first Israel's condition sets the stage for their sinfulness. After eating these fine foods and drinking the choice red wine, Israel the Righteous (see NIV mg. on Jeshurun) grew fat, that is, became affluent (the figurative language relates particularly to food) and then, rather than being thankful, reacted negatively—kicked! In the only other place where this verb is used, the Lord says to Eli, the high priest, "Why do you kick at my sacrifice?" which the NIV meaningfully translates "Why do you scorn my sacrifice?" (1 Sam 2:29). Here, however, the verb has no object. Only the reaction is given. Israel the Righteous—at least a tinge of sarcasm and possibly pathos is meant to be conveyed by this name—kicks! Where there should be thankfulness and obedience, there is open recalcitrance.

The last half of v.15 and on through v.18 shows how Israel kicked. Line two of v.15 goes back dramatically to the second person with three contiguous verbs without connectives: you grew fat (NIV, "filled with food"), you became heavy, you became obese ("sleek"). In this state Israel "abandoned," "rejected," "angered," "deserted," and "forgot" the Lord and "made him jealous." The God who had made Israel (v.15), who had fathered him and had given him birth (v.18), was maltreated this way. Though he was called "God" (*'elôah* ["Eloah," v.15] and *'ēl* ["El," v.18]), "Rock," "Savior," "Creator" (see v.6), and Sustainer of the nation, they made him jealous with their foreign gods and angered him with their detestable idols.

**16–18** The gods they turned to (rather than keeping allegiance to the Lord) were "foreign," "detestable idols," "demons," "no gods," and, "worthless idols" (the latter two in v.21). They were gods they had not before acknowledged. In contrast to the Lord who as Creator is the God of history and the God their fathers worshiped, these gods appeared recently and were gods their fathers had not feared (reverenced).

## Notes

**15** The hypocoristic "Jeshurun," a poetic appellation of endearment, appears three times in Deuteronomy (32:15; 33:5, 26) and once in Isaiah (44:2). See Craigie, p. 38; TWOT, 1:418.

The exact meaning of כָּשִׂיתָ (*kāśîṯā*), a *hapax legomenon*, is not clear. The NIV has followed a reconstruction based on Jer 5:28 and rendered it "sleek." Three verbs are used as parallels, probably not only suggesting affluent indulgence but also, as a result, stupidity.

**17** שֵׁדִים (*šēḏîm*, "demons") occurs only here and in Ps 106:37: "They sacrificed their sons and their daughters to demons," which might be reminiscent of this passage; it speaks of the same defection. The meaning is not certain. *Šēḏîm* are generally thought to be demons of a lesser rank and power than gods, but the evidence for this is late.

שְׂעָרוּם (*śeʿārûm*, "fear") is an uncommon word meaning "to be greatly frightened"; here it is probably referring to the usual attitude of people to "demons," though there may be overtones of worship involved.

## 9. *God's rejection of Israel*

### 32:19–30

19 The LORD saw this and rejected them
because he was angered by his sons and daughters.
20 "I will hide my face from them," he said,
"and see what their end will be;
for they are a perverse generation,
children who are unfaithful.
21 They made me jealous by what is no god
and angered me with their worthless idols.
I will make them envious by those who are not a people;
I will make them angry by a nation that has no
understanding.
22 For a fire has been kindled by my wrath,
one that burns to the realm of death below.
It will devour the earth and its harvests
and set afire the foundations of the mountains.

23 "I will heap calamities upon them
and spend my arrows against them.
24 I will send wasting famine against them,
consuming pestilence and deadly plague;
I will send against them the fangs of wild beasts,
the venom of vipers that glide in the dust.
25 In the street the sword will make them childless;
in their homes terror will reign.
Young men and young women will perish,
infants and gray-haired men.
26 I said I would scatter them
and blot out their memory from mankind,
27 but I dreaded the taunt of the enemy,
lest the adversary misunderstand
and say, 'Our hand has triumphed;
the LORD has not done all this.' "

28 They are a nation without sense,
there is no discernment in them.
29 If only they were wise and would understand this
and discern what their end will be!
30 How could one man chase a thousand,
or two put ten thousand to flight,
unless their Rock had sold them,
unless the LORD had given them up?

**19** In the Hebrew of v.19, the objective pronoun of the verb "rejected" is not written—a not uncommon Hebraic feature when the object is obvious. The indictment of both sons and daughters for angering the Lord is unusual since it is common to include both sexes under the term "sons" (which could be "children"), as at the end of v.20. Perhaps this more sharply indicates the total participation of the people in worshiping other gods—the women being implicated as much as the men. (For similar cases including sons and daughters in relation to God, see Isa 43:6 and Joel 2:28–29.)

**20** In his anger the Lord says, "I will hide my face from them," repeating what he had said to Moses and Joshua when he commanded them to write down the song (31:17–

18). At that time he spoke with even greater force (31:18). (For the significance of the hiding of his face, see the comment on 31:17–18.)

"I will . . . see what their end will be" (v.20) does not suppose that the Lord did not know what would transpire, even as Israel failed to understand (v.29). It is rather a declaration that he will see that those punishments do come. The two clauses—"I will hide my face from them" and "I will . . . see what their end will be"—are explicitly parallel. These two actions of the Lord follow from the condition of the people—from their being a perverse generation, unfaithful children. Their perversity stems not only from believing what is perverse and from perverse behavior that is concurrent but in indulging in prevarication (Prov 2:12, 14). Being children unfaithful to the Lord, they mouth lies.

**21** As the Lord has been raised to jealousy and anger by Israel's worship of worthless no-gods, so he will rouse Israel to jealousy and anger by humiliation by foolish, vile non-people. No specific nation seems to be intended, and several nations have fitted the description and fulfilled the prediction.

**22–23** The result of the Lord's anger (v.22) is described as a world-embracing cataclysm of fire adversely affecting three entities: the realm of death (whether the afterlife or the grave for dead bodies), the earth and its harvests (its productivity), and the very foundations of the mountains (Ps 18:7). In its context this is hyperbolical language to represent the frightful carnage to which Israel will be exposed because of infidelity to the Lord. The calamities of v.23 are those experiences that affect men adversely. These disasters or calamities will be heaped on Israel, and the Lord's arrows will be used up against his people.

**24** This general description is followed by specific calamities: famine, pestilence, plague, attacks by wild animals and snakes, as well as warfare. Each calamitous situation is further defined by appropriate descriptive words—not only famine (or hunger), but wasting famine (probably from desiccation, having all one's flesh and energy sucked out by total lack of fluids and of malnutrition); not only pestilence, but consuming pestilence (*rešep̱*, the word used here is the god of pestilence in Ugaritic literature). It is the fangs of the wild animals and the venom of vipers that will attack them.

**25–27** Moreover, the sword, that is, warfare, will reach Israel both "out in the streets" and "in their homes" (v.25), allowing them no place of safety. All ages will succumb; those who remain will be scattered so that no one will remember them as a nation (v.26).

This is the punishment the Lord said he would send the Israelites for their disloyalty. However, because Israel's enemies might understand what was happening and attribute the devastation of Israel to their own prowess in warfare, there seems to be an unvoiced suggestion that this would in a measure stay God's hand. The Lord's compassion for his people mentioned in v.36 also affects the full application of his anger.

**28–30** The poem from v.28 to v.33, or parts of it (esp. vv.32–33), has been interpreted as applying either to Israel or to Israel's enemies. Medieval Jewish commentators and some modern interpreters relate the passage to Israel. Most modern scholars apply at least vv.28–31 to Israel. Since what is expressed is elsewhere attributed to Israel, and since the transition from the focus on Israel to the enemies would be difficult and abrupt, Israel seems to be the subject of the section.

The conjunction *kî* ("for," untr. in NIV) beginning v.28 (and also v.31) suggests that the song now gives the reasons for the calamities described in the preceding section. These reasons are the obtuse stupidity on the part of Israel and the wickedness on the part of their enemies. Israel's stupidity derives from its lack of sagacity or wisdom, which the NIV well translates "without sense." Advice or counsel is the usual meaning. Sometimes, however, the ability to give good counsel or the character of good counsel is meant, which seems to be the sense here. The cognate verb of the noun in the parallel phrase "no discernment" indicates that they could not discern what their end would be.

Because of their lack of wisdom, the people could not detect or understand their destiny (v.29). It is a very singular obtuseness that is here attributed to Israel. This obtuseness could only result from total unbelief in what Moses had already told them and from a lack of faith that it really was the Lord who was the source of the miracles that brought them out of Egypt and through Sinai—providing for them for a whole generation. In later years, however, for a long while the people had insufficient knowledge of the message of Deuteronomy to make a sound judgment, though they were never wholly without some revelation from the Lord.

The rhetorical question of v.30 has no answer: those questioned would be silenced (whoever they may be and in whatever generation they heard or recited the song). If any answer could be given, it could only be, "There is no way one enemy warrior could chase a thousand Israelites, if the Lord was on Israel's side." So when this happened, it was obvious that their Rock who had fathered them (v.18), who was their Savior (v.15), and whom they had abandoned, rejected, deserted, and forgot (vv.15, 18), had now sold them (as Joseph was sold into slavery, Gen 37:36; 45:4–5) and "had given them up" (v.30). Israel was to experience this rejection of God over and over again in the settlement period of the judges (see Judg 2:14; 3:8; 4:2; 10:7).

## Notes

---

**19** The objects of the verbs for "saw" and "rejected" are assumed from the context (see GKC, sec. 117*f*).

**20** תַּהְפֻּכֹת (*tahpukōṯ,* "a perverse generation") occurs only here and nine times in Proverbs—almost always referring to speaking.

**21** נָבָל (*nāḇāl,* "fool," "foolish," "folly"; NIV, "no understanding") does not only describe noetic, judgmental deficiency but moral deficiency as well. Here it is parallel to הֲבָלִים (*hªḇālîm,* "worthless idols"). See Ps 14:1 NIV mg.

The apostle Paul applied the terms "not a nation" and "no understanding" to the Gentile nations generally in Rom 10:19 (cf. EBC, 10:114–15).

**22** אַפִּי (*'appî,* "my wrath"; lit., "my nostrils") is a common term for anger, appearing thirteen times in Deuteronomy alone.

**23** "I will heap" is more likely from יָסַף (*yāsaḇ,* "to add") rather than from אָסַף (*'āsaḇ,* "to gather").

**26** The verb פָּאָה (*pā'āh,* "scatter") is elsewhere unknown, but the cognate noun "corners" or "side" occurs often. The parallel with "blot out their memory" is congenial to the idea of thrust aside or scatter. For further discussion see S.R. Driver, *Deuteronomy*, p. 369 note; Gibson, *Canaanite Myths*, p. 162; and also KB (s.v.), which suggests "cleave in pieces."

---

## 10. *The punishment of Israel's enemies*

### 32:31–35

31 For their rock is not like our Rock,
as even our enemies concede.
32 Their vine comes from the vine of Sodom
and from the fields of Gomorrah.
Their grapes are filled with poison,
and their clusters with bitterness.
33 Their wine is the venom of serpents,
the deadly poison of cobras.

34 "Have I not kept this in reserve
and sealed it in my vaults?
35 It is mine to avenge; I will repay.
In due time their foot will slip;
their day of disaster is near
and their doom rushes upon them."

**31** The antecedent of "their" changes from Israel to the enemies of Israel as the NIV's change of capitalization indicates. The pronoun "their" in v.30 is Israel; in v.31 it is the enemies. In v.30 "their Rock" is the Lord; in v.31 "their rock" is the enemies' god, and even the enemies concede that the Lord is superior to "their rock."

This admission of the enemies looks back to the experience of the Egyptians just prior to the Exodus, especially as recorded in Exodus 14:25, and to the Balaam oracles where the Lord led Balaam, an enemy, to bless and not to curse Israel (Num 23–24). In later Israelite history the power of the enemies' god is touted as superior to that of the Lord. See particularly the Assyrian diatribes in 2 Kings 18:19–25, 31–35, and 2 Chronicles 32:10–19.

**32–33** Under the figure of vines, grapes, and wine, the wickedness of Israel's enemies is described. Their vine (character) has its source in the vine of Sodom and Gomorrah—those cities so wicked that they were annihilated by the Lord with cataclysmic force (Gen 19:24–25). The grapes from their vine were filled with poison, bitterness, and snake venom—synonyms significant of their patently evil and dangerous nature.

**34** Once more the text of the song reverts to the first person, with the Lord speaking directly of himself, asking a question to elicit a desired affirmation. The Lord has kept in reserve the history of the acts of wicked nations against his people. That wickedness has just been described in vv.32–33. "This" has as its antecedent the wickedness of the enemies (vv.27, 32–33). The Lord has sealed this wicked history in his vaults, just as Hosea later says that Ephraim's guilt is stored up till God's time of reckoning comes (Hos 13:12).

God's avenging wrath rests on his sense of righteousness. He will mete out righteous judgment whether in punishment or in defense. Requital and recompense stem from his inherent divine virtue. In this the attitude of the Lord God differs from human reactionary vengeance that seeks retaliation because of wounded pride or overweening resentment.

**35** The NIV places the emphasis where it belongs—"It is mine to avenge"—with the stress on "mine." "I," God says, "will repay." The enemies may think that it was their decision and their strength that brought terrible punishment on the Lord's people (v.27), but that was not really so. They were only the instruments of God's punishment. But because they willfully and wickedly acted within the providence of God, their time of punishment would also come. Isaiah expounded this theme in a denunciation of Assyria, whom he declared was the rod of the Lord's anger. "But . . . this is not what he intends," Isaiah says of Assyria, "his purpose is to destroy" (Isa 10:7). So Assyria too would be punished.

That punishment would come when the Lord's time for it had arrived, the time when their foot slips. This metaphor in these words occurs several times in the Psalms. In Psalm 17:5 the psalmist says, "My steps have held to your paths;/ my feet have not slipped"; and in Psalm 38:16 the petitioner cries out, "Do not let them gloat/ or exalt themselves over me when my foot slips." In Psalm 94:18 the psalmist testifies to the Lord's help: "When I said, 'My foot is slipping,'/ your love, O Lord, supported me." In each instance the slip of the foot describes a definite change in situation. One of the well-known sermons in American history was preached by Jonathan Edwards in 1741 from this verse and particularly from this clause: "In due time their foot will slip." The sermon subject was "Sinners in the Hands of an Angry God." Edwards thought that the verse was directed at the unbelieving Israelites, but his application of it reached to all wicked people.

The first clauses of v.35 are interpreted in Romans 12:19 and Hebrews 10:30 as teaching that revenge against any wickedness is precluded on the basis that the Lord says in this place, "It is mine to avenge; I will repay." In Hebrews 10:30 the wickedness is the rejection of Christ and his atonement. Hebrews 10:30 also quotes from the next verse (v.36): "The Lord will judge his people."

The time when God acts against the wicked is indicated as near and soon. Even though he is a God of patience with quite a different view of time than that of men (Ps 90:4; Isa 55:8), he nevertheless is said to move quickly to punish the wicked. "In due time" does not contradict "their day of disaster is near" or "their doom rushes upon them" but rather explains it. When their foot slips, disaster and doom rush in (Heb 2:3).

## Notes

**28–33** S.R. Driver (*Deuteronomy,* p. 370) suggests that these references speak of "Israel's inveterate inability to discern its true welfare."

**32–33** Keil and others suppose that vv.32–33 refer to Israel and point out that the figures of vine, grapes, and wine, and likeness to Sodom and Gomorrah are elsewhere used of Israel. Figures like these, however, are commonly used in various ways, and the context certainly favors the enemies being meant. The third person plural of "their vine," etc., surely has its antecedent in "their rock" in v.31.

The word תַּנִּינִם (*tannînim*) for serpents is a general one. The פֶּתֶן (*peṯen*, "cobra") is the Egyptian cobra (*naja haje*) found in the area south of Beersheba. Its bite may cause death within a half-hour. See *Fauna and Flora*, p. 72.

34 "Kept . . . in reserve" translates the *hapax legomenon* כָּמֻס (*kāmus*). The meaning is determined by the parallel line, ancient versions, and tradition.

---

## 11. *The Lord's compassion toward Israel and vengeance on the enemies* 32:36–43

36 The LORD will judge his people
and have compassion on his servants
when he sees their strength is gone
and no one is left, slave or free.
37 He will say: "Now where are their gods,
the rock they took refuge in,
38 the gods who ate the fat of their sacrifices
and drank the wine of their drink offerings?
Let them rise up to help you!
Let them give you shelter!

39 "See now that I myself am He!
There is no god besides me.
I put to death and I bring to life,
I have wounded and I will heal,
and no one can deliver out of my hand.
40 I lift my hand to heaven and declare:
As surely as I live forever,
41 when I sharpen my flashing sword
and my hand grasps it in judgment,
I will take vengeance on my adversaries
and repay those who hate me.
42 I will make my arrows drunk with blood,
while my sword devours flesh:
the blood of the slain and the captives,
the heads of the enemy leaders."

43 Rejoice, O nations, with his people,
for he will avenge the blood of his servants;
he will take vengeance on his enemies
and make atonement for his land and people.

**36** Here the focus of the song turns again to Israel. First it speaks of the Lord's vindication and compassion for them when the nation has been reduced to utter impotence, and the song reminds them of the impotence of the gods they had followed after their rejection of the Lord.

"The Lord will judge his people" is not here a declaration of punishment. It expresses the Lord's vindication of his people, having compassion on them and making atonement for both his land and his people (v.43). This vindication is portrayed in Genesis 30:6, where the same word is used. When Rachel's maidservant, Bilhah, gave birth to Dan, whose name means "he has vindicated" (see NIV mg.), Rachel said, "God has vindicated me." Part of the Lord's vindication of his people lies in his feeling of sorrow and sympathy for them in their deplorable state. The word for compassion is strongly anthropopathic, reflecting the feelings of sorrow and pity.

In the Hebrew, the first two lines of v.36 are quoted verbatim in Psalm 135:14—a psalm that has other likenesses to Deuteronomy. The Lord's vindication comes when his people have no more strength and, hyperbolically, no longer exist—neither those in slavery nor those who might still be considered free (actually, they would no longer exist as a nation). The Hebrew word for "strength," concretely "arm," a frequent figure for support or strength, indicates the utter impotence of Israel (no strength). From the following verses "no strength" doubtless labels the gods that they had relied on as likewise utterly impotent.

"Slave or free" is but one of many translations possible. But regardless of what the precise background and meaning of these gnomic words are, the sense conveyed is surely that the nation is so decimated that all classes of people are destroyed.

**37–38** The Lord asks his people, in this dreadful condition, where those gods are—those gods they took refuge in, those gods they thought were a rock, those gods that they worshiped with the fat of sacrifices and the wine of drink offerings, which supposedly the gods ate and drank. The fat of sacrifices and wine of drink offerings should have been offered to the Lord instead of to gods that could not help them. In a proper and effective bit of irony, the Lord suggests that those gods should arise and help them and give them shelter.

**39** As the song moves toward its climax, the Lord speaks of himself as the only true God who controls all life and history, especially as related to the fate of nations in battle with him and his people.

This section of the song (vv.39–42) begins with a strong personal assertion on the part of the Lord reiterating the assertions of 4:35, 39 that relate to the first commandment (5:7). The form of the first assertion suggests strong feeling on God's part. "See now," he said. The word for "see" here means "understand" or "grasp this mentally." In the same way David, in speaking to Saul after he had cut off a corner of his robe, emphatically called on Saul to "see" (using the imperative of see twice, which the NIV translates, "See, my father, look") and then added, "understand and recognize," the word "recognize" being another translation of "see" in parallel with "understand" (1 Sam 24:11).

What was Israel to understand? That the Lord is God! This statement is made the more impassioned and emphatic by the repetition of the first personal pronoun, "I, even I" (Isa 43:11; 51:12), and the simple but profound assertion, "I am he" (also repeated by Isaiah in 41:4; 43:10, 13; 46:4; 48:12)—an assertion of the reality and uniqueness of the Lord as God, readily seen in the line that follows, which asserts that no other God exists.

The reality of the Lord's deity is seen in what he does: he puts to death at his will and he gives life—a reference to his creative power and his power to rescue from death illustrated by his rescue of the nation of Israel when no one remains (v.36).

The Lord stated that he was the one who had wounded Israel and that he would also heal his people. Moreover, no one would be able to rescue Israel's enemies from his "hand" (i.e., power, a common Hebrew idiom). Isaiah expatiates on this in his prophecy against Babylon in Isaiah 43:10–15. That God delivers, rescues, and saves his people from their enemies is a frequent declaration in the OT and one of the major themes of the settlement narratives, particularly in the Book of Judges. The specific statement that no one can remove another from God's power occurs elsewhere also (see Job 10:7; Isa 43:13; Hos 5:14).

**40** In a strong anthropomorphism the Lord applied to himself the taking of an oath by raising the hand toward heaven (Gen 14:22; Exod 6:8; Num 14:30) and declaring, "As the LORD lives, I will" (cf. Judg 8:19; 1 Sam 14:39; et al.). Now, however, the formula is adjusted to the occasion by the Lord himself authenticating his oath by lifting his hand and declaring, "As surely as I live forever" (cf. Num 14:21, 28; Isa 49:18; Jer 22:24; Ezek 5:11; et al.).

**41–42** What the Lord declared as he used this strong figure must be taken as a statement of absolute certainty and received with the greatest seriousness. The Lord presented himself as a warrior, and the dramatic portrayal represented the terrible punishment to be meted out to his enemies. When he grasps his sharpened, flashing sword, it devours flesh, the heads of the enemy leaders; and he makes his arrows drunk with the blood, not only of those slain, but of the captives as well—signifying that no one will escape. In v.42 line three expounds line one while line four completes line two. The arrows that were before spent against Israel (v.23) now are turned on his enemies with devastating effect.

The sword that devours (2 Sam 2:26; 11:25) reaches to "the heads of the enemy leaders" (the long-haired heads of the enemy, which probably means the heads of the strong ones, i.e., the leaders, long hair being figurative for strong and vigorous leaders [cf. Samson, Judg 16:17]). This superior strength will be to no avail. It is in keeping with the theme of the Lord's devastation of the enemy to depict his arrows as destroying the heads of the strongest, the most virile of men—the ones who are the enemy leaders. None can withstand the Lord.

**43** The song ends with a call to the nations to rejoice with Israel because the Lord will punish his enemies for what they have done against his land and his people.

## Notes

**37** The word חָסָה (*ḥāsāh*, "take refuge") appears many times in the Psalms for taking refuge in the Lord (Pss 2:12; 5:11; et al.).

**38** The Hebrew for "Let them rise up" is singular; viz., "Let it be." The NIV follows the parallelism of the lines and the plural of other major, ancient translations.

The feminine noun סִתְרָה (*siṯrāh*, "shelter") appears only here. The masculine noun often is used adjectivally and adverbially as "secretly" and sometimes as a hiding place. See Ps 32:7: "You are my hiding place." Sometimes it is translated as shelter: "He who dwells in the shelter of the Most High" (Ps 91:1). See also Pss 27:5 and 61:4 (5 MT).

**41** The Hebrew אִם (*'im*), normally hypothetical, sometimes becomes equal to "when" (or better, perhaps, "whenever"), implying here that whenever the time for retribution comes, the Lord will be prepared with the implements of punishment in his hands.

Hebrew poetry is very succinct. "My hand grasps in judgment" has no pronominal object, but "it" is understood.

"My flashing sword" is in Hebrew "the lightning of my sword."

**43** A number of textual and interpretive problems occur here.

1. The causative form of the verb ordinarily means "cause to rejoice." However, the call to rejoice in this way appears also in Pss 32:11 and 81:1 (2 MT), where the NIV has "sing" and "sing for joy" respectively. See also the quotation in Rom 15:10.

2. The Hebrew is very concise with no definite indication of the relation of the verb to the following two nouns, which stand alone without prepositions or conjunctions. The sense, however, seems clear from the context. The same general structure is exhibited in the last clause of the verse.

3. Considerable variation is seen in ancient versions, especially in the LXX, which has a longer text that has some support in the DSS and is quoted from the LXX in Heb 1:6. See Albright, "Some Remarks," pp. 339–41; Cross, *Ancient Library,* pp. 182–83; and Skehan, "Qumran Fragment," pp. 12–15.

---

## 12. *Moses' presentation of the song and his exhortation to obey the law* 32:44–47

**44 Moses came with Joshua son of Nun and spoke all the words of this
song in the hearing of the people. 45 When Moses finished reciting all
these words to all Israel, 46 he said to them, "Take to heart all the words I
have solemnly declared to you this day, so that you may command your
children to obey carefully all the words of this law. 47 They are not just
idle words for you—they are your life. By them you will live long in the
land you are crossing the Jordan to possess."**

**44–47** The narrative about the Song of Moses comes to its conclusion here, which repeats 31:30 with an additional admonition to the people to command their children to obey "all the words of this law" (v.46). In 31:30 Moses is said to have recited "the words of this song." In 32:44 Moses, with Joshua son of Nun, spoke "all the words of this song" (the Hebrew says, "he and Joshua son of Nun"). In v.45 Moses finished his recitation. It is evident that Joshua had been with Moses, since, at the command of the Lord, Moses had called Joshua and the two of them had presented themselves before the Lord at the Tent of Meeting for Joshua's commissioning.

Moses' spiritual emphasis again appears in his admonition that the people "take to heart" (v.46) all that he had said. In like manner he had said before that they should seek the Lord with all their heart (4:29), love the Lord with all their heart (6:5; 13:3; 30:6), serve him with all their heart (10:12; 11:13), and fix his (Moses') words in their heart (11:18).

Previously Moses had said that the Lord was the people's life (30:20); here he said that "all the words I have solemnly declared to you," "all the words of this law" (v.46), are their "life" (v.47). This was so because by adherence to the revelation the Lord had given them, they were to live under his covenant in the land across the Jordan.

These words were not to be taken lightly, as though the people could follow them or disregard them with no great change in their welfare in either case. Not so! The revelation in covenant-treaty form was to be obeyed in all its detail, with a willing adherence and devotion both to the words and spirit of the law and to its giver—the Lord their God. He was their life, and his words were their life. Without the words there would be insufficient knowledge of him or of his way of life for them. Commitment to the Lord and to his word would insure a long national life for Israel in the Promised Land.

### Notes

---

**44** The MT has "Hoshea" for "Joshua" as in Num 13:8, 16. Elsewhere it is always "Joshua" for the son of Nun.

**45–46** Reciting their history, including the stipulations of the covenant, to their children was an important part of Israel's observance of the Deuteronomic legislation (6:7; 11:19; 31:13).

**47** דָּבָר רֵק (*dāḇār rēq,* "idle words") are empty, worthless, unprofitable words, i.e., words without meaningful content. *Rēq* frequently describes things but more often persons (Gen 37:24; Judg 7:16; 9:4; 2 Sam 6:20).

---

## C. *Directives for Moses' Death*

### 32:48–52

[48]On that same day the LORD told Moses, [49]"Go up into the Abarim Range to Mount Nebo in Moab, across from Jericho, and view Canaan, the land I am giving the Israelites as their own possession. [50]There on the mountain that you have climbed you will die and be gathered to your people, just as your brother Aaron died on Mount Hor and was gathered to his people. [51]This is because both of you broke faith with me in the presence of the Israelites at the waters of Meribah Kadesh in the Desert of Zin and because you did not uphold my holiness among the Israelites. [52]Therefore, you will see the land only from a distance; you will not enter the land I am giving to the people of Israel."

**48** Moses' ministry was over. All that remained was the patriarchal and prophetic blessing he was to bestow on the tribes, appropriately placed between the Lord's directives to Moses concerning his death and the carrying out of those directives. Within those directives, however, was one to soften Moses' great disappointment—the disappointment of not entering the Promised Land with his people. He was not to enter that land but was to look at it from an advantageous position—and die. Did ever exuberance of satisfaction, promise, and victory mix with disappointment and pathos more dramatically?

There was no lapse of time. On the very same day that the song was recited, the Lord's directives were received. Whether the beginning of chapter 34 should be translated as a temporal conjunctive with the imperfect verb marking the continual flow of the narrative, the force of the narrative seems to allow for no greater lapse of time than would fit into any day mentioned.

**49** The Lord's command to Moses to ascend Mount Nebo, look over the land, and then die there also appears in Numbers 27:12–14, with some slight variations. Mount Nebo is in the Abarim Mountains, a range running in a general north and south direction about ten miles east of the most northern part of the Dead Sea, rising to about 4,000 feet above the Dead Sea, which would be about 2,700 feet above the Mediterranean (sea level). Nebo is 2,631 feet above sea level. From Nebo Moses could see Canaan in the north beyond Lake Galilee, on the west the mountains of Judea, and toward the south as far as the area south of the Dead Sea (Zoar).

**50** On Nebo Moses was to die "and be gathered to" his people (an idiom for death; see Gen 25:8, 17; 35:29; 49:33; Num 20:24, 26; 31:2), as Aaron had died on Mount Hor (Num 20:22–29; 33:37–39).

**51–52** The reason for the prohibition against Moses' entrance into the Promised Land is more explicit here than that given for Aaron in Numbers 20:24, where it is simply stated that Moses and Aaron had rebelled against the Lord's command at the waters of

Meribah. Here it is said that they "broke faith" with the Lord in Israel's presence and did not uphold his holiness among the Israelites (v.51). Moses and Aaron were culpable because they had not properly conveyed the Lord's message or followed the way the Lord intended to supply water to the thirsty Israelites at Meribah Kadesh. Instead of speaking to the rock, they called the people rebels and struck the rock twice. The Lord denounced this action on the spot as a failure to trust him enough to honor him as holy. Because of this they would not be permitted to bring Israel into the land (Num 20:7–12; Ps 106: 32–33). Moses was to see the land only "from a distance" (v.52).

## Notes

**48** The stated time, "On that same day," relates specifically to when the Lord told Moses to ascend Mount Nebo, but the narrative flow suggests that Moses immediately obeyed.

**49** The name "Abarim" (meaning "places beyond") may stem from the position of this range beyond the Dead Sea near the Jordan.

**49, 52** For the location and the view from Nebo, see 34:1–4 and *World of the Bible,* 1:299. Perhaps Moses was to view the land as an element in the legal transfer of property (Gen 13:14–17; Deut 3:27; 34:1). It has been suggested that in Jesus' parable of the great banquet, the man who said that he had just bought a field and so must go and see it was also to look over the field as part of taking legal possession (Luke 14:18).

**50** The exact location of Mount Hor is not known but is most likely to be identified with Jebel Hadurah on the northwest border of what was Edom, about fifteen miles northeast of Kadesh. In 10:6 Aaron is said to have died in Moserah, the location of which is also unknown. However, according to the context of 10:6, it was between the wells of the Jaakanites and Gudgodah, which were in the vicinity of Kadesh (ZPEB, 3:201; WBE, 1:809; Y. Aharoni and M. Avi-Yonah, *Macmillan Bible Atlas* [New York: Macmillan, 1968], p. 41 map 51).

**51** מָעַל (*mā'al,* "to break faith with") is used to describe a wife's unfaithfulness to her husband (Num 5:12), the treachery of Israel when she forsook the Lord (Lev 26:40), and Achan's "breaking faith" with the Lord (Josh 22:16, 20).

**52** For the use of מִנֶּגֶד (*minneged*) to mean "from a distance," see 2 Kings 4:25.

## D. *The Blessing of Moses on the Tribes (33:1–29)*

### 1. *Introduction*

#### 33:1–5

1 This is the blessing that Moses the man of God pronounced on the Israelites before his death. 2 He said:

"The LORD came from Sinai
  and dawned over them from Seir;
  he shone forth from Mount Paran.
He came with myriads of holy ones
  from the south, from his mountain slopes.
3 Surely it is you who love the people;
  all the holy ones are in your hand.
At your feet they all bow down,
  and from you receive instruction,

[4]the law that Moses gave us,
the possession of the assembly of Jacob.
[5]He was king over Jeshurun
when the leaders of the people assembled,
along with the tribes of Israel.

**1** The blessings that Moses pronounced on the tribes is placed after the Song of Moses and between the directives of God to Moses regarding his death and the narrative of that death. Chapter 33 presents these blessings as recorded by someone other than Moses. In v.1 and in the formulaic introductions to the individual tribal blessings, we read in the third person: "About . . . he said" (vv.7, 8, 12, et al.). While a person speaking or writing of himself in the third person is not unknown in Deuteronomy and elsewhere, this chapter has every appearance of being reported by one other than the speaker. The respective blessings on the tribes are preceded by a formal expression of high praise to the Lord (vv.2–5) and are followed by another such encomium (vv.26–29).

The whole, as well as the parts, of the chapter has been subjected to much debate, resulting in much difference of opinion relative to the period of its formation and authorship. The generally salutary character of the blessings is said to demand a period of affluence and peace, for it is impossible to show that Moses could not hope for a period of success for Israel in the Promised Land. The contrasts between the promises of blessing and the warnings and even threats to Israel for apostasy are not far distant from one another anywhere in the messages ascribed to Moses. Moreover, a dying great leader's hopes of his people tend toward remembering the best in the characterizations of his nation. Above all, the development of the theme of the Lord's sovereign will as seen in Jacob's blessings on his sons is even more clearly seen in Moses' blessings on the tribes that have issued from Jacob's sons. The denial of the possibility of prophetic insight underlies a great number of the difficulties supposed in the denial of the Mosaic source of the blessings. Some additions or changes may have crept into the text that now exists, but this would not invalidate the text as a whole. No evidence suggests the name of the editor who wrote down the blessing together with its introduction and its conclusion.

The introductory statement very fittingly calls Moses "the man of God." Never before in the Pentateuch had this designation been used. The second occurrence also is a reference to Moses as the man of God (Josh 14:6). Subsequently, messengers of God (prophets especially) are called men of God (Judg 13:6, 8, and more often in 1 and 2 Kings). Moses is again designated as the man of God in the superscription to Psalm 90.

**2** The encomium to the Lord, as the introduction to the blessings, begins with the theophany at Sinai, as do other Scriptures portraying that event (Deut 1:6; 4:15; Judg 5:4–5; Ps 68:7–8). Deuteronomy usually speaks of Horeb as the mountain of the giving of the law, but here it is Sinai.

The verbs that the NIV translates as "came . . . dawned . . . shone forth" indicate that the coming of the Lord on Mount Sinai was like the sun flooding the desert area bounded by Sinai on the south, Seir on the northeast, and Paran on the north. The locations, particularly Paran, are not certain. It may be that the reference is to the presence of the Lord with them as they moved about during the forty-year existence in the desert. This idea, however, does not harmonize with the contextual situation of the giving of the law. The figure could be taken from the surrounding mountains and metaphorically related to the giving of the law on Mount Sinai with its thunder, lightning, earthquake, and darkness. In these meteorological elements the Lord is presented as the brightness of light. As it shone as though from the whole area bounded by the peripheral mountains, so the Lord shone on the people as they were stationed in the Sinai area. This figure promotes the grandeur of the Lord's theophanic presence.

The Lord came, however, not only as the light-giving sun but from the tens of thousands of his holy ones, that is, from heaven—or with myriads of his angels. Whether the preposition is one of source or one of association (with or without reconstruction), it is impossible to determine with certainty. The NIV together with many others (NEB, Beck, Craigie, et al.) opt for association. The difficulty in either case is the lack of support for this angelology in the narratives of the Lord's appearances on Sinai, but the poetic representations in theophanies often carry figures hyperbolically used while the experience is rooted in history and geography (Gen 28:12).

The last line of v.2 is especially difficult and consequently has had many greatly divergent translations and interpretations. The NIV has interpreted the first phrase (Heb., "from his right hand") as a geographical one meaning "from the south," a rather common usage (1 Sam 23:19, 24; Ps 89:12, and a cognate from Exod 26:18, 35; 27:9; et al.). It may be that Keil (p. 497) is right in supposing that the phrase means "flashes of lightning," which would be supported by the description of the Lord's presence on Sinai (Exod 19:16).

**3** The encomium moves on to state the Lord's love toward his people and their worshipful response to his instruction. It is the Lord, not some other god, who loves his people, the holy ones that are in his hand—a hand that both controls and supports them. At his feet they bow down and worship, and at his feet they receive the law that Moses gave them—the law that was their possession.

**4** Moses spoke of himself in the third person here, a fairly common practice of ancient leaders in this kind of literature.

**5** In praise of the Lord, his kingship at the assembly at Sinai is declared—his kingship over Jeshurun, Israel the Righteous. As suzerain over the vassal state, the Lord was king and ruler over the leaders and tribes when they assembled to receive and adopt the covenant-treaty at Sinai.

The Lord's kingship assumes supreme importance in the Mosaic economy. The effective implementation of this kingship became a very great practical problem in Israel. Without a hereditary monarchy or any other means than direct revelatory selection by the Lord, the Israelites had no way of recognizing a leader with the exception of the leadership invested in the high priest—a leadership that did not cover the power and responsibilities of Moses. Succession to Moses was established charismatically by the Lord's choice of Joshua, but no evidence exists that the Lord revealed to Joshua who was to be his successor. He, however, was careful to urge the people to be subservient to the Lord.

In the period of the judges, the leaders were all charismatically chosen by the Lord; and this was revealed to the people in a variety of ways.

When the people wanted to make Gideon king, he refused with a historic declaration: "I will not rule over you, nor will my son rule over you. The LORD will rule over you" (Judg 8:23). Not until the later years of Samuel did those who desired a king "such as all the other nations have" (1 Sam 8:5) succeed in installing a kingship other than that of the Lord's kingship in Israel. The Lord as king without any titular, earthly king to represent or embody him was of supreme importance to early Israel.

## Notes

---

**1–2** That chapter 33 was spoken by Moses and written down by someone else follows the pattern of the blessings of Isaac and Jacob (Gen 27:27, 39; 48:15, 20; 49:1, and many examples of benedictions in Nuzu literature; see R.K. Harrison, *Archaeology of the Old Testament* [Grand Rapids: Eerdmans, 1962], pp. 28–29).

**2** These same geographical representations in Judg 5:4 and Hab 3:3 are probably reminiscent of this passage.

In conformity with the preceding phrases, the NIV renders the end of v.2 topographically: "from his mountain slopes." The cue for the end of the line has been taken from Num 21:15, where אֶשֶׁד (*'ešed*, "slope") is translated "the slopes of." For other reconstructions and interpretations of the latter part of v.2, see source materials in Craigie, p. 392 n.1.

**3** The second half of v.3 is especially difficult and the translation tentative, but the basic meaning that the people are subservient to the Lord is surely correct.

**4** מוֹרָשָׁה (*môrāšāh*, "possession") is used only here of the law of Israel's possessions. Elsewhere the land or various people are a possession.

**5** For the meaning and occurrence of "Jeshurun," see the NIV margin, v.26, and 32:15.

This subject of kingship in Israel has been debated at great length in recent years. See Brueggemann, pp. 161–85; Mendenhall, *Law and Covenant;* id., *Tenth Generation;* and Weinfeld ("Review," pp. 99–108).

---

### 2. *Reuben*

33:6

> [6]"Let Reuben live and not die,
> nor his men be few."

**6** The order of the tribes in the blessings is not the order of the patriarchal blessings of Jacob, nor the order of birth of the tribal fathers, nor the order of their encampments, nor the order of either list in the census narratives in Numbers, nor the order of their tribal allotments in Transjordan and Canaan. For various reasons—some known and some unknown—all these differ from one another.

As in Jacob's blessings, Reuben, the eldest, is mentioned first, though he had lost his birthright because of fornication with Bilhah, his father's concubine (Gen 35:22; 49:4). Then comes Judah, who had been given the birthright, and then the other sons of Jacob and his wives, Rachel and Leah, followed by the sons of Jacob and the handmaids. Simeon is not mentioned. The Simeonites for the most part found their future together with Judah and never realized a tribal patrimony except for certain cities in Judah (Josh 19:1–9). The Simeonites were swallowed up in Judah. At least some of the Simeonites, however, did continue their tribal identity, as 1 Chronicles

## TRIBAL LISTS

| Jacob's Blessing | Order of Birth | Census | | Camps | Moses' Blessing | Allotments | |
|---|---|---|---|---|---|---|---|
| *Genesis* 49 | *Gen* 29:31–30:24; 35:16–18 | *Numbers* 1:5–15 | *Numbers* 1:20–42 | *Numbers* 2:1–33 | *Deut* 33 | *Deut* 3:12–17; *Josh* 13:15–31 | *Josh* 15:1–19:48 |
| Reuben | Reuben | Reuben | Reuben | Judah | Reuben | Reuben | |
| Simeon & | Simeon | Simeon | Simeon | Issachar | Judah | Gad | |
| Levi | Levi | Judah | Gad | Zebulun | Levi | Half-tribe of | |
| Judah | Judah | Issachar | Judah | — | Benjamin | Manasseh | |
| Zebulun | Dan | Zebulun | Issachar | Reuben | Joseph | — | |
| Issachar | Naphtali | Ephraim | Zebulun | Simeon | Ephraim | | Judah |
| Dan | Gad | Manasseh | Ephraim | Gad | Manasseh | | Ephraim |
| Gad | Asher | Benjamin | Manasseh | — | Zebulun | | The Rest |
| Asher | Issachar | Dan | Benjamin | Levi | Issachar | | Manasseh |
| Naphtali | Zebulun | Asher | Dan | — | Gad | | Benjamin |
| Joseph | Joseph | Gad | Asher | Ephraim | Dan | | Simeon |
| Benjamin | Benjamin | Naphtali | Naphtali | Manasseh | Naphtali | | Zebulun |
| | | — | | Benjamin | Asher | | Issachar |
| | | | | — | | | Asher |
| | | | | Dan | | | Naphtali |
| | | | | Asher | | | Dan |
| | | | | Naphtali | | | |

4:24–43 shows, even though they did not become as numerous as the people of Judah (1 Chron 4:27).

Though the tribe of Reuben lost its preeminent position, it was not to die but continued to live, though reduced numerically. Much difference of opinion arises from the last clause of v.6. Is the prayer that Reuben's descendants be few—or not few? Does the negation "not die" in the second clause carry over into the next line of the Hebraic structure? The NIV says that it does but in the margin admits the possibility that it does not, and the plea is that Reuben will have few descendants. The poetic structure of the Hebrew favors the NIV text on two counts: the parallelism of thought and the carryover of the negation. Such a repetition of an idea from one line meant to be included in the thought of the next line (though not included in the wording of the next line) is not uncommon in Hebrew, though often missed by expositors.

### 3. *Judah*

#### 33:7

7 And this he said about Judah:

"Hear, O LORD, the cry of Judah;
  bring him to his people.
With his own hands he defends his cause.
  Oh, be his help against his foes!"

**7** As with Reuben, so with Judah, the blessing of Moses comes as a prayer couched in very general expressions, which can be illustrated but not confined to specific historical experiences—either in the past or in what was still their future. The cry of Judah, the defense by his own hands, and the plea for the Lord's help all suggest a military situation. The hand of Judah, according to Jacob's blessing, was to be on the neck of his enemies, and for this victory his brothers would praise him. The prayer of Moses that Judah should be brought to his people may relate to his victorious return to his people from battle.

### 4. *Levi*

#### 33:8–11

8 About Levi he said:

"Your Thummim and Urim belong
  to the man you favored.
You tested him at Massah;
  you contended with him at the waters of Meribah.
9 He said of his father and mother,
  'I have no regard for them.'
He did not recognize his brothers
  or acknowledge his own children,
but he watched over your word
  and guarded your covenant.
10 He teaches your precepts to Jacob
  and your law to Israel.
He offers incense before you
  and whole burnt offerings on your altar.
11 Bless all his skills, O LORD,
  and be pleased with the work of his hands.

Smite the loins of those who rise up against him;
strike his foes till they rise no more."

**8–10** In Jacob's blessing, Simeon and Levi are considered together. In Moses' blessing, however, the status of Levi has changed remarkably because of the choice of Levi as the priestly tribe, the only appointment that gives every person in the tribe a special position in Israel. Not only all the men, but the women and the children too become beneficiaries of the state through the support generated by the tithes and other emoluments. But the blessing of Moses does not speak of these advantages. It speaks of Levi's status of caretaker, teacher, and revealer of the covenant and will of God, and of the bearing of the priestly responsibility of offering the sacrifices of the ritual system; that is, the Levities were both to represent the people before the Lord and to represent the Lord and his revelation to the people. That revelation of the Lord involved taking care of the written Book of the Law and the means of determining the Lord's will through the use of the Thummim and Urim that were deposited in the breastpiece of the high priest. Not only were the Levites (particularly the priests, the sons of Aaron) to have charge of the physical, inscriptured word placed beside the ark of the covenant and of the Thummim and Urim, they were also to teach that word to the people at regular intervals (Lev 10:11; Deut 31:9–13). The one that the Thummim and Urim belonged to is called the godly man or the man God favored (v.8).

The tribe of Levi is identified in the blessing by those certain acts that portrayed its loyal adherence to the Lord and to the covenant. The strife that arose at Massah and Meribah over water points out the difficulties that Moses, Aaron, the leaders of Israel, and the leaders of the tribe of Levi suffered on the journey from Egypt to Moab. The special devotion of Levi to the Lord is said to be portrayed by the action of the Levites in purging the community of sin by killing many of their own relatives after they had worshiped the golden calf (Exod 32:26–29). Because of the Levites' loyalty to the Lord on that occasion, they were set apart to him as the priestly tribe (Exod 32:29; Deut 10:8).

Offering incense and whole offerings to the Lord are together descriptions of the whole sacrificial system (v.10).

**11** Moses concluded his blessing on Levi with a prayer that Levi's use of his skills may be blessed with accomplishments that result in the Lord's being pleased with him. Moses also prayed that the power of Levi's enemies would be destroyed—never to rise again.

## Notes

8 Everywhere else the order is Urim and Thummim. On the use of Urim and Thummim, see Exod 28:30; Lev 8:8; Num 27:21; 1 Sam 28:6; Ezra 2:63; Neh 7:65; and WBE, pp. 1401, 1761; ZPEB, 5:450ff.

10 The Hebrew for "offers incense" is idiomatically anthropomorphic, viz., "bring incense to your nose."

11 חַיִל (*ḥāyil*, "skills") may be skills, abilities, strength, power, valor, or even substance, wealth, or army. The lines might read thus: "Bless all his powers, O LORD, and be pleased with what he has done."

"Loins" used in poetry signifies strength or ability (Job 40:16; Prov 31:17 [NIV, "arms"]).
In מִן־יְקוּמוּן (*min-yᵉqûmûn*, "till they rise no more"), *min* is used as an indefinite interrogative (NEB) as in Ugaritic (W.F. Albright, "The Old Testament and Canaanite Language and Literature," CBQ 7 [1945]: 23, n. 64).

---

## 5. *Benjamin*

### 33:12

12About Benjamin he said:

"Let the beloved of the LORD rest secure in him,
for he shields him all day long,
and the one the LORD loves rests between his shoulders."

**12** The blessing for Benjamin has a tenderness that differs markedly from the description of the Benjamites in Jacob's last words, in which Benjamin in strong metaphor is a ravenous wolf devouring prey (Gen 49:27). Moses asked that Benjamin as the one loved of the Lord and shielded continually by him would have a secure rest between the Lord's shoulders, that is, on his shoulders, as a father might carry a son—a figure already used to describe how the Lord carried the Israelites all through the desert journeys (1:31). "The one the LORD loves" in the third line of the NIV text is a repetition of "the beloved of the LORD" in line one, a device to signify the subject of the last line, which in English would be unclear without the noun instead of the pronoun.

## Notes

---

**12** The force of the verb יִשְׁכֹּן (*yiškōn*, "Let . . . rest") may be descriptive rather than cohortative and be translated thus: "The beloved of the LORD will rest [or rests] in him."

Some exegetes suppose that the references to Benjamin relate to God's dwelling in the locale of the Jerusalem temple, resting between the mountains that are near Jerusalem. This then would be indicative of a later date for its composition. But the tone of the passage is most probably due to the relationship that Jacob had to Benjamin (cf. Gen 35:18; 44:20).

---

## 6. *Joseph (Ephraim and Manasseh)*

### 33:13–17

13About Joseph he said:

"May the LORD bless his land
with the precious dew from heaven above
and with the deep waters that lie below;
14with the best the sun brings forth
and the finest the moon can yield;
15with the choicest gifts of the ancient mountains
and the fruitfulness of the everlasting hills;
16with the best gifts of the earth and its fullness
and the favor of him who dwelt in the burning bush.

Let all these rest on the head of Joseph,
  on the brow of the prince among his brothers.
17 In majesty he is like a firstborn bull;
  his horns are the horns of a wild ox.
With them he will gore the nations,
  even those at the ends of the earth.
Such are the ten thousands of Ephraim;
  such are the thousands of Manasseh."

**13–16a** When Jacob blessed his sons just prior to his death, he included Joseph rather than Ephraim and Manasseh, even though he had placed his blessing on them and had made a particular point of indicating that these two sons of Joseph were to be reckoned as his (Gen 48:5–20; 49:22–26). Moses also, however, mentioned the two tribes at the end of his statement about Joseph (v.17).

The first part of the Joseph blessing (vv.13–16a) is a prayer for the agricultural prosperity of his land while the second part (v.16b–17) describes his status and his military strength.

The blessing desired for Joseph is expressed in considerable poetic beauty. Some of the phrases and allusions are from Genesis 49:22–26. The word *meged* ("best" or "choicest") occurs five times in vv.13–16a. It is translated in the NIV in ways appropriate to its relation with the words it modifies and to English style. The phrases are "the precious dew from heaven," "the best the sun brings," "the finest the moon can yield," "the fruitfulness of the everlasting hills," and "the best gifts of the earth." In this list the words "precious," "best," "finest," "fruitfulness," and "best gifts" are all from the same Hebrew phrase, *mimmeged*. In the Song of Songs the lover using the same word describes the fruits in his beloved's garden as "choice" fruits (4:13, 16); and the beloved tells her lover that every "delicacy" was at their door (7:13). All these expressions in vv.13–16a elucidate the first clause of Moses' blessing on Joseph: "May the Lord bless his land."

This blessing would be achieved by the application of the precious things from heaven and from under the earth (vv.13–14)—the dew, the springs, and the rivers. The dew is used poetically for all precipitation from air and sky. The deep waters are the source of all waters exuding from the earth, both springs and rivers. The best and finest of the sun and moon are the products of the soil that the sun and the moon nurture.

The "ancient mountains" and "the everlasting hills" exemplify the land of the Joseph tribes across the middle of Canaan. The fertility of the land would cover the mountains with eternal productivity.

All this is summed up in v.16a—"with the best gifts of the earth"—and with the further explanation that this productivity would be in all fullness possible, as in 1 Chronicles 16:32; Psalm 24:1; 50:12; and about ten other places, relating to everything in the land and translated by "and everything in it." The fullest productivity is predicated for the Joseph tribes. The Lord, the one who presented himself to Moses in the burning bush, is the one who will favor Joseph with this blessing of abundance (see Exod 3).

**16b–17** The remainder of the Joseph blessing describes the character and prowess of these two tribes. The blessing is to rest as a crown on the head and brow of Joseph, "the prince among his brothers" (v.16b).

The NIV (KJV, NEB, JB) ascribes v.17 to the Joseph tribes as a whole; others identify the firstborn bull with Ephraim because Jacob gave first place to him rather than to Manasseh. But the reference to the majesty of the firstborn bull links v.17 with Joseph being prince among his brothers (v.16b). And the end of v.17 explicitly says that the goring of the nations by the one metaphorically called the firstborn bull and wild ox refers to both Ephraim and Manasseh. However, contrary to the usual poetic usage of citing thousands before ten thousands (1 Sam 18:7), the ten thousands of Ephraim are mentioned before the thousands of Manasseh. So it is obvious that Moses recognized the superiority of Ephraim, though Joseph, not Ephraim, is the firstborn bull.

Manasseh was really the firstborn son; but here, as in Jeremiah 31:9, this prominence has become Ephraim's later prominence. Ephraim became the dominant tribe in the northern kingdom and was often militarily the more powerful kingdom in Canaan in the ninth, eighth, and seventh centuries B.C. The goring of the nations is thought by some rabbinic authorities to be fulfilled in the conquests under Joshua, who was an Ephraimite (see Reider, p. 335). The extent of the military victories of Joseph, however, should best be taken as poetic hyperbole signifying the greater relative strength and prowess predicated of the Joseph tribes.

## Notes

---

**15** If the suggestion that מֵרֹאשׁ (*mērō'š*, "choicest gifts") be changed to מִמֶּגֶד (*mimmeḏeḏ*, "best," "finest," "best gifts") is followed, to conform with the series from v.14 through v.16a, there would be six occurrences of *mimmeged*, and "choicest gifts" would be added to the list. This conjecture is built on internal reconstruction; it is devoid of textual support. Nevertheless, the internal evidence is very strong and may be correct. If *mērō'š* is correct, the translation "From the tops of the ancient mountains" (KJV, "For the chief things") would be correct.

**16** The notion that שָׁכַן (*šāḵan*, "to dwell or inhabit") suggests a more permanent dwelling than the episode of Exod 3 would seem to indicate has no validity. It is used, for instance, to designate the presence of the cloud that guided Israel through the desert. When the cloud stopped, Israel was to stop and remain there until the cloud moved again, even though the stay might be very limited in time (Num 9:17–18). The certainty and reality of the Lord's presence are meant.

**17** The רְאֵם (*re'ēm*) was probably *bos primigenius*, the aurochs, a "wild ox," a species of wild cattle that became extinct in the seventeenth century A.D. It had notable, long horns that grew sideways from its head and then forward and upward. The aurochs were hunted by the Assyrian kings (*Fauna and Flora of the Bible*, p. 63; EB, s.v.).

וְהֵם . . . וְהֵם (*wehēm . . . wehēm*, "such are . . . such are") certainly shows that both Ephraim and Manasseh are like the firstborn bull and wild ox that will gore the nations.

---

### 7. *Zebulun and Issachar*

#### 33:18–19

18 About Zebulun he said:

"Rejoice, Zebulun, in your going out,
and you, Issachar, in your tents.
19 They will summon peoples to the mountain
and there offer sacrifices of righteousness;

> they will feast on the abundance of the seas,
> on the treasures hidden in the sand."

**18** Zebulun and Issachar, the last two sons of Leah, are mentioned together and in the same order as they are in Jacob's blessing, the younger being placed first. What is asserted of these two tribes speaks of them together as a unit. The poetic parallelistic structure of the first two lines is to be understood as a play on the fairly common expression of one's daily activity as "going out and coming in," with "in your tents" equivalent to "coming in." So then the sense is "Rejoice, Zebulun, and you, Issachar, in all your activities."

**19** These tribes together were to "summon peoples to the mountain" and "there offer sacrifices of righteousness." It is not clear who the peoples are or what mountain is meant, if, indeed, a particular mountain is meant at all. "Mountain" may simply be used—especially in poetry—to designate a place of sacrifice and worship. It was common in the ancient Near East (as also elsewhere) to worship on hills or mountains or at least on high places.

The peoples would certainly include other Israelites but may not be limited to them. Their sacrifices would be those of the sacrificial system Moses had given to them. No other sacrifices could be called righteous sacrifices, nor could righteous acts by themselves apart from the sacrificial system be considered as sacrifices at this time. And they would be limited to sacrifices offered at "the place the LORD your God will choose" (12:5). Sacrifices offered in the right spirit and with spiritual understanding are surely meant. This would be in harmony with the spirit of the sacrificial system given them by the Lord through Moses. Those sacrifices were never merely ritual; they were to be practiced with the understanding of their spiritual and theological meaning. They were righteous sacrifices.

These two tribes were to feast on "the abundance of the seas" and "the treasures hidden in the sand." The attempt to identify these items as particular sources of riches (e.g., glass) is ill advised. The pattern of these blessings is general in nature rather than particular. The boundaries of Zebulun and Issachar as allotted by Joshua did not give either Zebulun or Issachar access to the Mediterranean; but Moses is in harmony with the vision of Jacob, who saw Zebulun living by the seashore, a haven for ships, with his border extending toward Sidon (Gen 49:13). The influence of the tribes and the actual boundaries did not always remain where the original allotment placed them. Josephus (Antiq. V, 84 [i.22]) reports that Zebulun's lot included land that "belonged to Carmel and the sea." Zebulun and Issachar were to enjoy "the abundance of the seas" and "treasures hidden in the sand." Since sand is almost invariably the sand of the sea, that is, the seashore, it is likely that the two phrases are in synonymous parallelism referring to the same source of riches, namely, maritime wealth.

### 8. *Gad*

#### 33:20–21

20 About Gad he said:

> "Blessed is he who enlarges Gad's domain!
> Gad lives there like a lion,
> tearing at arm or head.

21 He chose the best land for himself;

the leader's portion was kept for him.
When the heads of the people assembled,
he carried out the LORD's righteous will,
and his judgments concerning Israel."

**20** The blessing on Gad focuses first on the Lord himself, who enlarges Gad's territory by giving the tribe what it requested after the conquest of the area east of the Jordan, which had been under the Amorite rulers Sihon and Og (Num 21:21–35; 32:33; Deut 3:1–20; 29:7–8). Gad was known as warlike and aggressive. The tribe was able to hold onto the territory and to keep its tribal identification on the east of Jordan until it succumbed to Tiglath-pileser in the latter part of the eighth century B.C. (1 Chron 5:23–26). This warlike character is portrayed as a lion that tears an arm and even the head of its prey. Jacob too saw Gad attacking its enemies (Gen 49:19), and 1 Chronicles describes some Gadites as having faces of lions (12:8); the least of them "was a match for a hundred, and the greatest for a thousand" (1 Chron 12:14).

**21** Gad chose the best (the first choice) of the land, or the leader's part. The word for leader stems from the idea of the one who gives commands. It definitely suggests that the land that fell to Gad was reckoned as the finest of all. Moreover, Gad was to fulfill the Lord's righteous will that the assembly of Israel had required of Reuben, Gad, and the half-tribe of Manasseh, that is, their cooperation in subduing the peoples of Canaan before they returned home to their territories east of Jordan (Num 32:1–33; Deut 3:18–20; Josh 1:12–18; 22:1–8).

## Notes

**20** By a slight variation from the MT, the translation could be thus: "Blessed be the expansive lands of Gad" (cf. NEB and Craigie, p. 440).

**21** In חֶלְקַת מְחֹקֵק (*ḥelqaṯ m$^{e}$ḥōqēq*, "the leader's portion"), *m$^{e}$ḥōqēq* is the Poel participle of חָקַק (*ḥāqaq*), which means "to engrave or inscribe," and so "a prescriber of laws," i.e., a commander, ruler, or, more generally, leader. In Gen 49:10, *m$^{e}$ḥōqēq* is a ruler's staff (on the basis of its parallelism with שֵׁבֶט [*šēḇeṭ*, "staff"]). In Num 21:18 in parallel with שַׂר (*śār*, "prince") and נָדִיב (*nāḏîḇ*, "noble"), *m$^{e}$ḥōqēq* is a noble's scepter, while in Judg 5:14 it is "captains" and in Isa 33:22, "lawgiver," parallel with "judge" and "king."

### 9. *Dan*

33:22

22About Dan he said:

"Dan is a lion's cub,
springing out of Bashan."

**22** The blessing on Dan is a metaphor describing at least the inherent, ravenous character of a lion's cub that springs on its prey. Jacob had likened Dan to a serpent, a viper, and it may be that Bashan of the MT should be read as the Ugaritic word for viper and so be in harmony with Jacob's blessing. The reference to Bashan, however, is not to Dan directly but to the lions of Bashan, an area somewhat removed from the area around Laish that was later occupied by Dan. Moreover, the suggestion that "laish," meaning "lions," could be the reason for the mention of a lion's cub seems odd. If the meaning of Laish was in mind, why was a different word for lion used? The meaning is clear: Moses saw the Danite tribe leaping out of ambush like a ravenous lion to secure its prey.

## Notes

**22** On "Bashan" see Craigie, p. 401; and Cross and Freedman, "Blessing of Moses," pp. 191–201.

גּוּר אַרְיֵה (*gûr 'aryēh,* "lion's cub") occurs also in Gen 49:9, describing Judah. לַיִשׁ (*layiš,* "laish") as lion appears in Job 4:11; Prov 30:30; and Isa 30:6, meaning "a strong or full grown lion."

### 10. *Naphtali*

33:23

[23]About Naphtali he said:

"Naphtali is abounding with the favor of the LORD
and is full of his blessing;
he will inherit southward to the lake."

**23** As with Dan, little is said of Naphtali; but while what is said of Dan may be either prowess or censure, what is said of Naphtali is approval. Naphtali will have the Lord's favor in abundance and will be full of blessing—blessing that will be his because of the excellent and fertile land the tribe will inherit. His land will extend from the north of Galilee to the area west and south of the lake.

## Notes

**23** It is true that יָם (*yām,* "sea") also may mean "west" and that a word for direction would fit well with דָּרוֹם (*dārôm,* "south"). However, the description of Naphtali's area relative to the Lake of Galilee is still quite general and apt.

### 11. *Asher*

33:24–25

[24]About Asher he said:

"Most blessed of sons is Asher;
let him be favored by his brothers,
and let him bathe his feet in oil.
[25]The bolts of your gates will be iron and bronze,
and your strength will equal your days.

**24–25** Asher, declared to be a most blessed of sons, is to be favored above his brothers. Bathing his feet in olive oil (probably mixed with various fragrant unguents) and having a secure residence behind gates bolted with iron and bronze bars, the tribe of Asher will grow in strength as its days increase in number.

## Notes

---

**24** For oil as ointment, see ZPEB, 4:515–18.

**25** Iron and bronze were the two hardest and strongest metals available for this purpose, though Israel herself did not have access to the techniques of iron metallurgy at this time.

דָּבָא (*dāḇā'*, "strength") occurs only here, and no Hebrew cognate gives any real assistance to determining its meaning. However, the Ugaritic *db'at,* meaning "strength," and the support of meaning from the LXX et al. makes strength the most likely meaning.

---

## 12. *Peroration of God and Israel, his people*

### 33:26–29

26 "There is no one like the God of Jeshurun,
who rides on the heavens to help you
and on the clouds in his majesty.
27 The eternal God is your refuge,
and underneath are the everlasting arms.
He will drive out your enemy before you,
saying, 'Destroy him!'
28 So Israel will live in safety alone;
Jacob's spring is secure
in a land of grain and new wine,
where the heavens drop dew.
29 Blessed are you, O Israel!
Who is like you,
a people saved by the LORD?
He is your shield and helper
and your glorious sword.
Your enemies will cower before you,
and you will trample down their high places."

**26** The conclusion of the blessing is like the introduction. Moses' final blessing returns to Israel as a whole—commencing, however, with praise to the Lord as the God of Jeshurun, a designation conforming to that of v.5 in the introductory encomium to the Lord as the king of Jeshurun (righteous Israel). The God of Jeshurun has a unique greatness—he rides on the heavens and on the clouds in his majesty to help his people. The heavens or the clouds elsewhere are the vehicle of God (see Pss 18:9; 68:33; Isa 19:1).

**27–28** The "eternal God" is the one who in the past was the God of their fathers (v.27). In many places Moses emphasized that he was sent by the God of their fathers. The Lord is God the Creator of all things, the God of history, and the God of the promises to the patriarchs.

Here Moses declared that the Lord was the dwelling of his people and his everlasting arms were beneath them to keep them from harm, discouragement, and failure. They would not be left to rely on only their own strength. The Lord was to drive out the enemy before them with the command "Destroy!"

The promise that God would go before Israel to conquer the land has always in it the participation of the people in obedience to the Lord's commands, but that participation is always to be understood as effective only as the Lord works with them and through them. The result will be victory that will leave Israel as a secure nation living in "safety" (v.28), without the interference or support of other nations, relying rather on the Lord, who would give them victory and would sustain them.

Israel, Jacob's spring, that is, the descendants that flowed from Jacob, would live safely and securely in the land whose supply of grain and wine was symbolic of rich productivity and where the dew of heaven, representative of sufficient precipitation, would nourish their crops.

**29** The blessing of Moses on the tribes ends with an exclamation, a rhetorical question, and an affirmation of the Lord's strength and help and of Israel's triumph over her enemies. The exclamation "Blessed are you, O Israel!" (v.29) comes as a fitting climax to these last words of Moses. The rhetorical question reinforces the exclamation by its obvious answer: no other nation was like Israel, the nation saved by the Lord. And the affirmation that follows reinforces the thrust of both the exclamation and the question. This twofold affirmation says, first, that the Lord is their shield, helper, and glorious sword and, second, that they will subdue their enemies.

As shield and helper, the Lord would defend them; as their sword of majesty or glory, he would give them victory over their enemies, thus indicating Israel's superiority. The enemies will present themselves as vanquished in battle and consequently as inferior to their conquerors.

In the same fashion David later said, when the Lord had delivered him from all his enemies, "Foreigners cringe before me" (Ps 18:44; cf. superscription to Ps 18). Israel will trample under foot the high places of their enemies, representative of their strongest refuges, which will be totally destroyed.

Moses closed his ministry and life on a positive note: Israel would be victorious over the enemies they would face on the other side of the Jordan.

## Notes

---

**26** The vowel pointing of the MT has Jeshurun here as vocative—"like God, O Jeshurun." The NIV follows the LXX, Syriac, Vulgate, both the Onkelos and the Psuedo-Jonathan Targums, and other versions, which read כְּאֵל (*kᵉʼēl*, "like a god") rather than כָּאֵל (*kāʼēl*, "like the God").

In Aqhat and other Baal myths, Baal is called "the Rider on the Clouds" (Coogan, p. 41) or the one who mounts the clouds (Thomas, p. 129). In Deuteronomy Moses was saying that the Lord, not Baal, was God who rides on the heavens or the clouds, governing the elements.

**27** קֶדֶם (*qeḏem*, "eternal") is variously used, meaning "before" either temporally or spatially. Spatially it is in front of or to the east; temporally it is former or ancient time. Here it refers to God as God of all time past; and since his arms are עוֹלָם (*ʻôlām*, "everlasting"), he is also the God of the future, as the rest of the section shows. In v.15 the *qeḏem* ("ancient") mountains are parallel to the *'ôlām* ("everlasting") hills.

This verse has been subject to considerable debate (as some modern translations indicate!). "Underneath" is said to refer to the earth as corollary to the mention of God as God of the heavens and the clouds, and therefore it says that on the earth his everlasting arms are around his people.

**29** The NIV margin reading "will tread upon your bodies" (or backs), which is supported by the Ugaritic *bmt,* may be the true idea of the text. This would refer to the ancient custom of placing representative leaders of defeated nations underfoot (see Kitchen, *Ancient Orient,* p. 164; Pfeiffer, p. 60; and *The World of the Bible,* 1:297, where Rameses III is seen treading on the bodies of defeated enemies).

---

## E. *The Death of Moses and the Succession of Joshua*

### 34:1–12

1 Then Moses climbed Mount Nebo from the plains of Moab to the top
of Pisgah, across from Jericho. There the LORD showed him the whole
land—from Gilead to Dan, 2 all of Naphtali, the territory of Ephraim and
Manasseh, all the land of Judah as far as the western sea, 3 the Negev
and the whole region from the Valley of Jericho, the City of Palms, as far
as Zoar. 4 Then the LORD said to him, "This is the land I promised on oath
to Abraham, Isaac and Jacob when I said, 'I will give it to your
descendants.' I have let you see it with your eyes, but you will not cross
over into it."

5 And Moses the servant of the LORD died there in Moab, as the LORD
had said. 6 He buried him in Moab, in the valley opposite Beth Peor, but
to this day no one knows where his grave is. 7 Moses was a hundred and
twenty years old when he died, yet his eyes were not weak nor his
strength gone. 8 The Israelites grieved for Moses in the plains of Moab
thirty days, until the time of weeping and mourning was over.

9 Now Joshua son of Nun was filled with the spirit of wisdom because
Moses had laid his hands on him. So the Israelites listened to him and
did what the LORD had commanded Moses.

10 Since then, no prophet has risen in Israel like Moses, whom the
LORD knew face to face, 11 who did all those miraculous signs and
wonders the LORD sent him to do in Egypt—to Pharaoh and to all his
officials and to his whole land. 12 For no one has ever shown the mighty
power or performed the awesome deeds that Moses did in the sight of
all Israel.

**1–4** Before he died, Moses climbed from the plains of Moab up to the top of the Pisgah range, to the top of Mount Nebo, and from there the Lord showed him the whole land. The description indicates the area one would see from Nebo when looking first northward (from Gilead to Dan), turning his gaze northwest (all of Naphtali; the territory of Ephraim and Manasseh), and west (all the land of Judah as far as the western sea), and then looking southward (the Negev and the whole region from the Valley of Jericho, the City of Palms, as far as Zoar).

As Moses viewed Canaan from the top of Mount Nebo, the Lord told him that this was the land he had promised to Abraham's descendants (see Gen 12:7; 13:14–17; 15:18; 17:8; 26:3; 28:4, 13, where the promise to Abraham, Isaac, and Jacob is recorded). "I will give it to your descendants" (v.4) is exactly as the promise is given in Exodus 33:1; its substance is in Deuteronomy 1:8.

The Lord said he would let Moses see the land with his eyes but that he would not be able to cross over the Jordan into it. At 120 years of age, Moses looked out over the land with eyes that "were not weak" (v.7), and—though he was still vigorous—his mission came to an end.

What drama! What pathos! What inward pain! What sense of accomplishment mixed with disappointment must have been in Moses' mind as he looked over the land the Lord had promised to Israel! Egyptian bondage had gone into history. The painful, difficult, formative years of the new nation's experience in the deserts were past. The Promised Land lay before him—but his mission was over. His desire had led him to plead again and again that the Lord would relent and let him enter that land, but this final report of the Lord's decree does not mention Moses' prayer. Had he at last quietly acquiesced to the will of God? Had he bowed to the inevitable? The certainty everyone faces? The end of his pilgrimage? That end had come.

**5–8** The "servant of the LORD" (v.5) died and was buried in an unknown way, in an unknown grave, in the valley facing Beth Peor, where the Israelites were encamped (3:29). The thirty-day mourning for Moses (v.8) conformed to the mourning period for Aaron (Num 20:29).

**9** Before the writer closed his remarks about Moses with a final eulogy, he made mention of Joshua the successor as one whose ability to lead rested on his ordination by Moses, an ordination that filled him with the spirit of wisdom. So Israel listened to (obeyed) Joshua—doing what the Lord had commanded them to do through Moses.

**10–12** Deuteronomy closes eulogizing Moses as the greatest of all prophets, the one whom the Lord knew intimately, and the greatest miracle worker. The acts of the Lord through Moses are said to be miraculous signs, wonders, and awesome deeds performed with mighty power. These were done before Pharaoh, his officials, his people, and in the sight of all Israel. These were done to accomplish the task the Lord had called Moses to do in Egypt and on the journey to Canaan.

Not until the Lord Jesus Christ came (the one whom Moses spoke about, John 5:46) was there anyone greater than Moses, the emancipator, prophet, lawgiver, and father of his country.

## Notes

**1–3** כָּל (*kol,* "all"), appearing three times in this description, is often used hyperbolically. In actuality Moses would have seen a large part of the land, including a large part of Naphtali, Ephraim, and Manasseh. However, he would not have been able to see the Mediterranean because the mountains of Judah are higher than Nebo—though he would have been able to see a large part of Judah, which did extend to the Mediterranean. It is not necessary to suppose that the Lord gave some special sight to Moses so that he could see over the mountains or through them; for these terms occur elsewhere, not in conformity to the demands of a scientific age that wants more precision than ancient usage gave—though even in the twentieth century words like "all" are often used in grandiose fashion.

**1** "Pisgah" might not be a proper noun; פִּסְגָּה (*pisgāh*) means "cleft," "ridge," or "range." The top of *pisgāh* might mean the highest point of the ridge of mountains rising in Moab east of the Dead Sea.

Though the Dan mentioned here is almost universally thought to be the Dan north of the Waters of Merom, which was so named after the Danite conquest of Laish during the period of the judges, it seems more likely that the Dan of Gen 14:14 and here (and possibly in 2 Sam 24:6) was a place in the north of Gilead. While such a place called Dan is not known from other sources, it would not be alone in that category. The Genesis narrative does not fit well at all with the Dan that had been Laish. It would have been quite out of the way for Abraham in his pursuit of the raiding party that had captured Lot. A Dan in Gilead better fits the description here, since the Dan north of the Waters of Merom could not be seen from Nebo.

**3** Zoar has not been located, but a place south of the Dead Sea is most likely (Gen 14:2, 8; 19:22–23, 30).

**6** The Qal imperfect with an indefinite subject, יִקְבֹּר (*yiqbōr*, "bury"), may be translated either as the NIV, "He buried him," or with an indefinite subject, "They buried him." The latter supposes some additional persons or powers buried Moses. This contradicts the general thrust of the narrative. Ibn Ezra suggested that Moses buried himself! The NIV translation is better, for the Hebrew phrase immediately preceding speaks of the Lord.

**7** The noun לֵחֹה (*lēḥōh*, "strength") appears only here, but the adjective לַח (*lāḥ*, "strong") occurs six times in the OT with the sense of fresh, moist, or green (tree). As a reference to sexual vigor (or physical health), see W.F. Albright, "The 'Natural Force' of Moses in the Light of Ugaritic," BASOR 94 (1944): 32–35.

**9** רוּחַ חָכְמָה (*rûaḥ ḥoḵmāh*, "the spirit of wisdom") is the equipment that makes it possible for one to do what the Lord delegates him to do. The skilled workmen who made the priestly garments for Aaron and his sons were given wisdom to make those garments (Exod 28:3). The spirit of wisdom for Joshua was the military and administrative ability necessary for the task the Lord had laid on him as well as the spiritual wisdom to rely on and be committed to the Lord.

**11–12** The terms used in this final description of Moses' ministry are common in the narratives of the Exodus and the desert journeys (see Exod 7:3; Num 14:11, 22; Deut 4:34; 6:22; 7:19; 11:3; 26:8; 29:3).

---

# JOSHUA

Donald H. Madvig

# JOSHUA

## Introduction



### 1. Background

The Book of Joshua deals with one very important stage in the fulfillment of God's great plan to provide salvation for the whole world. The people of Israel had to be settled in the Promised Land to prepare for the coming of another Joshua, viz., Jesus Christ, who was to live and die in that same land as Savior, not only of Israel, but of the entire human race.

The Pentateuch provides the background both historically and theologically for the Book of Joshua. The call of Abraham was God's initial response to the predicament of mankind as portrayed in Genesis 1–11. God was preparing a people through whom the Messiah would come. As part of that preparation, God promised to give them a land of their own (Gen 12:7; 13:14–17; 15:7; et al.). The fulfillment of that promise is the primary focus of the Book of Joshua.

The person and work of Moses are the most prominent features in this background. The author of Joshua has gone to great lengths to demonstrate that the work of Moses and the work of Joshua are related to each other as preparation and fulfillment. Joshua is presented always in the shadow of his great predecessor. Moses is the "servant of the LORD" while Joshua is only "Moses' aide." Not until the very end of the Book of Joshua is Joshua privileged to bear the high title "the servant of the LORD" (24:29). Many parallels are intentionally drawn between the lives of these two men, as will be pointed out in this commentary.

The Book of Joshua is closely related to the Book of Deuteronomy; even the language is similar. Deuteronomy seeks to prepare Israel for entry into the Promised

Land; Joshua describes that entry. This profound interrelationship, involving both language and theme, continues through the books of Judges, Samuel, and Kings.

Genesis and Deuteronomy provide respectively the prologue and the conclusion for Exodus, Leviticus, and Numbers, where the focus is on the law and the covenant. Moreover, it is not the possession of the land but the law and the covenant that constitute Israel as a nation, though admittedly possessing a land is necessary to being recognized as a nation. The books of Joshua and Judges view themselves as separate from the Pentateuch. They refer to the Pentateuch as a completed entity and as normative for them. The linguistic affinities between Deuteronomy and Joshua-Kings are thought by some to be the work of a seventh-century B.C. editor. This would also account for the many similarities with Jeremiah. Even if a seventh-century style has been imposed in the process of editing, the material itself is much earlier. Deuteronomy is forward looking. It explains how the law given to a specific generation is binding on all subsequent ones.

Moses was called by God to mold the people into a mighty nation and to lead them out of slavery. The central feature in Moses' leadership was the mediation of the law on Sinai. This law was so intimately identified with his person that it came to be known as the law of Moses. The "Book of the Law" of Moses was to be the guide for Joshua and Israel in the Conquest (1:7–8). Israel's success would always be dependent on reverence for and obedience to that law.

The Book of Joshua begins with the appointment of Joshua as Moses' successor. Though his career was not as colorful as Moses', Joshua's position as leader involved him, like Moses, in matters religious, military, civil, and social. His preparation for these important roles is described in the Pentateuch.

Joshua was prepared for spiritual leadership early in his life. He alone was privileged to accompany Moses to the top of Mount Sinai, where Moses received the tablets of the law from God (Exod 24:12–13). Joshua was Moses' attendant at the Tent of Meeting, where great theophanies occurred. He often remained in that holy place when Moses had to return to the camp of the Israelites (Exod 33:7–11).

Joshua was being prepared for military leadership when he was placed in charge of the Israelite forces in the battle with the Amalekites (Exod 17:8–16). Moreover, he participated in the first reconnaissance of the land of Canaan (Num 13:1–25). Thus he became intimately acquainted with the land that he later led Israel to conquer and that he divided among the tribes (Num 32:28–29; 34:17; Josh 1:6).

Though the book begins with Joshua's installation as leader, he had been commissioned for that task already while Moses was still living (Num 27:12–23; Deut 31:1–8).

The date of the Conquest continues to be debated. The traditional date (c. 1400 B.C.) is based on 1 Kings 6:1, which specifies that the fourth year of Solomon's reign was the "four hundred and eightieth year" after the Exodus. It is fairly well established that the fourth year of Solomon's reign was around 966 B.C. This would put the Exodus at about 1446 B.C. and the Conquest forty years later. These figures appear to be corroborated also by the total number of years that the various judges ruled.

On the other hand, while the Israelites were in Egypt, they built the city of Rameses (Exod 1:11). If this city was named for the Pharaoh, Rameses II, it is argued that the Exodus could not have occurred before 1290 B.C. Proponents of this later date regard the 480 years of 1 Kings 6:1 as an approximate figure representing twelve generations. They argue that the twenty-five years more nearly correspond to a generation so that twelve generations would be only around 300 years. By this method of reckoning, the Exodus would have occurred around 1260 B.C. and the Conquest about 1220 B.C.

Conservative scholars are divided on this issue. For this reason one scheme of dating cannot be called conservative and the other liberal. Nevertheless, Ronald Youngblood,[1] in a review of recent publications dealing with this problem, observes a trend toward the earlier dating. Among the things he reports are D.N. Freedman's arguments based on the Ebla Tablets that the date for Abraham must be moved back in history. Of course the dates for Abraham and for the Exodus are intertwined (cf. Gen 15:16; Exod 12:40). If an earlier date is given for Abraham, earlier dates for the Exodus and the Conquest must be given, too.

Various evidences from archaeological research are used in support of one date or the other. Archer (SOTI, pp. 253–59) devotes much attention to the many references in the Amarna Letters (c. 1400–1350 B.C.) to the *Ḫabiru*, a band of nomadic people who were invading the land of Canaan.

If the earlier date for the Conquest is correct, then it took place in the period when the Amarna Letters were written. These letters, which were sent to the king of Egypt by petty kings in Canaan, reflect a political situation very similar to that which prevailed when Israel entered the land. Egypt's influence over the region had deteriorated, and the country was divided into independent city-states.

Supporters of the later date appeal to other archaeological evidence, such as the explorations of Nelson Glueck in Transjordan, which indicate that that region was uninhabited from 1900 B.C. to 1300 B.C. If this is correct, then the defeat of the Amorite kings Og and Sihon could not have occurred prior to 1300 B.C. Moreover, supporters of the later dating contend that while there is ample evidence for the destruction of cities in Palestine in the thirteenth century there is little or none for the earlier date (cf. discussion in Wiseman, EBC, 1:317–18).

A re-evaluation of the archaeological discoveries at Tell es-Sultan (identified as ancient Jericho) has been published by Wood (pp. 44–57). His keen observations bring fresh insights to the debate concerning the date of the Conquest. Wood's careful analysis of the pottery, scarabs, and stratigraphy points to a date around 1400 B.C. for the destruction of Jericho reported in the biblical account. The responses to Wood's article indicate that it would be premature to conclude that the issue has been resolved (cf. BAR 16, 5 [1990]: 45–49, 68–69.)

## 2. Unity of Composition

Wellhausen found it inconceivable that the literary sources of the Pentateuch (JEDP) would not have included an account of the Conquest. He and others have attempted to trace those same sources in Joshua. Their inability to achieve anything approaching a consensus calls the whole theory into question. On the other hand, Martin Noth was impressed by the unified theological outlook that runs throughout the books of Deuteronomy through Kings. He proposed that these books formed a Deuteronomic history. There are good reasons for serious reservations about both of these positions. Ancient tradition has always made a sharp distinction between the Torah—the first five books—and the rest of the OT. While the Book of Joshua

[1] "A New Look at an Old Problem: The Date of the Exodus," *Christianity Today* (December 17, 1982): 58–60.

emphasizes the close relationship between the persons and work of Moses and Joshua, it makes clear that Joshua was not another Moses. Nowhere in Scripture is he given status approaching that of Moses. Though intimately related to the Pentateuch, the Book of Joshua has always been separate from it.

Nor is there any evidence of a separate literary entity composed of Deuteronomy through Kings. The similarities in theology and language may indicate no more than that the authors of the historical books were very thoroughly versed in the style and theology of Deuteronomy.

It is clear that the author did not include materials of the kinds nor in the proportions that we expect to find in an account of a military campaign such as the Conquest. This in itself is not indicative of disparate or inadequate sources. The author, whose purpose was primarily theological, deliberately described the Conquest in terms of a few decisive battles. It is safe to assume that he was acquainted with many more events than the few he chose to narrate.

The fact that most of the events in chapters 3–8 occurred in geographical areas that later were in the territory of Benjamin and which center around Gilgal has led some to the opinion that the author was working basically with Benjamite traditions that he was able to supplement with a few miscellaneous materials.

The presupposition of this commentary is that the author of Joshua drew from a wide collection of traditions. He selected and reshaped certain of these traditions to demonstrate from Israel's history that the Lord always blesses his people when they obey his law.

Admittedly, some of these traditions may have been etiologies—stories created to explain unusual names, places, or some other phenomena. This does not deny their historical credibility, nor does it repudiate the possibility that the author had some more important reason for including them.

What some have attributed to a hodge-podge of contradictory sources has more recently been explained as characteristic of Hebrew narrative style. Thematic concerns rather than chronology control the arrangement. At times the element of suspense, which was part of the living experience, is recreated for the reader by shifting the order of events. The use of proleptic summary statements before the detailed recitation of events makes the account seem repetitive, as does the retelling of certain matters from the standpoint of each of two or more different themes (cf. Woudstra, pp. 13–16).

The theology of the author has given a profound unity to the final form of the Book of Joshua and a remarkable consistency in point of view.

## 3. Authorship

In the Talmud (*Baba Bathra* 14b) Joshua is named as the author of the Book of Joshua. This view is appealing because the book bears his name. Furthermore, it lends more credibility to the narratives if they are the report of an eyewitness. Those who hold this view attribute to Eleazer or Phinehas the account of the death of Joshua and other short passages that Joshua could not have written.

The book itself does not specify who the author was, nor is the author named anywhere else in the OT. There are many other books in the OT that do not bear the name of the author. For example, few would want to argue that 1 and 2 Samuel were written by Samuel. The use of the first person plural pronoun in Joshua 5:1, 6 is not proof that the author was an eyewitness of the events narrated, since later generations were taught to regard their national history as consisting of events in which they too had participated (see the comment on 24:7). The name of the book is derived from the principal character, Joshua (*yᵉhôšûaʿ*), whose name means either "Save, Yahweh!" or "Yahweh saves." It is an appropriate name for the man Yahweh chose to lead his people triumphantly into the Promised Land. (His name occurs also in a shorter form, Hoshea [*hôšēaʿ*] in Num 13:8, 16; Deut 32:44 [NIV mg.]).

The Grecized form of Joshua is "Jesus" (*Iēsous*). There are two passages in the KJV of the NT where Joshua's name is actually spelled "Jesus" (cf. Gr. of Acts 7:45; Heb 4:8). Just as Joshua was instrumental in fulfilling God's promises to the Patriarchs, so everything that God promised in the entire OT is brought to fulfillment in Jesus (cf. Matt 1:21: "You are to give him the name Jesus, because he will save his people from their sins").

It is specifically stated in 8:32 and 24:26 that Joshua did some writing. In each case, however, it seems that what Joshua wrote was both different from and considerably less than the present book that bears his name.

## 4. Date

If Joshua was the author, then the date of writing the book is a fairly simple matter: it must have been written before his death and after the last event narrated in the book. Joshua was 110 years old when he died (24:29). If, as Woudstra (p. 209) suggests, Joshua was nearly the same age as Caleb, then his death and the writing of the book would have taken place about thirty years after the Conquest began. This would have been around 1370 B.C. according to the earlier dating. Other evidence, however, suggests a later date.

The phrase "to this day," which occurs frequently (4:9; 5:9; 6:25; 7:26; 8:28–29; 9:27; 10:27; 13:13; 15:63; 16:10; 23:9; cf. 22:3, 17), indicates the passing of time between the event and the recording of the event, though it was not necessarily a long period of time. In 6:25 it is stated that Rahab "lives among the Israelites to this day," which suggests that Rahab was still living at the time of this writing. Even this suggestion is not certain, for the statement may only mean that Rahab's descendants were still living among the Israelites.

Certain words and phrases are taken to indicate the time of Solomon's temple, such as "his treasury" (*'ôṣar YHWH;* lit., "the treasury of the LORD," 6:19) and "the treasury of the LORD's house" (*'ôṣar bêṯ-YHWH*, 6:24). These, however, may be modernizations introduced by a later editor. Some parts of the book could not have been written latter than the time of David and Solomon; e.g., Jebusites are said to still be living in Jerusalem (cf. 15:63 with 2 Sam 5:6–9) and Canaanites in Gezer (cf. 16:10 with 1 Kings 9:16).

## 5. Occasion and Purpose

Apparently the author had two complementary purposes in writing. The first was to show that God had been faithful in fulfilling his promise to Abraham to give the land of Canaan to him and to his descendants. The outline (q.v.) of the book shows how the author divided his material into two main divisions: a narration of the conquest of the land and a tedious and detailed description of the division of the land among the various tribes.

The author's second purpose was to demonstrate that the covenant-keeping God is also righteous. From Israel's own history at the time of the Conquest, he demonstrated that possession of the land was in part contingent on Israel's obedience to the law of Moses. God would not bless his covenant people unless they were obedient to his Word. This is clearly the main purpose of the book; for in the first part of the book (chs. 1–12) the author devoted less attention to Israel's military exploits than he did to the covenant and Israel's obedience or disobedience.

The inclusion of Joshua with the "Former Prophets" in the Jewish canon shows keen insight into the true function of the book. The author's intention was not to preserve history for its own sake, not even a prophetically interpreted history. He presented a careful selection of historical and traditional materials in order to preach. He wanted to proclaim that Israel was blessed at the time of the Conquest because she was faithful to her God and to his law and that this would be the secret of Israel's success and blessing in every generation.

This message would have special relevance at a time when the temptation to apostasy was strong or when Israel was suffering from a great national disaster. The period of the Judges nicely fits these criteria, as does the time of the early monarchy under Saul.

Obviously this message was appropriate also in the time of the Exile. This time is favored by those who argue for a Deuteronomic history. Such a history could not have been completed until after the fall of Jerusalem and would have been directed to the nation when it had been driven from the Promised Land into captivity in Babylonia. The Book of Joshua would speak emphatically to that situation by affirming that just as faithful obedience had been the prerequisite to Israel's conquest of the land in the first place, so now it was essential if the nation was to be restored to its land.

The unusual amount of attention given to Reuben, Gad, and the half-tribe of Manasseh suggests an occasion when the unity of the nation was in jeopardy. This fits the period of the Judges when individual tribes and groups of tribes acted independently. It could also apply to the time when Saul was attempting to unify the nation. The question of national unity was an especially obvious concern during the divided monarchy. The division experienced at that time, however, was between north and south, not east and west.

Since there is so much uncertainty about the date of this book, we must be careful not to allow matters of dating influence our interpretation.

## 6. Literary Form

The literary form of Joshua is a series of independent narratives, descriptions of tribal boundaries, and lists of towns, joined together by means of transitional paragraphs and summary statements that give unity and continuity to the whole. The structure is indicated in the Outline. There are two main sections to the book: God's promises to Israel were fulfilled in the conquest of the land (chs. 1–12), and God's promises were fulfilled also in the division of the land (chs. 13–22). The conclusion (chs. 23–24) is an exhortation to Israel to remain faithful to the Lord so as to enjoy the blessing of the land forever.

## 7. Theological Values

The Book of Joshua, like all other books of the Bible, is primarily a book of theology. Through it God has revealed himself and continues to do so.

God is the God of Israel. When he said, "I will take you as my own people, and I will be your God" (Exod 6:7; cf. Deut 4:20; 2 Sam 7:24; Jer 13:11; 30:22; 31:33; et al.), he entered into a covenant relationship with his people. In giving Israel the land, he was fulfilling the promises that he made to Abraham and which he reaffirmed to the people of Israel at the time of the Exodus. Thus he entered into covenant with some human beings, but not all. Here we see elements of a doctrine of election. Since God is the God of Israel, he was acting within his rights when he appointed Joshua as successor to Moses. By keeping his covenant with Israel, God reveals his great faithfulness.

God is holy. He does not tolerate wickedness and rebellion. The Canaanites were driven out because of their sin and disobedience. He treated Israel the same way. When one of their number violated the covenant with God, all progress in the Conquest was halted (ch. 7). God would not continue to bless his people unless that sin was dealt with. God rewards obedience. Whether God blesses or withholds his blessing is dependent on human response. He is no respecter of persons.

God is gracious. His grace, however, is not limited to Israel; for all who are willing to turn from their pagan ways and acknowledge him are spared (e.g., Rahab, the Gibeonites). Although God had given specific commands forbidding the assimilation of foreigners into Israel, his saving purpose prevailed: "Everyone who calls on the name of the Lord will be saved" (Rom 10:13).

God is the God of creation. All creation is subject to his sovereign control. Therefore he works mighty miracles: e.g., the drying up of the Jordan, the destruction of the walls of Jericho, the great hailstones that destroyed Israel's enemies, etc.

God is the God of the universe. The writer produced a beautiful testimony to God's universal reign from the mouth of the pagan woman Rahab, who said, "For the LORD your God is God in heaven above and on the earth below" (2:11). The land is his to take, and he can give it to whomever he pleases. In this same vein, J.L. Kelso sees the nature miracles as evidence of the Lord's victory over the gods of Canaan:

> The crossing of the Jordan at high flood and the cyclonic hail storm at Aijalon are of special theological significance, for Baal was the great Canaanite storm god who was supposed to control the rain, the hail, the snow and the floods of Palestine. These episodes proved that Baal was as powerless before Yahweh in Palestine as he had been in the episode of the plagues in Egypt.[2]

God is a man of war (cf. Exod 15:3). He fought for Israel: He commanded the attack; he provided the strategy; he assisted with supernatural acts; he hardened the hearts of the enemies so that they would not surrender; he gave victory to Israel. Joshua courted disaster when he neglected to consult with God before battle. The presence of the ark of the covenant with the Israelite army was truly the presence of God and a sign indicating that the Conquest was a religious event. In the Conquest God was marching triumphantly into Canaan to take possession of his land.

One of the many close links between Joshua and Deuteronomy is a common

[2] *Archaeology and Our Old Testament Contemporaries* (Grand Rapids: Zondervan, 1966), p. 53.

theological outlook in which the most distinctive element is the conviction that God rewards the faithful and punishes the wicked.

The book affirms both the complete fulfillment of all God's great promises and at the same time acknowledges the incomplete nature of the Conquest. This indicates that God had been faithful to his people and that the memory of his faithfulness was a promise for the future: he would complete the work he had begun.

The dangers of apostasy were ever present. In every act of covenant renewal, Israel was admonished to remain faithful. She was warned of the perils of unfaithfulness and informed how difficult it is to remain faithful.

Two themes from the Book of Joshua are developed in other parts of the Bible. The first is the promise of the land. Paul interpreted Romans 4:13–16 to mean that God promised to give the entire world to those who believe. Echoes of Joshua can be heard also in Jesus' beatitude: "Blessed are the meek, for they will inherit the earth" (Matt 5:5).

The second theme from Joshua that is developed elsewhere in Scripture is the concept of "rest." It refers to secure borders that eliminate all danger of attack from without. In the Epistle to the Hebrews, this rest is linked to the seventh day of Creation, which was a day of rest; and this rest is projected into the future when in the new creation Jesus will give rest to all believers.

## 8. Canonicity and Text

The inclusion of Joshua in the OT canon has never been disputed. Though it may be argued that the Jews accorded to the Pentateuch (the Torah) an authority above the rest of the Hebrew Scriptures, the prophetic books were not far behind in their estimation. The Book of Joshua stands at the very beginning of these prophetic writings.

Questions of authorship have been of prime importance in consideration of the canonicity of NT books. This test cannot be applied to the books of the OT, however. Joshua is only one of many OT books of uncertain authorship.

The Hebrew text used as the basis for the translation of Joshua in the NIV is the Codex Leningradensis, which is dated about A.D. 1008. This is the text presented by R. Meyer.[3] The text of Joshua is in an excellent state of preservation, and only a few emendations are suggested in the Notes in this commentary.

## 9. Special Problems

### a. *The Annihilation of the Canaanites*

The single greatest problem in the Book of Joshua is the extermination of the Canaanites. Men, women, and children were included among the things that were to be "devoted to the LORD" (6:17; cf. NIV mg.).

The Moabite Stone from the ninth century B.C. bears evidence that this practice was not unique to Israel in the ancient Near East. Inscribed on the stone is King Mesha's

---

[3] *Biblia Hebraica Stuttgartensia*, edd. K. Elliger and W. Rudolph (Stuttgart: Deutsche Bibelstiftung, 1976).

boastful report that he had destroyed all the inhabitants of Ataroth as a sacrifice to his god (ANET, p. 320).

This was not the first instance of the practice in Israel. In Numbers 21:2–3, the Israelites vowed to "totally destroy" (*ḥāram*) the cities of the Canaanites in the Negev if God would give Israel victory over them.

A common but unsatisfying explanation of this difficult moral problem is that Israel was mistaken in thinking that God had commanded such indiscriminate slaughter. It is pointed out that this practice was not carried out consistently in the Conquest (many exceptions are reported in Judges), nor was it practiced by Israel in later years.

This, however, does not explain the theology of Deuteronomy, Joshua, and Judges. The text (Josh 6:17, 21; Deut 20:17; Judg passim) clearly states that the command to destroy the Canaanites came from God himself, and the Israelites are reproved for their failure to obey it (cf. Ps 106:34–42).

God was careful to point out that he was not arbitrarily destroying the Canaanites just to give the land to Israel. The wickedness of the inhabitants of Canaan was the reason why God was removing them; and if Israel proved unfaithful, she too would be removed from the land (as happened in the Exile). Genesis 15:16 records a profound statement in which God tells Abraham that his descendants will have to wait four generations to take over the land because "the sin of the Amorites has not yet reached its full measure." God would not favor Israel in a way that was unfair to others.

A part of the wonderful omnipotence of God is that he works sovereignly in history to punish the wicked and to reward the righteous: "The Lord knows how to rescue godly men from trials and to hold the unrighteous for the day of judgment" (2 Peter 2:9).

The extermination of the Canaanites is but one of the many evidences in the Bible, as well as in real life, that evil is real and that the Devil exists. Evil does not flee at the snap of one's fingers. The struggle with sin and the Devil took the Son of God to the cross. There was no easy victory even for him. Only by his suffering and death has he overcome evil once and for all. Those who will not be separated from their sin by repentance will be destroyed with their sin, as Jesus said, "If you do not believe that I am the one I claim to be, you will indeed die in your sins" (John 8:24).

God's severity in his treatment of sin and of sinners is but the obverse side of his grace and love. Sin and evil destroy the people he loves and prevent the full establishment of his glorious kingdom.

One of the most telling objections to the slaughter of the Canaanites is raised against God's use of the Israelites as instruments of his judgment. Perhaps this was done to impress on the Israelites the truth that "the wages of sin is death" (Rom 6:23). The explanation given in the Wisdom of Solomon (12:3–11) is very thought provoking. It says that God chose to annihilate the Canaanites little by little, rather than all at once, to give them opportunity to repent.

The most difficult thing to understand is the slaughter of innocent children. We must remember that death is not the ultimate destiny of the human race, nor is it the greatest evil. Someday God will give a full explanation, which is something that only he can do.

### b. *Archaeology*

Archaeological research has given a mixed message with respect to the Book of Joshua. In some matters the biblical record has been confirmed. In others, however, questions have been raised. One unresolved issue is the dating of the Conquest, which we have already considered. Also unresolved is the identification of the sites of Ai and Jericho.

John Garstang discovered at Jericho a city that had been devastated and burned, and whose walls had fallen outward. He dated the fall of this city around 1400 B.C. and identified it with the Jericho of Joshua. This was an electrifying confirmation of the biblical account. However, subsequent research by Kathleen Kenyon seems to indicate that the ruins discovered by Garstang are from a much earlier date, and that any evidence of a city that may have existed at the time of the Conquest has been erased by primitive methods of earlier excavations and through the erosion of wind and rain. Woudstra (p. 69 n. 6) questions whether the site has been correctly identified as Jericho.

The location of Ai is also a perplexing problem. Ai has been identified with et-Tell, a little east of Bethel. Excavations at this site reveal that the city was uninhabited from about 2400 B.C. to the eleventh or tenth century B.C., when it was resettled by the Israelites. If so, then there would have been no fortified city there for Joshua to conquer. On the other hand, archaeological evidence indicates that Bethel was destroyed around 1250 B.C. Consequently, W.F. Albright suggested that the biblical story is really an account of the conquest of Bethel. It is safe to conclude that the final word has not been spoken. Perhaps Kenneth A. Kitchen is correct when he suggests that et-Tell is really Beth Aven and that the site of Ai has yet to be found.[4]

Butler (p. xxviii) makes the following observation:

> Archaeological research thus leaves confusion and unanswered questions for the present generation. This does not lead us to abandon archaeological research. It reminds us of the great difficulties which stand in our way when we seek to utilize discoveries for historical reconstruction. Archaeology can rarely name sites. Seldom, if ever, can it determine precisely who destroyed a site. It often cannot tell who occupied a site; it can place only relative dates on sites. Only rarely can it excavate an entire site and secure all the evidence.

## 10. Bibliography

### Books

Aharoni, Y. *The Land of the Bible.* Revised edition. Philadelphia: Westminster, 1979.

Albright, W.F. *From Stone Age to Christianity.* Revised edition. Garden City: Doubleday, 1957.

Baly, D. *The Geography of the Bible.* New York: Harper and Row, 1957.

Boling, R.G. *Joshua.* Anchor Bible. Garden City: Doubleday, 1982.

Bright, J. *Joshua.* Interpreter's Bible. Edited by G. Buttrick. Nashville: Abingdon, 1953.

______. *The Authority of the Old Testament.* Nashville: Abingdon, 1967.

______. *A History of Israel.* Revised Edition. Philadelphia: Westminster, 1981.

Butler, T.C. *Joshua.* Word Biblical Commentary. Waco: Word, 1983.

Calvin, J. *Commentaries on the Book of Joshua.* Grand Rapids: Eerdmans, 1949.

Goslinga, C.J. *Joshua, Judges, Ruth.* Bible Student's Commentary. Grand Rapids: Zondervan, 1986.

Gray, J. *Joshua, Judges and Ruth.* New Century Bible. London: Nelson, 1967.

Hall, J. *Contemplations on the Old and New Testaments.* London: T. Nelson and Sons, 1859.

[4]*Ancient Orient and Old Testament* (Chicago: InterVarsity, 1966), p. 63.

Hamlin, J. *Joshua: Inheriting the Land.* International Theological Commentary. Grand Rapids: Eerdmans, 1983.

Keil, C.F., and Delitzsch, F. *Joshua, Judges, Ruth.* Grand Rapids: Eerdmans, 1950.

Kenyon, Kathleen. *Excavations at Jericho.* New York: Praeger, 1957.

Miller, J.M., and Tucker, G.M. *The Book of Joshua.* Cambridge Bible Commentary. New York: Cambridge University Press, 1974.

Soggin, J.A. *Joshua.* Old Testament Library. Philadelphia: Westminster, 1972.

Woudstra, M. *The Book of Joshua.* New International Commentary. Grand Rapids: Eerdmans, 1981.

Yadin, Y. *The Art of Biblical Warfare.* 2 volumes. New York: McGraw-Hill, 1963.

## Articles

Albright, W.F. "The Israelite Conquest of Canaan in the Light of Archaeology." *Bulletin of the American Schools of Oriental Research* 74 (1939): 11–23.

Lewis, A. "Joshua." *The NIV Study Bible.* Edited by K. Barker. Grand Rapids: Zondervan, 1985.

Martin, W.J. " 'Dischronologized' Narrative in the Old Testament." Supplement. *Vetus Testamentum* 17 (1969): 179–86.

Wood, Bryant G. "Did the Israelites Conquer Jericho?" *Biblical Archaeology Review* 16, 2 (1990): 44–59. See also the letters in response: *Biblical Archaeology Review* 16, 5 (1990): 45–49, 68–69.

## 11. Outline

- I. Conquering the Promised Land (1:1–12:24)
  - A. A New Leader for Israel (1:1–18)
    - 1. Joshua's commission (1:1–9)
    - 2. Joshua's orders to the officers (1:10–11)
    - 3. Joshua's orders to the Transjordanian tribes (1:12–15)
    - 4. Joshua confirmed as leader (1:16–18)
  - B. Gaining a Foothold: Jericho and Ai (2:1–8:35)
    - 1. Rahab and the spies (2:1–24)
      - a. Sending the spies (2:1–7)
      - b. Rahab's covenant with the spies (2:8–21)
      - c. The report of the spies (2:22–24)
    - 2. Crossing the Jordan (3:1–4:24)
      - a. Instructions for crossing (3:1–13)
      - b. Crossing on dry ground (3:14–17)
      - c. Memorials to the Crossing (4:1–24)
        - 1) Twelve stones from the riverbed (4:1–9)
        - 2) The flow of the Jordan restored (4:10–18)
        - 3) The significance of the stones (4:19–24)
    - 3. Renewing the covenant with Israel (5:1–15)
      - a. The covenant sign (5:1–9)
      - b. The covenant meal (5:10–12)
      - c. The true leader of the covenant people (5:13–15)
    - 4. The conquest of Jericho (6:1–27)
      - a. The Lord's instructions (6:1–5)
      - b. The attack on Jericho (6:6–21)
      - c. Rahab rescued and Jericho cursed (6:22–27)
    - 5. The conquest of Ai (7:1–8:29)
      - a. Achan's sin (7:1–26)
        - 1) Israel's defeat at Ai (7:1–5)
        - 2) Joshua's intercession (7:6–9)
        - 3) The Lord's answer (7:10–15)
        - 4) The culprit discovered and punished (7:16–26)
      - b. The second attack on Ai (8:1–29)
        - 1) Commands for the second attack (8:1–9)
        - 2) Israel's victory (8:10–29)
    - 6. Covenant renewal at Mount Ebal (8:30–35)
  - C. The Southern Campaign (9:1–10:43)
    - 1. The Gibeonite deception (9:1–27)
      - a. The treaty with Israel (9:1–15)
      - b. The ruse discovered (9:16–27)
    - 2. Israel's victory over the southern coalition (10:1–43)
      - a. The rescue of the Gibeonites (10:1–15)
      - b. The execution of the five Amorite kings (10:16–28)
      - c. The completion of the southern campaign (10:29–43)
  - D. The Northern Campaign (11:1–15)
    - 1. The northern coalition formed (11:1–5)
    - 2. The major battle (11:6–9)
    - 3. The capture of the northern cities (11:10–15)

- E. A Summary of the Conquest (11:16–23)
- F. A List of Defeated Kings (12:1–24)
    - 1. Kings whom Moses defeated (12:1–6)
    - 2. Kings whom Joshua defeated (12:7–24)

II. Dividing the Promised Land (13:1–21:45)
- A. The Command to Divide the Land (13:1–7)
- B. Division of the Land East of the Jordan (13:8–33)
    - 1. Introduction (13:8–14)
    - 2. The inheritance of Reuben (13:15–23)
    - 3. The inheritance of Gad (13:24–28)
    - 4. The inheritance of the half-tribe of Manasseh (13:29–31)
    - 5. Summary (13:32–33)
- C. Division of the Land West of the Jordan (14:1–19:51)
    - 1. Introduction (14:1–5)
    - 2. The inheritance of Judah (14:6–15:63)
        - a. Caleb's inheritance (14:6–15)
        - b. The borders of Judah (15:1–12)
        - c. The inheritance of Caleb's daughter (15:13–19)
        - d. The towns of Judah (15:20–63)
    - 3. The inheritance of the Joseph tribes (16:1–17:18)
        - a. Introduction (16:1–4)
        - b. The inheritance of Ephraim (16:5–10)
        - c. The inheritance of Manasseh (17:1–13)
            - 1) Introduction (17:1–2)
            - 2) The inheritance of the daughters of Zelophehad (17:3–6)
            - 3) The boundaries of Manasseh (17:7–13)
        - d. The complaint of the Joseph tribes (7:14–18)
    - 4. Division of the rest of the land (18:1–19:51)
        - a. Joshua's rebuke of the seven tribes (18:1–10)
        - b. The inheritance of Benjamin (18:11–28)
            - 1) The borders of Benjamin (18:11–20)
            - 2) The towns of Benjamin (18:21–28)
        - c. The inheritance of Simeon (19:1–9)
        - d. The inheritance of Zebulun (19:10–16)
        - e. The inheritance of Issachar (19:17–23)
        - f. The inheritance of Asher (19:24–31)
        - g. The inheritance of Naphtali (19:32–39)
        - h. The inheritance of Dan (19:40–48)
    - 5. Joshua's inheritance (19:49–51)
- D. The Cities of Refuge (20:1–9)
    - 1. The rationale (20:1–6)
    - 2. The selection (20:7–9)
- E. Towns for the Levites (21:1–42)
    - 1. Assignment of the towns by lot (21:1–8)
    - 2. The towns of the Kohathites (21:9–26)
        - a. Towns of the descendants of Aaron (21:9–19)
        - b. Towns of the remaining Kohathites (21:20–26)

3. The towns of the Gershonites (21:27–33)
4. The towns of the Merarites (21:34–40)
5. Summary of the Levitical towns (21:41–42)

F. God's Promises Fulfilled in the Division of the Land (21:43–45)

III. Preparation for Life in the Promised Land (22:1–24:33)
A. The Eastern Tribes Return Home (22:1–34)
1. The dismissal of the eastern tribes (22:1–9)
2. The altar of witness (22:10–34)
a. The crisis (22:10–14)
b. The confrontation (22:15–20)
c. The explanation (22:21–29)
d. The resolution (22:30–34)

B. Joshua's Farewell to the Leaders (23:1–16)
1. God's blessing: the reward for faithfulness (23:1–11)
2. God's judgment: the consequences of unfaithfulness (23:12–16)

C. The Covenant Renewed at Shechem (24:1–28)
1. A recitation of Israel's sacred history (24:1–13)
2. Joshua's charge and the people's response (24:14–24)
3. Sealing the covenant (24:25–28)

D. Three Burials in the Promised Land (24:29–33)

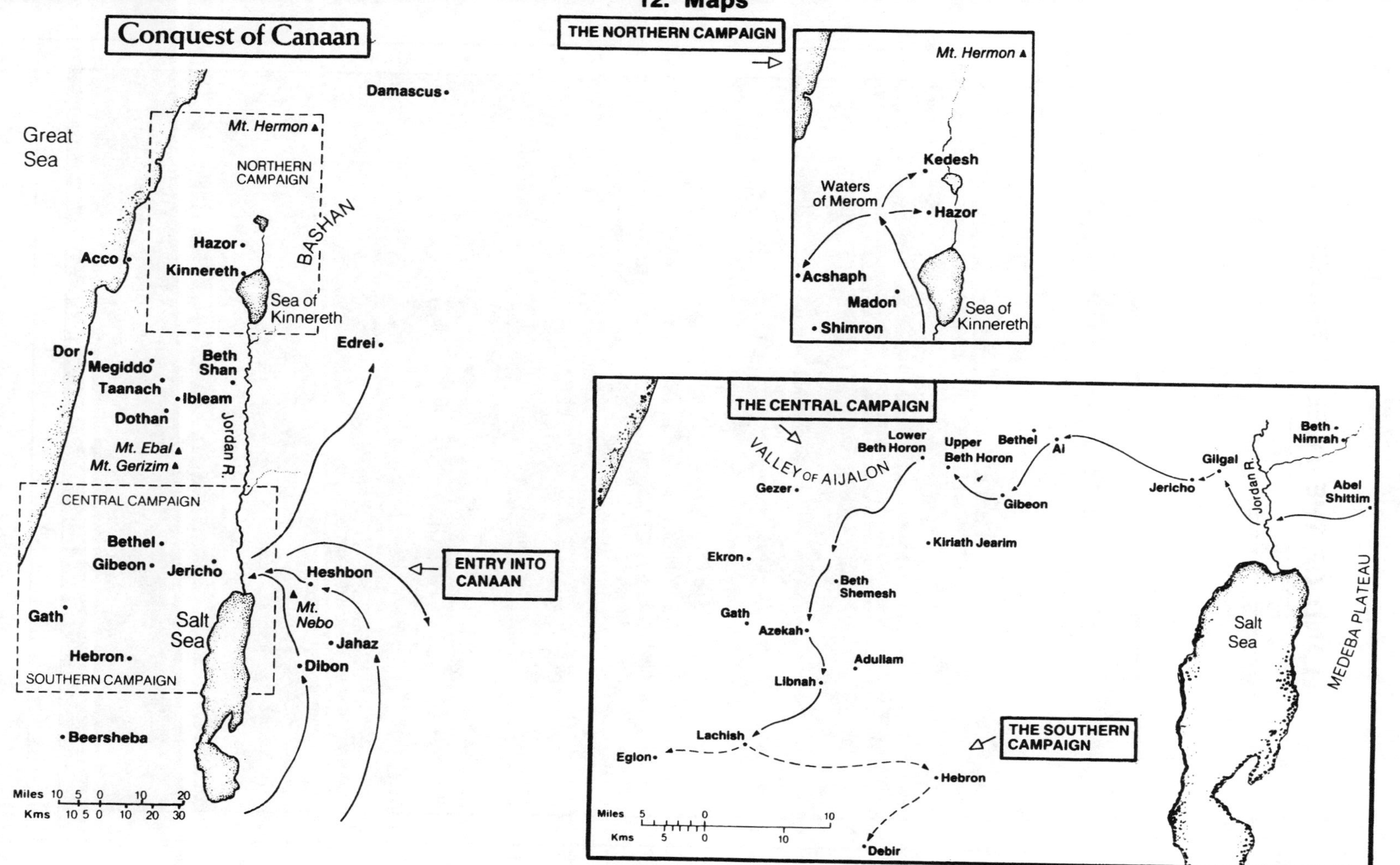
Conquest of Canaan
Damascus
Great Sea
Mt. Hermon
NORTHERN CAMPAIGN
BASHAN
Hazor
Acco
Kinnereth
Sea of Kinnereth
Edrei
Dor
Megiddo
Beth Shan
Taanach
Ibleam
Dothan
Jordan R.
Mt. Ebal
Mt. Gerizim
CENTRAL CAMPAIGN
Bethel
Gibeon
Jericho
Heshbon
ENTRY INTO CANAAN
Gath
Salt Sea
Mt. Nebo
Jahaz
Hebron
Dibon
SOUTHERN CAMPAIGN
Beersheba
Miles 10 5 0 10 20
Kms 10 5 0 10 20 30
THE NORTHERN CAMPAIGN
Mt. Hermon
Kedesh
Waters of Merom
Hazor
Acshaph
Madon
Shimron
Sea of Kinnereth
THE CENTRAL CAMPAIGN
Lower Beth Horon
Upper Beth Horon
Bethel
Ai
Beth Nimrah
Gilgal
Abel Shittim
VALLEY OF AIJALON
Gezer
Gibeon
Jericho
Jordan R.
Kiriath Jearim
Ekron
Beth Shemesh
MEDEBA PLATEAU
Gath
Azekah
Salt Sea
Adullam
Libnah
Lachish
THE SOUTHERN CAMPAIGN
Eglon
Hebron
Miles 5 0 10
Kms 5 0 10
Debir

# LAND OF THE TWELVE TRIBES

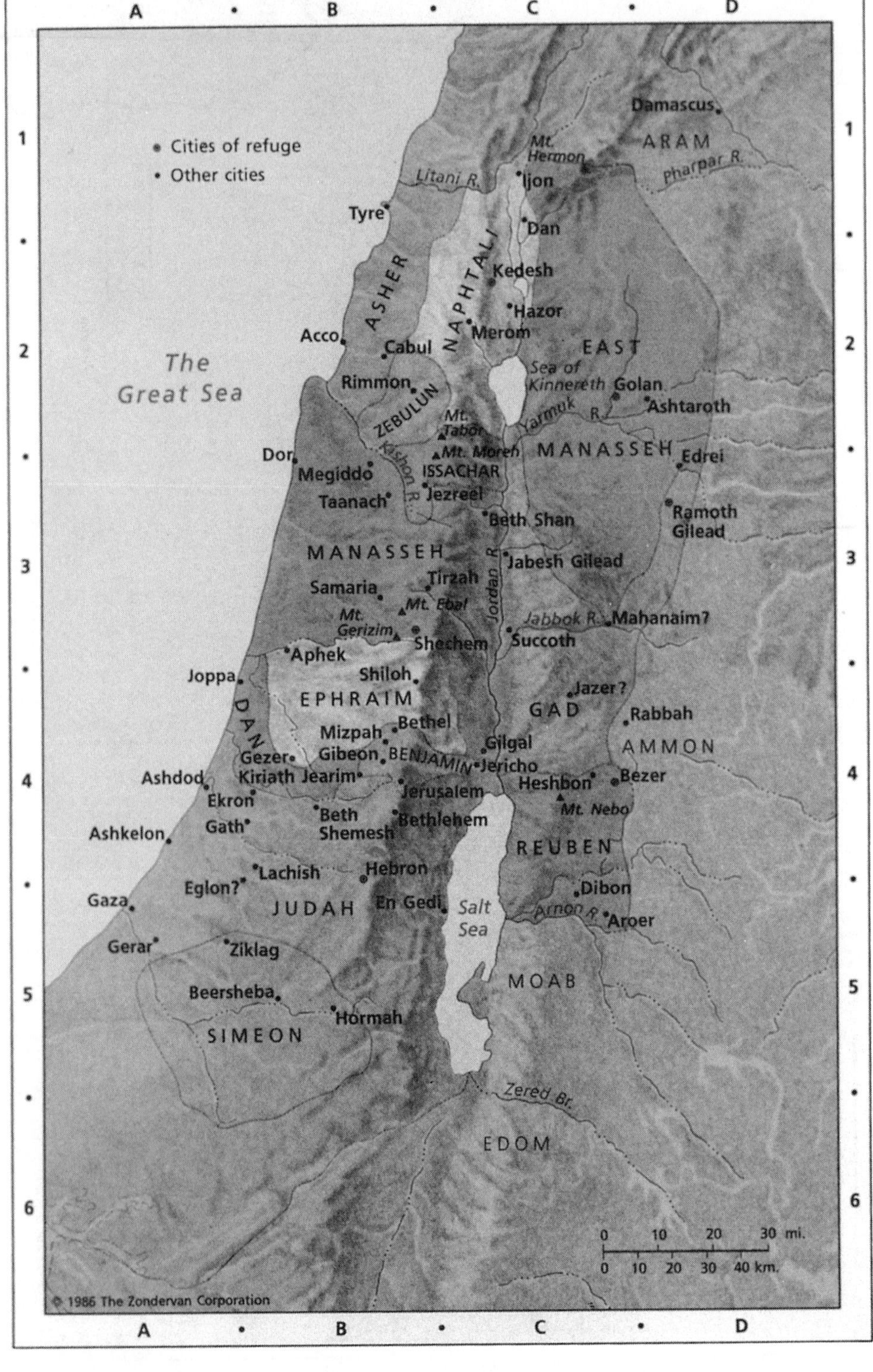

# Text and Exposition

## I. Conquering the Promised Land (1:1–12:24)

### A. *A New Leader for Israel (1:1–18)*

#### 1. *Joshua's commission*

1:1–9

1 After the death of Moses the servant of the LORD, the LORD said to
Joshua son of Nun, Moses' aide: 2 "Moses my servant is dead. Now then,
you and all these people, get ready to cross the Jordan River into the
land I am about to give to them—to the Israelites. 3 I will give you every
place where you set your foot, as I promised Moses. 4 Your territory will
extend from the desert to Lebanon, and from the great river, the
Euphrates—all the Hittite country—to the Great Sea on the west. 5 No
one will be able to stand up against you all the days of your life. As I was
with Moses, so I will be with you; I will never leave you nor forsake you.
6 "Be strong and courageous, because you will lead these people to
inherit the land I swore to their forefathers to give them. 7 Be strong and
very courageous. Be careful to obey all the law my servant Moses gave
you; do not turn from it to the right or to the left, that you may be
successful wherever you go. 8 Do not let this Book of the Law depart
from your mouth; meditate on it day and night, so that you may be
careful to do everything written in it. Then you will be prosperous and
successful. 9 Have I not commanded you? Be strong and courageous.
Do not be terrified; do not be discouraged, for the LORD your God will be
with you wherever you go."

**1** The opening words announce the death of Moses. It would be difficult to overestimate the importance of Moses to Israel. For forty years he had been their leader in religious, domestic, judicial, military, and civic concerns. With Moses' death one epoch ended and another began.

Moses' death separates the Book of Joshua from the Pentateuch, for, obviously, Moses' leadership had ended. A close relationship to the Pentateuch, however, is maintained because everything Joshua accomplished was the fulfillment of what God had begun with Moses. Observe the many links between Moses and Joshua in this chapter alone (vv.1, 3, 5, 7–8, 13–15, 17).

"Servant of the LORD" is a title of honor shared by Abraham, David, and the Servant of the Lord in Isaiah. (It is used most frequently of Moses: Exod 14:31; Num 12:7–8; Deut 34:5; and thirteen times in Joshua; "my servant" occurs twice.) The term "servant" was used to designate even the highest officials of a king. With the words "The LORD said to Joshua," leadership is transferred from Moses to Joshua. Joshua was specifically prepared and divinely appointed for this moment (see Introduction, p. 240; Num 27:15–23 and Deut 3:28; 31:1–8). Joshua is called the "son of Nun" ten times in this book (here, 2:1, 23; 6:6; 14:1; 17:4; 19:49, 51; 21:1; 24:29). Nothing is known about Joshua's father. Already in the Pentateuch Joshua was called "Moses' aide" (Exod 24:13; 33:11; Num 11:28). Only at the end of his life was he honored with the title "servant of the LORD" (24:29).

**2** Because of his disobedience, Moses was not allowed to lead the people of Israel into the Promised Land (Num 27:12–14). His death was the occasion for God to renew his command for Israel to enter the land. The crossing of the Jordan marked Israel's entrance to the Promised Land, just as crossing the Red Sea had marked their departure from Egypt. Flood conditions and the presence of the enemy on the other shore made this a formidable undertaking. The land was always considered to be God's gift to Israel (vv.3, 6, 11, 13, 15, et al.). The promise of the land, which was first given to Abraham in Genesis 12:7, is a major theme throughout patriarchal history and the Exodus, especially in the Book of Deuteronomy. The fulfillment of that promise is one of the major themes in Joshua.

**3** In the Hebrew text nearly the same wording is found in vv.3–5a as in Deuteronomy 11:24–25a. This is another of the many ties between Joshua and the Pentateuch, especially Deuteronomy. The author has taken pains to demonstrate that the work of Joshua is the fulfillment of the Pentateuch.

**4** The promise in Deuteronomy 11:24 (cf. Deut 1:6–8) is reiterated here, although the territory that Joshua and Israel actually conquered was not nearly so vast. The literal and complete fulfillment of this promise was not experienced by Israel until the reigns of David and Solomon (see 1 Kings 4:21, 24) and then once again in the time of Uzziah and Jeroboam. Though this vast area on both sides of the Jordan was promised to Israel (Deut 11:24), there is another tradition that regards only the land west of the Jordan as the Promised Land. According to this latter tradition, the territory possessed by the two and one-half tribes east of the Jordan lay outside the Promised Land (Josh 22:19). In Deuteronomy 12:10, for example, Moses stated that Israel would arrive at the land God promised them *after* they had crossed the Jordan. The word "desert" refers to the Negev in the south, and "Lebanon" (lit., "the Lebanon") refers to the Lebanese mountains. Palestine was referred to as "the Hittite country" by both Egypt and Babylonia even after the Hittites had withdrawn from the area (cf. Judg 1:26; cf. NIV Study Bible, p. 292 n. 1:4). "The Great Sea" is the Mediterranean.

**5** The conditions for the promise, "No one will be able to stand up against you," are stated in vv.6–9. It was Israel's failure to observe these conditions that caused their humiliating defeat at Ai (7:1–5). God's promise, "I will be with you," is most comforting and comprehensive (cf. Deut 31:6–8). The secret of Moses' success had been God's presence with him. It would be the secret of Joshua's success also, and it continues to be the secret of success for the church (cf. Matt 28:19–20). The conditions for this promise are found in vv.7–8 (cf. 7:12). The statement "I will never leave you nor forsake you" is an example of the doubling of synonyms for emphasis, a common feature in this chapter (cf. vv.7–9, 18).

**6** The command to be "strong and courageous" is repeated three times in God's charge to Joshua (vv.6–9) and again in the people's reply to Joshua (v.18). Perhaps Joshua was intimidated by the greatness of his predecessor Moses and the awesomeness of his own responsibility. For this reason courage is emphasized in the Lord's charge to him. This passage introduces the two major parts of the book: the conquest of the land (chs. 1–12) and the division of the land (chs. 13–21).

**7** "The law my servant Moses gave you" was probably some part or all of the Book of Deuteronomy (cf. Deut 1:5 where the contents of Deuteronomy are specifically called "this law," and see Deut 31:9–13). The many material and verbal parallels with

Deuteronomy show that the author of Joshua was familiar with its contents. The covenant relationship between Israel and God as given at Sinai was contingent on Israel's obedience to the law. The expression "to the right or to the left" is a vivid way of stating that no deviation would be permitted.

**8–9** Verse 8 is the theme verse of Joshua. Throughout the rest of the book, the author draws illustrations from this crucial period in Israel's history to demonstrate that God blesses his people when they obey him. The book may have been written in a period of apostasy and national disaster in an effort to call the people back to obedience (see Introduction, p. 244). The phrase "from your mouth" refers to the custom of muttering while studying or reflecting. The Hebrew word translated "meditate" (*hāḡāh*) literally means "mutter." When one continually mutters God's Word to himself, he is constantly thinking about it. Knowledge of God's law is not enough; one must also "be careful to do" what it commands. Thus the law of God is to control all thought and action. "Everything written in it" must be observed, because obedience to certain parts only is no obedience at all. As the Epistle of James (2:8–13) explains, such a practice shows respect for certain parts of the law only, but not for the Lawgiver.

## 2. *Joshua's orders to the officers*

### 1:10–11

10So Joshua ordered the officers of the people: 11"Go through the
camp and tell the people, 'Get your supplies ready. Three days from now
you will cross the Jordan here to go in and take possession of the land
the LORD your God is giving you for your own.'"

**10** Joshua had a well-organized chain of command by which orders quickly could be passed to the people. In this chain of command, of course, the Lord was always above Joshua.

**11** The supplies would have included the manna that God continued to provide until Israel crossed into the land (5:12). Each man was responsible for his own supplies since there was no regular quartermaster's corps. Once the Israelites were in the land, they found a ready food supply standing in the fields, because the invasion was begun during the harvest season (3:15). "Three days" is a stereotyped phrase that is common throughout the Bible. It simply means "the day after tomorrow" or "in a few days" (2:16, 22; 3:2; 9:16). It is difficult, if not impossible, to correlate all the references to "three days" in chapters 1–3.

## 3. *Joshua's orders to the Transjordanian tribes*

### 1:12–15

12But to the Reubenites, the Gadites and the half-tribe of Manasseh,
Joshua said, 13"Remember the command that Moses the servant of the
LORD gave you: 'The LORD your God is giving you rest and has granted
you this land.' 14Your wives, your children and your livestock may stay in
the land that Moses gave you east of the Jordan, but all your fighting
men, fully armed, must cross over ahead of your brothers. You are to
help your brothers 15until the LORD gives them rest, as he has done for
you, and until they too have taken possession of the land that the LORD

**your God is giving them. After that, you may go back and occupy your own land, which Moses the servant of the LORD gave you east of the Jordan toward the sunrise."**

**12** Throughout the book special attention is given to "the Reubenites, the Gadites and the half-tribe of Manasseh" (4:12–13; 13:8–32; 22:1–34). In his concern to guard against any possible estrangement of the two and one-half tribes from the rest of Israel, the author takes great pains to emphasize that all twelve tribes participated in the Conquest (cf. 22:24–25). Although their territory was included in the larger boundaries promised to Israel (1:3–4), the narrative at times seems to place the two and one-half tribes outside the Promised Land, strictly speaking, as is the case here (cf. 22:19). Later history demonstrated the consequences that resulted from their being cut off from the rest of Israel by the Jordan River and from their being exposed to their enemies through lack of natural boundaries.

**13** Moses' command is recorded in Deuteronomy 3:18–20 (cf. Num 32:20–22). The single quotation marks around part of v.13 suggest that that part is a direct quotation from Moses. It is possible, however, that all of vv.13b–15 is a rather free quotation of Deuteronomy 3:18–20. "Rest" implies secure borders and peace with all their enemies. It is an important concept in the OT (cf. Ruth 1:9; 3:1 NIV mg.). In the NT it is a type of spiritual salvation (Heb 4:1–11).

**14** It is necessary to interpret the phrase "all your fighting men," because Numbers 26:7, 18, 34 indicates that these tribes had as many as 110,000 men capable of bearing arms. Nevertheless, Joshua 4:13 states that only 40,000 warriors from the two and one-half tribes entered Canaan. Perhaps only the ablest fighting men participated in the Conquest while the others cared for the women, children, elderly, and domestic animals (cf. 22:8). The ablest men were to lead the march because they were not encumbered with families and livestock.

**15** For the return of these tribes to their own land, see 22:1–4. The account of Moses' assigning Transjordan as their inheritance is in Numbers 32.

### 4. *Joshua confirmed as leader*

#### 1:16–18

**16Then they answered Joshua, "Whatever you have commanded us we will do, and wherever you send us we will go. 17Just as we fully obeyed Moses, so we will obey you. Only may the LORD your God be with you as he was with Moses. 18Whoever rebels against your word and does not obey your words, whatever you may command them, will be put to death. Only be strong and courageous!"**

**16** It seems that this paragraph deals with all Israel, not just the Transjordanian tribes. The concern of this chapter is the transfer of leadership to Joshua, and we would expect the climax to be reached when the entire nation jubilantly acknowledged Joshua as Moses' successor (cf. 1 Sam 11:15, where the people ratified God's choice of Saul).

**17** The people pledged to Joshua the same allegiance that they had shown Moses. It is not clear whether the words "may the LORD your God be with you" are meant as a condition for their allegiance or whether they are meant as a prayer. They seem to be saying, "We will follow your leading so long as there is evidence that you are being led by God."

**18** The severity of the punishment threatened was in keeping with the military situation where strict discipline was required. This punishment was actually carried out in the case of Achan (ch. 7).

## B. *Gaining a Foothold: Jericho and Ai (2:1–8:35)*

### 1. *Rahab and the spies (2:1–24)*

#### a. *Sending the spies*

2:1–7

[1]Then Joshua son of Nun secretly sent two spies from Shittim. "Go, look over the land," he said, "especially Jericho." So they went and entered the house of a prostitute named Rahab and stayed there.
[2]The king of Jericho was told, "Look! Some of the Israelites have come here tonight to spy out the land." [3]So the king of Jericho sent this message to Rahab: "Bring out the men who came to you and entered your house, because they have come to spy out the whole land."
[4]But the woman had taken the two men and hidden them. She said, "Yes, the men came to me, but I did not know where they had come from. [5]At dusk, when it was time to close the city gate, the men left. I don't know which way they went. Go after them quickly. You may catch up with them." [6](But she had taken them up to the roof and hidden them under the stalks of flax she had laid out on the roof.) [7]So the men set out in pursuit of the spies on the road that leads to the fords of the Jordan, and as soon as the pursuers had gone out, the gate was shut.

**1** Why does the text specify that the spies were sent "secretly"? Any spy mission would have to be kept secret from the enemy. Perhaps Joshua was determined to keep it secret even from the Israelites because a negative report, such as the one brought back from an earlier spy mission (Num 13–14), might demoralize the people. The sending of spies was not an act of unbelief. The promise of divine aid never rules out human responsibility. Throughout the Book of Joshua, we find a bewildering interweaving of human action and divine intervention. Evidence suggests that Joshua sent spies before every major battle (cf. 7:2). The words "especially Jericho" indicate that this espionage mission was focused on Jericho, which was a formidable fortress guarding the pass leading westward into the mountainous region. Jericho was particularly important as the scene of Israel's first military engagement in the Promised Land.

Josephus (Antiq. V, 8 [i.2]) sought to clear the spies of any suspicion for having stayed at the house of a prostitute by calling Rahab an "innkeeper" (cf. NIV mg.). "Innkeeper" and "prostitute," however, were synonymous terms in that culture (cf. TWOT, p. 246). Rahab's house was the only place where the men could stay with any hope of remaining undetected and where they would be able to gather the information they were seeking. Moreover, her house afforded an easy way of escape since it was located on the city wall (v.15). There is no indication that Rahab was a temple prostitute.

The Hebrew word translated "stayed" (*šāḵaḇ*) can mean "lie down to sleep" or "lie down for sexual intercourse." Our text gives little help in clarifying this ambiguity. In view of the spies' very precarious circumstances, it seems highly unlikely that they engaged Rahab's professional services.

**2** For the most part the towns of Palestine were independent city-states at this time, and their rulers were called kings. The spies had failed in their attempt to remain undetected. The king was always first to be informed about such important matters. The report that "some of the Israelites have come" was the worst news conceivable. Rahab indicated that all her fellow citizens were in terror of the Israelites (vv.9–11; cf. Exod 15:15c). The word "tonight" must refer to late afternoon, because the spies would not have been able to enter the city after dark.

**3** The king would have assumed that the spies were staying with Rahab. In antiquity too, as in modern times, prostitutes frequently were involved in intelligence activities. The king expected Rahab to do her patriotic duty and turn the spies in. The ancient law code of Hammurabi contains the following provision: "If felons are banded together in an ale-wife's [prostitute's or innkeeper's] house and she has not haled [them] to the palace, that ale-wife shall be put to death" (S.R. Driver and J.C. Miles, *The Babylonian Laws* [Oxford: Clarendon, 1956], 2:45).

**4** In 6:17 Joshua explained that Rahab was to be spared because she hid the spies. Rahab lied as much in what she did as in what she said. Deception is an important strategy in warfare. Espionage would be impossible without it. When Rahab hid the spies, she sided with Israel against her own people. It was an act of treason!

**5** Rahab told the king's men to "go after them quickly." She made it clear that if the king's men tarried, the spies would escape. She did not want to take a chance on having her house searched, because she knew that anyone suspected of collaborating with the spies would be put to death.

**6** The flat-roofed houses of that era were suitable for drying grain or stalks. Rahab used her flax stalks to good advantage.

**7** The road mentioned here led from Jerusalem to Jericho and then eastward across the Jordan River (Aharoni, p. 60). The "fords" were places where the river was normally shallow enough to cross on foot. Though the river was at flood stage, the spies were able to cross without a miracle. When the pursuers went out, "the gate was shut"; i.e., it was closed again (see v.5). This detail is added to underscore the predicament of the spies, who were trapped inside the city.

## Notes

**4** The Hebrew has a singular suffix "him" on וַתִּצְפְּנוֹ (*wattiṣpᵉnô*, "and she hid him"). The LXX has αὐτοὺς (*autous*, "them"). Whether this difference reflects a different source document or an emendation by the translators to conform to the context is unknown.

**6** The editors of the NIV have enclosed v.6 in parentheses to indicate that this action took place earlier. Hebrew narrative is often written thematically and does not follow rigid rules of chronology.

There is another spelling of the pronoun הִיא (*hîʾ*, "she") that is common in the *Kethiv* of the Pentateuch—הִוא (*hîwʾ*; cf. Gen 4:22; 20:5; 38:25; et al.)—but is not found anywhere in Joshua. This detail indicates that the Book of Joshua is separate from the Pentateuch and not part of a Hexateuch.

---

## b. *Rahab's covenant with the spies*

### 2:8–21

8 Before the spies lay down for the night, she went up on the roof 9 and
said to them, "I know that the LORD has given this land to you and that a
great fear of you has fallen on us, so that all who live in this country are
melting in fear because of you. 10 We have heard how the LORD dried up
the water of the Red Sea for you when you came out of Egypt, and what
you did to Sihon and Og, the two kings of the Amorites east of the
Jordan, whom you completely destroyed. 11 When we heard of it, our
hearts melted and everyone's courage failed because of you, for the
LORD your God is God in heaven above and on the earth below. 12 Now
then, please swear to me by the LORD that you will show kindness to my
family, because I have shown kindness to you. Give me a sure sign
13 that you will spare the lives of my father and mother, my brothers and
sisters, and all who belong to them, and that you will save us from
death."

14 "Our lives for your lives!" the men assured her. "If you don't tell
what we are doing, we will treat you kindly and faithfully when the LORD
gives us the land."

15 So she let them down by a rope through the window, for the house
she lived in was part of the city wall. 16 Now she had said to them, "Go to
the hills so the pursuers will not find you. Hide yourselves there three
days until they return, and then go on your way."

17 The men said to her, "This oath you made us swear will not be
binding on us 18 unless, when we enter the land, you have tied this
scarlet cord in the window through which you let us down, and unless
you have brought your father and mother, your brothers and all your
family into your house. 19 If anyone goes outside your house into the
street, his blood will be on his own head; we will not be responsible. As
for anyone who is in the house with you, his blood will be on our head if
a hand is laid on him. 20 But if you tell what we are doing, we will be
released from the oath you made us swear."

21 "Agreed," she replied. "Let it be as you say." So she sent them away
and they departed. And she tied the scarlet cord in the window.

The large amount of space the author devotes to Rahab's bargaining with the spies shows that this is his primary interest in this chapter.

**8** The spies may have intended to "[lie] down for the night," but their rest was interrupted. These words must mean "before they had settled in for the night" or "before they had fallen asleep," since they would have had to have been lying down already to have been hidden under the flax.

**9** It is truly remarkable how much Rahab knew about Israel's history and God's plans for Israel's future. One of God's great purposes in the Exodus had been to make these same facts known to Pharaoh and the Egyptians (Exod 7:5). Rahab spoke of the takeover of the land as if it were an accomplished fact: "I know that the LORD *has given* this land to you" (emphasis mine). What God had done for Israel in Egypt and in Transjordan convinced Rahab that God was able to give Israel this land, too. The "great fear" that had fallen on all the people was predicted in Exodus 15:15b–16:

> The people of Canaan will melt away;
> terror and dread will fall upon them.
> By the power of your arm
> they will be as still as a stone—
> until your people pass by, O LORD,
> until the people you bought pass by.

**10** On the Lord's drying up the "Red Sea," see Exodus 14:21–31. For "Sihon and Og," see Numbers 21:21–35. "Amorites" is a general term designating the inhabitants of the mountainous regions on both sides of the Jordan. "Completely destroyed" is the translation of the Hebrew word *ḥerem,* which is a technical term for the ancient practice of completely destroying the spoils of warfare as a way of devoting them to a deity (cf. 6:17).

**11** Morale is always a major factor in warfare. Gideon excused all who were fearful from serving in his army (Judg 7:3). Fear is contagious and can even cause the defeat of an army that is superior in all other respects. The high point of this chapter is Rahab's confession of her faith. Her statement, "The LORD your God is God in heaven above and on the earth below," is remarkable for a pagan and is evidence of her conversion to faith in Israel's God.

**12** "Kindness" represents the Hebrew word *ḥeseḏ,* which is often translated "love" in the NIV, especially in the Psalms. In contexts like this, *ḥeseḏ* designates a reciprocal relationship of caring. This is clearly seen in Rahab's words: "you will show kindness to my family, because I have shown kindness to you." In delivering the spies from the king's officers, she risked her life and set herself against her own people. In return for this she deserved to be assured of her own safety and the safety of her family. The words "Give me a sure sign" should be included in the main sentence in v.12. They form the following parallel: "swear to me . . . give me a sure sign." Verse 13 should begin with the imperative, "Spare the lives."

**13** When Rahab requested that the spies "spare the lives" of her family, she may have been asking no more than that they be taken alive as prisoners (cf. LXX: *zōgrēsete,* "to capture alive"). Eventually, however, they were assimilated into the nation (6:25). In Scripture salvation is frequently a family matter: the Israelites celebrated the Passover by families (Exod 12:3); Joshua decided for his whole family that they would serve the Lord (24:15; cf. "you and your household" in Acts 16:31). The family members would demonstrate their personal faith by gathering in Rahab's house and remaining there (see excursus on p. 264). The phrase "all who belong to them" is ambiguous in Hebrew and may refer to their entire households or to all their possessions or to both.

**14** In the statement "If you don't tell" the pronoun is plural: Rahab and her entire family would have to guard this secret.

**15** Houses, such as Rahab's, constructed within the wall have been discovered by archaeologists in the ruins of ancient Jericho (Wood, p. 56).

**16** The translators of the NIV have used the past perfect "she had said" to indicate that the conversation in vv.16–21 occurred before Rahab lowered the spies to the ground. Hebrew narrative is often governed by thematic concerns rather than precise chronology. For the expression "three days," see the comment on 1:11. The hills to the west of Jericho are a barren wasteland. The king's officers had gone in the opposite direction.

**17–21** The spies laid down three conditions: (1) the scarlet cord must be placed in Rahab's window (v.18a); (2) Rahab's whole family must stay in her house (vv.18b–19); and (3) the covenant between Rahab and the spies must be kept secret (v.20). These were practical ways for Rahab and her family to demonstrate their faith.

Perhaps in v.17 we should read "the men *had said* to her," as in v.16. It is not likely that this lengthy conversation took place with Rahab at the window and the men shouting from below. Here and elsewhere elements of the story are so arranged as to intensify the suspense.

The "scarlet cord" (v.18) would identify Rahab's house. The spies, who were unaware of the mighty miracle that God would perform, were anticipating a house-to-house battle in which the Israelites would have been instructed to spare the house so marked. Though the scarlet cord reminds us of the blood of Christ, no typological relationship is stated anywhere in Scripture. There are striking similarities to the Passover: compare the scarlet cord with the sprinkled blood and the requirement that Rahab's family remain in the house with the command that the Passover be eaten in family units and that no one was to leave the house (Exod 12:21–23). In both cases faith was expressed through obedience.

The statement "his blood will be on his own head" (v.19) means that whoever disobeys the instruction to stay in the house will be responsible for his own death.

Since the spies did not know that God would use a miracle to capture the city, they may have arranged a plan by which Rahab would deliver the city into Israel's hands. This could be what Rahab was not to tell anyone (v.20). The statement "she tied the scarlet cord in the window" (v.21) forms a fitting conclusion for this section because it points to Rahab's faith in action.

## Notes

**14** In the MT תַּגִּידוּ (*taggîḏû*, "[you] tell") is second person plural. The reference may be to Rahab and her whole family. Other Hebrew MSS have the singular form referring to Rahab alone (cf. v.20).

**15** The presence of the article in בַּחֶבֶל (*baḥeḇel*)—literally, "*the* rope"—is surprising inasmuch as this is the first mention of any rope. Could it have been a rope for some special purpose such as pulling the flax to the roof (cf. GKC, 126*r*)?

### c. *The report of the spies*

#### 2:22–24

**22When they left, they went into the hills and stayed there three days,
until the pursuers had searched all along the road and returned without
finding them. 23Then the two men started back. They went down out of
the hills, forded the river and came to Joshua son of Nun and told him
everything that had happened to them. 24They said to Joshua, "The LORD
has surely given the whole land into our hands; all the people are
melting in fear because of us."**

**22** It is remarkable that the spies trusted Rahab so implicitly as to follow her instructions.

**23** Since the spies "told him everything," we must assume that v.24 is only a summary of what the spies said.

**24** The narrative ends triumphantly. The spies learned two very important facts: God had been faithful to his promise, and the inhabitants of the land were totally demoralized.

## Excursus: The Conversion of Rahab

Rahab's bold act of hiding the Israelite spies is interpreted by the NT as evidence of saving faith (Heb 11:31; James 2:25). We may call this her conversion experience because she turned from her pagan gods and from her people to identify with Israel and Israel's God. There are a number of "negative" points about her conversion: She was a prostitute by profession; she lied to protect the spies; she was motivated by fear; and she struck a shrewd bargain with the spies. Nevertheless, the glorious outcome of it all is indicated by the inclusion of her name in the genealogy of Jesus (Matt 1:5).

In considering Rahab's lie we must remember that she did not deceive with words alone but also by her actions. All espionage involves deception. Indeed, deception and surprise are two of the most effective strategies in warfare. The Hebrew concept of truth is not only conformity with fact but also faithfulness. Rahab chose to be faithful to the Israelites and their God. In so doing she committed an act of treason against her own people. Psalm 25:3 speaks of those "who are treacherous without excuse," which suggests that there may be times when treason is justified.

The spies violated God's explicit command that none of the people living in the land were to be spared (Deut 7:1–6; 20:16–18). Rahab, however, turned to God and sought deliverance. Her experience is proof of the gracious saving purpose of God. His overarching decree is that "everyone who calls on the name of the LORD will be saved" (Joel 2:32). This is one of the most dramatic examples of grace in the OT and is set in bold relief by the questionable aspects of Rahab's profession and conversion.

The salvation of Rahab is an example of what God would have done for others also. The king and the other citizens of Jericho knew all that she knew, but they did not turn to Israel's God for mercy. The fear that drove her to beg for mercy drove them in their stubborn rebellion. Accordingly, the others are called "the disobedient" in Hebrews 11:31 (cf. the story of the Gibeonites in ch. 9).

## 2. *Crossing the Jordan (3:1–4:24)*

The great climactic event in the Book of Joshua—crossing the Jordan—comes near the beginning. It marks the completion of God's redemptive act that began with the Exodus. This is made clear by the parallels between these two events. Psalm 114 refers to them as the crucial events through which God formed Israel as his own people.

### a. *Instructions for crossing*

3:1–13

1 Early in the morning Joshua and all the Israelites set out from Shittim
and went to the Jordan, where they camped before crossing over. 2 After
three days the officers went throughout the camp, 3 giving orders to the
people: "When you see the ark of the covenant of the LORD your God,
and the priests, who are Levites, carrying it, you are to move out from
your positions and follow it. 4 Then you will know which way to go, since
you have never been this way before. But keep a distance of about a
thousand yards between you and the ark; do not go near it."
5 Joshua told the people, "Consecrate yourselves, for tomorrow the
LORD will do amazing things among you."
6 Joshua said to the priests, "Take up the ark of the covenant and pass
on ahead of the people." So they took it up and went ahead of them.
7 And the LORD said to Joshua, "Today I will begin to exalt you in the
eyes of all Israel, so they may know that I am with you as I was with
Moses. 8 Tell the priests who carry the ark of the covenant: 'When you
reach the edge of the Jordan's waters, go and stand in the river.'"
9 Joshua said to the Israelites, "Come here and listen to the words of
the LORD your God. 10 This is how you will know that the living God is
among you and that he will certainly drive out before you the
Canaanites, Hittites, Hivites, Perizzites, Girgashites, Amorites and Jebusites. 11 See, the ark of the covenant of the Lord of all the earth will go
into the Jordan ahead of you. 12 Now then, choose twelve men from the
tribes of Israel, one from each tribe. 13 And as soon as the priests who
carry the ark of the LORD—the Lord of all the earth—set foot in the
Jordan, its waters flowing downstream will be cut off and stand up in a
heap."

**1** The journey from Shittim to the Jordan (c. ten miles) must have taken the better part of the day.

**2** "After three days" is a Hebrew idiom meaning "on the third day" (see commentary on 1:11).

**3** "The ark of the covenant" is the most prominent feature in these two chapters. The presence of the ark indicates that the crossing of the Jordan was much more than a military maneuver: It was a religious procession. The ark was a portable shrine built as a rectangular box, twenty-seven inches wide by twenty-seven inches high by forty-five inches long. It was overlaid with gold. The cover of the ark had a golden cherub on each end facing toward the middle. It was between these two cherubs that God met with Israel (Exod 25:10–22). The ark symbolized God's presence among his people. When the ark was carried across the Jordan, the Lord was marching in to claim his land. The expression "the priests, who are Levites" is redundant since all legitimate priests in Israel were Levites (cf. Num 3:5–13). The priests alone were permitted to carry the ark. The phrase "from your positions" is a reference to the specific locations that were assigned to the various tribes whenever they set up camp (cf. Num 2).

**4** The people were warned to "keep a distance" away from the ark because it was very holy. To maintain this distance of about "a thousand yards" while crossing the Jordan, they would have had to cross one-half mile upstream or one-half mile downstream. It is reasonable to suppose that they maintained this distance only until the priests were stationed with the ark in the middle of the river.

**5** The people were to be holy because God is holy, the ark was holy, and the event itself was holy. Consecration involved bathing, washing one's clothing, and abstinence from sexual activity (cf. Exod 19:14–15). "Amazing things" are miraculous things.

**6** The priests were commanded to take up the ark and cross over, but they were not told how they would be enabled to cross the river, which was overflowing its banks (v.15). In a similar way the Lord led Israel to the Red Sea without indicating how they would get across. Very often God waits for us to step out in faith before he opens the way for us.

**7** The appointment of Joshua as leader of the people would now be confirmed in action. One major reason for the great miracle was to demonstrate that God was with Joshua as surely as he had been with Moses.

**8** With the command "Go and stand in the river," the narrator builds the suspense. There is still no indication how the people will get through the water.

**9–10** There is no article in Hebrew in the phrase "the living God" (v.10). Without the article emphasis is placed on the fact that Israel's God is *living*. Joshua is not simply stating that the living God is *with* them. He is affirming that the God who marches with Israel is one who is able to act and to perform mighty deeds in contrast to the pagan gods that have eyes but cannot see, etc. (cf. Ps 115:3–7). Either term, "Canaanites" or "Amorites," can be used to designate the whole population of Canaan. Strictly speaking the Canaanites were the people living in the lowlands of the sea coast and the Jordan valley (Num 13:29), while the Amorites lived in the mountainous areas ("their name perhaps signifying mountain dwellers," TWOT, p. 56). For "Hittites" see 1:4. The emissaries from Gibeon are called "Hivites" in 9:7. Some Hivites were living also at the foot of Mount Hermon near Mizpah (11:3). Shechem, who fell in love with Jacob's daughter, Dinah, was called a Hivite also (Gen 34:2). The "Perizzites" lived in the central highlands in the time of Abraham and Jacob (Gen 13:7; 34:30). The "Gergashites" are mentioned here although they are not always included in the lists of the Canaanite populations. Their inclusion makes the number of nations seven—the number of completeness. The "Jebusites" inhabited Jerusalem (15:63), which was formerly called Jebus. Jebusites lived also in the hill country of northern Palestine (11:3).

**11** The way the people would cross the Jordan still had not been revealed. The ark would go before them, which signifies that God would go with them and prepare the way.

**12** The command to "choose twelve men" seems out of place here. It interrupts the flow of the narrative, and there is no explanation of why they were to be chosen or what they were to do. Perhaps this verse indicates when the men were actually selected, and 4:2–3, where the command is repeated, is the point in the narrative where the mission of the twelve was carried out.

**13** In the phrase "the LORD—the Lord of all the earth," observe the difference in the way the word "lord" is printed. Whenever it is printed with one large and three small capitals, it represents the sacred name "Yahweh." The Jews, out of reverence for God's holy name, regularly substituted the Hebrew word "Lord" (*'ᵃḏōnāy*) when they came to the name "Yahweh" (*YHWH*) in reading the Scriptures. The second occurrence of "Lord" in our verse, printed with one capital and the rest small letters, represents that Hebrew word (*'ᵃḏōn*), which actually means "lord," "ruler," or "owner." One of the great themes in both the Exodus and the Conquest is that Israel's God is the Lord of all the earth (cf. Exod 9:29). This gave Israel the right to take over the land. Moreover, Israel's victories were proof of their God's sovereignty over all the earth. Here, at last, we are told how the people would be able to cross. The regular flow of the river would be cut off upstream where the waters would collect in a heap. We must carefully observe all the clues in the text when attempting to visualize what actually happened.

## Notes

3 The LXX has τοὺς ἱερεῖς . . . καὶ τοὺς Λευίτας (*tous hiereis . . . kai tous Levitas*, "the priests and the Levites") for the MT's וְהַכֹּהֲנִים הַלְוִיִּם (*wᵉhakkōhᵃnîm halwîyim*, "and the priests, who are Levites").

4 In Hebrew the warning to stay far away from the ark comes first and gives greater emphasis to the sacredness of the ark. The same order in English would be confusing. It would seem to say that they would know the way to go by keeping away from the ark rather than by following it.

11 The article on הַבְּרִית (*habbᵉrîṯ*, lit., "the covenant") is difficult to interpret. GKC (128*c*) calls it an interpolation. Perhaps, however, אֲדוֹן כָּל־הָאָרֶץ (*'ᵃḏôn kol-hā'āreṣ*, "the Lord of all the earth") is in apposition to אֲרוֹן הַבְּרִית (*'ᵃrôn habbᵉrîṯ*, "the ark of the covenant") and means "the ark of the covenant," i.e., "the Lord of the whole earth."

### b. *Crossing on dry ground*

#### 3:14–17

**¹⁴**So when the people broke camp to cross the Jordan, the priests carrying the ark of the covenant went ahead of them. **¹⁵**Now the Jordan is at flood stage all during harvest. Yet as soon as the priests who carried the ark reached the Jordan and their feet touched the water's edge, **¹⁶**the water from upstream stopped flowing. It piled up in a heap a

**great distance away, at a town called Adam in the vicinity of Zarethan,**
**while the water flowing down to the Sea of the Arabah (the Salt Sea) was**
**completely cut off. So the people crossed over opposite Jericho. 17 The**
**priests who carried the ark of the covenant of the LORD stood firm on dry**
**ground in the middle of the Jordan, while all Israel passed by until the**
**whole nation had completed the crossing on dry ground.**

**14–16a** After the Israelites "broke camp," the priests led the way bearing the ark of the covenant (v.14). In stating that the Jordan was at "flood stage" (v.15), the narrator skillfully builds the suspense by suggesting the natural impossibility of what was about to happen. The statement that "as soon as . . . their feet touched the water's edge, the water . . . stopped flowing" (vv.15–16a) may be an example of narrative heightening, i.e., a kind of exaggeration or hyperbole used to convey a true sense of wonder at the great miracle that was taking place. The flow of the water had to have stopped upstream prior to the moment that the priests approached the river, or else it would have taken time for the water to flow away downstream after they stepped into the river's edge.

**16b** The flow of the river was interrupted, and the waters began to collect "in a heap" upstream. "Adam" was a city located about twenty miles upstream from where the Israelites crossed the Jordan. Aharoni (p. 34) states that "the vicinity of Adam was famous for the occasional landslides which dammed the floods of the Jordan." There is some ambiguity in the Hebrew preposition ḇ, which is translated "at" here: it could mean "from" (see Notes). Such a translation would suggest that the water was stopped near the place where the Israelites were and was backed up all the way to Adam. "At" seems to be the better translation. In that case, however, the water stopped too far upstream for the Israelites to have seen it, and the timing had to be perfect for the waters to be exhausted at the precise moment that the priests stepped into the river. "The Sea of the Arabah" is the Dead Sea. With the water from upstream "completely cut off," the water flowing downstream was soon emptied into the Dead Sea.

**17** The Hebrew term for "dry ground" (*ḥārāḇāh*) does not require that the riverbed be powdery dry but simply means that it was no longer covered with water. This indicates terra firma as contrasted to the flooding river (cf. 4:18, where the term "dry ground" is used to distinguish the bank from the riverbed).

## Notes

**14** The words הָאָרוֹן הַבְּרִית (*hā'ārôn habb*$^{e}$*rîṯ*, "the ark of the covenant") usually occur in a construct relationship (cf. v.11), but not here. Either *habb*$^{e}$*rîṯ* is an attributive so that the phrase means "the covenant ark" or it is an appositive, and the phrase means "the ark," i.e., "the covenant."

**16** The *Kethiv* has באדם (*b'dm*, lit., "at Adam"); the *Qere* has מֵאָדָם (*mē'āḏām*, "from Adam"). See the comment on this verse.

### c. *Memorials to the Crossing (4:1–24)*

#### 1) *Twelve stones from the riverbed*

4:1–9

1 When the whole nation had finished crossing the Jordan, the LORD
said to Joshua, 2 "Choose twelve men from among the people, one from
each tribe, 3 and tell them to take up twelve stones from the middle of
the Jordan from right where the priests stood and to carry them over
with you and put them down at the place where you stay tonight."
4 So Joshua called together the twelve men he had appointed from the
Israelites, one from each tribe, 5 and said to them, "Go over before the
ark of the LORD your God into the middle of the Jordan. Each of you is to
take up a stone on his shoulder, according to the number of the tribes of
the Israelites, 6 to serve as a sign among you. In the future, when your
children ask you, 'What do these stones mean?' 7 tell them that the flow
of the Jordan was cut off before the ark of the covenant of the LORD.
When it crossed the Jordan, the waters of the Jordan were cut off. These
stones are to be a memorial to the people of Israel forever."
8 So the Israelites did as Joshua commanded them. They took twelve
stones from the middle of the Jordan, according to the number of the
tribes of the Israelites, as the LORD had told Joshua; and they carried
them over with them to their camp, where they put them down. 9 Joshua
set up the twelve stones that had been in the middle of the Jordan at the
spot where the priests who carried the ark of the covenant had stood.
And they are there to this day.

**1** The frequent repetition of the phrase "the LORD said to Joshua" emphasizes the fact that everything was done in obedience to God's commands.

**2** If the narrative followed a strict chronological order, it would mean that these men crossed all the way over and were then sent back into the riverbed. The command was actually given, however, before the people began to cross; and it is recorded here at the point in the narrative when the men actually picked up the stones on their way across the river (see commentary on 3:12).

**3** Stones taken from the middle of the riverbed were remarkable evidence that the river had actually stopped flowing to allow Israel to cross over.

**4–6a** The Hebrew word *lip̱nê* often means "before" in the sense of "ahead of," but another common meaning, "in the presence of," is preferable here in v.5. The twelve men found their stones near the place where the priests carrying the ark were standing. The stones were "to serve as a sign" for future generations (v.6a).

**6b–9** The raising of stones as a memorial is common in the OT (cf. 7:26; 24:26–27; Gen 28:18–22; 31:45–47; 1 Sam 7:12). These memorials were intended to provoke questioning so that the story of God's miraculous interventions might be told over and over. The miracles would not be repeated—in fact, there is an economy of miracles in Scripture. Remembering was a way for future generations to participate in the great acts that God had done for Israel.

## Notes

**2–3** The plural imperatives קְחוּ (*qᵉḥû*, "choose") and וְצַוּוּ (*wᵉṣawwû*, "and tell") are unexpected. The divine commands to Joshua are usually expressed in the singular. The LXX, Syriac, and Vulgate all have the singulars.

**9** From a grammatical standpoint the translation in the NIV footnote is preferable: "Joshua also set up twelve stones [in the middle of the Jordan]." In Hebrew there is no article on the word "stones," אֲבָנִים, in the phrase וּשְׁתֵּים עֶשְׂרֵה אֲבָנִים (*ûštêm ʿeśrēh ʾᵃḇānîm*, "twelve stones)." If the author had been referring to the same twelve stones, an article would have been expected. The LXX seeks to clarify by adding the word "other" (*allous*): "twelve *other* stones." Some commentators assume that only one memorial was set up and argue that two variant accounts have been combined here. According to one account, the memorial was set up in the river. According to the other, it was placed on the shore. The NIV translators have opted for one memorial. The Hebrew text, however, states that Joshua erected two memorials, one of which was in the middle of the river where it could be seen whenever the river was low.

### 2) *The flow of the Jordan restored*

#### 4:10–18

10Now the priests who carried the ark remained standing in the
middle of the Jordan until everything the LORD had commanded Joshua
was done by the people, just as Moses had directed Joshua. The people
hurried over, 11and as soon as all of them had crossed, the ark of the
LORD and the priests came to the other side while the people watched.
12The men of Reuben, Gad and the half-tribe of Manasseh crossed over,
armed, in front of the Israelites, as Moses had directed them. 13About
forty thousand armed for battle crossed over before the LORD to the
plains of Jericho for war.
14That day the LORD exalted Joshua in the sight of all Israel; and they
revered him all the days of his life, just as they had revered Moses.
15Then the LORD said to Joshua, 16"Command the priests carrying the
ark of the Testimony to come up out of the Jordan."
17So Joshua commanded the priests, "Come up out of the Jordan."
18And the priests came up out of the river carrying the ark of the
covenant of the LORD. No sooner had they set their feet on the dry
ground than the waters of the Jordan returned to their place and ran at
flood stage as before.

**10** The statement "just as Moses had directed Joshua" reminds us again that Joshua's ministry was subservient to that of Moses. There is no record that Moses gave Joshua explicit instructions for crossing the Jordan, although such a crossing is implied in Deuteronomy 31:7. "The people *hurried* over" because the river was stopped for a limited time only.

**11** The clause "while the people watched" is an interpretation of the Hebrew words *lipnê hāʿām* (lit., "before the people"). It is clear that the priests did not march out of the river until *after* the people had crossed over. Therefore the word "before" must be understood in a spatial sense, i.e., "in the sight of."

**12** Again we see how important it was to our writer to emphasize that the Transjordanian tribes had a primary role in the conquest of the land of Canaan (cf. comment on 1:12). They went ahead of the other Israelites.

**13** For "forty-thousand," see comment on 1:14. They were "armed for battle" and thus were prepared in the event that the inhabitants of the land should attack while Israel was crossing the river.

**14** "The LORD exalted Joshua" as he had promised (3:7). Joshua was now firmly established as leader in the place of Moses. The parallel to Exodus 14:31 is striking.

**15–18** The following order is customary in Joshua: The Lord told Joshua (vv.15–16), Joshua told the people (v.17), and the command was obeyed (v.18). In this way the writer emphasizes that obedience is the prerequisite for God's blessing.

The Hebrew word for "dry ground" (*ḥārābāh,* v.18) is the same as in 3:17. Here it refers to the river bank as distinct from the riverbed. The miraculous element is heightened by stressing that the waters were cut off just long enough for Israel to cross over and then they "returned to their place."

## Notes

---

**18** The variation between the *Kethiv* בעלות (*b'lwt*) and the *Qere* כַּעֲלוֹת (*ka'alôṯ*) makes no difference in the meaning "when [the priests] came up."

---

### 3) *The significance of the stones*

### 4:19–24

[19]On the tenth day of the first month the people went up from the
Jordan and camped at Gilgal on the eastern border of Jericho. [20]And
Joshua set up at Gilgal the twelve stones they had taken out of the
Jordan. [21]He said to the Israelites, "In the future when your descendants
ask their fathers, 'What do these stones mean?' [22]tell them, 'Israel
crossed the Jordan on dry ground.' [23]For the LORD your God dried up
the Jordan before you until you had crossed over. The LORD your God
did to the Jordan just what he had done to the Red Sea when he dried it
up before us until we had crossed over. [24]He did this so that all the
peoples of the earth might know that the hand of the LORD is powerful
and so that you might always fear the LORD your God."

**19** The parallels between Moses and Joshua are obvious (cf. "the tenth day" here and in Exod 12:3). "Gilgal" was strategically located. The Jordan provided security on one side, and the open plain prevented any surprise attack from the other side. An abundant water supply was provided by the river. Gilgal was Israel's base of operations for some time (cf. 10:15, 43; 14:6).

**20** Joshua may have piled the stones in a heap, as in 7:26, or he may have placed them in a circle. Gilgal sounds like the Hebrew word for circle.

**21–23** Joshua foresaw the importance of this stone heap for future generations, as a memorial to the miraculous crossing (vv.21–22). Again the term "dry ground" is mentioned to emphasize the supernatural aspect of the crossing. Notice the pronoun "you" (v.23). Subsequent generations are to be told the story as if the event had happened to them personally so that they could participate in all that God had done for Israel (cf. the fluctuation of pronouns between second and third persons in 24:5–13). The crossings of the Red Sea and the Jordan were mighty miracles that were to be celebrated by Israel forever (cf. Ps. 114). They marked Israel's exodus from the land of bondage and entrance into the Land of Promise. They were a sign of Israel's transition from slavery to freedom.

**24** This verse gives two additional reasons for this great miracle: to impress the power of Israel's God on the nations and to confirm Israel's reverence for their God.

## Excursus: The Nature of the Miracle

It is possible that a landslide caused by an earthquake stopped the flow of the Jordan River. Landslides are common in the soft clay banks of the Jordan. At least two such landslides, each of which resulted in a damming of the river, are recorded in history: in A.D. 1267 and again in 1927. In the latter instance the slide occurred near the town of Adam (cf. 3:16), and the flow of the river was interrupted for about twenty-one hours. The Jordan Valley lies along one of the major faults on the earth's surface. Evidences of earthquake activity have been found in the excavations of Jericho. Moreover, there are indications in the Bible that earthquakes accompanied Israel's march into the Promised Land:

> O LORD, when you went out from Seir,
> when you marched from the land of Edom,
> *the earth shook*, the heavens poured,
> the clouds poured down water.
> *The mountains quaked* before the LORD, the One of Sinai,
> before the LORD, the God of Israel.
> (Judg 5:4–5, emphasis mine)

Psalm 114, which celebrates both the crossing of the Red Sea and the crossing of the Jordan, states:

> The sea looked and fled,
> the Jordan turned back;
> *the mountains skipped* like rams,
> the hills like lambs.
> . . . . . . . . . . . . . . . . . . . . . . . . . .
> *Tremble*, O earth, at the presence of the LORD.
> (Ps 114:3–4, 7, emphasis mine)

If an earthquake was responsible for stopping the Jordan River, it was still a miracle. The discovery of secondary causes only serves to explain how God did what he did, and only God's intervention can account for the miraculous timing. This must have been a remarkable example of what H.L. Ellison (*Joshua–2 Samuel* [Grand Rapids: Eerdmans, 1966], p. 7) calls "the supernatural use of the natural."

## 3. *Renewing the covenant with Israel (5:1–15)*

### a. *The covenant sign*

#### 5:1–9

1Now when all the Amorite kings west of the Jordan and all the
Canaanite kings along the coast heard how the LORD had dried up the
Jordan before the Israelites until we had crossed over, their hearts
melted and they no longer had the courage to face the Israelites.
2At that time the LORD said to Joshua, "Make flint knives and
circumcise the Israelites again." 3So Joshua made flint knives and
circumcised the Israelites at Gibeath Haaraloth.
4Now this is why he did so: All those who came out of Egypt—all the
men of military age—died in the desert on the way after leaving Egypt.
5All the people that came out had been circumcised, but all the people
born in the desert during the journey from Egypt had not. 6The Israelites
had moved about in the desert forty years until all the men who were of
military age when they left Egypt had died, since they had not obeyed
the LORD. For the LORD had sworn to them that they would not see the
land that he had solemnly promised their fathers to give us, a land
flowing with milk and honey. 7So he raised up their sons in their place,
and these were the ones Joshua circumcised. They were still uncircumcised because they had not been circumcised on the way. 8And after the
whole nation had been circumcised, they remained where they were in
camp until they were healed.
9Then the LORD said to Joshua, "Today I have rolled away the reproach
of Egypt from you." So the place has been called Gilgal to this day.

**1** The same formula, "Now when . . . heard," introduces chapters 9, 10, and 11. This transitional verse sums up the effect that the miraculous crossing of the Jordan had on the inhabitants of Canaan and explains how Israel could have been secure enough to observe the covenant ceremonies that follow. For Amorite and Canaanite, see comment on 3:10. News traveled fast, even in those times (cf. how much Rahab knew of Israel's history, 2:9–10). The use of the pronoun "we" cannot be taken as unmistaken evidence of an eyewitness report (see Notes). Later generations identified with the past events in Israel's history as if they themselves had actually been there. "Their hearts melted" with fear, but this did not result in their conversion as it did in the cases of Rahab and the Gibeonites (cf. 2:9–11; 9:9–11).

**2** This was the Bronze Age, when bronze implements were common; yet Joshua was commanded to make "flint knives." Religious ceremonies tend to preserve ancient customs. When God reaffirmed his covenant with Abraham, promising him the land of Canaan, he warned him that anyone who was not circumcised would be violating the covenant (Gen 17:7–14). Consequently, Israel could not claim the covenant land until the sign of the covenant had been restored. Here is another parallel between Moses and Joshua: When called to lead the covenant people out of Egypt, Moses had to restore the the covenant of circumcision in his own family (Exod 4:24–26). In the instructions God gave Moses for the Passover meal, no uncircumcised males were allowed to participate (cf. Exod 12:48–49). Circumcision may have been a puberty rite in some nations, but for Israel it marked one's entrance into the covenant community. In Hebrew this verse is redundant; it says, "Circumcise the Israelites again, a second time." There is no record that Joshua conducted any mass circumcision prior to this, nor was anyone to be circumcised over again. Joshua was reinstituting circumcision after it had been neglected during the forty years in the desert.

**3** The name "Gibeath Haaraloth" has a rather grotesque meaning: "the hill of the foreskins." Throughout the Promised Land there were monuments and place names that served to remind Israel of their history.

**4–5** It is strange that none of the males who were born in the desert were circumcised. The fact that Israel was always on the move is not an adequate explanation. Perhaps the sign of the covenant had been suspended while a whole generation rejected the covenant in disobedience and unbelief.

**6** Israel had disobeyed the Lord thirty-eight years earlier when they stood on the southern border of the Promised Land. Discouraged by the report of their spies, they did not believe God and would not obey his command to invade the land (Num 13–14). The stereotyped phrase "a land flowing with milk and honey" was used to describe the fruitfulness of the land (cf. Deut 11:9–12).

**7** God was fulfilling his promise in Numbers 14:31: "As for your children that you said would be taken as plunder, I will bring them in to enjoy the land you have rejected." This was a new beginning for the nation: The crossing of the Jordan symbolizes death and rebirth, and the renewal of circumcision constituted Israel anew as the people of God.

**8** The Conquest had to be delayed until the men recovered, for the Israelite warriors were temporarily rendered helpless by circumcision (cf. Gen 34:25). That circumcision had to be performed at this crucial moment shows how foundational the covenant relationship was between God and Israel. It is possible that a few males were living who had been circumcised in Egypt and who were under the age of twenty at the time of Israel's disobedience (cf. v.6).

**9** Since the Egyptians practiced circumcision, it is not likely that "the reproach of Egypt" refers to any inability to practice this rite in that land (cf. v.5). It probably means that the Israelites, now reestablished as the covenant people in the Land of Promise, had been delivered from their national disgrace of enslavement and homelessness. The name "Gilgal" sounds like the Hebrew word *gālal*, which means "to roll" (cf. the explanation given in the comment on 4:20). There are other instances in Scripture where a certain locality was given the same name on more than one occasion (cf. Gen 21:31 with Gen 26:33; and Gen 28:19 with Gen 35:14–15).

## Notes

---

1 The *Qere* reads עָבְרָם (*'oḇrām*), "until *they* crossed over" (emphasis mine). This provides logical consistency, but see the commentary.

---

### b. *The covenant meal*

#### 5:10–12

**[10]On the evening of the fourteenth day of the month, while camped at Gilgal on the plains of Jericho, the Israelites celebrated the Passover. [11]The day after the Passover, that very day, they ate some of the produce of the land: unleavened bread and roasted grain. [12]The manna stopped the day after they ate this food from the land; there was no longer any manna for the Israelites, but that year they ate of the produce of Canaan.**

**10** It was the first month (cf. 4:19); consequently "the fourteenth day" was the official day for observing the Passover (see Exod 12:2, 6, 18). Israel celebrated the Passover in the Land of Promise on the same day of the year as they first celebrated it before leaving the land of slavery. Though it had been observed at Sinai (Num 9:1–5), the Passover had been neglected during the years of rejection and wandering, just as circumcision had been. Many years later another "Joshua" ate the Passover with his disciples and constituted them as the new people of God under the new covenant (Matt 26:26–28).

**11** Another sign of a new beginning was that "they ate some of the produce of the land." "Unleavened bread" was prescribed for the entire week following the Passover (Exod 12:14–20); and, of course, they had no leaven at this time. For nearly forty years they had been living on manna and quail.

**12** When it was no longer needed, "the manna stopped." In the providence of God, extraordinary means are only temporary. Now the Israelites would experience the miracle of regular harvests in the land of milk and honey. The miracle of the manna prefigures the miraculous feedings by Jesus (Mark 6:30–44; 8:1–10 and parallels). Jesus' miracles were evidence of God's presence and were not intended to be regular sustenance (John 6:26–27).

### c. *The true leader of the covenant people*

#### 5:13–15

**[13]Now when Joshua was near Jericho, he looked up and saw a man standing in front of him with a drawn sword in his hand. Joshua went up to him and asked, "Are you for us or for our enemies?"**

**[14]"Neither," he replied, "but as commander of the army of the LORD I have now come." Then Joshua fell facedown to the ground in reverence, and asked him, "What message does my Lord have for his servant?"**

**[15]The commander of the LORD's army replied, "Take off your sandals, for the place where you are standing is holy." And Joshua did so.**

**13** On the eve of Israel's attack on Jericho, Joshua personally surveyed the area surrounding the city and inspected the fortifications. The words "he looked up" convey the element of surprise. "A man" is what Joshua thought he was seeing, but subsequent events reveal that it was no ordinary man. The man's "drawn sword" was symbolic of God's participation in the coming battle. Seeing the man standing there ready for combat provoked Joshua to inquire whether he was friend or foe.

**14** The stranger's response put everything in proper perspective. God is sovereign. It is never a question whether God is on our side but whether we are on God's side. The stranger came as "commander of the army of the LORD"; Joshua was to be subservient to him. Though he does not reappear in the story of the Conquest, the stranger was a heavenly being who fought behind the scenes in the spiritual realm. His presence was a sign that the Lord was the real military leader of the Conquest. Many identify this person as the angel of the Lord, who sometimes cannot be distinguished from the Lord himself (cf. Exod 3:2–4:17; Judg 6:11–23; et al.) The army of the Lord was an angelic host, and they assured victory to Israel if Israel was obedient (cf. Gen 32:1–2; 2 Kings 6:17). Though "Joshua fell facedown," we cannot be sure that he realized he was in the presence of a supernatural being. In that culture persons would prostrate themselves before anyone in authority. Moreover, when Joshua said "Lord," he used the Hebrew word *'ᵃḏônî*, which was used to address human beings. He did not use the divine name "Yahweh," which is translated "LORD" in English, written with small capitals (see comment on 3:13).

The paragraph division in the NIV suggests that the instructions for the conquest of Jericho (6:2–5) were the content of the stranger's message to Joshua. However, the encounter with the stranger is complete in vv.13–15, and a new episode is begun in 6:1. The purpose of this encounter was not to impart commands but to inspire Joshua with humility and reverence and to instill in him the confidence that God was with him and was in control (cf. 1:9).

**15** The command "Take off your sandals" does not indicate that this incident occurred at an ancient shrine. Rather, any place where God reveals himself is hallowed by that revelation (cf. Jacob at Bethel, Gen 28:10–22). The similarity to Moses' experience at the burning bush is obvious (Exod 3:1–6). These many parallels to the experiences of Moses confirm that Joshua is Moses' divinely chosen successor.

The events of this chapter are further evidence that the Conquest was to be accomplished by God's power, not man's. From a human point of view, it would have been wiser to fulfill the rituals of circumcision and the Passover on the other side of the Jordan where the Israelites were not exposed to their enemies. Celebrating them in the Promised Land, however, symbolized that the covenant relationship between God and Israel was a prerequisite for possessing the land. With this encounter the preparation for the Conquest was completed.

## Notes

---

**13** בִּירִיחוֹ (*bîrîḥô*, "near Jericho") literally means "in Jericho." Obviously, Joshua did not go inside the walled city of Jericho. He was only in the outlying agricultural lands.

**14** The word translated "neither" is the regular Hebrew negative לֹא (*lō'*, "no"). The LXX has ὁ δὲ εἶπεν αὐτῷ (*ho de eipen autō*, "and he said to him"). Apparently the LXX reads this as לוֹ (*lô*, "to him"). As a matter of fact, these two Hebrew words are often used interchangeably.

---

## 4. *The conquest of Jericho (6:1–27)*

### a. *The Lord's instructions*

#### 6:1–5

> [1]Now Jericho was tightly shut up because of the Israelites. No one went out and no one came in.
> [2]Then the LORD said to Joshua, "See, I have delivered Jericho into your hands, along with its king and its fighting men. [3]March around the city once with all the armed men. Do this for six days. [4]Have seven priests carry trumpets of rams' horns in front of the ark. On the seventh day, march around the city seven times, with the priests blowing the trumpets. [5]When you hear them sound a long blast on the trumpets, have all the people give a loud shout; then the wall of the city will collapse and the people will go up, every man straight in."

**1** The inhabitants of Jericho were paralyzed by fear of the Israelites and of Israel's invincible God (cf. 2:9–11; 5:1). The phrase "tightly shut up" represents two different participial forms of the same Hebrew verb (*sāgar*) and may be a device for emphasis (on this use of synonyms, see the comment on 1:5). Other translations attempt to give distinct meanings to each (e.g., the LXX uses Greek words that mean "shut up and fortified"; see Notes). The RSV has "shut up from within and from without," which is parallel to the statement "No one went out and no one came in." Fear of infiltration or trickery by the enemy would keep them from allowing anyone to enter. That no one was let out indicates how desperate the situation was. It was not uncommon in a time of siege to send warriors out to harass the enemies or to engage them in battle. Sometimes a small party was sent out secretly in search of help or supplies. They may have been too frightened to attempt any of these strategies, and they may have wanted to prevent the city from being weakened by defectors or deserters.

**2** Keil and Delitzsch (p. 64) interpret the instructions given here as the message of the commander of the army of the Lord to Joshua (see comment on 5:13–15). With the words "I have delivered Jericho," Joshua was reminded that victory comes only from the Lord. Compare Psalm 108:12–13:

> Give us aid against the enemy,
> for the help of man is worthless.
> With God we will gain the victory,
> and he will trample down our enemies.

Moreover, the tense of the verb (past perfect in English) indicates that the battle has already been won (cf. Rahab's words to the spies, 2:9).

The conquest of a walled city was a major challenge. Yadin (1:16–18) has listed five ways that a walled city could be captured: (1) by going over the wall using ladders, ramps, etc.; (2) by digging a tunnel under the wall; (3) by smashing a hole through the wall; (4) by laying siege until the city is starved into submission; (5) by some sort of subterfuge (e.g., the use of the wooden horse by the Greeks to conquer Troy and the use of an ambush and decoy by the Israelites in capturing Ai, 8:1–23). The Israelites had not encountered walled cities prior to this; and after their many years of wandering in the desert, they were not equipped for such an undertaking. High walls had discouraged the spies forty years earlier (Num 13:28). In Hebrew the phrase "fighting men" (*gibbôrê heḥāyil*) stands in apposition to "Jericho . . . with its king": the citizens and the king were all great warriors. The city of Jericho was strategically located as an imposing fortress guarding the fords across the Jordan and the passes into the hill country.

**3** The command to "march around the city once" seems senseless and required faith that God would keep his promise to deliver the city into their hands (Heb 11:30). The stratagem of waiting seven days has a number of parallels: Moses waited on Mount Sinai until the seventh day before God spoke to him (Exod 24:16). At one time the armies of Syria and Israel camped opposite each other for seven days before engaging in battle (1 Kings 20:29). On another occasion the army of Israel took a roundabout journey of seven days on the way to attack Moab (2 Kings 3:9). Job's friends sat with him for seven days before they began to speak (Job 2:11–13). When transported to the exiled Israelites, Ezekiel also sat in silence for seven days (Ezek 3:15).

Inside Jericho all routine pursuits had been given up, and every effort was aimed at defense. When Israel merely marched around the city day after day, the vigilance may have been relaxed and people may have turned their attention to such things as eating, sleeping, etc. On the other hand, this senseless marching may have completely demoralized the defenders, who would have been totally confused about what was going on. We must not overlook the possibility that the march around the city was another expression of God's grace giving the people one last opportunity to repent. Only "the armed men" were involved. The women, children, and livestock remained in the camp.

**4** Seven is the number of divine perfection or completeness. The emphasis on the number seven (fourteen times in this chapter), the use of ceremonial trumpets (made from ram's horns), the presence of priests, and the prominence of the ark all indicate that the conquest of Jericho was more than a military campaign; it was a religious event. Israel must always remember that the land was God's gift to them.

**5** "A long blast" was a signal distinct from the continual blowing of the trumpets. The phrase "all the people" means "the whole army." In this case women and children were not included. The "loud shout" was a war cry (see v.10) intended to encourage their fellows and intimidate the enemy. In v.10 we are informed that Joshua had ordered the people to be silent during all the marching up to this point. The way that God would give them the city is now revealed. "The wall of the city will collapse" is an appropriate translation of the Hebrew that says literally "will fall down in its place." The fact that "every man [went] straight in" has led to the supposition that the wall fell completely flat and that no one had to detour in the least to enter the city. This is not stated in the text, and, of course, the part of the wall that included Rahab's house was still standing. This passage is telling us that from their positions around the city, the Israelites were able to go directly in—though not necessarily in a perfectly straight line—so that the city would be attacked in every quarter at the same time.

## Notes

---

1 For סֹגֶרֶת וּמְסֻגֶּרֶת (*sōgeret ûm^esuggeret,* "was tightly shut up") the LXX reads *συγκεκλεισμένη καὶ ὠχυρωμένη* (*synkekleismenē kai ōchyrōmenē*, "shut up and fortified").

## b. *The attack on Jericho*

### 6:6–21

6So Joshua son of Nun called the priests and said to them, "Take up
the ark of the covenant of the LORD and have seven priests carry
trumpets in front of it." 7And he ordered the people, "Advance! March
around the city, with the armed guard going ahead of the ark of the
LORD."
8When Joshua had spoken to the people, the seven priests carrying
the seven trumpets before the LORD went forward, blowing their
trumpets, and the ark of the LORD's covenant followed them. 9The armed
guard marched ahead of the priests who blew the trumpets, and the rear
guard followed the ark. All this time the trumpets were sounding. 10But
Joshua had commanded the people, "Do not give a war cry, do not raise
your voices, do not say a word until the day I tell you to shout. Then
shout!" 11So he had the ark of the LORD carried around the city, circling
it once. Then the people returned to camp and spent the night there.
12Joshua got up early the next morning and the priests took up the
ark of the LORD. 13The seven priests carrying the seven trumpets went
forward, marching before the ark of the LORD and blowing the trumpets.
The armed men went ahead of them and the rear guard followed the ark
of the LORD, while the trumpets kept sounding. 14So on the second day
they marched around the city once and returned to the camp. They did
this for six days.
15On the seventh day, they got up at daybreak and marched around
the city seven times in the same manner, except that on that day they
circled the city seven times. 16The seventh time around, when the
priests sounded the trumpet blast, Joshua commanded the people,
"Shout! For the LORD has given you the city! 17The city and all that is in it
are to be devoted to the LORD. Only Rahab the prostitute and all who are
with her in her house shall be spared, because she hid the spies we
sent. 18But keep away from the devoted things, so that you will not bring
about your own destruction by taking any of them. Otherwise you will
make the camp of Israel liable to destruction and bring trouble on it.
19All the silver and gold and the articles of bronze and iron are sacred to
the LORD and must go into his treasury."
20When the trumpets sounded, the people shouted, and at the sound
of the trumpet, when the people gave a loud shout, the wall collapsed;
so every man charged straight in, and they took the city. 21They devoted
the city to the LORD and destroyed with the sword every living thing in
it—men and women, young and old, cattle, sheep and donkeys.

**6** Though repetitious, the account is not tedious. The narrator skillfully builds the suspense until it reaches its climax in v.20. The orders Joshua was to pass on to the people are summarized here (cf. vv.2–5).

**7** Separate orders were given to the priests and to the people. The *Qere* reads "they ordered" (see Notes) and preserves the idea of the chain of command whereby orders were passed from Joshua to the people through intermediaries (cf. 1:10–11; 3:2–3). The order to "advance" (*ʿiḇrû*) means literally "to cross over." It was an order to march from the camp to Jericho.

**8** The phrase "before the LORD" is a vivid reminder that the ark symbolized God's presence. The parallel statement in v.4 says that the seven priests were to carry seven horns *before the ark*. A few MSS and versions have added the word "ark" here also to make it read "before the ark of the LORD."

**9** Of course, "the rear guard" was armed also. The presence of warriors before and behind the ark is an indication that, contrary to the opinion of many, there was fighting to be done by the Israelites. Perhaps the "armed guard" consisted of warriors from the two and one-half tribes from Transjordan (cf. 4:12–13). Because of the privileges granted them, these tribes were to lead the others into every battle (a different order of march is prescribed in Num 2).

**10** These instructions were part of the orders Joshua had given earlier (vv.6–7, q.v.; cf. v.5).

**11** No details are given as to how the march was conducted (i.e., how many marched abreast or how long the column was). Jericho occupied only about five or six acres of land. Even though the Israelites must have maintained sufficient distance from the city to be safely beyond the range of bow and arrow, it is possible that the head of the column had arrived back at the camp before the last of the rear guard left.

**12–14** The repetitious narrative of the "next morning" (v.12) conveys something of the tedium of marching around the city day after day for six days.

**15** On the seventh day the Israelites set out "at daybreak" because of all that needed to be accomplished that day. Considering the size of Jericho and the number of Israelite troops, it is likely that when "they circled the city seven times," the column doubled over on itself again and again until the city was surrounded many columns deep.

**16** The eagerly awaited command to shout was given. Before telling us what happened, the narrator increases our suspense by inserting (vv.17–19) details concerning commands that Joshua must have given the people earlier (vv.6–7). It is difficult to conceive how Joshua could have given these detailed instructions when the army was spread all around the city.

**17** "Devoted" represents the Hebrew word *ḥerem* that is translated "completely destroyed" in 2:10. It designates a custom that is unfamiliar in the modern world (see NIV mg.). The annihilation of the Canaanites is one of the most perplexing moral problems in the Bible (see Introduction, pp. 246–47). The command given by Moses required only the extermination of all the inhabitants and their gods (Deut 7:1–6, 25–26; 20:16–18). When Israel destroyed the Amorites living west of the Jordan, they kept the livestock and the plunder for themselves (Deut 2:32–35; 3:3–7). The command in Exodus 23:31–33; and 34:11–14 did not require that the inhabitants be destroyed but only that they be driven out of the land. Jericho, however, was Israel's first conquest in the land of Canaan, a kind of firstfruits; therefore everything in it was holy—humans, animals, and property—and was to be consecrated to the Lord.

Though it is not stated explicitly, Rahab must have abandoned her profession before she was assimilated into Israel (v.25) and was married into the royal family (Matt 1:5). Her profession continues to be mentioned here and in vv.22 and 25 to emphasize that she was a trophy of God's grace. Her hiding of the spies is stated as the reason for her deliverance, and the NT interprets that action as evidence of her faith (cf. Heb 11:31; James 2:25). The interweaving of the deliverance of Rahab with the command to devote the entire city to destruction gives greater prominence to her deliverance, which is a major concern of the writer. The themes of judgment and salvation often appear side by side in Scripture: e.g., the salvation of Noah from the judgment of the Flood (Gen 6–8) and the salvation of Lot from the destruction of Sodom (Gen 19:1–29; see also John 3:16–21).

**18** The expressions "bring about your own destruction" and "make the camp of Israel liable to destruction" mean literally "to make into a thing devoted to destruction." The whole nation could be devoted to destruction through the action of a single person. One of the persistent themes of the OT is that the sin of an individual has consequences for the family and the community. This verse prepares us for the story of Achan in the next chapter. "Bring trouble" translates the Hebrew word *'āḵar,* which appears again in the name of the Valley of Achor (7:26).

**19** Metals are not destroyed by fire. They must be removed from common use by being placed in the treasury of the sanctuary where they would provide for the necessities of the sanctuary and the priests.

**20** The narrative, which has been interrupted by the instructions concerning the things devoted to destruction, is now resumed. To emphasize the divine intervention, no secondary causes for the collapse of the wall are mentioned. It would be no less a miracle were we to find that God used an earthquake to bring the walls down. (See the excursus at the end of the commentary on ch. 4.)

**21** The destruction of the defenders of the city together with their women and children involved the Israelites in hand-to-hand combat. Their enemies were not able to fight effectively because they were demoralized, outnumbered, and taken by surprise. Everything in the city was devoted to the Lord (the word "living" in the NIV is not attested in the Heb.).

## Notes

**7** In the *Kethiv* the verb is plural, ויאמרו (*wyy'mrw,* "and they said"), thus making the narrative follow this pattern: God spoke to Joshua (v.2), Joshua spoke to the priests (v.6), and the priests spoke to the army (v.7). Since the priests normally do not command the people in this book, the singular of the *Qere,* וַיֹּאמֶר (*wayyō'mer,* "and he said"; NIV, "and he ordered"), is preferable.

**12** The LXX adds τῇ ἡμέρᾳ τῇ δευτέρᾳ (*tē hēmera tē deutera,* "the second day"). The MT has no word for "next," but it is clearly implied in the context.

**18** An emendation suggested in the footnotes of BH is appealing. The change from תַּחֲרִימוּ (*taḥ[a]rîmû,* "bring about destruction") to תַּחְמְדוּ (*taḥm[e]ḏû*) is very simple and results in the translation "So that you will not covet and take any of them." The very same combination of verbs is found in 7:21.

### c. *Rahab rescued and Jericho cursed*

#### 6:22–27

[22]Joshua said to the two men who had spied out the land, "Go into the prostitute's house and bring her out and all who belong to her, in accordance with your oath to her." [23]So the young men who had done the spying went in and brought out Rahab, her father and mother and brothers and all who belonged to her. They brought out her entire family and put them in a place outside the camp of Israel.

[24]Then they burned the whole city and everything in it, but they put the silver and gold and the articles of bronze and iron into the treasury of the LORD's house. [25]But Joshua spared Rahab the prostitute, with her family and all who belonged to her, because she hid the men Joshua had sent as spies to Jericho—and she lives among the Israelites to this day.

[26]At that time Joshua pronounced this solemn oath: "Cursed before the LORD is the man who undertakes to rebuild this city, Jericho:

"At the cost of his firstborn son
  will he lay its foundations;
at the cost of his youngest
  will he set up its gates."

[27]So the LORD was with Joshua, and his fame spread throughout the land.

**22** Evidently the part of the wall where Rahab's house was located was miraculously preserved. The text does not require that every foot of the wall was leveled (cf. comment on v.5). The scarlet cord is not mentioned here.

**23** Rahab and her family were put in "a place outside the camp" as a kind of ritual quarantine. The camp of Israel was holy, and nothing unclean could be allowed to enter (cf. Lev 13:46; Num 5:3; 31:19; Deut 23:3, 14). After the passage of time and the observance of appropriate rituals, they were received into the congregation (see v.25).

**24** The term "the LORD's house" (*bêṯ-YHWH*) is generally applied only to the temple. Its use here for the tabernacle may be an anachronism (cf. 1 Sam 1:9). The application of later terminology to an earlier institution is not uncommon and does not detract from the veracity of the account.

**25** The statement "she lives among the Israelites to this day" could be evidence that the account was written during Rahab's lifetime, but probably what it means is that "she lives on in her posterity." In this chapter the two themes of chapter 2 are concluded: the capture of Jericho and the salvation of Rahab.

**26** "To rebuild" is a common English rendering for *bānāh,* which basically means "to build." The city of Jericho was to remain an object lesson of God's great victory in Israel's very first battle. The city was soon resettled (18:21; Judg 3:13–14; 2 Sam 10:5); but the curse was not fulfilled until the time of King Ahab, when Hiel, a resident of Bethel, rebuilt the wall around Jericho to make it a fortress once again (1 Kings 16:34). It is not clear whether the curse was fulfilled by a plague or an accident or whether Hiel offered his sons as sacrifices.

**27** Joshua was firmly established as leader in Israel (cf. 1:1–9; 2:9–11; 4:14; 5:1–3). The statement "The LORD was with Joshua" marks the climax of his rise to leadership. It is the fulfillment of God's promise in 1:5. The people had pledged their loyalty to Joshua on the condition that the Lord would be with him (1:17). This triumphant summary statement in no way prepares us for the disaster that is related in chapter 7.

### 5. *The conquest of Ai (7:1–8:29)*

#### a. *Achan's sin (7:1–26)*

##### 1) *Israel's defeat at Ai*

7:1–5

> 1 But the Israelites acted unfaithfully in regard to the devoted things;
> Achan son of Carmi, the son of Zimri, the son of Zerah, of the tribe of
> Judah, took some of them. So the LORD's anger burned against Israel.
> 2 Now Joshua sent men from Jericho to Ai, which is near Beth Aven to
> the east of Bethel, and told them, "Go up and spy out the region." So
> the men went up and spied out Ai.
> 3 When they returned to Joshua, they said, "Not all the people will
> have to go up against Ai. Send two or three thousand men to take it and
> do not weary all the people, for only a few men are there." 4 So about
> three thousand men went up; but they were routed by the men of Ai,
> 5 who killed about thirty-six of them. They chased the Israelites from the
> city gate as far as the stone quarries and struck them down on the
> slopes. At this the hearts of the people melted and became like water.

**1** As is common in Hebrew narrative, a summary statement of the event is given first (v.1) and then a more detailed account follows. Israel's sin was serious; it was a violation of their covenant with the Lord. Though the crime was committed by one person, the whole nation was considered guilty. The nation was responsible for the obedience of every citizen and was charged with the punishment of every offender.

The apostle Paul saw the same principle of solidarity at work in the church (1 Cor 5:6–13). Unjudged sin contaminated the whole assembly—"Don't you know that a little yeast works through the whole batch of dough?" (v.6).

However unfair it may seem, experience shows that the wrongdoing of a single individual has adverse effects on others (cf. Deut 5:9). Moreover, this was a time of war, and strict discipline had to be maintained. For "the devoted things," see the comments on 6:17–19. God's judgment on sin was viewed as his anger (cf. Rom 1:18–32, where the degradation of the heathen is another manifestation of God's wrath). The dreadfulness of sin and the justice of God are clearly seen here. God's judgment on the Canaanites was not arbitrary; it was the consequence of their sin, and now, when God's chosen people sin, they too must be judged. This is the reverse side of the theme of the book: God's people will not succeed if they are disobedient.

**2** "Ai" means "a ruins." In Hebrew it is always accompanied by the define article: "the ruins." This may not have been the name of the city, since it is a term that could be applied to any ruins. To specify which Ai, or ruins, is meant, the text states that it was near Bethel (cf. 12:9). (For the archaeological problems associated with Ai, see the Introduction, p. 248.)

The name "Beth Aven" means "house of wickedness." Hosea used it as a disparaging nickname for Bethel (cf. Hos 4:15; 5:8; 10:5). Joshua confined most of his military exploits to the mountainous areas where the inhabitants were unable to use chariots. The conquest of Ai and Bethel seems to be part of a plan to divide the central mountains in the middle and thus prevent any united defense.

In planning his strategy of attack, Joshua sent out spies as he had done earlier at Jericho. This was the first time in the Conquest that Joshua did anything on his own initiative, and it was doomed to failure. It is ominous that nothing is said about Joshua seeking guidance from the Lord. The great victory at Jericho made him overly confident of God's help.

**3** The total population of Ai was estimated to be only about twelve thousand men and women (8:25). Keil and Delitzsch (p. 77) conclude that a city of this size would be able to muster fewer than three thousand warriors. With armies of equal size, the defenders inside the city walls would have a considerable advantage. The confidence of the spies was inspired by their memory of Israel's great victory over Jericho and of God's intervention. Though it was only about fifteen miles from Jericho to Ai, the great difference in elevation (Jericho: 800 ft. below sea level; Ai: 2,500 ft. above) made this journey a rigorous climb.

**4** In spite of the fact that Joshua sent the larger number of troops suggested by the spies, the Israelites suffered a humiliating defeat.

**5** By modern standards thirty-six casualties out of three thousand troops would not be a great loss. Nevertheless, it was symbolic of Israel's resounding defeat. In the type of warfare that was fought in those days, it was not uncommon for the victor to have no casualties at all (cf. Num 31:48–49). The very same words that Rahab used to describe the demoralized population of Jericho (2:9, 11; cf. 5:1) are here applied to Israel.

## Notes

**2** Ai is mentioned in Gen 12:8 and 13:3. It is impossible to know whether a city by that name existed already or whether a name from a later period has been transferred back. The name "Beth Aven" is missing from the LXX.

### 2) *Joshua's intercession*

7:6–9

6 Then Joshua tore his clothes and fell facedown to the ground before
the ark of the LORD, remaining there till evening. The elders of Israel did
the same, and sprinkled dust on their heads. 7 And Joshua said, "Ah,
Sovereign LORD, why did you ever bring this people across the Jordan to
deliver us into the hands of the Amorites to destroy us? If only we had
been content to stay on the other side of the Jordan! 8 O Lord, what can I
say, now that Israel has been routed by its enemies? 9 The Canaanites
and the other people of the country will hear about this and they will
surround us and wipe out our name from the earth. What then will you
do for your own great name?"

**6** The actions described here—"tore his clothes and fell facedown. . . . and sprinkled dust on their heads"—are all appropriate for persons in mourning. Joshua and the elders were expressing their great grief at Israel's defeat. Joshua's first reaction was to turn to God. Therefore it was an act of faith when he fell down "before the ark." Joshua was able to approach the ark more freely than the high priest (cf. Lev 16:2). He, not the high priest, was responsible to intercede for the people. The "elders of Israel" are mentioned here for the first time. Through them Joshua exercised leadership over the nation. The actions of Joshua and the elders were not indications of repentance; they were expressions of anger, frustration, and distress.

**7** Joshua addressed God in a reverent manner, but that did not keep him from arguing with God. If victory was to be attributed to God's help, then defeat must come from God's failure to intervene. Joshua accused God of wanting to destroy his people. So soon after the miraculous victories over the Jordan and Jericho, Joshua was plunged into deep despair by Israel's first defeat. This is not the murmuring of unbelief and rebellion. It was the struggle of a man of faith who was brutally honest with God and was seeking answers to his urgent questions. When Joshua wished that Israel had been content to dwell on the east of the Jordan (cf. Exod 16:3), he came dangerously close to the way Israel had reasoned at Kadesh Barnea (Num 14:1–4). Had he forgotten that God himself had commanded them to cross over into Canaan? In self-pity Joshua charged God with capriciousness. Though Joshua could not be expected to know about Achan's sin, confidence in God's faithfulness should have made him look elsewhere for the reason for Israel's defeat.

**8** Joshua believed that the defeat of Israel meant the end of his leadership.

**9** Joshua was well aware that the report of Israel's victories had demoralized and immobilized the people of Canaan. The worst part of defeat was that Israel had lost this great advantage; now her enemies would be encouraged to fight back. Moreover, if Israel was destroyed, God's name would be disgraced. In OT times a name was more than just an identity. It stood for the person himself and his reputation. This was not special pleading; Joshua was showing genuine concern (cf. the intercession of Moses, Exod 32:12–13; Num 14:13–19; Deut 9:26–29). Verses 7–9 summarize the way Joshua prayed all afternoon.

## Notes

---

**7** "Sovereign LORD" is the way the NIV translates אֲדֹנָי יהוה (*'ᵃḏōnāy YHWH*), which is literally "Lord Yahweh."

---

### 3) *The Lord's answer*

**7:10–15**

[10]The LORD said to Joshua, "Stand up! What are you doing down on
your face? [11]Israel has sinned; they have violated my covenant, which I
commanded them to keep. They have taken some of the devoted things;

they have stolen, they have lied, they have put them with their own
possessions. [12]That is why the Israelites cannot stand against their
enemies; they turn their backs and run because they have been made
liable to destruction. I will not be with you anymore unless you destroy
whatever among you is devoted to destruction.
[13]"Go, consecrate the people. Tell them, 'Consecrate yourselves in
preparation for tomorrow; for this is what the LORD, the God of Israel,
says: That which is devoted is among you, O Israel. You cannot stand
against your enemies until you remove it.
[14]"'In the morning, present yourselves tribe by tribe. The tribe that the
LORD takes shall come forward clan by clan; the clan that the LORD takes
shall come forward family by family; and the family that the LORD takes
shall come forward man by man. [15]He who is caught with the devoted
things shall be destroyed by fire, along with all that belongs to him. He
has violated the covenant of the LORD and has done a disgraceful thing
in Israel!'"

**10** The Lord's command for Joshua to "stand up" seems like a rebuke. It was simply a response to an honest, if not altogether reverent, prayer. This was no time for self-pity; it was time for action.

**11** Joshua should have known that defeat was not due to any fickleness on God's part. The gift of the land was part of God's covenant with Israel; consequently the Conquest could not continue while Israel was not faithful to the covenant. In God's eyes the whole nation was implicated in the sin of Achan; his crime was their crime: "Israel has sinned; they . . . they . . . they . . . they. . . ." The repetition of the pronoun is further emphasized in the Hebrew by the inclusion of the word *gam* ("also") in each instance. Though *gam* is not represented by any word in the NIV, its force is preserved in the crisp, staccato style of this statement. For "the devoted things," see the comments on 6:18–19. Israel shared even in Achan's hypocrisy: "they have lied." The height of their offense was to take things that had been dedicated to God as their own. Ethical considerations alone will not explain the narrative if we fail to take God's honor into consideration.

**12** The warning in 6:18 came true: "they have been made liable to destruction," which means that they too must be devoted to destruction. No more dreadful threat is imaginable than that God would no longer be with Israel. The climax of chapters 1–6 comes in 6:27, which says, "So the LORD was with Joshua." Now, in the very next chapter, that relationship is threatened. At one time Moses had refused to lead the people unless God went with him (Exod 33:15). If the people will take action to "destroy whatever among you is devoted," they will demonstrate their innocence and preserve their relationship with God (cf. 2 Cor 7:5–12, esp. v.11c).

**13** The people must be consecrated again (cf. comment on 3:5). This procedure was necessary whenever God was going to act in some special way. He was going to come in judgment to remove the defilement from his people.

**14** The people would present themselves to the Lord by appearing before the sanctuary. The terms "tribe," "clan," "family," and "man" indicate various divisions in a society that was organized tribally. The Hebrew words are not used consistently in the OT, and it is difficult to find suitable equivalents in English. "Family" was a larger unit than our nuclear family, and the term "man" includes both wife and children. There is no specific statement as to how the Lord would single out the culprit (cf. 1 Sam 10:19–24). In a similar case (1 Sam 14:36–43), the guilty party was selected by casting lots. The use of lots eliminated any possibility of favoritism or manipulation. The decision was placed solely in the hands of God (cf. Prov 16:33). It is interesting to notice that the cause of defeat was revealed by the oracle, but lots were cast to find the offender.

**15** Though corporate responsibility was stressed, individual responsibility and guilt were not overlooked: The culprit "shall be destroyed." The nation would be absolved of guilt when the guilty individual was ferreted out and punished. The death penalty was made even more offensive by burning the offender's body (cf. Gen 38:24; Lev 21:9). The expression "all that belongs to him" is ambiguous. In v.24 it is clear that both persons and possessions were included.

### 4) *The culprit discovered and punished* 7:16–26

16Early the next morning Joshua had Israel come forward by tribes,
and Judah was taken. 17The clans of Judah came forward, and he took
the Zerahites. He had the clan of the Zerahites come forward by families,
and Zimri was taken. 18Joshua had his family come forward man by
man, and Achan son of Carmi, the son of Zimri, the son of Zerah, of the
tribe of Judah, was taken.

19Then Joshua said to Achan, "My son, give glory to the LORD, the God
of Israel, and give him the praise. Tell me what you have done; do not
hide it from me."

20Achan replied, "It is true! I have sinned against the LORD, the God of
Israel. This is what I have done: 21When I saw in the plunder a beautiful
robe from Babylonia, two hundred shekels of silver and a wedge of gold
weighing fifty shekels, I coveted them and took them. They are hidden in
the ground inside my tent, with the silver underneath."

22So Joshua sent messengers, and they ran to the tent, and there it
was, hidden in his tent, with the silver underneath. 23They took the
things from the tent, brought them to Joshua and all the Israelites and
spread them out before the LORD.

24Then Joshua, together with all Israel, took Achan son of Zerah, the
silver, the robe, the gold wedge, his sons and daughters, his cattle,
donkeys and sheep, his tent and all that he had, to the Valley of Achor.
25Joshua said, "Why have you brought this trouble on us? The LORD will
bring trouble on you today."

Then all Israel stoned him, and after they had stoned the rest, they
burned them. 26Over Achan they heaped up a large pile of rocks, which
remains to this day. Then the LORD turned from his fierce anger.
Therefore that place has been called the Valley of Achor ever since.

**16–18** In the selection process each tribe, clan, and family was represented by a single individual. To us the procedure seems to leave everything up to chance. For them it left everything in the hands of God, and, in the final analysis, the right person was chosen.

**19** "My son" may be the customary way of addressing a subordinate. Though Joshua deals gently and fairly with him, some indignation and vindictiveness are apparent in v.25. The expression "give glory to the LORD" is found also in John 9:24. In both instances it is an appeal for an honest confession. The same verbal root in Hebrew means "to praise" and "to confess"; therefore "give him the praise" could be translated "confess to him" (cf. KJV, which reads "make confession unto him"). Confession of sin is a way of honoring God. Joshua did not rely solely on the selection by lot. Personal confession and the gathering of evidence were also required (vv.22–23).

**20** Achan confessed his sin but was not forgiven because he did not confess willingly (cf. Ps 32; 1 John 1:9). His silence during the long process of casting lots is evidence of the hardness of his heart. As the selection came closer and closer to him—first his tribe, then his clan, then his family—he obviously hoped to avoid detection. His confession is not indicative of repentance because he would not have confessed if he had not been caught. True confession goes beyond the admission of what one has done. It includes recognition of guilt and true remorse.

**21** Achan called what he took "plunder." He viewed it as something customarily divided among the victors. Perhaps he was opposed to having everything put under the ban. The word "shekel" indicates a measure of weight, not a coin. Money was not coined until the seventh century. The weights are only approximate. "Wedge" indicates an ingot or a bar (RSV). Coveting is often the beginning of a sinful action. The tenth commandment is "You shall not covet" (Exod 20:17). The same three verbs "I saw," "I coveted," "I took" are found in the story of the Fall (Gen 3:6; the words "desirable" and "covet" are from the same Heb. root *ḥāmaḏ*; cf. James 1:13–15). Achan hid the things he took because he knew he had sinned. The gold is not mentioned at the end of this verse or in v.22. Silver may have been an inclusive term for both precious metals.

**22–23** The messengers located the hidden booty, brought it to Joshua, and spread everything "before the LORD" (v.23), i.e., at the Tent of Meeting (cf. v.14), because he is the final Judge.

**24** Representatives of the entire nation participated in the punishment of Achan in order to remove the guilt from all the people. Apparently Achan did not have a wife at this time; only "his sons and daughters" are mentioned. The punishment of children for the sin of their father is an offense to our sense of justice. Achan's family was implicated in his crime because he could not have hidden his loot in the ground under his tent without their knowing it. Moreover, this punishment is an example of the severe discipline that was necessary in time of war. Special severity was required also because Israel was God's agent in bringing severe judgment on the Canaanites. Achan was a wealthy man, possessing "cattle, donkeys and sheep." He had little need for what he stole.

"The Valley of Achor" has been identified with the Buqei'ah, about ten miles west of Qumran, high above the Dead Sea (cf. ZPEB, 1:38). In Hebrew "Achor" means "disaster." It is easily confused with Achan's name (1 Chron 2:7 gives Achar as Achan's name), and it is obvious that a play on words is intended.

**25** Once again "all Israel" refers to representatives from the whole nation. They were acting in accord with their promise to Joshua in 1:18. In the phrase "stoned him," the third person singular pronoun is used to point to Achan as the main offender; but the others were included. Then they were burned, and stones were heaped on them.

**26** The last action of v.25 is enlarged on in v.26 with the additional statement that this enormous heap of stones was still standing when this story was recorded. After Achan's sin had been judged, "the LORD turned from his fierce anger"; and Israel was restored to favor. The story of Achan and the story of Ananias and Sapphira (Acts 5; see Notes) are very similar. Hall (p. 99) explains, "God's first revenges are so much more fearful, because they must be exemplary."

## Notes

---

**17** The Hebrew reads "he had the family of the Zerahites come forward *man by man*" (לַגְּבָרִים [*lagg*$^{e}$*ḇārîm*]). This seems to be an error in transcription. The NIV follows a few Hebrew MSS and the Syriac, which have לַבָּתִּים (*labbāttîm*, "by families"; cf. v.14).

**26** L. Goppelt (*Typos* [Grand Rapids: Eerdmans, 1982], p. 119) states, "Ananias's lie (Acts 5:1ff.), like Achan's theft (Josh 7:1ff.), was an embezzlement of things dedicated to God. In both instances [LXX for Josh 7:1ff.] the word ἐνοσφίσατο [*enosphisato*, 'he took for himself'] is used, which occurs only one other time in the NT (Titus 2:10)."

---

### b. *The second attack on Ai (8:1–29)*

### 1) *Commands for the second attack*

#### 8:1–9

1 Then the LORD said to Joshua, "Do not be afraid; do not be
discouraged. Take the whole army with you, and go up and attack Ai.
For I have delivered into your hands the king of Ai, his people, his city
and his land. 2 You shall do to Ai and its king as you did to Jericho and
its king, except that you may carry off their plunder and livestock for
yourselves. Set an ambush behind the city."
3 So Joshua and the whole army moved out to attack Ai. He chose
thirty thousand of his best fighting men and sent them out at night 4 with
these orders: "Listen carefully. You are to set an ambush behind the
city. Don't go very far from it. All of you be on the alert. 5 I and all those
with me will advance on the city, and when the men come out against
us, as they did before, we will flee from them. 6 They will pursue us until
we have lured them away from the city, for they will say, 'They are
running away from us as they did before.' So when we flee from them,
7 you are to rise up from ambush and take the city. The LORD your God
will give it into your hand. 8 When you have taken the city, set it on fire.
Do what the LORD has commanded. See to it; you have my orders."
9 Then Joshua sent them off, and they went to the place of ambush
and lay in wait between Bethel and Ai, to the west of Ai—but Joshua
spent that night with the people.

**1** Joshua and all Israel had been demoralized by their defeat in the first attack on Ai. Now that the sin of Achan had been dealt with, God assured Israel of his presence and help (cf. 1:9). This time they had the divine promise of victory, a much larger army, and a far better strategy. The intertwining of miracle and human effort is hard to unravel in the Book of Joshua. Even with God's help, common sense and the best military strategy could not be neglected.

It is not clear how many men constituted "the whole army." The numbers given in this chapter are confusing (cf. vv.3, 12). When Transjordanian tribes were commanded to muster all their fighting men (1:14), they sent about 40,000 troops (4:13) out of approximately 110,580 men of military age (cf. Num 26:7, 18, 34). Using the same proportions the Twelve Tribes could have mustered an army of 200,000 to attack a city of 12,000 counting both men and women. Does it seem reasonable to suppose that if Joshua had come against the city with a massive force of 200,000 men, he would have been able to lure the inhabitants into attacking him? E.J. Young (*Introduction to the Old Testament* [Grand Rapids: Eerdmans, 1960], p. 176) suggests that the 30,000 in v.3 is the size of the whole army whereas the 5,000 in v.12 is the number of troops who were to lie in ambush. The rest of the army would have been held in reserve.

**2** Only the king and the people were to be devoted to destruction (cf. 6:17); the plunder and livestock from Ai and all subsequent cities could be kept by Israel and would be their means of support throughout the years of conquest. God explicitly commanded Joshua to "set an ambush." This is a form of deception and raises profound ethical and theological questions. Deception and surprise are necessary strategies in warfare. God cannot involve himself in war without being involved in these elements also. With the gate of the city on the north (v.11), "behind the city" would indicate the south side. Verse 12, however, places the ambush on the west, which was the far side (and thus behind) from Israel's base of operations and perhaps, for this reason, was least suspected by the king of Ai.

**3** Joshua sent "thirty thousand of his best fighting men" with orders to set an ambush. Perhaps only five thousand of them constituted that ambush. It would be difficult even for a detachment of five thousand men to avoid detection between Ai and Bethel. We must admit that this narrative is difficult to unravel largely because of the repetitious nature of Hebrew style. Possibly vv.10–13 report the carrying out of what was commanded in vv.3–9. The movement of troops "at night" was one of Joshua's successful strategies (cf. 10:9).

**4** Joshua's men were to be ready to move at a moment's notice. Israel's new strategy required careful coordination and quick action.

**5** The strategy of decoy was used to draw a sufficient number of the defenders away from the city to make its capture relatively easy. This involved a great risk, because a fleeing army was far more likely to suffer casualties.

**6** The ruse depended on making the attack appear similar to the previous one. To have approached the city this time with a vastly larger army of several hundred thousand troops would have put the king on his guard.

**7** The troops waiting in ambush were to move in when the defenders were drawn from the city. Verses 18–19 suggest that the troops waited for a signal from Joshua.

**8** The troops in ambush were to "set it on fire" to notify Joshua and the Israelites that the city had been taken. This would also demoralize the enemy. With their wives and children killed and their homes destroyed, what would they have left to fight for? Verse 28 records the total desolation of the city by fire. This time the Israelites must "do what the LORD has commanded." The account of the first attack was strangely silent about any commands from the Lord.

**9** Joshua set up the ambush "between Bethel and Ai" to avoid the main route between the two cities. He did not try to prevent Bethel from assisting Ai, because any engagement with the army from Bethel would have exposed the ambush. Joshua spent the night with the main army (the Heb. word *'am* frequently means "army" as it does here).

### 2) *Israel's victory*

#### 8:10–29

[10]Early the next morning Joshua mustered his men, and he and the
leaders of Israel marched before them to Ai. [11]The entire force that was
with him marched up and approached the city and arrived in front of it.
They set up camp north of Ai, with the valley between them and the city.
[12]Joshua had taken about five thousand men and set them in ambush
between Bethel and Ai, to the west of the city. [13]They had the soldiers
take up their positions—all those in the camp to the north of the city
and the ambush to the west of it. That night Joshua went into the valley.
[14]When the king of Ai saw this, he and all the men of the city hurried
out early in the morning to meet Israel in battle at a certain place
overlooking the Arabah. But he did not know that an ambush had been
set against him behind the city. [15]Joshua and all Israel let themselves be
driven back before them, and they fled toward the desert. [16]All the men
of Ai were called to pursue them, and they pursued Joshua and were
lured away from the city. [17]Not a man remained in Ai or Bethel who did
not go after Israel. They left the city open and went in pursuit of Israel.
[18]Then the LORD said to Joshua, "Hold out toward Ai the javelin that is
in your hand, for into your hand I will deliver the city." So Joshua held
out his javelin toward Ai. [19]As soon as he did this, the men in the
ambush rose quickly from their position and rushed forward. They
entered the city and captured it and quickly set it on fire.
[20]The men of Ai looked back and saw the smoke of the city rising
against the sky, but they had no chance to escape in any direction, for
the Israelites who had been fleeing toward the desert had turned back
against their pursuers. [21]For when Joshua and all Israel saw that the
ambush had taken the city and that smoke was going up from the city,
they turned around and attacked the men of Ai. [22]The men of the
ambush also came out of the city against them, so that they were caught
in the middle, with Israelites on both sides. Israel cut them down,
leaving them neither survivors nor fugitives. [23]But they took the king of
Ai alive and brought him to Joshua.
[24]When Israel had finished killing all the men of Ai in the fields and in
the desert where they had chased them, and when every one of them
had been put to the sword, all the Israelites returned to Ai and killed
those who were in it. [25]Twelve thousand men and women fell that day—
all the people of Ai. [26]For Joshua did not draw back the hand that held
out his javelin until he had destroyed all who lived in Ai. [27]But Israel did
carry off for themselves the livestock and plunder of this city, as the
LORD had instructed Joshua.
[28]So Joshua burned Ai and made it a permanent heap of ruins, a
desolate place to this day. [29]He hung the king of Ai on a tree and left him
there until evening. At sunset, Joshua ordered them to take his body

from the tree and throw it down at the entrance of the city gate. And they raised a large pile of rocks over it, which remains to this day.

**11** It was night when "they set up camp" (cf. v.3); so the army's presence was not detected until the next morning.

**12** Though the numbers are difficult to harmonize, this verse repeats the action that is described more fully in vv.3–9.

**13** Joshua went into the valley when everything was in readiness. The main army and the troops in ambush were in position. Apparently Joshua spent the night scouting the valley in preparation for battle the next day (cf. 5:13–15).

**14** Eager for victory and overly confident, the king "hurried out." The Hebrew word translated "at a certain place" (*lammô'ēḏ*) usually means an agreed upon time or place. Perhaps it refers to a place specified in Israel's battle plans. The "Arabah" is a desert area (this word commonly refers to the Jordan Valley).

**15** "Toward the desert" might also be translated "the way of the desert." It refers to a road leading from the vicinity of Ai (or Bethel) to Aphek (See map on p. 253).

**16–17** The proximity of Ai to Bethel may have encouraged the army of Bethel to come to the aid of Ai. The Israelite ambush had to be hidden from the main road to keep the troops coming from Bethel from discovering them. In their confidence of an easy victory, "they left the city open" (v.17) without anyone there to defend it.

**18** Joshua's use of the javelin is another indication that God was directing the army of Israel. It reminds us of Exodus 17:8–12, where the army of Israel was victorious as long as Moses was holding up the staff of God. Joshua did not bring his hand down until the victory over Ai was complete (v.26). There is no hint of magic. This action symbolizes that victory comes from the Lord.

**19** The narrative implies that holding out the javelin was a prearranged signal. The men in ambush would not have been able to see it, but they could have had scouts posted, as Keil and Delitzsch (p. 88) have suggested.

**20–21** The statement "they had no chance to escape in any direction" (v.20) literally says that "they had no hands to flee this way or this way." "No hands" may mean "no place to flee" (cf. LXX); but more likely it means "no strength," i.e., they lost their will to fight when they saw that their families and possessions were gone. The smoke rising from Ai was the signal to Joshua that the ambush had been successful (v.21).

**22–23** We should not seek to find any distinction between the words "survivors" and "fugitives." This is another example of synonyms used for emphasis, i.e., "they left no survivors at all!" (See the comment on 1:5.) The key captive, "the king" (v.23), was not killed in the battle but was taken to Joshua.

**24** We are surprised to learn that there were survivors in the city. Evidently the troops in ambush did not wait to destroy all the inhabitants before setting the city on fire.

**25** The chapter is strangely silent about what happened to the army from Bethel. They must have been destroyed at this time also (cf. 12:16 and the Notes on v.17).

**26** The word "destroyed" is once again the Hebrew term *ḥerem,* which means "devoted to the LORD by destruction" (see comment on 6:17).

**27** Joshua was careful to do everything in conformity with God's commands. Clearly the Lord was in control this time.

**28** "Heap" represents the Hebrew word *tel,* which is found in the names of many places in modern Israel, e.g., "Tel Aviv." It normally refers to a particular kind of mound that is formed by the ruins of a walled city. Such a mound can easily be distinguished from a natural hill by its truncated cone shape. The phrase "to this day" indicates that Ai had not been rebuilt at the time the narrative was composed. So far as we know, it was never rebuilt, though Joshua did not pronounce any curse to warn against the refortification of Ai as he had done in the case of Jericho (6:26).

**29** Though the king of Ai was not executed by hanging, his dead body was hung or impaled on a tree or pole to add to his disgrace (cf. KD, *The Pentateuch,* 3:204–5). To display the lifeless body of the king whom they had feared was another way of bolstering the morale of the Israelites. They were forbidden to leave a body hanging overnight because it would desecrate the land (Deut 21:23). This law required also that the body be buried the same day. The king of Ai's body was entombed in a pile of rocks so that it might serve as a vivid object lesson for future generations. Again, it is strange that the king of Bethel is not mentioned.

## Notes

**13** Two minor changes would make the end of this verse identical to the end of v.9: וַיֵּלֶךְ (*wayyēlek̲,* "and he went") to וַיָּלֶן (*wayyālen,* "and he spent the night") and הָעֵמֶק (*hāʿēmeq,* "the valley") to הָעָם (*hāʿām,* "the people").

**17** This is the only reference to the army of Bethel in the Book of Joshua. This, together with the fact that the chapter does not say anything about what happened to the king of Bethel or his army, has led some to suppose that "Bethel" is a later insertion. W.F. Albright took this as his clue that the story was originally about Bethel, not Ai ("The Israelite Conquest of Canaan in the Light of Archaeology," BASOR 74 [April 1939]: 16–17).

## 6. *Covenant renewal at Mount Ebal*

### 8:30–35

30 Then Joshua built on Mount Ebal an altar to the LORD, the God of
Israel, 31 as Moses the servant of the LORD had commanded the Israelites.
He built it according to what is written in the Book of the Law of
Moses—an altar of uncut stones, on which no iron tool had been used.
On it they offered to the LORD burnt offerings and sacrificed fellowship
offerings. 32 There, in the presence of the Israelites, Joshua copied on
stones the law of Moses, which he had written. 33 All Israel, aliens and

> citizens alike, with their elders, officials and judges, were standing on both sides of the ark of the covenant of the LORD, facing those who carried it—the priests, who were Levites. Half of the people stood in front of Mount Gerizim and half of them in front of Mount Ebal, as Moses the servant of the LORD had formerly commanded when he gave instructions to bless the people of Israel.
>
> [34]Afterward, Joshua read all the words of the law—the blessings and the curses—just as it is written in the Book of the Law. [35]There was not a word of all that Moses had commanded that Joshua did not read to the whole assembly of Israel, including the women and children, and the aliens who lived among them.

**30** The building of this altar and the ceremony that followed were commanded by Moses (Deut 27–28). By this act Joshua acknowledged the Lord as the source of every victory and blessing. Like Abraham, who built altars wherever he traveled throughout the land, Joshua was claiming this territory in the name of the Lord. It was an appropriate time to worship now that Israel had established a foothold in the central highlands that divided the north from the south. (Compare Exod 17:15 where Moses built an altar after his victory over the Amalekites.)

Because the narrative says nothing about any Israelite conquest of the area around Mount Ebal and Mount Gerizim, perhaps the inhabitants were friendly to Israel (this is the area that was subdued by Simeon and Levi, cf. Gen 34). Since the narrator only relates a few of the major battles, it is possible that the battle of Ai is symbolic of the conquest of the entire mountainous area in central Palestine. The Israelites could celebrate this ritual of covenant renewal in peace because God had placed the fear of Israel in the hearts of the natives. "Mount Ebal" became the central place of worship at this time in Israel's history.

**31** The use of "uncut stones" in constructing the altar (cf. Exod 20:25) may have been a reaction to pagan culture or another example of the conservatism of religion (see comment on 5:2), since the use of iron tools was a recent innovation.

**32** The law was "copied on stones" to give it a prominent and permanent place in the land. It was to be the basis of Israel's life in this land. The people's faithfulness to this law would determine their fortunes. The word "stones" has an article in Hebrew and refers to special stones covered with plaster that Moses had commanded to be prepared for this purpose (Deut 27:4).

**33** "Aliens and citizens alike" were included in Israel and participated in the covenant renewal. The religion of Israel at its best has always been a missionary religion. From the time of the Exodus, aliens who chose to live with Israel and worship her God were assimilated into the nation as, for example, Rahab and her family (cf. 1 Kings 8:41–43). "The ark of the covenant" was placed in the center of the assembly as a symbol of God's presence while the covenant was being renewed. For the expression "the priests, who were Levites," see the comment on 3:3. Everything was done as Moses "had formerly commanded" (cf. Deut 11:29; 27:11–26). The ceremony is summarized as "instructions to bless," placing the emphasis on the positive, even though Moses' command included both blessing and cursing (cf. v.34).

**34** The public reading of the law had a practical as well as a ceremonial function. It impressed the people with their responsibility to obey.

**35** Emphasis is placed again on the critical importance of obedience to the whole law. The Israelites were always to be considerate of "the aliens who lived among them" because they too had been aliens living in slavery in Egypt (Exod 22:21; 23:9; Deut 24:17–22).

## Notes

---

**30** According to the Samaritan Pentateuch, this altar was to be built on Mount Gerizim (Deut 27:4–5). This is the basis for the claim that the Samaritan temple built on that site is the only legitimate sanctuary (cf. John 4:20).

---

### C. *The Southern Campaign (9:1–10:43)*

### 1. *The Gibeonite deception (9:1–27)*

### a. *The treaty with Israel*

9:1–15

[1]Now when all the kings west of the Jordan heard about these
things—those in the hill country, in the western foothills, and along the
entire coast of the Great Sea as far as Lebanon (the kings of the Hittites,
Amorites, Canaanites, Perizzites, Hivites and Jebusites)—[2]they came
together to make war against Joshua and Israel.
[3]However, when the people of Gibeon heard what Joshua had done to
Jericho and Ai, [4]they resorted to a ruse: They went as a delegation
whose donkeys were loaded with worn-out sacks and old wineskins,
cracked and mended. [5]The men put worn and patched sandals on their
feet and wore old clothes. All the bread of their food supply was dry and
moldy. [6]Then they went to Joshua in the camp at Gilgal and said to him
and the men of Israel, "We have come from a distant country; make a
treaty with us."
[7]The men of Israel said to the Hivites, "But perhaps you live near us.
How then can we make a treaty with you?"
[8]"We are your servants," they said to Joshua. But Joshua asked,
"Who are you and where do you come from?"
[9]They answered: "Your servants have come from a very distant
country because of the fame of the LORD your God. For we have heard
reports of him: all that he did in Egypt, [10]and all that he did to the two
kings of the Amorites east of the Jordan—Sihon king of Heshbon, and
Og king of Bashan, who reigned in Ashtaroth. [11]And our elders and all
those living in our country said to us, 'Take provisions for your journey;
go and meet them and say to them, "We are your servants; make a treaty
with us."' [12]This bread of ours was warm when we packed it at home on
the day we left to come to you. But now see how dry and moldy it is.
[13]And these wineskins that we filled were new, but see how cracked
they are. And our clothes and sandals are worn out by the very long
journey."

> [14]The men of Israel sampled their provisions but did not inquire of the LORD. [15]Then Joshua made a treaty of peace with them to let them live, and the leaders of the assembly ratified it by oath.

**1–2** All the city-states in mountainous regions joined forces against Joshua. No longer would he be able to conquer one city at a time as he had done at Jericho and Ai. Perhaps these kings were encouraged by the initial defeat of Israel at Ai. No longer would the reports of earlier victories lead them to suppose that Israel was invincible. In resisting Israel, however, they were resisting God. Their stubborn rebellion against God was eloquent testimony that the sin of the Amorites had reached its full measure (cf. Gen 15:16).

**3** The Gibeonite league included the city of Gibeon and the surrounding dependencies that are named in v.17 (q.v.). The city of Gibeon has been identified with modern el-Jib on the central mountain range about eight miles northwest of Jerusalem. It is compared with a royal city, for it was larger than Ai and had an excellent army (10:2).

**4** The Gibeonites spared no effort in trying to convince Joshua and Israel that they lived in a faraway country.

**5** Perhaps their bread was "dry and crumbly" rather than "dry and moldy," since dry bread is not likely to become moldy.

**6** "Gilgal" is where Israel had had its base of operations since first entering the land (4:19). It is surprising that Joshua continued to use Gilgal as his base camp even after he had established a foothold in the mountainous region at Ai because of the arduous climb from Gilgal to the central mountain range. Perhaps Gilgal provided a more secure place for their families and livestock. Some have suggested that there was a second Gilgal in the vicinity of Shechem, but there is no indication of this in the text. The phrase "men of Israel" refers to the same group of officers who are called "leaders of the assembly" in vv.15 and 18 and "elders" in 8:33. The elaborate and rather bizarre preparations of the Gibeonites were designed to create the impression that they had come on a long journey "from a distant country." Somehow they knew that God had forbidden Israel to make any treaties or to save alive any of the inhabitants of the land (Deut 7:1–3; 20:16–18). When asked to "make a treaty," Israel should have become suspicious. The Gibeonites would have had little reason to seek a treaty with Israel had they really come from a distant country.

**7** The narrator identifies the inhabitants of Gibeon as "Hivites." Possibly they were "Horites, an ethnic group living in Canaan related to the Hurrians of northern Mesopotamia" (NIV Study Bible, p. 303 n.). This was one of the nations God had promised to drive out of the land before Israel (3:10). The leaders' question—"perhaps you live near us"—indicates suspicion.

**8** When the Gibeonites said, "We are your servants," they were offering to become Israel's vassals. In return they expected Israel, the stronger party, to protect them from their enemies (cf. 10:6). Their offer provoked Joshua to ask, "Where do you come from?" Notice how persistent Joshua and the leaders were in their attempt to carry out the Lord's command, even though they did not seek the Lord's guidance.

**9** The Gibeonites' statement that they had come "because of the fame of the LORD your God" is the key statement in the entire episode. "Fame" represents the Hebrew word *šēm,* which is commonly translated as "name." It includes the idea of fame but is a much richer concept. The name stands for the character of the person (7:9). The theology of the entire OT can be summarized in one sentence from the prophet Joel: "And everyone who calls on the name of the LORD will be saved" (2:32a).

Though the incident is filled with tension and contradiction, the Gibeonites were drawn by the great name ("fame," NIV) of Yahweh and were spared. When they said, "We have heard reports of him," they indicated that God's mighty acts on behalf of Israel had made his great name known far and wide. There are striking parallels with the story of Rahab (cf. 2:9–11). Just as Rahab had done, the Gibeonites believed the reports about the God of Israel; and fear drove them, as it had driven her, to seek to come under his protection and to scheme in order to escape annihilation at the hand of the Israelites (see Notes). In rehearsing the mighty acts of the Lord, the Gibeonites were careful to omit recent events that they would not have known about had they really come from a far country. The matters they omitted were the very things that motivated them to earnestly seek a treaty with Israel (cf. v.3).

**10** For "The two kings of the Amorites . . . Sihon . . . and Og," see Numbers 21:21–35 and Deuteronomy 2:26–3:17.

**11** The Gibeonites spoke of their "elders," but not their king. This may be evidence that, in contrast to the other cities, they actually had no king.

**12–13** The Gibeonites presented their contrived evidence to the Israelites to prove that they had come a very long way.

**14** It is strange that the Israelites "sampled their provisions" in spite of the fact that they were dry and moldy (or crumbly, see comment on v.5). Eating together was often a part of making a treaty (cf. Gen 31:54). How tragic it was that Israel was so impressed by the Gibeonites' stale provisions that they failed once again to seek God's guidance! Ironically, of all people, Joshua failed to inquire of the Lord. Joshua had gone up the mountain of revelation with Moses (Exod 24:13–14); and in his preparation for leadership, he had been trained in the use of the Urim and Thummim for determining the will of God (Num 27:18–21). How easy it is even in the service of the Lord to take God's guidance and blessing for granted!

**15** The NIV's "Joshua made a treaty of peace with them to let them live" is actually two clauses in Hebrew: (1) "he made an alliance with them" (*wayya'aś lāhem yᵉhôšuaʿ šālôm;* lit., "and Joshua made peace with them"), and (2) "he concluded a treaty with them to protect their lives" (*wayyiḵrōṯ lāhem bᵉrîṯ lᵉḥayyôṯām;* lit., "he made a covenant with them to cause them to live"). As the next chapter shows, this treaty committed Israel to more than simply sparing the Gibeonites' lives. Israel would have to come to their defense in all kinds of danger. The heads of government in Israel always ruled with the consent of the people. Hence, the treaty Joshua made was not valid until "the leaders of the assembly ratified it."

## Notes

---

**1** The LXX adds *καὶ οἱ Γεργεσαῖοι* (*kai hoi Gergesaioi*, "and the Gergashites") to agree with 3:10 et al.

**4** The translation in the RSV of וַיִּצְטַיָּרוּ (*wayyiṣṭayyārû;* NIV has "they went as a delegation") as "they made ready provision" is very appealing. It is based on a simple emendation of ר (*r*) to ד (*d*), which is a common orthographic error in copying, thus yielding וַיִּצְטַיָּדוּ (*wayyiṣṭayyāḏû*). The infinitive of this same verb occurs in v.12 where the NIV translates "when we packed it."

**6** The phrase אִישׁ יִשְׂרָאֵל (*'îš yiśrā'ēl*), though singular in form (viz., "man of Israel"), seems to function as a collective or plural here (viz., "men of Israel") and in the next verse.

**7** The NIV translates the *Kethiv* וַיֹּאמְרוּ (*wayyō'meᵉrû*, lit., "and they said") as "The men of Israel said," which seems preferable to the *Qere* וַיֹּאמֶר (*wayyō'mer*, "and he said"). For *'îš yiśrā'ēl* ("man of Israel") as a plural, see note 6 above.

**9** The invitation for all Gentiles to seek the Lord was voiced by Solomon at the dedication of the temple when he prayed:

> "As for the foreigner who does not belong to your people Israel but has come from a distant land because of your name—for men will hear of your great name and your mighty hand and your outstretched arm—when he comes and prays toward this temple, then hear from heaven, your dwelling place, and do whatever the foreigner asks of you, so that all the peoples of the earth may know your name and fear you, as do your own people Israel, and may know that this house I have built bears your Name." (1 Kings 8:41–43)

---

### b. *The ruse discovered*

#### 9:16–27

[16]Three days after they made the treaty with the Gibeonites, the Israelites heard that they were neighbors, living near them. [17]So the Israelites set out and on the third day came to their cities: Gibeon, Kephirah, Beeroth and Kiriath Jearim. [18]But the Israelites did not attack them, because the leaders of the assembly had sworn an oath to them by the LORD, the God of Israel.

The whole assembly grumbled against the leaders, [19]but all the leaders answered, "We have given them our oath by the LORD, the God of Israel, and we cannot touch them now. [20]This is what we will do to them: We will let them live, so that wrath will not fall on us for breaking the oath we swore to them." [21]They continued, "Let them live, but let them be woodcutters and water carriers for the entire community." So the leaders' promise to them was kept.

[22]Then Joshua summoned the Gibeonites and said, "Why did you deceive us by saying, 'We live a long way from you,' while actually you live near us? [23]You are now under a curse: You will never cease to serve as woodcutters and water carriers for the house of my God."

[24]They answered Joshua, "Your servants were clearly told how the LORD your God had commanded his servant Moses to give you the whole land and to wipe out all its inhabitants from before you. So we feared for our lives because of you, and that is why we did this. [25]We are now in your hands. Do to us whatever seems good and right to you."

26 So Joshua saved them from the Israelites, and they did not kill them.
27 That day he made the Gibeonites woodcutters and water carriers for
the community and for the altar of the LORD at the place the LORD would
choose. And that is what they are to this day.

**16** "Three days" (see comment on 1:11) may have been no later than the morning of the second day. There is irony in this statement, for scarcely had the treaty been concluded when the Israelites learned that they had been deceived. As their "neighbors," the Gibeonites were some of the very people whom Israel had been commanded to exterminate and with whom they were to make no treaties, lest they be tempted into idolatry (Deut 7:1–6; 20:16–18; see comment on v.7).

**17** When "the Israelites set out," their motive was more than curiosity. They were intent on violence but were restrained by their leaders (v.18). They arrived at Gibeon on "the third day," i.e., within a day or two. It was not far. In fact, the Israelite army was able to reach it after an all-night forced march from Gilgal (10:9). The cities of the Gibeonites were Gibeon (v.3), Kephirah (Khirbet el-kefireh, a few miles east of Gibeon), Beeroth (Khirbet el Burj, a few miles northeast of Gibeon), and Kireath Jearim (Deir el-'Azar, about six miles east of Jerusalem).

**18** Possibly "the whole assembly grumbled" because they were resentful of the plunder that had been denied them. On the other hand, they may have been fearful of another judgment like that at Ai, because they had failed to keep God's command.

**19** The "oath" was made in the name of the Lord. Consequently fidelity was owed, not to the Gibeonites, but to the Lord. The form of the oath called on the Lord to punish the Israelites if they failed to keep their agreement (cf. vv.18–20). This explains why Israel felt bound to the treaty even though it had been made under false pretenses (cf. Gen 27:35; Ps 15:4).

**20** The Hebrew word *qeṣeḇ* ("wrath") usually has the idea of divine retribution that inevitably follows the violation of some divine decree. In 22:20 this same word (*qāṣeḇ*) is used to describe the divine judgment on Israel for Achan's sin (cf. Num 1:53; 18:5). Many years later wrath did fall on Israel when King Saul violated this treaty with the Gibeonites (2 Sam 21:1–9).

**21** The Gibeonites were reduced to menial service as "woodcutters and water carriers." Moses' instructions were that if any city outside the Promised Land surrendered to Israel, its citizens should be permitted to live and be subjected to forced labor (Deut 20:10–15; cf. Josh 16:10; 17:13; Judg 1:28, 30, 33, 35). There is some confusion whether they were to serve "the entire community" (as here) or to serve "the house of my God" (v.23). In v.27 both ideas are combined. Possibly they were to cut the wood and draw the water needed for the temple ritual, a duty that normally fell to the community.

**22** At first Joshua's question seems humorous, if not ridiculous. Obviously the Gibeonites did what they did to save their lives! To Joshua, however, an honorable death was preferable to degrading subservience.

**23** Even the curse does not seem to be serious, since the Gibeonites had escaped the sentence of death. For pagans to come and serve at the Lord's sanctuary is surely a blessing (cf. Ps 84:10). The phrase "the house of my God" is not an anachronism; it could be applied to the tabernacle as well as to the temple.

**24** The Gibeonites did not anticipate the degrading sentence imposed on them, but they preferred to live. As in the case of Rahab, it was fear that led to their salvation. The same knowledge and fear that caused Rahab and the Gibeonites to humble themselves and sue for peace moved their contemporaries to obstinate resistance and destruction.

**25** In the ancient Near East, this posture of helplessness was really a position of security. It was a matter of personal honor to protect anyone who had surrendered himself for safekeeping. The statement "Do to us whatever seems good and right to you" was not simple resignation on the part of the Gibeonites. They knew the Israelites would be duty bound to treat them kindly.

**26–27** Joshua, being a leader of integrity, accepted the Gibeonites' surrender (v.26). The phrase "at the place that the LORD would choose" or its equivalent occurs twenty times in Deuteronomy. Worship was to be limited to one central sanctuary as a testimony to the fact that there was only one Lord (Deut 6:4) and in order to preserve the unity of the nation. This central sanctuary was located successively at Shechem, Shiloh, and Gibeon. Ultimately, of course, the site of the one sanctuary was to be Jerusalem.

It is difficult to determine whether the treaty with the Gibeonites should be viewed positively or negatively (cf. 1 Kings 8:41–43). There is no record that the Gibeonites ever became a snare to Israel, as was true in the case of other nations whom they failed to drive out (Judg 3:5–6). Judgment fell on Israel because of Achan's disobedience. Now, however, Israel was threatened with judgment if they broke this covenant with Gibeon. (God's wrath did come on Israel years later when King Saul violated this covenant, 2 Sam 21:1–9.) Moreover, the treaty with the Gibeonites gave Israel a decided military advantage in the south. This fact was recognized by Adoni-Zedek, king of Jerusalem, who tried to break up the alliance (10:1–5). The Gibeonites lived peaceably in Israel for many years. Nehemiah 3:7 and 7:25 suggest that ultimately they were fully assimilated. This is another example of the omnipotence of God, for his divine purpose was served even by the foolish error of his people. Whoever earnestly seeks deliverance from God always receives it.

### 2. *Israel's victory over the southern coalition (10:1–43)*

#### a. *The rescue of the Gibeonites*

10:1–15

1 Now Adoni-Zedek king of Jerusalem heard that Joshua had taken Ai
and totally destroyed it, doing to Ai and its king as he had done to
Jericho and its king, and that the people of Gibeon had made a treaty of
peace with Israel and were living near them. 2 He and his people were
very much alarmed at this, because Gibeon was an important city, like
one of the royal cities; it was larger than Ai, and all its men were good
fighters. 3 So Adoni-Zedek king of Jerusalem appealed to Hoham king of
Hebron, Piram king of Jarmuth, Japhia king of Lachish and Debir king of

Eglon. [4]"Come up and help me attack Gibeon," he said, "because it has
made peace with Joshua and the Israelites."
[5]Then the five kings of the Amorites—the kings of Jerusalem, Hebron,
Jarmuth, Lachish and Eglon—joined forces. They moved up with all
their troops and took up positions against Gibeon and attacked it.
[6]The Gibeonites then sent word to Joshua in the camp at Gilgal: "Do
not abandon your servants. Come up to us quickly and save us! Help us,
because all the Amorite kings from the hill country have joined forces
against us."
[7]So Joshua marched up from Gilgal with his entire army, including all
the best fighting men. [8]The LORD said to Joshua, "Do not be afraid of
them; I have given them into your hand. Not one of them will be able to
withstand you."
[9]After an all-night march from Gilgal, Joshua took them by surprise.
[10]The LORD threw them into confusion before Israel, who defeated them
in a great victory at Gibeon. Israel pursued them along the road going
up to Beth Horon and cut them down all the way to Azekah and
Makkedah. [11]As they fled before Israel on the road down from Beth
Horon to Azekah, the LORD hurled large hailstones down on them from
the sky, and more of them died from the hailstones than were killed by
the swords of the Israelites.
[12]On the day the LORD gave the Amorites over to Israel, Joshua said to
the LORD in the presence of Israel:

"O sun, stand still over Gibeon,
O moon, over the Valley of Aijalon."
[13]So the sun stood still,
and the moon stopped,
till the nation avenged itself on its enemies,

as it is written in the Book of Jashar.
The sun stopped in the middle of the sky and delayed going down
about a full day. [14]There has never been a day like it before or since, a
day when the LORD listened to a man. Surely the LORD was fighting for
Israel!
[15]Then Joshua returned with all Israel to the camp at Gilgal.

**1** One of the principal kings in the south gathered the whole region together to fight against Israel. Adoni-Zedek means "Lord of Righteousness" (cf. Melchi-Zedek, "King of Righteousness," Gen 14:18). News of Israel's victories at Jericho and Ai, with the extermination of all their inhabitants, struck fear into the heart of Adoni-Zedek. "Jerusalem," formerly called Jebus (Judg 19:10), was a stronghold of the Jebusites, one of the seven nations the Israelites were to drive out of the land (3:10). Though the king and his army were killed by Joshua and Israel, the city itself was not captured until after Joshua's death (Judg 1:8). Years later David captured it again (2 Sam 5:6–9) and made it his royal city.

**2** The defection of the Gibeonites was cause for great alarm for three reasons: (1) it was discouraging to see such a large city with an excellent army surrender to the enemy, (2) without Gibeon the southern coalition was severely weakened, and (3) they constituted a fifth column that would fight with Israel in time of war. Though it had no king (see comment on 9:11), Gibeon was "like one of the royal cities"; it was just as strong and influential as any city-state (cf. 11:12). There is a wordplay between "Gibeon" and "good fighters," which is literally *gibbōrîm*. Boling (p. 279) defines *gibbōrîm* as "men trained in combat and prosperous enough to afford armament, squire, and leisure time for such activity."

**3** "Hebron," known also as Kiriath Arba (20:7; cf. Gen 23:2; 35:27), was located about twenty miles south of Jerusalem. "Jarmuth" is modern Khirbet Yarmuk, about sixteen miles west of Jerusalem. "Lachish," modern Tell ed-Duweir, about twenty-five miles southwest of Jerusalem, guarded the valley that led to Hebron. "Eglon," about seven miles west of Lachish, is modern Tell el-Hesi on the edge of the foothills. "Debir," about thirty miles southwest of Jerusalem, is familiar in the OT as a place name but is also mentioned here as the name of the king of Eglon.

**4–5** Gibeon had to be punished to prevent any further defections to Israel and also to eliminate the threat of their siding with Israel in time of war (v.4). So the coalition of kings moved against Gibeon (v.5).

**6** The Gibeonites turned to Joshua for help because the treaty of peace (9:15) obligated Joshua to defend his vassals.

**7** The Hebrew word *'ālāh* (lit., "to go up") is the regular word for marching into battle. The march from Gilgal to Gibeon involved an ascent of 3,300 feet. It is not clear whether "all the best fighting men" is descriptive of the whole Israelite army or only a special division of elite troops (see comment on v.2).

**8** In Number 27:21 it is mentioned that Joshua was to receive answers from the Lord on the basis of the Urim and Thummim. Perhaps that is involved in this rather stereotyped form "The LORD said to Joshua" (cf. 1:1; 3:7; 4:1; et al.). The present situation was urgent, and God's word of encouragement and his promise of victory were welcome.

**9** A forced march under the cover of darkness was another of Joshua's well-planned strategies. The march, which covered a distance of about twenty miles, would have taken eight to ten hours.

**10** By means of a forced march, Joshua took the enemy by surprise; and the Lord used this to create disorder. This is another instance where human efforts and divine intervention worked hand in hand. "Beth Horon" is modern Beit 'Ur. It was composed of two parts: The upper town (Beit 'Ur el-Faqa) was about five miles northwest of Gibeon and the lower town (Beit 'Ur et-Taḥta) was about two miles farther (ZPEB, 1:536). The pass at Beth Horon was an important point of access to the hill country and Jerusalem. "Azekah" is modern Tel Zakariyeh in the Valley of Elah about seventeen miles south of Beth Horon. Joshua pursued his enemy along the ancient road that went from Lachish to the Valley of Aijalon. The site of "Makkedah" has not been determined. In disarray the enemy fled down from the mountains through the pass at Beth Horon and headed south.

**11** When God intervened on behalf of his people with "large hailstones," the accomplishments of Israel's army were dwarfed by comparison. It was the Lord who won the victory. The Canaanites, who worshiped nature deities, must have thought that their own gods were aiding the Israelites.

**12** This miracle is often called "Joshua's long day." It is the third and last great miracle in the book and the most bewildering. No final word can be said about the exact nature of the miracles when scholars disagree on the meaning of vv.12–13. The NIV is correct in arranging vv.12b–13a as poetic, and they must be interpreted accordingly. The LXX has attempted to remove any suggestion that Joshua addressed the sun and moon as pagan deities by making Joshua address the Lord: "Then Joshua said to the Lord . . . Let the sun. . . ." The word translated "stand still" is often translated "be silent." Joshua may have been requesting that the sun not shine with its normal brightness and heat. Cloud cover could have been a by-product of the hail storm (v.11). Joshua desired favorable conditions so as to be able to make the most of the victory. After an all-night march, the sun's heat would have sapped the strength of the weary Israelites; and relief from that heat would have helped just as much as extended daylight. This does not explain the mention of the moon. Perhaps it merely provides a poetic parallel to the sun. (On the various aspects of this event, see Goslinga, pp. 189–93.)

**13** The Hebrew word *'āmaḏ* ("stand," "stand still," or "stop") is used for the moon in parallel with *dāmam* for the sun. The word *'āmaḏ* was used in 3:16 to say that the waters of the Jordan "stopped flowing." In a poetic passage like this, it could mean "stop moving" or even "stop shining." "The Book of Jashar" (i.e., "the book of the righteous") is mentioned also in 2 Samuel 1:18. Like "the book of the annals of the kings of Israel" (1 Kings 14:19) and "the book of the annals of the kings of Judah" (1 Kings 14:29), this bit of ancient Hebrew literature has been lost. Perhaps it was a collection of heroic songs. All of vv.12–15 may have been quoted from that source. The final statement in this verse clearly favors the notion that the sun stood still or that it slowed down in its course across the sky. In either event the problem for geophysics are so great that some other solution has been eagerly sought by scholars both liberal and conservative. John S. Holladay ("The Day[s] the *Moon* Stood Still," JBL 87 [1968]: 166) lists a few suggestions:

> Modern interpreters, on the other hand, usually seek to place the events of the poem, taken as poetic hyperbole, meaningfully in the proper order. Thus H.H. Rowley speaks of a prayer that the dawn not come too soon. R.B.Y. Scott suggests that it is a request that the clouds hold (Josh 10:11) in order that the heat of the day not interfere with the pursuit of the enemy. John Bright in turn sees in the poem a prayer that the sun not dissipate the early morning mist in the valley before the surprise attack can take place, and Immanuel Velikovsky interprets the unique phenomena as the consequence of a radical alteration in the orbit of the planet Venus—surely the most elaborate attempt yet made at "taking the Bible seriously" as a unique scientific and historical record.

Holladay seeks to understand this poetic passage in the context of Joshua's time. After an extensive examination of ancient literature, he concludes that Joshua was asking for a favorable omen in the skies. Similar investigations led R.D. Wilson ("What Does 'The Sun Stood Still' Mean?" *Moody Monthly* 21 [October, 1920]: 67) to propose that the passage refers to an eclipse of the sun. He translated vv.12b–14 as follows:

> Be eclipsed, O sun, in Gibeon,
> And thou moon in the valley of Aijalon!
>
> And the sun was eclipsed and the moon turned back, while the nation was avenged on its enemies. Is it not written upon the book of Jashar?

And the sun stayed in the half of the heaven,
And set not hastily as when a day is done.

And there never was a day like that day before or since, in respect to Jehovah's hearing the voice of a man.

Reverence for God's Word should encourage us to suspend judgment until more evidence is available. In the meantime no single explanation can be made a test of orthodoxy.

**14** "There has never been a day like it before" is a stereotyped expression found also in 2 Kings 18:5 and 23:25. Something very spectacular occurred that day that elevated Joshua as a man of God: his prayers were unusually effective. This is another parallel between Moses and Joshua. Moses is described as one with whom God spoke "face to face" (cf. Num 12:6–8). This episode reminds us again that Israel was not winning the land by their own strength; God was giving it to them.

**15** This verse seems out of place here. The events of vv.16–27 are part of the battle, and it is very unlikely that Joshua returned to Gilgal in the middle of it all. Perhaps this verse concludes the quotation from the Book of Jashar. On the other hand, in Hebrew narrative style vv.7–14 may describe the battle in terms of the supernatural assistance provided by the Lord, and then vv.16–42 go over the same ground supplying details about the fate of the various kings and of their respective cities. In this case v.15 and v.43 would be describing the same event.

### b. *The execution of the five Amorite kings*

#### 10:16–28

16Now the five kings had fled and hidden in the cave at Makkedah.
17When Joshua was told that the five kings had been found hiding in the
cave at Makkedah, 18he said, "Roll large rocks up to the mouth of the
cave, and post some men there to guard it. 19But don't stop! Pursue
your enemies, attack them from the rear and don't let them reach their
cities, for the LORD your God has given them into your hand."
20So Joshua and the Israelites destroyed them completely—almost to
a man—but the few who were left reached their fortified cities. 21The
whole army then returned safely to Joshua in the camp at Makkedah,
and no one uttered a word against the Israelites.
22Joshua said, "Open the mouth of the cave and bring those five kings
out to me." 23So they brought the five kings out of the cave—the kings
of Jerusalem, Hebron, Jarmuth, Lachish and Eglon. 24When they had
brought these kings to Joshua, he summoned all the men of Israel and
said to the army commanders who had come with him, "Come here and
put your feet on the necks of these kings." So they came forward and
placed their feet on their necks.
25Joshua said to them, "Do not be afraid; do not be discouraged. Be
strong and courageous. This is what the LORD will do to all the enemies
you are going to fight." 26Then Joshua struck and killed the kings and
hung them on five trees, and they were left hanging on the trees until
evening.
27At sunset Joshua gave the order and they took them down from the
trees and threw them into the cave where they had been hiding. At the
mouth of the cave they placed large rocks, which are there to this day.

28 That day Joshua took Makkedah. He put the city and its king to the sword and totally destroyed everyone in it. He left no survivors. And he did to the king of Makkedah as he had done to the king of Jericho.

**16** "The five kings" are named in v.3.

**17–18** "Large rocks" (v.18) were placed at the entrance of the cave to prevent the kings who "had been found hiding" (v.17) there from escaping and thus to free the warriors to pursue the enemy.

**19** The warriors were encouraged to fight hard, "for the LORD your God has given them into your hand." The human agents are fully involved and their efforts are essential, but the final outcome is determined by the Lord. As many as possible of the enemy were to be slain in the open fields, because it would be nearly impossible to capture them once they had reached their fortified cities.

**20** With the phrase "almost to a man," the translators apparently have sought to ease the tension between the first and last parts of the verse. Literally, the verse says, "Now when Joshua and the sons of Israel finished smiting them with a very great slaughter until they were completely destroyed, then what survivors there were entered the fortified cities." It is another example of the use of hyperbole for emphasis.

**21** The statement that "The whole army then returned safely" implies that the Israelites suffered no casualties. In the warfare of that time, it was not unusual for the victor to suffer few casualties or none at all. Apparently the campaign took longer than this extremely abbreviated account might lead one to suppose. In vv.27 and 32 there are other indications that the campaign took several days, or perhaps weeks (cf. 11:18). The observation that "no one uttered a word" provides another parallel in the careers of Moses and Joshua. Moses told Pharaoh that the Egyptians would wail over the death of their firstborn, "but among the Israelites not a dog will bark at any man or animal" (Exod 11:7).

**22–24** The five kings were humiliated before they were killed (vv.22–23). Joshua did all he could to bolster the morale of his troops. When the officers placed their feet on the necks of these great and powerful kings (v.24), they recognized that they were frail human beings like everyone else. This practice was widespread in ancient times and is pictured in the paintings and reliefs of Egypt and Assyria (cf. the phrase "to put his enemies under his feet," 1 Kings 5:3; Ps 110:1; cf. Ps 8:6).

**25** The words "be strong and courageous" remind us of chapter 1 (vv.6–7, 9, 18).

**26** Joshua's subordinates may have slain the kings. We similarly say that a contractor built a house, though he himself may not have driven a single nail. The bodies of the kings were hung on trees to make them an example and to add to their humiliation (cf. 8:29). The Hebrew word *'ēṣ* means both "tree" and "pole"; consequently these kings may have been impaled on five poles erected for that very purpose.

**27** The bodies were taken down "at sunset" to keep from defiling the land (cf. Deut 21:23). The cave provided a convenient place for the burial of the slain kings; and by piling large rocks at the entrance, a memorial was created to keep alive the memory of another victory God enabled Israel to win.

**28** "That day" may mean "at that time" and not refer to a literal twenty-four hour period. For "totally destroyed" see the comment on 6:17. This comparison with the king of Jericho is strange because no details were given as to how Joshua treated him (cf. 6:20–21, 24).

### c. *The completion of the southern campaign*

#### 10:29–43

[29]Then Joshua and all Israel with him moved on from Makkedah to
Libnah and attacked it. [30]The LORD also gave that city and its king into
Israel's hand. The city and everyone in it Joshua put to the sword. He left
no survivors there. And he did to its king as he had done to the king of
Jericho.
[31]Then Joshua and all Israel with him moved on from Libnah to
Lachish; he took up positions against it and attacked it. [32]The LORD
handed Lachish over to Israel, and Joshua took it on the second day.
The city and everyone in it he put to the sword, just as he had done to
Libnah. [33]Meanwhile, Horam king of Gezer had come up to help
Lachish, but Joshua defeated him and his army—until no survivors
were left.
[34]Then Joshua and all Israel with him moved on from Lachish to
Eglon; they took up positions against it and attacked it. [35]They captured
it that same day and put it to the sword and totally destroyed everyone in
it, just as they had done to Lachish.
[36]Then Joshua and all Israel with him went up from Eglon to Hebron
and attacked it. [37]They took the city and put it to the sword, together
with its king, its villages and everyone in it. They left no survivors. Just
as at Eglon, they totally destroyed it and everyone in it.
[38]Then Joshua and all Israel with him turned around and attacked
Debir. [39]They took the city, its king and its villages, and put them to the
sword. Everyone in it they totally destroyed. They left no survivors. They
did to Debir and its king as they had done to Libnah and its king and to
Hebron.
[40]So Joshua subdued the whole region, including the hill country, the
Negev, the western foothills and the mountain slopes, together with all
their kings. He left no survivors. He totally destroyed all who breathed,
just as the LORD, the God of Israel, had commanded. [41]Joshua subdued
them from Kadesh Barnea to Gaza and from the whole region of Goshen
to Gibeon. [42]All these kings and their lands Joshua conquered in one
campaign, because the LORD, the God of Israel, fought for Israel.
[43]Then Joshua returned with all Israel to the camp at Gilgal.

**29** "Libnah" may be modern Tell Bornat, about six miles northwest of Lachish. Libnah, Makkedah, and Debir were not included in the coalition. Joshua was beginning to secure the foothills before invading the mountains. Libnah became one of the Levitical cities (21:13).

**30** Though the technical term *ḥērem* is not used, Joshua devoted the entire population to God by destruction (cf. v.28).

**31** For "Lachish" see the comment on v.3.

**32** The words "On the second day" are another clue that the campaign in the south may have continued for several days or weeks, but there is insufficient data to develop a detailed chronology.

**33** "Gezer" is modern Tell Jezer, near the entrance to the Valley of Aijalon, about a day's march north of Lachish. Joshua destroyed the king and his army, though he did not follow through to capture the city itself (cf. 16:10). In the time of Solomon, the king of Egypt captured Gezer and gave it to his daughter when she was married to Solomon (1 Kings 9:16). Gezer became a Levitical town (21:21).

**34–35** For "Eglon" see the comment on v.3.

**36** For "Hebron" see the comment on v.3. Leaving the foothills Joshua moved into the highlands and captured the two principal cities.

**37** The words "together with its king" may refer to v.26. It is possible, however, that Hebron had already enthroned a new king. The surrounding villages were subject to the king of Hebron and looked to that city for refuge and protection in time of emergency. Joshua "totally destroyed it and everyone in it." In 14:6–15; 15:15–19; and Judges 1:10–13, it is recorded that Caleb and men of Judah captured Hebron and Debir. It need not surprise us that a number of cities changed hands several times.

**38–39** "Debir" may be modern Khirbet Rabud, about seven and one-half miles south of Hebron (see Aharoni, p. 278 n. 78).

**40** This comprehensive statement of Joshua's victories in the south demonstrates that the accounts of the capture of a few cities is only a sketchy summary of the more important victories in a far more extensive campaign. "The hill country" is the central mountain range principally in Judah and Ephraim. "The Negev" is the desert in southern Palestine. "The western foothills," also called the Shephelah, is the area between the hill country of Judah and the coastal plain. "The mountain slopes" refers to the steep descent from the mountains to the Jordan Valley. We know, however, that Jerusalem was not conquered at this time (Judg 1:8); and although Jarmuth was also one of the cities in the southern coalition, its capture is not recorded here either. It appears that the Conquest was extensive enough to give Israel control of the area but not possession of every city. For "He totally destroyed" see the comment on 6:17. Probably the expression "all who breathed" did not include the livestock, which the Israelites were permitted to take as booty.

**41** The phrase "from Kadesh Barnea to Gaza" denotes a large area in southern Palestine. "Goshen" was a region between the hill country and the Negev. Obviously it was not the Goshen in Egypt.

**42** We have no way of determining the length of this "one campaign," but it must have taken a considerable amount of time. Victory in the south clearly demonstrated that "the LORD, the God of Israel, fought for Israel."

**43** The Israelites did not occupy these cities immediately. Instead they returned to their families and livestock in their base camp "at Gilgal."

## D. *The Northern Campaign (11:1–15)*

### 1. *The northern coalition formed*

11:1–5

> [1]When Jabin king of Hazor heard of this, he sent word to Jobab king of Madon, to the kings of Shimron and Acshaph, [2]and to the northern kings who were in the mountains, in the Arabah south of Kinnereth, in the western foothills and in Naphoth Dor on the west; [3]to the Canaanites in the east and west; to the Amorites, Hittites, Perizzites and Jebusites in the hill country; and to the Hivites below Hermon in the region of Mizpah. [4]They came out with all their troops and a large number of horses and chariots—a huge army, as numerous as the sand on the seashore. [5]All these kings joined forces and made camp together at the Waters of Merom, to fight against Israel.

**1** "Jabin" was still the name of the king of Hazor years later (cf. Judg 4:2). For this reason it has been suggested that the Judges account (4:2) and this one are two different versions of a single event. Jabin may have been a dynastic name assumed by all kings of Hazor. "Hazor" is modern Tell el-Qedah, about ten miles north of the Sea of Galilee. It was by far the most imposing city in all of Palestine, covering about two hundred acres (cf. the five or six acres of Jericho).

Hazor with its allies and armaments confronted Joshua and Israel with their last and most awesome challenge. Jabin may have heard of all Israel's mighty exploits from the crossing of the Red Sea (cf. 9:9–10) or simply of Israel's victories in Palestine (cf. 10:1).

The traditional location of "Madon," west of the Sea of Galilee near modern Qarn Haṭṭin, is now suspect. Aharoni (p. 117) suggests that the correct name is Merom (cf. LXX: *marrōn*). "Shimron" is Khirbet Sammuniyeh in the Plain of Esdraelon north of Megiddo. The precise location of "Acshaph" is uncertain.

**2** The cities named in v.1 were south of Hazor, but Jabin also summoned "the northern kings." The thirty-one kings named in 12:9–24 are probably only the more important ones. "The Arabah" is the valley through which the Jordan River flows. "Kinnereth" is either the Sea of Galilee or the city of Kinnereth on the northwestern shore. "Naphoth Dor" may refer to the coastal plain south of Mount Carmel where Dor was the principal city.

**3** Since "Canaanite" was a generic term for all who lived in the lowlands, "the Canaanites in the east" must refer to the people living in the Jordan Valley (cf. Num 13:29). The Amorites, Hittites, Perizzites, and Jebusites lived in the hill country. The inhabitants of Jerusalem were Jebusites. Joshua destroyed the army of the "Jebusites" (10:9–14) and killed Adoni-Zedek their king (10:22–27), but he did not capture their city. Possibly survivors from the southern campaign rallied to the support of the northern coalition. "Hermon" is the highest mountain in the Anti-Lebanon range. "Mizpah" means "watchtower"; consequently there are a number of cities with that name. This one was at the foot of Mount Hermon.

**4** Though Palestine at this time was made up of independent and hostile city-states, the presence of a common enemy caused them to rally to Jabin's call. The northern coalition was Israel's most formidable foe in terms of both numbers and weaponry. Each successive battle that Israel fought was more difficult than the last. "Horses and chariots" posed an awesome challenge to the Israelites whose army was made up solely of foot soldiers. All previous battles had been on terrain where the use of chariots was not feasible. "As numerous as the sand on the seashore" is a hyperbolic and stereotyped expression used in the OT to describe a vast multitude; but, of course, it is not an infinite number.

**5** The "Waters of Merom" is now thought to be Wadi Merron, which flows from the northern mountains into the Sea of Galilee. This is a mountainous area (elevation 4,000 ft.) and unsuitable for the use of chariotry. Perhaps the kings of the north planned only to meet here to develop their strategy.

## 2. *The major battle*

### 11:6–9

**6The LORD said to Joshua, "Do not be afraid of them, because by this time tomorrow I will hand all of them over to Israel, slain. You are to hamstring their horses and burn their chariots."**
**7So Joshua and his whole army came against them suddenly at the Waters of Merom and attacked them, 8and the LORD gave them into the hand of Israel. They defeated them and pursued them all the way to Greater Sidon, to Misrephoth Maim, and to the Valley of Mizpah on the east, until no survivors were left. 9Joshua did to them as the LORD had directed: He hamstrung their horses and burned their chariots.**

**6, 9** Before this last and most challenging battle, Joshua did not fail to consult the Lord (v.6). Horses were hamstrung by cutting the Achilles tendon on the hind legs to render them unfit for military use. Disabling the horses and burning the chariots (v.9) showed disdain for modern weaponry; Israel's confidence was to be in God alone (cf. Ps 20:7). Early Israelite tradition is consistently negative toward the use of horses and chariots (cf. Deut 17:16; 2 Sam 8:4; Isa 31:1).

**7** Joshua again resorted to a surprise attack (cf. 10:9). The enemies were caught unprepared and were driven into the mountains where chariots could not be used.

**8** Once again victory was God's gift to Israel. The defeated enemy fled in a northerly direction. Sidon is on the Phoenician coast north of Mount Carmel. Greater Sidon was on the mainland, whereas Lesser Sidon was an island fortress. The identification of "Misrephoth Maim" with modern Ain Misherifeh is questioned by Aharoni (p. 238). "The Valley of Mizpah" must have been in the north in the vicinity of Sidon and Misrephoth Maim. Perhaps it is to be identified with the Mizpah (v.3) at the foot of Mount Hermon.

## 3. *The capture of the northern cities*

### 11:10–15

**10At that time Joshua turned back and captured Hazor and put its king to the sword. (Hazor had been the head of all these kingdoms.)**

[11]Everyone in it they put to the sword. They totally destroyed them, not
sparing anything that breathed, and he burned up Hazor itself.
[12]Joshua took all these royal cities and their kings and put them to the
sword. He totally destroyed them, as Moses the servant of the LORD had
commanded. [13]Yet Israel did not burn any of the cities built on their
mounds—except Hazor, which Joshua burned. [14]The Israelites carried
off for themselves all the plunder and livestock of these cities, but all the
people they put to the sword until they completely destroyed them, not
sparing anyone that breathed. [15]As the LORD commanded his servant
Moses, so Moses commanded Joshua, and Joshua did it; he left nothing
undone of all that the LORD commanded Moses.

**10** The phrase "at that time" may denote the same day or several days later. Joshua "turned back" from pursuing his enemies in the north and concentrated on Hazor. As in the southern campaign, Joshua first defeated the combined armies and then captured the individual cities. The execution of the king is always mentioned separately. Perhaps the kings were killed with some special ceremony as in 10:22–27. Because of its size, Hazor had been the predominant city in the area for a long time.

**11** With almost monotonous regularity our writer reminds us that Joshua faithfully carried out the command that all the inhabitants of the land be devoted to the Lord by totally destroying them. As in 10:40, "anything that breathed" refers only to human beings. Archaeological excavations indicate that Hazor was destroyed sometime in the late fourteenth century B.C. and was not rebuilt until the time of Solomon (cf. 1 Kings 9:15).

**12** The "royal cities" were city-states each of which had its own king (cf. 10:2). We are reminded again that Joshua was completing the work that Moses had begun.

**13–14** The burning of the cities had not been commanded by God (cf. Deut 7:1–6; 20:16–18); consequently they were ready immediately for reoccupation by Israel. As the Lord had promised, the Israelites would live in cities they did not build and would have food that they had not provided (Deut 6:10–11).

**15** At the end of the Conquest, our writer reminds us again of his theme: Victory and blessing are the outcome of obedience. Joshua has done everything the Lord commanded Moses. The writer uses extravagant language—"he left nothing undone"—to celebrate Joshua's obedience and Israel's great victories even though he does not hesitate in succeeding chapters to indicate that the Conquest was still incomplete (cf. 13:1–5, 13; 15:63; 16:10; 17:12).

## E. *A Summary of the Conquest*

### 11:16–23

[16]So Joshua took this entire land: the hill country, all the Negev, the
whole region of Goshen, the western foothills, the Arabah and the
mountains of Israel with their foothills, [17]from Mount Halak, which rises
toward Seir, to Baal Gad in the Valley of Lebanon below Mount Hermon.
He captured all their kings and struck them down, putting them to
death. [18]Joshua waged war against all these kings for a long time.
[19]Except for the Hivites living in Gibeon, not one city made a treaty of
peace with the Israelites, who took them all in battle. [20]For it was the

Lord himself who hardened their hearts to wage war against Israel, so
that he might destroy them totally, exterminating them without mercy,
as the Lord had commanded Moses.
[21]At that time Joshua went and destroyed the Anakites from the hill
country: from Hebron, Debir and Anab, from all the hill country of
Judah, and from all the hill country of Israel. Joshua totally destroyed
them and their towns. [22]No Anakites were left in Israelite territory; only
in Gaza, Gath and Ashdod did any survive. [23]So Joshua took the entire
land, just as the Lord had directed Moses, and he gave it as an
inheritance to Israel according to their tribal divisions.
Then the land had rest from war.

**16** When the writer says that "Joshua took this entire land," he means that he gained control of the whole region even though he did not take every city. The last of the Canaanites were not subjected to Israel's authority until the reign of David. "The hill country" is the southern part of the central highlands that run through Palestine from north to south. "The Negev" is the desert area in the south. For "Goshen" see comment on 10:41. The "western foothills" also extended throughout Palestine from north to south between the central highlands and the coastal plain. The "Arabah" is the valley in which the Jordan River and the Dead Sea are found, and it continues on to the Gulf of Aqabah. The "mountains of Israel" refers to the central highlands in central Palestine that are called the hills of Ephraim. The coastal plains where the Canaanites were able to employ their chariots are not mentioned (cf. 9:1) because Joshua did not conquer those areas (cf. 17:16; Judg 1:19). The southern coastland was the stronghold of the Philistines, who continued to harass Israel until they were finally subdued by David.

**17** "Mount Halak" is modern Jebel Halaq about twenty-seven miles south of Beersheba. "Seir" is the name for the mountains of Edom southeast of the Dead Sea. "Baal Gad" may be modern Baalbek in the Beqa' Valley between the Lebanon and Anti-Lebanon mountains.

**18** Though the style of the narrative creates the impression of a lightning-quick campaign, our author does not conceal the fact that it really took "a long time." (In Exod 23:29–30, it is clearly stated that the takeover of the land would a be slow process over a period of many years.) Undoubtedly the Conquest involved many battles that are not mentioned.

**19** The surrender of the Gibeonites was one small exception to the general rule of totally annihilating the population of Canaan.

**20** God hardened the Canaanites' hearts, not to keep them from repenting, but to prevent them from surrendering to Israel in unrepentance. The examples of Rahab and the Gibeonites demonstrate the unchanging purpose of God that "Everyone who calls on the name of the Lord will be saved" (Rom 10:13). As in the case of Pharaoh, God may be said to harden the hearts of those who harden their own (cf. Exod 8:32 with Exod 9:12). God was patient as long as there was any hope of repentance (Rom 2:4), but the sin of the Amorites had reached its full measure (Gen 15:16). The writer celebrated the annihilation of the Canaanites, which is so offensive to the modern mind, because he knew there was no other way that God's gracious purpose could be fulfilled.

**21** It was the report of Anakites in the land that had discouraged Israel from entering from Kadesh Barnea (Deut 1:19–33). It is appropriate now in summarizing the victories of the Israelites to tell of their triumph over these very same people. Joshua as leader of the army is credited with the accomplishments of his subordinates (cf. 15:13–14, 17–19). "Anab" is Khirbet ʿAnab es-Seghireh, southwest of Debir.

**22** "Gaza, Gath and Ashdod" were three of the five Philistine cities that were located in the southern coastal plain. This verse places that whole region outside Israelite territory.

**23** On the statement "Joshua took the entire land," see the comment on v.16. "He gave it as an inheritance" is a transitional statement: with the Conquest completed (chs. 1–12), the author turns to the division of the land (chs. 13–19).

"Then the land had rest from war" is a profound declaration and a fitting conclusion for the first section of the book. It is prophetic of the "rest" that will come when all evil has been conquered and Christ is made King of Kings and Lord of Lords (Rev 11:15; 19:16).

## F. *A List of Defeated Kings (12:1–24)*

### 1. *Kings whom Moses defeated*

12:1–6

[1]These are the kings of the land whom the Israelites had defeated and whose territory they took over east of the Jordan, from the Arnon Gorge to Mount Hermon, including all the eastern side of the Arabah:

[2]Sihon king of the Amorites,
who reigned in Heshbon. He ruled from Aroer on the rim of the
Arnon Gorge—from the middle of the gorge—to the Jabbok River,
which is the border of the Ammonites. This included half of Gilead.
[3]He also ruled over the eastern Arabah from the Sea of Kinnereth to
the Sea of the Arabah (the Salt Sea), to Beth Jeshimoth, and then
southward below the slopes of Pisgah.

[4]And the territory of Og king of Bashan,
one of the last of the Rephaites, who reigned in Ashtaroth and
Edrei. [5]He ruled over Mount Hermon, Salecah, all of Bashan to the
border of the people of Geshur and Maacah, and half of Gilead to
the border of Sihon king of Heshbon.

[6]Moses, the servant of the LORD, and the Israelites conquered them. And Moses the servant of the LORD gave their land to the Reubenites, the Gadites and the half-tribe of Manasseh to be their possession.

**1** The Conquest is summarized by listing the kings that Israel defeated. East of the Jordan there were only two kings, each of whom ruled a wide area with many cities. The land west of the Jordan was divided into individual city-states. Israel's conquests on both sides of the Jordan are mentioned together here to emphasize the unity of the nation. The conquests summarized in this chapter do not begin to reach the boundaries of the Promised Land as stated in 1:4. The "Arnon Gorge" is modern Wadi el-Mujib. The Arnon River flows through this gorge and drops 3,500 feet in thirty-eight miles to enter the Dead Sea at about its midpoint north and south. This gorge formed the northern boundary of Moab. "From the Arnon Gorge to Mount Hermon" defines the territory in terms of its farthest extremes south and north. For "the Arabah" see the comment on 11:16.

**2** Most of the territory east of the Jordan is either mountainous or high plateau; accordingly the inhabitants are called Amorites (cf. comment on 3:10). Sihon and Og are called the two kings of the Amorites (2:10; 9:10). The defeat of Sihon is recorded in Numbers 21:21–31 and Deuteronomy 2:26–37. "Heshbon" is modern Tell Heshban, about fifteen miles east of where the Jordan flows into the Dead Sea. "Aroer" is modern ʿAraʿir on the edge of the desert, guarding the highway passing through the Arnon. The "Jabbok River" is modern Nahr ez-Zerqa, a tributary of the Jordan that drops 3,200 feet as it makes its way through the mountains of Gilead. The "Ammonites" lived east of Gilead. "Gilead" is the mountainous area east of the Jordan both north and south of the Jabbok.

**3** "The Sea of Kinnereth" is the Sea of Galilee, and "the Sea of the Arabah" is the Dead Sea. "Beth Jeshimoth" is modern Tell el-ʿAzeimeh on the northeastern shore of the Dead Sea. "Southward" is literally either "from Teman" or "in the direction of Teman." Teman is in Edom about midway between the Dead Sea and the Gulf of Aqabah. It is not clear whether "the slopes of Pisgah" refers to a single peak or to the entire range of the Abarim Mountains overlooking the northeastern shore of the Dead Sea. It was from here that Moses was permitted to view the Promised Land (Deut 34:1). "The slopes" refers to the steep descent into the Jordan Valley.

**4–5** Israel's victory over Og is recorded in Numbers 21:33–35 and Deuteronomy 3:1–11. "Bashan" (v.4) is the rich pastureland east of the Sea of Galilee, bordered by the Yarmuk River on the south, Mount Hermon on the north, and Salecah on the east. Og was one of the last of a race of giants called "Rephaites" (cf. Gen 14:5). The dimensions of his huge iron bed were thirteen feet by six feet (Deut 3:11). "Ashtaroth" is modern Tell ʿAshtarah and "Edrei" is modern Derʿa. They are located in eastern Bashan on tributaries of the Yarmuk River. Og ruled the "half of Gilead" (v.5) north of the Jabbok.

"Salecah" (v.5) is modern Salkhad, southeast of Ashtaroth at the base of Jebel Druze. "The people of Geshur and Maacah" are two groups of Arameans living on the frontier of Israelite Territory east of the Sea of Galilee.

**6** Moses is mentioned at the end of vv.1–6 and Joshua at the beginning of vv.7–24 to place them side by side and highlight the way the work of Joshua complemented the work of Moses. The statements about them are parallel: each speaks of the conquest and disposition of a certain part of the land. For "gave their land," see Numbers 32 and Deuteronomy 3:12–20.

## 2. *Kings whom Joshua defeated*

### 12:7–24

**7**These are the kings of the land that Joshua and the Israelites conquered on the west side of the Jordan, from Baal Gad in the Valley of

Lebanon to Mount Halak, which rises toward Seir (their lands Joshua
gave as an inheritance to the tribes of Israel according to their tribal
divisions—8 the hill country, the western foothills, the Arabah, the
mountain slopes, the desert and the Negev—the lands of the Hittites,
Amorites, Canaanites, Perizzites, Hivites and Jebusites):

9 the king of Jericho — one
the king of Ai (near Bethel) — one
10 the king of Jerusalem — one
the king of Hebron — one
11 the king of Jarmuth — one
the king of Lachish — one
12 the king of Eglon — one
the king of Gezer — one
13 the king of Debir — one
the king of Geder — one
14 the king of Hormah — one
the king of Arad — one
15 the king of Libnah — one
the king of Adullam — one
16 the king of Makkedah — one
the king of Bethel — one
17 the king of Tappuah — one
the king of Hepher — one
18 the king of Aphek — one
the king of Lasharon — one
19 the king of Madon — one
the king of Hazor — one
20 the king of Shimron Meron — one
the king of Acshaph — one
21 the king of Taanach — one
the king of Megiddo — one
22 the king of Kedesh — one
the king of Jokneam in Carmel — one
23 the king of Dor (in Naphoth Dor) — one
the king of Goyim in Gilgal — one
24 the king of Tirzah — one

thirty-one kings in all.

**7** For "Mount Halak" see the comment on 11:17.

**8** The "Negev" is the desert area south of Beersheba; so perhaps "the desert" designates the southern extreme of the Negev (cf. 15:61–62, where cities of the desert are named). For "Hittites" et al., see comment on 3:10. The Girgashites are omitted from this list of the nations of Palestine as in 9:1 and 11:3.

**9–13a** This is a catalog of the kings mentioned in chapters 6–10. The kings and armies of Jerusalem, Jarmuth, and Gezer were killed, but the cities were not captured. This may have been true of other cities also (e.g., Taanach, Dor, and Megiddo; cf. Judg 1:27).

**9** The necessity to specify that Ai was "near Bethel" suggests that there were other ruins with this same name (see comment on 7:2).

**13** The names of four of these southern cities—"Geder" (v.13b), "Hormah" and "Arad" (v.14), and "Adullam" (v.15b)—do not appear in the narratives of chapters 6–10, which confirms our suspicion that the author has only recorded a few of the battles.

"Geder" is modern Khirbet Jedur located in the hill country about five miles north of Hebron.

**14** "Hormah" means "destruction." This name was given to a number of cities that had been destroyed (cf. Num 14:44–45; 21:1–3; Judg 1:16–17). The "Hormah" that is mentioned here is modern Khirbet el Meshash, southeast of Beersheba. "Arad" is modern Tell 'Arad in the northern Negev east of Hormah.

**15** For "Libnah" see 10:29–30. "Adullam" is modern Tell esh-Sheikh Madhkur, about twelve miles northwest of Hebron.

**16** For "Makkedah" see 10:28. For "Bethel" see 8:16–17. According to 8:17, the army of Bethel participated in the battle of Ai, but the account does not record the killing of either king or army. The conquest of Bethel is reported in Judges 1:22–26. As we have seen, however, some cities were conquered more than once. With the name of Bethel, the list turns to cities in central and northern Palestine.

**17** "Tappuah" is modern Sheikh Abu Zarad, about eight miles southwest of Nablus. "Hepher" was in Sharon Valley, on the border of Ephraim and Manasseh.

**18** "Aphek" is modern Ras el 'Ain, about twelve miles northeast of Haipha. Since there were several Apheks (in Phoenicia, Asher, and Bashan), it is likely that "Lasharon" is not the name of a city but locates Aphek "in Sharon."

**19–20** For "Madon," "Hazor," "Shimron," and "Acshaph," see 11:1.

**21** "Taanach" is modern Tell Ti'innik in the Valley of Esdraelon. Excavations have produced evidence that rich and poor lived here side by side in the twelfth century B.C. This corresponds with the picture in Judges 1:27 of Canaanites living alongside Israelites whose standard of living was much lower than theirs. Taanach became a Levitical town (21:25). "Megiddo" is Tell el-Muteiellin in the Valley of Esdraelon. It became an important city in later Israelite history.

**22** "Kedesh" is probably in reference to Kedesh in Naphtali (modern Khirbet Qedish), northwest of Lake Huleh. "Jokneam in Carmel" is modern Tell Qeimun on the river Kishon.

**23** For "Dor" see 11:2. "Goyim" is the Hebrew word for "nations" or "Gentiles." Woudstra (p. 206, n. 6) proposes a slight emendation of the text to read "Galilee of the Gentiles" as in Isaiah 9:1. If "Gilgal" is the correct reading, it may be modern Jiljulieh, about four miles north of Aphek.

**24** "Tirzah" is modern Tell el-Far'ah, a few miles northeast of Nablus. It was the capital of the northern kingdom of Israel until the time of Omri (1 Kings 14:17; 15:21, 33; 16:6–24). "Thirty-one kings" is the correct total as the list stands. If "Lasharon" is not the name of a city (v.18) but locates Aphek "in Sharon," there would be one less.

Then by taking "Shimron Meron" as two separate names—Shimron and Meron—the full number would be restored.

## II. Dividing the Promised Land (13:1–21:45)

### A. *The Command to Divide the Land*

#### 13:1–7

> 1When Joshua was old and well advanced in years, the LORD said to him, "You are very old, and there are still very large areas of land to be taken over.
>
> 2"This is the land that remains: all the regions of the Philistines and Geshurites: 3from the Shihor River on the east of Egypt to the territory of Ekron on the north, all of it counted as Canaanite (the territory of the five Philistine rulers in Gaza, Ashdod, Ashkelon, Gath and Ekron—that of the Avvites); 4from the south, all the land of the Canaanites, from Arah of the Sidonians as far as Aphek, the region of the Amorites, 5the area of the Gebalites; and all Lebanon to the east, from Baal Gad below Mount Hermon to Lebo Hamath.
>
> 6"As for all the inhabitants of the mountain regions from Lebanon to Misrephoth Maim, that is, all the Sidonians, I myself will drive them out before the Israelites. Be sure to allocate this land to Israel for an inheritance, as I have instructed you, 7and divide it as an inheritance among the nine tribes and half of the tribe of Manasseh."

**1** "Joshua was old and well advanced in years" is a stereotyped expression that occurs again in 23:1–2 when Joshua was still older than he was at this time. Perhaps Joshua was about the same age as Caleb, whose age is given as eighty-five years in 14:10. This notice concerning Joshua's advanced age is more evidence that the Conquest took a long time. It seems that Israel had experienced a letdown after the widespread victories recorded in the first part of this book. The Lord had to remind Joshua of his unfinished task. The division of the land (v.7) was a part of his original commission from the Lord (1:6; Deut 31:7), and it had to be completed before Joshua died. This is one of the many places in Joshua where a fulfilled promise is set side by side with a promise that was yet to be fulfilled.

**2** A description follows of large areas that remain unconquered along the coast and in the far north. The many cities scattered here and there that had not been captured are not taken into consideration here. "The regions of the Philistines and Geshurites" is the southern coastland along the Mediterranean Sea. The Philistines came originally from Caphtor (Crete) as part of the migration of the "Sea Peoples" who invaded Egypt and Palestine in 1200 B.C. (see ZPEB, 4:767). They continued to oppress and harass the Israelites throughout the period of the Judges and the reign of Saul, until they were subdued by David. The Romans derived the name Palestine from Philistine. Geshur is the southernmost part of the Philistine plain and must not be confused with Geshur in Gilead (v.11). When David lived in exile among the Philistines, he made raids on the Geshurites (1 Sam 27:8).

**3** In the Egyptian language "Shihor" means "the Pool of Horus." In Isaiah 23:3 and Jeremiah 2:18, Shihor designates a branch of the Nile. Here (and in 1 Chron 13:5)

Shihor refers to the Wadi el-ʿArish, i.e., the River of Egypt, which flows from the Sinai Peninsula into the Mediterranean Sea about forty-five miles southwest of Gaza and marks the boundary between Egypt and Palestine.

"Ekron" is modern Khirbet el-Muqannaʿ. It was the farthest north of the five major Philistine cities, about twelve and a half miles northeast of Ashdod. Ekron was regarded as "Canaanite," for although the Philistines were not Canaanite, they had taken this area from the Canaanites. The five major cities of the Philistines are named: Gaza, Ashdod, and Ashkelon were near the coast, whereas Gath and Ekron were farther inland. "Gaza" is modern Ghazzeh. "Ashdod" is modern Esdud about three and a half miles southeast of modern Ashdod. "Ashkelon" is modern ʿAsqalan and "Gath" is Tell eṣ-Ṣafi. The rulers of these cities were not kings. In the Hebrew text they are called *seranîm,* which is a loan word from Greek. It is the word *tyrannos* ("tyrant"). In Deuteronomy 2:23 "the Avvites" are said to have been the original residents of the Philistine coastland whom the Philistines dispossessed. Apparently some of them still lived among the Philistines.

**4** Canaanite is used here in its broader sense to refer to any people, irrespective of origin, who lived in the lowlands. It refers to the inhabitants of the northern seacoast (cf. 5:1). "Sidonian" usually designates an inhabitant of Sidon or the surrounding area, but here it includes all the residents of the northern coastal plains. "Arah" is unknown. "Aphek" is modern Afqa near the sources of the River Ibrahim, southeast of Byblos. It is not to be confused with the Aphek on the Plains of Sharon (12:18). When used with reference to an area in the north, "Amorites" may refer to the people known as "Amurru," who are mentioned frequently in fourteenth- and thirteenth-century Egyptian and Hittite documents. We know of no time when Israel governed this far north along the Phoenician coast.

**5** "Gebal," also known as Byblos, is modern Jebail on the Phoenician coast north of Sidon. For "Baal Gad" see 11:17 and 12:7. "Lebo Hamath" is often translated "the entrance of Hamath." It is modern Lebweh, an important city on the Orontes River, along the border of Hamath (cf. 2 Kings 14:25). This area in the north was included in the territory defined in 1:4, but it extended far beyond the territory allotted to the nine and one-half tribes.

**6–7** The Lord reaffirmed his promise to drive out the inhabitants of the land (cf. 3:10). From this point on, however, further conquests would be the concern of the individual tribes. Moreover, the promise was conditional and was never completely fulfilled due to the incompleteness of Israel's obedience (cf. v.13). For "Misrephoth Maim" see 11:8. Israel had pursued her enemies into this territory and had defeated them. Evidently they did not fight with the natives of this area. Joshua was to divide all the land promised to Israel whether or not Israel possessed all of it at this time. The word translated "allocate" is the Hebrew word *happilehā* ("he caused it to fall") and refers to the casting of lots. The use of lots placed everything in the hands of God and freed Joshua and the elders from any possible charge of favoritism (cf. comment on 7:14). The concept of "inheritance" was very important in Israelite society. One's inheritance was a piece of real estate that was the inalienable possession of his family. A large portion of OT legislation is dedicated to regulating and protecting the rights of inheritance (cf. 17:3–6).

## Notes

---

**4** To read "from Arah" it was necessary to make a slight change in the vocalization from מְעָרָה ($m^e$'*ārāh*) to מֵעָרָה (*mē'ārāh*). No town by the name of Mearah is known either. The word means "cave." It is possible that it refers to an important cave in this area or a town by that name. Nevertheless, the reading "from Arah" is preferred because it preserves the customary designation of the two extremes of the area "from Arah to Aphek."

---

## B. *Division of the Land East of the Jordan (13:8–33)*

### 1. *Introduction*

13:8–14

[8]The other half of Manasseh, the Reubenites and the Gadites had received the inheritance that Moses had given them east of the Jordan, as he, the servant of the LORD, had assigned it to them.

[9]It extended from Aroer on the rim of the Arnon Gorge, and from
the town in the middle of the gorge, and included the whole plateau
of Medeba as far as Dibon, [10]and all the towns of Sihon king of the
Amorites, who ruled in Heshbon, out to the border of the Ammonites. [11]It also included Gilead, the territory of the people of Geshur
and Maacah, all of Mount Hermon and all Bashan as far as
Salecah—[12]that is, the whole kingdom of Og in Bashan, who had
reigned in Ashtaroth and Edrei and had survived as one of the last
of the Rephaites. Moses had defeated them and taken over their
land. [13]But the Israelites did not drive out the people of Geshur and
Maacah, so they continue to live among the Israelites to this day.

[14]But to the tribe of Levi he gave no inheritance, since the offerings made by fire to the LORD, the God of Israel, are their inheritance, as he promised them.

**8** The Transjordanian tribes receive a disproportionate amount of attention in this book that records the Conquest and division of the land *west* of the Jordan (cf. 1:12–15; 4:12; 12:1–6; 13:8–33; 22:1–34). The author was eager to uphold the unity of the Twelve Tribes in spite of the geographic separation and an undercurrent of feeling that only the land west of the Jordan was truly the Promised Land.

**9** For "Aroer on the rim of the Arnon Gorge," see the comment on 12:1–2. For "the town in the middle," see the comment on 12:2. The "plateau of Medeba" extended from the Arnon River on the south to the city of Heshbon in the north. It varied in elevation from 2,000 to 2,400 feet. "Medeba" is about seven miles south of Heshbon. "Dibon" is modern Dhiban about three les north of the Arnon. It later became the capital of Moab (cf. Isa 15:2; Jer 48:18, 22) and was the most important town on the road north of the Arnon River.

**10** For "Sihon" see 12:2. For "the border of the Ammonites," see 12:2.

**11** For "Gilead" see 12:2. "Geshur and Maacah" were Aramean states northeast of the Sea of Galilee. For "Bashan" see 12:4. For "Salecah" see 12:5.

**12** For "Ashtaroth and Edrei" see 12:4. For "Rephaites" see 12:4. For Moses' victory over Og and Sihon, see Numbers 21:21–35; Deuteronomy 2:26–37.

**13** Though this book celebrates God's great promises and Israel's mighty victories, it does not conceal the fact that sometimes the fulfillment of the promises was limited by Israel's failure to fully obey.

**14** The Levites were set apart for the service of the tabernacle and the altar (Exod 32:29; 38:21; Num 3:45). In order to preserve the full twelve tribes, without counting the Levites, the tribe of Joseph was divided into two tribes: Ephraim and Manasseh (cf. 14:3–4). Now, as the writer explained that the two and one-half tribes did not receive any inheritance west of the Jordan, he also explains that Levi received no inheritance at all.

## Notes

**14** This verse and v.33 are almost identical in the Hebrew. The major difference is that v.14 has the word אִשֵּׁי (*'iššê*, "offerings made by fire") and v.33 has the name מֹשֶׁה (*mōšeh*, "Moses"). Perhaps אִשֵּׁי is a scribal error.

### 2. *The inheritance of Reuben*

#### 13:15–23

15 This is what Moses had given to the tribe of Reuben, clan by clan:

16 The territory from Aroer on the rim of the Arnon Gorge, and from
the town in the middle of the gorge, and the whole plateau past
Medeba
17 to Heshbon and all its towns on the plateau, including
Dibon, Bamoth Baal, Beth Baal Meon,
18 Jahaz, Kedemoth, Mephaath,
19 Kiriathaim, Sibmah, Zereth Shahar on the hill in the
valley,
20 Beth Peor, the slopes of Pisgah, and Beth Jeshimoth
21 — all the towns on the plateau and the entire realm of Sihon king of
the Amorites, who ruled at Heshbon. Moses had defeated him and
the Midianite chiefs, Evi, Rekem, Zur, Hur and Reba—princes allied
with Sihon—who lived in that country.
22 In addition to those slain
in battle, the Israelites had put to the sword Balaam son of Beor,
who practiced divination.
23 The boundary of the Reubenites was
the bank of the Jordan. These towns and their villages were the
inheritance of the Reubenites, clan by clan.

**15** Beginning with Reuben in the south, a slightly more detailed description is given of the inheritance of each of the two and one-half tribes. The distribution "clan by clan" is in agreement with the principle laid down that the larger tribes were to receive a larger territory (see Num 26:52–56).

**17** For "Dibon" see v.9. "Bamoth Baal" was near Medeba. It is one of the places from which Balaam attempted to curse Israel (Num 22:41). "Beth Baal Meon" is modern Ma'in, about five miles southwest of Hesban.

**18** "Jahaz" was east of Medeba. It may be modern Khirbet el-Medeiyineh. It is where Sihon fought with Israel (Num 21:23; Deut 2:32). "Kedemoth" was selected to be a Levitical town (21:37). "Mephaath" may be modern Tell ej-Jawah, about five miles south of Amman.

**19** "Kiriathaim" may be modern Qaryat el-Mekhaiyet, the ruin of twin cities about six miles northwest of Dibon. It is the Shaveh Kiriathaim of Genesis 14:5 (Aharoni, p. 55). "Sibmah" may be modern Khirbet el-Qibah, about three miles southwest of Hesban. "Zereth Shahar" may be modern ez-Zarat on Mount 'Attarus overlooking the Dead Sea.

**20** "Beth Peor" was another place from which Balaam tried to curse Israel (Num 23:28). It was here that the Israelites engaged in sexual immorality with Moabite women and in idolatry (Num 25:1–3). This was the place Moses delivered his farewell address to Israel (Deut 3:29), and he was buried nearby (Deut 34:6). For "the slopes of Pisgah, and Beth Jeshimoth," see 12:3.

**21** All the territory and cities given to Reuben were from the realm of Sihon. Reuben did not receive "all" of Sihon's kingdom because a portion of it went to Gad (cf. v.27). The defeat of the "Midianite chiefs" is recorded in Numbers 31:8, where they are called "kings."

**22** When the Israelites were traveling north from the desert into Transjordan, Balaam was hired by Balak king of Moab to curse them. Each time he tried, the Lord made him bless Israel instead (Num 22–24; cf. Josh 24:9–10). Balaam's death is reported in Numbers 31:8. Though the OT does not give the reason why Balaam was slain, Revelation 2:14 makes him responsible for the sin of Israel recorded in Numbers 25:1–5 (cf. Deut 23:4–5; Neh 13:2; Mic 6:5).

**23** The Hebrew word *g*[e]***b̲***û*l* occurs twice in this verse and is translated "boundary" and "bank." It also means "frontier"; so it would be possible to translate: "The frontier of the Reubenites was the area along the Jordan." The word "villages" often refers to unwalled settlements outside a fortified city. Few of the cities in Transjordan had walls; therefore it is more likely that it refers to land around the city that was under cultivation or was used for raising livestock.

## Notes

---

**21** The Hebrew word נָכָה (*nāk̲āh,* "defeated") often means "killed."

---

### 3. *The inheritance of Gad*

#### 13:24–28

[24]This is what Moses had given to the tribe of Gad, clan by clan:

**[25]The territory of Jazer, all the towns of Gilead and half the**
**Ammonite country as far as Aroer, near Rabbah; [26]and from**
**Heshbon to Ramath Mizpah and Betonim, and from Mahanaim to**
**the territory of Debir; [27]and in the valley, Beth Haram, Beth Nimrah,**
**Succoth and Zaphon with the rest of the realm of Sihon king of**
**Heshbon (the east side of the Jordan, the territory up to the end of**
**the Sea of Kinnereth). [28]These towns and their villages were the**
**inheritance of the Gadites, clan by clan.**

**24** Gad received the central region in Transjordan.

**25** "Jazer" became a Levitical town (21:39). Since the Israelites had been forbidden to take any of the Ammonite territory (Deut 2:19, 37), "half the Ammonite country" may refer to land first taken from the Ammonites by Sihon and then taken from Sihon by the Israelites. If this is true, it would account for the later dispute between Jephthah and the Ammonites (Judg 11:13–27). "Rabbah" was the principal city of the Ammonites, about twenty-two miles east of the Jordan. "Aroer" here is not to be confused with the Aroer on the rim of the Arnon Gorge, some thirty miles farther south (12:2; 13:9, 16; see map on p. 254).

**26** "Mizpah" means "look-out," and there were many cities with this name. "Ramath Mizpah" may be the Ramoth in Gilead that was selected to be a city of refuge (20:8). "Betonim" is modern Khirbet Baṭneh, about four miles southwest of eṣ-Ṣalt. "Mahanaim" is modern Tell edh-Dhahal el-Gharbi on the Jabbok River on the border between Gad and Manasseh (see v.30). The location of "Debir" is unknown. It is not to be confused with the Debir west of the Jordan (12:13).

**27–28** "Beth Haram" (v.27) is modern Tell Iktanu near the place where the Wadi Ḥesban enters the Jordan Valley. Beth Nimra is modern Tell el-Bleibil, near the place where the Wadi Sa'eb enters the Jordan Valley. "Succoth" is modern Tell Der 'Alla, north of the place where the Jabbok River turns south. "Zaphon" is modern Tell es-Sa'idizeh, north of Succoth. "With" is not found in the Hebrew, and the phrase "the rest of the realm of Sihon" is probably in apposition to the preceding so that the towns named made up the rest of Sihon's territory (cf. v.21). "Sea of Kinnereth" is the Sea of Galilee.

## Notes

---

**26** A slight change in vocalization of לִדְבִר (*lid^e^bir*, "to Debir") would result in the reading לוֹ דְבָר (*lô d^e^bār*, "Lo Debar"), a town in Transjordan (2 Sam 9:4; 17:27).

---

### 4. *The inheritance of the half-tribe of Manasseh*

### 13:29–31

**[29]This is what Moses had given to the half-tribe of Manasseh, that is, to**
**half the family of the descendants of Mahasseh, clan by clan:**

30The territory extending from Mahanaim and including all of
Bashan, the entire realm of Og king of Bashan—all the settlements
of Jair in Bashan, sixty towns, 31half of Gilead, and Ashtaroth and
Edrei (the royal cities of Og in Bashan). This was for the descendants of Makir son of Manasseh—for half of the sons of Makir, clan by clan.

**29** The territory allocated to the half-tribe of Manasseh is the northern part of Transjordan and is not described in as much detail as the territories of Reuben and Gad.

**30** "Jair" and "Makir" (v.31) were prominent members of the tribe of Manasseh (Num 32:39–41). "The settlements of Jair" were tent cities that Jair had captured (cf. Num 32:41; 1 Chron 2:22–23).

**31** For "Makir" see 17:1 (cf. Gen 50:23). Here the name of Makir is used to designate the tribe of Manasseh.

### 5. *Summary*

13:32–33

32This is the inheritance Moses had given when he was in the plains of
Moab across the Jordan east of Jericho. 33But to the tribe of Levi, Moses
had given no inheritance; the LORD, the God of Israel, is their inheritance, as he promised them.

**32–33** Verse 32 brings down the curtain on the account of the distribution of the land east of the Jordan. Verse 33 repeats the statement in v.14, because of its importance.

## C. *Division of the Land West of the Jordan (14:1–19:51)*

### 1. *Introduction*

14:1–5

1Now these are the areas the Israelites received as an inheritance in
the land of Canaan, which Eleazar the priest, Joshua son of Nun and the
heads of the tribal clans of Israel allotted to them. 2Their inheritances
were assigned by lot to the nine-and-a-half tribes, as the LORD had
commanded through Moses. 3Moses had granted the two-and-a-half
tribes their inheritance east of the Jordan but had not granted the
Levites an inheritance among the rest, 4for the sons of Joseph had
become two tribes—Manasseh and Ephraim. The Levites received no
share of the land but only towns to live in, with pasturelands for their
flocks and herds. 5So the Israelites divided the land, just as the LORD had
commanded Moses.

The amount of space devoted to the description of the territory of each of the tribes and the order of presentation correspond to the importance of each particular tribe in Israel's history. Accordingly, Judah—the tribe of David, Solomon, and their successors—is treated most thoroughly. Then the tribes of Joseph are considered, who so predominated the northern kingdom that Ephraim became one of its names. The third and last tribe to be given special treatment is Benjamin, the tribe of Saul, Israel's first king.

**1** Only the territory west of the Jordan was called the land of Canaan. This is the land that God had promised to give Abraham (Gen 17:8). Here is where Abraham, Isaac, and Jacob lived and where God established his covenant with them (Exod 6:4). Though at times the dimensions of the land promised to Israel are described as reaching from the River of Egypt to the river Euphrates (e.g., 1:4), there is a strong, persistent tradition that the Promised Land was much more restricted. It was with great reluctance that Moses assigned the two and one-half tribes their inheritance in Transjordan. He was afraid it would be displeasing to the Lord because Transjordan was not a part of the land of Canaan (Num 32). The crossing of the Jordan is presented as Israel's triumphant march into the Land of Promise, just as the crossing of the Red Sea marked Israel's escape from the land of bondage.

"Eleazar the priest" was to assist Joshua in dividing the land. Eleazer is named first because he had the predominant role. As priest he was the one who wore the ephod with the Urim and Thummim by means of which the will of God was determined (Num 27:21; see Num 34:17, where once again Eleazar is named first). "The heads of the tribal clans" had been chosen by Moses, as commanded by the Lord, to help in the division of the land (Num 34:17–29).

**2** The land was to be "assigned by lot." The rabbis have a tradition that the names of the tribes were placed in one bowl and slips describing the various sections of the land in another. These were matched up by drawing one slip from each bowl. It seems certain, however, that the priest Eleazar employed the Urim and Thummim (cf. Num 27:21; 34:17). For Israel the use of lots left the choice completely in the hands of God (see comment on 7:14). The old refrain "as the Lord had commanded through Moses" is repeated again to drive home the point that obedience is the key to God's blessing.

**3** The repetition of background material that has been given several times already (1:15; 12:6; 13:8–32) suggests that this section of the book may have been once an independent unit.

**4** The Levites had been set apart to serve in the tabernacle. Therefore each of the sons of Joseph—"Ephraim and Manasseh"—was treated as a separate tribe to preserve the full number twelve (cf. Gen 48:5). The instructions God gave Moses about the Levites are recorded in Numbers 35:1–8. They were to be apportioned towns and agricultural lands throughout the territories of all the other tribes (ch. 21).

**5** Typical of OT narrative style, the introduction ends in a statement summarizing what the following account relates in detail.

## 2. *The inheritance of Judah (14:6–15:63)*

### a. *Caleb's inheritance*

14:6–15

6 Now the men of Judah approached Joshua at Gilgal, and Caleb son
of Jephunneh the Kenizzite said to him, "You know what the LORD said
to Moses the man of God at Kadesh Barnea about you and me. 7 I was
forty years old when Moses the servant of the LORD sent me from Kadesh
Barnea to explore the land. And I brought him back a report according
to my convictions, 8 but my brothers who went up with me made the

hearts of the people melt with fear. I, however, followed the LORD my
God wholeheartedly. [9]So on that day Moses swore to me, 'The land on
which your feet have walked will be your inheritance and that of your
children forever, because you have followed the LORD my God wholeheartedly.'
[10]"Now then, just as the LORD promised, he has kept me alive for forty-
five years since the time he said this to Moses, while Israel moved about
in the desert. So here I am today, eighty-five years old! [11]I am still as
strong today as the day Moses sent me out; I'm just as vigorous to go
out to battle now as I was then. [12]Now give me this hill country that the
LORD promised me that day. You yourself heard then that the Anakites
were there and their cities were large and fortified, but, the LORD helping
me, I will drive them out just as he said."
[13]Then Joshua blessed Caleb son of Jephunneh and gave him Hebron
as his inheritance. [14]So Hebron has belonged to Caleb son of Jephunneh the Kenizzite ever since, because he followed the LORD, the God of
Israel, wholeheartedly. [15](Hebron used to be called Kiriath Arba after
Arba, who was the greatest man among the Anakites.)
Then the land had rest from war.

**6** Caleb and Joshua were the two faithful spies who believed God was able to give Israel the land (Num 14:6–9, 30). The receiving of their inheritances frames the story of the dividing of the land among the nine and a half tribes, with Caleb's at the beginning and Joshua's at the end. Caleb and Joshua are living examples of God's faithfulness in fulfilling his promises made more than forty years earlier. In Genesis 15:19 the Kenizzites are listed as one of the pagan nations whose land God was giving to Israel. It is true that many foreigners were assimilated into Israel; but when Caleb is called a Kenizzite, it may mean no more than that one of Caleb's ancestors was named Kenaz (cf. 15:17; 1 Chron 4:13, 15). This title of honor "man of God" is ascribed to Moses also in Deuteronomy 33:1, Ezra 3:2, and in the title of Psalm 90. For what God said to Moses about Caleb and Joshua, see Numbers 14:30.

**7** "Kadesh Barnea" is modern 'Ain el-Qudeirat. The spy mission in which Caleb participated is recorded in Numbers 13. Caleb's report was characterized by bold confidence in God (Num 13:30; 14:6–9).

**8** The statement "I . . . followed the LORD my God wholeheartedly" is found three times in this brief passage (vv.9, 14). It describes Caleb as one who really lived out the theme of this book. It is the reason he was still alive and would inherit part of the land (v.9).

**9** Caleb asserted, "Moses swore to me." This promise is found in Deuteronomy 1:36, but it is not stated there nor anywhere else in the OT that Moses made an oath to him (cf. Num 20–24).

**10–11** Of all who were twenty years and older when Israel left Egypt, only Caleb and Joshua lived to enter the Promised Land. Caleb was now "eighty-five years old" (v.10). From this we can calculate the approximate number of years involved in the Conquest. Forty years old at the time of the spy mission plus thirty-eight years of wandering leaves seven years for the Conquest.

**12** These factors—"hill country . . . Anakites . . . cities . . . large and fortified"—are the very things that the ten faithless spies used to discourage the Israelites from entering the Promised Land (Num 13:28–29). Caleb viewed them as a challenge. In Deuteronomy 9:1–3, Moses assured Israel of God's help in dispossessing the Anakites. By faith Joshua and Caleb triumphed over the very formidable foe who intimidated the unbelieving Israelites.

**13–14** Some believe that when Joshua blessed Caleb, he bestowed on him the spiritual qualities needed for this dangerous venture.

**15** In Hebrew "Arba" means "four." "Arba" may have been the name of the fourth child in a family, similar to the Latin names Segundus, Tertius, and Octavius. The statement "Then the land had rest from war" appears also at the end of chapter 11 at the conclusion of the Conquest. It may be evidence that Caleb's conquest of Hebron actually took place as a part of the southern campaign. In Judges 1:9–10 the conquest of Hebron is credited to the men of Judah. Hebron is only one of many cities that had to be captured more than once (e.g., Jerusalem).

### b. *The borders of Judah*

#### 15:1–12

1 The allotment for the tribe of Judah, clan by clan, extended down to
the territory of Edom, to the Desert of Zin in the extreme south.
2 Their southern boundary started from the bay at the southern
end of the Salt Sea, 3 crossed south of Scorpion Pass, continued on
to Zin and went over to the south of Kadesh Barnea. Then it ran
past Hezron up to Addar and curved around to Karka. 4 It then
passed along to Azmon and joined the Wadi of Egypt, ending at the
sea. This is their southern boundary.
5 The eastern boundary is the Salt Sea as far as the mouth of the
Jordan.
The northern boundary started from the bay of the sea at the
mouth of the Jordan, 6 went up to Beth Hoglah and continued north
of Beth Arabah to the Stone of Bohan son of Reuben. 7 The
boundary then went up to Debir from the Valley of Achor and
turned north to Gilgal, which faces the Pass of Adummim south of
the gorge. It continued along to the waters of En Shemesh and
came out at En Rogel. 8 Then it ran up the Valley of Ben Hinnom
along the southern slope of the Jebusite city (that is, Jerusalem).
From there it climbed to the top of the hill west of the Hinnom
Valley at the northern end of the Valley of Rephaim. 9 From the
hilltop the boundary headed toward the spring of the waters of
Nephtoah, came out at the towns of Mount Ephron and went down
toward Baalah (that is, Kiriath Jearim). 10 Then it curved westward
from Baalah to Mount Seir, ran along the northern slope of Mount
Jearim (that is, Kesalon), continued down to Beth Shemesh and
crossed to Timnah. 11 It went to the northern slope of Ekron, turned
toward Shikkeron, passed along to Mount Baalah and reached
Jabneel. The boundary ended at the sea.
12 The western boundary is the coastline of the Great Sea.
These are the boundaries around the people of Judah by their clans.

**1** Judah, the tribe of the great Davidic dynasty, was the first tribe to receive its allotted territory in Canaan. God had commanded that when the land was divided the size of the territory should correspond to the size of the respective tribe or clan (Num 33:54). In the process of carrying out the command, Joshua gave Judah a territory larger than her numbers merited (19:9). No explanation is given as to why or how this happened. The territory of Edom was east of the Arabah. Here, however, Edom may refer to Amalekites living in the Sinai Peninsula and the southern Negev (cf. Gen 36:12, where Amalek is listed as a descendant of Esau). "The Desert of Zin" is the desert area around Kadesh Barnea (Num 20:1). Judah's lot was "in the extreme south." The description of Judah's southern boundary is in close agreement with the southern boundary of Canaan as described in Numbers 34:3–5.

**2** The Hebrew word for "the bay" is *hallāšōn* (lit., "the tongue"). This word usually refers to the Lisan, the peninsula that extends into the Dead Sea from the eastern shore. Here and in v.5, however, it refers to the extreme northern and southern ends of the Dead Sea. "The Salt Sea" is the Dead Sea.

**3** The "Scorpion Pass" has not been identified with certainty. Apparently "Zin" is a locality within the Desert of Zin from which the whole area was named. "Kadesh Barnea" was also in the Desert of Zin. It would have been the staging point for the Israelite's invasion of the land of Canaan had they trusted in God (cf. Num 13:26–33).

**4** "The Wadi of Egypt" is the Wadi el-ʿArish, i.e., the River of Egypt that flows from the Sinai Peninsula into the Mediterranean Sea at the southern extremity of Palestine. "The sea" is the Mediterranean.

**5** For "the bay" see the comment on v.2. "The northern boundary" of Judah corresponds to the southern boundaries of Benjamin (18:14–19) and Dan (19:41–46).

**6** Though serving to define the northern boundary of Judah, "Beth Hoglah" and "Beth Arabah" were assigned to Benjamin (18:19, 21–22).

**7** Because of the orientation of our maps with north at the top, we customarily think that to "go up" means to go north and to "go down" means to go south. These expressions are used in the OT with reference to elevation. Here the border of Judah ascends from the Valley of Achor, which borders on the Dead Sea. "Debir" is not to be confused with the Debir in vv.15, 49, and 10:38. There is little agreement as to the location of "the Valley of Achor." "Gilgal" is not the Gilgal on the plains of Jericho that Joshua made his base of operation when he entered Canaan (4:19). "The Pass of Adummim" is modern Talʿat ed-Damm. "The gorge" is modern Wadi Qelt. "En Shemesh" is modern Ain el-Ḥod, about two miles east of Jerusalem. "En Rogel" is modern Bir Ayyub, south of Jerusalem.

**8** "The Valley of Ben Hinnom" is the wide, deep valley on the south and east of the old city Jerusalem. "The hill" is modern Abu Tur. "The Valley of Rephaim" is modern Wadi el-Ward, west of Jerusalem.

**9** The name of the spring "the waters of Nephtoah" probably preserves the name of Merneptah, one of the Pharaohs of Egypt. "Baalah" is modern Deir el-ʿAzar. The border around Jerusalem is described in greater detail, perhaps to make clear that Jerusalem was not included in the territory of Judah.

**10** "Mount Seir" was on the west side of Jerusalem and must not be confused with Mount Seir in Edom, southwest of the Dead Sea. "Mount Jearim" is at modern Kesla, about ten miles west of Jerusalem. "Beth Shemesh" is modern Tell er-Rumeileh. In 19:41 it is called "Ir Shemesh." "Timnah" is prominent in the stories of Samson. It is modern Tell Baṭashi.

**11** For "Ekron" see 13:3. "Mount Baalah" may be el-Mughar, a steep incline two miles northwest of "Shikkeron," which is modern Tell el-Ful. "Jabneel," which came to be known as Jamnia, is modern Yebna.

**12** "The Great Sea" is the Mediterranean. With the Mediterranean as her western boundary, Judah's allotment included Philistine and Geshurite territory that had not been conquered yet (cf. 13:1–3). This was in conformity with the Lord's command (13:6) that the entire land of Palestine be allotted in the confidence that some day all would belong to Israel.

### c. *The inheritance of Caleb's daughter*

#### 15:13–19

**13**In accordance with the LORD's command to him, Joshua gave to Caleb son of Jephunneh a portion in Judah—Kiriath Arba, that is, Hebron. (Arba was the forefather of Anak.) **14**From Hebron Caleb drove out the three Anakites—Sheshai, Ahiman and Talmai—descendants of Anak. **15**From there he marched against the people living in Debir (formerly called Kiriath Sepher). **16**And Caleb said, "I will give my daughter Acsah in marriage to the man who attacks and captures Kiriath Sepher." **17**Othniel son of Kenaz, Caleb's brother, took it; so Caleb gave his daughter Acsah to him in marriage.

**18**One day when she came to Othniel, she urged him to ask her father for a field. When she got off her donkey, Caleb asked her, "What can I do for you?"

**19**She replied, "Do me a special favor. Since you have given me land in the Negev, give me also springs of water." So Caleb gave her the upper and lower springs.

**13** For "the LORD's command," see 14:6–9. God promised Caleb that he would inherit the land he had explored (14:9; Num 14:24). In the providence of God, this area fell within the borders of his own tribe. Once again "Arba" appears in the text as the name of a person (cf. 14:15).

**14** The names of "the three Anakites" were Ahiman, Sheshai, and Talmai (Num 13:22). They were living in Hebron at the time of the first spy mission. There are three accounts of the defeat of the Anakites: 11:21–22; 14:10–15; and 15:13–14. Each adds information not given in the preceding account (in Judg 1:9–10 this victory is credited to the men of Judah, but Judg 1:20 specifies that it was Caleb who actually did it).

**15** Notice that Caleb led the attack on Debir although Othniel captured it (v.17). As in the case of Hebron, this victory is also credited to Joshua as commander in chief (10:36–39; also in the summary in 11:21).

**16** It was not uncommon to offer special incentives for acts of bravery (cf. 1 Sam 17:25; 18:17, 25; 1 Chron 11:6).

**17** "Othniel" later became one of the judges of Israel (Judg 3:7–11). The expression "son of Kenaz" may indicate that his father or some other male ancestor was named Kenaz, or it may simply mean that he was a Kenizzite (see comment on 14:6). "Caleb's brother" may have been his blood brother or a member of the same clan or tribe. The Hebrew word *'āḥ* can mean "brother," "relative," or "ally." Judges 1:13 and 3:9 seem to favor the idea of blood brother, for Othniel is called "Caleb's younger brother."

**18–19** The Hebrew word translated "a special favor" (v.19) is *bᵉrāḵāh,* which is commonly translated "blessing." Perhaps Caleb's daughter was asking her father for a wedding gift. She needed "springs of water." Land in the Negev is of little value without water, but it is very productive when irrigated. Othniel recognized the validity of her request. The word translated "springs" is the Hebrew *gullôṯ,* which may mean "reservoirs" or "cisterns."

## Notes

---

**18** The alternative reading in the NIV margin makes good sense: Othniel urged his wife, and she went to ask her father.

---

### d. *The towns of Judah*

15:20–63

[20]This is the inheritance of the tribe of Judah, clan by clan:

[21]The southernmost towns of the tribe of Judah in the Negev toward the boundary of Edom were:
Kabzeel, Eder, Jagur, [22]Kinah, Dimonah, Adadah, [23]Kedesh,
Hazor, Ithnan, [24]Ziph, Telem, Bealoth, [25]Hazor Hadattah, Kerioth
Hezron (that is, Hazor), [26]Amam, Shema, Moladah, [27]Hazar Gaddah,
Heshmon, Beth Pelet, [28]Hazar Shual, Beersheba, Biziothiah,
[29]Baalah, Iim, Ezem, [30]Eltolad, Kesil, Hormah, [31]Ziklag, Madman-
nah, Sansannah, [32]Lebaoth, Shilhim, Ain and Rimmon—a total of
twenty-nine towns and their villages.

[33]In the western foothills:
Eshtaol, Zorah, Ashnah, [34]Zanoah, En Gannim, Tappuah, Enam,
[35]Jarmuth, Adullam, Socoh, Azekah, [36]Shaaraim, Adithaim and
Gederah (or Gederothaim)—fourteen towns and their villages.
[37]Zenan, Hadashah, Migdal Gad, [38]Dilean, Mizpah, Joktheel,
[39]Lachish, Bozkath, Eglon, [40]Cabbon, Lahmas, Kitlish, [41]Gederoth,
Beth Dagon, Naamah and Makkedah—sixteen towns and their
villages.
[42]Libnah, Ether, Ashan, [43]Iphtah, Ashnah, Nezib, [44]Keilah, Aczib
and Mareshah—nine towns and their villages.
[45]Ekron, with its surrounding settlements and villages; [46]west of
Ekron, all that were in the vicinity of Ashdod, together with their
villages; [47]Ashdod, its surrounding settlements and villages; and

Gaza, its settlements and villages, as far as the Wadi of Egypt and the coastline of the Great Sea.

48 In the hill country:
Shamir, Jattir, Socoh, 49 Dannah, Kiriath Sannah (that is, Debir),
50 Anab, Eshtemoh, Anim, 51 Goshen, Holon and Giloh—eleven
towns and their villages.
52 Arab, Dumah, Eshan, 53 Janim, Beth Tappuah, Aphekah,
54 Humtah, Kiriath Arba (that is, Hebron) and Zior—nine towns and
their villages.
55 Maon, Carmel, Ziph, Juttah, 56 Jezreel, Jokdeam, Zanoah,
57 Kain, Gibeah and Timnah—ten towns and their villages.
58 Halhul, Beth Zur, Gedor, 59 Maarath, Beth Anoth and Eltekon—
six towns and their villages.
60 Kiriath Baal (that is, Kiriath Jearim) and Rabbah—two towns
and their villages.

61 In the desert:
Beth Arabah, Middin, Secacah, 62 Nibshan, the City of Salt and En
Gedi—six towns and their villages.
63 Judah could not dislodge the Jebusites, who were living in
Jerusalem; to this day the Jebusites live there with the people of Judah.

**20** Bright, Boling, and others hold that the following list of towns in the territory assigned to Judah comes from an administrative register where the southern kingdom of Judah was divided into twelve districts for such purposes as taxation and military conscription (cf. R.H. Smith, "Joshua," *The Interpreter's One-volume Commentary on the Bible*, ed. Charles M. Laymon [Nashville: Abingdon, 1971], p. 131). The towns of Judah made up ten and one-half districts and the towns of Benjamin made up the other one and one-half (cf. 18:11, 21).

A modern reader may question the value of a long list of names of towns like this, but for the Judahite it described the homeland that God had given to his tribe. It is another evidence of the historical, down-to-earth nature of God's redemptive program. The sending of the Savior was also very down to earth; remember: "The Word became flesh and made his dwelling among us" (John 1:14).

**21** "The southernmost towns" are mostly towns in the Negev (esp. those in vv.26–32) that are also ascribed to Simeon in 19:1–9. There it is stated that the territory given to Judah was "more than they needed" (19:9). Consequently some of it was reassigned to Simeon. The distribution of the land was not all completed at once; rather it took place over an extended period of time (see 18:1–10). "Kabzeel" was the hometown of Benaiah, one of David's outstanding warriors (2 Sam 23:20; 1 Chron 11:22).

**23** "Kedesh" is not Kadesh Barnea, nor is it the Kedesh mentioned in 12:22. "Hazor" is not the Hazor in 11:10. Since "Hazor" is a Hebrew word that means "the surrounding agricultural land," perhaps we should read this as "Hazor Ithnan," i.e., "the agricultural lands of Ithnan."

**24** "Ziph" may be modern ez-Zeifeh. It is not the Ziph in v.55. "Bealoth" may be the same as Baalath Beer in 19:8.

**28** "Biziothiah" (*bizyôṯᵉyāh*) is emended by some to read *ûḇᵉnōṯêhā* ("and the surrounding villages"). This would help to reduce the number of towns bringing it closer to the number stated in v.32. It would be strange, however, in such a long list of towns to have this additional element only in the case of this one town.

**30** "Hormah" is modern Tell el-Meshash, southeast of Beersheba.

**31** "Ziklag" is the town that Achish, king of Gath, gave David as a place for him and his men to live during his time of exile from King Saul (1 Sam 27:6). This must be another town that was assigned to Judah but not occupied by them until years later. "Madmannah" is modern Khirbet Tatrit. "Sansannah" is modern Khirbet esh-Shamsaniyat.

**32** There are thirty-six towns named in the NIV translation of vv.21–32. Even if some of the names are combined, such as Hazor Ithnan (v.23) and Ain Rimmon (v.32), or accounted for in other ways (e.g., Biziothiah; see comment on v.28), it would be impossible to reduce the list to "twenty-nine towns." Goslinga suggests that twenty-nine was a copyist's mistake or that "a few names of villages were added that should not be included among the twenty-nine towns" (p. 127). The solution to the problem is not clear.

**33** "Zorah" is modern Ṣarʿah. It is the highest point in the Shephelah. Zorah and Eshtaol were the scenes of some of Samson's exploits (Judg 13:25; 16:31). Both are assigned to Dan in 19:41.

**34** "Zanoah" is Khirbet Zanuʿ, a little south of modern Zanoah. "En Gannim" is not to be confused with the En Gannim in Issachar (19:21). "Tappuah" is not to be confused with the Tappuah in Ephraim (12:17; 16:8) or with Beth Tappuah in v.53.

**35** For "Jarmuth" see 10:3. This city is not the Jarmuth in Issachar that became a Levitical city (21:29). For "Adullam" see 12:15. "Socoh" is modern Khirbet ʿAbbad. It is to be distinguished from the Socoh in v.48. For "Azekah" see 10:10.

**36** "Gederah" is modern Jedireh.

**39** For "Lachish" see 10:3–5. For "Eglon" see 10:3.

**41** "Beth Dagon" is to be distinguished from the Beth Dagon in Asher (19:27). The name means "house of Dagon." Dagon was the god of the Philistines (see 1 Sam 5:2–7). For "Makkedah" see 10:10, 28.

**42** For "Libnah" see 10:29.

**43** "Ashnah" is modern Idhnah, near Mareshah. "Nezib" is modern Khirbet Beit Neṣib, between Beth Zur and Mareshah.

**44** "Keilah" is modern Khirbet Qila, about eight miles northwest of Hebron. "Aczib" is modern Tell el-Beida, southwest of Adullam. "Mareshah" is modern Tell Ṣandaḥannah, about fourteen miles west northwest of Hebron.

**45–47** "Ekron," "Ashdod," and "Gaza" were three of the five major Philistine cities (see 13:3). These towns were assigned to Judah but were not possessed until many years later. The style of these three verses differs markedly from all the others in this list of towns assigned to Judah, both in the inclusion of the phrase "its surrounding settlements and villages" and in the omission of the concluding statement that gives the total number of cities. Ashdod and Ekron were nearly straight west of Jerusalem, Ekron near the foothills and Ashdod near the coast. Gaza was near the coast also but far south in the coastal plain.

**48** "Shamir" is modern Khirbet es-Samara, about twelve and one-half miles west southwest of Hebron. "Jattir" is modern Khirbet ʿAttir. It became a Levitical town (21:14). "Socoh" is modern Khirbet Shuweiket er-Ras and should not be confused with Socoh in v.35.

**50** For "Anab" see 11:21. "Eshtemoh" became a Levitical town (21:14).

**51** For "Goshen" see 10:41. "Holon" is modern Khirbet ʿIllin, near Beth Sur.

**52** "Arab" is modern er-Rabiyeh. "Dumah" is modern Deir ed-Domeh.

**53** "Beth Tappuah" is modern Taffuḥ, about three miles west of Hebron.

**54** For "Hebron" see 10:3. Hebron became a city of refuge (20:7) and a Levitical town (21:11). "Zior" is modern Ṣiʿir, about five miles east northeast of Hebron.

**55** "Maon" is modern Khirbet Maʿin, about eight miles south of Hebron. "Carmel" is not to be confused with Mount Carmel on the Mediterranean seacoast. It is modern Khirbet el-Kirmil, about seven and one-half miles south southeast of Hebron. "Ziph" is modern Tell Ziph. It is to be distinguished from Ziph in v.24. "Juttah" is modern Yaṭṭa, about five and one-half miles southwest of Hebron. It became a Levitical town (21:16).

**56** "Jezreel" is not to be confused with the town of the same name in the Valley of Esdraelon.

**57** "Kain" may be modern en-Nabi Yaqin, a few miles northeast of Ziph. For "Timnah" see v.10.

**58** "Halhul" is modern Ḥalḥul. "Beth Zur" is modern Khirbet eṭ-Ṭubeiqah, about four miles north of Hebron. "Gedor" is modern Khirbet Jedur.

**59** "Beth Anoth" is modern Khirbet Beit ʿAinun.

At this point the LXX supplies the names of eleven additional towns and in this way makes up the full twelve administrative districts from Judah alone (see comment on v.20).

**60** For "Kiriath Baal [Jearim]" see 9:17. "Rabbah" is not to be confused with Rabbah, the capital of Ammon.

**61** "The desert" refers to the desert area on the eastern border of Judah along the shore of the Dead Sea. In the title of Psalm 63, it is called "the Desert of Judah" (cf. 12:8). "Secacah" may be modern Khirbet es-Samrah in the center of the Buqei'ah.

**62** "Nibshan" may be modern Khirbet el-Maqari, far south in the Buqei'ah. "The City of Salt" may be Khirbet Qumran, the center of the Essene community made famous through the discovery of the Dead Sea Scrolls. "En Gedi" is modern Tell el-Jurn near the midpoint of the Dead Sea.

**63** The statement "Judah could not dislodge the Jebusites" is strange because Jerusalem was part of the territory assigned to Benjamin (18:28), and the description of the northern border of Judah so carefully excludes Jerusalem (see comment on v.9). Judges 1:8 records that the men of Judah did capture the city. Then in v.21 we have, almost word for word, the same statement as here, only it states that Benjamin did not capture Jerusalem. The final conquest of Jerusalem was accomplished under the direction of King David (2 Sam 5:6–10). The little information that we have does not provide a clear picture of the vicissitudes of this city. It is necessary to suppose that some cities, at least, changed hands several times before they were securely in Israel's control. The admission that Judah was unable to dislodge the Jebusites is even more strange in a book that exalts the supernatural power of God, which gives the victory to his people over all their enemies. In Joshua there is a remarkable mixture of miracle and human effort, a combination of divinely aided victory and failure that results from Israel's disobedience and unbelief. Thus God is revealed as sovereign. He responds to the needs of his covenant people but is not subject to their whims.

## Notes

**28** BHS suggests that וּבִזְיוֹתְיָה (*ûḇizyôṯyāh*, "and Bizyothiah") be emended to read וּבְנוֹתֶיהָ (*ûḇᵉnôṯeyhā*, "and the surrounding villages"; lit., "and her daughters").

### 3. *The inheritance of the Joseph tribes (16:1–17:18)*

#### a. *Introduction*

16:1–4

[1] The allotment for Joseph began at the Jordan of Jericho, east of
the waters of Jericho, and went up from there through the desert
into the hill country of Bethel. [2] It went on from Bethel (that is, Luz),
crossed over to the territory of the Arkites in Ataroth, [3] descended
westward to the territory of the Japhletites as far as the region of
Lower Beth Horon and on to Gezer, ending at the sea.
[4] So Manasseh and Ephraim, the descendants of Joseph, received their
inheritance.

**1** "The allotment for Joseph" was divided between the tribe of Ephraim (vv.5–10) and the half-tribe of Manasseh (17:1–13). The other half-tribe of Manasseh received its land east of the Jordan River (13:8–13). The tribe of Joseph was divided into two tribes to compensate for the tribe of Levi, which received no territorial allotment (14:3–4). The importance of the tribe of Joseph is reflected in their lot being drawn second and in the comparatively large amount of space devoted to the description of their territory. The sons of Joseph became the dominant tribes in the northern kingdom during the divided monarchy, so much so that the name Ephraim became one of the names for that kingdom (cf. Isa 7:2). The southern border of Joseph, which is described here, is actually the northern borders of Benjamin (18:11–14) and Dan (19:40–48).

"The Jordan of Jericho" designates the Jordan near Jericho. The NIV margin suggests this may have been another name for the Jordan River. "The waters of Jericho" are probably to be identified with 'Ain es-Sultan. Jericho itself was in the allotment of Benjamin (18:12). "The desert" is called "the desert of Beth Aven" in 18:12. Woudstra (p. 258) describes it as rising "precipitously out of the Jordan Valley." Although "Bethel" is on the border of Judah, it is assigned to Benjamin in 18:22.

**2** The NIV follows the LXX when it translates "Bethel (that is Luz)" in accordance with 18:13 where Bethel and Luz are clearly identified (cf. Gen 28:19; Judg 1:23). The Hebrew says literally "from Bethel to or toward Luz," unless this is simply a feminine form of the proper name (having both a masculine and feminine form). It has been suggested that originally the name Bethel referred only to the spot where God appeared to Jacob (Gen 28:10–19) while the nearby city continued to be called Luz (see Woudstra, p. 258). The "Arkites" were a non-Israelite clan about which nothing is known except that David's counselor Hushai was from that clan (2 Sam 15:32; 16:16). "Ataroth" is called Ataroth Addar in v.5 and 18:13. It is to be distinguished from Ataroth on the northern border of Ephraim (v.7).

**3** The "Japhletites" were another non-Israelite clan about which nothing is known (but cf. Japhlet, descendant of Asher, 1 Chron 7:32–33). For "Lower Beth Horon" see comment on 10:10. For "Gezer" see 10:33. "The Sea" is the Mediterranean.

**4** The order in which "Manasseh and Ephraim" are mentioned is the actual order of birth. The order in which their respective territories are described reflects the ascendancy of Ephraim (cf. Gen 48:12–20). The descriptions of the inheritances of the Joseph tribes differ from all the others in that they contain no lists of towns.

## Notes

---

1 "Began" translates וַיֵּצֵא (*wayyēṣē'*), which commonly means "and it came out." Some interpret this word here as referring to the lot: "and the lot came out for Joseph" (cf. 18:11: "The lot came up"; but here, however, the verb is וַיַּעַל [*wayya'al*]).

2 מִבֵּית־אֵל לוּזָה (*mibbêṯ-'ēl lûzāh*) is literally "from Bethel *to* Luz." The LXX treats it as all one name: Βαιθὴλ Λουζά (*Baithēl Louza*, "Bethel-Luz") and has the preposition εἰς (*eis*, "to"), whereas the MT has מִן (*min*), which usually means "from."

---

## b. *The inheritance of Ephraim*

### 16:5–10

5This was the territory of Ephraim, clan by clan:

The boundary of their inheritance went from Ataroth Addar in the
east to Upper Beth Horon 6and continued to the sea. From
Micmethath on the north it curved eastward to Taanath Shiloh,
passing by it to Janoah on the east. 7Then it went down from
Janoah to Ataroth and Naarah, touched Jericho and came out at the
Jordan. 8From Tappuah the border went west to the Kanah Ravine
and ended at the sea. This was the inheritance of the tribe of the
Ephraimites, clan by clan. 9It also included all the towns and their
villages that were set aside for the Ephraimites within the inheritance of the Manassites.

10They did not dislodge the Canaanites living in Gezer; to this day the
Canaanites live among the people of Ephraim but are required to do
forced labor.

**5–9** Although a disproportionate amount of space is devoted to Ephraim and Manasseh, the description of their territories is fragmentary and difficult to follow. Apparently vv.5–6a are a severely abbreviated restatement of the southern boundary. Then, beginning at Michmethath, the point farthest north, the boundary is traced east and south until it joins the southern boundary forming the eastern border (vv.6b–7). Beginning again at the far north, the northern boundary is followed to the Mediterranean Sea (v.8). Though not specified, the Mediterranean forms the western border.

For "Ataroth Addar" (v.5) see v.2. For "Upper Beth Horon" see comment on 10:10. "Michmethath" (v.6) is modern Khirbet Makhneh el-Foqa south of Shechem. "Taanath Shiloh" is modern Khirbet Ta'nah el-Foqa, about seven miles east of Shechem. "Janoah" is modern Khirbet Yanun southeast of Shechem. The "Ataroth" in v.7 is different from Ataroth in vv.2, 5, and 18:13. "Naarah" is modern Khirbet el-Ayush. "Tappuah" (v.8) is modern Sheikh Abu Zarad located south of Michmethath. "The Kanah Ravine" is modern Wadi Qana that flows into the Yarkon River and forms the border between Ephraim and Manasseh from Tappuah to the Mediterranean.

**10** On Israel's failure to "dislodge the Canaanites," see the comment on 15:63. The king and the army from "Gezer" were defeated by Joshua (10:30). Many of the natives of Canaan who survived were conscripted as "forced labor" to do menial tasks for Israel (Judg 1:28–30, 33, 35), but in the narrator's opinion this was the result of a serious failure on the part of the Israelites. The commands of God allowed them to subject the people from cities outside Palestine to forced labor, but the population of the cities inside the Promised Land—men, women, and children—were to be put to death without pity and without exception (Deut 20:10–18). As a result of this failure, the Israelites were corrupted by intermarrying with these pagans and engaging in their perverse and idolatrous worship (Judg 2:1–3; 3:5–6; 10:6).

We cannot be sure of the exact time reference of the phrase "to this day," but it seems that Gezer was not subjected to Israel until the time of Solomon (1 Kings 9:15–17).

### c. *The inheritance of Manasseh (17:1–13)*

#### 1) *Introduction*

17:1–2

> [1]This was the allotment for the tribe of Manasseh as Joseph's firstborn, that is, for Makir, Manasseh's firstborn. Makir was the ancestor of the Gileadites, who had received Gilead and Bashan because the Makirites were great soldiers. [2]So this allotment was for the rest of the people of Manasseh—the clans of Abiezer, Helek, Asriel, Shechem, Hepher and Shemida. These are the other male descendants of Manasseh son of Joseph by their clans.

**1** Manasseh was "Joseph's firstborn" son (Gen 41:51). This is another of the many OT examples where the rights of the firstborn were given to another (see comment on 16:4). "Makir" is called "Manasseh's firstborn" when, as it appears, Makir was Manasseh's only son (Gen 50:23). At times Makir's name is used to designate the half-tribe of Manasseh that settled east of the Jordan. In this verse Gilead designates both a people and a geographical area. As the name of a people, it designates the half-tribe of Manasseh east of the Jordan. For "Gilead and Bashan" see 13:29–31. The reason for their being given land in Gilead and Bashan was that they "were great soldiers." In Numbers 32:1–5 a different reason is given for their settling in Transjordan: They had large flocks and herds, and that land was suitable for livestock. Both reasons are applicable.

**2** From the records we have (Num 26:29–34; cf. 1 Chron 7:14–19), it is difficult to unravel the genealogy of Manasseh. The phrase "the rest of the people of Manasseh" designates the half-tribe that did not receive its inheritance in Transjordan. According to Numbers 26:29–33 (cf. 1 Chron 7:14–19), however, the six clans that are named here seem to account for all of the sons of Gilead, i.e., the whole tribe of Manasseh. Who then made up the half-tribe that settled in Gilead and Bashan? "Abiezer" is the clan to which Gilead belonged (Judg 6:11, 24, 34). It is called the Iezerite clan in Numbers 26:30. "Male descendants" are specified because the following paragraph deals with the inheritance of the daughters of Zelophehad.

#### 2) *The inheritance of the daughters of Zelophehad*

17:3–6

> [3]Now Zelophehad son of Hepher, the son of Gilead, the son of Makir, the son of Manasseh, had no sons but only daughters, whose names were Mahlah, Noah, Hoglah, Milcah and Tirzah. [4]They went to Eleazar the priest, Joshua son of Nun, and the leaders and said, "The LORD commanded Moses to give us an inheritance among our brothers." So Joshua gave them an inheritance along with the brothers of their father, according to the LORD's command. [5]Manasseh's share consisted of ten tracts of land besides Gilead and Bashan east of the Jordan, [6]because the daughters of the tribe of Manasseh received an inheritance among the sons. The land of Gilead belonged to the rest of the descendants of Manasseh.

**3** "Hepher" (cf. 12:17) and "Tirzah" (cf. 12:24) were also the names of Canaanite towns whose kings Joshua killed. The presence of those same names in the genealogy of Manasseh is viewed as evidence that Canaanites were assimilated into Israel.

**4** In the four instances in this book where Joshua and Eleazar are mentioned together, Eleazar is always named first, perhaps out of respect for his crucial role as high priest in the casting of lots (see 14:1; 19:51; 21:1). Though a different word (*nāśî'*) is used here for "leader," these are the same tribal representatives who were called "heads of the tribal clans" (*rā'šê '$^{a}$ḇôṯ hammaṭṭôṯ*) in 14:1 and 21:1. The daughters of Zelophehad based their claim on what "the LORD commanded Moses." Whether it was primarily the rights of the father or the rights of the daughters that were being protected, an unusual privilege and a remarkable measure of equality were granted to these women. In actual fact the daughters of Zelophehad had no "brothers" (cf. v.3), which is why the inheritance was passed on to them. The Hebrew word *'āḥ* can refer to any male relative, and it should be understood as "kinsman" or "tribesman" here.

**5–6** The "ten tracts" (v.5) are one each for five of Gilead's sons and one each for the five daughters of his sixth son. These ten tracts did not include any part of Gilead or Bashan.

### 3) *The boundaries of Manasseh*

#### 17:7–13

7 The territory of Manasseh extended from Asher to Micmethath
east of Shechem. The boundary ran southward from there to
include the people living at En Tappuah. 8 (Manasseh had the land
of Tappuah, but Tappuah itself, on the boundary of Manasseh,
belonged to the Ephraimites.) 9 Then the boundary continued south
to the Kanah Ravine. There were towns belonging to Ephraim lying
among the towns of Manasseh, but the boundary of Manasseh was
the northern side of the ravine and ended at the sea. 10 On the south
the land belonged to Ephraim, on the north to Manasseh. The
territory of Manasseh reached the sea and bordered Asher on the
north and Issachar on the east.

11 Within Issachar and Asher, Manasseh also had Beth Shan,
Ibleam and the people of Dor, Endor, Taanach and Megiddo,
together with their surrounding settlements (the third in the list is
Naphoth).

12 Yet the Manassites were not able to occupy these towns, for the
Canaanites were determined to live in that region. 13 However, when the
Israelites grew stronger, they subjected the Canaanites to forced labor
but did not drive them out completely.

**7** The description of "the territory of Manasseh" is very confusing. It provides little more than a clearer definition of the border with Ephraim. Opinions are divided on the proper interpretation of "Asher" here. It may refer to the tribe of Asher (cf. 19:24–31), it could be emended so as to be translated "slopes" (Boling, pp. 409, 412), or it may be a reference to some town—perhaps Yasir. For "Michmethath" see 16:6.

"Shechem" is between Mount Ebal and Mount Gerazim. It is mentioned frequently in the patriarchal stories in Genesis. Shechem was chosen to be a Levitical town (21:21) and one of the cities of refuge (20:7). Joshua gathered all Israel in Shechem for his farewell address and covenant renewal (ch. 24). "En Tappuah" is the same as "Tappuah" (see 16:8).

**8** "Tappuah" was one of several towns within the boundaries of Manasseh that belonged to Ephraim (cf. 16:9).

**9** For "the Kanah Ravine" see 16:8.

**10** For "bordered Asher on the north," see 19:24–31. For "Issachar on the east," see 19:17–23.

**11–13** Manasseh's northern boundary was the Valley of Esdraelon (v.11). Nevertheless a few towns belonged to Manasseh that lay "within Issachar and Asher." "Beth Shan" is Tell el-Ḥusn near modern Beisan. "Ibleam" is Tell Belʿameh near Jenin. For "Dor" see 11:2. "En Dor" is about seven miles southeast of Nazareth. For "Taanach" see 12:21. For "Megiddo" see 12:21. The statement "the third in the list is Naphoth" represents two Hebrew words that are difficult to translate (*šᵉlōše̱t hannāp̱e̱t*). On this Woudstra (p. 266) comments: "Although a number of different translations have been proposed, the rendering [i.e., 'the three-heights country'] does correspond accurately to the geographical situation of the last three cities mentioned, each of which was situated near a mountain ridge."

Though these cities were assigned to Manasseh, they were not conquered until many years later (v.12; cf. Judg 1:27). On v.13 see 16:10.

## Notes

7 The emendation is from אָשֵׁר (*'āšēr*, "Asher") to אָשֵׁד (*'āšēḏ*, "slopes"). The substitution of "resh" for "daleth" is a common scribal error.

### d. *The complaint of the Joseph tribes*

### 17:14–18

[14]The people of Joseph said to Joshua, "Why have you given us only one allotment and one portion for an inheritance? We are a numerous people and the LORD has blessed us abundantly."

[15]"If you are so numerous," Joshua answered, "and if the hill country of Ephraim is too small for you, go up into the forest and clear land for yourselves there in the land of the Perizzites and Rephaites."

[16]The people of Joseph replied, "The hill country is not enough for us, and all the Canaanites who live in the plain have iron chariots, both those in Beth Shan and its settlements and those in the Valley of Jezreel."

[17]But Joshua said to the house of Joseph—to Ephraim and Manasseh—"You are numerous and very powerful. You will have not only one allotment [18]but the forested hill country as well. Clear it, and its farthest limits will be yours; though the Canaanites have iron chariots and though they are strong, you can drive them out."

**14** The relative sizes of the various tribes as recorded in Numbers 26 indicate that Ephraim and Manasseh should have qualified for one allotment each. When one looks at a map, however, and considers the relative size of the territory granted to each tribe, it becomes apparent that the first two lots in the territory west of the Jordan were disproportionately large (i.e., Judah and Joseph). In terms of square miles, the Joseph tribes had little reason to complain. Moreover, the land they were given was the most fertile in all Palestine. Joshua was certainly justified in resisting their request.

**15** The Joseph tribes based their request on their great numbers. Joshua turned this around to challenge them to occupy the area already assigned to them. "The hill country of Ephraim" is the central mountainous region. The "Rephaites," like the Anakites, were a people of unusually large stature (cf. 12:4). As Caleb defeated the Anakites, so, with God's help, a great tribe like Ephraim should be able to conquer the Rephaites.

**16** The Joseph tribes' response shows that their difficulty was not the size of the allotment nor the forested condition of the highlands; it was the presence of other inhabitants whom they felt unable to drive out. Their foot soldiers were no match for the Canaanites' "iron chariots," which were actually constructed of wood with iron points and iron reinforcements. For "Beth Shan and . . . the Valley of Jezreel" (i.e., the Valley of Esdraelon), see comment on v.11 and Judges 1:27.

**17–18** Joshua recognized that the Joseph tribes did not need more land, but he reminded them that they were "numerous and very powerful" (v.17) and able to provide for their needs within the area already assigned to them.

## 4. *Division of the rest of the land (18:1–19:51)*

### a. *Joshua's rebuke of the seven tribes*

#### 18:1–10

[1]The whole assembly of the Israelites gathered at Shiloh and set up
the Tent of Meeting there. The country was brought under their control,
[2]but there were still seven Israelite tribes who had not yet received their
inheritance.
[3]So Joshua said to the Israelites: "How long will you wait before you
begin to take possession of the land that the LORD, the God of your
fathers, has given you? [4]Appoint three men from each tribe. I will send
them out to make a survey of the land and to write a description of it,
according to the inheritance of each. Then they will return to me. [5]You
are to divide the land into seven parts. Judah is to remain in its territory
on the south and the house of Joseph in its territory on the north. [6]After
you have written descriptions of the seven parts of the land, bring them
here to me and I will cast lots for you in the presence of the LORD our
God. [7]The Levites, however, do not get a portion among you, because
the priestly service of the LORD is their inheritance. And Gad, Reuben
and the half-tribe of Manasseh have already received their inheritance
on the east side of the Jordan. Moses the servant of the LORD gave it to
them."
[8]As the men started on their way to map out the land, Joshua
instructed them, "Go and make a survey of the land and write a
description of it. Then return to me, and I will cast lots for you here at
Shiloh in the presence of the LORD." [9]So the men left and went through
the land. They wrote its description on a scroll, town by town, in seven
parts, and returned to Joshua in the camp at Shiloh. [10]Joshua then cast
lots for them in Shiloh in the presence of the LORD, and there he
distributed the land to the Israelites according to their tribal divisions.

**1** "The whole assembly" refers to the seven tribes who had not yet received their inheritance (cf. v.3). "Shiloh" is modern Khirbet Seilun, about twelve miles south of Shechem. The Tent of Meeting is mentioned explicitly only twice in Joshua (cf. 22:19 where it is called "the LORD's tabernacle"). The expression "in the presence of the LORD" occurs a number of times (e.g., vv.6, 8, 10) and means "before" or "near the ark of the covenant," which was housed in the "Tent of Meeting." When the Israelites moved the Tent of Meeting to Shiloh, they moved the ark of the covenant there, too. This is where the ark remained until it was captured by the Philistines in the time of Eli the priest (1 Sam 4:1–11). Shiloh became the center of national life, and it was here that the final allotments of land were made. The transfer of the ark from Gilgal to Shiloh was symbolic of the completion of the Conquest because Gilgal was only on the edge of the Promised Land but Shiloh was in the center. Though the Israelites had the land "under their control," they still did not possess it all. They had not subdued all the Canaanites. Judges 1:30–36 states that enclaves were still holding out in Zebulun, Asher, Naphtali, and Dan.

**2** The statement "there were still seven Israelite tribes who had not yet received their inheritance" implies that a significant amount of time had elapsed. Throughout the Book of Joshua, events that took a considerable amount of time are compressed into a few verses. Apparently the remaining tribes had grown complacent. They were satisfied with nomadic life in the fertile land of Ephraim and Manasseh and were not eager to be involved in the warfare required to claim their own territory.

**3** The word "Israelites" refers only to those tribes who had not received their land. Joshua reproved them for the ingratitude and unbelief manifested in their failure to take the territory God had already given to them. Joshua was eager to complete his commission, which included, not only the conquest of the land, but also its division among the tribes.

**4** The appointment of "three men from each tribe" was part of a new system devised for dividing the remainder of the land. This new system may have been Joshua's response to the dissatisfaction of the Joseph tribes. Although the land had been divided by lot according to divine command, the area assigned to Judah was too large; and the Joseph tribes complained that theirs was too small. The phrase "according to the inheritance of each" means that the land was to be divided into equitable portions that could then be assigned by lot.

**5** Whatever inequities there might have been, the assignments already made were to stand.

**6** The casting of lots was done under Joshua's authority, but Eleazar the priest would be the one who actually did it (14:1–2; 19:51; cf. Num 27:21). When Joshua said that he would cast lots for the people "in the presence of the LORD," he was indicating that the lots would be cast near the ark of the covenant.

**7** The repetition of information previously given is a clue to the episodal nature of the narrative (cf. 13:14; 14:4; concerning the two and one-half tribes, cf. 13:8–32; 14:3). The two and one-half tribes from east of the Jordan must have become impatient to have the division of the land completed so that they could return home to their families and possessions.

**8–9** The men were to describe each area "town by town" (v.9) because the number and nature of the towns were more important to them than the precise borders or the number of square miles.

**10** Once again the word "Israelites" refers only to the seven tribes who as yet had not received any inheritance (cf. v.1).

### b. *The inheritance of Benjamin (18:11–28)*

#### 1) *The borders of Benjamin*

18:11–20

[11]The lot came up for the tribe of Benjamin, clan by clan. Their allotted territory lay between the tribes of Judah and Joseph:

[12]On the north side their boundary began at the Jordan, passed
the northern slope of Jericho and headed west into the hill country,
coming out at the desert of Beth Aven. [13]From there it crossed to
the south slope of Luz (that is, Bethel) and went down to Ataroth
Addar on the hill south of Lower Beth Horon.

[14]From the hill facing Beth Horon on the south the boundary turned south along the western side and came out at Kiriath Baal (that is, Kiriath Jearim), a town of the people of Judah. This was the western side.

[15]The southern side began at the outskirts of Kiriath Jearim on
the west, and the boundary came out at the spring of the waters of
Nephtoah. [16]The boundary went down to the foot of the hill facing
the Valley of Ben Hinnom, north of the Valley of Rephaim. It
continued down the Hinnom Valley along the southern slope of the
Jebusite city and so to En Rogel. [17]It then curved north, went to En
Shemesh, continued to Geliloth, which faces the Pass of Adummim,
and ran down to the Stone of Bohan son of Reuben. [18]It continued
to the northern slope of Beth Arabah and on down into the Arabah.
[19]It then went to the northern slope of Beth Hoglah and came out at
the northern bay of the Salt Sea, at the mouth of the Jordan in the
south. This was the southern boundary.

[20]The Jordan formed the boundary on the eastern side.
These were the boundaries that marked out the inheritance of the clans of Benjamin on all sides.

**11** Benjamin was not the largest of the seven tribes who were receiving their allotments; yet their territory is described in greater detail than that of the others. Some commentators assume that this is because the author had more information about Benjamin. On the other hand, if these lists came from an administrative register (cf. comment on 15:20), that in itself might account for the amount of detail. It is also possible that the author was more specific in describing the territory of Benjamin because of its importance as the tribe of Saul, the first king of Israel.

**12** "The north side" of Benjamin corresponds to the southern border of Ephraim (16:1–3).

**13** For "Luz (that is, Bethel)" see 16:1–2. For "Ataroth Addar" see 16:2. For "Lower Beth Horon" see 10:10; 16:2–3. Beth Horon belonged to Ephraim.

**14** "Along the western side" means the western boundary of Benjamin. "Kiriath Baal" (see 15:60) belonged to Judah. It was also known as Kiriath Jearim.

**15** "The southern side" of Benjamin was the northern boundary of Judah (15:5–9). For "the waters of Nephtoah," see 15:9.

**16** For "the Valley of Ben Hinnom" see 15:8. For "the Valley of Rephaim" see 15:8. For "En Rogel" see 15:7.

**17** For "En Shemesh" see 15:7. On "Geliloth" compare Gilgal in 15:7. For "Stone of Bohan" see 15:6.

**18** For "Beth Arabah" see 15:6, 61. "The Arabah" refers to the Jordan Valley.

**19** For "Beth Hoglah" see 15:6. For "the northern bay" see 15:5.

### 2) *The towns of Benjamin*

18:21–28

21 The tribe of Benjamin, clan by clan, had the following cities:
Jericho, Beth Hoglah, Emek Keziz, 22 Beth Arabah, Zemaraim,
Bethel, 23 Avvim, Parah, Ophrah, 24 Kephar Ammoni, Ophni and
Geba—twelve towns and their villages.
25 Gibeon, Ramah, Beeroth, 26 Mizpah, Kephirah, Mozah, 27 Rek-
em, Irpeel, Taralah, 28 Zelah, Haeleph, the Jebusite city (that is,
Jerusalem), Gibeah and Kiriath—fourteen towns and their villages.
This was the inheritance of Benjamin for its clans.

**21** The towns allotted to Benjamin are divided into two lists. One records twelve cities in the east (vv.21–24) and the other fourteen cities in the west (vv.25–28). The majority of the towns of Judah are divided into ten similar lists (15:21–44, 48–62). Many commentators believe that the author or editor has utilized an official list of cities divided into twelve administrative districts, perhaps from the time of David and Solomon (cf. comment on 15:20). For "Beth Hoglah" see 15:6.

**22** For "Beth Arabah" see 15:6. For "Bethel" see 7:2 (cf. Judg 1:22–23).

**23** "Parah" is modern Khirbet ʿAin Farah, northeast of Anathoth. "Ophrah" is modern et-Taiyibeh, about four miles northeast of Bethel.

**25** For "Gibeon" see 9:17. "Ramah" is modern er-Ram, about five miles north of Jerusalem. For "Beeroth" see 9:17.

**26** For "Kephirah" see 9:17. "Mozah" is modern Qalunyah, about four miles northwest of Jerusalem near the waters of Nephtoah.

**28** "Zelah" is where Saul was buried (2 Sam 21:14). For "the Jebusite city" see 10:1; 15:8, 63. "Gibeah" is modern Tell el-Ful. It must not be confused with Gibeah in Judah (15:57). "Kiriath" (see 9:17) may be the same as Kiriath Jearim.

### c. *The inheritance of Simeon*

19:1–9

1The second lot came out for the tribe of Simeon, clan by clan. Their inheritance lay within the territory of Judah. 2It included:

Beersheba (or Sheba), Moladah, 3Hazar Shual, Balah, Ezem,
4Eltolad, Bethul, Hormah, 5Ziklag, Beth Marcaboth, Hazar Susah,
6Beth Lebaoth and Sharuhen—thirteen towns and their villages;
7Ain, Rimmon, Ether and Ashan—four towns and their villages—
8and all the villages around these towns as far as Baalath Beer (Ramah in the Negev).

This was the inheritance of the tribe of the Simeonites, clan by clan.
9The inheritance of the Simeonites was taken from the share of Judah, because Judah's portion was more than they needed. So the Simeonites received their inheritance within the territory of Judah.

**1** All the towns allotted to Simeon had been given first to Judah. This situation has led some commentators to conclude that this list is artificial. The text clearly states (v.9) that it was because Judah's portion was too large that some of the towns were reassigned to Simeon. According to the blessing Simeon and Levi received from Jacob their father shortly before his death (Gen 49:7), their descendants were destined to be scattered among the other tribes as punishment for the violent revenge Simeon and Levi had taken against the Shechemites (Gen 34). Judges 1:3 records that Judah and Simeon cooperated in subduing pockets of Canaanites living within their territory. The towns of Simeon are listed in two groups: the first (vv.2–6) has thirteen towns, all of which are in the Negev; the second (vv.7–8) has four towns, two in the Negev and two in the foothills.

**2** "Beersheba" was an important fortress on Judah's southern border in the time of the divided kingdom. For "Moladah" see 15:26.

**3–6** For the towns listed in these verses, see 15:28–32. "Balah" (v.3) is Baalah in 15:29. "Bethul" (v.4) is Kesil in 15:30. For "Ziklag" (v.5) see 15:31. "Sharuhen" (v.6) is modern Tell el-Far'ah on the Philistine plain east of Beersheba. It is mentioned in Egyptian records as the place where the Hyksos retreated when they were expelled from Egypt. "Beth Lebaoth" is Lebaoth in 15:32.

**7–8** "Ain" and "Rimmon" (v.7) are unknown. Perhaps this should be read as one name: "Ain Rimmon," in which case the number of towns would be three, not four. "Ether" is modern Khirbet el-'Ater. "Baalath Beer" (v.8) is Bealoth in 15:24.

**9** All the towns assigned to Simeon were located within the borders of Judah with the consequence that Simeon was soon assimilated by Judah. Apparently 1 Kings 19:3 reflects a period when the assimilation was complete, because Beersheba, which had been given to Simeon, is called Beersheba in Judah.

### d. *The inheritance of Zebulun*

#### 19:10–16

[10]The third lot came up for Zebulun, clan by clan:
The boundary of their inheritance went as far as Sarid. [11]Going
west it ran to Maralah, touched Dabbesheth, and extended to the
ravine near Jokneam. [12]It turned east from Sarid toward the sunrise
to the territory of Kisloth Tabor and went on to Daberath and up to
Japhia. [13]Then it continued eastward to Gath Hepher and Eth
Kazin; it came out at Rimmon and turned toward Neah. [14]There the
boundary went around on the north to Hannathon and ended at the
Valley of Iphtah El. [15]Included were Kattath, Nahalal, Shimron,
Idalah and Bethlehem. There were twelve towns and their villages.
[16]These towns and their villages were the inheritance of Zebulun, clan
by clan.

**10** Though Zebulun was the younger brother of Issachar, he received his inheritance first (cf. Ephraim received his inheritance before Manasseh; see comment on 17:1). "Sarid" is modern Tell Shadud, south of Nazareth.

**11** "Maralah" may be modern Tell Thorah. "Dabbesheth" may be modern Tell esh-Shammam. "Jokneam" is Tell Qeimun near modern Yokne'am. The ravine is Wadi Musrarah, a tributary of the Kishon.

**12** "Kisloth Tabor" is modern Iksal, about four miles west of Mount Tabor. It is called Kesulloth in v.18. "Daberath" is modern Daburiyeh northwest of Mount Tabor. "Japhia" is modern Yafa southeast of Nazareth.

**13** "Gath Hepher" is modern Khirbet ez-Zurra', about three miles northeast of Nazareth. "Rimmon" is modern Tell el-Bedeiwiyeh. It guarded the western end of the valley of Beth Netopha (Sahl el-Baṭṭof).

**14** "The Valley of Iphtah El" is Wadi el-Malik on the border of Zebulun and Asher (v.27).

**15–16** For "Shimron" (v.15), see 11:1. "Bethlehem" is Beth Lahm east of Mount Carmel and should not be confused with Bethlehem in Judah. To arrive at a total of "twelve towns," some of the towns named in defining the border of Zebulun would have to be included.

### e. *The inheritance of Issachar*

#### 19:17–23

[17]The fourth lot came out for Issachar, clan by clan. [18]Their territory
included:
Jezreel, Kesulloth, Shunem, [19]Hapharaim, Shion, Anaharath,
[20]Rabbith, Kishion, Ebez, [21]Remeth, En Gannim, En Haddah and
Beth Pazzez. [22]The boundary touched Tabor, Shahazumah and
Beth Shemesh, and ended at the Jordan. There were sixteen towns
and their villages.
[23]These towns and their villages were the inheritance of the tribe of
Issachar, clan by clan.

**17** No description of the borders of Issachar is given, only a list of towns. Their inheritance lay mostly in the plain of Jezreel and was bounded on the west by Zebulun, on the north by Naphtali, on the east by the Jordan River, and on the south by Manasseh.

**18** "Jezreel" is modern Zere'in at the foot of Mount Gilboa. "Kesulloth" is the same as Kisloth Tabor in v.12. "Shunem" is modern Solem, about nine miles north of Jenin.

**19** "Hapharaim" is modern et-Taiyibeh. "Anaharath" may be Tell el-Mukharkhash, five miles southeast of Mount Tabor.

**20** "Kishion" is modern Khirbet Qasyun. It is listed as a Levitical town in 21:28.

**21** "Remeth" is modern Kokaab el-Hawa. "En Gannim" may be modern Khirbet Beit Jann near Jenin. It is listed as a Levitical town in 21:29. "En Haddah" is modern el-Hadatheh.

**22** "Beth Shemesh" is to be distinguished from Beth Shemesh in Judah (15:10) and Beth Shemesh in Naphtali (v.38).

### f. *The inheritance of Asher*

19:24–31

[24]The fifth lot came out for the tribe of Asher, clan by clan. [25]Their territory included:

Helkath, Hali, Beten, Acshaph, [26]Allammelech, Amad and Mishal.
On the west the boundary touched Carmel and Shihor Libnath. [27]It
then turned east toward Beth Dagon, touched Zebulun and the
Valley of Iphtah El, and went north to Beth Emek and Neiel, passing
Cabul on the left. [28]It went to Abdon, Rehob, Hammon and Kanah,
as far as Greater Sidon. [29]The boundary then turned back toward
Ramah and went to the fortified city of Tyre, turned toward Hosah
and came out at the sea in the region of Aczib, [30]Ummah, Aphek
and Rehob. There were twenty-two towns and their villages.

[31]These towns and their villages were the inheritance of the tribe of Asher, clan by clan.

**24** Asher's territory was located primarily on the western slopes of the mountains of Galilee.

**25** "Helkath" may be modern Tell el-Qasis. It is listed as a Levitical town in 21:31. "Hali" is modern Khirbet Ras 'Ali. "Beten" may be modern Khirbet Ibṭin. "Acshaph" may be modern Khirbet el-Harbaj.

**26** "Mishal" may be modern Tell Kisan. It is listed as a Levitical town in 21:30. "Shihor Libnath" may be a reference to the mouth of the Kishon River.

**27** "Cabul" is modern Kabul, about nine miles east of Acco. For "the Valley of Iphtah El," see v.14.

**28** “Abdon” is modern Khirbet ‘Abdeh, about four miles east of Achzib. “Hammon” is modern Umm el-‘Awamid. “Rehob” may be Tell el-Bir el-Gharbi. “Kanah” is modern Qana, about seven miles southeast of Tyre.

**29** “Aczib” is modern ez-Zib, about nine miles north of Acco.

**30** “Ummah” is considered to be an error for Acco, modern Tell el-Fukhkhar. “Aphek” is modern Tell el-Kurdaneh, about six miles southeast of Acco.

### g. *The inheritance of Naphtali*

19:32–39

32The sixth lot came out for Naphtali, clan by clan:
33Their boundary went from Heleph and the large tree in
Zaanannim, passing Adami Nekeb and Jabneel to Lakkum and
ending at the Jordan. 34The boundary ran west through Aznoth
Tabor and came out at Hukkok. It touched Zebulun on the south,
Asher on the west and the Jordan on the east. 35The fortified cities
were Ziddim, Zer, Hammath, Rakkath, Kinnereth, 36Adamah, Ramah, Hazor, 37Kedesh, Edrei, En Hazor, 38Iron, Migdal El, Horem,
Beth Anath and Beth Shemesh. There were nineteen towns and
their villages.
39These towns and their villages were the inheritance of the tribe of
Naphtali, clan by clan.

**32** The territory given to Naphtali lay between Asher and the Jordan.

**33** “Heleph” is modern Khirbet ‘Irbadeh at the foot of Mount Tabor. The “large tree in Zaanannim” is mentioned again in Judges 4:11. “Adami Nekeb” is modern Khirbet et-Tell. “Jabneel” is modern Tell en-Na‘am. “Lakkum” is modern Khirbet el-Manṣurah.

**34** “Aznoth Tabor” is modern Khirbet el-Jebell at the foot of Mount Tabor at the place where Zebulun, Issachar, and Naphtali came together.

**35** “Rakkath” is modern Khirbet el-Quneitireh. “Kinnereth” is modern Tell el-‘Oreimeh on the northwest shore of the Sea of Galilee.

**36** “Adamah” was built on top of Qarn Ḥaṭṭin and was the “largest and strongest” town in this region. “Ramah” is modern er-Ramah in the valley of Beth Kerem (esh-Shagur), which was the northernmost of four valleys that cut through the mountains of Galilee from east to west. It is to be distinguished from Ramah on the border of Asher (v.29). For “Hazor” see 11:10.

**37** “Kedesh” is modern Tell Qades. It is listed as a Levitical town in 21:32. It was also one of the cities of refuge (20:7). “Edrei” is to be distinguished from Edrei in Bashan (13:12).

**38** “Beth Anath” may be modern Ṣafed el-Baṭṭikh. “Beth Shemesh” may be modern Khirbet Tell er-Ruweisi and is to be distinguished from Beth Shemesh on Judah’s northern border (15:10) and from Beth Shemesh in Issachar (v.22).

## h. *The inheritance of Dan*

### 19:40–48

[40]The seventh lot came out for the tribe of Dan, clan by clan. [41]The territory of their inheritance included:

Zorah, Eshtaol, Ir Shemesh, [42]Shaalabbin, Aijalon, Ithlah, [43]Elon, Timnah, Ekron, [44]Eltekeh, Gibbethon, Baalath, [45]Jehud, Bene Berak, Gath Rimmon, [46]Me Jarkon and Rakkon, with the area facing Joppa.

[47](But the Danites had difficulty taking possession of their territory, so they went up and attacked Leshem, took it, put it to the sword and occupied it. They settled in Leshem and named it Dan after their forefather.)

[48]These towns and their villages were the inheritance of the tribe of Dan, clan by clan.

**40** The inheritance of Dan lay between the inheritance of Judah and that of Ephraim. To form this territory Judah gave up some of its northern towns and Ephraim gave up some of its southern towns. Dan's allotment overlapped Philistine territory, a situation that is reflected in the Samson stories.

**41** "Ir Shemesh" is Beth Shemesh on Judah's northern border (15:10). It is listed as a Levitical town in 21:16. "Zorah" and "Eshtaol" were received from Judah (see 15:33; cf. Judg 13:2, 25).

**42** "Shaalabbin" is modern Selbit. It is spelled Shaalbim in Judges 1:35. "Aijalon" (cf. 10:12 and 21:24), which is listed as a Levitical town in 21:24, is modern Yalo.

**43** "Timnah" is on Judah's northern border (cf. 15:10). This town is well known from the exploits of Samson (Judg 14:1). For this reason its location is thought to be in the Philistine territory. Aharoni (p. 312) suggests that the following name, Ekron, is given to distinguish this Timnah from others (e.g., in Judah; see 15:10, 57). The full name then would be "Timnath-Ekron."

**44** "Eltekeh" is listed as a Levitical town in 21:23. "Gibbethon" is modern Tell Malat, about five miles north of Khirbet el-Muqenna'. It is listed as a Levitical town in 21:23. "Baalath" is to be distinguished from the Baalah in 15:10.

**45** "Jehud" is modern el-Yehudiyeh about three miles north of Petaḥ Tikvah. "Bene Berak" is modern Ibn-Ibraq west of Yehudiyeh. "Gath Rimmon" is listed as a Levitical town in 21:24.

**47** "Leshem" is also known as Laish (Judg 18:29). The rather gruesome tale of the capture of this town by men from the tribe of Dan is related in Judges 18.

## 5. *Joshua's inheritance*

### 19:49–51

[49]When they had finished dividing the land into its allotted portions, the Israelites gave Joshua son of Nun an inheritance among them, [50]as the LORD had commanded. They gave him the town he asked for—

**Timnath Serah in the hill country of Ephraim. And he built up the town and settled there.**
**51 These are the territories that Eleazar the priest, Joshua son of Nun and the heads of the tribal clans of Israel assigned by lot at Shiloh in the presence of the LORD at the entrance to the Tent of Meeting. And so they finished dividing the land.**

**49** The description of the inheritances allotted to Caleb and Joshua, the two faithful spies, provided a framework within which land was allotted to the nine and one-half tribes. They were men of faith; therefore this arrangement symbolizes the spiritual truth that the gift of the land to Israel is predicated on faith.

**50** The words "as the LORD had commanded" must be a reference to Numbers 14:24, 30. "Timnath Serah" is modern Khirbet Tibnah near the Valley of Elah.

**51** The dividing of the land among the various tribes was complete (chs. 13–19). All that remained to be done was to designate the cities of refuge (ch. 20) and the Levitical towns (ch. 21).

This summary is very similar to the introduction in 14:1 with which the division of the land began.

### D. *The Cities of Refuge (20:1–9)*

#### 1. *The rationale*

20:1–6

**1 Then the LORD said to Joshua: 2 "Tell the Israelites to designate the cities of refuge, as I instructed you through Moses, 3 so that anyone who kills a person accidentally and unintentionally may flee there and find protection from the avenger of blood.**
**4 "When he flees to one of these cities, he is to stand in the entrance of the city gate and state his case before the elders of that city. Then they are to admit him into their city and give him a place to live with them. 5 If the avenger of blood pursues him, they must not surrender the one accused, because he killed his neighbor unintentionally and without malice aforethought. 6 He is to stay in that city until he has stood trial before the assembly and until the death of the high priest who is serving at that time. Then he may go back to his own home in the town from which he fled."**

**1–2** Murder is regarded as a very serious crime in the OT. One of the Ten Commandments is devoted to its prohibition (Exod 20:13; Deut 5:17). Capital punishment is prescribed in all cases of murder in a context that upholds the sanctity of all life, both human and animal (Gen 9:4–6). The land itself is defiled whenever murder goes unpunished (Num 35:33). Blood vengeance is an ancient custom that can be traced back to the early chapters of Genesis (e.g., Cain expected to be killed in revenge for the murder of his brother Abel [Gen 4:13–14]). The custom was still in force in the time of the monarchy (2 Sam 2:18–23; 3:27). Though the right of sanctuary was respected widely in the ancient Near East, the provision of "cities of refuge" (v.2) was a practice without parallel (Soggin, p. 198). The provision was made to distinguish between murder and accidental killing (manslaughter) and to grant the right of trial to suspected murderers. In Hebrew the pronoun "you" is plural and refers to instructions given for all the people (Num 35:6–34; Deut 19:1–13).

**3** A distinction was to be made between willful murder and manslaughter, i.e., "killing accidentally and unintentionally" (Num 35:6–34; Deut 19:1–13). In either case one had to leave his family and possessions and go immediately to the place of asylum to avoid being killed without a proper hearing. The elders of the cities of refuge were to provide protection and a trial for all suspected murderers (Num 35:25). Even though the law made provision for a strong centralized government or "state" to enforce the laws, at various times in Israel's history this was lacking, as in the period of Joshua and the judges. Thus the responsibility to protect rights to property or to avenge a murder fell to the victim's closest relative, who was called "the avenger of blood." Vengeance was to be a deterrent to murder.

**4** The city gate was an elaborate structure designed to control all traffic in or out and to thus facilitate the defense of the city. Normally there were benches in this area where the elders of the city would sit to adjudicate cases of various kinds (cf. Ruth 4:1–12). The accused must "state his case," for sanctuary was not to be granted indiscriminately. A person was to be regarded innocent until proven guilty, and a minimum of two witnesses was required to condemn one accused of murder (Num 35:30). The elders of these cities must "admit him . . . and give him a place to live." Apparently this included providing a means of livelihood, also.

**5** The command that "they must not surrender" indicates that he is assumed to be innocent. "Without malice aforethought" is a good translation for the literal Hebrew: "he did not hate him in the past."

**6** Protection from the avenger of blood was promised only so long as the accused remained in the city of refuge (Num 35:26–28). Even if he was only guilty of manslaughter, he had to remain in the city of refuge "until the death of the high priest." One who killed another accidentally was held responsible and had to forfeit his freedom for a period of time. (In Num 35:24–25 provision is made for the accused to stand trial before the assembly in the city where the crime was committed.) It is difficult to understand why the death of the high priest was chosen as the time for the sentence to be ended. This seems rather arbitrary and would inevitably result in certain inequities. The death of the high priest may have been a time of general amnesty (Boling, p. 474). The words "then he may go back" suggest that his old situation awaited him on his return. Nothing is said about what would be done for his family and his possessions while he was detained.

## 2. *The selection*

### 20:7–9

[7]So they set apart Kedesh in Galilee in the hill country of Naphtali, Shechem in the hill country of Ephraim, and Kiriath Arba (that is, Hebron) in the hill country of Judah. [8]On the east side of the Jordan of Jericho they designated Bezer in the desert on the plateau in the tribe of Reuben, Ramoth in Gilead in the tribe of Gad, and Golan in Bashan in the tribe of Manasseh. [9]Any of the Israelites or any alien living among them who killed someone accidentally could flee to these designated cities and not be killed by the avenger of blood prior to standing trial before the assembly.

**7** Three cities of refuge were selected in the territory west of the Jordan. They were strategically located so that wherever a person might be, he would have ready access to one of them. "Kedesh" (see 12:22) is in the north, "Shechem" (see comment and note on 8:30; cf. 8:33; Judg 9:7) in the center, and "Kiriath Arba" (see 14:15) in the south. Kiriath Arba (Hebron) was given to Caleb as a reward for his unwavering faithfulness (14:6–14). In 21:12 we are told that the territory around Kiriath Arba, the agricultural land and the villages, remained in Caleb's possession. Perhaps Caleb shared the city with the Levites (see comment on 21:1).

**8** The cities of refuge in Transjordan had already been selected by Moses (Deut 4:41–43). This passage may refer to the implementation of Moses' selection. Once again the distribution of the three cities is strategic. This time they are named from south to north (as in Deut 4:43). "Bezer" was in the south; it may be modern Umm el-ʿAmad. "Ramoth in Gilead," modern Tell Ramith, was in the center. "Golan" was in the north.

**9** Asylum in the cities of refuge was offered also to "any alien" living within the borders of Israel. The care shown to aliens is based on the memory of Israel's many years as aliens in Egypt. It is also testimony to God's care for all humanity. He is not partial or unfair in his dealings with mankind. Though the Israelites stood against the pagan societies around them, their hearts were to be open to receive any foreigner who would adopt their religion and their customs.

### E. *Towns for the Levites (21:1–42)*

#### 1. *Assignment of the towns by lot*

21:1–8

[1]Now the family heads of the Levites approached Eleazar the priest, Joshua son of Nun, and the heads of the other tribal families of Israel [2]at Shiloh in Canaan and said to them, "The LORD commanded through Moses that you give us towns to live in, with pasturelands for our livestock." [3]So, as the LORD had commanded, the Israelites gave the Levites the following towns and pasturelands out of their own inheritance:

[4]The first lot came out for the Kohathites, clan by clan. The Levites who were descendants of Aaron the priest were allotted thirteen towns from the tribes of Judah, Simeon and Benjamin. [5]The rest of Kohath's descendants were allotted ten towns from the clans of the tribes of Ephraim, Dan and half of Manasseh.

[6]The descendants of Gershon were allotted thirteen towns from the clans of the tribes of Issachar, Asher, Naphtali and the half-tribe of Manasseh in Bashan.

[7]The descendants of Merari, clan by clan, received twelve towns from the tribes of Reuben, Gad and Zebulun.

[8]So the Israelites allotted to the Levites these towns and their pasturelands, as the LORD had commanded through Moses.

**1** Now that all the land had been apportioned to the various tribes, "the family heads of the Levites" felt it was time for them to be given towns to live in. It is generally believed that the Levites lived in these towns without actually owning them, because it is stated repeatedly that the inheritance of the Levites would not be land but the service of God (cf. 14:4). The Levites may have lived in these towns side by side with members of the particular tribe from whose territory the town had been selected. Eleazar is named before Joshua as in other passages dealing with the division of land. "The heads of the other tribal families" complete the group of elders entrusted with this important task.

Some towns were assigned to the Levites even though they were still held by the Canaanites. This is the reason why some have argued that the institution of Levitical towns arose years later, perhaps in the time of the monarchy. Joshua, however, assigned many portions of the land that had not yet been conquered. He was confident that God would give Israel possession of these areas, also.

Four towns from each tribe were set apart for the Levites with the exception that only three were from Naphtali and nine were selected from the combined territories of Judah and Simeon (actually all the towns of Simeon were from the original allotment of Judah; cf. 19:1–9). Though Levitical towns were selected from every tribe, they were not evenly distributed throughout the land. They seem to have been clustered on the frontiers and in other endangered areas.

**2–3** "Shiloh" was the religious and political center for the Israelites at this time (cf. 18:1; 22:9). The Lord's command to Moses concerning towns for the Levites is found in Numbers 35:1–8. The fact that Joshua had to be reminded of this duty may reflect his advanced age. In Numbers 35:4–5, it is specified that more than half a square mile of pasture was to be assigned to the Levites with each town.

**4** The will of the Lord was determined by lot (see comment on 7:14 and 14:2). The "descendants of Aaron" are Kohathites; nevertheless they are treated separate from the rest of the tribes because they were the family of the high priest. Inasmuch as the temple would be built in Jerusalem, the towns of the high priest's family were conveniently located in the territories of Judah, Simeon, and Benjamin. Some see this as evidence that the Levitical towns were not selected until after Jerusalem was chosen as the site of the temple. Much to the contrary, it is evidence of God's providence. The number of towns set apart for the descendants of Aaron is indicative of God's providence also. At the time of selection, there were only three or, at most, four generations of the descendants of Aaron; and they would scarcely have needed thirteen towns.

**4–8** The number of towns for each clan (thirteen, ten, thirteen, twelve) was cleverly arranged without dividing the towns from any one tribe other than Manasseh, which had already been divided into two half-tribes.

### 2. *The towns of the Kohathites (21:9–26)*

#### a. *Towns of the descendants of Aaron*

21:9–19

[9]From the tribes of Judah and Simeon they allotted the following towns
by name [10](these towns were assigned to the descendants of Aaron who
were from the Kohathite clans of the Levites, because the first lot fell to
them):

[11]They gave them Kiriath Arba (that is, Hebron), with its surrounding pastureland, in the hill country of Judah. (Arba was the

forefather of Anak.) [12]But the fields and villages around the city
they had given to Caleb son of Jephunneh as his possession.
[13]So to the descendants of Aaron the priest they gave Hebron (a
city of refuge for one accused of murder), Libnah, [14]Jattir,
Eshtemoa, [15]Holon, Debir, [16]Ain, Juttah and Beth Shemesh, together with their pasturelands—nine towns from these two tribes.
[17]And from the tribe of Benjamin they gave them Gibeon, Geba,
[18]Anathoth and Almon, together with their pasturelands—four
towns.
[19]All the towns for the priests, the descendants of Aaron, were thirteen,
together with their pasturelands.

**9–10** We cannot be sure whether "the first lot fell" (v.10) to the descendants of Aaron deliberately out of respect for their honored position or whether it just happened that way in the providence of God. There was no question in the minds of the Israelites that God controlled the outcome of the casting of lots.

**11** For "Kiriath Arbah" see the comment on 14:15. For "Anak" see 11:21 and 14:12.

**12** On the inheritance of Caleb, see 14:6–15. The "villages" were the small settlements outside the walls of the towns.

**13** On the "cities of refuge," see chapter 20. Numbers 35:6 states specifically that the six cities of refuge were to be assigned to the Levites.

**15** "Holon" is spelled Hilen in 1 Chronicles 6:58.

**16** In place of "Ain," 1 Chronicles 6:59 has Ashan. "Juttuh" is not found in the MT of 1 Chronicles.

**17** "Gibeon" does not occur in the MT of 1 Chronicles 6:60.

**18** "Anathoth" is modern Ras el-Kharrubeh. It was the hometown of Jeremiah, and he too was a priest (Jer 1:1). "Almon" is modern Khirbet ʽAlmit. In 1 Chronicles 6:60 it is called Alemeth.

### b. *Towns of the remaining Kohathites*

21:20–26

[20]The rest of the Kohathite clans of the Levites were allotted towns from
the tribe of Ephraim:
[21]In the hill country of Ephraim they were given Shechem (a city
of refuge for one accused of murder) and Gezer, [22]Kibzaim and
Beth Horon, together with their pasturelands—four towns.
[23]Also from the tribe of Dan they received Eltekeh, Gibbethon,
[24]Aijalon and Gath Rimmon, together with their pasturelands—four
towns.
[25]From half the tribe of Manasseh they received Taanach and
Gath Rimmon, together with their pasturelands—two towns.
[26]All these ten towns and their pasturelands were given to the rest of the
Kohathite clans.

**22** "Kibzaim" does not occur in the list of towns in the MT of 1 Chronicles 6, where Jokmeam is found instead (v.68).

**23** "Eltekeh" and "Gibbethon" are not found in the list of towns in 1 Chronicles 6, where Aijalon and Gath Rimmon are added to the four towns from Ephraim (v.69). Woudstra (p. 310) comments that Eltekeh and Gibbethon never really came into the possession of the Israelites.

**25** Instead of "Taanach" and "Gath Rimmon," 1 Chronicles 6:70 has Aner and Bileam. Gath Rimmon was already listed in v.24 as from the tribe of Dan.

### 3. *The towns of the Gershonites*

21:27–33

27The Levite clans of the Gershonites were given:
from the half-tribe of Manasseh,
Golan in Bashan (a city of refuge for one accused of murder) and
Be Eshtarah, together with their pasturelands—two towns;
28from the tribe of Issachar,
Kishion, Daberath, 29Jarmuth and En Gannim, together with their
pasturelands—four towns;
30from the tribe of Asher,
Mishal, Abdon, 31Helkath and Rehob, together with their pasturelands—four towns;
32from the tribe of Naphtali,
Kedesh in Galilee (a city of refuge for one accused of murder),
Hammoth Dor and Kartan, together with their pasturelands—
three towns.
33All the towns of the Gershonite clans were thirteen, together with their pasturelands.

**27** "Be Eshtarah" is Ashtaroth in 1 Chronicles 6:71. Perhaps it is a contraction of Beth Eshterah, which means "House of Asherah." The Israelites felt no need to expunge the names of pagan deities from the names of their towns.

**28** "Kishion" is Kedesh in 1 Chronicles 6:72.

**29** "Jarmuth" is Ramoth in 1 Chronicles 6:73, and "En Gannim" is Anem.

**30** "Mishal" is Mashal in 1 Chronicles 6:74.

**31** "Helkath" is Hukok in 1 Chronicles 6:75.

**32** "Hammoth Dor" is Hammon in 1 Chronicles 6:76, and "Kartan" is Kiriathaim.

### 4. *The towns of the Merarites*

21:34–40

34The Merarite clans (the rest of the Levites) were given:
from the tribe of Zebulun,
Jokneam, Kartah, 35Dimnah and Nahalal, together with their
pasturelands—four towns;

36 from the tribe of Reuben,
Bezer, Jahaz, 37 Kedemoth and Mephaath, together with their pasturelands—four towns;
38 from the tribe of Gad,
Ramoth in Gilead (a city of refuge for one accused of murder), Mahanaim, 39 Heshbon and Jazer, together with their pasturelands—four towns in all.
40 All the towns allotted to the Merarite clans, who were the rest of the Levites, were twelve.

**34** "Jokneam" is missing in the MT of 1 Chronicles 6; and instead of "Kartah" in 1 Chronicles 6:77, we find Tabor.

**35** In place of "Dimnah," in 1 Chronicles 6:77 we find Rimmono; and there is no equivalent of "Nahalal" in 1 Chronicles.

**36** Somehow the author failed to mention that "Bezer" from the tribe of Reuben was a city of refuge (cf. 20:8). Nevertheless it is mentioned first in its subdivision as are all the other cities of refuge.

### 5. *Summary of the Levitical towns*

21:41–42

41 The towns of the Levites in the territory held by the Israelites were forty-eight in all, together with their pasturelands. 42 Each of these towns had pasturelands surrounding it; this was true for all these towns.

**41–42** No new information is given in this summary of the preceding verses.

## F. *God's Promises Fulfilled in the Division of the Land*

21:43–45

43 So the LORD gave Israel all the land he had sworn to give their forefathers, and they took possession of it and settled there. 44 The LORD gave them rest on every side, just as he had sworn to their forefathers. Not one of their enemies withstood them; the LORD handed all their enemies over to them. 45 Not one of all the LORD's good promises to the house of Israel failed; every one was fulfilled.

**43** The statement "the LORD gave Israel" emphasizes God's sovereign action. Israel's obedient participation was essential, but it was always secondary. The land was God's gift to Israel. All of Canaan was not yet in Israel's possession, nor were all the enemies destroyed; nevertheless Israel was in control of "all the land." It was securely in their hands. The promise of the land is a prominent theme in the history of the Patriarchs beginning with the call of Abraham (Gen 12:1–7). God's oath to Abraham had now been fulfilled. The words "they took possession of it and settled there" speak of the fulfillment of the hopes and aspirations of God's people. It is appropriate that the account of the Conquest and the division of the land begins (1:6) and ends on this note.

**44** The "rest" that "the LORD gave them" was a cessation of hostilities with the result that the people dwelt securely and serenely in the land (cf. Deut 12:9–10). This theme is taken up by the writer to the Hebrews (4:1–11), who indicates that a deeper rest that can only be fulfilled in Jesus Christ is typified. "Not one of their enemies withstood them" is a generalized statement that must not be pressed in detail. Chapters 6–11 are an account of sweeping victories. The Gibeonite deception and the pockets of resistance still holding out do not contradict the fact that Israel was victorious over every enemy that they faced in battle. As Keil and Delitzsch (p. 216) point out, "God had not promised the immediate and total destruction of the Canaanites, but only their gradual extermination (Exod 23:30; Deut 7:22)."

**45** "Not one of all the LORD's good promises . . . failed." On this note of victory and celebration, the story of the Conquest and the division of the land is completed.

## III. Preparation for Life in the Promised Land (22:1–24:33)

### A. *The Eastern Tribes Return Home (22:1–34)*

#### 1. *The dismissal of the eastern tribes*

22:1–9

1 Then Joshua summoned the Reubenites, the Gadites and the half-
tribe of Manasseh 2 and said to them, "You have done all that Moses the
servant of the LORD commanded, and you have obeyed me in everything
I commanded. 3 For a long time now—to this very day—you have not
deserted your brothers but have carried out the mission the LORD your
God gave you. 4 Now that the LORD your God has given your brothers rest
as he promised, return to your homes in the land that Moses the servant
of the LORD gave you on the other side of the Jordan. 5 But be very
careful to keep the commandment and the law that Moses the servant of
the LORD gave you: to love the LORD your God, to walk in all his ways, to
obey his commands, to hold fast to him and to serve him with all your
heart and all your soul."
6 Then Joshua blessed them and sent them away, and they went to
their homes. 7 (To the half-tribe of Manasseh Moses had given land in
Bashan, and to the other half of the tribe Joshua gave land on the west
side of the Jordan with their brothers.) When Joshua sent them home,
he blessed them, 8 saying, "Return to your homes with your great
wealth—with large herds of livestock, with silver, gold, bronze and iron,
and a great quantity of clothing—and divide with your brothers the
plunder from your enemies."
9 So the Reubenites, the Gadites and the half-tribe of Manasseh left
the Israelites at Shiloh in Canaan to return to Gilead, their own land,
which they had acquired in accordance with the command of the LORD
through Moses.

**1** The role played by the eastern tribes in the Conquest and their place in the nation and in the worship of Yahweh are prominent concerns throughout the Book of Joshua. Verses 1–8 together with 1:12–15 form a framework around the entire account of the Conquest and the division of the land. The Jordan River was a formidable natural barrier that isolated the two and one-half tribes from the rest of Israel. In later history this isolation was a serious threat to the political and religious unity of the nation. Seeds of disunity are already apparent in this chapter and demonstrate that the author had good reason to be concerned.

**2–3** The use of the phrase "Moses the servant of the LORD" (v.2) may be intended to remind the reader of 1:1, 2, and 7. The commission given in 1:12–15 is brought to its conclusion, and we are reminded again that obedience to a God-ordained leader is really obedience to God. Moses granted the request of these tribes to be allowed to settle east of the Jordan on condition that their armed men participate in the conquest of Canaan (Num 32:20–22: cf. 1:12–15). Consequently, Joshua's words "you have obeyed me" are reminiscent of the fact that they had accepted Joshua as Moses' rightful successor (cf. 1:16–18). Joshua commended the two and one-half tribes for the great sacrifice they had made. They had been separated from their families for a long time and had been unable to begin work on their newly acquired lands (v.3). What they had done for their fellow Israelites was regarded as service to God.

**4** "Rest" means the freedom to live in one's own land without the fear of war with any of the surrounding nations (see 21:44). Moses assigned the inheritances of the two and one-half tribes before Israel crossed the Jordan into the Promised Land (Num 32). "Your homes" translates the Hebrew word *'ohel,* which is commonly translated "tent" but has a much broader usage. When the Israelites settled in the land, they began to live in houses. It would be difficult to overestimate the importance of the Jordan River as a natural barrier that divided the land into "this side" and "the other side of the Jordan."

**5** "Be very careful to keep" (*šimrû meʾōḏ laʿaśôṯ*) is a common expression in Deuteronomy. This is the key verse in this chapter. It is another statement of the theme of the book that the people must be faithful to the Lord and obey his laws if they wish to be blessed and live in the land. In order to urge the Transjordanian tribes to continue to be faithful, Joshua reminded them of the way God had rewarded their faithfulness during the Conquest. This law or book of the law is probably all or part of the Book of Deuteronomy (see comment on 1:7). The emphasis here on loving the Lord and serving him with the whole heart is reminiscent of Deuteronomy 6:1–5. Legalism is rigid obedience to law for its own sake. The law, however, is an expression of God's will for his people and must be obeyed with wholehearted devotion. Jesus said, "If you love me, you will obey what I command" (John 14:15). To "hold fast to him" means to remain true to him in worship and obedience. These verses describe a close personal relationship between God and his people. Loyalty to Yahweh and an abhorrence of all foreign gods and idolatry is another theme that is dominant in both Deuteronomy and Joshua.

**6** Ritual blessing was viewed as an effective means of guaranteeing the well-being of another. It was not regarded as a magic incantation; rather, the one pronouncing the blessing was acting on behalf of God. It is apparent that the people did not go to their homes at this point. Hebrew narrative style often begins with a summary of the entire event and then presents the incident in detail.

**7** The reference to the two divisions of the tribe of Manasseh is strange here. It is another reason why some have concluded that all references to Manasseh in this chapter are later additions. The writer may have felt that the circumstance of a tribe being given land on both sides of the Jordan was unusual enough to merit special mention. Perhaps the shorter form "Reubenites and Gadites" (vv. 25, 32–34) is merely a more convenient way of referring to the two and one-half tribes.

**8** The Israelites had been enriched with the spoils taken in battle. The command "divide with your brothers" may mean that they were to take their rightful share of the spoils along with the other tribes who were settling in Canaan. It is more likely, however, that they were being commanded to share the booty with those who had remained in Transjordan to guard the women, children, and elderly and to care for the livestock (see comment on 1:14). The same arrangement was followed by Moses in dividing the spoils taken from the Midianites (Num 31:27; cf. 1 Sam 30:23–25).

**9** "Shiloh" was in the hill country of Ephraim. During the apportioning of the land to the various tribes, Shiloh had been selected as the place of worship. The Tent of Meeting had been set up there (18:1), and it was still in Shiloh in the time of Eli the priest and Samuel the prophet (1 Sam 1:3; 3:21; et al.). The name "Gilead" is used here to designate all of Israel's land east of the Jordan including Bashan. The word "Israelites" is the customary way of designating a major portion of the Israelites as distinguished from some smaller portion (e.g., "the Israelites grieved for their brothers, the Benjamites," Judg 21:6). It was appropriate that Joshua emphasized the fact that their land had been given to them by the Lord. For just as the crossing of the Jordan (chs. 3–4) was regarded as Israel's entrance into the Promised Land, so now some of the people believed that the warriors of the two and one-half tribes were leaving God's land when they crossed the Jordan to return home.

### 2. *The altar of witness (22:10–34)*

#### a. *The crisis*

22:10–14

[10]When they came to Geliloth near the Jordan in the land of Canaan, the Reubenites, the Gadites and the half-tribe of Manasseh built an imposing altar there by the Jordan. [11]And when the Israelites heard that they had built the altar on the border of Canaan at Geliloth near the Jordan on the Israelite side, [12]the whole assembly of Israel gathered at Shiloh to go to war against them.

[13]So the Israelites sent Phinehas son of Eleazar, the priest, to the land of Gilead—to Reuben, Gad and the half-tribe of Manasseh. [14]With him they sent ten of the chief men, one for each of the tribes of Israel, each the head of a family division among the Israelite clans.

**10** "Geliloth" is taken as a place name in the NIV. On the other hand, it may be a reference to Galilee or Gilgal. All these names are derived from the same Hebrew root. The land of Canaan lay exclusively on the west of the Jordan. In Hebrew the phrase "an imposing altar" literally means "an altar large in appearance." It was essential that the altar was large enough to be seen easily, because its function was to be a witness and not a place for sacrifice.

**11** The text does not say how much time elapsed before "the Israelites heard" about this project. We do know, however, that the warriors had had time to complete the altar and return to Gilead (v.15).

**12** "The whole assembly" refers only to representatives of the nine and one-half tribes. Since Israel was a theocracy at this time, "Shiloh" was the political as well as the religious center. The whole assembly was ready immediately "to go to war." They were not unmindful of the fact that the Transjordanian tribes served them at great personal sacrifice; nevertheless, they would not tolerate for a moment what appears to be a flagrant act of apostasy. They expected dire consequences for the entire nation (vv.17–20) if they did not obey Moses' command to deal severely with any such acts (cf. Lev 17:8–9; Deut 13:12–15).

**13** The zeal of the Israelites for the honor of God and the purity of his worship might have ended in terrible disaster had they not obeyed God's command to always investigate carefully before taking action (Deut 13:14). In this episode Phinehas, not Joshua or Eleazar, is the central figure. Phinehas had already distinguished himself as a zealous defender of true worship when Israel was entangled in immorality and idolatry at Peor (Num 25:6–18; Ps 106:30; Ecclus 45:23). The reputation he had gained may have been the reason that he was chosen for this important mission.

**14** Every tribe was represented because the investigation and any subsequent action were concerns for the whole nation.

### b. *The confrontation*

#### 22:15–20

[15]When they went to Gilead—to Reuben, Gad and the half-tribe of
Manasseh—they said to them: [16]"The whole assembly of the LORD says:
'How could you break faith with the God of Israel like this? How could
you turn away from the LORD and build yourselves an altar in rebellion
against him now? [17]Was not the sin of Peor enough for us? Up to this
very day we have not cleansed ourselves from that sin, even though a
plague fell on the community of the LORD! [18]And are you now turning
away from the LORD?

"'If you rebel against the LORD today, tomorrow he will be angry with
the whole community of Israel. [19]If the land you possess is defiled, come
over to the LORD's land, where the LORD's tabernacle stands, and share
the land with us. But do not rebel against the LORD or against us by
building an altar for yourselves, other than the altar of the LORD our God.
[20]When Achan son of Zerah acted unfaithfully regarding the devoted
things, did not wrath come upon the whole community of Israel? He was
not the only one who died for his sin.'"

**15–16** For "the whole assembly" (v.16), see the comment on v.12. The same Hebrew words (*māʿal maʿal*) are found here ("break faith") and in v.20 ("acted unfaithfully"). The building of this altar was viewed as an act of unfaithfulness to the God of Israel. We see here the value of immediate and open confrontation. When the nine and one-half tribes pressed for repentance and reconciliation before declaring war, it gave the others an opportunity to explain. Tragedy was averted by the willingness of both sides to dialogue. They did not accuse these men of turning away from the Lord to serve other gods but of deviating from the revealed will of the Lord. Even sacrifices offered in the name of the Lord were viewed as acts of rebellion when they were offered on an unapproved altar. The great sin of Jeroboam in later years was that he set up rival altars for the worship of Yahweh (1 Kings 12:26–30). Worship had been conducted at various places during the Conquest—Gilgal (5:10), Mount Ebal (8:30), and Shiloh (18:1). Moreover, in Judges and 1 Samuel sacrifices were offered on altars in a number of different places. Apparently all these altars were considered legitimate places for sacrifices.

**17** The mistakes of the past are appealed to here and in v.20. The "sin of Peor" drew some of the Israelites into pagan worship and immorality. About 24,000 died in a plague that the Lord sent as judgment on their sin. When they said, "We have not cleansed ourselves from that sin," they meant that the consequences of that sin continued to be experienced. Israel had to struggle continually against idolatry among her own people (cf. 24:23).

**18** The Israelites' concern was that, as at Peor, the whole community would be judged for the sin of a few.

**19** The word "defiled" (*ṭᵉmēʾāh*) is a technical term for ritual uncleanness and does not necessarily imply anything inherently evil or sinful. The question "If the land you possess is defiled" insinuates that Transjordan lay outside the sphere of the Lord's blessing and that the two and one-half tribes were building the altar to offer sacrifices and to sanctify it. When the nine and one-half tribes called the land of Canaan "the LORD's land," it is clear that they did not regard Transjordan as a part of the Promised Land (see also Num 32:6–9). The presence of "the LORD's tabernacle" was further evidence to them that the land west of the Jordan was especially blessed. Their willingness to "share the land" reveals a beautifully generous spirit and is proof of the sincerity of their concern for orthodox worship.

**20** For "the devoted things" see the comment on 6:17. The Israelites, who feared that the sin of a few would bring divine judgment once again "upon the whole community of Israel," manifested a strong sense of corporate responsibility. If the unfaithfulness of a single individual had such dire consequences (7:5, 24–26), what would happen when two and one-half tribes rebelled?

### c. *The explanation*

#### 22:21–29

21Then Reuben, Gad and the half-tribe of Manasseh replied to the
heads of the clans of Israel: 22"The Mighty One, God, the LORD! The
Mighty One, God, the LORD! He knows! And let Israel know! If this has
been in rebellion or disobedience to the LORD, do not spare us this day.
23If we have built our own altar to turn away from the LORD and to offer
burnt offerings and grain offerings, or to sacrifice fellowship offerings
on it, may the LORD himself call us to account.

24"No! We did it for fear that some day your descendants might say to
ours, 'What do you have to do with the LORD, the God of Israel? 25The
LORD has made the Jordan a boundary between us and you—you
Reubenites and Gadites! You have no share in the LORD.' So your
descendants might cause ours to stop fearing the LORD.

26"That is why we said, 'Let us get ready and build an altar—but not
for burnt offerings or sacrifices.' 27On the contrary, it is to be a witness
between us and you and the generations that follow, that we will
worship the LORD at his sanctuary with our burnt offerings, sacrifices
and fellowship offerings. Then in the future your descendants will not
be able to say to ours, 'You have no share in the LORD.'

[28]"And we said, 'If they ever say this to us, or to our descendants, we will answer: Look at the replica of the LORD's altar, which our fathers built, not for burnt offerings and sacrifices, but as a witness between us and you.'

[29]"Far be it from us to rebel against the LORD and turn away from him today by building an altar for burnt offerings, grain offerings and sacrifices, other than the altar of the LORD our God that stands before his tabernacle."

**21–22** The warriors from Transjordan appealed to God as their witness, using a name that emphasizes his omnipotence and sovereignty (cf. Ps 50:1). The repetition of this solemn name indicates how serious they considered the situation to be. If they were guilty, they would not object to being punished.

**23** The Transjordanians agreed that any departure from the pure worship of the Lord deserved severe judgment; however, they fervently rejected the idea that they had built an altar of their own as a rival to the altar at Shiloh.

**24** Joshua was afraid that the isolation caused by the Jordan might lead to the Transjordanians' turning from the worship of Yahweh (v.5). On the other hand, they were afraid that this isolation might cause their descendants to be rejected by the rest of Israel. Neither fear was unfounded. Keil and Delitzsch (p. 221) comment: "For, inasmuch as in all the promises and laws Canaan alone (the land on this side of Jordan, Num 34:1–12) is always mentioned as the land Jehovah would give to His people for their inheritance, it was quite a possible thing that at some future time the false conclusion might be drawn from this, that only the tribes who dwelt in Canaan proper were the true people of Jehovah." One of the tragedies of denominational and confessional isolation in present-day Christianity is that it is the cause of suspicion and misunderstanding.

**25** The Jordan River was an important natural barrier impeding communication and socialization. In the future it might be viewed as a boundary that God had ordained to mark off his own people from outsiders. For the omission of the half-tribe of Manasseh in "you Reubenites and Gadites," see the comment on v.7.

**26–27** The very presence of the altar would be a silent witness that the Transjordanian tribes had every right to be included in the people of Israel and the worship of Yahweh (cf. 24:27, where a stone serves as a witness).

**28–29** The altar was a "replica" of the Lord's altar because its shape was an integral part of its witness, linking it to the true altar at the Tent of Meeting. Apparently the design of an altar indicated what deity was worshiped at that altar. Many years later, in order to worship the god of the Syrians, King Ahaz had to have an altar constructed in Jerusalem patterned after the altar in Damascus (2 Kings 16:10–16; 2 Chron 28:22–25).

### d. *The resolution*

#### 22:30–34

[30]When Phinehas the priest and the leaders of the community—the heads of the clans of the Israelites—heard what Reuben, Gad and

Manasseh had to say, they were pleased. 31 And Phinehas son of
Eleazar, the priest, said to Reuben, Gad and Manasseh, "Today we
know that the LORD is with us, because you have not acted unfaithfully
toward the LORD in this matter. Now you have rescued the Israelites from
the LORD's hand."
32 Then Phinehas son of Eleazar, the priest, and the leaders returned
to Canaan from their meeting with the Reubenites and Gadites in Gilead
and reported to the Israelites. 33 They were glad to hear the report and
praised God. And they talked no more about going to war against them
to devastate the country where the Reubenites and the Gadites lived.
34 And the Reubenites and the Gadites gave the altar this name: A
Witness Between Us that the LORD is God.

**30** The Israelites "were pleased" when they realized that no bloodshed would be necessary. This proves that they were not motivated by a vengeful spirit but were distressed by what appeared to be a flagrant act of apostasy.

**31** The faithfulness and unity of God's people were taken as evidence of God's presence and blessing.

**32–33** No doubt the leaders of Israel returned from their Transjordanian meeting with joy in their hearts and were eager to inform the rest of the community of the good news (v.32). Not only were the people "glad to hear the report," but they also "praised God" (v.33). All talk of war ceased.

**34** Many years before, in this same land of Gilead, a memorial had been erected as a witness between Jacob and Laban, his father-in-law (Gen 31:43–54). In that instance, however, the memorial was not a symbol of unity but a warning to keep either party from crossing over to harm the other.

This altar was intended to be a witness that the Lord was the God of both the Transjordanian tribes and the rest of Israel, and, therefore, they were all brothers who shared a common form and place of worship. Though a single organizational structure may not be possible or even desirable for the church, the memory of a single cross is the symbol of unity that will ultimately destroy all divisiveness.

Later history reveals that the Israelites living in Transjordan were subject to repeated attacks by enemy armies and that they were tempted to worship foreign deities. Ultimately their land was taken from them and their few survivors were assimilated into the rest of Israel.

## Notes

---

**33–34** The LXX includes the words *καὶ τοῦ ἡμίσους φυλῆς* Μανασση (*kai tou hēmisous phylēs Manassē*, "and the half-tribe of Manasseh"), which are strangely absent from the MT in both verses.

---

## B. *Joshua's Farewell to the Leaders (23:1–16)*

Chapters 23 and 24 are so similar that some regard them as variant accounts of a single event. There are, however, marked differences between them. From a literary standpoint each chapter is complete in itself and independent. Chapter 23 is Joshua's personal farewell, in which he did all the speaking. In chapter 24 he led the people in a renewal of the covenant, and the people participated with appropriate responses. The theme of Joshua's farewell is a reiteration of the call to be faithful to the Lord and to obey his law. This would be the secret of victory for Israel over the pockets of resistance that remained.

### 1. *God's blessing: the reward for faithfulness*

#### 23:1–11

**1 After a long time had passed and the LORD had given Israel rest from
all their enemies around them, Joshua, by then old and well advanced in
years, 2 summoned all Israel—their elders, leaders, judges and
officials—and said to them: "I am old and well advanced in years. 3 You
yourselves have seen everything the LORD your God has done to all these
nations for your sake; it was the LORD your God who fought for you.
4 Remember how I have allotted as an inheritance for your tribes all the
land of the nations that remain—the nations I conquered—between the
Jordan and the Great Sea in the west. 5 The LORD your God himself will
drive them out of your way. He will push them out before you, and you
will take possession of their land, as the LORD your God promised you.
6 "Be very strong; be careful to obey all that is written in the Book of
the Law of Moses, without turning aside to the right or to the left. 7 Do
not associate with these nations that remain among you; do not invoke
the names of their gods or swear by them. You must not serve them or
bow down to them. 8 But you are to hold fast to the LORD your God, as
you have until now.
9 "The LORD has driven out before you great and powerful nations; to
this day no one has been able to withstand you. 10 One of you routs a
thousand, because the LORD your God fights for you, just as he
promised. 11 So be very careful to love the LORD your God.**

**1** It is not clear exactly what the words "After a long time" refer to. The NIV seems to take them to mean a long time after Joshua had assumed leadership in Israel. It is possible, however, that the Hebrew means "a long time *after* ['*aḥ$^{a}$rê*] the LORD had given Israel rest." The events of chapters 23 and 24 probably occurred shortly prior to Joshua's death at the age of 110 (24:29). At least twenty-five years had passed since the end of the Conquest because Joshua was the same age as or younger than Caleb (see comment on 14:10).

"Rest" is a common theme in Joshua; it was the goal of the Conquest. This rest was realized when the major battles were ended and Israel was settled in the land (11:23). They were at peace with "all their enemies" even though all those enemies had not yet been driven out (cf. vv.4–5).

**2** Chapters 23 and 24 both begin with Joshua assembling the representatives of the people. In chapter 22 (v.12; cf. v.16) "the whole assembly of Israel" designated representatives of the nine and one-half tribes. It is reasonable to suppose that 22:1–8 is Joshua's farewell to the Transjordanian tribes and that here again the words "all Israel" refer only to those tribes living west of the Jordan. The NIV correctly understands "all Israel" to mean "their elders, leaders, judges and officials." It would have been impossible for Joshua to address the whole nation at one time. Perhaps the leaders, judges, and officials were subdivisions of the elders (cf. 24:1). The place of assembly is not stated. It is not safe to assume that they gathered at Shiloh as in chapter 22, because a number of years must have elapsed between chapters 22 and 23. In chapter 24 we are told that they gathered at the tabernacle ("they presented themselves before God," v.1), but there is no similar reference in chapter 23. Joshua's advanced age was his reason for delivering his farewell address at this time.

**3** The Israelites were eyewitnesses of God's mighty acts. The importance of this is brought out in 24:31. The theme of Joshua's address is a call for loyalty to the Lord because of all he had done for Israel. Ultimately it was the Lord who defeated and dispossessed the Canaanites. In this holy war the Israelites did participate with sword and shield; nevertheless the victory was credited to God alone (cf. Deut 1:30; 3:22; 20:4).

**4** In 13:1–7 the Lord commanded Joshua to divide all of Canaan among the nine and one-half tribes even though much of it was yet to be conquered. Israel's lethargy in driving out the last of their enemies is difficult to understand, but it contributed to the fulfillment of God's promise to drive them out "little by little" (Exod 23:30). Joshua confined his remarks to the land "between the Jordan and the Great Sea" (which is further support of the supposition that this chapter deals only with the nine and one-half tribes).

**5** For the statement "as the LORD your God promised you," see comment on 13:6 and Exodus 23:23–33.

**6** The command "Be very strong" is reminiscent of the words of encouragement directed to Joshua several times in chapter 1 (cf. vv.6–7, 9, 18). The exhortation to courage and obedience to the Book of the Law of Moses in 1:7 is repeated here almost word for word. Joshua passed on to Israel the secret of success and prosperity that the Lord had given him at the beginning of the Conquest. God's promise was not unconditional; Israel's faithfulness was required. The law that must be obeyed "is God's gracious provision for a life of covenant fellowship between himself and the people" (Woudstra, p. 334).

**7** For the first time in Joshua, we find an explicit warning against intermingling with the native population whose immorality and degradation were closely tied to their religious practices. Because Israel replaced a people whose culture was far more advanced than their own, the temptation to worship the gods of the Canaanites must have been overwhelming. Yet if the Israelites were to adopt their wicked practices, they too would be subject to punishment (Deut 8:19–20). God does not show any partiality. Israel was to remain separate from the nations living in the land of Canaan (Exod 34:12, 15; cf. Deut 20:16 with 20:15); nevertheless, strangers from other nations were welcome to live with Israel and to worship the Lord (cf. 20:9, where the right of sanctuary is extended to resident aliens). "Invoke the names," "swear," "serve," and "bow down" are four expressions of worship that are specified here to show that no form of worship whatsoever must be accorded to these pagan deities.

**8** The Hebrew word translated "hold fast" (*dāḇaq*) is used in Genesis 2:24 to describe the intimate and binding relationship between husband and wife. It is used several times in Deuteronomy to describe a close relationship between God and man (4:4; 10:20; 11:22; 13:4). In spite of occasional lapses, Israel's behavior was characterized as holding fast to the Lord.

**9–10** The motive for faithfulness to the Lord was that he was the God who had given Israel the land. The statement "no one has been able to withstand you" (v.9) seems to overlook the early successes of the army of Ai. This circumstance, however, was not due to the superiority of that army but to Israel's unfaithfulness. Only when Israel was faithful would the Lord fight for them (v.10). Here is an instance where the exception clearly proves the rule.

**11** The command to "love the LORD" that was given to the Transjordanian tribes in 22:5 (see comment) is repeated here for the rest of Israel.

### 2. *God's judgment: the consequences of unfaithfulness*

#### 23:12–16

[12]"But if you turn away and ally yourselves with the survivors of these
nations that remain among you and if you intermarry with them and
associate with them, [13]then you may be sure that the LORD your God will
no longer drive out these nations before you. Instead, they will become
snares and traps for you, whips on your backs and thorns in your eyes,
until you perish from this good land, which the LORD your God has given
you.

[14]"Now I am about to go the way of all the earth. You know with all
your heart and soul that not one of all the good promises the LORD your
God gave you has failed. Every promise has been fulfilled; not one has
failed. [15]But just as every good promise of the LORD your God has come
true, so the LORD will bring on you all the evil he has threatened, until he
has destroyed you from this good land he has given you. [16]If you violate
the covenant of the LORD your God, which he commanded you, and go
and serve other gods and bow down to them, the LORD's anger will burn
against you, and you will quickly perish from the good land he has given
you."

**12** The danger of apostasy was Joshua's great concern here. Indeed, the message of this entire book is a warning against apostasy. "Ally yourselves" translates the same Hebrew word (*dāḇaq*) that was used for holding fast to the Lord in v.8. The devotion that belongs exclusively to the Lord must not be directed to any other. Intermarriage always posed a powerful threat to religious purity. It caused Solomon's downfall (1 Kings 11:1–8). Alliances with other nations frequently involved intermarriage (cf. Gen 34:9–10). Because of the great danger involved in intermarriage with these corrupt people, it was strictly prohibited for Israel (Exod 34:12–16; Deut 7:1–6).

**13** "The LORD your God will no longer drive out" was language that Moses also had used in warnings against apostasy (cf. Exod 23:30–33; 34:11–12; Num 33:55). Just as faithfulness had been essential for Israel to acquire the land, so now it was indispensable if they were to continue to live in the land.

**14** "The way of all the earth" is an interesting idiom for death. It emphasizes the universality of death in human experience (cf. 1 Kings 2:2; Rom 5:12). "All the good promises" of the Lord had indeed come true. Israel's victories had been so all pervasive that pockets of resistance remaining in the land did not detract from their appreciation of God's faithfulness. It is necessary to keep one's eyes on the big picture.

**15** God's faithfulness to his promises is proof positive that he will keep his threats as well. Israel should not suppose that being the recipients of God's blessings made them immune to his judgment. The words "he has threatened" are not represented in the Hebrew but have been supplied appropriately by the translators in keeping with the flow of the passage. The threat contained in this verse and the following one was fulfilled in the Babylonian exile.

**16** Although the concept of a covenant between Yahweh and Israel is foundational to the Book of Joshua, the word "covenant" does not occur often. The ark of the covenant predominates the account of the crossing of the Jordan (chs. 3–4) and the narrative about the conquest of Jericho (ch. 6). In chapter 5 the covenant rites of circumcision and Passover are reinstated before the covenant people take possession of the Land of Promise. After the initial victories at Jericho and Ai, a ceremony of covenant renewal is observed on Mount Ebal and Mount Gerizim (8:30–35). Finally, the concluding chapter (24) contains another ritual of covenant renewal. All this indicates that the Conquest was a religious event and not simply a military exploit: The Lord, the God of Israel, was marching into his own land with his own people.

## C. *The Covenant Renewed at Shechem (24:1–28)*

### 1. *A recitation of Israel's sacred history*

24:1–13

1 Then Joshua assembled all the tribes of Israel at Shechem. He
summoned the elders, leaders, judges and officials of Israel, and they
presented themselves before God.
2 Joshua said to all the people, "This is what the LORD, the God of
Israel, says: 'Long ago your forefathers, including Terah the father of
Abraham and Nahor, lived beyond the River and worshiped other gods.
3 But I took your father Abraham from the land beyond the River and led
him throughout Canaan and gave him many descendants. I gave him
Isaac, 4 and to Isaac I gave Jacob and Esau. I assigned the hill country of
Seir to Esau, but Jacob and his sons went down to Egypt.
5 " 'Then I sent Moses and Aaron, and I afflicted the Egyptians by what
I did there, and I brought you out. 6 When I brought your fathers out of
Egypt, you came to the sea, and the Egyptians pursued them with
chariots and horsemen as far as the Red Sea. 7 But they cried to the LORD
for help, and he put darkness between you and the Egyptians; he
brought the sea over them and covered them. You saw with your own
eyes what I did to the Egyptians. Then you lived in the desert for a long
time.
8 " 'I brought you to the land of the Amorites who lived east of the
Jordan. They fought against you, but I gave them into your hands. I
destroyed them from before you, and you took possession of their land.
9 When Balak son of Zippor, the king of Moab, prepared to fight against
Israel, he sent for Balaam son of Beor to put a curse on you. 10 But I

would not listen to Balaam, so he blessed you again and again, and I
delivered you out of his hand.
11 " 'Then you crossed the Jordan and came to Jericho. The citizens of
Jericho fought against you, as did also the Amorites, Perizzites,
Canaanites, Hittites, Girgashites, Hivites and Jebusites, but I gave them
into your hands. 12 I sent the hornet ahead of you, which drove them out
before you—also the two Amorite kings. You did not do it with your own
sword and bow. 13 So I gave you a land on which you did not toil and
cities you did not build; and you live in them and eat from vineyards and
olive groves that you did not plant.'

**1** There are three important elements that are new in chapter 24 and have no counterpart in chapter 23: (1) the review of Israel's history from the call of Abraham until the present, (2) the responses by the people with their solemn pledge to be faithful to Yahweh, and (3) the covenant that Joshua drew up for the Israelites (Karl Gutbrod, *Das Buch vom Landes Gottes* [Stuttgart: Calwer, 1951], pp. 156–57). These form the heart of chapter 24 and are evidence of its independence from chapter 23. Perhaps "all the tribes" refers only to the tribes that settled west of the Jordan (cf. comment on 23:2).

"Shechem" is modern Tell Balaṭa. Located in the hill country of Ephraim, it was one of the towns of Ephraim that were given to the Levites (21:21); it was also a city of refuge (20:7). There is no account of the conquest of Shechem in the Book of Joshua. This has led to the assumption that Shechem and the surrounding area were already populated with Israelites who were there before Joshua entered Canaan and welcomed him with open arms. We must remember, however, that the list of kings and towns that Israel conquered (12:9–24) gives an incomplete picture and includes the names of other towns for which there is no record of their conquest in the Book of Joshua.

Shechem may have been chosen as the site for Joshua's last great act of covenant renewal because of its illustrious history. This is where the Lord first promised the land of Canaan to Abraham and his descendants (Gen 12:6–7). Here Jacob buried all the idols found in his entourage in preparation for meeting the Lord at Bethel (Gen 35:4). In both accounts an oak tree is prominent. The fact that they presented themselves "before God" suggests that the tabernacle and the ark of the covenant were in Shechem at this time (cf. v.26, which mentions a "holy place" [*miqdāš*] in Shechem). Scholars are divided on this issue. Many insist that the sanctuary was still in Shiloh (cf. 18:1; 22:9, 12). It is possible that the ark had been brought just for this occasion and was placed in a temporary sanctuary. There is no clear evidence one way or the other. The essential point is that the people were made to feel accountable to God.

**2** This ceremony of covenant renewal is very similar in form to the suzerainty treaties that were common in the ancient Near East. Notice the following parallels: The preamble named the suzerain and the contracting parties (v.2a). The historical prologue recounted all the ways in which the suzerain had benefitted his subjects (vv.2b–13). The stipulations demanded of the vassal nations were stated (vv.14–15; vv.16–24 record the response of the people). Directions were given for the public reading and disposition of the text of the treaty (v.26; no public reading is described here). The treaty was attested by the seals of witnesses (vv.22, 27). Finally, there was a list of blessings for faithfulness in keeping the covenant and curses for unfaithfulness (vv.19–20).

"The River" is the Euphrates (see NIV mg.), but precisely where the forefathers lived is not indicated. Genesis 11:31 specifies Ur in Chaldea. Genesis is strangely silent about the existence of any pagan gods (except for Laban's "household gods" [Gen 31:19 et al.]); so it comes as a surprise when we are told they "worshiped other gods." Terah's name may be derived from a Hebrew word meaning "moon." The moon was the patron deity of Ur.

**3** Abraham was brought up in pagan idolatry; therefore, his call is an example of God's sovereignty and grace. We know none of the details of his conversion to the worship of the Lord. Abraham's call required that he go "from the land." The OT affirms that the whole earth belongs to the Lord (Ps 24:1) and does not endorse the view that he can be worshiped only in a certain geographical area. Nevertheless there are certain instances, like this one, where people who moved to a new location also changed their worship. Observe that "Canaan" is specified as the land to which he was led (see comment on 1:4). Abraham was constantly on the move in a land where all he ever possessed was the Cave of Machpelah, which he bought as a place of burial (Gen 23). There is a note of suspense in this recital. Land and "many descendants" were the major elements in God's promise to Abraham (Gen 15:5, 7, et al.), but neither materialized for several generations.

**4** The mountains of Seir are south of the Dead Sea in the land of the Edomites, the descendants of Esau. The suspense builds as Esau is given a land of his own while Jacob and his sons leave the land they expect to possess and go into bondage in Egypt. The mention of Jacob and Esau calls attention once again to God's sovereignty (see Rom 9:10–13).

**5** The entire narrative accentuates God's sovereign action in redemptive history. God said, "I took," "I gave," "I assigned," "I sent," "I afflicted," etc. Moses and Aaron were the principal figures in the deliverance from Egypt (Exod 3:1–4:17). The second person pronoun is surprising in the statement "I brought you out." Though some of his audience may have experienced the Exodus, most of them had not. In the very next sentence the reference is changed to "your fathers." A bewildering oscillation between second and third persons follows until the climax is reached in the words "you saw with your own eyes" (v.7, q.v.).

**6** The "sea" is the Red Sea. The Hebrew word for Red Sea (*yam sûp̱*) is literally "the Sea of Reeds" (NIV mg.; see comment on 2:10).

**7** Though Joshua says, "You saw with your own eyes," most of those listening to him had not seen these things. The alternation of pronouns from second to third person is indicative of Joshua's conviction that all Israel participated in every crucial event in their national history, whether or not they had actually been present. The profound effect that these events had on subsequent generations can be expressed only in language that speaks of those later generations as actually present. Forty years after God had made the covenant of Sinai, Moses said to the people, "It was not with our fathers that the LORD made this covenant, but with us" (Deut 5:3). Though the exact opposite was literally true, yet the words have a profound spiritual application. The events during the forty years of wandering are covered in a single sentence: "you lived in the desert for a long time." Perhaps Joshua's narration of Israel's history included many more details that the author of the book has eliminated to give us an abbreviated account.

**8** For the defeat of the Amorites, see Numbers 21 and Deuteronomy 2 and 3.

**9–10** Balak did not actually fight with Israel. The only resistance he offered was the hiring of Balaam to curse them (Num 22–24; Deut 23:4–5). In the NT Balaam is the epitome of a very evil person (2 Peter 2:15; Rev 2:14).

**11** It is strange that Joshua did not mention the miracles involved in crossing the Jordan and conquering Jericho. In Hebrew the phrase "citizens of Jericho" (*ba'*$^a$*lê-y*$^e$*rîḥô*) is literally the "lords" or "owners" of Jericho. They may have been the free citizens or the landowners. The fact that they fought against Israel is information that is not reported in chapter 6, and it runs counter to the viewpoint of some that in holy war the human agents do not actually fight. The picture in chapter 6 is the miraculous destruction of the walls so that the Israelites might have easy access to the town ("the people will go up, every man straight in," 6:5). The Israelites were responsible to destroy all the human beings and all the livestock (6:21). The words "as did also" have been added by the translators. The list of these seven nations stands in apposition to "the citizens of Jericho." For "Amorites" et al., see the comment on 3:10.

**12** John Garstang (*Joshua–Judges* [London: Constable and Co., 1931], pp. 258–60) explains the "hornet" as a reference to the Pharaoh of Egypt whose many campaigns into Canaan left the population seriously weakened when Israel invaded the land. In an alternative view, the hornet is the terror that the Lord sent to demoralize and immobilize the enemy (cf. 2:9–11, 24; 5:1). The two Amorite kings are examples of those who were driven out by the hornet. The mention of Sihon and Og at this point jars our sense of order. Hebrew narrative, however, often proceeded thematically and was not governed strictly by chronology. The statement "you did not do it with your own sword and bow" does not mean that they did not do any fighting (cf. v.11). Their efforts alone, however, would not account for the victory—it was a gift from God.

**13** "A land on which you did not toil," etc., is clearly in fulfillment of Deuteronomy 6:10–11.

### 2. *Joshua's charge and the people's response*
### 24:14–24

14 "Now fear the LORD and serve him with all faithfulness. Throw away
the gods your forefathers worshiped beyond the River and in Egypt, and
serve the LORD. 15 But if serving the LORD seems undesirable to you, then
choose for yourselves this day whom you will serve, whether the gods
your forefathers served beyond the River, or the gods of the Amorites, in
whose land you are living. But as for me and my household, we will
serve the LORD."
16 Then the people answered, "Far be it from us to forsake the LORD to
serve other gods! 17 It was the LORD our God himself who brought us and
our fathers up out of Egypt, from that land of slavery, and performed
those great signs before our eyes. He protected us on our entire journey

and among all the nations through which we traveled. [18]And the LORD
drove out before us all the nations, including the Amorites, who lived in
the land. We too will serve the LORD, because he is our God."
[19]Joshua said to the people, "You are not able to serve the LORD. He is
a holy God; he is a jealous God. He will not forgive your rebellion and
your sins. [20]If you forsake the LORD and serve foreign gods, he will turn
and bring disaster on you and make an end of you, after he has been
good to you."
[21]But the people said to Joshua, "No! We will serve the LORD."
[22]Then Joshua said, "You are witnesses against yourselves that you
have chosen to serve the LORD."
"Yes, we are witnesses," they replied.
[23]"Now then," said Joshua, "throw away the foreign gods that are
among you and yield your hearts to the LORD, the God of Israel."
[24]And the people said to Joshua, "We will serve the LORD our God and
obey him."

**14** At this point the Lord's message to Israel had ended. It was Joshua who said, "Fear the LORD." Some prefer to translate, "Revere the LORD," feeling that fear ought not be part of a believer's relationship to God. Fear, however, may either be destructive or saving. If we fear God, we will not need to fear his judgment (cf. Heb 12:28–29). The very first commandment is "You shall have no other gods before me" (Deut 5:7), because the worship of the Lord cannot be combined with idolatry. We are shocked to learn, then, that it was necessary for Joshua to command the Israelites to "throw away the gods" here at the end of his career as political and spiritual leader.

It is hard to imagine that the Israelites would still be worshiping idols after they had experienced so many of the Lord's great miracles and victories. While Achan's disobedience could not be tolerated for a moment, this sin had not been challenged until now. Joshua called the people to give undivided loyalty to the Lord as the only way to experience his presence and blessing in the future. For "the gods your forefathers served beyond the River," see the comment on v.2. The prophet Ezekiel also mentions Israel's unfaithfulness in Egypt (20:7; 23:3, 8). There is no explicit reference to the worship of Egyptian idols in the narratives of the Exodus, though Moses did question whether the Israelites were acquainted with the God of their fathers (Exod 3:13).

**15** Joshua was calling Israel to honesty and commitment. He wanted them to show singleness of heart. He wanted them to be honest with themselves and declare their allegiance. Though Joshua said, "Choose for yourselves," he did not intend to encourage idolatry. He was confident that the very thought of making a commitment to an idol would be so abhorrent to them that they would take a stand against all such worship.

The fertility cult of the Amorites with its many corrupt and immoral practices held a special appeal to the Israelites, who were settling down to agricultural life after so many years of wandering. This cult continued to be a strong temptation for many years. Our individualistic approach to salvation must be modified by the fact that here (and in Acts 16:31) individuals are challenged to involve their entire households.

**16–18** Joshua's appeal produced the effect he was looking for: "Far be it from us" (v.16) was a response involving both the will and the emotions. In denying the charge of idolatry, the Israelites asserted that the Lord had always been and always would be the object of their worship (v.18). The people added their personal affirmation to Joshua's recitation of the mighty acts God had done for them. With the words "brought us and our fathers" (v.17), they identified themselves with their fathers in God's saving purpose.

**19** Joshua's response, "You are not able," is unexpected. After encouraging the Israelites to make a commitment to the Lord, he told them they would be unable to keep it. There is irony in his statement. His purpose was not to discourage them but to lead them to count the cost and to mean what they said (cf. Luke 14:25–35). Some interpreters, however, take these words literally—the people cannot serve the Lord. They are not in the right state of mind. They are in need of NT grace. The fact is, however, they did serve God faithfully for many years (cf. v.31). Of course, they were only able to do this by the grace of God: OT grace. To be God's people they too must be holy—set apart (cf. "Be holy, because I am holy," Lev 11:44). Because the Lord "is a jealous God," he will not tolerate any rival deities or condone apostasy (Exod 20:5; 34:14; Deut 5:9).

The statement "he will not forgive" is hyperbole and is contrary to the nature of God, who is presented throughout the OT as a God of forgiveness and grace. The Lord revealed himself to Moses as "The LORD, the LORD, the compassionate and gracious God, slow to anger, abounding in love and faithfulness, maintaining love to thousands, and forgiving wickedness, rebellion and sin" (Exod 34:6–7a).

Though God forgives, he does not deal superficially with sin. Joshua wanted to caution the people not to speak carelessly, because God would hold them accountable. This is very much like God's word to Israel in the prophecy of Amos:

> "You only have I chosen
> of all the families of the earth;
> therefore I will punish you
> for all your sins." (3:2)

**21** When the people said, "No! We will serve the LORD," Joshua could see that his exhortation was producing the desired result.

**22** The people's own words would condemn them if at any time in the future they turned from the commitment that they had made that day.

**23–24** The matter of their idols had been raised by Joshua already in v.14. Now he called for action to substantiate the Israelites' commitment to the Lord. Nothing could be tolerated that might lead to their return to idolatry. The outward expression of discarding their idols was essential, but it had to be accompanied by loyalty from their hearts.

### 3. *Sealing the covenant*

#### 24:25–28

[25]On that day Joshua made a covenant for the people, and there at Shechem he drew up for them decrees and laws. [26]And Joshua recorded these things in the Book of the Law of God. Then he took a large stone and set it up there under the oak near the holy place of the LORD.

[27]"See!" he said to all the people. "This stone will be a witness against us. It has heard all the words the LORD has said to us. It will be a witness against you if you are untrue to your God."
[28]Then Joshua sent the people away, each to his own inheritance.

**25** The covenant Joshua made was likely a copy of the law of Moses (1:8; 22:5; 23:6). We have no other record of a covenant or law originating with Joshua.

**26** Commitments are too easily forgotten. Too soon the intensity of feeling fades away. Joshua memorialized this important transaction in both the written word and a visible object to preserve the memory for future generations, also. "The Book of the Law of God" was a collection of the laws or regulations that Joshua delivered to the people and as such was distinct from "the Book of the Law of Moses" (1:8 et al.). Many years prior in the same place, Joshua had written the word of the law of Moses on the stones of an altar (8:32). The reference to "the holy place" suggests that they had erected the Tent of Meeting here temporarily for this very occasion (cf. comment on v.1).

**27–28** Obviously the stone had not seen or heard anything. Its presence, however, would be a constant reminder (witness) of the covenant promises made by Israel that day. It may have borne some appropriate inscription, though nothing is stated in the text.

## D. *Three Burials in the Promised Land*

### 24:29–33

[29]After these things, Joshua son of Nun, the servant of the LORD, died
at the age of a hundred and ten. [30]And they buried him in the land of his
inheritance, at Timnath Serah in the hill country of Ephraim, north of Mount Gaash.
[31]Israel served the LORD throughout the lifetime of Joshua and of the elders who outlived him and who had experienced everything the LORD had done for Israel.
[32]And Joseph's bones, which the Israelites had brought up from Egypt, were buried at Shechem in the tract of land that Jacob bought for a hundred pieces of silver from the sons of Hamor, the father of Shechem. This became the inheritance of Joseph's descendants.
[33]And Eleazar son of Aaron died and was buried at Gibeah, which had been allotted to his son Phinehas in the hill country of Ephraim.

**29** Just how much time elapsed is not indicated. For the first time the title "the servant of the LORD" was granted to Joshua. He was elevated close to the stature of Moses. The author reports that when Joshua died, he was ten years younger than Moses, thus indicating that Joshua never became fully equal to Moses. With Joshua's death a certain style of leadership came to an end. The Book of Joshua began with the words "After the death of Moses" and then described the transfer of leadership to Joshua. The Book of Judges begins similarly ("After the death of Joshua," Judg 1:1) but names no one as Joshua's successor.

**30** The words "in the land of his inheritance" present an important contrast with Abraham and Jacob, who possessed nothing more than a few burial plots in a land where they lived as aliens. Now the Israelites lived in a land of their own. "Timnath Serah" is modern Khirbet Tibneh, twelve miles northeast of Lydda.

**31** That the people were faithful "throughout the lifetime of Joshua" is eloquent testimony to the power of Joshua's influence and the effectiveness of personal experience. The memorials, confessions, and rituals of covenant renewal were designed to keep the people loyal, but these were not adequate forever. What happened in the next generation is described in Judges 2:10–15.

**32** The burial of "Joseph's bones" symbolized the completion of an era and the fulfillment of God's promises to the Patriarchs. When he gave instructions for his remains to be buried in Canaan, Joseph manifested great faith in the promises of God (Gen 50:24–25; cf. Exod 13:19: in both passages Joseph's remains are a symbol of God's promise being fulfilled; cf. Heb 11:22). "Bones" is probably shorthand for dead body or remains, since Joseph's body had been mummified (Gen 50:26). The burial plots purchased by Abraham and Jacob were symbolic of their faith that God would give the whole land to their descendants. The burial of Joseph's remains provides a fitting conclusion to the long saga that began with the call of Abraham.

**33** When "Eleazar son of Aaron died," the whole generation of those who had left Egypt came to an end; an epoch had reached completion. In Hebrew "Gibeah" (*giḇʿaṯ pînᵉḥās*) is literally "Gibeah of Phinehas" and may be the full name of the town (cf. "Gibeah of Saul," 1 Sam 11:4). The term "hill country of Ephraim" may have been applied to a range of hills that extended into the territory of Benjamin, so that Gibeah would be the same as Geba in 21:17.

# JUDGES

Herbert Wolf

# JUDGES

## Introduction

1. Title
2. Historical Background
3. Authorship and Unity
4. Date
5. Purpose
6. Literary Form
7. Theological Values
8. Text
9. Special Problems
10. Bibliography
11. Outline

### 1. Title

The English title of this book reflects the MT (*šōpᵉṭîm,* "judges"), the LXX (*kritai,* "judges"), and the Vulgate (*Liber Judicum,* "Book of Judges") titles. God brought these "judges" (as the term is used in this book and in 1 Sam 1–7) to deliver Israel from oppression. Although they were divinely empowered leaders, they did not become hereditary rulers.

The noun *šōp̱ēṭ* appears only in 2:16–19, where it is used six times of those God raised up to "rescue" or "save" Israel from her enemies. Eight men are said to have "judged" or "led Israel" (3:10; 10:2–3; 12:7, 8–9, 11, 13–14; 15:20; 16:31). Even though others, such as Ehud (3:12–30) and Gideon (6:1–8:32), were judges, it is not specifically said that they "judged" or "led" Israel. Also "judging" or "leading" Israel was one woman, Deborah, to whom the people brought their disputes for a decision (4:4–5). Only in this last case is the concept of judicial decision applied to a judge, though this may have been a common function of these leaders after their military triumphs. In 11:27, Jephthah appealed to the Lord as "the Judge" to settle the quarrel between Israel and Ammon.

Elsewhere in Scripture the leaders of this period (from Joshua's death to the monarchy) are also called "judges" (Ruth 1:1; 2 Sam 7:11). Eli and Samuel were the last two judges, and their activities are related only in 1 Samuel. In all there were fifteen judges, if Barak is considered a co-judge with Deborah and if Eli and Samuel are added to the thirteen judges in the Book of Judges.

Outside Israel "judge" was a name for an Akkadian official (*šāpiṭu*) and also for rulers of Phoenicia and Carthage. The Carthaginian officials were termed *sufetes,* with responsibilities similar to the later Roman consuls. In the recently discovered

Ebla tablets, judges (Sumerian *di-ku*) served under governors in the overall administration of that powerful city during the middle of the third millennium B.C.[1]

## 2. Historical Background

The Book of Judges covers the period from the death of Joshua to the dawn of the monarchy. Political and religious turmoil accompanied Israel's attempts to occupy the land that had been conquered and divided by lot under the leadership of Joshua. Apart from the struggle against the Canaanites at the time of Deborah, Israel's adversaries came from outside the land. Most of these, such as Moab, Midian, and Ammon, periodically plundered the land. The Philistines, however, who at this time entered Palestine in greater numbers, contested with Israel for permanent possession of the land.

Tragically, the Israelites even fought among themselves. Ephraim was ravaged by Manasseh (ch. 12), and Benjamin was almost annihilated by the other tribes (chs. 20–21). Between the days of Joshua and Samuel, Israel plummeted to moral and spiritual disaster. Over and over the pattern of sin followed by oppression was repeated. Occasionally God raised up a Deborah or a Gideon to turn the people back to himself, but the intervals of revival were all too brief.

Judges falls directly within the heroic age, a time when divinely provided leaders were called on to save the day by personal exploits. It was an unstable period characterized by tribal migrations and lack of central authority. People led dangerous yet simple lives in which warlike pursuits alternated with ordinary peacetime activities.

The events narrated in Judges cover a period of 410 years if viewed consecutively. Such a lengthy time does not, however, fit any accepted chronology of the early history of Israel. Consequently some of the judgeships must have overlapped. Samson and Jephthah, for example, may have ruled simultaneously—one in the west, in Canaan, the other in the east, in Transjordan (10:7). The extent to which one telescopes these periods of years depends on the date assigned to the Exodus.[2] There are two major views of that date: 1446 B.C. and 1290 B.C. The latter date is the majority opinion, and among its adherents are many evangelical scholars. It requires that the 410 years be compressed into about a century and a half by assuming a large number of overlapping periods.[3] Judges itself, however, gives little evidence for so drastic a comparison.

Scholars who hold a late date often appeal to archaeological evidence, such as the Tell el-Amarna letters of the fourteenth century B.C. or the evidences of destruction at Hazor, Lachish, and elsewhere in the late thirteenth century B.C. Most of this evidence, however, is ambiguous. The Amarna letters contain names that do not always correspond closely with those in Joshua and Judges, but the events described can fit in quite smoothly at times (see coment on 3:8). Furthermore, the destruction levels at Hazor could be the result of liberation wars during the period of the judges and not of the conquest of Canaan under Joshua. Kathleen Kenyon holds that, judging

[1]See Giovanni Pettinato, *The Archives of Ebla* (Garden City, N.Y.: Doubleday, 1981), p. 122.
[2]See Leon Wood, *A Survey of Israel's History* (Grand Rapids: Zondervan, 1970), p. 207.
[3]Cf. K. Kitchen, *Ancient Orient and Old Testament* (Chicago: InterVarsity, 1966), pp. 73–75.

from the pottery, the biggest change in Palestinian culture comes around 1400 B.C., a date that favors a mid-fifteenth century Exodus.[4]

Bimson has reevaluated the biblical and archaeological evidence and favors a date of 1470 B.C. for the Conquest. Through meticulous analysis of the many lines of argument presented by proponents of the 1446 and 1290 B.C. dates, Bimson believes that he can solve a number of problems that continue to plague the other two views.[5]

A stele of Pharaoh Merneptah, dated about 1220 B.C., states that he defeated Israel, but this does not tell us how long Israel had been in Palestine. Generally the Egyptian forces stayed away from Palestine after 1400 B.C. This is attested in the Amarna letters, which record Israel's futile appeals for Egyptian help. A treaty between Hattusilis III and Rameses II kept the Hittite and Egyptian empires at peace during much of the thirteenth century B.C. Yet the king of Upper Mesopotamia did venture into Palestine to oppress the Hebrews (3:8–10).

## 3. Authorship and Unity

The writer of the Book of Judges is unknown, and the whole question of its authorship is complicated by the tripartite structure of the book. The wars of occupation[6] summarized in 1:1–2:5 seem to break the natural connection between Joshua 24 and Judges 2:6–9, where the death of Joshua is again recorded (v.8). The unity of 2:6–16:31 is, however, generally accepted because of a remarkable cyclical pattern that unfolds here. Six times the expression "the Israelites did evil in the eyes of the LORD" is found, introducing the major periods of oppression in the book (3:7, 12; 4:1; 6:1; 10:6; 13:1). The author used sources in his work, such as the Song of Deborah (ch. 5), but he succeeded in molding his material into a unified whole.

Chapters 17–21 form a double appendix sometimes relegated to a priestly author of the exilic period. Yet even these nonchronological chapters have a close connection with the rest of the book. The story concerning the tribe of Dan (chs. 17–18) follows immediately the Samson cycle (chs. 13–16) with its Danite origin. Both concluding episodes (chs. 19–21) deal with corruption even among the Levites and bring to a climax the grim recital of sin throughout the book.

Chapter 1 is a fitting prelude to the book, because it shows some of the failures of the tribes in their efforts to occupy the land. The problems that developed in these wars of conquest are symptomatic of the difficulties faced in the later wars of liberation. The apparent repetition of Othniel's heroics (1:11–15; cf. Josh 15:15–19) introduces the reader to the first judge. Mention of the Kenites (v.16) anticipates the important part played by Jael in 4:11–21.

Liberal scholars build Judges around a Deuteronomic core tied in with Pentateuchal criticism (cf. R.K. Harrison, IOT, pp. 682–83). Oral tradition is emphasized for the period from 1200–1000 B.C., with initial writing coming in the next two centuries, possibly by the authors of J (who knew God as "Yahweh") and E (who knew God as "Elohim"). A Deuteronomic recension in the late seventh century put the book in its basic form, though final editing is reserved for the postexilic period. This theory of

---

[4]See Bruce Waltke, "Palestinian Artifactual Evidence," BS 129 (1972): 36.

[5]John J. Bimson, *Redating the Exodus and the Conquest*, JSOT suppl. series 5 (Sheffield: University of Sheffield Press, 1978).

[6]For the significance of this crucial term, see Yehezkel Kaufmann, *The Biblical Account of the Conquest of Palestine* (Jerusalem: Magnes, 1953), pp. 65–66.

authorship depends largely on the accuracy of the whole JEDP formulation, a hypothesis now under attack by some scholars (see R.K. Harrison, "Historical and Literary Criticism of the Old Testament," EBC, 1:231–50). Greenspahn has argued that Judges largely lacks the characteristic Deuteronomic style and the emphasis on the centralization of worship. Except for chapters 2, 3, and 10, Greenspahn does not see the book as Deuteronomic.[7]

We should not eliminate, however, the possibility of editorial additions to the book. Although its main author may have been an associate of Samuel, unlike Samuel, he did not focus attention on the dangers inherent in the monarchy.

## 4. Date

Several factors show that the author lived and wrote during the early monarchy. The hectic events in the Book of Judges are viewed from the perspective of a united, stable rule: "In those days Israel had no king; everyone did as he saw fit" (21:25; cf. 18:1; 19:1). This statement suits the time of the united kingdom best; and 1:21 points to a period before David's capture of Jerusalem, for the Jebusites were living there "to this day." The mention of Canaanite control of Gezer (1:29) implies that the king of Egypt had not yet captured the city and given it to Solomon as a dowry for his Egyptian bride (c. 970 B.C.).

Reference to the "captivity of the land" in 18:30 has led many (e.g., Boling, p. 266) to connect at least the later chapters with the Assyrian devastation of Samaria (733–732 and 721 B.C.) or the Babylonian captivity itself (586 B.C.). Others would emend "land" to "ark" (*'āreṣ* to *'ārôn*) since the consonantal texts are very similar.[8] The ark of the covenant was captured by the Philistines the day Eli died (c. 1075 B.C.), as Israel's forces were crushed. When the glory "departed" from Israel that day (1 Sam 4:21), the word used is from the same root as "captivity" (*gālāh,* "to remove into exile"). It is unlikely that the idolatrous priests who served at Dan would have enjoyed an uninterrupted ministry, especially from the early period of the judges until 722 B.C. Such a situation could scarcely have been tolerated during David's godly reign.

## 5. Purpose

The primary purpose of the Book of Judges is to show that Israel's spiritual condition determined its political and material situation. When the nation turned to God in obedience, God graciously sent deliverers to rescue the people from oppression. When they disregarded Joshua's warnings and worshiped the gods of Canaan, the nation came under the control of tyrants and invaders.

As the book progresses, Israel's plight worsens. The stunning victories of Deborah and Barak and of Gideon are followed by the less decisive efforts of Jephthah and of Samson. Jephthah's victory over Ammon failed to prevent civil war. Samson's personal heroics did not throw off the Philistine yoke. By the end of the book, the stories of sin and all-out civil war depict the nation's desperate need for unity and order. The repeated references to a time when Israel had no king (18:1 et al.)

[7] Frederick Greenspahn, "The Theology of the Framework of Judges," VetTest 36, 4 (1986): 385–96.

[8] E.g., E.J. Young, *An Introduction to the Old Testament,* rev. ed. (Grand Rapids: Eerdmans, 1958), p. 180.

emphasize the author's intentions to show the advantages of a monarchy over anarchy. The implication is that a nation led by a godly king would experience prosperity under the blessing of God.

The Book of Judges shows that Israel failed to realize her divinely intended goal without a king. Israel was unable to govern herself according to the Mosaic law and thereby proved that she needed a king. In light of the leadership role assigned to Judah in both the prologue and the epilogue (1:1–2; 20:18), it is not surprising that eventually Judah emerged as the tribe that produced the Davidic dynasty.

The events recorded in Judges also serve in general to fill in the gap between the time of Joshua and that of Samuel. By recounting the fortunes of Israel during those three hundred difficult years, the author gives the student of Scripture a connected history of Israel at this time.

## 6. Literary Form

The Book of Judges might be called "epic" literature, a form associated with the heroic age (cf. Historical Background). Cyrus H. Gordon has noted many parallels between Judges and the Greek epics, the *Iliad* and the *Odyssey*.[9] Cycles about individual heroes characterize both literatures. The *Iliad*'s description of the wrath of Achilles can be compared with Samson's anger and revenge.

Epic literature of a heroic kind deals with military and romantic themes, giving details of both. For example, the "epic blow" describes a fatal wound administered against the enemy, such as the sword thrust of Ehud (3:21–22) or the tent peg hammered into Sisera's head by Jael (4:21). Little is left to the imagination. Relations between men and women are not so prominent in Judges as in heroic literature, though the marriage of Othniel and Acsah is mentioned in 1:13–15, and the immoral escapades of Samson are an important feature of chapters 13–16.

The cyclical pattern of the book can also be compared with the view of history held by the Hittites of Asia Minor. A Hittite king named Telepinus, who lived about 1500 B.C., wrote a proclamation in which he reviewed the sad sequence of events that befell his disunited country. His edict established a clear law of succession to the throne to avoid civil war and chaos, two of the evils the author of Judges wanted to see eliminated from Israel. This Hebrew-Hittite parallel is significant for the similar historical consciousness of the two peoples. They were the earliest to produce genuine works of history.[10]

## 7. Theological Values

Few books portray so complete a picture of human depravity as does Judges. A nation that before Joshua solemnly swore to obey God quickly intermarried with pagans and turned to other gods. Morality sank to great depths as son stole from mother (17:2–3) and a whole tribe condoned homosexuality and a rape-murder (19:22–30).

---

[9] *The Common Background of Greek and Hebrew Civilizations* (New York: W.W. Norton, 1965), pp. 222–26, 283–84.

[10] Cf. A. Malamat, "Causality in Hittite and Biblical Historiography," VetTest 5 (1955): 1–12.

Israel's sin made God angry; so he turned her over to her enemies. The nation that broke the covenant felt the wrath of a righteous God (2:20). He could not condone the people's behavior; and every time they lapsed into sin, judgment followed. God even strengthened the forces arrayed against Israel (3:12).

Over and over the suffering of the people led to repentance and a cry for mercy, and God's gracious response demonstrated his love and patience. Israel was his own special people, and he did not abandon them. When they prayed earnestly, he sent someone to rescue them, just as he had responded to the anguished cry of the Israelites in Egypt and sent Moses to rescue them from bondage (Exod 2:23–25).[11] Hebrews 11:32 praises the faith of Gideon, Barak, Samson, and Jephthah, each of whom God sovereignly prepared to meet specific crises. Often the Spirit of the Lord stirred the judges to action (3:10; 6:34; 11:29). To prove that victory was his doing, the Lord sent a flash flood to stop Sisera's mighty chariots and used Gideon's tiny army of three hundred to overwhelm the hosts of Midian.

Israel failed to drive out the Canaanites, but even here God revealed his sovereignty: he trained the younger generation in warfare (3:1–2). Samson's lustful infatuation with a Philistine woman was also used by the Lord to weaken the Philistines' domination over Israel (14:4).

## 8. Text

The text of Judges is generally in good condition, ranking with the Pentateuch among the best preserved parts of the OT. The Song of Deborah in chapter 5, however, is an ancient poem with several textual problems stemming from the obscurity of its vocabulary.

The LXX is useful in solving the problems in 14:15 and 16:13; it fills in details lacking in the Hebrew MSS (see Notes in loc.).

There are two distinct Greek versions of Judges represented by Codex Alexandrinus and Codex Vaticanus. Apparently they go back to divergent Hebrew texts.

Fragments of Judges have been found among the DSS of Cave 1 and Cave 4. Chapters 6, 9, and 21 are best represented and indicate that occasionally the DSS favor readings reflected in the Greek versions (cf. Boling, pp. 38–40).

## 9. Special Problems

One problem that perplexes the reader of Judges is the apparent approval of cruelty and killing. Ehud saved Israel by assassinating the king of Moab; Jael became a heroine by hammering a tent peg into Sisera's skull; Gideon executed the two kings of Midian; and Jephthah may have taken the life of his own daughter. These acts are not necessarily approved either by the author or by the Lord. Jael's deed reminds us of the attitude found in the imprecatory psalms (cf. 109:6–13), where Israel's enemy is viewed as God's enemy, and Jael's deed becomes the means of glorifying God. Wicked, murdering leaders deserved to die themselves.

Certain actions, however, cannot be defended from Scripture. If Jephthah did indeed offer his only daughter as a sacrifice, he committed a terrible sin even though

[11] Greenspahn, "Framework of the Judges," pp. 392–93.

he sincerely thought he was pleasing God (cf. comments on 11:31, 34–40). Long neglect of the Mosaic law had left the Israelites with many mistaken notions about God's will.

Another problem closely related to the above is how God's Spirit could use men like Jephthah and Samson, whose motives and behavior were open to such serious question. Samson's case is most acute because, in spite of his Nazirite vow, he gave free rein to his appetites and became involved with a number of women. Undisciplined and immoral, his credentials as a man of God were few.

The fact that God worked through Samson need not denote approval of his lifestyle. In God's sovereignty the Holy Spirit came on men for particular tasks, and this enduing was not necessarily proportionate to one's spirituality. The Spirit's power enabled men to inspire Israel (6:34; 11:29) and to perform great feats of strength (14:6, 19; 15:14). But it was a temporary enduement, and Samson and later Saul tragically discovered that the Lord had left them. The NT experience of the permanent indwelling of the Holy Spirit was not known in OT times.

## 10. Bibliography

Armerding, Carl E. "The Heroic Ages of Greece and Israel: A Literary-Historical Comparison." Ann Arbor, Mich.: University Microfilms, 1968.

Boling, Robert G. *Judges*. Anchor Bible. Garden City, N.Y.: Doubleday, 1975.

Bowling, Andrew C. "Judges." *Evangelical Commentary on the Bible*. Edited by Walter A. Elwell. Grand Rapids: Baker, 1989.

Bruce, F.F. "Judges." *The New Bible Commentary: Revised*. Edited by D. Guthrie et al. Grand Rapids: Eerdmans, 1970.

Burney, C.F. *The Book of Judges With Introduction and Notes*. 1918. Reprint. New York: Ktav, 1970.

Cohen, Abraham, editor. *Joshua, Judges*. London: Soncino, 1950.

Cundall, Arthur E., and Morris, Leon. *Judges, Ruth*. Chicago: InterVarsity, 1968.

Dalglish, Edward R. "Judges." *The Broadman Bible Commentary*. Vol. 2. Nashville: Broadman, 1970.

Davis, J.J. *Conquest and Crisis: Studies in Joshua, Judges, and Ruth*. Grand Rapids: Baker, 1969.

Garstang, John. *The Foundations of Bible History. Joshua, Judges*. London: Constable, 1931.

Goslinga, C.J. *Joshua, Judges, Ruth*. Bible Student's Commentary. Translated by Ray Togtman. Grand Rapids: Zondervan, 1986.

Keil, C.F., and Delitzsch, F. *Joshua, Judges, Ruth*. KD. 1887. Reprint. Grand Rapids: Eerdmans, 1950.

McKenzie, John L. *The World of the Judges*. Englewood Cliffs, N.J.: Prentice Hall, 1966.

Moore, G.F. *A Critical and Exegetical Commentary on Judges*. ICC. New York: Charles Scribner's Sons, 1900.

Myers, Jacob M., and Elliott, Phillip P. "Judges." *The Interpreter's Bible*. Edited by G.A. Buttrick. Vol. 2. New York: Abingdon, 1953.

Patterson, Richard. "The Song of Deborah." *Tradition and Testament*. Edited by John S. and Paul D. Feinberg. Chicago: Moody, 1981, pp. 123–60.

Wood, Leon J. *Distressing Days of the Judges*. Grand Rapids: Zondervan, 1975.

## 11. Outline

I. The Success and Failure of the Tribes in Canaan (1:1–2:5)
   A. The Capture of Adoni-Bezek (1:1–7)
   B. The Capture of Jerusalem, Hebron, and Debir (1:8–15)
   C. The Additional Success of Judah and Simeon (1:16–18)
   D. A Summary of Success and Failure (1:19–21)
   E. The Capture of Bethel (1:22–26)
   F. Additional Failures of the Tribes (1:27–36)
   G. Disobedience Condemned by the Angel of the Lord (2:1–5)

II. The Rule of the Judges (2:6–16:31)
   A. Introduction (2:6–3:6)
      1. The passing of godly leaders (2:6–9)
      2. The pattern of the period of the judges (2:10–23)
      3. The people left to test Israel (3:1–6)
   B. The Victory of Othniel Over Cushan-Rishathaim (3:7–11)
   C. The Victory of Ehud Over Moab (3:12–30)
      1. Israel oppressed by Moab (3:12–14)
      2. King Eglon slain by Ehud (3:15–25)
      3. The Moabites defeated by Ehud (3:26–30)
   D. The Victory of Shamgar Over the Philistines (3:31)
   E. The Victory of Deborah and Barak Over Jabin and Sisera (4:1–5:31)
      1. The prose account (4:1–24)
         a. The oppression (4:1–3)
         b. Deborah's challenge to Barak (4:4–10)
         c. Jael's husband introduced (4:11)
         d. Sisera's army routed by Barak (4:12–16)
         e. Sisera slain by Jael (4:17–24)
      2. The poetic version—the Song of Deborah (5:1–31)
         a. Praise to God for his intervention (5:1–5)
         b. Conditions during the oppression (5:6–8)
         c. Challenge to recount the Lord's victory (5:9–11)
         d. The roles of the individual tribes (5:12–18)
         e. The battle described (5:19–23)
         f. Jael praised for her deed (5:24–27)
         g. Sisera's mother's futile wait (5:28–30)
         h. Conclusion (5:31)
   F. The Victory of Gideon Over the Midianites (6:1–8:32)
      1. Israel's land devastated by the Midianites (6:1–6)
      2. Israel's disobedience condemned by a prophet (6:7–10)
      3. Gideon challenged by the angel of the Lord (6:11–24)
      4. The altar of Baal destroyed and Gideon's life imperiled (6:25–32)
      5. Gideon's army (6:33–35)
      6. The fleece (6:36–40)
      7. Gideon's army reduced (7:1–8a)
      8. Gideon's victory confirmed by a dream (7:8b–14)
      9. Preparation for the battle (7:15–18)

10. The Midianites routed (7:19–25)
11. The Ephraimites' complaint (8:1–3)
12. Lack of cooperation from Succoth and Peniel (8:4–9)
13. The capture of the kings of Midian (8:10–12)
14. Retaliation against Succoth and Peniel (8:13–17)
15. The Midianite kings slain (8:18–21)
16. Gideon's ephod (8:22–27)
17. Gideon's accomplishments and death (8:28–32)

G. The Brief Reign of Abimelech (8:33–9:57)
   1. Apostasy after Gideon's death (8:33–35)
   2. Abimelech's rise to power (9:1–6)
   3. Jotham's fable (9:7–21)
   4. The revolt of Gaal and Shechem (9:22–29)
   5. Gaal's defeat (9:30–41)
   6. The capture of Shechem and the tower of Shechem (9:42–49)
   7. The death of Abimelech (9:50–57)

H. The Rule of Tola and Jair (10:1–5)

I. The Victory of Jephthah Over the Ammonites (10:6–12:7)
   1. Oppression and supplication (10:6–16)
   2. Gilead's predicament (10:17–18)
   3. Jephthah's exile and recall (11:1–11)
   4. Jephthah's presentation of Israel's territorial claim (11:12–28)
   5. Jephthah's vow and victory over Ammon (11:29–33)
   6. Jephthah's vow fulfilled (11:34–40)
   7. Jephthah's defeat of Ephraim (12:1–7)

J. The Rules of Ibzan, Elon, and Abdon (12:8–15)
   1. Ibzan (12:8–10)
   2. Elon (12:11–12)
   3. Abdon (12:13–15)

K. Samson's Victory Over the Philistines (13:1–16:31)
   1. The angelic announcement of Samson's birth (13:1–14)
   2. The angel's miracle (13:15–23)
   3. The birth and growth of Samson (13:24–25)
   4. Samson's engagement to a Philistine (14:1–9)
   5. The marriage feast and the riddle (14:10–20)
   6. Samson's revenge for the loss of his wife (15:1–8)
   7. Samson's victory at Lehi (15:9–20)
   8. Samson's feat of strength at Gaza (16:1–3)
   9. Samson and Delilah (16:4–20)
   10. The capture and punishment of Samson (16:21–22)
   11. Samson's final revenge at the feast of Dagon (16:23–31)

III. Two Appendixes (17:1–21:25)

A. Micah's Priest and the Migration of Dan (17:1–18:31)
   1. Micah's mother and idolatry (17:1–6)
   2. Micah's Levite (17:7–13)
   3. Danite spies and Micah's priest (18:1–6)
   4. The report of the spies (18:7–10)
   5. The abduction of Micah's priest (18:11–21)

6. Micah's futile pursuit (18:22–26)
7. The capture of Laish (18:27–31)

B. The Atrocity at Gibeah and Civil War (19:1–21:25)
1. The reconciliation of the Levite and his concubine (19:1–8)
2. The journey to Gibeah (19:9–15)
3. The hospitality of the old man (19:16–21)
4. The sexual perversion of the Gibeahites (19:22–28)
5. The crime report to Israel (19:29–20:7)
6. Israel and Benjamin: preparations for war (20:8–18)
7. The first battle (20:19–23)
8. The second battle (20:24–28)
9. The third battle (20:29–41)
10. The flight of Benjamin (20:42–48)
11. Concern for Benjamin's survival (21:1–4)
12. Wives from Jabesh Gilead (21:5–14)
13. Wives from Shiloh (21:15–23)
14. Conclusion (21:24–25)

# Text and Exposition

## I. The Success and Failure of the Tribes in Canaan (1:1–2:5)

### A. *The Capture of Adoni-Bezek*

1:1–7

**[1]After the death of Joshua, the Israelites asked the LORD, "Who will be
the first to go up and fight for us against the Canaanites?"
[2]The LORD answered, "Judah is to go; I have given the land into their
hands."
[3]Then the men of Judah said to the Simeonites their brothers, "Come
up with us into the territory allotted to us, to fight against the
Canaanites. We in turn will go with you into yours." So the Simeonites
went with them.
[4]When Judah attacked, the LORD gave the Canaanites and Perizzites
into their hands and they struck down ten thousand men at Bezek. [5]It
was there that they found Adoni-Bezek and fought against him, putting
to rout the Canaanites and Perizzites. [6]Adoni-Bezek fled, but they
chased him and caught him, and cut off his thumbs and big toes.
[7]Then Adoni-Bezek said, "Seventy kings with their thumbs and big
toes cut off have picked up scraps under my table. Now God has paid
me back for what I did to them." They brought him to Jerusalem, and he
died there.**

**1–2** The first chapter presents supplementary material on the conquest of Canaan viewed from the standpoint of individual tribes. Most of the episodes occurred after the death of Joshua (v.1; cf. Introduction: Historical Background). Before conducting further military action, the people consulted the Lord, probably through the Urim and Thummim handled by the high priest (Num 27:21). As in the order of march in the wilderness, Judah was designated to be first (Num 2:9). Judah was also the tribe leading the march against Benjamin in the civil war (Judg 20:18). Though the Joseph tribes (Ephraim and Manasseh) received the birthright (1 Chron 5:1), Judah was destined to lead the nation (Gen 49:10).

"Canaanites" applies to all the peoples found in the land of Palestine, but at times it is restricted to the inhabitants of the valleys and coastal plains (Num 13:29). In v.4 they are linked with the Perizzites, an ethnic group often included in lists of the people of Canaan (3:5).

God's promise that he had "given the land into their hands" (v.2) parallels his encouraging words to Joshua after the death of Moses (Josh 1:3). Since Joshua himself had died, the same great promise held true for Judah.

**3** Judah invited their full-brother tribe Simeon to join them, especially since Simeon's territory was surrounded by Judah's inheritance (Josh 19:1). The tribe of Simeon was greatly reduced in numbers during the wilderness wanderings, probably as punishment for their sins of idolatry and fornication in Moab (Num 25:1–14). Simeon was partially absorbed by the larger and more powerful Judah.

**4–5** The scene of Judah's great victory at Bezek has not been positively identified. Bezek is also mentioned in 1 Samuel 11:8 as a site where Saul assembled an army. Khirbet Bezqa, near Gezer, may preserve the ancient name. Adoni-Bezek means "lord of Bezek," and some have identified him with the similar "Adoni-Zedek" of Joshua 10:1–3. The latter, however, was the king of Jerusalem, and the details of his defeat at the hands of Joshua do not match the events here. Adoni-Bezek did die in Jerusalem (v.7), but Adoni-Zedek was killed at Makkedah (Josh 10:21–26).

**6–7** The severing of Adoni-Bezek's thumbs and big toes incapacitated him as a warrior and as a priest, a dual function common to many kings. In their ordination service the priests had blood applied to their thumbs and big toes (Lev 8:23–24). Adoni-Bezek admitted that he had similarly mutilated the thumbs and toes of seventy kings (rulers of cities), making beggars out of them; so he deserved to be paid back.

This is a good illustration of lex talionis, the law of retaliation demanding an "eye for eye, tooth for tooth, hand for hand, foot for foot" (Exod 21:24; cf. Christ's reference to this law in the Sermon on the Mount, Matt 5:38).

## Notes

---

**4** Some (e.g., Boling, p. 54) interpret "Perizzites" to mean "residents of unwalled cities," those living in the hills. Joshua 11:3 and 17:15 identify them with the hill country and a wooded area. The cognate פְּרָזוֹן (*p*$^e$*rāzôn*) is translated "village life" in 5:7.

---

## B. *The Capture of Jerusalem, Hebron, and Debir*

### 1:8–15

[8]The men of Judah attacked Jerusalem also and took it. They put the
city to the sword and set it on fire.
[9]After that, the men of Judah went down to fight against the
Canaanites living in the hill country, the Negev and the western foothills.
[10]They advanced against the Canaanites living in Hebron (formerly
called Kiriath Arba) and defeated Sheshai, Ahiman and Talmai.
[11]From there they advanced against the people living in Debir
(formerly called Kiriath Sepher). [12]And Caleb said, "I will give my
daughter Acsah in marriage to the man who attacks and captures
Kiriath Sepher." [13]Othniel son of Kenaz, Caleb's younger brother, took
it; so Caleb gave his daughter Acsah to him in marriage.
[14]One day when she came to Othniel, she urged him to ask her father
for a field. When she got off her donkey, Caleb asked her, "What can I
do for you?"
[15]She replied, "Do me a special favor. Since you have given me land
in the Negev, give me also springs of water." Then Caleb gave her the
upper and lower springs.

**8** The city of Jerusalem did not become an integral part of Israel until David and Joab stormed the fortress of the Jebusites (2 Sam 5:7). Hence the successful attack of Judah was either a temporary or partial capture. Later on (9:45, 49) a distinction is made between Abimelech's capture and razing of Shechem and his conquest of the tower of Shechem. The inner citadel represents the final line of defense, and the men of Judah probably failed to penetrate the Jebusite fortress itself.

The problem is complicated by the reference in v.21 to the Benjamites' failure to drive the Jebusites out of Jerusalem. Joshua 15:63 is almost identical to v.21, except for the substitution of "Judah" for "Benjamin." The solution lies in the location of Jerusalem, directly on the border between Judah and Benjamin. It properly belonged to Benjamin (Josh 18:16), but both tribes had strong interests there.

**9** From Jerusalem the men of Judah went south and west to continue their conquest. The three areas mentioned are the major geographical divisions of southern Palestine. The "hill country" is the central mountainous region extending south to Hebron and Arad, the "Negev" is the "dry ground" in the southern sections, and the "western foothills," the Shephelah, represents the region between the mountains and the coastal plain.

**10** Hebron, some nineteen miles south of Jerusalem, has the highest elevation (three thousand feet) of any city in Judah and is famous as the home of Abraham. This important city had discouraged the men sent by Moses to spy out Canaan because of the size of the Anakim living there (Num 13:22–33). Sheshai, Ahiman, and Talmai were descendants of Anak, who had frightened the spies, but this time the men of Judah conquered them. Fittingly, it was Caleb, one of the two believing spies, who was allotted Hebron as his inheritance (Josh 14:13–14) and who directed its capture (Judg 1:20).

The ancient name of Hebron (Kiriath Arba) means the "city of Arba." Arba was one of the greatest leaders of the Anakites (Josh 14:15). The capture of Hebron and Debir is also described in Joshua 15:13–19.

**11** Debir, often identified with Tell Beit Mirsim, is located eleven miles southwest of Hebron. Its king was listed among the thirty-one kings captured by Joshua (Josh 12:13). The well-fortified city was destroyed by fire about 1200 B.C. Its older name (Kiriath Sepher) means "city of the scroll" or "book." Like Hebron it was a residence of some Anakites (Josh 11:21).

**12–13** Debir was captured by Caleb's younger brother Othniel after Caleb offered his daughter Acsah as the prize (v.12). Normally young men paid a bride-price to the father of the bride, but the military triumph was considered payment enough. Saul made the same arrangement with David, requiring one hundred Philistine foreskins to win the hand of Michal (1 Sam 18:25).

As relatives of Kenaz, Othniel and Caleb were apparently associated with an Edomite clan (Gen 36:11). Their rise to prominence in Judah and Israel demonstrates the degree to which other people were assimilated by the chosen nation.

**14–15** Caleb's daughter needed the permission of her husband before she could ask her father for a gift (v.14). Since Caleb had given them land in the arid Negev, she requested a field with "springs of water" (v.15). Caleb agreed, and this gift may have been her dowry.

## Notes

**10** "Kiriath Arba" may also mean "city of four" (אַרְבַּע, *'arba'* = "four"), pointing to a group of four cities. "Hebron" (חֶבְרוֹן, *ḥeḇrôn*) likely means "association," "federation."

**11** "Kiriath Sepher," as "city of the book" or "records" (סֵפֶר, *sēper*), may have had an official library or archive of some kind. The attempt to relocate Debir south of Hebron at Tell Rubad has not yet been generally accepted (cf. Boling, p. 56).

**13** The Hebrew construction permits Othniel to be either Caleb's brother or nephew. The Masoretes preferred the former. Marriage with one's niece was not forbidden by the law (see KD, p. 157).

**14** The LXX and Vulgate assume a masculine form ("he urged") on the ground that Othniel was pressing Acsah to ask for the favor. The parallel in Josh 15:18, however, has the feminine.

**15** בְּרָכָה (*berākāh*, "special favor") is literally "blessing." It means "gift" also in 1 Sam 25:27 and "present" in 30:26.

---

## C. *The Additional Success of Judah and Simeon*

### 1:16–18

**16**The descendants of Moses' father-in-law, the Kenite, went up from the City of Palms with the men of Judah to live among the people of the Desert of Judah in the Negev near Arad.

**17**Then the men of Judah went with the Simeonites their brothers and attacked the Canaanites living in Zephath, and they totally destroyed the city. Therefore it was called Hormah. **18**The men of Judah also took Gaza, Ashkelon and Ekron—each city with its territory.

**16** The Kenites, an ancient Canaanite people (Gen 15:19) connected with the Amalekites, had been friendly to Israel during the wilderness wanderings. Moses had, in fact, married a Kenite girl. The Kenites left Jericho, the "City of Palms" (3:13), and joined some people of Judah living near Arad, an important city sixteen miles directly south of Hebron. Moses had defeated the king of Arad as Israel skirted southern Palestine (Num 21:1–3), and Joshua later counted Arad's king among his victims (Josh 12:14).

**17** Judah together with Simeon successfully captured Zephath, renaming it Hormah. Hormah was allotted to Simeon by Joshua (Josh 19:4). Since the name means "total destruction," it may be the same Hormah demolished by Moses near Arad (Num 21:1–3). The complete destruction recalls the Lord's command to wipe out the Canaanites and their livestock and give all the articles of silver and gold to the sanctuary (Deut 7:1–2; 20:16–17; Josh 6:17–19).

**18** The capture of Gaza, Ashkelon, and Ekron by Judah must have been temporary (cf. v.19). These were Philistine cities along the coast, though the main migration of the Philistines did not reach Palestine till 1200 B.C. The order of the three cities suggests an invasion from the south.

## Notes

---

**17** The Hiphil יַחֲרִים (*yaharîm*) means "to put under the ban [חֵרֶם (*hērem*)]," "to devote to destruction." The word occurs again in Judges only in 21:11, but it appears often in Joshua (2:10; 6:21; et al.).

**18** The LXX supplies a negative—viz., "Judah did not take"—in an attempt to solve the problem of why in Samson's time the cities were once again under Philistine control (cf. 14:19; 16:21; 1 Sam 5:10; et al.). But the answer no doubt lies in the fact that Judah's overpowering of the three cities was only temporary.

---

## D. *A Summary of Success and Failure*

### 1:19–21

19 The LORD was with the men of Judah. They took possession of the
hill country, but they were unable to drive the people from the plains,
because they had iron chariots. 20 As Moses had promised, Hebron was
given to Caleb, who drove from it the three sons of Anak. 21 The
Benjamites, however, failed to dislodge the Jebusites, who were living in
Jerusalem; to this day the Jebusites live there with the Benjamites.

**19** While notably successful in the hilly regions of central Palestine, Judah failed to control the plains. The Israelites were no match for the iron chariots that functioned effectively on the level terrain along the coast. In chapters 4–5 the importance of these Canaanite chariots is dramatically shown.

**20** Taking Hebron represented the key achievement of Judah, and v.20 attributes its capture to Caleb (see comment on v.10). Hebron was also a city of refuge belonging to the priests (Josh 20:7; 21:11), but its fields and suburbs were Caleb's own possession (Josh 21:12).

**21** Benjamin's main city was Jerusalem, but neither Benjamin nor Judah could dislodge the Jebusites (see comment on v.8). An alternate name for Jerusalem is "Jebus" (19:10), which attests to the long attachment of the Jebusites to this natural stronghold. Many associate them with the Hurrians, who were particularly influential in Mesopotamia and Asia Minor during the second millennium B.C.

## E. *The Capture of Bethel*

### 1:22–26

22 Now the house of Joseph attacked Bethel, and the LORD was with
them. 23 When they sent men to spy out Bethel (formerly called Luz),
24 the spies saw a man coming out of the city and they said to him,
"Show us how to get into the city and we will see that you are treated
well." 25 So he showed them, and they put the city to the sword but
spared the man and his whole family. 26 He then went to the land of the
Hittites, where he built a city and called it Luz, which is its name to this
day.

**22** Next to Judah, the most important tribe was Ephraim; and vv.22–29 describe the activities of Ephraim and his brother, Manasseh. The two tribes may have cooperated in the capture of Bethel, since the attack is attributed to "the house of Joseph"; but the city lay within Ephraim's territory. Bethel means "house of God," a name given by Jacob after God's revelation to him there (Gen 28:19). As God promised to protect the patriarch, so he "was with" the Joseph tribes here. About twelve miles north of Jerusalem, Bethel was to become a key religious center during the divided kingdom. The Canaanites called the site "Luz" (Josh 18:13).

**23–25** To capture Bethel, Israel followed the strategy used earlier at Jericho. Spies were sent there (v.23), and they found a man willing to show them the entrance to the city. This may have been a secret tunnel, perhaps connected with the water system. Later Jerusalem was probably captured through a tunnel leading from the Gihon spring (2 Sam 5:8).

In return for his cooperation, the spies promised safety for the informer, just as Rahab and her family had been protected at Jericho. The idiom "to treat well" (cf. v.24) uses the word *ḥeseḏ*, which refers to "loyalty" to the terms of an agreement. Exactly the same idiom is applied to Rahab in Joshua 2:12 ("kindness"). The word often is used of God's faithfulness to his covenant promises. When the Israelites captured the city, they released the man and his family (v.25).

**26** These survivors headed north, "to the land of the Hittites." This is a term applied to Syria (Josh 1:4). The Hittite Empire was based in Asia Minor but extended its control over wide areas west of the Euphrates. Mesopotamian sources (cf. ANET, pp. 275, 277) referred to Syria and Palestine as the land of "Hatti" long after the Hittite Empire had collapsed. This new "Luz" in Hittite territory has not been located.

### F. *Additional Failures of the Tribes*

#### 1:27–36

**27** But Manasseh did not drive out the people of Beth Shan or Taanach
or Dor or Ibleam or Megiddo and their surrounding settlements, for the
Canaanites were determined to live in that land. **28** When Israel became
strong, they pressed the Canaanites into forced labor but never drove
them out completely. **29** Nor did Ephraim drive out the Canaanites living
in Gezer, but the Canaanites continued to live there among them.
**30** Neither did Zebulun drive out the Canaanites living in Kitron or
Nahalol, who remained among them; but they did subject them to
forced labor. **31** Nor did Asher drive out those living in Acco or Sidon or
Ahlab or Aczib or Helbah or Aphek or Rehob, **32** and because of this the
people of Asher lived among the Canaanite inhabitants of the land.
**33** Neither did Naphtali drive out those living in Beth Shemesh or Beth
Anath; but the Naphtalites too lived among the Canaanite inhabitants of
the land, and those living in Beth Shemesh and Beth Anath became
forced laborers for them. **34** The Amorites confined the Danites to the hill
country, not allowing them to come down into the plain. **35** And the
Amorites were determined also to hold out in Mount Heres, Aijalon and
Shaalbim, but when the power of the house of Joseph increased, they
too were pressed into forced labor. **36** The boundary of the Amorites was
from Scorpion Pass to Sela and beyond.

**27** The remainder of chapter 1 records the inability of the other tribes to occupy territory. Manasseh's allotment included several key cities in the Valley of Jezreel, which extended from the Sea of Galilee to the Mediterranean. Joshua 17:16 mentions the chariot problems in this area where the Canaanite "tanks" ("iron chariots") maneuvered freely. Beth Shan was an important fortress controlling a trading route across the Jordan. Egyptian troops were stationed there well into the twelfth century.

Taanach was five miles southeast of Megiddo, and the two cities frequently are mentioned together (cf. 5:19). Megiddo, located on the main route from Egypt to the north (the "way of the sea"), controlled the pass at the entrance to the Jezreel Valley. It too remained under Egyptian domination till about 1150 B.C. Dor lies along the

Mediterranean coast south of Carmel; Ibleam is situated at the southern end of the Jezreel Valley near Dothan.

Joshua had defeated the kings of Taanach, Megiddo, and Dor (Josh 12:21, 23), but a permanent Israelite occupation did not follow. The Canaanites, like the Amorites in vv.34–35, were determined to keep their living areas and resist Israel.

**28** The most the Israelites could do was to exploit the Canaanites as a cheap labor force. Moses earlier had instructed the nation to use the residents of peaceful cities near Canaan as forced laborers, but the peoples of Canaan were to be totally destroyed (Deut 20:11–17).

**29** Ephraim failed to gain possession of Gezer, a city strategically located in the foothills, eighteen miles west of Jerusalem. Gezer guarded the approaches to the foothills and Jerusalem from the northwest, as Lachish did from the southwest. Gezer was one of the last major cities to come under full control of Israel (see Introduction: Date).

**30** Zebulun's territory was north of Manasseh's. Although the cities of Kitron and Nahahol have not been positively identified, they likely were situated on the northern edge of the Jezreel Valley.

**31–32** The tribe of Asher experienced wide setbacks against Acco, Achzib, and Sidon, regions on the Mediterranean north of Mount Carmel, and against the other towns somewhat farther inland. The northern part of their territory became known as Phoenicia. Here the cities of Tyre and Sidon led a strong Canaanite culture with its vigorous Baal worship. Their culture and religion had a strong influence on Israel, especially during the reigns of Solomon and Ahab.

**33** The Naphtalites, whose region lay to the east of Asher, failed to dislodge the residents of two cities—Beth Shemesh and Beth Anath. Beth Shemesh, which means "house of the sun," may have had a sanctuary devoted to the worship of the sun god. Another and more famous Beth Shemesh was located in Judah (1 Sam 6). The name of the other city, Beth Anath, contains the name of Anath, the Canaanite goddess of war and both consort and sister of Baal. Beth Anath has been identified with modern el-Ba'neh near Naphtali's western border (cf. ISBErev, 1:463).

**34–36** The fortunes of the tribe of Dan have a certain prominence in Judges (see ch. 18). Their difficulties stemmed from Amorite pressure to keep them out of the plains and valleys (v.34), where most of their inheritance lay. The Amorites, normally found in the hill country (Num 13:29), are at times associated with the Philistines (1 Sam 7:14). They kept control of Aijalon, eleven miles northwest of Jerusalem, and nearby Shaalbim (v.35, or Shaalabbin). Mount Heres ("sun" mountain) is probably the Beth Shemesh fifteen miles west of Jerusalem. In Joshua 19:41–42, Ir Shemesh (*'îr šāmeš*, "city of the sun") is listed right before Shaalabbin and Aijalon. After the Danites migrated north, the nearby tribe of Ephraim finally subjugated the Amorites.

The final statement in the chapter (v.36) shows how much land was in the hands of the Amorites. The "Ascent of Akrabbim" (cf. NIV mg.), or "Scorpion Pass," is located south of the Dead Sea, at the southern border of the Promised Land (Josh 15:2–3).

## Notes

**27** The "surrounding settlements" of these cities are literally "her daughters" (בְּנֹתֶיהָ [*b*$^{e}$*nōṯeyhā*])—viz., the "villages" or "outposts" dependent on the main city.

### G. *Disobedience Condemned by the Angel of the Lord*

2:1–5

**1** The angel of the LORD went up from Gilgal to Bokim and said, "I
brought you up out of Egypt and led you into the land that I swore to
give to your forefathers. I said, 'I will never break my covenant with you,
**2** and you shall not make a covenant with the people of this land, but you
shall break down their altars.' Yet you have disobeyed me. Why have you
done this? **3** Now therefore I tell you that I will not drive them out before
you; they will be ⌊thorns⌋ in your sides and their gods will be a snare to
you."

**4** When the angel of the LORD had spoken these things to all the
Israelites, the people wept aloud, **5** and they called that place Bokim.
There they offered sacrifices to the LORD.

**1–2** The deplorable spiritual condition of the Israelites, not their lack of chariots, lay behind their failure to dispossess the Canaanites. To expose Israel's sinfulness, the "angel of the Lord" appeared to them (v.1). This angel, who is frequently identified with God himself (6:22; 13:21–22), was perhaps a preincarnate form of the Second Person of the Trinity. His announcements to Gideon and to Samson's parents promised deliverance at crucial points in Israel's history.

The move from Gilgal to Bokim may signify the relocation of the tabernacle. Gilgal, situated between the Jordan and Jericho, had been the initial religious center (Josh 4:19–20). The LXX adds "and to Bethel" after "Bokim" in an attempt to identify the new site. In 20:18–28 and 21:1–4, Bethel is identified with the sanctuary.

The angel of the Lord charged Israel with breaking their covenant with God in spite of his great acts of deliverance on their behalf (v.2). God had led them from slavery in Egypt to the fertile land of Canaan, fulfilling his promises to Abraham, Isaac, and Jacob. He would "never break [his] covenant" (cf. Lev 26:42–44; Deut 7:9); and out of gratefulness for his beneficence, Israel was expected to obey him. Yet they entered into agreements with the Canaanites, including marriage covenants (Prov 2:17), and did not tear down their altars as God had directed (Exod 34:12–13).

**3** God therefore did not help the Israelites drive out their enemies but left some to trap them through pagan customs and religions. Israel had been repeatedly warned that the Canaanites could become irritants in their eyes and thorns in their sides (Num 33:55; Josh 23:13).

**4–5** The response of the people to the angel's sad pronouncement was to weep loudly (v.4). Like the weeping of Numbers 14:1, when the spies announced that Canaan could not be captured, here the crying does not necessarily imply repentance. They offered sacrifices (v.5), however; and the burnt offerings and fellowship offerings sacrificed at Bethel not long after (21:1–4) did connote national mourning. "Bokim" means "weeping."

## Notes

1 The angel spoke of "my covenant," an expression that closely resembles the "messenger of the covenant" in Mal 3:1 (viz., "my messenger"). The Hebrew word מַלְאָךְ (*mal'āḵ*) can be translated either "angel" or "messenger." The reference in Malachi is messianic and relates to Christ.

3 The term צִדִּים (*ṣiddîm*) may be cognate to the Akkadian *ṣaddu*, which means "trap," "snare." Normally in Hebrew it means "sides" afflicted with thorns (Num 33:55) or "whips" (Josh 23:13). One of the two could be implied here. A third alternative is to follow the LXX, Latin, and Vulgate, which read צָרִים (*ṣārîm*, "enemies").

## II. The Rule of the Judges (2:6–16:31)

### A. *Introduction (2:6–3:6)*

#### 1. *The passing of godly leaders*

2:6–9

**6 After Joshua had dismissed the Israelites, they went to take possession of the land, each to his own inheritance. 7 The people served the LORD throughout the lifetime of Joshua and of the elders who outlived him and who had seen all the great things the LORD had done for Israel.**
**8 Joshua son of Nun, the servant of the LORD, died at the age of a hundred and ten. 9 And they buried him in the land of his inheritance, at Timnath Heres in the hill country of Ephraim, north of Mount Gaash.**

After a chapter that summarizes the incomplete wars of occupation, the reader is introduced to the threatening wars of liberation that characterize the period of the judges. To explain how Israel fell prey to powerful oppressors, the author reviews events since the death of Joshua. Verses 6–9 almost parallel Joshua 24:28–31.

**6–9** Just before his death, Joshua had led the people in renewing the covenant with the Lord. Then he sent them away to finish occupying the land (v.6). What they did about this is described in chapter 1. Joshua was buried on the land allotted to his family in Timnath Heres (v.9), probably the site of Tibneh, ten miles northwest of Bethel. He received the exalted title of "servant of the LORD." This phrase is reserved for devoted men of God such as Moses, David, and the prophets. Only here in v.8 (and the parallel in Josh 24:29) is Joshua called "the servant of the LORD."

During the lifetime of Joshua and the leaders who outlived him, Israel was relatively faithful to the Lord. These men had experienced God's miracles on behalf of Israel. Verse 7, unlike Joshua 24:31, adds the adjective "great" to describe God's works.

## Notes

9 "Timnath Heres" is spelled "Timnath Serah" in Josh 19:50 and 24:30. Apparently a scribe reversed the *ḥ* and the *s*.

## 2. *The pattern of the period of the judges*

### 2:10–23

10After that whole generation had been gathered to their fathers,
another generation grew up, who knew neither the LORD nor what he
had done for Israel. 11Then the Israelites did evil in the eyes of the LORD
and served the Baals. 12They forsook the LORD, the God of their fathers,
who had brought them out of Egypt. They followed and worshiped
various gods of the peoples around them. They provoked the LORD to
anger 13because they forsook him and served Baal and the Ashtoreths.
14In his anger against Israel the LORD handed them over to raiders who
plundered them. He sold them to their enemies all around, whom they
were no longer able to resist. 15Whenever Israel went out to fight, the
hand of the LORD was against them to defeat them, just as he had sworn
to them. They were in great distress.

16Then the LORD raised up judges, who saved them out of the hands of
these raiders. 17Yet they would not listen to their judges but prostituted
themselves to other gods and worshiped them. Unlike their fathers, they
quickly turned from the way in which their fathers had walked, the way
of obedience to the LORD's commands. 18Whenever the LORD raised up a
judge for them, he was with the judge and saved them out of the hands
of their enemies as long as the judge lived; for the LORD had compassion
on them as they groaned under those who oppressed and afflicted
them. 19But when the judge died, the people returned to ways even
more corrupt than those of their fathers, following other gods and
serving and worshiping them. They refused to give up their evil
practices and stubborn ways.

20Therefore the LORD was very angry with Israel and said, "Because
this nation has violated the covenant that I laid down for their
forefathers and has not listened to me, 21I will no longer drive out before
them any of the nations Joshua left when he died. 22I will use them to
test Israel and see whether they will keep the way of the LORD and walk
in it as their forefathers did." 23The LORD had allowed those nations to
remain; he did not drive them out at once by giving them into the hands
of Joshua.

**10** When Joshua's contemporaries had joined him in death, the new generation accelerated down the highway to destruction. They did not know God in a vital way. They had not seen the miracles their fathers had talked about. People cannot thrive on the spiritual power of their parents; each generation must personally experience the reality of God.

**11–13** The cyclical nature of Judges has been alluded to earlier under "Literary Form" (see p. 379). History repeated itself as Israel went through the fivefold pattern of sin, slavery, supplication, salvation, and silence (cf. Introduction: Theological Values).

The *sin* phase is always introduced with the words of v.11: "The Israelites did evil in the eyes of the LORD." Six times this blunt sentence is found (3:7, 12; 4:1; 6:1; 10:6; 13:1). Israel deserted the very God who had delivered them from Egypt and had saved them from Pharaoh and his host (cf. v.1). They worshiped Baal (v.13) or "the Baals." Baal is an epithet of the Canaanite storm god Hadad son of Dagon, the god of rain and agriculture, and the leading deity in the pantheon. There were also "Baals" associated with particular places, like the Baal of Peor (Num 25:3) or Baal-Berith

(Judg 9:4); and this may account for the plural form. Israel's earlier encounter with the Baal of Peor had been disastrous (Num 25).

The "Ashtoreths" (v.13) were deities such as Astarte, who was goddess of the evening star and renowned for her beauty. She was a goddess of fertility, love, and war, often linked with Baal (10:6). Ashtaroth's name and functions are sometimes confused with Asherah and Anath (cf. 1:33). Ugaritic literature has many references to the Astartes and their often degrading exploits (cf. W.F. Albright, *Archaeology and the Religion of Israel* [Baltimore: Johns Hopkins Press, 1953], pp. 74–78).

**14–15** The Lord became angry at Israel's apostasy and turned the Israelities over to their enemies (v.14), thus initiating the *slavery* phase of the cycle. God "sold them" as one sells a slave (3:8; Deut 32:30). Israel's crops, supposedly guaranteed by the worship of Baal, were carried off year after year. The strong hand of the Lord, which had released them from slavery in Egypt (Exod 13:3), now acted to secure Israel's "defeat" (v.15), just as God had warned through Moses (Deut 28:25). In their distress the people cried out to the Lord. Though not mentioned explicitly until v.18, this supplication is assumed as a result of their agony.

**16–19** Salvation came through the judges raised up by God (v.16). (For the significance of the title "judges," see the Introduction: Title.) Some fifteen individuals could claim this designation, though six are "minor" judges who are mentioned only briefly (Shamgar, Tola, Jair, Ibzan, Elon, and Abdon). Often a form of the verb *yāša'* ("to save") is used in conjunction with their work. In 3:15 the participle is translated "deliverer." The primary meaning is military victory.

Not long after gaining Israel's freedom, the judges would find the people newly enmeshed in sin. Their religious prostitution (v.17) meant that they were forsaking the nation's true "husband," the Lord, in favor of other gods. Significantly, "Baal" (*ba'al*) means "husband" or "owner." Moreover, the worship of the Canaanite gods literally involved sexual conduct with temple prostitutes supposedly to promote the fertility of the soil.

The Lord spared the people throughout the lifetime of a given judge, even though they deserved to be resubjugated. The divine compassion was as great as it had been in rescuing the people from Egypt, where they had "groaned" (cf. Exod 2:24; 6:5) under the severe "oppression" of Pharaoh (cf. Exod 3:9). The language of v.18 clearly looks back to the Egyptian bondage. But after the death of a judge, the corruption of the people increased.

Verse 19 indicates that the people's evil ways became progressively worse as the period of the judges continued. The word "stubborn" (*qāšāh*) was applied to Israel when Aaron made the golden calf (Exod 32:9; 33:3, 5; NIV, "stiff-necked"). The Israelites were stiff-necked in the wilderness, but they were even more obstinate in the Promised Land. A new environment, alas, did not mean a new attitude.

**20–23** For the third time since v.11, the anger of the Lord is mentioned (v.20; cf. vv. 12, 14). There is a note of contempt as the Lord addressed the people as "this nation" rather than as "my nation" (cf. Hag 1:2 ["These people"]). The summary in vv.20–23 closely resembles the stern pronouncement of vv.1–3 by the angel of the Lord. Violating the covenant meant a slower conquest of Canaan. The nations would be left there to test Israel's desire to obey the Lord (v.22). The constant pressure from a pagan culture would prove who the genuine believers really were.

## Notes

**18** The verb נָחַם (*nāḥam*, "to have compassion") can mean "to be sorry." Elsewhere in Judges it is used only in 21:6 and 15, where the other tribes "grieved" over the destruction of Benjamin.

**20** The word "to break" the covenant is עָבַר (*'āḇar*, "to cross over, overstep"). It is the same root from which the word "Hebrew" is derived (עִבְרִי [*'iḇrî*]), probably meaning one who "crossed" the river (Euphrates).

### 3. *The people left to test Israel*

### 3:1–6

**[1]These are the nations the Lord left to test all those Israelites who had not experienced any of the wars in Canaan [2](he did this only to teach warfare to the descendants of the Israelites who had not had previous battle experience): [3]the five rulers of the Philistines, all the Canaanites, the Sidonians, and the Hivites living in the Lebanon mountains from Mount Baal Hermon to Lebo Hamath. [4]They were left to test the Israelites to see whether they would obey the Lord's commands, which he had given their forefathers through Moses.**

**[5]The Israelites lived among the Canaanites, Hittites, Amorites, Perizzites, Hivites and Jebusites. [6]They took their daughters in marriage and gave their own daughters to their sons, and served their gods.**

**1–2** This section deals with the identity and function of the nations left in Canaan to test Israel (v.1). These nations afforded practical experience in warfare for the generations following Joshua. These new generations of Israelites had not participated in Joshua's wars of occupation and needed to learn how to fight (v.2). Israel would one day confront major powers like Egypt and Assyria; so the smaller wars against the nations of Canaan provided valuable training. David, for example, not only fought against the Philistines but lived among them and learned their military skills.

It seems strange to find God using the Canaanites both to punish and to teach Israel. Yet this was part of his sovereign action (see Introduction: Theological Values). The Canaanite presence in the land also kept the Israelites from being overrun with wild animals (Exod 23:29–30).

**3–4** The Philistines are mentioned first (v.3), perhaps because they were to become the primary opponents of Israel. Their five-city cluster along the Mediterranean included Gaza, Ashdod, Ashkelon, Gath, and Ekron (see 1:18 and Josh 13:3). Each city was ruled by a *seren*, a word probably cognate to the Greek *tyrannos* and familiar to us in the English derivative "tyrant." The Philistines migrated from Caphtor of the Aegean area (perhaps "Crete") and were among the "Sea Peoples" who ravaged Asia Minor and Ugarit before succumbing to Egypt about 1190 B.C. (Wood, *Israel's History*, pp. 59–60). The term *s^erānîm* for "rulers" is used only for the Philistines.

The "Sidonians" refers to the Phoenicians, whose leading port city was Sidon. After 1100 B.C. Tyre began to eclipse Sidon in importance (cf. 1:31).

The Hivites were located in northern Israel in Joshua 11:3, but Shechem (cf. Gen 34:2) and Gibeon (Josh 9:3, 7) in central Palestine were also Hivite cities. The Hivites are sometimes identified with the "Horites" or "Hurrians" (see comment on 1:21; cf.

Gen 36:2, 20; ZPEB, 3:172). "Mount Baal Hermon" is given as a border of the tribe of Manasseh in 1 Chronicles 5:23. Some (cf. J.B. Scott, ZPEB, 1:436) identify it with Baal Gad, a town at the foot of Mount Hermon (Josh 11:17) denoting the northern limits of Joshua's conquests (Josh 13:5). Lebo Hamath is likely the same as modern Lebweh, fourteen miles northeast of Baalbek.

**5–6** The Hittites may not be the same north Syrians of 1:26 but another Canaanite people well known at Hebron in the hills of Judah (Gen 23). The link between these Hittites and the Anatolian Empire is also problematic (cf. H. Hoffner, "Some Contributions of Hittitology to Old Testament Study," *Tyndale Bulletin* 20 [1969]: 28–29).

Intermarriage with the peoples of Canaan had been forbidden (Josh 23:12) since it would lead directly to idolatry. It was into that very trap, however, that the nation fell (cf. 2:1–3).

## Notes

---

3 "Lebo Hamath" may also mean "the entrance [לְבוֹא (*l*e*b̲ô'*, lit., "to go in, enter")] of Hamath," marking the southern border of the territory held by the kingdom of Hamath.

---

### B. *The Victory of Othniel Over Cushan-Rishathaim*

### 3:7–11

7The Israelites did evil in the eyes of the LORD; they forgot the LORD
their God and served the Baals and the Asherahs. 8The anger of the
LORD burned against Israel so that he sold them into the hands of
Cushan-Rishathaim king of Aram Naharaim, to whom the Israelites were
subject for eight years. 9But when they cried out to the LORD, he raised
up for them a deliverer, Othniel son of Kenaz, Caleb's younger brother,
who saved them. 10The Spirit of the LORD came upon him, so that he
became Israel's judge and went to war. The LORD gave Cushan-Rishathaim king of Aram into the hands of Othniel, who overpowered him.
11So the land had peace for forty years, until Othniel son of Kenaz died.

**7** The first cycle, though brief, follows the pattern delineated in chapter 2. Israel sinned by forgetting God and worshiping foreign deities. Asherah appears in Ugaritic literature as the wife of both El and Baal, and some confuse her with Ashtaroth/Astartes (2:13). An "Asherah" was also a symbol of the goddess, a sacred tree (Deut 16:21) or a carved pole set up beside an altar to Baal (Judg 6:25; cf. Albright, *Archaeology and the Religion of Israel*, p. 78). These components of the Canaanite "high places" became a regular feature of Israelite worship, and only the most godly kings tried to eradicate them (2 Chron 17:6).

**8** Israel's sin angered the Lord, who sent Cushan-Rishathaim, king of Upper Mesopotamia, to oppress them. Literally, the name of the country means "Aram [or 'Syria'] of the two rivers." D.J. Wiseman has identified it with modern eastern Syria and northern Iraq (NBD, p. 811; cf. J.J. Finkelstein, "Mesopotamia," JNES 21 [1962]: 73–92). The rivers are most likely the Tigris and Euphrates.

The king's name seems to mean "Cushan of double evil," a rather strange designation but perhaps intended to be an intimidating one. It could also be a caricature of the actual name, somewhat like Baal-Zebub ("lord of flies"; cf. 2 Kings 1:2–3). "Cush" (Gen 10:8) was the father of Nimrod, founder of Babylonian civilization, and people called "Kassites" ruled Babylon from 1500–1200 B.C. The name "Kashtiliash" used by several of their kings is similar to "Cushan."

Cushan-Rishathaim is otherwise unknown in historical annals, but M. Kline ("The Ha-Bi-Ru—Kin or Foe of Israel?" WTJ 20 [Nov 1957]: 54–61) has related his invasion to the much discussed Habiru oppression. The Habiru forces invaded Palestine mainly during the reign of the Pharaoh Akhenaton (1384–1367 B.C.), and it is tempting to connect Cushan with them. In light of the fact that the Mitanni Empire was beginning to crumble about this time, John H. Walton has suggested that Cushan-Rishathaim might have been one of their leaders (private communication). The kingdom of Mitanni was located in Upper Mesopotamia.

**9–10** When the Israelites appealed to God for help, Othniel was commissioned to rescue them (v.9). This relative of the illustrious Caleb has already been introduced in 1:11–15 as a successful warrior. The selection of Othniel shows that the oppression followed Joshua's death quite closely, perhaps about 1375–1367 B.C. When the Spirit of the Lord came on him, Othniel won a great victory (v.10). The empowering of the Spirit is crucial in Judges (see Introduction: Special Problems), and down to the time of David it remained the mark of God's chosen man.

**11** Othniel's triumph ushered in a forty-year peace, the first of several peace periods given in multiples of forty (v.30; 5:31; 8:28). Those favoring a late-date theory use this "round number" to reduce the actual years involved.

## Notes

---

8 Some scholars (cf. ZPEB, 1:1048) emend רִשְׁעָתַיִם (*riš'āṯayim*, "Rishathaim") to רֹאשׁ תֵּמָן (*rō'š tēmān*, "Rosh Teman"), which means "leader of Teman," a city located in Edom. The rendering אֲרָם (*'ărām*, "Aram") is then changed slightly to אֱדוֹם (*'ĕḏōm*, "Edom"). The evidence, however, makes these emendations unnecessary.

---

### C. *The Victory of Ehud Over Moab (3:12–30)*

#### 1. *Israel oppressed by Moab*

3:12–14

12 Once again the Israelites did evil in the eyes of the LORD, and
because they did this evil the LORD gave Eglon king of Moab power over
Israel. 13 Getting the Ammonites and Amalekites to join him, Eglon came
and attacked Israel, and they took possession of the City of Palms. 14 The
Israelites were subject to Eglon king of Moab for eighteen years.

**12–14** When Israel fell into sin, God used their perennial enemy Moab to subdue them (v.12). Usually the Lord gave power or strength to the Israelites (e.g., Samson, 16:28). Here, however, the Lord was on the side of Israel's foe. In Moses' day the Moabites had attempted to thwart Israel by hiring Balaam to curse them, and along with the Midianites they had actually involved God's people in idolatry (Num 25). But now Moab had allies such as the Amalekites (v.13), who had bitterly opposed Israel in the wilderness (Exod 17:8–16).

Moabite forces crossed the Jordan and occupied Jericho, the City of Palms. This means that they had first defeated the tribe of Reuben, which had inherited territory east of the Dead Sea. Because of their locale, the Transjordanian tribes were especially vulnerable to enemy attack. Jericho had been cursed by Joshua (Josh 6:26) and was probably unoccupied when King Eglon moved in. Garstang identified the small, unwalled city from the last half of the fourteenth century with Eglon's temporary occupation of it (but cf. Bimson, *Redating the Exodus*, pp. 124–25; Bryant G. Wood, "Did the Israelites Conquer Jericho? A New Look at the Archaeological Evidence," *Bibical Archaeology Review* 16, 2 [March/April 1990]: 44–58). From this strategic base Eglon dominated the Israelites for eighteen years (v.14).

## 2. *King Eglon slain by Ehud*

### 3:15–25

15Again the Israelites cried out to the LORD, and he gave them a
deliverer—Ehud, a left-handed man, the son of Gera the Benjamite. The
Israelites sent him with tribute to Eglon king of Moab.
16Now Ehud had
made a double-edged sword about a foot and a half long, which he
strapped to his right thigh under his clothing.
17He presented the tribute
to Eglon king of Moab, who was a very fat man.
18After Ehud had
presented the tribute, he sent on their way the men who had carried it.
19At the idols near Gilgal he himself turned back and said, "I have a
secret message for you, O king."
The king said, "Quiet!" And all his attendants left him.
20Ehud then approached him while he was sitting alone in the upper
room of his summer palace and said, "I have a message from God for
you." As the king rose from his seat,
21Ehud reached with his left hand,
drew the sword from his right thigh and plunged it into the king's belly.
22Even the handle sank in after the blade, which came out his back.
Ehud did not pull the sword out, and the fat closed in over it.
23Then
Ehud went out to the porch; he shut the doors of the upper room behind
him and locked them.
24After he had gone, the servants came and found the doors of the
upper room locked. They said, "He must be relieving himself in the inner
room of the house."
25They waited to the point of embarrassment, but
when he did not open the doors of the room, they took a key and
unlocked them. There they saw their lord fallen to the floor, dead.

**15** God's choice to end the Moabite oppression was a man from Benjamin, a tribe whose territory was adjacent to the enemy's stronghold at Jericho. The hero was Ehud, a left-handed man of the same mold as the seven-hundred expert slingers, all left-handed, who fought in the civil war (see comments on 20:13b–16, 43–47). The sad events in chapters 19–21 probably occurred prior to Moab's invasion and may even have precipitated it. Benjamin had a large number of ambidextrous warriors as late as David's day (1 Chron 12:2).

**16–17** Ehud's task was ostensibly to make the yearly tribute payment to Eglon to assure him of Israel's subjection for another year (v.17). Since the payment was carried by a number of men, it may have been food or wool. For the occasion Ehud had made a small sword or dagger, about eighteen inches long (v.16). It was well concealed, and the fact that he was left-handed enhanced his stratagem.

**18–23** Apparently Ehud and his men left Jericho before Ehud returned alone to strike his fatal blow (v.18). "The idols" (v.19) most likely were a well-known landmark, though the reference may actually be to "stone quarries" (NIV mg.) rather than "idols." The "Gilgal" located near this landmark is perhaps the one mentioned in Joshua 15:7 on the border between Benjamin and Judah. It lies between Jericho and Jerusalem north of the Pass of Adummim, whereas the more famous Gilgal is east of Jericho and not on the way to the hill country (cf. vv.26–27).

After the other Israelites were safely en route home, Ehud came back to seek a private audience with Eglon. Since Ehud was alone, the likelihood of treachery was even more remote. The king wanted to hear this secret message; so his request for silence was a signal for his officials and attendants to leave (v.19). Eglon was sitting in the cool upper room of his palace as Ehud presented the "message from God" (v.20). The king stood up reverently to hear the divine oracle, and Ehud drew his sword and delivered the fatal "message." Perhaps the huge size of the king (cf. v.17) and the unexpected use of the left hand prevented him from seeing Ehud's move, for it is clear that no cry of alarm was heard outside. The stark details of vv.21–22 are characteristic of the "epic blow." Ehud left the dagger completely buried in Eglon's abdomen and made his escape, locking the doors of the room to prevent quick detection of his crime (v.23).

**24–25** Eglon's officials hesitated to unlock the doors, assuming that their master might be seeing to his bodily needs (v.24). Finally they became suspicious and took a key to remove the bolt from the doors (v.25). They found the king lying on the floor, the victim of assassination.

The "key" may have been a flat piece of wood with pins that corresponded to the pins in a hollow bolt. The bolt was inside the door, and the lock was a piece of wood above the bolt from which the pins fell into the holes of the bolt. When the key was inserted, the pins in the bolt were raised and the bolt could be removed (NBC, p. 242).

As stated in the Introduction (Special Problems), God did not necessarily approve of the method used by Ehud. It may be significant that the Spirit of the Lord did not come on Ehud and that he was never described as "judging Israel." Sometime later David condemned the assassination of "an innocent man in his own house" (2 Sam 4:11). Yet the innocence or righteousness of Eglon is open to question, and Joshua's earlier policy at Jericho was to kill virtually the entire population (Josh 6:21, 25).

## Notes

**15** The word בֶּן־הַיְמִינִי (*ben-hay$^{e}$mînî*, "Benjamite") means "the son of the right hand"; so the left-handed ability of Ehud and other Benjamites seems strange. The expression אִטֵּר יַד־יְמִינוֹ

('*iṭṭēr yaḏ-yᵉmînô,* "left-handed") literally means "restricted as to his right hand." Since seven hundred men are so described (20:16), it is unlikely that this means "crippled."

**17** מִנְחָה (*minḥāh,* "tribute") is also the word for "gift" or "grain offering" (13:19). The payment was not optional, however, and a nation that withheld the "tribute" was considered rebellious (2 Kings 18:7, 14).

**22** וַיֵּצֵא הַפַּרְשְׁדֹנָה (*wayyēṣē' happaršᵉḏōnāh,* "which came out his back") is a difficult expression. The noun occurs only here. The KJV and RSV translate "and the dirt came out," implying an intestinal discharge caused by the sword thrust. Koehler-Baumgartner relates the word to the Akkadian *parašdinum* ("hole"), meaning that Ehud went out through an "escape hole." The construction is very similar to "Ehud went out to the porch" in v.23.

**24** מֵסִיךְ אֶת־רַגְלָיו (*mēsîḵ 'eṯ-raglāyw,* "relieving himself") is literally "[he] is covering his feet." This euphemism occurs also in 1 Sam 24:3 (4 MT).

---

## 3. *The Moabites defeated by Ehud*

### 3:26–30

[26]While they waited, Ehud got away. He passed by the idols and
escaped to Seirah. [27]When he arrived there, he blew a trumpet in the hill
country of Ephraim, and the Israelites went down with him from the
hills, with him leading them.
[28]"Follow me," he ordered, "for the LORD has given Moab, your
enemy, into your hands." So they followed him down and, taking
possession of the fords of the Jordan that led to Moab, they allowed no
one to cross over. [29]At that time they struck down about ten thousand
Moabites, all vigorous and strong; not a man escaped. [30]That day Moab
was made subject to Israel, and the land had peace for eighty years.

**26** The reluctance of the Moabite officials to break into the king's room gave Ehud the time he needed to escape. He followed the same route he had started to take earlier (cf. v.19 and comment), heading for the unidentified "Seirah." His goal was to reach the hill country of Ephraim, more than three thousand feet higher than Jericho. Ephraim was one of the most powerful tribes of Israel and occupied the territory adjacent to Benjamin on the north. Doubtless the people of Ephraim also had chafed under Moab's oppression.

**27–29** Ehud knew that the death of Moab's king would throw the officials and troops at Jericho into confusion—an opportune time to strike the hated invaders and end their rule. Using the ancient alarm system of a trumpet (Num 10:9), Ehud quickly assembled Israelite men to help him follow up his personal triumph (v.27). In 6:34 Gideon also sounds a trumpet to muster troops against the Midianites.

Ehud's bravery and enthusiasm inspired a large following, for all sensed that the Lord was handing over the enemy to them. Under Ehud's command the Israelites took control of the fords of the Jordan and cut off Moab's line of retreat (v.28). Gideon used the same strategy to slow down the Midianites (7:24), and Jephthah captured forty-two thousand Ephraimites at key fords (12:5–6). Ehud led the rout of ten thousand Moabites, who may have represented Eglon's crack troops (v.29). The expression *'îš ḥāyil* ("man of strength" or "courage") is also used to describe the "valiant fighters" of Benjamin in 20:44 and 46.

**30** Israel's victory restored her independence as Moab was "made subject" or "subdued." The verb *kāna'* ("to humble, subdue") is used at the end of several cycles in Judges (4:23; 8:28; 11:33) to indicate a thorough defeat. Eighty years of peace (1309–1229?), the longest "rest" in the book, followed Ehud's triumph. Some authorities connect this lengthy period with the revival of Egyptian strength and the famous peace treaty between Hattusilis III of the Hittites and Rameses II of Egypt (cf. Wood, *Israel's History*, p. 215). This pact between the two leading powers secured the peace of the Near East for much of the thirteenth century B.C.

## Notes

---

**29** The word שָׁמֵן (*šāmēn*, "vigorous") is literally "fat," a term also used of fertile soil and rich food. It denotes health and vitality. When Eglon was called "fat" in v.17, בָּרִיא (*bārî'*) was used. This word likewise is connected with prosperity (Ps 73:4) and health (Dan 1:15).

---

## D. *The Victory of Shamgar Over the Philistines*

### 3:31

> 31 After Ehud came Shamgar son of Anath, who struck down six hundred Philistines with an oxgoad. He too saved Israel.

**31** The reference to Shamgar is brief but intriguing. As with the other minor judges, there is no mention of the sin of Israel (10:1–5; 12:8–15). Unlike those judges, however, Shamgar's work was explicitly military. He won an astonishing victory over the Philistines by means of an oxgoad, rivaling Samson's exploits with the jawbone of a donkey (15:16). An oxgoad is a stout stick tipped with bronze and used for prodding animals. Shamgar's use of this weapon implies that the Philistines were already disarming neighboring people (cf. 5:8; 1 Sam 13:19–22).

Shamgar is a foreign name, perhaps of Hurrian origin. Anath is a fierce Canaanite goddess of war (cf. comment on 1:33), but "son of Anath" probably means "house of Anath"—"Beth Anath." Cities with that name were found in Naphtali (1:33) and Judah (Josh 15:59). Others interpret "son of Anath" to mean a person who is like Anath, that is, of warlike character (cf. Cyrus Gordon, *The Ancient Near East* [New York: W.W. Horton, 1965], p. 151).

In 5:6 Shamgar is mentioned, along with Jael, as a hero of Israel. Shamgar may have been a contemporary of Ehud, since the latter's death is not cited till 4:1.

## Notes

---

**31** "Ben Anath" may equal "Beth Anath," just as "Hadadezer son of Rehob" apparently means "Hadadezer from Beth Rehob" (2 Sam 8:3).

---

## E. *The Victory of Deborah and Barak Over Jabin and Sisera (4:1–5:31)*

### 1. *The prose account (4:1–24)*

Somewhat in the form of Hebrew parallelism, Judges has two supplementary accounts of the victory over the Canaanites. The first is in narrative fashion; the second is a majestic poem. Chapter 5 has received numerous plaudits for its artistic beauty, but scholars are beginning to recognize the artistry of the narrative account also (see esp. John H. Stek, "The Bee and the Mountain Goat: A Literary Reading of Judges 4," in *A Tribute to Gleason Archer,* edd. Walter C. Kaiser, Jr., and Ronald F. Youngblood [Chicago: Moody, 1986], pp. 53–86).

#### a. *The oppression*

4:1–3

**[1]After Ehud died, the Israelites once again did evil in the eyes of the**
**LORD. [2]So the LORD sold them into the hands of Jabin, a king of Canaan,**
**who reigned in Hazor. The commander of his army was Sisera, who**
**lived in Harosheth Haggoyim. [3]Because he had nine hundred iron**
**chariots and had cruelly oppressed the Israelites for twenty years, they**
**cried to the LORD for help.**

**1–3** The next major oppression came at the hands of a coalition of Canaanite forces led by Jabin and Sisera, and it affected primarily the northern tribes. Jabin lived in Hazor, once the largest city in Palestine, some nine miles north of the Sea of Galilee and located on the main route between Egypt and Mesopotamia. Joshua had defeated a Jabin king of Hazor, who had been the leader of the powerful northern coalition (Josh 11:1–11), and the Israelites had burned the city. Some scholars (cf. IB, 2:12–24) believe that chapters 4–5 are another version of that battle. Yet it is not unusual for several kings to use a dynastic name like "Jabin" (cf. K. Kitchen, *Ancient Orient and Old Testament* [Chicago: InterVarsity, 1966], p. 68).

Since the thirteenth-century destruction level at Hazor (Stratum I of the plateau, c. 1230 B.C.) shows no evidence of the burning required by Joshua 11:11, it is possible to identify Stratum III (c. 1400 B.C.) with Joshua's victory (Wood, *Distressing Days,* p. 102, and Waltke, "Palestinian Evidence," pp. 43–44). Stratum I could then be related to the Jabin of Judges 4–5.

"Harosheth Haggoyim" (v.2; lit., "Harosheth of the nations") has been identified with Tell el-Harbaj, just south of the Kishon River at Mount Carmel (Wood, *Israel's History,* p. 216 n. 39). Another possibility is Tell el-ʿAmr, twelve miles northwest of Megiddo. Sisera's strength lay in his 900 chariots, a sizable force for this early period, though Thutmosis III in the fifteenth century B.C. claimed to have seized 924 chariots at Megiddo (cf. ANET, p. 237). With this military advantage, Sisera terrorized the tribes living near the Valley of Jezreel.

#### b. *Deborah's challenge to Barak*

4:4–10

**[4]Deborah, a prophetess, the wife of Lappidoth, was leading Israel at**
**that time. [5]She held court under the Palm of Deborah between Ramah**
**and Bethel in the hill country of Ephraim, and the Israelites came to her**
**to have their disputes decided. [6]She sent for Barak son of Abinoam from**
**Kedesh in Naphtali and said to him, "The LORD, the God of Israel,**

commands you: 'Go, take with you ten thousand men of Naphtali and
Zebulun and lead the way to Mount Tabor. 7I will lure Sisera, the
commander of Jabin's army, with his chariots and his troops to the
Kishon River and give him into your hands.'"
8Barak said to her, "If you go with me, I will go; but if you don't go
with me, I won't go."
9"Very well," Deborah said, "I will go with you. But because of the
way you are going about this, the honor will not be yours, for the LORD
will hand Sisera over to a woman." So Deborah went with Barak to
Kedesh, 10where he summoned Zebulun and Naphtali. Ten thousand
men followed him, and Deborah also went with him.

**4–5** Throughout the time of the judges, women played an important role, and Deborah was the most outstanding of them (v.4). She was a prophetess, like Miriam (Exod 15:20) and Huldah (2 Kings 22:14), and also a judge (cf. Introduction: Title). Because the rule of women was not normal in Israel, her prominence implies a lack of qualified and willing men. Deborah sat as judge some fifty miles from Jezreel at the southern end of Ephraim's territory. But the Lord commanded her to challenge Barak of Naphtali to confront Sisera's troops. Deborah's involvement in the conflict indicates that the effects of the Canaanite oppression were felt even in Ephraim and Benjamin.

The reference to a palm tree (v.5) may allude to the stateliness and gracefulness of women (S of Songs 7:7–8). The palm is associated with prosperity in Psalm 92:12 and leadership in Isaiah 9:14.

**6** Barak lived in Kedesh, probably the same as Khirbet Qedish at the southern end of the Sea of Galilee (cf. Y. Aharoni, *Land of the Bible* [Philadelphia: Westminster, 1962], p. 204). Naphtali and Zebulun, the first tribes to be summoned, covered most of Israel's territory north of the Jezreel Valley. Cone-shaped Mount Tabor, at the boundary of the two tribes, rises some thirteen hundred feet from the valley and affords an unmistakable meeting place.

Barak was told to "lead the way" to Mount Tabor, a translation of the same Hebrew word (*māšak̲*) rendered "lure" in the next verse. If Barak did his part, God would lead the enemy into the trap. Literally *māšak̲* means "to draw along," and it is used of the sounding of the ram's horn (Exod 19:13). Since Ehud and Gideon blew such trumpets to assemble troops, Barak may have done likewise. Verse 10 says only that he "summoned" the tribes but does not tell us precisely how.

**7** Deborah revealed that the site of the battle would be near the Kishon River. This river, originating in the hills south and east of Taanach, flowed in a northwesterly direction through the Valley of Jezreel and emptied into the Mediterranean north of Carmel. During the summer months it dwindled to a mere stream. The surrounding valley was excellent terrain for deploying chariots. During the spring, however, the rains caused the river to overflow its banks and flood the low-lying areas nearby. Mount Tabor lay ten miles east of the Kishon.

**8–10** In response to the challenge, Barak expressed his willingness to go, but only if Deborah accompanied him (v.8). Her presence as a prophetess would assure contact with the Lord, just as the presence of Moses and the ark of the covenant brought victory in battle (Num 10:35) while their absence meant defeat (Num 14:44). Barak's lack of faith prompted Deborah to predict that the honor of killing Sisera would belong to a woman (v.9), namely Jael, wife of Heber the Kenite (see v.11). So Deborah went along, and her support helped Barak raise the necessary troops (v.10). They began the search for troops in Kedesh, Barak's hometown.

## Notes

**6** A better-known Kedesh, located about seven miles north of Hazor, cannot be the correct site if Sisera was fleeing to Hazor (cf. vv.11, 17).

**9** The alternate translation in the NIV—"on the expedition you are undertaking"—is the result of the ambiguous phrase עַל־הַדֶּרֶךְ (*'al-hadderek̲*). The preposition *'al* can mean either "on" or "on account of," and *derek̲* can mean "way" or "road." With that interpretation "expedition" is an excellent synonym.

### c. *Jael's husband introduced*

4:11

**[11]Now Heber the Kenite had left the other Kenites, the descendants of Hobab, Moses' brother-in-law, and pitched his tent by the great tree in Zaanannim near Kedesh.**

**11** This seemingly intrusive verse acquaints the reader with the family of the woman Deborah had just alluded to in v.9. As the narrative well shows, she was Jael. She belonged to the nomadic Kenites, most of whom lived in the arid regions of southern Judah (1:16). As relatives of Moses, the Kenites had a strong tie with Israel.

The "great tree" in Zaanannim is mentioned also in Joshua 19:33 as a landmark on the border of Naphtali. It lay on the escape route taken by Sisera after the battle.

## Notes

**11** Hobab is called Reuel's son in Num 10:29; so "brother-in-law" is a most likely rendering. חֹתֵן (*ḥōt̲ēn,* "father-in-law") can be חָתָן (*ḥāt̲ān,* "brother-in-law") with no change in consonants.

### d. *Sisera's army routed by Barak*

4:12–16

**[12]When they told Sisera that Barak son of Abinoam had gone up to**
**Mount Tabor, [13]Sisera gathered together his nine hundred iron chariots**
**and all the men with him, from Harosheth Haggoyim to the Kishon River.**
**[14]Then Deborah said to Barak, "Go! This is the day the LORD has given**
**Sisera into your hands. Has not the LORD gone ahead of you?" So Barak**
**went down Mount Tabor, followed by ten thousand men. [15]At Barak's**
**advance, the LORD routed Sisera and all his chariots and army by the**
**sword, and Sisera abandoned his chariot and fled on foot. [16]But Barak**

pursued the chariots and army as far as Harosheth Haggoyim. All the troops of Sisera fell by the sword; not a man was left.

**12–14** When Sisera learned of Israel's troop movements at the northeastern end of the valley, he called out his entire chariot force and a large army to advance against them from the west (vv.12–13). The presence of a sizable force at Mount Tabor cut off the line of communication between Sisera and King Jabin in Hazor. The main road from Megiddo to Hazor ran along the edge of Mount Tabor. Humanly speaking Barak's hastily gathered army had no chance against such might, but Deborah said that this was the opportune moment (v.14). She encouraged Barak by announcing that "the LORD [had] gone ahead of [him]." This reference to going ahead is a technical term used of a king marching at the head of his army (1 Sam 8:20). The Lord would take the lead in striking down the enemy (2 Sam 5:24).

**15–16** The Lord's role is even clearer in v.15 as he threw Sisera's army into confusion. The word *hāmam* ("routed") is used also of the panic that engulfed Pharaoh's chariots in the Red Sea (Exod 14:24, "confusion") and that which the Philistines arrayed against Samuel (1 Sam 7:10, "panic"). The last passage mentions God's thunder (cf. also Josh 10:10–11); and Deborah's song (5:20–21) shows that a sudden downpour overwhelmed Sisera's chariots, as the swelling river turned the ground to mud that clogged the wheels. Deborah may have pointed to the gathering storm clouds as she sent Barak into battle. The main conflict took place at Taanach, some five miles south of Megiddo (5:19).

The Lord's control of the forces of nature showed his superiority over Baal, the Canaanite storm god. Sisera would not have tried to depend on chariots during the rainy season; so this storm probably struck some time after the spring rains that normally end in May. In Palestine rain is almost unheard of from June through September.

The lightly armed Israelites quickly demoralized the bogged-down Canaanites, who turned and fled westward to Harosheth Haggoyim (v.16). It was a decisive victory, for the Canaanites never again formed a coalition against Israel. Even Sisera was forced to abandon his useless chariot and flee north, away from the heated action.

### e. *Sisera slain by Jael*

#### 4:17–24

17 Sisera, however, fled on foot to the tent of Jael, the wife of Heber the Kenite, because there were friendly relations between Jabin king of Hazor and the clan of Heber the Kenite.

18 Jael went out to meet Sisera and said to him, "Come, my lord, come right in. Don't be afraid." So he entered her tent, and she put a covering over him.

19 "I'm thirsty," he said. "Please give me some water." She opened a skin of milk, gave him a drink, and covered him up.

20 "Stand in the doorway of the tent," he told her. "If someone comes by and asks you, 'Is anyone here?' say 'No.'"

21 But Jael, Heber's wife, picked up a tent peg and a hammer and went quietly to him while he lay fast asleep, exhausted. She drove the peg through his temple into the ground, and he died.

22 Barak came by in pursuit of Sisera, and Jael went out to meet him. "Come," she said, "I will show you the man you're looking for." So he

**went in with her, and there lay Sisera with the tent peg through his temple—dead.**

**[23]On that day God subdued Jabin, the Canaanite king, before the Israelites. [24]And the hand of the Israelites grew stronger and stronger against Jabin, the Canaanite king, until they destroyed him.**

**17** Sisera headed north away from the main line of pursuit. He may have hoped to reach Hazor eventually, but his strength was running out. When he arrived at Zaanannim, he decided to take advantage of the hospitality of the friendly Kenites. He knew of their cordial relationship with Jabin but was clearly unaware of their intermarriage with Israel (v.11).

**18–20** Jael greeted Sisera as "lord," in deference, he thought, to his lofty military title (v.18). Her offer of refuge was tempting, for who would search for him in a woman's tent? Besides, the law of hospitality among nomads guaranteed the safety of one's guests. To this day Arabs will not allow anyone visiting them to be harmed while in their tent.

Jael put a covering over the exhausted leader and, instead of the water he asked for, gave him some milk from a skin (v.19). It was probably a kind of yogurt or curdled milk (5:25)—a drink called *leben,* which is still commonly used by the Arabs. The liquid was kept in animal skins, just as skins were also used for storing wine (Josh 9:4, 13). Though Jael's kindness convinced Sisera of his safety, he took one more precaution by asking her to mislead any potential searching party (v.20).

**21** When Sisera had fallen into a deep sleep, Jael picked up a wooden mallet and a tent peg and drove the peg into his temple. In her eagerness to kill the hated oppressor, Jael used enough force to hammer the tent peg into the ground. The blows resemble the extreme force with which Ehud stabbed Eglon (3:22). Women normally did the work of putting up and taking down the tents; so Jael knew how to handle her tools.

Although Jael's action was a startling violation of the law of hospitality, Sisera was a man who had "cruelly oppressed the Israelites for twenty years" (4:3). Since he had had no mercy on God's covenant people, Sisera probably lay under the sentence of "total destruction" placed on the Canaanites in general (Deut 7:2; Josh 6:17 [cf. NIV mg.]). Centuries later Ahab was denounced for setting free Ben-Hadad, king of Damascus, a man God "had determined should die" (1 Kings 20:42). Similarly, King Saul was censored for sparing the life of the Amalekite king Agag, whom Samuel himself put to death (1 Sam 15:33). Victory over the enemy was usually not considered complete until the leaders were eliminated, and in specific cases the Lord demanded that their lives be taken.

**22** When Barak finally tracked Sisera down, Jael showed him the dead commander. Again there is a close similarity with Eglon, for both leaders were "dead" (*nōp̄ēl mēṯ,* lit., "fallen dead"; cf. 3:25). Deborah's prediction had come true; Barak lost the honor of vanquishing his chief rival. Sisera had died at the hands of a woman—in that culture a disgraceful death (cf. 9:54).

**23–24** The rout of Sisera's army broke the power of Jabin, king of Canaan (v.23). Without his commanding general, Jabin succumbed to the Israelite forces (v.24). His eventual destruction doubtless includes the loss of his capital at Hazor.

## Notes

**18** The precise meaning of שְׂמִיכָה (*śᵉmîḵāh,* "covering") is not known. KB (s.v.) suggests a "curtain"; BDB (s.v.) has "rug"; Cundall (in loc.) favors a "fly-net."

**21** The root תָּקַע (*tāqa',* "to drive") is the same one used in 3:21 of Ehud's sword thrust. The detailed description is another example of the "epic blow."

Sisera must have been totally exhausted when he reached Jael's tent. The word נִרְדָּם (*nirdām,* "fast asleep") describes Jonah sleeping through the raging storm (Jonah 1:5). In Gen 2:21 it is used of Adam when God removed his rib.

### 2. *The poetic version—the Song of Deborah (5:1–31)*

The victory over the Canaanites was also commemorated in a poem of rare beauty. Called the "Song of Deborah," this masterpiece expresses heartfelt praise to God for leading his people in triumph. It is a hymn of thanksgiving, a song of victory like Exodus 15 or Psalm 68. The poetry itself is magnificent, featuring many examples of climactic (repetitive) parallelism (vv.7, 19–20, 27) and onomatopoeia (v.22). Climactic parallelism is also well known from Ugaritic, a fact that suits the ancient character of this song that contains archaic language and a host of difficult forms.

Few deny that the ode was written by an eyewitness soon after the events it celebrates. Deborah is usually considered the author; the connection between prophetess and music is a natural one (cf. the reference to Miriam in Exod 15:20–21). Verses 1 and 7 support Deborah's authorship, though it is grammatically correct to translate v.7 as either "I" or "you."

#### a. *Praise to God for his intervention*

5:1–5

1 On that day Deborah and Barak son of Abinoam sang this song:

2 "When the princes in Israel take the lead,
when the people willingly offer themselves—
praise the LORD!

3 "Hear this, you kings! Listen, you rulers!
I will sing to the LORD, I will sing;
I will make music to the LORD, the God of Israel.

4 "O LORD, when you went out from Seir,
when you marched from the land of Edom,
the earth shook, the heavens poured,
the clouds poured down water.
5 The mountains quaked before the LORD, the One of Sinai,
before the LORD, the God of Israel.

**1** A prose verse similar in form to Exodus 15:1 introduces the song. "Moses and the children of Israel" parallels "Deborah and Barak." In each case the author is likely the first person who is mentioned. Both songs also commemorate the supernatural overthrow of horses and chariots.

**2** The opening line is one of the most obscure in the song. It could also be translated "When locks of hair grow long in Israel," alluding to the practice of leaving hair uncut to fulfill a vow (Num 6:5, 18). This would connote dedication to the Lord in participating in a "holy war." Deuteronomy 32:42 may refer to long-haired soldiers, though "leaders" is also a possibility there. The willingness of the people to fight for the Lord is emphasized in the parallel line. The Hithphael of *nāḏaḇ* ("willingly offer") normally refers to those making voluntary contributions for the building of the sanctuary (Ezra 2:68), though the military sense is also present in 2 Chronicles 17:16 (cf. Ps 110:3 also). "Praise" is literally from the verb "to bless" (*bāraḵ*).

**3** Out of deep gratitude for God's motivating work among the people, Deborah lifted her heart to the One worthy of praise. She wanted kings and rulers to hear about the God of Israel and his magnificent victory. The word for "rulers" (*rōzᵉnîm*) denotes high officials. It is also found parallel to "kings" in Habakkuk 1:10 and Psalm 2:2.

The song is directed to Yahweh (the LORD), the name of God that expresses his covenant relationship with Israel. It is accompanied by musical instruments, though "make music" could mean "compose music."

**4–5** These two verses describe a theophany (a visible, temporal manifestation of God), a characteristic of songs of victory (Ps 68:7–8 [MT 8–9]). God's intervention is compared with his awesome appearance at Sinai (v.5), where the covenant with Israel was established to the accompaniment of thunderstorm and earthquake (Exod 19:16–18). This is an apt reference, for it was the rains that had been Sisera's undoing and again revealed God's transcendent power.

"Seir" (v.4) is a name for the mountains of Edom, a region between the Dead Sea and the Gulf of Aqaba. The same relationship between Edom and Sinai occurs in Deuteronomy 33:2.

## Notes

**2** The evidence for taking the root פרע (*pr'*) as "leader" is the Arabic *fr'* ("top" or "chief") and the Ugaritic *pr'* (possibly "chief" or "first"). The word "Pharaoh" (*par'ōh*) is also related to this root. If long hair is correct for *pr'*, it would parallel the "long-haired" Achaeans often referred to in Homer.

**5** "The One of Sinai" also occurs in Ps 68:8. זֶה (*zeh*) is used like the old relative pronoun זוּ (*zû*) from the Arabic *ḏû* ("owner," "the one belonging to").

For helpful insights on vv.1–5, see Claus Westermann, *The Praise of God in the Psalms* (Richmond, Va.: John Knox, 1961), pp. 90–101. An analysis of metrical patterns and strophic arrangements for vv.2–3 and 17–30 is found in Frank Moore Cross, Jr., *Studies in Ancient Yahwistic Poetry* (Baltimore: Johns Hopkins University Press, 1950), pp. 27–41.

### b. *Conditions during the oppression*

5:6–8

6"In the days of Shamgar son of Anath,
in the days of Jael, the roads were abandoned;
travelers took to winding paths.
7Village life in Israel ceased,
ceased until I, Deborah, arose,

arose a mother in Israel.
8 When they chose new gods,
war came to the city gates,
and not a shield or spear was seen
among forty thousand in Israel.

**6** Conditions were deplorable as Canaanite robbers roamed the highways, making travel dangerous. Commercial trading was likewise stopped, and the economy was adversely affected. "Caravans" may in fact be referred to if *'orāḥôṯ* ("roads") is changed to *'ōreḥôṯ*. In Isaiah 21:13 it clearly means "caravans." These difficulties existed in the time of Shamgar and Jael. These two heroes may have been contemporaries, and both were non-Israelites (3:31 and 4:11).

**7–8** Agriculture also was disrupted by the marauders. Life in unwalled villages was unsafe, and crops had to be abandoned (v.7). This lamentable situation continued until Deborah came on the scene. Her deep concern for the nation and her abilities as prophetess and judge inspired the people to take action. But first they had to give up the "new gods" they had chosen (v.8). God had sent war and oppression because of their sin; now they were being effectively disarmed as well (cf. comment on 3:31). The last part of v.8 might also mean that a potential army of forty thousand was too cowardly to use their available weapons.

## Notes

**6** On the name "Anath," see Peter Craigie, "Deborah and Anat: A Study of Poetic Imagery (Judges 5)," ZAW 90 (1978): 374–81.

**7** קַמְתִּי (*qamtî*, "I arose") could be an archaic second feminine singular: "you arose." The same ambiguity between "I" and "you" occurs in שָׁבַרְתִּי (*šāḇartî*, "you broke") in Jer 2:20.

It is possible that פְּרָזוֹן (*pirāzôn*, "village life") refers to "warriors" and not "villages" in view of its meaning in v.11. פְּרָז (*perez*), a close cognate, seems to mean warriors in Hab 3:14.

### c. *Challenge to recount the Lord's victory*

5:9–11

9 My heart is with Israel's princes,
with the willing volunteers among the people.
Praise the LORD!
10 "You who ride on white donkeys,
sitting on your saddle blankets,
and you who walk along the road,
consider 11 the voice of the singers at the watering places.
They recite the righteous acts of the LORD,
the righteous acts of his warriors in Israel.
"Then the people of the LORD
went down to the city gates.

**9** Though the function of vv.9–11 is difficult to determine, these verses pick up the encouraging theme of v.2. Oppression and defeat have given way to triumph, as travelers can once more move about freely and normal activities are resumed. The author's heart goes out to the volunteers and leaders whose courage made this possible. The "princes" (*ḥôqāqîm*) are individuals with authority (Deut 33:21 ["leader"]); in v.14 they are called "captains."

**10–11** All classes of travelers are told to listen as the singers recount God's great acts (v.11). The wealthy often rode female donkeys, and sometimes kings used their colts (v.10; cf. Gen 49:11; Zech 9:9). Whether rich or poor, all would stop at the wells and have an opportunity to hear about the Lord's "righteous acts."

The final two lines of v.11 present the reverse of v.8. Instead of war coming to the gates, people would congregate there for normal judicial and business activities. "Gates" may be used by metonymy for "cities" (Jer 14:2).

## Notes

---

**10** צְחֹרוֹת (*ṣᵉḥōrôṯ*), the word for "white," occurs only here. KB (s.v.) prefers "yellowish-red."

**11** In place of "singers" some explain the unusual מְחַצְצִים (*mᵉḥaṣᵉṣîm*) as a denominative verb from חֵץ (*ḥēṣ*, "arrow"). KD (in loc.) translates it "archers."

---

### d. *The roles of the individual tribes*

5:12–18

12 'Wake up, wake up, Deborah!
  Wake up, wake up, break out in song!
Arise, O Barak!
  Take captive your captives, O son of Abinoam.'
13 "Then the men who were left
  came down to the nobles;
the people of the LORD
  came to me with the mighty.
14 Some came from Ephraim, whose roots were in Amalek;
  Benjamin was with the people who followed you.
From Makir captains came down,
  from Zebulun those who bear a commander's staff.
15 The princes of Issachar were with Deborah;
  yes, Issachar was with Barak,
  rushing after him into the valley.
In the districts of Reuben
  there was much searching of heart.
16 Why did you stay among the campfires
  to hear the whistling for the flocks?
In the districts of Reuben
  there was much searching of heart.
17 Gilead stayed beyond the Jordan.
  And Dan, why did he linger by the ships?
Asher remained on the coast
  and stayed in his coves.
18 The people of Zebulun risked their very lives;
  so did Naphtali on the heights of the field.

To throw off the Canaanite yoke, it was important for the tribes to cooperate in battle. Those who participated are commended, while the tribes who shirked their responsibility are condemned.

**12** The section begins with a call to Deborah herself to awake. Normally "wake up" is a plea to take action (Ps 44:23; Isa 51:9), and apparently Deborah had to be roused from her complacency as a judge in southern Ephraim (4:5). The song she is asked to "break out in" may have been a war song (cf. 2 Sam 1:18). Barak too is called on to take captives, implying a convincing victory. The same imagery is applied to God in Psalm 68:18 and to Christ as Conqueror in Ephesians 4:8.

**13** The response of the people is given here, and the opening line indicates that the years of oppression took a heavy toll in lives. The verse may reflect a two-stage gathering of troops. First, volunteers may have joined their tribal leaders, before journeying together to the rallying point at Mount Tabor. The last phrase could be translated "against the mighty," meaning the enemy. The ambiguous preposition *b* is handled that way in v.23.

**14** Ephraim and Benjamin, two southern tribes, are mentioned first, perhaps because of their association with Deborah. The reference to Amalek is probably a geographical one. In 12:15 part of Ephraim is called "the hill country of the Amalekites," the former inhabitants of that area.

Makir usually refers to the half-tribe of Manasseh east of the Jordan, but here the western half is clearly intended (Josh 13:30–31) since the battle occurred within its borders.

Zebulun is mentioned in vv.14 and 18 and is highly praised for its bravery. Along with Naphtali, Zebulun had responded to Barak's initial summons (4:10).

**15a** Issachar, located at the eastern end of the Jezreel Valley, also participated enthusiastically as Barak led the charge from Mount Tabor.

**15b–16** Several tribes somewhat distant from the problem area earned the author's wrath for their inactivity. Apparently Reuben at least seriously considered sending some men, for their "searching of heart" is mentioned twice. The tribes from Transjordan had made an important contribution to the conquest under Joshua, but pressure from the Moabites may have influenced Reuben's decision. The mention of campfires and flocks presents a tranquil picture, however, in contrast with war cries and clashing armies.

**17** Gilead was a grandson of Manasseh, but the term "Gilead" is more commonly used as a geographical designation for much of Transjordan. The tribe of Gad possessed most of Gilead (Josh 13:24–25), though the half-tribe of Manasseh also lived there (Josh 13:31). "Reuben" and "Gilead" would thus include all three of the tribes across the Jordan.

The tribe of Dan had encountered difficulty in taking possession of their inheritance ever since the time of Joshua (cf. 1:34). It is not surprising, then, that they did not help solve this largely northern problem. The reference to "ships" implies that Dan had not yet migrated to the north.

Asher, situated along the coast north of Carmel, had also failed to dislodge the

Canaanites. Yet Asher was close enough to the oppressed area to have offered some assistance.

**18** The aloofness of these tribes is sharply contrasted with the wholehearted efforts of Zebulun and Naphtali. The connection of Napthali with the "heights of the field" may stem from the description of that tribe as a "doe set free" in Genesis 49:21.

Judah and Simeon are not mentioned in this catalog of tribes, presumably because of their location far to the south.

## Notes

---

**14** On the difficult expression שָׁרְשָׁם בַּעֲמָלֵק (*šoršām baʿamālēq,* "whose roots were in Amalek"), see Patterson's discussion in "The Song of Deborah," pp. 135–36.

שֵׁבֶט סֹפֵר (*šēḇeṭ sōp̄ēr,* "commander's staff") is literally "the staff of a scribe," implying an officer who recorded the names of the volunteers.

**15** פְּלַגּוֹת (*pᵉlaggôṯ,* "districts") sometimes means "streams" (Job 20:17) that "divide" the terrain. Either meaning fits, though "streams" would blend nicely with the imagery of v.16.

**16** The word מִשְׁפְּתַיִם (*mišpᵉṯayim,* "campfires") is problematic. It appears elsewhere only in Gen 49:14. "Saddlebags" (KB) or "sheep-pens" are other possibilities.

---

### e. *The battle described*

5:19–23

19 "Kings came, they fought;
the kings of Canaan fought
at Taanach by the waters of Megiddo,
but they carried off no silver, no plunder.
20 From the heavens the stars fought,
from their courses they fought against Sisera.
21 The river Kishon swept them away,
the age-old river, the river Kishon.
March on, my soul; be strong!
22 Then thundered the horses' hoofs—
galloping, galloping go his mighty steeds.
23 'Curse Meroz,' said the angel of the LORD.
'Curse its people bitterly,
because they did not come to help the LORD,
to help the LORD against the mighty.'

The vividness of the poetry increases as the author uses repetition, satire, and concrete imagery to paint a lively picture. "Fought" occurs four times; "river" three times; and the words "kings," "Kishon," and "galloping" occur twice. This poetic account should be closely compared with the description of the battle in 4:12–16.

**19** The armies clashed at Taanach, near Megiddo, and the kings of Canaan were supremely confident of victory. With a touch of sarcasm, the author says that this time there was no plunder. They had robbed and oppressed the Israelites for the last time.

**20–22** The Canaanites' downfall came as God intervened. In v.20 the stars are personified, doubtless in reference to the cloudburst sent by the Lord of hosts. The reference to the participation of the stars may be a slap at astrological readings used by the Canaanites. As the rains fell, the river Kishon overflowed its banks; and chariots and riders were swept away (v.21a).

The surging river encouraged the Israelites to "march on" (*dāra<u>k</u>*) in pursuit of the enemy (v.21b). The same word is used of "trampling down" the high places of the enemy in Deuteronomy 33:29 and of "overrunning" the foe in Judges 20:43. The mighty horses of the foe were no match for the people of the "mighty One" of Israel. In the context "thundering hoofs" (cf. v.22) seems to relate to the frantic retreat. Or it may refer generally to the supposedly invincible chariot corps. The repetition of "galloping" (*dahᵃrô<u>t</u>*) in the Hebrew is a striking example of onomatopoeia.

**23** The city of Meroz, perhaps the same as Khirbet Maurus, seven miles south of Kedesh Napthali, came under God's curse for failing to fight. The curse was pronounced by the angel of the Lord, who is mentioned here for the first time since 2:4. Meroz was undoubtedly located in the heart of the oppressed area; so the condemnation of that community was more severe than that of the distant tribes. Since elsewhere in Judges cities refusing to participate in urgent battles were destroyed by the Israelites (8:15–17; 21:8–10), Meroz may have shared the same fate.

## Notes

---

**19** בֶּצַע (*beṣa'*, "plunder") is more precisely "dishonest gain" and is associated with bribes (1 Sam 8:3) and extortion (Jer 22:17).

**21** Cross (*Ancient Yahwistic Poetry*, pp. 35–36) emends the third line, תִּדְרְכִי נַפְשִׁי עֹז (*ti<u>d</u>rᵉ<u>k</u>î na<u>p</u>šî 'ōz*, "March on, my soul; be strong!"), to read *tidrᵉkan(na) paršê 'uzzō* ("his mighty chargers pounded [the ground]"). The "resh" may have been lost by haplography because of its close similarity to "pe" in early Hebrew epigraphy.

**23** "Curse . . . bitterly" is actually a cognate construction, an imperative—ארו (*'ōrû*)—followed by the infinitive absolute—אָרוֹר (*'ārôr*). The form expresses great severity.

---

### f. *Jael praised for her deed*

### 5:24–27

24 "Most blessed of women be Jael,
the wife of Heber the Kenite,
most blessed of tent-dwelling women.
25 He asked for water, and she gave him milk;
in a bowl fit for nobles she brought him curdled milk.
26 Her hand reached for the tent peg,
her right hand for the workman's hammer.
She struck Sisera, she crushed his head,
she shattered and pierced his temple.
27 At her feet he sank,
he fell; there he lay.
At her feet he sank, he fell;
where he sank, there he fell—dead.

**24** In sharp contrast to the curse against Meroz is the blessing reserved for Jael, a woman who refused to remain neutral in this crucial conflict. Probably the blessing is pronounced by the poet rather than the Lord, for Jael's method of disposing of the enemy was certainly questionable (cf. Introduction: Special Problems). The details included in this poetic section have already been discussed in the prose account of 4:19–21.

**25–26** Jael treated Sisera in accord with his "noble" standing (v.25). The same word *'addîr* is used of the nobles of Israel in v.13. But this once magnificent leader was quickly struck down as four powerful verbs in v.26 describe the action. The first verb, "struck" (*hālᵉmāh*), was translated "thundered" when applied to horses' hoofs in v.22. The thundering steeds of Sisera proved no match for the hammering blows of Jael. This heroine is compared to an expert archer also, for the verbs "shattered" and "pierced" are used of arrows in Numbers 24:8 and Job 20:24.

**27** Verse 27 is an outstanding example of climactic parallelism. The words "sank" and "fell" occur three times each, and "feet" occurs twice. This repetition builds up to the final and climactic word of the verse. "Dead" is literally "destroyed" (*šāḏûḏ*). Sisera had been a mighty and devastating force against Israel, but now the destroyer was himself destroyed (cf. Isa 33:1).

## Notes

---

**26** Cross (*Ancient Yahwistic Poetry*, p. 37) revocalizes תִּשְׁלַחְנָה (*tišlaḥnāh*, "reached") to *tišlaḥan(na)*, taking the nun as an energic nun of a singular form.

The word מָחֲקָה (*māḥᵃqāh*, "crushed") appears only here and, joined with מָחֲצָה (*māḥᵃṣāh*, "shattered"), is an effective example of assonance.

**27** The combination כָּרַע נָפַל (*kāra' nāpal*, "he sank, he fell") occurs also in Ps 20:8, where those who depend on horses and chariots fall before those who trust in the Lord.

---

### g. *Sisera's mother's futile wait*

5:28–30

28 "Through the window peered Sisera's mother;
behind the lattice she cried out,
'Why is his chariot so long in coming?
Why is the clatter of his chariots delayed?'
29 The wisest of her ladies answer her;
indeed, she keeps saying to herself,
30 'Are they not finding and dividing the spoils:
a girl or two for each man,
colorful garments as plunder for Sisera,
colorful garments embroidered,
highly embroidered garments for my neck—
all this as plunder?'

**28–30** The scene shifts from Jael's tent to the luxurious home of Sisera. With a skillful, dramatic touch, the author reflects on the agonized waiting of Sisera's mother for the return of her son (v.28). The long delay could mean that the illustrious warrior had tasted defeat, but his mother and her ladies-in-waiting console themselves with visions of plunder (vv.29–30). It was common for soldiers to carry off beautiful maidens as trophies of victory (cf. 21:12). The word for "girl" (*raḥam,* v.30) normally means "womb," brusquely suggesting the lustful treatment each one could expect.

"Garments" (v.30) were a special prize of war (cf. Josh 7:21; Zech 14:14), and Sisera as commander was sure to secure the most beautiful for his family. The "colorful" garments were of dyed material (Job 38:14), and the embroidered cloth was the possession of brides (Ezek 16:10, 13) and princesses (Ps 45:14).

The suffering and longing of Sisera's mother resembles the agony of Hector's wife and mother described in the *Iliad.* Both scenes are moving and powerful.

## Notes

**28** The lapse of time expressed in line three is derived from the Polel form בֹּשֵׁשׁ (*bōšēš,* "so long"), a verb normally meaning "to be ashamed." As in Exod 32:1, it denotes keen disappointment at a lengthy delay.

**30** At the end of the verse, the MT has "for the necks of plunder." The NIV rightly repoints the construct צַוְּארֵי (*ṣawwᵉʾrê*) to צַוָּארַי (*ṣawwᵉʾrî*), meaning "my neck."

### h. *Conclusion*

5:31

> 31 "So may all your enemies perish, O LORD!
> But may they who love you be like the sun
> when it rises in its strength."
>
> Then the land had peace forty years.

**31** As in another song of victory (Ps 68:1–2), there is rejoicing over the fall of the wicked. The language reflects the statement made every time the sacred ark of the covenant was carried into battle (Num 10:35). Reference to the sun and its strength closely parallels Psalm 19:4b–6 and Malachi 4:2.

The stunning defeat of Sisera resulted in forty years of peace for Israel.

## Notes

**31** The NIV follows the Syriac and Vulgate, which have אֹהֲבֶיךָ (*ʾōhᵃḇeyḵā,* "they who love you"). The MT has אֹהֲבָיו (*ʾōhᵃḇāyw,* "they who love him").

### F. *The Victory of Gideon Over the Midianites (6:1–8:32)*

The Gideon cycle, extending to one hundred verses, is the longest segment of the book, with four more verses than those given to the Samson episodes. Chapter 9 might also be counted as part of the Gideon story, since it describes the rule of his son. Under the inspiring leadership of Gideon, the Israelites won a victory even more astonishing than that of Deborah and Barak.

### 1. *Israel's land devastated by the Midianites*

6:1–6

1 Again the Israelites did evil in the eyes of the LORD, and for seven
years he gave them into the hands of the Midianites. 2 Because the
power of Midian was so oppressive, the Israelites prepared shelters for
themselves in mountain clefts, caves and strongholds. 3 Whenever the
Israelites planted their crops, the Midianites, Amalekites and other
eastern peoples invaded the country. 4 They camped on the land and
ruined the crops all the way to Gaza and did not spare a living thing for
Israel, neither sheep nor cattle nor donkeys. 5 They came up with their
livestock and their tents like swarms of locusts. It was impossible to
count the men and their camels; they invaded the land to ravage it.
6 Midian so impoverished the Israelites that they cried out to the LORD for
help.

**1–4** For the fourth time in Judges, the Israelites fell into sin (v.1). This time they found themselves at the mercy of the invading Midianites. These desert dwellers, descended from Abraham and Keturah (Gen 25:2), lived generally to the south of Palestine. They were allied with the Moabites in an attempt to impede the Israelites under Moses (Num 22:7; 25:6), but Moses later routed them (Num 31:8).

Seven years the camel-riding Midianites swept across the Jordan into the Valley of Jezreel at harvest time. With their speedy, wide-ranging mounts, they roamed all the way to Gaza, helping themselves to crops and animals (v.4). The Midianites were joined by the Amalekites—who had earlier assisted King Eglon of Moab (3:12–13)—and by other eastern peoples (v.3). Israel was helpless to resist the invaders and literally took to the hills to save their lives (v.2). It was a time of judgment comparable to the Day of the Lord (Isa 2:12, 19; 9:4).

**5–6** The destruction was so great that it could be described in terms of a plague of locusts or grasshoppers (v.5). Both in numbers and in effect, the invasion of the nomads matched the work of those devastating insects earlier mentioned as the inevitable outcome of disobedience (Deut 28:38; cf. Joel 1:4). Barley and wheat, grapes and olives, the staple products of the land, were no doubt hard hit by this yearly destruction (cf. Joel 1:11). The loss of sheep, cattle, and donkeys was another curse predicted in Deuteronomy 28:31.

The main areas affected were those that had borne the brunt of the preceding Canaanite oppression. Manasseh suffered most, along with the other tribes adjacent to the Jezreel Valley: Asher, Zebulun, and Naphtali (v.35).

## Notes

**3** The "eastern peoples" were the בְּנֵי־קֶדֶם (*b$^{e}$nê-qeḏem,* lit., "the sons of the east"), who lived east and northeast of Palestine (Gen 29:1). It is a general term much like the word "Arabs" in current usage.

**5** A vast army is also compared to locusts in the Ugaritic "Kret Epic," line 103.
**6** The verb דָּלַל (*dālal*, "to impoverish") is the root of the common adjective דַּל (*dal*, "weak," "humble," "poor"), often used of the poor and needy in Israel (Amos 2:7; 4:1). In v.15 it is translated "weakest." The whole country was reduced to poverty.

---

## 2. *Israel's disobedience condemned by a prophet*

### 6:7–10

7 When the Israelites cried to the LORD because of Midian, 8 he sent
them a prophet, who said, "This is what the LORD, the God of Israel, says:
I brought you up out of Egypt, out of the land of slavery. 9 I snatched you
from the power of Egypt and from the hand of all your oppressors. I
drove them from before you and gave you their land. 10 I said to you, 'I
am the LORD your God; do not worship the gods of the Amorites, in
whose land you live.' But you have not listened to me."

**7–10** In their distress the Israelites once more cried out to the Lord (v.7). The last time this happened, God used the prophetess Deborah to bring deliverance (4:3–4). On this occasion the Lord sent a "prophet" (v.8a) to pinpoint the cause of the oppression in words similar to those of the angel of the Lord in 2:1–4.

Once again God reminded the people of their release from Egypt's slavery (vv.8b–9), which should have resulted in perpetual devotion to the Lord. Instead, the Israelites worshiped the gods of the Amorites (v.10a). Here "Amorites" is used generally of all the inhabitants of Palestine (cf. Gen 15:16), though it can sometimes be restricted to the hill country folk (cf. comment on 1:35). Israel refused "to listen to" the Lord (cf. v.10b), a Hebrew idiom for disobedience (cf. 2:2).

### Notes

---

**8** בֵּית עֲבָדִים (*bêṯ ʿᵃḇāḏîm*, "the land of slavery") is literally "the house of slaves." The phrase occurs also in Josh 24:17 and emphasizes the horrible conditions of life in Egypt (cf. Exod 13:3, 14).
**10** יָרֵא (*yārēʾ*, "worship") is literally "fear," expressive of the reverential awe inherent in genuine worship.

---

## 3. *Gideon challenged by the angel of the Lord*

### 6:11–24

11 The angel of the LORD came and sat down under the oak in Ophrah
that belonged to Joash the Abiezrite, where his son Gideon was
threshing wheat in a winepress to keep it from the Midianites. 12 When
the angel of the LORD appeared to Gideon, he said, "The LORD is with
you, mighty warrior."
13 "But sir," Gideon replied, "if the LORD is with us, why has all this
happened to us? Where are all his wonders that our fathers told us
about when they said, 'Did not the LORD bring us up out of Egypt?' But
now the LORD has abandoned us and put us into the hand of Midian."

14 The LORD turned to him and said, "Go in the strength you have and
save Israel out of Midian's hand. Am I not sending you?"
15 "But Lord," Gideon asked, "how can I save Israel? My clan is the
weakest in Manasseh, and I am the least in my family."
16 The LORD answered, "I will be with you, and you will strike down all
the Midianites together."
17 Gideon replied, "If now I have found favor in your eyes, give me a
sign that it is really you talking to me. 18 Please do not go away until I
come back and bring my offering and set it before you."
And the LORD said, "I will wait until you return."
19 Gideon went in, prepared a young goat, and from an ephah of flour
he made bread without yeast. Putting the meat in a basket and its broth
in a pot, he brought them out and offered them to him under the oak.
20 The angel of God said to him, "Take the meat and the unleavened
bread, place them on this rock, and pour out the broth." And Gideon did
so. 21 With the tip of the staff that was in his hand, the angel of the LORD
touched the meat and the unleavened bread. Fire flared from the rock,
consuming the meat and the bread. And the angel of the LORD
disappeared. 22 When Gideon realized that it was the angel of the LORD,
he exclaimed, "Ah, Sovereign LORD! I have seen the angel of the LORD
face to face!"
23 But the LORD said to him, "Peace! Do not be afraid. You are not
going to die."
24 So Gideon built an altar to the LORD there and called it The LORD is
Peace. To this day it stands in Ophrah of the Abiezrites.

**11** The Lord's instrument of deliverance was a young man from the tribe of Manasseh named Gideon. While he was threshing wheat in Ophrah, a site perhaps to be identified with et-Tayibah, eight miles northwest of Beth Shan (1:27), the angel of the Lord appeared to him. The angel sat under the oak tree, or terebinth, located there (cf. 4:5).

To hide the wheat and himself from the Midianites, Gideon was threshing in a winepress, a pit carved out of rocky ground. Normally threshing floors were located in exposed areas so that the wind could easily blow away the chaff.

**12** The angel's words seem out of line with the timid actions of Gideon, and Gideon himself challenged their validity. Actually, the promise of the Lord's presence was intended to encourage Gideon, just as the same assurance led Moses to take the Israelites out of Egypt. "The LORD is with you" is in fact the basic meaning of the name Yahweh (YHWH), revealed to Moses at Mount Sinai (Exod 3:12–14). If God is with us, who can resist us (cf. Isa 7:14; 8:8–10; Rom 8:31)?

Gideon was called a "mighty warrior," perhaps in anticipation of his remarkable bravery. The term *gibbôr heḥāyil* is the familiar "mighty man of valour" of the KJV. Often it is applied to fighting men (Josh 1:14; 10:7), but it can also refer to prominent men of wealth like Boaz in Ruth 2:1 (cf. Armerding, pp. 240–47). Some scholars understand the term to mean the upper class, the warriors who became the landed aristocracy. Gideon did have at least ten servants (v.27), which indicates the status of his father's family.

**13** Gideon did not recognize the visitor and complained that the oppression proved that the Lord was not with Israel. Like the psalmist, Gideon contrasted the miracles everyone had heard about with the current inactivity of the Lord (Ps 44:1–3, 9–16). Apparently Gideon was unaware of the prophet's explanation in vv.8–10.

**14** Here the heavenly guest is identified as the Lord himself, and something of his glory may have been revealed as he turned to face Gideon. The Lord was sending Gideon, as he had sent Moses (Exod 3:12) and would later send Isaiah (Isa 6:8–9). The strength Gideon possessed was the promise of the Lord's presence with him. Gideon could exchange his weakness for God's strength.

**15** It is difficult to know whether to translate *'ᵃḏōnāy* ("adonay") "sir" or "Lord," for it can mean either; and Gideon gradually came to recognize the supernatural character of the visitor. Gideon's excuses resemble the reluctance of Moses (Exod 3:11) or Saul (1 Sam 9:21). Gideon belonged to the weak clan of Abiezer, and his own position in his family division was not a prominent one. Yet the Bible contains many illustrations of the elevation to leadership of unlikely candidates such as Jephthah or David. God delights to use those who are young or humble and bring them to prominence (see 1 Cor 1:26–27).

**16** Gideon's fears were somewhat relieved by the reassurance that with the Lord's help the Midianites could be defeated. The comparison with "but one man" (*kᵉ'îš 'eḥāḏ;* NIV, "together") may mean that Gideon would conquer them as easily as one person can be eliminated or that they would fall all at once (i.e., at the same time). See Numbers 14:15 for the same idiom.

**17–21** To make sure of divine approval, Gideon requested that his guest perform a miraculous sign (v.17), the first of three signs Gideon was to see. He wanted proof that God or his messenger was really talking to him. First, however, Gideon received permission to bring his guest an offering (v.18).

Since "offering" (v.18) can mean "gift," the food prepared by Gideon was partially an expression of hospitality. In 13:15–20 Samson's parents cooked a young goat as a meal for their unknown guest, though the angel turned it into a burnt offering. Unleavened bread (v.19) is, of course, involved in many offerings; but it is sometimes served in quickly prepared meals (Gen 19:3). This was a substantial meal for such a time of scarcity, since the "ephah" of flour was about half a bushel. The angel instructed Gideon (v.20) to use the rock—perhaps part of the winepress—as an altar. The fiery consumption of the meat and bread indicated the acceptance of Gideon's offering and, together with the disappearance of the angel, provided the sign Gideon was seeking (v.21).

**22–24** Gideon's response was one of fright, however, for he knew that no one could see God face to face and live (v.22; Exod 33:20). Samson's parents expected a similar fate after an angelic visit (13:22). In both cases, however, the theophany brought blessing, not death. Gideon was quickly assured that he would live, since the Lord promised him "peace" (*šālôm*) and well being ("you are not going to die," v.23). This peace included not only his personal welfare but also the restoration of Israel's freedom and prosperity. Gratefully, Gideon built an altar to commemorate the Lord's promise (v.24).

## Notes

---

**11** גִּדְעוֹן (*giḏ'ôn,* "Gideon") is an unusual name. The closest to it is גִּדְעֹנִי (*giḏ'ōnî,* "Gideoni"), whose son Abidan was the leader of the tribe of Benjamin (Num 1:11; 2:22).

**13** נִפְלְאֹת (*nipleʾōṯ*), the word for "wonders," contains the root for the name given to the angel of the Lord in 13:18: פִּלְאִי (*pilʾî*, "beyond understanding," "wonderful"). Gideon himself witnessed a miracle performed by this wonder-working God.

**15** אֶלֶף (*ʾelep̱*, "clan") is literally "thousand." It means "clans" also in Num 1:16 and Josh 22:14. Apparently it is a synonym for מִשְׁפָּחָה (*mišpāḥāh*, "family," "tribe").

**19** The word מָרָק (*mārāq*, "broth") appears elsewhere only in Isa 65:4, with reference to eating the broth of unclean meat in pagan rituals.

---

## 4. *The altar of Baal destroyed and Gideon's life imperiled*

### 6:25–32

25That same night the LORD said to him, "Take the second bull from
your father's herd, the one seven years old. Tear down your father's altar
to Baal and cut down the Asherah pole beside it. 26Then build a proper
kind of altar to the LORD your God on the top of this height. Using the
wood of the Asherah pole that you cut down, offer the second bull as a
burnt offering."
27So Gideon took ten of his servants and did as the LORD told him. But
because he was afraid of his family and the men of the town, he did it at
night rather than in the daytime.
28In the morning when the men of the town got up, there was Baal's
altar, demolished, with the Asherah pole beside it cut down and the
second bull sacrificed on the newly built altar!
29They asked each other, "Who did this?"
When they carefully investigated, they were told, "Gideon son of
Joash did it."
30The men of the town demanded of Joash, "Bring out your son. He
must die, because he has broken down Baal's altar and cut down the
Asherah pole beside it."
31But Joash replied to the hostile crowd around him, "Are you going
to plead Baal's cause? Are you trying to save him? Whoever fights for
him shall be put to death by morning! If Baal really is a god, he can
defend himself when someone breaks down his altar." 32So that day
they called Gideon "Jerub-Baal," saying, "Let Baal contend with him,"
because he broke down Baal's altar.

**25–26** Almost immediately the Lord asked Gideon to respond to his call to deliver Israel from Midian by taking decisive action in his own family (v.25). Even his father had espoused the Baal cult, leading the community in the worship of this pagan deity. Through Moses, God had said that altars to Baal and their accompanying Asherahs (see comment on 3:7) must be torn down (Exod 34:12–13; Deut 7:5; cf. Judg 2:2). Baal worship was popular, however, and Gideon knew he was risking his life by obeying the Lord.

Part of Gideon's task was to sacrifice a bull on a new altar dedicated to the Lord. Bull worship was closely associated with Baal and his father, El, and this particular bull was doubtless reserved for the Baal cult. There is a question as to whether one or two bulls are referred to in v.25. The Hebrew text mentions "the second bull, the one seven years old," perhaps corresponding to the seven years of the oppression. The NASB renders v.25 thus: "Take your father's bull and a second bull seven years old." But "second" is translated "full-grown" (cf. NIV mg.) by some scholars and taken in apposition to the first bull. If two bulls were intended, one might have been used to break down the pagan altar.

The altar of the Lord was to be set up on top of a "height" (v.26, i.e., a "bluff" or "stronghold"), a prominent place where the city residents may have found refuge from the Midianites. Pieces of wood from the sacred pole would supply fuel for the burnt offering.

**27–30** Gideon followed the Lord's orders at night (v.27), correctly anticipating that his deeds would arouse the anger of the populace and his own relatives. Apparently one of Gideon's ten servants revealed the identity of Baal's enemy to the townspeople, and they demanded Gideon's death (vv.29–30). How different from Deuteronomy 13:6–10, where Moses commanded that even close relatives must be stoned for idolatry! The heresy had become the main religion.

**31** Joash refused to put his son to death, arguing that a deity like Baal could defend himself. To interfere was an insult to Baal punishable by death. Joash's seemingly honest appeal to Baal may reflect his own doubt in the power of a deity who could not deliver them from the Midianites.

**32** Gideon was probably called "Jerub-Baal" as a derogatory name, indicating the certain judgment the people expected him to face. When no harm came to him, the name became a reminder of Gideon's great victory over Baal.

## Notes

---

**25** The name of Gideon's father, יוֹאָשׁ (*yô'āš*, "Joash"), contains the "Yahweh" element in the first syllable. This may mean that a syncretism between the worship of Yahweh and Baal was practiced. Even Ahab, an avowed worshiper of Baal, named his sons Ahaziah and Jehoram, both compounded with "Yahweh."

The evidence for "full-grown" (NIV mg.) comes from the Arabic *taniyun* (KB, p. 998), which could correspond to שָׁנִי (*šānî*). The MT has the common שֵׁנִי (*šēnî*), meaning "second."

**32** The name "Jerub-Baal" becomes "Jerub-Besheth" in 2 Sam 11:21. Other names containing Baal were also changed later on. "Ish-Baal" ("man of Baal") is better known as "Ish-Bosheth," meaning "man of shame" (2 Sam 3:14). "Jerub" comes from the root רִיב (*rîḇ*), which is translated "plead [Baal's] cause," "fights [for him]," and "defend [himself]" in v.31. When Baal could not defend himself, he was proven to be a weak god indeed.

---

### 5. *Gideon's army*

#### 6:33–35

[33]Now all the Midianites, Amalekites and other eastern peoples joined
forces and crossed over the Jordan and camped in the Valley of Jezreel.
[34]Then the Spirit of the LORD came upon Gideon, and he blew a trumpet,
summoning the Abiezrites to follow him. [35]He sent messengers throughout Manasseh, calling them to arms, and also into Asher, Zebulun and
Naphtali, so that they too went up to meet them.

**33** The crisis in Ophrah was soon eclipsed by the annual invasion of the Midianite coalition. This was their eighth incursion into the fertile Valley of Jezreel, and it came during the wheat harvest in May or June (v.11).

**34–35** This time, however, the enemy was not to feast without a fight. The Spirit of the Lord came on Gideon, already encouraged by his initial obedience. Literally the Spirit "clothed" (v.34; NIV, "came upon") Gideon, an idiom used of Zechariah son of Jehoiada, who condemned the idolatry of King Joash and was killed for his boldness (2 Chron 24:20–21). Isaiah 51:9 speaks of being "clothe[d] . . . with strength," and apparently the power of the Spirit is in view in Judges also (cf. Luke 24:49).

Like Ehud (3:27), Gideon sounded the trumpet of alarm to gather the troops (v.35). The men of his own clan of Abiezer were the first to follow him—an indication that they now shared Gideon's attitude toward Baalism. Then the rest of Manasseh and the other northern tribes came to oppose the Midianites. Ephraim was not invited, perhaps because Gideon feared that this powerful "brother" tribe would not accept his leadership (cf. 1:22; 8:1–3).

## Notes

---

**34** The only other example of being "clothed" with the Spirit occurs in 1 Chron 12:18 (19 MT), where Amasai is inspired to speak in support of David. Also see 3:10 and the Introduction: Special Problems.

---

### 6. *The fleece*

#### 6:36–40

36Gideon said to God, "If you will save Israel by my hand as you have
promised—37look, I will place a wool fleece on the threshing floor. If
there is dew only on the fleece and all the ground is dry, then I will know
that you will save Israel by my hand, as you said." 38And that is what
happened. Gideon rose early the next day; he squeezed the fleece and
wrung out the dew—a bowlful of water.

39Then Gideon said to God, "Do not be angry with me. Let me make
just one more request. Allow me one more test with the fleece. This time
make the fleece dry and the ground covered with dew." 40That night
God did so. Only the fleece was dry; all the ground was covered with
dew.

**36–38** Gideon's confidence in God's promises was far from complete and needed to be bolstered frequently. As in the previous instance (v.17), Gideon again asked for a sign to confirm God's favor and word (v.36). His request resembles the behavior of Abraham's servant, who also made rather presumptuous demands of the Lord to be sure of the will of God (Gen 24:12–14). Gideon felt that if the fleece only was wet with dew (v.37) and not the surrounding ground, that meant the Lord was with him. As Gideon requested, so it was: the fleece was saturated with dew (v.38), but the ground was dry.

**39–40** The wool fleece would absorb the dew more readily than the hard ground of the threshing floor; so the second test required an even greater miracle (v.39). The dry fleece was strong evidence of God's hand (v.40). When Gideon made the second request, he knew the Lord would be unhappy with his weak faith. The wording of v.39 is remarkably close to Abraham's final plea as he interceded on behalf of Sodom (Gen 18:32).

Like Gideon, many a modern-day believer whose faith needs bolstering has "put out the fleece" to help him find the Lord's will. If this "fleece" consists of a careful observation and interpretation of God's leading through circumstances, the procedure can be a healthy one. But Gideon's method was to make purely arbitrary demands of God and insist on immediate guidance. Such an approach can hardly be recommended for Christians today. In Luke 1:18 Zechariah, the father of John the Baptist, doubted the words of Gabriel and was struck dumb (v.20). Despite Gideon's lack of faith and insistence on a second sign, God in mercy not only chose to withhold punishment but condescended to answer him.

### 7. *Gideon's army reduced*

#### 7:1–8a

1 Early in the morning, Jerub-Baal (that is, Gideon) and all his men
camped at the spring of Harod. The camp of Midian was north of them
in the valley near the hill of Moreh. 2 The LORD said to Gideon, "You have
too many men for me to deliver Midian into their hands. In order that
Israel may not boast against me that her own strength has saved her,
3 announce now to the people, 'Anyone who trembles with fear may turn
back and leave Mount Gilead.'" So twenty-two thousand men left, while
ten thousand remained.

4 But the LORD said to Gideon, "There are still too many men. Take
them down to the water, and I will sift them for you there. If I say, 'This
one shall go with you,' he shall go; but if I say, 'This one shall not go
with you,' he shall not go."

5 So Gideon took the men down to the water. There the LORD told him,
"Separate those who lap the water with their tongues like a dog from
those who kneel down to drink." 6 Three hundred men lapped with their
hands to their mouths. All the rest got down on their knees to drink.

7 The LORD said to Gideon, "With the three hundred men that lapped I
will save you and give the Midianites into your hands. Let all the other
men go, each to his own place." 8 So Gideon sent the rest of the
Israelites to their tents but kept the three hundred, who took over the
provisions and trumpets of the others.

**1** With his hastily assembled army, Gideon set up camp at En-Harod, the "spring of trembling," probably the modern ʿAin Jalud at the foot of Mount Gilboa. The Midianite hordes were located some four miles north of them in the Jezreel Valley, at a place about ten miles west of the Jordan. The invaders knew about this 32,000-man army and their leader (v.14), but apparently they did not view them as a serious threat.

**2–3** The Lord's instructions (v.2) probably came as a surprise to Gideon, who was already outnumbered four to one. But the size of the army was not the crucial factor: God could give victory to a few men as easily as to a large army (1 Sam 14:6). Lest Israel take credit for her achievements, the Lord began to remove all ground for boasting.

The first stage in the troop reduction was to allow the cowardly to go back home (v.3). Their fear might prove contagious and ruin the campaign. Indeed, Deuteronomy 20:8 specifies this exact procedure. More than two-thirds of Gideon's army took the chance to disengage themselves.

**4–6** The Lord, however, informed Gideon that the army had to be reduced even further (v.4). A special "screening" was set up based on the way the 10,000 drank water (v.5). This strange procedure netted a total of 300 men who apparently crouched down to scoop up water by using their hands as a dog uses its tongue (v.6). All the others dropped to their knees before drinking.

**7–8a** Possibly the 300 displayed a greater alertness in staying on their feet, but in actuality they may have been no more courageous than the 9,700 others. When v.8a says that Gideon "kept" (*heḥ*$^e$*zîq b*$^e$, lit., "to take fast hold") the 300, it implies that they too had a strong urge to vanish with their colleagues. This idiom is used again in 19:4, where a man is detained against his will, and in Exodus 9:2 Pharaoh forcibly "held on to" (NIV, "continue to hold") his Hebrew slaves. The idiom occurs also in Job 2:9, where Job's wife asks, "Are you still holding on to your integrity?" If these 300 men were beginning to tremble, the need for God's intervention became even greater.

Before departing the 9,700 gave the remaining soldiers their provisions and their trumpets. The large number of trumpets that Gideon acquired (cf. v.18) implies that a surprise attack was in the planning. The provisions were probably kept in the jugs that were later used so strategically.

## Notes

**3** The expression וַיִּצְפֹּר מֵהַר הַגִּלְעָד (*w*$^e$*yiṣpōr mēhar haggil'āḏ*, "and leave Mount Gilead") is difficult. The verb translated "leave" is a *hapax legomenon* (it occurs only here in the Bible). Moreover Mount Gilead is located on the wrong side of the Jordan. Some authorities understand it as a scribal error for "Gilboa," where the army was situated. Since Gilead was a grandson of Manasseh (Josh 17:3), the name could have been used in both sectors of that tribe's inheritance. In 5:14 the name "Makir" is applied atypically to part of Manasseh west of the Jordan.

**4** "Sift" is from the root צרף (*ṣārap̱*), which normally means "to test" or "refine" metals by smelting.

**8a** The mention of "tents" does not mean that the Israelites were not yet living in houses. The expression "to your tents" was still used after Solomon's time (1 Kings 12:16). Also see the Notes on 19:8.

### 8. *Gideon's victory confirmed by a dream*

7:8b–14

Now the camp of Midian lay below him in the valley. 9 During that night
the LORD said to Gideon, "Get up, go down against the camp, because I
am going to give it into your hands. 10 If you are afraid to attack, go
down to the camp with your servant Purah 11 and listen to what they are

**saying. Afterward, you will be encouraged to attack the camp." So he**
**and Purah his servant went down to the outposts of the camp. 12The**
**Midianites, the Amalekites and all the other eastern peoples had settled**
**in the valley, thick as locusts. Their camels could no more be counted**
**than the sand on the seashore.**
**13Gideon arrived just as a man was telling a friend his dream. "I had a**
**dream," he was saying. "A round loaf of barley bread came tumbling**
**into the Midianite camp. It struck the tent with such force that the tent**
**overturned and collapsed."**
**14His friend responded, "This can be nothing other than the sword of**
**Gideon son of Joash, the Israelite. God has given the Midianites and the**
**whole camp into his hands."**

**8b–11** With less than 1 percent of his original army, Gideon's faith again began to waver. For the third time God gave him a sign, and at last Gideon was thoroughly convinced (vv.9–10). Any promise of action repeated three times was regarded as the surest confirmation (16:15; Num 24:10). Before he attacked, Gideon and his aide Purah, who was probably his armor-bearer (9:54), paid a visit to the Midianite camp (v.11). What he was to hear would "strengthen his hands" (NIV, "be encouraged," v.11 [lit., "your hands will be strong"]), a Hebrew idiom for encouragement (1 Sam 23:16 [NIV, "find strength"]).

**12** At first the view was disconcerting, for the foe seemed innumerable (cf. Josh 11:4; 1 Sam 13:5). The descendants of Abraham also had been described in similar terms (Gen 22:17). On this occasion, however, Gideon could count the available Israelites all too easily.

**13–14** Gideon and his servant overheard two of the enemy soldiers discussing a dream (v.13). In the ancient world dreams were considered an important means of divine communication, particularly to leaders, and God used them often in the OT (1 Sam 28:6). He spoke to the Philistine king Abimelech in a dream (Gen 20:3–6), and the end of Genesis contains several symbolic dreams (37:6–7; 40:8–19; 41:1–32). Joseph's skill as an interpreter of dreams was matched by the enemy soldier's ability to predict the victory of Gideon (v.14).

Barley bread (v.13) could represent Israel as a cultivator of the soil. It was a staple food of the poorer classes, to which virtually the entire nation belonged. The key to the interpretation of the dream is that the word translated "tumbling" (*miṯhappēḵ*) can be applied also to swords. It literally means "overturning," and the feminine form is used of the flaming sword, "which turned every direction" (NASB), wielded by the angel at the entrance to the Garden of Eden (Gen 3:24). The verb "overturned" in v.13 is from the same root (*hāp̱aḵ*) and describes the overthrow of Sodom and Gomorrah (Gen 19:21, 25, 29). The "overturning" or "overthrow" of the tent represented the collapse of the nomadic forces.

## Notes

11 קְצֵה הַחֲמֻשִׁים (*qeṣēh haḥamušîm*, "outposts") is literally "the edge of the armed men." This obscure word for "soldiers" also occurs in Josh 1:14.

12 On the significance of "grasshoppers" or "locusts," see the comment on 6:5.
13 The meaning "round loaf" is uncertain since צְלִיל (*ṣᵉlîl*) is a *hapax legomenon;* KB suggests "slice of bread, disk."

The Hithpael מִתְהַפֵּךְ (*miṯhappēḵ,* "tumbling") need not represent precisely the same kind of motion when applied to a sword, but some sort of continual turning is meant.

---

## 9. *Preparation for the battle*

### 7:15–18

[15]When Gideon heard the dream and its interpretation, he worshiped God. He returned to the camp of Israel and called out, "Get up! The LORD has given the Midianite camp into your hands." [16]Dividing the three hundred men into three companies, he placed trumpets and empty jars in the hands of all of them, with torches inside.

[17]"Watch me," he told them. "Follow my lead. When I get to the edge of the camp, do exactly as I do. [18]When I and all who are with me blow our trumpets, then from all around the camp blow yours and shout, 'For the LORD and for Gideon.'"

**15** Gideon realized that what he had heard was far more than a coincidence; so he immediately prostrated himself in grateful worship before the Lord. Gideon was ready to fight and returned to prepare his men for the historic battle. Perhaps he shared with them the dream he had just overheard.

**16–18** The only orthodox part of Gideon's instructions was to divide the men into three groups (v.16). Saul and David later used the same successful strategy (1 Sam 11:11; 2 Sam 18:2). By spreading out around the Midianites, Gideon's troops would create the impression of being a much larger army.

The "trumpets" (*šôp̱ārôṯ,* "shofars") were the same ram's horn type used by Ehud and Gideon to summon the troops. Their value was not as musical instruments but as noise-making devices. Only the leaders would give signals on the trumpets; so three hundred trumpets normally represented a sizable army. When Joshua captured Jericho, only seven priests had trumpets (Josh 6:6).

The empty jars were used to hide the light of the torches until the proper moment arrived. Samson also used torches to frustrate the enemy in 15:4–5. The soldiers may have been mystified as to the actual purpose of such unusual weapons, but their orders were to follow Gideon's example carefully (v.17). After blowing the trumpets, they were to shout the war cry (v.18), given in its full form in v.20. The sequence of trumpet blast and war cry was also used at Jericho.

## Notes

---

**15** שֶׁבֶר (*šeḇer,* "interpretation") literally means "breaking," as one would "break a code."

The word for "worship" is a Hishtaphel form from the root חוה (*ḥwh*). It means "to fall face down to the ground" (cf. 2:12, 17, 19; Josh 5:14).

---

## 10. *The Midianites routed*

### 7:19–25

**19 Gideon and the hundred men with him reached the edge of the
camp at the beginning of the middle watch, just after they had changed
the guard. They blew their trumpets and broke the jars that were in their
hands. 20 The three companies blew the trumpets and smashed the jars.
Grasping the torches in their left hands and holding in their right hands
the trumpets they were to blow, they shouted, "A sword for the LORD and
for Gideon!" 21 While each man held his position around the camp, all
the Midianites ran, crying out as they fled.**

**22 When the three hundred trumpets sounded, the LORD caused the
men throughout the camp to turn on each other with their swords. The
army fled to Beth Shittah toward Zererah as far as the border of Abel
Meholah near Tabbath. 23 Israelites from Naphtali, Asher and all Manasseh were called out, and they pursued the Midianites. 24 Gideon sent
messengers throughout the hill country of Ephraim, saying, "Come
down against the Midianites and seize the waters of the Jordan ahead of
them as far as Beth Barah."**

**So all the men of Ephraim were called out and they took the waters of
the Jordan as far as Beth Barah. 25 They also captured two of the
Midianite leaders, Oreb and Zeeb. They killed Oreb at the rock of Oreb,
and Zeeb at the winepress of Zeeb. They pursued the Midianites and
brought the heads of Oreb and Zeeb to Gideon, who was by the Jordan.**

**19–20** Gideon and his men disrupted the Midianite camp sometime between ten o'clock and midnight, striking just after new guards had been posted (v.19). The guards were not ready to respond alertly to the commotion that developed. The Israelites' main weapon was noise; and between the trumpet blasts and the smashing of jars, they achieved the intended effect of demoralizing the Midianites. Once the jars were broken, three hundred torches lit up the night, apparently at the head of vast columns of troops. To add to the nightmare, a ringing battle cry pierced the night air (v.20).

**21–22** These startling developments quickly produced panic (v.21), a normal occurrence when God led his people into battle (cf. comment on 4:15–16 and Peter C. Craigie, *The Book of Deuteronomy*, NICOT [Grand Rapids: Eerdmans, 1976], p. 270). The Midianites were convinced that a powerful army was about to massacre them. According to v.21, the people ran about, shouting and trying to escape as fast as possible. In all the confusion they began fighting among themselves, thinking that enemy forces were already in their camp (v.22). Finally, to avoid the slaughter, the Midianite hordes fled toward the Jordan and the safety of the desert beyond.

The rout of the Midianites was not the first time that the element of surprise had been effectively used by Israel. Joshua had defeated an Amorite coalition after an all-night march (Josh 10:9). Several centuries later a Syrian army abandoned the siege of Samaria because the Lord produced the noise of thundering horses and chariots (2 Kings 7:6–7). These sound effects sent them fleeing into the night like the Midianites.

King Jehoshaphat likewise led an Israelite army that watched the enemy destroy itself. The greatly outnumbered Judean forces stood as motionless as Gideon's three hundred while civil war raged among an enemy coalition (2 Chron 20:17, 22–23).

The Midianites' line of flight was toward the southeast, past Beth Shan and across the Jordan. The location of the places mentioned in v.22 is uncertain, though Zererah may be the same as Zerethan, ten miles south of Jabesh Gilead. Abel Meholah was the hometown of Elisha (1 Kings 19:16), but this may be a different site with the same name in Transjordan.

**23–25** To help in the pursuit, Gideon summoned reinforcements (v.23), perhaps including many of his original 32,000. Their courage restored, they gladly rushed after the foe. Gideon also called on the powerful tribe of Ephraim to cut off the Midianites at the fords of the Jordan (v.24; cf. 3:28). Many of the enemy forces had not yet crossed when the men of Ephraim attacked them and captured Oreb (meaning "raven") and Zeeb ("wolf"), probably leading generals of the army (v.25). The two were promptly put to death at sites later named to commemorate the occasion. The "rock of Oreb" is mentioned again in Isaiah 10:26 in connection with the slaughter of Midian. When the Ephraimites met with Gideon in 8:1–3, they brought along the heads of the vanquished enemies.

## Notes

---

**22** The phenomenon of allied armies fighting among themselves also characterizes the eschatological wars against Gog (Ezek 38:18–21) and the armies surrounding Jerusalem (Zech 14:13–14) at the second coming of Christ.

**25** The relationship between the two "princes" (שָׂרִים [*śārîm*]), Oreb and Zeeb, and the two kings (מְלָכִים [*melāḵîm*]), Zebah and Zalmunna, may be the same as that between Sisera and Jabin. The same words are used in 4:2 for the Canaanite commander and king.

Gideon was probably east of the Jordan already. "By" is מֵעֵבֶר לְ (*mē'ēḇer le*, lit., "across"), which usually means Transjordan (Josh 13:32).

---

### 11. *The Ephraimites' complaint*

### 8:1–3

[1]Now the Ephraimites asked Gideon, "Why have you treated us like this? Why didn't you call us when you went to fight Midian?" And they criticized him sharply.

[2]But he answered them, "What have I accomplished compared to you? Aren't the gleanings of Ephraim's grapes better than the full grape harvest of Abiezer? [3]God gave Oreb and Zeeb, the Midianite leaders, into your hands. What was I able to do compared to you?" At this, their resentment against him subsided.

**1–3** The tribe of Ephraim had a proud heritage (see comment on 1:22) and felt insulted by Gideon's failure to call on them earlier (v.1). They had cooperated honorably with Ehud (3:26–29) and Barak (5:13–14a) and wondered why they were left out this time. Perhaps they were eager for some of the rich Midianite plunder that went to the victor.

Gideon might have questioned the Ephraimites' motives by asking them why they had not taken action on their own during the long seven-year oppression; but, unlike Jephthah (12:1–3), he adopted a course of appeasement. He praised them for their great victory over Oreb and Zeeb, assuring them that in comparison his accomplishments were small (vv.2–3). In a sense Ephraim received the "leftovers" (NIV, "gleanings"). These, however, were more substantial than the initial victory ("harvest") won by his little Abiezrite clan. Gideon's flattery calmed their anger and avoided the civil war that later flared up between Ephraim and Manasseh (12:4–6). His wise action admirably illustrates Proverbs 15:1: "A gentle answer turns away wrath."

## Notes

---

1 The word רִיב (*rîḇ*, "criticize") is also used of Israel's vigorous complaining to Moses in Num 20:3 (NIV, "quarreled"). The same root is part of Gideon's alternate name "Jerub-Baal" (6:32). See James Limburg, "The Root רִיב (*rîḇ*) and the Prophetic Lawsuit Speeches," JBL 88 (1969): 293–94, 297–99.

3 רוּחַ (*rû$^a$ḥ*, "resentment") is literally "spirit." It has the connotation of "temper" also in Prov 16:32 and Eccl 10:4.

---

## 12. *Lack of cooperation from Succoth and Peniel*

### 8:4–9

4 Gideon and his three hundred men, exhausted yet keeping up the
pursuit, came to the Jordan and crossed it. 5 He said to the men of
Succoth, "Give my troops some bread; they are worn out, and I am still
pursuing Zebah and Zalmunna, the kings of Midian."
6 But the officials of Succoth said, "Do you already have the hands of
Zebah and Zalmunna in your possession? Why should we give bread to
your troops?"
7 Then Gideon replied, "Just for that, when the LORD has given Zebah
and Zalmunna into my hand, I will tear your flesh with desert thorns and
briers."
8 From there he went up to Peniel and made the same request of them,
but they answered as the men of Succoth had. 9 So he said to the men of
Peniel, "When I return in triumph, I will tear down this tower."

**4–6** The chronological relationship between vv.1–3 and 4–9 is unclear. In any event, this new paragraph shifts back to the exploits of the "three hundred" (v.4). Gideon is faced with an attitude exactly the opposite of Ephraim's as two cities completely rejected his request for help (vv.5–6). The tiny army was now some forty miles from the hill of Moreh when they came to Succoth, just north of the Jabbok River. Worn out from the long chase, Gideon asked these residents of Gad for some provisions. The men of Succoth reasoned that the fleeing Midianites would soon regroup and easily defeat the makeshift army thrown together by Gideon. Any assistance given to Gideon would implicate Succoth and bring certain retaliation from the feared nomads.

The question in v.6 apparently refers to the custom of cutting off the hands of dead victims as a convenient body count. Saul required David to produce one hundred Philistine foreskins to prove he had killed that number (1 Sam 18:25; cf. Judg 1:6).

**7** The sarcastic, unpatriotic response of the leaders of Succoth brought a sharp retort from Gideon. Perhaps the tribes of Transjordan could be excused for failing to aid Deborah and Barak (5:17), but neutrality was impossible when the conflict was on their soil (cf. 5:23). Gideon promised that when he returned in victory, he would severely punish the city.

**8–9** Moving six miles east, Gideon received the same response from the people of Peniel (v.8). In the very place where Jacob had met with God and had his name changed to Israel (Gen 32:28–30), these descendants of his refused to believe that God could give victory over the Midianites. Gideon vowed that he would soon demolish the fortified tower that had made Peniel an important city (v.9).

## Notes

---

5 זֶבַח (*ze<u>b</u>ah*, "Zebah") means sacrifice, implying that he was born on the day of an important sacrifice (KB). The significance of Zalmunna is uncertain.

6 The word כַּף (*kap*) is often translated "palm." Here it is treated as a collective noun: "hands."

7 The exact nature of the punishment is unclear. דּוּשׁ (*dûš*, "tear") usually means "thresh," and it may indicate that the victims were dragged over thorns or laid on thorns. In Amos 1:3, Damascus is condemned for threshing Gilead with iron instruments.

9 שָׁלוֹם (*šālôm*, "triumph") means "peace." Gideon was to win a complete victory over Midian, but it meant anything but "peace" for Peniel.

---

## 13. *The capture of the kings of Midian*

### 8:10–12

**10Now Zebah and Zalmunna were in Karkor with a force of about fifteen thousand men, all that were left of the armies of the eastern peoples; a hundred and twenty thousand swordsmen had fallen. 11Gideon went up by the route of the nomads east of Nobah and Jogbehah and fell upon the unsuspecting army. 12Zebah and Zalmunna, the two kings of Midian, fled, but he pursued them and captured them, routing their entire army.**

**10–12** True to his word, Gideon pressed farther into Transjordan, following the caravan trail taken by the Midianites. By this time the remnants of the Midianite army were in Karkor (v.10), located perhaps in the Wadi Sirhan, east of the Dead Sea. Gideon passed Jogbehah (v.11), about fifteen miles southeast of Peniel and seven miles northwest of modern Amman. No doubt the Midianites believed they were safely out of range of the pursuing armies, but again Gideon surprised them and routed them (v.12).

Gideon's main goal was the capture of Midian's two kings, for without leadership the eastern hordes were not likely to resume their raids to the west. The two kings probably belonged to different tribal groups. Multiple rule in Midian was also the practice earlier, for Moses killed five Midianite kings (Num 31:7–8).

## Notes

**11–12** הֶחֱרִיד (*heheriḏ*, "routing") is more precisely "terrifying." The entire conflict began at "the spring of Harod" (7:1), where Gideon's men "trembled with fear" (חָרֵד [*ḥārēḏ*, cf. v.3]—cognate to this verb). How fitting that it should end with a terror-stricken Midian! The Hiphil is also used of an exhausted, easily frightened army in 2 Sam 17:2. It is associated with a "complacent" (בֶּטַח [*beṭah*], as in v.11) people in Ezek 30:9.

## 14. *Retaliation against Succoth and Peniel*

### 8:13–17

[13]Gideon son of Joash then returned from the battle by the Pass of Heres. [14]He caught a young man of Succoth and questioned him, and the young man wrote down for him the names of the seventy-seven officials of Succoth, the elders of the town. [15]Then Gideon came and said to the men of Succoth, "Here are Zebah and Zalmunna, about whom you taunted me by saying, 'Do you already have the hands of Zebah and Zalmunna in your possession? Why should we give bread to your exhausted men?'" [16]He took the elders of the town and taught the men of Succoth a lesson by punishing them with desert thorns and briers. [17]He also pulled down the tower of Peniel and killed the men of the town.

**13–17** The resounding victory over Midian did not deter Gideon from severely disciplining these two delinquent cities. He returned to Succoth "by the Pass of Heres" (v.13), meaning the pass of the "sun" (cf. comment on 1:35). A young man from Succoth was compelled to write down the names of the "princes" or "elders" (v.14). Unless this youth was a scribe, his ability to write attests to a high degree of popular literacy. He may have scratched the names on a piece of pottery.

The seventy-seven men who were registered on this death list heard Gideon repeat their earlier taunt before carrying out the punishment (v.15). Like their neighbors in Peniel, the men of Succoth doubtless died for their guilt (vv.16–17).

## Notes

**14** A. Demsky and M. Kochavi argue that the "young man" was probably a local official familiar with the names of the taxpayers (cf. "An Alphabet From the Days of the Judges," *Biblical Archaeology Review* 4, 3 [Sept–Oct 1978]: 28).

**16** The form ידע (*yōḏa'*), translated "taught . . . a lesson," is disputed. Some ancient versions favor יָדָשׁ (*yāḏāš*, "thresh"), which would agree with v.7. But the versions are not unanimous, and the Hiphil of ידע also occurs in Num 16:5, where Korah received his final "lesson" from the Lord.

**17** The word נָתַץ (*nāṯaṣ*, "pulled down") is the same one used when Gideon "broke down" the altar of Baal (6:31–32). Gideon felt a divine compelling in both cases. The defiance of the altars was interpreted as a חֵרֵף (*ḥērēp̱*, "taunt"; cf. v.15), not only against him, but against the living God (cf. Isa 37:4, 17).

## 15. *The Midianite kings slain*

### 8:18–21

[18]Then he asked Zebah and Zalmunna, "What kind of men did you kill
at Tabor?"
"Men like you," they answered, "each one with the bearing of a
prince."
[19]Gideon replied, "Those were my brothers, the sons of my own
mother. As surely as the LORD lives, if you had spared their lives, I would
not kill you." [20]Turning to Jether, his oldest son, he said, "Kill them!"
But Jether did not draw his sword, because he was only a boy and was
afraid.
[21]Zebah and Zalmunna said, "Come, do it yourself. 'As is the man, so
is his strength.'" So Gideon stepped forward and killed them, and took
the ornaments off their camels' necks.

**18** The scene probably shifts across the Jordan, so that Gideon could display his captives to the main body of Israelites. The presence of his young son, Jether, who likely did not accompany his father in the rigorous pursuit, also points to a location nearer home. After viewing the vengeance taken by Gideon on fellow Israelites, the Midianite kings did not hold out much hope for their own survival. In fact, they seemed to prefer death by admitting they had killed Gideon's full brothers, who shared his impressive appearance. This slaughter may have occurred during one of their earlier campaigns, when opportunity for revenge seemed remote.

**19** Gideon had considered sparing the kings' lives, but the additional element of personal revenge made their death certain. Moreover, the death of enemy leaders almost always accompanied total military victory (3:21–25; 4:21–22; 9:55; Josh 10:26).

**20–21** Gideon gave the honor of executing the kings to his firstborn son, Jether (v.20). The lad shunned this gruesome task, and the kings quickly pointed out that this was a man's job (v.21). For them it would be more honorable and less painful to be killed by a renowned warrior like Gideon. Death at the hands of a boy or a woman was considered a disgrace (5:24–27; 9:54). Gideon complied with their final request and slew the kings as Samuel slew Agag (1 Sam 15:33).

The crescent-shaped "ornaments" (lit., "little moons") on the camels' necks are still in common use among the Arabs. Made of silver or gold, they are mentioned again in Isaiah 3:18 ("crescent necklaces") among articles highly prized by women. The Midianites, along with many other Semitic people, probably worshiped the moon-god.

## Notes

---

**18** The word תֹּאַר (*tō'ar,* "bearing") describes the impressive appearance ("fine-looking") of David in 1 Sam 16:18. According to Isa 52:14 and 53:2, this physical quality was not possessed by the Servant of the Lord.

## 16. *Gideon's ephod*

### 8:22–27

22The Israelites said to Gideon, "Rule over us—you, your son and
your grandson—because you have saved us out of the hand of Midian."
23But Gideon told them, "I will not rule over you, nor will my son rule
over you. The LORD will rule over you." 24And he said, "I do have one
request, that each of you give me an earring from your share of the
plunder." (It was the custom of the Ishmaelites to wear gold earrings.)
25They answered, "We'll be glad to give them." So they spread out a
garment, and each man threw a ring from his plunder onto it. 26The
weight of the gold rings he asked for came to seventeen hundred
shekels, not counting the ornaments, the pendants and the purple
garments worn by the kings of Midian or the chains that were on their
camels' necks. 27Gideon made the gold into an ephod, which he placed
in Ophrah, his town. All Israel prostituted themselves by worshiping it
there, and it became a snare to Gideon and his family.

**22–23** Gideon's celebrated victory brought him an invitation to become king over Israel and establish a ruling dynasty (v.22). Under unified rule, the Israelites felt they could better prevent any future oppression. It is to Gideon's credit that he rejected the offer, insisting that theocracy, not monarchy, was best for Israel (v.23). God was their king, and the people needed to renew their allegiance to him.

Some scholars think that Gideon would have become king had he been more confident of support from Ephraim (cf. v.1) and other key tribes. He did in fact assume many of the prerogatives of a king; he established a large harem (v.30), amassed a fortune (v.26), acquired royal robes, and made an ephod to consult God (v.27). The name of his son Abimelech ("my father is king") probably does not mean that Gideon regarded himself as monarch. In personal names "my father" normally refers to God; so Gideon could have been reemphasizing the assertion of v.23.

**24–26** While refusing the throne, Gideon did accept gifts from his grateful soldiers (v.24). The weight of the rings totaled between thirty-five and seventy-five pounds, depending on the size of the shekel at that time. Most of the items given to Gideon often were worn by women in Israel. The "earrings" (*nezem*) were sometimes rather "noserings" for brides (Gen 24:47; Ezek 16:12). "Pendants" (*nᵉṭip̱ôṯ*, v.26) occurs in the same list of women's ornaments with regard to v.21 (Isa 3:19, "earrings"). The word for "chains" (*ʿᵃnāqôṯ*) is rendered "necklace" in Song of Songs 4:9. This vast repertoire of jewelry may have been a factor in Gideon's subsequent accumulation of wives.

Verse 24 contains the only reference in Judges to the Ishmaelites. Apparently this was an inclusive term for Israel's nomadic relatives and alternated freely with "Midianites," as evidenced by Genesis 37:25–28 and 39:1 (cf. Derek Kidner, *Genesis* [Chicago: InterVarsity, 1967], pp. 182–83).

**27** With the gold Gideon surprisingly made an ephod that was to lead Israel into idolatry. The ephod was an apronlike garment worn by the high priest and was made of linen; blue, purple, and scarlet yarn; and gold thread (Exod 39:2–5). Two shoulder straps and a waistband held it secure. The breastpiece of judgment, containing the mysterious Urim and Thummim (Exod 28:28–30), was attached to the ephod. It was used to consult God (1 Sam 23:9–10), and this may have been Gideon's purpose in making a golden replica. The priesthood had fallen on bad times (cf. 17:8–13); so Gideon may wrongly have assumed priestly functions.

The ephod is associated with images and idols in 17:5 and 18:14, 17. Perhaps it was not expressly viewed as an idol. Nevertheless, like Aaron's golden calf, it served an idolatrous purpose and is described in the same terms as the gods of Canaan (2:2, 17). Gideon, who had boldly broken up his father's altar to Baal, was now setting a trap for his own family.

## Notes

---

**27** The writer again uses the metaphor of marital unfaithfulness. The same verb, זָנָה (*zānah*, "to prostitute, commit fornication"), is likewise rendered "prostituted themselves" in 2:17.

---

### 17. *Gideon's accomplishments and death*

#### 8:28–32

**28Thus Midian was subdued before the Israelites and did not raise its head again. During Gideon's lifetime, the land enjoyed peace forty years.**

**29Jerub-Baal son of Joash went back home to live. 30He had seventy**
**sons of his own, for he had many wives. 31His concubine, who lived in**
**Shechem, also bore him a son, whom he named Abimelech. 32Gideon**
**son of Joash died at a good old age and was buried in the tomb of his father Joash in Ophrah of the Abiezrites.**

**28–31** Verse 28, which sums up this cycle, states that Midian had been thoroughly disgraced and caused no further trouble. Like an animal no longer able to toss its horns and charge against the foe, Midian could not "raise its head" (v.28; cf. Pss 83:2; 92:10). Gideon himself spent the remainder of his life in Ophrah (vv.29, 32). His many wives and sons reflected his prosperity (v.30). As wealth and prestige increased, so did one's harem. King Ahab also had seventy sons (2 Kings 10:1), and even some of Gideon's successors had thirty (10:4; 12:9) or forty (12:14) sons each. The hatred and murder that plagued Gideon's family are characteristic of OT polygamous situations.

Among Gideon's wives was a concubine from Shechem (v.31). Apparently she continued to live in her hometown and remained under the authority of her father. In such marriage relationships the husband was expected to visit from time to time (cf. 15:1). It is the son of this low-ranking wife who rises to prominence in the next chapter.

**32** Gideon's death notice further attests his importance; only he and Samson are said to have been buried in the tomb of their fathers. To die "at a good old age" implies a long and full life. Elsewhere in the OT the expression is used only of Abraham (Gen 15:15; 25:8) and David (1 Chron 29:28).

## Notes

**32** שֵׂיבָה (*śêḇāh,* "old age") literally means "gray-headed."

### G. *The Brief Reign of Abimelech (8:33–9:57)*

#### 1. *Apostasy after Gideon's death*

**8:33–35**

**[33]No sooner had Gideon died than the Israelites again prostituted themselves to the Baals. They set up Baal-Berith as their god and [34]did not remember the LORD their God, who had rescued them from the hands of all their enemies on every side. [35]They also failed to show kindness to the family of Jerub-Baal (that is, Gideon) for all the good things he had done for them.**

**33** Abimelech is not called a judge. Nor was he raised up by God to rescue Israel. Therefore this section differs from the other cycles. Since Abimelech was the son of Gideon, this period stands in a unique relationship with the preceding one. The introduction follows the common pattern quite closely in recording Israel's sin. Again the Israelites became enamored with Baal worship, and particularly Baal-Berith (v.33; cf. 2:11), whose worship was centered at Shechem. Baal-Berith means "Baal [or 'lord'] of the covenant" and may indicate that they had made a covenant with Baal or that Baal was the god who "watches over agreements" (so KB, s.v.). The deity is called "El-Berith" in 9:46, providing an interesting interchange between the head of the pantheon, El, and his more famous son, Baal.

**34–35** By worshiping "Baal-of-the-covenant," Israel deserted the God who had made a covenant with them at Sinai and who had repeatedly been their Savior (v.34). They also quickly forgot the benefits won for the nation by Gideon (v.35). The double name may be used to recall Baal's inability to "defend himself" (Jerub-Baal) against Gideon.

## Notes

**33** The form בַּעֲלֵי בְּרִית (*ba'ᵃlê bᵉrîṯ,* "allied with") occurs in Gen 14:13 to describe Abraham's allies, who were literally "possessors of a covenant" with him.

#### 2. *Abimelech's rise to power*

**9:1–6**

**[1]Abimelech son of Jerub-Baal went to his mother's brothers in Shechem and said to them and to all his mother's clan, [2]"Ask all the citizens of Shechem, 'Which is better for you: to have all seventy of Jerub-Baal's sons rule over you, or just one man?' Remember, I am your flesh and blood."**

[3]When the brothers repeated all this to the citizens of Shechem, they were inclined to follow Abimelech, for they said, "He is our brother." [4]They gave him seventy shekels of silver from the temple of Baal-Berith, and Abimelech used it to hire reckless adventurers, who became his followers. [5]He went to his father's home in Ophrah and on one stone murdered his seventy brothers, the sons of Jerub-Baal. But Jotham, the youngest son of Jerub-Baal, escaped by hiding. [6]Then all the citizens of Shechem and Beth Millo gathered beside the great tree at the pillar in Shechem to crown Abimelech king.

**1** In a polygamous society the relatives of one's mother can provide refuge and support for an ambitious prince. Abimelech was probably spurned by his half-brothers because of his mother's lowly status (cf. 11:1–2); so he appealed to his mother's brothers for help. After he killed his half-brother Amnon, Absalom too took refuge with his mother's family in Geshur (2 Sam 13:37–38).

Shechem (Tell Balatah) had been a prominent city since the days of the patriarchs. Situated in central Palestine between Mount Ebal and Mount Gerizim, it lay on important caravan routes running north and south and also from the Jordan to the Mediterranean. Jacob's sons had treacherously captured the city, killing the young prince Shechem and his father, Hamor (Gen 34). Shechem was also important as the burial place of Joseph (Josh 24:32). Jacob had promised to give the city to Joseph and his family (cf. Gen 48:22). Since no mention is made of the capture of Shechem during Joshua's conquest of Canaan, some scholars feel that a treaty was made with that city soon after the invasion (Cundall, p. 126). Joshua 8:30–35 records the covenant renewal ceremony held at Mount Ebal and Mount Gerizim after the defeat of Ai, and Joshua's final words of challenge were delivered at Shechem (Josh 24:1–27).

The people of Shechem maintained a link with the Canaanite founders of the city (v.28), and perhaps Abimelech's mother herself was a Canaanite. Gideon's relations with her may have stemmed from a desire to gain the support of this city on the southern border of Manasseh, which belonged to the troublesome Ephraimites (cf. 8:1–3).

**2–4** Abimelech's appeal was based on the tenuous claim that his brothers' rule would not have Shechem's best interests at heart (vv.2–3). In fact, it is unlikely that Gideon's sons intended to dominate an area thirty miles south of Ophrah. The residents of Shechem, however, agreed to his plan and provided a substantial sum to carry it out (v.4). Temple treasures were often used for military and political ends (cf. 1 Kings 15:18).

The individuals hired were a worthless band (*rêqîm*, "empty"; NIV, "reckless adventurers"), comparable to the "adventurers" under Jephthah's command (11:3) or the "worthless scoundrels" who misled Rehoboam (2 Chron 13:7).

**5–6** Treacherous and unstable, these mercenaries helped Abimelech commit wholesale fratricide (v.5a). The reference to "one stone" may be compared with the large stone on which Saul slaughtered the animals captured from the Philistines (1 Sam 14:33–35).

Mass murders are rarely a total success. Jotham managed a narrow escape (v.5b), as did the young Joash from the hand of Queen Athaliah (2 Chron 22:10–12). Nevertheless, Abimelech became the first person ever to be crowned as king in Israel. His abortive rule, however, ran roughshod over the divine requirements for that office (cf.

Deut 17:14–20). His coronation ironically took place near the tree in Shechem where Joshua had solemnly placed the "Book of the Law" (Josh 24:26).

Beth Millo (v.6), literally the "house of the fill," may be the same as the "tower of Shechem" of v.46. "Millo" is also used of a fortress in Jerusalem for defense purposes (cf. NIV mg. on 2 Sam 5:9 and 1 Kings 9:15). The word "fill" comes from the huge earthen platform on which these structures were built (cf. Boling, p. 171).

## Notes

---

**2** "Citizens" is בְּעָלִים (*b*$^{e}$*'ālîm*), the "baals" or "lords" of the city. It is equivalent to "the men of Shechem" (cf. vv.46 and 49; 20:5 and 1 Sam 23:11–12).

The Hebrew idiom is actually "flesh and bone," not "blood." See also Gen 29:14 and Luke 24:39.

**4** פֹּחֲזִים (*pōḥ*$^{a}$*zîm*, "adventurers") is used of Reuben (Gen 49:4), who was as uncontrollable or "turbulent" as water, and of "treacherous" prophets (Zeph 3:4).

**6** The translation "pillar" is uncertain. מֻצָּב (*muṣṣāḇ*) refers to something that is set up, perhaps an "outpost" or "siege work" (Isa 29:3). A stone or a pillar may be intended (cf. LXX and Josh 24:26).

---

### 3. *Jotham's fable*

#### 9:7–21

7When Jotham was told about this, he climbed up on the top of Mount
Gerizim and shouted to them, "Listen to me, citizens of Shechem, so
that God may listen to you. 8One day the trees went out to anoint a king
for themselves. They said to the olive tree, 'Be our king.'
9"But the olive tree answered, 'Should I give up my oil, by which both
gods and men are honored, to hold sway over the trees?'
10"Next, the trees said to the fig tree, 'Come and be our king.'
11"But the fig tree replied, 'Should I give up my fruit, so good and
sweet, to hold sway over the trees?'
12"Then the trees said to the vine, 'Come and be our king.'
13"But the vine answered, 'Should I give up my wine, which cheers
both gods and men, to hold sway over the trees?'
14"Finally all the trees said to the thornbush, 'Come and be our king.'
15"The thornbush said to the trees, 'If you really want to anoint me
king over you, come and take refuge in my shade; but if not, then let fire
come out of the thornbush and consume the cedars of Lebanon!'
16"Now if you have acted honorably and in good faith when you made
Abimelech king, and if you have been fair to Jerub-Baal and his family,
and if you have treated him as he deserves—17and to think that my
father fought for you, risked his life to rescue you from the hand of
Midian 18(but today you have revolted against my father's family,
murdered his seventy sons on a single stone, and made Abimelech, the
son of his slave girl, king over the citizens of Shechem because he is
your brother)—19if then you have acted honorably and in good faith
toward Jerub-Baal and his family today, may Abimelech be your joy, and
may you be his, too! 20But if you have not, let fire come out from
Abimelech and consume you, citizens of Shechem and Beth Millo, and
let fire come out from you, citizens of Shechem and Beth Millo, and
consume Abimelech!"

**[21]Then Jotham fled, escaping to Beer, and he lived there because he was afraid of his brother Abimelech.**

The sole survivor of Abimelech's purge delivered an incisive evaluation of his half-brother's rule. Presented in allegorical form, this story of the trees effectively lays bare Abimelech's true character and the utter disregard of the people of Shechem for Gideon's memory.

**7–9** Jotham traveled to Shechem and climbed Mount Gerizim's eight-hundred-foot slope south of the city (v.7). There, at a safe distance from his audience, he pronounced a powerful curse (cf. v.57). Earlier, Mount Gerizim had been a place to recite blessings (Deut 27:12), but its splendid acoustics served a different purpose on this occasion.

The introduction to the fable in v.7 contains an unusual reference to God as the One who listened to them. By this statement Jotham may be asking the hearers to present to God a response to his arguments. God is viewed as the Judge in Jotham's lawsuit against Shechem.

The use of a fable is similar to the riddle spoken by Samson in 14:14. This symbolic style was more extensively developed by the prophets, Ezekiel in particular (chs. 15, 17, 23, et al.). In the NT the same literary technique was effectively used in the parables of Christ. The comparison of kings to trees occurs also in Isaiah 10:33–34, where the king of Assyria is referred to as a cedar tree.

In recognition of Israel's lowly status, Jotham began, not with a cedar, but with an olive tree (vv.8–9). Olives were used for food, ointment, and medicine. They were one of Israel's most valued crops (Deut 11:14). Olive oil kept the lamps in the Holy Place burning constantly, thus "honoring" the Lord. In view of its important functions, the olive tree declined the offer to become king.

**10–11** The fig tree likewise passed up the opportunity to rule. Like olives, figs were a key agricultural product. Israel's picture of the ideal age was for every man to sit under his vine and under his fig tree (Mic 4:4; cf. 2 Kings 18:31).

**12–13** Predictably, the vine also refused. Its fruit was the main beverage of the land, and libations of wine accompanied many sacrifices at the sanctuary (Num 15:10). "Wine makes life merry" (Eccl 10:19). Jotham referred to the view common in his day, that "the gods" shared many of the activities of men (v.13). Ugaritic literature portrays the god El holding a cup of wine as he blessed the hero Kret (Cyrus Gordon, *The Common Background of Greek and Hebrew Civilizations* [New York: The Norton Library, 1965], pp. 144–45).

**14–15** At last the thornbush was called on; and, having nothing better to do, the surprised shrub gladly agreed to reign. The thorn was a menace to agriculture and had the quality of burning quickly (Ps 58:9). Since it provided little if any shade, its refuge is spoken of sarcastically. It could only threaten to destroy, if its rule were not accepted.

**16–20** By this time Jotham's main point was clear, but he gave a detailed interpretation in vv.16–20. Gideon probably represented one of the good trees invited to become king (8:22), though exact identifications are not needed. Noble, capable leaders like Gideon believed that the theocracy, not a monarchy, was the best form of government. This is quite different from the situation described in Isaiah 3, where qualified men are scarce and no one wishes to assume control of a monarchy already fallen into deep decay.

Abimelech was the thornbush king. Along with the Shechemites, he was guilty of a terrible crime against Gideon, who had saved them at the risk of his own life (vv.16–17). Abimelech really had nothing to offer the people and even hurled threats if he were not accepted (cf. Gerhard von Rad, *Wisdom in Israel* [London: SCM, 1972], p. 43). Any government founded on this kind of "good faith" would soon collapse. Abimelech's mother is called a "slave girl" (v.18), a term usually referring to a wife's servant who is also a concubine, such as Hagar or Bilhah (Gen 21:12; 30:3).

The reference to acting "honorably and in good faith" (v.19) with Gideon and his family implies that an agreement of some kind had been made with Gideon (cf. 8:35). The combination of *'ᵉmet̲* and *tāmîm* also occurs in Joshua 24:14, where Israel is instructed to serve the Lord "with all faithfulness." A judge and his family had certain privileges that the revolt completely ignored.

The supposition in v.20 is actually a grim prediction that the parties to the crime would mutually destroy each other. True to its nature, the thornbush would ignite a deadly blaze.

**21** Before the hostile audience could intercept him, Jotham ended his short speech and fled to Beer, which means "well." Since many sites bore that name, it cannot be positively identified.

## Notes

---

**7** ראשׁ (*rō'š*, "top") might refer to the ridge of the mountain. Possibly Jotham stood somewhere below the actual summit so that he could be heard more easily.

**8** The unusual imperatival form מלוכה (read as מָלְכָה [*molk̲āh*, "Be our king"]) is matched by forms in 1 Sam 28:8 and Isa 32:11.

**9** The plural אֱלֹהִים (*'ᵉlōhîm*, "gods") can equally well be translated "God," but the parallel in v.13 favors the plural form in both places.

**17** וַיַּשְׁלֵךְ אֶת־נַפְשׁוֹ (*wayyašlēk̲ 'et̲-nap̲šô*, "[and he] risked his life") is literally "threw away his life." שָׁלַךְ (*šālak̲*) is often used of throwing away dead bodies (Josh 8:29); so Jotham was emphasizing that Gideon had a close brush with death.

---

### 4. *The revolt of Gaal and Shechem*
### 9:22–29

22 After Abimelech had governed Israel three years, 23 God sent an evil
spirit between Abimelech and the citizens of Shechem, who acted
treacherously against Abimelech. 24 God did this in order that the crime
against Jerub-Baal's seventy sons, the shedding of their blood, might be
avenged on their brother Abimelech and on the citizens of Shechem,
who had helped him murder his brothers. 25 In opposition to him these
citizens of Shechem set men on the hilltops to ambush and rob
everyone who passed by, and this was reported to Abimelech.

**[26]Now Gaal son of Ebed moved with his brothers into Shechem, and its citizens put their confidence in him. [27]After they had gone out into the fields and gathered the grapes and trodden them, they held a festival in the temple of their god. While they were eating and drinking, they cursed Abimelech. [28]Then Gaal son of Ebed said, "Who is Abimelech, and who is Shechem, that we should be subject to him? Isn't he Jerub-Baal's son, and isn't Zebul his deputy? Serve the men of Hamor, Shechem's father! Why should we serve Abimelech? [29]If only this people were under my command! Then I would get rid of him. I would say to Abimelech, 'Call out your whole army!' "**

**22** Abimelech's rule was a brief one, and it apparently did not extend beyond Manasseh. Along with Shechem it included the nearby cities of Arumah (v.41) and Thebez (v.50). The word for "governed" (*yāśar;* cf. "struggled" in Hos 12:4) is unique to the book and is perhaps chosen to distinguish Abimelech's ill-fated rule from that of the true judges. Abimelech was more like a tyrant than a king, and he soon encountered opposition in Shechem itself.

**23–25** The Lord was at the source of the conflict, for he "sent an evil spirit" (v.23) to disrupt the relationship between Abimelech and Shechem. If "spirit" is to be taken in the sense of a supernatural being, this situation would be comparable to Saul's. Because of sin, God allowed an evil spirit to torment Israel's first king (1 Sam 16:14; cf. 1 Kings 22:19–23). Shechem and Abimelech had committed murder, and the friction between them arose as a result of their guilt. The men of Shechem had literally "strengthened his hands" by supporting and encouraging the atrocity (v.24; cf. Neh 2:18; Jer 23:14).

"To act treacherously" (*bāgaḏ,* v.23) is to break an agreement with someone. The rejection of one's wife and God are so described in Malachi 2:11–14. Shechem's citizens betrayed Abimelech by ambushing the caravans that passed through the ideally located city. No longer could Abimelech receive revenue from these welcomed traders. With travel so dangerous, the economy would suffer greatly (cf. 5:6).

**26–27** In v.26 a certain Gaal arrived on the scene to exploit the situation and to deepen the rift between Abimelech and Shechem. He was probably a Canaanite deadly opposed to Israelite rule. Gaal and his men came to Shechem near the time of the summer harvest, when the Canaanites had a religious festival similar to Israel's Feast of Tabernacles (Lev 23:34–43). The Canaanite celebration often included excessive drinking and immorality, hardly conducive to true religious expression. Yet the "festival" of v.27 is literally a "praise" or "rejoicing" (*hillûlîm*), when the gods would be honored for providing an abundant harvest (cf. 16:24). In Shechem the primary deity was Baal-Berith (cf. v.4).

**28–29** Gaal took advantage of the occasion to advocate open rebellion against Abimelech. Whereas Abimelech had earlier stressed his descent from a woman of Shechem (vv.1–2), Gaal noted that Abimelech's father was an Israelite. How could a city that traced its heritage back to the Hivite prince Hamor (Gen 34:2) give its allegiance to an Israelite intruder? Gaal boldly asserted that he would be a far better leader and threw out a challenge to Abimelech. It was a clever speech; Absalom later used the same strategy to win over Israel (2 Sam 15:1–6).

Part of Gaal's appeal lay in the fact that Abimelech did not reside in Shechem. He had appointed Zebul to govern the city, and the Shechemites may have resented this. The name "Zebul" (*zeḇul*), however, could be a Canaanite name meaning "prince." In Ugaritic it is an epithet of Baal.

## Notes

**24** In Hebrew vengeance is described as "putting their blood"—דָּמָם לָשׂוּם (*dāmām lāśûm*)—on the guilty. The blood of the slain must be avenged (2 Sam 4:11).

**25** During the fourteenth century B.C., Labayu, the Habiru prince of Shechem, regularly raided the territory and caravans of neighboring regions (cf. ANET, p. 485).

**26** The "brothers" of Gaal were probably members of the same tribal or ethnic group. Compare the reference to the tribe of Dan in 14:3 (cf. 13:2).

**27** The influence of the fruit of the vine in the revolt against Abimelech had been subtly alluded to by Jotham. Abimelech and the people of Shechem were to bring "joy" (שָׂמֵחַ [*śāmēaḥ*]) to each other (v.19), just as wine "cheers [same word] . . . both gods and men" (v.13). In reality the merrymaking of the festival increased the celebrants' hatred of Abimelech.

הִלּוּלִים (*hillûlîm*, "festival") occurs elsewhere in the OT only in Lev 19:24, where the fruit of Canaan was given to the Lord as an "offering of praise."

**29** צֵאָה (*ṣē'āh*, "call out") is an emphatic imperative as Gaal intensified the challenge to "come out" (v.33).

## 5. *Gaal's defeat*

### 9:30–41

30 When Zebul the governor of the city heard what Gaal son of Ebed
said, he was very angry. 31 Under cover he sent messengers to
Abimelech, saying, "Gaal son of Ebed and his brothers have come to
Shechem and are stirring up the city against you. 32 Now then, during
the night you and your men should come and lie in wait in the fields.
33 In the morning at sunrise, advance against the city. When Gaal and his
men come out against you, do whatever your hand finds to do."

34 So Abimelech and all his troops set out by night and took up
concealed positions near Shechem in four companies. 35 Now Gaal son
of Ebed had gone out and was standing at the entrance to the city gate
just as Abimelech and his soldiers came out from their hiding place.

36 When Gaal saw them, he said to Zebul, "Look, people are coming
down from the tops of the mountains!"

Zebul replied, "You mistake the shadows of the mountains for men."

37 But Gaal spoke up again: "Look, people are coming down from the
center of the land, and a company is coming from the direction of the
soothsayers' tree."

38 Then Zebul said to him, "Where is your big talk now, you who said,
'Who is Abimelech that we should be subject to him?' Aren't these the
men you ridiculed? Go out and fight them!"

39 So Gaal led out the citizens of Shechem and fought Abimelech.
40 Abimelech chased him, and many fell wounded in the flight—all the
way to the entrance to the gate. 41 Abimelech stayed in Arumah, and
Zebul drove Gaal and his brothers out of Shechem.

**30–33** When Zebul heard about Gaal's slanderous remarks aimed at Abimelech and him, he moved quickly before the rebel forces could decide to restrict his activities. He secretly sent messengers to inform Abimelech of the dangerous situation and to offer some sound advice (v.31). If Abimelech struck quickly, he could still save the day; for Gaal had not yet had time to organize the Shechemites into a solid army. Zebul recommended an ambush (vv.32–33)—a strategy that had worked at Ai (Josh 8:2) and in the civil war against the tribe of Benjamin (Judg 20:37).

**34** Abimelech took Zebul's advice and also used the tactics of his father, Gideon, of moving at night and dividing his forces into several companies. By morning Abimelech's army was ready to make a sudden dash to Shechem and surprise the enemy.

**35–37** Gaal, in his new role of leader of Shechem, was stationed at the city gate when he noticed the approaching men (v.35). But Zebul was there to ease Gaal's fears in an effort to keep him from preparing his troops (v.36). Finally, it was clear that people were coming from all over, including a company from the soothsayers' tree (v.37). Gaal may have wished he could have consulted a practitioner there, though his fate seemed sealed already.

**38–39** At this point Zebul reminded Gaal of his earlier taunt and challenged him to make good his boast (v.38). Gaal probably was not prepared for a siege; so he had little choice but to leave the city walls behind and confront Abimelech in the open (v.39). It is difficult to know whether Gaal had the support of the fighting men of Shechem in the battle or had to rely only on his personal supporters. The alternate translation of v.39 (NIV mg.: "Gaal went out in the sight of the citizens of Shechem") is equally valid. Shechem's residents were mainly involved in battles on the following day (vv.42–45).

**40–41** Whatever its composition, Gaal's army soon headed back to the city, and many more were killed or wounded along the way (v.40). Abimelech himself did not try to enter the city, but his capable governor drove the disgraced Gaal and his remaining men out of Shechem (v.41).

## Notes

**31** בְּתָרְמָה (*b^e^tormāh*, "under cover") is taken by the NIV from the root רמה (*rmh*), which means "to deceive"; cf. תַּרְמִית (*tarmît*, "deceitfulness"). Zebul used some sort of deception or "cover" to get word to Abimelech. Some authorities, such as KB, emend the text to בָּארוּמָה (*bā'rûmāh*, "in Arumah"), the city where Abimelech resided (cf. v.41). Versional support for this change is not strong, however.

"Stirring up" translates צָרִים (*ṣārîm*), a participle from צוּר (*ṣûr*), normally meaning "to besiege." In this instance *ṣûr* is to be understood as צרר (*ṣrr*, "to show hostility toward"; so Keil). The interchange between ayin waw and double ayin roots is common.

**32–33** The correlation between אָרַב (*'ārab*, "ambush," "lie in wait") and פָּשַׁט (*pāšaṭ*, "advance against," "make a dash") occurs also in 20:37.

**37** The obscure טַבּוּר (*ṭabbûr*, "the center of") occurs with אֶרֶץ (*'ereṣ*, "earth," "land") also in Ezek 38:12. There it may mean "the center" or "navel" of the earth. A well-known landmark may be intended.

**38** The word "big" is added before "talk" by the translators and is precisely the idiom intended (cf. Dan 7:8, "spoke boastfully").

---

## 6. *The capture of Shechem and the tower of Shechem* 9:42–49

42The next day the people of Shechem went out to the fields, and this
was reported to Abimelech. 43So he took his men, divided them into
three companies and set an ambush in the fields. When he saw the
people coming out of the city, he rose to attack them. 44Abimelech and
the companies with him rushed forward to a position at the entrance to
the city gate. Then two companies rushed upon those in the fields and
struck them down. 45All that day Abimelech pressed his attack against
the city until he had captured it and killed its people. Then he destroyed
the city and scattered salt over it.
46On hearing this, the citizens in the tower of Shechem went into the
stronghold of the temple of El-Berith. 47When Abimelech heard that
they had assembled there, 48he and all his men went up Mount Zalmon.
He took an ax and cut off some branches, which he lifted to his
shoulders. He ordered the men with him, "Quick! Do what you have
seen me do!" 49So all the men cut branches and followed Abimelech.
They piled them against the stronghold and set it on fire over the people
inside. So all the people in the tower of Shechem, about a thousand
men and women, also died.

Apparently the people of Shechem were eager to resume their normal activities. Abimelech, however, wanted to punish them further for their lack of loyalty. His vindictive action, however, destroyed the main city of his "kingdom" and left him with little to rule (cf. Prov 30:21–22).

**42–44** Since the fields were outside the city, the people had to leave it to bring in the rest of the harvest (v.42). It is not likely that they had any military plans. Nor did they anticipate further difficulty from Abimelech—at least not so soon. However, for the second day in a row, Abimelech set an ambush and surprised the people in the fields (v.43). He cut off their line of retreat to the city while the rest of his troops slaughtered those who were stranded (v.44).

**45** Already weakened by the loss of so many able-bodied men, the people left in Shechem were unable to ward off Abimelech's full-scale attack. He forced his way into the city and put the rest of the people to the sword. Then he tore down the main buildings and sowed the ground with salt to symbolize the utter destruction of the city and its perpetual infertility (Deut 29:23; Ps 107:34). Indeed, Shechem was not rebuilt until the reign of Jeroboam I, almost two centuries later (1 Kings 12:25).

**46** The tower of Shechem was probably the same as Beth Millo (see comment on v.6). Normally the tower or fortress was located within the city proper, as at Thebez (v.51). At Shechem the fortress-temple of El-Berith (or Baal-Berith; cf. comment on 8:33) may have been this inner citadel. The temple was a Late Bronze structure built on the ruins of a massive Middle Bronze temple (cf. G. Ernest Wright, *Shechem, the*

*Biography of a Biblical City* [New York: McGraw Hill, 1965], pp. 123–28). It has been identified with a building sixty-eight feet wide and eighty-four feet long situated in the upper part of the city. People could have taken refuge within its walls to defend the citadel independently of the rest of the city (cf. comment on 1:8).

Cundall (p. 134) admits that the tower of Shechem might be outside the walls of Shechem proper, perhaps on the slopes of Mount Ebal. This would fit the narrative nicely, but it does not correlate as well with the geographical and archaeological data.

**47–49** This time Abimelech decided to build a huge fire to destroy his victims. He and his men got some branches or brushwood from nearby Mount Zalmon ("the black or dark hill") and carried them to the tower. Abimelech's command to have his soldiers follow his example sounds like Gideon (7:17), who himself had destroyed a tower at Peniel (8:17). After the usual long, rainless summer, the wood was like tinder; so a blazing fire was soon underway. The temple gave the people no more protection than the house of Baal did when Jehu slaughtered Baal's devotees there (2 Kings 10:19–25). With the collapse of the fortress, all resistance at Shechem came to an end.

## Notes

---

**42–43** The Hebrew word עָם (*'am*) is translated "people" and "men" in these verses. Since it can mean "army," the implication may be that the soldiers of Shechem were sent out to complete the harvest in case new fighting broke out.

**46** The צְרִיחַ (*ṣerîaḥ*, "stronghold") appears as a hiding place again in 1 Sam 13:6 ("pits"), where it may mean "cellar" (cf. KB).

**48** Mount Zalmon (צַלְמוֹן [*ṣalmôn*]) is mentioned again in Ps 68:14 as a snow-capped mountain. Possibly two different hills are intended. "Zalmon" probably is derived from צלם (*ṣlm*, " to be dark"; cf. Akkadian *ṣalāmu*).

---

### 7. *The death of Abimelech*

#### 9:50–57

50 Next Abimelech went to Thebez and besieged it and captured it.
51 Inside the city, however, was a strong tower, to which all the men and
women—all the people of the city—fled. They locked themselves in and
climbed up on the tower roof. 52 Abimelech went to the tower and
stormed it. But as he approached the entrance to the tower to set it on
fire, 53 a woman dropped an upper millstone on his head and cracked his
skull.

54 Hurriedly he called to his armor-bearer, "Draw your sword and kill
me, so that they can't say, 'A woman killed him.' " So his servant ran him
through, and he died. 55 When the Israelites saw that Abimelech was
dead, they went home.

56 Thus God repaid the wickedness that Abimelech had done to his
father by murdering his seventy brothers. 57 God also made the men of
Shechem pay for all their wickedness. The curse of Jotham son of
Jerub-Baal came on them.

**50–53** Dissatisfaction with Abimelech's rule was evidently widespread, for he next traveled ten miles northeast of Shechem to punish Thebez (v.50). The city proper was easily taken, but a strong fortress within it proved more formidable. The people of Thebez heard of Abimelech's strategy at Shechem; so they climbed to the roof where they could offer some resistance (v.51). When Abimelech tried to set another fire (v.52), he was struck by a millstone thrown with amazing accuracy by a woman (v.53). The "upper millstone" (*pelaḥ reḵeḇ*) was an easily held stone, about ten inches long, that rode back and forth over the larger lower millstone as the grain was crushed (cf. Deut 24:6). Grinding wheat was the work of women, and the woman doubtless took the stone with her as a potential weapon. Her success was as surprising as the arrow that pierced Ahab's armor (1 Kings 22:34). It was unmistakably a divine retribution.

**54** Since dying at the hand of a woman was considered a disgrace (cf. 4:17–24), Abimelech, realizing that a woman had thrown the millstone, commanded his armor-bearer to kill him immediately. Yet long after his death, the credit continued to be given to the woman (cf. 2 Sam 11:21). Saul was another who asked his armor-bearer to kill him, lest the Philistines humiliate him (1 Sam 31:4).

**55** With Abimelech dead, the Israelites gave up their campaign and returned home. Similarly, later in Israel's history, the slaying of a leader led to the disintegration of Sheba's revolt against David (2 Sam 20:22) and to the dispersal of Ahab's armies at Ramoth Gilead (1 Kings 22:34–36). Each example illustrates the power of individual leaders and the desperate need for godly, capable rulers.

**56–57** The final two verses of chapter 9 summarize God's intervention in the downfall of Abimelech and Shechem. Both parties were guilty of murder and ultimately had to pay for their crimes. Jotham's curse was fulfilled in a remarkably literal way. The fire that destroyed the tower of Shechem may have been partially fed by thornbushes, the very designation used for Abimelech in the fable. Verse 48 states that Abimelech had put the wood for the fire on his "shoulder," which is "Shechem" (*š$^{e}$ḵem*) in Hebrew. Thus the name of the city held prophetic import for its own destruction.

## Notes

---

**54** The Polel imperative מוֹתְתֵנִי (*môṯ$^{e}$ṯēnî*, "kill me") is used in a similar context in 2 Sam 1:9.

**57** The literal idea behind "made . . . pay for" is "brought back on their head" (הֵשִׁיב בְּרֹאשָׁם [*hēšîḇ b$^{e}$rō'šām*]). The idiom is used at the death of wicked Nabal in 1 Sam 25:39 and of Joab in 1 Kings 2:32–33. Joab had needlessly killed Abner and Amasa.

---

## H. *The Rule of Tola and Jair*

### 10:1–5

**1** After the time of Abimelech a man of Issachar, Tola son of Puah, the
son of Dodo, rose to save Israel. He lived in Shamir, in the hill country of
Ephraim. **2** He led Israel twenty-three years; then he died, and was buried
in Shamir.

3 He was followed by Jair of Gilead, who led Israel twenty-two years.
4 He had thirty sons, who rode thirty donkeys. They controlled thirty
towns in Gilead, which to this day are called Havvoth Jair. 5 When Jair
died, he was buried in Kamon.

**1–2** Little is known about the rule of the minor judges mentioned here and in 12:8–15. The reference to "save" (v.1) implies a military victory over some oppressor. Except in the reference to Shamgar (3:31), none of the references to the other minor judges identify the oppressor of Israel. Since the word "led" (or "judged") appears most often with the lesser judges, some scholars (e.g., Boling, pp. 186–87) believe that the function of these judges was to handle judicial decisions and not fight wars. The last time "led" (*šāpaṭ*, v.2) occurred, it was applied to Deborah in this nonmilitary sense (4:4).

Tola son of Puah was, like his father, named after one of the sons of Issachar (Gen 46:13). "Tola" (*tôlā'*) means "scarlet," "purple," a sign of luxury (Lam 4:5). The location of Shamir is not known, though some have connected it with "Samaria" (*šimrôn*), which also happens to be the name of the last son of Issachar (Gen 46:13). But v.1 places Shamir in Ephraim's territory, while Samaria is in Manasseh. Both "Shamir" and "Shimron" were fairly common names (cf. Josh 11:1; 15:48). By maintaining a base in central Palestine, Tola may have exercised control over much of the land.

**3–5** Tola's twenty-three-year rule probably overlapped that of Jair, though Tola's began first. Jair was in charge of Gilead (v.4), east of the Jordan, and his rule provides a transition to the more important exploits of another Gileadite, Jephthah. Like Tola, Jair was named after a renowned figure—Jair son of Segub, the great-great-grandson of Manasseh who captured sixty cities in Bashan (Num 32:39–41; 1 Chron 2:22–23). These cities were called "Havvoth Jair" (the "tent cities" or "settlements of Jair"), and thirty of them were still controlled by Jair the judge.

That Jair had a total of thirty sons shows he was wealthy (cf. 8:30), as does his possession of thirty donkeys. Kings rode donkeys of this kind (Gen 49:11; Zech 9:9).

The city where Jair was buried, "Kamon" (v.5), has not been identified.

## Notes

1 The שָׁמִיר (*šāmîr*, "Shamir") of Josh 15:48 was located in the hill country of Judah.

4 On עֲיָרִים (*'ayārîm*, "donkeys"), see comment on 5:10. The word for "towns" is spelled exactly like that for "donkeys." This may be a textual error or an intentional wordplay (cf. BDB, s.v.). Usually "towns," "cities" is עָרִים (*'ārîm*).

## I. *The Victory of Jephthah Over the Ammonites (10:6–12:7)*

### 1. *Oppression and supplication*

10:6–16

6 Again the Israelites did evil in the eyes of the LORD. They served the
Baals and the Ashtoreths, and the gods of Aram, the gods of Sidon, the

gods of Moab, the gods of the Ammonites and the gods of the
Philistines. And because the Israelites forsook the LORD and no longer
served him, 7he became angry with them. He sold them into the hands
of the Philistines and the Ammonites, 8who that year shattered and
crushed them. For eighteen years they oppressed all the Israelites on
the east side of the Jordan in Gilead, the land of the Amorites. 9The
Ammonites also crossed the Jordan to fight against Judah, Benjamin
and the house of Ephraim; and Israel was in great distress. 10Then the
Israelites cried out to the LORD, "We have sinned against you, forsaking
our God and serving the Baals."

11The LORD replied, "When the Egyptians, the Amorites, the Ammonites, the Philistines, 12the Sidonians, the Amalekites and the Maonites
oppressed you and you cried to me for help, did I not save you from their
hands? 13But you have forsaken me and served other gods, so I will no
longer save you. 14Go and cry out to the gods you have chosen. Let
them save you when you are in trouble!"

15But the Israelites said to the LORD, "We have sinned. Do with us
whatever you think best, but please rescue us now." 16Then they got rid
of the foreign gods among them and served the LORD. And he could bear
Israel's misery no longer.

For the first time in Judges, the scene of oppression and victory shifts to Transjordan as the Ammonites exerted tremendous pressure from the east. The author uses the occasion of this renewed suffering to detail the phases of the cycle, as he did in 2:6–3:6. These verses also introduce the Philistine oppression, which probably ran concurrently with the Ammonite invasion (cf. v.7 and Introduction: Background).

**6–7** This is the final and most extensive list of Israel's sins. It may apply to the whole period. The Baals and Ashtoreths (v.6; cf. 2:11–13) were worshiped by most of the nations mentioned here, but other deities also were found. Moab's main god was Chemosh (Num 21:29), while Ammon served Milcom (1 Kings 11:5, NIV mg.). Dagon was the leading deity of the Philistines (16:23). By mentioning the gods of the Ammonites and the Philistines last, the author emphasizes that Israel deserved to be enslaved to these two nations (v.7).

**8–9** The opening clause of v.8 refers to the Ammonites and their severe oppression against Israel. "That year" can be placed about 1096 B.C. The oppression lasted as long as the Moabite one (3:14) and was concentrated in Gilead, a term for central and northern Transjordan (cf. 5:17). Tribes in south-central Palestine also came under Ammonite domination, and the mention of Ephraim (v.9) is important for the understanding of 12:1–3.

**10–14** Faced with mounting difficulties, Israel finally confessed her sin and cried out for help (v.10). The Lord, however, is not to be called on only in emergencies (vv.11–12); so he withheld assistance (v.13). After all, he had repeatedly rescued them only to have them turn quickly to other gods. The Lord's explanation in vv.13–14 closely resembles the message of the angel in 2:3 and of the prophet in 6:8–10. Israel did not deserve God's saving intervention.

The Lord contrasted Israel's disobedience with his own faithfulness in delivering them from at least seven oppressors. He released them from Egypt's iron furnace and enabled them to defeat Sihon and Og, the two kings of the Amorites (Josh 2:10) who lived in Transjordan. The Ammonites had earlier aided the Moabites (3:13), and Shamgar was renowned for defeating the Philistines (3:31). The Sidonians may have helped Jabin and Sisera during the "Canaanite" oppression (4:1–3), and the Amalekites already opposed Israel twice in Judges, supporting the Moabites (3:13) and the Midianites (6:3). The Midianites themselves may be the seventh nation mentioned, though the best Hebrew MSS have "Maon." This may refer to the Meunites, a people who later opposed Israel along with the Philistines and Arabians in 2 Chronicles 26:7. Some LXX MSS support the reading "Midian."

**15–16** Israel demonstrated the genuineness of her repentance by throwing out the idols she was worshiping and by being willing to return to God on his terms. Persistent prayer finally brought an answer from Israel's compassionate Lord (cf. 2:18). Expressed anthropomorphically God became "impatient" or "could bear [them] no longer" (*wattiqṣar nap̱šô,* lit., "and his soul became short") as he watched them suffer.

## Notes

**6** "Milcom," the god of the Ammonites (1 Kings 11:5, NIV mg.), is the same deity often called "Molech" (Lev 18:21). The consonants מלך (*mlḵ*) are given the vowels of בֹּשֶׁת (*bōšeṯ,* "shame"), just as "Jerub-Baal" becomes "Jerub-Besheth" (see Notes on 6:32).

**8** The juxtaposition of the roots רעץ (*r'ṣ,* "shattered") and רצץ (*rṣṣ,* "crushed") is an impressive example of assonance. רעץ occurs again only in Exod 15:6. וַיְרֹצְצוּ (*wayᵉrōṣᵉṣû,* "and [they] crushed") is a Polel form. The Hiphil was used in 9:53, where Abimelech's skull was "cracked."

**9** בֵּית אֶפְרָיִם (*bêṯ 'ep̱rāyim,*"house of Ephraim") recalls the more common "house of Joseph" (1:22).

**12** מָעוֹן (*mā'ôn,* "Maon") and מִדְיָן (*miḏyān,* "Midian") look very similar and could have been confused by a scribe. "Maon" is definitely the harder reading.

**16** The idiom וַתִּקְצַר (*wattiqṣar,* "and he could bear . . . no longer") is used of Israel in Num 21:4 when she "grew impatient" during the wilderness wanderings. Isaiah 42:14 also speaks of God's "restraining himself" (NIV, "held myself back") before taking action.

### 2. *Gilead's predicament*

**10:17–18**

[17]When the Ammonites were called to arms and camped in Gilead, the Israelites assembled and camped at Mizpah. [18]The leaders of the people of Gilead said to each other, "Whoever will launch the attack against the Ammonites will be the head of all those living in Gilead."

**17–18** Israel's deliverance came in the campaign that followed. At first, however, it looked as if another Ammonite victory was imminent. The Ammonite army had once more assembled to attack Israel, perhaps to carry off crops and livestock as the Midianites used to do. The Israelites, determined to stop the Ammonites, gathered at Mizpah to plan their strategy (v.17). The location of Mizpah is difficult to determine. The name, meaning "watchtower" or "lookout point," is a common one. There is a famous "Mizpah" in Benjamin, another north of the Jabbok (Gen 31:49), and a Ramath Mizpah in Gilead (Josh 13:26). Based on 11:29, this particular Mizpah was located near the territory of the Ammonites, whose capital, Rabbath Ammon, is the modern Amman, Jordan.

The leaders of Gilead had no outstanding general; so as an incentive they offered to make any commander who proved successful against the Ammonites the ruler of their entire territory (v.18; cf. 11:9). In their desperation they turned to Jephthah (11:5).

## Notes

---

**17** The Niphal of צעק (*ṣʿq*, "to gather, call to arms") is also used in 7:23–24 and 12:1.

**18** "Leaders" is שָׂרֵי (*śārê*), a term used of General Sisera (4:2), the "princes" of Issachar (5:15), and the governor of a city (9:30). Probably it includes all the military and political leaders. In chapter 11 the word "elders" (זְקֵנִים, *zᵉqēnîm*) is consistently applied to these leaders (vv.5, 8, 10).

"Launch the attack" is literally "begin to fight." The Hiphil of חלל (*ḥll*) appears also in 13:5 to describe Samson, the man who began the deliverance from the Philistines.

---

### 3. *Jephthah's exile and recall*

11:1–11

1Jephthah the Gileadite was a mighty warrior. His father was Gilead;
his mother was a prostitute. 2Gilead's wife also bore him sons, and
when they were grown up, they drove Jephthah away. "You are not
going to get any inheritance in our family," they said, "because you are
the son of another woman." 3So Jephthah fled from his brothers and
settled in the land of Tob, where a group of adventurers gathered
around him and followed him.
4Some time later, when the Ammonites made war on Israel, 5the
elders of Gilead went to get Jephthah from the land of Tob. 6"Come,"
they said, "be our commander, so we can fight the Ammonites."
7Jephthah said to them, "Didn't you hate me and drive me from my
father's house? Why do you come to me now, when you're in trouble?"
8The elders of Gilead said to him, "Nevertheless, we are turning to you
now; come with us to fight the Ammonites, and you will be our head
over all who live in Gilead."
9Jephthah answered, "Suppose you take me back to fight the
Ammonites and the LORD gives them to me—will I really be your head?"
10The elders of Gilead replied, "The LORD is our witness; we will
certainly do as you say." 11So Jephthah went with the elders of Gilead,
and the people made him head and commander over them. And he
repeated all his words before the LORD in Mizpah.

**1–3** The opening paragraph is a parenthesis introducing the reader to the hero, Jephthah son of Gilead. Like Tola and Jair (10:1, 3), Gilead too was named after a famous ancestor, in this case the grandson of Manasseh. Without doubt his family belonged to the "upper class," one reason why Jephthah was called a "mighty warrior" (v.1) or "man of valor" (*gibbôr ḥayil*; cf. comment on 6:12). Jephthah was certainly a capable fighter, but his social position also was important. Because of his mother's status, he was an illegitimate son and ranked at the bottom of his family (v.2). Nevertheless, it was a prominent family. Jephthah's origins are even more clouded than Abimelech's, whose mother was at least a concubine. In spite of the fact that Jephthah was an illegitimate child, the Lord saw fit to use him in a remarkable way.

Apparently Gilead was not a polygamist. Only one wife is mentioned in v.2, and the reason for Jephthah's expulsion was that he was the son of "another woman." His half-brothers had little sympathy for him, especially in the matter of inheritance. Sarah had the same reasoning in her desire to drive Ishmael away from Isaac (Gen 21:10).

Unlike Abimelech, Jephthah did not have the protection of his mother's family; so he was forced to flee to Tob (v.3), which is probably to be identified with et-Taiyibeh, some fifteen miles east of Ramoth Gilead. In this desolate region Jephthah roamed with a band of "adventurers" (*rêqîm*) and fellow misfits. The same word is used in 9:4 of the men Abimelech hired. Jephthah, however, resembled David in his association with malcontents (1 Sam 22:2), for both of them molded a difficult group into an effective fighting force. Exile in the wilderness became excellent preparation for more significant service.

**4–6** Jephthah established such a reputation as a skilled fighter and leader that the men of Gilead turned to him in their search for a commander. Presumably "some time later" (v.4) brings the reader back to 10:17–18 and the Mizpah gathering. A number of Gilead's leaders extended an invitation to Jephthah to assume command of their army as *qāṣîn* ("commander," "chief," or "ruler") (vv.5–6). This term is used of military and political leaders (Josh 10:24; Isa 1:10) and is cognate to the Arabic *qāḍin* ("judge"). Perhaps *qāṣîn* was equivalent to *šôpēṭ,* the usual word for "judge" in the book.

**7–11** With understandable bitterness, Jephthah reminded the leaders of Gilead of his ostracism (v.7). His complaint about being appealed to as a last resort is almost identical to the words of the Lord in 10:14. The elders assured Jephthah that his banishment was over and that they would in fact make him ruler over all Gilead after the battle (v.8). This offer astonished Jephthah, but he was convinced by their willingness to take an oath (v.10).

Jephthah's years of wandering had served to deepen his faith in the Lord. If victory lay ahead, it would be from the Lord's hand. When Jephthah returned with the leaders to Mizpah, he also confirmed his intentions "before the LORD" (v.11) as the agreement with Gilead was sealed. The ceremony at Mizpah had the makings of a coronation as the people installed their new leader.

## Notes

**1** Jephthah might have been the oldest son, but even so his expulsion was not illegal. Deuteronomy 21:15–17 would not apply in his case.

**2** The Piel of גָּרַשׁ (*gāraš,* "to drive out") is used both in this verse and in Gen 21:10.

**9** Jephthah's surprise was expressed in the emphatic pronoun אָנֹכִי (*'ānōḵî,* "I"): "Will I really be your head?"

**10** שֹׁמֵעַ (*šōmēaʿ*, "witness") is literally "hearer." God had heard the elders' promises and would judge any violation (cf. Prov 21:28).

## 4. *Jephthah's presentation of Israel's territorial claim*

### 11:12–28

12Then Jephthah sent messengers to the Ammonite king with the
question: "What do you have against us that you have attacked our
country?"
13The king of the Ammonites answered Jephthah's messengers,
"When Israel came up out of Egypt, they took away my land from the
Arnon to the Jabbok, all the way to the Jordan. Now give it back
peaceably."
14Jephthah sent back messengers to the Ammonite king, 15saying:

"This is what Jephthah says: Israel did not take the land of Moab or
the land of the Ammonites. 16But when they came up out of Egypt,
Israel went through the desert to the Red Sea and on to Kadesh.
17Then Israel sent messengers to the king of Edom, saying, 'Give us
permission to go through your country,' but the king of Edom
would not listen. They sent also to the king of Moab, and he
refused. So Israel stayed at Kadesh.
18"Next they traveled through the desert, skirted the lands of
Edom and Moab, passed along the eastern side of the country of
Moab, and camped on the other side of the Arnon. They did not
enter the territory of Moab, for the Arnon was its border.
19"Then Israel sent messengers to Sihon king of the Amorites,
who ruled in Heshbon, and said to him, 'Let us pass through your
country to our own place.' 20Sihon, however, did not trust Israel to
pass through his territory. He mustered all his men and encamped
at Jahaz and fought with Israel.
21"Then the LORD, the God of Israel, gave Sihon and all his men
into Israel's hands, and they defeated them. Israel took over all the
land of the Amorites who lived in that country, 22capturing all of it
from the Arnon to the Jabbok and from the desert to the Jordan.
23"Now since the LORD, the God of Israel, has driven the Amorites
out before his people Israel, what right have you to take it over?
24Will you not take what your god Chemosh gives you? Likewise,
whatever the LORD our God has given us, we will possess. 25Are you
better than Balak son of Zippor, king of Moab? Did he ever quarrel
with Israel or fight with them? 26For three hundred years Israel
occupied Heshbon, Aroer, the surrounding settlements and all the
towns along the Arnon. Why didn't you retake them during that
time? 27I have not wronged you, but you are doing me wrong by
waging war against me. Let the LORD, the Judge, decide the dispute
this day between the Israelites and the Ammonites."

28The king of Ammon, however, paid no attention to the message
Jephthah sent him.

**12–13** Jephthah's first move as commander was to get in touch with the Ammonites in an attempt to negotiate peace (v.12). Perhaps diplomacy would work, particularly since Ammon would learn from the messengers that a strong commander now headed the forces of Gilead. The reply from the king of the Ammonites contained hope for peace (v.13), but only on the condition that Israel return "occupied territory."

**14–15** Since the disputed land lay between the Arnon and the Jabbok rivers, Jephthah sent back a detailed explanation of how Israel obtained possession of that region. This historical summary attempts to prove that Israel captured this land from the Amorites without violating the territorial rights of either Moab or Ammon.

Throughout the message reference is repeatedly made to the kingdom of Moab. Ammon is not mentioned again until v.27. This is because Sihon king of the Amorites had taken away some land once belonging to Moab (Num 21:26). In all likelihood the Moabites were now allied with the Ammonites, as they had been before (cf. 3:13).

**16–18** Jephthah first referred to Israel's stay at Kadesh (v.16), when they requested permission to travel through Edom (Num 20:14–17) and Moab (v.17). The Pentateuch itself does not record this petition to Moab. Neither Edom nor Moab allowed Israel to pass through; so the people detoured south of Edom and then east of Moab, stopping at the eastern end of the Arnon River (v.18). The Lord specifically commanded Israel not to fight against Edom, Moab, and Ammon because these peoples were all related to Israel; and God had given them their own territory (Deut 2:5, 9, 19).

**19–22** No such prohibition applied to Sihon, however. So when the Amorite king also refused the Israelites passage, there was a battle at Jahaz, which is probably located near Medeba, south of the capital of Heshbon (vv.19–20). God gave the Israelites a decisive victory (v.21), and they took possession of the precise parcel of land then claimed by the king of Ammon (v.13).

One wishes that Jephthah would have defined the eastern boundary more clearly since Ammonite territory lay in that direction. According to Numbers 21:24, however, Moses' conquest reached up to the Ammonite border but did not include any of their land. Yet some of the kingdom of Sihon may have once belonged to the Ammonites, since the tribe of Gad was allotted "half the Ammonite country" in Joshua 13:25. Based on the borders at the time of Israel's conquest, Jephthah's case is a strong one. Moses had seized only Amorite territory and had avoided any open conflict with either Moab or Ammon.

**23–24** In OT times war often was viewed as a contest between the gods of the nations involved (cf. v.27). The Lord had clearly defeated the gods of the Amorites, giving Israel clear title to the land. The Ammonites, therefore, had no right to take it away (v.23). They should have been content with the territory Chemosh had given to them (v.24). Indeed, land itself was considered the property of the deity (cf. 2 Kings 5:17). Ammon was thus guilty of stealing real estate belonging to the God of Israel.

Jephthah's reference to Chemosh raises a problem, since Chemosh was the god of Moab while Milcom was the Ammonites' deity. One solution, implied in the comment on vv.14–15, was the close association of Moab and Ammon. The Ammonites may have joined in the worship of Moab's gods, just as the Midianites did in Numbers 25. Possibly "Chemosh" and "Milcom" were viewed as alternate names of the same deity. "Chemosh" is called "Ashtar-Chemosh" in line 17 of the Moabite Stone, and he may also have been identified with the Baal of Peor (Num 25:1–3).

Another possibility is that Jephthah confused the two names. As leader of a group of outlaws, he was hardly an expert in matters of history and comparative religion. His later action in offering up his daughter reveals a clear misunderstanding of Scripture. Inspiration guarantees an accurate account of Jephthah's message, but does it guarantee that all his statements are true? In favor of a wholly reliable account is the amazing accuracy of Jephthah's other historical statements. This would indicate that "Chemosh" was not an error.

A further problem stems from the apparent equality of Chemosh and Israel's God. Again, it is difficult to understand the depth of Jephthah's theological perception. He may have viewed Chemosh as a god who really existed, or he may have referred to him only for the sake of argument. Chemosh was certainly a reality in the minds of his worshipers. In actuality, of course, all the possessions of Moab and Ammon came from the one true God (Deut 2:9, 19; Amos 9:7).

**25–26** Jephthah's final argument is based on the length of time Israel had possessed the disputed territory. Balak was the king of Moab who hired Balaam to curse the Israelites. After the curses turned out to be repeated blessings (Num 24:10), Balak made no attempt to regain the area held by Sihon and then Israel (v.25). He clearly recognized the legitimacy of Israel's claim to the land. During the next "three hundred years," neither Moab nor Ammon succeeded in retaking the land (v.26). Did not such a long occupancy prove Israel's right to that area?

The mention of the 300 years fits in neatly with an early date for the Conquest (cf. Introduction: Background). Those favoring the late-date theory view it as a round number denoting several generations (like 480 in 1 Kings 6:1) or as a total of what were actually overlapping periods. The number of years given thus far for the periods of oppression and peace comes to 301, not counting the 18 years of Ammonite oppression.

**27–28** Insisting on his innocence, Jephthah appealed to the Lord to decide the issue (v.27). Wars between nations, as well as individual disputes (1 Sam 24:15), were regarded as ordeals that vindicated the claims of one party. This is the only explicit reference in the book to the Lord as judge.

Jephthah's detailed arguments failed to impress the king of Ammon (v.28). Convinced that at least might was on his side, the king prepared for war with Israel.

## Notes

---

**13** The antecedent of אֶתְהֶן (*'e<u>t</u>hen,* "them"; tr. collectively as "it" in NIV) would be the cities that made up the land. The gender of "cities" (עָרִים, *'ārîm*) is also feminine.

**24** The link between Chemosh and Milcom may be the "Ashtar" of the Moabite Stone. Ashtar is called "tyrant" or "king" in Ugaritic (ANET, p. 140, lines 53–56); and "Milcom" is clearly derived from מֶלֶךְ (*mele<u>k</u>*), the usual word for "king."

**26** Heshbon and Aroer were on the important King's Highway that ran some twelve to fifteen miles east of the Dead Sea. Heshbon was opposite the northern end of the Dead Sea, while Aroer lay twenty-five miles south of Heshbon. Both were allotted to the tribe of Reuben.

On "surrounding settlements" see the Notes on 1:27.

**27** חָטָאתִי (*ḥāṭā'<u>t</u>î,* "I have wronged") is literally "I have sinned," which further illustrates the religious nature of warfare.

---

### 5. *Jephthah's vow and victory over Ammon*

11:29–33

[29]Then the Spirit of the LORD came upon Jephthah. He crossed Gilead
and Manasseh, passed through Mizpah of Gilead, and from there he
advanced against the Ammonites. [30]And Jephthah made a vow to the
LORD: "If you give the Ammonites into my hands, [31]whatever comes out

**of the door of my house to meet me when I return in triumph from the Ammonites will be the LORD's, and I will sacrifice it as a burnt offering."**
**32 Then Jephthah went over to fight the Ammonites, and the LORD gave them into his hands. 33 He devastated twenty towns from Aroer to the vicinity of Minnith, as far as Abel Keramim. Thus Israel subdued Ammon.**

**29** As in the case of Gideon (6:34), the Spirit of the Lord empowered Jephthah in preparation for battle. Strengthened by this divine designation, he traveled north through Transjordan, gathering troops from the tribes of Gad and Manasseh. These two tribes actually split Gilead between them (Josh 13:25, 31), with Gad receiving the larger share.

**30–31** Jephthah's desire to defeat the Ammonites was so intense that he made a special "vow to the Lord" (v.30). Though intended as an act of devotion, it showed a lack of faith in God's enabling power. Scholars continue to debate whether or not Jephthah had a human sacrifice in mind. The masculine gender could be translated "whatever comes out" (v.31) or "whoever comes out" and "I will sacrifice it," but it is hard to see how a common animal sacrifice would express unusual devotion.

Human sacrifice was strictly forbidden by the Mosaic law (Lev 18:21; Deut 12:31); so Jephthah should have known that God's favor could not be gained in this terrible way. Yet Israel's neighbors—ironically, especially the Ammonites—sacrificed their children; and this custom might have influenced Jephthah. The most notable example was the slaughter of the crown prince at the hands of the king of Moab (2 Kings 3:27). In his desperation the king was willing to pay the ultimate price for victory. Although Jephthah did not originally plan to sacrifice his daughter, he would gladly have offered up anyone else if it helped bring victory.

**32–33** The Lord gave Israel a stunning victory over Ammon, and Israel was able to capture twenty cities. These included Aroer, at Reuben's southern border just north of the Arnon, and Abel Keramim, tentatively located about five miles north of Heshbon. Thus the bulk of the region between the Arnon and the Jabbok once again belonged to Israel. Verse 33 indicates that a very large number of Ammonites died in the battle.

## Notes

---

**31** The words בְּשׁוּבִי בְשָׁלוֹם (*bešûḇî ḇešālôm,* "when I return in triumph") are identical with those of Gideon in 8:9, as he grimly promised death to the men of Peniel.

The NASB connects the last two clauses with "or" instead of "and" (NIV) in an attempt to provide one option for a human, the other for an animal. While it is true that the conjunction וְ (*we*) can mean "or" occasionally, the writer knows of no case where it joins clauses so diverse in structure and has the meaning "or." The specified word for "or," אוֹ ('*ô*), would be expected, as in v.34.

**33** "Minnith" may be the same as Μααυιθ (*Maanith*) of Eusebius' *Onomasticon,* which town was located some four miles northeast of Heshbon. The "wheat of Minnith" is mentioned in Ezek 27:17.

---

### 6. *Jephthah's vow fulfilled*

#### 11:34–40

34When Jephthah returned to his home in Mizpah, who should come
out to meet him but his daughter, dancing to the sound of tambourines!
She was an only child. Except for her he had neither son nor daughter.
35When he saw her, he tore his clothes and cried, "Oh! My daughter!
You have made me miserable and wretched, because I have made a vow
to the LORD that I cannot break."
36"My father," she replied, "you have given your word to the LORD. Do
to me just as you promised, now that the LORD has avenged you of your
enemies, the Ammonites. 37But grant me this one request," she said.
"Give me two months to roam the hills and weep with my friends,
because I will never marry."
38"You may go," he said. And he let her go for two months. She and
the girls went into the hills and wept because she would never marry.
39After the two months, she returned to her father and he did to her as
he had vowed. And she was a virgin.
From this comes the Israelite custom 40that each year the young
women of Israel go out for four days to commemorate the daughter of
Jephthah the Gileadite.

**34–35** The flush of victory gave way to bitter despair when Jephthah was greeted by his daughter, leaping and dancing (v.34), like Miriam and the women of Israel who had celebrated the triumph of the Red Sea (Exod 15:20). But as the first to leave his house, she came under the terms of his vow. How strange for this happy young girl to notice the response of her father! He behaved like a defeated soldier, not the victorious commander he really was. Jephthah quickly realized what he had done; for his daughter was an only child, and her death would mean the end of his family line.

Jephthah's lamentable words in v.35 describe the situation as an unmitigated disaster. Both he and the Ammonites were humiliated and subdued. His own daughter unknowingly brought calamity to herself and her father.

**36–39** Jephthah's daughter sensed the implications of her father's vow but made no attempt to get him to break it. Her willingness to yield herself resembled that of another only child, Isaac, who faced almost certain death when he allowed his father to tie him to an altar (Gen 22). Even if victory over Ammon meant her life, it was worth it; and she gently encouraged her father to perform his vow (v.36).

First, however, Jephthah's daughter requested a two-month period in which she could literally "bewail her virginity" (v.37). The goal of every Hebrew girl was to marry and have children (Gen 30:1), but Jephthah's daughter would do neither. Accompanied by her friends, she spent two months on the mountains, weeping and meditating, preparing for her ordeal (v.38). When she returned, Jephthah carried out his solemn vow (v.39).

**40** The yearly commemoration of this noble girl makes sense only if she died at the hands of her father. The view that she served at the sanctuary (Exod 38:8) in lifelong ministry would not demand this kind of lamenting. And, sad to say, not all the women "at the entrance to the Tent of Meeting" remained virgins either (1 Sam 2:22).

The death of this innocent girl came because of a rash vow. Jephthah knew that it was a sin to break a vow (Num 30:2), but in this case it was a greater sin to fulfill it. Jephthah was treating his daughter as a "person devoted to destruction" (Lev 27:29).

This punishment was a strong curse reserved for the enemies of God (cf. Josh 6:17), but Jephthah's daughter had done nothing to deserve such a fate. According to Proverbs 26:2, "an undeserved curse does not come to rest." Perhaps an analogy may be drawn from the oath Saul took and Jonathan inadvertently violated. Saul concluded that his son must die, but the people rescued the popular prince (1 Sam 14:28, 43–45). Likewise, though Jephthah sincerely believed God required him to go through with his promise, he was badly mistaken.

## Notes

---

**34** Women customarily greeted military heroes in this way; so it seems strange that Jephthah was taken by surprise. The תֻּפִּים (*tuppîm,* "tambourines") and מְחֹלוֹת (*m$^{e}$ḥōlôṯ,* "dancing") are also mentioned in Exod 15:20 and 1 Sam 18:6.

**35** Gideon used the same interjection אֲהָהּ (*'$^{a}$hāh,* "oh") when he was afraid he would die (6:22).

Ironically, the root כָּרַע (*kāra',* translated "made miserable," here in the Hiphil) is used of Sisera's "bowing down" at the feet of Jael (5:27).

עָכַר (*'āḵar,* "to grieve, trouble"; NIV, "wretched") appears in Josh 7:25, where Achan "brought trouble" on all Israel. Also compare 1 Sam 14:29.

**39** "She was a virgin" is literally "she did not know a man." יָדַע (*yāḏa',* "to know") is used as a euphemism for sexual intercourse (cf. 19:25; 21:11).

A thorough discussion of the problem of this passage is found in James Mathisen's "Jephthah's Vow and Jephthah's Daughter's Fate" (Master's thesis, Wheaton College, 1969). For a summary of arguments in favor of the view that Jephthah's daughter was not put to death, see Gleason Archer, *A Survey of Old Testament Introduction* (Chicago: Moody, 1974), pp. 284–85.

---

### 7. *Jephthah's defeat of Ephraim*

#### 12:1–7

1 The men of Ephraim called out their forces, crossed over to Zaphon
and said to Jephthah, "Why did you go to fight the Ammonites without
calling us to go with you? We're going to burn down your house over
your head."
2 Jephthah answered, "I and my people were engaged in a great
struggle with the Ammonites, and although I called, you didn't save me
out of their hands. 3 When I saw that you wouldn't help, I took my life in
my hands and crossed over to fight the Ammonites, and the LORD gave
me the victory over them. Now why have you come up today to fight
me?"
4 Jephthah then called together the men of Gilead and fought against
Ephraim. The Gileadites struck them down because the Ephraimites had
said, "You Gileadites are renegades from Ephraim and Manasseh."
5 The Gileadites captured the fords of the Jordan leading to Ephraim,
and whenever a survivor of Ephraim said, "Let me cross over," the men
of Gilead asked him, "Are you an Ephraimite?" If he replied, "No," 6 they
said, "All right, say 'Shibboleth.'" If he said, "Sibboleth," because he
could not pronounce the word correctly, they seized him and killed him
at the fords of the Jordan. Forty-two thousand Ephraimites were killed
at that time.

**7 Jephthah led Israel six years. Then Jephthah the Gileadite died, and was buried in a town in Gilead.**

The proud and powerful tribe of Ephraim had earlier denounced Gideon for failing to invite them to participate in the victory over Midian (8:1–3). Gideon had soothed them by involving them in the campaign and praising their contribution. Once more Ephraim challenged another general of Manasseh, and this time the exchange did not end so amicably. Jephthah was not about to be bullied by his ungrateful neighbors, and a tragic civil war broke out between these two tribes descended from Joseph.

**1–3** The Ephraimites voiced their complaint after crossing the Jordan and coming to Zaphon, a town about five miles north of Succoth (v.1). They threatened to burn down Jephthah's house, as if he were no more than a petty prince (cf. 15:6).

Understandably, Jephthah was greatly irritated by the Ephraimites' arrogance. During the eighteen-year oppression, the people of Gilead had doubtless asked for help from Ephraim and other affected tribes (cf. 10:9), but no assistance was forthcoming (v.2). In the recently completed campaign, there was no mention of an invitation to Ephraim (11:29), though Jephthah indicated that a general call may have gone out. The fight against the Ammonites was a perilous one at best. Yet Jephthah defeated them and gave God the credit (v.3). Why should the Ephraimites complain about a victory accomplished through God's intervention for the benefit of all the tribes? It was a strange jealousy that spurred on Ephraim.

**4–6** The civil war was triggered when the men of Ephraim called the Gileadites "fugitives" or "renegades" (v.4). This insult may have been partially aimed at Jephthah's former position as a brigand chief, but more likely it stemmed from the division between the eastern and western tribes (cf. 5:15–17). Half of Manasseh lay east of the Jordan, occupying Gilead along with the tribe of Gad. Ephraim looked down on these relatives across the river, who no longer even spoke the same dialect (v.6).

For the third time in Judges, the capture of the fords of the Jordan was crucial (v.5; 3:28; 7:24–25). Apparently these were the same fords where the Ephraimites had cut down the Midianites in chapter 7. But this time Jephthah's army slaughtered the Ephraimites who were trying to flee from the skillful Gileadite fighters. The army of Ephraim turned out to be the fugitives. "Survivor" (*pālîṭ*, v.5) is the same word translated "renegades" in v.4.

The clever test faced by the disgraced soldiers was to pronounce the word "Shibboleth" (*šibbōleṯ*), which means either "an ear of grain" or "a flowing stream." The Ephraimites were identified when they managed to say only "Sibboleth" (*sibbōleṯ*). Their pronunciation, like Peter's accent in Matthew 26:73, gave them away. This dialectal difference provides interesting material for linguists. The sibbilants are notoriously difficult in Semitic languages. During World War II, the Nazis identified Russian Jews by the way they pronounced the word for corn: "kookoorooza."

With the loss of 42,000 men, Ephraim's military capability was virtually wiped out (cf. Num 1:33). Jephthah was vindicated and his position as leader of Gilead was strengthened. Nevertheless, the intertribal warfare illustrated the serious problems that confronted the nation as a whole.

**7** Jephthah "led" or "judged" Israel for only six years and most likely ruled only in Transjordan. He was buried in Gilead, perhaps in Mizpah where he had made his home.

## Notes

**4** The translation "from" for בְּתוֹךְ (*b^e^t̲ôḵ*) makes excellent sense. בְּ (*b^e^*) frequently means "from" in Ugaritic.

**7** Some MSS of the LXX read בְּעִירוֹ (*b^e^'îrô,* "in his city") for בְּעָרֵי (*b^e^'ārê,* "in the cities of" Gilead). This reading would also point to Mizpah as Jephthah's burial place.

### J. *The Rules of Ibzan, Elon, and Abdon (12:8–15)*

Before his detailed discussion of Samson's life, the author inserts brief notices about the last three minor judges. They ruled for comparatively short periods of time and were probably contemporaries.

#### 1. *Ibzan*

12:8–10

> **8After him, Ibzan of Bethlehem led Israel. 9He had thirty sons and thirty daughters. He gave his daughters away in marriage to those outside his clan, and for his sons he brought in thirty young women as wives from outside his clan. Ibzan led Israel seven years. 10Then Ibzan died, and was buried in Bethlehem.**

**8** Ibzan ruled from Bethlehem, which may refer to the famous town south of Jerusalem or to a city in the territory of Zebulun, located about ten miles north of Megiddo (Josh 19:15). The Zebulun location is favored because the southern city is usually identified as "Bethlehem in Judah" (17:7–9; 19:1–2, 18). If the northern site is correct, however, it means that two judges from Zebulun are treated in succession.

**9–10** Ibzan's large family reveals his wealth and polygamous practices (cf. 8:30; 10:4). The meaning of "outside his clan" is not certain, and the words "his clan" are not found in the Hebrew text. In its only other occurrence in a similar context, "outside" (*ḥûṣāh*) refers to outside the immediate family (Deut 25:5). "Clan" may well be correct, for marriages were often contracted within one's tribe (14:3). The fact that Ibzan's marriage policy is mentioned, however, may indicate a break with tradition.

## Notes

**9** According to Deut 25:5, a brother-in-law is to marry a young widow, lest she go "outside" the family (הַחוּצָה, *haḥûṣāh*).

## 2. *Elon*

### 12:11–12

**[11]After him, Elon the Zebulunite led Israel ten years. [12]Then Elon died, and was buried in Aijalon in the land of Zebulun.**

**11–12** Elon ranks with Tola (10:1–2) as a judge about whom almost nothing is known. Like Tola, he was named after one of the sons of the founder of the tribe (Gen 46:14). The city where he was buried may in fact have been named for his famous forebear, since the consonants for "Aijalon" are the same as for "Elon" (*'yln*). Tola had lived in a site named after a son of Issachar (cf. 10:1–2). The name "Aijalon" could have arisen because of the well-known city and valley of that name west of Jerusalem (cf. Josh 10:12).

## Notes

---

**11–12** The LXX has Αἰλωμ (*Ailōm*) for both the name of the man and the name of the place.

---

## 3. *Abdon*

### 12:13–15

**[13]After him, Abdon son of Hillel, from Pirathon, led Israel. [14]He had forty sons and thirty grandsons, who rode on seventy donkeys. He led Israel eight years. [15]Then Abdon son of Hillel died, and was buried at Pirathon in Ephraim, in the hill country of the Amalekites.**

**13** Pirathon is probably the same as modern Far'ata, located about six miles southwest of Shechem. It was the home of Benaiah, one of David's mighty men (1 Chron 11:31) from Ephraim (1 Chron 27:14). The site is close to the border between Ephraim and Manasseh, and its connection with "the hill country of the Amalekites" (v.15) has been discussed with reference to 5:14.

**14–15** The mention of Abdon's forty sons and thirty grandsons seems out of proportion with his short period as judge (v.14). Counting sons and grandsons, Abdon's offspring equaled Gideon's (8:30).

For the significance of the donkeys, see the comment on 10:4.

## K. *Samson's Victory Over the Philistines (13:1–16:31)*

From chapters 13 to 18, the author concentrates on the tribe of Dan, which had been one of the largest and most prominent tribes during the wilderness march (Num 2:25–31). In the period of the judges, however, Dan seemed helpless against the Amorites (1:34) and moved northward to find new territory (chs. 17–18). Contrasted with these failures are the exploits of Samson, whose personal achievements are detailed in four chapters. Yet his own life was a strange mixture of the strength and weakness that epitomized the tragic conditions within the tribe itself.

### 1. *The angelic announcement of Samson's birth*

#### 13:1–14

1 Again the Israelites did evil in the eyes of the LORD, so the LORD delivered them into the hands of the Philistines for forty years.

2 A certain man of Zorah, named Manoah, from the clan of the Danites, had a wife who was sterile and remained childless. 3 The angel of the LORD appeared to her and said, "You are sterile and childless, but you are going to conceive and have a son. 4 Now see to it that you drink no wine or other fermented drink and that you do not eat anything unclean, 5 because you will conceive and give birth to a son. No razor may be used on his head, because the boy is to be a Nazirite, set apart to God from birth, and he will begin the deliverance of Israel from the hands of the Philistines."

6 Then the woman went to her husband and told him, "A man of God came to me. He looked like an angel of God, very awesome. I didn't ask him where he came from, and he didn't tell me his name. 7 But he said to me, 'You will conceive and give birth to a son. Now then, drink no wine or other fermented drink and do not eat anything unclean, because the boy will be a Nazirite of God from birth until the day of his death.'"

8 Then Manoah prayed to the LORD: "O Lord, I beg you, let the man of God you sent to us come again to teach us how to bring up the boy who is to be born."

9 God heard Manoah, and the angel of God came again to the woman while she was out in the field; but her husband Manoah was not with her. 10 The woman hurried to tell her husband, "He's here! The man who appeared to me the other day!"

11 Manoah got up and followed his wife. When he came to the man, he said, "Are you the one who talked to my wife?"

"I am," he said.

12 So Manoah asked him, "When your words are fulfilled, what is to be the rule for the boy's life and work?"

13 The angel of the LORD answered, "Your wife must do all that I have told her. 14 She must not eat anything that comes from the grapevine, nor drink any wine or other fermented drink nor eat anything unclean. She must do everything I have commanded her."

**1** The primary introduction to this cycle was in 10:6–16, where it was linked with the sins that brought on the Ammonite invasion. Now the author, having described the defeat of Ammon, turns to the enemy that proved to be a thorn in Israel's side until David mastered them.

The Philistines had lived in Palestine since Abraham's time (Gen 21:32–34; 26:1–6); but since 1200 B.C., they had settled along the coast in increasing numbers (cf. 3:3). Shamgar had won a great victory over them (3:31), halting their advance at least temporarily.

The Philistines, however, were warlike and powerful, and by 1100 B.C. they were exerting considerable pressure from their five cities in the west. The start of their forty-year oppression of Israel—the longest in the book—followed about five years later, and the tribes of Dan and Judah were the first to come under Philistine rule (cf. 15:11).

**2–5** The epic story of Samson begins in the city of Zorah (v.2), located in the foothills about fifteen miles west of Jerusalem, on the northern edge of the valley of Sorek.

Zorah is mentioned five more times in the book, always in conjunction with nearby Eshtaol (v.25; 16:31; 18:2, 8, 11).

The plight of Manoah's wife was one shared earlier by the renowned Sarah and Rachel (Gen 11:30; 29:31). Since the Israelites considered children as a gift of God (cf. Ps 127:3), they viewed barrenness as a mark of divine disfavor. To die childless was tragic indeed (cf. 11:37–40). Manoah's wife would have been overjoyed to have just an ordinary baby, but the angel of the Lord informed her that she would have a special son (v.3). An angelic visitor had also appeared to Hagar (Gen 16:11). Moreover, God appointed the angel Gabriel to announce to Mary that she would be the mother of Jesus (Luke 1:26–38). On each occasion the angel used similar terminology to announce the birth of a son: "you are going to conceive and have a son" (vv.3, 5). It was a formula of blessing used also in Isaiah 7:14.

The son promised to Manoah's wife would be a Nazirite (*nāzîr*, v.5), a word meaning "dedicated" or "consecrated." According to Numbers 6:1–12, the Nazirite vow was voluntarily taken for a limited time, but Samson's was lifelong. A Nazirite had three special restrictions: (1) he was to abstain totally from wine and beer ("fermented drink") and could not eat any grapes or raisins; (2) he could not have his hair cut during the time of the vow; and (3) he could not come near a corpse. Violation of all these requirements plays an important part in Samson's life, though the second restriction is particularly emphasized.

Samson's mother was also commanded to observe the Nazirite vow (v.4), at least during the course of her pregnancy. The prohibition against eating unclean food applied to all Israelites. It was, however, especially important for her because carcasses were used as food and could contaminate—or make ceremonially unclean—whatever they came in contact with (cf. Lev 11:32–40). This related directly to the third restriction.

The dedication of the child was to have military implications also, for he would gain victories over the Philistines. Yet since he would only "begin the deliverance" (v.5), the conquest would be an incomplete one.

**6–7** Manoah's wife shared the amazing news with her husband but had difficulty describing the visitor (v.6). "A man of God" is a term normally applied to prophets such as Moses (Deut 33:1) or Samuel (1 Sam 9:6). David, a king as well as a prophet, received the same designation (2 Chron 8:14). The man's impressive and majestic appearance caused her to wondered whether he was an angel. "Awesome" (*nôrā'*), or "fear-producing," is often descriptive of deity (Pss 66:5; 76:12).

To establish the authenticity of the message, it was important to know the name of the messenger (cf. Exod 3:13). Manoah's wife was afraid to ask, but her husband tried to find out his name in vv.17–18.

**8–14** Manoah's motivation in praying for a second visit by the man of God apparently lay in his anxiety about rearing so unusual a child (v.8). He seemed overwhelmed by the responsibility, which may explain why his wife had said nothing to him about the child's involvement with the Philistines. Possibly Manoah was suspicious that his wife had been imagining things, and he wanted confirmation of her story.

In any event, the Lord answered Manoah's prayer and sent the angel back, though again he appeared only to the woman initially (v.9). This time, however, Manoah was able to confer with him (vv.11–18). Yet the angel said nothing more about how to raise the child; the boy's manner of life and his mission in life had been adequately explained in v.5. Verse 14 does, however, add the detail about avoiding any product of the grapevine, not just wine (cf. Num 6:3). The fact that the angel did not directly answer Manoah's question may imply that his request for a confirming visit showed lack of faith. Like Gideon (6:36–40), Manoah was not easily convinced by the word of God.

## Notes

---

**4** The word שֵׁכָר (*šēk̲ār,* "fermented drink") is cognate to the Akkadian *šikaru,* a kind of beer.

**5** The use of הִנֵּה (*hinnēh,* "behold"; untr. in NIV) with הָרָה (*hārāh,* "conceive") provides important evidence that the same construction can mean "a virgin will become pregnant," not "is pregnant," in Isa 7:14. An announcement of this kind could be part of a marriage ceremony as a blessing on the new relationship. For a fuller discussion of these passages, see the writer's article "The Immanuel Prophecy in Isaiah 7:14–8:22," JBL 91 (1972): 450, 456.

---

### 2. *The angel's miracle*

### 13:15–23

15 Manoah said to the angel of the LORD, "We would like you to stay
until we prepare a young goat for you."
16 The angel of the LORD replied, "Even though you detain me, I will not
eat any of your food. But if you prepare a burnt offering, offer it to the
LORD." (Manoah did not realize that it was the angel of the LORD.)
17 Then Manoah inquired of the angel of the LORD, "What is your name,
so that we may honor you when your word comes true?"
18 He replied, "Why do you ask my name? It is beyond understanding."
19 Then Manoah took a young goat, together with the grain offering, and
sacrificed it on a rock to the LORD. And the LORD did an amazing thing
while Manoah and his wife watched: 20 As the flame blazed up from the
altar toward heaven, the angel of the LORD ascended in the flame. Seeing
this, Manoah and his wife fell with their faces to the ground. 21 When the
angel of the LORD did not show himself again to Manoah and his wife,
Manoah realized that it was the angel of the LORD.
22 "We are doomed to die!" he said to his wife. "We have seen God!"
23 But his wife answered, "If the LORD had meant to kill us, he would
not have accepted a burnt offering and grain offering from our hands,
nor shown us all these things or now told us this."

**15–17** Proper attitude demanded that Manoah provide a meal for his guest (v.15), as Abraham had done on a similar occasion (Gen 18:1–8). So Manoah prepared a young goat, the same kind of animal Gideon offered to his heavenly visitor (6:17–19). Since Manoah and his wife had not fully realized who the angel was, they did not intend to sacrifice the goat. When the angel asked that a burnt offering be presented to the Lord (v.16), Manoah wondered about the identity of this man (v.17). A knowledge of his name would provide a clue to his nature also. Besides, Manoah wished to "honor" or "reward" the man who predicted the birth of the long sought after son. The same Hebrew term is used of Balak's promise to reward Balaam richly for cursing Israel (Num 22:17, 37).

**18–22** The angel avoided a direct answer to the question, as he had done with Jacob centuries before (Gen 32:29). In the phrase "beyond understanding" (v.18), however, there is a clear indication of his divine nature. The phrase is a translation of the word *pil'î*, which can also be rendered "wonderful." The same root occurs in "an amazing thing" in v.19 and in "wonders" in 6:13. In Isaiah 9:6 the closely related noun *pele'* is translated "Wonderful (Counselor)," a title for Christ himself.

Proof that this was the angel of the Lord came when Manoah presented the burnt offering and its accompanying grain offering (v.19). As the flame rose, the angel ascended in it before the couple's startled eyes (v.20). This was even more spectacular than the disappearance of the angel who talked with Gideon (6:21). Manoah's reaction to the miracle, however, matched Gideon's; Manoah too thought he would die as a result of seeing God (vv.21–22; cf. Gen 16:13 and comment on 6:22).

**23** It was the Lord who calmed Gideon's fear of dying (6:23), but it was Manoah's wife who relieved his anxiety. Using good common sense, she reasoned that the Lord would not have taken the trouble to come down twice and promise them a child if they were to die immediately. Besides, the Lord had requested and accepted an offering from them. The acceptance may again have been evident if the fire was supernaturally lit, though this point is not as clear as it was in 6:21.

## Notes

---

**19** The word צוּר (*ṣûr*, "rock") also occurred as the site of Gideon's sacrifice (6:21). In 13:20 an altar is also mentioned, whereas Gideon did not build one until afterwards (6:24).

The Hiphil of פלא (*pl'*, "amazing") is used of surprising or marvelous activity also in 2 Chron 26:15 (NIV, "greatly") and Isa 29:14.

---

### 3. *The birth and growth of Samson*

13:24–25

**24**The woman gave birth to a boy and named him Samson. He grew
and the LORD blessed him, **25**and the Spirit of the LORD began to stir him
while he was in Mahaneh Dan, between Zorah and Eshtaol.

**24–25** The faith of Manoah's wife was rewarded when the Lord blessed the couple with a baby boy (v.24). The name "Samson" is formed from the word for "sun" (*šemeš*), perhaps to signify that God, like the sun, had brought new light into their lives (cf. Mal 4:2). A possible factor in the naming of Samson was the location of Beth Shemesh ("house of the sun") on the southern edge of the Sorek Valley, directly opposite Zorah. Samson's name was given by his mother, which compares with Hagar's naming of Ishmael (Gen 16:11; cf. Isa 7:14).

The early years of Samson's life are covered swiftly (cf. Luke 1:80; 2:40, 52). God gave him a sound mind and a strong body as he grew to maturity. For a while at least he lived in Mahaneh Dan (v.25), which means "camp of Dan." It may have been a temporary home due to Philistine pressure on the cities. In 18:12 Mahaneh Dan is located west of Kiriath Jearim. Eshtaol lay a mile and a half northeast of Zorah and is always linked with that city (cf. comment on v.2).

More than any other judge, Samson was moved by the Spirit of God (v.25; also 14:6, 19; 15:14). On this occasion an unusual verb describes the Spirit's activity. Elsewhere the word is used of men whose spirits are disturbed by dreams, such as Pharaoh (Gen 41:8) and Nebuchadnezzar (Dan 2:1, 3). Perhaps the Lord used the same means to speak to Samson and to stir him to "begin the deliverance . . . from the hands of the Philistines" (v.5).

Contrasted with Jephthah, Samson had every advantage as a boy. His birth was predicted by an angel; he had godly parents who loved him greatly; he was uniquely dedicated to God as a Nazirite; and he experienced the power of God's Spirit as a young man. Despite all these favorable factors, Samson's life as it unfolds in the next three chapters is marked by tragedy.

## Notes

**25** This is the only verse where the Qal of פעם (*p'm*, "to stir, trouble") is used. The Niphal stem occurs in Gen 41:8 and Dan 2:3 and the Hithpael in Dan 2:1.

### 4. *Samson's engagement to a Philistine*

#### 14:1–9

1 Samson went down to Timnah and saw there a young Philistine
woman. 2 When he returned, he said to his father and mother, "I have
seen a Philistine woman in Timnah; now get her for me as my wife."
3 His father and mother replied, "Isn't there an acceptable woman
among your relatives or among all our people? Must you go to the
uncircumcised Philistines to get a wife?"
But Samson said to his father, "Get her for me. She's the right one for
me." 4 (His parents did not know that this was from the LORD, who was
seeking an occasion to confront the Philistines; for at that time they
were ruling over Israel.) 5 Samson went down to Timnah together with
his father and mother. As they approached the vineyards of Timnah,
suddenly a young lion came roaring toward him. 6 The Spirit of the LORD
came upon him in power so that he tore the lion apart with his bare
hands as he might have torn a young goat. But he told neither his father
nor his mother what he had done. 7 Then he went down and talked with
the woman, and he liked her.
8 Some time later, when he went back to marry her, he turned aside to
look at the lion's carcass. In it was a swarm of bees and some honey,
9 which he scooped out with his hands and ate as he went along. When
he rejoined his parents, he gave them some, and they too ate it. But he
did not tell them that he had taken the honey from the lion's carcass.

**1–2** The saga of Samson begins and ends the same way, with Samson displaying a fatal weakness for Philistine women. In this first episode Samson traveled some four miles southwest of Zorah to Timnah (v.1), a city on the border between Judah and Dan, which apparently was assigned to the latter tribe (Josh 15:10; 19:43).

The presence of Philistines at Timnah reveals their occupation of Israelite territory. Philistine rule was more subtle and peaceful than the other periods of oppression, since Samson and presumably others were free to intermarry with the Philistines. Even the tribe of Judah was content to let the Philistines control them, a sign that a fairly normal life was possible (15:11).

At Timnah a Philistine woman captivated Samson, and he wished to marry her (v.2). Normally in Israel parents decided whom their children should marry (Gen 24:4; Exod 21:9), or at least they had an important voice in the decision (Gen 28:1–2). The parents were responsible for making arrangements with the bride's parents (Gen 24:34–38). Samson was willing to let his parents approach the woman's parents as long as he selected the woman. In Genesis 34:4 Shechem had asked his father, Hamor, to get Jacob's daughter as his wife.

**3–4** Samson's parents objected strenuously to his choice (v.3). Israel had been warned not to intermarry with the Canaanites (Deut 7:1–3; cf. Judg 3:6). Although the Philistines were not listed among the seven nations of Canaan in Deuteronomy 7:1–3, the same objections given there applied to the Philistines also. They were foreigners whose idolatry would lead their spouses astray. How much better to marry a "relative," someone from the tribe of Dan, or at least an Israelite girl! Mixed marriages were uniformly disastrous early (Gen 26:34–35) and late (Neh 13:27) in Israel's history. Moreover, the Philistines were the one nation near Israel that did not practice circumcision of any kind. In Egypt, Moab, and elsewhere, circumcision was often associated with reaching puberty or with premarital rites; but at least it was circumcision. Samson himself later used "uncircumcised" as an epithet for the pagan Philistines (15:18; cf. 2 Sam 1:20).

The pleading of Samson's parents did not sway him. His emphatic reply might be paraphrased, "She's the one I want and that's it!" Reluctantly his parents gave in, convinced that he would regret the decision and ruin his life. From the divine perspective, however, Samson's contact with the Philistines gave an opportunity for God to use him (v.4). It seems paradoxical that the Lord would work through Samson's willful decision, but this aspect of God's sovereignty appeared before in Judges (cf. 3:1–2 and Introduction: Theological Values).

**5–6** Samson and his reluctant parents were traveling to Timnah to discuss marriage arrangements when his great strength was first displayed (v.5). He had evidently left his parents briefly and rejoined them later on the main road (cf. v.6 and vv.8–9). Attacked by a lion, Samson was enabled by the Spirit of God to kill the lion easily. This is the first time in the OT that *ṣālaḥ* is linked with the Spirit's work. The verb means "to rush upon" and is used of a fire in Amos 5:6. In 1 Samuel the Spirit came powerfully on Saul, enabling him to prophesy (10:6, 10) or to prepare for battle (11:6). David experienced the "rush" of the Spirit when he was anointed as king (1 Sam 16:13). For Samson the presence of God's Spirit meant tremendous physical strength (cf. 14:19; 15:14).

Other figures in pagan literature, such as Enkidu, companion of Gilgamesh, and the Greek hero Heracles were renowned for killing lions with their bare hands. David rescued lambs from the mouths of bears and lions, though he apparently "struck" them with his shepherd's staff (1 Sam 17:34–37).

Samson said nothing to his parents about his feat because his contact with the dead lion violated his Nazirite vow (cf. Num 6:6, 9). This is made clearer by the repetition in v.9. The mention of the vineyards in v.5 may mean that Samson broke another Nazirite law by eating some grapes (Num 6:3).

**7–9** This additional meeting with the woman reinforced Samson's desire to marry her; so at the specified time he returned to Timnah for the wedding feast (vv.7–8a). On the way he took the same path he had followed in v.5 and noticed that there was a honeycomb in the lion's carcass (v.8b). Heedless of the Nazirite vow, he scooped out some delicious honey and shared it with his parents (v.9). It was the unusual location of the honey that gave Samson the idea for the riddle of vv.12–14.

## Notes

**1** Timnah has been identified with Tell el-Batash, about four miles northwest of Beth Shemesh (cf. Boling, p. 229). Evidence of Philistine occupation has been found there.

**1–2** The verb וַיֵּרֶד (*wayyēreḏ*, "[and he] went down," vv.1, 5, 10) fits the lower elevation of Timnah. Conversely, וַיַּעַל (*wayya'al*, "[and he] returned") in v.2 is literally "went up."

**3** The NIV's "she's the right one for me" renders the idiom יָשְׁרָה בְעֵינָי (*yāšᵉrāh ḇᵉ'ênāy*), which is literally "she is right in my eyes." Another version of the same idiom is found in v.7: "he liked her." The same Hebrew words are behind the last verse in Judges: "Everyone did as he saw fit." Samson was conforming to the undisciplined life-style of his age.

**4** תֹּאֲנָה (*tō'ᵃnāh*, "occasion") occurs only here. A verb from the same root (אנה, *'nh*) is used of an accidental homicide in Exod 21:13, where God "lets it happen." Again, God's permissive will is in view.

## 5. *The marriage feast and the riddle*

### 14:10–20

[10] Now his father went down to see the woman. And Samson made a
feast there, as was customary for bridegrooms. [11] When he appeared, he
was given thirty companions.
[12] "Let me tell you a riddle," Samson said to them. "If you can give me
the answer within the seven days of the feast, I will give you thirty linen
garments and thirty sets of clothes. [13] If you can't tell me the answer, you
must give me thirty linen garments and thirty sets of clothes."
"Tell us your riddle," they said. "Let's hear it."
[14] He replied,

> "Out of the eater, something to eat;
> out of the strong, something sweet."

For three days they could not give the answer.
[15] On the fourth day, they said to Samson's wife, "Coax your husband
into explaining the riddle for us, or we will burn you and your father's
household to death. Did you invite us here to rob us?"
[16] Then Samson's wife threw herself on him, sobbing, "You hate me!
You don't really love me. You've given my people a riddle, but you
haven't told me the answer."
"I haven't even explained it to my father or mother," he replied, "so
why should I explain it to you?" [17] She cried the whole seven days of the
feast. So on the seventh day he finally told her, because she continued
to press him. She in turn explained the riddle to her people.

18Before sunset on the seventh day the men of the town said to him,

"What is sweeter than honey?
What is stronger than a lion?"

Samson said to them,

"If you had not plowed with my heifer,
you would not have solved my riddle."

19Then the Spirit of the LORD came upon him in power. He went down
to Ashkelon, struck down thirty of their men, stripped them of their
belongings and gave their clothes to those who had explained the
riddle. Burning with anger, he went up to his father's house. 20And
Samson's wife was given to the friend who had attended him at his
wedding.

**10** Arriving at Timnah, Samson made preparations for the wedding feast. The only other such feast in the OT was given by Laban, the father of Leah, at her marriage to Jacob (Gen 29:22). It too was seven days long (29:27–28), reflecting the leisurely pace of an Eastern culture that was accustomed to lengthy celebrations. "Feast" (*mišteh*) is literally "a place of drinking," and doubtless the forbidden fruit of the vine passed between the lips of Samson the Nazirite.

Samson's father is singled out, perhaps because he was paying for the feast, or perhaps because he was a witness to this marriage covenant (cf. Gen 24:50; Ezek 16:8). Witnesses were asked to sign deeds of purchase in legal transactions (Jer 32:12), and this may have included marriage contracts also (cf. Wolf, "Immanuel Prophecy," pp. 450–53).

**11** The thirty companions were probably provided by the bride's family. These "companions" correspond to the "guests of the bridegroom" mentioned in Matthew 9:15 and Mark 2:19. Perhaps Samson broke with tradition by failing to bring along his own attendants; so Philistine ones were invited. Some commentators suggest that these companions were a kind of bodyguard for protection against marauders. At this feast their function, however, was to match wits with Samson.

**12–13** Though the riddle was designed as a form of entertainment, it may have been related to the lack of proper wedding attire also (cf. Matt 22:11–12). Samson's offer was an attractive one, since clothes were highly regarded in the Near East, and the men had a whole week to solve the riddle. The word for "sets" of good clothes (lit., "changes of" [*ḥᵃlip̱ōṯ*] clothes) is used along with silver to designate gifts of great value in Genesis 45:22 and 2 Kings 5:22. By accepting the challenge, the Philistines may have wanted to prove that they were smarter than the Israelites. When the Queen of Sheba visited Solomon, she tested him with "hard questions" (*ḥîḏôṯ*, the word translated "riddle" here) (1 Kings 10:1).

**14** The riddle was set forth in concise Hebrew parallelism, a couplet that translates into good English verse due to the accidental rhyme. Solving the riddle turned out to be more difficult than anticipated; so by the middle of the week the Philistines realized what this wedding might cost them. Samson may have given them a fighting chance to solve the riddle, because the word "lion" in Hebrew (*'ᵃrî*) is almost identical to an Arabic word for "honey" (*'ary*). Some of the Philistines may have been aware of this, but none of the thirty were.

**15–17** In desperation the Philistines threatened Samson's wife (v.15), and the festal atmosphere turned into a battle of nerves. The bride was asked to use any means possible to get the answer from Samson, or she and her family faced death. Their threat of burning down her father's house had to be taken seriously, as 15:6 shows. To save her family Samson's wife pled for him to show his love by confiding in her and then wore him down by weeping for a week (vv.16–17). It was a strategy that Delilah also used with success (cf. 16:15). Samson was good at keeping secrets (cf. vv.6, 9), but he eventually gave in to his wife's nagging.

**18–20** Given the answer by Samson's wife, the Philistines triumphantly presented it before the deadline (v.18). Samson replied with another bit of verse that showed how they got the answer. Heifers were not normally used for plowing; so the thirty had not played fair. In retaliation Samson traveled over twenty miles to the coastal city of Ashkelon, one of the five key Philistine centers (v.19). There, again empowered by the Spirit (v.6), he waylaid thirty well-dressed men and robbed them of their clothes to pay off the debt. Apparently he hoped to conceal his actions by going such a long distance from Timnah.

Still angry with his wife, Samson avoided her for a time and returned to his father's home. If Samson had not had relations with his wife, the marriage was not fully legal; and the bride's father wondered whether it ever would be consummated. Therefore, because he did not want his daughter to be abandoned in disgrace so soon after the wedding, he gave her to Samson's best man (v.20; cf. 1 Sam 25:44).

## Notes

---

**15** The reading "fourth" found in the LXX and the Syriac has much to commend it (see NIV mg.). In Hebrew "fourth" differs from "seventh" only in the first letter: רְבִיעִי (*r<sup>e</sup>ḇîʿî*) or שְׁבִיעִי (*šeḇîʿî*).

"Coax," a Piel imperative from פַּתָּה (*pāṯāh*), normally has a bad connotation. It is used of "seducing" a virgin (Exod 22:16) and "enticing" to sin (Prov 1:10).

---

### 6. *Samson's revenge for the loss of his wife*

**15:1–8**

1 Later on, at the time of wheat harvest, Samson took a young goat
and went to visit his wife. He said, "I'm going to my wife's room." But
her father would not let him go in.
2 "I was so sure you thoroughly hated her," he said, "that I gave her to
your friend. Isn't her younger sister more attractive? Take her instead."
3 Samson said to them, "This time I have a right to get even with the
Philistines; I will really harm them." 4 So he went out and caught three
hundred foxes and tied them tail to tail in pairs. He then fastened a torch
to every pair of tails, 5 lit the torches and let the foxes loose in the
standing grain of the Philistines. He burned up the shocks and standing
grain, together with the vineyards and olive groves.
6 When the Philistines asked, "Who did this?" they were told,
"Samson, the Timnite's son-in-law, because his wife was given to his
friend."

**So the Philistines went up and burned her and her father to death.**
**[7]Samson said to them, "Since you've acted like this, I won't stop until I get my revenge on you." [8]He attacked them viciously and slaughtered many of them. Then he went down and stayed in a cave in the rock of Etam.**

**1–2** Samson's anger eventually subsided, and he decided to reclaim his wife (v.1). The wheat harvest occurred in early June and was a time of festivity. Because the word "visit" is used, many scholars feel that Samson's marriage was of the *beena* (an Akkadian word) or "visit" type, in which the wife would stay in her father's house and be visited periodically by her husband (cf. 8:31 and de Vaux, AIs, pp. 28–29). By this arrangement the Philistine bride would avoid the in-law problems her presence in an Israelite household would cause.

If this was a "visit" marriage, the young goat was considered an acceptable present for the enjoyment of marital relations (Gen 38:17). Samson also wanted to atone for apparently deserting his wife. When he announced his intention of going to her room and consummating the marriage, her father told him that she was no longer his wife (v.2). Knowing that Samson had legally purchased his bride, the father offered him his more beautiful younger daughter. Unlike Jacob, Samson was not impressed with the "Rachel" of this family and flatly rejected the offer.

**3–6** Samson's claim of innocence may have been correct (v.3). Even the Philistines still referred to him as "the Timnite's son-in-law" (v.6). True, he had not immediately consummated the marriage, but was this sufficient ground for the divorce effected by the father? Later on David did not hesitate to take back his wife Michal forcibly, though Saul had given her to another man (1 Sam 25:44; 2 Sam 3:13–15).

Samson held all the Philistines responsible for the affront and took revenge. His anger is reminiscent of the *mênis* motif of the heroic age (See Introduction: Historical Background). The wrath of Achilles erupted when his beloved Briseis was taken away; and, like Samson, the Greek hero was involved in several acts of vengeance before his rage abated (cf. Cyrus Gordon, *The Common Background of Greek and Hebrew Civilizations* [New York: Norton, 1965], pp. 270–71, 298, and Armerding, p. 251).

The "foxes" (v.4) Samson used may actually have been jackals, a closely related animal that moves in packs and can be more readily caught. Either animal would, however, be difficult to catch in such quantities. The fire spread with incredible speed, and soon the Philistines' crops were ruined (v.5). The fire destroyed the sheaves of stacked grain and also the grain ready to be harvested in the fields (Deut 23:25). Grapevines and olive trees were also ruined.

Under the law (Exod 22:6), burning crops and fields was considered a serious offense; and the Philistines were distressed at this blow to their economy (v.6). They retaliated by burning Samson's wife and her father, a fate that ironically she had tried to avoid by wheedling out of Samson the key to his riddle (14:15). When David's son Absalom later set Joab's barley field on fire, it proved an effective way of achieving his purpose (2 Sam 14:29–32).

**7–8** Quickly the feud with the Philistines assumed national proportions as Samson sought to avenge the death of his wife. Though he intended to "stop" when he got even (v.7), neither side quit seeking revenge till Samson and thousands of Philistines were dead (v.8; cf. 16:28). How rapidly the effects of sin and hatred spread! Presumably the slaughter took place in the Timnah area, but it served to arouse all Philistia.

Anticipating the Philistines' reaction, Samson took refuge in a "cave" or cleft of a rock (v.8). The same combination of *s*[e]*ʿîp̱* ("cave") and *selaʿ* ("rock") occurs in Isaiah 2:21, which speaks of men fleeing to the hills to escape the terror of the Day of the Lord. Samson doubtless found an inaccessible crag where capture would be most difficult. "Etam" may have been a town in southern Judah (cf. 1 Chron 4:32), though a city by that name was located near Bethlehem and Tekoa (2 Chron 11:6).

## Notes

---

**1** Compare the visit-type marriage in Middle Assyrian Law 27 (ANET, p. 182).

**2** The two infinitive absolutes אָמֹר (*'āmōr*, "so sure"; untr. in NIV) and שָׂנֹא (*śānō'*, "thoroughly hate") make the opening statement very emphatic. Her father had no doubt that Samson had lost all love for his wife.

**8** "Viciously" is an attempt to render שׁוֹק עַל־יָרֵךְ (*šôq ʿal-yārēḵ*, "leg on thigh"), an obscure proverbial statement. The preposition *ʿal* is also used after נָכָה (*nāḵāh*, "attack") in Gen 32:11 (12 MT) in the sense of "along with." Perhaps it means that Samson killed them "one after another." Cundall (in loc.) thinks the expression "leg and thigh" may be associated with wrestling.

---

### 7. *Samson's victory at Lehi*

#### 15:9–20

9 The Philistines went up and camped in Judah, spreading out near
Lehi. 10 The men of Judah asked, "Why have you come to fight us?"
"We have come to take Samson prisoner," they answered, "to do to
him as he did to us."
11 Then three thousand men from Judah went down to the cave in the
rock of Etam and said to Samson, "Don't you realize that the Philistines
are rulers over us? What have you done to us?"
He answered, "I merely did to them what they did to me."
12 They said to him, "We've come to tie you up and hand you over to
the Philistines."
Samson said, "Swear to me that you won't kill me yourselves."
13 "Agreed," they answered. "We will only tie you up and hand you
over to them. We will not kill you." So they bound him with two new
ropes and led him up from the rock. 14 As he approached Lehi, the
Philistines came toward him shouting. The Spirit of the LORD came upon
him in power. The ropes on his arms became like charred flax, and the
bindings dropped from his hands. 15 Finding a fresh jawbone of a
donkey, he grabbed it and struck down a thousand men.
16 Then Samson said,

"With a donkey's jawbone
  I have made donkeys of them.
With a donkey's jawbone
  I have killed a thousand men."

17When he finished speaking, he threw away the jawbone; and the place
was called Ramath Lehi.
18Because he was very thirsty, he cried out to the LORD, "You have
given your servant this great victory. Must I now die of thirst and fall into
the hands of the uncircumcised?" 19Then God opened up the hollow
place in Lehi, and water came out of it. When Samson drank, his
strength returned and he revived. So the spring was called En Hakkore,
and it is still there in Lehi.
20Samson led Israel for twenty years in the days of the Philistines.

**9–13** Aroused by Samson's outbursts, the Philistines assembled as an army and moved into Judah near "Lehi" (v.9; lit., "jawbone"), the name given to the area after Samson's victory. The presence of an army prompted a quick investigation; for the men of Judah were anxious to keep the peace (v.10). Aware of Samson's hideout, three thousand men went to extradite him (v.11). Their action betrays the strange complacency with the status quo that made them willing to accept the continued domination of the godless Philistines. Here was an opportunity for them to rally around their hero and march against the Philistines. Instead, they meekly bowed to Philistine wishes and handed Samson over to face almost certain death (v.12). Observe that Samson's justification of his behavior in v.11 was the same one used by the Philistines: They deserved to be paid back!

Samson agreed to let the men of Judah tie him up after being assured that they would not harm him (v.13). He had no desire to fight and kill his own countrymen. Uncertain of his attitude toward them, they tied him securely with new ropes.

**14–15** The Philistines' battle cry was a sign that they sensed victory over their hated foe (v.14). Israel was later to raise a shout as they pursued the Philistines staggered by Goliath's death (1 Sam 17:52). Shouting provided a psychological advantage over the enemy (cf. 1 Sam 4:5). In this instance the shouting only served to arouse Samson. Empowered again by the divine Spirit (cf. 14:6), Samson easily snapped the ropes that bound him. He seized a fresh jawbone of a donkey, one that was moist and not brittle, and killed a thousand men (v.15). Any of the Philistines who survived probably fled the scene in astonishment. Again, the men of Judah had a chance to follow up this victory and throw off Philistine domination, but they remained strangely inactive.

**16–17** To commemorate the triumph, Samson composed another short poem (v.16). Like the couplet in 14:18, this poem uses repetition. It is difficult to interpret. Verse 2 apparently contains a wordplay based on the similar sound of *ḥᵃmôr*, ("donkey") and *ḥōmer* ("pile" or "heap"). The NIV chooses "donkey" and does not rule out the possibility of a double meaning (NIV mg.). The carcasses of donkeys were usually thrown outside the city wall (Jer 22:19), and this kind of disgraceful burial had befallen the Philistines.

Samson's single-handed victory resembled the method and results of Shamgar, who had slain six hundred Philistines with an oxgoad (3:31). Eleazer and Shammah, two of David's heroes, were later to wield deadly swords against the Philistines (2 Sam 23:9–12). The importance of the jawbone and the fact that Samson left it at the scene of the battle accounts for the name "Jawbone Hill" (v.17 NIV mg.).

**18–19** Samson's weariness after the battle may be compared with the fatigue of Eleazer (2 Sam 23:10) or especially that of Elijah (1 Kings 19:4), who had won a signal triumph over the prophets of Baal only to feel near death shortly after. Samson acknowledged that God was responsible for his victory, but, like Elijah, Samson was physically and emotionally drained following the conflict (v.18).

As he had done for the Israelites in the wilderness (Exod 17:6), God provided water for Samson. The strength-restoring flow came from the "hollow" (v.19) or "mortar" in Lehi. This was most likely a feature of the terrain that resembled the deep, bowllike shape of a mortar. The spring was thereafter called "Caller's Spring" (*'ên haqqôrē'*, "En Hakkore") because of God's wonderful answer to prayer.

Samson's tenure as "judge" may have fallen between 1075–1055 B.C., a time when Samuel's ministry was also underway. Although Samson may not have exercised judicial functions as such, the people may have turned to him as their leader during the years after Lehi. This early reference to his twenty-year prominence (cf. 16:31 also) indicates that his effectiveness ended prior to the tragic events of chapter 16.

## Notes

---

**10, 12** "To take prisoner" and "to tie up" represent the same Hebrew word, אָסַר (*'āsar*). Thus the men of Judah were cooperating with the Philistines to the fullest extent.

**16** The translation "heaps upon heaps" (KJV et al.) is partially based on Exod 8:14 (10 MT), where חֳמָרִם חֳמָרִם (*ḥ*$^{o}$*mārim ḥ*$^{o}$*mārim*, "heaps, heaps") has that meaning. The NIV rendering handles the problematic חֲמֹרָתָיִם (*ḥ*$^{a}$*mōrāṯāyim*, "two heaps"[?]) as חֲמַרְתִּים (*ḥ*$^{a}$*mārtîm*, "made donkeys"), a denominative verb from the noun "donkey." The similar denominative use of חמר II (BDB) in Exod 2:3 ("coated it with tar") supports this interpretation.

**19** "Opened up" translates וַיִּבְקַע (*wayyiḇqa'*), which is literally "split."

A mortar, מַכְתֵּשׁ (*maḵtēš*, "hollow place") is a deep bowl, usually made of basalt or limestone, in which materials are pounded. A place in or near Jerusalem is named "Mortar" (Zeph 1:11 NIV mg.).

---

### 8. *Samson's feat of strength at Gaza*

#### 16:1–3

**1 One day Samson went to Gaza, where he saw a prostitute. He went in to spend the night with her. 2 The people of Gaza were told, "Samson is here!" So they surrounded the place and lay in wait for him all night at the city gate. They made no move during the night, saying, "At dawn we'll kill him."**

**3 But Samson lay there only until the middle of the night. Then he got up and took hold of the doors of the city gate, together with the two posts, and tore them loose, bar and all. He lifted them to his shoulders and carried them to the top of the hill that faces Hebron.**

**1–3** The final episodes in Samson's story confirm his great physical strength and his great weakness for women. A number of years passed before Samson ventured into Philistine territory again. This time he went to Gaza (v.1), some forty miles west of Hebron and twelve miles south of Ashkelon. Even at this southernmost Philistine city, his reputation was well known; and the residents showed great caution in their attempt to capture him.

Samson's sensual nature led him to involvement with a prostitute, one of many at centers such as Gaza. Still not married, Samson was particularly susceptible to temptations of the flesh (cf. Gen 38:12–15). Thinking they had him trapped, the men of Gaza hid outside and made plans to surprise Samson in the morning (v.2). Their lack of activity implies that many of them fell asleep, confident that the locked city gates had hemmed in their prisoner.

Sometime during the middle of the night, when the Philistines least expected it, Samson left his shelter and tore loose the city gate as easily as one would pull out a tent peg (v.3). He carried off the heavy wooden doors, the posts on which they hung, and the crossbar of wood or metal that reinforced the doors. While the men watched in amazement, he proceeded to haul the whole gate assembly to a hill opposite Hebron.

## Notes

---

**1** The exact location of Gaza is disputed, though it was on the road to Egypt and only a few miles from the Mediterranean. Tell el 'Ajjul is one suggested site.

**2** "Made no move" is literally "they kept quiet." It is the only Hithpael occurrence of חָרֵשׁ (*ḥārēš*).

**3** The hill was near Gaza, not Hebron. עַל פְּנֵי (*'al* $p^{e}$*nê*, lit., "before the face of") means "facing" or "toward" also in Gen 18:16.

---

## 9. *Samson and Delilah*

### 16:4–20

4 Some time later, he fell in love with a woman in the Valley of Sorek
whose name was Delilah. 5 The rulers of the Philistines went to her and
said, "See if you can lure him into showing you the secret of his great
strength and how we can overpower him so we may tie him up and
subdue him. Each one of us will give you eleven hundred shekels of
silver."
6 So Delilah said to Samson, "Tell me the secret of your great strength
and how you can be tied up and subdued."
7 Samson answered her, "If anyone ties me with seven fresh thongs
that have not been dried, I'll become as weak as any other man."
8 Then the rulers of the Philistines brought her seven fresh thongs that
had not been dried, and she tied him with them. 9 With men hidden in the
room, she called to him, "Samson, the Philistines are upon you!" But he
snapped the thongs as easily as a piece of string snaps when it comes
close to a flame. So the secret of his strength was not discovered.
10 Then Delilah said to Samson, "You have made a fool of me; you lied
to me. Come now, tell me how you can be tied."
11 He said, "If anyone ties me securely with new ropes that have never
been used, I'll become as weak as any other man."
12 So Delilah took new ropes and tied him with them. Then, with men
hidden in the room, she called to him, "Samson, the Philistines are
upon you!" But he snapped the ropes off his arms as if they were
threads.
13 Delilah then said to Samson, "Until now, you have been making a
fool of me and lying to me. Tell me how you can be tied."

He replied, "If you weave the seven braids of my head into the fabric
⌊on the loom⌋ and tighten it with the pin, I'll become as weak as any other
man." So while he was sleeping, Delilah took the seven braids of his
head, wove them into the fabric and tightened it with the pin.
Again she called to him, "Samson, the Philistines are upon you!" He
awoke from his sleep and pulled up the pin and the loom, with the
fabric.
[15]Then she said to him, "How can you say, 'I love you,' when you
won't confide in me? This is the third time you have made a fool of me
and haven't told me the secret of your great strength." [16]With such
nagging she prodded him day after day until he was tired to death.
[17]So he told her everything. "No razor has ever been used on my
head," he said, "because I have been a Nazirite set apart to God since
birth. If my head were shaved, my strength would leave me, and I would
become as weak as any other man."
[18]When Delilah saw that he had told her everything, she sent word to
the rulers of the Philistines, "Come back once more; he has told me
everything." So the rulers of the Philistines returned with the silver in
their hands. [19]Having put him to sleep on her lap, she called a man to
shave off the seven braids of his hair, and so began to subdue him. And
his strength left him.
[20]Then she called, "Samson, the Philistines are upon you!"
He awoke from his sleep and thought, "I'll go out as before and shake
myself free." But he did not know that the LORD had left him.

**4–5** Samson's downfall came in a series of events much like those in chapter 14. Once again a woman led him to divulge a secret. Delilah lived near Samson's hometown, for Zorah and Mahaneh Dan (cf. 13:25; the site is unknown) were situated by the Sorek Valley (v.4). "Sorek" (*śōrēq*) means "choice vine," perhaps a hint that the Nazirite vow was in grave danger. Delilah is never called a Philistine woman (cf. 14:1–2), but her proximity to the Philistine-occupied area and her close contact with their leaders indicate that she probably was one of them. Foreign women had a peculiar fascination for Samson (14:1; 16:1).

The Philistine leaders were determined to find out the secret of Samson's strength. Instead of threatening the woman he was infatuated with, as the wedding guests had done (14:15), the five rulers (cf. 3:3) promised Delilah a fortune (v.5). Eleven hundred shekels of silver was a substantial sum (cf. 17:2). It would total at least 140 pounds in weight; no wonder Delilah did not give up till she had discovered the secret of Samson's strength.

The Philistines' goal was to "subdue" Samson (v.5); they hoped to harness his strength and put it to good use. The verb "subdue" (*ʿinnāh*) is used of the hard labor the Egyptians imposed on the Israelites in Genesis 15:13 and Exodus 1:11–12.

**6–9** Delilah's objective must have been obvious to Samson (v.6). He knew how "well" his Philistine wife had kept a secret (14:17) of far less importance than this one. Confident that he would never tell her the truth, he toyed with her for his own amusement (v.7). The first clue dealt with "thongs" ("bowstrings," NIV mg.) made from animal intestines. These were *laḥîm* ("fresh"), a word that sounds much like *lᵉḥî*, the fresh "jawbone" he so effectively had used in battle (15:15). But their moistness was of no more help than the perfect number seven as Samson easily broke them, and the Philistines made no attempt to seize him (vv.8–9). The ease with which Samson snapped the cords is described in terms similar to those in 15:14. The "string" (v.9) is literally "tow," the highly flammable (cf. Isa 1:31) fibers that are shaken off flax when it is beaten. As soon as tow comes near fire, it disintegrates.

Though the account mentions that Samson fell asleep only before the last two tests, it is also likely that Delilah waited for him to doze off before trying to tie him on the first two occasions.

**10–12** Delilah claimed that Samson deceived or cheated her (v.10). Pharaoh had long before incurred the same charge by deceiving Moses into thinking he would release the Israelites (Exod 8:29). Samson's second clue was a variation of the first one (v.11), though the Philistines should have learned from previous experience that new ropes could not shackle him (15:13). Perhaps they felt that the men of Judah had not tied him securely enough the first time. But special tying was ineffective as Samson once more broke free (v.12).

**13–14** Again Delilah complained of being mistreated (v.13), and her third plea to Samson took on a new intensity. The omission in v.13 of the Hebrew particle of entreaty (*nā'*) used in v.6 (untr. in NIV) and v.10 ("Come now") suggests that Delilah shouted, "Tell me!" as Samson's irritation grew. This time he came dangerously close to the truth as he linked his strength with his hair, and his explanation was so different that it might have given Delilah hope that he was not lying. (His seven braids may have looked like those of the statue of Apollo in the National Archaeological Museum in Athens.)

It is difficult to determine the kind of loom Samson's hair was woven to. Both horizontal and vertical looms were used at the time. The fact that Samson was sleeping suggests the horizontal kind (IBD, 1:652), which normally had two beams supported by four pegs driven into the ground. Having woven Samson's hair into the fabric and fastened it with a pin, Delilah thought she had him trapped. Ironically, the words "tightened it with [= 'drove'] the pin" (*tiṯqa' bayyāṯēḏ*, v.14) are the same ones used of Jael, who drove the tent peg into Sisera's head (4:21). Though Delilah did not kill Samson in the same way, she was to become as important a heroine among the Philistines as Jael had been in Israel.

Samson had no more difficulty "pulling up" the pin and the whole loom (cf. v.14) than he had "tearing loose" the gate of Gaza (cf. v.3). The word *nāsa'* is used in both places.

**15–17** By this time Delilah was frustrated. Yet though she had failed to learn the secret and the Philistines had grown impatient and had gone home (cf. v.18), she was not yet ready to give up (vv.15–16). Instead, she did as Samson's wife had done and began to question his love (cf. 14:16). He might have challenged her on the same grounds, for her own love was anything but clear.

Samson's continued deception disturbed Delilah because it confirmed his intention to keep the secret. Lying once or twice might have been forgiven, but this was the third time (on the significance of the number three, cf. comment on 7:8b–11). But Delilah kept after Samson, who became so tired of her nagging (v.16) that he finally gave in (v.17), as he had during the wedding feast (14:17). Rather than break his relationship with Delilah, he allowed it to break him.

Samson's career as a Nazirite was an inconsistent one. He had been careless about keeping his distance from the fruit of the vine or from dead bodies (cf. 14:6–10). Yet he kept his long hair as the symbol of his dedication to God. This was the specific point the angel had spoken of (13:5), and it may have superseded the other Nazirite restrictions in importance (cf. 1 Sam 1:11).

**18–20** Knowing that she had finally arrived at the truth, Delilah persuaded the Philistine rulers to return so that she might betray him to them (v.18). While they knew that shaving beards and pulling out hair was a sign of mourning (cf. Jer 41:5), they hardly dared believe what cutting off Samson's hair would do to him.

The denouement of the story of Samson's life is one of the great movements in OT literature. Verse 20 in a few poignant strokes portrays the hero's downfall; the rest of the chapter is high tragedy, commemorated by Milton in his dramatic poem *Samson Agonistes.*

Samson himself could not believe the inevitable, planning to elude the Philistines as always. But the bonds of sin are not so easily shaken off. When the Spirit of the Lord leaves someone, the results are indeed disastrous. King Saul was another who forfeited the right to the power of the Spirit (1 Sam 16:14) and ended his life in tragedy.

## Notes

---

**4** שֹׂרֵק (*śōrēq,* "Sorek") apparently means "bright red." This high quality vine is symbolic of an Israel planted by God (Isa 5:2; Jer 2:21).

The meaning of "Delilah" is uncertain. The personal name "Dalili" occurs in Ugaritic, perhaps related to the root *dll* ("to be poor, lowly").

**9** The "hidden" men—אֹרֵב (*'ōrēb̲*)—are those who "lie in wait" to ambush. In v.2 the men of Gaza are so described.

Samson's ability to "snap" thongs or ropes (v.12) symbolizes the God-given freedom he enjoyed. נתק (*ntq*) in the Piel is used in Ps 2:3 of the desire of nations to break loose from God (cf. Jer 2:20).

The word נְעֹרֶת (*ne'ōret̲,* "string") is derived from the same root as "shake" used in v.20. What seemed so easy in v.9 became impossible in v.20.

**13–14** The words included in the LXX and other ancient versions, which were adopted by the NIV, are probably authentic. Apparently their omission from the MT occurred when the scribe's eye inadvertently dropped from וְתָקַעַתְּ (*wet̲āqa'at,* "[if you] tighten [it]") to וַתִּתְקַע (*wattit̲qa',* "and [she] tightened [it]").

**15** "You won't confide in me" is literally "your heart is not with me." "Everything" in vv.17–18 is similarly "all his heart."

---

### 10. *The capture and punishment of Samson*

16:21–22

**[21]Then the Philistines seized him, gouged out his eyes and took him down to Gaza. Binding him with bronze shackles, they set him to grinding in the prison. [22]But the hair on his head began to grow again after it had been shaved.**

**21–22** Moving in quickly, the Philistines seized Samson and blinded him (v.21). The Jews considered loss of eyesight a terrible curse. Rebellious children deserved to be blinded (Prov 30:17). The residents of a whole city were threatened with the loss of their right eyes as a special insult (1 Sam 11:2).

Samson's feet were fettered by bronze shackles (cf. 2 Sam 3:34), and he was forced to work in a prison in Gaza, the very city from which he had once escaped (v.3). Grinding at the mill was a woman's job (9:53), which added to Samson's humiliation. It is unclear whether he used a small hand-mill or was forced to turn a large circular stone, a job normally given to donkeys. The latter task would avenge Samson's earlier treatment of the Philistines (15:16). Centuries later a fate similar to Samson's was suffered by King Zedekiah when the Babylonians blinded and shackled him and threw him into prison (Jer 52:11).

The Philistines allowed Samson's hair to grow again (v.22), perhaps desirous of using what they then thought was his "controllable" strength.

## Notes

---

**21** Gouging out eyes is also referred to in an argument between Moses and rebels in Israel (Num 16:14). In both passages either the Qal or Piel of נקר (*nqr*) is used.

---

## 11. *Samson's final revenge at the feast of Dagon*

### 16:23–31

23 Now the rulers of the Philistines assembled to offer a great sacrifice
to Dagon their god and to celebrate, saying, "Our god has delivered
Samson, our enemy, into our hands."
24 When the people saw him, they praised their god, saying,

> "Our god has delivered our enemy
> into our hands,
> the one who laid waste our land
> and multiplied our slain."

25 While they were in high spirits, they shouted, "Bring out Samson to
entertain us." So they called Samson out of the prison, and he
performed for them.
When they stood him among the pillars, 26 Samson said to the servant
who held his hand, "Put me where I can feel the pillars that support the
temple, so that I may lean against them." 27 Now the temple was
crowded with men and women; all the rulers of the Philistines were
there, and on the roof were about three thousand men and women
watching Samson perform. 28 Then Samson prayed to the Lord, "O
Sovereign Lord, remember me. O God, please strengthen me just once
more, and let me with one blow get revenge on the Philistines for my
two eyes." 29 Then Samson reached toward the two central pillars on
which the temple stood. Bracing himself against them, his right hand on
the one and his left hand on the other, 30 Samson said, "Let me die with
the Philistines!" Then he pushed with all his might, and down came the
temple on the rulers and all the people in it. Thus he killed many more
when he died than while he lived.
31 Then his brothers and his father's whole family went down to get
him. They brought him back and buried him between Zorah and Eshtaol
in the tomb of Manoah his father. He had led Israel twenty years.

**23–25** The capture of Samson led to great rejoicing; and the Philistines had a national festival in honor of Dagon, their god of grain and chief deity (v.23). Dagon was also worshiped by the West Semitic residents of Mari on the Euphrates, and a temple to "Dagan" (= Dagon) existed at Ugarit. In some texts from Ugarit, Baal is called "the son of Dagan." Among the Philistines there were temples to this god in Gaza and Ashdod (1 Sam 5:1–7).

The Philistines attributed Samson's downfall directly to Dagon (v.24), and it was this theological error that led to the destruction of Dagon's temple. Samson fell into their hands, not because Dagon had defeated the Lord, but because Samson's sinfulness had caused the God of Israel to abandon him.

How vividly the Philistines remembered Samson's "reign of terror"! It had been a time of devastation and death, and even Dagon's grain was put to the torch (15:5). But this was replaced by laughter and feasting as the drunken Philistines called for the once invincible Samson to appear before them (v.25). The word translated "entertain" (*ṣāḥaq*) is literally "play with," "amuse." It turned out to be as deadly as the "war games" that were played in 2 Samuel 2:14. Clearly the Philistines intended to mock Samson as he performed for their amusement (cf. Gen 21:9).

**26–30** From the noise around and above him, Samson could tell that he was near the center of the building. With help from the young man assigned to attend him, Samson located the main columns of the temple (v.26). It was Samson's turn to get revenge on the Philistines (15:7); so he called on the Lord for assistance (v.28), as he had done at Lehi years earlier (15:18). The Philistines apparently had no inkling of Samson's intentions. Indeed, he may not have fully regained his strength until the Lord empowered him one last time.

With a mighty effort Samson dislodged the pillars from their bases, bringing down the roof on top of the dignitaries assembled inside (v.30). Thousands of spectators on the roof (v.27) also perished in the fall, and the number killed proved to be Samson's greatest slaughter. He gladly died with them rather than continue his pitiful existence among them.

**31** The "brothers" who buried Samson may have been relatives from the tribe of Dan (cf. 14:3). The "father's family" was a more restricted group than a clan but broader than our Western conception of a family. Samson was laid to rest in the region where he had grown up and was given the honor of burial in his father's tomb (cf. 8:32).

Samson was ranked among the heroes of the faith (Heb 11:32). Yet he failed to live up to his great gifts. Unable to conquer himself, he was ruined by his own lusts. He stands as a tragic example of a man of great potential who lacked stability of character. Still, God in his sovereignty used him. Samson did much to hamper the oppressive actions of the Philistines, and his final victory in the temple of Dagon may have been a factor in the defeat of the Philistines at Mizpah shortly thereafter (1 Sam 7:7–14).

## Notes

**25** The opening clause is literally "while their heart was good," an idiom that occurs also in 18:20 and 19:6, 22, with the sense of "enjoying oneself." In 1 Sam 25:36, Nabal's "heart was good" when he was drunk (NIV, "in high spirits").

The two spellings of the verb "to play"—שׂחק (*śḥq*) and צחק (*ṣḥq*)—provide another illustration of variation among the sibilants (cf. 12:6).

**26** "Feel" comes from one of two roots. The *Kethiv* supports ימשׁ (*ymš*) and the *Qere* favors מושׁ (*mûš*), both of which mean "feel," "touch."

**29** The exact way Samson dislodged the pillars is not known. לפת (*lpṯ*, "reached") occurs only here in the Qal. In the Niphal it seems to mean "twist."

---

## III. Two Appendixes (17:1–21:25)

The final five chapters of Judges constitute two nonchronological appendixes to the book, omitting any reference to judges or times of oppression. Both episodes recounted in this section occurred early in the whole period of the judges and illustrate the moral and religious decay that led many to call for the appointment of a king. The key expression in these chapters is "In those days Israel had no king" (17:6; 18:1; 19:1; 21:25; cf. Introduction: Authorship and Unity).

### A. *Micah's Priest and the Migration of Dan (17:1–18:31)*

As suggested in the introduction to the Samson cycle (cf. p. 460), chapters 17–18 continue the emphasis on the tribe of Dan. Their migration to the north had left their original tribal allotment vulnerable to Philistine occupation. It may also explain why Samson received so little help from his fellow Danites; for only part of the tribe remained in the south. The events related in these two chapters probably occurred after the episodes recorded in chapters 19–21.

#### 1. *Micah's mother and idolatry*

17:1–6

[1]Now a man named Micah from the hill country of Ephraim [2]said to his mother, "The eleven hundred shekels of silver that were taken from you and about which I heard you utter a curse—I have that silver with me; I took it."

Then his mother said, "The LORD bless you, my son!"

[3]When he returned the eleven hundred shekels of silver to his mother, she said, "I solemnly consecrate my silver to the LORD for my son to make a carved image and a cast idol. I will give it back to you."

[4]So he returned the silver to his mother, and she took two hundred shekels of silver and gave them to a silversmith, who made them into the image and the idol. And they were put in Micah's house.

[5]Now this man Micah had a shrine, and he made an ephod and some idols and installed one of his sons as his priest. [6]In those days Israel had no king; everyone did as he saw fit.

**1–2** The bizarre and violent events in the appendixes are closely linked with the hills of Ephraim (v.1), the highlands of central Palestine beginning some twelve miles north of Jerusalem. This region also played an important role in the success of Ehud, Deborah, and Gideon (3:27; 4:5; 7:24). In tune with the moral chaos of the day, a man named Micah stole a substantial sum of silver from his own mother (v.2). The eleven hundred shekels—about twenty-eight pounds (NIV mg.)—is an amount mentioned in 16:5 also. Compared with a yearly wage of ten shekels (v.10), its value represents a fortune. No wonder Micah's mother cursed the thief! Since a well-founded curse was dreadfully effective—even within one's own family (Gen 9:25)—Micah was frightened into confessing his guilt. Immediately his mother pronounced a blessing on him to undo the curse that threatened him. In Malachi 2:1–2 God nullified the effects of priests' blessings by turning their words into curses.

**3–4** Out of gratitude for getting her silver back, Micah's mother decided to consecrate it to the Lord (v.3; cf. Exod 28:38). Yet the desire to make an idol was diametrically opposed to God's command and, in fact, made Micah's mother liable to God's curse (Deut 27:15). Strangely, she dedicated only two hundred of the original eleven hundred shekels (v.4). Both her motivation and her activity are questionable.

With the two hundred shekels of silver, the silversmith made an idol—or idols—for Micah's mother. Verse 3 and also 18:14, 17–18 imply that at least two idols were made, but in the Hebrew text of 18:30–31 only one is mentioned. If it was only one idol, it may have been cast in the form of a calf (cf. the golden calf Aaron fashioned at Mount Sinai, Exod 32:4). Later the same idol was associated with the city of Dan (cf. 18:30; 1 Kings 12:29).

**5–6** In v.5 the word "teraphim" is used for "idols." Though plural in form, "teraphim" can refer either to one or more "household idols" (Gen 31:19; 1 Sam 19:13, 16). Scripture consistently condemns the use of teraphim (cf. 1 Sam 15:23). Like the ephod (cf. 8:27), with which they are also linked in 18:14, 17–18, the teraphim could be used for divination purposes (Ezek 21:21).

Since the ephod (in this case probably a linen waist cloth; cf. 1 Sam 2:18; 2 Sam 6:14) was a priestly garment, Micah went one step further by ordaining one of his sons as priest (v.5). The word for "installed" (*millē' 'et-yad*, "to fill the hand") is a technical term used of Aaron and his sons when they presented the wave offering during the ordination ceremonies (cf. Exod 29:9, 24). So Micah boldly set up a shrine (lit., a "house of God") right in his home. It was a sad perversion of the true worship, leading the author of Judges to bemoan the fact that in those days everyone did as he saw fit (v.6; cf. Notes on 14:3). The sobering assessment also ends the Book of Judges (21:25).

## Notes

1 Micah is called מִיכָיְהוּ (*mîḵāyehû*) in vv.1 and 4, but elsewhere the shorter form מִיכָה (*mîḵāh*) is used. The name means "Who is like Yahweh?"

3 The terms for "image" and "idol" are פֶּסֶל (*pesel*) and מַסֵּכָה (*massēḵāh*). The former is normally carved from wood or chiseled from rock, but it can also be poured or cast (Isa 40:19; 44:10). Isaiah 40:19 describes the "casting" of an idol that is then plated or overlaid with gold. The same process may have been used here, substituting silver for gold. These two terms for idols occur together also in Deut 27:15 and Nah 1:14.

5 The enigmatic תְּרָפִים (*terāp̄îm*, "idols") is possibly derived from the Hittite word *tarpi*, meaning a good or evil "demon." See Harry A. Hoffner, Jr., "The Linguistic Origins of Teraphim," BS 124 (1967): 230–38.

## 2. *Micah's Levite*

### 17:7–13

7 A young Levite from Bethlehem in Judah, who had been living within
the clan of Judah, 8 left that town in search of some other place to stay.
On his way he came to Micah's house in the hill country of Ephraim.
9 Micah asked him, "Where are you from?"
"I'm a Levite from Bethlehem in Judah," he said, "and I'm looking for
a place to stay."
10 Then Micah said to him, "Live with me and be my father and priest,
and I'll give you ten shekels of silver a year, your clothes and your food."
11 So the Levite agreed to live with him, and the young man was to him
like one of his sons. 12 Then Micah installed the Levite, and the young
man became his priest and lived in his house. 13 And Micah said, "Now I
know that the LORD will be good to me, since this Levite has become my
priest."

**7–9** The law had specified that priests were to come from the tribe of Levi; so Micah was quick to "upgrade" his religious establishment when the opportunity arose. The Levite he hired had been living in Bethlehem (v.9), a town that also figures prominently in the grim account beginning in 19:1. Ironically, Bethlehem was to be the birthplace of King David, whose righteous rule contrasted sharply with the perversions associated with the town in Judges.

Bethlehem was not one of the forty-eight Levitical cities assigned by Moses. The Levites were doubtless scattered because of lack of support, a situation that prevailed all too often in Israel's history (cf. Neh 13:10). In an attempt to improve his situation (v.8), the young Levite traveled north and found Micah eager to hire a more "legitimate" priest.

**10–12** The Levite became both a "father" and a "son" to Micah (vv.10–11). "Father" is a term of honor used of Joseph's position in Egypt (Gen 45:8) and of Elisha as a respected prophet (2 Kings 6:21; 13:14). The salary of ten shekels of silver a year may not, however, have matched the lofty position (cf. 16:5; 17:2–3). Micah promised to give him enough to live on, including the clothes needed to carry on his priestly functions. Content with these terms, the Levite agreed to serve Micah, who thereupon carried out the second ordination ceremony in the chapter (v.12; cf. v.5). The new priest was called Jonathan son of Gershom, a descendant of Moses (18:30). Since the priesthood was restricted to the descendants of Aaron, Jonathan's attempt to minister was abortive.

**13** Equipped with a shrine, a Levitical priest, and an assortment of idols, Micah somehow felt that this strange combination would bring God's blessing. His smug assertion ranks with Aaron's announcement about a "festival to the LORD" the day after the golden calf was made (Exod 32:5). Both Aaron and Micah were sadly mistaken in their expectations.

## Notes

---

7 The full expression "Bethlehem in Judah" also appears in 19:1–2, Ruth 1:1–2, and 1 Sam 17:12. This may distinguish it from a Bethlehem in Zebulun (cf. 12:8).

מִשְׁפַּחַת (*mišpaḥaṯ,* "family," "clan") is used in the sense of tribe in 13:2.

The consonants for "who had been living [there]"—גרשם (*gršm*)—are the same as those of the name "Gershom" (גֵּרְשֹׁם [*gēršōm*]; cf. 18:30 and Cundall, p. 186).

**8** The expression לַעֲשׂוֹת דַּרְכּוֹ (*la'ᵃśôṯ darkô,* "on his way") is literally "to make his way." The idiom does not occur elsewhere; so the alternate translation "to carry on his profession" (NIV mg.) is possible. BDB (p. 203) favors "journey" over "profession."

**10** "Clothes" is עֵרֶךְ בְּגָדִים (*'ēreḵ beḡāḏîm*), an "arrangement" or "suit" of clothes. The term *'ēreḵ* is used of the loaves of bread set on the table in the tabernacle (Exod 40:23).

---

## 3. *Danite spies and Micah's priest*

### 18:1–6

1In those days Israel had no king.
And in those days the tribe of the Danites was seeking a place of their
own where they might settle, because they had not yet come into an
inheritance among the tribes of Israel. 2So the Danites sent five warriors
from Zorah and Eshtaol to spy out the land and explore it. These men
represented all their clans. They told them, "Go, explore the land."
The men entered the hill country of Ephraim and came to the house of
Micah, where they spent the night. 3When they were near Micah's
house, they recognized the voice of the young Levite; so they turned in
there and asked him, "Who brought you here? What are you doing in
this place? Why are you here?"
4He told them what Micah had done for him, and said, "He has hired
me and I am his priest."
5Then they said to him, "Please inquire of God to learn whether our
journey will be successful."
6The priest answered them, "Go in peace. Your journey has the LORD's
approval."

**1** The opening sentence occurs four times in these final chapters (17:6; 19:1; 21:25) and reveals the standpoint of the monarchy. The chaos described in chapters 17–21 had to be stopped; and despite the monarchy's drawbacks, kingly rule improved general conditions at least temporarily.

The plight of the tribe of Dan was first mentioned in 1:34–35, where the Amorites prevented the Danites from taking possession of their inheritance. Caught in a squeeze between the Amorites and the Philistines to the west and the territory of Judah to the south, the Danites sought out a new homeland. They clearly felt that the boundary lines had not fallen for them "in pleasant places" (Ps 16:6). Their desire to move revealed a lack of faith in the Lord who had allotted to them their original territory.

**2–3** Five spies were sent from the same area where Samson grew up, Zorah and Eshtaol (v.2; cf. 13:2). They were assigned to search for a new location to the north, much like the twelve men commissioned by Moses (Num 13:2). En route they stopped at Micah's house, which must have been near a main road. They were attracted by the voice of the recently hired Levite (v.3). Their questions imply that they knew him personally, but perhaps it was his southern "Judean" accent that caught their attention (cf. 12:6). The repetitive questions reveal their surprise at finding a Levite in that locale.

**4–6** When they learned his occupation and resources, the Danites decided to consult the Lord through the Levite. Both the ephod and the teraphim might have been used for that purpose (cf. 1:1 [NIV Study Bible note]; 17:5). The inquiry was successful, for "Go in peace" (v.6) implies they would be victorious over the enemy (cf. Notes on 8:9).

## Notes

**1** The Danite migration is summarized also in Josh 19:47.

**2** The "warriors" were בְּנֵי־חַיִל (*bᵉnê-ḥayil*), a term translated "able-bodied men" in Deut 3:18 (cf. Judg 3:29).

רַגֵּל (*raggēl*, "spy out") is used also in Josh 2:1 and 6:25. Such reconnoitering was contrived to help the conquest of enemy territory (1 Chron 19:3).

**6** The NIV's "your journey has the LORD's approval" basically renders נֹכַח יהוה דַּרְכְּכֶם (*nōḵaḥ YHWH darkᵉḵem*), which is literally "your way is before the LORD." He would view their actions with favor (cf. Ezek 14:3).

### 4. *The report of the spies*

18:7–10

[7]So the five men left and came to Laish, where they saw that the people were living in safety, like the Sidonians, unsuspecting and secure. And since their land lacked nothing, they were prosperous. Also, they lived a long way from the Sidonians and had no relationship with anyone else.

[8]When they returned to Zorah and Eshtaol, their brothers asked them, "How did you find things?"

[9]They answered, "Come on, let's attack them! We have seen that the land is very good. Aren't you going to do something? Don't hesitate to go there and take it over. [10]When you get there, you will find an unsuspecting people and a spacious land that God has put into your hands, a land that lacks nothing whatever."

**7** The spies traveled straight north till they arrived at the city of Laish, some one hundred miles from their original inheritance and farther north than any territory allotted to the tribes of Israel. There, at the foot of Mount Hermon, they discovered a highly desirable location, a long distance from potential enemies and furnished with an excellent supply of water—springs that formed one of the sources of the Jordan River. The Lebanon range protected it from interference from either Syria or Phoenicia. The residents of Laish enjoyed their secure position and had not built any defenses against invaders. It was an ideal situation for the land-hungry Danites.

**8–10** The account the spies gave to the rest of the tribe was most promising (vv.8–9). Their positive and unanimous report, recommending an immediate attack, contrasted sharply with the pessimistic majority opinion of the spies sent by Moses to explore the entire land (cf. Num 13:25–33). The claim of divine approval (v.10), however, based on the consultation of v.6, was hardly justifiable.

## Notes

---

7 לַיִשׁ (*layiš*, "Laish") means "lion" and has been identified with Tell el-Qadi, a prominent mound a half mile in diameter. "Laish" is called "Leshem" in Josh 19:47. For a summary of excavations at Dan, see Avram Biran, "Tel Dan," BA 37, 3 (May 1974): 26–51.

The concept of "unsuspecting and secure"—שֹׁקֵט וּבֹטֵחַ (*šōqēṭ ûḇōṭēaḥ*)—is often used of cities that have a false sense of security (8:11; Ezek 16:49; 38:11). These terms can be used, however, to describe the safety of those who trust in the Lord (Isa 32:17).

אָדָם (*'āḏām*, lit., "man"; NIV, "anyone else") was understood by some early versions as אֲרָם (*'ărām*, "Aram" or "Syria"). This slight change in the text makes excellent sense.

10 "Spacious" renders רַחֲבַת יָדַיִם (*raḥăḇaṯ yāḏayim*), which is literally "broad of hands"; hence the land stretched "wide to right and left" (Moore, p. 393). This expression was used by the leaders of Shechem in an attempt to convince the people that there was room for the family of Jacob to live among them (Gen 34:21).

---

### 5. *The abduction of Micah's priest*

#### 18:11–21

11 Then six hundred men from the clan of the Danites, armed for
battle, set out from Zorah and Eshtaol. 12 On their way they set up camp
near Kiriath Jearim in Judah. This is why the place west of Kiriath Jearim
is called Mahaneh Dan to this day. 13 From there they went on to the hill
country of Ephraim and came to Micah's house.
14 Then the five men who had spied out the land of Laish said to their
brothers, "Do you know that one of these houses has an ephod, other
household gods, a carved image and a cast idol? Now you know what to
do." 15 So they turned in there and went to the house of the young Levite
at Micah's place and greeted him. 16 The six hundred Danites, armed for
battle, stood at the entrance to the gate. 17 The five men who had spied
out the land went inside and took the carved image, the ephod, the
other household gods and the cast idol while the priest and the six
hundred armed men stood at the entrance to the gate.
18 When these men went into Micah's house and took the carved
image, the ephod, the other household gods and the cast idol, the priest
said to them, "What are you doing?"
19 They answered him, "Be quiet! Don't say a word. Come with us, and
be our father and priest. Isn't it better that you serve a tribe and clan in
Israel as priest rather than just one man's household?" 20 Then the
priest was glad. He took the ephod, the other household gods and the
carved image and went along with the people. 21 Putting their little
children, their livestock and their possessions in front of them, they
turned away and left.

**11–12** Responding to the challenge of the spies, the Danites quickly set out for this new "promised land." Yet one wonders why only six hundred are mentioned (v.11). Were they only part of a larger migrating group, or does this low number reflect the toll taken by their wars with the Philistines and Amorites? From the Samson narratives it is clear that not all the Danites moved north. The claim of v.19 implies that the whole tribe was involved, but this may have been an exaggeration to impress the Levite.

The first stop on the journey was near Kiriath Jearim (v.12), a city about eight miles from their original homeland of Zorah and Eshtaol (see comment on 13:2). "Mahaneh Dan" ("Dan's camp," NIV mg.) was mentioned in 13:25 also.

**13–17** The next leg of the journey brought the Danites to the home of Micah (v.13). They had recalled the favorable oracle of v.6 and were planning to make more extensive use of the priest and his paraphernalia. Their intentions are made quite clear at the end of v.14. The young Levite must have been surprised to see the men again, and at first he was dismayed at the theft of the ephod and idols (vv.16–17; cf. 17:4–5). With a six-hundred-man army poised outside, there was little the priest could do to prevent the robbery.

**18–21** The priest's mild protest was countered by an offer that he join the Danites and enjoy an expanded ministry to an entire tribe (vv.18–19). With the prospect of a higher salary and increased influence, he quickly forgot his loyalty to Micah and agreed to their terms (v.20). Instead of losing his religious equipment and perhaps his life, he gained a new position. No wonder he "cheered up" so quickly. His fickle and mercenary attitude reflects the state of the priesthood during this period. Equally deplorable is the fact that one tribe would steal from another with apparent impunity. The treacherous behavior of the tribe of Dan in dealing with Micah and the city of Laish illustrates the "serpent" nature predicted by Jacob in Genesis 49:17.

## Notes

---

**12** Kiriath Jearim had been one of the four cities of the Gibeonite confederacy (Josh 9:17). אַחֲרֵי (*'aḥ$^a$rê*, "west") is literally "behind," since one always faced east when noting directions.

**15** וַיִּשְׁאֲלוּ־לוֹ לְשָׁלוֹם (*wayyiš'$^a$lû-lô l$^e$šālôm*, "[and they] greeted him") is literally "[and they] asked him about his welfare"; i.e., they asked him how he was (cf. Exod 18:7).

**16** A gate is normally at the entrance to a city, not a house; but cf. Exod 32:26–27, where a camp has "gates" (NIV, "entrance").

**19** See the comment on 17:10 on the use of "father and priest." The reference to "clan" may allude to the fact that the tribe of Dan consisted of the one "Shuhamite" clan (Num 26:42).

**20** "Glad" reflects the idiom יָטַב לֵב (*yāṭaḇ lēḇ*, "the heart was glad"). The Levite's spirit was cheered when he heard the Danites' proposal (cf. Notes on 16:25 and cf. Esth 1:10).

**21** "Possessions" is כְּבוּדָּה (*k$^e$ḇûddāh*), meaning "heavy goods" in the sense of "valuables." The cognate *kāḇōḏ* ("glory") means "wealth" in Gen 31:1.

---

### 6. *Micah's futile pursuit*

#### 18:22–26

22 When they had gone some distance from Micah's house, the men
who lived near Micah were called together and overtook the Danites.
23 As they shouted after them, the Danites turned and said to Micah,
"What's the matter with you that you called out your men to fight?"

[24]He replied, "You took the gods I made, and my priest, and went away. What else do I have? How can you ask, 'What's the matter with you?'"

[25]The Danites answered, "Don't argue with us, or some hot-tempered men will attack you, and you and your family will lose your lives." [26]So the Danites went their way, and Micah, seeing that they were too strong for him, turned around and went back home.

**22–24** When Micah discovered the loss of his idols and his priest, he hastily gathered some friends and pursued the thieves. The Danites were forced to travel at a moderate pace because of the children and the livestock; so they were easily overtaken by Micah and his men (v.22; cf. Gen 31:23). The Danites pretended to be innocent of the charge hurled by Micah; but, unlike Jacob in Genesis 31:31–32, they did not invite a search. Micah's protest in v.24 has an almost humorous ring to it. He had good reason to be upset, and the Danites knew it.

**25–26** With their superior manpower, the Danites threatened to attack Micah's forces and put an end to his complaints. They claimed to be fierce or desperate men, as dangerous as a bear robbed of her cubs (2 Sam 17:8). Faced with almost certain defeat and death, Micah sadly gave up the cause and returned home. His failure is in marked contrast to the stunning victory gained by Abraham and his small army when they overtook the coalition of kings who had captured Lot and the wealth of Sodom and Gomorrah (Gen 14:10–16). The God of Abraham proved stronger than the idol deities fashioned by Micah. Like the gods of Babylon, Micah's gods were taken captive, unable to effect their own escape (cf. 6:31; Isa 46:1–2).

## Notes

**22** The word וַיַּדְבִּיקוּ (*wayyadbîqû*, "and [they] overtook") is also used of Laban's pursuit of Jacob and his own daughters (Gen 31:23).

**25** מָרֵי נֶפֶשׁ (*mārê nepeš*, "hot-tempered") is literally "bitter of soul." In Job 3:20 and Prov 31:6 it is used of those on the verge of perishing.

To "lose your lives" is actually to "gather up your soul." This same idiom is often used of one who is "gathered [אָסַף (*'āsap*)] to his people" in death (Num 20:24). If Micah wanted to die a natural death, retreat was the best policy.

### 7. *The capture of Laish*

18:27–31

[27]Then they took what Micah had made, and his priest, and went on to Laish, against a peaceful and unsuspecting people. They attacked them with the sword and burned down their city. [28]There was no one to rescue them because they lived a long way from Sidon and had no relationship with anyone else. The city was in a valley near Beth Rehob.

The Danites rebuilt the city and settled there. [29]They named it Dan after their forefather Dan, who was born to Israel—though the city used to be called Laish. [30]There the Danites set up for themselves the idols, and Jonathan son of Gershom, the son of Moses, and his sons were priests for the tribe of Dan until the time of the captivity of the land.

31 They continued to use the idols Micah had made, all the time the house of God was in Shiloh.

**27–28** Moving straight north, the Danites successfully attacked and destroyed Laish (v.27). It is not clear whether the residents were under the Canaanite curse, but the burning of the city suggests that the Danites thought so. Their actions are reminiscent of Abimelech's revenge against Shechem and the tower of Shechem (9:45–49). Because of the isolated location of Laish, the people could not find help against the invaders (v.28). Perhaps some soldiers from Beth Rehob could have assisted them if they had had an alliance with them. In 2 Samuel 10:6 the Syrians of Beth Rehob were hired as mercenaries.

**29–30** The new city was renamed "Dan" (v.29) and became the northernmost outpost of Israel in the proverbial "from Dan to Beersheba." There Micah's idols were set up and Jonathan son of Gershom served as priest (v.30). Gershom was a son of Moses (Exod 2:21–22), but the Masoretes inserted the letter "nun" in his name so that "Manasseh" was read instead (see Notes). Their intention was doubtless to remove any taint of idolatry from Moses' revered name, but one only has to read about the golden calf of his brother Aaron to realize the family's potential for idolatry!

Dan and Bethel were selected by Jeroboam I as sites for his golden-calf worship for the northern kingdom (1 Kings 12:28–29). He may simply have continued the idolatrous tradition introduced at the founding of Dan.

The reference to "captivity" has already been dealt with in the Introduction (cf. Date). If the reference is to the deportation by Tiglath-pileser III in 733–732 B.C., the verse may be a later editorial addition. Archer (SOTI, pp. 281–82) favors the view that this was a local captivity in the area around Dan after a border defeat during the latter period of the judges. Cundall (p. 192) prefers to relate this captivity to the widespread Philistine control of Israel after the death of Saul (2 Sam 2:8–11).

**31** The mention of Shiloh lends support to the theory of an earlier captivity, since the house of God was no longer at Shiloh after the destruction of that city by the Philistines around 1075 B.C. (cf. Jer 7:12–15). The tabernacle had been set up at Shiloh, some twenty miles north of Jerusalem, by Joshua (Josh 18:1); and the site continued as a religious center during the period of the judges. In those days Israel had no king and no Jerusalem sanctuary to unify the people.

## Notes

**28** There was a "Rehob" that marked the most northerly city seen by the twelve spies (Num 13:21). A city by that name lay in the territory of Asher (Judg 1:31).

**30** In the consonantal text the difference between Moses—מֹשֶׁה (*mōšeh*)—and "Manasseh"—מְנַשֶּׁה (*m*e*naššeh*)—is only the one letter. The nun (נ) was raised above the line to show that it was a later editorial insertion.

## B. *The Atrocity at Gibeah and Civil War (19:1–21:25)*

The second appendix relates one of the most shocking episodes of Israel's history. It occurred early in the period of the judges, because Phinehas, the grandson of Aaron, was still ministering as high priest (20:28; cf. Num 25:7, 11), and because the tribes were still able to function as a unit (cf. Josh 22:9–34). There is also a need for a long time span between the disgraceful behavior of the tribe of Benjamin and the choice of a Benjamite as king in the eleventh century. Saul was in fact from the same town of Gibeah (cf. 1 Sam 10:26)!

### 1. *The reconciliation of the Levite and his concubine*

#### 19:1–8

1In those days Israel had no king.
Now a Levite who lived in a remote area in the hill country of Ephraim
took a concubine from Bethlehem in Judah. 2But she was unfaithful to
him. She left him and went back to her father's house in Bethlehem,
Judah. After she had been there four months, 3her husband went to her
to persuade her to return. He had with him his servant and two donkeys.
She took him into her father's house, and when her father saw him, he
gladly welcomed him. 4His father-in-law, the girl's father, prevailed upon
him to stay; so he remained with him three days, eating and drinking,
and sleeping there.
5On the fourth day they got up early and he prepared to leave, but the
girl's father said to his son-in-law, "Refresh yourself with something to
eat; then you can go." 6So the two of them sat down to eat and drink
together. Afterward the girl's father said, "Please stay tonight and enjoy
yourself." 7And when the man got up to go, his father-in-law persuaded
him, so he stayed there that night. 8On the morning of the fifth day,
when he rose to go, the girl's father said, "Refresh yourself. Wait till
afternoon!" So the two of them ate together.

**1–2a** As in the story of chapters 17–18, the major characters come from the hill country of Ephraim and from Bethlehem Judah (v.1). This time it was the Levite who lived in Ephraim and had a concubine from Bethlehem. Evidently she was unhappy with her status as a secondary wife; for she committed adultery and then returned to the refuge of her father's home in Bethlehem rather than face an angry husband (v.2a).

**2b–4** Four months later (v.2b), the Levite attempted to recover his concubine (v.3). Using tender, comforting words, he tried to persuade her that reconciliation was the best policy. Her father was very happy to see him, probably because the breakup of the relationship had meant social disgrace for the family. Anxious to please his son-in-law, the father insisted that the Levite stay in Bethlehem a few days (v.4). In the East such an offer of hospitality was a common occurrence (cf. Gen 24:55). As a matter of fact, the laws of hospitality play an extremely important role as the story unfolds (cf. 4:17–23).

**5–8** The Levite's attempt to get an early start on both the fourth and fifth day was thwarted by his father-in-law. The language used in v.5 is similar to Abraham's offer to his unexpected guests (Gen 18:5). In Abraham's case the "something to eat" (*paṯ-leḥem*) turned out to be a sumptuous meal. The enjoyment mentioned in vv.6 and 9 is often associated with food and drink (cf. v.22 and Notes on 18:20).

The concubine was apparently not present during the meals, for "the two of them" (vv.6, 8) refers to the Levite and the father. She is ignored through most of the narrative, and there is no indication that she even wanted to rejoin her husband.

The delay on the fifth day proved to be as dangerous as Lot's hesitation in Genesis 19:16.

## Notes

---

**2a** וַתִּזְנֶה (*wattizneh,* "but she was unfaithful") is translated "became angry" by the LXX (A, which is a proto-Lucianic text here) and the Vulgate. They may have read it as *wattiznaḥ,* which means "to reject" in Hos 8:5 (NIV, "throw out"). Either interpretation makes good sense.

**3** "To persuade her" is literally "to speak to her heart." It is used of Shechem seeking to comfort Dinah whom he wished to marry (after he had raped her) in Gen 34:3. Joseph (Gen 50:21) and Boaz (Ruth 2:13) also spoke words of encouragement.

**4** The redundant expression חֹתְנוֹ (*ḥōṯenô,* "his father-in-law") occurs here and in v.9. It can easily be confused with חָתָן (*ḥāṯān,* "son-in-law"). See Notes on 4:11.

**5** סְעָד לִבְּךָ (*se'āḏ libbeḵā,* "refresh yourself") is literally "sustain your heart."

**8** The father's speech is full of Bedouin terminology. In v.8 "afternoon" is literally "the pitching [נְטוֹת (*neṭôṯ*)] of the day," as one would pitch a tent for the night. In v.9 he spoke of the "camping" (חֲנוֹת [*ḥanôṯ*]) of the day (NIV, "almost evening") and described the Levite's home as a אֹהֶל (*'ōhel,* "tent").

---

### 2. *The journey to Gibeah*

#### 19:9–15

**9**Then when the man, with his concubine and his servant, got up to
leave, his father-in-law, the girl's father, said, "Now look, it's almost
evening. Spend the night here; the day is nearly over. Stay and enjoy
yourself. Early tomorrow morning you can get up and be on your way
home." **10**But, unwilling to stay another night, the man left and went
toward Jebus (that is, Jerusalem), with his two saddled donkeys and his
concubine.

**11**When they were near Jebus and the day was almost gone, the
servant said to his master, "Come, let's stop at this city of the Jebusites
and spend the night."

**12**His master replied, "No. We won't go into an alien city, whose
people are not Israelites. We will go on to Gibeah." **13**He added, "Come,
let's try to reach Gibeah or Ramah and spend the night in one of those
places." **14**So they went on, and the sun set as they neared Gibeah in
Benjamin. **15**There they stopped to spend the night. They went and sat in
the city square, but no one took them into his home for the night.

**9–10** When his father-in-law requested that the Levite delay his departure for a third time, the Levite refused the offer and insisted on leaving (see Notes on v.8). Perhaps he felt that he had stayed too long already. Unfortunately it was the kindness of the girl's father that led to her fatal overnight stay in Gibeah. The travelers headed north toward Jerusalem, six miles from Bethlehem. They must have left mid to late afternoon, since daylight was almost gone when they reached Jerusalem.

**11–14** The road the Levite and his company took passed just to the west of Jebus; so it would have been a convenient lodging place (v.11). But the Levite refused his servant's suggestion due to the foreign residents of the city (v.12; cf. 1:8, 21). He feared the possibility of danger there and wanted to reach an Israelite city where, ironically, he expected good hospitality (v.13). Gibeah lay four miles beyond Jebus. Both cities belonged to the tribe of Benjamin, as the author makes clear in vv.14 and 16. Up to that time apparently the Benjamites' immorality was not well known, or else the news simply had not reached the Levite's "remote" home area (cf. v.1).

Gibeah has been identified with Tell el-Ful. It is often called "Gibeah of Saul" since the first king of Israel established his modest capital there (1 Sam 10:26; 14:2).

**15** The city square was an open area just inside the city gate, and it was the logical place for visitors to wait. They would have had to spend the night there if no invitation was forthcoming (cf. Gen 19:2). After the lavish hospitality of Bethlehem, it must have seemed strange that no one offered them lodging. But it was too late to venture out onto the dark roads.

## Notes

---

**15** The word מְאַסֵּף (*me'assēp̱*, "took [in]") is from the same root used in 18:25 to refer to the "gathering in" or "losing" of one's life. For the concubine the two ideas were closely related.

---

### 3. *The hospitality of the old man*

19:16–21

[16]That evening an old man from the hill country of Ephraim, who was
living in Gibeah (the men of the place were Benjamites), came in from
his work in the fields. [17]When he looked and saw the traveler in the city
square, the old man asked, "Where are you going? Where did you come
from?"
[18]He answered, "We are on our way from Bethlehem in Judah to a
remote area in the hill country of Ephraim where I live. I have been to
Bethlehem in Judah and now I am going to the house of the LORD. No
one has taken me into his house. [19]We have both straw and fodder for
our donkeys and bread and wine for ourselves your servants—me, your
maidservant, and the young man with us. We don't need anything."
[20]"You are welcome at my house," the old man said. "Let me supply
whatever you need. Only don't spend the night in the square." [21]So he
took him into his house and fed his donkeys. After they had washed
their feet, they had something to eat and drink.

**16–17** In a culture where inns or hostels were nonexistent, it was incredible that anyone would refuse hospitality to a stranger. Yet the Levite and his party were ignored till an old man from the same tribal area as the Levite came on the scene (v.16). This Ephraimite was residing in Gibeah on a temporary basis, somewhat as Lot had been living in Sodom (Gen 19:9). Like Lot, the old man did not share the morals of the townspeople.

**18–19** The Levite explained the situation, though he added that he was going to the house of the Lord (v.18), which was then located at either Bethel or Shiloh. Perhaps he planned to offer a sacrifice of thanksgiving for the return of his concubine. He made it clear that he had plenty of provisions; so the old man would not find his visit burdensome. Normally the host supplied the needs of the traveler (Gen 24:25), but the Levite was taking no chances.

**20–21** The old man warmly welcomed the Levite to alleviate his nervousness about the strange reception of Gibeah. Spending the night in the square was far too dangerous; so the three were taken into his house. The crisis was over—or so it seemed. The friendly man performed the normal duties of a host, politely refusing the Levite's offer to use his own supplies. The old man fed the animals and provided water for the trio to wash their feet (cf. Gen 18:4; 24:25). Then they enjoyed a meal together.

## Notes

**16** "Living" translates גָּר (*gār*), the same word applied in a mocking way to Lot in Gen 19:9. A resident alien did not have all the rights of a full citizen.

**18** In place of "house of the LORD," the LXX has "my house," which would be simpler to interpret. The final yod of בֵּיתִי (*bêṯî*) may have been misunderstood as the abbreviation of יהוה (*YHWH*, "Yahweh" or "LORD"): בֵּית יהוה (*bêṯ YHWH*).

**19** The expression אֵין מַחְסוֹר כָּל־דָּבָר (*'ên maḥsôr kol-dāḇār*), which is rendered "we don't need anything," is almost identical to 18:10's "a land that lacks nothing." The Levite's need was actually far greater than he thought.

### 4. *The sexual perversion of the Gibeahites*

#### 19:22–28

22While they were enjoying themselves, some of the wicked men of
the city surrounded the house. Pounding on the door, they shouted to
the old man who owned the house, "Bring out the man who came to
your house so we can have sex with him."
23The owner of the house went outside and said to them, "No, my
friends, don't be so vile. Since this man is my guest, don't do this
disgraceful thing. 24Look, here is my virgin daughter, and his concubine. I will bring them out to you now, and you can use them and do to
them whatever you wish. But to this man, don't do such a disgraceful
thing."
25But the men would not listen to him. So the man took his concubine
and sent her outside to them, and they raped her and abused her
throughout the night, and at dawn they let her go. 26At daybreak the
woman went back to the house where her master was staying, fell down
at the door and lay there until daylight.
27When her master got up in the morning and opened the door of the
house and stepped out to continue on his way, there lay his concubine,
fallen in the doorway of the house, with her hands on the threshold.
28He said to her, "Get up; let's go." But there was no answer. Then the
man put her on his donkey and set out for home.

**22–24** Before long it became evident that the Levite and his company had relaxed prematurely, and the Levite must have immediately understood why no one else had offered hospitality. Gibeah had imbibed the morals of Canaan and had become another Sodom. Just as the worship of Baal had brought about a near catastrophe in the plains of Moab (Num 25:1–9), so the Baal cult was probably responsible for subverting the Benjamites. This must have been comparatively soon after the earlier incident, for the same priest Phinehas intervened on both occasions (Num 25:7–8; Judg 20:28).

The "wicked men" (v.22) are literally "sons of Belial"—worthless scoundrels bent on evil. They were active homosexuals engaging in practices plainly condemned in Scripture (Lev 18:22; 20:13). The old man felt a deep sense of responsibility to protect his principal guest, and in desperation he offered the townspeople his own daughter and the Levite's concubine instead of letting them assault his guest (v.23). Lot had been willing to commit his daughters to a similar fate (Gen 19:8), but the angels had rescued them. In those days the place of a woman was often very lowly, and the "disgraceful thing" (v.24) was to molest the man. Nevertheless, the Israelites normally considered the rape of a woman disgraceful (Gen 34:7), and women who were promiscuous were also condemned to death for their behavior (Deut 22:21). In each of these passages the same word (*n^e^b̲ālāh*) is used.

**25–26** One can easily see why the concubine had left her husband in the first place. She was virtually sacrificed to save his skin as the men sexually "abused" (*hit̲ʿallēl*) her all night (v.25). Saul had fallen on his sword rather than suffer abuse at the hands of the Philistines (1 Sam 31:4, where the same word is used). The concubine survived till dawn, but by actual sunrise the ordeal had taken her life (v.26).

**27–28** The Levite had not anticipated the mass assault his concubine had succumbed to, but his words in v.28 seem callous nonetheless. Should he not have shown concern for her long before daybreak? And did he really expect her to be in any condition to travel? It is little wonder that he is called impersonally her "master" rather than "husband" in vv.26–27 (cf. v.11 also).

The night of horror made a powerful impact on the nation, and centuries later the prophet Hosea recalled the depth of Gibeah's corruption (Hos 9:9; 10:9).

## Notes

**22** בְּלִיַּעַל (*b^e^lîyaʿal*, lit., "Belial"; NIV, "wicked") may mean "without profit." It is parallel to "death" in Ps 18:4–5. Nabal is called a "wicked man" in 1 Sam 25:25, and his name meant "disgrace" (cf. vv.23–24).

The actual term behind "have sex" is the verb יָדַע (*yād̲aʿ*, "to know"), expressing intimate carnal knowledge. The same word is translated "raped" in v.25 (cf. Gen 19:5).

**24** עַנּוּ (*ʿannû*, "use them") is translated "violated" in a similar context in Deut 22:24, 29. The basic idea is to "afflict" or "humble" (cf. Gen 34:2).

### 5. *The crime report to Israel*

#### 19:29–20:7

29When he reached home, he took a knife and cut up his concubine,
limb by limb, into twelve parts and sent them into all the areas of Israel.
30Everyone who saw it said, "Such a thing has never been seen or done,
not since the day the Israelites came up out of Egypt. Think about it!
Consider it! Tell us what to do!"
20:1Then all the Israelites from Dan to Beersheba and from the land of
Gilead came out as one man and assembled before the LORD in Mizpah.
2The leaders of all the people of the tribes of Israel took their places in
the assembly of the people of God, four hundred thousand soldiers
armed with swords. 3(The Benjamites heard that the Israelites had gone
up to Mizpah.) Then the Israelites said, "Tell us how this awful thing
happened."
4So the Levite, the husband of the murdered woman, said, "I and my
concubine came to Gibeah in Benjamin to spend the night. 5During the
night the men of Gibeah came after me and surrounded the house,
intending to kill me. They raped my concubine, and she died. 6I took my
concubine, cut her into pieces and sent one piece to each region of
Israel's inheritance, because they committed this lewd and disgraceful
act in Israel. 7Now, all you Israelites, speak up and give your verdict."

**29** The shocking murder influenced the Levite to take drastic action himself. His concubine had been sacrificed to the lust of the men of Gibeah. He cut up her body as one divides the carcass of a sacrificial animal (Exod 29:17; Lev 1:6) and then sent a part of her body to each of the Twelve Tribes, including the leaders of the offending tribe, Benjamin. Apparently the recipients of this gruesome parcel were expected to respond to the appeal or else risk being struck with the sword themselves (cf. 21:10). The same technique was used at Gibeah by King Saul, who cut up oxen and circulated them throughout Israel to raise an army (1 Sam 11:7).

**30–20:1** Predictably, the nation reacted with burning indignation (v.30). The Israelites had been guilty of numerous sins since the Exodus, but never of anything so repulsive as this. They needed to appraise the situation and then plan a course of action. As in the case of Saul's appeal in 1 Samuel 11:7, the nation "came out as one man" (20:1). They came even from the distant borders of Israel, including many from Gilead in Transjordan. Mizpah, an important religious center in the days of Samuel (1 Sam 7:5, 16), was the rallying center. It may have been selected since it was only a few miles from Gibeah.

**2–3** Israel was "the people of God" (v.2), though the actions of Benjamin belied that title. The leaders bore the solemn responsibility of meting out the proper punishment for the crime, and a large army supported them. Some have questioned the accuracy of the numbers given here, but the pattern seems to be consistent. Benjamin's forces of 26,700 (v.15) were proportionate to the 400,000, and the 40,000 men lost by Israel (20:21, 25) represented 10 percent of the total. In 12:6 the single tribe of Ephraim had a fighting force of 42,000. Though the Benjamites were aware of the army being assembled at Mizpah, they had chosen to boycott the conference.

**4–7** The Levite related the shocking details of the murder, claiming that his own life had been in danger that night (vv.4–5). He may have exaggerated this point to place himself in the best possible light before the assembly. Then he explained his decision to dismember the concubine's dead body lest the deed go unnoticed (v.6). Such "lewd" (*zimmāh*) behavior as that of the men of Gibeah deserved swift and harsh punishment, and the Levite pled that the leaders would hand down a guilty verdict (v.7).

## Notes

---

**29** The word for "knife," מַאֲכֶלֶת (*ma'ᵃkelet*, "the devourer," from *'ākal*, "to eat"), was also used in Gen 22:6, 10, where Abraham was on the verge of sacrificing Isaac.

**30** The last two words in the verse, עֻצוּ (*'uṣû*, "Consider it") and דַּבֵּרוּ (*dabbērû*, "Tell us [what to do]"), also occur together in Isa 8:10, where the nations are devising and proposing plans against Judah. The nouns cognate to these verbs are used in Judg 20:7.

**20:1** The use of "Dan" does not mean that the migration of that tribe must have occurred prior to this episode. In Gen 12:8 there are references to Abraham at "Bethel" even though that particular name originated with Jacob one hundred years later (Gen 28:19).

Mizpah is usually identified with Tell en-Nasbeh, eight miles north of Jerusalem, but some scholars favor Nebi Samwil, only five miles northwest of Jerusalem.

**2** The word פִּנּוֹת (*pinnôt*, "leaders") means "corners" or, idiomatically, "cornerstones." See 1 Sam 14:38; Isa 19:13; and Zech 10:4.

**6** זִמָּה (*zimmāh*, "lewd") is usually related to sexual immorality (Job 31:11; Jer 13:27). In Hos 6:9 it is applied to murder without any sexual connotation.

---

## 6. *Israel and Benjamin: preparations for war*

### 20:8–18

8 All the people rose as one man, saying, "None of us will go home. No,
not one of us will return to his house. 9 But now this is what we'll do to
Gibeah: We'll go up against it as the lot directs. 10 We'll take ten men out
of every hundred from all the tribes of Israel, and a hundred from a
thousand, and a thousand from ten thousand, to get provisions for the
army. Then, when the army arrives at Gibeah in Benjamin, it can give
them what they deserve for all this vileness done in Israel." 11 So all the
men of Israel got together and united as one man against the city.

12 The tribes of Israel sent men throughout the tribe of Benjamin,
saying, "What about this awful crime that was committed among you?
13 Now surrender those wicked men of Gibeah so that we may put them
to death and purge the evil from Israel."

But the Benjamites would not listen to their fellow Israelites. 14 From
their towns they came together at Gibeah to fight against the Israelites.
15 At once the Benjamites mobilized twenty-six thousand swordsmen
from their towns, in addition to seven hundred chosen men from those
living in Gibeah. 16 Among all these soldiers there were seven hundred
chosen men who were left-handed, each of whom could sling a stone at
a hair and not miss.

17 Israel, apart from Benjamin, mustered four hundred thousand
swordsmen, all of them fighting men.

18 The Israelites went up to Bethel and inquired of God. They said,
"Who of us shall go first to fight against the Benjamites?"

The LORD replied, "Judah shall go first."

**8–10** The response to the Levite's plea was a positive one, and all Israel resolved to take punitive action against Gibeah (v.8). This decision was clearly God's will, though they cast lots to find out which tribe should lead the way (v.9; also cf. v.18). Ten percent of the troops were set apart to gather supplies in case a lengthy campaign was necessary. No effort was to be spared to deal with the "vileness" (v.10) or "disgraceful act" (cf. 19:23–24) of the men of Gibeah.

**11** For the third time in the chapter, the expression "as one man" occurs (cf. vv.1, 8). The Israelites were knit together as a unit, in marked contrast to the days of Deborah and Barak (5:15–17).

**12–13a** As originally intended, the anger of the nation was directed only against Gibeah. Since Gibeah belonged to the tribe of Benjamin, however, the leaders of that tribe were of necessity involved. According to Deuteronomy 13:5 and 21:21, idolaters or rebellious sons had to be "cleaned out" or "purged" from Israel. Capital punishment was clearly prescribed, and the Israelites confronted the Benjamites with the Mosaic passages.

**13b–16** Rather than surrender the guilty men, the leaders of the tribe chose to be loyal to the town of Gibeah. What had begun as a punitive operation against one city now turned into full-scale civil war. Later the tribes of Ephraim and Manasseh were to engage in bitter fighting (12:4–6), but here the eleven tribes were all pitted against Benjamin. The men of Benjamin had a good reputation as excellent soldiers, true to the prediction of Jacob in Genesis 49:27. Their prowess with the bow and the sling was well known, and even in the time of Saul some Benjamites could use the sling with either hand (1 Chron 8:40; 12:2). Their superior skill was expected to offset the numerical advantage of the other tribes. If many of the soldiers of Gibeah were among the elite slingers, one can understand why the whole tribe would be reluctant to hand them over without a battle. The term "left-handed" (v.16) was also used of Ehud of Benjamin (3:15).

Apparently seven hundred slingers formed a unit within the army, much like the chariotry or the light infantry. They formed an important component in the armies of Jehoram (2 Kings 3:25) and Uzziah (2 Chron 26:14) several centuries later. Stones propelled at speeds up to ninety miles per hour were extremely effective. David proved this in his victory over Goliath.

**17–18** The forces of Israel comprised a powerful army, the largest the nation had ever assembled (cf. v.2). As described in 1:1, the nation sought guidance from God; and again the Lord directed that the prominent tribe of Judah should lead the way (cf. Num 2:9). Gibeah's proximity to the territory of Judah insured familiarity with the terrain.

The mention of Bethel poses a problem, since the tabernacle was located at Shiloh (cf. 18:31). Some have suggested that the Israelites inquired of "the house of God" at Shiloh, but normally this is expressed by *bê<u>t</u> 'ᵉlōhîm* and not *bê<u>t</u> 'ēl*. Besides, the city Bethel is clearly intended in 20:31 and 21:19. Bethel had been a revered location ever since the Lord revealed himself to Jacob at that site (Gen 28:11–19); so, like Mizpah (v.1), Bethel could have been one of several suitable holy places. The ark of the covenant may have been moved from Shiloh to Bethel (cf. vv.26–27) to be nearer to the scene of battle. The ark frequently accompanied Israel into battle (cf. Num 10:35).

Since Phinehas the high priest stayed with the ark, it was possible to inquire of the Lord wherever Phinehas happened to be. In 2 Chronicles 1:3–4 it is plain that at the start of Solomon's reign the tabernacle was at Gibeon while the ark was in Jerusalem.

## Notes

---

**8** The interchange between "tent" (אהל ['*hl*, tr. "home"]) and "house" is the same found in 19:9 and 29.

**10** עָם (*'am*, "army") is literally "people."

"Gibeah" is actually "Geba" (גֶּבַע [*geba'*]) in the MT, but the two are easily confused; and Gibeah is clearly intended. First Sam 13:16 should also probably be "Gibeah" (cf. NIV mg.).

**12** The form שִׁבְטֵי (*šibṭê*, "tribes") looks plural but must be singular in context. It may preserve an archaic genitive ending.

**13a** To "purge" is literally to "consume" or "burn." This Piel of בער (*b'r*) is also found in Deut 17:7, 12; 19:13, 19; and elsewhere.

**15** In the LXX readings, B has 23,000 and A 25,000 rather than the 26,000 of the MT.

**16** The word יַחֲטִא (*yahᵃṭi'*, "[he would] miss") contains the root of the common verb "to sin." In Isa 65:20 it means "to fail to reach" the age of one hundred.

---

### 7. *The first battle*

### 20:19–23

19The next morning the Israelites got up and pitched camp near
Gibeah. 20The men of Israel went out to fight the Benjamites and took
up battle positions against them at Gibeah. 21The Benjamites came out
of Gibeah and cut down twenty-two thousand Israelites on the battlefield that day. 22But the men of Israel encouraged one another and
again took up their positions where they had stationed themselves the
first day. 23The Israelites went up and wept before the LORD until
evening, and they inquired of the LORD. They said, "Shall we go up again
to battle against the Benjamites, our brothers?"
The LORD answered, "Go up against them."

**19–21** Confident of victory, the Israelites moved their forces and equipment near Gibeah and lined up for battle (v.19). But the hilly terrain gave the advantage to the defending Benjamites, who used their expert slingers and swordsmen to kill 22,000 of the enemy (v.21). The men of Benjamin fought with the determination of those who knew that their very existence as a tribe was at stake. Apparently they struck quickly and withdrew into the city, leaving the Israelites to mourn their losses the rest of the day.

**22–23** The startling defeat brought Israel to its knees. On other occasions such slaughter had followed blatant national sin (Num 25:6; Deut 1:45), and it may be that the corrupting practices of Canaan had affected other tribes also. Israel as well as Benjamin may have needed some purging. The tribes wondered whether the defeat was punishment for attacking a "brother" tribe—perhaps they had misinterpreted the Lord's will. So this time they asked the question the answer to which they had assumed in v.18.

The Lord, however, again answered affirmatively, and the army received a much-needed boost to their morale (cf. 1 Sam 4:9; 2 Sam 10:12).

## Notes

---

**21** The Hiphil הִשְׁחִית (*hišhîṯ*,"cut down") is literally "ruin" or "destroy" and is used of killing people (1 Sam 26:9) or destroying cities (Gen 18:28). It occurs also in vv.25, 35, and 42.

**22** Logically this verse follows v.23. See 1:4–6 where the same inverted order of verses occurs.

The Hithpael יִתְחַזֵּק (*yiṯḥazzēq*, "encourage one another") is literally "to strengthen one another" (2 Chron 12:13).

---

### 8. *The second battle*

20:24–28

[24]Then the Israelites drew near to Benjamin the second day. [25]This
time, when the Benjamites came out from Gibeah to oppose them, they
cut down another eighteen thousand Israelites, all of them armed with
swords.

[26]Then the Israelites, all the people, went up to Bethel, and there they
sat weeping before the LORD. They fasted that day until evening and
presented burnt offerings and fellowship offerings to the LORD. [27]And
the Israelites inquired of the LORD. (In those days the ark of the covenant
of God was there, [28]with Phinehas son of Eleazar, the son of Aaron,
ministering before it.) They asked, "Shall we go up again to battle with
Benjamin our brother, or not?"

The LORD responded, "Go, for tomorrow I will give them into your hands."

**24–25** Early the next day a more determined Israelite army took the field only to fall back once more before the invincible men of Benjamin. This time somewhat fewer were killed, but the eighteen thousand casualties brought the two-day total to a staggering forty thousand, 10 percent of their entire force! It seemed catastrophic; but by reducing the size of the army, God was showing them that numbers alone did not guarantee victory. They needed to trust God to accomplish the impossible, as he did for Gideon's three hundred (cf. 7:7).

**26** Deeply discouraged the army retreated eight miles north to Bethel. The weeping and fasting revealed their desperation, for it appeared that the Lord was ignoring their just cause. Earlier the nation had also wept and sacrificed to the Lord when judgment was threatened (2:4–5). Later King David fasted and wept as he begged the Lord to spare the life of Bathsheba's child (2 Sam 12:21–22).

The combination of burnt offerings and fellowship offerings was usually an expression of devotion and commitment. Solomon offered both kinds of sacrifices at the dedication of the temple (1 Kings 8:64), and Joshua had built an altar on Mount Ebal as the nation renewed its allegiance to the Lord (Josh 8:31). The absence of any sin offering implies that the people were innocent of wrongdoing.

**27–28** Ministering at Bethel was Phinehas, the zealous grandson of Aaron who had stopped the terrible plague on the plains of Moab, where 24,000 Israelites had perished in the worship of the Baal of Peor (Num 25:9). Once more he was called on to intercede in a time of national disaster. The sacred ark was also there, symbolizing the presence and power of God (cf. 1 Sam 4:3). This is the only mention of the ark in Judges.

The Israelites were prepared to give up the fight against Benjamin, but the Lord again advised them to attack. This time he gave assurance of victory!

---

### 9. *The third battle*

#### 20:29–41

29 Then Israel set an ambush around Gibeah. 30 They went up against
the Benjamites on the third day and took up positions against Gibeah as
they had done before. 31 The Benjamites came out to meet them and
were drawn away from the city. They began to inflict casualties on the
Israelites as before, so that about thirty men fell in the open field and on
the roads—the one leading to Bethel and the other to Gibeah.
32 While the Benjamites were saying, "We are defeating them as
before," the Israelites were saying, "Let's retreat and draw them away
from the city to the roads."
33 All the men of Israel moved from their places and took up positions
at Baal Tamar, and the Israelite ambush charged out of its place on the
west of Gibeah. 34 Then ten thousand of Israel's finest men made a
frontal attack on Gibeah. The fighting was so heavy that the Benjamites
did not realize how near disaster was. 35 The LORD defeated Benjamin
before Israel, and on that day the Israelites struck down 25,100
Benjamites, all armed with swords. 36 Then the Benjamites saw that they
were beaten.
Now the men of Israel had given way before Benjamin, because they
relied on the ambush they had set near Gibeah. 37 The men who had
been in ambush made a sudden dash into Gibeah, spread out and put
the whole city to the sword. 38 The men of Israel had arranged with the
ambush that they should send up a great cloud of smoke from the city,
39 and then the men of Israel would turn in the battle.
The Benjamites had begun to inflict casualties on the men of Israel
(about thirty), and they said, "We are defeating them as in the first
battle." 40 But when the column of smoke began to rise from the city, the
Benjamites turned and saw the smoke of the whole city going up into
the sky. 41 Then the men of Israel turned on them, and the men of
Benjamin were terrified, because they realized that disaster had come
upon them.

**29** In the ancient Near East, the third time for any event or activity was often the decisive time (cf. comments on 7:8b–11 and 16:15–17). If Israel lost this battle, the war against Benjamin would have ended in disgrace. To strengthen their attack, the Israelites changed their strategy. They decided to set an ambush, a strategy successfully used by Joshua at Ai (Josh 8:2) and by Abimelech at Shechem (Judg 9:33–44). The men of Benjamin were overconfident after two easy victories, and the ruse might work.

**30–36a** For the third consecutive day, the Israelites lined up against Gibeah, and once again the Benjamites sensed victory (v.30). They pursued the men of Israel, who were retreating to the north, and thirty more soldiers died (v.31). The death of these men actually made the strategy more effective. When most of the defenders were some distance from Gibeah, the ten thousand men in ambush attacked the city (v.34). This sizable force (twice that of Joshua at Ai [Josh 8:12]) was well able to capture Gibeah (v.36a). It is unclear whether any heavy fighting occurred at Gibeah itself. Where the main forces were located, however, the battle raged. Yet the success of the ambush turned the tide of the battle.

**36b–41** In characteristic Hebrew fashion the writer repeats himself as he adds details about the ambush and its effect (v.36b). The sudden assault on Gibeah brought death to all in the city (v.37). Gibeah was quickly set on fire to signal that the city had been captured (v.38). When they saw the smoke, the other Israelites turned and began to fight in earnest (vv.39–41). They probably pointed to the fire so that the Benjamites would turn around and see what had happened. As in the case of Ai (Josh 8:20), the psychological impact was tremendous. The Benjamites could not believe their eyes, and they lost all incentive to fight. Disaster (lit., "evil") had caught up with them because of their evil deeds.

The word for "whole" (*kālîl,* v.40) is often used of "whole burnt offerings" (Deut 33:10) and is in fact used of burning a town whose people have become involved in idolatry (Deut 13:16). The entire town literally became a burnt offering!

## Notes

**29** At Ai the Lord himself commanded the use of an ambush (Josh 8:2).

**31** Some scholars (e.g., Cundall, Burney) feel that "Gibeah" should be "Geba," a city a few miles to the northeast (cf. Notes on v.10). Others (e.g., Dalglish) suggest that nearby "Gibeon" was intended.

**33** Baal Tamar ("Possession of Palms") is otherwise unknown.

"West" (מַעֲרָב [*maʿarab̲*]) is a reading of the LXX, Vulgate, and Syriac. If the MT's מַעֲרֵה (*maʿareh*) is correct, it may mean "bare space" (BDB) or "vicinity" (KB).

**37** On פָּשַׁט (*pāšaṭ,* "make a dash"), see the Notes on 9:32–33. The context there also relates to an ambush.

מָשַׁךְ (*māšak̲,* "spread out") means to "draw out" (cf. comment on 4:6).

**38** The use of a fire signal or "cloud" (מַשְׂאַת [*maśʾat̲*]) occurs also in Jer 6:1.

The form הֶרֶב (*hereb̲,* "great") may be a Hiphil imperative or an alternate form of the infinitive absolute הַרְבֵּה (*harbēh*). See BDB (p. 915) and Ps 51:4 (2 EV; NIV, "all"). It might also be handled as a Hiphil perfect, הִרְבָּה (*hirbāh*), paralleling the construction in v.40.

**41** The amazement of the Benjamites ("were terrified") compares with the shock of Joseph's brothers when they realized that he was still alive (Gen 45:3) and with Saul's reaction when he contacted the deceased Samuel (1 Sam 28:21). בהל (*bhl*) is used in each case.

## 10. *The flight of Benjamin* 20:42–48

[42]So they fled before the Israelites in the direction of the desert, but they could not escape the battle. And the men of Israel who came out of the towns cut them down there. [43]They surrounded the Benjamites, chased

**them and easily overran them in the vicinity of Gibeah on the east.**
**44 Eighteen thousand Benjamites fell, all of them valiant fighters. 45 As**
**they turned and fled toward the desert to the rock of Rimmon, the Israelites cut down five thousand men along the roads. They kept pressing after the Benjamites as far as Gidom and struck down two thousand more.**
**46 On that day twenty-five thousand Benjamite swordsmen fell, all of**
**them valiant fighters. 47 But six hundred men turned and fled into the**
**desert to the rock of Rimmon, where they stayed four months. 48 The**
**men of Israel went back to Benjamin and put all the towns to the sword, including the animals and everything else they found. All the towns they came across they set on fire.**

**42** Caught between the inspired main force of Israelites and the ten thousand troops used in the ambush, the Benjamites' only recourse was to flee. They headed east toward the desert area extending from Bethel to Jericho (cf. Josh 16:1). Perhaps they hoped to cross the Jordan and escape into the deserts beyond, but the sheer numbers of Israelites made this impossible. The pursuing forces were augmented by men from nearby cities. Whenever Israel had the enemy on the run, it seemed that volunteers flocked to join in the pursuit. The Midianites (7:23–24) and Philistines (1 Sam 14:22) were also routed by rapidly growing armies.

**43–47** The Benjamites were surrounded not far from Gibeah and suffered tremendous losses as the Israelites seemed intent on wiping them out. The term "cut down" (v.45) means "glean" (*ʿālal*), with the idea of killing or capturing the enemy down to the last man (cf. Deut 24:21 [NIV, "go over"]; Jer 6:9). In one day some 25,000 elite warriors died (v.46). The total slain, given more exactly as 25,100 in v.35, still does not seem to account for the 26,700 mentioned in v.15. If only 600 survived, 26,100 must have been killed. The other 1,000 men apparently died during the first two days of fighting, where the author of Judges only supplies the number of Israelites who were killed.

The last 600 men of Benjamin found refuge at the rock of Rimmon (v.47), a conical limestone hill surrounded by wadis and located about four miles east of Bethel. Numerous caves provided hiding places from the relentless pursuers. Modern Rammun preserves the name of the ancient site.

**48** Methodically, the Israelite soldiers captured and destroyed the defenseless towns of Benjamin. Sihon's Amorite kingdom had suffered the same harsh treatment during the Conquest (Deut 2:34). According to Deuteronomy 13:12–18, any Israelite city that harbored idolaters was to be burned—people as well as animals. The sin of Gibeah was considered as serious as idolatry. The prime offenders here were guilty on both counts, which may explain the terrible extent of the retribution.

## Notes

---

**42** The second clause is literally "the battle overtook them." In v.45 the same word (דבק [*d̲bq*] in the Hiphil) is rendered "pressing after" (cf. 18:22 also).

On "cut down" see vv.21 (cf. Notes in loc.) and 25.

**43** "Easily" is an attempt to translate מְנוּחָה (*m^enûḥāh*, "resting place"). There was no relief for the weary soldiers. The LXX MS B reads ἀπο Νουα (*apo Noua*, "from Noua"), understanding the term as a proper name.
**44** On אַנְשֵׁי־חָיִל (*'anšê-ḥāyil*, "valiant fighters"), see the comment on 3:29.
**45** "Rock of Rimmon" means either "Pomegranate Rock" or "Roaring Rock." The god Ramanu was known to the Assyrians as "the thunderer."
"Gidom" is not mentioned anywhere else.
**48** "All the towns" translates עִיר מְתֹם (*'îr m^etōm*). Probably מְתִם (*m^etim*), from מַת (*mat*, "male") is intended. In Deut 2:34 and 3:6, *'îr m^etîm* is found in contexts identical to this one. All males and females were killed in the slaughter.

---

## 11. *Concern for Benjamin's survival*

### 21:1–4

[1]The men of Israel had taken an oath at Mizpah: "Not one of us will give his daughter in marriage to a Benjamite."

[2]The people went to Bethel, where they sat before God until evening, raising their voices and weeping bitterly. [3]"O LORD, the God of Israel," they cried, "why has this happened to Israel? Why should one tribe be missing from Israel today?"

[4]Early the next day the people built an altar and presented burnt offerings and fellowship offerings.

**1–2** Unlike most victorious armies, the men of Israel mourned rather than celebrated. The terrible judgment against Benjamin had all but eliminated that tribe. So Israel went to Bethel to weep before the Lord (v.2), just as they had done after being defeated in the two earlier battles (20:23, 26). Did the nation suddenly realize that the punishment had gone further than they intended, or were they simply lamenting the judgment that the Benjamites fully deserved?

It appeared that the tribe would become extinct because of the oath that had been taken when the Israelite army assembled at Mizpah (v.1; cf. 20:1–2). The low morality exhibited at Gibeah was sufficient reason for banning intermarriage with that tribe. The men of Benjamin had become Canaanites (cf. 3:6). But, as in Jephthah's case (11:35), the people later regretted that they had taken an oath.

**3** When Israel had won battles in the past, sometimes very few men were missing in action (cf. Num 31:49). No wonder they bemoaned the fact that an *entire tribe* was missing after this conflict. The tribes of Israel were twelve in number, but Jacob's youngest son was about to lose his posterity completely.

**4** To renew their commitment to the Lord and to seek his help, the people presented the same kinds of offerings mentioned in 20:26. This time they built another altar, as Gideon did during another national crisis (6:24, 28).

## Notes

---

1 Customs of intermarriage are also discussed in the Samson narrative in 14:1–4.

**2** The meaning of "bitterly" is derived from the cognate accusative בְּכִי (*b^eki̇̂*, "weeping") modified by the adjective "great" (גָּדוֹל, *gāḏôl*; cf. 2:4 also).

---

## 12. *Wives from Jabesh Gilead*

### 21:5–14

**5**Then the Israelites asked, "Who from all the tribes of Israel has failed to assemble before the LORD?" For they had taken a solemn oath that anyone who failed to assemble before the LORD at Mizpah should certainly be put to death.

**6**Now the Israelites grieved for their brothers, the Benjamites. "Today
one tribe is cut off from Israel," they said. **7**"How can we provide wives
for those who are left, since we have taken an oath by the LORD not to
give them any of our daughters in marriage?" **8**Then they asked, "Which
one of the tribes of Israel failed to assemble before the LORD at Mizpah?"
They discovered that no one from Jabesh Gilead had come to the camp
for the assembly. **9**For when they counted the people, they found that
none of the people of Jabesh Gilead were there.

**10**So the assembly sent twelve thousand fighting men with instructions to go to Jabesh Gilead and put to the sword those living there,
including the women and children. **11**"This is what you are to do," they
said. "Kill every male and every woman who is not a virgin." **12**They
found among the people living in Jabesh Gilead four hundred young women who had never slept with a man, and they took them to the camp at Shiloh in Canaan.

**13**Then the whole assembly sent an offer of peace to the Benjamites at
the rock of Rimmon. **14**So the Benjamites returned at that time and were
given the women of Jabesh Gilead who had been spared. But there were not enough for all of them.

**5–7** The dilemma posed by the first oath was partially solved by reflecting on another, more important oath the Israelites had taken. When the limbs of the concubine had been sent throughout Israel, the implication was that any city that did not respond to deal with this atrocity would itself be subject to death (cf. comment on 19:29). If it had not been for their grief over Benjamin, the Israelites might never have discovered which regions were delinquent.

**8–9** The search revealed that the city of Jabesh Gilead was guilty. This town was located nine miles southeast of Beth Shan and two miles east of the Jordan. Perhaps these residents of Manasseh refused to oppose a tribe related to them through Rachel. Later on Saul of Benjamin rescued Jabesh Gilead from invaders (1 Sam 11), and they in turn risked their lives to save his body from disgrace (1 Sam 31:11–13). These close ties probably came as a result of the intermarriage in Judges 21.

**10–12** In any event, the leaders of Israel decided that Jabesh Gilead deserved the same fate as the cities of Benjamin in 20:48 (v.10). According to Numbers 31:17–18, it was permissible in a war of revenge to save the lives of the virgins (v.11). They alone could be spared, and it was this provision that was used to secure wives for Benjamin. Four hundred girls were taken to Shiloh on the Canaan side of the Jordan River (v.12).

Shiloh, which figures prominently in this chapter (cf. vv.19–21), was the place where the tabernacle was located (cf. 18:31 comment). Situated about nine miles north of Bethel and the rock of Rimmon, Shiloh afforded a temporary refuge where the captive girls could mourn the loss of their loved ones.

**13–14** Four months had passed since the six hundred Benjamites had been in hiding. The anger stirred by the war had now subsided, and the men were doubtless eager to give up their precarious existence. When the offer of peace was combined with a promise of wives, the men of Benjamin decided it was safe to accept the terms. Thus the sole survivors of a city were married to the remaining refugees of a tribe. Since there were only four hundred women, however, two hundred men were still left without spouses.

## Notes

---

**5** The "solemn" oath is literally the "great" or "big" one—הַגְּדוֹלָה (*hagg*$^{e}$*ḏôlāh*). This is the only time in the OT that *gāḏôl* modifies "oath."

The use of the Qal infinitive absolute מוֹת (*môṯ*) with the Hophal imperfect יוּמָת (*yûmāṯ*) is quite common (cf. Exod 19:12). The NIV renders the combination as "should certainly be put to death."

**6** On "grieved" see the Notes on 2:18.

Literally "their brothers, the Benjamites" is "their brother Benjamin." The singular emphasizes the importance of each son of Jacob. In Gen 42:38 the very prospect of losing Benjamin had brought deep grief to Jacob.

נִגְדַּע (*nigda'*, "cut off") is parallel to נִשְׁבָּרָה (*nišbārāh*, "broken") in Jer 48:25, where the horn of Moab is cut off.

**8** מַחֲנֶה (*maḥ*$^{a}$*neh*, "camp") is translated "army" in 4:16 and 8:10–12 (cf. Num 2:3).

**11–12** בְּתוּלָה (*b*$^{e}$*ṯûlāh*, "virgin") occurs only in v.12, while vv.11–12 both have the idiom "young women who had never slept with a man" (NIV renders it "virgin in v.11; cf. Num 31:17–18). Codex Vaticanus inserts "But spare the virgins" at the end of v.11, probably copying the style of Num 31:18.

**13** וַיִּקְרְאוּ לָהֶם שָׁלוֹם (*wayyiqr*$^{e}$*'û lāhem šālôm*, "sent an offer of peace") is actually "called peace to them." Deuteronomy 20:10 uses the same idiom, adding *l*$^{e}$ before *šālôm*. Fifty MSS include *l*$^{e}$ here also.

**14** The quantitative use of כֵּן (*kēn*, "so," "enough") is also reflected in 1 Kings 10:12.

---

## 13. *Wives from Shiloh*

### 21:15–23

15 The people grieved for Benjamin, because the LORD had made a gap
in the tribes of Israel. 16 And the elders of the assembly said, "With the
women of Benjamin destroyed, how shall we provide wives for the men
who are left? 17 The Benjamite survivors must have heirs," they said, "so
that a tribe of Israel will not be wiped out. 18 We can't give them our
daughters as wives, since we Israelites have taken this oath: 'Cursed be
anyone who gives a wife to a Benjamite.' 19 But look, there is the annual
festival of the LORD in Shiloh, to the north of Bethel, and east of the road
that goes from Bethel to Shechem, and to the south of Lebonah."

20 So they instructed the Benjamites, saying, "Go and hide in the
vineyards 21 and watch. When the girls of Shiloh come out to join in the
dancing, then rush from the vineyards and each of you seize a wife from

the girls of Shiloh and go to the land of Benjamin. 22When their fathers
or brothers complain to us, we will say to them, 'Do us a kindness by
helping them, because we did not get wives for them during the war,
and you are innocent, since you did not give your daughters to them.'"
23So that is what the Benjamites did. While the girls were dancing,
each man caught one and carried her off to be his wife. Then they
returned to their inheritance and rebuilt the towns and settled in them.

**15–18** As in v.6, the grief of the nation is mentioned (v.15); and it seems as if the leaders were unaware of the four hundred women obtained from Jabesh Gilead (v.16). Perhaps the plan to abduct the maidens of Shiloh was formed before the outcome of the campaign against Jabesh Gilead was known. After the four hundred Jabesh Gilead virgins arrived on the scene, it would be difficult to worry about the tribe being "wiped out" (v.17). By v.22 the results of the war with Jabesh Gilead had become available.

The "gap" (v.15) was literally a "breach" (*pereṣ*), usually associated with an outburst of the Lord's anger (2 Sam 6:8). It also refers to a break in a wall, suggesting the incompleteness of Israel without Benjamin. For the third time in the chapter, reference is made to the oath that forbade the giving of daughters to Benjamin (v.18; cf. vv.1, 7). In the absence of wives, the breach seemed irreparable.

**19** A solution was suggested by the approaching festival in Shiloh, when a large number of people would gather. During the celebration perhaps the Benjamites could find the girls they needed. The festival was likely the Feast of Tabernacles since vineyards are mentioned and the grape harvest comes in August and September. One of the purposes of the fall Tabernacles Feast was to rejoice over the summer fruit that had been gathered. Samuel's parents traveled annually to Shiloh to worship the Lord (1 Sam 1:3). Some scholars believe that the Passover is intended, for the dancing could imitate the celebrating of Miriam and the women of Israel after the Exodus (cf. Exod 15:20–21).

The detailed directions about Shiloh's location may have been given to assist the Benjamites in making the fastest escape possible. Probably they were not familiar with the region, since it lay in the middle of Ephraim's territory to the north. In view of the spiritual condition of Gibeah and most of Benjamin, it is unlikely that they had bothered to attend any recent religious festival in Shiloh. The road from Bethel to Shechem was, however, a major north-south highway. Lebonah, modern el-Lubban, was located three miles north of Shiloh.

**20–23** Ironically, the men of Benjamin were told to set an ambush ("hide," v.20) for the girls, the same technique used by the Israelites against the Benjamites at Gibeah (20:37). The strategy worked flawlessly, and each man obtained his wife.

This highly unorthodox method of obtaining a wife was sure to disturb the relatives of the wives greatly. Fathers and brothers usually received a bride price from the prospective groom and had an important voice in arranging the marriage (cf. Gen 24:50–53). The Israelites promised to intercede for Benjamin on the grounds that there was no other way to save the devastated tribe. The action against Jabesh Gilead had brought forth only four hundred wives, and more were needed. Besides, the fact that the Benjamites *stole* the maidens absolved the parents from the curse against giving their daughters to Benjamin! These arguments may have been less than convincing, but the leaders of Israel prevented the relatives from retaliating against the Benjamites (cf. 18:22–26).

Restored to their property, the surviving Benjamites began the long task of rebuilding and repopulating their cities. It is a tribute to their hard work and to the resiliency of Israel as a whole that a member of the Benjamite tribe was selected to be the first king (1 Sam 9:1–2).

## Notes

**17** The word יְרֻשָּׁה (*yᵉruššāh*, "heirs") is normally translated "possession," referring to land, but see Lev 25:45–46 and Num 18:20.

**19** Shiloh was about two miles east of the Bethel-Shechem road.

**21** The feminine plural "girls" is linked with the masculine plural verb יֵצְאוּ (*yēṣᵉʾû*, "come out"; cf. 1 Kings 11:3 and GKC, 145*p*).

חָטַף (*ḥāṭap̱*, "seize") is used in Ps 10:9 of the wicked who is waiting in ambush to catch the helpless man.

Greek tradition tells of the Messenians who stole girls from Laconia during a festival of Artemis (cf. Boling, p. 294).

**22** On רִיב (*rîḇ*, "complain"), see the Notes on 8:1.

"Do us a kindness" is an attempt to render חָנּוּנוּ אוֹתָם (*ḥonnûnû ʾôṯām*). BDB (p. 336) suggests "favor us with them," which refers the "them" to the girls rather than the Benjamites.

The words כָּעֵת תֶּאְשָׁמוּ (*kāʿēṯ teʾšāmû*), used here with the negative *lōʾ* to give the rendering "you are innocent," literally mean "now you are guilty," implying that if the parents had willingly married their daughters to Benjamin, the sanctions of the oath would have applied (cf. the use of *kāʿēṯ* in 13:23 [NIV, "now"]).

**23** גָּזָלוּ (*gāzālû*, "caught") occurs in Gen 31:31, where Jacob worried that Laban would "take [back his daughters] by force."

## 14. *Conclusion*

### 21:24–25

[24]At that time the Israelites left that place and went home to their tribes and clans, each to his own inheritance.
[25]In those days Israel had no king; everyone did as he saw fit.

**24–25** Since the Israelites had dealt with the sin of Benjamin (cf. 20:8) and yet had provided for the future of that defeated tribe, the soldiers felt free to disband (v.24). The task had been far more difficult than they had anticipated, and the whole affair constituted one of the most tragic chapters of Israel's history.

The last verse (v.25) repeats the somber words with which these appendixes began in 17:6 (cf. Notes on 14:3). From the standpoint of the monarchy, the period of the judges was indeed a time of anarchy and upheaval. The often leaderless people wallowed in idolatry, immorality, and hatred. Sin abounded on both a personal and a national level, and God repeatedly allowed the enemy to overwhelm his people. The reigns of David and Solomon were a far happier time. Yet it was the last of the judges, Samuel, whom God used to call the people to repentance.

# RUTH

F.B. Huey, Jr.

# RUTH

## Introduction



### 1. Background

By any standards the Book of Ruth is a classic short story. It has been called the most beautiful short story ever written. It deals with a plot that naturally emerges through conversations between the major characters: Ruth, Naomi, and Boaz.

The setting of the book is the time of the judges. Chronological uncertainties, however, make it impossible to date this period more precisely than the last third of the second millennium B.C. The date of the judges hinges on the date of the Exodus, a question scholars have long debated. For many years a thirteenth-century date has been widely accepted.[1] Recently, however, the issue has been reopened with arguments for a date about 1470 B.C.[2] Hans Goedicke has proposed a date of 1477 B.C., but for different reasons.[3]

The period of the judges was between the initial conquest of Palestine under Joshua and the establishment of the monarchy under Saul. It was a time of moral and political chaos in Israel. There was no strong central government or leader, the people repeatedly turned away from God, and neighboring peoples constantly harassed and invaded the disorganized nation (Judg 2:14–15; 21:25).

In later Judaism, at least since the twelfth century A.D., the Book of Ruth became one of five books (called the Megilloth) read at the various Jewish festivals. Ruth was read during the Feast of Weeks (known also as Shabouth or Pentecost), which marked the end of grain harvest. The other books of the Megilloth are Song of Songs (read at

[1] E.g., John Bright, *A History of Israel*, 3d ed. (Philadelphia: Westminster, 1981), p. 123.

[2] See John J. Bimson, *Redating the Exodus and Conquest*, JSOT, Suppl. Series 5 (Sheffield: University of Sheffield Press, 1978).

[3] See Hershel Shanks, "The Exodus and the Crossing of the Red Sea According to Hans Goedicke," BAR 7 (Sept.–Oct. 1981): 42–50; see also D.J. Wiseman's discussion in this series, EBC, 1:317–18.

Passover), Lamentations (read on the ninth of Ab), Ecclesiastes (read during the Feast of Booths), and Esther (read during Purim).

The Book of Ruth's historicity has been both defended (Archer, Harrison, May, Slotki) and denied (Eissfeldt, Gressman, Gunkel, R. Pfeiffer). The story has been called a folktale (Sasson [i.e., pure fiction]) that became associated with David at a later time. Yet it seems unlikely that David would have been linked to a Moabite ancestry unless the tradition were true. No Israelite would have created such a detested family connection. Apparently David's ancestry was too well known to hide, even if he had desired to do so. Campbell perceptively observes that a better question to ask about Ruth than historicity is plausibility and concludes that the book is "eminently plausible" (*Ruth*, p. 10).

The story of Ruth has also been interpreted as a disguised fertility cult myth with Elimelech and Naomi representing Tammuz and Ishtar.[4] This interpretation, however, has been almost universally rejected (e.g., Eissfeldt, R. Pfeiffer, Weiser). The story is plausible, contemporary circumstances and customs are accurately reflected, and nothing is gained by denying its historicity.

## 2. Unity

No serious attempts have been made to fragment the Book of Ruth into a number of originally separate sources. Scholars have generally conceded it to be a single composition without seam or any additions except for 4:17b and the formal genealogy in 4:18–22. For years critical scholars generally agreed that these two passages were additions to the original story and summarize the fuller genealogy of 1 Chronicles 2:3–15 (e.g., Childs, Eissfeldt, Fohrer). There is today, however, a tendency among critical scholars to insist that even these concluding verses were integral parts of the original written story designed to preserve the ancestral links of David with the Moabites (Fichtner, Gerleman, Lamparter).

## 3. Authorship

Jewish tradition in the Talmud (*Baba Bathra* 14b) accepted Samuel as the author of the Book of Ruth, but scholars today do not take that tradition seriously. The similarity of the language of Ruth to that of Judges and Samuel was probably responsible for linking it to Samuel. There is nothing in the Book of Ruth itself that helps us to identify the author. All we can say is that he was a literary artist and a skillful teacher.

## 4. Date

The Book of Ruth in its written form has been dated from the time of Samuel (a Jewish tradition preserved in the Talmud) to the early monarchical period (Archer, Hals, Keil, Young) to a date after the Exile (Eissfeldt, Fohrer, R. Pfeiffer, Weiser; Campbell [*Ruth*, pp. 24–28] discusses the arguments for a late date but concludes

[4]W.E. Staples, "The Book of Ruth," AJSL 53 (April 1937): 145–57; cf. p. 150.

that it was written in the ninth century B.C.). It could not have been earlier than David because it contains his genealogy (unless only the genealogy was a later addition).

Arguments for an early date include familiarity with ancient customs characteristic of the period of the judges and the use of some identifiable archaic language (e.g., the *n* endings; see Myers, p. 20). The style is markedly different from those books known to be postexilic (e.g., Ezra, Esther). These stylistic characteristics, however, have been explained as the narrator's art, an intentional effort to "archaize" the book, much as a skillful writer of a historical novel today carefully researches and reflects the customs and language of the period his story is set in (Gordis, Gray; but denied by Myers, p. 32).

Arguments for a late date include alleged Hebrew modes of expression and Aramaic words characteristic of the postexilic period (see Morris, pp. 232–33). Yet at best this evidence is questionable. The confusion of gender, for example, has been presented as evidence for a late date. There are seven instances in Ruth where a masculine plural suffix is used with a feminine plural antecedent. However, this anomaly may be an archaic feminine dual ending. Aramaisms as proof of a late date are no longer in vogue; and, in fact, there are very few Aramaic words in Ruth. Since Aramaic was an international language in the preexilic period, and since one can never be sure whether the Aramaic word is original or a redactor's revision, Aramaisms are no longer indisputable evidence for late dating.[5] The location of Ruth in the *Keṯûḇîm* ("The Writings"; see Place in the Canon) has also been used to support a late date of composition, but the argument is not valid (Gray, p. 398). Morris (p. 231) cites some early evidence that Ruth was not originally included among the *Keṯûḇîm*.

Those who propose a late date for the writing of Ruth do not, however, necessarily deny the antiquity or authenticity of the original story. Some scholars believe that Ruth was a story that was first told in poetic, oral form during the time of the judges (Myers, p. 64). Then it was put into prose, as early as the tenth century (during Solomon's reign) to the eighth century, and finally edited into its present form after the Exile (c.450–250 B.C.). This theory, however, has not gone unchallenged (e.g., Campbell, *Ruth*, p. 8).

## 5. Purpose

Scholars do not agree as to the purpose of the Book of Ruth (see Leggett, pp. 163–72). Many (e.g., Bertholet, Rost, Weiser), following a theory first proposed in 1857 by Abraham Geiger, once believed that the Book of Ruth served as a protest against the narrow nationalism and exclusivism of Ezra and Nehemiah (who strenuously objected to marriage with foreigners) by pointing out that an ancestor of the revered David married a foreigner. However, the story is too forthright and simple to contain such a subtle polemic; in fact, most readers would have missed the implication. Also, Ruth was not just a foreigner. She was a convert to the Israelite faith; so she could hardly have been used as an argument in favor of mixed marriages.

Other scholars believe that the purpose of the book was to give an account of the

---

[5]Archer, SOTI, pp. 127–31; F.F. Bruce, *The Books and the Parchments* (Westwood, N.J.: Fleming H. Revell, 1963), p. 48; Hals, p. 68; Harrison, IOT, p. 1061; K.A. Kitchen, *Ancient Orient and Old Testament* (Chicago: InterVarsity, 1966), p. 145.

ancestry of David, since it was not included in 1 and 2 Samuel.[6] Therefore 4:18–22 becomes the climax rather than an afterthought to the story. Though the author's main purpose may not have been to provide an account of David's genealogy, it is uncertain that the book would ever have become part of the canon except for its association with him.

Hals believes that the purpose of Ruth is to show how God is totally and continuously in control of all human events (p. 18), though in an unperceived way, and compares the hidden causality of God in Ruth to the Joseph story (Gen 37–50) (pp. 34–44) and to the succession history of David (2 Sam 9–20) (pp. 21–34). Gray, Haller, Hertzberg, and Rudolph also support divine providence as the principal emphasis in Ruth.

Other suggested purposes of the book are so numerous that they can only be listed without comment: Ruth shows how anyone can become a believer and experience the blessings of God;[7] the rewards are great to those who perform deeds of kindness for others (Slotki, p. 38); it shows how a person or nation can best be loyal to God; its only purpose was for entertainment;[8] it was written as a plea for racial tolerance and a demonstration that true religion exceeds the bounds of nationality;[9] the writer wanted to teach a number of spiritual and moral truths (Slotki, p. 39); it was intended to awaken the people of God to their high privilege and responsibility (Herbert, p. 316); it was a polemic against the exclusion of the Moabites from the community of Israel (ibid.); it was a story in praise of the loyalty and worth of Ruth (Gunkel, Gressmann); it was written to explain why David took his parents to Moab while he was in flight from Saul (Budde); its purpose was to emphasize the laws of levirate marriage and the redemption of a kinsman's property;[10] and, finally, it has been suggested that its primary purpose was to celebrate friendship[11] or faithfulness.[12]

With so many proposed purposes of the Book of Ruth (and the above list is not exhaustive), it is obvious that the book has something for everyone. So it would be presumptuous to choose only one purpose to the exclusion of all others. The inability to agree on a single purpose for Ruth may reflect the exegetes' failure to formulate or use hermeneutical rules for the interpretation of historical literature.

## 6. Literary Form

Many scholars use the technical term "novella" (e.g., Fohrer, Hals) or short story (Campbell, Gray) to describe closely knit short stories such as Ruth, Esther, the Joseph story of Genesis 37–50, and similar narratives in the OT. Ruth has been called an idyllic tale (Goethe) and also a parable (Herbert). Its simple, clear style and deft touch in delineating a character or painting a scene with a minimum of words shows the writer's literary skill, as does the remarkable symmetrical design of its structure.

[6]Harrison, IOT, p. 1063; J. Alberto Soggin, *Introduction to the Old Testament*, Old Testament Library (Philadelphia: Westminster, 1976), p. 395.

[7]Smith, IB, 2:831.

[8]R.H. Pfeiffer, *Introduction to the Old Testament* (New York: Harper, 1941), p. 719.

[9]Harrison, IOT, p. 1063.

[10]Cited by Gray, p. 401, but denied by Morris, p. 242.

[11]Smith, IB, 2:831; Morris, p. 241.

[12]Eissfeldt, p. 482, cites an obvious parallel with Job, where God restores blessing on the one who has endured suffering and affliction.

The literary devices the writer used are many and varied: chiasmus, merismus, repetition (esp. of key words), assonance, inclusio, and wordplay. The language has affinities with certain narratives of the Pentateuch and the narratives of Joshua, Judges, 1 and 2 Samuel, and 1 and 2 Kings.

Myers believes that the book was originally composed in poetic form, probably for the purpose of oral transmission. Later it was transferred to a prose form with its poetic format still visible. Myers identified all or part of thirty-three verses as of poetic origin. Campbell (*Ruth*, p. 12) denies that the book was originally written in poetic form and that the present version is a relic of the original poem. Sasson (p. 222) also warns against speaking of the "poetry" of Ruth without stretching the definition of poetry.

## 7. Theological Values

The Book of Ruth does not deal with the major events or the institutions in Israel's history but with the problems and concerns of a single family in Bethlehem. The story form, however, should not blind the reader to the book's theological values, chief of which is the emphasis on the providence of God. Through the story of the experiences of this family, Ruth presents unobtrusively but powerfully the concept of divine providence, called by Hals "divine causality" (p. 77). There are no direct conversations with God or appeals to him, though three names for God are found in the book (Yahweh, Elohim, Shaddai), and the solemn oath "As surely as the LORD lives" (3:13) is invoked. One who rejects belief in divine providence will argue that everything that happens in the book is by chance—the famine, the deaths, Ruth's choice of Boaz's field as a place to glean, his attraction to her, and their eventual marriage. Though God appears hidden throughout the story, he, rather than Naomi, Ruth, or Boaz, has been called the key figure in the book (Rudolph) and the "primary actor in the drama" (Campbell). Hals says that "with virtually his every word the author is endeavoring to present the providence of God" (p. 8).

The covenant relationship that bound the people of Israel to God and to one another underlies much of the book, though it is never mentioned, nor are the tabernacle and the sacrifices. Though the word "covenant" is not found in Ruth, it is a significant factor in the book's unfolding plot. Ruth's eloquent commitment to the God of her mother-in-law (1:16–17) was her acceptance of a relationship voiced earlier by Israel at Mount Sinai: "Everything the LORD has said we will do" (Exod 24:3). When Boaz commended Ruth's loving care of Naomi—"May you be richly rewarded by the LORD" (2:12)—he was echoing Deuteronomic theology: "All these blessings will come upon you and accompany you if you obey the LORD your God" (Deut 28:2). Even Naomi's bitter complaint, "the LORD has afflicted me" (1:21), was based on the presupposition of his faithfulness and trustworthiness by reason of his covenant relationship with his people.

Other theological ideas found in the book include "redemption" (there are twenty-three occurrences of the word *gā'al* in Ruth). "Covenant loyalty" (*ḥeseḏ;* NIV, "kindness"), though found only three times (1:8; 2:20; 3:10), is a prominent idea emphasizing that loyalty is rewarded. God's sovereignty in the affairs of his people is frequently expressed (1:21) or implied (he brings famine and turns barrenness into fertility).

## 8. Place in the Canon

Ruth's place in the canon was never seriously questioned (as was, e.g., Esther). Its connection with David, the frequent mention of God, and the exemplary morality of its leading characters were sufficient to secure its place in the canon.

In the Jewish Bible Ruth appears in the third division, the *Keṯûḇîm,* though not always in the same position. In the Talmud (*Baba Bathra* 14b), it was the first book in the *Keṯûḇîm,* followed by the Book of Psalms. It was later transfered to the Megilloth, five books grouped together in the *Keṯûḇîm* (the other four being Song of Songs, Ecclesiastes, Lamentations, and Esther); but its position there has varied also. Sometimes it appears as the first of the Megilloth; but in most printed Hebrew Bibles today it stands second, after Song of Songs (following the chronological order of the Jewish festivals in which one of the books of the Megilloth is read). Ruth is read during the Feast of Weeks (Pentecost).

Scholars who understand the *Keṯûḇîm* to be the last section of the OT to be canonized use Ruth's inclusion in that section of the Hebrew Bible as evidence for the late date of the book. Many evangelical scholars reject this concept of canonization outright and argue for progressive recognition of the books as authoritative as they came from the hands of the writers. Ruth's inclusion in the *Keṯûḇîm* can be explained as a transfer from an older section to join it to the other books of the Megilloth.

The LXX, followed by the Vulgate and subsequent Western versions, placed Ruth after the Book of Judges because of the similar setting of the two books established in Ruth 1:1: "In the days when the judges ruled."

## 9. Text

The Hebrew text of Ruth contains relatively few problems. It does have a number of words not found elsewhere in the OT, and it is written in a classical form of Hebrew that reminds the reader of Samuel and Kings. There are some unusual textual variants and a few textual problems, but they are not numerous. The LXX agrees closely with the MT; the differences are not of major significance. Some problems occur in 1:21; 2:7; and 4:5 because of the obscurity of the text. The Masoretes suggested several variant readings, and these will be discussed as they are encountered.

## 10. Special Problems

The problems associated with the Book of Ruth are largely matters of interpretation. Questions concerning the difference in the application of the levirate law in Ruth from Deuteronomy 25:5–10 have not been resolved satisfactorily.[13] Naomi's relationship to the family land that was sold is not clear. The reasons for the nearest kinsman's refusal to marry Ruth remain in question (see Leggett, pp. 209–53; Sasson, pp. 136–40). Scholars have differed about the morality of the events at the threshing floor. W.E. Staples[14] and H.G. May[15] argue that sacred prostitution at the high place in Bethlehem was involved. De Waard and Nida (p. 50) say it is not clear whether an

[13]See Millar Burrows, "The Marriage of Boaz and Ruth," JBL 49 (December 1940): 445–54; G.R. Driver and John C. Miles, *The Assyrian Laws* (Oxford: Clarendon, 1935), pp. 244ff.; Morgenstern, pp. 175ff.; Rowley, pp. 171–94.

[14]"The Book of Ruth," AJSL 53 (1937): 145–57.

[15]"Ruth's Visit to the High Place at Bethlehem," *Journal of the Royal Asiatic Society* (1939): 75–78.

euphemism for sexual intercourse was involved. Campbell (*Ruth*, p. 138) concludes that nothing improper occurred.

## 11. Bibliography

### Books

Baldwin, J.G. "Ruth." *The New Bible Commentary: Revised.* Edited by D. Guthrie et al. Grand Rapids: Eerdmans, 1970, pp. 277–83.

Beattie, D.R.G. *Jewish Exegesis of the Book of Ruth.* Journal for the Study of the Old Testament. Supplement Series 2. Sheffield, England: University of Sheffield, 1977.

Campbell, Edward F., Jr. *Ruth: A New Translation With Introduction and Commentary.* The Anchor Bible. Vol. 7. Garden City, N.Y.: Doubleday & Co., 1975.

———. "The Hebrew Short Story: A Study of Ruth." *A Light Unto My Path: Old Testament Studies in Honor of Jacob M. Myers.* Edited by Howard N. Bream et al. Philadelphia: Temple University Press, 1974, pp. 83–101.

Cooke, George A. *The Book of Ruth.* The Cambridge Bible for Schools and Colleges. Cambridge: University Press, 1913.

Gerleman, Gillis. *Ruth. Das Hohelied.* Biblischer Kommentar: Alten Testaments. Neukirchen-Vluyn: Neukirchener Verlag, 1965.

Gray, John. *Joshua, Judges, and Ruth.* The Century Bible New Edition. London: Thomas Nelson and Sons, 1967.

Hals, Ronald M. *The Theology of the Book of Ruth.* Facet Books. Biblical Series 23. Philadelphia: Fortress, 1969.

Herbert, A.S. "Ruth." *Peake's Commentary on the Bible.* Edited by Matthew Black and H.H. Rowley. London: Thomas Nelson and Sons, 1962, pp. 316–17.

Hubbard, Robert L., Jr. *The Book of Ruth.* New International Commentary on the Old Testament. Grand Rapids: Eerdmans, 1988.

Keil, C.F., and F. Delitzsch, *Biblical Commentary on the Old Testament: Joshua, Judges, Ruth.* Reprint edition. Translated by James Martin. Grand Rapids: Eerdmans, 1956.

Kenneday, A.R.S. *The Book of Ruth. The Hebrew Text With Grammatical Notes and Vocabulary.* New York: Macmillan; London: SPCK, 1937.

Knight, George A.F. *Ruth and Jonah: The Gospel in the Old Testament.* The Torch Bible Commentaries. London: SCM, 1950.

Lawson, George. *Expositions of Ruth and Esther.* Evansville, Ind.: Sovereign Grace, 1960.

Leggett, Donald A. *The Levirate and Goel Institutions in the Old Testament With Special Attention to the Book of Ruth.* Cherry Hill, N.J.: Mack, 1974.

Morris, Leon. "Ruth." *Judges and Ruth.* Tyndale Old Testament Commentaries. Edited by D.J. Wiseman. London: Tyndale, 1968, pp. 217–318.

Myers, Jacob M. *The Linguistic and Literary Form of the Book of Ruth.* Leiden: E.J. Brill, 1955.

Rowley, Harold H. "The Marriage of Ruth." *The Servant of the Lord and Other Essays on the Old Testament.* 2d edition. Edited by H.H. Rowley. Oxford: Basil Blackwell, 1965, pp. 169–94.

Rudolph, Wilhelm. *Das Buch Ruth, Das Hohelied, Die Klagelieder.* Kommentar zum Alten Testament. Gütersloh: Gütersloher Verlagshaus Gerd Mohn, 1962.

Sasson, Jack M. *Ruth: A New Translation With a Philological Commentary and a Formalist-Folklorist Interpretation.* Baltimore: Johns Hopkins Press, 1979.

Slotki, Judah J. "Ruth." *The Soncino Books of the Bible: The Five Megilloth.* Edited by A. Cohen. London: Soncino, 1946, pp. 34–65.

Smith, Louise Pettibone. "The Book of Ruth: Introduction and Exegesis." *The Interpreter's Bible.* Vol. 2. Edited by G.A. Buttrick et al. New York and Nashville: Abingdon, 1953, pp. 827–52.

Trible, Phyllis. *God and the Rhetoric of Sexuality.* Overtures to Biblical Theology. Philadelphia: Fortress, 1978, pp. 166–99.

Waard, Jan de, and Eugene A. Nida. *A Translator's Handbook on the Book of Ruth.* Helps for Translators 15. London: United Bible Societies, 1973.

## Periodicals

Ap-Thomas, D.R. "The Book of Ruth." *Expository Times* 79 (September 1968): 369–73.

Beattie, D.R.G. "Kethibh and Qere in Ruth IV 5." *Vetus Testamentum* 21 (October 1971): 490–94.

Morgenstern, Julian. "The Book of the Covenant: Part II." *Hebrew Union College Annual* 7 (1930): 19–258, esp. 162–83.

Thompson, Thomas, and Dorothy Thompson. "Some Legal Problems in the Book of Ruth." *Vetus Testamentum* 18 (January 1968): 79–99.

## 12. Outline

I. An Israelite Family's Sojourn in Moab (1:1–5)
   1. Famine in Judah (1:1–2)
   2. Deaths of Naomi's Husband and Children (1:3–5)

II. Naomi's Return to Judah (1:6–22)
   1. Naomi's Appeal to Her Daughters-in-law (1:6–15)
   2. Ruth's Pledge to Remain With Naomi (1:16–18)
   3. Arrival of Naomi and Ruth in Bethlehem (1:19–22)

III. Ruth the Gleaner (2:1–23)
   1. In the Fields of Boaz (2:1–3)
   2. Boaz's Notice of Ruth (2:4–7)
   3. Boaz's Provision for Ruth (2:8–16)
   4. Ruth's Conversation With Naomi About Boaz (2:17–23)

IV. Encounter at the Threshing Floor (3:1–18)
   1. Naomi's Advice to Ruth (3:1–5)
   2. Ruth at the Feet of Boaz (3:6–13)
   3. Ruth's Return to Naomi (3:14–18)

V. A Transaction at the City Gate (4:1–12)
   1. A Kinsman's Refusal to Redeem Naomi's Land (4:1–6)
   2. Boaz's Purchase of the Land (4:7–12)

VI. Birth of a Son to Boaz and Ruth (4:13–17)

VII. The Genealogy of David (4:18–22)

# Text and Exposition

## I. An Israelite Family's Sojourn in Moab (1:1–5)

### 1. *Famine in Judah*

1:1–2

> [1]In the days when the judges ruled, there was a famine in the land, and a man from Bethlehem in Judah, together with his wife and two sons, went to live for a while in the country of Moab. [2]The man's name was Elimelech, his wife's name Naomi, and the names of his two sons were Mahlon and Kilion. They were Ephrathites from Bethlehem, Judah. And they went to Moab and lived there.

**1** With only nineteen carefully chosen Hebrew words, the author establishes the time and circumstances of a Hebrew family's migration to a foreign land. These words set the stage for the subsequent story of the Book of Ruth. The narrative begins with *wayᵉhî* (lit., "and it was"), traditionally rendered "now it came to pass" (KJV) but rightly omitted altogether in some translations (e.g., NIV, JB, RSV; see T.O. Lambdin, *Introduction to Biblical Hebrew* [London: Darton, Longman and Todd, 1973], p. 123). This phrase introduces eight OT books: Joshua, Judges, 1 and 2 Samuel, Ezekiel, Jonah, Ruth, and Esther. It was quite typical of Hebrew to begin a sentence or a book with "and" and without any syntactical connection with what preceded.

The story, though written at a later time, opens during "the days when the judges ruled" (lit., "in the days of the judging of the judges"), which has been determined to have been during the last third of the second millennium B.C. Unresolved questions of Hebrew chronology make it impossible to date the time of the judges more precisely (see discussion of date in Introduction: Background).

The judges functioned as military leaders in times of crisis; they also served as local rulers, administering political and legal justice (Judg 4:4–5). The time of the judges was a period of lawlessness and chaos in Israel when "everyone did as he saw fit" (Judg 21:25).

The story begins in a time of famine, a natural catastrophe that occurred often in Palestine, where crops were dependent on the rainfall in its proper season. Deuteronomy 28:15, 23–24, 38–40 gives a theological explanation for the famines Israel experienced. Famine could also be the result of the devastation of the land by an enemy, such as was inflicted by the Midianites (Judg 6:3–6). *Bā'āreṣ* ("in the land") could only mean the land of Canaan, which God had given his people. The famine was probably widespread and not limited to the region of Bethlehem.

"Bethlehem in Judah" is to be distinguished from a lesser-known town of the same name in the territory of Zebulun (Josh 19:15). Located about six miles south of Jerusalem, Bethlehem in Judah is over twenty-three hundred feet above sea level. The name means "house of bread" and suggests the fertility of the region. Attempts have been made to link its name to the Assyrian deity Lakhmu, thereby making it mean "house of Lakhmu" (cf. Beth Dagon [Josh 15:41; 19:27]). Bethlehem is best known as the birthplace of both David and Jesus Christ. Rachel had been buried near there (Gen 35:19).

The severity of the famine caused a certain man and his family to leave their home in Bethlehem and to journey to Moab in the expectation of a fuller life. Permanent migration was not their intention; the word *gûr* ("to live for a while"; KJV, "to sojourn") denotes the status of a resident alien that usually included protection under the laws of the host land. People migrated to other lands only in the direst circumstances; for abandonment of one's homeland meant severance from one's family, clan, and deity.

The family's destination was "the country of Moab" (lit., "the fields of Moab"), a land that lay east of the Dead Sea. A large area of Moab is fertile and receives adequate rain. The exact part of Moab where the family migrated cannot be determined (cf. William L. Reed, "Translation Problems in the Book of Ruth," *The College of the Bible Quarterly* 41 [April 1964]: 4–7; R.K. Harrison, "Moab, Moabites," ZPEB, 4:257–66).

**2** The head of the family was Elimelech, whose name means "God is king" or "my God is king." As a kinsman of Boaz, his ancestry could be traced to the tribe of Judah (2:1; 4:20–21; Num 1:7). His wife's name, Naomi, derives from a word that means "pleasant" or "lovely." Transliterated it would be spelled *Noʿ$^{o}$mî*. The meaning of the first son's name, Mahlon, is uncertain. It has been linked to the root "to be sterile," "to be weak, ill," "crown," or "to pierce." The other son's name, Kilion (which rhymes with Mahlon), is perhaps from the root *klh* ("to be finished," "at an end," or perhaps "weakening" or "pining"), but its meaning is uncertain (Campbell, *Ruth*, p. 54).

In the Bible the names of the members of this family occur only in the Book of Ruth and in the genealogical notice in Matthew 1:5. In ancient times names often reflected religious beliefs or personality traits. In the face of etymological uncertainties, however, it is best not to read too much hidden significance into the names of Elimelech's family.

The family is identified as Ephrathites from Bethlehem in Judah. Bethlehem was also known as Ephrath (Gen 35:19) and as Bethlehem Ephrathah (Ruth 4:11; Mic 5:2). Ephrathah has been understood to have been either an older settlement that became absorbed into Bethlehem or the district where Bethlehem was located. It has also been linked to Ephraim, which may suggest that members of that tribe settled in Bethlehem.

## Notes

**1** The LXX$^{BL}$ and some other LXX MSS omit "in the days." The Syriac reads "in the days of the judges."

The LXX$^{BL}$ and the Syriac omit "two" in the phrase "his two sons."

Many scholars feel that the word שְׂדֵי (*ś$^{e}$ḏê*, "country") is not a plural construct, as it appears to be, but is singular, probably from an older, poetic form.

**2** The LXX$^{BL}$ read "Elimelech" as "Abimelech." There are several Abimelechs in the OT but only one Elimelech.

## 2. *Deaths of Naomi's Husband and Children*

### 1:3–5

[3]Now Elimelech, Naomi's husband, died, and she was left with her two sons. [4]They married Moabite women, one named Orpah and the other

**Ruth. After they had lived there about ten years, 5both Mahlon and Kilion also died, and Naomi was left without her two sons and her husband.**

**3** We are not told how long the family was in Moab before Elimelech died. A later rabbinic tradition says he was punished because of greed or because he forsook his homeland.

**4a** Naomi's sons "married" (lit., "lifted up to themselves"; an expression used elsewhere only in postexilic books: 2 Chron 13:21; 24:3; Ezra 9:2, 12; 10:44; Neh 13:25) Moabite wives named Orpah and Ruth (4:10 reveals that Ruth was married to Mahlon). Marriages with Moabites were not specifically forbidden by the law (Deut 7:1, 3), though Moabites were not allowed in the congregation of the Lord to the tenth generation (Deut 23:3; Neh 13:1–3). No satisfactory explanation for either of the wives' names has been proposed. "Orpah" is usually derived from *ʿōrep̱* ("back of the neck" = stiff-necked, i.e., one who turned her back on her mother-in-law). It has also been linked to "mane," "cloud," "perfume," "aroma," "kindness," or "a handful of water." "Ruth" is traditionally derived from *rāʿāh* ("friend" or "friendship"), but *rāwāh* ("to water abundantly," "to be saturated") also has its advocates (Gray; Harvey, IDB).

**4b–5** The Hebrew is not clear whether the sons lived in Moab for ten years or whether they were married for ten years (v.4b) before their deaths (v.5). Rabbinic tradition says their deaths were punishment for leaving Judah and for marrying non-Jews. For a woman to be "left without" (lit., "left from") her husband and "her . . . sons" (*yelāḏeyhā*, ordinarily this word is used of young children; only here in the OT is it explicitly used of married men) was serious enough in her own community, but in another land she would be in desperate straits. It was only natural that Naomi's thoughts would turn to her homeland at such a time. As in Job's time of calamity, the question "Why?" looms large in the reader's mind at this point in the story.

## Notes

4 The Syriac renders Ruth as "woman companion" throughout the book.

5 The use of יְלָדִים (*yelāḏîm*, "sons") instead of the usual word for sons, בָּנִים (*bānîm*), anticipates 4:16, where Naomi will take a new יֶלֶד (*yeleḏ*, "child"; i.e., Obed) to her bosom.

The frequent use of chiasmus (the reversal of the order of words or phrases for rhetorical effect) in Ruth is illustrated in v.3 (husband and sons) and v.5 (sons and husband).

## II. Naomi's Return to Judah (1:6–22)

### 1. *Naomi's Appeal to Her Daughters-in-law*

1:6–15

**6When she heard in Moab that the LORD had come to the aid of his people by providing food for them, Naomi and her daughters-in-law**

prepared to return home from there. 7 With her two daughters-in-law she
left the place where she had been living and set out on the road that
would take them back to the land of Judah.
8 Then Naomi said to her two daughters-in-law, "Go back, each of you,
to your mother's home. May the LORD show kindness to you, as you have
shown to your dead and to me. 9 May the LORD grant that each of you will
find rest in the home of another husband."
Then she kissed them and they wept aloud 10 and said to her, "We will
go back with you to your people."
11 But Naomi said, "Return home, my daughters. Why would you come
with me? Am I going to have any more sons, who could become your
husbands? 12 Return home, my daughters; I am too old to have another
husband. Even if I thought there was still hope for me—even if I had a
husband tonight and then gave birth to sons— 13 would you wait until
they grew up? Would you remain unmarried for them? No, my
daughters. It is more bitter for me than for you, because the LORD's hand
has gone out against me!"
14 At this they wept again. Then Orpah kissed her mother-in-law good-
by, but Ruth clung to her.
15 "Look," said Naomi, "your sister-in-law is going back to her people
and her gods. Go back with her."

**6** Naomi heard that the Lord "had come to the aid of" (*pāqaḏ*, "visited" [KJV, RSV, NASB], a word that can mean "punish" [Exod 32:34; Amos 3:2] but also can express God's kindness [Exod 4:31; Ps 8:4]) his people. She made preparations for returning to Judah. Orpah and Ruth did not question their duty to accompany their mother-in-law, though it meant leaving their own land.

**7–8** Apparently the party had not traveled far on the road to Judah (v.7) when Naomi realized the difficulties that faced her "daughters-in-law" (the word *kallāh* can also mean "bride"). Therefore she released them from all obligation to her by encouraging them to return to their "mother's home" (v.8). As returning to their "father's house" (Gen 38:11; Lev 22:13; Judg 19:2–3) would have been more usual, the reference here is probably to the women's quarters of the home where comfort would be forthcoming and preparations for another marriage initiated.

Naomi's parting wish was that the Lord (not Chemosh, a principal Moabite deity) would "show kindness" to her daughters-in-law as they had to her. The Hebrew word for "kindness" (*ḥeseḏ*) is difficult to translate uniformly by a single English word. It is usually associated with loyalty to covenant obligations and has been translated "keep faith" (NEB) and "be good" (TEV). *Ḥeseḏ* encompasses deeds of mercy performed by a more powerful party for the benefit of the weaker one (see Katharine Doob Sakenfeld, *The Meaning of Hesed in the Hebrew Bible: A New Inquiry* [Missoula, Mont.: Scholars, 1978]).

**9** Naomi also expressed the hope that her daughters-in-law would find rest in the home of another husband. "Rest" here refers to the security in the ancient Near Eastern culture that marriage gave a woman, not to freedom from work. Naomi kissed them in a parting gesture, but they began to weep loudly (lit., "they lifted up their voice and wept").

**10** ***Kî*** (usually tr. "surely," "indeed," "that," or "for") here functions properly as an adversative—"no" (JB, NASB, RSV; NIV does not translate it).

Both Orpah and Ruth refused to be separated from Naomi. They pledged themselves to return to Judah with her. Their devotion, while remarkable in the light of what they were giving up to remain with Naomi, was at the same time high commendation of Naomi's character. By following her, they were abandoning their families, friends, homeland, deities, and prospects for remarriage.

**11** Naomi attempted to show her daughters-in-law the irrationality of their determination to remain with her. The verse assumes the law of levirate marriage (Lat. *levir,* "brother-in-law") and cannot be understood apart from it. The levirate law (Deut 25:5–10) provides for the marriage of a childless widow to a brother-in-law. If the daughters-in-law went with Naomi, as foreigners there would be little or no hope for them of remarriage and homes of their own. Naomi reminded them that she was not pregnant with sons who, as the younger brothers of Mahlon and Kilion, would be obligated to marry their widowed sisters-in-law according to the levirate law. Naomi's rebuke of their offer was not harsh but considerate. Observe her tender address: "my daughters." Her unselfish placing of her daughters-in-law's welfare above her own shows her noble character.

**12–13** Naomi pointed out further absurdities of the situation they were creating. She presented hypothetical cases in v.12, each more implausible than the preceding. First, she reminded them that she was too old to find a husband. Then, even if she did find one and married that same night, it would be asking too much for them to wait till her sons were grown in order to marry them.

Having sized up the situation, Naomi concluded that her lot was far more bitter than that of her daughters-in-law. Because of their younger ages, they could remarry and find happiness and security in their homeland. But the true bitterness of Naomi's lot was that she believed the Lord was punishing her. Underlying the Book of Ruth and the theology of the entire OT is the belief that nothing happens by chance. God is sovereign and does whatever he desires. Naomi offered no explanation as to why she thought God was her enemy. Perhaps, like Job, she could not really understand the calamities that had struck her.

**14** The daughters-in-law wept again because of the hopeless situation Naomi had described to them. Orpah took leave of her mother-in-law with a parting kiss. Ruth, however, refused to leave Naomi. Orpah has frequently been described as unfeeling and stiff-necked because she deserted Naomi; but a careful reading of the text shows that, though reluctant to leave, she obeyed Naomi's wishes. Nevertheless, by returning to her land she returned to her gods (v.15). So she stood in marked contrast to Ruth's faith (v.16). Later tradition, probably reflecting a critical attitude toward Orpah, made her an ancestor of David's foe, Goliath. Verse 14 is another example of the terse manner in which action and emotion can be expressed in Hebrew; there are only ten Hebrew words in this verse.

The verb used to describe Ruth's response, *dāḇaq* ("clung to"), elsewhere expresses the ideal closeness that can be experienced in the marriage relationship (Gen 2:24; 1 Kings 11:2). The Hebrew word order places the noun "Ruth" ahead of the verb *dāḇaq,* thus emphasizing the contrast between the responses of the two women: "Orpah kissed . . . good-by, but Ruth clung."

**15** In ancient times it was believed that a deity had power only in the geographical region occupied by his worshipers. Thus to leave one's land meant separation from one's god(s). Naomi, though a worshiper of Yahweh, encouraged Ruth to join her sister-in-law and return to her land and to her own "gods" (NIV, KJV, NEB, RSV; "god," JB, TEV, NAB; *'ᵉlōhîm* may be translated "a god" or "gods" or "God," depending on the context). The OT does not acknowledge the genuine existence of other gods, but it does admit their reality as objects of worship.

## Notes

**6** The LXX, OL, and Syriac say "two daughters-in-law."

The LXX has "and they returned" whereas the Hebrew is "and she returned," thereby keeping focus on Naomi.

**8** Some LXX MSS have "father's house"; the Syriac has "your parents."

עִמָּכֶם (*'immāḵem*, "with you") has a masculine plural pronominal suffix when the feminine form would have been expected. This substitution of a masculine for a feminine pronoun has been explained as a peculiarity of the language, influenced by the dominant male role; but it may have been an early feminine suffix (Campbell, *Ruth*, p. 65; Sasson, p. 23).

**12** יֵשׁ (*yēš*, "hope") expresses the idea of trust, eager expectation, or confident waiting for something to happen.

**13** The meaning of לָהֵן (*lāhēn*) in this verse is unresolved. In Hebrew and perhaps Aramaic it means "therefore"; but it probably should be emended to read לָהֶם (*lāhem*, "for them"), in agreement with the LXX, Syriac, Targum, OL, and Vulgate (see Campbell, *Ruth*, pp. 68–69).

אַל (*'al*, "no") occurs rarely as an independent negative (cf. Gen 19:18; Judg 19:23; 2 Sam 13:16; 2 Kings 3:13; 4:16 for other examples).

**14** After Orpah kissed her mother-in-law, the Syriac adds "and she turned and went"; the LXX adds "and she returned to her people." The meaning is clear without these explanations.

**15** The LXX adds "Naomi said to Ruth." Hebrew is not so precise as Greek in naming speakers.

## 2. *Ruth's Pledge to Remain With Naomi*

### 1:16–18

**16** But Ruth replied, "Don't urge me to leave you or to turn back from you. Where you go I will go, and where you stay I will stay. Your people will be my people and your God my God. **17** Where you die I will die, and there I will be buried. May the LORD deal with me, be it ever so severely, if anything but death separates you and me." **18** When Naomi realized that Ruth was determined to go with her, she stopped urging her.

**16–17** Ruth's answer to Naomi has become a classic expression of devotion and loyalty and is sometimes recited as part of a marriage vow. Ruth's commitment to go and "stay" (v.16; lit., "lodge" or "spend the night") wherever Naomi went was not limited to the journey back to Bethlehem but was a commitment to share her home and circumstances, whatever they might be, after they returned to Judah. Ruth's renunciation of her people and gods was total. The Hebrew is terse: "your people my people; your God my God."

By first naming the people and then God, Ruth revealed that she could not relate to God apart from his people. Nothing but death would separate her from Naomi. She swore a solemn curse on herself if she did not keep her promise ("May the LORD deal with me" [v.17], a formula found here and in eleven passages in Samuel and Kings, e.g., 1 Sam 3:17; 14:44; 1 Kings 2:23; 2 Kings 6:31; lit., "Thus may the LORD do to me and thus may he add"). Ruth invoked the covenant name of God for the first and only time in this self-imprecation. Her commitment of no separation even by death probably refers to the Israelite custom of burying members of the same family in a family tomb.

Ruth's unselfish devotion has often been praised and justly so. But Naomi's character and life during her years in Moab must not be overlooked. Naomi's consistent living must have so impressed her daughter-in-law to cause her to abandon her homeland and her gods.

**18** Naomi obviously realized the determination of her daughter-in-law and saw that it would do no good to argue further with her. The solemnity of Ruth's curse was itself sufficient to deter Naomi from further protestations.

## Notes

---

**16** Since אֱלֹהִים (*'ᵉlōhîm*) can be rendered "gods" or "God," Ruth may have been saying, "Your gods are my gods," if, in fact, she had little or no knowledge of the religion of the Hebrews. However, this seems unlikely because her prior relationship with Naomi would have made it impossible for her to be unaware of Naomi's belief in one God.

**18** The verb מִתְאַמֶּצֶת (*miṯ'ammeṣeṯ,* "was determined") literally means "having strengthened herself" and is a Hithpael form of a verb meaning "to be strong."

---

### 3. *Arrival of Naomi and Ruth in Bethlehem*

#### 1:19–22

[19]So the two women went on until they came to Bethlehem. When they arrived in Bethlehem, the whole town was stirred because of them, and the women exclaimed, "Can this be Naomi?"

[20]"Don't call me Naomi," she told them. "Call me Mara, because the Almighty has made my life very bitter. [21]I went away full, but the LORD has brought me back empty. Why call me Naomi? The LORD has afflicted me; the Almighty has brought misfortune upon me."

[22]So Naomi returned from Moab accompanied by Ruth the Moabitess, her daughter-in-law, arriving in Bethlehem as the barley harvest was beginning.

**19** Nothing is told of events along the road back to Bethlehem; but considering that thieves frequently lurked along the roads, it must have been a dangerous trip for two unaccompanied women (cf. Ezra 8:22, 31; Jer 3:2; Luke 10:30). Observe the providential care of God that is implied so frequently throughout the Book of Ruth.

The root of the word used to describe the town's reaction on the arrival of the two women—*hûm* ("was stirred")—is onomatopoeic and could be translated "the town *hummed* with the news of their arrival" (cf. also 1 Sam 4:5; 1 Kings 1:45; Mic 2:12). The commotion caused by Naomi's return may have been from the joy of seeing her again or may describe the women's shocked whispering about her abject, changed appearance. The NIV's "Can this be Naomi?" suggests the latter, for the harsh treatment of the years had certainly altered her appearance. If the prefixed *hª* of *hªzō'ṯ* is exclamatory instead of interrogative, it could be translated "This indeed is Naomi!" (Sasson, p. 32). The word "women" is not in the Hebrew, but the verbal form of "exclaimed" is feminine plural and therefore warrants the clarified translation. Some scholars have suggested that the men were working in the fields and therefore were not present when Naomi arrived.

**20** Naomi's reply to the women involves a play on names. Following a common practice in the ancient Near East of changing a name to reflect changed circumstances (cf. Gen 17:5, 15; 32:28; 35:18; 41:45; Num 13:16; 2 Kings 24:17; Dan 1:7), Naomi asked that her name be changed from Naomi ("Pleasant") to Mara ("Bitter"). The spelling of *mārā'* with a final ' (aleph) instead of an *h* (he) has been explained as an Aramaized spelling, but it may be only an orthographic change that occurred in the course of scribal transmission. Her reason for changing her name was that God had "made [her] life very bitter" (cf. Job 27:2, where Job made a similar accusation). The name for God used in this verse is "the Almighty" (*šadday*, "Shaddai"; cf. Notes). This was the name of God the patriarchs knew before he revealed himself to Moses (Exod 6:3). Naomi's concept of the sovereignty of God caused her to attribute her ill fortune to him, not to chance or to other gods. She did not mean it as an accusation but as an acknowledgment of his total control of all things.

**21** Naomi further contrasted her former and current states: "I went away full" (i.e., rich, not in possessions, but in a husband and sons). The position of "I" is emphatic and is intended to heighten the contrast with her current condition caused by the Lord—"empty" (i.e., widowed, childless, and poor).

Portraying herself as a defendant in a legal action, Naomi insisted that she should not be called "Pleasant" since the Lord himself had "afflicted" ("testified against," NIV mg.) her. She believed that God was showing his displeasure with her by the misfortunes she had experienced. Naomi probably shared the Israelite belief that God blessed the righteous and brought calamity on the unrighteous (Deut 28:1–2, 15; Job 11:13–20). Again she named "the Almighty" ("Shaddai") as the one who had brought misfortune (lit., "caused evil") on her.

**22** This verse summarizes the preceding events of the first chapter with one additional bit of information—the two women "returned" (a verb found twelve times in the first chapter) in the beginning of the season of barley harvest. According to the Gezer calendar—the oldest-known calendar yet found in Palestine—barley harvest was the eighth month of the agricultural calendar (i.e., April/May). Wheat harvest followed a few weeks later. The verse prepares the reader for the events to follow in the harvest field in chapter 2.

## Notes

**19** A few LXX MSS use a singular verb. Thus it is Naomi who asks, "Is it Naomi?" and then proceeds to give her ironic answer.

**20** "Mara" is the only name of one of the principal characters in the Book of Ruth that is translated in the LXX into Greek: *Pikran*. Apparently the LXX saw the other names as purely personal names, without emphasis on the meaning of the Hebrew word (Beattie, *Ruth*, p. 10).

שַׁדַּי (*šadday*, "Shaddai," "the Almighty") as a name for God occurs forty-eight times in the OT, especially in Job, where it occurs thirty-one times. It is often combined with אֵל (*'ēl*, "God") and translated "God Almighty." *Šadday* has been linked etymologically to "mountain," "breast," "ruler," or "devastating power"; but no clear connection has been generally accepted by scholars (cf. E.C.B. MacLaurin, "Shaddai," *Abr-Nahrain* 3 [1961–1962]: 99–118; Frank M. Cross, "Yahweh and the God of the Patriarchs," HTR 55 [1962]: 225–59; Morris, pp. 264–68; Norman Walker, "A New Interpretation of the Divine Name 'Shaddai,'" ZAW 72 [1968]: 64–66; Victor P. Hamilton, "שַׁדַּי [*shadday*]," TWOT, p. 907).

The JB attempts to preserve the play on words by translating "Call me Mara, for Shaddai has marred me bitterly." Moffatt has "Call me Mara, for the Almighty has cruelly marred me."

**21** רֵיקָם (*rêqām*, "empty") is actually an adverb, "emptily," "empty-handed(ly)," found also in 3:17. William Holladay, *A Concise Hebrew and Aramaic Lexicon of the Old Testament* (Grand Rapids: Eerdmans, 1971), s.v., gives "without property, without family" as the sense in this verse.

The MT pointing of עָנָה as a Qal perfect, *'ānāh*, means "answer." Repointed as a Piel, *'innāh*, it means "afflicted" (NIV, with LXX, Syr., Vul.). NIV's marginal note reflects the MT: "has testified against" (cf. BDB, s.v., I and III).

The LXX[A] omits the words meaning "the Almighty has brought misfortune upon me."

**22** The masculine plural form is used—בָּאוּ (*bā'û*, lit., "they came")—when the feminine would be expected. The NIV's "arriving in" avoids the pronoun altogether. Some scholars interpret it as an emphasizing particle found in Ugaritic as *hm*/*hmt* (Campbell, *Ruth*, p. 78). But see the objections by J.C. deMoor, "Ugaritic *hm*—Never 'Behold,'" *Ugarit-Forschungen* 1 (1969): 201–2.

Part of this verse is also found in 2:6 and has been interpreted by some as an accidental insertion in 1:22 and by others as an intentional insertion to emphasize that Ruth had returned to the true God. It cannot be proved, however, that one is the source of the other rather than a deliberate literary device of the author.

---

## III. Ruth the Gleaner (2:1–23)

### 1. *In the Fields of Boaz*

#### 2:1–3

**1** Now Naomi had a relative on her husband's side, from the clan of Elimelech, a man of standing, whose name was Boaz.

**2** And Ruth the Moabitess said to Naomi, "Let me go to the fields and pick up the leftover grain behind anyone in whose eyes I find favor."

Naomi said to her, "Go ahead, my daughter." **3** So she went out and began to glean in the fields behind the harvesters. As it turned out, she found herself working in a field belonging to Boaz, who was from the clan of Elimelech.

**1** This chapter opens a window on the hardships of the poor in ancient Palestine. The first verse immediately establishes the relationship of Boaz to Naomi. He was a "relative" of Elimelech ("acquaintance," Sasson; "kinsman," KJV, RSV; the Hebrew word is from the verb *yāḏa'* ["to know"] and is found only here and in Prov 7:4; Ruth 3:2 has a different form of the same word). He was a "man of standing" (the phrase *'îš* *gibbôr* was used of warriors [Judg 6:12; 11:1] but could also mean a distinguished, honored person; cf. NIV; "a property holder," Sasson; "well-to-do," NEB, JB; "prominent," NAB; "mighty man of wealth," KJV. In 2 Kings 15:20 the phrase describes a wealthy person).

The most important fact revealed here about Boaz is that he was a kinsman of Elimelech; i.e., he was from his "clan." *Mišpāḥāh* is best translated as "clan" (NIV), which was the link between the family and the larger unit, the tribe.

The etymology of Boaz is uncertain. It has been taken from *bô'az* ("in him [is] strength"), from *ben 'az* ("son of strength"), or from an Arabic word for "lively," "vigorous." Ras Shamra discoveries have strengthened support for the meaning "Baal is strong." The name of one of the pillars in front of Solomon's temple, "Boaz" (1 Kings 7:21), has been examined for its relationship to the Boaz of the Book of Ruth. Scholars, however, have not agreed on its meaning. One proposal is that it was the first word of a dynastic formula, "In the strength of [*b*ᵉ'*ōz*] Yahweh shall the king rejoice" (R.B.Y. Scott, "The Pillars of Jachin and Boaz," JBL 58 [June 1939]: 143–50). Another is that the pillars were named for two of Solomon's ancestors; if so, the meaning of the second pillar, Jachin, is otherwise unknown.

**2** Ruth requested that Naomi allow her to go into the fields to "pick up" (*lāqaṭ*, "glean," "gather up"; it is used of stones [Gen 31:46] and of money [Gen 47:14]) the leftover "grain" ("corn," KJV, JB, NEB; "corn" is the British equivalent of "grain"). The law expressly allowed the poor the right to glean in the fields (Lev 19:9–10; 23:22; Deut 24:19–21), but the owners of the fields were not always cooperative. A hard day's work under the hot sun frequently netted only a small amount of grain (cf. Isa 17:5–6).

Ruth seemed to be aware of the attitude of the landowners and hoped she would find a field to glean in where she would "find favor" (the expression is always used by a person of inferior status in reference to a superior). The sentence construction could mean that she especially had Boaz in mind (cf. vv.10, 13); but the usual interpretation, based on v.3, is that chance (Providence) led her to Boaz's field. Her desire to find a field where she would be favorably received may have reflected her knowledge of how the poor were frequently treated by hostile landowners, or it may have shown her awareness of being a foreigner. Of twelve occurrences of the name "Ruth" in the book, "the Moabitess" is added five times as a reminder that she was an alien.

Naomi granted Ruth's request and added an affectionate "my daughter" (found eight times altogether in the book). No reason is given for Naomi not joining Ruth in the fields as might have been expected of one in her dire circumstances.

**3** By chance (Heb., "her chance chanced" or "she happened to happen on"; NIV, "As it turned out"; cf. Eccl 2:14, where the same verb [*qrh*] is used) Ruth found herself gleaning in the fields that belonged to Boaz. The suggestion that Ruth's encounter with Boaz was by blind chance is offset by the emphasis throughout the story on God's providential guidance. From the perspective of Ruth and Boaz, the meeting was accidental, but not from God's perspective. Perhaps the writer was subtly expressing his theological conviction that God directs even the "accidental" (see Hals for an excellent study of God's providence in the Book of Ruth). Once again the writer reminds the reader that Boaz was from the family of Elimelech.

## Notes

1 See C.U. Wolf, "Tribe," IDB, 4:698–701, and R. de Vaux, AIs, 1:3–8, 19–21, for further discussion of tribal relations.

The *Kethiv* of "relative" is מְיֻדָּע, a Pual participle, and would be read *m*ᵉ*yuddā'*, a word that denotes a close or intimate friend in other OT occurrences. The *Qere* is מוֹדַע (*mô*<u>*d*</u>*a'*), a noun meaning "kinsman." Both the *Kethiv* and the *Qere* come from the root יָדַע (*yā*<u>*d*</u>*a'*, "to know").

The LXX and OL spell Boaz as Boos/Booz.

2 Ruth's request to go to the fields is a cohortative verbal form with a participle of polite entreaty—נָא (*nā'*)—that could be translated "*Please* let me go!" (the particle is usually translated by KJV as "I pray thee" but in this verse as "now"). It has also been understood as a particle of determination as a logical consequence of the general situation in which it is spoken or of an immediately preceding statement ("I want to go out" or "I am going out"; cf. Lambdin, *Biblical Hebrew*, p. 170).

---

## 2. *Boaz's Notice of Ruth*

### 2:4–7

4 Just then Boaz arrived from Bethlehem and greeted the harvesters, "The LORD be with you!"

"The LORD bless you!" they called back.

5 Boaz asked the foreman of his harvesters, "Whose young woman is that?"

6 The foreman replied, "She is the Moabitess who came back from Moab with Naomi. 7 She said, 'Please let me glean and gather among the sheaves behind the harvesters.' She went into the field and has worked steadily from morning till now, except for a short rest in the shelter."

**4** Boaz came from Bethlehem to see how the work was going. He greeted his workers with a typical Israelite greeting: "The LORD be with you!" which gives immediate insight into his character (cf. Judg 6:12; Ps 129:8). They responded with a similar greeting. This kind of salutation would rarely be heard in the fields today! The use of *hinnēh* to introduce the verse is difficult. Its exact meaning has never been determined (see Lambdin, *Biblical Hebrew*, pp. 168–70, for a discussion of this word). Traditionally translated as "lo," "behold!" (KJV), it is here translated as "just then" (NIV).

**5** The Hebrew is abrupt without a transition that would be expected in good English literary style. It is not necessary to conclude that Boaz's next words after his greeting were a question about Ruth. Boaz's question to his foreman, "Whose young woman is that?" does, however, suggest an attraction to Ruth, a woman he had not noticed previously working in his fields. The question suggests that he was seeking information about her ancestry or clan (cf. Gen 32:17–18; 1 Sam 17:55–58; 30:13). It has also been understood as the storyteller's device to move the story forward and, if so, could be paraphrased, "Where does this young woman fit in?"

**6–7** The "foreman" (v.6; lit., "the young man standing over the reapers") identified Ruth as the Moabitess who had returned with Naomi. Boaz had surely heard about the return of the two women, though he apparently had not yet encountered them. The foreman further told of Ruth's courteous request for permission to glean after the reapers had completed their work (v.7), even though the law allowed her the right to glean (cf. v.15, which makes it clear that the privilege of collecting grain from among the sheaves could only be granted by the field's owner). He described her as hard working, taking little time to rest.

The difficulty of translating the last phrase of v.7 is shown by the various ways it has been rendered. These fall into two categories: (1) those that say Ruth took no time for rest and (2) those that say she took time off for rest (cf. "except for a short rest in the shelter" [NIV]; "she tarried a little in the house" [KJV]; "she must have spent little time at home" [Sasson]). The Hebrew says, "This her sitting [in] the house a little." The word "house" is not clear in this verse. Was it Ruth's own home she shared with Naomi, or was it a shelter in the fields where the workers could rest? Temporary shelters, made of upright poles and covered with leafy branches or straw, were quite common in the ancient Near East.

## Notes

---

**5** Some LXX MSS and the OL rephrase the question: "Who is this young woman?" The Syriac reads: "What is the good of this young woman?"

**7** The LXX reads: "She has not rested in the field a little." The Vulgate reads: "Not even for a moment has she returned to the house." See Campbell (*Ruth*, pp. 94–96) for an extensive discussion of some of the problems of translating this verse. The NIV captures the likely meaning of this elusive phrase by translating הַבַּיִת (*habbayiṯ*) as "the shelter."

---

## 3. *Boaz's Provision for Ruth*

### 2:8–16

8 So Boaz said to Ruth, "My daughter, listen to me. Don't go and glean
in another field and don't go away from here. Stay here with my servant
girls. 9 Watch the field where the men are harvesting, and follow along
after the girls. I have told the men not to touch you. And whenever you
are thirsty, go and get a drink from the water jars the men have filled."
10 At this, she bowed down with her face to the ground. She
exclaimed, "Why have I found such favor in your eyes that you notice
me—a foreigner?"
11 Boaz replied, "I've been told all about what you have done for your
mother-in-law since the death of your husband—how you left your
father and mother and your homeland and came to live with a people
you did not know before. 12 May the LORD repay you for what you have
done. May you be richly rewarded by the LORD, the God of Israel, under
whose wings you have come to take refuge."
13 "May I continue to find favor in your eyes, my lord," she said. "You
have given me comfort and have spoken kindly to your servant—though
I do not have the standing of one of your servant girls."
14 At mealtime Boaz said to her, "Come over here. Have some bread
and dip it in the wine vinegar."
When she sat down with the harvesters, he offered her some roasted
grain. She ate all she wanted and had some left over. 15 As she got up to

**glean, Boaz gave orders to his men, "Even if she gathers among the sheaves, don't embarrass her. [16]Rather, pull out some stalks for her from the bundles and leave them for her to pick up, and don't rebuke her."**

**8–9** The good report the foreman gave concerning Ruth could only increase Boaz's interest in her. His greeting—"My daughter" (v.8)—reminds the reader of the disparity of their ages. He encouraged her, not to go to other fields to glean, but to remain with his servant girls and work alongside them. The men wielded the sickles, and the women followed along, tying the sheaves in bundles (v.9). As further proof of his concern for her and his desire to protect her from harm, Boaz told Ruth that he had ordered the men not to "touch" her (*nāga'*, "to reach to," "to strike"; NEB, "molest"). She could also drink from the "water jars" (*kēlîm*, "vessels," not so specific as NIV) that the men had filled for their use. This was a privilege not ordinarily permitted the gleaners. The liquid is not specified in the Hebrew; water was probably intended, as every other occurrence of the verb *šā'aḇ* ("to draw") in the OT is used exclusively for drawing water.

**10** Ruth's response is typical of ancient Near Eastern expressions of gratitude and humility that may seem exaggerated to us (Josh 7:6; Judg 13:20; 1 Sam 20:41; 25:23; 2 Sam 14:4). She bowed herself with her face to the ground before Boaz and asked in amazement why she, a foreigner, had found favor in his eyes.

At this point there is a play on words not apparent in the EVV and an assonance that emphasizes the consonants *n* and *k* (*lᵉhakkîrēnî wᵉ'ānōḵî noḵrîyyāh*, lit., "to notice me, and I a foreigner"). The word for "foreigner" (*noḵrî*) comes from a word that means "to recognize" (i.e., be conspicuous).

**11** Although Boaz did not recognize Ruth when he first saw her (v.5), he had already heard about her. He informed Ruth that he knew of her kindness to Naomi and of her abandonment of her own people and land in order to come to live with a people whom she had not previously known (cf. Gen 12:1, where Abraham was asked to go to a land he did not know). The reader is not told where Boaz learned all this; but in a community the size of Bethlehem, it would have been impossible for him not to have known about Ruth.

**12** Boaz pronounced a blessing on Ruth, not only for her sacrificial loyalty to Naomi, but especially for her acceptance of the God of Israel. A vivid idiom describes her faith: "under whose wings you have come to take refuge." It pictures a tiny bird snuggling under the wings of its mother (cf. Deut 32:11). The word for "wing" is also the word for the "skirt" or "robe" of a man (cf. 3:9, where it is so used). Figuratively the idiom symbolizes God as the Protector (Pss 36:7; 57:1; 91:4).

**13** Ruth responded with true humility and undoubtedly with some surprise that Boaz could speak such comforting and kind words to one who did not even have the standing of a servant girl before him. The optative translation, "May I continue to find favor" (NIV; cf. KJV, JB, NAB), has been questioned by Sasson (in loc.). Ruth's calling Boaz "my lord" was a common way of showing respect; "lord" (*'ᵃḏōnî*) is the equivalent of "sir." The phrase "have spoken kindly" is literally "spoken on the heart of." It may be understood as an expression of confidence about the future (cf. Gen

50:21; Isa 40:2). Ruth was not pleading with Boaz to be kind; she was grateful that he was kind.

Scholars are divided as to whether *šip̱ḥāh* ("servant," NIV) should be distinguished from *'āmāh* (3:9; "servant," NIV) or is synonymous with it (cf. Sasson, p. 53; Campbell, *Ruth*, p. 101). Some believe a *šip̱ḥāh* was a woman on the lowest social level whereas there is evidence that an *'āmāh* was a woman who could become the wife or concubine of a freeman. In her humility Ruth added that she did not even occupy the position of Boaz's lowliest *šip̱ḥāh*.

**14** Boaz showed his increasing interest in Ruth by inviting her to share the noon meal with his reapers. The meal consisted of bread (or in a broader sense, food), wine vinegar, and roasted grain. The grain was roasted over a fire; then its husks were removed; and it was eaten at once. Grain so prepared is still served today. Boaz himself served her as she sat with his reapers, an act interpreted by some as ceremonial. Ruth ate till she was satisfied, with food left over. Then she left to return to the fields. In NT times Jews refused to eat with Gentiles (cf. Acts 10:28), but the Israelite attitude toward foreigners was apparently not so rigid in the time of the judges.

**15–16** After Ruth went back to continue her work, Boaz ordered his reapers to let her glean among the sheaves (not just picking up grain that they accidently dropped as they reaped) and not to "embarrass" her (v.15; "reproach," KJV; "insult," NASB; "scold," NEB; "rebuke," NAB). Moreover, they were to pull stalks from their bundles that had not yet been tied up by the women and leave them for her to pick up (v.16). Boaz's instructions were generous beyond the requirements of the law that allowed the gleaners in the fields only after the reapers had finished their work. His actions showed that he already had a special interest in Ruth.

## Notes

8 Elsewhere in this chapter the eleven occurrences of the verb לקט (*lqṭ*, "to glean") are in the Piel stem. Here it is a Qal stem. No satisfactory explanation has yet been given for this different vocalization. E. Jenni (*Das hebräische Pi'el* [Zürich: EVZ Verlag, 1968], pp. 188–89) argued that this verb in the Qal stem normally expresses gleaning with little effort because of the abundant supply, whereas the Piel implies gleaning that is difficult and therefore thorough. Since the word occurs only in Ruth in 2:8 following a negative, he concluded that the negation places the emphasis on the result rather than on the effort and that therefore the Piel would be inappropriate.

11 The verb נגד (*ngd*) appears first as a Hophal infinitive absolute (*huggēḏ*), followed by the Hophal perfect (*huggaḏ*), a construction that emphasizes the modal idea ("I've been told all about," NIV; "it hath fully been shewed me," KJV; "I have had a complete account," NAB). See Josh 9:24 for the same expression.

The Hebrew idiom for "a people you did not know *before*" is "know yesterday three [days ago]"; cf. Exod 5:8; Deut 4:42.

13 The LXX, OL, and Syriac omit the negative in "I am not one of your maidservants" (RSV).

14 "Offered" is from the Hebrew root צָבַט (*ṣāḇaṭ*), which occurs only here in the OT. It is found in Ugaritic as "tongs," "handles."

The LXX[L] has "my bread" for "the bread"; the OL has "your bread."

חֹמֶץ (*ḥōmeṣ*, "wine vinegar," NIV; "vinegar," KJV; "milk," Syriac) was a drink of sour wine mixed with a little oil. It was a by-product of winemaking and an effective thirst quencher. Since the Nazirite was prohibited from drinking it as part of his vow (Num 6:3), it was probably considered a desirable drink (cf. William L. Reed, "Translation Problems in the Book of Ruth," *The College of the Bible Quarterly* 41 [April 1964]: 8–10, for further discussion).

**16** צְבָתִים (*ṣᵉḇāṯîm*) occurs only here in the OT but is probably another form of the word צֶבֶט (*ṣāḇaṭ*) found in v.14. Translated as "bundles" (NIV, RSV) and "handfuls" (KJV, NAB), its meaning is still uncertain. It may refer to bundles not yet tied up.

---

## 4. *Ruth's Conversation With Naomi About Boaz*

### 2:17–23

17So Ruth gleaned in the field until evening. Then she threshed the
barley she had gathered, and it amounted to about an ephah. 18She
carried it back to town, and her mother-in-law saw how much she had
gathered. Ruth also brought out and gave her what she had left over
after she had eaten enough.
19Her mother-in-law asked her, "Where did you glean today? Where
did you work? Blessed be the man who took notice of you!"
Then Ruth told her mother-in-law about the one at whose place she
had been working. "The name of the man I worked with today is Boaz,"
she said.
20"The LORD bless him!" Naomi said to her daughter-in-law. "He has
not stopped showing his kindness to the living and the dead." She
added, "That man is our close relative; he is one of our kinsman-
redeemers."
21Then Ruth the Moabitess said, "He even said to me, 'Stay with my
workers until they finish harvesting all my grain.'"
22Naomi said to Ruth her daughter-in-law, "It will be good for you, my
daughter, to go with his girls, because in someone else's field you might
be harmed."
23So Ruth stayed close to the servant girls of Boaz to glean until the
barley and wheat harvests were finished. And she lived with her mother-
in-law.

**17** Ruth gleaned in the field till evening and then beat out what she had gleaned (i.e., she separated the grain from the chaff). Her gleanings measured about an ephah of barley, about one-half to two-thirds a bushel (also estimated as twenty-nine to fifty pounds). Such a large quantity could not have been acquired in a day by an ordinary gleaner. It shows how Boaz's instructions to his reapers aided Ruth and also how diligently Ruth had worked. Since the ration of a male worker in ancient Mari was about one to two pounds of grain per day, Ruth probably gathered enough to last Naomi and her for several weeks.

**18** Ruth returned to Bethlehem and proudly showed her mother-in-law what she had gleaned that day (lit., "her mother-in-law saw what she had gleaned"). Ruth also gave Naomi some of the food she had saved from her noon meal with the reapers.

**19** Naomi must have been amazed by what she saw, for her words tumbled out in rapid succession. There was a question concerning where Ruth had worked (actually two questions, but they occur as synonymous parallels) and a hasty blessing pronounced on the benefactor, unknown as yet to Naomi. Ruth identified him as Boaz, already known to the reader; but the narrator intentionally heightened the dramatic suspense by withholding the name till the end of the sentence.

Hals (pp. 4, 7) points out that every prayer in the book is a prayer of blessing and that every prayer is answered.

**20** On learning the name of their generous benefactor, Naomi pronounced a second blessing on him but acknowledged that it was the Lord who had not stopped showing his "kindness" (*ḥeseḏ;* the same word used in 1:8) to the living and the dead (cf. Gen 24:27; 2 Sam 2:5). This interpretation hinges on understanding the antecedent of the relative particle *'ašer* ("who"; NIV, "he") to be the Lord; some take the antecedent to be Boaz. Naomi added for Ruth's benefit that Boaz was a "close relative."

Naomi's reference to "the dead" may show that she was already anticipating the outcome of the events. As a kinsman-redeemer (*gō'ēl,* the first occurrence of this word in Ruth), under the levirate law Boaz could fulfill the duty of preserving the name of the dead by marrying Ruth. The root of *gō'ēl* means "to redeem, buy back." The responsibilities of the *gō'ēl* included avenging the death of a murdered relative (Num 35:19), marrying a childless widow of a deceased brother (Deut 25:5–10), buying back family land that had been sold (Lev 25:25), buying a family member who had been sold as a slave (Lev 25:47–49), and looking after needy and helpless members of the family (Lev 25:35). It is difficult to know how conscientiously this law was observed since the the Israelites broke most of the covenant laws, but Jeremiah 32:6–25 indicates that it was still binding in the sixth century B.C.

**21** Apparently interrupted by Naomi before her account was complete, Ruth continued by telling of Boaz's instruction to her to remain close to his servants till the harvest was finished.

**22** Naomi expressed approval ("It will be good," NIV) that Ruth was allowed the protection of going to the fields with Boaz's maidens. She was aware that a woman of Ruth's status could meet with harm if she worked alone in other fields (lit., "that they do not meet you in another field"; the verb *pāga'* can mean "meet" or "encounter," e.g., Exod 5:20; 1 Sam 10:5; but it is also used to mean "strike down" or "attack violently," e.g., Exod 5:3; 1 Sam 22:17–18; 1 Kings 2:25, 29).

**23** Ruth accepted Naomi's counsel and stayed close to Boaz's servant girls in the fields till both barley and wheat harvests were finished. She continued living with her mother-in-law, to whom she returned from the fields each evening. The two harvest seasons would have lasted for about seven weeks (cf. Deut 16:9), normally from late April to early June.

## Notes

---

17 שְׂעֹרִים (*śe'ōrîm,* "barley") is plural in Hebrew. GKC (124*m*) explains this as a "plural of result," i.e., parts that are detached from the whole.

**18** The LXX supports the Hebrew—"and her mother-in-law saw"—but the Syriac and Vulgate read a causative—"and she showed her mother-in-law," a reading adopted by JB, NAB, RSV, TEV. A change in subject is not unusual in Hebrew, and there is no reason to modify the translation here (cf. NIV, KJV, NASB, NEB).

**19** The Syriac arranges the words so that Boaz comes first in Ruth's reply; but the effect, probably intentional, is diminished by not saving his name till the end of the account.

**20** "The living and the dead" has been interpreted both as a reference to Naomi and Ruth ("the living") and Elimelech, Mahlon, and Kilion ("the dead") and as a merism (the equivalent of "everyone").

R. Laird Harris (TWOT, 1:144) helpfully points out that "one difference between this root [*gā'al*] and the very similar root *pādâ*, 'redeem,' is that there is usually an emphasis in *gā'al* on the redemption being the privilege or duty of a near relative."

**21** The LXX and OL omit "the Moabitess" and add "to her mother-in-law."

הַנְּעָרִים (*hannᵉʿārîm*, "my workers") is masculine plural and is taken by some scholars as an intentional reference to the unusual instructions given by Boaz to his men that allowed Ruth to work near them. Others believe this is another example of the use of the masculine gender to include both male and female servants of Boaz. Some LXX MSS and the OL use the feminine plural to harmonize it with Naomi's statement in v.22 (cf. v.8).

**22** For "someone else's field," the Syriac reads "in the field of someone you do not know."

**23** For "lived with" the Vulgate and a few Hebrew MSS read "returned to."

---

## IV. Encounter at the Threshing Floor (3:1–18)

### 1. *Naomi's Advice to Ruth*

#### 3:1–5

**[1]One day Naomi her mother-in-law said to her, "My daughter, should I not try to find a home for you, where you will be well provided for? [2]Is not Boaz, with whose servant girls you have been, a kinsman of ours? Tonight he will be winnowing barley on the threshing floor. [3]Wash and perfume yourself, and put on your best clothes. Then go down to the threshing floor, but don't let him know you are there until he has finished eating and drinking. [4]When he lies down, note the place where he is lying. Then go and uncover his feet and lie down. He will tell you what to do."**

**[5]"I will do whatever you say," Ruth answered.**

**1** The reader is not told how much time lapsed between the closing of chapter 2 and Naomi's question to Ruth in 3:1. Naomi asked whether she should "try to find a home" (*mānôᵃḥ*, "find rest") for her daughter-in-law. "Rest" here (cf. another form of the same word in 1:9) implies the security and benefits found in marriage by a woman in the ancient Near East. It was customary for parents (or, in this case, Naomi) to arrange marriages (Gen 24:3–4; 34:4; Judg 14:2).

Naomi's motive was unselfish: "where you will be well provided for" (NIV; lit., "that it will be well to you"; "I seek for you a happy future," Sasson [in loc.]). If Ruth remained an unprotected widow in a foreign land, life could go very hard for her.

**2** Naomi knew that Boaz was a kinsman (but not the nearest, as v.12 reveals; cf. a similar word in 2:1) who could satisfy the levirate law of marriage. She interpreted Boaz's kindness to Ruth that allowed her to work alongside his maidservants as an indication of a favorable disposition on his part toward Ruth and possibly a willingness to do the kinsman's part.

One must resist an inclination to caricature Naomi as a "matchmaker," but obviously she had been giving the matter some thought. She knew that Boaz was going to winnow barley at the threshing floor that same night, and she had devised a plan whereby he might know of Ruth's willingness to marry him.

Threshing floors were nothing more than level places of smooth rock or pounded earth located on a hill, where the grain could be separated from the chaff by tossing the threshed grain into the wind that rose in the evening from the Mediterranean. The grain, being heavier, fell to the ground as the chaff was blown away.

**3** Naomi instructed Ruth to beautify herself according to the custom of the times by washing (cf. Isa 1:16) and perfuming herself ("anoint," NASB). Then after putting on her "best clothes" (NIV, RSV; however, it is unlikely that an impoverished Ruth would have had best clothes; the Hebrew means only a "garment" or "mantle"; cf. Ezek 16:9–13 for a description of a bride's preparations), she was to "go down" to the threshing floor (Bethlehem stood on the ridge of a hill that was higher than the threshing floor; however, the LXX has "go up"). Naomi cautioned Ruth not to reveal herself to Boaz till he had finished eating and drinking.

Commentators have speculated about Boaz's presence at the threshing floor. It seems unusual that a man as important and wealthy as Boaz would have been guarding his grain through the night from thieves, as some suggest (Morris, p. 285), when a trusted servant would have been expected to perform that duty. Also, to avoid falling asleep, one who planned an all-night vigil would not likely have filled himself with food and drink (and, as a matter of fact, Boaz did fall asleep). Some scholars have interpreted his actions as ceremonial, perhaps as preparation for some cultic festival; but this interpretation finds no support in the rest of the story. Whatever Boaz's motive may have been for spending the night at the threshing floor, his presence there reveals an unpretentious man, one who enjoyed all aspects of life associated with the land.

**4** Naomi further instructed Ruth to "note" (lit., "know") where Boaz lay down and then to go in, uncover his feet, and lie down. She would then wait for Boaz to tell her what to do. Naomi probably had in mind that Boaz would recognize Ruth's action as an appeal to marry her as the next of kin. Many scholars point out that the word "feet" is frequently used as an euphemism for the sexual organs and is so used here (cf. Exod 4:25; Judg 3:24; 1 Sam 24:3; Isa 6:2; 7:20; Ezek 16:25). Others caution against rashly accusing Naomi of encouraging Ruth to such an act of boldness and immorality. The verb *šāḵaḇ* ("lie down") frequently refers to sexual intercourse, but again that interpretation is not unequivocal here. Staples ("Ruth," pp. 150, 156–67) interpreted Ruth's act as an example of sacred prostitution at the high place in Bethlehem, but the extreme cultic interpretation he gives the book has been almost universally rejected as without foundation.

**5** Ruth agreed to do exactly as her mother-in-law had instructed her (cf. Exod 19:8; 24:3; 2 Kings 10:5). Verse 9 suggests, however, that Ruth did not wait for Boaz to tell her what to do after he awoke, as Naomi had instructed her. Divine providence does not eliminate human activity.

## Notes

---

**1** The imperfect verb here אֲבַקֶּשׁ (*'ᵃḇaqqeš*) could be understood as the active and continuing efforts of Naomi on behalf of Ruth: "Have I not been seeking?" GKC (107*a*) says the imperfect "represents actions . . . as still continuing or in the process of accomplishment."

**2** On מֹדַעְתָּנוּ (*mōḏa'tānû*), see Notes on 2:1 for a different form of the same word and comments there.

No satisfactory explanation can be offered for Boaz's winnowing barley because 2:23 indicates that both the barley harvest and the wheat harvest, which followed it, had passed. שְׁעָרִים (šᵉ'ārîm, "gates") has been proposed for שְׂעֹרִים (*śᵉ'ōrîm*, "barley"). The translation would be: "He is winnowing at the threshing floor near the gate" (cf. 1 Kings 22:10).

הַלַּיְלָה (*hallāylāh*) should probably be understood here as "the evening" rather than "the night" because the wind needed for winnowing usually arose in the afternoon and lasted till shortly after sunset.

**3** Naomi's series of instructions to Ruth are not the expected imperatives but a series of perfects with ו (*w*, waw), a normal construction in Hebrew that can also express a command (GKC, 112*aa*).

The word for "anointing" here ("perfume," NIV) is סוּךְ (*sûḵ*,"pour") instead of מָשַׁח (*māšaḥ*, "rub" or "smear"), from which "Messiah" comes.

The LXX[L] adds "and rub yourself with myrrh" after "anoint yourself."

**4** In recognition of the sexual innuendos of Ruth's uncovering Boaz's feet, the LXX, Vulgate, and Syriac were all careful in their translations to make it clear that only the place of Boaz's feet was involved.

**5** Before the last word of this verse in the MT, there is a space that contains only the vowels ֵ (*ṣērê*) and ַ (*paṯaḥ*). The *Qere* instructs the reader to supply the consonants אלי (*'ly*), thus reading אֵלַי (*'ēlay*, "to me"). See the same occurrence in v.17.

---

### 2. *Ruth at the Feet of Boaz*

3:6–13

6So she went down to the threshing floor and did everything her
mother-in-law told her to do.
7When Boaz had finished eating and drinking and was in good spirits,
he went over to lie down at the far end of the grain pile. Ruth
approached quietly, uncovered his feet and lay down. 8In the middle of
the night something startled the man, and he turned and discovered a
woman lying at his feet.
9"Who are you?" he asked.
"I am your servant Ruth," she said. "Spread the corner of your
garment over me, since you are a kinsman-redeemer."
10"The LORD bless you, my daughter," he replied. "This kindness is
greater than that which you showed earlier: You have not run after the
younger men, whether rich or poor. 11And now, my daughter, don't be
afraid. I will do for you all you ask. All my fellow townsmen know that
you are a woman of noble character. 12Although it is true that I am near
of kin, there is a kinsman-redeemer nearer than I. 13Stay here for the
night, and in the morning if he wants to redeem, good; let him redeem.
But if he is not willing, as surely as the LORD lives I will do it. Lie here
until morning."

**6** The verses that follow describe how Ruth carried out the plan that Naomi had proposed to her and Boaz's response to it. The kaph (*k*) in "did everything" ("did according to all," NASB) has been interpreted by some scholars (e.g., Campbell, *Ruth*, p. 121, following David Noel Freedman) as a *kap̱ veritatis*, and thus the phrase would be translated as "did everything exactly as."

**7** As Naomi had anticipated, Boaz ate and drank. He was happy and contented ("in good spirits," NIV; "his heart was merry," KJV, RSV; "at peace with the world," NEB; "in a happy mood," JB; lit., "his heart was good"; the phrase does not necessarily mean he was drunk and does not have this meaning in Judg 18:20, 1 Kings 21:7, or Eccl 7:3; but cf. 1 Sam 25:36; 2 Sam 13:28; Esth 1:10). Boaz lay down at the end of the pile of grain that had been threshed and winnowed and went to sleep. Ruth entered "quietly" (lit., "in secrecy"; cf. Judg 4:21; 1 Sam 24:4), uncovered his feet, and lay down.

**8** Some time must have passed between v.7 and v.8, though the reader is not told at what time Ruth entered the threshing floor. At midnight (lit., "in the half of the night"), Boaz awoke suddenly (perhaps from a bad dream or from the cold caused by his uncovered feet) and discovered that a woman was lying at his feet. A Targum interpretation says, "His flesh became weak like a turnip!" In the darkness he did not immediately recognize Ruth. If he shared the widespread belief in demons in the ancient Near East, he might have feared that the figure was that of a night demon and "turned" himself away (*lap̱aṯ* means "to turn" or "twist away," "touch," "look around," "bend forward"; it is found elsewhere only in Judg 16:29; Job 6:18) in haste to escape the clutches of the supposed demon. The important thing is that in turning himself, Boaz discovered the woman lying at his feet.

**9** Boaz recognized the shadowy figure as a woman, as his question "Who are you?" uses the feminine singular pronoun *'āt*. Ruth immediately identified herself as his "servant" Ruth (here *'āmāh* is used, not *šip̱ḥāh;* cf. comment on 2:13). Then she asked him to spread the corner of his "garment" (*kānāp̱,* "wing"; KJV, RSV, "skirt"; cf. comment on 2:12) over her since he was a *gō'ēl* (cf. comment on 2:20). Ruth's request has been interpreted as a request for protection or for marriage ("marry me," TEV). Deuteronomy 22:30 (23:1 MT) and Ezekiel 16:8 support the interpretation that the request suggests marriage. Marriage, however, was only one function of the *gō'ēl* (cf. comment on 2:20); he was also to serve as protector of needy members of the family. It would be an arbitrary judgment to insist that Ruth was proposing marriage, though it is true that the custom of placing the corner of a garment over a maiden as a symbol of marriage is known among the Arabs. It may be significant that she said, "You are a kinsman-redeemer," rather than, "You are my kinsman-redeemer," as there was a closer kinsman (3:12; 4:1). Naomi could not have been ignorant of the existence of the nearer kinsman, though Ruth may have been.

**10** Boaz was flattered by Ruth's kindness in seeking him out ("greater than that which you showed earlier," a reference to Ruth's kindness to Naomi in not forsaking her; cf. 2:11). If there had been doubt earlier about his age, it is now clear that Boaz was much older than Ruth, though *baḥûrîm* ("younger men," lit., "choice ones") may only mean men of means or those qualified to serve as *gō'ēl.* It pleased him that she turned trustingly to him rather than to a younger man, "whether rich or poor" (perhaps a merism for people from all walks of life).

It is increasingly clear that Boaz interpreted Ruth's bold actions as a request for marriage. Some commentators have cynically described the entire episode as an example of the wily ways of a woman to get her man. This kind of interpretation shows a lack of sensitivity to the chain of events that are unfolding in the story.

**11** Boaz allayed Ruth's concern that she might have acted presumptuously or offended him by her forwardness. He assured her that he would do all that she requested. Everyone in Bethlehem knew (lit., "all the gate of my people know"; perhaps a reference to the influential people, as they were the ones who sat in the city gate to settle civil disputes, or it could be understood as synecdoche) that she was a "woman of noble character" (the same phrase is found in Prov 31:10; a similar phrase is used to describe Boaz in Ruth 2:1). He assured her that all would know there was nothing wrong in the fact that Ruth had come to him with the request to marry him.

**12** Boaz then informed Ruth that there was a barrier to his serving as *gō'ēl*—viz., there was already a nearer kinsman on whom the legal duty to serve as *gō'ēl* fell. As already suggested, Naomi could not have been unaware of the other kinsman, though Ruth probably may not have known of his existence. Why Naomi sent Ruth to Boaz instead of to the other man can only be surmised. Naomi may have preferred Boaz or for some reason did not feel free to approach the other kinsman directly and hoped that Boaz would serve as a "go between." Though the reader already knows through the subtleties of the storyteller's art that Boaz loved Ruth, it is clear that as an honorable man he was going to adhere strictly to the laws of his people.

**13** Boaz requested that Ruth remain at the threshing floor the rest of the night after assuring her that he would contact the near kinsman the next morning to see whether he would accept his obligation to her. If he would not, Boaz swore with an oath ("as surely as the LORD lives," the most solemn and binding oath a Hebrew could take on himself) that he would be Ruth's *gō'ēl* ("I will do it"; the Hebrew adds an emphatic pronoun to the verb: "I will claim you myself," NAB). Not to carry through his commitment after invoking the Lord's name would have been a violation of the third commandment (Exod 20:7).

Scholars are not agreed as to whether anything improper took place at the threshing floor between Ruth and Boaz. Those who interpret a sexual relation in the events reflect their twentieth-century cultural conditioning of sexual permissiveness. They fail to appreciate the element of Ruth's trust that Boaz would not dishonor her whom he wanted for his wife. They fail to appreciate the cultural taboos of Ruth's time that would have prevented a man of Boaz's position from taking advantage of Ruth, thereby destroying her reputation and perhaps endangering his own. Biblical writers were not squeamish about describing sexual encounters, but the writer of Ruth has deliberately refrained from saying there was a liaison between Ruth and Boaz. If read carefully and with sensitivity, it becomes clear that he was saying just the opposite. Both Ruth and Boaz acted virtuously in a situation they knew could have turned out otherwise. Chastity was not an unknown virtue in the ancient world.

## Notes

**7** The LXX$^{BL}$ omit "and drinking." The LXX$^{B}$ omits "and (she) lay down."

**9** The same Hebrew word כָּנָף (*kānāp̱*, "the corner of your garment") is found in 2:12, where it is translated "wings." In both passages the idea of protective care is intended; it is therefore likely that the repetition of the word in 3:9 is intentional (see Hals, p. 7 n. 14).

**12** The opening phrase וְעַתָּה כִּי אָמְנָם כִּי אם (*weʿattāh kî 'omnām kî 'm*, "Although it is true that") is difficult. The MT has no vowels on *'m*, an indication by the Masoretes that, though written, it should not be read. See Sasson (pp. 88–89) and Campbell (*Ruth*, p. 125) for a discussion of the textual problems here.

**13** The ל (*l*, lamed) or the נ (*n*, nun) in the word לִינִי (*lînî*, "stay here") is written with a larger script in some MSS, and the *n* is smaller than normal in others. No acceptable explanation has been given for these vagaries of the MT.

הַלַּיְלָה (*hallaylāh*, "the night") after the verb לִינִי (*lînî*, which means "to spend the night") is redundant.

The Syriac lacks Boaz's oath—"as surely as the LORD lives."

---

## 3. *Ruth's Return to Naomi*

### 3:14–18

[14]So she lay at his feet until morning, but got up before anyone could be recognized; and he said, "Don't let it be known that a woman came to the threshing floor."

[15]He also said, "Bring me the shawl you are wearing and hold it out." When she did so, he poured into it six measures of barley and put it on her. Then he went back to town.

[16]When Ruth came to her mother-in-law, Naomi asked, "How did it go, my daughter?"

Then she told her everything Boaz had done for her [17]and added, "He gave me these six measures of barley, saying, 'Don't go back to your mother-in-law empty-handed.'"

[18]Then Naomi said, "Wait, my daughter, until you find out what happens. For the man will not rest until the matter is settled today."

**14** Ruth remained at Boaz's feet till morning but arose to leave before daybreak with Boaz's encouragement, lest it be known that "a woman" (Heb., "the woman") had spent the night there. He knew that if it became known, town gossips would put the worst construction on the incident, just as some modern commentators do, thereby destroying Ruth's reputation and perhaps his own.

**15** Before he allowed her to leave, Boaz asked Ruth to hold out the "shawl" she was wearing ("cloak," JB, NAB, NEB; "mantle," RSV; the Hebrew word *miṭpaḥaṯ* is found elsewhere only in Isa 3:22, and its exact meaning is uncertain). He filled it with six "measures" of barley; six ephahs is understood, but the exact quantity of barley is unknown as the ephah measure varied in ancient times. Then she returned to the city. Some have interpreted the gift of grain as a bridal price, the *môhar;* but this is unlikely. Others interpret it as some kind of message intended for Naomi, perhaps a gift in recognition of her part in bringing Ruth to him or to secure her consent to the marriage. It has also been interpreted as a gift for sexual favors or as a "cover" for Ruth so that, should anyone chance to see her, it would appear that she had been at work gathering grain. Others see it simply as a gift from a man to a woman whom he hoped to make his wife.

**16–17** Naomi's question to Ruth (v.16) on the daughter-in-law's return seems strange: "Who are you, my daughter?" (lit. tr. of Heb.; cf. v.9, where "my daughter" is omitted from the question). It could be understood as initial lack of recognition in the early morning darkness. The meaning of the question, however, probably is "How did it go?" (NIV). An interesting suggestion by Sasson (in loc.) is that the question means "Who are you now?" i.e., "Are you still Mahlon's widow or are you Boaz's wife?" This interpretation is supported by the reading in the Qumran Cave 2 MS b: "What are you?" (cf. Deut 4:7; Judg 13:17; Mic 1:5, where *mî* is translated "what").

Ruth told her mother-in-law all that had happened. She pointed to the barley Boaz had given her (v.17) and repeated his admonition, "Don't go back to your mother-in-law empty-handed" (the same word used by Naomi in 1:21 to describe herself; her "empty" days were about to end). These are the last recorded words of Ruth in the book.

**18** On learning what had happened, Naomi advised, "Wait" (NIV, JB, NAB, NEB; "Sit still," KJV; "Sit tight," Campbell [*Ruth*, pp. 116, 129]; "Stay put," Sasson) "until you find out what happens" (NIV; Heb., "how the matter will fall"). She was convinced that Boaz was the kind of person who would not rest till the matter was settled that day—the matter of the right of the nearer kinsman. Subsequent events prove she knew her kinsman well. Also, her advice to "wait" reveals a stance of faith—a confident, expectant belief that only God could bring the venture to a successful conclusion.

## Notes

---

**14** The Hebrew literally says, "before a man could recognize his companion," an idiom for "before dawn."

**15** Most Hebrew MSS have "he returned," while the Vulgate, Syriac, and some Hebrew MSS have the feminine form: "she returned." Either reading makes good sense, though from 4:1 it is argued that Boaz went later.

**16** The LXX[B] omits "How did it go?"

**18** The first occurrence of דָּבָר (*dāḇār*, "matter," KJV; "what happens," NIV) without the article here is unusual, especially as it appears later in the verse with the article ("the matter"). The Vulgate omits "today."

---

## V. A Transaction at the City Gate (4:1–12)

### 1. *A Kinsman's Refusal to Redeem Naomi's Land*

4:1–6

[1]Meanwhile Boaz went up to the town gate and sat there. When the
kinsman-redeemer he had mentioned came along, Boaz said, "Come
over here, my friend, and sit down." So he went over and sat down.
[2]Boaz took ten of the elders of the town and said, "Sit here," and they
did so. [3]Then he said to the kinsman-redeemer, "Naomi, who has come
back from Moab, is selling the piece of land that belonged to our
brother Elimelech. [4]I thought I should bring the matter to your attention

and suggest that you buy it in the presence of these seated here and in the presence of the elders of my people. If you will redeem it, do so. But if you will not, tell me, so I will know. For no one has the right to do it except you, and I am next in line."

"I will redeem it," he said.

5 Then Boaz said, "On the day you buy the land from Naomi and from Ruth the Moabitess, you acquire the dead man's widow, in order to maintain the name of the dead with his property."

6 At this, the kinsman-redeemer said, "Then I cannot redeem it because I might endanger my own estate. You redeem it yourself. I cannot do it."

**1** Naomi was correct in her assessment of Boaz's determination to settle the matter as quickly as possible. He went to the city gate, a kind of outdoor court, the place where judicial matters were resolved by the elders and those who had earned the confidence and respect of the people (Deut 22:15; 2 Sam 15:2; Prov 22:22; Jer 38:7; Amos 5:10). The location also served as a place for transacting business and as a kind of forum or public meeting place. Boaz waited for the nearer kinsman, who had prior rights and duties toward Naomi and Ruth, to pass that way. In a town the size of Bethlehem, the best place to encounter friends was to station oneself at the city gate. Sooner or later everyone passed that way.

Boaz did not have long to wait. He saw the man he was seeking and hailed him. The salutation "my friend" (NIV) or "man" (JB) misses the Hebrew idiom *p$^e$lōnî 'almōnî*, which would best be translated "Mr. So-and-so." The idiom was used when the writer did not deem it essential to give the person's name (cf. 1 Sam 21:2; 2 Kings 6:8). It does not mean that Boaz did not know his name.

The use of this idiom here has also been interpreted as deliberate on the part of the storyteller. As it was shameful not to fulfill the role of kinsman-redeemer, the kinsman was unworthy of mention by name. His attention gained by Boaz's greeting, the man stopped and sat down at the gate with Boaz.

**2** Boaz called ten elders who were already nearby to serve as witnesses to the legal brief he was about to set forth. (Years later ten became the number of men required to constitute a synagogue.) The elders (from *zāqān*, "to have a beard") exercised important roles—both judicial and political—in all the periods of Israel's history (see Deut 19:12; 21:2; 22:15; 25:7–9; Josh 20:4; Judg 11:7–8; 1 Kings 8:3; 21:8; Ezra 10:8; Isa 37:2 ["leading (priests)"]; Joel 1:14). In matters of dispute they sat and listened to the opposing parties present their cases, heard witnesses, weighed evidence, and then made their decision. In the matter between Boaz and the other kinsman, they primarily were serving as witnesses rather than as jurors settling a dispute.

**3–4** Boaz proceeded to set forth his case. He explained that Naomi, who had returned from Moab, was selling a piece of land that belonged to their "brother" (*'āḥ*, a word that often means simply "a relative" or "kinsman"), Elimelech. The reader is not told why she was selling it or what her legal claim to it was. How could she sell land that according to law passed from a man to his son or to his kinsmen? Property could pass from father to daughter if there was no son, but the law did not make specific provision for passing an inheritance from husband to wife. (For an extensive discussion of the various problems and solutions associated with Naomi selling the land, see Sasson, pp. 108–15.)

It was extremely important in Israel that land remain within the family (cf. Lev 25:23–28; Num 27:1–11; 36:1–12; Deut 19:14; 1 Kings 21; Jer 32). Boaz urged the kinsman to make his intentions known before the people and before the elders who were witnessing the exchange. Would he redeem the property as nearest kinsman? Boaz acknowledged that the other kinsman's claim preceded his own. The man immediately agreed to redeem the property. He must have felt that it would be to his advantage to buy it (his reply uses the emphatic pronoun "I"; translated literally the phrase would read: "I, I will redeem").

**5** The kinsman's reply dashed all hopes that Boaz may have entertained for marrying Ruth, but Boaz did not show it. He reminded the kinsman of a condition he must satisfy to redeem the land. He must marry (*qānāh*, "buy," "acquire," "redeem") Ruth the Moabitess (Heb., "buy the field from the hand of Naomi and from Ruth") to bear children to restore the name of Elimelech to his inheritance in accordance with the levirate law (see Deut 25:5–6). The firstborn son of their marriage would legally be Mahlon's son.

It is difficult to know whether the kinsman must buy Ruth (with JB, NAB, NASB, NEB, RSV, TEV, following the Vul. and Syr.) or buy from Ruth (with KJV, NIV, following the MT). Furthermore, this case differs from the levirate law on several counts: (1) here a more distant relative than a brother was expected to marry the widow; (2) the kinsman removed his own shoe instead of the rejected widow doing it; and (3) apparently no disgrace was involved, as the significance of removing the shoe here was to seal a legal transaction.

Boaz probably hoped to discourage the kinsman from buying the land by reminding him that the purchase of the land obligated the kinsman to marry Ruth, though he gave the kinsman every opportunity to do just that.

**6** On hearing Boaz's inclusion of Ruth in the transaction, the kinsman refused to redeem the land. His justification was that it would "endanger" (*šāḥaṯ*, "spoil," "ruin," "damage") his own estate. In the presence of the witnesses, he forfeited his right of redemption to Boaz, the next nearest kinsman, by refusing to honor his obligation (the Hebrew is emphatic: "redeem for you, you, my right of redemption").

Most scholars interpret the kinsman's refusal as an awareness that he would be paying part of what should be his own children's inheritance to buy land that would revert to Ruth's son as a legal heir of Elimelech. Some think he was reluctant to intermarry with a Moabite woman (cf. Deut 23:3–4). If an alternate interpretation is correct (that Boaz was offering the kinsman the opportunity to buy Elimelech's land at the same time Boaz was marrying Ruth; cf. Notes on v.5), the kinsman still faced the prospect of returning the land to Naomi if she had a "son" through Ruth and Boaz.

## Notes

---

1 In Hebrew Boaz as the subject of the verb עָלָה (*'ālāh*, "went up") is in a position that suggests that a contrast is intended with the preceding verse (3:18), which concerned Ruth and Naomi (cf. Campbell, *Ruth*, p. 140). If so, a good translation would be: "As for Boaz, he

went up," or (with NIV) "Meanwhile Boaz went up." However, it may communicate a sense of immediacy (Sasson, p. 104).

For a discussion of the role of the gate in the ancient Near East, see Ludwig Köhler, *Hebrew Man* (New York and Nashville: Abingdon, 1956), pp. 127–50, on "Justice in the Gate."

וְהִנֵּה (*wᵉhinnēh,* "behold"; untr. in NIV) suggests the immediacy of the situation, i.e., no sooner had Boaz seated himself than he saw the man he was seeking. Its occurrence here may be a subtle reminder of God's providence working behind the scenes in the whole affair.

Why the writer did not name the גֹּאֵל (*gō'ēl,* "kinsman-redeemer") in this verse remains obscure. Did the writer not know his name? Did he think it was unimportant to give his name? Did he think the *gō'ēl* was unworthy to be mentioned by name because of his shameful refusal to fulfill his obligation? Many plausible explanations have been offered for the omission of his name (e.g., Sasson, pp. 106–7; Campbell, *Ruth,* pp. 141–43), but none commends itself above the others. There are numerous examples in the Bible where a person's name is not given when the reader might have expected it (e.g., the Pharaoh, Exod 1; a prophet, 1 Kings 13; the wise men, Matt 2:1 [NIV, "magi"]; a centurion, Matt 8:5).

Boaz's commands—"Come over here" and "sit down"—are both emphatic imperatives.

4 The statement "I thought I should bring the matter to your attention" reflects a colorful Hebrew idiom: אֲנִי אָמַרְתִּי אֶגְלֶה אָזְנְךָ (*'ᵃni 'āmartî 'eg̱leh 'oznᵉḵā,* "I said I will uncover your ear," here with the emphatic pronoun *'ᵃni,* "I"); it was perhaps originally coined when confidential information was told to someone by lifting the hair that covered the ear. The OT contains many similar symbolic gestures (e.g., "weaken the face," i.e., "curry favor," Prov 19:6; "lifted up the hand," i.e., "swore," Ezek 20:5–6; "do not inhale," i.e., "take no delight"; NIV, "cannot stand," Amos 5:21).

The MT reads, "But if he will not [redeem]." Most translations follow the LXX, Syriac, and Vulgate: "But if you will not [redeem]."

5 The *Kethiv* is first person—קָנִיתִי (*qānîṯay,* "I have purchased" or "am purchasing")—but the *Qere* and context require a second masculine singular—קָנִיתָה (*qānîṯāh,* "you have purchased" or "are purchasing"). Sasson (pp. 119–36) defends the *Kethiv* and discusses the interpretation of this crucial verse at length. He insists that the purchase of the land and the marriage with Ruth were two separate matters. He concludes that the kinsman refused to buy the land on learning that Boaz planned to marry Ruth and then to declare their firstborn son as Mahlon's legal son and heir. There would then be no advantage to the kinsman to buy Elimelech's land, for it would revert to Mahlon's levirate son. Sasson denies that the kinsman refused to buy land because it entailed an obligation to marry Ruth; he does not believe levirate marriage was the issue at stake. Sasson's argument ignores Boaz's statement in 3:13, that he would be *gō'ēl* only if the nearer kinsman-redeemer refused.

---

## 2. *Boaz's Purchase of the Land*

### 4:7–12

[7](Now in earlier times in Israel, for the redemption and transfer of property to become final, one party took off his sandal and gave it to the other. This was the method of legalizing transactions in Israel.)

[8]So the kinsman-redeemer said to Boaz, "Buy it yourself." And he removed his sandal.

[9]Then Boaz announced to the elders and all the people, "Today you are witnesses that I have bought from Naomi all the property of Elimelech, Kilion and Mahlon. [10]I have also acquired Ruth the Moabitess, Mahlon's widow, as my wife, in order to maintain the name of the dead with his property, so that his name will not disappear from among his family or from the town records. Today you are witnesses!"

[11]Then the elders and all those at the gate said, "We are witnesses. May the LORD make the woman who is coming into your home like Rachel and Leah, who together built up the house of Israel. May you have standing in Ephrathah and be famous in Bethlehem. [12]Through the offspring the LORD gives you by this young woman, may your family be like that of Perez, whom Tamar bore to Judah."

**7** "In earlier times" ("in former times," JB, KJV, RSV; cf. 1 Sam 9:9, where the same phrase is found) introduces the author's parenthetical insertion to describe a custom that was no longer practiced at the time the book was written (cf. Jer 32:9–12, where written, attested documents for transfer of land were in use). The origin of the custom has been traced to an ancient practice of taking possession of property by walking on the soil that was being claimed (cf. Deut 1:36; 11:24; Josh 1:3; 14:9). There was also a similar custom in Nuzu. Removing the sandal and handing it to another became a symbol of the transfer of the land.

**8** In the presence of the gathered witnesses, the kinsman renounced his right to the land and invited Boaz to buy it. In a time when few written records were kept, attestation by a number of witnesses made transactions legally secure.

The Hebrew is not clear as to whose sandal was transferred. Some say it was Boaz's; others, that it was the kinsman's. The practice of removing a sandal described here is different from that described in Deuteronomy 25:9 (which suggests contempt for a husband's brother who refused to fulfill the duty of a brother-in-law to the widow), unless in both cases it symbolized no more than a release from a social obligation. Here it appears to be a ritual used to confirm the ratification of a transaction. Most scholars believe that it was the kinsman who removed his sandal and gave it to Boaz to symbolize the completion of the transaction (this interpretation is supported by some Greek versions and by the Vulgate). Those who say it was Boaz's sandal believe the sandal was the "price" by which Boaz purchased the right to Ruth, but this interpretation seems unlikely.

See Deuteronomy 25:7–10 concerning the humiliation of the man who chose not to accept his role as redeemer (*gō'ēl*). None of the disgrace of that regulation seems to be suggested in the encounter between Boaz and the other kinsman.

**9–10** Boaz addressed the elders and all the people who had assembled and reminded them that they were witnesses to what had transpired. He had "bought" (v.9; *qānā*, "acquired," "possessed," not necessarily by purchase; cf. the same verb in v.10) all that belonged to Elimelech and to his sons, Kilion and Mahlon (cf. the order in which the sons are named in 1:2, 5), from Naomi. In addition he "acquired" Ruth to become his wife in order to "maintain the name of the dead with his property" so that his name would not disappear from among his people (cf. 2 Sam 18:18; Isa 56:4–5). Only in v.10 is the reader told that Ruth had been Mahlon's wife.

Boaz began and ended his remarks to the elders and the people with the same words: "Today you are witnesses" (vv.9–10; cf. Josh 24:22). The writer never theologizes on the story he was telling. Yet he may have wanted to suggest that if a mere human being could love an outcast, redeem her, and bring her into fellowship with himself, God could love all the outcasts of the world, redeem them, and bring them into fellowship with himself.

**11–12** The people answered with what must have been an established legal response: "We are witnesses" (v.11; cf. 1 Sam 12:5). Moreover, they pronounced a blessing of fertility on Ruth, that she would be like Rachel and Leah, who had twelve sons between them (Gen 29:31–30:24).

The people then pronounced a dual blessing on Boaz, the first of which has been given two interpretations. "May you have standing" (NIV; Heb., "May you make strength") may refer to a wish for fertility, i.e., the increase of Boaz's family, with material prosperity as a secondary meaning. Most translations, however, understand the first blessing on Boaz as a desire that he achieve wealth.

The second blessing on Boaz was that he would become "famous" (*qᵉrā'-šēm*, lit., "call a name") in Bethlehem.

In a parallel blessing of fertility, but extended to the entire family of Boaz in v.12, the people wished that his family would be like the family of Perez, whom Tamar bore to Judah (cf. Gen 38:29; 1 Chron 2:5; 4:1; cf. Job 1:2; 42:13; Ps 127:4–5). Perez is intentionally named because he was an ancestor of the house of Judah (Gen 38:26, 29).

As it was understood that the first son would be reckoned as Mahlon's, the people were expressing a hope that Boaz would have many other children, who would legally be his.

## Notes

**7** לְפָנִים (lᵉp̱anîm, "in earlier times") can indicate a previous time of close proximity (Judg 3:2; Neh 13:5; Job 42:11) or of long ago, even mythic antiquity (1 Chron 9:20; Ps 102:25).

לְקַיֵּם (*lᵉqayyēm*, "to become final") has frequently been interpreted as an Aramaism, but it may be a form from an old Hebrew dialect.

שָׁלַף (*šālap̱*, "took off"), a perfect form of the verb, is usually construed as an iterative, which is quite unusual for a perfect. One proposed solution has been to revocalize as שָׁלוֹף (*šālôp̱*), an infinitive absolute that could have an iterative function. Another solution has been to posit an original waw consecutive prefixed to the verb, which would give the perfect an imperfect meaning, which normally may express the iterative.

תְּעוּדָה (*tᵉ'ûḏāh*, "testimony") occurs elsewhere only in Isa 8:16, 20, where it parallels תּוֹרָה (*tôrāh*, "law"), but the meaning in Ruth is different. It has been translated "method of legalizing transactions" (NIV), "ratification" (JB), "attestation" (NAB, NASB, NEB).

The LXX reads "buy my redemption responsibility" instead of "buy it."

The LXX and OL add "and gave it to him" at the end of the verse.

**9** The Syriac omits "all the property of Elimelech." The OL omits "all the property of Kilion and Mahlon."

**10** The NIV translates מִשַּׁעַר מְקוֹמוֹ (*miššaʻar mᵉqômô*, "from the gate of his place") as "from the town records." The phrase probably refers to Mahlon's legal rights or to the fact that the deceased's name would be perpetuated in his community.

**11** The LXX has the people agreeing to be witnesses and the elders pronouncing the blessing whereas the Syriac and OL, with the MT, have the two groups acting together as witnesses and pronouncers of blessing.

**12** Tamar and Ruth are among the four women listed in the ancestry of Jesus in Matt 1:1–16. These four included harlots (Tamar, Rahab), a foreigner (Ruth), and a not unwilling adulteress (Bathsheba).

## VI. Birth of a Son to Boaz and Ruth

### 4:13–17

13 So Boaz took Ruth and she became his wife. Then he went to her,
and the LORD enabled her to conceive, and she gave birth to a son. 14 The
women said to Naomi: "Praise be to the LORD, who this day has not left
you without a kinsman-redeemer. May he become famous throughout
Israel! 15 He will renew your life and sustain you in your old age. For your
daughter-in-law, who loves you and who is better to you than seven
sons, has given him birth."
16 Then Naomi took the child, laid him in her lap and cared for him.
17 The women living there said, "Naomi has a son." And they named him
Obed. He was the father of Jesse, the father of David.

**13** The events of at least nine months are described in one sentence of fifteen Hebrew words, including five verbs. We are given no details concerning the kind of marriage ceremony that united Boaz and Ruth. Neither are we told how much time elapsed between their marriage and the birth of their first son. Attributing to the Lord Ruth's conception after ten years of sterility may be the writer's subtle way of explaining why Mahlon, living in a land that worshiped Chemosh, was unable to have children. Both fertility and barrenness were attributed to the Lord (Gen 29:31; 30:2).

**14** The women of the community who earlier had witnessed Naomi's bitter lament now gathered around her to share her happiness. They praised the Lord, giving him credit for providing a redeemer (*gō'ēl*) for Naomi. Some scholars believe Boaz was the *gō'ēl*, but most understand the child to be the *gō'ēl* (v.15 supports this interpretation). It was the child who took away Naomi's reproach of childlessness and would take care of her in her old age. Those who insist that Boaz was the *gō'ēl* argue that he was consistently anticipated as the *gō'ēl* (2:20; 3:9, 12–13; 4:10). Therefore it would be unusual for that responsibility now to be suddenly transferred to a baby. Reference to the child as Naomi's *gō'ēl* should be understood in the context as a blessing pronounced over the child, just as the men had previously prayed for blessing on Boaz (v.11).

The women blessed the child and expressed a hope that he would become famous throughout Israel (Heb., "his name will be called or proclaimed in Israel"). Some have argued unconvincingly that the last phrase refers to the Lord or to Boaz, not to the child.

**15** The women foresaw the child in his *gō'ēl* role as a restorer of life for Naomi and as one who would sustain her in her old age. They also had a word of praise for Ruth; she was better to Naomi than seven sons might have been. In the Bible the number seven symbolizes completion. The tribute to Ruth is striking in light of the importance placed on sons in the OT. One who possessed many sons would be assured of support in her old age and a continuation of her family line (cf. 1 Sam 1:8; 2:5; Job 1:2; 42:13).

**16** Naomi took the newborn child, laid him in her bosom ("lap," NIV), and became his nurse. The word translated "nurse" (*'āman*, "cared for him") means guardian rather than wet nurse (cf. Esth 2:7, where the masculine form of the word is used of Mordecai [NIV, "he had brought up"]; 2 Kings 10:1, 5, where it describes the guardians of Ahab's sons; also see Num 11:12; Isa 49:23 for the masculine form).

Many scholars have taken Naomi's act as a formal adoption, though there is no biblical evidence for such a ceremony (cf. Gen 30:3; 50:23). If it was a legal adoption, Naomi became the child's legal mother, just as Mahlon was his legal father. If the scene does not describe formal or symbolic adoption, then nothing more is intended in this verse than a description of a grandmother delighting in her first grandchild.

**17** It may be important to the interpretation to suggest that the women of v.14 and v.17 may not be the same, as different Hebrew words are used. The word *nāšîm* (v.14) is a general term for women, whereas *šᵉkēnôt* (v.17) means "neighborhood women."

This verse gives the only example in the OT of a child being named by someone other than the immediate family (cf. Exod 2:10). Because the naming of children by others than the parents was so unusual (cf. Luke 1:59), many scholars want to emend the text here. There is, however, no valid reason for abandoning the MT reading. The women who named the child said, "A son has been born to Naomi" (RSV), which may be no more than a way of saying that she had a grandchild; or it may be interpreted as a continuation of an adoption formula suggested in v.16.

The name given the child was Obed ("servant"; perhaps it meant he would serve his grandmother in the capacity of *gō'ēl*). The name was frequently combined with another word: e.g., Ebedmelech ("servant of the king"), Obadiah ("servant of Yahweh"), Obed-edom ("servant of Edom"). Many scholars believe Obed is a shortened form of Obadiah (not to be confused with the prophet of the same name).

A genealogical fragment concludes the verse by linking Obed to David as the father of Jesse and thus as the grandfather of David. Some scholars have questioned whether the statement is a genuine part of the original narrative.

The story of Ruth has shown how a Moabite woman obtained an exalted place in Hebrew history. There is later evidence that David did not forget his Moabite roots. During the period of flight from Saul's wrath, David asked the king of Moab to let his parents stay there for refuge (1 Sam 22:3–4). A later Jewish tradition says David took vengeance on the Moabites (2 Sam 8:2) because the Moabite king betrayed David and put his parents to death.

## Notes

---

13 An unusual word for marriage לָקַח (*lāqaḥ*, "to take") is found here (cf. Exod 2:1; 21:10; 34:16; Deut 24:1).

The LXX[B] omits "and she became his wife. Then he went to her" after "So Boaz took Ruth."

וַתְּהִי־לוֹ (*wattᵉhî-lô*, "and he went to her") is the usual OT way of referring to sexual relations (cf. Gen 16:2; Deut 22:13; 2 Sam 16:21). It may have originally referred to the custom of the bridegroom going into the marriage tent.

15 מֵשִׁיב נֶפֶשׁ (*mēšîḇ nepeš*, "renew your life") is literally "one who causes life [*nepeš*] to return." Perhaps the author intended to show that Naomi's complaint of 1:21 ("caused me to return emptily," MT) had been resolved.

---

## VII. The Genealogy of David

### 4:18–22

18 This, then, is the family line of Perez:

Perez was the father of Hezron,
19 Hezron the father of Ram,
Ram the father of Amminadab,
20 Amminadab the father of Nahshon,
Nahshon the father of Salmon,
21 Salmon the father of Boaz,
Boaz the father of Obed,
22 Obed the father of Jesse,
and Jesse the father of David.

**18** For years scholars seemed to agree that the genealogy of ten names that concludes the Book of Ruth was a later addition. They insisted that in its earliest form the story had nothing to do with David or his ancestry. The source of this "postscript" has been attributed to a priestly writer by those who do not accept the unity of the book. They argue that the addition was made because the only importance of the book was its association with David, and his ancestry therefore needed a fuller account. Since 1 Chronicles 2:4–15 is similar to Ruth 4:18–22, it was believed that the Ruth passage was copied from Chronicles sometime after 400 B.C. Some scholars, however, now believe that Chronicles copied from Ruth or that both go back to an original temple source. Other scholars insist that vv.18–22 cannot be dismissed as an addition simply because it uses the *'ēlleh tôl^e^d̲ôt̲* form ("these are the generations"; NIV, "This . . . is the family line") that critical scholars attribute to priestly redactors.

Perez, the son of Tamar (Gen 38:29), and Hezron are mentioned in Genesis 46:12 (cf. Matt 1:3). The genealogy in Ruth is traced back to Perez, who was the founder of a family of Judah that was named for him, called the Perezites (Num 26:20), to which Elimelech and Boaz belonged. The list is composed of ten names. It appears that there are gaps (i.e., unimportant names are omitted) in order to preserve the number ten. Even if there are some omissions in the genealogy, its authenticity is attested by the unlikeliness of a Jewish scribe creating an ancestry for David that included a Moabitess without a valid basis. The first five names cover the period from the time of the entry into Egypt (Perez, Gen 46:12) to the time of Moses (Nahshon, Exod 6:23; Num 1:7), while the remaining five belong to the period of the early settlement in Canaan to the closing years of the judges.

**19** Hezron, the son of Perez, is mentioned in Genesis 46:12; Numbers 26:21; 1 Chronicles 2:5, 9, 18, 21, 24–25; 4:1; Matthew 1:3; and Luke 3:33. In 1 Chronicles 2:25, 27, Ram appears as the son of Jerahmeel and the grandson of Hezron, not his son. Ram is mentioned again only in 1 Chronicles 2:9–10 as a brother of Jerahmeel and grandfather of Nahshon. He is the Arni of Luke 3:33 (NIV mg.).

**20** Amminadab (son of Ram, 1 Chron 2:10) was the father-in-law of Aaron (Exod 6:23) and thus a contemporary of Moses. He was the father of Nahshon (Num 1:7; 2:3; 7:12, 17; 10:14; 1 Chron 2:10). He is mentioned in Matthew 1:4 and Luke 3:33.

Nahshon was a prince of the house of Judah in Moses' time (Num 1:7; 2:3; 7:12, 17; 10:14) and the son of Amminadab (Exod 6:23; 1 Chron 2:10). He assisted Moses in taking the census of Israel (Num 1:7). He is also mentioned in the genealogy of Matthew 1:4 and Luke 3:32 (in the latter he is Naasson [Gr.]).

**21** Salmon is spelled Salma in v.20 (cf. NIV mg.) and in 1 Chronicles 2:11, 51, 54. According to the genealogy in Matthew 1:4–5, he married Rahab, the harlot of Jericho. He is called Sala in Luke 3:32 (NIV mg.).

With the naming of Boaz, the rest of the genealogy falls into focus. Neither Mahlon nor Elimelech is included, however, as the "legal" father of Obed; instead, Boaz, his natural father, is listed.

**22** The link to David has now been established. Obed is presented as the father of Jesse and thus the grandfather of David.

It is difficult to know why the Book of Ruth ends with a genealogy. It is unlikely that the only purpose of the story was to lead up to the genealogy, and yet it is improbable that the Book of Ruth would have found its way into the OT canon apart from its connection with David. Perhaps the genealogy was included to remind the reader of the hand of God in the direction and continuity of history. Two people brought together by a highly unlikely series of circumstances became ancestors of the great king of Israel, David, who in turn for Christians provides an integral link in the genealogy of our Lord.

## Notes

**18** The familiar but archaic "begat" (KJV) has been rendered in various ways by modern translations: "was the father of" (JB, NAB, NEB, NIV, RSV, TEV), "bore" (Sasson), "begot" (Campbell), "to . . . was born . . ." (NASB).

Sasson (pp. 178–87) discusses at length the genealogy of vv.18–22 and defends it as an integral part of the narrative.

Most LXX traditions, OL, and the Vulgate have "Hezrom" instead of "Hezron." The exchange between *n* and *m* occurs in other Hebrew names, e.g., Gershon/m.

**22** The LXX[A], Syriac, and OL add "the king" to "David"; cf. Matt 1:6.

# 1, 2 SAMUEL

Ronald F. Youngblood

# 1, 2 SAMUEL

## Introduction



### 1. Title

In the Jewish canon the two books of Samuel were originally one. There is no break in the MT between 1 and 2 Samuel, and the Masoretic notes at the end of 2 Samuel give a total of 1,506 verses for the entire corpus and point to 1 Samuel 28:24 as the middle verse of the "book" (*spr,* sing.). Like Kings and Chronicles, each of which is slightly longer than Samuel, the scroll of Samuel was too unwieldy to be handled with ease and so was divided into two parts in early MSS of the LXX. Not until the fifteenth century A.D. was the Hebrew text of Samuel separated into two books, and the first printed Hebrew Bible to exhibit the division is the Bomberg edition published in Venice in 1516/17.

It is understandable that the ancient Hebrew title of the book was *šᵉmû'ēl,* since the prophet Samuel is the dominant figure in the early chapters. A major theme of the work, however, led the LXX translators to group Samuel together with *mᵉlāḵîm* ("Kings") and to refer to them collectively as *Bibloi Basileiōn* ("Books of Kingdoms"). Jerome modified the title slightly to *Librī Rēgum* ("Books of Kings") so that Samuel and Kings, each divided into two parts, became known as 1, 2, 3, and 4 Kings respectively. To this day Catholic commentators and translators often refer to 1 and 2 Samuel as "1 and 2 Kings" (cf. the version by Ronald Knox), a practice that has caused no end of confusion, even if only temporary, to non-Catholic users of their works. Protestants have uniformly reverted to labeling the books after their ancient Hebrew name.

### 2. Authorship and Date

According to the Babylonian Talmud, "Samuel wrote the book that bears his name" (Baba Bathra 14b). The same Talmud also asserts that the first twenty-four chapters of

1 Samuel were written by Samuel himself (1 Sam 25:1 reports his death) and that the rest of the Samuel corpus was the work of Nathan and Gad (Baba Bathra 15a). First Chronicles 29:29 is doubtless the source of the latter rabbinic assessment: "As for the events of King David's reign, from beginning to end, they are written in the records of Samuel the seer, the records of Nathan the prophet and the records of Gad the seer." Samuel, Nathan, and Gad may not have been the authors of the "records" that bear their names, however; and, in any event, 1 Chronicles 29:29 appears to be listing sources used by the Chronicler and therefore should not be understood as having anything to say about the authorship of the books of Samuel. Although the priests Ahimaaz (cf. 2 Sam 15:27, 36; 17:17, 20; 18:19, 22–23, 27–29) and Zabud (cf. 1 Kings 4:5), among others, have been proposed as possible candidates, arguments in their favor fail to convince. In sum, we must remain content to leave the authorship of Samuel—and, for that matter, of other OT books such as Joshua, Judges, Kings, and Chronicles—in the realm of anonymity. Ultimately, of course, the Holy Spirit is the Author who prompted the inspired narrator and gave his work the "omniscient" quality often remarked upon.[1]

Although the statement that "Ziklag . . . has belonged to the kings [pl.] of Judah ever since" (1 Sam 27:6) implies that Samuel was not written until after the division of the kingdom of Israel following the death of Solomon in 931 B.C., the possibility of a modest number of later editorial updatings and/or modernizations of the original work cannot be ruled out. In any case, "one imagines the writer of Samuel or the Chronicler as authors, not redactors, rather much as one might assume that any anonymous text, whatever its history might have been, implies an 'author' and a 'reader' whose narrative strategies and response may be inferred from the 'work.' "[2] With respect to the date of the books of Samuel, all that can be said for certain is that since they report "the last words of David" (2 Sam 23:1), they could not have been written earlier than the second quarter of the tenth century B.C. (David died c. 970).

## 3. Historical Context

Because of its setting during the period of the judges, the Book of Ruth was inserted between Judges and Samuel at least as early as the translation of the LXX and continues to occupy that position in most versions to the present time. In the Jewish canon, however, Ruth is one of the five festal "scrolls" (*m^egillôṯ*) and therefore appears closer to the end of the Hebrew Bible in a section called *k^eṯûḇîm* ("Writings"). When Ruth is thus displaced, Samuel follows immediately upon Judges.

After the conquest of Canaan by Joshua, the people of Israel experienced the normal range of problems that face colonizers of newly occupied territory. Exacerbating their situation, however, was not only the resilience of the conquered but also the failures—moral and spiritual as well as military—of the conquerors. Their rebellion against the covenant that God had established with them at Sinai brought divine retribution, and the restoration that resulted from their repentance lasted only until they rebelled again (cf. Judg 2:10–19; Neh 9:24–29). The dreary cycle of rebellion—retribution—repentance—restoration—rebellion is repeated over and over again

[1] Cf. Shimon Bar-Efrat, "Literary Modes and Methods in the Biblical Narrative in View of 2 Samuel 10–20 and 1 Kings 1–2," *Immanuel* 8 (Spring 1978): 20.

[2] Burke O. Long, "Framing Repetitions in Biblical Historiography," JBL 106, 3 (1987): 386.

throughout the Book of Judges, which in many respects rehearses the darkest days of Israel's long history.

By the end of Judges the situation in the land had become intolerable. Israel was *in extremis*, and anarchy reigned: "Everyone did as he saw fit" (Judg 17:6; 21:25). A series of judges, upon whom the Spirit of the Lord "came" (Judg 3:10; 6:34; 11:29) with energizing "power" (Judg 14:6, 19; 15:14), provided little more than a holding action against Israel's enemies within and without, who were both numerous and varied. More than three centuries of settlement (cf. Judg 11:26) did not materially improve Israel's position, and thoughtful people must have begun crying out for change.

If theocracy implemented through divine charisma was the hallmark of the period of the judges (cf. Judg 8:28–29), theocracy mediated through divinely sanctioned monarchy would characterize the next phase in the history of the Israelites. In the days of the judges "Israel had no king" (Judg 17:6; 18:1; 19:1; 21:25), and it was becoming apparent to many that she desperately needed one. Judgeship did not end with Samson, however. The priest Eli and the prophet Samuel both served as judges (cf. 1 Sam 4:18; 7:6, 15, 17). Not until the accession of Saul did the people have a king in the truest sense of the word—and even then they expected him to "judge" them (cf. 1 Sam 8:5–6, 20).

Edwin R. Thiele has succeeded in establishing 931/30 B.C. as the year when the division of the monarchy took place following Solomon's death.[3] If we interpret the biblical figures literally, Solomon reigned from 970 to 931 (forty years, 1 Kings 11:42), David from 1010 to 970 (forty years and six months, 2 Sam 5:5), and Saul from 1052 to 1010 (forty-two years, 1 Sam 13:1). Assuming that Samuel was about thirty years old when he anointed Saul as king of Israel, we arrive at the approximate dates of 1080 (the birth of Samuel) to 970 B.C. (the death of David) as the time span covered in the books of Samuel.

## 4. Literary Context and Unity

Joshua, Judges, Samuel, and Kings constitute the first half of *nᵉḇî'îm* ("Prophets"), the middle section of the Jewish canon. As the so-called Former Prophets, the four books present a carefully selected series of narratives that summarize the history of God's people during a period spanning well over eight centuries: from the beginning of the conquest of Canaan (c. 1405 B.C.) to the end of the monarchy and beyond (c. 561 B.C., "the thirty-seventh year of the exile of Jehoiachin king of Judah" [2 Kings 25:27]). Told from a prophetic viewpoint (cf. 2 Kings 18:13, 17–37; 19:1–20:19 = Isa 36:1–38:8; 39:1–8; cf. 2 Kings 25:27–30 = Jer 52:31–34), the story proclaims the central truth that Israel could anticipate the Lord's blessing only so long as she remained

[3]*A Chronology of the Hebrew Kings* (Grand Rapids: Zondervan, 1977), pp. 15, 31. Although he objects to certain aspects of Thiele's overall tour de force, William Hamilton Barnes settles on 932 B.C. as the most likely year for the beginning of the divided monarchy; cf. *Studies in the Chronology of the Divided Monarchy of Israel*, Harvard Semitic Monograph 48 (Atlanta: Scholars, 1991), pp. 153–54. Whether arguments in favor of an earlier (e.g., 945; cf. E.W. Falstich, *History, Harmony, and the Hebrew Kings* [Spencer: Chronology Books, 1986], pp. 202–3) or later date (e.g., 927; cf. John H. Hayes and Paul K. Hooker, *A New Chronology for the Kings of Israel and Judah and Its Implications for Biblical History and Literature* [Atlanta: John Knox, 1988], pp. 18–19) will succeed in winning the day remains to be seen.

faithful to the stipulations of the Sinai covenant and to the laws and decrees that explicated them.

It has long been recognized that the four books of the Former Prophets expand on the parenetic exhortations of Moses enshrined in the Book of Deuteronomy, itself a covenant renewal document of the first order.[4] That the Lord rewards the righteous and punishes the wicked is only to be expected in light of the covenant blessings and curses detailed in Deuteronomy 27:9–28:68. One of the many interrelationships shared by the five books is a theology of monarchy, well summarized by Raymond B. Dillard: "Deuteronomy also provided for the day that the people would want a king (17:14–20), so the [Deuteronomic] historian reports what life was like both without a king (Joshua, Judges) and with a king (Samuel, Kings); it is largely a record of the disobedience of the people and the faithfulness of God."[5]

Building on the impressively "Deuteronomic" qualities of Joshua, Judges, Samuel, and Kings, Martin Noth concluded that Deuteronomy should be detached from the Pentateuch (the remaining four books—Genesis, Exodus, Leviticus, Numbers—thus constituting a "Tetrateuch") and added to Joshua through Kings, thus forming a five-part continuous work that he called the "Deuteronomistic History" and that he claimed was compiled during the exilic period.[6] Its author made use of a number of independent literary units (including Deuteronomy itself), which he interwove with his own contributions to produce the finished product. Strictly speaking, the term "Deuteronomic" refers to the writer(s) of Deuteronomy, and the term "Deuteronomistic" is used of the compiler(s) of the great historical narrative that stretches from Deuteronomy through 2 Kings. Since the second term is so cumbersome, however, the first is often used in both senses and will be thus employed throughout the following commentary.

How are we to evaluate Noth's theory? Undoubted similarities among the various books make it attractive indeed. Even the casual reader cannot fail to observe that Joshua begins with "After the death of Moses," Judges with "After the death of Joshua," and 2 Samuel with "After the death of Saul," and that 2 Kings begins similarly, although the corresponding phrase sits differently in its context and is therefore rendered in a slightly different way: "After Ahab's death." It would therefore appear that the narrator deliberately signaled to his readers as sharp a break at 2 Samuel 1:1 and at 2 Kings 1:1 (breaks later confirmed by whoever it was that divided the scrolls of Samuel and Kings into two books each) as he had at Joshua 1:1 and Judges 1:1. Numerous other stylistic, linguistic, and thematic features are shared by the books of Deuteronomy through Kings so that references to the "Deuteronom(ist)ic historian" are de rigueur in scholarly discussion, no matter what the theological persuasion of the participants.

A word of caution is in order, however. My use of the term "Deuteronomic" does not imply a late date for Deuteronomy (which I believe to have come from the hand of Moses) or an exilic date for Joshua, Judges, or Samuel (which I believe to have been written relatively soon after the events that they record). Whether there was in fact a

[4]Cf. especially Meredith G. Kline, *Treaty of the Great King. The Covenant Structure of Deuteronomy: Studies and Commentary* (Grand Rapids: Eerdmans, 1963).

[5]"David's Census: Perspectives on II Samuel 24 and I Chronicles 21," in *Through Christ's Word: A Festschrift for Dr. Philip E. Hughes*, edd. W. Robert Godfrey and Jesse L. Boyd III (Phillipsburg: Presbyterian and Reformed, 1985), p. 100; cf. also Gerbrandt, pp. 189–94.

[6]*Überlieferungsgeschichtliche Studien*, 2d ed. (Tübingen: Max Niemeyer, 1957), pp. 1–110. English translation: *The Deuteronomistic History*, JSOT suppl. 15 (Sheffield: JSOT, 1981).

"Deuteronomic" historian who lived during the Exile and who gathered together the books of the Former Prophets, collating them into a continuous narrative and adding his own editorial touches to reflect the Mosaic theology enshrined in the Book of Deuteronomy, remains moot. In the following commentary, therefore, "Deuteronomic" is used descriptively rather than prescriptively.[7]

In the Jewish canon the Latter Prophets (Isaiah, Jeremiah, Ezekiel, the Twelve [Minor Prophets]) follow immediately after the historical narratives known as the Former Prophets and strengthen the rabbinic tradition that Joshua, Judges, Samuel, and Kings were written from a prophetic perspective (see above). The LXX translators, on the other hand, placed Chronicles immediately after the Latter Prophets. In so doing they honored the fact that the Chronicler, writing late in the fifth century B.C. during the era of restoration following exile, summarized the narratives of Genesis through Kings in much briefer detail. Greater attention, however, is paid by the Chronicler to the period of the monarchy, especially to those aspects of the Davidic dynasty that he considered admirable. Among the literary sources used extensively by Chronicles were the books of Samuel and Kings. The chapters of 1 Chronicles most indebted to Samuel are 3, 10–11, 13–15, and 17–21; and comparisons between the two parallel accounts will be noted in the commentary.[8]

## 5. Purpose

From the beginning of the Book of Joshua to its end, Joshua and the Israelites are commanded to obey the "Book of the Law" (Josh 1:8; 23:6), probably Deuteronomy (cf. esp. Josh 8:31, where Deut 27:5–6 is cited along with Exod 20:25; cf. also Josh 14:9, which echoes Deut 1:36). Although the conqueror of Canaan, Joshua knows full well that the Lord gives the victory (cf. Josh 1:2–3, 5, 9, 11, 13, 15; 2:9–11, 14, 24; 3:10; et al.). He thus prefigures the coming monarchy, whose kings are to submit to divine leadership as they rule over Israel under God.

Judges is permeated by the same theme: When Israel was oppressed by the enemy and cried out to God for help, the Lord delivered them by raising up "judges, who saved them out of the hands of these raiders" (Judg 2:16). When "the kings of Canaan fought" against the people (Judg 5:19), they were no match for Israel's God: "From the heavens the stars fought, from their courses they fought against Sisera" (Judg 5:20). Because the enemies of Israel were also the enemies of the Lord, their doom was sealed (cf. Judg 5:31). Like Joshua, the judges therefore also foreshadow the kings who would succeed them.

In the books of Samuel, monarchy becomes a reality. Three dominant figures—Samuel the kingmaker, Saul the abortive king, David the ideal king—highlight its agonies as well as its ecstasies.

> According to the Deuteronomist the political success or failure of a king was entirely dependent upon the degree to which Israel obeyed the covenant. Political success could thus only be achieved by a king through fulfilling his responsibility

[7] Cf. similarly Dillard, "David's Census," p. 99 and n. 15; Howard, "The Case for Kingship," p. 19 and n. 2; id., "Review of Gerbrandt," p. 101 and n. 3; p. 103 and n. 5.

[8] For detailed comparisons between the Hebrew text of Samuel and its parallels in 1 Chronicles and Psalm 18 (as well as elsewhere in the OT), cf. especially Bendavid, pp. 31–70; for detailed comparisons in English, cf. Crockett, pp. 106–41; Newsome, pp. 23–79.

> as covenant administrator. Given this view, it is also clear that military success was not a major accomplishment of a king, but the act of Yahweh in his role as protector of the people. The king's role in this was to trust Yahweh to deliver, and then to be obedient to his word. (Gerbrandt, p. 194)

A major purpose of Samuel, then, is to define monarchy as a gracious gift of God to his chosen people. Their desire for a king (1 Sam 8:5) was not in itself inappropriate, despite Samuel's initial displeasure (v.6). Nor were they necessarily wrong in wanting a king like "all the other nations" had (vv.5, 20). Their sin consisted in the fact that they were asking for a king "to lead us and to go out before us and to fight our battles" (v.20). In other words, they refused to believe that the Lord would grant them victory in his own time and according to his own good pleasure (contrast 2 Sam 8:6, 14). They were willing to exchange humble faith in the protection and power of "the LORD Almighty" (1 Sam 1:3) for misguided reliance on the naked strength of "the fighting men of Israel" (2 Sam 24:4).

## 6. Literary Form

Justifiable concern for the inspired truth and moral excellence of Scripture should not be permitted to blind us to its consummate beauty. For the most part the books of Samuel are composed of prose narratives that serve well in presenting a continuous, historical account of the advent, establishment, and consolidation of monarchy in Israel. It is possible to isolate various literary units within the larger whole—Ark Narratives (1 Sam 4:1b–7:17), Rise of Saul (chs. 8–12), Decline of Saul (chs. 13–15), Rise of David (16:1–28:2), David's Accession to Kingship (Over Judah, 2 Sam 1:1–3:5; Over Israel, 3:6–5:16), David's Powerful Reign (5:17–8:18), David's Court History (chs. 9–20), Epilogue (chs. 21–24)—although debate is vigorous concerning the parameters of many of them.

In recent years various sections of the books of Samuel have been subjected to close reading in order to uncover aspects of Samuel's exquisite literary structure. While manufacturing chiasms where there are none is a constant temptation that the exegete must avoid at all costs, the author of Samuel seems to have used the technique on numerous occasions. A clear example is the Epilogue, in which the Song of David (2 Sam 22) and David's Last Words (23:1–7) nestle between two warrior narratives (21:15–22; 23:8–39) that are framed in turn by reports of divine wrath against the people of God (21:1–14; ch. 24).

Second Samuel 1–20 displays a four-part architectonic structure that is impressive indeed. David's Accession to Kingship Over Judah (1:1–3:5) ends with a four-verse listing of the sons born to David in Hebron (3:2–5); David's Accession to Kingship Over Israel (3:6–5:16) ends with a four-verse listing of the children born to him in Jerusalem (5:13–16); David's Powerful Reign (5:17–8:18) and David's Court History (chs. 9–20) each end with a four-verse roster of his officials (8:15–18; 20:23–26). A symmetrical literary edifice of such magnitude can hardly be accidental. Similar examples, for many of which I am indebted to the monographs listed in the Bibliography as well as to other books and articles, are noted in the commentary (cf. also John A. Martin, pp. 131–45).

When poetry punctuates the corpus here and there, it does so in memorable and striking ways. David's Lament for Saul and Jonathan (2 Sam 1:1–17) not only underscores his genuine esteem for Saul and his heartfelt love for Jonathan but also serves as a means of opening the Second Book of Samuel on a poignantly lyrical note. The Song of Hannah and the Song of David—the first near the beginning of the work (1 Sam 2:1–11) and the second near its end (2 Sam 22)—remind us that the two books were originally one by framing their main contents, by opening and closing in similar ways, and by highlighting the messianic horizons of the Davidic dynasty through initial promise (1 Sam 2:10) and eternal fulfillment (2 Sam 22:51).

## 7. Canonicity and Text

> The three sections of the [Hebrew Bible] have a descending order of sanctity. The Torah was believed to be the direct word of God, spoken to Moses on top of Mount Sinai. . . . The books of the prophets [*sic*] were believed to have been revealed to them in the "spirit of prophecy." The message is from God, but the words are the prophet's own words. The Writings were believed to have been written in the "holy spirit." They were inspired by God but had a human authorship. . . . The books of the Prophets and the Writings exist for inspirational purposes, but actual Jewish law and practice is derived solely from the five books of the Torah.[9]

Despite Judaism's trilevel theory of inspiration, the canonicity of the books of Samuel has rarely if ever been disputed by Jews or Christians. Although 1 Samuel is not quoted in the NT, and although citations from 2 Samuel appear there only a few times (cf. 2 Sam 7:8, 14 in 2 Cor 6:18; 7:14 in Heb 1:5; 22:50 in Rom 15:9), Samuel and David in particular are mentioned frequently in its pages. In addition the OT stories about Hannah and Peninnah, Samuel and Eli, Saul and David, David and Jonathan, David and Goliath, Samuel and the medium at Endor, David and Bathsheba, Amnon and Tamar, David and Absalom, and numerous other pericopes have proven to be rich resources for countless sermons, lectures, and lessons throughout the centuries.

For reasons unknown, the MT of Samuel has suffered more in scribal transmission than any other OT book.[10] Fortunately the DSS, the Lucianic recension of the LXX (together with proto-Lucianic versions), the LXX itself (esp. the Vaticanus MS), and parallels in 1 Chronicles and Psalm 18 are often helpful in attempts to recover the original text. When two or more non-MT readings agree as over against the MT, careful attention should be paid to the evidence they present.

Cave 4 at Qumran yielded three priceless MSS of Samuel: (1) 4QSam[b], dating from the middle of the third century B.C. and containing fragments of 1 Samuel; (2) 4QSam[c], from the early first century B.C. and containing fragments of 1 Samuel 25; 2 Samuel 14–15; (3) 4QSam[a], the best-preserved of the biblical MSS from Cave 4, a large scroll dated in the third quarter of the first century B.C. and containing fragmentary parts of much of 1 and 2 Samuel. Since all three MSS are a thousand years older than any previously known Hebrew MS, their value for the textual criticism of Samuel is obvious. Although the technical literature on the Samuel DSS is extensive,[11] the recent release of photographs of all unpublished DSS for scholarly

[9]Stephen M. Wylen, *Settings of Silver: An Introduction to Judaism* (Mahwah: Paulist, 1989), p. 12.

[10]In almost fifty separate instances in the books of Samuel, the NIV footnotes indicate preference for a reading other than that of the MT.

[11]Cf. Frank Moore Cross, Jr., "The Contribution of the Qumrân Discoveries to the Studies of the Biblical Text," in *Qumran and the History of the Biblical Text*, edd. Frank Moore Cross and Shemaryahu Talmon

examination will greatly enhance DSS research through provision of materials that up to this point have been granted to only a privileged few.

With respect to the various MSS and recensions of the LXX (including the Lucianic), the BH and BHS notes are not always trustworthy. Since the text edited by Alfred Rahlfs is incomplete (*Septuaginta* [Stuttgart: Württembergische Bibelanstalt, 1962]), for serious LXX textual research with respect to the books of Samuel it is necessary to make use of *The Old Testament in Greek According to the Text of Codex Vaticanus*. Volume II: The Later Historical Books. Part I: I and II Samuel, edd. Alan England Brooke and Norman McLean with Henry St. John Thackeray (Cambridge: Cambridge University Press, 1927).

All things considered, resource materials for textual criticism of 1 and 2 Samuel have never been more abundant or accessible. Their judicious use can assist scholars in making substantial strides toward restoring the original Hebrew text. Caution remains the watchword, however, and changes should always and only be suggested on a case-by-case basis. The observation of Carlson is both typical and apropos: "The LXX text of the Books of Samuel is of outstanding value, though emendation and correction of the Masoretic text demands careful and thorough consideration" (p. 37).[12]

## 8. Theological Values

In terms of the political scene, Israel at the beginning of 1 Samuel was a loosely organized federation of anemic tribal territories scarcely able to keep the Philistines and other enemies at bay. By the end of 2 Samuel, however, Israel under David had become the most powerful kingdom in the eastern Mediterranean region, strong at home and secure abroad. As far as the religious picture is concerned, the opening chapters of 1 Samuel find Israel worshiping at a nondescript shrine presided over by a corrupt priesthood. The last chapter of 2 Samuel, however, records David's purchase of a site in Jerusalem upon which the temple of Solomon, one of the most magnificent buildings in the ancient world, would soon be erected. Sweeping change, then, is a hallmark of the Samuel narratives—change guided and energized by the Lord himself through fragile vessels of the likes of Samuel, Saul, and David.

"Perhaps God's major act in 1 and 2 Samuel is his electing or choosing" (John A.

---

(Cambridge: Harvard University Press, 1975), pp. 278–92; id., "The History of the Biblical Text in the Light of Discoveries in the Judaean Desert," in *Qumran and the History of the Biblical Text*, pp. 177–95; id., "The Oldest Manuscripts from Qumran," JBL 74, 3 (1955): 147–72; id., "The Ammonite Oppression of the Tribes of Gad and Reuben: Missing Verses from 1 Samuel 11 Found in 4QSamuel[a]," in *History, Historiography and Interpretation: Studies in Biblical and Cuneiform Literatures*, edd. H. Tadmor and M. Weinfeld (Leiden: Brill, 1984), pp. 148–58; id., "II: Original Biblical Text Reconstructed from Newly Found Fragments," *Bible Review* 1, 3 (1985): 26–35; Ralph W. Klein, *Textual Criticism of the Old Testament: The Septuagint After Qumran* (Philadelphia: Fortress, 1974); Eugene Charles Ulrich, Jr., "4QSam[c]: A Fragmentary Manuscript of 2 Samuel 14–15 From the Scribe of the *Serek Hay-yaḥad* (1QS)," BASOR 235 (Summer 1979): 1–25; id., *The Qumran Text of Samuel and Josephus*.

[12]Cf. also J. Barton Payne, "The Sahidic Coptic Text of I Samuel," JBL 72, 1 (1953): 60–62; Bruce M. Metzger, "Lucian and the Lucianic Recension of the Greek Bible," NTS 8, 3 (1962): 193–200; Gleason L. Archer, "A Reassessment of the Value of the Septuagint of 1 Samuel for Textual Emendation, in the Light of the Qumran Fragments," in *Tradition and Testament: Essays in Honor of Charles Lee Feinberg*, edd. John S. and Paul D. Feinberg (Chicago: Moody, 1981), pp. 234–40; cf. especially Stephen Pisano, *Additions or Omissions in the Books of Samuel: The Significant Pluses and Minuses in the Massoretic, LXX, and Qumran Texts*, Orbus Biblicus et Orientalis 57 (Göttingen: Vandenhoeck and Ruprecht, 1984), pp. 1–16, 283–85.

Martin, p. 309). The Lord's elective purposes embraced Samuel (cf. 1 Sam 1:19–20), Saul (cf. 10:20–24), and David (cf. 16:6–13). As the theological centerpiece of the Deuteronomic corpus, 2 Samuel 7 describes the choice of the Davidic dynasty, through which the future kings of Judah (including the Messiah) would come. In 2 Samuel 7, kingship and covenant kiss each other.

Reversal of fortune as an index of divine sovereignty is another significant motif. The Song of Hannah is programmatic in this regard:

> The LORD brings death and makes alive;
> he brings down to the grave and raises up.
> The LORD sends poverty and wealth;
> he humbles and he exalts.
>
> He raises the poor from the dust
> and lifts the needy from the ash heap;
> he seats them with princes
> and has them inherit a throne of honor.
> (1 Sam 2:6–8)

A formerly barren woman (cf. 1 Sam 1:5–6) becomes the mother of six children (cf. 2:21); men of privilege (cf. 2:12–16), Eli's sons, die in shame (cf. 4:11); an unheralded donkey wrangler (cf. 9:2–3) and an obscure shepherd boy (cf. 16:11) are anointed as the first two rulers of Israel (cf. 10:1; 16:13). The overall structure of each of the books of Samuel makes its contribution in this respect as well: Just as the literary and theological midpoint of 1 Samuel foresees the divinely energized transition from Saulide to Davidic rule (cf. 1 Sam 16:13–14), so also does the prophetic rebuke at the literary and theological crux of 2 Samuel besmirch David's kingship with an indelible stain (cf. 2 Sam 12:9–10).

A key theme of the ark narratives (1 Sam 4–7) is that God refuses to be manipulated. Carrying the ark into battle does not guarantee an Israelite victory (cf. 4:3–11), placing the ark in a Philistine temple does not insure divine blessing (cf. 5:1–6:12), and looking into the ark brings death (cf. 6:19; cf. also 2 Sam 6:6–7). If the ark's exile at Kiriath Jearim (cf. 1 Sam 6:21–7:2) coincided with the end of the period of the judges, its triumphal entry into Jerusalem (cf. 2 Sam 6:16) confirmed that a new day had dawned for God's people.

As repository of the tablets of the covenant, the ark reminded the Israelites of God's demands on their lives. The priesthood, however, continued to preside over the divine oracles, the lots known as Urim and Thummim, to which penitents and supplicants alike resorted in time of need. Oracular inquiry brought Saul to the people's attention (cf. 1 Sam 10:20–24), determined the best time for military attack (cf. 14:36–37; 23:1–4; 30:8; 2 Sam 2:1; 5:19–25), and provided assistance for David (cf. 1 Sam 22:9–15). Forsaken by dreams, Urim, and prophets, the desperate Saul resorted to a medium for guidance (cf. 28:6–25).

The offices of king and prophet arose simultaneously in Israel. Saul, the first king (cf. 1 Sam 10:24), was anointed by Samuel, who stands at the head of the prophetic line (cf. 9:6–10, 19; Acts 3:24; 13:20; Heb 11:32) as promised to Moses (cf. Deut 18:15–18). If the task of the king was to administer the covenant, that of the prophet was to interpret its demands. In matters relative to God's will as revealed through his word, the submission of kings to prophets was self-understood (cf. 1 Sam 13:13; 15:22–23; 2 Sam 12:7–14). To the end of the monarchy, the prophets protected with holy zeal their divinely authorized claims over kingship.

Theocracy through monarchy was an ideal that fared better in proclamation than in practice. What Samuel had warned about (cf. 1 Sam 8:10–18), the people continued to lust after (cf. vv.19–20). In any event, Saul's failure brought about not a new dispensation but a different king, a man "better than" him (15:28), a man after God's own heart (cf. 13:14). To the extent that David understood that his role as human king was to implement the mandates of the Divine King, blessing would follow (cf. 2 Sam 6:11–15, 17–19; cf. esp. 7:27–29). When he deliberately flouted God's will, however, he could count equally on the fact that he would be under the curse (cf. 12:1–18). And so it would be with his descendants on the throne: If the Davidic covenant was eternal in the sense that his line would continue forever (cf. 7:12–16, 25–29; 23:5; Ps 89:27–29, 33–37), it was also conditional in that individual participants in it would be punished when they sinned (cf. 1 Kings 2:4; 8:25; 9:4–5; Pss 89:30–32; 132:12).[13]

"Uneasy lies the head that wears a crown," wrote William Shakespeare (KH IV, 2.3.1). Royal perquisites are often overbalanced by seemingly intractable problems. When enemies lift the siege, family members engage in betrayal; when voyeurism ceases to beckon and panic subsides, ambitious sons rebel. At such times begging for God's mercy becomes a daily exercise, and psalms of petition and lament are written and sung. And when all is said and done, the towering figure of David continues to alternately attract and repel. He is the Lord's anointed, and therefore we pay him rightful homage; he is insulated from mundane matters and oblivious to his people's needs, but because of his divine appointment we fault him for not following the highest possible standard.

> O hard condition,
> Twin-born with greatness, subject to the breath
> Of every fool, whose sense no more can feel
> But his own wringing! What infinite heart's-ease
> Must kings neglect, that private men enjoy!
>
> (KH V, 4.1)

## 9. Bibliography

### A. *Commentaries*


Ackroyd, Peter R. *The First Book of Samuel.* Cambridge Bible Commentary on the New English Bible. Cambridge: Cambridge University Press, 1971.

Anderson, A.A. 2 *Samuel.* Word Biblical Commentary 11. Dallas: Word, 1989.

Baldwin, Joyce G. *1 & 2 Samuel.* Downers Grove: InterVarsity, 1988.

Brueggemann, Walter. *First and Second Samuel.* Interpretation: A Bible Commentary for Teaching and Preaching. Louisville: John Knox, 1990.

Driver, S.R. *Notes on the Hebrew Text and the Topography of the Books of Samuel.* Second edition, revised and enlarged. Oxford: Clarendon, 1913.

Eslinger, Lyle M. *Kingship of God in Crisis: A Close Reading of 1 Samuel 1–12.* Bible and Literature 10. Sheffield: Almond, 1985.

Fokkelman, Jan P. *King David (II Sam. 9–20 & I Kings 1–2).* Volume 1 of *Narrative Art and Poetry in the Books of Samuel: A Full Interpretation Based on Stylistic and Structural Analyses.* Assen: Van Gorcum, 1981.


[13]Cf. similarly Howard, "Review of Gerbrandt," pp. 102, 113–14.

Goldman, S. *Samuel: Hebrew Text and English Translation With an Introduction and Commentary*. London: Soncino, 1951.
Gordon, Robert P. *I and II Samuel: A Commentary*. Grand Rapids: Zondervan, 1986.
Hertzberg, Hans Wilhelm. *I and II Samuel: A Commentary*. Old Testament Library. Philadelphia: Westminster, 1964.
Keil, C.F., and F. Delitzsch. *Biblical Commentary on the Books of Samuel*. Grand Rapids: Eerdmans, 1956.
Kirkpatrick, A.F. *The First Book of Samuel*. CBSC. Cambridge: Cambridge University Press, 1880.
———. *The Second Book of Samuel*. CBSC. Cambridge: Cambridge University Press, 1891.
Klein, Ralph W. *1 Samuel*. Word Biblical Commentary 10. Waco: Word, 1983.
McCarter, P. Kyle, Jr. *I Samuel: A New Translation With Introduction, Notes & Commentary*. AB 8. Garden City: Doubleday, 1980.
———. *II Samuel: A New Translation With Introduction, Notes and Commentary*. AB 9. Garden City: Doubleday, 1984.
Miscall, Peter D. *1 Samuel: A Literary Reading*. Bloomington: Indiana University Press, 1986.
Patrick, Symon. *A Commentary Upon the Two Books of Samuel*. London: Chiswell, 1703.
Smith, Henry Preserved. *A Critical and Exegetical Commentary on the Books of Samuel*. ICC. Edinburgh: T. and T. Clark, 1904.

## B. *General Works*

Ackerman, James S. "Knowing Good and Evil: A Literary Analysis of the Court History in 2 Samuel 9–20 and 1 Kings 1–2." JBL 109, 1 (1990).
Aharoni, Yohanan. *The Land of the Bible*. Revised edition. Philadelphia: Westminster, 1979.
Alter, Robert. *The Art of Biblical Narrative*. New York: Basic, 1981.
Bailey, Randall C. *David in Love and War: The Pursuit of Power in 2 Samuel 10–12*. Journal for the Study of the Old Testament Supplement 75. Sheffield: JSOT, 1990.
Barrick, W. Boyd, and John R. Spencer, edd. *In the Shelter of Elyon: Essays on Ancient Palestinian Life and Literature in Honor of G.W. Ahlström*. Journal for the Study of the Old Testament Supplement 31. Sheffield: JSOT, 1984.
Barthélemy, Dominique, et al., edd. *Preliminary and Interim Report on the Hebrew Old Testament Text Project*. Volume 2: *Historical Books*. Stuttgart: United Bible Societies, 1976.
Bendavid, Abba. *Parallels in the Bible*. Jerusalem: Carta, 1972.
Berlin, Adele. *Poetics and Interpretation of Biblical Narrative*. Sheffield: Almond, 1983.
Birch, Bruce C. *The Rise of the Israelite Monarchy: The Growth and Development of 1 Samuel 7–15*. SBL Dissertation 27. Missoula: Scholars, 1976.
Bright, John. *A History of Israel*. 3d ed. Philadelphia: Westminster, 1981.
Brueggemann, Walter. *David's Truth in Israel's Imagination and Memory*. Philadelphia: Fortress, 1985.
———. *Power, Providence, and Personality: Biblical Insight Into Life and Ministry*. Louisville: Westminster/John Knox, 1990.
Campbell, Antony F. *Of Prophets and Kings: A Late Ninth-Century Document (1 Samuel 1–2 Kings 10)*. CBQ Monograph 17. Washington: Catholic Biblical Association of America, 1986.
Carlson, R.A. *David the Chosen King: A Traditio-Historical Approach to the Second Book of Samuel*. Stockholm: Almqvist and Wiksell, 1964.
Conroy, Charles. *Absalom Absalom! Narrative and Language in 2 Sam 13–20*. Analecta Biblica 81. Rome: Pontifical Biblical Institute, 1978.
Crockett, William Day. *A Harmony of the Books of Samuel, Kings, and Chronicles*. London: Revell, 1897.
Cross, Frank Moore. *Canaanite Myth and Hebrew Epic: Essays in the History of the Religion of Israel*. Cambridge: Harvard University Press, 1973.

Cross, Frank Moore, and David Noel Freedman. "A Royal Song of Thanksgiving: II Samuel 22 = Psalm 18." JBL 72, 1 (1953).

Curtis, John Briggs. "'East Is East. . . .'" JBL 80, 4 (1961).

Eslinger, Lyle, and Glen Taylor, edd. *Ascribe to the Lord: Biblical and Other Studies in Memory of Peter C. Craigie.* Journal for the Study of the Old Testament Supplement 67. Sheffield: JSOT, 1988.

Flanagan, James W. *David's Social Drama: A Hologram of Israel's Early Iron Age.* Journal for the Study of the Old Testament Supplement 73. Sheffield: Almond, 1988.

Freedman, David Noel. "Divine Names and Titles in Early Hebrew Poetry." *Magnalia Dei: The Mighty Acts of God. Essays on the Bible and Archaeology in Memory of G. Ernest Wright.* edd. Frank Moore Cross, Werner E. Lemke, and Patrick D. Miller, Jr. Garden City: Doubleday, 1976.

Garsiel, Moshe. *The First Book of Samuel: A Literary Study of Comparative Structures, Analogies, and Parallels.* Ramat-Gan: Revivim, 1985.

Gerbrandt, Gerald Eddie. *Kingship According to the Deuteronomic History.* Society of Biblical Literature Dissertation Series 87. Atlanta: Scholars, 1986.

Gnuse, Robert Karl. *The Dream Theophany of Samuel: Its Structure in Relation to Ancient Near Eastern Dreams and Its Theological Significance.* Lanham: University Press of America, 1984.

Gordon, Robert P. "David's Rise and Saul's Demise." *Tyndale Bulletin* 31 (1960).

Gunn, David M. *The Story of King David: Genre and Interpretation.* Journal for the Study of the Old Testament Supplement 6. Sheffield: JSOT, 1978.

———. *The Fate of King Saul: An Interpretation of a Biblical Story.* Journal for the Study of the Old Testament Supplement 14. Sheffield: JSOT, 1980.

———, ed. *Narrative and Novella in Samuel: Studies by Hugo Gressmann and Other Scholars 1906–23.* Journal for the Study of the Old Testament Supplement 116. Sheffield: Almond 1991.

Howard, David M., Jr. "The Case for Kingship in the Old Testament Narrative Books and the Psalms." *Trinity Journal* 9 (1988).

———. "Review of Gerbrandt, *Kingship According to the Deuteronomistic History.*" *Westminster Theological Journal* 52 (1990).

Humphreys, W. Lee. "From Tragic Hero to Villain: A Study of the Figure of Saul and the Development of 1 Samuel." *Journal for the Study of the Old Testament* 22 (1982).

Ishida, Tomoo, ed. *Studies in the Period of David and Solomon and Other Essays.* Winona Lake: Eisenbrauns, 1982.

Jones, Gwilym H. *The Nathan Narratives.* Journal for the Study of the Old Testament Supplement 80. Sheffield: JSOT, 1990.

Lewis, Theodore J. *Cults of the Dead in Ancient Israel and Ugarit.* Harvard Semitic Monograph 39. Atlanta: Scholars, 1989.

McCarter, P. Kyle, Jr. "'Plots, True or False': The Succession Narrative as Court Apologetic." *Interpretation* 35, 4 (1981).

Martin, John A. "Studies in 1 and 2 Samuel. Part 1: The Structure of 1 and 2 Samuel." *Bibliotheca Sacra* 141, 1 (1984).

Merrill, Eugene H. *Kingdom of Priests: A History of Old Testament Israel.* Grand Rapids: Baker, 1987.

Mettinger, Tryggve N.D. *King and Messiah: The Civil and Sacral Legitimation of the Israelite Kings.* Lund: Gleerup, 1976.

Miller, Patrick D., Jr., Paul D. Hanson, and S. Dean McBride, edd. *Ancient Israelite Religion: Essays in Honor of Frank Moore Cross.* Philadelphia: Fortress, 1987.

Neufeld, Edward. "Hygiene Conditions in Ancient Israel [Iron Age]." *Biblical Archaeologist* 34, 2 (1971).

Newsome, James D., Jr., ed. *A Synoptic Harmony of Samuel, Kings, and Chronicles With Related Passages From Psalms, Isaiah, Jeremiah, and Ezra.* Grand Rapids: Baker, 1986.

Noth, Martin. *Überlieferungsgeschichtliche Studien*. 2d ed. Tübingen: Max Niemeyer, 1957. English translation: *The Deuteronomistic History*. Journal for the Study of the Old Testament Supplement 15. Sheffield: JSOT, 1981.

Polzin, Robert. *Samuel and the Deuteronomist*. San Francisco: Harper, 1989.

Preston, Thomas R. "The Heroism of Saul: Patterns of Meaning in the Narrative of the Early Kingship." *Journal for the Study of the Old Testament* 24 (1982).

Rasmussen, Carl G. *Zondervan NIV Atlas of the Bible*. Grand Rapids: Zondervan, 1989.

Rosenberg, Joel. *King and Kin: Political Allegory in the Hebrew Bible*. Bloomington: Indiana University Press, 1986.

Rost, Leonhard. *The Succession to the Throne of David*. Translated by Michael D. Rutter and David M. Gunn. Sheffield: Almond, 1982.

Segal, J.B. "Numerals in the Old Testament." *Journal of Semitic Studies* 10, 1 (1965).

Segal, M.H. "The Composition of the Books of Samuel," in *The Pentateuch: Its Composition and Its Authorship and Other Biblical Studies*. Jerusalem: Magnes, 1967.

Snaith, Norman H. *Notes on the Hebrew Text of 2 Samuel xvi–xix*. London: Epworth, 1945.

Stek, John. *The Former Prophets: A Syllabus*. Unpublished, 1985.

Sternberg, Meir. *The Poetics of Biblical Narrative: Ideological Literature and the Drama of Reading*. Bloomington: Indiana University Press, 1987.

Talmon, Shemaryahu. *King, Cult, and Calendar in Ancient Israel: Collected Studies*. Jerusalem: Magnes, 1986.

Ulrich, Eugene Charles, Jr. *The Qumran Text of Samuel and Josephus*. Harvard Semitic Monograph 19. Missoula: Scholars, 1978.

Vannoy, J. Robert. *Covenant Renewal at Gilgal*. Cherry Hill, N.J.: Mack, 1978.

Waltke, Bruce K., and M. O'Connor. *An Introduction to Biblical Hebrew Syntax*. Winona Lake: Eisenbrauns, 1990.

Watson, Wilfred. "Shared Consonants in Northwest Semitic." *Biblica* 50, 4 (1969).

Whybray, R.N. *The Succession Narrative: A Study of II Sam. 9–20 and I Kings 1 and 2*. Studies in Biblical Theology 9. London: SCM, 1968.

Wiseman, D.J., ed. *Peoples of Old Testament Times*. Oxford: Clarendon, 1973.

Yadin, Yigael. *The Art of Warfare in Biblical Lands in the Light of Archaeological Discovery*. London: Weidenfeld and Nicolson, 1963.

Youngblood, Ronald F. *The Amarna Correspondence of Rib-Haddi, Prince of Byblos* (EA 68–96). Ann Arbor: University Microfilms, 1973.

## 10. Outline

### First Samuel

I. Prelude to Monarchy in Israel (1:1–7:17)
  A. The Childhood of Samuel (1:1–4:1a)
    1. The birth and dedication of Samuel (1:1–28)
    2. The Song of Hannah (2:1–11)
    3. The wicked sons of Eli (2:12–26)
    4. The oracle against the house of Eli (2:27–36)
    5. The call of Samuel (3:1–4:1a)
  B. The Ark Narratives (4:1b–7:17)
    1. The capture of the ark (4:1b–11)
    2. The death of Eli (4:12–22)
    3. The Lord's affliction of the Philistines (5:1–12)
    4. The return of the ark (6:1–7:1)
    5. Samuel the judge (7:2–17)

II. Advent of Monarchy in Israel (8:1–15:35)
  A. The Rise of Saul (8:1–12:25)
    1. The demand for a king (8:1–22)
    2. The anointing of Saul (9:1–10:16)
    3. The choice of Saul by lot (10:17–27)
    4. The defeat of the Ammonites (11:1–11)
    5. The confirmation of Saul as king (11:12–12:25)
  B. The Decline of Saul (13:1–15:35)
    1. The rebuke of Saul (13:1–15)
    2. The struggle against the Philistines (13:16–14:23)
    3. The cursing of Jonathan (14:24–46)
    4. Further wars of Saul (14:47–52)
    5. The rejection of Saul (15:1–35)

III. Establishment of Monarchy in Israel (16:1–31:13)
  A. The Rise of David (16:1–28:2)
    1. The anointing of David (16:1–13)
    2. The arrival of David in the court of Saul (16:14–23)
    3. The death of Goliath (17:1–58)
    4. The jealousy of Saul (18:1–30)
    5. David the refugee (19:1–24)
    6. Jonathan's friendship (20:1–42)
    7. David and the priest of Nob (21:1–9)
    8. David the fugitive: Gath, Adullam, Mizpah (21:10–22:5)
    9. The slaughter of the priests of Nob (22:6–23)
    10. The rescue of Keilah (23:1–6)
    11. The pursuit of David (23:7–29)
    12. Sparing Saul's life (24:1–22)
    13. David, Nabal, and Abigail (25:1–44)
    14. Sparing Saul's life again (26:1–25)
    15. Achish the Philistine (27:1–28:2)
  B. The End of the Reign of Saul (28:3–31:13)
    1. Saul and the medium at Endor (28:3–25)

2. The dismissal of David (29:1–11)
3. The defeat of the Amalekites (30:1–31)
4. The death of Saul and Jonathan (31:1–13)

## Second Samuel

I. Consolidation of Monarchy in Israel (1:1–20:26)
  A. David's Accession to Kingship Over Judah (1:1–3:5)
    1. The death of Saul and Jonathan (1:1–16)
    2. David's lament for Saul and Jonathan (1:17–27)
    3. David anointed king over Judah (2:1–7)
    4. War between Saul's house and David's house (2:8–3:1)
    5. Sons born to David in Hebron (3:2–5)
  B. David's Accession to Kingship Over Israel (3:6–5:16)
    1. Abner's defection to David (3:6–21)
    2. The murder of Abner (3:22–39)
    3. The murder of Ish-Bosheth (4:1–12)
    4. David anointed king over Israel (5:1–5)
    5. David's conquest of Jerusalem (5:6–12)
    6. Children born to David in Jerusalem (5:13–16)
  C. David's Powerful Reign (5:17–8:18)
    1. The Philistines defeated (5:17–25)
    2. The ark brought to Jerusalem (6:1–23)
    3. The Lord's covenant with David (7:1–17)
    4. David's prayer to the Lord (7:18–29)
    5. David's enemies defeated (8:1–14)
    6. David's officials (8:15–18)
  D. David's Court History (9:1–20:26)
    1. Kindness to Mephibosheth (9:1–13)
    2. The Ammonites defeated (10:1–19)
    3. David's sin against Bathsheba (11:1–5)
    4. The murder of Uriah (11:6–27)
    5. Nathan's rebuke (12:1–25)
    6. The Ammonites defeated (12:26–31)
    7. Amnon's sin against Tamar (13:1–22)
    8. The murder of Amnon (13:23–39)
    9. The wise woman of Tekoa (14:1–20)
    10. Absalom's return to Jerusalem (14:21–33)
    11. Absalom's conspiracy (15:1–12)
    12. David's flight (15:13–37)
    13. Kindness to Ziba (16:1–4)
    14. Shimei's curse (16:5–14)
    15. Ahithophel's advice (16:15–17:29)
    16. Absalom's death (18:1–18)
    17. David's mourning for Absalom (18:19–19:8)
    18. David's return to Jerusalem (19:9–43)
    19. Sheba's rebellion (20:1–22)
    20. David's officials (20:23–26)

- II. Epilogue (21:1–24:25)
  - A. The Lord's Wrath Against Israel (21:1–14)
  - B. David's Heroes (21:15–22)
  - C. David's Song of Praise (22:1–51)
  - D. David's Last Words (23:1–7)
  - E. David's Mighty Men (23:8–39)
  - F. The Lord's Wrath Against Israel (24:1–25)

# Text and Exposition

## I. Prelude to Monarchy in Israel (1:1–7:17)

The theme of the books of Samuel is the beginning of Israel's monarchy in the eleventh century B.C. The LXX translators recognized this and titled the books *Basileiōn* ("Concerning Kingdoms"), a title that includes the books of the Kings. First Samuel introduces us to Israel's last two judges (Eli, a failure; Samuel, a success) and first two kings (Saul, a failure; David, a success).

### A. *The Childhood of Samuel (1:1–4:1a)*

Appropriately the story of Israel's monarchy begins with an account of the early life of Samuel: prophet, priest, judge, and, most significantly, king-maker. God chose Samuel to anoint both Saul and David, Israel's first two kings. Each was to be the "leader" (*nāgîḏ*) over his people (10:1; 13:14; 16:13).

#### 1. *The birth and dedication of Samuel*

1:1–28

1 There was a certain man from Ramathaim, a Zuphite from the hill
country of Ephraim, whose name was Elkanah son of Jeroham, the son
of Elihu, the son of Tohu, the son of Zuph, an Ephraimite. 2 He had two
wives; one was called Hannah and the other Peninnah. Peninnah had
children, but Hannah had none.
3 Year after year this man went up from his town to worship and
sacrifice to the LORD Almighty at Shiloh, where Hophni and Phinehas,
the two sons of Eli, were priests of the LORD. 4 Whenever the day came
for Elkanah to sacrifice, he would give portions of the meat to his wife
Peninnah and to all her sons and daughters. 5 But to Hannah he gave a
double portion because he loved her, and the LORD had closed her
womb. 6 And because the LORD had closed her womb, her rival kept
provoking her in order to irritate her. 7 This went on year after year.
Whenever Hannah went up to the house of the LORD, her rival provoked
her till she wept and would not eat. 8 Elkanah her husband would say to
her, "Hannah, why are you weeping? Why don't you eat? Why are you
downhearted? Don't I mean more to you than ten sons?"
9 Once when they had finished eating and drinking in Shiloh, Hannah
stood up. Now Eli the priest was sitting on a chair by the doorpost of the
LORD's temple. 10 In bitterness of soul Hannah wept much and prayed to
the LORD. 11 And she made a vow, saying, "O LORD Almighty, if you will
only look upon your servant's misery and remember me, and not forget
your servant but give her a son, then I will give him to the LORD for all the
days of his life, and no razor will ever be used on his head."
12 As she kept on praying to the LORD, Eli observed her mouth.
13 Hannah was praying in her heart, and her lips were moving but her
voice was not heard. Eli thought she was drunk 14 and said to her, "How
long will you keep on getting drunk? Get rid of your wine."
15 "Not so, my lord," Hannah replied, "I am a woman who is deeply
troubled. I have not been drinking wine or beer; I was pouring out my
soul to the LORD. 16 Do not take your servant for a wicked woman; I have
been praying here out of my great anguish and grief."
17 Eli answered, "Go in peace, and may the God of Israel grant you
what you have asked of him."

18She said, "May your servant find favor in your eyes." Then she went
her way and ate something, and her face was no longer downcast.
19Early the next morning they arose and worshiped before the LORD
and then went back to their home at Ramah. Elkanah lay with Hannah
his wife, and the LORD remembered her. 20So in the course of time
Hannah conceived and gave birth to a son. She named him Samuel,
saying, "Because I asked the LORD for him."
21When the man Elkanah went up with all his family to offer the
annual sacrifice to the LORD and to fulfill his vow, 22Hannah did not go.
She said to her husband, "After the boy is weaned, I will take him and
present him before the LORD, and he will live there always."
23"Do what seems best to you," Elkanah her husband told her. "Stay
here until you have weaned him; only may the LORD make good his
word." So the woman stayed at home and nursed her son until she had
weaned him.
24After he was weaned, she took the boy with her, young as he was,
along with a three-year-old bull, an ephah of flour and a skin of wine,
and brought him to the house of the LORD at Shiloh. 25When they had
slaughtered the bull, they brought the boy to Eli, 26and she said to him,
"As surely as you live, my lord, I am the woman who stood here beside
you praying to the LORD. 27I prayed for this child, and the LORD has
granted me what I asked of him. 28So now I give him to the LORD. For his
whole life he will be given over to the LORD." And he worshiped the LORD
there.

**1–2** In the MT the beginning of the description of Samuel's father, Elkanah, is identical to that of Samson's father, Manoah, in Judges 13:2. Each description begins with the statement "There was a certain man," followed by the name of his hometown, his own name, the tribe he comes from or is living with, and a reference to his marital status. The strong similarity between the two passages is probably intentional and highlights the dedication of both Samson and Samuel as Nazirites to the Lord from birth (see below).

The word "Ramathaim"—the name of the town of Samuel's birth, official residence, and burial—is dual in form and appears to mean "Two Heights." It is probably not intended as a grammatical dual, however, but rather possesses locative force (cf. Aharoni, *Land of the Bible*, p. 120). Elsewhere the town is called simply Ramah (1:19; 2:11; 7:17; et al.). Of the several Israelite towns bearing that name, Ramah ("height") of Ephraim (mentioned in the Bible more often than any other Ramah) is perhaps to be identified with the NT Arimathea (Matt 27:57; John 19:38) and the modern Rentis, sixteen miles east of Joppa on the west slope of the hill country of Ephraim.

Samuel's Ramah is probably not to be equated with the Ramah of Joshua 18:25, since the latter is specifically located in the tribal territory of Benjamin (Josh 18:21, 28). Nebi Samwil (Arabic for "Prophet Samuel"), visible from the outskirts of Jerusalem high on the horizon to the northwest, is the traditional site of Samuel's tomb; but there is no certain basis for this identification.

Samuel's father is called a Zuphite, doubtless because of his descent from Zuph (v.1). The same family line (with minor variations) is recorded twice in 1 Chronicles 6 (vv.26–27, 34–35 [in reverse order]). The Chronicles genealogies identify Samuel as a member of the Kohathite branch of the tribe of Levi and an ancestor of tabernacle and temple musicians (1 Chron 6:16, 22, 31–33). The reference to Samuel's father as an Ephraimite, then, relates to the territory where he lived rather than to his tribal origin. Allotted no patrimony of their own, the Levites lived among the other tribes (see Josh 21:20–22, where, however, Ramah is not specifically mentioned as a Levitical town).

"Elkanah" was a popular name in ancient Israel, shared by at least five different OT men (two of whom were Samuel's father's ancestors; see 1 Chron 6:22–27). The name means "God has created [a son]"—tantalizingly prophetic of what was soon to occur in Hannah's womb.

Elkanah must have been a man of some means, for he is the only commoner in the books of Samuel and Kings specifically mentioned as having more than one wife. Although polygamy was not God's intention for mankind (cf. the sing. "wife" and "one flesh" in Gen 2:24; cf. Mal 2:15), having "two wives" (v.2) accords with the polygamous culture of the ancient world (cf. de Vaux, AIs, pp. 24–26). Lamech, the seventh descendant in the line of Cain, is the first-mentioned polygamist in the Bible (Gen 4:19). Although polygamy is never explicitly condemned in Scripture, its complications and unsavory results are everywhere apparent.

Hannah (*ḥannāh,* lit., "Grace") initially has pride of place in v.2, probably because she was Elkanah's favorite. Later in the same verse, however, Peninnah (*p^eninnāh,* lit., "Ruby") is mentioned first, no doubt because she was a prolific childbearer (cf. v.4, "all her sons and daughters"). Barrenness in ancient times was the ultimate tragedy for a married woman, since her husband's hopes and dreams depended on her providing him with a son to perpetuate his name and inherit his estate (cf. Gen 11:30; 15:2–4; 16:1–2; 17:15–16; 21:1–2; 25:5).

**3–8** Three times a year all Israelite men were required to be at the central or most important sanctuary to offer sacrifices in observance of the main religious festivals (Exod 34:23; Deut 12:5–7; see also Luke 2:41). Elkanah was no exception (vv.3, 21; 2:19). For some time Shiloh (modern Seilun, sixteen miles east of Ramah) had been the location of the tabernacle and the ark of the covenant (4:3–4; Josh 18:1; Judg 18:31). Eli ("Exalted is [the Lord]"), the priest at Shiloh (v.9; 2:11) and a judge in Israel (4:18; cf. NIV mg.), was descended from Aaron's son Ithamar, if the Ahimelech who was Eli's great-grandson and successor (14:3; 22:20) is the one mentioned in 1 Chronicles 24:3. Each of Eli's two reprobate sons—unfortunately also priests—had an Egyptian name: Hophni ("Tadpole") and Phinehas ("The Nubian"). The latter should not be confused with his earlier, godly namesake, a son of Aaron's son Eleazar (Exod 6:25; Num 25:10).

The festival in view here is probably the Feast of Tabernacles (as also in Judg 21:19–21), celebrated in the fall. Sacrifices were offered to the "the LORD Almighty" (v.3; *YHWH ṣ^eḇā'ôṯ,* lit., "the LORD of hosts"). This is the first OT occurrence of "Almighty/hosts" being added to a divine name. One connotation of the title is that he is "the God of the armies of Israel" (17:45; in this case the Heb. word for "armies" is different from that for "hosts"). But since "hosts" can mean not only human armies (Exod 7:4, "divisions") but also celestial bodies (Deut 4:19, "array") or heavenly creatures (Josh 5:14), the NIV everywhere translates the word as "Almighty" in the sense of "he who is sovereign over all the 'hosts' (powers) in heaven and on earth, especially over the 'hosts' (armies) of Israel" (NIV preface, p. ix). It is noteworthy that this majestic name for God, appearing at the inception of the Israelite monarchy, describes him in a way that is much more royal than military (cf. J.P. Ross, "Jahweh *Ṣ^eḇā'ôṯ* in Samuel and Psalms," VetTest 17, 1 [1967]: 76–92).

Festival celebrations were times of rejoicing in God's blessings, especially that of a bountiful harvest. Elkanah distributed portions of sacrificial meat (cf. Exod 29:26; Lev

7:33; 8:29) to Peninnah and her children, since family members shared in certain of the sacrificial offerings brought to the Lord (cf. Deut 12:17–18; 16:13–14). Elkanah provided Hannah with a double portion because of his love for her. He perhaps also knew, along with the narrator, that his wife's barrenness was by divine providence (vv.5–6; cf. Gen 15:3; 16:2; 20:18; 30:2).

Hannah's sterility likely prompted Elkanah to take Peninnah as his second wife (cf. the actions of Sarai, Gen 16:2; Rachel, 30:3; and Leah, 30:9). Peninnah thus became Hannah's "rival" (*ṣārāh,* v.6; *ṣar* ["adversary," "enemy"] was used in this sense as early as the time of Moses [Lev 18:18] and as late as the intertestamental period [Ecclus 37:11]). She "kept provoking" (v.6) Hannah, culminating in "grief" (v.16; the repetition of the root *k's* underscores the connection). Peninnah intended to "irritate" (*rā'am,* lit., to "thunder against") Hannah (cf. 2:10, where Hannah declares that the Lord will "thunder against" [*rā'am*] all who oppose him, doubtless including Peninnah). The devout Hannah, in the spirit of Deuteronomy 32:35, is content to allow the Lord to avenge the wrong committed against her (cf. David's statement in 2 Sam 3:39).

Elkanah's family "went up" (in the technical sense of journeying to a sacred place; cf. v.3; Exod 34:24) yearly to the "house of the LORD" (v.7). This term refers to the tabernacle but apparently also includes more permanent auxiliary structures that had doors (3:15) and therefore doorposts (v.9). These sacred buildings are called "the LORD's temple" (cf. 3:3). Hannah's rival took special delight in using the annual pilgrimage to Shiloh as an occasion for continued provocation, badgering Hannah to the point of tears.

Elkanah, mindful of Hannah's grief, asked her, "Why are you downhearted?" (v.8). More literally the question is, "Why is your heart bad?" The only other precise OT parallel for this phrase is Deuteronomy 15:10: "Do so without a grudging heart" (lit., "May your heart not be bad when you do so!" [i.e., when you give generously to the Lord]). To do something "with a bad heart" means to do it resentfully (or grudgingly; so NIV on Deut 15:10). Thus Elkanah is not so much asking Hannah why her heart is sad ("Why are you downhearted?") but why her heart is bad ("Why are you resentful?"). Are you angry or full of spite because you do not have children? "Don't I"—your husband, who loves you very much—"mean more to you than ten sons?" ("ten," like seven, represents completeness or fullness; viz., the Ten Commandments; cf. Exod 26:1, 16; 34:28; et al.; cf. also 2:5; Ruth 4:15; cf. Edward F. Campbell, Jr., *Ruth,* AB 7 [Garden City: Doubleday, 1975], p. 164; M.H. Pope, IDB [K-Q], 3:565–66).

**9–11** Hannah's misery peaked at Shiloh during an annual pilgrimage. Eli, "the LORD's priest in Shiloh" (14:3), the chief religious official, was sitting on "a chair" (lit., "the chair," in the sense of "his chair"; cf. 4:13, 18; cf. also Judg 3:20) near the worship complex (which included the tabernacle; cf. NIV mg.). The earlier Sumero-Akkadian cognate of the word translated "temple" means "palace" and thus reminds us that the tabernacle and temple in the Israelite theocracy were residences symbolically inhabited by the Divine King.

Hannah's sadness and "bitterness of soul" (v.10, a favorite concept of Job: see 3:20; 7:11; 10:1; 21:25; see also "discontented" in 1 Sam 22:2) led her to pray and make a vow to the Lord. On behalf of her hoped-for son, she made "a special vow, a vow of separation to the LORD" (Num 6:2). The Nazirite vow included (1) abstaining from the use of grapes in any form, (2) not shaving the hair on one's head, and (3) avoiding dead bodies (Num 6:3–7). Although the term "Nazirite" is absent in 1 Samuel, it is surely presupposed. The text states that "no razor will ever be used on his head" (v.11), an expression used elsewhere only of the Nazirite Samson (Judg 13:5; 16:17; see also Num 6:5, which, however, renders a different Heb. phrase). The LXX inserts "and he will not drink wine or any intoxicating beverage."

A DSS fragment 4QSam[a] states at the end of v.22: "[I g]ave him (to be) a Nazirite forever all the days of [his life]" (for a photograph of the Heb. text, see Frank M. Cross, Jr., "A New Qumran Biblical Fragment Related to the Original Hebrew Underlying the Septuagint," BASOR 132 [1953]: 17; cf. also Cross's transcription on p. 18 and in context on p. 26, col. I, lines 3–4). Samuel is described in the Apocrypha as "a Nazirite of the LORD in the prophetic office" (Ecclus 46:13 Heb. text). Josephus states that Samuel drank only water (Antiq. V, 347 [x.3]). The Mishnah argues that Samuel was indeed a Nazirite (*Nazir* 9.5). The Nazirite vow was not usually taken by proxy and was rarely lifelong; the only other biblical parallels to Samuel's Naziriteship are Samson (Judg 13:5) and perhaps John the Baptist (Luke 1:15).

Hannah humbly calls herself "your servant" (v.11), a submissive way of referring to oneself in the presence of a superior in ancient Near Eastern culture (cf. v.16; 3:9–10). Her request that God "look upon [her] misery" recalls Leah's grateful response after the birth of her firstborn son, Reuben (Gen 29:32; see NIV mg.). David later uses the same expression in a time of crisis (2 Sam 16:12). Hannah's plea to the Lord to "remember" her was soon answered (v.19). God's remembrance is not a matter of recalling to mind but of paying special attention to or lavishing special care on one (cf. Ps 8:4, where the same Heb. verb is rendered "are mindful of" in parallelism with "care for"). Hannah recognizes that children are always a gift of God, the Great Enabler of conception and childbirth (cf. Ruth 4:13). If he will "give" her a son, in gratitude she will "give" him back to the Lord—which in a broader sense was a covenant requirement for every Israelite mother (Exod 22:29).

**12–18** Hannah's prayer reveals her conscious, intimate relationship with God. She prayed "to" (*lip̱nê,* lit., "in the presence of"; cf. 1 Kings 8:28 ["in your presence"]) the Lord (v.12); she prayed "in her heart" (v.13, i.e., to herself; cf. Abraham's servant in Gen 24:45); and she prayed silently. Eli, observing the scene, misunderstood Hannah's actions. Prayer in the ancient world was almost always audible (cf. Pss 3:4; 4:1; 6:9 [and passim in the Psalms, the prayerbook of ancient Israel]; Dan 6:10–11), and drunkenness was not an uncommon accompaniment of festal occasions (including esp. the Feast of Tabernacles [cf. de Vaux, AIs, p. 496] and perhaps also Pentecost, Acts 2:13).

Eli—who, after all, was the chief priest at Shiloh—can hardly be excused for his spiritual insensitivity. He should have realized that Hannah's moving lips signified earnest prayer rather than intoxicated mumbling. He therefore mistakenly rebukes her, "How long will you make a drunken spectacle of yourself?" (v.14, pers. tr.).

Hannah justly protests that she has been drinking neither wine nor beer—which, when imbibed in sufficient quantities, produce drunkenness (Isa 28:7). Far from pouring herself too many drinks, she had been "pouring out [her] soul to the LORD" (v.15), a vivid idiom for praying earnestly (cf. Pss 42:4; 62:8; Lam 2:19). She declares herself to be "deeply troubled" (*qᵉšaṯ-rûᵃḥ,* lit., "burdened in spirit"; cf. Job 7:11); and under no circumstances does she want Eli to mistake her for a "wicked woman" (*baṯ-bᵉlîyāʿal,* lit., "daughter of worthlessness," v.16; cf. the description of Hophni and Phinehas as "wicked men"—*benê-beliyā'al,* lit., "sons of worthlessness"—in 2:12).

Satisfied with Hannah's explanation, Eli tells her to "go in peace" (v.17, a common biblical expression of farewell; cf. 25:35; Mark 5:34). Eli's hope that God would grant Hannah's request is soon fulfilled in the birth of Samuel (v.27; cf. 2:20). Godly Hannah, God's willing servant (v.18; cf. Deut 10:12; Mic 6:8), would receive the desire of her heart from God's gracious hand. Being assured by Eli's response, she breaks her self-imposed fast, and her face is "no longer downcast" (*lō'-lāh 'ôd;* lit., "no longer to her [as it had been previously]").

**19–20** The next day Elkanah's family worshiped the Lord, an experience with special meaning for Hannah this time. After their return from Shiloh to Ramah, Elkanah "lay with" (*wayyēda',* lit., "and he knew," a common OT euphemism for sexual intimacy; cf. Gen 4:1, 17, 25) Hannah. The Lord, as she had earnestly prayed (v.11), "remembered her" (v.19; see comment on v.11)—just as he had remembered her ancestor Rachel (Gen 30:22)—by enabling her to bear a son. Hannah called him Samuel (lit., "Name of God") and then punned on the name (a common ancient practice; cf. NIV mg. at Gen 11:9; Exod 2:10) by saying that she had "asked" the Lord for him (interestingly, all three consonants in Heb. *š'l,* "ask," are found in the same order in *šmw'l,* "Samuel").

**21–23** After Samuel was born, Elkanah continued his custom of taking his family with him annually to Shiloh to sacrifice to the Lord (1:3; 2:19). On at least one occasion he had the additional purpose of fulfilling a "vow" (v.21), perhaps in support of Hannah's earlier vow (v.11)—although it was not unusual for sacrifice and vow to accompany each other (Deut 12:11). In any case, Hannah decided not to make the trip to Shiloh this time (v.22). She preferred to wait until Samuel was weaned. Then she could leave him there to serve the Lord at the tabernacle for the rest of his life, as she had promised.

In the ancient world a child was breast-fed for two or three years (cf. 2 Macc 7:27) before it was considered old enough to spend extended periods of time away from home. After Samuel's weaning, Hannah intended to "present him before the LORD" (v.22; see Notes). Elkanah agreed with his wife's desire to follow through with her vow (v.23).

**24–28** The big day finally arrived, and Hannah was ready. We are not told whether the family waited for an official annual festival. For the trip from Ramah to Shiloh, they took ample provisions with them (v.24). The three-year-old bull, in the prime of life, was doubtless meant to be sacrificed to the Lord (v.25). The purpose of the flour and wine, however, remains obscure. The Hebrew word for "flour" used here (*qemaḥ*) occurs in a sacrificial context only once in the OT—and that in a special situation unaccompanied by the sacrifice of an animal (Num 5:15). It is possible, therefore, that the flour here was to be baked into loaves or cakes of unleavened bread (cf. 28:24; Judg 6:19) and used as food, along with the wine ("skin[s] of wine" always refers only to food: 10:3; 25:18; 2 Sam 16:1; Jer 13:12).

When "they" (doubtless the official slaughterers at the tabernacle; the Heb. for "they had slaughtered the bull" should be construed as an impersonal passive; viz., "the bull had been slaughtered") had sacrificed the bull, "they" (in this case, Hannah and Elkanah) brought Samuel before Eli the priest (v.25). In addressing Eli, Hannah used a common oath formula: "As surely as you live" (*ḥê napšᵉkā*, lit., "By the life of your soul" = "By your life," v.26; cf. 20:3; see also 17:55; 25:26; 2 Sam 11:11; 14:19). She thus solemnly affirms that she is indeed the same woman he first had met a few years earlier and that the boy Samuel, given in answer to her prayers, is now to be given back to the Lord for the rest of his life. Her words to Eli in v.27 echo his to her in v.17, the main difference being that Eli referred to Hannah's benefactor as "the God of Israel" while she used his more intimate, covenant name: "the LORD." Eli responded to Hannah's brief remarks by worshiping the God whom they both served (v.28).

## Notes

---

**1** צוֹפִים (*ṣôp̱îm*) is interpreted by the NIV as "Zuphite" (*ṣûp̱î*) with reference to Elkanah's descent from a man named Zuph. The *m* on *ṣôp̱îm* must thus be understood either (1) as dittography (from the following word, which in Heb. begins with *m*) or (2) as an example of the so-called enclitic *m*, which is not infrequently appended to words in several Semitic languages, including Hebrew. The NIV margin suggests the less plausible (because grammatically difficult) reading "Ramathaim Zuphim," understanding the phrase as a compound proper name that would relate the town of Ramah to the "district of Zuph" (1 Sam 9:5). For additional details concerning the location of Ramah/Ramathaim, see J. Albright, "Ramah," *Biblical Illustrator* 9, 4 (1983): 23–26; R.A. Spencer, "Arimathea," *Biblical Illustrator* 10, 3 (1984): 77–78.

קָנָה (*qānāh*), the verbal root underlying the name Elkanah, occurs in the OT as early as Gen 4:1 ("brought forth"), where it puns on the name "Cain," קַיִן (*qayin*). The verb also appears in Gen 14:19, 22, where "God Most High" (*'ēl 'elyôn*) is called "Creator [קֹנֵה, *qōnēh*] of heaven and earth." Similar titles were also frequently applied to El, the chief Canaanite deity, in ancient times (for details cf. M.H. Pope, *El in the Ugaritic Texts*, VetTest suppl. 2 [Leiden: Brill, 1955], pp. 50–54).

אֶלְקָנָה (*'elqānāh*, "Elkanah") appears on an unpublished seal decorated with the figure of an ibex; see Nahman Avigad, *Ancient Israelite Religion: Essays in Honor of Frank Moore Cross*, edd. P.D. Miller, Jr., P.D. Hanson, and S.D. McBride (Philadelphia: Fortress, 1987), fig. 4, p. 200. Two other seals mentioned by Avigad and containing the same verbal root are pertinent here: (1) *qnyw*, "Yahweh Has Created"; and especially (2) *mqnyw*, "The Creation of Yahweh" (ibid., pp. 197–98). The latter name is the same as that of Mikneiah (1 Chron 15:18), who, like Elkanah's descendants, was a tabernacle/temple musician (1 Chron 15:21). It has long been recognized (BDB, pp. 888–89) that the root *qny* in various Semitic languages often means "create," especially when a deity is its subject; cf. KB, p. 843; N. Habel, "'Yahweh, Maker of Heaven and Earth': A Study in Tradition Criticism," JBL 91 (1972): 321–37; U. Cassuto, *Biblical and Oriental Studies* (Jerusalem: Magnes, 1975), 2:55; P.D. Miller, Jr., "El, the Creator of Earth," BASOR 239 (1980): 43–46; Joseph Aistleitner, *Wörterbuch der Ugaritischen Sprache* (Berlin: Akademie, 1963), p. 229. Contrast, however, B. Vawter, "Yahweh: Lord of the Heavens and the Earth," CBQ 48 (1968): 461–67.

**2** The names "Hannah" and "Peninnah" appear only in the first two chapters of 1 Samuel in the OT. A Hebrew seal from the Lachish area dating to the period of 725–675 B.C., however, displays the name Hannah (*ḥnh*); cf. J.R. Bartlett, "The Seal of *Ḥnh* From the Neighbourhood of *Tell ed-Duweir*," PEQ 108 (1976): 59–60. In the NT a prophetess named Hannah is mentioned in Luke 2:36. Unfortunately the KJV spelling "Anna" in that verse has become traditional; the only recent EVV that spell the name correctly (and therefore maintain continuity with the OT counterpart) are those of Lamsa, Moffatt, and Smith-Goodspeed (cf. NASB mg.).

The name "Peninnah" may be related to a similar Arabic word meaning "woman with luxuriant hair" (cf. KB, 2:768). But it is perhaps better to assume it to be the feminine singular form of the masculine plural פְּנִינִים (*p*[e]*nînîm*), which means something like "coral(s)" or "rubies." The latter is the consistent translation of the NIV; cf. Job 28:18; Prov 3:15; 8:11; 20:15; 31:10; Lam 4:7. With the exception of Prov 20:15, all the other texts describe something or someone as being better than rubies. Similarly, Hannah ("Grace")—at least in Elkanah's eyes—was better than Peninnah ("Ruby"; cf. 1 Sam 1:5).

**5** Although clearly a dual noun, אַפָּיִם (*'appāyim*, "double") elsewhere always means either "face" ("nose," "nostril" in the sing.) or "anger." On the basis of LXX evidence, it is often emended to אֶפֶס (*'epes*) and, combined with the following כִּי (*kî*), translated as "nevertheless," "although" (for details and the resulting understanding of v.5, cf. S.R. Driver, *Notes on the Books of Samuel*, p. 8). David Aberbach retains the consonantal MT (*'pym*) but interprets it as *pym* (a measure of weight; see comment on 13:21) prefixed by prosthetic *aleph* and thus interprets the gift Elkanah gave to Hannah as "one portion, a *pim* in value" ("מנה אחת אפים [1 Sam. I 5]: A New Interpretation," VetTest 24, 3 [1974]: 350–53). Ferdinand Deist successfully criticizes Aberbach, but his own proposal—to emend the already emended *'epes* to *'*[a]*bûs(āh)* ("fattened") and to understand the resulting phrase as "one portion (of) fattened (meat)" but to translate it as "one selected portion" on the basis of a targum on Samuel—heaps conjecture on conjecture and therefore fares no better ("*'Appayim* [1 Sam. I 5] < **pym*?" VetTest 27, 2 [1977]: 205–9).

Preferable is the suggestion of Barthélemy et al., who state that the literal meaning of *'appāyim* ("face") designates Hannah's portion as one that "was particularly large and honourable." They would therefore translate the phrase as "a worthy portion" (2:146). But the NIV's "double" remains the best rendering of *'appāyim*. The word is after all a dual—"two nostrils," "two sides of the face"—and in this context would mean simply "two times." I have argued elsewhere that "overwhelmingly in Hebrew a part of the body is used to represent 'time' in this sense" (Youngblood, *The Amarna Correspondence*, p. 17). The entire phrase in v.5 should thus be translated "one portion two times," hence "a double portion."

**9** The word translated "doorpost," מְזוּזָה (*m*[e]*zûzāh*), is rendered "doorframe" in Exod 12:7; Deut 6:9; 11:20. The last two of these passages is the basis for the Jewish tradition of placing a small wooden, metal, or glass case, called a *mezuzah*, about five feet from the floor to the right of the entrance on the doorframe of the home. Inside the *mezuzah* is a tiny parchment on which is written the words of Deut 6:4–9 (the *Shema*, Judaism's confession of faith, proclaiming God's unity); see Deut 11:13–21. On entering his home, the devout Jew touches the *mezuzah* and is thereby reminded of his belief in the sanctity of the house in which he lives.

**15** שֵׁכָר (*šēkār*) is the etymological and semantic equivalent of the Akkadian *šikaru* ("beer"). The Hebrew word was rendered almost exclusively as "strong drink" in earlier EVV; the NIV, however, translates the word correctly as "beer" or "fermented drink" throughout. For a thorough treatment of the Akkadian materials, see especially L.F. Hartman and A.L. Oppenheim, "On Beer and Brewing Techniques in Ancient Mesopotamia," JAOS suppl. 10 (Baltimore: Johns Hopkins, 1950).

**16** The etymology of בְּלִיַּעַל (*b*[e]*lîya'al*), translated here as "wicked," has long been disputed. Modern scholars tend to derive it from the root *bl'* ("to swallow"), referring to personified Death or Sheol as the Great Swallower (e.g., Prov 1:12); cf. D. Winton Thomas, *Biblical and Patristic Studies*, edd. J.N. Birdsall and R.W. Thomson (New York: Herder, 1963), pp. 11–19; Mitchell Dahood, *Psalms I* (Garden City: Doubleday, 1965), p. 105, n. 5. The most transparent etymology is *b*[e]*lî* + *ya'al*, "without value," "worthless(ness)" (so BDB, p. 116). Another attractive possibility, however, is to understand the second element in the word, *y'l*, as an imperfect/jussive form of the root *'ly* ("to go/come up") and to translate "[the place from which] none comes up," a euphemism for Sheol expressing a motif not unknown in the OT (cf. Job 7:9; 10:21; 16:22; cf. Cross and Freedman, "A Royal Song of Thanksgiving," p. 22, n. 16). *Ben belîya'al* would then mean "son of perdition," "hellion." In any case, although its etymology remains uncertain, the word came into the NT as Belial, a proper name virtually synonymous with Satan, the very personification of wickedness (2 Cor 6:15).

**20** The NIV margin on the name Samuel, although superficially true, has little if anything to do with the argument of the text itself. שמע (*šm'*, "hear") is found only once in 1 Samuel 1 (v.13, "heard"), but not in connection with the birth, naming, or dedication of the child. On the other hand, שאל (*š'l*, "ask") is found seven times in 1 Sam 1 (v.17, "request" [NIV, "what"]; v.17, "asked"; v.20, "asked"; v.27, "request" [NIV, "what"]; v.27, "asked"; v.28, "give"; v.28, "given")—each time in connection with the birth, naming, or dedication of the child. Although שְׁמוּאֵל (*šemû'ēl*) means "Name of God" on the analogy of other proper nouns like Penuel or Peniel ("Face of God," cf. Gen 32:30–31; cf. NIV mg.), Reuel ("Friend of God," Exod 2:18), and Jeruel (perhaps "Foundation of God," 2 Chron 20:16), the narrator chose to pun on the name by using the verb *š'l* ("ask") rather than to connect it in any way with the verb *šm'* ("hear") or the noun *šm* ("name").

Those scholars (e.g., Ackroyd [*First Book of Samuel*], Mauchline, McCarter [*I Samuel*]) who see in the frequent use of *š'l* in 1 Sam 1 an attempt to explain the origin of the name Saul (the last of the seven occurrences—*šā'ûl*, "given," in v.28—is precisely the Heb. spelling of "Saul") would do better to reckon with the likelihood that the continued association of the root of Saul's name, not with Saul but with Samuel, is the narrator's subtle way of reminding us that throughout most of Saul's reign, the Lord's will for his people was channeled through Samuel the king-maker, not Saul the king, who soon demonstrated his inability to rule over Israel under God. Only the "Name of God"—that is, the Divine Presence—was to be sovereign over his people. This fact diminishes W.J. Martin's suggestive proposal that the name Samuel "was probably part of a sentence spoken by Hannah at his birth. The full sentence would have been in some such form as: 'I asked for him *a godly name*' " (NBD, p. 1134). The word "Name" in "Name of God" refers to God's name, not Samuel's.

**22** וְנִרְאָה אֶת־פְּנֵי יהוה (*wenir'āh 'et-pene YHWH*, lit., "and he will appear before the LORD") is a technical expression used in reference to the requirement of all male Israelites to attend the three annual religious festivals at the central sanctuary (cf. Exod 34:23–24; Deut 16:16; 31:11).

**23** The NIV margin reads "your" (instead of "his") from the DSS and the LXX (the Syr. reading probably derives from the LXX). More specifically, 4QSam[a] and the LXX read "what goes forth from your mouth" instead of the MT's "his word." Since no divine word has been mentioned thus far in 1 Sam, 4QSam[a] (dutifully followed by the LXX) was probably trying to smooth out a difficulty by equating the word with Hannah's vow. Earlier commentators (e.g., KD) resolved the problem by referring the divine word to the statement of Eli in v.17, who presumably was speaking on God's behalf. There, however, the birth of Samuel is in view—and by v.23 Samuel has already been born (v.20). At the same time, why would a scribe change an original "your (word)" to "his (word)"? It seems best to assume an earlier word of the Lord not recorded in our text. Interestingly, the JB read "your" in v.23, but the New JB (commendably) reverts to the MT's "his."

**24** For over a century most commentators have read פר משלש (*pr mšlš*, "a three-year-old bull") with the LXX (cf. also Gen 15:9) instead of the MT's פר[י]ם שלשה (*pr[y]m šlšh*, "three bulls"), assuming that the *m* on *pr[y]m* was misplaced. The LXX reading has now been confirmed by 4QSam[a]: *[pr bn] bqr mšlš*. For parallel usage at Nuzi, where (as here and in Gen 15:9) the animal's age specifies maturity for purposes of sacrifice, see E.A. Speiser, "The Nuzi Tablets Solve a Puzzle in the Books of Samuel," BASOR 72 (1938): 15–17.

**27–28** Near the end of 1 Samuel 1, the narrator clusters four of the seven times he uses the root שאל (*š'l*, "ask") as a pun on the name "Samuel" (שמואל, *šmw'l*). Twice in v.27 it has its usual meaning ("a/the request," translated as "what" and "asked" in the NIV). Twice in v.28, however, it bears the derived meaning "allow to ask," "lend on request," hence "give." The son Hannah requested God gave, and she gratefully gives her gift back to the Giver.

---

## 2. *The Song of Hannah*

### 2:1–11

1 Then Hannah prayed and said:

"My heart rejoices in the Lord;
in the Lord my horn is lifted high.
My mouth boasts over my enemies,
for I delight in your deliverance.

2 "There is no one holy like the Lord;
there is no one besides you;
there is no Rock like our God.

3 "Do not keep talking so proudly
or let your mouth speak such arrogance,
for the Lord is a God who knows,
and by him deeds are weighed.

4 "The bows of the warriors are broken,
but those who stumbled are armed with strength.
5 Those who were full hire themselves out for food,
but those who were hungry hunger no more.
She who was barren has borne seven children,
but she who has had many sons pines away.

6 "The Lord brings death and makes alive;
he brings down to the grave and raises up.
7 The Lord sends poverty and wealth;
he humbles and he exalts.
8 He raises the poor from the dust
and lifts the needy from the ash heap;
he seats them with princes
and has them inherit a throne of honor.

"For the foundations of the earth are the Lord's;
upon them he has set the world.
9 He will guard the feet of his saints,
but the wicked will be silenced in darkness.

"It is not by strength that one prevails;
10 those who oppose the Lord will be shattered.
He will thunder against them from heaven;
the Lord will judge the ends of the earth.

"He will give strength to his king
and exalt the horn of his anointed."

11 Then Elkanah went home to Ramah, but the boy ministered before the Lord under Eli the priest.

**1–2** Although 1 Samuel 2:1–10 is a prayer, as v.1 indicates and the NIV section head acknowledges, it is commonly referred to as the "Song of Hannah" because of its lyrical qualities and similarities to other ancient OT hymns (e.g., the Songs of Moses and Miriam, Exod 15:1–18, 21; the Song of Moses, Deut 32:1–43; the Song of Deborah, Judg 5; and esp. the Song of David, 2 Sam 22). Robert Lowth, eighteenth-century doyen of Hebrew poetic structure, called it a "thanksgiving ode" (*Lectures on* *the Sacred Poetry of the Hebrews* [London: Chadwick, 1847], p. 216). Sigmund Mowinckel called it a psalm of thank offering, stating that it was sung in celebration of victory over enemies (*Samuelsboken* [Oslo: Aschehoug, 1936], p. 152). Like the Song of Hannah, Jonah's song of thanksgiving (though much later) is also called a prayer (Jonah 2:1, 7, 9).

Willis has shown that the Song of Hannah is a royal song of victory/triumph that is to be classified among the other ancient hymns listed above, all of which reflect traditional combat motifs, are composed in the first person singular, and emphasize the Lord's everlasting and universal power and sovereignty. In terms of poetic style, all contain repetitive parallelism in both bicola and tricola, exhibit a staccato effect, and tend to repeat important words in sequence (see Notes on v.3). Characteristic expressions and ideas also recur in these victory hymns; those that appear in both 2:1–10 and 2 Samuel 22 will be especially noted in the commentary. First Samuel 2:1–10 may have originated as a song of triumph at the Shiloh sanctuary in connection with Israel's victory over an enemy. Such songs would then have been taught to worshipers, and this one perhaps became a personal favorite of Hannah. Therefore, when she brought Samuel to Shiloh to dedicate him to the Lord, she sang it as a means of expressing her gratitude and praise to the Giver of life (cf. esp. v.5). For additional details, see John T. Willis, "The Song of Hannah and Psalm 113," CBQ 25, 2 (1973): 139–54.

The Song of Hannah appears near the beginning of 1 Samuel, and the Song of David appears near the end of 2 Samuel. These two remarkably similar hymns of praise thus constitute a kind of *inclusio,* framing the main contents of the books and reminding us that the two books were originally one. Both begin by using "horn" (1 Sam 2:1; 2 Sam 22:3) as a metaphor for "strength," referring to God as the "Rock," and reflecting on divine "deliverance/salvation" (1 Sam 2:1–2; 2 Sam 22:2–3). Both end by paralleling "his king" with "his anointed" (1 Sam 2:10; 2 Sam 22:51).

It may well be that Hannah's song is the seedplot for Mary's Magnificat (Luke 1:46–55; cf. also the Song of Zechariah in vv.68–79). The two hymns begin similarly, and certain themes in the Song of Hannah recur in the Song of Mary (cf. 1 Sam 2:4, 7–8 with Luke 1:52; 1 Sam 2:5 with Luke 1:53; notice also that Luke 1:48a—"for he has been mindful of the humble state of his servant"—is obviously dependent on 1 Sam 1:11 LXX: "if you will only look upon the humble state of your servant"). Both Hannah and Mary became pregnant miraculously (though admittedly in quite different ways), in due course each presented her firstborn son to the Lord at the central sanctuary (1:22; Luke 2:22), and both sang a hymn of thanksgiving and praise (Hannah after the birth of Samuel [1 Sam 2:1–10], Mary before the birth of Jesus [Luke 1:46–55]).

The songs of Hannah and Mary, together with their contexts, have in turn influenced a second-century-A.D. pseudepigraphal work known as the *Protevangelium of James.* It tells the story of Mary's elderly parents independently praying for a child. The old woman vows that the child will be "a gift to the Lord my God" (cf. 1 Sam 1:11). Mary is born in response to the prayers, and at the age of three she is presented by her parents to the priests in the temple at Jerusalem. The name of Mary's aged mother? Anna—the same as that of Samuel's aged mother, Hannah.

The Song of Hannah begins on a note of grateful exuberance: "Heart, strength, mouth—all that she thinks and does and says is centered in the great act of God on her behalf" (David A. Hubbard, "The Song of Hannah, A Bible Study," *Theology, News and Notes* [1974]: 13). Like that of the psalmist (Ps 9:1–2; cf. also 5:11), Hannah's heart rejoices in the Lord—and in his deliverance (or salvation) as well (see Pss 9:14; 13:5; 35:9; Isa 25:9). The metaphor of one's horn being lifted high (see also Pss 89:17, 24; 112:9) perhaps comes from the animal world, where members of the *Cervidae* family (deer, et al.) use their antlers in playful or mortal combat (cf. Deut 33:17; Ps 92:10). "Horn" thus symbolizes strength (see NIV mg.). Whereas here Hannah is grateful that her own "horn" is lifted high (i.e., that Samuel has been born—cf. 1 Chron 25:5 NIV mg.; so McCarter, *I Samuel*), in 2 Samuel 22:3 David refers to God himself as "the horn of my salvation."

For Hannah, the Lord is holy, unique, and mighty (v.2). She therefore celebrates God's holiness, his otherness, in righteous victory (as in Exod 15:11; Ps 99:3, 5, 9; Isa 5:16). She then connects his uniqueness with the metaphor of the Rock, exactly as David later does (2 Sam 22:32). However rocklike others—human or divine—may consider themselves, "their rock is not like our Rock" (Deut 32:31). God as the Rock is one of the most recognizable and familiar images of divine refuge and strength, not only in the OT (cf. Gen 49:24; Deut 32:4; Isa 26:4; Hab 1:12; frequently in the Psalms), but also in Christian hymnody ("Rock of Ages," "O Safe to the Rock That Is Higher Than I," et al.).

**3–8d** After describing God in his majesty and power, Hannah warns all (the verbs in v.3 are plural) who would vaunt themselves in their pride (including, of course, Peninnah). In the light of all that God is and does, arrogance is both foolish and futile (Pss 31:18; 75:4; 138:6; Isa 5:15–16). Using the same verb used earlier of her (*rby*), Hannah contrasts the fact that she "kept" praying (1:12) with her rebuke to Peninnah (among others) not to "keep" talking so proudly. The doubling of *g*[e]*ḇōhāh* ("proudly"), rendered "so proudly" in NIV, is a literary feature characteristic of the most ancient Hebrew poetry and helps us date the Song of Hannah early rather than late. God, who knows the heart, judges and weighs it rather than external appearances (16:7; 1 Kings 8:39; Prov 16:2; 21:2; 24:12).

The informal contrasts here presented by Hannah prepare us for the series of seven formal contrasts in vv.4–7 (v.8a–d simply expands on the two contrasts in v.7): (1) strong and weak, (2) full and hungry, (3) barren and fertile, (4) dead and alive, (5) sick and well, (6) poor and rich, and (7) humble and exalted. So classic and striking are these opposing qualities and characteristics that Lowth uses them as a paradigm for what he calls antithetic parallelism (*Lectures*, pp. 215–16). As Hubbard puts it, God "turns losers into winners and winners into losers" ("Song of Hannah," p. 13).

The "broken" bows of v.4 are echoed by the "shattered" opponents of v.10, since the Hebrew root (*ḥtt*) is the same. And if the verb translated "bend" (*niḥaṯ*) in 2 Samuel 22:35 is derived from the same root (as one Heb. MS indicates), we have yet another connection between the Song of David and the Song of Hannah. In any case, the phrase "armed with strength" in v.4 reappears in 2 Samuel 22:40 as well as in a Qumran text of 22:33 (see NIV mg. in loc.). Making the strong weak and the weak strong is what God does in Hebrews 11:32–34, a text that includes both Samuel and David as the recipients of divine deliverance.

The last half of v.5 had special meaning for Hannah. Like the mother of Samson, another lifelong Nazirite, the mother of Samuel had once been barren (cf. Judg 13:2–3). "Seven" here means simply "many" (cf. Ruth 4:15), as the parallel line shows (for a similar phenomenon, cf. comment on 1 Sam 1:8). At the same time, seven—as a number symbolizing completion—also represents the ideal (cf. Job 1:2; 42:13). Just as she who has had many "pines away" (*'umlālāh*), so also the mother of seven will "grow faint" (Jer 15:9; same Heb. word). The formerly barren Hannah eventually had a total of six children (v.21)—one short of the ideal.

Verses 6–8 make explicit what was only implicit in vv.4–5: The Sovereign God, according to his own good pleasure, ultimately blesses some and curses others (cf. vv.9c–10c). Verse 6a contrasts death with life, and possibly the second half does too (so McCarter, *I Samuel*). However, the second half may refer rather to rescue from the brink of death after a serious illness and therefore contrast sickness with health. Deuteronomy 32:39 and 2 Kings 5:7 have the same two sets of contrasts (death/life, sickness/health). In addition, bringing up from the grave in Psalm 30:2–3 clearly refers to healing rather than resurrection.

The Lord can—and does—reverse the fortunes of poor and rich (Zech 9:3–4), of the humble and the proud (Job 5:11; Ps 75:7; and esp. 2 Sam 22:28). He can lift a Baasha "from the dust" and later consume him (1 Kings 16:2–3); he can ensconce a Job on an ash heap (Job 2:8) and later restore him (Job 42:10).

The MT of the first three lines of v.8 is almost identical to that of Psalm 113:7–8a. If (as seems likely) Psalm 113 is later than Hannah's song, the psalmist has added an exquisite touch in the light of Hannah's situation: "He [the Lord] settles the barren woman in her home/ as a happy mother of children" (113:9).

**8e–10** Though the underlying Hebrew text is different, 2 Samuel 22:16 also makes reference to the "foundations of the earth." There, as here and elsewhere (cf. similarly Job 38:4; Pss 75:3; 82:5; 104:5; Isa 24:18; 48:13; 51:13, 16), such phrases refer pictorially to the firmness and stability of God's creation—which, however, is always under his sovereign control, for good or ill. How much more is he able to protect his people (Prov 3:26) and confound his (and their) enemies (Deut 32:35)!

The word *ḥāsîḏ*, often translated "saint" (as in v.9), means "one to whom the Lord has pledged his covenant love," his *ḥeseḏ*. As here, it frequently appears in the Psalms in opposition to the wicked: cf. Psalms 12:1 ("godly"), 8; 50:5 ("consecrated ones"), 16; 97:10 ("faithful ones"); 145:10, 20 (for discussion cf. Willis Judson Beecher, *The Prophets and the Promise* [Grand Rapids: Baker, 1963], pp. 313–43; for messianic implications in the present passage, cf. esp. p. 325). The final destiny of the ungodly, however, is the silence of Sheol, the grave, the netherworld, where all is darkness (Job 10:21–22; 17:13; 18:18; Ps 88:12; Prov 20:20; cf. also Matt 8:12; for further details, cf. Ronald F. Youngblood, "Qoheleth's 'Dark House' [Eccl 12:5]," JETS 29, 4 [1986]: 397–410).

Hannah learned that in the battles of life it is not physical strength that brings victory (cf. also Ps 33:16–17; Jer 9:23). Had Moses depended on such resources against the Amalekites, he would not have defeated them ("winning" in Exod 17:11 is from the same Heb. root as "prevails" here [*gbr*]). But whether through human agency or directly, God always shatters the enemy (v.10; cf. Exod 15:6; Ps 2:9). Peninnah may have "thundered against" (see comment on 1:6 above) Hannah, but never mind: Hannah knew full well that the Lord would ultimately "thunder against" Peninnah and all others who oppose him (v.10; 2 Sam 22:14), including Israel's inveterate enemies, the Philistines (1 Sam 7:10).

The Song of Hannah ends as it began, concluding the *inclusio* by again using the word "horn" metaphorically in the sense of "strength" (as the parallel in the preceding line demonstrates). Hannah voices the divine promise of strength to the coming "king"—initially David, who will found a dynasty with messianic implications ("king" is used in a messianic sense in, e.g., Ps 2:6; Isa 32:1; Jer 23:5; Ezek 37:22, 24; Hos 3:5; Zech 9:9). The king—the "anointed" one—will rule by virtue of God's command and will therefore belong to him body and soul. The king will be "his" (v.10; 2 Sam 22:51).

**11** With Samuel's dedication and Hannah's song complete, the family returned to Ramah—except for Samuel, who began what was to be a continuing ministry (so the verb forms imply; cf. S.R. Driver, *Notes on the Books of Samuel*, pp. 28, 151) as a priest (2:18; 3:1; so *šrt* intends when "the LORD" is its grammatical object; see BDB, p. 1058).

## Notes

**3** 4QSam[a] reads דעת (*dʿt*, sing.) instead of the MT's דעות (*dʿwt*, pl.), thus describing God simply as a God of "knowledge." But the Qumran text also has חתה (*ḥth*, sing.) instead of the MT's חתים (*ḥtym*, pl.) in v.4, thereby exhibiting a tendency toward the singular in this hymn. It would therefore seem best to read אֵל דֵּעוֹת (*ʾēl dēʿôṯ*) with the MT here and to translate something like "the all-knowing God" (so BDB, p. 42).

**5** The MT underlying the translation "hunger no more" is fraught with difficulties. The meaning of the verb is uncertain, its connection with the following particle is unclear, and the Masoretic punctuation is suspect. But since the verb חדל (*ḥdl*) in several other places (e.g., Judg 20:28; Jer 40:4; Ezek 2:5, 7; 3:11; Zech 11:12) seems to mean "to not do something," where the "something" is the preceding verb in question (so NIV in all the passages), it is perhaps best to translate the first two lines of v.5 as follows: "Those who were full hire themselves out for food,/ but the hungry do not do so anymore." This was the solution of several early Jewish exegetes and has been argued most recently and forcefully by Theodore J. Lewis, "The Songs of Hannah and Deborah: *ḤDL*–II ('Growing Plump')," JBL 104, 1 (1985): 105–8.

**6** שְׁאוֹל (*šeʾôl*) is usually translated "the grave" in the NIV (cf. R. Laird Harris, *The NIV: The Making of a Contemporary Translation*, ed. Kenneth L. Barker [Grand Rapids: Zondervan, 1986], pp. 58–71). In a few instances, however, it is rendered "the realm of death" or the equivalent (e.g., Deut 32:22) as a vivid image of the netherworld, the place of the departed spirits of the dead (cf. Nicholas J. Tromp, *Primitive Conceptions of Death and the Nether World in the Old Testament* [Rome: Pontifical Biblical Institute, 1969], pp. 10, 70, 129–51, 167–96). The two concepts are not mutually exclusive since the grave, a literal tomb, can also be viewed figuratively as the portal through which the deceased gains admission to the afterlife.

**10** In the common expression "ends of the earth," אַפְסֵי (*ʾap̱sê*, "ends of") derives ultimately from the Sumerian *ab.zu* via the Akkadian *apsû* ("fresh water"), referring to the fresh waters that were believed to surround the earth in ancient cosmology. The Sumerian word is also the origin of the Greek *ἀβύσσος* (*abyssos*), the Abyss of Luke 8:31; Rev 9:1–2, 11; 11:7; 17:8; and 20:1, 3.

The NIV rightly scans v.10b–c as a couplet, but the translation "against them" is highly suspect at best. One would not expect "the LORD" in the second line to be paralleled by "he" in the first line (the reverse would be the normal pattern). The parallel passage in 2 Sam 22:14 is helpful at this point: "The LORD thundered from heaven;/ the voice of the Most High resounded." More literally the second line reads: "The Most High gave his voice"—i.e., "the Most High" is the subject of the second line, paralleling "the LORD" as the subject of the first. "Most High" here is עֶלְיוֹן (*ʿelyôn*). Some fifty years ago H.S. Nyberg observed that the alternate forms עלו/עלי/על (*'l/'ly/'lw*) were used as a divine name cognate to *'elyôn* and also meaning "Most High" in several OT poetic passages as well as elsewhere in the ancient Near East; cf. "Studien zum Religionskampf im Alten Testament," *Archiv für Religionswissenschaft* 35 (1938): 329–87. The NIV acknowledges this usage in 2 Sam 23:1; Ps 7:8, 10; and Hos 7:16; 11:7. עלו (*'lw*) should be translated "Most High" in 1 Sam 2:10 as well (as Nyberg already recognized): "The Most High will thunder from heaven/the LORD will judge the ends of the earth." The Hebrew name is formally similar to that of Eli, which (as indicated above in the comment on 1:3) means something like "Exalted is [the Lord]" or "The Most High [is the Lord]." For additional details see Mitchell Dahood, "The Divine Name *'Ēlî* in the Psalms," *Theological Studies* 14, 3 (1953): 452–57; Freedman, "Divine Names," pp. 55–107.

מָשִׁיחַ (*māšîaḥ*, "anointed") underlies our word "Messiah" and reminds us that great David's greater Son, Jesus the Christ—Greek *Christos* ("anointed")—would some day culminate David's royal line (cf. this typological, eschatological use of "anointed" here as well as in v.35; 2 Sam 22:51; 2 Chron 6:42; Pss 2:2; 89:38, 51; 132:10, 17). For a fine summary statement of this interpretation, see Franz Delitzsch, *Old Testament History of Redemption*, reprint ed. (Peabody: Hendrickson, 1988), p. 79; for the possibility that v.10 originally had in mind a local "king" of an Israelite city-state or tribe, and that therefore the Song of Hannah comes from a promonarchic circle of the premonarchic period who felt that the Lord's kingship was not jeopardized by an earthly king, cf. Willis, "Song of Hannah," pp. 148–49.

The Song of Hannah is commonly dated during the period of the monarchy (tenth century B.C. or later) because of the reference to a future king in v.10. On the basis of stylistic phenomena, however, W.F. Albright (cited in Freedman below) dated it to the late eleventh century (i.e., only slightly later than the time of Hannah herself); and on the basis of divine names and titles, Freedman places it in the eleventh or tenth century ("Divine Names," pp. 55, 96). When all is said and done, then, there would seem to be no insuperable reason not to assume that Hannah's song is contemporary with her. Her celebration of the Lord's victory (v.1), uniqueness (v.2), power (vv.3–8), and judgment (vv.9–10; Hubbard, "Song of Hannah," pp. 12–14) demonstrates her earnest desire to praise God for blessings past, present, and future.

---

## 3. *The wicked sons of Eli*

### 2:12–26

12 Eli's sons were wicked men; they had no regard for the LORD. 13 Now
it was the practice of the priests with the people that whenever anyone
offered a sacrifice and while the meat was being boiled, the servant of
the priest would come with a three-pronged fork in his hand. 14 He would
plunge it into the pan or kettle or caldron or pot, and the priest would
take for himself whatever the fork brought up. This is how they treated
all the Israelites who came to Shiloh. 15 But even before the fat was
burned, the servant of the priest would come and say to the man who
was sacrificing, "Give the priest some meat to roast; he won't accept
boiled meat from you, but only raw."

16 If the man said to him, "Let the fat be burned up first, and then take
whatever you want," the servant would then answer, "No, hand it over
now; if you don't, I'll take it by force."

17 This sin of the young men was very great in the LORD's sight, for they
were treating the LORD's offering with contempt.

18 But Samuel was ministering before the LORD—a boy wearing a linen
ephod. 19 Each year his mother made him a little robe and took it to him
when she went up with her husband to offer the annual sacrifice. 20 Eli
would bless Elkanah and his wife, saying, "May the LORD give you

**children by this woman to take the place of the one she prayed for and
gave to the LORD." Then they would go home. 21 And the LORD was
gracious to Hannah; she conceived and gave birth to three sons and two
daughters. Meanwhile, the boy Samuel grew up in the presence of the
LORD.**

**22 Now Eli, who was very old, heard about everything his sons were
doing to all Israel and how they slept with the women who served at the
entrance to the Tent of Meeting. 23 So he said to them, "Why do you do
such things? I hear from all the people about these wicked deeds of
yours. 24 No, my sons; it is not a good report that I hear spreading among
the LORD's people. 25 If a man sins against another man, God may
mediate for him; but if a man sins against the LORD, who will intercede
for him?" His sons, however, did not listen to their father's rebuke, for it
was the LORD's will to put them to death.**

**26 And the boy Samuel continued to grow in stature and in favor with
the LORD and with men.**

**12–17** This account of the sin of Eli's sons is followed immediately by a statement concerning Samuel's ministry before the Lord (v.18), as is the subsequent account (vv.27–36) of the prophecy against Eli's house (3:1). Thus the narrator highlights the sharp contrast between Eli and his sons and Samuel. In addition, the reference to Hophni and Phinehas as "wicked men" (v.12) contrasts them with Hannah, who did not consider herself a "wicked woman" (1:16)—as Eli himself acknowledged (1:17). Finally, the sons of Eli "had no regard for" (*lō' yāḏ$^{e}$ʿû;* lit., "they did not know") the Lord—unlike Samuel, who "did not yet know" (3:7) the Lord (implying that he would come to know him in the future).

Attempts are made to distinguish the priestly practice/custom described in vv.13–14 from the obvious priestly violation depicted in vv.15–16 (e.g., Eslinger, *Kingship of God;* McCarter, *I Samuel*). But by comparing vv.13–14 with Deuteronomy 18:3, Garsiel has shown that "the 'ordinance of the priests' here, like the 'ordinance of the king' later on (8:11)," is an ironic opening "whose point is the antithesis between the actual and the desirable, or (to put it differently) between the murky reality and the requirements of the law" (pp. 38–39). Not content with the specified portions of the animals that the sacrificer is to "give" (so lit. in Deut 18:3) to the priests (cf. also Lev 7:34), each of Eli's sons "would take for himnself whatever the fork brought up" (v.14). And not only that, "even [*gam*] before the fat was burned" (v.15), as the law mandated (Lev 7:31), Hophni and Phinehas demanded raw meat. In fact, on occasion they even preferred roasted meat to boiled—as if in mockery of the necessarily hasty method of preparing the first Passover feast (Exod 12:8–11). They wanted their unlawful portion before the Lord received what was rightfully his (cf. Delitzsch, Driver, Hertzberg, Klein). Their rebellion, impatience, and impudence (v.16) are described as a "very great" sin (v.17). Like their postexilic counterparts (Mal 1:6–14), these premonarchic priests treated the Lord's offerings with contempt. Such conduct, especially when practiced by God's ministers, can only lead to disaster (cf. Num 16:30–32).

**18–26** Even as a young apprentice priest under Eli's supervision, Samuel wore the linen ephod characteristic of that ministry. Anthony Phillips, primarily on the basis of 2 Samuel 6:14, attempted to prove that Samuel's ephod "is not to be understood as a special priestly garment but a brief loincloth suitable for young children" ("David's Linen Ephod," VetTest 19, 4 [1969]: 487). But Phillips fails to explain why David

(2 Sam 6:14) would wear a child's garment, and he resorts to the LXX omission of "linen" in 1 Samuel 22:18 to confirm his belief that the eighty-five priests slaughtered by Doeg are not described there as "wearing" ephods but as "carrying" an "oracular instrument" (another meaning for *'ēpôḏ*). N.L. Tidwell ("The Linen Ephod: 1 Sam. II 18 and 2 Sam. VI 14," VetTest 24, 4 [1974]: 505–7) rightly criticizes Phillips's view in favor of the traditional interpretation: "Linen ephod" always refers to a priest's garment, whether worn by a youth or by an adult. Indeed, the little "robe" that Samuel's mother made for him annually as he was growing up (v.19) may well have been an example of the "robe of the ephod" mentioned in Exodus 28:31 (the Heb. word for "robe" is the same in both passages). Although David is not described as wearing such a robe in 2 Samuel 6:14, he is so depicted in the parallel text of 1 Chronicles 15:27.

The use of *š'l* twice in v.20 (here translated "the one she prayed for," "gave") echoes its sevenfold use in chapter 1 (see Notes on 1:20) and reminds us of Hannah's vow. By providing Hannah with additional children, the Lord continued to be gracious to her, as he had been to her ancestress Sarah centuries earlier (Gen 21:1). The narrator's description of Samuel's continued growth in the Lord's presence (v.21), as well as in stature and in favor with God and men (v.26), is echoed in Luke's portrayal of Jesus' youth (Luke 2:40, 52). The narrator's description also frames the account of further sinful activity by Eli's sons (vv.22–25) and thus extends the contrast between them and Samuel.

The hapless Eli, whose advanced age is stressed in the text from this point on (v.22; 4:15, 18), was unable to restrain the sinful conduct of his sons. To their earlier callous treatment of their fellow Israelites (vv.13–16) they added sexual promiscuity—and with the women who served at the tabernacle (cf. Exod 38:8) at that. Such ritual prostitution (if indeed it was; Eslinger, *Kingship of God*, pp. 122–23, expresses doubts), though common among Israel's Canaanite neighbors, was specifically forbidden to the people of God (Num 25:1–5; Deut 23:17; Amos 2:7–8). Eli's rebuke, justified in the light of widespread and public reports of his sons' evil deeds, fell on deaf ears. His theological arguments, weak at best, were to no avail, especially since God had already determined to put Hophni and Phinehas to death (v.25).

The most familiar and notable case of divine judicial hardening against defiant refusal to repent is that of the Pharaoh of the oppression (Exod 4:21–14:17); for a summary explanation, see Ronald F. Youngblood, *Exodus* (Chicago: Moody, 1983), pp. 45–46. Numerous sensitive discussions (cf. Matitiahu Tsevat, "The Death of the Sons of Eli," *Journal of Bible and Religion* 32, 4 [1964]: 355–58; Eslinger, *Kingship of God*, pp. 126–27), while admirable, do not materially advance our understanding beyond the traditional view (cf. Delitzsch). What is eminently clear is that God's decision to end the lives of Eli's sons was irrevocable. Hannah had already expressed her willingness to leave such decisions within the sphere of divine sovereignty (v.6)—and so must we!

## Notes

13 Three-pronged forks, dating to the Late Bronze age and apparently used as sacrificial implements, have been excavated at Gezer (cf. Neufeld, pp. 53–54).

**20** This verse contains two excellent examples of how Qumran readings may confirm earlier suggestions for changes in the MT. 4QSam[a] reads ישלם (*yšlm*, "restore," "repay") instead of the MT's ישם (*yśm*, "give," "grant"), thus reinstating the idiom שַׁלֵּם תַּחַת (*šillēm taḥaṯ*, "repay in exchange for") as in Exod 21:36. The purpose of Eli's blessing is that the Lord might restore children to Elkanah in exchange for the loss of Samuel, whom Hannah had given to the Lord in faithfulness to her vow (cf. similarly Eslinger, *Kingship of God*, p. 121). 4QSam[a] also reads the more grammatically correct השאיל[ה] (*hš'yl[h]*, "she gave") instead of the MT's שָׁאַל (*š'l*, "he asked"). Both readings were proposed eighty years ago, partly on the basis of the LXX, in BDB (pp. 964, 982).

**25** As the NIV margin indicates, we cannot always be sure whether אֱלֹהִים (*'ᵉlōhîm*) means "God" or "(the) judges" in certain contexts. In Exod 21:6 and 22:8–9, the NIV places "judges" in the text, "God" in the margin; in 22:28 the situation is reversed. In Pss 82:1, 6; 138:1, on the other hand, the NIV renders "gods" (in quotation marks) to bring out the idea of prideful self-deification on the part of arrogant rulers. Here in v.25, and in the Exodus passages, it is perhaps best to leave the question moot, since in any case the "judges" (if such they be) are viewed as God's representatives who reflect his will and carry out his desires.

---

## 4. *The oracle against the house of Eli*

### 2:27–36

27 Now a man of God came to Eli and said to him, "This is what the
LORD says: 'Did I not clearly reveal myself to your father's house when
they were in Egypt under Pharaoh? 28 I chose your father out of all the
tribes of Israel to be my priest, to go up to my altar, to burn incense, and
to wear an ephod in my presence. I also gave your father's house all the
offerings made with fire by the Israelites. 29 Why do you scorn my
sacrifice and offering that I prescribed for my dwelling? Why do you
honor your sons more than me by fattening yourselves on the choice
parts of every offering made by my people Israel?'

30 "Therefore the LORD, the God of Israel, declares: 'I promised that
your house and your father's house would minister before me forever.'
But now the LORD declares: 'Far be it from me! Those who honor me I
will honor, but those who despise me will be disdained. 31 The time is
coming when I will cut short your strength and the strength of your
father's house, so that there will not be an old man in your family line
32 and you will see distress in my dwelling. Although good will be done
to Israel, in your family line there will never be an old man. 33 Every one
of you that I do not cut off from my altar will be spared only to blind your
eyes with tears and to grieve your heart, and all your descendants will
die in the prime of life.

34 "'And what happens to your two sons, Hophni and Phinehas, will be
a sign to you—they will both die on the same day. 35 I will raise up for
myself a faithful priest, who will do according to what is in my heart and
mind. I will firmly establish his house, and he will minister before my
anointed one always. 36 Then everyone left in your family line will come
and bow down before him for a piece of silver and a crust of bread and
plead, "Appoint me to some priestly office so I can have food to eat."'"

**27–36** After the contrasting and transitional v.26 (see above), the chapter concludes by expanding on the Lord's intention to put Eli's sons to death (v.25). The prophetic oracle to (and against) Eli uses the messenger formula ("This is what the LORD says") and mediates the divine word through a "man of God" (v.27). The term "man of God" occasionally refers to an angel (cf. Judg 13:3, 6, 8–9), but it is usually employed as a synonym for "prophet" (cf. esp. 1 Sam 9:9–10). In the ancient world it was used in extrabiblical literature as well; for example, a seal of a prophet of the god Melqart reads: "Belonging to Baal-yaton, the man of God, who depends on Melqart" (cf. Walter Beyerlin, ed., *Near Eastern Religious Texts Relating to the Old Testament* [Philadelphia: Westminster, 1978], p. 247).

Though almost always identified by name, in v.27 the man of God is anonymous. He reminds Eli that God had revealed himself to his ancestor Levi's house (in Aaron; see Exod 4:14–16) before the Exodus. Indeed, Aaron had been the object of special divine election (v.28) to serve the Lord as the first in a long line of priests (Exod 28:1–4). Aaron would go up "to" the Lord's altar (or, perhaps better, "upon" one or more steps next to it, since archaeologists have frequently unearthed ancient stepped altars in Israel; cf. also Lev 9:22) and would wear the ephod in the course of his divinely ordained work (v.28; cf. Lev 8:7). Recipients of such privilege, Eli and his sons (see NIV mg.; Qumran and LXX use a singular verb here, but cf. "yourselves" later in the verse) nevertheless "scorn" the Lord's prescribed sacrifices (v.29).

The verb translated "scorn" here (*bāʿaṭ*, v.29) means literally "to kick" and is found only once elsewhere in the OT: "Jeshurun [a poetic name for Israel; cf. Isa 44:1–2] grew fat and kicked;/ filled with food, he became heavy and sleek" (Deut 32:15). Although the Hebrew words for "fat" and "heavy" are different there than the word for "fattening" here, the parallel is striking: Like Israel centuries earlier, the house of Eli has "kicked at" the Lord's offerings by gorging themselves on the best parts of the sacrifices brought by the Israelites (vv.13–17). By condoning the sin of Hophni and Phinehas (however reluctantly), Eli has demonstrated that he loves his sons more than he loves God and that he is therefore unworthy of the Lord's continued blessing (see Matt 10:37). Was Eli's participation in his sons' gluttony one of the reasons why, at the time of his death, he had become "heavy" (4:18; yet a fourth Heb. root)?

The Lord had promised that Aaron's descendants would always be priests (v.30; cf. Exod 29:9), and he had confirmed that promise on covenant oath (Num 25:13). They would "minister before"—*hālaḵ*, literally, "walk (back and forth) before" (as did Enoch, Gen 5:22, 24; Noah, 6:9; and Abraham, 17:1)—the Lord forever. But because of flagrant disobedience, the house of Eli, like the house of Saul later (13:13–14), would be judged by God. Although the Aaronic priesthood was perpetual, individual priests who sinned could thereby forfeit covenant blessing. The Lord honors (*kāḇēḏ*, lit., "makes heavy") those who honor him, but he disdains (*qālāh*, lit., "makes light") those who despise him. Eli had honored his sons (v.29) more than he honored God (v.30). The description of divine judgment in v.31, when translated literally, is vivid indeed: "I will chop off your arm and the arm of your father's house" (*zᵉrōaʿ*, "arm," is often used as a metaphor for "strength" in the OT). Eli would be the last "old man" in his family line, because God's fulfillment of his death sentence would be swift and sure (4:11, 18; 22:17–20; 1 Kings 2:26–27).

Examples of the predicted distress in God's "dwelling" (v.32; the tabernacle is meant) are the capture of the ark by the Philistines (4:11) and the destruction of Shiloh (cf. Jer 7:12, 14; 26:6, 9). Although in Eli's line there would "never" (lit., "not . . . all the days") be an old man, in the line that would replace his there would "always" (lit., "all the days," v.35) be a faithful priest. The only member of Eli's line to "be spared" (v.33) was Abiathar, and in any case he was removed from the priesthood (1 Kings 2:26–27).

Hophni and Phinehas would die "on the same day" (v.34; fulfilled in 4:11), a prophetic sign to Eli not only of his own impending death but also of the fulfillment of the other components in the oracle of the man of God. The Lord would bring a "faithful" priest on the scene, who would be privy to the very thoughts of God and obedient to him (v.35).

*Ne'ᵉmān* ("faithful," v.35) contrasts strongly with the rebellion of Eli's sons and plays an important role in the succeeding context, both near and remote. In this same verse the Lord says, "I will firmly establish his house"—literally, "I will build for him a faithful house" (cf. 2 Sam 7:27 with respect to David's dynasty)—in which "firmly" translates the same Hebrew word (*ne'ᵉmān* ). In 25:28 "lasting dynasty" (lit., "faithful house") is used of David, and 1 Chronicles 17:23 records a similar promise concerning David and his house, where "established" is *yē'āmēn.* In the present context the faithful priest whose house the Lord would firmly establish refers initially to Samuel (3:1; 7:9; 9:12–13; cf. esp. 3:20, where it states that all Israel knew that Samuel "was attested"—*ne'ᵉmān*—as a prophet). Later, however, the line of Zadok son of Ahitub would replace that of Abiathar, Eli's descendant (2 Sam 8:17; 15:24–29; 1 Kings 2:35), a replacement that would constitute a greater fulfillment of the oracle of the man of God. Zadok and his descendants would thus "always" minister before the Lord's "anointed one"—David's son Solomon (1 Kings 2:27, 35) and his descendants. Nevertheless, "the prophecy of the man of God was fulfilled in Zadok and Solomon, but was not exhausted" there (Delitzsch, *Old Testament History,* p. 79).

Ultimate fulfillment would come only in Jesus the Christ, the supremely Anointed One, "designated by God to be high priest" (Heb 5:10) "forever, in the order of Melchizedek" (6:20), the ancient priest-king of Jerusalem (Gen 14:18; Heb 7:1). Although Zadok and Melchizedek were clearly two different people, the obvious connection between their names may not be unintentional. In his high-priestly office, Jesus brings the ministry of both men to full fruition.

As for the members of Eli's house, once fattened on priestly perquisites (v.29), soon not even the least benefit of priestly office would be theirs (v.36). The magnificent chiastic structure of 1 Samuel 2 must not be missed:

A. The song of Hannah, concluding with reference to the Lord's anointed (2:1–10)
  B. Samuel ministers before the Lord (2:11)
    C. The sins of Eli's sons (2:12–17)
      D. Samuel ministers before the Lord (2:18–19)
        E. Eli blesses Samuel's parents (2:20–21a)
      D′. Samuel grows in the Lord's presence (2:21b)
    C′. The sins of Eli's sons (2:22–25)
  B′. Samuel grows in the Lord's presence (2:26)
A′. The oracle of the man of God, concluding with reference to the Lord's anointed (2:27–36)

At the center of the chiasm is Eli's blessing of Elkanah and Hannah, who now disappear from the narrative. The blessing is framed by references to the ministry and growth of their son and Eli's successor, which in turn prepare us for references to Samuel's ministry (3:1) and growth (3:19) in the next chapter. For a similar analysis and additional details, see Michael Fishbane, "I Samuel 3: Historical Narrative and Narrative Poetics," *Literary Interpretations of Biblical Narratives,* ed. K.R.R. Gros Louis and J.S. Ackerman (Nashville: Abingdon, 1982), 2:194–96.

## Notes

**29** BDB (p. 733) pronounces מָעוֹן (*mā'ôn*) in vv.29 and 32 "unintelligible." But the ancient versions provide no variants by way of help, and Barthélemy declares the translation "dwelling" to be one of three possible, acceptable renderings in both verses (pp. 153–55; cf. also Delitzsch).

**33** The Hebrew form of the verb translated "to grieve," לַאֲדִיב (*la'ᵃḏîḇ*), is morphologically suspect; and in any case its root, אדב (*'db*), is unique in the OT. Leviticus 26:16 reads in part מְכַלּוֹת עֵינַיִם וּמְדִיבֹת נָפֶשׁ (*mᵉḵallôṯ 'ênayim ûmᵉḏîḇōṯ nāp̱eš*, "destroy your sight and drain away your life"), providing an excellent parallel to the phrase here: לְכַלּוֹת אֶת־עֵינֶיךָ וְלַאֲדִיב אֶת־נַפְשֶׁךָ (*lᵉḵallôṯ 'eṯ-'êneyḵā wᵉla'ᵃḏîḇ 'eṯ-nap̱šeḵā*, "to blind your eyes with tears and to grieve your heart"). It is therefore advisable to assume a scribal error in v.33 and to change the incorrect form *la'ᵃḏîḇ* to *lᵉhāḏîḇ* (לְהָדִיב), Hiphil infinitive construct of דוב (*dûḇ*), just as מְדִיבֹת (*mᵉḏîḇōṯ*) is a Hiphil feminine plural participle from the same root (cf. similarly S.R. Driver, *Notes on the Books of Samuel*, in loc.). The 1 Samuel passage could just as well be translated, to conform with the Leviticus passage, as "to destroy your sight and drain away your life" (perhaps to be understood figuratively). Such, in any case, was to be Eli's literal fate (4:15, 18).

**36** אֲגוֹרָה (*'ᵃgôrāh*, "piece") is found only here in the OT. Its obvious reference to a very small amount of silver made it suitable to serve as the modern Hebrew word to denote the smallest Israeli coin.

---

## 5. *The call of Samuel*

### 3:1–4:1a

[1]The boy Samuel ministered before the LORD under Eli. In those days
the word of the LORD was rare; there were not many visions.
[2]One night Eli, whose eyes were becoming so weak that he could
barely see, was lying down in his usual place. [3]The lamp of God had not
yet gone out, and Samuel was lying down in the temple of the LORD,
where the ark of God was. [4]Then the LORD called Samuel.

Samuel answered, "Here I am." [5]And he ran to Eli and said, "Here I
am; you called me."

But Eli said, "I did not call; go back and lie down." So he went and lay down.

[6]Again the LORD called, "Samuel!" And Samuel got up and went to Eli
and said, "Here I am; you called me."

"My son," Eli said, "I did not call; go back and lie down."

[7]Now Samuel did not yet know the LORD: The word of the LORD had not
yet been revealed to him.

[8]The LORD called Samuel a third time, and Samuel got up and went to
Eli and said, "Here I am; you called me."

Then Eli realized that the LORD was calling the boy. [9]So Eli told
Samuel, "Go and lie down, and if he calls you, say, 'Speak, LORD, for
your servant is listening.'" So Samuel went and lay down in his place.

[10]The LORD came and stood there, calling as at the other times,
"Samuel! Samuel!"

Then Samuel said, "Speak, for your servant is listening."

[11]And the LORD said to Samuel: "See, I am about to do something in
Israel that will make the ears of everyone who hears of it tingle. [12]At that
time I will carry out against Eli everything I spoke against his family—
from beginning to end. [13]For I told him that I would judge his family
forever because of the sin he knew about; his sons made themselves

contemptible, and he failed to restrain them. 14Therefore, I swore to the
house of Eli, 'The guilt of Eli's house will never be atoned for by
sacrifice or offering.'"
15Samuel lay down until morning and then opened the doors of the
house of the LORD. He was afraid to tell Eli the vision, 16but Eli called him
and said, "Samuel, my son."
Samuel answered, "Here I am."
17"What was it he said to you?" Eli asked. "Do not hide it from me.
May God deal with you, be it ever so severely, if you hide from me
anything he told you." 18So Samuel told him everything, hiding nothing
from him. Then Eli said, "He is the LORD; let him do what is good in his
eyes."
19The LORD was with Samuel as he grew up, and he let none of his
words fall to the ground. 20And all Israel from Dan to Beersheba
recognized that Samuel was attested as a prophet of the LORD. 21The
LORD continued to appear at Shiloh, and there he revealed himself to
Samuel through his word.
4:1And Samuel's word came to all Israel.

The literary genre of 1 Samuel 3 has usually been considered a prophetic-call narrative in the grand tradition of Exodus 3 (Moses), Isaiah 6, Jeremiah 1, and the like. Recently, however, on the basis of ancient Near Eastern parallels, Gnuse has theorized that 1 Samuel 3 is best analyzed as an auditory message dream theophany. Although he sometimes tilts the evidence in his direction (e.g., he translates *šāḵaḇ* "sleep" in vv.2–3 but is content to render it in its more common sense of "lie down" in the rest of the chapter), his arguments are impressive (see on p. 249 his summary of ten characteristics that Samuel's experience shares with accounts of other ancient Near Eastern dreams). In any event, the literary genre in this case is not destructive of the historicity of the event being narrated (contrary to Gnuse; cf. pp. 219–23, 250). Of course, the genre could turn out to be a blend of both types (a not uncommon feature of OT literature)—prophetic-call narrative plus auditory message dream theophany. But the advantage of Gnuse's analysis is that it deals adequately with the fact that the Lord speaks to Samuel at night—a matter not handled convincingly by the theory that 1 Samuel 3 is a prophetic-call narrative and nothing more.

**1** The introductory verse informs us of the rarity of special revelation in the days of the judges. There were not "many" visions in the sense that the few visions that did exist were not widely known (in 2 Chron 31:5 the same Heb. root speaks of an order that "went out"—i.e., it was disseminated far and wide). Amos 8:11–12 tells of similar days of spiritual famine that were soon to come, a prophecy fulfilled not only as a result of the disaster of 722 B.C. but also in the exilic and postexilic periods (Ps 74:9; Ezek 7:26). The word "vision(s)" is a technical term for "divine revelation mediated through a seer" (*ḥôzeh,* one of the two Heb. words for "seer," has the same root as that for "vision," *ḥāzôn*; *mar'āh,* the other word for "vision" in this chapter (v.15), also is used in the sense of "vision as a means of divine revelation" and has the same root as *rô'eh,* the other word for "seer"). *Ḥāzôn* appears in the title verse of three OT prophetic books (Isaiah, Obadiah, Nahum).

**2** "In that day" is used here in the general sense of "at that time," justifying the NIV contextual rendering "One night." Eli's aging eyes were so "weak" (contrast Moses in Deut 34:7) that he could barely "see" (he would eventually go completely blind; cf.

4:15). How different from Samuel, whose eyes saw clearly in a physical and a spiritual sense (v.15)!

**3** The lamps on the seven-branched lampstand (Exod 25:31–37) were filled with olive oil, lit at twilight (30:8), and kept burning "before the LORD from evening till morning" (27:20–21; cf. Lev 24:2–4; 2 Chron 13:11). Thus Samuel's encounter with the Lord on his bed in the tabernacle compound (v.3; cf. comment on 1:7 above) took place during the night, since the "lamp of God had not yet gone out."

**4–10** Although Samuel did not yet know that it was the Lord who was speaking to him (v.7), his answer was typical of the servant who hears and obeys the divine call: "Here I am" (v.4; see Gen 22:1, 11; Exod 3:4; Isa 6:8). Samuel's openness to serving God would soon enable him to know the Lord (v.7) in a way that Eli's sons never did (2:12). Although the word of the Lord had not yet been revealed to Samuel, that would take place very soon (v.11); and as God continued to speak to Samuel through the years (v.21), the Lord's word would so captivate him that it would be virtually indistinguishable from "Samuel's word" (4:1). Samuel the priest, God's minister, would become Samuel the prophet (v.20), God's spokesman.

Samuel—on that fateful night—thought that Eli was calling him. Twice Eli told Samuel to go back to bed, but the third time it finally dawned on the aged priest that it must be God who was calling the boy (vv.5–8). He therefore told Samuel that he should respond the next time by saying, "Speak, LORD, for your servant is listening" (v.9).

This time the Lord "came and stood there" (v.10), suggesting that Samuel could see him as well as hear him (cf. similarly Gen 18:22 and NIV mg.). Again the Lord called out Samuel's name twice, imparting a sense of urgency and finality (cf. Gen 22:11; Exod 3:4; Acts 9:4). Samuel responded as Eli had instructed, repeating Eli's words verbatim—with one notable exception: he left out the word "LORD" (whether through caution, ignorance, or accident, it is impossible to say; cf. again v.7).

**11–14** The Lord's word to Samuel (vv.11–14), like the man of God's oracle to Eli (2:27–36), not only had immediate reference to Eli's house but also pointed forward to the more remote future. The disaster to overcome Eli and his sons (including the destruction of Shiloh, the location of the central sanctuary) would "make the ears of everyone who hears of it tingle" (v.11)—a striking expression used only here (at the beginning of the monarchy) and in 2 Kings 21:12; Jeremiah 19:3 (at the end of the monarchy, when Jerusalem and the central sanctuary were destroyed). The Lord would carry out his judgment against Eli and his sons "from beginning to end" (v.12), an idiom implying the accomplishment of his full purpose (BDB, p. 320). Death was the penalty for showing contempt for the priesthood (Deut 17:12) as well as for disobeying one's parents (21:18–21), and Eli was implicated because he did not restrain Hophni and Phinehas (v.13).

If the NIV margin gives the correct reading (as seems likely; the MT reading is grammatically difficult), the sins of Eli's sons are compounded: Blaspheming the divine name was always a capital sin (Lev 24:11–16, 23). The house of Eli had committed blatant sins against God and showed no signs of remorse. Having passed the point of no return, they were subject to the divine death sentence (2:25; cf. Heb 12:16–17); no sacrifice or offering could atone for their guilt (v.14). Centuries later the same fate, and for much the same reasons, would overtake Jerusalem (Isa 22:14).

**15–18** When Samuel arose in the morning, he opened the doors of the tabernacle compound (v.15) and doubtless busied himself with other tasks to avoid telling Eli what he had seen and heard. The aged priest was not to be denied, however, and demanded a full report (vv.16–17). Indeed, he swore an oath of imprecation (cf. 2 Sam 3:35), calling down God's judgment on Samuel if the boy refused to tell everything he knew. The chiastic structure of v.17 focuses our attention on Eli's oath (pers. tr.):

A. "The word that he spoke to you,
  B. you hide from me;
    C. (the oath)
  B′. you hide from me,
A′. the word that he spoke to you."

(See Wilfred G.E. Watson, "The Structure of 1 Sam 3," *Biblische Zeitschrift* 29, 1 [1985]: 93.) The narrator, in describing Samuel's obedient response to Eli (v.18), echoes key words from v.17 (pers. tr.): "Samuel told him all the words; he did not hide [anything] from him." Eli's reaction is both devout and submissive (like that of Job in Job 2:10): "Let him do [better, 'he does'; the verb is imperfect rather than jussive and is identical to the form translated 'deal' in v.17] what is good in his eyes" (v.18). Eli resigns himself to divine sovereignty, realizing that it would be futile to do otherwise.

**3:19–4:1a** As the Lord's presence would later be with David (16:18; 18:12), so the Lord was with Samuel (v.19), a fact evident to all the Israelites (v.20). That God "let none of [Samuel's] words fall" (v.19) means that he made sure that everything Samuel said with divine authorization came true (the idiom is translated "Do not neglect anything you have recommended" in Esth 6:10); the same idea is expressed differently in 9:6. Although earlier God's word had not been revealed to Samuel (v.7), it now was; and as the Lord had appeared to him earlier (vv.10–14), so he "continued to appear at Shiloh" (v.21). As stated above, the Lord's word (v.21) became equivalent to "Samuel's word" (4:1), which is here introduced with the same formula that appears throughout the books of the Prophets with respect to the word of the Lord: It "came" to its recipients (cf. Jer 1:2, 4, 11, 13; Hos 1:1; Mic 1:1).

The expression "from Dan to Beersheba" (v.20) represents the northern and southern boundaries respectively of the united monarchy under David and Solomon (1 Kings 4:25). This expression occurs frequently in the narratives about David (2 Sam 3:10; 17:11; 24:2, 15).

It is demonstrable, not only contextually, but also by the fact that many Hebrew MSS of 1 Samuel display a section interval after "Israel," that the literary unit under consideration here ends at 4:1a. The entire unit (3:1–4:1a) is arranged in chiastic fashion:

A. Absence of divine oracles (3:1)
  B. Eli's fading powers (3:2)
    C. Three divine calls to Samuel (3:3–9)
      D. A divine oracle to Samuel (3:10–15)
    C′. Eli's request for Samuel's report (3:16–18)
  B′. Samuel's growing stature (3:19a)
A′. Return of divine oracles (3:19b–4:1a)

(cf. similarly Fishbane, "I Samuel 3," p. 193).

The focus of the section is thus the Lord's sentence of judgment against the house of Eli. The boy Samuel, having become a "man of God" (vv.19–20; 9:6–14), has confirmed in no uncertain terms the prophecy earlier proclaimed by the anonymous "man of God" (2:27–36).

## Notes

---

**20** Yohanan Aharoni suggests that two impressive city gates having the same basic plan, one excavated at the ancient site of Dan and the other at Beersheba, should be dated to the time of David. He further proposes that since the external limits of the land had been fortified by David, it was necessary for Solomon to fortify only certain strategically located internal cities (Hazor, Gezer, Megiddo, Jerusalem, et al.; cf. 1 Kings 9:15–19). For a summary of Aharoni's position (not shared by Avraham Biran, Dan's excavator—although his date differs from that of Aharoni by scarcely fifty years), see "King David as Builder," *Biblical Archaeology Review* 1, 1 (1975): 13–14.

---

### B. *The Ark Narratives (4:1b–7:17)*

### Excursus

Recent research has questioned the proper parameters of the narratives about the ark of the covenant in the books of Samuel. More than sixty years ago, Rost implied that 1 Samuel 4:1b–7:1 and 2 Samuel 6 were the only remaining excerpts from a longer and continuous ark narrative (cf. pp. 6–34). Until a few years ago, his theory was widely accepted; and indeed Antony F. Campbell (*The Ark Narrative [1 Sam 4–6; 2 Sam 6]: A Form-Critical and Traditio-Historical Study* [Missoula: Scholars, 1975]) has vigorously defended Rost's basic thesis. In a study entitled "Chronological Sequence in Two Hebrew Narratives" (BT 29, 3 [1978]), Robert Dorn also takes the demarcations of Rost and Campbell for granted (p. 317).

Now, however, two other careful studies of the matter have attracted attention. Franz Schicklberger (*Die Ladeerzählungen des ersten Samuel-Buches: Eine literaturwissenschaftliche und theologiegeschichtliche Untersuchung* [Wurzburg: Echter, 1973]) wants to limit the ark narratives to 1 Samuel 4:1–6:16, while Patrick D. Miller, Jr., and J.J.M. Roberts (*The Hand of the Lord: A Reassessment of the "Ark Narrative" of 1 Samuel* [Baltimore: Johns Hopkins Press, 1977]) opt for 1 Samuel 2:12–17, 22–25, 27–36; 4:1b–7:1. These in turn have provoked a spirited response from Antony F. Campbell ("Yahweh and the Ark: A Case Study in Narrative," JBL 98, 1 [1979]: 31–43), who rightly points out that the delimiting of the extent of the text is strongly dependent on estimates of its theological intention.

In any case, John Willis ("An Anti-Elide Narrative Tradition From a Prophetic Circle at the Ramah Sanctuary," JBL 90 [1971]: 288–308) has argued for the essential integrity of the first seven chapters of 1 Samuel as an overall literary unit, without of course precluding the possibility of subunits within those chapters. Since the debate continues without a resolution in sight, I advance the proposal, which I attempt to justify in the ensuing comments, that the ark narrative begins at 1 Samuel 4:1b with the first of the Israelite-Philistine wars and ends at 7:17 with the brief notice of Samuel's judgeship following the last of the Israelite-Philistine wars before Israel's demand for a king. It is impossible for us to know whether 2 Samuel 6, which resumes the story of what happened to the ark after David became king, was at one time part of a longer narrative.

## 1. *The capture of the ark*

### 4:1b–11

Now the Israelites went out to fight against the Philistines. The
Israelites camped at Ebenezer, and the Philistines at Aphek. 2 The
Philistines deployed their forces to meet Israel, and as the battle spread,
Israel was defeated by the Philistines, who killed about four thousand of
them on the battlefield. 3 When the soldiers returned to camp, the elders
of Israel asked, "Why did the LORD bring defeat upon us today before the
Philistines? Let us bring the ark of the LORD's covenant from Shiloh, so
that it may go with us and save us from the hand of our enemies."

4 So the people sent men to Shiloh, and they brought back the ark of
the covenant of the LORD Almighty, who is enthroned between the
cherubim. And Eli's two sons, Hophni and Phinehas, were there with the
ark of the covenant of God.

5 When the ark of the LORD's covenant came into the camp, all Israel
raised such a great shout that the ground shook. 6 Hearing the uproar,
the Philistines asked, "What's all this shouting in the Hebrew camp?"

When they learned that the ark of the LORD had come into the camp,
7 the Philistines were afraid. "A god has come into the camp," they said.
"We're in trouble! Nothing like this has happened before. 8 Woe to us!
Who will deliver us from the hand of these mighty gods? They are the
gods who struck the Egyptians with all kinds of plagues in the desert.
9 Be strong, Philistines! Be men, or you will be subject to the Hebrews,
as they have been to you. Be men, and fight!"

10 So the Philistines fought, and the Israelites were defeated and every
man fled to his tent. The slaughter was very great; Israel lost thirty
thousand foot soldiers. 11 The ark of God was captured, and Eli's two
sons, Hophni and Phinehas, died.

**1b** The Philistines, inveterate enemies of Israel during the latter half of the period of the judges and the early years of the Israelite monarchy, are mentioned nearly 150 times in 1 and 2 Samuel alone. They were so entrenched and dominant in the coastal areas and the foothills of Canaan that they eventually gave their name (Palestine) to the entire land. Although their connections with various Aegean cultures have been verified through decades of intensive research, their origins remain somewhat obscure. The OT relates them to Caphtor (Gen 10:14 = 1 Chron 1:12; Jer 47:4; Amos 9:7), which was probably Crete. The aggressive, expansionist ancestors of the Philistines of the time of Samuel apparently arrived in Canaan shortly after 1200 B.C. For details see especially Trude Dothan, *The Philistines and Their Material Culture* (New Haven: Yale University, 1982), pp. 13–16, 21–24, 289–96.

It is impossible to say who was the aggressor in this first-recorded battle between Israel and the Philistines. The Philistines camped at Aphek (modern Ras el-Ain, in the plain of Sharon ten miles east and slightly north of Joppa), an important site inhabited during the entire biblical period (in NT days it was called Antipatris; cf. Acts 23:31). Ebenezer, where the Israelites camped, is probably to be identified with modern Izbet Sarteh, about two miles east of Aphek on the road to Shiloh. Izbet Sarteh, a primitive Israelite outpost, was occupied for only about two centuries (c. 1200–1000 B.C.) (cf. Moshe Kochavi and Aaron Demsky, "An Israelite Village from the

Days of the Judges," *Biblical Archaeology Review* 4, 3 [1978]: 19–21; id., "An Alphabet From the Days of the Judges," pp. 23–30). Although the Ebenezer in 7:12 may not be the same as the one in 4:1, the presence of the name in both verses is surely not accidental and helps us to identify the parameters of the overall literary unit known as the ark narratives (4:1b–7:17). Aphek is mentioned again in the books of Samuel only in 1 Samuel 29:1.

**2–3** The Israelites were defeated not once but twice in this chapter (vv.2, 10). Not until 7:10–11 did they defeat the Philistines on the battlefield and then only (as always) with divine help. The Israelites lost "four thousand" men (v.2), a terrible tragedy no matter how that number is understood. Segal ("Numerals," p. 12) observes that the numbers 400, 4,000, and 40,000 are sometimes "associated with flight and with battles." In addition to being a round number, then, "four thousand" here is perhaps a metaphor for "a large number of military casualties." Another complicating factor is that *'elep̱* ("thousand") is often used in a more general sense in reference to a military "unit" (cf. 17:18; 29:2; 2 Sam 18:4). Perhaps "four thousand" here means "four units of soldiers." Thus a measure of uncertainty often obtains when the word for "thousand" or "unit" is used in a military context in the OT. (See Ronald Allen's extensive discussion of the problem of large numbers in his Introduction to the Book of Numbers, EBC, 2:680–91.) "Soldiers" (v.3) translates *'am,* the common word for "people" (as in v.4). The NIV frequently and correctly renders it "soldiers" or "troops" in military settings.

The Israelite elders (who make their next appearance at the beginning of the following literary unit; see 8:4) were puzzled by the debacle on the battlefield (v.3). Their solution was to bring the ark of the covenant into the camp to guarantee the Lord's presence with his people. Clearly the ark is a significant thematic element in this section; of the sixty-one occurrences of the word "ark" in the books of Samuel, all but twenty-five appear in 1 Samuel 4:1b–7:2.

The elders doubtless remembered the account of Joshua's victory over Jericho, in which the ark was a highly visible symbol of divine help and strength (Josh 6:2–20; cf. also Num 10:35). It would accompany Israel's army on at least one other occasion in the future as well (2 Sam 11:11). What the elders failed to understand, however, was that the ark was neither an infallible talisman nor a military palladium that would insure victory. If God willed defeat for his people, a thousand arks would not bring success. Marten H. Woudstra has well stated concerning attempts to manipulate the ark: "The offenses against the ark as pledge of Yahweh's presence appear to be mainly of two kinds: (1) a misplaced reliance on the ark, and (2) an irreverent disregard for the ark" (*The Ark of the Covenant from Conquest to Kingship* [Philadelphia: Presbyterian and Reformed, 1965], p. 55). The elders understood clearly that if God was not "with" them, defeat was inevitable (Num 14:42; Deut 1:42). They mistakenly assumed, however, that wherever the ark was, the Lord was.

**4–9** So men were sent to Shiloh from the Israelite camp at Ebenezer (vv.4–5; 5:1) to bring back the ark, here impressively described as "the ark of the covenant of the LORD Almighty [see comment on 1:3], who is enthroned between the cherubim" (cf. 2 Sam 6:2; 2 Kings 19:15 = Isa 37:16; 1 Chron 13:6; Pss 80:1; 99:1). Over fifty years ago W.F. Albright demonstrated that cherubim were winged sphinxes—that is, winged lions with human heads ("What Were the Cherubim?" BA 1, 1 [1938]: 1–3). In ancient Near Eastern art a king was often pictured sitting on a throne supported on each side by a cherub. It appears then that one function of the ark of the covenant was to serve as the symbolic cherub-throne of the invisible Great King. If so, the two cherubim on the ark stood parallel to each other, faces turned slightly inward (Exod 25:20). By comparing v.4 with 2 Samuel 6:2, 1 Chronicles 13:6, and Isaiah 37:16, W.F. Albright further suggests that "[Name of] Yahweh of Hosts, Enthroned on the Cherubim" was the official name given to the ark. He visualizes Hezekiah's prayer in Isaiah as having been "addressed to the invisible Presence which hovered above" the ark inside the Most Holy Place in the temple (review of B.N. Wambacq, *L'Épithète Divine Jahvé Seba'ôt: Étude Philologique Historique et Exégétique* [Bruges: Desclée, 1947], in JBL 67 [1948]: 379). While such a name would certainly have been appropriate during the period of the monarchy, Albright's theory remains unproven.

The ark, accompanied by Hophni and Phinehas, caused a great commotion upon reaching the Israelite camp (v.5). The people gave a loud shout, reminiscent of the battle cry at Jericho's demise (Josh 6:5, 20). The uproar aroused the Philistines camped nearby, and their superstitious response echoed that of the Israelite elders (vv.6–8). They believed that the arrival of the ark heralded the coming of whatever god (v.7) or gods (v.8) its owners worshiped. To avoid being enslaved by the Hebrews, as the Hebrews had been by them (cf. Judg 13:1), they encouraged one another to be strong and fight like men (v.9).

**10–11** The result of the ark's presence was another Israelite defeat, this one far more severe than the previous and described as a *makkāh* ("slaughter," v.10)—echoing the same word used of the Egyptian "plague(s)," whose memory had so impressed the Philistines (v.8). The Philistines' own turn would come (14:13; 19:8; 23:5), but in the meantime Israel suffered heavy losses. The sins of Eli's sons produced appalling casualties among Israel's foot soldiers (cf. Deut 28:15, 25). As foretold by the man of God (2:34), Hophni and Phinehas died (v.11). The elders' folly was revealed as the Philistines captured the ark (a doleful refrain occurring in vv.17, 19, 21, 22), and the destruction of Shiloh—and perhaps the tabernacle itself—was not far behind (cf. Ps 78:56–64; Jer 7:12, 14; 26:6, 9).

## Notes

1 In the late 1970s an ostracon containing a five-line inscription was recovered from an Early Iron Age grain silo in the ruins of Izbet Sarteh. The fifth line was soon identified as an alphabet, but the first four lines remained undeciphered until recently. According to William H. Shea, they read as follows: "Unto the field we came, (unto) Aphek from Shiloh. The Kittim took (it [the ark of the covenant] and) came to Azor, (to) Dagon lord of Ashdod, (and to) Gath. (It returned to) Kiriath Jearim. The companion of the foot soldiers, Hophni, came to tell the elders, 'A horse has come (and) upon (it was my) brother for us to bury' " ("The 'Izbet Ṣarṭah Ostracon," *Andrews University Seminary Studies* 28, 1 [1990]: 62). Shea (p. 81) observes that eleven of the key words in the inscription appear in the parallel account of the capture of the ark in chapters 4–6: "Aphek" (4:1), "field" (4:2), "elders" (4:3), "Shiloh" (4:3–4), "Hophni" (4:4, 11, 17), "foot soldiers" (4:10), "take/capture" (4:11ff.), "tell" (4:13), "Ashdod" (5:1–7), "Gath" (5:8), "Kiriath Jearim" (written "Jearim Kiriah"; 6:21). If Shea's reading holds up under further analysis, the Izbet Sarteh ostracon contains the earliest known extrabiblical references to an OT event (the capture of the ark by the

Philistines) and an OT person (Hophni) (cf. William H. Shea, "Ancient Ostracon Records Ark's Wanderings," *Ministry* [1991]: 14).

**2** The verbal root in the difficult phrase וַתִּטֹּשׁ הַמִּלְחָמָה (*wattiṭṭōš hammilḥāmāh,* "and as the battle spread") is נָטַשׁ (*nāṭaš*), which means "leave," "abandon." Mitchell Dahood suggests that the verb is a by-form of לָטַשׁ (*lāṭaš,* "sharpen") and translates the phrase "and when the clash grew sharp" (cf. "Hebrew-Ugaritic Lexicography VI," *Biblica* 49, 3 [1968]: 361–62). The interchange of the dentals *n* and *l* occurs elsewhere in Hebrew, and the root *lṭš* is used figuratively in Job 16:9: "My opponent fastens on me his piercing eyes."

**3** The origin of the word בְּרִית (*b^erîṯ,* "covenant") is disputed. Likely it derives from the Akkadian *birīt* ("between"), emphasizing the indispensable quality of relationship that inheres in every covenant (see Ronald F. Youngblood, "The Abrahamic Covenant: Conditional or Unconditional?" *The Living and Active Word of God: Essays in Honor of Samuel J. Schultz,* edd. Morris Inch and Ronald Youngblood [Winona Lake: Eisenbrauns, 1983], pp. 34–35).

The NIV text "it" and the margin "he" should probably be reversed. God, not the ark, is "with" his people to avert defeat in Num 14:42 and Deut 1:42. God, not the ark, "saves" his people "from the hand of" the enemy; see Judg 6:14 and 2 Kings 16:7 where, as here, the Hebrew idiom is הוֹשִׁיעַ מִכַּף (*hôšî^a' mikkaḇ,* "save from the hand of").

---

## 2. *The death of Eli*

### 4:12–22

12That same day a Benjamite ran from the battle line and went to Shiloh, his clothes torn and dust on his head. 13When he arrived, there was Eli sitting on his chair by the side of the road, watching, because his heart feared for the ark of God. When the man entered the town and told what had happened, the whole town sent up a cry.

14Eli heard the outcry and asked, "What is the meaning of this uproar?"

The man hurried over to Eli, 15who was ninety-eight years old and whose eyes were set so that he could not see. 16He told Eli, "I have just come from the battle line; I fled from it this very day."

Eli asked, "What happened, my son?"

17The man who brought the news replied, "Israel fled before the Philistines, and the army has suffered heavy losses. Also your two sons, Hophni and Phinehas, are dead, and the ark of God has been captured."

18When he mentioned the ark of God, Eli fell backward off his chair by the side of the gate. His neck was broken and he died, for he was an old man and heavy. He had led Israel forty years.

19His daughter-in-law, the wife of Phinehas, was pregnant and near the time of delivery. When she heard the news that the ark of God had been captured and that her father-in-law and her husband were dead, she went into labor and gave birth, but was overcome by her labor pains. 20As she was dying, the women attending her said, "Don't despair; you have given birth to a son." But she did not respond or pay any attention.

21She named the boy Ichabod, saying, "The glory has departed from Israel"—because of the capture of the ark of God and the deaths of her father-in-law and her husband. 22She said, "The glory has departed from Israel, for the ark of God has been captured."

**12–18** No sooner was the second battle with the Philistines over than the tragic news of Israel's defeat reached Shiloh. The apprehensive question, "What happened?" (*meh-hāyāh haddāḇār,* v.16) occurs elsewhere only in 2 Samuel 1:4 and telegraphs the narrator's intention to compare this account and the one that begins 2 Samuel. Here a Benjamite (v.12) reports Israel's flight from and slaughter by the Philistines as well as the death of two prominent Levites (v.17); there an Amalekite (2 Sam 1:8) reports Israel's flight from and slaughter by the Philistines as well as the death of two prominent Benjamites (2 Sam 1:4). In both cases (v.12; 2 Sam 1:2) the messenger arrived with his clothes "torn and dust on his head" (identical Heb. phrase both places), a sign of anguish and distress (cf. Josh 7:6; Neh 9:1).

Eli is as he was when we first met him (v.13; 1:9), and there he will be when he dies: sitting on his chair (v.18). In 1:9 he was near an entrance to the Lord's house; now he simply sits beside the road. Perhaps no longer considering himself to be the priest he once was, Eli nevertheless trembles with fear (for this nuance of the verb, cf. Judg 7:3) for the ark's safety.

The messenger first told his story to the townspeople at Shiloh, who "sent up a cry" (v.13) when they learned that the ark had not brought them victory and was no longer with them. The later reaction of the Ekronites was similar but for the opposite reason: Philistine possession of the ark was causing an epidemic of tumors among the people (5:9–12). Mere possession of the ark enabled neither Israelite nor Philistine to manipulate the God whose presence it symbolized.

Hearing the uproar in the city, Eli wanted to know its meaning. Ninety-eight years old, obese (v.18), and totally blind (v.15; the Heb. phrase translated "eyes were set" occurs again only in 1 Kings 14:4 [Ahijah's "sight was gone"]), Eli was probably unable to go into town without considerable help; so the messenger went to him (v.14). The verb *biśśar* ("bring news") and its cognate noun *bᵉśōrāh* ("news") almost always connote news that is good—or at least neutral. In v.17, however, the verb is used in the sense of bringing bad news, the only such case in the OT. The news was bad indeed, and the messenger concludes by reporting that the ark of God had been captured.

The news that Hophni and Phinehas were dead did not seem to faze Eli, who may have already given them up as hopeless. But the shock of hearing that the ark had been captured was too much for him. He "fell" off his chair, broke his neck, and died (v.18), a tragic parody of the results of Israel's second encounter (v.10) with the Philistines (lit., "thirty thousand foot soldiers fell"; same Heb. verb). The corpulence that contributed to Eli's death may have been partly due to his participation in the gluttony of his sons (see comment on 2:30 above). The tragedy of Eli's life thus matches that of Saul: sometimes serving God faithfully, at other times not measuring up to even the most moderate of standards. Priest at Shiloh for most of his adult life, he had judged (cf. NIV mg.) Israel for forty years. Following him as both priest and judge (7:6, 15–17) was his young protégé, Samuel.

**19–22** Eli's death did not end the tragedy, even in his own family. The message of Eli's and Phinehas's deaths, combined with the report of the ark's capture (given pride of place in v.19; cf. also v.22), caused Phinehas's pregnant wife to go into premature labor. As a disturbing vision would later cause Daniel to be "overcome with anguish" (Dan 10:16), so a distressing report caused her to be "overcome by her labor pains" (same Heb. expression). In her case, however, the combination was fatal: She died in childbirth. The narrator patterns the account after that of Rachel's death (the Heb. for "Don't despair" here is more literally translated "Don't be afraid" in Gen 35:17).

Before she died Phinehas's wife named her newborn son Ichabod (lit., "no glory," v.21 NIV mg.; cf. 14:3). Verse 21 gives a general reason for the naming, but v.22 is more specific: "The glory has departed [lit., 'has gone into exile'; so also v.21] from Israel, for the ark of God has been captured." After the Exodus the Lord promised to consecrate the tabernacle by his glory (Exod 29:43); after it was set up, his glory filled it and the cloud covered it (Exod 40:34–35). The term "glory" represents the Presence of God dwelling—*škn*—in the tabernacle (Ps 26:8; cf. also Exod 25:8; 29:44–46), giving rise to the later theological term *šᵉkînāh*, sometimes called the "Shek(h)inah Glory." Hebrews 9:5 clarifies the connection between the ark and the Divine Presence: "Above the ark were the cherubim of the Glory, overshadowing the atonement cover." Perhaps the wife of Phinehas, in her dying hour, spoke better than she knew.

## Notes

**18** Segal remarks: "40 years represents the period of a complete generation. . . . The rule of Eli, of David, and of Solomon each lasted 40 years; so also did the rule of Saul. . . . But it is, of course, the 40 years of Israel's wanderings in the Wilderness that left the most vivid mark on the Old Testament" ("Numerals," p. 11). In at least a few of these cases "forty years" should be understood as a rough approximation or perhaps even as a figure of speech for a generation, as Segal suggests (cf. also Ps 95:10).

**21** אִי־כָבוֹד (*'î-kāḇôḏ*, "no glory") uses a rare form of the Hebrew negative particle, the only other clear case occurring in Job 22:30 ("not innocent"). The same particle, however, is used more frequently in Ugaritic and Phoenician. Since *zbl* ("Prince") is an epithet of Baal in Ugaritic, it is quite likely that the Hebrew form of the name of the Phoenician princess Jezebel, אִיזֶבֶל (*'îzeḇel*), means "No Prince" in reference to the myth of Baal's death (as recorded, for example, in the epic literature of Ugarit). The Ugaritic text CTA 6:III–IV:29, 40 reads as follows: *iy zbl b'l arṣ*, "There is no prince, lord [= Baal] of the earth" (cf. Gordon, UT, p. 356). Another possibility is to read *iy* as the interrogative "Where?" and to translate *iy zbl* as "Where is the prince?" (cf. Baruch Margalit, *A Matter of "Life" and "Death": A Study of the Baal-Mot Epic [CTA 4–5–6]* [Neukirchen-Vluyn: Neukirchener, 1980], p. 169). In either case *iy zbl* (= Jezebel) would imply the (at least temporary) nonexistence of "Prince" Baal.

## 3. *The Lord's affliction of the Philistines*

### 5:1–12

1After the Philistines had captured the ark of God, they took it from
Ebenezer to Ashdod. 2Then they carried the ark into Dagon's temple
and set it beside Dagon. 3When the people of Ashdod rose early the next
day, there was Dagon, fallen on his face on the ground before the ark of
the LORD! They took Dagon and put him back in his place. 4But the
following morning when they rose, there was Dagon, fallen on his face
on the ground before the ark of the LORD! His head and hands had been
broken off and were lying on the threshold; only his body remained.
5That is why to this day neither the priests of Dagon nor any others who
enter Dagon's temple at Ashdod step on the threshold.
6The LORD's hand was heavy upon the people of Ashdod and its
vicinity; he brought devastation upon them and afflicted them with
tumors. 7When the men of Ashdod saw what was happening, they said,

"The ark of the god of Israel must not stay here with us, because his hand is heavy upon us and upon Dagon our god."
[8]So they called together all the rulers of the Philistines and asked them, "What shall we do with the ark of the god of Israel?"

They answered, "Have the ark of the god of Israel moved to Gath." So they moved the ark of the God of Israel.

[9]But after they had moved it, the LORD's hand was against that city, throwing it into a great panic. He afflicted the people of the city, both young and old, with an outbreak of tumors.
[10]So they sent the ark of God to Ekron.

As the ark of God was entering Ekron, the people of Ekron cried out, "They have brought the ark of the god of Israel around to us to kill us and our people."
[11]So they called together all the rulers of the Philistines and said, "Send the ark of the god of Israel away; let it go back to its own place, or it will kill us and our people." For death had filled the city with panic; God's hand was very heavy upon it.
[12]Those who did not die were afflicted with tumors, and the outcry of the city went up to heaven.

**1–5** From the battlefield at Ebenezer, the Philistines took the ark of the covenant to Ashdod (v.1), apparently the chief city of their pentapolis (6:17). Ashdod, the only extensively excavated Philistine capital, was located three miles from the Mediterranean coast about thirty miles southwest of Ebenezer. The ark was brought into the temple of Dagon, the Philistine national deity (v.2), and placed near a large idol representing him. The next day the statue of Dagon had fallen facedown, vanquished by Israel's God (as the Philistine champion Goliath would later be defeated by David; see 17:49) and prostrate before the ark in a posture of worship. The people of Ashdod put the idol back in its "place" (the people of Ekron, filled with panic, would soon demand that the ark be returned to "its own place"; see v.11). The next morning Dagon was again facedown before the ark—this time its head and hands were "broken off" (v.4), just as Goliath's head would later be "cut off" by David (17:51; same Heb. verb).

In the ancient world severed heads (cf. Goliath; see also 29:4) and hands (cf. Judg 8:6) were battlefield trophies that assisted the victor in establishing the correct body count (see Antony F. Campbell, *The Ark Narrative*, p. 86, n. 1). The Lord had therefore vanquished Dagon in his own temple, a premonition of things to come. At the temple of Dagon in Gaza, the power of God—symbolized by the hair on Samson's head and the strength in his earlier hands—had defeated the Philistines and their god (Judg 16:21–30). On yet another occasion, however, the Philistines enjoyed a notable victory: They hung up the severed head of Israel's king Saul in a temple of Dagon (1 Chron 10:10), perhaps at Beth Shan (cf. 1 Sam 31:10).

The head and hands of Dagon's statue landed on the temple threshold, rendering it sacred (in the minds of his worshipers) and therefore untouchable (v.5). Zephaniah describes "idolatrous priests" (Zeph 1:4) and their followers as those who "avoid stepping on the threshold" (v.9). They, like the superstitious Philistines before them, were ripe for punishment.

**6–12** With the reference to Dagon's hands being rendered helpless, the narrator introduces a major motif in the account: the hand of the Lord. This motif is so thematic within the ark narratives that Miller and Roberts have perceptively used it as the title of their monograph on the subject. They find it (or its equivalent) eight times in the narrative: 4:8; 5:6, 7, 9, 11; 6:3, 5, 9 (*The Hand of the Lord: A Reassessment of the*

*"Ark Narrative" of 1 Samuel*, p. 48; their ninth citation [5:4] admittedly relates to the hands of Dagon's statue). Because they end the ark narratives at 7:1, they omit from their list of citations the important reference in 7:13, which summarizes the theme.

The first reference here to the hand of the Lord comes from the lips of the Philistines, who related the divine hand to the plagues of Egypt (4:8)—and rightly so (see Exod 9:3; cf. also Jer 21:5–6). They did not take lightly the possibility that the fate of the Egyptians might befall them also (6:6). In the ancient world sickness and plague were often specifically described as the baleful effects of the "hand" of a god (cf. J.J.M. Roberts, "The Hand of Yahweh," VetTest 21, 2 [1971]: 244–51). In addition every characteristic expression relating to the hand of the Lord in the ark narratives has a strikingly similar Akkadian parallel (cf. pp. 248–49 n. 6).

Tumors were one of the many potential curses that would be inflicted on the Israelites if they disobeyed God (Deut 28:58–60). Here that affliction descended on the Philistines (v.6), who realized that the hand of the Lord was heavy on them (v.7; cf. v.11). Their five rulers (6:18) advised them to get rid of the ark (v.8)—which all recognized as the visible surrogate for the Israelite deity and therefore the cause of the plague—by moving it to Gath (modern Tell es-Safi, about twelve miles east-southeast of Ashdod). Thus the Lord's hand was against Gath (v.9; cf. 7:13) and brought "an outbreak of tumors" on its inhabitants. The Hebrew word for "outbreak" is found only here and was apparently interpreted by the LXX as "groin," yielding the translation "tumors in the groin" (see NIV mg.)—a common symptom of bubonic plague.

The ark was quickly shipped to Ekron (modern Khirbet el-Muqanna, about six miles due north of Gath; for a survey of recent archaeological discoveries at Ekron during its peak of development in the time of Samuel, cf. Trude Dothan, "Ekron of the Philistines. Part I: Where They Came From, How They Settled Down, and the Place They Worshiped In," *Biblical Archaeology Review* 16, 1 [1990]: 26–36). But the arrival of the ark in Ekron had the same effect there as the news of its capture had in Shiloh: The people sent up a cry for help (vv.10, 12; see 4:13–14), fearful that the God of Israel would "kill" them—a power that he certainly possessed (cf. 2:6, 25). As the Pharaoh's officials had urged him to let the Israelites go in order to stop the series of plagues engulfing them (Exod 10:7; cf. 12:31–33), so also the people of Ekron told their rulers to send the ark away (v.11). Even those who did not die were afflicted with tumors (v.12); no one escaped the dreaded plague.

The lesson of chapters 4 and 5 is clear: Neither Israelites nor Philistines—not even Dagon himself—can control or resist the will of the sovereign Lord, whose Presence, though enthroned between the cherubim surmounting the ark of the covenant, is not limited by that location and therefore cannot be manipulated by the whim of whoever happens to be in possession of it at any particular time.

## Notes

---

2 The older etymology of דָּגוֹן (*dāgôn*) from דָּג (*dāg*, "fish")—assuming either that Dagon was a fish-god or that he was the god of a maritime people—has now been almost universally abandoned in favor of a derivation from דָּגָן (*dāgān*, "grain"). Ugaritic epic literature claims that Dagon was the father of Baal, the storm-god of fertility, a paternity compatible with his

role as a grain-god. From early times he was worshiped widely by the Semitic peoples of the Levant. Numerous towns were named after him, including Beth Dagon in Judah (Josh 15:41) and Beth Dagon in Asher (Josh 19:27), neither of which has been located.

5 The phrase עַד הַיּוֹם הַזֶּה (*ʿaḏ hayyôm hazzeh,* "to this day"), here and elsewhere in Samuel (e.g., 6:18; 27:6 ["ever since"]; 30:25; 2 Sam 4:3; 6:8; 18:18), indicates that the narrator lived some time later than the events he recorded.

6 "Tumors" (vv.6, 9, 12; 6:4, 5, 11, 17; cf. also Deut 28:27) translates two different words in the MT (often marginal readings): עֳפָלִים (*ʿᵒp̱ālîm,* "swellings") and טְחֹרִים (*ṭᵉḥōrîm,* perhaps "hemorrhoids"; hence KJV, "emerods"). Of the numerous suggested identifications of the specific malady that struck the Philistines, bubonic plague remains the most likely: "It is a disease characterized by an epidemic occurrence, by the appearance of tumours, by the production of panic amongst the affected population, by a high mortality rate, and by an association with mice or rats" (John Wilkinson, "The Philistine Epidemic of I Samuel 5 and 6," ET 88, 5 [1977]: 137). The attempt of Geyer to resurrect the theory that the plague was dysentery and that the tumors were a late symptom uses hopelessly tortuous arguments, makes questionable textual choices, and finds no causal connection between the plague and the rats (he seems not to have been aware of Wilkinson's fine article) (John B. Geyer, "Mice and Rites in 1 Samuel V–VI," VetTest 31, 3 [1981]: 293–304). The LXX addition to v.6 (see NIV mg.), which makes the connection, doubtless rests on reliable tradition, and the guilt offering described in chapter 6 demonstrates that the Philistines were aware of the link as well. The causal connection between rats and plague was not conclusively demonstrated until 1908 (Wilkinson, "The Philistine Epidemic," p. 139). That fleas, hosted by rats, are the actual transmitters of plague is now widely known; for details, cf. Nicole Duplaix, "Fleas: The Lethal Leapers," *National Geographic* 173, 5 (1988): 672–94. In 1630–31 French artist Nicolas Poussin produced a remarkable painting entitled "The Plague at Ashdod"; for a reproduction see Robert R. Stieglitz, "Ancient Records and the Exodus Plagues," *Biblical Archaeology Review* 13, 6 (1987): 48. Whether 1 Sam 5–6 records the first occurrence of bubonic plague in history is impossible to say. Accounts of earlier plagues abound (cf. Ronald F. Youngblood, "Amorite Influence in a Canaanite Amarna Letter [EA 96]," BASOR 168 [1962]: 24–27), but information concerning whether they were bubonic is lacking.

8 סֶרֶן (*seren,* "ruler"), used in the OT only of Philistine rulers, is perhaps related to *τύραννος* (*tyrannos*), from which "tyrant" is derived, and/or to the Hittite *tarwanas,* "judge" (cf. K.A. Kitchen, "The Philistines," *Peoples of Old Testament Times,* ed. D.J. Wiseman [Oxford: Oxford University Press, 1973], pp. 67, 77 n. 110).

---

## 4. *The return of the ark*

### 6:1–7:1

[1]When the ark of the LORD had been in Philistine territory seven
months, [2]the Philistines called for the priests and the diviners and said,
"What shall we do with the ark of the LORD? Tell us how we should send
it back to its place."
[3]They answered, "If you return the ark of the god of Israel, do not
send it away empty, but by all means send a guilt offering to him. Then
you will be healed, and you will know why his hand has not been lifted
from you."
[4]The Philistines asked, "What guilt offering should we send to him?"
They replied, "Five gold tumors and five gold rats, according to the
number of the Philistine rulers, because the same plague has struck
both you and your rulers. [5]Make models of the tumors and of the rats
that are destroying the country, and pay honor to Israel's god. Perhaps
he will lift his hand from you and your gods and your land. [6]Why do you
harden your hearts as the Egyptians and Pharaoh did? When he treated

them harshly, did they not send the Israelites out so they could go on
their way?
7"Now then, get a new cart ready, with two cows that have calved and
have never been yoked. Hitch the cows to the cart, but take their calves
away and pen them up. 8Take the ark of the LORD and put it on the cart,
and in a chest beside it put the gold objects you are sending back to him
as a guilt offering. Send it on its way, 9but keep watching it. If it goes up
to its own territory, toward Beth Shemesh, then the LORD has brought
this great disaster on us. But if it does not, then we will know that it was
not his hand that struck us and that it happened to us by chance."
10So they did this. They took two such cows and hitched them to the
cart and penned up their calves. 11They placed the ark of the LORD on
the cart and along with it the chest containing the gold rats and the
models of the tumors. 12Then the cows went straight up toward Beth
Shemesh, keeping on the road and lowing all the way; they did not turn
to the right or to the left. The rulers of the Philistines followed them as
far as the border of Beth Shemesh.
13Now the people of Beth Shemesh were harvesting their wheat in the
valley, and when they looked up and saw the ark, they rejoiced at the
sight. 14The cart came to the field of Joshua of Beth Shemesh, and there
it stopped beside a large rock. The people chopped up the wood of the
cart and sacrificed the cows as a burnt offering to the LORD. 15The
Levites took down the ark of the LORD, together with the chest
containing the gold objects, and placed them on the large rock. On that
day the people of Beth Shemesh offered burnt offerings and made
sacrifices to the LORD. 16The five rulers of the Philistines saw all this and
then returned that same day to Ekron.
17These are the gold tumors the Philistines sent as a guilt offering to
the LORD—one each for Ashdod, Gaza, Ashkelon, Gath and Ekron.
18And the number of the gold rats was according to the number of
Philistine towns belonging to the five rulers—the fortified towns with
their country villages. The large rock, on which they set the ark of the
LORD, is a witness to this day in the field of Joshua of Beth Shemesh.
19But God struck down some of the men of Beth Shemesh, putting
seventy of them to death because they had looked into the ark of the
LORD. The people mourned because of the heavy blow the LORD had dealt
them, 20and the men of Beth Shemesh asked, "Who can stand in the
presence of the LORD, this holy God? To whom will the ark go up from
here?"
21Then they sent messengers to the people of Kiriath Jearim, saying,
"The Philistines have returned the ark of the LORD. Come down and take
it up to your place."
7:1So the men of Kiriath Jearim came and took up the ark of the LORD.
They took it to Abinadab's house on the hill and consecrated Eleazar his
son to guard the ark of the LORD.

**1–6** Chapter 4 tells of the capture of the ark, chapter 5 of its movement from place to place in Philistia, and chapter 6 of its return to Israel after being in Philistine territory for several months (v.1; "seven" is perhaps a figurative number or an approximation, as "three" is in a similar situation in 2 Sam 6:11). The Philistines, eager to rid themselves of the ark and its sinister influence, and not possessed of the same scruples concerning divination as the Israelites were (cf. Deut 18:14; Isa 2:6), sought supernatural guidance as to the best way of sending the ark back to "its [proper] place" (v.2). "Tell us [*hōḏi'unû*, lit., 'make known to us'; see 'you will know,' v.3, *w$^e$nôḏa' lāḵem*, lit., 'it will be made known to you,' from the same Hebrew root, *yd'*] how," they said to their pagan counselors.

Ancient religious protocol mandated that the worshiper not approach his god(s) empty-handed (cf. Exod 23:15; Deut 16:16). Thus the Philistine priests and diviners advised that a guilt offering (which, in Israel at least, served as payment to atone for unintentional sins; see Lev 5:14–19) accompany the ark back to Israel (v.3). Although such an offering was normally an animal sacrifice, occasionally money or other valuables were acceptable (even in Israel; see 2 Kings 12:16). If the Lord accepted the Philistines' offering, their people would be healed; then they would know that his hand had been responsible for their misery (see also v.9).

Verse 4, by linking tumors, rats, and plague, strengthens the theory that the tumors were symptoms of bubonic plague spread by an infestation of rats, which, like human invaders, were capable of destroying a country (v.5; cf. Jer 36:29; Dan 11:16). The Philistine advisers recommended gold models of tumors and rats to serve as the guilt offering to placate the God of Israel. Perhaps the Philistines intended the models to function in the realm of sympathetic magic also, so that by sending them out of their land the genuine articles would depart as well. Apart from the present context, the only other references to rats/mice in the OT are Leviticus 11:29 and Isaiah 66:17, where they are numbered among ceremonially unclean animals.

The Hebrew word for "plague" (*maggēp̱āh,* v.4) is also used to describe the Egyptian plagues in Exodus 9:14, further heightening the parallel between the earlier disaster and this (cf. again v.6). The lesson is clear: Hardening one's heart (same Heb. expression in Exod 8:15, 32; 9:34) only brings divine retribution, resulting in the victory of God's people over their enemies (Exod 12:31–32). The Philistines are thus well advised to cut their losses as soon as possible.

**7–12** A new cart (as in 2 Sam 6:3) pulled by two cows "that have calved and have never been yoked" (translating *'ālôṯ 'ᵃšer lō'-'ālāh 'ᵃlêhem 'ōl*—a remarkable example of assonance, v.7) was to be used to transport the ark. The cows would later be sacrificed by the Israelites (v.14) in faint reminiscence of the slaughter of the red heifer by Eleazar (Num 19:2–3; cf.—coincidentally?—the Eleazar consecrated to guard the ark at the end of its long journey [7:1]; cf. further Deut 21:1–9). The Philistines were to "take" the calves from their mothers (v.7), "send" the gold objects as a guilt offering to the Lord (vv.8, 17), and "return" the ark to him and his people (v.21; the verbs are all forms of the same stem of the same Heb. root *šûb*).

The first destination of the ark was Beth Shemesh (modern Tell er-Rumeileh, about nine miles east-southeast of Ekron), just inside Israelite territory. Listed among the priestly cities (Josh 21:13–16; 1 Chron 6:57–59), Beth Shemesh had a pagan past (its name means "Temple of the Sun-God"). Large quantities of Philistine pottery found in its ruins attest to Philistine cultural influence there during the period of the judges. The Philistines of Samuel's day, however, acknowledged that Beth Shemesh was under Israelite control. They hoped that the cows would take the ark there, reasoning that if cows new to the yoke would desert their newborn calves—even temporarily—to pull a cart all the way to Beth Shemesh, that would be a supernatural sign that the divine owner of the ark had sent the plague against them. But if the ark did not reach Beth Shemesh, they would take that fact as proof that the Lord's hand had not struck them (v.9; for the same expression see Job 1:11; 2:5; 19:21) and that mere chance was responsible (for the biblical distinction between divine providence and pagan belief in chance, cf. Gustav Friedrich Oehler, *Theology of the Old Testament,* 4th ed. [New York: Funk and Wagnalls, 1883], pp. 121–22).

Against nature ("lowing all the way" because their calves were not with them [v.12]) and under divine compulsion (not turning "to the right or to the left"—i.e., staying on the main road; see Deut 2:27), the cows pulled the cart straight to Beth Shemesh (vv.11–12a). The five Philistine rulers, following the cows to the border, stayed only long enough to make sure that the ark was securely in Israelite hands (vv.12b, 16).

**6:13–7:1** The ark arrived at Beth Shemesh in June, during wheat harvest (v.13), after the spring rains (cf. 12:16–18). Rejoicing to see the ark, the people decided to use the cart for fuel and to sacrifice the cows as a burnt offering. They "chopped up the wood" (v.14), a phrase that also describes the preliminaries for another memorable burnt offering a thousand years earlier (Gen 22:3; "cut enough wood" is the same Heb. expression). (The idiom "sacrifice/offer up a burnt offering" appears also in 7:9–10, another indication that the ark narratives continue through to the end of ch. 7.)

A large rock in a field belonging to Joshua of Beth Shemesh (not to be confused with Joshua son of Nun, Moses' successor) became the temporary locale for the ark (vv.14–15, 18). The Levites, who alone were permitted to handle the ark (cf. Josh 3:3; 2 Sam 15:24), had removed it from the cart and set it on the rock (v.15), which served as a witness of the ark's homecoming until at least the time of the narrator ("to this day," v.18).

Meanwhile, the five Philistine rulers returned to their pentapolis (v.17), all five cities of which are mentioned elsewhere only in Joshua 13:3. Gaza, the southernmost of the five, was located about three miles from the Mediterranean coast and about twenty-two miles southwest of Ashdod, while Ashkelon was on the coast about halfway between Ashdod and Gaza. Each of the five fortified towns was supported by a number of nearby "country villages" (v.18; cf. similarly Deut 3:5 ["unwalled villages"]; Esth 9:19 ["rural . . . villages"]).

Divine retribution continued to overtake those who misused the ark. This time some men of Beth Shemesh "looked into" the ark (v.19), a sin punishable by instant death (Num 4:5, 20; cf. also 2 Sam 6:6–7). The mourners sensed that the ark symbolized the presence of a "holy God" (v.20; cf. Lev 11:44–45), whose sanctity they could not approach. They therefore hoped he would depart from them (the unexpressed subject of "go up" could be either "the ark" or "God"; perhaps both are intended).

Kiriath Jearim (v.21; modern Deir el-Azar, about ten miles northeast of Beth Shemesh) was the ark's location for the next twenty years (7:2; for details cf. Joseph Blenkinsopp, "Kiriath-jearim and the Ark," JBL 88, 2 [1969]: 143–56). More specifically, it resided at "Abinadab's house on the hill" (7:1; 2 Sam 6:3; cf. also NIV mg. on 2 Sam 6:4). Eleazar (whose name has perhaps survived in the modern Arabic name of Kiriath Jearim; viz., Deir el-Azar) son of Abinadab was then consecrated to guard it. The downgraded status of the ark may have been partially due to the Philistine destruction of Shiloh (not referred to in this context but presupposed by Ps 78:60; Jer 7:12, 14; 26:6, 9) and perhaps the tabernacle as well (which would then have been rebuilt later), c. 1050 B.C. Not until David's accession as king in Jerusalem would the ark once again be restored to its rightful place of honor (2 Sam 6).

## Notes

**3** The NIV translation of the last sentence of this verse makes good sense of the relationship between the two clauses; cf. similarly Aelred Cody's review of Miller and Roberts' *The Hand of the Lord,* in CBQ 40 (1978): 98, which provides a convincing parallel with the Hittite Plague Prayers of Mursilis.

**5** "Pay honor" and "harden" (v.6) are renderings of the root כבד (*kbd,* "heavy"), and "lift" translates the root קלל (*qll,* "light"). This echoes the same pair of roots in 2:30 ("honor" and "disdain" respectively; see comment there) and highlights the ironic contrast between the refusal of two Aaronic (and therefore legitimate) priests to obey God and the willingness of Philistine (and therefore illegitimate) priests to do everything necessary to placate God.

**8** אַרְגָּז (*'argaz,* "chest"; elsewhere only in vv.11, 15) is a word "possibly of southwestern Anatolian, Cilician, or Illyrian origin" (Dothan, *The Philistines and Their Material Culture,* p. 23) and was therefore probably brought to the Canaanite mainland by the Philistines.

**18** The main difference between the text and the margin is the reading אֶבֶן (*'eben,* "rock"; see vv.14–15), with a few Hebrew MSS, as opposed to אָבֵל (*'ābēl,* apparently to be understood as a proper name), with most Hebrew MSS. The latter reading may have arisen due to the occurrence of the same root in the next verse ("mourned"). For the possibility that "Great Mourning" is in fact the correct reading and had become a name for the large rock, cf. Antony F. Campbell, *Ark Narrative,* p. 117, n. 2.

**19** The margin reading, "50,070," is attested in all the major ancient versions and is therefore textually secure. The number is far too large, however, to have constituted only "some" of the men of Beth Shemesh; at the same time, the death of "seventy" would hardly be described as a "heavy blow," especially in the light of 4:10 (where "thirty thousand" men died in a "slaughter" that was "very great" [excluding "very," the Heb. is the same as that for "heavy blow"]). A suggested solution is to change ויך בעם שׁבעים איש חמשים אלף איש (*wyk b'm šb'ym 'yš ḥmšym 'lp 'yš,* "He struck down among the people seventy men [and] fifty thousand men") to read ויך בעם שׁבע ים איש חמשׁ ים אלף איש (*wyk b'm šb' ym 'yš ḥmš ym 'lp 'yš,* "He struck down the people for seven days, men for five days, a thousand men") (cf. R. Althann, "Consonantal *ym:* Ending or Noun in Isa 3:13; Jer 17:16; 1 Sam 6:19," *Biblica* 63, 4 [1982]: 563–65). The number slain at Beth Shemesh then becomes a "thousand" rather than "seventy" or "50,070." Although the proposal is attractive, the resulting Hebrew text is awkward and difficult grammatically, even in the poetic format in which Althann casts it.

---

## 5. *Samuel the judge*

### 7:2–17

2 It was a long time, twenty years in all, that the ark remained at Kiriath
Jearim, and all the people of Israel mourned and sought after the LORD.
3 And Samuel said to the whole house of Israel, "If you are returning to
the LORD with all your hearts, then rid yourselves of the foreign gods and
the Ashtoreths and commit yourselves to the LORD and serve him only,
and he will deliver you out of the hand of the Philistines." 4 So the
Israelites put away their Baals and Ashtoreths, and served the LORD only.
5 Then Samuel said, "Assemble all Israel at Mizpah and I will intercede
with the LORD for you." 6 When they had assembled at Mizpah, they drew
water and poured it out before the LORD. On that day they fasted and
there they confessed, "We have sinned against the LORD." And Samuel
was leader of Israel at Mizpah.
7 When the Philistines heard that Israel had assembled at Mizpah, the
rulers of the Philistines came up to attack them. And when the Israelites
heard of it, they were afraid because of the Philistines. 8 They said to

Samuel, "Do not stop crying out to the LORD our God for us, that he may
rescue us from the hand of the Philistines." [9]Then Samuel took a
suckling lamb and offered it up as a whole burnt offering to the LORD. He
cried out to the LORD on Israel's behalf, and the LORD answered him.
[10]While Samuel was sacrificing the burnt offering, the Philistines
drew near to engage Israel in battle. But that day the LORD thundered
with loud thunder against the Philistines and threw them into such a
panic that they were routed before the Israelites. [11]The men of Israel
rushed out of Mizpah and pursued the Philistines, slaughtering them
along the way to a point below Beth Car.
[12]Then Samuel took a stone and set it up between Mizpah and Shen.
He named it Ebenezer, saying, "Thus far has the LORD helped us." [13]So
the Philistines were subdued and did not invade Israelite territory again.
Throughout Samuel's lifetime, the hand of the LORD was against the
Philistines. [14]The towns from Ekron to Gath that the Philistines had
captured from Israel were restored to her, and Israel delivered the
neighboring territory from the power of the Philistines. And there was
peace between Israel and the Amorites.
[15]Samuel continued as judge over Israel all the days of his life. [16]From
year to year he went on a circuit from Bethel to Gilgal to Mizpah,
judging Israel in all those places. [17]But he always went back to Ramah,
where his home was, and there he also judged Israel. And he built an
altar there to the LORD.

Although it is generally assumed that 7:1 concludes the ark narratives (at least the 1 Samuel portion of them), I have argued in the foregoing pages that the account continues to the end of chapter 7 (see esp. the comment on 4:1b–7:17). To summarize: Mention of the ark and Kiriath Jearim links v.2 tightly to v.1; the thematic word "hand" appears throughout (vv.3, 8, 13, 14 [in the last verse "power" is the same Heb. word]); "rulers of the Philistines" occurs in v.7 (and not again until 29:2); "burnt offering" (vv.9–10) reprises 6:14–15; the Philistines continue to attack Israel (vv.10–11), but they are defeated in a decisive campaign that rounds out this series of battles (v.13); the memorial stone in v.12 recalls the large rock in 6:14–15, 18; and Ebenezer (v.12), even if it represents a different place, echoes Ebenezer in 4:1; 5:1 (the only other two places in the Bible where the name occurs).

A recent attempt to parallel 1 Samuel 7 with Exodus 17 (J. Ernest Runions, "Exodus Motifs in First Samuel 7 and 8," EQ 52, 3 [1980]: 130–31) collapses when the details of the alleged similarities are carefully compared. Runions's comments concerning Samuel's career and role as generally analogous to those of Moses, however, are helpful indeed.

**2–4** The "twenty years" that the ark remained at Kiriath Jearim (v.2) may be figurative for "half a generation" (cf. Segal, "Numerals," p. 11, n. 14), during which time the "people" (lit., "house," as in v.3, in the sense of "family," "community") of Israel "mourned" (the Heb. verb *nāhāh,* different from the far more common one represented in 6:19 [*'āḇal*] occurs only twice elsewhere: Ezek 32:18 ["wail"] and Mic 2:4 ["taunt"]), apparently with sincere remorse. They were bemoaning the reduced status of the ark, no longer housed in a tabernacle. Samuel encouraged them to repent and to serve the Lord wholeheartedly (v.3), as he would again (12:20, 24).

Like Jacob (Gen 35:2, 4) and Joshua (Josh 24:14, 23) before him, Samuel urged the people to get rid of the foreign gods (idols) that they were so prone to worship (cf. also Deut 12:3; Judg 10:16; 2 Chron 19:3; 33:15). "Foreign gods and . . . Ashtoreths" (v.3) is essentially synonymous with "Baals and Ashtoreths" (v.4; 12:10, Judg 2:13; 10:6), as the people's response in v.4 to Samuel's counsel in v.3 indicates. Baal and Ashtoreth (or, alternatively, Asherah; cf. Judg 3:7) were the chief god and goddess, respectively, in the Canaanite pantheon during this period; so the phrases in vv.3–4 signify "gods and goddesses" (cf. the corresponding Akkadian expression *ilū u ištarātu*). Local manifestations (idols) of such deities in hundreds of Canaanite towns and villages provide yet another reason for the frequent use of their names in the plural.

Baal, god of fertility and the storm, was believed to be the son of Dagon, god of grain (see Notes on 5:2). Ashtoreth, goddess of love and fertility, vied for supremacy with Asherah, mother-goddess and consort of El (the creator-god in the earlier Canaanite pantheon but now displaced by Baal). The association of Baal, Asherah, and Ashtoreth with fertility, particularly as expressed in depraved sexual ritual at Canaanite shrines, made them especially abominable in the Lord's eyes. The name "Baal" was often linked with *bōšeṯ* ("shame[ful]") in the biblical text (cf. Jer 11:13; Hos 9:10), and the two words occasionally interchanged in proper names (e.g., Ish-Bosheth in 2 Sam 2:8 = Esh-Baal in 1 Chron 8:33 [see NIV mg.]). The name "Ashtoreth" (originally "Ashtart[u]") has been revocalized to rhyme with *bōšeṯ* and thus stigmatize her with Baal's shame.

Samuel's plea is light years away from the depraved paganism of Canaanite religion: "Commit yourselves [lit., 'your hearts'; cf. earlier in the same verse] to the LORD" (v.3). God's people are to serve him exclusively (vv.3–4; see esp. Deut 6:13, quoted by Jesus in Matt 4:10 = Luke 4:8).

**5–6** The assembly of "all Israel" (v.5) did not necessarily include every single Israelite living in the land but probably consisted of representatives from all the tribal territories. A common phrase in the books of Samuel, it is of course sometimes used in an all-inclusive way (cf. 3:20) as determined by context. Convocations at Mizpah (modern Tell en-Nasbeh, about fourteen miles south-southwest of Shiloh) in Benjamin were not uncommon in the days of the judges and early monarchy (cf. 10:17; Judg 20:1; 21:8). There Samuel prayed for the people (for Samuel as a man of prayer, cf. also vv.8–9; 8:6; 12:19, 23; 15:11; Jer 15:1), and there they "poured . . . out [water] before the LORD" (v.6). Although the meaning of this latter act (the expression is unique) is somewhat uncertain (BDB, p. 1049, is perhaps correct in calling it a "symbol of contrition" in this setting), David later "poured out" water before the Lord (2 Sam 23:16; the Hebrew verb, however, is different) as a libation in the context of the heroism of his three companions.

The notice of Samuel's judgeship (v.6; see NIV mg.) is followed immediately by a report of Philistine intention to attack Israel. We are thus reminded that the function of a "judge" during this period was more executive than judicial. "Judge" often paralleled "ruler" or "prince" in contemporary Canaanite literature as well as in the OT itself (cf. Exod 2:14), and one of the most common roles of the judge was to repel invaders (v.8; Judg 2:16, 18).

**7–9** Cowed by Philistine might, Israel typically reacted with fear to news of impending warfare with them (v.7; 17:11; 28:5). But when the Philistines "came up" to attack, Samuel prayerfully "offered . . . up" (v.9; same Heb. root in both cases, *'ālāh*) a burnt offering to the Lord (for Samuel as priest, cf. 9:12; 11:14–15; 16:2; Ps 99:6). The sacrifice was a suckling lamb at least eight days old (cf. Lev 22:27).

**10–12** While the sacrifice was still in progress, the Philistine troops marched forward. Before the battle could be joined, however, the Lord "thundered" against the enemy (v.10; see 2:10; 2 Sam 22:14–15). In so doing he demonstrated that he, not the Philistine Dagon, not the Canaanite Baal son of Dagon, was truly the God of the storm, the only one able to control the elements whether for good or ill (cf. 12:17–18). The NIV translation "with loud thunder" for the more literal "with a great voice" (v.10) highlights the vivid OT image of thunder as the voice of God (see Ps 29:3–9).

The ensuing panic in their ranks (cf. 2 Sam 22:14–15) drove the Philistines into full retreat, enabling the Israelites to pursue and slaughter them (v.11). The location of Beth Car (perhaps meaning "House of the Lamb"; cf. 15:9) is unknown, as is that of Shen ("Tooth," v.12). The best suggestion for the latter is that of Delitzsch (cf. also Klein), who reads it as a common noun referring to the sharp overhang of a cliff (as in 14:4–5; Job 39:28). Another possibility, although hardly necessary, is to emend *haššēn* ("The Tooth") to *yešānāh* ("The Old One") on the basis of readings in the ancient versions (cf. also 2 Chron 13:19). In either case the Ebenezer of v.12 is almost certainly not the Ebenezer of 4:1 and 5:1, since the latter is too far to the northwest for Mizpah to be used as a benchmark for its location.

The stone set up by Samuel is reminiscent of other commemorative stelae (cf. Gen 35:14; Josh 4:9; 24:26; for details see Carl F. Graesser, "Standing Stones in Ancient Palestine," BA 35, 2 [1972]: 34–63). *'Eḇen hā'āzer* ("The Stone of [Divine] Help"; see NIV mg.) pays tribute to the God apart from whom victory is inconceivable.

**13–17** These verses echo "the formulae which mark the end of the story of a judge (cf. Judg. 3:30; 8:28)" (Dennis J. McCarthy, "The Inauguration of Monarchy in Israel: A Form-Critical Study of I Samuel 8–12," Int 27 [1973]: 402). A new paragraph should therefore start at the beginning of the verse, not in the middle (as in NIV). At the same time the second half of the verse assumes continued Philistine pressure (though greatly reduced) against Israel and thus cautions us not to understand the first half as meaning that the Philistines no longer bothered the Israelites in any way (cf. esp. 9:16). The Amorites (the Heb. term is cognate to Akkadian *amurrû*, "westerner"), who preferred to live in the hilly regions of the land (cf. Num 13:29; Deut 1:7) as compared to the Philistines who lived along the coast, were also relatively nonbelligerent during this period (v.14; cf. further 2 Sam 21:2). The Hebrew for the phrase "peace between" (*šālôm bên*) occurs only twice elsewhere (Judg 4:17 ["friendly relations between"]; 1 Kings 5:12 ["peaceful relations between"]); the latter text suggests that the Israelites and Amorites had signed a mutual nonaggression pact.

The circuit of Samuel's judgeship (v.16) was relatively restricted: Bethel (perhaps modern Beitin), Gilgal (perhaps modern Khirbet el-Mefjer), and Mizpah were all within a few miles of one another. All three towns served as shrine centers at one time or another, as did Ramah, Samuel's hometown (cf. the mention of the altar in v.17). The latter was not far from the other three (about fourteen miles northwest of Mizpah). The narrator reminds us again of the local nature of judgeship in ancient Israel to subtly introduce us to the need—however ambiguous and contradictory—for a king "such as all the other nations have" (8:5, 20).

## Notes

9 טָלֵה (*ṭāleh*, "lamb") occurs only twice elsewhere (Isa 40:11; 65:25) and emphasizes the young age of the animal. The Aramaic cognate means not only "young lamb" but also "young boy"; Jesus uses the feminine form of the word in the story of the resurrection of a twelve-year-old girl (Mark 5:41).

## II. Advent of Monarchy in Israel (8:1–15:35)

Monarchy was a significant factor in God's plans for his people from the days of Abraham (Gen 17:6, 16). The blessing of Jacob hints at the establishment of a continuing dynasty (Gen 49:10). Israel was to be "a kingdom of priests and a holy nation" (Exod 19:6). Balaam's fourth oracle refers to monarchical rule (Num 24:17–19), and Moses outlines the divine expectations Israel's kings were to meet (Deut 17:14–20).

However, from the earliest days it was recognized that ultimately God himself was King (Exod 15:18; Num 23:21; Deut 33:5); he alone possessed absolute power and authority (Exod 15:6, 11; Judg 5:3–5; cf. also Judg 8:22–23). Any king of Israel would have to appreciate from the outset that he was to rule over Israel under God. Only on the basis of this fundamental theological premise can the narratives of the advent of monarchy in Israel be properly understood. Those narratives consist of the accounts of the rise (8:1–12:25) and decline (13:1–15:35) of Saul, Israel's first king.

### A. *The Rise of Saul (8:1–12:25)*

Many commentators routinely assert that chapters 8–12 are a literary pastiche of diametrically opposed promonarchical and antimonarchical source materials. The claim is often made that the former originated in preexilic times and that the latter arose in the bitterness and disappointment of Exile some time (whether sooner or later) after the destruction of Jerusalem in 586 B.C. The chapters therefore do not provide reliable historical information but constitute a mixture of contradictory tracts for different times. It is becoming increasingly clear, however, that the account of the beginnings of Israel's monarchy is partly a reflection of the ambiguity toward kingship in general in the light of the excesses that characterized monarchy among Israel's neighbors (cf. I. Mendelsohn, "Samuel's Denunciation of Kingship in the Light of the Akkadian Documents From Ugarit," BASOR 143 [1956]: 17–22). "Israel failed in so far as she sought earthly power and political influence, and succeeded only in so far as she realized her divine destiny" (Hugh J. Blair, "Kingship in Israel and Its Implications for the Lordship of Christ Today," EQ 47, 2 [1975]: 71).

Many of the nations surrounding Israel considered their kings to be gods, whether by divine adoption or through self-deification (cf. Isa 14:4, 13–14; Ezek 28:2, 6, 9). In Israel such a claim was unthinkable since the king possessed neither deity nor absolute authority (2 Kings 5:7)—but the temptation and danger were ever present. To be sure, Israel's king was to exercise "political and military power, but he stood under the authority and judgment of God" (Waylon Bailey, "The King and the Sinai Covenant," *Biblical Illustrator* 10, 3 [1984]: 39). Finally, discussion of monarchy among God's people must take into account God's will. J. Barton Payne's comments are helpful in this regard:

> It *was not* God's will for Israel to have a king in the way they were asking for it. Still, God's resultant precept, what His "permissive will" came to be, was to direct Samuel to anoint Saul as king out of the tribe of Benjamin. . . . Three important distinctions are here to be observed. (1) God changed His preceptive will, but only because men had changed (cf. 8:3–5). In fact, it was because God's standard of righteousness had not changed that His precept had to change. . . . (2) God performed the very act that men wanted; but, while their motive was wrong and in this act they became guilty, God's motive was right and in the very same act He did not become guilty. . . . (3) God was grieved over men's apostasy (v.7); and their act called forth His divine love. In spite of the sin-inspired situation of Saul, and in fact through it, God ministered a number of deliverances (9:16; 10:9, 24; 11:13). Saul had thus been a part of God's decree from the first, and He used the wrath of men to praise Him (Ps. 76:10). ("Saul and the Changing Will of God," BS 129 [1972]: 323)

Ronald E. Clements summarizes:

> The sharpness of the criticism of the kingship expressed here is not in order to reject the institution altogether, which would make nonsense of the sequel in Yahweh's acceding to the request. Rather it is to condemn the precipitate action of the people in pressing their desire, when Yahweh himself was able to do all that was necessary in order to ensure the people's salvation, as the preceding Deuteronomistic narrative of the victory won by Samuel over the Philistines illustrates. ("The Deuteronomistic Interpretation of the Founding of the Monarchy in I Sam. VIII," VetTest 24, 4 [1974]: 406–7)

Clearly these five chapters constitute a literary unit, for they are immediately preceded by the formula that marks the end of the story of a judge (7:13–17) and immediately followed by the formula that marks the beginning of the account of a reign (13:1; cf. McCarthy, "The Inauguration of Monarchy," p. 402). The divisions of the unit (as determined here) alternate between negative and positive attitudes toward monarchy (not as contradictory but as complementary): 8:1–22, negative; 9:1–10:16, positive; 10:17–27, negative; 11:1–11, positive; 11:12–12:25, negative (cf. McCarthy, "The Inauguration of Monarchy," pp. 401–2, who characterizes the alternating sections as "reports" and "stories"; for a full discussion of the entire problem, cf. Vannoy, pp. 197–239).

### 1. *The demand for a king*

#### 8:1–22

**1When Samuel grew old, he appointed his sons as judges for Israel.**
**2The name of his firstborn was Joel and the name of his second was**
**Abijah, and they served at Beersheba. 3But his sons did not walk in his**
**ways. They turned aside after dishonest gain and accepted bribes and perverted justice.**

**4So all the elders of Israel gathered together and came to Samuel at**
**Ramah. 5They said to him, "You are old, and your sons do not walk in**
**your ways; now appoint a king to lead us, such as all the other nations have."**

6But when they said, "Give us a king to lead us," this displeased Samuel; so he prayed to the LORD. 7And the LORD told him: "Listen to all that the people are saying to you; it is not you they have rejected, but they have rejected me as their king. 8As they have done from the day I brought them up out of Egypt until this day, forsaking me and serving other gods, so they are doing to you. 9Now listen to them; but warn them solemnly and let them know what the king who will reign over them will do."

10Samuel told all the words of the LORD to the people who were asking him for a king. 11He said, "This is what the king who will reign over you will do: He will take your sons and make them serve with his chariots and horses, and they will run in front of his chariots. 12Some he will assign to be commanders of thousands and commanders of fifties, and others to plow his ground and reap his harvest, and still others to make weapons of war and equipment for his chariots. 13He will take your daughters to be perfumers and cooks and bakers. 14He will take the best of your fields and vineyards and olive groves and give them to his attendants. 15He will take a tenth of your grain and of your vintage and give it to his officials and attendants. 16Your menservants and maidservants and the best of your cattle and donkeys he will take for his own use. 17He will take a tenth of your flocks, and you yourselves will become his slaves. 18When that day comes, you will cry out for relief from the king you have chosen, and the LORD will not answer you in that day."

19But the people refused to listen to Samuel. "No!" they said. "We want a king over us. 20Then we will be like all the other nations, with a king to lead us and to go out before us and fight our battles."

21When Samuel heard all that the people said, he repeated it before the LORD. 22The LORD answered, "Listen to them and give them a king."

Then Samuel said to the men of Israel, "Everyone go back to his town."

**1–3** Although Samuel's death is not recorded until 25:1, the narrator begins to refer to his advanced age (vv.1, 5; 12:2). The old order (of the judges) is passing, the new (of the monarchy) is dawning. The root *špṭ* ("judge") is frequent in this chapter (v.1, "judges"; v.2, "served"; v.3, "justice"; vv.5–6, 20, "lead" [NIV mg., "judge"]; vv.9, 11, "what . . . will do"), further strengthening the chapter's function as transition as well as linking judgeship closely to the coming monarchy. While Samuel continued as judge at Ramah and nearby towns (7:15–17), he appointed his two sons to serve in the same capacity at Beersheba (v.2) on the southern boundary of the land (cf. 3:20). Their actions and reputations (v.5) belied their names—Joel ("The Lord is God"), Abijah ("My [Divine] Father is the Lord")—but at least their geographical distance from Samuel (Beersheba is about fifty-seven miles south-southwest of Ramah) absolved him from any direct complicity in their evil deeds (so Eslinger, *Kingship of God,* p. 252).

Whether Samuel should have appointed his sons as judges in the first place is highly questionable, since judgeship was usually a divine charisma (cf. Judg 2:16, 18; 3:10, 15; 6:12; 11:29; 13:25). In any event, they did not follow in their father's footsteps (v.3). "Turned aside" and "perverted" are identical in the Hebrew text and tie the three sins—"dishonest gain and accepted bribes and perverted justice"—together. Failing to emulate their father (12:3–4) or their God (Deut 10:17), Joel and Abijah accepted bribes, a crime inseparable from the perversion and denial of justice (Prov 17:23). Moses condemned these common offenses again and again (Exod 23:6,

8; Deut 16:18–19; 24:17; 27:19; cf. also Ps 15:5; Lam 3:35; Amos 2:7). Ironically, Samuel's two sons were as wicked in their own way as were Eli's two sons.

**4–9** Old men ("elders," v.4) confront an old man (Samuel, v.4) and—perhaps unwittingly—remind him of the cruel parallel between himself and the aged (and now deceased) Eli, Samuel's predecessor as priest and judge (v.5; cf. 2:22). Because of Samuel's age, and because they want nothing to do with a dynastic succession that would include his rebellious sons, the elders in their collective wisdom decide that a king would best suit their needs. "Samuel experiences what Moses, the prophets, and even Jesus experience: 'We do not want this man to reign over us' (Luke 19.14)" (Hertzberg, p. 72). Samuel had "appointed" his sons as "judges" (v.1); the elders wanted him to "appoint" a king to "judge" (see NIV mg.) Israel (v.5). Samuel's reluctant compliance with their request would—ironically—twice include the Hebrew verb "appoint," but in a harsher sense: "make them serve" (v.11), "assign" (v.12).

The elders wanted a king "such as all the other nations have" (v.5). Verse 20 reveals their hidden agenda: The king would "go out before us and fight our battles." They were looking for a permanent military leader who would build a standing army powerful enough to repulse any invader. Moses clearly foresaw the elders' demand (Deut 17:14) and warned of the grave dangers involved in pursuing such a course of action (Deut 17:15–17). Samuel, fully aware of those dangers, was "displeased" with the elders' request (v.6)—and he was convinced that the Lord too was displeased (12:17; cf. also 15:11).

Nevertheless, Samuel, seeking God's mind in the matter, was doubtless surprised when the Lord told him to "listen to" (lit., "obey"; vv.7, 9, 22) the people's request mediated through their elders. As in the desert centuries earlier (Exod 16:8), Israel was not rejecting the Lord's chosen leader but the Lord himself (v.7; see also 10:19). Since the days of the Exodus—that mighty act of corporate and personal redemption—the people had consistently preferred other gods and other leaders to God himself and his chosen servants (v.8).

But why does the Lord exclude Samuel from the people's rejection in v.7 and then include him in it in v.8? Delitzsch asserts that by rejecting Samuel (God's representative), the people are in effect rejecting God himself. That is clearly not the most obvious meaning of the passage, however. Scott L. Harris ("1 Samuel VIII 7–8," VetTest 31, 1 [1981]: 79–80) proposes *gm-mlk* ("also a king") instead of *gm-lk* ("also to you") at the end of v.8. The MT error would have occurred by simple haplography (writing once what should have been written twice) of the *m*, and the new reading yields the translation "so they are also making a king." The "now" (*w*[e]*'attāh*) that begins the next verse is then reprised in 10:19b ("So now") and 12:13, both times in contexts that begin—as here—with a rehearsal of Israel's sins during the days of the Exodus and conclude with their impetuous demand for a king (10:18–19a; 12:6–12). Although Harris's suggestion lacks textual evidence, the conjectural emendation has much to commend it in the overall context of the larger unit (chs. 8–12).

God, graciously condescending to the people's desire (a desire not in itself wrong but sullied by the motivation behind it), told Samuel to warn them what the "regulations of the kingship" (10:25; cf. the almost identical phrase in vv.9, 11 ["what the king . . . will do"]) would demand of them. The phrase "will reign over them" (vv.9, 11) highlights the loss of freedom in (absolute) monarchy and is a sad commentary on Israel's renunciation of their Divine King.

**10–18** The "regulations of the kingship" described by Samuel (with God's prompting and approval, v.10) were totally bereft of redeeming features and consisted only of oppressive requirements. Among the latter was the corvée (forced labor), including compulsory induction ("make them serve," v.11) of both raw recruits (cf. Saul's policy, 14:52) and laborers in field and foundry (v.12). Although common in the ancient world generally, the corvée was unknown in Israel during the time of the judges and was introduced there under the monarchy (cf. Mendelsohn, "Samuel's Denunciation of Kingship," p. 21, n. 33; id., "On Corvée Labor in Ancient Canaan and Israel," BASOR 167 [1962]: 33).

The palace-to-be would acquire horses in great numbers (contrary to Deut 17:16), and the king's chariots would need front runners (v.11; cf. the practice of Absalom [2 Sam 15:1] and Adonijah [1 Kings 1:5]). Reference (v.12) to commanders "of thousands and . . . of fifties" (probably shorthand for "thousands, hundreds, fifties and tens"; cf. Exod 18:21, 25; Deut 1:15) implies a huge standing army. The term "weapons of war" (v.12) would become so immediately recognizable that David would be able to use it as a figure of speech in his elegy for Saul and Jonathan (2 Sam 1:27). Women would not be exempt from conscription into royal service (v.13). Even in desperate times the king would always get his share (Amos 7:1)—a minimum of 10 percent of the income from field and flock (vv.15, 17).

Key words in the "regulations of the kingship" are "take" (vv.11, 13–17) and "best" (vv.14, 16). By nature royalty is parasitic rather than giving, and kings are never satisfied with the worst. Although Israelite rulers were prohibited from expropriating family property (cf. Ezek 46:18), no such scruples applied to Canaanite rulers—as Ahab learned in the sordid case of Naboth's vineyard (1 Kings 21:7). Garsiel (pp. 69–70) observes that although the king "takes" everything, Samuel reminds the people that he himself has "taken" nothing (12:3–4).

Samuel's "regulations of the kingship," which would not benefit the average Israelite, followed contemporary semifeudal Canaanite society. "In view of the evidence from the Akkadian texts from Ugarit it seems obvious that the Samuel summary of 'the manner of the king' does not constitute 'a rewriting of history' by a late opponent of kingship but represents an eloquent appeal to the people by a contemporary of Saul not to impose upon themselves a Canaanite institution alien to their own way of life" (Mendelsohn, "Samuel's Denunciation of Kingship," p. 22). Various aspects of the "regulations" would be implemented by Saul (22:6–19) and Absalom (2 Sam 15:1–6)—although Solomon would become the most notable offender. In the light of Samuel's own record of fairness and honesty during his judgeship (cf. esp. 12:3–5), it is no wonder that he was alarmed at the prospect of setting up a typical Oriental monarchy in Israel.

If the "regulations of the kingship" attained full authority, the average Israelite would soon be little more than a chattel at the disposal of his monarch. The frequent occurrence of *'eḇeḏ* ("servant," "slave") thus sounds an especially ominous note (vv.14–15, "attendants"; v.16, "menservants"; v.17, "slaves"). In v.17 Samuel warned the people that they would "become" their king's "slaves," terminology employed elsewhere of bondage imposed by a conqueror (17:9, "become . . . subjects"; 27:12, "be . . . servant"; 2 Sam 8:2, 6, "became subject to"). Too late the Israelites would cry out to a God who would not answer (v.18)—unlike the days when Samuel was judge (7:8–9).

**19–22** Samuel's best efforts were futile. Despite his totally negative delineation of the royal "regulations," the people refused to "listen to" (v.19; i.e., "obey"; see comment on v.7) him. They wanted a king—a demand that Samuel hurled back in their teeth twice in the context of their rejection of divine rule (10:19; 12:12). They clung doggedly to their original request (v.5): "We [emphatic in Heb.] will be like all the other [pagan] nations" (v.20). The implicit military component of their idea of monarchy now becomes explicit: Their king would "fight our battles"—although a godly Israelite king would know from the outset that it was the Lord's joyful duty to do just that for his people (2 Chron 32:8).

As the Lord had told Samuel earlier (v.7), so he told him now: "Listen to [= obey] them and give them a king" (v.22). On that negative (for Samuel) note the chapter ends and Samuel's farewell oration to Israel begins (12:1).

The eight speeches in chapter 8 constitute a remarkable chiasm in which the second element in each pair reverses the roles of speaker and addressee:

A. The people to Samuel (v.5)
  B. Samuel to the Lord (v.6)
    C. The Lord to Samuel (vv.7–9)
      D. Samuel to the people (vv.10–18)
      D′. The people to Samuel (vv.19–20)
    C′. Samuel to the Lord (v.21)
  B′. The Lord to Samuel (v.22a)
A′. Samuel to the people (v.22b)

Eslinger (*Kingship of God,* pp. 258–59) helpfully notes: "At the centre of this inversion we see that the opposition between two groups is really between Samuel and the people—not between the people and Yahweh as would be expected. The structural opposition supports and confirms a fact that appears during the course of the unfolding dialogue: Yahweh, though not liking the request, does not deny it; instead, he simply subverts it."

## Notes

**2** The names of Samuel's two sons occur again only in 1 Chron 6:28, 33 (both in v.28, Joel alone in v.33). In 1 Chron 6:28 the word יוֹאֵל (*yô'ēl,* "Joel") was omitted in Hebrew manuscripts (see NIV mg.) after the word שְׁמוּאֵל (*šᵉmû'ēl,* "Samuel") due to the scribal error known as *homoioteleuton* ("same ending").

**6** Except for the change of verb, "Give us a king to lead us" is a verbatim citation of "Appoint a king to lead us" (v.5). The Bible often follows the practice, common in the ancient world, of approximating direct quotations instead of citing *ipsissima verba.*

**16** In context "cattle" rather than "young men" (see NIV mg.) is clearly the better reading. The MT's בַּחוּרֵיכֶם הַטּוֹבִים (*baḥûrêḵem haṭṭôḇîm,* "the best of your young men") perhaps arose under the influence of בָּחוּר וָטוֹב (*bāḥûr wāṭôḇ,* "an impressive young man," 9:2).

The word "best" modifies only "cattle/young men" in the MT; NIV's extension to "donkeys" is contextually apt.

## 2. *The anointing of Saul*

### 9:1–10:16

1 There was a Benjamite, a man of standing, whose name was Kish son
of Abiel, the son of Zeror, the son of Becorath, the son of Aphiah of
Benjamin. 2 He had a son named Saul, an impressive young man without
equal among the Israelites—a head taller than any of the others.
3 Now the donkeys belonging to Saul's father Kish were lost, and Kish
said to his son Saul, "Take one of the servants with you and go and look
for the donkeys." 4 So he passed through the hill country of Ephraim and
through the area around Shalisha, but they did not find them. They went
on into the district of Shaalim, but the donkeys were not there. Then he
passed through the territory of Benjamin, but they did not find them.
5 When they reached the district of Zuph, Saul said to the servant who
was with him, "Come, let's go back, or my father will stop thinking about
the donkeys and start worrying about us."
6 But the servant replied, "Look, in this town there is a man of God; he
is highly respected, and everything he says comes true. Let's go there
now. Perhaps he will tell us what way to take."
7 Saul said to his servant, "If we go, what can we give the man? The
food in our sacks is gone. We have no gift to take to the man of God.
What do we have?"
8 The servant answered him again. "Look," he said, "I have a quarter
of a shekel of silver. I will give it to the man of God so that he will tell us
what way to take." 9 (Formerly in Israel, if a man went to inquire of God,
he would say, "Come, let us go to the seer," because the prophet of
today used to be called a seer.)
10 "Good," Saul said to his servant. "Come, let's go." So they set out
for the town where the man of God was.
11 As they were going up the hill to the town, they met some girls
coming out to draw water, and they asked them, "Is the seer here?"
12 "He is," they answered. "He's ahead of you. Hurry now; he has just
come to our town today, for the people have a sacrifice at the high
place. 13 As soon as you enter the town, you will find him before he goes
up to the high place to eat. The people will not begin eating until he
comes, because he must bless the sacrifice; afterward, those who are
invited will eat. Go up now; you should find him about this time."
14 They went up to the town, and as they were entering it, there was
Samuel, coming toward them on his way up to the high place.
15 Now the day before Saul came, the LORD had revealed this to
Samuel: 16 "About this time tomorrow I will send you a man from the
land of Benjamin. Anoint him leader over my people Israel; he will
deliver my people from the hand of the Philistines. I have looked upon
my people, for their cry has reached me."
17 When Samuel caught sight of Saul, the LORD said to him, "This is the
man I spoke to you about; he will govern my people."
18 Saul approached Samuel in the gateway and asked, "Would you
please tell me where the seer's house is?"
19 "I am the seer," Samuel replied. "Go up ahead of me to the high
place, for today you are to eat with me, and in the morning I will let you
go and will tell you all that is in your heart. 20 As for the donkeys you lost
three days ago, do not worry about them; they have been found. And to
whom is all the desire of Israel turned, if not to you and all your father's
family?"
21 Saul answered, "But am I not a Benjamite, from the smallest tribe of
Israel, and is not my clan the least of all the clans of the tribe of
Benjamin? Why do you say such a thing to me?"

22Then Samuel brought Saul and his servant into the hall and seated
them at the head of those who were invited—about thirty in number.
23Samuel said to the cook, "Bring the piece of meat I gave you, the one I
told you to lay aside."

24So the cook took up the leg with what was on it and set it in front of
Saul. Samuel said, "Here is what has been kept for you. Eat, because it
was set aside for you for this occasion, from the time I said, 'I have
invited guests.'" And Saul dined with Samuel that day.

25After they came down from the high place to the town, Samuel
talked with Saul on the roof of his house. 26They rose about daybreak
and Samuel called to Saul on the roof, "Get ready, and I will send you on
your way." When Saul got ready, he and Samuel went outside together.
27As they were going down to the edge of the town, Samuel said to Saul,
"Tell the servant to go on ahead of us"—and the servant did so—"but
you stay here awhile, so that I may give you a message from God."

10:1Then Samuel took a flask of oil and poured it on Saul's head and
kissed him, saying, "Has not the LORD anointed you leader over his
inheritance? 2When you leave me today, you will meet two men near
Rachel's tomb, at Zelzah on the border of Benjamin. They will say to
you, 'The donkeys you set out to look for have been found. And now
your father has stopped thinking about them and is worried about you.
He is asking, "What shall I do about my son?"'

3"Then you will go on from there until you reach the great tree of
Tabor. Three men going up to God at Bethel will meet you there. One
will be carrying three young goats, another three loaves of bread, and
another a skin of wine. 4They will greet you and offer you two loaves of
bread, which you will accept from them.

5"After that you will go to Gibeah of God, where there is a Philistine
outpost. As you approach the town, you will meet a procession of
prophets coming down from the high place with lyres, tambourines,
flutes and harps being played before them, and they will be prophesying. 6The Spirit of the LORD will come upon you in power, and you will
prophesy with them; and you will be changed into a different person.
7Once these signs are fulfilled, do whatever your hand finds to do, for
God is with you.

8"Go down ahead of me to Gilgal. I will surely come down to you to
sacrifice burnt offerings and fellowship offerings, but you must wait
seven days until I come to you and tell you what you are to do."

9As Saul turned to leave Samuel, God changed Saul's heart, and all
these signs were fulfilled that day. 10When they arrived at Gibeah, a
procession of prophets met him; the Spirit of God came upon him in
power, and he joined in their prophesying. 11When all those who had
formerly known him saw him prophesying with the prophets, they asked
each other, "What is this that has happened to the son of Kish? Is Saul
also among the prophets?"

12A man who lived there answered, "And who is their father?" So it
became a saying: "Is Saul also among the prophets?" 13After Saul
stopped prophesying, he went to the high place.

14Now Saul's uncle asked him and his servant, "Where have you
been?"

"Looking for the donkeys," he said. "But when we saw they were not
to be found, we went to Samuel."

15Saul's uncle said, "Tell me what Samuel said to you."

16Saul replied, "He assured us that the donkeys had been found." But
he did not tell his uncle what Samuel had said about the kingship.

**1–2** Scholarly studies of Saul, the first king of Israel, have depicted him as (among other things) villain, tragic figure, flawed ruler, naive farm-boy, degenerate madman, fate-driven pawn, reluctant king—the list goes on and on. Such characterizations are at least partially true; Saul was surely one of the most complex persons described in Scripture.

Notice that almost all the above portrayals are decidedly negative. Historically writers have focused on the darker side of Saul's nature. While not wishing to deny that side, I am sympathetic with those scholars (still in the minority, to be sure) who attempt to portray Saul more fairly by means of a closer reading of the text itself. Fresh winds are blowing in Saulide scholarship, and Israel's first king is undergoing a long-overdue rehabilitation. Although at times moody, impulsive, suspicious, violent, insincerely remorseful, out of control, and disobedient to God, at other times he was kind, thoughtful, generous, courageous, very much in control, and willing to obey God. My commentary from this point to the end of 2 Samuel 1, while by no means neglecting Saul's undoubted negative qualities and actions, will nevertheless praise him wherever justified.

Humphreys (pp. 95–117) outlines the biblical story of Saul as a drama in three acts: Saul becomes king (essentially chs. 9–14), Saul is rejected (essentially chs. 15–27), and dénouement (essentially chs. 28–31). The progressive deterioration in Saul's character and career, clear enough in the basic outline, becomes even more evident as the parallel scenes in each act unfold (the divisions and basic titles are essentially those of Humphreys, the elaborations are mine): Act I, Scene 1: Saul meets Samuel, who anoints him (9:3–10:16); Act II, Scene 1: Saul meets Samuel, who condemns him (ch. 15); Act III, Scene 1: Saul meets Samuel, who dooms him (ch. 28). Act I, Scene 2: Success in battle, with the help of God (ch. 11); Act II, Scene 2: Success in battle, with the help of David (chs. 17–18); Act III, Scene 2: Suicide in battle (ch. 31). Act I, Scene 3: Saul's failure, before Samuel and Jonathan (chs. 13–14); Act II, Scene 3: Saul's failure, before David (chs. 19–26). For Humphreys's fuller summary, see his p. 98.

As Samuel's father, Elkanah, was given a formal and stereotyped introduction in 1:1 (see comment there), so Saul's father, Kish, is introduced in a strikingly similar way in 9:1. To highlight the comparison even further, a few Hebrew MSS add *'eḥāḏ* ("certain"; see 1:1) before "Benjamite." David is later given a similar formal introduction, though much abbreviated (17:12). Kish is called a "man of standing," a characteristic title used also of Boaz (Ruth 2:1) and Jeroboam I (1 Kings 11:28). The term often has military connotations and is translated "brave man" in Saul's servant's description of David (16:18). It is nowhere used of Saul himself. The names of the ancestors of Kish are undistinguished; most are not found elsewhere, the only exception being Abiel (see 1 Chron 11:32). The family line is from Benjamin, the smallest of the tribes. Israel's first king came from these humble origins.

The Hebrew root for the name "Saul," which means "Asked (of God)," occurs in 8:10, where the people were "asking" for a king (cf. Notes on 1:20 concerning "given" in 1:28). "Though God actually appointed Saul, Saul did not in the final analysis represent God's choice, but the people's choice. . . . The Israelites . . . wanted . . . one who was grand in appearance and in whom they could rejoice with fleshly pride (I Sam. 8:20). So God picked for them the man who in all Israel came nearest to fulfilling their idea of what a king should be" (G. Coleman Luck, "The First Glimpse of the First King of Israel," BS 123 [1966]: 61). As another Saul (Acts 13:9) later summarized: "The people asked for a king, and [God] gave them Saul son of Kish" (Acts 13:21). A name closely related to that of Saul is Shealtiel ("I Have Asked of God"), a descendant of David and ancestor of Jesus (Matt 1:12).

Saul is introduced as an "impressive" young man (v.2). The Hebrew adjective is *ṭôḇ* ("good"), translated "handsome" with respect to David when he is introduced into the narrative (16:12). It is also used of the baby Moses ("fine") at his introduction (Exod 2:2).

In v.2 *ṭôḇ* is used again of Saul: He was "without equal" (lit., there was "none better than he") among the Israelites. That would eventually change, however; his kingdom would be torn from him and given to "one better than" he—to David (15:28). Since the word originally meant "good" in general and "good-looking" only by extension, it is a "two-faced epithet. Does Saul owe his election to his being the best or the best-looking of the Israelites? Since the two possibilities are compatible . . . the question remains submerged for the time being" (Sternberg, p. 355).

Saul was also "a head taller" than his fellow Israelites (v.2), a characteristic noteworthy enough to be mentioned again (10:23–24). Of regal stature, he had the potential of being every inch a king. Saul's subsequent failure as king makes the well-known divine admonition in 16:7 all the more poignant: "Do not consider his appearance or his height, for I have rejected him." An attractive appearance is desirable, of course, especially in leaders (cf. Gen 39:6 of Joseph; 2 Sam 14:25 of Absalom). Luck observes ("First Glimpse," p. 63) that another Saul (also from Benjamin), though lacking the externals (2 Cor 10:10), possessed the internal, spiritual qualities that made him one of the greatest men who ever lived.

**3–14** The Lord used straying donkeys, of all things, to bring Saul into contact with Samuel. The first and last occurrences of the donkeys in this context (v.3; 10:16) serve as a frame for the larger literary unit. A gentle irony: Just as Saul son of Kish was sent to "look for" donkeys that temporarily could not be "found" (vv.3–4, 20; 10:2, 14, 16), so also the people intent on making him king "looked for" the bashful and reluctant Saul son of Kish, who temporarily could not be "found" (10:21).

Searching for the lost donkeys, Saul and his servant crisscrossed the borderlands between Benjamin and Ephraim, but to no avail (v.4). The locations of Shalisha and Shaalim remain uncertain; the connection, if any, between Shalisha and Baal Shalishah (2 Kings 4:42) is equally obscure. Aharoni (*Land of the Bible*, p. 244) suggests that Shaalim and Shalisha are related respectively to Shual and Shilshah, the names of Asherite clans (1 Chron 7:30, 36–37) "associated with the border districts of Benjamin and Ephraim" (for a region named Shual, cf. also 13:17). It is also possible that the names of two relatively unknown regions were chosen because of their euphony with the name *šā'ûl* ("Saul").

Because the "hill country of Ephraim" (v.4) was a relatively large area, we cannot be sure of the route taken by Saul and the servant. But they began and ended their search there since Zuph (v.5)—whether a geographic name (as here; its precise location is unknown) or personal name—is associated with the hill country of Ephraim in 1:1 (see Notes there). The unnamed town in v.6 is therefore probably Ramah.

Saul, not wishing to cause his father needless worry, wants to give up the search and return to Benjamin (v.5). The servant, however, points out that there is a "man of God" nearby who might be able to tell them which route to take to complete their mission (v.6). The servant appears to be more persistent and imaginative than Saul himself (cf. also v.8)—a fact that may not speak well for Saul's future attempts at leadership. Although the man of God is not named at first (probably to heighten suspense), we are later informed that he is indeed Samuel (v.14).

The term "man of God," common in the OT, is also found occasionally elsewhere in the ancient Near East (see comment on 2:27). In Israel it generally (but cf. its application to David in 2 Chron 8:14) is synonymous with "prophet" or "seer" (e.g., Moses, Deut 33:1; Elijah, 1 Kings 17:18; Elisha, 2 Kings 4:16), as in vv.9–10. The true man of God can be characterized as a man of virtue (he is "highly respected," v.6, a description applied to David in 22:14; cf. the sarcastic use of the same Heb. verb by Michal in 2 Sam 6:20 ["has distinguished himself"], followed by David's devastating reply to her in v.22, concluding with the same verb: "I will be held in honor"). The true man of God is also, equally appropriately, a man of victory ("everything he says comes true," v.6; cf., with respect to Samuel himself, 3:19: The Lord "let none of his words fall to the ground").

Saul continued to protest (v.7), reminding the servant that they had no gift for the prophet; their "sacks" (lit., "vessels"; the word *k*[e]*lî* usually refers to solid containers, less frequently to bags or sacks [e.g., 17:40, 49; Gen 42:25]) were empty. When consulting a prophet, it was common courtesy to bring a gift (Amos 7:12), whether modest (1 Kings 14:3) or lavish (2 Kings 8:8–9). The prophet, of course, reserved the right to refuse it (2 Kings 5:15–16). Obviously the custom suffered considerable abuse (Jer 6:13; 8:10; Ezek 22:25 [see NIV mg.]; Mic 3:5, 11).

The servant responded that he had "a quarter of a shekel of silver" to give to the prophet (v.8). Although coinage was not invented until the seventh century B.C., it is likely that much earlier there were pieces of silver of fixed weight (in this case, about three grams; see NIV mg.) for use in trade and commerce (cf. Baruch Kanael, "Ancient Jewish Coins and Their Historical Importance," BA 26, 2 [1963]: 39).

Verses 9–10 bring together in one place the three main terms to describe the prophetic office: "seer," "prophet," "man of God." The narrator has chosen an especially appropriate context for this, since Samuel is often (and fittingly) called the "last of the judges and first of the prophets"—the latter in the sense that the formal office of prophet began with the monarchy and ended shortly after the monarchy did (for Samuel's unique role, cf. 2 Chron 35:18; Ps 99:6; Jer 15:1; and esp. Acts 3:24; 13:20; Heb 11:32).

Verse 9 has been called the only example in the OT of semantic change (explanatory substitution of one word for another: "The prophet of today used to be called a seer"; cf. Werner Weinberg, "Language Consciousness in the OT," ZAW 92, 2 [1980]: 185–86). The word "seer" translates two different Hebrew words: *rō'eh*, as here, and *ḥōzeh*. Although the latter appears to be the more technical synonym for "prophet" (its cognate nouns are used almost exclusively in the sense of "[divine communication through] vision/revelation"), the two words for "seer" are used interchangeably (cf. esp. Isa 30:10, where they appear in parallel lines; to avoid redundancy in English, *ḥōzîm* is rendered "prophets"). *Rō'eh* was not completely replaced by "prophet" (cf. MT of Isa 30:10). In addition to the present context, Samuel is called a seer also in 1 Chronicles 9:22; 26:28; and *ḥōzeh* and "prophet" both describe Gad in 2 Samuel 24:11.

"Seer" means just what its Hebrew (and English) root implies: one who sees—but with spiritual eyes—beneath the surface of the obvious, focusing on the divine dimension. A seer was a man of (spiritual) vision (cf. Isa 1:1; 6:1–5; Jer 1:11–19; Amos 7:7–9; 8:1–2; Zech 1:7–6:8).

The word "prophet" (*nāḇî'*) occurs more than three hundred times in the OT. The prophet, more specifically, was "called" in the sense of being "summoned by God to be a spokesman for God" (cf. Exod 7:1–2, where Aaron is called Moses' "prophet" just as Moses is God's prophet [who says everything God commands him to say], and

Exod 4:16, where it is said of Aaron: "He will speak to the people for you, and it will be as if he were your mouth and as if you were God to him"). The prophet was to be God's "mouth"; that was his "calling." In other words, the prophet, as God's spokesman, was a man (or woman; several prophetesses are attested in the OT) of vocation. Prophecy was by calling, not by choice. It is therefore not surprising that prophetic-call narratives play such a prominent role in the Bible (e.g., Exod 3:1–4:17, Moses; 1 Sam 3:4–18; Isa 6; Jer 1:4–19; Ezek 1–3; Hos 1:2–3:5; Amos 7:14–15; Jonah 1:1–2; 3:1–2).

Saul and his servant went "up the hill" (v.11) to the town (probably Ramah, which means "height"). It was early evening, since some girls were coming out to the well to draw water (see Gen 24:11; cf. also v.19). When asked whether the seer was there, they informed the men that he had arrived only recently to participate in a sacrificial ritual at the *bāmāh* ("high place," v.12). Almost always on conspicuous elevations and often located outside of town (vv.14, 25), high places were open-air sanctuaries, sometimes with shrines or other buildings (v.22), where worship was conducted. The Lord was occasionally worshiped there (as here; cf. also 1 Kings 3:2, 4–5), but their habitual use for idolatry and other pagan practices (1 Kings 12:31–32) brought them under divine condemnation (1 Kings 13:1–2). Kings of the divided monarchy were often judged by whether they had destroyed the high places (cf. 2 Kings 12:1–3; 14:1–4; 18:1–4; 23:4–15). The association of high places with idolatry had contributed to the divine rejection of Shiloh and the capture of the ark (Ps 78:58–61).

Verses 12–13 are charged with urgency: "He's ahead of you. Hurry now; he has just come. . . . Go up now." The same is true of 13:8–9, where Saul's impatience compels him to act precipitously. Then, just as "he finished making the offering, Samuel arrived" (13:10). Gunn astutely observes: "Saul's haste in the one scene leads to success, in the other to disaster. In chapter 13 he decides to wait no longer for the prophet. The remark in chapter 9 comes back to haunt us: 'for the people will not eat till he comes, since he must bless the sacrifice'" (*The Fate of King Saul*, p. 62).

H. Mowvley ("The Concept and Content of 'Blessing' in the Old Testament," *Bible Translator* 16 [1965]: 78) sees an act of consecration in v.13: "In blessing the sacrifice Samuel set it apart for divine use." Baruch M. Bokser more appropriately understands the expression to refer to a blessing said before eating food that happened to be part of a sacrificial animal about to be offered to the Lord ("*Ma'al* and Blessings Over Food: Rabbinic Transformation of Cultic Terminology and Alternative Modes of Piety," JBL 100, 4 [1981]: 557; cf. also Delitzsch). Such thanksgiving prayers became more common during the intertestamental period and are reflected in the NT as well (Matt 26:26–27; Mark 6:41; 8:6–7; Luke 24:30).

**15–24** Bruce C. Birch ("The Development of the Tradition on the Anointing of Saul in I Sam 9:1–10:16," JBL 90, 1 [1971]: 55–68) believes that v.15 begins a modified version of the formal literary structure known as the "call narrative" (often used to describe the calls of the classical prophets). The elements in this case are (1) divine confrontation, v.15; (2) introductory word, vv.16–17; (3) objection, v.21; (4) commission, 10:1; (5) sign, 10:1 (reading with LXX; cf. NIV mg.), 5–7a; (6) reassurance, 10:7b. The divine encounter with Saul was mediated through Samuel, to whom the Lord had "revealed" (v.15; lit., "uncovered the ear of," as if to speak in secret) his will (the same idiom is used of David in 2 Sam 7:27; 1 Chron 17:25).

As Birch points out, the language of 10:1 (if the longer LXX reading is followed; cf.

NIV mg.) is largely paralleled in vv.16–17, which constitute the introductory word of the call narrative. As an act of gracious condescension to the people's request (Acts 13:21), the Lord would send an obscure Benjamite to Samuel (v.16), emphasizing the divine initiative in the matter. Samuel was to "anoint" him (with oil; cf. 10:1; cf. also 15:1, 17; with respect to David, see 16:3, 12–13; 2 Sam 2:4, 7; 3:39; 5:3, 17; 12:7); the verb is *māšaḥ,* from which *māšîaḥ* ("anointed [one], messiah") is derived.

Anointing was by prophet and/or people, both acting as agents of the Lord (cf. in David's case 16:12–13; 2 Sam 2:4; 5:3). It symbolized the coming of the Holy Spirit in power (16:13; Isa 61:1–3). (For a thorough study see E. Kutsch, *Salbung als Rechtsakt im Alten Testament und im alten Orient,* BZAW 88 [Berlin: Töpelmann, 1963].) Especially at the beginning of the monarchy, anointing was to the office of *nāgîḏ* ("leader," "ruler") rather than *meleḵ* ("king"; cf. v.16; 10:1; of David, cf. 13:14; 25:30; 2 Sam 5:2; 6:21; 7:8). Beyond the likelihood that it represents Samuel's understandable reluctance to establish a full-fledged kingship (with all its negative implications; cf. again 8:10–18), the term *nāgîḏ* (lit., "[one] given prominence, [one] placed in front") might have been a title for "king-designate, king-elect" (cf. 2 Chron 11:22) with military connotations (v.16).

In language strongly reminiscent of the Exodus (v.16), God had looked on the people of Israel (cf. Exod 2:25), whose cry had reached him (cf. Exod 3:9). The new leader would have the potential of delivering Israel from the Philistines (cf. the earlier flawed strategy of the elders, 4:3)—although some (troublemakers, to be sure) seriously doubted that Saul would be able to accomplish that formidable task (10:27). Blenkinsopp notes that the Philistines were not subdued during the rest of Samuel's lifetime (7:13; 10:5; 13:3–22; 14:46) and beyond (31:1–10) ("Kiriath-Jearim and the Ark," p. 145).

The verb *rā'āh* ("to see") is prominent in these verses. Samuel the "seer" (vv.18–19) "caught sight of" Saul (v.17), raised up as leader because God had "looked upon" his people (v.16). "This is the man," the Lord said to Samuel (v.17), in a scene that would be replayed with only modest variations a few years later, this time with David as the subject (16:12). The string of parallels can be extended to Isaiah 42:1–4 ("Here is my servant") and John 19:5 ("Here is the man"), 14 ("Here is your king"), all of which refer to Jesus the "Christ," the "Anointed" par excellence, who neither disappoints nor fails and whose kingdom has no end (Luck, "First Glimpse," p. 66).

The Lord identified Saul for Samuel (v.17), who then identified himself to Saul (vv.18–19). As the Lord had promised to "send" (v.16) Saul to Samuel, so Samuel would soon "let" Saul "go" (v.19; lit., "send" him on his way, as in v.26; same Heb. root) after his divine commissioning (10:9). Samuel the seer authenticated his prophetic role by revealing Saul's inmost thoughts and relieved Saul's mind by informing him that his father's donkeys had been found (vv.19–20). He then told Saul that all Israel was eagerly awaiting his benevolent reign.

In the manner of Moses (Exod 3:11; 4:10) and Jeremiah (Jer 1:6), Saul respectfully demurred (v.21). He pointed out that Benjamin, his tribe, was the smallest in all Israel (doubtless due to the terrible massacre decades earlier; cf. Judg 20:46–48) and that, like Gideon (Judg 6:15), his clan was the weakest in his tribe. Saul's humility, here and elsewhere (cf. 10:22), was thus in the grand tradition of prophets and judges.

Samuel, however, knowing that Saul was God's choice, brushed aside his objections and led him and his servant into a "hall" in a building on the high place outside Ramah (v.22). The Hebrew word for "hall" (*liškāh*) almost always denotes a room in a sanctuary or temple. Such rooms were normally used as apartments for sanctuary personnel or as storerooms (cf. Neh 10:39; Jer 35:2, 4). The hall at Ramah was large enough to seat thirty people, a figure Segal ("Numerals," p. 19) suggests is used to express "minimum decemplurality"—that is, an approximate number in the low tens (cf. Judg 14:11; 2 Sam 23:13, 24; the LXX reads "seventy" here, a somewhat larger approximation).

Saul and his servant, guests of honor, were seated at the head of the table. The special "piece of meat" (v.23) brought to Saul was perhaps the "share" of the sacrifice normally reserved for priests (cf. Lev 7:33, same Heb. word [*mānāh*]; "leg" in v.24 and "thigh" in Lev 7:33 both translate *šôq*). If so, Samuel may have been treating Saul as though he were a fellow priest. It was a special "occasion" (v.24; lit., "appointed time") indeed, a time for celebration—unlike a future "set time" (13:8, 11) when Saul's impatience and disobedience would initiate his downfall (13:13–14).

**25–27** After what must have been a sumptuous if solemn meal, eaten in a house of worship on a sacred site, Samuel, Saul, and Saul's servant retired to Ramah and conversed for awhile on the "roof" of Samuel's house (v.25). Fateful events, also with profound implications for monarchical rule, would later take place on the "roof" of David's palace (2 Sam 11:2; 16:22). But for now Samuel was preparing Saul for his divine commissioning as ruler of Israel. Sleeping overnight on the roof of a house (v.26) is a common practice even today in the Middle East. In ancient times wealthy householders occasionally constructed a small bedroom on the roof to provide comfort, privacy, and protection for their guests (2 Kings 4:10).

The following morning Samuel told Saul to dismiss his servant temporarily (v.27; see 10:14). Saul himself, however, was to stay briefly at Ramah (10:2) to receive a communication from God (v.27) and to be anointed leader over the Lord's inheritance (10:1).

**10:1–8** Saul's rise to kingship over Israel took place in three distinct stages: He was (1) anointed by Samuel (9:1–10:16), (2) chosen by lot (10:17–27), and (3) confirmed by public acclamation (11:1–15). Scholarly proclivity to fragment longer texts into shorter ones in a search for earlier documents has tended to parcel out these three accounts into two or more sources. Such a procedure is unnecessary here, however, since the accounts describe three separate actions that are complementary rather than contradictory. Christian E. Hauer, Jr., tantalizingly suggests that the stories themselves reflect the successive extensions of Saul's dominion, whether by enthusiastic public approval or by conquest. Corresponding to the above three stages, in Hauer's view the expansion would have been from (1) Gibeah of God to (2) Mizpah to (3) Gilgal (the latter including modest acquisitions in Transjordan as a result of the defeat of the Ammonites). Although one might quibble over details, Hauer's theory has the advantage of being paralleled in the similar successive accessions of David to kingship (Ziklag to Hebron to Jerusalem), involving clear territorial increments ("Does I Samuel 9:1–11:15 Reflect the Extension of Saul's Dominions?" JBL 86, 3 [1967]: 306–10).

The Lord had told Samuel to anoint Saul as leader over his people Israel (9:16). Samuel now proceeded to fulfill that command, being careful to inform Saul that the anointing was from the Lord (v.1). The Israelites are here called the Lord's "inheritance" (see also 26:19; 2 Sam 20:19; 21:3) in the sense that they inhabited his territorial patrimony and belonged uniquely to him as Creator, Redeemer, and Conqueror (Deut 4:20; 9:26; 32:8–9; Ps 78:70–71). The anointing oil that Samuel poured on Saul's head was a distinctive formula, not to be used for any other purpose (Exod 30:23–33); it was "sacred" oil (Ps 89:20). Samuel also kissed Saul as an act of respect and in recognition of his new role as ruler of Israel (cf. Ps 2:11–12).

Zafrira Ben-Barak ("The Mizpah Covenant [I Sam 10:25]—The Source of the Israelite Monarchic Covenant," ZAW 91, 1 [1979]: 38) has helpfully summarized various aspects and features of the anointing ritual: (1) The anointer of the chosen one is either a prophet or a priest (or both, as here; cf. 16:13; 1 Kings 1:39; 2 Kings 9:1–6; 11:12); (2) the chosen one was sometimes anointed privately (9:25–10:1; 2 Kings 9:6), with public acclaim coming only later; (3) *nāgîḏ* ("ruler," "leader") was often the title conferred by this act (v.1; 13:14; 2 Sam 5:2–3; 1 Kings 1:35); (4) the anointing oil was poured from a flask or horn (v.1; 16:13; 1 Kings 1:39; 2 Kings 9:1).

The expansionist LXX text of v.1 (see NIV mg.) calls for a "sign" (sing.) confirming the Lord's choice of Saul as authenticated by his anointing. Verses 7 and 9, however, speak of "signs" (pl.)—of which there were three. The first (v.2) was the promise that Saul would "meet" (the root is *māṣā'*, which figures prominently throughout the rest of this section: "found," v.2; "meet," v.3; "finds," v.7; cf. also the comment on "found" at 9:3) two men who would verify that Kish's donkeys had indeed been found and that therefore Saul's father could now devote his attention to his son's welfare.

The second sign (vv.3–4) was that three men would meet Saul and offer him two loaves of bread, which he would accept. Like Moses before them (Exod 19:3), the men were "going up to God" to worship and commune with him. On their way they would "greet" Saul (lit., "ask concerning" his "well being/welfare"; the same idiom is used in 17:22; 30:21; 2 Sam 8:10; cf. 25:5–6). The verbal root is *šā'al* ("ask"), yet another example of the familiar pun on the name *šā'ûl* ("Saul").

The third and final sign (vv.5–7), because of its significance, is described at greater length. Whereas the first sign involved two men and the second involved three men, the third focused on a "procession"—a larger band or group—of prophets (vv.5, 10). Saul would meet them outside "Gibeah of God" (v.5), so-called perhaps because a high place was nearby. The location of a "Philistine outpost" there identifies it with Geba in Benjamin (13:3), modern Jeba, about five miles north-northeast of Jerusalem (cf. Aharoni, *Land of the Bible*, pp. 275, 286, 317 n. 2; for an unsuccessful attempt to locate "Gibeah of God" at Gibeon, cf. Aaron Demsky, "Geba, Gibeah, and Gibeon—An Historico-Geographic Riddle," BASOR 212 [1973]: 26–31).

The beginnings of the Israelite monarchy witnessed the emergence of a prophetic movement known as the "sons of the prophets" (cf. 1 Kings 20:35). "Sons" is used here in the sense of "members of a group," and the NIV therefore often translates the Hebrew idiom "sons of the prophets" as "company of the prophets" (cf. 2 Kings 2:3, 5, 7, 15). They served as a refreshing counterpoise to the potential despotism of the monarchy and the tendency toward formalism in the priesthood. The bands or companies (vv.5, 10; 19:20; 2 Kings 2:15–17) were often large in number ("fifty," 2 Kings 2:7; "one hundred," 1 Kings 18:4, 13; 2 Kings 4:43). They were frequently associated with time-honored places, often at or near shrines, such as Ramah (19:18–20), Bethel (2 Kings 2:3), Jericho (2:5), and Gilgal (4:38).

The characteristic activity of the prophetic bands was "prophesying" (v.5), usually interpreted in these contexts to mean "uttering ecstatic praises/oracles" or the like (BDB, Delitzsch, Klein). A strong case can be made in vv.5–13 and 19:20–24, however, for the meaning "being in" or "falling into a possession trance":

> In the first passage the behavior is accompanied, perhaps fostered, by music. It is interpreted as a radical transformation of the personality, and may confer extraordinary powers on the person so affected. According to the second it may entail stripping off one's clothes, and may issue in a coma. In both its onset is described as an invasion, or at least as visitation, by a divine spirit. It is a group behavior and is contagious. It seems clear that we have to do with some kind of trance state, or altered state of consciousness. (Simon B. Parker, "Possession Trance and Prophecy in Pre-exilic Israel," VetTest 28, 3 [1978]: 272)

Parker (ibid., p. 274) notes that studies of similar phenomena in other cultures, both ancient and modern, have shown that possession trance can be either personal/compensatory (as here) or mediumistic (involving communication between God and man or between persons). A classic example of mediumistic possession trance in the eleventh century B.C. (contemporary with Samuel) is that witnessed by the Egyptian official Wenamun at Byblos in Phoenicia (cf. Hans Goedicke, *The Report of Wenamun* [Baltimore: Johns Hopkins Press, 1975], pp. 53–57). Parker ("Possession Trance," pp. 275–78) further observes that possession by "the Spirit of the Lord" (v.6), in whose name Saul has just been anointed leader over Israel (v.1), confirms and legitimates that appointment—a function of possession trance attested elsewhere in the OT (Num 11:16–17, 24–29) as well as in other cultures. To ask "Is Saul also among the prophets [*nᵉḇî'îm*]?" (vv.11–12), then, is to question his qualifications and legitimacy as Israel's ruler. The denominative verbs *nibbā'/hiṯnabbē'* ("act like a prophet or ecstatic"—*nāḇî'*) will therefore mean either "prophesy" or "be in" or "fall into" a "possession trance," depending on the context.

As in v.5, the actions and activities of prophetic bands elsewhere were sometimes accompanied by music or minstrels (2 Kings 3:15; 1 Chron 25:1–7). "Lyres" and "harps" (see also 16:16, 23) render the words *nēḇel* (the same word also refers to a "skin" of wine, as in v.3) and *kinnôr* respectively, although some scholars feel that the English definitions of the two Hebrew words should be reversed. The ancient lyre was a three-to-twelve-stringed instrument played with the fingers or a plectrum, while the harp was much larger, a ten-to-twenty-stringed instrument usually played without a plectrum. The ancient tambourine, probably very similar to its modern counterpart, was typically played by women (and therefore not used in temple worship in Israel). It almost certainly did not have small metal disks or rings attached to its frame (cf. David W. Music, "Tabrets," *Biblical Illustrator* 10, 3 [1984]: 79–81). The flute (or, more precisely, single or double clarinet, oboe, or shawm) had one or more mouthpieces and was played with its shaft(s) extended straight ahead rather than to the side. (For details on these and other instruments, cf. Ovid R. Sellers, "Musical Instruments of Israel," BA 4, 3 [1941]: 33–47.) All four musical instruments are mentioned in Isaiah 5:12 in a context of drunken banqueting; three of them (plus two more) appear in 2 Samuel 6:5 in a context of joyful celebration before the Lord. As always music could be used for good or ill, which is true of other phenomena associated with prophecy.

Individual or group prophesying, ecstatic or not, was often induced when the Spirit of the Lord came on a person in power (v.6; 19:20, 23; Num 11:25, 29). At such times the prophet would experience an altered state of consciousness and would be "changed into a different person" (cf. also v.9). Such ecstasy was often contagious (v.10; 19:20–24). Similar ecstatic phenomena, though in a negative sense, were sometimes induced when an "evil" or "injurious" spirit came on a person (18:10; cf.

also 16:14–16, 23). Members of prophetic bands were often young (2 Kings 5:22; 9:4); they frequently lived together (2 Kings 6:1–2), ate together (2 Kings 4:38), and were supported by the generosity of their fellow Israelites (2 Kings 4:42–43). Such characteristics led the church father Jerome to refer to them as the "monks of the OT"—although celibacy was not a requirement for membership (2 Kings 4:1). Samuel provided guidance and direction for the movement in its early stages, as Elijah and Elisha did later. At the head of a particular group of prophets would be the "father" (v.12; 2 Kings 2:12) or "leader" (19:20).

The "sons of the prophets" and their distinguished mentors performed yeoman service for their fellow Israelites. They served as counselors of kings, historians of the nation, and instructors of the people (2 Kings 4:13; 6:9; 1 Chron 29:29). Although they have left us no readily identifiable written legacy, they were the precursors of the classical canonical prophets (Isaiah through Malachi).

Samuel told Saul that after three signs had been fulfilled, he was to do whatever his hand found to do (v.7), a sound bit of advice strongly recommended by the Teacher (Qoheleth) as well (Eccl 9:10). Samuel assured Saul that God was with him, implying that therefore he could not fail (cf. Josh 1:5).

Then came a sober warning: At a later time Samuel would meet Saul at Gilgal (about eleven miles east-northeast of Gibeah of God) in the Jordan Valley (and therefore "down" with respect to Gibeah; v.8). A preliminary meeting would first be held there to reaffirm Saul's kingship (11:14–15), with the appropriate fellowship offerings and accompanying celebration. Then on a later occasion Samuel would meet Saul again at Gilgal, this time to sacrifice burnt offerings (cf. Lev 1:3–17; 6:8–13) and fellowship offerings (cf. Lev 3:1–17; 7:11–21). On this latter occasion Saul was to wait seven days, until Samuel came and told him what to do. Saul faithfully fulfilled the former obligation (13:8), but impatience got the better of him. He failed to await Samuel's arrival with further instructions, and his act of disobedience was the beginning of the end for his kingdom (13:9–14).

**9–16** Meanwhile, however, Saul was open to Samuel's instructions and the Lord's leading. He "turned" to leave (v.9)—literally, "turned his shoulder" to leave, a symbol of having reached the point of no return, whether in resoluteness or retreat (cf. the similar idiom in Ps 21:12, where the Heb. word for "shoulder" is translated "backs" in context)—and when he did so, God "changed Saul's heart" (v.9), as Samuel had predicted would happen in connection with the fulfillment of the third sign (v.6). The arrival of Saul and his servant ("they," v.10) at Gibeah of God (cf. v.5) was followed by the Spirit of God coming on Saul in power, resulting in his joining the prophetic band in their ecstatic behavior. The same powerful accession of God's Spirit would energize Saul to lead his troops into battle against the Ammonites some time later (11:6).

Gibeah of God (more commonly called Geba, modern Jeba) was scarcely four miles northeast of Gibeah of Saul (more commonly called Gibeah in Benjamin or simply Gibeah, modern Tell el-Ful), the hometown of the new Israelite ruler. When his fellow townsmen learned of Saul's arrival, they turned out in force to see what had happened to the "son of Kish" (v.11). Since the peculiar way of referring here to Saul follows a pattern sometimes used in a disparaging or contemptuous sense (cf. "son of Jesse" used of David, 20:27; "sons of Zeruiah" used of Joab and Abishai, 2 Sam 16:10; "son of Remaliah" used of Pekah, Isa 7:4), Saul's acquaintances may have been insulting him by calling him "son of Kish" (so perhaps BDB). It is more likely, however, that they, longtime residents of the area, knew the young Saul primarily as the son of his father (cf. the detailed discussion of D.J.A. Clines, "X, X *Ben* Y, *Ben* Y: Personal Names in Hebrew Narrative Style," VetTest 22, 3 [1972]: 282–85). A thousand years later another Prophet, the "carpenter's son," would be similarly criticized by his fellow citizens and would declare himself to be "without honor"—and that "in his hometown and in his own house" (Matt 13:53–57).

In any case, the following sentence—"Is Saul also among the [ecstatic] prophets?" (v.11)—is surely to be understood as a rhetorical question demanding a negative answer. The Spirit of the Lord, coming on Saul in power, authenticated him as Israel's next ruler and produced the visible evidences of ecstatic behavior (see comment on v.5). To question the genuineness of that behavior was to question Saul's legitimacy in his new office. John Sturdy's suggestion ("The Original Meaning of 'Is Saul Also Among the Prophets?' [1 Samuel x 11, 12; xix 24]," VetTest 20, 2 [1970]: 206–13) that the saying represents later Davidic propaganda against Saul is based on its supposedly late and legendary setting and is therefore unverifiable conjecture.

A.S. Herbert ("The 'Parable' [*Māšāl*] in the Old Testament," SJT 7, 2 [1954]: 182–83) points out that the "saying" (v.12, *māšāl*, "proverb," "parable") reported here and in 19:24 is not a typical example of popular wisdom. It is a scornful phrase and should be understood as such. Other popular proverbs used in similarly mocking or despondent ways are recorded in Ezekiel 12:22–23 and 18:2–3.

In terms of literary structure, the use of this particular proverb in vv.11–12 and then later in 19:24 brackets the narrative at the descriptions of Saul's first and last encounters with the Spirit of God. "The first comes just before he attains kingship, the last just before his full descent from kingship into madness and death" (Humphreys, p. 37 n. 41).

"And who is their father?" (v.12) was asked to find out the identity of the leader of the "procession of prophets" (vv.5, 10; cf. 2 Kings 2:12). Although perhaps prompted by the reference to Saul as "son of Kish" (v.11), the question was not so banal as to be requesting information about Saul's physical paternity (despite ancient versional support for the reading "his" instead of "their"—in which case the inquirer would still have been asking about who Saul's spiritual father was).

Verses 14–16 conclude the theme of Kish's concern for Saul's whereabouts and welfare (see v.2; 9:6). Saul's "uncle" (v.14; the word specifically means "father's brother") was doubtless seeking information for Kish and himself. Although the uncle is not identified by name here, he may have been Ner the father of Abner, later the commander of Saul's army (14:50–51). The story of finding Kish's lost donkeys is once again related, but Saul did not tell his uncle anything about Samuel's view of kingship or his own participation in it (v.16; cf. 8:6–22). Rule over Israel would soon be his in truth (11:14), but it would not be long before he would be convinced that he was about to lose it to a man after God's own heart (18:8).

## Notes

---

**9:7** תְּשׁוּרָה (*tešûrāh*, "gift") is not found elsewhere; its meaning has been determined by context. Mitchell Dahood suggests "food for a journey," deriving it from Hebrew-Ugaritic *š(w)r* ("to travel"; "Hebrew-Ugaritic Lexicography XI," *Biblica* 54, 3 [1973]: 354; "Hebrew-Ugaritic

Lexicography XII," *Biblica* 55, 3 [1974]: 392–93). Shalom M. Paul ("1 Samuel 9:7: An Interview Fee," *Biblica* 59, 4 [1978]: 542–44), agreeing with several earlier Jewish commentators that the word is derived from שׁוּר (*šûr,* "to see") and therefore means "interview fee," substantiates that derivation by comparing Akkadian *nāmurtu/tāmartu* ("audience fee," "interview present") from *amāru* ("to see"). Since the Akkadian noun had that meaning in the twelfth century B.C., the comparison with its Hebrew semantic equivalent is especially appropriate.

**9** Although we cannot be certain, the Hebrew word נָבִיא (*nāḇî'*, "prophet") is probably a Qal passive participle from a verbal root cognate to Akkadian *nabû* ("to summon, call a person [to exercise a function]," "to appoint a person to an office"; CAD 11, 1 [1980]: 35–37). The Akkadian adjective *nabû/nabī'u* means simply "called" (ibid., p. 31). John Briggs Curtis has recently suggested that v.7, where נָבִיא (*nāḇî'*) is a Hiphil first person plural imperfect ("we bring/give") of בּוֹא (*bô'*, "to enter"), provides us with a folk etymology of its homograph in v.9. *Nāḇî'* in the sense of "prophet" would then have popularly meant something like a "person to whom we bring gifts to obtain oracles" ("A Folk Etymology of *Nāḇî'*," VetTest 29, 4 [1979]: 491–93). It is much more likely, however, that the form in v.7 resulted from the narrator's indulging his love of wordplay or punning, a common phenomenon in the OT (cf. 25:25; for selected examples see Weinberg, "Language Consciousness," pp. 198–200).

**24** הֶעָלֶיהָ (*he'āleyhā,* "what was on it") is a grammatical anomaly, being the only known OT instance of a preposition preceded by a definite article functioning as a relative pronoun (BDB, p. 209). The form is therefore commonly emended to הָאַלְיָה (*hā'alyāh,* "the fat tail"). Every occurrence of the latter, however (Exod 29:22; Lev 3:9; 7:3; 8:25; 9:19), is in a sacrificial context; the fat tail was always offered to the Lord, never eaten as part of a meal. 4QSam[a] reads [ה]עלינה (*[h]'lynh,* "the upper"; McCarter, *I Samuel,* p. 170), which could conceivably modify the preceding הַשּׁוֹק (*haššôq,* "the thigh," a feminine noun; see Lev 7:33). But since the "upper thigh" is not attested as a cut of meat elsewhere, it is best to read with the MT here.

**10:1** In 1988 archaeologists uncovered in the bottom of a three-foot-deep pit near Qumran, at the northwestern end of the Dead Sea, a five-inch-diameter clay flask wrapped in a nest of palm fibers and containing a small amount of well-preserved reddish oil, probably distilled from balsam. Dating from the first century A.D., the oil may be the only surviving sample of its kind and may be similar to that used to anoint ancient Israelite kings (cf. provisionally *Los Angeles Times,* San Diego edition [16, 1989], Part I, p. 11; *National Geographic* 176, 4 [1989]: 562; and especially Joseph Patrich, "Hideouts in the Judean Wilderness," *Biblical Archaeology Review* 15, 5 [1989]: 34–35).

**2** The location of Zelzah, the site of Rachel's tomb, is unknown. Rachel, who died in childbirth, was buried "on the way to Ephrath (that is, Bethlehem)" (Gen 35:19; cf. also Gen 48:7), a reference that describes the location only generally. Jeremiah 31:15 offers no help, since the word "Rachel" there is used metaphorically and Ramah is merely a representative town where some of the exiles were living (Jer 40:1). The shrine enclosing Rachel's tomb on the road northwest of Bethlehem dates only to the Crusader period and in any case is simply a guess as to the tomb's location. Attempts to equate Zelzah with Zela (2 Sam 21:14), the site of the tomb of Kish (Saul's father), are philologically unconvincing.

**3** Similarly, the location of אֵלוֹן תָּבוֹר (*'ēlôn tāḇôr,* "the great tree of Tabor") is unknown. It is tempting to identify it with אַלּוֹן בָּכוּת (*'allôn bāḵûṯ,* "Oak of Weeping," Gen 35:8; see NIV mg. in loc.), where Rebekah's nurse Deborah (דְּבֹרָה, *d[e]ḇōrāh*) was buried, and also with תֹּמֶר דְּבוֹרָה (*tōmer d[e]ḇôrāh,* "The Palm of Deborah," Judg 4:5; cf. the punning proximity of הַר תָּבוֹר [*har tāḇôr,* "Mount Tabor"] in the next verse). As their contexts suggest, all three trees were near Bethel. Proposed connections between any two of the sites, however, are tenuous at best.

**5** In 1969 Moshe Dothan excavated a tenth-century B.C. pottery stand at Ashdod in the first post-Philistine stratum at the site. The stand is decorated with five figures: (1) a tambourine player, (2) a flute player, (3) a lyre player, (4) a woman (musician?), and (5) a male (musician?). Although the interpretation of the last two figures remains uncertain because they are partially destroyed, Dothan immediately noticed the striking relationship between this scene and the one depicted in v.5 (cf. Bathja Bayer, "The Finds That Could Not Be," *Biblical Archaeology Review* 8, 1 [1982]: 32).

**14** Except for the poorly supported reading of one or two MSS in 27:10 (see BHS there for details), אָן (*'ān*, "where") is anomalous in v.14. Elsewhere אָנָה (*'ānāh*) is the normal word used to express "where" in the sense of "whither" (cf. 2 Sam 2:1; 13:13). If the vocalization of the MT is incorrect in v.14, one could account for the consonantal text by assuming defective writing of the final long vowel in the original word. It is also possible that the consonantal text simply exhibits the phenomenon of shared consonants, in this case the ה (*h*) at the beginning of the next word doing double duty by being assumed at the end of the MT's אָן (cf. Watson, "Shared Consonants," p. 531).

---

## 3. *The choice of Saul by lot*

### 10:17–27

17 Samuel summoned the people of Israel to the LORD at Mizpah 18 and said to them, "This is what the LORD, the God of Israel, says: 'I brought Israel up out of Egypt, and I delivered you from the power of Egypt and all the kingdoms that oppressed you.' 19 But you have now rejected your God, who saves you out of all your calamities and distresses. And you have said, 'No, set a king over us.' So now present yourselves before the LORD by your tribes and clans."

20 When Samuel brought all the tribes of Israel near, the tribe of Benjamin was chosen. 21 Then he brought forward the tribe of Benjamin, clan by clan, and Matri's clan was chosen. Finally Saul son of Kish was chosen. But when they looked for him, he was not to be found. 22 So they inquired further of the LORD, "Has the man come here yet?"

And the LORD said, "Yes, he has hidden himself among the baggage."

23 They ran and brought him out, and as he stood among the people he was a head taller than any of the others. 24 Samuel said to all the people, "Do you see the man the LORD has chosen? There is no one like him among all the people."

Then the people shouted, "Long live the king!"

25 Samuel explained to the people the regulations of the kingship. He wrote them down on a scroll and deposited it before the LORD. Then Samuel dismissed the people, each to his own home.

26 Saul also went to his home in Gibeah, accompanied by valiant men whose hearts God had touched. 27 But some troublemakers said, "How can this fellow save us?" They despised him and brought him no gifts. But Saul kept silent.

**17–24** We have observed that the major literary units comprising the narrative of the rise of Saul (chs. 8–12) alternate between negative (8:1–22; 10:17–27; 11:12–12:25) and positive (9:1–10:16; 11:1–11), the former being antimonarchical and the latter promonarchical. Verses 17–27, though mostly negative, contain certain positive elements (esp. in vv.20–24; cf. Bruce C. Birch, "The Choosing of Saul at Mizpah," CBQ 37, 4 [1975]: 447–57). Birch (pp. 452–54) appropriately analyzes the literary structure of vv.17–19 as follows: (1) call to assembly, v.17; (2) messenger formula, v.18a; (3) recitation of saving acts, v.18b; (4) accusation, v.19a; (5) announcement, v.19b.

Assembling the Israelites at Mizpah (modern Tell en-Nasbeh, about four miles northwest of Gibeah of God), the site of other noteworthy convocations (see comment on 7:5), Samuel addresses them (v.18) in words strongly reminiscent of those of the prophet in Judges 6:8–9a. The messenger formula identifies the Lord, in expansive terms, as specifically the God of his chosen people Israel. The Lord then speaks in the first person, using the emphatic pronoun "I" (v.18) in strong contrast to the emphatic "But you" of v.19. The familiar Exodus redemption formula is followed by a reminder that God delivered his people not only from Egypt but also from the "kingdoms" (such as Bashan, Num 32:33; Deut 3:4, 10, 13; cf. also Deut 3:21; 28:25; Josh 11:10) that "oppressed" them (such as Egypt itself, Exod 3:9; Canaan, Judg 4:3; Sidon, Amalek, Maon, Judg 10:12; cf. Judg 2:18). Although the Lord has saved them out of all their "calamities and distresses" (v.19; for the same Heb. expression, see Deut 31:17, 21, "disasters and difficulties"; Ps 71:20, "troubles many and bitter"), they have rejected him (echoing 8:7; cf. also Num 11:20). The Israelites continued to insist in no uncertain terms that they wanted a king (see 8:5, 19)—a demand not outside God's will (Deut 17:14–15) but one sinfully motivated. Samuel, reluctantly acquiescing, told the people to present themselves before the Lord (cf. the assembly at Shechem after Joshua's conquest of Canaan, Josh 24:1) by their tribes and clans.

The procedure of casting sacred lots, here to pinpoint Saul as Israel's king (vv.20–21; cf. also 14:41–42), was used earlier to isolate Achan as the thief of Israel's plunder (Josh 7:14–18; the Heb. verb translated "chosen" here is rendered "taken" there). The lots, known as Urim ("Curses," providing negative responses) and Thummim ("Perfections," providing positive responses), were stored in the breastplate attached to the ephod of the high priest (Exod 28:28–30) and were brought out and cast whenever a simple "yes" or "no" would suffice (as here, where the process of elimination could be used effectively; cf. also 23:2, 4, 9, 11–12; Num 27:21). Although casting lots was perhaps not unlike throwing dice, the results were not left to chance since God himself guided the decisions (Prov 16:33). Verses 20–21 show that Benjamin was chosen by lot from the Twelve Tribes, Matri (unknown elsewhere) from the Benjamite clans, and Saul—God's man for this season—from the Matrite families. Ironically, like the lost donkeys that had earlier consumed so much anxious time for their searchers (9:3–5, 20; 10:2, 14–16), "when they looked for [Saul], he was not to be found" (v.21).

Another divine oracle was therefore necessary, but this time the question demanded more than a "yes" or "no" answer. So in a more direct way the people "inquired" (the root is *šā'al*, another example of the familiar pun on Saul's name) of the Lord to discover Saul's whereabouts. The reluctant "leader" was subsequently found hiding among the "baggage" (v.22; the Heb. word in this specific sense is elsewhere translated "supplies," always in a military context, perhaps hinting at the major task that the people hoped Saul would enthusiastically assume; cf. 17:22; 25:13; 30:24; Isa 10:28).

Anxious to hail their new king, the people ran to bring him out from his hiding place (v.23). He came out and "stood"—presented himself—in their midst (the verbal root is the same as that translated "present yourselves" in v.19). His impressive height is again stressed, as it had been earlier (9:2). Samuel reminded the Israelites that the Lord had "chosen" Saul (the Heb. verb is different from that used in vv.20–21, distinguishing direct and personal divine choice from the indirect and impersonal decisions of Urim and Thummim). The verb "choose" in similar contexts is used most often of God's choice of David (16:8–10; 2 Sam 6:21; 1 Kings 8:16; 1 Chron 28:4; 2 Chron 6:5–6; Ps 78:70). "Like Saul (10:17–26), David (16:1–13) is selected by Yahweh even though he seems the least likely candidate" (Humphreys, p. 107).

C.J. Labuschagne has noted that the vocabulary of incomparability to describe a newly appointed king of Israel was significant because only he—to the exclusion of all others—had a claim to the throne (cf. Solomon, 1 Kings 3:12–13; Neh 13:26; Hezekiah, 2 Kings 18:5; Josiah, 2 Kings 23:25) (*The Incomparability of Yahweh in the Old Testament* [Leiden: Brill, 1966], p. 10). At the same time, of course, such language is most appropriate to the incomparable God himself, as David recognized (2 Sam 7:22).

The public acclamation—"Long live the king!" (v.24, used also of the pretenders Absalom [2 Sam 16:16] and Adonijah [1 Kings 1:25] as well as of kings David [1 Kings 1:31], Solomon [1 Kings 1:34, 39], and Joash [2 Kings 11:12 = 2 Chron 23:11])—has survived virtually to modern times. It represents now, as it did then, the enthusiastic hopes of the citizenry that their monarch may remain hale and hearty in order to bring their fondest dreams to fruition. The people of Saul's day "shouted" their approval—and the verb the narrator used to describe their praise surfaces in Zechariah 9:9, where the prophet advises Jerusalem to "shout" in recognition of the coming of a righteous and saving king (ultimately the Messiah, the Christ; see Matt 21:4–5; John 12:12–15).

**25–27** After the people's acclamation of Saul as their king, Samuel outlined for them the "regulations of the kingship" (*mišpaṭ hammᵉlu<u>k</u>āh,* v.25). My commentary on 8:10–18 takes for granted the equation of this phrase with "what the king . . . will do" (*mišpaṭ hammele<u>k</u>*) in 8:9, 11. The time has come for me to defend that position.

Some commentators contend that the two phrases must be distinguished from each other and that they have different referents (cf. Vannoy, pp. 229–33). Others agree but prefer to extend the distinction still further by giving "what the king . . . will do" a different nuance in 8:9 ("manner of the king"—i.e., how a [benevolent] king should conduct himself) from that in 8:11 ("custom of the king"—i.e., how a [despotic] king will conduct himself; cf. Eslinger, *Kingship of God,* pp. 352–55). This latter position usually assumes that God told Samuel to instruct—and warn—the Israelites about what they could expect if they persisted in their demand to have a king (8:9) but that when Samuel relayed the divine word to them he either deliberately skewed it in a decidedly negative direction or at least selectively emphasized the obvious problems inherent in monarchy while omitting or downplaying its potential benefits (8:11–18; cf. Polzin, *Samuel and the Deuteronomist* pp. 86–88—a section of his book that Polzin suggestively entitles "Why Samuel's *Mišpaṭ* Is Only Half the Story").

It is difficult, however, to maintain a distinction between 8:9 and 8:11, especially considering 8:10: "Samuel told *all* the words of the LORD to the people" (emphasis mine). Furthermore, insisting on the equation of 8:9, 11 with 10:25 is at least as old at the LXX, which reads *to dikaiōma tou basileōs* ("the regulation[s]/requirement[s] of the kingship") in all three verses. Hertzberg, however, is doubtless correct in observing that the written document in 10:25 "was not intended to contain just the complicating factors mentioned as a warning to the people in ch. 8" (p. 90; cf. also Polzin, *Samuel and the Deuteronomist,* p. 86, who correctly asserts that "both the rights *and* the duties of the king appear to be what Samuel would have 'written in a book and laid before the LORD' [10:25]; surely one without the other would have ill-served both God and the community" [emphasis his]).

Talmon, in an extended discussion of "The Rule of the King" (pp. 53–67), insists on the virtual identity of the *mišpaṭ* mentioned in 8:9, 11 with that in 10:25: "Samuel's speech was political in tone in the interests of persuasion, his remarks addressed only to controversial issues. Only later, after the anointing ceremony had taken place, was the 'Rule of the King' presented in complete form and properly formulated. Then Samuel 'told the people of the rule of the kingdom, and wrote it in a book, and laid it up before the Lord' (1 Sam 10:25)" (p. 61). Says Talmon, "There is no distinction between משפט המלך [*mšpṭ hmlk*] and משפט המלוכה [*mšpṭ hmlwkh*]; they are not to be set up as separate concepts" (p. 61 n. 27; cf. also Henry Preserved Smith, *A Critical and Exegetical Commentary on the Books of Samuel* [ICC], p. 74; de Vaux, AIs, pp. 94, 98).

I heartily agree with such assessments. The "kingship" of 10:25 is the same as the "kingship" of v.16, the negative aspects of which Samuel warns the people about in chapter 8. That the description in 10:25 implies a somewhat fuller document than is warranted in Samuel's earlier summary is clear enough, but to claim that the two sets of regulations are completely different is not justified by either the language or the context. H.P. Smith expresses the relationship well in his commentary on 10:25: "The *custom of the king* already recited in 8[9–18]. . . was threatened as the penalty of the people's choice. As they have persisted in their choice, the threat will be carried out. The document is laid up before Yahweh as a testimony, so that when they complain of tyranny they can be pointed to the fact that they have brought it upon themselves" (*Commentary on the Books of Samuel*, p. 74).

Eslinger translates *mišpaṭ hammᵉlukāh* as "monarchic constitution" (*Kingship of God*, p. 355), while the title of Ben-Barak's study, "The Mizpah Covenant (I Sam 10:25)—the Source of the Israelite Monarchic Covenant," attempts to define it even more precisely. But "constitution," with all its modern connotations, is an overtranslation of *mišpaṭ;* and despite Ben-Barak's best efforts to elicit comparisons between this document and the covenants of Exodus 19–24 and Joshua 24, he surely extracts more from a single verse than could have been found there were it not for the fuller Exodus and Joshua "parallels." Ben-Barak himself admits that the 1 Samuel 10:25 document is not called a *bᵉrîṯ* ("covenant") in the OT (ibid., p. 33). It is perhaps best to be content with the more modest rendering of the NIV: "regulations of the kingship" (which included, but were not restricted to, those mentioned in 8:11–18). The closest parallel is the "law and . . . decrees" of the king(dom) outlined in Deuteronomy 17:14–20 (cf. esp. v.19). For the possible relationship between 1 Samuel 8 and 10:17–27, and Deuteronomy 17:14–20, see S.R. Driver, *A Critical and Exegetical Commentary on Deuteronomy*, ICC (Edinburgh: T. and T. Clark, 1895), pp. 212–13, and especially Gerbrandt, p. 108.

After Samuel explained to the people the monarchic regulations (v.25), he wrote them down on a scroll, a common method used throughout the OT period to record important matters (Exod 17:14; Josh 18:9) in perpetuity (Job 19:23–24; Isa 30:8). He deposited the scroll in a safe place "before the LORD"—i.e., in the tabernacle, which was probably located at Mizpah at that time (cf. v.17)—in order (1) to preserve it for future reference (cf. similarly 2 Kings 22:8) and (2) that it might serve as a witness against the king and/or people should its provisions ever be violated (cf. similarly Deut 31:26; Josh 24:26–27).

Samuel then permitted all the people to return to their homes (v.25). Saul, the recently anointed king, went to his home in Gibeah (v.26; see also 14:2; 22:6; 26:1), also known as Gibeah of Saul (11:4; 15:34) and Gibeah in Benjamin (13:2, 15; 14:16) to distinguish it from other towns bearing the same name ("Gibeah" means "hill"). The site, modern Tell el-Ful, is three miles north of Jerusalem, whose modern skyline is clearly visible from the tell. Located about four miles southeast of Mizpah (v.17), Tell el-Ful was excavated by William F. Albright, who in 1922 and 1933 cleared the remains of what might possibly be Saul's citadel. Though little survived, at the time of its discovery the site was the "oldest datable Israelite fortification of Iron I" (*The Archaeology of Palestine* [Harmondsworth: Penguin, 1949], p. 120; cf. also fig. 30 on p. 121, updated in Yohanan Aharoni, *The Archaeology of the Land of Israel* [Philadelphia: Westminster, 1982], p. 191 fig. 56).

With the formal festivities over, two opposing reactions to Israel's new leader surface: "Valiant men" (v.26), apparently eager to affirm God's choice ("whose hearts God had touched"; cf. v.24), accompanied Saul to Gibeah, while "troublemakers" (v.27; the same Heb. expression is translated "wicked men" in 2:12) despised him. The latter group unwittingly echoed to Saul the earlier words of Gideon about himself: "How can I save Israel?" (Judg 6:15). Neither Gideon nor the troublemakers understood—at least not at first—that it is God, not man, who saves (Judg 6:16; 1 Sam 10:19).

In contemptible violation of ancient custom about seeking the favor or help of prophet (9:7–8) or king (1 Kings 10:25; 2 Chron 17:5), the troublemakers, despising Saul, "brought him no gifts" (v.27). Saul, however, always reticent, kept his silence (as he had before; cf. v.16).

## Notes

**19** אֶלֶף (*'eleḇ*, lit., "thousand") is infrequently used in the metaphorical sense of "clan" (as here; cf. also 23:23; Josh 22:14; Judg 6:15; Mic 5:2). Numbers 31:5 is especially instructive in this connection, for there the Hebrew word is appropriately translated both as "thousand" and as "clan."

**26** "Valiant men" translates הַחַיִל (*haḥayil*, "valor") by synecdoche. 4QSam[a], however, reads בני החיל (*bny hḥyl*, "sons/men of valor"; cf. also LXX's *υἱοὶ δυνάμεων* [*huioi dynameōn*]), probably correctly, since it forms a better parallel with בְּנֵי בְלִיַּעַל (*b[e]nê ḇ[e]lîya'al*, "sons/men of worthlessness") in v.27.

**27** Based on 4QSam[a] and the LXX, many read the last two Hebrew words of v.27—וַיְהִי כְּמַחֲרִישׁ (*way[e]hî k[e]maḥ[a]rîš*, lit., "and/but he was like one being silent")—as וַיְהִי כְּמוֹ חֹדֶשׁ (*way[e]hî k[e]mô ḥōḏāš*, lit., "and it was about a month [later]"; for the idiom and construction, cf. Gen 38:24) and attach it to the beginning of chapter 11 (cf. the similar suggestion of BDB [p. 294] long before the DSS were discovered). Barthélemy (p. 168), however, prefers to retain the MT, rendering the phrase "and he was as one who imposed silence on himself" (cf. NIV, "But Saul kept silent"). Since the MT is contextually appropriate (see commentary on v.27 above), there is no compelling reason to abandon it here.

### 4. *The defeat of the Ammonites*

#### 11:1–11

1 Nahash the Ammonite went up and besieged Jabesh Gilead. And all the men of Jabesh said to him, "Make a treaty with us, and we will be subject to you."

2 But Nahash the Ammonite replied, "I will make a treaty with you only on the condition that I gouge out the right eye of every one of you and so bring disgrace on all Israel."

3 The elders of Jabesh said to him, "Give us seven days so we can
send messengers throughout Israel; if no one comes to rescue us, we
will surrender to you."
4 When the messengers came to Gibeah of Saul and reported these
terms to the people, they all wept aloud. 5 Just then Saul was returning
from the fields, behind his oxen, and he asked, "What is wrong with the
people? Why are they weeping?" Then they repeated to him what the
men of Jabesh had said.
6 When Saul heard their words, the Spirit of God came upon him in
power, and he burned with anger. 7 He took a pair of oxen, cut them into
pieces, and sent the pieces by messengers throughout Israel, proclaiming, "This is what will be done to the oxen of anyone who does not
follow Saul and Samuel." Then the terror of the LORD fell on the people,
and they turned out as one man. 8 When Saul mustered them at Bezek,
the men of Israel numbered three hundred thousand and the men of
Judah thirty thousand.
9 They told the messengers who had come, "Say to the men of Jabesh
Gilead, 'By the time the sun is hot tomorrow, you will be delivered.'"
When the messengers went and reported this to the men of Jabesh, they
were elated. 10 They said to the Ammonites, "Tomorrow we will
surrender to you, and you can do to us whatever seems good to you."
11 The next day Saul separated his men into three divisions; during the
last watch of the night they broke into the camp of the Ammonites and
slaughtered them until the heat of the day. Those who survived were
scattered, so that no two of them were left together.

**1–2** "If any chapter of 1 Samuel gives even the most conservative reader cause for textual emendation of the MT, it is chap. 11" (Robert Polzin, "On Taking Renewal Seriously: 1 Sam 11:1–15," in *Ascribe to the Lord: Biblical and Other Studies in Memory of Peter C. Craigie*, JSOT suppl. 67, edd. Lyle Eslinger and Glen Taylor [Sheffield: JSOT, 1988], p. 493). For "But Saul kept silent" in 10:27, 4QSam$^a$—the most fully preserved of the biblical scrolls from Qumran cave 4—substitutes the following extensive passage: "[Na]hash king of the Ammonites sorely oppressed the Gadites and the Reubenites, and he gouged out a[ll] their right [e]yes and struck ter[ror and dread] in [I]srael. Not a man was left among the Israelites bey[ond Jordan who]se right eye was no[t go]uged out by Naha[sh king] of the [A]mmonites, except that seven thousand men [fled from] the Ammonites and entered [J]abesh Gilead. About a month later"—at which point the scroll continues with "Nahash the Ammonite went up" (11:1 MT).

Obviously 4QSam$^a$ contains valuable background information and provides a helpful rationale for what otherwise is an abrupt and vicious threat by the Ammonite king against the inhabitants of Jabesh Gilead. Cross points out that the vengeful punishment insisted on by Nahash is best explained by the 4QSam$^a$ additional paragraph, viz., the Jabeshites were giving aid and comfort to Ammon's ancestral enemies, the Reubenites and Gadites, who occupied territory traditionally claimed by the Ammonites; therefore the Jabeshites should receive the same harsh treatment earlier meted out to the Reubenites and Gadites (cf. "Ammonite Oppression," pp. 148–58; id., "II: Original Biblical Text," pp. 26–35). Josephus' account of Nahash's aggression (Antiq. VI, 68–72 [v.1]) also presupposes some such prologue as described in the 4QSam$^a$ paragraph. The above considerations, and others like them (cf. Terry L. Eves, "One Ammonite Invasion or Two? 1 Sam 10:27–11:2 in the Light of 4QSam$^a$," WTJ 44 [1982]: 308–26, esp. 318–21—but notice the assumptions that Eves is forced to make about how the MT reading arose [p. 324]), have led the NRSV (although alone among modern EVV) to include it in its text of 1 Samuel 10:27.

The Qumran addition, however, should not be accorded primacy simply because of its contextual attractiveness. OT narrative often appears inexplicably terse—especially from our modern perspective. Indeed, 4QSam[a] strips the standardized account of its leanness and elegance. As Polzin admits: "Although providing important background for the key events of this chapter, 4QSam[a] adds little else to the esthetic and ideological dimensions of the story as found in the MT" ("On Taking Renewal Seriously," p. 493 n. 1). Furthermore, why would Nahash's mutilation of the Jabeshites suddenly "bring disgrace on all Israel" (v.2) if he had been mutilating Reubenites and Gadites all along? And why could not the "background" information provided by 4QSam[a] be just as easily an indication of its secondary character—inserted later to "explain" the abruptness of Nahash's actions—as of its originality? "The wise course for the present, therefore, is to reserve judgement on the status of these additional lines in 4QSam[a]" (Gordon, *I & II Samuel*, p. 64; cf. further Alexander Rofé, "The Acts of Nahash According to 4QSam[a]," IEJ 32 [1982]: 129–33).

As for the broader historical context of 1 Samuel 11, commentators have long recognized the resemblance between a tribal call to arms represented by Saul's dismembering of a pair of oxen and the disposition of the pieces (v.7) and the dismemberment of the Levite's concubine and the disposition of the parts (Judg 19:29). The similarities between Judges 19–21 and 1 Samuel 11 are even more extensive, as Polzin ("On Taking Renewal Seriously," pp. 500–501) observes:

(1) Jabesh Gilead is paired with Gibeah in Benjamin in both passages. In Judges, Jabesh Gilead refuses to join Israel's call against sinful Gibeah; in Samuel, Saul at Gibeah issues Israel's call to deliver besieged Jabesh.

(2) The narrative in Judges is framed by emphatically premonarchic statements—"In those days Israel had no king" (Judg 19:1; 21:25)—while in Samuel the account is embellished by distinctively monarchic statements: "Then Samuel said to the people, 'Come, let us go to Gilgal and there reaffirm the kingship.' So all the people went to Gilgal and confirmed Saul as king in the presence of the LORD" (11:14–15).

(3) The ubiquitous Benjamin (*binyāmin*, "right son") in the Judges account sends forth "paronomastic rays" (Polzin's suggestive term) to the Samuel narrative, where Nahash threatens (v.2) to gouge out every "right eye" (*'ên yāmîn*) of the Jabeshites, who later respond to the Ammonites (v.10): "Do to us whatever seems good to you" (lit., "good in your eyes")—a phrase in turn reminiscent of the conclusion of Judges 21: "Everyone did as he saw fit" (v.25; lit., "did what was fitting in his eyes").

(4) The phrase *t[e]nû hā'[a]nāšîm ûn[e]mîṯēm* occurs only in 1 Samuel 11:12 ("Bring these men . . . and we will put them to death") and in Judges 20:13 ("Surrender those . . . men . . . so that we may put them to death") in the entire OT.

Polzin concludes ("On Taking Renewal Seriously," p. 503), "That the men of Jabesh-Gilead had earlier refused to honour their tribal obligations at Mizpah makes their present treachery in offering covenantal peace to Ammon without a fight (v 1) simply characteristic." However, it also must be pointed out that by liberating Jabesh Gilead from Ammonite oppression, Saul gained the support and gratitude of Israel's Transjordanian regions. In particular, the people of Jabesh remained loyal to Saul even after his death, risking their own lives at the hands of the Philistines to rescue the bodies of Saul and his sons and to give them proper burial (31:11–13; cf. 2 Sam 21:11–14). Saul's successor, David, recognizing the strategic importance of Transjordan, courted the favor of the men of Jabesh by implying that he would protect them just as Saul had (2 Sam 2:4–7; for additional details, see Curtis, "East Is East . . . ," pp. 356–57).

During the time of the judges, the Ammonites, descendants of Lot's son Ben-Ammi (Gen 19:36–38), encroached on Israelite territory on more than one occasion (Judg 3:13; 10:6–9; 11:4). Their belligerence against Jabesh Gilead ("Dry [Soil] of Gilead")—probably modern tell el-Maqlub (Aharoni, *Land of the Bible*, pp. 127–28; the nearby Wadi Yabis preserves the element Jabesh in the ancient name) located about twelve miles southeast of the prominent mound of Beth Shan—in the days of Saul was thus not unexpected.

The royal name Nahash (v.1), although usually (and not inappropriately) taken to mean "Snake" (*nāḥāš*), is understood by Cross ("II: Original Biblical Text," p. 26) to be an abbreviation of *nḥš ṭwb* ("Good Luck"; the verbal root *nḥš* means "to practice divination" or "to look for omens," as in Gen 44:5, 15). "Nahash" appears elsewhere in the OT only in the books of Samuel and in a parallel passage in 1 Chronicles (1 Sam 12:12; 2 Sam 10:2 [with which cf. 1 Chron 19:1–2]; 17:27 [cf. also v.25]). Apart from 1 Samuel 12:12, we cannot know for certain whether the other men named Nahash are the same as the Nahash of 1 Samuel 11 since the name may have been an Ammonite dynastic title.

The Ammonite siege of Jabesh Gilead produced a conciliatory response in its inhabitants. They asked Nahash to "make a treaty" (v.1, lit., "cut a covenant") with them, as a result of which they would recognize him as their suzerain and become his vassals (cf. similarly Ezek 17:13–14). The phrase "cut a covenant" is almost universally understood to refer to the sacrifice ("cutting") of one or more animals as an important element in covenant solemnization ceremonies in ancient times. That "cut" in the formula harks back to the method of slaughtering an animal can hardly be denied (cf. Jer 34:18: "The men who . . . have not fulfilled the terms of the covenant they *made* [lit., 'cut'] . . . I will treat like the calf they *cut* in two and then walked between its pieces" [italics mine], in which the two occurrences of "cut" are identical in Heb.). Robert Polzin, however, in "*HWQY*' and Covenantal Institutions in Early Israel" (HTR 62 [1969]: 227–40), proposes an alternative interpretation—viz., that "cut," "kill," "dismember," and similar verbs in covenantal contexts refer to vividly acting out the fulfillment of the self-maledictory curse spoken by participants in covenants rather than to the ritual sacrifice of an animal.

Although, of course, the two interpretations are not necessarily mutually exclusive, Polzin's suggestion is attractive. As Polzin himself observes, Saul's threat in v.7 ("This is what will be done to the oxen [i.e., cutting them into pieces] of anyone who does not follow Saul and Samuel") "brings to mind the conditional curse oaths of treaty ratification ceremonies" ("*HWQY*' and Covenantal Institutions in Early Israel," p. 240). Upon receiving the pieces of Saul's oxen brought to them by messengers, the various Israelite tribes are to honor the mutual-protection clauses of their covenant in defense of Jabesh Gilead. (Diana Edelman's theory ["Saul's Rescue of Jabesh-Gilead (I Sam 11 1–11): Sorting Story From History," ZAW 96, 2 (1984): 195–209] that Jabesh Gilead was not Israelite during the days of Saul can be maintained only at the unacceptable expense of claiming that several verses in 1 Samuel 11 are later additions [p. 205]; cf. also that the Jabeshites were numbered among the Israelites at least as early as the time of the judges [Judg 21:8].)

Cross ("Ammonite Oppression," pp. 156–57 and n. 23) sees an additional implication as well. Nahash's threat to gouge out the right eye of every Jabeshite (v.2) may imply their rebellion against a previously established overlordship (at least as understood from Nahash's perspective), especially considering such texts as Numbers 16:13–14; Judges 16:21; 2 Kings 25:7 (cf. Jer 39:6–7; 52:10–11); and Zechariah 11:17. In the ancient Near East, the physical mutilation, dismemberment, or death of an animal or human victim could be expected as the inevitable penalty for treaty violation. Thus "make" (= "cut," v.1), "gouge out" (v.2), and "cut . . . into pieces" (v.7) all belong to what Cross calls "a single ideological complex" (*Canaanite Myth and Hebrew Epic*, p. 266; less likely is the "sacramental" explanation proposed by W. Robertson Smith, *Lectures on the Religion of the Semites*, 2d ed. [London: A. and C. Black, 1894], p. 402 n. 3).

**3** Nahash's threat (v.2) received a plaintive response from the elders of Jabesh, who functioned in their normal responsibility as representatives of the community (cf. 4:3; 8:4; 16:4). They tried to buy some time: "Give us seven days" (lit., "Leave us alone [for] seven days"; cf. same Heb. verb in 2 Kings 4:27) to send for help. Although the text is silent about Nahash's reaction, the implication is that he acceded to the elders' request, apparently sure of his own military superiority.

The language of the elders' plea uses two key verbal roots that are thematic throughout the rest of the chapter. The first is *yš'*, translated "rescue[d]" here and in v.13 and "delivered" in v.9. Human rescue is desperately yearned for in v.3, but Saul recognizes the coming of that hoped-for deliverance as deriving from God himself (v.13; its origin is [deliberately?] ambiguous in v.9; in 19:5 and 2 Sam 23:10, 12, the same root is rendered "victory," the source of which is clearly stated to be divine). Although human beings are often deputized to fight God's battles in the OT, the victory—whether mediated through human agency or not—is always his and his alone (cf. Exod 15:1–10; Judg 5:20; 2 Sam 8:6, 14; Pss 60:12; 144:10; Prov 21:31; Isa 10:5; Jer 51:20–23).

The second verbal root is *yṣ'* ("to go out"). Here and in v.10 it is translated "surrender" (viz., to the Ammonites; cf. similarly 2 Kings 18:31 = Isa 36:16; Jer 38:17, 21), while in v.7 it is rendered "follow" (Saul and Samuel) and "turned out" (as one man). For the Israelites generally and the Jabeshites specifically, doing nothing was not an option. They would either "go out" to the enemy in defeat and humiliation or "go out" in victory under the divinely authorized leadership of Saul and Samuel.

**4** When the Jabeshite messengers arrived at Gibeah of Saul (modern Tell el-Ful, three miles north of Jerusalem) with the terms of Nahash's demands, its people "wept aloud" (lit., "raised their voice[s] and wept"), a common Israelite display of helplessness, grief, distress, or remorse (cf. Judg 2:4; 1 Sam 24:16; 2 Sam 3:32; 13:36). Apparently Saul's fellow citizens in his own hometown despaired of leadership at this critical juncture in their history.

**5–6** But at that very moment, Saul was returning from plowing in the fields, and he asked two questions: "What is wrong with the people? Why are they weeping?" (v.5). Upon hearing the Jabeshites' report, Saul was energized by a powerful accession of God's Spirit (v.6). He had already experienced a similar accession earlier, enabling him to "prophesy" (10:6–10). This time, however, in the tradition of the judges from Othniel (Judg 3:10) to Samson (Judg 14:19), the Spirit of God filled Saul with divine indignation ("he burned with anger"; cf. Judg 14:19) and empowered him as a military leader. Although the earlier accession had been temporary, this one was somewhat more permanent, apparently lasting until Samuel anointed David to replace Saul as king (16:13–14; cf. Leon J. Wood, *The Holy Spirit in the Old Testament* [Grand Rapids: Zondervan, 1976], pp. 50, 60–63). The pouring out of the Holy Spirit in the OT often symbolized and accompanied the anointing of the recipient to an important position of leadership, whether as prophet, army commander, king (16:1, 13), or preacher/proclaimer (Isa 61:1).

**7** Rallying the troops to defend a covenant suzerain, vassal, or brother was a common stipulation in ancient treaties. Like the Levite before him who had issued a call to arms by cutting up his dead concubine and sending the parts to each of the various Israelite tribes (Judg 19:29; 20:6), Saul cut two of his oxen into pieces and sent them throughout Israel as a graphic illustration of what would happen to any tribe that failed to commit a contingent of troops (cf. Judg 21:5, 10). As Elisha the plowman slaughtered a pair of oxen and served a meal to his friends at the time of his prophetic call (1 Kings 19:21), so Saul the plowman slaughtered a pair of oxen as a means of rallying the people to his side at the onset of his service as their king. The "terror of the LORD" that here fell on the people is not to be understood as fear of divine punishment. Keil and Delitzsch well summarize its true intent: "In Saul's energetic appeal the people discerned the power of Jehovah, which inspired them with fear, and impelled them to immediate obedience" (p. 112).

**8** The mustering or counting of the troops (cf. 13:15; 14:17; 2 Sam 24:2, 4) took place at Bezek (modern Khirbet Ibziq, about seventeen miles west of Jabesh Gilead), which is mentioned elsewhere in the Hebrew text of the OT only in Judges 1:4–5. There, at the beginning of the period of the judges, two tribes cooperated to rout the Canaanites and Perizzites at Bezek; here, at the beginning of the Israelite monarchy, Bezek becomes a staging ground for a united Israelite attack that will lead to the defeat of the Ammonites. As in 1 Samuel 4:2, 10, so also here in v.8, we cannot be sure whether *'eleḇ* means "thousand" or is used in a more general sense to refer to a military "unit" (as in 17:18; 29:2; 2 Sam 18:4; see comment on 1 Sam 4:2). Nor can the possibility of hyperbole be discounted (cf. 18:7; 21:11). In any case, the numbers in this verse represent substantial contingents of troops. Their being listed separately as "men of Israel" and "men of Judah" either anticipates the eventual division of the kingdom into north and south or reflects authorship (or later modest editorial updating) of this section of the books of Samuel in the days of the divided monarchy (i.e., after 931 B.C.; cf. similarly the implications of the reference to "all Israel from Dan to Beersheba" in 3:20).

**9** Saul and his troops told the messengers to return to Jabesh Gilead and inform its frightened citizens that divine deliverance (cf. v.13; cf. also 19:5; 2 Sam 23:10, 12) would come to them the very next day. It would take place "by the time the sun is hot" (for this expression, cf. Exod 16:21 ["when the sun grew hot"]; Neh 7:3), a phrase that almost surely refers to high noon, the hottest and brightest time of day (cf. similarly Ps 37:6; Amos 8:9; cf. esp. v.11 with 2 Sam 4:5). The messengers' report caused the men of Jabesh to become "elated," an emotion experienced also by those who gathered at Gilgal after the Ammonite defeat to confirm Saul as king in recognition of his military prowess under God's direction (v.15; "held a . . . celebration" translates the same Heb. verb as "were elated" in v.9).

**10** Confident of victory, the Jabeshites—tongue in cheek—promised the Ammonites that they would surrender to them the following day and that the Ammonites would then be free to do "whatever seems good to you" (lit., "whatever seems good in your eyes," the narrator's ironic pun on Nahash's earlier threat to gouge out the right eye of any rebellious Jabeshite; cf. the same idiom in 14:36).

**11** Saul wasted no time in deploying "his men" (lit., "the people," a noun often meaning "troops" in OT military contexts) for the attack on Ammon. "The next day" probably refers to the evening of the day on which Saul's message reached the Jabeshites (v.9), since among the Israelites each new day began after sunset (rather than after midnight as in the modern Western world). Saul, following a military strategy common in those days (see 13:17–18; Judg 7:16; 9:43; 2 Sam 18:2), divided his men into three groups: Offensively, it gave the troops more options and greater mobility, while defensively it lessened the possibility of losing everyone to a surprise enemy attack. The Israelites under Saul's leadership broke into the Ammonite camp "during the last watch of the night," reminiscent of the beginning of the end for another of Israel's ancient enemies as well (see Exod 14:24, the only other place where the phrase in quotes is used).

The Mesopotamian practice of dividing the night into three "watches" (first [cf. Lam 2:19], middle [Judg 7:19], and last), each about four hours long, was followed throughout western Asia in the pre-Christian period; the last or morning watch included the transition from darkness to dawn. Saul's attack obviously caught the Ammonites by surprise, and—as promised (v.9)—by high noon God had defeated them and delivered his people, routing the enemy survivors by scattering them in every direction (cf. also Num 10:35; Ps 68:1).

## Notes

5 The second question—"Why are they weeping?"—contains an example of the relatively infrequent use of כִּי (*kî*) as an interrogative particle following the more common interrogatives, such as מַה־ (*mah-*) and מִי (*mî*). Since *kî* is often causal, it is usually translated "that" (here and in similar sequences), especially in the KJV tradition (cf. ASV, RSV, NASB, NKJV). However, when a *kî* clause occurs after an interrogative clause that demands the reason for an exceptional event or situation, it often functions as a logical (and not necessarily causal) follow-up question itself (cf. Gen 20:9; Exod 3:11; 32:21; Num 11:12–13; 16:13; 22:28; Judg 9:28; 11:12; 1 Sam 17:26; 18:18; Isa 36:5; cf. similarly Anneli Aejmelaeus, "Function and Interpretation of כִּי in Biblical Hebrew," JBL 105, 2 [1986]: 201–2, who tends to "regard these cases as a special group within the causal function of כִּי"). In any event, the emotion-freighted contexts in which the above examples occur would seem to demand vigorous, staccatolike sequences of short questions rather than the bland, question-plus-causal-statement renderings usually encountered in English translations—including the NIV (except here and in Num 11:12; 16:13).

9 In vv.9–11, in several places where the MT has plural verbal forms, one or more MSS of the LXX use singular forms: "They told" (v.9), LXX "He told"; "they broke into" (v.11), LXX "he broke into"; "[they] slaughtered" (v.11), LXX "he slaughtered." Although the plural form in v.9 could conceivably be understood as an impersonal passive in terms of its meaning, the forms in the MT of v.11 obviously have Saul's troops as their subject. The LXX

singular renderings, then, are perhaps intended to highlight Saul's leadership by attributing the victory over the Ammonites to him personally.

A similar phenomenon may be observed in vv.12–15—but this time its effect is to stress Samuel's role, especially in the confirmation of Saul as king: "Bring [pl.]" (v.12), LXX "Bring [sing.]"; "Saul said" (v.13), LXX "Samuel said"; "[they] confirmed" (v.15), LXX "Samuel confirmed"; "they sacrificed" (v.15), LXX "he sacrificed"; "Saul and all the Israelites" (v.15), LXX "Samuel and all the Israelites." In all these cases in vv.9–15, however, it seems evident that the LXX renderings represent not so much a translation as a commentary or interpretation.

---

## 5. *The confirmation of Saul as king*

### 11:12–12:25

12 The people then said to Samuel, "Who was it that asked, 'Shall Saul
reign over us?' Bring these men to us and we will put them to death."
13 But Saul said, "No one shall be put to death today, for this day the
LORD has rescued Israel."
14 Then Samuel said to the people, "Come, let us go to Gilgal and
there reaffirm the kingship." 15 So all the people went to Gilgal and
confirmed Saul as king in the presence of the LORD. There they
sacrificed fellowship offerings before the LORD, and Saul and all the
Israelites held a great celebration.
12:1 Samuel said to all Israel, "I have listened to everything you said to
me and have set a king over you. 2 Now you have a king as your leader.
As for me, I am old and gray, and my sons are here with you. I have been
your leader from my youth until this day. 3 Here I stand. Testify against
me in the presence of the LORD and his anointed. Whose ox have I
taken? Whose donkey have I taken? Whom have I cheated? Whom have
I oppressed? From whose hand have I accepted a bribe to make me shut
my eyes? If I have done any of these, I will make it right."
4 "You have not cheated or oppressed us," they replied. "You have not
taken anything from anyone's hand."
5 Samuel said to them, "The LORD is witness against you, and also his
anointed is witness this day, that you have not found anything in my
hand."
"He is witness," they said.
6 Then Samuel said to the people, "It is the LORD who appointed Moses
and Aaron and brought your forefathers up out of Egypt. 7 Now then,
stand here, because I am going to confront you with evidence before the
LORD as to all the righteous acts performed by the LORD for you and your
fathers.
8 "After Jacob entered Egypt, they cried to the LORD for help, and the
LORD sent Moses and Aaron, who brought your forefathers out of Egypt
and settled them in this place.
9 "But they forgot the LORD their God; so he sold them into the hand of
Sisera, the commander of the army of Hazor, and into the hands of the
Philistines and the king of Moab, who fought against them. 10 They cried
out to the LORD and said, 'We have sinned; we have forsaken the LORD
and served the Baals and the Ashtoreths. But now deliver us from the
hands of our enemies, and we will serve you.' 11 Then the LORD sent
Jerub-Baal, Barak, Jephthah and Samuel, and he delivered you from the
hands of your enemies on every side, so that you lived securely.
12 "But when you saw that Nahash king of the Ammonites was moving
against you, you said to me, 'No, we want a king to rule over us'—even
though the LORD your God was your king. 13 Now here is the king you
have chosen, the one you asked for; see, the LORD has set a king over

you. 14If you fear the LORD and serve and obey him and do not rebel
against his commands, and if both you and the king who reigns over you
follow the LORD your God—good! 15But if you do not obey the LORD, and
if you rebel against his commands, his hand will be against you, as it
was against your fathers.

16"Now then, stand still and see this great thing the LORD is about to
do before your eyes! 17Is it not wheat harvest now? I will call upon the
LORD to send thunder and rain. And you will realize what an evil thing
you did in the eyes of the LORD when you asked for a king."

18Then Samuel called upon the LORD, and that same day the LORD sent
thunder and rain. So all the people stood in awe of the LORD and of
Samuel.

19The people all said to Samuel, "Pray to the LORD your God for your
servants so that we will not die, for we have added to all our other sins
the evil of asking for a king."

20"Do not be afraid," Samuel replied. "You have done all this evil; yet
do not turn away from the LORD, but serve the LORD with all your heart.
21Do not turn away after useless idols. They can do you no good, nor
can they rescue you, because they are useless. 22For the sake of his
great name the LORD will not reject his people, because the LORD was
pleased to make you his own. 23As for me, far be it from me that I should
sin against the LORD by failing to pray for you. And I will teach you the
way that is good and right. 24But be sure to fear the LORD and serve him
faithfully with all your heart; consider what great things he has done for
you. 25Yet if you persist in doing evil, both you and your king will be
swept away."

**12–15** Saul's gracious refusal to execute his erstwhile enemies seems to tie v.13 (and therefore also v.12) more closely with vv.14–15—and chapter (ch. 12)—than with vv.1–11 (see NIV sectional heading at v.12). Vannoy, however, considers 1 Samuel 11:14–12:25 to be a single literary unit, as the subtitle of his work shows. I fully agree that 1 Samuel 12 describes a covenant renewal ceremony (cf. also Klaus Baltzer, *The Covenant Formulary* [Philadelphia: Fortress, 1971], pp. 66–68; William J. Dumbrell, *Covenant and Creation* [Nashville: Thomas Nelson, 1984], p. 135; Eslinger, *Kingship of God*, pp. 37, 383–428 passim) at Gilgal. I nevertheless see no compelling reason not to begin the major compositional unit at 11:12 rather than at v.14. In any case, the conjunctions the NIV uses—correctly, I believe ("But," v.13; "Then," v.14; "So," v.15)—obviously tie vv.12–15 together as a coherent section within the larger compositional unit of 11:12–12:25 and do not commend a sharp break at v.14.

The substance of v.12 finds an eerie echo at the end of Jesus' parable of the ten minas: " 'But those enemies of mine who did not want me to be king over them—bring them here and kill them in front of me' " (Luke 19:27). Saul's troops and the people of Jabesh Gilead, having witnessed God's victory over Ammon under Saul's leadership, demanded from Samuel the death penalty (v.12) for all the troublemakers who had questioned his ability to save them from foreign rule (10:27).

Saul, however, showing how magnanimous he could be when given the opportunity, asserted that the divine deliverance was a cause for gratitude, not vengeful retribution (v.13). Perhaps Jonathan's later rebuke of his father, Saul, in a somewhat similar situation, was inspired by the events recorded here, and perhaps Saul's ready agreement to what his son was saying (19:1–6) was because he then remembered his own earlier statesmanlike declaration of generosity. In any event, Saul's words would later echo in a rhetorical question asked by his successor, David, with the result that the life of the miserable Shimei was spared: "Should anyone be put to death in Israel today?" (2 Sam 19:22).

Saul's demonstration of the leadership qualities necessary to be Israel's king led Samuel to convoke an important meeting at Gilgal (v.14), perhaps modern Khirbet el-Mefjer (about thirty-eight miles southwest of Jabesh Gilead and eight miles north of the Dead Sea west of the Jordan). Vannoy points out (pp. 82–83) that Gilgal was an appropriate site for such a meeting because of its covenant-renewal associations at the beginning of the Conquest period (Josh 4–5). The OT records three meetings of Samuel and Saul at Gilgal, each fateful for Saul: (1) In the flush of his victory over Ammon, Saul was reaffirmed as king (11:14–15); (2) because of his impatience while awaiting Samuel's arrival, Saul was rebuked by his spiritual mentor (13:7–14); and (3) because of his disobedient pride after the defeat of the Amalekites, Saul was rejected as king (15:10–26).

The purpose of the first meeting is to "reaffirm the kingship" (v.14) of Saul, who had already been anointed at Ramah (10:1) and chosen by lot at Mizpah (10:17–25). The reaffirmation of Saul's kingship is a confirmation by public acclamation (v.15) and is the last of the three stages comprising his rise to monarchy over Israel. The verb *ḥiddēš*, appropriately translated "reaffirm" in the NIV, means "make new, renew," and is perhaps used here to "refer to the initiation of the final stage of the coronation process—an 'inauguration' in the sense of launching the third and final stage of the kingship rite" (Edelman, "Saul's Rescue," p. 199).

Samuel's invitation to the people to reaffirm Saul as king was greeted with enthusiasm (v.15). "In the presence of the LORD" they confirmed their earlier choice, and "before the LORD" (same Heb. expression) they brought their sacrifices. As in an earlier ceremony of covenant ratification (Exod 24:5), so also here fellowship offerings were the appropriate response of the people of Israel, who by sacrificing them were expressing their desire to rededicate themselves to God in covenant communion and allegiance. Saul's ascent to the throne was now complete, and the "great celebration" that accompanied the sacrificial ritual more than matched Israel's earlier elation upon their receiving the messengers' report of the imminent doom of the Ammonites (v.9).

**12:1** Chapter 12 concludes the account of the rise of Saul to kingship over Israel, a story that began in chapter 8 with the people's demand for a king. In the broader sweep of the Deuteronomic presentation, however, chapter 12 is appropriately included among those passages that "stand at the turning points of Israel's history: the beginning and the end of the conquest, of the era of the judges, and of the monarchy" (Dennis J. McCarthy, "II Samuel 7 and the Structure of the Deuteronomistic History," JBL 84 [1965]: 131). McCarthy rightly observes (p. 137) that in the total scheme of things, the Deuteronomic history provides three programmatic chapters and then uses six of its key passages "to show how these programs worked or failed in subsequent history . . . as follows" (slightly modified):

| | |
|---|---|
| A. Moses commands the conquest and distribution of the land (Deut 31). | A¹. Joshua undertakes the conquest (Josh 2). |
| | A². Joshua conquers and prepares the distribution (Josh 11–13). |
| B. Joshua commands the covenant, the program for life in the land (Josh 23). | B¹. The people break the covenant (Judg 2). |

B[2]. The people reject the Lord for a human king (1 Sam 12).

C. Nathan's promise (2 Sam 7).

C[1]. The promise fulfilled in Solomon (1 Kings 8).

C[2]. Final failure of the kingship (2 Kings 17).

(p. 137)

It is immediately evident that 1 Samuel 12 plays a prominent role in the Deuteronomic formulation of Israel's history from the Mosaic period through the end of the monarchy (for additional details, see Walter C. Kaiser, Jr., *Toward an Old Testament Theology* [Grand Rapids: Zondervan, 1978], pp. 64–66, 123–24). McCarthy's schema is moderately deficient, however, in failing to include Joshua 24 together with Joshua 23 as the two-chapter ending of the Conquest period. That Joshua 24 should be included becomes clear when one observes (1) that Judges 2:6–9 reprises Joshua 24:28–31 and (2) that Joshua 23–24, like 1 Samuel 12, constitutes the farewell of an Israelite leader combined with a covenant renewal ceremony. Thus Joshua 23–24 describes covenant renewal, Judges 2 summarizes covenant violation, and 1 Samuel 12 describes covenant renewal again. Joshua 23–24 and 1 Samuel 12 serve as a literary frame for the narrative of the judges. The prophet Samuel, the "last of the judges," here at Gilgal delivers his *apologia pro vita sua* in the context of covenant renewal (cf. Baltzer, *The Covenant Formulary*, pp. 66–68; Gerbrandt, p. 143; Vannoy) and formally (if grudgingly) ushers in the period of the monarchy, which begins with the formulaic description of the length of Saul's reign in 13:1.

Literary analysis enables us to divide chapter 12 into four roughly equal parts, arranged chiastically, with v.13 serving as the hinge:

A. Samuel vindicates his covenant faithfulness before the people as witnessed by the Lord and his newly anointed king (vv.1–5).
  B. Samuel summarizes the righteous acts of the Lord during the periods of the Exodus and the judges to demonstrate divine reign through human leaders (vv.6–12).
    C. Samuel observes that the Lord has granted the people's selfish and apostate desire for a king (v.13).
  B′. Samuel summarizes the prospect of blessing for covenant obedience and of curse for covenant disobedience, confirming the ominous side of that prospect by a divinely sent miracle (vv.14–19).
A′. Samuel calls the people, the king, and himself to continued covenant faithfulness (vv.20–25).

Although Vannoy outlines vv.14–25 differently (p. 131), his isolation of v.13 as a separate unit calls attention to its central importance in the chapter (cf. p. 41 n. 95: "I Sam. 12:13 with its juxtaposition of the people's request and Yahweh's response points to the resolution of the kingship issue which has been the focal point of the narratives of 1 Sam. 8–12").

As chapter 12 opens, Samuel begins his *apologia* by reminding the people of Israel that he has "listened to" them and has set a king over them. The phrase "listened to" (in the sense of "obeyed"; cf. vv.14–15) echoes 8:7, 9, 22, and highlights Samuel's commitment to God's will despite his own personal reservations. After all, Saul is "the man the LORD has chosen," the king affirmed by public acclamation (10:24).

**2** However reluctantly, Samuel formally acknowledges the transfer of Israel's leadership from himself to Saul. Although Samuel has been the recognized "leader" of the people from his youth until the present (cf. 3:10; 3:19–4:1; 7:15–17), King Saul is now their "leader." Both "as . . . leader" and "have been . . . leader" translate the common idiom "walk before" (cf. Gen 17:1), an expression that can mean, among other things, "to minister before" (as in 2:35) and "to walk in front of as leader" (as here)—that is, in this context "living in the public eye, under constant scrutiny" (Baldwin, p. 99). Samuel's reference to himself as "old and gray" is probably a modest claim to wisdom (cf. Job 15:9–10), which was often an expectation attaching to elders' years of experience. His mention of his sons emphasizes the length of time it has been his privilege to serve the people of Israel—and perhaps also provides them with an unwelcome reminder of their earlier refusal to allow his sons to succeed him as judge (8:5).

**3** The NIV's "Here I stand" (reminiscent—though with a different nuance and in a different situation—of Martin Luther's reputed *Hier stehe/bin ich*) translates *hinᵉnî*, which is literally "Here I am," and echoes an important servant motif (e.g., Gen 22:1, 11) in Samuel's first recorded words (cf. 3:4, 5, 6, 8, 16). Samuel invites the people to "testify against" (respond [negatively] to, witness against) him about covenant stipulations he might have violated. As though in a courtroom, the inquiry takes place "in the presence of" Samuel's heavenly and earthly superiors: "the LORD and his anointed" (Saul, cf. 10:1; for the entire phrase in reference to God and the king, cf. the NIV mg. on Ps 2:2).

Aware that testifying on his own behalf could well result in self-incrimination (cf. 2 Sam 1:16), Samuel nevertheless launches into a brief series of protestations of innocence. The key verb is "taken" ("accepted" renders the same Heb. word), which Samuel consciously uses as a powerful means of contrasting his admirable behavior with the potentially oppressive demands of a (despotic) king that he had earlier warned about (8:11, 13–17; cf. Eslinger, *Kingship of God*, p. 388; Garsiel, pp. 69–70; Vannoy, p. 16). Doubtless alluding to the covenant stipulations of Exodus 20:17, Samuel challenges the people to accuse him of having taken from any of them so much as an ox or a donkey (contrast 8:16; 22:19; 27:9). His claim of exemplary conduct in this regard may be compared to that of Moses (Num 16:15) and Paul (Acts 20:33).

Samuel goes on to affirm that he has neither "cheated" nor "oppressed" anyone (v.3). The parallel use of these two verbs in the poetry of Amos 4:1, where they are translated "oppress" and "crush" respectively (cf. also Hos 5:11, "oppressed . . . trampled"; Deut 28:33, where the NIV translates the two verbs as a hendiadys: "cruel oppression"), shows that they are approximately synonymous. Samuel's refusal to cheat/oppress others looks backward to his specific denial of having engaged in bribery. The Book of the Covenant in Exodus 23:8 (repeated almost verbatim in Deut 16:19) issues a general warning against accepting bribes, pointing out that doing so "blinds" (distorts) a judge's ability to make fair and just decisions. Although in v.3 the word for "bribe" is different from that used in the Covenant Code and means literally "ransom," "price for life" (the same word is translated "bribes" in Amos 5:12; Ecclus 46:19), and although "make me shut my eyes" is a different expression than "blinds" in the Covenant Code, the intent there and here is virtually identical. Accepting bribes is universally condemned in Scripture, and Samuel carefully distances himself from a practice that has already made his own sons infamous (8:3; cf. further Ps 15:5; Amos 5:12). "If I have done any of these," though not in the MT, is necessary in

English to prepare for Samuel's conclusion: "I will make it right" (lit., "I will restore to you"; cf. 2 Sam 9:7).

**4** The people readily accepted and agreed with Samuel's declaration. Like Elisha after him (2 Kings 5:16–17)—and unlike Elisha's servant Gehazi (2 Kings 5:20)—Samuel declared his determination not to make merchandise of the prophetic office (cf. further Mic 2:6–11; 3:11).

**5** After solemnly affirming his innocence of any wrongdoing, Samuel—using characteristic covenant-renewal terminology (cf. Josh 24:21–22, 27)—declares that the Lord and Saul (cf. v.3) are witnesses to the truthfulness of his words. As Achish would later absolve David of any fault attributed to him by his detractors (29:3, 6; cf. David's concurrence in v.8), so Samuel here denies—under implied oath—that he is guilty of crimes against his fellow Israelites. The people's response, "He is witness," could refer either to the Lord or to Saul and may be intentionally ambiguous. Less likely, though not impossible, would be the translation "They are witness[es]" (so Vannoy, p. 18).

**6** Joshua 24:2–15, in proper covenant-renewal fashion, summarizes the history of God's people from the time of Abraham through the conquest of Canaan, stressing divine leadership and the people's idolatrous disloyalty while challenging them to covenant faithfulness. Similarly vv.6–12 summarize the history of Israel from the time of Moses and the Exodus through the period of the judges and their sinful request for a king, stressing divine leadership and Israel's idolatrous disloyalty while challenging them to the same covenant faithfulness (for a brief analysis of these and other similar passages, cf. W. Gordon Robinson, "Historical Summaries of Biblical History," EQ 47, 4 [1975]: 195–207). Such historical prologues are common features in suzerainty covenant documents throughout the Near East in the second millennium B.C. (cf. George E. Mendenhall, "Law and Covenant in Israel and the Ancient Near East," BA 17, 3 [1954]: 58).

By highlighting the name YHWH from the outset (v.6), Samuel leaves no doubt that, in the final sense, Israel's leader has always been the Lord. The NIV's "appointed" attempts to translate *'āśāh 'eṯ-*, a difficult phrase in this context. The best solution is "worked with" (cf. BDB, p. 794), which compares 14:45 (where the semantic equivalent *'āśāh 'im-* obviously has that sense; cf. NIV's "did this . . . with God's help"). The meaning would then be that God, working through and in concert with Moses and Aaron, freed his people from Egyptian bondage (cf. Exod 6:13, 26–27; for the same idea, cf. the NIV mg. of Rom 8:28: "God works together with those who love him to bring about what is good"; cf. also the expression "God's fellow workers" in 1 Cor 3:9).

The exodus of Israel from Egypt during the days of Moses was remembered as the greatest of all divine acts of redemption for the nation. "I am the LORD your God, who brought you out of Egypt, out of the land of slavery" stands in Exodus 20:2 as the elegantly brief preamble-plus-historical-prologue that precedes the Ten Commandments—the covenant stipulations to be obeyed unquestioningly by God's people—and its modified form therefore serves here as an appropriate opening to Samuel's summary (cf. also v.8). Kaiser estimates that similar formulaic reminders of the Exodus redemption occur throughout the OT "about 125 times" (*Toward an Old Testament Theology*, p. 59).

**7** Samuel continues to use the language of the courtroom as he commands the people to "stand" at attention and in anticipation before the bar of God's justice (cf. v.16 and Exod 14:13). He intends to "confront [them] with evidence" (lit., "enter into judgment/litigation with/against" them, using the Niphal of *špṭ,* followed by *'ēṯ;* cf. Prov 29:9, "goes to court with") of God's blessing on their history, all the more casting their apostasy in darker relief. The contrast is heightened by using *'itt[e]ḵem* twice, first as a particle of disadvantage (NIV, "confront you"; lit., "against you") and then as a particle of advantage ("for you"; see Theophile J. Meek, "Translating the Hebrew Bible," *Bible Translator* 16 [1965]: 144). Samuel's evidence is "the righteous acts performed by the LORD" (*ṣiḏqôṯ YHWH;* cf. Judg 5:11; Dan 9:16; Mic 6:5; cf. further Rev 15:4), virtually synonymous with the *magnalia Dei,* the "mighty acts" of God for his people (cf. Exod 6:6; 7:4; Pss 106:2; 145:4, 12; 150:2 ["acts of power"]; cf. esp. Ps 71:16, 24).

**8** Verses 8–12 recapitulate and expand on 8:7–8. In 12:8 "Jacob" refers not only to the patriarch himself but also, by extension, to the nation of Israel (as often in the OT). The Lord (cf. also v.10) graciously answered (Exod 2:25) their cry for help (Exod 2:23–24). He sent his servants Moses (Exod 3:10) and Aaron to lead Israel out of Egypt (cf. 1 Sam 10:18)—a fact acknowledged even by their enemies (1 Sam 6:6)—and to bring them to the borders of the Promised Land.

**9** The language of vv.9–11 is heavily dependent on terminology characteristic of the Book of Judges. The dreary cycle of rebellion-retribution-repentance-restoration described throughout that book (cf. also the summary in Neh 9:26–31) is reprised here: rebellion (v.9a), retribution (v.9b), repentance (v.10), and restoration (v.11).

Rebelling against their God, the Israelites "forgot" (v.9; cf. Judg 3:7) what he had done for them in the past and ignored him personally as they worshiped other gods (cf. v.10). In response to his people's apostasy and in retribution against them for their sin, the Lord "sold them" (cf. Judg 2:14; 3:8)—as though on the slave market—"into the hand[s] [i.e., 'power'] of" their enemies, including Sisera (Judg 4:2; cf. Ps 83:9), the commander of the army of the city of Hazor (modern Tell el-Qedah, about nine miles north of the Sea of Galilee; cf. Ronald F. Youngblood, "Hazor," in *Major Cities of the Biblical World,* ed. R.K. Harrison [Nashville: Thomas Nelson, 1985], pp. 119–29), the Philistines (Judg 3:31; 10:7; 13:1), and Eglon king of Moab (Judg 3:12–14).

**10** Verse 10, part of which summarizes Judges 10:15–16, describes repentant Israel sporadically throughout the period of the judges. Although they often forsook the Lord and violated his covenant with them by serving the Baals (male deities; cf. commentary on 7:4; cf. also Judg 2:11; 3:7; 10:6, 10) and the Ashtoreths (female deities; cf. commentary on 7:3–4; cf. also Judg 2:13; 10:6), they pled for his deliverance and promised to serve him alone if only he would release them from the shackles of enemy oppression.

**11** God did restore the Israelites to their former covenant relationship by sending judges to their rescue. Jerub-Baal, another name for Gideon (cf. NIV mg.), is perhaps mentioned first (1) because he is the central figure in the Book of Judges and arguably the most important of the judges themselves, (2) because his very name (cf. Judg 6:32 and NIV mg. there) means "Let Baal Contend" and thus explicitly contradicts the Israelite tendency to worship the shameful (cf. 2 Sam 11:21, where Gideon is called

Jerub-Besheth, a scornful scribal variant that means "Let Shame Contend") god Baal (cf. v.10), and (3) because he specifically refused to establish dynastic as opposed to divine rule over his countrymen (Judg 8:22–23)—for which refusal he must surely have been one of Samuel's heroes (cf. v.13).

Reference is next made to Barak, Deborah's general in the successful war against Sisera's Canaanite army (Judg 4:6–7). Barak is followed by Jephthah (Judg 11:1), victor over the Ammonites—who had been aided and abetted by the Philistines to establish hegemony over Israel in Transjordan (Judg 10:7–8). (One would have expected Samuel to refer also to Ehud, the judge who led Israel's troops against the "king of Moab" [v.9; cf. Judg 3:26–30], but perhaps allusion to the implied defeat of "the gods of Moab" alongside "the gods of the Ammonites and the gods of the Philistines" in the Jephthah narratives [Judg 10:6] was considered sufficient.)

Finally, Samuel mentions himself as the last of the judges as well as the most recent victor over the Philistines (7:6, 11–15). He then summarizes the Lord's triumphant deliverance of his people, through his chosen leaders, from "your enemies on every side, so that you lived securely" (v.11; the underlying Heb. is a clear echo—and here a fulfillment—of the divine promise recorded in Deut 12:10, which the NIV translates: "your enemies around you so that you will live in safety").

**12** Three times in these chapters the antithetical negative *lō' kî* (lit., "no, but"; for details cf. GKC, sec. 163) is used to stress the people's determination not to have God as their King but rather to have a human king like "all the other nations" (8:5–7): (1) after Samuel's earlier warning about the dangers inherent in their demand (8:19–20), (2) during the public assembly at Mizpah (10:19), and (3) in the face of the Ammonite threat (12:12). Later in v.12 the poignancy of Samuel's sadness is brought out even more starkly by the syntax, as Daniel Lys observes: "The *waw* connecting the two parts of this verse indicates a strong opposition: 'when [whereas, even though] the Lord your God was your king' " ("Who Is Our President? From Text to Sermon on I Samuel 12:12," Int 21, 4 [1967]: 410). Their sinful demand proved them to be totally unlike Jerub-Baal/Gideon (Judg 8:23), the paradigm judge (v.11).

**13** Serving as the hinge of the chapter, this verse focuses once again on the gracious, permissive will of God, who has "given" (lit.; NIV, "set"; cf. Gen 41:41, "put . . . in charge") his people the king they "asked for" (*š'l;* yet another pun on the name "Saul," *šā'ûl;* cf. also vv.17, 19). Over and over Israel had requested—yea, demanded—a king (e.g., 8:5–6, 22; 10:19; 12:1), and Saul in successive stages had acceded to that office. The Lord's eventual rejection of the very king the people demanded is eerily echoed later in a similar situation in Hosea 13:10–11 (cf. esp. v.11: "In my anger I gave you a king,/ and in my wrath I took him away").

**14–15** Certain key phrases in v.14 ("fear the LORD and serve," "both you and the king who reigns over you") are echoed in vv.24–25 ("fear the LORD and serve," "both you and your king") and frame the last half of the chapter (vv.14–25).

Verses 14–15 represent the blessings and curses sections respectively that were part of ancient suzerainty covenants. As such the structure of each balances and parallels that of the other—but not as usually thought. The NIV sides with most translations and commentators, who assume an aposiopesis (here a suppressed apodosis) at the end of v.14, which must then be contextually supplied to complete the sense (hence NIV's "good!" for which there is no equivalent in the Heb.).

However, Vannoy points out that "the two verses display a remarkably close parallelism in wording and structure, and because the apodosis is introduced in verse 15 with והיתה [*whyth*], the parallelism strongly supports beginning the apodosis of verse 14 with והיתם [*whytm*]" (p. 42). The resulting translation of vv.14–15 would then be: "If you fear the LORD and serve and obey . . . and do not rebel . . . , then both you and the king who reigns over you will follow the LORD your God. But if you do not obey the Lord, and if you rebel . . . , then his hand will be against you, as it was against your fathers." Vannoy summarizes this new understanding of v.14 thus: "Israel must not replace her loyalty to Yahweh by loyalty to her human ruler. . . . If Israel fears Yahweh, . . . then she will show that even though human kingship has been introduced into the structure of the theocracy, she continues to recognize Yahweh as her sovereign" (p. 44; cf. similarly Antony F. Campbell, *The Study Companion to Old Testament Literature: An Approach to the Writings of Pre-Exilic and Exilic Israel* [Wilmington: Michael Glazer, 1989], pp. 156–57 and n. 15).

The blessings-and-curses terminology of Deuteronomy and Joshua permeates vv.14–15. To "fear the LORD and serve" him (v.14; Josh 24:14) brings his blessing; to "rebel against his commands" (v.15; Deut 1:26, 43; 9:23; Josh 1:18) brings his curse. "Fear of God/the LORD" (*yir'aṯ 'ᵉlōhîm/YHWH*), a common expression in OT wisdom literature (cf. Job 28:28; Prov 1:7; 9:10), was the generic term for "religion" in ancient Israel; the Akkadian phrase *pulḫti ili* ("fear of God") is the semantic equivalent. As is well known, in the OT fearing God had more the connotation of reverence and awe (cf. Deut 17:19) than of terror or dread—although the latter was not totally lacking. To "serve" means not only to work and minister but also to worship (cf. already 7:3–4). If Israel and her new king would fear, serve, and obey God (v.14) by carefully following his law, they would receive his blessing (for the king, see Deut 17:18–20). Disobedience and rebellion "against his commands" (v.15), however—including especially forgetting or forsaking him and serving other gods (cf. Deut 8:19; Josh 24:20)—would result in his curse (symbolized by his powerful "hand") against them in the future (cf. 1 Kings 13:21–26; Lam 1:18) as it had been against their "fathers" in the past (cf. Num 20:24–26; 27:12–14).

**16** Verses 16–19 continue the theme of covenant curse established in v.15. Earlier (v.7) Samuel had told the people to "stand" before the bar of divine justice and be confronted with the evidence of God's righteous acts in the past on their behalf. Now (v.16) he commands them to "stand" and be awed by divine omnipotence, to "see this great thing the LORD is about to do before your eyes" (cf. also Exod 14:31). The divine act then results in what Raymond C. van Leeuwen appropriately calls a "cosmic inversion": "Rain and thunder appear during the dry season of wheat harvest" ("Proverbs 30:21–23 and the Biblical World Upside Down," JBL 105, 4 [1986]: 604). In that part of the world not only is "rain in harvest . . . not fitting" (Prov 26:1), it is so totally unexpected that it could easily be interpreted as a sign of divine displeasure.

**17** "Thunder" is literally "voices" (cf. also Exod 9:33–34), a metaphor that represents thunder as the loud and powerful voice of God manifested in storms (cf. 7:10; cf. also esp. Ps 29:3–9). The narrator's use of "voices" in the sense of thunder might well have been intended to echo its use in the account of the establishment of the Sinaitic covenant (Exod 19:16; 20:18; cf. similarly Vannoy, p. 51 and n. 118). The driving rain that often accompanied such thunder could be especially destructive to crops (Prov 28:3), and when it occurred unseasonably, it could leave those who depended on it destitute. By destroying Philistine grain during wheat harvest, Samson had understood fully that he could inflict serious harm on his enemies (Judg 15:1–5). Before the Exodus, a plague of hail accompanied by thunder and rain devastated a recalcitrant pharaoh's fruit trees, flax, and barley (Exod 9:22–32). Thus Samuel's rhetorical question—"Is it not wheat harvest now [lit., 'today']?"—served as an ominous reminder to the people that all their hard work had the potential of being wiped out in an equally brief period of time. In any event, the display of divine power in the rainstorm would force the people to "realize" (lit., "know and see"; the same Heb. phrase echoes later in Saul's desire to "find out" [14:38] what sin had been committed) how evil their motives had been when they had "asked" (a pun on the name "Saul"; also v.19) for a king.

**18–19** Samuel's prayer for a storm out of season was answered "that same day," and all the people "stood in awe" (lit., "feared"; same Heb. root in v.14) of both God and Samuel (v.18). A similar statement in Exodus 14:31 pairs God and Moses as the objects of Israel's fear and trust after the miracle at the Sea of Reeds. The reputation of Moses and Samuel as being especially close to God's counsel (Jer 15:1) was justly deserved: Although the Hebrew verbs are different, the people's plea to Samuel—"Pray to the LORD" (v.19)—is a clear echo of a pharaoh's cry to Moses (and Aaron) centuries earlier in a similar situation (Exod 9:28). That the people should ask Samuel to pray to the Lord "your" God (rather than "our" God) may be an index of their perception of their own apostate condition. Reflecting Samuel's words in v.17, they admit that asking for a king was an evil that "added to" (v.19)—and thus perhaps superseded—all their other sins (cf. similarly 2 Chron 28:13; Job 34:37; Isa 30:1).

The people's concern that they should not die—in the broad context of the entire chapter but especially in the narrow context of unseasonable thunder and rain that might be expected to destroy their wheat before it could be harvested—prompted Tremper Longman III to propose correctly that vv.16–19 should be interpreted "as the outworking of a covenant curse which motivates the Israelites to repent of their past sin and to keep the sanctions which had just been presented to them by Samuel" ("1 Samuel 12:16–19: Divine Omnipotence or Covenant Curse?" WTJ 45 [1983]: 171). Longman observes (pp. 170–71) that covenant curses due to general apostasy are often described elsewhere in the OT in terms of drought, famine, and the like (cf. Lev 26:19–20; Deut 28:22–24, 38–42).

**20** The literary coherence of vv.20–25 (cf. also McCarthy, "II Samuel 7 and Deuteronomic History," p. 135) is established by key words and phrases in the MT of vv.20 and 24–25 to frame it: "Be afraid" (v.20); "fear" (v.24); "you" (emphatic; vv.20, 24 [second occurrence in Heb.]); "evil" (vv.20, 25); and especially "serve . . . with all your heart" (vv.20, 24). Samuel concludes his address to the people of Israel by encouraging them to do good (vv.20–24) and warning them not to do evil (v.25).

Samuel reminds the people that they (emphatic "you," v.20) were the ones who asked for—yea, demanded—a king (cf. v.19); thus they have only themselves to blame if Saul proves to be either weak or despotic. All is not lost, however, if only the people will acknowledge that their true King is the Lord himself: "Do not ['*al*] turn away." Samuel further urges Israel to "serve the LORD with all your heart," an often expressed covenant requirement (e.g., Deut 10:12–13; 11:13–14; cf. also 30:9–10).

**21** By contrast, says Samuel, the people are not to follow "useless" (*tōhû*, the word rendered "formless" in Gen 1:2) things/people. Although idols are described as *tōhû* in Isaiah 41:29 (NIV, "confusion"; cf. also 44:9, "nothing"), hence NIV's "useless idols" here, the reference in this context is perhaps broader and denotes any defection from serving the Lord—including, of course, preference for a human king (so Eslinger, *Kingship of God*, pp. 418–19; cf. similarly Vannoy, p. 55). Only God can do the people good; no one else can "rescue" (cf. NIV, "deliver[ed]" in vv.10–11; 10:18).

**22** The Lord's elective purposes for his people would not be denied. His intention to make Israel his own covenant people (Exod 19:5; cf. 1 Peter 2:9) was not because of any merit on their part (Deut 7:6–7). Far from it, he chose them because of his love for them and to fulfill the oath that he had sworn to their forefathers (Deut 7:8–9; cf. Gen 15:4–6, 13–18; 22:16–18). In addition, and perhaps most important of all, he chose them "for the sake of his great name" (cf. also Josh 7:9–11, where the Lord's "great name" is linked to the Sinaitic covenant)—that is, based on the integrity of his self-revelation (cf. Vannoy, p. 56). In this last clause of v.22, says McCarthy, "the problems raised in the pericope are finally solved. The kingship has been integrated into the fundamental relationship between Yahweh and the people and that relationship reaffirmed" ("The Inauguration of Monarchy," p. 412).

**23** Taking his rightful place among such giants of intercession as Moses (Exod 32:30–32), Daniel (Dan 9:4–20), Paul (Rom 1:9–10; Col 1:9; 1 Thess 3:10; 2 Tim 1:3), and Jesus (Isa 53:12; Rom 8:34; Heb 7:25), Samuel declares his unwillingness to sin against God (cf. Saul's command in 14:33–34) by failing to pray for Israel (cf. also v.19; 7:5, 8–9; 8:6; 15:11; Jer 15:1). To help the people live a life pleasing to God, Samuel promises to "teach" (the Heb. root is *yrh*, the same as in *tôrāh*, "instruction," "law") them "the way that is good and right" (cf. also 1 Kings 8:36 = 2 Chron 6:27; Pss 25:8; 32:8; Prov 4:11).

**24–25** The rest is up to the people themselves; so chapter 12 ends with encouragement to faith and obedience (v.24, which summarizes Deut 10:20–21) and warning against the consequences of disobedience (v.25) appropriate to a covenant renewal document. Samuel's admonition in v.24a is strikingly similar to that of "the Teacher, son of David, king in Jerusalem" (Eccl 1:1): "Here is the conclusion of the matter: Fear God and keep his commandments" (Eccl 12:13). After all, the Lord had done "great things" for his people (v.24b), which should have been a cause for rejoicing on their part (Ps 126:2–3; Joel 2:21). Samuel feels constrained to remind them, however, that pursuing their penchant for evil will surely result in their destruction: "You and your king will be swept away" (v.25). The verbal root is *sph*, which appears again in 26:10, where David predicts that the Lord would cause Saul's demise, that perhaps Saul would go into battle and "perish"—and so it happened (31:1–5). Thus the final words of Samuel's address and the final days of Saul's kingship, passages that frame the account of Saul's reign (chs. 13–31), are suffused with the stench of death.

## Notes

**14–15** Vannoy, in a lengthy and carefully reasoned argument, insists that מְלוּכָה (*m*[e]*lûḵāh*, "kingship," v.14) here refers to God's kingdom rather than to human monarchy and that v.15

is the first reference in 1 Samuel to Saul's actually becoming king as but one aspect of Israel's continued recognition of the kingship of God over his people (pp. 61–82). The immediate context of v.14, however, uses the root מלך (*mlk*), not of God, but of Saul ("reign," v.12; "confirmed . . . as king," v.15; "set a king," 12:1; "king," 12:2). Furthermore, of the twenty-four times that the word *m$^{e}$lûḵāh* occurs in the OT, it refers to divine kingship only twice at best (Ps 22:28; Obad 21)—as Vannoy himself acknowledges (p. 76 n. 44). Fifteen of the twenty-four occurrences are in Samuel and Kings, and in all fifteen cases—unless v.14 is the exception—it means human rather than divine kingship (cf. 10:16, 25; 14:47; 18:8). Although there can be no doubt that Saul was supposed to rule under God's direction, divine superintendence of Israel's monarchy should not be read into the word *m$^{e}$lûḵāh* in v.14.

**12:3** Ecclesiasticus 46:13–20, a passage that praises Samuel, includes a summary of 1 Sam 12:1–5 in 46:19, in which the MT's אַעְלִים (*'a'lîm*, "make me shut") is replaced by נעל[י]ם (*n'l[y]m*, "[pair of] sandal[s]"). The Hebrew text of Ecclus 46:19 thus reads, in part: "From whom have I accepted a bribe, even so much as a [pair of] sandal[s]?" (i.e., the most trifling bribe; cf. Gen 14:23; Amos 2:6; 8:6). The LXX's ὑποδημα[των] (*hypodēma[tōn]*, "sandal[s]") dutifully follows this (or a similar Heb. variant) in both 1 Samuel and Ecclesiasticus. However, the MT idiom העלים עיני (*h'lym 'yny*, "shut/close [one's] eyes"), in the sense of "refuse to help/protest/get involved," is well established in the OT (Lev 20:4; Prov 28:27; Ezek 22:26) and fits admirably in the present context.

**5** The NIV's "they said" at the end of the verse either translates the plural verb found in many Hebrew MSS (also in the LXX) or else understands the MT singular form as a collective with "people" as the implied subject (cf. v.6).

**11** Three of the four proper names in this verse deserve further comment. The narrator's explanation of the name Jerub-Baal in Judg 6:32—"Let Baal Contend"—may be, as often in the Bible, a wordplay, considering the context. Names such as Irēba-Adad ("Adad Substitutes") and Rīb-Haddi ("The Compensation of Hadad"), rulers of Assyria and Byblos respectively during the Amarna age, might well lead to the conclusion that "Baal Substitutes" was the original meaning of Jerub-Baal—especially when it is recognized that Hadad and Baal were two different names for the same god (*hd* and *b'l* are often parallel to each other in Ugaritic; cf. UT, II AB vii:35–37). Jerub-Baal would thus be an *Ersatzname*, one of a class of names that indicates the previous loss of a child in the family. Although there is no evidence for the meaning "substitute" or "compensate" for the verb רִיב (*rîḇ*) in the OT, since proper names tend to preserve archaic usages, it may well be that a name like Jerub-Baal (and, for that matter, Jeroboam) is an *Ersatzname* survival from an earlier era (for additional details, cf. Youngblood, *The Amarna Correspondence*, pp. 5–8).

"Barak" is the reading in some LXX MSS and also in the Syriac; the MT has "Bedan," Hebrew בְּדָן (*b$^{e}$ḏān;* cf. NIV mg.). Attempts to equate Bedan with Samson (understanding *bdn* to be an abbreviation for "son of Dan," "Danite") or with the minor judge Abdon (Judg 12:13, 15) are rightly rejected by Y. Zakovitch, "יפתח = בדן," VetTest 22, 1 (1972): 123–24. His own solution, however—namely, that Bedan is another name for Jephthah based on an argument derived from the occurrence of the name Bedan in 1 Chron 7:17—depends on the unlikely suggestion that later scribes twice emended the text to insert Jephthah's name smoothly into it (pp. 124–25). Nor does the proposal of Vannoy (p. 33 n. 66), who accepts the suggestion that Bedan is another name for Barak, fare any better, since there is no evidence to support it. The best solution remains that of most commentators: The versional "Barak" is correct, and the MT בדן (*bdn*) is an early transcriptional error for ברק (*brq*). Confusion between *d* and *r* and between *n* and *q* was not of infrequent occurrence in the ancient West Semitic scripts, especially in the tenth–ninth centuries B.C. In any case, the sequence "Jerub-Baal, Barak, Jephthah and Samuel" (v.11) appears to be alluded to in Heb 11:32: "Gideon, Barak, . . . Jephthah, . . . Samuel."

The Syriac and Lucianic reading "Samson" for the Hebrew "Samuel" as the final name in the list (cf. NIV mg.) may have been intended to protect Samuel from the accusation of pride. Such third-person references to oneself are not uncommon in the OT, however, and were a frequent narrative device. Furthermore, that Samuel would mention himself in his roles as the last of the judges and the most recent conqueror of the Philistines is not at all unexpected.

---

## B. *The Decline of Saul (13:1–15:35)*

Although the story of Saul's decline begins in chapter 13 and is highlighted in chapters 13–15, it continues sporadically to the end of 1 Samuel and is inextricably intertwined with the story of David's rise (16:1–28:2). The entire account of the interaction between the two processes as recorded in 1 Samuel 13–31 is aptly termed "the crossing fates" by Jan P. Fokkelman (*Narrative Art and Poetry in the Books of Samuel: A Full Interpretation Based on Stylistic and Structural Analyses;* vol. 2, *The Crossing Fates [I Sam. 13–31 and II Sam. I]* [Assen: Van Gorcum, 1986]). Elsewhere Jan P. Fokkelman states, "As one man's fate goes down, the other's goes up" ("Saul and David: Crossed Fates," *Bible Review* 5, 3 [1989]: 25).

Chapters 13–15, which constitute a separate unit apart from the preceding and following chapters, focus our attention on Saul's reign after the problem of kingship is resolved in chapters 8–12. Chapter 13 begins with the typical Deuteronomic formula for introducing the reign of a southern Israelite king (see below for details), chapter 15 ends with a final breach between Samuel and Saul, and chapter 16 begins with God's command to Samuel to anoint a son of Jesse of Bethlehem to replace Saul as king. Gerbrandt summarizes: "The narrative in 1 Samuel 13–15 thus performs the important function of being a bridge between 1 Samuel 8–12 and 1 Samuel 16ff, and also provides the Deuteronomist with the opportunity to emphasize some key elements of his understanding of the role of the king in this new era" (p. 158).

The literary structure of chapters 13–15 is chiastic:

A. The rebuke of Saul (13:1–15)
  B. The struggle against the Philistines (13:16–14:23)
    C. The cursing of Jonathan (14:24–46)
  B′. Further wars of Saul (14:47–52)
A′. The rejection of Saul (15:1–35)

Samuel's initial rebuke of Saul (A) parallels God's final rejection of Saul (A′); and Saul's victory against the Philistines (B) parallels his victories against various enemies, including the Philistines (B′). The hinge of the section is Saul's determination, however reluctant, to execute his firstborn son, Jonathan, heir to the throne (C).

### 1. *The rebuke of Saul*

13:1–15

1Saul was ⌊thirty⌋ years old when he became king, and he reigned over
Israel ⌊forty-⌋ two years.
2Saul chose three thousand men from Israel; two thousand were with
him at Micmash and in the hill country of Bethel, and a thousand were
with Jonathan at Gibeah in Benjamin. The rest of the men he sent back
to their homes.
3Jonathan attacked the Philistine outpost at Geba, and the Philistines
heard about it. Then Saul had the trumpet blown throughout the land
and said, "Let the Hebrews hear!" 4So all Israel heard the news: "Saul

has attacked the Philistine outpost, and now Israel has become a stench
to the Philistines." And the people were summoned to join Saul at
Gilgal.
5 The Philistines assembled to fight Israel, with three thousand
chariots, six thousand charioteers, and soldiers as numerous as the
sand on the seashore. They went up and camped at Micmash, east of
Beth Aven. 6 When the men of Israel saw that their situation was critical
and that their army was hard pressed, they hid in caves and thickets,
among the rocks, and in pits and cisterns. 7 Some Hebrews even crossed
the Jordan to the land of Gad and Gilead.
Saul remained at Gilgal, and all the troops with him were quaking with
fear. 8 He waited seven days, the time set by Samuel; but Samuel did not
come to Gilgal, and Saul's men began to scatter. 9 So he said, "Bring me
the burnt offering and the fellowship offerings." And Saul offered up the
burnt offering. 10 Just as he finished making the offering, Samuel
arrived, and Saul went out to greet him.
11 "What have you done?" asked Samuel.
Saul replied, "When I saw that the men were scattering, and that you
did not come at the set time, and that the Philistines were assembling at
Micmash, 12 I thought, 'Now the Philistines will come down against me at
Gilgal, and I have not sought the LORD's favor.' So I felt compelled to
offer the burnt offering."
13 "You acted foolishly," Samuel said. "You have not kept the
command the LORD your God gave you; if you had, he would have
established your kingdom over Israel for all time. 14 But now your
kingdom will not endure; the LORD has sought out a man after his own
heart and appointed him leader of his people, because you have not
kept the LORD's command."
15 Then Samuel left Gilgal and went up to Gibeah in Benjamin, and
Saul counted the men who were with him. They numbered about six
hundred.

1 The RSV rendering of v.1 might be the most courageous translation of a biblical verse ever made: "Saul was . . . years old when he began to reign; and he reigned . . . two years over Israel" (footnotes inform the reader that the lacunae represent numbers that have dropped out during the course of transmitting the text). Although the KJV tried to make the best of a bad situation by translating the Hebrew as it stood ("Saul reigned one year; and when he had reigned two years over Israel," followed by the main clause beginning v.2), scholars generally agree that since "something has happened to the Hebrew text of 1 Samuel 13:1, the length of Saul's reign can only be estimated" (K.A. Kitchen, *Ancient Orient and Old Testament* [Downers Grove: InterVarsity, 1966], p. 75). In any event, omission (whether accidental or not) of year-dates from official regnal documents was not uncommon in ancient times (cf. ibid., p. 75 n. 65).

Verse 1 is doubtless the defective remnant of the formal introduction of Saul's reign. Such formulas are common in later portions of the Deuteronomic history but—beginning with David, 2 Samuel 5:4—always and only concerning southern kings: Rehoboam, 1 Kings 14:21; Jehoshaphat, 22:42; Jehoram, 2 Kings 8:17; Ahaziah, 8:26; Joash, 11:21–12:1; Amaziah, 14:2; Azariah/Uzziah, 15:2; Jotham, 15:33; Ahaz, 16:2; Hezekiah, 18:2; Manasseh, 21:1; Amon, 21:19; Josiah, 22:1; Jehoahaz, 23:31; Jehoiakim, 23:36; Jehoiachin, 24:8; and Zedekiah, 24:18. Each of the above kings from Rehoboam through Zedekiah is honored by a similar formula in 2 Chronicles; none of the northern Israelite kings beginning with Jeroboam I—who are considered both illegitimate and apostate—is so honored in either history. It is not immediately apparent why the 2 Samuel 5:4 formula for David is not repeated in 1 Chronicles; nor can we be sure why neither Abijah nor Asa, the second and third southern kings during the divided monarchy—not to mention Solomon, son of David—was recognized by such a formula.

Two notable exceptions to the southern orientation of the regnal formula must be mentioned: that of Saul in v.1 and that of Ish-Bosheth son of Saul (2 Sam 2:10). The latter verse is especially suggestive since it ends as follows: "The house of Judah, however, followed David." After the murder of Ish-Bosheth (2 Sam 4), the regnal formula is reserved exclusively for southern kings. As for Saul, the mutilated condition (whether deliberate or accidental) of v.1 may reflect later scribal antipathy or indifference toward him.

The two NIV footnotes to v.1 summarize the text-critical reasons for the numbers the NIV restores there. The reference to Saul's having ruled "forty years" (Acts 13:21) is strengthened by the notation in Josephus (Antiq. VI, 378 [xiv.9]) to the effect that he ruled "eighteen years while Samuel was alive, and two [and twenty] years after his death." Other attempts to solve the problem of the lacunae are numerous, and none is more certain than any other. In light of the above discussion, however, all attempts based on the supposed integrity of the present Hebrew text are doomed to failure (cf. the suggestion of Edward A. Niederhiser to the effect that Saul spent one year exercising his kingship and two years being officially anointed king: "One More Proposal for 1 Samuel 13:1," *Hebrew Studies* 20 [1979]: 44–46).

**2–10** The background of v.2 appears to be an occasion when Saul was dispersing the mustered troops of Israel (J. Maxwell Miller, "Saul's Rise to Power: Some Observations Concerning 1 Sam 9:1–10:16; 10:26–11:15; and 13:2–14:46," CBQ 36, 2 [1974]: 161). The people had "chosen" a king to lead them into battle (8:18–20), and now their king obliged them: Saul "chose" three thousand Israelite men (v.2) to serve in his standing army (cf. Samuel's warning in 8:11–12). Two thousand were under his command at Micmash (modern Mukhmas) and in the high country at Bethel (modern Beitin), while one thousand were at Gibeah in Benjamin (his hometown, modern Tell el-Ful, three miles north of Jerusalem) under the command of his son Jonathan (which means "The LORD Has Given"; this is the first mention of Jonathan in the Bible). Micmash was almost five miles southeast of Bethel and about four miles northeast of Gibeah. Apparently feeling confident in the size of his two military units, Saul sent the rest of the men home.

The smaller unit under Jonathan started a war against the Philistines by attacking their outpost at Geba in Benjamin (v.3), modern Jeba (called "Gibeah of God" in 10:5), about five miles north-northeast of Jerusalem. Saul, ultimately responsible for the attack (v.4) and realizing that the main Philistine army had heard about it, entertained second thoughts about his own troop strength. He therefore had the ram's-horn trumpet blown throughout Israel to summon additional men (cf. Judg 3:27; 6:34). The verb "hear[d]," used three times in vv.3–4, heightens narrative suspense as it stresses the awareness of all the antagonists who have a stake in the upcoming hostilities. Since "Hebrew" was commonly used by non-Israelites as a synonym for "Israelite" (cf. 4:5–10), it is understandable that the two terms should alternate throughout the narratives of the Philistine wars in chapters 13–14.

To state that Israel had now become a "stench to the Philistines" (v.4) was tantamount to affirming that Philistia would muster her troops to fight Israel (cf. 2 Sam 10:6 = 1 Chron 19:6; Gen 34:30; Exod 5:21)—and so she did (v.5). In the meantime,

Saul's call to arms (v.3) was answered by the "people" (v.4; *'am* is used here in the technical sense of "soldiers," "[fighting] men," as in vv.2, 5). They assembled at Gilgal, perhaps modern Khirbet el-Mefjer (about eleven miles east-northeast of Geba).

The Philistines were feared far and wide for their wooden chariots armed with iron fittings at vulnerable and strategic points. Although there is no mention of Philistine chariots or charioteers in the account of Saul's death in chapter 31, the Amalekite who reported the event to David introduced them into his story (2 Sam 1:6), presumably to enliven it and to impress David with his own courage in the face of enemy fire. Similarly, the present account (v.5) uses hyperbole to emphasize the magnitude of the Philistine threat. Besides being able to put three thousand two-man chariots into the field, the enemy had summoned troops "as numerous as the sand on the seashore"—a simile not only familiar to a believing community who traced their allegiance to the Lord back to the Abrahamic covenant (Gen 22:17; cf. also 1 Kings 4:20–21) but also useful in describing huge numbers of fighting men (2 Sam 17:11; Josh 11:4) and their animals (Judg 7:12).

Since the Philistines set up camp at Micmash, Saul either hastily retreated to Gilgal or perhaps had earlier decided to make his headquarters there (vv.4, 7). Beth Aven ("Temple of Wickedness"), although elsewhere used as a pejorative nickname for Bethel ("Temple of God"; cf. Hos 4:15; 5:8; 10:5; and NIV mg. to those verses), here in v.5 (and 14:23) refers to a site (possibly Tell Maryam) just west of Micmash. This Beth Aven (perhaps originally vocalized as Beth On, "Temple of Strength"; cf. the name of the Benjamite town Ono in 1 Chron 8:12; Ezra 2:33; Neh 7:37; 11:35) is distinguished from Bethel in Joshua 18:12–13 and is said to be east of Bethel in Joshua 7:2.

The Philistine deployment at Micmash caused mass desertions in the Israelite army. Like their ancestors before them (Judg 6:2), some of the Israelites hid in whatever out-of-the-way places they could find (v.6; 14:11, 22). Others fled eastward across the Jordan River (v.7), seeking safety in Gad and Gilead (both Transjordanian regions were between the Sea of Galilee and the Dead Sea, Gad being smaller than and south of Gilead during this period; cf. Barry J. Beitzel, *The Moody Atlas of Bible Lands* [Chicago: Moody, 1985], p. 120; cf. also 2 Sam 24:5–6). David would later discover that caves (23:23; 24:3, 7–8, 10)—and one in particular (22:1; 2 Sam 23:13)—would afford especially safe protection from Saul and other enemies.

The greatly reduced number of men who remained with Saul at Gilgal were understandably frightened (v.7). Saul, remembering Samuel's earlier command (10:8), waited seven days for his arrival (v.8). When the prophet failed to appear at the appointed time, even more of Saul's troops began to defect. Desperate, Saul decided to seek the Lord's favor (v.12) by sacrificing the offerings (v.9) that Samuel had told him he himself would make. It may be overly analytical to point out that Samuel prescribed "burnt offerings" (pl., 10:8) while Saul mentions "burnt offering" (sing., v.9; cf. also vv.10, 12) since Samuel could have been speaking in general terms or the singular form could be understood as a collective. Nevertheless, it is perhaps significant that the text indicates that Samuel arrived on the scene just after Saul had offered up the burnt offering but before he had had time to sacrifice the fellowship offerings (v.10). "The narrator wants the reader to infer that Samuel was in fact close by, waiting to catch Saul and then to reprove him, as Samuel immediately does" (Preston, p. 34). The fact that upon Samuel's arrival Saul went out to "greet" (lit., "bless"; cf. Gen 47:7 and NIV mg. there; cf. also 2 Kings 4:29; 10:15) him would not mollify him in this situation any more than his similar statement in similar circumstances would later (15:13).

Saul's sin was not that as king he was forbidden by God's law to sacrifice burnt offerings and fellowship offerings under any and all circumstances. Later David (2 Sam 24:25) and Solomon (1 Kings 3:15) made the same kinds of offerings, and there is no hint of divine rebuke in either case. Saul sinned because he disobeyed God's word through the prophet Samuel (v.13)—a sin that he would commit again (15:26).

**11–15** Saul's motivation to offer the sacrifice seems genuine and appropriate: The Philistines were gathering for battle against Israel, his men were deserting him, and Samuel had not arrived on the scene when he had said he would (v.11). Saul therefore felt the urgent need to seek God's favor—or at least that was his excuse (v.12). What he apparently failed to realize, however, is that animal sacrifice is not a prerequisite for entreating God. In the OT there is no clear case of *ḥillāh 'eṯ-pᵉnê* ("sought the favor of [God/the LORD]") in a context where sacrifice was a necessary accompaniment (cf. Exod 32:11; 1 Kings 13:6; 2 Kings 13:4; 2 Chron 33:12; Ps 119:58; Jer 26:19; Dan 9:13; Zech 7:2; 8:21–22; Mal 1:9; notwithstanding K. Seybold to the contrary, TDOT, 4:408–9). The fact is that Saul had not heeded the divine word through the prophet, and obedience is always better than sacrifice (15:22).

But there is more. It would seem that in ancient Israel rituals associated with the holy war were not to be performed by the king unless a prophet was present. Both in chapter 13 and in chapter 15 Saul acted without the presence of Samuel, and in both cases his transgression was related to holy war ritual (vv.11–12; 15:3 [see also NIV mg. there], 7–11, 17–19). For these offenses he was rebuked by Samuel and rejected by God (cf. further Gerbrandt, pp. 156–57).

Wolfgang M.W. Roth has perceptively observed that the four Niphal occurrences of *skl* ("act foolishly," v.13; 2 Sam 24:10 = 1 Chron 21:8; 2 Chron 16:9) belong together:

> They refer to the action of an "anointed one of the LORD" (Saul, David, Asa) in conflict situations, when military or political considerations stand against certain prophetical concepts connected with Holy War, they occur either in the first or second person sing. as accusations or confessions, and they mark the breaking point in the conflict between prophet and king. ("A Study of the Classical Hebrew Verb *ṣkl*," VetTest 18, 1 [1968]: 74)

The basic thrust of the verb is that of intellectual inability or incapability, and the Niphal brings out the reflexive-tolerative aspect and leads to the meaning "act foolishly in self-reliance" (ibid., pp. 76–78). In Saul's case acting foolishly meant to disobey the divine command mediated through a prophet (v.13; cf. also 15:19, 23, 26; contrast Hezekiah's obedience in 2 Chron 29:25).

Had Saul obeyed, his "kingdom" (*mamlāḵāh*) over Israel would have been divinely established *'aḏ-'ôlām* ("in perpetuity," "for all time," v.13). Such a promise presents a difficulty in light of the Davidic covenant since the Lord affirms that David's throne will be established "forever" (2 Sam 7:13, 16; cf. also Gen 49:10). It is possible, of course, that God's original choice of Saul (9:15–17; 10:1, 24), which appears in any case to have been intended as a foil to David, carried with it a genuine (though hypothetical) promise of a continuing dynasty that was never in danger of being fulfilled, given Saul's character.

A more helpful solution, however, is to compare the case of Saul with that of

Jeroboam I, who in 1 Kings 11:38 is promised an "enduring dynasty" (*bayiṯ-ne'ᵉmān*) like that already promised to David ("lasting dynasty," 25:28; cf. also 2 Sam 7:16: "Your house and your kingdom will endure forever"). It is clear that Jeroboam's dynasty would not replace David's but would exist alongside it. Similarly, Saul's kingdom/dynasty could theoretically have been established alongside that of David without endangering or contradicting the enduring character of the latter (cf. Howard, "The Case for Kingship," p. 23 n. 14).

But Saul, reminded twice that he had not obeyed the Lord's command (vv.13–14), is told in no uncertain terms that he would be replaced by a man after God's own heart (v.14; Acts 13:22), a man who truly has God's interests at heart. Saul would be replaced by a neighbor of his, a neighbor better than him (15:28). He would later become so distraught over this prospect that he would beg David not to cut off his descendants or wipe out his name from his father's family (24:21). Daniel Lys observes that Saul's "kingdom" would soon be ruled over by a "leader" (*nāg̱îḏ*, the transitional title used at the onset of monarchy in Israel; cf. also 25:30) appointed by God ("Who Is Our President? From Text to Sermon on I Samuel 12:12," Int 21, 4 [1967]: 409). "The Israelite king was rightly king only as far as he was the representative of *the* King; otherwise the Lord would reject him" (ibid., p. 417).

In v.15 the MT has Samuel leaving Gilgal and going to Gibeah while Saul apparently stays in Gilgal. The LXX, however, has Samuel leaving Gilgal and going on his way while Saul and his troops go to Gibeah (see NIV mg.). Since Saul has already arrived at Gibeah in v.16, the LXX text perhaps preserves a genuine tradition about the sequence of events. In any case, Saul takes a census of his fighting men to assess their numerical strength (cf. 11:8; 14:17). In spite of the original two thousand men (or three thousand, if he was already in Gibeah and the count would therefore include Jonathan's troops) mentioned earlier (v.2) and the general call to arms to supplement them (vv.3–4), wholesale defections had reduced his troops to "about six hundred" (cf. 14:2). The books of Judges and Samuel often specify units of six hundred men (Judg 3:31; 18:11, 16–17; 1 Sam 23:13; 27:2; 30:9; 2 Sam 15:18), which Segal describes as a "modest military force" ("Numerals," p. 13). Fokkelman observes: "The reduction of Saul's troops to 600 men is a literary way of telling us that he has an opportunity to become another Gideon, to achieve victory with only a small contingent of courageous followers" ("Saul and David," p. 27).

## Notes

---

8 A few Hebrew MSS insert אמר (*'mr*) before שמואל (*šmw'l*, "Samuel") in the difficult phrase למועד אשר שמואל (*lmw'd 'šr šmw'l*), yielding the meaning "until the time that Samuel set" (cf. NIV). Thus the MT's reading might have resulted either from haplography of *'mr* after *'šr* or of *śm* before *šmw'l*.

---

## 2. *The struggle against the Philistines*

### 13:16–14:23

16 Saul and his son Jonathan and the men with them were staying in Gibeah of Benjamin, while the Philistines camped at Micmash.

17 Raiding parties went out from the Philistine camp in three detachments. One turned toward Ophrah in the vicinity of Shual, 18 another
toward Beth Horon, and the third toward the borderland overlooking the
Valley of Zeboim facing the desert.

19 Not a blacksmith could be found in the whole land of Israel, because
the Philistines had said, "Otherwise the Hebrews will make swords or
spears!" 20 So all Israel went down to the Philistines to have their
plowshares, mattocks, axes and sickles sharpened. 21 The price was two
thirds of a shekel for sharpening plowshares and mattocks, and a third
of a shekel for sharpening forks and axes and for repointing goads.

22 So on the day of the battle not a soldier with Saul and Jonathan had
a sword or spear in his hand; only Saul and his son Jonathan had them.

23 Now a detachment of Philistines had gone out to the pass at
Micmash. 14:1 One day Jonathan son of Saul said to the young man
bearing his armor, "Come, let's go over to the Philistine outpost on the
other side." But he did not tell his father.

2 Saul was staying on the outskirts of Gibeah under a pomegranate
tree in Migron. With him were about six hundred men, 3 among whom
was Ahijah, who was wearing an ephod. He was a son of Ichabod's
brother Ahitub son of Phinehas, the son of Eli, the LORD's priest in
Shiloh. No one was aware that Jonathan had left.

4 On each side of the pass that Jonathan intended to cross to reach
the Philistine outpost was a cliff; one was called Bozez, and the other
Seneh. 5 One cliff stood to the north toward Micmash, the other to the
south toward Geba.

6 Jonathan said to his young armor-bearer, "Come, let's go over to the
outpost of those uncircumcised fellows. Perhaps the LORD will act in our
behalf. Nothing can hinder the LORD from saving, whether by many or by
few."

7 "Do all that you have in mind," his armor-bearer said. "Go ahead; I
am with you heart and soul."

8 Jonathan said, "Come, then; we will cross over toward the men and
let them see us. 9 If they say to us, 'Wait there until we come to you,' we
will stay where we are and not go up to them. 10 But if they say, 'Come up
to us,' we will climb up, because that will be our sign that the LORD has
given them into our hands."

11 So both of them showed themselves to the Philistine outpost.
"Look!" said the Philistines. "The Hebrews are crawling out of the holes
they were hiding in." 12 The men of the outpost shouted to Jonathan and
his armor-bearer, "Come up to us and we'll teach you a lesson."

So Jonathan said to his armor-bearer, "Climb up after me; the LORD
has given them into the hand of Israel."

13 Jonathan climbed up, using his hands and feet, with his armor-
bearer right behind him. The Philistines fell before Jonathan, and his
armor-bearer followed and killed behind him. 14 In that first attack
Jonathan and his armor-bearer killed some twenty men in an area of
about half an acre.

15 Then panic struck the whole army—those in the camp and field,
and those in the outposts and raiding parties—and the ground shook. It
was a panic sent by God.

16 Saul's lookouts at Gibeah of Benjamin saw the army melting away in
all directions. 17 Then Saul said to the men who were with him, "Muster
the forces and see who has left us." When they did, it was Jonathan and
his armor-bearer who were not there.

18 Saul said to Ahijah, "Bring the ark of God." (At that time it was with
the Israelites.) 19 While Saul was talking to the priest, the tumult in the
Philistine camp increased more and more. So Saul said to the priest,
"Withdraw your hand."

**20**Then Saul and all his men assembled and went to the battle. They found the Philistines in total confusion, striking each other with their swords. **21**Those Hebrews who had previously been with the Philistines and had gone up with them to their camp went over to the Israelites who were with Saul and Jonathan. **22**When all the Israelites who had hidden in the hill country of Ephraim heard that the Philistines were on the run, they joined the battle in hot pursuit. **23**So the LORD rescued Israel that day, and the battle moved on beyond Beth Aven.

**16–22** The combined forces of Saul and Jonathan at Gibeah (v.16) numbered only in the hundreds (14:2), while those of the Philistines at Micmash scarcely four miles to the northeast numbered in the thousands (v.5). Philistine "raiding parties" (v.17; 14:15; lit., "the destroyer," thus bent on destruction and pillage) left camp in three detachments, a common military strategy in those days (11:11; Judg 7:16; 9:43; 2 Sam 18:2) since it provided more options and greater mobility. The final destruction of each detachment is left deliberately vague, the word "toward" having the general meaning "in the direction of" (as in Judg 20:42). They headed off in three different directions: One group went toward Ophrah in Benjamin (cf. Josh 18:23; modern et-Taiyibeh, six miles north of Micmash) in the region of Shual (otherwise unknown, unless related to Shaalim in 9:4; see comment there), a second (v.18) went toward (Upper) Beth Horon in Ephraim (cf. Josh 16:5; modern Beit Ur el-Foqa, ten miles west of Micmash) on the border of Benjamin, and the third went an undetermined distance eastward toward the Valley of Zeboim (location unknown).

Peter R. Ackroyd is correct in his contention that vv.19–22 provide an introduction to "a heroic tale of the exploits of Jonathan" and that their purpose is to describe the humiliation of Israel "with a corresponding exaltation of the power of Israel's God." But his further assumption that the passage has nothing to do with ironworking as an index of Philistine military superiority ("Note to **parzon* 'Iron' in the Song of Deborah," JSS 24, 1 [1979]: 19–20) is surely wide of the mark. For decades archaeologists working at many different sites have unearthed iron artifacts in bewildering number and variety dating from the period of greatest Philistine power and leading to the general consensus that the metal was introduced into Canaan—at least for weapons, agricultural tools, and jewelry—by the Philistines (cf. G. Ernest Wright, "Iron in Israel," BA 1, 2 [1938]: 5–8; James D. Muhly, "How Iron Technology Changed the Ancient World—And Gave the Philistines a Military Edge," *Biblical Archaeology Review* 8, 6 [1982]: 40–54). Megiddo, Beth Shemesh, Gezer, Tell Qasileh, and other sites have yielded iron tools of various kinds (cf. Yigael Yadin, "Megiddo of the Kings of Israel," BA 33, 3 [1970]: 78–79, 95). Perhaps most intriguing of all is the iron plowpoint from the time of Saul found at his citadel in Gibeah (cf. Lawrence A. Sinclair, "An Archaeological Study of Gibeah [Tell el-Fûl]," BA 27, 2 [1964]: 55–57).

As an effective method of denying weapons to the beleaguered Israelites, the Philistines had apparently deported all the Israelite blacksmiths (v.19; cf. similarly 2 Kings 24:14, 16; Jer 24:1; 29:2). Hebrew fighting men were not to have swords or spears (Saul and Jonathan, either with Philistine permission or by subterfuge, were the sole exceptions; v.22).

Although the precise nature of some of the agricultural tools named in vv.20–21 remains uncertain (for a typical attempt to identify them from an archaeological standpoint, cf. G. Ernest Wright, "I Samuel 13:19–21," BA 6, 2 [1943]: 33–36), the intention of the passage became clear when Samuel Raffaeli discovered that *pîm*

(NIV, "two thirds of a shekel," v.21) refers to a unit of weight (cf. O.R. Sellers and W.F. Albright, "The First Campaign of Excavation at Beth-zur," BASOR 43 [1931]: 9). Made of stone and other materials, weights marked *pym* have turned up in various excavations (cf. George L. Kelm and Amihai Mazar, "Excavating in Samson Country: Philistines and Israelites at Tel Batash," *Biblical Archaeology Review* 15, 1 [1989]: 49). The *pym* has proven to be two-thirds of a shekel in weight. If silver was the medium of exchange in v.21, the Philistines charged the Israelites an exorbitant price for sharpening and repointing their tools.

Since Philistia was located on the coastal plains west of the foothills of Judah, Israelites who visited the Philistines for any purpose "went down" to them (v.20; see Judg 14:19; 16:31; Amos 6:2). The word for "plowshares," occurring again in the messianic oracle found in Isaiah 2:2–4 (= Mic 4:1–3; see also Joel 3:10), probably means more precisely "plowpoints," since plowshares themselves were made of wood in ancient times. The word "axes" is used elsewhere in contexts of cutting down trees and chopping wood (Judg 9:48; Ps 74:5; Jer 46:22). A cognate form of the word for "goads," which is found only here and in Ecclesiastes 12:11 in the OT, is apparently now attested in Ugaritic (see Mitchell Dahood, "*ebrew-Ugaritic Lexicography II," *Biblica* 45 [1964]: 404).

As in the days of Deborah (Judg 5:8), the Israelites were woefully outgunned as the battle against the enemy loomed before them (v.22). Despite their lack of weapons, however, with God's help (14:6) they would rout the mighty Philistines just as David would later defeat the giant Goliath (17:45, 47).

**13:23–14:14** The stage having been set in 13:16–22, the drama of Israel's victory over Philistia begins with a remarkably courageous attack by two men, who win a skirmish with a heavily armed enemy against overwhelming odds.

A "detachment" (the Heb. word is different from that in 13:17 and is translated "outpost" in 14:1, 4, 6, 11, 15) of Philistines had left their main camp at Micmash (13:16) and had gone out (v.23) to defend a pass leading to it. As in 13:3, so also in 14:1, it is Saul's son Jonathan, rather than Saul himself, who takes the initiative against the enemy. He suggests to his armor-bearer that they attack the recently established Philistine outpost. Armor-bearers in ancient times had to be unusually brave and loyal, since the lives of their masters often depended on them. David would later serve Saul in that capacity (16:21); and Saul's final valiant stand against the Philistines at Mount Gilboa would take place alongside his faithful armor-bearer, who would die with him (31:4–6). In the present situation the function of Jonathan's armor-bearer was especially important because of the scarcity of weapons in Israel (13:22). Jonathan decided not to tell his father about his plans, perhaps not to worry him needlessly or because he felt that Saul would forbid him to go.

Meanwhile, Saul's modest army of six hundred men (v.2; 13:15) was with him near Gibeah, his hometown. Although the statement that Saul himself was sitting "under a pomegranate tree" contrasts his timidity and relative ease/luxury (the pomegranate was a highly prized fruit; cf. Num 20:5; Deut 8:8; S of Songs 4:13; 6:11; 7:12; Joel 1:12; Hag 2:19) with Jonathan's willingness to sacrifice his very life for Israel, it may simply be intended as an allusion to his role as leader (cf. Judg 4:5). The specific location of Migron (v.2) and its relationship to the Migron of Isaiah 10:28 remain unclear.

Among the men with Saul was the priest Ahijah ("Brother of the LORD"), son of Ahitub ("Covenant Brother"; for the root *ṭwb* used as a legal term in covenant contexts, cf. Michael V. Fox, "*Ṭôḇ* as Covenant Terminology," BASOR 209 [1973]: 41–42), grandson of Phinehas and great-grandson of Eli (v.3). Reference to Ahijah's ancestors recalls the divine curse on the house of Eli (2:30–33) and the deaths of Eli (4:18)—who had been "the LORD's priest in Shiloh," a city so recently destroyed by the Philistines (cf. Ps 78:60; Jer 7:12, 14; 26:6, 9)—and Phinehas (4:11). Later the text will describe the deaths of Ahitub and his fellow priests (22:11–18)—including perhaps Ahijah, if Ahimelech is another name for Ahijah (22:9–11)—at the command of Saul himself. Especially poignant is the reference to Ahijah's "wearing an ephod" (v.3), a priestly description (cf. 2:28) stressed by the narrator as he reports the massacre of eighty-five descendants of Eli (22:18).

The apparently needless reference to Ichabod ("No Glory"; cf. NIV mg. to 4:21) recalls yet another tragedy in Eli's family. Thus the rebuked king Saul is in the company of the priest Ahijah of the rejected house of Eli, and neither is "aware" that the courageous Jonathan son of Saul is on his way to fight the Philistines. David Jobling summarizes: "His own royal glory gone, where else would we expect Saul to be than with a relative of 'Glory gone'?" ("Saul's Fall and Jonathan's Rise: Tradition and Redaction in 1 Sam 14:1–46," JBL 95, 3 [1976]: 368).

The names of the cliffs flanking the Micmash pass (v.4; cf. Isa 10:28–29) were doubtless intended to pinpoint the site of the Philistine outpost, but their own locations are no longer known. "Cliff" (v.5) translates a Hebrew phrase that means literally "tooth of a cliff" (cf. Job 39:28, "rocky crag"), perhaps emphasizing the sharp and jagged nature of the rock formation. If the two cliffs are mentioned in the same order in vv.4 and 5, Bozez was on the north and Seneh was on the south. Bozez ("Shining"?) would then perhaps be so named because its face, being on the south, would catch the rays of the sun. As for Seneh ("Thornbush"[?]; cf. a similar Heb. word in Exod 3:2–4; Deut 33:16), it may have been so-called because of thornbushes growing on or near its face (cf. Josephus' reference to "the Valley of Thorns, close to a village named Gibeah of Saul," Wars V, 51 [ii.1]). The suggestion of J. Maxwell Miller (among others) that the "modern name, Wadi eṣ-Ṣuweinît [*sic*], is probably based on the same root" ("Saul's Rise to Power," p. 163 n. 17) fails to account for the different sibilants in the two words or for the *ṭ* in the modern name. In any case, the Wadi eṣ-Ṣuweiniṭ (seven miles northeast of Jerusalem) is indeed the deep gorge near which the Philistine outpost was located (for general orientation cf. Yohanan Aharoni and Michael Avi-Yonah, *The Macmillan Bible Atlas* [New York: Macmillan, 1968], p. 60).

When Jonathan repeated his suggestion of v.1 to his armor-bearer, he made a significant change by calling the Philistines "those uncircumcised fellows" (v.6), a term of reproach used elsewhere of Goliath (17:26, 36) and other Philistines (31:4 = 1 Chron 10:4; 2 Sam 1:20) and serving to designate them as nonparticipants in the Abrahamic covenant (Gen 17:9–11).

Jonathan is confident that the Lord will fight for Israel and that nothing can keep God from saving them (cf. David's taunt to Goliath in 17:47). He knows that with God on his side even an insignificant number of men can achieve victory (v.6; cf. Judg 7:4, 7). Other parallels with the story of Gideon commend themselves as well: the hero accompanied by only one servant (v.7; cf. Judg 7:10–11); the sign (vv.9–10; cf. Judg 7:13–15); the panic (v.15; cf. Judg 7:21); the confusion, causing the enemy soldiers to turn on "each other with their swords" (v.20; cf. Judg 7:22); reinforcements from the "hill country of Ephraim" (v.22; cf. Judg 7:24); and the pursuit (v.22; cf. Judg 7:23; cf. similarly Jobling, "Saul's Fall and Jonathan's Rise," p. 369 n. 7; cf. further Garsiel, pp. 87–93).

The armor-bearer's response to Jonathan (v.7) shows the extent of his loyalty: "Do all that you have in mind" (*bilᵉḇāḇeḵā,* lit., "in your heart") finds its counterpoint in "I am with you heart and soul" (*kilᵉḇāḇeḵā,* lit., "according to your heart," translated as hendiadys by the NIV). Their two hearts beating as one, the men will march into battle together. The verse is later echoed (almost verbatim in the Heb.) in a striking parallel (2 Sam 7:3) when the prophet Nathan says to David, "Whatever you have in mind, . . . do it"—but this time the counterpoint (though not as verbally pleasing) is much superior: "The LORD is with you."

A brief comment by Jonathan (v.8) introduces the sign (vv.9–10) and its sequel (vv.11–14). As the dew on the fleece would give Gideon the faith to believe that God would save Israel by Gideon's hand (Judg 6:36–37), so the appropriate Philistine response to the approach of Jonathan and his armor-bearer would give Jonathan the faith to believe that the Lord would give the enemy into their hands (vv.9–10).

When the Philistines caught sight of the two men (v.11), they assumed them to be Israelite deserters who had earlier hidden in caves and holes (13:6). Confident that they had nothing to fear, the Philistines shouted the fateful words: "Come up to us" (v.12). Goliath would learn the folly of saying "Come here" (17:44) to a mere boy who seemed to pose no threat. Like the Philistine outpost at the Micmash pass, he would feel the fatal sting of the God who had the power to give Israel's enemies into her hands (v.12; cf. 17:47). Wasting no time, Jonathan and his companion climbed up to the outpost and began the slaughter. The use of the rare Polel of *mûṯ* ("killed," v.13) invites further comparison to the account of David's victory over Goliath, where the same stem of the verb is used (17:51). Although outnumbered about ten to one, Jonathan and his armor-bearer dispatched "some twenty men" (v.14) in a "[furrowed] area" (*maʿᵃnāh;* cf. Ps 129:3) of a field small enough to be plowed by a yoke of oxen in half a day (cf. NIV mg. here and at Isa 5:10)—that is, the Philistines were killed in a brief time and a short distance.

**15–23** Confusion struck the Philistine troops (v.15; cf. vv.20, 22) whatever their location: in the camp at Micmash (13:16), out in the field, at the various outposts, with one or another of the three raiding parties (13:17–18). The panic, sent by God (cf. also 2 Kings 7:6–7), was of the kind promised to Israel against her enemies when the people trusted him (Deut 7:23) but also part of the covenant curse against Israel herself when she was apostate (Deut 28:20). During such times of terror, the ground may shake, as when the Lord led his people through the Sea of Reeds while at the same time overthrowing the Egyptians (Ps 77:18), or as an accompaniment to a theophany (2 Sam 22:8 = Ps 18:7), or—again—as a manifestation of God's displeasure against apostate Israel (Amos 8:8).

So total was the Philistine panic and so noisy their flight (*hāmôn,* "army," in v.16 is translated "tumult" in v.19) that Saul's watchmen on the walls at Gibeah could see—and perhaps hear—many of the enemy soldiers as they scattered in all directions. The "melting [away]" of an enemy force is a vivid metaphor describing full retreat (cf. Isa 14:31; cf. also Exod 15:15; Josh 2:9, 24). Curious about what was causing the Philistine flight, and perhaps considering the possibility of helping to turn it into a total rout, Saul decided once again to take a census of his troops (v.17; see 13:15)—but this time to see whether any of them had left the camp and were perhaps responsible for the Philistine panic. Amazingly enough, it was not until the census was complete that Saul became aware of the absence of Jonathan, his own son.

Still not quite ready to go to Jonathan's aid, however, Saul told the priest Ahijah to bring the ark of God before him (v.18). The LXX has "ephod" (doubtless reading *'pwd* instead of *'rwn;* cf. v.3 and NIV mg. here) instead of "ark of God"; the verb "bring" (*higgîš*) is used of the ephod (23:9; 30:7) but not of the ark, and lots are cast later in the chapter (vv.41–42). On the other hand, the MT of v.18 uses the phrase "ark of God" twice (translated "it" by the NIV the second time; cf. also 3:3; 4:11, 13), a special point is made of the fact that it was "with the Israelites" at that time (presumably having been brought to Gibeah—temporarily, at least—from Kiriath Jearim; cf. 7:2), and Saul may well have wanted to carry it into battle against the Philistines in a superstitious attempt to guarantee victory (cf. 4:3–7). In any event, "the near-unanimous preference of older critics for 'ephod' of the LXX over 'ark' has now been reversed, and most recent authorities retain 'ark' as *lectio difficilior*" (Jobling, "Saul's Fall and Jonathan's Rise," p. 369 n. 6; cf. Miscall, p. 92; Garsiel, p. 87).

Hearing the increasing tumult in the Philistine camp, Saul apparently changed his mind about the need to make use of the ark and told Ahijah to stop the ritual proceedings (v.19). Together with his men he then marched into battle (v.20), presumably without benefit of priestly blessing of any kind. The Philistines, meanwhile, had become filled with total "confusion" (*m[e]hûmāh,* a word assonant with *hāmôn,* "tumult," in the previous verse). Brother was wielding sword against brother, a scene to be repeated in the eschaton (Ezek 38:21).

Saul, Jonathan, and the Israelite army were soon joined by two groups of reinforcements, distinguished from each other by the occurrence of *gam-hēmmāh* (lit., "also they") in vv.21 and 22. Some were Hebrews who had previously gone to the Philistine camp (v.21), perhaps either to have their agricultural tools sharpened (cf. 13:20) or, disgruntled with Israelite rule, to hire themselves out as mercenaries (cf. David among the Philistines in 29:6). In any event, it is not necessary to insist that "Hebrews" here should be differentiated from "Israelites" (see comment on 13:3) or that it stands for *'apirū,* a nonethnic designation for members of disparate groups of uprooted persons who exchanged their services for supplies and shelter (cf. Barry J. Beitzel, "Hebrew [People]," in ISBErev., 2:657). The second group of reinforcements (v.22) consisted of Israelite deserters who had been hiding (cf. 13:6) in the hill country of Ephraim, a large, partially forested plateau (Josh 17:15–18) north and west of Micmash. Saul himself would have known the area well (9:3–4). The "hot pursuit" of the combined Israelite forces under Saul and Jonathan would be tragically reversed in the final relentless attack of the Philistines against the king and his son (31:2 = 1 Chron 10:2).

The Hebrew expression translated "So the LORD rescued Israel that day" (v.23) is a verbatim quotation of Exodus 14:30 (NIV, "That day the LORD saved Israel") in the narrative of the Sea of Reeds. Its deliberate use stresses the importance of Saul's victory while also giving all the glory to God (as Saul apparently also did; cf. v.39). The Israelite forces, however, were not satisfied with the results of their own efforts until they had driven the Philistines some distance west of Beth Aven (v.23) toward their own homeland beyond Aijalon (v.31).

## Notes

---

**13:16** J. Maxwell Miller has attempted to prove that "Geba, Geba of Benjamin, Gibeah, Gibeah of Saul, and, probably, Gibeath-elohim [Gibeah of God] were essentially identical and are to be associated with the site of present-day Jeba'" ("Geba/Gibeah of Benjamin," VetTest 25, 2 [1975]: 165). But by the simple expedient of assuming גבע (*gb'*, "Geba") to be an orthographic variant of גבעה (*gb'h*, "Gibeah") in a very few passages, the NIV successfully maintains the traditional distinction between Geba (in Benjamin)/Gibeah of God, on the one hand, and Gibeah (in Benjamin/of Saul), on the other (cf. NIV mg. to v.16; Judg 20:10, 33).

---

## 3. *The cursing of Jonathan*

### 14:24–46

24 Now the men of Israel were in distress that day, because Saul had
bound the people under an oath, saying, "Cursed be any man who eats
food before evening comes, before I have avenged myself on my
enemies!" So none of the troops tasted food.
25 The entire army entered the woods, and there was honey on the
ground. 26 When they went into the woods, they saw the honey oozing
out, yet no one put his hand to his mouth, because they feared the oath.
27 But Jonathan had not heard that his father had bound the people with
the oath, so he reached out the end of the staff that was in his hand and
dipped it into the honeycomb. He raised his hand to his mouth, and his
eyes brightened. 28 Then one of the soldiers told him, "Your father
bound the army under a strict oath, saying, 'Cursed be any man who
eats food today!' That is why the men are faint."
29 Jonathan said, "My father has made trouble for the country. See
how my eyes brightened when I tasted a little of this honey. 30 How much
better it would have been if the men had eaten today some of the
plunder they took from their enemies. Would not the slaughter of the
Philistines have been even greater?"
31 That day, after the Israelites had struck down the Philistines from
Micmash to Aijalon, they were exhausted. 32 They pounced on the
plunder and, taking sheep, cattle and calves, they butchered them on
the ground and ate them, together with the blood. 33 Then someone said
to Saul, "Look, the men are sinning against the LORD by eating meat that
has blood in it."
"You have broken faith," he said. "Roll a large stone over here at
once." 34 Then he said, "Go out among the men and tell them, 'Each of
you bring me your cattle and sheep, and slaughter them here and eat
them. Do not sin against the LORD by eating meat with blood still in it.'"
So everyone brought his ox that night and slaughtered it there.
35 Then Saul built an altar to the LORD; it was the first time he had done
this.
36 Saul said, "Let us go down after the Philistines by night and plunder
them till dawn, and let us not leave one of them alive."
"Do whatever seems best to you," they replied.
But the priest said, "Let us inquire of God here."
37 So Saul asked God, "Shall I go down after the Philistines? Will you
give them into Israel's hand?" But God did not answer him that day.
38 Saul therefore said, "Come here, all you who are leaders of the
army, and let us find out what sin has been committed today. 39 As surely
as the LORD who rescues Israel lives, even if it lies with my son Jonathan,
he must die." But not one of the men said a word.
40 Saul then said to all the Israelites, "You stand over there; I and
Jonathan my son will stand over here."
"Do what seems best to you," the men replied.
41 Then Saul prayed to the LORD, the God of Israel, "Give me the right
answer." And Jonathan and Saul were taken by lot, and the men were

cleared. 42 Saul said, "Cast the lot between me and Jonathan my son." And Jonathan was taken.

43 Then Saul said to Jonathan, "Tell me what you have done."

So Jonathan told him, "I merely tasted a little honey with the end of my staff. And now must I die?"

44 Saul said, "May God deal with me, be it ever so severely, if you do not die, Jonathan."

45 But the men said to Saul, "Should Jonathan die—he who has brought about this great deliverance in Israel? Never! As surely as the LORD lives, not a hair of his head will fall to the ground, for he did this today with God's help." So the men rescued Jonathan, and he was not put to death.

46 Then Saul stopped pursuing the Philistines, and they withdrew to their own land.

In this central section of chapters 13–15, the already developed contrast between Saul and Jonathan reaches its zenith. In vv.1–46 "Saul . . . is not so much wicked as foolish and frustrated. His intentions are good, indeed thoroughly pious, but he pursues them in self-defeating ways, and events thwart them" (Jobling, "Saul's Fall and Jonathan's Rise," p. 368).

**24–30** The scenes recorded here constitute a flashback to events simultaneous with the battle description in vv.20–23. Saul (v.24) had bound the "people" (*'am,* "troops" in this context, as often in Samuel; cf. the same word translated as "troops" later in the verse) under an oath of abstaining from food for the entire day of the battle, an understandable religious demand in a "holy war" context. The result, however, was that they were "in distress" (the same Heb. verb is translated "hard pressed" in 13:6) from hunger. Thus Saul's motivation, however praiseworthy, resulted in his men's becoming "faint" (v.28) and "exhausted" (v.31). Perhaps this is why the narrator uses the Hiphil verbal form *wayyō'el* ("had bound . . . under an oath," from *'ālāh*), since the form itself conjures up the root *y'l,* which means "acted foolishly" in the Niphal stem, or for that matter the root *'wl,* a noun form of which means "fool" (*'ᵉwîl*) and is found often in Proverbs. Jobling ("Saul's Fall and Jonathan's Rise," p. 374 and n. 32) sees here a deliberate pun that highlights Saul's "foolish oath" and that may be reflected in the double translation of the LXX: "Saul acted very foolishly . . . and laid a curse on the people." Accompanying the fulfillment of the oath, intended to implement a religiously motivated fast that would energize the men and fill them with a fighting zeal, would be the opportunity for Saul to take vengeance on his enemies (cf. similarly Samson's prayer in Judg 16:28). It was not uncommon for Israel's leaders to formally pronounce curses on friend and foe alike (cf. 26:19; Josh 6:26).

Just as a riddle about eating honey in a Philistine context got Samson into trouble (Judg 14:8–20), so also tasting honey in a Philistine context almost cost Jonathan his life. Upon entering a forest (v.25; perhaps in the hill country of Ephraim [cf. comment on v.22]), Saul's troops noticed a honeycomb (cf. v.27) on the ground. Although it was filled with honey, no one so much as tasted any of it because they "feared" the oath (v.26)—that is, they took it seriously; they respected it (cf. Prov 13:13; cf. further Fox, "*Ṭôḇ* as Covenant Terminology," p. 41). But Jonathan, unaware of the oath (v.27), used the end of his staff (perhaps to avoid being stung by bees) to dip some honey from the comb (compared with date honey, bees' honey was especially sweet and was virtually a luxury food; cf. S of Songs 4:11; 5:1). When Jonathan ate it, his eyes "brightened" ("shone," "lit up"), implying renewal of strength (cf. NIV mg.; cf. Ezra

9:8; Ps 13:3). Especially instructive in this regard are the metaphors in Psalm 19:8–10: "The commands of the LORD are radiant,/ giving light to the eyes. . . ./ The ordinances of the LORD . . . are sweeter than honey,/ than honey from the comb."

One of Jonathan's fellow soldiers warned him about his father's oath (v.28), adding the observation that obeying it had caused the troops to become "faint" (the same verbal form is translated "exhausted" in v.31; cf. also Judg 4:21; 2 Sam 21:15). Jonathan's rebuttal, based on his refreshment after eating food, is that Saul "has made trouble [*'āḵar*] for the country" (v.29). The verb "*'kr* specifically means 'to bring into cultic jeopardy' " (Jobling, "Saul's Fall and Jonathan's Rise," p. 370, though "cultic" may be an overtranslation), here in the context of holy war (cf. Josh 6:18; 1 Kings 18:17–18; cf. similarly 1 Macc 3:5; 7:22). Of particular interest is the story of Achan, whose name (in the form Achar) became a wordplay on the root *'kr* (Josh 7:25; 1 Chron 2:7; and NIV mg.) and after whom the Valley of Achor was named (Josh 7:26 and NIV mg.; Isa 65:10; Hos 2:15 and NIV mg.). Concerning Jonathan, Jobling summarizes: "He, not his father, has correctly interpreted Yhwh's will" ("Saul's Fall and Jonathan's Rise," p. 370). Jonathan concludes (v.30) by arguing that even more Philistines would have been killed if Saul's men had eaten some of the food they "took" as plunder from the enemy. The verb *māṣā'* in this context means "found [with the intention of taking]" (cf. also Judg 5:30; 21:12; 2 Chron 20:25; Ps 119:162).

**31–35** "That day" (v.31) is doubtless the same as "that day" in v.24, but Saul's men were no longer under his oath of abstinence (v.32) because it was after evening and the Philistines were totally routed. The Israelites had devastated them and driven them westward all the way to Aijalon (modern Yalo, about sixteen miles west of Micmash and seven miles southwest of [Upper] Beth Horon [cf. 13:18]), which had originally been assigned to the tribal territory of Dan (Josh 19:40–42) but which, after the Canaanites had prevented the Danites from coming into their full inheritance (Judg 1:34; 18:1), was now in the hill country of Ephraim (1 Chron 6:67–69).

Echoes of vv.32–35 reverberate throughout chapter 15: "pounce[d] on the plunder" (v.32; 15:19—the only two occurrences of the denominative verbal root *'yṭ* in the OT), sheep and cattle (v.32; 15:9, 14–15, 21), cattle and sheep (v.34; 15:3, translating a different pair of Heb. words than in the preceding set), sin(ning)/sinned (vv.33–34; 15:24, 30), "bring me" (v.34; 15:32—identical Heb. in the two verses). Saul's commendable attempt to engage in proper ceremonial practice in vv.32–35 contrasts with his total failure in the same arena in chapter 15.

Famished, the Israelite troops seized sheep, cattle, and calves from the Philistine plunder, butchered them, and ate the meat without waiting for the blood to drain from it (v.32). Since eating meat with the blood still in it was forbidden to the people of God throughout their history (cf. Lev 17:10–14; 19:26; Deut 12:16, 23–24; Ezek 33:25; Acts 15:20), it is not surprising that Saul, on hearing of his men's sinful deed, would immediately act to absolve them of guilt. He first accused them of having betrayed their promise to God, of having "broken faith" (v.33; the root *bgd* is strikingly used five times in succession in Isa 24:16: "The treacherous betray!/ With treachery the treacherous betray!"). He then demanded that a large stone be rolled over to him so that animals could be properly slaughtered on it, not on the ground as before (v.32)—perhaps because the ground was reserved for receiving the drained blood (cf. Deut 12:16, 24).

Although Klein claims that the "large stone" in v.33 should be compared to that in 6:14, "which served as an altar for sacrifice at Beth-shemesh when the ark was returned from the Philistines" (*1 Samuel,* p. 139), we observe that nothing is said in either chapter about a rock on which sacrifice was offered. In fact, 6:15, 18 state specifically that the "large rock" (the Heb. phrase thus translated in ch. 6 is the same as that for "large stone" in v.33) was used as a temporary pedestal for the ark. In any case, the issue in vv.32–34 is slaughtering animals for food, not sacrificing animals for atonement. We cannot even be sure that the large stone was incorporated into the altar that Saul built later (v.35), as asserted by some (e.g., Kirkpatrick, p. 136).

Saul demanded that each of his men "bring" (v.34) their animals to him for slaughter. The same Hebrew phrase so translated appears on Saul's lips also in the account of his rebuke by Samuel (13:9) and on Samuel's lips in the account of Saul's rejection by God (15:32). Here in v.34 it poignantly underscores Saul's commendable attempt to right a sinful wrong perpetrated by his understandably hungry troops—a hunger originally caused by a well-intended but ill-advised oath that Saul had imposed on them. Spiritually sensitive Israelite leaders built altars as a matter of routine (cf. Samuel, 7:17; David, 2 Sam 24:25; 1 Chron 21:18; Gideon, Judg 6:24). In Saul's case a special point is made of the fact that this was the "first time" he had done so (v.35), probably a negative comment directed at Saul's lack of piety.

**36–46** The literary integrity of this unit is highlighted by the *inclusio* that frames it: "Go down after the Philistines" (v.36) is mirrored by "stopped pursuing the Philistines" (v.46; lit., "went up from after the Philistines"). Initially Saul determined to plunder and slaughter them until nothing and no one remained. The decision to attack at night and plunder till dawn (v.36) reflects the common practice of conducting military operations in the dead of night, when the number of attackers was small and therefore the element of surprise was important (cf. 2 Sam 17:22; Judg 16:3). Saul's men, apparently satisfied that he had their best interests at heart, were ready to follow him (vv.36, 40).

The priest Ahijah, however, sensed the need to "inquire of" God (v.36; lit., "draw near to"; cf. Zeph 3:2), perhaps by making use of the sacred lots stored in the ephod (v.3; cf. further vv.41–42). Agreeing, Saul "asked" (v.37; yet another Heb. pun on the name "Saul") the Lord whether the defeat of the enemy was imminent (cf. similarly 7:8–9; Judg 20:23). When he received no answer, he sensed that something was amiss in the army (v.38). Much later, after his rejection by God, Saul would understand that no approach or technique, however authorized in other contexts, would bring a divine response, however desperate his need (28:6, 15).

Saul called for the army "leaders" (v.38; cf. Judg 20:2; lit., "corner[stone]s"; cf. Isa 19:13; Zech 10:4) to come before him to ascertain what sin had been committed (v.38) and who had committed it (v.39). Pronouncing the solemn asseverative oath "As surely as the LORD lives," which is used very often (though not always) in contexts where life and death hang in the balance (cf. v.45; 19:6; 20:3, 21; 25:34; 26:10, 16; 28:10; 2 Sam 4:9–10; 12:5; 14:11; 15:21), Saul affirmed that whoever had sinned "must die" (v.39; the Heb. construction underlying this phrase is translated "will surely die" in Gen 2:17 and is echoed verbatim in v.44). If necessary, he was even prepared to give up the life of his son Jonathan (vv.39, 44; cf. similarly Abraham and Isaac, Gen 22:10, 12, 16; Heb 11:17; Reuben and his two sons, Gen 42:37; Jephthah and his daughter, Judg 11:31, 39). Respectful even in the face of Saul's shocking announcement, knowing that Jonathan had (however innocently) violated his father's imposed oath, aware that the brave Jonathan would likely die though no fault of his own, doubtless sympathizing with Jonathan's position as over against Saul's folly—

none of his men "said a word" (lit., "was answering him") during those dramatic moments.

Anticipating the casting of lots to determine by the process of elimination (cf. 10:19–21 and comments there; Josh 7:11–12, 14–18) who had committed the sin that imperiled further war against Philistia (v.41), Saul made the "first binary division" (Klein, *1 Samuel*, p. 140) by lining up his troops on one side and himself and Jonathan on the other (v.40). Again the text stresses the tenseness of the scene by noting the acquiescence of Saul's men.

At best, "Give me the right answer" in the MT of v.41 is difficult. A. Toeg, after surveying several attempts to maintain its authenticity—including reference to supposed Mesopotamian analogies such as *kettam šuknā* ("Put right"; i.e., "Grant me a clear and true response")—concludes that the longer LXX version (see NIV mg.) is the more original text ("A Textual Note on 1 Samuel XIV 41," VetTest 19, 4 [1969]: 493–98; cf. also F.F. Bruce, "The Old Testament in Greek," *Bible Translator* 4, 4 [1953]: 159). In any event, mention of the priestly ephod in v.3 and of the casting of lots in vv.41–42 (no Heb. equivalent for "lot" is found in the text in either verse, but in both cases the NIV correctly supplies the word based on the context, as it does also in Job 6:27) provides a strong presumption for the accuracy of the tradition underlying the LXX text at this point, if not of its precise wording. The MT's *tāmîm* (rendered "right answer" in v.41) should surely be vocalized *tummîm* ("Thummim") with the LXX.

The casting of lots proceeds swiftly, and the rest of the men are eliminated as "Jonathan and Saul" are taken (v.41; that Jonathan's name appears first is an ominous sign). As the final lot is cast, Saul is cleared and Jonathan taken (v.42). Saul's statement to Jonathan echoes Joshua's to Achan centuries earlier: "Tell me what you have done" (v.43; Josh 7:19). The NIV translation of Jonathan's response makes him sound more indignant than the Hebrew text warrants: "I merely tasted a little honey with the end of my staff. And now must I die?" A more literal rendering reveals his willingness to accept the consequences of his action: "I indeed tasted a little honey with the end of my staff. I am ready to die" (cf. also Jobling, "Saul's Fall and Jonathan's Rise," p. 370; Klein, *1 Samuel*, p. 131). Even more solemn than the oath Saul had taken earlier (v.39) is the one he now takes (v.44; cf. also 25:22; Ruth 1:17; 1 Kings 2:23), and it seems that Jonathan's doom is sealed.

Unable to contain themselves any longer in the face of gross injustice, Saul's men remind him of how cruel it would be to execute Israel's deliverer (v.45). Jonathan would remember their cry of "Never!" as he later encouraged David (20:2). Because he was able to achieve victory with God's help (cf. Gen 4:1), not a single hair of his head would fall to the ground (so also of the son of the wise woman from Tekoa, 2 Sam 14:11; of Adonijah, 1 Kings 1:52; of the men with Paul in the boat about to be shipwrecked, Acts 27:34). Finally persuaded, Saul rescinds his order, and thus Jonathan is "rescued" (lit., "ransomed"; cf. Job 6:23) by the fervent pleas of the troops. Distracted by his determination to execute his own son, Saul loses his best opportunity to deal the Philistines a lethal blow (v.46).

### 4. *Further wars of Saul*

#### 14:47–52

47After Saul had assumed rule over Israel, he fought against their
enemies on every side: Moab, the Ammonites, Edom, the kings of

**Zobah, and the Philistines. Wherever he turned, he inflicted punishment**
**on them. 48 He fought valiantly and defeated the Amalekites, delivering**
**Israel from the hands of those who had plundered them.**
**49 Saul's sons were Jonathan, Ishvi and Malki-Shua. The name of his**
**older daughter was Merab, and that of the younger was Michal. 50 His**
**wife's name was Ahinoam daughter of Ahimaaz. The name of the**
**commander of Saul's army was Abner son of Ner, and Ner was Saul's**
**uncle. 51 Saul's father Kish and Abner's father Ner were sons of Abiel.**
**52 All the days of Saul there was bitter war with the Philistines, and**
**whenever Saul saw a mighty or brave man, he took him into his service.**

Just before the account of the divine rejection of Saul in chapter 15, the end of his reign is marked by an editorial summary of his career (Jobling, "Saul's Fall and Jonathan's Rise," p. 371 n. 15). Like other similar royal summaries (cf. that concerning Jeroboam II, 2 Kings 14:28), it includes a brief statement about his military victories over his enemies (vv.47–48, 52). The names and relationships of important members of his family (vv.49–51) are also given.

**47–48** The ambiguity (perhaps intentional) of the statement that Saul "assumed rule over" Israel (v.47) may be illustrated by the assertion in BDB, p. 540, that it refers to "Saul's seizing the kingdom, i.e., acquiring it actually by force of arms," as opposed to BDB, p. 574, where we read that the phrase here simply means to "assume sovereignty over" the land. The verb *lāḵad* ("seize," "take") is used in vv.41–42 in the sense of being "taken" by lot. Although for the most part we do not know the times or extent of Saul's wars against his enemies, we read that he was successful wherever he turned: against the Transjordanian triad of Ammon (cf. 11:1–11), Moab, and Edom (northeast, east, and southeast of the Dead Sea respectively); against the Aramean kingdom of Zobah (north of Damascus), where David was similarly successful (2 Sam 8:3–12; 10:6–19); and—last but not least—against the Philistines. In anticipation of Saul's fiasco in chapter 15, the narrator reserves the Amalekites (who inhabited large tracts of land southwest of the Dead Sea) for special attention (v.48).

On one or more occasions (otherwise unrecorded) during his reign, Saul "fought valiantly" against Amalek (v.48; other occurrences of the idiom associate it with God's help; "gain the victory," Ps 60:12 = 108:13; "has done mighty things," 118:15–16) and defeated them. Saul also saved Israel from the hands of "those who had plundered" them (the phraseology echoes the grand tradition of the judges; cf. Judg 2:16, where the same Heb. participle is translated "raiders"). But Saul's incomplete victory in chapter 15, caused by his disobedience, led to divine rejection and the loss of his kingdom (15:28; 28:17–18).

**49** The names of Saul's children are recorded in v.49 and those of other family members appear in vv.50–51. In addition to his firstborn, Jonathan, Saul had at least two other sons: Ishvi (meaning unknown), who is probably to be identified with Ish-Bosheth, since the latter was not killed (31:2) in Saul's last battle (2 Sam 2–4; = Esh-Baal, 1 Chron 8:33 = 9:39), and Malki-Shua ("My King Is Noble," 31:2 = 1 Chron 10:2; 1 Chron 8:33 = 9:39). Each of the four references listed for Malki-Shua also includes the name of a fourth son, Abinadab ("My Father Is Noble"); why he is not mentioned here in v.49 is unknown. Saul's two daughters, Merab (2 Sam 21:8; better Merob, which perhaps means "Substitute," "Compensation" [see comment on Jerub-Baal in 12:11]; cf. the Qumran and LXX vocalization of the name; cf. esp. Robert B. Lawton, "1 Samuel 18: David, Merob, and Michal," CBQ 51, 2 [1989]: 423–25) and

Michal (perhaps contracted from Michael, "Who Is Like God?"; cf. 19:11–17; 2 Sam 6:16–23), are listed in their proper genealogical order (cf. similarly Gen 29:16). Both would later be offered in marriage to David (18:17–27).

**50–51** Saul's wife (v.50) was Ahinoam ("My Brother Is Pleasant") daughter of Ahimaaz (meaning unknown); nothing further is known of Ahimaaz (for Ahinoam see comment on 25:43). Saul also had a concubine named Rizpah (2 Sam 3:7). The commander of Saul's army was his cousin Abner (spelled Abiner in the Heb. only here), which means either "My Father is Ner" (he is called "son of Ner") or "My Father Is the Lamp" (a metaphor for God himself; cf. 2 Sam 22:29; cf. further Robert Houston Smith, "The Household Lamps of Palestine in Old Testament Times," BA 27, 1 [1964]: 21–22). Saul's father, Kish (v.51), and uncle Ner were both sons of Abiel ("My Father Is God"; cf. 9:1).

**52** Chapter 14 concludes with reminders of the never-ending and all-pervasive Philistine threat and of the king's continuing need for fresh troops (the latter of which Samuel had warned the people about when they had originally demanded a king; 8:11). The final verse of the chapter also sends forth literary rays into the future. One of the "brave" men Saul will conscript is David (18:17); and David himself, after committing adultery with the wife of Uriah, would doom him by having him sent to the battlefront "where the fighting is fiercest" (2 Sam 11:15; the Heb. phrase is translated "bitter war" here in v.52). Once the husband of Bathsheba was dead, David "had her brought to" his house to become his wife (2 Sam 11:27; the Heb. phrase is translated "took him into his service" here in v.52).

## Notes

**25** One Hebrew MS has הָעָם (*hā'ām*, "the people"; NIV, "army") instead of the MT's הָאָרֶץ (*hā'āreṣ*, "the land"; cf. NIV mg.).

**30** We would expect הַמַּכָּה (*hammakkāh*, "the slaughter"; thus NIV) instead of the MT's מַכָּה (*makkāh*, without the definite article). Perhaps the MT reading illustrates the phenomenon of shared consonants, the ־ה (*h-*) of the definite article being shared with the same letter that ends the preceding word (so Watson, "Shared Consonants," p. 531).

**32** The correctness of the *Qere* reading וַיַּעַט (*wayya'aṭ*, "[and] pounced on") is confirmed by the occurrence of the same rare verb in the same phrase in 15:19. There is thus no need to connect the *Kethiv* reading וַיַּעַשׂ (*wayya'aś*, lit., "and he did/made") with a presumed Arabic cognate meaning "turn," as does D. Winton Thomas, who does not mention the *Qere* ("Translating Hebrew *'āsāh*," *Bible Translator* 17, 4 [1966]: 192).

### 5. *The rejection of Saul*

#### 15:1–35

1 Samuel said to Saul, "I am the one the LORD sent to anoint you king
over his people Israel; so listen now to the message from the LORD. 2 This
is what the LORD Almighty says: 'I will punish the Amalekites for what
they did to Israel when they waylaid them as they came up from Egypt.
3 Now go, attack the Amalekites and totally destroy everything that

belongs to them. Do not spare them; put to death men and women,
children and infants, cattle and sheep, camels and donkeys.'"
4So Saul summoned the men and mustered them at Telaim—two
hundred thousand foot soldiers and ten thousand men from Judah.
5Saul went to the city of Amalek and set an ambush in the ravine. 6Then
he said to the Kenites, "Go away, leave the Amalekites so that I do not
destroy you along with them; for you showed kindness to all the
Israelites when they came up out of Egypt." So the Kenites moved away
from the Amalekites.
7Then Saul attacked the Amalekites all the way from Havilah to Shur,
to the east of Egypt. 8He took Agag king of the Amalekites alive, and all
his people he totally destroyed with the sword. 9But Saul and the army
spared Agag and the best of the sheep and cattle, the fat calves and
lambs—everything that was good. These they were unwilling to destroy
completely, but everything that was despised and weak they totally
destroyed.
10Then the word of the LORD came to Samuel: 11"I am grieved that I
have made Saul king, because he has turned away from me and has not
carried out my instructions." Samuel was troubled, and he cried out to
the LORD all that night.
12Early in the morning Samuel got up and went to meet Saul, but he
was told, "Saul has gone to Carmel. There he has set up a monument in
his own honor and has turned and gone on down to Gilgal."
13When Samuel reached him, Saul said, "The LORD bless you! I have
carried out the LORD's instructions."
14But Samuel said, "What then is this bleating of sheep in my ears?
What is this lowing of cattle that I hear?"
15Saul answered, "The soldiers brought them from the Amalekites;
they spared the best of the sheep and cattle to sacrifice to the LORD your
God, but we totally destroyed the rest."
16"Stop!" Samuel said to Saul. "Let me tell you what the LORD said to
me last night."
"Tell me," Saul replied.
17Samuel said, "Although you were once small in your own eyes, did
you not become the head of the tribes of Israel? The LORD anointed you
king over Israel. 18And he sent you on a mission, saying, 'Go and
completely destroy those wicked people, the Amalekites; make war on
them until you have wiped them out.' 19Why did you not obey the LORD?
Why did you pounce on the plunder and do evil in the eyes of the LORD?"
20"But I did obey the LORD," Saul said. "I went on the mission the LORD
assigned me. I completely destroyed the Amalekites and brought back
Agag their king. 21The soldiers took sheep and cattle from the plunder,
the best of what was devoted to God, in order to sacrifice them to the
LORD your God at Gilgal."
22But Samuel replied:

"Does the LORD delight in burnt offerings and sacrifices
as much as in obeying the voice of the LORD?
To obey is better than sacrifice,
and to heed is better than the fat of rams.
23For rebellion is like the sin of divination,
and arrogance like the evil of idolatry.
Because you have rejected the word of the LORD,
he has rejected you as king."

24Then Saul said to Samuel, "I have sinned. I violated the LORD's
command and your instructions. I was afraid of the people and so I gave
in to them. 25Now I beg you, forgive my sin and come back with me, so
that I may worship the LORD."

26But Samuel said to him, "I will not go back with you. You have
rejected the word of the LORD, and the LORD has rejected you as king
over Israel!"
27As Samuel turned to leave, Saul caught hold of the hem of his robe,
and it tore. 28Samuel said to him, "The LORD has torn the kingdom of
Israel from you today and has given it to one of your neighbors—to one
better than you. 29He who is the Glory of Israel does not lie or change
his mind; for he is not a man, that he should change his mind."
30Saul replied, "I have sinned. But please honor me before the elders
of my people and before Israel; come back with me, so that I may
worship the LORD your God." 31So Samuel went back with Saul, and
Saul worshiped the LORD.
32Then Samuel said, "Bring me Agag king of the Amalekites."
Agag came to him confidently, thinking, "Surely the bitterness of
death is past."
33But Samuel said,

"As your sword has made women childless,
so will your mother be childless among women."

And Samuel put Agag to death before the LORD at Gilgal.
34Then Samuel left for Ramah, but Saul went up to his home in
Gibeah of Saul. 35Until the day Samuel died, he did not go to see Saul
again, though Samuel mourned for him. And the LORD was grieved that
he had made Saul king over Israel.

Chapter 15, which concludes the account of Saul's decline (chs. 13–15), is the classic exposition of the theme of "prophetic opposition to reliance on anybody or anything but the LORD who alone leads Israel's Holy War" (Wolfgang M.W. Roth, "A Study of the Classical Hebrew Verb *ṣkl*," VetTest 18, 1 [1968]: 74–75). As in chapter 13 Saul's offering of an unauthorized sacrifice in the context of holy war led to Samuel's initial rebuke, so in chapter 15 Saul's intention to offer an unauthorized sacrifice in the context of holy war leads to God's final rejection. If at that earlier time Saul was denied a dynasty, now he is denied his kingship. Thus chapter 15 is climactic. "Saul's loss of kingship and kingdom are irrevocable; the rest of 1 Samuel details how in fact he does lose it all" (Miscall, p. 98).

**1–3** The emphatic position of the independent pronoun—"I am the one"—stresses Samuel's role as the representative through whom God anointed Saul and through whom he now proclaims a further message to him (v.1). As Miscall correctly observes (pp. 98–99), Saul is here described for the first time as having been anointed *meleḵ* ("king"; see also v.17); previously the transitional term *nāgîḏ* ("leader") is used at his anointing (9:16; 10:1). His fall from grace thus becomes all the more stark—and that of David in a similarly tragic situation (2 Sam 12:7–10) mirrors the scene that unfolds in this chapter.

Soon to wrest the kingship from Saul's grasp, the Lord—the only true King in Israel's theocratic monarchy—is described as "the LORD Almighty" (v.2), a specifically royal name (see comment on 1:3). His message to Saul is that the time has come for the final destruction of the Amalekites, predicted and reiterated long ago (Exod 17:8–16; Num 24:20; Deut 25:17–19). The summary of Saul's wars at the end of chapter 14 includes his defeat of Amalek on one or more otherwise unrecorded occasions (14:48), casting the failure of chapter 15 in even sharper relief. The geographical clues scattered throughout the chapter make it clear that the Amalekites referred to here are the traditional southern marauders rather than a smaller

Amalekite enclave occupying an area in the hills of western Samaria. The only way that the northern Amalekite theory can be maintained is by the unacceptable means of assuming that all the clues are secondary insertions (cf. Diana Edelman, "Saul's Battle Against Amaleq [1 Sam. 15]," JSOT 35 [1986]: 71–84).

The significance and uniqueness of the divine command to annihilate the Amalekites is underscored by *ḥrm*, "the irrevocable giving over of things or persons to the LORD, often by totally destroying them" (NIV mg., v.3). Although the root appears often enough elsewhere in the OT in contexts of holy war, it occurs in the books of Samuel only here in chapter 15. The verb ("completely/totally destroyed") is found, however, a total of seven times in this one chapter (vv.3, 8, 9 [bis], 15, 18, 20), while its cognate noun ("what was devoted to God") appears once (v.21). The precise meaning of the verb in this context is secured by the verbs associated with it at its first occurrence in v.3: "attack," "do not spare," "put to death." Although all the verbs except one in v.3 are in the singular, Saul is not expected to accomplish the grisly task himself. The key verb "totally destroy" is plural and thus implicates the Israelite troops as well (in two MT MSS "totally destroy" is also singular, obviously an attempt to harmonize it with the other verbs).

It is furthermore clear that "everything that belongs to them" (v.3) here means "everything among them that breathes" (cf. strikingly, Deut 20:16–17). Representative pairings of animate creatures doomed to destruction conclude the verse. This list is ominously echoed—almost verbatim—in 22:19, where Saul exterminates all the inhabitants of the town of Nob. Fokkelman observes that "in killing everyone in Nob, including Yahweh's priests, Saul takes his revenge against God. Saul does to a town of Yahweh's priests what God through Samuel had ordered Saul to do to the Amalekites" ("Saul and David," p. 28). The command in v.3 is specific: "Do not spare them"—Saul, however, rationalized the disobedience of that command (vv.9, 15).

We should not be surprised that Saul did not flinch at the prospect of killing ostensibly innocent women and children. Although outside of Israel the root *ḥrm* in the sense here outlined occurs only in line 17 of the Mesha inscription (Rudolf Smend and Albert Socin, *Die Inschrift des Königs Mesa von Moab* [Freiburg: J.C.B. Mohr, 1886], pp. 12, 23), wars in the ancient Near East always had a religious dimension, and the battlefield was an arena of divine retribution. The Amalekites, in their persistent refusal to fear God (Deut 25:18), sowed the seeds of their own destruction. God is patient and slow to anger, "abounding in love and faithfulness" (Exod 34:6); he nevertheless "does not leave the guilty unpunished" (v.7).

The agent of divine judgment can be impersonal (e.g., the Flood or the destruction of Sodom and Gomorrah) or personal (as here), and in his sovereign purpose God often permits entire families or nations to be destroyed if their corporate representatives are willfully and incorrigibly wicked (cf. Josh 7:1, 10–13, 24–26). For further discussion of this sensitive issue, see especially the nuanced treatments of Peter C. Craigie, *The Problem of War in the Old Testament* (Grand Rapids: Eerdmans, 1978); John W. Wenham, *The Enigma of Evil: Can We Believe in the Goodness of God?* (Grand Rapids: Zondervan, 1985), pp. 99–101, 119–25, 165–68.

**4–9** Saul's preparations for battle against the Amalekites are outlined in vv.4–6. He "summoned" (lit., "caused to hear"; cf. "called up" in 23:8) from Judah "ten thousand" men (v.4); the number probably denotes "the least number for a complete fighting force" (Segal, "Numerals," pp. 5–6; thus there were only "ten thousand foot soldiers" left in the decimated army of Jehoahaz, 2 Kings 13:7). In addition Saul mustered "two hundred thousand foot soldiers," probably from Israel (on the analogy of 11:8; cf. comment there). Saul's troop strength had declined considerably since the battles against Nahash and the Ammonites (11:8), but it was more than adequate for the present task. Although the precise location of the mustering site (Telaim, probably = Telem in the Negev, Josh 15:21, 24) is unknown, it has been suggested recently that the "city of Amalek" (v.5) is modern Tel Masos (about seven miles east-southeast of Beersheba) and that a destruction layer there attests to the successful ambush of Saul's troops (cf. Ze'ev Herzog, "Enclosed Settlements in the Negeb and the Wilderness of Beer-Sheba," BASOR 250 [Spring 1983]: pp. 43, 47).

Before Saul's main attack against the Amalekites (vv.7–9), he urged the Kenites living in or near Amalekite territory (cf. 27:10; 30:29) to move out (at least temporarily) to avoid getting killed in the crossfire. Saul's regard for the welfare of the Kenites is in recognition of the fact that they "showed kindness" to the Israelite spies centuries earlier and had thus been spared in return (Josh 2:12–14; so Miscall, pp. 100–101).

The Israelites attacked the Amalekites throughout their homeland—from Havilah (location unknown but perhaps in northern Arabia) to Shur (on the eastern border of the Nile delta, v.7; cf. also 27:8; Exod 15:22)—an extensive area that had formerly been settled by descendants of Ishmael (Gen 25:17–18). The powerful assonance evident in "totally destroyed [*ḥrm*] with the sword [*ḥrb*]" is not unique to v.8 (cf. Deut 13:15; Josh 6:21; Isa 34:5). The description of the total destruction of "all" the people (v.8) is hyperbolic, since the Amalekites as a whole survived to fight again (cf. 30:1). In any event, Saul spared Agag—but perhaps with the intent of later putting him to death, since the idiom "take alive" often describes an action preparatory to subsequent execution (cf. 2 Kings 10:14; 2 Chron 25:12; and esp. Josh 8:23, 29). It is noteworthy that Samuel nowhere berates Saul for having (temporarily?) preserved Agag's life.

Although Numbers 24:7 with its reference to "Agag" may be a specific prediction of the events in chapter 15, it is equally possible that Agag was a dynastic royal name among the Amalekites and that Numbers 24:7 merely speaks in general terms of the historical domination of Amalek by Israel. That Haman the "Agagite" (Esth 3:1, 10; 8:3, 5; 9:24) was an Amalekite is taken for granted by Josephus, who states that Haman's determination to destroy all the Jews in Persia was in retaliation for Israel's previous destruction of all his ancestors (Antiq. XI, 211 [vi.5]).

Besides sparing Agag, Saul and his troops also set aside the best of the enemy's animals while destroying those that were worthless and weak (v.9). When reproved by Samuel for not slaughtering even the best animals (vv.14, 19), he gave the excuse that his "soldiers" (vv.15, 21) intended to sacrifice them to the Lord. If Saul is sincere at this point, his reluctance to accept responsibility and his haste to shift the blame to his men is disquietingly reminiscent of similar situations in the past (Gen 3:12–13; Exod 32:21–24). The text, however, states that Saul and his men were "unwilling" to destroy—a verb specifically linked elsewhere with the sin of rebellion (Deut 1:26).

**10–21** In truth, "the word of the LORD was rare" in those days (3:1). The phrase "the word of the LORD came to" is used of God's revelation to a prophet only three times in the books of Samuel—once in blessing (through Nathan to David, 2 Sam 7:4) and twice in judgment (through Samuel to Saul, v.10; through Gad to David, 2 Sam 24:11). In each of two stages in this section (vv.10–15, 16–21), Samuel brings the condemning word of God to Saul for having disobeyed the divine command.

The use of the Niphal of the verb *nāḥam* ("repent") in chapter 15 presents something of a problem because it appears to involve God in contradictory actions. In v.11 the Lord says, "I have repented" (NIV, "I am grieved"); in v.29 Samuel says twice of him that he does not "repent" (NIV, "change his mind"); and in v.35 the narrator says of him that he "repented" (NIV, "was grieved"). Terence E. Fretheim, in an otherwise excellent article, speaks of "limited divine knowledge of the future," of "what God has learned, and how God adjusts in view of such learning" ("Divine Foreknowledge, Divine Constancy, and the Rejection of Saul's Kingship," CBQ 47, 4 [1985]: 595, 602). Much better is the analysis of John Goldingay:

> To speak of God changing his mind about an act or regretting it suggests the reality of his interacting with people in the world. . . . His reactions to the deeds of others reflect a coherent pattern rather than randomness. Further, whereas human beings make their decisions unaware of all their consequences, so that those consequences can catch them out, God (so the OT assumes) can foresee not only the consequences of his own actions but also the nature of the responses they will meet with and the nature of other human acts, so that he can in turn formulate his response to these in advance. So the interaction between divine and human decision-making is real (there are genuine human acts to foresee), yet God is not caught out by the latter, and in this sense he does not have to change his mind. (*Theological Diversity and the Authority of the Old Testament* [Grand Rapids: Eerdmans, 1987], pp. 16–17)

Walter C. Kaiser, Jr. (*Toward Old Testament Ethics* [Grand Rapids: Eerdmans, 1983], p. 250) remarks, "God can and does change in his actions and emotions towards men so as not to be fickle, mutable, and variable in his nature or purpose" (see further Page H. Kelley, "The Repentance of God," *Biblical Illustrator* 9, 1 [1982]: 12–13). The NIV's "am/was grieved" in vv.11, 35 is, of course, justifiable (cf. H. Van Dyke Parunak's contention that *nḥm* means "suffer emotional pain" not only here but also in Gen 6:6–7; Judg 21:6, 15; Jer 31:19 [NIV, "repented"], "A Semantic Survey of *NḤM*," *Biblica* 56 [1975]: 519). In such contexts the connection between "regret, suffer remorse, be grieved" and "repent, relent, reconsider" (cf. Exod 32:11–14; Jer 18:8, 10) is not far to seek.

Whether Samuel had by this time become reconciled—however reluctantly—to Saul's kingship is difficult to say. After all, God's role in making Saul king is stressed over and over in these chapters (9:17; 10:1, 24; 12:13; 13:13; 15:1). Although Samuel did not yet know it, Saul had "turned away" (v.11) from the Lord, an action fraught with the most serious of consequences (cf. Num 14:43; 32:15; Josh 22:16, 18, 23, 29; 1 Kings 9:6–7); to fail to carry out God's "instructions" (lit., "words") is to become his enemy (cf. Pss 50:16–17; 119:139). The Lord's "word" to Samuel in v.11 was clearly disturbing to him. It caused him to be "troubled" (lit., "angry"; cf. 18:8; 2 Sam 3:8; and esp. 2 Sam 6:8, where the divine execution of Uzzah makes David "angry") and to cry out (for help, often for someone else; cf. 7:8–9; 12:8, 10) to the Lord all night long.

Was Samuel, sympathetic to Saul's plight, trying to persuade God to forgive Saul and retain him as king? Or was Samuel, antagonistic toward Saul, pleading with God to maintain somehow Samuel's credibility (since it was Samuel who had anointed Saul as king)? Although the text is noncommittal on this point, attempts to explain Samuel's sense of urgency along these and similar lines are legion (cf. Fretheim, "Divine Foreknowledge," p. 601; Miscall, p. 103). Whatever the reason(s) for Samuel's distress/anger, and whatever the content of his cries for help, it was during his nightlong wrestling with God in prayer that he received the divine message of irreversible doom for Saul's kingdom (cf. v.16). God has now spoken; throughout the rest of the chapter Samuel mediates the divine word to the rejected Saul.

Wherever it was that Samuel expected to find Saul when he went out to meet him (v.12) and declare to him the message of doom, he was told that Saul had gone to Carmel (modern Khirbet el-Kirmil in the hill country of Judah [cf. 25:2, 5, 7, 40; Josh 15:48, 55] eight miles south-southeast of Hebron, not the northern Carmel on the Mediterranean coast). There Saul set up a monument (probably an inscribed victory stele) "in his own honor" (apparently not giving credit to the Lord). The word for "monument" is *yāḏ* ("hand"), used in the same sense concerning the equally egotistical Absalom (2 Sam 18:18). Having built the monument, Saul then "turned" (preparatory to leaving; cf. v.27) and went to Gilgal—the very place where Samuel had earlier rebuked him but that at the same time had in Saul's mind become associated with sacrifice (13:7–14; cf. v.21).

When Samuel arrived at Gilgal, Saul—either genuinely or pretending innocence—greeted him in the traditional way (v.13; cf. 23:21; 2 Sam 2:5; Ruth 2:19–20; 3:10) and then told him that he had carried out the Lord's "instructions" (lit., "word"—does he avoid saying "words" [cf. comment on v.10] because of having spared Agag and the best animals?). But Samuel, not to be denied, wanted to know why he heard the "bleating" of sheep and the "lowing" (lit., in both cases, "voice") of cattle in the background (v.14). The terms used in Samuel's question will soon return to haunt Saul when Samuel says to him that "obeying" (lit., "hearing") the "voice" of the Lord pleases him more than bringing sacrifices to him (v.22; cf. also v.19 and the comment on v.24). Thus Saul's meek retort in v.15 fails on two counts: (1) However commendable his declared motive, Saul was told to destroy every living thing and therefore should not have spared even the best of the animals; (2) even if his soldiers were primarily responsible for saving the animals, Saul was their leader and therefore should not have tried to shift the blame to them. Especially stark is the contrast between "they spared" and "we totally destroyed." Notice that in speaking to Samuel, Saul referred to "the LORD your God" (rather than "the LORD our God"; cf. vv.21, 30)—even though he had just invoked the name of the Lord in a personal way and had claimed to have obeyed him (v.13).

Samuel would have none of Saul's self-righteous protestations. With all the force of divine authority, he told Saul to "stop" (v.16; the same Heb. verb is translated "be still" in Ps 46:10)—a command analogous to "you acted foolishly" in 13:13 (so Miscall, p. 105)—and to listen to what God had revealed to him the previous night. He reminded Saul (v.17) that despite the fact that Saul had once considered himself too insignificant to be Israel's ruler (cf. 9:21; 10:22), the Lord had nevertheless anointed him as king. He then summarized (v.18) the divine commission of vv.2–3, emphasizing the intractable sinfulness of the Amalekites by calling them "wicked people" (lit., "[habitual] sinners," the same Heb. word used in Ps 1:1, 5) and reiterating the irrevocable, divine intention to destroy them completely (cf. similarly 2 Sam 22:38 = Ps 18:37; 1 Kings 22:11 = 2 Chron 18:10; Jer 9:16). Quick to condemn his troops for having "pounced on the plunder"—including especially "sheep and cattle"—after defeating the Philistines (14:32–33), Saul discovered that to "pounce on the plunder" (v.19)—including especially "sheep and cattle" (v.21)—is to "do evil in the eyes of the LORD" (an echo of Israel's sinful demand for a king in the first place; cf. 12:17).

Saul has no better defense against Samuel's onslaught than to repeat in detail (vv.20–21) what he had already said in summary (v.13). Although he stresses his own obedience by speaking in the first person several times in v.20, he also tries to justify the actions of his troops (v.21) by attributing to them the worthy intention to sacrifice to the Lord the animals they had spared. Saul's terminology in v.21 and Samuel's in v.22 link the disobedience of Saul and his men to the earlier wickedness of Eli and his reprobate sons. As the latter had sinfully fattened themselves on the "choice parts" of Israel's offerings (2:29), so Saul's troops had stubbornly kept the "best" of the plundered animals in order to sacrifice them (v.21; the Heb. word in the two passages is identical and is not the same as the word for "best" in vv.9, 15). As the doom of Hophni and Phinehas was sealed because it was the Lord's "will" to put them to death (2:25), so the rejection of Saul is irreversible because the Lord does not "delight" in willful disobedience (v.22; same Heb. root in both verses).

**22–31** The poetic format of Samuel's well-known condemnation of Saul's objection (vv.22–23) in no way blunts its severity (cf. similarly v.33). As at the time of the Fall (Gen 2–3), the matter at stake is one of obedience, and Saul failed as miserably as did Adam and Eve.

Verse 22, a classic text on the importance of obedience, moral conduct, and proper motivation vis-à-vis animal sacrifice, has a striking parallel in the Egyptian Instruction for Meri-ka-Re, written a millennium earlier: "More acceptable is the character of one upright of heart than the ox of the evildoer" (ANET, p. 417). If nothing else, the Egyptian parallel eviscerates the shopworn argument that v.22 and other biblical texts that have the same emphasis (e.g., Pss 40:6–8; 51:16–17; Isa 1:11–15; Jer 7:21–23; Hos 6:6; Mic 6:6–8; Mark 12:32–33) pit the prophetic stress on obeying the divine word against the priestly commitment to sacrificial ritual. Samuel, himself both prophet (3:20) and priest (cf. 2:35 and comment; cf. also 3:1), not only received and proclaimed the word of God (vv.10–11, 16–17) but also brought sacrifices to the Lord (7:9; 9:12–13; 10:8). The issue here is not a question of either/or but of both/and. Practically speaking, this means that sacrifice must be offered to the Lord on his terms, not ours. Saul's postponement of the commanded destruction, however well meaning, constituted flagrant violation of God's will.

Verse 22a asks a rhetorical question that is then answered in v.22b. The seriousness of disobedience is underscored in v.23a, and devastating application is made to Saul's situation in v.23b. The vocabulary of v.22 reverberates throughout Isaiah 1:11: "The LORD" takes no "pleasure" (same Heb. root as "delight" in v.22) in "sacrifices" or "burnt offerings," in "rams" or the "fat" of other animals. On the other hand, mutual "delight" between God and his children can be expected when the righteous among them meditate on his law (Ps 1:2) and heed his words as mediated through his prophets.

For the sake of clarity in English, the NIV has transformed the metaphors of v.23a into similes. In neither line is "like" represented in the Hebrew text, which is thus all the more blunt. The lexicon of disobedience is repulsive indeed. The open insurrection known as "rebellion" and the pushy presumption called "arrogance" (cf. Gen 19:9, where the same Heb. root has the wicked men of Sodom "bringing pressure" on the hapless Lot) are the equivalents of the sins of "divination" (found in association not only with other forms of spiritism but also with human sacrifice in Deut 18:10) and "idolatry" (the superstitious worship of household gods, *t<sup>e</sup>rāpîm;* contrast the godly purge initiated by Josiah in 2 Kings 23:24). The alternative to obedience is costly: Selfish refusal to submit to the commands of the sovereign Lord results in slavery to malign forces in the demonic realm.

Just as Saul's earlier impetuous disobedience had brought the full force of Samuel's rebuke (13:14), so now his halfhearted fulfillment of the divine command removes him from royal office. Rejection begets rejection (v.23b), and the doleful refrain echoes throughout the rest of the chapter and beyond (v.26; 16:1).

The note of finality in Samuel's voice finally brings Saul to his senses. To read his plea of remorse in vv.24–25 in connection with Exodus 10:16–17 is to recognize that Saul, perhaps unwittingly, is echoing the sentiments of an earlier beleaguered ruler, the Pharaoh of the Exodus (cf. also Exod 9:27). Like Balaam before him (Num 22:34) and like David after him (2 Sam 12:13; 24:10, 17 [cf. 1 Chron 21:8, 17]; Ps 51:4), Saul says—twice—"I have sinned" (vv.24, 30). He confesses to having "violated the LORD's command" (v.24), apparently not having learned the lesson of his earlier failure (13:13). Such action has no hope of success (Num 14:41; 22:18; 24:13). Fearing the people more than God (always a dubious enterprise; cf. Prov 29:25; Isa 51:12–13), Saul "gave in to them"—literally, "obeyed them"—when all along he should have been obeying the voice of God through the prophet (vv.19, 22).

At first Saul's plea to Samuel for forgiveness (v.25) falls on deaf ears (v.26). As far as Samuel is concerned, the conversation is over; so he turns to leave the scene (v.27). At this point "Saul" (not in the MT but supplied by 4QSam[a], the LXX, and the NIV in the interests of clarity) in desperation seizes the hem of Samuel's robe. Saul may not have been aware of the full implications of his act, which seems to have been spontaneous and unpremeditated. But since a man's robe may symbolize his power and authority (cf. 2:19 and comment; cf. also 18:4 and esp. 24:11), perhaps the narrator is telling us that the tearing of Samuel's robe implies an irreparable breech between Saul and Samuel as well as the more obvious sundering of the kingdom from Saul's personal rule and that of his descendants (v.28; cf. similarly 1 Kings 11:11–13, 29–31), dashing whatever ambitions his sons Jonathan (18:1–5; 23:16–18) and Ish-Bosheth (2 Sam 2:8–9) and his grandson Mephibosheth (2 Sam 16:3) might eventually have had.

The "neighbor" destined to receive Saul's kingdom (v.28; cf. also 13:14) is David, whose identity is clearly revealed to Saul once and for all by the robed apparition of Samuel (28:14, 17–18). As obedience is "better than" sacrifice (v.22), so David is "better than" Saul. It goes without saying that the new ruler should be "better than" his or her predecessor (cf. Esth 1:19), and it is ironic that Saul himself had originally been considered "better than" (NIV, "without equal among," 9:2) his peers.

The general statement in Numbers 23:19 concerning the immutability of God's basic nature and purpose (cf. the helpful summary article by Billy Graham, "God Has Not Changed," *Decision* 30, 10 [1989]: 1–3) is now applied in v.29. Fretheim ("Divine Foreknowledge," pp. 597–98) makes a strong case for referring this verse to God's irrevocable decision to give the kingdom to David rather than to God's irreversible determination to reject Saul, pointing out that the verb "lie" was used in Davidic covenant contexts (cf. "betray" in Ps 89:33; Fretheim's reference to "lie" in 89:35 [cf. his n. 9] is to a different, though semantically equivalent, Heb. verb). In any event, Samuel gives to the unchangeable God a unique name by calling him the "Glory" (*nēṣaḥ*) of Israel (the word is also used once as an attribute of God; cf. NIV's "majesty" in 1 Chron 29:11).

Although some may attempt to assert that God is beyond gender since he is "not a man" (v.29; cf. also Num 23:19; Hos 11:9), John W. Miller correctly insists that the contrast in all three texts is not between a God beyond gender and man as male but between a God who is truthful and compassionate and man who is deceitful and merciless ("Depatriarchalizing God in Biblical Interpretation: A Critique," CBQ 48, 4

[1986]: 612–13). Miller summarizes by stating that it cannot be argued "on the basis of these texts that a 'masculine label' for deity was thought to be dangerous or that a depatriarchalizing principle was at work in biblical religion" (ibid., p. 613).

Perhaps by now reconciled to the irreversible divine determination (for another example, cf. Ezek 24:14) to reject him finally as king of Israel, Saul poignantly repeats (in summary fashion, v.30) his earlier statements of confession and of his desire for Samuel to "come back" with him (vv.24–25), whether back to Gilgal (v.33) or simply because Samuel was again about to leave (cf. v.27). Saul wanted to save face before the elders and people of Israel by publicly worshiping the Lord and so demonstrating his allegiance to him. Samuel—a man, not God—this time relented (v.31).

**32–35** There was one piece of business still to take care of, however. Using the language common to the ritual procedure of sacrifice (v.32), Samuel said, "Bring me [a verbatim echo of the same Heb. phrase in 13:9] Agag"—whom he then further describes as "king of the Amalekites," thus again underscoring Saul's failure to destroy them completely. In Samuel's mind Agag is an offering to be sacrificed to the Lord. Whatever Agag's physical condition or state of mind (he is brought before Samuel *maʿᵃḏannōṯ*, which probably means "in chains" [see Notes below for details]; the NIV renders "confidently"; NIV mg., "trembling"), he apparently feels that his life will be spared—although "Surely the bitterness of death is past" could perhaps be understood as a statement of resignation to his fate.

Quickly dispelling whatever optimism Agag might have felt, Samuel's couplet (which rhymes in Heb.) applies the lex talionis to the Amalekite king (cf. similarly Judg 1:7 and the statement of Jesus in Matt 7:2) and reminds him that bloodshed begets bloodshed (Gen 9:6; for a contrasting application of "like for like," cf. David's statement to Saul in 26:24). Without further ado Samuel then executes Agag, probably by hacking him in pieces (see Notes below; for the treaty violation implications of such an act, cf. 11:12 and comment). Following the death of Agag, Samuel and Saul go their separate ways—Samuel to his hometown of Ramah (v.34), just as he does after anointing David (16:13), and Saul to his hometown of Gibeah. "Until the day of [one's] death" or its equivalent often has negative connotations in the OT, as here in the case of Saul (v.35) and in 2 Samuel 6:23 in the case of Saul's daughter Michal. Although after this time Saul would go to see Samuel again on more than one occasion (19:23–24; 28:10–11), never again would Samuel initiate such a meeting. Samuel nonetheless "mourned" for Saul (cf. also 16:1), the narrator using the verb that is normally used for lamenting for the dead (*'bl*). Gunn observes, "As far as Samuel is concerned, Saul is a dead man" (*The Fate of King Saul*, p. 147).

The chapter ends with a doleful echo of v.11: "The Lord was grieved that he had made Saul king." Saul's rejection of God's word through his prophet had led to God's rejection of Saul's rule over his people. To end this part of our discussion on a relatively positive note, however, we do well to remember, with Fretheim ("Divine Foreknowledge," p. 597), that the divine rejection of the kingship of Saul does not imply a rejection of the person of Saul.

## Notes

---

9 The NIV translates the MT's משנים (*mšnym*, "second things") as "fat calves," presumably reading שׁמנים (*šmnym*) with one Hebrew MS (cf. the root *šmn* used similarly in Neh 8:10

["choice food"]; Ezek 34:16 ["sleek (sheep)"]; cf. also LXX's ἐδεσμάτων (*edesmatōn*, "foods," "meats"). The margin reading "grown bulls" may be an attempt to render the MT; cf. Barthélemy, who states that "seconds" refers to "those animals which were kept and fattened after the first-born had been given to God" (p. 181).

12 יָד (*yād*, "hand") in the sense of "monument" is found also in Isa 56:5 ("memorial") and Ezek 21:19 ("signpost"). The Isa 56:5 reference in full, יָד וָשֵׁם (*yād wāšēm*, "a memorial and a name") has given the name Yad Vashem to the main Holocaust monument in modern Jerusalem, which contains records of systematic extermination of millions of Jews in concentration camps throughout eastern Europe during World War II. The use of the term "hand" to designate an inscribed stele occurs not only in v.12 (and perhaps also in 1 Chron 18:3; cf. comment on 2 Sam 8:3) but also a century earlier in an apology of Hattusilis III (cf. Edelman,"Saul's Battle," pp. 76, 82 n. 17). Various theories proposed for calling such a monument a "hand" include (1) its roughly handlike shape (an upright shaft with a rounded top), (2) the fact that some stelae have one or more hands engraved on their sides, and (3) the use of *yd* in the sense of "phallus" at Qumran (and also at least once in the OT; cf. Isa 57:8; NIV,"nakedness"); cf. esp. M. Delcor, "Two Special Meanings of the Word יד in Biblical Hebrew," JSS 12, 2 (1967): 230–40.

18 "Wicked people" is in apposition to Amalekites," making the two terms virtually synonymous. Later Judaism equated "sinner" with "Gentile" (= "pagan"; cf. Karl Heinrich Rengstorf, "ἁμαρτωλός," TDNT, 1:324–26), a fact reflected in the NT (cf. Matt 5:47 with Luke 6:32; Matt 26:45 with Luke 18:32; and esp. Gal 2:15). The connection is already implied, however, in such OT texts as Ps 9:17, where "the wicked" and "the nations" are found in synonymous parallelism.

32 מַעֲדַנֹּת (*maʿadannōṯ*) has been derived from three different roots: (1) עדן (*ʿdn*, "luxuriate"; cf. "reveled," Neh 9:25), thus NIV's "confidently" here; (2) מעד (*mʿd*, "totter"; cf. "wavering," Ps 26:1), thus the NIV mg., "trembling" (LXX, *tremōn*) here; (3) by metathesis ענד (*ʿnd*, "bind"; cf. Prov 6:21). Since *maʿadannōṯ* occurs elsewhere in the OT only in Job 38:31, where it parallels מֹשְׁכוֹת (*mōšekôṯ*, "cords"), it most likely means "chains," "fetters" here as well as there (cf. second NIV mg. note at Job 38:31) (so McCarter, *I Samuel*, p. 264 n. 32). For a full discussion of the options, see Robert G. Bratcher, "How Did Agag Meet Samuel? (1 Sam. 15:32)," *Bible Translator* 22, 4 (1971): 167–68 (but notice the caveat of Barthélemy, p. 182).

33 The targumic rendering of שסף (*ššp*), a *hapax legomenon* in the OT, is פשח (*pšḥ*, "tear in pieces"; cf. the Heb. cognate in Lam 3:11, "mangled"). The NIV's "put . . . to death" is more cautious and not without reason; *ššp* has been analyzed as a Shaphel (causative) of סוף (*swp*, "come to an end"), thus meaning "put an end to" (cf. Dahood, "Hebrew-Ugaritic Lexicography XI," p. 362).

---

## III. Establishment of Monarchy in Israel (16:1–31:13)

Although monarchy in the person of Saul had long since arrived in Israel by the time of the events recorded in chapter 16, only with the anointing and rapid rise of David can it be said to have been truly established. Unlike Saul's abortive rule, a complex admixture resulting from popular demand and divine choice, David's reign was sovereignly instituted by God alone. Already in chapter 14 it is clear that Saul would not father a royal dynasty; for that chapter gives the distinct impression that the rift begun there between the king and his firstborn son, Jonathan, would only widen with the passing of the years. In fact, chapters 16–31 are as much the story of the decline and ultimate fall of Saul and Jonathan as they are the rise of David, although the beginnings of that decline and fall were already evident in chapters 13–15.

Looking at the Deuteronomic history as a whole, Gerbrandt observes that "a total of

40 [*sic*] chapters (1 Samuel 16–1 Kings 1) have [*sic*] David as the center of attention whereas the whole history from David to the end of the two kingdoms is dealt with in only 46 chapters. . . . Literally the David stories are right at the center of the history" (p. 158). Although this latter statement is somewhat imprecise, the basic centrality and dominance of David in the Deuteronomic history is beyond reasonable question. Despite his obvious faults, he is the man after God's own heart, the key figure in the story, the ideal king against whom the characters and careers of his royal descendants on the throne are constantly measured.

P. Kyle McCarter, Jr. ("The Apology of David," JBL 99, 4 [1980]: 489–504) sees in 1 Samuel 16:14–2 Samuel 5:10 "an old, more or less unified composition describing David's rise to power" (p. 493), which "in its original formulation was of Davidic date" (p. 502). Together with Herbert M. Wolf ("The Apology of Hattušiliš Compared With Other Ancient Near Eastern Political Self-Justifications" [Ph.D. diss., Brandeis University, 1967]: 99–117) and Harry A. Hoffner, Jr. ("Propaganda and Political Justification in Hittite Historiography," in *Unity and Diversity: Essays in the History, Literature, and Religion of the Ancient Near East*, edd. H. Goedicke and J.J.M. Roberts [Baltimore: Johns Hopkins University Press, 1975], pp. 49–62), McCarter sees the so-called apology of the Hittite king Hattusilis III (thirteenth cent. B.C.)—which tells of his rise to power, his rebellion against his nephew and predecessor, and his ascription of success to his patron deity—as a useful model for determining the literary genre of the biblical account of David's rise ("The Apology of David," pp. 495–99). But while there may be some justification for McCarter's assertion that the "Apology of David" ends at 2 Samuel 5:10 (which concludes with the expression "the LORD God Almighty was with him"; cf. v.18), there is little reason for his assumption that it does not begin until 1 Samuel 16:14, since the two halves of chapter 16 are clearly of a piece (cf. S.D. Walters, "The Light and the Dark," in *Ascribe to the Lord: Biblical and Other Studies in Memory of Peter C. Craigie*, edd. Lyle Eslinger and Glen Taylor [Sheffield: JSOT, 1988], pp. 567–89).

## A. *The Rise of David (16:1–28:2)*

Just as the story of the advent of Israelite monarchy (chs. 8–15) begins with an account of the rise of Saul (chs. 8–12), so also the story of the establishment of that monarchy begins with an account of the rise of David. In this case, however, the rise of the latter is so intimately connected with the decline of the former that it occupies much more space in the telling. If at times the stories of Saul and David intersect, at other times they go their own way—only to interlace again and again in what Fokkelman refers to as *The Crossing Fates*. The result makes for one of the most fascinating and engrossing sections of the entire Samuel corpus.

### 1. *The anointing of David*

#### 16:1–13

[1]The LORD said to Samuel, "How long will you mourn for Saul, since I have rejected him as king over Israel? Fill your horn with oil and be on your way; I am sending you to Jesse of Bethlehem. I have chosen one of his sons to be king."

[2]But Samuel said, "How can I go? Saul will hear about it and kill me."

The LORD said, "Take a heifer with you and say, 'I have come to
sacrifice to the LORD.' 3 Invite Jesse to the sacrifice, and I will show you
what to do. You are to anoint for me the one I indicate."
4 Samuel did what the LORD said. When he arrived at Bethlehem, the
elders of the town trembled when they met him. They asked, "Do you
come in peace?"
5 Samuel replied, "Yes, in peace; I have come to sacrifice to the LORD.
Consecrate yourselves and come to the sacrifice with me." Then he
consecrated Jesse and his sons and invited them to the sacrifice.
6 When they arrived, Samuel saw Eliab and thought, "Surely the LORD's
anointed stands here before the LORD."
7 But the LORD said to Samuel, "Do not consider his appearance or his
height, for I have rejected him. The LORD does not look at the things man
looks at. Man looks at the outward appearance, but the LORD looks at the
heart."
8 Then Jesse called Abinadab and had him pass in front of Samuel. But
Samuel said, "The LORD has not chosen this one either." 9 Jesse then
had Shammah pass by, but Samuel said, "Nor has the LORD chosen this
one." 10 Jesse had seven of his sons pass before Samuel, but Samuel
said to him, "The LORD has not chosen these." 11 So he asked Jesse,
"Are these all the sons you have?"
"There is still the youngest," Jesse answered, "but he is tending the
sheep."
Samuel said, "Send for him; we will not sit down until he arrives."
12 So he sent and had him brought in. He was ruddy, with a fine
appearance and handsome features.
Then the LORD said, "Rise and anoint him; he is the one."
13 So Samuel took the horn of oil and anointed him in the presence of
his brothers, and from that day on the Spirit of the LORD came upon
David in power. Samuel then went to Ramah.

One of the many indications that the two halves (vv.1–13, 14–23) of chapter 16 are closely related is that each section is framed by an *inclusio:* "Horn with/of oil" is found in vv.1 and 13, and the phrase "Spirit . . . departed from" constitutes the first words of v.14 and the last words of v.23 (see the MT; cf. Walters, "The Light and the Dark," pp. 569–73, for this and other similarities between the two halves).

In addition to being the middle chapter of 1 Samuel, chapter 16 is pivotal in another way as well: Its first half (vv.1–13), ending with a statement concerning David's reception of the Spirit of God, describes David's anointing as ruler of Israel to replace Saul; its second half (vv.14–23), beginning with a statement concerning Saul's loss of the Spirit and its replacement with an "evil spirit" sent by God, describes David's arrival in the court of Saul. Thus the juxtaposition of vv.13 and 14 delineates not only the transfer of the divine blessing and empowerment from Saul to David but also the beginning of the effective displacement of Saul by David as king of Israel. The transition at vv.13–14 can thus be arguably defined as the literary, historical, and theological crux of 1 Samuel as a whole.

**1–5** After an indeterminate period of time, chapter 16 begins where chapter 15 ends: Samuel is still mourning for Saul (v.1)—perhaps over his loss of kingdom and dynasty, perhaps because of his disobedience, or perhaps for him personally. Ironically, the divine "how long" serves as a prophetic rebuke to the prophet Samuel (so Martin Kessler, "Narrative Technique in 1 Sm 16:1–13," CBQ 32, 4 [1970]: 547 and n. 21). God has rejected Saul as king over Israel (13:13–14; 15:23, 26); thus a change of leadership is in order. The Lord tells Samuel to go to "Jesse of Bethlehem" (v.1), a phrase that appears again in 17:58 and is thus used as an *inclusio* to frame and tie together chapters 16 and 17 (the only other occurrence of the expression is in v.18, where Saul's servant gives a summary description of the young David). At Bethlehem one of Jesse's sons would become the next ruler of Israel by being anointed with oil (as Saul had been anointed earlier, 9:16; 10:1; cf. also 2 Kings 9:1, 3, 6). Jesse of the tribe of Judah (cf. Ruth 4:12, 18–22) and his hometown, Bethlehem in Judah, would forever become associated with the Messiah (Isa 11:1–3, 10; Mic 5:2; Matt 1:1, 5–6, 16–17; 2:4–6).

The Lord also tells Samuel that he has "chosen" (v.1, lit., "seen"; for another case of "see" in the sense of "choose" in connection with the divine election of a king, cf. 2 Kings 10:3) a son of Jesse. Miscall (pp. 115, 118; cf. similarly Kessler, "Narrative Technique in 1 Sm 16:1–13," p. 549) points out that various forms of the root *r'h* ("see") occur throughout the chapter: v.1 ("chosen"), v.6 ("saw"), v.12 ("features"), v.17 ("find"), v.18 ("seen"), and, remarkably, a total of four times in v.7 ("appearance," "look[s] at" [ter] [Heb.]). The contrasting expressions in 8:22 (lit., "make for them a king") and 16:1 (lit., "I have seen . . . for myself a king") stress that while Saul was in reality the people's king, David would become the Lord's king (so Gunn, *The Fate of King Saul,* p. 125; Baldwin, p. 121; cf. similarly "for me" in v.3).

Samuel was understandably afraid that the rejected Saul would kill him if he learned that Samuel was on the way to Bethlehem to anoint Saul's successor (v.2) (for an excellent treatment, cf. John Murray, *Principles of Conduct: Aspects of Biblical Ethics* [Grand Rapids: Eerdmans, 1957], pp. 139–41). The Lord therefore reminded Samuel of an accompanying (if secondary) reason for making the journey: to sacrifice a heifer (presumably as a fellowship offering; cf. Lev 3:1) in conjunction with the ritual of anointing (cf. similarly 9:11–10:1; 11:15). It is unnecessary to refer to God's advice as a "pretext" (or other word with negative connotations) as Calvin (cited in KD, p. 168), Gordon (*I & II Samuel,* p. 150), and others do.

The sacrificial ceremony was for a select few (including Jesse, his sons, and the elders of Bethlehem, vv.4–5) and was therefore by invitation only (v.3; cf. similarly 9:24). God's promise to Samuel—"I [emphatic] will show you what to do"—echoes an early classic passage about prophetic enabling: "I [emphatic] . . . will teach you what to do" (Exod 4:15; cf. also Jesus' assurance to Paul in Acts 9:6). Samuel is left with no doubt concerning God's sovereign role in the choice of Saul's successor: Samuel must anoint for the Lord the one whom the Lord indicates (v.3; cf. Deut 17:15).

Obedient to the Lord's command (v.4), Samuel went to Bethlehem (four miles south-southwest of Jerusalem). Perhaps awed by his formidable reputation (had they heard of the recent execution of Agag [15:33]?), the town elders "trembled when they met him" (as the priest Ahimelech would tremble later when meeting David, 21:1; the same Heb. verb is translated "quaking with fear" in 13:7). They asked Samuel the customary question in such circumstances: "Do you come in peace?" (cf. similarly 1 Kings 2:13; 2 Kings 9:22). Samuel's cordial response allayed their fears as he told them (part of) the reason he had come (v.5). In preparation for entering into God's presence, he had the elders consecrate themselves; then he personally consecrated the specially designated celebrants (Jesse and his sons). Such ceremonial cleansing, whether or not self-administered, was often accompanied by putting on fresh garments to heighten the symbolism (Gen 35:2–3; Exod 19:10–14).

**6–10** Samuel, apparently eager to get on with the anointing of Israel's next king (v.6), "saw" Eliab (meaning "My God Is Father"), "David's oldest brother" (17:28), and felt sure that he was the Lord's chosen one, his "anointed" (*māšîaḥ*; see Notes on 2:10). As though in a courtroom, Samuel sees Eliab as standing "before" the Lord, the Judge (cf. 12:3, where the same Heb. word is translated "in the presence of"). Later hindsight, however, makes it clear that David, not Eliab or any other of Jesse's sons, will occupy a throne that will endure "before" the Lord forever (Ps 89:35–37).

Indeed, the divine response to Samuel's musings (v.7) immediately eliminates Eliab as Israel's future king. God rejects him (as he had rejected Saul, v.1), knowing that Samuel is impressed by Eliab's physique (including especially his "height"—cf. the reference to Saul's height in 9:2 and Samuel's assumption that visible attributes of that kind are important in a king, 10:23–24). What Samuel "saw" externally (v.6) was Eliab's "appearance" (v.7; the same Heb. word underlies both words), but what man "looks at" is not what God "looks at" (again the Heb. root is the same as that in "saw"; "looks at" is used three times in v.7). That God is not man is emphasized here, as it was in 15:29. "Man looks at the outward appearance"—an insight appreciated even by the notorious Machiavelli ("Men in general judge more from appearances than from reality"). Representing a different Hebrew root than earlier in the verse, the second occurrence of the word "appearance" means literally "eyes" (so also v.12; Lev 13:55). Human beings are impressed—and therefore often deceived—by what their eyes tell them, while God looks at the "heart" (cf. also 1 Kings 8:39; 1 Chron 28:9; cf. further 2:3; Isa 11:3; 55:8–9), a contrast highlighted also by Jesus (Luke 16:15).

Abinadab and Shammah, the second and third sons of Jesse (17:13), fared no better than Eliab had. When Abinadab ("My [Divine] Father Is Noble") passed by, Samuel said, "The LORD has not chosen this one either" (v.8), a statement repeated verbatim in the MT with respect to Shammah in v.9 (modified slightly by the NIV, apparently for stylistic variation). The name Shammah is probably an abbreviation of its alternate forms, Shimea and Shimeah (2 Sam 13:3, 32; 21:21 = 1 Chron 20:7; 2:13), and thus means something like "Heard [by God]."

Verse 10 summarizes the rest of the proceedings with respect to the divine rejection of David's brothers. None of the seven is acceptable. It is clear not only from this context but also from 17:12–14 that David is the eighth. First Chronicles 2:13–15, however, lists and numbers Jesse's sons and calls David the "seventh"—an assessment that Josephus apparently agrees with in his account of David's anointing (Antiq. VI, 161 [viii.1]). Walters thus suggests that the reference to David as the eighth son in connection with his anointing is "a witness to an eschatological reading. Since the world was created in seven days, eight is a suitable number to symbolize the beginning of a new order" ("The Light and the Dark," p. 585). The Syriac version of 1 Chronicles 2:15, attempting to harmonize it with 1 Samuel, lists "Elihu" as Jesse's seventh son and David as the eighth. Although an Elihu is named as a "brother of David" in 1 Chronicles 27:18, "Elihu" there may be a variant of "Eliab," or "brother" may be used in its broader sense of "relative." All things considered, it may be best to assume that one of David's seven older brothers died without offspring and is therefore omitted from the genealogy in 1 Chronicles 2:13–15.

**11–13** Samuel, knowing God's determination that one of Jesse's sons will be king (v.1), but also knowing that God has not chosen any of the first seven (v.10), asks Jesse whether he has any other sons (v.11). Jesse informs him that there is one more, the "youngest" (cf. also 17:14), the Hebrew for which can also be translated "smallest."

Perhaps the ambiguity is deliberate here, and a contrast is being drawn not only with Eliab (vv.6–7) but also with Saul (9:2; 10:23; so Kessler, "Narrative Technique in 1 Sm 16:1–13," p. 550). In 11QPs[a] 151, a Hebrew pseudo-Davidic psalm that differs in important essentials from its LXX equivalent, David says, "Smaller was I than my brothers, the youngest of my father's sons. So he made me shepherd of his flock. . . . He sent his prophet to anoint me, Samuel to make me great. My brothers went out to meet him, handsome of figure and of appearance. Though they were tall of stature, handsome because of their hair, the LORD God chose them not" (for the Heb. text, cf. J.A. Sanders, *The Psalms Scroll of Qumran Cave 11 [11QPs[a]]* in *Discoveries in the Judaean Desert of Jordan IV* [Oxford: Clarendon, 1965], p. 55).

Although the NIV translates *w[e]hinnēh* as "but" (v.11), it can just as easily (and thus less negatively and perhaps more appropriately) be rendered "and (in fact)." When we first meet Saul, he is looking for his father's donkeys (9:2–3); when we first meet David, he is tending his father's sheep. Since the metaphors of shepherd and flock for king and people respectively were widespread in the ancient world (cf. references to the king of Babylon as shepherd in the prologue to the Code of Hammurapi, eighteenth century B.C.), Jesse is speaking better than he knows as he unwittingly introduces his youngest son as Israel's next king. In the words of Walters ("The Light and the Dark," p. 574 n. 17): "The shepherd/flock image is a kind of *Leitmotif* for David from this point on. . . . The book's last story shows David deeply concerned for the flock [2 Sam 24:17]" (cf. further 17:15, 20, 28, 34, 40; 2 Sam 5:2; 7:8; cf. also Ezek 34:23).

At Samuel's request, Jesse sends someone to bring David in from the fields (v.12). Ironically, David, while presumably not a tall man, immediately presents a striking appearance. Although physical attractiveness is by no means a necessary attribute for a king, it is here elevated to the status of an important characteristic, if not a prerequisite. David is "ruddy" (cf. also 17:42; elsewhere the Heb. word appears only in Gen 25:25 ["red"], where it describes Esau [= Edom, "Red"] at his birth), not the "pink-cheeked babyface" of Robert North's bizarre translation, which, according to North, makes David suitable as a "therapist for Saul in his advancing insanity" ("David's Rise: Sacral, Military, or Psychiatric?" *Biblica* 63, 4 [1982]: 543).

David has "a fine appearance" (v.12; lit., "beautiful eyes"; cf. v.7 and comment) and "handsome features." Since the phrases are virtually synonymous, their elements are therefore interchangeable (e.g., "fine" plus another word for "appearance" is translated "handsome" in describing David in 17:42). Good looks, while often desirable, contain their obvious pitfalls (cf. Absalom's "handsome appearance," 2 Sam 14:25, or the "very beautiful" Bathsheba, 2 Sam 11:2). Indeed, the most instructive example is the narrator's comparison between Saul and David in his use of *ṭôḇ* ("good") in the sense of "handsome" (David, v.12) and of "impressive" and, negatively, "without equal" (Saul, 9:2). By using the same adjective, "the narrator carefully associates David with Saul and suggests that the 'rise-fall' pattern will be repeated in David" (Preston, p. 38).

No sooner was David brought into Samuel's presence than the Lord commanded Samuel to anoint him as Israel's next ruler (v.12). "He is the one" is literally "He is this one," reminiscent not only of "not . . . this one," "not . . . these" of vv.8–10 with respect to David's older brothers, but also of "This is the man [who] . . . will govern" (9:17) with respect to Saul. If Saul at one time had been God's choice, David is now surely the chosen one.

In v.13 David is mentioned for the first time by name in the books of Samuel. His name was once thought to be related to a supposed *dawidum* ("chief[tain]") found in the Mari letters and elsewhere. It is now known, however, that the reading *da-Wi-du-um* is a syllabic writing for Akkadian *dabdûm* ("defeat," "massacre"; cf. *Assyrian Dictionary*, ed. A. Leo Oppenheim [Chicago: Oriental Institute, 1959], 3:14) and therefore has nothing to do with David's name. It is perhaps best to understand *dāwiḏ* to be a defectively written Qal passive participle of *dwd*, thus meaning "Beloved [of the LORD]" (cf. the similar name Jedidiah [*yᵉḏîḏᵉyāh*], the other name of David's son Solomon [2 Sam 12:25], formed from the Qal passive participle of the byform *ydd* and thus likewise meaning "Beloved of the LORD"). *Dwdh* in line 12 of the Mesha inscription might then be not only a longer (Moabite) form of David's name but also an extrabiblical reference to King David himself (cf. John C.L. Gibson, *Hebrew and Moabite Inscriptions*, vol. 1, in *Textbook of Syrian Semitic Inscriptions* [Oxford: Clarendon, 1971], p. 80).

The narrator links Samuel's anointing of David ("in the presence of his brothers," so that there might be witnesses and also to make it clear that David, although the youngest of Jesse's sons, is truly God's choice) with David's accession of the Spirit of the Lord (v.13). Anointing with oil thus symbolized anointing with the Holy Spirit (cf. Isa 61:1). In David's case the divine accession was permanent ("from that day on"; cf. the similar expression in 30:25, "from that day to this"), while elsewhere the same Hebrew verb allows for the Spirit to come and go (twice for Saul, 10:6, 10; 11:6; three times for Samson, Judg 14:6, 19; 15:14).

Although the work of the Holy Spirit in David's life appears to be qualitatively different from that in the lives of other OT saints, it is often claimed that the normal experience of the Spirit in the OT was external and temporary as compared to the permanent indwelling of the Spirit beginning on the Day of Pentecost (Acts 2:1–4). As Daniel I. Block points out, however, such a view overlooks the indispensable animating role of the Spirit in effecting spiritual renewal in the OT (cf. Deut 30:6), disregards the witness of Psalm 51:10–12 (where David's continued acceptance in the Divine Presence and the salvific work of the Spirit within him represent his only hope), ignores Jesus' rebuke of Nicodemus for being ignorant of the regenerating power of the Spirit (John 3:8–10), and misses the point of Ezekiel 36:25–29, which anticipates the day when the transforming work of the Spirit in the lives of people will be the rule rather than the exception ("The Prophet of the Spirit: The Use of *rwḥ* in the Book of Ezekiel," JETS 32, 1 [1989]: 40–41; cf. also Walter C. Kaiser, Jr., *Toward Rediscovering the Old Testament* [Grand Rapids: Zondervan 1987], pp. 135–41, who emphasizes further the connection of the Holy Spirit with Christ as a distinguishing feature of the NT experience when compared with that of the OT).

Verse 13 concludes with Samuel's prophetic departure for his home in Ramah. Although he makes additional appearances later on, he no longer plays an active role in the books that bear his name. The anointing of David was the capstone to Samuel's career.

## Notes

1 Anointing oil is specially stated to have been poured from an animal "horn" (קֶרֶן, *qeren*) only in the case of David (vv.1, 13) and Solomon (1 Kings 1:39), kings of the united

monarchy during Israel's golden age (cf. also the intricate metaphor, lit., "horn, son of oil," in Isa 5:1 [NIV, "fertile hillside"]). Horns served as convenient receptacles for other precious substances as well (cf. Job 42:14 for the name of Job's third daughter, Keren-Happuch, which means "Horn of Antimony").

7 לֹא אֲשֶׁר יִרְאֶה הָאָדָם (*lō' 'ᵃšer yir'eh hā'āḏām*, lit., "not what man looks at") is translated by the NIV as "[the LORD] does not look at the things man looks at," which correctly assumes an ellipsis (cf. KJV, RSV, and KD, p. 169). Barthélemy suggests an even briefer ellipsis: "‹It is› not ‹a matter of› what man sees" (p. 183). In any case, it is not necessary to assert, with Cross (on the basis of his restoration in 4QSam[b]), that "the phrase יראה האלהים appears to have fallen out by haplography due to *homoioarkton*" ("Oldest Manuscripts," p. 166).

11 Since the Hebrew text of Ecclus 32:1 uses the verb סבב (*sbb*, "surround," "gather around") in the same sense of "sit down," it is not necessary for the NIV footnote to cite "some LXX MSS" as justification for such a rendering.

---

## 2. *The arrival of David in the court of Saul*

### 16:14–23

[14]Now the Spirit of the LORD had departed from Saul, and an evil spirit from the LORD tormented him.

[15]Saul's attendants said to him, "See, an evil spirit from God is tormenting you. [16]Let our lord command his servants here to search for someone who can play the harp. He will play when the evil spirit from God comes upon you, and you will feel better."

[17]So Saul said to his attendants, "Find someone who plays well and bring him to me."

[18]One of the servants answered, "I have seen a son of Jesse of Bethlehem who knows how to play the harp. He is a brave man and a warrior. He speaks well and is a fine-looking man. And the LORD is with him."

[19]Then Saul sent messengers to Jesse and said, "Send me your son David, who is with the sheep." [20]So Jesse took a donkey loaded with bread, a skin of wine and a young goat and sent them with his son David to Saul.

[21]David came to Saul and entered his service. Saul liked him very much, and David became one of his armor-bearers. [22]Then Saul sent word to Jesse, saying, "Allow David to remain in my service, for I am pleased with him."

[23]Whenever the spirit from God came upon Saul, David would take his harp and play. Then relief would come to Saul; he would feel better, and the evil spirit would leave him.

As noted above, the two halves (vv.1–13, 14–23) of chapter 16 are linked together in various ways and therefore constitute a literary unit. One link is the position of David's name. "In each of its first appearances it is the object of a verb: in v.13 the spirit of YHWH 'seizes' (*ṣālaḥ*) David, and in v.19 Saul asks Jesse to 'send' (*šālaḥ*) David to him. . . . The two verbs are very similar in sound, being distinguished only as the two sibilants *ṣ* and *š* are distinguished" (Walters, "The Light and the Dark," pp. 572–73).

In addition, however, the hinge of the chapter underscores, as described in the title of an excellent article by David M. Howard, Jr., "The Transfer of Power From Saul to David in 1 Sam 16:13–14" (JETS 32, 4 [1989]: 473–83). "The movements of the figures here—YHWH's Spirit, Samuel, the evil spirit—in relationship to each other effectively tell the story of the transfer of political power and spiritual power from Saul to David" (ibid., p. 477).

**14–18** The relationships of four movements in vv.13–14 are clarified in the following chart, which exhibits an ABB′A′ pattern:

| | | |
|---|---|---|
| (1) The Spirit of YHWH | comes upon | David (v.13c) |
| (2) Samuel | leaves | David (v.13d) |
| (3) The Spirit of YHWH | leaves | Saul (v.14a) |
| (4) An evil spirit | comes upon | Saul (v.14b) |

Howard summarizes: "When YHWH's Spirit came upon David his anointer left, leaving him in good hands. When YHWH's Spirit left Saul an evil spirit came upon him, leaving him in dire straits" (ibid., p. 481).

The Spirit's coming on David and the Spirit's leaving Saul were two climactic events that occurred in close sequence to each other (cf. esp. 18:12: "The LORD was with David but had left Saul"). Just as the accession of the Spirit by David was an expected accompaniment of his anointing as Israel's next ruler (v.13), so the departure of the Spirit from Saul (v.14) should be understood as the negation of effective rule on his part from that time on. No longer having access to Samuel's counsel, Saul eventually was forced to resort to the desperate expedient of consulting a medium because God had "turned away" from him (28:15; the Heb. verb is the same as the one rendered "departed" in v.14).

The "evil spirit" (v.14), the divinely sent scourge that "tormented" (lit., "terrified," "terrorized") Saul, returned again and again (18:10; 19:9). Just as God had sent an evil spirit to perform his will during the days of Abimelech (Judg 9:23), so also he sent an evil spirit on Saul—"both of whom proved to be unworthy candidates for the office" of king in Israel (Howard, "The Transfer of Power," p. 482). In both instances it was sent in response to their sin, which in Saul's case was particularly flagrant (13:13–14; 15:22–24). Although the "evil" spirit may have been a demon that embodied both moral and spiritual wickedness, it may rather have been an "injurious" (so NIV mg.) spirit that "boded ill for Saul, one that produced harmful results for him" (Howard, "The Transfer of Power," p. 482 n. 36). It was thus doubtless responsible for the mental and psychological problems that plagued Saul for the rest of his life.

That God used alien spirits to serve him is taken for granted in the OT (cf. esp. 2 Sam 24:1 with 1 Chron 21:1). On occasion God's people "were not very concerned with determining secondary causes and properly attributing them to the exact cause. Under the divine providence everything ultimately was attributed to him; why not say he did it in the first place?" (Walter C. Kaiser, Jr., *Hard Sayings of the Old Testament* [Downers Grove: InterVarsity, 1988], p. 131; cf. also Gleason L. Archer, *Encyclopedia of Bible Difficulties* [Grand Rapids: Zondervan, 1982], p. 180: "Saul's evil bent was by the permission and plan of God. We must realize that in the last analysis all penal consequences come from God, as the Author of the moral law and the one who always does what is right [Gen. 18:25]"; cf. Fredrik Lindstrom, *God and the Origin of Evil* [Lund: Gleerup, 1983]).

As French *marechal* ("blacksmith") developed into marshal, and as *chambellan* ("bedchamber attendant") developed into chamberlain, so also *'eḇeḏ* ("servant") came to mean "attendant," "official" in royal circles in Israel, beginning during the days of Saul. The title was conferred on high officials and is found inscribed on their seals. It was also employed side by side with the use of the term as a conventional way of referring to oneself while addressing a superior (cf. conveniently Talmon, p. 64 and nn. 34–36). Thus Saul's "attendants," aware that their king was being tormented by an evil spirit (v.15), referred to themselves as his "servants" (same Heb. word) who were ready and eager to help (v.16; cf. v.17; 17:32, 34, 36; 18:5 ["officers"], 22, 24; 19:1; 28:7).

Perhaps sensing that "music hath charms to soothe the savage breast," Saul's attendants offered to look for someone to play the "harp" (*kinnôr;* cf. comment on 10:5) to make their master "feel better" (v.16). Pictorial representations of the asymmetrical harp or lyre ranging from the twelfth to seventh centuries B.C. can help us visualize what David's harp looked like (cf. *Biblical Archaeology Review* 8, 1 [1982]: 22, 30, and esp. 34). Walters ("The Light and the Dark," p. 582) points out that of the fifteen OT occurrences of *niggēn* ("play [an instrument]"), seven appear in this section of 1 Samuel (vv.16 [bis], 17, 18, 23; 18:10; 19:9) and thus serve at the outset to highlight the reputation of David as "Israel's singer of songs" (2 Sam 23:1).

Saul agreed with his attendants' counsel (v.17), and one of his "servants" (lit., "young men," a different Heb. word than that rendered "attendants" in v.15 and "servants" in v.16) suggested that a certain son of Jesse would meet Saul's needs admirably (v.18). In the course of doing so, the servant gave—in a series of two-worded Hebrew phrases—as fine a portrayal of David as one could wish. Understandably he began with a characterization of him as a musician and then continued by describing him as a "brave man" (the same Heb. phrase is used of Saul's father, Kish, and is translated "man of standing" in 9:1), a "warrior" (translated "fighting man" of Goliath in 17:33 and "experienced fighter" of David in 2 Sam 17:8), a discerning and articulate speaker, and a handsome man as well. The servant's final descriptive phrase—set off from what precedes by a major disjunctive accent in the MT—reminds us that just as the Lord was with Samuel (3:19), so also he was with David. This latter attribute becomes yet another *Leitmotif* for David (17:37; 18:12, 14, 28; 2 Sam 5:10; so Walters, "The Light and the Dark," pp. 570–71; McCarter, "The Apology of David," pp. 499, 503–4). Although unwittingly, Saul's servant has just introduced us to Israel's next king.

A modern assessment of David's character and career sees him as "giant-slayer, shepherd, musician, manipulator of men, outlaw, disguised madman, loyal friend and subject, lover, warrior, dancer and merrymaker, father, brother, son, master, servant, religious enthusiast, and king" and then asks, "What are we to make of this enormous portrait? Where do we begin?" (Kenneth R.R. Gros Louis, "King David of Israel," in *Literary Interpretations of Biblical Narratives*, edd. Kenneth R.R. Gros Louis and James S. Ackerman [Nashville: Abingdon, 1982], 2:205). The rest of our commentary can only tentatively analyze these and other aspects of the personality and deeds of this most complex of all Israelite kings. For now, a gentle irony: Although Saul's servant agreed with the positive contemporary consensus that kings and courtiers should be "fine-looking" (v.18), the same Hebrew word is preceded by a negative particle in its description of great David's greater Son as one who had "no beauty" (Isa 53:2).

**19–23** Again Saul, influenced by a servant's suggestion, sent for the man described: Jesse's son—here, for only the second time so far, identified by the name David (v.19). Saul's reference to David as being "with the sheep" thus identifies him as a shepherd and uses "language which refers allusively to him as a kingly figure"

(Walters, "The Light and the Dark," p. 575). Like Jesse earlier (cf. v.11 and comment), Saul unwittingly characterizes David as Israel's next king.

It is often stated that numerous inconsistencies, especially in matters of detail, exist in the early stories of David and Saul (for a typical list, see Emmanuel Tov, "The Composition of 1 Samuel 16–18 in the Light of the Septuagint Version," in *Empirical Models for Biblical Criticism*, ed. Jeffrey H. Tigay [Philadelphia: University of Pennsylvania, 1985], pp. 121–22). The appropriate response to such alleged discrepancies is not, however, to seek refuge in the fact that in chapters 16–18 "the Masoretic Text has 80 percent more verses than does the LXX" (ibid., p. 99) and thus to attribute the differences to an attempt by the standardizers of the present Hebrew text to include variant readings whether or not they could be harmonized. Nor should one assume the prior existence of two or more different narratives of how David rose to power, along the lines of the now discredited documentary hypothesis (for a lively survey of this approach, cf. North, "David's Rise," pp. 524–44). Much to be preferred is the method of examining each so-called discrepancy on its own merits in an attempt to determine whether it is more apparent than real.

A case in point: If Saul recognizes David as Jesse's son in v.19, why does he later ask him whose son he is (17:58)? In the light of the differing contexts in the two chapters, a possible solution comes to mind. In chapter 16 Saul's initial interest in David was as a harpist, while in chapter 17 he is interested in him primarily as a warrior (according to his customary policy, 14:52). Saul's question in 17:58, in any event, is only a leadoff question; his conversation with David continued far beyond the mere request for his father's name (18:1). He probably wanted to know, among other things, "whether there were any more at home like him" (Archer, *Encyclopedia of Bible Difficulties*, p. 175). It is of course not beyond the realm of possibility that Saul simply forgot the name of David's father during the indeterminate period between chapters 16 and 17.

A firm believer in the truth later expressed in Proverbs 18:16—"a gift opens the way for the giver/and ushers him into the presence of the great"—Jesse sent David to take bread, wine, and a young goat (staple items; cf. 10:3) to Saul (v.20). Obviously impressing Saul (v.21), David "entered his service" (*wayya'ᵃmōḏ lᵉp̱ānāyw*, lit., "stood before him," a common idiom in the ancient Near East [cf. v.22, "remain in my service"]; the Akkadian semantic equivalent is *uzuzzu pani*) as an armor-bearer. Although skilled men can expect to be pressed into service by kings (Prov 22:29), Saul also "liked" David personally (the same Heb. verb describes Jonathan's relationship to David and is translated "loved"; cf. 18:1, 3; 20:17). At the same time the narrator may well be playing on the ambiguity of the verb *'āhēḇ* ("love") in these accounts, since it can also have political overtones in covenant/treaty relationships (so J.A. Thompson, "The Significance of the Verb *Love* in the David-Jonathan Narratives in 1 Samuel," VetTest 24, 3 [1974]: 335).

Obviously delighted with David, Saul engages him as one of his servants (v.22). Sandwiched between the two occurrences of the noun *rûᵃḥ* ("spirit") in v.23 is the verb *rāwaḥ* ("relief would come"). The noun and the verb both come from the same root (*rwḥ*) and thus constitute an elegant wordplay, stressing that David's skill as a harpist brings soothing "relief" that drives the evil "spirit" from the disturbed king (cf. similarly Walters, "The Light and the Dark," p. 578).

The chapter ends with a gifted young man, Israel's future king, coming to serve a rejected and dejected ruler who is totally unaware of the implications of his welcoming David into his court. Not just "a handsome yokel with a rustic lyre," Jesse's son is the anointed king (ibid., p. 581).

## Notes

16 יֹדֵעַ מְנַגֵּן (*yōḏēaʿ menaggēn*, lit., "knows how, plays"; NIV, "can play") is a difficult grammatical construction. Since one MS reads נַגֵּן (*naggēn*) here, and since v.18 reads יֹדֵעַ נַגֵּן (*yōḏēaʿ naggēn*, lit., "knows how to play"; so NIV), it is better to understand the *m* on *mngn* in v.16 to be a misplaced enclitic from the end of the preceding word than to assume that *ydʿ mngn* is a conflation of *ydʿ (l)ngn* and *mngn* (cf. GKC, sec. 120*b* n. 1).

### 3. *The death of Goliath*

#### 17:1–58

1Now the Philistines gathered their forces for war and assembled at
Socoh in Judah. They pitched camp at Ephes Dammim, between Socoh
and Azekah. 2Saul and the Israelites assembled and camped in the
Valley of Elah and drew up their battle line to meet the Philistines. 3The
Philistines occupied one hill and the Israelites another, with the valley
between them.
4A champion named Goliath, who was from Gath, came out of the
Philistine camp. He was over nine feet tall. 5He had a bronze helmet on
his head and wore a coat of scale armor of bronze weighing five
thousand shekels; 6on his legs he wore bronze greaves, and a bronze
javelin was slung on his back. 7His spear shaft was like a weaver's rod,
and its iron point weighed six hundred shekels. His shield bearer went
ahead of him.
8Goliath stood and shouted to the ranks of Israel, "Why do you come
out and line up for battle? Am I not a Philistine, and are you not the
servants of Saul? Choose a man and have him come down to me. 9If he
is able to fight and kill me, we will become your subjects; but if I
overcome him and kill him, you will become our subjects and serve us."
10Then the Philistine said, "This day I defy the ranks of Israel! Give me a
man and let us fight each other." 11On hearing the Philistine's words,
Saul and all the Israelites were dismayed and terrified.
12Now David was the son of an Ephrathite named Jesse, who was
from Bethlehem in Judah. Jesse had eight sons, and in Saul's time he
was old and well advanced in years. 13Jesse's three oldest sons had
followed Saul to the war: The firstborn was Eliab; the second, Abinadab;
and the third, Shammah. 14David was the youngest. The three oldest
followed Saul, 15but David went back and forth from Saul to tend his
father's sheep at Bethlehem.
16For forty days the Philistine came forward every morning and
evening and took his stand.
17Now Jesse said to his son David, "Take this ephah of roasted grain
and these ten loaves of bread for your brothers and hurry to their camp.
18Take along these ten cheeses to the commander of their unit. See how
your brothers are and bring back some assurance from them. 19They are
with Saul and all the men of Israel in the Valley of Elah, fighting against
the Philistines."
20Early in the morning David left the flock with a shepherd, loaded up
and set out, as Jesse had directed. He reached the camp as the army

was going out to its battle positions, shouting the war cry. 21 Israel and
the Philistines were drawing up their lines facing each other. 22 David
left his things with the keeper of supplies, ran to the battle lines and
greeted his brothers. 23 As he was talking with them, Goliath, the
Philistine champion from Gath, stepped out from his lines and shouted
his usual defiance, and David heard it. 24 When the Israelites saw the
man, they all ran from him in great fear.

25 Now the Israelites had been saying, "Do you see how this man
keeps coming out? He comes out to defy Israel. The king will give great
wealth to the man who kills him. He will also give him his daughter in
marriage and will exempt his father's family from taxes in Israel."

26 David asked the men standing near him, "What will be done for the
man who kills this Philistine and removes this disgrace from Israel?
Who is this uncircumcised Philistine that he should defy the armies of
the living God?"

27 They repeated to him what they had been saying and told him, "This
is what will be done for the man who kills him."

28 When Eliab, David's oldest brother, heard him speaking with the
men, he burned with anger at him and asked, "Why have you come
down here? And with whom did you leave those few sheep in the
desert? I know how conceited you are and how wicked your heart is;
you came down only to watch the battle."

29 "Now what have I done?" said David. "Can't I even speak?" 30 He
then turned away to someone else and brought up the same matter, and
the men answered him as before. 31 What David said was overheard and
reported to Saul, and Saul sent for him.

32 David said to Saul, "Let no one lose heart on account of this
Philistine; your servant will go and fight him."

33 Saul replied, "You are not able to go out against this Philistine and
fight him; you are only a boy, and he has been a fighting man from his
youth."

34 But David said to Saul, "Your servant has been keeping his father's
sheep. When a lion or a bear came and carried off a sheep from the
flock, 35 I went after it, struck it and rescued the sheep from its mouth.
When it turned on me, I seized it by its hair, struck it and killed it. 36 Your
servant has killed both the lion and the bear; this uncircumcised
Philistine will be like one of them, because he has defied the armies of
the living God. 37 The LORD who delivered me from the paw of the lion
and the paw of the bear will deliver me from the hand of this Philistine."

Saul said to David, "Go, and the LORD be with you."

38 Then Saul dressed David in his own tunic. He put a coat of armor on
him and a bronze helmet on his head. 39 David fastened on his sword
over the tunic and tried walking around, because he was not used to
them.

"I cannot go in these," he said to Saul, "because I am not used to
them." So he took them off. 40 Then he took his staff in his hand, chose
five smooth stones from the stream, put them in the pouch of his
shepherd's bag and, with his sling in his hand, approached the
Philistine.

41 Meanwhile, the Philistine, with his shield bearer in front of him, kept
coming closer to David. 42 He looked David over and saw that he was
only a boy, ruddy and handsome, and he despised him. 43 He said to
David, "Am I a dog, that you come at me with sticks?" And the Philistine
cursed David by his gods. 44 "Come here," he said, "and I'll give your
flesh to the birds of the air and the beasts of the field!"

45 David said to the Philistine, "You come against me with sword and
spear and javelin, but I come against you in the name of the LORD
Almighty, the God of the armies of Israel, whom you have defied. 46 This
day the LORD will hand you over to me, and I'll strike you down and cut

off your head. Today I will give the carcasses of the Philistine army to
the birds of the air and the beasts of the earth, and the whole world will
know that there is a God in Israel. 47All those gathered here will know
that it is not by sword or spear that the LORD saves; for the battle is the
LORD's, and he will give all of you into our hands."

48As the Philistine moved closer to attack him, David ran quickly
toward the battle line to meet him. 49Reaching into his bag and taking
out a stone, he slung it and struck the Philistine on the forehead. The
stone sank into his forehead, and he fell facedown on the ground.

50So David triumphed over the Philistine with a sling and a stone;
without a sword in his hand he struck down the Philistine and killed him.

51David ran and stood over him. He took hold of the Philistine's sword
and drew it from the scabbard. After he killed him, he cut off his head
with the sword.

When the Philistines saw that their hero was dead, they turned and
ran. 52Then the men of Israel and Judah surged forward with a shout
and pursued the Philistines to the entrance of Gath and to the gates of
Ekron. Their dead were strewn along the Shaaraim road to Gath and
Ekron. 53When the Israelites returned from chasing the Philistines, they
plundered their camp. 54David took the Philistine's head and brought it
to Jerusalem, and he put the Philistine's weapons in his own tent.

55As Saul watched David going out to meet the Philistine, he said to
Abner, commander of the army, "Abner, whose son is that young man?"

Abner replied, "As surely as you live, O king, I don't know."

56The king said, "Find out whose son this young man is."

57As soon as David returned from killing the Philistine, Abner took
him and brought him before Saul, with David still holding the Philistine's head.

58"Whose son are you, young man?" Saul asked him.

David said, "I am the son of your servant Jesse of Bethlehem."

Just as Samuel's anointing of Saul (10:1) was followed by Saul's defeat of Nahash and the Ammonites (11:1–11), so also Samuel's anointing of David (16:13) was followed by David's defeat of Goliath and the Philistines (ch. 17). Although lacking time frames, the impression in both instances is that the Israelite victory occurred fairly soon after the anointing and thus demonstrated the courage, determination, and military expertise of the newly anointed leader.

The exciting story of David and Goliath is an excellent example of an attempt at representative warfare effected by means of a contest of champions. The purpose of such contests was "to obviate the necessity of a general engagement of troops which would spill more blood than necessary to resolve the dispute" (Harry A. Hoffner, Jr., "A Hittite Analogue to the David and Goliath Contest of Champions?" CBQ 30 [1968]: 220). Whether this kind of radical limitation on warfare is ever sincerely accepted by either side remains in itself a matter of dispute (for a nuanced treatment of the issue, cf. George I. Mavrodes, "David, Goliath, and Limited War," *Reformed Journal* 33, 8 [1983]: 6–8). It is clear, however, that contests of champions (to be carefully distinguished from duels, which are individual combats not representing larger groups) such as that between David and Goliath or between Menelaus and Paris (Homer *Iliad* bk. 3) were not uncommon in ancient times (for additional examples, see Hoffner, "A Hittite Analogue," pp. 220–25).

Partly because the LXX text of chapter 17 is shorter than the MT, some assert that the David-Goliath story weaves together two or more separate accounts without regard to possible discrepancies (cf. Emmanuel Tov, "The David and Goliath Saga: How a Biblical Editor Combined Two Versions," *Bible Review* 11, 4 [1986]: 35–41).

But David W. Gooding, among others, argues for the unity and integrity of the chapter in spite of the alleged differences between the LXX and the MT ("An Approach to the Literary and Textual Problems in the David–Goliath Story: 1 Sam 16–18," in Dominique Barthélemy, David W. Gooding, Johan Lust, and Emmanuel Tov, *The Story of David and Goliath: Textual and Literary Criticism* [Göttingen: Vandenhoeck and Ruprecht, 1986], pp. 55–86, 99–106, 114–20, 145–54). Indeed, close readings of the text in recent years have tended to regard the finished canonical narrative as an exquisitely structured whole. For example, T.A. Boogaart ("History and Drama in the Story of David and Goliath," *Reformed Review* 38 [1985]: 205) perceptively observes that vv.1–54 constitute a cycle of confrontation-challenge-consternation repeated three times:

I. Goliath's Challenge (vv.1–11)
   A. Confrontation: Philistines and Israelites Face Each Other; Goliath Appears (vv.1–7)
   B. Challenge: Goliath Defies the Ranks of Israel (vv.8–10)
   C. Consternation: Saul and Israel Are Dismayed and Terrified (v.11)

II. David Witnesses Goliath's Challenge (vv.12–39)
   A. Confrontation: David Appears in the Israelite Camp; Philistines and Israelites Face Each Other (vv.12–22)
   B. Challenge: David Hears Goliath Defying the Ranks of Israel (v.23)
   C. Consternation: David Converses With the Fearful Israelites, His Angry Brother, and an Indecisive Saul (vv.24–39)

III. David Meets Goliath's Challenge (vv.40–54)
   A. Confrontation: David and Goliath Face Each Other (vv.40–41)
   B. Challenge: David and Goliath Summon Each Other; David Kills Goliath (vv.42–51a)
   C. Consternation: Philistines Flee From Israelites (vv.51b–54)

This commentary will assume the validity of Boogaart's basic structure without following it slavishly.

**1–3** The imminent battle against the Philistines described in this chapter is only one of many that involved Saul's troops (cf. 13:12–14:46 and the summary statement in 14:47) since the Philistines were his inveterate enemies throughout his reign (14:52). On this occasion (v.1) the Philistines gathered "their forces" (lit., "their camps"; v.53 ends with the same Heb. phrase [NIV, "their camp"], thus forming an *inclusio* around the narrative) between Socoh and Azekah, two towns in the western foothills of Judah (Josh 15:20, 33, 35).

Modern Khirbet Abbad (seventeen miles west-southwest of Jerusalem) is the location of ancient Socoh, which was two and one-half miles southeast of Azekah (modern Khirbet Tell Zakariyeh). The latter town later became famous as one of the last two (the other being Lachish) to fall to Nebuchadnezzar II before the destruction of Jerusalem by the Babylonians in 586 B.C. (Jer 34:7; Lachish letter 4:10–13). The precise location of Ephes Dammim (called Pas Dammim in 1 Chron 11:13; cf. also 2 Sam 23:9 and comment), the Philistine campsite, is unknown but was probably on the southern slopes of the Valley of Elah (v.2; the modern Wadi es-Sant) and about a mile south of Azekah. The Israelite camp, on the northern slopes of the valley and perhaps less than a mile northeast of Socoh, was thus less than three miles east of Ephes Dammim.

The contest between David and Goliath took place on the floor of the valley itself, about halfway between (v.3) the two opposing campsites. (For a map of the area showing the major routes and locations, cf. Rasmussen, p. 113.)

**4–7** The portrayal of Goliath may well be "the most detailed physical description of any found in scripture" (Boogaart, "The Story of David and Goliath" p. 207). In agreement with the non-Semitic background of the Philistines, the name "Goliath" (*golyaṯ*) is best connected with such Indo-European names as the Lydian *Aluattēs* (cf. William F. Albright, CAH[3], 2.2.33, p. 513 n. 8; Kitchen, "The Philistines," p. 67). In vv.4 and 23 Goliath is called a "champion" (*'îš-habbēnayim*). The Hebrew phrase, found nowhere else in the OT, means literally "the man between two [armies]" (BDB, p. 108) and is attested at Qumran in the sense of "infantryman." In Ugaritic a similar expression, *bnš bnny*, means "middleman," "intermediary," "representative" (William F. Albright, "Specimens of Late Ugaritic Prose," BASOR 150 [1958]: 38 n. 12). Gath (modern Tell es-Safi), Goliath's hometown, was located five miles due west of Azekah.

By any standard of measure, the Philistine champion was a giant of a man (v.4). Some LXX MSS give his height as "four cubits and a span" (so also 1QSam[a]; Jos. Antiq. VI, 171 [ix. 1]), others "five cubits and a span." The MT reads "six cubits and a span" (thus NIV mg.), making him "over nine feet tall." Other comparable heights in the OT are those of "an Egyptian who was seven and a half feet tall" (1 Chron 11:23) and Og king of Bashan, whose size is not specified but whose bed/sarcophagus was "more than thirteen feet long" (Deut 3:11). The MT account of Goliath's height is paralleled in modern times by reports concerning Robert Pershing Wadlow, who was eight feet eleven inches tall at the time of his death on July 15, 1940, at the age of twenty-two (*Insight* [18, 1985]: 51).

Goliath's armor and weapons are described at length (vv.5–7; for a useful summary together with photographs and drawings of Philistine and similar weaponry, see especially Yadin, *The Art of Warfare*, pp. 265–66, 336–41, 344, 354–55). The Hebrew term for "helmet" in vv.5, 38 (*k/qôḇa'*) is doubtless a loanword from Hittite *kupaḫ(ḫ)i* (T.C. Mitchell, "Philistia," in *Archaeology and Old Testament Study*, ed. D. Winton Thomas [Oxford: Clarendon, 1967], p. 415).

A coat of mail such as Goliath's was fashioned from several hundred small bronze plates (cf. Yadin, *The Art of Warfare*, pp. 196–97) that resembled fish scales (the Heb. masc. pl. word for "scale" in v.5 is used of fish scales in its fem. sing. form in Lev 11:9–10, 12; Deut 14:9–10) and had to meet the needs of protection, lightness, and freedom of movement (ibid., p. 354). The weight of Goliath's armor is thus all the more impressive (NIV mg., "about 125 pounds"). David, however, scorned both helmet and armor, finding his ultimate protection in God himself (vv.38–39, 45).

Like his helmet and coat of mail, the rest of Goliath's defensive armor was also made of bronze (v.6). Greaves protected the legs below the knee, and javelins were probably used to fend off attackers as often as they were used in offensive maneuvers. Goliath's most formidable offensive weapon seems to have been his spear (v.7), whose heavy "point" (lit., "flame," referring to its shape) was made of iron (a metal monopolized by the Philistines and denied to the Israelite troops; cf. comment on 13:19–22). Its shaft was "like a weaver's rod" (cf. also 2 Sam 21:19 = 1 Chron 20:5; 11:23), the leash rod of a loom (a block of wood separating the threads of the warp to offer passage for the threads of the woof), in that it had a loop and a cord wound around it so that the spear "could be hurled a greater distance with greater stability by virtue of the resultant spin" (Yadin, *The Art of Warfare*, pp. 354–55). Goliath's sword, although not mentioned until later in the chapter (vv.45, 51), doubtless had an iron blade. Receiving added protection from the large shield (*ṣinnāh;* cf. 1 Kings 10:16 = 2 Chron 9:15; cf. further de Vaux, AIs, pp. 244–45) carried by his aide, the Philistine giant must have felt—and appeared—invincible.

**8–11** Goliath hurls the challenge of representative combat into the teeth of the Israelite army (vv.8–10). Priding himself on his Philistine heritage, he addresses the Israelites as Saul's "servants" (v.8), an ambiguous term that can mean either "officials" or "slaves" (cf. comment on 16:15–16). What Goliath intends by it becomes readily apparent, however, in v.9, when he uses the same Hebrew word in the clear sense of "subjects" and then follows it with the verb "serve" (again from the same Heb. root). The Philistines (so Goliath thinks) will win a quick and easy victory over Israel, who will then be enslaved by them. But although Goliath means to "defy the ranks of Israel" (v.10; cf. v.25), David sees him as defying "the armies of the living God" (vv.26, 36)—yea, even God himself (v.45, although the relative *'ᵃšer* ["whom"] could also be translated "which" and thus refer again to the armies).

Having thrown down the gauntlet, the Philistine challenger at first had no takers. In fact, Saul and his troops (v.11) were "dismayed and terrified" (a common Heb. verbal pairing, elsewhere always reversed; cf. "be afraid . . . be discouraged" in Deut 1:21; 31:8; Josh 8:1; 10:25; 1 Chron 22:13; 28:20; 2 Chron 20:15, 17; 32:7; "be afraid or terrified" in Jer 23:4; Ezek 2:6; 3:9; "fear . . . be dismayed" in Jer 30:10; 46:27). Barring the response of an Israelite hero, Goliath would win by default, and the Philistines would continue to be Israel's masters.

**12–16** Again we are introduced to David, Jesse's son (v.12; see comment on 16:19). Jesse, like Elimelech during the days of the judges (Ruth 1:1–2), was an Ephrathite from Judahite Bethlehem. It is clear from Genesis 35:19; 48:7; Joshua 15:59a LXX; Ruth 4:11; and Micah 5:2 that Ephrath(ah) was another name for Bethlehem in Judah (as opposed to Bethlehem in Zebulun, Josh 19:10, 15). Jesse, already an "old" man (perhaps an "elder"; see Notes) during Saul's reign, had eight sons, the first three of whom are again named here (v.13; cf. 16:6–11 and comment).

Jesse's three oldest sons, loyal warriors all, "followed" Saul into battle (vv.13–14). The MT emphasizes this fact by repeating the verb (lit., "walked [after]") three times in the two verses (NIV omits it once in v.13 for stylistic reasons). By contrast David—"the youngest" (v.14)—"went back and forth [lit., 'was walking and returning'] from Saul" (v.15). Although having entered Saul's service earlier (16:21), David was currently engaged in his main task, tending his father's sheep—in preparation for a more important shepherding task later (cf. comments on 16:11, 19; cf. further the similar description of Moses in Exod 3:1). Scornful of all such activity, Goliath came forward twice a day (v.16) for forty days (a month and then some; cf. Segal, "Numerals," pp. 10–11) in continuing, taunting defiance. He "took his stand," like the kings of the earth in Psalm 2:2 (same Heb. verb), "against the LORD and against his anointed one" (Ps 2:2 NIV mg.).

**17–22** Boogaart ("The Story of David and Goliath," p. 204) notes that Jesse's command to David was threefold: (1) to take provisions to David's brothers and their unit commander, (2) to find out how his brothers were getting along, and (3) to bring back a token (cf. v.18 NIV mg.) of their welfare (vv.17–18). He further observes that David fulfilled the first two parts of the command upon arriving at the camp (v.22; cf. also v.23) but the third part not until the end of the account when he took Goliath's head and armor as trophies of war (v.54).

The urgency of Jesse's command ("Hurry," v.17; cf. 20:6; lit., "run," as in vv.22, 48, 51—in each case stressing the youthful eagerness and energy that characterized David in this chapter) underscores his concern for his sons' well-being and safety (cf. similarly Jacob in Gen 37:13–14). Jesse sent along the staple items of roasted grain (cf. Ruth 2:14) and bread for David's brothers, while for the commander of their unit he provided a gift of "ten cheeses" (v.18; cf. Segal, "Numerals," p. 5). Jesse's observation that David's brothers and their comrades-in-arms were "fighting against the Philistines" (v.19) was doubtless spoken with pride and intended as a gentle rebuke to David.

The rest of chapter 17 describes David's transformation from being a shepherd of flocks to becoming a leader of people. He "left" his father's flock with a "shepherd" (v.20; lit., "keeper"), and he "left" his "things" with the "keeper" of the "supplies" (v.22; the term is used in the sense of "military supplies" in 25:13; 30:24; cf. the comment on "baggage" in 10:22). In v.20 the rare word translated "camp" (*ma'gāl;* elsewhere in this sense only in 26:5, 7) means literally "wagon-wheel track" and probably refers to the "tracks" made by supply wagons that outlined the perimeter of the camp. David used the word metaphorically in the Shepherd Psalm ("paths of righteousness," Ps 23:3).

When he reached the battle lines, David "greeted" (v.22) his brothers (lit. Heb., "asked concerning [their] welfare/well-being [*šālôm*]," the same word used by Jesse in v.18: "how [they] are"; cf. the comment at 10:4; cf. also the English greeting "How are you?").

**23–30** Even from a distance Goliath's defiant challenge appears to have been loud enough to interrupt David's conversation with his brothers (v.23). The mere sight of the giant was enough to cause the men of Israel to flee in disorder and panic ("ran" in v.24 [lit., "fled"] does not translate the same verb as in v.22; unlike his fellow Israelites, who "ran from" Goliath, David "ran . . . to meet him" [v.48] and "ran and stood over him" [v.51]). The narrator reminds us that nothing has changed in more than a month (v.16): The same Hebrew phrase translated "terrified" in v.11 is translated "in great fear" in v.24.

Boogaart ("The Story of David and Goliath," pp. 208–9) points out the strong contrast between "the soldiers' words of resignation" (v.25) and "David's words of indignation" (v.26): The men of Israel call Goliath "this man," David calls him "this uncircumcised Philistine"; they say that Goliath has come out to "defy Israel," David says that he has come out to "defy the armies of the living God"; they refer to Goliath's potential victor as "the man who kills him," David refers to him as "the man who kills this Philistine and removes this disgrace from Israel." In short, the men of Israel "see an insuperable, fearsome giant who is reproaching Israel; David sees merely an uncircumcised Philistine who has the audacity to reproach the armies of the living God" (ibid., p. 208).

Giving one's daughter in marriage as a reward for faithful service (v.25) was not unprecedented in Israel (cf. Josh 15:13–17, where, again, the foe consisted of men of unusually tall stature, in this case the Anakites; cf. Num 13:32–33; Deut 1:28; 2:10,

21; 9:2). In addition, Saul promised great wealth to Goliath's victor as well as making his father's family *ḥop̱šî* ("exempt") in Israel. Although N.P. Lemche has recently suggested that here this term refers to receiving "supplies from the royal household" ("חפשי in 1 Sam. xvii 25," VetTest 24, 3 [1974]: 374), such an offer would be anticlimactic in light of the "great wealth" mentioned earlier in the verse. Considering all the evidence from within the OT itself ("free[d]"; Exod 21:2, 5, 26–27; Deut 15:12, 18; Job 3:19; Isa 58:6; Jer 34:9–11, 14, 16) as well as from elsewhere in the ancient Near East (the *ḫupšū,* mentioned in the Nuzi documents, Ugaritic literature, Amarna tablets, Assyrian laws, and Late Assyrian texts, were "free-born people" who "engaged primarily in agricultural pursuits as small land-holders and tenant-farmers" [I. Mendelsohn, "New Light on the *ḫupšū,*" BASOR 139 (1955): 11]), the NIV's "exempt his father's family from taxes" remains the best understanding of the passage in this context (cf. de Vaux, AIs, p. 88; McCarter, *I Samuel,* p. 304; Talmon, pp. 65–66).

In righteous indignation David implicitly offers himself to fight Goliath (v.26), an offer that becomes explicit in v.32. Nahash the Ammonite had intended to "bring disgrace on all Israel" (11:2), and in David's eyes the presence of Goliath the "uncircumcised Philistine" (cf. comment on 14:6) has already brought on Israel disgrace that must be removed (cf. further Isa 25:8). The Hebrew root for "disgrace" in v.26 is the same for "defy" later in the verse: Goliath is disgracing/defying Israel, and David—with God's help—intends to remove that disgrace/defiance. Since "defy" in v.26 answers to "defy" in v.25 (Boogaart, "The Story of David and Goliath," p. 208), the last sentence in v.26—especially in light of *kî* introducing a clause after an interrogative clause—should doubtless be translated as follows: "Who is this uncircumcised Philistine? Why should he defy the armies of the living God?" (cf. comment on 11:5). Despite what the Philistines may think or believe, their god Dagon is a destroyed, dead idol (5:3–4). By contrast "the LORD is the true God;/ he is the living God, the eternal King" (Jer 10:10; cf. also Deut 5:26; 2 Sam 22:47; Jer 23:36).

Verses 27–30 constitute a literary unit framed by *wayyō'mer . . . kaddāḇār hazzeh* (lit., "And said . . . according to this word"), translated "repeated . . . what they had been saying" in v.27 and "brought up the same matter" in v.30. Both framing verses respond to David's desire to know what would be done for the man who killed Goliath (v.26), the details of which had been given in v.25.

Just as Joseph's older brothers reacted with jealous hatred to his dreams of sovereignty over them (Gen 37:4–36), so also David's oldest brother, Eliab, misunderstood and angrily questioned David's motives for coming down to the battlefield. Eliab, angered at David's seeming irresponsibility, unknowingly underscored David's transition from shepherd to ruler when he referred to the fact that David would "leave" a few sheep (v.28; see comment on "left" in v.20). David's response to Eliab was respectful but firm (v.29).

**31** David's expressions of bravado were reported to Saul, who then decided that he wanted to talk to the young shepherd. "Sent for" and "took" (v.40) translate the same Hebrew verb and are probably intended to form an *inclusio* circumscribing this pericope (for other unifying features of the passage, cf. Anthony R. Ceresko, "A Rhetorical Analysis of David's 'Boast' [1 Samuel 17:34–37]: Some Reflections on Method," CBQ 47, 1 [1985]: 61–62).

**32–33** Knowing that the Lord is on his side, David offers to fight Goliath (v.32) in spite of the overwhelming odds against him (cf. Deut 20:1–4). His confident statement, "Let no one lose heart," is made all the more specific by the overly eager LXX (and some OL MSS): "Let not the king lose heart." But Saul, unimpressed, insists that a fight between David and Goliath would be a mismatch (v.33): "You" (emphatic pronoun) are "only a boy," while "he" (emphatic pronoun) has been a "fighting man" ever since his boyhood days. Goliath, of course, would agree with Saul's assessment and would despise David because he was "only a boy" (v.42). David would also agree with Saul's "You are not able to go out" against the Philistines—but not in the sense that Saul intended. "I," says David, "cannot go" (v.39; the Heb. echoes Saul's warning) wearing this heavy armor because I am not used to it. As for Goliath's reputation as a "fighting man," David has already been referred to as a "warrior" (same Heb. phrase) earlier in the text (16:18). The odds are therefore much more even than either Saul or Goliath might imagine, especially when the divine element is added to the equation.

**34–35** In vv.34–37 David demonstrates beyond cavil that he "speaks well" (16:18). Though others may flee from lions and bears (Amos 5:19), David does not. It would not be at all inappropriate to compare Goliath with "a roaring lion or a charging bear" (Prov 28:15). As a shepherd "keeping his father's sheep" (v.34; cf. 16:11), David often rescued them from the mouths of dangerous animals (v.35; cf. also Amos 3:12). When they turned to attack him, he "struck . . . and killed" (v.35) them. As a newly established leader of his Father's people, David soon "struck . . . and killed" the dangerous Goliath (v.50).

**36–37** The comparison between David as a herder of sheep and David as a leader of people ("The armies [flock] of the living God [father] were being threatened by a predator [Goliath]," Boogaart, "The Story of David and Goliath," p. 209) is made even more explicit in vv.36–37. Goliath will be "like" (v.36) the lion or the bear, both of whom David had killed. As God had delivered David from the "paw" (lit., "hand") of the lion and of the bear, so he (an emphatic pronoun, untr. in NIV but answering to the "he" of v.33 [used there of Goliath], is the subject of the verb) would also deliver him from the "hand" of the Philistine (v.37; cf. further Exod 18:9–10). Another more subtle comparison is also evident: As David routinely "rescued" sheep from wild animals (v.35), so also God had "delivered" David from them and would thus "deliver" him from Goliath (v.37; same Heb. verb). Indeed, deliverance from enemies depicted as predatory animals is a not uncommon motif in Scripture (Ps 22:21; cf. also 2 Tim 4:17).

Saul, again impressed by David's bravado (cf. v.31), now tells him to "Go" (v.37)—a command he was not initially willing to give him (v.33). Saul's added expression of encouragement ("the Lord be with you") echoes the original description of David given by Saul's servant (16:18) and unwittingly calls attention to the tragically disparate spiritual conditions of Saul and David (16:13–14).

**38–40** Saul, desirous of giving David every advantage, clothed him in the same kind of armor and crowned him with the same kind of helmet that Goliath wore (v.38; cf. v.5). He also gave him his own "tunic" (v.38) and "sword" (v.39). Since it was believed that to wear the clothing of another was to be imbued with his essence and to share his very being (cf. Johs. Pedersen, *Israel: Its Life and Culture. I–II* [London:

Oxford, 1926], pp. 302–3), these latter acts were probably calculated to so bind Saul to David that Saul would be able to take credit for, or at least to share in, David's victory over the Philistine giant. In a similar way Jonathan would soon give David, among other things, his own "tunic" and "sword" (18:4) as visible tokens of his covenant love for him (18:3).

David, however, denied Saul his potential moment of glory. Saul had said "Go" (v.37); but David, after "walking around," insisted that he could not "go" while wearing Saul's armor (v.39; same Heb. verb in all three cases) because, not being used to it, he would be weighed down and therefore slowed down by it. After taking the armor off, he selected five sling stones (v.40) from the streambed in the Valley of Elah. Such stones were part of the normal repertoire of weapons in the ancient world (cf. 2 Chron 26:14) and were usually balls two or three inches in diameter and manufactured from flint (Ovid R. Sellers, "Sling Stones in Biblical Times," BA 2, 4 [1939]: 41–42, 45). David, however, had a ready supply of naturally spherical stones of the right size at hand. The sling itself "consisted of two long cords with a pocket in the center. The slinger placed a stone in the pocket, grasped the ends of the cords, whirled the stone, and shot by releasing one of the cords" (ibid., p. 42; cf. Judg 20:16; 1 Chron 12:2; cf. further Yadin, *The Art of Warfare*, pp. 9–10, 364). Armed only with his shepherd's staff and the five sling stones "in the pouch of his shepherd's bag" (v.40), David the Israelite shepherd strides forth to do battle with Goliath the Philistine champion.

**41–42** Together with his aide carrying a large shield (v.41; cf. v.7 and comment there), the huge Goliath must have considered himself invincible. He failed to understand, however, that he and his shield bearer were no match for David and his God. Goliath's observation merely echoed Saul's opinion that David, far from being a worthy opponent, was "only a boy" (v.42; cf. v.33). The Philistine, who "despised" David, was not impressed that he was "ruddy and handsome" (cf. 16:12). Goliath, unfortunately, did not reckon with the truth that such egotistical pride "goes before destruction,/ a haughty spirit before a fall" (Prov 16:18).

**43–44** Apparently not noticing David's sling, or at least discounting its potential lethal effectiveness against his full suit of armor, Goliath perceived that David was coming to fight against him with "sticks" (v.43; the singular form of the same Heb. word is translated "staff" in v.40). Such weapons, he implied, would be appropriate for beating a "dog" (*keleḇ*), the lowest of animals (cf. similarly 24:14; 2 Sam 3:8; 9:8; 16:9; in Deut 23:18 the word is an epithet applied to a male prostitute; Akkadian *kalbu* and Ugaritic *klb* are used in similarly pejorative senses), but would be of no use whatever in trying to defeat a champion like himself. He therefore cursed David "by" (i.e., "by invoking," "in the name of"; cf. 2 Kings 2:24) his "gods" (or "god," as the Heb. word may also be translated; perhaps the reference is to Dagon, the main Philistine deity during this period; cf. comment and Notes on 5:2). Part of the content of his curse was that he intended to give David's flesh to the "birds of the air and the beasts of the field" (v.44)—a curse that, in typical Near Eastern fashion, David promptly hurled back into his teeth (v.46; cf. also Jer 34:20).

**45–47** David's responding taunt begins and ends with reference to the ineffectiveness and irrelevance of "sword and spear" (vv.45, 47; in short supply in Israel in any case; cf. 13:19, 22) when the God of Israel is involved in the battle (for other rhetorical features binding these three verses together, cf. Ceresko, "David's 'Boast,'" pp. 73–74 n. 56). "You" (Goliath; v.45, emphatic pronoun) and "I" (David; emphatic pronoun) possess weapons that belong to totally different realms (cf. 2 Chron 32:7–8; 2 Cor 10:3–4). David fights Goliath "in the name of" the Lord—that is, "as his representative" (BDB, p. 102; cf. 25:5, 9; 2 Sam 6:18; Exod 5:23; Deut 10:8; 2 Chron 14:11). One of the names of the "God of the armies of Israel" is the regal name "LORD Almighty" (lit., "LORD of Hosts/Armies"—although the Heb. word for "armies" is different in the two expressions and therefore "armies of Israel" cannot be used, without further ado, to define "Hosts" in the name "LORD Almighty"; cf. comment on 1:3 for details). Goliath is on perilous ground: To defy "the armies of Israel" (v.45) is to defy "the armies of the living God" (v.36; cf. comment on v.10) and is tantamount to defying God himself (the relative pronoun "whom," which the NIV takes as referring to God in v.45, could also be translated "which" in reference to "armies").

Anxious to get on with the contest (v.48), David asserts (v.46) that Goliath will be killed "this day," "today" (same Heb.). The Lord, says David to Goliath, will "hand you over to me" (lit., "deliver you into my hand"; cf. 24:18; 26:8, the only other occurrences of the Heb. idiom using the Piel). David threatens to "cut off" the giant's head (lit., "remove," translating a different Heb. verb from that used in v.51). David's next words may reflect that section of the Ugaritic Baal epic

> in which Anath threshes the death-god, Mot. We are there told (*a*) that Mot's body will be food for the birds of the air, and, subsequently, (*b*) that El receives a sign that Baal "lives" and "exists." Thus the narrative of the combat between David and Goliath may be a polemical allusion to these features: David's victory will leave the foe slain on the battlefield as food for the birds, and thus "all the earth may know that God exists [*yēš*] for Israel," which is how the final words in the quotation may also be translated. (Tryggve N.D. Mettinger, *In Search of God: The Meaning and Message of the Everlasting Names* [Philadelphia: Fortress, 1988], p. 87)

The contrast would then be between dead idols—like the Philistine god Dagon—and the living God (cf. also Isa 37:4, 17, 19; Jer 10:1–16). Even though *kol-hā'āreṣ* ("the whole world," v.46) should perhaps be here translated "the whole land" (i.e., the land of Israel, as often; cf. "All those gathered here," v.47), the point remains the same: All who hear will know that the God of Israel is the only true God. In addition, they will know that the Lord, not weapons of war (cf. also Ps 44:3, 6–7) or a human instrument, is the true Deliverer (v.47), a fact understood by Jonathan as well (14:6). "The battle" belongs to him alone (2 Chron 20:15).

David began his taunt to Goliath by referring to "you" and "I" (v.45), emphatic singular pronouns that echoed Goliath's challenge in v.44. He concludes by warning that God would give "you" (pl.) into "our" (pl.) hands (v.47), thus reminding Goliath of his own earlier intention that their battle was indeed representative warfare, the results of which would have profound implications for the Philistines and Israelites as a whole (vv.8–9).

**48–49** Undeterred, Goliath moved closer to "attack" (v.48) David, who in turn wasted no time in running (cf. also vv.22, 51) forward to "meet" him (same Heb. verb). One sling stone sufficed; it felled the Philistine, who—like the idol of his god Dagon in an earlier episode—toppled to the ground facedown (v.49; cf. 5:4). As inevitably as a prisoner sinks into the mud at the bottom of a cistern (Jer 38:6), so David's stone sank into Goliath's forehead.

**50–51a** With only a sling and a stone, not with a sword, David vanquished Goliath. As David had earlier "struck . . . and killed" wild animals threatening his father's sheep (v.35), so now he "struck down the Philistine and killed him" (v.50). The Hebrew of vv.50–51 is ambiguous (probably unintentionally) concerning whether David killed Goliath with a sling stone or with Goliath's own sword. Boogaart's analysis ("The Story of David and Goliath," p. 214 n. 8) seems best: Verse 50 is the narrator's personal comment, stating that David "killed" Goliath (eventually) and anticipating "the death of Goliath which is not recorded until verse 51." David did not kill Goliath with an Israelite sword (v.50); irony of ironies, he did it with Goliath's own sword (v.51; cf. similarly Benaiah's exploit in 2 Sam 23:21). Baldwin summarizes: "The stone had stunned the giant, and now the sword must kill him" (p. 128; cf. Ariella Deem, " 'And the Stone Sank Into His Forehead': A Note on 1 Samuel xvii 49," VetTest 28, 3 [1978]: 350).

The fact that David "ran" (v.51a) to the Philistine after felling him indicates that he wanted to kill Goliath before he regained consciousness. Whether David first despatched him by plunging the sword into his heart and then decapitating him or whether beheading him was the manner of his execution is impossible to say. In either case, as he had promised (v.46), he cut off the Philistine's head (v.51; cf. similarly 31:9; 2 Sam 20:22), reminiscent of the earlier decapitation of the statue of the Philistine god Dagon (5:4). Goliath's head was later displayed as a trophy of war (v.54); his sword as well became a battlefield trophy (owned by David; cf. 21:9).

Marking the beginning of the end for the Philistines, David's victory over Goliath has frequently been celebrated in art and literature. Michelangelo's magnificent statue of the encounter, made from a block of marble discarded by another sculptor, stands on a hilltop overlooking Florence in Italy. The LXX Psalm 151 well summarizes David's daring feat: "I went out to meet the Philistine, and he cursed me by his idols. But I drew his own sword; I beheaded him, and I removed reproach from the people of Israel" (vv.6–7). Ceresko's theological recapitulation is very much to the point: "David's defeat of the Philistine champion affirms the superiority of trust in Yahweh over any purported marvels of human technology or skill" ("David's 'Boast,' " p. 72).

**51b–54** The death of Goliath produced panic in the Philistine ranks, and "they" (doubtless including Goliath's shield bearer) fled in disorder (v.51b). Goliath's original defiant challenge—that the winner of the battle between himself and his Israelite counterpart would thus decide the future ruler-subject relationship between the two nations (v.9)—was now forgotten or ignored or both. The men of "Israel" and "Judah" (by now a traditional distinction made by the narrator; cf. comment on 11:8), with a shout of triumph (v.52; cf. God's exultation in Ps 60:8 = 108:9), set out in hot pursuit, chasing the Philistines all the way to Gath (Goliath's hometown, v.4) and Ekron (modern Khirbet el-Muqanna, about six miles north of Gath). Shaaraim (in the western foothills of Judah, Josh 15:21, 33, 36; location unknown, but perhaps modern Khirbet Sairah northeast of Azekah; cf. Rasmussen, p. 113) was perhaps chosen by the narrator as a reference point because it means "Two Gates," thus alluding to the "entrance" of Gath and the "gate(s)" of Ekron (v.52).

On returning from the slaughter of the Philistines, the Israelite army plundered the enemy camp (v.53) at Ephes Dammim (v.1). This common ancient practice is illustrated not only elsewhere in the OT (e.g., 2 Kings 7:16) but also in other Near Eastern literature (e.g., the Egyptian Sinuhe, after defeating a "mighty man of Retenu," says: "What he had planned to do to me I did to him. I took what was in his tent and stripped his encampment" [ANET, p. 20]). David's role in the plundering operation is perhaps summarized in v.54b, which informs us that he put Goliath's weapons in "his" own tent. The NIV assumes that David's tent is intended here ("his own"), but it is unlikely that David, a visitor to the battlefield, would have had his own tent. James K. Hoffmeier ("The Aftermath of David's Triumph Over Goliath: 1 Samuel 17:54 in Light of Near Eastern Parallels," *Archaeology in the Biblical World* 1, 1 [1991]: 18–19) makes a strong case for the possibility that Goliath's tent is meant and that Goliath's weapons and tent alike were David's share of the plunder.

Humiliating one's enemies by cutting off and displaying the heads of their vanquished heroes was commonly practiced in the ancient Near East (cf. 1 Chron 10:10; for a pictorial representation, cf. ANEP, no. 236). Thus David proceeded to put Goliath's head on public display. Some consider the fact that he took it to Jerusalem (v.54), a city not yet under Israelite control (cf. 2 Sam 5:6–10), to be a "hopeless anachronism" (cf. Simon J. DeVries, "David's Victory Over the Philistine as Saga and as Legend," JBL 92, 1 [1973]: 24 n. 3). Hoffmeier suggests that David was probably "putting the Jebusites on notice that just as the Philistine had fallen victim to David, Jerusalem's demise was only a matter of time" ("The Aftermath of David's Triumph," p. 22). Perhaps under cover of night to avoid detection, David may have affixed Goliath's head to Jerusalem's wall (cf. 31:10 for the similar treatment of Saul's body by the Philistines).

**55–58** The events recorded in v.54 postdate vv.55–58, as v.57 makes clear. Indeed, vv.55–56 synchronize with v.40, while vv.57–58 follow immediately on v.51a. For the difficulty posed by Saul's ignorance of the name of David's father in v.58, see the comment on 16:19. Psychologically, Saul's reaction to David in vv.55–58 as a whole may also be explained as "haughtiness fed by envy" (Herman M. van Praag, "The Downfall of King Saul: The Neurobiological Consequences of Losing Hope," *Judaism* 35, 4 [1986]: 421).

Three times (vv.55, 56, 58) Saul expresses a desire to know who this "young man" is, using the ordinary word *na'ar* in vv. 55 and 58 but the extremely rare word *'elem* (found elsewhere only in 20:22 and perhaps emphasizing the strength and vigor of youth) in v.56 (cf. KB, p. 709; cf. also the frequently attested Ugaritic cognate *ġlm* ["young man"]; Aistleitner, *Wörterbuch der Ugaritischen Sprache,* no. 2150). Abner, Saul's cousin and the commander of his army (14:50–51), could not of course be expected to know all of Saul's court favorites (v.55). Abner therefore uses the common oath formula—"As surely as you live" (see comment on 1:26)—to underscore his inability to answer the king's question.

Determined to know who the boy is, however, Saul says to Abner, "Find out" (v.56; lit., "You [emphatic pronoun] ask" [*šᵉ'al,* yet another wordplay on Saul's name]). Immediately after David "returned" from his triumph over Goliath, therefore, Abner brought him to Saul (v.57), and David identified himself as the son of "Jesse of Bethlehem" (v.58; for the significance of this phrase as terminating a literary unit, cf. comment on 16:1). David's fellow warriors (including Saul) would soon be "returning" home from the battlefield itself (18:6)—and Saul's misunderstanding of the welcome they received from the women of Israel would trigger a long-standing and ultimately self-defeating jealousy toward David (18:7–9).

## Notes

**8** It is not necessary to assume (with BDB, p. 136; S.R. Driver, *Notes on the Books of Samuel*, p. 140) that the MT's בְּרוּ (*b^erû*, "Eat," root *brh*) is a scribal error for בחרו (*bḥrw*). The NIV's "Choose" can just as well be a translation of a revocalized בֹּרוּ (*bōrû*, root *brr;* cf. the participial forms rendered "choice," "chosen" in 1 Chron 7:40; 9:22; 16:41; Neh 5:18).

**12** "Old and well advanced in years" usually translates זָקֵן בָּא בַּיָּמִים (*zāqēn bā' bayyāmîm,* lit., "old, coming [along] in[to] the days"; cf. Gen 24:1; Josh 13:1; 23:1). Here, however, the Hebrew reads זָקֵן בָּא בַאֲנָשִׁים (*zāqēn bā' ba'^anāšîm,* lit., "old, coming among men"). Barthélemy (p. 184) suggests "an elder, notable/distinguished among men," a proposal made all the more attractive when one compares 1 Chron 4:38, הַבָּאִים בְּשֵׁמוֹת (*habbā'îm b^ešēmôṯ,* lit., "the ones coming with names"; NIV, "the men listed . . . by name"), perhaps to be understood as "the men distinguished by name" (later in the same verse they are called "leaders of their clans"). One would have expected Jesse to be a "man of standing" (cf. Saul's father, Kish, in 9:1), especially since his grandfather Boaz is described in those terms (Ruth 2:1).

**18** חֲרִצֵי הֶחָלָב (*h^ariṣê heḥālāḇ* , "cheeses") means literally "cut(ting)s of milk." For the possible role that *ḥārîṣ* (found only here in the OT in the sense of "cheese") played in the popular (mis)understanding of the name of Jerusalem's Tyropoeon Valley ("Valley of the Cheese-makers"), see A. van Selms, "The Origin of the Name Tyropoeon in Jerusalem," ZAW 91, 2 (1979): 170–76 (according to van Selms, *tyropoiōn* means "cutting[s]," "moat[s]").

עֲרֻבָּה (*'^arubbāh,* "assurance"; NIV mg., "*some token;* or *some pledge of spoils*"), although found elsewhere in the OT only in Prov 17:18 ("security"), is one of a number of cognate nouns derived from the relatively common verb עָרַב (*'āraḇ,* "pledge," "exchange"). Long a crux in this passage (the Targum on the Prophets, e.g., understands the phrase "bring back some assurance" to mean "bring back the divorce certificates of their wives," implying that before they went to war, Saul's soldiers granted conditional divorces to their wives and thus made it possible for them to remarry if the men died in battle and no proof of their death was forthcoming), the word is probably best understood in the sense of "token" (so NIV mg.) and refers in anticipation to Goliath's armor (v.54).

**34** The NIV translates the difficult וּבָא הָאֲרִי וְאֶת־הַדּוֹב (*ûḇā' hā'^arî w^e'eṯ-haddôḇ*) as "When a lion or a bear came," which in any event is clearly the basic intended sense of the clause. One Hebrew MS omits the *nota accusativi* אֶת (*'eṯ*) in an attempt to resolve the grammatical difficulty it poses. Ceresko perhaps has outlined a better solution (based on an earlier proposal by Felix Perles). He revocalizes the consonantal text as אָתָא (*'āṯā*), defective writing for אָתָה (*'āṯāh*), and translates the resulting clause as "Whenever a lion came or a bear attacked" (see "David's 'Boast,'" pp. 60, 63–64, for details).

**43** Aspects of Goliath's sarcastic question—"Am I a dog, that you come at me with sticks?"—are paralleled in Akkadian omen literature (e.g., Maqlu 5:43: "[May they chase the sorceress away] *kīma kalbi ina ḫaṭṭi* [like a dog with a stick]"), in the Amarna letters (e.g., EA 71:16–19, *Mīnu 'Abdi-'Aširta ardu kalbu u yilqu mat šarri ana šâšu,* "Who is Abdi-Ashirta, the slave, the dog, that he takes the land of the king for himself?"), and in the Lachish ostraca (e.g., 2:3–4, *'bdk klb,* "your slave, the dog"); for additional details, cf. Youngblood, *The Amarna Correspondence*, pp. 92–93.

**49** Medieval Jewish commentators wondered (1) how David's stone could have sunk into Goliath's "forehead," which was presumably covered by his helmet, and (2) why, if struck on the forehead, Goliath would have fallen "facedown" instead of on his back. Deem ("'And the Stone Sank Into His Forehead,'" pp. 349–51) suggests that מֵצַח (*mēṣaḥ*), the ordinary Hebrew word for "forehead," should here be translated "greave" (cf. מִצְחַת נְחֹשֶׁת [*miṣḥaṯ neḥōšeṯ*, "greaves made of bronze"] in v.6). David's sling stone would thus have struck Goliath on or near his knee, just above one of his two greaves, causing him to fall facedown and enabling David to rush forward and behead him with his own sword. Deem points out that such a reading has an interesting parallel in T Judah 3:1: "I ran out alone against one of the kings, struck him on his leg armor, knocked him down, and killed him" (translation of H.C. Kee in *The Old Testament Pseudepigrapha: Apocalyptic Literature and Testaments*, ed. James H. Charlesworth [Garden City: Doubleday, 1983], 1:796). But Deem admits (1) the occasional possibility of the exposure of the forehead in helmets similar to that worn by Goliath, (2) the weight of Goliath's frontal armor and the momentum of his forward movement would surely have been enough to cause him to fall facedown rather than backward, and (3) a sling stone sinking "into his greave" seems much less threatening than one sinking "into his forehead."

**52** The first occurrence of "Gath" here assumes the correctness of some LXX MS readings; instead of גַּת (*gaṯ*), the MT has גַּיְא (*gay'*, "valley"; cf. NIV mg.). Nor is the referent of "Gath" in this verse certain; it is possible that Gittaim (modern Ras Abu Humeid, four miles northwest of Gezer) is intended (cf. G. Ernest Wright, "Fresh Evidence for the Philistine Story," BA 29, 3 [1966]: 80; Aharoni, *Land of the Bible*, p. 271).

---

## 4. *The jealousy of Saul*

### 18:1–30

[1]After David had finished talking with Saul, Jonathan became one in
spirit with David, and he loved him as himself. [2]From that day Saul kept
David with him and did not let him return to his father's house. [3]And
Jonathan made a covenant with David because he loved him as himself.
[4]Jonathan took off the robe he was wearing and gave it to David, along
with his tunic, and even his sword, his bow and his belt.

[5]Whatever Saul sent him to do, David did it so successfully that Saul
gave him a high rank in the army. This pleased all the people, and Saul's
officers as well.

[6]When the men were returning home after David had killed the
Philistine, the women came out from all the towns of Israel to meet King
Saul with singing and dancing, with joyful songs and with tambourines
and lutes. [7]As they danced, they sang:

> "Saul has slain his thousands,
> and David his tens of thousands."

[8]Saul was very angry; this refrain galled him. "They have credited
David with tens of thousands," he thought, "but me with only thou-
sands. What more can he get but the kingdom?" [9]And from that time on
Saul kept a jealous eye on David.

[10]The next day an evil spirit from God came forcefully upon Saul. He
was prophesying in his house, while David was playing the harp, as he
usually did. Saul had a spear in his hand [11]and he hurled it, saying to
himself, "I'll pin David to the wall." But David eluded him twice.

[12]Saul was afraid of David, because the LORD was with David but had
left Saul. [13]So he sent David away from him and gave him command
over a thousand men, and David led the troops in their campaigns. [14]In
everything he did he had great success, because the LORD was with him.
[15]When Saul saw how successful he was, he was afraid of him. [16]But all
Israel and Judah loved David, because he led them in their campaigns.

[17]Saul said to David, "Here is my older daughter Merab. I will give her
to you in marriage; only serve me bravely and fight the battles of the

LORD." For Saul said to himself, "I will not raise a hand against him. Let
the Philistines do that!"
18But David said to Saul, "Who am I, and what is my family or my
father's clan in Israel, that I should become the king's son-in-law?" 19So
when the time came for Merab, Saul's daughter, to be given to David,
she was given in marriage to Adriel of Meholah.
20Now Saul's daughter Michal was in love with David, and when they
told Saul about it, he was pleased. 21"I will give her to him," he thought,
"so that she may be a snare to him and so that the hand of the
Philistines may be against him." So Saul said to David, "Now you have a
second opportunity to become my son-in-law."
22Then Saul ordered his attendants: "Speak to David privately and
say, 'Look, the king is pleased with you, and his attendants all like you;
now become his son-in-law.'"
23They repeated these words to David. But David said, "Do you think it
is a small matter to become the king's son-in-law? I'm only a poor man
and little known."
24When Saul's servants told him what David had said, 25Saul replied,
"Say to David, 'The king wants no other price for the bride than a
hundred Philistine foreskins, to take revenge on his enemies.'" Saul's
plan was to have David fall by the hands of the Philistines.
26When the attendants told David these things, he was pleased to
become the king's son-in-law. So before the allotted time elapsed,
27David and his men went out and killed two hundred Philistines. He
brought their foreskins and presented the full number to the king so that
he might become the king's son-in-law. Then Saul gave him his
daughter Michal in marriage.
28When Saul realized that the LORD was with David and that his
daughter Michal loved David, 29Saul became still more afraid of him,
and he remained his enemy the rest of his days.
30The Philistine commanders continued to go out to battle, and as
often as they did, David met with more success than the rest of Saul's
officers, and his name became well known.

A slight disruption in chronological order, a feature of chapter 17 (see comment on 17:55), characterizes chapter 18 as well. For example, Saul's promotion of David to a high rank in Israel's army, since it is introduced by "Whatever Saul sent him to do" (v.5), postdates the army's return from the battlefield after David had killed Goliath (v.6). At the same time v.5 illustrates Saul's increasingly schizophrenic behavior, since his jealous fear of David (v.9) obviously on occasion abated long enough for him to appreciate David's service and reward him accordingly.

Up to the events recorded in chapter 18, Saul had apparently been favorably disposed toward David. The scene that unfolds in vv.6–9, however, changed all that. Concerning Saul's progressive disintegration, Gunn observes that "from this point on the negative side of his character comes increasingly to the surface" (*The Fate of King Saul*, p. 80).

**1–4** Some time after David's conversation with Saul that concludes chapter 17, Saul's son Jonathan entered into a covenant with David (v.3). The ambiguous verb "loved" describes the relationship (vv.1, 3). Tom Horner (*Jonathan Loved David: Homosexuality in Biblical Times* [Philadelphia: Westminster, 1978]) asserts that the relationship between David and Jonathan was homosexual (cf. esp. pp. 20, 26–28, 31–39). But the verb *'āhēḇ* ("love") is not used elsewhere to express homosexual desire or activity, for which the OT employs *yāḏa'* ("know"), in the sense of "have sex with" (Gen 19:5; Judg 19:22). The latter verb is never used of David's relationship with Jonathan.

Rather, as conveniently summarized by Thompson ("The Significance of the Verb *Love,*" pp. 334–38), "love" has political overtones in diplomatic and commercial contexts. Indeed, "we may suspect that already in 1 Samuel xvi 21 [NIV, "Saul liked (David)"] the narrator is preparing us for the later political use of the term" (p. 335). A clear example of the treaty/covenant use of "love" is 1 Kings 5:1, which says that Hiram king of Tyre "had always 'loved' David" (appropriately rendered in the NIV as "had always been on friendly terms with David"). To summarize: In vv.1, 3 the narrator probably uses "the ambiguous word *love 'āheḇ* because it denoted more than natural affection however deep and genuine this may have been" (ibid., p. 336; cf. also vv.16, 20, 22 [NIV, "like"], 28; 20:17; 2 Sam 1:26).

The intimate friendship enjoyed by David and Jonathan—a friendship that has become proverbial—is further characterized by the phrase *nep̱eš niqšerāh benep̱eš* ("became one in spirit with," v.1; lit., "spirit bound with spirit"). The closest parallel is Genesis 44:30: *nep̱eš qešûrāh benep̱eš* ("life . . . closely bound up with . . . life"), describing Jacob's profound love for his youngest son, Benjamin (cf. Gen 44:20). Peter R. Ackroyd makes the important observation that just as *'āhēḇ* in chapter 18 is intentionally ambiguous so also "there is another verbal subtlety in 1 Sam. xviii 1 in the use of the root *qšr*" ("The Verb Love—*'Āhēḇ* in the David-Jonathan Narratives—A Footnote," VetTest 25, 2 [1975]: 213). In its various conjugations the root can mean either "bind," "tie," or "conspire" (whether positively or negatively) depending on context. Ackroyd summarizes: "The use here of another term which has both a nonpolitical and a political meaning is a further indication of the way in which an overtone is being imparted to what might at first sight appear to be a straightforward piece of narrative" (ibid., pp. 213–14). Indeed, the word *nep̱eš* ("life," "soul," "spirit," "self") occurs twice in "became one in spirit with" and once in "he loved him as himself" (v.1; so also in v.3; 20:17), thus linking the two phrases together.

David's close relationship with Jonathan made Saul all the more determined to make David a permanent member of the royal household (v.2). The covenant between Jonathan and David (v.3; 20:8) was only one of many such agreements "made" (lit., "cut"; cf. comment on 11:1) over a long period of time, until David's kingship was firmly established (20:16–17; 23:18; 2 Sam 3:13, 21; 5:3; cf. Thompson, "The Significance of the Verb *Love,*" p. 334). And when Jonathan took off his robe (a symbol of the Israelite kingdom; cf. 15:27–28 and comment) and gave it to David (v.4), he was in effect transferring his own status as heir apparent to him (cf. Gunn, *The Fate of King Saul,* p. 80). Saul had earlier tried to put his tunic and armor on David, but to no avail (17:38–39). Jonathan now gives his own tunic and armor (including a type of belt that was often used to hold a sheathed dagger; cf. 2 Sam 20:8) to David, who apparently accepts it without further ado. "David can receive from Jonathan what he cannot receive from Saul" (ibid., p. 80).

**5** This verse anticipates and summarizes David's continued successes as a warrior after his victory over Goliath (cf. the similarity with v.30). The root *śkl,* used to describe David's triumphs, combines the virtues of success and wisdom (cf. vv.14–15, 30, and NIV mgs.). Having experienced repeated military success himself (14:47), Saul appreciated its importance and honored David accordingly by giving him command over one or more army units (cf. also v.13; cf. similarly Joseph's elevation to the position of vizier over the land of Egypt in Gen 41:33, 40–43). David's skill as a warrior "pleased" (lit., "was good in the eyes of," in contrast to the song of the Israelite women, which "galled"—lit., "was bad in the eyes of"—Saul; v.8) all the *'am* ("people"; here more precisely "troops," as in v.13). After David became Israel's king, his ability to please his subjects would continue (2 Sam 3:36).

**6–8** When David the conquering hero returned to the Israelite camp (17:57) after killing Goliath, here (v.6) called simply "the Philistine" (par excellence; so also frequently in ch. 17; cf. further 19:5), and after the Israelite army had defeated their Philistine counterparts (17:52–53), all the troops (including Saul) returned home to be greeted by their fellow countrymen. Such victory celebrations were normally led by women, who came to meet the triumphant warriors with "dancing" accompanied by "tambourines" (cf. Exod 15:20; Judg 11:34; Ps 68:24–25; 149:3; Jer 31:4) as well as with "singing" (cf. similarly Exod 15:21; Judg 5:1).

The term *šālišîm,* derived from the Hebrew word "three" and found here uniquely in a context of celebration (elsewhere it means something like "third man in a chariot," hence "chariot officers," e.g., Ezek 23:15, 23), is translated "lutes" by the NIV (whether because of their supposed triangular shape or perhaps because they had three strings). Another possibility, however, is that it designates a song pattern, since there are three beats in each line of the Hebrew original of the song quoted in v.7 (cf. Sellers, "Musical Instruments of Israel," p. 45): "Saul has slain his thousands,/ and David his tens of thousands." It was sung by the women as they "danced" (different Heb. root from v.6; "celebrated" would be preferable, as in 2 Sam 6:5, 21).

Saul's reaction to the contents of the refrain was not surprising: He became angry (cf. 20:7), assuming that David was receiving ten times more praise than himself (v.8). But entirely apart from the fact that the refrain gives him pride of place (his name is mentioned before David's ), "thousand . . . ten thousand" is a stock parallel pair in the OT (cf. Ps 91:7; Mic 6:7) as well as in Ugaritic (cf. "a thousand fields, ten thousand acres" [V AB D 82; ANET, p. 137]). Each element in the pair is hyperbolic for a large number (cf. G.B. Caird, *The Language and Imagery of the Bible* [Philadelphia: Westminster, 1980], p. 133), and there is therefore no inherent necessity to interpret the second as greater than the first. It may well be that the song lavishes equal praise on both Saul and David (so also Stanley Gevirtz, *Patterns in the Early Poetry of Israel* [Chicago: Oriental Institute, 1963], p. 24; for the possibility that the refrain is intentionally ambiguous, see Gunn, *The Fate of King Saul,* p. 149 n. 8). In any case, Saul now fears for his kingdom, as well he might—but not because of his misunderstanding of an innocently sung victory hymn. After Absalom's death David's men would later affirm that David was worth "ten thousand" of them (2 Sam 18:3), perhaps an intentional echo of a refrain that by their time had become proverbial (21:11; 29:5).

**9–16** Just as "from that day on" signals a major literary break in 16:13, so also does the similar expression "from that time on" in v.9. David's military prowess made him Saul's equal, at the very least, in the perception of their fellow Israelites, and Saul's formerly positive attitude toward his young armor-bearer now became decidedly negative: He "eyed" him (a unique expression; the NIV rendering "kept a jealous eye on" should perhaps be modified to "kept a fearful eye on" in light of vv.12, 15, 29).

Saul's paranoia concerning David was exacerbated by the frequent arrival of "an evil spirit from God" (v.10; see comment on 16:14). On more than one occasion in the past, Saul had received an accession of the Spirit of God, which "came upon him in power" (10:10; 11:6), but now the evil spirit "came forcefully upon" him (same Heb. verb in all cases). Whether good or evil, such accessions sometimes induced "prophesying," often resulting in an altered state of consciousness (see comment on 10:5–6), accompanied at times by bizarre behavior (19:23–24). To bring relief to Saul when an evil spirit was tormenting him, David would play the harp (16:15–16, 23; cf. 19:9). The MT of v.10 states that David was playing the harp "with his hand" and then notes that there was a spear "in Saul's hand," underscoring the contrast between David's helpful service and Saul's murderous designs.

There would be at least one other time (cf. "twice," v.11) when Saul would try to pin David to the wall with a spear (19:10). Although Jonathan at first could not believe that Saul was determined to kill David (20:9), Saul's attempt to impale even his own son finally convinced him (20:32–33). Later given a similar opportunity to pin Saul to the ground with a spear, David declared that he would never "lay a hand on the LORD's anointed" (26:8–11).

Apparently fearful (*yr'*, vv.12, 28–29; in v.15 a different Heb. verb is used) because God was with David (Jonathan had no such fears; cf. 20:13) but had "left" him (cf. esp. 16:13–14 and comment), Saul "sent away" David (v.13; "left" and "sent away," from the same Heb. root). He made him commander of a "thousand" (probably a round number signifying a military unit; cf. 17:18 and NIV mg. in loc.), something he was sure David would never do for the men of Benjamin (22:7). Saul's purpose, however, was sinister: He intended to place David at the head of the front rank of troops, where he would be sure to be killed by the Philistines (v.17; cf. David's similar treatment of Uriah in 2 Sam 11:14–15).

For his part David "led the troops in their campaigns" (v.13; lit., "went forth and came back at the head of the troops"; cf. also v.16). "To go forth and come back" is frequently used with military connotations (cf. Num 27:16–17; cf. also 1 Sam 29:6 [NIV, "to have you serve (with me in the army)"]; Josh 14:11 ["to go out (to battle)"]; cf. further Thompson, "The Significance of the Verb *Love*," p. 337 n. 1). David's military exploits, possible only because the Lord was "with him" (v.14), bound him all the more closely to "Israel and Judah" (v.16; for this phrase see comment on 11:8) in covenant relationship ("loved"; see v.1 and comment). By contrast Saul "was afraid of" David (v.15; the Heb. verb *gwr* often means "be terrified," as in Num 22:3) because of his success on the battlefield.

**17–19** As a further means of assuring David's death at the hands of the Philistines, Saul offered him the distraction of his "older daughter Merab" (better "Merob"; see comment on 14:49) in marriage (v.17). But just as David's ancestor Jacob preferred Laban's younger daughter Rachel to her older sister Leah (Gen 29:16–18), so also David declined to marry Merob (v.18) and later became the husband of her younger sister Michal (vv.26–28). Jacob's love for Rachel (Gen 29:11, 18, 20, 30), however, is not paralleled in David, who is never described as loving Michal. In fact, Michal loved David (vv.20, 28), a circumstance so unusual that Alter affirms it to be "the only instance in all biblical narrative in which we are explicitly told that a woman loves a man" (*The Art of Biblical Narrative,* p. 118; cf. similarly Adele Berlin, "Characterization in Biblical Narrative: David's Wives," JSOT 23 [1982]: 70). Although Alter's statement is not quite accurate (cf. S of Songs 1:7; 3:1–4), the mention of Merob in v.17 reminds us of Leah and Rachel and "sets up a parallel which underscores what David lacks in his relationship with Michal: love" (Lawton, "1 Samuel 18: David, Merob, and Michal," p. 425).

Saul's mandate to David in v.17—essentially "be brave and fight"—echoed the common battle cries of those days (cf. 4:9). David had already proven himself to be just the sort of man that Saul was eager to press into service in his army (14:52). Saul apparently understood that to fight Israel's battles (8:20) was in reality to fight the Lord's battles (cf. also 25:28; 2 Chron 32:8). His duplicity, however, is evident in his intention not to raise his own hand against David but to place him in situations that would guarantee his death at "the hand of the Philistines" (v.17 MT; also in vv.21, 25).

David's self-effacing statement of reluctance to marry Merob (v.18) reprises Saul's earlier modest questioning of his own background and abilities (9:21). In spite of everything, whether intentionally or unintentionally, whether innocently or through carefully planned strategy, David would indeed soon become "the king's son-in-law" (22:14)—but because Michal, not Merob, would be his wife (v.27). For her part Merob was given by Saul to another man (v.19), to whom she eventually bore five sons (2 Sam 21:8).

**20–26a** The literary structure of vv.20–26a is chiastic (cf. similarly Gunn, *The Fate of King Saul*, pp. 149–50 n. 10):

A. Michal's love for David pleases Saul (v.20).
  B. Saul wants David to fall at the Philistines' hands (v.21).
    C. Saul sends a message to David (vv.22–23a).
    C′. David sends a message to Saul (vv.23b–24).
  B′. Saul wants David to fall at the Philistines' hands (v.25).
A′. Becoming the king's son-in-law pleases David (v.26a).

The middle verses (vv.22–24) continue the tug-of-war concerning whether David will become Saul's son-in-law, with Saul playing the role of the suitor and David the role of the one being courted.

Every time either Merob or Michal appears in this chapter, she is referred to as the "daughter" of Saul (vv.17, 19–20, 27–28). David's marriage to one or both could not escape the political implications of their being the daughters of the reigning king: If Saul (and Jonathan) should die, David's claim on the throne of Israel would be all the stronger if he were married to one of its princesses. In addition the symbolism of David marrying Saul's daughter should not be missed: When political marriages were arranged, it was usually the daughter of the ostensibly weaker ruler who married the stronger (cf. Gen 34:9; 1 Kings 3:1; 2 Chron 18:1). David's relentless climb to Israel's throne proceeds apace.

Michal's "love" for David (vv.20, 28) parallels that of Jonathan (vv.1, 3) and, while doubtless genuine, perhaps carries the same covenantal nuances. What is certain is that these two siblings "show more love and loyalty to their father's competitor than to their father. The biblical author further invites the comparison by juxtaposing their stories in 1 Sam. 18–20" (Berlin, "Characterization in Biblical Narrative," p. 70).

Saul and David were both "pleased" (vv.20, 26) at the prospect of Michal's marriage to David, but for different reasons. As Moses had been a "snare" to the Egyptian Pharaoh (Exod 10:7) in the sense of tripping him up at every turn and keeping him off guard, so also Saul intended that Michal would be a "snare" to David (v.21) in the sense that Saul's demanded bride-price of a hundred Philistine foreskins would prove to be his undoing (v.25). David, on the other hand, brought back "two" hundred foreskins (v.27) and thus—ironically—capitalized on the "second opportunity" (v.21) that Saul gave him.

Saul, to confirm to David his desires concerning Michal, sent further word through his "attendants" (v.22, lit., "servants"; see comment on 16:15–16). They were to approach David "privately" to make it appear as though they were speaking to him on their own rather than at Saul's command. They stressed their own loyalty to him (on "like" in v.22; cf. comment on 16:21), which matched that of the people as a whole (v.16).

David's response to them (v.23), however, once more emphasizes his humble origins (cf. v.18). He again demonstrates that he "speaks well" (16:18), this time by using a Hebrew wordplay captured by the NIV in "small matter" (from *qll;* cf. Isa 49:6) and "little known" (from *qlh;* cf. Prov 12:9, "a nobody"), each of which translates the same underlying consonantal text (*nqlh*). In addition David refers to himself as a "poor man," a description that will come back to haunt him in Nathan's parable (2 Sam 12:1–4).

Saul, however, would not allow David to plead poverty as an excuse to get out of marrying Michal. A mere "hundred Philistine foreskins" would suffice as compensation for her (v.25). The Hebrew term *mōhar* ("bride-price"; elsewhere only in Gen 34:12; Exod 22:16[15 MT]) refers to payment made by the groom to the bride's father (cf. similarly Deut 22:29) and is paralleled in other Semitic cultures from the earliest times (cf. W. Robertson Smith, *Kinship and Marriage in Early Arabia* [Cambridge: Cambridge University Press, 1885], pp. 78–80; id., *The Prophets of Israel and Their Place in History to the Close of the Eighth Century* B.C., 2d ed. [London: A. & C. Black, 1919], pp. 171, 410 n. 13). But "the *mohar* seems to be not so much the price paid for the woman as a compensation given to the family, and, in spite of the apparent resemblance, in law this is a different consideration. The future husband thereby acquires a right over the woman, but the woman herself is not bought and sold" (de Vaux, AIs, p. 27). Under certain circumstances, as here (cf. also Josh 15:16), "heroic deeds could be substituted for the *mohar*" (I. Mendelsohn, "The Family in the Ancient Near East," BA 11, 2 [1948]: 27).

In asking David to kill one hundred Philistines, Saul of course was hoping that David himself would be killed. Saul gave another reason, however, for his demand: that he might "take revenge" on his enemies (v.25) by decimating them (cf. 14:24; Judg 15:7; and 16:28 for other examples of avenging oneself on the Philistine foe). Ironically, as Gunn observes (*The Fate of King Saul*, p. 150 n. 10), David himself has become one of Saul's "enemies" (v.29; cf. also 19:17; 20:13; 24:4, 19; 25:26, 29).

**26b–29** The word *hayyāmîm* (lit., "the days") occurs at the end of v.26b ("allotted time") and of v.29, thus forming a frame around this section. "Presented the full number" (v.27) echoes "elapsed" in v.26b (the same Heb. root underlies both expressions), thus further linking v.26b with what follows rather than with what precedes.

David's "men," later to become his loyal companions during the days of their mutual flight from Saul (cf. 23:3, 5; 24:3; 25:12–13), are first mentioned in v.27. The verbs "went out," "killed," and "brought" are singular in number, stressing David's leadership in fulfilling Saul's demand. "Presented," however, has a plural subject and involves David's men, without whose help he surely would have failed, in the overall success of his venture. For the MT's "two hundred" the LXX has "one hundred," which is sometimes assumed to be the correct reading on the basis of 2 Samuel 3:14. The latter verse, however, simply quotes Saul's original figure (v.25) as the price of Michal's hand. Saul, true to his word, gave his daughter to his enemy (v.27). "He is thus even more enmeshed with David: indebted to him for his harp-playing/healing and his military service, and tied to him through Jonathan's love and his daughter's marriage" (Gunn, *The Fate of King Saul*, p. 81).

The combination of the evidence of God's help for and presence with David (v.28; cf. vv.12, 14 and comment on 16:18) and of Michal's love for David (vv.20, 28) increased Saul's fear of David (v.29; cf. v.12), with the result that "he" (Saul) remained "his" (David's) enemy for the rest of his "days" (cf. 23:14).

**30** The final verse of chapter 18 repeats the theme of David's success (cf. vv.5, 14–15). He soon proved that he was more than a match for the Philistine commanders; and even when they later joined in common cause against Saul, they would justifiably remain wary of David (29:3–4, 9). In contrast to David's own earlier protestations concerning his unworthiness and obscurity (v.23), the text observes that his name was now "well known" (lit., "precious," as in Ps 139:17; Isa 43:4). The superlatives heaped on him are reminiscent of the earlier description of Saul (9:2), as if to remind us that David had become what Saul could no longer be.

## Notes

**7** In an Egyptian victory hymn of the fifteenth century B.C., Thutmose III says, "I bind the barbarians of Nubia by ten-thousands and thousands, the northerners by hundred-thousands as living captives" (ANET, p. 374). The Egyptian word for "hundred thousand," *hfnw*, "also has the abstract meaning 'great quantity' " (James K. Hoffmeier, "Egypt As an Arm of Flesh: A Prophetic Response," in *Israel's Apostasy and Restoration: Essays in Honor of Roland K. Harrison*, ed. Avraham Gileadi [Grand Rapids: Baker, 1988], p. 86). Hoffmeier suggests that the Egyptian couplet may be a parallel to "thousands, . . . tens of thousands" in v.7 (p. 95 n. 67).

**18** חַיַּי (*ḥayyay*, "my life") should probably be repointed here as חַיִּי (*ḥayyî*) in the unique sense of "my family" (thus NIV). S.R. Driver (*Notes on the Books of Samuel*, p. 153) is perhaps correct in assuming that the following "my father's clan" is a scribal explanation of this rare term.

Perhaps כִּי (*kî*) should here be translated by the interrogative "why" instead of the NIV's "that" (see comment on 11:5).

**21** Saul's statement to David at the end of v.21, "Now you have a second opportunity to become my son-in-law," is probably to be understood as "a formal declaration over David which secures his betrothal to Michal, 'Today you shall be my son-in-law.' . . . We find the head of his house acting unilaterally without recourse to the courts to bring about a change in legal status which as in divorce and adoption is effected by a specific spoken formula" (Anthony Phillips, "Another Example of Family Law," VetTest 30, 2 [1980]: 241). The initial בִּשְׁתַּיִם (*bištayim*, "with a second [opportunity]" [hence NIV]) could also be rendered (with approximately the same meaning) "in a second way" (cf. Job 33:14; so KD, p. 192).

**27** On an interior wall of his mortuary temple at Medinet Habu, Rameses III (c. 1198–1166 B.C.) commissioned scenes depicting the counting of hands severed from his enemies in battle as a means of establishing a body count (cf. ANEP, no. 348). Elsewhere on the same temple walls is a panel that has been interpreted as picturing a pile of foreskins collected for the same purpose, perhaps from Philistines (whose armies were driven out of Egypt by Rameses III).

## 5. *David the refugee*

### 19:1–24

[1]Saul told his son Jonathan and all the attendants to kill David. But
Jonathan was very fond of David [2]and warned him, "My father Saul is
looking for a chance to kill you. Be on your guard tomorrow morning;
go into hiding and stay there. [3]I will go out and stand with my father in
the field where you are. I'll speak to him about you and will tell you what
I find out."

[4]Jonathan spoke well of David to Saul his father and said to him, "Let
not the king do wrong to his servant David; he has not wronged you,
and what he has done has benefited you greatly. [5]He took his life in his
hands when he killed the Philistine. The LORD won a great victory for all
Israel, and you saw it and were glad. Why then would you do wrong to
an innocent man like David by killing him for no reason?"

[6]Saul listened to Jonathan and took this oath: "As surely as the LORD
lives, David will not be put to death."

[7]So Jonathan called David and told him the whole conversation. He
brought him to Saul, and David was with Saul as before.

[8]Once more war broke out, and David went out and fought the
Philistines. He struck them with such force that they fled before him.

[9]But an evil spirit from the LORD came upon Saul as he was sitting in
his house with his spear in his hand. While David was playing the harp,
[10]Saul tried to pin him to the wall with his spear, but David eluded him
as Saul drove the spear into the wall. That night David made good his
escape.

[11]Saul sent men to David's house to watch it and to kill him in the
morning. But Michal, David's wife, warned him, "If you don't run for
your life tonight, tomorrow you'll be killed." [12]So Michal let David down
through a window, and he fled and escaped. [13]Then Michal took an idol
and laid it on the bed, covering it with a garment and putting some
goats' hair at the head.

[14]When Saul sent the men to capture David, Michal said, "He is ill."

[15]Then Saul sent the men back to see David and told them, "Bring
him up to me in his bed so that I may kill him." [16]But when the men
entered, there was the idol in the bed, and at the head was some goats'
hair.

[17]Saul said to Michal, "Why did you deceive me like this and send my
enemy away so that he escaped?"

Michal told him, "He said to me, 'Let me get away. Why should I kill
you?'"

[18]When David had fled and made his escape, he went to Samuel at
Ramah and told him all that Saul had done to him. Then he and Samuel
went to Naioth and stayed there. [19]Word came to Saul: "David is in
Naioth at Ramah"; [20]so he sent men to capture him. But when they saw
a group of prophets prophesying, with Samuel standing there as their
leader, the Spirit of God came upon Saul's men and they also
prophesied. [21]Saul was told about it, and he sent more men, and they
prophesied too. Saul sent men a third time, and they also prophesied.
[22]Finally, he himself left for Ramah and went to the great cistern at
Secu. And he asked, "Where are Samuel and David?"

"Over in Naioth at Ramah," they said.

[23]So Saul went to Naioth at Ramah. But the Spirit of God came even
upon him, and he walked along prophesying until he came to Naioth.
[24]He stripped off his robes and also prophesied in Samuel's presence.
He lay that way all that day and night. This is why people say, "Is Saul
also among the prophets?"

Although Saul is earlier described as desiring David's permanent residence at the palace (18:2), chapter 19 records the final break—however ambiguous from Saul's point of view (vv.6–7)—between the two men. Now determined once and for all to kill David, Saul forces David's flight, and the vocabulary of the refugee suffuses the chapter ("go into hiding," v.2; "eluded," v.10; "made good his escape," v.10; "run for your life," v.11; "fled and escaped," v.12; "escaped," v.17; "get away," v.17; "fled and made his escape," v.18).

**1–7** "A king delights in a wise servant,/ but a shameful servant incurs his wrath" (Prov 14:35). The Hebrew root translated "wise" in the proverb is used to describe David's "success" in 18:5, 14–15, 30 (see comment on 18:5), a success that brought varied and inconsistent responses from Saul. Although Saul's wise and successful "servant" (v.4), David is the object, not of the king's delight, but of his murderous intent: He commands his "attendants" (v.1; lit., "servants"; see comment on 16:15–16), as well as his son Jonathan, to kill David. Saul's tortured duplicity becomes more and more evident as we recall that he had earlier ordered his attendants to tell David privately that the king was "pleased with" him (18:22). The narrator now states that Jonathan is "fond of" David (identical Heb. expression) and that Jonathan will therefore do everything in his power to save the life of his covenanted friend (cf. 18:1–3 and comment).

The NIV's "warned" (vv.2, 11; lit., "told") appropriately links the concern of Jonathan with that of his sister Michal, both of whom want no harm to come to David. Saul's determination, on the other hand, is relentless: He "is looking" for an opportunity to kill David, he "tried" again to pin him to the wall with his spear (v.10), and he "plans" to destroy the town of Keilah because of David (23:10; same Heb. verb in all three passages). So Jonathan warns his friend, "Be on your guard" (v.2; cf. 2 Sam 20:10 for the danger of ignoring such advice), using the same Hebrew verb as in v.11, where Saul's men are told to "watch" David's house one night to prevent him from escaping so that they could kill him in the morning. God's servant must always be alert, because his enemy will surely be (1 Peter 5:8).

Jonathan also tells David to "go into hiding and stay there" (v.2; lit., "stay in a secret place and hide"). From this time on and for a long period of time, the man after God's own heart would be a hunted fugitive. He would hide from his best friend's father at the beginning of his career and from his own son near its end (2 Sam 17:9). Miscall observes (p. 126) that David's hiding from Saul in a secret place "foreshadows his sin with Bathsheba 'in a secret place' (2 Sam. 12:12)."

Jonathan's personal interest in helping David is underscored by use of the emphatic pronoun in the phrases "I will go out," "I'll speak" (v.3). Jonathan promised to stand "with" (lit., "at the hand of") his father, Saul, as David's advocate (cf. v.4). By doing so, Jonathan was sure that he would be acting in the king's best interests (cf. 1 Chron 18:17, "at the king's side" [lit., "hand"]; Neh 11:24, "the king's agent" [lit., "at the king's hand"]). The venue was the "field" where David was hiding (cf. also 20:5, 11, 24, 35), perhaps a location not far from Saul's fortress in Gibeah. Jonathan further promised to keep David fully informed (cf. David's fears expressed in 20:10).

The plea of Jonathan in vv.4–5 begins and ends with his hope that Saul would not "do wrong to" David, especially since the latter had not "wronged" the king (cf. also 24:11; in all cases the Heb. verb is *ḥāṭā'*, lit., "sinned [against]"). Jonathan further reminds his father that David's deeds have helped Saul, that David "took his life in his hands" (v.5; for the idiom cf. further 28:21; Judg 12:3; Job 13:14; Ps 119:109) when he escaped Goliath's challenge, and that Saul himself had been pleased with the outcome (17:55–58). There is therefore no reason to kill "an innocent man," and such a crime could only bring bloodguilt on Saul (Deut 21:8–9). "Why" would his father want to do David harm, Jonathan asks—a question that he would later find it necessary to repeat (20:32). The works of David should bring him praise, not death (cf. Prov 31:31).

Through David's initial success on the battlefield the Lord had "won a great victory" for all Israel (v.5), just as through Saul's earlier similar success the Lord had "rescued" Israel (see 11:13 and comment; same Heb. idiom). But whereas in chapter 11 Saul refused to allow his detractors to be put to death, in chapter 19 he orders the execution of one of his courtiers. Fortunately, Jonathan's rebuke of his father brought him to his senses, at least temporarily: He "listened to" (v.6; lit., "obeyed") Jonathan and took the most solemn of all oaths (cf. 14:39 and comment; cf. also Jer 4:2; Hos 4:15), promising that David would not be put to death—a promise that he quickly and conveniently forgot (v.11). In the meantime, however, David was once again made a member of Saul's court in good standing (v.7; cf. 16:21; 18:2).

**8–10** David's continued military success against the Philistines (v.8) evoked the repetition of a familiar scene (vv.9–10; see comment on 16:14, 16; 18:10–11).

**11–17** Verse 10 ends by stating that "David made good his escape" and v.18 begins with "When David had fled and made his escape," the two expressions thus framing the account (vv.11–17) of Michal's helping David to escape (cf. Gunn, *The Fate of King Saul*, p. 83) from Saul's "men" (lit., "messengers"; vv.11, 14–16). The account itself, structurally held together also by the repeated use of *šlḥ* ("send"; vv.11, 14–15, 17), is one of a series of deception stories "in which the response to the opening situation is a deception. These stories have the following common structure or pattern: (1) a difficult situation provides the necessity for a party to act; (2) that party performs a deception to escape the situation; (3) the immediate threat of the opening situation is removed" (Robert C. Culley, "Themes and Variations in Three Groups of OT Narratives," *Semeia* 3 [1975]: 5). Other examples given by Culley are Abram's deceiving the Egyptian Pharaoh (Gen 12:10–20), Lot's daughters' conceiving sons through their father (Gen 19:30–38), Tamar's conceiving a son through Judah (Gen 38), the midwives' deceiving the Egyptian Pharaoh (Exod 1:15–21), the Gibeonites' deceiving the Israelites (Josh 9:3–15), and Ehud's killing the king of Moab (Judg 3:12–30).

Tradition ascribes vv.11–17 as the original setting of Psalm 59, which includes in its title "When Saul had sent men to watch David's house in order to kill him," using the language and vocabulary of v.11. Although the mission of Saul's men was to kill David "in the morning," God's strength and love preserved him "in the morning" (Ps 59:16).

The human agent assuring David's rescue was Michal, his loving wife (18:20, 28). After warning him to flee the home they shared (v.11), she helped him escape by lowering him "through a window" (v.12; for other examples cf. Josh 2:15; 2 Cor 11:33). To give David time to put sufficient distance between himself and his pursuers, Michal fashioned a crude dummy to take his place in his bed (v.13). She further stalled for time by telling Saul's men that her husband was ill (v.14), thus implying that they should not disturb him.

Michal's dummy is described in connection with *t^e^rāp̄îm* (cf. NIV mg. on v.13), usually translated "idols," "household gods" (thus NIV's "idol" in vv.13, 16 and "idolatry" in 15:23). Since *terāp̱îm* is always plural, and since the idols they denote are presumably always small (Gen 31:19, 34–35; Judg 17:5; 18:14, 17–18, 20; 2 Kings 23:24; Ezek 21:21; Hos 3:4; Zech 10:2), the dummy was almost certainly not a single, man-sized idol. Michal's ruse was probably effected by piling clothing, carpets, or the like on David's bed and covering it with a garment, allowing only the goats' hair at the head to show. She did not place the household idols "on" or "in" (NIV, vv.13, 16) the bed but "at" or "beside" it (*'el* often has this meaning; cf. BDB, p. 40 sec. 8) to enhance the impression of David's illness (cf. similarly Ackroyd, *First Book of Samuel*, pp. 157–58). The Hebrew root of *terāp̱îm*, although unknown, may have been *rph* ("sink," "drop," "be weak") or *rp'* ("heal"; for an excellent summary, cf. Aubrey R. Johnson, *The Cultic Prophet in Ancient Israel* [Cardiff: University of Wales Press, 1944], p. 31 n. 3).

Michal's use of household idols doubtless reflects pagan inclination or ignorance on her part. But the narrator also employs her actions to make yet another connection between David's wife Michal and Jacob's wife Rachel (see comment on 18:17). Each woman deceived her father by using teraphim (cf. Gen 31:33–35) and thus demonstrated that she was "more devoted to her husband than to her father" (Lawton, "1 Samuel 18: David, Merob, and Michal," p. 425). Another final (though more remote) link between the two accounts is the use of the rare word *mera'ašôṯ* (lit., "place[s] at the head") in vv.13, 16 and Genesis 28:11, 18 (the term occurs elsewhere only in 1 Sam 26:7, 11–12, 16; 1 Kings 19:6).

Michal's ruse worked to perfection; Saul's men were deceived (v.14). Saul, however, not satisfied with their report, sent his men back for another look, this time with orders to "bring [David] up" to Gibeah, bed and all, so that he might be killed there (v.15). By the time they arrived (v.16), of course, David was long gone. Near the end of his reign over Israel, Saul would command the medium at Endor to "bring up" Samuel (28:8, 11), with equally distressing results.

In v.5 Saul's son asks him "why" he would want to kill David, and in v.17 Saul asks his daughter "why" she would "deceive" (lit., "betray"; cf. 1 Chron 12:17; Lam 1:19) him and keep David from being killed. Michal's response repeats a key verb in Saul's question: Her "get away" and his "send . . . away" both translate *šlḥ* (cf. further the comment on v.11). In addition, she brings the entire matter full circle by echoing her earlier words to David in v.11, where she warned him that if he did not flee he would "be killed." Alter observes: "Michal coolly turns around her own words to David and her actions of the previous night and pretends that David threatened her, saying, 'Help me get away or I'll kill you'" (*The Art of Biblical Narrative*, p. 120).

Saul's own words identify David as his mortal "enemy" (v.17; cf. 18:29), barring forever his return to Saul's court at Gibeah. David's days as an outlaw, now begun in earnest, would continue until Saul's death.

**18–24** Verse 18 reverts to the time when David had escaped after Michal's warning (v.12). He went to Ramah, Samuel's hometown (far to the northwest of Gibeah; see comment on 1:1), to inform the prophet about what Saul had done. Perhaps to escape detection, he and Samuel then went to Naioth (v.18) at Ramah (v.19). Naioth, possibly a common noun ("habitations") rather than a place name, may refer to the compound of dwellings in Ramah where Samuel's "group of prophets" (v.20) lived (cf. 2 Kings 6:1–2).

In relentless pursuit of David, Saul sends men to Naioth to capture him. The Spirit of God, however, protects David by causing first three successive contingents of Saul's messengers (vv.20–21) and finally Saul himself to prophesy (vv.22–23). Saul's men "saw" (not "heard") Samuel's disciples "prophesying" (v.20), which—as in a similar situation earlier (10:5–6, 9–11)—probably means that the prophesying was in the form of succumbing to a divinely induced possession trance rather than of speaking a divinely given word (see comment on 10:5 for details). Each such group of prophets had a "leader" (as here, v.20) or "father" (10:12; 2 Kings 2:12), in this case Samuel.

Finally realizing that his men were not going to apprehend David, Saul took matters into his own hands by going to Ramah himself (v.22). Stopping at Secu (mentioned only here; meaning and location unknown), he "asked" (*šā'al*, yet another pun on his name) for the exact whereabouts of Samuel and David. Told they had gone to Naioth, Saul continued on his way and began "prophesying" after receiving an accession of the Spirit of God (v.23).

An accompaniment of Saul's prophesying was that he, like those who had arrived before him (implied by "also," omitted by the NIV at the beginning of v.24), "stripped off" his garments. Since *'ārōm* in context with *pāšaṭ* ("strip off") is elsewhere rendered "naked" (cf. Job 22:6; Hos 2:3), the NIV's discreet translation "that way" is unnecessary. In fact, the implication is that Saul, minus the robes symbolic of his rule (cf. comment on 2:19; 15:27)—yea, naked—demonstrates once again his forfeiture of any claim to be Israel's king. In addition, the rhetorical question demanding a negative answer—"Is Saul also among the prophets?"—underscores that forfeiture and thus takes an ironic twist: To question the genuineness of Saul's prophetic behavior was to question his legitimacy as king of Israel (see comment on 10:11).

The use of this proverb first in 10:11–12 and now here brackets the narrative descriptions of Saul's first and last encounters with Samuel as well as with the Spirit of God. Neither legitimate king nor genuine prophet, Saul continues to stumble toward his doom at the hands of the Philistines, when he will be "stripped" of his garments for the last time (31:8–9).

## Notes

**10** According to Waltke and O'Connor, "the anarthrous phrase *blylh hw'* 'in that night' (Gen 19:33; 30:16; 32:23) is both anomalous and textually suspect" and should probably be amended to *blylh hhw'* on the basis of the Samaritan Pentateuch (*Biblical Hebrew Syntax*, p. 313 n. 22). But the same anarthrous phrase occurs here, and similar phenomena are attested elsewhere in the OT and in Moabite (cf. GKC, sec. 126*y*). Emendation of the MT therefore seems unnecessary.

**13** William F. Albright proposed "old rags" as a translation of תְּרָפִים (*t^erāp̱îm*) in vv.13, 16 (*Archaeology and the Religion of Israel*, 4th ed. [Baltimore: Johns Hopkins Press, 1956], p. 207 n. 63), especially since no man-sized idols have turned up in archaeological excavations in Palestine (p. 114; so also Ronald F. Youngblood, "Teraphim," in WBE, p. 1685). But since *t^erāp̱îm* always means "(household) idols" elsewhere in the OT, it seems best to keep that sense here as well.

## 6. *Jonathan's friendship*

### 20:1–42

1Then David fled from Naioth at Ramah and went to Jonathan and
asked, "What have I done? What is my crime? How have I wronged your
father, that he is trying to take my life?"
2"Never!" Jonathan replied. "You are not going to die! Look, my
father doesn't do anything, great or small, without confiding in me. Why
would he hide this from me? It's not so!"
3But David took an oath and said, "Your father knows very well that I
have found favor in your eyes, and he has said to himself, 'Jonathan
must not know this or he will be grieved.' Yet as surely as the LORD lives
and as you live, there is only a step between me and death."
4Jonathan said to David, "Whatever you want me to do, I'll do for
you."
5So David said, "Look, tomorrow is the New Moon festival, and I am
supposed to dine with the king; but let me go and hide in the field until
the evening of the day after tomorrow. 6If your father misses me at all,
tell him, 'David earnestly asked my permission to hurry to Bethlehem,
his hometown, because an annual sacrifice is being made there for his
whole clan.' 7If he says, 'Very well,' then your servant is safe. But if he
loses his temper, you can be sure that he is determined to harm me. 8As
for you, show kindness to your servant, for you have brought him into a
covenant with you before the LORD. If I am guilty, then kill me yourself!
Why hand me over to your father?"
9"Never!" Jonathan said. "If I had the least inkling that my father was
determined to harm you, wouldn't I tell you?"
10David asked, "Who will tell me if your father answers you harshly?"
11"Come," Jonathan said, "let's go out into the field." So they went
there together.
12Then Jonathan said to David: "By the LORD, the God of Israel, I will
surely sound out my father by this time the day after tomorrow! If he is
favorably disposed toward you, will I not send you word and let you
know? 13But if my father is inclined to harm you, may the LORD deal with
me, be it ever so severely, if I do not let you know and send you away
safely. May the LORD be with you as he has been with my father. 14But
show me unfailing kindness like that of the LORD as long as I live, so that
I may not be killed, 15and do not ever cut off your kindness from my
family—not even when the LORD has cut off every one of David's
enemies from the face of the earth."
16So Jonathan made a covenant with the house of David, saying,
"May the LORD call David's enemies to account." 17And Jonathan had
David reaffirm his oath out of love for him, because he loved him as he
loved himself.
18Then Jonathan said to David: "Tomorrow is the New Moon festival.
You will be missed, because your seat will be empty. 19The day after
tomorrow, toward evening, go to the place where you hid when this
trouble began, and wait by the stone Ezel. 20I will shoot three arrows to
the side of it, as though I were shooting at a target. 21Then I will send a
boy and say, 'Go, find the arrows.' If I say to him, 'Look, the arrows are
on this side of you; bring them here,' then come, because, as surely as
the LORD lives, you are safe; there is no danger. 22But if I say to the boy,
'Look, the arrows are beyond you,' then you must go, because the LORD
has sent you away. 23And about the matter you and I discussed—
remember, the LORD is witness between you and me forever."
24So David hid in the field, and when the New Moon festival came, the
king sat down to eat. 25He sat in his customary place by the wall,
opposite Jonathan, and Abner sat next to Saul, but David's place was

empty. 26 Saul said nothing that day, for he thought, "Something must
have happened to David to make him ceremonially unclean—surely he
is unclean." 27 But the next day, the second day of the month, David's
place was empty again. Then Saul said to his son Jonathan, "Why hasn't
the son of Jesse come to the meal, either yesterday or today?"
28 Jonathan answered, "David earnestly asked me for permission to go
to Bethlehem. 29 He said, 'Let me go, because our family is observing a
sacrifice in the town and my brother has ordered me to be there. If I have
found favor in your eyes, let me get away to see my brothers.' That is
why he has not come to the king's table."
30 Saul's anger flared up at Jonathan and he said to him, "You son of a
perverse and rebellious woman! Don't I know that you have sided with
the son of Jesse to your own shame and to the shame of the mother who
bore you? 31 As long as the son of Jesse lives on this earth, neither you
nor your kingdom will be established. Now send and bring him to me,
for he must die!"
32 "Why should he be put to death? What has he done?" Jonathan
asked his father. 33 But Saul hurled his spear at him to kill him. Then
Jonathan knew that his father intended to kill David.
34 Jonathan got up from the table in fierce anger; on that second day
of the month he did not eat, because he was grieved at his father's
shameful treatment of David.
35 In the morning Jonathan went out to the field for his meeting with
David. He had a small boy with him, 36 and he said to the boy, "Run and
find the arrows I shoot." As the boy ran, he shot an arrow beyond him.
37 When the boy came to the place where Jonathan's arrow had fallen,
Jonathan called out after him, "Isn't the arrow beyond you?" 38 Then he
shouted, "Hurry! Go quickly! Don't stop!" The boy picked up the arrow
and returned to his master. 39 (The boy knew nothing of all this; only
Jonathan and David knew.) 40 Then Jonathan gave his weapons to the
boy and said, "Go, carry them back to town."
41 After the boy had gone, David got up from the south side ⌊of the
stone⌋ and bowed down before Jonathan three times, with his face to the
ground. Then they kissed each other and wept together—but David
wept the most.
42 Jonathan said to David, "Go in peace, for we have sworn friendship
with each other in the name of the LORD, saying, 'The LORD is witness
between you and me, and between your descendants and my descendants forever.'" Then David left, and Jonathan went back to the town.

The chronological continuation of chapter 20 from the preceding chapter is secured by the reference to "Naioth at Ramah" in v.1 (found elsewhere only in 19:18–23). The frequent repetition of key terms and motifs throughout chapter 20, which will be pointed out in the comments below, also guarantees its integrity as a cohesive literary unit. Especially noteworthy is the expression "The LORD is witness between you and me forever" (vv.23, 42), which concludes each of the chapter's roughly equal halves (cf. Polzin, *Samuel and the Deuteronomist*, pp. 191–93; M.H. Segal, *The Pentateuch: Its Composition and Its Authorship and Other Biblical Stories* [Jerusalem: Magnes, 1967], p. 183).

**1–4** Polzin observes that the first half of chapter 20 contains a

> preponderance of definite, forceful, strident, and emotionally charged language. . . . The finite verb is strengthened or emphasized by a preceding infinitive absolute of the same stem no fewer than seven times in verses 1–21; both David and Jonathan frequently invoke the LORD's name in solemn oath, self-imprecation

> or blessing; the partners repeatedly protest, implore, and react in the strongest of terms; and they frequently punctuate their statements with the deictic *hinnēh*, "behold." (*Samuel and the Deuteronomist,* pp. 191, 264 nn. 10–13)

The brief interchange between David and Jonathan recorded in vv.1–4 is bracketed by David's question, "What have I done . . . that he is trying to take my life [lit., 'soul']?" (v.1), and Jonathan's words of assurance, "Whatever you [lit., 'your soul'] want me to do, I'll do for you" (v.4). David's flight from Saul at Naioth takes him back to the Gibeah fortress and to his friend (v.1), the only one he can trust. Like his ancestor Jacob before him (Gen 31:36; cf. similarly Abimelech's plea in Gen 20:9 and Obadiah's question in 1 Kings 18:9), David wants to know the nature of the terrible sin he has supposedly committed that would bring on such frantic pursuit of him. The naked truth that Saul was "trying to take" (lit., "seeking") his life would be repeated over and over by himself and others (22:23; 23:15; 25:29; 2 Sam 4:8).

But to Jonathan, trusting son as well as loyal friend, it was incredible to think that Saul really intended to harm David (vv.2, 9; cf. also Saul's oath in 19:6)—until it became painfully obvious to him (v.33). Jonathan, reminded of how his comrades-in-arms had come to his defense with their "Never!" in the face of Saul's murderous intentions toward his own son (14:45), encouraged David with the same interjection (vv.2, 9). He assured him that Saul did nothing without "confiding in me" (lit., "uncovering/opening my ear," an idiom used by Jonathan again in vv.12–13 [NIV, "let you know"]).

David, however—more sensitive to Saul's unpredictability and changes of mood—responds to Jonathan's "Look. . . . Why would he hide this from me?" (v.2) with his own "Look, . . . let me go and hide in the field" (v.5). He swears (v.3; cf. also vv.17, 42) with the most solemn of oaths (cf. also v.21; 19:6; see comment on 14:39) that there is "only a step" between him and death at the hands of Saul. As Abigail would later do in a similar situation (25:26), David strengthens the assertion even further by adding "and as you live" (cf. also 17:55; for its significance see comment on 1:26). He thus affirms that Saul, who "knows" of the high regard in which Jonathan holds David (cf. v.29), does not want his son to "know" of his evil designs on David's life or he would be "grieved" (cf. v.34). One major emphasis of the chapter concerns who knows (or does not know) this or that matter—and therefore, as Polzin observes, in chapter 20 "words using the root *YD'*, 'to know,' occur more often (twelve times) than in any other chapter in the book" (*Samuel and the Deuteronomist,* p. 194).

**5–7** Verses 5–23 constitute a three-act drama structured around ten "if-then" statements (vv.6, 7a, 7b, 8, 9, 10, 12, 13, 21, 22; cf. ibid., pp. 192, 264 n. 16, who discerns an eleventh [v.14]). The acts are arranged in chiastic order:

A. David's plan to help Jonathan know (vv.5–7)
 B. David and Jonathan's mutual covenant (vv.8–17)
A′. Jonathan's plan to tell David that he now knows (vv.18–23)

The vocabulary of v.5 (which begins the drama) is echoed in that of v.24 (which begins the second half of the chapter). David's plan (vv.5–7) is simple: If Saul accepts Jonathan's explanation for David's absence from the forthcoming New Moon festival celebration, then David is safe; but if Saul becomes angry, then Jonathan will know that Saul is bent on harming David.

The monthly burnt offerings at the appearance of the new moon (Num 28:14) were accompanied by celebration and rejoicing (Num 10:10). David's emphatic "I" (v.5) probably contains an element of surprise that he should be invited and also of trepidation in the knowledge of what would happen to him if he attended. He therefore plans to hide in a "field" (near Saul's fortress in Gibeah; see 19:3 and comment) until the evening of the third day, by which time he would presumably expect to receive word from Jonathan concerning Saul's reaction toward his absence from the festival.

David's excuse for not attending (v.6) is relayed by Jonathan to Saul in vv.28–29 (with some additional details). The verb "asked permission" (vv.6, 28, the rare Niphal of *šā'al* attested elsewhere only in Neh 13:6) provides yet another opportunity to pun on the name "Saul." David's desire to participate in an "annual sacrifice" with his family would not have been considered unusual (1:21; 2:19). During Samuel's boyhood days the normal venue was Shiloh (1:3), the site of the tabernacle. By David's time, however, Shiloh had been destroyed (see comment on 4:11), and the tabernacle had no fixed location. Thus it was only to be expected that annual sacrifices would be offered in the celebrants' hometowns.

Understandably, David was risking Saul's wrath by pretending to substitute a competing festival for the one the king had invited him to. Perhaps Bethlehem, his hometown, had the additional stigma of being outside Saul's domain (as argued by G.W. Ahlström, "Was David a Jebusite Subject?" ZAW 92, 2 [1980]: 285–87). In any case, David surely was not serious in asserting that Saul's ready agreement to allow him to go to Bethlehem would mean that he would then be back in the king's good graces (v.7)—"unless, of course, his entire strategy in having Jonathan lie about his absence is to provoke Saul to an angry outburst that would remove Jonathan's misconceptions, not his own" (Polzin, *Samuel and the Deuteronomist*, p. 189). David knew that Saul was determined to kill him (v.7); and although Jonathan had not yet brought himself to admit that cold fact (vv.9, 13), he soon would (v.33).

**8–17** Covenant terminology ("show kindness," vv.8, 14; "brought him into a covenant," v.8; "do not ever cut off your kindness," v.15; "made a covenant," v.16; "reaffirm his oath," v.17; "love[d]," v.17), used by both David and Jonathan, links together vv.8–17. Reminding Jonathan of the covenant that they had made (18:3), David asks him to demonstrate covenant loyalty, *ḥeseḏ* ("kindness," v.8)—conduct required in "the mutual relationship of rights and duties between allies" (Nelson Glueck, *Ḥesed in the Bible* [Cincinnati: Hebrew Union College, 1967], pp. 46–47). David's willingness to die "if I am guilty" would later be echoed by his son Absalom (2 Sam 14:32), though neither man believed himself worthy of death. David voiced his preference for dying at the hand of his covenanted friend Jonathan ("yourself" is emphatic) instead of his sworn enemy Saul. But Jonathan avowed that if he "had the least inkling" (v.9; lit., "knew at all") that his father intended to harm David, he would surely "tell" his friend. David, still wary, wants to know whether Jonathan would really "tell" (v.10) him if Saul answered "harshly" (a not uncommon quality in royal speech; cf. Gen 42:7, 30; 1 Kings 12:13 = 2 Chron 10:13) when he learned the reason for David's absence.

Cain had said to his brother Abel, "Let's go out to the field" (Gen 4:8), using the privacy it afforded to kill him. By contrast Jonathan said the same thing to his covenant brother David (v.11), using the privacy the field afforded to assure him of his undying loyalty. The fact that David and Jonathan went to the field "together" (lit., “the two of them”) underscores their close relationship and is reminiscent of the description of Abraham and Isaac at Moriah (Gen 22:6, 8).

The New Moon festival would be celebrated “tomorrow” (v.5), at which time Saul would react in one way or another to David’s absence (v.7). In accord with David’s wishes to learn of Saul’s response by “the evening of the day after tomorrow” (v.5), Jonathan promises on oath to send David word no later than that time—whether the news is favorable (v.12) or unfavorable (v.13). In either case, Jonathan says, “I . . . [will] send you away safely” (lit., “I will send you away, and you will go in peace”; cf. v.42 for the fulfillment of Jonathan’s promise). “May the LORD deal with me, be it ever so severely” (cf. also 3:17; 14:44; lit., “May the LORD do thus to me, and thus may he add”) was perhaps “accompanied by a suggestive gesture such as feigning to slit one’s throat” (William Sanford LaSor, David Allan Hubbard, and Frederic Wm. Bush, *Old Testament Survey: The Message, Form, and Background of the Old Testament* [Grand Rapids: Eerdmans, 1982], p. 240 n. 40). To the assessment of others concerning the Lord’s presence “with” David (see 16:18 and comment; 17:37; 18:12, 14, 28), Jonathan now adds his own prayer to the same end (v.13). In so doing he parallels David’s divine calling with that of Saul and thus recognizes—again (see comment on 18:4)—that David, and not he himself (Saul’s disobedience had long since forfeited an enduring kingdom for himself and his descendants, 13:13–14), will be the next king of Israel.

In vv.14–15 covenant friendship is the basis of Jonathan’s plea that neither he nor his descendants be executed by David after he becomes king. The link between these two verses and 2 Samuel 9 is established by comparing *ḥesed̲ YHWH* (“the kindness of the LORD”; NIV, appropriately, “unfailing kindness like that of the LORD,” v.14) with *ḥesed̲ ʾᵉlōhîm* (“the kindness of God”; i.e., “kindness like that of God,” preferable to the NIV’s “God’s kindness,” 2 Sam 9:3; cf. 2 Sam 9:1, 7). Norman H. Snaith suggests that since the divine name is sometimes used to denote the superlative, *ḥesed̲ YHWH* in v.14 perhaps means “the greatest possible loyalty.” In any case, “the word *chesed* plus the Sacred Name is used in 1 Sam 20:14 to express the close bond between David and Jonathan, the Hebrew equivalent of Roland and Oliver, Aeneas and Achates, Orestes and Pylades, the ‘faithful friends’ of history and romance and legend” (“The Meanings of a Word,” *Bible Translator* 16 [1965]: 47).

Jonathan’s plea to David not to “cut off” (v.15) his kindness from Jonathan’s “family” (lit., “house,” paralleling “house” in v.16) forms a Hebrew wordplay not only with “cut off . . . from the face of the earth” (v.15; for the idiom see Zeph 1:3) but also with “made [lit., ‘cut’; see comment on 11:1] a covenant” in v.16. By now Jonathan surely perceives that among David’s “enemies” (v.15; cf. also v.16) whom he predicts will be cut off is his own father, Saul (cf. 18:29; 19:17).

Thus Jonathan, on behalf of his family/house/descendants, extends in perpetuity (“ever,” v.15; cf. vv.23, 42) his previous covenant with David (see 18:3 and comment; cf. also 22:8) to the house/family/descendants of the latter (v.16). In so doing he prays that the Lord may “call David’s enemies to account” (lit., “demand an accounting [for the shedding of innocent blood] from the hand of David’s enemies”; cf. 2 Sam 4:11; for a parallel idiom, cf. Gen 9:5). Since covenants by nature and definition involve reciprocal obligations (v.42), Jonathan also has David reaffirm his side of the agreement (v.17), in context with the covenant language of 18:1, 3: “He loved him as [he loved] himself.”

**18–23** Jonathan's suggested ruse (vv.18–22) begins by echoing the time and place of the venue that David had originally proposed (v.5). He agrees that David will be "missed" because his seat will be "empty" (v.18; same Heb. in both cases). On the third day (v.19) David is to go to the field where he hid (David's suggestion as well, v.5) "when this trouble began" (probably referring to Saul's plans to kill him, 19:2). There he is to "wait" (lit., "sit"; instead of occupying a "seat" at Saul's religious festival [v.18], David will "sit" by himself in a nearby field) by a stone called Ezel (mentioned only here; location unknown).

Jonathan himself (the "I" at the beginning of v.20 is emphatic) will then aim three arrows at the stone, "shooting" (lit., "sending," a key verb in this section; cf. vv.21–22) as though at a target. The boy dispatched to find the arrows will be told either that the arrows are "on this side of" him (v.21) or "beyond" him (v.22). If the former is the case, David is "safe" (v.21), which, of course, is Jonathan's intention (v.13) and in which case David may return to the fortress at Gibeah. But if the arrows are beyond where the boy is at the time of Jonathan's shout, then David's life is in danger, and he must flee in response to the will of "the LORD" (v.22).

The first literary half of the chapter closes with Jonathan's reminder to David of the eternal nature of the covenant of friendship that bound them (v.23; cf. also v.42). Jonathan was especially concerned that David (the first "you" is emphatic) and his dynasty keep his promise, made on oath, not to break covenant with Jonathan (emphatic "I") and his descendants (vv.15–17). He therefore invokes the Lord as witness "between" the two men in a manner reminiscent of the ancient agreement between Jacob and Laban (Gen 31:48–53).

**24–34** Playing out the charade to humor his friend, David hid in the field (v.24 echoes v.5). When the celebrants gathered for the New Moon festival, Saul took his customary seat "by the wall" (v.25), where he could feel relatively secure from surprise attack. Jonathan and Abner, Saul's army commander (and cousin) (14:50; 17:55), occupied places of honor at the table, but David's place was "empty" (as Jonathan and David had planned, v.18).

Saul's ignorance of what was really taking place (he "said nothing," v.26) matched that of the boy sent by Jonathan to retrieve the arrows (he "knew nothing," v.39). When David did not appear on the first day of the New Moon festival, Saul assumed that something had happened to make him "ceremonially unclean" (v.26; cf. Lev 15:16, 18) and therefore disqualified from participating in a religious feast (cf. Num 9:6). But when David's seat was empty on the second day of the *ḥōḏeš* ("New Moon festival," v.27, as in vv.5, 18, 24; NIV's "month," vv.27, 34, while possible, causes unnecessary confusion; for the likelihood that the New Moon was celebrated for at least two days, cf. de Vaux, AIs, p. 470) also, Saul naturally wanted to know why. In referring to David as the "son of Jesse" (vv.27, 30–31; cf. also 22:7–9, 13, and esp. 25:10), Saul probably intended at least a mild insult (see comment on 10:11).

Jonathan's response to Saul's question (vv.28–29) reflects the language of David's original plan (v.6) but with the addition of a few details. Polzin (*Samuel and the Deuteronomist*, p. 264 n. 14), among others, calls attention to a wordplay in vv.27–28: David would rather celebrate with his humble family in "Bethlehem" (*bêṯ lāḥem*, v.28) than risk coming to a king's "meal" (*lāḥem*, v.27). Because of his wariness of Saul's paranoia, David's excuse is also a lie. He knows, however, that he can trust Jonathan: "I have found favor in your eyes" (v.3, quoted by Jonathan in v.29). A subtle irony in David's desire to "get away" (*mālaṭ*) to see his brothers is evident in the frequent use of the verb in its more common sense of "flee," "escape" with respect to his flight from Saul (e.g., 19:10, 12, 17–18), thus signaling yet another aspect of his fugitive status. Though Saul's grandson will always be welcome at King David's "table" (2 Sam 9:7–13), David feels unwelcome at the "table" of King Saul (v.29).

As David had feared (v.7), Saul became violently angry (v.30) when Jonathan told him the reason for David's absence. For all intents and purposes, Jonathan and David were indistinguishable to Saul as he exploded in "foul-mouthed anger" (Hertzberg, p. 175). The vile epithet Saul hurled at his son Jonathan, which the NIV translates euphemistically as "You son of a perverse and rebellious woman," is difficult to render without being equally vulgar—although TEV's "You bastard!" and NJB's "You son of a rebellious slut!" come close. Saul, of course, is cursing Jonathan, not Jonathan's mother, as the rest of the verse makes clear. He accuses Jonathan of having "sided with" (lit., "chosen") David, and that not only to his own shame but also the shame of the "mother who bore you" (lit., "nakedness of your mother," a phrase that elsewhere has sexual connotations; cf. the MT of Lev 18:7).

Saul further reminded Jonathan that so long as David remained alive, neither Jonathan (emphatic "you," v.31) nor Jonathan's kingdom could survive. History would prove Saul's fears to be prophetic beyond his worst nightmares: Although the kingdom of Saul and his son would not be established (13:13–14), the kingdom of David and his son would be (2 Sam 7:16, 26; 1 Kings 2:12, 46). The word *bēn* ("son"), used twice by Saul in v.30, occurs twice again on Saul's lips in v.31. Its second occurrence is hidden in the NIV's "must die": *ben-māwe<u>t</u>* (lit., "son of death" = a person characterized by or deserving of death). The idiom appears elsewhere only twice, both times in the books of Samuel (26:16; 2 Sam 12:5), and its last occurrence—on the lips of David himself—will recoil to haunt him for the rest of his life as the prophet Nathan identifies David as the one worthy of death: "You are the man!" (2 Sam 12:7).

Saul's demand for David's death (v.31) brings a predictable response from Jonathan: "Why?" (v.32; cf. 19:5). Jonathan's further question, "What has he done?" reflects his earlier reminder to Saul that David's actions had benefited the king (19:4). But Saul, though placated before (19:6), would not be denied this time. Saul, not having David as his target as on two previous occasions (18:10–11; 19:9–10), tried to pin David's surrogate Jonathan to the wall with his spear (v.33). Jonathan needed no further convincing that Saul indeed intended to kill David (something David had obviously known much earlier; cf. v.7) and that the spear had really been meant for his covenanted friend. In Saul's eyes, Jonathan and David had momentarily become one.

It was Jonathan's turn to fly into a rage (the Heb. phrase translated "fierce anger" in v.34 elsewhere describes the highest levels of disappointed human fury; cf. Exod 11:8; 2 Chron 25:10; Isa 7:4). Knowing of his father's murderous designs on and mistreatment of David caused Jonathan to be "grieved" (v.34), a response that his friend had foreseen (v.3). On the second day of the New Moon festival, neither David (v.27) nor Jonathan (v.34) ate at the king's table (vv.29, 34).

**35–40** The final section of chapter 20 (vv.35–42) is divided into two unequal parts, each of which ends with "back to [the] town" (vv.40, 42).

Verses 35–40 describe the fulfillment of the ruse proposed earlier (vv.18–22). Jonathan had told David to wait by the stone Ezel on the second day of the New Moon festival "toward evening" (v.19). Jonathan had left unspecified the time of the shooting of the three arrows (v.20), which he now begins on the following morning (v.35), presumably because the flight of an arrow is more easily seen in daylight. The boy Jonathan takes with him (vv.21–22) is here described as being "small" (v.35) and thus less likely to ask embarrassing questions about the orders he is given.

Although the MT reads "arrows" (pl.) the first time the word appears in vv.36–38 and "arrow" (sing.) the other four times (so also NIV), the number of arrows that Jonathan actually shot remains uncertain. Except for the last of the four occurrences of the singular (where, in any event, many MSS join the *Qere* in reading the pl.), the word for "arrow" is very rare (found elsewhere only in 2 Kings 9:24) and in each case is read as a plural in two or more Hebrew MSS. The four plural readings, however, may be a misguided scribal attempt to harmonize vv.36–38 with the "[three] arrows" of vv.20–22. Jonathan tells the boy to find the "arrows" he shoots (v.36a); but, since his aim is true, he discovers that he needs to shoot only one "arrow" (v.36b).

The arrow's landing beyond the running lad, loudly confirmed by Jonathan (v.37) so that David would be sure to hear it, was a signal to David that it was God's will for him to remain a fugitive from Saul (v.22). Jonathan's urgent commands to the boy (v.38) were obviously intended for David instead, but the boy of course did not know the reason behind the shooting of the arrow(s) in the first place (v.39). He therefore interpreted his master's words as a command to retrieve the arrow(s) and return to him. Jonathan then sent him back to town with all the weapons (v.40), assuming (and doubtless hoping) that David might want a private moment to bid his friend farewell.

**41–42** Getting up from his hiding place near "the stone" (v.41, implied from v.19), David bowed down more than once (a not uncommon practice in ancient times; cf. Gen 33:3 and often in the Amarna letters [Youngblood, *The Amarna Correspondence*, pp. 15–19]) to acknowledge Jonathan's (covenant) superiority ("with his face to the ground"; cf. further 24:8; 25:23, 41; 28:14). Their mutual kissing and weeping (v.41), though in expectation of their coming farewell (v.42), is reminiscent of the poignantly emotional scene involving Joseph and his brothers (Gen 45:14–15).

Jonathan's "Go in peace" (*lēḵ lᵉšālôm,* v.42) reflects the "safe(ly)" of vv.7, 13, 21 (see comment on vv.13, 21) and is generally spoken by a superior to an inferior (cf. 1:17; 25:35). At the same time Jonathan magnanimously uses the emphatic "we" as he reminds David of their mutual—and everlasting—oath of friendship (cf. vv.17, 23). They had sworn to each other "in the name of the LORD" (cf. Deut 6:13; 10:20), thus employing an oath that the Decalogue solemnly warned the ancient Israelite not to "misuse" (Exod 20:7 = Deut 5:11; cf. also Lev 19:12). The covenant between Jonathan and David included their "descendants forever" (cf. v.15 and comment; cf. also 24:21).

The two friends parted after Jonathan's farewell speech. Apart from one other brief meeting (23:16–18), this was the last time they would see each other.

## Notes

---

1 Perhaps כִּי (*kî*) should here be translated by the interrogative "why" instead of the NIV's "that" (see comment on 11:5).

3 The opening words, וַיִּשָּׁבַע עוֹד דָּוִד (*wayyiššāḇaʿ ʿôḏ dāwiḏ,* lit., "But David took an oath again"), present a difficulty since no previous oath is mentioned. The LXX and Syriac omit

*'ôḏ* (so also the NIV), as does Driver (assuming dittography at both ends of the word). Others preserve *'ôḏ* but revocalize *wyšb'* as וַיָּשֶׁב (*wayyāšeḇ*, "But he replied"), assuming the MT's final ' to be dittography (so Gordon, *I & II Samuel*, in loc.; cf. similarly Hertzberg, Klein, McCarter, Smith). Barthélemy, however, prefers the MT, apparently either willing to allow the difficulty to remain or understanding "again" as a way of expressing the addition of David's oath to his strong assertion of v.1.

**10** The difficult phrase אוֹ מַה־יַּעַנְךָ אָבִיךָ קָשָׁה (*'ô mah-yya'ankā 'āḇîḵā qāšāh*) has provoked numerous suggestions for emendation (see the commentaries). But since *'ô* ("or") occasionally means "if," "when" (as in Lev 26:41), and since *mah* sometimes functions as a relative pronoun meaning "what(ever)" (as in 19:3), "if what your father answers you is harsh" (cf. similarly NIV) solves the problem nicely.

**14** The best way to make sense out of the first two occurrences of וְלֹא (*wᵉlō'*, "and not") in v.14 is to repoint the consonantal text as וְלֻא (*wᵉlu'*, "and if only"; cf. לוּא [*lû'*, "if (only)"] in 14:30). Verse 14 would then read literally: "And if only you, as long as I am alive—indeed, if only you would show me the kindness of the LORD—that I may not die!" (cf. NIV; cf. also KD, p. 210).

**19** Although difficult, תֵּרֵד מְאֹד (*tērēḏ mᵉ'ōḏ*, lit., "you/she will go down exceedingly") can hardly be separated from וְהַיּוֹם רַד מְאֹד (*wᵉhayyôm raḏ mᵉ'ōḏ*, lit., "and the day went down exceedingly"; Judg 19:11; NIV, "and the day was almost gone"). McCarter, who correctly links the two passages, nevertheless reads in v.19, "you will wander [from the verb רוד (*rûḏ*)] exceedingly" = "you will be long gone" (*I Samuel*, p. 337 n. 19). But comparison with Isa 38:8, הַשֶּׁמֶשׁ . . . יָרָדָה (*haššemeš . . . yārāḏāh*; lit., "the sunlight . . . had gone down") makes resort to the rare verb *rûḏ* unnecessary. In the phrase in v.19 *tērēḏ* is correctly vocalized from the root *yrd* and has as its subject the unexpressed feminine noun *šemeš*: "[the sun] goes down exceedingly" = "[the sun] has almost set." The NIV's "toward evening" expresses the same idea idiomatically.

**25** The MT's וַיָּקָם יְהוֹנָתָן (*wayyāqom yᵉhônāṯān*, "and Jonathan got up"; cf. NIV mg.) is doubtless due to contamination from v.34. The NIV text of v.25 follows the LXX, which reads "and he was in front of Jonathan," implying וַיְקַדֵּם (*wayyᵉqaddēm*; cf. S.R. Driver, *Notes on the Books of Samuel*, p. 169, for details; cf. also Barthélemy, p. 192).

---

## 7. *David and the priest of Nob*

### 21:1–9

**1** David went to Nob, to Ahimelech the priest. Ahimelech trembled when he met him, and asked, "Why are you alone? Why is no one with you?"

**2** David answered Ahimelech the priest, "The king charged me with a certain matter and said to me, 'No one is to know anything about your mission and your instructions.' As for my men, I have told them to meet
me at a certain place. **3** Now then, what do you have on hand? Give me five loaves of bread, or whatever you can find."

**4** But the priest answered David, "I don't have any ordinary bread on hand; however, there is some consecrated bread here—provided the men have kept themselves from women."

**5** David replied, "Indeed women have been kept from us, as usual whenever I set out. The men's things are holy even on missions that are
not holy. How much more so today!" **6** So the priest gave him the consecrated bread, since there was no bread there except the bread of the Presence that had been removed from before the LORD and replaced by hot bread on the day it was taken away.

**7** Now one of Saul's servants was there that day, detained before the LORD; he was Doeg the Edomite, Saul's head shepherd.

> [8]David asked Ahimelech, "Don't you have a spear or a sword here? I haven't brought my sword or any other weapon, because the king's business was urgent."
> [9]The priest replied, "The sword of Goliath the Philistine, whom you killed in the Valley of Elah, is here; it is wrapped in a cloth behind the ephod. If you want it, take it; there is no sword here but that one."
> David said, "There is none like it; give it to me."

The last sentence in the NIV rendering of 20:42 is 21:1 in the MT, accommodating the traditional one-verse numbering difference between the Hebrew and the English texts throughout chapter 21. The commentary follows the English numbering system.

Chapters 21–22 apparently record events later than those in the preceding chapters since by this time David has gathered around him a sizable body of "men" (21:2, 4–5; 22:6) and has become their "leader" (22:2). The two chapters comprise a literary unit of three sections arranged in chiastic order. Chapters 21:1–9 and 22:6–23 are concerned with the priestly compound at Nob in Benjamin while the central section (21:10–22:5) summarizes David's flight to Gath in Philistia, Adullam in Judah, and Mizpah in Moab. Chapter 21:1–9, in turn, describes how David receives food (vv.1–6) and weapons (vv.8–9) from Ahimelech the priest, two sections that frame a brief notice regarding the presence in Nob of Doeg, one of Saul's servants (v.7).

**1–6** David, needing help in his continued flight from Saul, went to Nob (perhaps modern el-Isawiyeh, one and one-half miles northeast of Jerusalem [cf. Isa 10:32] and two and one-half miles southeast of Gibeah of Saul). The site of a large contingent of priests (22:11, 18–19), Nob may have been the location of the tabernacle (though not the ark of the covenant; cf. comment on 7:2) for a time. Ahimelech, one of the more prominent of Nob's priests and mentioned several times in these chapters, "trembled" when he "met" David (v.1), thus fearing his reputation and perhaps also recognizing his authority (cf. 16:4 for the similar reaction of Bethlehem's elders when confronted by Samuel).

Ahimelech's two questions—"Why are you alone?" and "Why is no one with you?"—may seem to be saying much the same thing, but David answers them separately. He is alone because there is a secret matter that he wishes to discuss with the priest (v.2a), and his men are not with him because he will meet them later (v.2b). Polzin (*Samuel and the Deuteronomist*, p. 195) suggests that the unnamed "king" in David's first answer is—in the narrator's mind, at least—not Saul but the Lord, who "charged" David with a certain matter and gave him "instructions" (v.2), just as he had earlier "appointed" him leader of his people to replace the discredited Saul (13:14; same Heb. root in all three cases). Polzin's proposal is attractive in that the name Ahimelech means "The King [i.e., God] Is My Brother" and that the narrator is thus perhaps engaging in wordplay in v.2. In addition Jonathan had been convinced that the Lord had "sent" David away (20:22), just as the Divine King has now asserted to David that no one is to know about "your mission" (v.2; lit., "the mission that I am sending you on"). David's statement concerning his meeting his men at a "certain" place is a rare Hebrew idiom that is used when one either does not know the name of a person or place or when he is deliberately trying to conceal it from his audience (Ruth 4:1, "my friend" [KJV, "such a one"]; 2 Kings 6:8, "such and such").

David next asks Ahimelech two questions (vv.3, 8), each of which is followed by the priest's answer (vv.4, 9a) and then David's response (vv.5, 9b). The questions are parallel in that both use the same rare idiom: "What do you have on hand?" (lit.,

"What is that under your hand/control?" v.3) and "Don't you have a spear or a sword here?" (lit., "Isn't there here a spear or sword under your hand/control?" v.8). David follows up his first question with a request: "Give me [lit., 'Give into my hand'] five loaves of bread"—a modest amount at best (cf. 17:17).

Echoing David's request, Ahimelech tells him what he has and does not have "on hand" (v.4): No "ordinary" (lit., "common") bread is available, but "there is" (for other examples of the rare emphatic position of *yēš*, see the MT of Judg 19:19; Isa 43:8) some "consecrated" (lit., "holy") bread that David and his men may eat. There was a condition, however: The men must not recently have had sexual relations with women, which would have rendered them ceremonially unclean (Exod 19:14–15; Lev 15:18) and therefore temporarily unfit to partake of the holy food.

David assured Ahimelech that women had indeed been "kept" (v.5; different Heb. verb than in v.4) from himself and his men, his customary practice whenever he "set out" to do battle (for *yāṣā'* in this specialized sense, cf. 8:20; 17:20). Uriah the Hittite would later refuse to sleep with his wife, Bathsheba, while on military duty (2 Sam 11:11). The sharp distinction between the "holy" (*qōḏeš*) and the "common" (*ḥōl;* cf. Lev 10:10; Ezek 22:26; 42:20; 44:23; 48:14–15) observed in v.4 is maintained in v.5. Even on "missions" (different Heb. word than in v.2) that are "not holy" (*ḥōl*), the "bodies" (see NIV mg.) of David's men are "holy" (*qōḏeš*). How much more so, then, during this particular venture—though we are not told what David's mission is. (He may well have made up the story out of whole cloth, either to deceive Ahimelech into supplying his needs or to protect the priest from any accusation of complicity in his flight from Saul.)

Satisfied with David's rationale, Ahimelech gives him the consecrated/holy bread, now identified specifically as the bread of the (divine) "Presence" (*pānîm,* v.6; cf. the mandate of placing the bread regularly "before" [*lip̱nê,* lit., "in the presence of"] the Lord [Lev 24:8]). Such bread (Exod 25:30; 35:13; 39:36; 40:23; Lev 24:5–8; 1 Kings 7:48 = 2 Chron 4:19), after it had performed its symbolic function, became "a most holy part" of the customary share given to the priests, who were to eat it in a "holy" place (Lev 24:9).

Since priestly perquisites were for priests and their families only (cf. Exod 29:32–33; Lev 22:10–16), how could Ahimelech in good conscience give the consecrated bread to David and his men, who were not priests? The answer provided by Jesus (Matt 12:1–8; Mark 2:23–28; Luke 6:1–5), the authoritative "Lord of the Sabbath," seems to be that "human need takes priority over ceremonial law" (F.F. Bruce, *The Hard Sayings of Jesus* [Downers Grove: InterVarsity, 1983], p. 33) and that it is always "lawful" on the Sabbath "to do good" (Mark 3:4). Possibly the incident recorded in vv.1–6 took place on a Sabbath day, since v.6 could imply that the consecrated bread being given to David had been replaced with a fresh supply ("hot bread") not long before (cf. Lev 24:8).

The reference to Abiathar (rather than to his father, Ahimelech) in Mark 2:26 is also puzzling (KD [p. 218 n. 1] calls it "an error of memory" on Mark's part). Perhaps John W. Wenham has the best solution. He observes that *epi tou batou* ("in the account of the bush," Mark 12:26) may be paralleled in *epi Abiathar archiereōs* in Mark 2:26, which should then be translated "in the account of Abiathar the high priest" ("Mark 2:26," JTS 1 [1950]: 156), especially since Abiathar was the only survivor of the slaughter of the priests of Nob (22:20) and in fact became much more noteworthy than his father (cf. chs. 22–30; 2 Sam 15–20; 1 Kings 1–4 [passim]; for a different [though related] solution, cf. Archer, *Encyclopedia of Bible Difficulties*, p. 362).

**7** Doeg the Edomite, perhaps a mercenary pressed into service as a result of Saul's war(s) against Edom (14:47), is introduced parenthetically in anticipation of his sinister role later (22:18–19). He had been detained "before the LORD" (i.e., at the tabernacle), probably for an undisclosed ceremonial reason (KD [p. 219] suggests that he may have been a proselyte "who wished to be received into the religious communion of Israel"). The verb "detained" echoes "kept" in v.5, both coming from the same Hebrew root. Doeg's official role in Saul's employ was as his "head shepherd" (cf. Joseph's brothers in Gen 47:6: "Put them in charge of my own livestock"; lit., "Make them chiefs [i.e., 'chief herdsmen,' thus NEB] of my own livestock").

**8–9** David's request for bread (v.3) is followed by one for weapons (v.8). David's question to Ahimelech—"Don't you have?" (lit., "Isn't there under your hand?")—is mirrored in his further statement, "I haven't brought" (lit., "I haven't taken in my hand"). What is not in David's hand he hopes is in Ahimelech's. The urgency of the "king's business" (v.8; cf. v.2, where the Heb. word for "business" is translated "a certain matter") is David's excuse for his lack of weapons. As in v.2 (see comment there), the identity of the king remains shrouded in studied ambiguity.

The only weapon Ahimelech has to offer to David is the sword of Goliath, whom—as was apparently widely known—David had killed in the "Valley of Elah" (v.9; cf. 17:2, 19, 48–51). Although he first took the giant's sword as part of his share of the Philistine plunder (17:54), he must have eventually brought it to the sanctuary of the Lord (for a Hittite parallel, cf. Hoffner, "A Hittite Analogue," p. 225). Ahimelech thus tells David that it is in a storage place behind the "ephod" (the priestly garment that held the breastpiece containing the sacred lots; cf. Exod 28:28, 30), where David can find it protected in a "cloth" (v.9; lit., "garment," often used as wrapping material in ancient times; cf. Exod 12:34; Judg 8:25).

Although David had not "brought" (v.8; lit., "taken") his own sword, Ahimelech was able to supply one: If you "want" (v.9; lit., "will take for yourself") Goliath's sword, then "take" it. As David had earlier said concerning the bread, "Give me five loaves" (v.3), he now says concerning the sword, "Give it to me" (v.9).

Ahimelech says of Goliath's mighty weapon, "There is no sword . . . but that one"; and David responds, "There is none like it" (v.9). David thus echoes Samuel's earlier description of Saul, the newly chosen king: "There is no one like him" (10:24). Polzin (*Samuel and the Deuteronomist*, p. 197) makes the important observation that

> the priestly transfer to David of the sword . . . speaks of the holy and mysterious transfer of royal power from Saul to David. . . . Once David is installed as king in Jerusalem and the matter of his "everlasting" kingship revealed in the vision of Nathan, it is no accident that David prays to the LORD in words that recall the very sword of Goliath, even as they tie together the unique choice of David with the unique LORD [2 Sam 7:22].

Polzin (ibid., p. 265 n. 23) also calls attention to the prayer of David's son Solomon in 1 Kings 8:23.

## Notes

---

**2** David's response to Ahimelech's first question is chiastically arranged, the first half of the chiasm occurring in his opening statement and the second half in his quotation of the Lord's words. A literal translation is "The King *charged* me with a *mission* and said to me, 'No one is to know anything about the *mission* that I am sending you on and that I have *charged* you with.' "

**6** The MT plural form הַמּוּסָרִים (*hammûsārîm,* "that had been removed") is probably a mistake for singular הַמּוּסָר (*hammûsār;* thus 4QSam$^{b}$) and arose by attraction to the preceding הַפָּנִים (*happānîm;* cf. Cross, "Oldest Manuscripts," p. 168).

---

### 8. *David the fugitive: Gath, Adullam, Mizpah*

#### 21:10–22:5

10 That day David fled from Saul and went to Achish king of Gath.
11 But the servants of Achish said to him, "Isn't this David, the king of the
land? Isn't he the one they sing about in their dances:

> " 'Saul has slain his thousands,
> and David his tens of thousands'?"

12 David took these words to heart and was very much afraid of Achish
king of Gath. 13 So he pretended to be insane in their presence; and
while he was in their hands he acted like a madman, making marks on
the doors of the gate and letting saliva run down his beard.
14 Achish said to his servants, "Look at the man! He is insane! Why
bring him to me? 15 Am I so short of madmen that you have to bring this
fellow here to carry on like this in front of me? Must this man come into
my house?"
22:1 David left Gath and escaped to the cave of Adullam. When his
brothers and his father's household heard about it, they went down to
him there. 2 All those who were in distress or in debt or discontented
gathered around him, and he became their leader. About four hundred
men were with him.
3 From there David went to Mizpah in Moab and said to the king of
Moab, "Would you let my father and mother come and stay with you
until I learn what God will do for me?" 4 So he left them with the king of
Moab, and they stayed with him as long as David was in the stronghold.
5 But the prophet Gad said to David, "Do not stay in the stronghold.
Go into the land of Judah." So David left and went to the forest of
Hereth.

Gath in Philistia (21:10–15), Adullam in Judah (22:1–2), and Mizpah in Moab (22:3–5) are presented in sequence as three of the places of refuge that David resorted to in his continuing flight from Saul.

**10–15** Immediately after departing from Nob ("That day," v.10) with the sword of Goliath, David went to Gath (ironically Goliath's hometown, 17:4), possibly to seek employment as a mercenary soldier. The king of Gath was Achish son of Maoch (*mā'ôḵ,* 27:2), perhaps an alternate form of Maacah (*ma'$^{a}$ḵāh,* 1 Kings 2:39), in which case Achish would have been the ruler of Gath for over forty years. In the title of Psalm 34, he is called Abimelech, possibly a Philistine royal or dynastic title (cf. Gen

20:2; 21:32; 26:1). The name Achish occurs in proto-Philistine and Philistine contexts outside the OT (e.g., Akashu, Ikausu; cf. Kitchen, "The Philistines," p. 67).

Whatever David's intentions in going to Gath, the "servants" (perhaps in the sense of "officers" or "attendants"; cf. comment on 16:15) of Achish (v.11) were sufficiently impressed by David's reputation—as reflected in the ditty composed after he and Saul had defeated the Philistines (18:7; cf. esp. 29:4–5)—to be wary of him. Calling him "king of the land," however, may have been belittling his importance by considering him only one among many such local rulers (cf. Josh 12:7, 9–24).

David took the servants' words seriously (v.12; cf. same Heb. idiom in Job 22:22). Having fled "from" (*mippenê*) Saul (v.10 [11 MT]), David was now very much afraid "of" (*mippenê*) Achish (v.12 [13 MT]). "Sensing danger [David] extracts himself from the situation by feigning madness. It creates a nice contrast. David controls madness. Madness controls Saul" (Gunn, *The Fate of King Saul*, p. 86).

In v.13 the verb translated "he acted like a madman" is used elsewhere to describe behavior resulting from drunkenness (Jer 25:16; 51:7) or terror (Jer 50:38) or to drive a chariot furiously or recklessly (Jer 46:9; Nah 2:4). The manifestations of David's pretended insanity were "making marks" (Heb. verb used elsewhere only in Ezek 9:4) on the doors of the (city) gate and letting saliva run down his beard—hardly the picture of a recently anointed king (contrast the positive image of oil running down the beard of Aaron in Ps 133:2).

Achish has seen enough. Sarcastically declaring that he already has sufficient madmen of his own, he makes it clear that he wants nothing more to do with this Israelite refugee (vv.14–15). David's deception of Achish has worked—as it would again (ch. 27) and again (ch. 29).

**22:1–2** Leaving Gath (v.1) David "escaped" (probably a reference to his continuing flight from Saul; cf. 27:1) to a cave near Adullam (in the western foothills of Judah, Josh 15:35; perhaps modern Khirbet esh-Sheikh Madhkur, about ten miles east-southeast of Gath). His brothers and other family members went "down" (presumably from the higher ground at Bethlehem, their hometown; cf. also Gen 38:1; 2 Sam 23:13 = 1 Chron 11:15) to join him there. They may have feared royal reprisal if they remained in Bethlehem, where Saul would be sure to come looking for the fugitive David.

It is possible, though by no means certain, that David's relatives joined "those" (v.2; lit., "a man," repeated three times in the verse; cf. also "men" near the end of the verse) who "gathered" around him (perhaps in anticipation of military action, as in 7:7 ["assembled"]). Numbering about "four hundred" (in itself a formidable force; cf. 25:13; 30:10, 17; Gen 33:1) even in the beginning, the ranks of David's men eventually swelled to as many as six hundred (23:13; 27:2; 30:9; cf. also 13:15 and comment; 14:2; 2 Sam 15:18; Judg 3:31; 18:11, 16–17). United by adverse circumstances of all sorts (e.g., the Heb. phrase translated "discontented" means literally "bitter of soul"; cf. 1:10), they were attracted to the charismatic David as their "leader" (v.2, a word with military connotations, often in contexts of raiding/looting; cf. 2 Sam 4:2; 1 Kings 11:24). Such bands of malcontents and other social misfits were not uncommon in the ancient Near East (cf. Judg 9:4; 11:3) and were often elsewhere known as *ʿapirū* (cf. Edward F. Campbell, Jr., "The Amarna Letters and the Amarna Period," BA 23, 1 [1960]: 14; cf. similarly David O'Brien, "David the Hebrew," JETS 23, 3 [1980]: 204).

**3–5** The section begins and ends with reference to place names not found elsewhere in the OT. The location of the "forest of Hereth" (v.5) is unknown (except that it was somewhere in Judah), while this particular "Mizpah" (v.3, *miṣpeh,* "Watchtower"; cf. 2 Chron 20:24, "place that overlooks"; Isa 21:8) was located on one of the heights of the tableland east of the Dead Sea. It was understandable that David should seek refuge for his "father and mother" in Moab (which he would later conquer, 2 Sam 8:2), since Moabite blood flowed through the veins of his ancestors on his great-grandmother's side (Ruth 1:4; 4:13, 16–17). In being solicitous of the needs of his parents, David was following common ancient practice (Josh 2:13, 18; 6:23; 1 Kings 19:20) as well as obeying the fifth commandment (Exod 20:12; Deut 5:16). In addition, his desire to conform to God's will (v.3) not only finds precedent in his previous conduct (cf. 17:35–37, 45–47) but also would become increasingly evident throughout his days as a fugitive from Saul (cf. 23:1–2, 4, 10–11; 25:32; 26:11, 23). David's "stronghold" (vv.4–5; cf. 24:22; 2 Sam 5:17; 23:14 = 1 Chron 11:16), whose location is unknown, could not have been the Cave of Adullam (contra Ackroyd, Hertzberg, Driver, McCarter, et al.) since the "stronghold" was not in Judah (v.5). David's true stronghold, of course, was ultimately God himself (2 Sam 22:2–3 = Ps 18:2).

As the prophet Samuel had helped and advised Saul, so from now on "the prophet Gad" (v.5), among others, would perform the same functions for David (cf. 2 Sam 24:11, where Gad is called "David's seer"). It was through such prophets that the word of God was mediated to Israel's leaders during the days of the monarchy, and it was often by such prophets that records of the royal reigns were written down (1 Chron 29:29).

## Notes

---

**13** The traditional title of Psalm 34, which includes the phrase "he pretended to be insane" (lit., "he changed/disguised his judgment/sense/taste"), places the psalm in the context of David's experience recorded in vv.10–15 (cf. esp. v.13). Although some have felt that the occurrence of the word "taste" in Ps 34:8 attracted later traditionalists to make a literary link with the wording of v.13, several verses in the psalm itself make a historical connection between the two texts plausible if not certain (cf. "fear[s]" in 34:4, 7, and deliverance from "troubles" in 34:6, 17, 19). Indeed, the psalm as a whole is appropriately tied to the episode in David's life described in vv.10–15.

Somewhat less close is the relationship between David's experience and Psalm 56. Verse 13 in our text states that David was "in their hands," at best a tenuous parallel to "the Philistines had seized him" in the title of the psalm. At the same time its general tenor lends itself to connection with the event in Gath (cf. "many are attacking me," Ps 56:2; "I will not be afraid," 56:4; "you have delivered me from death," 56:13); and it is therefore understandable that traditionalists might have linked the two passages.

**4** The MT's וַיַּנְחֵם (*wayyanḥēm,* "and he led them"; root נחה [*nḥh*]) has been vocalized as וַיַּנִּחֵם (*wayyanniḥēm,* root נוח [*nwḥ*]) by the NIV to yield the more likely meaning "he left them" (cf. the same problem and solution in 2 Kings 18:11, "settled them").

---

## 9. *The slaughter of the priests of Nob*
### 22:6–23

6 Now Saul heard that David and his men had been discovered. And
Saul, spear in hand, was seated under the tamarisk tree on the hill at

Gibeah, with all his officials standing around him. [7]Saul said to them, "Listen, men of Benjamin! Will the son of Jesse give all of you fields and vineyards? Will he make all of you commanders of thousands and commanders of hundreds? [8]Is that why you have all conspired against me? No one tells me when my son makes a covenant with the son of Jesse. None of you is concerned about me or tells me that my son has incited my servant to lie in wait for me, as he does today."

[9]But Doeg the Edomite, who was standing with Saul's officials, said, "I saw the son of Jesse come to Ahimelech son of Ahitub at Nob. [10]Ahimelech inquired of the LORD for him; he also gave him provisions and the sword of Goliath the Philistine."

[11]Then the king sent for the priest Ahimelech son of Ahitub and his father's whole family, who were the priests at Nob, and they all came to the king. [12]Saul said, "Listen now, son of Ahitub."

"Yes, my lord," he answered.

[13]Saul said to him, "Why have you conspired against me, you and the son of Jesse, giving him bread and a sword and inquiring of God for him, so that he has rebelled against me and lies in wait for me, as he does today?"

[14]Ahimelech answered the king, "Who of all your servants is as loyal as David, the king's son-in-law, captain of your bodyguard and highly respected in your household? [15]Was that day the first time I inquired of God for him? Of course not! Let not the king accuse your servant or any of his father's family, for your servant knows nothing at all about this whole affair."

[16]But the king said, "You will surely die, Ahimelech, you and your father's whole family."

[17]Then the king ordered the guards at his side: "Turn and kill the priests of the LORD, because they too have sided with David. They knew he was fleeing, yet they did not tell me."

But the king's officials were not willing to raise a hand to strike the priests of the LORD.

[18]The king then ordered Doeg, "You turn and strike down the priests." So Doeg the Edomite turned and struck them down. That day he killed eighty-five men who wore the linen ephod. [19]He also put to the sword Nob, the town of the priests, with its men and women, its children and infants, and its cattle, donkeys and sheep.

[20]But Abiathar, a son of Ahimelech son of Ahitub, escaped and fled to join David. [21]He told David that Saul had killed the priests of the LORD. [22]Then David said to Abiathar: "That day, when Doeg the Edomite was there, I knew he would be sure to tell Saul. I am responsible for the death of your father's whole family. [23]Stay with me; don't be afraid; the man who is seeking your life is seeking mine also. You will be safe with me."

Verses 6–23 serve the dual function of (1) describing the penultimate fulfillment of the Lord's promised judgment against the priestly house of Eli (see comment on 2:31–33; for the ultimate fulfillment see 1 Kings 2:26–27) and (2) demonstrating the complete contrast between the rejected king Saul's contempt for a priesthood that he considered to be treacherous and the elected king David's respect for and gratitude toward a priesthood that he considered to be an important mediator of God's will to his anointed.

The section begins with Saul the king "seated" (*yôšēḇ*, v.6) under a tree, with possible pagan connotations, and concludes with Abiathar the priest of the Lord being advised by David: "Stay [*šeḇāh*] with me" (v.23). The pericope as a whole has a chiastic arrangement:

A. Saul berates his officials (vv.6–8).
B. Doeg informs on Ahimelech (vv.9–10).
C. Saul condemns Ahimelech and his fellow priests (vv.11–17).
B′. Doeg kills Ahimelech and his fellow priests (vv.18–19).
A′. David protects Ahimelech's son (vv.20–23).

**6–8** Christian E. Hauer, Jr., perceptively observes that whereas the information gatherers of King David's administration were adroit on the foreign field but inept at home, Saul seems to have been poor at gathering information from abroad but was adept at coping with internal security matters (cf. 23:7, 19, 25, 27; 24:1; 26:1). In the present context (v.6) Saul "knew both David's whereabouts and the identity of the men with him" ("Foreign Intelligence and Internal Security in Davidic Israel," *Concordia Journal* 7, 3 [1981]: 96). David and his men "had been discovered" (lit., "were known"; cf. Prov 10:9, "will be found out"). The description of Saul with "spear in hand" reminds us of what a constant threat he was to friend and foe alike (cf. 18:10–11; 19:9–10; 20:33). Although the location of a "tamarisk tree" could have neutral (31:13) or even positive (Gen 21:33) connotations, the "hill" outside Gibeah may well have been a place given over to pagan worship (cf. Ezek 16:24–25, 31, 39, where the same Heb. word is translated "lofty shrine[s]" in a chapter devoted to apostasy of the most detestable kind). Saul's officials were dutifully "standing around him" (cf. v.9), ostensibly at his beck and call (cf. 4:20, "attending her").

Saul demands of his fellow Benjamites an answer to the question of whether the "son of Jesse" (v.7, a pejorative way of referring to David; cf. vv.8, 13; cf. comment on 20:27) can provide for them more possessions and privileges than they already have as associates of Saul himself. Does David have the power of a Samuel or a Saul to appoint them to high positions (cf. 8:1; 18:13)? Would David be able to make them "commanders of thousands and commanders of hundreds" (v.7, which, if true, would mean that David had become king; cf. 8:12 and comment; cf. also 17:18 NIV mg.)? After all, David himself was merely a "leader" (v.2, translating the same Heb. word here rendered "commander") of a few hundred men.

In his paranoia Saul assumes that all his men (v.8)—indeed, the priest Ahimelech as well (v.13)—are co-conspirators with David against him. By using the verb *qāšar* ("conspired"), the narrator may be subtly implying that soldiers and priests alike had become "one in spirit with" David (see 18:1 and comment). Saul complains that no one "tells" (lit., "opens the ear of"; see comment on "confiding in me," 20:2) him about his son Jonathan's perceived acts of treachery: making a covenant with David (cf. 18:3; 20:16) and inciting David to ambush Saul. All this, Saul insists, demonstrates his servants' lack of concern for their master.

**9–10** Like Saul's officials (v.6), Doeg the Edomite was "standing" (v.9) near him. Imitating Saul's reference (v.7) to David as the (despised) "son of Jesse," Doeg informs Saul that he witnessed David's meeting with Ahimelech at Nob (see 21:7). In this chapter Ahimelech is referred to several times as "son of Ahitub" (vv.9, 11, 12, 20) to highlight his membership in the condemned family of the high priest Eli (see 14:3 and comment, where it is suggested that Ahimelech might be another name for Ahijah).

Doeg reports to Saul that Ahimelech had "inquired" (v.10; root *š'l;* yet another wordplay on the name Saul; cf. vv.13, 15; 23:2, 4) of the Lord for David, a fact not mentioned in 21:1–9 but readily admitted to by the priest (v.15). In addition, Doeg continues, Ahimelech gave David "provisions" and "the sword of Goliath the Philistine" (cf. 21:6, 9; both expressions are in emphatic position in their respective clauses, stressing Doeg's opinion that Ahimelech was committing treasonable acts by assisting Saul's enemy).

According to its traditional title, Psalm 52 contains David's tirade against Doeg on this occasion. In the first stanza (52:1–4) David appears to accuse Doeg of falsehood, while in the second (vv.5–7) he foretells divine judgment on him. After David proclaims his confidence in God's unfailing love on his behalf (v.8), the psalm concludes with praise to the Lord for his deeds and his presence ("name," v.9).

**11–17** Doeg's report to Saul resulted in the king's sending for Ahitub's "whole" priestly family (v.11), who "all" responded by coming from Nob to Gibeah, scarcely two miles to the northwest ("whole" and "all" emphasize the almost total annihilation about to take place). Upon their arrival Saul addressed Ahimelech in words that echo his statements to his officials in vv.7–8: "Listen . . . son of Ahitub" (v.12). The epithet "son of Ahitub" is not only the pejorative equivalent of "son of Jesse" (vv.7–9, 13), demonstrating Saul's anger over what Ahimelech has done, but also forms a suitable literary parallel to his earlier reference to his officials as "men [lit., 'sons'] of Benjamin" (v.7). In response Ahimelech's "Yes, my lord" is appropriately servile and obedient.

Saul's retort in v.13 combines the elements of Doeg's report in v.10 ("inquiring of God" for David as well as providing him with "bread" and "a sword") and the substance of his own accusations against his officials in v.8 ("conspired against me," "lies in wait for me," "as he does today"; cf. also "incited," v.8, and "rebelled," v.13, both of which are translations of forms of *qûm*, "rise up"). But whereas Saul was of the opinion that his men had conspired among themselves, he insists that Ahimelech is overtly in league with his enemy David ("you and the son of Jesse," v.13).

Ahimelech's response to Saul (vv.14–15) is polite but firm. He defends David's character by suggesting that none of the king's servants is as "loyal" (v.14) as David (cf. comment on "faithful," describing Samuel, in 2:35). After all, David is Saul's "son-in-law" (cf. 18:18). In addition, he is the captain of Saul's "bodyguard" (the word is later used of David's own bodyguard in 2 Sam 23:23 = 1 Chron 11:25) and "highly respected" (cf. comment on 9:6, again describing Samuel; cf. further the characterization of Benaiah, a valiant fighter in charge of David's bodyguard, in 2 Sam 23:22–23, "held . . . in honor").

Having evaluated David's reputation positively to his own satisfaction, Ahimelech emphatically denies that this was the first time he had consulted God on David's behalf (the essential element of the Heb. idiom rendered "Of course not!" in v.15 is translated "Never!" in 14:45; 20:2, 9). Saul should therefore not "accuse" (a strong verb in such contexts; elsewhere rendered "slander," Deut 22:14, 17; "charges," Job 4:18) Ahimelech or his father's family. In any case, Ahimelech claims to know nothing "at all" (lit., "small or great") of the crimes that Saul attributes to David. Believing Ahimelech to be a liar, however, Saul tells him that he and his family "will surely die" (v.16; cf. Saul's intention concerning his own son Jonathan in 14:39, 44). Polzin observes: "Ahimelech is playing here a kind of Jonathan role in the particular conjunction of death and ignorance that permeates their speech in chapters 20 and 22. In 20:2 Jonathan responded to David's worries, 'You shall not die. Behold, my father does nothing either great or small without disclosing it to me.' . . . In Jonathan's formulation, knowledge of things great and small goes with life; in Ahimelech's case, ignorance of matters great or small will lead to death" (*Samuel and the Deuteronomist*, p. 199).

As good as his word, Saul issues orders for the execution of the priests of Nob. He first commands the "guards" (v.17; lit., "runners," cf. comment on 8:11) "at his side" (lit., "the ones standing around/with him," as in vv.6, 9) to "turn" (preparatory to acting; cf. v.18; cf. also 15:12, 27) and kill them. The priests' crime was that although they knew David was fleeing, they did not "tell" Saul about it (cf. the similar reticence of his own men, v.8). More serious, however, is the fact that the priests "too" (along with David's followers, v.2—and perhaps also [some of] Saul's men?) are in league with David. But Saul's orders fall on deaf ears, thwarted by the religious scruples of his officials. They refuse to raise "a hand" (lit., "their hand," echoing the terminology used earlier in the verse to describe the priests, who "have sided with" [lit., "their hand is with"] David) against the priests of the Lord. The fugitive David would later say, "I will not lift my hand against my master [Saul], because he is the LORD's anointed" (24:10), and after Saul's death he would rebuke an Amalekite for insensitivity in the same respect (2 Sam 1:14).

Saul's officials are adamant: They are "not willing" to kill the Lord's priests (v.17). The same Hebrew verb is used later to describe David's unwillingness, as well as that of Saul's armor-bearer, to harm the Lord's anointed ("would not," 26:23; 31:4). Miscall appropriately compares what Doeg the Edomite was about to do to the priests with what Saul and his men had earlier refused to do to the Amalekites (15:9, "were unwilling"): "Through the hand of a foreigner, Saul perpetrates upon Israelites, priests of the Lord, what he himself did not perpetrate upon foreigners, the Amalekites" (p. 136).

**18–19** When Saul, not to be denied, issues his ominous order to Doeg, the doom of the priests is sealed. An Edomite, Doeg has no qualms about killing Israelite priests. The MT uses the emphatic pronoun "he" in connection with the verb "struck . . . down" (v.18), paralleling the emphatic "You" earlier in the verse and stressing the willingness of a foreigner to do what Saul's Israelite officials refused to do. The number of priests murdered surely qualifies the deed as a massacre, and reference to them as wearing the "linen ephod" links the act to the prophecy against the house of Eli delivered by an unnamed man of God (2:28; cf. also 14:3 and the comment on "linen ephod" in 2:18).

Not satisfied with killing the eighty-five priests of Nob, Doeg extends the slaughter by putting the entire town "to the sword" (v.19; cf. the similar threat against Jerusalem recorded in 2 Sam 15:14). The doleful list of victims at the end of the verse recalls once again the contrast to Saul's earlier reluctance to totally destroy the Amalekites (see comment on 15:3). "Put to the sword" is the usual NIV rendering of the MT's "strike with the edge [lit., 'mouth'] of the sword," perhaps a vivid description of the sickle-shaped blades of swords commonly used throughout much of the OT period (cf. Yadin, *Art of Warfare*, pp. 204, 206–7).

**20–23** Probably unknown to Saul at the time, "a" (v.20; lit., "one," stressing the fact that he was the sole survivor) son of Ahimelech "escaped" (the same verb is frequently used of David; cf. 19:10, 12, 17–18) and joined David's fugitive band. Abiathar ("The [Divine] Father Is Excellent") by name (cf. Moses' father-in-law, the priest Jethro, whose name means "His Excellency"), he performed priestly functions for David for the rest of David's life (cf. 23:6, 9; 30:7; 2 Sam 8:17), eventually to be replaced by Zadok under Solomon's reign (1 Kings 2:27, 35; for the reference to Abiathar in Mark 2:26, see comment on 21:6). When he informs David that Saul had issued orders resulting in the massacre of all the priests of Nob except himself (v.21), David tells him (v.22) that he had anticipated Doeg's act of betrayal ever since their earlier encounter at Nob (cf. 21:7). David then confesses that he himself, however unwittingly, is ultimately accountable for the massacre. In saying "I am responsible," David uses a form of the same Hebrew verb translated "turn," "turned" in v.18. Although it was Doeg the Edomite who "turned" and killed the priests, it was David who, through his earlier presence at Nob, was "responsible" for causing their death. He therefore offers refuge to Abiathar, telling him not to "be afraid" (v.23; cf. Jonathan's similar reassurance to David in 23:17). Abiathar may count on David's protection: "You" (emphatic), David says, "will be safe with me." Saul now seeks the life (see comment on 20:1) of both of them; so they become partners in flight. King-elect and priest-elect have joined forces as fellow fugitives.

## Notes

6 Saul may have chosen a tamarisk tree, which is "found abundantly in deserts, dunes and salt marshes" (*Fauna and Flora of the Bible* [London: United Bible Societies, 1972], p. 182) but is not native to the hill country of Gibeah, to officiate under because its anomalous presence (like that of the palm tree under which Deborah sat [Judg 4:5]) would have made it instantly recognizable from a distance. In addition, it provides delightful shade that is cooler than that of other trees (cf. Nogah Hareuveni, *Tree and Shrub in Our Biblical Heritage* [Kiryat Ono: Neot Kedumim, 1984], pp. 24–26).

"Tamarisk" as the correct meaning of אֵשֶׁל (*'ešel*) is defended by James Barr, who vigorously critiques other ancient and modern renderings such as "measure of length," "plot of land," "grove" ("Seeing the Wood for the Trees? An Enigmatic Ancient Translation," JST 13, 1 [1968]: 11–20). Although the NEB translates *'ešel* as "strip of ground" as its preferred rendering in Gen 21:33, the 1989 REB prefers "tamarisk tree" in conformity with 1 Sam 22:6; 31:13 (the only two other places in the OT where the Heb. word appears).

14 "Captain" translates שַׂר (*śar*), probably the original reading (cf. the LXX's *ἄρχων*, *archōn*), for which the MT's סָר (*sār*, "turning [aside], departing") is doubtless an aural scribal error. Restoration of *śar* in this verse strengthens its function as a *Leitwort* throughout the chapter (cf. vv.2 ["leader"], 7 ["commanders"]).

## 10. *The rescue of Keilah*

### 23:1–6

1 When David was told, "Look, the Philistines are fighting against
Keilah and are looting the threshing floors," 2 he inquired of the LORD,
saying, "Shall I go and attack these Philistines?"
The LORD answered him, "Go, attack the Philistines and save Keilah."
3 But David's men said to him, "Here in Judah we are afraid. How
much more, then, if we go to Keilah against the Philistine forces!"
4 Once again David inquired of the LORD, and the LORD answered him,
"Go down to Keilah, for I am going to give the Philistines into your
hand." 5 So David and his men went to Keilah, fought the Philistines and
carried off their livestock. He inflicted heavy losses on the Philistines

**and saved the people of Keilah. 6(Now Abiathar son of Ahimelech had brought the ephod down with him when he fled to David at Keilah.)**

Chapters 23 and 24 are linked together by the frequent occurrence of the word "hand," which appears twenty times in the two chapters. It is found nine times in chapter 23 (vv.4, 6 ["with him" = lit., "in his hand"], 7, 11 ["to him" = lit., "into his hand"], 12 ["to Saul" = lit., "into the hand of Saul"], 14, 16 ["helped him find strength" = lit., "strengthened his hand"], 17, 20) and eleven times in chapter 24 (vv.4, 6, 10 [bis], 11 [bis, the second occurrence being "I am not guilty" = lit., "there is not in my hand"], 12, 13, 15, 18, 20). In chapter 23 the issue is usually that of the effective (or ineffective) use of "power" (a frequent metaphorical meaning of "hand"), while in chapter 24 the stress is more on the restraint of power than on its use (cf. Miscall, p. 139). The two unequal halves of chapter 23 (vv.1–6, 7–29) have in common David's use of the priestly ephod to inquire of the Lord (vv.6, 9), first to save the people of Keilah from the Philistines (vv.1–6) and then to save himself from Saul (vv.7–29).

**1–6** The Philistine threat, relegated to the background for several chapters, returns to menace a town in Judah (v.1). Keilah, prominent in this chapter, is mentioned elsewhere in the OT only in Joshua 15:44 (which locates it in the western foothills of Judah; cf. Josh 15:21, 33) and Nehemiah 3:17–18 (where it gave its name to an administrative district of Judah after the Babylonian exile; it had apparently also been an important town much earlier, as references to *Qīltu* in the fourteenth-century Amarna letters indicate; cf. ANET, pp. 487, 489). Ancient Keilah is usually identified with the modern site of Khirbet Qila, located about eighteen miles southwest of Jerusalem and three miles southeast of Adullam.

Just as Saul had saved Israel from "those who had plundered" them (see 14:48 and comment), so also David would save the people of Keilah from the Philistines who were "looting" (v.1) their threshing floors (same Heb. verb). In ancient Near Eastern towns, threshing floors often served as storage areas (2 Kings 6:27; Joel 2:24).

David's repeated inquiries to God concerning whether he should go to Keilah and attack the Philistines, together with their divine responses (vv.2, 4), are reminiscent of similar inquires and responses during the period of the judges (Judg 20:23, 28). Such inquiries usually made use of the sacred lots, the Urim and Thummim, stored in the priestly ephod (cf. v.6; see comment on 14:36, 40–42). When "David's men" (v.3; see comment on 18:27) learned that the Lord had responded affirmatively to his first inquiry, they demurred. After all, they said, even in the relative security of certain parts of Judah—for example, the forest of Hereth (22:5–6)—"we" are afraid (v.3; the emphatic "we" balances and contrasts with the emphatic "they," the subject of "are looting" in the MT of v.2). But going to Keilah, closer to Philistines who were in battle array and armed to the teeth, would be even worse—in fact, it would be too frightening to contemplate.

David therefore inquired of the Lord again (v.4), and this time God told him that he himself (the "I" is emphatic) would guarantee David's victory over the Philistines (the Lord's earlier response [v.2] had not spelled out the means by which David would "save Keilah"). The promise of divine help apparently reassured David's men, who then joined him in defeating the enemy. All the verbs in v.5, however, are singular in number, reflecting either (1) the lack of faith of David's men or (2) the common attribution of success to the leader, even though it was clearly understood that he could not have succeeded on his own. Thus David "saved" the people of Keilah (v.5), as God had commanded (v.2) and promised (v.4). The account of the victory concludes with the parenthetical note that Abiathar had earlier brought the priestly ephod with him when he had fled from Nob and joined David (v.6; cf. 21:9; 22:20). As in chapter 17, so also here the Lord chooses not the rejected king but the fugitive king-elect to deliver his people from the Philistines.

### 11. *The pursuit of David*

#### 23:7–29

[7]Saul was told that David had gone to Keilah, and he said, "God has handed him over to me, for David has imprisoned himself by entering a town with gates and bars." [8]And Saul called up all his forces for battle, to go down to Keilah to besiege David and his men.

[9]When David learned that Saul was plotting against him, he said to Abiathar the priest, "Bring the ephod." [10]David said, "O LORD, God of Israel, your servant has heard definitely that Saul plans to come to Keilah and destroy the town on account of me. [11]Will the citizens of Keilah surrender me to him? Will Saul come down, as your servant has heard? O LORD, God of Israel, tell your servant."

And the LORD said, "He will."

[12]Again David asked, "Will the citizens of Keilah surrender me and my men to Saul?"

And the LORD said, "They will."

[13]So David and his men, about six hundred in number, left Keilah and kept moving from place to place. When Saul was told that David had escaped from Keilah, he did not go there.

[14]David stayed in the desert strongholds and in the hills of the Desert of Ziph. Day after day Saul searched for him, but God did not give David into his hands.

[15]While David was at Horesh in the Desert of Ziph, he learned that Saul had come out to take his life. [16]And Saul's son Jonathan went to David at Horesh and helped him find strength in God. [17]"Don't be afraid," he said. "My father Saul will not lay a hand on you. You will be king over Israel, and I will be second to you. Even my father Saul knows this." [18]The two of them made a covenant before the LORD. Then Jonathan went home, but David remained at Horesh.

[19]The Ziphites went up to Saul at Gibeah and said, "Is not David hiding among us in the strongholds at Horesh, on the hill of Hakilah, south of Jeshimon? [20]Now, O king, come down whenever it pleases you to do so, and we will be responsible for handing him over to the king."

[21]Saul replied, "The LORD bless you for your concern for me. [22]Go and make further preparation. Find out where David usually goes and who has seen him there. They tell me he is very crafty. [23]Find out about all the hiding places he uses and come back to me with definite information. Then I will go with you; if he is in the area, I will track him down among all the clans of Judah."

[24]So they set out and went to Ziph ahead of Saul. Now David and his men were in the Desert of Maon, in the Arabah south of Jeshimon. [25]Saul and his men began the search, and when David was told about it, he went down to the rock and stayed in the Desert of Maon. When Saul heard this, he went into the Desert of Maon in pursuit of David.

[26]Saul was going along one side of the mountain, and David and his men were on the other side, hurrying to get away from Saul. As Saul and his forces were closing in on David and his men to capture them, [27]a messenger came to Saul, saying, "Come quickly! The Philistines are raiding the land." [28]Then Saul broke off his pursuit of David and went to

**meet the Philistines. That is why they call this place Sela Hammahlekoth. 29 And David went up from there and lived in the strongholds of En Gedi.**

In contrast to David's seeking and receiving divine guidance, which brings him victory (vv.1–6), Saul relies totally on human messages and reports (cf. vv.7, 13, 19, 25, 27), which bring him frustration and failure (vv.7–29). Ironically, the Hebrew verb translated "inquired" in vv.2 and 4 is *šā'al,* a wordplay on Saul's name.

The section describes Saul's pursuit of David from Keilah (vv.7–13) to the Desert of Ziph (vv.14–24a) to the Desert of Maon (vv.24b–28) and concludes with David's flight to the strongholds of En Gedi (v.29).

**7–13** The statements "Saul was told that David had gone to Keilah" (v.7) and "Saul was told that David had escaped from Keilah" (v.13) frame the literary unit. Whether sincerely or in a false display of piety, Saul affirms that God has "handed" David over to him (v.7; cf. v.20—where, however, the Heb. verb is different). Saul assumes that David is trapped, that he has "imprisoned himself" (cf. Ezek 3:24, "shut yourself") in a walled town from which there may be only one exit (the same Heb. verb underlies the renderings "surrender" in vv.11–12 and "handing . . . over" in v.20). "Gates and bars" is literally "two doors [cf. Isa 45:1 MT] and a bar." Keilah perhaps had only one gateway in its wall, its two reinforced wooden doors hinged to posts at the sides of the entrance, meeting in the center, and secured with a heavy metal bar spanning the entrance horizontally (for a possible parallel, cf. Judg 16:3). Preparing to attack David at Keilah, Saul "called up" (v.8) his troops (the Heb. verb is the common *šāma'* ["heard"] in its rare Piel form, the only other occurrence in the OT being in 15:4 [see comment there]).

David soon found out (v.9) that Saul was "plotting" (lit., "thinking/planning evil"; cf. the same idiom in Prov 3:29, "plot harm") against him. He therefore told Abiathar to bring the ephod so that he might use the Urim and Thummim to inquire of the Lord (as he had in vv.1–6; cf. also 30:7–8). The verb "bring" is commonly used in cultic or ceremonial contexts (cf. 14:18; see 14:34 and comment).

David begins and concludes his plea (vv.10–11) with the words "O LORD, God of Israel," acknowledging the Lord as the true Sovereign of his people. Just as Saul earlier was "looking for a chance" to kill him (19:2) and had "tried" to pin him to a wall (19:10), David now expresses his concern that Saul "plans" to destroy Keilah because of him (v.10; same Heb. verb in all three cases).

Although David asks two questions (v.11), the Lord answers only the second one. David therefore repeats the first question (v.12), this time expressing his concern for the safety of his men also. The Lord now answers it as well. In each case the divine response consists of only one Hebrew word, which the NIV appropriately translates as tersely as possible. That the citizens of Keilah would even think of surrendering their deliverer and his men to Saul might seem like the height of ingratitude, but perhaps they feared royal retribution if they harbored fugitives. In any case, because the Lord's answers to David's questions bode ill for David and his men, they leave Keilah and frequently change their location (v.13; for some of the places they eventually went, cf. 30:27–31, where the verb "had roamed" renders the same Heb. verb as "kept moving" does here). Although since the last count (22:2) the number of his men has increased to "about six hundred" (cf. also 25:13; 27:2; 30:9; see also comment on 13:15), David understandably feels that they are still no match for Saul and his army (cf. the reference to Saul's "three thousand chosen men" in 24:2). For his part, Saul changes his mind about going to Keilah when he learns that the fugitives have left.

**14–24a** Just as references to Keilah frame vv.7–13, so also references to Ziph frame vv.14–24a. Mentioned elsewhere only in v.15 and 26:2, the Desert of Ziph (v.14) was doubtless located east of Ziph (v.24), which had been allotted to Judah in the hill country west of the Dead Sea after Joshua's conquest of Canaan (Josh 15:48, 55). The modern site of the ancient town is Tell Zif, located twelve miles southeast of Keilah. Knowing that Saul was relentlessly continuing his search for him (vv.14, 25), David hid in various "strongholds" in the Desert of Ziph (vv.14, 19) and elsewhere (v.29).

Despite the careful description of the location of Horesh and its strongholds (vv.15, 19), the exact site is unknown (although Khirbet Khuresa, less than two miles from Tell Zif, may preserve the ancient name). In spite of God's gracious and providential care (v.14), David was afraid, because Saul came out to take his life "while David was at Horesh in the Desert of Ziph" (v.15; see Notes). So Saul's son Jonathan went to Horesh to remind David of the Lord's concern for him and to encourage him (v.16). Jonathan said (v.17), "Don't be afraid, because" (*'al-tîrā' kî*, echoing *wayyirā' kî* in v.15) Saul will not "lay a hand on you."

This was not, of course, the first time that Saul had "come out" against David to "take/seek his life" (v.15; cf. 20:1; 22:23)—nor would it be the last (25:29; 26:20). Miscall (p. 141) observes that Jonathan's helping David "find strength in God" (v.16) in this situation is paralleled by a similar crisis later: "David found strength in the LORD his God" when his own men were talking about stoning him (30:6). Jonathan's "Don't be afraid" (v.17) is mirrored—ironically—by David's earlier "don't be afraid" to the fugitive Abiathar in the face of the same threat (22:23). Miscall (p. 142) notes that Jonathan's assurance to David that Saul's murderous intent would come to naught has an earlier analogy (20:2).

Jonathan vigorously continues to encourage David: "You [emphatic] will be king," while "I [emphatic] will be second to you"—an inevitable truth that Saul also knows (v.17). Although "second" in contexts of this kind means primarily "second-in-command," "next in rank" (1 Chron 16:5; 2 Chron 28:7; 31:12; Esth 10:3; Jer 52:24), Miscall makes the suggestive observation that it can also mean "double" or "copy" (Gen 43:12; Deut 17:18) and that therefore Jonathan is at the same time David's "copy, his equal" (p. 142). "The two of them" (v.18)—as equals—then make a covenant in the presence of the Lord, perhaps invoking his blessing and taking an oath in his name. While it is possible that this constitutes a reaffirmation of the earlier covenant initiated by Jonathan between the two men (18:3; 20:8), it is better understood as a fresh, bilateral covenant defining their new relationship (see comment on 18:3). Having comforted his friend, Jonathan returns home to Gibeah—perhaps never to see David again (no further meetings between the two men are recorded).

Certain "Ziphites" (anarthrous in v.19 in all but two Heb. MSS) go to Gibeah and reveal David's whereabouts, perhaps to ingratiate themselves to Saul. Their words to him—"Is not David hiding among us?"—are repeated verbatim in the title of Psalm 54, whose traditional setting is thus the narrative in vv.19–24a. In the psalm David prays for deliverance (Ps 54:1–2); complains that ruthless, ungodly men are seeking his life (v.3); pleads that their evil deeds will recoil on them (v.5); and promises a freewill offering to the Lord in gratitude for God's faithfulness in delivering him (vv.6–7). The psalm's centering verse (v.4) focuses on David's assurance that the Lord is his help and sustainer.

The Samuel narrative locates David's hiding place on the hill of Hakilah (cf. 26:1, 3), an unknown location south of Jeshimon (cf. v.24; 26:1, 3), whose location is also unknown except generally as a "wasteland" (so the Heb. word; cf. Num 21:20; 23:28) between Ziph and the Dead Sea. The Ziphites invite Saul to come to them "whenever it pleases you" (v.20; lit., "according to all the desire of your soul," a rare idiom found also in Deut 12:15, 20, 21 ["as much . . . as you want"]; 18:6 ["in all earnestness"]; Jer 2:24 ["in her craving"]), at which time they promise to hand David over to him.

Saul's reply to the Ziphites, "The LORD bless you" (v.21), is a stereotyped expression (see comment on 15:13) that tells nothing about his piety (or lack of it; see v.7 and comment). His gratitude for their "concern" for him recalls the earlier episode where he "spared" Agag—like himself, a doomed king—and the best of the Amalekite livestock (15:9, 15) in direct violation of God's command through Samuel (15:3; same Heb. verb; cf. the similar observation in Polzin, *Samuel and the Deuteronomist*, p. 204). The NIV's "make further preparation" (v.22) is not on target in this context; "make sure once more" (NAB) is much better (cf. also NASB, NEB, RSV). Always the investigator relying on human ability, Saul tells the Ziphites to "find out" (vv.22–23; cf. 14:38; lit., "know and see") where David usually hides. David will later hurl Saul's phrase back at him ("understand and recognize," 24:11) in protestation of his own innocence (cf. further "See [how]" in 1 Kings 20:7; 2 Kings 5:7).

Saul is determined to track David down no matter where he goes or what it takes (vv.22–23; cf. Hushai's similar advice to Absalom against his father, David, in 2 Sam 17:12–14). Under no circumstances will he permit the "crafty" David to outwit him (v.22; cf. Gen 3:1 where the same Heb. root describes the serpent). The Ziphites are to pinpoint every potential hiding place that David might use and then report back to Saul "with definite information" (v.23; same Heb. root as that for "make . . . preparation" in v.22; see Notes). Obedient to their presumed overlord, they return to Ziph and begin to comb the area in search of David and his men (v.24a).

**24b–29** *Hālaḵ* ("went"), the basic Hebrew verb of movement, gives unity to vv.25–28, for each verse contains the verb at least once (v.25, "began"; v.26, "was going," "to get away"; v.27, "Come"; v.28, "went"). Verse 28 in the MT concludes chapter 23; v.29 of the EVV is 24:1 in the MT.

On the run as usual (v.13), David and his men go to "the Desert of Maon, in the Arabah south of Jeshimon" (v.24b; for Jeshimon see comment on v.19). Although "Arabah" is usually thought of as the name of the desert flatlands stretching for more than a hundred miles from the southern end of the Dead Sea to the northern end of the Gulf of Aqaba, in some contexts (as here) it clearly refers to northward extensions of those flatlands west and east of the Dead Sea and beyond, all the way to the southern end of the Sea of Galilee (for details cf. S. Cohen, IDB, 1:177–79; H.G. Andersen, ZPEB, 1:233–36). Like the Desert of Ziph (see comment on v.14), the Desert of Maon was named for a town that had been allotted to Judah in the hill country west of the Dead Sea after Joshua's conquest of Canaan (Josh 15:48, 55). Modern Khirbet Main, five miles south of Ziph, marks the location of the ancient site, and the Desert of Maon would thus most likely have been south of the Desert of Ziph (cf. the map in Rasmussen, p. 114).

Upon hearing that Saul had once again embarked on his relentless "search" for him (v.25; cf. v.14), David retreated with his men to "the rock" (soon to be given a name, v.28) in the Desert of Maon. Informed of this (probably by the Ziphites), Saul pursued his quarry. He probably divided "his forces" (v.26) into two groups so that they could attack both flanks of David's men "on the other side" of the mountain, thus "closing in" on them. Although David had been able to "get away" from Saul on several occasions (cf. 18:11; 19:10), it appears that this time all was lost—at least from a human standpoint. Providentially, however, a messenger arrived with the unsettling news that Philistines were raiding (v.27) part of Saul's sovereign territory. Sensing a greater threat from the Philistines, Saul had no choice but to postpone his pursuit of David (v.28). The "rock" (*sela'*, v.25) from which Saul and his men marched out to engage the Philistines in battle was called "Sela Hammahlekoth." The name originally may have meant "Smooth/Slippery Rock" (the same Heb. root is used to describe David's five "smooth stones" in 17:40). By popular etymology it came to mean "The Rock of Parting" (see NIV mg.; the same Heb. root is translated "scatter[ed]" in Gen 49:7; Lam 4:16), apparently referring to the timely retreat of Saul's men from David's men on that occasion (for other examples of topographical features receiving memorable names, cf. 7:12; 2 Sam 2:16; Josh 5:3; Judg 15:17, 19).

God used the distraction of Philistines, rather than the aid of Ziphites or other Judahites, to rescue David from the tentacles of Saul (cf. similarly Miscall, p. 143). For his part David moved himself and his men to strongholds in the vicinity of the En Gedi oasis (v.29; modern Ain Jidi, near Tell ej-Jurn on the western shore of the Dead Sea fourteen miles east of Ziph). Known also as Hazazon Tamar (2 Chron 20:2; cf. Gen 14:7), En Gedi's powerful, perennial spring provided abundant water for vineyards (S of Songs 1:14) and played a prominent role in Ezekiel's vision of a restored Israel (Ezek 47:10, 18–19; 48:28).

## Notes

---

7 The NIV's "God has handed him over to me" translates נִכַּר אֹתוֹ אֱלֹהִים בְּיָדִי (*nikkar 'ōṯô 'ᵉlōhîm bᵉyāḏî*, "God has delivered him into my hand[s]"). For *nikkar* the LXX reads *πέπρακεν* (*pepraken*, "sold"), giving rise to the suggestion that *nikkar* is a scribal error for מָכַר (*mākar*; see Smith, p. 212 and cf. Judg 4:9 for the idiom). סִכַּר (*sikkar*, "hand over") has also been proposed on the basis of Isa 19:4 (see S.R. Driver, *Notes on the Books of Samuel*, p. 184; Klein, p. 228; McCarter, *I Samuel*, pp. 369–70). James Barr defends the existence of a rare verb *nkr* (which he defines as "acquire," "sell"), points to the use of וָאֶכְּרֶהָ (*wā'ekkᵉrehā*) in Hos 3:2 as a parallel example from the same root (although *wā'ekkᵉrehā* is usually derived from כָּרָה [*kārāh*]; cf. BDB, p. 500), and adduces Ugaritic *nkr* (*Comparative Philology and the Text of the Old Testament* [Oxford: Clarendon, 1968], p. 331; cf. also John Gray, *The Legacy of Canaan: The Ras Shamra Texts and Their Relevance to the Old Testament*, 2d rev. ed. [Leiden: Brill, 1965], p. 141 n. 1; cf. p. 260; Johannes C. de Moor, *An Anthology of Religious Texts From Ugarit* [Leiden: Brill, 1987], p. 153 n. 24). Attention should also be called to Akkadian *nukkuru* ("to transfer/reassign/move someone to another location"), which has the added advantage of being in the same stem as *nikkar* (cf. CAD, 11:169, for examples).

9 4QSam[b] preserves a fragmentary text of vv.9–17 (cf. Cross, "Oldest Manuscripts," pp. 169–71). Although it presents a few modest deviations from the MT, one or two of which may be closer to the autographs of 1 Samuel, none is significant enough to require attention for the purposes of this commentary.

The so-called long forms of the Hebrew masculine singular imperative, which end in ה ָ (normally *â,* but in this series *āh*), perhaps originally functioned as ventives, like Akkadian verbal forms ending in *-a(m).* The ventive expresses action from the standpoint of its destination: "here," "to me," and so forth (Wolfram von Soden, *Grundriss der Akkadischen Grammatik* [Rome: Pontifical Biblical Institute, 1952], pp. 1007–8; K. Riemschneider, *An Akkadian Grammar,* tr. Thomas A. Caldwell, John N. Oswalt, and John F.X. Sheehan [Milwaukee: Marquette University Press, 1974], pp. 51–52). Thus הַגִּישָׁה (*haggîšāh*) would have originally expressed fully the idea "bring to me" and only later—when the ventive nuance had been lost—would have required the kind of explicit expansion found in 30:7 (MT).

**15** חֹרֶשׁ (*ḥōreš*) means "forest" (cf. 2 Chron 27:4 ["wooded areas"]; Isa 17:9 ["thickets"]; Ezek 31:3); so the trees of Horesh would have provided additional cover for David and his men.

In the light of the overall context, the MT's וַיַּרְא כִּי (*wayyar' kî,* "and he saw that"; NIV, "he learned that") is to be repointed as וַיִּרָא כִּי (*wayyirā' kî,* "and he was afraid, because"; so virtually all recent commentators; e.g., Baldwin, Driver, Gordon, Klein, McCarter). *Wayyar'* in 26:3 should not be used to justify the MT vocalization here because there the context demands "when he saw."

**23** "At Nacon" (see NIV mg.) understands אֶל־נָכוֹן (*'el-nāḵôn*) as containing a proper name (cf. the similar situation in 26:4). But although Nacon is clearly a place-name in 2 Sam 6:6 (see comment there for the alternate form "Kidon" in the 1 Chron 13:9 parallel), it seems best to understand it here as a common noun from the root כּוּן (*kûn,* "be firm, definite, prepared, sure") in light of the use of the same root in v.22 (see comment in loc.).

---

## 12. *Sparing Saul's life*

### 24:1–22

[1]After Saul returned from pursuing the Philistines, he was told, "David
is in the Desert of En Gedi." [2]So Saul took three thousand chosen men
from all Israel and set out to look for David and his men near the Crags
of the Wild Goats.
[3]He came to the sheep pens along the way; a cave was there, and Saul
went in to relieve himself. David and his men were far back in the cave.
[4]The men said, "This is the day the LORD spoke of when he said to you, 'I
will give your enemy into your hands for you to deal with as you wish.' "
Then David crept up unnoticed and cut off a corner of Saul's robe.
[5]Afterward, David was conscience-stricken for having cut off a corner
of his robe. [6]He said to his men, "The LORD forbid that I should do such a
thing to my master, the LORD's anointed, or lift my hand against him; for
he is the anointed of the LORD." [7]With these words David rebuked his
men and did not allow them to attack Saul. And Saul left the cave and
went his way.
[8]Then David went out of the cave and called out to Saul, "My lord the
king!" When Saul looked behind him, David bowed down and prostrated himself with his face to the ground. [9]He said to Saul, "Why do you
listen when men say, 'David is bent on harming you'? [10]This day you
have seen with your own eyes how the LORD delivered you into my hands
in the cave. Some urged me to kill you, but I spared you; I said, 'I will not
lift my hand against my master, because he is the LORD's anointed.'
[11]See, my father, look at this piece of your robe in my hand! I cut off the
corner of your robe but did not kill you. Now understand and recognize
that I am not guilty of wrongdoing or rebellion. I have not wronged you,
but you are hunting me down to take my life. [12]May the LORD judge
between you and me. And may the LORD avenge the wrongs you have
done to me, but my hand will not touch you. [13]As the old saying goes,
'From evildoers come evil deeds,' so my hand will not touch you.

14 “Against whom has the king of Israel come out? Whom are you
pursuing? A dead dog? A flea? 15 May the LORD be our judge and decide
between us. May he consider my cause and uphold it; may he vindicate
me by delivering me from your hand.”
16 When David finished saying this, Saul asked, “Is that your voice,
David my son?” And he wept aloud. 17 “You are more righteous than I,”
he said. “You have treated me well, but I have treated you badly. 18 You
have just now told me of the good you did to me; the LORD delivered me
into your hands, but you did not kill me. 19 When a man finds his enemy,
does he let him get away unharmed? May the LORD reward you well for
the way you treated me today. 20 I know that you will surely be king and
that the kingdom of Israel will be established in your hands. 21 Now
swear to me by the LORD that you will not cut off my descendants or wipe
out my name from my father’s family.”
22 So David gave his oath to Saul. Then Saul returned home, but David
and his men went up to the stronghold.

As noted earlier (see comment on intro. to ch. 23), chapter 24 follows naturally on chapter 23 from a literary standpoint in that the word “hand” appears frequently in each chapter. In addition, chapter 24 begins where chapter 23 ends: David is in the desert strongholds of En Gedi. Finally, Saul’s relentless pursuit of David in chapter 23 continues in chapter 24. The linkage between the two chapters is thus secured.

At the same time, however, it is equally clear that chapters 24–26 form a discrete literary unit within 1 Samuel. Chapters 24 and 26 are virtually mirror images of each other, beginning with Saul’s receiving a report about David’s latest hiding place (24:1; 26:1), focusing on David’s refusal to lift a hand against Saul, “the LORD’s anointed” (24:6, 10; 26:11), and concluding with the words of a remorseful Saul and his returning home from his pursuit of David (24:17–22; 26:21, 25). The two chapters form a frame around the central chapter 25, where the churlish Nabal functions as an alter ego of the rejected Saul. In addition, divine protection that keeps David from shedding innocent blood runs as a unifying thread through all three chapters. In the words of Gordon: “From 24:1 to 26:25 we have a three-part plot in which there is incremental repetition of the motif of blood-guilt and its avoidance” (“David’s Rise,” p. 53).

The last verse of chapter 23 in the NIV constitutes the first verse of chapter 24 in the MT, accommodating the traditional one-verse numbering difference between the Hebrew and the English texts throughout chapter 24 (for a similar phenomenon in chapter 21, see comment on intro. to ch. 21). Chapter 24 itself divides naturally into three roughly equal sections arranged in chiastic order:

A. David spares Saul’s life (vv.1–7)
  B. David’s *apologia* (vv.8–15)
A′. David agrees to spare Saul’s descendants (vv.16–22)

**1–7** On a previous occasion when the Israelites “returned from chasing the Philistines,” they plundered their camp (17:53). This time, after Saul “returned from pursuing the Philistines” (v.1; cf. 23:28), he was told about David’s general location (the desert west of En Gedi; see comment on 23:29) and set out with “three thousand chosen men” (v.2; see also 26:2) that outnumbered David’s motley band (see 22:2 and comment) five to one (23:13; 25:13; 27:2; 30:9). The term “chosen men” refers to warriors who were especially skilled (Judg 20:16) and courageous (Judg 20:34, “finest men”). Saul narrowed his search to an area near the Crags of the Wild Goats (location unknown, although the reference to "wild goats" stresses the inaccessibility of the site—cf. Job 39:1, "mountain goats"; Ps 104:18—and thus sets up a contrast with En Gedi, which means "Spring of the [Tame] Young Goat").

The "sheep pens" Saul "came to" (v.3) probably consisted of one or more enclosures made of low stone walls flanking the entrance to a cave. Thus Saul would have entered the pens to gain access to the cave ("came" and "went in" translate the same Heb. verbal form). His purpose in going into the cave was to "relieve himself" (lit., "cover his feet"; cf. other expressions such as "go outside" [Deut 23:12] and "sit down outside" [Deut 23:13], both translated "relieve yourself" by the NIV). The narrator may have chosen this particular euphemism for defecation because it occurs elsewhere only in Judges 3:24, where it is used of Eglon king of Moab who, "alone in the upper room of his summer palace" (Judg 3:20), was killed by the judge Ehud. Saul king of Israel, going inside the cave in search of privacy, is similarly unaware that he is placing himself in mortal danger.

Unknown to Saul, David and his men were "far back in" that very cave (lit., "in the deepest recesses of"; cf. Jonah 1:5, where the same Heb. word is translated "below [deck]"). The traditional titles of Psalms 57 and 142 connect those psalms with this incident. In Psalm 57 David prays for divine help (Ps 57:1–5), crying out for deliverance from "those who hotly pursue" him (v.3) and whom he describes metaphorically as "lions" and "ravenous beasts" (v.4). In the latter half of the psalm (vv.6–11), he praises the Lord for his great "love" and "faithfulness" (v.10), which give him the assurance of the deliverance he seeks. Psalm 142 similarly voices David's prayer for divine rescue from "those who pursue" him (v.6) as well as his plea for release from his "prison" (v.7, perhaps a reference to the cave). He is grateful for the anticipated deliverance that will take place because of the "goodness" of God (v.7). In both psalms David cries out for divine "mercy" (57:1; 142:1), and in both he affirms that the Lord, not the cave, is his true "refuge" (57:1; 142:5).

If the titles of Psalms 57 and 142 preserve an authentic tradition concerning their setting, David must have composed them long before Saul arrived on the scene, because David's men see in the presence of Saul inside the cave a golden opportunity to get rid of him once and for all (v.4). Whether we choose the NIV text (which would refer to a divine promise to David not mentioned previously) or the footnote (which would refer to God's providence working through present circumstances), the end result is the same: David now has a chance to eliminate his "enemy" (vv.4, 19; see also 18:29 and comment; the word is similarly used by Saul of David in 19:17).

Out of respect for Saul's divine anointing, and therefore not willing to kill him, but at the same time wanting to let him know that he was not in control of his own destiny, David crept up behind him "unnoticed" (cf. "quietly," translating the same Heb. word, in the sinister context of Judg 4:21). In cutting off the corner of Saul's robe, David may have been symbolically depriving Saul of his royal authority and transferring it to himself (cf. v.11; see also comment on 15:27–28 and 18:4). At the very least, parallels from cuneiform texts found at Mari and Alalakh "may imply that David's act in cutting off the 'wing' or hem of Saul's garment was an act of rebellion for which he was later repentant" (D.J. Wiseman, "Alalakh," in *Archaeology and Old Testament Study*, ed. D. Winton Thomas [Oxford: Clarendon, 1967], p. 128).

The fact that David was "conscience-stricken" (v.5) for what he had done is to be understood as recognition on his part that he had sinned (cf. 2 Sam 24:10, the only other occurrence of the expression in the OT). A literary echo of this scene appears in 25:31, where Abigail's warning to David reminds him that vengeance belongs to God and that, if he were to kill Nabal and his men, the guilt resulting from needless bloodshed would be on his "conscience."

Using a solemn oath (v.6; the essence of this verse is summarized in the parallel context in 26:11), David affirms to his men that he will never "do" (same Heb. verb translated "deal [with]" in v.4) harm to his master Saul, who is "the LORD's anointed" (used seven times in chs. 24 and 26: 24:6 [bis], 10; 26:9, 11, 16, 23). Made the anointed of the Lord by divine appointment and human ministration (see 9:16 and comment; 10:1; cf. also 12:3, 5), Saul is king. David—himself also the Lord's anointed, and thus perhaps not wanting to do anything that could provide a precedent for his own murder later (Polzin, *Samuel and the Deuteronomist*, p. 210)—will not lay a hand on Saul (vv.6, 10; cf. also 26:9, 11, 23). Indeed, using metaphorically a strong verb that means literally "tear apart" (Lev 1:17; Judg 14:6), David "rebuked" his men for even so much as thinking otherwise (v.7), and Saul leaves the cave none the wiser.

**8–15** The brief *apologia* of David recorded here should be compared with that of Samuel (ch. 12)—not so much in terms of precise literary parallels as in terms of persuasive power. At the same time David's *apologia* is echoed at the end of chapter 26, where it functions in much the same way as that of Samuel, serving as a kind of farewell speech to Israel's king.

After Saul left the cave (v.7), David, after a short time, himself emerged and "called out" to Saul (v.8; the verb often implies physical distance between sender and receiver, as in 20:37). Addressing Saul as his acknowledged superior ("My lord the king!" echoed in 26:17, 19), David "bowed down and prostrated himself with his face to the ground"—the same expression used of Saul doing obeisance to an apparition of the deceased Samuel (28:14).

David begins his protestation and defense with a "Why?" (v.9) that echoes that of Saul, who had earlier accused David of conspiracy (22:13). He assures Saul that he is not intent on "harming" him (v.9), nor is he guilty of "wrongdoing" (v.11; same Heb. word in both cases). Unlike those who spread false rumors about his murderous plans, David refuses to listen to all who would incite him to vengeance against Saul (v.10). Indeed, the king himself knows that David has just now had a unique opportunity to kill him, but David has refused to seize it.

Pressing his advantage, three times David says to Saul, *r*ᵉ*'ēh*: "See, . . . look. . . . recognize" (v.11). When he addresses Saul as "my father," he is probably not simply using a term of respect but is reminding the king that he is, after all, Saul's son-in-law (cf. 18:17–27; 22:14) and thus holds him in high regard (Saul will later respond to David as "my son," v.16). Taking another tack, Gunn (*The Fate of King Saul*, pp. 94–95) suggests that by calling Saul his father "David has usurped Jonathan's sonship; symbolically he requires Saul as father in order for his future kingship to be (symbolically) legitimate," and "even the cutting of the robe . . . confirms symbolically that Saul's status—as king *and* father (i.e., dynast)—is in effect transferred to David." The "piece/corner of [Saul's] robe," mentioned four times in this chapter (vv.4–5, 11 [bis]) and now in David's hand (v.11), is a "symbol of Samuel, of the kingdom, and of Saul's rejection" and, in addition, "points ahead to a future date when the Lord tears the kingdom from the hand of Solomon, David's son" (Miscall, p. 148; cf. comment on 15:27–28; 19:24; cf. also 28:14, 17; 1 Kings 11:11–13, 29–31).

Continuing to protest his innocence, David wants Saul to "understand and recognize" (v.11; lit., "know and see"; cf. comment on "find out" in 23:22–23) that he is not guilty of "wrongdoing," a plea that he will repeat later ("wrong" in 26:18

translates the same Heb. word; see also comment on v.9 and note especially Abigail's warning to David in 25:28b). Using the same verbal root as in 20:1, David reminds Saul that he has not "wronged" (lit., "sinned [against]") him (cf. also Jonathan's strong objections to his father in 19:4). There is therefore no reason, says David, that Saul should be "hunting" him down (the verb, used elsewhere only in Exod 21:13, means "act with malicious intent"; cf. the related noun in Num 35:20, 22: "[un]intention[ally]"). Unwilling to submit their dispute to human arbitration, David prays that the only fair and impartial Judge (cf. Judg 11:27), the Lord himself, might "judge between you and me" (v.12), a request repeated almost verbatim in the Hebrew of v.15 (there translated "decide between us"). But no matter what happens, David assures his king, "My hand will not touch you" (vv.12–13). After all, evil deeds are perpetrated only by evildoers, as an ancient proverb affirms (v.13). The proverb may in fact be double-edged, vindicating the righteous David's refusal to harm Saul while at the same time condemning the wicked Saul for his malicious pursuit of David (cf. similarly A.S. Herbert, "The 'Parable' [*Māšāl*] in the Old Testament," SJT 7, 2 [1954]: 183–84).

Earlier EVV (KJV, ASV, RSV, NEB) understood the two brief phrases at the end of v.14 as noninterrogative statements of fact or as exclamations. The meaning would then be that Saul should not waste his time chasing David, who is as insignificant as a "dead dog" (cf. also 2 Sam 9:8; 16:9), a "single flea" (MT; echoed in 26:20). More recent versions (including NIV), however, tend to treat the phrases as questions (NASB, REB) and thus as veiled threats to Saul: If he thinks that David will be easy to vanquish, he had better think again (cf. similarly Gunn, *The Fate of King Saul*, p. 154 n. 6).

David concludes his apology by entreating the Lord to decide between himself and Saul (v.15; the rare Heb. word translated "judge" is not the same as that in v.12 and occurs elsewhere only in Ps 68:5 ["defender"], where it again describes God). Confident of the outcome, David affirms his belief that the Lord will "uphold" his "cause" against Saul, using a phrase that he would use again after the death of Nabal, Saul's alter ego (25:39; cf. Gordon, "David's Rise," p. 48). He prays to the Lord to "vindicate me [by delivering me] from" Saul (the words in brackets are supplied by the NIV to fill what would otherwise be an English ellipsis; for another way of treating the same Heb. idiom, cf. 2 Sam 18:19, 31, where David is informed that God has "delivered him from" his enemies—this time including Abaslom, his son).

**16–22** Saul's remorseful response to David (vv.17–21) is framed by transitional v.16 and concluding v.22. It is no more necessary to deny Saul's sincerity here than it is in the parallel passage in 26:21, 25. In each case Saul begins with the plaintive "Is that your voice, David my son?" (v.16; 26:17; cf. also 26:21, 25). For the significance of "my son" here, see the comment on "my father" in v.11. Speaking later to Nabal, David refers to himself as "your son David" (25:8), strengthening the suggestion that Nabal functions as Saul's alter ego (cf. Gordon, "David's Rise," pp. 47–48). Miscall makes the important observation that Saul "will soon act to end David's status as royal son-in-law by giving Michal [Saul's daughter and David's wife, 18:27] to Palti (1 Sam 25:44)" (p. 146). Meanwhile Saul, distressed and conscience-stricken, "wept aloud" when confronted by David's innocence. "Saul's weeping and his address to David as 'my son' will be echoed . . . when David weeps over the death of . . . Absalom, who has attempted to seize the throne from David, as Saul perceives David trying to do from him" (Preston, p. 35; cf. 2 Sam 15:1–12; 18:33).

Mirroring Judah's words concerning his daughter-in-law Tamar (Gen 38:26), Saul says to his son-in-law David, "You are more righteous than I" (v.17). He then draws a contrast between David's exemplary conduct (emphatic "You") and his own deplorable actions (emphatic "I"). David has treated Saul "well" (v.17), Saul admits that what David has done to him is "good" (v.18), and Saul desires that the Lord will reward David "well" for what he has done (v.19), since a man never lets his enemy get away "unharmed" (lit., "in a good way"; same Heb. word in all four cases). Saul admits to David, "I have treated you badly" (v.17; Heb. idiom elsewhere only in Gen 50:17; Prov 3:30 ["done you . . . harm"]; Isa 3:9 ["brought disaster upon"]). Gordon ("David's Rise," p. 48) notes the same contrast in David's words concerning Nabal: "He has paid me back evil for good" (25:21).

Saul's recognition that the Lord had "delivered" him into David's hands (v.18; different Heb. verb in v.10) is later echoed by Abishai (26:8; cf. also David's confident challenge to Goliath in 17:46: "The LORD will hand you over to me"). Understanding that David has every right not to let his "enemy" (v.19; cf. v.4) get away, Saul—with words reminiscent of Boaz's to Ruth (Ruth 2:12)—prays that God will reward David richly for what he has done.

Earlier Samuel had told Saul that, because of his rebellion against God, his "kingdom" would not endure but would be given to a man after God's own heart (13:14)—"and now" (v.20; see Notes) Saul emphatically acknowledges that David will be ruler over the "kingdom" of Israel (cf. also 15:28; 18:8). Saul says "I know" that David will be king (v.20), an observation that Jonathan had earlier made about his father's knowledge (23:17).

Like Jonathan before him (see comments on 20:15, 42), Saul is concerned that David not "cut off" his "descendants" (v.21). And as David had sworn that he would show unfailing kindness to Jonathan and his family (20:14–17), so now he swears that he will not harm Saul's offspring or wipe out his name (vv.21–22). Because "name is inextricably bound up with existence" in the ancient world, "to cut off a name . . . is to end the existence of its bearer" (R. Abba, IDB, p. 501).

Having secured David's oath, Saul returns to Gibeah. David, however, wisely continues to distrust Saul and therefore retreats to his "stronghold" (v.22; see 22:4–5 and comment).

## Notes

---

**7** (8 MT) This verse ends with two common Hebrew words, וַיֵּלֶךְ בַּדָּרֶךְ (*wayyēlek̲ baddārek̲*, "and went his way"), that appear elsewhere in this section only in v.2 ("and set out") and v.3 ("the way"). Two other verbs that help to tie the section together are עָשָׂה (*'āśāh*) in v.4 (5 MT) ("deal") and v.6 (7 MT) ("do") and קוּם (*qûm*) in v.4 (5 MT) ("crept up") and v.7 (8 MT) ("attack," "left").

**8** (9 MT) The word אַחֲרֵי (*'aḥ$^a$rê*, "after," "behind") occurs seven times in vv.8–15 (three times in v.8 [9 MT] and four in v.14 [15 MT]), here usually left untranslated by the NIV to accommodate English idiom. It serves, however, not only to give cohesion to the literary unit but also to frame all but its last verse.

**10** (11 MT) The NIV's "I spared" is elliptical for "my eye spared," a common OT idiom (cf. Deut 7:16; 13:8; 19:13 ["look on with pity," "show pity"]). Although the Hebrew word for "eye" (feminine in gender) does not appear as the subject of the verb "spared" in v.10, the third person feminine singular verb (וַתָּחָס [*wattāḥos*]) implies it, as the Vulgate recognizes (*pepercit . . . oculus meus*) and as several translations (e.g., ASV, KJV, NASB) and commentators agree (e.g., Klein, Keil, McCarter). Although Saul has seen with his own "eyes" that the Lord has delivered him into David's hands, David's "eye" has spared Saul.

**13** (14 MT) The NIV's "the old saying" renders מְשַׁל הַקַּדְמֹנִי (*m^e šal haqqaḏmōnî*, lit., "the proverb of the ancient one"). A DSS fragment (cf. BHS) reads the second word as a plural (cf. also Watson, "Shared Consonants," p. 532), probably to smooth out the awkwardness of the phrase. The MT, however, is just as smooth if the singular *haqqaḏmōnî* is understood as a collective (observed already long ago by KD, p. 236), a common phenomenon in nouns of the gentilic type (Waltke and O'Connor, *Biblical Hebrew Syntax*, p. 115).

**14** (15 MT) The meaning "flea" for פַּרְעֹשׁ (*par'ōš*), a rare word at best, is secured by the various forms of its Akkadian cognate—*pu/irša'u, puru'su*—which also mean "flea" (Benno Landsberger, *Die Fauna des alten Mesopotamiens nach der 14. Tafel der Serie ḪAR.RA = ḫubullu* [Leipzig, 1934], p. 126).

**20** (21 MT) The MT of v.20 begins with וְעַתָּה (*w^e'attāh*, "And now"), which, as Polzin observes (*Samuel and the Deuteronomist*, pp. 206, 268 n. 6), occurs twelve times in chapters 24–26 (24:20–21 [21–22 MT]; 25:7, 17, 26 [bis], 27; 26:8, 11, 16, 19–20) and only twenty-one times in the rest of 1 Samuel. In these three chapters in particular the narrator records matters of emphasis, persuasion, and conviction that he tags by the use of *w^e'attāh*, not always expressed in translation by the NIV because of its stylistic redundancy in English.

---

## 13. *David, Nabal, and Abigail*

### 25:1–44

[1]Now Samuel died, and all Israel assembled and mourned for him; and they buried him at his home in Ramah.

Then David moved down into the Desert of Maon. [2]A certain man in Maon, who had property there at Carmel, was very wealthy. He had a thousand goats and three thousand sheep, which he was shearing in Carmel. [3]His name was Nabal and his wife's name was Abigail. She was an intelligent and beautiful woman, but her husband, a Calebite, was surly and mean in his dealings.

[4]While David was in the desert, he heard that Nabal was shearing sheep. [5]So he sent ten young men and said to them, "Go up to Nabal at Carmel and greet him in my name. [6]Say to him: 'Long life to you! Good health to you and your household! And good health to all that is yours!

[7]"'Now I hear that it is sheep-shearing time. When your shepherds were with us, we did not mistreat them, and the whole time they were at Carmel nothing of theirs was missing. [8]Ask your own servants and they will tell you. Therefore be favorable toward my young men, since we come at a festive time. Please give your servants and your son David whatever you can find for them.'"

[9]When David's men arrived, they gave Nabal this message in David's name. Then they waited.

[10]Nabal answered David's servants, "Who is this David? Who is this son of Jesse? Many servants are breaking away from their masters these days. [11]Why should I take my bread and water, and the meat I have slaughtered for my shearers, and give it to men coming from who knows where?"

[12]David's men turned around and went back. When they arrived, they reported every word. [13]David said to his men, "Put on your swords!" So they put on their swords, and David put on his. About four hundred men went up with David, while two hundred stayed with the supplies.

[14]One of the servants told Nabal's wife Abigail: "David sent messengers from the desert to give our master his greetings, but he hurled

insults at them. 15 Yet these men were very good to us. They did not
mistreat us, and the whole time we were out in the fields near them
nothing was missing. 16 Night and day they were a wall around us all the
time we were herding our sheep near them. 17 Now think it over and see
what you can do, because disaster is hanging over our master and his
whole household. He is such a wicked man that no one can talk to him."

18 Abigail lost no time. She took two hundred loaves of bread, two
skins of wine, five dressed sheep, five seahs of roasted grain, a hundred
cakes of raisins and two hundred cakes of pressed figs, and loaded
them on donkeys. 19 Then she told her servants, "Go on ahead; I'll follow
you." But she did not tell her husband Nabal.

20 As she came riding her donkey into a mountain ravine, there were
David and his men descending toward her, and she met them. 21 David
had just said, "It's been useless—all my watching over this fellow's
property in the desert so that nothing of his was missing. He has paid
me back evil for good. 22 May God deal with David, be it ever so severely,
if by morning I leave alive one male of all who belong to him!"

23 When Abigail saw David, she quickly got off her donkey and bowed
down before David with her face to the ground. 24 She fell at his feet and
said: "My lord, let the blame be on me alone. Please let your servant
speak to you; hear what your servant has to say. 25 May my lord pay no
attention to that wicked man Nabal. He is just like his name—his name
is Fool, and folly goes with him. But as for me, your servant, I did not see
the men my master sent.

26 "Now since the LORD has kept you, my master, from bloodshed and
from avenging yourself with your own hands, as surely as the LORD lives
and as you live, may your enemies and all who intend to harm my master
be like Nabal. 27 And let this gift, which your servant has brought to my
master, be given to the men who follow you. 28 Please forgive your
servant's offense, for the LORD will certainly make a lasting dynasty for
my master, because he fights the LORD's battles. Let no wrongdoing be
found in you as long as you live. 29 Even though someone is pursuing
you to take your life, the life of my master will be bound securely in the
bundle of the living by the LORD your God. But the lives of your enemies
he will hurl away as from the pocket of a sling. 30 When the LORD has
done for my master every good thing he promised concerning him and
has appointed him leader over Israel, 31 my master will not have on his
conscience the staggering burden of needless bloodshed or of having
avenged himself. And when the LORD has brought my master success,
remember your servant."

32 David said to Abigail, "Praise be to the LORD, the God of Israel, who
has sent you today to meet me. 33 May you be blessed for your good
judgment and for keeping me from bloodshed this day and from
avenging myself with my own hands. 34 Otherwise, as surely as the LORD,
the God of Israel, lives, who has kept me from harming you, if you had
not come quickly to meet me, not one male belonging to Nabal would
have been left alive by daybreak."

35 Then David accepted from her hand what she had brought him and
said, "Go home in peace. I have heard your words and granted your
request."

36 When Abigail went to Nabal, he was in the house holding a banquet
like that of a king. He was in high spirits and very drunk. So she told him
nothing until daybreak. 37 Then in the morning, when Nabal was sober,
his wife told him all these things, and his heart failed him and he
became like a stone. 38 About ten days later, the LORD struck Nabal and
he died.

39 When David heard that Nabal was dead, he said, "Praise be to the
LORD, who has upheld my cause against Nabal for treating me with

contempt. He has kept his servant from doing wrong and has brought
Nabal's wrongdoing down on his own head."
Then David sent word to Abigail, asking her to become his wife. 40His
servants went to Carmel and said to Abigail, "David has sent us to you to
take you to become his wife."
41She bowed down with her face to the ground and said, "Here is your
maidservant, ready to serve you and wash the feet of my master's
servants." 42Abigail quickly got on a donkey and, attended by her five
maids, went with David's messengers and became his wife. 43David had
also married Ahinoam of Jezreel, and they both were his wives. 44But
Saul had given his daughter Michal, David's wife, to Paltiel son of Laish,
who was from Gallim.

Chapter 25 is the central panel in the triptych that comprises chapters 24–26. As such it not only anchors the literary unit but also facilitates the fact that chapters 24 and 26 mirror each other. Beginning with the death of David's friend Samuel, it ends with Saul's giving David's wife Michal to another man and thus considering David as good as dead. It is therefore possible to interpret chapter 25 as marking the low point in David's fortunes. At the same time, however, in the chapter David acquires a wise wife (Abigail) who had successfully persuaded him not to harm a quintessential fool (Nabal). Saul, who figures largely in chapters 24 and 26, appears only in the last verse of chapter 25. But it is hard to escape the implication that in chapter 25 Saul, though physically absent, is nonetheless figuratively present in Nabal, his alter ego.

This chapter is structured chiastically as follows (cf. Stek, *The Former Prophets*, p. 65A):

A. Samuel dies (v.1a).
  B. David the fugitive is in the vicinity of the wealthy Nabal and his beautiful wife Abigail (vv.1b–3).
    C. Hearing of Nabal's situation and later rebuffed by him, David prepares to avenge the insult (vv.4–13).
      D. Abigail prepares food to take to David (vv.14–19).
        E. David meets Abigail (vv.20–35).
      D′. Abigail returns home to find Nabal gorging himself on food (vv.36–38).
    C′. Hearing of Nabal's death, David praises the Lord for having upheld his cause against Nabal (v.39a).
  B′. David the fugitive has taken the beautiful Abigail as his second wife (vv.39b–43).
A′. Saul treats David as though he were dead (v.44).

Detailed comparisons between the sets of parallel sections will be pointed out in the commentary.

**1a** "Saul's public recognition of David's coming kingship [24:20] is the cue for Samuel to leave the scene" (Gunn, *The Fate of King Saul*, p. 95). The notice of Samuel's death in v.1 apparently marks the point at which, according to Talmudic tradition, authorship of the books of Samuel passed from the prophet himself (who supposedly wrote 1 Samuel 1–24) to Nathan and Gad (who supposedly wrote 1 Samuel 25–31 and all of 2 Samuel; cf. Baba Bathra 14b–15a). This tradition, however, is based on a misunderstanding of 1 Chronicles 29:29 and therefore has little to commend it (cf. McCarter, *I Samuel*, pp. 3–4; S. Szikszai, IDB, 4:203; contrast H. Wolf, ZPEB, 5:260–61).

Loved and respected by his people, Samuel was mourned by them at his death. Elements of the laconic statement in v.1 are repeated in 28:3 ("all Israel," "mourned for him," "buried him," "Ramah"). "Assembled" is also echoed in 28:4, but with a sinister twist: In v.1 all Israel "assembled" to lament Samuel's death, while in 28:4 the Philistines "assembled" to fight all Israel. The Hebrew roots of "assembled" and "buried"—*qbṣ* and *qbr* respectively—provide a fine example of alliteration and assonance in v.1.

"Buried" appears in 1 Samuel only here, in its echo in 28:3, and in 31:13 (the last verse in 1 Samuel). Notices of the burials of Samuel and Saul in v.1 and 31:13 thus serve as a kind of *inclusio* framing the final seven chapters of the book. Although local tradition places Samuel's tomb in Nebi Samwil northwest of Jerusalem, such tradition depends on the unlikely identification of Nebi Samwil with Ramah (see comment on 1:1; for details cf. S.R. Driver, HDB, 4:198).

**1b–3** The difference in social status between David and Nabal becomes immediately apparent (Stek, *The Former Prophets*, p. 65C): David "moved down" to the "Desert of Maon" (v.1; for the location of Maon and the desert named after it, see comment on 23:24), but he told his men to "go up" (v.5) to Nabal at "Carmel" (which means "Vineyard Land," "Garden Spot"; for its location see comment on 15:12). Like David's later friend Barzillai (2 Sam 19:32), Nabal was very "wealthy" (v.2; lit., "great," as in 2 Sam 3:38). The Hebrew word translated "property" here (so also REV, NAB) often means "occupation," "work" (Gen 46:33; 47:3; Judg 13:12; Isa 54:16) and is therefore rendered "business" in some modern translations (e.g., RSV, NASB, JB). The observation that Nabal had "three thousand" sheep may be yet another attempt to present him as the alter ego of Saul, who had "three thousand chosen men" (24:2; 26:2; cf. Stek, p. 65G). Sheepshearing, a time for celebration (cf. 2 Sam 13:23–24), took place "after the summer grazing when the profits were distributed" (Ralph Gower, *The New Manners and Customs of Bible Times* [Chicago: Moody, 1987], p. 143). Plucking by hand and/or with the help of bronze combs sufficed for shearing sheep until the Iron Age, when iron shears came into use (Nina Hyde, "Wool—Fabric of History," *National Geographic* 173, 5 [1988]: 557).

The contrast between Nabal and his wife Abigail (v.3) could scarcely be more stark. Not only "beautiful" (lit., "lovely in form"; the same expression is used to describe Rachel in Gen 29:17 and Esther in Esth 2:7), Abigail was also "intelligent" (lit., "good in understanding"; cf. 2 Chron 30:22; Ps 111:10; Prov 13:15). Nabal, however, was "mean" (lit., "evil")—and thus a polarity between "good" (*ṭôḇ*) and "evil" (*ra'*) is set up at the beginning of chapter 25. As Gunn observes (*The Fate of King Saul*, pp. 96, 154 n. 7), each of the two terms ("good" or "do good"; "evil" or "do evil") appears seven times in the chapter ("good," vv.3, 8 ["festive"], 15, 21, 30–31 ["brought . . . success"], 36 ["high"]; "evil," vv.3, 17 ["disaster"], 21, 26 ["harm"], 34 ["harming"], 39 [bis: "wrong," "wrongdoing"]). Together they underscore one of the major themes of the story: Good brings its own reward, while evil recoils on the head of the wicked.

The names of Abigail ("My [Divine] Father Is Joy") and Nabal ("Fool"; cf. v.25 and comment) well describe the characters of the couple. Nabal's parents, however, are not likely to have given their son the name "Fool." The Hebrew word *nāḇāl* may therefore also have had one or more positive meanings (for examples cf. Jon D. Levenson, "I Samuel 25 as Literature and History," *Literary Interpretations of Biblical Narratives*, vol. 2; ed. Kenneth R.R. Gros Louis [Nashville: Abingdon, 1982], p. 222), but it also is possible that Nabal was a deliberately pejorative nickname applied to the man in later life rather than a praenomen given to him at birth. According to the MT vocalic text, Nabal was a "Calebite" (*kālibbî*), a word with the same root as *keleḇ* ("dog"), hence "doglike"—a description that is anything but complimentary (see comment on 17:43). According to the MT consonantal text, however, Nabal was "like his heart" (*k^e libbô*), which is almost certainly "an allusion to Psalm 14:1 (53:2): 'The fool [*nāḇāl*] has said in his heart [*b^e libbô*], "There is no God." ' If this is correct, then we have here an instance of scribal sarcasm. The consonantal text alludes to the prideful and ultimately stupid and arrogantly unperceptive character of this man, who seems to have recognized no authority other than his own" (ibid., p. 223).

The beautiful and intelligent Abigail, though mismatched with Nabal, is a perfect match for David, whose commendable qualities complement hers (cf. 16:12, 18). In all respects she is David's equal (ibid., p. 228; Stek, p. 65D). In fact, she should perhaps be identified with one of David's two sisters, the only other Abigail mentioned in the Bible (1 Chron 2:15–16). According to 2 Samuel 17:25, David's sister Abigail was the daughter of Nahash, who was perhaps the Ammonite ruler of 11:1–2 and 12:12. This identification would help to explain the friendship between Nahash and David (2 Sam 10:2). At the same time, since David was the son of Jesse, Abigail would then have been only his half sister (cf. similarly KD, *The Book of Chronicles*, pp. 62–63, although Keil apparently understands Nahash to have been a woman), which would have made it possible for him to marry her (v.42; cf. similarly Gen 20:12). If the two Abigails are thus identified (cf. G.R.H. Wright, "Dumuzi at the Court of David," *As on the First Day: Essays in Religious Constants* [Leiden: Brill, 1987], p. 52), her first husband would have been Jether (2 Sam 17:25; 1 Chron 2:17)—perhaps Nabal's real name (Jon D. Levenson and Baruch Halpern, "The Political Import of David's Marriages," JBL 99, 4 [1980]: 511–12).

**4–13** After hearing that Nabal is shearing sheep (v.4), David sends "ten" (a number often used to represent "the smallest effective group" [Segal, "Numerals," p. 5]) young men (*n^e ʿārîm*) to him (v.5). Later Abigail, again proving herself to be a "fit partner" for David (Stek, p. 65E), goes to him attended by her "five" (a "modest" number [Segal, "Numerals," p. 9]) young women (*naʿ^a rōṯeyhā*, v.42).

David's message to Nabal through his men (vv.5–8) begins by telling them to "greet him" (lit., "inquire of him concerning [his] well-being/welfare"; see comment on 10:4) in David's name (i.e., as his representative; cf. also v.9, and see comment on 17:45). The boon of "well-being/welfare/peace/good health" is expressed in v.5 by the word *šālôm*, which reappears three times in v.6 ("Good health to you and [good health to] your household! And good health to all that is yours!"). Nabal's foolish rejection of David's friendly overtures (vv.10–11) evokes a threefold response from David in v.13, this time repeating the word *ḥereḇ* ("sword": " 'Put on your swords!' So they put on their swords, and David put on his [sword]"). The opposition between *šālôm* and *ḥereḇ* found here is a striking prefiguration of Jesus' statement: "I did not come to bring peace, but a sword" (Matt 10:34).

"[And] now" (v.7)—David continues in his persuasive tone (see comment and Notes on 24:20) as he seeks a favor from Nabal. He senses that sheep-shearing time would put Nabal in a good mood, because it is a "festive" occasion (v.8). Utilizing the ancient equivalent of the protection racket (cf. Gunn, *The Fate of King Saul*, p. 96), David observes that his men did not mistreat Nabal's shepherds or steal anything from them (v.7; cf. Samuel's *apologia* in 12:4–5), perhaps implying that there were plenty of opportunities to do so. One of Nabal's servants would later confirm to Abigail the claims of David (vv.14–15; cf. also v.8) and would express his gratitude for the protection provided by David's men (v.16; cf. also David's complaint in v.21). David's concern for the welfare of Nabal's shepherds had in fact extended over a long period of time (vv.7, 15–16).

David's request that Nabal should "be favorable toward my young men" (v.8; lit., "the young men find favor in your eyes") is the epitome of courtesy (cf. 1:18; 20:29; 27:5). The season for sheep-shearing provides opportunity for a "festive time" (lit., "good day"; cf. Esth 8:17 ["celebrating"]; 9:19 ["joy and feasting"], 22 ["day of celebration"]; cf. also T Asher 4:4, where "good day" means "festival" [*The Apocryphal Old Testament*, ed. H.F.D. Sparks (Oxford: Clarendon, 1984), p. 579 n. 3]). As Stek observes (p. 65G), Nabal's negative response (vv.10–11) on a "good day" results in the likelihood of a time of "evil" (NIV, "disaster," v.17) for him. David is simply requesting for himself and his men "whatever" supplies (primarily food; cf. v.11) Nabal might be willing to give them, since they depend on the generosity of others for the protection they provide (v.16). David's curious reference to himself as Nabal's "son" (v.8) makes sense if Nabal is functioning as Saul's literary surrogate in this chapter.

Arriving in Carmel, David's men act as faithful messengers by reporting to Nabal "this message" (lit., "according to all these words," v.9; the same Heb. expression is translated "every word" in v.12) in the name of their leader. The verb rendered "waited" (lit., "rested") can also be translated "stopped" (cf. Num 10:36, "came to rest"), here in the sense of "stopped speaking," implying that they did not add anything to David's words.

Possibly these "ten young men" (v.5) sent to Nabal by David were officers in his small army, since they are called his "servants" at the beginning of v.10 (for "servant" in the sense of "officer," see comment on 16:15–16; cf. also 18:5; 29:3). Nabal clearly uses the same word of them in the same verse with its most basic meaning. His repeated "Who?" is uttered with scorn, like that of David with respect to Goliath (17:26). Nabal also uses "son of Jesse" in an insulting and belittling way, as did Saul before him (see 20:27 and comment; 22:7). In so doing Nabal rejects David's courteous reference to himself as Nabal's "son" (v.8). The rebel Sheba would later dismiss the "son of Jesse" with similar contempt (2 Sam 20:1; cf. Levenson, "I Samuel 25 as Literature and History," p. 237).

Nabal's contention that "many servants are breaking away from their masters these days" (v.10) is at least double-edged and perhaps even triple-edged: (1) He may be referring to David, who is fleeing from his master Saul; (2) he may be subtly suggesting to David's servants that they would be well advised to break away from their master, possibly even to join Nabal's household; and (3), ironically, he speaks better than he knows, since "he is about to find *himself* in the role of a master whose slaves break away, telling their mistress of her husband's stupidity and ethical vacuity" (Levenson, "I Samuel 25 as Literature and History," p. 225 [emphasis his]; cf. vv.14–17). Gunn makes an additional observation about v.10: "This scathing dismissal is strongly reminiscent of Saul's sarcastic outburst against David in chapter 22" (*The Fate of King Saul*, p. 97; cf. 22:7–8).

Nabal is even unwilling to give to David and his men "bread and water" (v.11), the most basic food and drink (Num 21:5; Deut 9:9, 18; 1 Kings 13:8–9, 16–17; cf. the similar refusal of the officials of Succoth to the request of Gideon for his men, Judg 8:4–6, 15)—much less the meat he had slaughtered for his workers. Nabal telegraphs his egotism in the MT of v.11, which uses "I" and "my" a total of eight times (four times apiece): "I take," "I slaughtered," "I give," "I know"; "my bread," "my water," "my meat," "my shearers."

Upon receiving Nabal's response, David's men "turned" (the verb is often used of an [abrupt] about-face, especially in military contexts; cf. Judg 20:39, 41; Ps 78:9) and reported back to David (v.12). His immediate reaction was to retaliate by arming himself and his men with swords (v.13; for the literary function of the triple mention of "sword" in the MT here see comment on v.6; cf. similarly Miscall, p. 151)—a poignant contrast to his earlier repudiation of the sword before his contest with Goliath (17:39, 45, 47). Splitting his six hundred men into two groups of unequal size, David sets out for Carmel with four hundred (a number often "associated with flight and with battles" [Segal, "Numerals," p. 12]) and leaves the rest behind with the "supplies" (a term with military connotations; see comment on "baggage" in 10:22 and on "supplies" in 17:22). The two hundred who "stayed with the supplies" are not to be considered in any way inferior and were expected to share in whatever plunder would be seized (cf. 30:24; for an identical deployment of David's men on a later occasion—though for a different reason—cf. 30:9–10).

**14–19** The section begins with "told" (v.14) and ends with "did not tell" (v.19). In the MT in each case the clause starts with its object ("Abigail" in v.14, "her husband Nabal" in v.19), making the *inclusio* around the whole appear all the more striking and deliberate. The parallel section (vv.36–38) uses the same verb twice as well, this time beginning with a negative construction ("told . . . nothing," v.36) and ending with a positive construction ("told," v.37; cf. similarly Stek, *The Former Prophets*, p. 65B).

Nabal's servant describes to Abigail (v.14) the shoddy treatment David's men received at Nabal's hands. David had sent messengers to "give" Nabal "his greetings" (the verb "greet" here [cf. 2 Sam 8:10 = 1 Chron 18:10] literally means "bless," "praise," as in vv.32–33, 39) but had been crudely rebuffed by him. Abigail's response to her meeting with David, by contrast, was a "gift" (lit., "blessing," v.27) of substantial proportions (v.18). Nabal, as we might suspect, "hurled insults" at David's men.

Nabal's servant continues to apprise Abigail of his favorable impression of David and his men (v.15), repeating some of their terminology (cf. v.7). He especially stresses the physical proximity of Nabal's shepherds to David's men ("near them," vv.15–16) during "the whole time" (v.15; "all the time," v.16) they were in the fields. Like the fortress "wall" enclosing a city (v.16; the same metaphor is used of God in Zech 2:5), the protection provided by David and his men continued around the clock ("night and day"). Afraid that the "good" deeds (v.15) of David's men will be repaid by "disaster" (v.17) against Nabal and his household because of his moral obtuseness, his servant appeals to Abigail for help. "Think it over and see," he says to her (lit., "know and see," a common phrase in 1 Samuel; see comment on "realize" in 12:17 and on "find out" in 23:22–23), pleading with her to make up for her husband's dereliction. "Disaster is determined/inevitable" (*kāl^eṯāh hārā'āh;* NIV, "disaster is hanging [over]"; cf. 20:7, 9 ["determined to harm"]; Esth 7:7 ["decided (his) fate"]), because Nabal is a "wicked man" (*ben-b^elîya'al;* cf. 2:12 of Eli's sons; cf. also 10:27 ["troublemakers"]; see comment and Notes on "wicked woman" in 1:16; cf. further *'îš b^elîya'al* in v.25). The servant concludes his appeal by observing that no one can talk to Nabal, implying that perhaps his wife Abigail may be able to persuade him of the folly of his ways.

Nabal's sloth is more than compensated for by Abigail's speed in meeting David's needs: She "lost no time" (v.18), she acted "quickly" (vv.23, 34, 42; same Heb. verb in all four cases). Nabal's stinginess is counterbalanced by his wife's generosity; her itemized tally of foodstuffs for David and his men surpasses the size of a later similar list drawn up for the same purpose (2 Sam 16:1). "Cakes of raisins" and "cakes of pressed figs" (v.18) were especially prized, not only for their sweetness and nutritive value, but also because they could be kept for some time without spoiling (cf. 30:1, 11–12).

David had earlier asked Ahimelech the priest for "five loaves of bread," or "whatever you can find" (21:3), and Ahimelech had responded—however reluctantly—by giving him consecrated bread, the only food available (21:6). When David's servants asked Nabal for "whatever you can find" (v.8; similar though not identical Heb. in 21:3), he refused to give them any "bread" at all (v.11). Now, in response to David's need, Abigail supplies him with "two hundred loaves of bread" in addition to large amounts of other provisions (v.18). Levenson observes that when Abigail finally tells Nabal about her gift to David (v.37; cf. v.19), his heart fails him "over a negligible loss"—the loss of "various perishables and exactly five sheep [v.18] out of his three thousand [v.2]" ("I Samuel 25 as Literature and History," p. 227). Perhaps a further irony is that among Abigail's provisions for David are two "skins" (*niḇlê*) of wine—a possible wordplay on *nāḇāl* ("Nabal").

**20–35** Possessing its own literary unity, this central section of chapter 25 begins and ends with three-verse paragraphs (vv.20–22, 32–34) that reflect each other and frame the speech of Abigail, which constitutes the heart of the chapter (vv.24–31). Except for the suffix, the Hebrew rendered "toward her" (v.20) is the same as that translated "to meet me" (vv.32, 34). In addition vv.22 and 34 each begin with an oath and end with the Hebrew phrase translated "one male." Verse 23 (which introduces Abigail's speech) and v.35 (which concludes the whole) in the MT also share certain words: "See" (untr. in NIV; it appears before "I have heard" in v.35) answers to "saw" (v.23), and "your request" (lit., "your face," v.35) echoes "her face" (v.23).

Having sent her servants ahead with the provisions for David and his men, Abigail follows on a donkey (v.20; cf. also vv.23, 42), a common means of transportation in ancient times (Exod 4:20; Josh 15:18 = Judg 1:14; 2 Chron 28:15). She intercepts David near a mountain "ravine," an out-of-the-way place reminding us that he is still a hunted fugitive (same Heb. word translated "hiding" in 19:2). He and his men are on their way to punish Nabal for his incivility. The MT is ambiguous concerning whether Abigail has heard David's words recorded in vv.21–22 (NIV's "had just said" implies that she has not). In any case, David feels cheated ("It's been useless," lit., "for deception/disappointment") by Nabal's action (or inaction). Although guaranteeing that none of the property of "this fellow" (spoken in a scornful tone of voice; cf. 21:15) was "missing" (cf. also vv.7, 15), David has been "paid . . . back evil for good" (an expression implying betrayal or cruelty; cf. Gen 44:4; Prov 17:13; Jer 18:20; cf. also especially the Davidic Pss 35:12; 38:20; 109:5). David, intending to retaliate in the heat of his anger, will later praise the Lord for having "brought Nabal's wrongdoing [= evil] down on his own head" (v.39; the Heb. verb rendered "brought . . . down" is translated "paid . . . back" in v.21). With a strong oath of self-imprecation (v.22; see comment on 20:13), David swears that he will kill every male in Nabal's household by daybreak—although he later expresses his gratitude that the Lord (and Abigail) kept him from doing so (vv.33–34).

In preparation for responding at some length to David's threat against her husband (vv.24–31) and in contrast to Nabal's treatment of David and his men (vv.10–11), Abigail bows down respectfully before him (v.23). As D.M. Gunn has pointed out ("Traditional Composition in the 'Succession Narrative,'" VetTest 26, 2 [1976]: 221–22), details of both form and content relating to Abigail's speech are paralleled in the account of the interview between David and the wise woman of Tekoa in 2 Samuel 14:1–20. With respect to content, both scenes involve a woman interceding with David for herself and her family, and both are concerned with themes of bloodguilt and revenge. With respect to form, the following details stand out (translating the Heb. literally and disregarding the order of the elements):

| 1 Samuel 25 | 2 Samuel 14 |
|---|---|
| And she fell before David with her face to the ground, and she bowed down, . . . and she said (vv.23–24) | And she fell with her face to the ground, and she bowed down, and she said (v.4) |
| "On me, my lord, is the blame" (v.24) | "On me, my lord the king, is the blame" (v.9) |
| "Please let your servant speak in your ears, and hear the words of your servant" (v.24) | "Please let your servant speak a word to my lord the king" (v.12) |
| And he said to her, "Go up in peace to your home; see, I have heard your voice and granted your request" (v.35) | And the king said to the woman, "Go to your home, and I will issue an order in your behalf" (v.8) |

Abigail's speech is a masterpiece of rhetoric, appealing not only to reason and the emotions, but also to her own credibility (Kenneth W. Shoemaker, "The Rhetoric of Abigail's Speech [1 Sam. 25:24–31]" [paper given at 1987 SBL annual meeting, rhetorical criticism section], 6). Beginning with a formal exordium (v.24) and ending with a formal conclusion (v.31b), the main body of the speech treats matters of the past (v.25), present (vv.26–28a; vv.26a, 26b, and 27 all begin with "And now" in the MT), and future (vv. 28b–31a; v.30 begins with "And it will be" in the MT; cf. ibid., pp. 20–21).

Riding alone "into a troop of four hundred armed men bent on violence [vv.20–22]" (ibid., p. 4), the defenseless Abigail knows that she has very little time to change their minds. She immediately demonstrates an attitude of submission to David, referring to him as "my lord/master" in every verse of her speech and to herself as "your servant" in all but vv.26, 29, and 30 (cf. Hannah to Eli in 1:15–16; Ruth to Boaz in Ruth 2:13). The contrast between her attitude toward David and that of Nabal could hardly be more striking. Gunn observes: "For Nabal, David is 'servant' [v.10]; for Abigail, he is 'master'" (*The Fate of King Saul*, p. 99). In addition, although Nabal is "such a wicked man that no one can talk to him" (v.17), Abigail pleads for an opportunity to "speak to" David.

Abigail, the consummate diplomat, knows that she has to be careful "neither to exculpate Nabal nor to appear disloyal to him. . . . In short, she must win David without betraying Nabal. Abigail devises the perfect solution to the dilemma: she intercedes on behalf of Nabal (v.24), although conceding that he has no case and no hope of survival (vv.25–26). In other words, while overtly defending him, she covertly dissociates herself from him" (Levenson, "I Samuel 25 as Literature and History," p. 230). To save Nabal's life, she assumes his guilt (v.24). Her admission is "unacceptably lame, but it has succeeded in buying further time" (Shoemaker, "Abigail's Speech," p. 10). The urgency and insistence clearly detectable throughout her speech is modulated by a tone of courtesy and politeness, evidenced in her frequent use of the particle *nā'* ("please," vv.24, 25 [omitted in NIV], 28).

Abigail's characterization of Nabal as a "wicked man" and a "fool" (v.25) has often been misunderstood as a heartless and self-serving denunciation of her husband. The contrary is the case, however: Her action is one of "wit and tactical maneuvering. . . . It is very unlikely that David would have been eager to marry [vv.39–40, 42] any woman known for disloyalty, even though wealthy and beautiful, since such a treacherous woman in the royal chambers would be a constant threat. A wife's self-sacrificial loyalty to her spouse, on the other hand, would be a virtue prized by any husband" (Shoemaker, "Abigail's Speech," pp. 13–14). At the same time her integrity prevents her from pulling any punches. Since Nabal is a "wicked man" (see comment on v.17; cf. also 2 Sam 20:1, where the same Heb. expression ["troublemaker"] is used of Sheba—who referred disparagingly to David as "son of Jesse," as Nabal had done earlier [v.10; cf. Levenson, "I Samuel 25 as Literature and History," p. 237]), one should "pay no attention" (cf. also 4:20) to him (Shoemaker, "Abigail's Speech," p. 7, suggests "not . . . take . . . seriously"; the same Heb. phrase is translated "do not worry" in 9:20 and "won't care" in 2 Sam 18:3).

Abigail's statement that Nabal (*nāḇāl*, "Fool") "is just like his name" is perhaps the best biblical illustration of the ancient perception that a name was not simply a label for distinguishing one thing from another but that "a more profound connection between the name and its bearer" should be sought (Mettinger, *In Search of God*, p. 7). In other words, "name" equals "person" (cf. Isa 30:27), and "Nabal"—whether name or epithet (cf. similarly Prov 21:24; see also commentary on v.3)—equals "Fool" with all the nuances implied in that term (cf. Isa 32:6, which says of the fool that, among other things, "the hungry he leaves empty/ and from the thirsty he withholds water"—a description that characterizes Nabal precisely [v.11], as observed by Levenson, "I Samuel 25 as Literature and History," pp. 221–22). Thus "his name is Fool, and folly [*nᵉḇālāh*] goes with him." That the root *nbl* basically means "be foolish," "fool," "folly," is secured not only by numerous references in the OT (for a complete list, cf. BDB, pp. 614–15) but also by versional renderings (LXX, Vul.) as well as Hebrew-Greek equivalences in Ecclesiasticus (cf. 4:27; 21:22). At the same time the various Hebrew roots (including *nbl*) thus translated in the OT have not so much to do with people who are stupid, ignorant, or even naive as they do with those who are "morally deficient" (NIV mg. at Prov 1:7). Tellingly and ironically, David's wife Ahinoam (v.43) bore his first son, Amnon, who proved to be "one of the wicked fools" (*nᵉḇālîm*, 2 Sam 13:13) capable of doing a "wicked thing" (*nᵉḇālāh*, 2 Sam 13:12; cf. Stek, *The Former Prophets*, p. 65E; cf. also Josh 7:15, "disgraceful thing"). Although the Hebrew root is different, 26:21 records Saul's admission that he "acted like a fool," strengthening the observation that in chapter 25 Nabal functions as Saul's alter ego.

Although assuming her husband's blame (v.24), Abigail disavows having seen the "men" (v.25) David had sent to him (v.5, where the same Heb. word is translated "young men"). She senses that God has "kept" (v.26) David from harming Nabal and his men, a truth that David acknowledges (v.34—though placing the emphasis on not harming Abigail). At the same time David asserts the important role of Abigail herself in keeping him from "bloodshed" (v.33), recognizing in her the mediator of the Lord's intentions. Since vengeance belongs to God alone (Deut 32:35), David must not avenge himself (vv.26, 31, 33). To do so would be to usurp God's prerogatives, "act the fool and violate the wisdom" of Proverbs 20:22: "Do not say, 'I'll pay you back for this wrong!'/ Wait for the LORD, and he will deliver you" (thus Stek, p. 65E, who observes that the Heb. for "deliver" in Prov 20:22 is the same as that for "avenging/avenged" in vv.26, 31, 33). With the same double asseveration used earlier by David (see 20:3 and comment), Abigail expresses her desire that David's "enemies" (among whom Saul counts himself, 18:29; cf. also 26:8) and all who "intend to harm" him (the same Heb. phrase is translated "bent on harming" in 24:9) might "be like Nabal" (v.26)—thus apparently anticipating the death of her husband and also, by implication, foreshadowing the death of Saul (cf. Gordon, "David's Rise," p. 49), of whom Nabal is the alter ego.

Though Nabal may be stingy, not so Abigail: She describes the generous supply of food that she brings to David and his men as a "gift" (v.27), literally a "blessing" (cf. 2 Kings 5:15; the same Heb. word is translated "present" in 30:26; Gen 33:11 and "special favor" in Josh 15:19 = Judg 1:15). The narrator will later (v.42) demonstrate Abigail to be a fit partner for David by portraying her as "attended by her five maids" (*n'rwt*, lit., "her five maids walking at her feet"), an echo of her description of David's contingent as "the men [*n'rym*] who follow you" (lit., "the men who walk at the feet of my master"; cf. Stek, p. 65E).

Continuing to accept the blame for Nabal's folly, Abigail begs David's forgiveness for her own "offense" (v.28; the same Heb. root is translated "rebellion" in David's disclaimer in 24:11). In fact, Abigail's burden in v.28 is to plead with David not to do anything rash—anything that might endanger or even destroy the "lasting dynasty" (*bayiṯ ne'ᵉmān*; cf. 1 Kings 11:38, where the same Heb. expression is translated "dynasty as enduring") that God will give him. So clearly is Abigail's statement in this regard an adumbration of Nathan's prophecy in 2 Samuel 7:16 ("Your house . . . will endure" [*ne'man bêṯkā*]; cf. also 1 Chron 17:23) that the rabbis of Talmudic times counted Abigail "among seven women who they believed had been graced by the holy spirit, the source of prophecy" (Levenson, "I Samuel 25 as Literature and History," p. 231). Unlike the king desired by the people of Samuel's day, a king who would "fight our battles" (8:20), David is to be a man who "fights the LORD's battles" (v.28)—as Saul had insincerely and hypocritically asked David to do (18:17).

Abigail warns David not to let "wrongdoing be found" in him (v.28)—a flaw that David's son Solomon would later use ("evil is found" [1 Kings 1:52] translates the same Heb. phrase) as a reason/excuse to execute his half-brother Adonijah, a rival claimant to David's throne (1 Kings 2:24–25). Shoemaker understands "as long as you live" (lit., "from your days") in the sense of "any of your days" ("from" with partitive force), arguing that the possibility of evil conduct on David's part "subtly includes the present day's affairs" ("Abigail's Speech," p. 7).

Although the "good/evil" terminology (see comment on v.3) is not used in v.29, the contrast is nonetheless evident: Abigail assures David that his life is safe but that the lives of his enemies are doomed. The "someone" intending to "take [David's] life" is of course Saul (see 20:1 and comment; see also 22:23 ["seeking your life . . . seeking mine"]; 23:15). But neither Saul nor anyone else will be able to wrest David from the protection of the Lord his God, who secures him in the "bundle" of the living (the word translated "bundle" is found elsewhere in the sense of a "pouch/purse" containing money [Gen 42:35; Prov 7:20] or a "sachet" containing myrrh [S of Songs 1:13]). Conversely, the same Lord will "hurl away" into oblivion the enemies of David as though from the pocket of a "sling"—a clear echo of David's divinely empowered victory over Goliath (in its only other occurrence in the Piel, the Heb. verb for "hurl away" is rendered "slung" in 17:49, while the noun "sling" appears in 17:40, 50). G.M. Mackie suggests the possibility that Abigail's imagery serves the additional function of contrasting the two pouches used by the shepherd, the "bundle of the living" referring to the pouch that held food (symbolizing life) and the "pocket of a sling" the pouch that held the stone (symbolizing death; *Bible Manners and Customs* [New York: Revell, 1898], p. 33).

Continuing to look into the future, Abigail again alludes to the Davidic covenant of 2 Samuel 7 (see comment on v.28 above). On the basis of Akkadian *ṭābūta dabābu* ("to discuss good/friendly relations," "to establish a [favorable] treaty"; cf. *Chicago Assyrian Dictionary* [1959], 3:8), the idiom *dibbēr ṭôḇāh* ("speak/promise good thing[s]") is often best translated in the same way (cf. 1 Kings 12:7, where "establish a covenant with them" is preferable to the NIV's "give them a favorable answer"; thus perhaps also similarly in 2 Kings 25:28 = Jer 52:32). In the context of 2 Samuel 7, "established this covenant with" is better than "promised these good things to" in v.28 (= 1 Chron 17:26). Likewise, Abigail refers to the time when the Lord will have done for David "according to every good thing that he spoke/promised" (*k^e^ḵōl 'ᵃšer-dibber 'eṯ-haṭṭôḇāh,* v.30; cf. NIV), that is, "according to everything in the covenant that he (will have) established" with David (cf. Fox, "*Ṭôḇ* as Covenant Terminology," p. 42).

Although God has already "appointed him leader" (v.30), a fact earlier announced to Saul by Samuel (see 13:14 and comment), David would not exercise effective rule over Israel until after Saul's death. In the meantime, however, Abigail does not want David to do anything to jeopardize his future or endanger his throne. In a literary echo of 24:5 (see comment in loc.), she warns him not to burden his "conscience" (v.31; lit., "heart"; cf. Eccl 7:22) with "needless bloodshed" against Nabal (cf. Jonathan's admonition to Saul in 19:5; cf. 1 Kings 2:31). Such a burden, unnecessary from the outset, would be "staggering" indeed, bringing David distress like that of the kind of chronic drunkenness that causes leaders to "stumble when rendering decisions" (Isa 28:7).

As Joseph had concluded his conversation with the Pharaoh's cupbearer by requesting that he "remember" Joseph when all "goes well" with him (Gen 40:14), so also Abigail ends her plea by asking that David "remember" her when the Lord "has brought . . . success" to him (v.31; same Heb. verbs in both verses). Levenson, observing that Abigail is alone with David throughout her address, interprets the phrase "remember your servant" in a highly personal sense: "She offers victuals to David's men; to David, she offers herself" ("I Samuel 25 as Literature and History," p. 230; cf. v.42).

David's three-verse response (vv.32–34) to the rhetorical brilliance of Abigail mirrors the three-verse paragraph (vv.20–22) with which this literary unit begins (see comment on vv.20–22). In addition, the response has its own literary symmetry: The phrases "the LORD, the God of Israel" and "to meet me" both occur in vv.32 and 34.

Although David was on his way to destroy Nabal's household, Abigail's sevenfold use of the divine name YHWH (vv.26 [bis], 28 [bis], 29, 30, 31) has perhaps reminded him of the spiritual dimensions of his calling—or, as Shoemaker puts it, "David's Yahwistic perspective has been refocused" ("Abigail's Speech," p. 16). David sees in Abigail the Lord's envoy: "Praise be to the LORD [v.32; cf. v.39] . . . who has sent you." "Praise be to" (v.32) and "May . . . be blessed" (v.33) translate the same Hebrew root (*brk;* NIV almost always avoids "bless" where God is the object). David recognizes that "good judgment" is an admirable quality in a woman (cf. Prov 11:22 ["discretion"]). He also understands that God has used Abigail to keep him from bloodshed and from attempting to avenge himself (v.33; the Heb. verb rendered "keeping" [cf. Ps 119:101], however, is different from that in vv.26, 34). The oath "As surely as the LORD . . . lives" (v.34) is frequently used where life and death hang in the balance (see comment on 14:39). Mass killings of the kind that David had contemplated often occurred at night, giving point to his statement that not a male in Nabal's household would have survived till "daybreak" (v.34; cf. v.22; 14:36).

This lengthiest of pericopes in the chapter (vv.20–35) concludes with David's grateful acceptance of Abigail's gift of food for himself and his men (v.35). He makes it clear that she has succeeded in assuaging his wrath: "Go [lit., 'Go up,' usually to higher ground; cf. Gen 44:17, 'go back'] . . . in peace." That he has been impressed and influenced by her impassioned arguments is clear from his acknowledgment: "I have heard your words" (lit., "I have listened to your voice"), an idiom that often implies obedience. In any event, his final words must have been like music to her ears: "I have . . . granted your request" (lit., "lifted up your face"; cf. Job 42:8–9, "accept[ed] his [Job's] prayer"), guaranteeing that he would not be the instrument of Nabal's death. The basic elements of the idioms here used by David are reminiscent of the Aaronic benediction: "The LORD turn [lit., 'lift up'] his face toward you" in blessing and peace (Num 6:24–26).

**36–38** The repetition of three crucial words gives unity to this brief paragraph: "heart" (vv.36 ["spirits"], 37), "died" (vv.37 ["failed"], 38), and "told" (vv.36–37; for the literary significance of this verb in the section, see the comment on its structural parallel in vv.14–19).

Abigail went to Nabal's "house" (v.36), doubtless in Carmel (cf. v.40), where his sheep-shearing celebration was taking place (see v.2 and comment on vv.7–8). He was presiding at a banquet fit for a "king"—a cruel irony when it is remembered that his wife has just declared her allegiance to Israel's king-elect. At his feast Nabal proved to be "a fool [*nāḇāl*] who is full of food" (Prov 30:22), something the very earth cannot tolerate (Prov 30:21). Through overindulgence in wine he was "in high spirits" (lit., "his heart is good/merry"; cf. Judg 16:25; Esth 1:10; cf. also David's firstborn son, Amnon, in 2 Sam 13:28). Realizing that Nabal was in no condition to understand what she might say to him, Abigail decided to tell him "nothing" (lit., "nothing small or great"; see 22:15 ["nothing at all"] and comment) until "daybreak"—the time by which, ominously, David had originally sworn to kill every male in Nabal's household (v.34; cf. also v.22).

As it turns out, of course, Nabal's folly was his own worst enemy. By the next morning "Nabal was sober" (v.37; lit., "the wine had gone out of Nabal"). Levenson observes that the consonants of Nabal's name can be vocalized as *nēḇel* ("wineskin"; cf. v.18) and that the narrator may well be using a wordplay: "In short, the man is equated with his bladder" ("I Samuel 25 as Literature and History," p. 227; cf. also

Levenson and Halpern, "The Political Import of David's Marriages," p. 514 n. 18; Gordon, "David's Rise," p. 51).

Feeling that the time is now ripe, Abigail tells her husband "all [so a few Heb. MSS] these things." When David's men had earlier given Nabal "this message" (v.9; lit., "all these things"), he insulted them and David. When they returned to David and reported to him "every word" (v.12; lit., "all these things"), he and his men prepared to march into battle against Nabal. Now, when Nabal hears from his wife "all these things" (v.37)—perhaps the entire story of her meeting with David, but doubtless including the list of provisions that she had so generously given him and that Nabal would surely begrudge (see v.18 and comment)—the shock is too much for him in his materialistic greed. Nabal the "fool," Nabal the "wineskin," who was very drunk and "was in high spirits" (lit., whose "heart was good") just a day earlier (v.36), now suffers from a heart that goes bad: "His heart failed him" (v.37; lit., "died in him"). Since the heart is the seat of courage (cf. David's statement to Saul: "Let no one lose heart on account of this Philistine," 17:32), Nabal is depicted as a coward as well.

The description of Nabal's becoming "like a stone" ("petrified," BDB, p. 7) should not be diagnosed as a specific illness (heart attack, stroke, etc.) but understood figuratively (cf. Exod 15:16, where Moses affirms that God's enemies will be "as still as a stone"). Indeed, reference to a "stone" may be yet another allusion to the Goliath narrative (cf. 17:50; see comment on v.29; cf. similarly Miscall, p. 154; Polzin, *Samuel and the Deuteronomist*, pp. 211–12). At the same time, it is equally possible that the narrator looks at Nabal as receiving a "heart of stone" in exchange for his heart of flesh—the reverse of the promise in Ezekiel 36:26 (Levenson, "I Samuel 25 as Literature and History," p. 227).

Though not immediate, Nabal's death was not long in coming. After about ten days "the LORD struck" him (v.38). The same Hebrew phrase is used in 26:10 of the ultimate fate of Saul, of whom Nabal was the alter ego (cf. similarly Gordon, "David's Rise," p. 49). Thus Nabal "died" at God's hand. As Stek observes, *wayyāmōṯ* ("and [it/he] died," vv.37 ["failed"], 38) forms an "inclusio that frames the account of Nabal's end" (*The Former Prophets*, p. 65F).

**39a** David greets the news of Nabal's death with an outburst of praise, echoing that in v.32. As he had earlier entreated the Lord to "uphold" his "cause" against Saul (24:15), so now he expresses his gratitude to the Lord for having "upheld his cause" against Saul's alter ego (cf. similarly Gordon, "David's Rise," who notes that these "are the only occurrences of the root ריב, in its forensic sense, in 1 Samuel," p. 48). Nabal's having treated David with "contempt" also makes him like Goliath, who brought "disgrace" on Israel (17:26; same Heb. word in both cases). The Lord's dealings with David and Nabal could hardly be more diverse: As for David, God has "kept his servant from doing wrong" (cf. the almost identical language in the Davidic Ps 19:13), while in Nabal's case he has "brought [his] wrongdoing down on his own head" (for the same idiom, cf. Judg 9:57 ["made (them) pay for all their wickedness"]; 1 Kings 2:44 ["repay you for your wrongdoing"]; cf. also similarly Joel 3:4, 7 ["return on your own heads what you have done"]).

**39b–43** Striking similarities between the occurrence, sequence, and subject(s) of verbs in this passage and in its parallel earlier in the chapter have already been noted (see Notes on vv.4–13). The most important feature giving internal literary unity to the section is the phrase *lô leʾiššāh* (lit., "to him as a wife") at the end of vv.39b, 40, and 42. It serves also to highlight David's marriage to Abigail as the theme of the pericope.

Nabal now dead, David "sent" his servants to Abigail to "take" her to become his wife (vv.39b–40). Miscall notes that David here "sends and takes, as he does with another woman at a future time (2 Sam. 11:4)" (p. 156). Abigail, by no means unwilling, nevertheless continues to characterize herself as David's "maidservant" (v.41, using the same Heb. word translated "servant" in vv.24–25, 28, 31)—one of the many persons/things Samuel had warned Israel that their king would "take" (8:16; see comment on 8:11). Adopting the same posture of servile obedience with which she had first met him (v.23), Abigail then expresses her readiness to go so far as to "wash the feet of my master's servants" (v.41). Since foot-washing normally was a self-administered act (Gen 18:4; 19:2; 24:32; 43:24; Judg 19:21; 2 Sam 11:8; S of Songs 5:3), Abigail demonstrates her joyful willingness to be "slave of all" (Mark 10:44; cf. John 13:5–17). As Rebekah, accompanied by her maids, had returned with Abraham's servant to become Isaac's wife (Gen 24:61–67), so also Abigail, "attended by her five maids" (v.42), hurries back with David's messengers to become his wife (though she was probably his half sister; see comment on v.3).

Like its literary parallel (vv.1b–3), v.43 calls attention to a geographical site ("Jezreel," a southern town of unknown location in the hill country of Judah near Maon and Carmel, v.2; cf. Josh 15:21, 48, 55–56). The NIV translation "David had also married [pluperfect] Ahinoam," which implies that his marriage to Ahinoam occurred before he took Abigail as his wife, is doubtless correct, since Ahinoam is always mentioned before Abigail when the two names occur together (27:3; 30:5; 2 Sam 2:2; 3:2–3 = 1 Chron 3:1–4). The only other Ahinoam mentioned in the Bible is the wife of Saul (14:50), and it has therefore been plausibly suggested that, before David took Abigail to become his wife, he had already asserted his right to the throne of Israel by marrying Queen Ahinoam—a tactic perhaps hinted at in Nathan's speech to David (2 Sam 12:8; cf. Levenson, "I Samuel 25 as Literature and History," pp. 241–42; cf. also, however, the caution of Gordon, "David's Rise," p. 44).

David's polygamy, at first blush inconsistent with the description of him as a man after God's own heart (13:14), finds a typical ancient rationalization in the Qumran Damascus Document: "David had not read the sealed book of the Law which was in the ark. . . . And the deeds of David rose up, . . . and God left them to him" (CD 5:3–6, as tr. by G. Vermes, *The Dead Sea Scrolls in English*, rev. ed. [Baltimore: Penguin, 1965], p. 101). Thus the Qumran Covenanters might argue that David cannot be blamed for his polygamy because he was ignorant of God's intentions (cf. similarly Lucetta Mowry, "The Dead Sea Scrolls and the Background for the Gospel of John," BA 17, 4 [1954]: 97). The truth, of course, lies elsewhere (see comments on 1:2 and 2 Sam 12:8).

**44** Whether or not Ahinoam of Jezreel is to be identified with the wife of Saul, he "had given" (pluperfect, v.44; thus also Alter, *The Art of Biblical Narrative*, p. 121) his daughter Michal, David's wife, to another man. From a literary standpoint the narrator may be describing Saul's intention to treat David as being as good as dead, thus balancing the account of Samuel's death at the beginning of the chapter (v.1a; cf. Stek, *The Former Prophets*, p. 65B). Conversely, Alter may be right in assuming that, since Michal is after all "David's wife" (v.44; cf. 18:27), Saul's motive may be "to demonstrate, however clumsily, that David has no bond of kinship with the royal family and hence no claim to the throne" (*The Art of Biblical Narrative*, p. 121). The name of Michal's second husband was Paltiel, who was from Gallim. Although its location is unknown, it may be the same Gallim of Isaiah 10:30 (near Gibeah and Anathoth, and thus a few miles north of Jerusalem), which appears in association with Laishah, an expanded form of the name of Paltiel's father, Laish.

Thus chapter 25, whose main burden is a move by David to kill a man (Nabal) and later to marry his wife (Abigail), comes to a close. Second Samuel 11, the story of David, Uriah, and Bathsheba, is the only other chapter in the books of Samuel with the same theme. First Samuel 25 is thus "a proleptic glimpse, within the context of David's ascent, of his fall from grace" (Levenson, "I Samuel 25 as Literature and History," p. 237).

## Notes

**1** The NIV's "Maon" is based on the LXX (cf. NIV mg.). The MT reads פָּארָן (*pā'rān*, "Paran"), as do a few LXX MSS, but the Desert of Paran is much too far south to figure in this context (cf. also "Maon" in v.2).

**4–13** Several key verbs in this section are echoed in the same order in its parallel passage (vv.39–42), usually with the same subject: וַיִּשְׁמַע (*wayyišma'*, "[David] heard," vv.4, 39); וַיִּשְׁלַח (*wayyišlaḥ*, "[David] sent," vv.5, 39); וַיָּבֹאוּ (*wayyāḇō'û*, "[David's men/servants] arrived/went," vv.9, 40); וַיְדַבְּרוּ (*wayᵉḏabbᵉrû*, "[David's men/servants] spoke/said," vv.9, 40); and וַיֹּאמֶר/וַתֹּאמֶר (*wayyō'mer/wattō'mer*, "[Nabal/Abigail] answered/said," vv.10, 41) (cf. similarly Stek, *The Former Prophets*, p. 65B).

**6** The NIV's "Say to him: 'Long life to you!' " renders וַאֲמַרְתֶּם כֹּה לֶחָי (*wa'ᵃmartem kōh leḥāy*, lit., "And you shall say thus: 'To the life!' "). It is perhaps preferable to read לְאָחִי (*lᵉ'āḥî*) instead of *lᵉḥāy*, assuming elision of א (cf. בָּנוּ [*bānû*] for בָּאנוּ [*bā'nû*, "we come"] in v.8). The entire expression would then be translated (lit.): "And you shall say thus to my brother" (cf. Vul., *et dicetis sic fratribus meis*).

**14** The verb עִיט (*'îṭ*, "hurl insults," "scream," "shriek"), although unique to this verse, is cognate with the more common עַיִט (*'ayiṭ*, "bird of prey"). Its homonym, also found only in 1 Samuel, means "pounce" (14:32; 15:19).

**22** Instead of the MT's "David's enemies," the NIV here reads "David" (with the LXX; cf. NIV mg.), doubtless correctly (cf. also Barthélemy, p. 199), since the common formula of self-imprecation is used and since "David's enemies" scarcely makes sense here (cf., however, KD, p. 242). McCarter suggests that since David's threat is in fact never carried out, "a scribe has changed David's words [in the MT] to protect him (or his descendants!) from the consequences of the oath" (*I Samuel*, p. 394, n. 22).

The NIV's euphemistic "one male" translates מַשְׁתִּין בְּקִיר (*maštîn bᵉqîr*, "one who urinates against a wall"). Outside this chapter the expression is used only in 1 Kings 14:10; 16:11; 21:21; 2 Kings 9:8, each time (as here) in a context where the extermination of an entire family or household is in view.

**33** The Hebrew translated "May you be blessed for your good judgment" reads literally, "May your good judgment be blessed and may you be blessed." For other examples of blessing invoked on inanimate objects, cf. Deut 28:5 ("basket," "kneading trough"); Prov 5:18 ("fountain").

**44** פַּלְטִי (*palṭî*, "Palti"; see NIV mg.), which means "My Deliverance," is the hypocoristicon (shortened form) of the theophoric name פַּלְטִיאֵל (*palṭî'ēl*; lit., "God Is My Deliverance/Deliverer," 2 Sam 3:15).

## 14. *Sparing Saul's life again*

### 26:1–25

1 The Ziphites went to Saul at Gibeah and said, "Is not David hiding on
the hill of Hakilah, which faces Jeshimon?"
2 So Saul went down to the Desert of Ziph, with his three thousand
chosen men of Israel, to search there for David. 3 Saul made his camp
beside the road on the hill of Hakilah facing Jeshimon, but David stayed
in the desert. When he saw that Saul had followed him there, 4 he sent
out scouts and learned that Saul had definitely arrived.
5 Then David set out and went to the place where Saul had camped. He
saw where Saul and Abner son of Ner, the commander of the army, had
lain down. Saul was lying inside the camp, with the army encamped
around him.
6 David then asked Ahimelech the Hittite and Abishai son of Zeruiah,
Joab's brother, "Who will go down into the camp with me to Saul?"
"I'll go with you," said Abishai.
7 So David and Abishai went to the army by night, and there was Saul,
lying asleep inside the camp with his spear stuck in the ground near his
head. Abner and the soldiers were lying around him.
8 Abishai said to David, "Today God has delivered your enemy into
your hands. Now let me pin him to the ground with one thrust of my
spear; I won't strike him twice."
9 But David said to Abishai, "Don't destroy him! Who can lay a hand on
the LORD's anointed and be guiltless? 10 As surely as the LORD lives," he
said, "the LORD himself will strike him; either his time will come and he
will die, or he will go into battle and perish. 11 But the LORD forbid that I
should lay a hand on the LORD's anointed. Now get the spear and water
jug that are near his head, and let's go."
12 So David took the spear and water jug near Saul's head, and they
left. No one saw or knew about it, nor did anyone wake up. They were all
sleeping, because the LORD had put them into a deep sleep.
13 Then David crossed over to the other side and stood on top of the
hill some distance away; there was a wide space between them. 14 He
called out to the army and to Abner son of Ner, "Aren't you going to
answer me, Abner?"
Abner replied, "Who are you who calls to the king?"
15 David said, "You're a man, aren't you? And who is like you in Israel?
Why didn't you guard your lord the king? Someone came to destroy
your lord the king. 16 What you have done is not good. As surely as the
LORD lives, you and your men deserve to die, because you did not guard
your master, the LORD's anointed. Look around you. Where are the
king's spear and water jug that were near his head?"
17 Saul recognized David's voice and said, "Is that your voice, David
my son?"
David replied, "Yes it is, my lord the king." 18 And he added, "Why is
my lord pursuing his servant? What have I done, and what wrong am I
guilty of? 19 Now let my lord the king listen to his servant's words. If the
LORD has incited you against me, then may he accept an offering. If,
however, men have done it, may they be cursed before the LORD! They
have now driven me from my share in the LORD's inheritance and have
said, 'Go, serve other gods.' 20 Now do not let my blood fall to the
ground far from the presence of the LORD. The king of Israel has come
out to look for a flea—as one hunts a partridge in the mountains."
21 Then Saul said, "I have sinned. Come back, David my son. Because
you considered my life precious today, I will not try to harm you again.
Surely I have acted like a fool and have erred greatly."

[22]"Here is the king's spear," David answered. "Let one of your young
men come over and get it. [23]The LORD rewards every man for his
righteousness and faithfulness. The LORD delivered you into my hands
today, but I would not lay a hand on the LORD's anointed. [24]As surely as I
valued your life today, so may the LORD value my life and deliver me from
all trouble."
[25]Then Saul said to David, "May you be blessed, my son David; you
will do great things and surely triumph."
So David went on his way, and Saul returned home.

The striking similarities between chapters 24 and 26, already noted briefly (see comment at introduction to 24:1–22) and expanded on below, have led some scholars to assume that the same incident is in view. But the differences are equally striking. Therefore it is best to conclude with Mauchline that "there is no difficulty in supposing that there may have been two occasions, in different circumstances, when David spared Saul's life" (p. 173; cf. KD, pp. 247–49). The most fundamental difference between the two chapters is expressed by Miscall: "Chapter 24 was a study in David's restraint when given an opportunity to harm or kill Saul. Chapter 26 is a demonstration of David's ability to put himself in the position to kill Saul" (p. 158; cf. p. 162).

The chapter narrates the final confrontation between Saul and David, and its speeches are animated by the mutual irreconcilability of the two men (cf. Gordon, "David's Rise," p. 59). Its literary structure is arranged chiastically:

A. Saul searches for David, who then responds (vv.1–5).
  B. David keeps his man Abishai from killing Saul (vv.6–12).
  B′. David rebukes Saul's man Abner for not protecting Saul (vv.13–16).
A′. Saul talks to David, who then responds (vv.17–25).

**1–5** The common verb *bô'* ("come," "enter") is a unifying feature of this section, appearing in all but one of its verses ("went," v.1 [a different word is used for "went" in v.2]; "followed," v.3; "arrived," v.4; "went," v.5). It occurs elsewhere in the chapter only in vv.7, 10, and 15.

Verse 1 is an abbreviated and slightly modified echo of 23:19 (see comment there concerning Hakilah and Jeshimon; for the location of Ziph, see comment on 23:14). Since there were "strongholds" (23:19) at Hakilah, it was an especially secure place for a fugitive to hide and was therefore doubtless used often by David and his men. Substituting for the specific "south of" in 23:19, the more flexible Hebrew idiom *'al pᵉnê* (lit., "near the face of"; cf. "near," 24:2) describes the general location of Hakilah in v.1 ("which faces"; "facing," v.3).

Having heard the report of the Ziphites, Saul goes "down" (v.2) from the high ground at Gibeah (v.1) with his "three thousand chosen men" (see 24:2 and commentary) to the "Desert of Ziph" (for its general location see comment on 23:14). There he continues to "search . . . for" David, as he had done earlier (23:14, 25; cf. 24:2, "look for"). David, sensing that Saul has followed him to the desert (v.3), sends scouts to confirm that fact (v.4; for the NIV mg.'s "had come to Nacon," see comment and Notes on 23:23).

After his scouts have pinpointed the exact location of Saul's camp, David waits until Saul and his men have retired for the night ("had lain down," "was lying," v.5) and then goes to look over the situation for himself. Saul's apparent invulnerability is detailed: (1) Abner, his cousin (see comment on 14:50–51) and the commander of "his" (MT) army, is lying beside him; (2) he is safely inside the "camp" (vv.5, 7, lit., "wagon-wheel track"; see comment on 17:20); and (3) the rest of his army is encamped "around him" (v.5; cf. v.7). Nevertheless Gunn observes that "despite these impossible odds," David goes down to the camp (*The Fate of King Saul*, p. 102).

**6–12** Not to be confused with Ahimelech the priest (cf. ch. 21), "Ahimelech the Hittite" (v.6), mentioned only here, was one among many mercenaries who formed a part of David's burgeoning army (for a later similar example, cf. Uriah the Hittite, 2 Sam 11:3). Together with "Abishai son of Zeruiah, Joab's brother," he is asked whether he is willing to join David in going down to Saul's camp. Zeruiah, David's sister, was the mother of Abishai and Joab (1 Chron 2:15–16), who both figure prominently in 2 Samuel, especially after David becomes king following Saul's death.

Portending his later importance, Abishai (rather than Ahimelech the Hittite) volunteers to go down with David into the camp of Saul. The two men arrive after dark ("by night," v.7), when everyone is asleep, and leave before anyone wakes up (v.12). Since Saul and his men are in a "deep sleep" brought on by the Lord (v.12; cf. Gen 2:21; 15:12), David and Abishai can move about undetected and speak to one another without being heard. Like a scepter symbolizing the royal presence, a "spear" (v.7)—"that spear which is a hall-mark of Saul" (Gunn, *The Fate of King Saul*, p. 102; cf. 18:10; 19:9–10; 20:33; 22:6)—is stuck in the ground near his head. Abishai, anxious to be rid of Saul once and for all, wants to kill him with "the spear" (v.8 MT; NIV's "my spear" is unwarranted and detracts from the ironic potential of Saul's being assassinated with his own spear, an understanding preferred by many commentators [e.g., Baldwin, Driver, Hertzberg, Klein, Smith]).

Abishai's sense of urgency (a characteristic of the chapter as a whole) is conveyed by his "Today" and his "Now" (v.8; lit., "And now," for which cf. David's words in vv.11, 16 [MT, "And now look around you"], 19–20; see comment and Notes on 24:20). His words to David are strikingly reminiscent of David's to Goliath in 17:46: "This day [= 'Today' in v.8] the LORD will hand you over to me" (lit., "will deliver you into my hand"; see comment in loc.; cf. 24:18). In addition, Gunn (*The Fate of King Saul*, p. 102) points out the similarity between the beginning of Abishai's speech and that of David's men in 24:4—although a different Hebrew verb (lit., "give") is used there (as also here in v.23 [NIV, "delivered"]). All these cases, however, attest to a common theme: It is the sovereign Lord who brings deliverance, whether potential or actual, to his king-elect.

Abishai, however, envisions himself as the instrument of divine deliverance: "Let me pin him to the ground" (v.8). In so speaking he echoes—probably unwittingly—the narrator's description of Saul's murderous intentions against David (see 18:10–11 and comment; 19:10; cf. 20:33). Not characterized by restraint, Abishai is always quick to act (cf. his later proposals to kill Shimei on the spot [2 Sam 16:9–10; 19:21–23]; cf. further Miscall, p. 159). He is also confident about his strength, claiming that he will be able to execute Saul without having to "strike him twice" (v.8; cf. the similar description of the brute strength of Abishai's brother Joab against the hapless Amasa in 2 Sam 20:10).

As in chapter 24, David does not allow any of his men to press their advantage against the unsuspecting Saul. Because he is the "LORD's anointed" (v.9; see 24:6 and comment), no one—including David himself—is to "lay a hand on" him (vv.9, 11, 23; cf. "lift my hand against" in 24:6, 10). Jonathan's earlier question—"Why then would you do wrong to an innocent [*nāqî*] man like David by killing him?" (19:5)—receives a faint echo in that of David: "Who can [kill Saul] . . . and be guiltless [*wᵉniqqāh*]?" David's command to Abishai—"Don't destroy him!" (v.9)—may be the origin of the familiar *'al-tašḥēṯ* ("Do Not Destroy") in the titles of the Davidic Psalms 57–59, two of which have David's fugitive days as their traditional background (Pss 57; 59; cf. the title of the Asaphite Ps 75).

In v.10 David intones the solemn oath—"As surely as the LORD lives"—that is often used where matters of life and death are at stake (cf. v.16; see comment on 14:39). Then, in a series of three clauses separated by *'ô . . . 'ô* (which the NIV translates as "either . . . or," assuming that the first clause governs the next two in the sense that the second and third clauses describe ways in which the Lord might put Saul to death; so also Gordon, "David's Rise," p. 49; Klein; McCarter), David describes potential ways that Saul might die. It is equally possible, however, that the phrase here means "or . . . or" and that v.10 outlines three options rather than two (thus Driver, Keil, Mauchline, Smith; cf. also Gunn, *The Fate of King Saul*, p. 103; Miscall, p. 159; Polzin, *Samuel and the Deuteronomist*, p. 212): (1) The Lord will "strike" him (with a fatal disease, as he did his alter ego Nabal, 25:38), "or" (2) when his "time" comes (lit., "day"; for the expression cf. Jer 50:27, 31; Ezek 21:25, 29; and esp. Davidic Ps 37:13) he will die (i.e., a natural death), "or" (3) he will "perish" (lit., "be swept away," as in 12:25; for the same verb cf. 27:1, "be destroyed") in battle. Under either understanding, of course, the Lord is the ultimate cause of Saul's death, not only because of his sovereign will, but also because vengeance belongs to him, as Abigail reminded David (25:26, 31) and as he himself acknowledged (25:32, 39). The last of David's suggestions turned out to be a presentiment of Saul's fate (cf. 31:1–6).

Reflecting the language of 24:6, David uses another oath (v.11) to underscore his refusal to kill Saul. In 24:4 he had taken "a corner of Saul's robe," a symbol of royal authority (see comment there). Here he orders Abishai to take Saul's spear (a symbol of his authority but also of death) and water jug (a symbol of life; cf. 1 Kings 19:4–6). As Saul was unprotected and unsuspecting in 24:3, so also here—indeed, he and his men are unable to awaken because of divinely induced slumber. Thus David and Abishai, unseen and unheard, steal away into the night (v.12).

Although Abishai doubtless obeyed David's command to take the spear and the water jug (v.11), he did so on David's behalf—and so the text attributes the act to David (v.12). Polzin contrasts the scene in this chapter to a similar episode in 22:6–23: "Whereas David's taking of bread and the sword of Goliath caused Saul to murder the priests of Nob, here his taking of water and the spear of Saul embodies a refusal to murder" (*Samuel and the Deuteronomist*, p. 212).

**13–16** In addition to the single-minded theme of this section (David's rebuke of Abner), another unifying feature is the subtle *inclusio* formed by the occurrence of the root *r'š* in vv.13 ("top") and 16 ("head").

After leaving Saul's camp, David places a safe distance between himself and his enemy. The idiom *'āmaḏ mērāḥōq* ("stand/stay at a distance"; NIV, "stood . . . some distance away," v.13) means to distance oneself for reasons of fear, awe, respect, caution, etc. (cf. Exod 20:18, 21; 2 Kings 2:7; Isa 59:14; and the Davidic Ps 38:11, "stay far away"). On a later occasion Shimei would similarly leave a valley between himself and David in order to curse him and throw stones at him with impunity (2 Sam 16:13).

David calls out to Saul's army in general and to its commander, Abner, in particular (and thus by association to "the king" himself, v.14). David's question implies that he had to call several times, perhaps because the men were sleeping (v.12). Abner finally replies, "Who are you who calls [*qārā'tā*] to the king?" (v.14). McCarter contends that David's reply to Saul in v.20 echoes Abner's question in v.14 (*I Samuel*, p. 408): David stands on a "mountain" (v.13; NIV, "hill") calling (v.14), and he later complains to Saul that he is comparing David to a "partridge" (*qōrē'*, lit., "caller") being hunted in "mountains" (v.20; cf. a similar wordplay in Judg 15:18–19, where En Hakkore probably meant "Spring of the Partridge").

David's first two questions in v.15 seem to be scornful, although it is also possible that they were uttered with incredulous pity. His third question rebukes Abner for dereliction of duty, a failing in which he also implicates Abner's men (v.16): Not to protect the king, "the LORD's anointed," is inexcusable—indeed, is worthy of death (for the phrase "deserve to die" [lit., "are sons of death"], see comment on "must die" in 20:31; cf. similarly "those condemned to die/death" in Pss 79:11; 102:20; for the circumstances leading to Abner's death, cf. 2 Sam 3:22–27). The "someone" (lit., "one of [David's] soldiers") who came to "destroy" (v.15) the king was of course Abishai (v.9), whom David had already kept from doing so.

Whereas Jethro's stern rebuke of his son-in-law Moses had been nonetheless helpful (Exod 18:17), David's echo of it is a condemnation of Abner ("What you [sing.] have done is not good," v.16). Gunn calls attention to the irony that follows: "As Yahweh *lives*, you deserve to *die*" (*The Fate of King Saul*, p. 156 n. 14).

**17–25** The final section of chapter 26 consists of a conversation between Saul and David, with Saul beginning and ending the interchange but with David doing most of the talking: Saul (v.17a), David (vv.17b–20), Saul (v.21), David (vv.22–24), Saul (v.25). The king addresses the fugitive as *bᵉnî dāwiḏ* ("my son David") in the first, middle, and last verses (vv.17, 21, 25), thus giving literary unity to the section. Saul's initial question—"Is that your voice, David my son?" (v.17)—is a verbatim echo of 24:16. But whereas there David had addressed Saul not only as "my lord the king" (24:8) but also as "my father" (see 24:11 and comment), here Saul is simply "my lord the king" (v.17; cf. v.19). Saul has already acknowledged/designated David as his legitimate successor (24:20), and therefore David no longer needs the rejected "king" as his "father" (Gunn, *The Fate of King Saul*, p. 104).

David, recognizing his continuing fugitive status, begins and ends his first response to Saul with the verb *rāḏaṗ* ("pursuing," v.18; "hunts," v.20). His "What have I done" (v.18) is later mirrored by Saul's "you will do" (v.25). As before, so also now he is firm in his conviction that he is innocent of any "wrong[doing]" (v.18; cf. 24:11). Just as "I am not guilty of wrongdoing" (24:11) would be more literally translated as "there is no wrongdoing in my hand," so also here its echo—"what wrong am I guilty of?"—is more literally "what wrong is in my hand?" The latter expression, in turn, is mirrored in v.23, where David tells Saul that the lord delivered him "into my hands" (cf. "in my hand" in v.18). By deciding again not to "lay a hand" on the Lord's anointed (v.23), David refuses to make his guiltless hands guilty of wrongdoing.

In vv.19–20a David sets forth two possible sources of Saul's dogged pursuit of him. First, God may have "incited" Saul (as he later "incited" David to take a census, 2 Sam 24:1) against him (v.19). In that case David hopes to appease God by bringing him an offering that he may "accept" (lit., "smell"; cf. Gen 8:20–21). (Gunn [*The Fate of King Saul*, p. 156 n. 15] points out that Saul's earlier perception was that his son

Jonathan had "incited" David [22:8, different Heb. verb] to lie in wait for Saul. Thus David and Saul interpreted their mutually hostile relationship quite differently.)

Second, men may be at fault. In that case David pronounces a solemn oath against them: "May they be cursed before the LORD!" (cf. Josh 6:26). David's sense of urgency in v.19 is underscored by his use of "now" (lit., "today," as in vv.21, 23–24): He is concerned that his fugitive status would prevent his participation in "the LORD's inheritance" (i.e., the land of Israel; cf. 2 Sam 20:19; 21:3). In ancient times it was commonly believed that to be driven from one's homeland was tantamount to leaving one's god(s) and being forced to "serve other gods," the gods of the alien territory of exile (cf. Ronald F. Youngblood, *Faith of Our Fathers* [Glendale: Regal, 1976], p. 84; for a more general treatment, see Daniel Isaac Block, *The Gods of the Nations: Studies in Ancient Near Eastern National Theology* [Jackson: Evangelical Theological Society, 1988]). David thus prays that Saul will not cause him to die "far from the presence of the LORD" (v.20)—in this case, Philistia (see ch. 27). Gunn observes that Saul's pursuit of David is forcing him "to break the first and greatest commandment" (*The Fate of King Saul,* p. 104).

In a reprise of 24:14, David concludes his statement to Saul by stressing the incongruity of Saul's enterprise (v.20b): The most powerful man in the land ("king of Israel") has taken it upon himself to "come out" (cf. also 23:15) to look for something trivial, something unworthy of his time and energy—a single "flea." In 24:14 the "flea" reference is in the form of a question and thus serves as a veiled threat. Here, however, the context is quite different: Looking for a single flea is compared to hunting a single "partridge" (lit., "caller"; see comment on v.14) in the mountains, something no one in his right mind would take the time or make the effort to do. Since the sand partridge (*Ammoperdix heyi*) is the only partridge found in the desert areas west of the Dead Sea, David's comparison of it to himself is particularly apt: "This partridge is a great runner and speeds along the ground when it is chased, until it becomes exhausted and can be knocked down by the hunter's stick" (*Fauna and Flora of the Bible,* p. 64).

Saul responds to David (v.21) with words that he has felt a need to utter before: "I have sinned" (cf. 15:24; contrast David's description of his own conduct in 24:11). Recognizing that David has "considered" his "life precious" (for the idiom cf. 2 Kings 1:13–14, "have respect for . . . life"; cf. Ps 72:14, "precious is their blood in his sight"), Saul promises not to harm him. Apparently Saul's repentance is sincere this time: He admits that he has erred "greatly" (*harbēh me'ōḏ*, "very greatly") and that—like his alter ego Nabal (see comment on 25:25)—he has "acted like a fool" (cf. Samuel's rebuke of Saul in 13:13). David's later confession to the Lord in 2 Samuel 24:10 (= 1 Chron 21:8) is ironically and sadly reminiscent of Saul's words in v.21.

David's retort to Saul offers to return his spear (v.22), the symbol of death, but not the water jug, the symbol of life. Miscall suggests that keeping the jug "could be a sign of David's control" over the situation (p. 161). The argument of David to the effect that God "rewards" (v.23; cf. similarly 2 Sam 16:12) all who are characterized by "righteousness and faithfulness" (for the pairing of *ṣeḏāqāh* and *'emûnāh*, cf. Prov 12:17 ["truthful . . . honest"]; Isa 59:4 ["justice . . . integrity"]; Jer 5:1; Hab 2:4) is perhaps as much a condemnation of Saul's conduct as it is a commendation of his own. As before (24:10; see comment on 22:17; cf. further 31:4 = 1 Chron 10:4), so also now David refuses to lay a hand on Saul, the Lord's anointed. It is the Lord who has "delivered" Saul into David's hands (v.23), and as recompense for his respect for

Saul's life he prays that the Lord will "deliver" him (v.24; different Heb. verbs) from "all trouble."

Although David has valued Saul's life, he does not ask Saul to reciprocate. Instead, he places in God's hand whatever worth his life might have (cf. similarly Gunn, *The Fate of King Saul*, p. 105). Likewise, deliverance from "all trouble" (cf. 2 Sam 4:9 for David's confident assertion about God's past deliverance in every negative circumstance) will come from God, not from Saul—who in fact has been the major cause of "trouble" for David in any case.

Strangely enough, Saul's final words to David (v.25) are good wishes for his greatness and triumph. Three times Saul has called David his "son" (vv.17, 21, 25), and Saul now apparently knows that David will be his successor on Israel's throne as well (cf. similarly 24:19–20). His blessing on David virtually assures as much. David had prayed that any potential enemies of his might be "cursed" (v.19); Saul now leaves David after praying that he might be "blessed" (v.25; cf. David's words to Abigail in 25:33). Since there is now nothing more to be said, David and Saul part (cf. 24:22), never to see each other again.

## Notes

---

**6** Two Hebrew bullae (clay seal impressions) from the late seventh or early sixth century B.C. display the name יהואב (*yhw'b*, "Jehoab"), which is "the first known instance of the full form of the biblical name Joab" (Nahman Avigad, *Hebrew Bullae From the Time of Jeremiah: Remnants of a Burnt Archive* [Jerusalem: Israel Exploration Society, 1986], p. 43).

That Abishai, Joab, and Asahel (2 Sam 2:18) are consistently referred to as sons of their mother Zeruiah rather than as sons of their father is unusual. It is perhaps best explained in light of the reference to the tomb of Asahel's father in 2 Sam 2:32, which suggests that he had already died "while his sons were children" (F.H. Cryer, "David's Rise to Power and the Death of Abner: An Analysis of 1 Samuel xxvi 14–16 and Its Redactional-Critical Implications," VetTest 35, 4 [1985]: 388 n. 9).

**8** The MT's בחנית ובארץ (*bḥnyt wb'rṣ*, lit., "with the spear and into the ground") is difficult at best. Perhaps the words should be divided differently: *bḥnytw b'rṣ* ("with his spear into the ground"; see comment in loc.).

**12** Two MT MSS insert אֲשֶׁר (*'ᵃšer*, "that [are/were]") before מראשתי (*mr'šty*, "near [Saul's] head"), in conformity with the same phrase in vv.11, 16. The *Qere* in v.12, however, vocalizes *mē-* ("from"; cf. LXX, ἀπὸ [*apo*]), instead of as the nominal prefix *mᵉ-* (as in vv.11, 16). Keil is therefore probably correct in asserting that the *m-* does double duty in v.12 (*mē-* standing for *mim[ᵉ]-*, KD, p. 250; cf. similarly Watson, "Shared Consonants," p. 532).

**15** The idiom שָׁמַר אֶל־ (*šāmar 'el-*, "watch over"; NIV, "guard"; cf. 2 Sam 11:16, "had . . . under siege") has recently been thus interpreted in the Lachish ostraca and used to argue in favor of the view that they were draft letters written from, rather than to, Lachish (for detail's cf. Oded Borowski, "Yadin Presents New Interpretation of the Famous Lachish Letters," *Biblical Archaeology Review* 10, 2 [1984]: 77).

**19** David's way of addressing Saul—"Now let my lord the king listen to his servant's words"—finds an exact parallel in a seventh-century B.C. ostracon found at Mesad Hashavyahu, a fortress near Yavneh Yam ten miles south of Tel Aviv. Like David, the supplicant begins his plea to redress a wrong as follows: "Let my lord the governor listen to his servant's word" (cf. Alan R. Millard, "The Question of Israelite Literacy," *Bible Review* 3, 3 [1987]: 27).

---

## 15. *Achish the Philistine*

### 27:1–28:2

[1]But David thought to himself, "One of these days I will be destroyed by the hand of Saul. The best thing I can do is to escape to the land of the Philistines. Then Saul will give up searching for me anywhere in Israel, and I will slip out of his hand."

[2]So David and the six hundred men with him left and went over to Achish son of Maoch king of Gath. [3]David and his men settled in Gath with Achish. Each man had his family with him, and David had his two wives: Ahinoam of Jezreel and Abigail of Carmel, the widow of Nabal. [4]When Saul was told that David had fled to Gath, he no longer searched for him.

[5]Then David said to Achish, "If I have found favor in your eyes, let a place be assigned to me in one of the country towns, that I may live there. Why should your servant live in the royal city with you?"

[6]So on that day Achish gave him Ziklag, and it has belonged to the kings of Judah ever since. [7]David lived in Philistine territory a year and four months.

[8]Now David and his men went up and raided the Geshurites, the Girzites and the Amalekites. (From ancient times these peoples had lived in the land extending to Shur and Egypt.) [9]Whenever David attacked an area, he did not leave a man or woman alive, but took sheep and cattle, donkeys and camels, and clothes. Then he returned to Achish.

[10]When Achish asked, "Where did you go raiding today?" David would say, "Against the Negev of Judah" or "Against the Negev of Jerahmeel" or "Against the Negev of the Kenites." [11]He did not leave a man or woman alive to be brought to Gath, for he thought, "They might inform on us and say, 'This is what David did.'" And such was his practice as long as he lived in Philistine territory. [12]Achish trusted David and said to himself, "He has become so odious to his people, the Israelites, that he will be my servant forever."

[28:1]In those days the Philistines gathered their forces to fight against Israel. Achish said to David, "You must understand that you and your men will accompany me in the army."

[2]David said, "Then you will see for yourself what your servant can do."

Achish replied, "Very well, I will make you my bodyguard for life."

Technically speaking, the story of the rise of David continues beyond Saul's death (ch. 31) and through the accounts of David's elimination of other rivals to his divinely granted rule over Israel (2 Sam 1–5). At the same time, however, there is a distinct literary break at 28:3, which begins the narrative that describes Saul's final hours. The vignette depicting David's settling in Philistia (27:1–28:2), therefore, is a convenient point to bring to an end—in a more restricted sense and in conformity with our overall outline—the story of David's rise (16:1–28:2), which, as we have seen, interlaces and oscillates with the story of Saul's decline. God's name is not mentioned either in chapter 31 or 27:1–28:2, perhaps suggesting that Saul entered his final battle against the Philistines without God's help (cf., ominously, 28:6) and that David did not consult God (maybe believing that he could not do so because he was no longer in Israel, his homeland; see comment on 26:19–20) when he decided to escape to Philistine territory.

**27:1–12** Chapter 27 occupies the lion's share of the account of David's relationship to Achish of Gath (27:1–28:2). Long a fugitive, David decides to flee to Philistia where he will be free of Saul's relentless pursuit once and for all. The chapter thus exudes permanence and stability and is characterized by such words as *yāšaḇ* ("live," vv.3 ["settled"], 5 [bis], 7, 8, 11), *yôm* ("day," vv.1, 6, 6 ["since"], 7 [untr. in NIV], 7 ["year"], 10 ["today"], 11 ["as long as"]), and *'ôlām* ("forever," vv.8 ["ancient times"], 12). As Polzin observes (*Samuel and the Deuteronomist*, p. 216), the chapter "ends with the narrator revealing the inner thoughts of Achish (as the inner thoughts of David were divulged at the beginning)": David "thought to himself" (v.1; lit., "said to/in his heart"; cf. Gen 8:21), Achish "said to himself" (v.12; lit., "saying," the context implying "to himself").

David knows that it is only a matter of time before he will be "destroyed" (lit., "swept away"; cf. 12:25; 26:10 ["perish"]) by Saul (v.1). Polzin notes correctly that "the use of *sāp̱āh* ['sweep away'] in 1 Samuel indicates a close connection between the fates of king and people" (*Samuel and the Deuteronomist*, p. 269 n. 1). In v.1 David, in whom—by Saul's own testimony—the fate of the people of Israel resides (24:20), is in danger of being swept away by the king himself. David thus comes to the conclusion that "the best thing I can do is" (lit., "there is nothing better for me than"; for the idiom, cf. Eccl 3:12; 8:15) to "escape" (emphatic; the same verb, echoed later in the verse, is there translated "slip out") to Philistia. He feels that if he does so, Saul will "give up" his pursuit (lit., "despair in," "find hopeless"; cf. Job 6:26; Isa 57:10; Jer 2:25 ["It's no use"]; 18:12). David's confidence that he will then be able to "slip out of/escape from his hand" (cf. 2 Chron 16:7; Jer 32:4; 34:3; 38:18, 23; Dan 11:41, in each of which passages the idiom connotes deliverance from mortal danger) is confirmed when Saul stops "searching" for him (vv.1, 4), as he had relentlessly done while David was still in Israelite territory (23:14, 25; 24:2; 26:2, 20). "Thus a cycle is complete: David had come into Saul's life in large part through the Philistines (chapter 17), and now he moves out of Saul's life through the agency of the Philistines. The difference is that in the first place he had defeated them whereas now he joins them" (Gunn, *The Fate of King Saul*, p. 106).

So David and his "six hundred men" (v.2; for the significance of the number, see comment on 13:15; 23:13) seek refuge in Philistia with Achish son of Maoch king of Gath, to whom David had earlier fled for help (see 21:10 and comment for details concerning the names of Achish and his father). Since Gath is some thirty rugged miles northwest of the Desert of Ziph, where David had been hiding earlier (26:1–2), the task of moving himself, his two wives Ahinoam and Abigail (see comment on 25:3, 43), and his men and their families (v.3) must have involved considerable hardship.

David's settlement in Gath would doubtless be temporary, however, since he is not sure that it would be advisable to live with a man who had earlier given him reason to fear him (21:11–12). David therefore hopes that if he has "found favor" in the "eyes" of Achish (v.5)—implying that Achish can now trust him (see comment on 20:29)—the Philistine ruler will not insist that he live in the "royal city" (v.5), a term stressing the size, importance, and dominance of the city so described (cf. similarly 2 Sam 12:26 ["royal citadel"]; Josh 10:2; *āl šarrūti* is the Akkadian equivalent [*The Assyrian Dictionary* (Chicago: Oriental Institute, 1964), 1.1.382], *āl šarri* in Amarna Akkadian [ibid., p. 386; J.A. Knudtzon, *Die el-Amarna-Tafeln* (Leipzig: J.C. Hinrichs, 1915), 2:1368]). David would be content to be assigned a country town; so Achish gives him Ziklag (v.6), which originally had been part of the tribal patrimony of Simeon "within the territory of Judah" (cf. Josh 19:1, 5; cf. Josh 15:21, 31). The modern site of ancient

Ziklag is probably Tell esh-Shariah, about twenty-three miles south-southwest of Gath, although Tell Halif (in Judah, ten miles east of Tell esh-Shariah) has also been suggested (J. Simons, *The Geographical and Topographical Texts of the Old Testament* [Leiden: Brill, 1959], p. 145; [no author listed], "Digging in '89," *Biblical Archaeology Review* 15, 1 [1989]: 28). In any event, Achish doubtless placed David in Ziklag to protect Philistia against marauders from the south. David's settlement there anticipates the subsequent ownership of Ziklag by the "kings of Judah" (v.6), of whom he would become the ideal dynastic ancestor (2 Sam 2:4). Altogether David lived in Philistine-controlled territory (vv.6, 11) for "a year" (lit., "days," translated "annual" in 1:21, 2:19; 20:6) "and four months" (v.7).

While vv.1–7 describe David's settlement in Philistia, vv.8–12 outline his raiding operations, in connection with which—for the second time—he succeeds in deceiving Achish (cf. 21:12–15). Since the Philistines themselves were often raiders (23:27), it is not surprising that a Philistine vassal or ally like David would also engage in raiding campaigns (vv.8, 10; the Heb. verb here and in 23:27 means "to strip off"). Among those whom David and his men raided were the Geshurites (a southern people mentioned elsewhere only in Josh 13:2 and not to be confused with the northern Geshurites, for which see comment on 2 Sam 3:3), the Girzites (*Kethiv*, mentioned only here and otherwise unknown; *Qere* "Gizrites" would be the inhabitants of Gezer, which is, however, too far north to fit the present context), and the Amalekites (themselves characterized as raiders in 30:1, 14 [cf. 14:48]; see also comment on 15:7 for their connection with Shur). All these peoples had lived in southern Canaan and northern Sinai "from ancient times" (v.8, perhaps a reference to the early confrontation between Amalek and Israel reported in Exod 17:8–16; for a close parallel to this nuance of *mē'ôlām*, see Jer 28:8 ["from early times"], making it unnecessary to read a posited *mṭlm*, "from Tela[i]m" [cf. 15:4], with the LXX, Garsiel, Driver, Gordon, McCarter, Klein, et al. [contrast KD, RSV]). Saul had conducted a fateful campaign against the Amalekites (ch. 15), and David would soon fight them again (ch. 30).

David's "practice" (v.11) whenever he attacked an area was not to "leave a man or woman alive" (vv.9, 11). Unlike the situation in 15:3, however (see comment there), where total annihilation of the population was for religious purposes, David here kills everyone so that no survivors would be left to report to Achish what has really happened (v.11). In addition to garments, he "took" as plunder (v.9; cf. the use of the verb in that sense also in 30:16, 18–20; Gen 14:11 ["seized"]; 1 Kings 14:26) only animals, a procedure to be expected as a matter of course from kings (8:16), but not from prophets (see comment on 12:3).

Although David was raiding Geshurites, Girzites, and Amalekites (v.8), he told Achish that he was raiding various subdistricts of the Negev (v.10) that belonged to or were controlled by Judah (30:26–29): the "Negev of Judah" (in southern Judah near Beersheba; Joab would later complete David's census there [cf. 2 Sam 24:7]), the "Negev of Jerahmeel" (probably in southern Judah in the eastern Negev basin), the "Negev of the Kenites" (see comment on 15:6; probably in the northeastern Negev basin near Arad; cf. Rasmussen, p. 246 and the map on p. 114). Far enough away from Gath so that Achish would be ignorant of his movements, David can lie to him with impunity—especially by leaving no survivors who might be able to contradict him. David thus has the best of both worlds: He implies to Achish that Judahite hostility toward David is increasing, and at the same time he gains the appreciation and loyalty of Judah toward himself by raiding their desert neighbors.

To his detriment, Achish trusts David (v.12) and is therefore deceived by his report. He is confident that David the Israelite has become "odious" to his own people (see comment on "stench" in 13:4; cf. 2 Sam 10:6; 16:21) and will thus be forced to be a "servant" of Achish the Philistine. But "like Nabal, Achish seriously underestimates David by regarding him as a servant or slave" (Miscall, p. 165; cf. Gunn, *The Fate of King Saul*, p. 107). Another Philistine from Gath had likewise prematurely predicted much the same fate for David's fellow Israelites (17:9). The term *'ôlām* ("forever") means "for life" in this context (as in Exod 21:6; Lev 25:46; Deut 15:17) and is thus a virtual synonym of *kol-hayyāmîm* (lit., "all the days") in 28:2.

**28:1–2** The brief paragraph that concludes this account of David's relationship with Achish is framed by "In those days" (v.1) and "all the days" (v.2; NIV, "for life").

Still laboring under the assumption that David is his faithful vassal, Achish forcefully reminds him ("must" is emphatic) that he and his men are expected to "accompany" (v.1; lit., "go/march out with") the Philistines to fight against Israel. David appears to acquiesce by responding that Achish would then "see" (echoing Achish's "understand," v.1; identical Heb. verb) for himself what David was capable of doing (v.2). In referring to himself as Achish's "servant," David reflects the thoughts of Achish concerning him (27:12)—although David intends nothing more than a polite expression equivalent to the personal pronoun "I" (cf. BDB, p. 714).

Continuing to misjudge David, Achish announces his desire to make him "my bodyguard" (lit., "guard/watcher for my head"). As Miscall observes, this is the same David who had "once cut off the head of another Philistine from Gath and whom the Philistine generals fear will reconcile himself to Saul 'with the heads of the men here' (1 Sam. 29:4)" (p. 167). Achish, however, fails to "see" (v.2) that David and his men constitute a dangerous fifth column inside Philistine territory.

## Notes

---

**8** "The peoples had lived" translates הֵנָּה יֹשְׁבוֹת (*hēnnāh yōšᵉḇôṯ*). Although the feminine plural appears to be unprecedented, feminine singular forms are not unusual with reference to countries or populations of a country (cf. S.R. Driver's comment on ותערך [*wt'rk*, "were drawing up"] in 17:21, *Notes on the Books of Samuel*, p. 143).

**10** Although KD attempts to make sense of the MT's אַל (*'al*, "not") by construing it like μή (*mē*) in an interrogative sense ("You have not gone raiding today, have you?"), it is perhaps better to read אָן (*'ān*, "Where?"; cf., however, note on 10:14), with one or two MSS and the NIV (cf. BDB, p. 39). 4QSam[a] at this point unfortunately breaks off immediately after its reading על (*'l*, "Against" [?]) and therefore cannot be used to support the LXX's ἐπὶ τίνα (*epi tina*, "Against whom?").

---

## B. *The End of the Reign of Saul (28:3–31:13)*

First Samuel concludes decisively with an account of the end of King Saul's reign, contrasting Saul with David for the last time. The four-chapter narrative is arranged chiastically:

A. Saul's final night (28:3–25)
B. David's dismissal by the Philistines (29:1–11)
B′. David's destruction of the Amalekites (30:1–31)
A′. Saul's final day (31:1–13)

The section as a whole is framed by notices of the burials of Samuel (28:3) and Saul (31:13; see also comment on 25:1a).

## 1. *Saul and the medium at Endor*

### 28:3–25

3 Now Samuel was dead, and all Israel had mourned for him and
buried him in his own town of Ramah. Saul had expelled the mediums
and spiritists from the land.
4 The Philistines assembled and came and set up camp at Shunem,
while Saul gathered all the Israelites and set up camp at Gilboa. 5 When
Saul saw the Philistine army, he was afraid; terror filled his heart. 6 He
inquired of the LORD, but the LORD did not answer him by dreams or Urim
or prophets. 7 Saul then said to his attendants, "Find me a woman who is
a medium, so I may go and inquire of her."
"There is one in Endor," they said.
8 So Saul disguised himself, putting on other clothes, and at night he
and two men went to the woman. "Consult a spirit for me," he said,
"and bring up for me the one I name."
9 But the woman said to him, "Surely you know what Saul has done.
He has cut off the mediums and spiritists from the land. Why have you
set a trap for my life to bring about my death?"
10 Saul swore to her by the LORD, "As surely as the LORD lives, you will
not be punished for this."
11 Then the woman asked, "Whom shall I bring up for you?"
"Bring up Samuel," he said.
12 When the woman saw Samuel, she cried out at the top of her voice
and said to Saul, "Why have you deceived me? You are Saul!"
13 The king said to her, "Don't be afraid. What do you see?"
The woman said, "I see a spirit coming up out of the ground."
14 "What does he look like?" he asked.
"An old man wearing a robe is coming up," she said.
Then Saul knew it was Samuel, and he bowed down and prostrated
himself with his face to the ground.
15 Samuel said to Saul, "Why have you disturbed me by bringing me
up?"
"I am in great distress," Saul said. "The Philistines are fighting
against me, and God has turned away from me. He no longer answers
me, either by prophets or by dreams. So I have called on you to tell me
what to do."
16 Samuel said, "Why do you consult me, now that the LORD has turned
away from you and become your enemy? 17 The LORD has done what he
predicted through me. The LORD has torn the kingdom out of your hands
and given it to one of your neighbors—to David. 18 Because you did not
obey the LORD or carry out his fierce wrath against the Amalekites, the
LORD has done this to you today. 19 The LORD will hand over both Israel
and you to the Philistines, and tomorrow you and your sons will be with
me. The LORD will also hand over the army of Israel to the Philistines."
20 Immediately Saul fell full length on the ground, filled with fear
because of Samuel's words. His strength was gone, for he had eaten
nothing all that day and night.
21 When the woman came to Saul and saw that he was greatly shaken,
she said, "Look, your maidservant has obeyed you. I took my life in my

hands and did what you told me to do. 22 Now please listen to your
servant and let me give you some food so you may eat and have the
strength to go on your way."
23 He refused and said, "I will not eat."
But his men joined the woman in urging him, and he listened to them.
He got up from the ground and sat on the couch.
24 The woman had a fattened calf at the house, which she butchered at
once. She took some flour, kneaded it and baked bread without yeast.
25 Then she set it before Saul and his men, and they ate. That same night
they got up and left.

The strange story of the meeting of Saul with Endor's "witch" (so called traditionally; better "necromancer" or "medium" [NIV]), resulting in the announcement that Saul would die at the hands of the Philistines (v.19), is preceded (27:1–28:2) and followed (29:1–11) by accounts of David's friendly relationships with the Philistines through Achish king of Gath. After an introductory verse that sets the stage for what follows (v.3), the chapter continues with a brief description of the problem Saul faces (vv.4–6), narrations of his conversations with the medium (vv.7–14) and with Samuel (vv.15–19), and the story of his final meal (vv.20–25).

**3** Since v.3a reprises 25:1a (see comment there), the pluperfect "had mourned" is appropriate. The reminder that Samuel had died is coupled with the observation that Saul (perhaps in obedience to the Law of Moses, viz., Lev 19:31; 20:6–7; Deut 18:11) had expelled the mediums and spiritists from Israel; both events figure prominently in the rest of the chapter. Although the basic meaning of *'ôḇ* was probably "spirit" (v.8; cf. the rendering "ghost" in Isa 29:4), by metonymy it came to mean "medium" (2 Kings 21:6 [= 2 Chron 33:6]; 23:24; 1 Chron 10:13; Isa 19:3) in the technical sense of one who consulted "the dead on behalf of the living" (Isa 8:19). Harry A. Hoffner makes the intriguing suggestion that *'ôḇ* originally meant "sacrificial pit," which was personified as $^{D}$A-a-bi, the god of the netherworld (TDOT, 1:130–34). The term *yiddeʿōnî* ("spiritist"; lit., "one who has [occult?] knowledge") is always found in association with *'ôḇ(ôṯ)* ("medium[s]").

**4–6** "The wording of this introduction (28:4f.) is notable, for it is strongly reminiscent of two other fateful confrontations between Saul and the Philistines, the first at Michmash/Gilgal (13:5f.), the second at Socoh/Elah (17:1f., 11)" (Gunn, *The Fate of King Saul*, p. 108). In addition, the first two words of the Hebrew consonantal text of v.4—*wyqbṣw plštym*, "the Philistines assembled/gathered"—echo v.1 and remind us yet again of the ever-present Philistine threat throughout Saul's reign.

Skillfully and tersely, v.4 describes the opposing forces: The Philistines "assembled" (*wyqbṣw*) and "set up camp" at Shunem, while Saul "gathered" (*wyqbṣ*) his forces and "set up camp" (same Heb. root tr. "army" in v.5) at Gilboa. Located in the northern tribal territory of Issachar (Josh 19:17–18), Shunem (modern Solem, at the southern foot of Mount Moreh, nine miles east-northeast of Megiddo) is mentioned in the fifteenth-century B.C. roster of Canaanite towns drawn up by Thutmose III, in the fourteenth-century Amarna letters, and in the tenth-century topographical list of Sheshonk. It was the hometown of Abishag, a young virgin who attended King David (1 Kings 1:3), and of a well-to-do woman who assisted the prophet Elisha (2 Kings 4:8, 12). Gilboa, a mountain (modern Jebel Fuquah) ten miles south-southeast of Shunem, is referred to elsewhere in the OT only as the site of Saul's death (31:1, 8 = 1 Chron 10:1, 8; 2 Sam 1:6, 21; 21:12).

When Saul "saw" the Philistines, he became "afraid" (v.5; both verbs translate the Heb. consonants *wyr'* and thus constitute a wordplay)—not the first time that the appearance or approach of the Philistines had struck fear in Israelite hearts (17:11, 24; 23:3). Given the situation, it is understandable that Saul "inquired of" the Lord (v.6; *wayyiš'al šā'ûl,* lit., "and Saul asked," yet another pun on Saul's name). Although 1 Chronicles 10:14 states that Saul "did not inquire" of the Lord, a different verb (*drš*) is used. In addition, "it may be correctly remarked that Saul's attempts at inquiry were of so unworthy a nature that it would be an abuse of language to speak of him as really 'inquiring of Jehovah' " (John W. Haley, *An Examination of the Alleged Discrepancies of the Bible,* reprint ed. [Grand Rapids: Baker, 1958], pp. 359–60; cf. further KD, p. 173). For all Saul's efforts—whether desperate, sincere, or otherwise—to receive an "answer" (v.6; cf. v.15) from the Lord, none came (a disquieting echo of 14:37; see comment there). The normal modes of divine communication were silent: "dreams" (cf. v.15), "Urim" (the sacred lots stored in the priestly ephod; cf. comment on 23:6, 9; cf. also NIV mg. on 14:41 and comment in loc.), "prophets" (cf. v.15).

**7–14** Under such circumstances it is not surprising that Saul, even if out of sheer desperation, would resort to a forbidden source of information—indeed, to a "medium" (v.7), a necromancer of the sort that he himself had earlier expelled from the land (v.3). Fearful of Philistine strength, he wanted to know how to proceed (v.15) and thus was willing to go to any lengths to find out what to do.

The fascinating story of the medium at Endor was long remembered in ancient Israel (cf. its brief summary in 1 Chron 10:13–14) and has been the subject of intense debate since the earliest times: "Was the woman actually able to raise up the righteous dead (i.e., Satan having power over the saints) or was her craft one of mere delusion? Was Samuel resuscitated or was this a demon? Did Samuel appear due to the necromancer's craft or did God intervene and raise Samuel himself?" (Lewis, *Cults of the Dead,* p. 115 n. 39). Individual proponents of one or more of these views, as well as of others of a similar nature, are not far to seek (e.g., Hoffner, TDOT, 1:133–34; Haley, *Alleged Discrepancies,* pp. 194–95; Archer, *Encyclopedia of Bible Difficulties,* pp. 180–81; *Seventh-day Adventists Believe . . .* [Washington: General Conference of Seventh-day Adventists, 1988], p. 355).

Early church fathers, fearful of affirming that the prophet Samuel was a shade in Sheol, that a medium was an appropriate intermediary between the divine and human worlds, and that necromancy is efficacious, "proceeded to undermine the literal text with one of two arguments: either sorcery is just demonic deceit, and what appeared was not really Samuel, but a demon in his guise; or, Samuel was not really in Hades but had been sent by God to announce Saul's fate" (Patricia Cox, "Origen and the Witch of Endor: Toward an Iconoclastic Typology," AThR 61, 2 [1984]: 139). As for Origen, in his typical fashion he was not bothered by what appears to be the plain, literal meaning of the text (that Samuel was really in the netherworld and that the medium really had the power to bring him up). Without denying that literal meaning, by tortuous allegorizing Origen's fertile mind came to the conclusion that the story is also typological of the mediating work of Christ, who voluntarily descended into hell, prophesied to souls in the depths, is a mediatorial figure who breaks the barrier between the netherworld and this world, and has the power to bring back the inhabitants of Hades and usher them through the flaming sword that guards the way to the Tree of Life (ibid., pp. 140–44).

My own sympathies lie with the judgment of Gregory of Nazianzus, who was content to leave the text in its ambiguity: "Samuel was raised, *or so it seems,* by the woman having a familiar spirit" (*Invective Against Julian* 1.54; emphasis mine). An element of mystery suffuses 1 Samuel 28, and it would be presumptuous to claim to have successfully plumbed its depths.

Having received no answer from the Lord (v.6), Saul sent his "attendants" (v.7, lit., "servants"; see comment on 16:15–16) for help from another quarter. "Find" a medium (lit., "Seek"; the verb has been used frequently of Saul's search for David, and now Saul uses it for the last time [cf. Gunn, *The Fate of King Saul,* p. 108]), the king says, thus violating his own earlier intention (v.3). Endor is probably not related to Dor on the Mediterranean coast but is rather to be sought inland from Taanach and Megiddo (Josh 17:11; Ps 83:9–10). It is almost certainly to be identified with modern Khirbet Safsafeh, located four miles northeast of Shunem and thus dangerously close to where the Philistines were encamped (v.4). On the basis of Ugaritic parallels, Othniel Margalith suggests that Endor means "Spring of the Oracular Sanctuary" ("Dor and En-Dor," ZAW 97, 1 [1985]: 111), a fitting name in light of the medium's reference to Samuel's apparition as a "god" (see comment on v.13). That Saul should prefer a "woman" as a medium (v.7) is not surprising (cf. Nah 3:4, where the pagan city of Nineveh is compared to a "mistress of sorceries" enslaving nations "by her witchcraft"; cf. also Akkadian *šā'iltu,* "she who asks questions [of the gods]"; see esp. A. Leo Oppenheim, "The Interpretation of Dreams in the Ancient Near East," *Transactions of the American Philosophical Society* 46, 3 [1956]: 221). The narrator, perhaps deliberately, uses a different Hebrew word for "inquire of " in v.7 than he does in v.6, where the Lord is the object.

Although Saul was obviously convinced that if he "disguised himself" (v.8) he would be able to conceal his identity, he was wrong (v.12)—and in any event the information he received through (or in spite of) the medium's efforts was hardly what he wanted to hear (vv.17–20). Centuries later King Ahab of Israel and King Josiah of Judah would reap similarly negative benefits from disguising themselves in order to gain the anonymity that they hoped would protect them (1 Kings 22:30, 34–35 = 2 Chron 18:29, 33–34; 2 Chron 35:22–24).

Since the netherworld is a place of darkness (Job 10:21–22; 17:13; Pss 88:12; 143:3; for details cf. Youngblood, "Qoheleth's 'Dark House,'" pp. 401–10), "night" (v.8) provided the proper setting for communicating with one of its denizens (cf. Lewis, *Cults of the Dead,* p. 114). In addition, necromancers may well have preferred to do their work at night (cf. Hoffner, TDOT, 1:133), and Saul would have found it easier to conceal his identity under cover of darkness. Taking two men with him, the king went to the woman and asked her to "consult" a "spirit" (*'ôḇ,* v.8; see comment on v.3) on his behalf. The root of the Hebrew word for "consult" is *qsm,* other forms of which are elsewhere translated "diviners," "divination," a practice universally condemned as a pagan abomination (6:2) to be scrupulously avoided by Israel (Deut 18:10, 14; 2 Kings 17:17). Saul's earlier rebellion against the Lord had been so heinous that Samuel had compared it to the "sin of divination" (15:23). Nevertheless, Saul is now commanding a diviner, a necromancer, to "bring up" for him (v.8; cf. vv.11, 13, 15) one who dwells in the "realm of death below" (Deut 32:22).

Not yet recognizing Saul, the woman reminds him that Israel's king has "cut off" (v.9) all the land's mediums and spiritists. Her words to Saul drip with irony: "You know" (*yāḏa'tā*) that "spiritists" (*yidde'ōnî*) are no longer allowed here. Saul will later compound the irony by asking the wraith that he believes to be Samuel "to tell me" (*lehôḏî'ēnî*) what to do (v.15). Meanwhile the woman wonders why her nocturnal visitor would want to put her life in jeopardy by begging her to do what royal decree has forbidden. Although "cut off" may not necessarily have implied death (cf. "expelled" in v.3), the execution of diviners was not without precedent in Israel (Josh 13:22).

In promising the woman that she would not be punished, Saul uses the most solemn of oaths by swearing to her in the Lord's name (v.10; see comment on 14:39). As Miscall observes, "This is the last time that Saul will speak the name of the Lord" (p. 168).

Saul's response to the medium's question (v.11) is very specific: He wants her to bring up "Samuel" (the word is in emphatic position). Although Saul and Samuel had worked at cross-purposes throughout much of their time together, the king now desires a final word from his prophet. How—and whether—the woman engaged the dead we are not told. "Even the Rabbis did not speculate as to her technique in conjuring up Samuel, but simply stated 'she did what she did, and she said what she said, and raised him'" (Lewis, *Cults of the Dead,* p. 115).

Whether she saw Samuel in the flesh or an apparition or simply an internal vision, the medium's reaction when Samuel appeared was one of shock and surprise: She "cried out" (v.12), an emotional outburst often linked with feelings of fear and dismay (cf. 4:13; 5:10). "The incident does not tell us anything about the veracity of claims to consult the dead on the part of mediums, because the indications are that this was an extraordinary event for her, and a frightening one because she was not in control" (Baldwin, p. 159). At the very least the woman must have been clairvoyant, because while in her trancelike state she was able to penetrate Saul's disguise and recognize him (cf. KD, p. 262).

The irony continues: Saul, previously afraid because of the Philistine threat (v.5) and soon to be afraid "because of Samuel's words" (v.20), tells the necromancer not to be afraid (v.13). He then asks her what she sees, thus indicating that he is not privy to the apparition itself. She responds that she sees "a spirit"—literally "[a] god[s]" (*'ᵉlōhîm,* a different Heb. word than that used in v.8). A living prophet could be compared to God in the sense that he was God's mouthpiece and therefore spoke with God's authority (cf. Exod 7:1–2; Deut 18:17–18). Here the situation is quite different, however. It seems that in ancient times the deceased could be referred to as "gods" in that they lived in the realm of the preternatural (cf. Lewis, *Cults of the Dead,* pp. 115–16; Tromp, *Primitive Conceptions of Death,* pp. 176–78). Indeed, the apparition of Samuel is seen coming up out of "the ground"—*hā'āreṣ*—a word often used in the ancient Near East to refer to the netherworld, the realm of the dead (cf. Lewis, *Cults of the Dead,* p. 114; Tromp, *Primitive Conceptions of Death,* pp. 23–46; for Akkadian *erṣetu* in the same sense, see *The Assyrian Dictionary* [Chicago: Oriental Institute, 1958], 4:310–11). Ironically, although Saul had attempted to drive all the mediums and spiritists "from the land" (vv.3, 9), a medium now sees an apparition coming up "out of the ground/netherworld" (v.13; same Heb. phrase in all three verses). This understanding of v.13 lends credence to the interpretation of Endor as "Spring of the Assembly of the Gods," "Spring of the Oracular Sanctuary" (see comment on v.7).

Saul, unable himself to see the "spirit," wants to know what he looks like (v.14). When the medium describes him as "an old man wearing a robe," Saul is convinced that the apparition is Samuel, who in Saul's mind has always worn the robe of the prophet (15:27; cf. already 2:18–19). "Samuel is clothed in a dead man's robe as he foretells the imminent death of Saul and his sons. The robe as shroud enfolds Saul's death as well as Samuel's" (Polzin, *Samuel and the Deuteronomist,* p. 219). That Saul now "knew" it was Samuel (v.14) plays on the medium's earlier statement to him: "Surely you know" (see comment on v.9). In a verbatim reprise of 24:8, in the context of which David had Saul's robe—and destiny—in his grasp (24:4), Saul "bowed down and prostrated himself with his face to the ground" (v.14). The intimate connection between the two passages has not been lost on Polzin: "It would appear that as David bowed down before Saul, the one who by now ought to be dead, so Saul now bows down before Samuel, the one who is really dead" (*Samuel and the Deuteronomist,* p. 271 n.7).

**15–19** Having concluded his conversation with the medium (vv.7–14), Saul now speaks (probably via the medium) to what he believes to be Samuel (or the "spirit" of Samuel). The apparition begins the interchange by complaining that Saul has "disturbed" him (v.15; the same Heb. verb is translated "is astir" in Isa 14:9, where the spirits of the departed in Sheol are pictured as being roused at the arrival of another denizen). Saul's response—that he is in "distress" because of the Philistines—uses the same Hebrew phrase earlier translated "their situation was critical," describing Israel's plight when facing a similar Philistine threat (13:6). Saul's claim to be in "great" distress reflects his desperate emotional state. Though speaking to a "spirit" (*'ᵉlōhîm,* v.13), he knows full well that "God" (*'ᵉlōhîm,* v.15) has abandoned him. Saul has felt it necessary to consult "[a] god[s]" because of the silence of the one true "God" (cf. similarly Lewis, *Cults of the Dead,* p. 116), who "has turned away from" him (vv.15–16)—a fate that the Lord had consigned to Saul years before at the time of David's anointing (see comment on 16:14; cf. also 18:12).

The "not yet" of the Lord's revelation to Samuel (3:7) finds its bitter echo in the "no longer" of the Lord's response to Saul (v.15; thus approximately, Polzin, *Samuel and the Deuteronomist,* p. 220). In v.6 the narrator observes that the Lord did not answer Saul "by dreams or Urim or prophets." In v.15 Saul tells "Samuel" that God does not answer him "either by prophets or by dreams," perhaps omitting "Urim" to hide from Samuel his slaughter of the priests of Nob (22:11–19; cf. similarly Polzin, *Samuel and the Deuteronomist,* p. 270 n. 4) and perhaps listing "prophets" first in his hope that the prophet Samuel will now fill that vacuum. In a sense Samuel obliges: Saul has complained that God no longer speaks "by" (lit., "by the hand of") prophets, and Samuel says that the Lord has done what he predicted "through" (lit., "by the hand of") Samuel himself (v.17). Meanwhile Saul wants Samuel to "tell" him (lit., "cause to know"; for the irony of his request, see the comment on v.9; for the function of pagan diviners in this regard, cf. 6:2) what to do—though he had paid little attention to Samuel's counsel up to this point (cf. 10:8 with 13:8–14).

Whether the "Samuel" of this chapter is the prophet himself or an apparition, his statements to Saul in vv.16–19 are in full agreement with what we know of Samuel in other contexts. As he had punned on Saul's name before (cf. 12:17, "asked"), so he does now (v.16, "consult"; for another example see the comment on "inquired of" in v.6). Although Saul uses the general word "God" in v.15, Samuel characteristically refers to "the LORD" in vv.16–19—seven times in all (the number of completion/perfection [see comment on 2:5]; cf. also independently Miscall, p. 169; Brueggemann, *First and Second Samuel,* p. 195).

The prediction in v.17 refers back to 15:28 and echoes much of the terminology found there. The imagery of tearing a kingdom away from one Israelite ruler and giving it to another is repeated with respect to the division of the monarchy in connection with Solomon's death (1 Kings 11:11–13, 31; 14:8; 2 Kings 17:21).

Samuel had told Saul that the Lord had given the kingdom of Israel to "one of your neighbors—to one better than you" (see 15:28 and comment). The prophet now repeats that language verbatim (v.17) but specifies precisely the referent of the final phrase: "to David" (a fact that Saul himself had already admitted earlier, however; cf. 24:20, where Saul says that the kingdom would be established "in your [David's] hands," reflected here in v.17, which affirms that the kingdom would be torn "out of your [Saul's] hands"). Ironically the prophet Nathan would later tell King David that, because of his sins against Bathsheba and Uriah, the Lord would take David's wives and give them to "one who is close to you" (i.e., Absalom; 2 Sam 12:11; cf. 2 Sam 16:20–22), the Hebrew for which is translated "one of your neighbors" in 15:28 and 28:17.

Verse 18 summarizes the two fateful decisions made by Saul that prompted the Lord to wrench the kingdom from his grasp: (1) He disobeyed the Lord's command through his prophet (see ch. 13), and (2) he refused to fully "carry out" (lit., "do"; cf. similarly Isa 48:14) the divine wrath against the Amalekites (see ch. 15). Saul had not been willing to "do" God's wrath against Amalek; therefore God has "done" (v.18) his will against Saul. Obeying God had never been easy for Saul (cf. 15:19, 22), and his impatient insistence on his own way cost him the kingdom.

Although throughout Samuel's lifetime the Israelites had been delivered "out of the hand/power of the Philistines" (cf. 7:3, 14), the Lord would now "hand over" Israel to them (v.19). On the last night of Saul's life, Samuel euphemistically predicts the slaughter on Mount Gilboa: "Tomorrow you and your sons will be with me" (in the netherworld, the realm of death; cf. David's plaintive words in 2 Sam 12:23). Samuel's last-recorded words, describing the fate of "both Israel and you [Saul]" (v.19), reprise the final words of his *apologia:* "Both you [Israel] and your king [Saul] will be swept away" (12:25). Thus did Samuel, in the words of George Gordon, Lord Byron, rise "from the grave, to freeze once more/ The blood of monarchs with his prophecies" (*Don Juan*, lines 82–83).

Apart from v.20, Samuel does not appear again in the two OT books named after him. His importance and influence, however, continue to leave their mark throughout the rest of the Bible. His family tree appears twice in the Chronicler's genealogies (1 Chron 6:25–28, 33–38). If Moses is rightly celebrated as Israel's lawgiver par excellence, so also Samuel is justly heralded as the prototypical prophet (1 Chron 11:3; 2 Chron 35:18; Ps 99:6; Jer 15:1), standing at the head of the prophetic line (Acts 3:24; 13:20; Heb 11:32). Bearing the titles of both "prophet" and "seer" (1 Chron 9:22; 26:28; cf. 1 Sam 9:9, 19), he shared in recording the events of King David's life (1 Chron 29:29). As priest, judge, prophet, counselor, and anointer of Israel's first two rulers, Samuel takes his place as one of ancient Israel's greatest and most godly leaders (cf. the encomium in honor of Samuel in Ecclus 46:13–20).

**20–25** The chapter races to its conclusion: "Immediately" (v.20) and "at once" (v.24) are both forms of the verb *mhr* ("hasten"). His strength gone (vv.20, 22), King Saul falls on the ground "full length" (v.20), the narrator ironically using a word ("length/height") that qualifies a man for kingship in the eyes of his fellows but not in the eyes of God (16:7; cf. 10:23–24). Fearful earlier because of the Philistine threat (v.5), Saul is now "filled with fear" because of Samuel's words of doom. In addition he lacks physical strength because he has eaten no food "all that day and night," an expression used elsewhere in a ritualistic setting (19:24). Since eating nothing is also often a religious act (a "fast" [BDB, p. 37]; cf. Ezra 10:6), Lewis may be correct in his inference that "Saul's going without food 'all that day and night' in verse 20 is due to the requirements of the ritual" of necromancy (*Cults of the Dead*, p. 114).

The medium, politely referring to herself as Saul's "(maid)servant" (for the idiom see 1:11 and comment; 25:27), reminds him that she risked her own safety when she "took [her] life in [her] hands" (v.21; see comment on 19:5). The verb *šmʿ* ("hear," "obey," "listen to") plays a prominent role in this section: The medium "obeyed" Saul (v.21) when she "did" (lit., "listened to") what he told her to do; she now wants him to "listen to" her (v.22) and eat some food; although he at first refused, he finally "listened to" her (v.23) when his men joined her in urging him. To meet Saul's acknowledged need for food, the woman deftly uses the tactic of demanding reciprocity: "I took" (v.21) and "let me give" (v.22) both translate forms of *śîm* ("put," "set"; cf. "set" in its first occurrence in 9:24), and after the phrase "please listen" in v.22 the MT includes the words "also you" (emphatic pronoun). The medium is thus determined that Saul respond to her on a *quid pro quo* basis. Her offer to give him "some food" (v.22; lit., "a piece of bread"; see 1 Kings 17:11 for the same Heb. expression) belies her intention to serve him a more sumptuous meal (vv.24–25).

In the light of Samuel's fateful words, Saul's response is understandably negative: He refuses to eat (v.23). Polzin (*Samuel and the Deuteronomist*, p. 271 n. 10) calls attention to the contrast in the way food functions at the beginning and at the end of 1 Samuel: When Hannah could not yet have a child, she "would not eat" (1:7); when Saul learns that he and his sons will soon die, he "will not eat." (The account of David's reaction to the news of his son's fatal illness comes to mind as well [2 Sam 12:15–23].) It is only when Saul's men join their voices of encouragement to that of the woman that he gets up from the ground and agrees to have a meal.

The activity described in v.24 is very similar, even in the choice of vocabulary, to the scenes of hospitality depicted in Genesis 18:6–7 and 19:3 (for a concise description of ancient Near Eastern hospitality, cf. Youngblood, *Faith of Our Fathers*, pp. 41–42). "Fattened calf" was a delicacy (cf. Jer 46:21; Mal 4:2 ["calves released from the stall"]) available only to the wealthy (Amos 6:4; cf. also Luke 15:22–30). That the woman had a calf "at/in the house" is not surprising in light of archaeological evidence that domestic stables were probably located inside residences and not separate from them (for details see Philip J. King, *Amos, Hosea, Micah—An Archaeological Commentary* [Philadelphia: Westminster, 1988], pp. 149–51; cf. also the wording of Jephthah's vow in Judg 11:30–31).

Brueggemann (*First and Second Samuel*, p. 196) summarizes: "Read at its best, this meal is a kind of last supper, one final meal for a king (cf. 25:36) who will not be a king much longer. It is as though the woman wants one last regal gesture for Saul when no one else will give it (cf. Mark 14:3–9)." Having eaten, Saul and his men go out into the night—"that same night" (v.25) in which Samuel's words have sealed the fate of a doomed king.

## Notes

---

8 With minor exceptions, the practice of "putting on other clothes" was virtually unknown among the ordinary population in ancient Israel, being restricted to royalty (2 Sam 12:20;

2 Kings 22:14 = 2 Chron 34:22), the priesthood (Lev 6:11; Ezek 42:14; 44:19), and probably the very rich (cf. Neufeld, p. 53 n. 31).

**10** "You will not be punished" translates אִם־יִקָּרֵךְ עָוֹן (*'im-yiqqᵉrēḵ 'āwōn*, lit., "punishment will not befall [קרה (*qrh*)] you." The *dagesh* in *yiqqᵉrēḵ* is *dagesh forte dirimens* and serves to make the shewa more audible (cf. GKC, sec. 20*h*). For other examples in 1 Samuel, see 1:6 (הַרְּעִמָהּ [*harrᵉ'imāh*]); 10:11 (מֵאִתְּמוֹל [*mē'ittᵉmôl*]).

**13** The NIV margin on אֱלֹהִים (*'ᵉlōhîm*, "spirits/gods") recognizes not only the fact that *'ᵉlōhîm* itself is a plural noun but also that its accompanying verb עֹלִים (*'ōlîm*, "coming up") is plural. Since *'ᵉlōhîm* in the sense of "God" normally takes singular verbs (cf. Gen 1:1), the construction in v.13 leads to the conclusion that "god(s)" rather than "God" is meant.

**16** The rare עָר (*'ār*, "enemy," found elsewhere in the OT only in Ps 139:20 ["adversaries"]) may be a dialectal variant of צַר (*ṣar*). Perhaps the narrator chose it as an anticipatory pun on רֵעַ (*rēaʿ*, "neighbor") in v.17.

**17** The MT reads literally: "The LORD has done for him(self) what he predicted," the phrase "for himself" (לוֹ [*lô*]) to be understood as a dative of advantage (cf. the *dativus ethicus* of GKC, sec. 119*s*; Waltke and O'Connor, *Biblical Hebrew Syntax*, p. 208). It is therefore unnecessary to read לך (*lk*, "to you") with a few MSS and versions (for details cf. BHS).

**19** Many modern commentators (e.g., Driver, Mauchline, McCarter) assert that the last sentence of this verse is a variant of its first clause and that therefore one or the other should be omitted as repetitive (for details cf. Lewis, *Cults of the Dead*, p. 110). But in stating that the "army/camp" of Israel would "also" be handed over to the Philistines, the last sentence adds information not present earlier. Baldwin summarizes: "The people and their army are bound up with their king, and they too will suffer defeat as the result of Saul's disobedience" (p. 160). KD takes a slightly different tack but with the same basic result: The "camp" of Israel was plundered (p. 264; apparently in contrast to earlier references in the verse, which refer to the death of Saul, his people, and his sons).

**23** "Urging" renders the root פרץ (*prṣ*), which many commentators assume is a mistaken metathesis of פצר (*pṣr*; cf. Lewis, *Cults of the Dead*, p. 111). But although *pṣr* is indeed attested in the sense of "urge" (cf. 2 Kings 5:16), it is no more common than *prṣ* with the same meaning (2 Sam 13:25, 27; 2 Kings 5:23). In fact, metatheses of consonants in roots with liquids and/or sibilants are relatively frequent in the Semitic languages, including Hebrew (for other examples cf. Waltke and O'Connor, *Biblical Hebrew Syntax*, pp. 94, 424–25). In any event, Hebrew *prṣ* ("urge") is probably cognate to Akkadian *parāṣu* ("penetrate, pierce, bring pressure on"; for the root *pṣr* in the latter sense, cf. Gen 19:9) and perhaps also to Arabic *faraḍa* ("establish, stipulate, resolve, decide, impose"; cf. peculiarly BDB, p. 823, which asserts that Heb. *pṣr* is "perh[aps] related" to the above Akkadian and Arabic roots "by transp[osition]" and then goes on to suggest that *prṣ* here and in 2 Sam 13:25, 27; 2 Kings 5:23 should "prob[ably]" be read as though from *pṣr*; cf. BDB, p. 829)—a tortuous argument at best.

**24** The elision of א (') in ותפהו (*wtphw*), from אפה (*'ph*, "bake"), also occurs elsewhere in first-radical-' verbs in the books of Samuel (cf. J. Stek, "What Happened to the Chariot Wheels of Exod 14:25?" JBL 105, 2 [1986]: 293).

---

## 2. *The dismissal of David*

### 29:1–11

[1]The Philistines gathered all their forces at Aphek, and Israel camped by the spring in Jezreel. [2]As the Philistine rulers marched with their units of hundreds and thousands, David and his men were marching at the rear with Achish. [3]The commanders of the Philistines asked, "What about these Hebrews?"

Achish replied, "Is this not David, who was an officer of Saul king of
Israel? He has already been with me for over a year, and from the day he
left Saul until now, I have found no fault in him."
4 But the Philistine commanders were angry with him and said, "Send
the man back, that he may return to the place you assigned him. He
must not go with us into battle, or he will turn against us during the
fighting. How better could he regain his master's favor than by taking
the heads of our own men? 5 Isn't this the David they sang about in their
dances:

> "'Saul has slain his thousands,
> and David his tens of thousands'?"

6 So Achish called David and said to him, "As surely as the LORD lives,
you have been reliable, and I would be pleased to have you serve with
me in the army. From the day you came to me until now, I have found no
fault in you, but the rulers don't approve of you. 7 Turn back and go in
peace; do nothing to displease the Philistine rulers."
8 "But what have I done?" asked David. "What have you found against
your servant from the day I came to you until now? Why can't I go and
fight against the enemies of my lord the king?"
9 Achish answered, "I know that you have been as pleasing in my eyes
as an angel of God; nevertheless, the Philistine commanders have said,
'He must not go up with us into battle.' 10 Now get up early, along with
your master's servants who have come with you, and leave in the
morning as soon as it is light."
11 So David and his men got up early in the morning to go back to the
land of the Philistines, and the Philistines went up to Jezreel.

Although chapter 29 plays an important literary role in the story of the end of Saul's reign (see comment on 28:3–31:13), it is also reminiscent of the events recorded in 27:1–28:2, as the following commentary attempts to demonstrate. Thus 27:1–28:2 and chapter 29 frame the account of Saul and the medium at Endor (28:3–25), isolating it as a separate literary unit. In addition chapter 29, the narrative of David's third deception of Achish king of Gath (cf. 21:12–15; 27:8–12), introduces the report of David's defeat of the Amalekites (ch. 30), a stark contrast to Saul's earlier fateful failure (ch. 15) and his forthcoming death during a final battle against his nemesis, the Philistines (ch. 31).

Brief as it is, the chapter itself is nonetheless exquisitely crafted. It begins and ends at "Jezreel" (vv.1, 11), hard by the site of Saul's suicide. Its repeated use of other key words and phrases, which will be noted as they appear, is impressive. Finally, Achish's triple vindication of David's honor and dependability is spaced evenly throughout (vv.3, 6, 9).

**1–11** The chapter begins by recalling the muster of Philistine and Israelite armies described in 28:4 (cf. 28:1). In reconciling the differences between the place names in v.1 and in 28:4, the summary of Aharoni (*Land of the Bible*, pp. 290–91) is helpful: "The Philistine rulers assembled their forces at Aphek at the sources of the Yarkon (1 Sam. 29:1) preparatory to marching on Jezreel (vs. 11). Saul's troops 'were encamped by the fountain which is in Jezreel' (vs. 1); on the eve of the battle they ranged themselves on Mount Gilboa. The Philistines made camp across from them at Shunem (1 Sam. 28.4)."

Verse 1, like its counterpart (28:4), describes the opposing forces in a terse and balanced way: The Philistines gathered their "forces" (lit., "camps") at Aphek, and Israel "camped" near Jezreel. Aphek, modern Ras el-Ain at the point where the

Philistine plain meets the plain of Sharon, is mentioned in the books of Samuel only here and in 4:1. It was thus the staging area for Philistine troop deployment in the first and last battles between Israel and Philistia recorded in 1 Samuel. Jezreel (not to be confused with the southern site of the same name; see 25:43 and comment), located in the tribal territory of Issachar (Josh 19:17–18), is modern Zerin, on a spur of Mount Gilboa three miles south of Shunem. News about the death of Saul and Jonathan would soon be relayed from Jezreel (2 Sam 4:4), which was to play a key (if ambiguous) role in the unfolding history of the northern kingdom (cf. 1 Kings 21:1; Hos 1:4–5; 2:22–23).

The personal involvement of the Philistine "rulers" (vv.2, 6–7; see comment and Notes on 5:8) demonstrates their perception that the present battle was crucial. Most commentators distinguish between "rulers" and "commanders" (vv.3–4, 9) in this chapter (cf. Baldwin, Gordon, Klein, McCarter, Smith), although a few hesitate to commit themselves on the matter (cf. Ackroyd, Hertzberg). Others, however (e.g., KD, Mauchline), equate the two terms—and, indeed, comparing vv.3–4 with v.6 provides little justification for making the distinction.

The resolute Philistines march out in traditional military units of "hundreds" and "thousands" (cf. 2 Sam 18:4), numbers that in such cases should probably be understood figuratively rather than literally (see comments on 4:2; 11:8). David and his men, mercenaries in the Philistine army (cf. 28:1), fall in behind at the behest of Achish king of Gath (see comment on 21:10).

The Philistine commanders, understandably wary of David (cf. 18:30), question the wisdom of including "Hebrews" (v.3) in the army ("Hebrew" was commonly used by non-Israelites as a synonym for "Israelite"; cf. 4:5–10; 13:19; 14:11; see also comments on 13:3; 14:21–22). But Achish, who had earlier made David his "bodyguard for life" (28:2), rises to his defense: (1) Although David had at one time been an "officer" of Saul (lit., "servant"; for the nuance "officer, official," cf. 1 Kings 11:26; 2 Kings 25:8; Isa 36:9), he "left" Saul (lit., "fell away from"; cf. Jer 39:9, where "those who had gone over to" [lit., "the falling ones who had fallen to"] expresses the idea of transfer of allegiance). (2) Having fled from Saul, David has now been with Achish for "over a year" (lit., "these days or these years," an idiom meaning something like "a year or two"; cf. 27:7, which notes that David lived in Philistine-controlled territory "a year and four months") and has therefore had sufficient time to demonstrate his loyalty. (3) During this entire period ("until now," vv.3, 6, 8) Achish has found "no fault" in David (v.3, a sentiment repeated by Achish in v.6 and shared [cynically?] by David himself in v.8). The words "no fault" (lit., "nothing," "not . . . anything"), reflecting David's presumed innocence of wrongdoing, echo not only his earlier protestations in the story of Nabal and Abigail (25:7, 21) but also Samuel's self-justification in his *apologia* (12:5).

Unconvinced, the Philistine commanders demand that Achish "send" David "back" (v.4), a verb (*šwb*) repeated in various forms and to the same end throughout the rest of the chapter (vv.4 ["return"], 7 ["turn back"], 11 ["go back"]). They insist that he return to "the place (Achish) assigned him"—that is, Ziklag (see 27:6 and comment), to which David indeed eventually goes (vv.11; 30:1). They do not want David to go with them "into battle" (vv.4, 9) for fear that he will turn against them "during the fighting" (same Heb. for both expressions). They are concerned that he might "turn against" them (lit., "become an adversary against"; the word for "adversary" [*śāṭān*] was later specialized to refer to "the Adversary [par excellence]"—namely, "Satan" [cf. Job 1–2; 1 Chron 21:1]; for the idiom used here, cf.

Num 22:22 ["oppose"]; 2 Sam 19:22). As a potential fifth column in the Philistine ranks, David might kill some of them and take their "heads" as trophies of war (cf., ironically, 31:9; see also comment on 28:2). In so doing he would regain "his master's" (i.e., Saul's; cf. v.3) favor.

The Philistine commanders conclude their critique by reminding Achish of the victory refrain (v.5)—by now well known (see 18:7–8 and comment; 21:11)—sung by the women of Israel in honor of (Saul and) David. As the commanders do so, they sarcastically hurl Achish's own words back at him: "Isn't this the David" (identical Heb. to "Is not this David," v.3; cf. 21:11). In addition, the Philistines "take the song as a celebration of solidarity between David and Saul. Saul and David are linked in the Philistine perception in common military exploits. Obviously such a man cannot fight with the Philistines against Saul" (Brueggemann, *First and Second Samuel*, p. 198).

Achish, not willing to buck his peers on this point, tells David about the commanders' concern but without sharing any details with him (vv.6–7, 9). To assure David of the truth of what he is about to say, he takes a solemn oath in the name of David's God (v.6; see comment on 14:39). As far as Achish is aware (but cf. 27:8–11), David has been "reliable" (lit., "upright," as in Job 1:1). Thus, says Achish, "I would be pleased" (lit., "it would be pleasing in my eyes," as in v.9) to have you (David) "serve" (lit., "go forth and come back"; see comment on 18:16) in the army. The contrast between the attitude of Achish toward David and that of the other Philistine rulers toward him could not be more stark: "The rulers don't approve of" him (v.6; lit., he is "not pleasing in the eyes of the rulers")—indeed, David is in danger of doing something that will "displease" them (v.7; lit., be "displeasing in the eyes of" them). "Pleasing" (*ṭôḇ*, "good") and "displeasing" (*rā'*, "evil") set up the classic confrontation that began in the Garden of Eden (Gen 2:9, 17: 3:4, 22).

The narrator describes the perceptions of Achish and his fellow Philistine rulers in terms of black and white: In the mind of Achish, David is good ("I have found no fault [*rā'āh*, a different word than that used in v.3] in you"), while the other commanders consider him to be evil. Seeing no hope of reconciling the two opposing viewpoints, Achish advises David to "go in peace" (v.7), a cordial expression of farewell (2 Sam 15:9; cf. 2 Sam 15:27). Furthermore, Achish is doubtless concerned about "the lucrative booty he is receiving from David [cf. 27:9]. He readily accepts the generals' demand, because he does not want to jeopardize the relationship he has with David" (Miscall, p. 174).

David's response (v.8) echoes in part some of Achish's own words (cf. v.6). In addition, David wants to know "what [he has] done" to deserve such suspicion, again playing the role of the innocent victim, as he earlier had before his brother Eliab (17:29), his friend Jonathan (20:1), and his master Saul (26:18). He wants to fight (or pretends that he does) against the enemies of his "lord the king" (v.8)—Achish, at least in this context. But, as Miscall asks, is David's true lord and king Achish or Saul or both or neither? "Is David being ironic?" (p. 175).

For the third time (v.9; cf. vv.3, 6) Achish vindicates David's honor and dependability. Brueggemann (*First and Second Samuel*, p. 200) sees in this a possible parallel to Pilate's threefold declaration concerning Jesus: "I find no basis for a charge against him" (John 18:38; 19:4, 6; cf. Luke 23:22). In Achish's eyes David is like "an angel of God," an epithet used elsewhere (cf. 2 Sam 14:17, 20; 19:27; Zech 12:8) in "metaphorical reference to the king in court-etiquette fashion" (Talmon, p. 30 n. 67). The name of God is used only twice in this chapter (vv.6, 9), both times by Achish rather than David, perhaps implying that while David was in Philistine territory, he did not consult the Lord (for a similar phenomenon see the comment on 27:1–28:2).

"Now" (v.10) echoes the beginning of v.7 (the MT also starts with "now"). The opening word of both verses thus underscores the urgency of Achish's request to David to return to Ziklag before he needlessly angers the Philistine rulers even further. David is to take with him his "master's" (Saul's; see comment on "my lord the king" in v.8) servants and "get up early/leave in the morning" (same Heb. expression). To go "as soon as it is light" would be to take advantage of the cool morning hours (cf. similarly Gen 44:3), especially if the journey was long (Ziklag was fifty miles from Aphek). That David and his men go back to the "land of the Philistines" (v.11) reflects the narrator's judgment that Aphek, strictly speaking, is not in Philistine territory.

Thus David, doubtless relieved, avoids fighting against his own countrymen—and does so with Philistine blessing. Brueggemann observes a further irony: "The very same Philistines who will finally dispose of Saul (ch. 31) are the ones who unwittingly rescue David" (*First and Second Samuel,* p. 199).

## Notes

**1** עַל (*'al*) is the most common way of expressing "by" in association with bodies of water (cf. Ps 1:3). As here, however, in a few cases ־בְּ (*b-*) is used (cf. Ezek 10:15, 20).

**2** Usually "march" (in a military sense) is rendered in Hebrew by יָצָא (*yāṣā'*, "go [out]"; cf. 2 Sam 18:6 and esp. 18:4). Here, however, the narrator twice chose עֹבְרִים (*'ōḇᵉrîm,* "passing [over/by/through]"; NIV, "marched," "were marching"), perhaps as an anticipatory pun on עִבְרִים (*'iḇrîm,* "Hebrews") in v.3.

**4** "Go into battle" in this verse (as also in 26:10) is literally "go down into battle" (cf. 30:24). But when Achish later repeats the Philistine commanders' statement, he quotes them as saying "go up . . . into battle" (v.9; cf. v.11; 7:7). S.R. Driver's resolution of the apparent discrepancy is probably correct: "The narrator must here allow the Philistines to speak from the *Israelite* point of view (cf. v.6, where Achish is represented as swearing by *Yahweh*), who would 'go down' from the mountainous country of Judah to fight against the Philistines in their plains. . . . Here [in v.9] the Philistines speak from the point of view which would be natural to them, when they were invading the high central ground of Canaan" (*Notes on the Books of Samuel,* pp. 219–20).

**10** After "come with you" the LXX inserts several clauses, which the NRSV takes to be original and therefore includes in its text, translating as follows: "and go to the place that I appointed for you. As for the evil report, do not take it to heart, for you have done well before me" (cf. similarly JB, NJB, NAB, NEB, REB; cf. Ackroyd, Driver, Hertzberg, Klein, Mauchline, McCarter, Smith). But together with v.9, v.10 just as it stands adequately answers David's questions (v.8). In addition, apart from "do not take it to heart," the insertion adds no new information and looks more like a characteristic LXX expansion than a mistaken MT omission.

### 3. *The defeat of the Amalekites*

#### 30:1–31

**1 David and his men reached Ziklag on the third day. Now the**
**Amalekites had raided the Negev and Ziklag. They had attacked Ziklag**
**and burned it, 2 and had taken captive the women and all who were in it,**

both young and old. They killed none of them, but carried them off as
they went on their way.
3When David and his men came to Ziklag, they found it destroyed by
fire and their wives and sons and daughters taken captive. 4So David
and his men wept aloud until they had no strength left to weep. 5David's
two wives had been captured—Ahinoam of Jezreel and Abigail, the
widow of Nabal of Carmel. 6David was greatly distressed because the
men were talking of stoning him; each one was bitter in spirit because
of his sons and daughters. But David found strength in the LORD his
God.
7Then David said to Abiathar the priest, the son of Ahimelech, "Bring
me the ephod." Abiathar brought it to him, 8and David inquired of the
LORD, "Shall I pursue this raiding party? Will I overtake them?"
"Pursue them," he answered. "You will certainly overtake them and
succeed in the rescue."
9David and the six hundred men with him came to the Besor Ravine,
where some stayed behind, 10for two hundred men were too exhausted
to cross the ravine. But David and four hundred men continued the
pursuit.
11They found an Egyptian in a field and brought him to David. They
gave him water to drink and food to eat— 12part of a cake of pressed
figs and two cakes of raisins. He ate and was revived, for he had not
eaten any food or drunk any water for three days and three nights.
13David asked him, "To whom do you belong, and where do you come
from?"
He said, "I am an Egyptian, the slave of an Amalekite. My master
abandoned me when I became ill three days ago. 14We raided the Negev
of the Kerethites and the territory belonging to Judah and the Negev of
Caleb. And we burned Ziklag."
15David asked him, "Can you lead me down to this raiding party?"
He answered, "Swear to me before God that you will not kill me or
hand me over to my master, and I will take you down to them."
16He led David down, and there they were, scattered over the
countryside, eating, drinking and reveling because of the great amount
of plunder they had taken from the land of the Philistines and from
Judah. 17David fought them from dusk until the evening of the next day,
and none of them got away, except four hundred young men who rode
off on camels and fled. 18David recovered everything the Amalekites had
taken, including his two wives. 19Nothing was missing: young or old,
boy or girl, plunder or anything else they had taken. David brought
everything back. 20He took all the flocks and herds, and his men drove
them ahead of the other livestock, saying, "This is David's plunder."
21Then David came to the two hundred men who had been too
exhausted to follow him and who were left behind at the Besor Ravine.
They came out to meet David and the people with him. As David and his
men approached, he greeted them. 22But all the evil men and troublemakers among David's followers said, "Because they did not go out
with us, we will not share with them the plunder we recovered. However,
each man may take his wife and children and go."
23David replied, "No, my brothers, you must not do that with what the
LORD has given us. He has protected us and handed over to us the forces
that came against us. 24Who will listen to what you say? The share of the
man who stayed with the supplies is to be the same as that of him who
went down to the battle. All will share alike." 25David made this a statute
and ordinance for Israel from that day to this.
26When David arrived in Ziklag, he sent some of the plunder to the
elders of Judah, who were his friends, saying, "Here is a present for you
from the plunder of the LORD's enemies."

**[27]He sent it to those who were in Bethel, Ramoth Negev and Jattir;**
**[28]to those in Aroer, Siphmoth, Eshtemoa [29]and Racal; to those in the**
**towns of the Jerahmeelites and the Kenites; [30]to those in Hormah, Bor**
**Ashan, Athach [31]and Hebron; and to those in all the other places where**
**David and his men had roamed.**

Even when all seems lost, David continues to prosper. Although he arrives in Ziklag and finds it destroyed, through God's help he tracks the Amalekites down and recovers all the people and plunder they had taken. He then ingratiates himself to his troops and his neighbors by sharing his good fortune with them. Chapter 30 is a case study of the qualities that make for strong and compassionate leadership: persistence, empathy, faith in God, commitment to a cause, integrity, decisiveness, generosity. Saul, disobeying God's prophet, defeated the Amalekites but lost his kingdom (ch. 15); David, seeking God's will, defeats the Amalekites and embarks on his reign (ch. 30).

The chapter displays a chiastic arrangement:

A. David reaches destroyed Ziklag and finds it plundered (30:1–3).
  B. David and his men are promised the Lord's help (30:4–8).
    C. David defeats the Amalekites (30:9–20).
  B′. David shares the Lord's plunder with his men (30:21–25).
A′. David returns to Ziklag and distributes the remaining plunder (30:26–31).

**1–3** The section is framed by the notice that "David and his men reached/came to" (same Heb. verb in both cases) Ziklag (vv.1, 3). Having been dismissed by Achish, David and his men begin the long trek from Aphek (29:1) to Ziklag (see comment on 27:6) in "the land of the Philistines" (29:11) and arrive there on the "third day" (v.1). The narrator observes that in the meantime the Amalekites (Israel's agelong enemies, who inhabited large tracts of land southwest of the Dead Sea) had "raided the Negev and Ziklag," a summary statement that is given more detailed definition in v.14. "Raided" here and in v.14 means literally "stripped," the verb used in 31:9 of the Philistines' ignominious treatment of the vanquished Saul. The Amalekites took advantage of David's absence from Ziklag, raiding the town in retaliation for when David had earlier "raided" them (27:8). They "attacked" Ziklag (v.1), and so—again *quid pro quo*—David later "fought" them (v.17; same Heb. verb). Their burning of Ziklag (vv.1, 3, 14) would be tragically echoed in the Philistines' burning of the bodies of Saul and his sons (31:12).

The Amalekites had also "taken captive" (vv.2–3) everyone who lived in the town, from the youngest to the oldest (vv.2, 19). The captured "women" receive pride of place in v.2, probably because David's two wives were included among them (v.5). Killing no one, the Amalekites "carried them off" (lit., "drove them," as in v.20, where the same Heb. verb is used in reference to livestock; cf. also 23:5). The allusion to "sons and daughters" in v.3 receives added emphasis in v.6, where they are the objects of special concern on the part of David's men (cf. v.19, where the same Heb. phrase is translated "boy or girl").

**4–8** Weeping aloud is an understandable reaction when the situation seems hopeless (see comment on 11:4). But the abject sorrow of David and his men (v.4) would soon be replaced by confident expectation as a result of the Lord's assurance of victory (v.8). David mourns the apparent loss of his two wives (v.5), Ahinoam of Jezreel and

Abigail of Carmel (see comment on 15:12; 25:3, 43), whom he had moved to Ziklag after Achish had assigned the town to him (cf. 27:3–6).

Added to David's grief is the fact that he is "greatly distressed" (v.6) because his men blame him for their plight. Pointing to an earlier parallel where Saul is pictured as being "in great distress" (see 28:15 and comment), Brueggemann comments: "Both David and Saul are portrayed as persons in deep crises of leadership, and both are deeply at risk. What interests us is the difference of response. . . . Saul seeks refuge in a medium," while David inquires of the Lord (*First and Second Samuel,* p. 201). In the meantime, however, David's men consider "stoning him"—a much more serious threat than the later frivolous action of Shimei (even though the same Heb. verb is used; cf. 2 Sam 16:6, 13). Convinced that they will never see their children again, the men are "bitter in spirit" (v.6; cf. 1:10, "in bitterness of soul"; 2 Kings 4:27, "in bitter distress"). While in 22:2 people who were "discontented" (same Heb. in all these cases) flocked to David's leadership, here his men are so distraught that they cannot think clearly and are prepared to do him harm.

David's spiritual discernment now comes to the fore: He "found strength" (v.6) in the right Person (cf. similarly Ezra 7:28, "took courage"; Dan 10:19). Concerning the last sentence in v.6, Brueggemann observes that it "anticipates Paul's wondrous two-sided statement of Philippians 2:12–13: 'Work out your own salvation . . . for God is at work.' David counts heavily on God's being at work. At the same moment David is boldly at work on the rescue mission" (*First and Second Samuel,* p. 202). Although the Hebrew phrase translated "had no strength" in v.4 is not from the same root, the contrast is nonetheless striking. By using the expression "the LORD his God," the narrator emphasizes David's intimate relationship with the One who from the beginning has always been "with him" (see 16:18 and comment).

As at Keilah, so also at Ziklag, David says to Abiathar the priest (v.7), "Bring me the ephod" (see comment on 23:6, 9; see also 22:20 and comment), which David then uses to inquire of the Lord (v.8; see 23:2, 4 and comment; see also comments on 14:36, 41–42). When the rejected Saul inquired of the Lord, no answer came (28:6); when the "man after [God's] own heart" (13:14) does the same, the Lord answers specifically and with precision (as here; cf. also 23:2, 4). In this case David asks whether he should "pursue" the Amalekite raiders and, if so, whether he would be able to "overtake" them. The Lord's response is immediate, clear, and full of encouragement: David is commanded to "pursue," he will "certainly overtake" (infinite absolute plus finite verb), and in addition—the divine bonus—he will "succeed in the rescue" (again, infinitive absolute plus finite verb). True to his promise, the Lord makes sure that David has "recovered" everything, including the captives and plunder (vv.18, 22; "recovered" is from the same Heb. verb as "rescue" in v.8).

**9–20** The staging area for the campaign against the Amalekites is the Besor Ravine, mentioned only in this chapter. Today called the Wadi Ghazzeh, it empties into the Mediterranean Sea about four miles south of Gaza. (Since the Wadi Ghazzeh in this area is not very deep, to call it a "ravine" is somewhat misleading; cf. Rasmussen, p. 212 n. 18.) Of David's "six hundred men" (v.9; for the significance of the number, see comment on 13:15; cf. 27:2), two hundred are too "exhausted" (vv.10, 21) to continue the rigorous march. David and the four hundred others, however, press on (for an identical deployment of David's men on an earlier occasion—though for a different reason—see 25:13 and comment).

Finding a starving Egyptian in a field (v.11), they give him water and food, including cakes of raisins and of pressed figs (v.12), items especially suitable for men on the march (see 25:18 and comment). His enforced three-day fast has apparently weakened him, because after eating he is "revived" (v.12; lit., "his spirit/strength returned to him," as with Samson in a similar situation: "his strength returned" [Judg 15:19; "revived" there renders a different Heb. verb]).

David's questions to the Egyptian (v.13) are reminiscent of Nabal's to David's servants in 25:10–11 (cf. Jonah 1:8)—although the selfish stinginess of Nabal, who had no intention of sharing his food and water with strangers, is no match for the generosity of David. While Nabal gave nothing to the "servants" of a fellow Israelite (for possible referents of "servants," see comment on 25:10), David supplies the needs of a hated Amalekite's Egyptian "slave" (v.13; same Heb. word in both passages), whose cruel master had left him for dead simply because he had become ill.

The emphatic "we" at the beginning of v.14 suggests that the slave participated personally in the Amalekites' raids. The summary statement in v.1—"the Negev and Ziklag"—is now given definition: Among the pillaged regions were the Negev of the Kerethites ("probably S Philistine Plain area and W Negev region E and NE of Gaza" [Rasmussen, p. 246 and map on p. 114]), an undefined portion of Judahite territory (the MT does not justify the NIV's use of "the" before the "territory" in v.14), and the Negev of Caleb (named after the clan that occupied it and of which Nabal was a member [25:3], it was doubtless located in the "Hill Country of Judah, S of Hebron but NE of Beersheba" [ibid., p. 246]; for other subdistricts of the Negev, see the comment on 27:10). Last of all, says the Egyptian, "Ziklag we burned" (the word order in the MT—which, when combined with Ziklag's placement at the end of the list, makes the town doubly emphatic as the focus of the Amalekite attack).

The Egyptian agrees to show David where the Amalekite raiding party has gone if David will swear not to kill him or "hand [him] over to" his master (lit., "deliver [him] up to the hands of"; cf. 23:11–12 ["surrender . . . to"], 20; see comment on "imprisoned himself" in 23:7). Miscall observes, "There is poignancy to his speech, since it intones both Saul's earlier request for an oath from David not to kill him (1 Sam. 24:22 [EV v.21]) and Saul's death on Mt. Gilboa" (p. 180).

Although in the earlier episode David "gave his oath" (24:22), the present text is silent concerning whether he does the same in this case. In any event, the Egyptian leads David down to the Amalekite bivouac (v.16). The raiders are not only "eating" and "drinking"—in contrast to the former plight of the Egyptian slave (vv.11–12), who had considered himself one of their number (vv.13–14)—but also "reveling" (the Heb. verb usually means "go on pilgrimage," "celebrate a [religious] festival"; cf. "festive" in Ps 42:4). After all, they had recently "taken" great quantities of plunder (cf. vv.18–20; see also comment on 27:9). Brueggemann characterizes the scene: "The Amalekites are presented . . . with an extra rhetorical flourish designed to make them as unattractive as possible. They are 'eating and drinking and dancing,' surely the marks of a degenerate people who practice excessive self-indulgence (cf. Ex. 32:6)" (*First and Second Samuel*, pp. 202–3).

David and his men are more than a match for the Amalekites, who must have been much more numerous than the Israelites. Even after a full night and day of fighting (v.17), during which large numbers of Amalekites must have fallen (cf. the hyperbolic "none of them got away"), "four hundred"—the same figure used to describe David's original army (v.10)—are still able to get away. Like an earlier horde of Midianite raiders (Judg 6:3–5), the Amalekites rode on camels (the mount of choice of many Eastern peoples; cf. Isa 21:7), this time in order to make good their escape.

Emphasizing the completeness of the rout and the scope of David's victory, the narrator reports that everything the Amalekites had "taken" (vv.16, 18–19) David "took" back (v.20), including (most important of all) "his two wives" (v.18). Indeed, "nothing was missing" (v.19). As in 23:5 (during the rescue of Keilah, the account of which has much in common with that of the rescue of Ziklag), so also here the Hebrew verbs are in the singular ("fought," v.17; "recovered," v.18; "brought . . . back," v.19; "took," v.20), rightly attributing success to David as the leader of his men (see comment on 23:5). The latter in fact refer to the retrieved spoil as "David's plunder" (v.20). Gunn, noting that the rest of chapter 30 "is devoted to one theme—the spoil taken from the Amalekites" (*The Fate of King Saul*, p. 110), makes the further observation that "Samuel's words of rejection still ring in our ears (15:19) . . .: 'Why did you not obey the voice of Yahweh?'" (ibid., pp. 110–11). Brueggemann summarizes: "The Amalekites are resented for taking spoil; Saul is rejected for taking spoil; David is saluted and championed for doing the same" (*First and Second Samuel*, p. 203).

**21–25** David, of course, understands that the plunder is ultimately not his but the Lord's (vv.23, 26), and he must therefore exercise the utmost care in its disposition. Returning to the Besor Ravine, he and his troops are met by the two hundred men who had remained behind (v.21; cf. vv.9–10). As was his custom on such occasions (17:22; 25:5–6), David "greeted" them (lit., "asked about" their "well-being/welfare"; see comment on 10:4).

As Saul had his "troublemakers" (10:27; see comment on 25:17) at the beginning of his reign, so also David has his (v.22). They declare their unwillingness to share the plunder with men who had not participated in the campaign against the Amalekites, and even their concession to allow the two hundred to receive their families back is marred by the verb they use ("take" is literally "drive," "lead," ordinarily used to express forced movement, as with livestock [v.20]; see comment on v.2).

David, generously calling the troublemakers "my brothers" (v.23; cf. Jesus' polite use of "friend" in Matt 20:13), reminds them that the booty is not, as they think, "the plunder we recovered" (v.22) but rather "what the LORD has given us" (v.23). God has enabled them to defeat the "forces" (the same Heb. word is translated "raiding party" in vv.8, 15) that came against them. However exhausted the men who remained behind might have been, they deserve a reward for staying with and guarding the "supplies" (v.24; see comment on "baggage" in 10:22). They are thus not to be considered inferior and are to share equally in the plunder (cf. similarly 25:13) with those who "went down to the battle" (see Notes on 29:4). Like his ancestor Abraham (Gen 14:24), the magnanimous David—who knows full well that he has been divinely deputized to distribute the Lord's plunder as he wishes (cf. similarly Matt 20:14–15)—makes sure that loyal service is suitably compensated (cf. further 1 Cor 3:8). "The basis of distribution is not risk or victory or machismo but simply membership in the community" (Brueggemann, *First and Second Samuel*, p. 205).

The last word of the sentence "All will share alike" (v.24c) reappears as a grisly echo in 31:6, which reports that Saul and all his comrades died "together" (same Heb. word). David (v.25) makes the principle of equal sharing of plunder a "statute and ordinance" (a technical term for divinely established laws, as in Exod 15:25, "a decree and a law"; Josh 24:25, "decrees and laws"; cf. also Ps 81:4, "decree . . . ordinance") for Israel in perpetuity ("from that day to this"; cf. the action of Joseph, with similar long-term effects, in Gen 47:26).

**26–31** The final section of chapter 30 begins as does the first: "David arrived in/reached Ziklag" (vv.1, 26; same Heb. verb in both verses). The fact that David sends some of the plunder to Judah (v.26) leads Brueggemann to characterize him as a "giver, not a taker [see comment on 8:11, 13–17]. It is his propensity to give that makes his new kingdom possible" (*First and Second Samuel*, p. 206). Representing Judah, the elders (cf. 2 Sam 19:11) receive a "present" (lit., "blessing") from David, who thus reciprocates the earlier generosity of Abigail, who gave a "gift" (lit., "blessing") to David and his men (see 25:27 and comment). The Judahite elders, who are David's "friends" (v.26), stand in contrast to the Amalekite raiders, who are "the LORD's"—and therefore David's—"enemies."

Concluding the chapter, vv.27–31 list the specific places where David's "present" was distributed and give additional information concerning the areas raided by the Amalekites. Bethel (v.27, not the famous site in Benjamin at modern Beitin twelve miles north of Jerusalem, for which see 7:16; 10:3; 13:2), whose location is unknown, is probably the Judahite Kesil (Josh 15:30, LXX[B] *Baithēl*), alternately called Bethul (Josh 19:4) or Bethuel (1 Chron 4:30), "House of God," doubtless because a temple had been built there. Ramoth Negev ("Heights of the Negev"), probably the same as Ramah in the Negev (Josh 19:8), is mentioned in one of the Arad ostraca and is perhaps to be located at modern Khirbet Ghazzeh (cf. Yohanan Aharoni, "Arad: Its Inscriptions and Temple," BA 31, 1 [1968]: 17–18) twenty miles south-southeast of Hebron. Jattir, a town for the Levites (Josh 21:14; 1 Chron 6:57) in the hill country of Judah (Josh 15:48), is modern Khirbet Attir thirteen miles south-southwest of Hebron.

Aroer (not the same as the Reubenite Aroer, Josh 13:16; 1 Chron 5:8) is modern Khirbet Ararah (probably = *'aḏ'āḏāh* in Josh 15:22 [cf. LXX[B] *Arouēl*] with Heb. *d* mistakenly written for *r*; cf. Aharoni, *Land of the Bible*, p. 117), fifteen miles south of Jattir. The location of Siphmoth, mentioned only here, is unknown. Eshtemoa/Eshtemoh, modern es-Semu nine miles south-southwest of Hebron, was (like Jattir) a town for the Levites in the hill country of Judah (Josh 15:50; 21:14; 1 Chron 6:57).

The word "Racal" (v.29), otherwise unknown, may be a scribal error for "Carmel" (ZPEB, 5:17; cf. LXX[B] *Karmēlō*), the modern Khirbet el-Kirmil four miles northeast of Eshtemoa. Various "towns of the Jerahmeelites and the Kenites" (v.29; see comment on 27:10) are also objects of David's generosity.

Although the location of Hormah (v.30) is uncertain (for details cf. Aharoni, *Land of the Bible*, pp. 215–16), it is probably modern Khirbet el-Meshash four miles north of Aroer and is mentioned in connection with Kesil/Bethul/Bethuel in Joshua 15:30; 19:4; and 1 Chronicles 4:30 (see comment on Bethel in v.27). Hormah had been the site of an early Amalekite victory over Israel (Num 14:45), who later attacked and destroyed it (Num 21:3; Josh 12:14; Judg 1:17). Bor Ashan, mentioned only here, is probably the same as Ashan, like Jattir and Eshtemoa, a Judahite town (Josh 15:42; 19:7) for the Levites (1 Chron 6:59), perhaps to be identified with modern Tell Beit Mirsim about twelve miles southwest of Hebron (cf. Aharoni, *Land of the Bible*, pp. 261–62, 354). The word "Athach," otherwise unknown, may be a scribal error for "Ether" (Josh 19:7; cf. already KD; cf. Josh 15:42, where LXX[B] reads *Ithak*), probably modern Khirbet el-Ater fifteen miles northwest of Hebron.

Although v.31 concludes with a general statement concerning "other places where David and his men had roamed" (see 23:13 and comment), the list of specific sites that began in v.27 ends here with Hebron, the most important city where plunder was sent (cf. also Josh 10:3; for the significance of the similar position of Ziklag in an earlier list, see v.14 and comment). While this is the only mention of Hebron in 1 Samuel, it plays a key role in 2 Samuel, where it appears about twenty-five times (most of the occurrences are clustered in chs. 2–5). Located in the hill country of Judah (Josh 15:54), twenty-seven miles northeast of Ziklag, Hebron was the seat of David's rule for seven years and six months (2 Sam 5:5) before he made Jerusalem, eighteen miles to the north-northeast, his political and religious capital.

David thus ingratiates himself to the elders and other inhabitants of Judah by sharing with them the plunder recovered from the Amalekites. And even before David the king-elect has finished currying favor with Israelites living in the south, King Saul has died while fighting the Philistines in the north, a story vividly and tersely related in the last chapter of 1 Samuel.

## Notes

---

**2** The MT does not read "and all," but the NIV is justified in filling the ellipsis because the context demands some such phrase (cf. vv.3, 6, 19). Indeed, the LXX *ad sensum* reads *καὶ πάντα* (*kai panta*), and the NASB inserts "and all" in italics.

**5** "Widow" here and in 27:3 renders אִשָּׁה (*'iššāh*) contextually in the sense of "[former] wife [of a deceased man]." The common Hebrew word for "widow" is אַלְמָנָה (*'almānāh*).

**14** Elsewhere in the books of Samuel, the Kerethites always appear alongside the Pelethites, both groups together constituting a corps of foreign mercenaries used as David's bodyguard (2 Sam 8:18; 20:7, 23; cf. de Vaux, AIs, p. 123). "Kerethites" later served as a synonym of "Philistines" (Ezek 25:16; Zeph 2:5). Although "Kerethite" almost surely means "Cretan" (cf. K.A. Kitchen, *Peoples of Old Testament Times*, ed. D.J. Wiseman [Oxford: Clarendon, 1973], p. 56), it is remotely possible that it is a common noun meaning "executioner" or the like from כרת (*krt*, "cut"; for details cf. M. Delcor, "Les Kéréthim et les Crétois," VetTest 28, 4 [1978]: 420).

**15** An episode in the story of Esther provides an eerie if unintentional parallel to the present account. Like the Egyptian slave, Esther is an unwilling foreigner in unfamiliar surroundings. Like him, she does not "eat or drink for three days, night or day" (Esth 4:16). Like him she then goes to a king (or king-elect). And like him, in so doing she places her very life at risk.

**21** The NIV's "people" presumably intends to include the Israelite captives mentioned in vv.18–19. Elsewhere in the chapter, however, עָם (*'am*) is always used in the technical sense of "troops" (as commonly in the books of Samuel) and is therefore translated "men" (vv.4, 6). In fact, the phrase that the NIV translates "the people with him"—הָעָם אֲשֶׁר־אִתּוֹ (*hā'ām 'ašer-'ittô*)—is rendered in v.4 "his [i.e., David's] men." Indeed, *hā'ām* near the end of v.21 itself is translated "his men." Thus "men" would be better than "people" in this context.

**22** The NIV translates *ad sensum* "with us" (cf. a few Heb. MSS), as do the LXX and Vulgate. The MT reads "with me," explained (however improbably) by KD as referring to "the person speaking."

**25** שִׂים מִשְׁפָּט (*śîm mišpāt*, "make/establish an ordinance," "lay down a ruling") corresponds to the Mari expression *šipṭam nadānum/šakānum* (cf. Abraham Malamat, "Mari," BA 34, 1 [1971]: 19).

**27** In Josh 19:8 the NIV implies that Ramah in the Negev is the same as Baalath Beer (cf. Marten H. Woudstra, *The Book of Joshua*, NICOT [Grand Rapids: Eerdmans, 1981], p. 281).

The identification is not certain, however; compare Rasmussen, p. 228, where the two sites are equated, with p. 128, where a map locates them more than twenty miles apart.

28 A silver hoard discovered recently in the ruins of Eshtemoa was at first thought to be part of the booty that David sent to the town. The clay jugs in which the silver was found, however, were made at least a century after the event took place (cf. Ze'ev Yeivin, "The Mysterious Silver Hoard From Eshtemoa," *Biblical Archaeology Review* 13, 6 [1987]: 41–43).

---

## 4. *The death of Saul and Jonathan*

### 31:1–13

1 Now the Philistines fought against Israel; the Israelites fled before
them, and many fell slain on Mount Gilboa. 2 The Philistines pressed
hard after Saul and his sons, and they killed his sons Jonathan,
Abinadab and Malki-Shua. 3 The fighting grew fierce around Saul, and
when the archers overtook him, they wounded him critically.
4 Saul said to his armor-bearer, "Draw your sword and run me
through, or these uncircumcised fellows will come and run me through
and abuse me."
But his armor-bearer was terrified and would not do it; so Saul took
his own sword and fell on it. 5 When the armor-bearer saw that Saul was
dead, he too fell on his sword and died with him. 6 So Saul and his three
sons and his armor-bearer and all his men died together that same day.
7 When the Israelites along the valley and those across the Jordan saw
that the Israelite army had fled and that Saul and his sons had died, they
abandoned their towns and fled. And the Philistines came and occupied
them.
8 The next day, when the Philistines came to strip the dead, they found
Saul and his three sons fallen on Mount Gilboa. 9 They cut off his head
and stripped off his armor, and they sent messengers throughout the
land of the Philistines to proclaim the news in the temple of their idols
and among their people. 10 They put his armor in the temple of the
Ashtoreths and fastened his body to the wall of Beth Shan.
11 When the people of Jabesh Gilead heard of what the Philistines had
done to Saul, 12 all their valiant men journeyed through the night to Beth
Shan. They took down the bodies of Saul and his sons from the wall of
Beth Shan and went to Jabesh, where they burned them. 13 Then they
took their bones and buried them under a tamarisk tree at Jabesh, and
they fasted seven days.

"Chapters 30 and 31 gain in poignancy and power if we regard their events as simultaneous. In the far south, David is anxious about his own and about spoil, while in the far north Saul and the Israelite army perish [cf. also 2 Sam 1:1–4]. . . . While David smites (*hikkah*) ['fought,' 30:17] the Amalekites, and they flee (*nus*) [30:17], the Philistines smite (*hikkah*) ['killed,' v.2] Saul and his sons, and Israel flees (*nus*) [vv.1, 7]" (Miscall, pp. 181–82). Consonant with a narrative suffused with violence and death, most of the verbs in chapter 31 reflect the carnage at Mount Gilboa. Having consigned Saul to his inexorable fate, God is not mentioned in the chapter (cf. the same phenomenon in 27:1–28:2 and see comment there).

In slightly abbreviated form, chapter 31 is repeated in 1 Chronicles 10:1–12, where it serves as an introduction to the Chronicler's story of David, which comprises the rest of 1 Chronicles. The commentary below will note only those places where the differences between the two texts are significant or where the Chronicler makes his own unique contribution.

Focusing on Saul's death, the narrator of chapter 1 works quickly and sparsely. The chapter divides most naturally into two parts: Verses 1–7 describe the battle itself, while vv.8–13 relate its aftermath. Verses 1 and 8 (the initial verses in each section) contain the only references in the chapter to the "slain" (NIV, "dead" in v.8) who fell "on Mount Gilboa."

**1–7** The Philistine threat has hung like a pall over Israel throughout 1 Samuel almost from the beginning (cf. 4:1–2), and the end is not yet. Even now, "as Samuel promised, the Philistines fight Israel (cf. 28:19)" (Brueggemann, *First and Second Samuel*, p. 207)—and, as all too often under Saul's erratic leadership, "many" Israelites "fell slain" (v.1). The present scene stands in marked contrast to David's killing of Goliath, which galvanized the Israelite army with the result that the Philistine "dead were strewn" along the roadside (17:52; the Heb. phrase is the same as that for "fell slain" in v.1). Symbolizing defeat for Israel, the verb "fell" appears three times in this section (vv.1, 4–5; cf. also "fallen" in v.8). Mount Gilboa would always be remembered as the place where Saul and his sons died (see comment on 28:4).

Although Saul and Jonathan had earlier engaged "in hot pursuit" of the Philistines (14:22), now the tables are tragically turned: The Philistines "pressed hard" after Saul and his sons (v.2; same Heb. phrase; cf. also 2 Sam 1:6, "almost upon him"; Judg 20:45). Of the four sons of Saul (for details see comment on 14:49), three (including Jonathan, who should have been the heir apparent) are killed (vv.2, 6, 8) before Saul himself commits suicide. The other son, Esh-Baal/Ish-bosheth, may not have been present on the battlefield (he makes his first appearance in the narrative in 2 Sam 2:8).

With Saul helpless and virtually alone, the Philistines moved in for the kill. As the fighting grew "fierce" around him (v.3, lit., "heavy"; cf. Judg 20:34), the archers "overtook him" (lit., "found him" in the sense of finding their mark, as an ax head might "hit" [Deut 19:5, lit., "find"] and kill a man), and he was badly wounded.

Saul does not want the Philistines, "these uncircumcised fellows" (v.4; see comment on 14:6), to finish him off and "abuse" him (cf. Judg 19:25; "Saul is afraid of being tortured before he dies" [McCarter, *I Samuel*, p. 443]). Relying on his armor-bearer to do as he is told (for the importance of an armor-bearer to his master, see comment on 14:1), Saul tells him, "Draw your sword and run me through" (v.4). David had earlier drawn Goliath's sword from its scabbard and used it to kill the Philistine giant (17:51), but Saul's armor-bearer—like David before him (26:23)—"would not" kill the Lord's anointed (see comment on "not willing" in 22:17). Miscall observes: "Saul, in his last moment, is not supported by his armor-bearer—this one or his earlier armor-bearer. 'David came to Saul . . . and became his armor-bearer' (1 Sam. 16:21–22). Again we are subtly reminded that David is not there at Mt. Gilboa" (p. 182). Since Saul is determined to die on his own terms, he has no alternative but to take his own sword and fall on it. Just as Eli, a failed priest for forty years, died by falling off "his" (lit., "the") chair (4:18), so also Saul, a hapless king for forty years (Acts 13:21), dies by falling on "his" (lit., "the") sword. Polzin suggests yet another comparison:

> Wounded in battle, both Abimelech and Saul ask their armor bearers to kill them lest they bear the ignominy of being killed by one who is uncircumcised (in Abimelech's case by a woman, in Saul's by the Philistines). The differing responses of their armor bearers is significant: Abimelech's young man thrusts him through

> (Judg. 9:54), but Saul's is unwilling to kill his master, forcing the king to commit suicide. (*Samuel and the Deuteronomist*, p. 224)

Although one could conceivably read into Saul's suicide the decision of a desperate man who was as good as dead, the narrative itself provides its own rationale. "There is a reasoned and controlled quality in this final act—'lest these uncircumcised come and slay me and make mockery of me' (31:4)—that stands in marked contrast to his earlier rashness (14:18, 24)" (Humphreys, p. 98).

> Saul thus kills himself for a noble reason, the same reason in essence that David had given earlier for refusing to kill Saul. . . . Saul dies on the battlefield, doing the job he had been anointed and elected to do—leading the army of Israel against her enemies. Through all the reluctance, failure, and madness, he kept his bargain to the end, dying as the military king. (Preston, p. 37)

But in another sense the Philistines do in fact kill Saul, since their archers wound him beyond hope of recovery. Thus the man who had originally been introduced as the one who would "deliver [God's] people from the hand of the Philistines" (9:16) meets his end by dying at their hands.

Seeing that his king is dead, the armor-bearer follows his example and falls on his own sword (v.5). Perhaps in order to stress the camaraderie and mutual loyalty within the Israelite army, the narrator states that all the warriors—Saul, his sons, his armor-bearer, his men—die "together" (v.6; see comment on "alike" in 30:24). Miscall observes that "Saul and his sons, like Eli and his sons, die on the same day, a day on which the Philistines defeat Israel" (p. 170; cf. 2:34; 4:10–12, 17–18). Although many Israelites not directly involved in the fighting manage to escape the Philistine onslaught, the extent of the enemy victory is impressive: They occupy deserted Israelite towns in "the valley" (v.7; doubtless the Valley of Jezreel, as in Judg 7:1, 8, 12 [cf. Judg 6:33]) and in Transjordan.

The three stanzas of *Song of Saul Before His Last Battle* by George Gordon (Lord Byron) imaginatively reconstruct Saul's last words to his men, his armor-bearer, and his son Jonathan:

> Warriors and chiefs! should the shaft or the sword
> Pierce me in leading the host of the Lord,
> Heed not the corse, though a king's in your path:
> Bury your steel in the bosoms of Gath!
>
> Thou who art bearing my buckler and bow,
> Should the soldiers of Saul look away from the foe,
> Stretch me that moment in blood at thy feet!
> Mine be the doom which they dared not to meet.
>
> Farewell to others, but never we part,
> Heir to my royalty, son of my heart!
> Bright is the diadem, boundless the sway,
> Or kingly the death, which awaits us to-day!

**8–13** The following day (v.8) the Philistines come back to the battlefield to "strip the dead"; on a later occasion David's men would return the favor (2 Sam 23:9–10). Brueggemann (*First and Second Samuel*, p. 208) suggests that the Philistines might have been able to identify Saul's body "not only by his height but by his special armor (17:38)." As David had earlier cut off the head of the Philistines' champion (see 17:51

and comment), they now cut off the head of Israel's king (v.9), soon to put it on display in the temple of Dagon as a trophy of war (1 Chron 10:10; see comment on 5:4). They also strip Saul of his armor, soon to display it in the temple of their goddesses (v.10; for "Ashtoreths" meaning "goddesses" see comment on 7:3–4; cf. also "gods" in the parallel passage in 1 Chron 10:10, in this case probably meaning "goddesses," for which Heb. had no specific word). Messengers are sent to "proclaim the news" of the resounding victory and its aftermath—good news, but only from the Philistine standpoint (see 4:17 and comment; cf. 2 Sam 1:20; 4:10).

The report is to be broadcast throughout Philistia but especially "in the temple of their idols" (v.9). Whether the various temples mentioned in vv.9–10 and in the parallel texts in 1 Chronicles are different designations for the same building or refer to more than one building is impossible to say (although at least two buildings seem intended). It is indeed ironic, however, that a book that begins at the "house/temple of the LORD at Shiloh" (1:24; cf. 1:9; see also comment on 1:7) ends at the "house/temple" of one or more pagan deities. With respect to archaeological excavations at Beth Shan, T.C. Mitchell comments: "In level V (*c.* 11th century) two temples were uncovered, one (the S) dedicated to the god Resheph and the other to the goddess Antit, and [A.] Rowe [field director of the excavations from 1925–28] has suggested that these are the temples of Dagon and Ashteroth in which Saul's head and armour were displayed by the Philistines" ("Bethshean, Bethshan," NBD, 2d ed. [Wheaton: Tyndale House, 1982], p. 136; for a brief description of the excavation results, cf. G.M. FitzGerald, "Beth-shean," *Archaeology and Old Testament Study*, ed. D. Winton Thomas [Oxford: Clarendon, 1967], pp. 193–96).

As for the mutilated bodies of Saul and his sons (Saul's suicide did not in fact prevent his body from being abused, v.4), the Philistines fasten them to Beth Shan's wall (vv.10, 12, probably to the face of it; for a parallel cf. the following from a stela of Amenhotep II in the temple of Amada in Nubia: "Six men of these enemies were hanged on the face of the wall of Thebes. . . . Then the other foe was . . . hanged to the wall of Napata, to show his majesty's victories" [John A. Wilson, ANET, p. 248]). Beth Shan is modern Tell el-Husn, an impressive and picturesque mound of ruins fifteen miles south-southwest of the Sea of Galilee at the junction of the Jezreel and Jordan valleys. The name of the ancient city is preserved in that of the nearby town of Beisan.

At the beginning of his reign, Saul's first military action had been to rescue the people of Jabesh Gilead (see comment on 11:1) from the Ammonites (11:1–11). At the end of his reign, after his final military action (which cost him his life), the grateful people of Jabesh (v.11) pay tribute to Saul and his sons by retrieving their bodies from Beth Shan and giving them an honorable burial (vv.12–13; 2 Sam 2:4–5). The "valiant men" of Jabesh (v.12; the Heb. idiom implies unusual courage; cf. 2 Sam 11:16, "strongest defenders"; 23:20 *Qere*, "valiant fighter"), doubtless at great personal risk (cf. Brueggemann, *First and Second Samuel*, p. 209), travel by night (probably to increase their chances of avoiding detection [cf. 2 Sam 2:29, 32; 4:7], especially since they have to cross the Jordan) to Beth Shan, about twelve miles to the northwest. There they lovingly remove the bodies of Saul and his sons and take them to Jabesh, where they burn them (perhaps to avoid "risk of infection from the quickly decomposing bodies," Baldwin, p. 171; cf. Amos 6:10).

"In the end, Saul is humiliated and then honored" (Brueggemann, *First and Second Samuel*, p. 208; cf. also Hertzberg, p. 234). The last verse of 1 Samuel describes the Jabeshites' two final acts of respect: They "buried" (see comment on 25:1a; 28:3–

31:13) Saul and his sons, and they "fasted." The bones were interred "under a [MT 'the'] tamarisk tree" (called "the great tree" in 1 Chron 10:12)—an ironic twist on Saul's position of haughty authority "under the tamarisk tree" at Gibeah, his hometown (22:6). The fasting of the men of Jabesh for Saul and his sons would be repeated by David and his men, though for a shorter period of time (2 Sam 1:12). "Seven days" is frequently associated with "ceremonies involving ritual uncleanness" (Segal, "Numerals," pp. 15–16; cf. Lev 13:4–6, 21, 26–27, 31–34, 50–51, 54; 14:8–9, 38–39; 15:13, 19; Num 6:9; 12:14–15; 19:11–12). In this case it may have been a period of mourning as well as fasting (cf. Lewis, *Cults of the Dead,* pp. 44–45; cf. Gen 50:10; Ecclus 22:12).

In its final chapter 1 Samuel thus ends on a high note "by putting aside allusion to Saul's dark and clouded days. It closes . . . with pathos, with a memory of Saul's finest hour" (Miscall, p. 182). Though Saul "was predestined to fail and he did, as a commander, a father, a friend, the founder of a monarchy," he nevertheless "perseveres in the mission for which he was chosen, the protection of Israel from annihilation by the surrounding enemies. Therein lies his greatness. Though he lost favor in the eyes of the Lord of Israel, yet Saul continued to feel compassion for the Children of Israel" (van Praag, "The Downfall of King Saul," p. 424).

At best, however, Saul remains a complex and enigmatic figure, at once hero and villain. "What [R.B.] Sewall [*The Vision of Tragedy* (New Haven: Yale University Press, 1962), p. 32] says of *Oedipus the King* can be said of the tragedy of King Saul as well: 'At the end . . . much remains to praise, much to blame, and much to wonder at' " (Humphreys, p. 102). Perhaps the fittest conclusion to the story of Saul, as well as the most appropriate transition from 1 Samuel to 2 Samuel, is the Chronicler's inspired coda: "Saul died because he was unfaithful to the LORD; he did not keep the word of the LORD and even consulted a medium for guidance, and did not inquire of the LORD. So the LORD put him to death and turned the kingdom over to David son of Jesse" (1 Chron 10:13–14).

The king is dead.

Long live the king!

## Notes

3 "They wounded him critically" renders וַיָּחֶל מְאֹד מֵהַמּוֹרִים (*wayyāḥel me'ōḏ mēhammôrîm,* lit., "he was wounded exceedingly by the archers"). Unpointed, ויחל (*wyḥl*) may be parsed as a Qal imperfect from חול (*ḥwl*) or חלל (*ḥll*), one of which in this case is probably a byform of the other; see especially רַב מְחוֹלֵל (*raḇ meḥôlēl,* "an archer who wounds," Prov 26:10), in which *meḥôlēl* is either a Po'el participle from *ḥll* or a Po'lel participle from *ḥwl* (cf. מְחוֹלֶלֶת [*meḥôleleṯ,* "who pierced"], a similarly ambiguous form in Isa 51:9). Given the root *ḥll* in v.1 ("slain") and v.8 ("dead"), it would seem best to assume that root here as well. The MT apparently understands *wayyāḥel* from *ḥwl*/*ḥyl* in the sense of "he was in anguish," "he was afraid"; cf. the possible semantic parallels in v.4: יָרֵא מְאֹד (*yārē' me'ōḏ,* "was terrified") and 28:5: וַיֶּחֱרַד לִבּוֹ מְאֹד (*wayyeḥeraḏ libbô me'ōḏ,* "terror filled his heart"; lit., "his heart was afraid exceedingly"). Very few commentators (e.g., KD, Klein) and versions (e.g., ASV) translate the passage in that way, however, and the NIV rendering is contextually preferable (cf. also Driver, Hertzberg, Mauchline, McCarter, Smith, LXX, KJV, NKJV, NASB, RSV, NEB/REB, TEV).

4 הָעֲרֵלִים ... הִתְעַלְּלוּ (*hā'ᵃrēlîm* . . . *hiṯ'allᵉlû,* "uncircumcised fellows will . . . abuse") is a fine example of assonance.

6 By substituting "all his house died together" for "his armor-bearer and all his men died together," 1 Chron 10:6 perhaps stresses the faithfulness of the warriors who stood with Saul to the end. In either case "all" is hyperbolic since many Israelites were not involved in the battle (v.7) and since Saul's son Ish-Bosheth, a member of Saul's "house," would not die until later (2 Sam 4:7–8).

10 Beth Shan is spelled בֵּית שַׁן (*bêṯ šan*) here and in 2 Samuel 21:12, בֵּית שְׁאָן (*bêṯ šᵉ'ān*) elsewhere (Josh 17:11, 16; Judg 1:27; 1 Kings 4:12; 1 Chron 7:29). Although the name would appear to mean "Temple of [the God] Shan," a divine name Shan/Sha'an is thus far unattested. Beth Shan should perhaps therefore be analyzed as Akkadian *bītu ša Ani* ("Temple of Anu"; cf. the writing of Beth Shan as *bīt[u] ša-a-ni* in Tell el-Amarna letter 289:20). For Anu, the Sumero-Babylonian god of the heavens, cf. Herman Wohlstein, *The Sky-God An-Anu: Head of the Mesopotamian Pantheon in Sumerian-Akkadian Literature* (Jericho: Paul Stroock, 1976).

12 Since the bones of Saul and his sons remained after the Jabeshites burned their bodies, cremation (which reduces a corpse to ashes) is not in view. Nor should "burned them" be understood as meaning "burned spices for them" or "anointed them with spices" (cf. NEB) on the basis of 2 Chron 16:14; 21:19; Jer 34:5 (NIV, "make a fire in [one's] honor"), where the Hebrew idiom is quite different (as pointed out long ago by KD).

---

# Second Samuel

## I. Consolidation of Monarchy in Israel (1:1–20:26)

The overriding theme of the books of Samuel is the beginning of Israel's monarchy in the eleventh century B.C. Having discussed its prelude (1 Sam 1:1–7:17), advent (1 Sam 8:1–15:35), and establishment (1 Sam 16:1–31:13), the author next turns to its consolidation under David, Israel's greatest king.

Many scholars assume that the story of David's rise that begins in 1 Samuel 16:1 does not end until 2 Samuel 5:10 (cf. McCarter, "The Apology of David," pp. 489–504; id., *II Samuel,* pp. 142–43; Brueggemann, *First and Second Samuel,* pp. 236, 244) or perhaps until the early chapters of 2 Samuel (for a summary listing, cf. Charles Mabee, "David's Judicial Exoneration," ZAW 92, 1 [1980]: 89 n. 1). The Deuteronomic historian himself, however, has provided an important clue that contravenes all such assessments. If—as seems likely—the books of Joshua, Judges, Samuel, and Kings were written/compiled/edited by the same individual(s), it is surely to the point to observe that just as Joshua begins with "After the death of Moses" and Judges begins with "After the death of Joshua," so also 2 Samuel begins with "After the death of Saul." (Although 2 Kings begins similarly, the corresponding phrase sits differently in the verse and is therefore appropriately rendered in a slightly different way by the NIV: "After Ahab's death.") In other words, the narrator telegraphed to his readers as sharp a break at 2 Samuel 1:1 as he had at Joshua 1:1 and Judges 1:1 (a break later confirmed by whomever it was that divided the scroll of Samuel into two books).

In addition, as my overall outline of 2 Samuel indicates (see section 10 of the introduction), the first twenty chapters constitute a carefully crafted literary masterpiece that divides into four sections of varying length, each of which ends with a four-verse list of names. The first two sections (1:1–3:5; 3:6–5:16) conclude respectively with a list of sons born to David in Hebron (3:2–5) and children born to David in Jerusalem (5:13–16), while each of the last two sections (5:17–8:18; 9:1–20:26) concludes with a list of David's officials (8:15–18; 20:23–26). Such a structure bears every indication of being deliberate rather than accidental (for a similar—though not identical—analysis arrived at independently, see John A. Martin, pp. 37–39; for 2 Sam 1:1 as the start of "the narration of events centered solely around David," cf. Mabee, "David's Judicial Exoneration," p. 90 and n. 3; for chs. 1–20 as a single literary unit, cf. Baldwin, p. 176).

Beginning with the list of sons born to David in Hebron (3:2–5), much of 2 Samuel is paralleled in 1 Chronicles (a process already begun in 1 Samuel 31; see comment on 1 Sam 31:1–13):

| 2 Samuel | 1 Chronicles |
|---|---|
| 3:2–5 | 3:1–4a |
| 5:1–3 | 11:1–3 |
| 5:4–5 | 3:4b; 29:26–27 (cf. 1 Kings 2:11) |
| 5:6–10 | 11:4–9 |
| 5:11–12 | 14:1–2 |
| 5:13–16 | 3:5–8; 14:3–7 |
| 5:17–25 | 14:8–16 |
| 6:1–11 | 13:5–14 |
| 6:12b–19a | 15:25–16:3 |
| 6:19b–20a | 16:43 |
| 7:1–17 | 17:1–15 |
| 7:18–29 | 17:16–27 |
| 8:1–14 | 18:1–13 (cf. 1 Kings 11:23b–24a) |
| 8:15–18 | 18:14–17 |
| 10:1–19 | 19:1–19 |
| 11:1 | 20:1a |
| 12:29–31 | 20:1b–3 |
| 21:18–22 | 20:4–8 |
| 23:8–23 | 11:11–25 |
| 23:24–39 | 11:26–41a |
| 24:1–9 | 21:1–6 |
| 24:10–17 | 21:7–17 |
| 24:18–25 | 21:18–27 |

In addition, chapter 22 is paralleled in Psalm 18. For detailed comparisons between the MT of 2 Samuel and its parallels in 1 Chronicles and Psalm 18 (as well as elsewhere in the OT), see especially Bendavid, pp. 31–70; for detailed comparisons in English, see Crockett, pp. 106–41, and especially Newsome, pp. 23–79. The commentary below will note only those places where the differences between 2 Samuel and parallel texts are significant or where the parallel text makes its own contribution. Given the fact that the Chronicler, in order to highlight the enduring values of David's reign, tends to omit those episodes in 2 Samuel that are unflattering to David, comparisons between 2 Samuel and 1 Chronicles have continued to hold a special fascination for generations of readers of the OT.

## A. *David's Accession to Kingship Over Judah (1:1–3:5)*

The story of David's rise to the kingship of Judah begins with an account of the decimation of Saul's line (1:1–16) and ends with a summary of David's fecundity (3:2–5). Nestled in the center of the literary unit is the narrative of David's anointing as king over Judah (2:1–7), signaling the replacement of Saul and his house in southern Canaan.

### 1. *The death of Saul and Jonathan*

#### 1:1–16

1 After the death of Saul, David returned from defeating the Amalekites
and stayed in Ziklag two days. 2 On the third day a man arrived from
Saul's camp, with his clothes torn and with dust on his head. When he
came to David, he fell to the ground to pay him honor.
3 "Where have you come from?" David asked him.
He answered, "I have escaped from the Israelite camp."
4 "What happened?" David asked. "Tell me."
He said, "The men fled from the battle. Many of them fell and died.
And Saul and his son Jonathan are dead."
5 Then David said to the young man who brought him the report, "How
do you know that Saul and his son Jonathan are dead?"
6 "I happened to be on Mount Gilboa," the young man said, "and there
was Saul, leaning on his spear, with the chariots and riders almost upon
him. 7 When he turned around and saw me, he called out to me, and I
said, 'What can I do?'
8 "He asked me, 'Who are you?'
" 'An Amalekite,' I answered.
9 "Then he said to me, 'Stand over me and kill me! I am in the throes of
death, but I'm still alive.'
10 "So I stood over him and killed him, because I knew that after he
had fallen he could not survive. And I took the crown that was on his
head and the band on his arm and have brought them here to my lord."
11 Then David and all the men with him took hold of their clothes and
tore them. 12 They mourned and wept and fasted till evening for Saul and
his son Jonathan, and for the army of the LORD and the house of Israel,
because they had fallen by the sword.
13 David said to the young man who brought him the report, "Where
are you from?"
"I am the son of an alien, an Amalekite," he answered.
14 David asked him, "Why were you not afraid to lift your hand to
destroy the LORD's anointed?"
15 Then David called one of his men and said, "Go, strike him down!"
So he struck him down, and he died. 16 For David had said to him, "Your
blood be on your own head. Your own mouth testified against you when
you said, 'I killed the LORD's anointed.' "

Second Samuel begins as 1 Samuel ends—with an account of the death of King Saul and his son Jonathan, the heir apparent. But while 1 Samuel 31 describes the events as they actually occurred, 2 Samuel 1:1–16 consists of a report of the events filtered through the not disinterested words of an Amalekite alien. The section displays a chiastic arrangement:

A. David strikes down the Amalekites (1:1).
  B. David questions an Amalekite (1:2–5).
    C. The Amalekite tells David his story (1:6–10).

C′. David and his men react to the Amalekite's story (1:11–12).
B′. David questions the Amalekite again (1:13–14).
A′. David strikes down the Amalekite (1:15–16).

**1** Verses 1 and 15–16 frame the literary unit by referring to David's "striking down" (Hiphil of *nāḵāh*) the Amalekite(s) (v.1, "defeating"; v.15, "struck him down" ["strike him down" earlier in the verse is from the Heb. root *pg'*]). Verse 1 and 8:13 also form an *inclusio* surrounding a larger section (chs. 1–8) that immediately precedes the court history (chs. 9–20): David "returned from defeating" the Amalekites (v.1); David "returned from striking down" the Edomites (8:13). David's earlier successful returning home from battle (1 Sam 17:57) had aroused Saul's jealousy (1 Sam 18:6-9)—and the resulting paranoia had contributed to his decline and ultimate demise.

**2–5** Saul's defeat and death at the hands of the Philistines and David's victory over the Amalekites occurred at approximately the same time (as the syntax of vv.1–2 indicates; cf. KD). The distance from Mount Gilboa (v.6; see comment on 1 Sam 28:4) to Ziklag (v.1; see comment on 1 Sam 27:6) is more than eighty miles, a three-day trip for the Amalekite fugitive (v.2). His arrival in Ziklag is underscored by the use of three different forms of the same Hebrew verb (tr. "arrived," v.2; "came," v.2; "come," v.3), and the place he fled from is called "Saul's camp" by the narrator (v.2) and "the Israelite camp" by the Amalekite himself (v.3).

The story in vv.2–5 echoes the similar account of the Benjamite fugitive's report in 1 Samuel 4:12–17 (cf. "his clothes torn and [with] dust on his head," v.2; 1 Sam 4:12; "What happened?" v.4; 1 Sam 4:16) and should be compared with it (see comment on 1 Sam 4:12; cf. also independently Garsiel, pp. 102–6). Garsiel summarizes:

> The author of Samuel established a deliberate connection between the two stories in order to set up an analogy between the fates of Saul's house and of Eli's. . . . The comparison indicates that there is a clear rule of law which connects a leader's conduct with his fate and the fate of his house. A degenerate leader, whether it is himself who has sinned or his sons, will ultimately be deposed . . . or come to a tragic end, just as Eli and his sons die on the same day, and so do Saul and his. (p. 106)

Torn clothes (v.2; cf. v.11) and dust on one's head are signs of anguish and distress (cf. 15:32; Josh 7:6; Neh 9:1), appropriate and understandable behavior in a man who has so recently witnessed a battlefield scene of suffering and death. Like Abigail before him (1 Sam 25:23), the man demonstrates his submission to David by prostrating himself in his presence.

David's desire to know where the man has come from (v.3) is doubtless prompted by the man's forlorn and unkempt appearance (cf. similarly 1 Sam 30:13). His response—that he has escaped from the Israelite camp—makes David all the more curious; so he demands that the man "tell" him what has happened (v.4). Continuing to characterize the man, the participial form of the verb *ngd* ("tell"; cf. 18:11) is rendered "who brought . . . the report" in vv.5, 13 (cf. similarly 4:10; NIV leaves the word untranslated in v.6 in deference to English style). Rendered elsewhere as "messenger" (cf. 15:13; Jer 51:31), the term in this context thus reduces the function of the Amalekite to that of a bearer of news. His report reveals that the Israelites "fled" from the battle against the Philistines and that many of them "fell and died" (v.4; cf. 1 Sam 31:1). What is more, continues the man—who obviously thinks that he is bringing David good news (4:10)—"Saul and his son Jonathan are dead." David of course wants to know how the messenger can be so sure of this latter assertion (v.5); so the man tells his story (vv.6–10).

**6–10** The Amalekite's account of Saul's death deviates in several important respects from that given in 1 Samuel 31. Bill T. Arnold gives a concise summary of the most obvious differences: "In 1 Samuel 31 . . . the king committed suicide, here the Amalekite killed him; there he was wounded by archers, here his enemies were charioteers; there the Philistines took his armor, here the Amalekite brought his crown and armlet to David" ("The Amalekite's Report of Saul's Death: Political Intrigue or Incompatible Sources?" JETS 32, 3 [1989]: 209).

Most of the proposed solutions to the problem—e.g., that the narrator has transmitted two mutually contradictory accounts, or that the Amalekite's story is true (which would mean that the report in 1 Sam 31 is false), or that the so-called contradictions can be dissolved by postulating separate literary sources in vv.1–16 (a theory effectively answered by Arnold, ibid., pp. 290–94)—only serve to further complicate it. Commentators have therefore tried to harmonize the two accounts. Typical is the early reconstruction by Josephus. He claimed that when Saul's armor-bearer refused to kill him, the king tried to fall on his own sword but was too weak to do so. Saul then turned and saw the Amalekite, who, upon the king's request, complied by killing him. After the Amalekite had taken the king's crown and armband and fled, Saul's armor-bearer killed himself (Jos. Antiq. 6, 370–72 [xiv.7]). Josephus's attempt at conflation, while commendable and in some respects helpful, errs in his basic assumption that the Amalekite was telling the truth.

The messenger begins his report to David (v.6) by stating that he "happened" (better something like "just happened" to bring out the force of the Heb. infinitive-absolute-plus-finite-verb construction) to be on Mount Gilboa (the scene of Saul's last battle, 1 Sam 31:1; see comment on 28:4). There he encountered the wounded Saul, who was supporting himself by "leaning on his spear"—a parable of his tendency to rely on human effort rather than on divine resources (cf. Isa 10:20; 31:1, where "rely" translates the same Heb. verb as "leaning" does here). Philistine "chariots and riders," feared far and wide (see comment on 1 Sam 13:5), were "almost upon him" (see comment on 1 Sam 31:2, where "pressed hard" renders the same Heb. verb).

Seeing the Amalekite nearby, Saul called out to him (v.7). The man replied with the response commonly used by servants: "What can I do?" (*hinnēnî;* lit., "Behold me," "Here I am" [cf. Gen 22:1, 11; Isa 6:8], in this case "How can I [possibly] help you?"). Perhaps to be sure that the man was not a Philistine, who might abuse the Israelite king if he had the chance (cf. 1 Sam 31:4), Saul asked the man to identify himself (v.8). His answer—that he was an "Amalekite"—gives to the account an ironic touch, since David had recently returned to Ziklag after defeating an Amalekite raiding party (v.1; cf. 1 Sam 30).

Satisfied as to the general identity of the young man, Saul uttered words reminiscent of the earlier description of David's dispatching of Goliath: "Stand over me and kill me" (v.9; cf. 1 Sam 17:51). Although in mortal agony and wanting to die, Saul was unable—or (at least temporarily) unwilling (cf. 1 Sam 31:4)—to take his own life.

Apparently happy to oblige, the Amalekite claims to have fulfilled Saul's wish to the letter (v.10). He "knew" that the fallen king could not survive, and—since he himself had killed him—he could also "know" for certain (v.5) that Saul was dead. After killing the king, the Amalekite took Saul's "crown" (*nēzer*), the primary symbol of his royal authority (cf. 2 Kings 11:12 = 2 Chron 23:11), as well as a band (there is no definite article in the MT) that he was wearing on his arm. The armlet (*'eṣ'āḏāh*) may have been made of gold (cf. the same Heb. word in Num 31:50) and was perhaps another symbol of royalty. Arnold surmises:

> In the Joash enthronement passage (2 Kgs 11:12) we read that "then they brought out the king's son, and put the crown (*nēzer*) upon him, and gave him the testimony (*hā'ēdût*)." *BHK* and many commentators read *haṣ'ādôt* ("the armlets") for "the testimony," thus providing a perfect illustration of the crown and armlet as the primary royal insignia. ("The Amalekite's Report," p. 296)

But although the proposed emendation is both attractive and modest (requiring the addition of only one Heb. consonant), and although the form *haṣṣᵉ'āḏôṯ* does in fact occur in Isaiah 3:20 (NIV, "ankle chains," perhaps better "armlets"), the NIV's "copy of the covenant" in 2 Kings 11:12 (= 2 Chron 23:11) faithfully translates *hā'ēḏûṯ* there and makes equally good sense in context. In any case, Arnold's plausible reconstruction of the sequence of events is not dependent on the Joash enthronement passage:

> After Saul's serious wound, and in light of the imminent arrival of the Philistines and his armor-bearer's reluctance to mercifully kill him, he committed suicide. In the ensuing chaos the Amalekite, whose connections with the Israelite camp are unknown, took the royal insignia from the king's corpse. The next morning the Philistines found Saul's body and stripped him of his armor. But the most substantial spoils of war, the royal crown and armlet, were already being carried to Ziklag with the message that Saul was dead. (ibid., pp. 296–97)

**11–12** Having once been a valued member of Saul's court, David undoubtedly recognizes the crown and armlet in the hands of the Amalekite. But the messenger could scarcely have been prepared for the response of David and his men, who tear their clothes (v.11) for much the same reason that the Amalekite had earlier torn his (see comment on v.2). With genuine and heartfelt expressions of grief over Saul and Jonathan (cf. also vv.17–27) and the other fallen Israelite warriors, David and his men mourn (v.12; cf. 11:26; 1 Sam 25:1; 28:3) and weep (cf. also v.24). They also fast, but only "till evening," which was apparently David's usual practice in such situations (cf. 3:35; contrast the week-long fast of the Jabeshites for Saul and his sons [see comment on 1 Sam 31:13]). Their sorrow extends to the "house of Israel" (v.12), a reference to the people as a whole ("house" in the sense of "family," "community"; see comment on 1 Sam 7:2), since all Israel has suffered tragic and irreparable loss in the death of their king.

**13–14** Apparently after the period of mourning (vv.11–12) is over, David questions the messenger again (cf. vv. 2–5). David's "Where are you from?" (v.13) does not repeat his earlier "Where have you come from?" (v.3), which is concerned with the man's most recent location (cf. "Where do you come from?" in 1 Sam 30:13). Here David wants to know something of the man's background, probing even more deeply than Saul's "Who are you?" in v.8. Thus, in addition to repeating the information that he is an Amalekite (v.13; cf. v.8), the man affirms that he is the son of an "alien."

It would seem that David has now learned all that he needs to know concerning the Amalekite. Since his father is a resident alien, living in Saul's realm, the young man can be expected to have at least minimal knowledge about Israel's basic traditions, including the inviolability of "the LORD's anointed" (vv.14, 16). David's question to him (v.14) is therefore entirely in order. By the Amalekite's own testimony (cf. v.16), he had lifted his hand (see comment on 1 Sam 22:17) to "destroy" (see comment on 1 Sam 26:9; for another example of "destroy" with a human object, cf. 2 Sam 14:11) the Lord's anointed king, something David had never done—though he had had more than one opportunity to do so (see 1 Sam 24:6 and comment; 24:10; 26:9 and comment; 26:11).

**15–16** Far from receiving the reward that he thinks David will surely give him because of the "good news" he thought he was bringing (4:10), the Amalekite's callous bravado (v.14) has sealed his own doom. As David would later order his men to execute the murderers of Ish-Bosheth son of Saul (4:12), so now he calls one of his "men" (v.15, lit., "young men") to strike down the "young man" (v.13) who claims to have killed Saul. The command of execution—"Strike him down!" (v.15)—was all too common in the early days of Israel's monarchy (cf. 1 Sam 22:18; 1 Kings 2:29). In this case the subsequent statement, "So he struck him down," uses a different verb from that used earlier in the verse, probably to form an *inclusio* with v.1 (see comment there; the latter verb is the same as that used of David's striking down Goliath in 1 Sam 17:50).

The Amalekite's own words—that he had "killed" (v.16; cf. v.10) Saul—proved to be his undoing. Before the Amalekite's summary execution, David told him, "Your blood be on your own head," a stock phrase pronounced to protect the one who authorizes an execution by clearing him of bloodguilt against the murdered man (cf. 1 Kings 2:31–33)—in this case Saul, of whose death David (soon to become the de facto king of Israel) thus declares himself innocent. A gentle irony: The Amalekite, hoping for a reward by bringing to David the crown that had been on Saul's "head" (v.10), discovers—too late—that his claim to have killed Saul has brought bloodguilt against the Lord's anointed down on his own "head" (v.16).

The story ends as it began: David "strikes down" one or more hated "Amalekites" (see comment on v.1). Although he acts in accord with the messenger's own words, we have no way of knowing whether David in fact believes them. In the light of 1 Samuel 31, it is clear that the young man's claim to have killed Saul was false, however much the rest of his story may appear to have the ring of truth. Arnold's summary statement is apropos: "The events described in 1 Samuel 31 and 2 Samuel 1 are historically consistent if it is assumed that the Amalekite messenger was attempting to deceive David" ("The Amalekite's Report," p. 298).

## Notes

1 The MT's הָעֲמָלֵק (*hā'ᵃmālēq*, "the Amalek") is unique in the OT and should doubtless be vocalized to be read as the gentilic הָעֲמָלֵקִי (*hā'ᵃmālēqî*, "the Amalekite[s]") with several Hebrew MSS (cf. BDB, Driver).

**9** "I am in the throes of death" is literally "the שָׁבָץ [*šāḇāṣ*, a *hapax legomenon* of unknown meaning] has seized me." If the word is related to the root *šḇṣ* used in various forms elsewhere of the fabrication of priestly garments in the sense of "[intricately] weave [cloth]," "mount/set [gems]" (Exod 28:4, 11, 13, 14, 20, 25, 39; 39:6, 13, 16, 18), the rendering "throes [of death]," with its implications of (intricate?) convulsion, may be close to what the narrator intended.

The sentence כִּי־כָל־עוֹד נַפְשִׁי בִּי (*kî-ḵol-ʿôḏ nap̱šî bî*, "But I'm still alive"; lit., "But my life is still in me") finds a striking parallel in Job 27:3: כִּי־כָל־עוֹד נִשְׁמָתִי בִי (*kî-ḵol-ʿôḏ nišmāṯî ḇî*, "As long as I have life within me").

**12** The LXX reads Ἰούδα (*Iouda*, "Judah," apparently from a Heb. text that had יהודה [*yhwdh*] instead of the MT's יהוה [*YHWH*, "the LORD"]), thus paralleling "army [lit., 'people'] of Judah" and "house of Israel" (for the significance of similar pairings in the books of Samuel, see the comment on 1 Sam 11:8). Siegfried Herrmann observes, however, that "עם יהוה refers to the tribal levies, but בית ישראל refers to the totality represented by the 'people of the Lord', or, in other words, to the 'state' of Israel" ("King David's State," in W. Boyd Barrick and John R. Spencer, edd., *In the Shelter of Elyon: Essays on Ancient Palestinian Life and Literature in Honor of G.W. Ahlström*, JSOT suppl. series 31 [Sheffield: JSOT, 1984], p. 269; for full argumentation see pp. 268–72).

---

## 2. *David's lament for Saul and Jonathan*

### 1:17–27

17 David took up this lament concerning Saul and his son Jonathan,
18 and ordered that the men of Judah be taught this lament of the bow (it is written in the Book of Jashar):

19 "Your glory, O Israel, lies slain on your heights.
How the mighty have fallen!

20 "Tell it not in Gath,
proclaim it not in the streets of Ashkelon,
lest the daughters of the Philistines be glad,
lest the daughters of the uncircumcised rejoice.

21 "O mountains of Gilboa,
may you have neither dew nor rain,
nor fields that yield offerings ⌊of grain⌋.
For there the shield of the mighty was defiled,
the shield of Saul—no longer rubbed with oil.
22 From the blood of the slain,
from the flesh of the mighty,
the bow of Jonathan did not turn back,
the sword of Saul did not return unsatisfied.

23 "Saul and Jonathan—
in life they were loved and gracious,
and in death they were not parted.
They were swifter than eagles,
they were stronger than lions.

24 "O daughters of Israel,
weep for Saul,
who clothed you in scarlet and finery,
who adorned your garments with ornaments of gold.

25 "How the mighty have fallen in battle!
Jonathan lies slain on your heights.
26 I grieve for you, Jonathan my brother;
you were very dear to me.

Your love for me was wonderful,
 more wonderful than that of women.

27 "How the mighty have fallen!
 The weapons of war have perished!"

"David's lament over Saul and Jonathan is powerful, passionate poetry commonly regarded as being directly from David's hand" (Brueggemann, *First and Second Samuel*, p. 213). That David was the author of this remarkable poem and that its date of composition was therefore about 1000 B.C. or slightly earlier is universally recognized (cf. Freedman, "Divine Names," pp. 55, 57, 72, 96; Stanley Gevirtz, "David's Lament Over Saul and Jonathan," in *Patterns in the Early Poetry of Israel*, Studies in Ancient Oriental Civilization 32 [Chicago: University of Chicago Press, 1963], p. 72; William L. Holladay, "Form and Word-Play in David's Lament Over Saul and Jonathan," VetTest 20, 2 [1970]: 154). The poem is strikingly secular, never once mentioning God's name or elements of Israel's faith (see comment on v.21). Although OT laments over individuals are not uncommon (cf. 1 Kings 13:30; Jer 22:18; 34:5; Ezek 28:12–19; 32:2–15), the only other such recorded lament by David is that over Abner in 3:33–34.

It is generally agreed that vv.19–27 constitute the limits of the poem, secured by the *inclusio* formed by "How the mighty have fallen!" in vv.19 and 27. Although a few scholars would begin the poem with v.18, it is possible to do so only by resorting to radical and extensive emendation (cf. Gevirtz, "David's Lament," pp. 73–76; Holladay, "Form and Word-Play in David's Lament," pp. 162–68). My treatment of David's lament itself will thus begin with v.19 and will assume that vv.17–18 establish its historical and literary context.

The most satisfying structural outline of vv.19–27 to date is that of William H. Shea ("Chiasmus and the Structure of David's Lament," JBL 105, 1 [1986]: 13–25). He understands the body of the poem to consist of five stanzas (vv.20, 21, 22–23, 24–25, 26) framed by vv.19 and 27. In addition "the lament was composed in an overall chiasm by form in which the poetic units of the piece lengthen progressively toward its center and then decrease progressively after having reached that point" (ibid., p. 14). Although I agree with much of Shea's analysis, it breaks down in his poetic scansion of the central section as well as in his combining v.24 and v.25 into one stanza. I also disagree, however, with the NIV scansion, which incorrectly combines v.22 with v.21. In my judgment Shea has proven that vv.22 and 23 belong together.

My seven-stanza outline, which focuses on the reference in each verse to Saul and/or Jonathan (named or unnamed), exhibits a basically chiastic arrangement (though less pristine than that of Shea):

A1. 1:19: Jonathan (unnamed)
 A2. 1:20: both men (unnamed)
  B. 1:21: Saul (named)
   C. 1:22–23: Jonathan and Saul (both named)
  B′. 1:24: Saul (named)
 A1′. 1:25–26: Jonathan (named)
A2′. 1:27 both men (unnamed)

**17–18** "Took up . . . lament" (v.17) renders the cognate accusative construction *qyn . . . qînāh* (cf. also Ezek 32:16 [NIV, "chant"]; 2 Sam 3:33 omits the noun, while Jer 9:10; Ezek 28:12; 32:2; Amos 5:1 use the verb *nś'* for "take up"). The term *qînāh* in the OT "is used of a formal utterance which expresses grief or distress. It . . . could be learned [cf. v.18] and practiced" (David L. Zapf, "How Are the Mighty Fallen! A Study of 2 Samuel 1:17–27," *Grace Theological Journal* 5, 1 [1984]: 116). The Irish word "keen," which is a funeral song accompanied by wailing, may derive ultimately from the Hebrew root *qyn*. Since 3:2 meter is commonly (though not exclusively) employed in OT poems of the lament genre (cf. often in the Book of Lamentations), the 3:2 pattern is sometimes called *qinah* meter. All attempts to find *qinah* rhythm in vv.19–27, however, have thus far proven unsuccessful.

The NIV added "this lament of the" (v.18) in deference to the needs of English translation. Zapf points out that *qšt* (["The] Bow") is probably the title of the lament (ibid., p. 116; cf. also KD). The word appears in v.22 as a weapon used by Jonathan, who was probably a skilled bowman (cf. 1 Sam 20:18–22, 35–40), and Saul had been mortally wounded by archers (1 Sam 31:3).

Like Joshua's poetic address to the sun and moon (Josh 10:12–13), David's lament was eventually written down in the "Book of Jashar" (v.18; cf. also 1 Kings 8:13 [LXX 8:53], where the LXX adds: "It is written in the book of the song [*tēs ōdēs*]," the last two words of which are generally believed to be based on a Heb. text that read *hšyr*, a transcriptional error for *hyšr* ["Jashar"]). Hebrew *hayyāšār* means literally "the upright," perhaps an overall descriptive term for the contents of the poetic collection. Freedman suggests that the earliest editions of the "Book of the Wars of the LORD" (Num 21:14) and the Book of Jashar "may well go back to the time of the judges, but the final published form must be dated in the monarchic period" ("Divine Names," p. 99 n. 18).

**19** Shea observes ("Chiasmus and the Structure of David's Lament," p. 20) that the *inclusio* formed by vv.19 and 27 displays "How the mighty have fallen!" in the second colon of v.19 and in the second-to-last colon of v.27, thus providing an additional element of symmetry to the poem. "How" followed immediately by a verb in the perfect tense often signals the beginning of a lament, the best known example being Lamentations 1:1. Holladay ("Form and Word-Play in David's Lament," pp. 166–67) expects *gibbôrîm* ("[the] mighty") to be paralleled by *ḥayil* ("power[ful]"), as often elsewhere in the OT (for examples cf. Gevirtz, "David's Lament," p. 89), and therefore sees irony in the fact that *ḥālāl* ("slain") appears instead of *ḥayil*. In v.22, however, "blood of the slain" is parallel to "flesh of the mighty," and in that verse there can be no question of emending "slain" to "power(ful)" since the phrase "blood of the slain" is secured by its occurrence in Numbers 23:24 ("blood of his victims"). In any event "mighty" in v.19 is probably best understood as being parallel to "glory," and thus "slain" is parallel to "fallen" (cf. similarly in v.25, and note especially the phrase "fell slain" in 1 Sam 31:1 [see also comment there]). The word *gibbôrîm* ("mighty") appears in another ancient poem, the Song of Deborah (Judg 5:13, 23), and the root *gbr* is thematic of David's lament, occurring no less than six times in its nine verses: vv.19, 21, 22, 23 ("stronger"), 25, 27.

*Bāmôṯ* usually means "high places" in the sense of open-air worship sites (authorized or not; see comment on 1 Sam 9:12), but "heights" in the more general sense of topographical elevations is also common for *bāmôṯ*, especially in poetry (cf. Deut 32:13; Hab 3:19). "Heights" here refers to Gilboa (v.21), located in "Israel," which was Saul's main realm and to whose people David's lament is addressed. Not yet king over all Israel, David orders that the lament be taught only to the men of

"Judah" (v.18), where he has already gained considerable influence (see 1 Sam 30:26–31 and comment).

According to David Noel Freedman, *haṣṣᵉḇî* ("Your glory," v.19 [NIV]) should be translated "the gazelle" as a nickname or sobriquet for Jonathan. He summarizes: "In our opinion, 'Jonathan' in vs. 25 explicates 'the gazelle' in vs. 19" ("The Refrain in David's Lament Over Saul and Jonathan," in *Ex Orbe Religionum: Studia Geo. Widengren*, part 1 [Leiden: Brill, 1972], p. 120). Freedman is surely correct in his analysis: "Gazelle" is used as a simile for a fleet-footed warrior in the immediate context (2:18; cf. also 1 Chron 12:8), Saul and Jonathan are compared to "eagles" and "lions" in v.23, and the simile of a deer is employed in connection with "heights" in 22:34 (cf. Hab 3:19). That Jonathan should be compared to a gazelle is entirely appropriate (cf. 1 Sam 14:4–5, 10, 12–13).

Although Saul and Jonathan are each named four times in David's lament (Saul, vv.21, 22, 23, 24; Jonathan, vv.22, 23, 25, 26), Jonathan is given pride of place when the two are first mentioned together (v.22) and is featured in the false coda (v.25). It is therefore not surprising that he is alluded to, even if not by name, at the beginning of the poem. Zapf's translation of *haṣṣᵉḇî* ("the gazelle/glory") arises from his conclusion that it "is probably purposely ambiguous both in reference and meaning" ("How Are the Mighty Fallen!" p. 117). If Zapf's reasoning that led him to his decision is somewhat convoluted (see ibid., pp. 106–7), his summary is nonetheless helpful: "Saul is not slighted, but Jonathan is given a certain preference" (p. 107). In the first stanza of his lament, therefore, David serves notice to the reader that he intends to highlight his relationship to "the gazelle," his "dear" friend (v.26), Jonathan.

**20** The second stanza begins and ends with assonance: *taggîḏû ḇᵉgaṯ* ("Tell . . . in Gath"; cf. Mic 1:10 and NIV mg. there); *pen-taʿᵃlōznāh bᵉnôṯ hāʿᵃrēlîm* ("lest the daughters of the uncircumcised rejoice"). The Hebrew verbs rendered "tell" and "proclaim" occur together again in 4:10 ("told," "bring good news"; for other examples cf. Gevirtz, "David's Lament," p. 83), recalling the frequent use of *ngd* ("tell") in the story concerning the Amalekite earlier in the chapter (see comment on v.4). The verb translated "proclaim" almost always implies good news—in this case, of course, only from the standpoint of the Philistines (see comment on 1 Sam 31:9), who can be expected to spread the report of Saul's death like wildfire. "Gath, standing at the eastern edge of Philistine territory near the hill country of Israel, and Ashkelon by the sea represent all of Philistine territory" (Zapf, "How Are the Mighty Fallen!" p. 113). The words of an Akkadian proverb are apt in this context: "Secret knowledge is not safeguarded by an enemy" (ANET, p. 425 [1.14–15]).

The "daughters of the Philistines/uncircumcised" (cf. 1 Sam 31:1, 4; see also comment on 1 Sam 14:6), from whom the news of the Israelite defeat is to be kept if at all possible, will "be glad" and "rejoice" if they hear of it (the Heb. verbs are paralleled also in Prov 23:15–16; Jer 50:11; Zeph 3:14; cf. Gevirtz, "David's Lament," p. 84). In David's lament they appear in poetic opposition to the "daughters of Israel," who are commanded to "weep for Saul" (v.24).

**21** The alleged difficulties in the third stanza have attracted more attention from commentators than the rest of the verses in the poem combined, especially the phrase that the NIV renders "nor fields that yield offerings ⌊of grain⌋." Despite references in ancient Egyptian literature to the "Field of Offerings," a kind of paradise, the goal of the deceased (cf. Leonard H. Lesko, "Some Observations on the Composition of the

*Book of Two Ways*," JAOS 91, 1 [1971]: 30–43), perhaps similar to the "Elysian field(s)" of Greek mythology, the heavenly destination of Saul and Jonathan is not in view here. The verse consists of something more mundane: a curse on the "mountains of Gilboa," the site of the Israelite defeat (cf. comment on v.6), which is described topographically by Shea:

> Gilboa is not a solitary mountain peak, nor a series of peaks, but a ridge some eight miles long and three to five miles wide running southeast and south from Jezreel. It forms the watershed between the plain of Esdraelon and the plain around Beth-shean, dropping away sharply to the north and east. It slopes gradually to the west, however, and on this gentle fertile terrain, barley, wheat, figs and olives are grown . . . [It was] this western slope to which rain and dew were denied by the curse of this poem. ("Chiasmus and the Structure of David's Lament," pp. 141–42)

Other texts demonstrating that the land is affected adversely by murderous acts include Psalm 106:38 and Hosea 4:2–3. For a defense of "O field of heights," the most likely rendering of the disputed phrase, see the Notes.

The parallelism between "dew" and "rain" occurs also in 1 Kings 17:1—again in a context in which their absence signifies a curse against the land (the two words are paralleled also, but in reverse order, in Deut 32:2; Job 38:28). In Hebrew thought, dew was often a symbol of resurrection or the renewing of life (cf. Ps 110:3; Isa 26:19; cf. also the name Abital [2 Sam 3:4], "My [Divine] Father is Dew" or "[Divine] Father of Dew"; for parallels elsewhere in the ancient Near East, cf. Magnus Ottosson, "The Prophet Elijah's Visit to Zarephath," in *In the Shelter of Elyon*, pp. 190–91).

The Hebrew root *mgn* (usually "shield") on occasion seems to mean "king," "sovereign," "donor," or the like (cf. Gen 15:1; Pss 47:9; 84:9; 89:18 and NIV mgs.; for details see esp. M. O'Connor, "Yahweh the Donor," *Aula Orientalis* 6 [1988]: 47–60). Although "there are cases in which it is impossible to decide clearly between *māgēn*, 'shield', and *mgn*, 'donor' " (ibid., p. 52), the context in v.21 tips the scales in favor of "shield." Whether *nig'al* means "defiled" (NIV) in the sense that, in the words of Shea ("Chiasmus and the Structure of David's Lament," p. 142), "the Philistines treated [Saul's shield as they wished] like the Israelites did Goliath's armor and sword" (cf. 1 Sam 17:54; 21:9), or whether it means "rejected (with loathing)" in the sense that, in the words of S.R. Driver (*Notes on the Books of Samuel*, p. 237), the shield is pictured "as lying upon the mountains, no longer polished and ready to be worn in action, but cast aside as worthless, and neglected," the verb is more suited to shields than to sovereigns.

The rendering "sovereign" in v.21 is not without its proponents (cf. Mitchell Dahood, "Northwest Semitic Notes on Genesis," *Biblica* 55, 1 [1974]: 78), but it can only be justified by assuming that "rubbed [lit., 'anointed'] with oil" refers to Saul and thus by translating *b^elî* ("no longer") asseveratively in the sense of "surely," "firmly," "duly" (cf. O'Connor, "Yahweh the Donor," pp. 57–58; Freedman, "The Refrain in David's Lament," pp. 122–23)—a questionable procedure at best. In favor of "shield" is the appearance of "bow" and "sword" in v.22 (cf. the sequence "bow" [NIV, "arrows"], "shield," "sword" in Ps 76:3 [observed also by Shea, "Chiasmus and the Structure of David's Lament," p. 142 n. 5]). In addition to Isaiah 21:5, which urges the Babylonians to "anoint/oil the shields" (to keep them in good condition), an

Old Babylonian text from Tell Asmar lists "one sila of oil to rub shield(s)" (cf. Alan R. Millard, "Saul's Shield Not Anointed With Oil," BASOR 230 [1978]: 70).

**22–23** Shea has demonstrated conclusively that vv.22 and 23 together constitute a stanza that resides at the center of the poem (cf. also Fokkelman, "Saul and David," p. 30; Holladay, "Form and Word-Play in David's Lament," p. 179). Each of the two verses refers to both Saul and Jonathan by name, the only verses in the lament to do so. Verse 22 mentions Jonathan before Saul (thereby giving Jonathan pride of place), while v.23 reverses the names. In addition, the MT of the first two lines of v.22 parallels that of the last two lines of v.23 in striking ways: Both units employ pairs of the preposition *min* ("from . . . from" in v.22, "than . . . than" in v.23); the last noun of the first unit ("the mighty") and the last verb of the second unit ("they were stronger") come from the same root (*gbr*); and *ḥᵃlālîm* ("the slain," v.22) and *qallû* ("they were swifter," v.23) convey somewhat similar sounds (Shea, "Chiasmus and the Structure of David's Lament," p. 17). Holladay makes the further observation that the ubiquitous word *lō'* ("not") occurs three times in vv.22–23 and nowhere else in the lament (ibid., p. 179 n. 5).

In no uncertain terms verses 22–23 summarize the bravery, the determination, the comradeship, and the ability of King Saul and his son Jonathan. Verse 22 reflects the language of Deuteronomy 32:42, a verse that concludes the words of the Lord in another ancient Israelite poem, the Song of Moses. There "the blood of the slain" (a singular collective; for the exact phrase found here, cf. Num 23:24 ["the blood of his victims"], which concludes Balaam's second oracle) is mentioned, and we are told that "arrows" drink "blood" and that the "sword" devours "flesh" (cf. similarly Isa 34:5–6). Likewise here Jonathan's "bow" did not turn back from "blood" and Saul's "sword" did not return (to its sheath; cf. Ezek 21:5) "unsatisfied" (literally, "empty[-handed]"; cf. Isa 55:11; Jer 14:3 ["unfilled"]; 50:9) from "flesh" (literally, "fat," translating a different Heb. word from that in Deut 32:42). (For the parallelism between "blood" and "fat," cf. again Isa 34:6–7, where a battle is compared to an animal sacrifice; cf. also Jer 46:10; Ezek 39:17–19; cf. Gevirtz, "David's Lament," p. 88; Holladay, "Form and Word-Play in David's Lament," p. 177.)

The MT of v.23 juxtaposes "in life" (lit., "during their lifetime[s]; cf. 18:18) with "and in death," placing the two phrases between "they were loved and gracious" and "they were not parted." The effect is to suggest that both verbal clauses pertain to both temporal expressions: The king and his son, inseparable in life as in death, will continue to be honored in death as in life. The Hebrew roots underlying "loved" and "gracious," applied here to Saul and Jonathan, are in v.26 applied to Jonathan alone, though in reverse order ("dear" and "love"; cf. independently Gevirtz, "David's Lament," p. 91). "Swifter than eagles" recurs in Jeremiah 4:13 and Lamentations 4:1 (for other examples of the eagle simile/metaphor, cf. Deut 28:49; Jer 48:40; 49:22; Hos 8:1), and "stronger than lions" reprises Judges 14:18 (but with a different Heb. verb for "stronger"; cf. also Num 23:24; 24:9; Isa 38:13; Jer 51:38; Lam 3:10; Ezek 22:25). Ironically, the other two places in the OT where "swift" and "strong" are parallel (Amos 2:14 uses a different Heb. word for "strong"—though the sentiment is much the same) may be applied to the tragic end of Saul and Jonathan: "The race is not to the swift/or the battle to the strong" (Eccl 9:11); "The swift cannot flee/nor the strong escape" (Jer 46:6).

**24** The central stanza of David's lament (vv.22–23) is flanked by the only two stanzas that mention Saul alone and by name (vv.21, 24). Verse 24 mirrors v.20: There David deplores the likelihood that the news of the Israelite defeat at Gilboa will spread throughout Philistia, causing the "daughters of the Philistines/uncircumcised" to "be glad/rejoice"; here David calls on the "daughters of Israel" to "weep" for Saul, as he and all his men had done (v.12). Weeping for/over a person (or a personified place) was a universal custom in ancient Israel (3:34; Job 30:25; Jer 22:10; 48:32; Ezek 27:31).

Although it is possible that the "daughters of Israel" in this case were professional mourners (cf. the "daughters of the nations" who chant a lament in Ezek 32:16; cf. also the professional "wailing women" of Jer 9:17 in the context of the command, "Teach your daughters how to wail," in Jer 9:20), the reference is probably rather to the wealthy women of the land since Saul is described as having lavished fine clothes and expensive jewelry on them. The rare word *ʿᵃḏānîm,* here translated "finery," occurs elsewhere in the OT only twice, in both cases used of food or drink ("delights," Ps 36:8; "delicacies," Jer 51:34). It was perhaps used in this verse because of its assonance with *ʿᵃḏî* ("ornament[s]"). Gevirtz observes ("David's Lament," p. 93) that "scarlet" and "ornaments of gold" are paralleled again in Jeremiah 4:30 ("jewels of gold"; cf. also Jer 2:32 for "jewelry" as a rendering of *ʿᵃḏî*). The Hebrew words for "scarlet" and "garments/clothes" are found in close association also in the poem concerning the wife of noble character that concludes the Book of Proverbs (cf. Prov 31:21–22). The literary artistry in the MT of the last two lines of v.24 is commented on by Shea, who points out that "the verb for 'clothe' occurs at the beginning of the first colon, and the noun for 'clothes' appears at the end of the second" ("Chiasmus and the Structure of David's Lament," p. 18).

**25–26** Verses 25–26, which are the only two verses in which Jonathan appears alone by name, combine to form a stanza. Verse 25 reflects v.19 (where Jonathan is called "the gazelle"; see comment there). "How the mighty have fallen" is a verbatim echo of v.19 and at first gives the impression that the lament concludes at this point. The addition of "in battle," however, signals the possibility that v.25 is a false ending, a possibility that is confirmed as the poem continues. Verse 25 is best described as a false/fake coda that David uses to heap further praise on his friend Jonathan. Indeed, "the separate treatment of Jonathan in a fake coda subtly shows David's preference for him [over Saul]" (Zapf, "How Are the Mighty Fallen!" p. 121). The two lines of v.25 reverse the elements of v.19, its mirror image. As in v.19, so also in v.25, "your heights" refers to Israel's heights on the slopes of Mount Gilboa.

The relatively common idiom *ṣar lᵉ-* ("to be in distress"; cf. 1 Sam 13:6; lit., "it is distressing to/for") occurs only twice in 2 Samuel, both times on the lips of David (1:26 ["I grieve"]; 24:14). Its placement in the first and last chapters serves as a kind of *inclusio* that highlights the lament theme with which the book begins and ends. With respect to the structure of v.26 itself, Shea observes that in the MT "the suffixed preposition *lî* . . . occurs in first position ['I'] in the first colon, in second position ['to me'] in the second colon, in third position ['for me'] in the third colon, and it does not appear at all in the fourth colon. This distribution appears to be more by design than by accident" ("Chiasmus and the Structure of David's Lament," p. 20).

David's grief in v.26 is for Jonathan, his "brother"—not in the sense of "brother-in-law" (a true enough description; cf. 1 Sam 18:27 and comment) but of "treaty/covenant brother" (as in Num 20:14; 1 Kings 9:12–13; 20:32–33; for Akkadian examples, cf.

CAD, 1.1.200–201). David's further statement that Jonathan's "love" for him was "more wonderful than that of women," although occasionally (and perversely) understood in a homosexual sense, should rather be understood to have covenantal connotations, "love" in such contexts meaning "covenantal/political loyalty" (see comment on 1 Sam 18:1–4; cf. also Robert North, "Social Dynamics From Saul to Jehu," *Biblical Theology Bulletin* 12, 4 [1982]: 112). Indeed, the Hebrew word for "love" is translated "friendship" in a similar context (Ps 109:4–5).

The Hebrew roots underlying the words "dear" and "love" in v.26 are repeated from v.23 but in reverse order ("loved and gracious"). "The first word bespeaks physical attraction, a trait [Jonathan] shared with David himself (cf. I Sam. 16:12). The second word expresses an elemental devotion, a devotion he shared distinctively with David. Taken together the two words articulate a peculiar and precious bonding with David" (Brueggemann, *First and Second Samuel*, pp. 216–17). Since *n'm* ("gracious," "dear," "pleasant," "beloved") does not occur in 1 Samuel 16:12, Brueggemann might better have called attention to 2 Samuel 23:1, where David is described as Israel's "beloved" (*n*[e]*'îm*) singer (see NIV mg. in loc.).

**27** Just as Jonathan is hidden in a metaphor ("the gazelle") in the first line of David's lament (see v.19 and comment), so also Saul and Jonathan are hidden in a metaphor ("the weapons of war"; see comment on 1 Sam 8:12; cf. also Gevirtz, "David's Lament," p. 95) in its last line (v.27). The first and last lines (highlighting respectively the slaying of Jonathan and the perishing of Saul and Jonathan) not only support but also frame the *inclusio*—"How the mighty have fallen!"—which is the theme of the entire poem (cf. also v.25).

"The artful execution of this work serves as a fitting tribute both to its esteemed author and to those whom he commemorated by composing it" (Shea, "Chiasmus and the Structure of David's Lament," p. 25). In addition, the lament of David for Saul and Jonathan is characterized by both passion and restraint. While giving full vent to his feelings upon hearing the report of their death, David displays no bitterness toward his mortal enemy Saul. As Holladay remarks: "The judgment of T.H. Robinson is certainly justified: 'We know nothing of David which presents him in a better light'" ("Form and Word-Play in David's Lament," p. 189).

Carlson (p. 48) rightly calls attention to the similarity between v.18, where David orders that the men of Judah be "taught" his lament for Saul and Jonathan, and Deuteronomy 31:19 (cf. also 31:22), where the Lord commands Moses to write down a song (Deut 32:1–43) and "teach" it to the Israelites. Apparently the epic hymns of Israel's history were intended to be taught and applied from generation to generation. David's lament may well have been a favorite, if 1 Maccabees 9:21 is a reliable indication. There we read that the lamentation for the slain Judas Maccabeus, leader of the Jewish rebellion against their Seleucid overlords, began with these words: "How the mighty has fallen!"

## Notes

---

**18** Among the best known English "translations" of an allegedly genuine Hebrew "Book of Jashar" is *The Book of Jasher* (the KJV spelling of the word) by Jacob Ilive (Bristol: Philip

Rose, 1829), originally published in London in 1751. Ilive claimed that Alcuin, abbot of Canterbury, had found the Hebrew text in Gazna, Persia, and had then translated it into English. That Ilive—a known plagiarist and opportunist—himself wrote the book out of whole cloth, however, is clear from the patent absurdity of its contents. The text of the Hebrew "Book of Jashar" has apparently been irretrievably lost.

**21** For the interruption caused by ־בּ (*b-*) in the construct phrase הָרֵי בַגִּלְבֹּעַ (*hārê baggilbōaʿ*, "the mountains of Gilboa"), a not uncommon phenomenon in the OT, see also 10:9: בְּחוּרֵי בְיִשְׂרָאֵל (*beḥûrê byiśrāʾēl*, "the best troops in Israel").

Mitchell Dahood translates the first three lines of v.21 as follows:

O mountains of Gilboa,
  no dew and no rain upon you,
O upland fields!

("Hebrew-Ugaritic Lexicography X," *Biblica* 53, 3 [1972]: 398; cf. also Freedman, "The Refrain in David's Lament," pp. 121–22; Jan P. Fokkelman, "שדי תרומת in II Sam 1:21a—A Non-Existent Crux," ZAW 91, 2 [1979]: 290–93; Zapf, "How Are the Mighty Fallen!" pp. 108, 118; Shea, "Chiasmus and the Structure of David's Lament," p. 15). תְּרוּמָה (*terûmāh*, "offering," "contribution") is almost always found elsewhere in sacral contexts (cf. BDB, p. 929, for a complete list of passages), the only apparent exception being Prov 29:4 ("[greedy for] bribes"). In this otherwise thoroughly secular lament, therefore, it seems best to assume that *terûmāh* (from רום [*rûm*, "to be high"]) at one time had a wider semantic range and to understand וּשְׂדֵי תְרוּמֹת (*ûśedê terûmōt*) as "O [vocative use of the conjunction; for details cf. Dahood, 'Hebrew-Ugaritic Lexicography X,' p. 398] fields of heights!" (cf. the cognate expression מְרוֹמֵי שָׂדֶה (*merômê śādeh*, "the heights of the field," in the similar battle context of Judg 5:18) parallel to "O mountains of Gilboa." Fokkelman defends the parallelism on the basis of the overall chiastic structure of v.21:

O mountains of Gilboa,
  no dew
  and no rain on you,
O high fields!

For there was defiled [כִּי שָׁם נִגְעַל (*kî šām nigʿal*)]
  the shield of the mighty,
  the shield of Saul—
no longer rubbed with oil [בְּלִי מָשִׁיחַ בַּשָּׁמֶן (*belî māšîaḥ baššāmen*)].

Fokkelman observes: "In v.21b the alliteration *šam ni- . . . šamen* contributes to the chiasmus" ("שדי תרומת in II Sam 1:21a," p. 291).

Despite the valiant efforts of T.L. Fenton to salvage it ("Comparative Evidence in Textual Study: *M. Dahood on 2 Sam. i 21 and CTA 19 [1 Aqht], I, 44–45*," VetTest 29, 2 [1979]: 162–70), H.L. Ginsberg's celebrated emendation of וּשְׂדֵי תְרוּמֹת (*ûśedê terûmōt*) on the basis of its supposed Ugaritic exemplar must be given up. Rendering Ugaritic *bl ṭl bl rbb bl šrʿ thmtm* as "No dew, no rain; no welling-up of the deep," he proposed reading the MT *ʾl-ṭl wʾl-mṭr wśdy trwmt* similarly, assuming transcriptional error in the last two words ("A Ugaritic Parallel to 2 Sam 1:21," JBL 57 [1938]: 209–13; "Ugaritic Studies and the Bible," BA 8, 2 [1945]: 56–57; ANET, p. 153 n. 34). The emendation was summarily adopted by, among others, the RSV and numerous commentators (cf. Holladay, "Form and Word-Play in David's Lament," pp. 170–72; Gevirtz, "David's Lament," pp. 85–86). Since שרע [*šrʿ*] is not sufficiently similar graphically to שדי [*śdy*], however, Robert Gordis invented a new Hebrew word (שְׁדִי [*šedi*]); claimed it to have cognates in Arabic, Syriac, and Aramaic; and gave it the meaning "outpouring" ("The Biblical Root *ŠDY-ŠD:* Notes on 2 Sam. i. 21; Jer. xviii. 14; Ps. xci. 6; Job v. 21," JTS 41, 1 [1940]: 36). But the supposed parallel between the Ugaritic and OT texts breaks down syntactically as well: Ugaritic *bl . . . bl . . . bl* is quite different from the MT's *ʾl . . . wʾl . . . w-*, in which the last *w-* would surely be followed by *ʾl* if "nor" were intended. In any event, few translations and commentators agree with Ginsburg today; the NRSV, e.g., renders "bounteous fields" (cf. also Walter Harrelson, "Recent Discoveries and Bible Translation," *Religious Education* 85, 2 [Spring 1990]: 192–93; cf. similarly Gonzálo Báez-Camargo, "Biblical Archaeology Helps the Translator," *The Bible Translator* 31, 3 [1980]: 319—although he vacillates between other options as well).

Uncertainty as to whether to read מָשִׁיחַ (*māšîᵃḥ*) with most MT MSS or מָשׁוּחַ (*māšûᵃḥ*) with about twenty MSS should probably be decided in favor of the latter. Although both words are passive participles of the verb meaning "anoint," the first is used again and again in the books of Samuel to refer to the "anointed" leader of the Lord's people (cf. 1 Sam 2:10, 35; 12:3, 5; 24:6, 10; 26:9, 11, 16, 23; 2 Sam 1:14, 16; 19:21; 22:51; 23:1). The latter form, differing slightly from the former, would thus heighten the grisly wordplay in the verse: Saul, anointed with oil at the beginning of his reign (cf. 1 Sam 10:1), has now at the end of his reign lost his shield, "no longer rubbed with oil." In addition, as Holladay observes ("Form and Word-Play in David's Lament," p. 175), שָׁאוּל (*šā'ûl*, "Saul") and *māšûᵃḥ* share the same vowel pattern and thus display assonance.

**22** Holladay (ibid., p. 178) calls attention to "the most remarkable assonantal symmetry of the whole verse": *ḥl* in the last word of line one (חללים [*ḥllym*, "slain"]), *ḥlb* in the first word of line two ("flesh"), *ḥr* in the last word of line three (אחור ['*ḥwr*, "back"]), and *ḥrb* in the first word of line four ("sword").

**24** Although referring to the same object ("daughters of Israel"), הַמַּלְבִּשְׁכֶם (*hammalbišḵem*, "who clothed you") and לְבוּשְׁכֶן (*lᵉḇûšḵen*, "your garments") display different pronominal suffixes (second person masc. pl. and fem. pl. respectively). Some Hebrew MSS level the two words out in one direction, others in another (cf. BHS). But the masculine suffixed pronoun is often used for a feminine antecedent, and in fact the same alternation between masculine and feminine suffixes in v.24 is attested in Isa 3:16–17 (with "daughters" as the antecedent): "The women [lit., 'daughters'] of Zion are haughty, . . . with ornaments jingling on their [masc. pl.] ankles. Therefore the LORD will bring sores on the heads of the women [lit., 'daughters'] of Zion; the LORD will make their [fem. pl.] scalps bald."

**26** The anomalous form נִפְלְאַתָה (*nip̱lᵉ'aṯāh*, "was wonderful") has occasioned considerable discussion. If it was intended as a feminine singular participle, we would have expected נִפְלֵאת (*nip̱lē'ṯ*), as in Deut 30:11. If, however, it was intended as a third-person feminine perfect (as seems more likely), we would have expected נִפְלְאָה (*nip̱lᵉ'āh*) or, as in Ps 118:23, נִפְלָאת (*nip̱lā'ṯ*). But, as Holladay observes, "We may have here an archaic form because of the assonance with *'ahᵃbāṯᵉkā* which follows; so it is best to leave the vocalization as the MT gives it" ("Form and Word-Play in David's Lament," p. 183).

---

## 3. *David anointed king over Judah*

### 2:1–7

1 In the course of time, David inquired of the LORD. "Shall I go up to
one of the towns of Judah?" he asked.
The LORD said, "Go up."
David asked, "Where shall I go?"
"To Hebron," the LORD answered.
2 So David went up there with his two wives, Ahinoam of Jezreel and
Abigail, the widow of Nabal of Carmel. 3 David also took the men who
were with him, each with his family, and they settled in Hebron and its
towns. 4 Then the men of Judah came to Hebron and there they anointed
David king over the house of Judah.
When David was told that it was the men of Jabesh Gilead who had
buried Saul, 5 he sent messengers to the men of Jabesh Gilead to say to
them, "The LORD bless you for showing this kindness to Saul your
master by burying him. 6 May the LORD now show you kindness and

**faithfulness, and I too will show you the same favor because you have done this. 7 Now then, be strong and brave, for Saul your master is dead, and the house of Judah has anointed me king over them."**

In many respects chapters 2–8 form

> the crux of the book. Here the fertility motif reaches a peak. The thesis of the author—that Israel is blessed with fertility when the nation (and the epitome of the nation, the king) is following the covenant—is demonstrated in these chapters. The king, the ark (representing the presence of God and the Word of God, the covenant), and fertility are all intertwined in a beautifully artistic way. (John A. Martin, p. 37)

Nestled in the heart of the literary unit that describes David's triumph over the remnant of Saul's house (1:1–3:5), 2:1–7 divides most naturally into two roughly equal sections (vv.1–4a, 4b–7), each of which ends with a statement declaring that the house of Judah has anointed David to be king over them (vv.4a, 7b; cf. similarly Carlson, p. 49).

**1–4a** King Saul now dead and buried, the time has come for the private anointing of David (1 Sam 16:13) to be reprised in public (see Notes on v.1). Saul's death made it possible for David and his men to move about more freely; so he decides to leave Ziklag (1:1)—but not without seeking divine guidance. Unlike Saul (cf. 1 Chron 10:14; see comment on 1 Sam 28:6), David "inquired of the LORD" (v.1), doubtless by asking his friend Abiathar the priest to consult the Urim and Thummim stored in the ephod that he had brought with him from Nob (1 Sam 22:20; 23:6; see comment on 1 Sam 14:36, 40–42; 23:2). This is not the first time that David had inquired of God in so formal a way (cf. 1 Sam 23:1–4, 9–12; 30:7–8), nor would it be his last (cf. 5:19, 23–24).

David wants to know whether he should "go up" (v.1) to one of the towns in the hill country of Judah (the Heb. verb, thematic of the section, appears a total of five times in vv.1–3: "go up" [bis], "go," v.1; "went up," v.2; "took" [lit., "caused to go up"], v.3). By means of the sacred lots, the Lord responds affirmatively. When David then asks for a more precise destination, the lots (through the process of elimination; see comment on 1 Sam 10:20–21) pinpoint Hebron as the place. Located twenty-seven miles northeast of Ziklag, Hebron was the most important city David sent plunder to after defeating the Amalekites (see 1 Sam 30:31 and comment) and looms large in chapters 2–5. Obedient to the divine command, David severs his ties with Philistine Ziklag (see comment on 1 Sam 27:6) and, with his two wives Ahinoam and Abigail (27:3; 30:5; see comment on 1 Sam 25:3, 43), moves to Judahite Hebron (v.2). He also takes with him the army of men who have rallied to his leadership (see 1 Sam 22:2 and comment), and they together with their families settle in Hebron and its nearby villages (v.3). The nucleus of his future government now his loyal neighbors, David is publicly anointed by the "men of Judah" (perhaps the elders; cf. 5:3; cf. also 1 Sam 30:26) as king over the "house of Judah" (v.4; cf. also vv.7, 10–11), the people of Judah as a whole ("house" in the sense of "family," "community"; see comment on 1:12). David's elevation to kingship, however, though administered by men, is fundamentally due to divine anointing (5:3, 12; 12:7; 1 Sam 15:17; see comment on 1 Sam 15:1; 16:13).

**4b–7** Word eventually reaches David that the men of Jabesh Gilead (see comment on 1 Sam 11:1) had given Saul a decent burial (v.4; 1 Sam 31:11–13). Since Jabesh is an Israelite (not Judahite) town and therefore presumably still loyal to Saul's house (in speaking to the Jabeshites, David twice refers to "Saul your master" [vv.5, 7]), David realizes that he must try to win them over to his side. He therefore sends messengers to them with overtures of peace and friendship, an approach that stands in sharp contrast to the tactics used by David's men in the rest of the chapter. Brueggemann's summary is apropos: "The much later crisis of I Kings 12 suggests that the Davidic hold on the north is never deeply established. In our chapter we are given two episodes of David's attentiveness to the north. One (vv.4b–7) is a peaceable act of friendship. The other (vv.8–32) is an act of confrontation and hostility" (*First and Second Samuel,* p. 220).

Although "The LORD bless you" was a traditional form of greeting (see comment on 1 Sam 15:13), it here further "expresses appreciation and praise for the outstanding loyalty of the Jabesh-Gileadites to their dead king" (Anderson, p. 29). The Jabeshites are commended for "showing kindness" (in the sense of demonstrating loyalty; cf. 3:8, where "I am loyal" translates the same Heb. idiom) to Saul (v.5). "Kindness" (*ḥesed̲;* see comment on 1 Sam 20:8, 14–15) of this sort ultimately derives from God, as David himself recognizes (cf. 9:1, 3, 7; cf. also 1 Kings 3:6). Indeed, he invokes the Lord's "kindness and faithfulness" on the Jabeshites (v.6; cf. 15:20; Gen 32:10; cf. esp. Exod 34:6, where "love and faithfulness" [rendering the same Heb. phrase] are part of the very nature of God himself).

"Love/kindness and faithfulness" are part and parcel of all genuine covenant relationships, and David stresses his eagerness (the "I" in v.6 is emphatic) to transfer the Jabeshites' covenant loyalty from Saul to himself. He offers to "show you the same favor" (*'eʿᵉśeh 'ittᵉk̲em haṭṭôb̲āh hazzō't̲,* lit., "do with you this good [thing]") that Saul had shown them. The "favor/good thing" in this case is a "treaty of friendship" (cf. Delbert R. Hillers, "A Note on Some Treaty Terminology in the Old Testament," BASOR 176 [1964]: 47; cf. Deut 23:6; see also comment on 1 Sam 25:30), since *ʿāśāh ṭôb̲ā* ("do [a] good [thing]") here corresponds to Akkadian *ṭābūta epēšu* and Sefire *ʿbd ṭbt'* with the same meaning (for which cf. W.L. Moran, "A Note on the Treaty Terminology of the Sefire Stelas," JNES 22 [1963]: 173–76; for additional bibliography, cf. esp. Edelman, "Saul's Rescue," p. 202 n. 30). This understanding obviously has implications for the proper exegesis of the phrase rendered "promised these good things" in 7:28 (see comment there).

Just as in v.6 David had said that "I" (emphatic) would make the same treaty of friendship with the Jabeshites that Saul had made with them, so also in v.7 he reminds them that Saul their master is now dead and that the house of Judah has anointed "me" (emphatic) king. "David wishes to take Saul's place as suzerain of Jabesh-Gilead. Since treaties did not automatically continue in force when a new king took the throne, it was necessary for David actively to seek a renewal of the pact" (Hillers, "Treaty Terminology," p. 47). David's enthusiasm is also demonstrated in his repeated use of "now [then]" in vv.6–7 (in the MT, the word occurs at the beginning of both verses).

David concludes his offer to enter into a covenant relationship with the Jabeshites by encouraging them to "be strong and brave" (v.7). The Hebrew phrase rendered "be strong" means literally "let your hands be strong" (as in Zech 8:9, 13; cf. also 2 Sam 16:21), an idiom that often means "be encouraged" (cf. Judg 7:11). "Be brave" is literally "become sons of power/might" (cf. also 13:28; in 1 Sam 18:17 the same

Heb. phrase is translated "serve . . . bravely"), the term "son of might" implying "one characterized by might"—that is, a "brave man/soldier" (17:10; 1 Sam 14:52). With Saul dead and David anointed king over Judah, David invites the Jabeshites to enter into a mutual defense treaty with him. But there is more than one fly in the ointment, as the rest of the chapter clearly suggests.

## Notes

---

1 וַיְהִי אַחֲרֵי־כֵן (*wayehî 'aḥarê-ḵēn*, lit., "And it was after this"; cf. 2 Chron 20:1), rendered by NIV as "In the course of time," recurs in 8:1; 10:1; 13:1; and, somewhat unexpectedly, 21:18. With the exception of 1 Sam 24:5 ("Afterward"), all other instances of the formula *wyhy 'ḥry-kn* in the OT, including those in 2 Samuel, "appear at the beginning of episodes in the accounts of the reign of a particular individual. . . . The formula's function is controlled, not by the genre of the material it introduces, but rather by the redactor's intention, positing a sequence of events internal to a reign" (Bailey, *David in Love and War*, pp. 56–57).

---

## 4. *War between Saul's house and David's house*

### 2:8–3:1

8 Meanwhile, Abner son of Ner, the commander of Saul's army, had
taken Ish-Bosheth son of Saul and brought him over to Mahanaim. 9 He
made him king over Gilead, Ashuri and Jezreel, and also over Ephraim,
Benjamin and all Israel.
10 Ish-Bosheth son of Saul was forty years old when he became king
over Israel, and he reigned two years. The house of Judah, however,
followed David. 11 The length of time David was king in Hebron over the
house of Judah was seven years and six months.
12 Abner son of Ner, together with the men of Ish-Bosheth son of Saul,
left Mahanaim and went to Gibeon. 13 Joab son of Zeruiah and David's
men went out and met them at the pool of Gibeon. One group sat down
on one side of the pool and one group on the other side.
14 Then Abner said to Joab, "Let's have some of the young men get up
and fight hand to hand in front of us."
"All right, let them do it," Joab said.
15 So they stood up and were counted off—twelve men for Benjamin
and Ish-Bosheth son of Saul, and twelve for David. 16 Then each man
grabbed his opponent by the head and thrust his dagger into his
opponent's side, and they fell down together. So that place in Gibeon
was called Helkath Hazzurim.
17 The battle that day was very fierce, and Abner and the men of Israel
were defeated by David's men.
18 The three sons of Zeruiah were there: Joab, Abishai and Asahel.
Now Asahel was as fleet-footed as a wild gazelle. 19 He chased Abner,
turning neither to the right nor to the left as he pursued him. 20 Abner
looked behind him and asked, "Is that you, Asahel?"
"It is," he answered.
21 Then Abner said to him, "Turn aside to the right or to the left; take
on one of the young men and strip him of his weapons." But Asahel
would not stop chasing him.

22 Again Abner warned Asahel, "Stop chasing me! Why should I strike
you down? How could I look your brother Joab in the face?"
23 But Asahel refused to give up the pursuit; so Abner thrust the butt of
his spear into Asahel's stomach, and the spear came out through his
back. He fell there and died on the spot. And every man stopped when
he came to the place where Asahel had fallen and died.
24 But Joab and Abishai pursued Abner, and as the sun was setting,
they came to the hill of Ammah, near Giah on the way to the wasteland
of Gibeon. 25 Then the men of Benjamin rallied behind Abner. They
formed themselves into a group and took their stand on top of a hill.
26 Abner called out to Joab, "Must the sword devour forever? Don't
you realize that this will end in bitterness? How long before you order
your men to stop pursuing their brothers?"
27 Joab answered, "As surely as God lives, if you had not spoken, the
men would have continued the pursuit of their brothers until morning."
28 So Joab blew the trumpet, and all the men came to a halt; they no
longer pursued Israel, nor did they fight anymore.
29 All that night Abner and his men marched through the Arabah. They
crossed the Jordan, continued through the whole Bithron and came to
Mahanaim.
30 Then Joab returned from pursuing Abner and assembled all his
men. Besides Asahel, nineteen of David's men were found missing.
31 But David's men had killed three hundred and sixty Benjamites who
were with Abner. 32 They took Asahel and buried him in his father's tomb
at Bethlehem. Then Joab and his men marched all night and arrived at
Hebron by daybreak.
3:1 The war between the house of Saul and the house of David lasted a
long time. David grew stronger and stronger, while the house of Saul
grew weaker and weaker.

Saul may be dead, but Saulide interests are very much alive. With the future of "all Israel" (v.9) at stake, it is understandable that there should be rival claimants for the tribal territories. Although the story of the struggle between Saul's house and David's house begins in 2:8 and does not end until 5:3, the main outlines are established in 2:8–32 and the inevitable outcome is summarized in 3:1. The literary structure of 2:8–32 is chiastic:

A. Ish-Bosheth is king in Mahanaim; David is king in Hebron (vv.8–11).
   B. Abner suggests that hostilities begin (vv.12–17).
      C. Abner kills Asahel (vv.18–23).
   B′. Abner suggests that hostilities cease (vv.24–28).
A′. Ish-Bosheth's men return to Mahanaim; David's men return to Hebron (vv.29–32).

**2:8–11** "Abner son of Ner, the commander of Saul's army" (v.8; cf. also 1 Sam 17:55; 26:5) and Saul's cousin (see comment on 1 Sam 14:50), had either avoided or escaped from the battle on Mount Gilboa that had resulted in the death of "Saul and his three sons" (1 Sam 31:8). Still ostensibly loyal to the dead king, Abner had taken a fourth son, Ish-Bosheth, and "brought him over" (eastward across the Jordan; cf. v.29, where the same Heb. verb is translated "crossed") to Mahanaim ("Two Camps"; see Gen 32:2 and NIV mg.), far away from the continuing Philistine threat. Located just north of the Jabbok River in the tribal territory of Gad (Josh 13:26, 30; 21:38), ancient Mahanaim is probably the modern Tell edh-Dhahab el-Gharbi about seven miles east of the Jordan. Later in David's reign, Mahanaim would serve as a place of refuge for him during the rebellion of his son Absalom (17:24, 27; 19:32; 1 Kings 2:8).

Ish-Bosheth ("Man of Shame"), mentioned only in chapters 2–4, is perhaps to be identified with Ishvi in 1 Samuel 14:49 (see comment there). Not killed in Saul's last battle (cf. 1 Sam 31:2), he may have been something of a coward. In any event, "it is Abner, not Ishbosheth, who holds the real power" (Brueggemann, *First and Second Samuel*, p. 221). Scribal tradition often substituted the word *bōšeṯ* ("shame") for the hated name of the Canaanite god Baal (cf. Jer 3:24; 11:13 ["shameful god(s)"]; Hos 9:10 ["shameful idol"]). Thus Ish-Bosheth's real name was E/Ish-Baal, "Man of Baal" (cf. 1 Chron 8:33; 9:39 and NIV mg.), Mephibosheth's (4:4) was Merib-Baal (1 Chron 8:34; 9:40 and NIV mg.), and Jerub-Besheth's was Jerub-Baal (11:21 and NIV mg.; cf. also Judg 6:32 and NIV mg.). Since *ba'al* is also a common noun meaning "lord," "owner," or "master" and could therefore be used occasionally in reference to the one true God (cf. Hos 2:16 and NIV mg.), it is possible that Saul did not intend to honor the Canaanite god Baal when he named his son Ish-Baal (which would mean "The Man of the Lord")—especially since the name of his firstborn son Jonathan means "The LORD Has Given." The scribes who transmitted the Hebrew Scriptures, however, alert to the dangers of ambiguity in such names, provided a *caveat lector* in the instances noted above.

Although David became king over "the house of Judah" by popular anointing (v.4), Abner singlehandedly makes Ish-Bosheth king over "all Israel" (v.9), thus demonstrating that he is the real power behind the throne of Israel now that Saul is dead. The first three names in v.9 are of regions, each introduced by the preposition *'el* ("to," "over") and the last three are of tribal territories, each introduced by the preposition *'al* ("upon," "over"). Gilead, the area east of the Jordan between the southern end of the Sea of Galilee and the northern end of the Dead Sea, included the town of Jabesh Gilead (v.4), which was located thirteen miles north of Mahanaim (v.8)—indicating something of the difficulty David faced in attempting to win the Jabeshites over to his side. The location of Ashuri (mentioned only here) remains unknown and is hardly the tribal territory of Asher (cf. NIV mg.), since tribal names are restricted to the last triad in the verse (KD, p. 295, declares that the reading "Ashuri[tes]" is "decidedly faulty" and is content to affirm that "the true name cannot be discovered"; cf. similarly S.R. Driver, *Notes on the Books of Samuel*, p. 241). Jezreel is the extensive valley that separates the hill country of Manasseh from that of Galilee and is the region in which the town of Jezreel was located (cf. 4:4; see also comment on 1 Sam 29:1).

The territories of Ephraim and Benjamin are probably selected to represent those areas within Israel that could be reasonably considered to have been under Saul's control ("all [emphatic] Israel" [v.9] is an obvious hyperbole for the northern tribes; cf. similarly 4:1). Ephraim was the largest tribal territory in the north, and Benjamin (cf. also vv.15, 25, 31) was the homeland of Saul (1 Sam 9:1–2). A.D.H. Mayes makes the helpful observation that

> the Song of Deborah [Judges 5] and the event it commemorates presuppose a national consciousness, and self-identification as the people of Yahweh, which could have appeared surely not long before the Israelite monarchy under Saul. The area over which Saul reigned, described in 2 Sam. 2.9, is almost exactly that from which contingents came, or were expected to come, to the help of Deborah and Barak against Sisera. (*Judges*, Old Testament Guides [Sheffield: JSOT, 1985], p. 87)

It is this realm that Ish-Bosheth son of Saul now inherits—with the ambitious Abner son of Ner pulling the strings behind the scenes.

The formal notice summarizing the reign of Ish-Bosheth (v.10) follows the typical pattern of the regnal formula (cf. 1 Kings 14:21; see also comment on 1 Sam 13:1) by recording (1) his age when he became king and (2) the length of his reign. After the murder of Ish-Bosheth (ch. 4), the regnal formula is reserved exclusively for southern kings (beginning with David, 5:4)—and, indeed, even v.10, written ostensibly to honor Ish-Bosheth, ends as follows: "The house of Judah, however, followed David." Since David is the man after God's own heart (see comment on 1 Sam 13:14), following David implies following the Lord (see esp. comment on 1 Sam 12:14). "Followed" (v.10) renders *hāyû 'aḥ^a^rê*, literally "were/went after." It is therefore sadly ironic that when the united kingdom was torn in two after the death of David's son Solomon and when Jeroboam was made king over "all Israel" (the northern tribes), only the tribe of Judah "remained loyal to" (*hāyāh 'aḥ^a^rê*) the house of David (1 Kings 12:20).

It is conceivable that "the distinctive concepts of 'Judah and Israel' evolved during David's kingdom in Hebron, and after a period of reunification these entities were allowed to live on in the United Monarchy, though without an official division" (Zechariah Kallai, "Judah and Israel—A Study in Israelite Historiography," IEJ 28, 4 [1978]: 257). In any event, during the coexistence of Ish-Bosheth's and David's reigns "Israel" is referred to several times in contrast/opposition to "Judah" (2:10–11, 17, 28; 3:8, 10, 12, 17–19, 21, 37–38; 4:1). Since David became king of Israel shortly after Ish-Bosheth's death (4:12–5:3), and since David's reign in Hebron was more than five years longer than Ish-Bosheth's in Mahanaim (2:10–11; cf. also 5:5), it must have been several years after Saul's death before Ish-Bosheth had gained enough support to become king over the northern tribes. Thus Ish-Bosheth's two-year reign would have coincided with the last two years of David's seven-and-one-half-year reign over Judah.

**12–17** It is only to be expected that David and Ish-Bosheth would each attempt to seize the other's kingdom. Full-scale warfare was not the only way to accomplish such a goal, however. "A general engagement of troops could . . . be avoided by the substitution of a contest of teams of champions. It appears that such was the case with the two teams of twelve men each who fought for David and Ishbaal at the pool of Gibeon" (Hoffner, "A Hittite Analogue," p. 221; cf. also F. Charles Fensham, "The Battle Between the Men of Joab and Abner as a Possible Ordeal by Battle?" VetTest 20, 3 [1970]: 356–57).

During the days of Joshua, Gibeon (v.12) "was an important city, like one of the royal cities" (Josh 10:2). Allotted to the tribe of Benjamin (Josh 18:21, 25), the ancient site is today known as el-Jib (an abbreviation that reflects the original name), six miles northwest of Jerusalem. Although Gibeon was located in Saulide territory, the fact that the combat between the Israelites and the Judahites took place there "might not be accidental, because from another part of the book of Samuel it is clear that Saul during his life acted treacherously to the Gibeonites by breaking the treaty in Jos. ix (cf. 2 Sam. xxi). It is thus to be expected that the Gibeonites should side with David and not with the Saulites" (ibid., p. 357). Once again the hand of God can be seen working on David's behalf.

So Saul's cousin Abner, together with Ish-Bosheth's men (v.12), meet David's nephew Joab (see comment on 1 Sam 26:6), together with David's men, at the "pool of

Gibeon" (v.13), apparently a well-know site (perhaps the same as the "great pool in Gibeon" of Jer 41:12). It is often identified with the round, rock-cut pool excavated on the northeast side of el-Jib in 1956 by an archaeological expedition directed by James B. Pritchard. The pool is a cylindrical shaft thirty-seven feet in diameter and thirty-five feet deep. Its five-feet-wide spiral stairway, which winds downward around the inside wall of the pool in a clockwise direction, continues below the floor level to an additional depth of forty-five feet. "From the fill of the pool came two jar handles bearing the name 'Gibeon' inscribed in good Hebrew script. . . . This discovery would seem to make the identification of the site of el-Jib with the biblical Gibeon certain" (James B. Pritchard, "The Water System at Gibeon," BA 19, 4 [1956]: 70; for additional details, cf. id., "Industry and Trade at Biblical Gibeon," BA 23, 1 [1960]: 23–24; id., *Gibeon, Where the Sun Stood Still: The Discovery of the Biblical City* [Princeton: Princeton University Press, 1962], pp. 64–74).

Ish-Bosheth's men and David's men sit down on opposite sides of the pool of Gibeon, probably facing each other (v.13). Abner makes a proposal, which Joab accepts, that some of the young men in one group "fight hand to hand" with some in the other (the verb *śiḥaq*, "play, make sport of," is in this case a euphemistic technical term for hand-to-hand combat; cf. Y. Sukenik, "Let the Young Men, I Pray Thee, Arise and Play Before Us," *Journal of the Palestine Oriental Society* 21 [1948]: 110–16; cf. also Brueggemann, *First and Second Samuel*, p. 222). Twelve from each group are "counted off" (v.15, *ya'aḇrû b<sup>e</sup>mispār*, lit., "they pass/cross over by number," an idiom drawn from the practice of making animals pass under a shepherd's rod or hand as they are being counted; cf. Lev 27:32; Jer 33:13; Ezek 20:37; cf. similarly Exod 30:13–14; 38:26). The number twelve here doubtless stands for the twelve tribes of "all Israel" (v.9), whose fate hangs in the balance: "12 of the men of Ishbosheth fought 12 of the men of David to decide the succession to the throne" (Segal, "Numerals," p. 7).

The initial skirmish ends quickly (v.16). Each man "grabbed" (forcibly; cf. 13:11; 1 Sam 17:35 ["seized"]) his opponent by the head, thrusting a dagger into his side. Just as all the men had met at the pool "together" (v.12 [untr. in NIV]), so also all the men now fall down "together" (v.16). From that day forward the site of the mutual massacre was called Helkath Hazzurim, which means either "Field of Daggers" (from *ṣûr/ṣōr*, "rock," "flint"; cf. Exod 4:25; Josh 5:2–3; Ps 89:43 ["edge (of his sword)"]; Ezek 3:9; the word for "dagger" in v.16 is *ḥereḇ*, usually translated "sword" as in Ps 89:43; its plural is rendered "knives" in Josh 5:2–3) or "Field of Hostilities" (from *ṣrr*, "be hostile toward"; cf. NIV mg.). In this case "the context ended in a draw with each man slaying his opponent [v.16], so that a general engagement ensued [v.17]" (Hoffner, "A Hittite Analogue," p. 221). Thus v.17, the middle verse in the chapter, not only looks backward to the standoff in vv.12–16 but also—and supremely—looks forward to the resounding defeat of the "men of Israel" (summarized in vv.30–31). "The battle . . . was very fierce" (v.17) is eerily reminiscent of "The fighting grew fierce" (1 Sam 31:3)—fighting that led to the defeat and death of Saul king of Israel.

In an ancient Hittite account of representative combat, the gods are described as having given "the verdict by an ordeal on the guilty party. . . . Although nowhere in the narrative of 2 Sam. ii 12ff." is the Lord "*expressis verbis* called in as Judge to decide the ordeal by battle, the role of the Lord who has chosen David and rejected Saul is clearly discernable [*sic*] in the background" (Fensham, "The Battle Between the Men of Joab and Abner," p. 357).

**18–23** The word *'aḥ^a^rê* ("after," "behind," "rear part") occurs a total of fifteen times in chapter 2, usually left untranslated by the NIV in the interests of English idiom. In addition to its appearance in v.1 (see Notes in loc.) and v.10 (see comment there), it is found—remarkably—at least once in ten consecutive verses (vv.19–28) as well as in v.30. A particle implying pursuit, it thus gives unity and texture to the theme of chase that dominates vv.19–28: "chased [after]," "pursued [after]," v.19; "behind," v.20; "chasing [after]," v.22; "butt," "back," v.23; "pursued [after]," v.24; "behind," v.25; "pursuing [after]," v.26; "pursuit of [/after]," v.27; "pursued [after]," v.28 (cf. also "pursuing [after]" in v.30).

The "sons of Zeruiah" (v.18) are "the ruthless devotees of David who always smell blood (cf. I Sam. 26:6–9; II Sam. 3:39; 16:9)" (Brueggemann, *First and Second Samuel,* p. 222; cf. also 18:14; for additional details see Rosenberg, pp. 164–71). Of the three sons mentioned here, only Asahel ("God Has Made/Done") appears for the first time (see Notes on 1 Sam 26:6). Like Jonathan (see comment on 1:19), Asahel is compared to a gazelle (whether *Gazella dorcas,* with yellowish-brown fur, or *Gazella arabica,* with grey fur, is impossible to say), whose "only means of defence are its colour and the speed with which it can escape" (*Fauna and Flora of the Bible,* p. 34; cf. 1 Chron 12:8; Prov 6:5). Though "fleet-footed" (v.18; cf. Amos 2:15), Asahel's speed as a runner would eventually prove to be his undoing (cf. v.23).

The initial combat between Ish-Bosheth's men and David's men, which had ended in a draw (vv.12–16), now broadens and becomes more dangerous. Abner, not spoiling for a fight and eager to get out of harm's way, flees the scene of the massacre. Asahel, however, is determined to overtake and kill Abner, nothing deterring him ("turning neither to the right nor to the left," v.19). After identifying his pursuer to his own satisfaction (v.20), Abner tells Asahel to "turn aside to the right or to the left" (i.e., give up the chase, v.21). He advises him to appease his desire for vengeance in another—perhaps less deadly—way: "Take on" (lit., "seize," "grab," as in v.16) one of the young men fleeing from Gibeon and "strip him" (cf. similarly Judg 14:19) of his weapons. The single-minded Asahel, however, is adamant (v.21).

Abner then issues a final warning: Unless he stops chasing Abner, Asahel will be the one who dies (v.22). Why would he want Abner to strike him "down" (lit., "to the ground"; cf. 18:11)? And if Abner kills Asahel, how could he "look" Asahel's brother Joab "in the face"? The Hebrew idiom means literally "lift up one's face," sometimes "without shame" (Job 11:15), in this case probably without fear—and Abner's fear of Joab proves to be not unfounded (cf. 3:27, 30).

Asahel, however, refuses to listen. Continuing to run full speed ahead, he closes the gap between himself and Abner, and the latter suddenly turns to face his pursuer. Asahel's momentum hurls him onto the butt of the spear of Abner, who thrusts it through Asahel's "stomach" (v.23; cf. the similar fate of Abner himself [3:27], of Ish-Bosheth [4:6], and of Absalom's army commander Amasa ["belly," 20:10]), killing him on the spot. "Every man" who "stopped when he came" to the place where Asahel had died (v.23) does not refer to travelers or others who stop to pay their respects, as many commentators believe (e.g., Baldwin, Hertzberg), but to David's men, Asahel's pursuers, who stand transfixed in horror at the death of a fallen comrade (see Gordon, McCarter; cf. the similar situation in 20:12, where "everyone who came . . . stopped" renders the same Heb. phrase). If some "stop" (v.23; 20:12) because of fear or revulsion, others continue to "pursue" (v.24; 20:13) in order to right a wrong. The same Hebrew verb translated "stopped" in v.23 is rendered "came to a halt" in v.28, where it again refers to Joab's men.

Asahel, though dead because of his headlong pursuit of Abner, would be long remembered in Israel. He is listed first among the "Thirty," David's military elite (23:24 = 1 Chron 11:26). Commander of the fourth of David's army divisions, Asahel's untimely death early in David's reign made it necessary for his son to succeed him in that post (1 Chron 27:7). It would only be a matter of time, however, before Asahel's brother Joab would avenge his great loss (3:30).

**24–28** Although others may come to a halt—even if only momentarily—at the sight of their dead comrade, Joab and Abishai continue their pursuit of Abner (v.24). At sunset they (and presumably a contingent of troops with them, v.27) arrive at (and probably, to get a better view of the surrounding countryside, climb to the top of) the hill of Ammah near Giah (both of which are otherwise unmentioned; locations unknown) somewhere in the wasteland east of Gibeon. Confronting them, the Israelites (here called "men of Benjamin" [v.25; cf. also vv.9, 15, 31], probably because they were the largest contingent as well as because Benjamin was Saul's [and thus Ish-Bosheth's] tribal homeland) take their stand "on top of a [nearby] hill"—an ideal vantage point from which to direct or engage in battle if necessary (cf. Exod 17:9–10).

Just as Abner had earlier proposed that hostilities begin (v.14), so also—doubtless sensing the hopelessness of his situation—he now proposes that they cease (v.26). Across the valley between the two hills on which their respective troop contingents are deployed, Abner calls out to Joab: "Must the sword devour forever?" Brueggemann makes a helpful observation at this point:

> It is striking that the phrase, "sword devouring," is twice addressed to Joab. In the first usage, by Abner, the warning causes Joab to stop the killing. In the second usage (11:25), by David, the words are flippant and dismissive. The two uses of the phrase are realistic about the bloody dimensions of royal power. They mock Joab as the man at the center of the killing. (*First and Second Samuel*, p. 224)

The phrase itself may derive from the shape of the blades of swords used throughout much of the OT period (see comment on 1 Sam 22:19).

"How long" (v.26) commonly introduces questions implying a rebuke (see comment on 1 Sam 16:1; cf. also 1 Sam 1:14; Hos 8:5; Zech 1:12), and Abner uses it to good effect. He cleverly baits Joab by referring to the two groups of antagonists as "brothers"—and Joab bites by accepting the identification (v.27). He suggests that Joab's men "stop pursuing" Abner's—and the end result was that Joab "returned from pursuing" Abner (v.30; same Heb. expression). When brothers fight brothers, the result can only be "bitterness" (v.26) and shame (Obad 10).

Commentators differ on their understanding of Joab's response in v.27 (after the introductory oath formula, for which see comment on 1 Sam 14:39). Some connect Joab's reply to v.14 (cf. KD, p. 298: "'*If thou hadst not spoken* [*i.e.* challenged to single combat, ver. 14], *the people would have gone away in the morning, every one from his brother,*' *i.e.* there would have been no such fratricidal conflict at all"; cf. similarly first NIV footnote on v.27). But the NIV text (and that of the second footnote), in assuming that Joab is responding to Abner's words in the nearer context (v.26), is the more natural reading of the Hebrew original. The verb *na'ᵃlāh,* translated "gone away" by KD, is elsewhere rendered "took oneself away" in the sense of lifting a siege (Jer 37:5, 11 ["withdraw"]). Joab calls off the chase (v.28), and Abner's timely plea thus leads to results remarkably similar to those described in 1 Samuel 25:34.

Three times in 2 Samuel Joab blows the ram's-horn trumpet (v.28; 18:16; 20:22), and on each occasion his act signals the cessation of hostilities.

**29–32** Paralleling vv.8–11, which begin by bringing Ish-Bosheth to Mahanaim and end with David in Hebron, vv.29–32 begin by returning Abner's (= Ish-Bosheth's) men to Mahanaim and end by returning Joab's (= David's) men to Hebron. In each case the men march all night to reach their respective home bases (vv.29, 32). It was customary for armies to travel at night, probably to be as inconspicuous as possible (see comment on 1 Sam 31:12).

The Arabah (v.29; cf. also 4:7) refers here to the Jordan Valley between the Dead Sea and the Sea of Galilee. Marching eastward across the Jordan, Abner and his men continue through the Bithron (not mentioned elsewhere; location unknown) and arrive at Mahanaim, more than thirty miles from the wasteland east of Gibeon.

Including Asahel, a total of twenty of David's men are "missing" in action (v.30), presumably all dead. The body count of Ish-Bosheth's men, however, is "three hundred and sixty" (v.31). The eighteen-to-one ratio in favor of David demonstrates how terrible was the cost of Abner's arrogance (v.14) and how thoroughly "Abner and the men of Israel were defeated by David's men" (v.17).

Joab's men "took" (v.32, lit., "lifted up"; the same Heb. verb is used in 4:4 with the crippled Mephibosheth as its object) Asahel's body to Bethlehem, the hometown of David and his clan (1 Sam 20:6), where Asahel—Joab's brother and David's nephew (see comment on v.13)—would soon be given a proper burial in "his father's tomb." During much of ancient Israelite history, multiple burials in family tombs cut into the underlying rock of the slopes of hills were commonplace (cf. Robert E. Cooley, "Gathered to His People: A Study of a Dothan Family Tomb," in *The Living and Active Word of God: Studies in Honor of Samuel J. Schultz*, edd. Morris Inch and Ronald Youngblood [Winona Lake: Eisenbrauns, 1983], pp. 49–58). Having left the body of their fallen comrade in Bethlehem, Joab and his men continue on their way to Hebron, more than twenty miles southwest of the wasteland east of Gibeon.

**3:1** The first verse of chapter 3 serves as a summary of 2:8–32. Together with v.6 it also brackets the list of sons born to David while he was king in Hebron (vv.2–5). Though virtually unmentioned up to this point, at least in the sense of ruling dynasties, the "house of Saul" and the "house of David" (cf., however, comment on 1 Sam 20:16) figure prominently in the next several chapters (cf. esp. ch. 7 for David's "house"). War—almost inevitable when rivals aspire to the same throne—continues between them "a long time" (at least for the two years of Ish-Bosheth's reign over Israel [v.10] and perhaps longer). But Ish-Bosheth's weakness is no match for David's strength, and the outcome is a foregone conclusion. Indeed, as if to emphasize David's invincible, divinely given power (cf. 5:10), the narrator pits David alone, who "grew stronger and stronger" (sing. Heb. verbs), against the entire "house of Saul," who "grew weaker and weaker" (pl. Heb. verbs). As Gideon had learned in an earlier era, weakness is an asset only when God's presence accompanies it (Judg 6:15–16). Long ago the Spirit of the Lord had come upon David and departed from Saul (see comment on 1 Sam 16:14).

## Notes

---

**8** Another way of handling the problem of the name "Baal" occurring in proper names was to substitute the generic word אֵל (*'ēl*, "God"; cf. "Eliada" [5:16] for "Beeliada" [1 Chron 14:7 and NIV mg.]).

**12** Apart from the two occurrences of "young men" (נְעָרִים [*neʿārîm*]) in vv.14, 21, various terms for "men" (in the sense of able-bodied men who can fight in a battle) occur more than a dozen times in vv.12–32, always in carefully articulated patterns. The "men" of Ish-Bosheth (v.12) or of David (vv.13, 15 [untr. in NIV], 17, 30–31) are called עֲבָדִים (*ʿabāḏîm*, lit., "servants"), reflecting their submissive obedience to the kings of their respective realms (see comment on 1 Sam 17:8). The "men" of Israel (v.17) or of Abner (vv.29, 31 [untr. in NIV]) are אֲנָשִׁים (*'anāšîm*), the ordinary word for "men," while the "men" of Joab (vv.26–28, 30) are called עָם (*ʿam*, "people"), commonly used in the books of Samuel in the sense of "soldiers" or "troops"; here the difference in terminology may be intended to highlight—subtly, to be sure—the fact that Joab's mighty "soldiers" are sure to defeat Abner's mere "men." Not until the battle is over and Israel has been overwhelmingly defeated (v.31) are the victors, Joab's "men" (v.32), called *'anāšîm*. The only other place in the chapter where the word "men" is reflected in a Hebrew equivalent is in reference to the "men" of Benjamin in v.25, where בָּנִים (*bānîm*, "sons") is used (probably to exploit its euphony with "Benjamin").

**23** The Hebrew for "died on the spot" means literally "died under him" (i.e., "died [on the place that was] under him"). The closest parallel elsewhere in the OT is Jer 38:9, "where he will starve to death" (lit., "and he will die [on the place that is] under him because of starvation").

**24** The proper name גִּיחַ (*gîaḥ*, "Giah") is probably related to a water source of some kind (Aharoni, *Land of the Bible*, p. 109). The Hebrew root is used of movement of or in water (cf. "surge," Job 40:23; "thrashing about," Ezek 32:2). Gihon, an expanded form of the same word, is the name of one of the four rivers of Eden (Gen 2:13) as well as of a major spring located outside the eastern wall of Jerusalem (1 Kings 1:33) that even today provides water to its citizens.

**29** בִּתְרוֹן (*biṯrôn*), perhaps not a place name, may have meant "ravine" or "morning" or the like (see NIV mg.). For the latter cf. W.R. Arnold, who translates "forenoon" on the basis of what he perceives as parallelism with "night" earlier in the verse ("The Meaning of בתרון," AJSL 28 [1911–12]: 274–83; cf. also NAB, NASB, NJB, REB, RSV, TEV).

**31** The NIV's "Benjamites who were with Abner" understands מבנימן ובאנשי אבנר (*mbnymn wb'nšy 'bnr*, lit., "from Benjamin and among/from the men of Abner") in the sense of "from Benjamin—namely, from Abner's men." The NIV rendering is supported by 4QSam[a], which reads מאנשי (*m'nšy*, "from the men of") instead of the MT's *wb'nšy*, thus clarifying the sense of the preposition and eliminating the ambiguous copula entirely (cf. also NAB, McCarter). In any case, the interchangeability of the two prepositions is clear from other passages in 2 Samuel (see Notes on 5:13; 13:30; 17:12; 22:9; cf. esp. Nahum M. Sarna, "The Interchange of the Prepositions *Beth* and *Min* in Biblical Hebrew," JBL 78, 4 [1959]: 310–13).

---

## 5. *Sons born to David in Hebron*

### 3:2–5

2 Sons were born to David in Hebron:
His firstborn was Amnon the son of Ahinoam of Jezreel;
3 his second, Kileab the son of Abigail the widow of Nabal of Carmel;
the third, Absalom the son of Maacah daughter of Talmai king of Geshur;

> 4the fourth, Adonijah the son of Haggith;
> the fifth, Shephatiah the son of Abital;
> 5and the sixth, Ithream the son of David's wife Eglah.
> These were born to David in Hebron.

The fact that vv.2–5 are flanked by references to "the war between the house of Saul and the house of David" (vv.1, 6) not only confirms the literary unity of the section but also highlights its function: to portray the growing strength of David's house in contradistinction to that of Saul (for other examples of this technique in the books of Samuel and the various purposes it serves, cf. Long, "Framing Repetitions," pp. 385–99). The verses have their own *inclusio* as well ("were born to David in Hebron," vv.2, 5; given the clear Pual in v.5, the debate between Niphal [*Qere*] and syncopated Pual [*Kethiv*] in v.2 as the original Heb. verbal stem underlying "were born" should perhaps be settled in favor of the latter, the *Qere* Niphal then being viewed as a scribal harmonization with 5:13).

Verses 2–5 are paralleled in 1 Chronicles 3:1–4a.

**2–5** Anointed king over Judah in Hebron, David settled down with his two wives Ahinoam and Abigail and began to build a substantial family during his seven-and-a-half-year rule there (vv.2–3; cf. 2:1–2, 4, 11). His firstborn son Am(i)non ("Faithful"; for the alternate spelling, cf. the MT of 13:20), the son of Ahinoam, would ultimately be killed by the men of Absalom (13:28–29), David's third son (v.3). His second son, Kileab, whose mother was Abigail (v.3), is mentioned only here and apparently died before he was able to enter the fray to determine who would be David's successor as king of Israel.

Ab(i)s(h)alom ("My [Divine] Father Is Peace" or "[Divine] Father of Peace"; for the alternate spelling [although a different Absalom is in view], cf. 1 Kings 15:2, 10 and NIV mg.) was the son of Maacah (v.3), a Geshurite princess, whom David may have married as part of a diplomatic agreement with Talmai, the Geshurite king. Fearing royal reprisal over the murder of Amnon, Absalom would eventually flee to the protection of his grandfather and stay in Geshur for three years (13:37–38). Although it is tempting to equate Maacah's homeland with the southern Geshur mentioned in 1 Samuel 27:8 (see comment in loc.), Talmai's Geshur was a small Aramean kingdom (cf. 15:8) northeast of the Sea of Galilee and often associated with the neighboring kingdom of Maacah (Deut 3:14; Josh 12:5; 13:11, 13), the namesake of Talmai's daughter. Another Absalom would later name his own daughter Maacah, who would become the wife of Rehoboam son of Solomon (1 Kings 15:2, 10; 2 Chron 11:20–22).

Adonijah ("My Lord Is the LORD," v.4) the son of Haggith ("Festal One"; cf. Haggai, a masculine form of the same name) would figure prominently in the struggle for David's throne (cf. 1 Kings 1–2), eventually to be assassinated in favor of Solomon. Of Shephatiah ("The Lord Judges") the son of Abital ("My [Divine] Father Is Dew" or [Divine] Father of Dew"; see comment on 1:21) and of Ithream (perhaps "[My Divine] Kinsman Is Abundance") the son of Eglah ("Heifer") nothing further is known. That Eglah alone is called "David's wife" (v.5) may be due to the fact that she is the last in the list and that her relationship to David therefore summarizes that of the other women. David's polygamy, begun with Ahinoam and Abigail (see comment on 1 Sam 25:43), continues unabated—indeed, it increases—in Hebron.

In addition to summarizing David's fecundity in Hebron (one or more of David's wives bore him other children as well; cf. Absalom's sister Tamar, 13:1), vv.2–5 also have their political ramifications. Brueggemann observes that the important names in the section are "Amnon (v.2; cf. chs. 13–14), Absalom (v.3; cf. chs. 15–19), and Adonijah (v.4; cf. I Kings 1–2). The sequence of Amnon, Absalom, and Adonijah provides an outline for the coming drama" (*First and Second Samuel,* p. 255).

## Notes

---

3 Commentators often assume a relationship between כִּלְאָב (*kil'āḇ*) and כָּלֵב (*kālēḇ,* "Caleb") in light of the Calebite ancestry of Nabal (1 Sam 25:3), the deceased husband of Abigail. But apart from the fact that the intrusive א (') is then difficult to explain, the last three letters of *kl'b* ("Kileab") coincide with the first three letters of *l'bygl* ("[the son] of Abigail"), which immediately follows *kl'b* in the MT. The suspicion of dittographic corruption in the MT at this point is therefore strong (cf. Driver, Kirkpatrick). In addition, the parallel text in 1 Chronicles 3:1 reads "Daniel" instead of "Kileab," and both 4QSam[a] and the LXX display *d* rather than *k* as the first consonant in the name of David's second son. Another possibility is that Kileab and Daniel were alternate names for the same man (thus KD). Symon Patrick provides a typical explanation:

> And the Hebrew Doctors give this Reason for both Names. He called him, say they, when he was born *Daniel* (which was his *Fundamental,* that is, his primary Name) because, said he, *God hath judged,* or *vindicated* me from *Nabal.* And afterwards he called him *Chileab,* as much as to say, *like to his Father:* Because in his Countenance he resembled *David.* And this he did, for this reason, to silence the Mockers of that Age: Who said *Abigail* had conceived by *Nabal,* whose Son this was. For the confuting of which Calumny, God was pleased to order that the Fashion of his Face should be perfectly like to *David's.* (p. 345)

Archaeologists working at Tell Hadar northeast of the Sea of Galilee have unearthed an eleventh-century beer strainer in the burnt debris of a building tentatively identified as a palace. They interpret their discovery as confirming "the Biblical narrative that the land of Geshur existed during the period between the careers of Joshua and King David" (Timothy Renner and Ira Spar, "The Land of Geshur Project," *New Jersey Archaeological Consortium Newsletter* 3 [1988]).

---

### B. *David's Accession to Kingship Over Israel (3:6–5:16)*

The story of how David became king of all Israel follows, in most essentials, the same outline already established in the account of his accession to kingship over Judah (1:1–3:5). Both begin with a warrior trying to curry David's favor (an unnamed Amalekite, 1:1–13; Saul's army commander Abner, 3:6–21) and continue with the execution or murder of the warrior (1:14–16; 3:22–32), which is followed by a lament uttered by David (over Saul and Jonathan, 1:17–27; over Abner, 3:33–34). Near the center of each literary unit is a brief report of the anointing of David as king (over Judah, 2:1–7; over Israel, 5:1–5). David and his men are then successful in defeating their enemies (2:8–3:1; 5:6–12), and each unit concludes with a list of sons/children born to David (in Hebron, 3:2–5; in Jerusalem, 5:13–16). The similarities between the two sections point to the careful craftsmanship of a single author, who now sets about to tell his readers that just as the house of David has replaced Saul and his house in southern Canaan (1:1–3:5), so also David's house is about to replace that of Saul in the rest of the land as well (3:6–5:16).

### 1. *Abner's defection to David*

#### 3:6–21

6 During the war between the house of Saul and the house of David,
Abner had been strengthening his own position in the house of Saul.
7 Now Saul had had a concubine named Rizpah daughter of Aiah. And
Ish-Bosheth said to Abner, "Why did you sleep with my father's
concubine?"
8 Abner was very angry because of what Ish-Bosheth said and he
answered, "Am I a dog's head—on Judah's side? This very day I am
loyal to the house of your father Saul and to his family and friends. I
haven't handed you over to David. Yet now you accuse me of an offense
involving this woman! 9 May God deal with Abner, be it ever so severely,
if I do not do for David what the LORD promised him on oath 10 and
transfer the kingdom from the house of Saul and establish David's
throne over Israel and Judah from Dan to Beersheba." 11 Ish-Bosheth
did not dare to say another word to Abner, because he was afraid of
him.
12 Then Abner sent messengers on his behalf to say to David, "Whose
land is it? Make an agreement with me, and I will help you bring all Israel
over to you."
13 "Good," said David. "I will make an agreement with you. But I
demand one thing of you: Do not come into my presence unless you
bring Michal daughter of Saul when you come to see me." 14 Then David
sent messengers to Ish-Bosheth son of Saul, demanding, "Give me my
wife Michal, whom I betrothed to myself for the price of a hundred
Philistine foreskins."
15 So Ish-Bosheth gave orders and had her taken away from her
husband Paltiel son of Laish. 16 Her husband, however, went with her,
weeping behind her all the way to Bahurim. Then Abner said to him, "Go
back home!" So he went back.
17 Abner conferred with the elders of Israel and said, "For some time
you have wanted to make David your king. 18 Now do it! For the LORD
promised David, 'By my servant David I will rescue my people Israel from
the hand of the Philistines and from the hand of all their enemies.'"
19 Abner also spoke to the Benjamites in person. Then he went to
Hebron to tell David everything that Israel and the whole house of
Benjamin wanted to do. 20 When Abner, who had twenty men with him,
came to David at Hebron, David prepared a feast for him and his men.
21 Then Abner said to David, "Let me go at once and assemble all Israel
for my lord the king, so that they may make a compact with you, and that
you may rule over all that your heart desires." So David sent Abner
away, and he went in peace.

The devastating defeat of Ish-Bosheth's men by David's men (2:30–31) has made its impact on Saul's cousin Abner. Ruthless and ambitious, Abner is a canny politician who sees the handwriting on the wall. He therefore sets about to transfer Ish-Bosheth's kingdom over to David—and Ish-Bosheth can only sit by helplessly and watch the inevitable unfold (vv.9–11). A key word in the narrative, used only and always by Abner, is *yāḏ* ("hand"): Although Abner has not yet "handed" Ish-Bosheth "over to" (lit., "caused [him] to be found in the hand of") David (v.8), he will soon "help" (lit., "[his] hand will be with"; see comment on 1 Sam 22:17) David to bring all Israel over to him (v.12). The Lord had earlier promised that "by" (lit., "by the hand of") David he would rescue Israel from the "hand" of the Philistines—indeed, from the "hand" of all her enemies (v.18). Doubtless hoping for a prominent place in David's kingdom, Abner wants to be the divinely chosen agent in delivering Israel to David's rule.

**6** Echoing v.1a, v.6a is thematic of the rest of chapter 3 and all of chapter 4 in its reminder of the continuing struggle between the Saulides and the Davidides. Echoing v.1b, v.6b parallels Abner's "strengthening" position in Saul's house with David's "stronger and stronger" control of his own fortunes, both of which contrast sharply with Ish-Bosheth's "weaker and weaker" hold on Israel's throne. Verse 6 also implies that Abner is not only well positioned to wrest Israel's kingdom from the hapless Ish-Bosheth but also to do with it whatever he pleases—including deliver it to David. It may therefore not be inappropriate to observe yet another contrast in the wider context: While Abner was "strengthening his own position" (*hthẓq*) in the house of Saul, it was characteristic of David that he "found strength" (*hthẓq*) in the Lord his God (1 Sam 30:6).

**7–11** Ish-Bosheth's surprise question to Abner—"Why did you sleep with my father's concubine?" (v.7)—arrives like a bolt from the blue. "It springs on us a situation where one agent reproaches another for a full-blown and explosive affair of which we have had no inkling, let alone any queries" (Sternberg, p. 241).

Saul's concubine, Rizpah daughter of Aiah, is mentioned elsewhere only in 21:8–11 (where she protects the exposed corpses of seven of Saul's male descendants [including two of her own sons] from the ravages of wild animals). "Sleep with" is literally "come to," a common Hebrew euphemism for sexual intercourse. Ish-Bosheth accuses Abner of "coming to" King Saul's concubine (and now presumably Ish-Bosheth's, since Saul is dead)—an act by Abner that probably is intended to assert his claim to Saul's throne (cf. vv.8–10; 16:20–22; 1 Kings 1:1–4; 2:13–22; cf. Levenson and Halpern, "The Political Import of David's Marriages," p. 508; Brueggemann, *First and Second Samuel*, pp. 225–26). Later Abner "came to" David at Hebron (v.20), offering to deliver to him the kingdom that apparently he considered his to dispose of as he wished (v.21).

But for now Abner responds indignantly (v.8) to Ish-Bosheth: "Am I a dog's head?" (Although unique, the expression is clearly to be taken as self-depreciating and uncomplimentary; see comment on 1 Sam 17:43.) How can Ish-Bosheth possibly think that Abner would defect to Judah? Abner protests that although "this very day" he is loyal to Saul's house, Ish-Bosheth is accusing him "now" (same Heb. word in both cases). "I am loyal" translates the same Hebrew covenant idiom rendered "showing kindness" in 2:5 (see comment there) and makes all the more reasonable Abner's forthcoming request of David to "make an agreement" with him (v.12; cf. vv.13, 21). Abner compounds his arrogance by claiming allegiance not only to Saul but also to his "family" (lit., "brothers/relatives") and "friends" (for the same two terms in parallelism, cf. Prov 19:7). After all, he continues, he has not "handed" Ish-Bosheth "over to" (cf. Zech 11:6; lit., "caused [him] to be found in the hand of") David. He therefore pretends not to be able to understand how Ish-Bosheth can "accuse" him "of an offense" involving Rizpah—a bold protestation indeed, since the Hebrew phrase rendered "accuse of offense" is elsewhere rendered "punish for sin/guilt/wickedness" in a number of key theological texts (Exod 20:5 = Deut 5:9; Exod 34:7; Lev 18:25; Num 14:18; Isa 13:11; 26:21; Jer 25:12; 36:31; Amos 3:2).

Far from denying Ish-Bosheth's accusation, however, Abner takes a strong oath of self-imprecation (v.9; cf. v.35; see comment on 1 Sam 20:13), vowing that he will become God's instrument in bringing about what the Lord had promised to David (the reference is perhaps to 1 Sam 15:28 and/or 16:1)—namely, transferring Saul's kingdom to him. "David's throne" (v.10), already established over Judah (2:4) and soon to be established over Israel, would some day soon be occupied by David's son Solomon (1 Kings 2:12, 24, 45), later be discredited by Solomon's reprobate descendants who would be destroyed by the Lord himself (Jer 13:13–14; 29:16–17), and eventually be inherited by the Lord's Messiah, who will reign forever in peace and with justice and righteousness (Isa 9:6–7). For now, however, during his lifetime David would rule over "Israel and Judah" (cf. 5:5; 12:8; 24:1; see also comment on 2:10) all the way "from Dan to Beersheba" (cf. 17:11; 24:2, 15; see comment on 1 Sam 3:20). Cowardly (see comment on 2:8) and powerless, Ish-Bosheth for his part can do nothing to stem the tide of Abner's ambitions (v.11).

**12–16** Divided into two parts by the expression "sent messengers" (vv.12, 14; cf. MT paragraph indicators), vv.12–16 constitute the central section of the present literary unit (vv.6–21) and focus on David's recovery of and reunion with his wife Mical.

The preliminary meeting between Abner and David takes place through messengers rather than face to face. Abner's rhetorical question, "Whose land is it?" (v.12), is perhaps intentionally ambiguous. It could mean "The land of Israel is mine to give" (and therefore David should make an agreement "with me"), or it could mean "The land of Israel is yours because of God's promise" (and therefore Abner will act as God's agent and "help you bring all Israel over to you"). Abner's ambition tips the scales in favor of the former interpretation. Indeed,

> it may be that Abner, as *de facto* ruler of all Israel, offered David his allegiance in exchange for the position of *śar ṣābā'* [commander of the army], the equivalent of his office in Eshbaal's army and the post currently held by Joab. V.12 suggests something of the sort when it speaks of a *personal* deal between these two men. (James Vanderkam, "Davidic Complicity in the Deaths of Abner and Eshbaal: A Historical and Redactional Study," JBL 99, 4 [1980]: 531–32)

In either case it is clear that the Lord is working behind the scenes to deliver the northern tribes into David's hands (the Heb. expression rendered "bring . . . over to" is translated "turn[ed] . . . over to" in 1 Chron 10:14; 12:23, the process in both cases occurring because of divine initiative). "Make an agreement" is literally "Cut your covenant" (for the idiom "cut a covenant/treaty," see comments on 1 Sam 11:1; 18:3) and emphasizes the personal nature of the deal that Abner wants to strike with David.

For his part, David is willing to accept Abner's proposal only on one condition: that he bring Michal, Saul's younger daughter (see comment on 1 Sam 14:49), with him when he comes to Hebron (v.13). David is adamant, warning Abner not to "come into my presence" (lit., "see my face") without bringing Michal when he comes to "see me" (lit., "see my face," repeating the same Heb. phrase for emphasis).

Clines points out that David chooses his words carefully in vv.13–14 ("X, X *Ben* Y, *Ben* Y," p. 271). When speaking to Abner he refers to Michal as "daughter of Saul" (v.13), thus reminding Abner that if he agrees to bring her with him he has turned his back on Ish-Bosheth for good and has assented to David's succession to Saul's throne. When speaking to Ish-Bosheth, however, David calls Michal "my wife" (v.14), thus reminding Ish-Bosheth that she is David's wife, not Paltiel's, and that the responsibility for her being now with Paltiel is Ish-Bosheth's, since he is the son and heir of Saul (Ish-Bosheth is mentioned several times in ch. 3, but only in v.14 is he called "son of Saul"), who wrongfully gave her to Paltiel in the first place (1 Sam 25:44).

Alter makes the further observation that Paltiel

> is called twice in close sequence [vv.15, 16] Michal's man or husband (*'ish*), a title to which at least his feelings give him legitimate claim, and which echoes ironically against David's use in the preceding verse [v.14] of *'ishti*, my wife or woman, to describe a relationship with Michal that is legal and political but perhaps not at all emotional on his side. (*The Art of Biblical Narrative*, p. 122)

Now that Saul's death has given him a free hand, David wants to strengthen his claim to Saul's throne by retrieving the woman for whom, after all, he had earlier paid the demanded bride-price of "a hundred Philistine foreskins" (v.14)—indeed, he had paid double what had been required of him (see comments on 1 Sam 18:25–27).

Michal's guardian and brother Ish-Bosheth, powerless as ever, readily consents to David's demand and takes Michal away from her husband "Paltiel son of Laish" (v.15; see comment and note on 1 Sam 25:44). When Abner and Michal depart for Hebron, the heartsick and weeping Paltiel tags along as far as Bahurim (v.16, mentioned elsewhere only in Davidic contexts: 16:5; 17:18; 19:16; 1 Kings 2:8), where Abner orders him to go back home (probably to Mahanaim). Although the precise location of Bahurim is uncertain (somewhere near the Mount of Olives, however; cf. 15:30, 32; 16:1, 5), it is perhaps the modern site of Ras et-Tumeim about one and a half miles northeast of Jerusalem and thus almost twenty miles southwest of Mahanaim.

And so it is that Michal is added to David's roster of wives. His repossession of her does not violate the terms of Deuteronomy 24:1–4, "since his separation from his wife was involuntary. The right of a husband to reclaim his wife . . . is well entrenched in Mesopotamian law, and may be assumed to have operated in Israel" (Gordon, *I & II Samuel*, p. 219).

**17–21** Like the previous section (vv.12–16), so also vv.17–21 divide into two roughly equal halves. In vv.17–19 Abner tries to convince the elders of Israel and the Benjamites that the time is ripe for them to make David their king. In vv.20–21 Abner arrives in Hebron, offers to facilitate a compact between all Israel on the one hand and David on the other, and then departs. The theme of the opening and closing verses of the section—that Israel would soon make David their king—is echoed and summarized in the terminology of 5:3: "the elders of Israel" (v.17; 5:3), "make/made a compact" (v.21; 5:3).

The time when Abner "conferred" (v.17, to gain support for his cause; cf. 1 Kings 1:7) with Israel's elders was probably antecedent to the events of vv.15–16 (thus Kirkpatrick), since the elders were doubtless headquartered for the most part in Mahanaim and served as Ish-Bosheth's advisors there, while it is equally clear that Abner escorted Michal to Hebron (cf. vv.13, 16). Abner's counsel to the elders is straightforward: There is no reason to delay any longer in making David king over all Israel (vv.17–18). God had promised David that he would be divinely endowed to "rescue/deliver my people Israel from the hand of the Philistines" (v.18), a word originally spoken concerning Saul—who, however, failed miserably in that endeavor (see 1 Sam 9:16 and comment). In any event, God himself is the true Deliverer of his people (cf. esp. 1 Sam 7:8) and thus sovereignly chooses whom and when he will. David is called the Lord's "servant" (v.18) more than thirty times in the OT, usually in reference to the historical David (cf. 7:5, 8, 26, and the titles of Pss 18; 36) but also to the eschatological, messianic David (cf. Ezek 34:23–24; 37:24–25).

On his way to Hebron, Abner pays special attention to the Benjamites, who are Saul's (and Ish-Bosheth's) kinsmen. He "spoke" to them "in person" (v.19) and then continued on to "tell" David (the Heb. idiom underlying both expressions means literally "speak into the ears of") what Israel and Benjamin wanted to do. Though counted among the northern tribes and an indispensable part of the kingdom of Israel, the "house of Benjamin" (v.19) would eventually become inextricably linked to the house of Judah (cf. 1 Kings 12:21–23).

Arriving in Hebron with Michal, Abner and his twenty men sit down to a feast prepared for them by David (v.20). Whether the feast is in celebration of David's (re)marriage to Michal (cf. similarly Vanderkam, "Davidic Complicity in the Deaths of Abner and Eshbaal," p. 532; cf. further Gen 29:21–22; Judg 14:10; Matt 22:2) or is part of the protocol of covenants recently made (vv.12–13; cf. Abraham Malamat, "Organs of Statecraft in the Israelite Monarchy," BA 28, 2 [1965]: 35; cf. further Gen 26:28–30; 31:44, 53–54) is difficult to say, although the latter is perhaps more likely (cf. vv.20–21 with Gen 26:28–31).

With his offer to bring "all Israel" into a covenant relationship with David (v.21), Abner's defection to the house of Judah is complete. The earlier "agreement" between the two men (vv.12–13) was personal and is not to be confused with the national "compact" (v.21; cf. also 5:3) now to be made between north and south, even though *b$^{e}$rîṯ*, usually translated "covenant," underlies both words. Abner assures David that the end result of the compact would be that "you may/will rule over all that your heart desires," a phrase ironically echoed in the Lord's words to Jeroboam in prediction of the rupture of the united kingdom after the death of Solomon (1 Kings 11:37). To David's kingdom the ten northern tribes would soon be added; from his son Solomon's kingdom the ten northern tribes would eventually be taken away.

Abner's mission now complete, David sends him away and he goes "in peace" (v.21). The phrase is repeated in vv.22–23, perhaps to emphasize the fact that David had promised Abner safe conduct (cf. REB; cf. also 15:27; Gen 26:29, 31). The promise, if such it was, would prove to be tragically meaningless, as the next section demonstrates.

## Notes

7 Although the name Ish-Bosheth does not appear in the MT of v.7, the NIV correctly supplies it in context (cf. v.8). It in fact occurs in a few Hebrew MSS, and 4QSam$^{a}$, LXX, and Syriac seem to reflect a Hebrew text that read "Ish-Bosheth son of Saul" (cf. BHS).

8 Early Jewish commentators (e.g., Rashi, Kimchi) frequently understood the phrase "dog's head" to mean "head/commander over dogs." Abner thus accuses Ish-Bosheth of treating him, "the commander of Saul's army" (2:8), as though he were merely the captain of a pack of dogs (cf. Symon Patrick, p. 347).

16 בָּכֹה אַחֲרֶיהָ עַד־בַּחֻרִים (*bāḵōh 'aḥ$^{a}$reyhā 'aḏ-baḥurîm*, "weeping behind her . . . to Bahurim") is a fine example of assonance in the MT.

**18** The NIV's "I will rescue" renders the MT's הוֹשִׁיעַ (*hôšîaʿ*, "to rescue" [Hiphil infinitive construct] or "he rescued" [Hiphil third person masc. sing. perfect]). Although many Hebrew MSS here read אוֹשִׁיעַ (*ʾôšîaʿ*, "I will rescue" [Hiphil first person sing. imperfect]; cf. also the ancient versions), Barthélemy remarks that "the infinitive here may be interpreted as a decision to save, 'I will save'" (p. 214). It is also possible that the MT form is a mispointed Hiphil infinitive absolute (for examples cf. GKC, sec. 53*k*) used as a finite verb.

---

## 2. *The murder of Abner*

### 3:22–39

[22]Just then David's men and Joab returned from a raid and brought
with them a great deal of plunder. But Abner was no longer with David
in Hebron, because David had sent him away, and he had gone in peace.
[23]When Joab and all the soldiers with him arrived, he was told that
Abner son of Ner had come to the king and that the king had sent him
away and that he had gone in peace.
[24]So Joab went to the king and said, "What have you done? Look,
Abner came to you. Why did you let him go? Now he is gone! [25]You
know Abner son of Ner; he came to deceive you and observe your
movements and find out everything you are doing."
[26]Joab then left David and sent messengers after Abner, and they
brought him back from the well of Sirah. But David did not know it.
[27]Now when Abner returned to Hebron, Joab took him aside into the
gateway, as though to speak with him privately. And there, to avenge the
blood of his brother Asahel, Joab stabbed him in the stomach, and he
died.
[28]Later, when David heard about this, he said, "I and my kingdom are
forever innocent before the LORD concerning the blood of Abner son of
Ner. [29]May his blood fall upon the head of Joab and upon all his father's
house! May Joab's house never be without someone who has a running
sore or leprosy or who leans on a crutch or who falls by the sword or
who lacks food."
[30](Joab and his brother Abishai murdered Abner because he had
killed their brother Asahel in the battle at Gibeon.)
[31]Then David said to Joab and all the people with him, "Tear your
clothes and put on sackcloth and walk in mourning in front of Abner."
King David himself walked behind the bier. [32]They buried Abner in
Hebron, and the king wept aloud at Abner's tomb. All the people wept
also.
[33]The king sang this lament for Abner:

"Should Abner have died as the lawless die?
[34] Your hands were not bound,
your feet were not fettered.
You fell as one falls before wicked men."

And all the people wept over him again.
[35]Then they all came and urged David to eat something while it was
still day; but David took an oath, saying, "May God deal with me, be it
ever so severely, if I taste bread or anything else before the sun sets!"
[36]All the people took note and were pleased; indeed, everything the
king did pleased them. [37]So on that day all the people and all Israel
knew that the king had no part in the murder of Abner son of Ner.
[38]Then the king said to his men, "Do you not realize that a prince and
a great man has fallen in Israel this day? [39]And today, though I am the
anointed king, I am weak, and these sons of Zeruiah are too strong for
me. May the LORD repay the evildoer according to his evil deeds!"

Chapter 3 concludes with a detailed account of the events preceding, including, and following the death of Abner. It centers on v.30, a parenthetical statement that explains why Joab found it necessary to kill his northern counterpart. Various elements in the two halves of the section parallel one another, producing a symmetrical outline:

A. Joab kills Abner (3:22–27).
  B. David protests his innocence of Abner's death (3:28).
    C. David curses Joab (3:29).
    [The narrator summarizes (3:30)].
A′. David mourns Abner's death (3:31–35).
  B′. Everyone acknowledges David's innocence (3:36–37).
    C′. David praises Abner and curses Joab (3:38–39).

**22–27** Key verbs in vv.22–27 are *bô'* ("come"; v.22 ["returned," "brought"], v.23 ["arrived," "had come"], v.24 ["went," "came"], v.25 ["came," "movements"]) and *yāḏa'* ("know"; v.25 ["know," "observe," "find out"], v.26). Three verses in succession conclude with the report that David sent Abner away, and Abner went "in peace" (vv.21–23). In the middle of this otherwise tranquil scene (v.22) the narrator states that David's men and Joab "returned" from a raid (the verb is singular, stressing Joab's leadership), the theme in this case being not "peace" but "plunder" (the word is in emphatic position in its clause).

Arriving in Hebron and learning that Abner has already come and gone (v.23), Joab goes to David and demands to know why he released Abner—the only genuine obstacle to David's sitting on Israel's throne—when he had him firmly in his grasp (v.24). After all, the man whom David has allowed to leave is not just any "Abner" (v.24); he is "Abner son of Ner" (v.25), a cousin of Saul who must therefore be an opponent of David (cf. Clines, "X, X *Ben* Y, *Ben* Y," pp. 274–75). Indeed, Abner has doubtless come to Hebron for the sole purpose of learning everything that might well prove useful in the future (cf. similarly the mission of the envoys of Merodach-Baladan king of Babylon in the days of Hezekiah, 2 Kings 20:12–18 = Isa 39).

"Movements" (v.25) is the NIV rendering of the merism "going(s) out and coming(s) in," a common OT expression capable of a wide range of applications (cf. Deut 28:6, 19) that probably originated in such mundane activities as going out to the fields in the morning and returning at night and that was eventually pressed into service as a *terminus technicus* for the "exits and entrances" of buildings (cf. Ezek 43:11; 44:5). Joab's accusation that David allowed Abner to "deceive" him (v.25) is ironic in light of his own subsequent treachery (v.27). The principle elucidated in Proverbs 24:28–29 is surely apropos: "Do not . . . use your lips to deceive. Do not say, 'I'll do to him as he has done to me;/ I'll pay that man back for what he did.'"

"A striking feature of the scene in which Joab excoriates his royal master (2 Sam 3:24–25) is the complete silence of David" (Vanderkam, "Davidic Complicity in the Deaths of Abner and Eshbaal," p. 533 n. 39)—who, however, is realistic enough to recognize that he is still too weak to risk a showdown with the sons of Zeruiah (v.39). The brash Joab thus feels free to leave David without so much as waiting for a response to his rebuke (v.26); nor is David told that Joab's men pursue Abner and bring him back from the "well" (better "cistern"; cf. NAB, RSV; cf. similarly NJB) of Sirah (mentioned only here, perhaps to be identified with modern Sirat el-Ballai about two and a half miles north of Hebron; for details cf. Simons, *The Geographical and Topographical Texts*, p. 330; cf. also McCarter, *II Samuel*).

Joab's deception of Abner is chillingly similar to Cain's treachery toward his brother Abel (Gen 4:8). Pretending that he wants to discuss a private matter with him, Joab takes Abner "into" (v.27, lit., "to the midst of") the gateway, doubtless to a relatively secluded area within what was often a beehive of activity. Then, "to avenge" (*bᵉ-*, lit., "[in exchange] for"; cf. v.14, where the same Heb. preposition is translated "for the price of") the blood of his brother Asahel, Joab kills Abner. The method used—he "stabbed him in the stomach" (v.27)—is the same used in Abner's killing of Asahel (see comment on 2:23) and thus illustrates the lex talionis ("principle of retaliation in kind"; cf. Exod 21:23–25).

**28** The expansive phrase *mē'aḥᵃrê ḵēn* ("later," lit., "from after this") lends a touch of formality to David's protestation of innocence (the idiom occurs only twice elsewhere: 15:1 ["in the course of time"]; 2 Chron 32:23 ["from then on"]). In addition, Clines observes that from here to the end of the chapter Abner is given his legal/formal title "Abner son of Ner" only in vv.28 and 37 (cf. "X, X *Ben* Y, *Ben* Y," p. 275 for details). Furthermore, David's use of "forever" adds to the solemnity of his statement (cf. 1 Kings 2:33).

Upon hearing of Abner's murder, David declares himself—and his kingdom, doubtless including his future royal heirs—innocent of all personal responsibility for Abner's death. The motif of David as "innocent" is first recorded in the assessment of his friend Jonathan (1 Sam 19:5) and recurs in the Davidic psalms (cf. Pss 19:13; 26:6; 64:4). Needless to say, that opinion is not shared by disaffected Israelites, who hold David accountable for the massacre of the Saulides and continue to think of him as a "man of blood" (cf. 16:7–8).

**29** For his part, however, David disavows all such responsibility. He places the blame squarely where it belongs by cursing the "head of Joab" (cf. the words of Solomon in 1 Kings 2:33) and devoutly hoping that Abner's blood will "fall" (lit., "swirl"; cf. Jer 23:19; 30:23) upon it—that is, that Joab's bloodguilt will eventually bring about his own destruction (see comment on 1:16 for the similar expression, "Your blood be on your own head") through the medium of divine vengeance (cf. v.39). Just as David had absolved himself and his "kingdom" of all guilt in the matter (v.28), so also now he includes Joab's "father's house" in Joab's condemnation.

That the land of Israel could be adversely affected by murderous acts is clear from 1:21 (see comment there). "Apart from the land, blood pollution also affects persons directly (Gen 42:22; Judg 9:24; 2 Sam 3:28–29; 16:7–8; 1 Kings 2:33; Jer 26:15; 51:35; Ezek 16:38; 22:4; 23:45; 35:6; Joel 4:19, 21 [3:19, 21 MT]; Lam 4:13)" (David P. Wright, "Deuteronomy 21:1–9 as a Rite of Elimination," CBQ 49, 3 [1987]: 395 n. 24).

As he weaves the tapestry of his curse against Joab, David's penchant for colorful language is given full rein. He pleads that Joab's house "may never be without" (v.29; lit., "may there never be cut off from Joab's house"; cf. the similar curse context of Josh 9:23 where Joshua uses the same Heb. idiom in telling the Gibeonites that they "will never cease" to be servants of the Israelites) people who would suffer in five categories: (1) someone who has a "running sore" (the Heb. word is often translated "bodily discharge" [cf. Lev 15:2; 22:4] and refers to such infectious conditions as diarrhea and urethral emissions); (2) someone who has "leprosy" (the Heb. term is elsewhere sometimes translated "infectious skin disease" and does not always necessarily mean "leprosy"; see NIV mg.; cf. also Lev 14:3 and NIV mg.);

(3) someone who "leans on a crutch" (*pelek*, here translated "crutch," occurs elsewhere only once [Prov 31:19], where it means "spindle" [cf. Akkadian *pilakku*]); (4) someone who falls by the sword (the fate of Israel's army at Mount Gilboa, 1:12); (5) someone who lacks food (cf. 1 Sam 2:36; Prov 12:9; Amos 4:6). The first three curses relate to physical ailments, the fourth to war, and the fifth to famine—a deadly triad in the ancient world (cf. "sword, famine and plague," which occurs fifteen times in Jeremiah alone: 14:12; 21:7, 9; 24:10; 27:8, 13; 29:17, 18; 32:24, 36; 34:17; 38:2; 42:17, 22; 44:13).

**30** The central verse in this literary unit implicates Abishai in Joab's murder of Abner, as does the final verse ("sons of Zeruiah," v.39). Since "the blood of a kinsman must be avenged by the death of the one who shed it" (de Vaux, AIs, p. 11), Joab and Abishai invoked the hoary custom of the blood feud as a rationale for murdering Abner (who, after all, had killed "their brother Asahel"). Abner, however, had killed Asahel "in the battle," and it is therefore questionable whether the blood vengeance of Joab and Abishai was justified in this case. Indeed, David later excoriates Joab for having shed the blood of Abner "in peacetime as if in battle" (1 Kings 2:5). Joab, of course, may have had an ulterior motive in wanting Abner out of the way: the fear that Abner, the "commander of Saul's army" (2:8), might supersede him as commander of David's army (8:16; 20:23; 1 Kings 1:19; 11:15, 21).

**31–35**

> We need not doubt David's genuine respect for Abner, but the funeral is also a media event. It is like a U.S. president with the returned body of a soldier from an unauthorized war. The president must lead national mourning, which is genuine, but at the same time must stage a media event designed to legitimate policy. (Brueggemann, *First and Second Samuel*, p. 230)

Thus David issues commands concerning Abner's funeral (v.31). The murderer Joab is required to attend, as are all his men, referred to seven times in vv.31–37 as "all the people" (vv.31, 32, 34, 35 ["they all"], 36 ["all the people," "them"], 37; that the phrase means Joab's men is clear from their description as being "with him" at their first appearance [v.31] and as being distinguished from "all Israel" at their last [v.37]; cf. also 2:26–28, 30 and Notes on 2:12).

David's weeping and mourning over a slain family member, comrade, or friend is not only a concession to custom but also—and far more significantly—an indication of his tender heart (cf. 1:12; 13:36–37; 18:33; 19:1–4). Joab and his men are ordered to walk in front of the funeral procession, with David bringing up the rear as he walks behind the "bier" (translating the most common Heb. word for "bed/couch," as in 1 Sam 19:13, 15–16).

> David is in charge and Joab is humiliated. . . . The narrator seems to grasp the dramatic power of this moment, for he refers to David as "King David" (v.31). While David had previously been identified as "king" (2:4, 7, 11; 3:17, 21–24), this is the first formal use linking personal name and royal office. It is when the threat of the north has been decisively eliminated in the death of Abner that the throne is secure enough to warrant this powerful phrase. (ibid., p. 230)

Although Abner was a Benjamite (1 Sam 9:1; 14:50–51) and under ordinary circumstances would have been taken to his hometown for burial, David honors him by burying him in the royal city of Hebron (v.32; 4:12). Expressing his grief, the king "wept aloud" (lit., "raised his voice and wept"; see comment on 1 Sam 11:4) at Abner's tomb.

The weeping of Joab's men ("all the people," vv.32, 34; see comment on v.31) frame David's brief lament for Abner (vv.33b–34) together with its introduction (v.33a). As did his only other recorded lament (1:19–27), David's lament (see commentary on 1:17) for Abner again demonstrates the emotive powers of his literary genius. An exquisitely crafted quatrain, it is arranged chiastically: The two outer lines bemoan Abner's unjust death, while the two inner lines celebrate his unfettered life. Lines one and four begin with an infinitive construct preceded by the preposition *k-* ("as"); lines two and three begin with rhyming words (*yāḏeḵā*, "your hands"; *ragleyḵā*, "your feet") followed immediately by *lō'* ("not"). In addition, as Holladay observes, v.33 "plays on *'abnēr* and *nābāl*" ("Form and Word-Play in David's Lament," p. 156; cf. also id., *Jeremiah: A Fresh Reading* [New York: Pilgrim, 1990], pp. 21–22).

The rhetorical question that begins the lament requires a negative answer. Hands not bound and feet not fettered, Abner was surely not "lawless" (*nāḇāl*, recalling Nabal, whose name Abigail said means "Fool, and folly goes with him" [1 Sam 25:25; see comment there], and whose alter ego was Saul [see comment on introduction to 1 Sam 25], not Abner). The parallel to "lawless" (v.33) in v.34 is "wicked men" (*b^e^nê-'awlāh*, cf. also 7:10 ["wicked people"]), literally "sons of wickedness"—again reminiscent of Nabal, whom Abigail called a "wicked man" (*ben-b^e^lîya'al*, lit., "son of wickedness" [see 1 Sam 25:17 and comment]).

As in the case of Saul and Jonathan and their comrades in arms, so also for Abner: David fasts till evening (v.35; see 1:12 and comment). Try as they might, Joab's men are unable to induce David (who takes a strong oath of self-imprecation; cf. v.9 and see comment on 1 Sam 20:13) to eat the customary funeral meal (cf. Jer 16:5, 7; Ezek 24:17) "before the suns sets." Although David could not have been completely unhappy about the death of his most powerful rival for control, his grief is genuine. If he mourned at length for Saul and Jonathan, he mourns no less for Abner.

**36–37** David's magnanimity impresses Joab's men and is sure to draw them ever closer to his inner circle of advisors. Indeed, in their eyes he can do no wrong (v.36). Even more important in the immediate circumstance, however, is the clear understanding not only of Joab's men but also of "all Israel" that David was not an accessory to Abner's death (v.37). His protestation of innocence (v.28), believable then to his own cohorts, is ratified now by the northern tribes. Appropriately regal, David stands above the fray.

**38–39** The chapter concludes with David's final brief encomium for Abner (v.38) and final imprecation against Joab and Abishai (v.39), both of which are directed to his own men. Just as it was important that all Israel "knew" that David was innocent of the death of Abner (v.37), so also David wants his men to "realize" that in Abner a great man has been lost to Israel (v.38; same Heb. verb). The NIV translation of the Hebrew phrase (*śar w^e^gāḏôl*) that David uses to describe Abner—"a prince and a great man"—is as old as the KJV and has been used as a eulogy in countless funerals for generations. Its closest OT parallel (although in a negative context) is Micah 7:3, where "judge" (*šōp̱ēṭ*) is flanked by *śar* ("ruler") and *gāḏôl* ("powerful"). But since *śar* is frequently used elsewhere of Abner in the sense of "commander" (see 2:8 and comment), it is surely better to understand *śar wᵉgāḏôl* in the present context as a hendiadys and to render it "a great commander"—a title whose significance could not have been lost on Joab (who, however, may not have been within earshot on this occasion).

"This day" (v.38) and "today" (v.39) connect the two verses and lend a note of immediacy to them. David harbors no illusions about the fact that although he is "the anointed king" (lit., "anointed [as] king"; cf. 2:4; for the unusual form *māšûaḥ*, see comment and Notes on 1:21), he is nevertheless "weak" (cf. 1 Chron 22:5; 29:1, where he uses the same Heb. word to describe his son Solomon as "inexperienced"). By contrast Joab and Abishai (the "sons of Zeruiah" [cf. 2:18], constant thorns in David's side; cf. 16:10; 19:22) are "strong"; and David, exercising commendable caution, realizes that he is not presently able to rebuke them with any semblance of authority. In the hearing of his own men (v.38), however, he repeats the curse against Joab (cf. v.29, where no hearers are mentioned), perhaps this time including Abishai—although the language of the imprecation is nonspecific: "May the LORD repay the evildoer according to his evil deeds!" (v.39; cf. Solomon's prayer in 1 Kings 8:32; cf. also Pss 18:20, 24; 28:4 [both are Davidic psalms]; in the NT, cf. 2 Tim 4:14; Rev 20:12–13).

## Notes

**29** For בית אביו (*byt 'byw*, "his father's house"), 4QSamᵃ reads בית יואב (*byt yw'b*, "Joab's house"). Although this makes equally good sense, the Qumran reading is doubtless in anticipation of the same phrase a few words later in the verse. The MT is thus *lectio difficilior* and should therefore be retained (so also LXX, McCarter).

Although McCarter (*II Samuel*, p. 118) claims that *plkm* in the Phoenician Karatepe inscription means "crutches," the context there (lines 26–27) also allows "spindles" as a possible translation (thus, e.g., Franz Rosenthal in ANETSup, p. 654 n. 4). In any event, although translations and commentators are divided here between "staff/crutch" (ASV, KJV; Hertzberg, KD, Kirkpatrick, McCarter, Smith) and "spindle/distaff" (which would imply effeminacy, or at least doing the work of women; NAB, NASB, NJB, REB, RSV, TEV; Anderson, Baldwin, Driver, Gordon, Mauchline), the context favors "staff/crutch" (see comment above).

### 3. *The murder of Ish-Bosheth*

#### 4:1–12

1 When Ish-Bosheth son of Saul heard that Abner had died in Hebron,
he lost courage, and all Israel became alarmed. 2 Now Saul's son had
two men who were leaders of raiding bands. One was named Baanah
and the other Recab; they were sons of Rimmon the Beerothite from the
tribe of Benjamin—Beeroth is considered part of Benjamin, 3 because
the people of Beeroth fled to Gittaim and have lived there as aliens to
this day.

4 (Jonathan son of Saul had a son who was lame in both feet. He was
five years old when the news about Saul and Jonathan came from

Jezreel. His nurse picked him up and fled, but as she hurried to leave, he
fell and became crippled. His name was Mephibosheth.)
5 Now Recab and Baanah, the sons of Rimmon the Beerothite, set out
for the house of Ish-Bosheth, and they arrived there in the heat of the
day while he was taking his noonday rest. 6 They went into the inner part
of the house as if to get some wheat, and they stabbed him in the
stomach. Then Recab and his brother Baanah slipped away.
7 They had gone into the house while he was lying on the bed in his
bedroom. After they stabbed and killed him, they cut off his head.
Taking it with them, they traveled all night by way of the Arabah. 8 They
brought the head of Ish-Bosheth to David at Hebron and said to the
king, "Here is the head of Ish-Bosheth son of Saul, your enemy, who
tried to take your life. This day the LORD has avenged my lord the king
against Saul and his offspring."
9 David answered Recab and his brother Baanah, the sons of Rimmon
the Beerothite, "As surely as the LORD lives, who has delivered me out of
all trouble, 10 when a man told me, 'Saul is dead,' and thought he was
bringing good news, I seized him and put him to death in Ziklag. That
was the reward I gave him for his news! 11 How much more—when
wicked men have killed an innocent man in his own house and on his
own bed—should I not now demand his blood from your hand and rid
the earth of you!"
12 So David gave an order to his men, and they killed them. They cut
off their hands and feet and hung the bodies by the pool in Hebron. But
they took the head of Ish-Bosheth and buried it in Abner's tomb at
Hebron.

Saul the king is dead, Jonathan the heir apparent is dead, Abinadab and Malki-Shua (two of Jonathan's brothers) are dead (1 Sam 31:2), Abner the commander of the army is dead—and no other viable claimants or pretenders continue to block David's accession to the throne except Saul's son Ish-Bosheth and Jonathan's son Mephibosheth. Chapter 4 removes them from the scene, one explicitly and the other implicitly. The chapter is a masterpiece of literary artistry, as the following outline demonstrates:

- A. The *dramatis personae* (4:1–4)
  1. Ish-Bosheth, Baanah, Recab (4:1–3)
  2. Mephibosheth, lame in both feet (4:4)
- B. The deed (4:5–8)
  1. The murder of Ish-Bosheth (4:5–7)
  2. His head brought to David (4:8)
- C. The consequences (4:9–12)
  1. The verdict of David (4:9–11)
  2. The execution of Recab and Baanah, whose hands and feet are cut off (4:12)

Each of the three main sections contains four verses, further divided into a three-verse unit followed by a one-verse conclusion (each of which features one or more parts of the body). Verses 1 and 12 form an *inclusio,* the common elements of which are "Ish-Bosheth" (see Notes on v.1), "Abner" (mentioned only in vv.1, 12 in this chapter), "Hebron," and "hands" (used in the plural only in vv.1, 12 in this ch.; see comment on v.1).

**1–3** When David "heard" that Abner had died, he declared his own innocence and cursed Abner's murderer (3:28–29). When Ish-Bosheth "heard" that Abner had died, "he lost courage" (v.1; lit., "his hands became weak/limp," a common and picturesque idiom; cf. 17:2; 2 Chron 15:7 ["give up"]; Neh 6:9; Isa 13:7; Jer 6:24; 50:43; Ezek 7:17; 21:7; Zeph 3:16)—a typical and expected reaction (cf. 3:11). Abner's death left a power vacuum in the north, and it is therefore not surprising that all Israel became "alarmed" (the Heb. verb is translated "shaken" in 1 Sam 28:21).

Among the opportunists eager to take charge are two of Ish-Bosheth's men who are "leaders of raiding bands" (v.2; in the singular the phrase is translated "leader of a band of rebels" in 1 Kings 11:24). Such groups functioned under David's authorization as well (3:22; 1 Chron 12:18) and were not uncommon elsewhere during the early days of Israel's monarchy (cf. 1 Sam 30:1, 8, 15). Ish-Bosheth's men, Baanah and Recab, were Beerothites (for another prominent Beerothite, who became Joab's armor-bearer, cf. 23:37 = 1 Chron 11:39) from Beeroth in Benjamin, Ish-Bosheth's tribal homeland. A town of the Gibeonite tetrapolis (Josh 9:17) assigned to Benjamin (Josh 18:21, 25), ancient Beeroth is probably modern Khirbet el-Burj located four and a half miles northwest of Jerusalem. Its indigenous population had become "aliens" (v.3; cf. 1:13) in Gittaim (modern Ras Abu Humeid, seventeen miles northwest of Beeroth) at the edge of Philistine territory, doubtless because they were driven out by invading Benjamites. Beeroth is thus considered "part of" Benjamin (v.2)—unlike Gibeonites proper who, although Saul had tried to annihilate them, were not a "part of" Israel (21:2) because Joshua had earlier "made a treaty of peace with them to let them live" (Josh 9:15).

Though from Beeroth, Baanah and Recab were members of the tribe of Benjamin and thus ostensibly loyal to Saul (and Ish-Bosheth). It is therefore incorrect to state that their plot against Ish-Bosheth is "an effort at revenge for the violence with which Saul had apparently treated the Gibeonites, Israel's treaty partners" (Vanderkam, "Davidic Complicity in the Deaths of Abner and Eshbaal," p. 534 n. 40). McCarter notes that the treachery of Baanah and Recab "is born not of revenge but of crass opportunism and the hope of a reward from David" (*II Samuel*, p. 128).

**4** Jonathan's son Mephibosheth is introduced parenthetically to demonstrate that his youth and physical handicap disqualify him for rule in the north. Symon Patrick provides another possible reason: "to show, what it was that emboldened these Captains [Banaah and Recab] to do what follows: Because he, who was the next Avenger of Blood, was very young; and besides was lame and unable to pursue them" (p. 364).

In brief compass the verse provides information concerning why the boy is "lame in both feet" (the same Heb. phrase is echoed in 9:3 ["crippled in both feet"]). Soon after the death of Saul and Jonathan (1 Sam 31:2–6), news concerning the tragedy was relayed from Jezreel (see comment on 1 Sam 29:1) to the remaining members of the Saulide clan, probably by Israelites fleeing the battlefield (1 Sam 31:7). When the nurse of Jonathan's son learned that the boy's father had been killed, she too decided to flee with the boy to a safer location. In her headlong flight (cf. the similar incident in 2 Kings 7:15) the boy fell from her grasp and became permanently crippled (for Mephibosheth's subsequent history, cf. ch. 9; 16:1–4; 19:24–30; 21:7). Five years old when his father died, Mephibosheth would still have been only twelve (cf. 2:11) at the time of the assassination of his uncle Ish-Bosheth.

**5–7** The story of that assassination is the focus of the chapter. Mabee helpfully entitles vv.5–8 "The Deed" and vv.9–12 "Consequence" ("David's Judicial Exoneration," p. 100; cf. similarly my outline in comment on 4:1–12), although his insistence on a judicatory backdrop in the account is overdone. Baanah's name appears before that of Recab in v.2, perhaps because he was the older of the two men. In the rest of the chapter, however, Recab's name always occurs first (vv.5–6, 9), probably indicating that he is the prime instigator of the murder of Ish-Bosheth.

The two brothers go to the "house of Ish-Bosheth" (v.5; doubtless in Mahanaim; cf. 2:8, 12, 29) and arrive there at the time of siesta in "the heat of the day" (i.e., high noon; cf. Gen 18:1; see esp. 1 Sam 11:9, 11 and comment), knowing full well that Ish-Bosheth would be sleeping. As Abner had been murdered in the "midst/inner part" of the gateway at Hebron (see comment on "into" in 3:27), so Ish-Bosheth would be murdered in the "inner part" of his house (v.6; the same Heb. word). As Joab had lured Abner to his death ("as though to speak with him privately," 3:27), so Recab and Baanah would gain access to Ish-Bosheth's sanctum through subterfuge ("as if to get some wheat"). And Ish-Bosheth would die as Abner had died: In each case the assailant(s) "stabbed him in the stomach" (v.6; 3:27)—a technique rapidly becoming the preferred method of killing during David's reign (see comment on 2:23).

Ish-Bosheth is assassinated while lying on "the bed in his bedroom" (v.7), luxuries available only to the wealthy or to royalty in those days (Exod 8:3; 2 Kings 6:12; Eccl 10:20). "The narrative uses three verbs to characterize [the murderers'] action (v.7). They strike, they kill, they decapitate (cf. I Sam. 17:46 [also 17:50]). Ish-Bosheth, pitiful creature bereft of Abner, is three times dead" (Brueggemann, *First and Second Samuel*, p. 234). The verb "cut off" (cf. also 16:9; 2 Kings 6:32) is literally "remove" and evokes a crude and grisly image. Recab and Baanah had entered Ish-Bosheth's house as if to "get" (v.6, lit., "take") wheat; they are now "taking" (v.7; cf. also v.12) Ish-Bosheth's head to David as a trophy of their vile deed. To avoid easy detection they travel through the night by way of the Arabah (see comment on 2:29) from Mahanaim to Hebron, a distance of almost thirty miles.

**8** Presenting the head of Ish-Bosheth to David, Recab and Baanah remind him that Ish-Bosheth's father, Saul, had been David's "enemy" (see comments on 1 Sam 18:29; 19:17; 24:4). Indeed, Saul had "tried to take" (lit., "sought") David's "life" on many occasions (see comment on 1 Sam 20:1). But now, say the assassins, the Lord himself—to whom belongs all vengeance (cf. David's words to Saul in 1 Sam 24:12; cf. also Deut 32:35; Rom 12:19; Heb 10:30)—has "avenged" (cf. 22:48–49a = Ps 18:47–48a) David not only against Saul but also against Saul's "offspring" (including Ish-Bosheth, the last viable scion of the Saulide line). And now that none of Saul's descendants remains an obstacle to Davidic pretensions or ambitions, "the gift of Ish-Bosheth's head [to David] is at the same time the gift of the kingdom" (David M. Gunn, "David and the Gift of the Kingdom [2 Sam 2–4, 9–20, 1 Kings 1–2]," *Semeia* 3 [1975]: 17).

**9–11** The assassins' offer (v.8) and the king's response (vv.9–11) are the only direct quotations in the chapter. Agreeing that it is the Lord who avenges and rescues, David takes an oath in his name (v.9; see esp. 1 Sam 14:39 and comment). The MT of David's entire statement in v.9 is echoed verbatim in 1 Kings 1:29 (where the NIV renders "every trouble" instead of "all trouble," as here). The two asseverations form an *inclusio* surrounding the timespan of David's reign as king in Jerusalem, the first being spoken just after his rival Ish-Bosheth is killed and the last just before his own son Solomon becomes king. "Delivered me" is literally "redeemed/ransomed my life," a phrase commonly used by Israel's psalmists (e.g., Pss 34:22; 49:8, 15; 55:18;

71:23). To the assassins' reminder that Saul had tried to take David's "life" (v.8) the king responds that the Lord delivers his "life" (v.9) out of "all trouble" (including the difficulties he had faced when he was a fugitive from Saul's wrath; see comment on 1 Sam 26:24).

Like the Amalekite who claimed to have killed Saul (1:10), Recab and Baanah can hardly have expected David's blistering response to their murder of Saul's son Ish-Bosheth (vv.10–11; see 1:14, 16). The man who had "told" David that Saul was dead (v.10) was of course the Amalekite (see comment on 1:4). Although he thought he was bringing "good news" (see comments on 1:20; 1 Sam 31:9), he brought about only his own death at David's headquarters in Ziklag (cf. 1:1). Expecting a "reward" for his news (cf. 18:22), he received death instead. "While Paul's discussion of the rights of the Christian preacher is based on different premises in 1 Corinthians 9:1–18, his references to his personal 'reward' for his preaching of the 'good news' (vv.16–18) could hint at the custom reflected here" (Gordon, *I & II Samuel*, p. 223).

If David condemned the Amalekite for delivering the *coup de grâce* to the mortally wounded Saul on the battlefield, the a fortiori—"how much more" (v.11; cf. 1 Sam 14:30; 21:5; 23:3)—is self-evident in this context: (1) Recab and Baanah, "wicked men," have killed Ish-Bosheth, an "innocent" (lit., "righteous") man (cf. similarly Solomon's condemnation of Joab for killing Abner and Amasa, both of whom were more "upright" [1 Kings 2:32; same Heb. word] than he). Mabee further observes:

> The criminality of the defendants is clearly shown in their designation as רשעים [*rš'ym*], while the deceased is termed צדיק [*ṣdyq*]. . . . Therefore the crime is not regicide—even though it is a king who is murdered. . . . Although Ish-Bosheth was crowned king, he was not anointed (II Sam 2 9). Thus, there is an implicit denial of Ish-Bosheth's kingship at the point where David refers to him as a "righteous man." Of course, the case is quite different at II Sam 1 14. ("David's Judicial Exoneration," p. 104 and n. 48)

(2) Although Saul was killed in a context of danger and violence in battle, Ish-Bosheth was murdered in what should have been the secure and peaceful serenity of "his own house and on his own bed" (v.11; since David is aware of this detail, the assassins must have told him more than the summary statement of v.8 implies). David's outrage (whether real or pretended) over the circumstances of Recab and Baanah's assassination of Ish-Bosheth causes him to "demand his blood from your hand"—that is, hold them accountable for his death (see comment on 1 Sam 20:16; cf. similarly Gen 9:5; Ezek 3:18, 20; 33:6, 8). Again and again Saul had "tried to take" (v.8, lit., "sought") David's life; now David is in a position to "demand" (lit., "seek") the blood of Saul's son Ish-Bosheth from the hands of his assassins.

**12** "All who draw the sword will die by the sword," said Jesus (Matt 26:52). Death begets death: The Amalekite claimed to have killed Saul, and in retaliation David "put him to death" (v.10); Recab and Baanah have "killed" Ish-Bosheth (v.11), so David gives the order that they in turn be "killed" (v.12; same Heb. verb in all three cases).

As Adoni-Bezek had been mutilated by having "his thumbs and big toes" (lit., "the thumbs of his hands and of his feet") "cut off" (Judg 1:6), so David's men mutilate the dead bodies of Recab and Baanah by "cut[ting] off" (same Heb. verb) their "hands" (see comment at the introduction to vv.1–12; cf. v.1 and comment) and "feet" (cf. v.4).

Symon Patrick makes the quaint observation that this was done "by *David's* Order no doubt: They having slain their Master with their *hands,* made their escape from Justice with their *feet*" (p. 366; cf. similarly KD).

Since the object of "hung" is left unexpressed in the MT, commentators are divided concerning whether it is "hands and feet" (e.g., Kirkpatrick, Mauchline, Smith) or "bodies" (supplied by the NIV; cf. also Anderson, Gordon, KD). The latter is preferable, however, since it was the ancient custom to expose to public view the entire corpse of the victim (whether mutilated or not) whenever possible (cf. 21:9–10; 1 Sam 31:9–10; Deut 21:22–23; Josh 10:26–27; Esth 2:23). It is ironic indeed that the prolonged struggle between Ish-Bosheth's men and David's men begins and ends by the placid waters of a pool. Although the location of the "pool of Gibeon" is almost certainly known (see comment on 2:13), that of the "pool of Hebron" remains obscure (for discussion cf. Anderson, p. 72).

The contrast between the treatment of the remains of the assassins and of Ish-Bosheth could hardly be more striking. The Hebrew word for "head" is in emphatic position in v.12b, justifying the NIV's "But" at the beginning of the sentence. While the dead bodies of Recab and Baanah are impaled in a public setting to disgrace them and deter others, Ish-Bosheth's head is given an honorable burial in Abner's tomb at "Hebron"—the headquarters of David, their political rival. "Just as Abner takes (לקח) Ish-Bosheth and makes him king (2 8–9), now David and his men take (לקחו) the head of Ish-Bosheth and bury it" (Mabee, "David's Judicial Exoneration," p. 105; Ish-Bosheth's head is also the object of the verb "taking" in v.7). Erstwhile comrades in life, Abner and Ish-Bosheth sleep in the same tomb in death. If at Abner's funeral David walked behind the dead man's "bier" (*miṭṭāh,* 3:31), David now oversees the funeral of Ish-Bosheth, ruthlessly killed while lying peacefully in "bed" (*miṭṭāh,* v.7).

With the death of Ish-Bosheth, no other viable candidate for king remains for the elders of the northern tribes. Meanwhile David sits in regal isolation, above the fray as always, innocent of the deaths of Saul, Jonathan, Abner, and now Ish-Bosheth. The way is open for his march to the throne of Israel.

## Notes

---

1 As in 3:7 (see Notes in loc.), so also here (and in v.2) the name "Ish-Bosheth" is not present in the MT. Although it is possible that "a deliberate excision of the offensive name is to be presumed" in vv.1–2 (Clines, "X, X *Ben* Y, *Ben* Y," p. 286), a more satisfactory solution has been given by Frank Moore Cross, Jr.:

> In II Sam. 4:1, 2 the *MT* reads *wyšm' bn š'wl . . . hyw bn š'wl. . . .* The latter phrase makes no sense whatever; the former is not happy. In both the *LXX* and 4QSam[a] the reading is *wyšm' mpybšt bn š'wl* [v.1], which grammatically makes perfect sense. However, Mephibosheth is an obvious blunder. Ishbosheth is meant in both instances. The reviser of the text did not replace the erroneous reading with the correct one; rather he excised the mistake and left the text standing. In the case of *hyw lmpybšt bn š'wl* [v.2], he cut out not only *mpybšt* but also *l* and forgot to replace it before *bn šwl* [*sic*], leaving nonsense. (*The Ancient Library of Qumran and Modern Biblical Studies* [Garden City: Doubleday Anchor, 1961], p. 191 n. 45)

3 Gittaim ("Two Gaths"), mentioned by its full name elsewhere only in Neh 11:33, may be the same as the Gath of 1 Chron 7:21 and 8:13.

4 Since children in ancient Israel were normally weaned by the age of three (see comment on 1 Sam 1:22), Mephibosheth's "nurse" was not a wet nurse but a hired attendant who "cared for" him (as the samae Heb. verb is translated of Naomi's relationship to Obed in Ruth 4:16).

As scribal tradition often substituted "Ish-Bosheth" (which means "Man of Shame") for "E/Ish-Baal" (which means "Man of Baal"; see comment on 2:8), so also Mephibosheth's real name was Merib-Baal (cf. 1 Chron 8:34; 9:40; and NIV mg.). Although מְרִיב בַּעַל (*m$^{e}$rîḇ ba'al*) is usually translated "Baal Defends [My] Case" (cf. Albright, *Archaeology and the Religion of Israel,* p. 113) or the like, it should probably rather be considered an *Ersatzname* and rendered "Baal Substitutes" (for details see Notes on Jerub-Baal in 1 Sam 12:11). The second occurrence (left untr. in NIV) of Merib-Baal's name in 1 Chron 8:40 is spelled מְרִי־בַעַל (*m$^{e}$rî-ḇa'al;* all LXX recensions also exhibit only one *b* in Meri[b]-Baal in 1 Chronicles), which perhaps means "Rebel[lion] of Baal" (cf. מְרִי [*m$^{e}$rî,* "rebellion"] in 1 Sam 15:23). As for מְפִיבֹשֶׁת (*m$^{e}$p̄îḇōšeṯ*), "One Who Scatters Shame" is the probable meaning (for details cf. Werner Weinberg, "Language Consciousness in the OT," ZAW 92, 2 [1980]: 201 n. 40)—although revocalizing the MT to read מִפִּיבֹשֶׁת (*mippîḇōšeṯ*) would produce the translation "From the Mouth of Shame."

6 The MT's הֵנָּה (*hēnnāh,* "here," "they," or revocalized as הִנֵּה [*hinnēh,* "behold"]) at the beginning of the verse is superfluous in English and is therefore justifiably omitted by the NIV. Considering v.7 a doublet of v.6, many translations (e.g., NAB, NJB, REB, RSV, TEV) and commentators (e.g., Driver, Gordon, Hertzberg, Kirkpatrick, Mauchline, McCarter, Smith; cf. also BHK) have been attracted to the LXX version of v.6: "And behold, the woman guarding the house had been cleaning wheat, and she had nodded off and fallen asleep. So Recab and his brother Baanah slipped in." The MT, however, yields good sense as it stands (esp. if v.7 is rendered in the pluperfect) and has therefore been retained by many translations (e.g., KJV, ASV, NASB, NIV) and commentators (e.g., KD, Anderson, Baldwin [although hesitantly]; cf. BHS, Barthélemy). In any event, repetition of information in successive verses (as in vv.6–7) is a common feature of Hebrew narrative and is attested here in the immediate context (3:22–23—which, interestingly, also begins with "Behold" [NIV, "Just then"]).

7 BHS's אֶל (*'al*) is a typographical error for עַל (*'al,* "on"; cf. BHK).

The custom of possessing a severed head as a victory trophy was common in ancient times and was practiced by Sumerians, Egyptians, Assyrians, and Romans (among others). An excellent example of such a trophy is the head of the Elamite king Teumman. Reliefs from the reign of Ashurbanipal (669–626 B.C.) picture Teumman being decapitated, his head being transported in a captured Elamite mule-drawn wagon, and his preserved (perhaps embalmed) head attached to a large ring suspended from the upper branches of a pine tree (for details, including photographs of the reliefs, cf. Pauline Albenda, "Landscape Bas-Reliefs in the *Bīt-Ḫilāni* of Ashurbanipal," BASOR 225 [1977]: 29–33).

9 The idiom "redeem/ransom [one's] life" (see comment) is almost always translated "redeem [one's] soul" in the KJV. Although in the present context the phrase does not have salvific significance, Derek Kidner is surely on target in his comment on Ps 34:22: "At whatever level David himself understood his affirmation of 22a, *the Lord redeems the life . . . ,* the whole verse is pregnant with a meaning which comes to birth in the gospel, and which is hardly viable in any form that falls short of this" (*Psalms 1–72: An Introduction and Commentary on Books I and II of the Psalms* [Downers Grove: InterVarsity, 1973], pp. 141–42).

---

## 4. *David anointed king over Israel*

### 5:1–5

1 All the tribes of Israel came to David at Hebron and said, "We are
your own flesh and blood. 2 In the past, while Saul was king over us, you

**were the one who led Israel on their military campaigns. And the LORD said to you, 'You will shepherd my people Israel, and you will become their ruler.'"**

**3 When all the elders of Israel had come to King David at Hebron, the king made a compact with them at Hebron before the LORD, and they anointed David king over Israel.**

**4 David was thirty years old when he became king, and he reigned forty years. 5 In Hebron he reigned over Judah seven years and six months, and in Jerusalem he reigned over all Israel and Judah thirty-three years.**

Just as the account of the anointing of David as king over Judah (2:1–7) nestles near the center of the first major literary unit of 2 Samuel (1:1–3:5), so also the report of his anointing as king over all Israel (5:1–5) is located near the center of the second major unit (3:6–5:16). And just as 2:1–7 divides naturally into two roughly equal sections (vv.1–4a, 4b–7), so also does 5:1–5 (vv.1–3, 4–5). "All the tribes of Israel came to David at Hebron" (v.1) forms an *inclusio* with "When all the elders of Israel had come to King David at Hebron" (v.3), and vv.3 and 5 end by referring to David as *mlk* ("king," v.3; "reigned," v.5) "over (all) Israel" (cf. similarly Carlson, p. 52).

The rationale for the division is further strengthened by the fact that vv.1–3 are paralleled in 1 Chronicles 11:1–3 while vv.4–5 are paralleled in 1 Chronicles 3:4b; 29:26–27 (cf. also 1 Kings 2:11).

**1–3** That the kingdom about to be established under King David is intended as a truly united monarchy is underscored by the use of the word "all" three times (vv.1, 3, 5). The "elders" of Israel (v.3; cf. 17:4, 15; 1 Sam 4:3; 8:4; 15:30), representing the "tribes" (v.1), come to David at Hebron with the express purpose of submitting to his rule. Preliminary consultations with the elders had already been initiated by Abner (3:17), but his death had postponed further discussion. In any event, David may have preferred not to pursue the matter until after Ish-Bosheth's abortive reign was no longer a factor. The eagerness of the elders to make David the king over all Israel without further delay is reflected in the consistent double expression of personal subject (explicit in the MT) throughout their brief plea to David: "We [ourselves] are" (v.1), "you [yourself] were" (v.2a), "you [yourself] will" (v.2b), "you [yourself] will" (v.2c).

At the very least, the elders' reference to themselves as "your own flesh and blood" (lit., "your bone and your flesh," v.1) signifies their sense of kinship with him (cf. Wilfred G.E. Watson, "Some Additional Word Pairs," in *Ascribe to the Lord: Biblical and Other Studies in Memory of Peter C. Craigie*, JSOT suppl. 67, edd. Lyle Eslinger and Glen Taylor [Sheffield: JSOT, 1988], p. 186; cf. also 19:12–13; Gen 2:23; 29:14; Judg 9:2). Thus the elders declare their first reason for desiring David as their king: He is a "brother Israelite" (Deut 17:15; so already Symon Patrick, p. 367). In addition, however, Walter Brueggemann has argued that "[We are your] bone and flesh" is "a statement of loyalty in initiating and affirming a treaty relationship . . . a covenant formula which describes the commitments of partners to each other who have obligations to each other in all kinds of circumstances, thick and thin (*'ṣm* and *bśr*)" ("Of the Same Flesh and Bone [Gn 2,23a]," CBQ 32, 4 [1970]: 536, 538; cf. pp. 532–42 for full discussion; cf. also id., *First and Second Samuel*, p. 237). The elders' affirmation to David, then, anticipates the covenant-making scene of v.3.

The elders' second reason is that during Saul's reign David was Israel's best army officer—a fact recognized even by the Philistines (1 Sam 29:3, 5; cf. Brueggemann, *First and Second Samuel*, p. 237). Indeed, David was "the one who led Israel in their military campaigns" (v.2), the rendering of a Hebrew phrase that means literally "the one who led out and the one who brought back Israel" (cf. Num 27:17, 21; see also comment on 1 Sam 18:13, 16). In the days of the prophet Samuel, the elders of Israel (1 Sam 8:4) had demanded "a king to lead us and to go out before us and fight our battles" (1 Sam 8:20). Saul was to some extent such a king, but David would be supremely so—as events would soon demonstrate (vv.6–12, 17–25).

Their understanding that the Lord has chosen David (a perception that had been shared by Abner; cf. 3:18) is the elders' third reason for wanting him to ascend to Israel's throne. They sense that the Lord has invested David with the titles of "shepherd" and "ruler" (v.2) as well as "king" (v.3). With respect to the term "shepherd," Symon Patrick is technically correct in his observation that this is "the first time we find a Governour described by this Name in Scripture" (p. 368). Apart from God himself (Gen 48:15; 49:24), David is the first example of a specific person being called a "shepherd," although the idea in principle antedates him by several centuries (cf. Num 27:17). Moreover, the motif of David as shepherd was prefigured at his earliest anointing (see comment on 1 Sam 16:11; for details cf. the fine summary by Walters, "The Light and the Dark," pp. 574–75).

Understanding that the figure of the shepherd would be immediately familiar to their subjects and that they would readily associate it with gentleness, watchfulness, and concern, ancient Near Eastern rulers commonly referred to themselves as "the shepherd" (see Notes). Since it is the shepherd's task to lead, feed, and heed his flock, the shepherd metaphor was a happy choice for benevolent rulers and grateful people alike (cf. Jer 3:15; 23:4). David thus becomes the paradigm of the shepherd-king (cf. Ps 78:70–72; Ezek 34:23; 37:24), and it is not surprising that "great David's greater son," Jesus Christ, should be introduced frequently and glowingly in the NT as the "good shepherd" (John 10:11, 14), the "great Shepherd" (Heb 13:20), and the "Chief Shepherd" (1 Peter 5:4), the one who provides for his sheep all things needful for the abundant life.

Needless to say, a benevolent shepherd can change into a tyrannical despot. Forgetting that he is supposed to lead his sheep to verdant pastures, he can drive them mercilessly and trample them underfoot (Jer 23:1–2; Ezek 34:1–10; Zech 11:4–17). "It is not accidental that Nathan's parable utilizes the shepherd-sheep metaphor to indict David (12:1–4). In the episode of Bathsheba and Uriah, David misuses his role as shepherd and at enormous cost works only to enhance his own situation" (Brueggemann, *First and Second Samuel*, p. 238). In the beginning David could do no wrong (3:36), but with the passing of time his power would become increasingly seductive and intoxicating—to the detriment of himself, his family, and his people.

In addition to being called "shepherd," David is called *nāg̱îḏ* ("ruler") as well. Carlson notes that "the 'shepherd' motif is also connected with the term *nāg̱îḏ* in 7:8" (p. 53; more precisely, 7:7–8), thus linking the two passages together. The title "ruler, leader" provided a convenient transition between judgeship on the one hand and kingship on the other. Although more than a judge, the *nāg̱îḏ* was not yet a king in the full sense of that term (see comment on 1 Sam 9:16).

Dale Patrick suggests that "there is only one account in Biblical literature of a covenant being made between a human king and his subjects where sovereignty itself was at issue: 2 Sam. v 1–3" ("The Covenant Code Source," VetTest 27, 2 [1977]: 152; cf. also Patrick's helpful comparisons between covenant-making elements in the narrative framework [Exod 19:3–8; 24:3–8] and similar elements in vv.1–3 [ibid., pp. 152–53]). David's sovereignty is underscored by the threefold reference to him as "king" in v.3. He does not go to Israel's elders in Mahanaim; they come to him in Hebron. Their need for him is greater than his for them—although the stakes are enormous on both sides.

Abner had suggested earlier that Israel "make a compact" with David (see 3:21 and comment; lit., "cut a covenant/treaty," for which see comments on 1 Sam 11:1; 18:3). But now that the moment for such an agreement has arrived, it is the king who initiates the compact with his (future) subjects, not the other way around (v.3; cf. similarly Jer 34:8). At the same time, however, the covenant should not be understood as bestowing on David the role of all-powerful suzerain and dooming the Israelites to become his craven vassals. "The evident meaning is that David bound himself formally to certain contractual obligations toward the Israelites" (McCarter, *II Samuel*, p. 132; cf. similarly Brueggemann, *First and Second Samuel*, p. 239). The covenant-making formalities take place "before the LORD" (v.3), acknowledging that the proceedings are under his guidance and enjoy his blessing (v.12; see 1 Sam 11:15 and comment).

As David had earlier been anointed king over Judah (see 2:4 and comment), so now he is anointed king over Israel, "as the LORD had promised through Samuel" (1 Chron 11:3; cf. 1 Sam 15:28; 16:13). "There is, thus, a duality in the kingship of David, a duality which reasserted itself in the breaking free of Israel from Judah and the Davidic dynasty after the death of Solomon" (Cross, *Canaanite Myth and Hebrew Epic*, p. 230; cf. "all Israel and Judah," v.5). The news of the anointing would soon become well enough known to cause concern in the hearts of the Philistines (v.17). Although for a while David would bask in the afterglow of his divine unction, his failure to live up to God's expectations for it and demands connected with it would evoke prophetic wrath (12:7)—just as in the case of his predecessor Saul (1 Sam 15:17–19).

**4–5** Before its use to characterize David's reign, the regnal formula—"So-and-so was *x* years old when he became king, and he reigned *y* years" (v.4)—was used of Saul (1 Sam 13:1) and of Ish-Bosheth son of Saul (2 Sam 2:10), after whom it was reserved exclusively for kings headquartered in Judah (for details see comments on 1 Sam 13:1).

As Jacob's son Joseph had become vizier of Egypt at the age of thirty (Gen 41:46), so Jacob's descendant David became king in Hebron when he was thirty years old (v.4)—the approximate age of Jesus "when he began his ministry" (Luke 3:23). David's overall reign of forty years matches that of his predecessor Saul (cf. Acts 13:21; see also comment on 1 Sam 13:1) as well as that of his son and successor Solomon (1 Kings 11:42). If thirty years represents the age when a man reached his maturity and could thus (if from the tribe of Levi) enter service at the Israelite tabernacle (Num 4:47), forty years "represents the period of a complete generation" (Segal, "Numerals," p. 11; cf. Ps 95:10). David's total life span matches the psalmist's ideal: "The length of our days is seventy years" (Ps 90:10).

The forty-year reign of David consisted of seven and a half years in Hebron over Judah alone (v.5; 2:11; 1 Chron 3:4; the seven years of 1 Kings 2:11 and 1 Chron 29:27 is intended only as a round number) and thirty-three years in Jerusalem over all Israel and Judah. Although Jerusalem had not been unknown to David before the elders of Israel anointed him (see 1 Sam 17:54 and comment), he is now determined to make it his capital.

## Notes

**2** מוֹצִיא וְהַמֵּבִי (*môṣî' wᵉhammēḇî*) should be corrected to הַמּוֹצִיא וְהַמֵּבִיא (*hammôṣî' wᵉhammēḇî'*, "the one who led out and the one who brought back") on the basis of the *Qere* and 1 Chron 11:2. In the MT the loss of the ה (*h*) at the beginning of the first word and of the א (') at the end of the second was due either to haplography or to the phenomenon of shared consonants (for the latter cf. Watson, "Shared Consonants," p. 531).

In the prologue to his celebrated code of laws, Hammurapi of Babylon (c. 1792–1750 B.C.) refers to himself as "the shepherd, called by Enlil," and as "the shepherd of the people"; in the epilogue he speaks of the people "whose shepherding Marduk had committed to me," calls himself "the beneficent shepherd," and pronounces a blessing upon his successor if the latter heeds the words of Hammurapi's statutes: "May he shepherd his people in justice!" (cf. ANET, pp. 164–65, 177–78).

The etymological origins of עַם (*'am*, "people") remain obscure despite a recent attempt of Robert McClive Good, *The Sheep of His Pasture: A Study of the Hebrew Noun* 'Am(m) *and Its Semitic Cognates*, Harvard Semitic Monograph 29 (Chico: Scholars, 1983): "The noun *'am(m)* represents the sound made by caprine beasts and originally signified 'flock' " (p. 2). Good's theory is especially tantalizing in light of OT references to shepherding of people, but his philological arguments are based primarily on hypothetical evidence derived from a supposed Arabic cognate—and Hebrew-Arabic isoglosses are distressingly few in number at best. Reviewers of Good's thesis have been understandably skeptical (cf. Carol Meyers in CBQ 48, 1 [1986]: 106–8; J.J.M. Roberts in JBL 105, 2 [1986]: 325–26).

Although it is well known that Matt 2:6 quotes Mic 5:2 (see NIV mg. on Matt 2:6), it is not commonly recognized that the latter half of Matt 2:6 also cites the present passage, "doubtless due to the suggestion in Mic 5:4" (Robert L. Reymond, *Jesus, Divine Messiah: The Old Testament Witness* [Ross-shire: Christian Focus, 1990], p. 56; cf. also Homer Heater, Jr., "Matthew 2:6 and Its Old Testament Sources," JETS 26, 4 [1983]: 395–97; A.J. Petrotta, "A Closer Look at Matt 2:6 and Its Old Testament Sources," JETS 28, 1 [1985]: 47–52).

### 5. *David's conquest of Jerusalem*

#### 5:6–12

6 The king and his men marched to Jerusalem to attack the Jebusites,
who lived there. The Jebusites said to David, "You will not get in here;
even the blind and the lame can ward you off." They thought, "David
cannot get in here." 7 Nevertheless, David captured the fortress of Zion,
the City of David.

8 On that day, David said, "Anyone who conquers the Jebusites will
have to use the water shaft to reach those 'lame and blind' who are
David's enemies." That is why they say, "The 'blind and lame' will not
enter the palace."

9 David then took up residence in the fortress and called it the City of
David. He built up the area around it, from the supporting terraces
inward. 10 And he became more and more powerful, because the LORD
God Almighty was with him.

11 Now Hiram king of Tyre sent messengers to David, along with cedar
logs and carpenters and stonemasons, and they built a palace for David.
12 And David knew that the LORD had established him as king over Israel
and had exalted his kingdom for the sake of his people Israel.

In the MT *wayyēlek* ("he went") stands at the beginning of v.6 ("marched") and v.10 ("became"), thus forming an *inclusio* around vv.6–10. Other verbs that tie the section together are *yšb* ("live," "take up residence," vv.6, 9) and *bw'* ("get in," "enter," vv.6 [bis], 8). The terms "fortress" (vv.7, 9) and "the city of David" (vv.7, 9) are repeated as well. That vv.6–10 constitute a literary unit separate from vv.11–12 emerges also from the fact that vv.6–10 are paralleled in 1 Chron 11:4–9 while vv.11–12 are paralleled in 1 Chron 14:1–2. The larger section is further divisible into the account of how David conquered Jerusalem (vv.6–8) and how he then settled in the city and built it up (vv.9–10).

The separation between 1 Chron 11:4–9 and 14:1–2 opens up the possibility that the order of events from 2 Sam 5:6 onward may be thematic rather than chronological. Eugene H. Merrill argues that such is in fact the case. Concerning chapter 5 he observes:

> 2 Sam. 5:1–9a can . . . be confidently assigned to [David's accession] year. The commencement of building activities (9b) must also have taken place then, but it is inconceivable that they were completed within the year (5:11–12) and that David's becoming "more and more powerful" (5:10) and his accumulation of a large family all transpired in that brief time (5:13–16). The Philistine wars (5:17–25), on the other hand, almost certainly preceded the conquest of the city and yet, as the historian emphasizes, followed David's accession to the Saulide throne (5:17). The reason for the inclusion of the Philistine campaigns here no doubt lies in the fact that the ark—the subject of chapter 6—was in Philistine territory at Kiriath-jearim and the defeat of the Philistines would explain how the ark could be safely removed from there to Jerusalem. ("The 'Accession Year' and Davidic Chronology," *Journal of the Ancient Near Eastern Society* 19 [1989]: 108)

Thus David's palace (v.11) may not have been built until as long as twenty-five years after the wars against the Philistines (vv.17–25) and the conquest of Jerusalem (vv.5–8; cf. Merrill, *Kingdom of Priests*, p. 244). Although one might quibble with one or more details of Merrill's analysis, he demonstrates conclusively that the author/compiler of 2 Samuel did not intend to provide a strictly chronological narrative. Indeed, vv.6–16 highlight key events of David's entire reign and are followed by summaries of his experiences in the military (vv.17–25), cultic (ch. 6), and theological (ch. 7) arenas.

**6–8** "These verses are among the most difficult in the books of Samuel" (Brueggemann, *First and Second Samuel*, p. 239). Jones, however, has greatly advanced their understanding and, by building on the suggestions of earlier interpreters, has cleared up many problems (pp. 119–41).

The catchword "Jerusalem" (v.6) links vv.6–8 to the previous section (Carlson, p. 55; cf. v.5). Jerusalem, although usually thought to mean "Foundation of [the God] Shalem" (cf. IDB, 2:843), probably means "City of [the God] Shalem" (cf. Ronald F. Youngblood, "Ariel, 'City of God,'" in *Essays on the Occasion of the Seventieth Anniversary of the Dropsie University [1909–1979]*, edd. Abraham I. Katsh and Leon Nemoy [Philadelphia: Dropsie, 1979], p. 460; cf. independently Mauchline, p. 216). Far and away the most important city in the Bible, Jerusalem is mentioned there more often than any other. Geographically and theologically it is located "in the center of the nations" (Ezek 5:5). Known also by its abbreviated name "Salem" (Ps 76:2), it makes only one appearance in the OT before the time of Joshua (Gen 14:18; cf. also Heb 7:1–2, where *šālēm* is defined as "peace," *šālôm,* through wordplay).

The gloss in 1 Chronicles 11:4 (cf. also Josh 15:8; 18:28; Judg 19:10) explains that Jerusalem was also known as Jebus (meaning unknown), whose pre-Israelite, pagan inhabitants were thus called Jebusites, probably of Hurrian/Hittite origin (Ezek 16:3, 45; for details cf. Harry A. Hoffner, Jr., "The Hittites and Hurrians," in *Peoples of Old Testament Times,* ed. D.J. Wiseman [Oxford: Clarendon, 1973], p. 225). Since the earlier inhabitants of Jerusalem were Amorites (Josh 10:5; cf. also Ezek 16:3, 45), "it appears that Jerusalem was not Jebusite till the time of the Israelite Conquest" under Joshua (Benjamin Mazar, "Jerusalem in the Biblical Period," in *Jerusalem Revealed: Archaeology in the Holy City 1968–1974,* ed. Y. Yadin [Jerusalem: Israel Exploration Society, 1975], p. 4). In any event, "the Jebusite settlement in Jerusalem . . . was so firmly established in the city that it could not be dislodged by the Israelites, but remained as a foreign enclave in their midst when they settled in the land and persisted in this way until David conquered Jerusalem" (Jones, p. 122).

Soon after being anointed king over all Israel and Judah (v.5), David deploys his men for a march on Jerusalem "to attack the Jebusites, who lived in the land" (v.6; NIV, "lived there"). The phrase "in the land" is problematic since the Jebusites seem to have been confined to Jerusalem (and only part of the city at that). Wilfred G.E. Watson has thus suggested that *hayᵉḇusî yôšēḇ hā'āreṣ* ("the Jebusites, who lived in the land") be translated "the Jebusite ruler of the city" ("David Ousts the City Ruler of Jebus," VetTest 20, 4 [1970]: 501–2). But (1) 1 Chronicles 11:4 clearly understands the singular form "Jebusite" in v.6 as a collective by following it with the plural form *yōšᵉḇê,* and (2) that *'ereṣ* ever means "city" in the OT remains to be proven and should therefore not be used to promote a rendering that is suspect on other grounds.

The solution proposed by Jones (pp. 125–26) is much to be preferred: Jerusalem was the name for the Jebusite settlement on two hills, one of which was heavily defended (the "fortress of Zion," v.7) and was located in the southeast sector of the present city while the other consisted of unprotected open country located in the southwest. In addition, the "threshing floor of Araunah the Jebusite" (24:16), where the temple of Solomon would eventually be built (2 Chron 3:1), was north of the fortress in an open area. It is clear, therefore, that many Jebusites lived outside the fortress and could be referred to as being "in the land"—either in the sense of living in the open country, or by synecdoche: "Because they inhabited the region around the south-eastern hill, the text is correct; but it lacks precision in that it uses the name of the whole for the part, and does not specify that, when David went up to Jerusalem, he was going to attack the fortress on the south-eastern hill" (ibid., p. 126).

The two-site location of Jebusite Jerusalem also explains the apparent contradiction between Joshua 15:63 and Judges 1:8. The former text states that at the time of the conquest Israel "could not dislodge the Jebusites, who were living in Jerusalem" (cf. also Judg 1:21)—a reference to the fortress on the southeastern hill. The latter text asserts that the men of Judah "attacked Jerusalem . . . and took it. They put the city to the sword and set in on fire"—a reference to the open settlement on the southwestern hill. It may even be the case that the OT name of Jerusalem, *yᵉrûšāla[y]im* (lit., "Two Jerusalems"), referred to the two distinct sites of the Jebusite city.

The interchange about the "blind" and the "lame" in vv.6 and 8, although interpreted in numerous ways (for a convenient summary, cf. Gilbert Brunet, "Les Aveugles et Boiteux Jebusites," in *Studies in the Historical Books of the Old Testament,* VetTest suppl. 30, ed. J.A. Emerton [Leiden: Brill, 1979], p. 72), is best understood as "an example of pre-battle verbal taunting, somewhat similar to the exchanges between the Rabshakeh and the Jerusalemites in 2 Kgs 18.19–27" (Jones, p. 125). Thus in v.6 the Jebusites smugly claim that even disabled people can withstand any attack on their fortress, while in v.8 David retaliates in kind by characterizing all Jebusites—"David's enemies"—as "lame and blind" (whether the defenders of the fortress could hear all or part of David's rejoinder is impossible to say).

The overconfident Jebusites, however, reckon without the skill and determination of David, who captures the fortress of Zion and renames it the "city of David" (vv.7, 9; cf. Jones, p. 123). Its conqueror, he also becomes its owner and gives it his name. But David's defeat of the Jebusites does not mean that he wiped them out.

> On the evidence of the friendly negotiations between David and Araunah in 2 Sam. 24.18–25, and David's insistence on paying a fair price for the Jebusite's threshing-floor rather than taking possession of it as conqueror, it can be suggested that there was no outright slaughter of the Jebusites or an attempt to oust them from their stronghold. . . . Jerusalem is usually described as a city-state, and the position envisaged after its storming by David and his troops is that it remained a city-state; the coming of David meant only a change of city ruler. . . . The inhabitants remained, but their fortress had now become the personal possession of David and was under his control. (ibid., p. 135)

Although occurring more than 150 times in the OT, the name "Zion" (meaning unknown) appears only six times in the historical books (beginning here [= 1 Chron 11:5]; cf. also 1 Kings 8:1 = 2 Chron 5:2; 2 Kings 19:21, 31). Referring in v.7 to the Jebusite citadel on the southeastern hill, the name is also used elsewhere of the temple mount (e.g., Isa 10:12) or of the entire city of Jerusalem (e.g., Isa 28:16).

Up to this time Jerusalem had been on the border between Judah in the south (Josh 15:1, 5, 8) and Benjamin in the north (Josh 18:11, 16). Tied to no tribe, the City of David (a name that the southeastern hill continued to bear long after David's time, Isa 22:9; cf. also Isa 29:1) could champion its neutrality, central location, and virtual impregnability as qualities that made it and its environs the ideal capital for David's newly established, united kingdom.

Since v.7 describes the fortress of Zion as already captured and v.8 records David's instructions to its potential captor, "said" (v.8) is better rendered as a pluperfect ("had said," as in 1 Chron 11:6). The "one who conquers the Jebusites" (v.8) would turn out to be Joab, who would be rewarded with the position of commander-in-chief of the armies of united Israel as a result (1 Chron 11:6). Exactly how the fortress was captured remains unclear because the meaning of *ṣinnôr* is uncertain. Here translated "water shaft," it is rendered "waterfalls" in its only other occurrence in the OT (Ps 42:7; cf. perhaps also *ṣanṯ*ᵉ*rôṯ* ["pipes (for pouring out oil)," in Zech 4:12]). Assuming that "water shaft" or the like is correct, Joab (perhaps assisted and accompanied by his men) would then have either (1) climbed up through a tunnel that led from a water source outside the city to a location somewhere within the city or (2) cut off the citadel's water supply and thus forced the "lame and blind"—the Jebusite defenders—to surrender. Despite its attractiveness, the earlier theory that the Jebusite *ṣinnôr* is to be identified with the water shaft that leads from the Gihon spring to the southeastern hill and that was discovered by Charles Warren in 1867 remains unproven (cf. Anderson, p. 84; Kathleen M. Kenyon, *The Bible and Recent Archaeology*, rev. ed. [Atlanta: John Knox, 1987], p. 92; Philip J. King's review of Harry

Thomas Frank, *Discovering the Biblical World,* ed. James F. Strange; rev. ed. [Maplewood: Hammond, 1988], in *Biblical Archaeology Review* 15, 1 [1989]: 13).

David's declaration that the Jebusites, the "lame and the blind," are his enemies eventually gave rise to an epigram: "The 'blind and lame' will not enter the palace" (v.8), which would be built at an indeterminate time in the future (v.11). The revulsion of David for the Jebusites barred them from associating with him from that day onward. Carlson's observation that in its context the saying expresses "the idea that Mephibosheth is disqualified by his lameness from filling the functions of the sacral king in the palace and the temple" (p. 57) forges a useful link between v.8 and related texts (cf. Lev 21:18; Deut 15:21; Mal 1:8, 13). At the same time, however, David would eventually welcome the lame Mephibosheth (9:13) into the royal palace, and in the messianic age the blind and the lame would be special recipients of divine favor (cf. Isa 35:5–6; Jer 31:8; Matt 12:22; 21:14; Acts 3:7–8). "In the old Jerusalem of this text, the blind and lame are excluded and despised. In the new Jerusalem envisioned by the gospel, all are welcomed. . . . David, the provoked warrior, might exclude. David, the embodiment of Israel's best hope, will eventually include" (Brueggemann, *First and Second Samuel,* pp. 241–42; cf. also esp. M. Dennis Hamm, *The Beatitudes in Context: What Luke and Matthew Meant* [Wilmington: Michael Glazier, 1990], pp. 90–91, 105).

**9–10** David thus "took up residence" (v.9) in Jerusalem where the Jebusites "lived" (v.6; same Heb. verb). Expropriating the "fortress" (of Zion, v.7; see comment there) as his private property, he renamed it "the City of David" (v.9; see comment on v.7). He then set about to repair the surrounding areas "from the supporting terraces inward." The term rendered "supporting terraces" is Millo (see NIV mg.), which means "fill(ing)." Depending on the topography, fill on which other structures could be erected (in Judg 9:6 and 2 Kings 12:20, the proper name Beth Millo means "House of [i.e., built on] Fill") might consist of rock, tamped earth, or a combination. In the present case "the term *Millo* refers to stone-filled terraces . . . supported by the retaining walls located along the eastern slope of the southeastern ridge" (W. Harold Mare, *The Archaeology of the Jerusalem Area* [Grand Rapids: Baker, 1987], p. 65; cf. also Kathleen Kenyon, *Royal Cities of the Old Testament* [New York: Schocken, 1971], pp. 33–35). As the city expanded, the terraces would expand accordingly (1 Kings 9:15, 24; 11:27) and in any event would be in constant need of repair and reinforcement (2 Chron 32:5). First Chronicles 11:8 observes that, in addition to David's building activities, Joab (David's commander-in-chief and the point man in Jerusalem's conquest) "restored the rest of the city" (parts of which were doubtless damaged or destroyed as a result of Joab's attack to capture it).

The assertion that David "became more and more powerful" (v.10) is reminiscent of 3:1 (see comment there). Now as earlier, however, David himself is not the source of his strength. The narrator is quick to remind his readers that "the LORD God Almighty" (a title for God that is more royal than military; see comment on 1 Sam 1:3), the true King of Israel, grants his power and, as always, is "with him" (see 1 Sam 16:18 and comment; cf. also 1 Sam 17:37; 18:12, 14, 28).

**11–12** The fact that vv.6–10 are paralleled in 1 Chronicles 11:4–9 while vv.11–12 are not paralleled until 1 Chronicles 14:1–2 hints at the possibility that the events described in vv.11–12 occurred a long time after those recorded in vv.6–10. That possibility becomes a certainty when it is noted that Hiram (v.11) did not become king of Tyre until about 980 B.C. (and thus more than twenty years after David was anointed king over Israel and conquered Jerusalem). Hiram continued his friendly relations with Israel's royal house well into the reign of David's son Solomon (1 Kings 5:1–12; 9:10–14). Hiram's name, an abbreviation of Ahiram, means "Brother of the Exalted (God)," as does the variant spelling Huram, which occurs often in Chronicles (see the NIV mg. on 2 Chron 2:3). Located just beyond the border of the tribal territory of Asher (Josh 19:24, 29) more than fifty miles north of Jerusalem, Tyre ("Rock") was a well-fortified island in the Mediterranean Sea with a supply depot (called Ushu by the Assyrians) on the coast nearby. The former island is now joined to its mainland sister, and the two sites exist as eṣ-Ṣur today.

During the latter part of David's reign and much of Solomon's, Hiram traded building materials (which Israel lacked) for agricultural products (which Phoenicia lacked). Thus Hiram sends to David logs of "cedar" (v.11; *Cedrus libani,* whose "fragrant wood is much sought after for building purposes, as it does not easily rot" [*Fauna and Flora of the Bible,* p. 108]; cf. 1 Kings 5:6–10; 6:9–10; 9:11; 1 Chron 22:4; 2 Chron 2:3, 8), doubtless lashed into rafts and floated down the Mediterranean coast to Joppa, from which they would be transported overland to Jerusalem (cf. 1 Kings 5:8–9; Ezra 3:7). He also sends David carpenters and stonemasons (cf. also 2 Kings 12:11–12; 1 Chron 22:15), both of which were in short supply in Israel (cf. 1 Kings 5:6, 18).

All this activity would eventuate in a "palace for David" (v.11)—a palace that would fill him with a certain unease (7:1–2). Brueggemann puts his finger on at least a part of the problem that David faces:

> David has joined the nations. David is a practitioner of alliances and accommodations. . . . Jeremiah later sees that cedar and its accompanying opulence will talk Judean kings out of justice (Jer. 22:13–18). Verse 11 sounds like a historical report, but it is in fact an ominous act of warning. (*First and Second Samuel,* p. 246)

For now, however, David—witnessing God's evident blessing on his life—once again acknowledges the Lord's role in establishing "him as king over Israel" (v.12). Indeed, David's throne and dynasty would be established forever (7:11b–16; 22:51; 1 Sam 25:28), culminating in the eternal reign of great David's greater Son (Luke 1:30–33). As Israel's ideal ruler, David has the privilege of seeing his kingdom "exalted" (v.12; "highly exalted," 1 Chron 14:2) by the Lord himself. All this is not for his own sake alone but also—and primarily—for the sake of "his" (i.e., God's) people.

## Notes

---

**6** Symon Patrick (p. 371) calls attention to the following commonly-held theory (among others):

> A great many by *the blind and the lame* understand the Images of their Gods. . . . As if they had said, our Gods, whom ye call blind and lame, that have Eyes and see not, Feet and walk not (as it is CXV. *Psal.*) they shall defend us: And you must overcome them, before you overcome us. *Luther* himself thus explains the Sense; *These blind and lame,* saith he, *were the Idols of the Jebusites; which to irritate David, they set upon*

*their Walls, as their Patrons and Defenders: And they did as good as say, thou dost not fight with us, but with our Gods; who will easily repel thee.*

Similar to this is a Hittite soldiers' oath calculated to strike terror into the hearts of all who would presume to oppose the Hittite rulers:

> They parade in front of them a (blind woman) and a deaf man and [you speak] as follows: "See! here is a blind woman and a deaf man. Whoever does evil to the king (and) the queen, let the oaths seize him! Let them make him blind! Let them [ma]ke him [deaf]! . . . Let them [annihilate him], the man (himself) together with his wife, [his children] (and) his kin!" (ANET, p. 354).

7 In 1983 archaeologist Yigal Shiloh uncovered what is probably the base of the Jebusite citadel, the "fortress of Zion." Built no later than the fourteenth century B.C., the substructure itself is immense, covering more than 2,150 square feet of space (cf. Norman Kempster, *Los Angeles Times* [August 16, 1983]: 1; Hershel Shanks, "The City of David After Five Years of Digging," *Biblical Archaeology Review* 11, 6 [1985]: 25–26).

8 The fact that צִנּוֹר (*ṣinnôr*) means "water duct/pipe/spout" in Mishnaic and modern Hebrew supports the interpretation given in the comment on v.8. The NIV margin ("scaling hooks") is based primarily on an Aramaic cognate, as are similar renderings offered by a few versions (e.g., REB) and commentators (e.g., William F. Albright, "The Old Testament and Archaeology," in *Old Testament Commentary*, edd. Herbert C. Alleman and Elmer E. Flack [Philadelphia: Muhlenberg, 1948], p. 149; Merrill F. Unger, "Archaeology and the Reign of David," BS 111, 441 [1954]: 13–14; Yadin, *The Art of Warfare*, p. 268). Other translations have also been proposed (for a typical list cf. Gilbert Brunet, "David et le *Ṣinnôr*, " in *Studies in the Historical Books of the Old Testament*, p. 74 n. 9).

"David's enemies" renders either the *Kethiv* שָׂנְאוּ נֶפֶשׁ דָּוִד (*śānᵉʾû nep̱eš dāwiḏ* ("they hate David's soul") or the *Qere* revocalized שֹׂנְאֵי נֶפֶשׁ דָּוִד (*śōnᵉʾê nep̱eš dāwiḏ*, "haters of David's soul"). The NIV margin ("hated by David") translates the *Qere* שְׂנֻאֵי נֶפֶשׁ דָּוִד (*śᵉnuʾê nep̱eš dāwiḏ*, "hated of/by David's soul"). 1QSam[a] reads the verb as שׂנאה (*śnʾh*), resulting in the translation "David's soul hates," making active the passive *Qere* reading. Although any of the readings makes good sense, the epigram in v.8b gives a slight edge to the NIV margin.

9 בָּיְתָה (*bāyᵉṯāh*), here translated "inward" (cf. Exod 28:26 = 39:19 ["inside"]; 1 Kings 7:25 = 2 Chron 4:4 ["toward the center"]), could also be translated "to the palace," especially since בַּיִת (*bayiṯ*) means "palace" in vv.8, 11. Fortunately both renderings lead to the same result.

11 Although Alberto R. Green places Hiram's accession to the throne of Tyre too early (c. 1000 B.C.), his detailed treatment of all the data available for determining the date is invaluable ("David's Relations With Hiram: Biblical and Josephan Evidence for Tyrian Chronology," in *The Word of the Lord Shall Go Forth: Essays in Honor of David Noel Freedman in Celebration of His Sixtieth Birthday*, ASOR special vol. series 1, edd. Carol L. Meyers and M. O'Connor [Winona Lake: Eisenbrauns, 1983], pp. 373–97). Whereas Green gives Hiram a reign of a half century (pp. 389–91), other representative scholars whose calculations Green records (p. 392) assign the Tyrian king a total of thirty-four regnal years ranging from as early as 980–947 B.C. to as late as 962–929 B.C.

The phrase translated "stonemasons," חָרָשֵׁי אֶבֶן קִיר (*ḥārāšê ʾeḇen qîr*), means literally "craftsmen of stone of wall," in which the word for wall refers to the wall of a building (as opposed to a city wall). The parallel in 1 Chron 14:1 omits *ʾeḇen* ("stone").

---

## 6. *Children born to David in Jerusalem*

### 5:13–16

**13After he left Hebron, David took more concubines and wives in Jerusalem, and more sons and daughters were born to him. 14These are**

**the names of the children born to him there: Shammua, Shobab, Nathan, Solomon, 15 Ibhar, Elishua, Nepheg, Japhia, 16 Elishama, Eliada and Eliphelet.**

As the list of sons born to David in Hebron (3:2–5) concludes the account of his accession to kingship over Judah (1:1–3:5), so the roster of children born to David in Jerusalem concludes the narrative of his accession to kingship over Israel (3:6–5:16). The two lists may originally have been parts of one (as in 1 Chron 3:1–8) and only later separated, as the phrase "After he left Hebron" (v.13) suggests (cf. 3:5b: "These were born to David in Hebron"). In any case and at the very least, "After he left Hebron" indicates that the lists are chronologically sequential.

**13–16** In violation of the divine decree to Israel's future kings not to "take many wives" (Deut 17:17), David takes "more" concubines and wives (v.13)—that is, in addition to his wives Ahinoam and Abigail (see comment on 1 Sam 25:43) and to the wives he had already taken in Hebron (see comment on 3:5). This is the first time that concubines are mentioned in connection with David (cf. also 1 Chron 3:9)—and it is also the only time that the phrase "concubines and wives" occurs in the Bible (the usual order is "wives and concubines"; cf. 19:5; 1 Kings 11:3; 2 Chron 11:21; Dan 5:2–3, 23). By placing the word "concubines" in emphatic position, the narrator is perhaps deploring David's proclivity for the trappings of a typical Oriental monarch, including a harem.

David fathered many "sons and daughters" (v.13) in Jerusalem. Although vv.14–16 list only sons born to him by his wives (as 1 Chron 3:9 states), the name of at least one of David's daughters has survived (Tamar, the sister of Absalom; cf. 13:1; 1 Chron 3:9).

Verses 13–16 are paralleled in 1 Chronicles 3:5–8 and 14:3–7. The following chart prepared by James W. Flanagan (*David's Social Drama: A Hologram of Israel's Early Iron Age,* JSOT suppl. series 73 [Sheffield: Almond, 1988], p. 348) is useful for comparing the three passages:

| 2 Sam 5:14–16 | 1 Chron 3:5–8 | 1 Chron 14:4–7 |
|---|---|---|
| Shammua | Shimea | Shammua |
| Shobab | Shobab | Shobab |
| Nathan | Nathan | Nathan |
| Solomon | Solomon | Solomon |
| Ibhar | Ibhar | Ibhar |
| Elishua | Elishama | Elishua |
| | Eliphelet | Elpelet |
| | Nogah | Nogah |
| Nepheg | Nepheg | Nepheg |
| Japhia | Japhia | Japhia |
| Elishama | Elishama | Elishama |
| Eliada | Eliada | Beelida [*sic*] |
| Eliphelet | Eliphelet | Eliphelet |

The most obvious difference among the three lists is the omission of two names (El[i]p[h]elet, Nogah) in 2 Samuel 5. Scribal error is the probable cause, since the names from Ibhar to the end are correctly added up as nine in 1 Chronicles 3:8. The first of the two names may have been omitted either because of its similarity to

Elishua, which immediately precedes it, or its identity to Eliphelet (the last name in the list). As for Nogah, it may have dropped out by haplography because of its similarity to Nepheg, which immediately follows it.

Apart from the two omissions, the list in 2 Samuel 5 is almost identical to that in 1 Chronicles 14. The only exception is Eliada ("God Knows," v.16) in place of Beeliada ("Baal Knows," 1 Chron 14:7), which—although doubtless the original name—was considered shameful by one or more of the scribes who transmitted 2 Samuel and was therefore altered (for a similar phenomenon see comment on Ish-Bosheth in 2:8). It is likely, therefore, that 1 Chronicles 14 is the most accurate of the three lists, faithfully preserving the correct forms of the names of all thirteen of David's sons who were born in Jerusalem.

The 1 Chronicles 3 list, on the other hand, is the most poorly transmitted of the three, although with only modest variations from the other two. Shimea (1 Chron 3:5) is an alternate form of Shammua, both names meaning "Heard (by God)." While 2 Samuel 5:15 and 1 Chronicles 14:5 have Elishua ("My God Is Salvation"), 1 Chronicles 3:6 reads Elishama ("My God Hears"), a duplicate of the antepenultimate name in all three lists. And while 1 Chronicles 14:5 has Elpelet ("God Is Deliverance"), 1 Chronicles 3:6 contains the variant Eliphelet ("My God Is Deliverance"), a duplicate of the last name in all three lists. In addition, 1 Chronicles 3:5 also misspells Bathsheba as "Bathshua" (see NIV mg. on 1 Chron 3:5–6 for details on this and other related matters).

The first four names in the list (v.14) are of sons born to David by Bathsheba (1 Chron 3:5), two of whom appear elsewhere in the biblical narratives (the only two among the thirteen sons in the lists to do so; cf. Baldwin, p. 199). Nathan ("[God] Gives"; not to be confused with the famous prophet of the same name) is mentioned in Luke 3:31 in the genealogy of Jesus. Solomon ("[God Is] His Peace"), appearing here for the first time in the Bible and David's tenth son overall (David himself was an eighth son), would eventually outlast his rivals for the throne and rule over the united kingdom (cf. 1 Kings 1:28–39).

It is worth noting that at least four of David's sons born in Jerusalem (five, if Beeliada/Eliada is included) had names containing the element El ("God")—Elishua, Elpelet (1 Chron 14:5), Elishama, Eliphelet—while none of the names contained the element Yah ("LORD"). Of the sons born to David in Hebron, however, none bore El names while two—Adonijah, Shephatiah (3:4)—had names containing Yah. The relatively high proportion (a third of the total at each site) seems to be deliberate and may reflect the often claimed preference of Judahites for the name Yah(weh) and of Israelites (members of the northern tribes) for the name El(ohim) respectively. If so, David may have had political considerations in mind by catering to northern predilections in naming his Jerusalem sons.

A final observation: The two main claimants to David's throne in his later years were Absalom (his third-born, 3:3) and Solomon (his tenth-born). Although the first means "(Divine) Father of Peace" and the second "(God Is) His Peace," it is hardly accidental that each of the two men was anxious to rule over Jerusalem—a city whose name, dominated by the same basic root (*šlm*), probably means "City of (the God) Shalem" (see comment on v.6; cf. similarly Jones, p. 127; Talmon, p. 152 n. 19).

## Notes

---

**13** "In Jerusalem" translates מִירוּשָׁלַם (*mîrûšālaim,* lit., "from Jerusalem"). That מִן (*min,* "from") means "in" here is clear, however, from the parallel in 1 Chron 14:3, which reads בִּירוּשָׁלָם (*bîrûšālāim;* for other examples cf. Sarna, "The Interchange of *Beth* and *Min,*" pp. 312–13).

**16** The alternation between Eliada (v.16) and Beeliada (1 Chron 14:7) is strikingly paralleled in the Book of Judges. A god named Baal-Berith appears in Judg 8:33, and the "temple of Baal-Berith" is mentioned in Judg 9:4. But the same building is later called the "temple of El-Berith" (Judg 9:46). In this case, however, the variation in name was an intra-Canaanite issue: "El was the nominal head of the Canaanite pantheon, but his position was virtually taken over by Baal, the great, active god, in a process taking many generations" (Arthur E. Cundall, *Judges: An Introduction and Commentary* [Chicago: InterVarsity, 1968], p. 135).

---

### C. *David's Powerful Reign (5:17–8:18)*

As the story of David's accession to kingship over Judah (1:1–3:5) parallels that of his accession to the throne of Israel (3:6–5:16), each concluding with a list of his sons (3:2–5; 5:13–16), so the account of his powerful reign (5:17–8:18) parallels that of his court history (chs. 9–20), each concluding with a roster of his officials (8:15–18; 20:23–26).

The narrative before us is especially representative of those early chapters of 2 Samuel that Carlson describes as "David under the blessing" (p. 39). A key verse in this respect, highlighting as it does the manifest blessing of the Lord upon David and his activities, is 7:29, containing the final, emphatic words of David's prayer: "Now be pleased to bless the house of your servant, that it may continue forever in your sight; for you, O Sovereign LORD, have spoken, and with your blessing the house of your servant will be blessed forever."

Excluding the appendix (8:15–18), 5:17–8:18 exhibits a chiastic structure:

A. The Philistines defeated (5:17–25)
  B. The ark brought to Jerusalem (6:1–23)
    C. The Lord's covenant with David (7:1–17)
  B′. David's prayer (7:18–29)
A′. David's enemies defeated (8:1–14)

The section detailing the provisions of the Davidic covenant is of supreme importance and therefore occupies pride of place at the center of the literary unit.

#### 1. *The Philistines defeated*

5:17–25

**[17]When the Philistines heard that David had been anointed king over
Israel, they went up in full force to search for him, but David heard about
it and went down to the stronghold. [18]Now the Philistines had come and
spread out in the Valley of Rephaim; [19]so David inquired of the LORD,
"Shall I go and attack the Philistines? Will you hand them over to me?"
The LORD answered him, "Go, for I will surely hand the Philistines over
to you."
[20]So David went to Baal Perazim, and there he defeated them. He
said, "As waters break out, the LORD has broken out against my enemies**

**before me." So that place was called Baal Perazim. [21]The Philistines
abandoned their idols there, and David and his men carried them off.
[22]Once more the Philistines came up and spread out in the Valley of
Rephaim; [23]so David inquired of the LORD, and he answered, "Do not go
straight up, but circle around behind them and attack them in front of
the balsam trees. [24]As soon as you hear the sound of marching in the
tops of the balsam trees, move quickly, because that will mean the LORD
has gone out in front of you to strike the Philistine army." [25]So David did
as the LORD commanded him, and he struck down the Philistines all the
way from Gibeon to Gezer.**

Paralleled in 1 Chronicles 14:8–16 (which contains a few significant and helpful differences), 5:17–25 describes two Israelite victories over the Philistines, their agelong enemies. The two confrontations (vv.17–21, 22–25) are similar in several ways: (1) The Philistines are the aggressors (they "went up/came up [same Heb. verb] . . . and spread out," vv.17–18, 22); (2) the locale is the same ("the Valley of Rephaim," vv.18, 22); (3) David's response to the challenge is the same (he "inquired of the LORD," vv.19, 23); (4) David obeys God's command ("So David went/did," vv.20, 25); (5) the battles end in the same way (David "defeated/struck down" [the same Heb. verb] the enemy, vv.20, 25); (6) "YHWH—not David—is prominent as Israel's ultimate warrior" (Howard, "The Case for Kingship," p. 113; cf. vv.19, 24). Although by no means the only battles King David fought against the Philistines (cf. 8:1), these serve as a paradigm to summarize the continuing conflict.

**17–21** "David's capture of Jerusalem . . . has been placed [by commentators] before, after, and between the two Philistine incursions on the valley of Rephaim" (Christian E. Hauer, Jr., "Jerusalem, the Stronghold, and Rephaim," CBQ 32, 4 [1970]: 571; cf. similarly Jones, p. 121). Although Hauer himself argues that the events in chapter 5 are roughly chronological and that David seized Jerusalem "immediately after his anointment as king over all Israel" ("Jerusalem, the Stronghold, and Rephaim," pp. 572–75), KD is surely correct in its observation that both of David's victories over the Philistines "belong in all probability to the interval between the anointing of David . . . and the conquest of the citadel of Zion" (p. 323). It is as soon as the Philistines learn "that David had been anointed" that they become concerned (v.17), not at a later time. Furthermore, they go to "search" for him, an unnecessary task if David had already occupied the formidable fortress of Zion.

Both armies rely on military intelligence reports as they deploy their forces: The Philistines "heard" and "went up," and then David "heard" and "went down" (v.17). The tentacles of David's intelligence system were evidently widespread and effective (10:7, 17; cf. Hauer, "Foreign Intelligence," p. 97).

The "stronghold" (*mᵉṣûḏāh*, v.17) to which David retreats is not the "fortress" of Zion (*mᵉṣuḏāh*, vv.7, 9), in spite of the fact that the two Hebrew words are morphologically identical. That the first is here written *plene* and the second defectively suggests that the author intends to make a distinction between them. Also David "went down" to the stronghold, an act that cannot describe the ascent necessary to reach the hill on which Zion rests. Although the cave of Adullam is a possible candidate for the "stronghold" (thus Hauer, "Jerusalem, the Stronghold, and Rephaim," pp. 575–78; Carlson, p. 56 n. 2), the latter, while sometimes mentioned in association with Adullam (23:13–14; 1 Sam 22:1–5), is never equated with the cave itself and in at least one case cannot be so equated (see comment on 1 Sam 22:4–5).

The precise identification and location of David's stronghold must therefore remain uncertain.

The NIV pluperfect "had come" (v.18) is correct, both grammatically (cf. N.L. Tidwell, "The Philistine Incursions Into the Valley of Rephaim," in *Studies in the Historical Books of the Old Testament,* suppl. to VetTest 30 [Leiden: Brill, 1979], p. 206) and contextually (the Philistine action in v.18 is antecedent to that of David in v.17). In 1 Chronicles 14:9, 13, the verb "raided," which is substituted for "spread out" in the present section (vv.18, 22), merely indicates that the Philistines have more than one purpose in mind and should not be used to argue that vv.18–21 were originally written to describe a less momentous occasion and only later became displaced into the present context (as asserted by Tidwell, ibid., pp. 195–98, 205, 211–12). If "spread out" is often used in scenes suggestive of plunder (cf. Judg 15:9), it is also used in a more general sense (cf. Isa 16:8).

The locale of the two battles is the "Valley of Rephaim" (vv.18, 22; cf. also 23:13 and comment), west-southwest of Jerusalem on the border between the tribal territories of Judah and Benjamin (Josh 15:1, 8; 18:11, 16). A relatively flat area, its fertile land produced grain that not only provided food for Jerusalem (Isa 17:5) but also attracted raiding parties. It is known today as el-Baqʿa, "through which the modern railway achieves its Jerusalem terminus" (Hauer, "Jerusalem, the Stronghold, and Rephaim," p. 573 n. 10).

Bruce K. Waltke (ZPEB, 5:64–66) asserts that *rᵉp̱āʾîm,* from *rp*ʾ ("heal") and/or *rph* ("sink," "relax," thus "sunken/powerless ones"), is used in the OT in three distinct senses, the relationship between which is obscure: (1) Inhabitants of the netherworld ("dead," "departed spirits," "spirits of the dead/departed": Job 26:5; Ps 88:10; Prov 2:18; 9:18; Isa 14:9; 26:14, 19). "The most that can be said with certainty about this use of *rephaim* is that the Israelites applied the term to people who were dead and gone" (ibid., p. 64). (2) Pre-Israelite inhabitants of Transjordan ("Rephaites": Gen 14:5; 15:20; Deut 2:11, 20; 3:11, 13; Josh 12:4; 13:12; 17:15), noted for their great height (Deut 2:10–11; 3:11). (3) Giants who were descendants of Rapha, the eponymous ancestor of one distinct group of Rephaim (21:16, 18, 20, 22; 1 Chron 20:4 ["Rephaites"], 6, 8). Goliath, the Philistine giant (1 Sam 17:4), may have been such a "Rephaite" (21:19; 1 Chron 20:5). It is impossible to know whether the Valley of Rephaim was named after one of these three groups (cf., however, Tidwell, "Philistine Incursions," pp. 203–4).

To meet the Philistine threat David, as always, "inquired of the LORD" (v.19) by consulting the Urim and Thummim through a priest (see comments on 2:1; 1 Sam 14:36, 40–42; 23:2; for structural similarities between several of these passages, cf. Tidwell, ibid., p. 208). Having gone "down" to the stronghold (v.17), David now asks the Lord (1) whether he should "go" (lit., "go up") and attack the Philistines and (2) whether the Lord will hand them over to him (v.19). The divine answer is emphatically affirmative to both questions ("Go" is again literally "Go up").

In obedience to God's command, David "went" (the verb is singular, v.20; the parallel in 1 Chron 14:11 uses a plural verb, which the NIV translates by adding "and his men" after "David" [see also comment on v.25]) to engage the Philistines in battle at Baal Perazim (location unknown, although modern ez-Zuhur, four miles southwest of Jerusalem, has been suggested). Meaning "The Lord [in this case Yahweh, not Baal] Who Breaks Out" (see NIV mg.), Baal Perazim was so named because of David's affirmation following the Philistine defeat: "As waters break out, the LORD has broken out against my enemies before me" (v.20). The phrase "before me" underscores the divine initiative in the Lord's fighting on David's behalf, as does "in front of you" in v.24 (same Heb. in both instances). Purposeful divine wrath may "burst/break out" at any time, not only against God's enemies, but also against his own people (Exod 19:22, 24; 1 Chron 15:13; Job 16:14; Ps 60:1; 106:29). A string of names involving the element Perez began early in Israel's history when Judah's son was named Perez ("Breaking Out"; see NIV mg. on Gen 38:29) because he had "broken out" of his mother's womb. In addition to Baal Perazim, another place name—Perez Uzzah ("The Outbreak Against Uzzah"; see NIV mg. at 6:8)—would soon arise, this time from the Lord's anger breaking out against a disobedient Israelite (6:8 = 1 Chron 13:11).

In full retreat from the forces of Israel, the Philistines abandon "their idols" (v.21), which they had probably brought onto the battlefield as protective talismans (see comment on 1 Sam 4:3 concerning a similar use of the ark by the Israelites). Although other renderings have been suggested for *ʿaṣabbêhem* in this case (e.g., vessels or containers for carrying plunder [Tidwell, "Philistine Incursions," p. 211]; scimitars as religious images [F. Willesen, "The Philistine Corps of the Scimitar From Gath," JSS 3, 4 (1958): 333–34]), the traditional translation is preferable in light of 1 Chronicles 14:12, where the parallel has "their gods" (cf. also LXX, OL). The purpose of carrying the Philistine idols away from the battlefield (v.21; cf. similarly 2 Chron 25:14) was so that, at David's command and in accordance with Mosaic prescription (Deut 7:5, 25), they could be burned up (1 Chron 14:12).

**22–25** On an indeterminate subsequent occasion ("once more," v.22), the Philistines again "came up" (cf. "went up," v.17). The narrator echoes the first battle account by stating that they "spread out in the Valley of Rephaim" (see v.18 and comment). As before (v.19), David inquires of the Lord (v.23). Unlike earlier, however, this time David is told not to "go (straight) up" (v.23; see comment on v.19, where "go" renders the same Heb. verb). Apparently the first confrontation was with a smaller contingent of Philistines, whereas now a flanking movement ("circle around behind them") is strategically preferable. The Israelite attack is apparently to take place in front of a grove of "balsam" trees, although the identification of the kind of tree/shrub (*beḵāʾîm*) remains uncertain (KJV, e.g., renders "mulberry"; REB, "aspen"; NAB, "mastic"; cf. Hertzberg, "mastic terebinth"). It may well be that the Valley of Baca (*bāḵāʾ*), obviously in the vicinity of Jerusalem (Ps 84:5–6), received its name from the event recorded here.

The Lord instructs David to "move quickly" (v.24) as soon as he hears the sound of "marching" in the treetops. Related to a Hebrew root meaning "step, pace, march," the noun translated "marching" nevertheless occurs only here. Chaim Herzog and Mordechai Gichon make the intriguing suggestion that David, "aware of the fact that the daily breeze from the sea reaches the Jerusalem area at about noon, . . . timed his attack for this hour, so that the rustle of the trees would cover the steps of the stealthily approaching Israelites" (*Battles of the Bible* [New York: Random House, 1978], p. 80). However that may be, the significance of the sound in the treetops again stresses the divine initiative: "The LORD has gone out in front of you" (v.24), an almost verbatim echo of Judges 4:14, "Has not the LORD gone ahead of you?" (Carlson, pp. 56–57; cf. also Gerbrandt, p. 148). Indeed, Howard calls attention to the contrast between the present text "and 1 Sam 8:20, where Israel had asked for a king who would 'go out before us and fight our battles'" ("The Case for Kingship," p. 113).

It is stated of David that, acting at God's command (a common OT response; cf. Gen

50:12; Exod 7:10, 20; Num 8:3; Josh 4:8; Ezek 12:7), "he struck down" (the parallel in 1 Chron 14:16 includes David's men by reading "they struck down") the Philistines (v.25, echoing "strike" in v.24; see comment on "defeated" in v.20). In describing the complete rout of the enemy, the narrator uses a common idiom of retreat in stating that they were pursued "all the way from" (cf. 1 Sam 15:7) Gibeon (six miles northwest of Jerusalem; see comment on 2:12) to Gezer. A city in the northern foothills in the tribal territory of Ephraim just east of the Philistine plain, Gezer remained a Canaanite enclave because of the ultimate failure of the Israelites to drive out its inhabitants (Josh 16:3, 10; Judg 1:29). Today called both Tell Jezer and Tell Abu Shusheh, Gezer is located fifteen miles due west of Gibeon and is one of the most important archaeological sites in the entire region. Philistine as well as Israelite remains have been unearthed there (cf. the early summary articles by H. Darrell Lance, "Gezer in the Land and in History," and William G. Dever, "Excavations at Gezer," in BA 30, 2 [1967]: 34–62).

"The biblical record does not claim that David actually conquered Philistia. He merely pushed the Philistines out of his territory as far as Gezer. . . . Without conquering, David was still able to maintain nominal control over Philistia" (Hoffmeier, "Egypt as an Arm of Flesh," p. 82). It is to David's credit that, under the Lord's direction, he knew when and how much to conquer. He has thus taken his place in history among those warriors who were at one and the same time courageous, clever, and compassionate. "Medieval chivalry chose David as one of its main paragons from among *les neuf-preux*. . . . The nine exemplary knights of Christendom, consisting of Joshua, David, Judas Maccabeus, Hector, Alexander, Caesar, Arthur, Charlemagne and Godefroi of Bouillon" (Herzog and Gichon, *Battles of the Bible*, pp. 75, 230–31 n.1).

## Notes

**18** Ancient mythological texts from Ugarit refer to *rpum*, "a (semi-)divine guild of chariot-riding warriors" (B. Margulis, "A Ugaritic Psalm [RS 24.252]," JBL 89, 3 [1970]: 301; Tidwell, "Philistine Incursions," p. 204; cf. contra Marvin Pope, "The Cult of the Dead at Ugarit," in *Ugarit in Retrospect: Fifty Years of Ugarit and Ugaritic,* ed. Gordon Douglas Young [Winona Lake: Eisenbrauns, 1981], p. 174). A striking parallel between the Ugaritic *rpum* and the biblical Rephaites is that both are stated to have been headquartered at Ashtaroth and Edrei in Transjordan (Josh 12:4; 13:12; cf. Margulis, "A Ugaritic Psalm [RS 24.252]," pp. 293–94; Pope, "The Cult of the Dead at Ugarit," p. 172 n. 40).

**21** עזב (*'zb*, "abandon") and עצב (*'ṣb*, "idol") provide an excellent example of alliteration and assonance in the Hebrew text.

**24** Symon Patrick (pp. 377–78) makes the quaint suggestion that בְּרָאשֵׁי (*berā'šê*) "should not be rendered *in the tops* (for Men do not walk on the Trees) but *in the beginnings;* in the very entrance of the place, where the Mulberry Trees were planted: Where God intended to make a sound, as if a vast number of Men were marching to fall upon the *Philistines.*" But ראשׁ (*rō'š*) does in fact refer to the top(s) of trees elsewhere (Isa 17:6; Ezek 17:4, 22), and when it is used in the sense of "beginning," it is almost always temporal rather than spatial. In any event, it is never a synonym for "entrance."

**25** The MT's גֶּבַע (*geḇa'*,"Geba") is a scribal error for גִּבְעוֹן (*giḇ'ôn*, "Gibeon"; cf. LXX; cf. also 1 Chron 14:16), as virtually all commentators agree (cf. NIV mg.; KD; in any case, Geba's location about five miles north-northeast of Jerusalem effectively removes it from the present context). Many assume further that Isa 28:21 refers to the event(s) here recorded (cf. Carlson, p. 56 n. 3; Blenkinsopp, "Kiriath-Jearim and the Ark," p. 151 no. 30), although the episode related in Josh 10:10–14 is another possible referent for the Isaiah passage.

---

## 2. *The ark brought to Jerusalem*

### 6:1–23

1David again brought together out of Israel chosen men, thirty
thousand in all. 2He and all his men set out from Baalah of Judah to
bring up from there the ark of God, which is called by the Name, the
name of the LORD Almighty, who is enthroned between the cherubim
that are on the ark. 3They set the ark of God on a new cart and brought it
from the house of Abinadab, which was on the hill. Uzzah and Ahio,
sons of Abinadab, were guiding the new cart 4with the ark of God on it,
and Ahio was walking in front of it. 5David and the whole house of Israel
were celebrating with all their might before the LORD, with songs and
with harps, lyres, tambourines, sistrums and cymbals.
6When they came to the threshing floor of Nacon, Uzzah reached out
and took hold of the ark of God, because the oxen stumbled. 7The
LORD's anger burned against Uzzah because of his irreverent act;
therefore God struck him down and he died there beside the ark of God.
8Then David was angry because the LORD's wrath had broken out
against Uzzah, and to this day that place is called Perez Uzzah.
9David was afraid of the LORD that day and said, "How can the ark of
the LORD ever come to me?" 10He was not willing to take the ark of the
LORD to be with him in the City of David. Instead, he took it aside to the
house of Obed-Edom the Gittite. 11The ark of the LORD remained in the
house of Obed-Edom the Gittite for three months, and the LORD blessed
him and his entire household.
12Now King David was told, "The LORD has blessed the household of
Obed-Edom and everything he has, because of the ark of God." So
David went down and brought up the ark of God from the house of
Obed-Edom to the City of David with rejoicing. 13When those who were
carrying the ark of the LORD had taken six steps, he sacrificed a bull and
a fattened calf. 14David, wearing a linen ephod, danced before the LORD
with all his might, 15while he and the entire house of Israel brought up
the ark of the LORD with shouts and the sound of trumpets.
16As the ark of the LORD was entering the City of David, Michal
daughter of Saul watched from a window. And when she saw King David
leaping and dancing before the LORD, she despised him in her heart.
17They brought the ark of the LORD and set it in its place inside the tent
that David had pitched for it, and David sacrificed burnt offerings and
fellowship offerings before the LORD. 18After he had finished sacrificing
the burnt offerings and fellowship offerings, he blessed the people in
the name of the LORD Almighty. 19Then he gave a loaf of bread, a cake of
dates and a cake of raisins to each person in the whole crowd of
Israelites, both men and women. And all the people went to their homes.
20When David returned home to bless his household, Michal daughter
of Saul came out to meet him and said, "How the king of Israel has
distinguished himself today, disrobing in the sight of the slave girls of
his servants as any vulgar fellow would!"
21David said to Michal, "It was before the LORD, who chose me rather
than your father or anyone from his house when he appointed me ruler
over the LORD's people Israel—I will celebrate before the LORD. 22I will
become even more undignified than this, and I will be humiliated in my
own eyes. But by these slave girls you spoke of, I will be held in honor."

**23And Michal daughter of Saul had no children to the day of her death.**

Apart from its appearance in 1 Samuel 14:18 (see comment there), the ark of the covenant has not been mentioned in the books of Samuel since 1 Samuel 7:2, where the narrator comments that it remained at Kiriath Jearim for twenty years. Although it is impossible to say whether 6:1–23 was originally a part of a longer narrative that began in 1 Samuel 4 (see comment on 1 Sam 4:1b–7:17), the two accounts (compare esp. 1 Sam 6 with 2 Sam 6) are

> similar enough to suggest the lineaments of a type-scene: in both, there is a triumphal procession; in both, there is great rejoicing and the offering of thanksgiving sacrifices; in both, there is a wagon and oxen; in both, there is retribution for unwarranted proximity to the Ark; and in both, the itinerant Ark proves its sufficiency against its enemies and against the hazards of travel. (Rosenberg, p. 116)

Thus the story of the ark is now resumed in 2 Samuel 6. Since the "twenty years" of 1 Samuel 7:2 perhaps "refers to the period between the ark's return from Philistia [1 Sam 6:21–7:1] until the battle reported in" 1 Samuel 7:7–13 (Klein, *1 Samuel*, p. 65)—or alternatively until the end of Samuel's judgeship (1 Sam 7:15)—to the twenty years must be added at least the forty years of Saul's reign (see comment on 1 Sam 13:1) plus a few years into the reign of David, leading to a grand total of more than sixty years that the ark languished in exile (for a similar estimate based on "the well-established view that Shiloh was destroyed about 1050 B.C. and that David began to reign around the turn of the millennium," see Blenkinsopp, "Kiriath-Jearim and the Ark," p. 145).

The account of the ark's arrival in Jerusalem is entirely consonant with similar ceremonies elsewhere in the ancient Near East.

> In light of . . . Akkadian and Phoenician parallels . . . we are in a position to understand 2 Samuel 6 as the record of a historically unique cultic event, viz., the ritual dedication of the City of David as the new religious and political capital of the Israelites, the people of Yahweh. The purpose of the ceremony was the sanctification of the City of David for the installation of the ark in the hope that Yahweh's presence would assure the success of David's government and the welfare of the people. (P. Kyle McCarter, Jr., "The Ritual Dedication of the City of David in 2 Samuel 6," in *The Word of the Lord Shall Go Forth*, p. 276; cf. similarly Brueggemann, *First and Second Samuel*, p. 249)

So David adds to political centralization in Jerusalem a distinctly religious focus by bringing to the city the most venerable and venerated object of his people's past: the Lord's ark—repository of the covenant, locus of atonement, throne of the invisible Yahweh. It is no wonder that the story of the ark's solemn procession is told not only in 2 Samuel 6 but also in 1 Chronicles 13, 15–16, where the Chronicler, true to his affection for matters liturgical and Levitical, preserves numerous details not found in the more concise and matter-of-fact Samuel account. Close parallels between the two narratives, however, are nonetheless frequent: 1 Chronicles 13:5–14 echoes vv.1–11; 1 Chronicles 15:25–16:3 reprises vv.12b–19a, and 1 Chronicles 16:43 is the equivalent of vv.19b–20a. The Chronicler omitted the confrontation between David and Michal in vv.20b–23, perhaps because he construed it as presenting David in a somewhat unfavorable light.

Furthermore, direct quotations as well as reminiscences of 2 Samuel 6 and 1 Chronicles 13, 15–16 are scattered throughout several psalms. The Davidic Psalms 24 and 68 reflect on the ceremonial procession of the ark, probably for a later festival commemorating the event (cf. Ps 24:7–10, the last verse of which uses the name "LORD Almighty" [cf. 2 Sam 6:2]; Ps 68:16–17, 24–27, 29, 35). Psalm 132, a song of ascents perhaps used at royal coronation ceremonies (cf. 132:18), appears to summarize events beginning with David's reign (including the arrival of the ark in Jerusalem: cf. 132:6–9 and especially the reference to Kiriath Jearim in 132:6 ["Jaar"]) and continuing through the early decades of Israel's monarchy (cf. the quotation of 132:8–10 in 2 Chron 6:41–42). The 2 Samuel 6 ark narrative (and its parallels in 1 Chronicles) may also have influenced the Korahite Psalm 47 (see esp. 47:5, 8) and the anonymous Psalm 99 (see esp. 99:1–2, 9).

Particularly impressive is David's psalm of thanks in 1 Chronicles 16:8–36, which has almost verbatim parallels in three additional anonymous psalms (1 Chron 16:8–22 = Ps 105:1–15; 1 Chron 16:23–33 = Ps 96; 1 Chron 16:34–36 = Ps 106:1, 47–48). It has been suggested that the difficult Song of Songs 6:12 be translated "I knew not my heart; it made of me the chariots of Ammi-nadab" (cf. NIV mg. on S of Songs 6:12) in metaphorical reference to the "new cart(s)" that the "sons of Abinadab" (2 Sam 6:3) used to transport the ark (for details cf. Raymond Jacques Tournay, *Word of God, Song of Love: A Commentary on the Song of Songs* [Mahwah: Paulist, 1988], pp. 98–106). All things considered, then, David's bringing the ark of the covenant of the Lord to the City of David in Jerusalem made a notable impact on Israel's history as reflected in substantial portions of several sections of the OT.

In addition to 2 Samuel 6 and 1 Chronicles 13:5–14; 15:25–16:3, 43, a third Hebrew text—4QSam[a]—witnesses to the events recorded here. Ulrich ranks the three texts as follows: 4QSam[a] is "the best," 1 Chronicles is "a close second," and the MT of Samuel, in this chapter as elsewhere, "retains its reputation as a poorly preserved text" (*The Qumran Text*, p. 197; cf. also pp. 220–21). The NIV margin notes on vv.3–5 confirm the overall accuracy of Ulrich's analysis, and the commentary below will make use of the helpful readings from 4QSam[a] and 1 Chronicles elsewhere in the chapter as well.

In the overall structure of the larger narrative describing David's powerful reign (5:17–8:18), the story of the ark's journey to Jerusalem parallels the moving prayer of David as recorded in 7:18–29 (see comment on 5:17–8:18). My analysis of 2 Samuel 6 is based on the following symmetrical outline, which attempts to divide the chapter into its natural components:

A. David's unsuccessful attempt to transport the ark (6:1–5)
  B. Judgment against Uzzah (6:6–11)
A′. David's successful attempt to transport the ark (6:12–19)
  B′. Judgment against Michal (6:20–23)

**1–5** The parallel passage in 1 Chronicles 13:5–8 is preceded by a paragraph (vv.1–4) in which David confers with his army officers (v.1) before announcing to the "whole assembly of Israel" (vv.2, 4) his plans to bring the "ark of our God" (v.3) to Jerusalem in accordance with the "will of the LORD our God" (v.2). The "territories of Israel" (v.2) to which the joyful news was sent included the area "from the Shihor River" (v.5; probably either the northeast section of the Pelusiac branch of the Nile in the eastern part of Egypt's delta or a frontier canal at the delta's edge) "to Lebo Hamath" (modern Lebweh, forty-five miles north of Damascus in the Beqa' of Lebanon).

Kiriath Jearim (see comment on 1 Sam 6:21) is located about halfway "between Jerusalem and Gezer, which David had reached when pursuing his enemies, 5:25. Here we have the associative point of departure for the incorporation of the account of the transfer of the Ark to Jerusalem, 6:1–23" (Carlson, p. 58). Thus the rout of the Philistines "all the way . . . to Gezer" (5:25) enables David to consider the possibility of bringing Israel's most sacred object to the political nerve center of his realm.

For the third time ("again," v.1; cf. 5:17–21, 22–25) David assembles his troops (cf. similarly Blenkinsopp, "Kiriath-Jearim and the Ark," p. 151), here to serve as a military escort for the ark of the covenant. David's "chosen men" (cf. 10:9 = 1 Chron 19:10) are reminiscent of Saul's elite corps of soldiers (see comment on 1 Sam 24:2)—although David's troops outnumber Saul's by a factor of ten, perhaps to underscore the significance and solemnity of David's mission (cf. Carlson, pp. 64–65). While "thirty thousand" (cf. also 1 Sam 4:10) perhaps means rather "thirty units of soldiers" here (see comment on 1 Sam 4:2), it is also possible that the number is to be taken literally in this context.

Just as Kiriath Arba was an earlier name of Hebron (Josh 14:15; 15:13) and Kiriath Sepher of Debir (Josh 15:15), so also Kiriath Jearim ("City of Forests") was doubtless the original name of "Baalah of Judah" (v.2 and first NIV mg. note; cf. 1 Chron 13:6; cf. similarly Blenkinsopp, "Kiriath-Jearim and the Ark," pp. 146–47). In summary, Kiriath Jearim (Josh 9:17; 15:9; 1 Chron 13:5–6) = Kiriath Baal (Josh 15:60; 18:14) = Baal(ah) (Josh 15:9–10) = Baal(ah) of Judah (v.2; 1 Chron 13:6). Furthermore, Jaar (Ps 132:6) is an abbreviated form of Kiriath Jearim (see NIV mg. on Ps 132:6; cf. also 132:8). Blenkinsopp observes (1) that Kiriath Jearim occupied the nodal point on the boundaries of Judah, Benjamin, and Dan (ibid., pp. 147–48) and (2) that expressions such as "Mount Jearim" (Josh 15:10), "Mount Baalah" (Josh 15:11), and "fields of Jaar" (Ps 132:6) suggest that the name Kiriath Jearim "may have covered a fairly large area" (ibid., p. 147 n. 16). In any event, for half a century or more the ark of the covenant had been sequestered in "the house of Abinadab, which was on the hill" (v.3; see comments on 1 Sam 7:1), either inaccessible to the Israelites because of Philistine control of the region or languishing in neglect (perhaps partially because King Saul had shown no interest in it; cf. 1 Chron 13:3).

The solemnity of the scene that unfolds in chapter 6 is enhanced by the grandiose description of the ark and the repeated references to it. As in 1 Samuel 4:4 (see comment there), the ark is depicted in v.2 as the seat of authority of "the LORD Almighty" (see comment on 1 Sam 1:3), "who is enthroned between the cherubim" (cf. 2 Kings 19:15 = Isa 37:16; Pss 80:1; 99:1).

It is also referred to as the "ark of God" (vv.2, 3, 4, 6, 7, 12 [bis]) and the "ark of the LORD" (vv.9, 10, 11, 13, 15, 16, 17). Although there is no discernible reason for the alternation in the divine names in these expressions, it is noteworthy that in the chapter each of the names occurs seven times (the number of completion/perfection) in connection with the ark. Indeed, the ark "is called by the name/Name" (v.2), an idiom denoting ownership (BDB, p. 896; cf. 12:28 ["will be named after"]; 1 Kings 8:43 ["bears your Name"]; 2 Chron 7:14; Jer 25:29 ["bears my Name"]) and thus here emphasizing that the ark is the Lord's property. The term "Name" (unmodified grammatically with a divine title following it), appearing in the books of Samuel only here and in 7:13, not only refers to the Lord's name but also stands for his presence (cf., e.g., Exod 23:21; Lev 24:11, 16; see also comment on 1 Sam 25:25) and is especially common in Deuteronomy in connection with the centralized place of worship that the Lord would choose for his people in the Promised Land (Deut 12:5, 11, 21; 14:23–24; 16:2, 6, 11; 26:2). "From this deeper meaning of 'the name of God' we may probably explain the repetition of the word שֵׁם [*šēm*, 'name'], which is first of all written absolutely (as at the close of Lev. xxiv.16), and then more fully defined as 'the name of the Lord of hosts'" (KD, p. 330).

David's intention to "bring up" (v.2; cf. v.15) the ark to the City of David (cf. v.12) is of course not only commendable but also entirely appropriate (cf. 1 Kings 8:1, which records Solomon's desire to "bring up" the ark from the City of David to the temple). At the same time, however, his first attempt to do so follows Philistine rather than Levitical procedure. David and his men "brought" (v.3, lit., "carried"; cf. v.13) the ark from Abinadab's house by transporting it on a "new cart," the method earlier used by the Philistines (see 1 Sam 6:7–8 and comments). If Abinadab had not already died, he was surely an elderly man by this time. It is therefore possible that Uzzah and Ahio were Abinadab's grandsons rather than his "sons" (v.3; the Heb. word for "son" often means "grandson," as in 9:9–10; 19:24). Their task was to guide the cart, Ahio walking in front (v.4) and Uzzah presumably bringing up the rear.

With David taking the lead, the whole "house of Israel" (v.5, "house" being used here in the sense of "family," "community"; see comment on 1 Sam 7:2) begins "celebrating" (though sometimes associated with dancing [cf. 1 Chron 15:29], celebrating is not identical to it; see comment on "danced" in 1 Sam 18:7). In this context "before the LORD" (v.5; cf. v.14) is virtually tantamount to "before the ark" (a literal translation of "in front of it," v.4). "With all (their) might" is echoed verbatim in v.14 ("with all [his] might"; cf. Gunn, *The Story of King David*, pp. 73–74) and contributes to the enthusiastic abandon that characterizes the chapter as a whole.

"Songs" (perhaps of victory; see comment on 1 Sam 18:6), the singular of the Hebrew for which is sometimes equivalent to "music" (cf. 1 Chron 25:6–7), introduces the list of accompanying musical instruments that follows. "Harps, lyres, tambourines" were staple elements on such joyful occasions (see comments on 1 Sam 10:5; 16:16; 18:6). The sistrum, mentioned only here in the OT, was used widely throughout the ancient Near East, especially in Egypt. It consisted of a handle fitted to "a metal loop with holes through which pieces of wire were inserted and bent at the ends. Since the holes were larger than the wire, the instrument produced a jingling sound when shaken. The Hebrew word comes from a verb which means 'shake;' so it is reasonable to suppose that the *mena'an'im* were sistra" (Sellers, "Musical Instruments of Israel," pp. 44–45). "Cymbals" were of two kinds, one set of which were struck vertically (harsh/noisy cymbals) and the other horizontally (clear cymbals). The former may be reflected in the "clash of cymbals" and the latter in the "resounding cymbals" of Psalm 150:5. The cymbals here were probably clear cymbals (similar to but smaller than their modern descendants), bronze examples of which (cf. 1 Chron 15:19) archaeologists have found at several sites in Israel (e.g., Beth Shemesh [cf. ibid., p. 46, fig. 12:c]; Hazor [cf. Bayer, "The Finds That Could Not Be," p. 24]). While not mentioning sistrums, the parallel passage in 1 Chronicles 13:8 concludes the list with "trumpets," resulting in a total of six different musical instruments used to accompany the first attempt to bring the ark from Kiriath Jearim to Jerusalem.

**6–11** Just as "David and the whole house of Israel" (*dāwiḏ wᵉḵol-bêṯ yiśrā'ēl*) begins the last verse of the previous section (vv.1–5), so also "Obed-Edom and his entire household" (*'ōḇēḏ 'ᵉḏōm wᵉ'eṯ-kol-bêṯô*) ends the last verse of the present section (vv.6–11). The contrast is stark: David and Israel's house celebrate while the ark is being mishandled, whereas Obed-Edom and his house are blessed because the ark is under his protection.

Since threshing floors were often places of sanctity (cf. 24:16, 18, 21, 24–25; Gen 50:10; 1 Kings 22:10; Hos 9:1), the "threshing floor of Nacon" (v.6) may also have been a holy site (cf. J.R. Porter, "The Interpretation of 2 Samuel VI and Psalm CXXXII," JTS 5 [1954]: 171). Unfortunately, it is mentioned only here ("Nacon" as a proper noun is a secondary reading in 1 Sam 23:23; 26:4; see NIV mgs. there and see Notes on 1 Sam 23:23), its location is unknown, and even the spelling of its name is uncertain (1 Chron 13:9, e.g., reads "Kidon" instead of "Nacon"). "Two verbs with which *nacon* could be connected are *kûn*, 'to be fixed or prepared', or *nāḵāh*, 'to smite'; indeed the latter occurs in verse 7 ['struck him down']. The name may have been coined to encapsulate memories of the disaster, witnessed by the great company of worshippers" (Baldwin, pp. 207–8; cf. similarly Carlson, p. 78).

In any event, the threshing floor is fraught with peril for Uzzah (whose name, ironically, means "Strength," from the same Heb. root translated "might" in v.5). Sensing that the oxen pulling the cart were stumbling (v.6) and might therefore cause the ark to fall to the ground, Uzzah "reached out" (elliptical for "reached out his hand," as in 1 Chron 13:9, 4QSam[a], and several ancient versions; cf. Ulrich, *The Qumran Text*, p. 195, and BHS) to steady the ark. In so doing he "took hold of" it, and thus his doom was sealed despite whatever good intentions he may have had.

The wrath of divine judgment fell on Uzzah "because of his irreverent act" (v.7), a phrase that is unique in the OT (for discussion cf. Carlson, p. 79) and that is understood in 1 Chronicles 13:10 to mean in this context "because he had put his hand on the ark" (cf. also probably 4QSam[a]; Ulrich, *The Qumran Text*, p. 195). Although this in itself would have been enough to condemn him, (1) Uzzah was transporting the ark in a cart rather than carrying it on his shoulders, and (2) there is no evidence that he was a Kohathite Levite in any event (cf. Num 4:15; cf. similarly Terence Kleven, "Hebrew Style in II Samuel vi" [presented at the Evangelical Theological Society annual meeting in New Orleans, November 1990], p. 6, who calls attention as well to such related texts as Exod 25:12–15; Num 3:29–31; 7:9; Deut 10:8). Just as God had "struck down" and put to death some of the men of Beth Shemesh for looking into the ark (1 Sam 6:19; cf. Num 4:20), so also God "struck [Uzzah] down" (v.7) for touching the ark.

It is sometimes claimed that the ark, a wooden chest overlaid inside and out with gold (Exod 25:10–11), functioned as a huge Leyden jar that produced enough static electricity while bumping along the rocky road to electrocute Uzzah when he touched it. But it is also conceivable that a member of the ark's military escort used his spear (one Heb. word for which is *kîḏōn* [cf. Jer 50:42], the name of the threshing floor according to 1 Chron 13:9) to dispatch Uzzah. In any event, the Lord was the ultimate cause of Uzzah's death, whether or not he used secondary means to accomplish the act of judgment.

As if to emphasize the threshing floor as the locale of Uzzah's death, the narrator states not only that Uzzah died "there" but also that God struck him down "there" (omitted by NIV in the interests of English style). An additional irony is that he died "beside" (*'im*, usually "with," but cf. similarly "near" in 1 Sam 10:2) the ark, which he had been attempting to rescue from real or imagined harm ("beside the ark of God" [v.7] and "with the ark of God" [v.4] translate the same Heb. phrase). John H. Stek observes that the fate of Uzzah brings to mind "the deaths of Nadab and Abihu, Lev.

10:1, 2; Achan, Josh. 7; and Ananias and Sapphira, Acts 5:1–11; all of whom failed to take Yahweh's rule seriously—at the dawn of new eras in the history of the kingdom of God" (*The Former Prophets*, p. 69).

The Lord's anger (v.7) causes David to react first with anger of his own (v.8) and then with fear (v.9). David is understandably indignant that the divine "wrath" (v.8, lit., "breaking out") has broken out against Uzzah and resulted in his death, a seemingly harsh penalty for so small an infraction. Indeed, it may have been David himself who named the place of Uzzah's death Perez Uzzah (v.8), "The Outbreak Against Uzzah" (see NIV mg.; see also comment on Baal Perazim in 5:20).

It is not surprising that David's anger against God should be mingled with fear of him (v.9). His fear was experienced "that day" (i.e., the day of Uzzah's death, as opposed to "this day" [v.8], the time of the narrator of 2 Samuel; see comment on 1 Sam 6:18), in the light of which he questions whether the ark can "ever" (implied in the context, though not explicitly represented in the MT) come to him. Although written from a different perspective, Blenkinsopp's observation ("Kiriath-Jearim and the Ark," p. 151 n. 33) is surely correct: "The question of David . . . is answered in the liturgy of Ps 24 (vss. 4f.)."

David decides that a cooling-off period is in order before he is willing to give further consideration, if at all, to taking the ark to be "with him" (remembering what happened when it was with Uzzah) in the "City of David" (v.10, the new name so recently given to the fortress of Zion; see comment on 5:7). Instead, he gives the ark a temporary home in the house of "Obed-Edom" ("Servant of Edom," in which "Edom" is probably the name of either a god or a tribe; cf. S.R. Driver, *Notes on the Books of Samuel,* in loc.) the Gittite.

While it is true that "Gittite" can refer to someone whose hometown was the Philistine city of Gath (cf. Goliath in 1 Sam 17:4, 23; 2 Sam 21:19), it is unlikely that David would entrust the ark to the care of a Philistine. Since *gaṯ* is the ordinary word for "(wine)press," the epithet "Gittite" can be used with respect to any activity (cf. the enigmatic feminine form *gittîṯ* in the titles of Pss 8; 81; 84) or place name (cf. Gath Hepher, Josh 19:13; 2 Kings 14:25; Gath Rimmon, Josh 19:45; 21:24–25; 1 Chron 6:69) related to winepresses. Indeed, it is even possible that Obed-Edom was originally from Gittaim ("Two [Wine]presses"; see Notes on 4:3).

In any case, despite the skepticism of some commentators (e.g., McCarter, Smith), Obed-Edom was a Levite (1 Chron 15:17–18, 21, 24–25; 16:4–5, 38; Jos. Antiq. 7, 83 [iv.2])—in fact, he was a Kohathite Levite if Gath Rimmon in Dan or Manasseh was his hometown (Josh 21:20, 24–26; 1 Chron 6:66, 69; cf. Kirkpatrick). The house of Obed-Edom was probably located "somewhere on the southwestern hill of Jerusalem" (Carlson, p. 79; on the two-site location of Jebusite Jerusalem see comment on 5:6). There the ark remained for three months (v.11), during which time the Lord blessed the house of Obed-Edom, soon to be reflected in the confidence of David that the Lord would bless the house of David forever (7:29). In the case of Obed-Edom, the divine blessing (as often in the OT) would ultimately come in the form of numerous descendants: "62 in all" (1 Chron 26:8; cf. "For God had blessed Obed-Edom" [1 Chron 26:5]).

**12–19** That vv.12–19 constitute a literary unit is strengthened by the fact that vv.12b–19a are paralleled in 1 Chronicles 15:25–16:3. In addition v.12 begins with a reference to the Lord blessing the household of Obed-Edom while v.20, which starts the next unit, begins with a reference to David blessing his own household. Finally, *wayyēlek* ("went") in vv.12, 19 serves to frame the whole (NIV's unjustifiable translation "went down" in v.12 needlessly muffles the echo in v.19).

True to form, the Chronicler precedes his parallel narrative with a lengthy account that details the functions of the Levites with respect to the triumphal procession of the ark (1 Chron 15:1–24). In the center of his addendum, the Chronicler summarizes the reasons for the failure of the initial attempt to bring the ark to the City of David: "It was because you, the Levites, did not bring it up the first time that the LORD our God broke out in anger against us. We did not inquire of him about how to do it in the prescribed way" (1 Chron 15:13).

Eventually David is told of the Lord's blessing on the house of Obed-Edom "because of the ark" (v.12). Sensing that it is therefore now safe to bring the ark up to the fortress, David proceeds to do so. In this endeavor he is accompanied by "the elders of Israel and the commanders of units of a thousand" (1 Chron 15:25). Although David's leadership role is emphasized by the use of verbs in the singular number ("he sacrificed," v.13; "David sacrificed," v.17), the Chronicler is at pains to point out that David had help ("they sacrificed," 1 Chron 15:26 [obscured by the NIV's rendering in the passive]; 16:1). If in the case of the first attempt there was celebration and singing (v.5), now there is "rejoicing" (v.12).

> Vss 13–14 are the central verses in the chapter which mark the changes David makes in the transportation of the ark. . . . First, individuals are now carrying the ark. . . . Second, . . . after the procession has marched six steps, David sacrifices. . . . Third, . . . David wears a linen ephod. . . . Each of the changes are [*sic*] a clue that laws for the transport of the ark are now being obeyed. The ark was not to be moved in the manner of the Philistines, but as enjoined by Israelite law. (Kleven, "Hebrew Style in II Samuel vi," pp. 8–9)

"Those who were carrying the ark" (v.13) were of course (Kohathite) Levites (1 Chron 15:26; cf. also 2 Sam 15:24). Although v.13 may intend to state that when the Levites had taken six steps a bull and a fattened calf were sacrificed, after which the procession continued uninterrupted on its way to the City of David, Assyrian parallels make it more likely that sacrifices were offered every six steps (cf. McCarter, "Ritual Dedication," pp. 273–74, 277 n. 1; cf. also Carlson, pp. 80, 86). Given the proximity of the house of Obed-Edom to the City of David (see comment on v.10), such a procedure would not have been needlessly cumbersome or time-consuming. The six-step ritual may have been memorialized in the six steps of David's son Solomon's throne, where a total of twelve lions standing on the steps (1 Kings 10:19–20) probably symbolized Israel's twelve tribes.

Oxen/bulls (v.13) were commonly sacrificed as "burnt offerings and fellowship offerings" (vv.17–18; cf. Lev 1:4–6; 4:10; 9:4, 18), and the "fattened calf" (v.13) would be sacrificed with increased frequency during Solomon's reign (1 Kings 1:9, 19, 25; cf. also Luke 15:23–30). The "seven bulls and seven rams" of 1 Chronicles 15:26 are perhaps also to be understood as part of the overall picture of burnt offerings and fellowship offerings here described (for the use of rams as sacrifices, cf. Lev 9:2, 4).

Prefiguring the priestly functions of King David (v.14), the prophet Samuel had earlier worn a "linen ephod" (see 1 Sam 2:18 and comment; cf. also 1 Sam 22:18). First Chronicles 15:27 states that, in addition to the ephod, David was "clothed in a robe of fine linen," doubtless the "robe of the ephod" that was worn under the ephod itself (cf. Exod 28:31). During the time of the Israelite monarchy, kings occasionally officiated as priests (cf. 24:25; 1 Kings 8:64; 9:25). At the same time, however,

> we must note that the instances where the king's personal action is beyond question are all very special or exceptional: the transference of the Ark, the dedication of the altar or sanctuary, the great annual festivals. Ordinarily, the conduct of worship was left to the priest (2 K 16:15). Anointing did not confer on the king a priestly character. . . . he was not a priest in the strict sense. (de Vaux, AIs, p. 114)

"With all his might" (v.14; cf. also v.5) David "danced" (or "[was] dancing," as in v.16; in both cases the verb is a participle) "before the LORD"—in this case before the ark, the symbol of the Divine Presence (see comment on v.5). The Hebrew verb here translated "danced/dancing" is unique to this chapter, although it occurs in Ugaritic with the same meaning (cf. G.W. Ahlström, "*KRKR* and *ṮPD*," VetTest 28, 1 [1978]: 100–101, responding to Y. Avishur, "KRKR in Biblical Hebrew and Ugaritic," VetTest 26, 3 [1976]: 257–61, who argues that the verb means "play").

As "David and the whole house of Israel" (v.5) had celebrated during the earlier procession of the ark, so "he and the entire house of Israel" (v.15; the MT is the same in both cases) now "brought up" (or "were bringing up," a participial form; cf. "was entering," "leaping," "dancing" in v.16) the ark from the house of Obed-Edom. The scene is punctuated with "shouts" (of excitement and triumph, as on a similar earlier occasion; see 1 Sam 4:5–6 and comment; cf. also 2 Chron 15:14: Ezra 3:11–13) and with the sound of ram's-horn "trumpets" (or perhaps "a trumpet," since the form is singular; cf. also Ps 47:5, which may be a reference to this event). First Chronicles 15:28 has "rams' horns and trumpets" (cf. the similar distinction between rams' horns and trumpets in Ps 98:6) as well as cymbals, lyres, and harps (instruments used also during the first procession of the ark; cf. v.5).

Halfway through the literary unit (vv.12–19) the narrator pauses to inject a discordant note (v.16). "Michal daughter of Saul" (so described because here and in v.20 she is depicted as being critical of David and is therefore "acting like a true daughter of Saul"; Clines, "X, X *Ben* Y, *Ben* Y," p. 272) "watched" the proceedings "from a window" (cf. Sisera's mother, Judg 5:28; Jezebel, 2 Kings 9:30; the Heb. phrase is the same in all three cases). The "Frau im Fenster" ("woman at the window") may be

> the best-known motif in the Phoenician tradition of art, certainly the most common of the Phoenician ivory motifs. . . . There is only one example at Samaria, but it appears frequently at Nimrud and Khorsabad in Assyria, at Arslan Tash in Syria, and in Cyprus. Adorned with an Egyptian wig or headdress, the woman peers through a window within recessed frames overlooking a balcony balustrade (a low railing) supported by voluted (scroll-shaped) columns. (King, *Amos, Hosea, Micah*, p. 146; cf. also Porter, "The Interpretation of 2 Samuel VI and Psalm CXXXII," p. 166; ANEP, figs. 131, 799)

Perhaps still smarting from her earlier separation from her former husband Paltiel (cf. 3:13–16), Michal looks at her present husband, David, with something less than the love she at one time had for him (see 1 Sam 18:20 and comment). Seeing him "leaping and dancing" (the same Heb. verbs in the Piel stem are not found in the OT outside the present context [for "dancing" see comment on v.14]; 1 Chron 15:29 ["dancing and celebrating"] substitutes two Heb. verbs more commonly attested)—

even though "before the LORD"—she reacts with disgust. Once Michal had helped David escape through a window (1 Sam 19:12); now, peering at him through a window, she despises him "in her heart" (v.16).

Although later returning to the encounter between David and Michal (vv.20–23), the narrator first concludes the story of the ark's procession into the City of David. The ark is brought in and "set" (the same Heb. verb is used similarly in 1 Sam 5:2) in its predetermined place "inside the tent David had pitched for it" (v.17; cf. 2 Chron 1:4). David had apparently pitched the tent at some time prior to his appointment of and conference with the personnel who accompanied the procession (compare 1 Chron 15:1, 3 with 16:1). "This construction of a new tabernacle to house the ark . . . was necessitated by the destruction of the original Mosaic tent, evidently when the Philistines overran Shiloh about 1050 B.C. and carried away the ark" (Unger, "Archaeology and the Reign of David," p. 20; see also comment on 1 Sam 4:11). Apparently at a somewhat later date, another tabernacle was constructed and installed at the high place in Gibeon (1 Kings 3:4; 1 Chron 16:39; 21:29; 2 Chron 1:3, 5, 13), about six miles northwest of Jerusalem (see comment on 2:12). Thus there were in effect two tabernacles: The one in Jerusalem served as the repository for the ark (1 Chron 16:37), while the one in Gibeon housed the other tabernacle furnishings (1 Chron 16:39–40; cf. 1 Kings 1:39; 2:28–30; 3:4). Nowhere in the books of Samuel, Kings, or Chronicles is the ark associated with Gibeon or with a sanctuary there. Just before Solomon's prayer at the dedication of the temple, the priests "brought up the ark of the LORD ['from Zion, the City of David,' 1 Kings 8:1] and the Tent of Meeting and all the sacred furnishings in it [from Gibeon]" (1 Kings 8:4). Although reference to the Gibeon tabernacle as the one that "Moses the LORD's servant had made in the desert" (2 Chron 1:3; cf. 1 Chron 21:29) may mean that the original Mosaic tabernacle had survived for over four hundred years, the phrase can also be taken in a metaphorical sense (i.e., the Gibeon tabernacle was made in strict accordance with the Mosaic pattern).

During the time that the Mosaic tabernacle was in not in use (for whatever reason), various offerings continued to be sacrificed without necessary benefit of the bronze altar of burnt offering. Thus David sacrifices "burnt offerings and fellowship offerings" (v.17; cf. also 24:25; 1 Sam 13:9) as an act of gratitude (cf. 1 Sam 6:14–15) and consecration (cf. 1 Kings 8:63–64) "before the LORD" (i.e., honoring the Divine Presence symbolized by the ark). In particular, the fellowship offering (traditionally "peace offering"; see NIV mg.) signified the desire of the worshipers to rededicate themselves to God in covenant allegiance and to reaffirm their king as God's covenanted temporal ruler (see comment on 1 Sam 11:15). It is therefore possible that the present ritual procedures also imply David's formal (re)investiture as king over Israel in Jerusalem, especially in light of Mesopotamian *sulmānû* ("peace offering") parallels (cf. James W. Flanagan, "Social Transformation and Ritual in 2 Samuel 6," in *The Word of the Lord Shall Go Forth*, pp. 368–69).

After bringing an unspecified number of offerings (vv.17–18), David blesses the *'am* ("people" [v.18] in this case rather than "troops," since "both men and women" are included [v.19]). Because the act of blessing was a function of spiritual leadership (cf. 1 Sam 2:20; cf. also Gen 14:18–19), David once again performs the role of a priest (see comment on v.14). As he had challenged Goliath "in the name of the LORD Almighty" (see comment on 1 Sam 1:3)—that is, as the Lord's representative (see comment on 1 Sam 17:45)—so he blesses Israel in the same powerful name (v.18). Carlson observes: "Just as the removal of the Ark from Kiriath-jearim was begun with the calling out of the divine name over the Ark [v.2], so the enterprise was concluded with a blessing pronounced in the same divine name" (p. 89). Thus "the name of the LORD Almighty" (vv.2, 18) forms a literary and theological *inclusio* that frames the account of the procession of the ark of the covenant of the Lord.

David adds to his blessing the distribution of food (v.19), an association also found in Psalm 132:15 (an ark-procession Psalm [see comment on 6:1–23]; cf. Porter, "The Interpretation of 2 Samuel VI and Psalm CXXXII," p. 168). The universal nature of the royal largesse could hardly be stated more explicitly in the MT: "to all the people [the phrase is omitted in the NIV in the interests of English style], to the whole crowd of Israelites, both men and women, to each person." Although staple foods, at least one of the three items given by David to the people ("cake of raisins") is found once in a ritual context (Hos 3:1). "Cake of dates" as the meaning of *'ešpār*, which is attested only here (and in the parallel in 1 Chron 16:3), is secured by an Arabic cognate (cf. Ludwig Koehler, "Problems in the Study of the Language of the Old Testament," JSS 1, 1 [1956]: 15; KB, p. 95). The italics in the KJV rendering ("good piece *of flesh*") in this case demonstrate uncertainty (for a defense of the KJV, as well as for a critique of an even more fanciful interpretation ["sixth part of a bullock"], cf. Symon Patrick, p. 388). To summarize:

> The blessing of the people and the giving out of cakes made with fruit (an Oriental fertility motif) was [*sic*] a sign to the people that now that God was in their midst and now that they were dedicated to living according to the covenant there would be fertility in the land. Such was the significance of David's sending each one to his own house (6:19). (John A. Martin, p. 38)

**20–23** Just as the preceding section (vv.12–19) began with a blessing on a household (v.12), so also does the present section. Having blessed the Israelites who witnessed the procession of the ark (v.18), David returns home to "bless" his own household (v.20). Although the Hebrew verb sometimes means "greet" (preferred here by Alter, *The Art of Biblical Narrative*, p. 124), Carlson is surely correct in stating that such a connotation in this context "is far too weak" (p. 92 n. 3)—especially in light of the frequent use of the verb earlier in the chapter (vv.11–12, 18). Indeed, the contrast between the inevitable success of the Lord's blessing on the household of Obed-Edom (see v.11 and comment) and the failure of David's aborted blessing on his own household (see comment on v.23) is striking.

When a warrior returned victorious from battle, the women of his hometown would come out to meet him and would celebrate with music and dancing (see comment on 1 Sam 18:6). David might have expected his wife, "Michal daughter of Saul" (see comment on v.16), to celebrate his similar triumph in much the same way. If so, he is quickly disappointed: "Until the final meeting between Michal and David, at no point is there any dialogue between them—an avoidance of verbal exchange particularly noticeable in the Bible, where such a large part of the burden of narration is taken up by dialogue. When that exchange finally comes, it is an explosion" (Alter, *The Art of Biblical Narrative*, p. 123).

Although only one sentence long (v.20), Michal's words drip with the "How" of sarcasm (cf. Job 26:2–3; Jer 2:23): David, the "king of Israel" (an office once occupied by her father Saul), has "distinguished himself" (lit., "honored himself," as in v.22 ["be held in honor"]; see comment on "highly respected" in 1 Sam 9:6). Michal punctuates her disdain by doubly emphasizing the time of the event (in the MT "today" appears again after "disrobing") as well as by underscoring the act itself three times (in addition to NIV's "disrobing," the final clause of the verse reads literally: "as any vulgar fellow, disrobing, would disrobe"; for the uniqueness of infinitive construct followed by infinitive absolute, cf. S.R. Driver, *Notes on the Books of Samuel*, p. 272). It may be that the "repeated expression indicates continual action: 'uncovered himself like [vulgar fellows] go and uncover themselves'" (Carlson, p. 91). To what extent David's state of undress was scandalous is impossible to say (earlier he had been wearing at least a "linen ephod" [v.14] and a "robe of fine linen" [1 Chron 15:27])—although Josephus claims that, at least by the time of Michal's outburst, he was "naked" (*gymnoumenos*, Jos. Antiq. 7, 87 [iv.3]). Hints of this sort (including also mention of "slave girls" in vv.20, 22) have led some commentators to detect orgiastic overtones in David's dancing and/or to assume that "it was a prelude to the sacred marriage" rite (Porter, "The Interpretation of 2 Samuel VI and Psalm CXXXII," p. 166). Such extreme interpretations, however, do not tally with David's own explanation of his actions in vv.21–22. Far from the kind of "vulgar fellow" (v.20, lit., "empty, worthless person"; cf. Judg 9:4 ["adventurers"]; 11:3; 2 Chron 13:7) who would be an exhibitionist in the sight of the slave girls of his "servants" (or "officers," another possible rendering of *'ᵃḇāḏîm;* see comment on 1 Sam 16:15–16), David makes it clear that he is very much concerned about how the Lord evaluates his actions.

The centerpiece in the literary unit in which it appears, David's response (vv.21–22) to Michal (not called "daughter of Saul" in v.21, perhaps because "attention now focuses on David, who is the subject of the sentence," Clines, "X, X *Ben* Y, *Ben* Y," p. 272) is honest and direct. He begins and ends his first sentence (v.21) by insisting that he is celebrating "before the LORD" (noted also by Brueggemann, *First and Second Samuel*, p. 252; cf. vv.14, 16), not before the slave girls. In his rebuke of Michal, David is at pains to dissociate himself from Saul ("your father") and the Saulides by asserting that God had chosen him rather than them, a sentiment shared by the representatives of Israel's tribes (5:2). David, of course, knows that the Lord had in fact chosen Saul (see 1 Sam 10:24 and comment), but he also knows that Saul's abortive kingship has been replaced by his own (cf. 1 Sam 16:8–13; 1 Kings 8:16 = 2 Chron 6:5–6; 1 Chron 28:4; Ps 78:70). David is "ruler" (*nāḡîḏ*) over Israel by divine appointment (see 1 Sam 13:14 ["leader"] and comment; cf. also 1 Sam 25:30), as his son Solomon would be after him (cf. 1 Kings 1:35). The phrase "ruler over the LORD's people Israel" (v.21) contains distinct echoes of "my people Israel, and you will become their ruler" in 5:2 (Gunn, *The Story of King David*, p. 74). Thus David, in a spirit of gratitude and dedication, is quick to "celebrate before the LORD" (v.21), as he had been during the first (unsuccessful) attempt to bring the ark to Zion (see v.5 and comment; cf. further Deut 12:7; 16:1).

David now preempts the verb *kāḇēḏ* (lit., "be heavy") used by Michal in v.20 ("distinguished himself") and opposes it to the verb *qālal* (lit., "be light"). He revels in the fact that he will become even more "undignified" (*qll*, v.22) than he now appears, to the extent that he will be "humiliated" (lit., "low"; cf. similarly Mal 2:9) in his own "eyes" (as opposed to the "sight" of the slave girls [v.20]; the same Heb. noun in both cases). But by those same slave girls (v.22), whom Michal herself has already mentioned (v.20)—"by them" (emphatic; *'immām*, left untr. in NIV)—David will be "held in honor" (*kbd;* cf. the description of David's mighty men in 23:19, 23).

The counterpoise between *kbd* and *qll* appears elsewhere in the books of Samuel as well. In 1 Samuel 2:30 the Lord says, "Those who honor [*kbd*] me I will honor [*kbd*], but those who despise me will be disdained [*qll*].” And in the earlier ark narrative in 1 Samuel 6, the Philistine priests and diviners suggest to their questioners that they should “pay honor [*kbd*] to Israel’s god. Perhaps he will lift [*qll*] his hand from you. . . . Why do you harden [*kbd*] your hearts as the Egyptians and Pharaoh did?” (1 Sam 6:5–6). In such passages there is something of “the exalted being humbled and the humbled being exalted (Matt. 23:12; Luke 14:11; 18:14). David is indeed the one who humbles himself and who, by the power of God, is exalted” (Brueggemann, *First and Second Samuel*, p. 253).

The chapter ends on a somber note: “Michal daughter of Saul” remains childless to her dying day (v.23). The use of the patronymic in this case “presumably means: ‘Here is the punishment for an opponent of David the divinely chosen king’, and perhaps also: ‘So David fails to legitimise his succession to Saul’s throne through Michal’ ” (Clines, “X, X *Ben* Y, *Ben* Y,” p. 272). In ancient times childlessness, whether natural or enforced, was the ultimate tragedy for a woman (see comment on 1 Sam 1:2). Negative connotations are also implied in the expression “to the day of (one’s) death” (cf. 1 Kings 15:5; see also 1 Sam 15:35 and comment).

Josephus states that Michal, “after her later marriage to the man on whom her father Saul bestowed her, . . . bore five children” (Jos. Antiq. 7, 89 [iv.3]). Verse 23 clearly asserts that Michal’s childless state was perpetual. While the Lord’s blessing on Obed-Edom resulted in a large number of descendants for him (see comment on v.11), David’s intended blessing on his own household (v.20) was effectively nullified by Michal’s tragic criticism of her husband. Her resulting childlessness “gave David the opportunity to pass the leadership on to his sons by other wives. . . . The return of Michal and her barrenness serve as the pivot upon which the transition of ruling houses turned” (Flanagan, “Social Transformation and Ritual in 2 Samuel 6,” p. 367).

At the same time, David’s treatment of Michal is less than exemplary. In this respect Alter’s summary is worth pondering:

> The writer . . . does not question the historically crucial fact of David’s divine election, so prominently stressed by the king himself at the beginning of his speech; but theological rights do not necessarily justify domestic wrongs, and the anointed monarch of Israel may still be a harsh and unfeeling husband to the woman who has loved him and saved his life. (*The Art of Biblical Narrative*, pp. 124–25; cf. 1 Sam 18:20, 28; 19:11–17)

## Notes

---

1 The two Hebrew words that begin the narrative of David’s first attempt to transport the ark (vv.1–5) echo those that begin the narrative of his second battle against the Philistines (5:22–25): Compare וַיֹּסִפוּ עוֹד (*wayyōsipû ʿôḏ*, “Once more,” 5:22, lit., “They added again”; root *ysp*) with וַיֹּסֶף עוֹד (*wayyōsep ʿôḏ*, “again brought together,” 6:1; root *ʾsp*).

That the MT’s וַיֹּסֶף (*wayyōsep*, “added,” an auxiliary verb) stands for וַיֶּאֱסֹף (*wayyeʾesōp*, “brought together”) is clear from the parallel in 1 Chron 13:5, where the text reads וַיַּקְהֵל (*wayyaqhēl*, “assembled”). The elision of א (ʾ) also occurs elsewhere in first-radical-ʾ verbs in the books of Samuel (e.g., 20:9; 1 Sam 28:24; cf. Stek, “What Happened to the Chariot Wheels?” p. 293).

כָּל־בָּחוּר בְּיִשְׂרָאֵל (*kol-bāḥûr beyiśrā'ēl,* "every chosen man in Israel"; NIV, "out of Israel chosen men," v.1) and כָּל־בֵּית יִשְׂרָאֵל (*kol-bêṯ yiśrā'ēl,* "the whole house of Israel," v.5) form an *inclusio* that gives literary unity to the first five verses of the chapter.

2 Although the first NIV note states that בַּעֲלֵי יְהוּדָה (*ba'alê yehûḏāh*) is "a variant of *Baalah of Judah*" (cf. 1 Chron 13:6), it is surely better to assume, with Segal, that the "final *yod* [on בעלי (*b'ly*)] was dittographed from the initial *yod* in the next word [יהודה (*yhwdh*)]" (*The Pentateuch,* p. 199 n. 24). The resulting "Baal of Judah" would then be another way of expressing "Kiriath Baal (that is, Kiriath Jearim), a town of the people of Judah" (Josh 18:14; cf. also Ulrich, *The Qumran Text,* p. 204; S.R. Driver, *Notes on the Books of Samuel,* pp. 265–66).

As the second NIV note indicates, the MT's שֵׁם (*šēm,* "[the] name") appears only once in the LXX and Vulgate (and probably also in 4QSam[a]; cf. Ulrich, *The Qumran Text,* p. 194). Instead of the first occurrence, many MSS have שָׁם (*šām,* "there"), which, however, makes less sense and in any case is probably influenced by מִשָּׁם (*miššām,* "from there") earlier in the verse.

3 Although the name Ahio could be revocalized to mean "his brother/brothers," Ahio ("Brother/Kinsman of the LORD") is attested as a proper name elsewhere in the OT (1 Chron 8:31; 9:37).

4 At the beginning of the verse, the MT repeats "and brought it from the house of Abinadab, which was on the hill" from v.3. The dittography in the MT—doubtless caused by the fact that "new cart," which appears before the two clauses in v.3, recurs at the end of that verse—is not found in 4QSam[a] (cf. Ulrich, *The Qumran Text,* p. 195) or in some LXX MSS (see NIV mg. on vv.3–4).

5 The MT's בְּכֹל עֲצֵי בְרוֹשִׁים (*bekōl 'aṣê berôšîm,* "with all [kinds] of wood[en instruments made] of pine") is doubtless a scribal error for בְּכָל־עֹז וּבְשִׁירִים (*bekol-'ōz ûbešîrîm,* "with all [their] might, with songs"; cf. NIV mg.; cf. also Ulrich, *The Qumran Text,* p. 195), especially since "with all [his] might" (v.14) echoes v.5.

צֶלְצְלִים (*ṣelṣelîm,* "cymbals") appears elsewhere in the OT only in Ps 150:5 (bis). The parallel text in 1 Chron 13:8 substitutes מְצִלְתַּיִם (*meṣiltayim*), a dual form found frequently in Chronicles and once each in Ezra and Nehemiah. Although the latter has understandably been considered an apparently later equivalent of *ṣelṣelîm* (BDB, p. 853), its attestation in Ugaritic (*mṣltm*) opens up the possibility of early origin and a northern provenance (cf. Stanley Gevirtz, "Of Syntax and Style in the 'Late Biblical Hebrew'—'Old Canaanite' Connection," JANES 18 [1986]: 25–26 and n. 7).

6 For the MT's נכון (*nkwn*), the parallel in 1 Chron 13:9 reads כידן (*kydn*) and 4QSam[a] reads either נודן (*nwdn*) or נידן (*nydn;* cf. Ulrich, *The Qumran Text,* p. 195). The letters ד (*d*), כ (*k*), and נ (*n*) are similar enough to one another not only to account for all the readings but also to make it difficult if not impossible to choose between them (ibid., p. 213).

7 שַׁל (*šal*), the key word in עַל־הַשַּׁל (*'al-haššal,* "because of his irreverent act") may be cognate to the Aramaic שָׁלוּ (*šālû,* "neglect"; Ezra 4:22; 6:9 ["fail"]; Dan 6:4 ["negligent"]; cf. Carlson, p. 79). If so, שׁל (*šl*) should perhaps be read as שׁלו (*šlw*), the ו (*w*) on the following word (וימת [*wymt*]) doing double duty (cf. Watson, "Shared Consonants," p. 531).

16 At the beginning of the verse, the MT reads והיה (*whyh*), which usually means "and it will be." 4QSam[a] and 1 Chron 15:29, however, read correctly ויהי (*wyhy,* "and it was"; cf. LXX's καὶ ἐγένετο [*kai egeneto*]).

---

## 3. *The Lord's covenant with David*

### 7:1–17

**1 After the king was settled in his palace and the LORD had given him**
**rest from all his enemies around him, 2 he said to Nathan the prophet,**

"Here I am, living in a palace of cedar, while the ark of God remains in a
tent."
[3]Nathan replied to the king, "Whatever you have in mind, go ahead
and do it, for the LORD is with you."
[4]That night the word of the LORD came to Nathan, saying:

[5]"Go and tell my servant David, 'This is what the LORD says: Are
you the one to build me a house to dwell in? [6]I have not dwelt in a
house from the day I brought the Israelites up out of Egypt to this
day. I have been moving from place to place with a tent as my
dwelling. [7]Wherever I have moved with all the Israelites, did I ever
say to any of their rulers whom I commanded to shepherd my
people Israel, "Why have you not built me a house of cedar?"'
[8]"Now then, tell my servant David, 'This is what the LORD Almighty
says: I took you from the pasture and from following the flock to be
ruler over my people Israel. [9]I have been with you wherever you
have gone, and I have cut off all your enemies from before you. Now
I will make your name great, like the names of the greatest men of
the earth. [10]And I will provide a place for my people Israel and will
plant them so that they can have a home of their own and no longer
be disturbed. Wicked people will not oppress them anymore, as
they did at the beginning [11]and have done ever since the time I
appointed leaders over my people Israel. I will also give you rest
from all your enemies.
"'The LORD declares to you that the LORD himself will establish a
house for you: [12]When your days are over and you rest with your
fathers, I will raise up your offspring to succeed you, who will come
from your own body, and I will establish his kingdom. [13]He is the
one who will build a house for my Name, and I will establish the
throne of his kingdom forever. [14]I will be his father, and he will be
my son. When he does wrong, I will punish him with the rod of men,
with floggings inflicted by men. [15]But my love will never be taken
away from him, as I took it away from Saul, whom I removed from
before you. [16]Your house and your kingdom will endure forever
before me; your throne will be established forever.'"

[17]Nathan reported to David all the words of this entire revelation.

Although it is helpful to consider chapter 7 as an integral whole in the sense that 7:18–29 is David's prayerful response to Nathan's oracle (7:4–17), which in turn is introduced by a temporal and spatial backdrop (7:1–3), there is virtually unanimous agreement among scholars that 7:1–17 constitutes a discrete literary unit within the Deuteronomic history. As such it is the center and focus of (1) the narrative of David's powerful reign over Israel (see comment on 5:17–8:18), (2) the story of David's life as a whole (cf. similarly Gerbrandt, p. 160), and indeed (3) the Deuteronomic history itself (cf. similarly Carlson, p. 127; Dennis J. McCarthy, "II Samuel 7 and the Structure of the Deuteronomic History," JBL 84, 2 [1965]: 131, 134, 137; see comment on 1 Sam 12:1–5). In fact, from a theological standpoint 7:1–17 (or 7:1–29) is the "highlight of the Books of Samuel . . . if not of the Deuteronomistic History as a whole" (Anderson, p. 112; cf. also Brueggemann, *First and Second Samuel*, p. 253). Cross "finds it surprising that more attention has not been given to the Deuteronomistic idiom of the chapter. It fairly swarms with expressions found elsewhere in works of the Deuteronomistic school," many of which will be noted below (*Canaanite Myth and Hebrew Epic*, p. 252). "[Second] Samuel 7 is rightly regarded as an 'ideological summit', not only in the 'Deuteronomistic History' but also in the Old Testament as a whole" (Gordon, *I & II Samuel*, p. 235). Heinz Kruse enumerates more than forty separate texts that may have been influenced by Nathan's prophecy, ranging widely through the Pentateuch, the Former and Latter Prophets, and the Writings—and including a few references in the books of the Apocrypha as well ("David's Covenant," VetTest 35, 2 [1985]: 139–41). Other passages could easily be added to the list (cf. Clements, "The Deuteronomistic Interpretation," p. 399 n. 3). Given such statistics, it would be difficult to dispute the contention of Jon D. Levenson that the Lord's covenant with David "receives more attention in the Hebrew Bible than any covenant except the Sinaitic" ("The Davidic Covenant and Its Modern Interpreters," CBQ 41, 2 [1979]: 205–6).

"This chapter was to become the source of the messianic hope as it developed in the message of prophets and psalmists" (Baldwin, p. 213; cf. also Gordon, *I & II Samuel*, p. 236; Brueggemann, *First and Second Samuel*, p. 257; Carlson, p. 127). Judging from 4QFlor(ilegium), a midrash on 7:10b–14a, the Qumran sectarians also detected clear messianic overtones in Nathan's oracle (see commentary below). It remained for the NT, however, to fully exploit the messianic implications inherent in 7:4–17. While it is true that direct citations of chapter 7 are few and far between (vv.8, 14 in 2 Cor 6:18; v.14 in Heb 1:5), various elements of the Davidic covenant are alluded to in the NT again and again, as the commentary will demonstrate. Indeed, Stephen concludes his summary of Israel's history with transparent references to the divine promise to David, "who enjoyed God's favor and asked that he might provide a dwelling place for the God of Jacob. But it was Solomon who built the house for him. . . . 'What kind of house will you build for me? says the Lord. Or where will my resting place be?'" (Acts 7:46–47, 49).

Although chapter 7 nowhere contains the word "covenant," it is universally recognized that it describes the Lord's covenant with David (cf. its inclusion among the covenants listed under *bᵉrîṯ* ["covenant"] in BDB, p. 136). Several OT texts do in fact refer to Nathan's oracle as the exposition of a "covenant" established by the Lord with his servant (cf. 23:5; 1 Kings 8:23; 2 Chron 13:5; Pss 89:3, 28, 34, 39; 132:12; Isa 55:3; Jer 33:21; cf. also Ecclus 45:25), and covenant terminology appears at various points in the chapter as well (e.g., see comments on "love" in v.15 and "good things" in v.28).

The precise nature of the Davidic covenant, long a matter of dispute (usually cast in terms of whether it is "conditional," "unconditional," or a combination of the two), has been illuminated by M. Weinfeld's important distinction:

> Two types of official judicial documents had been diffused in the Mesopotamian cultural sphere from the middle of the second millennium onwards: the political treaty which is well known to us from the Hittite empire and the royal grant, the classical form of which is found in the Babylonian *kudurru* documents (boundary stones). . . . The structure of both types of these documents is similar. Both preserve the same elements: historical introduction, border delineations, stipulations, witnesses, blessings and curses. Functionally, however, there is a vast difference between these two types of documents. While the "treaty" constitutes an obligation of the vassal to his master, the suzerain, the "grant" constitutes an obligation of the master to his servant. In the "grant" the curse is directed towards the one who will violate the rights of the king's vassal, while in the treaty the curse is directed towards the vassal who will violate the rights of his king. In other words, the "grant" serves mainly to protect the rights of the *servant*, while the treaty comes to protect the rights of the *master*. What is more, while the grant is a reward for loyalty and good deeds already performed, the treaty is an inducement for future

> loyalty. ("The Covenant of Grant in the Old Testament and in the Ancient Near East," JAOS 90, 2 [1970]: 184–85, italics his)

Weinfeld goes on to assert that the Davidic covenant is of the grant and not the vassal type. As the promissory covenant included gifts bestowed on the vassal for loyally serving his master, so "David was given the grace of dynasty because he served God with truth, righteousness and loyalty (I Kings III, 6; cf. IX, 4, XI, 4, 6, XIV, 8, XV, 3)" (ibid., p. 185).

Although it would be tempting to characterize the treaty/obligatory/law type of covenant as "conditional" and the grant/promissory/oath type as "unconditional" without further ado, the truth of the matter is far more complex (cf. Ronald F. Youngblood, "The Abrahamic Covenant: Conditional or Unconditional?" in *The Living and Active Word of God: Essays in Honor of Samuel J. Schultz,* edd. Morris Inch and Ronald Youngblood [Winona Lake: Eisenbrauns, 1983], pp. 31–46). Weinfeld himself admits to a conditional element within the Davidic covenant ("The Covenant of Grant," p. 196), although he attributes it (needlessly, in my judgment) to "the Deuteronomist, the redactor of the Book of Kings" (ibid., p. 195). That the grant type of covenant, by its very nature, tends toward unconditionality by no means eliminates the possibility of its having conditions or obligations, which in any case are of the essence of the covenant concept itself (cf. Youngblood, "The Abrahamic Covenant," pp. 33, 35, 37–38, 45). It is not surprising, therefore, that many commentators find one or more conditional elements in Nathan's oracle (Kruse, "David's Covenant," p. 159; Gerbrandt, pp. 166–69; Carlson, p. 126 and n. 5; Mettinger, *In Search of God,* pp. 143–45; E. Theodore Mullen, Jr., "The Sins of Jeroboam: A Redactional Assessment," CBQ 49, 2 [1987]: 216 n. 12; *The Scofield Reference Bible,* ed. C.I. Scofield [New York: Oxford University Press, 1909], p. 362 n. 2; Ronald W. Pierce, "Spiritual Failure, Postponement, and Daniel 9," *Trinity Journal* 10, NS 2 [Fall 1989]: 219 n. 34; William J. Dumbrell, "The Prospect of Unconditionality in the Sinaitic Covenant," in *Israel's Apostasy and Restoration: Essays in Honor of Roland K. Harrison,* ed. Avraham Gileadi [Grand Rapids: Baker, 1988], p. 154 n. 1; Avraham Gileadi, "The Davidic Covenant: A Theological Basis for Corporate Protection," in *Israel's Apostasy and Restoration,* p. 159).

Bruce K. Waltke notes, on the one hand, that "YHWH's grant to David places no obligations on David for its enactment or perpetuation. It is unilateral, and in that sense unconditional" ("The Phenomenon of Conditionality Within Unconditional Covenants," in *Israel's Apostasy and Restoration,* p. 130). On the other hand, however, "the explicit condition put upon the Davidic covenant, extending the irrevocable grant only to a faithful son who keeps the obligations of the treaty, is found not only in putative D[euteronomist] (compare 1 Kgs 2:4; 6:12–13; 8:25; 9:4ff.) but also in the apparently ancient Psalm 132 [vv.11–12]" (ibid., p. 132). To summarize:

> In reiterating the terms of the Davidic covenant to Solomon (1 Kgs 9:4–9), eminently clear conditions are laid down by God. The tension between divine commitment to an unalterable promise on the one hand and the inexorable human bent toward sin on the other is explored in Psalm 89 and in 132:11–12. . . . The fact that a covenant that is everlasting from the divine standpoint may in the course of time be broken by sinful human beings need not give us pause (cf. Isa 24:5). (Youngblood, "The Abrahamic Covenant," p. 41)

Outside the OT, the closest ancient Near Eastern parallels to the Davidic covenant of grant are Hittite and neo-Assyrian documents (Weinfeld, "The Covenant of Grant," p. 189; cf. also id., "Addenda to JAOS 90 [1970], pp. 184ff.," JAOS 92, 3 [1972]: 468–69) rather than the Egyptian *Königsnovelle* ("King's Letter"; contrast Martin Noth, *The Laws in the Pentateuch and Other Studies* [Philadelphia: Fortress, 1967], p. 257 and n. 23). Within the OT itself, the grant type of covenant includes the Noahic (Gen 9:8–17) and Abrahamic (Gen 12:1–3; 15:1–21; 17:1–27) as well as the covenant with Phinehas (Num 25:10–13). Relationships between the Abrahamic and Davidic covenants are especially close (cf. Ronald E. Clements, *Abraham and David: Genesis 15 and Its Meaning for Israelite Tradition,* Studies in Biblical Theology, Second Series 5 [London: SCM, 1967], pp. 47–60; James Freeman Rand, "Old Testament Fellowship With God," BS 109, 433 [1952]: 52).

The most important OT covenant of the treaty type is the Mosaic/Sinaitic (Exod 19–24). Of course, differences between the two covenant types should not be allowed to obscure their similarities or to set them in opposition to each other. Waltke argues: "YHWH's grants and treaty do not rival or exclude, but complement one another. . . . YHWH irrevocably committed himself to the house of David, but rewarded or disciplined individual kings by extending or withholding the benefits of the grant according to their loyalty or disloyalty to His treaty" ("The Phenomenon of Conditionality," pp. 125, 135; cf. also Clements, *Abraham and David,* p. 53; McCarthy, "II Samuel 7 and Deuteronomic History," p. 136; Youngblood, "The Abrahamic Covenant," p. 42; Levenson, citing Ps 78:68–72 ["The Davidic Covenant," p. 218]). The period of the judges, with its recurring cycle of rebellion/retribution/repentance/restoration (cf. Judg 2:11–19; Neh 9:26–29), made it clear that Israel's corporate vassalage to Yahweh as divine Suzerain was virtually impossible to realize. Thus

> the Davidic covenant did away with the necessity that all Israel—to a man—maintain loyalty to YHWH in order to merit his protection. In the analogy of suzerain-vassal relationships, David's designation as YHWH's "son" and "firstborn" (2 Sam 7:14; Pss 2:6–7; 89:27) legitimized him as Israel's representative—as the embodiment of YHWH's covenant people, also called his "son" and "firstborn" (Exod 4:22). . . . Henceforth, the king stood as proxy between YHWH and his people. (Gileadi, "The Davidic Covenant," p. 160)

Indeed, Frederick C. Prussner finds in the conjunction of the Sinaitic and Davidic covenants the theological center of OT faith ("The Covenant of David and the Problem of Unity in Old Testament Theology," in *Transitions in Biblical Scholarship,* Essays in Divinity 6, ed. J. Coert Rylaarsdam [Chicago: University of Chicago Press, 1968], pp. 29–41).

The location of chapter 7 in its present position is doubtless thematic rather than chronological. Nathan's oracle came to David after "the LORD had given him rest from all his enemies around him" (v.1)—but the account of David's defeat of his enemies is related in 8:1–14 (cf. also 23:9–17). As Merrill observes: "It was not until these kingdoms [Philistia, Moab, Zobah, Damascus, Ammon, Amalek, Edom] were actually subdued that David turned wholeheartedly to religious pursuits" (*Kingdom of Priests,* p. 243). Along similar lines, David's "palace" (v.1) was probably not constructed until relatively late in his reign (see comment on 5:11).

Pursuing his proposal that the Davidic covenant describes a grant recognizing prior loyal vassalage, Weinfeld suggests that chapter 7 follows chapter 6 because "the promise of dynasty to David is to be seen as a reward for his devotion" ("The Covenant of Grant," p. 187 n. 28), while Porter sees the link between the two chapters as springing from the posited mutual relationship to Psalm 132 ("The Interpretation of 2 Samuel VI and Psalm CXXXII," p. 169). And whereas Kruse asserts that if the Davidic covenant was a reward "we may suppose that it was given before David proved himself unworthy of it by his sin against Uriah (2 Sam. xi)" ("David's Covenant," p. 150), Waltke proposes more plausibly that by placing chapter 11 after chapter 7 the narrator "subtly instructs us that the beneficiaries' darkest crimes do not annul the covenants of divine commitment" ("The Phenomenon of Conditionality," p. 131).

The literary structure of 7:1–17 may be outlined as follows:

A. Setting (7:1–3)
B. Nathan's oracle (7:4–17)
  1. Introduction (7:4)
  2. Body (7:5–16)
    a. God's questions (7:5–7)
    b. God's promises (7:8–16)
      (1) to be realized during David's lifetime (7:8–11a)
      (2) to be fulfilled after David's death (7:11b–16)
  3. Conclusion (7:17)

Second Samuel 7:1–17 is paralleled in 1 Chronicles 17:1–15.

**1–3** Settled in his royal house and victor over his enemies (v.1), David's regal status is now beyond question. "The shepherd boy in his tent has become a king, enthroned in his palace" (Carlson, p. 97). David is thus referred to as "the king" three times in three successive verses in the MT (vv.1–3; NIV uses "he" in v.2 in deference to English style) and is not called by his personal name until v.5 (the Chronicler, however, substitutes "David"—to him, the human name above all others—for "the king" in all three places in the MT [1 Chron 17:1–2]).

David decides that the time has finally come for him to do what any self-respecting king worthy of the name should do: build a house for his God. The contrast between his own house and that of the Lord is stark: The human king ("I," v.2; emphatic) is "living" (*yšb*, translated "was settled" in v.1) in a sumptuous "palace" (vv.1–2, lit., "house"), while the "ark of God" (v.2, emphatic)—the symbolic throne of the Divine King (see 1 Sam 4:4 and comment)—"remains" (*yšb*) in a mere tent. Constructed of the finest materials and with the best available workmanship (see 5:11 and comment), David's palace overwhelms in size and splendor the relatively simple "tent" (see Notes on v.2). To David's credit he recognizes that the imbalance needs to be rectified.

Safe within his well-fortified palace and behind secure frontiers, the king would doubtless have plenty of time for a major construction project. The Lord has "given him rest from all his enemies around him" (v.1; cf. v.11; cf. similarly 1 Kings 5:4; 1 Chron 22:9, 18; 23:25; 2 Chron 14:7; 15:15; 20:30), fulfilling during David's reign a promise he had made to Israel centuries earlier (cf. Deut 3:20; 12:10; 25:19; Josh 1:13, 15) and had already fulfilled during the lifetime of Joshua (Josh 21:44; 22:4; 23:1). "David completed what Joshua had begun: the taking possession of Canaan. It is this completion of Joshua's work which is reflected in II Sam. 7:1, 11. Now David plans to build a temple as the sequel of the LORD's having granted him rest from his enemies" (Wolfgang Roth, "The Deuteronomic Rest Theology: A Redaction-Critical Study," *Biblical Research* 21 [1976]: 8). Verse 1 may also be characterized "as a fulfillment of the prayer with which [the royal psalm in 1 Sam 2:1–19] concludes: 'May he (Yahweh) give strength to his king, and exalt the power of his anointed,' v.10b" (Carlson, pp. 99–100; see comment on 1 Sam 2:10). The expansionist LXX text of 1 Samuel 10:1 suggests that the task of saving the people "from the power of their enemies round about" (see NIV mg. on 1 Sam 10:1) "was first of all given to Saul and later transferred to David" (Carlson, p. 90; see comment below on v.15).

That David had determined to build a "palace of cedar" (*byt 'rzym,* v.2; see 5:11 and comment) for himself is not unexpected (cf. Jer 22:14–15). But "the plushness of the proposed temple [v.7, 'house of cedar' (*byt 'rzym*)] contradicts Yahweh's self-understanding. Yahweh will not be bought off, controlled, or domesticated by such luxury" (Brueggemann, *First and Second Samuel,* p. 254). For the Ugaritic Baal, building a "house of cedar" (*bt arzm*) for himself might serve the function of "guaranteeing the future existence of the cosmos" (Carlson, p. 98; cf. de Moor, *Anthology of Religious Texts,* p. 55). The Lord, however, requires no such assurances. If a house is to be built for him—not that he needs it to dwell in, of course (cf. 1 Kings 8:27; Isa 66:1–2; Acts 7:48; 17:24–25; Heb 8:1–2; 9:24; Sib Oracles 4:8–11), but as a symbol of his presence among his people—he himself will name the time, the place, and the builder (vv.5–7).

Just as Saul had been advised by Samuel, who had been "attested as a prophet" (1 Sam 3:20; for the etymology and meaning of the Heb. word for "prophet," see comment on 1 Sam 9:9), so also David would be helped and counseled by various prophets (see comment on 1 Sam 22:5). The most important and famous of these was "Nathan the prophet" (v.2), who appears here for the first time in the text. In addition to being the recipient of the divine oracle outlining the Davidic covenant (vv.4–17), Nathan ("[God] Gives") confronts David after his sin with Bathsheba (ch. 12) and plays a prominent role in the anointing of Solomon (rather than Adonijah) as David's successor (1 Kings 1). He was also responsible for recording many of the events of the reigns of David (1 Chron 29:29) and Solomon (2 Chron 9:29).

With respect to David's implied desire to build a temple to house the ark of God (v.2), Nathan agrees that the king should do whatever he has "in mind" (v.3). The statement is that of a loyal subject following customary protocol (see 1 Sam 14:7 and comment) and, in the case of Nathan, has "no bearing whatever on (his) later judgment or oracle as Yahweh's prophet" (Cross, *Canaanite Myth and Hebrew Epic,* p. 242; cf. also Noth, *The Laws in the Pentateuch,* pp. 257–58; Kruse, "David's Covenant," p. 147; Baldwin, p. 217; Brueggemann, *First and Second Samuel,* p. 254). In any event, "for all his prompt complaisance, Nathan is not to be compared with the kind of fawning time-servers who surrounded Ahab and told him what he wanted to hear (1 Ki. 22:6); his subsequent behaviour here, as also in ch. 12, puts him in a different class" (Gordon, *I & II Samuel,* p. 237). Indeed, Nathan understands that David will ultimately follow the path of obedient servanthood (v.5) because "the LORD is with" him (v.3; cf. v.9; see also 5:10; 1 Sam 16:18 and comments; cf. further Cross, *Canaanite Myth and Hebrew Epic,* p. 250 n. 130; p. 252).

**4** Nathan's oracle proper (vv.5–16) is framed by an introduction (v.4) and a summary statement (v.17). Of the three times the phrase "the word of the LORD came to" is used of God's revelation to a prophet in the books of Samuel (see comment on 1 Sam 15:10), only here does it appear in an oracle of blessing. In all three cases, however, the oracle came during the night, as Carlson observes (p. 108; cf. 24:11; 1 Sam 15:10, 16). Here it is referred to as a *ḥizzāyôn* ("revelation/vision" [v.17]), which was often received at night (cf. Job 4:13 ["dreams"]; 7:13–14; 20:8; 33:15). Nathan's oracle thus serves as a counterpoise to Samuel's dream theophany (see comment at introduction to 1 Sam 3:1–4:1a).

**5–7** The messenger formula ("This is what the LORD says," v.5) pinpoints Nathan as the mediator of the divine oracle to David. In contrast to his title as "the king" in the opening verses of the chapter (see comment on vv.1–3), David is now referred to by the Lord as "my servant David" (vv.5, 8; see comment on 3:18; cf. also 1 Kings 11:13, 32, 34, 36, 38, 14:8; 2 Kings 19:34; 20:6; Jer 33:21–22, 26; Ezek 34:23–24), a description that he willingly and humbly accepts (v.26).

> The only other occurence [*sic*] of this precise phrase, "my servant N.," in the whole of the Deuteronomic work is "my servant Moses" in the words of Yahweh to Joshua when he takes over the leadership of Israel [Josh 1:2, 7]. Not even Joshua himself merits the title. . . . This calls attention to David's importance—he merits comparison with Moses—and the important new thing, the institution of the Davidic monarchy, which begins with him. (McCarthy, "II Samuel 7 and Deuteronomic History," p. 132; cf. Gerbrandt, p. 170)

The substantive contents of the present literary unit (vv.5–7) are framed by two questions asked by the Lord, both of which pertain to building a temple for him (vv.5, 7). The first—"Are you the one to build me a house to dwell in?"—has been interpreted in a variety of ways (for a typical list, cf. Gerbrandt, p. 162). After examining a number of ancient extrabiblical Near Eastern texts that deal with the building/rebuilding/repairing of temples, Michiko Ita concludes:

> The real issue is that both the initiative to build a temple and the choice of the person for the task must come from God and not from an individual king. . . . First, God has not commanded the building of a temple either to any of the past leaders or to David himself (vss 6–7). Second, the choice of the person is God's affair. God's denial—put in the interrogative form (vs 5)—concerns the person of David and not the temple itself. The emphatic position of the pronoun (*h'th*) makes this point more than clear. Moreover, this denial of David results in the positive choice of his successor in vs 13, where the emphatic *hw' ybnh* ["He is the one who will build"] is to be noted as a counterpart of the emphatic denial in vs 5. ("A Note on 2 Sam 7," in *A Light Unto My Path: Old Testament Studies in Honor of Jacob M. Myers*, Gettysburg Theological Studies 4; edd. Howard N. Bream, Ralph D. Heim, and Carey A. Moore [Philadelphia: Temple University, 1974], p. 406; cf. Carlson, p. 109).

That the question in v.5 expects a negative answer is clear not only from the succeeding context but also from the LXX's *Ou sy* ("Not you") and from the Chronicler's parallel: "You are not the one" (1 Chron 17:4).

Needless to say, the prohibition of v.5 is merely temporary. "This is confirmed by the later verses in the chapter, by verses such as 1 Kgs 5:3–5, as well as by the positive emphasis on the temple throughout the remainder of the history" (Gerbrandt, p. 162). David's son Solomon (see comments on vv.12–13) would eventually build the Lord's house (cf. 1 Kings 5:3–5; 6:1). In the broader context, at least two reasons are given for the fact that David himself did not build the temple: (1) He is too busy waging war with his enemies (1 Kings 5:3); (2) he is a warrior who has shed much blood (1 Chron 22:8; 28:3). The reasons are complementary rather than contradictory, the first being practical and the second theological (cf. similarly Walter C. Kaiser, Jr., "The Blessing of David: The Charter for Humanity," in *The Law and the Prophets: Old Testament Studies Prepared in Honor of Oswald Thompson Allis,* ed. John H. Skilton [Nutley: Presbyterian and Reformed, 1974], p. 304 n. 21). Neither reason dims David's vision, however (cf. similarly Ps 132:1–5), and before his death he makes extensive preparations for the temple that would eventually be built by Solomon (cf. 1 Chron 22:2–5; 28:2).

But the time for construction has not yet arrived. The tabernacle still suffices as the Lord's dwelling (v.6). Although David is "living" (*yšb*) in a palace (v.1), the Lord has never "dwelt" (*yšb;* thus also "dwell" in v.5) in a permanent house, not "from the day" (cf. Judg 19:30) he "brought the Israelites up out of Egypt" (v.6)—a common phrase recalling the miracles of the Exodus redemption (cf. 1 Sam 8:8; 10:18; Deut 20:1; Josh 24:17; for additional examples cf. Cross, *Canaanite Myth and Hebrew Epic,* p. 253; see comment on 1 Sam 12:6). The Lord has been content with "moving from place to place" (*hthlk;* cf. v.7, "moved"; cf. also Deut 23:14, "moves about"), demonstrating his continuing desire to "walk" (*hthlk*) among his people (Lev 26:12; cf. Gen 3:8).

Referred to as "tent(-curtain[s])" in v.2 (see Notes), the tabernacle is called both a "tent" (*'ōhel*) and a "dwelling" (*miškān*) in v.6. The latter term is commonly translated "tabernacle" in the OT (cf. Exod 25:9) and occurs elsewhere in association with the former (cf. Exod 26:12–13), especially in the phrase "tent over the tabernacle" (Exod 26:7; 36:14; 40:19). The irony in v.6 must not be missed: Although God condescends to accompany his people on their journey with a tent as his dwelling (v.6b), a tent carried by them, all along they have in fact been carried by him (v.6a).

Like the first, the second question in the present literary unit (vv.5–7) expects a negative answer (see comment on v.5). Beginning with the word "did," it implies that the Lord never required the Israelites to build him a "house of cedar" (v.7; see comment on v.2). "Any of their rulers" translates *'aḥaḏ šiḇṭê yiśrā'ēl,* which is literally "one of the tribes of Israel." Since the same Hebrew phrase occurs in 15:2 in its literal sense, Philippe de Robert wants to translate it the same way here ("Judges ou Tribus en 2 Samuel VII 7?" VetTest 21, 1 [1971]: 116–18; cf. also the LXX's *phylēn* ["tribe"]). As S.R. Driver had already pointed out long ago, however (*Notes on the Books of Samuel,* p. 274), there is no example of any tribe having been divinely commissioned to "shepherd" (see 5:2 and comment; cf. also 24:17) Israel (but cf. Kirkpatrick, who suggests that "tribes" may be understood "of the different tribes which through the Judges and leaders chosen from them successively attained the supremacy, as Ephraim in the time of Joshua, Dan in the days of Samson, Benjamin in the reign of Saul" [*The Second Book of Samuel,* p. 98; cf. 1 Chron 28:4; Ps 78:67–68]). Many commentators therefore substitute *šōpṭê* ("judges," "leaders") for *šiḇṭê* on the basis of 1 Chronicles 17:6 (where the LXX, however, has *phylēn*) and the subsequent context (vv.10–11; cf. McCarthy, "II Samuel 7 and Deuteronomic History," p. 133 and n. 7; S.R. Driver, *Notes on the Books of Samuel,* in loc.).

The best solution to the problem would seem to be that of Patrick V. Reid, who suggests revocalizing the MT's *šiḇṭê* as *šōḇṭê,* "a denominative qal participle . . . of *šēḇeṭ,* meaning 'the one who wields a staff,'" thus "staff bearers," which "fits the imagery of the passage much better than 'judges.' One would expect that the persons bearing the shepherd's staff would be commissioned 'to shepherd'" ("*šbṭy* in 2 Samuel 7:7," CBQ 37, 1 [1975]: 18; cf. pp. 17–20 for full argumentation; cf. similarly McCarter, *II Samuel;* cf. also the use of *šēḇeṭ* ["scepter"] as a metaphor for authoritative rule in the messianic texts Gen 49:10; Num 24:17). The NIV's "rulers" (v.7; "ruler" in v.8 renders a different Heb. word) is a term general enough to capture the basic idea.

"People" used with reference to Israel is an important *Leitmotif* in the chapter (cf. independently Carlson, p. 118), employed four times in each half (vv.7, 8, 10, 11; vv. 23 [ter], 24; see also comment on 6:21). "The people of God is one of the most prominent themes in the Bible" (John Goldingay, *Theological Diversity and the Authority of the Old Testament* [Grand Rapids: Eerdmans, 1987], p. 59; for full discussion cf. pp. 59–96). "I will be your God, and you will be my people" or the equivalent is doubtless the most characteristic covenant expression in the entire OT (cf. v.24; Exod 6:7; Lev 26:12; Deut 26:17–18; Jer 7:23; 30:22; 31:1, 33; 32:38; Ezek 34:30; 36:28; 37:23; Hos 1:9–10; 2:23; cf. also Heb 8:10).

**8–11a** The repetition of the messenger formula (see comment on v.5) marks v.8 as the start of a new section of Nathan's oracle. Here, however, the word "LORD" (v.5) has been augmented by "Almighty," a regal title (see comment on 1 Sam 1:3) that stresses the Lord's function as covenant Suzerain of David, his "servant" vassal (see comment on v.5). Characteristically, David in his response to God willingly acknowledges both roles (vv.26–27). In Paul's citation of v.14a in 2 Corinthians 6:18, he similarly acknowledges the solemnity and importance of "Almighty" in describing the Lord in this context.

The divine grant to David is divided into two parts: "promises to be realized during David's lifetime (2 Sam 7:8–11a) and promises to be fulfilled after his death (7:11b–16)" (Waltke, "The Phenomenon of Conditionality," p. 130). Verses 7b–8a constitute a brief historical prologue in which the Lord reviews his earlier blessings on his servant David. He begins by reminding David of where he found him: "I [emphatic] took you . . . from following the flock" (v.8). At the time of David's earlier private anointing, Samuel had said, "Send for him" (1 Sam 16:11; lit., "Send and take him"); the Lord now observes that it was he himself who "took" David. As in the case of Amos, the Lord took him "from following the flock" (Amos 7:15, "from tending the flock"; same Heb. expression in both passages). Once a mere shepherd boy (see comments on 5:2; 1 Sam 16:11), David has been given a much weightier responsibility: to be "ruler" over the Lord's people Israel (see comments on 5:2; 6:21; 1 Sam 9:16; 10:1; cf. also Hezekiah in 2 Kings 20:5 ["leader"]). "Yahweh could use David, not because he was a great military leader, but because he was faithful. In this way a good king can be an agent by which the people are blessed" (Gerbrandt, p. 171).

Verse 9 is linked to v.6 through the use of the durative form *wā'ehyeh* ("I have been"): As the Lord had been "moving from place to place" with his people (v.6; cf. also v.7), so he has been "with" (v.9; see v.3 and comment; cf. also Carlson, p. 114) David "wherever" he has gone (cf. v.7; 8:6, 14; Josh 1:7, 9). The Lord had promised to "cut off" David's enemies from before him (cf. also 1 Sam 20:15).

Verses 9b–11a contain three elements: The Lord will (1) make David's "name great" (v.9b), (2) "provide a place" for Israel (v.10), and (3) give David "rest" from all his enemies (v.11a; Carlson, pp. 114–15). The divine promise to make the name of David great is a clear echo of the Abrahamic covenant (cf. Gen 12:2), which in turn stands in sharp contrast to the self-aggrandizing boasts of the builders of the tower of Babel: "so that we may make a name for ourselves" (Gen 11:4). An example of David's name becoming great is 8:13, where the narrator reports that David "became famous" (lit., "made a name"; cf. 1 Kings 1:47) after defeating the Edomites (cf. similarly 1 Sam 18:30). But again David testifies to his reliance on God's power as he affirms that redemption takes place in the context of God's determination to "make a name for himself" (vv.23, 26; cf. Jer 13:11; 32:20; see 1 Sam 12:22 and comment).

That God would provide a "place" for his people (v.10) had been predicted long ago: "Every place where you set your foot will be yours: Your territory will extend from the desert to Lebanon, and from the Euphrates River to the western sea" (Deut 11:24; cf. Josh 1:3–4). "Since this promise is identical with that given to Abraham in Gen. 15:18 . . . the introduction of the *māqōm* ['place'] idea in 7:10 [cf. also 1 Sam 12:8] implies that the Covenant made with Abraham is fulfilled through David" (Carlson, p. 116; cf. 8:1–4). And far from being temporary, the "place" that God would provide would be the land where he would "plant" them (v.10; cf. Exod 15:17; Pss 44:2; 80:8; Isa 5:2; Jer 2:21; Amos 9:15). Plant imagery is frequently applied to David's dynasty in the OT (e.g., Ps 80:15; Isa 11:1, 10; Jer 23:5; 24:5–6; 33:15; Ezek 19:10–14; Zech 3:8; 6:12; cf. Talmon, p. 218 n. 26).

Having a home of their own, David and his countrymen will no longer "be disturbed" (v.10; i.e., "tremble" in fear [Deut 2:25; same Heb. verb in both cases]) by "wicked people" (lit., "sons of wickedness" [see comment on "wicked men" in 3:34], which contrasts with "Israelites" [lit., "sons of Israel"] in vv.6–7). Indeed, "wicked people will not oppress them anymore" (a phrase echoed in Ps 89:22), as had been their fate earlier in their history ("at the beginning"; cf. Gen 15:13, where the Lord predicts that Abraham's descendants would be "mistreated" [thus also Deut 26:6; same Heb. verb as that rendered "oppress" here] four hundred years—yet another link between the Abrahamic and Davidic covenants [cf. Carlson, p. 118]). Although oppression had been virtually endemic in Israel during the entire period of the "judges" (v.11; NIV mg.), such would no longer be the case.

"David and his line are presented as the true successors of the judges who will bring on the lasting rest from Israel's enemies which the earlier leaders were unable to achieve" (McCarthy, "II Samuel 7 and Deuteronomic History," p. 133; cf. Gerbrandt, p. 171 n. 186; Roth, "The Deuteronomic Rest Theology," p. 8; Howard, "The Case for Kingship," p. 113 n. 36). As always, of course, the ultimate Giver of the rest is God himself (v.11; see v.1 and comment). The Chronicler's parallel notes that the method the Lord would use to "give [David] rest from" all his enemies would be to "subdue" them (1 Chron 17:10).

**11b–16** Just as the divine pronouncements in vv.5–7 and 8–11a are introduced with the messenger formula "This is what the LORD [Almighty] says," so also vv.11b–16 begin with the oracular preface "The LORD declares to you" as a means of introducing God's promises to David's descendants: a "house" (= dynasty, vv.11b, 16; cf. "offspring," v.12); a throne (vv.13, 16) and kingdom (vv.12–13, 16) that will last forever (vv.13, 16); a "house" (= temple, v.13); and a Father-son relationship (v.14) including a covenant love that will never be taken away (v.15). The importance of "house" in the sense of "dynasty" in Nathan's oracle is underscored by its appearance at the beginning (v.11b) and end (v.16) of the literary unit, thus serving to frame the whole.

That "house" is used with two different meanings in these verses is clear from the verbs used with it: In v.11b the verb is *'śh* ("establish"; lit., "make"; cf. 1 Kings 2:24, where "made a house" is translated "founded a dynasty"), while in v.13 the verb is *bnh* ("build," as in v.5; see comment there). Although David is not to build a "house" (temple) for the Lord (v.5), the Lord will establish a "house" (dynasty) for David (v.11; cf. similarly Brueggemann, *First and Second Samuel,* p. 255). It is David's "offspring" (v.12) who will build the Lord's temple (v.13).

All the promises in this section would be fulfilled after David's death, after his being laid to "rest" (v.12; lit., "lie down"; a different Heb. verb is used for "rest" in vv.1, 11) with his "fathers" (cf. 1 Kings 1:21; 2:10)—an expression used of Moses (Deut 31:16) and others (cf. Gen 47:30). It reflects the ancient Israelite practice of having multiple burials in family tombs (see comment on 2:32).

"Like Abraham, David is receiving promises concerning a son yet unborn" (Gordon, *I & II Samuel,* p. 239). Saul's earlier plea to David not to cut off "my descendants" (lit., "my seed after me," 1 Sam 24:21; cf. Ruth 4:12 for "seed/offspring" applied to David's ancestor[s]) is reprised in the Lord's determination with respect to David to "raise up your offspring to succeed you" (lit., "your seed after you"; cf. similarly 1 Kings 15:4). The emphasis that David's offspring would "come from your own body" (lit., "loins" as the locus of procreation, v.12) forges yet another striking line to the Abrahamic covenant (cf. Gen 15:4), as does the repeated reference to Abraham's "seed/descendants after you/him" in Genesis 17:7–10, 19.

Although Carlson (p. 122) assumes that the offspring of v.12 is Absalom because of the occurrence of "is of my own flesh" (lit., "has come from my own loins") in 16:11, Symon Patrick long ago understood that the future tense in v.12 "shows that he speaks of one, who was not yet born, *viz. Solomon:* And that *Absalom, Adonijah,* and the rest who pretended to the Kingdom, were not designed for it: Being already proceeded from him" (p. 395; cf. 3:2–5, which lists the sons born to David in Hebron). Furthermore, the Lord promises to "establish" (vv.12–13, 16; see 5:12 and comment; the verb is *kwn,* different from that used in v.11 [see comment there]) the "kingdom" and throne of Solomon, not Absalom. Although Saul's kingdom could earlier have been theoretically "established" alongside that of David (see 1 Sam 13:13 and comment), such was not to be (cf. v.15).

The possibility of understanding "seed" ("offspring," NIV) as either singular or plural (cf. Ps 89:4, 29, 36, where the Heb. word for "seed" is translated "line" in connection with the Davidic covenant) is exploited by Paul in Galatians 3:16: "The promises were spoken to Abraham and to his seed. The Scripture [Gen 12:7; 13:15; 24:7] does not say 'and to seeds,' meaning many people, but 'and to your seed,' meaning one person, who is Christ" (cf. also "the Seed" [= Christ] in Gal 3:19 and "Abraham's seed" [= Christians] in Gal 3:29). The trajectory from the Abrahamic covenant through the Davidic covenant to the new covenant in Christ is strengthened by the repetition of words such as "seed" used in a messianic sense (cf. similarly John M.G. Barclay, *Obeying the Truth: A Study of Paul's Ethics in Galatians* [Edinburgh: T. and T. Clark, 1988], p. 89; cf. also John 7:42 and NIV mg. there; Acts 13:23 ["descendants"]; cf. further Dale Goldsmith, "Acts 13 33–37: A *Pesher* on II Samuel 7," JBL 87, 3 [1968]: 321–24).

Unlike vv.11 and 16, v.13 uses "house" in the sense of a building (cf. also vv.1–2 ["palace"], 5–7), in this case a house of worship, a temple. David's offspring (v.12)—"he" (emphatic, v.13), answering to the emphatic "you" (David) of v.5 (see comment there)—has been designated to build a temple for the Lord's "Name" (i.e., his presence, v.13 [for "name" = "presence" cf. John 1:12]; see comment on 6:2; cf. also

1 Kings 3:2; 5:3, 5; 8:16, 18–19, 44, 48; 9:7). "Within the [Deuteronomic] History this ['he'] is an obvious reference to Solomon. This verse could be interpreted both as a justification for Solomon's building the temple, and as a sign legitimating his rise to the throne (the one who builds the temple is the God-chosen successor to David)" (Gerbrandt, p. 163; cf. Brueggemann, *David's Truth*, pp. 75–76). Indeed, "1 Kings 6–8 is the fulfilment of the oracular promise in 7:13a, cf. 1 Kings 8:14–21, 24" (Carlson, p. 120; Gerbrandt, p. 165). As for v.13b, it promises that the Davidic dynasty, throne, and kingdom will endure "forever" (a fact mentioned seven times in ch. 7: vv.13b, 16a, 16b, 24, 25, 29a, 29b; cf. also 22:51; 1 Kings 2:33, 45; 1 Chron 22:10; Ps 89:4).

Not the least because they are cited twice in the NT (2 Cor 6:18; Heb 1:5), the Lord's words in v.14a are doubtless the best known as well as the most solemn in the entire chapter: "I [emphatic] will be his father, and he [emphatic] will be my son." In its original setting the son is Solomon, as the subsequent context makes clear (cf. also 1 Chron 22:9–10). The statement in the first instance was not a formula of begetting but of adoption (Edmond Jacob, *Theology of the Old Testament* [New York: Harper, 1958], p. 236; cf. also Pss 2:7; 89:26; Shalom M. Paul, "Adoption Formulae: A Study in Cuneiform and Biblical Legal Clauses," *Maarav* 2, 2 [1980]: pp. 173–85; Anthony Phillips, "Another Example of Family Law," VetTest 30, 2 [1980]: 240–41). The formula "provides both the judicial basis for the gift of the eternal dynasty (compare Pss 2:7–8; 89) and the qualification that disloyal sons will lose YHWH's protection (compare 1 Kgs 6:12–13; 9:4, 6–7)" (Waltke, "The Phenomenon of Conditionality," p. 131; cf. Weinfeld, "The Covenant of Grant," p. 190).

Because of its typological use in 2 Corinthians 6:18 and Hebrews 1:5, v.14a has long been considered messianic in a Christological sense. The Qumran text known as 4Q Florilegium, an eschatological midrash primarily on vv.10b–14a (although other OT passages, including Ps 2:1, are also treated in it), demonstrates that the Dead Sea sectarians also understood v.14a to be messianic (for text cf. J.M. Allegro, "Fragments of a Qumran Scroll of Eschatological *Midrāšîm*," JBL 77, 4 [1958]: 350–54; Yigael Yadin, "A Midrash on 2 Sam. vii and Ps. i–ii [4Q Florilegium]," IEJ 9 [1959]: 95–98; for a literate and readily accessible translation, cf. Vermes, *The Dead Sea Scrolls in English*, pp. 245–47). William R. Lane observes that 4Q Florilegium divides naturally into two parts, the first of which concentrates mainly on vv.10b–14a and deals with "the establishment of the true house of Israel under the Davidic Messiah and the subsequent era of peace" and the second with "the wicked and their affliction of the elect during the final struggle" ("A New Commentary Structure in 4Q Florilegium," JBL 78, 4 [1959]: 344).

Needless to say, the Qumran sectarians interpreted the OT "prooftexts" according to their own agenda. The fact that they understood v.14a messianically, however, is surely significant for the NT passages that do the same. No longer is it possible to insist that the NT writers overstepped their bounds in claiming that the divine sonship of the Messiah (in their case, Jesus) is adumbrated in 2 Samuel 7, Psalm 2, and elsewhere. They were making use of well-established, exegetical methodologies that had long been recognized in Jewish scholarly circles. Indeed, 4Q Florilegium "suggests that the Qumran community . . . inherited a messianic reading of [Nathan's] oracle from earlier times. . . . Christian and Qumran interpreters shared a basic approach to the verses, but their exegesis led in rather different directions" (Donald Juel, *Messianic Exegesis: Christological Interpretation of the Old Testament in Early Christianity* [Philadelphia: Fortress, 1988], pp. 61–62; cf. also pp. 87–88).

At the same time, what is particularly striking about the 4Q Florilegium commentary is that it

> betrays no embarrassment regarding the use of father-son imagery in v.14. That is notable only in light of later targumic and rabbinic tradition that took great pains to ensure that the imagery from this text be understood as figurative. Later tradition was hesitant to use "son" to speak of the Messiah; the Qumran interpreter shows no such reservations. (ibid., p. 68.; cf. also p. 78)

Like 4Q Florilegium, Hebrews 1:5 also quotes v.14a and Psalm 2 (this time, however, Ps 2:7: "You are my Son; today I have become your Father"). The author of Hebrews uses the two texts to demonstrate that Jesus, the Son of God, "became as much superior to the angels as the name he has inherited is superior to theirs" (Heb 1:4) when he "sat down at the right hand of the Majesty in heaven" (Heb 1:3). Furthermore, "the 'Son of God' is a title applied to Jesus by the gospel writers to highlight his messianic and divine origin as the fulfilment of such Old Testament prophecies as Psalm 2:7 and 2 Samuel 7:14" (Craig L. Blomberg, *The Historical Reliability of the Gospels* [Downers Grove: InterVarsity, 1987], p. 251). And such passages as Luke 1:32–33 reverberate with echoes of Nathan's oracle: "[Jesus] will be great and will be called the Son of the Most High. The Lord God will give him the throne of his father David, and he will reign over the house of Jacob forever; his kingdom will never end."

At the same time, "son" in v.14a could be understood by NT writers in a collective sense, as 2 Corinthians 6:18 demonstrates: "I will be a Father to you,/ and you will be my sons and daughters,/ says the Lord Almighty" (see NIV mg.). Murray J. Harris notes: "What God promised to Solomon through David and to Israel through Solomon (cf. Jer 31:9) finds its fulfillment in what God is to the community of believers through Christ (Gal 3:26; 4:6)" (EBC, 10:360). Father-son imagery representing God's relationship to the people of Israel is common in the OT. Besides Jeremiah 31:9, it is found in such texts as Exodus 4:22–23; Deuteronomy 14:1; 32:6, 19; Isaiah 1:2; 30:1; 43:6; 45:10; 63:16; 64:8; Jeremiah 3:19; Hosea 1:10; 11:1; and Malachi 1:6; 2:10.

A further aspect of the father-son metaphor is its covenant setting. In Mesopotamia, for example, "employment of familial metaphors to express political ties was . . . a well-known phenomenon in the diplomatic lexicon of the second millennium. Thus *abbūtu* 'fathership' signifies suzerainty, *mārūtu* 'sonship'—vassalship" (Paul, "Adoption Formulae," p. 177). The use of "father" for God and "son" for Solomon in v.14a is thus entirely appropriate in what has justifiably come to be known as the Davidic covenant. At the same time the most characteristic of all covenant formulas—"I will be your God, and you will be my people"—is taken from "the sphere of marriage/adoption legal terminology like its Davidic counterpart in II Sam. VII, 14" (Weinfeld, "The Covenant of Grant," p. 200).

Although the Davidic king was to enjoy the unique relationship of being the Lord's "son," he would thereby be brought "all the more firmly within the constraints of Yahweh's fatherly discipline" (Gordon, *I & II Samuel*, p. 239), as v.14b indicates. The Lord would use men as agents of divine judgment on Solomon (and his dynastic successors) "when he does wrong" (cf. Solomon's words in 1 Kings 8:47 in their context). It is not an idle promise: "The rod" (v.14b; cf. also Ps 89:32) of divine wrath would fall on Jerusalem and her citizens because of the sins of David's descendants (cf. Lam 3:1). The Chronicler's parallel leaves out v.14b entirely because of his characteristic desire to display the Davidic dynasty in the best possible light. His omission of the negative threat makes it tempting to assume that Hebrews 1:5, referring to the sinless Christ, cites 1 Chronicles 17:13 rather than 2 Samuel 7:14 (cf. Reymond, *Jesus, Divine Messiah,* p. 11 n. 6). Symon Patrick, however, prefers to call v.14 "a mixt [*sic*] Prophecy, some part of which belongs to Christ, and the other part to *Solomon,* and his Successors in the Kingdom of *Israel*" (p. 395).

But neither expedient seems necessary. Although the NT leaves no doubt that v.14a is fulfilled typologically in Jesus, it is also clear that in its original setting the entire verse refers to the Lord's adoption of Solomon (and his royal descendants) as his son/vassal: "The son given into adoption has the duties of a son (= respecting his parents) but also has the privileges of a son: he has to be treated like the son of a free citizen and not like a slave. . . . What is then meant in II Sam. VII, 14 is that when David's descendants sin they will be disciplined like rebellious sons by their father but they will not be alienated" (Weinfeld, "The Covenant of Grant," pp. 192–93). Such an understanding in no way denies the interpretation that Solomon, the type, prefigures Jesus, the antitype.

Taken together, vv.14b–15 have often been understood to mean that the Davidic covenant is unconditional: No matter what David's descendants do (v.14b), the Lord's love will "never be taken away" from them (v.15). But although the verses "may point in that direction, it is striking that a passage so clearly grounded in the royal cults of that time would emphasize that Yahweh will punish the king for disobeying the law. This must be seen as at least qualifying the promise if not making it conditional. These verses point out that kings are not to use the Davidic promise as a justification for any style of behavior" (Gerbrandt, p. 164).

At the same time, however, the "When" of v.14b gives way to the "But" of v.15. Brueggemann remarks:

> Sound interpretation requires us to recognize that while the covenantal "if" is silenced in this theology, it has not been nullified. Therefore, interpretation must struggle with the tension of "if" and "nevertheless" that is present in the Bible, in our own lives, and in the very heart of God. . . . The historical process teaches us about the reality of judgment and condition, so that we know about the "if" of reality from our own experience. The other side of the tension, God's unconditional commitment, will be operative in biblical faith only if Nathan's bold oracle of "nevertheless" is sounded as the gospel. (*First and Second Samuel,* p. 259)

All three verbs in v.15 ("be taken away," "took . . . away," "removed") are forms of the verb *swr* ("turn aside"), the second and third occurrences of which are identical (*hᵃsirōṯî*). The Lord promises that although he "turned aside" his love from Saul (whom the Chronicler in his parallel, reluctant to mention Saul by name, simply calls David's "predecessor" [1 Chron 17:13]), David's mortal enemy whom the Lord "turned aside" from before him, the divine love will never "turn aside" from David's seed ("offspring," v.12), David's son Solomon (and his descendants)—and ultimately great David's greater Son, Jesus Christ. Carlson notes that "the emphasized *hēsîr* element in v.15 derives from the previous description of Saul and David, cf. 1 Sam. 16:14, 18:12, 28:15 f." (p. 122; see comments on 1 Sam 16:14; 28:15–16). In addition *lō'-yāsûr* ("will never be taken away") echoes the same phrase in Genesis 49:10 ("will not depart"; cf. Carlson, p. 108).

God's covenant with David assures him that his covenant "love" (*ḥeseḏ,* v.15; see comments on 2:6; 1 Sam 20:8, 14–15; cf. Roger T. Beckwith, "The Unity and Diversity of God's Covenants," *Tyndale Bulletin* 33 [1987]: 102 n. 26) will never leave David's son as it had left Saul. An important emphasis in v.15 is the fact that it constitutes "an endorsement of the Davidic claim to the throne over against the Saulide and any others that may emerge" (Levenson, "The Davidic Covenant," p. 217). The word *ḥesed̲* becomes a virtual synonym for *b^e^rît̲* ("covenant") in later allusions to the Davidic covenant (cf. 22:51 ["unfailing kindness"]; 1 Kings 3:6 ["kindness"]; 2 Chron 6:42 ["great love"]; Ps 89:28, 33, 49; Isa 55:3; 1 Macc 2:57 [for the last reference, cf. Kruse, "David's Covenant," p. 148, who observes that *eleos* ("mercy") = *ḥesed̲* in this context; cf. further Pierre Bordreuil, "Les 'Graces de David' et 1 Maccabees ii 57," VetTest 31, 1 [1981]: 73–76).

With respect to Isaiah 55:3 (cited in Acts 13:34 to demonstrate that Jesus' resurrection was further proof of God's covenant love to David), Walter C. Kaiser, Jr., makes the helpful observation that "the phrase *ḥasd̲ê dāwid̲ hanne'emānîm* ['faithful love promised to David'] . . . echoes 2 Sam. 7.15–16: 'My *ḥesed̲* I will not remove from him. . . . Sure [*ne'man*] are your house and your kingdom before me forever" ("The Unfailing Kindnesses Promised to David: Isaiah 55:3," JSOT 45 [1989]: 92). Verse 16 itself reprises earlier promises in the near context in summary fashion (for "house/dynasty" see comment on v.11b; for "kingdom" and "throne"—which are linked contextually to "house/dynasty"—and "forever" see comment on v.13b; for "established" see comment on v.12).

That David's "house" would "endure" (v.16) echoes Abigail's insight in 1 Samuel 25:28 (see comment on "lasting dynasty" there; see also comment on "firmly [established his] house" in 1 Sam 2:35; cf. 1 Kings 11:38 ["dynasty as enduring"]—the Heb. expression is virtually the same in all four passages). *N'mn* ("enduring," "true," "established," "confirmed") is applied also to the divine promises made to David (1 Kings 8:26; 1 Chron 17:23; 2 Chron 1:9; cf. further Mettinger, *In Search of God*, pp. 144–45, who calls attention to the fact that "Isaiah's address to the Davidide Ahaz [Isa 7:9] . . . contains a play on the Nathan prophecy"; cf. similarly Gordon, *I & II Samuel*, p. 240), which comprise the covenant itself (which "will never fail," Ps 89:28). Through Solomon (cf. 1 Chron 22:6–11; 28:5–7) and his descendants, David's throne would "be established" (*kwn*, v.16; cf. 1 Kings 2:45 ["remain secure"]; Ps 89:37).

When A.G. Hebert wrote a book that he subtitled *A Study of the Fulfilment of the Old Testament in Jesus Christ and His Church*, he could think of no better main title than *The Throne of David* (London: Faber and Faber, 1941). More than any other, Christ fulfills the promises of the Davidic covenant. "The failure of the kings generally leads not to disillusion with kingship but to the hope of a future king who will fulfill the kingship ideal—a hope which provides the most familiar way of understanding the significance of Jesus of Nazareth, the *Christ* coming in his *kingdom*" (Goldingay, *Theological Diversity and the Authority of the Old Testament*, p. 70). That the throne of David will remain "forever" (v.16) refers ultimately to "none but Christ, for *David*'s Kingdom had an end, but Christ's hath none" (Symon Patrick, p. 396; cf. Luke 1:31–33). In the words of Martin Luther, "his kingdom is forever."

**17** Nathan's oracle (vv.5–16) having come to an end, a summary statement functions, together with the introduction (v.4), to frame the oracle itself. It was incumbent on a prophet to report "all the words" that the Lord commissioned him to proclaim (cf. Jer

42:4 ["everything"]), and Nathan keeps nothing back. "The task of the prophet, to convey the message of the Lord faithfully and accurately, is carried out by Nathan, though it involved contradicting what he had already said to David by way of personal opinion" (Baldwin, p. 217; see v.3 and comment).

The Lord's "revelation/vision" (*ḥizzāyôn,* see v.4 and comment) to Nathan concerning David and his dynasty is perhaps referred to in Psalm 89:19 ("vision," *ḥāzôn*), which may allude also to the divine communication to Samuel in 1 Samuel 16:12.

## Notes

---

**2** "In a tent" is literally "inside the curtain(s)" and refers to "the" tent earlier pitched by David and "inside" which he had set the ark in its place (6:17). As in Exod 26:1–13, the noun translated "curtain(s)" almost always refers to the curtains of the tabernacle (for which see comment on 6:17).

**6** The NIV's "with a tent as my dwelling" (lit., "in a tent and in a dwelling") is rendered as a hendiadys also by Carlson ("in a tent-dwelling," p. 106). The Chronicler captures the durative aspect of the entire sentence ("I have been moving from place to place with a tent as my dwelling") with a creative rendering of the hendiadys: "I have moved from one tent site to another, from one dwelling place to another" (1 Chron 17:5). Cross (*Canaanite Myth and Hebrew Epic,* pp. 242–43) observes that the pair of words surfaces in Ps 78:60 ("tabernacle," "tent") in reference to its abandonment by the Lord at Shiloh (see comment on 1 Sam 4:11).

**7** The NIV's "did I ever say" apparently vocalizes the first word דבר דברתי (*dbr dbrty*) as the infinitive absolute דַּבֵּר (*dabbēr*) rather than following the MT cognate accusative דָּבָר (*dāḇār*). Although Cross (ibid., p. 253) affirms the MT vocalization and lists many other examples of *dbr* in cognate accusative constructions from elsewhere in the Deuteronomic corpus, all of them interpose one or more graphemes (e.g., *'šr*) between the verbal form and its object and are thus not true parallels to *dbr dbrty.* The juxtaposition of the two forms in the present verse, as well as the LXX's *εἰ λαλῶν ἐλάλησα* (*ei lalōn elalēsa,* "speaking have I ever spoken") both here and in the parallel in 1 Chron 17:6, make the infinitive absolute construction the better choice.

**9** A few commentators have attempted to equate David's promised "great name" (שֵׁם גָּדוֹל, *šēm gāḏôl*) with its literal Egyptian equivalent, *ren wer.* But since the Egyptian phrase is a technical term referring to a fivefold royal titulary and is never used in the sense of "fame" or "renown," it is entirely different from its Hebrew counterpart (cf. Kitchen, *Ancient Orient,* pp. 110–11).

**12** One of the two pillars standing in front of Solomon's temple was named "Jakin" (1 Kings 7:21; 2 Chron 3:17). R.B.Y. Scott ("The Pillars Jachin and Boaz," JBL 58, 2 [1939]: 143–49) has plausibly suggested on the basis of ancient Near Eastern parallels that יָכִין (*yāḵîn,* "he establishes, he will establish") may well be the first word of a royal dynastic oracle on the basis of such texts as vv.12–13, 16, thus explaining why it was customary for kings of Judah to stand "by the pillar" on ceremonial occasions (2 Kings 11:14; 23:3). The entire sentence may have been "The Lord will establish your throne forever" or the like (cf. Albright, *Archaeology and the Religion of Israel,* p. 139; D.J. Wiseman and C.J. Davey, NBDrev., p. 545).

**16** The reading "before me" (i.e., the Lord) with a few Hebrew MSS and the LXX is clearly preferable to the MT's "before you" (i.e., David; see NIV mg.), which "may have been subject to secondary influence from the expressions in vv.26 and 29 ['in your sight'], with which it stands in a factual connexion" (Carlson, p. 108). On the other hand, the MT reading לפניך (*lpnyk*) might have arisen from dittography, since the following word begins with כ (*k*).

---

## 4. *David's prayer to the Lord*

### 7:18–29

18 Then King David went in and sat before the LORD, and he said:

"Who am I, O Sovereign LORD, and what is my family, that you
have brought me this far? 19 And as if this were not enough in your
sight, O Sovereign LORD, you have also spoken about the future of
the house of your servant. Is this your usual way of dealing with
man, O Sovereign LORD?

20 "What more can David say to you? For you know your servant,
O Sovereign LORD. 21 For the sake of your word and according to
your will, you have done this great thing and made it known to your
servant.

22 "How great you are, O Sovereign LORD! There is no one like
you, and there is no God but you, as we have heard with our own
ears. 23 And who is like your people Israel—the one nation on earth
that God went out to redeem as a people for himself, and to make a
name for himself, and to perform great and awesome wonders by
driving out nations and their gods from before your people, whom
you redeemed from Egypt? 24 You have established your people
Israel as your very own forever, and you, O LORD, have become their
God.

25 "And now, LORD God, keep forever the promise you have made
concerning your servant and his house. Do as you promised, 26 so
that your name will be great forever. Then men will say, 'The LORD
Almighty is God over Israel!' And the house of your servant David
will be established before you.

27 "O LORD Almighty, God of Israel, you have revealed this to your
servant, saying, 'I will build a house for you.' So your servant has
found courage to offer you this prayer. 28 O Sovereign LORD, you are
God! Your words are trustworthy, and you have promised these
good things to your servant. 29 Now be pleased to bless the house of
your servant, that it may continue forever in your sight; for you, O
Sovereign LORD, have spoken, and with your blessing the house of
your servant will be blessed forever."

The heartfelt response of King David to the oracle of the prophet Nathan is one of the most moving prayers in Scripture (other nonpsalmic prayers of a similar genre are 1 Kings 3:6–9; 8:22–53; 1 Chron 29:10–19; Ezra 9:6–15; Neh 1:4–11; 9:5–38; Job 42:2–6; Jer 32:16–25; Dan 9:4–19; Jonah 2:2–9; Matt 6:9–13; Luke 2:29–32; 10:21–22). In it he humbly expresses his gratitude to the Lord for revealing his will to him through Nathan and declares his own desire that the divine promises might indeed be fulfilled to the greater glory of God.

In the overall chiastic arrangement of the narrative of David's powerful reign over Israel (see comment on 5:17–8:18), David's prayer parallels the story of the procession of the ark into the city of Jerusalem (ch. 6). The literary structure of vv.18–29 may be outlined as follows (cf. similarly C.F.D. Erdmann, "The Books of Samuel," in *Commentary on the Holy Scriptures: Critical, Doctrinal, and Practical*, ed. John Peter Lange [Grand Rapids: Zondervan, n.d.], 5:433, 435, 437):

A. The present: gratitude for divine favor (7:18–21)
B. The past: praise for what God has already done (7:22–24)
C. The future: prayer for divine fulfillment of covenant promises (7:25–29)

Second Samuel 7:18–29 is paralleled in 1 Chronicles 17:16–27.

**18–21** In response to the Lord's promises as mediated through Nathan, David "went in" (v.18, probably into the tent he had pitched for the ark) and sat "before the LORD" (i.e., before the ark; see 6:17 and comment). Since the customary posture of prayer was standing or kneeling, the fact that David "sat" before the Lord was perhaps "in accordance with the prerogative of the Davidic kings (*cf.* Ps. 110:1)" (Gordon, *I & II Samuel,* p. 241).

Beginning his prayer with appropriate humility and deference ("Who am I . . . that you have brought me this far?"), David addresses God with a title unique to the books of Samuel—"Sovereign LORD"—which he employs seven times (vv.18, 19 [bis], 20, 22, 28, 29). As Carlson notes, the name is "used by Abraham when addressing his God in Gen. 15:2, 8" (p. 127). A further link between the Davidic and Abrahamic covenants is thus established. Kaiser calls attention to five additional earlier attestations of the name, each "in a prayer to God as in this passage: Moses' prayers in Deut. 3:24; 9:26; Joshua's prayer in Josh. 7:7; Gideon's prayer in Judges 6:22; and Samson's prayer in Judges 16:28" ("The Unfailing Kindnesses Promised to David," p. 310 n. 43). And if God is sovereign to David, he recognizes his own status as vassal by referring to himself ten times as the Lord's "servant" (vv.19, 20, 21, 25, 26, 27 [bis], 28, 29 [bis]; see comments on v.5; 3:18; 1 Sam 1:11; 25:24).

The central theme of the prayer is David's *bayiṯ* ("house/dynasty"). Like the special name David uses to address the Lord, it too appears in the first and last verses of the prayer and occurs seven times (vv.18 ["family"], 19, 25, 26, 27, 29 [bis]; cf. Cross, *Canaanite Myth and Hebrew Epic,* p. 247). Though his household is insignificant at present (v.18), David is confident that it will become great in the future because of the proven reliability of God and his promises.

That the Lord has brought him to this point in his experience (v.18) would be sufficient for David, but he gratefully recognizes that in God's eyes it is "not enough" (v.19; *qṭn,* lit., "small"). The Lord has even better things in store for him in the future. The NIV rendering "Is this your usual way of dealing with man?" although barely possible, remains problematic (see Notes).

"Confessing that to say more would be as inadequate as it would be unnecessary (vs.20; cf. Ps 139,4; Isa 65,24), David yet continues with gratitude for the divine message" (Tsevat, "The House of David in Nathan's Prophecy," p. 354). The Lord has honored his servant (cf. 1 Chron 17:18) beyond measure, and David asserts that there is scarcely anything more that he can say. He affirms that the Lord "know[s]" his servant (v.20), which perhaps includes the fact that he has "chosen" him (cf. Gen 18:19, where the Heb. verb is the same; cf. similarly Amos 3:2). David had earlier reminded Michal that the Lord "chose" him (6:21—where, however, a different Heb. verb is used) rather than anyone from Saul's household (cf. also 1 Sam 16:1).

Recognizing the unconditional aspect of the Lord's covenant with him (v.21), David "accepts the promises as certain, with no obligations imposed on him" (Waltke, "The Phenomenon of Conditionality," p. 131). If David earlier knew that the Lord had blessed him "for the sake of" his people Israel (5:12), he now confesses that the Lord has done a great thing simply "for the sake of" his "word" (v.21). The Lord has also acted according to his "will" (lit., "heart"), a blessing that David later echoes in claiming that he himself has found "courage" (lit., "his heart") to offer his prayer to God (v.27).

The greatness of God and his deeds overwhelm David, who refers to the "great thing" the Lord has done (v.21; cf. "great deeds" in the Davidic Ps 145:6; cf. also Ps 92:5), to how "great" the Sovereign Lord is (v.22; cf. Ps 104:1), to the "great" wonders the Lord has performed in the past (v.23), and to how "great" the Lord's name is (v.26; the parallel in 1 Chron 17:19 adds to the list by substituting "made known all these great promises" for "made it known to your servant" in v.21). And the God who "know[s]" his servant (v.20) is also the God who makes his great deeds "known" to his servant (v.21).

**22–24** Verse 22 is only one among many OT texts describing God as unique, as *sui generis* (for details cf. esp. Labuschagne, *The Incomparability of Yahweh,* pp. 8–30, 64–123). That there is "no one like" the Lord is a major theme in the Song of Hannah (1 Sam 2:2) as well as a point of comparison used by the prophet Samuel as he presents Saul to the people as their first king (see 1 Sam 10:24 and comment). That there is "no God but/except/besides/apart from" the Lord rings like a refrain throughout the words of psalmist (cf. 22:32 = Ps 18:31) and prophet alike (cf. Isa 45:5, 21; 64:4; Hos 13:4; for the importance of the prophetic proclamations of the unity and uniqueness of the God of Israel in Isaiah 40–48, cf. Menahem Haran, "The Literary Structure and Chronological Framework of the Prophecies in Is. XL–XLVIII," *Supplements to VetTest* 9 [Leiden: Brill, 1963], p. 134).

> From Deut. 33:29, II Sam. 7:23 and Deut. 4:7 [cf. also Deut 4:8, 33–34] it appears that there is a close connection between Yahweh's incomparability and that of his people. Because Yahweh is incomparable, it follows that the people He elected as His own and with whom He entered into communion, who of themselves had no qualities worthy of this attribute, may also be considered incomparable. The application of a divine attribute to the nation does not denote their deification, and there is no evidence whatsoever that Israel regarded herself deified as a result of the application to herself of an attribute of Yahweh. (Labuschagne, *The Incomparability of Yahweh,* pp. 149–50)

Three times in v.23 Israel is referred to as God's "people" (*'am*), the one elect "nation" (*gôy*) out of all the "nations" (*gôyim*). Israel's powerful "God" is contrasted with the nations' impotent and ineffective "gods" (same Heb. word in both cases).

Israel's matchless Lord, who brooks no rivals, has gone out to do three things for his grateful people: "redeem" them (cf. Deut 7:8; 9:26; 13:5; 15:15; 21:8; 24:18; Neh 1:10; Jer 31:11), "make a name" for himself (see comment on v.9; cf. also v.26), and "perform great and awesome wonders" (cf. Deut 10:21; cf. also Deut 7:21; 10:17; Neh 9:32; Pss 99:3; 106:22; 145:6; Isa 64:3; Dan 9:4; Joel 2:31 ["great and dreadful"]; Mal 4:5 ["great and dreadful"]) by driving out the enemy.

In connection with "perform great and awesome wonders," the MT includes the phrase "for you," "on your behalf" (pl.; omitted by NIV, apparently in the interests of economy of style in English), indicating that divine victories for Israel's ancestors continue to bless the people of David's time. Indeed, in vv.23–24 the Sinaitic covenant is cited in support of the Davidic (for details cf. Gileadi, "The Davidic Covenant," p. 160). The ancient establishment of Israel as God's own people "forever" (v.24) is now to be channeled through David and his dynasty, which will continue "forever" (vv.25, 29 [bis]; see also v.13 and comment). The old Abrahamic and Sinaitic covenant formula—"I will be your God, and you will be my people"—undergoes yet another variant (see comment on "I will be his father, and he will be my son" in v.14) as David emphasizes that the Lord has "become their [Israel's] God" (v.24; cf. Gen 17:7–8; 28:21; Exod 6:7; 29:45; Lev 11:45; 22:33; 25:38; 26:12, 45; Num 15:41; Deut 26:17; 29:13). Thus the OT manifestation of the kingdom of God is now to be mediated through the Davidic monarchy (vv.24–25).

**25–29** That the concluding verses of David's prayer constitute a literary unit in their own right is clear not only from the multiple use of the word "forever" (vv.25, 26, 29 [bis]) but also from the fact that *w'th* ("And now") begins vv.25, 28 (untr. by NIV), and 29. David is very much concerned about the permanence of the "promise" the Lord has "made" (v.25, lit., "promised," as at the end of the verse; cf. also 1 Kings 6:12; 8:24–26) concerning the Davidic dynasty. ***Dibbēr*** ("speak") in the special sense of "promise" is common in the Deuteronomic corpus (Cross, *Canaanite Myth and Hebrew Epic*, p. 254; cf. Deut 1:11; 6:3; 9:3, 28; 10:9 ["told"]; 11:25; 12:20; 15:6; 18:2; 26:18; 27:3; 29:13; Josh 13:14, 33; 22:4; 23:5, 10).

The covenanted establishment of David's house (v.26; cf. v.16) would be a visible sign of the greatness of God's name. Indeed, "LORD Almighty" (vv.26–27) would become widely known as the appropriate royal title of the Great King, the God of Israel (see comments on v.8; 1 Sam 1:3). In the light of God's sovereignty, David willingly and humbly refers to himself seven times as the Lord's "servant" (vv.25, 26, 27 [bis], 28, 29 [bis]; see comment on v.5).

David is grateful that God has "revealed . . . to" him (v.27, lit., "uncovered the ear of"; see 1 Sam 9:15 and comment; cf. also 1 Sam 20:2 ["confiding in"], 12–13 ["let . . . know"]; 22:8 ["tells" (bis)], 17 ["tell"]) his plans and purposes: "I will build a house for you" (see comment on a similar expression in 1 Sam 2:35), which reprises v.11 (though the verb is different; see comment there). He acknowledges that the Sovereign Lord alone is God (v.28; "you" is emphatic), as the prayers of Elijah and Hezekiah would also confess (1 Kings 18:37; 2 Kings 19:15, 19; cf. also Neh 9:6–7). Just as the widow at Zarephath would affirm that the "word" of the Lord from Elijah's mouth is the "truth" (1 Kings 17:24), so also David now states that the "words" of the Lord are "trustworthy" (v.28; same Heb. terms in both cases). Although 2 Samuel 7 never uses the term "covenant" (*b[e]rîṯ*) of God's promises to David, "good things" (*ṭôḇāh*, v.28) is a technical term synonymous with "covenant" in contexts like this (cf. Fox, "Ṭôḇ as Covenant Terminology," pp. 41–42; Malamat, "Organs of Statecraft in the Israelite Monarchy," p. 64; see 2:6 and comment; 1 Sam 25:30 and comment). It is possible (if not probable) that *way[e]ḏabbēr 'ittô ṭōḇôṯ* ("He spoke kindly to him"; 2 Kings 25:28 = Jer 52:32) should rather be rendered "He established a covenant with him."

David concludes his prayer with a request (expressed in the form of a command) to the Lord to "be pleased" (v.29, softened in the 1 Chron 17:27 parallel: "you have been pleased"; cf. 1 Sam 12:22; Job 6:28 ["be so kind as"]) to bless the Davidic dynasty. The root *brk* ("bless"), which occurs three times as a summarizing *Leitmotif* in v.29, often relates to the propagation of numerous descendants (e.g., Ps 115:14–15; see 6:11 and comment; cf. also 6:12). "Through the descendants of Abraham the nations of the earth would acquire blessing for themselves. . . . It is not unimportant, therefore, that one of Israel's royal psalms [Ps 72:17] gives voice to the hope that the Davidic king will become a symbol of blessing to the nations" (Clements, *Abraham and David*, pp. 58–59).

Since it is the Sovereign Lord himself who has promised ("you" is emphatic), David speaks with the calm assurance of a man who knows that his house will continue forever "in your sight" (v.29; same Heb. expression translated "before you" in v.26). The prayer of David thus ends on a note of confident contentment.

## Notes

19 וְזֹאת תּוֹרַת הָאָדָם (*wezō't tôrat hā'ādām*) is literally "And this is the law of man" (NIV, "Is this your usual way of dealing with man?"). Not only is the customary Hebrew sign of the interrogative ה (*h*) lacking, but also the translation of *tôrat* as "usual way of dealing with," however "frequent in rabbinic Hebrew" (Matitiahu Tsevat, "The House of David in Nathan's Prophecy," *Biblica* 46 [1965]: 354 n. 1), would be unique to this passage as far as the OT is concerned (cf. BDB, p. 436; the expected word is מִשְׁפָּט [*mišpāṭ*], as in 1 Sam 2:13 ["practice"]; 27:11 ["practice"]). While it is not quite true that the phrase as a whole has "defied the wits of the exegetes" (Kruse, "David's Covenant," p. 157 n. 44), all proposed emendations of the MT here, whether or not based on the parallel in 1 Chron 17:17 ("You have looked on me as though I were the most exalted of men"), are unsatisfactory, as recognized long ago by S.R. Driver (*Notes on the Books of Samuel,* p. 277).

The best suggestion to date is that of Kaiser ("The Blessing of David: The Charter for Humanity," pp. 311–15). He chooses the nuance "charter" because the continuance of David's house into the future is "the plan and prescription for God's kingdom whereby the whole world shall be blessed with the total content of the promise doctrine. It [the Davidic covenant] is a grant conferring powers, rights, and privileges to David and his seed for the benefit of all mankind" (ibid., p. 314). Indeed, the phrase *tôrat hā'ādām* may find its cognate reflex in Akkadian *têrēt nišī,* "oracular decisions given to man" (cf. *The Assyrian Dictionary,* edd. John A. Brinkman, Miguel Civil, Ignace J. Gelb, A. Leo Oppenheim, and Erica Reiner [Chicago: Oriental Institute, 1980], 11/2:284; cf. Henri Cazelles, "Shiloh, the Customary Laws and the Return of the Ancient Kings," in *Proclamation and Presence: Old Testament Essays in Honour of Gwynne Henton Davies,* edd. John I. Durham and J.R. Porter, reprint [Macon: Mercer, 1983], who renders the Heb. and Akkadian phrases "the decree concerning humanity in general" [p. 250]; cf. also Carlson, p. 125 and n. 4; Anderson, pp. 126–27). The promises of the Abrahamic covenant, already universal in scope (cf. Gen 12:3), are thus confirmed in the Davidic as well.

21 The parallel in 2 Chron 17:19 reads עבד (*'bd,* "servant") instead of the MT's דבר (*dbr,* "word"; cf. also δοῦλον [*doulon*], "servant," in some LXX MSS). The MT, however, should be retained as *lectio difficilior.* In addition, the variant "servant" can be explained as *lapsus calami* under the influence of the same word at the end of the verse as well as near the end of the previous verse. Finally, David's use of "servant" ten times in his prayer (see comment on v.19) may be intentional and would thus allow no further occurrences.

23 When used of the God of Israel, אֱלֹהִים (*'elōhîm*) usually takes singular agreement, while when used of pagan gods it takes the plural agreement. There are a few exceptions to this general rule, however, and הָלְכוּ (*hālekû,* "went out" [pl.]) is a case in point (the parallel in 1 Chron 17:21 uses the singular form). For discussion of honorific plural nouns, cf. Waltke and O'Connor, *Biblical Hebrew Syntax,* pp. 122–24.

The difference between text and margin readings in the NIV focuses on one Hebrew word. The MT's לארצך (*l'rṣk,* "for your land") is surely to be read לגרש (*lgrš,* "by driving out"), with the parallel in 1 Chron 17:21 (cf. also LXX).

25 Though not uncommon elsewhere in the OT, the compound divine title "LORD God" occurs only here in the books of Samuel, and for unknown reasons. In any case, the MT vocalization indicates that the Hebrew name is to be pronounced in the same way as the compound

Hebrew title translated seven times as "Sovereign LORD" (see comment on v.18)—viz., *’ᵃḏōnāy ’ᵉlōhîm.*

27 In the MT "offer . . . prayer" is a cognate accusative construction (lit., "pray . . . prayer"; cf. 1 Kings 8:28–29).

---

## 5. *David's enemies defeated*

### 8:1–14

1In the course of time, David defeated the Philistines and subdued
them, and he took Metheg Ammah from the control of the Philistines.
2David also defeated the Moabites. He made them lie down on the
ground and measured them off with a length of cord. Every two lengths
of them were put to death, and the third length was allowed to live. So
the Moabites became subject to David and brought tribute.
3Moreover, David fought Hadadezer son of Rehob, king of Zobah,
when he went to restore his control along the Euphrates River. 4David
captured a thousand of his chariots, seven thousand charioteers and
twenty thousand foot soldiers. He hamstrung all but a hundred of the
chariot horses.
5When the Arameans of Damascus came to help Hadadezer king of
Zobah, David struck down twenty-two thousand of them. 6He put
garrisons in the Aramean kingdom of Damascus, and the Arameans
became subject to him and brought tribute. The LORD gave David victory
wherever he went.
7David took the gold shields that belonged to the officers of
Hadadezer and brought them to Jerusalem. 8From Tebah and Berothai,
towns that belonged to Hadadezer, King David took a great quantity of
bronze.
9When Tou king of Hamath heard that David had defeated the entire
army of Hadadezer, 10he sent his son Joram to King David to greet him
and congratulate him on his victory in battle over Hadadezer, who had
been at war with Tou. Joram brought with him articles of silver and gold
and bronze.
11King David dedicated these articles to the LORD, as he had done with
the silver and gold from all the nations he had subdued: 12Edom and
Moab, the Ammonites and the Philistines, and Amalek. He also
dedicated the plunder taken from Hadadezer son of Rehob, king of
Zobah.
13And David became famous after he returned from striking down
eighteen thousand Edomites in the Valley of Salt.
14He put garrisons throughout Edom, and all the Edomites became
subject to David. The LORD gave David victory wherever he went.

Recapitulating David's military victories during his years as king over Israel and Judah in Jerusalem, vv.1–14 parallel the account of the defeat of the Philistines (5:17–25) in the overall structure of the narrative of David's powerful reign (5:17–8:18; see comment there). The summary may not be intended as all-inclusive, since other wars and skirmishes are mentioned later in the book (cf. ch. 10; 21:15–22; 23:8–23).

The section leaves no doubt about the fact that David's armies were invincible and that no nation, however numerous or powerful its fighting men, could hope to withstand the Israelite hosts. The account teems with verbs denoting military action: *nkh* ("defeat/fight/strike down," vv.1, 2, 3, 5, 9, 10 ["(gain) victory"], 13); *kn'* ("subdue," v.1); *lqḥ* ("take," vv.1, 7, 8); *hyh l'bdym* ("become subject," vv.2, 6, 14); *lkd* ("capture," v.4); *lḥm* ("[do] battle," v.9); *kbš* ("subdue," v.11).

At the same time, however, a striking summary statement appears twice in the section as if to emphasize that the reader—and David himself—must never forget the identity of the real Conqueror: "The LORD gave David victory wherever he went" (vv.6, 14).

Geographical arrangement of the conquered foes seems intentional and produces the following outline:

A. Enemies defeated in the west (v.1)
B. Enemies defeated in the east (v.2)
C. Enemies defeated in the north (vv.3–12)
D. Enemies defeated in the south (vv.13–14)

Second Samuel 8:1–14 is paralleled in 1 Chronicles 18:1–13 (cf. also 1 Kings 11:23b–24a).

1 The formula "In the course of time" is used often in 2 Samuel to denote narrative sequence, whether chronological or thematic (see 2:1 and Notes in loc.). It is impossible to know for certain whether the divine promises of chapter 7 preceded or followed the divine victories of chapter 8 (cf. 7:1, "After . . . the LORD had given him rest from all his enemies around him"; 7:11, "I will also give you rest from all your enemies"). At the same time, however, Merrill (*Kingdom of Priests*, p. 247) plausibly argues that "David was occupied by military affairs throughout his early years; not until after the subjugation of Rabbah [in Ammon; cf. v.12; ch. 10; 11:1; 12:26–27, 29] did he move the ark and make any plans for a temple" (and thus, presumably, receive and respond to Nathan's oracle [ch. 7]). Carlson, on the other hand, argues that the Lord's promise to "provide a place" for his people (7:10) is fulfilled by David's conquests described in chapter 8 (pp. 115–16). Although in my judgment Merrill's overall treatment of the chronological problems (*Kingdom of Priests*, pp. 243–48) is more persuasive, final resolution must await further evidence (if any).

In any event, it would seem that the account of the Philistine defeat (v.1) is intended by the narrator to resume the story told in 5:17–25 (cf. Baldwin, p. 219; Gordon, *I & II Samuel*, p. 242). The verb *nkh* ("strike," 5:24; "struck down," 5:25) is echoed in v.1 ("defeated"). As for the verb *kn'* ("subdued," v.1), Carlson is of the opinion that the expression alludes "to the greatest triumph in the period of the Judges, 4:23" (p. 57; cf. also Deut 9:3; 1 Chron 17:10; Neh 9:24; Ps 81:14). It is better, however, to relate it to 1 Samuel 7:13, which reports that during Samuel's judgeship "the Philistines were subdued and did not invade Israelite territory again"—especially since additional terms in v.1 reprise the same context in 1 Samuel: *lqḥ* ("took," v.1) is rendered "had captured" in 1 Samuel 7:14, and "from the control [*yaḏ*] of the Philistines" (v.1) is translated as "from the power [*yaḏ*] of the Philistines" in 1 Samuel 7:14.

Exactly what it was that David "took" from the Philistines cannot be determined with certainty. If *meṯeg hā'ammāh* is a place name (NIV, "Metheg Ammah"), it occurs nowhere else, and attempts to relate it to "the hill of Ammah" (2:24) simply compare one obscure/unknown site to another. The word *meṯeg* elsewhere means "bit, halter" (2 Kings 19:28 = Isa 37:29; Ps 32:9; Prov 26:3), and *'ammāh* may here be cognate to *'ēm* ("mother"). The phrase *meṯeg hā'ammāh* would then mean "the authority of the mother-city/metropolis" (BDB, p. 52; S.R. Driver, *Notes on the Books of Samuel*, in loc.; cf. 20:19, which refers to a "city that is a mother ['ēm] in Israel"). Most commentators agree that this is the general sense of the phrase, noting that the parallel in 1 Chronicles 18:1 interprets it to refer to "Gath and its surrounding villages" (lit., "its daughters"). Kirkpatrick's summary is typical:

> The most probable explanation of this obscure expression is *took the bridle of the metropolis out of the hand of the Philistines,* i.e. wrested from them the control of their chief city. This is equivalent to the statement in I Chr. xviii.I that "David took Gath and her towns out of the hand of the Philistines"; and it may be noticed that the metaphor of the "mother-city" is employed there, for the word translated "towns" literally means *daughters.* (*The Second Book of Samuel,* p. 105)

A less-acceptable solution is that of Hertzberg, who prefers to understand *'ammāh* in its more common sense of "forearm, cubit" and to render the phrase "the reins of the forearm, the leading reins" (p. 288 n. b). Thus "up to this point, the Philistines were in the saddle in Palestine; from now on it is Israel, i.e. David" (ibid., p. 290).

The importance of the conquest of Philistia by David can scarcely be overestimated: "The Philistines considered themselves the legitimate heirs of the Egyptian rule in Palestine and their defeat by David implied the passage of the Egyptian province of Canaan into the hands of the Israelites" (Abraham Malamat, "The Kingdom of David & Solomon in Its Contact With Egypt and Aram Naharaim," BA 21, 4 [1958]: 100).

**2** As David "defeated" the Philistines (v.1), so also he "defeated" the Moabites (v.2). Why he fought against Moab is unknown, especially since the Moabitess Ruth was his ancestress (cf. Ruth 4:10, 13, 16–17) and Moab had at one time sheltered his parents (see comment on 1 Sam 22:3–4). "A Jewish tradition relates that the king of Moab betrayed his trust and murdered David's parents" (Kirkpatrick, *The Second Book of Samuel,* p. 105). If it be true that David is presaged in the messianic promise of Numbers 24:17 (see comment on 7:7), Symon Patrick may be correct in asserting that the Moabite defeat fulfills that prophecy (p. 402; cf. Kirkpatrick, *The Second Book of Samuel,* p. 105).

David's method of executing a specified number of prisoners of war is not attested elsewhere (McCarter, *II Samuel*). Making them lie down on the ground and then measuring them off with a length of cord, he puts two-thirds of them to death. Since the terminology in this description is often used of the measuring and allocation of land (cf. Josh 19:51; Pss 16:6; 60:6 = 108:7; 78:55; Amos 7:17; Mic 2:5), a few earlier commentators assumed that "made them lie down" is to be understood metaphorically as "laying level their strong Holds and fortified Places" (Symon Patrick, p. 402) and that, after the country was carefully surveyed ("measured . . . off"), two-thirds of it was depopulated. Although the end result would be the same under either interpretation, the consensus among recent commentators strongly favors the rendering adopted by the NIV. David's destruction of Moab means that only a third of its inhabitants are "allowed to live"—ironically, a more humane treatment than his earlier attacks on other areas, during which he did not "leave" anyone "alive" (see 1 Sam 27:9, 11 and comment; same Heb. verb in both passages). Characteristically, the parallel in 1 Chronicles 18:2 omits the account of David's atrocity in v.2.

Like the Arameans (v.6) and Edomites (v.14), the Moabites "became subject to" David (v.2). In the case of Moab and Aram, vassalage to David explicitly included bringing tribute to him (vv.2, 6; cf. D.J. Wiseman, "'Is It Peace?'—Covenant and Diplomacy," VetTest 32, 3 [1982]: 313). Although not stated in the text, bringing of tribute may be implied in the Edomite subjugation as well. The Hebrew word for "tribute" often means "gift(s)/offering(s)" presented as sacrifices (cf. 1 Chron 16:29; Ps 96:8; Ezek 20:31), which are thus understood as tribute brought into the throne room of the Great King. After David's death, nations conquered by him would continue to bring tribute to his son Solomon (1 Kings 4:21) and his successors. The Moabite contribution to King Ahab would be substantial: "a hundred thousand lambs and . . . the wool of a hundred thousand rams" (2 Kings 3:4).

**3–12** Despite the limited information available about Aram during David's reign, the space given to its conquest in this chapter testifies to its overall significance in the scheme of things.

> The kingdom of Aram Zobah, . . . whose strength is difficult to estimate from the fragmentary evidence found in the Bible, expanded during the reign of its king Hadadezer . . . over vast territories. In the south it apparently reached the frontier of Ammon, as can be deduced from the intervention of Aramaean troops on the side of the Ammonites in their war with David (II Samuel 10:6 ff.). In the northeast the kingdom of Zobah extended to the river Euphrates and even to territories beyond it (II Sam. 8:3; 10:16). In the east it touched the Syrian desert and in the west it included Coelesyria. (Malamat, "The Kingdom of David and Solomon," p. 100)

(See also Benjamin Mazar, "The Aramean Empire and Its Relations With Israel," BA 25, 4 [1962], which locates the focal point of the Zobah kingdom "probably in the northern part of the Lebanon valley," p. 102.) The events in this section are sometimes interrelated with those of 10:1–11:1 and 12:26–31 by seeing them as describing the same situation or by viewing them as sequential. It is probably best, however, to understand 8:3–12 as a record of battles that occurred after the campaigns reported in chapters 10–12 (cf. Bright, p. 202 n. 38; Leon J. Wood, *A Survey of Israel's History*, rev. ed. [Grand Rapids: Zondervan, 1986], p. 226).

As David had "defeated" the Philistines (v.1) and Moabites (v.2), so he also "fought" (v.3) and "defeated" (v.9) the Arameans (same Heb. verb in each case). His main adversary is "Hadadezer [vv.3, 5, 7–10, 12; 10:16, 19; 1 Kings 11:23] son of Rehob" (the mention of Rehob only in vv.3, 12 serves to form an *inclusio* that demarcates the literary unit). Hadadezer ("[The God] Hadad Is [My] Help") is the Hebrew form of an Aramean dynastic royal title that appears in transcription in Assyrian annals as *(H)adad-(ʿ)idri* (cf. ANET, p. 279), which reflects the *ḏ* › *d* shift in Aramaic (cf. the name of Saul's son-in-law Adriel ["My Help Is God"; 21:8; 1 Sam 18:19], which corresponds to the name Azriel in Hebrew [1 Chron 5:24; 27:19; Jer 36:26]). This particular Hadadezer was king of Zobah (vv.3, 5, 12; 10:6, 8; 23:36; title of Ps 60), an Aramean nation that Saul had earlier fought against with success (see 1 Sam 14:47 and comment). Hadad was the most common personal name of the Canaanite storm-god, better known by the appellative title *baʿal*, which means "lord." During the Hyksos period (seventeenth–sixteenth centuries B.C.) he was identified with the Egyptian storm-god Seth, and it was probably at that time that Baal came into use as a personal name for Hadad (cf. William F. Albright, *Yahweh and the Gods of Canaan: A Historical Analysis of Two Contrasting Faiths* [Garden City: Doubleday, 1968], p. 124).

The ambiguous pronoun "he" (v.3), whose antecedent could be either David or Hadadezer, has puzzled scholars for centuries (cf. Symon Patrick, p. 404). Most recent commentators, however, prefer Hadadezer (cf. KD, p. 358: "The subject . . . must be Hadadezer and not David; for David could not have extended his power to the Euphrates before the defeat of Hadadezer"). The phrase "restore [cf. 9:7; 16:3 ('give . . . back')] his control" translates *l^ehāšîḇ yāḏô,* for which the parallel in 1 Chronicles has *l^ehaṣṣîḇ yāḏô,* rendered "establish his control" in the NIV. But the latter expression surely means "set up his monument," referring to "the erection of a victory stele" (Gordon, *I & II Samuel,* p. 243; cf. S.R. Driver, *Notes on the Books of Samuel,* p. 281; see 1 Sam 15:12 and comment; cf. esp. Hoffner, "A Hittite Analogue," p. 222 n. 6). Such monuments were located in prominent places (cf. 18:18), such as near the "Euphrates River" (v.3), the greatest river in western Asia (and therefore sometimes called simply "the River" [par excellence]). Marking the eastern reaches of David's realm, the Euphrates was also one of the fixed boundaries of the land promised to Abraham (Gen 15:18). Reference to it here thus forges yet another link between the Abrahamic and Davidic covenants (cf. also Deut 1:7; 11:24; Josh 1:4; 1 Kings 4:21, 24).

The general tenor of the account implies that David drove back the forces of Hadadezer all the way to the Euphrates. In so doing he captured substantial numbers of chariots, charioteers, and foot soldiers (v.4). Philistine chariots and riders/charioteers were feared far and wide (see comments on 1:6; 1 Sam 13:5), and there is no reason to assume that Aramean chariots and riders were feared any the less. The number of Aramean foot solders was about twenty thousand (cf. also 10:6), which, although a standard figure for a large army (cf. Segal, "Numerals," pp. 6–7), is nevertheless smaller than the number that Saul was able to muster against the Amalekites (1 Sam 15:4). In any event, since *'elep̱* ("thousand") sometimes means "(military) unit" in battle contexts (see comment on 1 Sam 4:2), a measure of uncertainty obtains for at least some of the occurrences of *'elep̱* in chapter 8.

David's seizure of a thousand Aramean chariots included the capture of the chariot horses that pulled them. He "hamstrung" most of the horses (i.e., severed the large tendon above and behind their hocks to disable them; cf. also Josh 11:6, 9). Although it is often assumed that David did so because he did not understand the value of chariots in warfare and that not until the days of Solomon did chariot squadrons become an integral part of Israel's armed forces, Yadin makes a good case for David's use of chariots despite the present hamstringing incident: David's own chariot units may have already been up to full strength, he could not have successfully fought a formidable Aramean chariot force far from home without comparable vehicles of his own, and "the Biblical references to the chariots of Abasalom [15:1] and Adonijah [1 Kings 1:5] show that they must have [also] been a common sight in the army of David" (*The Art of Warfare,* p. 285).

Damascus (v.5), a key player in the Aramean league of nations (cf. Merrill F. Unger, *Israel and the Arameans of Damascus* [London: James Clarke, 1957], pp. 38–51) that included Zobah (v.3) and (Beth) Rehob (10:6, 8), sends a huge contingent of troops to "help" (*'zr*) Hadadezer. The obvious wordplay on Hadadezer's name (see comment on v.3) is especially poignant, since his god Hadad is clearly of no help to him. Indeed, David strikes down "twenty-two thousand" of the Damascus reinforcements, a number used in the OT to represent a "large national force" (cf. Segal, "Numerals," p. 7, for details). He then puts "garrisons" (v.6; cf. also v.14) throughout the Aramean kingdom of Damascus, with the result that the Arameans become tributary to him.

Since *n$^{e}$ṣîḇ* ("garrison"; cf. also 1 Sam 10:5; 13:3 ["outpost"]) can also mean "monument/pillar" (Gen 19:26) or "governor" (1 Kings 4:19), it is possible that "governors" is intended here (and in v.14; cf. Mazar, "The Aramean Empire," p. 104). Larry E. McKinney, however, observes that the various nuances are not necessarily mutually exclusive and cogently argues that the word "likely encompasses something of each of these possible meanings" ("David's Garrisons in Edom," *Biblical Illustrator* 10, 1 [Fall 1983]: 62). The "garrison," then, would have served as a "monument" to David's control over Aram and would have been commanded by a "governor."

A characteristic formula stressing divine enablement recurs (with variations) throughout the Book of Judges: "Then the Lord raised up judges, who saved [*yšʿ*] them out of the hands of these raiders" (Judg 2:16; cf. Judg 2:18; 3:9, 31; 6:14; 10:1; et al.). Talmon (p. 51 n. 36) plausibly suggests that "the author of the Book of Samuel employed this formula in reference to David, but with an interesting change: 'And the Lord gave victory [*yšʿ*] to David wherever he went' " (vv.6, 14; see also comments on "rescue[d]" [*yšʿ*] in 3:18; 1 Sam 14:23). In the present section the sentence (v.6b, repeated in v.14b) serves to frame the rest of the story of David's conquests (cf. Long, "Framing Repetitions," pp. 387, 398) and in so doing stresses that God, not David, is the true Savior of his people. Indeed, the Lord not only grants victory to David but is also with him "wherever" he goes (vv.6, 14; see 7:9 and comment).

Part of the tribute that David "took" (vv.7–8) from Hadadezer was his officers' "gold shields" (v.7). Though they "belonged to" (or were "carried by," as the parallel in 1 Chron 18:7 states) the officers, they were obviously ceremonial or decorative shields and were not used in battle (cf. S of Songs 4:4; Ezek 27:11). Whether they were made of solid gold or simply bossed with gold or supplied with golden fittings is impossible to say (contrast the shields mentioned in 1 Kings 10:16–17; 14:26). Brought to Jerusalem and eventually placed in Solomon's temple where they remained for well over a century, the shields now "belonged to" David (2 Kings 11:10). Brueggemann notes that David's rapacious ways, as evidenced by the verb "took" (vv.7–8), were not limited to shields and similar items of booty: He also sent messengers to Bathsheba "to get her" (11:4; lit., "and he took her"; *David's Truth*, p. 81).

Three towns that belonged to Hadadezer (Tebah, Berothai [v.8], and Cun [cf. the 1 Chron 18:8 parallel]) yielded a "great quantity of bronze" to King David. *Harbēh m$^{e}$'ōḏ* ("great quantity," v.8) is echoed in 12:2, where the prophet Nathan intimates that David is a rich man who has a "very large number" of sheep and cattle. From this later perspective the Chronicler adds to v.8 the note that Solomon used the bronze "to make the bronze Sea, the pillars and various bronze articles" for his temple (1 Chron 18:8; cf. 1 Kings 7:13–47). It is therefore ironic that the identical bronze items became booty in the hands of the Babylonians when Solomon's temple was destroyed in 586 B.C. (cf. 2 Kings 25:13–14).

The MT's "Betah" (v.8) is doubtless a metathesized form of Tebah (cf. Tibhath, another form of the same name in the parallel in 1 Chron 18:8 [see NIV mg. there]; cf. also some LXX MSS [see NIV mg. here]), the Tubikhi of Egyptian inscriptions (cf. ANET, p. 477 and n. 31; exact location unknown). Tebah appears in a list of Abraham's descendants (Gen 22:24) in association with Aram (Gen 22:21). The ancient site of Berothai (probably the same as Berothah in Ezek 47:16) is doubtless modern Bereitan, thirty miles north-northwest of Damascus. Ancient Cun is perhaps modern Ras Baalbek, thirty miles north-northeast of Berothai. All three towns were therefore located in the northern part of the Lebanese Beqa'. References to Berothai and Cun have apparently been found in close association with each other in an Eblaite gazetteer (cf. Mitchell Dahood, "Philological Observations on Five Biblical Texts," *Biblica* 63, 3 [1982]: 390–91; for additional details on all three sites, cf. McCarter, *II Samuel*, p. 250).

The news of David's defeat of the entire army of Hadadezer eventually reaches the ears of Tou king of Hamath (v.9). The capital city of a nation with the same name, ancient Hamath is modern Hama (on the middle Orontes River about 120 miles north of Damascus). Added to the fact that David had already pursued Hadadezer "as far as Hamath" (1 Chron 18:3), it is understandable that Tou would want to make peace with the conquering Israelite king. He therefore sends his son to "greet" David (v.10, lit., "ask about the well-being/welfare of"; cf. 1 Sam 10:4; 30:21; see comments on 1 Sam 17:22; 25:5) and to "congratulate" him (lit., "bless"; cf. 1 Kings 1:47; see comment on "give . . . greetings" in 1 Sam 25:14) on his "victory" (from *nkh*, "strike down," a different root than the one used in vv.6, 14; see comment on v.6) over Hadadezer. Indeed, the Aramean king has been "at war with" Tou (lit., "a man of battles of/against"; cf. S.R. Driver, who interprets the idiom to mean "a man engaged often in conflict with" [*Notes on the Books of Samuel*, p. 282]; cf. also "those who wage war against," Isa 41:12 [same Heb. phrase as here]). The word *ṣbh* ("Zobah") in Aramean script has been found on bricks excavated at Hamath and dating from as early as the tenth century B.C., a discovery that probably testifies to "an ancient connection between Zobah and Hamath" (Malamat, "The Kingdom of David and Solomon," p. 101 n. 22).

Joram, the name of Tou's son, means "The Lord Is Exalted." His original Aramean name, Hadoram (i.e., *Haddu-rām*, "Hadad Is Exalted"; cf. NIV mg., LXX, and the parallel in 1 Chron 18:10), may have been modified by David. If so, it is not implausible "to see a certain Israelite influence on internal affairs in Hamath" (cf. Yutaka Ikeda, "Solomon's Trade in Horses and Chariots in Its International Setting," in *Studies in the Period of David and Solomon and Other Essays*, ed. Tomoo Ishida [Winona Lake: Eisenbrauns, 1982], p. 237 and n. 126). Although Joram brings "articles of silver and gold and bronze" to David (v.10), this does not necessarily mean that Hamath was now tributary to Israel in a formal sense but should probably be understood as a voluntary gift to gain David's goodwill (cf. similarly 1 Kings 15:18–19; contrast Wiseman, "'Is It Peace?'" p. 319; Mazar, "The Aramean Empire," p. 103; Malamat, "The Kingdom of David and Solomon," p. 101—who, however, admits that "the country of Hamath, of course, was not really annexed to Israel, and therefore it is often mentioned in the Biblical literature in connection with the northern frontier of the Israelite kingdom" [ibid., p. 101 n. 23]). Since silver was often rarer (and therefore more valuable) than gold in the ancient Near East (cf. R.J. Forbes, *Studies in Ancient Technology* [Leiden: Brill, 1964], 8:209–26 passim), the mention of silver before gold in vv.10–11 (cf. also 21:4) may indicate their relative value during David's time (cf., however, the parallel in 1 Chron 18:10, where the order is reversed).

In grateful acknowledgment of divine blessing, David dedicates all the articles—whether received as gift, tribute, or plunder—to the Lord (vv.11–12). Although v.12 concludes the relatively lengthy account of his campaigns against the north (Aram), the narrator also includes in it a summary of David's conquest of neighboring nations in every direction: south (Edom; cf. also vv.13–14), east (Moab [cf. v.2] and Ammon [cf. also chs. 10–12, esp. 12:29–31 (cf. Bailey, *David in Love and War*, p. 78); see also

1 Sam 11:1 and comment]), west (Philistia; cf. v.1), and southwest (Amalek; cf. also 1:1; 1 Sam 30; see also comments on 1 Sam 14:48; 15:2; 28:18).

**13–14** The statement in v.13 that David "returned from striking down" the Edomites echoes the assertion in 1:1 that David "returned from striking down" the Amalekites and with it forms an *inclusio* that surrounds a large literary section of 2 Samuel (see comment on 1:1; cf. also 1 Sam 17:57; 18:6). At the same time *nkh* ("striking down") not only serves to introduce the present literary unit (as it does the other three in this section: v.1 ["defeated"], v.2 ["defeated"], v.3 ["fought"]) but also forms an *inclusio* with the same verb in v.1, thus helping to demarcate the narrative of the defeat of David's enemies in vv.1–14. Although Abishai son of Zeruiah (see 1 Sam 26:6 and comment) did the actual "striking down" (cf. the parallel in 1 Chron 18:12), David is the supreme commander and thus gets the credit ("became famous" [v.13] = literally "made a name"; cf. 1 Kings 1:47; see comment on 7:9).

Abishai strikes down 18,000 Edomites (v.13), while his brother Joab, commander of Israel's army (v.16), strikes down 12,000 (cf. the title of Ps 60), apparently in the same battle. Whether the 12,000 should be added to the 18,000 or are part of them is impossible to say. Symon Patrick's proposal is as typical as it is attractive: "*Abishai*, who began the Fight, perhaps slew six Thousand, and then *Joab* coming in with his Reserve slew twelve Thousand more; which in all make eighteen Thousand" (p. 408). The "Valley of Salt" (cf. also 2 Kings 14:7; 2 Chron 25:11) was perhaps either the Wadi el-Milh (Arabic for "valley of salt") east of Beersheba or was located in the es-Sebkha region south of the Dead (Salt) Sea.

Having conquered the Edomites, David (through Abishai; cf. 1 Chron 18:12–13) "put garrisons throughout Edom" (literally and emphatically "put in Edom garrisons, in all Edom he put garrisons," v.14) as he did similarly in the Aramean kingdom of Damascus (see comment on "garrisons" in v.6). McKinney points to Umm el-Bayyara (near Petra) and Ezion Geber (at the northern end of the Gulf of Aqaba) as the most likely candidates for Israelite garrisons and suggests the possibility that "David's desire to exploit Edom's abundant copper mines was a chief cause of his war with the Edomites" ("David's Garrisons in Edom," pp. 64–65). The narrator's summary, which replicates v.6b (see comment there), concludes the section on a note of triumph—"The LORD gave David victory wherever he went"—and serves again to remind the reader that it is because God is with him that David prospers.

Malamat observes that the "unprecedented territorial expansion" of David's realm "may be explained by assuming that David's kingdom based itself on comprehensive political organizations which had existed before and which, through David's victories over their rulers, passed into his hands with their complex systems intact" ("The Kingdom of David and Solomon," p. 100). It was also made possible by the power vacuum left by the decline and/or fall of the great empires (Hittite, Egyptian, Babylonian, Assyrian) in the twelfth and eleventh centuries B.C. (cf. Mazar, "The Aramean Empire," p. 102). By any method of calculation, the regions added to David's realm through the defeat of the nations surrounding him more than doubled the territory of Israel. The successful military campaigns described in chapter 8 initiated the golden age of Israelite history.

David's new boundaries, resulting from his conquest of Philistia (v.1), Moab (v.2), Cis-Euphrates (vv.3–4), Aram of Damascus (vv.5–12), Ammon, Amalek (v.12), and Edom (vv.13–14), correspond to those outlined in the divine promise to Abraham: "To your descendants I give this land, from the river of Egypt to the great river, the

Euphrates" (Gen 15:18; cf. also Deut 11:24; Josh 1:4). Yet another link is thus forged between the covenants of Abraham and David. Indeed, as Carlson expresses it, "the Covenant made with Abraham is fulfilled through David" (p. 116; cf. also 1 Kings 4:21, where David's realm as bequeathed to his son Solomon is described in similar terms).

## Notes

1 According to Carlson, אַמָּה (*'ammāh*) "should probably be interpreted as an Akkadianism, *ammatu,* 'land' " (p. 116 n. 1). Akkadian *ammatu* in this sense, however, is very rare (cf. *ammatu B* in *The Assyrian Dictionary,* ed. Miguel Civil et al. [Chicago: Oriental Institute, 1968], 1/2:75). Indeed, *ammatu* in Akkadian can just as readily be a synonym for *ummu,* "mother" (cf. *ammatu C* in ibid.; see comment on v.1).

3 The NIV's "Euphrates" reads with the *Qere* rather than with the *Kethiv,* which omits the consonants of פְּרָת (*pᵉrāṯ*). The Hebrew form derives from Akkadian *Purattu,* ultimately from Sumerian B/PURANUN. English "Euphrates" transliterates Greek Εὐφράτης (*Euphratēs*), which in turn also comes from Akkadian *Purattu* via Old Persian *Ufratu.*

4 The NIV's "captured a thousand of his chariots, seven thousand charioteers" reflects the wording of the parallel in 1 Chron 18:4 as well as the LXX and the probable reading in 4QSam[a] (for additional reasons justifying the NIV mg. and departure from the MT, cf. Ulrich, *The Qumran Text,* pp. 56–57).

9 The MT's תֹּעִי (*tō'î,* "Toi"; cf. NIV mg.) is a variant spelling of Tou, as the ancient versions make clear (cf. McCarter, *II Samuel,* p. 245; cf. also 1 Chron 18:9–10).

12–13 The NIV's "Edom(ites)" instead of "Aram(eans)" is not only based on the parallels in 1 Chron 18:11–12 but also has the support of the LXX and Syriac as well as of some Hebrew MSS (see NIV mg.). Because of the similarity between ד (*d*) and ר (*r*), אדם (*'dm*) and ארם (*'rm*) were often confused in scribal transmission.

13 The Valley of Salt may have been known earlier as the Valley of Siddim (Gen 14:3, 8, 10; cf. Rasmussen, p. 44). It has been suggested that שִׂדִּים (*śiddîm*) is derived from the Hittite *siyantas,* "salt" (ZPEB, 5:426).

### 6. *David's officials*

#### 8:15–18

> [15]David reigned over all Israel, doing what was just and right for all his people. [16]Joab son of Zeruiah was over the army; Jehoshaphat son of Ahilud was recorder; [17]Zadok son of Ahitub and Ahimelech son of Abiathar were priests; Seraiah was secretary; [18]Benaiah son of Jehoiada was over the Kerethites and Pelethites; and David's sons were royal advisers.

The first twenty chapters of 2 Samuel divide rather naturally into four sections of varying length, each of which ends with a four-verse list of names (see outline in section 10 of commentary). Each of the last two sections (5:17–8:18; chs. 9–20) concludes with a list of David's officials (8:15–18; 20:23–26). After a brief but majestic introduction (v.15), the present list proper (vv.16–18) includes the names, patronymics, and offices of the men in David's cabinet.

Second Samuel 8:15–18 is paralleled in 1 Chronicles 18:14–17.

**15** A mighty warrior (vv.1–14), King David now reigns over "all" Israel (the description perhaps includes many if not most of the conquered territories) and administers justice and equity to "all" his people. Just as the statement that David "reigned over all Israel" is followed by a list of his officials, so also is the statement that his son Solomon "ruled over all Israel" (1 Kings 4:1) followed by a similar list (1 Kings 4:2–6).

"Doing what was just and right" was the hallmark of a strong king in the ancient Near East and included such reforms as the elimination of oppression and exploitation (cf. esp. Ps 72). Finding a precise parallel in Akkadian *kittum u mīšarum* (cf. *The Assyrian Dictionary*, ed. Miguel Civil et al. [Chicago: Oriental Institute, 1971], 8:470–71; ibid. [1977], 10/2:117–18), *mišpāṭ ûṣᵉḏāqāh* ("just[ice] and right[eousness]") are qualities that the Great King himself exemplifies (cf. Ps 103:6) and that he expects in his people as well as in his rulers (cf. Isa 5:7; Amos 5:7, 24; 6:12). In the *eschaton* the Messiah will demonstrate and implement them in their fullness (Isa 9:7).

**16–18** "David's officialdom . . . has been shown to have been organized in part at least on Egyptian models . . . doubtless . . . through Phoenician or other intermediaries," especially in differentiating between the recorder (v.16) and secretary (v.17; Unger, "Archaeology and the Reign of David," p. 17; cf. also McCarter, *II Samuel*, p. 255). As expected, the commander of David's army (v.16; cf 20:23; 1 Kings 1:19) is Joab son of Zeruiah (see 1 Sam 26:6 and comment; cf. also 2:13). Jehoshaphat ("The Lord Judges") son of Ahilud (cf. 20:24) is recorder and remains so into the reign of Solomon (1 Kings 4:3). The function of the recorder (cf. also 2 Kings 18:18, 37; 2 Chron 34:8) was apparently either to have oversight of state records and documents or to serve as a royal herald, equivalent to the Egyptian *whm.w* ("speaker"), whose role was to make reports to the king and transmit royal decrees (cf. Anderson, p. 136; McCarter, *II Samuel*, p. 255).

The identity and function of each of the three officials mentioned in v.17 swarm with problems, as commentaries, special studies, and monographs amply attest. Though appearing here by name for the first time, Zadok ("Righteous") was probably one of the preliminary fulfillments of the oracle of the man of God in 1 Samuel 2:35 (see comment there; cf. also Jones, p. 133; Saul Olyan, "Zadok's Origins and the Tribal Politics of David," JBL 101, 2 [1982]: 183 n. 34). It is striking, and perhaps intentional, that Jehoshaphat (*yhwšpṭ*, v.16) and Zadok (*ṣdwq*, v.17) should be listed in sequence so soon after David is described as doing what is "just [*mšpṭ*] and right [*ṣdqh*]" (v.15).

The root *ṣdq* is found in the names of priests and kings of Jerusalem from the earliest times (cf. Melchizedek, Gen 14:18; Adoni-Zedek, Josh 10:1), and Zedekiah was the last king of Judah before Jerusalem was destroyed by Nebuchadrezzar II in 586 B.C. One of the postexilic priests in Jerusalem bore the name J(eh)ozadak (1 Chron 6:14–15; Ezra 3:2, 8; 5:2; 10:18; Neh 12:26; Hag 1:1, 12, 14; Zech 6:11). In Ezekiel's theocracy, centering around Jerusalem, the "sons of Zadok" are "the only Levites who may draw near to the LORD to minister before him" (Ezek 40:46; cf. also 43:19; 44:15; 48:11), while the Sadducees, the aristocratic priestly party headquartered at the Jerusalem temple beginning as early as the second century B.C., almost certainly derive their name from Zadok. Partly because of the frequent use of *ṣdq* in names of priests/kings associated with Jerusalem, Zadok's origins are often linked to the so-called Jebusite hypothesis, which seeks to demonstrate that Zadok was the Jebusite priest of God Most High (like Melchizedek, Gen 14:18) in Jerusalem before the conquest of the city of David (cf. H.H. Rowley, "Zadok and Nehushtan," JBL 68, 2 [1939]: 113–41; Christian E. Hauer, Jr., "Who Was Zadok?" JBL 82, 1 [1963]: 89–94).

It is clear, however, that "Zadok son of Ahitub" (v.17) is not a Jebusite but a Levite (cf. 1 Chron 6:1, 8, 52–53), not to be confused with the later Zadok son of Ahitub (1 Chron 6:12; Zadok and Ahitub were both common priestly names [for Ahitub cf. 1 Sam 14:3; 22:9, 11–12, 20; for Zadok cf. 1 Chron 9:11; Neh 11:11]). Indeed, he should perhaps be identified with the Levite Zadok mentioned in 1 Chronicles 12:28 as a contemporary of David (cf. J. Barton Payne, EBC, 4:378). Cross (*Canaanite Myth and Hebrew Epic*, p. 214 n. 72) translates *na'ar* as "aide" in the phrase *na'ar gibbôr ḥāyil* (1 Chron 12:28), which the NIV renders "brave young warrior." Cross would thus understand the entire phrase to imply that Zadok was a "noteworthy/powerful aide" (or the like) in the service of the Levite Jehoiada (1 Chron 12:27; cf. Olyan, "Zadok's Origins," pp. 188–89 and n. 50; for *na'ar* in the sense of "aide," cf. Neh 6:5). Benaiah (v.18), another of David's officials, was probably the son of this same Jehoiada (for details cf. ibid., p. 185).

In any event, Zadok was not from the line of Eli (see comment on 1 Sam 2:35), whose only remaining descendant was apparently Abiathar (see 1 Sam 22:20 and comment). Since Abiathar was the son of an Ahimelech who did not survive Doeg's slaughter of the priests of Nob (1 Sam 22:16, 20), many commentators follow the Syriac version and read "Abiathar son of Ahimelech" (cf. also 1 Sam 23:6; 30:7) instead of "Ahimelech son of Abiathar" in v.17. But there is no reason why the principle of papponymy (naming a child after its grandfather), a widespread practice in ancient times (cf. 1 Chron 6:9b–10a; 7:20), should not apply here. In addition, "Ahimelech son of Abiathar" as the name of one of David's priests is firmly attested elsewhere (cf. 1 Chron 18:16 [where the reading "Abimelech" is clearly secondary; see NIV mg. there]; 24:6). The young Ahimelech may have sometimes substituted for his father, Abiathar (cf. 15:24; 20:25), when the latter was unable to serve because of illness or the like (for discussion of various possibilities, cf. KD, pp. 365–67).

"Zadok a descendant of Eleazar [cf. 1 Chron 6:4–8] and Ahimelech a descendant of Ithamar" (1 Chron 24:3) shared priestly duties during at least part of the reign of David. Whether Zadok at first represented the southern half of the kingdom (originally headquartered in Hebron) and Ahimelech (or, alternatively, Abiathar) the northern (centered in Jerusalem after its capture by David), as some assert (cf. Cross, *Canaanite Myth and Hebrew Epic*, pp. 214–15; Olyan, "Zadok's Origins," p. 183), it is impossible to say. During the early years of David's reign, Zadok may have been appointed to offer sacrifices at the tabernacle in Gibeon (cf. 1 Chron 16:39–40) and Abiathar/Ahimelech to minister before the ark of the covenant in Jerusalem (so also independently KD, p. 365; see comment on 6:17 for the likelihood that there were two tabernacles during the reign of David).

The function of Seraiah ("The Lord Prevails") as "secretary" (v.17) was as much that of a secretary of state as it was that of a royal scribe (cf. de Vaux, AIs, p. 131). In the parallel in 1 Chronicles 18:16, David's secretary is called Shavsha, while other secretaries bear the names of "Sheva" (20:25) and "Shisha" (1 Kings 4:3) respectively. The similarity of the latter three names (which indeed might be alternate spellings of the same name and therefore refer to the same person) and their dissimilarity to that of Seraiah (which, unlike the others, contains a ר [*r*]) have led Aelred Cody to make the tantalizing suggestion that they reflect eighteenth/nineteenth dynasty Egyptian *sš-š't* or *sḫ-š't*, a compound expression that combines words meaning "scribe" and "official message," hence a term for a government scribe. He notes that the word translated into cuneiform appears in an Amarna letter addressed to the Egyptian court ("Le Titre Égyptien et le Nom Propre du Scribe de David," RB 72 [1965]: 387) and concludes that in its OT occurrences it is simply the Egyptian equivalent of the Hebrew word for "secretary"—a proposal that makes sense in light of the fact that David's cabinet may have been patterned after Egyptian models (see comment on v.16). Attractive though the suggestion is, however, it would leave the secretary unnamed/unidentified (and thus unique) in each list in which the term appears. Although Shavsha (1 Chron 18:16) may be an alternate name for Seraiah in v.17, it is equally possible that he served as secretary in Seraiah's absence (for whatever reason).

Benaiah ("The Lord Builds") is the son of Jehoiada (v.18), perhaps the same Jehoiada who was an older colleague of Zadok (v.17; cf. again 1 Chron 12:27–28 and esp. 27:5, where Jehoiada is called a "priest"). In charge of David's bodyguard (23:22–23), Benaiah would eventually become a royal executioner (cf. 1 Kings 2:25, 34, 46; cf. also 2 Sam 23:20–21) and rise to the position of commander-in-chief of Israel's army (1 Kings 4:4). In the present context he is in charge of the "Kerethites and Pelethites" (v.18). The Kerethites are " 'Cretans' without qualms" (Kitchen, "The Philistines," p. 56), while the Pelethites are doubtless Philistines, the word *pᵉlēṯî* being formed on the analogy of *kᵉrēṯî* (Pelethites are never mentioned apart from Kerethites [v.18; 15:18; 20:7, 23; 1 Kings 1:38, 44; 1 Chron 18:17]). Some of the Kerethites had apparently settled in or near Philistine territory (see comment on 1 Sam 30:14). Together with the Pelethites, the Kerethites constituted a corps of foreign mercenaries employed as David's bodyguard (for details see Notes on 1 Sam 30:14; cf. also D. Huttar in ZPEB, 1:787; for full discussion, cf. Delcor, "Les Kéréthim et les Crétois," pp. 409–22). "It seems likely that David sought to protect his kingship by having a bodyguard of foreign mercenaries who were independent of inner tensions in the court. They were professional soldiers, who are called 'David's mighty men' [*gibbôrîm;* NIV, 'special guard'] in 1 Kgs. 1.8" (Jones, p. 43; cf. also Brueggemann, *David's Truth,* p. 83).

The list of David's officials concludes by reporting that his sons (how many and who they were is not stated) were *kōhᵃnîm* (the word is in emphatic position), which NIV translates as "royal advisers." In v.17, however, with reference to Zadok and Ahimelech, the same word is rendered "priests" in the NIV (cf. also NIV mg. on v.18). Indeed, in another list of David's officials, Zadok and Ahimelech are called "priests" (20:25), after which the text continues by stating that Ira the Jairite was David's "priest" (20:26). These and similar considerations have led Carl Edwin Armerding, among others, to assert that there were "priests in early Israel who were (1) connected with the royal house, (2) not of the Levitical order, and (3) serving a function that is still largely unknown to us" ("Were David's Sons Really Priests?" in *Current Issues in Biblical and Patristic Interpretation: Studies in Honor of Merrill C. Tenney Presented by His Former Students,* ed. Gerald F. Hawthorne [Grand Rapids: Eerdmans, 1975], p. 76).

Although the validity of Armerding's three points would seem beyond dispute, two interrelated questions still remain: (1) Does the performance of priestly functions on occasion (cf. 24:25; 1 Kings 8:64) automatically make the performer a "priest" in the strict sense of that word? I have argued earlier that it does not (see comment on 6:14; cf. similarly Rowley, "Zadok and Nehushtan," p. 129 n. 44). (2) Does *kōhēn* in contexts such as the present always mean "priest"? Not necessarily. Although in v.17

the LXX rightly refers to Zadok and Ahimelech as *hiereis* ("priests"), in v.18 it calls David's sons *aularchai* ("princes of the court"; cf. KJV, "chief rulers"). The parallel to v.18 in 1 Chronicles 18:17 understands *kōh*$^{a}$*nîm* to mean "chief officials at the king's side." After listing Zadok and Abiathar as "priests" in the Solomonic court (1 Kings 4:4), the narrator describes Zabud son of Nathan as "a priest and personal adviser to the king" (1 Kings 4:5), a phrase that would perhaps be better translated as "a priest—that is, a personal adviser to the king" (there is no "and" in the text), the latter phrase thus explaining what "priest" (*kōhēn*) means in this case. Similarly, Ira was probably David's "royal adviser" (*kōhēn*) rather than his "priest" (20:26). In a note on 1 Chronicles 18:17, J. Barton Payne defines *kōh*$^{a}$*nîm* as "a term that by Ezra's time was restricted to 'priests' but that in Samuel preserves an older, broader meaning of 'official ministers'" (EBC, 4:399; cf. BDB, p. 434, which defines *kōhēn* in certain situations as a chieftain/prince exercising priestly functions). In short, then, *kōhēn* does not always mean "priest" *sensu strictu.*

The relationship between vv.15–18 and 20:23–26 is discussed in the comment on the latter passage.

## Notes

**18** The NIV's "over" translates על (*'l*), which appears in only one Hebrew MS but occurs in several ancient versions (cf. BHS) as well as in the parallel in 1 Chron 18:17. Its absence in the MT may be partially explained on the basis of haplography, since the previous word ends in ע (').

Although it does not deal adequately with the appearance of כהן (*khn*) in 20:26 and 1 Kings 4:5, the suggestion that כהנים (*khnym*, "priests") may be a transcriptional error for סכנים (*sknym*, "stewards") in v.28 is otherwise attractive. The parallel in 1 Chron 18:17 might then be attempting to explain the rare word סכן (*sōḵēn*), which is found elsewhere in the OT only in Isa 22:15, where it is defined as one who is "in charge of the palace." The latter expression is used of Ahishar in the list of Solomon's cabinet officers (1 Kings 4:6; for additional details, cf. G.J. Wenham, "Were David's Sons Priests?" ZAW 87, 1 [1975]: 79–82).

### D. *David's Court History (9:1–20:26)*

The lengthy account of the court history of David that begins in chapter 9 is "the earliest and greatest example of Hebrew historiography" (Jared J. Jackson, "David's Throne: Patterns in the Succession Story," *Canadian Journal of Theology* 11, 3 [1965]: 195). Robert H. Pfeiffer's justifiably glowing description of these chapters is often quoted:

> Ahimaaz, or whoever wrote the early source in Samuel, is the "father of history" in a much truer sense than Herodotus half a millennium later. As far as we know, he created history as an art, as a recital of past events dominated by a great idea. . . . David's biographer was a man of genius. Without any previous models as guide, he wrote a masterpiece, unsurpassed in historicity, psychological insight, literary style, and dramatic power. (*Introduction to the Old Testament*, rev. ed. [New York: Harper, 1948], p. 357)

(See also Jackson, "David's Throne," p. 183 n. 4; James A. Wharton, "A Plausible Tale: Story and Theology in II Samuel 9–20, I Kings 1–2," Int 35, 4 [1981]: 341; R.N. Whybray, *The Succession Narrative: A Study of II Samuel 9–20; I Kings 1 and 2*, Studies in Biblical Theology, Second Series 9 [London: SCM, 1968]: 10.) Indeed, David's court history has been claimed to function as the worthy conclusion to one of the greatest epics of all time (cf. Robert H. Pfeiffer and William G. Pollard, *The Hebrew Iliad: The History of the Rise of Israel Under Saul and David* [New York: Harper, 1957], pp. 86–120).

Ever since Rost's isolation of 2 Samuel 9–20 and 1 Kings 1–2 as a discrete literary unit (pp. 65–114, esp. pp. 84–87), it has been customary to refer to the account as the Succession Narrative (cf. Jackson, "David's Throne," p. 183; Whybray; Walter Brueggemann, "On Trust and Freedom: A Study of Faith in the Succession Narrative," Int 26, 1 [1972]: 3–4). But while there can be no doubt that the succession to David's throne is a prominent theme in these chapters, "the title *Court History* is preferable to *Succession History* (or the like) because the latter term focuses attention too narrowly upon one of its concerns, which, while it is extremely important, is hardly the only one. Thus a neutral title such as *Court History* more adequately reflects the contents" (Vanderkam, "Davidic Complicity in the Deaths of Abner and Eshbaal," p. 522 n. 2). In a closely reasoned treatment James W. Flanagan suggests that the bulk of chapters 9–20 constitutes a court history of David to which certain Solomonic sections, including 1 Kings 1–2, were later added, the end result comprising a succession narrative ("Court History or Succession Document? A Study of 2 Samuel 9–20; 1 Kings 1–2," JBL 91, 2 [1972]: 172–81).

Flanagan's study raises the issue of the beginning and the ending of the narrative, including—but not restricted to—the question of whether 1 Kings 1–2 is part of it. Although most commentators would contend that 2 Samuel 9–20; 1 Kings 1–2 constitute a continuous literary unit (cf. Jackson, "David's Throne," p. 195; Ackerman, p. 57; Leo G. Perdue, "'Is There Anyone Left of the House of Saul . . . ?': Ambiguity and the Characterization of David in the Succession Narrative," JSOT 30 [1984]: 79), many would begin the story earlier than 2 Samuel 9 and/or conclude it later than 1 Kings 2 and/or remove from the chapters certain sections under the assumption that they are not part of the original account. In any event, it is becoming increasingly clear that "it is difficult to think of I Kings 1–2, in which the urgency of the succession question is obvious, as deriving from the same hand as II Samuel 9–20, where it is not" (P. Kyle McCarter, Jr., "'Plots, True or False': The Succession Narrative as Court Apologetic," Int 35, 4 [1981]: 361). Flanagan points out that while there are literary similarities between 2 Samuel 9–20 and 1 Kings 1–2, there are differences as well ("Court History or Succession Document?" p. 173). Although his attempt is not entirely successful, it demonstrates the unity of theme and purpose in the section as a whole. He concludes that 1 Kings 1–2 (plus the Bathsheba episode in 2 Sam 11–12) were added to the court history by a later hand (ibid., p. 181; cf. similarly McCarter, "'Plots, True or False,'" pp. 361–62, 365–66).

Detailed characterizations of *dramatis personae*, intimate descriptions of human flaws and foibles, lengthy episodes instead of summary vignettes—these and other features lend to chapters 9–20 an impression of verisimilitude and unmistakably eyewitness quality (cf. Stuart Lasine, "Fiction, Falsehood, and Reality in Hebrew Scripture," *Hebrew Studies* 25 [1984]: 28). The entire account must have been written late in the reign of David or early in the reign of Solomon (cf. Jackson, "David's Throne," pp. 183–84; Whybray, *The Succession Narrative*, pp. 54–55), and the author, whether Ahimaaz or Abiathar or someone else (cf. Jackson, "David's Throne," p. 190 and n. 27; Rost, p. 106), must himself have been a major player in the events he recorded.

If we allow for understandable hyperbole, Jackson's opinion concerning the purpose of David's court history is helpful: "to display, in all their richness and depth, the varied relations of men who no longer walk by faith in the cultic religious symbols of the past but contend for temporal power and freedom of self-expression in the mundane world of daily, i.e. secular life" ("David's Throne," p. 185). According to Whybray and others, wisdom influence is prominent throughout the narrative. Since most of chapters 9–20 can be justifiably characterized as "David under the Curse" (Carlson, p. 25) because of the section's uncomplimentary portrayal of David, it is not surprising that the Chronicler's parallels to these chapters include only the account of David's victory over the Ammonites (10:1–11:1; 12:29–31 = 1 Chron 19:1–20:3; cf. similarly Perdue, "'Is There Anyone Left of the House of Saul. . . ?'" p. 82 n. 15). Conspicuous by their absence in 1 Chronicles are the Bathsheba/Uriah episodes (11:2–12:25).

Despite Flanagan's valiant attempt ("Court History or Succession Document?" pp. 177–81), no persuasive or convincing overall literary structure for chapters 9–20 has yet emerged. The most that can be suggested is a series of interlocking themes that weave their way throughout the tapestry of the text: rebukes delivered to David (Jackson, "David's Throne," p. 187), sexual escapades (ibid., pp. 189, 193 n. 31; John A. Martin, p. 39), news reports (Jackson, "David's Throne," p. 193 n. 33), the difficulty of distinguishing between good and evil (Ackerman, pp. 42, 53), deception/treachery (Harry Hagan, "Deception as Motif and Theme in 2 Sm 9–20; 1 Kgs 1–2," *Biblica* 60, 3 [1979]: 301–26). The narrator calls attention to divine purpose and activity only rarely, as for example in 11:27; 12:24; 17:14 (cf. Rost, p. 106; Jackson, "David's Throne," pp. 184–85; Brueggemann, "On Trust and Freedom," p. 9; Gerhard von Rad, "The Beginnings of Historical Writing in Ancient Israel," in *The Problem of the Hexateuch and Other Essays*, reprint [London: SCM, 1984], pp. 198–201; Whybray, *The Succession Narrative*, p. 64). In numerous other instances the characters themselves express their belief that God is—or is not—at work.

As the previous literary unit (5:17–8:18) ends with a list of David's officials (8:15–18), so do chapters 9–20 (20:23–26). And as the succeeding literary unit (chs. 21–24) begins with a narrative concerning the survivors in Saul's family (21:1–14), so do chapters 9–20 (ch. 9; cf. esp. the reference to the "house" of "Saul" in the first verse of each unit [9:1; 21:1]).

### 1. *Kindness to Mephibosheth*

#### 9:1–13

[1]David asked, "Is there anyone still left of the house of Saul to whom I can show kindness for Jonathan's sake?"

[2]Now there was a servant of Saul's household named Ziba. They called him to appear before David, and the king said to him, "Are you Ziba?"

"Your servant," he replied.

[3]The king asked, "Is there no one still left of the house of Saul to whom I can show God's kindness?"

Ziba answered the king, "There is still a son of Jonathan; he is crippled in both feet."

4 "Where is he?" the king asked.
Ziba answered, "He is at the house of Makir son of Ammiel in Lo
Debar."
5 So King David had him brought from Lo Debar, from the house of
Makir son of Ammiel.
6 When Mephibosheth son of Jonathan, the son of Saul, came to
David, he bowed down to pay him honor.
David said, "Mephibosheth!"
"Your servant," he replied.
7 "Don't be afraid," David said to him, "for I will surely show you
kindness for the sake of your father Jonathan. I will restore to you all the
land that belonged to your grandfather Saul, and you will always eat at
my table."
8 Mephibosheth bowed down and said, "What is your servant, that you
should notice a dead dog like me?"
9 Then the king summoned Ziba, Saul's servant, and said to him, "I
have given your master's grandson everything that belonged to Saul
and his family. 10 You and your sons and your servants are to farm the
land for him and bring in the crops, so that your master's grandson may
be provided for. And Mephibosheth, grandson of your master, will
always eat at my table." (Now Ziba had fifteen sons and twenty
servants.)
11 Then Ziba said to the king, "Your servant will do whatever my lord
the king commands his servant to do." So Mephibosheth ate at David's
table like one of the king's sons.
12 Mephibosheth had a young son named Mica, and all the members
of Ziba's household were servants of Mephibosheth. 13 And Mephibosheth lived in Jerusalem, because he always ate at the king's table, and
he was crippled in both feet.

Two themes dominate the section: showing kindness (vv.1, 3, 7) and eating at the king's table (vv.7, 10–11, 13). Meeting in the middle verse of the chapter (v.7), they lead to the following chiastic outline (cf. similarly Kiyoshi K. Sacon, "A Study of the Literary Structure of 'The Succession Narrative,' " *Studies in the Period of David and Solomon and Other Essays* [Winona Lake: Eisenbrauns, 1982], pp. 48–49):

A. David intends to favor the survivors in Saul's family (9:1).
  B. David speaks to Saul's servant Ziba (9:2–5).
    C. David expresses favor to Mephibosheth (9:6–8).
  B′. David speaks to Saul's servant Ziba (9:9–11a).
A′. David implements favor to survivors in Saul's family (9:11b–13).

**1** Now that he is the undisputed king, a fact emphasized again and again in this chapter (vv.2, 3, 4, 5, 9, 11), David can afford to be magnanimous. Although during his days as a fugitive from Saul David would have had no compunctions about killing all who were still "left" of his foes, whether real or imagined (cf. 1 Sam 25:34), and although during his early and somewhat tenuous years as king in Hebron he considered all members of the "house of Saul" his mortal enemies (cf. 3:1, 6, 8, 10), he now actively seeks out anyone "still left of the house of Saul" (vv.1, 3) so that he might bestow the royal largesse on him.

To any remaining members of Saul's family David desires to show kindness "for Jonathan's sake" (vv.1, 7). The "kindness" (*ḥeseḏ*) he speaks of (vv.1, 3, 7) derives from his long-standing covenant relationship with the deceased Jonathan. David had asked Jonathan to show him kindness (see 1 Sam 20:8 and comment), and for his part Jonathan had echoed the same request (see 1 Sam 20:14 and comment). Just as the

Jabeshites had shown kindness to Saul by burying him (see 2:5 and comment), so also now David wishes to show kindness to Saul's house.

**2–5** Contact between David and the house(hold) of Saul is made through one of its servants, a man named Ziba (v.2; cf. 19:17). Called to appear before the king, he answers David's question concerning his identity with the customary submissive response of an inferior to his superior: "Your servant" (see comment on 1 Sam 25:24).

In a virtual echo of his question in v.1, David asks Ziba (v.3) whether Saul's house "still" has a survivor to whom David would be able to "show kindness like that of God" (a translation preferable to NIV's "God's kindness"; see 1 Sam 20:14 and comment). Ziba responds that there "still" remains one of Jonathan's sons, a man who is "crippled in both feet" (v.3; for possible implications of this description, see comment on 4:4, where NIV renders the same Heb. phrase "lame in both feet").

David's question concerning the whereabouts of Jonathan's son brings a response that is both immediate and precise: A specific town and a specific house in that town are named. The house belongs to Makir son of Ammiel (vv.4–5; cf. also 17:27). Although Ammiel ("My [Divine] Kinsman Is God") was also the name of Bathsheba's father (1 Chron 3:5; in 2 Sam 11:3 he is given the variant name Eliam ["The (Divine) Kinsman Is My God"]), there is no reason to identify the two men.

As for Makir, every reference to his earlier namesake calls him either the (firstborn) son of Manasseh (Gen 50:23; Num 26:29; 27:1; 32:39–40; 36:1; Josh 13:31; 17:1, 3; 1 Chron 7:14; in Judg 5:14 Makir is doubtless a synonym for Manasseh) or the father of Gilead (Num 26:29; 1 Chron 2:21, 23; 7:14–17; cf. Deut 3:15), thus establishing his Transjordanian provenance. The town of Lo Debar (vv.4–5) was also located east of the Jordan River, as indicated by its association with Mahanaim (formerly the headquarters of Saul's now-deceased son Ish-Bosheth; see 2:8 and comment), Rabbah, Rogelim (cf. 17:27), and Karnaim (cf. Amos 6:13). The various spellings of Lo Debar in the MT—*lô ḏᵉḇār* (vv.4–5), *lōʾ ḏᵉḇār* (17:27), *lōʾ ḏāḇār* (Amos 6:13)—make its meaning ambiguous and prompt Ackerman to refer to the name as "an interesting designation, which can imply 'no thing' (*lōʾ ḏāḇār*), or 'he has a word/thing,' that is, up his sleeve (*lô ḏāḇār*)" (pp. 42–43). Although the exact location of Lo Debar is uncertain, a likely identification is with modern Umm ed-Dabar ten miles south-southeast of the Sea of Galilee.

**6–8** In this central and pivotal section of the chapter, David meets "Mephibosheth son of Jonathan, the son of Saul" (v.6; for the meaning of Mephibosheth see Note on 4:4). The double patronymic is used here because "the ancestry of Mephibosheth is fundamental to the narrative" (Clines, "X, X *Ben* Y, *Ben* Y," p. 275). In the rest of the chapter the unadorned name is employed.

As in v.2, so also in v.6 David's pronouncing of the name of his visitor evokes the response "Your servant." Here, however, the visitor bows down to pay honor to David, and here in addition Mephibosheth prefaces "your servant" with the word "Behold" (untr. in NIV).

Doubtless knowing that what had happened to his uncle Ish-Bosheth (cf. 4:5–8), Mephibosheth is understandably apprehensive. To put him at ease David tells Mephibosheth not to be afraid (v.7; cf. the identical reassurances uttered by David [1 Sam 22:23] and Jonathan [1 Sam 23:17]). True to his earlier promise (vv.1, 3), David declares emphatically that he will show Mephibosheth kindness for Jonathan's sake (see comment on v.1). David's specific expressions of covenant loyalty to Saul's grandson would consist of (1) restoring to him all the land that had belonged to Saul and (2) welcoming him as a perennial guest at the royal table.

As for the first demonstration of the king's generosity, Ziba's later statement that Mephibosheth hopes that "the house of Israel will give me back my grandfather's kingdom" (16:3) may reflect wishful thinking on Mephibosheth's part right from the start ("restore" in v.7 and "give . . . back" in 16:3 both render the same Heb. verb)—or at least a misunderstanding of David's intentions. It is clear that by "land" (lit., "field," v.7; cf. 19:29) David means "(farm)land" (lit., "ground," v.9), not "land" that one rules over ("kingdom," 16:3).

As for the second demonstration—that Mephibosheth would always "eat at my table" (vv.7, 10; the MT reads "eat food at my table" in both verses)—a similar ambiguity exists. "Given David's loathing for 'the lame and the blind' since the war against the Jebusites (2 Sam 5:6–8), one is brought up short by his decision to give Jonathan's son Mephibosheth, 'lame in both feet' (9:3, 13), a permanent seat at the royal table. . . . Is David willing to undergo such a daily ordeal just in memory of his friendship with Jonathan, as he himself declares, or as the price for keeping an eye on the last of Saul's line? Considering David's genius for aligning the proper with the expedient, he may be acting from both motives" (Sternberg, p. 255; cf. similarly Ackerman, p. 43; Perdue, " 'Is There Anyone Left of the House of Saul. . . ?' " p. 75; Curtis, "East Is East . . . ," p. 357). What is beyond dispute is that "eating (food) at the (king's) table" (cf. also vv.11, 13; 19:28) can be understood as a metaphor referring to house arrest (cf. 2 Kings 25:29 = Jer 52:33). Indeed, David himself had experienced what it was like to feel somewhat unwelcome at the table of a king (see comment on 1 Sam 20:29).

The central section of the chapter ends as it began: Mephibosheth "bowed down" (vv.6, 8) and, speaking to the king, referred to himself as "your servant" (vv.6, 8). He was grateful that David should "notice" him (*pānāh 'el-* ["pay/give attention to"]; cf. 1 Kings 8:28 = 2 Chron 6:19). Becoming more craven still in his submission to David, Mephibosheth referred to himself as a "dead dog" (v.8; cf. 3:8; see also the comment and Notes on 1 Sam 17:43)—an epithet earlier applied by David to himself (1 Sam 24:14) and later hurled by Abishai at Shimei, "a man from the same clan as Saul's family" (16:5, 9).

**9–11a** Like its parallel section (vv.2–5), the present literary unit states that Ziba is "summoned" into David's presence (v.9; "called" in v.2 translates the same Heb. verb). Ziba is here referred to as the *na'ar* ("steward") of Saul (cf. 16:1; 19:17; NIV's "servant" in v.9 obscures the fact that everywhere else in the chapter "servant" renders *'eḇeḏ*).

David announces to Ziba that he has turned over to Mephibosheth the property belonging to Saul and his "family" (lit., "house," v.9; the announcement thus echoes "house of Saul," "Saul's household" in vv.1–3). As if to stress the extent of the royal bounty, David uses the word *kōl* ("all") twice in v.9: "everything," "entire family/house" ("entire" untr. in NIV). He then gives Ziba the responsibility to "farm" (*'āḇaḏ*, lit., "serve," "work"; cf. Gen 2:5; 3:23; 4:2, 12) the land on Mephibosheth's behalf (v.10). Ziba is also to "bring in the crops" (the object, contextually implicit in the Heb. verb, is made explicit by the NIV; cf. Neh 13:15; Hag 1:6 ["harvested"]) so that Saul's grandson may "be provided for" (lit., "have food and eat it"—a phrase that seems to cast a cloud over David's generous pledge that Mephibosheth would always "eat [food] at [the king's] table" [vv.7, 10, 11, 13], since it appears that Mephibosheth would be supplying some if not most of his own provisions). In any event, Ziba's "fifteen sons and twenty servants" (v.10; 19:17), all of whom were in turn servants of Mephibosheth (v.12), would comprise a sufficient work force to help Ziba carry out the king's commands (v.11a).

**11b–13** David's intention to show kindness to Saul's survivors (v.1) is now implemented. The literary section begins and ends with the reminder that Mephibosheth always "ate" (lit., "was eating," emphasizing the habitual and continuing nature of the activity) at the king's table (vv.11b, 13).

Some time has passed since the earlier mention of Mephibosheth in 4:4, when he was no more than twelve years of age (see comment on 4:4). He is now old enough to have a "young son" named Mica(h) (v.12), whose descendants are listed in 1 Chronicles 8:35–38; 9:41–44. The meaning of Micah's name, which is the same as that of the famous prophet, is "Who Is Like (Yahweh)?"—quite a contrast to the meaning of the name of Mephibosheth himself (see Notes on 4:4).

And so Mephibosheth was moved from Lo Debar (vv.4–5) to Jerusalem (v.13), where he from that day on "lived" continually (lit., "was living"; see comment on v.11b). The chapter concludes with a final—and perhaps ominous—reminder that he was "crippled in both feet" (cf. 19:26; see comments on v.3; 4:4).

## Notes

4 The MT's לִדְבִר (*lidbir*) in Josh 13:26 (NIV, "Debir") should probably be revocalized as לֹדְבָר (*lōd$^e$bār;* cf. BHS) and equated with the Transjordanian Lo Debar (cf. S.R. Driver, *Notes on the Books of Samuel*, p. 286). As in 2 Sam 17:27, so also in Josh 13:25–26, it shares proximity with Rabbah and Mahanaim.

11 The NIV correctly reads "David's table" (with the LXX; see margin) for the MT's "my table" (which KD labels a "mistake," p. 371). To read "As for Mephibosheth, *said the king*, he shall eat at my table" (KJV) is contextually awkward. The reading "my table" in v.11 probably arose by contamination from the same phrase in vv.7, 10.

### 2. *The Ammonites defeated*

10:1–19

1 In the course of time, the king of the Ammonites died, and his son
Hanun succeeded him as king. 2 David thought, "I will show kindness to
Hanun son of Nahash, just as his father showed kindness to me." So
David sent a delegation to express his sympathy to Hanun concerning
his father.
When David's men came to the land of the Ammonites, 3 the Ammonite
nobles said to Hanun their lord, "Do you think David is honoring your
father by sending men to you to express sympathy? Hasn't David sent
them to you to explore the city and spy it out and overthrow it?" 4 So
Hanun seized David's men, shaved off half of each man's beard, cut off
their garments in the middle at the buttocks, and sent them away.
5 When David was told about this, he sent messengers to meet the
men, for they were greatly humiliated. The king said, "Stay at Jericho till
your beards have grown, and then come back."

6When the Ammonites realized that they had become a stench in
David's nostrils, they hired twenty thousand Aramean foot soldiers from
Beth Rehob and Zobah, as well as the king of Maacah with a thousand
men, and also twelve thousand men from Tob.
7On hearing this, David sent Joab out with the entire army of fighting
men. 8The Ammonites came out and drew up in battle formation at the
entrance to their city gate, while the Arameans of Zobah and Rehob and
the men of Tob and Maacah were by themselves in the open country.
9Joab saw that there were battle lines in front of him and behind him;
so he selected some of the best troops in Israel and deployed them
against the Arameans. 10He put the rest of the men under the command
of Abishai his brother and deployed them against the Ammonites.
11Joab said, "If the Arameans are too strong for me, then you are to
come to my rescue; but if the Ammonites are too strong for you, then I
will come to rescue you. 12Be strong and let us fight bravely for our
people and the cities of our God. The LORD will do what is good in his
sight."
13Then Joab and the troops with him advanced to fight the Arameans,
and they fled before him. 14When the Ammonites saw that the Arameans
were fleeing, they fled before Abishai and went inside the city. So Joab
returned from fighting the Ammonites and came to Jerusalem.
15After the Arameans saw that they had been routed by Israel, they
regrouped. 16Hadadezer had Arameans brought from beyond the River;
they went to Helam, with Shobach the commander of Hadadezer's army
leading them.
17When David was told of this, he gathered all Israel, crossed the
Jordan and went to Helam. The Arameans formed their battle lines to
meet David and fought against him. 18But they fled before Israel, and
David killed seven hundred of their charioteers and forty thousand of
their foot soldiers. He also struck down Shobach the commander of
their army, and he died there. 19When all the kings who were vassals of
Hadadezer saw that they had been defeated by Israel, they made peace
with the Israelites and became subject to them.
So the Arameans were afraid to help the Ammonites anymore.

Chapters 10–12 constitute a distinct literary unit within the Court of History of David (chs. 9–20), as demonstrated by several factors: (1) 10:1 and 13:1 both begin with "In the course of time," a phrase that always inaugurates a new section (cf. Wolfgang Roth, "You Are the Man! Structural Interaction in 2 Samuel 10–12," *Semeia* [1977]: 4; John I. Lawlor, "Theology and Art in the Narrative of the Ammonite War," *Grace Theological Journal* 3, 2 [1982]: 193); (2) 10:1–11:1; 12:26–31 describe Israel's military victories over the Ammonites, thus forming a frame around the central narrative of David-Bathsheba-Uriah-Nathan-Solomon (11:12–12:25; cf. Bailey's summary description of these chapters in the title of his book *David in Love and War: The Pursuit of Power in 2 Samuel 10–12*); (3) the parallel in Chronicles (1 Chron 19:1–20:3) is the equivalent of 10:1–11:1 plus 12:29–31, thus spanning chapters 10–12 while at the same time omitting the unsavory picture of David that forms the heart of the section; (4) the *Leitwort šālaḥ* ("send") appears twenty-three times in chapters 10–12 (it is found only twenty-one times in the rest of the Court History and only thirteen times in chs. 1–8, 21–24). Its concentration in these chapters probably represents "a conscious development of a power motif" (Lawlor, "Theology and Art," p. 196; cf. Bailey's similar insight in the subtitle of his book *David in Love and War: The Pursuit of Power in 2 Samuel 10–12*).

The story of the Ammonite wars is the only extensive narrative in the Court History that casts David in a favorable light. To be sure, elsewhere the narrator of the history sometimes views David positively—or at least sympathetically—in briefer sections (cf. 12:13, 22–23; 18:32–33; 19:38–39). On the whole, however, chapters 9–20 deserve the label given by Carlson to the last two-thirds of 2 Samuel: "David under the Curse" (pp. 7, 25, 140).

It may well be that various episodes in chapters 10–12 are not set forth in chronological order. The events cover a period of at least two years, which raises the legitimate question as to whether Joab's military campaigns against the Ammonites would have lasted all that time. As Lawlor states, the reports in 10:1–11:1; 12:26–31 might be "an example of deliberate narrative framing without concern for linear chronology/sequence" ("Theology and Art," p. 204 n. 33). With respect to their chronological relationship to events narrated elsewhere in 2 Samuel, it is probably best to see the episodes of chapters 10–12 as having occurred earlier than those recorded in 8:3–12 (see comment there; cf. also Carlson, p. 146 n. 4).

Attempts to discern a comprehensive literary structure (often chiastic) for chapters 10–12 fail to convince, nor does the rather straightforward narrative of chapter 10 itself yield readily to literary analysis. At the same time, internal considerations (discussed below) lead to a tripartite division of the chapter:

A. The Ammonites humiliate David's delegation (10:1–5).
B. The Ammonites and their Aramean allies flee from Joab (10:6–14).
C. David defeats the Arameans (10:15–19).

Second Samuel 10:1–19 is paralleled in 1 Chronicles 19:1–19.

**1–5** The opening formula "In the course of time" (v.1) is often used in 2 Samuel to introduce narrative sequence, whether chronological or thematic. It does not necessarily imply that what follows it is chronologically later than what precedes it (see Notes on 2:1 and comment on 8:1). Indeed, the relationship between chapter 10 and chapter 9 is literarily associative in that chapter 10 echoes key words from chapter 9: "Cf. the expression 'show kindness' in 10:2 (*bis*) and 9:1, 3, 7. Among other *verba associandi* in this connexion may be named 'servant', 10:2–4 [NIV "men"] to 9:10–12, and Zobah, 10:6, 8, *ṣā<u>b</u>ā* ('host'), 10:7, 16, 18 [NIV, 'army'], to Ziba in 9:2–3, 9–12" (Carlson, p. 145 n. 3).

The deceased "king of the Ammonites" (v.1) was Nahash (v.2; cf. 1 Sam 12:12). If his name means "Snake" (see comment on 1 Sam 11:1), then that of his son Hanun—although generally understood to mean "Favored (by God)" or the like (cf. BDB, p. 337)—might, in the eyes of the OT narrator and his readers, mean "Loathsome" (cf. Bailey, *David in Love and War*, p. 163 n. 99), as the same Hebrew root is translated in Job 19:17. When political power is based on dynastic rule, a king about to die can reasonably expect his son to succeed him as king (cf. 2 Kings 13:24). Thus Hanun becomes king of Ammon as a result of his father's death.

Assuming that the Nahash of v.2 is the same Ammonite king defeated by Saul (1 Sam 11:1–11), the kindness he showed to David may have been expressed during David's days as a fugitive from the Israelite royal court. David now wants to reciprocate by showing kindness to Nahash's son, thereby cementing the alliance already existing between Israel and Ammon. As David showed "kindness" (*ḥese<u>d</u>*) to Mephibosheth for the sake of his father Jonathan (9:7), with whom he had established a covenant relationship many years earlier (see comments on 1 Sam 20:8, 14), so he also shows "kindness" to Hanun for the sake of his father Nahash, with whom he had probably already concluded a prior treaty arrangement (cf. Lawlor, "Theology and

Art," p. 194 n. 3). The former act promoted domestic harmony and solidified David's own position inside Israel, and the latter is calculated to maintain the viability of one of David's international agreements and strengthen his position outside Israel (cf. similarly Pinhas Artzi, "Mourning in International Relations," in *Death in Mesopotamia: Papers Read at the XXVI*[e] *Rencontre Assyriologique Internationale*, Copenhagen Studies in Assyriology 8; ed. Bendt Alster [Copenhagen: Akademisk Forlag, 1980], p. 169 n. 18).

The means chosen by David to show kindness to his deceased ally's son is sending a delegation to "express his sympathy" (*nḥm*, vv.2–3). Fokkelman observes that this " 'comforting' alliterates with *Nāḥāš* as well as *Ḥānūn* and connects them both" (*King David*, p. 43). Artzi provides extrabiblical examples of acts of official mourning over the demise of a foreign king and notes that, although they are insufficient as a means of solving crises, they express solidarity in common human fate and may thus contribute to peaceful coexistence ("Mourning in International Relations," pp. 161–70). He suggests further that such mourning belongs to the same level of graciousness as that expressed in the sending of a delegation to convey wishes of good health "on the eve of recovery from a dangerous illness" (ibid., p. 167; cf. p. 170 n. 24, where Merodach-Baladan's apparent concern for Hezekiah [2 Kings 20:12] is cited as an example). The verb "sent" (v.2), used frequently throughout this chapter (vv.3 [bis], 4, 5, 6 [NIV's "hired" is literally "sent and hired"], 7, 16 [NIV's "had . . . brought" is literally "sent and caused . . . to go out"]), reflects in most cases the deliberate maneuvering for power that is taking place during these days (see comment on 10:1–19).

Upon the arrival of David's delegation to the land of the Ammonites, the Ammonite "nobles" (*śārîm*, v.3; perhaps here "[army] commanders," as in 1 Sam 29:3 [cf. Gordon, *I & II Samuel*, p. 250]) share their suspicions with Hanun. "They mistrust David's motives and urge a harsh response (cf. a parallel of advisers in I Kings 12:6–11)" (Brueggemann, *First and Second Samuel*, p. 270). Citing yet another parallel—the reaction of Joab to Abner's visit in 3:24–25—Gunn observes that "in the political world of Joab and the courtiers suspicion is the order of the day. An unsolicited offer of friendship belongs to unreality" (*The Story of King David*, p. 97).

Hanun's men are sure that David's delegation, like the Danite warriors of Judges 18:2, have been sent into alien territory to "explore" and "spy out" the region. In this case the focus of their interest is said to be "the city" (v.3; probably Rabbah [cf. 11:1], the capital city, today known as Amman [the capital of the Hashemite Kingdom of Jordan] and located about forty miles east-northeast of Jerusalem)—although the parallel in Chronicles hints at the possibility that the Ammonites are accusing David's men of having designs on "the country" (*hā'āreṣ*) as a whole (1 Chron 19:3). In either case the Israelites have come to "overthrow" the Ammonite birthright (the same Heb. verb elsewhere almost always has the Lord as its subject; cf. Gen 19:21, 25, 29; Deut 29:23; Job 9:5 ["overturns"]; 12:15 ["devastate"]; 34:25; Jer 20:16; Lam 4:6; Amos 4:11; Hag 2:22 [twice: "overturn," "overthrow"]).

Accepting the assessment of his men, Hanun decides to refuse David's cordial overtures and to humiliate David's messengers. He (probably through his henchmen rather than personally) begins shaving off "half of each man's beard" (v.4; 1 Chron 19:4 summarizes by stating simply that he shaved "them"), no doubt vertically rather than horizontally to make them look as foolish as possible. Although voluntarily shaving off one's beard was a traditional sign of mourning (Isa 15:2; Jer 41:5; 48:37), forcible shaving was considered an insult and a sign of submission (cf. Isa 7:20).

Hanun then cuts off their garments "in the middle at the buttocks" (whether vertically or horizontally in this case is difficult to say) and then sends them on their way. Forced exposure of the buttocks was a shameful practice inflicted on prisoners of war (cf. Isa 20:4).

Hanun's treatment of David's men was clearly a violation of "the courtesies normally extended to the envoys of other states" in ancient times (Wiseman, " 'Is It Peace?' " p. 315). Indeed, the indignities heaped on them are a grotesque parody of the normal symbolic actions that accompanied mourning (cf. similarly Artzi, "Mourning in International Relations," p. 170 n. 22).

Introductory formulas located at strategic points throughout chapter 10 almost certainly refer to intelligence data gathered by David's scouts to keep him informed of significant developments on the international scene: "When David was told about/of this" (vv.5, 17), "On hearing this" (v.7; cf. Hauer, "Foreign Intelligence," pp. 97–98). Knowing that the maltreatment of his men by Hanun is causing them to be "greatly humiliated" (v.5; cf. Num 12:14 ["have been in disgrace"]; Ps 74:21 ["in disgrace"]), David sends messengers to tell them to stay at Jericho (modern Tell es-Sultan, six miles west of the Jordan River and just north of a major ancient highway leading from Rabbah to Jerusalem) until their beards have grown back. Only after remaining there (presumably out of public view) for a suitable length of time are they obliged to return to Jerusalem.

As the hair on Samson's shorn head ultimately grew back (Judg 16:22) and proved to be a bad omen for the Philistines, so also the regrowth of the beards of David's men would portend disaster for the Ammonites. Hanun's foolish miscalculation would bring about his own defeat. "The misfortune of the comforting delegation of David is the actual cause of the (already looming) war against the Ammonite-Aramean coalition" (Artzi, "Mourning in International Relations," p. 166).

**6–14** Verses 6 and 14 both begin with the same statement—"When the Ammonites saw [NIV, 'realized' in v.6] that"—thus forming an *inclusio* that frames the literary unit (cf. Fokkelman, *King David*, p. 46; the major variation in the two verses is that they use two different Qal forms of the same Heb. verb). The Ammonites' perception of themselves is accurate: They have become a "stench" in David's nostrils (v.6)—not necessarily a situation to be deplored (cf. 16:21), although in the present case it is tantamount to affirming that David would almost surely be expected to declare war against Ammon (see 1 Sam 13:4 and comment). In anticipation of that likelihood the Ammonites, at enormous cost, hire a large army of Arameans to supplement their own troops. Although *'elep̱* sometimes means "(military) unit" (see comments on 8:4; 1 Sam 4:2), the huge amount of silver (see 1 Chron 19:6 and footnote) expended in the Ammonites' enlistment and supply of the Arameans makes it virtually certain that the word is intended in its ordinary sense of "thousand" throughout this chapter.

The hiring of mercenaries, who thus owed their livelihood and security to their master, was not uncommon in ancient times (cf. 2 Kings 7:6; 2 Chron 25:6). In the present situation Arameans are hired from Beth Rehob (v.6, called simply Rehob in v.8; an Aramean district north of Laish/Dan [Judg 18:28; cf. also Num 13:21], probably located in the Beqa' region of Lebanon), Zobah (cf. the title of Psalm 60; for the location see comment on 8:3), Maacah (assigned to the tribal territory of East Manasseh [Josh 13:8, 11] but not conquered by Israel [Josh 13:13]; comprises the northeast portion of the Huleh Valley and the northwestern Golan Heights region), and Tob (a town and district where the judge Jephthath found protection [Judg 11:3,

5; cf. perhaps also 1 Macc 5:13; 2 Macc 12:17]; modern et-Taiyibeh, located forty-five miles northeast of Rabbah). For a map showing the relative locations of these four regions, see Rasmussen, p. 117. From the fact that the Ammonites choose to hire Arameans, it is possible to infer the earlier expansion of Aram to the borders of Ammon itself (cf. Malamat, "The Kingdom of David & Solomon," p. 100).

The parallel account of the Aramean muster recorded in 1 Chronicles 19:6–7 differs in several particulars from the narrative in v.6. Assuming that the numbers have been transcribed accurately in both accounts, we can nevertheless harmonize the two passages as follows: "Aram Naharaim" (i.e., Northwest Mesopotamia; cf. 1 Chron 19:6 and margin) includes Beth Rehob and Tob in v.6; "the king of Maacah with his troops" (1 Chron 19:7) are "the king of Maacah with a thousand men" of v.6; and "thirty-two thousand chariots and charioteers/horsemen" (1 Chron 19:7; cf. also 1 Chron 19:6) represent the numerical strength of the chariot force hired by Hanun and equal the "twenty thousand foot soldiers" plus the "twelve thousand men" of v.6. Apparently "charioteer/horseman," used here in the sense of "rider" (an infantryman conveyed from place to place in a chariot), could be interchanged with "foot soldier" in both 2 Samuel and 1 Chronicles (cf. Zane C. Hodges, "Conflicts in the Biblical Account of the Ammonite-Syrian War," BS 119, 475 [1962]: 241–42; see also the comment on v.18 below).

Upon learning that the Ammonite-Aramean coalition has been formed, David takes no chances: He sends out the entire army, under the leadership of his commander Joab, to engage them (v.7). While the Ammonites prepare to defend their city (probably Rabbah, the capital) by amassing at its most vulnerable point, the "entrance to their city gate" (v.8; cf. similarly Judg 9:40), the troops from the various Aramean districts (each army apparently led by its own king; cf. 1 Chron 19:9) are deployed in "the open country" (lit., "the field[s]"; cf. 11:23 ["the open"]; 18:6). The scene is described in solemn, formal terms: The Ammonites "came out and drew up in battle formation," an expression that echoes Goliath's taunt in 1 Samuel 17:8 by using the same Hebrew phrase ("Why do you come out and line up for battle?").

Before the battle is joined, Joab decides on strategy (vv.9–10) and encourages his brother Abishai (vv.11–12; see 1 Sam 26:6 and comment). Just as the double assertion that the Ammonites "saw" (vv.6, 14) frames the longest literary unit in the chapter (see comment on v.6), so also the statement that Joab "saw" (v.9) begins the crucial central paragraph (vv.9–12) of that unit. Joab perceives enemy "battle lines" (*p^e^nê hammilḥāmāh*, lit., "the face[s] of the battle") "in front of him" (*mippānîm*, lit., "from face[s]") and behind him (cf. similarly 2 Chron 13:14), thus recognizing that he must divide his army if he is to prevail. Sensing that the Arameans are the stronger of the two forces in the enemy coalition, he "selected" some of the "best troops" (the root is *bḥr* in both cases; see Notes on "chosen men" in 6:1 and comment on 1 Sam 24:2) and decided to lead them personally to fight against the Arameans (cf. Herzog and Gichon, *Battles of the Bible*, p. 83). The rest of the "men" (v.10; lit., "people," often used in the sense of "troops" in military contexts in the books of Samuel [cf. v.13]) he puts under the command of Abishai, who leads them against the Ammonites. "Deployed" (vv.9–10; cf. also 1 Sam 4:2) is the same verb of action (*'rk*) rendered "drew up" in v.8 and "formed" in v.17.

Joab's heartening speech to his brother (vv.11–12) uses the verb *ḥzq* ("be strong") twice in each verse (the second occurrence in v.12 is rendered "let us fight bravely"). Failing to size up one's opponent adequately, for whatever reason, can prove disastrous (cf. 1 Kings 20:23). Joab therefore stresses vital communication between the two commanders so that either can come to the other's "rescue" if necessary (v.11)—an outcome that the Ammonites and Arameans would be unable to accomplish with respect to each other (cf. v.19, where "to help" renders the same Heb. verb translated "to rescue" in v.11b).

Shouts and cheers calculated to raise the spirits of one's comrades and urge them on to success and victory have resounded from the earliest times. Joab's "Be strong" (v.12) is clearly reminiscent not only of the ringing words of encouragement of Moses and the Lord to Joshua and to all Israel (Deut 31:6–7, 23; Josh 1:6–7, 9) but also of those of the Transjordanian tribal leaders to Joshua (Josh 1:18). Joab's "let us fight bravely" echoes the Philistines' "be strong" in 1 Samuel 4:9 (same Heb. verbal form in both texts). Joab senses that he is responsible not only for the people of Israel but also for "the cities of our God" (for an attempt at identification with sites in southern Transjordan, cf. Raphael Giveon, " 'The Cities of Our God' [II Sam 10 12]," JBL 83, 4 [1964]: 415–16). Like Eli before him (see 1 Sam 3:18 and comment), Joab resigns himself to divine sovereignty: "The LORD will do what is good in his sight" (v.12).

Leading Israel's finest troops and convinced of the Lord's guidance, Joab marches into battle against the Arameans, who turn tail and flee (v.13). As soon as the Ammonites learn of Aram's headlong retreat, they flee to the protection of the walls of Rabbah (v.14). Apparently unable to pursue his advantage against the Ammonites by besieging the city—for now, at least—Joab returns to Jerusalem.

**15–19** That the Arameans are "routed by/before Israel" (v.15) is reminiscent of an earlier episode in which the Philistines were "routed before the Israelites" (1 Sam 7:10), especially since in both cases the Lord played the key role in the enemy retreat. Undeterred by what they consider a minor setback, however, the Arameans regroup their forces. Hadadezer (v.16; see 8:3 and comment) sends for Aramean reinforcements from beyond the eastern side of the Euphrates River (cf. Malamat, "The Kingdom of David & Solomon," p. 102), and his army commander Shobach (later killed in battle, v.18) leads them to Helam (possibly modern Alma, about seven miles north of Tob; cf. perhaps also Alema in 1 Macc 5:26, 35 [cf. Gordon, *I & II Samuel*, pp. 251–52]).

When David's intelligence network informs him of the exact location of the Aramean forces (v.17), he musters his entire army and crosses the Jordan River eastward to engage the Arameans in battle. Although the Arameans "regrouped" (v.15), the Israelites that David "gathered" (v.17) would prove to be more than a match for them (same Heb. verb). The contrast between David's leading his own army (cf. also 12:29) in this situation and his remaining behind in Jerusalem in the next episode (11:1) is noteworthy (cf. Lawlor, "Theology and Art," p. 195).

No braver than the Aramean mercenaries hired by the Ammonites, Hadadezer's reinforcements also flee from the Israelites (v.18; cf. v.13). This time, however, David and his men press their advantage and inflict huge numbers of casualties on the enemy. Unless an error in transcription has occurred, the discrepancy between "seven hundred of their charioteers" here (v.18) and "seven thousand of their charioteers" in the parallel passage (1 Chron 19:18) is perhaps best resolved by understanding *rekeḇ* in v.18 to mean "(men of) chariots" or "(men of) chariot divisions" and in 1 Chronicles 19:18 to mean "charioteers" (cf. Hodges, "Conflicts in the Biblical Account," p. 242 n. 6; Symon Patrick, p. 425). As to the "foot soldiers" in 1 Chronicles 19:18, where v.18 has the Hebrew word for "horsemen" (see NIV mg.), the two texts can be reconciled by assuming either that the terms were interchangeable (see comment on v.6) or that foot soldiers and horsemen "were mixed together . . .: And that in all there were slain forty thousand of them, part Horsemen, and part Footmen" (Symon Patrick, p. 425). In any event, these texts clearly distinguish not only between "charioteers" and "foot soldiers" (cf. also 8:4) but also between "charioteers" and "horsemen" (cf. the MT of v.18).

The forty thousand horsemen/foot soldiers (cf. also Judg 5:8) probably represents four armies of troops (cf. Segal, "Numerals," p. 12). Carlson makes the intriguing observation that the numbers four and seven, here boding ill for Aram, are reprised in the passing of judgment on David in chapter 12 (p. 146; cf. 12:6, 18).

Noting that the MT of v.19 features verbs with the same consonants (*wyr'w*)—though with different meanings ("saw," "were afraid")—at the beginning and near the end, Fokkelman (*King David*, p. 50) suggests the following (slightly modified) outline for the verse:

A. When saw the kings—
B. the vassals (*'bd*) of Hadadezer—
C. their defeat by Israel,
C′. they made peace with Israel
B′. and became subject (*'bd*) to them.
A′. Therefore were afraid the Arameans.

The "kings" refers back to v.8 (cf. 1 Chron 19:9, which makes the reference explicit). The defeat of the Arameans at the hands of Israel leaves them no option: They sue for peace (cf. Wiseman, "'Is It Peace?'" p. 313; cf. similarly Josh 10:1, 4; cf. also Deut 20:12; Josh 11:19) and become subject to the Israelites (cf. 8:6; for implications see comment on 8:2). By substituting "David" for "the Israelites" and "him" for "them," 1 Chronicles 19:19 highlights the personal role of the king in the proceedings (cf. also 22:44).

Aram's fear of going to the aid of the Ammonites after the present debacle may have sprung at least partly from the first-rate intelligence system that David enjoyed (cf. Hauer, "Foreign Intelligence," p. 98). In any case, the Ammonites, to their detriment, are now on their own (cf. 11:1; 12:26–31).

## Notes

9 Because בישראל (*byiśr'l*, "in Israel") follows immediately after a construct noun, many Hebrew MSS exhibit a *Qere* reading that omits the preposition (cf. BHS). It is not unusual, however, for a prepositional phrase to stand after a construct participle, as here (cf. Waltke and O'Connor, *Biblical Hebrew Syntax*, p. 165).

15–19 The MT of the final section of chapter 10 begins and ends similarly: וַיַּרְא אֲרָם (*wayyar' 'ᵃrām*, "After the Arameans saw," v.15); וַיִּרְאוּ אֲרָם (*wayyir'û 'ᵃrām*, "So the Arameans were afraid," v.19b). In addition v.19a echoes v.15a: "After/When . . . saw that they had been routed/defeated by Israel" (the same Heb. verb is contextually rendered "routed" in v.15 and "defeated" in v.19). The total effect is to form an *inclusio* that frames the literary unit. At the same time, v.15—"After . . . saw"—echoes the beginning of the previous section: "When . . . realized/saw" (see v.6 and comment; cf. Fokkelman, *King David*, pp. 48–49).

**15** Instead of the MT's ויאספו יחד (*wy'spw yḥd*, "they gathered themselves together"; NIV, "they regrouped"), two MSS read the final word in the verse as יחדו (*yḥdw;* cf. BHS). Although the translation remains the same in either case, it may well be that the MT intends the reading *yḥdw* by sharing the ו (*w*) with which the next verse begins (cf. Watson, "Shared Consonants," p. 531).

**16** הדדעזר (*hdd'zr*, "Hadadezer") is erroneously spelled הדרעזר (*hdr'zr*, "Hadarezer") in 1 Chron 18:3, 5, 7–10; 19:16, 19, doubtless due to similarity between the consonants ד (*d*) and ר (*r*). שׁוֹבַךְ (*šôḇaḵ*, "Shobach") is spelled alternately שׁוֹפַךְ (*šôpaḵ*, "Shophach") in 1 Chron 19:16, 18. The interchange between *b* and *p* is fairly widespread in all the Semitic languages (cf. Anton C.M. Blommerde, *Northwest Semitic Grammar and Job*, Biblica et Orientalia 22 [Rome: Pontifical Biblical Institute, 1969], pp. 5–6); cf. דְּבַשׁ (*dᵉḇaš*, "honey") with Akkadian *dišpu* ("honey"); נֹפֶת (*nōpeṯ*, "honey [from the comb]") with Akkadian *nūbtu* ("honeybee") and Ugaritic *nbt* ("honey") (cf. KB, pp. 203, 628).

---

## 3. *David's sin against Bathsheba*

### 11:1–5

[1]In the spring, at the time when kings go off to war, David sent Joab out with the king's men and the whole Israelite army. They destroyed the Ammonites and besieged Rabbah. But David remained in Jerusalem.

[2]One evening David got up from his bed and walked around on the roof of the palace. From the roof he saw a woman bathing. The woman was very beautiful, [3]and David sent someone to find out about her. The man said, "Isn't this Bathsheba, the daughter of Eliam and the wife of Uriah the Hittite?" [4]Then David sent messengers to get her. She came to him, and he slept with her. (She had purified herself from her uncleanness.) Then she went back home. [5]The woman conceived and sent word to David, saying, "I am pregnant."

Although chapter 11 is a discrete unit in a larger complex consisting of chapters 10–12 (see comment on 10:1–19), references to David, Joab, the Ammonites, Rabbah, and Jerusalem in 11:1 and in 12:26–31 make it likely that chapters 11–12 constitute an integral section within that complex. A close reading of the section produces the following chiastic outline (cf. similarly Samuel A. Meier, *The Historiography of Samuel* [master's thesis, Dallas Theological Seminary, 1978], pp. 8–9; for a comparable though slightly divergent analysis, cf. Sacon, " 'The Succession Narrative,' " pp. 42–44):

A. David sends Joab to besiege Rabbah (11:1).
  B. David sleeps with Bathsheba, who becomes pregnant (11:2–5).
    C. David has Uriah killed (11:6–17).
      D. Joab sends David a message (11:18–27a).
        E. The Lord is displeased with David (11:27b).
      D′. The Lord sends David a messenger (12:1–14).
    C′. The Lord strikes David's infant son, who dies (12:15–23).
  B′. David sleeps with Bathsheba, who becomes pregnant (12:24–25).
A′. Joab sends for David to besiege and capture Rabbah (12:26–31).

The contrast between the folly of David (as played out in chs. 11–12) and the "wisdom of Solomon" (1 Kings 10:4; cf. 1 Kings 4:29–34) is masterfully explicated by Carole Fontaine, "The Bearing of Wisdom on the Shape of 2 Samuel 11–12 and 1 Kings 3," JSOT 34 (1986): 61–77. In the course of his downward slide from temptation into sin, David manages to disobey three of the Ten Commandments: "You shall not covet your neighbor's wife"; "You shall not commit adultery"; "You shall not murder" (Exod 20:17, 14, 13). His execrable conduct in chapter 11 is a parade example of the truths expressed in James 1:14–15: "Each one is tempted when, by his own evil desire, he is dragged away and enticed. Then, after desire has conceived, it gives birth to sin; and sin, when it is full-grown, gives birth to death."

**1** "The story of David and Bathsheba has long aroused both dismay and astonishment; dismay that King David, with his manifest piety, could stoop to such an act, and astonishment that the Bible narrates it with such unrelenting openness, although the person involved is David, the great and celebrated king, the type of the Messiah" (Hertzberg, p. 309). David's sin against Bathsheba, while described in the most laconic fashion imaginable, is none the less significant for all that. Indeed, "the David-Bathsheba episode . . . is pivotal to our understanding of his reign" (Rosenberg, p. 125).

The story, continuing the account begun in chapter 10, is set "in the spring, at the time when kings go off to war" (v.1; cf. 1 Kings 20:22, 26). "The month of March, named after Mars the Roman god of war, affords a parallel" (Gordon, *I & II Samuel*, p. 252). Springtime, which marks the end of the rainy season in the Middle East, assures that roads will be in good condition (or at least passable), that there will be plenty of fodder for war horses and pack animals, and that an army on the march will be able to raid the fields for food (cf. de Vaux, AIs, pp. 190, 251). Less likely is the theory that "the spring" (lit., "the [re]turn of the year") in this case refers to "a particular historical date (one year after the kings of Aram went forth to join the Ammonites against Israel)" (an option proposed by Sternberg, p. 194; cf. 10:6; 1 Chron 19:9).

David "sent" (v.1; for the importance of *šlḥ* in chs. 10–12, see comment on 10:2, and for its importance in ch. 11 in particular, cf. Uriel Simon, "The Poor Man's Ewe-Lamb: An Example of a Juridical Parable," *Biblica* 48, 2 [1967]: 209) his army commander Joab, his "men" (lit., "servants," doubtless the mercenary troops), and the "whole Israelite army" (the tribal muster) to continue the battle against Ammon. The result is the mass slaughter of the Ammonites and the siege of Rabbah, their capital city (see comment on 10:3), the reduction and capture of which is yet to come (cf. 12:26–29).

The narrator thus leaves the impression that every able-bodied man in Israel goes to war—everyone, that is, except the king himself: "But David remained in Jerusalem." The contrast between David and his men could hardly be expressed in starker terms. Staying home in such situations was not David's usual practice, of course (cf. 5:2; 8:1–14; 10:17). Indeed, leading his troops into battle was expected to be the major external activity of an ancient Near Eastern ruler (see 1 Sam 8:5–6, 20 and comments). Although therefore reprehensible in itself, David's conduct on this occasion opens the way for royal behavior that is more despicable still.

**2–5** Yet another contrast is now in evidence: Although King David's army marches off to war "at the time when kings" do so (v.1), King David himself gets out of bed "one evening" (v.2; lit., "at the time of evening"). Perhaps because of the oppressive heat of a spring sirocco, he has apparently lengthened his afternoon siesta into the cooler part of the day (cf. Gen 24:11). Getting up "from" (lit., "from upon") his bed and taking a stroll, "from" (lit., "from upon") the roof of his palace he sees a woman bathing. As Bailey notes, the other occurrences of *hthlk* ("walked around") used of David occur in contexts with a negative flavor, and we are therefore probably justified in assuming that here as well "some questionable conduct is about to occur" (*David in Love and War,* p. 86; cf. 1 Sam 23:13 ["moving from place to place"]; 25:15 ["were"]; 30:31 ["roamed"]). The roof of the royal palace in Jerusalem would later become the focus of yet another sinful act (cf. 16:22; cf. similarly Dan 4:29–30; see also 1 Sam 9:25–26 and comment).

"Remember all the commands of the LORD, that you may obey them and not prostitute yourselves by going after the lusts of your own hearts and eyes" (Num 15:39). Failing to heed the warning expressed in that and/or similar texts, David "saw" a woman (v.2) and wanted her. Concerning Matthew 5:29, Bruce observes that "Matthew places this saying immediately after Jesus's words about adultery in the heart, and that is probably the original context, for it provides a ready example of how a man's eye could lead him into sin" (*The Hard Sayings of Jesus,* p. 54).

The woman David sees is "very beautiful," which translates a Hebrew phrase reserved for people of striking physical appearance (e.g., Rebekah [Gen 24:16; 26:7], Vashti [Esth 1:11], Esther [Esth 2:7], and—not to discriminate against men—David himself [see comment on 1 Sam 16:12, where a cognate Heb. expression is used]). The woman David sees is bathing, and the sight of her naked body arouses him. His virgin-conceived descendant would one day condemn such voyeurism for the sin that it is: "Anyone who looks at a woman lustfully has already committed adultery with her in his heart" (Matt 5:28).

For now, however, the heat of an unusually warm spring day has not only extended David's normal siesta period and then brought him outdoors for a refreshing walk on the palace roof; it has also forced the woman to bathe outside to escape the suffocatingly hot atmosphere of her house. Such heat makes people more susceptible to sexual encounters (cf. H. Hirsch Cohen, "David and Bathsheba," *Journal of Bible and Religion* 33, 2 [1965]: 144), and in his vulnerability David succumbs. Continuing the use of a key verb as established earlier in the chapter, the narrator states that David "sent" (v.3; see comment on v.1) someone to find out about the woman and then, having learned her identity, "sent" (v.4) messengers to get her.

In addition to simply stating her given name—Bathsheba ("Daughter of an Oath" or "Daughter of Seven" [i.e., perhaps "Seventh Daughter/Child"])—the man sent to identify the woman tells David that she is the daughter of Eliam (given the variant name Ammiel in 1 Chron 3:5; for the meaning of names, see comment on 9:4) and the wife of Uriah the Hittite (v.3). The rhetorical "Isn't this Bathsheba?" perhaps intentionally echoes the earlier "Isn't this David?" (cf. 1 Sam 21:11; 29:3, 5). The reference to Eliam probably reflects Bathsheba's upper-class pedigree, because Eliam was the son of Ahithophel (23:34), who was in turn David's counselor (see 15:12 and comment; cf. Hayim Tadmor, "Traditional Institutions and the Monarchy: Social and Political Tensions in the Time of David and Solomon," in *Studies in the Period of David and Solomon,* p. 247). Since Eliam was one of David's warriors and thus perhaps a foreign mercenary, and since Bathsheba is listed along with the pagan ancestresses of Jesus (Matt 1:3–6), we "have to reckon with the possibility that [she] was of non-Israelite origin" (Jones, pp. 43–44; cf. Fontaine, "The Bearing of Wisdom," p. 66).

As for Uriah the Hittite, in spite of his mercenary status as another of David's warriors (cf. 23:39) he was apparently a worshiper of the Lord (his name probably means "Yahweh Is My Light"; for the less likely possibility that it is of Hurrian derivation and is related to that of Araunah the Jebusite, cf. C.J. Mullo Weir, "Nuzi," in *Archaeology and Old Testament Study,* ed. D. Winton Thomas [Oxford: Clarendon, 1967], p. 82). Like Ahimelech the Hittite before him (see 1 Sam 26:6 and comment), Uriah depends on his master David for sustenance and support. In return he gives total loyalty to "king, nation, and fellow warriors. . . . This loyalty of a foreigner is emphasized twice more in the behavior of Ittai and Hushai" (Perdue, " 'Is There Anyone Left of the House of Saul . . . ?' " p. 76; cf. chs. 15–18). An attempt to define Uriah's Hittite origins is made, among others, by Richard H. Beal: "Although Uriah may have been a free-lance soldier from one of the numerous north-Syrian Syro-Hittite states, he more likely was a descendant of those Hittite refugees who more than a century earlier had settled in the land of Palestine, in flight from the collapsing Hittite Empire" ("The Hittites After the Empire's Fall," *Biblical Illustrator* 10, 1 [1983]: 81).

It is the wife of this trusted servant that David is about to violate, and v.4 mercifully tells the story in the briefest possible compass. Master of all he surveys, David has everything—and yet does not have enough (for a useful comparison with Adam's/Everyman's sin in the Garden of Eden, cf. Walter Vogels, "David's Greatness in His Sin and Repentance," *The Way* 15, 4 [1975]: 245). David sends messengers to "get" (lit., "take") her. "The ironic contrast with 2 Sam 2–4 is marked: the king who was content to be given his kingdom must seize by force (against Uriah if not Bathsheba) a wife" (Gunn, "David and the Gift," p. 19; cf. also p. 35). Upon being summoned, Bathsheba "came to him, and he slept with her" (v.4; cf. the same Heb. idiom in Gen 19:34 ["go in and lie with him"]; the verb *bô'* ["enter," "come in"] is often used by itself [governing various prepositions] with the nuance "have sexual intercourse," although a man is almost always the subject [cf. BDB, p. 98]). The parallel section near the end of the narrative repeats the scene, but this time David is the subject of both verbs: "He went [lit., 'came'] to her and lay with her" (12:24). If in the latter case Bathsheba is already David's wife, in the former the relationship is blatantly adulterous. "Gratifying the desire conceived as he walked about on his palace roof (*wayyithallēk,* 11:2), David lies with the wife of a trusted and trusting servant (*wayyiškab 'immāh,* 2 Sam. 11.4), thereby rejecting the teachings of wisdom on adultery in Proverbs 6.22, teachings which 'will lead you when you walk (*b*ᵉ*hithalleka̅*)' and 'watch over you when you lie down (*b*ᵉ*šokb*ᵉ*kā*)' " (Fontaine, "The Bearing of Wisdom," p. 65).

The parenthetic sentence—"She had purified herself from her uncleanness"—is a circumstantial clause (S.R. Driver, *Notes on the Books of Samuel,* p. 289) that describes "Bathsheba's condition at the time of the action, and is thus to be rendered in English by a perfect tense (i.e. it is something that happened before but about which the reader only learns now)" (Berlin, "Characterization in Biblical Narrative," p. 80). Its purpose is

> to inform the reader that Bathsheba was clearly not pregnant when she came to David, since she had just been "purified from her uncleanness". Shortly thereafter she found that she was, and that leaves no doubt that the child is David's, since her husband had been out of town during the interlude between the bath and her visit to the palace. Moreover, the phrase may also alert the reader to the fact that Bathsheba was, at this time in her cycle, most likely to become pregnant. (ibid.)

(See also Simon, "The Poor Man's Ewe-Lamb," p. 213; Fokkelman, *King David,* p. 52; cf. already W. Robertson Smith, *Kinship and Marriage in Early Arabia,* pp. 275–76.) Referring to her menstrual period (cf. Lev 15:25–26, 30; 18:19; Ezek 36:17), Bathsheba's "uncleanness" is ceremonial rather than hygienic—although the two are not necessarily unrelated (cf. the English proverb "Cleanliness is next to godliness"; cf. also the Mishnaic saying "Heedfulness leads to physical cleanliness, and physical cleanliness leads to ritual purity" [*Soṭah* 9.15], quoted by Neufeld, p. 64).

Verse 5 begins and ends with the same verb, thus emphatically implicating David: "The woman conceived [lit., 'became pregnant'] . . . 'I am pregnant.'" Of all the fateful conceptions recorded in the OT (cf. Hagar, Gen 16:4–5; Lot's daughters, Gen 19:36; Rebekah, Gen 25:21; Tamar, Gen 38:18; Jochebed, Exod 2:2), Bathsheba's ranks near the top of the list in terms of future repercussions. As Lawlor notes, the message she sends to David—"I am pregnant"—are her "only words in the entire narrative. . . . The only recorded speech of Bathsheba, brief though it is, sets in motion a course of action which ultimately results in her husband's death" ("Theology and Art," p. 197).

## Notes

---

1 "Kings" renders the *Qere,* which assumes a reading מלכים (*mlkym*) along with many Hebrew MSS and several versions (cf. BHS). The MT's מלאכים (*ml'kym,* "messengers") is clearly inferior (though not without its supporters; cf. Fokkelman, *King David,* pp. 50–51), especially in light of the unequivocal testimony of the parallel text (1 Chron 20:1) and of the fact that "it applies the time-indicator to the season of the year appropriate for campaigning and not to the sending of messengers, an operation in which the seasonal time factor is of no significance" (Simon, "The Poor Man's Ewe-Lamb," p. 209 n. 1). Rosenberg suggests—more cleverly than convincingly, however—that the two readings may be due to studied and deliberate ambiguity, in which "we find ourselves with an oddly convoluted inversion of kingly function in the king's preference of agents to represent him. In this transition of a sedentary monarchy, the agent within the king and the king within the agent seem at war with each other" (p. 126).

2 A pottery figurine of a woman bathing in an oval bathtub, found at Aczib in 1942 and dating from the eighth or seventh century B.C., illustrates the domestic bathtub of the kind that Bathsheba might have used. Royal families and the wealthy also had luxurious bathrooms in their elaborate houses (cf. Neufeld, pp. 41, 51–52).

4 The NIV margin is contextually invalid (see comment above). The proposal of Martin Krause, that Lev 15:19–28 helps us to pinpoint David's sexual liaison with Bathsheba to a time subsequent to the fourteenth day after she began menstruating ("II Sam 11 4 und das Konzeptionsoptimum," ZAW 95 [1983]: 434–37), is somewhat too precise.

---

### 4. *The murder of Uriah*

#### 11:6–27

[6]So David sent this word to Joab: "Send me Uriah the Hittite." And
Joab sent him to David. [7]When Uriah came to him, David asked him how
Joab was, how the soldiers were and how the war was going. [8]Then
David said to Uriah, "Go down to your house and wash your feet." So
Uriah left the palace, and a gift from the king was sent after him. [9]But

Uriah slept at the entrance to the palace with all his master's servants and did not go down to his house.

10When David was told, "Uriah did not go home," he asked him, "Haven't you just come from a distance? Why didn't you go home?"

11Uriah said to David, "The ark and Israel and Judah are staying in tents, and my master Joab and my lord's men are camped in the open fields. How could I go to my house to eat and drink and lie with my wife? As surely as you live, I will not do such a thing!"

12Then David said to him, "Stay here one more day, and tomorrow I will send you back." So Uriah remained in Jerusalem that day and the next. 13At David's invitation, he ate and drank with him, and David made him drunk. But in the evening Uriah went out to sleep on his mat among his master's servants; he did not go home.

14In the morning David wrote a letter to Joab and sent it with Uriah. 15In it he wrote, "Put Uriah in the front line where the fighting is fiercest. Then withdraw from him so he will be struck down and die."

16So while Joab had the city under siege, he put Uriah at a place where he knew the strongest defenders were. 17When the men of the city came out and fought against Joab, some of the men in David's army fell; moreover, Uriah the Hittite was dead.

18Joab sent David a full account of the battle. 19He instructed the messenger: "When you have finished giving the king this account of the battle, 20the king's anger may flare up, and he may ask you, 'Why did you get so close to the city to fight? Didn't you know they would shoot arrows from the wall? 21Who killed Abimelech son of Jerub-Besheth? Didn't a woman throw an upper millstone on him from the wall, so that he died in Thebez? Why did you get so close to the wall?' If he asks you this, then say to him, 'Also, your servant Uriah the Hittite is dead.'"

22The messenger set out, and when he arrived he told David everything Joab had sent him to say. 23The messenger said to David, "The men overpowered us and came out against us in the open, but we drove them back to the entrance to the city gate. 24Then the archers shot arrows at your servants from the wall, and some of the king's men died. Moreover, your servant Uriah the Hittite is dead."

25David told the messenger, "Say this to Joab: 'Don't let this upset you; the sword devours one as well as another. Press the attack against the city and destroy it.' Say this to encourage Joab."

26When Uriah's wife heard that her husband was dead, she mourned for him. 27After the time of mourning was over, David had her brought to his house, and she became his wife and bore him a son. But the thing David had done displeased the LORD.

As in the earlier verses of chapter 11 (vv.1, 3, 4, 5), so also in vv.6–27, the verb *šlḥ* ("to send") continues to be prominent (vv.6 [ter], 12, 14, 18, 22, 27 ["had her brought"]) as an index of royal power (see comments on v.1 and introduction to 10:1–19). But another verb now rears its ugly head: *mwt* ("to die," vv.15, 17, 21 [bis], 24 [bis], 26)—the ever-present potential fate of the powerless victims of royal sending run amok. Uriah the Hittite, loyal subject and servant of King David, is soon to die by regnal fiat, his only crime being that he gets in the way of royal lust and power through no fault of his own.

**6–17** Early in Israel's history an Egyptian pharaoh had concocted a three-phase plan to solve what he considered a serious problem: the strength and large numbers of Israelites in his kingdom. Each phase was more ruthless than the preceding: (1) The Egyptian slave masters oppressed the Israelites with forced labor (Exod 1:11–14). When that did not work, (2) the Hebrew midwives were commanded to kill every newborn Hebrew male infant (Exod 1:15–21). When the midwives disobeyed the Pharaoh's edict, (3) all the Egyptians were ordered to throw every newborn male into the Nile (Exod 1:22).

In a similar way, David hatches a three-phase scheme to solve the serious problem of Bathsheba's pregnancy, each phase more ruthless than the preceding. But although the Pharaoh's best efforts failed, David succeeds—temporarily at least—in concealing his sin. Vogels ("David's Greatness," p. 246) refers to David's effort as a series of three "cover-ups": a "clean" one (vv.6–11), a "dirty" one (vv.12–13), and a "criminal" one (vv.14–17).

As Bathsheba had sent word to David informing him of the problem (v.5), David now sends word to Joab to begin the process of seeking a solution (v.6). At David's command Joab sends him "Uriah the Hittite," the full description once again underscoring Uriah's mercenary status and therefore presumably also his loyalty to David (see comment on v.3). Having been "sent" for by David, Uriah "came to him" (v.7), just as Bathsheba had come under similar circumstances (v.4).

David begins his conversation with Uriah in an apparently solicitous and cordial way by asking about the welfare/progress (*šālôm;* see 1 Sam 10:4; 17:22 and comments) of Joab, the soldiers, and the war (v.7). Such queries by the king would later return to haunt him (cf. 18:29, 32, where "safe" renders the same Heb. idiom containing the word *šālôm*).

Ostensibly satisfied concerning how things are going on the battlefield, David tells Uriah to go down to his house and "wash" his "feet" (v.8). Although usually an expression describing an act affording refreshment and relaxation in a land where dusty roads are the rule (see 1 Sam 25:41 and comment; cf. also Luke 7:44; 1 Tim 5:10), the phrase may well be intended here as a double entendre, given the euphemistic use of "feet" in the sense of "genitals" (cf. Exod 4:25; Deut 28:57 [NIV, "womb"]; Isa 7:20 [NIV, "legs"]). David would thus be suggesting to Uriah that he "enjoy his wife sexually" (Gale A. Yee, "'Fraught With Background': Literary Ambiguity in II Samuel 11," Int 42, 3 [1988]: 245; cf. Simon, "The Poor Man's Ewe-Lamb," p. 214). Thus Bathsheba's washing ("bathing," v.2; same Heb. verb) and Uriah's washing would both involve or eventuate in sexual cohabitation.

In any event, Uriah "left" (v.8; lit., "went out," *yṣ'*) the palace, and a royal gift "was sent" (lit., "went out," not *šlḥ*, the usual verb translated "send"; see v.1 and comment) after him. *Maś'ēṯ* (lit., "that which rises/is lifted"; cf. BDB, p. 673, for its various nuances) means "gift" in other contexts as well, especially where granted by a superior to an inferior (cf. Gen 43:34 ["portion(s)"]; Esth 2:18; Jer 40:5 ["present"]).

"And Uriah slept" (v.9; possible tr.). "For a moment it looks as though the king's plan is going to work, but the text immediately veers around" (Sternberg, p. 200). The ambiguous conjunction that begins the verse must therefore be rendered adversatively: "But Uriah slept" (thus correctly NIV)—not with Bathsheba, as David had hoped, but "at the entrance to the palace with all his master's [doubtless David's] servants." Foiling David's plan (cf. v.8), Uriah steadfastly refuses to "go down to his house" (v.9; cf. also vv.10 ["go home" (bis)], 13 ["go home"]; same Heb. expression).

The next day, when David learns that Uriah did not in fact go down to his house (and therefore did not sleep with his wife), he obviously wants to know why (v.10). He reminds Uriah that he has just come from a "distance" (lit., "way"), a term that sometimes means "military campaign" (cf. Judg 4:9 [NIV mg., "expedition"]; 1 Sam 21:5 ["missions"]; 1 Kings 8:44 ["wherever," lit., "on the way/campaign where"]). Thus "David's importunings to Uriah . . . can also be taken to reflect the celibacy devolving on those going into battle" (Simon, "The Poor Man's Ewe-Lamb," p. 214). Uriah's retort in v.11, then, becomes "doubly trenchant, if we take it not as an open defiance but as an indirect, unconscious rebuke. The sting of the words is accordingly palpable only to David. Uriah is not ready to do legitimately what [David] has done criminally" (ibid.; on the question of whether Uriah might be expected to have known about David's liaison with Bathsheba, cf. esp. Sternberg, pp. 201–9).

Just as David and his men had always "kept themselves from women" whenever they set out to do battle (1 Sam 21:4–5; see comment there), so now Uriah refuses to sleep with his wife, even while on a brief furlough from military duty (v.11). Unlike David, who "remained" (*yšb*) in Jerusalem (see v.1 and comment), the ark (for the practice of carrying the ark of the covenant out to the battlefield, see comment on 1 Sam 4:3) and the tribal musters from Israel and Judah (equivalent to the "whole Israelite army" in v.1; see comment there) are "staying" (*yšb*) at military campsites. NIV's "in tents" (*bassukkôṯ*) should doubtless be rendered "in Succoth" (as in the NIV mg. at 1 Kings 20:12, 16). Succoth (modern Tell Deir Alla, a Transjordanian site almost forty miles northeast of Jerusalem) was evidently the forward base that served as a suitable staging area for Israel's battles against the Ammonites (and against the Arameans as well; cf. Yadin, *The Art of Warfare*, pp. 274–75, where additional reasons—not the least of which is the fact that the ark was ensconced in an *'ōhel* ["tent"; see 6:17 and comment] rather than in a *sukkāh* ["hut"]—are given for rejecting the translation "tents" in this context; cf. also McCarter, *II Samuel*, p. 287). Although "master" and "lord(s)" (v.11) render the same Hebrew noun, the NIV is probably correct in distinguishing the first (Joab) from the second (David) since "my lord's men" (lit., "the servants of my lord") are in all likelihood the same as "the king's men" (lit., "his servants," the mercenary corps) in v.1 (see comment there). Thus each unit in v.11 (with the exception of the ark) has its correspondent in v.1 (as might be expected prima facie). It is understandable that Uriah would speak of Joab as "my master Joab" (v.11), which "is indeed how one makes a deferential reference to one's [immediate] commanding officer" (Sternberg, p. 204).

In light of the fact that David's entire army is on the battlefield, how could Uriah in good conscience "eat" and "drink" and "lie" with his wife (v.11; all three verbs would be used again with telling effect in Nathan's rebuke [see comment on 12:3])? David had already "slept/lain" with Uriah's wife (v.4; same Heb. verb as in v.11)—a matter about which Uriah probably has no knowledge—while Uriah himself has "slept" and would "sleep" only among David's servants (vv.9, 13). Indeed, both David and Bathsheba had sinned when she "came [*bw'*] to him, and he slept [*škb*] with her" (v.4), while Uriah refuses to "go" (*bw'*) to his house and "lie" (*škb*) with his wife (v.11; cf. similarly Fokkelman, *King David*, p. 55). That he calls Bathsheba "my wife" could hardly have failed to rebuke David, who had callously violated the relationship between Uriah and the person most precious to him.

Uriah concludes his statement to David by emphatically rejecting the king's offer. Taking a solemn oath, which translates literally as "By your life, and by the life of your soul" (NIV condenses the two expressions into one: "As surely as you live"; cf. similarly 14:19; 15:21; see also comments on 1 Sam 1:26; 20:3), Uriah swears that he will not so much as think of doing the unthinkable. "Uriah's name turns out to be Yahwist, after all. In the heart of the imperial phalanges we find an orthodox Israelite, quietly observing the wartime soldier's ban against conjugal relations (cf. I Sam. 21:4–7)" (Rosenberg, p. 132).

Failing in his first attempt to cover up his sin, David tries again: " 'Stay [*yšb*] here one more day'. . . . So Uriah remained [*yšb*]" (v.12)—indeed, against his better judgment Uriah "remained in Jerusalem" at the behest of the king who had earlier (perhaps selfishly) done the same thing (v.1), and with disastrous results.

Although Uriah will not go to his own house to eat and drink (v.11), he has no such scruples in the king's house (v.13). When David gets him drunk, he assumes that Uriah's inhibitions will be overcome (cf. Hab 2:15) and that he will automatically go home, sleep with Bathsheba, and thus absolve David of any charge of her child's paternity. At first it appears that David's plan will succeed: "Indeed, 'in the evening he went out to lie on his bed' [v.13]—on his bed at home? With his wife? No, on his bed of the past two nights, 'with the servants of his lord, and did not go down to his house'" (Sternberg, p. 201).

His second attempt at covering up his affair with Bathsheba having failed, David senses that he has exhausted his options and so decides to have Uriah killed. The narrative is ambiguous concerning what David thinks Uriah knows (for a penetrating discussion of possible hypotheses, cf. Sternberg, pp. 209–13). In any event, David takes no chances: In the morning he "wrote a letter to Joab and sent it with [*wayyišlaḥ beyaḏ;* lit., 'sent by the hand of'; see comment on 12:25] Uriah" (v.14). Doubtless unknown to him, Uriah carries to Joab his own death warrant.

Comparison of the contents of David's letter to those of the infamous Jezebel's letters concerning Naboth (cf. 1 Kings 21:9–11) is not out of place, since in both cases an innocent man is executed at an Israelite monarch's whim. David orders Joab to put Uriah in the front line of battle against the Ammonites where "the fighting is fiercest" (v.15)—a phrase that echoes the "bitter war" against the Philistines in the days of Saul (see 1 Sam 14:52 and comment; same Heb. expression). Uriah is then to be abandoned to his fate: He will be "struck down [*nkh*] and die."

"Cursed is the man who kills [*nkh*] his neighbor secretly [*bassāṯer*]," intones Deuteronomy 27:24. David "struck down [*nkh*]" Uriah and took his wife (12:9), and these things were done "in secret [*bassāṯer*]" (12:12). The implication is obvious: David's heinous actions are punishable under the divine curse (cf. Carlson, p. 141).

At this point in the account, however, Uriah is still alive. When Joab receives David's letter, he recognizes the fact that to isolate Uriah as the only fatality in the attack would cast suspicion on David's motives. He therefore "makes improvements on the plan, implementing it in spirit rather than to the letter. . . . He realized that the saving in casualties, however desirable in itself, is also the weak spot in the king's plan. It is better for many to fall, he decides, than for the conspiracy to stand revealed" (Sternberg, p. 214). Joab thus besieges "the city" (v.16)—that is, Rabbah, the Ammonite capital (cf. v.1)—and puts Uriah at a "place" where its best troops are defending it (for "place" as a technical term in battle narratives, cf. Josh 8:19 ["position"]; Judg 20:33). But he also sends other "men" (*'ām,* lit., "people," a term often used in the sense of "soldiers" in military contexts; see comment on 1 Sam 11:11) in David's "army" (lit., "servants" and thus mercenaries, like Uriah himself; see comment on v.1) to accompany Uriah into the heat of battle (v.17).

And so it is that "some" (vv.17, 24) of the mercenaries are sacrificed so that one, relatively unnoticed, might die. The literary unit closes with David's criminal purpose finally accomplished—"Uriah the Hittite was dead"—a doleful refrain repeated in the rest of chapter 11, each time emphasizing not only a brave warrior's mercenary status but also his unswerving loyalty to his liege lord: "Your servant Uriah the Hittite is dead" (v.21), "Your servant Uriah the Hittite is dead" (v.24; cf. also v.26). The poignancy and pathos of his death are not dimmed by the matter-of-fact way in which the reports of it—whether by the narrator, by Joab, or by Joab's messenger—are treated as an addendum: "Moreover" (v.17), "Also" (v.21), "Moreover" (v.24; in each case *gam*).

**18–27a** "Joab has performed his task so well that he got Uriah killed without giving the show away. Now he must effectively disguise his report to the king, concealing from the messenger the true purpose of his mission. While the messenger believes that he is carrying news about the abortive battle, Joab smuggles into the message the crucial item about Uriah's death" (Sternberg, p. 215). Sending a complete "account of the battle" (vv.18–19) to David through a messenger, Joab warns the latter that the king's anger may "flare up" (v.20; same Heb. verb used of the Lord's anger in 2 Chron 36:16 ["was aroused"])—presumably when he learns of the high casualty count. Indeed, says Joab, David may ask a series of questions designed to reveal the stupidity (in his opinion) of Joab's battle plans against Rabbah.

Sternberg may well be correct in his evaluation of Joab's hypothetical reconstruction of David's words as suggesting "a picture of a general who not only gives his messenger the contents of the king's anticipated response but also acts the part of the king, expressively mimicking the intonations and speech patterns of royalty in rage" (p. 219). At the same time, however, the potential response as recorded is a literary masterpiece in miniature, chiastically arranged:

A. Why did you get so close (*ngš*) to the city (v.20b)?
  B. Didn't you know they would shoot from (*m'l*) the wall (v.20c)?
    C. Who killed Abimelech (v.21a)?
  B′. Didn't a woman throw something from (*m'l*) the wall (v.21b)?
A′. Why did you get so close (*ngš*) to the wall (v.21c)?

David's supposed questions thus focus attention on the central issue in the parallel: "Who (really) killed Abimelech" (= Uriah)?

To get too near a city wall in ancient times was to flirt with mortal danger, since arrows and other missiles rained down from protected positions. Joab thus senses that when David hears about the casualties he will want to know why his men needlessly risked their lives. In fact, Joab surmises, David—an acknowledged expert in military lore—will probably also remind Joab's messenger of the story of the death of Abimelech son of Gideon, who lost his life because of his foolhardiness (v.21; cf. Judg 9:50–54). In the days of the judges, during the siege of Thebez (exact location unknown, although probably a few miles northeast of Shechem; for possible identifications, cf. Aharoni, *Land of the Bible,* p. 265) "a woman dropped [*hšlyk;* cf. v.21 ("throw")] an upper millstone on [Abimelech's] head and cracked his skull" (Judg 9:53).

As Sternberg notes (pp. 219–22), the parallels between Abimelech on the one hand and Uriah and David on the other are multifaceted. Abimelech and Uriah are "struck down/killed" (*nkh,* vv.15, 21) because of a woman—and David falls because of a woman as well. The story of Abimelech conjures up the image of disgrace brought on royalty because of a woman's hand and an attempt to cover up the disgrace for fear that rumors would spread among the people (cf. Judg 9:53–54). Of course

> David, God's anointed and a great king, is otherwise poles apart from a petty thug like Abimelech. . . . [But] that David is likened to Abimelech has—because of the very distance between them—the effect of diminishing his image. The more so

> since Abimelech fell at a woman's hands while at the head of his army: David falls at a woman's hands precisely because he plays truant from war. (Sternberg, pp. 221–22)

Arriving in Jerusalem, Joab's messenger tells David "everything" his master has sent him to communicate (v.22). He apparently elaborates somewhat on the words of Joab, however, by giving (or concocting) a few additional details. The powerful Ammonites, says the messenger, "came out" from Rabbah (v.23; cf. v.17) to engage the Israelites in "the open," but David's men were able to drive them back to "the entrance to the city gate" (for the tactical significance of these locations, see 10:8 and comment). If wisdom influence has made an impact on chapters 11–12, the observation of Fontaine is apropos: "Unlike Wisdom at the gate, bringing life through her teachings (Prov. 1.20ff.; 8.1ff.), the woman at the wall of Thebez brings death, and the allusion to the incident conjures up a feminine shadow of death hovering over Uriah at the gate of Rabbah (2 Sam. 11.23b), all because of his failure to stand father to David's child" ("The Bearing of Wisdom," p. 65).

As the messenger completes the fulfillment of his mission to David, his words remind us that the tragedy has come full circle: The archers' death volley has been fired "from" (*mēʿal,* lit., "from upon") the wall (v.24; cf. also vv. 20–21), echoing the same prepositional phrase used earlier in the chapter (see comment on v.2). And it is not the guilty king, safe in his fortress palace in Jerusalem, who suffers; the enemy's arrows find their mark in his innocent "servants" (v.24), in his innocent "men" (lit., "servants"), who are sacrificed so that David can inconspicuously dispose of his ultimate target, his "servant" Uriah the Hittite.

The verbal element of the initial clause of David's response to Joab through the messenger—"May this thing/matter not be evil in your eyes" (v.25; NIV, "Don't let this upset you")—reverberates suggestively throughout the various ambivalent attitudes toward monarchy in the books of Samuel. The Israelite elders' original request for a king had "displeased" Samuel (see 1 Sam 8:6 and comment), and David's popularity had "galled" Saul (1 Sam 18:8). In the present context, although David tries to placate Joab with the assurance that the casualties among the mercenaries should not be allowed to "upset" him, "the thing David had done displeased the LORD" (v.27; cf. also 12:9; for additional examples, cf. Carlson, p. 151 and n. 3).

Temporarily oblivious to the divine displeasure, David resorts to a platitude: "The sword devours one as well as another" (see 2:26 and comment; see also comment on 18:8 [lit., "the forest devoured more lives . . . than the sword devoured"]). From his own selfish perspective the king is basically saying that what is done is done, that it cannot be helped, and that innocent people will often get caught in the crossfire when vital goals are pursued. What is more, David further masks his true concerns by telling the messenger to authorize Joab to "press" the attack against Rabbah (cf. in addition 12:26–31) as part of the royal message that will "encourage" him (v.25; same Heb. verb).

When the news of Uriah's death reaches Bathsheba, she mourns for him— probably with more feeling than formality (cf. v.26, which reads literally "When Uriah's wife heard that her husband Uriah was dead, she mourned for her husband," a sentence that also implicitly condemns David's adultery by stressing three times the husband-wife relationship between Uriah and Bathsheba). Although David had "mourned and wept and fasted" for the fallen Saul and Jonathan and their troops, as well as for Israel as a whole (see 1:12 and comment), unlike Bathsheba he apparently sheds no tears for Uriah (not to mention the other mercenaries).

The husband of Bathsheba now dead and the period of her mourning now over, the way is open for David to bring her to his house. The Hebrew phrase translated "had her brought" (v.27) is literally "sent and collected her" and emphasizes the abuse of royal power that David is increasingly willing to exercise (see comments on v.1; 10:1–19; the same Heb. verb is rendered "took . . . into his service" in 1 Sam 14:52 [see comment there]).

Bathsheba becomes David's wife, and in due course a son is born of their earlier adulterous act. That the child is not named is perhaps because "his life was so short and he died within seven days after birth [see 12:18 and comment], which was before the time for giving him a name (cf. Lk. 1:59)" (Jones, p. 112). Although short-lived and unnamed, however, he would not be unloved during the days of his fatal illness (cf. 12:16–24).

**27b** Serving as the hinge of chapters 11–12 (see comment on 11:1–5), v.27b looks backward to v.25 (see comment there) and forward to 12:9. It thus functions not as a later "redactional link" (as suggested by Jones, p. 96) but takes its rightful place as an integral part of the original narrative.

David's third cover-up, the death of Uriah, "is not the end: the last word belongs to Someone else: 'But what David had done displeased Yahweh'" (Vogels, "David's Greatness," p. 247). This is the only reference to "the LORD" in the entire chapter, but it is nevertheless ironic that "Yahweh does not act. Rather, 'the deed' . . . is subject of the verb. The deed did evil 'in the eyes of Yahweh.' Yahweh does not act or move or intervene or assert himself. *He is simply there*" (Brueggemann, "On Trust and Freedom," p. 10; italics his). The Lord's people are confident that he himself will "do what is good in his sight" (10:12), even though all too often they do the reverse (cf. Gen 38:10; Isa 59:15 ["was displeased"]). David would later confess that his sin with Bathsheba is known to God and is therefore deserving of divine judgment: "Against you, you only, have I sinned/ and done what is evil in your sight" (Ps 51:4).

## Notes

---

**20** W.F. Albright reads *it-ta[g](!)-šu* in a damaged line on a cuneiform letter found at Taanach by Ernst Sellin in 1903–4 ("A Prince of Taanach in the Fifteenth Century B.C.," BA 94 [1944]: 22 n. 63). If his reading is correct (which seems likely in context), the resulting phrase—*ittagšu ana ālāni*—means literally "gets close to the cities" and reflects the same idiom as נִגַּשְׁתֶּם אֶל־הָעִיר (*niggaštem 'el-hā'îr*, "you get close to the city"). Thus the Taanach phrase, though ostensibly written in Akkadian, exhibits a strong Canaanite overlay and provides another example of *ngš* in the sense of "approach," "go near," as opposed to standard Akkadian *nagāšu*, which means "leave," "wander" (cf. *The Assyrian Dictionary*, [1980], 11:108).

**21** Abimelech was the son of Gideon, whose other name was Jerub-Baal (cf. NIV mg.; cf. also 1 Sam 12:11 and comment). For the rationale behind the pejorative Jerub-Besheth, see comments on 2:8; 1 Sam 12:11.

"Upper millstone" (cf. also Deut 24:6; Judg 9:53) is literally "millstone of riding," because it rides back and forth on top of its lower (and larger) counterpart (for details cf. IDB, 3:380–81; ZPEB, 4:227). For "lower millstone" as a simile of hardness, cf. Job 41:24.

**23** "But we drove them back" reads literally "But we were against them," the preposition in this case being of the kind that can exist "dependent on a verb (generally a verb of motion), which, for the sake of brevity, is not expressed, but in sense is contained in what is apparently the governing verb" (GKC, sec. 119*ee*).

**24** The *Kethiv* of the words rendered "archers" and "shot arrows" assumes the Aramaic form of the verb ירא (*yr'*), as in 2 Chron 26:15, whereas the *Qere* recognizes the א (') as superfluous and vocalizes on the basis of the more common Heb. form ירה (*yrh*), as in v.20; 1 Sam 20:20, 36, 37 ("had fallen"); 31:3. For examples of the same phenomenon in other verbs with ה (*h*) as the third radical, cf. GKC, sec. 75*rr*.

**25** The troublesome accusative particle אֶת־ (*'et-*) before הַדָּבָר הַזֶּה (*haddāḇār hazzeh*, "this thing/matter") is omitted by a few Hebrew MSS (cf. BHS), in effect making the phrase the subject of the sentence. S.R. Driver, however, understands it to be construed as an accusative *ad sensum* and gives additional examples (*Notes on the Books of Samuel*, p. 291).

Although זֹה (*zōh*, "this") is often considered to be late biblical Hebrew (cf. by implication BDB, p. 262), the phrase כָּזֹה וְכָזֶה (*kāzōh wᵉkāzeh*, "one as well as another"; lit., "like this and like this") demonstrates that "the corpus of what have been perceived to be uniquely LBH [Late Biblical Hebrew] traits is dwindling" (Gevirtz, "Of Syntax and Style," p. 26; cf. p. 25 n. 3; cf. also Judg 18:4 ["what"]; 1 Kings 14:5 ["such and such an answer"]).

---

## 5. *Nathan's rebuke*

### 12:1–25

[1]The LORD sent Nathan to David. When he came to him, he said, "There were two men in a certain town, one rich and the other poor. [2]The rich man had a very large number of sheep and cattle, [3]but the poor man had nothing except one little ewe lamb he had bought. He raised it, and it grew up with him and his children. It shared his food, drank from his cup and even slept in his arms. It was like a daughter to him.

[4]"Now a traveler came to the rich man, but the rich man refrained from taking one of his own sheep or cattle to prepare a meal for the traveler who had come to him. Instead, he took the ewe lamb that belonged to the poor man and prepared it for the one who had come to him."

[5]David burned with anger against the man and said to Nathan, "As surely as the LORD lives, the man who did this deserves to die! [6]He must pay for that lamb four times over, because he did such a thing and had no pity."

[7]Then Nathan said to David, "You are the man! This is what the LORD, the God of Israel, says: 'I anointed you king over Israel, and I delivered you from the hand of Saul. [8]I gave your master's house to you, and your master's wives into your arms. I gave you the house of Israel and Judah. And if all this had been too little, I would have given you even more. [9]Why did you despise the word of the LORD by doing what is evil in his eyes? You struck down Uriah the Hittite with the sword and took his wife to be your own. You killed him with the sword of the Ammonites. [10]Now, therefore, the sword will never depart from your house, because you despised me and took the wife of Uriah the Hittite to be your own.'

[11]"This is what the LORD says: 'Out of your own household I am going to bring calamity upon you. Before your very eyes I will take your wives and give them to one who is close to you, and he will lie with your wives

in broad daylight. 12You did it in secret, but I will do this thing in broad
daylight before all Israel.'"
13Then David said to Nathan, "I have sinned against the LORD."
Nathan replied, "The LORD has taken away your sin. You are not going
to die. 14But because by doing this you have made the enemies of the
LORD show utter contempt, the son born to you will die."
15After Nathan had gone home, the LORD struck the child that Uriah's
wife had borne to David, and he became ill. 16David pleaded with God
for the child. He fasted and went into his house and spent the nights
lying on the ground. 17The elders of his household stood beside him to
get him up from the ground, but he refused, and he would not eat any
food with them.
18On the seventh day the child died. David's servants were afraid to
tell him that the child was dead, for they thought, "While the child was
still living, we spoke to David but he would not listen to us. How can we
tell him the child is dead? He may do something desperate."
19David noticed that his servants were whispering among themselves
and he realized the child was dead. "Is the child dead?" he asked.
"Yes," they replied, "he is dead."
20Then David got up from the ground. After he had washed, put on
lotions and changed his clothes, he went into the house of the LORD and
worshiped. Then he went to his own house, and at his request they
served him food, and he ate.
21His servants asked him, "Why are you acting this way? While the
child was alive, you fasted and wept, but now that the child is dead, you
get up and eat!"
22He answered, "While the child was still alive, I fasted and wept. I
thought, 'Who knows? The LORD may be gracious to me and let the child
live.' 23But now that he is dead, why should I fast? Can I bring him back
again? I will go to him, but he will not return to me."
24Then David comforted his wife Bathsheba, and he went to her and
lay with her. She gave birth to a son, and they named him Solomon. The
LORD loved him; 25and because the LORD loved him, he sent word
through Nathan the prophet to name him Jedidiah.

With respect to literary structure and context, chapter 12 combines with chapter 11 to form an integral section (see comment on 11:1–5) within the larger complex consisting of chapters 10–12 (see comment on 10:1–19). As such it follows naturally and relentlessly upon the sins of David described so laconically in chapter 11 and provides the divine response to his adultery with Bathsheba and his murder of her husband, Uriah (together with the other mercenaries who were also innocent victims of David's desperate maneuvering). Each of the segments of the chapter is chiastically parallel to its corresponding segment in chapter 11 (cf. 12:1–14 with 11:18–27a, 12:15–23 with 11:6–17, 12:24–25 with 11:2–5, and 12:26–31 with 11:1 [see comment on 11:1–5]).

**1–14** The account of the Lord's sending the prophet Nathan to David to announce God's judgment on him includes Nathan's parable (vv.1–4), David's indignant reaction (vv.5–6), Nathan's two-word condemnation (v.7a MT), two divine oracles (vv.7b–12), David's confession (v.13a), and Nathan's announcement of judgment tempered by grace (vv.13b–14).

Although vv.1–4 exhibit characteristics of fable (George W. Coats, "Parable, Fable, and Anecdote: Storytelling in the Succession Narrative," Int 35, 4 [1981]: 368–82) and melodrama (Stuart Lasine, "Melodrama as Parable: The Story of the Poor Man's Ewe-Lamb and the Unmasking of David's Topsy-Turvy Emotions," *Hebrew Annual*

*Review* 8 [1984]: 101–24), the overall category of "parable" best defines the literary genre of Nathan's tale (cf. Adrian Graffy, "The Literary Genre of Isaiah 5, 1–7," *Biblica* 60, 3 [1979]: 404–6; Brad H. Young, *Jesus and His Jewish Parables: Rediscovering the Roots of Jesus' Teaching* [Mahwah: Paulist, 1989], pp. 5, 13 n. 11, 108–9, 241; Simon, "The Poor Man's Ewe-Lamb," pp. 220–42). In a later article Coats himself observes that "Nathan's response to the king's judgment makes the function of the fable as a parable explicit" ("II Samuel 12:1–7a," Int 50, 1 [1986]: 170). At the same time, however, it would seem best not to attempt a more restrictive definition, such as "juridical parable" (Simon, "The Poor Man's Ewe-Lamb," pp. 220–25) or "self-condemnation parable" (Graffy, "The Literary Genre of Isaiah 5, 1–7," p. 408) or "disguised parable" (Lawrence M. Wills, "Observations on 'Wisdom Narratives' in Early Biblical Literature," in *Of Scribes and Scrolls: Studies on the Hebrew Bible, Intertestamental Judaism, and Christian Origins. Presented to John Strugnell on the Occasion of His Sixtieth Birthday*, edd. Harold W. Attridge, John J. Collins, and Thomas H. Tobin [Lanham: University Press of America, 1990], p. 60). In any event, Simon ("The Poor Man's Ewe-Lamb," p. 221) and Graffy ("The Literary Genre of Isaiah 5, 1–7," pp. 404–8) agree that 14:1–20; 1 Kings 20:35–42/43; Isaiah 5:1–7; and Jeremiah 3:1–5 are four parables that resemble Nathan's parable in one or more ways (cf. similarly Wills, "Observations on 'Wisdom Narratives,'" p. 59). Graffy has identified four structural elements that appear in each of the five parables, and it is useful to set them forth as they occur in Nathan's parable and in the parable of the wise woman of Tekoa:

| | 12:1–7a | 14:1–20 |
|---|---|---|
| Introductory formula | v.1a | vv.1–5a |
| Presentation of the case | vv.1b–4 | vv.5b–7, 15–17 |
| Judgment of the case | vv.5–6 | vv.8–11 |
| True meaning revealed | v.7a | vv.12–14, 18–20 |

If chapter 11 is liberally flecked with the verb *šlḥ* ("send") as an index of human power (see comments on 10:1–19; 11:1), chapter 12 begins by using it with God as the subject: "The LORD sent Nathan to David" (v.1a). A few Hebrew MSS add "the prophet" to "Nathan" here, as does the LXX. In any case, it is clearly in his prophetic role that Nathan is sent by the Lord to proclaim his convicting word to the king (see comments on 7:2; 1 Sam 22:5).

Initially, the divine word takes the form of a parable. Briskly told, its vocabulary would later be used by the prophet Zechariah to describe the injustice of the "rich" (*'šr*) against the "flock" (*ṣ'n*) whose "buyers" (*qnh*) slaughter them and whose own shepherds do not "spare" (*ḥml*) them, with the result that the Lord would no longer "pity" (*ḥml*) the people of the land (Zech 11:4–6; cf. *'šr* [vv.1–2, 4]; *ṣ'n* ["sheep," vv.2, 4]; *qnh* ["bought," v.3]; *ḥml* ["refrained," v.4]; *ḥml* [in David's angry response, v.6]; cf. similarly Lasine, "Melodrama as Parable," p. 104 and n. 6). That Nathan's rebuke begins with a parable makes it none the less effective, since its verisimilitude is reflected in the modern Bedouin custom of *Adayieh* ("attack"), which clarifies "two motives in the parable: the urgency and supremacy of the duty of hospitality, on the one hand, and the reality of the emotional attachment of man to his beast—the ewe that was like a daughter" (Simon, "The Poor Man's Ewe-Lamb," p. 229; for additional details, cf. pp. 227–30).

The immediate use of the word "men" (*'anāšîm*) in v.1b and the triple occurrence of "man" ('*îš*) in the concluding verse of the parable (v.4: "rich man" [first occurrence], "poor man," "one"), combined with David's double use of the word "man" in v.5, prepare the reader for Nathan's powerful accusation in v.7a. Now a rich man, David should have remembered what it was like to be "poor" (v.1b) because by his own admission he himself had once been a "poor man" (see 1 Sam 18:23 and comment). The "very large number" of sheep and cattle owned by the rich man (= David; v.2) echoes the "great quantity" of bronze taken by David from the Arameans (see 8:8 and comment; same Heb. phrase). The "sheep and cattle" in the parable symbolize David's many wives, a fact clarified in the succeeding verses.

By contrast the "poor man" (= Uriah) has "nothing except" (*'ên-kōl kî 'im*) one little "ewe lamb" (= Bathsheba; v.3). The description is reprised in a similar tale of poverty, in which a poor widow announces that she has "nothing . . . except" a little oil (2 Kings 4:2; same Heb. expression). The verbs used of the ewe lamb in the rest of v.3 indicate that it is prized as a genuine member of the poor man's family: He "raised it" (lit., "caused it to live"; cf. Ezek 16:6), it "grew up" with the other family members (cf. 1 Sam 2:21; 3:19; Ezek 16:7), it "shared" (lit., "ate") his food and "drank" from his cup and "slept/lay" in his arms (the latter three verbs echo Uriah's refusal to "eat" and "drink" and "lie" with his wife in 11:11; cf. Lawlor, "Theology and Art," pp. 198, 201). "Food" (v.3) is literally "piece (of bread)," meager fare at best (cf. 1 Sam 2:36; see also 1 Sam 28:22 and comment). The expression "slept in his arms" (cf. "He gathers the lambs in his arms," Isa 40:11) is frequently used of a woman lying in a man's embrace or near him (cf. ironically 1 Kings 1:2 ["lie beside him"]; cf. also Mic 7:5). That the ewe lamb stands for Uriah's wife becomes clear at the end of v.3, where the narrator states that it "was like a daughter/*bat* (as in *bat-šeba'*) to him" (Ackerman, p. 44; for additional helpful details concerning the description of the lamb in human terms, cf. Coats, "Parable, Fable, and Anecdote," p. 371).

By no means the ordinary word for "traveler" (v.4, first occurrence), ***hēleḵ*** (lit., "walking, walker") appears elsewhere only once in the OT (1 Sam 14:26 ["oozing out"]; for a more common word for "traveler" [v.4, second occurrence], cf. Judg 19:17; Jer 9:2; 14:8). It is perhaps used here to remind the reader that David's trouble began in the first place because he had earlier "walked around" (*wayyiṯhallēḵ*) on the roof of his palace (see 11:2 and comment). Bound by culture and tradition to provide hospitality for his guest (see comment on 1 Sam 28:24), the rich man sets about to prepare a meal for him. Instead of slaughtering one of his own animals, however, he "took" (v.4) the poor man's one ewe lamb instead—just as David had sent messengers to "get" (lit., "take," 11:4) Bathsheba.

That the rich man "refrained" (*wayyaḥmōl*) from taking one of his own animals (v.4) is the key element in understanding the main point of Nathan's parable. David would soon condemn the man because "he had no pity" (*lō'-ḥāmāl*, v.6). Lasine's observations are perceptive:

> The prophet only says that the rich man spared ("had pity on") his own animals. He leaves it to the hearer to notice a connection between the villain's "pitying" of his own flocks and his lack of pity for the poor man's ewe. David not only notices this connection but focuses on it. . . . He shows that the rich man's "pity" for his own property equals "no-pity" for the poor man and his little lamb. But by correcting these perversions of justice and sensibility, David creates a *new* opposition between himself and the story, one involving *his* relationship to pity. His pity for the victims in the story is in stark contrast to his lack of pity for Uriah, his victim in

> real life. ("Melodrama as Parable," pp. 112–13, italics his; cf. similarly Lawlor, "Theology and Art," pp. 201–2)

Understandably, David's moral indignation against the rich man in Nathan's parable takes the form of burning anger (v.5) that will not be assuaged until justice is done (unlike the lack of resolution of David's anger following the incident of Amnon's rape of Tamar; see 13:21 and comment). As in 1 Samuel 26:16, David uses the Lord's name in a solemn oath (cf. 14:11; see 1 Sam 14:39 and comment), and as in 1 Samuel 26:16, David declares that someone "deserves to die" (lit., "is a son of death"; see comments at 1 Sam 20:31; 26:16), in this case "the man who did this"—David of course oblivious to the fact that he himself is "the man" (v.7a). Thus "David has been trapped by his own sentence" (Ackerman, p. 44).

Since theft of a lamb was not a capital crime, David's outburst is an exaggeration "designed to express the gravity of the sin involved in the callous ignoring of the poor man's attachment to his ewe" (Simon, "The Poor Man's Ewe-Lamb," p. 230). It "reflects the inadequacy of the civil law in this particular case. . . . The rich man deserved death for his callous act, but was protected by the law itself" (Anthony Phillips, "The Interpretation of 2 Samuel xii 5–6," VetTest 16, 2 [1966]: 243). Thus the man's penalty is that he must pay for the confiscated lamb "four times over" (v.6) as mandated by Exodus 22:1. His guilt is clear: He must make restitution "because [*'ēqeb̲ 'ᵃšer*] he did such a thing" (i.e., took the poor man's only ewe lamb)—just as David will soon be told that he is guilty "because [*'ēqeb̲ kî*] you . . . took the wife of Uriah the Hittite" (v.10). Unlike the Pharaoh's daughter, whose heart was so touched at the sight of the crying Hebrew baby that she "felt sorry" for him (Exod 2:6), the rich man (= David) had no "pity" (v.6; same Heb. verb; see also v.4 and comment). "The Egyptian princess, a person who held Moses in her power, a foreigner, not a member of the covenant community, has what David did not have. She has compassion for the baby" (Coats, "II Samuel 12:1–7a," p. 171).

Many have seen (correctly, in my opinion) in the fourfold restoration as applied to David "an allusion to the death of four of David's sons, namely Bathsheba's first child [v.18], Amnon [13:28–29], Absalom [18:14–15] and Adonijah [1 Kings 2:25]" (Jones, p. 103). Indeed, Ackerman observes that "the narrator has unobtrusively introduced a lamb motif as he describes [the last three] sons and their fate" (for details, cf. p. 50).

Up to this point in the MT, the narrator has used "man" and "men" six times—four times by Nathan (vv.1, 4 ["rich man," first occurrence; "poor man"; "one"]), twice by David (v.5). Now the identity of the culprit in the parable becomes explicit in the seventh appearance of the incriminating word as Nathan delivers his terse rebuke to David: "You are the man" (v.7a), a statement that J. Ian H. McDonald calls "the most dramatic sentence in the Old Testament" ("The Bible and Christian Practice," in *Theology and Practice*, ed. Duncan B. Forrester [London: Epworth, 1990], p. 24). On the broader horizon it can be affirmed that "David, royal judge, is shown to be a rich oppressor" whose dynasty has "sprung from an adulterously begun union" (Roth, "You Are the Man!" p. 10). In the shorter term, however, Nathan's abrupt application "draws a parallel between the rich man's exploitation of the poor on account of his superior status and the king's misuses of his own position of authority. Attention is thus focused not on the simple case of theft, but on the exploitation of the weak by one enjoying a superior position" (Jones, p. 100). Thus identification with the rich man implies that David is not merely "a man who deserves to die, but who can only be sued in tort: he is, by his murder of Uriah, an actual murderer who should suffer execution under Israel's criminal law. It is only due to Yahweh's direct pardon that David is to be spared (2 Sam. xii 13)" (Phillips, "The Interpretation of 2 Samuel xii 5–6," p. 244).

Appropriately, a few Hebrew MSS insert a closed paragraph marker after "This is the man" to separate v.7a from v.7b. Verses 7b–12, the divine oracles that continue Nathan's rebuke, divide naturally into two unequal sections separated by a closed paragraph marker (vv.7b–10 and 11–12), each section beginning with the prophetic messenger formula "This is what the LORD says" (cf. vv.7b, 11). In addition, "the two sections concentrate on different aspects of David's sin, the first being more concerned with the murder of Uriah and the second relating exclusively to David's adultery with Bathsheba" (Jones, pp. 101–2). Perhaps most significantly vv.9–10, the middle two verses of the six that make up the oracles, can be arguably defined as the literary, historical, and theological crux and center of 2 Samuel as a whole (see comment below).

After Nathan strengthens the basic messenger formula by referring to the Lord as "the God of [the entire nation of] Israel" (v.7b), the first section of the divine oracle begins with the two occurrences of the emphatic pronoun: "*I* anointed" and "*I* delivered." The Lord reminds David that it was he who anointed him king (more than once; see 1 Sam 16:13; 2 Sam 2:4a; 5:3 and comments) and that it was he who delivered him from Saul's clutches (more than once; see 1 Sam 24:15; 26:24; 27:1; 2 Sam 4:9 and comments). Just as Saul, the Lord's anointed, had fallen from grace, so also would David—though not in the same way or to the same degree (see comment on 1 Sam 15:1; cf. also 1 Sam 15:17–23).

In addition, the Lord who "gave" Saul's "house" (= family and property; see comments on 9:9–11a) and wives to David and who "gave" the "house" (= kingdom) of "Israel and Judah" (see comment on 5:3) to David (v.8) would soon "give" the wives to someone else (v.11). In light of the monogamous ideal outlined in Genesis 2:22–24, the gift of "wives" in vv.8, 11 would seem to be a divine concession to the polygamy that was relatively common (at least among the upper classes) in ancient Near Eastern culture (see comments on 1 Sam 1:2; 25:43). Saul's "wives" presumably included at least Ahinoam (see comment on 1 Sam 25:43; cf. also Levenson and Halpern, "The Political Import of David's Marriages," pp. 507, 513) and perhaps also his concubine Rizpah (cf. 3:7). The fact that they are given into David's "arms" (v.8) is an ironic allusion to Nathan's parable (cf. v.3; cf. also Mic 7:5 ["embrace"]). And the God whose generosity knows no bounds would have "given" (lit., "added") even more to David if he had considered it appropriate to do so.

But David's unbridled desire and willful murder have foreclosed any such options. The first section of the divine oracle (vv.7b–10) concludes with two verses (vv.9–10) that are closely tied to each other by their use of the terms "despise(d)," "Uriah the Hittite," "sword," and "took . . . wife . . . to be your own." The verses perform the same function for 2 Samuel as 1 Samuel 16:13–14 perform for 1 Samuel (see comment on 1 Sam 16:1–13): By leaving no doubt concerning the Lord's displeasure with the king's sins and his determination to punish him, vv.9–10 constitute the literary, historical, and theological center not only of the oracle itself but also of the entire book. To use Carlson's helpful rubric, David is now truly and undeniably "under the Curse" (pp. 7, 25, 140).

If Saul lost the kingdom through having "rejected the word of the LORD" (1 Sam 15:23), David is judged because he has decided to "despise the word of the LORD" (v.9). To despise the Lord's word is to break his commands and thus to incur guilt and punishment (cf. Num 15:31), and that without remedy (cf. 2 Chron 36:16). Proverbs 13:13 is apropos: "He who scorns/despises [though not having the same three consonants, the Hebrew verbs translated 'despise' here (*bwz*) and in v.9 (*bzh*) spring from the same biconsonantal root] instruction [*dbr*] will pay for it,/ but he who respects a command is rewarded." To despise the Lord's "word" (*dbr*) is to do "what is evil in his eyes" (v.9; see comment on 11:27b), a link that David later acknowledges when he confesses to God that he has done "what is evil in your sight, so that you are proved right when you speak [*dbr*]" (Ps 51:4). Taking 11:27b; 12:9; and Proverbs 13:13 together, Brueggemann argues that " 'in the eyes of Yahweh' can most plausibly be understood as that benevolent life-giving ordering upon which the wise reflected and which David in his foolishness violated" ("On Trust and Freedom," p. 11).

In v.9 the emphatic position of "Uriah the Hittite," "his wife," and "him"—objects that in each case precede their governing verbs—underscores the callous and heinous nature of David's sins against them. People who above all others he should have cherished and cared for became instead the degraded and destroyed targets of royal lust and caprice. The trusted mercenary Uriah is "struck down" (see 11:15 and comment) and "killed" by the sword of the enemy. Although the Lord "gave" and would have given "even more" (v.8), David "took" (see comment on v.4; see also 5:13 and comment) someone else's wife to be his own (vv.9–10). Unfeeling acquisitiveness is of the very nature of royalty (see 1 Sam 8:11, 13–17, and comment).

Despising the word of the Lord (v.9) is tantamount to despising the Lord himself (v.10). In doing both, David finds himself in unsavory company (cf. 1 Sam 2:29–30). With respect to the statement that "the sword will never depart from [David's] house," Carlson observes: "David's ominous words in . . . 11:25 ['the sword devours one as well as another'] recoil upon his own house in 12:10" (p. 158). David's "never" in his colorful curse against Joab's "house" in 3:29 also returns to haunt him in the inexorable language of divine judgment (v.10).

The second section of the Lord's oracle (vv.11–12) is relentless in the immediacy with which it threatens retaliation against the king. "Out of your own household" (v.11) renders the same Hebrew expression translated "from your house" in v.10. As David has done what is "evil" (v.9), so the Lord will bring "calamity" upon him (v.11; same Heb. word); and as David has done evil "in [the Lord's] eyes" (v.9), so the Lord will bring calamity upon the king "before [his] very eyes" (v.11). Indeed, the Hebrew grammatical construction translated "I am going to bring calamity" is perhaps better rendered "I am about to bring calamity" (as in, e.g., 1 Sam 3:11), emphasizing the imminence of the events described (cf. GKC, sec. 116*p*)—events such as Amnon's rape of Tamar (13:1–14), Absalom's murder of Amnon (13:28–29), Absalom's rebellion against David (15:1–12), and more. David's punishment for his crimes against Bathsheba and Uriah is a clear example of a conditional element in the Davidic covenant (see comment on 7:1–17; cf. Waltke, "The Phenomenon of Conditionality," p. 132).

As David "took" Uriah's wife (vv.9–10), so the Lord will "take" David's wives (v.11). As the Lord "gave" Saul's property and Israel's kingdom to David (v.8), so he says that he will now "give" David's wives to someone else, to "one who is close to you" (v.11)—ironically, an expression earlier used of David himself in similar circumstances (see 1 Sam 15:28; 28:17 ["one of your neighbors"] and comments). The "one who is close" to David turns out to be his own son Absalom: "David's voyeurism in 2 Sam 11:2 and Nathan's curse in 12:11 foreshadow Absalom's rooftop orgy (16:20–22)" (Levenson and Halpern, "The Political Import of David's Marriages," p. 514).

Although Uriah had refused to "lie" with his own wife (11:11), David had "slept" with her (11:4)—and soon Absalom would "lie" with David's wives (v.11; same Heb. verb). As the Lord would take David's wives "before [his] very eyes," so Absalom would lie with them "in broad daylight" (v.11; lit., "before the eyes of this sun").

David's despising of God (v.10) and his commands (v.9) resulted in his "doing" evil in the Lord's eyes (v.9). But although David "did" evil "in secret" (see comment on 11:15), the Lord would "do" his will against David "in broad daylight" (v.12; not the same expression as in v.11, it reads literally "before [*neged*] the sun"; cf. Num 25:4) and thus "before [*neged*] all Israel" (cf. the fulfillment "in the sight of all Israel" in 16:22). As it turns out, three of David's sons would prove themselves "unfit to rule by recapitulating, each in his turn, their father's sin. . . . Just as David willfully takes Bathsheba for himself (II Sam. 11:2–4), so Amnon forces Tamar (II Sam. 13:8–14), Absalom enters the royal harem (II Sam. 16:22), and Adonijah tries to claim his deceased father's concubine (I Kings 2:13–17)" (McCarter, " 'Plots, True or False,' " p. 359).

To his credit, David confesses to the prophet Nathan that he has broken God's law: "I have sinned against the LORD" (v.13a: cf. David's words in 24:10, 17 and especially in Ps 51:4: "Against you, you only, have I sinned"; for Saul's earlier agonized admission to the prophet Samuel in similar circumstances, see 1 Sam 15:24, 30 and comment). Though he could have vacillated or indignantly denied Nathan's accusation or ridded himself of Nathan in one way or another, David accepts full responsibility for his actions. "In his total and immediate response of repentance. . . , there is no hint in the narrative that this is anything less than an authentic, rightly intentioned confession. It is presented without irony or suspicion" (Brueggemann, "On Trust and Freedom," p. 8).

And, as might be expected, the prophet does not leave the king comfortless. Nathan comes to David with words of divine grace. "Only the man who accepts that he was wrong can be forgiven. 'Yahweh, for his part, forgives your sin [v.13b]' " (Vogels, "David's Greatness," p. 251). In judging the rich man for his cruelty (v.5), David had unwittingly chosen his own death penalty (cf. Lev 20:10; Deut 22:22). But the Lord, through his prophet, announces the forgiveness of David's "sin" (against Bathsheba) and preserves David's life: "You are not going to die." The fact that God does not hesitate to strike people down for what might be considered lesser infractions (see 6:7 and comment) makes his forbearance in David's case all the more noteworthy.

At the same time, however, the Lord is not yet through with David: "By doing this you have shown utter contempt for the LORD" (v.14 mg., which is doubtless the intention of the narrator and is preferable to the NIV text reading; see Notes below). In this respect David finds himself in the company of Eli's reprobate sons, who had been in the habit of "treating the LORD's offering with contempt" and whose sin was therefore "very great in the LORD's sight" (1 Sam 2:17; cf. "evil in his eyes," v.9). David would not "die" (v.13), but the son born to him will (v.14). Tit for tat: Having "show[n] utter contempt" (infinitive absolute plus finite verb) for the Lord, David's son will "die" (infinitive absolute plus finite verb; better, "surely die" [cf. Gen 2:17, where the same grammatical construction appears]). "When David slept with the woman and created new life, the woman did not belong to him but to Uriah. The child cannot belong to David. He cannot enrich himself through his sin, and in a sense, justice is done to Uriah" (Vogels, "David's Greatness," p. 251).

**15–23** The account of the death of David's infant son, a result of David's sin (vv.15–23), is paralleled by the story of Uriah's death, a crime of which David was guilty (11:6–17; see comment on 11:1–5). And just as in 11:15–26 the verb *mwt* ("to die") occurs numerous times (see comment on 11:6–27), so also it appears numbingly often in vv.15–23 (vv.18 [ter], 19 [ter], 21, 23).

Having fulfilled his prophetic mission, Nathan leaves the palace and goes home. The Lord then strikes Bathsheba's newborn son (v.15) with what proves to be a fatal illness (cf. 1 Sam 25:38; see also comment on 1 Sam 26:10). The phrase "the child that Uriah's wife has borne to David" underscores the fact that David's adultery and murder will claim yet another innocent victim.

Despite the prophet's pronouncement that the child's fate is sealed (v.14), David is not yet willing to resign himself to the death of his son. He therefore intercedes for the child's life (v.16). "Supplication is more humbling than resignation" (Simon, "The Poor Man's Ewe-Lamb," p. 239). Ostensibly as a symbol of mourning (see also v.20 and comment), he "fasted" (see comments on 1:12; 3:32–35; 1 Sam 31:13). Although the series of consecutive perfects beginning with "went" is correctly rendered as repeated action in the NIV (cf. also S.R. Driver, *Notes on the Books of Samuel*, in loc.), commentators in general seem not to have noticed that going "into (one's) house" and spending one's nights "lying on the ground" are incompatible activities, unless the house has a dirt floor—which was surely not the case in David's palace. In any event, the MT does not have "into his house" in v.16 (contrast "went to his [own] house" in v.20), and thus "went" (*bā'*) should probably be understood here as an auxiliary verb used to initiate action (cf. the analogous use of imperative *bô'* with auxiliary function in cohortative constructions as noted in Waltke and O'Connor, *Biblical Hebrew Syntax*, p. 574). Outside the royal palace, David "spent the nights lying on the ground"—ironically, just as Uriah and his fellow soldiers had done (cf. 11:9, 11; cf. Vogels, "David's Greatness," p. 261).

If Genesis 24:2 is any indication ("the chief/oldest servant in his household" is literally "his servant, the elder in his household"), "the elders of [David's] household" (v.17) must have been loyal servants to whom David had delegated important tasks. Concerned for his welfare, they stand "beside" (or "over," as in 1:9) him, urging him to get up and take care of his personal needs. He refuses, however, and will not so much as "eat" any food with them. Koehler argues cogently that the root *brh* (here written *br'*) "means 'eat invalid food, or the food of mourners'" ("Problems," p. 6; see also 3:35 and comment; cf. 13:6, 10).

The death of the child—son of Bathsheba, "Daughter of Seven" (see comment on 11:3); son of David, chosen above his seven brothers (see 1 Sam 16:10 and comment; cf. Vogels, "David's Greatness," p. 252)—takes place on "the seventh day" (v.18). Although it is impossible to know whether the day the child died was "the seventh Day after its Birth before it was circumcised; or the seventh after it fell sick" (Symon Patrick, p. 446), on balance the former is the more attractive (see comment on 11:27a). David's "servants" (vv.18–19, 21), doubtless to be identified with the "elders of his household" (see comment on v.17), are reluctant to tell him of the child's death for fear that their master may do something "desperate" (lit., "evil," "disastrous"; for the same idiom, cf. Jer 26:19; 41:11 ["crimes . . . had committed"]).

Aware of the whispering of his servants and thus realizing that the child is dead, David gives verbal expression to his own worst nightmare (v.19). Whether or not he voices it in the form of a question (two Heb. MSS do not exhibit the *he-* interrogative particle; cf. BHS), the servants finally affirm to him that the child is indeed dead.

Having admitted to himself the inevitable, David gets up from the ground (v.20). After he had "washed" (cf., ironically, 11:2, 8, where the Heb. verb is the same) and put on lotions (a procedure sometimes associated with the absence or cessation of mourning; cf. 14:2), he "changed his clothes." Although some have understood the latter act simply as a privilege of David's royal status (as opposed to that of commoners; cf. Neufeld, "Hygiene Conditions," p. 53 n. 31), it is surely better to see it as the shedding of mourning garb and the reverting back to normal clothing, especially since "lying in sackcloth (on the ground)" is the attested reading in v.16 in 4QSam[a], most LXX MSS (including the Lucianic recension), one OL MS, and Josephus (Antiq. VII, 154 [vii.4]) (for details cf. Ulrich, *The Qumran Text,* p. 100; cf. also Simon, "The Poor Man's Ewe-Lamb," p. 240 n. 1).

After entering the "house of the LORD" (the tabernacle; see 1 Sam 1:7 and comment) to worship him, apparently resigned to divine judgment against himself and his child, David then goes to "his own house" (v.20). There he breaks his fast (cf. v.16) and eats ordinary food (as opposed to the food of mourners that he had earlier rejected [see comment on v.17; the verb "ate" is here *'kl,* not *br'*]).

Understandably, David's servants are confused. While the child was alive, David—acting like a mourner—had "fasted and wept" (v.21; for the association of fasting and weeping with mourning, see 1:12; 3:31–35 and comments; cf. also Judg 20:26; Esth 4:3; Ps 69:10–11; Joel 2:12). Now that his son is dead, however, the king puts on garments befitting royalty and enjoys a good meal.

Concerning David's response to his perplexed servants (vv.22–23), Perdue asks: "Are these the words of a grief-stricken father, or of a callous ruler realizing he had failed to negate Nathan's prophecy predicting trouble from the king's own house, a prediction whose initial sign was the death of the child?" (" 'Is There Anyone Left?' " p. 77). Walter Brueggemann had already answered Perdue's question: "David's reaction to the death of his child . . . is an act of profound faith in the face of the most precious tabus of his people. . . . David had discerned, for whatever reasons, that the issues of his life are not to be found in cringing fear before the powers of death, but in his ability to embrace and abandon, to love and to leave; to take life as it comes, not with indifference but with freedom, not with callousness but with buoyancy" (*In Man We Trust: The Neglected Side of Biblical Faith* [Atlanta: John Knox, 1972], p. 36).

David readily admits that his conduct might have appeared peculiar, that his mourning might have seemed premature (v.22). But he was counting on the open door of the divine "perhaps": "Who knows?" (cf. similarly Joel 2:13–14; Jonah 3:9). "To be sure, David's hope in this instance was ill-founded, but his use of *mî yôdēa'* functions in the same way the prophetic *'ûlay* ('perhaps') does in Amos v 15 and comparable passages. The emphasis falls on the sovereignty of God, but human beings still dare to hope that compassion will gain the upper hand" (James L. Crenshaw, "The Expression *Mî Yôdēa'* in the Hebrew Bible," VetTest 36, 3 [1986]: 275; cf. also Simon, "The Poor Man's Ewe-Lamb," p. 239 n. 1).

Resigned to the death of his child, David asks his servants why he should "fast" (the participle is better rendered "continue fasting"). Since the netherworld is the "Land of No Return" (Akkad. *erṣet lā târi,* the name by which it was often described in ancient Mesopotamia; for OT observations of a similar nature, cf. Job 7:9 ["he who goes down to the grave (= Sheol) does not return"]; 10:21 ["place of no return"]; 16:22 ["journey of no return"]; Prov 2:18–19; Ezek 26:20; for discussion cf. Tromp, *Primitive Conceptions of Death,* pp. 189–90), the child "will not return" to David, and nothing that David can do will "bring him back again" (v.23). Indeed, David's only option for a reunion with his son is to "go to him" (cf. similarly Coats, "II Samuel 12:1–7a," p. 173). But however far this may fall short of Christian confidence in the eventual resurrection of the body and the life everlasting (cf. Kirkpatrick, *The Second Book of Samuel*, p. 131), all is not lost: "David comes to terms with his own mortality, and even in that finds hope, because he looks forward to being reunited with his child. The Lord who had sent Nathan to David had had the last word and, though David was bereft, he was content" (Baldwin, p. 241).

A final word: "By way of personal conclusion, one could read and meditate on Psalm 51. The biblical tradition has understood this psalm as reflecting the feelings and prayer 'of David, when the prophet Nathan came to him because he had been with Bathsheba'" (Vogels, "David's Greatness," p. 254).

**24–25** As noted above (see comment on 11:1–5), vv.24–25 mirror 11:2–5. At the beginning of the narrative, Bathsheba had been "the wife of Uriah the Hittite" (see 11:3 and comment), but as an outcome of the sin of King David she has become "his wife" (v.24). "David is able, but with apparent impunity now, to do precisely what he had done to set the story in motion: he can have sexual intercourse with Bathsheba, the woman of his desire (11:4; 12:24)" (Gunn, "David and the Gift," p. 20).

If Isaac's marriage to Rebekah helped him to find comfort after his mother's death (Gen 24:67), David "comforted" Bathsheba (who doubtless mourned her son's death) when he "went to her and lay with her" (v.24; see 11:4 and comment). In due course she gives birth to yet another son, later to be recognized as a "wise son" given to David by the Lord (1 Kings 5:7). The boy is named Solomon, which apparently means "(God Is) His Peace" (see comment on 5:14; for another possibility, cf. Jones, p. 113 ["His Replacement/Substitution"]). That his name contains the same Hebrew root (*šlm*) as does Jerusalem (see comment on 5:6) is probably not coincidental (cf. similarly Talmon, p. 152 n. 19).

The statement that the Lord "loved" Solomon (v.24; cf. Neh 13:26; cf. similarly Deut 4:37; 7:8; Ps 146:8; Prov 3:12; 15:9) perhaps has covenantal overtones and should therefore include the technical nuance that the Lord "honors his treaty commitments to the dynasty" (Brueggemann, "On Trust and Freedom," p. 13 and n. 32; for "love" in the sense of "covenantal/political loyalty," see comments on 1:26; 1 Sam 18:1–4). If so, the suggestion that the name Solomon means something like "His Submission (Is to the Lord)" becomes more attractive (for discussion, cf. Z.W. Falk, "Hebrew Legal Terms: II," JSS 12, 2 [1967]: 244).

On the basis of his love for Solomon, the Lord "sent word through" (lit., "sent by the hand of," v.25—an ironic touch; see 11:14 and comment) the prophet Nathan, who is thereby instructed to call David's newborn son Jedidiah ("Loved by the LORD" [see NIV mg.]; cf. *yᵉḏîḏ YHWH*, "the beloved of the LORD" [Deut 33:12], a phrase used to describe Benjamin), a name similar to that of David himself (for details see comment on 1 Sam 16:13). Why the boy was given two names is a question that has been much discussed. Since Jedidiah is an unambiguously orthodox name, Jones suggests that it was calculated to "satisfy the Israelite [as opposed to the Jebusite] element in Jerusalem" (p. 114). It seems more likely, however, that "Solomon" should be understood "as a throne name which David . . . conferred upon his son Jedidiah . . . so as to suggest his (future) appointment as king in (Jeru)salem" (Talmon, p. 152). The dual naming thus anticipates "the change of name which Solomon himself assumed when he succeeded to the throne" (ibid.).

If at the beginning of chapter 12 Nathan rebuked the king (vv.7–14), at its end he comforts him (v.25). But Nathan's ministry with respect to David and Solomon/Jedidiah is not yet finished. During David's last days Nathan would play a key role in making sure that Solomon would succeed his father as king of Israel (cf. 1 Kings 1:11–14, 24–27). In fact, Nathan would share in Solomon's anointing (1 Kings 1:34, 45), the most solemn act of all.

## Notes

**5** When Lasine states that "Nathan's tale evokes a vehement emotional response from David, who . . . does not view it as a melodrama" ("Melodrama as Parable," p. 103), he seriously undercuts his own analysis of the literary genre of Nathan's rebuke by claiming to understand the prophet's words better than David did. The Egyptian Tale of the Eloquent Peasant, which predates David by more than half a millennium, also excoriates anyone who would plunder the property of the poor: "Do not despoil a poor man of his possessions, a feeble man whom you know, for his possessions are (the very) breath to a poor man, and to take them away is to stop up his nose" (translation by R.O. Faulkner in *The Literature of Ancient Egypt: An Anthology of Stories, Instructions, and Poetry,* new edition; ed. William Kelly Simpson [New Haven: Yale University Press, 1973], p. 43).

**6** Although Josephus (Antiq. VII, 150 [vii.3]), the Lucianic recension of the LXX, and some Targum MSS join the MT in reading "four times," the LXX prefers "seven times." But

> while it is possible that the punitive damages were later increased, it is more likely that sevenfold is a later proverbial expression indicating that perfect restitution must be made. A later scribe might have altered the MT to conform to the law, but it would seem more probable that the LXX rendering is due to a recollection of the proverbial saying preserved in Prov. vi 31, which also reads sevenfold. As the amount of compensation was fixed by law, it is unlikely that David would need to resort to a proverbial saying. (Phillips, "The Interpretation of 2 Samuel xii 5–6," p. 243)

It is therefore unnecessary to insist that "the reading 'fourfold' must be taken (as most exegetes in fact do) to be secondary—and, we may add, post-Deuteronomic" (Carlson, p. 156).

**14** Since נִאֵץ (*ni'ēṣ*) is never causitive elsewhere in the OT (cf. BDB, p. 611), the NIV's "you have made the enemies of the LORD show utter contempt" is suspect from the outset. The margin reading, "you have shown utter contempt for the LORD," is clearly the author's intent—but it is not necessary to omit "the enemies of." Kitchen provides the solution: "The literal reading is no fault of the text, it is simply a euphemism to avoid saying 'having slighted the Lord. . .', by transferring the insult verbally to God's enemies. Remarkably enough, *exactly* the same euphemism has been noticed in an Egyptian decree of the seventeenth century B.C." (*Ancient Orient,* p. 166; italics his). For the same conclusion, cf. the detailed discussion of M.J. Mulder ("Un Euphémisme dans 2 Sam. xii 14?" VetTest 18, 1 [1968]: 108–14), who also calls attention to the possibility that "David's enemies" in 1 Sam 20:16; 25:22 is likewise a euphemism for David himself (p. 113; cf. NIV mg. on 1 Sam 25:22; cf. further McCarter, *II Samuel,* p. 296).

**16** That consultation of the dead was commonly practiced in the ancient world is beyond cavil (cf. the warnings in Deut 18:10–11; Isa 8:19; 57:9; 65:2, 4; see also 1 Sam 28:7–14 and comment), but the theory that אַרְצָה (*'ārṣāh,* "on the ground") here means "to/into the netherworld" and that David is therefore "ritually acting out a descent into the netherworld to try to bring his son back from the clutches of death" (Lewis, *Cults of the Dead,* p. 43) can only be described as eccentric.

## 6. *The Ammonites defeated*

### 12:26–31

[26]Meanwhile Joab fought against Rabbah of the Ammonites and captured the royal citadel. [27]Joab then sent messengers to David, saying, "I have fought against Rabbah and taken its water supply. [28]Now muster the rest of the troops and besiege the city and capture it. Otherwise I will take the city, and it will be named after me."

[29]So David mustered the entire army and went to Rabbah, and attacked and captured it. [30]He took the crown from the head of their king—its weight was a talent of gold, and it was set with precious stones—and it was placed on David's head. He took a great quantity of plunder from the city [31]and brought out the people who were there, consigning them to labor with saws and with iron picks and axes, and he made them work at brickmaking. He did this to all the Ammonite towns. Then David and his entire army returned to Jerusalem.

In the overall scheme of chapters 10–12, 10:1–11:1 and vv.26–31 describe Israel's military victories over Ammon and thus bracket the central narrative of David-Bathsheba-Uriah-Nathan-Solomon (11:2–12:25; see comment on 10:1–19). At the same time, however, in the light of the fact that chapters 11–12 constitute an integral section within the larger complex, vv.26–31 mirror 11:1 (see comment on 11:1–5) and bring to a successful conclusion the siege of Rabbah that was mounted at the beginning of chapter 11. Since it is unlikely that the siege itself lasted for the minimum of two years implied in the events of chapters 11–12, chronological considerations would appear to have yielded to literary and thematic concerns in the narrator's presentation. The NIV's "Meanwhile" in v.26 is therefore entirely in order.

The present literary unit (vv.26–31) divides naturally into two sections, the first (vv.26–28) with Joab as the major actor and the second (vv.29–31) featuring David. That only vv.29–31 are paralleled by the Chronicler (cf. 1 Chron 20:1b–3) is fully compatible with his interest in highlighting the positive aspects of David's reign.

**26–28** Tying three verses together is the verb *lkd* ("take," "capture," vv.26, 27, 28 [bis]). Intensifying the siege of Rabbah (the Ammonite capital city; see comment on 10:3), the onset of which is recorded in 11:1 (see comment there), Joab captures its "royal citadel" (*'îr hamm$^{e}$lûḵāh,* "city of royalty," v.26), probably the major fortification either within the city or guarding the approaches to it (for a similar expression, see comment on 1 Sam 27:5). The city now rendered defenseless, Joab sends word to David that he has fought against Rabbah and taken its "water supply" (*'îr hammāyim,* "city of water[s]," v.27). Although the latter expression is clearly to be linked in some way to the former (indeed, two Heb. MSS read *hamm$^{e}$lûḵāh* instead of *hammāyim* in v.27; cf. BHS), the "city of water[s]" is patently not the "beautiful harbor" of the Living Bible (Rabbah is seventy miles inland from the Mediterranean Sea). The phrase is doubtless elliptical for "citadel protecting the water supply" or the like (cf. Anderson, in loc.). Josephus (Antiq. VII, 159 [vii.5]) understood "took the city of waters" to refer to cutting off the main Ammonite water supply (noted by Symon Patrick, p. 451). McCarter summarizes: "Perhaps 'the Royal Citadel' [v.26] was the official name used by the narrator and 'the citadel of the water supply' [v.27] was not a name ('the Citadel of Waters') but rather Joab's descriptive way of identifying its strategic importance to David" (*II Samuel,* p. 310).

Rabbah now in dire straits, Joab advises David to muster the "rest of the troops" (lit., "people," v.28; see 10:10 and comment) and lead them in the final attack against the city. Joab warns that, if the king refuses to become personally involved, he himself will capture Rabbah, in which case it will be named after Joab rather than after David. Although the victor may not always have sole control of distributing the spoils, he apparently reserves for himself the privilege of renaming the conquered site (see comments on 5:7, 9; see also 6:2 and comment).

One of the most strategically significant cities in the Transjordanian region, Rabbah would now become part of David's domain. It was therefore vital that David, not Joab, be credited with seizing it. "Joab clearly discerned that it was important for David to preserve his mastery and domination in the east and that all possible ties be made with the king" himself (Curtis, "East Is East . . . ," p. 357; cf. Simon, "The Poor Man's Ewe-Lamb," p. 209).

**29–31** In vv.29 and 31, references to "David" and "the entire army" (lit., "all the people" [= troops; see comment on v.28]) form an *inclusio* that serves to frame the literary unit (NIV, "his" in v.31 is not represented in the MT and muffles its echo of v.29). The unit is paralleled by 1 Chronicles 20:1b–3.

Although 1 Chronicles 20:1b ("Joab attacked Rabbah and left it in ruins") seems intended as a summary of vv.26–28, it can also be viewed as functioning in much the same way as v.29—namely, to introduce the account of David's plunder of Rabbah and his forced levy of its people (vv.30–31). In any case, David finishes what Joab has begun: Having "mustered" the necessary troops (the same Heb. verb is rendered "gathered" in 10:17; see comment there), he captures the city (v.29). Of the many trophies seized by David, one of the most spectacular was a gold crown that had rested on the Ammonite king's head and was now transferred to David's (v.30). Set with "precious stones" (for possible examples cf. Ezek 28:13), the crown was of such enormous weight and value (see second NIV mg. note) that it was probably used only on ceremonial occasions.

"Plunder from the city" (v.30) and "the people [probably = troops, as throughout these verses] who were there" (v.31) are in emphatic position in their respective sentences, and both phrases are objects of the verb *hôṣî'* ("brought out"; rendered "took" in v.30). The "plunder" was in "great quantity" (*harbēh me'ōḏ*), the first word of which may be a subtle pun on *rabbāh* ("Rabbah"). As for the "people," earlier interpreters explained that David "put them under saws, and under harrows of iron, and under axes of iron, and made them pass through the brick-kiln" (v.31 KJV; cf. also Symon Patrick, pp. 452–53). That David was capable of such atrocities is not disputed (see 8:2 and comment). But "consigning them to labor with . . . and with . . . " is more likely to represent a correct rendering of the key preposition *b-* than "put them under . . . and under. . . . " Apparently David forced the defeated Ammonites to work on various building projects. The "saws," for example, were of the kind used to trim the faces of blocks of stone (cf. 1 Kings 7:9).

Only after David had extended the forced labor requirement to the other defeated Ammonite towns did he and his troops return to Jerusalem (v.31). The Israelite victory was thus both thoroughgoing and complete. David's accomplishment was all the more impressive when it is remembered that

> the number and strength of [the Ammonite] fortress dwellings . . . point to a dynamic civilization with a well-organized center of political authority. And the effectiveness of their defensive set-up is attested by the fact that, as far as we know,

only once in some six centuries of Ammonite history was the ring of defenses around their capital at Rabbah-ammon ever breached, and the capital itself besieged and taken: in the 10th century B.C., when Israelite military power was at its height, under the leadership of David and his commander Joab. (George M. Landes, "The Material Civilization of the Ammonites," BA 24, 3 [1961]: 74)

## Notes

---

**30** The MT's מלכם (*mlkm*) can be vocalized either as מַלְכָּם (*malkām,* "their king" [NIV text]) or as מִלְכֹּם (*milkōm,* "Milcom," a variant of the name of the chief Ammonite god Molech [first NIV mg. note]; cf. 1 Kings 11:5, 33). The same ambiguity obtains in the case of Jer 49:1, 3; Amos 1:15; Zeph 1:5, as attested by the NIV margin readings on those verses. Needless to say, the correct reading in each context must be judged on its own merits. Here "their king" is probably to be preferred, not only because it is unlikely that David would have worn the crown of a pagan idol, but also because the transfer of the crown from one head to another was doubtless emblematic of the transfer of sovereign authority over the Ammonites from the head of their king to that of David (cf. Baldwin, pp. 245–46 n. 1; for fallen crowns as symbols of the loss of royal authority, cf. Jer 13:18). An ornate limestone bust of an Ammonite king wearing a crown, dating from the ninth century B.C. and said to have been unearthed in the vicinity of Rabbah, is pictured on the cover of *Biblical Archaeology Review* 8, 5 (1982). In Egyptian style, the crown bears an ostrich feather on each side with flowered reliefs carved in front.

**31** "He made them work at brickmaking" is an attempt to render הֶעֱבִיר אוֹתָם בַּמַּלְבֵּן (*he'ᵉḇîr 'ōṯām bammalbēn,* reading the final word with the *Qere* rather than with the anomalous *Kethiv* במלכן [*bmlkn*]), a clause of uncertain meaning (see NIV mg.). That *malbēn* means something like "brickmaking" is secured by Jer 43:9 ("brick pavement") and Nah 3:14 ("brickwork"). The NIV text apparently assumes a scribal error and reads העביד (*h'byd,* "caused to work") instead of העביר (*h'byr,* "caused to pass (through)" (ד [*d*] and ר [*r*] are very similar in appearance). Precedent for such a variant is attested in Gen 47:21, where the Samaritan Pentateuch reads *h'byd 'tw l'bdym* ("reduced the people to servitude," NIV) for the MT's *h'byr 'tw l'rym* ("moved the people into the cities," NIV mg.). Forcing captive people to work hard in brickmaking was not uncommon in ancient times (cf. Exod 1:13–14).

---

### 7. *Amnon's sin against Tamar*

### 13:1–22

1 In the course of time, Amnon son of David fell in love with Tamar, the
beautiful sister of Absalom son of David.
2 Amnon became frustrated to the point of illness on account of his
sister Tamar, for she was a virgin, and it seemed impossible for him to
do anything to her.
3 Now Amnon had a friend named Jonadab son of Shimeah, David's
brother. Jonadab was a very shrewd man. 4 He asked Amnon, "Why do
you, the king's son, look so haggard morning after morning? Won't you
tell me?"
Amnon said to him, "I'm in love with Tamar, my brother Absalom's
sister."
5 "Go to bed and pretend to be ill," Jonadab said. "When your father
comes to see you, say to him, 'I would like my sister Tamar to come and

give me something to eat. Let her prepare the food in my sight so I may
watch her and then eat it from her hand.'"
6So Amnon lay down and pretended to be ill. When the king came to
see him, Amnon said to him, "I would like my sister Tamar to come and
make some special bread in my sight, so I may eat from her hand."
7David sent word to Tamar at the palace: "Go to the house of your
brother Amnon and prepare some food for him." 8So Tamar went to the
house of her brother Amnon, who was lying down. She took some
dough, kneaded it, made the bread in his sight and baked it. 9Then she
took the pan and served him the bread, but he refused to eat.
"Send everyone out of here," Amnon said. So everyone left him.
10Then Amnon said to Tamar, "Bring the food here into my bedroom so
I may eat from your hand." And Tamar took the bread she had prepared
and brought it to her brother Amnon in his bedroom. 11But when she
took it to him to eat, he grabbed her and said, "Come to bed with me,
my sister."
12"Don't, my brother!" she said to him. "Don't force me. Such a thing
should not be done in Israel! Don't do this wicked thing. 13What about
me? Where could I get rid of my disgrace? And what about you? You
would be like one of the wicked fools in Israel. Please speak to the king;
he will not keep me from being married to you." 14But he refused to
listen to her, and since he was stronger than she, he raped her.
15Then Amnon hated her with intense hatred. In fact, he hated her
more than he had loved her. Amnon said to her, "Get up and get out!"
16"No!" she said to him. "Sending me away would be a greater wrong
than what you have already done to me."
But he refused to listen to her. 17He called his personal servant and
said, "Get this woman out of here and bolt the door after her." 18So his
servant put her out and bolted the door after her. She was wearing a
richly ornamented robe, for this was the kind of garment the virgin
daughters of the king wore. 19Tamar put ashes on her head and tore the
ornamented robe she was wearing. She put her hand on her head and
went away, weeping aloud as she went.
20Her brother Absalom said to her, "Has that Amnon, your brother,
been with you? Be quiet now, my sister; he is your brother. Don't take
this thing to heart." And Tamar lived in her brother Absalom's house, a
desolate woman.
21When King David heard all this, he was furious. 22Absalom never
said a word to Amnon, either good or bad; he hated Amnon because he
had disgraced his sister Tamar.

Within the Court History of David (chs. 9–20), the longest definable literary section is the story of Absalom in chapters 13–20 (more precisely, 13:1–20:22; cf. Conroy, pp. v, 6 n. 31). Absalom's name appears in the OT approximately one hundred times, more than 90 percent of which occur in chapters 13–20. Although Absalom dies in chapter 18 (cf. 18:14–15), his memory and influence continue down to the end of the Court History (cf. 20:6).

If the integrity of chapters 13–20 as a literary unit of the highest order is beyond question (cf. Conroy, p. 1), it is equally clear that the section contains two readily distinguishable subsections: chapters 13–14, which may be characterized as exhibiting for the most part a "desire/fulfillment of desire" pattern, and chapters 15–20, which prefer a "departure/return" pattern (for details cf. ibid., pp. 89–93; for the same basic division, cf. Mats Eskhult, *Studies in Verbal Aspect and Narrative Technique in Biblical Hebrew Prose* [Stockholm: Almqvist and Wiksell, 1990], pp. 58–59; Carlson, p. 42).

Although my parameters for the four segments within chapters 13–14 (i.e., 13:1–22,

23–39; 14:1–20, 21–33) are more traditional than those of Conroy (i.e., 13:1–22, 23–38, 39–14:27 [14:25–27 he calls a "descriptive parenthesis," p. 92], 28–33) and thus differ slightly from them, his insight into the basic theme of the chapters is helpful and suggestive. Literary clues leading to the isolation of chapters 13–14 as a separate unit include (1) "In the course of time" at 13:1 (*way*[e]*hî 'aḥ*[a]*rê-ḵēn*) and 15:1 (*way*[e]*hî mē'aḥ*[a]*rê ḵēn*), signaling the start of a new section; (2) *l*[e]*'aḇšālôm* (lit., "to Absalom") at the beginning of 13:1 and the end of 14:33, forming an *inclusio* to frame the whole; and (3) the "two years" of 13:23, "three years" of 13:38, and "two years" of 14:28, specific time spans arranged in chiastic order and adding up to seven years, the number seven symbolizing completion (cf. similarly Carlson, p. 164).

The furies unleashed by David in chapter 11, having already taken their toll in the death of the unnamed infant son of David and Bathsheba (12:19), continue unimpeded in the rape and desolation of David's daughter Tamar (13:14, 20), the murder of David's son Amnon (13:28–29), and the enforced exile and quarantine of David's son Absalom (13:34, 37–38; 14:28). Chapters 13–14 are thus aptly characterized as "family tragedies" (Eskhult, *Studies in Verbal Aspect and Narrative Technique*, pp. 58–59).

> Clearly we are expected to see in chapter 13 a recapitulation of what had gone before in chapter 11. David had seen a beautiful woman, had taken her and lain with her; then, in order to prevent discovery through the birth of an obviously illegitimate child, he had attempted to trick the husband into a false paternity and, failing this, had finally engaged in an intrigue which led to Uriah's death. Amnon, David's son, desires a beautiful girl, he conspires to trick her into a position where he can seize and lie with her, but is in turn conspired against and murdered. David finds, coming to expression within his own family, the elements of his own earlier experience. . . . His sin has come home to roost. (Gunn, *The Story of King David*, pp. 98–99; cf. also Ackerman, p. 49; Preston, p. 41)

George P. Ridout has provided a detailed chiastic outline of vv.1–22 (*Prose Compositional Techniques in the Succession Narrative [2 Samuel 7, 9–20; 1 Kings 1–2]* [Ann Arbor: University Microfilms, 1985], pp. 50–56), reproduced here with slight modifications:

- A. Amnon in love with Tamar (13:1–2)
  - B. Intervention of Jonadab (13:3–5)
    - C. Tamar's arrival (13:6–9a)
      - D. Amnon's servants ordered to leave (13:9b)
        - E. Amnon's command to Tamar to come to bed with him; her unavailing plea (13:10–14a)
          - F. Amnon's rape of Tamar; the turning of love to hatred (13:14b–15a)
        - E′. Amnon's command to Tamar to depart; her unavailing plea (13:15b–16)
      - D′. Amnon's servant recalled (13:17)
    - C′. Tamar's departure (13:18–19)
  - B′. Intervention of Absalom (13:20)
- A′. Absalom's hatred for Amnon (13:21–22)

Although it is relatively easy to indulge in minor quibbles with Ridout's attempt (cf. Conroy, p. 20; Fokkelman, *King David*, pp. 100–101), his analysis has the advantage of showing how a narrative that begins with love (vv.1–2) and ends with hatred (vv.21–22) centers on an act of violence that turns love into hatred (vv.14b–15a). His outline will therefore be followed here. Fokkelman's modest rearrangement of and additions to the chain-structure outline by Shimon Bar-Efrat ("Some Observations on the Analysis of Structure in Biblical Narrative," VetTest 30, 2 [1980]: 162–63]) leads to the same broadly chiastic conclusion (*King David,* pp. 101–2):

*love/hatred* (vv.14b–15a)<br>
Tamar – Amnon (vv.8–16)<br>
(v.7) David – Tamar  Amnon – servant (v.17)<br>
(v.6) Amnon – David  servant – Tamar (v.18)<br>
(vv.3–5) Jonadab – Amnon  Tamar – Absalom (vv.19–20)<br>
(vv.1–2) *love*  *hatred* (vv.21–22)

**1–2** That vv.1–22 constitute a pericope with literary integrity is clear: "The three personal names (Absalom, Tamar, and Amnon) form an *inclusion* between v.1 and v.22b. The beginning and end . . . are also linked by way of a reversal: Amnon loves . . . at v.1, he is hated . . . at v.22" (Conroy, p. 17). The transitional formula "In the course of time" does not "mark a completely new beginning but rather a new episode which shares something with the foregoing" (ibid., p. 41). Although not necessarily signifying chronological sequence (see Notes on 2:1 and comments on 8:1; 10:1), the phrase in this context appears in any case to introduce an account of events occurring later than those in chapters 10–12.

As an index of the fact that the story of Amnon's sin against Tamar is part of the larger narrative of Absalom's relentless march to usurp the throne of Israel now occupied by his father David, Absalom's name appears first in the Hebrew text of v.1. The half brothers "Absalom son of David" (David's third son) and "Amnon son of David" (David's firstborn; see 3:2–3 and comments) contextually surround Tamar (v.1), "sister to Absalom and object of desire to Amnon. . . . They move between protecting and polluting, supporting and seducing, comforting and capturing her" (Phyllis Trible, *Texts of Terror: Literary-Feminist Readings of Biblical Narratives* [Philadelphia: Fortress, 1984], p. 38). Tamar's name means "Palm Tree" (as in S of Songs 7:7–8, where a palm tree's height is compared to a woman's stature and its clusters of fruit to her breasts).

Sister of Absalom and half sister of Amnon, Tamar is "beautiful" indeed (v.1). Good looks were not at a premium in David's family: The "handsome" Absalom (14:25) would father a "beautiful" daughter also named Tamar (14:27)—probably in memory of his sister—and David himself was "handsome" (1 Sam 16:12; 17:42). In addition, David was attracted to "beautiful" women like Abigail (1 Sam 25:3) and, of course, Bathsheba (11:2; same Heb. word in all verses except the last). Thus it is not surprising that David's son Amnon "fell in love with" Tamar (cf. also v.4; for the ingressive mode of the verb, cf. Eskhult, "Studies in Verbal Aspect and Narrative Technique," p. 59).

As a "virgin" (v.2), however, strictly speaking "Tamar is protected property, inaccessible to males, including her brother" (Trible, *Texts of Terror*, p. 38). Amnon is therefore "frustrated" (or "distressed/in distress," as the same Heb. expression is translated in 24:14; 1 Sam 28:15; 30:6) to the extent that he becomes lovesick (cf. "faint with love" in S of Songs 2:5; 5:8; the Heb. root rendered "faint" is the same as that for "illness" in v.2). The statement that "it seemed impossible for him to do anything to her" is perhaps deliberately ambiguous since "the key verb's literal sense and its supporting syntax permit a double entendre: 'And it was awesome in the eyes of Amnon to do something to her' " (Rosenberg, p. 140). In general, *l<sup>e</sup>hippālē' min* normally means "to be beyond the powers of," "to be too hard/difficult for" someone (to do/contemplate; cf. Gen 18:14; Deut 30:11; Jer 32:17, 27), whereas *l<sup>e</sup>hippālē' b<sup>e</sup>'ênê* means "to be wonderful/marvelous in the eyes of" someone (cf. Ps 118:23; Zech 8:6 ["seem marvelous to"]; for additional details, cf. Rosenberg, p. 244 n. 51). Since the latter form of the Hebrew expression is used here, it may not at all seem "impossible" for Amnon to violate his half sister Tamar. Indeed, given her unusual beauty, it may in fact seem quite possible—perhaps even "awesome"—for him to do so.

**3–5** Jonadab's intervention on Amnon's behalf (vv.3–5) and Absalom's intervention on Tamar's behalf (v.20) are similar in that both begin with one or more questions (vv.4, 20a) and then continue with words of advice (vv.5, 20b). More immediately important from a structural standpoint, however, is a comparison between a literal rendering of the Hebrew texts of vv.1 and 3: "And to Absalom . . . a sister. . . , and her name Tamar" (v.1); "And to Amnon a friend, and his name Jonadab" (v.3; cf. similarly Trible, *Texts of Terror*, p. 39). Tamar may be "beautiful" (v.1), but Jonadab is "very shrewd/wise" (v.3). At first blush it would seem that Tamar is no match for Jonadab and that his counsel to Amnon will surely contribute to her undoing.

As the son of David's brother Shimeah (called Shammah in 1 Sam 16:9; 17:13 and Shimea in 1 Chron 2:13), Jonadab (a name that means "The LORD Is Noble" and that was perhaps deliberately chosen to reflect the name of Shimeah's older brother Abinadab, which means "My [Divine] Father Is Noble"; see 1 Sam 16:8 and comment) is Amnon's cousin, and thus all the people mentioned by name in vv.1–22 are members of the same family. Jonadab is also Amnon's "friend" (*rē<sup>a</sup>'*), perhaps in this case connoting

> a special office or association with the royal family (especially in light of his role as a counselor in David's cabinet; cf. 13:32–35). During Solomon's reign, Zabud son of Nathan has the title of priest and "king's friend" (*rē'eh hammelek*, 1 Kgs 4:5 [NIV, "personal adviser to the king"]). It may well be that with Jonadab (and others?) this cabinet post has its rudimentary beginnings in the Davidic monarchy. (Andrew E. Hill, "A Jonadab Connection in the Absalom Conspiracy?" JETS 30, 4 [1987]: 387; cf. perhaps also 16:16–17)

Since counsel was often sought from wise men and women during David's reign (cf. 14:2; 20:16), it is doubtless better to translate *ḥāḵām* by the more neutral "wise" than the more nuanced (and possibly incorrect) "shrewd" (v.3). Jonadab is then a wise man, and the ploy suggested by him "to Amnon for the seduction of Tamar was known to him by virtue of his standing in the royal court as a sage" (ibid., p. 388), as we shall see.

Jonadab begins by asking Amnon why he—who is, after all, the "king's son" (v.4)—looks so "haggard" all the time (the Heb. word has various shades of meaning, including "weak" [3:1; Ps 41:1] and "scrawny" [Gen 41:19]). Jonadab's urbane "Won't you tell me?" is much more polite than David's terse "Tell me" (1:4), a difference readily explained by observing who is speaking to whom. Amnon's response, as reported by the narrator, is a masterpiece of alliteration in the MT, all six words beginning with the same letter: *'eṯ-tāmār '<sup>a</sup>ḥôṯ 'aḇšālōm 'āḥî '<sup>a</sup>nî 'ōhēḇ* (lit.,

"Tamar, the sister of Absalom my brother, I love"). The alliteration in ' (*aleph*) "gives the impression of a succession of faltering sighs" (Conroy, p. 29 n. 38). The word "Tamar" is in emphatic position and is thus highlighted as referring to the object of Amnon's desire.

If Egyptian contacts with and influence on the Israelite united monarchy (attested for Solomon's reign; cf. 1 Kings 3:1; 4:30) began during the days of David, Jonadab's familiarity with Egyptian wisdom literature may have led him to reflect on the practical application of words like these (from an Egyptian love poem of the Nineteenth Dynasty [c. 1303–1200 B.C.]; the translation is by Michael V. Fox, *The Song of Songs and the Ancient Egyptian Love Songs* [Madison: University of Wisconsin Press, 1985], p. 13):

I will lie down inside,
and then I will feign illness.
Then my neighbors will enter to see,
and then (my) sister will come with them.
She'll put the doctors to shame
(for she) will understand my illness.

So strikingly similar to the above excerpt are certain elements of Jonadab's advice to Amnon in v.5—"Go to bed" (lit., "Lie down [cf. v.8] on your bed"), "pretend to be ill," "come to see," "my sister . . . to come"—that the relationship between the two texts can hardly be coincidental. Without comparing the boy in the Egyptian poem to Amnon (and therefore without referring to the fact that "illness" [lit., "making himself ill," v.2] and "pretend[ed] to be ill" [vv.5–6] are the only occurrences of Hithpael *ḥlh* in the OT), Fox says of the boy that "perhaps the illness he feigns is more real than he realizes, for the last line speaks of his illness as a real one that cannot be diagnosed by the physicians, but only by his beloved" (ibid., p. 13). The similarities between such Egyptian love songs and the story of Amnon and Tamar should not be allowed to obscure the differences, however: "There is a strong and effective contrast between the scenes of idyllic charm which are associated with the motif of love-sickness in Egyptian poetry and the act of brutal selfishness which will be the outcome of Amnon's love-sickness" (Conroy, p. 27; cf. Hill, "A Jonadab Connection," pp. 388–89).

Jonadab knows that when David hears of his son Amnon's "illness," he will come "to see" him (v.5; for another example of sickbed visitation, cf. Ps 41:6). At that point Amnon should tell his father that he wants Tamar to come and "give" him something "to eat" (for the rare verb *brh*, "[give to] eat" [in the sense of "eat food intended for mourners/sick people"; vv.5–6, 10] and its cognate noun *biryāh*, "food intended for mourners/sick people" [vv.5, 7, 10], cf. Koehler, "Problems," p. 6; see also 12:17 and comment). Tamar would also "prepare" (lit., "do") the food in Amnon's "sight" (v.5), a procedure that recalls the impossibility/awesomeness in Amnon's "eyes/sight" to "do" something to Tamar (see v.2 and comment; cf. Trible, *Texts of Terror*, p. 41). There is perhaps here also an echo of Nathan's parable, which included a privileged rich man who "prepared" a poor man's ewe lamb for a visiting traveler (12:4).

When Tamar arrives in his "sickroom," Amnon will surely want to "watch [her]" (v.5; an ambiguous phrase, since there is no object in the MT)—but in what sense? Trible suggests: "Though David must be made to think that Amnon wants to see the food being prepared, the reader knows that he wants to see Tamar" (ibid., p. 41). If so,

Amnon's desire to "watch" reprises his father's earlier voyeurism ("he saw" [see 11:2 and comment]; same Heb. verb).

Does Jonadab act alone in the advice he gives to Amnon? Perhaps not. Since Absalom is David's third son while Amnon is his firstborn, Absalom may be willing to sacrifice his sister in a power play for the throne. At the same time Jonadab may be attempting to secure his own political future by casting his lot with the ambitions of the aggressive Absalom, whom he sees as eventually winning out over the dissolute Amnon in any case. Jonadab would thus be a "co-conspirator with Absalom in the whole affair, since both men have much to gain" (Hill, "A Jonadab Connection," p. 389).

**6–9a** Tamar's arrival into Amnon's presence (vv.6–9a) is shaped by the verbs *bw'* ("come [in]," v.6) and *hlk* ("go/went," vv.7–8), while her departure from Amnon (vv.18–19) is described by the verbs *yṣ'* ("go out," v.18 ["put . . . out"]) and *hlk* ("went," v.19 [bis]). In addition Tamar's "hand" is to serve food to Amnon in v.6 (cf. also v.5) but symbolizes mourning and desolation in v.19.

Amnon readily accepts the advice of Jonadab, whom he perceives as acting in his best interests (v.6). But although on David's arrival Amnon at first quotes Jonadab's words verbatim ("I would like my sister Tamar to come," v.6; cf. also v.5), he inserts his own vocabulary in describing what he wants her to do after she actually comes: (1) The phrase "make some special bread" is an attempt to render the rare noun *lᵉbiḇôṯ* and its equally rare denominative verb *libbēḇ* (the words are found only here and in vv.8, 10). The fact that elsewhere the root *lbb* always means "heart" has led commentators to translate the noun in chapter 13 as "heart-shaped cakes" (Waltke and O'Connor, *Biblical Hebrew Syntax*, p. 412) or "heart-cakes . . . a heart-strengthening kind of pastry" (KD, p. 398) or—an especially felicitous rendering—"hearty dumplings" (McCarter, *II Samuel*, p. 322). Since the cognate verb is translated "you have stolen my heart" in Song of Songs 4:9 (for the connection between "heart" and "love" in ancient Israel, cf. also S of Songs 5:2; 8:6), it is possible that Amnon is being deliberately ambiguous: The cakes/dumplings will strengthen his heart (the nuance he hopes David will choose), but they will also reflect his amorous intentions (the true meaning under his hidden agenda). Indeed, the ambiguity is perhaps furthered by the explicit mention of "two" cakes/dumplings in the MT of v.6 (for details cf. Fokkelman, *King David*, pp. 105–6; Ackerman, p. 45). (2) Amnon plays on David's sympathies by using the verb *brh* ("eat [invalid food]") in the phrase "eat from her hand" (v.6) instead of *'kl*, the ordinary verb "eat," suggested by Jonadab in "eat . . . from her hand" (v.5).

Without hesitation Tamar obeys David's command to go to the house of her "brother Amnon" (vv.7–8; the constant repetition of "sister" [vv.2, 5–6, 11, 21] and "brother" [vv.7–8, 10, 12, 20] describing their relationship throughout ch. 13 heightens the tragedy about to ensue). As might be expected, Amnon is "lying down" (v.8), a "posture of power devastating for Tamar" (Trible, *Texts of Terror*, p. 43). Eskhult observes that "in vv.8b–9a the rapid succession of *wayyiqṭol*-clauses creates the impression of bustling activity" (*Studies in Verbal Aspect and Narrative Technique*, p. 59), a series of six verbs divided into two sets of three that, as Trible perceptively notes, not only "detail (Tamar's) activities" but also "focus on Amnon's eyes" (*Texts of Terror*, p. 43): "And she took some dough, and she kneaded it, and she made the bread *in his sight;* and she baked it, and she took the pan, and she served him the bread" (NIV slightly modified; italics mine). The verb "knead" and its object "dough" are sometimes used, whether literally or figuratively, in contexts where spiritual adultery is deplored (Jer 7:18; Hos 7:4).

Amnon's response to Tamar's six acts of solicitude on his behalf is a climactic seventh act of the capricious sort so characteristic of spoiled and pampered royalty: He "refused" to eat (v.9a; cf. vv.14, 16, where the Heb. verb, however, is different).

**9b** In vv.9b and 17, Amnon's initial commands in both cases are plural in number in the MT ("Send [everyone] out," v.9b; "Get [this woman] out," v.17) and include the expression *mēʿālay* ("out of here"; lit., "from upon me"). Although addressing an individual in v.17 (and perhaps also in v.9b), Amnon uses the indefinite/impersonal plural imperative (for similar phenomena cf. Waltke and O'Connor, *Biblical Hebrew Syntax*, p. 71). In v.9b "Send everyone out [*hôṣîʾû*] of here" is perfectly matched by its response: "So everyone left [*wayyēṣeʾû*, lit., 'went out'] him" (lit., "from upon him").

The peremptory command of Amnon in v.9b echoes verbatim that of Joseph centuries earlier: "Have everyone leave my presence!" (Gen 45:1; identical Heb. sentence). But while Joseph desired privacy so that he could be alone when he made himself known to his brothers, Amnon wants to be alone so that, unseen and unhindered, he can ravish his sister.

**10–14a** The structure of vv.10–14a and vv.15b–16 is similar in that each contains (1) a terse command addressed by Amnon to Tamar (vv.11, 15b), (2) a strong negative plea by Tamar (vv.12–13, 16a), and (3) the same concluding response by Amnon: "But he refused to listen to her" (vv.14a, 16b).

Once they are alone, Amnon tells Tamar to bring the "[invalid] food" to him so that he might "eat [the invalid food]" from her hand (v.10). The language Amnon uses is designed to perpetuate the charade of his pretended illness (cf. vv.5–6). Unsuspecting, Tamar brings the "bread" (see comment on v.6) to Amnon, her "brother" (see comment on v.7), in the "bedroom"—a locale usually reserved for rest and bliss but where betrayal and violence all too often hold sway (cf. 4:7).

As soon as the gullible Tamar was within arm's reach, Amnon "grabbed" her (v.11; forcibly, expressed by the Hiphil of *ḥzq;* see 2:16 and comment; the Qal of *ḥzq* is used in v.14, where Amnon is described as being "stronger" than Tamar). His lustful demand, however elegant from a literary standpoint, is both ominous and insensitive: "Come to bed with me, my sister" (*bôʾî šiḵᵉḇî ʿimmî ʾᵃḥôṯî*). "In v.11 the change to shorter sentences conveys the violence of Amnon's desire which is reflected too by the assonance in *-î* (four times) and by the staccato rhythm of his words" (Conroy, p. 30; cf. Trible, *Texts of Terror*, p. 59 n. 31).

> The dialogue in the story of Amnon and Tamar . . . looks like a conscious allusion to the technique used in the episode of Joseph and Potiphar's wife. Amnon addresses to his half-sister exactly the same words with which Potiphar's wife accosts Joseph—["Come to bed with me!" (Gen 39:7)]—adding to them only one word, the thematically loaded "sister" (2 Sam. 13:11). She responds with an elaborate protestation, like Joseph before her. (Alter, *The Art of Biblical Narrative*, p. 73)

"Come to bed" (v.11) is literally "Come, lie down," the latter verb (*škb*) being used in an entirely different way than in vv.5–6, 8 (see also 11:4 and comment; 12:24). The ambiguity of "my sister" is also notable, since Amnon may be simultaneously referring to Tamar not only as his half sister but also as his potential sexual companion (for the latter, cf. S of Songs 4:9–10, 12; 5:1–2; for "sister" in the same sense in Egyptian love poems, cf. Fox, *The Song of Songs*, pp. xii–xiii, 8, 136).

Tamar's immediate response to Amnon is indignant as well as frantic: "Don't" (v.12)—or, more simply, "No" (as in v.16; cf. 1 Sam 2:24; Judg 19:23). She matches his "my sister" with "my brother," but in the sibling rather than in the amorous sense. One by one, her short sentences bespeak her terror: "Don't force me" (v.12; cf. vv.14 ["raped"], 22 ["disgraced"], 32 ["raped"]; same Heb. verb). The Piel of *'ānāh* in the sense of "force a woman to have sexual intercourse" is attested both in legal contexts (Deut 21:14; 22:24, 29) and in narrative passages (Gen 34:2; Judg 19:24; 20:5; Lam 5:11; Ezek 22:10–11; for details cf. Beth Glazier-McDonald, "Malachi 2:12: *'ēr we'ōneh*—Another Look," JBL 105, 2 [1986]: 296).

The list of things that, in the minds of those who decide to make pronouncements on the subject, "should not be done" (v.12) is long enough (cf. Gen 20:9; 29:26; Lev 4:2, 13, 22, 27; 5:17), and sexual sins in particular are among those that should not be committed "in Israel" (vv.12–13; Gen 34:7; Deut 22:21; Judg 20:6, 10; Jer 29:23; cf. also Josh 7:15). Indeed, Tamar calls Amnon's intended act of rape a *neḇālāh* ("wicked thing," v.12), the kind of activity engaged in only by "wicked fools" (*neḇālîm*, v.13).

Anthony Phillips, among others, observes that *neḇālāh* ("folly," "disgraceful/outrageous thing," "vileness") appears in "connection with outrageous sexual offences" and adds to the above list Judges 19:23–24 ("*NEBALAH*–A Term for Serious Disorderly and Unruly Conduct," VetTest 25, 2 [1975]: 237). Pointing out that "*nebalah* is reserved for extreme acts of disorder or unruliness which themselves result in a dangerous breakdown in order, and the end of an existing relationship," he defines it as " 'an act of crass disorder or unruliness' or 'acting in an utterly disorderly or unruly fashion' " (ibid., p. 238). It is, in fact, "action which is to be utterly deplored" (ibid., p. 237), as its application to "that wicked man Nabal" indicates (see comment on "folly" in 1 Sam 25:25). Thus "Amnon's rape of his half-sister Tamar" violates "the ancient prohibition on casual sexual relations outside marriage with women whom one could expect to find living under the same family roof. . . . While Amnon could certainly have married Tamar with his father's consent. . . , to force her was indeed an act of crass disorder, extreme unruliness (*nebalah*), which inevitably led to bloodshed within the royal family" (ibid., p. 239).

The *casus pendens* constructions in v.13 ("What about me? . . . And what about you?") contribute to the staccato effect of Tamar's series of objections. As far as she herself is concerned, she wants to know "where" (cf. the plaintive cry of the similarly distraught Reuben, Gen 37:30) she could possibly get rid of her "disgrace" (*ḥerpāh:* cf. 1 Sam 25:39 ["contempt"]; Prov 6:32–33; Isa 47:3 ["shame"]; Ezek 16:57 ["scorned"]). And as far as Amnon is concerned, Tamar warns him that if he gives vent to his lustful desires, he will be like one of Israel's "wicked fools" (see comment on "lawless" in 3:33).

Having asked and answered her own rhetorical questions, Tamar voices her final plea (v.13): "Now then [omitted by NIV; see, however, comment on v.20]," she implores Amnon, "please speak to the king" (referring to him not as their father but by his title, since she anticipates his acting in an official capacity rather than as a family member). She is sure that David will not keep her from "being married to" Amnon (although the MT does not include the phrase in quotation marks, the NIV correctly supplies it). After all, had not her ancestor Abraham married his half sister Sarah (cf. Gen 20:12)?

Although we are not told whether Tamar would object to becoming Amnon's wife, she does not appear to be inherently opposed to such a prospect. What she is adamantly against is sexual intercourse with him outside the marriage relationship. "Marriage between a half-brother and half-sister is forbidden in Pentateuchal law (Lv. 18:9, 11; 20:17; Dt. 27:22), though whether such a law operated in this period is open to question" (Gordon, *1 & 2 Samuel,* p. 263). It would therefore seem likely that Amnon was about to become "guilty of rape, not of incest" (Conroy, p. 18 n. 4; cf. also Trible, *Texts of Terror,* p. 60 n. 37)—although if in her desperation Tamar is clutching at straws, incest is indeed a possible concomitant of Amnon's crimes (cf. KD, pp. 398–99; Baldwin, p. 248).

Tamar's most eloquent pleadings, however, are to no avail. Her three "Don't"s in v.12 and her three "And"s in v.13 (lit., "And as for me," "And as for you," "And now") meet with the same climactic seventh act—this time a paradigm of ominous insensitivity—as before: Amnon "refused to listen to her" (v.14a; see comment on v.9a).

**14b–15a** The center of the chiasm that structures this section (see comment on 13:1–22) focuses on Amnon's unspeakable violence against his half sister. He had "grabbed" her earlier (v.11), and he has apparently not released her throughout the entire dreary episode. He is, after all, "stronger" than she (v.14b; same Heb. verb in both cases). A painful irony is evident in comparing the story of David and Goliath with that of Amnon and Tamar: The young underdog David "triumphed over" the hitherto invincible Philistine (1 Sam 17:50), while David's firstborn son "was stronger than" his weak and innocent half sister (v.14b; identical Heb. verbal construction in both texts).

So Amnon "raped her"—literally, "forced her [see v.12 and comment] and laid her." The latter verb echoes v.11, where Amnon commands Tamar: "Come to bed with me"—literally, "Come, lie down [*škb*] with me." Here, however, the verb *škb* does not govern the particle of accompaniment *'im* ("with") but the accusative particle *'ēṯ,* hence "laid her" (cf. Trible, *Texts of Terror,* p. 46; cf. similarly Sternberg, pp. 536–37 n. 4). Whereas David had "slept/lain with [*škb 'm*]" Bathsheba (11:4), implying at least the possibility of consent on her part, Amnon "laid" (*škb 't*) Tamar, forcing her against her will (the same comparison between father and son, although highlighting other verbs in the two passages, is made by Gunn, *The Story of King David,* p. 100).

The immediate denouement of the rape (v.15a) is poignantly anticlimactic. A rapist's emotional response following the crime is unpredictable: If Shechem "loved" Dinah after he "violated" (*'nh*) her (Gen 34:2–3), Amnon "hated" Tamar after he "forced" (*'nh*) her (vv.14b–15a). Needless to say, hatred subsequent to the act of sexual intercourse is not confined to situations of rape; it can arise in the marriage bed as well (cf. Deut 22:13, 16; 24:3, where in each case "dislikes" is literally "hates").

Verse 15a (through "In fact, he hated her") includes a chiasm that, when translated literally, underscores the intensity of Amnon's newly found hatred for Tamar (cf. Fokkelman, *King David,* p. 107; cf. similarly Trible, *Texts of Terror,* p. 47; Conroy, p. 32):

A. Then Amnon hated her
  B. with a hatred
    C. great
      D. exceedingly;

D′. indeed,
C′. great
B′ was the hatred
A′. with which he hated her.

The latter sentence concludes with the phrase "more than the love with which he had loved her" (literal rendering). Thus the fourfold reference to "hate" that constitutes the subject matter of the chiasm is flanked (vv.1, 4; v.15a) by two sets of twofold references to "love." Although the fires of love may often burn away hatred (and perhaps even postpone death; cf. S of Songs 8:6), hatred may often extinguish the fires of "love"—especially when it takes on the nuance of "lust" (cf. similarly Trible, *Texts of Terror*, p. 47). Love in any form will not appear again in vv.15b–22, but hatred will (v.22).

**15b–16** Scarcely has Tamar had a chance to catch her breath after being ravished by Amnon before he delivers to her "a curt asyndetic pair of imperatives" (Conroy, p. 33): "Get up and get out!" (v.15b). The Hebrew expression (*qûmî lēḵî*), though only half as long as its counterpart in v.11b, is characterized by the same staccato rhythm as well as the same assonance in *-î*. It thus conveys the intensity of Amnon's hatred as vividly as his earlier commands had imparted the passion of his desire (see comment on v.11b). Before, consumed by lust, he had begun by begging Tamar to "come [in]"; now, repulsed by disgust, he concludes by banishing her with the words "get/go out." And Amnon's final word to Tamar also resonates within a wider literary context: It is "the same as the first word [*lky*, 'go'] spoken to her by the king in v.7" (Conroy, p. 33).

Although Tamar's response here (v.16) is much briefer than her earlier pleas (vv.12–13), she is no more ready to obey Amnon's commands now than she was before. And just as he dropped the seductive "my sister" (v.11) from his concluding terse statement (v.15b), so also she omits the plaintive "my brother" (v.12) from her final words to him. She begins in the same way as she had before, however: "No!" (v.16; see comment on v.12). As in the case of Samson's intention to do more "harm" to the Philistines than he had done before (Judg 15:3), Amnon's sending Tamar away would only add insult to injury by involving him in a greater "wrong" than the rape itself (v.16; same Heb. word in both passages).

For the third time, however, Amnon "refused" (vv.9, 14, 16)—and this time his rejection of Tamar's plea echoes the previous one almost verbatim (v.14a reads literally, "But he refused to listen to her voice [i.e., refused to obey her]").

**17** Although Amnon speaks to his personal servant, his first command to him is a plural imperative (as in the parallel in v.9b; see comment there). In v.9b he wanted everyone else out of his bedroom so that, without the presence of witnesses, he could have his own way with Tamar; here he wants Tamar out of his bedroom so that, in her absence, he will not be reminded unduly of the awful sin he has committed.

Brusque and impassive, Amnon wants to get rid of Tamar. "This woman" translates the unadorned feminine demonstrative *zō'ṯ*, the masculine equivalent of which (*zeh*) is often used in a derogatory sense (cf. 1 Sam 10:27, "this fellow" [= Saul]; 21:15, "this fellow," "this man" [= David]; 25:21, "this fellow" [= Nabal]). Thus perhaps *zō'ṯ* here is best rendered simply "this thing," reflecting the contempt in which

Amnon now holds Tamar: "One could hardly express more clearly Amnon's revulsion at his act, or the fact that he had treated his half-sister as a thing, not as a person" (Jackson, "David's Throne," p. 190; cf. Trible, *Texts of Terror*, p. 48). Like Pharaoh to Moses ("Get out of my sight [*mē'ālāy*, lit., 'from upon me']," Exod 10:28), so Amnon to Tamar ("Get this woman out of here [*mē'ālay*]"): Both are nervous at the prospect of seeing the face of an unwanted or rejected person at an undetermined time in the future.

Amnon's second command to his servant is to "bolt the door after her." The purpose of securing doors is all too often to prevent or conceal a questionable or evil deed—for example, a homosexual act in the case of Lot (cf. Gen 19:6), a murder in the case of Ehud (cf. Judg 3:21–24), a rape in the case of Amnon. Needless to say, a door keeps people not only out but also in, and thereon hangs an illustration: "On the surface, it is Tamar who is shut out, but upon Amnon too a door is closed. His fate is sealed from this moment" (Conroy, p. 33).

**18–19** Although Tamar's arrival into Amnon's presence was carefully orchestrated (vv.6–9a), her forced departure is abrupt indeed. Obedient to a fault, the servant of Amnon wastes no time: He "put her out" (v.18; same Heb. verb as in v.9b ["Send . . . out"; see also comment there]). Once the man (in this case Amnon) has satisfied his lustful desires, he discards the woman (cf. similarly Judg 19:25) as though she were so much refuse.

But Tamar is one of "the virgin daughters" (see comment on v.2) "of the king" (v.18), a status that should have made her doubly untouchable. By no means trash, she wears a "richly ornamented robe" that befits her regal position. Now no longer a virgin, she tears her robe (v.19) as a symbol of her ravished state: "Worn (v.18a), it signifies her status as an unmarried princess; torn (v.19a), it symbolizes the ruin of her life (v.20b)" (Conroy, p. 34). The act of tearing her garment also gives expression to her mourning over her irreparable loss (cf. v.31; 15:32), as do her putting "ashes on her head" (cf. similarly 1:2 and comment; 1 Sam 4:12 and comment; Esth 4:1) and her "weeping/crying aloud" (cf. 19:4). Tamar's putting her "hand" (see comment on v.6; perhaps better "hands" [cf. BHS]) on her head is probably emblematic not only of mourning (for details cf. de Vaux, AIs, p. 59) but also of exile or banishment (cf. Jer 2:37; for a relief at Medinet Habu depicting prisoners of Rameses III with their arms/hands on/over their heads, cf. ANEP, fig. 7). "In her plea to Amnon at v.13 Tamar asked, 'where shall I carry (*HLK* hif ['get rid of']) my shame'?; now in vv. 19f. she goes (*HLK* twice in v.19 ['went']) to her brother Absalom" (Conroy, p. 34).

**20** Absalom's advice to Tamar parallels Jonadab's counsel to Amnon (vv.3–5; see comment on 13:1–22), strengthening the suggestion that Jonadab and Absalom are working in concert (see comment on v.5; cf. also Rosenberg, pp. 156–59). In terms of literary structure, the verse is exquisitely ordered:

A. "her brother" (Absalom)
B. "your brother" (Amnon)
C. "my sister" (Tamar)
B′. "your brother" (Amnon)
A′. "her brother" (Absalom)

Bar-Efrat, from whom this beautiful observation is derived, points out how not only the substantives are concentrically arranged . . . but also in their possessive

> suffixes, indicating the 3rd, 2nd, 1st, 2nd, and 3rd person respectively. . . . Tamar stands in the centre and is, in the first place, surrounded and enclosed by her evil brother, but he is, in turn, surrounded and enclosed . . . by the good brother whose loving "my sister" originates in the centre. (Fokkelmann, *King David,* pp. 111–12)

At the same time, the narrator reminds his readers that the whole sordid episode is a family affair.

The advice of Absalom is both matter-of-fact and calculating. Choosing his words carefully, he asks Tamar whether Amnon (spelled "Aminon" in the MT only here; see comment on 3:2) has "been with" her—an expression that, though not sexually explicit, is at least suggestive of potential involvement (cf. Gen 39:10). He counsels her to be quiet about the matter "now" (cf. v.13 MT)—that is, "for the time being" (cf. Trible, *Texts of Terror,* p. 51). Since Amnon is Tamar's "(half) brother," the problem will be solved within the parameters of the family. Therefore Tamar should not "take this thing to heart" (i.e., pay undue attention to it or worry about it; cf. 1 Sam 4:20; 9:20, where the same Heb. idiom, or its equivalent, is used).

For the foreseeable future Tamar would live in her brother Absalom's "house" ("not . . . a residence removed from the royal palace but merely an area within it" [M. O'Connor, "The Grammar of Finding Your Way in Palmyrene Aramaic and the Problem of Diction in Ancient West Semitic Inscriptions," in *Focus: A Semitic/Afrasian Gathering in Remembrance of Albert Ehrman*; Current Issues in Linguistic History 58; ed. Yoel L. Arbeitman (Amsterdam/Philadelphia: John Benjamins, 1988), p. 356 n. 5]). There she would remain "desolate," which "includes the meanings 'unmarried' and 'childless': see Isa 54, 1. For a Hebrew woman it was a living death (cf. 2 Sam 20, 3)" (Conroy, p. 35 n. 70).

**21–22** David and three of his children (Amnon, Absalom, Tamar) are linked together in the final segment (vv.21–22) of the literary unit under review (vv.1–22), just as they were in the beginning segment (vv.1–2). There the interrelationships were reasonably positive, and love was the keynote (v.1); here, however, all semblance of harmony has dissolved, and emotions such as anger (v.21) and hatred (v.22) dominate.

When David hears about Amnon's rape of Tamar and its sequel, he is understandably "furious" (v.21)—just as he had "burned with anger" after learning of the despicable conduct of the rich man in Nathan's parable (see 12:5 and comment; same Heb. expression in both cases). But even though he is "King David" (the title is an ironic touch), he perhaps feels that he is powerless to act because he himself is guilty of a similar sin: his adultery with Bathsheba. If Dinah's brothers, hearing about the rape of their sister and thus becoming angry (Gen 34:7), proceeded to take what they considered to be the necessary steps to avenge her (Gen 34:25–29), David's guilt in an analogous situation paralyzes him.

Indeed, David's responses throughout chapter 13 are reactive rather than proactive (cf. vv.37, 39).

> The results of David's sin with Bathsheba become evident in his relations with his sons, for how can a father discipline his children when he knows that he has done worse than they? When David's son Amnon rapes Tamar . . . David is very angry (II Sam. 13:21), and yet David takes no action, for he, too, has committed his own sexual offense. The upshot is that Tamar's brother, Absalom, murders Amnon (II Sam. 13:29), but David again does nothing, for he, too, has a murder on his head.

(Paul J. and Elizabeth Achtemeier, *The Old Testament Roots of Our Faith* [Philadelphia: Fortress, 1979], p. 94)

(See also Ackerman, p. 48; Lasine, "Melodrama as Parable," p. 102.) David is as clearly unable to control his sons' passions as he is his own (cf. Jackson, "David's Throne," p. 189).

Meanwhile Absalom bides his time (v.22), saying nothing "either good or bad" to Amnon (cf. Gen 31:24, 29)—that is, nothing "one way or the other" (Gen 24:50; same Heb. idiom in all four texts). Absalom's remarkable forbearance, which would last two years (v.23), provides further evidence in favor of the conspiracy theory (see comment on v.5). He "remained silent and inactive, although [*kî*, untr. in NIV] he hated Amnon" (Conroy, p. 18 n. 6; cf. similarly W. Malcolm Clark, "A Legal Background to the Yahwist's Use of 'Good and Evil' in Genesis 2–3," JBL 88, 3 [1969]: 269 n. 14).

Amnon's acquired hatred for his half sister Tamar (v.15) is reprised in Absalom's acquired hatred for his half brother Amnon (v.22). The phrase *'al-d<sup>e</sup>ḇar 'ªšer* ("because") followed by a verb occurs only here and in Deuteronomy 22:24 (bis); 23:4 ("for"). "In the legal texts of Dt the phrase introduces the reason for a condemnation or sentence, and a similar nuance may be had at 2 Sam 13,22: Absalom's silence and separation from Amnon means that the latter has already been sentenced" (Conroy, p. 35 n. 74).

## Notes

3 Instead of the MT's "Jonadab" (first occurrence), "Jonathan" is read in 4QSam[a] and the Lucianic recension of the LXX, probably by contamination from 21:21 (where Jonathan, another son of Shimeah, is mentioned).

16 Although S.R. Driver declares אַל־אוֹדֹת (*'al-'ôḏōṯ*) to be "untranslateable" (*Notes on the Books of Samuel*, p. 298; cf. Kirkpatrick, Smith), KD suggests that "nothing more is needed than to supply תְּהִי [*t<sup>e</sup>hî*]" to arrive at the clear (lit. rendered) translation: "Do not become the cause of this great evil, (which is) greater than another that thou hast done to me, to thrust me away." Another possibility is to translate, with Goldman, "Not so, because this great wrong in putting me forth is worse than the other that thou didst unto me" (p. 260). Since many MSS read עַל (*'al*) instead of אַל (*'al*; cf. BHS), the MT may have originally read *'al 'al-'ôḏōṯ* ("No, because"), *'al* dropping out of some MSS because of haplography and *'al* out of others for the same reason (for *'al-'ôḏōṯ*, "because of," cf. Gen 21:11 ["because it concerned"], 25 ["about"]; Exod 18:8 ["for (the) sake (of)"]; Num 12:1; 13:24; Judg 6:7; Jer 3:8). In any case, emendations of the MT based on the LXX are uncalled for, since the LXX may have been translating *ad sensum* a Hebrew *Vorlage* identical to or close to the MT.

18 The meaning of פַּסִּים (*passîm*), which renders "(richly) ornamented" in vv.18–19 as well as in Gen 37:3, 23, 32, remains uncertain (see NIV mg. here and at Gen 37:3; cf. also the extended discussion in McCarter, *II Samuel*, pp. 325–26). The two most common translations are "long-sleeved" (based on the LXX renderings here) and "embroidered" (perhaps "based on one meaning of *pas* in Rabbinic Hebrew, viz., 'strip, stripe'—thus *k<sup>e</sup>tōnet passîm*, 'gown of strips' or 'striped gown' " [ibid., p. 325]; cf. Joseph's "coat of *many* colours" [KJV]). It is impossible to choose definitively between the two, nor do the "embroidered garments" worn by the royal bride in Ps 45:14 constitute an unassailable parallel since the phrase translates a different Hebrew word (cf. similarly Judg 5:30).

21 At the end of the verse, the NRSV appends "but he would not punish his son Amnon, because he loved him, for he was his firstborn." The added words (cf. already Jos. Antiq.

VII, 173 [viii.2]; JB; NAB; NEB; cf. also Barthélemy, pp. 234–35) "can be restored on the basis of the Greek and Old Latin texts and a fragment of the longer reading in a Hebrew manuscript from Qumran (4QSam[a])" (McCarter, " 'Plots, True or False,' " p. 366 n. 20; cf. similarly S.R. Driver, *Notes on the Books of Samuel*, p. 301, based on the LXX alone). Although the addition is attractive (cf. "His father had never interfered with [Adonijah]" in 1 Kings 1:6, which looks like a literary reminiscence of the versional "he would not punish his son" [same Heb. idiom in both cases]), Conroy issues a helpful caveat (pp. 152–53).

---

## 8. *The murder of Amnon*

### 13:23–39

23 Two years later, when Absalom's sheepshearers were at Baal Hazor
near the border of Ephraim, he invited all the king's sons to come there.
24 Absalom went to the king and said, "Your servant has had shearers
come. Will the king and his officials please join me?"
25 "No, my son," the king replied. "All of us should not go; we would
only be a burden to you." Although Absalom urged him, he still refused
to go, but gave him his blessing.
26 Then Absalom said, "If not, please let my brother Amnon come with
us."
The king asked him, "Why should he go with you?" 27 But Absalom
urged him, so he sent with him Amnon and the rest of the king's sons.
28 Absalom ordered his men, "Listen! When Amnon is in high spirits
from drinking wine and I say to you, 'Strike Amnon down,' then kill him.
Don't be afraid. Have not I given you this order? Be strong and brave."
29 So Absalom's men did to Amnon what Absalom had ordered. Then all
the king's sons got up, mounted their mules and fled.
30 While they were on their way, the report came to David: "Absalom
has struck down all the king's sons; not one of them is left." 31 The king
stood up, tore his clothes and lay down on the ground; and all his
servants stood by with their clothes torn.
32 But Jonadab son of Shimeah, David's brother, said, "My lord should
not think that they killed all the princes; only Amnon is dead. This has
been Absalom's expressed intention ever since the day Amnon raped
his sister Tamar. 33 My lord the king should not be concerned about the
report that all the king's sons are dead. Only Amnon is dead."
34 Meanwhile, Absalom had fled.
Now the man standing watch looked up and saw many people on the
road west of him, coming down the side of the hill. The watchman went
and told the king, "I see men in the direction of Horonaim, on the side of
the hill."
35 Jonadab said to the king, "See, the king's sons are here; it has
happened just as your servant said."
36 As he finished speaking, the king's sons came in, wailing loudly.
The king, too, and all his servants wept very bitterly.
37 Absalom fled and went to Talmai son of Ammihud, the king of
Geshur. But King David mourned for his son every day.
38 After Absalom fled and went to Geshur, he stayed there three years.
39 And the spirit of the king longed to go to Absalom, for he was
consoled concerning Amnon's death.

Bracketed by the "two years" of Absalom's silent waiting (v.23) and the "three years" of his voluntary exile (v.38), vv.23–39 constitute a distinct literary unit. Although it has been argued that v.39 is more closely linked to what follows it than to what precedes it (cf. Sacon, " 'The Succession Narrative,' " p. 42; Fokkelman, *King*

*David,* p. 126), at the very least it is better to treat it as a transitional verse connecting chapter 13 to chapter 14.

The entire unit divides most naturally into two main sections that describe, respectively, Amnon's murder (vv.23–29) and its aftermath (vv.30–38; cf. similarly Fokkelman, *King David,* p. 114). The former section refers to David exclusively as "the king" (vv.24, 25, 26; cf. also "the king's sons" [vv.23, 27, 29]), while the latter often uses the proper name (vv.30, 32, 37, 39 [MT; see NIV mg.]). Both sections appear to be arranged chiastically:

A. Absalom invites the king and his officials to the sheepshearing (13:23–24).
  B. Despite Absalom's urging, the king refuses (13:25).
    C. Absalom requests that Amnon alone be allowed to come (13:26a).
  B′. Due to Absalom's urging, the king agrees (13:26b–27).
A′. Absalom orders his men to kill Amnon (13:28–29).
A. David and his servants mourn (13:30–31).
  B. Jonadab speaks to David (13:32–33).
    C. Absalom alone flees (13:34).
  B′. Jonadab speaks to David (13:35).
A′. David and his servants mourn (13:36–39).

The latter chiasm is similar to certain elements of the analysis suggested by Sacon (" 'The Succession Narrative,' " pp. 41–42), who, however, needlessly complicates the outline by attempting to draw vv.23–29 into one large overall chiasm. The result is a top-heavy structure that parallels vv.23–29b with vv.37–38b. My proposal has the advantage of isolating the two main *dramatis personae:* Amnon the victim as the center of attention in v.26a, and Absalom the murderer as the focal point in v.34.

**23–24** Two full years having passed (v.23, lit., "And it was for two years, [namely] days"; for the same Heb. construction, cf. 14:28; see also comment on 13:1–22), Absalom determines that the time is ripe to avenge the rape of his sister Tamar. He chooses sheepshearing, a festive season (see comment on 1 Sam 25:2), as a suitable if macabre backdrop for the murder of his brother Amnon: As the sheep of Absalom would lose their wool (vv.23–24), so David's firstborn, the potential shepherd of Israel, would lose his life (vv.28–29).

The locale is Baal Hazor, perhaps the same as the Benjamite village of Hazor (cf. Neh 11:33) and identified with modern Jebel/Tel Asur (about fifteen miles north-northeast of Jerusalem), the highest peak (3,333 feet above sea level) in the hill country of Ephraim (cf. Rasmussen, p. 40; cf. also Aharoni, *Land of the Bible,* p. 29). A magnificent site, it is the place to which Absalom invites the king, together with all his sons and officials, to join in celebrating their mutual prosperity. Absalom's words to his father David (v.24) are well chosen in terms of both politeness and protocol. Referring to himself as "your servant," he continues his request: "Will the king and his officials [lit., 'servants'] please join me [lit., 'your servant']?"

**25** The king's two brief responses to Absalom, combined with the phrase "Absalom urged him," link v.25 to vv.26b–27 as parallel elements in the chiastic structure of vv.23–29. From a literary standpoint David's "No, my son" reprises Tamar's "No, my brother" (see v.12 and comment; cf. further Rosenberg, p. 147). From an exegetical standpoint, however, it is a much gentler rebuff (cf. Naomi's "No, my daughters" in Ruth 1:13) than Tamar's desperate cry for help. In any event, David knows that if his entire retinue would accompany Absalom, it would be "a burden to" him (lit., "heavy [up]on," as in Neh 5:18). Absalom's urging to the contrary notwithstanding, David refuses to go and gives him his "blessing" (or "farewell"; cf. NIV mg. on Gen 47:10).

**26a** After asking for the impossible (doubtless knowing that he would be refused), Absalom cannily requests that Amnon alone be allowed to come (for *wālōʾ* [lit., "and not"] in the sense of "if not," cf. 2 Kings 5:17). He probably realizes that David, knowing that Absalom may intend to harm Amnon because of what he did to Tamar, will not accede to his latter request any more than he did to the former. On the other hand, perhaps Absalom hopes that the two years that have elapsed since the rape have dimmed the event in his father's mind. In addition, Absalom refers to Amnon as "my brother" (only here in the entire chapter), apparently to assuage whatever lingering fears David may have.

**26b–27** To Absalom's chagrin, David does not agree immediately. His "Why . . . ?" (v.26b) smacks more of the suspicious than of the incredulous. This time, however, Absalom's urging (v.27; cf. the parallel in v.25) is successful—and perhaps beyond his wildest expectations: The indecisive king not only allows his son Amnon to go but also sends the rest of his sons along with him. "David puts himself at ease by giving Amnon the company of his brothers. For Absalom they are no hindrance, however, but a good cover needed to receive Amnon fittingly at his country-seat" (Fokkelman, *King David,* p. 116).

**28–29** Emboldened by his increasing success (in vv.24–27 he alternates between requesting and urging), Absalom now commands (the verb "order" is used of/by him three times in vv.28–29). He gets the attention of his men by telling them to "listen" (cf. also Ps 45:10; lit., "see/look," as in Exod 25:40; 2 Kings 6:32). To be "in high spirits from drinking wine" (v.28) is often to invite mischief at best (cf. Esth 1:10–11) and disaster at worst (see 1 Sam 25:36 and comment)—in this case mayhem ("Kill him"). Sandwiched between Absalom's words of encouragement and reassurance—"Don't be afraid" (see 9:7 and comment) and "Be strong and brave" (lit., "Be strong and become sons of power/might"; for the latter clause see 2:7 and comment)—is the "I" (emphatic) of potentially royal mandate.

As the daughter of Jephthah died because "he did to her as he had vowed" (Judg 11:39), so the brother of Absalom dies because "Absalom's men did to Amnon what Absalom had ordered" (v.29; similar Heb. euphemistic form of expression in both cases). Panic-stricken, the rest of the king's sons decide against waiting to find out whether Absalom's execution order will extend to them: They get on their "mules" (the mount of choice for royalty during the early monarchy; cf. 18:9; 1 Kings 10:25; 18:5) and flee for their lives.

Thus David's adultery with Bathsheba is mirrored in his son Amnon's rape of Tamar, and David's murder of Uriah is reprised in Absalom's execution of Amnon. "It will suffice here to conclude that Amnon and Absalom are chips off the old block" (Fokkelman, *King David,* p. 125). Applicable to the present situation, a principle enunciated by Paul is terser still: "A man reaps what he sows" (Gal 6:7).

**30–31** Before the princes arrive in Jerusalem, a false "report" comes to David (v.30), claiming that Absalom has killed "all the king's sons." It would seem that David's usually reliable intelligence network (see 10:5 and comment) has failed him this time.

Like far too many rumors, the one that reaches David is a gross exaggeration: As far as the king's sons are concerned, apart from Absalom "not one of them is left" (for the same Heb. expression, cf. Ps 106:11, where it is said of Israel's Egyptian pursuers in the days of the Exodus that "not one of them survived").

David's immediate reaction to the news is both predictable and understandable: He "stood up" in alarm (v.31), bolt upright, just as his sons had done when their brother Amnon was killed ("got up," v.29; same Heb. verb in both cases). Echoing the behavior of his disgraced daughter Tamar, who tore her robe to bewail the loss of her virginity, David tears his clothes as a sign of mourning (see v.19 and comment), and his "servants" dutifully follow suit (v.31; cf. also v.36 [the same Heb. word is translated "officials" in v.24; see 1 Sam 16:15–16 and comment]). As a further symbol of his grief, the king lies "on the ground" (v.31), just as he had done while pleading to God for the life of his illegitimate son (see comment on 12:16).

**32–33** The false "report" (*šᵉmuʿāh,* v.30) is quickly challenged by a wise man who may have been a member of David's cabinet (see comment on v.3): Jonadab son of "Shimeah" (*šimʿāh,* v.32; for the observation that the consonantal structure of the two Heb. words is the same, cf. Fokkelman, *King David,* p. 118). Jonadab's prior knowledge that "only Amnon is dead" (vv.32–33) and that his murder has been Absalom's expressed "intention" (cf. similarly KD, Anderson; *śûmāh* is attested only here) for the past two years lends further credence to the theory that Absalom and Jonadab had long ago hatched a plot to do away with Amnon, David's heir apparent and thus an obstacle to Absalom's pretensions. Although the erroneous report had stated that "Absalom" had struck down all the princes (v.30), Jonadab knows that "they [Absalom's men] killed" only Amnon (v.32 [cf. v.29]; cf. Hill, "A Jonadab Connection," p. 390). Jonadab's confident assertion being the true state of affairs, David should not "be concerned about the [false] report" that has come to him (v.33; lit., "lay [*śym,* cognate to and punning on *śûmāh* in v.32] the word upon his heart"; see comment on 1 Sam 21:12 ["took these words to heart"]).

**34** Whereas the king's sons had "fled" to avoid Amnon's fate (v.29), Absalom has meanwhile also "fled," in this case to escape royal retribution (v.34; different Heb. verbs). Although the other princes escape to the refuge of Jerusalem, Absalom flees across the Jordan, far from Jerusalem—a flight of such import that it is mentioned three times in the space of five verses (vv.34, 37, 38). Ironically, David himself would later "flee" to "escape from Absalom" (15:14; cf. also 1 Sam 19:12, 18; 22:17).

One of the watchmen atop the walls of Jerusalem sees a number of men "on" (for *min* ["from"] in the sense of "in, on," see Notes on 5:13) the road leading to the city from the west. He reports to David that they are "in the direction of Horonaim" (or "on the road from Horonaim"; cf. similarly "on the road down from Beth Horon" in Josh 10:11). Meaning literally "Two Horons," Horonaim here is not the Moabite town mentioned in Isaiah 15:5 and Jeremiah 48:3, 5, 34 (= *ḥwrnn* in lines 31–32 of the Mesha stele) but refers to the Levitical city (cf. Josh 21:20, 22; 1 Chron 6:66, 68) of Upper and Lower Beth Horon, modern Beit Ur el-Foqa and Beit Ur el-Tahta respectively, located in Ephraim two miles apart on a ridge ten to twelve miles northwest of Jerusalem. Fleeing from Baal Hazor (see comment on v.23), the royal party must have traveled "by way of Bethel and picked up the Horonaim road near Gibeon" (McCarter, *II Samuel,* p. 333).

**35** As Jonadab had earlier assured the king that of all his sons only Amnon was dead (see vv.32–33 and comments), so he now advises David to see with his own eyes that "the king's sons are here." He then adds a statement that is doubtless intended to ingratiate himself to David: "It has happened just as your servant said."

**36–39** The scene of mourning described in vv.36–39 balances that in vv.30–31. Appearing at the beginning of vv.36 ("finished") and 39 ("longed"), the verb *klh* frames the literary unit.

The Hebrew clause rendered "the king's sons came in" (v.36) echoes verbatim the one translated "See, the king's sons are here" in v.35. David's servants and sons join him in weeping and wailing "loudly" and "bitterly" (v.36; for other examples of David's mourning over a slain family member, comrade, or friend, see comment on 3:32). "Wailing loudly" is an idiomatic rendering of the picturesque phrase "raised their voice(s) and wept" (see comment on 1 Sam 11:4), while "wept . . . bitterly" (cf. also Judg 21:2) translates a cognate accusative construction that means literally "wept a great weeping." The effect of both expressions used together is to emphasize the pathos and sense of utter hopelessness that surrounds the tragic loss of a firstborn son.

For his part Absalom, David's third son, flees for his life to Geshur (v.37) in Aram (cf. 15:8) to find protection in the household of Talmai, his grandfather on his mother's side (see 3:3 and comments). "Like Jacob before him, Absalom fled to Aramaean kinsmen in the North-east" (Carlson, p. 164). "King David" (though the words are not in the MT, they appear in the LXX and are rightly supplied contextually by the NIV) continues to mourn for "his son"—doubtless Amnon, although the fact that the narrator does not name him leaves open the slight possibility that Absalom, "the favorite now in exile" (Sternberg, p. 231), is intended (David's later grieving for his son Absalom is one of the most poignant scenes in all of Scripture [cf. 18:33–19:4]). The depth of David's grief over Amnon's death is underscored in the statement that he mourned for his son "every day" (lit., "all the days"), an emphatic expression elsewhere translated "always" (cf. 1 Sam 2:35) and "for life" (cf. 1 Sam 28:2).

Meanwhile, "only after a three-year self-imposed exile in Geshur [v.38] . . . does [Absalom] return to Jerusalem [14:23] to make preparations for his own kingship by undermining popular allegiance to David. . . . Certainly this belies a carefully constructed strategy for seizing control of the monarchy and bespeaks a man of considerable foresight, determination and ability" (Hill, "A Jonadab Connection," pp. 389–90). "When revolt against David did finally come, it is not surprising that its roots were in the east. . . . One must wonder if Absalom did not expect to receive aid in his revolt from his eastern allies" (Curtis, "East Is East . . . ," pp. 357–58).

Absalom's rebellion, however, is still in the future. For now the narrator briefly explores David's attitude toward Absalom after the period of mourning for Amnon is over. The rendering represented by the NIV ("the spirit of the king longed to go to Absalom," v.39) "is opposed . . . to the conduct of David towards Absalom as described in ch. xiv.,—namely, that after Joab had succeeded by craft in bringing him back to Jerusalem, David would not allow him to come into his presence for two whole years" (KD, p. 405). Noting that *klh* is stronger than "long, yearn," meaning rather "fail, be finished, be spent" (cf. esp. Ps 84:2 ["faints"]; 143:7), McCarter translates: "The king's enthusiasm for marching out against [Absalom] was spent" (*II Samuel*, p. 344; cf. the alternate rendering in Barthélemy, p. 238). The Hebrew idiom *yṣ' 'l* ("go [out] to") is used in the sense of "march out against" in Deuteronomy 28:7 (NIV, "come at"). The first clause of v.39 thus asserts that "David is no longer openly hostile to [Absalom] and, therefore, ready to be prodded step by step towards a reconciliation" (McCarter, *II Samuel*, p. 344).

## Notes

23 S.R. Driver's linguistic arguments (*Notes on the Books of Samuel*, pp. 301–2; cf. also BDB, p. 68b sec. 6) for equating "Ephraim" here with the town of "Ephron" (*Qere* "Ephrain") in 2 Chron 13:19 are effectively negated by his own note: "But it is odd that the site of a conspicuous hill . . . should have to be defined by its nearness to a place . . . nearly 500 ft. in the valley below it" (p. 302). As for McCarter's observation that "the preposition *'im* means 'near, in the vicinity of,' not 'within' " (*II Samuel*, p. 333), the NIV rendering "near the border of" satisfactorily resolves the alleged difficulty, both linguistically and geographically.

25 For פרץ (*prṣ*) in the sense of "urge" here and in v.27, see Notes on 1 Sam 28:23. To see "error" in this root wherever it means "urge" (cf. Lewis, *Cults of the Dead*, p. 111) is unwise as well as unnecessary.

27 Barthélemy recommends an addendum: "And Absalom prepared a feast like a king's feast" (p. 235; cf. also JB, NAB, NEB, NRSV; for details regarding support from ancient versions and possibly also from 4QSam[a], cf. McCarter, *II Samuel*, p. 330). It would seem just as likely, however, that the putative Hebrew *Vorlage* of the versions has suffered from contamination from 1 Sam 25:36 as that the MT has lost a sentence through scribal error. In any case, sheepshearing was known as a time for celebration (see comment on 1 Sam 25:2), and therefore further elaboration is not called for every time it is mentioned.

30 נוֹתַר (*nôṯar*, "be left," "survive") is one among several verbs that may employ either -בְּ (*b*[e]-; cf. 17:12; Lev 8:32; 14:18) or מִן (*min*, as here; cf. also Lev 7:17; 14:29) as the subordinating preposition (for examples of other verbs, cf. Sarna, "The Interchange of *Beth* and *Min*," p. 312).

32 The fact that the Hebrew consonants of the words rendered "report" (v.30) and "Shimeah" (v.32) are identical in the MT (see comment on v.32) may have influenced the narrator's choice of "Shimeah" (rather than its variants "Shammah," "Shimea") here and in v.3 (see comment there).

34 The last sentence of the verse is based on the LXX and is not included in the MT (see the NIV margin note). As reconstructed the Hebrew *Vorlage* was probably something like this: ויבא הצפה ויגד למלך ויאמר אנשים ראיתי מדרך חרנים מצד ההר (*wyb' hṣph wygd lmlk wy'mr 'nšym r'yty mdrk ḥrnym mṣd hhr*, "The watchman went and told the king, 'I see men in the direction of Horonaim, on the side of the hill' "; cf. S.R. Driver, *Notes on the Books of Samuel*, in loc.; McCarter, *II Samuel*, p. 333), which dropped out of the MT when a scribe's eye skipped from the first occurrence of *mṣd hhr* ("from/on the side of the hill") to the second.

39 Since the verb rendered "longed" is feminine, the MT's "David" (דוד, *dwd*) cannot be its subject. "Spirit" (רוח, *rwḥ*), however, is almost always feminine and is therefore either the explicit (see NIV text) or implied subject of the verb (see NIV mg.; for details justifying the NIV text reading, cf. Ulrich, *The Qumran Text*, pp. 106–7).

### 9. *The wise woman of Tekoa*

#### 14:1–20

1Joab son of Zeruiah knew that the king's heart longed for Absalom.
2So Joab sent someone to Tekoa and had a wise woman brought from

there. He said to her, "Pretend you are in mourning. Dress in mourning
clothes, and don't use any cosmetic lotions. Act like a woman who has
spent many days grieving for the dead. 3Then go to the king and speak
these words to him." And Joab put the words in her mouth.
4When the woman from Tekoa went to the king, she fell with her face
to the ground to pay him honor, and she said, "Help me, O king!"
5The king asked her, "What is troubling you?"
She said, "I am indeed a widow; my husband is dead. 6I your servant
had two sons. They got into a fight with each other in the field, and no
one was there to separate them. One struck the other and killed him.
7Now the whole clan has risen up against your servant; they say, 'Hand
over the one who struck his brother down, so that we may put him to
death for the life of his brother whom he killed; then we will get rid of
the heir as well.' They would put out the only burning coal I have left,
leaving my husband neither name nor descendant on the face of the
earth."
8The king said to the woman, "Go home, and I will issue an order in
your behalf."
9But the woman from Tekoa said to him, "My lord the king, let the
blame rest on me and on my father's family, and let the king and his
throne be without guilt."
10The king replied, "If anyone says anything to you, bring him to me,
and he will not bother you again."
11She said, "Then let the king invoke the LORD his God to prevent the
avenger of blood from adding to the destruction, so that my son will not
be destroyed."
"As surely as the LORD lives," he said, "not one hair of your son's head
will fall to the ground."
12Then the woman said, "Let your servant speak a word to my lord the
king."
"Speak," he replied.
13The woman said, "Why then have you devised a thing like this
against the people of God? When the king says this, does he not convict
himself, for the king has not brought back his banished son? 14Like
water spilled on the ground, which cannot be recovered, so we must
die. But God does not take away life; instead, he devises ways so that a
banished person may not remain estranged from him.
15"And now I have come to say this to my lord the king because the
people have made me afraid. Your servant thought, 'I will speak to the
king; perhaps he will do what his servant asks. 16Perhaps the king will
agree to deliver his servant from the hand of the man who is trying to cut
off both me and my son from the inheritance God gave us.'
17"And now your servant says, 'May the word of my lord the king bring
me rest, for my lord the king is like an angel of God in discerning good
and evil. May the LORD your God be with you.'"
18Then the king said to the woman, "Do not keep from me the answer
to what I am going to ask you."
"Let my lord the king speak," the woman said.
19The king asked, "Isn't the hand of Joab with you in all this?"
The woman answered, "As surely as you live, my lord the king, no one
can turn to the right or to the left from anything my lord the king says.
Yes, it was your servant Joab who instructed me to do this and who put
all these words into the mouth of your servant. 20Your servant Joab did
this to change the present situation. My lord has wisdom like that of an
angel of God—he knows everything that happens in the land."

The "desire/fulfillment of desire" motif exhibited in chapter 13 continues in chapter 14, which itself contains additional literary clues that lead to the isolation of chapters 13–14 as a separate unit (for details see comment on 13:1–22) within the Court History of David (chs. 9–20). As a whole, chapter 14 is concerned with Joab's successful attempt to bring Absalom back to Jerusalem from his self-imposed exile in Geshur. Apart from the incidental reference to Absalom's daughter Tamar in v.27, Joab and Absalom are the only two *dramatis personae* named in the chapter. The other two players are "the king" (obviously David, though never referred to by name) and the wise woman from Tekoa. David at this point still commands the respect of his subjects (however grudgingly it may be in some cases) since each of the other three main characters in chapter 14 bows down, "face to the ground" (vv.4, 22, 33), before him.

Despite various suggestions concerning the division of chapter 14 into two or more subsections, the traditional bipartite analysis (vv.1–20, 21–33) remains the simplest and best. As a whole, the chapter is framed by an *inclusio* formed by the appearance of the name "Absalom" at the end of vv.1 and 33. The only other verse in chapter 14 ending with "Absalom" is v.21, which thus begins a subsection that mirrors the structure of the full chapter. As for the section constituted by vv.1–20, the verb that begins its first verse and concludes its last verse is *yd'* ("know"), reflecting the fact that Joab understands David's intentions (v.1) and David understands Joab's (cf. Jeanne Marie Leonard, "La Femme de Teqoa et le fils de David: Etude de 2 Samuel 14/1–20," *Communio Viatorum* 23, 3 [1980]: 143–44).

Helpful parallels between vv.1–20 and other episodes in the books of Samuel have often been observed. Echoes of David's meeting with Abigail in 1 Samuel 25:20–35 have been explored by David M. Gunn ("Traditional Composition in the 'Succession Narrative,'" VetTest 26, 2 [1976]: 221–22; for details see comment on 1 Sam 25:23) as well as by R. Bickert ["Die List Joabs und der Sinneswandel Davids," VetTest suppl. 30 [1979]: 42–43). Structural elements common to the story of the Tekoite woman and Nathan's parable (12:1–7a) have been noted by Graffy ("The Literary Genre of Isaiah 5, 1–7," pp. 406–7; cf. also Fokkelman, *King David*, pp. 141–42; for details see comment on 12:1–14), while similarities between the narrative of the "wise woman" of Tekoa and that of the "wise woman" of Abel Beth Maacah (20:14–22) have been pointed out by Claudia V. Camp ("The Wise Women of 2 Samuel: A Role Model for Women in Early Israel?" CBQ 43, 1 [1981]: 14–29). My commentary will elaborate on the various comparisons as they occur and where considered necessary.

The question of whether the narrator pictures wisdom as residing in the Tekoite woman or in Joab has been hotly debated. Whybray states flatly that the story of "Joab's use of the woman of Tekoa is really a story of Joab's wisdom rather than of the woman: Joab applied his wisdom 'in order to change the course of affairs' (v.20)" (*The Succession Narrative*, p. 59; for detailed argumentation, cf. George G. Nicol, "The Wisdom of Joab and the Wise Woman of Tekoa," ST 36, 2 [1982]: 97–104). Rebuttal is set forth by J. Hoftijzer ("David and the Tekoite Woman," VetTest 20, 4 [1970]: 419–44), who summarizes: "The author of the story does not present Joab as wise, but the woman. Her wisdom is that she was able to handle a very tricky case, a case that remained a real test case for her even if she was fully instructed" (p. 444 n. 1; cf. also Camp, "Wise Women of 2 Samuel," pp. 17–18 n. 8). It seems best, however, to admit that the dispute between the two views is not a matter of either/or but of both/and: Joab is wise in knowing whom to delegate to approach David and in knowing what to tell her to say, and the Tekoite woman is wise in knowing how to implement Joab's instructions in the midst of a delicate situation. If the scales must be tipped in one direction or the other, the woman gets the nod. She, after all, is the one who is called "wise" (v.2).

The pericope as a whole appears to be structured chiastically:

A. Joab "knew" (14:1).
  B. Joab instructs the wise woman (14:2–3).
    C. The woman makes a request of the king (14:4–5a).
      D. She makes her first appeal (14:5b–10).
        E. She successfully pleads for her son's life (14:11).
      D′. She makes her second appeal (14:12–17).
    C′. The king makes a request of the woman (14:18–19a).
  B′. She admits that Joab has instructed her (14:19b).
A′. The king "knows" (14:20).

**1** The full name "Joab son of Zeruiah" (see comment on 1 Sam 26:6) signals a new beginning in the narrative (Joab has not been mentioned since 12:27). "Longed for," intended by the NIV to continue the thought of 13:39 (see comment there), is represented in the MT only by the preposition *ʿal* ("on"). "The king's heart longed for Absalom" is therefore better rendered "The king's mind was on Absalom" (cf. Job 1:8, "Have you considered" [lit., "Have you set your heart/mind on"])—implying, in context, that Joab chooses a time when he knows that David is thinking about Absalom, "trying (presumably) to decide how to handle the matter" of potential reconciliation between father and son (McCarter, *II Samuel*).

**2–3** Determined to enlist an expert to help his cause, Joab sends for a "wise woman" (cf. the wise woman from Abel Beth Maacah, 20:15–16) to be brought to Jerusalem. His choice of a woman rather than a man is perhaps related to the nature of his mission, and his decision to engage a stranger rather than an intimate (such as Jonadab; see comments on 13:3, where "wise" is preferable to "shrewd") may be calculated to catch David off guard and therefore help him ultimately to view his relationship to Absalom more objectively. Speaking with the voice of authority and uttering proverbs are two traits, often associated with wisdom, that are exhibited by the wise woman from Tekoa and her counterpart from Abel (cf. Camp, "Wise Women of 2 Samuel," pp. 17–18). In the present narrative wisdom is mentioned again only in v.20 (see comment there) and thus (together with its appearance in v.2) strengthens the *inclusio* formed by the occurrences of the verb "know" in vv.1 and 20.

The woman is from Tekoa, the birthplace of one of the earliest of the writing prophets (Amos 1:1), a town located in the Desert of Judah (cf. 2 Chron 20:20) about ten miles south of Jerusalem at a site today called Khirbet Tequ. Upon her arrival in Jerusalem, Joab tells the woman (v.2) to pretend that she is in "mourning," to dress in "mourning" clothes, and to act as if she is "grieving" for the dead (all three words are forms of the same Heb. root). She is thus asked to play a fictitious role, to participate in a "dramatic fiction," as Luis Alonso Schökel labels the episode ("David y la Mujer de Tecua: 2 Sm 14 como Modelo Hermenéutico," *Biblica* 57, 2 [1976]: 192). By telling her to pretend that she has "spent many days grieving for the dead," Joab is—doubtless intentionally—comparing her with David, who "mourned for his son every day" (see 13:37 and comment; same Heb. verb). Indeed, the woman from Tekoa and the king of Israel are twice bereaved: She has lost her husband and a son, and he has lost an illegitimate son born through Bathsheba as well as Amnon his firstborn. The link between the woman's situation and David's earlier loss is highlighted by Joab's command to her not to "use any cosmetic lotions" (v.2; see 12:20 and comment).

Joab next orders the woman to go to the king and "speak these words" to him (v.3), the narrator here using a Hebrew idiom that can mean "give this advice" (cf. 17:6). But the contents of the message Joab wants the Tekoite to deliver are quite specific; so he "put[s] the words in her mouth" (cf. the woman's admission to that effect in the parallel passage [v.19b]). In cases where the context is clear, this phrase is always used when a superior instructs a subordinate (cf. Hoftijzer, "David and the Tekoite Woman," p. 419 n. 3; cf. Exod 4:15; Num 22:38; 23:5, 12, 16; Ezra 8:17 ["told them what (to say)"]). At the same time, however, the authority that inheres in the words put in someone's mouth should not be confused with the personal authority that the chosen vessel might carry (for a carefully nuanced treatment, cf. Camp, "Wise Women of 2 Samuel," p. 18 n. 8). Joab is to be commended for choosing a messenger who is perceptive (= "wise") enough to take the words he gives her and use them in the most persuasive way before the king.

**4–5a** Arriving at the royal court in Jerusalem, the woman of Tekoa gains an audience with David (v.4), as Joab had commissioned her to do (v.3). To pay the king due respect, she falls before him, "face to the ground," as Joab (v.22) and Absalom (v.33) would later do (cf. also 1:2; 18:28; 24:20; 1 Kings 1:23; see esp. 1 Sam 25:23 and comment). Her initial request—"Help me [*hôšiʿāh*], O King!"—would be echoed not only by another woman to another king of Israel (cf. 2 Kings 6:26; cf. also Matt 15:25) but also by the crowds on Psalm Sunday: "Hosanna to the Son of David!" (Matt 21:9 [see NIV mg.]; for discussion cf. Leonard, "La Femme de Teqoa," pp. 146–48).

In his role as judge and paramount (for the term cf. Elizabeth Bellefontaine, "Customary Law and Chieftainship: Judicial Aspects of 2 Samuel 14:4–21," JSOT 38 [1987]: 57–58), David asks the woman, "What is troubling you?" (v.5a). Although the Hebrew idiom (lit., "What to you?" [*mah-llā<u>k</u>*]) may seem harsh because of its terseness, it often carries with it elements of genuine concern: "What can I do for you?" (Caleb to his daughter Acsah, Josh 15:18); "What is it you want?" (David to Bathsheba, 1 Kings 1:16); "What's the matter?" (2 Kings 6:28, in response to "Help me, my lord the king!" [2 Kings 6:26; see comment on v.4 above]).

**5b–10** The woman begins her first appeal to David by identifying herself as a widow and then adding: "My husband is dead" (v.5b). The latter clause, which belabors the point and is clearly successive in the mind of the speaker, justifies Eskhult's description of the Tekoite as a "pretended widow" (*Studies in Verbal Aspect and Narrative Technique*, p. 60; cf. also Brueggemann, *First and Second Samuel*, p. 292). As the sequel indicates, she is a consummate actress and spins a tale that is eminently believable.

Using the submissive language of the ancient Near East in the presence of a superior, she refers to herself as David's "servant" (vv.6–7, 12, 15–17, 19; see 1 Sam 1:11 and comment; 1 Sam 28:21–22; and esp. 1 Sam 25:24–25, 27–28, 31, 41; 2 Sam 20:17). She states that her two sons "got into a fight," as brothers (or friends or kinsmen) often will (cf. Exod 2:13; 21:22; Lev 24:10; Deut 25:11). The goal of one of the sons was apparently mayhem, or perhaps even murder, and thus the battleground of choice was at some distance from their village—a field, where the presence of witnesses and/or rescuers would be unlikely (cf. Gen 4:8; Deut 21:1; 22:25–27).

There, says the Tekoite, one of the brothers "struck the other and killed him" (v.6), a fate that would some day claim Absalom himself (18:15; cf. similarly 1:15; 4:7; 21:17).

The "widow" then states that, after the slaying of her son, clan loyalty took over and demanded retribution against the murderer (v.7). Whether members of the clan who wanted revenge appealed to regulations such as those recorded in Exodus 21:12 and Numbers 35:18–19 (cf. Leonard, "La Femme de Teqoa," p. 136) is not stated. The Hebrew word here translated "clan" may have represented an association of extended families coextensive (or nearly so) with the village or town in which they lived (as perhaps also in 16:5 and 1 Sam 20:6; cf. Bellefontaine, "Customary Law and Chieftainship," p. 50). As such they would have been the local community that normally determined the penalty for such matters as homicide, perhaps on the basis of certain provisions of tribal law, elements of which would then have eventually been incorporated into covenant law. In any event, the Tekoite comes to David, not to dispute the general custom of blood vengeance (see comment on 3:30), but to question its strict application to her only surviving son. She wants the king to overrule the decision of the clan and to exhibit flexibility "on the basis of certain extenuating circumstances: there were no witnesses to the crime; it appeared to be unpremeditated; the mother's widowhood and dependence on the remaining son; and the role of her son as heir and preserver of the lineage" (ibid., pp. 54–55).

To fortify her claim that the entire clan has "risen up" (i.e., "rebelled"; see 1 Sam 22:13 and comment) against her (v.7), the woman of Tekoa makes up out of whole cloth the very words of their supposed demand. Her calculated deceit is similar to that reflected in Michal's statement to Saul: "(David) said to me, 'Let me get away. Why should I kill you?' " (1 Sam 19:17; see comment there; for discussion of various types of nonverifiable quoted speech, cf. Berlin, *Poetics and Interpretation of Biblical Narrative,* pp. 96–97).

Fabrication though it is, the Tekoite's story is persuasive enough to convince David that she is telling the truth. She claims that she has been ordered to "hand over" her other son, the accused murderer (cf. 20:21). The clan will then execute him "for" (i.e., "in exchange for," *bêt pretii,* as in 1 Sam 3:13 ["because of"]; cf. GKC, sec. 119*p*) having "killed" his brother (similarly, Joab and Abishai murdered Abner because he had "killed" their brother Asahel [3:30; see comment there]). The sad fact that David had earlier "killed" Uriah (12:9) is yet another example of unchecked power that uses murder to gain its own ends. Concluding her supposed citation of the clan's demands, the woman hints at the likelihood that their ulterior motive in putting her only surviving son to death was to get rid of the "heir" (cf. Jer 49:1) and thereby gain possession of the family property (cf. also v.16). She thus raises the issue of a possible conflict of interest on their part (cf. Bellefontaine, "Customary Law and Chieftainship," p. 55).

In a final personal plea (v.7), the wise woman of Tekoa uses a vivid figure of speech to add a note of pathos to her request. She accuses the clan members of wanting to extinguish, to "put out" (cf. similarly 21:17; Isa 42:3 ["snuff out"]), the only "burning coal" remaining to her (for Akkadian parallels, cf. Hoftijzer, "David and the Tekoite Woman," p. 422 n. 2). He is all she has "left," and when he is gone, her deceased husband will be without "descendant" (the two words are derived from the same Heb. root; for the latter word, cf. Gen 45:7 ["remnant"]). In addition her husband's "name" (cf. Deut 25:5–6; Isa 14:22)—and therefore his very existence (see 1 Sam 24:21 and comment)—will be blotted out and thus forgotten. Every memory of him will be expunged from "the face of the earth" (cf. 1 Sam 20:15; Zeph 1:2–3).

The wise woman from Tekoa has spun an admirable tale. Plausible enough for David to believe it, the situation it describes differs enough from his own (cf. already Symon Patrick, p. 470) to keep him from becoming suspicious of her true purposes. Her story prepares the groundwork for what Joab wants her to accomplish.

Although David surely has the power and authority to reverse the decision of the members of the woman's clan, he at first treads cautiously so as not to alienate a group that "forms part of his own power base" (Bellefontaine, "Customary Law and Chieftainship," p. 61). Unlike his earlier forceful and decisive response to Abigail ("Go home in peace. I have heard your words and granted your request," 1 Sam 25:35), his statement to the Tekoite is uncharacteristically vague: "Go home, and I will issue an order in your behalf" (v.8).

Undeterred, the woman is not to be dismissed quite so easily. Like Abigail before her, she makes a confession of guilt ("let the blame rest on me," v.9; cf. 1 Sam 25:24) in the hope that doing so will force David to take action. It seems probable, then, that in both situations the confession is meant to support the plea, so that "the central point of these texts is *not* who takes (or has to take) the responsibility in the case under consideration" (Hoftijzer, "David and the Tekoite Woman," p. 427). The Tekoite's desire that the king and this throne "be without guilt" (v.9; cf. Exod 21:28 ["not be held responsible"]) is merely a polite addendum to her main assertion. Surely David's throne, having begun a long and distinguished history (see comment on 3:10; cf. also 7:13, 16), is not to be sidetracked by a local family squabble.

Impressed by the woman's persistence, the king commits himself personally to make sure that no one who chose to interfere with the royal decision concerning her would ever "bother" her again (v.10; cf. Gen 26:11 ["molest"]; 1 Chron 16:22 ["touch"]).

**11** The center of the chiasm (see comment on 14:1–20) focuses on the successful plea of the "widow" for the life of her "son," which emboldens her to launch into her second plea (vv.12–17). It also contains the first of the woman's seven references to God (vv.11, 13, 14, 15, 17 [bis], 20) as well as David's only use of the divine name in the chapter.

Pleading that the king will pray to the Lord on her behalf, the Tekoite asks for divine help in preventing the "avenger of blood" from killing her only surviving son (for the function of the avenger of blood, cf. Num 35:6–28; Deut 19:1–13; Josh 20). She pretends that she wants to keep the avenger from "adding [*Qere harbaṯ*] to the destruction," from causing "a really 'big killing', so then she will not only have lost one son, but also the second, her last one" (Hoftijzer, "David and the Tekoite Woman," p. 429 n. 2). She wants to make sure, she says, "that my son will not be destroyed" (lit., "that they [i.e., the clan members] will not destroy my son"; cf. v.7, where "get rid of" translates the same Heb. verb rendered "destroyed" here; for another example of "destroy" with a human object, see comment on 1:14—where, however, a different Heb. verb is used [the one translated "destruction" in 14:11]).

Just as in his response to Nathan's parable, so also in the case of the Tekoite woman David uses the Lord's name in a solemn oath (see 12:5 and comment; see also 1 Sam 14:39 and comment). He promises her that not one hair of her "son" (the NIV rendering "son's head" clarifies the terse Heb. idiom) will "fall to the ground" (for other occurrences of this trope, see comment on 1 Sam 14:45). David's reference to the "hair" of the woman's "son" is both ironic and poignant: The hair of his own son

Absalom was not only an index of his handsome appearance (cf. vv.25–26) but would also contribute to his undoing (cf. 18:9–15).

Referring to the language of the Heidelberg Catechism in describing the secure refuge afforded by the gospel ("Jesus Christ . . . protects me so well that without the will of my Father in heaven not a hair can fall from my head"; cf. also Luke 21:18), Brueggemann goes on to make a striking comparison with our text (*First and Second Samuel*, p. 293): "Imagine, the protection of every hair on the head by a royal father who is utterly attentive and utterly powerful."

**12–17** Having received the assurance she needs, the woman is now ready to make her second appeal. Her words echo those of Abigail: "Let your servant speak" (v.12; cf. 1 Sam 25:24). When David gives the Tekoite permission to say whatever she wishes, she addresses him in an open and forthright way. In the light of his firm determination to intervene on behalf of the murderous sibling for whose life she has just pleaded, why has the king "devised" (v.13—or, more strongly, "done"; cf. Hoftijzer, who argues that when interpreting the verb *ḥšb*, "it is very difficult to make a clear cut division between devising and doing" ["David and the Tekoite Woman," p. 434]) a thing "like this" (a phrase that often has negative connotations; cf. 1 Sam 4:7)? Unlike her own situation, which involves only a relatively small clan, by allowing (or forcing) Absalom to remain in exile David has jeopardized the future welfare of all the "people of God" (cf. Judg 20:2; the term is equivalent to "people of the LORD" in the Deuteronomic corpus, as observed by Bickert, "Die List Joabs und der Sinneswandel Davids," p. 46 and nn. 55–56; cf. 6:21; 1 Sam 2:24; for related expressions, see also 1:12 and comment).

To make sure that David understands the ramifications of what she is saying, the woman points out that his willingness to help her "son" convicts the king himself because he has not "brought back" Absalom, his own banished son (the verb is used of straying sheep in Ezek 34:4, 16). Just as her first appeal had asked "that a fratricide go unpunished and that the offender be restored to his family and to his status as a son and heir (v.7)," so also the

> second appeal (by Joab through the woman) requests that another fratricide go unpunished and the offender be restored to "the people of God" (v.13) and, by implication, to his status as son and heir. In neither case is the murderer declared innocent, granted pardon or excused for his deed. But their actions with their consequences are weighed in the balance of a broader context, namely, the suffering and disaster which would befall others if due sanctions were imposed. (Bellefontaine, "Customary Law and Chieftainship," p. 63)

Like the wise woman of Abel Beth Maacah (cf. 20:18), the woman of Tekoa demonstrates her expertise and authority in the arena of wisdom (cf. Camp, "Wise Women of 2 Samuel," p. 18) by making use of a proverb (v.14), choosing the common identificational type (ibid., pp. 16, 20). Her selection in this case, referring as it does to water spilled on "the ground," may have been triggered at least partially by David's promise that not a hair of her son's head would fall to "the ground" (v.11). Although the exact application of the proverb is debatable (e.g., whether it means that life once lost cannot be recovered or that death is inevitable or that punishment for sin is irrevocable or something else), the image of wasted water is suggestive and therefore appropriate in any event (cf. similarly Job 11:16; Pss 22:14–15; 58:7; Prov 17:14). Just as in 12:14 the expression "will surely die" (see comment there) refers to "untimely death as a punishment for sins of others" (Hoftijzer, "David and the Tekoite Woman," p. 432 n. 2; p. 433 n. 1), so also "the people of God" (v.13)—"we" (v.14)—"must die" (or "will surely die"; same Heb. as in 12:14) an "untimely death, because they will be punished for the king's sin" (ibid., p. 433) in not bringing Absalom back from exile.

Despite the understanding of many commentators (cf. already Symon Patrick, p. 473), the NIV's "take away life" (v.14) would seem to be unprecedented for the relatively common expression *nś' npš*. In the present context it apparently means something like "dedicate himself" (cf. Hoftijzer, "David and the Tekoite Woman," pp. 436–37; Camp, "Wise Women of 2 Samuel," p. 16 n. 5; cf. Ps 24:4 ["lift up his soul" = "dedicate himself"]; Prov 19:18 ["be a willing party"]; Hos 4:8 ["relish" = "direct their activities toward"]). It is therefore best to translate v.14b (cf. also v.13b) as a rhetorical question: "But will not God dedicate himself, and will he not devise ways to make sure that a banished person does not remain banished/estranged from him?" It was commonly believed in ancient times that estrangement from God's presence was automatic—and potentially permanent—if a person was driven from his homeland (see 1 Sam 26:19–20 and comment). The Tekoite implies that God will effect Absalom's return from Aram to Israel. Although David has "devised" one thing (v.13), God "devises" another (v.14). The difference between the actions of the king and of the Lord is underscored as well by the two occurrences of *lᵉḇiltî* ("in order that not": "the king has not brought back his banished son" [v.13]; "so that a banished person may not remain estranged from him" [v.14]; cf. Schökel, "David y la Mujer de Tecua," pp. 200–201).

Having made her point, the woman concludes her second appeal by intermingling elements of it with those of her first appeal. Since the "people" (the "whole clan" [v.7]? the "people of God" [v.13]?) had "made [her] afraid" (v.15; cf. 2 Chron 32:18; Neh 6:9 ["frighten"]), she had nothing to lose by seeking an audience with the king. In her desire that "the king" would "do what his servant asks" (v.15), she unwittingly cements her relationship with her mentor Joab, who would later be grateful that "the king has granted his servant's request" (v.22; same Heb. in both cases). She hopes that the king will "deliver his servant [i.e. the woman herself] from the hand of" the avenger (v.16), and in so doing she uses a common idiom employed elsewhere of what a king is expected to do on a national scale (cf. 19:9; cf. similarly 1 Sam 8:20) or of what the Lord does on behalf of his chosen ones (cf. 22:1; 1 Sam 4:3; 2 Kings 20:6; 2 Chron 32:8, 11; Ezra 8:31).

The woman of Tekoa is afraid that her clan members will "cut off" (lit., "destroy"; see comment on v.11) her and her son from "God's inheritance" (NIV, "the inheritance God gave us," v.16), a term that, although found nowhere else, is doubtless equivalent to "the LORD's inheritance" (20:19; 21:3; 1 Sam 26:19) and may be interpreted as referring either to the land and people of Israel (see comment on 1 Sam 10:1 and the expansionist LXX text translated in the NIV mg. there; cf. also Hoftijzer, "David and the Tekoite Woman," p. 439 n. 3, where additional supporting references are cited; Harold O. Forshey, "The Construct Chain *naḥᵃlat YHWH/'ᵉlōhîm*," BASOR 220 [1975]: 51–53) or to an individual "family's landed property or its share in Yahweh's land" (Anderson, p. 189; cf. also Leonard, "La Femme de Teqoa," pp. 137–38, and the expression "the inheritance of my fathers" applied to Naboth's vineyard in 1 Kings 21:3–4). Bellefontaine observes that the avenger may have an ulterior motive in wanting to kill the woman's only surviving son: to "gain possession of the family property on the death of the heir" ("Customary Law and Chieftainship," p. 55).

The Tekoite introduces the final words of her second appeal by echoing verbatim what she had stated earlier: "Your servant thought/says" (vv.15, 17). She wants David's decision to bring her "rest"—that is, relief from a bad situation (cf. Hoftijzer, "David and the Tekoite Woman," p. 440; cf. Ruth 1:9; Isa 28:12; cf. esp. Jer 45:3). Like Achish before her (see 1 Sam 29:9 and comment) and Mephibosheth after her (cf. 19:27), she compares David to an "angel of God"—not merely to flatter him (contra Hoftijzer, "David and the Tekoite Woman," p. 441) but, more importantly, to recognize that in some respects at least the king is "the embodiment of the divine power. . . . Perhaps a bit of this is *Hofstil* (cf. 1 Sam 29:9), but solid reality stands behind it. The king was expected to give judgments of more than human wisdom" (Dennis J. McCarthy, "Compact and Kingship: Stimuli for Hebrew Covenant Thinking," in ***Studies in the Period of David and Solomon and Other Essays***, ed. Tomoo Ishida [Winona Lake: Eisenbrauns, 1982]: 82).

Like an angel of God, David is capable of "discerning [lit., 'hearing'; same Heb. verb as 'agree' in v.16] good and evil" (v.17), a merism (cf. Hoftijzer, "David and the Tekoite Woman," p. 441) that not only intends to encompass all moral knowledge (cf. 19:35 ["what is good and what is not"]; Gen 2:9, 17; 3:5, 22; Deut 1:39 ["good from bad"]; 30:15 ["prosperity . . . and destruction"]; Pss 34:14; 37:27; Isa 7:15–16 ["wrong and . . . right"]; Amos 5:14–15; cf. esp. 1 Kings 3:9) but also "presupposes God's moral inerrancy. . . . That the speaker means to praise David rather than God only underscores the powers of divinity, which so unthinkingly surface as an ideal norm and basis for comparison" (Sternberg, p. 90; see also comment on v.20). The woman's stated desire that the Lord might be "with" the king (v.17) not only expresses her hope that God will help him make the right decision(s) but also echoes a recurring *Leitmotif* for David in the books of Samuel (see comment on 1 Sam 16:18).

**18–19a** Balancing the woman's request of the king (cf. vv.4–5a), David now makes a request of her. Using language reminiscent of Eli's demand to the young Samuel (cf. 1 Sam 3:17), the king insists that the Tekoite not "keep" (v.18; lit., "hide") the truth from him. He senses that she is not acting entirely on her own initiative and wants to know whether Joab's "hand" is "with" her in what she is doing (v.19a)—that is, whether Joab is behind all this and is giving her support in what the king now recognizes is her (= Joab's ) effort to return Absalom to Jerusalem (for the Heb. idiom "hand is with" in the sense of "support," cf. 2 Kings 15:19; Jer 26:24).

**19b** To swear to the truth of what she is about to say, the woman takes a solemn oath that translates literally as "By the life of your soul" (cf. 15:21; 1 Sam 17:55; 25:26; see also comments on 2 Sam 11:11; 1 Sam 1:26; 20:3). She is firmly convinced that no one can turn "to the right or to the left" (for the idiom, cf. Isa 30:21) of anything David says, implying that the "king's words hit the mark precisely; he discerns the exact state of the case" (Kirkpatrick, *The Second Book of Samuel*, p. 146; cf. KD, pp. 410–11). Reprising v.3b, she readily admits that Joab engineered her deceptive gambit when he "put all these words in (her) mouth."

**20** Ultimately, of course, David is not fooled by the woman's/Joab's fictitious story. Although Joab "knew" (v.1), the king "knows" even more. Like an angel of God, David discerns good and evil (see v.17 and comment); like an angel of God, David knows "everything that happens in the land," the simile in this case presupposing God's omniscience (Sternberg, p. 90). If Joab has been able to "change" (*sabbēḇ*, lit., "turn around") the present situation, his ploy is transparent to David. The woman may be "wise" (v.2), but the "wisdom" of the king is compared to that of a divine messenger and, by implication, to that of God himself.

At the same time, however, the Tekoite's compliment is not without its backlash. Her ingratiating simile is "exposed as an empty superlative by way of opposition to reality past (the 'David did not know' formulas that punctuate the story of Abner's murder, or his falling into the trap set by Nathan's parable) and to come" (Sternberg, p. 93). Rounded off within itself, the account of the wise woman of Tekoa serves as a socio-political example of "the process by which the judicial authority of the chief [David] was expanded and strengthened while that of the autonomous local groups [clan members] was gradually weakened" (Bellefontaine, "Customary Law and Chieftainship," p. 64). In its wider context, the narrative depicts the kind of royal power that Absalom—and others—will either try to undermine or seek to usurp.

## Notes

4 "Went," attested in many MSS of the MT as well as in the LXX, Vulgate, and Syriac (cf. BHS; see also NIV mg.), answers to "go" in v.3. Although most MT MSS have וַתֹּאמֶר (*wattō'mer*, "said/spoke"; probably by contamination by the same word later in the verse), "went" would appear to be the superior reading (contra Barthélemy, p. 239).

5 The construction of the verse is strikingly similar to that of 2 Kings 4:14. In each case a speaker asks a solicitous question, which is then followed by a brief two-part response beginning with אֲבָל ('*ᵃḇāl*). Although "indeed" (v.5) and "well" (2 Kings 4:14) are possible translations of '*ᵃḇāl*, the latter seems more natural and would be equally appropriate here: "Well, I am a widow; my husband is dead."

13 Since all other occurrences of מִדַּבֵּר (*middabbēr*, "says") are clearly Hithpael forms (rendered "speaking" in Num 7:89; Ezek 2:2; 43:6), there is no compelling reason to take it as מִן (*min*, "from," "because of") plus Piel here (as is done by Hoftijzer, "David and the Tekoite Woman," p. 430 n. 1)—especially because the resulting translation would not improve on that of the NIV. Indeed, since in the other three cases the subject of the verb is the invisible God, the use of the Hithpael in v.13 adds to the solemnity and significance of the word of David, who is twice described by the Tekoite as being like "an angel of God" (vv.17, 20).

16 The NIV's "is trying" is supplied *ad sensum*, as in the LXX and Vulgate (for details cf. BHS). It is not necessary to assume that a word has dropped out of the MT (contra Forshey, "The Construct Chain," p. 52 n. 14).

נַחֲלַת אֱלֹהִים (*naḥᵃlaṯ 'ᵉlōhîm*, "the inheritance of 'God") is rendered "the inheritance of (one's) ancestors" by Lewis (*Cults of the Dead*, p. 178 n. 14). But although it is true that *'ᵉlōhîm* occasionally refers to human beings (cf. BDB, p. 43, for examples), translations other than "God," "god(s)" should be resorted to only when all else fails.

19 In context the NIV's "no one" is a possible translation of the MT's אִשׁ ('*š*) whether understood as defective writing of אִישׁ ('*yš*, "man"), with many MSS, or as a rare alternate spelling of יֵשׁ (*yš*, "there is"), with a few MSS (cf. BHS for details), as in Mic 6:10 (where, however, the NIV translates '*š* as a defectively written form of the verb נשה [*nšh*, "forget"]). The latter is preferable syntactically and has the support of 4QSam[c], which reads *yš* (cf. Ulrich, "4QSam[c]: A Fragmentary Manuscript," pp. 6, 12). The spelling with ' is normal in Ugaritic and Aramaic ('*ṯ*).

4QSam[a] and 4QSam[c] may now be added to the few MSS that insert א (') into its proper place (cf. BHS) in להשׂמא(י)ל (*lhśm'[y]l*, "turn . . . to the left"; cf. Ulrich, "4QSam[c]: A Fragmentary Manuscript," pp. 6, 9). The MT omits ', as also in Ezek 21:21 (EV 16).

---

## 10. *Absalom's return to Jerusalem*

### 14:21–33

21 The king said to Joab, "Very well, I will do it. Go, bring back the young man Absalom."

22 Joab fell with his face to the ground to pay him honor, and he blessed the king. Joab said, "Today your servant knows that he has found favor in your eyes, my lord the king, because the king has granted his servant's request."

23 Then Joab went to Geshur and brought Absalom back to Jerusalem.
24 But the king said, "He must go to his own house; he must not see my face." So Absalom went to his own house and did not see the face of the king.

25 In all Israel there was not a man so highly praised for his handsome appearance as Absalom. From the top of his head to the sole of his foot
there was no blemish in him. 26 Whenever he cut the hair of his head—he used to cut his hair from time to time when it became too heavy for him—he would weigh it, and its weight was two hundred shekels by the royal standard.

27 Three sons and a daughter were born to Absalom. The daughter's name was Tamar, and she became a beautiful woman.

28 Absalom lived two years in Jerusalem without seeing the king's
face. 29 Then Absalom sent for Joab in order to send him to the king, but Joab refused to come to him. So he sent a second time, but he refused
to come. 30 Then he said to his servants, "Look, Joab's field is next to mine, and he has barley there. Go and set it on fire." So Absalom's servants set the field on fire.

31 Then Joab did go to Absalom's house and he said to him, "Why have your servants set my field on fire?"

32 Absalom said to Joab, "Look, I sent word to you and said, 'Come here so I can send you to the king to ask, "Why have I come from Geshur? It would be better for me if I were still there!"' Now then, I want to see the king's face, and if I am guilty of anything, let him put me to death."

33 So Joab went to the king and told him this. Then the king summoned Absalom, and he came in and bowed down with his face to the ground before the king. And the king kissed Absalom.

As a whole, chapter 14 is framed by an *inclusio* formed by the occurrence of "Absalom" at the end of vv.1 and 33, and the subsection consisting of vv.21–33 is bracketed by an *inclusio* formed in the same way. But although the name "Absalom" appears prominently in the section (it is absent only from vv.22 and 26), the key player is clearly Joab, who mediates between the king and his son and is eventually the catalyst that brings about their reconciliation. Joab is the central figure in the two exchanges of direct discourse at the beginning and end of the pericope: (1) The king speaks (v.21), Joab speaks (v.22), the king speaks (v.24); (2) Absalom speaks (v.30), Joab speaks (v.31), Absalom speaks (v.32).

Like the first half of the chapter (see comment on vv.1–20), the second half appears to be structured chiastically:

A. The king tells Joab to bring Abraham back (14:21).
  B. The king refuses to grant Absalom a royal audience (14:22–24).
    C. Absalom is described as being handsome (14:25).
      D. Absalom periodically cuts his hair (14:26).
    C′. Absalom's daughter is described as being beautiful (14:27).
  B′. Absalom insists on a royal audience (14:28–32).
A′. The king summons Absalom into his presence (14:33).

**21** Although Joab may have been listening in as the woman of Tekoa wove the elaborate tapestry of her fictitious story, it is more likely that he was waiting in the wings to learn of its outcome (v.19 implies his absence from the audience room). In any case the king, impressed by the urgency and logic of the woman's arguments in her desire to save the life of her son, applies them to his own situation. David tells Joab that he will "do it" (lit., "do this thing")—that is, (give the order to) bring Absalom back from exile. Verse 21 thus serves an additional function as a transition between the two main sections of the chapter, since "do it" reprises "did this" (v.20) and anticipates "has granted (his servant's) request" (v.22, lit., "has done [his servant's] word/thing").

Since David will force Absalom to wait for a long time before allowing him to come into his presence (cf. vv.24, 28), his calling Absalom a "young man" (v.21) is doubtless more a reference to his immaturity and temperament than to his endearing qualities.

**22–24** Like the Tekoite before him (cf. v.4) and Absalom after him (cf. v.33), Joab falls, "face to the ground" (v.22), before the king (see comments on vv.1–20; v.4). The statement that Joab "blessed" David surely implies a prayer directed to God, a prayer that David would receive a divine blessing (as in Ps 72:15; for details and additional references, see TDOT, 2:291–92; see also 1 Sam 26:25 and comment). Continuing in an attitude of humility mingled with courtesy, Joab expresses his gratitude that he has "found favor" in the king's eyes" (v.22; cf. 16:4; 1 Sam 1:18; 16:22 ["pleased with"]; 20:3, 29; see also comments on 25:8 ["be favorable toward"]; 27:5), a perception suggested by the fact that David has "granted his servant's request" (see comment on "do what his servant asks" in v.15).

Through the good offices and personal mission of Joab, Absalom's three-year, self-imposed exile at Geshur in Aram (see 13:37–38 and comments) now comes to an end as he returns to Jerusalem (v.23). Not yet welcome in David's quarters or the royal court, however, Absalom must "go to his own house" within the palace precincts (v.24; see comment on 13:20). The verb "go" (*sbb*, lit., "go around") is a weak echo of "change" (*sabbēḇ*) in v.20 (see comment there) and reflects the reality that Joab's ultimate goal remains unfulfilled. David is still not ready to allow Absalom to "see" his "face"—that is, have an audience with him (cf. Exod 10:28; the Heb. expression "and did not see the face of the king" at the end of this unit [v.24] is repeated verbatim at the beginning of the parallel unit ["without seeing the king's face," v.28]; see also the comment on 3:13 ["come into my presence," "see me"]).

**25** Since he has a "handsome" father (1 Sam 16:12; 17:42) and a "beautiful" sister (see comments on 13:1), it is not surprising that Absalom himself should be "handsome." Although the expression "from the top of (one's) head to the sole of (one's) foot" or its equivalent usually encompasses the range or scope of a disease or injury (cf. Lev 13:12; Deut 28:35; Job 2:7; Isa 1:6), in Absalom's case it describes his striking appearance: Like the most ideal of priests (cf. Lev 21:17–18, 21, 23 ["defect"]) or the most desirable of women (cf. S of Songs 4:7 ["flaw"]), Absalom is totally without "blemish." Such uncommon good looks often attract fawning praise (cf. Gen 12:14–15—but contrast Prov 31:30), and so handsome is Absalom that in Israel he is the most "highly praised" of all.

Adonijah, a younger son of David, will reprise various aspects of Absalom's life (cf. McCarter, "'Plots, True or False,'" p. 365), including the characteristic of being "handsome" (1 Kings 1:6 [although the Heb. term is different]). A pleasing appearance, after all, was often considered to be "a prerequisite for royal leadership" (Long, "Framing Repetitions," p. 396)—but only from a human standpoint (see 1 Sam 16:7 and comment). If Absalom "is a type of David, it is a particularly hollow and romantic version, laden with posturing and public relations, and markedly heavy on the visual and superficial" (Rosenberg, p. 156).

**26** A child of the court, Absalom has learned to cultivate "a certain narcissism centered in the hair" (ibid.). Refraining from cutting one's hair was an emblem of Naziriteship (cf. Num 6:5) and, in the case of Samson, a badge of strength (cf. Judg 16:17). For Absalom, however, it is a sign of vanity, and he therefore cuts it only when it becomes too heavy for him, probably once a year (NIV, "from time to time" is literally "from end of days to the days"; for a similar expression rendered "year after year," "each year," cf. 1 Sam 1:3; 2:19; cf. BDB, p. 399; see also comment on "years" in 13:23). Its weight (see NIV mg.), if too great to be believable, should doubtless be attributed to hyperbole rather than to scribal error (contra KD, p. 412).

As the center of the chiasm in the first section of the chapter focuses on hair (see comment on v.11), so also here. What Absalom proudly considers his finest attribute will prove to be the vehicle of his ultimate downfall (cf. 18:9–15).

**27** Perhaps to mock Absalom's forthcoming pretensions to royalty, the narrator notes that children "were born to" him (the phrase occurs elsewhere in the books of Samuel only in 3:2 and 5:13, where the lists of King David's children in Hebron and Jerusalem are given). Since 18:18 indicates that Absalom had no sons to carry on his name, his three unnamed sons mentioned here may have died in infancy (cf. KD, p. 412; Gleason L. Archer, Jr., *Decision* [1980]: 14; Lewis, *Cults of the Dead*, p. 118). But the name of his daughter has been preserved, probably because it is the same as that of her aunt and namesake, the beautiful Tamar, Absalom's sister, whose beauty his daughter reflects (see 13:1 and comment). It is also possible, however, that Absalom named his daughter "Tamar" for an entirely different reason: "'Tamar,' after all, is the name of the dynastic mother (Gen. 38) of the Judahite line of Peretz, from which both David and Absalom have sprung. In naming his daughter 'Tamar,' Absalom may be expressing his own ambition to be a dynastic founder" (Rosenberg, p. 159). Tamar should not be confused with Maacah, the daughter of another Absalom (cf. 1 Kings 15:2, 10 and NIV mg.; see comment on 3:3).

In terms of the literary structure of vv.21–33, the fact that Tamar is "beautiful" (v.27) matches the description of her father as "handsome" in the parallel passage (v.25; same Heb. in both verses).

**28–32** Although Absalom's exile is over, he is forced to cool his heels in Jerusalem for "two years" (v.28; for the structural significance of the "two years" here and in 13:23 and the "three years" of 13:38, see comment on 13:1–22) before being invited to see "the king's face" (for the meaning of this phrase and its importance with respect to its parallel unit, see comment on v.24). The literary subsection under consideration (vv.28–32) is delimited by the phrases "without seeing the king's face" in v.28 and "I want to see the king's face" in v.32.

No more persuasive with Joab (v.29) than he had earlier been with David (cf. 13:25), Absalom decides to take drastic measures. In an act reminiscent of that of Samson against the Philistines (cf. Judg 15:3–6), he instructs his servants to torch a nearby field belonging to Joab (v.30) as a means of not only getting his attention but also of getting even for being slighted by him. The loss of an entire crop of barley was a tragedy in ancient times (cf. Exod 9:28–31; Joel 1:11), even in the best of circumstances. On the basis of the Mosaic law (cf. Exod 22:6), Joab would have every right to demand adequate compensation, especially since in this case the fire was set deliberately.

If Joab's indignant reaction (v.31) is understandable, Absalom has a ready answer. Joab has been unresponsive to Absalom's repeated pleas for his mediation, leaving Absalom with few alternatives. Unless the king grants him an audience soon, he might as well never have left Geshur (v.32; cf. v.23 in the parallel passage) in the first place (cf. similarly Exod 14:11–12; 16:3; 17:3; Num 11:5, 18, 20; 14:2–4; 20:3–5; 21:4–5; Judg 6:13). Echoing verbatim the earlier words of his father to his friend Jonathan ("if I am guilty"; see 1 Sam 20:8 and comment), Absalom declares himself ready to be "put . . . to death"—and thus he unwittingly reprises the penalty that the wise woman of Tekoa knew would be incurred by her only surviving "son" because of his alleged fratricide (cf. v.7).

**33** The three chief players (the king, Joab, Absalom) in the beginning of the drama (v.21) come together again at its end (v.33). Joab, suitably chastened by Absalom's rebuke, submits to his request and relays his desires to David. Summoned to the court, Absalom prostrates himself with his "face to the ground" (see comment on vv.1–20). He had wanted to see "the king's face" (v.32), and now he gets his wish: He humbles himself "before the king" (lit., "to the king's face"). But perhaps Absalom also gets the last laugh, at least for awhile: Although he has "bowed down" to King David and then has been "kissed" by the king (who acts according to royal protocol and not as Absalom's father; cf. 19:39), David's subjects would soon "bow down" before Absalom himself, who would then "kiss" them (15:5). Absalom would thus steal the hearts of the men of Israel (cf. 15:6) as a first step on his march to his father's throne.

## Notes

---

**26** "The royal standard" is literally "the stone of the king" (אֶבֶן הַמֶּלֶךְ ['eben hammelek]), in which "stone" refers to a specific weight (cf. "stone" as a fourteen-pound weight in the modern British system). Stones of various sizes, carefully polished and often sculpted and/or inscribed, were used as sets of weights in ancient times and frequently turn up in archaeological excavations. The phrase אבני מלכא (*'bny mlk'*, lit., "the stones of the king") occurs frequently in *Aramaic Papyri Discovered at Assuan,* ed A.H. Sayce (London: Alexander Moring, 1906; cf. A 7; B 14–15; C 15; D 14, 21; F 10; G 5, 6–7, 9, 10, 14–15, 34–35, 36; H 15; J 16).

**30** 4QSam[c] exhibits two divergences from the MT that are of interest. Instead of ולו (*wlw*, "and he has"), the Qumran text reads ולוא (*wlw'*, "but there was no"; cf. Ulrich, "4QSam[c]: A Fragmentary Manuscript," p. 7; some MT MSS have ולא [*wl'*]; cf. BHS), implying that Joab's barley field contained only stubble when it was set on fire. But torched barley stalks make Joab's reaction (v.31) much more understandable, and the MT *wlw* gains credence in light of the second of the significant Qumran readings in v.30. 4QSam[c] appends to the verse an entire sentence (cf. also LXX) that translates literally as follows: "Joab's young men went to him with their garments torn and said, 'Absalom's servants set the field on fire.'" Since the young men's statement duplicates the last sentence of v.30 in the MT, some assume that the MT omitted the 4QSam[c] material by haplography (cf. Ulrich, "4QSam[c]: A Fragmentary Manuscript," p. 14). The characteristic terseness of Hebrew prose, however, advises caution in such matters (the NAB is the only recent EV that includes the Qumran reading).

---

## 11. *Absalom's conspiracy*

### 15:1–12

1 In the course of time, Absalom provided himself with a chariot and horses and with fifty men to run ahead of him. 2 He would get up early and stand by the side of the road leading to the city gate. Whenever anyone came with a complaint to be placed before the king for a decision, Absalom would call out to him, "What town are you from?" He would answer, "Your servant is from one of the tribes of Israel." 3 Then Absalom would say to him, "Look, your claims are valid and proper, but there is no representative of the king to hear you." 4 And Absalom would add, "If only I were appointed judge in the land! Then everyone who has a complaint or case could come to me and I would see that he gets justice."

5 Also, whenever anyone approached him to bow down before him, Absalom would reach out his hand, take hold of him and kiss him. 6 Absalom behaved in this way toward all the Israelites who came to the king asking for justice, and so he stole the hearts of the men of Israel.

7 At the end of four years, Absalom said to the king, "Let me go to Hebron and fulfill a vow I made to the LORD. 8 While your servant was living at Geshur in Aram, I made this vow: 'If the LORD takes me back to Jerusalem, I will worship the LORD in Hebron.'"

9 The king said to him, "Go in peace." So he went to Hebron.

10 Then Absalom sent secret messengers throughout the tribes of Israel to say, "As soon as you hear the sound of the trumpets, then say, 'Absalom is king in Hebron.'" 11 Two hundred men from Jerusalem had accompanied Absalom. They had been invited as guests and went quite innocently, knowing nothing about the matter. 12 While Absalom was offering sacrifices, he also sent for Ahithophel the Gilonite, David's counselor, to come from Giloh, his hometown. And so the conspiracy gained strength, and Absalom's following kept on increasing.

Chapters 15–20 constitute the major part of the longest definable literary section (chs. 13–20; more precisely, 13:1–20:22) of the Court History of David (chs. 9–20; see comments on 13:1–22). Unlike chapters 13–14, which exhibit for the most part a "desire/fulfillment of desire" pattern, chapters 15–20 prefer a "departure/return" pattern. As such the section lends itself readily to chiastic analysis, variations on which are offered by most literary critics (cf. David M. Gunn, "From Jerusalem to the Jordan and Back: Symmetry in 2 Samuel xv–xx," VetTest 30, 1 [1980]: 109–13). Perhaps the most satisfying attempt overall has been made by Conroy, p. 89:

A. Rebellion breaks out (15:1–12)
  B. The king's flight: meeting scenes (15:13–16:14)
    C. Clash of counselors (16:15–17:23)
    C′. Clash of armies (17:24–19:9)
  B′. The king's return: meeting scenes (19:9–41)
A′. The king returns to Jerusalem, and the final stirrings of rebellion are crushed (19:42–20:22)

My own analysis, which coincides with that reflected in the NIV subheadings, differs from that of Conroy but nevertheless converges with his at several points:

A. Absalom rebels against David (15:1–12).
  B. David flees from Jerusalem (15:13–37).
    C. David expresses kindness to Ziba (16:1–4).
      D. Shimei curses David (16:5–14).
        E. Ahithophel offers advice to Absalom (16:15–17:29).
      D′. Joab's men kill Absalom (18:1–18).
    C′. David mourns for Absalom (18:19–19:8).
  B′. David returns to Jerusalem (19:9–43).
A′. Sheba rebels against David (20:1–22).

The brief summary narrative of Absalom's rebellion against his father (15:1–12) is happily characterized as a "diptych" by Fokkelman (*King David*, p. 165). Each of its two panels (vv.1–6, 7–12) begins with a time-lapse phrase: "In the course of time" (v.1), "At the end of four years" (v.7).

**1–6** In the light of 13:1 (see comment there; see also comment on 13:1–22), it might be expected that 15:1 should also begin with *wayᵉhî 'aḥᵃrê-ḵēn*, as 4QSamᶜ does (cf. Ulrich, "4QSamᶜ: A Fragmentary Manuscript," p. 7) and as Ulrich insists it should (ibid., pp. 14–15), rather than with *wayᵉhî mē'aḥᵃrê ḵēn*. One could also argue, however, that the slight difference in the two phrases is intentionally designed not only to maintain continuity between chapters 13–14 and chapter 15 but also to signal the substantially new beginning that occurs in 15:1 (cf. Conroy, p. 41; see also comment on vv.1–12). In any event, the expansive *mē'aḥᵃrê ḵēn* phrase is relatively rare (see comment on 3:28) and serves in this case to carry the narrative forward chronologically.

Immediately after the introductory formula, the text reads *wayya'aś . . . 'aḇšālôm* ("Absalom provided"), which combines with the same Hebrew phrase in v.6 (there rendered "Absalom behaved") to form an *inclusio* that brackets the intervening material. Absalom's providing himself with a "chariot and horses" and "men to run ahead of him" symbolizes his ambition to acquire the trappings of royalty (see 1 Sam 8:11 and comment; cf. Gen 41:43; see also comment on "guards" in 1 Sam 22:17) and would later (after Absalom's death) be imitated by another pretender to the throne, his younger brother Adonijah—even to the number of outrunners (cf. 1 Kings 1:5).

Absalom's plan to ingratiate himself to the people of Israel is as simple as it is subtle. Early each morning he takes up a position alongside the main road leading to Jerusalem's city gate (v.2), the place where disaffected citizens would be expected to bring their complaints for royal adjudication (cf. de Vaux, AIs, pp. 152–53, 155; cf. similarly Josh 20:4). He then asks such a person what town he is from, the sort of question a superior (especially a king) might be expected to ask an inferior (cf. 1:3, 13;

see 1 Sam 30:13 and comment). If the plaintiff responds that he is from "one of the tribes of Israel" (v.2; see comment on "any of their rulers" in 7:7), Absalom then assures him—apparently without further ado or investigation—that his claims are valid and "proper" (v.3; cf. Prov 8:9 ["right"]). He proceeds to commiserate with the person by deploring the fact that the king has no representative on hand to "hear" the case (cf. Deut 1:16–17; Job 31:35; cf. esp. 1 Kings 3:11 ["administering"])—although the wise woman of Tekoa had earlier made the observation that David is indeed capable of "discerning" good and evil (see comment on 14:17).

Needless to say, a solution for the plaintiff's dilemma is ready at hand: Absalom himself, he wistfully suggests ("If only," v.4; cf. 23:15 ["Oh, that someone would"]), should be appointed judge. Everyone could then come "to me" (emphatic), Absalom says, and he would personally see to it that justice was served. Continuing his royal posturing, Absalom proceeds to "take hold of" (probably forcibly, v.5; see comments on "grabbed" in 2:16; 13:11) and "kiss" (cf. also 19:39) anyone who approaches him to "bow down" to him (see 14:33 and comment). In everything he does Absalom implies that he himself, and not King David, is best suited to provide the people with the "justice" (*mišpāṭ*, v.6; cf. 1 Kings 3:11) they deserve (for other examples of the root *špṭ* in this section, cf. vv.2 ["decision"], 4 ["judge," "case" (cf. also Lam 3:59 ["cause"]; Num 27:5)]).

By means of such behavior—now flattering, now forceful—Absalom "stole the hearts" of the men of Israel (v.6; cf. "deceived" in Gen 31:20, 26), all the while successfully concealing his subversive activity from his father (cf. v.13). Absalom's

> approaching the people prior to their reaching the court seems propagandistic, intended (1) to turn them away in their quest convinced that their suit would not be heard; (2) to raise doubts about David's competence to rule; and (3) to sow seeds of yearning for Absalom to be chief judge . . . in Israel. Hence, 2 Sam. 15:2–6 is not a trustworthy statement of David's fulfillment of his role as judge. It does, however, demonstrate that Absalom's desire to be "judge" in Israel was due, not to a concern about justice, but to his ambition to replace his father as chief in the land. (Bellefontaine, "Customary Law and Chieftainship," p. 59)

Nevertheless, something must have gone awry with David's rule to explain the readiness with which the people were willing to abandon him and follow his son. Noting that the title of Psalm 3 attributes its writing to David "when he fled from his son Absalom," Midrash Tanḥuma calls attention to Psalm 3:2 ("Many are saying of me,/ 'God will not deliver him' ") and then observes: "They were saying of David: '(How) can there be salvation for a man who had taken the lamb captive and slew the shepherd [referring to David's affair with Bathsheba and the murder of Uriah] and who caused Israel to fall by the sword [criticizing David's ruthless military campaigns, in which countless Israelite soldiers must have lost their lives]?' " "Taking the two reasons given, . . . they would account realistically for the rebellion against [David] and the recourse to the machinery prepared by Absalom and ready to hand for his forceable removal from the throne" (J. Weingreen, "The Rebellion of Absalom," VetTest 19, 2 [1969]: 266; for the midrashic citation, cf. ibid., p. 264).

Absalom, of course, was by no means the only prince in ancient times to try to usurp power from his father. A striking Ugaritic parallel has been pointed out by Victor H. Matthews and Don C. Benjamin (*Old Testament Parallels: Laws and Stories From the*

*Ancient Near East* [Mahwah: Paulist, 1991], p. 205), describing Prince Yassib's challenge to King Keret:

> "Listen to me carefully!" Yassib threatens:
> "If enemies had invaded the land while you were ill,
> They would have driven you out,
> Forced you into the hills.
> Your illness made you derelict:
> You did not hear the case of the widow,
> You did not hear the case of the poor,
> You did not sentence the oppressor,
> You did not feed the orphan in the city,
> . . . nor the widow in the country. . . .
> Step down from the kingship,
> Allow me to reign.
> Relinquish your power,
> Let me sit on your throne."

**7–12** After he has lived in Jerusalem for four years, Absalom decides that the time has finally come for him to seize the kingdom. As a way of masking his true intentions, he asks David for permission to go to Hebron, where he intends to "fulfill a vow" (v.7; cf. Pss 50:14; 66:13; 116:14, 18) that he had made to the Lord. David Marcus observes (*Jephthah and His Vow* [Lubbock: Texas Tech, 1986], pp. 19–21) that Absalom's vow (vv.7–8) and the four other examples of vows recorded in the OT (Jacob's, Gen 28:20–22; Israel's, Num 21:2; Jephthah's, Judg 11:30–31; Hannah's, 1 Sam 1:11) share several characteristics: (1) Each is preceded by an introduction that contains the verb *ndr* ("to vow") and its cognate accusative (in this case "a vow I made," v.7; cf. also "I made this vow," v.8); (2) the deity to whom the vow is addressed is named (here "the LORD," v.7); (3) a form of the verb "to say" introduces the vow proper (here *lē'mōr*, v.8, rendered in this case simply as a colon); (4) a protasis introduced by "if" (v.8) contains (except for Jacob's vow) an infinitive absolute plus the finite verb in the imperfect (here *yāšôḇ yᵉšîḇēnî*, "[ever] takes me back," v.8); and (5) an apodosis is expressed by the perfect consecutive (here *wᵉʿāḇaḏtî*, "I will worship," v.8—that is, Absalom promises to offer sacrifices to the Lord in Hebron [cf. v.12]).

The statement that Absalom desires to go to "Hebron" (v.7), a city that figures largely in this passage (vv.8, 9, 10), reminds the reader that David had earlier been anointed king over Israel there (cf. 5:3). During the three years Absalom was "at Geshur in Aram" (v.8) he may have been attempting to drum up support among his eastern allies (see 13:38 and comment), looking forward to the time when he would rebel against his father. David, apparently unsuspecting (cf., however, Wiseman, "'Is It Peace?'" p. 324), tells his son to "go in peace" (v.9), a cordial expression of farewell (see comment on 1 Sam 29:7) that perhaps in this case also includes a promise of safe conduct (cf. v.27; see comment on 3:21).

Meanwhile Absalom sends "secret messengers" (v.10; cf. Num 21:32 ["spies"]; 1 Sam 26:4 ["scouts"]) throughout Israel. Their mission is to alert the various tribal territories that a prearranged signal ("the sound of the trumpets") is their mandate to declare Absalom king of Israel. A large contingent of men from Jerusalem, unsuspecting of Absalom's true intentions, has accompanied him to Hebron (v.11).

If the Lord's earlier reminder to Samuel to sacrifice a heifer in conjunction with the anointing of David was not a pretext to distract the rejected Saul (see 1 Sam 16:2 and comment), the same cannot be said for Absalom's offering of sacrifices (v.12) in connection with a supposed vow that he had previously made (see comments on vv.7–8). Realizing that if his designs on Israel's throne are to have any chance of success he will need all the expert advice he can get, he sends for David's own counselor, Ahithophel. The name means "My Brother Is Foolishness" (cf. v.31 [where, however, a different Heb. root is used]), the latter element of which is vocalized like *bōšeṯ* ("shame"; see comment on the name Ish-Bosheth, "Man of Shame," in 2:8). The scribal treatment of Ahithophel's name alludes "to his 'shameful' role as a deserter to Absalom and his death in degradation, 17:23" (Carlson, p. 252). Ahithophel's son Eliam (cf. 23:34) is doubtless to be identified with Bathsheba's father (see 11:3 and comment), and it is therefore understandable that "as Bathsheba's grandfather he [Ahithophel] was an enemy of David" (Hugo Gressmann, "The Oldest History Writing in Israel," in *Narrative and Novella in Samuel: Studies by Hugo Gressmann and Other Scholars, 1906–1923,* JSOT suppl. 116; ed. David M. Gunn [Sheffield: Almond, 1991], p. 39).

Years before, David had experienced the exhilaration of growing "stronger and stronger, while the house of Saul grew weaker and weaker" (3:1). Now, however, the shoe is on the other foot: To David's detriment, the evil alliance of Absalom's ambition and Ahithophel's advice makes it inevitable that Absalom's following will continue to increase (v.12).

## Notes

---

**7** Since the MT's "forty" is contextually impossible, the reading "four," attested in several ancient witnesses (see NIV mg.), surely represents the original text (cf. KD, pp. 415–16).

**8** Although the infinitive absolute יָשׁוֹב (*yāšôḇ*) and the following verb יְשִׁיבֵנִי (*y^e šîḇēnî*) are from two different roots (*yšb* and *šwb* respectively), the phenomenon is not unique to this text; cf. אָסֹף אָסֵף (*'āsōp̱ 'āsēp̱,* "I will sweep away" [Zeph 1:2]), in which the root of the first verb is *'sp* and the second *swp*. In Zeph 1:2 the infinitive absolute *'āsōp̱* was "chosen for assonance" (BDB, p. 692), and the same considerations were doubtless in view here as well.

Not in the MT, "in Hebron" is nevertheless at least implied in the context to avoid the impression that Absalom intends to worship the Lord in Jerusalem. The phrase in fact appears in some MSS of the LXX (see NIV mg.) in its Lucianic recension (cf. Driver, Mauchline, McCarter, Smith).

**12** Since the idiom "sent for" requires the addition of a form of קרא (*qr',* "called") to שלח (*šlḥ,* "sent"; cf. 1 Sam 22:11), the apparent supralinear restoration of ויקרא (*wyqr'*) after וישלח (*wyšlḥ*) in 4QSam^c (cf. Ulrich, "4QSam^c: A Fragmentary Manuscript," pp. 8, 16) probably reproduces the original text (cf. also LXX *καὶ ἐκάλεσεν* [*kai ekalesen*]; the MT does not have *wyqr'*).

The hometown of Ahithophel "the Gilonite" was Giloh, a town in the hill country of Judah (cf. Josh 15:48, 51). Although its exact location remains unknown, its association with Anab, Eshtemoh, and Anim (Josh 15:50), all of which were located south of Hebron, places it in that general vicinity, perhaps "at the southernmost end of the Judean mountains, close to the northern Negev" (Amihai Mazar, "Giloh: An Early Israelite Settlement Site Near Jerusalem," IEJ 31, 1-2 [1981]: 2). In any event, Ahithophel's hometown is not the site of the same name near Jerusalem that has recently been undergoing excavation (for which cf. ibid., pp. 1–36).

## 12. *David's flight*

### 15:13–37

13A messenger came and told David, "The hearts of the men of Israel
are with Absalom."
14Then David said to all his officials who were with him in Jerusalem,
"Come! We must flee, or none of us will escape from Absalom. We must
leave immediately, or he will move quickly to overtake us and bring ruin
upon us and put the city to the sword."
15The king's officials answered him, "Your servants are ready to do
whatever our lord the king chooses."
16The king set out, with his entire household following him; but he left
ten concubines to take care of the palace. 17So the king set out, with all
the people following him, and they halted at a place some distance
away. 18All his men marched past him, along with all the Kerethites and
Pelethites; and all the six hundred Gittites who had accompanied him
from Gath marched before the king.
19The king said to Ittai the Gittite, "Why should you come along with
us? Go back and stay with King Absalom. You are a foreigner, an exile
from your homeland. 20You came only yesterday. And today shall I make
you wander about with us, when I do not know where I am going? Go
back, and take your countrymen. May kindness and faithfulness be with
you."
21But Ittai replied to the king, "As surely as the LORD lives, and as my
lord the king lives, wherever my lord the king may be, whether it means
life or death, there will your servant be."
22David said to Ittai, "Go ahead, march on." So Ittai the Gittite
marched on with all his men and the families that were with him.
23The whole countryside wept aloud as all the people passed by. The
king also crossed the Kidron Valley, and all the people moved on toward
the desert.
24Zadok was there, too, and all the Levites who were with him were
carrying the ark of the covenant of God. They set down the ark of God,
and Abiathar offered sacrifices until all the people had finished leaving
the city.
25Then the king said to Zadok, "Take the ark of God back into the city.
If I find favor in the LORD's eyes, he will bring me back and let me see it
and his dwelling place again. 26But if he says, 'I am not pleased with
you,' then I am ready; let him do to me whatever seems good to him."
27The king also said to Zadok the priest, "Aren't you a seer? Go back
to the city in peace, with your son Ahimaaz and Jonathan son of
Abiathar. You and Abiathar take your two sons with you. 28I will wait at
the fords in the desert until word comes from you to inform me." 29So
Zadok and Abiathar took the ark of God back to Jerusalem and stayed
there.
30But David continued up the Mount of Olives, weeping as he went;
his head was covered and he was barefoot. All the people with him
covered their heads too and were weeping as they went up. 31Now David
had been told, "Ahithophel is among the conspirators with Absalom."
So David prayed, "O LORD, turn Ahithophel's counsel into foolishness."
32When David arrived at the summit, where people used to worship
God, Hushai the Arkite was there to meet him, his robe torn and dust on
his head. 33David said to him, "If you go with me, you will be a burden to
me. 34But if you return to the city and say to Absalom, 'I will be your
servant, O king; I was your father's servant in the past, but now I will be
your servant,' then you can help me by frustrating Ahithophel's advice.
35Won't the priests Zadok and Abiathar be there with you? Tell them
anything you hear in the king's palace. 36Their two sons, Ahimaaz son of

Zadok and Jonathan son of Abiathar, are there with them. Send them to me with anything you hear."
37So David's friend Hushai arrived at Jerusalem as Absalom was entering the city.

A narrative whose main subject is fleeing is likely to contain a large number of verbs of motion, and vv.13–37 are no exception. The most important of them are *'br* ("pass by, cross over, move on, march"), which occurs nine times (vv.18 [bis], 22 [bis], 23 [ter], 24 ["leaving"], 33 ["go"]); *šwb* ("return, go back") eight times (vv.19, 20, 20 ["take"], 25 ["take," "bring . . . back"], 27, 29 ["took . . . back"], 34); *bw'* ("come, enter, arrive") seven times (vv.13, 18 ["accompanied"], 20, 28, 32, 37 [bis]); and *hlk* ("go, walk, come") seven times (vv.14 ["leave"], 19, 20 [three times, two of which are rendered as portions of other idioms in the interests of English style], 22, 30 ["was barefoot," lit., "was walking barefoot"]).

In his discussion of the Court History of David, Wharton makes an especially noteworthy observation concerning vv.13–37:

> All the utterly real issues between people and people and between God and people that swirl throughout II Samuel 9–20, I Kings 1–2 also swirl about Jesus as he moves toward the cross. One must think that the Gospel writers were acutely aware of this when they depicted Jesus' Maundy Thursday walk to the Mount of Olives in ways so graphically reminiscent of the "passion" of the first *Meshiach* in II Samuel 15:13–37. Even the detail of Judas' betrayal of Jesus, and his subsequent suicide, have no remote parallel anywhere in Scripture, with the remarkable exception of Ahithophel, who betrayed the Lord's anointed and thus opened the door to suicidal despair (II Samuel 17:23). ("A Plausible Tale," p. 353)

The literary unit divides naturally into four roughly equal sections. A paragraph summarizing the preparations for and the beginning of the flight (vv.13–18) is followed by David's instructions to three of his supporters, one at the outset of the journey (Ittai, vv.19–23) and the other two en route (Zadok, vv.24–31; Hushai, vv.32–37).

**13–18** *Wayyāḇō'* ("came," "arrived") begins vv.13 and 37, thus becoming a part of an *inclusio* that brackets the entire literary unit (vv.13–37). The word rendered "messenger" (v.13; cf. Jer 51:31) is a participial form of *ngd* ("tell"; cf. 18:11) and refers to one who brings a report, usually a bearer of bad news (see comment on 1:5), as in this case: The hearts of the men of Israel are now "with" Absalom; they are following him with total devotion (for the idiom, cf. 1 Kings 11:4, where the heart of David's son Solomon is described as having been turned "after" other gods [same Heb. word in both cases]) because he "stole the[ir] hearts" (see v.6 and comment). Thus Israel's "gift of the kingdom to David is revoked. . . . The kingdom is now taken from him" (Gunn, "David and the Gift of the Kingdom," p. 22).

David sees no way out but to "flee" (v.14; cf. the title of Psalm 3), an activity that is not new to him (cf. 1 Sam 19:12, 18; 22:17)—and a cruelly ironic twist on Absalom's earlier flight from Jerusalem to escape his father (see 13:34, 37–38, and comment). To his officials David counsels the utmost speed (*mhr*, "immediately") since Absalom can be expected to "move quickly" (*mhr*). If Absalom succeeds in overtaking David and his men, they will be brought to ruin and Jerusalem will be "put . . . to the sword," a terrifying fate at best (see 1 Sam 22:19 and comment).

Loyal to a fault (v.15), the king's "officials" indicate that they, his "servants" (same

Heb. word; see comments on 1 Sam 1:11; 16:15–16), are ready to abide by whatever decision he "chooses" (*bḥr*, perhaps a deliberate wordplay on *brḥ* ["flee"] in v.14). And so it is (vv.16–17) that "the king set out, with" virtually everyone in the palace ("his entire household," v.16; "all the people," v.17) "following him." In addition to his numerous wives (see comments on 3:2; 12:8; 1 Sam 25:43), David also had many concubines (see 5:13 and comment), ten of whom he leaves behind to take care of the palace. Ahithophel would soon counsel the triumphant usurper, Absalom, to have sexual relations with David's concubines in full public view (cf. 16:21–22), as a result of which David would eventually put them under house arrest "till the day of their death" (20:3).

The first stop reached by the fleeing king and his retinue is a "place some distance away" (*bêṯ hammerḥāq*, v.17), perhaps the "last house" on the eastern edge of Jerusalem (cf. Anderson, Gordon, McCarter). David pauses temporarily as all his officials, together with his crack mercenary corps (the "Kerethites and Pelethites," v.18; see comment on 8:18), march on ahead. In addition, "six hundred" (cf. 1 Sam 23:13; 27:2; 30:9; for the significance of the number, see comment on 1 Sam 13:15) "Gittites" (originally citizens of the Philistine city of Gath [modern Tell es-Safi, about twenty-four miles west-southwest of Jerusalem]), doubtless also mercenaries, march before the king (cf. Herzog and Gichon, *Battles of the Bible*, p. 87). By any reckoning David has a sizable and dependable military force to protect him from whatever contingency might arise from Absalom's delusions of grandeur.

**19–23** The first high official in David's retinue to whom the king speaks is Ittai (v.19), the leader of the Gittite mercenaries, who is apparently considered trustworthy enough to share command of Israelite troops as well (see comment on 18:2). Apparently of Philistine origin, the name Ittai can hardly be separated from Itiya and Witiya, names of one or more governors of the Philistine city of Ashkelon who appear in several Amarna letters written almost four centuries before the time of David (cf. Delcor, "Les Kéréthim et les Crétois," pp. 412–13). Since the name is non-Semitic, it does not mean "(God Is) With Me" or the like. Although *'ittay* ("Ittai") is found in association with *'ittānû* ("with us," v.19) and *'ittô* ("with him," v.22), the appearance of the alternate forms *'immānû* ("with us") and *'immāḵ* ("with you," v.20) at a greater distance from "Ittai" make it more likely that the *'itt-* forms are wordplays than that they are attempts to define the name.

Addressing Ittai, David wants to know why "you" (v.19), of all people (the pronoun is emphatic), would wish to accompany him in his flight. "The king" (David) recommends that Ittai return to Jerusalem and stay with "the king" (thus the MT; the NIV renders "King Absalom" to resolve the ambiguity). It would seem that David considers Absalom's coup d'état a fait accompli (cf. v.34). Ittai has nothing to gain and everything to lose by remaining with David. After all, he is already a displaced person from his Philistine homeland. Because of Ittai's recent arrival on the scene, David is reluctant to make him "wander about" (v.20; cf. Ps 59:11), like the Israelites in the Sinai desert (cf. Num 32:13), on a journey of uncertain destination. Commending him to the "kindness and faithfulness" of God (for the importance of this phrase to covenant relationships, see 2:6 and comment), he therefore commands him to return to Jerusalem with his fellow Gittites.

Not to be dissuaded, however, Ittai takes the most solemn of oaths (v.21; see comments on 11:11; 1 Sam 14:39; 20:3; 25:26) as he swears undying loyalty to David. Like Ruth before him in a similar situation (cf. Ruth 1:16–17), Ittai pledges that he will never leave the king, whether in "life or death" (a Deuteronomic phrase, cf. Deut 30:15, 19). And as in the case of Naomi (cf. Ruth 1:18), David—however reluctantly—honors Ittai's determination and agrees to let him march on, together with all his men and "the families" that are with him (v.22, lit., "all the children," the latter term serving here as synecdoche; for details and additional references, cf. TDOT, 5:348–49).

Whatever problems certain citizens of Jerusalem and other towns may have with David (see comment on v.6), people living in the countryside see him in a different light. He is their king—and as he and his followers pass by, the people weep "aloud" (v.23; cf. 1 Sam 28:12 ["at the top of her voice"]) as an expression of their fear for an uncertain future. Prefiguring the passion of another anointed King centuries later (cf. John 18:1), David crosses the Kidron Valley, a stream bed east of Jerusalem that is dry most of the year. Large numbers of his followers continue on toward the northern part of the Desert of Judah, David and his immediate retainers apparently moving along at a somewhat slower pace (cf. 16:1).

Just as vv.30–31 serve as a transition between David's conversations with Zadok and Husahi, so also v.23 serves as a natural segue from David's discussion with Ittai to that with Zadok.

**24–31** Sharing priestly duties during at least part of the reign of David, Zadok and Abiathar (v.24; 20:25; for details see comments on 8:17; 1 Sam 22:20) decide to accompany him on his flight from Jerusalem. Not wanting to leave the ark of the covenant in the city and perhaps trusting in its supposed powers as a military palladium if war should break out (see 1 Sam 4:3–4 and comment), Levites carry it (see comments on 6:13; 1 Sam 6:15) across the Kidron. As during another procession of the ark (see 6:13 and comment), the Levites halt long enough for sacrifices to be offered. The ceremony continues until all the refugees have left Jerusalem (cf. similarly Josh 3:17; 4:11).

David's instructions to Zadok are divided into two parts, the first having to do with the return of the ark to Jerusalem (vv.25–26) and the second with the role of Zadok and Abiathar as listening posts there to keep David informed of important developments concerning Absalom's burgeoning rebellion (vv.27–29). Sensing no need for the ark to accompany him, David directs Zadok to take it back to the city (v.25). Like Gideon (cf. Judg 6:17), he hopes to "find favor in the LORD's eyes" (cf. also Gen 6:8). Indeed, he is prepared to resign himself to the will of God, to whatever seems good "to him" (v.26, lit., "in his eyes"). David is confident that if the Lord so chooses, he will bring him back to Jerusalem to see again not only the ark in its proper setting but also the Lord's "dwelling place" (v.25), probably in this context a reference to the city itself (cf. Isa 33:20, where Jerusalem is called a peaceful "abode" [same Heb. word in both cases]). But if the Lord declares that he is not "pleased" with David (v.26)—unlike during his many experiences of fleeing from his enemies, when he reveled in the fact that the Lord "delighted" in him (22:20; same Heb. word)—he will accept that also with equanimity. Like the Gibeonites in the presence of Joshua (cf. Josh 9:25, the wording of which is echoed here), David is "ready" to throw himself on the mercy of the court (the equivalent of *hin[e]nî* ["I am ready"], the characteristic response of the servant [often translated "Here I am"; cf. Gen 22:1, 11], is rendered simply "We are" in Josh 9:25). As the people of Gibeon were prepared to accept "whatever seems good" to Joshua, so David is resigned to "whatever seems good" to the Lord.

In both verses of his second statement to Zadok (vv.27–28), David begins with a form of the verb *r'h* ("see"; *rᵉ'û* ["See"] at the beginning of v.28 is omitted by the NIV in the interests of style). Although "Aren't you a seer?" (v.27) is a possible translation of *hrw'h 'th* (for the role of a seer in ancient Israel, see 1 Sam 9:9 and comment), the Hebrew phrase is not stated negatively. In addition, the presence of *r'w* in v.28 (the same word is translated "Listen!" in 13:28) makes it likely that the two expressions should be understood in the same way. "Do you see?" (in the sense of an imperative "See," "Look") would parallel nicely the "See" that begins v.28 (for a similar example compare *hr'h 'th* ["do you see," Ezek 8:6] with *hr'yt* ["do you see," "have you seen"] in the same context [Ezek 8:12, 15, 17]; cf. 1 Sam 10:24; 17:25). If it be argued that Zadok is here called a "seer" because his divinely imparted knowledge will enable him to "inform" David (v.28), it is necessary to point out that (1) ordinary human knowledge is sufficient to "inform" (the verb, a participial form of which occurs in v.13 ["messenger"; see comment there], commonly means simply "tell"); (2) more than one person will "inform" David (the "you" before "to inform" is plural); (3) when "Zadok does inform David, it is because he in his turn is informed by Hushai (2 Sam. xvii 15), not because of Zadok's position as oracle priest" (J. Hoftijzer, "A Peculiar Question: A Note on 2 Sam. xv 27," VetTest 21, 5 [1971]: 607; for additional details cf. pp. 606–9).

Zadok will be of more help to David back in Jerusalem than if he flees with him, so David tells him to return to the city with his son Ahimaaz and Abiathar's son Jonathan (v.27). "Ahimaaz" and "Jonathan" have occurred already in the books of Samuel as the names of other men (1 Sam 13:2; 14:50). (Zadok's son Ahimaaz as well as Abiathar have been suggested as possible authors of David's Court History [see comments on 9:1–20:26].) The specificity (and perhaps also the urgency) of David's request is underscored by his addendum: "your [pl.] two sons with you [pl.]" (v.27; the NIV prefaces the phrase with "You and Abiathar take" to clarify in English the Heb. intention). David wants to make sure that Zadok understands that the two priests and their two sons—all four of them—are to return to Jerusalem.

As for David himself, he will continue on his way and wait at the "fords [reading *'aḇrôṯ* with the *Kethiv;* cf. 17:16, where many MSS likewise read *'aḇrôṯ* (cf. BHS) instead of *'arḇôṯ* (thus *Qere* in v.28), "steppes"] in the desert" (v.28) on the west bank of the Jordan (cf. 17:16; cf. further 19:18). Although the exact site is unknown, "fords" is a more likely reading than "steppes" because "it gives a more specific location for the purpose of passing on the information" (Anderson, p. 201). David expects Zadok and Abiathar to be involved together in gathering data about Absalom's plans ("you" in v.28 is plural). Following David's instructions (v.29), the two men "took" (the verb is singular, stressing Zadok's primary responsibility) the ark back to Jerusalem (cf. vv.25–26) and "stayed" (pl.) there (cf. vv.27–28).

After dismissing Zadok and Abiathar, David ascends the storied hill east of Jerusalem (cf. 1 Kings 11:7; Ezek 11:23), the Mount of Olives (v.30)—eventually linked to Jesus' triumphal entry (cf. Luke 19:29, 37), his teaching ministry (the so-called Olivet discourse; cf. Mark 13:3), his agony at Gethsemane (cf. Luke 22:39), his ascension (cf. Acts 1:11–12), and his second advent (cf. Zech 14:4). Facing the eminence on which Solomon's temple was later built, the Mount of Olives is about twenty-seven hundred feet high and rises about two hundred feet above the city itself. As David and the people with him climb the hill, they express their sorrow and sense of love by "weeping" (v.30) and their despair and sense of foreboding by covering their heads (cf. Esth 6:12; 7:8; Jer 14:3–4). In addition, David walks barefoot to symbolize the shameful exile on which he is now embarking (cf. Isa 20:2–3; cf. similarly Mic 1:8).

"Uneasy lies the head that wears a crown," wrote William Shakespeare (KH IV, part 2, 3.1.31). A harried king feels surrounded by conspirators (cf. v.12; see comment on 1 Sam 22:8, 13), and David's intelligence network (see 10:5 and comment) informs David that Ahithophel (see v.12 and comment) is among them (cf. v.31). The news alarms David, and he turns to God for help. "It was clear to David . . . that Ahithophel as counsellor of the king not only held one of the highest court positions of confidence but also that whoever had the benefit of this advice in political or military matters would be successful. . . . This makes all the more understandable why David appealed as a last resort to the only power he thought able to intervene and to disqualify the counsel of a man considered practically infallible" (Roth, "A Study of the Classical Hebrew Verb *ṣkl*," p. 71): "O LORD, turn Ahithophel's counsel into foolishness" (v.31; cf. Isa 44:25 ["nonsense"]).

**32–37** The summit of the Mount of Olives was a place "where people used to worship God" (v.32)—and where false gods would later be worshiped (cf. 1 Kings 11:7). Upon arriving there David finds Hushai the Arkite waiting to "meet" him (*qr'*; cf. also 16:1), his robe "torn" (*qr'*; the wordplay is perhaps intentional) and dust on his head (signs of anguish and distress; see comments on 1:2; 13:19; 1 Sam 4:12). Hushai's clan, the Arkites (*'arkî*), lived near Ataroth (cf. Josh 16:2) "in NE Ephraim on the border with Manasseh" (Rasmussen, p. 227) and should not be confused with the Arkites (*'arqî*) who were one of the ten traditional tribal groups in the Canaanite orbit (cf. Gen 10:17) and who lived in Arqat (Irqata in the Amarna letters; for details cf. Youngblood, *The Amarna Correspondence*, pp. 104–5), modern Tell Arqa (about 120 miles north-northeast of the Sea of Galilee).

As in the case of Zadok and Abiathar (cf. vv.24–29), David is convinced that Hushai will be of more value to him back in Jerusalem than as a fellow refugee. Hushai will only be a "burden" to the king if he accompanies him (v.33; cf. 19:35 for Barzillai's perspective self-evaluation in the parallel section; cf. also Num 11:11, 17; Job 7:20). David therefore tells Hushai to return to the city and promise Absalom the same kind of faithful service that he had already given to David himself (v.34). By becoming a member of Absalom's inner council, Hushai would be able to assist David by "frustrating" Ahithophel's advice (a not uncommon role of competent and clever counselors in ancient times; cf. Ezra 4:5). David had already prayed that the Lord would turn Ahithophel's "counsel" into foolishness (v.31), and now he is convinced that Hushai can be a divinely empowered instrument to accomplish the goal of "frustrating" (and so it would be; cf. 17:14) Ahithophel's "advice" (v.34; same Heb. word as that for "counsel" in v.31). Hushai thus becomes a key link in David's resources of "statecraft and espionage in order to counter the sagacity of Ahithophel" (William McKane, *Prophets and Wise Men*, Studies in Biblical Theology 44 [Naperville: Allenson, 1965], p. 57).

Zadok and Abiathar are to be David's eyes and ears in the palace while the king is fleeing (see v.28 and comment), and he wants Hushai to collaborate with them by telling them anything he hears there (v.35; "you hear" is singular). The three men will then send the priests' two sons to David with whatever helpful information they have been able to gather (v.36; "Send" and "you hear" are plural).

And so it is that Absalom, the king's treasonous son, and Hushai, the king's loyal "friend" (v.37; 16:16; see Notes below), arrive at Jerusalem simultaneously.

## Notes

---

**19** לִמְקוֹמֶךָ (*limqômeḵā,* "from your homeland") provides an excellent example of ־לְ (*l-*) in the sense of "from," as the ancient versions understood it here (cf. BHS; for other examples, cf. Mitchell Dahood, "Hebrew-Ugaritic Lexicography IV," *Biblica* 47, 3 [1966]: 406).

**23** "Toward the desert" translates עַל־פְּנֵי־דֶרֶךְ אֶת־הַמִּדְבָּר (*ʿal-pᵉnê-ḏereḵ ʾeṯ-hammiḏbār,* lit., "over the face of the road/direction of the desert"). The particle ־אֶת (*ʾeṯ-*), whether it here means "with" or is understood as the sign of the definite accusative, is without analogy. Driver and others (e.g., Anderson, Mauchline, H.P. Smith) therefore assume it to be a scribal error for זַיִת (*zayiṯ,* "olive"), on the basis of the Lucianic recension of the LXX, and *dereḵ (haz)zayiṯ* is then read "the Olive Way" (McCarter, *II Samuel,* in loc.). But the difficulty in the MT is relieved considerably if *ʾeṯ-* is omitted (with many MSS) or if ־אֶל (*ʾel-,* "to, toward") is read in its place (with two MSS; cf. BHS). Emendation is thus unnecessary.

**24** וַיַּעַל (*wayyaʿal*) in the Qal would mean "went up" (see NIV mg.), while in the Hiphil it can mean "offered (sacrifices)" even without an object (cf. 24:22; in 1 Sam 2:28 "go up to my altar" can also be rendered alternatively "offer sacrifices on my altar"). The NIV text reading "offered sacrifices" is surely correct here, since "went up" would be contextually awkward (for details cf. Hertzberg, p. 343 n. a; Fokkelman, *King David,* p. 455).

**34** For a detailed study of the differences in vv.34–35 between the MT, the LXX, and the Lucianic recension of the LXX, cf. Julio Trebolle, "Espías contra Consejeros en la Revuelta de Absalón (II Sam., xv, 34–36): Historia de la Recensión como Método," RB 86, 4 (1979): 524–43. Although McCarter accepts the lengthy LXX addition in v.34 (*II Samuel,* p. 367), Anderson wisely advises caution (p. 201).

**37** "Friend" is used here and in 16:16, not in the sense of "acquaintance," but as a technical term for an important cabinet post (see comment on 13:3; the Heb. word is rendered "personal adviser" in 1 Kings 4:5, and Hushai himself is called the king's "friend" in a list of David's officials [1 Chron 27:33]; cf. NIV mg. on 1 Kings 1:8; for discussion, cf. McCarter, *II Samuel* p. 372).

---

### 13. *Kindness to Ziba*

#### 16:1–4

1 When David had gone a short distance beyond the summit, there was
Ziba, the steward of Mephibosheth, waiting to meet him. He had a string
of donkeys saddled and loaded with two hundred loaves of bread, a
hundred cakes of raisins, a hundred cakes of figs and a skin of wine.
2 The king asked Ziba, "Why have you brought these?"

Ziba answered, "The donkeys are for the king's household to ride on,
the bread and fruit are for the men to eat, and the wine is to refresh
those who become exhausted in the desert."
3 The king then asked, "Where is your master's grandson?"

Ziba said to him, "He is staying in Jerusalem, because he thinks,
'Today the house of Israel will give me back my grandfather's kingdom.'"
4 Then the king said to Ziba, "All that belonged to Mephibosheth is
now yours."

"I humbly bow," Ziba said. "May I find favor in your eyes, my lord the
king."

David now encounters Ziba (vv.1–4), the first of two men with links to the house of Saul (the other is Shimei [vv.5–14]). Although Ziba attempts to ingratiate himself to him and Shimei curses him, David treats each with courtesy. The brief account of the king's kindness to Ziba (vv.1–4) has obvious connections with the narrative of his kindness to Mephibosheth (ch. 9), many of which will be noted below.

The first verse establishes the backdrop for the next three, each of which begins with *wayyō'mer hammelek̲* ("And/Then the king said/asked").

**1** Proceeding beyond the summit of the Mount of Olives, David is met (see 15:32 and comment) by Ziba (see comment on 9:2), the steward of Saul's grandson Mephibosheth (cf. 9:6; see Notes on 4:4). Ziba's entourage includes donkeys loaded with all kinds of provisions, items especially suited for men on the march. Apparently Ziba wants to demonstrate his loyalty to David. Although *ṣemed̲* normally means "two" (cf. Judg 19:3, 10), "pair of" (cf. 1 Sam 11:7), the NIV rendering "string of" is probably contextually preferable here (v.2 seems to demand more than two donkeys) and receives support from the somewhat broad usage of Akkadian cognates *ṣimdu, ṣimittu* (cf. *The Assyrian Dictionary* [Chicago: Oriental Institute, 1962], 16:197–99). The foodstuffs for David and his men assembled years before by Abigail (see 1 Sam 25:18 and comments) surpassed in amount and variety those described here, but Ziba's gift is nonetheless generous—even though it may have come from Mephibosheth's resources rather than his own (cf. Brueggemann, *First and Second Samuel*, pp. 305–6). Indeed, Mephibosheth will later claim that he himself had "saddled" a donkey so that he might join David in his flight from Absalom—unlike the pretentious use made of "saddled" donkeys by the conniving Ziba, whom Mephibosheth will accuse of having "betrayed" him (19:26).

**2–4** Suspicious either of Ziba's motives or of the origin of the supplies he has brought, David asks, "Why have you brought these?" (v.2, lit., "What are these to/for you?" cf. similarly Gen 33:5, 8; Ezek 37:18). Ziba deftly dodges the question of whether he has a right to bring them and concentrates instead on their purposes, all of which are good and proper: The donkeys are for the king's household to ride on (and are therefore doubtless more than two in number; see comment on v.1; see also 1 Sam 25:20 and comment), and the foodstuffs are for nourishment and refreshment. The Hebrew word for "fruit" in v.2 is the same as that for "figs" in v.1, the NIV probably understanding the word in v.2 as encompassing the raisins and figs in v.1. People on an arduous journey quickly become "exhausted" and need special attention (v.2; cf. Judg 8:4, 15), particularly if they are fleeing for their lives. Ziba, whatever his ulterior motives may be, declares his willingness to help.

Still skeptical, David wants to know where Mephibosheth is (v.3), perhaps to speak directly to him to find out whether Ziba is telling the truth. Ziba's response—later indignantly denied by Mephibosheth (cf. 19:26–28)—is that the latter has decided to stay in Jerusalem in the belief that the house of Israel will return the kingdom (for a similar false hope, cf. 1 Kings 12:21 = 2 Chron 11:1) to the house of Saul and therefore to Mephibosheth himself. David had earlier agreed to "restore" to Mephibosheth all the land that belonged to Saul (see 9:7 and comment), but he had never agreed to "give . . . back" Saul's kingdom to him (v.3; same Heb. verb). Apparently Ziba either did not know or did not care that the kingdom of Israel had long ago been torn from Saul by divine decree and given to David (see 1 Sam 15:27–28 and comments). In any case, Ziba attributes to Mephibosheth words whose genuineness it is impossible to verify.

For the moment at least, David chooses to believe Ziba (v.4). Without hearing the other side of the story, David punishes Mephibosheth in absentia by giving Ziba everything that formerly belonged to his master. Not unexpectedly, Ziba's response is servile: "I humbly bow." Mephibosheth has taught him well (cf. 9:6, 8).

## Notes

3 Wordplay between ישׁב (*yšb*) and שׁוב (*šwb*), noted already in 15:8 (see Notes there), occurs also in 16:3 ("is staying," "give . . . back"; cf. Conroy [p. 121], who appropriately cites 15:19 ["go back," "stay"] and 15:29 ["took . . . back," "stayed"] as well).

## 14. *Shimei's curse*

### 16:5–14

5 As King David approached Bahurim, a man from the same clan as Saul's family came out from there. His name was Shimei son of Gera, and he cursed as he came out. 6 He pelted David and all the king's officials with stones, though all the troops and the special guard were on David's right and left. 7 As he cursed, Shimei said, "Get out, get out, you man of blood, you scoundrel! 8 The LORD has repaid you for all the blood you shed in the household of Saul, in whose place you have reigned. The LORD has handed the kingdom over to your son Absalom. You have come to ruin because you are a man of blood!"

9 Then Abishai son of Zeruiah said to the king, "Why should this dead dog curse my lord the king? Let me go over and cut off his head."

10 But the king said, "What do you and I have in common, you sons of Zeruiah? If he is cursing because the LORD said to him, 'Curse David,' who can ask, 'Why do you do this?'"

11 David then said to Abishai and all his officials, "My son, who is of my own flesh, is trying to take my life. How much more, then, this Benjamite! Leave him alone; let him curse, for the LORD has told him to. 12 It may be that the LORD will see my distress and repay me with good for the cursing I am receiving today."

13 So David and his men continued along the road while Shimei was going along the hillside opposite him, cursing as he went and throwing stones at him and showering him with dirt. 14 The king and all the people with him arrived at their destination exhausted. And there he refreshed himself.

The second Saulide encountered by David in chapter 16 (see introduction to vv.1–4) is Shimei, whose reaction to the king is diametrically opposite to that of Ziba. While the latter is ingratiating and submissive, Shimei is insulting and defiant.

The chiastic structure of the literary unit is exquisite, as demonstrated by George P. Ridout (*Prose Compositional Techniques in the Succession Narrative* [unpublished dissertation; Berkeley, Graduate Theological Union, 1971], pp. 56–70) and amplified by Walter Brueggemann, "On Coping With Curse: A Study of 2 Sam 16:5–14," CBQ 36, 2 (1974): 177 (the titles of the sections are my own):

A. David approaches Bahurim (16:5a).
  B. Shimei pelts David with stones (16:5b–6).
    C. Shimei curses David (16:7–8).
      D. Abishai wants to kill Shimei (16:9).

C′. David accepts Shimei's curses (16:10–12).
B′. Shimei pelts David with stones (16:13).
A′. David arrives at his destination (16:14).

Although Brueggemann does not organize the speeches of Shimei, Abishai, and David (vv.7–12) chiastically, such an arrangement seems transparent. The focus of the unit is thus Abishai's desire for Shimei's execution.

**5a** On the line of march of David and his party is Bahurim (for possible location see comment on 3:16). "Approached" (*ûḇā'*) and "arrived" (*wayyāḇō'*, v.14) form a suitable *inclusio* to frame the intervening verses.

**5b–6** Bahurim is the hometown of Shimei son of Gera (the latter name is clearly Benjamite; cf. Gen 46:21; Judg 3:15; 1 Chron 8:3, 5, 7), a member of one of the Saulide clans (v.5b). Shimei is in an ugly mood: As he comes out of the town, he curses David (cf. the parallel in v.13), much as Goliath had done years earlier (cf. 1 Sam 17:43). To curse a descendant of Abraham is to invite divine retribution (cf. Gen 12:3), and Shimei's headstrong actions will not ultimately go unpunished (1 Kings 2:8–9) in spite of his repenting of them (cf. 19:18–20). Not content with hurling curses at the king—a particularly heinous act in itself, the equivalent of blasphemy (cf. Exod 22:28)—Shimei pelts David and his officials with stones (v.6) as a palpable means of expressing his great displeasure (cf. similarly Exod 21:18). Fortunately for David, his armed escort is protecting him on all sides ("right and left," v.6; cf. similarly Ps 16:8).

**7–8** The three speeches that form the center of the literary unit (Shimei's, vv.7–8; Abishai's, v.9; David's, vv.10–12) contain the phrase *hēšîḇ YHWH* ("the LORD has repaid/will repay") twice (vv.8, 12) within the larger unit (cf. Brueggemann, "On Coping With Curse," p. 177). Shimei continues his curse by demanding that David get out of Benjamite territory (v.7). He refers to David not only as a "man of blood" (vv.7–8; cf. the plural form "bloodthirsty men" in Pss 5:6; 26:9; 55:23; 59:2; 139:19—ironically, all of them psalms of David; cf. also Prov 29:10 [a proverb of David's son Solomon]) but also as a "man of Belial" (NIV, "scoundrel," v.7; see Notes on 1 Sam 1:16; see also comments on 1 Sam 25:17, 25).

In the tradition of Nathan (cf. 12:10–12), Shimei tells David that his sins will be punished (v.8; cf. Brueggemann, "On Coping With Curse," p. 179). Although the referents Shimei has in mind in speaking of the "blood" that David has shed "in the household of Saul" (v.8) remain uncertain—whether "Meribaal, Abner, Ish-baal, Saul, Uriah" (ibid., p. 177), or, assuming a dischronologized narrative, the seven male descendants of Saul mentioned in 21:4–6, 8–9 (cf. Hertzberg, pp. 299, 381; Vanderkam, "Davidic Complicity in the Deaths of Abner and Eshbaal," pp. 537–39)—Shimei insists that David's ruin is inevitable because of it. Of course, David had earlier disavowed any responsibility for the "blood" of Abner (3:28), as one might expect (but see comment there). In addition, Shimei's curses ring somewhat hollow in the light of the fact that Saul's house itself is "blood-stained" (21:1). In any event, Shimei (and doubtless many if not most of his compatriots) are apparently ready to acknowledge David's son Absalom as their new king (v.8).

**9** The focus of the present literary unit centers on Abishai's rash suggestion that Shimei should be summarily put to death. Not characterized by cautious restraint, this "son of Zeruiah" (see comment on 1 Sam 26:6) is always quick to act, especially when he thinks execution is the best way to solve a problem (see 1 Sam 26:8 and comment). Indeed, the present situation is not the only time Abishai will recommend that Shimei should be killed for cursing the king (cf. 19:21).

Abishai cannot understand why a "dead dog" (a reference to the lowest of animals and therefore, with or without the qualifying adjective "dead," a term of reproach and insult; cf. 3:8; 1 Sam 24:14; see comments on 9:8; 1 Sam 17:43; see also Notes on 1 Sam 17:43) should be allowed to curse David with impunity. To get rid of a minor annoyance like Shimei, Abishai wants to "cut off his head"—the earlier fate of the Philistine Goliath (cf. 1 Sam 17:46) and the Saulide Ish-Bosheth (see 4:7 and comment).

**10–12** The words of Shimei's curse (vv.7–8) include his belief that God is not displeased with it (cf. v.8), and each verse of the parallel passage (vv.10–12) underscores David's conviction either that the Lord has told Shimei to curse him (vv.10–11) or that Shimei's curse finds its origin in the Lord himself (see comment on v.12).

Knowing that the "sons of Zeruiah" (v.10; cf. also 19:22) usually work in concert with one another, David's rebuke to Abishai apparently includes his brother Joab (cf. KD, p. 425; cf. already Symon Patrick, p. 503). "Sons of Zeruiah" is probably used in a disparaging or contemptuous sense here (see comments on 2:18 and 3:39; see also comments on "son of Kish" in 1 Sam 10:11 and "son of Jesse" in 1 Sam 20:27). "What do you and I have in common?" echoed verbatim in an identical context in 19:22, is literally "What to me and to you?" (the pronoun is plural here and in 19:22), a phrase that is often used elsewhere when the speaker senses a threat (cf. Judg 11:12 ["What do you have against us?"]; 1 Kings 17:18; 2 Chron 35:21 ["What quarrel is there between you and me?"]) or lack of common purpose (cf. 2 Kings 3:13 ["What do we have to do with each other?"]; cf. the Semitism in John 2:4 ["Why do you involve me?"] pointed out by Snaith, *The Hebrew Text of 2 Samuel xvi–xix* [London: Epworth, 1945], p. 14). David's long experience with God's intimate presence has taught him that if the Lord has prompted Shimei's curse, no one should question Shimei's motivation (cf. similarly Job 9:12; Eccl 8:4; cf. further Brueggemann, "On Coping With Curse," p. 184), however vindictive or otherwise unworthy it might be.

Widening his audience, David now addresses not only Abishai but also "his [David's] officials" (v.11; cf. v.6). The king knows that his throne is coveted by his son, a common threat in ancient times (cf. 2 Chron 32:21). The Lord's covenant with David had promised him that he would be succeeded by a son who would "come from [his] own body" (7:12; cf. Gen 15:4)—but that son would be Solomon (see comment on 7:12), not Absalom ("is of my own flesh," v.11; same Heb. in both cases). Indeed, Absalom is "trying to take [David's] life," as Saul had attempted to do on more than one occasion (see comments on 4:8; 1 Sam 20:1). It is not surprising, then, that the Saulide Shimei—"this Benjamite" (cf. 1 Sam 9:21; 1 Kings 2:8)—should be bent on David's ruin. But although centuries later another counselor would warn another king that it would not be in the king's best interests to "tolerate" a certain community of Jews (Esth 3:8), among whom were Benjamites (cf. Esth 2:5), David's mandate concerning Shimei is clear and forthright: "Leave him alone" (v.11; same Heb. verb).

Like Hannah before him (see comment on "look upon [my] misery" in 1 Sam 1:11), David hopes that the Lord will "see [his] distress" (v.12; same Heb. idiom) and "repay" him with good—the opposite of what Shimei's curse intends (cf. "has repaid" in v.8). The "good" that David yearns for (v.12) is perhaps a reflection on the contents of the Lord's covenant with him (see comment on "good things" in 7:28; cf. similarly Brueggemann, "On Trust and Freedom," p. 15 n. 33).

In any event, David realizes that the curse of Shimei is not an "undeserved curse" (Prov 26:2). The phrase "the cursing I am receiving" (v.12) is literally "his curse"—that is, God's curse, as Vanderkam correctly observes ("Davidic Complicity in the Deaths of Abner and Eshbaal," p. 536). Thus in all three verses of the literary unit David, while still pleading for divine mercy, reckons with the punishment that God is inflicting on him. His statements constitute "a confession of guilt" (ibid., p. 536) with respect to his crimes against the Saulides, and—especially in v.12—he expresses his confidence in the fact that although the Lord's "response cannot be anticipated or predicted it can be trusted" (Brueggemann, "On Coping With Curse," p. 189).

**13** Shimei's pelting David with stones and cursing him (cf. vv.5b–6) do not stop, as this verse makes clear. Shimei's persistence in such potentially dangerous activity bears eloquent witness to the depth of his anger and frustration. As David and his party continue slowly on their way, Shimei keeps pace along a hillside that parallels the road. The phrase "cursing as he went" echoes "cursed as he came out" in v.5b. In addition to his stone-throwing, Shimei begins "showering [David] with dirt," a colorful cognate accusative construction (lit., "dirting him with dirt") that uses a denominative Hebrew verb found only here in the OT.

**14** The king had "approached" Bahurim (v.5a), and now he has "arrived" at his destination (the same Heb. verb begins each of the two verses [see comment on v.5a]). With him are "all the people" (*'am;* cf. 17:22), here doubtless including not only "all the troops" (*'am*) but also "all the king's officials" and the "special guard" (v.6) as well as others in his retinue. Although their destination is not named in the text, it is "clear from ch. xvii. 18, that the halting-place was not Bahurim, but some place beyond it" (Kirkpatrick, *The Second Book of Samuel,* p. 161).

The physical and psychological stresses of the journey leave David and his company "exhausted" (cf. 17:29 ["tired"]; 1 Sam 14:28 ["faint"], 31), and he therefore takes the opportunity to "refresh" himself (the Heb. verb, a denominative from *nep̄eš,* "throat, being, breath, soul," includes the nuance of "catch one's breath," "rest," and is found elsewhere only in the Sabbath contexts of Exod 23:12 ["refreshed"] and 31:17 ["rested"]).

## Notes

---

**10** In its rendering "If . . . because. . . ," the NIV has chosen the *Kethiv* reading of the first particle and the *Qere* of the second. Although other options and permutations are possible (e.g., *Qere* "In this way" instead of "If" yields equally good sense; for a full discussion, cf. Vanderkam, "Davidic Complicity in the Deaths of Abner and Eshbaal," p. 536 and n. 44), *Qere* "because" is surely preferable to *Kethiv* "and if" in light of the repetition of "because the LORD said to him" in v.11 ("for the LORD has told him to").

**12** The NIV's "my distress" renders ענײ (*'nyy*) with a few MSS, a reading apparently presupposed also by the ancient versions (cf. BHS), as opposed to the MT *Kethiv* עוני (*'wny,* "my iniquity/guilt"). The *Qere* עיני (*'yny,* "my eyes") also has its adherents, who understand it in the sense of "my tears" (for discussion cf. Snaith, *The Hebrew Text of 2 Samuel xvi–xix*, pp. 16–17; Vanderkam, "Davidic Complicity in the Deaths of Abner and Eshbaal," p. 536 n. 45).

---

## 15. *Ahithophel's advice*

### 16:15–17:29

15Meanwhile, Absalom and all the men of Israel came to Jerusalem, and Ahithophel was with him. 16Then Hushai the Arkite, David's friend, went to Absalom and said to him, "Long live the king! Long live the king!"

17Absalom asked Hushai, "Is this the love you show your friend? Why didn't you go with your friend?"

18Hushai said to Absalom, "No, the one chosen by the LORD, by these people, and by all the men of Israel—his I will be, and I will remain with him. 19Furthermore, whom should I serve? Should I not serve the son? Just as I served your father, so I will serve you."

20Absalom said to Ahithophel, "Give us your advice. What should we do?"

21Ahithophel answered, "Lie with your father's concubines whom he left to take care of the palace. Then all Israel will hear that you have made yourself a stench in your father's nostrils, and the hands of everyone with you will be strengthened." 22So they pitched a tent for Absalom on the roof, and he lay with his father's concubines in the sight of all Israel.

23Now in those days the advice Ahithophel gave was like that of one who inquires of God. That was how both David and Absalom regarded all of Ahithophel's advice.

17:1Ahithophel said to Absalom, "I would choose twelve thousand men and set out tonight in pursuit of David. 2I would attack him while he is weary and weak. I would strike him with terror, and then all the people with him will flee. I would strike down only the king 3and bring all the people back to you. The death of the man you seek will mean the return of all; all the people will be unharmed." 4This plan seemed good to Absalom and to all the elders of Israel.

5But Absalom said, "Summon also Hushai the Arkite, so we can hear what he has to say." 6When Hushai came to him, Absalom said, "Ahithophel has given this advice. Should we do what he says? If not, give us your opinion."

7Hushai replied to Absalom, "The advice Ahithophel has given is not good this time. 8You know your father and his men; they are fighters, and as fierce as a wild bear robbed of her cubs. Besides, your father is an experienced fighter; he will not spend the night with the troops. 9Even now, he is hidden in a cave or some other place. If he should attack your troops first, whoever hears about it will say, 'There has been a slaughter among the troops who follow Absalom.' 10Then even the bravest soldier, whose heart is like the heart of a lion, will melt with fear, for all Israel knows that your father is a fighter and that those with him are brave.

11"So I advise you: Let all Israel, from Dan to Beersheba—as numerous as the sand on the seashore—be gathered to you, with you yourself leading them into battle. 12Then we will attack him wherever he may be found, and we will fall on him as dew settles on the ground. Neither he nor any of his men will be left alive. 13If he withdraws into a city, then all Israel will bring ropes to that city, and we will drag it down to the valley until not even a piece of it can be found."

14 Absalom and all the men of Israel said, "The advice of Hushai the
Arkite is better than that of Ahithophel." For the LORD had determined to
frustrate the good advice of Ahithophel in order to bring disaster on
Absalom.

15 Hushai told Zadok and Abiathar, the priests, "Ahithophel has
advised Absalom and the elders of Israel to do such and such, but I have
advised them to do so and so. 16 Now send a message immediately and
tell David, 'Do not spend the night at the fords in the desert; cross over
without fail, or the king and all the people with him will be swallowed
up.'"

17 Jonathan and Ahimaaz were staying at En Rogel. A servant girl was
to go and inform them, and they were to go and tell King David, for they
could not risk being seen entering the city. 18 But a young man saw them
and told Absalom. So the two of them left quickly and went to the house
of a man in Bahurim. He had a well in his courtyard, and they climbed
down into it. 19 His wife took a covering and spread it out over the
opening of the well and scattered grain over it. No one knew anything
about it.

20 When Absalom's men came to the woman at the house, they asked,
"Where are Ahimaaz and Jonathan?"

The woman answered them, "They crossed over the brook." The men
searched but found no one, so they returned to Jerusalem.

21 After the men had gone, the two climbed out of the well and went to
inform King David. They said to him, "Set out and cross the river at
once; Ahithophel has advised such and such against you." 22 So David
and all the people with him set out and crossed the Jordan. By
daybreak, no one was left who had not crossed the Jordan.

23 When Ahithophel saw that his advice had not been followed, he
saddled his donkey and set out for his house in his hometown. He put
his house in order and then hanged himself. So he died and was buried
in his father's tomb.

24 David went to Mahanaim, and Absalom crossed the Jordan with all
the men of Israel. 25 Absalom had appointed Amasa over the army in
place of Joab. Amasa was the son of a man named Jether, an Israelite
who had married Abigail, the daughter of Nahash and sister of Zeruiah
the mother of Joab. 26 The Israelites and Absalom camped in the land of
Gilead.

27 When David came to Mahanaim, Shobi son of Nahash from Rabbah
of the Ammonites, and Makir son of Ammiel from Lo Debar, and Barzillai
the Gileadite from Rogelim 28 brought bedding and bowls and articles of
pottery. They also brought wheat and barley, flour and roasted grain,
beans and lentils, 29 honey and curds, sheep, and cheese from cows'
milk for David and his people to eat. For they said, "The people have
become hungry and tired and thirsty in the desert."

The central unit of chapters 15–20 (more precisely, 15:1–20:22) deals with the conflicting advice of Ahithophel and Hushai (16:15–17:29; for the overall outline of chs. 15–20 see comment on 15:1–12). It begins by reprising the end of chapter 15, which describes the coming of Absalom and Hushai to Jerusalem (cf. 15:37; 16:15–16), and it ends as the previous section (16:5–14) ended: The king and all the people with him arrive at their destination "exhausted/tired" (17:29; see comment on 16:14). Three key verses, interspersed throughout (16:23; 17:14, 23), provide the clue for analyzing the section as three chiasms arranged within a larger chiastic structure, the clash between Ahithophel's advice and Hushai's advice serving as the focus of the whole:

A. Arriving in Jerusalem, Absalom is befriended (16:15–19).
  $B_1$. Ahithophel advises Absalom (16:20–22).
    $B_2$. Ahithophel is described in glowing terms (16:23).
  $B_3$. Ahithophel advises Absalom (17:1–4).
    $C_1$. Hushai advises Absalom (17:5–13).
      $C_2$. Hushai's advice is declared better than Ahithophel's (17:14).
    $C_3$. Hushai advises Zadok and Abiathar (17:15–16).
  $B_1'$. David crosses the Jordan (17:17–22).
    $B_2'$. Ahithophel commits suicide (17:23).
  $B_3'$. Absalom crosses the Jordan (17:24–26).
A′. Arriving in Mahanaim, David is befriended (17:27–29).

**15–19** Resuming the narrative that ends in 15:37, v.15 describes Absalom's arrival in Jerusalem with "all the men of Israel" (lit., "all the people/troops, the men of Israel"), the main Israelite army, together with Ahithophel, who had formerly been "David's counselor" (see comment on 15:12) but has now defected to Absalom—doubtless because he feels that the future lies with the son rather than with the father.

Enter Hushai (v.16; see 15:32 and comment), who will turn out to be the fly in Ahithophel's ointment, an integral member of David's fifth column in Absalom's fledgling court. He is again described as David's "friend" (*rēʿeh*), his official cabinet title (see Notes on 15:37). A Davidic loyalist, Hushai speaks to Absalom in words that are an exercise in studied ambiguity. If Absalom understands Hushai's "Long live the king!" (v.16; see 1 Sam 10:24 and comment) as a reference to himself, it is virtually certain that in his own mind Hushai is thinking of David.

Although the first part of Absalom's response to Hushai (v.17) may be intended as a question (the Heb. interrogative particle, though common, is not mandatory; cf. Waltke and O'Connor, *Biblical Hebrew Syntax*, p. 316 n. 1), it is also possible to read it as a caustic comment: "So this is the love you show your friend!" (cf. Snaith, *The Hebrew Text of 2 Samuel xvi–xix*, p. 21). Absalom is doubtless belittling Hushai's official title by sarcastically using the ordinary word for "friend, acquaintance," twice (*rēaʿ*; cf. de Vaux, AIs, p. 123; McCarter, *II Samuel* pp. 372, 384). He questions Hushai's "love," his covenant fidelity, to David (see 1 Sam 20:15 and comment). He also wonders aloud why the supposedly faithful Hushai did not "go with" David. After all, two hundred men had "accompanied" Absalom (15:11; same Heb. idiom)—however unknowingly—from Jerusalem to Hebron, had they not?

Hushai counters by ostensibly declaring his loyalty to Absalom. Beginning with the emphatic "No" (v.18; for other examples, cf. 24:24; 1 Sam 2:16; 10:19; 12:12), he affirms that he will remain with the one whom the Lord has "chosen" (the verb is singular, perhaps implying that the roles of the people and of the men of Israel in the choice of a king are being downplayed). By appearing to refer to the pretender Absalom, Hushai is engaging in flattery since nowhere is Absalom stated to be the Lord's choice. On the other hand, the OT fairly teems with references to David as the one whom God has chosen (cf. 6:21; 1 Sam 16:8–13; 1 Kings 8:16; 11:34; 1 Chron 28:4; 2 Chron 6:5–6; Ps 78:70)—and thus Hushai once again probably has David in mind, although of course he wants Absalom to think otherwise.

As Hushai concludes his assurances to Absalom, he becomes less ambiguous (v.19), although even here he avoids mentioning Absalom's name directly. David had earlier asked Hushai to offer the same service to Absalom that he had formerly performed for David (cf. 15:34), and Hushai now fulfills that request. To his own rhetorical question concerning whom he should serve, Hushai says, "Should I not serve the son?" (lit.,

"Should it not be before his son?"), and following his assertion that just as he has served "your father" (David), Hushai says, "So I will serve you" (lit., "so I will be before you"). The peculiar phraseology and careful indirection of Hushai's language enables him to have it both ways. Commenting on the question "Should it not be (before) his son?" Baldwin writes: "Indeed it should, if [Hushai] were loyal to [Absalom's] father. As it is, Hushai will serve Absalom while at the same time being loyal to Absalom's father. Hushai has kept his integrity, Absalom has been blinded by his own egoism, and the reader is permitted to see one example of the outworking of God's providence" (p. 264).

**20–22** The first of three chiasms in the present literary unit contains two pieces of advice given by Ahithophel to Absalom (16:20–22; 17:1–4) bracketing a highly complimentary description of Ahithophel himself (16:23). Having listened to Hushai's pledge of fealty (vv.16–19), Absalom turns his attention to a counselor whom he feels confident he can trust.

The idiom "Give . . . your advice" (v.20) occurs in Judges 20:7 ("give your verdict") in a context of hearing the evidence and then making the wisest and best judgment on the basis of it. Although other advisers may have been present ("give" is plural), Absalom is primarily interested in Ahithophel's observations concerning the current situation.

Ahithophel first suggests that Absalom preempt his father's harem and that he have sexual relations with the ten concubines whom David had left behind in Jerusalem to take care of the palace (v.21; see 15:16 and comment). David had illicitly slept with a woman who was not his wife (cf. 11:4), and now his son is counseled to follow in his father's footsteps. Doing so, Absalom would make himself a "stench" in David's nostrils—a fact not necessarily to be deplored, although not without its inherent dangers (see comments on 10:6; 1 Sam 13:4). In this case, however, Ahithophel clearly believes that the "hands" of Absalom's supporters would be "strengthened" (an idiom that often implies encouragement; see comment on 2:7) by such a bold move on his part.

Having the utmost confidence in Ahithophel's advice, Absalom agrees to it. A tent is pitched on the "roof" of the palace (v.22), doubtless the very roof on which his father had earlier committed an equally sinful act (see 11:2 and comment). The "tent" (*'ōhel*) may have been intended to symbolize the *ḥuppāh* ("pavilion") occupied by the bridegroom and bride on their wedding night (as in Ps 19:4–5; cf. Joel 2:16 ["chamber"]; for similar customs among modern nomadic Arabs, cf. the observations of W. Robertson Smith, *Kinship and Marriage*, pp. 167–69).

Thus with the full knowledge of the people of Israel, Absalom sleeps with his father's concubines—little remembering that to do so may well jeopardize his inheritance rights (cf. Gen 35:22; 49:3–4) and compel him to forfeit them to another (cf. Ronald F. Youngblood, *The Book of Genesis: An Introductory Commentary*, 2d ed. [Grand Rapids: Baker, 1991], p. 277). Nor would the concubines, however loudly they might protest their innocence, remain guiltless. Upon his return to Jerusalem, David would put them under house arrest where they would remain "till the day of their death, living as widows" (20:3).

**23** In theory, of course, Ahithophel's advice concerning David's concubines was entirely appropriate, since a king's harem was expected to be passed on to his successor (cf. 12:8). "Possession of the harem was a title to the throne" (de Vaux, AIs,

p. 116). It is therefore understandable that both David and Absalom should respect the "advice" (*'ēṣāh*) of Ahithophel (see comments on 15:31, 34) and regard it as equal to that of one who "inquires of God"—literally, "consults the word [*dāḇār*] of God." The value of Ahithophel's advice was like that of a priestly oracle divinely sent. "The *'ēṣā* which brings success is that of the sagacious statesman, and failure to heed it brings such consequences as are comparable with those resulting from a failure to obey God. God is represented as controlling history through the mediation of human decisions: that is, to neglect *'ēṣā* is to be exposed to the judgment of God" (McKane, *Prophets and Wise Men*, p. 56).

**17:1–4** Sensing that he has successfully shored up Absalom's claims to kingship over Israel, at least in the eyes of the citizens of Jerusalem (cf. 16:20–22), Ahithophel now suggests to Absalom a bold military expedition that he is convinced would result in David's death (17:1–4). Whether literally or figuratively, Ahithophel puts himself in the position of an army commander whose job it is to "choose" (v.1; cf. Josh 8:3) the right number of men to carry out the appropriate strategic goals. "I would choose . . . and set out . . . in pursuit of" renders a series of cohortative verbs that translate literally as "Let me choose . . . and let me set out . . . and let me pursue" (see NIV mg.). Ahithophel's militarily correct advice is thus both terse and urgent: "There is not a moment to lose, the only course is to hit David hard before he can regroup his forces, and the statement itself has no time for fancy rhetorical maneuvers" (Alter, *The Art of Biblical Narrative*, p. 74). "Twelve thousand" may be Ahithophel's way of asserting the need to muster at least one "thousand/unit" (see comment on 1 Sam 4:2) from each of the Twelve Tribes in order to demonstrate the involvement of all Israel in Absalom's rebellion.

Although the first-person verbal forms in vv.2–3 are more varied than in v.1 (see NIV text and mg. on v.2), the sense of urgency does not diminish. Ahithophel advises an attack on David while he is "weary" (v.2; cf. Deut 25:18) and "weak." The latter term is literally "limp/feeble of hands" (cf. Job 4:3; Isa 35:3)—an expression often implying discouragement (see comment on 4:1)—and appears to be in deliberate contrast to the earlier description of Absalom's followers whose "hands . . . will be strengthened" and who would thus be encouraged (see 16:21 and comment). The large number and mobility of the troops proposed by Ahithophel is calculated not only to "strike" David himself "with terror" (cf. similarly Ezek 30:9) but also to frighten his men into running for their lives (cf. Zech 1:21). Ahithophel's strategy involves a lightninglike surgical strike that would hopefully result in the death of only "the king" (v.2—a title that Ahithophel still uses for David [perhaps out of habit] but that surely does not please Absalom). All the other people would then be brought back to Jerusalem unharmed (v.3).

Absalom seems just as impressed by Ahithophel's advice on this occasion as he was earlier (cf. 16:20–22), an opinion shared by the "elders of Israel" (v.4)—upon whom, after all, the ultimate responsibility for entering into covenant with a new king devolves (see 3:17; 5:3 and comments). Nevertheless Absalom, realizing that whatever plan he adopts must be as nearly foolproof as possible, decides to get a second opinion.

**5–13** Absalom therefore summons Hushai the Arkite (see comment on 15:32), whom he knows to be a trusted confidant of David (see 16:16–17 and comments) but who—like Ahithophel (cf. 15:12)—has offered his services (even though in Hushai's case the offer may be more apparent than real; see 16:18–19 and comments). Before taking any action Absalom wants to "hear" (v.5; cf. Num 9:8 ["find out"]; Ps 85:8 ["listen to"]) "what [Hushai] has to say" (lit., "what is in his mouth"; cf. 1:16; cf. similarly 14:3, 19b). The phrase *gam-hû'* ("also he"), although perhaps implied in the NIV rendering, stresses Absalom's insistence on comparing Hushai's views with those of Ahithophel and should thus be represented in the translation (e.g., by adding "as well" to the end of v.5).

The root *dbr* in its nominal ("word") and verbal ("speak") functions appears four times in v.6 (in chiastic order: verb, noun, noun, verb) in Absalom's statement to Hushai, a literal translation of which reads as follows: "Ahithophel has spoken according to this word [see comment on 14:3]. Shall we do this word? If not, you [emphatic] speak." The effect of such a rendering is to highlight Absalom's apparent understanding of Ahithophel's advice as having the potential of being the equivalent of a divine oracle (see comment on 16:23). At the same time, however, it would seem that Absalom is open to giving Hushai's counsel the same standing.

In his response to Absalom, Hushai first of all denigrates Ahithophel's second piece of advice (vv.1–3) by asserting that it is "not good" (v.7)—a judgment that, although totally at odds with the narrator's (cf. v.14), reflects the Lord's determination to frustrate Ahithophel's counsel (cf. v.14). For all intents and purposes, the phrase "the advice Ahithophel has given" (lit., "has advised," v.7) echoes "the advice Ahithophel gave" (lit., "advised," 16:23) and once again calls attention to the difference between the narrator's positive evaluation (of Ahithophel's first piece of advice, to be sure) in the latter text as compared to Hushai's here. "Devise your strategy" (lit., "Advise advice"), the prophet thunders (Isa 8:10), "but it will be thwarted" (see 15:34 ["frustrating"] and comment)—because "God is with us" (Isa 8:10; cf. 2 Sam 17:14).

What follows (vv.8–13) is Hushai's "brilliant rhetorical contrivance," which counters Ahithophel's "militarily correct advice. . . . But rhetoric is not necessarily evil in the Bible, and the contrastive technique takes a dialectical turn here, for Absalom is, after all, a usurper, and Hushai, bravely loyal to David, is using his ability to deceive through words in order to restore the rightful king to his throne" (Alter, *The Art of Biblical Narrative,* p. 74). The two parts of Hushai's speech (vv.8–10, 11b–13)—separated by "So I advise you" (v.11a)—make use of the repetition of key words and/or ideas that have enabled Bar-Efrat to construct the following skeletal outline (with slight modifications; cf. "Some Observations on the Analysis of Structure," pp. 170–71):

A. "know your father . . . fighters" (v.8a)
  B. "as a wild bear" (v.8b)
    C. "the troops" (v.8c)
      X. "some other place" (*b'ḥd/t hmqwmt,* v.9a)
    C′. "the troops" (v.9b)
  B′. "like . . . a lion" (v.10a)
A′. "knows . . . your father . . . a fighter" (v.10b)
D. "all Israel . . . be gathered" (*yē'āsēp̱,* v.11b)
  E. "as the sand on the seashore" (v.11c)
    X′. "wherever" (*b'ḥt hmqwmt,* v.12a)
  E′. "as dew settles on the ground" (v.12b)
D′. "withdraws [*yē'āsēp̱*) . . . all Israel" (v.13)

The first part (A–A′) reveals the weak points (from Hushai's perspective, of course) in Ahithophel's advice, while the second (D–D′) offers Hushai's alternative plan, which is supposedly better. In the first section of the first part (A–C) Hushai shows why Ahithophel's plan will be unsuccessful, and in the second (C′–A′) he states that in fact it will do more harm than good. The first section of the second part (D–E) describes the elaborate preparations necessary before attacking David, and the second section (E′–D′) outlines the effects of the attack. The transitional clause (X) in the first part observes that "in one of the places" David remains "hidden," while the transitional clause (X′) in the second expresses the confidence that "in one of the places" he will be "found." And so it is that Hushai the Arkite uses rhetorical artistry of the highest order in his attempt to convince Absalom that the counsel of Ahithophel the Gilonite will result in a course of action that cannot but fail while his own advice, if followed, can only succeed.

Hushai makes capital of David's long-standing reputation as a "fighter" (*gibbôr*, vv.8, 10; cf. the early description of him as *gibbôr ḥayil* ["a brave man," 1 Sam 16:18]). Indeed, David and his men are as "fierce" (lit., "bitter of soul," v.8; see 1 Sam 1:10 and comment; cf. Judg 18:25 ["hot-tempered"]), and therefore as dangerous, as a "wild bear robbed of her cubs" (cf. Prov 17:12; Hos 13:8; cf. also 2 Kings 2:24). Due caution must be exercised in trying to outsmart or overpower David, whose fame as an "experienced fighter" (*'îš milḥāmāh*, lit., "man of war") is widely known (see comment on 1 Sam 16:18 ["warrior"]).

Although *yālîn* in v.8 could be understood as a Hiphil, with the resulting translation being something like "he will not let the troops rest overnight" (cf. Hertzberg, p. 347) in the sense that "none of them will be asleep and they will be ready, from an ambush, to cause some initial slaughter among Absalom's men" (Snaith, *The Hebrew Text of 2 Samuel xvi–xix*, p. 29), this would be the only case of Hiphil *lw/yn* in the OT (cf. BDB, p. 533). In addition the traditional Qal parsing of the verb, adopted by the NIV ("he [David] will not spend the night with the troops"), is better contextually in that it forges a more natural link with v.9: "Even now, he is hidden [see comment on 1 Sam 19:2] in a cave or some other place." David is a past master at knowing how—and where—to hide from pursuers (see 1 Sam 23:22–23 and comment). If indeed he is trying to escape from his son Absalom by cowering in a "cave" (cf. also Jer 48:28) that is hard to find, it is ironic that Absalom's final resting place will be a large "pit" in a forest (18:17; same Heb. noun).

Warning Absalom that David on the offensive would have the strategic advantage and would therefore draw first blood, Hushai points out that the exaggerated news of the initial defeat ("a slaughter," v.9; cf. 1 Sam 4:17 ["(heavy) losses"]) would cause uncontrollable panic among Absalom's troops (v.10). Absalom's "bravest soldier" (*ben-ḥayil*, lit., "son of power/might"; see 2:7 and comment) is no match for David's "brave" men (*b$^e$nê-ḥayil*, v.10), who in this regard emulate their leader (see 1 Sam 18:17 and comment). Though their hearts be like that of a lion, Absalom's troops will "melt" (cf. Ps 22:14; Ezek 21:7; Nah 2:10) with fear. David, after all, is a "fighter" (see comment on v.8) who has not flinched in the presence of lions (cf. v.10) or bears (cf. v.8), among the most dangerous of animals (see 1 Sam 17:34–37 and comment; cf. Prov 28:15; Hos 13:8).

After eloquently belittling Ahithophel's counsel, Hushai gives some advice of his own. If followed, his plan is so elaborate that it will consume enough time for Hushai to send instructions to David concerning what to do in the light of Absalom's troop movements. Hushai suggests to Absalom that he needs a much larger force than the mere "twelve thousand" men (see v.1 and comment) proposed by Ahithophel. Absalom must enlist every able-bodied Israelite, "from Dan to Beersheba" (v.11; see comments on 3:10; 1 Sam 3:20)—an enormous army, "as numerous as the sand on the seashore" (see 1 Sam 13:5 and comment). The ultimate flattery: Absalom will personally lead them into battle (v.11).

Apparently swept along by his own glibness, Hushai rhetorically joins in the fray himself: "We will fall" on David (*naḥnû,* from *nûaḥ* [cf. BDB, p. 59; KD, pp. 430–31; S.R. Driver, *Notes on the Books of Samuel,* p. 323; Snaith, *The Hebrew Text of 2 Samuel xvi–xix,* p. 32], not an alternate form of *'anaḥnû,* the independent personal pronoun "we") as "dew" settles on the ground (v.12; cf. similarly Ps 110:3 [NIV mg.]), a comparison that emphasizes total coverage (McCarter, *II Samuel*) and/or irresistibility (Leslie C. Allen, *Word Biblical Commentary: Psalms 101–150* [Waco: Word, 1983], p. 81). Neither David nor any of his men will be able to survive such an onslaught (cf. 1 Sam 14:36).

Adopt whatever tactics he will, David cannot possibly escape—not even if he "withdraws" (v.13, lit., "gathers himself"; same Heb. verb as translated "be gathered" in v.11; cf. Num 11:30 ["returned"]) into the presumed safety of a city. Using a vivid hyperbole, Hushai envisions the entire Israelite army attaching ropes to that city in order to "drag" it down into the valley. The Hebrew verb *sāḥab̲* is used elsewhere only in Jeremiah, where it always suggests the humiliation of being "dragged away" to destruction as if by an animal (cf. Jer 15:3; 22:19; 49:20b = 50:45b). David's supposed haven will be so thoroughly demolished that not a "piece" of it will be found (the Heb. word refers to a small "pebble"; cf. Amos 9:9).

**14** Verses 16:15–17:29 constitute the central section in the chiastic structure of chapters 15–20 (see comment on 15:1–12), and 17:5–16 is the central chiasm in the carefully crafted arrangement of literary units in 16:15–17:29 (see comment there). Since 17:14 is the focal point of vv.5–16, it serves also as the literary center of chapters 15–20.

The three key verses in 16:15–17:29 (16:23; 17:14, 23) are intimately linked to one another. The MT of all three verses makes use of the root *y'ṣ* ("advise, counsel") in its verbal and nominal forms (16:23, three times; 17:14, three times; 17:23, once). But whereas 16:23 and 17:23 refer only to Ahithophel's counsel, 17:14 compares the advice of Ahithophel with the advice of Hushai—and records the judgment of "Absalom and all the men of Israel" that the latter is better than the former. If the fortunes of Ahithophel rose to their zenith in 16:23, they have sunk to their nadir in 17:23.

The critical turning point is v.14. The delays inherent in Hushai's counsel give David and his troops time to escape across the Jordan and then regroup; thus Hushai's rhetoric wins the day. Absalom made his fateful choice, and Hushai becomes the point man in the Lord's determination to "frustrate" (see 15:34 and comment) Ahithophel's counsel. The admittedly "good advice of Ahithophel," described so glowingly in 16:23, and the forthcoming "disaster on Absalom," implied in and hastened by Ahithophel's suicide (17:23), thus flank the erroneous judgment of Absalom and his men as reported in v.14.

> It is intriguing to see Ahithophel's first counsel to Absalom accepted and executed, making the break between father and son final and public (2 Sam. xvi 20–22), but his second and more crucial advice (2 Sam. xvii 1–4) at once countered by Hushai's

> verbose arguments (xvii 5–13). If Absalom and his companions had followed Ahithophel's second advice as they had the first, the rebel would have defeated his father and won the kingdom, but, as the narrator affirms, "the LORD had ordained to defeat the good counsel of Ahithophel" (2 Sam. xvii 14 b). (Roth, "A Study of the Classical Hebrew Verb *ṣkl*," p. 71)

And the litany of the divinely sent "disaster" against Israel's royal house has only just begun (cf. 1 Kings 21:21, 29; 2 Kings 21:12; 22:16–17; Jer 4:6; 6:19).

**15–16** Having given Absalom advice that, if implemented, would turn out well for David (vv.5–13), Hushai now gives similar advice to the priests Zadok and Abiathar (vv.15–16; see 15:24 and comment), who are in a position to carry out Hushai's instructions through their sons Ahimaaz and Jonathan (see 15:35–36 and comment). He quickly rehearses the substance of Ahithophel's advice to "Absalom and the elders of Israel" (v.15; see vv.1–4 and comments) and then contrasts it with his own obviously superior counsel (cf. vv.5–13; the "I" in v.15 is emphatic).

Since there is no time to lose, Hushai's advice (vv.15–16) and its execution (vv.17–22) are suffused with an atmosphere of urgency ("immediately" [v.16], "quickly" [v.18], and "at once" [v.21] all render *meherah*). His message for David is that it would be too dangerous to spend even one more "night" (v.16; cf. v.1) at the "fords in the desert" (see 15:28 and comment). The king's only option is to "cross" the Jordan "without fail" (augmenting the finite verb, the infinitive absolute underscores the need for swift and decisive action). If he refuses to do so, he and his entire party will be "swallowed up" (cf. Job 37:20; Isa 9:16 ["led astray"]; for a discussion of the metaphor, cf. Conroy, p. 126 n. 51).

**17–22** The final internal chiasm (vv.17–26) in the present literary unit (see comment on 16:15–17:29) brackets the suicide of Ahithophel (v.23) with two accounts of royal figures crossing the Jordan (David the king, vv.17–22; Absalom the crown prince, vv.24–26). Gunn observes that the narrative in vv.17–22 shares a number of features with the story of the spies at Jericho in Joshua 2:

> There are two spies in or at a city. The king of the city learns of their presence and sends men to find them. They are hidden in a house (under something) by a woman. The king's men come to the house and demand the spies be given up. But the woman gives false directions, the pursuers go on their way, fail to find the spies, and return to the city. The spies escape. ("Traditional Composition in the 'Succession Narrative,'" p. 224)

But simply comparing shared features, however striking, between the two accounts in no way "argues strongly for their being derived from a common stereotype" (ibid., p. 225). The most one can surmise in such cases is that the narrator of the books of Samuel chose to stress elements in his episode that recalled similar elements in the Jericho story, perhaps to remind his readers that God provides similarly in corresponding situations. In any event, the differences between the two accounts far outweigh their common characteristics.

The messengers designated to bring word to David (cf. v.16) are Jonathan and Ahimaaz (v.17), sons of Abiathar and Zadok respectively (see 15:27–28, 36 and comments). In order not to be accused of attempting to subvert Absalom's plans originating in Jerusalem while at the same time wanting to be near enough to keep in touch with developments there, Jonathan and Ahimaaz are staying at En Rogel (v.17), a spring (modern Bir Ayyub ["The Well of Job"]) in the Kidron Valley on the border between Benjamin and Judah (cf. Josh 15:1, 7; 18:11, 16) less than a mile south-southeast of the capital city. Locale of the abortive coronation of David's son Adonijah (cf. 1 Kings 1:9, 25), its name (lit., "Washerman's Spring") derives from a Hebrew root that elsewhere means "spy." It thus forms a wordplay on the mutual spying and intrigue that take place throughout these chapters between Absalom's men and David's men (see comments on "secret messengers" in 15:10 and on "Rogelim" in 17:27).

David's need for up-to-date news is reflected in the frequent use of the verb *ngd* ("tell," vv.16–17; "inform," vv.17, 21). A servant girl from Jerusalem relays the necessary information to Jonathan and Ahimaaz, who cannot risk "being seen" entering the city (v.17)—but in spite of their caution a young man who "saw" them (v.18) reports their whereabouts to Absalom (ironically the verb *r'h* ["see"] plays an important role in 15:27–28 as well; see comments there). Knowing that they must act "quickly" (v.18; see comment on "immediately" in v.16), the two men leave En Rogel and go to Bahurim (about two miles to the northeast; see comment on 3:16; cf. also 16:5). There they climb down into a well in a residential courtyard (cf. Neh 8:16), and the wife of the house's owner keeps their presence secret by spreading a covering over (cf. similarly 2 Kings 8:15; Ps 105:39) the mouth of the well (v.19). She then scatters "grain" over the covering, ostensibly to dry it out (for discussion cf. Snaith, *The Hebrew Text of 2 Samuel xvi–xix*, p. 37; the Hebrew word here rendered "grain" appears elsewhere only in Prov 27:22). The ruse works, and the men's hiding place is kept secret.

When Absalom's men arrive in Bahurim and ask the woman where Ahimaaz and Jonathan are, she says that they have already left. Apparently not believing her, they search the area, returning to Jerusalem only after failing to find the two fugitives (v.20). As soon as Absalom's men are gone, the two climb out of the well and go to deliver Hushai's instructions (cf. vv.15–16) to David (v.21), who is presumably still at the unspecified "destination" mentioned in 16:14 (see comment there). They advise him to cross the Jordan (cf. v.22) "river" (*mayim*, lit., "water") and to do so "at once" (see comment on "immediately" in v.16) in the light of Ahithophel's advice (v.21) to Absalom to strike quickly and decisively (see comments on vv.1–4). Sensing that there is no time to lose, David and his entire party cross over to the eastern side of the Jordan River under cover of darkness (v.22; see comment on 1 Sam 14:36).

**23** If in 16:23 Ahithophel is described in glowing terms as being at the height of his power and influence because of the extraordinary brilliance and dependability of his "advice," the parallel passage in 17:23 (see comment on 16:15–17:29) depicts him as realizing that his "advice"—though not having lost any of its luster or suitability (see vv.1–4 and comments)—has not been followed this time. Knowing that the implementation of Hushai's advice will not result in the death of David, who will thus return to Jerusalem seeking revenge on his enemies, Ahithophel therefore decides that the only course of action open to him is suicide. After he has returned to Giloh, his hometown (see Notes on 15:12), and has "put his house in order" (cf. 2 Kings 20:1 = Isa 38:1; *way$^e$ṣaw 'el-bêṯô* is a phrase that implies the giving of one's last will and testament in anticipation of imminent death; cf. late and modern Hebrew *ṣawwā'āh,* "[verbal] will"), he strangles himself (*ḥnq;* cf. Job 7:15; Nah 2:12). Although the precise means that Ahithophel used to commit suicide by strangling is not specified (cf. Symon Patrick, who cites the bizarre interpretation of those who assert that "being full of Anguish, Anger and Vexation . . . these Passions cast him into so violent a Distemper, that he was strangled by it," p. 517), it was probably by hanging from a rope. Accounts of suicide are infrequent in the OT (see 1 Sam 31:4–5 and comments; cf. Judg 9:54; 1 Kings 16:18; cf. also 2 Macc 10:13; 14:41).

After his death Ahithophel is buried in his "father's tomb" (v.23), the normal place of interment in those days (see 2:32 and comment; cf. Judg 8:32; 16:31). As KD observes (p. 433), David's prayer (see 15:31 and comment) is now answered. And just as Ahithophel had betrayed an anointed king of Israel (see 15:12 and comment) and finished his days as a suicide, so also would the betrayer of another Anointed King come to the same inglorious end (cf. Matt 27:4–5; Acts 1:18; cf. *inter alia* Wharton, "A Plausible Tale," p. 353).

**24–26** The account of the crossing of the Jordan by Absalom parallels the similar narrative concerning David (vv.17–22; see comment on 16:15–17:29), who stays one step ahead of his pursuers by continuing on to Mahanaim (vv.24, 27), the earlier headquarters of his rival Ish-Bosheth about seven miles east of the river in the tribal territory of Gad (see 2:8 and comment). Since Joab had apparently accompanied David on his flight from Jerusalem (see comment on 16:10), Absalom had appointed another leader "over the army" (v.25; see 8:16 and comment) to replace him. The new commander is Amasa, whose name in emphatic position as the first word in the MT of v.25 attests to his notoriety if not his importance (cf. 19:11–13). His father was Ithra/Jether (see NIV mg.; cf. 1 Kings 2:5, 32), perhaps Nabal's real name (see comment on 1 Sam 25:3), and his mother was Nahash's daughter Abigal/Abigail (see NIV mg.; cf. 1 Chron 2:17), David's half sister (and probably his wife; see comment on 1 Sam 25:3) as well as the sister of Zeruiah—which makes Amasa a relative not only of David but also of Joab. Although the exact location of Absalom's camp is not specified, the "land of Gilead' (v.26) presumably encompassed Gad, and therefore Mahanaim, at this time—an ominous prospect for David and his men.

**27–29** As Absalom had been befriended upon his arrival in Jerusalem (16:15–19), so in the parallel passage David is befriended upon his arrival in Mahanaim (vv.27–29; see comment on 16:15–17:29). Three staunch allies come to his aid (v.27): the Ammonite Shobi (mentioned only here) son of Nahash (probably the Nahash of v.25, for which see comments on 1 Sam 11:1; 25:3) from Rabbah (see comment on 10:3), Mephibosheth's patron Makir from Lo Debar (see 9:4–5 and comment), and the Gileadite Barzillai ("Iron Man") from Rogelim (mentioned elsewhere only in 19:31, its location [though uncertain] is perhaps modern Bersinya or nearby Dhaharat Soqa, about ten miles east-southeast of Lo Debar and forty miles northwest of Rabbah). The Hebrew form of the word "Rogelim," which means "Washermen," is the plural of that of "Rogel" in the place-name En Rogel (v.17; see comment there).

In addition to various housekeeping items (v.28a), David's friends also bring essential foodstuffs to supply his needs and those of the people with him (vv.28b–29a; for similar lists see 16:1; 1 Sam 17:17–18; 25:18 and comments), flour (see 1 Sam 1:24 and comment; cf. 28:24) and roasted grain (see 1 Sam 17:17 and comment; cf. 25:18), beans and lentils (cf. Ezek 4:9; cf. also Gen 25:34), "honey and curds" (often food of last resort, eaten in times of political turmoil; cf. Isa 7:15, 22; cf. Ronald F. Youngblood, *Themes From Isaiah* [Ventura: Regal, 1984], p. 48), sheep, and "cheese from cows' milk" (*šᵉp̱ôṯ bāqār* [the first word is a *hapax legomenon*]). Knowing full well that the rigors of the desert flight have caused David and his party to become "tired" (see 16:14 ["exhausted"] and comment) and that they are "hungry and thirsty" (cf. Ps 107:4–5; cf. Ps 3, which may reflect this period in David's life), Shobi, Makir, and Barzillai want to give them the rest and provisions they need.

Refreshed, David and his troops will engage Absalom and his army. The battle will be joined in Transjordan, and the outcome there will determine which of the two men will rule over all Israel (cf. Curtis, "East Is East . . . ," p. 358).

## Notes

**18** The NIV reads "his" (לוֹ [*lô*]) with the *Qere* and the ancient versions. The *Kethiv*, לֹא (*lō'*, "no, not"), probably arose by contamination from "No" earlier in the verse.

**19** Although שֵׁנִית (*šēnîṯ*) means literally "(a) second (time)," the NIV's "furthermore" is clearly preferable here. For the same phenomenon with respect to the cognate Akkadian adverb *šanītam*, cf. discussion in Youngblood, *Amarna Correspondence*, pp. 47–48.

**23** "One who inquires" renders יִשְׁאַל (*yiš'al*, "he inquires"), with or without the *Qere* אִישׁ (*'îš*, "man," "one") that follows the verb. As S.R. Driver observes, the *Qere* "is not needed" (*Notes on the Books of Samuel*, p. 320).

**17:3** "The death of the man you seek will mean the return of all" renders a Hebrew clause that translates literally as "Like the return of all (is) the man whom you are seeking." The NIV thus includes "the death of" *ad sensum* in the light of v.2 (cf. similarly KD, p. 429). Emendations on the basis of the LXX are therefore as unnecessary, as are claims that the MT clause in question is "defective" (McCarter, *II Samuel* p. 381) or "unintelligible" (Snaith, *The Hebrew Text of 2 Samuel xvi–xix*, p. 26).

**9** As the lack of discussion in the commentaries attests, כִּנְפֹל בָּהֶם בַּתְּחִלָּה (*kinᵉp̄ōl bāhem battᵉḥillāh*, lit., "according to the fall of against/among them at the first") can be rendered with equal plausibility as "If he should attack your troops first" (NIV text; cf. Judg 1:1; 20:18; cf. Hertzberg, KD) and as "When some of the men fall at the first attack" (NIV mg.; cf. Anderson, Driver, McCarter).

**12** For the idiom נוֹתַר מִן/בְּ־ (*nôṯar min/bᵉ-*, "survive/be left among"), see the Notes on 13:30.

**16** Comparing the cognate Arabic verb *balaġa*, A. Guillaume makes a persuasive case for the meaning "suffer mishap, be afflicted, be distressed" for בלע (*bl'*, "be swallowed up") here and in a number of other OT texts ("A Note on the √ בלע," JTS 13 [1962]: 320–22; cf. also McCarter, *II Samuel* p. 388).

**19** "The opening of the well," פני הבאר (*pny hb'r*, lit., "the face/surface of the well"), is usually expressed by פי הבאר (*py hb'r*, lit., "the mouth of the well"; cf. Gen 29:2, 3, 8, 10), a reading that is found in some MT MSS and that is probably more original here also (but cf. Hertzberg, p. 348 n. b).

**20** "They crossed over the brook" renders עָבְרוּ מִיכַל הַמָּיִם (*'āḇrû mîḵal hammāyim*, lit., "They crossed over the brook of water," possibly a reference to the Jordan River; see comment on v.21), in which *mîḵal* ("brook"?) is a *hapax legomenon* of uncertain meaning (cf. the NIV mg.: "They passed by the sheep pen toward the water"). Perhaps the narrator chose the rare word *mîḵal* to recall the stratagem of David's wife Michal on a previous occasion (cf. 1 Sam 19:11–17).

**25** Despite the support of some LXX MSS, the MT's "Israelite" can hardly be the correct reading here and may have been influenced by the appearance of "Israel" in vv.24, 26. For the likelihood that "Jezreelite" (cf. some LXX MSS) was in the autograph because it best explains the readings "Israelite" and "Ishmaelite" (cf. 1 Chron 2:17 and some LXX MSS; see NIV mg.), see the discussion of Levenson and Halpern, "The Political Import of David's Marriages," pp. 511–12. In the light of 19:11–13 (see comment on 19:13), the Jezreel in question would be the southern town of unknown location in the hill country of Judah (see comment on 1 Sam 25:43).

**28** The Hebrew word translated "and roasted grain" appears twice in the MT of v.28. The second occurrence is probably due to dittography and is therefore omitted in most LXX MSS and in Syriac (see NIV mg.; cf. however KD, pp. 434–35).

---

## 16. *Absalom's death*

### 18:1–18

1 David mustered the men who were with him and appointed over
them commanders of thousands and commanders of hundreds. 2 David
sent the troops out—a third under the command of Joab, a third under
Joab's brother Abishai son of Zeruiah, and a third under Ittai the Gittite.
The king told the troops, "I myself will surely march out with you."
3 But the men said, "You must not go out; if we are forced to flee, they
won't care about us. Even if half of us die, they won't care; but you are
worth ten thousand of us. It would be better now for you to give us
support from the city."
4 The king answered, "I will do whatever seems best to you."
So the king stood beside the gate while all the men marched out in
units of hundreds and of thousands. 5 The king commanded Joab,
Abishai and Ittai, "Be gentle with the young man Absalom for my sake."
And all the troops heard the king giving orders concerning Absalom to
each of the commanders.
6 The army marched into the field to fight Israel, and the battle took
place in the forest of Ephraim. 7 There the army of Israel was defeated by
David's men, and the casualties that day were great—twenty thousand
men. 8 The battle spread out over the whole countryside, and the forest
claimed more lives that day than the sword.
9 Now Absalom happened to meet David's men. He was riding his
mule, and as the mule went under the thick branches of a large oak,
Absalom's head got caught in the tree. He was left hanging in midair,
while the mule he was riding kept on going.
10 When one of the men saw this, he told Joab, "I just saw Absalom
hanging in an oak tree."
11 Joab said to the man who had told him this, "What! You saw him?
Why didn't you strike him to the ground right there? Then I would have
had to give you ten shekels of silver and a warrior's belt."
12 But the man replied, "Even if a thousand shekels were weighed out
into my hands, I would not lift my hand against the king's son. In our
hearing the king commanded you and Abishai and Ittai, 'Protect the
young man Absalom for my sake.' 13 And if I had put my life in
jeopardy— and nothing is hidden from the king—you would have kept
your distance from me."
14 Joab said, "I'm not going to wait like this for you." So he took three
javelins in his hand and plunged them into Absalom's heart while
Absalom was still alive in the oak tree. 15 And ten of Joab's armor-
bearers surrounded Absalom, struck him and killed him.
16 Then Joab sounded the trumpet, and the troops stopped pursuing
Israel, for Joab halted them. 17 They took Absalom, threw him into a big
pit in the forest and piled up a large heap of rocks over him. Meanwhile,
all the Israelites fled to their homes.
18 During his lifetime Absalom had taken a pillar and erected it in the
King's Valley as a monument to himself, for he thought, "I have no son
to carry on the memory of my name." He named the pillar after himself,
and it is called Absalom's Monument to this day.

In the overall structure of 15:1–20:22, the story of Absalom's death (18:1–18) provides a counterpoise to that of Shimei's curse (16:5–14; see comment on 15:1–12). Just as in the earlier narrative an adversary of David (Shimei) curses him (vv.16:5, 7–8, 13), so also here an adversary of David (Absalom) opposes him in battle (vv.6–8); just as in the earlier account David demands that Shimei be spared (16:11), so also here David demands that Absalom be spared (vv.5, 12); and just as in the earlier episode a son of Zeruiah (Abishai) is ready to kill Shimei (16:9), so also here a son of Zeruiah (Joab, v.2) is ready to kill Absalom—and indeed wounds him, perhaps mortally (vv.14–15).

The literary unit is best divided into three sections of unequal length (cf. similarly Conroy, pp. 55–66): (1) David's mustering of his troops (vv.1–5); (2) the battle between David's men and Absalom's men (vv.6–8); (3) Absalom's death (vv.9–18).

**1–5** "The inclusions between vv. 1 ['commanders of thousands and commanders of hundreds'] and 4 ['units of hundreds and of thousands'] and between vv. 2 and 5 (the names of the generals) . . . interlock to give a firm unity to the passage" (Conroy, p. 55). The numbers in vv.1 and 4 are arranged chiastically as well. In addition *'am* ("men, troops") occurs at least once in each of the five verses.

Whether "thousands" and "hundreds" (vv.1, 4; cf. also v.3) are to be understood literally or figuratively (in the sense of "military units"; see comments on 1 Sam 4:2; 18:13; see also 1 Sam 17:18 and NIV footnote; cf. 1 Sam 8:12; 22:7), it is clear that David has formidable military strength at his disposal. Having "mustered" or "counted" his troops (v.1; see 1 Sam 11:8 and comment) and having separated them into three divisions (v.2, a common strategy in ancient times; see comment on 1 Sam 11:11; cf. 1 Sam 13:17–18), he sends them out under the "command" (lit., "hand"; cf. similarly Num 31:49) of Joab (the overall commander of David's army; see comments on 8:16; 1 Sam 26:6), his brother Abishai (see comment on 1 Sam 26:6), and Ittai respectively. Though a Philistine, Ittai the Gittite—who is leader of one of the most important of David's mercenary detachments (see 15:19 and comment)—is considered loyal enough to also share command of the Israelite regulars with Joab and Abishai. While David is mentioned by name in each of the first two verses, from v.2b to the end of the section (v.5) the narrator refers to him no less than five times as "the king," not only stressing the fact that he is the legitimate ruler of Israel, but also leaving no doubt concerning who is really in charge.

David announces to the assembled troops that he ("I myself," emphatic) intends to march out with them as well (v.2). Conroy observes in v.3 a reversal of 17:11: "Hushai who was not speaking for Absalom's good had urged him to lead his forces personally into battle, but David's men who are genuinely concerned for his welfare urge him to stay behind" (p. 57). The men point out that if they are forced to flee, or even if half of them are killed in battle, Absalom's soldiers "won't care" (v.3; see comment on "pay no attention" in 1 Sam 25:25) "about us" (the phrase, used twice in the MT of v.3, is omitted the second time by NIV in the interests of English style). But "you" (emphatic, referring to David), on the other hand, are "ten thousand" times as important as the troops. Since "ten thousand" men was "the smallest number appropriate to an army" (Segal, "Numerals," p. 6), the statement of David's men is tantamount to saying that he is equal to all of them put together. They are convinced that he will be of more help to them—in terms not only of morale but also of giving them a cause to fight for—if he remains behind in "the city" (i.e., Mahanaim, 17:24, 27).

Acquiescing to their wishes, David stands "beside the gate" (v.4) of the city, a prominent and visible location (cf. 15:2; Prov 8:3) from which to review the troops as they march off to battle. Their "units of hundreds and of thousands" (numbers that should perhaps be understood figuratively) might have brought back to David memories of his days as a mercenary in a Philistine army (see 1 Sam 29:2 and comment). His final order to his three commanders (v.5)—an order that all the troops hear as well—is that they be "gentle" (cf. Job 15:11; Isa 8:6), i.e., that they not deal too hastily (cf. Gen 33:14 ["slowly"]), with Absalom. David's reference to his son as "the young man" (cf. also vv.12, 29, 32) indicates, together with his words "for my sake," something of his paternal affection in spite of Absalom's destructive ambition, arrogance, and treachery.

**6–8** The brief account of the battle between the armies of David and Absalom is a tightly knit section, framed by an *inclusio* formed by the occurrence of "battle" and "forest" in vv.6, 8. While the repetition of "that day" (vv.7, 8) and of *'am* ("people," vv.6, 7 ["army"]; v.8 ["lives"]) serves to unify the section as well, the most striking feature is the use of *watt*ᵉ*hî* ("and it was") in all three verses ("took place," v.6; "were," v.7; part of the periphrastic expression "spread out," v.8). The resemblance in construction between vv.6b–7a ("and the battle took place in the forest of Ephraim. There the army of Israel was defeated by David's men") and 2:17 ("The battle that day was very fierce, and Abner and the men of Israel were defeated by David's men"), the middle verse in chapter 2 (see comment on 2:17), is also noteworthy (cf. Conroy, p. 59 n. 50).

The locale of the initial confrontation is "the field" (v.6), which provides ample room for large-scale troop movements (see comments on "the open [country]" in 10:8; 11:23). In spite of the fact that the "forested hill country" of Ephraim and Manasseh (cf. Josh 17:15, 17–18) was west of the Jordan River, the location of the armies of David and Absalom in Transjordan demands an eastern site for the specific "forest of Ephraim" mentioned here (v.6; cf. George Adam Smith, *The Historical Geography of the Holy Land*, 22d ed. [London: Hodder and Stoughton, n.d.], who observes that Ephraimites had settled "in Gilead in such large numbers that the western Ephraimites call the Gileadites fugitives from Ephraim [Judges xii. 4]" [p. 335 n. 2]; for full discussion cf. LaMoine DeVries, "The Forest of Ephraim," *Biblical Illustrator* 10, 1 [1983]: 82–85). A "pit in the forest" would prove to be the ignominious burial place of Absalom following his summary execution (v.17).

If in v.6 "army" (*'am;* lit., "people"; see comment on v.1) refers to David's troops, in v.7 it signifies Absalom's men. The "army of Israel" consists of "the levies from the northern tribes" (Siegfried Herrmann, "King David's State," in *In the Shelter of Elyon: Essays on Ancient Palestinian Life and Literature in Honor of G.W. Ahlström*, JSOT suppl. series 31; edd. W. Boyd Barrick and John R. Spencer [Sheffield: JSOT, 1984], p. 269) and is equivalent to the "army of the LORD" in 1:12 (see Notes in loc.). The verb "defeated" (see comments on 10:15 ["routed"]; 1 Sam 4:2; cf. 1 Sam 7:10 ["routed"]) and the noun "casualties" (see comment on 17:9 ["slaughter"]; cf. 1 Sam 4:17 ["losses"]) translate the same Hebrew root (*ngp*), which is used more often of plague or disease than in battle contexts (cf. Conroy, p. 59 n. 53) and thus highlights not only the total devastation that has befallen Absalom's troops but also the key role played by the Lord in their overthrow. The "twenty thousand" men killed by David's troops represents a "large army" (Segal, "Numerals," p. 6; see comment on "ten thousand" in v.3).

That the battle is spread out "over the whole countryside" (v.8) echoes 1 Samuel 30:16, where the narrator states that the Amalekites were scattered "over the countryside" celebrating the great amount of plunder they had seized in a raid (identical Heb. expression in both passages). The Hebrew sentence rendered "the forest claimed more lives . . . than the sword" may be literally translated as "the forest was greater to devour among the people than that which the sword devoured" (for the image of the devouring sword, see comments on 2:26; 11:25). Natural phenomena are often more deadly than human enemies (cf. Jos 10:11; cf. Conroy, p. 59 n. 54). Of the many suggestions concerning what it means that the forest would "devour" more than the sword, McCarter's seems best: The dense "forest of Ephraim" (v.6), characterized by uneven and dangerous terrain, was a battleground "where the numerically superior force of [Absalom's] conscript army would be at a disadvantage against David's more skilled private army, with its considerable experience of guerrilla warfare" (*II Samuel,* p. 405; see also comment on v.17).

**9–18** *Wayyiqqārē'* ("happened"), which begins v.9, is echoed as a homonym in v.18, where it means "is called." The two occurrences of the word thus form an *inclusio* that brackets the literary unit.

Verses 9–18 provide a macabre example of how a forest can "devour." Riding his "mule," a suitably regal animal (v.9, see comment on 13:29), Absalom gets his "head" caught in a tangle of "thick branches" (rendering a word found only here, although a word derived from the same Heb. root is translated "mesh" in parallelism with "net" in Job 18:8; for further examples cf. Conroy, p. 61 n. 59) growing out from a large oak tree as the mule passes under them and leaves its owner behind. Conroy's comment is appropriate: "The mule was a royal mount; losing his mule Absalom has lost his kingdom" (p. 60).

Although it is possible to understand Absalom's predicament as having gotten his neck caught in a fork formed by two of the branches, Conroy observes that "the reader who recalls 14,26 will almost certainly visualize Absalom's hair in connection with the entanglement . . . , and will easily draw a contrast between promise and pride on the one hand and humiliation and doom on the other" (p. 44 n. 4). Indeed, the word "head" is used as synecdoche for "hair" in 14:26 ("hair of his head" is literally "his head"; see also comment there). "In midair" is the NIV rendering of a colorful phrase that translates literally as "between heaven and earth" (cf. 1 Chron 21:16; Ezek 8:3; Zech 5:9).

Among David's "men" (v.9; lit., "servants/officers," as also in v.7) is "one of the men" (v.10, *'îš 'eḥāḏ*—i.e., "a certain man" [see 1 Sam 1:1 and comment; cf. Snaith, *The Hebrew Text of 2 Samuel xvi–xix,* p. 45])—who is the first to see Absalom hanging in the tree. In reporting to Joab what he has seen (v.10), the man is characterized as a *maggîḏ* (v.11; NIV, "who had told"), a messenger who ordinarily brings bad news (see comments on 1:5; 15:13). To Joab, however, the news is bad only in the sense that Absalom is still alive.

Whichever of the two main approaches one takes to translating the *hinnēh* in Joab's response, its call for violence and vengeance is totally in character. NIV's "What! You saw him?" or the like is preferred by Conroy as being the "stronger sense" and therefore preferable (p. 61 n. 61). Snaith, on the other hand, would read "If you saw him, . . ." (*The Hebrew Text of 2 Samuel xvi–xix,* p. 46), a construction that has precedent in the books of Samuel (cf. "If we go, . . ." [1 Sam 9:7]). In any event, Joab cannot understand why the man did not kill Absalom on the spot. Had he done so,

Joab says, it would have been incumbent on Joab ("I would have had" [v.11] is emphatic) to give the man ten shekels of silver (about four ounces [see NIV mg.], a not inconsiderable sum; cf. Judg 17:10, where it represents the annual stipend offered to a Levite in addition to his food and clothing) as well as a warrior's belt (cf. 1 Kings 2:5).

Not nearly so insensitive and unscrupulous as Joab, the man affirms that even a hundred times as much silver could not induce him to "lift" his "hand against" Absalom (v.12; see comments on "raise a hand" in 1 Sam 22:17 and on "lay a hand on" in 1 Sam 26:9), who is after all the "king's son." He had been among the troops who had heard David order his three commanders to "be gentle with the young man Absalom" (v.5, see comment there), and he now reminds Joab of that fact (v.12). He knows that if he had killed Absalom, Joab would not have defended him (v.13; for "kept your distance," cf. Exod 2:4; Obad 11 ["stood aloof"]), since ultimately "nothing is hidden from" David (see comment on 14:18; cf. Pss 69:5; 139:15; Hos 5:3), who, like an angel of God—indeed, like God himself—"knows everything that happens in the land" (14:20; see comment there). The king would therefore surely execute the murderer of his son.

Petulant and impatient, Joab declared his unwillingness to wait for his man to kill Absalom and decided to take matters into his own hands (v.14). Whether the weapons he used were "javelins" cannot be determined with certainty (the LXX reads *belē* ["darts"]). In any case, Joab "plunged" (cf. Judg 3:21; 4:21 ["drove"]) three sharp-pointed instruments of some kind into Absalom. They pierced his "heart" (i.e., "chest"; cf. Nah 2:7 ["breasts"]; cf. also Ps 37:15) while he was still alive in "the heart of" (NIV omits the Heb. expression in the interests of English style) the oak tree. Mortally wounded, Absalom was then "surrounded" (v.15; cf. Judg 16:2; 2 Kings 3:25; 6:15; Eccl 9:14) by ten of Joab's "young men" (Heb.), who finished the grisly task of striking and killing (see comment on 14:6) the "young man" Absalom (vv.5, 12). In so doing they performed one of the functions of "armor-bearers" (cf. 23:37), who were expected to be ready to fight and kill when the occasion arose (cf. Judg 9:54; 1 Sam 14:13–14; 31:4; see comment on 1 Sam 14:1). If "ten" shekels were Joab's spurned offer to pay for Absalom's death (v.11), "ten" armor-bearers (v.15) are prepared to assassinate the king's son for nothing. The death of Absalom brings to three the number of sons that David has lost as a result of his sins against Bathsheba and her husband Uriah the Hittite (see 12:6 and comment).

Israel's erstwhile leader now dead, Joab "sounded" the trumpet (v.16; the same Heb. verb is rendered "plunged" in v.14 and is a wordplay on it, as also in Judg 3:21, 27; cf. Conroy, pp. 63–64 n. 79) to recall his troops (see 2:28 and comment). Echoing Hushai's suggestion that perhaps David was hiding in a "cave" (see 17:9 and comment), the narrator states that after Absalom's death his corpse is thrown into a large "pit" (v.17; the Heb. noun is the same) in the "forest" (of Ephraim; see v.6 and comment). An enormous (*gāḏôl me'ōḏ* , "very large") heap of rocks is then piled up over him (a common practice to mark the graves of infamous people; cf. Josh 7:26; 8:29). The survivors among Absalom's troops have meanwhile fled to their "homes" (lit., "tents"; cf. 19:8; 20:1, 22; 1 Sam 4:10; 13:2).

The account of Absalom's demise concludes with a brief flashback summary of his self-serving attempt to perpetuate his name (v.18). From a literary standpoint it is linked closely to what precedes it, not only in the echo of the homonym *wayyiqqārē'* ("is called," from v.9; see comment there), but also in the use of "erected," which renders the Hiphil of *nṣb,* as does "piled up" in v.17. There are thus two monuments commemorating Absalom (the "heap of rocks" in v.17, the "pillar" in v.18), each in its own way as pitiable as the other.

If Saul and his son Jonathan were inseparable "in life" (1:23), Absalom's tragedy is compounded by the fact that "during his lifetime" (v.18; same Heb. expression) he had no son who was willing or able to memorialize him. Although the setting up of memorial pillars was not uncommon in ancient times (cf. Gen 28:18, 22, 31:13; 35:14), the only other example of a funereal pillar in the OT is the one that "marks Rachel's tomb" (Gen 35:20). The precise function of the pillar erected by Absalom has been long debated, since *hzkyr šmy*, here translated "carry on the memory of my name" (for the same expression and/or concept, cf. Gen 21:12; 48:16; Num 27:4; Deut 25:6–7; Ruth 4:5, 10; Ps 45:17; see also comments on 14:7; 1 Sam 24:21), might also be rendered "invoke my name" on the basis of cognate phrases in Akkadian and Aramaic (for discussion cf. Lewis, *Cults of the Dead*, pp. 96, 119, 173).

An additional factor is the comparison often made between v.18 and the role of the devoted son described in Ugaritic text *2 Aqht* (*CTA* 17) 1:27, 45: *nṣb skn ilibh bqdš* ("who erects the stele/monument of his *ilib* in the sanctuary"). If the comparison is justified and *ilib* means "ancestral spirit(s)" (cf. G.R. Driver, *Canaanite Myths and Legends*, Old Testament Studies 3 [Edinburgh: T. and T. Clark, 1956], p. 49), then ancestor worship may be in view (for discussion cf. Theodor H. Gaster, *Thespis: Ritual, Myth, and Drama in the Ancient Near East*, rev. ed. [New York: Harper, 1966], pp. 333–35). If, however, *ilib* means "ancestral god(s)" (cf. de Moor, *Anthology of Religious Texts*, p. 228), then idolatry would be implied (cf. Anson F. Rainey, "Institutions: Family, Civil, and Military," in *Ras Shamra Parallels: The Texts From Ugarit and the Hebrew Bible*, Analecta Orientalia 50, ed. Loren R. Fisher [Rome: Pontifical Biblical Institute, 1975], 2:78–79).

While there is nothing inherently inconceivable about the possibility of Absalom's having imbibed one or more of the customs of his pagan neighbors/relatives (his mother, after all, was the daughter of an Aramean king; see 3:3 and comment), it is far from certain that the Ugaritic text in question is in fact an apt parallel of v.18 (for discussion cf. Conroy, p. 65 n. 88). Indeed, apart from the example of filial piety (or, perhaps, the lack of same; see comment below), the only clearly shared element is the verb *nṣb* ("to erect"). Since Absalom sets up the monument "to himself" (thus NIV; *lô* is probably not intended as a dative of advantage ["ethical dative"] here), and since he names the pillar "after himself" (*ʿal-šᵉmô*, lit., "according to his [own] name"; cf. Gen 48:6 ["under the names of"]; Exod 28:21 ["with the name of"]), it is best to understand *hazkîr šᵉmî* in its normal sense of "carry on the memory of my name" (cf. Carl F. Graesser, "Standing Stones in Ancient Palestine," BA 35, 2 [1972]: 40). Like the equally egotistical Saul before him (see 1 Sam 15:12 and comment), Absalom decides to memorialize himself by erecting a monument (perhaps an inscribed stele of some sort) in his own honor. His plaint that he has "no son" to do it for him is usually understood to mean that all three of the unnamed sons mentioned in 14:27 had already died (see comment there). It is also possible, however, that one or more of his sons were unwilling (for whatever reason) to perpetuate their father's memory. If so, the monument stands as yet another poignant act of desperation by its builder (cf. similarly Stan Rummel, "Using Ancient Near Eastern Parallels in Old Testament Study," *Biblical Archaeology Review* 3, 3 [1977]: 10).

"Absalom's Monument" (lit., "Absalom's hand"; see comments on 8:3; 1 Sam 15:12; cf. also Isa 56:5 ["memorial"]; cf. M. Delcor, "Two Special Meanings of the Word יד in Biblical Hebrew," JSS 12, 2 [1967]: 230; Hoffner, "A Hittite Analogue," p. 222 n. 6), erected in the "King's Valley" (known also as the "Valley of Shaveh" [Gen 14:17], a place of uncertain location but probably near Jerusalem), could be seen "to this day" (v.18)—that is, the time of the narrator of 2 Samuel (cf. 4:3; 6:8; Gen 35:20; see also 1 Sam 6:18 and comment). The monument is not to be identified with the fifty-two-foot-high "Tomb/Pillar of Absalom," a monolith cut out of a cliff in the Kidron Valley east of Jerusalem that probably received its name because of its resemblance to a pillar. Its burial chamber "is reminiscent of Hellenistic and Roman sepulchers and is to be dated to the first part of the first century A.D." (W. Harold Mare, *The Archaeology of the Jerusalem Area* [Grand Rapids: Baker, 1987], p. 195).

## Notes

---

**2** "Will surely march out" renders a strengthening infinitive absolute construction. Although it is relatively infrequent with the verb יצא (*yṣ'*), the parallel literary section (16:5–14) contains another example ("as he came out," 16:5).

**3** The basic difference between the NIV text reading and margin reading of the verse is that between "you" (אַתָּה [*'attāh*]) and "now" (עַתָּה [*'attāh*]). "You," the choice of virtually all commentators, is the contextually superior variant. Although deciding in favor of "now," the KJV rendered correctly *ad sensum*: "But now *thou art* worth ten thousand of us." The first "now" in the MT of v.3 probably arose from contamination by the second occurrence of "now" later in the verse (cf. independently KD, p. 435).

"To give . . . support" renders either the Hiphil *Kethiv* לעזיר (*l'zyr*), for an original להעזיר (*lh'zyr*, "to provide help"; cf. GKC, sec. 53*q*), or the Qal *Qere* לעזור (*l'zwr*, "to help"). Since the existence of Hiphil *'zr* in the OT is suspect (the only other possible occurrence is the problematic מעזרם (*m'zrm*) in 2 Chron 28:23—where, however, the initial *m* is probably due to dittography [cf. BHS]), the Qal form is preferable (for discussion, cf. S.R. Driver, *Notes on the Books of Samuel*, p. 328).

**9** "He was left hanging" translates וַיֻּתַּן (*wayyuttan*, lit., "and he was put/placed," from נתן [*ntn*]). The same rendering results from what is doubtless the correct reading—ויתל (*wytl*, from תלה [*tlh*])—as demonstrated by 4QSam[a] and LXX (for details cf. McCarter, *II Samuel*, p. 401; cf. also תָּלוּי [*tālûy*, "hanging"] in v.10).

**12** Though attested in only two Hebrew MSS (cf. BHS), "for my sake" (לִי [*lî*]) is also assumed in several ancient versions (see NIV mg.) and has the advantage of echoing the same phrase in v.5. The NIV margin alternative attempts to make sense of MT מִי (*mî*, "who[ever]"; cf. further KD, p. 438).

**13** The text reading is based on the *Qere* "my life," whereas the margin rendering prefers the *Kethiv* "his life" (the Heb. may be translated literally as "And/Or if I had dealt falsely/recklessly with my/his life"; for discussion cf. Kirkpatrick, *The Second Book of Samuel*, p. 172; McCarter, *II Samuel*, pp. 397, 401).

**16** חָשַׂךְ (*ḥāśak*, "halted, held back") could also be rendered "spared" here (cf. BDB, p. 362; for discussion cf. Conroy, p. 62 n. 73).

---

## 17. *David's mourning for Absalom*

### 18:19–19:8

19 Now Ahimaaz son of Zadok said, "Let me run and take the news to
the king that the LORD has delivered him from the hand of his enemies."

20"You are not the one to take the news today," Joab told him. "You
may take the news another time, but you must not do so today, because
the king's son is dead."
21Then Joab said to a Cushite, "Go, tell the king what you have seen."
The Cushite bowed down before Joab and ran off.
22Ahimaaz son of Zadok again said to Joab, "Come what may, please
let me run behind the Cushite."

But Joab replied, "My son, why do you want to go? You don't have
any news that will bring you a reward."
23He said, "Come what may, I want to run."

So Joab said, "Run!" Then Ahimaaz ran by way of the plain and
outran the Cushite.
24While David was sitting between the inner and outer gates, the
watchman went up to the roof of the gateway by the wall. As he looked
out, he saw a man running alone. 25The watchman called out to the king
and reported it.

The king said, "If he is alone, he must have good news." And the man
came closer and closer.
26Then the watchman saw another man running, and he called down
to the gatekeeper, "Look, another man running alone!"

The king said, "He must be bringing good news, too."
27The watchman said, "It seems to me that the first one runs like
Ahimaaz son of Zadok."

"He's a good man," the king said. "He comes with good news."
28Then Ahimaaz called out to the king, "All is well!" He bowed down
before the king with his face to the ground and said, "Praise be to the
LORD your God! He has delivered up the men who lifted their hands
against my lord the king."
29The king asked, "Is the young man Absalom safe?"

Ahimaaz answered, "I saw great confusion just as Joab was about to
send the king's servant and me, your servant, but I don't know what it
was."
30The king said, "Stand aside and wait here." So he stepped aside
and stood there.
31Then the Cushite arrived and said, "My lord the king, hear the good
news! The LORD has delivered you today from all who rose up against
you."
32The king asked the Cushite, "Is the young man Absalom safe?"

The Cushite replied, "May the enemies of my lord the king and all who
rise up to harm you be like that young man."
33The king was shaken. He went up to the room over the gateway and
wept. As he went, he said: "O my son Absalom! My son, my son
Absalom! If only I had died instead of you—O Absalom, my son, my
son!"
19:1Joab was told, "The king is weeping and mourning for Absalom."
2And for the whole army the victory that day was turned into mourning,
because on that day the troops heard it said, "The king is grieving for
his son." 3The men stole into the city that day as men steal in who are
ashamed when they flee from battle. 4The king covered his face and
cried aloud, "O my son Absalom! O Absalom, my son, my son!"
5Then Joab went into the house to the king and said, "Today you have
humiliated all your men, who have just saved your life and the lives of
your sons and daughters and the lives of your wives and concubines.
6You love those who hate you and hate those who love you. You have
made it clear today that the commanders and their men mean nothing to
you. I see that you would be pleased if Absalom were alive today and all
of us were dead. 7Now go out and encourage your men. I swear by the
LORD that if you don't go out, not a man will be left with you by nightfall.

This will be worse for you than all the calamities that have come upon you from your youth till now."

[8]So the king got up and took his seat in the gateway. When the men were told, "The king is sitting in the gateway," they all came before him.

Meanwhile, the Israelites had fled to their homes.

Although the similarities between 18:19–19:8 and its counterpart (16:1–4) in the architectonic structure of chapters 15–20 (more precisely, 15:1–20:22) are not as numerous or convincing as are other parallel sections in that structure (see comment on 15:1–12), they are not totally absent. If in 16:2–4 David reveals his skepticism as he addresses a series of questions to Ziba concerning Mephibosheth, a pretender to the throne of Israel, in 18:28–32 he demonstrates equal skepticism as he questions Ahimaaz and a Cushite concerning Absalom, another pretender to Israel's throne. And if in 16:2–4 David's statements are introduced three times by the formulaic *wayyō'mer hammelek̲* ("And/Then the king said/asked"; see comment on 16:1–4), in the present section they are prefaced six times in the same way (cf. vv.25b, 26b, 27b, 29, 30, 32). Thus *wayyō'mer hammelek̲* occurs nine times in 16:1–4; 18:19–19:8—an impressive figure in the light of the fact that it is found only eight times in the rest of the larger literary complex (15:19, 25, 27; 16:10; 19:23, 33, 38; 20:4).

Two clearly distinguishable units comprise 18:19–19:8: (1) 18:19–33, which recounts in exquisite detail how two messengers relay the news of Absalom's death (indirectly, to be sure) to David; (2) 19:1–8, which records the words of Joab's rebuke to the mourning king. While the latter consists of a summary description of David's inconsolable grief (19:1–4) followed by Joab's rebuke and David's response to it (19:5–8), the former is divided into three sections arranged in chiastic order (as noted by Fokkelman, *King David*, p. 251 [the titles of the sections are mine]):

A. The messengers are sent to bring news to David (18:19–23)
 B. David anxiously waits for news concerning Absalom (18:24–27)
A′. David receives the messengers and their news (18:28–33)

Two key verbal roots recurring frequently throughout 18:19–33 are *rwṣ* ("run," vv.19, 21, 22 [bis: "run," "go"], 23 [ter], 24, 26 [bis], 27 [bis; NIV omits the second occurrence for stylistic reasons]), and *bśr* ("[bring] news," vv.19, 20 [ter: "take the news," "take the news," "do so"], 22, 25, 26, 27, 31). At least one of the two roots occurs in each verse from v.19 through v.27, and their interplay has the effect of slowing down the action while at the same time heightening the suspense. As noted by Gunn, 18:19–33 bears a certain resemblance to the messenger scene in 2 Kings 9:17–20 ("Traditional Composition," pp. 227–28).

**19–23** Jubilant over the fact that Absalom's army has been defeated by David's troops (cf. v.7), Ahimaaz (see comments on 15:27, 36) asks Joab for permission to report to the king: "Please let me run" (v.19; same Heb. expression as in v.22). His desire to "take the news" is doubtless prompted by his feeling that David will be as happy about the outcome of the battle as he himself is (the verb *bśr* and its cognate forms almost always connote news for David that is good; see comment on 1 Sam 4:17). What could be better news for David than that the Lord has "delivered him" (vv.19, 31; lit., "vindicated him [by delivering him]"; see 1 Sam 24:15 and comment) from the rebellious Israelite troops, who have therefore become "his" enemies (whether the antecedent is David or the Lord, the end result is the same; see comment on "the LORD's enemies" in 1 Sam 30:26)?

Joab, however, at first refuses to send Ahimaaz (v.20), perhaps because he does not want to endanger the life of a messenger who will in fact have brought bad news to the king. Three times he tells Ahimaaz that he is not to take the news "today" ("another time" is literally "another day"), the third time underscoring his point by using "today" in emphatic position (lit., "but today you must not take the news"). Whether at this juncture Ahimaaz knows that Absalom is dead is a moot point since, as McCarter observes (*II Samuel,* p. 408), the last clause in v.20 is probably the narrator's comment rather than a part of Joab's statement to Ahimaaz: "This was because the king's son was dead."

Another more likely messenger comes to Joab's attention: "a [lit., 'the'] Cushite" (v.21). To equate him with the Benjamite "Cush" in the title of Psalm 7, where the LXX reads *Chousi* ("Cushite"; cf. BHS there), is unproductive since the contents of the psalm imply that "Cush(i)" is David's enemy (as many if not most Benjamites were). As a gentilic the term "Cushite" can refer to a person born either in the upper Nile region (a Nubian [cf. Eli's son Phinehas; see comment on 1 Sam 1:3]) or in central and southern Mesopotamia (cf. Youngblood, *The Book of Genesis,* p. 130). In their relationships with the people of Israel, Cushites in the OT are alternately friendly (cf. Jer 38:7–13; 39:15–18) or hostile (cf. 2 Chron 14:9–15). After surveying several proposed identifications and interpretations of the Cushite in v.21, Conroy appropriately summarizes: "Rather than speculate on the possibly baleful significance . . . of the possibly black skin . . . of the possibly Nubian messenger, it is preferable to think that Joab chose the Cushite simply because he was an alien and hence, if the worst came to the worst, more expendable" (p. 69 n. 102). Thus Joab sends him on his way, instructing him simply to tell David what he has seen.

Undeterred and unafraid, Ahimaaz again requests permission to take the news to David, "come what may" (vv.22–23). "Please let me run" (v.22; see v.19 and comment), he says, "also me" (an emphatic expression omitted in the NIV, probably for stylistic reasons). As before, however, Joab tries to deter him. Whether "my son" (v.22) was a conventional way of addressing a messenger (cf. 1 Sam 4:16) is uncertain, although it is surely going too far to assert (with Conroy [p. 70 n. 106] and McCarter [*II Samuel,* p. 408]) that here it is condescending, patronizing, or ironic. In any event, Joab attempts to convince Ahimaaz that none of the news he has can be expected to "bring . . . a reward" (v.22, lit., "find [anything]"; cf. Job 31:25 ["had gained"]; Hos 12:8 ["have become"]; for *b*[e]*śôrāh* ["news"] in a similar context implying reward, see 4:10 and comment).

Persistent to the end, Ahimaaz pleads a third time—and Joab finally relents (v.23). So intent is Ahimaaz on performing his mission well that, even though the Cushite has a head start, Ahimaaz outruns him. If the forest of Ephraim (see comment on v.6) was along the eastern border of the "plain" (cf. Gen 19:17, 25)—i.e., the plain of the Jordan (see NIV mg.; cf. Gen 13:10–11; 1 Kings 7:46 = 2 Chron 4:17)—Ahimaaz's route, though less direct and therefore a mile or two longer than that of the Cushite, would be over smoother and more level ground than his and would therefore enable him to arrive at Mahanaim in less time (for a plausible reconstruction of the two routes, cf. the map of Yohanan Aharoni and Michael Avi-Yonah, *The Macmillan Bible Atlas,* rev. ed. [New York: Macmillan, 1977], p. 71). In addition Ahimaaz from the outset may have been stronger and more athletic than the Cushite (cf. 17:17–21).

**24–27** The scene shifts to Mahanaim, the temporary headquarters of David (v.24; see 17:24 and comment). There the king, waiting for news of the outcome of the battle, sits between "the inner and outer" (lit., "the two") gates of the city, perhaps in one of the guardrooms. A watchman, standing on the roof of the gateway complex that forms part of the city wall, looks out toward the horizon and catches sight of a lone runner approaching the city. When the watchman calls to the king below and reports what he has seen, the king assumes that if the runner is by himself "he must have good news" (v.25; lit., "good news must be in his mouth"; see comment on 17:5). But the narrator's observation that the man "came closer and closer," reprising as it does the earlier description of the Philistine Goliath who "kept coming closer" to David (1 Sam 17:41), has an unsettling and ominous ring. The watchman then sees another man running, and this time he calls the information down to the city "gatekeeper" (v.26), whose duties included the dissemination of news to interested parties (cf. 2 Kings 7:10–11). The king is thus duly notified, and his response is the same as before.

Ahimaaz's reputation as a superb athlete has preceded him, and the watchman recognizes his running style even before he has gotten close enough for his face to be visible (v.27). For the third time David responds favorably, characterizing Ahimaaz as a "good" man and the news he brings as "good" (the MT adds "good" [the explicit use of which with *bśr* is unnecessary; see comments on v.19; 1 Sam 4:17] to "news" only here in the entire narrative). If we agree for the sake of the argument that 1 Kings 1–2 is in fact a part of David's Court History (chs. 9–20; for discussion see comments on 9:1–20:26), the observation of Gunn is especially apt: "Just as the watchman's identification of Ahimaaz draws the comment from the king that 'He is a good man [*'yš ṭwb*] and comes with good news [*'l bśwrh ṭwbh ybw'*]', so in 1 Kgs i 42–3 the arrival of Jonathan the son of Abiathar with news for Adonijah prompts Adonijah to say, 'Come in [*b'*] for you are a worthy man [*'yš ḥyl*] and bring good news [*ṭwb tbśr*]' " ("Traditional Composition," p. 228). In the eyes of the recipients, however, in both cases the news turns out to be anything but good.

**28–33** Whereas in vv.19–23 Joab sends two messengers to bring news to David, in the parallel section (vv.28–33) David receives Joab's messengers and their news. The chiastic effect (see comment on 18:19–19:8) is enhanced by the fact that in the earlier passage the Cushite was sent before Ahimaaz while here Ahimaaz (who outran the Cushite) is received first. In addition the name "David" is used only once (v.24) in the entire literary unit (vv.19–33), and that in its central section (vv.24–27; see comment on 18:19–19:8). The bracketing sections (vv.19–23, 28–33) refer to him as "the king" consistently throughout. Cohesion is given to the present section by the striking wordplay between the three occurrences of *šālôm* (vv.28 ["All is well!"], 29 ["safe"], 32 ["safe"]) and the five occurrences of *'abšālôm* (vv.29, 32, 33 [ter]).

Arriving in Mahanaim, Ahimaaz first reassures the king with the common *šālôm* greeting (v.28; see 1 Sam 25:5–6 and comments). As the Cushite had bowed down before Joab (cf. v.21), Ahimaaz bows down before King David—but in the most respectful of ways, as Absalom himself had once done: "with his face to the ground" (v.28; cf. 14:33; see comment on 14:4). Beginning with an outburst of praise (see comment on 1 Sam 25:32), Ahimaaz informs David that the Lord has "delivered up" the king's enemies. The idiom is the same as that in 1 Samuel 17:46; 24:18; and 26:8, but here it is used absolutely (without "into the hand of"; see commentary on 1 Sam 17:46). In every case it is the sovereign Lord (cf. independently Conroy, p. 72 n. 118), not mighty armies, who brings deliverance.

But, with respect to the reports not only of Ahimaaz (v.28) but also of the Cushite (v.31), Conroy observes: "It is as if [David] had not really heard their words at all.

They were interested in the plural of the defeated forces; he is concerned only about the singular of his son" (p. 74). Again referring to Absalom as "the young man" (v.29; see comment on v.5), David insists on knowing whether he is "safe" (*šālôm*). Conroy's remark is to the point: "The insistence on *šlwm* here reminds the reader that the last word spoken to Absalom both by his father (15,9 ["peace"]) and by Ahithophel (17,3 ["unharmed"]) was *šlwm*" (p. 74). For his part Ahimaaz, who perhaps does not know that Absalom is dead (see comment on v.20), responds simply that he saw great "confusion" (v.29), a not uncommon phenomenon in battle situations (see comments on 1 Sam 14:19–20). Indeed, there was so much tumult that he does not "know what it was" (the NIV adds the last two words for clarity; Ahimaaz concludes his speech with *mh* ["what"], as in Prov 9:13: "without knowledge" [lit., "does not know what"]). His question unanswered, David tells Ahimaaz to step aside and "wait here" (v.30), echoing verbatim the command of Balaam to Balak centuries earlier (cf. Num 23:15 ["Stay here"; identical Heb. expression]).

After David dismisses Ahimaaz, the Cushite arrives with his report. He may have overheard the original request of Ahimaaz to Joab because he uses the same idiom to describe Israel's defeat: "The LORD has delivered you . . . from the hand of [your enemies]" (v.31; see comment on v.19 [the NIV here omits "the hand of"]). When the king asks him the same question he had asked Ahimaaz (v.32; see v.29 and comment), the Cushite responds—euphemistically, to be sure–that Absalom is dead: "May the enemies of my lord the king and all who rise up to harm you be like that young man." Garsiel perceptively observes:

> There is a clear rule of law which connects a leader's conduct with his fate and the fate of his house. A degenerate [*sic*] leader, whether it is himself who has sinned or his sons, will ultimately be deposed (see the story of Samuel and his sons) or come to a tragic end, just as Eli and his sons die on the same day, and so do Saul and his. This law holds true of David also; . . . just as in the stories of the death of Eli, Saul and their sons, in the story of Absalom there appears a runner who announces the evil tidings of his death in battle (II Sam. 18:19–32); and before that, in the story of Amnon's murder, a rumor comes to the king of the killing of all his sons, although it is found that only Amnon had been killed (II Sam. 13:30–36). With this, the criticism of all four leaders described in the book of Samuel, together with their sons, reaches its conclusion. (p. 106)

In the light of his obvious concern about his son, David's reaction to the news of Absalom's death is totally predictable: He is shaken (v.33), he mourns (19:1; for another example of parallelism between *rgz* ["shake," "tremble"] and *'bl* ["mourn"], cf. Amos 8:8; cf. Conroy, p. 75 n. 130). Seeking privacy to weep alone, he goes up to the room over the city gateway (see v.24 and comment) and laments as he goes: "O my son Absalom! My son, my son Absalom! If only I [emphatic] had died instead of you—O Absalom, my son, my son!" Totally unlike the otherwise similar complaint of certain grumbling Israelites on their trek through the desert following the Exodus ("If only we had died . . . in Egypt!" [Exod 16:3]), David's mournful cry is filled with the pathos of a father's grieving heart: "If only I had died instead of you."

By no means is this the first time that David weeps over the death of someone—a compatriot (cf. 3:32), a close friend (cf. 1:11–12), even a son (cf. 13:33, 35–36)—but here his grief knows no bounds, and his language is therefore unique. The

> extreme possibility of repetition, where the device has a totally dramatic justification as the expression of a kind of mental stammer, is bound to be relatively rare, especially in nondramatic literature, but it does occur occasionally in the Bible, most memorably when David is informed of Absalom's death. . . . The poet-king, who elsewhere responds to the report of death with eloquent elegies, here simply sobs, "Absalom, Absalom, my son, my son," repeating "my son" eight times in two verses [18:33; 19:4]. (Alter, *The Art of Biblical Narrative,* p. 92)

Writers as different as George Gordon Lord Byron and William Faulkner have been moved by David's poignant words to incorporate them into their own writings in one form or another. Indeed, in weeping and in addressing Absalom as "my son," David himself echoes an earlier occasion in which Saul had done the same with respect to him, even while perceiving David as one who was attempting to seize the throne of Israel—just as Absalom has tried to do (see 1 Sam 24:16 and comment).

But the narrative of the events immediately preceding and following Absalom's death as recorded in chapter 18 recalls another emotion-laden story as well.

> The description of Absalom's demise resonates with allusions to Abraham's binding of Isaac in Genesis 22. . . . Both Absalom and the ram are caught in a thicket (*śôbek/sĕbak*). Whereas Abraham is commanded not to send forth his hand (*'al tišlaḥ yadekā*) unto the lad (22:12), Joab's soldier refuses to send forth his hand (*lō' 'ešlaḥ yādî*) unto the son of the king (18:12). And finally, Abraham offers up the ram in place of his son (*taḥat bĕnô* [22:13]). It takes a while for David to help us perceive this analogy, but finally he makes it clear: "would that I had died in place of you (*taḥtekā*), O Absalom, my son, my son." (Ackerman, p. 50)

The last verse of chapter 18 in the NIV constitutes the first verse of chapter 19 in the MT, accommodating the traditional one-verse numbering difference between the Hebrew and English texts throughout chapter 19 (for the same phenomenon in 1 Sam 24, see comment on 1 Sam 24:1–22; for a similar phenomenon in 1 Sam 21, see comment on 1 Sam 21:1–9). The commentary below will follow the English numbering system.

Verses 1–8, which conclude the literary unit that begins at 18:19 (see comment on 18:19–19:8), themselves comprise a discrete subunit that uses an *inclusio* to frame the whole: "Joab was told, 'Behold [MT *hinnēh,* omitted by NIV for stylistic reasons], the king is weeping and mourning for Absalom'" (v.1); "The men were told, 'Behold [again omitted by NIV], the king is sitting in the gateway'" (v.8; cf. Fokkelman, *King David,* p. 269). Avoiding the personal name "David," the account employs "the king" throughout (see comment on 18:28–33 for the same phenomenon in certain sections of ch. 18). In vv.1–8 the "exclusive use of *hmlk* . . . (where David is most a father and least a king) is quite striking and could perhaps be taken as a deliberate contrast and an implied criticism on the part of the narrator" (Conroy, p. 81).

The subsection divides into two equal halves, vv.1–4 providing a summary description of David's grief and vv.5–8 recording Joab's lengthy rebuke and David's brief response. Verse 4 concludes by condensing the poignant lament with which chapter 18 ends, repeating verbatim its first ("O my son Absalom!") and last ("O Absalom, my son, my son!") clauses.

**19:1–4** Doubtless a beneficiary of David's intelligence network (see comment on 10:5), Joab is eventually "told" (v.1) of David's "weeping" (see comment on 18:33) and "mourning" for his son Absalom (see 13:37 and comment for David's similar reaction to the death of his son Amnon; see also comment on 14:2). It is not long before Joab's entire army hears of it as well (v.2), with the result that what should have been for them a great "victory" (brought about by the Lord; cf. 23:10, 12; see 1 Sam 19:5 and comment) has become a cause for "mourning" (a noun form from the same Heb. root used in v.1). Far from capitalizing on their triumph as an occasion for celebration, the men slink into Mahanaim like those who "steal in" (v.3; lit., "make themselves move around like thieves"; cf. similarly Snaith, *The Hebrew Text of 2 Samuel xvi–xix*, p. 54) because cowardice has forced them to flee the battlefield. Meanwhile David, with face "covered" (v.4; *lā'aṭ* is a byform of the verb *lwṭ*, used here in the sense of "cover with a burial cloth," as in Isa 25:7 ["the shroud that enfolds"]), continues to cry aloud (cf. 13:19) as he mourns for his dead son.

**5–8** Rosenberg aptly characterizes this subsection: "Joab, asserting the reasons of state security that demanded Absalom's death, accuses David of grave discourtesy to his supporters and friends—the words [vv.5–7] are extraordinarily frank and represent Joab's only open rebuke of the king throughout the entire Davidic history" (p. 166)—a rebuke that will cost him dearly (cf. v.13), at least temporarily.

Whereas the narrator employs *'am* ("people") to describe David's "army/troops/men" (vv.2, 3, 8), Joab uses *'ᵃḇāḏîm* ("servants")—a term implying loyalty, obedience, dependence—for the same purpose (vv.5, 6, 7). Stressing not only the thoughtless immediacy of the king's insensitivity but also the urgent need for prompt action, Joab makes use of the word "today" no less than five times (twice in v.5 ["Today," "just"], three times in v.6 [omitted once by the NIV for stylistic reasons]).

David's army commander begins by upbraiding him for humiliating the very men ("your men," v.5) who are responsible for having saved the king's life as well as the lives of all who are near and dear to him (*nep̱eš* ["life"], which appears four times in the verse, is omitted by the NIV before "[your] concubines"), including those of his "wives and concubines" (for which see comments on 5:13; 12:8; 1 Sam 25:43; see also 1 Sam 1:2 and comment). Joab is of course right: "David's men" (18:7) have in fact won the battle. But the heart of Joab's complaint is that David loves those who hate him and hates those who love him (v.6). Although Joab's accusation has been called a "colossal hyperbole" (Fokkelman, *King David*, p. 272), "it accurately reflects the topsy-turvy nature of the king's extreme emotions. Its similarity to the description of Amnon's swing from love to hatred (13:15) reminds the reader that such emotions are common to father and son, both of whom commit grave acts of injustice" (Lasine, "Melodrama as Parable," p. 117). Whatever else it may involve, at the very least "love" in this context surely implies covenant loyalty (see comments on 1:26; 1 Sam 16:21; 18:1–4; 20:17; cf. also Conroy, p. 79 and n. 151).

Joab has received the clear impression that the "commanders" (v.6, including himself, Abishai, and Ittai [cf. 18:5]) and their men mean nothing at all to the king. Indeed, in his present frame of mind David would trade Absalom's life for those of everyone else (ironically, "if [*lu'*] Absalom were alive" echoes 18:12: "if [*lu'*] a thousand shekels were weighed out into my hands, I would not lift my hand against the king's son"). Conroy observes on 18:33 that "David wished that he had died himself instead of Absalom, but here Joab accuses him of wishing Absalom were alive even if that meant the loss of the whole army" (p. 79). The ambiguity of David's behavior when issues of life and death are at stake is explored also in 12:18–23 (see comments there).

Joab's final statement in his rebuke begins and ends with "now" (v.7; see comment on "today" in vv.5–6). He swears on oath to David that if the king does not immediately go out and "encourage" (v.7; lit., "speak to the heart of"; cf. 2 Chron 32:6 ["encourage"]) his "men" (*'ᵃḇāḏîm*) by nightfall not a "man" (*'îš*) will remain loyal to him. The troops of Judah thus having deserted David, no greater calamity for him throughout his entire life could possibly be imagined.

However reluctantly, the king is prodded into action by Joab's harsh words. If David formerly sat in the gateway of Mahanaim awaiting news of the battle's outcome (cf. 18:24), he now takes his seat there in his official capacity of adjudicating the grievances (see 15:2 and comment; cf. also 1 Kings 22:10) of any and "all" of the "men" (lit., "people"; see comment on v.5) of Judah ("all," which appears twice in the MT of v.8, is omitted by the NIV after "When" for reasons of style). The literary unit ends by echoing the earlier report that the Israelites had "fled to their homes" (18:17; the NIV has wrongly placed v.8b, the contents of which constitute one of a series of concluding statements [cf. v.39; 18:17; 20:22; cf. also 1 Sam 2:11; 7:17; 10:25–26; 15:34; 24:22; 26:25], at the beginning of the next section).

## Notes

---

**20** *Qere* כִּי־עַל־כֵּן (*kî-'al-kēn,* lit., "because therefore") is the preferred reading. The omission of *kēn* in the *Kethiv* is doubtless due to haplography because of the following בֵּן (*ben,* "son of"; cf. KD, p. 440; S.R. Driver, *Notes on the Books of Samuel,* p. 331; McCarter, *II Samuel,* p. 402).

**26** "Look, another man" is literally "Look, a man," the NIV having inserted "another" *ad sensum.* Conroy's comment is apropos:

> One would almost have expected the word "another" in the sentinel's words (*hnh 'yš 'ḥr rṣ lbdw*), and indeed this is had by the ancient versions [cf. BHS], but the MT form without *'ḥr* has its own effect. It expresses well the impersonal attitude of the sentinel who reports just what he sees at this moment and makes no connection with what he has seen previously, and this contrasts with the king's impatient eagerness and anxiety. (p. 71)

**19:8** (9 MT) A gate complex and its pavement were built at Dan near the northern border of Israel at the end of the tenth century B.C. (cf. Avram Biran, "Tel Dan," BA 37, 2 [1974]: 49). Near the entrance to the gate itself was found an unusual structure, built of ashlars and originally having at its four corners small columns with decorated capitals or bases. "The columns may have supported a canopy which covered the structure. The use of this structure could not be determined archaeologically, but it is possible that it served as a base for a throne. . . . The reference in II Samuel 19:8 surely must refer to some special structure [at Mahanaim] where David sat and where the people could see him" (ibid., pp. 45, 47; cf. also p. 46 for photographs of the structure at Dan).

---

## 18. *David's return to Jerusalem*

### 19:9–43

9Throughout the tribes of Israel, the people were all arguing with each
other, saying, "The king delivered us from the hand of our enemies; he
is the one who rescued us from the hand of the Philistines. But now he
has fled the country because of Absalom; 10and Absalom, whom we

anointed to rule over us, has died in battle. So why do you say nothing
about bringing the king back?"

11King David sent this message to Zadok and Abiathar, the priests:
"Ask the elders of Judah, 'Why should you be the last to bring the king
back to his palace, since what is being said throughout Israel has
reached the king at his quarters? 12You are my brothers, my own flesh
and blood. So why should you be the last to bring back the king?' 13And
say to Amasa, 'Are you not my own flesh and blood? May God deal with
me, be it ever so severely, if from now on you are not the commander of
my army in place of Joab.'"

14He won over the hearts of all the men of Judah as though they were
one man. They sent word to the king, "Return, you and all your men."
15Then the king returned and went as far as the Jordan.

Now the men of Judah had come to Gilgal to go out and meet the king
and bring him across the Jordan. 16Shimei son of Gera, the Benjamite
from Bahurim, hurried down with the men of Judah to meet King David.
17With him were a thousand Benjamites, along with Ziba, the steward of
Saul's household, and his fifteen sons and twenty servants. They rushed
to the Jordan, where the king was. 18They crossed at the ford to take the
king's household over and to do whatever he wished.

When Shimei son of Gera crossed the Jordan, he fell prostrate before
the king 19and said to him, "May my lord not hold me guilty. Do not
remember how your servant did wrong on the day my lord the king left
Jerusalem. May the king put it out of his mind. 20For I your servant know
that I have sinned, but today I have come here as the first of the whole
house of Joseph to come down and meet my lord the king."

21Then Abishai son of Zeruiah said, "Shouldn't Shimei be put to death
for this? He cursed the LORD's anointed."

22David replied, "What do you and I have in common, you sons of
Zeruiah? This day you have become my adversaries! Should anyone be
put to death in Israel today? Do I not know that today I am king over
Israel?" 23So the king said to Shimei, "You shall not die." And the king
promised him on oath.

24Mephibosheth, Saul's grandson, also went down to meet the king.
He had not taken care of his feet or trimmed his mustache or washed his
clothes from the day the king left until the day he returned safely.
25When he came from Jerusalem to meet the king, the king asked him,
"Why didn't you go with me, Mephibosheth?"

26He said, "My lord the king, since I your servant am lame, I said, 'I will
have my donkey saddled and will ride on it, so I can go with the king.'
But Ziba my servant betrayed me. 27And he has slandered your servant
to my lord the king. My lord the king is like an angel of God; so do
whatever pleases you. 28All my grandfather's descendants deserved
nothing but death from my lord the king, but you gave your servant a
place among those who eat at your table. So what right do I have to
make any more appeals to the king?"

29The king said to him, "Why say more? I order you and Ziba to divide
the fields."

30Mephibosheth said to the king, "Let him take everything, now that
my lord the king has arrived home safely."

31Barzillai the Gileadite also came down from Rogelim to cross the
Jordan with the king and to send him on his way from there. 32Now
Barzillai was a very old man, eighty years of age. He had provided for the
king during his stay in Mahanaim, for he was a very wealthy man. 33The
king said to Barzillai, "Cross over with me and stay with me in
Jerusalem, and I will provide for you."

34But Barzillai answered the king, "How many more years will I live,
that I should go up to Jerusalem with the king? 35I am now eighty years
old. Can I tell the difference between what is good and what is not? Can

your servant taste what he eats and drinks? Can I still hear the voices of
men and women singers? Why should your servant be an added burden
to my lord the king? 36 Your servant will cross over the Jordan with the
king for a short distance, but why should the king reward me in this
way? 37 Let your servant return, that I may die in my own town near the
tomb of my father and mother. But here is your servant Kimham. Let him
cross over with my lord the king. Do for him whatever pleases you."

38 The king said, "Kimham shall cross over with me, and I will do for
him whatever pleases you. And anything you desire from me I will do for
you."

39 So all the people crossed the Jordan, and then the king crossed
over. The king kissed Barzillai and gave him his blessing, and Barzillai
returned to his home.

40 When the king crossed over to Gilgal, Kimham crossed with him. All
the troops of Judah and half the troops of Israel had taken the king over.

41 Soon all the men of Israel were coming to the king and saying to
him, "Why did our brothers, the men of Judah, steal the king away and
bring him and his household across the Jordan, together with all his
men?"

42 All the men of Judah answered the men of Israel, "We did this
because the king is closely related to us. Why are you angry about it?
Have we eaten any of the king's provisions? Have we taken anything for
ourselves?"

43 Then the men of Israel answered the men of Judah, "We have ten
shares in the king; and besides, we have a greater claim on David than
you have. So why do you treat us with contempt? Were we not the first
to speak of bringing back our king?"

But the men of Judah responded even more harshly than the men of
Israel.

In the overall structure of chapters 15–20 (more precisely 15:1–20:22), the literary unit describing the return of "King David" (v.11) to Jerusalem (vv.9–43) parallels that depicting his flight (15:13–37) caused by Absalom's rebellion (see comment on 15:1–12). If the earlier account included David's instructions to three of his supporters (Ittai, 15:19–23; Zadok, 15:24–31; Hushai, 15:32–37), the present narrative contains meetings with three representatives of "important constituencies with which David must come to terms" (Brueggemann, *First and Second Samuel,* p. 326): Shimei (vv.15b–23), Mephibosheth (vv.24–30), Barzillai (vv.31–39). The three sections are in turn bracketed by a prologue (vv.9–15a) and an epilogue (vv.40–43), each of which deals with the question of who—Israel or Judah—should escort the king on his triumphant return to his capital city (cf. the threefold repetition of *lhšyb 't-hmlk* ["to bring back the king"] in vv.10, 11, 12, echoed in v.43: *lhšyb 't-mlky* ["to bring back our (lit., 'my') king"]).

The resulting chiastic outline thus focuses on Mephibosheth (see comment on v.24):

A. Israel or Judah? (19:9–15a)
  B. Shimei the Benjamite (19:15b–23)
    C. Mephibosheth the Saulide (19:24–30)
  B′. Barzillai the Gileadite (19:31–39)
A′. Judah or Israel? (19:40–43)

In addition to structural similarities, a number of shared lexical elements link the two parallel sections, among which are references to Zadok and Abiathar (v.11; 15:24, 27, 29, 35, 36); the root *mhr* ("hurry," v.16; 15:14 ["immediately," "moved quickly"]);

the word "ford" (v.18; 15:28); the unusual expression *hāyāh lᵉmaśśā' 'el/'al* ("be a burden to," v.35; 15:33); and the idiom "do to/for" a person "whatever pleases/seems good to" him (vv.37–38; 15:26).

**9–15a** The use of "all" twice in v.9 (rendered once as "throughout") forges a transitional link with the final verse of the preceding section (see comment on v.8). Animated discussion ("arguing with each other," v.9) is the order of the day as some Israelites remind their countrymen that David, despite whatever flaws he may have, had in fact been their conquering hero in the past—indeed, "he is the one" (emphatic) who had long since rescued them from their perennial enemies, the Philistines (see 5:17–25; 8:1 and comments). At the same time, however, he has now "fled" (*bāraḥ*) the country (an activity to which David was no stranger; cf. 1 Sam 20:1) "because of" Absalom (*mē'al,* better, "from"; cf. Neh 13:28, where *w'bryḥhw m'ly* is rendered "And I drove him away [lit., 'caused him to flee'] from me"). David's partisans continue their apologia by pointing out that Absalom himself, whom Israel had "anointed" to rule over them (v.10, the only reference to Absalom's anointing), is now dead. They therefore insist ("now," omitted by NIV [before "why"] for stylistic reasons) on knowing why their fellow Israelites ("you," emphatic plural) "say nothing" (lit., "remain quiet/silent"; cf. 13:20) about returning David to his rightful place on the throne in Jerusalem.

If there are any doubts at this point in the account concerning who is really king, the narrator erases them by using the title "King David" (v.11). Sending word to his friends Zadok and Abiathar, the priests (cf. 15:27–29, 35; 17:15–16; see also 15:24 and comment), David tells them to ask the elders of Judah (whom he had counted as his friends many years before; see 1 Sam 30:26 and comment) why they should be the "last" to bring the king back to the city. The men of Israel would later chide the men of Judah by claiming that Israel, not Judah, was the "first" to speak of bringing the king back (v.43)—although of course the desire to do so was by no means unanimous throughout Israel (cf. v.10). In the meantime David is privy to the substance of the ongoing discussions, the news of which has reached him at his "quarters" in Mahanaim (v.11, lit., "house"; the same Heb. word refers to David's "palace" in Jerusalem earlier in the verse). At least partly because of his ancestry (cf. Ruth 4:12, 18–22), David senses a special tie between himself and the Judahite elders; so he repeats his incredulous question: "Why should you be the last to bring back the king?" (v.12b). His close relationship to them as he describes it in v.12a reads literally as follows: "My brothers are you [emphatic], my bone and my flesh are you [emphatic]."

> It can of course be argued that this is reference to blood ties. But such can be the case only in a most general sense. More likely, "brother" and "bone and flesh" refer to the sharing of covenant oaths. Pedersen [*Israel: Its Life and Culture I–II,* pp. 57–60] shows that "brother" refers to all those who have ties of community and commitments to solidarity. Thus David's reference here is not to blood ties, though they may be present, but rather that mutual covenant commitments must be honored because the vows assume fidelity through thick and thin. (Brueggemann, "Of the Same Flesh and Bone," p. 536)

"Bone and flesh," rendered by the NIV as "own flesh and blood" (v.12), describes a claim to relationship with David made earlier by the tribes of Israel as well (see 5:1

and comment). It is the men of Judah, however, who will try to convince the Israelites that David is more "closely related to us" (v.42) than he is to them.

To "Amasa" (emphatic, v.13) also—clearly a blood relative of David (see 17:25 and comment)—Zadok and Abiathar are to say, "Are you [emphatic] not my own flesh and blood?" Although Joab was also related to David (see 1 Sam 26:6 and comment), he was Absalom's chief executioner as well (cf. 18:14–15), and thus his position as David's army commander (cf. 18:2; see also comments on 8:16; 1 Sam 26:6) is in jeopardy (cf. in addition his recent rebuke of the king, however well received [see vv.5–8 and comments]). Echoing verbatim the strong oath of self-imprecation that he took earlier on another occasion (cf. 3:35; see comment on 1 Sam 20:13), David replaces Joab with Amasa as the commander of his army "from now on" (v.13; lit., "all the days"), an emphatic expression that the NIV translates "for life" in a similar context (1 Sam 28:2). Ironically, some time earlier "Absalom had appointed Amasa over the army [of Israel] in place of Joab" (17:25), and now Joab is ousted as Judah's army commander as well. "Still the practical politician, David sought by maintaining Amasa as commander-in-chief to placate the dissident elements in the east who had been allied with Absalom. . . . Thus David had met the challenge of Transjordanic Israel and had proved the master" (Curtis, "East Is East . . . ," p. 358).

Although it is impossible to know for certain whether it was David who "won over the hearts of all the men [*'îš*] of Judah" (v.14; the Lucianic recension of the LXX makes Amasa the subject), the end result is that they send word to the king to return to Jerusalem with all his "men" (*'aḇāḏîm*, lit., "servants," "officials"). Happy to comply with their request, David leaves Mahanaim and arrives at the Jordan River (v.15a). The question concerning whether Israel (vv.9–10) or Judah (vv.11–12) would "bring the king back" (vv.10, 11, 12) is resolved—at least temporarily—in favor of Judah.

**15b–23** Various other significant constituencies, however, also vie for David's approval. Shimei the Benjamite (vv.15b–23), Mephibosheth the Saulide (vv.24–30), and Barzillai the Gileadite (vv.31–39) are the three key figures that represent them (see comment on 19:9–43). Each section is characterized at the outset as a meeting scene: "Judah had come to Gilgal to go out and meet the king" (v.15b); "Mephibosheth, Saul's grandson, also went down to meet the king" (v.24); "Barzillai the Gileadite also came down from Rogelim to cross the Jordan with the king" (v.31). Eskhult correctly observes that the three episodes "are all commenced by a circumstantial clause of the type (*wə*)*subj–qṭl*" (*Studies in Verbal Aspect and Narrative Technique*, p. 67): *wîhûḏāh bā'* ("Now [the men of] Judah had come," v.15b); *ûmepiḇōšeṯ ben-šā'ûl yāraḏ* ("Mephibosheth, Saul's grandson, also went down," v.24); *ûḇarzillay haggil'āḏî yāraḏ* ("Barzillai the Gileadite also came down," v.31). That "Judah" in v.15b means "the men of Judah" (NIV) is clear in that it is flanked in vv.14, 16 by the phrase *'îš yehûḏāh* in reference to the same entity. They intend to bring the king "across the Jordan" (v.15b, cf. v.41) from the eastern side to Gilgal (perhaps modern Khirbet el-Mefjer, about four miles west of the Jordan and sixteen miles northeast of Jerusalem), from which he—like Joshua before him (cf. Josh 10:7)—would lead his followers to ultimate triumph over the land.

Accompanying the men of Judah is "Shimei son of Gera, the Benjamite from Bahurim" (v.16; see 16:5, 11 and comments). He who had earlier been quick to curse David and pelt him with stones (see 16:5–14 and comments) now hastens ("hurried," v.16; "rushed," v.17) to beg for mercy (vv.18b–20). With him are not only a "thousand" (perhaps here "military unit"; see comments on 18:1, 4; 1 Sam 4:2) of his countrymen but also "Ziba, the steward of Saul's household, and his fifteen sons and twenty servants" (v.17; see 9:1, 2, 9, 10 and comments). Shimei and his companions have come to take the king and his household westward across the "ford" of the Jordan (v.18; see 15:28 and comment). In addition, they are eager to "do whatever he wished" (lit., "do whatever is/was pleasing in his eyes")—just as Mephibosheth (v.27, "do whatever pleases you") and Barzillai (v.37, "Do . . . whatever pleases you") would later desire for David as well (same Heb. idiom in all three cases).

Because the reference to Ziba in v.17 has temporarily interrupted the story of Shimei, the latter is reintroduced in v.18b as "Shimei son of Gera" (cf. v.16). "The function of the full 'XbY' name form can be explained . . . as indicating the refocussing of attention on Shimei" (Clines, "X, X *Ben* Y, *Ben* Y," p. 276). Arriving in David's presence on the eastern side of the Jordan, Shimei, while fully admitting that earlier he "did wrong," begs that the king not hold him "guilty" (v.19, the verb and substantive are both forms of the root *'wh*). On another occasion David declares that anyone "whose sin (the LORD) does not count against him" is blessed (Ps 32:2), a statement that employs the same phrase here rendered "May (my lord) not hold me guilty." Although punishment is only to be expected when one "does wrong" (7:14; cf. 24:17), Shimei hopes that David will not "remember" (v.19) what he had done to the king on the day he left Jerusalem (see 16:5–14 and comments)—a plea that contrasts sharply with Abigail's request that David "remember" her and her good deeds on his behalf when the Lord has brought him success (1 Sam 25:31). Shimei earnestly desires that David "put . . . out of his mind" (v.19) the spiteful and foolish behavior of his servant; he does not want the king to "take it to heart" (as the Heb. idiom is elsewhere translated; cf. 1 Sam 21:12).

A short time ago Shimei had called David a "man of blood" (16:7–8), a "scoundrel" (16:7); now he addresses him respectfully—indeed, in an attitude of complete submission—as "my lord (the king)" and refers to himself as "your servant" (vv.19–20; see 1 Sam 25:24 and comment). Recognizing how inappropriate his earlier conduct was, he readily confesses, "I [emphatic] have sinned" (v.20). In so doing he echoes the similarly contrite words of Saul, his deceased fellow Benjamite (see 1 Sam 26:21 and comment). In Shimei's mind, however, his misdeeds are part of a past that he would just as soon forget. It is now "today," and he wants to be the "first of the whole house of Joseph" (v.20)—the "first" among all the Israelites (cf. v.43; for "house of Joseph" [the largest and most prominent of the northern bribes; cf. Gen 49:22–26; Josh 17:17] as synecdoche for "Israel," cf. Josh 18:5; Judg 1:22, 35; 1 Kings 11:28; Amos 5:6; Obad 18; Zech 10:6)—to "meet my lord the king" (implying his desire that David return to his rightful place in Jerusalem).

But "Abishai son of Zeruiah" (v.21), one of David's army commanders (see 18:2 and comment), will hear none of it. Because David, "the LORD's anointed" (see comments on 5:3; 1 Sam 16:13), had been "cursed" by Shimei (see 16:10–12 and comments), Abishai wants him "put to death," not only because such rashness is entirely in character for Abishai (see 16:9 and comment), but perhaps also because "to curse the king was considered a capital offense. . . , like cursing God (I Kings 21:10; cf. Ex 22:27 [EV v.28])" (Talmon, p. 30).

David's reply to Abishai (v.22) echoes verbatim his response to him in an identical context earlier: "What do you and I have in common, you sons of Zeruiah?" (see 16:10 and comments). By using *hayyôm* ("today," "this day") three times in rapid succession, David underscores the fact that he himself is in full control of the situation and that he alone will determine Shimei's fate. Although "you have become" is plural and it is therefore virtually certain that David is speaking to Joab as well as to Abishai (cf. "sons [pl.] of Zeruiah" earlier in the verse), it is equally clear that Abishai is the main addressee (*śāṭān* ["adversary"] is singular). The word for "adversary" was later specialized to refer to "the Adversary (par excellence)"—namely, Satan (see comment on 1 Sam 29:4).

In the present context "my adversary" probably means "a legal accuser on my behalf" since the language of both Shimei (vv.19–20) and Abishai (v.21) is demonstrably forensic (for discussion cf. Peggy L. Day, "Abishai the *śāṭān* in 2 Samuel 19:17–24," CBQ 49, 4 [1987]: 543–47). Wanting to know why Abishai thinks he has to stand up for the king's rights, David rhetorically asks whether anyone should be "put to death in Israel today"—that is, summarily executed. In reprising the similar statesmanlike declaration of his predecessor Saul (see 1 Sam 11:13 and comment), David exhibits "a flash of that magnanimity which marked him at his best" (Gunn, "David and the Gift," p. 32). As in the case of Saul's words to Jonathan in 1 Samuel 20:30, David's "Do I not know" is intended as a rebuke to Abishai. "In his earlier rejection of Abishai's desire to kill, David gave a theological reason (16:11–12). Now David gives a more practical reason. David ['I' is emphatic] is king over Israel' (v.22)" (Brueggemann, *First and Second Samuel,* p. 327). Turning to Shimei, he promises him on oath that his life will be spared (v.23). Although at the end of his days David will change his mind and strongly urge Shimei's execution (cf. 1 Kings 2:8–9), at least for now geopolitical considerations would seem to demand his "affirmation of Shimei as a larger strategic gesture to reclaim the loyalty of the north" (ibid.).

**24–30** The second—and central—of the three key men who come to meet David is "Mephibosheth, Saul's grandson" (v.24; see comments on 4:4; 9:6). The pericope that describes the meeting is delimited by the balanced statements "the king . . . returned [*bā'*] safely" (v.24) and "the king has arrived [*bā'*] . . . safely" (v.30).

David's exile from Jerusalem has encompassed many days if not weeks, and during that entire time ("from the day the king left until the day he returned," v.24) Mephibosheth has not cared for his feet, mustache, or clothes in a way befitting a guest of royalty (cf. 9:7, 10–12). That he has not "taken care of ['*āśāh*] his feet" probably means that he has not "trimmed his toenails" (cf. LXX; for discussion cf. McCarter, *II Samuel,* pp. 417, 421) since the following clause ("trimmed his mustache") also uses the verb *'āśāh.* Indeed, the two clauses are identical except for the object of the verb (*welō'-'āśāh raglāyw welō'-'āśāh śepāmô,* lit., "and he did not do his feet, and he did not do his mustache"). To "cover one's mustache" (NIV, "cover [the lower part of] one's face") was a sign of ceremonial uncleanness (cf. Lev 13:45), mourning (cf. Ezek 24:17, 22), or shame (cf. Mic 3:7). Mephibosheth's refusal to wash his clothes is likewise more than a matter of careless hygiene: It demonstrates his desire to remain ceremonially unclean during the king's absence (cf. Exod 19:10, 14).

Employing the verb translated "left" (*hlk*) in v.24, David wants to know why Mephibosheth decided not to "go" with him (v.25) when he was forced to flee from Absalom (cf. 1 Sam 30:22 for the potentially negative implications of not accompanying a king on risky ventures). Mephibosheth counters by stating that he had indeed wanted to "go" (*hlk,* v.26) with the king but that since he is "lame" (see comments on 5:8; 9:13; see also 4:4 and comment) he needed to have his donkey "saddled" so that he could "ride on" it. But his servant "Ziba" (not in the MT of v.26, the name is supplied by the NIV for purposes of clarity) had betrayed him. Mephibosheth may be implying that the string of donkeys Ziba had earlier "saddled" (see 16:1 and comment) and brought to David for his household to "ride on" (16:2) included Mephibosheth's own private mount, leaving him without means of transportation. He further accuses Ziba of having "slandered" (*rgl*) him in David's presence (v.27)—at the very time when Mephibosheth was experiencing discomfort and humiliation by not taking care of his "feet" (*rgl*, v.24).

Mephibosheth, however, consoles himself with "the confidence that David will not be fooled by the misrepresentation of Ziba, but will get to the bottom of the affair and separate truth from falsehood" (McKane, *Prophets and Wise Men*, p. 59). After all, he asserts, King David is "like an angel of God" (v.27) and therefore not only "knows everything that happens in the land" (14:20) but also exercises divine wisdom "in discerning good and evil" (14:17; see comments on 14:17, 20; 1 Sam 29:9). He readily admits that Saul's descendants—including, presumably, himself—"deserved" only "death" (v.28, lit., "were men of death"; cf. 1 Kings 2:26; see also comments on the Heb. expression "son[s] of death" in 12:5; 1 Sam 20:31; 26:16) from David, whose life Saul had persistently and mercilessly tried to take from him (see comments on 4:8; 1 Sam 20:1). By contrast, Mephibosheth is grateful that David has given him the privilege—at least as he himself understands it—of being among those who "eat at" the king's "table" (v.28; see comment on 9:7). He does not use his own "right(s)" (lit., "righteousness") as a basis for claiming royal reward (see comment on 1 Sam 26:23), nor does he sense that he deserves to make further "appeals" to the king (lit., "cries"; same Heb. root as in v.4).

David responds to Mephibosheth by ordering him and Ziba to divide "the fields" (v.29)—"the land" that he had originally restored to Mephibosheth (see 9:7 and comment; same Heb. word in both cases) but had later turned over to Ziba (cf. 16:4). Did David's decision to share the estate between the two men reflect "his conclusion that there was no possibility of ascertaining which of them was telling the truth" (McKane, *Prophets and Wise Men*, p. 59)? Or was it "a compromise taking the place of a judgement based on fact-finding, which might have been too troublesome at that time" (Z.W. Falk, "Hebrew Legal Terms: III," JSS 14, 1 [1969]: 41)? Probably neither. As David's son Solomon would later threaten to divide a living baby in order to discern which of two mothers was telling the truth (cf. 1 Kings 3:24–25), so David here demands the division of the fields in order to discern whether Mephibosheth or Ziba is the liar. David Damrosch observes that just as the real mother of the living baby offered the child to the false claimant in order to preserve its life (cf. 1 Kings 3:26), so also Mephibosheth offers the entire estate to Ziba (*The Narrative Covenant: Transformations of Genre in the Growth of Biblical Literature* [San Francisco: Harper, 1987], p. 247; cf. v.30).

Indeed, the comparison between the episodes of Solomon and David may be even closer. The Talmudic tractate Shabbat 56b records a comment of R. Judah: "When David said to Mephibosheth, 'Thou and Ziba divide the land,' a Heavenly Voice said to him, 'Rehoboam and Jeroboam shall divide the kingdom.'" If the baby remained undivided because Solomon had "wisdom from God" (1 Kings 3:28), and if the command of David (who was "like an angel of God," v.27) to "divide the fields" (v.29) became moot because of Mephibosheth's magnanimity (v.30), the death of Solomon would eventually bring about the division of the kingdom (cf. 1 Kings 11:11–13) and the divine assignment of ten of the twelve tribes of Israel to Jeroboam I (cf. 1 Kings 11:29–31; see also comment on v.43 below).

**31–39** The third and last of the three representatives to meet David at the Jordan is "Barzillai the Gileadite" from "Rogelim" (v.31; see 17:27 and comments). Verse 31, which speaks of Barzillai's leaving his hometown, and v.39, which records his return to his home, form an *inclusio* that frames the literary unit (the two verses also share the name "Barzillai," refer to "the king," and include the phrase "cross[ed] the Jordan"; in both cases the verbal form is *wayya'ᵃḇōr*). A chiastic outline characterizes the section (cf. similarly Fokkelman, *King David*, p. 305):

A. Introduction (19:31–32)
  B. David speaks to Barzillai (19:33).
    C. Barzillai speaks to David (19:34–37).
  B′. David speaks to Barzillai (19:38).
A′. Conclusion (19:39)

In some respects the presence of Barzillai at the Jordan is more significant than that of either Shimei or Mephibosheth. It is not only that he symbolizes the vast Transjordanian regions, the control of which were crucial to any Israelite king, but also that with respect to David he has the prestige ("eighty years of age," v.32; cf. Ps 90:10) and wherewithal ("very wealthy," v.32; cf. the description of Nabal in 1 Sam 25:2) to "send him on his way" back to Jerusalem (v.31; cf. 1 Sam 9:26). "He" (emphatic) it was, after all, who along with others "had provided for the king" (v.32) during the royal exile in Mahanaim (see 17:27–29 and comments).

David makes it clear, however, that he wants to repay Barzillai's kindness: "You [emphatic] cross over with me" (v.33, lit. tr.). David's goal is to induce his friend to take up residence with him in Jerusalem so that the king can "provide" for him (v.33) as he had earlier "provided" for the king (v.32; for discussion of *kwl* with a more inclusive meaning than simply "to feed," cf. Alan J. Hauser, *From Carmel to Horeb: Elijah in Crisis*, JSOT suppl. series 85 [Sheffield: Almond, 1990], pp. 14, 85 n. 9).

But Barzillai protests that the number of years left in his life is limited at best and that therefore it would make no sense for him to move to Jerusalem (v.34). He points out that he is "now" (v.35; lit., "today"—i.e., "at this very moment") eighty years old (see comment on v.32). In stating that he cannot tell the difference "between what is good and what is not" (lit., "between good and evil"), Barzillai may be implying that he is too old to appreciate the good life at David's court, since it is not necessarily only little children who are unable to distinguish good from bad (cf. Deut 1:39; Isa 7:15–16; Jonah 4:11).

At the same time, however, since Barzillai's words echo 14:17, Ackerman may be correct in asserting that

> these three passages [14:17, 20; 19:35] combine to articulate a theme that runs throughout the Court History: the role of the king involves a keen discernment that helps him judge between good and evil. It is almost a superhuman knowledge that is required, like that of the angel of God [see comment on v.27]—bridging the epistemological gap among humans, as well as between the human and the divine. Thus, the phrase heaped on the king [in 14:17, 20] is also a challenge—both to the king and to the reader—to read situation and text closely, to perceive what is going on and why. Can anyone—characters or reader—discern good and evil? (p. 42; see also comment on 14:17)

In any event, the aged Barzillai, like other elderly sages of his time and all times, observes that his taste buds have been dulled and his ability to "hear" singing (the Heb. verb intends, more precisely, "*listen to* . . . with satisfaction or enjoyment" [S.R. Driver, *Notes on the Books of Samuel,* p. 337]) has declined (v.35; cf. Eccl 12:4). Like Hushai in the parallel literary section (15:13–37; see comment on 15:1–12), Barzillai does not want to be a "burden" to David (v.35; see 15:33 and comment), perhaps in the sense that he would require constant care and attention (cf. Symon Patrick, p. 548). He wants only to accompany the king across the Jordan "for a short distance" (v.36) and has no desire for further rewards. He will then return to Rogelim, where he will die and be interred in the family burial site (v.37; see 2:32 and comment). If the king agrees, Kimham (probably one of Barzillai's sons, a tradition preserved in some LXX MSS [cf. BHS]; cf. 1 Kings 2:7) will be Barzillai's surrogate at the royal court. To the final request of Barzillai to David—"Do for him [Kimham] whatever pleases you [David]" (v.37)—the king replies, "I [emphatic] will do for him whatever pleases you [Barzillai]" (v.38; for this idiom as a lexical link to the parallel literary section, see comment on vv.9–43). David then adds that he is prepared to do for Barzillai anything his friend desires.

Formalities concluded, the crossing of the Jordan by the king and his party takes place (v.39) opposite Gilgal (v.40; see v.15b and comment). Before Barzillai returns to his home, David kisses him (for kissing as an act of royal protocol, see comment on 14:33) and gives him his "blessing" (or, perhaps better, "farewell"; see comment on 13:25; cf. the NIV mg. on Gen 47:10; for *nšq* used alone in the sense of "kiss good-by," cf. Gen 31:28; Ruth 1:14; 1 Kings 19:20).

**40–43** Like its counterpart (vv.9–15a; see comment on vv.9–43), vv.40–43 address the question of whether it is Israel or Judah that will accomplish the vital mission of bringing David back to Jerusalem. Further tying together the two sections is the use of "brothers" in the general sense of allies or compatriots (vv.12, 41; see comment on v.12). After a brief introduction (v.40), the "men of Israel" and the "men of Judah" speak alternately (v.41; v.42; v.43a), with the men of Judah having the final say—although exactly what they say is left unrecorded (v.43b).

David's escort had consisted of "all the troops of Judah" and "half the troops of Israel" (v.40). Since Israel had a much larger army to begin with (see 17:11 and comment), that only half its troops had participated in the crossing might be understood merely in terms of logistics. On the other hand, perhaps the narrator is subtly granting Judah pride of place (in any case, Judah, David's tribe, is mentioned first). The acrimony between the two groups increases when the men of Israel complain to the king that the men of Judah—ostensibly their "brothers" (v.41; see comment above)—might as well have "kidnapped" David and his men (as the verb here rendered "steal . . . away" is translated in Exod 21:16; Deut 24:7) to keep as many as possible of the men of Israel from sharing the privilege of accompanying the king westward to Gilgal.

The men of Judah have a ready answer, of course: As a member of their tribe, David is more "closely related" to Judah than he is to Israel (v.42). Thus there is no need for the men of Israel to be angry over what seems to the men of Judah to be perfectly natural. Nor have the latter taken advantage of their relationship to the king. Indeed, they strongly deny that they have either "eaten any" of his provisions or "taken anything" from his supplies (the force of both finite verbs in the MT is strengthened by a preceding infinitive absolute form).

But the men of Israel reject all such explanations. Judah is only one tribe, while Israel has ten "shares" (v.43, lit., "hands"; cf. Gen 47:24 ["fifths"]; 2 Kings 11:7 ["companies"]) in the king—that is ten tribes in the overall kingdom (for Ugar. *yd*, "hand," meaning "share" [pl. *ydt*, as in the Heb. of v.43 (v.44 MT)], cf. *ydty*, "my portions" [Baal V.i.21]; for Akkad. *qātu*, "hand," in the sense of "share [of an inheritance/estate]," cf. *The Assyrian Dictionary* [Chicago: Oriental Institute, 1982], 13:196–97). The fact that the only other occurrence of *'eśer yāḏôṯ* ("ten shares") is in Daniel 1:20 ("ten times"), where the figure ten is doubtless metaphorical, leads Conroy to the conclusion that "*'śr ydwt* is more likely to be a round figure expressing superiority . . . than a reference to the ten northern tribes" (p. 123 n. 32). Far more plausible, however, is comparison with "the tearing of Ahijah's mantle into twelve pieces giving Jeroboam ten (1 Kings 11:30–31, 35). In these last two texts [v.43; 1 Kings 11:30–31, 35] there is clearly a stylized reference to the restricted Israel, to the 'Ten Tribes' of the divided kingdom" (Kallai, "Judah and Israel," p. 256). Such elements in the narrative "point forward to, and possibly reflect awareness of, the later division of the kingdom" (Gordon, *I & II*, p. 293) and have obvious implications for the date of the writing of the books of Samuel (indeed, KD states categorically that "they were not written till after the division of the kingdom under Solomon's successor" [p. 11]).

Since the men of Israel "have ten shares in the king," they conclude that it logically follows ("besides," v.43) that they "have a greater claim on David" than Judah has. David's sizable land grant to Mephibosheth (cf. 9:7–13) and—even more impressive—the extensive tribal territories to which Ish-Bosheth fell heir (see 2:9–10 and comments) give substance to the assertion of Israel's men. They therefore want to know why the men of Judah "treat" them "with contempt" (v.43, lit., "humble" them; cf. Isa 9:1; 23:9), and they conclude their part of the debate by reminding the Judahites that they—the men of Israel—were the "first" to speak of returning David to his rightful place in Jerusalem (see v.20 and comment).

The words of the men of Israel, however, cause the men of Judah to respond more "harshly" still. By using the root *qšh*, the narrator not only echoes the earlier fears of David as he anticipated King Saul's wrath (cf. 1 Sam 20:10) but also foreshadows the foolish attitude of Rehoboam as he—king of Judah and potentially king of all Israel—irrevocably alienates the northern tribes (cf. 1 Kings 12:13 = 2 Chron 10:13).

## Notes

---

**9** (10 MT) "Arguing with each other" renders נָדוֹן (*nāḏôn*), a Niphal participle from דין (*dyn*, "judge, dispute"; cf. LXX *κρινόμενος* [*krinomenos*]). But since this would be the only example of Niphal *dyn* in the OT, perhaps the original reading was נָלוֹן (*nālôn*), a Niphal participle from לין II (*lyn*, "grumble, murmur"; cf. the Lucianic recension of the LXX *γογγύζοντες* [*gongyzontes*]), used with relative frequency of Israel's grumbling against the Lord's servants (cf. Num 16:41 [MT 17:6]: וַיִּלֹּנוּ [*wayyillōnû*], LXX *ἐγόγγυσαν* [*egongysan*]; cf. BHS) and employed once in the absolute sense (Ps 59:15: וילינו [*wylynw*, "howl"], LXX *γογγύσουσιν* [*gongysousin*]).

**13** (14 MT) The root of תֹּמְרוּ (*tōmerû*, "[you ] say") is אמר (*'mr*), the quiescent א (') of תֹּאמְרוּ (*tō'merû*) having dropped out in the orthography.

**18** (19 MT) "They crossed at the ford" (NIV) presumably assumes dittography of ה (*h*) in the MT ועברה העברה (*w'brh h'brh*) and defective writing of the verb in וְעָבְרוּ הָעֲבָרָה (*wᵉ'āḇᵉru hā'ᵃḇārāh,* "They crossed back and forth"; frequentative use of the perfect with waw consecutive, for which cf. GKC, sec. 112*e–o;* cf. similarly S.R. Driver, *Notes on the Books of Samuel,* p. 335, who states further that the words "will then describe the purpose with which Ziba and his attendants . . . came down to the Jordan").

**31** (32 MT) "From there" renders אֶת־בַּיַּרְדֵּן (*'et-bayyardēn*), a syntactically impossible construction in which the sign of the direct object (*'et-*) is followed by a phrase that means "in/from the Jordan." The best solution is perhaps to omit *'et-* (as a few Heb. MSS do; cf. BHS) and to translate "from the Jordan" (= NIV "from there") with the Lucianic recension of the LXX.

**32** (33 MT) שִׂיבָתוֹ (*šîḇāṯô*), translated "his stay," is a difficult form at best if derived from the root ישׁב (*yšb*), which is called for here. It is thus better to read the infinite construct form שִׁבְתּוֹ (*šiḇtô*) with some Hebrew MSS (cf. BHS).

**40** (41 MT) *Qere* העבירו (*h'byrw,* "had taken . . . over") is much to be preferred to the syntactically inept *Kethiv* ויעברו (*wy'brw*), which probably arose by contamination from the same form ("bring . . . across") in v.41 (42 MT) (where it is used correctly).

---

## 19. *Sheba's rebellion*

### 20:1–22

1 Now a troublemaker named Sheba son of Bicri, a Benjamite,
happened to be there. He sounded the trumpet and shouted,

"We have no share in David,
  no part in Jesse's son!
Every man to his tent, O Israel!"

2 So all the men of Israel deserted David to follow Sheba son of Bicri.
But the men of Judah stayed by their king all the way from the Jordan to
Jerusalem.
3 When David returned to his palace in Jerusalem, he took the ten
concubines he had left to take care of the palace and put them in a
house under guard. He provided for them, but did not lie with them.
They were kept in confinement till the day of their death, living as
widows.
4 Then the king said to Amasa, "Summon the men of Judah to come to
me within three days, and be here yourself." 5 But when Amasa went to
summon Judah, he took longer than the time the king had set for him.
6 David said to Abishai, "Now Sheba son of Bicri will do us more harm
than Absalom did. Take your master's men and pursue him, or he will
find fortified cities and escape from us." 7 So Joab's men and the
Kerethites and Pelethites and all the mighty warriors went out under the
command of Abishai. They marched out from Jerusalem to pursue
Sheba son of Bicri.
8 While they were at the great rock in Gibeon, Amasa came to meet
them. Joab was wearing his military tunic, and strapped over it at his
waist was a belt with a dagger in its sheath. As he stepped forward, it
dropped out of its sheath.
9 Joab said to Amasa, "How are you, my brother?" Then Joab took
Amasa by the beard with his right hand to kiss him. 10 Amasa was not on
his guard against the dagger in Joab's hand, and Joab plunged it into
his belly, and his intestines spilled out on the ground. Without being
stabbed again, Amasa died. Then Joab and his brother Abishai pursued
Sheba son of Bicri.
11 One of Joab's men stood beside Amasa and said, "Whoever favors
Joab, and whoever is for David, let him follow Joab!" 12 Amasa lay

wallowing in his blood in the middle of the road, and the man saw that
all the troops came to a halt there. When he realized that everyone who
came up to Amasa stopped, he dragged him from the road into a field
and threw a garment over him. 13After Amasa had been removed from
the road, all the men went on with Joab to pursue Sheba son of Bicri.
14Sheba passed through all the tribes of Israel to Abel Beth Maacah
and through the entire region of the Berites, who gathered together and
followed him. 15All the troops with Joab came and besieged Sheba in
Abel Beth Maacah. They built a siege ramp up to the city, and it stood
against the outer fortifications. While they were battering the wall to
bring it down, 16a wise woman called from the city, "Listen! Listen! Tell
Joab to come here so I can speak to him." 17He went toward her, and
she asked, "Are you Joab?"

"I am," he answered.

She said, "Listen to what your servant has to say."

"I'm listening," he said.

18She continued, "Long ago they used to say, 'Get your answer at
Abel,' and that settled it. 19We are the peaceful and faithful in Israel. You
are trying to destroy a city that is a mother in Israel. Why do you want to
swallow up the LORD's inheritance?"

20"Far be it from me!" Joab replied, "Far be it from me to swallow up
or destroy! 21That is not the case. A man named Sheba son of Bicri,
from the hill country of Ephraim, has lifted up his hand against the king,
against David. Hand over this one man, and I'll withdraw from the city."

The woman said to Joab, "His head will be thrown to you from the wall."

22Then the woman went to all the people with her wise advice, and
they cut off the head of Sheba son of Bicri and threw it to Joab. So he
sounded the trumpet, and his men dispersed from the city, each
returning to his home. And Joab went back to the king in Jerusalem.

The account of Sheba's rebellion against David serves as a counterpoise to the story of Absalom's conspiracy (15:1–12) in chapters 15–20, which constitute the major part of the narrative that comprises chapters 13–20 (more precisely, 13:1–20:22), the longest definable literary section of the Court History of David (chs. 9–20; see comments on 13:1–22; 15:1–12). David's statement to Abishai in v.6 highlights the comparison between the two episodes and underscores the seriousness of Sheba's revolt: "Now Sheba son of Bicri will do us more harm than Absalom did."

Since vv.1 and 22b both contain the phrases *wayyiṯqaʿ baššōp̱ār* ("he sounded the trumpet") and *'îš le'ōhālāyw* ("every man to his tent"/"each returning to his home"), the two verses form an *inclusio* that brackets the literary unit, which may be outlined chiastically:

A. Sheba deserts David (20:1–2).
 B. David takes steps to foil Sheba (20:3–7).
  C. Joab kills his rival Amasa (20:8–13).
 B′. The wise woman of Abel defeats Sheba (20:14–22a).
A′. Joab returns to David (20:22b).

**1–2** Mentioned eight times throughout the chapter, the rebel is always given his full name, "Sheba son of Bicri" (vv.1, 2, 6, 7, 10, 13, 21, 22; the NIV has added "Sheba" in vv.14, 15 for purposes of clarity), a highly unusual phenomenon that calls for explanation. In Jeremiah 2:23 the people of Judah are compared to "a swift she-camel [*biḵrāh*], running here and there" (i.e., rebellious), and Isaiah 60:6 speaks of "young camels [*bik̲rê*] of Midian and Ephah," mentioning also the land of "Sheba" in that context. Clines observes that

> the implication could perhaps be that Sheba is a true son of בֶּכֶר [*bek̲er*], stubborn, rebellious, and self-willed. It may be more than coincidental that in Isa. lx 6 Sheba is referred to as a region of camels (בכר [*bkr*]). Of course there is no real connection between the place name שְׁבָא [*šᵉb̲ā'*] and the personal name שֶׁבַע [*šeb̲a'*], but it is not impossible that a link between the refractory Sheba son of בֶּכֶר [*bek̲er*] and a well-known home of the בֶּכֶר was intended by the story-teller, who referred invariably to "Sheba b. Bichri" in order to reinforce his view of Sheba's character, which he blackens at the very beginning with the epithet "son [*sic*] of Belial" (xx 1). ("X, X *Ben* Y, *Ben* Y," p. 277)

Sheba is introduced as a "troublemaker" (v.1 [cf. 1 Sam 10:27; 30:22], lit., "man of Belial"; see comment on "scoundrel" in 16:7; see also note on 1 Sam 1:16 and comments on 1 Sam 25:17, 25), a "'reckless' person, one who disregards the proprieties or disturbs the *status quo*" (Gunn, *The Story of King David,* p. 140 n. 20). Reference to him as a "Benjamite" marks him as a northerner and perhaps a Saulide partisan as well (cf. 1 Sam 9:1). The narrator's statement that Sheba "happened" (v.1) to be at the scene of the debate that ends chapter 19 ties him contextually to Absalom, who "happened" to meet David's men (18:9) and thus lost his life (the Niphal of *qr'* in the sense of "happen," rare at best, occurs in only these two places in the books of Samuel). It is as though the text is telling its readers that Sheba picks up the baton dropped by Absalom.

Sounding a ram's-horn trumpet, Sheba delivers (perhaps even composes) a brief but powerful statement (v.1) that would become a rallying cry for future secessionists (cf. 1 Kings 12:16 = 2 Chron 10:16). He declares that he and his compatriots have no "share" in David's realm (i.e., David's inheritance; cf. Gen 31:14) and no "part" in "Jesse's son." Clines to the contrary notwithstanding ("X, X *Ben* Y, *Ben* Y," pp. 285–86), the phrase "Jesse's son" is doubtless used in a disparaging or contemptuous sense here (see comment on the parallelism between "David" and "son of Jesse" in 1 Sam 25:10; see also comments on 1 Sam 20:27; 22:7). Sheba, having lost patience with David, orders "every man to his tent" (i.e., his home; cf. v.22; 1 Kings 8:66; the phrase apparently derives "from a time when the nation dwelt actually in tents" [S.R. Driver, *Notes on the Books of Samuel,* p. 148]). Despite the fact that David had been divinely anointed king over "Israel" (v.1; cf. 19:21; see comments on 5:3; 12:7; 1 Sam 16:13), Sheba apparently suspects that David's loyalties basically lie in the south and therefore urges the representatives of the northern tribes to recommend secession.

Although the men of Judah "stayed by" their king (v.2; lit., "clung to" him; cf. Ruth 1:14; the verb is used figuratively "of loyalty, affection etc., [sometimes] with idea of physical proximity retained" [BDB, p. 179]), escorting him "all the way from the Jordan to Jerusalem," the "men of Israel"—following Sheba's lead—deserted David.

Gunn makes the important observation that "nowhere is it said that Sheba actually engaged in armed rebellion, merely that he called for the men of Israel to disband and go home, though of course the implication is secession" (*The Story of King David,* p. 140 n. 20). The time to secede is not yet ripe, however. "It is no coincidence that independence is declared in practically identical terms in the cry of 2 Sam 20:1b and 1 Kgs 12:16. Sheba ben Bichri was before his time—so a 'worthless fellow.' After Ahijah's intervention, the time had come" (Antony F. Campbell, *Of Prophets and Kings,* p. 83).

**3–7** The steps David takes to foil Sheba's rebellion involve three (groups of) people: concubines (v.3), Amasa (vv.4–5), Abishai (vv.6–7).

Before his flight from Jerusalem in the wake of Absalom's conspiracy, David had "left" ten concubines to "take care of" the palace (v.3; see comments on 15:16; 16:21). Returning now to his "palace," he takes the concubines who were supposed to care for the "palace" and puts them in a "house" under guard (same Heb. word in all three cases), virtually incarcerating them (indeed, the phrase *bêṯ-mišmereṯ,* here rendered "house under guard," is closely paralleled by *bêṯ mišmār,* "prison," in Gen 42:19). Although he "returned" (*bw'*) to the palace, David did not "lie" (*bw'*) with the concubines—as his treasonous son Absalom had done (see 16:21–22 and comments). To be sure, David makes certain that the concubines' needs are "provided" for (see comment on 19:33); but he also keeps them in confinement under house arrest, and they are forced to remain in that situation—as though "widows"—for the rest of their lives (v.3).

Brueggemann observes that

> the presence of concubines [at the palace in Jerusalem] suggests how much the monarchy has embraced the royal ideology of the Near East, which is inimical to the old covenant tradition. David takes a drastic step of confining the concubines and presumably having no more to do with them. His action is most likely a concession and conciliatory gesture to the north. . . . In making this move, David not only distances himself from his own former practice but also offers a contrast to the conduct of Absalom (16:21–22). (*First and Second Samuel,* p. 330)

The second step taken by David is to order Amasa (v.4), his new army commander (see 19:13 and comment), to "summon" the men of Judah (for military action; cf. Judg 4:10) to come to Jerusalem within three days, and Amasa is to be there personally as well ("yourself" is emphatic). Amasa, however, takes longer than the time allotted to him (v.5).

Apparently losing patience with Amasa (and perhaps also fearing that he may have defected), David takes the third step by giving a command to Abishai (v.6), another of his generals (see 18:2 and comment). After describing the danger if Sheba is left to do as he wishes (see comment on vv.1–22), David speaks directly and forcefully to Abishai (the MT places an emphatic "you" before "take" in v.6). He is to muster his "master's men" (i.e., David's men [cf. Hertzberg, p. 372], described further in v.7) and "pursue" Sheba (cf. vv.7, 10, 13). David is afraid that Sheba will "find" refuge in a fortified city (cf. Ps 107:4) and so "escape from us" (thus NIV, apparently following the Vul. and the Lucianic recension of the LXX; the MT *hiṣṣîl 'ênēnû* is best understood to mean "tear out our eye[s]," a metaphor meaning "do us serious injury" [cf. KD, p. 453]; for gouging out eyes as a cruel expedient, see 1 Sam 11:2 and comment; for full discussion of other options, cf. S.R. Driver, *Notes on the Books of Samuel,* p. 342).

That David ignores Joab in his planning is noteworthy (see 19:13 and comment). "Joab's men" (v.7; see 18:2 and comment) now march out "under the command of Abishai" (as the NIV justifiably renders *'aḥ$^{a}$rāyw,* lit., "after him"), who is also over the Kerethites and Pelethites (David's mercenary troops; see comments on 8:18; 15:18) as well as all the "mighty warriors" (*gibbōrîm,* perhaps also mercenaries), professional soldiers who are called David's "special guard" in 16:6; 1 Kings 1:8 (same Heb. word; see comment on 8:18) and are perhaps here to be identified with the Gittites of 15:18 (for discussion, cf. Kirkpatrick, *The Second Book of Samuel*, p. 153). The immediate task of Abishai's substantial army is to "pursue [see comment on v.6] Sheba son of Bicri" (v.7), a phrase repeated as a refrain in the next section.

**8–13** Focusing on the death of Amasa at the hands of Joab, his rival for power (see 19:13 and comment), the central section of the present literary unit (vv.1–22) divides naturally into two parts, each of which ends with the phrase "pursue[d] Sheba son of Bicri" (as does the preceding section; see v.7 and comment): Joab's murder of Amasa is reported in vv.8–10, and the removal of Amasa's body is described in vv.11–13.

The story of Amasa's death is eerily reminiscent of several other violent episodes recorded in chapters 2–4. Amasa belatedly joins Abishai's army at "the great rock [otherwise unknown; for tentative identifications, cf. McCarter, *II Samuel*, p. 429] in Gibeon" (v.8; modern el-Jib, six miles northwest of Jerusalem). Although located in the tribal territory of Benjamin, Gibeon was probably more likely to side with David than with the Saulides (see comment on 2:12). Joab is there, and he wears a "military tunic" that was doubtless much like that worn earlier by Jonathan, which included a type of belt often used to hold a sheathed dagger (see comment on 1 Sam 18:4). Not concealed, the dagger was fastened on over the tunic (cf. 1 Sam 17:39; 25:13) and was therefore in plain view. Wearing a sword or dagger at one's side did not hamper certain kinds of activity (cf. Neh 4:18).

And so it was that Joab "stepped forward" (v.8)—an ominous choice of terminology by the narrator, since the same Hebrew verb is translated "went out" and "marched out" in v.7 in a clearly military context. Joab contrives to allow his dagger to fall out of its sheath, and with "a natural motion, given such circumstances, he picks it up with his left hand and continues to greet Amasa" (Edward A. Neiderhiser, "2 Samuel 20:8–10: A Note for a Commentary," JETS 24, 3 [1981]: 210), referring to him as his "brother" (v.9, probably in the general sense of "comrade in arms" [see comment on 19:12], even though the two men were in fact blood relatives [see comment on 17:25]). Joab then "took" (lit., "seized") Amasa "by the beard" with his right hand, ostensibly to "kiss" him (v.9; for the kiss of greeting, cf. 14:33; 15:5; Gen 33:4) but in reality to kill him (cf. 1 Sam 17:35, where David is reported to have "seized" a lion "by its hair" [lit., "beard"] in order to strike and kill it). The kiss of Joab thus turns out to be the kiss of a Judas (cf. Luke 22:47–48).

"The 'accidentally' dropped sword dangling idly in [Joab's] left hand is not a recognizable danger" (Neiderhiser, "2 Samuel 20:8–10," p. 210), and therefore Amasa is "not on his guard" against it (i.e., he pays no attention to it, v.10; see comment on 1 Sam 19:2 for the importance of being vigilant). Before Amasa realizes what is happening, Joab has "plunged" the dagger into his "belly" in a frightening reprise of earlier events (see 2:23; 3:27; 4:6 and comments; in all four cases the Heb. verb is *nkh* ["thrust, stabbed, plunged"] and the noun is *ḥōmeš* ["stomach, belly"]). "Without being stabbed again" (v.10; the Heb. phrase echoes "won't strike him twice" in 1 Sam 26:8 [see comment there]), Amasa dies. "There is something almost cruelly comic about the portrait: Amasa was the man whose loss of a battle [17:25; 18:7] gained him a command [19:13], who failed to keep an appointment [20:4–5], and who could not spot the sword in his rival's hand" (Gunn, *The Story of King David*, p. 140 n. 21). After Amasa's murder, Joab and Abishai continue the pursuit of Sheba.

Even as one of Joab's men attempts to rally his comrades to the chase by linking loyalty to the discredited Joab (see comments on v.7; 19:13) with loyalty to David (v.11; cf. Exod 32:26; Josh 5:13; 2 Kings 10:6), a dramatic pause in the action is effected by the threefold use of *'āmaḏ* in vv.11 ("stood") and 12 ("came to a halt," "stopped"). The corpse of Amasa lies wallowing in its blood in the middle of the "road" (vv.12–13), right where Joab had killed him. Since the "road" (*m^e^sillāh*, "a prepared road leading across country" [TDOT, 3:278]) was doubtless a major highway used by David's troops, Amasa's body proves to be an unacceptable distraction that slows their progress as they stop to gawk. Seeing this, the man trying to rally the troops drags the body into a field and covers it with a "garment" (v.12). Only then is the pause in the action broken as all the men finally join Joab and continue the pursuit of Sheba (v.13).

**14–22a** The account of Sheba's defeat, which parallels the attempt of David to foil him (vv.3–7; see comment on vv.1–22), is divided into two unequal sections. The first episode (vv.14–15), which exhibits numerous verbal connections to the previous pericope (vv.8–13; see comments below), describes the violent siege of Abel Beth Maacah by the ruthless Joab. The second episode (vv.16–22a) relates the story of the subtler and more nuanced approach of the wise woman of Abel and illustrates the truism that less is more.

Trying to drum up support for his secessionist cause, Sheba stayed one step ahead of his pursuers as he "passed" (v.14; the same Heb. verb is rendered "went on" in v.13) throughout Israel, eventually arriving at Abel Beth Maacah, modern Abil el-Qamh, more than ninety miles north of the vicinity of Gilgal. Since Abel is four miles west of Dan (cf. 1 Kings 15:20) at the northernmost end of the land (see comment on 1 Sam 3:20), it was indeed necessary for Sheba to travel "through all the tribes of Israel" to reach it. Apparently, however, he was able to enlist only the "Berites" (v.14), who "gathered together" to follow his lead (for *qhl* [*Qere*] in the sense of assembling for mutual protection and/or [possible] warfare, cf. Josh 22:12; Judg 20:1; Esth 8:11; 9:2, 15 ["came together"], 16, 18; Ezek 38:7). Mentioned only here, *bērîm* is probably a scribal error for *biḵrîm* (LXX *en Charrei*), "Bicrites" referring to Sheba ben Bicri's own clan (cf. Baldwin, p. 280; Gordon, *I & II*, pp. 295, 362 n. 210; William White, Jr., ZPEB, 1:610). Compared to those who were ready to "follow Joab" (v.11), the number of men who "followed" Sheba (v.14) is pitiable indeed.

Lacking neither confidence nor desire when it comes to besieging cities (cf. 11:1), Joab leads his troops against Sheba in Abel Beth Maacah (v.15). If Joab is responsible for the fact that Amasa's intestines "spilled out" (*špk*) on the ground (v.10), he also takes credit for the fact that his men "built" (*špk*) a "siege ramp" at Abel (*sōl^e^lāh* ["siege ramp"] shares with *m^e^sillāh* ["highway," vv.12–13] the root *sll* ["lift up, construct"]). The ramp (cf. 2 Kings 19:32 = Isa 37:33; Jer 6:6; Ezek 4:2; 26:8) stands against the "outer fortifications" or ramparts (cf. Isa 26:1; Lam 2:8) of the city and serves as a means of access for attackers to pull down the city wall itself.

At this point a "wise woman" (unnamed, like her counterpart from Tekoa; see comment on 14:20) makes her appearance. As in 14:1–20, so also in 20:16–22a, the term "wise woman" (14:2; 20:16) is echoed at the end of its respective episode by the word "wisdom" (14:20; 20:22a ["wise advice"]), the four elements thus forming a double *inclusio* that brackets the whole. Calling out from the city (perhaps from the top of the wall), the woman of Abel pleads for patience as she shouts "Listen!" (pl.) twice to the besiegers (v.16) and speaks the same word (sing.) once to Joab (v.17). Having confirmed his identity (his name and reputation have obviously preceded him) and gained his attention, she submissively refers to herself as his "servant" (as her predecessor had earlier done to David; see 14:6 and comment). He in turn responds politely to her "Listen" by saying "I'm listening."

The wise woman now establishes the credentials of her city, her fellow citizens, and herself—not only as purveyors of wisdom but also as peacemakers. From antiquity Abel Beth Maacah has been justly famed as a place to which people resorted to find solutions for difficult problems (v.18). The woman therefore rebukes Joab for besieging the city as she speaks on behalf of its inhabitants: "We are [emphatic, lit., 'I am'] the peaceful [ones] and faithful [ones] in Israel" (v.19). Describing the admirable qualities of Abel's people, she uses language that reflects several Davidic psalms (cf. 7:4; 12:1; 31:23). By way of contrast ("You" is emphatic), she accuses Joab of trying to "destroy" (lit., "put to death") a city that is a "mother [see comment and Notes on Metheg Ammah in 8:1] in Israel." The epithet "mother in Israel" is applied elsewhere only to the prophetess Deborah (cf. Judg 5:7).

> Abel is characterized in the proverb [v.18] as a city with a long reputation for wisdom and faithfulness to the tradition of Israel. It is, therefore, a mother in the same way Deborah was: a creator and hence a symbol of the unity that bound Israel together under one God Yahweh. And it is the wise woman's implicit appeal to this unity that stops Joab in his tracks. (Camp, "Wise Women of 2 Samuel," p. 28)

The woman wishes to know why Joab would want to swallow up "the LORD's inheritance" (v.19; cf. 21:3; 1 Sam 26:19), a phrase referring either to the land and people of Israel or to the share of Abel Beth Maacah in that land (see 14:16 and comment).

Impressed by the logic of the woman's arguments as well as by her sincerity, Joab relents. In the strongest possible terms ("Far be it from me!" [v.20]; cf. 1 Sam 2:30; 12:23; cf. also 1 Sam 14:45; 20:2, 9 ["Never!"]; 22:15 ["Of course not!"]; 24:6; 26:11 ["The LORD forbid"]), he categorically denies that it is his intention either to "swallow up" (v.20; cf. v.19) or "destroy" (different Heb. verb from that used by the woman in v.19 [see comment there] but the same as the one rendered "battering" in v.15). He assures her that he is interested only in apprehending Sheba, whom he characterizes as being from the "hill country of Ephraim" (v.21), a large, partially forested plateau that extended into the tribal territory of Benjamin (cf. v.1) from the north. He asserts that Sheba has "lifted up his hand" against David, implying that his treachery with respect to the king must be punished. Since the relatively common idiom *nś' yd* is found only here and in 18:28 in the sense of "rise in rebellion" (cf. Conroy, p. 72 n. 119), Joab's use of it links the revolt of Sheba to that of Absalom and his fellow conspirators.

Joab tells the wise woman that if the citizens of Abel will release Sheba to him ("hand over" is plural; same Heb. verb as in 14:7, providing yet another parallel to the narrative of the wise woman of Tekoa), he and his men will pull back from the city. Promising Joab that Sheba's head will be thrown to him "from" the wall (*b*[e]*'aḏ*, v.21; perhaps better "through [an opening in]" the wall; cf. 6:16 ["from" in the sense of "through"]; 1 Sam 19:12; 2 Kings 1:2), the woman relays her proposal to the people of the city. Impressed by her "wise advice" (v.22, lit., "wisdom"; cf. 1 Kings 4:34), they proceed to cut off Sheba's head (see comments on 1 Sam 17:51; 31:9) and toss it out to Joab.

And so the rebellion of Sheba son of Bicri comes to an inglorious end, but with a surgical strike against one man rather than by destroying an entire city—and all because of the calming advice of the wise woman of Abel. "Sagacity, faithfulness, a commanding presence, and readily acknowledged influence with her peers—these are the attributes that clearly mark this woman" (Camp, "Wise Women of 2 Samuel," p. 26). Brueggemann has observed: "Wise words override ruthless policy. At the end, not only the woman and the city are saved; something of David's dignity and self-respect are also rescued from Joab's mad, obedient intent" (*First and Second Samuel,* p. 332).

**22b** By echoing the language of v.1 ("he sounded the trumpet," "each returning to his home"; see comment on vv.1–22), the narrator brings the story of Sheba's revolt to a fitting conclusion. Whereas Sheba had sounded a trumpet to rally secessionists, Joab does so to call off the siege of Abel and send his men on their way. Although the verb *pûṣ* in battle contexts normally means "scattered" after defeat (cf. 1 Sam 11:11; Num 10:35; Ps 68:1), here it bears the unusual sense of "dispersed, demobilized" after victory (cf. Conroy, p. 59 n. 52).

With Joab's return to the king in Jerusalem, the grand symphony known as the Court History of David reaches its conclusion for all practical purposes (at least as far as the books of Samuel are concerned; see comment on 9:1–20:26). The last four verses of chapter 20 constitute a suitably formal coda, serving the same function for the Court History that the last four verses of chapter 8 do for the narrative of David's powerful reign (see comment on 5:17–8:18).

## Notes

---

1 In addition to its occurrence in chapter 20, the personal name Sheba (שֶׁבַע [*šb'*]) appears on a Hebrew seal and on Samaria ostracon 2:6 as well as on a fragment of a bulla (seal impression) recently discovered in Jerusalem (cf. Avigad, *Hebrew Bullae,* p. 111).

3 אַלְמְנוּת חַיּוּת (*'almenûṯ ḥayyûṯ,* lit., "widowhood of life") is translated "living as widows" by the NIV, which apparently repoints the MT as אַלְמָנוֹת חַיּוֹת (*'almānôṯ ḥayyôṯ,* "living widows"; cf. LXX). Although the consonantal text, however vocalized, remains difficult (cf. S.R. Driver, *Notes on the Books of Samuel,* p. 341, for discussion), the NIV rendering is surely preferable to that of J.M. Allegro, who resorts to an Arabic cognate (often a dubious procedure at best) to arrive at his translation "widowhood of shame" ("The Meaning of *Ḥayyûṯ* in 2 Samuel 20, 3," JTS 3 [1952]: 40–41).

5 *Qere* ויוחר (*wywḥr,* "he took longer"; preferable to *Kethiv* וייחר [*wyyḥr*]) is from the root אחר (*'ḥr*). For other examples of this phenomenon in the books of Samuel, cf. ותחז (*wtḥz,* "took," v.9), from אחז (*'ḥz*) and see also Notes on 6:1; 19:13; 1 Sam 28:24.

14 Abel Beth Maacah would later be conquered by the Aramean king Ben-Hadad I (cf. 1 Kings 15:20 = 2 Chron 16:4 [where it is called Abel Maim]) and still later by the Assyrian ruler Tiglath-Pileser III (cf. 2 Kings 15:29), who referred to it in his annals as Abilakka (cf. ANET, p. 283) or, if a scribal lapse is assumed, Abil‹ma›akka (cf. Aharoni, *Land of the Bible,* p. 372). The NIV margin reading, "Abel, even Beth Maacah," analyzes the ־ו (*w-*) as *wāw explicativum* (for which cf. GKC, sec. 154*a* n. b), another example of which occurs in v.19 ("that is"). The name of the site was sometimes abbreviated to Abel, as in v.18 (cf. also *'-b-r,* no. 92 in Thutmose III's roster of Canaanite towns [cf. Aharoni, *Land of the Bible,* p. 162]).

19 "A city that is a mother" (עִיר וְאֵם [*'îr we'ēm*]) brings to mind the term "metropolis," which appears as a loanword (*mṭrpwls* ) in an Old Syriac sale deed found at Dura (cf. M. O'Connor, "The Arabic Loanwords in Nabatean Aramaic," JNES 45, 3 [1986]: 228 n. 94).

---

## 20. *David's officials*

### 20:23–26

**[23]Joab was over Israel's entire army; Benaiah son of Jehoiada was over the Kerethites and Pelethites; [24]Adoniram was in charge of forced labor; Jehoshaphat son of Ahilud was recorder; [25]Sheva was secretary; Zadok and Abiathar were priests; [26]and Ira the Jairite was David's priest.**

As the outline of 2 Samuel indicates (see Introduction), the first twenty chapters divide into four literary units of varying length, each of which ends with a four-verse list of names. Each of the last two units (5:17–8:18; chs. 9–20) concludes with a list of David's officials (8:15–18; 20:23–26) that provides the names, patronymics (for the most part), and offices of the men in David's cabinet. Despite the caveats of McCarter (*II Samuel*, p. 435), it seems best to understand the list in 8:15–18 as coming from the earlier years of David's reign and the present list as deriving from the later years.

Although the roster of officials in 8:15–18 begins with the statement that David "reigned over all Israel" and the list in 1 Kings 4:2–6 begins by informing the reader that his son Solomon "ruled over all Israel" (1 Kings 4:1), vv.23–26 do not begin with a reference to David's reign. While it may be overstating the case to "assume that by omitting David's name from it, the second list of David's high officials tells us, though implicitly, that the *de facto* ruler was then Joab, who ranked at the top of the list (2 Sam 20:23a)" (Tomoo Ishida, "Solomon's Accession to the Throne of David—A Political Analysis," in *Studies in the Period of David and Solomon and Other Essays*, ed. Tomoo Ishida [Winona Lake: Eisenbrauns, 1982], p. 185), at the very least the omission reflects David's weakened position in the wake of the rebellions of Absalom and Sheba.

All rivals for power (including Amasa; see v.10 and comment) now eliminated, Joab—as earlier (see 8:16 and comment)—is commander of "Israel's entire army" (v.23), while Benaiah (rather than Abishai, v.7) retains formal control over the Kerethite and Pelethite mercenaries (see comment on 8:18).

A new and ominous figure—Adoniram—makes his appearance in the royal cabinet (v.24). He is in charge of the corvée, the age-old institution (cf. ANET, p. 485 n. 7) that involved impressing prisoners of war into "forced labor" (*mas*) on such projects as the building of highways, temples, and palaces. Foreseen as early as the time of Moses (cf. Deut 20:10–11), it was apparently inaugurated in Israel's monarchy by David at least partially in anticipation of the construction of a temple by his son Solomon (see 7:12–13 and comments). In choosing Adoniram, however, "David had appointed a man who was to play a prominent part in the apostasy of the Northern Kingdom, 1 Kings 12:18 f." (Carlson, p. 180).

Just as he was earlier in David's reign, so also now Jehoshaphat is still recorder (see comments on 8:16). Apparently, however, Sheva has replaced Seraiah as secretary (v.25; for possible relationships between the names Sheva, Seraiah, Shisha [1 Kings 4:3], and Shavsha [1 Chron 18:16], see comment on 8:17). With respect to the substitution of "Zadok and Abiathar" (v.25) for "Zadok . . . and Ahimelech son of Abiathar" in the earlier list, as well as for discussion concerning possible relationships between the three men, see comment on 8:17. Although it is possible that Ira the Jairite (presumably either a descendant of Jair or an inhabitant of one of the settlements known as Havvoth Jair; cf. Num 32:41; 1 Kings 4:13) shared the priesthood with Zadok and Abiathar, it is perhaps better to understand *kōhēn* (rendered "priest" in v.26) in the sense of "royal adviser" (as in 8:18 [see comment there]; cf. Goldman, pp. 236, 319).

> The initial offer of Israel's throne was in the form of a covenant (5:1–3), but the presence of these officers tells against a covenantal version of royal power. The raw political strength that dominates this story of David's return to power presents the wise woman of 20:16–22 as an important contrast. . . . In the midst of Jerusalem's *Realpolitik*. . . she can still imagine that careful speech, peaceable treasuring, and secure trust offer another way in public life. There is more to public life than David's sexual politics or Joab's killing fields. (Brueggemann, *First and Second Samuel*, pp. 332–33)

## Notes

**23** "Kerethites" (כרתי [*krty*]) is the reading not only of the *Qere* but also of many Hebrew MSS and most versions (cf. BHS). "Carites" (כרי [*kry*], *Kethiv;* cf. also 2 Kings 11:4, 19) is doubtless incorrect since "Pelethites" is invariably preceded by "Kerethites" in the OT (cf. v.7; 8:18; 15:18; 1 Kings 1:38, 44; 1 Chron 18:17). The similarity between the two words, together with the fact that *krty* is found in parallelism with *kry* in Ugaritic (cf. M. Delcor, "Les Kéréthim et les Crétois," VetTest 28, 4 [1978]: 415), readily accounts for the *Kethiv* reading.

**24** Second Samuel 20:24; 1 Kings 4:6; 5:14; 12:18 = 2 Chron 10:18 in NIV all state that Adoniram ("My [Divine] Lord is Exalted") was in charge of forced labor under David/Solomon/Rehoboam. The MT of v.24, however, reads "Adoram" (although "Adoniram" is attested in some LXX MSS; cf. NIV mg.), as does the MT of 1 Kings 12:18 (although "Adoniram" appears in some LXX MSS as well as in Syr.; cf. NIV mg.). In 2 Chron 10:18, on the other hand, the MT reads "Hadoram"—which the NIV margin there explains as "a variant of Adoniram." But while it is indeed possible to understand Hadoram in 2 Chron 10:18 as a spelling variant of Adoram (which in turn would probably be a contracted form of Adoniram), in the light of 2 Sam 8:10 (see comment there) it is equally possible to explain it as a name in its own right with the meaning "Hadad Is Exalted." The name Adoram can also be analyzed, however, as meaning "Adad is Exalted" (for the alternate spellings of the divine name, cf. William F. Albright *Archaeology and the Religion of Israel,* 5th ed. [Garden City: Doubleday, 1968], pp. 157–58; for alternate spelling as a personal name, cf. the MT of 1 Kings 11:17, which translates literally as follows: "And Adad fled, he and some Edomite men who had been servants of his father with him, to go to Egypt; and Hadad was a small boy"). In that case "the Masoretes may thus have had good reason for using the more Canaanite-sounding form Adoram in 20:24 and 1 Kings 12:18, as against Adoniram in 1 Kings 4:6" and 5:14 (Carlson, p. 180).

**26** Instead of היארי (*hy'ry,* "the Jairite"), the Lucianic recension of the LXX reads ὁ Ιεθερ (*ho Iether,* "the Ithrite"), which, if correct, would identify the Ira of v.26 with one of David's elite "Thirty" (cf. 23:38).

## II. Epilogue (21:1–24:25)

If in fact the books of Samuel have as their basic theme the beginnings of Israel's monarchy in the eleventh century B.C., and if chapters 1–7 of 1 Samuel describe the prelude to that monarchy, chapters 8–15 its advent, chapters 16–31 its establishment, and chapters 1–20 of 2 Samuel its consolidation under David, then the last four chapters of 2 Samuel—which for all intents and purposes conclude the magisterial history of the judgeship of Samuel, the reign of Saul, and the reign of David—function as an epilogue to the books of Samuel as a whole.

Despite the miscellaneous character and dischronologized nature of chapters 21–24, many commentators have recognized the undoubted chiastic arrangement of their overall contents (cf. the discussion by Brueggemann, *First and Second Samuel,* p. 335). On this point Sternberg makes a useful observation: "It is suggestive that the most conspicuous and large-scale instance of chiasm in Samuel applies to a hodgepodge that has the least pretensions to literariness and, even with the artificial design thrown in, hardly coheres as more than an appendix" (p. 40). Indeed, it "deliberately subordinates expository to aesthetic coherence, business to pleasure" (ibid., p. 42).

At the same time, however, it would be a serious mistake to assume that the epilogue is disinterested in theological reflection or that it is otherwise inferior to the celebrated Court History (chs. 9–20) that immediately precedes it. The narrator's masterful use of prose and poetry alike provide a fitting conclusion to the career of Israel's greatest king. "In sum, the final four chapters, far from being a clumsy appendix, offer a highly reflective, theological interpretation of David's whole career adumbrating the messianic hope" (Brevard S. Childs, *Introduction to the Old Testament as Scripture* [Philadelphia: Fortress, 1979], p. 275).

The following literary analysis was arrived at independently:

A. The Lord's Wrath Against Israel (21:1–14)
B. David's Heroes (21:15–22)
C. David's Song of Praise (22:1–51)
C′. David's Last Words (23:1–7)
B′. David's Mighty Men (23:8–39)
A′. The Lord's Wrath Against Israel (24:1–25)

If it be claimed that an outline of this sort is more clever than credible, I would simply call attention to the double *inclusio* that links together the first and last sections—an *inclusio* that is all the more impressive since it interlocks the first verse of chapter 21 with the last verse of chapter 24: "a famine for three successive years" (21:1), "three years of famine" (24:13); "God/the LORD answered prayer in behalf of the land" (21:14; 24:25).

## A. *The Lord's Wrath Against Israel*

### 21:1–14

**1 During the reign of David, there was a famine for three successive**
**years; so David sought the face of the LORD. The LORD said, "It is on**
**account of Saul and his blood-stained house; it is because he put the**
**Gibeonites to death."**
**2 The king summoned the Gibeonites and spoke to them. (Now the**
**Gibeonites were not a part of Israel but were survivors of the Amorites;**
**the Israelites had sworn to ⌊spare⌋ them, but Saul in his zeal for Israel**
**and Judah had tried to annihilate them.) 3 David asked the Gibeonites,**
**"What shall I do for you? How shall I make amends so that you will bless**
**the LORD's inheritance?"**

4 The Gibeonites answered him, "We have no right to demand silver or
gold from Saul or his family, nor do we have the right to put anyone in
Israel to death."
"What do you want me to do for you?" David asked.
5 They answered the king, "As for the man who destroyed us and
plotted against us so that we have been decimated and have no place
anywhere in Israel, 6 let seven of his male descendants be given to us to
be killed and exposed before the LORD at Gibeah of Saul—the LORD's
chosen one."
So the king said, "I will give them to you."
7 The king spared Mephibosheth son of Jonathan, the son of Saul,
because of the oath before the LORD between David and Jonathan son of
Saul. 8 But the king took Armoni and Mephibosheth, the two sons of
Aiah's daughter Rizpah, whom she had borne to Saul, together with the
five sons of Saul's daughter Merab, whom she had borne to Adriel son
of Barzillai the Meholathite. 9 He handed them over to the Gibeonites,
who killed and exposed them on a hill before the LORD. All seven of them
fell together; they were put to death during the first days of the harvest,
just as the barley harvest was beginning.
10 Rizpah daughter of Aiah took sackcloth and spread it out for herself
on a rock. From the beginning of the harvest till the rain poured down
from the heavens on the bodies, she did not let the birds of the air touch
them by day or the wild animals by night. 11 When David was told what
Aiah's daughter Rizpah, Saul's concubine, had done, 12 he went and
took the bones of Saul and his son Jonathan from the citizens of Jabesh
Gilead. (They had taken them secretly from the public square at Beth
Shan, where the Philistines had hung them after they struck Saul down
on Gilboa.) 13 David brought the bones of Saul and his son Jonathan
from there, and the bones of those who had been killed and exposed
were gathered up.
14 They buried the bones of Saul and his son Jonathan in the tomb of
Saul's father Kish, at Zela in Benjamin, and did everything the king
commanded. After that, God answered prayer in behalf of the land.

The account of the Gibeonites' revenge (vv.1–14) begins with the Lord's wrath against Israel as expressed in a three-year famine (v.1) and ends with the Lord's answer to Israel's prayers by removing it (v.14). David's request (vv.1–4), Gibeon's demand (vv.5–6), David's acquiescence (vv.7–9), Rizpah's vigil (v.10), and David's final act of respect to the house of Saul (vv.11–14) constitute the various segments of the episode.

**1–4** Lengthy famines were common in the ancient world (cf. Gen 12:10; 26:1; 41:54–57; Ruth 1:1; 2 Kings 4:38), and it is therefore not surprising that at least one famine of unusual severity should occur at some point during the forty-year "reign of David" (v.1). The MT description is especially vivid, informing the reader that the famine continues for "three years, year after year" (NIV, "three successive years"). Since it is often only "in their misery" that God's people pray to him (Hos 5:15), it may well be that David has not "sought the face of the LORD" (v.1) until Israel is *in extremis* (cf. 2 Chron 7:14; cf. esp. the Davidic expressions of need recorded in 1 Chron 16:11; Pss 24:6; 27:8). "In the secular realm, [the idiom 'seek the face of'] is used in referring to the king, 'seek the face of the king' (Prov. 29:26; cf. 1 K. 10:24; 2 Ch. 9:23), evidently meaning to 'obtain the favor of the king'. . . . [The act] assumes the personal movement of the one seeking toward the one being sought" (TDOT, 2:237). David thus makes his way to the divine throne room, perhaps entering the tabernacle itself, in order to receive mercy and help for his people.

The Lord's answer is not long in coming: "Saul and his blood-stained house" are to blame, since "bloodshed pollutes the land" (Num 35:33; cf. Deut 19:10). Saul's crime is that he had "put the Gibeonites to death" (for the location of Gibeon, see comment on 20:8) and in so doing had violated the age-old "treaty with the Gibeonites" made with them by Joshua (Josh 9:16), one of the provisions of which was that the Israelites would "let them live" (Josh 9:15, 20–21). Despite the fact that Israel's people "did not kill them" (Josh 9:26), Israel's first king "put [some of them] to death" (v.1).

David, Israel's second king, is determined to right the wrong of Saul against the Gibeonites; so he summons them in order to discuss the matter with them. "Not a part of Israel" (v.2), the Gibeonites are characterized as "Hivites" (Josh 9:7; 11:19), as "survivors of the Amorites," a relatively nonbelligerent people during this period (see comment on 1 Sam 7:14). The statement that the Israelites had "sworn to spare them" (lit., "sworn an oath to them," v.2) echoes the language of the narrative in Joshua many times over (cf. Josh 9:15, 18, 19 and esp. 20: "We will let them live, so that wrath will not fall on us for breaking the oath we swore to them"). Although enthusiasm, when properly directed, is commendable (cf. Num 11:29), Saul's misplaced zeal for "Israel and Judah" (v.2; see comments on 5:3; 1 Sam 11:8; 15:4; 17:52) has now brought famine on the land. It is not the first time that Saul had "tried" to wipe out a real or supposed enemy (see comments on 1 Sam 19:2, 10; 23:10).

Wanting to rectify the situation, David asks the Gibeonites whether there is anything he can do to "make amends" (lit., "make atonement," v.3; cf. Exod 32:30; Num 16:46-47; 25:13).

> Since the verb *kipper* is used absolutely here, it is impossible to say from the construction alone whether it means to propitiate or to expiate. From the context, however, it is clear that it means both. David is seeking both to satisfy the Gibeonites and to "make up for" the wrong done to them. It is equally clear that he cannot achieve the latter without the former. There is no expiation without propitiation. (Paul Garnet, "Atonement Constructions in the Old Testament and the Qumran Scrolls," EQ 46, 3 [1974]: 134)

David pursues reconciliation with the Gibeonites "so that you will bless [an imperative used in a voluntative sense 'for the purpose of expressing with somewhat greater force the intention of the previous verb' (S.R. Driver, *Notes on the Books of Samuel*, p. 350); cf. precisely the same construction—with the same verbal root—in Gen 12:2: 'and (= so that) you will be a blessing'] the Lord's inheritance" (i.e., the land and people of Israel; see comments on 14:16; 20:19; 1 Sam 26:19). David apparently wants the Gibeonites, when their requirements have been met, to pray that God will bless David's people (cf. TDOT, 2:292; see also comment on 14:22).

The Gibeonites begin by indicating to David two things that they have no right to demand: (1) "silver or gold" from Saul's family (v.4; see comment on 8:11); (2) the death of "anyone ['*îš*, lit., 'a man'] in Israel" (for the custom of blood vengeance, see comments on 3:30; 14:7). They are asking neither for money from the extended clan of the man who murdered their fellow citizens nor for the execution of Israelites in general. It is only when David expands his initial question ("What shall I do for you?" v.3) to "What do you want me to do for you?" (lit., "What are you saying I should do for you?" v.4; cf. 1 Sam 20:4) that the Gibeonites become more specific in their demand.

**5–6** The Gibeonites' desire for vengeance concerns one "man" (*'îš*, v.5; see comment on v.4) and, since he is now dead, focuses on his descendants. Because of Saul, the Gibeonites have been "destroyed" (cf. 22:38; 1 Sam 15:18 ["wiped . . . out"]), plotted against, decimated, and deprived of a place in Israel. They therefore request that "seven" of Saul's male descendants be turned over to them (v.6), seven in this case not only being intended literally (cf. v.8) but also perhaps to be understood in the sense of full retribution (see 1 Sam 2:5 and comment). Saul's "bloodstained house" (v.1) would now be completely avenged (cf. Num 35:33; see comment on 16:7–8 for the possibility that Shimei's curse reflects the present situation).

While vv.1–9 surely constitute a parade example of the fact that "if the original offender was no longer alive vengeance could be exercised even upon his descendants" (Isaac Schapera, "The Sin of Cain," in *Anthropological Approaches to the Old Testament,* ed. Bernhard Lang [Philadelphia: Fortress, 1975], p. 28), it is also clear that much more than a simple blood feud is in view here. As stated earlier (see comment on v.1), David has discovered "that the famine was due to the breaking of the covenant between Gibeon and Israel, brought about by an act of Saul, years before. Propitiation could only be effected by the death of the sons of Saul at the hands of the Gibeonites" (F. Charles Fensham, "The Treaty Between Israel and the Gibeonites," BA 27, 1 [1964]: 99; for ancient Near Eastern parallels that report plague, drought, famine, and other disasters believed to result from breach of covenant, cf. p. 100).

Seven of Saul's descendants are therefore to be "killed and exposed" (v.6; cf. vv.9, 13; Num 25:4). The Hebrew verb designates "a solemn ritual act of execution imposed for breach of covenant," probably involving the "cutting up or dismembering [of] a treaty violator as a punishment for treaty violation" (Polzin, "*HWQY'* and Covenantal Institutions in Early Israel," pp. 229, 234; cf. Cross, *Canaanite Myth and Hebrew Epic,* p. 266). In addition to natural calamities such as those mentioned above (plague, drought, famine, etc.; cf. Fensham, "The Treaty between Israel and the Gibeonites," p. 100), Polzin singles out two other covenant curses attested in extrabiblical sources from the ancient Near East: "The progeny of the transgressor shall be obliterated; and the corpse of the transgressor will be exposed. All three of these curses are involved in 2 Sam 21:1–14" ("*HWQY'* and Covenantal Institutions in Early Israel," p. 228 n. 4).

As Agag was put to death "before the LORD" (1 Sam 15:33), so also Saul's descendants are to be killed and exposed "before the LORD" (v.6; cf. v.9), perhaps so that his blessing might be sought (see comments on 5:3; 1 Sam 11:15). Ironically, the act is to take place at "Gibeah of Saul" (modern Tell el-Ful, three miles north of Jerusalem), the hometown (see comment on 1 Sam 10:10) of the one who had "put the Gibeonites to death" (v.1) in the first place. The citizens of Gibeon then compound the irony by sarcastically referring to Saul as the Lord's "chosen one" (v.6), a descriptive title used often of God's people in general but applied specifically elsewhere only to Moses (cf. Ps 106:23), David (cf. Ps 89:3), and the servant of the Lord (cf. Isa 42:1). Saul, however, is in fact referred to as "the man the LORD has chosen" in 1 Samuel 10:24 (see comment there).

With whatever ulterior motives (if any; cf. Anderson, pp. 251–52; Mauchline, pp. 303–4), David acquiesces to the Gibeonites' request.

**7–9** Because of the "oath before the LORD" (v.7) sworn long ago between David and Saul's son Jonathan (see 1 Sam 20:42 and comment; cf. also 1 Sam 20:14–17), the king spares Jonathan's son Mephibosheth (see also 19:24–30 and comments), whose future is presumably now secure. Although he is never again mentioned in the OT, his namesake—a son of "Aiah's daughter Rizpah" (v.8), Saul's concubine (see 3:7 and comment)—has the misfortune of being one of the seven descendants of Saul to be handed over to the Gibeonites. The other six are Rizpah's son Armoni (brother of the hapless Mephibosheth) and the five sons of Saul's daughter Merab (better Merob, for which see comment on 1 Sam 14:49), whom she had borne to Adriel the Meholathite (cf. 1 Sam 18:19; Adriel's father Barzillai is not to be confused with David's friend Barzillai the Gileadite, for which see comment on 17:27).

After being delivered over to the Gibeonites by David, the seven are "killed and exposed . . . before the LORD" (v.9; see comments on v.6) on a hill where they could be easily seen. The verb "fell" is used to portray their execution in a picturesque way (cf. 11:17; 1 Sam 14:13) and is parallel to "were put to death" (v.9), an idiom that often implies summary execution (see comments on 19:22; 1 Sam 11:13; cf. also 1 Sam 19:6; 20:32). The time of year is carefully specified as "during the first days of harvest, just as the barley harvest was beginning," the latter phrase adding a touch of precision to the former. In ancient Israel, reapers began harvesting the barley crop (cf. Ruth 1:22) in late April (for discussion cf. Edward F. Campbell, Jr., *Ruth*, p. 108). So important was the time of barley harvest in the agricultural year that it served as one of the reference points in the tenth-century Gezer calendar (cf. G. Ernest Wright, ***Biblical Archaeology*** [Philadelphia: Westminster, 1957], pp. 180–84).

**10** Rizpah, bereft of two sons (cf. v.8), spreads "sackcloth" (a sign of mourning; cf. 3:31) on a rock, where she will stay day and night (cf. 1 Kings 21:27; Esth 4:3; Isa 58:5; Joel 1:13) for the foreseeable future. She intends to remain there at least until the "rain" comes down (lit., "water," as in Judg 5:4; Job 5:10)—probably an unseasonable late-spring or early-summer shower (cf. Gordon, McCarter) rather than the heavy rains of October (cf. Kirkpatrick). In either case she refuses to leave the exposed bodies of her sons and the other five victims until the drought ends as a sign that Saul's crime has been expiated. Furthermore, to allow the "birds of the air" and the "wild animals" to feast on the carcasses would be not only to subject them to the most ignominious treatment possible (cf. 1 Sam 17:44, 46; Ps 79:2; Jer 16:4) but also to resign them to the curse reserved for covenant violators (cf. Fensham, "The Treaty Between Israel and the Gibeonites," p. 100; cf. Jer 34:20).

Roland de Vaux has proposed that several features mentioned in vv.1–10 and paralleled in a Ugaritic text mark the account as one reporting "a human sacrifice to assure fertility" (***Studies in Old Testament Sacrifice*** [Cardiff: University of Wales, 1964], p. 61). "The Gibeonites are not Israelites, they are descendants of the old population of Canaan: with David's consent, they indulged in a Canaanite fertility rite" (ibid., p. 62). As McCarter correctly notes, however, such suggestions "disregard the reason for the execution offered by the text itself. The Saulides are crucified in propitiation of divine wrath arising from the violation of a treaty sanctioned by solemn oaths. . . . It is a matter of propitiatory justice, of restitution exacted upon those who bear the guilt for a gross breach of a divinely sanctioned oath" (*II Samuel*, p. 44).

**11–14** Upon being told of Rizpah's vigil (v.11)—and perhaps also of her implied desire to make sure that the remains of Saul's seven descendants be given a proper burial—David is conscience-stricken to follow her example. He makes the long journey to Jabesh Gilead (v.12, probably modern Tell el Maqlub about fifty miles northeast of Jerusalem; see comment on 1 Sam 11:1) to retrieve the bones of Saul and Jonathan from its citizens, who had buried them there (see 2:4b and comment) after having "taken them secretly" (lit., "stolen them") from Beth Shan's "public square" (apparently near the section of the city wall where the Philistines had hung the bodies of the two men after they had been struck down at Gilboa; see 1 Sam 31:8–13 and comments). Reinterment of bones was not uncommon in ancient times (for the odyssey of Joseph's bones, cf. Gen 50:25–26; Exod 13:19; Josh 24:32), and David now intends to give those of Saul and Jonathan an honorable—if secondary—burial (v.13; contrast the prediction of Jehoiakim's burial in Jer 22:19). The bones of the seven male descendants of Saul who had been "killed and exposed" (v.13; see comment on v.6) are also gathered up, perhaps to be interred near (or even with, as the LXX of v.14 states; cf. also Baldwin, KD, Mauchline, Smith) the bones of Saul and Jonathan.

And so Saul and his son Jonathan arrive at their final resting place, the tomb of "Saul's father Kish" (v.14; see comment on 1 Sam 9:1). Attempts to equate "Zelzah on the border of Benjamin," the location of "Rachel's tomb" (1 Sam 10:2), with "Zela in Benjamin" (v.14), where Kish was buried, are philologically unconvincing. Zela(h), mentioned elsewhere only in Joshua 18:28, is a site of unknown location.

As noted earlier (see comment on v.10), the three-year "famine" (v.1) caused by drought came to an end when God sent rain on the land. The execution of the seven had atoned for Saul's sin and propitiated the divine wrath. Thus the last sentence of v.14 not only reiterates the fact that the Lord has come to his people in grace but also serves to bring the section to a close: God has "answered prayer in behalf of the land" (for the significance of the echo of this phrase in the last verse of 2 Samuel, see comment on 21:1–24:25).

## Notes

---

1 Although most commentators are content to state that Saul's crime against Gibeon is mentioned nowhere else in the OT (for discussion cf. McCarter, *II Samuel*, p. 441), Jörn Halbe has suggested that the flight of the people of Beeroth to Gittaim (cf. 4:2–3) may have been a result of Saul's persecution of the Gibeonites ("Gibeon und Israel: Art, Veranlassung und Ort der Deutung ihres Verhältnisses in Jos. IX," VetTest 25 3 [1975]: 634). Joshua 9:17 locates Beeroth as within Gibeon's sphere of influence and therefore presumably under the protection of Israel's treaty with its citizens. For a defense of the years 996–993 B.C. as the most likely time for the three-year famine of vv.1–14, cf. Merrill, *Kingdom of Priests*, pp. 253–54.

6 "Be given" renders either *Qere* יֻתַּן (*yuttan*), a Qal passive form, or *Kethiv* ינתן (*yntn*), universally vocalized as a Niphal (יִנָּתֵן [*yinnāṯēn*]; cf. S.R. Driver, *Notes on the Books of Samuel*, p. 351). Given the fact that the Gibeonites were "survivors of the Amorites" (v.2), however, it is perhaps better to vocalize the *Kethiv* as יֻנְתַּן (*yuntan*), an unassimilated Qal passive form that, like *antinnu* ("I will . . . give/permit") in a Byblian Amarna letter of the fourteenth century B.C., "illustrates the Amorite tendency to avoid the assimilation of the consonant *n* to a following dental or sibilant" (Youngblood, "Amorite Influence," p. 26).

Although the root of הוקיע (*hwqyʻ*, "kill and expose") is clearly יקע (*yqʻ*, "be dislocated"; cf. Gen 32:25 ["wrenched"]), the byform נקע (*nqʻ*, "be severed/alienated") also provides helpful semantic background. The two roots are used synonymously in Ezek 23:18: "I turned away from her in disgust [*yqʻ*], just as I had turned away [*nqʻ*] from her sister." In Arabic the root *nqʻ* is employed to denote a plundered animal that is sacrificed and eaten after a raid but before the division of the rest of the booty. The practice seems to have served a ritual purpose (W. Robertson Smith, *Lectures on the Religion of the Semites,* 2d ed. [London: A. and C. Black, 1894], pp. 491–92; cf. also Polzin, "*HWQY*ʿ and Covenantal Institutions in Early Israel," p. 232).

7 "Oath" (שבעת [*šbʿt*]) forms a wordplay with "seven" in v.6 (שבעה [*šbʿh*]) and "seven of them" in v.9 (שבעת(י)ם [*šbʿt(y)m*]).

8 In the light of 1 Sam 18:19, "Merab/Merob" (cf. NIV) is surely to be preferred to "Michal" despite its weaker MS attestation (cf. NIV mg. for details). KJV's "the five sons of Michal the daughter of Saul, whom she brought up for Adriel" is apparently based (at least partially) on a Targumic explanation and ignores the fact that ילד ל־ (*yld l-*) means "bear to," not "bring up for." The tortuous attempt of Zafrira ben-Barak to retain "Michal" in the text by stating (among other things) that "Adriel" is the Aramaic equivalent of the Hebrew name "Paltiel" (3:15) is unconvincing ("The Legal Background to the Restoration of Michal to David," *Studies in the Historical Books of the Old Testament,* VetTest suppl. 30, ed. J.A. Emerton [Leiden: Brill, 1979], pp. 26–27).

9 "They were put to death" translates הם המתו (*hm hmtw, Kethiv*) where המה המתו (*hmh hmtw*) is expected (thus *Qere*). Perhaps the ה־ (*h-*) at the beginning of the verb was intended to be shared with that at the end of the pronoun (cf. Watson, "Shared Consonants," p. 531).

For בימי קציר בראשנים (*bymy qṣyr brʾšnym,* "during the first days of the harvest"), the Lucianic recension of the LXX reads ἐν ἡμέραις ζειῶν (*en hēmerais zeiōn,* "during the days of spelt"), a phrase that "at once arouses suspicion, for not only does it make little sense, but it also introduces a serious chronological difficulty, in that emmer, or spelt, was harvested *later* than barley" (S.P. Brock, "An Unrecognized Occurrence of the Month Name Ziw [2 Sam. xxi 9]," VetTest 23, 1 [1973]: 101; cf. Exod 9:31–32). Thus it may well be that *zeiōn* in the Lucianic text is a scribal error for ζειου (*zeiou,* "Ziv"), the second month (mid-April to mid-May). Since the MT, however, reads smoothly as is, it is unnecessary to emend it to conform to the Lucianic reading (contra Brock, ibid., p. 103).

---

## B. *David's Heroes*

### 21:15–22

[15]Once again there was a battle between the Philistines and Israel.
David went down with his men to fight against the Philistines, and he
became exhausted. [16]And Ishbi-Benob, one of the descendants of
Rapha, whose bronze spearhead weighed three hundred shekels and
who was armed with a new ⌊sword⌋, said he would kill David. [17]But
Abishai son of Zeruiah came to David's rescue; he struck the Philistine
down and killed him. Then David's men swore to him, saying, "Never
again will you go out with us to battle, so that the lamp of Israel will not
be extinguished."

[18]In the course of time, there was another battle with the Philistines,
at Gob. At that time Sibbecai the Hushathite killed Saph, one of the
descendants of Rapha.

[19]In another battle with the Philistines at Gob, Elhanan son of Jaare-
Oregim the Bethlehemite killed Goliath the Gittite, who had a spear with
a shaft like a weaver's rod.

[20]In still another battle, which took place at Gath, there was a huge
man with six fingers on each hand and six toes on each foot—twenty-
four in all. He also was descended from Rapha. [21]When he taunted
Israel, Jonathan son of Shimeah, David's brother, killed him.

[22]These four were descendants of Rapha in Gath, and they fell at the
hands of David and his men.

Parallel to the narrative of David's mighty men in 23:8–39 (see comment on 21:1–24:25), the present account summarizes four noteworthy battles that David and his men fought against his nemesis, the Philistines. How the various skirmishes are related chronologically to those mentioned in 5:17–25; 8:1, 12; 23:9–17—or, for that matter, to each other—is impossible to ascertain.

The first and last verses (vv.15, 22) of the literary unit refer to David and "his men" (*'ᵃḇāḏāyw*, lit., "his servants/officers"; in v.17 "men" renders *'anšê*) and thus serve to frame the whole. Verse 22, the epilogue that concludes the section, observes that the four slain Philistine champions were descendants of "Rapha," the eponymous ancestor of one distinctive group of Rephaim (see comment and Notes on 5:18). The rest of the unit, arranged chiastically, includes two shorter passages nestling at the center, each of which relates to a battle at "Gob" and begins with *wthy-'wd hmlḥmh* (lit., "And again there was the battle") while the two bracketing passages (vv.15–17, 20–21) each begin with *wthy-'wd mlḥmh* (lit., "And again there was a battle"):

A. Abishai kills Ishbi-Benob at an unnamed site (21:15–17).
  B. Sibbecai kills Saph at Gob (21:18).
  B′. Elhanan kills "Goliath" at Gob (21:19).
A′. Jonathan kills an unnamed opponent at Gath (21:20–21).

**15–17** Battles between Israel and the Philistines, Israel's agelong enemy, were not uncommon during the early years of the united monarchy period (cf. 1 Sam 4–7; 12–14; 17–19; 23; 28–31; see also comment above on 21:15–22). It was often necessary for David and his troops to go "down" (v.15) from the heights of his capital city to the Philistine foothills and plains (which were at a much lower elevation than Jerusalem). On this occasion the long march and the rigors of battle leave him "exhausted" (cf. also 1 Sam 14:31).

Ishbi-Benob (known only from this text) decides to take advantage of David's situation and kill him (v.16). The weight of his bronze spearhead (see NIV mg.), although only half that of Goliath's (cf. 1 Sam 17:7), nevertheless marks him as a man of unusual size and strength. *Qayin*, occurring as a noun only here and translated "spearhead," at the very least "signifies a sort of weapon, especially one used by a brute"—and it is therefore hardly coincidental that the name of the murderer Cain is spelled the same way in Hebrew (Yehuda T. Radday, "Humour in Names," *On Humour and the Comic in the Hebrew Bible*, JSOT suppl. 92; edd. Yehuda T. Radday and Athalya Brenner [Sheffield: Almond, 1990], p. 75). Ishbi-Benob is also "armed" with a "new" weapon of some sort, the nature of which is not specified in the text. The NIV supplies "sword," an excellent guess supported by the fact that (1) the Hebrew adjective rendered "new" is feminine and the Hebrew word for "sword" is likewise feminine, (2) several ancient versions add "sword" (cf. BHS), and (3) "armed" (lit., "girded") occurs in 20:8 ("was wearing") in relation to "sword" ("dagger"; compare also Judg 18:11, 16, 17 with Judg 18:27).

Like the other combatants, Ishbi-Benob is one of the "descendants" of "Rapha" (v.16; cf. vv.18, 20 and the summary statement in v.22). Although the Hebrew word translated "descendants" is used elsewhere of the progeny of huge ancestors (cf. "descendants of Anak" in Num 13:22, 28; Josh 15:14), and although "Rapha" (*rph*) seems clearly to be the forefather of at least one group of the "Rephaim" (*rp'ym;* cf. the spelling *rp'* for Rapha in 1 Chron 20:6, 8; see also comment and Notes on 5:18), quite different understandings have been proposed for each of the two words.

Willesen argues that *yālîḏ*, conventionally translated as "son," "descendant," never has that meaning "but always denotes a person of slave status. . . . So the *ylydy hrph* of II Sam. xxi were members of a corps called *hrph*" ("The Philistine Corps," p. 328). Following Willesen's lead, Conrad E. L'Heureux proposes that "the term *yālîḏ* does not designate a physical descendant, but one who is born into the group by adoption, initiation or consecration" and that in vv.15–22 the word should be rendered as "votaries"—although "with considerable reservation" ("The *yᵉlîḏê hārāpā'*—A Cultic Association of Warriors,".BASOR 221 [1976]: p. 84 and n. 15; cf. also McCarter, *II Samuel,* pp. 449–50).

As for "Rapha," Willesen asserts that the *h* on the front of the word is not the Hebrew definite article but is part of the root of the word itself. Because of the non-Semitic, Aegean origin of the Philistines, "it seems plausible to search Greek for an equivalent of *hrph,* and here the word *ἅρπη* 'sickle, scimitar' recommends itself. . . . To sum up, the Philistine *ylydy hrph* was a body of warriors dedicated to a deity whose symbol was the royal Syro-Palestinian scimitar" ("The Philistine Corps," pp. 331, 335). L'Heureux, correctly observing that "few Semitists are likely to be comfortable with *harpē* as the source of *hārāpāh,*" nevertheless agrees in principle that "the term *rp'* was a divine epithet" of some sort and thus translates the phrase in question "the votaries of Rapha," who "were fighting men initiated into an elite group whose patron was *(h)rp*'" ("The *yᵉlîḏê hārāpā',*" pp. 84–85).

Two decisive considerations, however, weigh heavily against all such interpretations: (1) The warriors in question are not simply referred to by the *terminus technicus yālîḏ* (vv.16, 18; 1 Chron 20:4) but, even more frequently, are described through the use of other forms of the verbal root *yld: yullaḏ*(v.20) and *yullᵉḏû* (v.22), both of which are probably Qal passive perfect forms; *nôlaḏ* (1 Chron 20:6) and *nûllᵉḏû* (1 Chron 20:8), both of which are Niphal perfects (for the anomaly of the latter, cf. GKC, sec. 69*t*). Indeed, *yālîḏ* itself is a Qal passive participle of the same root. (2) Although 2 Samuel consistently uses the root *rph* (cf. vv.16, 18, 20, 22), 1 Chronicles just as consistently uses *rp'* (cf. 1 Chron 20:4, 6, 8)—a root that can hardly be separated from the *rp'(m)* of the Ugaritic texts (cf. similarly ANET, p. 149 n. 2). In fact, 1 Chronicles 20:4 calls the warriors in question *yᵉliḏê hārᵉpā'îm* ("the descendants of the Rephaites"). All things considered, therefore, it is difficult to escape what seems to be an inevitable conclusion: The *ylydy (h)rph/(h)rp'(ym)* are descendants of Rapha, the eponymous ancestor of at least one group of Rephaites (see comment and Notes on 5:18).

Despite his unusual size, Ishbi-Benob (v.16) faces a formidable opponent in "Abishai son of Zeruiah" (v.17), who, totally in character (see 16:9; 19:21; 1 Sam 26:8 and comments), comes to David's "rescue" (lit., "help") by killing the Philistine. Sensing that the king has just experienced a close shave, his men swear to him that he will never again accompany them when they go out to battle (see comments on 11:1; 18:3). They want to make sure that David, the "lamp" of Israel—he who, with God's help, has brought the light of continued prosperity and well-being to the whole land (cf. 22:29; 1 Kings 15:4; Ps 132:17; cf. also Job 18:5–6; Prov 13:9)—will not be "extinguished" (see 14:7 and comment). The lamp imagery is probably derived from the seven-branched lampstand in the tabernacle (see 1 Sam 3:3 and comment).

**18** At this point the parallels between 2 Samuel and 1 Chronicles resume, to be continued sporadically throughout the rest of the book (for details see comment on 1:1–20:26). The commentary below will note only those places where the differences between vv.18–22 and 1 Chronicles 20:4–8 are significant or where the parallel text makes its own contribution. Since "In the course of time" normally marks a substantially new departure in the narrative (though not necessarily with chronological overtones; see Notes on 2:1 and comments on 8:1; 10:1; 13:1), its occurrence here is surprising. Its presence at the beginning of the second segment of its overall literary section (see comment on 21:15–22), however, may have played a part in the Chronicler's decision to omit the Ishbi-Benob pericope.

This time the location of the battle is "Gob" (*gôḇ*, vv.18–19), which it is tempting to read as "Nob" (*nôḇ*) in both verses, as many Hebrew MSS do (cf. BHS). Nob would echo nicely the name of Ishbi-Benob (v.16), which apparently means something like "Inhabitant of Nob," the "town of the priests" whose citizens Saul had massacred (see 1 Sam 21:1; 22:18–19 and comments). First Chronicles 20:4, however, seems to indicate that Gob (mentioned nowhere else in the OT) was "another name for Gezer" (Rasmussen, p. 237), which is located just east of the Philistine plain twenty miles west-northwest of Jerusalem (see comment on 5:25).

The Rephaite Saph (given the alternate name Sippai in 1 Chron 20:4) is killed by David's hero Sibbecai the Hushathite, known elsewhere as one of the Thirty (see comment and NIV mg. on 2 Sam 23:27; cf. 1 Chron 11:29) and also as a commander in charge of one of twelve army divisions, each of which consists of twenty-four thousand men (cf. 1 Chron 27:11). At the end of the parallel verse in Chronicles, the narrator adds the comment that the Philistines "were subjugated" (1 Chron 20:4), perhaps in part as a result of the death of Saph/Sippai.

**19** A third battle against the Philistines also takes place at Gezer/Gob (see comment on v.18). This time the Israelite hero is "Elhanan son of Jair" (cf. 1 Chron 20:5). Since it is universally recognized that the first occurrence of *'ōrᵉgîm* is an erroneous scribal insertion caused by the appearance of the word at the end of the verse (where it forms part of the expression rendered "weaver's rod"), the name "Jaare-Oregim" (and the NIV mg., which suggests the translation "Jair the weaver") can be safely scuttled. In the light of the well-known fact that David son of "Jesse of Bethlehem" (1 Sam 16:1, 18; 17:58) killed Goliath (cf. 1 Sam 17:51, 57; 18:6; 19:5; 21:9), it is often suggested that "David" is Elhanan's throne name and that "Elhanan son of Jaare" (*y'ry*) is a scribal error for "Elhanan son of Jesse" (*yšy;* cf. A.M. Honeyman, "The Evidence for Regnal Names Among the Hebrews," JBL 67, 1 [1948]: 23–24; Emanuel Tov in a letter to the editor, *Bible Review* 3, 3 [1987]: 6).

To attempt to answer the question of who killed Goliath by equating David with Elhanan, however, fails to reckon with the references to "David"—not "Elhanan"—that flank v.19 (vv.15, 17, 21, 22). Nor does it adequately address the parallel text: "Elhanan son of Jair killed Lahmi the brother of Goliath the Gittite" (1 Chron 20:5; cf. also NIV mg. on v.19). Although the MT of 1 Chronicles 20:5 (*'t-lḥmy 'ḥy glyt,* "[killed] Lahmi the brother of Goliath") appears to be original and the text of v.19 (*byt hlḥmy 't glyt,* "The Bethlehemite [killed] Goliath") seems to be a corruption of it, it is also possible that the original text read "the Bethlehemite [killed] the brother of Goliath"—or, for that matter, "the Bethlehemite [killed] Lahmi the brother of Goliath."

Whatever option one chooses, however, "the fact of the matter then is that David slew Goliath, and that Elhanan slew the brother of Goliath" (Edward J. Young, *An Introduction to the Old Testament,* rev. ed. [Grand Rapids: Eerdmans, 1960], p. 198; cf. KD, pp. 465–66; Archer, *Encyclopedia of Bible Difficulties,* pp. 178–79). That there was more than one Goliath (cf. Haley, *Alleged Discrepancies*, p. 336; Kirkpatrick, *The Second Book of Samuel*, p. 197) or that "Goliath" was a common noun that "had come to designate a type" (Hertzberg, p. 387) seems a less likely solution.

In any event, "Elhanan son of Jair the Bethlehemite" (if that is the correct reading) is to be distinguished from "Elhanan son of Dodo from Bethlehem" (23:24)—although an attempt to equate them on the part of a copyist of 2 Samuel may have resulted in the (incorrect?) reading "the Bethlehemite" in v.19 (cf. J. Barton Payne in EBC, 4:404; for a judicious and helpful survey of various possible resolutions of the differences between v.19 and 1 Chron 20:5; cf. D.F. Payne in NBCrev., pp. 318–19).

The main weapon of Goliath's brother, "a spear with a shaft like a weaver's rod," matched that of Goliath himself (see comment on 1 Sam 17:7). On another occasion one of David's men faced a similar spear, again wielded by a giant—this time an Egyptian (cf. 1 Chron 11:23).

**20–21** The last of the four battles against the Philistines takes place at "Gath" (v.20), the hometown of Goliath (cf. v.19; see 1 Sam 17:4 and comment), modern Tell es-Safi (see comment on 1 Sam 5:8), located about twelve miles south-southwest of Gezer. A nameless Rephaite, a "huge" man (cf. Num 13:32 ["of great size"]; 1 Chron 11:23 ["tall"]; Isa 45:14) with an extra digit on each hand and foot, taunts Israel (v.21, as Goliath had done many years earlier; see comment on 1 Sam 17:10 ["defy"]). He is soon dispatched, however, by "Jonathan [not to be confused with David's friend of the same name] son of Shimeah, David's brother" (for the various spellings of the name of Shammah, the third oldest brother of David, see comment on 1 Sam 16:9).

**22** Thus "four" Rephaite giants are killed (the number is omitted in 1 Chron 20:8, since the death of Ishbi-Benob is not recorded in 1 Chron 20:4–7) by David's men. If there is no indication in the text that David personally did battle with them, he nevertheless shares the credit for their death because he is king and his men act under his command. Relatively rare, the idiom "fall at/into the hands of" occurs again in 24:14 and therefore serves to enhance the *inclusio* effect discussed in the comment on 21:1–24:25.

## Notes

---

**21** Some LXX MSS read Ιωναδαβ (*Iōnadab*, "Jonadab") instead of "Jonathan" (cf. BHS), doubtless on the basis of 2 Sam 13:3 (see comment there). Since the LXX reading is otherwise unfounded, it is better to assume that "Jonathan and Jonadab were brothers" (McCarter, *II Samuel*, p. 449).

---

## C. *David's Song of Praise*

### 22:1–51

[1]David sang to the LORD the words of this song when the LORD delivered him from the hand of all his enemies and from the hand of Saul. [2]He said:

"The LORD is my rock, my fortress and my deliverer;

3 my God is my rock, in whom I take refuge,
my shield and the horn of my salvation.
He is my stronghold, my refuge and my savior—
from violent men you save me.
4 I call to the LORD, who is worthy of praise,
and I am saved from my enemies.

5 "The waves of death swirled about me;
the torrents of destruction overwhelmed me.
6 The cords of the grave coiled around me;
the snares of death confronted me.
7 In my distress I called to the LORD;
I called out to my God.
From his temple he heard my voice;
my cry came to his ears.

8 "The earth trembled and quaked,
the foundations of the heavens shook;
they trembled because he was angry.
9 Smoke rose from his nostrils;
consuming fire came from his mouth,
burning coals blazed out of it.
10 He parted the heavens and came down;
dark clouds were under his feet.
11 He mounted the cherubim and flew;
he soared on the wings of the wind.
12 He made darkness his canopy around him—
the dark rain clouds of the sky.
13 Out of the brightness of his presence
bolts of lightning blazed forth.
14 The LORD thundered from heaven;
the voice of the Most High resounded.
15 He shot arrows and scattered ⌊the enemies⌋,
bolts of lightning and routed them.
16 The valleys of the sea were exposed
and the foundations of the earth laid bare
at the rebuke of the LORD,
at the blast of breath from his nostrils.

17 "He reached down from on high and took hold of me;
he drew me out of deep waters.
18 He rescued me from my powerful enemy,
from my foes, who were too strong for me.
19 They confronted me in the day of my disaster,
but the LORD was my support.
20 He brought me out into a spacious place;
he rescued me because he delighted in me.

21 "The LORD has dealt with me according to my
righteousness;
according to the cleanness of my hands he has
rewarded me.
22 For I have kept the ways of the LORD;
I have not done evil by turning from my God.
23 All his laws are before me;
I have not turned away from his decrees.
24 I have been blameless before him
and have kept myself from sin.
25 The LORD has rewarded me according to my
righteousness,
according to my cleanness in his sight.

26 "To the faithful you show yourself faithful,
to the blameless you show yourself blameless,
27 to the pure you show yourself pure,
but to the crooked you show yourself shrewd.
28 You save the humble,
but your eyes are on the haughty to bring them low.
29 You are my lamp, O LORD;
the LORD turns my darkness into light.
30 With your help I can advance against a troop;
with my God I can scale a wall.

31 "As for God, his way is perfect;
the word of the LORD is flawless.
He is a shield
for all who take refuge in him.
32 For who is God besides the LORD?
And who is the Rock except our God?
33 It is God who arms me with strength
and makes my way perfect.
34 He makes my feet like the feet of a deer;
he enables me to stand on the heights.
35 He trains my hands for battle;
my arms can bend a bow of bronze.
36 You give me your shield of victory;
you stoop down to make me great.
37 You broaden the path beneath me,
so that my ankles do not turn.

38 "I pursued my enemies and crushed them;
I did not turn back till they were destroyed.
39 I crushed them completely, and they could not rise;
they fell beneath my feet.
40 You armed me with strength for battle;
you made my adversaries bow at my feet.
41 You made my enemies turn their backs in flight,
and I destroyed my foes.
42 They cried for help, but there was no one to save them—
to the LORD, but he did not answer.
43 I beat them as fine as the dust of the earth;
I pounded and trampled them like mud in the streets.

44 "You have delivered me from the attacks of my people;
you have preserved me as the head of nations.
People I did not know are subject to me,
45 and foreigners come cringing to me;
as soon as they hear me, they obey me.
46 They all lose heart;
they come trembling from their strongholds.

47 "The LORD lives! Praise be to my Rock!
Exalted be God, the Rock, my Savior!
48 He is the God who avenges me,
who puts the nations under me,
49 who sets me free from my enemies.
You exalted me above my foes;
from violent men you rescued me.
50 Therefore I will praise you, O LORD, among the nations;
I will sing praises to your name.
51 He gives his king great victories;
he shows unfailing kindness to his anointed,
to David and his descendants forever."

It has long been recognized that 2 Samuel 22 is not only one of the oldest major poems in the OT but also that, because Psalm 18 parallels it almost verbatim, it is a key passage for the theory and practice of OT textual criticism. "The importance of this poem for the study of textual transmission can scarcely be overemphasized. No other ancient piece of comparable length appears in parallel texts in the OT" (Cross and Freedman, "A Royal Song of Thanksgiving," p. 15).

Although defective spelling and the presence of other orthographic archaisms are more common in 2 Samuel 22 than in Psalm 18 (cf. ibid., pp. 15–17), the relatively poor scribal transmission of the text of Samuel renders moot the question of whether 2 Samuel 22 contains a more original text overall than does Psalm 18. Whereas Robert Alter voices his opinion that 2 Samuel 22 is "the probably more authentic text" (*The Art of Biblical Poetry* [New York: Basic, 1985], p. 29), the NIV margin notes declare four Psalm 18 readings superior to those of 2 Samuel 22 and only one Samuel reading superior to that of Psalm 18. Since the NIV chose not to footnote numerous other differences between the two texts, however, the four-to-one statistic is somewhat misleading. It is often difficult to decide between equally viable variant readings. In any event, it is quite likely that more than one version of David's poem was in circulation, and it is even possible (if not probable) that he himself produced more than one draft of the song. KD gives a typical summary:

> Neither of the two texts that have come down to us contains the original text of the psalm of David unaltered; but the two recensions have been made quite independently of each other, one for the insertion of the psalm in the Psalter intended for liturgical use, and the other when it was incorporated into the history of David's reign, which formed the groundwork of our books of Samuel. The first revision may have been made by David himself when he arranged his Psalms for liturgical purposes; but the second was effected by the prophetic historian, whose object it was . . . not so much to give it with diplomatic literality, as to introduce it in a form that should be easily intelligible and true to the sense. (p. 469)

The commentary below will note only the more significant differences between chapter 22 and Psalm 18.

Attempts have been made to demonstrate that David's psalm is combined from two separate and readily discernible psalms, the one spoken by an individual who celebrates victory over the enemy (vv.2–31) and the other by the monarch who celebrates the dispersion of the enemy (vv.32–51). Among others, however, J. Kenneth Kuntz makes a good case for the literary integrity and theological unity of the psalm by noting (1) that the "old gnomic quatrain (vv.26–27)," which is "located at the psalm's midpoint, fulfills a crucial pivotal function in effectively uniting the poem in its several parts" as it looks backward as well as forward, (2) the way in which divine names and appellatives are employed throughout the psalm (cf. *ṣûrî*, "my rock," used of God in the introductory and concluding words of praise [vv.3, 47]), and (3) the repeated use of various nouns and verbs within both halves ("Psalm 18: A Rhetorical-Critical Analysis," JSOT 26 [1983]: 19–21). In addition, Alter makes the observation that of the eight essentially synonymous lines in the psalm, "two occur at the very beginning [vv.2, 3a–b] and three at the very end [vv.49, 50, 51a–b] of the poem, leading one to suspect that the poet reserved this paradigmatic form of static parallelism for the purpose of framing, while parallelism in the body of the poem is preponderantly dynamic" (*The Art of Biblical Poetry*, p. 33).

Virtually unanimous agreement on such matters as genre and data is not far to seek.

Claus Westermann identifies the framework of the psalm as a "declarative psalm of praise (psalm of thanks) of the individual" (*The Praise of God in the Psalms* [Richmond: John Knox, 1965], pp. 103–4; for a penetrating discussion of the fact that the expression of thanks of God is a way of praising, cf. ibid., pp. 25–30), a more precise description than the traditional "(royal) psalm/song of thanksgiving" (cf. Kuntz, "Psalm 18," p. 3; Peter R. Ackroyd, "The Succession Narrative [so-called]," Int 35, 4 [1981]: 393; Kirkpatrick; Baldwin; Gordon; KD; Hertzberg; Mauchline; Anderson; cf. also the title of Cross and Freedman's article). It is also generally held that the psalm dates from the tenth century B.C. (cf. Cross and Freedman, "A Royal Song of Thanksgiving," pp. 20, 23 n. 13; Albright, *Yahweh and the Gods of Canaan*, p. 25; Freedman, "Divine Names," pp. 57, 96; Kuntz, "Psalm 18," p. 3) and that certain sections of it (esp. the theophany in vv.8–16) draw on still earlier sources (cf. Cross and Freedman, "A Royal Song of Thanksgiving," p. 21). In addition, internal attribution of authorship to David himself has held up well under scholarly scrutiny (cf. Freedman, "Divine Names," p. 76; KD; Kirkpatrick; Gordon; Baldwin).

The position of chapter 22 within 2 Samuel is appropriate indeed: "With its title referring to the deliverance of David from the power of all his enemies, [it] comes fittingly after the near-escape of David from death described in the hero section of 21:15–22" (Ackroyd, "Succession Narrative," p. 393). Located near the end of the books of Samuel, it nicely balances the Song of Hannah near the beginning (1 Sam 2:1–10) and shares several of its terms and themes (see comment on 1 Sam 2:1–2; cf. also Freedman, "Divine Names," pp. 75–76, 87, 89, 95). With respect to the wider context of the entire OT, "the attribution to David of a thanksgiving poem (II Sam. 22) followed by his 'last words' in 23:1–7 provides a correspondence to the placing of the Song and Blessing of Moses in Deuteronomy 32 and 33" (Ackroyd, "Succession Narrative," p. 393).

Apart from its setting (v.1), chapter 22 may be analyzed as follows (the minimal sections agree with the NIV scansion):

A. Introductory words of praise (22:2–4)
B. Reasons for praise (22:5–46)
   1. David's deliverance from his enemies (22:5–20)
      a. Though death threatened, the Lord heard me (22:5–7).
      b. Great is the Lord of heaven and earth (22:8–16).
      c. Though great in heaven, he saved me on earth (22:17–20).
   2. The basis of God's saving deliverance (22:21–30)
      a. The Lord saves those who are righteous (22:21–25).
      b. The Lord's justice is evident in his actions (22:26–30).
   3. The outworking of God's saving deliverance (22:31–46)
      a. The Lord, whose way is perfect, makes my way perfect (22:31–37).
      b. I gained the victory over my enemies (22:38–43).
      c. The Lord enabled me to gain the victory (22:44–46).
C. Concluding words of praise (22:47–51)

*Leitwörter* that characterize the psalm include *yšʿ* ("save, deliver"; cf. Alter, *The Art of Biblical Poetry*, p. 32) and *ṣûr* ("rock"; cf. Kuntz, "Psalm 18," pp. 20–21).

1 Psalm 18 agrees with chapter 22 that the psalm recorded in both books originates with David, who in Psalm 18 is called "the servant of the LORD." Although "of David"

in the title of the psalm doubtless implies authorship, the elasticity of the Hebrew preposition makes it hazardous to assume that proper names following it in other psalm titles are always the authors of their respective psalms (despite the fact that in many cases they surely are). The Lord is the eminently worthy recipient of David's song, but the narrator is probably not telling us that David "sang" it to him. In parallel contexts elsewhere *dbr* is more properly rendered "recited" (Deut 31:30) or "spoke" (Deut 32:44). When "song" (*šîr*) is the object of "sing" in similar situations, the normal way of expressing the Hebrew verb is to use the cognate *šyr* (cf. Exod 15:1; Ps 137:3).

If God's people tend to believe that the ark of the covenant (cf. 1 Sam 4:3; see, however, Notes in loc.) or the king of Israel (see comments on 14:16; 19:9) saves them from the hand of their enemies, David knows full well that the Lord is the one who has "delivered him." Exactly "when" the psalm was first recited is uncertain, although it must have been after the prophet Nathan's announcement of God's covenant with him (see comments on v.51; 7:1–17; see also comment on "given him rest from all his enemies around him" in 7:1).

**2–4** In his introductory words of praise, David affirms that the Lord is everything to him, that he is all he needs. Nine epithets underlining God's protecting presence are divided into three sets of three each: "my rock" (*sal'î*), "my fortress," "my deliverer" (v.2); "my rock" (*ṣûrî*), "my shield," "the horn of my salvation" (v.3a); "my stronghold," "my refuge," "my savior" (v.3b). The first two sets begin with synonyms for "rock"; the second two sets end with words derived from the root *yš'* ("save"), a *Leitwort* throughout the psalm (cf. also "you save me" [v.3b] and "I am saved" [v.4]); and the first and third sets end with the only two participles among the nine terms, both stressing the theme of rescue ("deliverer," "savior"). Each of the nine terms is personalized by adding the suffix *-î* ("my"), which also produces an impressive rhyming effect. A final participle, "worthy of praise" (*m^ehullāl*), begins v.4 in the MT and thus contributes a tenth and climactic epithet to the list.

Numerous words and phrases throughout David's poem are echoed again and again in the Book of Psalms, and the divine titles in vv.2–4 are no exception (the following examples are representative rather than exhaustive). "My rock" (*sal'î*) and "my fortress" (v.2) appear together in Davidic Psalm 31:3 (= Ps 71:3), while "my rock" occurs alone in Psalm 42:9. Remarkably, Davidic Psalm 144 displays five of the epithets: "my Rock" (*ṣûrî*, v.1), "my fortress," "my stronghold," "my deliverer," "my shield" (v.2). "My fortress" is found also in Psalm 91:2 and "my deliverer" (*m^epalṭî*) in Davidic Psalm 40:17 (= 70:5). In addition the root *plṭ* is echoed in v.44, where David gratefully asserts: "You have delivered me."

By virtue of their respective positions near the beginning of 1 Samuel and near the end of 2 Samuel, the Song of Hannah (1 Sam 2:1–10) and the Song of David constitute a kind of overall *inclusio*, framing the main contents of the books and underscoring the fact that the two books were originally one. Both hymns begin by using "horn" as a figure of speech for "strength" (see NIV mg. on v.3; see also comment on 1 Sam 2:1), by referring to God as the "rock," and by reflecting on divine "deliverance/salvation" (*yš'*; cf. 1 Sam 2:1–2; 2 Sam 22:3); and both hymns end by paralleling "his king" with "his anointed" (1 Sam 2:10; 2 Sam 22:51). In terms of inner *inclusios*, however, the hymns go their separate ways: The Song of Hannah concentrates on "horn" (1 Sam 2:1, 10), while the Song of David emphasizes "rock" (vv.3, 47 [bis]) and "salvation" (vv.3, 47 ["Savior"], 51 ["victories"]). God as David's "rock" (*ṣûr*) appears in Psalms 19:14; 28:1 as well (cf. also 92:15). Such a God, without peer as protector of his chosen servants, is one in whom David can confidently "take refuge" (v.3; cf. Davidic Pss 2:12; 11:1; 16:1; 31:1 [= 71:1]; cf. also 118:8–9).

The Lord as "shield" not only protects David from his enemies (vv.1, 3) but also insures the safety of all who are godly (cf. v.31). It is not always possible to tell whether *mgn,* used frequently of God (and sometimes of Israel's king) in the Psalms, should be translated "shield" or "sovereign" (cf. the NIV mg. notes on Davidic Pss 7:10; 59:11 as well as on Pss 84:9; 89:18; cf. also "kings" in Ps 47:9, where the mg. alternative is "shields"). When the former is intended, the root is *gnn* ("protect"); when the latter is in view, the root is apparently *mgn* ("give") as in Proverbs 4:9 ("present"; cf. also Ugar. *mgn,* "give, present"; cf. Aistleitner, *Wörterbuch der Ugaritischen Sprache,* pp. 178–79). The rendering "sovereign" in such cases is surely preferable to "donor" or the like (contrast O'Connor, "Yahweh the Donor," pp. 47–60; see also comment on 1:21). The association of "shield" with "salvation/victory" (*yš'*) is relatively common in the Psalms (cf. v.36; Pss 3:2 ["deliver"], 3; 7:10; cf. John S. Kselman, "Psalm 3: A Structural and Literary Study," CBQ 49, 4 [1987]: 576 n. 12).

"Stronghold/fortress" (*miśgāḇ*), a secure, lofty retreat that the enemy finds inaccessible, is a frequent metaphor for God in the Psalms (cf. Davidic Pss 9:9 ["refuge . . . stronghold"]; 59:9, 16, 17; 62:2, 6; 144:2 ["stronghold"]; cf. also Pss 46:7, 11; 48:3; 94:22). As such he is the "refuge" of his chosen one (cf. Davidic Ps 59:16; cf. also Jer 16:19). That the Lord is therefore eminently able to save him from "violent men" (v.3) is a theme to which David returns at the end of the poem (v.49), and that God delights to "give victory to" his people, to "save/rescue" them from all their enemies and from every calamity, is a prominent thread running throughout the books of Samuel (see comments on 3:18; 8:6; 1 Sam 10:19; 14:23; for *yš'* as an important *Leitwort* in ch. 22, cf. vv.3, 4, 28, 36, 42, 47, 51).

Having described at length the God who is strong to save, David states for the record what has become his habitual exercise: "I call to the LORD" (v.4; cf. v.7; Davidic Ps 86:3, 5, 7)—a practice he shares with saints of all times and places (cf. Job 27:10; Ps 50:15; Isa 55:6; Lam 3:57; Rom 10:12; 1 Peter 1:17). Such a God, supremely "worthy of praise" (cf. Davidic Ps 145:3; cf. also Pss 48:1; 96:4), specializes in assuring his people that they will ultimately be "saved/rescued" from their "enemies" (cf. Num 10:9; cf. similarly Jer 30:7).

**5–7** Among the reasons David gives for praising the Lord (vv.5–46) is, indeed, the fact that God has already delivered him from his enemies (vv.5–20). Whether in images watery (v.5) or terrestrial (v.6), "death" formed an all-encompassing *inclusio* (vv.5a, 6b) that threatened to swallow David. Like the modern Grim Reaper, death in ancient times was personified and/or localized through the use of proper nouns: *m[w]t* ("Death"), the Canaanite deity known from the Ugaritic epics (cf. similarly Job 28:22); *b^eliya'al* ("Destruction"), rendering a Hebrew word that came into the NT as "Belial," a name virtually synonymous with Satan (cf. 2 Cor 6:15; see Notes on 1 Sam 1:16); *š^e'ôl* ("Sheol"; see NIV mg.) or "The Grave," the realm of the afterlife, the place of departed spirits (see Notes on 1 Sam 2:6 [the Song of Hannah], where "death" and "the grave" are parallel, as they are here in v.6; cf. also Ps 116:3).

The metaphor of "waves" (v.5; lit., "breakers") as an instrument of divine judgment occurs elsewhere in psalmic literature as well (cf. Pss 42:7; 88:7; Jonah 2:3). "Swirled about" (*'pp,* v.5) and "coiled around" (*sbb,* v.6), parallel verbs in Jonah 2:5 ("engulfing," "surrounded"), are equally at home in the sea (*'pp:* Jonah 2:5; *sbb:* Ps

88:17; Jonah 2:5) and on land (*'pp:* Davidic Ps 40:12; Ps 116:3 ["entangled"]; *sbb:* Davidic Ps 22:12, 16; Pss 49:5; 118:10–11, 12 ["swarmed around"]; Hos 7:2). "Overwhelmed" (v.5, lit., "terrified, terrorized, frightened"; see comment on "tormented" in 1 Sam 16:14) is used of divine visitants again and again in the Book of Job (cf. Job 3:5; 9:34; 13:11, 21; 15:24 ["fill . . . with terror"]; 18:11 ["startle"]; 33:7 ["alarm"]; cf. also Isa 21:4 ["makes . . . tremble"]); and just as the snares of death "confronted" David (v.6), so did days of suffering "confront" Job (cf. Job 30:27).

In v.6, death is pictured as a hunter setting traps for his victims. If the "cords of the grave" and the "snares of death" confronted David with mortal danger, the "cords of death" and the "anguish of the grave" did the same to an unnamed poet in Psalm 116:3. The Book of Proverbs speaks of a "fountain of life"—the "teaching of the wise" (Prov 13:14), the "fear of the LORD" (Prov 14:27)—that neutralizes the "snares of death."

Just as calling to the Lord should be our lifelong response to an all-sufficient God (vv.2–3) who is worthy of praise (v.4), so also calling to the Lord should be our immediate reaction (v.7) when we are threatened by nameless dread or mortal danger (vv.5–6). When in "distress/trouble," David (v.7; cf. Ps 59:16)—and other afflicted saints (cf. Pss 66:14; 102:2)—knew to whom to turn. From his "temple," his heavenly dwelling (v.7; cf. Davidic Pss 11:4; 29:9; cf. also Isa 6:1; Mic 1:2; Hab 2:20; cf. Cross and Freedman, "A Royal Song of Thanksgiving," p. 23 n. 11), God heard the plea of David, whose "cry" for help (cf. Davidic Pss 39:12; 40:1; cf. also 1 Sam 5:12; Ps 102:1; Lam 3:56) reached the ears of the Lord.

**8–16** Situated at the center of David's paean of praise to God for having delivered him from his enemies (vv.5–20) is a magnificent theophany (vv.8–16) that shares motifs and vocabulary with other OT theophanic sections, both early (cf. Exod 19:16–20; Judg 5:4–5; Davidic Ps 68:4–8, 32–35) and late (cf. Isa 6:1–8; Hab 3:3–15; Ezek 1:4–28; 10:1–22). The "foundations of the earth" (v.16) answer to the "foundations of the heavens" (v.8), not only forming an *inclusio* that delimits the literary unit but also reminding us of God's greatness through the vast reaches of his creation. Another linkage that gives integrity to the section is the similarity between *geḥālîm bā'ᵃrû mimmennû* ("burning coals blazed out of it," v.9) and *bā'ᵃrû gaḥᵃlê-'ēš* ("bolts of lightning blazed forth," v.13; cf. also the repeated references to "his nostrils" [vv.9, 16]). Beginning with two tristichs (vv.8–9), the unit continues to the end in a series of eight distichs (vv.10–16), the total of ten matching the number of divine epithets in the introductory words of praise (vv.2–4). If the opening section concentrates on God's majestic being, the theophany focuses on his mighty omnipotence.

The poetic description of the divine self-manifestation is cast in terms of natural phenomena related to earthquake and storm. An earth set to quaking and trembling by the power of God (v.8) is a common motif (cf. Judg 5:4b = Davidic Ps 68:8a; Job 9:6; Pss 46:2; 77:18; Isa 13:13; Jer 51:29; see esp. 1 Sam 14:15 and comment). Serving as an appropriate counterpoise to the quaking earth is the shaking of the "foundations of the heavens" (v.8), probably a reference to the "mountains on which the vault of heaven seems to rest" (Kirkpatrick, *The Second Book of Samuel,* p. 201; cf. "vaulted heavens," Job 22:14; "pillars of the heavens," Job 26:11)—indeed, Psalm 18:7 reads "foundations of the mountains" (as do the Syr. and Vul. versions; see NIV mg.).

Earth and heaven alike tremble when the Lord is "angry" (cf. Isa 13:13) at the enemies of his people (cf. 1 Sam 14:15). The Hebrew idiom rendered "he was angry" (v.8) means literally "it burned for him," an expression that leads naturally into the terrifying portrait of God as a smoke-spewing, fire-breathing nemesis (v.9; the imagery is similar to that used of the leviathan in Job 41:18–21). Unlike the altar smoke and fire in the Isaianic theophany (cf. Isa 6:4, 6), the present context seems to define the "smoke" as storm clouds (compare Exod 19:16 with 20:18) and the "fire" and "burning coals" as flashes of lightning (in v.13, "bolts of lightning" is lit. "coals of fire"). "Smoke" in the Lord's "nostrils" (v.9) depicts the judgment of divine wrath against his enemies (cf. Isa 65:5; cf. also Ezek 38:18 ["my hot anger," lit., "my anger in/from my nostrils"]), and "burning coals" can metaphorically represent instruments of divine punishment (cf. Ezek 10:2).

In theophanic splendor the Lord "parted the heavens and came down" (v.10; Davidic Ps 144:5; cf. also Isa 64:1, where the more vigorous expression "rend the heavens" is used). "The sense of the root, *nṭy*, here must be, 'to spread out, to spread apart, to spread open (as curtains)'" (Cross and Freedman, "A Royal Song of Thanksgiving," p. 24 n. 23). When God "comes down/goes down/descends" from heaven, his appearance is awesome indeed (cf. Exod 19:11, 18, 20; Neh 9:13). Although on occasion he comes down to rescue (cf. Exod 3:8; Num 11:17), more often than not his descent is for the purpose of judgment (cf. Gen 11:5; 18:21; Isa 31:4; 64:1, 3; Mic 1:3). At such time his "feet" (v.10; cf. Nah 1:3; cf. similarly Exod 24:10; Hab 3:5 ["steps"]; Zech 14:4) are planted on "dark clouds," which signal the ominous approach and destructive power of a violent thunderstorm (cf. Deut 4:11; 5:22; Ps 97:2–4).

One or more "cherubim" (v.11; the Heb. word is sing.) are the metaphorical means of transportation that the Lord "mounted/rode" (*rkb*). If above the ark of the covenant the cherubim (winged sphinxes) support the throne from which God reigns over his people (see comments on 6:2; 1 Sam 4:4), in storm theophanies the cherubim support (or pull) a chariot, pictured in the form of swift clouds that scud across the heavens (cf. Davidic Ps 68:4, 33; Deut 33:26; Isa 19:1). As the seraphs in Isaiah's inaugural vision "flew" (cf. Isa 6:2, 6), so the cherubim in David's poem—and, with them, their divine passenger—"flew," in this case driven along on the "wings of the wind" (for the imagery cf. esp. Ps 104:3; cf. also Hos 4:19, where "whirlwind" is lit. "wind with its wings"). In the Ugaritic epic literature the Canaanite god Baal is described as the "rider of the clouds" (*rkb ʿrpt;* cf. ANET, pp. 130–31; for a sensitive treatment of such Ugaritic epithets and their parallels in the OT, cf. Peter C. Craigie, *Ugarit and the Old Testament* [Grand Rapids: Eerdmans, 1983], pp. 77–79).

Darkness shrouds the middle verse (v.12) of the theophany. The God of wind and rain is pictured as if dwelling in storm clouds, which form his "canopy" and from which he thunders (cf. Job 36:29 ["pavilion"]; cf. also Deut 5:23; Isa 40:22). Interfacing with the darkness is the "brightness" of the Lord's presence (*nōgah*, v.13), a "brilliant light" (Ezek 1:4, 27) or "radiance" (Ezek 1:28; 10:4) that surrounds him, a brightness that in lesser measure he condescends to share with his chosen rulers (cf. 23:4).

Thunder (v.14), lightning (v.15), and their effects (v.16) round out the theophany, the final three verses of which provide its only explicit references to the name of "the LORD" (vv.14, 16). "The efficacy of Yahweh's self-manifestation . . . is artfully imparted in vv.14–16 and a perceptible climax is reached" (Kuntz, "Psalm 18," p. 11). That God "thundered from heaven" against his enemies (v.14) is yet another example of a common OT motif (see comments on 1 Sam 2:10; 7:10; see also Notes on 1 Sam 2:10 and comment on 1 Sam 1:6). His "voice" is a vivid image of thunder, not only in the OT (for a representative listing cf. Moshe Held, "The *YQTL-QTL* [*QTL-*

*YQTL*] Sequence of Identical Verbs in Biblical Hebrew and in Ugaritic," in *Studies and Essays in Honor of Abraham A. Neuman*, edd. Meir Ben-Horin, Bernard D. Weinryb, and Solomon Zeitlin [Leiden: Brill, 1962], p. 287 n. 4) but also elsewhere in the ancient Near East (see comments on 1 Sam 7:10; 12:17; cf. also, in a Ugaritic poem with reference to Baal, "of the giving forth of his voice [*tn qlh*] in the clouds, of his letting loose the lightnings to the earth" [de Moor, *Anthology of Religious Texts*, p. 54]).

"The voice of the Most High resounded" (v.14) is literally "the Most High gave forth his voice" (*ytn qwlw*), the predicate of which is normally rendered by the verb "thunder" in the NIV (cf. Jer 25:30; Joel 2:11; 3:16; Amos 1:2). Alter suggests that the reason "thundered" occurs before "gave forth his voice" has to do with "the issue of consequentiality. I would assume that thunder precedes the voice of the Lord because that is the way it was experientially for the ancient Near Eastern imagination: first the awestruck observer heard the peal of thunder; then he realized that God must be speaking" (*The Art of Biblical Poetry*, p. 34).

"Arrows" as a figure of speech for "bolts of lightning" (v.15) appear also in Habakkuk 3:9 (cf. 3:11) and Zechariah 9:14. The context of Davidic Psalm 144:6, with which v.15 has much in common, indicates that the NIV is justified in understanding the masculine plural suffix on *wypyṣm* as referring to "enemies" in both verses (cf. similarly NAB; for discussion cf. KD, p. 475). Together with thunder, lightning is a common accompaniment of theophanies (cf. Exod 19:16; Ps 77:18; Ezek 1:13–14). And as thunder "routed" the Philistines in the days of Samuel (1 Sam 7:10), so lightning has "routed" David's enemies.

With its emphasis on cosmic phenomena, the closing verse of the theophany (v.16) reprises its opening (v.8). If the heavens respond to the earth in v.8, the "earth" (lit., "world") answers the "sea" in v.16. The phrase *'pqy ym* ("valleys of the sea") is related semantically (though not theologically) to the Ugaritic expression *apq thmtm* ("sources/channels of the [two] seas"; cf. G.R. Driver, *Canaanite Myths and Legends*, pp. 96–97, 108–9). In Psalm 18:15, therefore, *'pyqy mym* should probably be divided differently and read *'pyqy-mym*, the first *m* to be understood as an enclitic between the two elements of a construct phrase (cf. Cross and Freedman, "A Royal Song of Thanksgiving," p. 26 n. 41; Frank Moore Cross and David Noel Freedman, *Studies in Ancient Yahwistic Poetry*, SBLD series 21 [Missoula: Scholars, 1975], p. 28; Dahood, "Hebrew-Ugaritic Lexicography IV," p. 418). The reading *'pyqy mym* in Psalm 18 probably arose by being attracted to the same expression in Psalm 42:1; Song of Songs 5:12; and Joel 1:20, where it means "streams of water." That *mayim* ("water[s]") in Psalm 18:15 is intended in the sense of "sea" is a less plausible explanation for the variant. The word *'pyqy* with the meaning "valleys of" is attested in Joel 3:18, where it is translated "ravines of" and where "water" appears in the same clause.

However firm and stable the foundation of the "heavens" (v.8) and the "earth/world" (v.16) may be in the normal course of events (cf. Pss 93:1; 96:10; Prov 8:29; Isa 40:21; Jer 31:37; Mic 6:2), the Lord of the universe can shake them and lay them bare (v.16) in accordance with his sovereign will (cf. Ps 82:5; Isa 24:18–19; see also comment on 1 Sam 2:8e). Dislocation and exposure of so severe a kind takes place "at the blast of breath" from his nostrils, a display of divine wrath (cf. Exod 15:7–8; Job 4:9; Isa 30:27–28; 59:18–19). The parallel word "rebuke" (*g'r*) often takes on the nuance of "explosive blast" in contexts of "forceful and destructive movement of air accompanied by loud, frightening noise" (James M. Kennedy, "The Root *G'R* in the Light of Semantic Analysis," JBL 106, 1 [1987]: 59, 64; cf. Job 26:11; Pss 76:6; 80:16;

104:7; 106:9; Isa 50:2; 66:15; Nah 1:4). The rebuke of the Lord (v.16) as an index of his anger (v.8) has thus brought the theophany full circle.

**17–20** David concludes his overall description of deliverance from his enemies (vv.5–20) by asserting that the self-revealing, all-powerful Sovereign of the universe (vv.8–16) reached down from heaven and saved him on earth (vv.17–20). The Lord lives not only "on high" (v.17; cf. Mic 6:6 ["exalted"]) but also "with him who is contrite and lowly in spirit" (Isa 57:15), the better to rescue him from whatever danger befalls him. Just as the Pharaoh's daughter "drew" David's great predecessor, Moses, from the waters of the Nile (Exod 2:10), so also the Lord "drew" David (v.17; the Heb. verb *māšāh* occurs three times in the OT [cf. Ps 18:16 (17 MT)]) out of "deep waters" (*mayim rabbîm,* lit., "many waters"), a cosmic metaphor that symbolizes the most threatening of perils (cf. Davidic Pss 32:6 ["mighty waters"]; 144:7).

Although "powerful" (v.18; cf. Davidic Ps 59:3 ["fierce men"]), David's enemies were no match for God, who "rescued" him (v.18; different Heb. verb in v.20). If the snares of death "confronted" David without lasting effect (v.6), his foes "confronted" him in vain (v.19). In speaking of the "day of my disaster" (v.19), David uses a common expression that elsewhere refers to an experience of divinely-sent judgment, punishment, or vengeance (cf. Deut 32:35; Job 21:30 ["calamity"]; Prov 27:10 ["when disaster strikes"]; Jer 18:17; 46:21; Obad 13). The linguistic and cultural background of *'ê<u>d</u>* ("disaster") is perhaps to be sought in the widespread practice of the "river ordeal" (cf. *'ē<u>d</u>* ["streams"] in Gen 2:6; Job 36:27), a form of legal trial in which a suspected criminal was thrown into a river and his success or failure in attempting to swim to shore was interpreted as a divinely-sent index of his guilt or innocence. The semantic development of *'ē<u>d</u>/'ê<u>d</u>* would thus have been from "river, stream" to the specialized nuance "river ordeal" to the more general meaning "ordeal, calamity, distress" (cf. P. Kyle McCarter, "The River Ordeal in Israelite Literature," HTR 66, 4 [1973]: 403–12). In the present context the case for such a relationship is strengthened by the proximity of "day of my disaster" (v.19) to the "deep waters" that threatened David in v.17. Through every trial, the Lord himself was David's "support" (v.19), the Hebrew word for which (*miš'ān*) was recently found in Jerusalem as a personal name on a clay seal impression dating from the early sixth century B.C. It is "probably a shortened form of an unknown theophoric name, such as *Mish'aniyahu ['The Lord is My Support'], which expresses a desire for divine support of the new-born infant" and which is based on v.19 (Avigad, *Hebrew Bullae,* p. 78).

That the Lord safely "brought [David] out" (v.20) of the ordeals through which he had gone (cf. Ps 66:12) implies that he is the God who "sets [his chosen ones] free" from the worst their enemies can do to them (v.49; same Heb. verb). David was released into a "spacious place," a term that elsewhere suggests freedom from bondage and oppression (cf. Davidic Ps 31:8; Ps 118:5 ["setting . . . free"]; Hos 4:16 ["meadow"]).

**21–25** The fact that the Lord "delighted in" David (v.20; see 15:26 and comment) provides a convenient transition to the psalm's second main section, in which David describes the basis of God's saving deliverance (vv.21–30) as consisting of two main factors: the righteousness of those who are rescued by God (vv.21–25) and the justice of God himself (vv.26–30). The present unit clearly displays its own internal literary integrity by framing the whole with phrases repeated in vv.21, 25: "according to my righteousness," "has rewarded me," and—if the LXX, Vulgate, and Psalm 18:24 are followed (see NIV mg. on v.25)—"according to the cleanness of my hands" (cf. similarly the independent treatment of Kuntz, "Psalm 18," p. 12).

Is David saying that his "righteousness" (vv.21, 25) has earned God's favor? Hardly.

> The psalmist is not talking about justification by works, much less about sinless perfection, but about "a conscience void of offence toward God and men" (Acts 24:16). In the issue between himself and his opponents right was on his side, or Yahweh would not have savingly interposed. As verses 26–28 make clear, Yahweh may intervene for good or ill, and all depending upon the integrity or otherwise of the human element. (Gordon, *I & II*, p. 306)

Far from taking matters into his own hands, David had "kept the ways of the LORD" (v.22; cf. Gen 18:19; Judg 2:22; cf. also 1 Kings 2:3) and had waited for divine vindication against his enemies. "Now that vindication had come, and therefore he could safely conclude that he was right with God (*cf.* Ps. 66:18–19)" (Baldwin, p. 288). Not pretending to be perfectly righteous, David was simply laying claim "to sincerity and single-heartedness in his devotion to God. Compare his own testimony (I Sam xxvi. 23), God's testimony (I Kings xiv. 8), and the testimony of history (I Kings xi. 4, xv. 5), to his essential integrity" (Kirkpatrick, *The Second Book of Samuel*, pp. 204–5). It is in this context that David's self-evaluation in vv. 21–25 must be understood.

"Cleanness" (*bōr*) of hands, while intended here (and in Job 22:30) in a moral and spiritual sense (cf. the similar expression in Davidic Ps 24:4), is an idiom that derives ultimately from the practice of washing one's hands with "soda" (*bōr;* cf. Job 9:30; cf. Neufeld, p. 50). That the Lord was a God who "rewarded" people according to their righteousness (vv.21, 25) was a principle that David had embraced long before he became king (cf. 1 Sam 26:23).

Central in this section, as well as in David's concern, is his determination to keep God's laws before him so that he may not be tempted to turn away from the divine "decrees" (v.23; cf. Ps 89:31), as his son Solomon would later do (cf. 1 Kings 11:11). David's testimony that he has been "blameless" before the Lord (v.24; cf. Deut 18:13) is echoed later not only in the statement that God shows himself "blameless" to those who are "blameless" (v.26) but also in David's realization that the God whose way is "perfect" (v.31) makes "perfect" the way of his chosen one (v.33; same Heb. root).

As noted above (see comment on v.21), vv.21 and 25 form an *inclusio* that brackets the literary section, a fact that argues against the omission of v.25 on the grounds that it "seems out of place in the present context" (Cross and Freeman, "A Royal Song of Thanksgiving," p. 28 n. 59). The literary and theological summary of Kuntz is apropos: "As a meaningful sense unit, this strophe [vv.21–25] is committed to the assumption that as Yahweh's servant, the king's righteousness is firmly anchored in his unwavering commitment to Yahweh and his covenant. Accordingly, royal self-exultation is in no wise permitted" ("Psalm 18," p. 12).

**26–30** The second main factor in David's description of the basis of God's saving deliverance (vv.21–30; see comment on v.21) is the Lord's justice, which is evident in his actions (vv.26–30). At the precise center of the entire poem is "apparently an old gnomic quatrain" (Cross and Freedman, "A Royal Song of Thanksgiving," p. 28 n. 60), the first three cola of which are introduced by *'im* ("to") and exhibit God's positive, reciprocal response to those whose lives are holy, and the fourth colon of which is introduced by *wᵉʿim* ("but to") and exhibits God's negative response to the ungodly. To the "faithful" (*ḥāsîḏ*), the one who has appropriated the (covenant) love (*ḥeseḏ*) demonstrated to him by the Lord (see comments on 1 Sam 2:9; 20:8), God shows himself faithful (v.26a). To the "blameless" (*tāmîm*), the one who has been made "perfect" in God's eyes (see comment on v.24), the Lord shows himself blameless (v.26b; cf. Ps 84:11). To the "pure" (*nāḇār*), the one whose hands are characterized by "cleanness" (see comment on v.21; same Heb. root), God shows himself "pure" (v.27a; cf. Isa 52:11, where the same verb is used to describe those "who carry the vessels of the LORD"). But to the "crooked" (*ʿiqqēš*, v. 27b), the one whose words are "perverse" (cf. Prov 8:8; cf. also Davidic Ps 101:4; Prov 11:20; 17:20) and whose paths are littered with traps for the unwary (cf. Prov 22:5 ["wicked"]), the Lord shows himself "shrewd."

Although Psalm 18:26 preserves the correct form of the verb (*tiṯpattāl*, from the root *ptl;* cf. *ʿiqqēš ûp̄ᵉṯaltōl*, "warped and crooked" [Deut 32:5]; *nip̄tāl wᵉʿiqqēš*, "crooked or perverse" [Prov 8:8]), the anomalous form *tittappāl* (from the root *tpl*) in v.27 may be a deliberate wordplay on the name of David's enemy Ahithophel, which means "My Brother Is Foolishness" (see comment on 15:12). Thus for the Lord to show himself "shrewd" toward those who are "crooked" means—in the 2 Samuel 22 version of David's psalm—that he turns them into fools (cf. Carlson, pp. 251–52). At the hinge of the poem, therefore, David acknowledges himself (and his God) to be "faithful," "blameless," and "pure," whereas his enemies are "crooked" and are made to be "fools" by the same Lord who is David's deliverer.

The contrast established between the godly and the godless in vv.26–27 is summarized in v.28. Continuing to address God in the second person (a notable characteristic of vv.26–30), David asserts that the Lord saves the "humble" (cf. Prov 3:34; 16:19 ["oppressed"]) but that his eyes bring low the "haughty" (for the Ps 18:27 variant—"those whose eyes are haughty"—cf. Davidic Ps 131:1; Prov 6:17; 21:4; 30:13). In a similar context (Ps 147:6), God's sustenance of the "humble" is set over against the fact that he "casts" the wicked to the ground (same Heb. verb translated "bring . . . low" in v.28). More important still is the Song of Hannah's description of the Lord (see comment on 22:1–51) as one who "humbles" and "exalts" (1 Sam 2:7; same Heb. roots as those rendered "bring . . . low" and "haughty" in v.28).

David as the "lamp" of Israel (see comment on 21:17) merely reflects the blinding light of the glory of God, who is the "lamp" of David himself (v.29). "If the king could be regarded as a lamp or luminary, then God certainly could be also, as celestial gods were in the Canaanite tradition" (Robert Houston Smith, "The Household Lamps of Palestine in Old Testament Times," BA 27, 1 [1964]: 21). "You, O LORD, keep my lamp burning" (Ps 18:28) is probably an expansive variant of v.29a (for an explanation of how it might have entered the text, cf. Cross and Freedman, "A Royal Song of Thanksgiving," p. 29 n. 64).

With God on his side, David feels invincible (v.30). Since "scale a wall" is clearly the meaning of the second line of the verse (for *dillēg*, "scale," "leap [over]," cf. S of Songs 2:8; Isa 35:6), the alternative translation in the NIV margin ("run through a barricade") provides a more suitable parallel in the first line than "advance against a troop" (see Notes). Either reading, of course, reflects David's confidence that with the Lord's help he can accomplish anything, no matter how difficult.

**31–37** The psalm's third major section (vv.31–46), which expounds the outworking of God's saving deliverance, begins by describing the Lord as the enabler of his servant David (vv.31–37). Several of the epithets used of God in the introductory words of praise (vv.2–4) recur here.

God's name (*hā'ēl,* lit., "the God") is placed front and center ("As for God," v.31) as a means of foregrounding his presence and power (cf. vv.33 ["It is God"], 48 ["He is the God"]). The Lord, whose works and ways are "perfect" (v.31; Deut 32:4; see comment on v.24), makes David's "way perfect" (v.33) by providing him with everything he needs to ensure victory over his enemies. The Lord, whose "word" (cf. Ps 119:140 ["promises"]) is "flawless" in the sense that like precious metals in a refiner's furnace it has been "tested" to the point of proving its purity (Ps 119:140), is a "shield" who protects all who "take refuge" in him (see v.3 and comments; cf. also Prov 30:5, where Agur appears to quote the last three lines of v.31).

The Lord's irresistible and omnipotent ability is linked to his absolute incomparability. David's two rhetorical questions in v.32 demand the uncompromisingly negative answer "no one." There is no god "besides the LORD" (cf. Isa 43:11; 44:6; 45:21); there is no "Rock" apart from our God (see comments on v.3; 1 Sam 2:2; cf. also Deut 32:31 and esp. Isa 44:8). Uniquely beyond compare, the Lord brooks no rivals (cf. Labuschagne, *The Incomparability of Yahweh,* pp. 114–23; see also 7:22 and comment).

In the remainder of the present literary unit, David glorifies the God who readies him for battle against the enemy (vv.33–37). The Lord "arms [him] with strength" (v.33, a reading superior to that of the MT [see NIV mg. for details; cf. also v.40]; see 1 Sam 2:4 and comment), making him physically, mentally, and spiritually powerful. Kirkpatrick (*The Second Book of Samuel,* p. 207) observes "the analogy between the perfection of God's way (*v.*31) and His servant's" and invites comparison with Matthew 5:48: "Be perfect, therefore, as your heavenly Father is perfect."

Habakkuk borrows freely from the language and phraseology of v.34 in the last verse of the psalm that concludes his prophecy (cf. Hab 3:19). David is grateful to the Lord for giving him the sure-footedness of a deer, enabling him even to stand on the perilous "heights" (the final consonant of *bmwty,* otherwise difficult to explain, is perhaps a dittography of the first consonant of the following word) without fear of falling (cf. Deut 32:13; Isa 58:14). The Lord also "trains [David's] hands for battle" (v.35; cf. Davidic Ps 144:1) and strengthens his arms so that they are powerful enough to bend a bow of "bronze" (an hyperbole, since bows [whether simple or composite] were always made of wood; cf. Yadin, *The Art of Warfare,* pp. 6–8; for bronze as a symbol of strength, cf. Job 6:12; 40:18; Jer 1:18; 15:12, 20). The Hebrew phrase here translated "bow of bronze" is contextually rendered "bronze-tipped arrow" in Job 20:24.

The last two verses (vv.36–37) of David's description of God as enabler (vv.31–37) address the Lord directly. He gives David a "shield" that guarantees "victory" (v.36; for the association of "shield" with "salvation/victory" [*yš'*] in the Psalms, see v.3 and comment), and he condescends to "stoop down" (*'nh* III; cf. BDB, p. 776) in order to make David great. He also broadens the "path" beneath David's feet (lit., "step," v.37, here metonymy for "path"; cf. Lam 4:18, where "[our] step[s]" is parallel to "our streets"), so that his ankles do not "turn" (cf. Davidic Ps 37:31 ["slip"]; Job 12:5 ["slipping"]).

**38–43** Adequately strengthened and properly equipped by the Lord (vv.31–37), David was able to gain victory over his enemies with God's help (vv.38–43). As he describes the thoroughness of his triumph, he virtually exhausts the lexicon of Hebrew verbs that have to do with annihilation, several of which appear earlier in the books of Samuel. He "crushed" (v.38; cf. 21:5 ["decimated"]; 1 Sam 24:21 ["wipe out"]) his enemies "till they were destroyed" (see 21:5 and comment; *'aḏ-kallôṯām,* rendered "until you have wiped them out" in 1 Sam 15:18 [see comment there]). "Crushed" in v.39 (cf. Davidic Ps 68:21; cf. also Deut 32:39 ["wounded"]; 33:11 ["smite"]; Hab 3:13) translates a different Hebrew verb than in v.38 and is augmented (not in Ps 18:38, however) by a form of the same Hebrew verb rendered "destroyed" in v.38, resulting in the phrase "crushed them completely." Thus David's enemies "fell" (cf. 1:12, 19, 21; see 1 Sam 31:1 and comment), never to "rise" again (cf. Isa 43:17).

As in the last two verses (vv.36–37) of the previous section (vv.31–37), so also in the middle two verses (vv.40–41) of the present section (vv.38–43) David addresses the Lord directly. God has "armed" David "with strength" (v.40; see comment on v.33) and "made" his enemies "bow" before him in craven submission (cf. Davidic Ps 17:13 ["bring . . . down"]; cf. also Ps 78:31 ["cutting down"]). David's "adversaries" (lit., "those who rose" against him, v.40) will "rise" no more (v.39). If the Lord has broadened David's path "beneath" him (v.37), and if his enemies have fallen "beneath" his feet (v.39), David joyfully confesses that the Lord has caused them to bow "at my feet" (lit., "beneath me," v.40). The Lord has made David's enemies "turn their backs" (v.41; cf. Exod 23:27; Josh 7:8 ["has been routed"], 12; Jer 48:39) in flight, and David has thus "destroyed" (*ṣmt,* not the same Heb. verb as in v.38; cf. Davidic Pss 54:5; 69:4; 101:5, 8 ["put to silence"]; 143:12 ["silence"]; cf. also Pss 73:27; 94:23) his "foes" (lit., "those who hated" him; cf. Davidic Pss 68:1; 69:4; cf. also Deut 33:11).

Although the enemy tried to find relief from David's onslaught, there was "no one to save them" (v.42; see comment on "no one comes to rescue us" in 1 Sam 11:3; cf. also Deut 28:29, 31; Judg 12:3 ["wouldn't help"]; Isa 47:15). "Cried for help" renders *yšw'w* and is based on one Hebrew MS, ancient versions, and Psalm 18:41 (cf. BHS). But the MT *yš'w* ("looked," from the root *š'h)* may be an intentional wordplay on *yš'*, the most important *Leitwort* in David's psalm (cf. Alter, *The Art of Biblical Poetry,* p. 32), and may therefore be the more original reading.

Giving his enemies no quarter, David "beat" them (v.43; cf. Exod 32:6 ["grind"]; Job 14:19 ["wears away"]) as fine as the "dust" (cf. Deut 9:21; 2 Kings 23:6, 15) of the "earth" ("borne on the wind" in Ps 18:42 translates *'l-pny-rwḥ* and may be a scribal error imported from *'l-knpy-rwḥ* ["on the wings of the wind"] in v.11 [cf. Cross and Freedman, "A Royal Song of Thanksgiving," p. 32 n. 94]). He "trampled" them with his feet (cf. Ezek 6:11; 25:6) as though they were "mud in the streets" (cf. Mic 7:10; Zech 10:5). Mud, mire, and refuse in streets and alleys reflects conditions that were "not accepted as a matter of fact, but rather were referred to with a sense of shame and disgrace" (Neufeld, p. 45). The similes in v.43 thus portray David's enemies as objects of humiliation and contempt.

**44–46** Concluding the third main section (vv.31–46) of his reasons for praising the Lord (vv.5–46), David gives credit to God for enabling him to gain the victory over his enemies (vv.44–46). If earlier he had confessed that the Lord is his "deliverer," he now acknowledges the fact that God has "delivered" him (v.44) from "attacks" on all sides (cf. Davidic Ps 55:9 ["strife"]; cf. also Judg 12:2 ["struggle"]; Isa 41:11 ["(those who) oppose"]). Although it is possible to understand David as saying that he has been attacked by "my people" (*'ammî*), all other references in the present literary unit are to his external enemies. It is therefore better to read the suffix as an archaic genitive indicator (for another example see Notes on v.24) and to translate "the people" (as in Ps 18:43, where the MT reads *'ām*). A suitable parallel is thus supplied for the "nations" over whom David has been "preserved" as head (*šmr*) or been "made" the head (*śym*, the variant in Ps 18:43).

David's conquests resulted in large numbers of people he "did not know" becoming "subject to" him (v.44; see 8:2; 10:19 and comments; cf. also 8:6). Since the enemies of God can be expected to "cringe" before him (Pss 66:2; 81:15), there is no reason why foreigners under David's control should not "come cringing" to the Lord's anointed (v.45). Indeed, "as soon as they hear" (*lišmôaʻ/lᵉšēmaʻ 'ōzen* [for *lᵉšēmaʻ*, cf. Ps 18:44], lit., "at the hearing of an ear") they obey him. William Morrow argues forcefully that *šēmaʻ 'ōzen*, traditionally translated "the hearing of the ear," is better understood as "rumor" or "mere report." Thus in v.45 "the nations proffer their obeisance to Israel's king at the *šmʻ 'zn* concerning him. According to the psalmist, 'mere report' or 'rumor' of his might was enough to secure their fealty" ("Consolation, Rejection, and Repentance in Job 42:6," JBL 105, 2 [1986]: 220; cf. already KD, p. 483).

*Bny nkr* ("foreigners") begins vv.45 and 46, and the repetition would ordinarily not be infelicitous in English translation. But since the two lines of Psalm 18:44 are transposed (as compared to the parallel in 2 Sam 22:45), Psalm 18:44b, 45a both begin with *bny nkr*, resulting in a harsh juxtaposition when both are translated the same way. The NIV thus renders "They all" at the beginning of Psalm 18:45 (and therefore also 2 Sam 22:46) for stylistic reasons. David's power and reputation strike terror in subject and foreigner alike, and they all "lose heart" (v.46; cf. Exod 18:18 ["wear . . . out"]). Their only recourse is to "come trembling" (reading *wyḥrgw* with Ps 18:45 and certain ancient versions; see NIV mg.) from their "strongholds" (cf. Mic 7:17 ["dens"], where "come trembling" in a similar context renders the root *rgz* and secures the same meaning in David's psalm for the otherwise unattested root *ḥrg*). Utterly dejected, the peoples in and around David's realm cower before him and his God.

**47–51** The impressive coda to the Song of David consists of a joyful paean of praise. Although *ḥay-YHWH* (v.47) could be read as a solemn oath introducing the rest of the section ("As surely as the LORD lives"; cf. 1 Sam 14:39 and comment), it is probably better (with the NIV) to understand it as an exclamation—"The LORD lives!"—that echoes David's description of the Lord as "the living God" decades earlier (see 1 Sam 17:26 and comment).

From the fact that God is indeed alive springs the rest of David's words of exultation. He begins with a common outburst of praise to which he is no stranger (see 1 Sam 25:32 and comment; cf. also the words of Ahimaaz in 18:28), directing it to the omnipotent Lord who is his "Rock" (*ṣûr;* see comment on v.3). The God who is himself "exalted" (v.47; cf. Davidic Pss 21:13; 57:5, 11; cf. also Ps 46:10) has "exalted" his servant David (v.49; cf. Davidic Pss 9:13 ["lift . . . up"]; 27:5 ["set . . . high"]; Hos 11:7). If the second occurrence of "Rock" is retained (see, however, the Notes on v.47), then "the Rock, my Savior," is reprised in similar divine epithets elsewhere (cf. Deut 32:15; Pss 89:26; 95:1 ["Rock of our salvation"]). If, however,

"Rock" is omitted (as in Ps 18:46), the title "Savior" alone is echoed not only in several Davidic psalms (cf. Pss 24:5; 25:5; 27:9; 51:14 ["who saves me"]; 65:5) but also in numerous other passages (cf. Pss 79:9; 85:4; 88:1 ["who saves me"]; 1 Chron 16:35; Isa 17:10; Mic 7:7; Hab 3:18). In any event, the first occurrence of "Rock" and the reference to God as "Savior" remind his people that his mighty power works hand in hand with his redemptive grace.

When the Lord "avenges" his chosen king (v.48; see comment on 4:8), he "puts" the nations (Hiphil of *yrd;* cf. Davidic Ps 56:7 ["bring down"]; Ps 18:47 displays the Hiphil of *dbr,* "subdues," as a variant reading) "under" him (see comment on v.40) and "sets" him "free" from his enemies (lit., "brings" him "out," v.49; see comment on v.20). Indeed, David is exalted above his "foes" (lit., "those who rose" against him, v.49; see comment on "adversaries" in v.40) and is rescued from "violent men" (see comment on v.3; cf. Davidic Ps 140:1, 4, 11; Prov 3:31; 16:29).

Because of all that God has done for him, none of which he can possibly repay, David speaks to the Lord directly and annouces his determination to "praise" him "among the nations" (v.50; cf. Davidic Ps 108:3), to "sing praises" to his "name" (cf. Pss 92:1 ["make music"]; 135:3), the name of him who alone is worthy of praise (cf. Davidic Ps 8:1, 9; cf. also 1 Chron 16:10; 29:13 [both in Davidic psalms]; Ps 45:17 ["memory"]; 1 Kings 8:33, 35; Isa 26:13). That the nations of the world would share in David's praise to the Lord was a firm belief of the apostle Paul, who in Romans 15:9 quotes 2 Samuel 22:50: "Therefore I will praise you among the Gentiles, I will sing hymns to your name."

Like the Song of Hannah many years earlier, the magnificient Song of David ends with parallel references to the Lord's "king" and the Lord's "anointed" (v.51; 1 Sam 2:10; see comment on 1 Sam 2:1–2; cf. also Pss 2:2 [alternate reading in NIV mg.]; 89:38, 51; 132:10, 17). To his king the Lord gives great "victories" (see comments on 8:6; cf. 1 Sam 14:45; 19:5; cf. Hab 3:8), and to his anointed—to David and his "descendants" (cf. Jer 33:21–22, 26)—he shows "kindness" (see comment on 2:6; cf. 1 Kings 3:6).

God's covenant with David guarantees that the "kindness" here affirmed (*ḥesed*), the unfailing "love" that is given freely and knows no bounds (cf. Ps 89:28, 33), would continue to bring untold blessing to the Davidic line for all future generations (see 7:15 and comment; cf. also 7:13, 16, 25; 23:5; Ps 89:4, 29, 36). The "messenger of the covenant" (Mal 3:1), the Lord's representative and Messiah, would confirm and establish the Davidic covenant; the Lord's messianic servant, himself a "covenant for the people" (Isa 42:6; 49:8), would fulfill the Davidic covenant as king through unending days (cf. Isa 9:7; Luke 1:31–33). It is thus both serendipitous and satisfying that the Song of David, a psalm of impressive scope and exquisite beauty, should begin with "The LORD" (v.2), the Eternal One, and end with "forever" (v.51).

## Notes

2 Psalm 18 begins David's praise hymn with "I love you, O LORD, my strength" (v.2 MT), a verse that does not appear in 2 Samuel in the MT but is included in the Syriac as well as in the Lucianic recension of the LXX. "My deliverer" is enhanced by לִי (*lî*, "of/belonging to me") in v.2 but not in Ps 18:2 [3 MT]. Since *lî* occurs in the same expression in Ps 144:2,

however, it is doubtless original in 2 Samuel as well (cf. also צרי ואיבי לי [*ṣry w'yby ly,* "my enemies and my foes (belonging to me)"] in another Davidic psalm, Ps 27:2).

**3** The NIV vocalizes the MT אֱלֹהֵי (*'$^{e}$lōhê*) as אֱלֹהַי (*'$^{e}$lōhay,* "my God"), doubtless correctly (cf. אֵלִי [*'ēlî*] in Ps 18:2 [3 MT]; cf. also v.7). By the same token, therefore, the MT *'$^{e}$lōhê* in Ps 43:2 should be revocalized as *'$^{e}$lōhay,* the resulting line reading either "You are my God, my stronghold," or "You, my God, are my stronghold" (cf. *'$^{e}$lōhāy,* "my God," in 43:4–5).

After "my stronghold" Ps 18:2 [3 MT] omits "my refuge and my savior—from violent men you save me," resulting in a different poetic scansion of its lines from that in 2 Samuel (cf. Ps 18:2 NIV).

**5** Although אפפני (*'ppny*) is in the perfect "tense" and יבעתני (*yb'tny*) is in the imperfect, both are correctly translated as past-tense verbs ("swirled about," "overwhelmed"). The frequent alternation of perfect and imperfect verbs is "a technique of Hebrew poetic craft, without significance in meaning" (Kselman, "Psalm 3," p. 577 n. 13; cf. similarly Cross and Freedman, *Studies in Ancient Yahwistic Poetry,* p. 28).

Instead of "waves of death," Ps 18:4 (5 MT) reads "cords of death," doubtless a scribal error imported from "cords of the grave" in the next verse. "Waves" is a much better parallel for "torrents" than is "cords."

**7** Whereas v.7 reads "I called . . . I called . . . my cry," Ps 18:6 (7 MT) has "I called . . . I cried [for help] . . . my cry." A good case can be made for both variants, since in the original text the second element could have been intended as a reflection of either the first or the third.

The MT translates literally as "my cry . . . to his ears," the verb "came" being understood elliptically rather than expressed formally. תָּבוֹא (*tāḇô',* "came") occurs in the text of Ps 18:6 [7 MT]. For the possibility that it accidentally dropped out of the Samuel text and for a suggestion concerning how it might have happened, cf. Cross and Freedman, "A Royal Song of Thanksgiving," p. 23 n. 13.

**9** The antiquity of the theophanic description (vv.8–16) is well illustrated in its frequent use of -בּ (*b-*) in the sense of "from" (*b-* is the normal way of representing "from" in Ugaritic): "from his nostrils" (v.9), "from heaven" (Ps 18:13; 2 Sam 22:14 employs מִן [*min*]), "at/from the rebuke" (v.16; Ps 18:15 reads *min;* cf. Cross and Freedman, *Studies in Ancient Yahwistic Poetry,* pp. 27–28; Sarna, "The Interchange of the Prepositions *Beth* and *Min* in Biblical Hebrew," pp. 312–13).

**11** "Soared" (וידא [*wyd'*]), parallel to "flew," is clearly better than וירא (*wyr'*), "appeared" (for details see NIV mg.). The scribal error in most MSS of the MT is due to the similarity between ד (*d*) and ר (*r*) as well as to the rarity of the verb דָּאָה (*dā'â,* "soar," "swoop [down]"), which is found elsewhere only in Deut 28:49; Ps 18:10 [11 MT]; Jer 48:40; 49:22. It is also possible that ויראו (*wyr'w*), which begins v.16 in the MT, had its baleful influence on the errant scribe.

**12** The MT סכות (*skwt,* "canopies") is probably a scribal error caused by metathesis of סכתו (*sktw,* "his canopy"; for *sktw* cf. Ps 18:11 [12 MT]; cf. also similar readings in several Heb. MSS and in some ancient versions of v.12 as documented in BHS).

"Dark" (חשכת [*ḥškt*]), as in Ps 18:11 (12 MT), is surely the correct reading instead of the MT "massed" (חשרת [*ḥšrt*]; see NIV mg.), a word unattested elsewhere. For an attempt to connect *ḥšrt* with late Hebrew *ḥšrh* ("sieve") and therefore to understand the word as suggesting sieve-like clouds through which rainwater drops, see Cross and Freedman, "A Royal Song of Thanksgiving," p. 25 n. 33.

**13** "Bolts of lightning [lit., 'coals of fire'] blazed forth" answers to "burning coals blazed out" in v.9. "Clouds advanced" (עָבָיו עָבְרוּ [*'āḇāyw 'āḇ$^{e}$rû*]), added in Ps 18:12 (13 MT), was perhaps influenced by "clouds" in Ps 18:11 (12 MT) and a metathesis of "blazed" (בָּעֲרוּ [*bā'$^{a}$rû*]) in v.13. "With hailstones and" (בָּרָד וְ- [*bārāḏ w$^{e}$-*]), also added, possibly arose from a corruption of "blazed" as well, and the repetition of "with hailstones and bolts of lightning" in Ps 18:13 (14 MT) compounded the problem (see NIV mg. in loc.).

**14** For the probable parallelism between "LORD" and "Most High" in the Song of Hannah, see Notes on 1 Sam 2:10 (cf. also Freedman, "Divine Names," pp. 67, 90–91).

**15** The *Kethiv* ויהמם (*wyhmm*, "and routed them") is to be preferred over the suffixless *Qere* ויהם (*wyhm*), not only because of Ps 18:14 (15 MT), but also because of the similar reading in Ps 144:6.

**16** The version of David's poem in Psalm 18 personalizes the final phrases of the theophany by reading "your rebuke, O LORD," and "your nostrils" (Ps 18:15 [16 MT]) instead of "the rebuke of the LORD" and "his nostrils" respectively.

**17** "He reached down" is elliptical for "reached down his hand" (cf. Davidic Ps 144:7; cf. similarly Cross and Freedman, "A Royal Song of Thanksgiving," p. 26 n. 44).

**23** The MT of v.23b translates literally, "As for his decrees, I have not turned away [אָסוּר (*'āsûr*), Qal] from them" (מִמֶּנָּה [*mimmennāh*], to be analyzed either as the preposition plus third person feminine singular suffix, "her/it" [understood collectively], or as the preposition plus a remnant of the third person feminine plural suffix "from them" [for which cf. Cross and Freedman, "A Royal Song of Thanksgiving," p. 27 n. 55; cf. also LXX ἀπ' αὐτῶν [*ap' autōn*]). The MT of the parallel in Ps 18:22 (23 MT) translates literally, "His decrees I have not turned away [אָסִיר (*'āsîr*), Hiphil] from me" (מֶנִּי [*mennî*]), an alternate way of expressing the same idea.

**24** What appears to be a first person singular suffix (ִי [-*î*]) on "sin" is probably to be analyzed instead as "an old genitive case ending" (Cross and Freedman, "A Royal Song of Thanksgiving," p. 28 n. 58).

**28** Since the sign of the definite accusative is extremely rare in poetry, it is better to vocalize את (*'t*) as אַתְּ (*'attā*, "you"; cf. אַתָּה [*'attâh*] in Ps 18:27 [28 MT]; cf. also σύ [*sy*] in some MSS of the LXX) than as אֶת (*'et*) with the MT.

**30** Although גְּדוּד (*gᵉdûd*, "troop," "raiding band/party") is attested elsewhere in the books of Samuel (cf. 4:2; 1 Sam 30:8, 15, 23 ["forces"]), the Lucianic recension of the LXX reads πεφραγμένος (*pephragmenos*, "fenced, fortified, walled"), suggesting גָּדוּר (*gādûr*, "wall[ed]") in its Hebrew exemplar. The final ד (*d*) in the MT's גדוד (*gdwd*) is thus perhaps a scribal error for ר (*r*).

**33** Although the Hebrew MS evidence for וַיִּתֵּן (*wayyittēn*, "and makes") is extremely weak (cf. BHS), the NIV prefers it (perhaps because of Ps 18:32 [33 MT]) to the MT וַיַּתֵּר (*wayyattēr*), a Hiphil form of נתר (*ntr*), which means either "cause to tremble" (cf. Hab 3:6) or "let loose, release, set free, untie" (cf. Job 6:9; Pss 105:20; 146:7; Isa 58:6). Attempts to parse the form as though from יתר (*ytr*, "be affluent, rich"; cf. Mitchell Dahood, "Hebrew-Ugaritic Lexicography III," *Biblica* 46 [1965]: 325–26), from תור (*twr*, "spy out, go around"; cf. KD, p. 479), or from תאר (*t'r*, "trace out, draw in outline"; cf. McCarter, *II Samuel*, p. 459) are unconvincing.

**35** "Bend" translates נחת (*nḥt*, masc. sing.) here, נחתה (*nḥth*, fem. sing.) in Ps 18:34 (35 MT), neither form exhibiting concord with the Hebrew feminine plural word underlying "arms" (but cf. GKC, sec. 145*o* for the former, 145*k* for the latter). An alternative is to read with one Hebrew MS נחתת (*nḥtt*) from the root חתת (*ḥtt*), to understand "bow" as the subject, and to translate: "A bow of bronze is broken by my arms." Although the resulting text is somewhat more difficult grammatically, reading the root *ḥtt* has the advantage of forging yet another link between the Song of David and the Song of Hannah (see 1 Sam 2:4 and comment).

**36** Between "You give me your shield of victory" and "you stoop down to make me great," Ps 18:35 (36 MT) inserts the line "and your right hand sustains me," for the secondary nature of which see the discussion in McCarter, *II Samuel*, p. 460.

**38** "Crushed" (אשמידם [*'šmydm*]) and "overtook" (אשיגם [*'śygm*], Ps 18:37 [38 MT]) are "old variants" (Cross and Freedman, "A Royal Song of Thanksgiving," p. 31 n. 86).

**40** The form ותזרני (*wtzrny*, "You armed me") is contracted from ותאזרני (*wt'zrny;* cf. Ps 18:39). For other examples of the elision of first-radical א (') in Piel forms, see GKC, sec. 68*k* (see also Notes on 20:5).

**41** "You made" renders נָתַתָּה (*nātattāh*) from נתן (*ntn*) in Ps 18:40 (41 MT). Here in v.41 the form is simply תַּתָּה (*tattāh*), probably a scribal error for יָתַתָּ(ה) (*yātattā[h]*), "a Canaanite dialectal form (root, *ytn*), as in Ugar. and Phoen." (Cross and Freedman, "A Royal Song of

Thanksgiving," p. 32 n. 91). The loss of the ־י (*y*-) may have resulted from haplography, since the previous word ends in *y* (cf. also Watson, "Shared Consonants," p. 538).

43 "I pounded," parallel to "I beat," translates אדקם (*'dqm*) and is doubtless the correct reading. "I poured . . . out" (אריקם [*'ryqm*], Ps 18:42 [43 MT]) arose because of the common confusion between ד (*d*) and ר (*r*).

47 "Rock" appears in the second line of v.47 (but not in the second line of Ps 18:46 [47 MT]), perhaps repeated by mistake from the first line. In any case, if "Rock" is retained אֱלֹהֵי (*'elōhê*, "God") should be revocalized as אֱלֹהַי (*'elōhay*, "my God"), since the MT construct form is ungrammatical as it stands. The NIV has in fact performed the same revocalization in v.3 (see Notes there), and doing it here would thus enhance the *inclusio* already demonstrable between the two verses (see comment on vv.2–4).

---

## D. *David's Last Words*

### 23:1–7

1 These are the last words of David:

"The oracle of David son of Jesse,
  the oracle of the man exalted by the Most High,
the man anointed by the God of Jacob,
  Israel's singer of songs:

2 "The Spirit of the LORD spoke through me;
  his word was on my tongue.
3 The God of Israel spoke,
  the Rock of Israel said to me:
'When one rules over men in righteousness,
  when he rules in the fear of God,
4 he is like the light of morning at sunrise
  on a cloudless morning,
like the brightness after rain
  that brings the grass from the earth.'

5 "Is not my house right with God?
  Has he not made with me an everlasting covenant,
  arranged and secured in every part?
Will he not bring to fruition my salvation
  and grant me my every desire?
6 But evil men are all to be cast aside like thorns,
  which are not gathered with the hand.
7 Whoever touches thorns
  uses a tool of iron or the shaft of a spear;
  they are burned up where they lie."

Sharing with the Song of David (ch. 22) the center of the extensive structural chiasm that makes up chapters 21–24 (see comment on 21:1–24:25) are vv.1–7, characterized by the narrator as the "last words of David" (v.1). Like their counterpart in chapter 22, vv.1–7 are generally acknowledged to have been written by David himself (cf. Hertzberg, p. 400; Kruse, "David's Covenant," p. 148; G. Del Olmo Lete, "David's Oracle [2 Samuel xxiii 1–7]: A Literary Analysis," VetTest 34, 4 [1984]: 430 n. 40) and are therefore given a date in the tenth century B.C. (cf. Cross, *Canaanite Myth and Hebrew Epic*, p. 234; H. Neil Richardson, "The Last Words of David: Some Notes on II Samuel 23:1–7," JBL 90, 3 [1971]: 257; Freedman, "Divine Names," pp. 73, 88, 96).

Although it is common for students of David's elegant peroration to emphasize its undoubted wisdom motifs (cf. P.A.H. de Boer, "Texte et Traduction des Paroles Attribuées à David en 2 Samuel xxiii 1–7," in *Volume du Congres: Strasbourg 1956*, suppl. to VetTest 4 [Leiden: Brill, 1957], p. 48), Del Olmo Lete has made a good case for prophetic and royal-dynastic elements in addition to sapiential features (cf. "David's Oracle," pp. 434–37). Indeed, "the metaphors, 'morning of sunshine light' and 'fertilizing rain' [v.4], take in and synthesize the whole royal ideology of the Near East, adopted by Israel and reinterpreted conditionally according to the Yahwistic covenant system depending on behaviour" (ibid., p. 431; cf. Brueggemann, *Power, Providence, and Personality*, pp. 97–99; Johnson, *Sacral Kingship in Ancient Israel*, pp. 14–17; see also comments on 7:1–17).

After the narrator's superscript (v.1a), the poem itself begins. Two internal chiasms (vv.2a/3b, vv.5a/5de; cf. Richardson, "The Last Words of David," pp. 259, 262, 264 [following unpublished observations made by David Noel Freedman]) supplement the overall chiastic structure of David's oracle (cf. similarly Del Olmo Lete, "David's Oracle," pp. 424, 430):

A. David speaks in the third person about himself (23:1b–e).
  B. David speaks in the first person (23:2–3ab).
    C. The Lord speaks (23:3cd–4).
  B′. David speaks in the first person (23:5).
A′. David speaks in the third person about evil men (23:6–7).

By nestling the divine description of the ideal king in the middle of the poem, David's "last words" give God the central—and therefore the final—word.

**1a** As de Boer observes ("Texte et Traduction," p. 48), "Words of (דִּבְרֵי [*diḇrê*]) David" recalls Proverbs 30:1 with respect to Agur and Proverbs 31:1 with respect to King Lemuel (*diḇrê* is translated "sayings of" in both verses). Like Agur and King Lemuel, King David has gained the reputation of being a wise man—in his case, more than a wise man (see comments on 14:17, 19b, 20).

Even allowing for dischronologization in the books of Samuel, the phrase "last words" need not be understood in the sense of the last words David spoke during his lifetime but is doubtless used in a way analogous to "last will and testament" or the like. Verses 1b–7 summarize his final literary legacy to Israel.

**1b–e** David begins by identifying his poem as an "oracle" and by providing his listeners/readers with a laudatory self-description. Although the Hebrew word rendered "oracle" (*nᵉ'um*) is almost always applied to the Lord in reference to what he solemnly "declares" (cf. 1 Sam 2:30), in a few cases it is used of men in prophetic (cf. Balaam son of Beor, Num 24:3a, 15a) or wisdom settings (cf. Agur son of Jakeh, Prov 30:1a ["declared"]). Just as the fathers of Balaam and Agur are named in the texts cited, so David is here referred to as "David son of Jesse" (cf. also 1 Chron 10:14; 29:26; cf. esp. the editorial note in Ps 72:20: "This concludes the prayers of David son of Jesse"), and just as v.1b is paralleled in v.1c by beginning with the words "the oracle of the man" (*nᵉ'um haggeḇer*), so are the next lines in the verses cited (Num 24:3b, 15b ["the oracle of one"]: Prov 30:1b ["This man declared"]).

If in v.1c–e David awards himself three titles that appear grandiose, it is to his credit that two of them give the Lord the glory for David's success. David considers himself to be exalted by the "Most High" (*'āl*), an abbreviated divine epithet identified some fifty years ago in the Hebrew text (see Notes on 1 Sam 2:10; cf. also Hos 7:16; 11:7; cf. Freedman, "Divine Names," pp. 65, 73, 91; Dahood, "Hebrew-Ugaritic Lexicography III," p. 324; id., "The Divine Name *'Ēlî* in the Psalms," p. 452). David represents himself as a man "anointed" (see comments on 5:3; 1 Sam 16:13) by the "God of Jacob" (cf. Davidic Pss 20:1; 24:6; cf. also Pss 46:7, 11; 75:9; 76:6; 81:1, 4; 84:8; 94:7; Isa 2:3 = Mic 4:2).

Finally, David declares himself to be "Israel's singer of songs" (*neʿîm zemirôṯ yiśrā'ēl,* lit., "the pleasant one of the songs of Israel"; cf. S.R. Driver, *Notes on the Books of Samuel,* p. 357, for full discussion). Richardson asserts that *n'(y)m* is "an epithet for heroes and royal persons, as in Ugaritic" ("The Last Words of David," p. 261), and observes that it is "translated 'beloved' by H.L. Ginsberg" (see also NIV mg.) in ANET, p. 143 (Richardson, "The Last Words of David," p. 261 n. 19). But since *nā'îm* is used in a context of music in Psalm 81:2 (where it is rendered "melodious"), the traditional "singer" is both plausible and defensible.

As for *zemirôṯ* ("songs"), Theodor H. Gaster suggested long ago that, on the basis of context as well as of cognates in other Semitic languages (including especially Ugaritic), *zimrāṯ* in Exodus 15:2 (where it is traditionally rendered "song") means "protection" or the like ("Notes on 'The Song of the Sea' [Exodus xv.]," ExpT 48 [1936–1937]: 45). His proposal and its implications for v.1e have found widespread acceptance over the past half-century (cf. Richardson, "The Last Words of David," pp. 259, 261; Freedman, "Divine Names," p. 58; Anderson, p. 268). At the same time, however, the word is attested frequently in the sense of "song(s)" (cf. Job 35:10; Pss 95:2 ["music and song"]; 119:54; Isa 24:16 ["singing"]). For the entire phrase Lewis proposes "the bard of Israel's songs" (*Cults of the Dead,* p. 52). Although Del Olmo Lete prefers to render *zemirôṯ* "Defence" as a divine epithet ("David's Oracle," p. 425), he admits that "the possibility of 'word play' cannot be altogether discarded" (p. 416).

**2–3ab** David's fourfold ascription of divine origin (vv.2–3ab) to the revelation that comes to him (vv.3cd–4) is arranged chiastically. The MT of v.2a has the subject (a construct phrase) first, then the verb (*dibber*), then a prepositional phrase: "The-Spirit-of-the-LORD spoke through-me." The MT of its corresponding line (v.3b) reverses the elements by placing a prepositional phrase first, then the verb (again *dibber*), then the subject (a construct phrase), suggesting the following literal translation: "To-me spoke the-Rock-of-Israel." The end result is a tightly crafted *inclusio* that guarantees the unity of the section (cf. Richardson, "The Last Words of David," pp. 259, 262).

As the "Spirit of God came upon" Balaam and enabled him to utter the "words of God" (Num 24:2, 4; cf. similarly 1 Chron 12:18), so also "the Spirit of the LORD spoke through" David (v.2) and delivered to him the message that God wanted him to receive. That David spoke "by the Spirit" on another occasion is affirmed by Jesus himself (Matt 22:43), and David's use of the phrase "spoke through" represents a clear claim to divine inspiration (cf. Hos 1:2; cf. similarly Num 12:2; 1 Kings 22:28). David is conscious of the fact that the "word" of the Lord was on his "tongue" (cf. Davidic Ps 139:4; cf. also the description of the wife of noble character in Prov 31:26) and that the mighty "Rock of Israel" (see comments on 22:3; 1 Sam 2:2; cf. esp. Isa 30:29) had spoken to him.

**3cd–4** "Qualities of an Ideal King" could well be the caption of the Lord's portrait of royalty mediated through David. The root *mšl* ("rules," v.3) occurs only here in the books of Samuel and was perhaps chosen because of its frequent appearance in OT wisdom literature. "Fear of God," the generic term for "religion, piety" in ancient Israel (cf. similarly Freedman, "Divine Names," p. 62), was also a common wisdom motif (see comment on 1 Sam 12:14). Thus he who rules in the fear of God rules "in righteousness"—literally, "as a righteous one" (*ṣaddîq*), an epithet that has clear messianic connotations (cf. Jer 23:5; Zech 9:9).

As amply attested by numerous scholarly attempts to translate v.4 (cf. Richardson, "The Last Words of David," p. 259; David Noel Freedman, "II Samuel 23:4," JBL 90, 3 [1971]: 329–30), the terseness of the MT makes its syntax difficult to untangle. The basic outline of the verse is evident, however: The first half compares the rule of the righteous king to the benefits of sunlight, the second half to the fertilizing effects of rain. In so doing it is remarkably similar to Psalm 72, where the ideal ruler, characterized by "righteousness" (72:1–2), will endure as long as the "sun" (72:5) and will be like "rain" that waters the earth (72:6; cf. also Del Olmo Lete, "David's Oracle," pp. 435–36).

That a king should be compared to the sun, which was originally created to "govern" (*mšl*) the day (Gen 1:16, 18), is not surprising. Indeed, solar language was employed in royal ideology throughout the ancient Near East (cf. the detailed discussion in Hans-Peter Stähli, *Solare Elemente in Jahweglauben des alten Testaments*, Orbis Biblicus et Orientalis 66 [Göttingen: Vandenhoeck and Ruprecht, 1985]). The righteous king is like the first "light of morning" (*'ôr bōqer*, v.4), just after dawn (cf. 17:22 ["daybreak"]; 1 Sam 14:36 ["dawn"]; 25:34, 36) on a cloudless day at "sunrise." Carlson perceptively observes that "it is thus deeply symbolical that David is punished 'in the sight of the sun' " (p. 257; see comments on "in broad daylight" in 12:11–12).

The image of "brightness" is continued into the latter half of v.4— now related, however, not to sunshine but to the lightning that accompanies thunderstorms (see 22:13 and comment). It would therefore perhaps be better to translate "brightness associated with rain" (or the like) instead of "brightness after rain" (NIV). As the fructifying influence of rain helps the grass to grow (cf. Deut 32:2), so also the benevolent rule of a righteous king causes his people to flourish (cf. Ps 72:6–7). It may be instructive to observe that news of the death of King Saul evoked from David a curse against the mountains of Gilboa, imploring that they might no longer have dew or "rain" (1:21). If the presence of the ideal king produces health and prosperity, the absence of royal rule—of whatever sort—guarantees famine and drought.

**5** Just as the corresponding section is arranged chiastically (see comment on vv.2–3b), so also is the present section (cf. Richardson, "The Last Words of David," pp. 259, 264), which consists of a series of negative rhetorical questions expecting positive answers. The MT begins with *kî-lō'* ("Is not"), which is followed by a verb (or verbal adjective), "right/established"; the verse ends with *kî-lō'* followed by a verb ("Will he not bring to fruition"). ***Kî emphaticum*** ("surely" or the like) occurs twice more in the MT of v.5 and underscores the forcefulness of David's confidence (for other examples of ***kî emphaticum,*** cf. T. Muraoka, ***Emphatic Words and Structures in Biblical Hebrew*** [Jerusalem: Magnes], pp. 158–64; Dahood, "Hebrew-Ugaritic Lexicography III," p. 327; cf. also Aejmelaeus, "Function and Interpretation of כי in Biblical Hebrew," pp. 195, 208).

Encouraged by the possibilities for righteous leadership implied in the Lord's words, David speaks positively of his "house" (i.e., his family and dynasty; see comment on 7:11b), of the covenant that God had made with him, of the fruition of his salvation, and of the fulfillment of all his desires. He had been convinced that his "house" would be "established" (*kwn*) in God's presence (7:26), as Nathan the prophet had reported to him (cf. 7:11, where, however, "established" renders a different Heb. root), and he is now sure that his "house" is "right with God" (better, "established [*kwn*] in the presence of God").

An enduring dynasty was part of the "everlasting covenant" (*b*ᵉ*rîṯ 'ôlām*) that the Lord had made with David (v.5; cf. similarly with Noah, Gen 9:16; with Abraham, Gen 17:7; with Israel through Moses at Sinai, Exod 31:16 ["lasting covenant"]; Lev 24:8; with Aaron, Num 18:19; with Phinehas, Num 25:13 ["covenant of a lasting (priesthood)"]; with the new people of God, Jer 32:40; 50:5; Ezek 16:60; 37:26). Attempts by Freedman ("Divine Names," pp. 73–74, 92, 100 n. 39) and others (cf. Richardson, "The Last Words of David," pp. 259, 263–64) to read *'ôlām* as a divine epithet and translate the clause "Has not the Eternal made a covenant with me?" founder not only on the frequency of *b*ᵉ*rîṯ 'ôlām* as a *terminus technicus* in the OT but also on the common occurrence of its semantic equivalents elsewhere (for details cf. Weinfeld, "The Covenant of Grant," pp. 199–201). In addition, "forever" (*'aḏ-'ôlām, l*ᵉ*'ôlām*) looms large in chapter 7 (cf. vv.13, 16, 24, 25, 26, 29; see comment on 7:13b; see also 22:51 and comment).

After rejoicing in the fact that in every detail the Lord's covenant with him is "arranged" (cf. Job 13:18 ["prepared"]) and "secured" (cf. Deut 7:8 ["kept"], 12 ["keep"]), David expresses his assurance that God will bring his "salvation" to fruition (cf. the Davidic Ps 12:5 ["protect"]; Job 5:4, 11 ["safety"]; see 22:3 and comments) and grant him his "every desire" (as Hiram would later do for David's son Solomon; cf. 1 Kings 5:8 ["all you want"], 10; 9:11).

**6–7** If in v.1b–e David speaks in the third person about himself as a man blessed by God, in vv.6–7 by way of contrast he describes the fate of "evil men" (*b*ᵉ*lîya'al;* see comment on "troublemakers" in 1 Sam 30:22; see also Notes on 1 Sam 1:16). All of them are to be cast aside like "thorns" (cf. Ezek 28:24), whose sharp-pointed branches make them too dangerous to pick up with unprotected hands. Anyone touching them is well-advised to use a tool of "iron" (v.7; see comments on 1 Sam 13:19–22) or the "shaft of a spear"—both of which conjure up images of offensive weapons that can be used to kill an enemy (see comments on 1 Sam 17:7; see also 2 Sam 21:19 and comment). A parallel way of destroying thorns (or enemies) is to burn them up (cf. Ps 118:12; Isa 9:18; 33:12) "where they lie" (*baššāḇeṯ,* felicitously rendered "on the spot," "*in situ,*" by Johnson, *Sacral Kingship in Ancient Israel,* p. 17 and n. 8).

> It would be possible to see here a counter-replica of Jotham's famous apologue (Judg. ix 7–15), "the trees looking for a king", perhaps the most pungent criticism of the monarchy ever written. In contrast to the attitude of the "thorny shrub" (*'āṭāḏ*), the only pretender to kingship who commands everybody to come under this [*sic*] protection ("shadow") and threatens them otherwise with the "fire" that will come out from it, here the "thorn" (*qôṣ*) appears to be unapproachable to any but the unfriendly, and is itself allotted to the "fire" that will eat it up. (Del Olmo Lete, "David's Oracle," pp. 436–43)

If evil men are "cast aside" (v.6), the anointed of the Lord, God's Messiah, is "exalted" (v.1).

And thus David's "last words" (v.1) come to an end. Along with all his other poems, they represent a legacy and variety of hymns that are unparalleled elsewhere in Scripture. Israel's ideal king was also, indeed, "Israel's singer of songs," "Israel's beloved singer" (v.1). In the words of the fourth stanza of "Jerusalem, My Happy Home" (Joseph Bromehead, 1795):

There David stands with harp in hand
　As master of the choir:
Ten thousand times that man were blest
　That might this music hear.

## Notes

6 In BHS בְּקוֹץ (*b<sup>e</sup>qôṣ*) is a typographical error for כְּקוֹץ (*k<sup>e</sup>qôṣ*, "like thorns"; cf. BH; cf. Del Olmo Lete, "David's Oracle," p. 422 n. 23).

The unique form כֻּלָּהַם (*kullāham*, "all of them") is perhaps a combination of the consonants of כֻּלְּהֶם (*kull<sup>e</sup>hem*) and the vowels of כֻּלָּם (*kullām*; cf. similarly de Boer, "Texte et Traduction," p. 55).

7 P. de Boer suggests ("avec de grandes réserves," to be sure) that בַּשָּׁבֶת (*baššā<u>b</u>e<u>t</u>*, "where they lie"; usually parsed as from ישב [*yšb*]; see also comment above) derives from the root שבת (*šbt*, "cease, rest"), and thus he translates "dans l'air calme"—that is, "in a situation where destruction by fire presents no danger of spreading" (p. 55). Although his proposal is perhaps not as farfetched as it may at first appear, it is surely not an improvement over more traditional renderings. Dahood's "without cessation" fares no better, depending as it does on understanding ־בּ (*b-*) in the rare sense of "without" ("Hebrew-Ugaritc Lexicography X," p. 403).

### E. *David's Mighty Men*

### 23:8–39

[8]These are the names of David's mighty men:
Josheb-Basshebeth, a Tahkemonite, was chief of the Three; he raised
his spear against eight hundred men, whom he killed in one encounter.
[9]Next to him was Eleazar son of Dodai the Ahohite. As one of the three
mighty men, he was with David when they taunted the Philistines
gathered ⌊at Pas Dammim⌋ for battle. Then the men of Israel retreated,
[10]but he stood his ground and struck down the Philistines till his hand
grew tired and froze to the sword. The LORD brought about a great
victory that day. The troops returned to Eleazar, but only to strip the
dead.
[11]Next to him was Shammah son of Agee the Hararite. When the
Philistines banded together at a place where there was a field full of
lentils, Israel's troops fled from them. [12]But Shammah took his stand in
the middle of the field. He defended it and struck the Philistines down,
and the LORD brought about a great victory.
[13]During harvest time, three of the thirty chief men came down to
David at the cave of Adullam, while a band of Philistines was encamped
in the Valley of Rephaim. [14]At that time David was in the stronghold, and

the Philistine garrison was at Bethlehem. 15David longed for water and
said, "Oh, that someone would get me a drink of water from the well
near the gate of Bethlehem!" 16So the three mighty men broke through
the Philistine lines, drew water from the well near the gate of Bethlehem
and carried it back to David. But he refused to drink it; instead, he
poured it out before the LORD. 17"Far be it from me, O LORD, to do this!"
he said. "Is it not the blood of men who went at the risk of their lives?"
And David would not drink it.

Such were the exploits of the three mighty men.

18Abishai the brother of Joab son of Zeruiah was chief of the Three.
He raised his spear against three hundred men, whom he killed, and so
he became as famous as the Three. 19Was he not held in greater honor
than the Three? He became their commander, even though he was not
included among them.

20Benaiah son of Jehoiada was a valiant fighter from Kabzeel, who
performed great exploits. He struck down two of Moab's best men. He
also went down into a pit on a snowy day and killed a lion. 21And he
struck down a huge Egyptian. Although the Egyptian had a spear in his
hand, Benaiah went against him with a club. He snatched the spear from
the Egyptian's hand and killed him with his own spear. 22Such were the
exploits of Benaiah son of Jehoiada; he too was as famous as the three
mighty men. 23He was held in greater honor than any of the Thirty, but
he was not included among the Three. And David put him in charge of
his bodyguard.

24Among the Thirty were:

Asahel the brother of Joab,
Elhanan son of Dodo from Bethlehem,
25Shammah the Harodite,
Elika the Harodite,
26Helez the Paltite,
Ira son of Ikkesh from Tekoa,
27Abiezer from Anathoth,
Mebunnai the Hushathite,
28Zalmon the Ahohite,
Maharai the Netophathite,
29Heled son of Baanah the Netophathite,
Ithai son of Ribai from Gibeah in Benjamin,
30Benaiah the Pirathonite,
Hiddai from the ravines of Gaash,
31Abi-Albon the Arbathite,
Azmaveth the Barhumite,
32Eliahba the Shaalbonite,
the sons of Jashen,
Jonathan 33son of Shammah the Hararite,
Ahiam son of Sharar the Hararite,
34Eliphelet son of Ahasbai the Maacathite,
Eliam son of Ahithophel the Gilonite,
35Hezro the Carmelite,
Paarai the Arbite,
36Igal son of Nathan from Zobah,
the son of Hagri,
37Zelek the Ammonite,
Naharai the Beerothite, the armor-bearer
of Joab son of Zeruiah,
38Ira the Ithrite,
Gareb the Ithrite
39and Uriah the Hittite.

There were thirty-seven in all.

Mirroring the account of the memorable deeds of David's heros in 21:15–22 is the list of his mighty men in 23:8–39, which includes reports of several exploits that heighten the similarities between the two narratives and thus enhance the chiastic structure of chapters 21–24 (see comment on 21:1–24:25). The section divides naturally into two main segments, the first of which describes adventures experienced by warriors in the highest echelons of David's army (vv.8–23, paralleled in 1 Chron 11:11–25) and the second of which provides a list of notable fighting men who were among the "Thirty" (vv.24–39, paralleled in 1 Chron 11:26–41a). The first segment consists of three roughly equal parts, each of which summarizes one or more heroic exploits: (1) of the "Three" (vv.8–12); (2) of "three of the thirty chief men" (vv.13–17); (3) of two particularly notable fighters, of whom one was chief of the Three and the other was put in charge of David's bodyguard (vv.18–23).

While it is sometimes assumed that the Three were over the Thirty (cf. Merrill, *Kingdom of Priests*, p. 282), the precise relationships between the various power blocs in David's military administration remain debatable (for a useful survey cf. Benjamin Mazar, "The Military Elite of King David," VetTest 133 [1963]: 310–20). Needless to say, their composition and leadership varied through the years, as even the present section attests.

**8–12** The parallel in 1 Chronicles is introduced with the statement that David's mighty men and/or their chiefs "gave his kingship strong support to extend it over the whole land" (1 Chron 11:10). Since the context in 1 Chronicles is the anointing of David as king over Israel after his seven-year reign in Hebron (1 Chron 11:1–3) followed by the conquest of Jerusalem (1 Chron 11:4–9), vv.8–39 doubtless represent the organization of David's military command at a time relatively early in his reign over all Israel. Indeed, many of the events in the section should perhaps be dated even earlier in light of the fact that "the appearance of Asahel, brother of Joab, in the list of the heroes [v.24] sets a *terminus ad quem* for the list as a whole, since Asahel was murdered by Abner during the war between Eshbaal and David at the beginning of David's reign at Hebron" (Mazar, "The Military Elite," p. 318; see comment on 2:23). In most respects the account in vv.8–39 agrees with that in 1 Chronicles 11:11–41a "except that there are a considerable number of errors of the text, more especially in the names, which are frequently corrupt in both texts, so that the true reading cannot be determined with certainty" (KD, p. 491).

"These are the names of" (v.8) is a stock formula that echoes the opening words of the Book of Exodus (Exod 1:1). *Gibbōrîm*, elsewhere a general term for unusually strong and courageous soldiers (cf. 1 Sam 2:4 ["warriors"]; 17:51 ["hero"]), is here translated "mighty men" in a more specific sense, almost always in connection with the number "three" (vv.9, 16, 17, 22).

First to be mentioned is Jashobeam (1 Chron 11:11; the second element in the variant "Josheb-Basshebeth" in v.8 is probably a scribal error caused by vertical dittography from the end of v.7 [see comment and Notes in loc.; for other possibilities see NIV mg. on v.8]). His patronymic, Tahkemonite (otherwise unknown), is "probably a variant of Hacmonite" (of equally obscure origin) in 1 Chronicles 11:11 (see NIV mg.; cf. also "Hacmoni" in 1 Chron 27:32). Jashobeam, among others during David's long reign (cf., e.g., Abishai, v.18), was "chief of the Three" (v.8). Since the Hebrew words for "three" (*šlš, šlšh, šlšt*), "thirty" (*šlšym*), and "officer" (*šlyš*) are similar to each other, they are sometimes miscopied, and it is therefore not always possible to tell which one was intended by the author/compiler (cf. 1 Chron 11:11 and

NIV mg. there). Three and thirty are relatively common numbers in the OT, the former "used as a minimum plural" and the latter "to express . . . minimum decemplurality" (Segal, "Numerals," p. 19). In terms of David's military administration, the regular regiment of four hundred to six hundred men (see comments on 1 Sam 22:2; 23:13) "was divided into three units: Two fighting units and one unit to guard the weapons [see comments on 1 Sam 25:13; 30:9–10]. This division was most certainly based on ancient tradition. It presumably served as the basis for the emergence of David's three commanding officers or 'champions'" (Mazar, "The Military Elite," p. 314). As for the number thirty, it is already "found in the premonarchic Israelite tradition, where there is frequent mention of thirty champions, or sons, who were associated with a charismatic personality or with the head of a clan" (ibid., p. 310; cf. n. 2, where he cites Judg 10:4; 12:9; 14:11; 1 Sam 9:22; 1 Chron 11:42; cf., however, the caveat of McCarter, *II Samuel,* pp. 496–97).

Like Abishai (cf. v.18), the courageous Jashobeam "raised his spear against" a large number of men (v.8), whom he succeeded in killing in a single encounter. Although "eight hundred" may seem an exaggeration, there is no MS evidence that would warrant reducing it to the "three hundred" in the parallel text of 1 Chronicles 11:11, where it probably arose by contamination from the same figure in 1 Chronicles 11:20 (= 2 Sam 23:18).

Jashobeam, along with eleven other warriors in vv.9–30 (virtually in sequence), resurfaces in 1 Chronicles 27 as the commander of one of David's twelve army divisions: Jashobeam, v.8 (1 Chron 27:2); Dodai, v.9 (1 Chron 27:4); Benaiah son of Jehoiada, v.20 (1 Chron 27:5); Asahel, v. 24 (1 Chron 27:7); Shammah/Shammoth/Shamhuth, v.25 (1 Chron 27:8); Ira, v.26 (1 Chron 27:9); Helez, v.26 (1 Chron 27:10); Sibbecai, v.27 (1 Chron 27:11); Abiezer, v.27 (1 Chron 27:12); Maharai, v.28 (1 Chron 27:13); Benaiah the Pirathonite, v.30 (1 Chron 27:14); Heled/Heldai, v.29 (1 Chron 27:15).

Next to Jashobeam was Eleazar, the second of the "three mighty men" (v.9). Not to be confused with the man of the same name in 1 Samuel 7:1, Eleazar was the son of Dodai the "Ahohite," the same Benjamite clan (cf. Ahoah, 1 Chron 8:4) as that of Zalmon, one of the Thirty (cf. v.28). Unlike other Israelite troops, who "retreated" (lit., "went up/away," v.9; cf. 1 Kings 15:19 ["withdraw"]; 2 Kings 12:18; Jer 21:2) from a second epic battle against the Philistines near "Pas Dammim" (see NIV mg.; see comment on Ephes Dammim in 1 Sam 17:1, which begins the account of the first battle), Eleazar "stood his ground" (v.10) and joined David as, tit for tat, they "taunted" the enemy (v.9; see comment on 21:21; the same Heb. verb is translated "defy" in 1 Sam 17:10, 25–26, 36, 45; see also comments on 1 Sam 17:43–47). Eleazar struck down the Philistines with such fierceness that his hand "froze to the sword" (v.10; for a similar phenomenon in modern times, cf. Kirkpatrick, *The Second Book of Samuel,* p. 216) and thus "grew tired" (cf. Isa 40:30 ["grow . . . weary"] and contrast Isa 40:31 ["not grow weary"]). But there was victory nonetheless—a "great victory" that, as in the case of Shammah (cf. v.12), was brought about by the Lord (see comments on 19:2; 1 Sam 19:5). Although not participating in the battle itself, the troops who had fled (cf. v.9) returned in order to "strip" the dead (v.10). In so doing, David's men repaid the indignities perpetrated by the Philistines on an earlier occasion (see 1 Sam 31:8 and comment).

Third and last of the "three mighty men" (v.9) was "Shammah son of Agee" (v.11), who is not to be identified either with David's third brother (for which see 1 Sam 16:9 and comment) or with "Shammah the Harodite" (v.25). Shammah son of Agee was a

"Hararite" (a gentilic of unknown derivation) and is mentioned again in v.33 as the father of Jonathan, one of the Thirty (cf. also "Ahiam the Hararite," v.33). As fear of the Philistines had struck panic in the hearts of Israel's troops on other occasions (see comment on v.9), so also the Israelites fled when the Philistines "banded" together (v.11; cf. v.13) in a field full of "lentils" (a staple food crop; see 17:28 and comment). Depending on divine help for victory, however (see comment on v.10), Shammah took his stand in the middle of the field and defeated the enemy.

**13–17** Often correlated historically with the events described in 5:17–25 (cf. Tidwell, "Philistine Incursions," p. 198 and n. 33; Brueggemann, *In Man We Trust*, p. 36), the story of David and the three mighty men at the cave of Adullam is one of the most familiar and best loved in the entire corpus. An act of loyalty and unselfish bravery (v.16a) is matched by an act of gratitude and self-effacing chivalry (vv.16b–17), and the result is an account that highlights the most admirable qualities in all four men.

The "thirty chief men" (v.13) are doubtless to be equated with the "Thirty" (vv.23–24) who were already a part of David's growing military force when he was at Ziklag (cf. 1 Chron 12:1, 4; for David's days at Ziklag, cf. 1 Sam 27:6–12; 29:1–30:26). Early on, the Thirty had apparently "formed a kind of supreme command" under the leadership of David (Mazar, "The Military Elite," p. 310). Three of the thirty had now come "down" to him at the "cave of Adullam" (v.13; see 1 Sam 22:1 and comment), while a detachment of Philistines was camped in the "Valley of Rephaim" (see 5:18 and comment). That the "stronghold" (v.14), the "rock" (1 Chron 11:15), and the "cave" itself are various ways of referring to the same fortified area cannot be proven (see comments on 5:17; 1 Sam 22:4–5; cf. also 1 Sam 24:22).

At David's hometown of Bethlehem in Judah (see 1 Sam 16:1; 17:12 and comments), the Philistines had established a "garrison" (v.14; cf. 1 Sam 14:1, 4, 6, 11, 15 ["outpost"]). His throat parched, David expressed aloud his wistful longing (see comment on 15:4) for a drink of water from the well near Bethlehem's gate (v.15), where as a boy he had doubtless slaked his thirst on many occasions "during harvest time" (v.13). So loyal were David's three "mighty men" that his wish became their command: Heedless to the danger facing them, they marched the twelve miles from Adullam east-northeast to Bethlehem, "broke through" the Philistine lines (v.16; cf. similarly 5:20; cf. Tidwell, "Philistine Incursions," p. 198 n. 33), drew water from the well, and carried it back to David.

The account of the king's reaction to the bravery of his men (vv.16b–17) is framed by *w$^{e}$lō' 'āḇāh lištôṯām:* "But he refused to drink it" (v.16b), "And David would not drink it" (v.17). David acts and speaks within the boundaries of the *inclusio*. Instead of drinking the water, he "poured it out" before the Lord (v.16) as a libation offering (cf. Gen 35:14; Num 28:7; 2 Kings 16:13; Jer 7:18; Hos 9:4; see also 1 Sam 7:6 and comment). Instead of quenching his thirst, he solemnly and emphatically denied that he would even think of doing such a thing (v.17; see comments on 20:20; 1 Sam 22:15; 24:6) as he declared that the water symbolized the very blood of his men, who had served him "at the risk of" (i.e., "in exchange for," *bêt pretii;* see comment on 14:7; cf. also 3:14 ["for the price"]) their "lives" (v.17; cf. Num 16:38 ["at the cost of their lives"]; 1 Kings 2:23 ["pay with his life"]; Prov 7:23; cf. esp. Lam 5:9).

Thus David resisted the temptation to pull rank. "In an act of chivalry he pours the water on the ground, refusing to enjoy what his men have gotten him at great risk. He understands intuitively (and that is his greatness) that such a costly commodity is appropriately used only for a sacramental act . . . (note that the central motif is paralleled in John 12:1–8)" (Brueggemann, *In Man We Trust*, p. 37). And just as the gracious gesture of the woman who poured perfume on Jesus' head would be proclaimed everywhere "in memory of her" (Matt 26:13), so also the exploits (v.17) of the courageous warriors—whose self-denying loyalty prompted David to pour out an oblation to the Lord—would be remembered for all future generations.

**18–23** By this point in the Samuel corpus "Abishai the brother of Joab son of Zeruiah" (v.18) is well known to its readers as a brave if impetuous fighting man (see comments on 1 Sam 26:6; 2 Sam 2:18; 3:30; 16:9; 18:2; 19:21; 21:17). In light of the overall context of vv.18–19, it is more likely that, like Jashobeam (see comment on v.8), Abishai was chief of the "Three" (v.18) than of the "Thirty" (see NIV mg. for details). Also like Jashobeam (see v.8 and comment), Abishai "raised his spear against" and "killed" a large number of men. His prodigious feat of courage made him as "famous" as the Three themselves (v.18; cf. 8:13 with reference to David) and doubtless contributed to his being "held in greater honor" (cf. the variant "doubly honored," 1 Chron 11:21) than the Three (v.19; see comments on 6:20, 22; 1 Sam 9:6; and esp. 1 Sam 22:14). Indeed, although he was not included among them, he became their commander.

"Benaiah son of Jehoiada" (v.20) is likewise no stranger to readers of Samuel (see 8:18 and comment). From Kabzeel, a town somewhere in the southern Negev and originally allotted to the tribal territory of Judah (cf. Josh 15:21), he was a "valiant" fighter (like the men of Jabesh Gilead; see 1 Sam 31:12 and comment) who performed a number of exploits. Among other notable feats he struck down "Moab's two best men" (not "two of Moab's best men" [NIV], which would be expressed differently in Heb.) and, in the midst of adverse circumstances, killed a lion (thus emulating his king; see 1 Sam 17:34–37 and comment). In the eyes of the narrator, however, the most formidable of Benaiah's accomplishments (if space given to its telling is a reliable index) was apparently his encounter with a "huge" Egyptian (v.21; "seven and a half feet tall," according to 1 Chron 11:23). Armed with only a club, Benaiah snatched the Egyptian's spear from him and killed him with it.

Concluding the first main segment (vv.8–23) of its literary section (see comment on vv.8–39), vv.22–23 echo the terminology of vv.17–19 ("Such were the exploits," vv.17, 22; "as famous as the three/Three," vv.18, 22; "held in greater honor than," vv.19, 23; "not included amoung them/the Three," vv.19, 23). Since Benaiah was for a while "over the Thirty" (1 Chron 27:6)—a position occupied at other times by Ishmaiah the Gibeonite (cf. 1 Chron 12:4) and Amasai (cf. 1 Chron 12:18)—it is not surprising that he should be held in greater honor than the Thirty were (v.13). King David rewarded Benaiah by putting him in charge of his "bodyguard" (v.23), a position similar to that once occupied by David himself in the days of Saul (see 1 Sam 22:14 and comment). The term is perhaps here used in reference to the Kerethites and Pelethites (see 8:18 and comment; see also Notes on 1 Sam 30:14).

**24–39** A roster of notable warriors (vv.24–39, paralleled in 1 Chron 11:26–41a) is the second of the two main segments comprising the literary section that preserves the names and, in a few celebrated cases, the exploits of David's mighty men (vv.8–39). If the first segment (vv.8–23) focuses on the Three, the second concentrates on the Thirty.

The parallel list in Chronicles often varies from that in Samuel, especially in the last few verses. Many of the differences consist of minor spelling or transcription errors, a number of which are recorded in the NIV footnotes on vv.27–36. The total lack of NIV footnotes on 1 Chronicles 11:26–41 gives the misleading impression that all of the scribal slips are in the Samuel list, which is surely not the case. The twelve names in the list that reappear in 1 Chronicles 27 as those of commanders of David's army division have already been noted (see comment on vv.8–12). Reference to them in that role will therefore not be repeated below, nor will every variation between names in the three lists (ch. 23; 1 Chron 11; 27), which doubtless derive from different periods in David's reign, be commented on (for a comparison of corresponding names in the MT of the three lists, cf. S.R. Driver, *Notes on the Books of Samuel,* pp. 362–63).

Referred to as *gibbôrê haḥ$^{a}$yālîm* ("the mighty men") by the Chronicler (1 Chron 11:26; the term is used of David in 1 Sam 16:18 ["brave men"]; see also comment on 1 Sam 9:1), the "Thirty" (v.24) were perhaps "a kind of supreme army council which was largely responsible for framing the internal army regulations, deciding on promotions and appointments, and handling other military matters" (Yadin, *The Art of Warfare,* p. 277; see also comment on v.13). If the "sons of Jashen" (v.32) were only two in number, vv.24–39 enumerate thirty-two men who, together with Jashobeam (v.8), Eleazar (v.9), Shammah (v.11), Abishai (v.18), and Benaiah (v.20), account for the grand total of "thirty-seven" that sums up the whole (v.39). If, however, *bny* ("sons of," v.32) is a dittography of the last three letters of the previous word (*hš'lbny,* "the Shaalbonite"), and if Jashen's patronymic has dropped out of the text of v.32 (cf. BHS; cf. also "the Gizonite" in 1 Chron 11:34), then the number of men in vv.24–39 is thirty-one. To bring the total to thirty-seven an additional name must therefore be sought or implied (perhaps that of Joab, whose inclusion in the list is perhaps self-understood in light of his position "over the [entire] army" [8:16; 20:23]; cf. also the frequent incidental references to Joab in the overall section [vv.18, 24, 37]).

Some of the names in vv.24–39 are very familiar, some are less so, and some are otherwise unknown. Joab's brother Asahel (v.24), who plays a prominent role in chapter 2 (see comment on 2:18), was killed by Abner (cf. 2:23), Saul's cousin (cf. 1 Sam 14:50–51). Elhanan son of Dodo (v.24) is not to be confused with the Elhanan who killed Goliath's brother (see 21:19 and comment). Likewise Shammah the Harodite (v.25), who is called "Shammoth" in 1 Chronicles 11:27 and is probably to be identified with Shamhuth in 1 Chronicles 27:8, is not to be confused with other leaders named Shammah (see v.11 and comment).

Another Harodite was Elika (v.25), a name that probably means "God Has Guarded" (cf. Ran Zadok, "On Five Biblical Names," ZAW 89, 2 [1977]: 266). The hometown of Shammah and Elika may have been Harod (modern Ein Jalud, nine miles west-northwest of Beth Shan), whose nearby spring proved attractive to Gideon and his army before their battle against the Midianites (cf. Judg 7:1). Helez (v.26) is a name found also on a recently discovered seal impression (cf. Avigad, *Hebrew Bullae,* p. 57). Helez the Paltite (v.26) was doubtless from Beth Pelet, a town of unknown location in the Negev in the tribal territory originally allotted to Judah (cf. Josh 15:27).

Ira (v.26) is not the same as the Ira in v.38 (who is perhaps to be equated with Ira the Jairite; see comment and Notes on 20:26). Ira son of Ikkesh ("Crooked" [*'iqqēš*]; see comment on 22:27) was from Tekoa, hometown of the prophet Amos as well as of a notable wise woman (see 14:2 and comment), and Abiezer (v.27) was from Anathoth, hometown of the prophet Jeremiah (cf. Jer 1:1; for its location and pagan associations, cf. Ronald F. Youngblood, "The Call of Jeremiah," *Criswell Theological Review* 5, 1 [1990]: 100–102).

"Mebunnai" (*mbny,* v.27) is better read as "Sibbecai" (*sbky;* see NIV mg. for details). One of David's heroes mentioned in an earlier chapter, Sibbecai the Hushathite killed Saph, a descendant of Rapha (see 21:18 and comment). Like Eleazar son of Dodai, Zalmon (v.28) was an Ahohite (see v.9 and comment). Maharai (v.28) and Heled/Heleb (see NIV mg. on v.29) son of Baanah (not to be confused with the Baanah of 4:2) were both from Netophah (a town of uncertain location near Bethlehem; cf. 1 Chron 2:54; Ezra 2:22; Neh 7:26; cf. also Neh 12:28).

From Gibeah in Benjamin (Saul's hometown, modern Tell el-Ful [three miles north of Jerusalem; see comment on 1 Sam 13:2]), Ithai (*'yty,* 1 Chron 11:31) should not be confused with Ittai the Gittite (see 15:19 and comment) even though his name is spelled the same in v.29 (*'ittay*). Benaiah (v.30; not to be identified with Benaiah son of Jehoiada, v.20) was from Pirathon, hometown of the judge Abdon "in Ephraim, in the hill country of the Amalekites" (Judg 12:15). The ancient site is modern Farata, seven miles west-southwest of Shechem.

Hiddai/Hurai (v.30; see NIV mg.) was from the ravines of Gaash, a mountainous area north of which Joshua was buried at Timnath Serah/Heres (modern Khirbet Timnah, eighteen miles northwest of Jerusalem) in the hill country of Ephraim (cf. Josh 24:30 = Judg 2:9). Abi-Albon (v.31) was from Beth Arabah, a desert village somewhere on the border between Judah (cf. Josh 15:6, 61) and Benjamin (cf. Josh 18:18, 22), while Azmaveth the Barhumite (v.31) may have been from Bahurim (cf. "Baharumite" in 1 Chron 11:33), hometown of the rebel Shimei (see 3:16; 16:5b and comments).

Eliahba (v.32), which means "God Conceals (the Newborn Infant)," is constructed from the same root as Hubba ("Concealed [by God]"), a hypocoristic name found recently on a seal impression (cf. Avigad, *Hebrew Bullae,* p. 53). The hometown of Eliahba was Shaalabbin/Shaalbim (modern Selbit, nineteen miles southeast of Joppa), a town originally allotted to the tribal territory of Dan (cf. Josh 19:42; Judg 1:35; 1 Kings 4:9). The "son of" (v.33; see first NIV mg. note) Shammah the Hararite (one of the Three; see v.11 and comment) was Jonathan (v.32), obviously not to be equated with the famous son of Saul and friend of David. Also a Hararite was Ahiam son of Sharar/Sacar (v.33; see second NIV mg. note). Eliphelet (v.34), clearly not David's son who bore the same name (see 5:16 and comment), was from the Aramean district of Maacah (see 10:6 and comment), whose mercenary troops David decimated in a battle against the Ammonites (cf. ch. 10). Zobah, another kingdom of Aram defeated by David as well as by Saul before him (see comments on 8:3; 10:6; 1 Sam 14:47), is mentioned as the homeland of Igal (v.36) son of Nathan (not the famous prophet of the same name).

Especially interesting is the listing of "Eliam son of Ahithophel the Gilonite" (v.34). Father of Bathsheba (see 11:3 and comment), with whom David committed adultery, Eliam was also the son of Ahithophel, David's counselor who defected to Absalom (see 15:12 and comment)—perhaps inclined to do so because of David's sin against Ahithophel's granddaughter. Hezro (v.35) was from Carmel, a village in the hill country of Judah (see 1 Sam 15:12 and comment) that was the hometown of the infamous Nabal (cf. 1 Sam 25:2–3). Paarai was an Arbite, perhaps from Arab (also in the hill country of Judah; cf. Josh 15:52), whose modern location is possibly Khirbet er-Rabiya eight miles southwest of Hebron.

According to 1 Chronicles 11:38, the son of Hagri/Haggadi (v.36; see NIV mg.) was named Mibhar (*mbḥr*), a word that may have been accidentally omitted from 2 Samuel by haplography with the previous word (*mṣbh,* "from Zobah"). Zelek (v.37) was from Ammon east of the Jordan River, and Naharai, one of Joab's armor-bearers (see 18:15 and comment; David had once been Saul's armor-bearer [cf. 1 Sam 16:21]), was from Beeroth in Benjamin (see 4:2 and comment). Ira (v.38; not the same as the Ira in v.26) was an Ithrite, as was Gareb. Ira the Ithrite is probably to be identified with Ira the Jairite (see Notes on 20:26), who was either David's "priest" or his "royal adviser" (see comment on 20:26). "Ithrite" is perhaps the gentilic of Jattir, a Levitical town located thirteen miles south-southwest of Hebron (see comment on 1 Sam 30:27; cf. Olyan, "Zadok's Origins," p. 190).

For reasons unknown, the Chronicler omitted the total of the number of warriors at the conclusion of his list (unlike the "thirty-seven" of v.39) and added another sixteen names (cf. 1 Chron 11:41b–47). That vv.24–39 preserve the more original roster is clear from the *inclusio* formed by its first and last names. If Asahel the brother of Joab (v.24) came to an untimely end at the hands of Abner (cf. 2:23), Uriah the Hittite (v.39) met his tragic death because an adulterous king could find no other way to cover his sinful tracks (see 11:14–17 and comments). None would doubt that in virtually every other respect David, who often genuinely sought to do God's will, was an ideal king (see vv.3cd–4 and comments)—"except in the case of Uriah the Hittite" (1 Kings 15:5).

## Notes

---

**8** The abrupt (and ungrammatical) appearance of עדינו העצנו (*'dynw h'ṣnw*, "Adino the Eznite," otherwise unknown) in the MT probably arose as a corruption of עורר את־חניתו (*'wrr 't-ḥnytw*, "raised his spear"; cf. the 1 Chron 11:11 parallel; cf. also v.18 = 1 Chron 11:20; see NIV mg. on v.8).

**9** Although the *Qere* has the expected definite article (ה־ [*h-*]) on גִּבֹּרִים (*gibbōrîm*, "mighty men"), the *Kethiv* omits it, perhaps allowing the *h* on the end of the preceding word to perform double duty (cf. Watson, "Shared Consonants," p. 531).

**11** "Banded together," literally, "came together to/in a band" (לַחַיָּה [*laḥayyāh*]), is often read "came together at Lehi" (לֶחְיָה [*leḥyāh*]) on the basis of the Lucianic recension of the LXX (*ἐπὶ σιάγονα* [*epi siagona*], "at a jawbone") as well as of Judg 15:9, 14, 17 (see NIV mg.), 19 (cf. S.R. Driver, *Notes on the Books of Samuel*, p. 365). In v.13, however, חַיַּת (*ḥayyaṯ*) can only mean something like "group, band" (cf. Ps 68:10 ["people"]), making a revocalization of *laḥayyāh* in v.11 unnecessary.

First Chron 11:13 reads "barley" instead of "lentils" and attributes Shammah's feat of courage to Eleazar (and David; cf. 1 Chron 11:12–14). Apparently a scribe accidentally omitted in Chronicles the material found in 2 Sam 23:9b–11a (for details cf. KD, *The Books of the Chronicles*, pp. 176–77; cf. also KD, p. 495; S.R. Driver, *Notes on the Books of Samuel*, p. 365; Gordon, *I & II Samuel*, p. 312).

**15** The Hebrew word באר (*b'r*, "well," vv.15–16) is vocalized as though "cistern" (בור [*bwr*]) were intended (cf. 1 Chron 11:17–18, where *bwr* appears). In any event, the traditional site of "David's Well," half a mile north-northeast of Bethlehem (cf. H.B. Tristram, *Bible Places*, rev. ed. [London: SPCK, 1897], p. 99), is too far from the city to be the well/cistern mentioned here.

**20** "Best men" renders אראל (*'r'l*; 1 Chron 11:22 has אריאל [*'ry'l*]), a word of uncertain meaning. Although it is tempting to connect it with *'r'l* in line 12 of the (Moabite) Mesha inscription, doing so does not assist in elucidating its sense (cf. John C.L. Gibson, *Textbook of Syrian Semitic Inscriptions. Volume I: Hebrew and Moabite Inscriptions* [Oxford: Clarendon,

1971], p. 80). In the present context it forms a wordplay with אריה (*'ryh*, "lion"; 1 Chron 11:22 has ארי [*'ry*]) later in the verse.

**30** The lack of the definite article (ה- [*h-*]) on "Pirathonite" is probably due to haplography, since the preceding word ([בניה[ו] [*bnyh(w)*]) ends in *h* (cf. 1 Chron 11:31; cf. Watson, "Shared Consonants," p. 531).

---

## F. *The Lord's Wrath Against Israel*

### 24:1–25

1 Again the anger of the LORD burned against Israel, and he incited
David against them, saying, "Go and take a census of Israel and Judah."
2 So the king said to Joab and the army commanders with him, "Go
throughout the tribes of Israel from Dan to Beersheba and enroll the
fighting men, so that I may know how many there are."
3 But Joab replied to the king, "May the LORD your God multiply the
troops a hundred times over, and may the eyes of my lord the king see it.
But why does my lord the king want to do such a thing?"
4 The king's word, however, overruled Joab and the army commanders; so they left the presence of the king to enroll the fighting men
of Israel.
5 After crossing the Jordan, they camped near Aroer, south of the town
in the gorge, and then went through Gad and on to Jazer. 6 They went to
Gilead and the region of Tahtim Hodshi, and on to Dan Jaan and around
toward Sidon. 7 Then they went toward the fortress of Tyre and all the
towns of the Hivites and Canaanites. Finally, they went on to Beersheba
in the Negev of Judah.
8 After they had gone through the entire land, they came back to
Jerusalem at the end of nine months and twenty days.
9 Joab reported the number of the fighting men to the king: In Israel
there were eight hundred thousand able-bodied men who could handle
a sword, and in Judah five hundred thousand.
10 David was conscience-stricken after he had counted the fighting
men, and he said to the LORD, "I have sinned greatly in what I have done.
Now, O LORD, I beg you, take away the guilt of your servant. I have done a
very foolish thing."
11 Before David got up the next morning, the word of the LORD had
come to Gad the prophet, David's seer: 12 "Go and tell David, 'This is
what the LORD says: I am giving you three options. Choose one of them
for me to carry out against you.'"
13 So Gad went to David and said to him, "Shall there come upon you
three years of famine in your land? Or three months of fleeing from your
enemies while they pursue you? Or three days of plague in your land?
Now then, think it over and decide how I should answer the one who
sent me."
14 David said to Gad, "I am in deep distress. Let us fall into the hands
of the LORD, for his mercy is great; but do not let me fall into the hands of
men."
15 So the LORD sent a plague on Israel from that morning until the end
of the time designated, and seventy thousand of the people from Dan to
Beersheba died. 16 When the angel stretched out his hand to destroy
Jerusalem, the LORD was grieved because of the calamity and said to the
angel who was afflicting the people, "Enough! Withdraw your hand."
The angel of the LORD was then at the threshing floor of Araunah the
Jebusite.
17 When David saw the angel who was striking down the people, he
said to the LORD, "I am the one who has sinned and done wrong. These

are but sheep. What have they done? Let your hand fall upon me and my
family."
18On that day Gad went to David and said to him, "Go up and build an
altar to the LORD on the threshing floor of Araunah the Jebusite." 19So
David went up, as the LORD had commanded through Gad. 20When
Araunah looked and saw the king and his men coming toward him, he
went out and bowed down before the king with his face to the ground.
21Araunah said, "Why has my lord the king come to his servant?"
"To buy your threshing floor," David answered, "so I can build an
altar to the LORD, that the plague on the people may be stopped."
22Araunah said to David, "Let my lord the king take whatever pleases
him and offer it up. Here are oxen for the burnt offering, and here are
threshing sledges and ox yokes for the wood. 23O king, Araunah gives
all this to the king." Araunah also said to him, "May the LORD your God
accept you."
24But the king replied to Araunah, "No, I insist on paying you for it. I
will not sacrifice to the LORD my God burnt offerings that cost me
nothing."
So David bought the threshing floor and the oxen and paid fifty
shekels of silver for them. 25David built an altar to the LORD there and
sacrificed burnt offerings and fellowship offerings. Then the LORD
answered prayer in behalf of the land, and the plague on Israel was
stopped.

The books of Samuel close with the account of a plague sent by God against Israel because of David's sin in ordering a census of his troops. Displaying a double *inclusio* with its literary counterpart in 21:1–14 (see comment on 21:1–24:25), chapter 24 provides a fitting conclusion to the story of David by calling attention, once more and finally, not only to his ambition and pride, but also to his humility and remorse.

The chapter divides naturally into three approximately equal segments, each of which is constructed within its own *inclusio*. David's sin is the subject of vv.1–9, in which the command to take a census of "Israel and Judah" (v.1) results in a report of the total number of fighting men "in Israel . . . and in Judah" (v.9). David's confession is the subject of vv.10–17, at the beginning of which "David . . . said to the LORD, 'I have sinned' " and asked to be relieved of his "guilt" (*ʿ$^{a}$wōn*, v.10) and at the end of which "David . . . said to the LORD, 'I am the one who has sinned and done wrong [*heʿ$^{e}$wêṯî*, v.17].' " David's altar is the subject of vv.18–25, in which Gad's command to build "an altar to the LORD on the threshing floor of Araunah the Jebusite" (v.18) results in David's building "an altar to the LORD there" (v.25).

First Chronicles 21:1–6, 7–17, and 18–27 replicate vv.1–9, 10–17, and 18–25 respectively. Differences between the two parallel accounts are not only frequent but also, in a few instances, startling. Only the most important of them will be noted in the commentary that follows.

**1–9** Just as the Lord's anger had "burned against" Uzzah because of an irreverent act on his part (6:7), so also the anger of the Lord "burned against" Israel (v.1; cf. also Num 25:3; 32:13; Judg 2:14, 20; 3:8; 10:7; 2 Kings 13:3), in this case because of an unspecified sin. That it did so "again" would appear from a literary standpoint to be a reflection on the earlier outbreak of divine wrath that brought about the three-year famine of 21:1.

If the subject of "incited" in v.1 is surely the Lord, it is just as surely *śāṭān* in the parallel text of 1 Chronicles 21:1. The most recent thorough treatment of various attempts to explain the relationship between the two passages is that of John H.

Sailhamer ("1 Chronicles 21:1—A Study in Inter-Biblical Interpretation," *Trinity Journal* 10 [1989]: 33–48), who arranges them "under three headings: harmonistic, redactional, and exegetical" (p. 34). Although harmonistic approaches "all express important theological and biblical insights into the nature of the problem, none of the approaches find support within the immediate text itself. They are, in fact, not so much attempts to explain the difficulty of the text as attempts to explain it away" (p. 36). After thus dismissing the harmonistic method, he quickly (and rightfully) dispenses with the redactional explanation in a single paragraph (p. 37).

But Sailhamer's lengthy exegetical discussion, although stimulating and perceptive in many ways, ultimately fares no better. His rendering of *śāṭān* as "adversary" in 1 Chronicles 21:1 (cf. 19:22; see comment on 1 Sam 29:4) in reference to the enemies of Israel (ibid., pp. 42–44; cf. 1 Kings 5:4; 11:23, 25) fails to explain either (1) why the term is not used of Israel's enemies anywhere in Samuel or elsewhere in Chronicles or, especially, (2) how Israel's human "adversary, enemy" could be the subject of "incited" in 1 Chronicles 21:1.

On balance, then, the harmonistic approach remains the best of the available options (for rabbinic alternatives cf. Goldman, pp. 341–42). "The older record [v.1] speaks only of God's permissive action: the later [1 Chron 21:1] tells us of the malicious instrumentalilty of Satan. The case is like that of Job" (Kirkpatrick, *The Second Book of Samuel*, p. 223; cf. Job 1:12; 2:6–7, 10; cf. KD, p. 503; Archer, *Encyclopedia of Bible Difficulties*, pp. 186–88; Kaiser, *Hard Sayings of the Old Testament*, pp. 129–32). The difference between Samuel and Chronicles illustrates "the tendency to associate evil with Satan. . . . In the second-century (BC) book of Jubilees, for example, the action of God in testing Abraham (Gn. 22:1) is said to have been at the instigation of the Satan-figure 'Mastema' (Jub. 17:15–18:19)" (Gordon, *1 & 2 Samuel*, p. 317; cf. D.S. Russell, *The Old Testament Pseudepigrapha: Patriarchs and Prophets in Early Judaism* [Philadelphia: Fortress, 1987], p. 74; Baldwin, p. 294). However paradoxically, a divinely-sent affliction can be called a "messenger of Satan" (2 Cor 12:7; for discussion cf. Murray J. Harris in EBC, 10:396).

Thus the Lord through Satan "incited" David (see 1 Sam 26:19 and comment; cf. also Job 2:3; Jer 43:3) against Israel by commanding him to "take a census" of Israel and Judah (v.1). Since census-taking was not sinful in and of itself (cf. Exod 30:11–12; Num 1:1–2), what was the nature of David's transgression? After a survey of numerous possibilities, Dillard has recourse to

> two passages: (1) Joab's objection in the immediate context (I Chron. 21:3) that even if the count were a hundred times increased, they would all still be David's subjects, and (2) the explicit statement that Joab did not finish the count and did not "take the number of the men twenty years old or less because the Lord had promised to make Israel as numerous as the stars of the sky" (I Chron. 27:23–24). For the Chronicler in particular, . . . the arena of David's transgression appears to be that taking a census impugns the faithfulness of God in the keeping of His promises—a kind of walking by sight instead of by faith. ("David's Census," pp. 104–5)

Consistent with his tendency to portray David in the best possible light and therefore to revel in his name, the Chronicler frequently substitutes "David" for "the king" as he modifies the Samuel narrative (cf. v.2 with 1 Chron 21:2; v.9 with 1 Chron 21:5; v.20 with 1 Chron 21:21 [bis]; v.24 with 1 Chron 21:24 ["King David"]). The king tells Joab (who is "over the army" [8:16; cf. 20:23]) and the army commanders with him to "go" (v.2; cf. v.8), using a verb that means more specifically "go around" (cf. Num 11:8), "roam" (cf. Job 1:7; 2:2), in the sense of "range widely." David wants his officers to cover the length and breadth of the land of Israel from north to south, "from Dan to Beersheba" (see comments on 3:10; 17:11; 1 Sam 3:20). Concentrating only on the "fighting men" (vv.2, 3 ["troops"], 4, 9, 10, lit., "people"; see comment on "soldiers" in 1 Sam 4:3), they are not only to count them but also to "enroll" them (vv.2, 4), an act with purposes more military than statistical (cf. 1 Sam 11:8 ["mustered"]; 14:17; cf. esp. Num 1:2–3, where "take a census of the whole Israelite community" [v.2] is defined more precisely as "number by their divisions all the men in Israel twenty years old or more who are able to serve in the army" [v.3], the verb "number" rendering the same Heb. verb here translated "enroll").

Joab, sensing David's hidden agenda, immediately expresses his reservations. His hope that the Lord will "multiply" (v.3; cf. Deut 1:11 ["increase"]) the troops a hundred times over and that David's eyes will see it is doubtless voiced with reluctance since he wonders how the king could possibly "want" (lit., "be pleased"; cf. 1 Sam 28:22; see comment on 1 Sam 19:1) to do such a thing. Joab is further convinced that David's precipitous action will "bring guilt on Israel" (1 Chron 21:3). But the king is adamant. "Overruled" by David's word (v.4, lit., "overpowered"; cf. 3:1; see comments on 10:11; 13:4b ["was stronger than"]), Joab and the army commanders proceed to carry out his orders.

As the place names in vv.5–7 demonstrate, territories conquered by David are not included in the census. The muster of the militia involves only the "entire land" of Israel and Judah (v.8), and the survey follows its borders in a counterclockwise direction (for an excellent map of the itinerary, cf. Rasmussen, p. 119). Not to be confused with the town of the same name to which David sent part of the plunder from his victory over the Amalekites (see 1 Sam 30:28 and comment), Aroer (v.5, originally allotted to the tribal territory of Rueben; cf. Josh 13:15–16; 1 Chron 5:8) is modern Arair, about fourteen miles east of the Dead Sea on the northern bank of the Arnon River. Its location in the southeastern corner of Israel made it the ideal starting point for the census, which was to include all able-bodied men of military age living within the designated borders. The unnamed (and unknown) "town in the [middle of the] gorge" is invariably mentioned as being in the vicinity of Aroer (cf. Deut 2:36; Josh 13:9, 16).

Continuing northward, Joab's party moves on to Jazer, a Levitical town in the tribal territory of Gad (cf. Num 32:1, 3, 35; Josh 13:25; 21:39: 1 Chron 6:81). The modern site of Jazer is possibly Khirbet es-Sar, located about six miles west of Amman. North of Gad is the region known as Gilead (v.6), which was somewhat larger than Gad at this time (see 1 Sam 13:7 and comment). "Tahtim Hodshi" (*tḥtym ḥdšy*), otherwise unmentioned, is a town or region of unknown location somewhere between Gilead and Dan. On the basis of the Lucianic recension of the LXX, the MT is often emended to *hḥtym qdšh*), "[the region of] the Hittites, toward Kedesh [on the Orontes]"—which, however, is about a hundred miles northeast of Dan and is therefore much too distant to serve as the northern boundary of Israel (for discussion cf. S.R. Driver, *Notes on the Books of Samuel*, p. 374). If the MT text is corrupt at this point, the most likely solution is that of Patrick Skehan, who suggests *tḥt ḥrmwn*, "[the region] below [Mount] Hermon" ("Joab's Census: How Far North [2 Sm 24,6]?" CBQ 31, 1 [1969]: 45 and n. 19, pp. 47, 49; cf. similarly S.R. Driver, *Notes on the Books of Samuel*, p. 374; Aharoni, *Land of the Bible*, p. 318 n. 19; McCarter, *II Samuel*, pp. 504–5; cf. Josh 11:3, 17; 13:5).

"[To] Dan Jaan" (*dnh y'n*), also otherwise unmentioned, may be a village near the town of Dan or a fuller name for Dan itself. It is also possible that the MT is a corruption of *dnh [w]'ywn*, "to Dan and Ijon," two towns mentioned together also in 1 Kings 15:20 (= 2 Chron 16:4). The modern site of ancient Dan is Tell el-Qadi near the foot of Mount Hermon twenty-five miles north of the Sea of Galilee, and that of Ijon is Tell ed-Dibbin nine miles north-northwest of Dan on a direct line "toward Sidon" (v.6) on the coast of Lebanon.

Southeast of Sidon the census takers go toward the "fortress of Tyre" (v.7) on the Mediterranean just above the northwestern boundry of Israel (cf. Josh 19:29) in an area inhabited by "Hivites and Canaanites," who were among Israel's perennial enemies (cf. Exod 23:23; Josh 9:1; 12:8). At one time Canaanites had perhaps been ubiquitous in the land (cf. Alan R. Millard, "The Canaanites," in *Peoples of Old Testament Times,* ed. D.J. Wiseman [Oxford: Clarendon, 1973], pp. 36–38), while Hivites were a minor population group of whom nothing is known outside the OT (cf. D.J. Wiseman, "Introduction: Peoples and Nations," in *Peoples of Old Testament Times,* pp. xv–xvi). Some Hivites, however, may have been Hurrians (cf. Hoffner, "The Hittites and Hurrians," p. 225). In any event, Joshua 11:3 mentions Hivites who lived "below Hermon" (see comment on v.6) in southern Lebanon. Before returning to Jerusalem (v.8), Joab and his officers travel parallel to the Mediterranean coast and conclude their census at Beersheba in the "Negev of Judah" on Israel's southern border (v.7; see comment on 1 Sam 27:10). Modern Beersheba, gateway to and capital of the Negev, is located near the site of its ancient namesake forty-five miles southwest of Jerusalem.

As leader of his team, Joab transmits to David the results of their efforts. He reports the number of "able-bodied men" (v.9; the Heb. idiom implies unusual courage; cf. 11:16 ["strongest defenders"]; 23:20 ["valiant fighter"]; see comment on "valiant men" in 1 Sam 31:12) who can "handle a sword" (lit., "draw a sword," as in 1 Sam 17:51; 31:4; cf. Judg 8:10 ["swordsmen"]; 20:2 ["armed with swords"], 15, 17, 25, 35, 46; 2 Kings 3:26).

As is well known, the tally of fighting men recorded in Joab's report differs in the parallel accounts. According to v.9, the figures in Israel and Judah are 800,000 and 500,000 respectively, while in 1 Chron 21:5 they are 1,100,000 and 470,000 (or, in the LXX, 480,000; cf. BHS) respectively. To complicate matters further, "both Josephus and the Lucianic texts of Samuel show 900,000 for Israel and 400,000 for Judah in Samuel" (Dillard, "David's Census," p. 97), raising the possibility that the problem is at least partly text-critical in nature. In any event, "no theological reason can be suggested for the variation in the numbers; the inflationary glorification so often attributed to the Chronicler is totally absent" (ibid., pp. 97–98). Indeed, even in the present context the Chronicler's figure for Judah is lower than the corresponding figure in v.9. Nor can one solve the problem by observing that "Joab did not include Levi and Benjamin in the numbering" (1 Chron 21:6), since in that case the grand total in Chronicles—not Samuel—should be smaller. How, then, to untie the Gordian knot?

The best solution would seem to lie along lines proposed by J. Barton Payne ("Validity of Numbers in Chronicles," *Near East Archaeological Society Bulletin* 11 [1978]: 5–58), who notes that v.9 refers simply to "Israel" whereas 1 Chronicles 21:5 states that the census covers "all Israel" and that therefore "Chronicles' first sum is greater, perhaps because 'the regular army of 288,000 (I Chronicles 27:1–15) is included'" (ibid., p. 16, citing A.M. Renwick in NBC, p. 292). As for the difference between the 500,000 men of Judah in v.9 compared to the 470,000 in 1 Chronicles 21:5, it is quite likely that the figure in Samuel is rounded off while that in Chronicles is "more precise" (Payne, "Validity of Numbers," p. 23).

A second problem relates to the hugeness of the numbers themselves. Although Renwick admits that understanding them literally would "imply a population of at least six million in the small country of Palestine," he nevertheless defends them: "When the intense fertility of the land is considered, such a population is quite reasonable and this view is sustained by the innumerable ruins of cities and villages which still abound" (NBC, p. 292; cf. also Kirkpatrick, *The Second Book of Samuel*, p. 227; KD, pp. 505–6). Most commentators, however, sense that the numbers are inordinately large when interpreted literally. Payne therefore proposes to revocalize *'elep̱* ("thousand") as *'allup̱* ("specially trained warrior") in the light of their description as "able-bodied men who could handle a sword" ("Validity of Numbers," p. 39). But why it would take almost three hundred days (cf. v.8) to conduct a census of a total of "1,570 outstanding military figures" (Payne, EBC, 4:407) remains unclear. So it is perhaps best to understand *'elep̱* here in the sense of "military unit" (see comment on 1 Sam 4:2), a meaning admirably suited to the present setting (cf. Baldwin, p. 296; Gordon, *1 & 2 Samuel*, p. 319; Anderson, p. 285; McCarter, *II Samuel*, p. 510).

**10–17** Eventually coming to the realization that his command to take a census of Israel's fighting men had been not only "repulsive" to Joab (1 Chron 21:6) but also "evil in the sight of God" (1 Chron 21:7), David is "conscience-stricken" (v.10; see 1 Sam 24:5 and comment). As he had done earlier, so now also he confesses to the Lord: "I have sinned" (see 12:13 and comment)—but this time he adds the word "greatly" (*me'ōḏ*), perhaps having become more sensitive to the enormity of willful rebellion against God (cf. Ps 19:13). Not waiting for a prophetic word of absolution this time, David begs the Lord to "take away" his guilt (contrast 12:13). He realizes that he has done a "foolish" thing (*skl;* see comment on 1 Sam 13:13)—indeed, it is "very" (*me'ōḏ*) foolish. "David's confession . . . is the ideal repentance of the ideal king. . . . *ṣkl* ni. is here employed to reveal David's insight into the seriousness of his error in relying on numerical strength instead of on the LORD's power who can 'save by many or few' (1 Sam. xiv 6)" (Wolfgang Roth, "A Study of the Classical Hebrew Verb *ṣkl*," VetTest 18, 1 [1968]: 76).

Although David may not have needed a prophet to mediate the assurance of divine forgiveness to him, he apparently does need a prophet to outline for him his future options (v.12; cf. similarly the ministry of the prophetess Huldah to King Josiah in 2 Kings 22:11–20). If it is possible to read the verb in v.11b as a pluperfect ("had come"), it is equally possible—and perhaps even more likely—"that Yahweh's word to Gad was given after David had got up" (Alfons Schulz, "Narrative Art in the Books of Samuel," in *Narrative and Novella in Samuel: Studies by Hugo Gressmann and Other Scholars 1906–1923*, JSOT suppl. 116 [Sheffield: Almond, 1991], p. 128). As the "word of the LORD" had come to the prophets Samuel and Nathan in critical situations (see comments on 7:4; 1 Sam 15:10; cf. similarly 1 Kings 16:7; 18:1; 2 Kings 20:4), so also it comes to the prophet Gad (see 1 Sam 22:5 and comment; cf. 1 Chron 29:29, where Samuel, Nathan, and Gad are mentioned together as among the chroniclers of David's reign), who is David's "seer" (v.11; cf. 1 Chron 29:29; 2 Chron 29:25; see comment on 1 Sam 9:9).

Relayed to David through Gad, the Lord's "three options" (v.12) turn out to be "three punishments" (the MT of v.12 at this point has no noun of any kind in association with "three"): "three years of famine," "three months of fleeing," "three days of plague" (v.13). As the suggested periods decrease in length, the specific punishment linked with each period increases in severity. The choice is David's to make, however. Before Gad can bring back to the Lord an answer from the king, David must "think it over and decide" (lit., "know and see," for which see comments on 1 Sam 23:22–23 ["find out"]; 24:11 ["understand and recognize"]).

Since David is forced to choose among the least of three evils, he is in "deep distress" no matter what he does (v.14). But because the people of God have always confessed that his "mercy is great" (cf. Neh 9:19, 27, 31; Ps 119:156; Dan 9:18), David expresses his desire to fall into the hands of the Lord rather than of men. Entirely apart from the fact that he had already experienced famine (cf. 21:1–14) and war (cf. 21:15–22; 23:8–23), therefore, David chooses the three-day plague (v.15):

> War would place the nation at the mercy of its enemies: famine would make it dependent on corn-merchants, who might greatly aggravate the misery of scarcity: only in the pestilence—some form of plague sudden and mysterious in its attack, and baffling the medical knowledge of the time—would the punishment come directly from God, and depend immediately upon His Will. (Kirkpatrick, *The Second Book of Samuel*, p. 228)

Equally instructive is a rabbinic explanation of David's reasoning: "If I choose famine the people will say that I chose something which will affect them and not me, for I shall be well supplied with food; if I choose war, they will say that the king is well protected; let me choose pestilence, before which all are equal" (cited in Goldman, p. 345).

Divine judgment in the form of a plague was not long in coming. Indeed, it began "that morning" (v.15; cf. v.11). It probably did not continue for three days, however, since an amelioration of "the time designated" might have been effected by the Lord's intervention described in v.16. Furthermore, the Hebrew phrase rendered "until (the end of) the time designated" is understood to mean "until noon" in the LXX and "until the sixth hour" in the Syriac (see BHS for details). But however long or short the duration of the plague, "seventy thousand . . . died." If David, bent on conquest, had planned the census as a military muster (see comment on v.2), the Lord's response is not unexpected. "Wanting more land and more people to rule, David finds himself with 70,000 fewer subjects" (Dillard, "David's Census," p. 106).

Who, precisely, are the hapless victims of the plague? The NIV apparently considers them to have been ordinary Israelite "people" (vv.15–16, 17, 21). But since *'m* is translated "fighting men," "troops," everywhere else in chapter 24 (see comment on v.2), since *'yš* (lit., "man") implies "military man" each time it appears in the chapter (vv.9 [ter], 15), and since "from Dan to Beersheba" in v.15 echoes the geographical limits of the military muster ordered by David in v.2, it is preferable to translate *'m* as "fighting men" in vv.15–17, 21 as well. The "seventy thousand" who died should thus be understood as "seventy military units" in harmony with the suggested rendering of *'elep̱* in v.9 (see comment there).

As in the critical days of Sennacherib's attempted siege of Jerusalem (cf. 2 Kings 19:35 = Isa 37:36; cf. 2 Chron 32:21), so also in the days of David's extremity the "angel of the LORD" is the instrument of the divinely-sent plague (v.16). For centuries the identity of the angel of the Lord has been a subject of vigorous debate. Although many have taught that the angel was Jesus Christ in a preincarnate form (cf. J. Borland, *Christ in the Old Testament* [Chicago: Moody, 1978]; Reymond, *Jesus, Divine Messiah,* p. 1), such a view severely weakens (1) the uniqueness of the Incarnation and (2) the basic argument of Hebrews 1, which goes to great lengths to point out that Jesus is far superior to all of God's angels.

Since the Hebrew word for "angel" also means "messenger," it is perhaps better to understand the angel of the Lord as a special messenger from the court of heaven who bears all the credentials of the King of heaven and can therefore speak and act on his behalf. He can use the first person pronoun of himself as though he were the sender (cf. Judg 6:16), or he can use the third person pronoun in reference to the sender (cf. Judg 6:12; cf. esp. Judg 13:3–23 for various titles given to the angel of the Lord: "man of God," "angel of God," "man," "God," "the LORD"). In either case, he symbolizes the presence of the King who sends him. Thus when the angel of the Lord appears, the Lord himself is symbolically present (for discussion cf. Oehler, *Theology of the Old Testament,* pp. 129–34; Youngblood, *The Book of Genesis,* pp. 166–67). In any event, surely the angel and the Lord are not simply to be equated without further ado. Indeed, in v.16 they are clearly distinquished from each other ("the LORD . . . said to the angel"; cf. also the parallel text in 1 Chron 21:15, which states that "God sent an angel").

Having already killed a large number of men throughout the rest of the country (v.15), the angel now "stretched out his hand" to destroy the capital city itself (v.16; cf. Exod 9:15; Job 1:11, 12 ["lay a finger"]; see 1 Sam 6:9 and comment). At this juncture, however, the Lord is "grieved" (*nḥm*) because of the calamity (cf. Gen 6:6–7; Exod 32:12, 14 ["relent"]; Jer 18:8, 10 ["reconsidered"]; 26:3, 13, 19; 42:10; Joel 2:13; Jonah 4:2; for discussion of "grieving/relenting/repenting" with God as subject, see comment on 1 Sam 15:11). Divine judgment already more than adequate, the Lord says "Enough!" (*raḇ;* cf. Gen 45:28 ["I'm convinced!"]; Exod 9:28; 1 Kings 19:4) and orders the angel to "withdraw" his hand (cf. Exod 4:26 ["let . . . alone"]; Deut 4:31 ["abandon"]; 31:6, 8 ["leave"]; Josh 1:5; 10:6; 1 Chron 28:20 ["fail"]; Neh 6:3; Ps 138:8).

Visible to David's eyes, the angel and his destructive actions in "striking down" the men (v.17; cf. 1 Sam 4:8; 5:6, 9 ["afflicted"]) repulse the king. He again confesses that he has "sinned" (see comment on v.10) and "done wrong" (*'ānōḵî,* the emphatic "I," is used with each of the two verbs). The men who are being killed are merely "sheep," who are not guilty and for whom David feels responsible (cf. Jer 23:1–3; Ezek 24:5 ["flock"]; 34:2–10; Zech 11:7, 17). David's loving concern for and care of "sheep," whether literal or metaphorical, has characterized him from his first appearance in the books of Samuel (cf. 1 Sam 16:11) to his last. Rather than witness the further destruction of his men, he calls the wrath of God down on himself and his own family (cf. Moses' similar plea in Exod 32:32; cf. also Deut 9:26–27).

In preparation for the final pericope in the books of Samuel (vv.18–25), the narrator observes that the angel of the Lord is at the "threshing floor of Araunah the Jebusite" (v.16; for discussion of Jebusites as the pre-Israelite inhabitants of Jerusalem, see comment on 5:6). As will soon become clear in this case, threshing floors in ancient times were often places of sanctity (see comment on 6:6). The Jebusite fortress was on the southeastern hill of Jerusalem (see comment on 5:7), and the threshing floor belonging to Araunah "is usually thought to be north of it, and thus outside the fortified area" (Jones, p. 126).

Araunah's name is spelled in several different ways in the MT of Samuel and

Chronicles: *'rwnh*, vv.20–24; *'rnyh*, v.18; *'rnn*, 1 Chron 21:15–25; 2 Chron 3:1; and, significantly, *h'wrnh* (*Kethiv; h'rwnh, Qere*), v.16 (lit., "the Araunah"). The latter spelling, the first in sequence in chapter 24, opens up the possibility that "Araunah" was a title rather than a proper name, and the MT accents on *'rwnh hmlk* in v.23 lead to the conclusion that the phrase is "to be taken as a unity, indicating that Araunah was given the title *mlk* ['king'], and was in fact the last Jebusite king of the city. . . . *hmlk* is simply a gloss translating the foreign term into Hebrew for the reader's benefit" (N. Wyatt, " 'Araunah the Jebusite' and the Throne of David," ST 39 [1985]: 40). Although Wyatt argues at length that Araunah was in fact Uriah the Hittite, his treatment is unconvincing. With respect to the meaning and origin of the word "Araunah,"

> the parallel account in 1 Chronicles 21:14–30, as well as the LXX translation of both accounts [Ορνα (*Orna*)], suggests that the M.T. consonants *'rwnh* in 2 Samuel 24 have resulted from a transposition of the consonants *'wrnh*. The "name" (if it be not rather a title) of this Jebusite was the Hurrian word *ewri-ne*, "the lord". The same name (spelled *'wrn*) occurs in a text from Ugarit. (Hoffner, "The Hittites and Hurrians," p. 225)

**18–25** In response to David's urgent prayer (v.17), the angel of the Lord (1 Chron 21:18) orders the prophet Gad (see comment on v.11) to tell David to "go up" (v.18) to Araunah's threshing floor, which was doubtless located "on an elevated spot exposed to the wind" (G.B. Funderburk, ZPEB, 5:739). There David is to "build" (lit., "erect"; cf. 1 Kings 16:32 ["set up"]; 2 Kings 21:3 = 2 Chron 33:3) an altar to the Lord. Prompted by the divine command, David obeys (v.19).

After having "looked" (v.20, lit., "looked down"; cf. 1 Sam 13:18 ["overlooking"]; Lam 3:50) and seen David and "his men" (*'ᵃḇāḏāyw*, lit., "his officials/servants"; see comment on 1 Sam 16:15–16) coming over toward him, Araunah leaves the threshing floor (cf. 1 Chron 21:21) and pays homage to David, his acknowledged superior ("my lord the king," v.21), by bowing down before him with his "face to the ground" (v.20; cf. 14:4, 22, 33, 18:28; 1 Sam 20:41; 25:41; 28:14; see 1 Sam 24:8; 25:23 and comments). If Araunah himself had once been the Jebusite king of Jerusalem (see comment on v.18), he is now merely another "servant" of the Israelite king of Jerusalem (v.21; see comment on 1 Sam 1:11).

To Araunah's query concerning the purpose of David's visit, the king says that he wants to buy the threshing floor from him as a suitable place where he can "build" an altar to the Lord (the Heb. verb rendered "build" here and in v.25 is not the same as the one used in v.18; see comment there). He understands that sacrificing "burnt offerings and fellowship offerings" (v.25) will propitiate the divine wrath (cf. de Vaux, *Studies in Old Testament Sacrifice*, pp. 37–42; Leon Morris, *The Apostolic Preaching of the Cross* [Grand Rapids: Eerdmans, 1956], pp. 129–36) and bring the "plague" to an end (*maggēp̱āh*[see 1 Sam 6:4 and comment] here and in v.25 is not the same as the Heb. word translated "plague" in vv.13, 15). As a similarly devastating plague had been "stopped" in the days of Phinehas son of Eleazar son of Aaron (Num 25:7–8; Ps 106:30 ["checked"]), so David wants the plague on Israel to cease.

The conversation between David and Araunah is reminiscent of that between Abraham and Ephron (cf. Gen 23:3–15; cf. Youngblood, *The Book of Genesis*, pp. 193–94), and David's situation is just as desperate as Abraham's had been. Like Ephron, Araunah is willing to give whatever is needed (vv.22–23); like Abraham,

David insists on paying (v.24a); as in the case of Abraham and Ephron, David and Araunah finally agree on a purchase price (v.24b).

Although they usually toiled as draft animals (cf. 6:6), "oxen" (v.22) were also commonly sacrificed as burnt offerings and fellowship offerings (see 6:13, 17–18 and comments). Ordinarily used to separate heads of grain from husks and chaff (cf. Isa 41:15), "threshing sledges" could also serve as fuel. Commonly employed to guide animals engaged in plowing (cf. 1 Kings 19:19), "ox yokes" might also be burned at a barbecue (cf. 1 Kings 19:21) or an altar. Although oxen, threshing sledges, and ox yokes constitute the matériel of his livelihood, Araunah is prepared to give them to David for a higher purpose. He also expresses his hope that the Lord "your" God (v.23; it would seem that Araunah the Jebusite is deliberately distancing himself from what he considers to be an Israelite deity) will "accept" David (cf. Jer 14:10, 12; Ezek 20:40–41; Hos 8:13 ["(be) pleased with"]; cf. esp. Ezek 43:27).

To Araunah's gracious (though perhaps not totally disinterested) offer, David replies in characteristic fashion (cf. 23:16b–17), pointedly referring to the Lord as "my" God: "I will not sacrifice to the LORD my God burnt offerings that cost me nothing" (v.24). His emphatic "No" resonates with the sound of authority (see 16:18 and comment) as he insists on paying for the threshing floor (lit., "buying it . . . in exchange for [*bêt pretii;* see comments on 14:7; 23:17] a price"). The transaction is finalized as David agrees to pay Araunah "fifty shekels of silver" (see comment on 1 Sam 9:8) for the threshing floor and the oxen (v.24), an amount that balloons in the Chronicler's parallel to "six hundred shekels of gold"—a price, however, that doubtless includes the entire "site" (a much larger area, 1 Chron 21:25) and that may in fact have involved a subsequent purchase (cf. Kirkpatrick, *The Second Book of Samuel,* p. 232). Segal makes the tantalizing but unprovable suggestion that, since six hundred is twelve times fifty, "the Chronicler gives this incident a national significance" (encompassing the twelve tribes of Israel; "Numerals," p. 9).

And so, as Omri king of Israel would later buy the hill of Samaria and build his capital city on it (cf. 1 Kings 16:23–24), David king of Israel and Judah buys a threshing floor and builds an altar on it. He then sacrifices "burnt offerings and fellowship offerings" (v.25; see 6:17–18 and comments) as a means of seeking divine favor (see 1 Sam 13:9 and comment). The Lord's response? He "answered prayer in behalf of the land" (21:14; for literary significance see comment on 21:1–24:25). The angel of death having "put his sword back into its sheath" (1 Chron 21:27), divine judgment—the plague against Israel—is "stopped" (v.25; see v.21 and comment).

Although David appears content simply to build an altar on the threshing floor of Araunah the Jebusite, his son Solomon would eventually build the temple there (cf. 1 Chron 22:1) on the hill called Moriah (cf. 2 Chron 3:1; Gen 22:2; cf. Youngblood, *Book of Genesis,* pp. 187–88).

> At the same site where Abraham once held a knife over his son (Gen. 22:1–19), David sees the angel of the Lord with sword ready to plunge into Jerusalem. In both cases death is averted by sacrifice. The temple is established there as the place where Israel was perpetually reminded that without the shedding of blood there is no remission of sin (Heb. 9:22). Death for Isaac and for David's Jerusalem was averted because the sword of divine justice would ultimately find its mark in the Son of God (John 19:33). (Dillard, "David's Census," p. 107)

Small wonder, then, that the NT should begin with "a record of the genealogy of Jesus Christ the son of David, the son of Abraham. . . ."

## Notes

**1** In the first two chapters of Job (Job 1:6–9, 12; 2:1–4, 6, 7), Satan is called הַשָּׂטָן (*haśśāṭān*), literally, "the Accuser/Adversary (par excellence)" (see NIV mg. on Job 1:6). By the time of the Chronicler, however, the definite article has been dropped and *śāṭān* has become a proper name (1 Chron 21:1).

**2** In context, "Joab and the army commanders" is a better reading than the MT's "Joab the army commander" (for details see NIV mg.).

**12** "Giving" is literally "laying upon" (נטל על [*nṭl ʿl*]; cf. Lam 3:28). The parallel in 1 Chron 21:10 reads נטה על (*nṭh ʿl*), lit., "stretching out upon," which would be unique in the sense of "give/offer to" (cf. BDB, p. 640). Since some Hebrew MSS do in fact read *nṭl ʿl* in 1 Chron 21:10 (see BHS), *nṭl* is preferable in both passages.

**13** That "three years" is a better reading than the "seven years" of the MT is clear not only from the parallel in 1 Chron 21:12 and from the LXX evidence (see NIV mg.) but also from the symmetry of the three punishments themselves (for detailed discussion, cf. Carlson, pp. 204 n. 4). For the significance of the *inclusio* formed by "a famine for three successive years" (21:1) and "three years of famine" (v.13), see comment on 21:1–24:25.

**14** Instead of "Let us fall" the Chronicler reads "Let me fall" (1 Chron 21:13), perhaps to reflect his perception of David's selflessness and humility. For the literary significance of the use of the rare idiom "fall into/at the hands of" here, see comment on 21:22.

**17** Whereas the MT of v.17 reads ואנכי העויתי (*wʾnky hʿwyty*, "and I have done wrong") and that of 1 Chron 21:17 reads והרע הרעותי (*whrʿ hrʿwty*, "and I have surely done wickedly"), 4QSam[a] offers a text that appears to be more original in that it helps to explain the difference between the parallels in Samuel and Chronicles: ואנכי הרעה הרעתי (*wʾnky hrʿh hrʿty*, "and I, the shepherd, have done wickedly"; cf. Ulrich, *The Qumran Text*, pp. 86–87). The antithetical "These are but sheep" favors the Qumran reading as well (cf. Dillard, "David's Census," p. 97; for "shepherd/flock" as a kind of *Leitmotif* with respect to David, see 1 Sam 16:11 and comment).

**22** "Burnt offering" (singular) is often used in a collective sense. In the present context, for example, the parallel reads "burnt offerings" (1 Chron 21:23), and shortly thereafter the situation is reversed ("burnt offerings," v.24; "burnt offering," 1 Chron 21:24).

**23** In the MT, the first sentence translates literally as follows: "Everything he-gives Araunah the-king to-the-king." By legitimately rendering "the-king" as a vocative, the NIV reads, "All this Araunah gives, O king, to the king," whence the translation, "O king, Araunah gives all this to the king." In light of the MT accents, however, it is more natural to read "Araunah the king gives all this to the king" (see comment on v.16).